Preface

This dictionary has been designed as a reliable and user-friendly tool for use in all language situations. It provides accurate and up-to-date information on written and spoken German and English as they are used today.

Its 55,000 words and phrases and 80,000 translations give you access to German texts of all types. The dictionary aims to be as comprehensive as possible in a book of this size, and includes many proper names and abbreviations, as well as a selection of the most common terms from computing, business and current affairs.

Carefully constructed entries and a clear page design help you to find the translation that you are looking for fast. Examples (from basic constructions and common phrases to idioms) have been included to help put a word in context and give a clear picture of how it is used.

Vorbemerkung

Dieses Wörterbuch wurde als zuverlässiger und benutzerfreundlicher Begleiter für Schule, Beruf und Freizeit entwickelt. Es gibt schnell und präzise Auskunft über den aktuellen Wortschatz des Englischen und des Deutschen in seiner geschriebenen und gesprochenen Form.

55 000 Wörter und Ausdrücke mit ihren 80 000 Übersetzungen eröffnen den Zugang zu englischen Texten aller Art. Um dieses Nachschlagewerk innerhalb des vorgegebenen Umfangs so umfassend wie möglich zu gestalten, wurden zudem viele Eigennamen und Abkürzungen sowie eine Auswahl der gebräuchlichsten Begriffe aus den Bereichen EDV/Internet, Wirtschaft und Tagespolitik aufgenommen.

Mit großer Sorgfalt gestaltete Einträge und eine übersichtliche Seitengestaltung helfen dem Benutzer, die gesuchte Übersetzung schnell zu finden. Zusätzlich veranschaulichen zahlreiche Beispiele (von grammatischen Basiskonstruktionen und gebräuchlichen Kollokationen bis zu idiomatischen Wendungen) die Benutzung des betreffenden Wortes im Kontext.

Abkürzungen		Abbreviations
Akkusativ	A	accusative
Abkürzung	*abk / abbr*	abbreviation
abwertend	*abw*	pejorative
Adjektiv	*adj*	adjective
Verwaltung	ADMIN	administration
Adverb	*adv*	adverb
Flugwesen, Luftfahrt	AERON	aeronautics, aviation
Landwirtschaft	AGRIC	agriculture
amtssprachlich, formell	*amt*	official language
Anatomie	ANAT	anatomy
Archäologie	ARCHAEOL	archaeology
Architektur	ARCHIT	architecture
Astrologie	ASTROL	astrology
Astronomie	ASTRON	astronomy
Kfz-Technik	AUT(O)	automobile, cars
Hilfsverb	*aux*	auxiliary
Biologie	BIOL	biology
Botanik	BOT	botany
Chemie	CHEM	chemistry
Handel	COMM	commerce, business
ein zusammengestztes Substantiv bildend ein Substantiv, das zur näheren Bestimmung eines anderen dient z.B. **gardening** in **gardening book** oder **airforce** in **airforce base**	*comp*	compound-forming element a noun used to modify another noun, e.g. **gardening** in **gardenin[g] book** or **airforce** in **airforce base**
Komparativ	*compar*	comparative
Datenverarbeitung	COMPUT	computers
Konjunktion	*conj*	conjunction
Bauwesen	CONSTR	construction, building trade
Verlaufsform	*cont*	continuous
Kochkunst	CULIN	culinary, cooking
Dativ	*D*	dative
demonstrativ, hinweisend	*dem*	demonstrative
Determinant	*det*	determiner
Wirtschaft	ECON	economics
Datenverarbeitung	EDV	computers
eigentliche Bedeutung	*eigtl*	literal

LAROUSSE

TASCHEN-WÖRTERBUCH

DEUTSCH
ENGLISCH

ENGLISCH
DEUTSCH

ISBN 978-2-0354-2087-9

Sales: Houghton Mifflin Company, Boston
Library of Congress CIP Data
has been applied for

LAROUSSE

POCKET DICTIONARY

GERMAN ENGLISH

ENGLISH GERMAN

Für diese Ausgabe/For this edition

Helen Galloway Sigrid Koehler
Janice McNeillie

Für frühere Ausgaben/For the previous edition

Helen Bleck Alexander Behrens Joaquín Blasco
Anna Canning Lynda Carey Stuart Fortey
Helen Galloway Steffen Krug Elisabeth Lauer
Dörthe and Günther Lügenbuhl Friedman Lux
Úna ní Chiosáin Ruth Noble Elaine O'Donoghue
Christina Reinicke Stefan Rosenland Veronika Schilling
Ingrid Schumacher Alan Seaton Liliane Seifert
Katerina Stein Anna Stevenson Patrick White

Abkürzungen		Abbreviations
Elektrotechnik	ELEKTR/ELEC	electricity, electronics
etwas	*etw*	something
Interjektion	*excl*	exclamation
Femininum	*f*	feminine
umgangssprachlich	*fam*	informal
übertragene Bedeutung	*fig*	figurative
Finanzen	FIN	finance, financial
Flugwesen, Luftfahrt	FLUG	aeronautics, aviation
gehoben	*fml*	formal
Fotografie	FOTO	photography
Fußball	FTBL	football
Genitiv	*G*	genitive
gehoben	*geh*	formal
generell	*gen*	generally
Geografie	GEOGR	geography, geographical
Geologie	GEOL	geology, geological
Geometrie	GEOM	geometry
Grammatik	GRAMM	grammar
Geschichte	HIST	history
humorvoll	*hum*	humerous
Industrie	IND	industry
unbestimmt	*indef*	indefinite
umgangssprachlich	*inf*	informal
Interjektion	*interj*	exclamation
unveränderlich	*inv*	invariable
ironisch	*iron*	ironic
jemand	*jd*	someone (nominative)
jemandem	*jm*	someone (dative)
jemanden	*jn*	someone (accusative)
jemandes	*js*	someone (genitive)
Komparativ	*kompar*	comparative
Konjunktion	*konj*	conjunction
Kochkunst	KÜCHE	culinary, cooking
Rechtswesen	LAW	law
Linguistik	LING	linguistics
eigentliche Bedeutung	*lit*	literal
Maskulinum	*m*	masculine noun
Mathematik	MATH	mathematics
Medizin	MED	medicine
Meteorologie	METEOR	weather, meteorology

Abkürzungen		Abbreviations
Militärwesen	MIL	military
Musik	MUS	music
Mythologie	MYTH	mythology
Schifffahrt	NAUT	navigation
Schifffahrt	NAVIG	nautical, maritime
Norddeutsch	*Norddt*	northern German
Neutrum	*nt*	neuter noun (countries and towns) not used with an article
Zahlwort	*num*	numeral
ohne Plural	*ohne pl*	uncountable noun
sich	*o.s.*	oneself
Ostdeutsch	*Ostdt*	East German
Österreichisch	*Österr*	Austrian German
abwertend	*pej*	pejorative
Perfekt	*perf*	perfect
persönlich	*pers*	personal
Fotografie	PHOT	photography
Redewendung(en)	*phr*	phrase(s)
Physik	PHYS	physics
Plural	*pl*	plural
Politik	POL	politics
besitzanzeigend	*poss*	possessive
Partizip Perfekt	*pp*	past participle
Präposition	*präp*	preposition
Präsens	*präs*	present
Präteritum	*prät*	preterite
Vorsilbe	*pref*	prefix
Präposition	*prep*	preposition
Pronomen	*pron*	pronoun
Psychologie	PSYCH	psychology, psychiatry
Vergangenheitsform	*pt*	past tense
Warenzeichen	®	registered trademark
Eisenbahn	RAIL	railways
Rechtswesen	RECHT	law
reflexives Verb	*ref*	reflexive verb
regelmäßig	*reg*	regular
Religion	RELIG	religion
Redewendung(en)	*RW*	phrase(s)

Abkürzungen | Abbreviations

Abkürzungen		Abbreviations
salopp	*salopp*	very informal
jemand	*sb*	someone, somebody
Subjekt	*sbj*	subject
Schifffahrt	SCHIFF	navigation
Schule	SCHULE/SCH	school
Schweizerdeutsch	*Schweiz*	Swiss German
Singular	*sg*	singular
Slang	*sl*	slang
Sport	SPORT	sport
Börse	ST EX	stock exchange
etwas	*sthg*	something
Süddeutsch	*Süddt*	southern German
Superlativ	*superl*	superlative
Technik, Technologie	TECH	technology
Telekommunikation, Fernmeldewesen	TELEKOMM/TELEC	telecommunications
Fernsehen	TV	television
Druckwesen	TYPO	printing
Plural	*U*	uncountable noun
britisches Englisch	*UK*	British English
Universität	UNIV	university
unregelmäßig	*unr*	irregular
unveränderlich	*unver*	invariable
amerikanisches Englisch	*US*	American English
Verb	*v/vb*	verb
intransitives Verb	*vi*	intransitive verb
unpersönliches Verb	*vimp/v impers*	impersonal verb
salopp	*vinf*	very informal
vor Substantiv	*vor Subst*	before noun
transitives Verb	*vt*	transitive verb
vulgär	*vulg*	vulgar
Wirtschaft	WIRTSCH	economics
Zoologie	ZOOL	zoology
kulturelle Entsprechung	≃	cultural equivalent
Trennbarkeit des deutschen Verbs	|	indicates separable German verb

Lautschrift

Deutsche Vokale

[a] Affe, Banane
[a:] Arzt, Antrag
[e] Beton
[e:] edel
[ɛ] echt, Händler
[ɛ:] Rätsel, Dessert
[ə] Aktie
[i:] Vier
[i] Radio
[ɪ] Winter
[o] Melodie
[o:] apropos
[ɔ] sollen
[ø] ökologisch
[ø:] Öl
[œ] Köchin, Pumps
[u] Kuvert, aktuell
[u:] Kuh
[ʊ] Kunst
[y] Büchse, System
[y:] Tür

Deutsche Diphthonge

[ai̯] Deichsel
[aʊ̯] Auge
[ɔy̯] EuroCity

Deutsche Nasale

[ɑ̃] Chanson
[ɑ̃ :] Abonnement
[ɛ̃:] Pointe
[ɔ̃] Chanson

Phonetics

English vowels

[ɑ:] barn, car, laugh
[æ] pat, bag, mad
[ɒ] pot, log
[e] pet, tend
[ɜ:] burn, learn, bird
[ə] mother, suppose
[i:] bean, weed
[ɪ] pit, big, rid
[ɔ:] born, lawn
[u:] loop, loose
[ʌ] run, cut
[ʊ] put, full

English diphthongs

[aɪ] buy, light, aisle
[aʊ] now, shout, town
[eɪ] bay, late, great
[ɔɪ] boy, foil
[əʊ] no, road, blow
[ɪə] peer, fierce, idea
[eə] pair, bear, share
[ʊə] poor, sure, tour

Halbvokale		Semi-vowels
Jubiläum	[j]	you, spaniel
Hardware	[w]	wet, why, twin

Konsonanten		Consonants
Baby	[b]	bottle, bib
ich	[ç]	
Achse, Kaviar	[k]	come, kitchen
Duett, Medien	[d]	dog, did

Lautschrift		Phonetics
Gin	[dʒ]	jet, fridge
Fantasie, Vier	[f]	fib, physical
Algerien, gut	[g]	gag, great
Hobby	[h]	how, perhaps
alphabetisch, Laser	[l]	little, help
Material, Alarm	[m]	metal, comb
November, Angabe	[n]	night, dinner
singen	[ŋ]	sung, parking
Pony, Pappe	[p]	pop, people
Apfel	[pf]	
Revue, rot	[r]	right, carry
Slalom, Soße	[s]	seal, peace
Stadion, Schule	[ʃ]	sheep, machine
Toast, Volt	[t]	train, tip
Konversation	[ts]	
Chili	[tʃ]	chain, wretched
	[θ]	think, fifth
	[ð]	this, with
Vase, Wagen	[v]	vine, livid
Macht, lachen	[x]	
Soße, Sonne	[z]	zip, his
Etage	[ʒ]	usual, measure

Die Betonung der deutschen Stichwörter wird mit einem Punkt für einen kurzen betonten Vokal (z.B. **Berg**) und mit einem Strich für einen langen betonten Vokal (z.B. **Magen**) angegeben.

German headwords have the stress marked either by a dot for a short stressed vowel (e.g. **Berg**) or by an underscore for a long stressed vowel (e.g. **Magen**).

Der Hauptton eines englischen Wortes ist durch ein vorangestelltes [ˈ] markiert, der Nebenton durch ein vorangestelltes [ˌ].

The symbol [ˈ] indicates that the following syllable carries primary stress and the symbol [ˌ] that the following syllable carries secondary stress.

Das Zeichen [ʳ] zeigt in der englischen Phonetik an, dass der Endkonsonant „r" ausgesprochen wird, wenn das folgende Wort mit einem Vokal beginnt. Im amerikanischen Englisch wird dieses „r" so gut wie immer mitgesprochen.

The symbol [ʳ] in English phonetics indicates that the final "r" is pronounced only when followed by a word beginning with a vowel. Note that it is nearly always pronounced in American English.

Warenzeichen

Als Warenzeichen geschützte Wörter sind in diesem Wörterbuch durch das Zeichen ® gekennzeichnet. Die Markierung mit diesem Symbol, oder sein Fehlen, hat keinen Einfluss auf die Rechtskräftigkeit eines Warenzeichens.

Trademarks

Words considered to be trademarks have been designated in this dictionary by the symbol ®. However, neither the presence nor the absence of such designation should be regarded as affecting the legal status of any trademark.

Infinitive	Past Tense	Past Participle	Infinitive	Past Tense	Past Participle
arise	arose	arisen	drive	drove	driven
awake	awoke	awoken	eat	ate	eaten
be	was,	been	fall	fell	fallen
	were		feed	fed	fed
bear	bore	born(e)	feel	felt	felt
beat	beat	beaten	fight	fought	fought
begin	began	begun	find	found	found
bend	bent	bent	fling	flung	flung
bet	bet/	bet/	fly	flew	flown
	betted	betted	forget	forgot	forgotten
bid	bid	bid	freeze	froze	frozen
bind	bound	bound	get	got	got
bite	bit	bitten			(*US* gotten)
bleed	bled	bled	give	gave	given
blow	blew	blown	go	went	gone
break	broke	broken	grind	ground	ground
breed	bred	bred	grow	grew	grown
bring	brought	brought	hang	hung/	hung/
build	built	built		hanged	hanged
burn	burnt/	burnt/	have	had	had
	burned	burned	hear	heard	heard
burst	burst	burst	hide	hid	hidden
buy	bought	bought	hit	hit	hit
can	could	–	hold	held	held
cast	cast	cast	hurt	hurt	hurt
catch	caught	caught	keep	kept	kept
choose	chose	chosen	kneel	knelt/	knelt/
come	came	come		kneeled	kneeled
cost	cost	cost	know	knew	known
creep	crept	crept	lay	laid	laid
cut	cut	cut	lead	led	led
deal	dealt	dealt	lean	leant/	leant/
dig	dug	dug		leaned	leaned
do	did	done	leap	leapt/	leapt/
draw	drew	drawn		leaped	leaped
dream	dreamed/	dreamed/	learn	learnt/	learnt/
	dreamt	dreamt		learned	learned
drink	drank	drunk	leave	left	left

e	Past Tense	Past Participle	Infinitive	Past Tense	Past Participle
lend	lent	lent	sleep	slept	slept
let	let	let	slide	slid	slid
lie	lay	lain	sling	slung	slung
light	lit/	lit/	smell	smelt/	smelt/
	lighted	lighted		smelled	smelled
lose	lost	lost	sow	sowed	sown/
make	made	made			sowed
may	might	–	speak	spoke	spoken
mean	meant	meant	speed	sped/	sped /
meet	met	met		speeded	speeded
mow	mowed	mown/	spell	spelt/	spelt/
		mowed		spelled	spelled
pay	paid	paid	spend	spent	spent
put	put	put	spill	spilt/	spilt/
quit	quit/	quit/		spilled	spilled
	quitted	quitted	spin	spun	spun
read	read	read	spit	spat	spat
rid	rid	rid	split	split	split
ride	rode	ridden	spoil	spoiled/	spoiled/
ring	rang	rung		spoilt	spoilt
rise	rose	risen	spread	spread	spread
run	ran	run	spring	sprang	sprung
saw	sawed	sawn	stand	stood	stood
say	said	said	steal	stole	stolen
see	saw	seen	stick	stuck	stuck
seek	sought	sought	sting	stung	stung
sell	sold	sold	stink	stank	stunk
send	sent	sent	strike	struck	struck/
set	set	set			stricken
shake	shook	shaken	swear	swore	sworn
shall	should	–	sweep	swept	swept
shed	shed	shed	swell	swelled	swollen/
shine	shone	shone			swelled
shoot	shot	shot	swim	swam	swum
show	showed	shown	swing	swung	swung
shrink	shrank	shrunk	take	took	taken
shut	shut	shut	teach	taught	taught
sing	sang	sung	tear	tore	torn
sink	sank	sunk	tell	told	told
sit	sat	sat	think	thought	thought

Infinitive	Past Tense	Past Participle	Infinitive	Past Tense	Past Participle
throw	threw	thrown	weep	wept	wept
tread	trod	trodden	win	won	won
wake	woke/ waked	woken/ waked	wind	wound	wound
wear	wore	worn	wring	wrung	wrung
weave	wove/ weaved	woven/ weaved			

Infinitiv	Präsens	Präteritum	Perfekt
beginnen	beginnt	begann	hat begonnen
beißen	beißt	biss	hat gebissen
bitten	bittet	bat	hat gebeten
bleiben	bleibt	blieb	ist geblieben
bringen	bringt	brachte	hat gebracht
denken	denkt	dachte	hat gedacht
dürfen	darf	durfte	hat gedurft/dürfen
essen	isst	aß	hat gegessen
fahren	fährt	fuhr	hat/ist gefahren
finden	findet	fand	hat gefunden
fliegen	fliegt	flog	hat/ist geflogen
fließen	fließt	floss	ist geflossen
geben	gibt	gab	hat gegeben
gehen	geht	ging	ist gegangen
gelten	gilt	galt	hat gegolten
geschehen	geschieht	geschah	ist geschehen
gießen	gießt	goss	hat gegossen
greifen	greift	griff	hat gegriffen
haben	hat	hatte	hat gehabt
halten	hält	hielt	hat gehalten
heben	hebt	hob	hat gehoben
heißen	heißt	hieß	hat geheißen
helfen	hilft	half	hat geholfen
kennen	kennt	kannte	hat gekannt
kommen	kommt	kam	ist gekommen
können	kann	konnte	hat können/gekonnt
lassen	lässt	ließ	hat gelassen/lassen
laufen	läuft	lief	hat/ist gelaufen
leihen	leiht	lieh	hat geliehen
lesen	liest	las	hat gelesen
liegen	liegt	lag	hat gelegen
lügen	lügt	log	hat gelogen
messen	misst	maß	hat gemessen
mögen	mag	mochte	hat gemocht/mögen
müssen	muss	musste	hat gemusst/müssen
nehmen	nimmt	nahm	hat genommen
nennen	nennt	nannte	hat genannt

Infinitiv	Präsens	Präteritum	Perfekt
raten	rät	riet	hat geraten
reißen	reißt	riss	hat/ist gerissen
rennen	rennt	rannte	ist gerannt
riechen	riecht	roch	hat gerochen
rufen	ruft	rief	hat gerufen
schieben	schiebt	schob	hat geschoben
schießen	schießt	schoss	hat/ist geschossen
schlafen	schläft	schlief	hat geschlafen
schlagen	schlägt	schlug	hat/ist geschlagen
schließen	schließt	schloss	hat geschlossen
schneiden	schneidet	schnitt	hat geschnitten
schreiben	schreibt	schrieb	hat geschrieben
schreien	schreit	schrie	hat geschrie(e)n
schwimmen	schwimmt	schwamm	hat/ist geschwommen
sehen	sieht	sah	hat gesehen
sein	ist	war	ist gewesen
singen	singt	sang	hat gesungen
sitzen	sitzt	saß	hat gesessen
sprechen	spricht	sprach	hat gesprochen
springen	springt	sprang	hat/ist gesprungen
stehen	steht	stand	hat gestanden
stehlen	stiehlt	stahl	hat gestohlen
sterben	stirbt	starb	ist gestorben
stoßen	stößt	stieß	hat/ist gestoßen
streiten	streitet	stritt	hat gestritten
tragen	trägt	trug	hat getragen
treffen	trifft	traf	hat getroffen
treten	tritt	trat	hat getreten
trinken	trinkt	trank	hat getrunken
tun	tut	tat	hat getan
verlieren	verliert	verlor	hat verloren
waschen	wäscht	wusch	hat gewaschen
werden	wird	wurde	ist geworden/worden
werfen	wirft	warf	hat geworfen
wissen	weiß	wusste	hat gewusst
wollen	will	wollte	hat gewollt/wollen

DEUTSCH-ENGLISCH

GERMAN-ENGLISH

a, A (*pl* **a** ODER **-s**) [ɑː] *das* - **1.** [Buchstabe] a, A - **2.** MUS A.

Aal (*pl* **-e**) *der* eel.

aalglatt *adj abw* slippery.

a.a.O. (*abk für* **am angegebenen Ort**) loc. cit.

Aas (*pl* **-e** ODER **Äser**) *das* - **1.** *(pl Aase)* [Kadaver] carrion *(U)* - **2.** *(pl Äser) salopp abw* [Luder] devil; **kein Aas** *salopp* not a damned single person.

ab ◇ *präp (+ D)* - **1.** [zeitlich] from; **ab 8 Uhr** from 8 o'clock; **ab 18 (Jahren)** over (the age of) 18 - **2.** [räumlich] from; **ab Werk** ex works; **9.30 ab Köln** leaving Cologne at 9.30 - **3.** [bei einer Reihenfolge] over; **Einkünfte ab 15 000 Euro** incomes over 15,000 euros. ◇ *adv* - **1.** [räumlich] off; **weit ab gelegen** situated a long way away - **2.** [auffordernd]: **ab ins Bett!** get to bed! - **3.** [elliptisch] off; **Hut ab!** *fig* hats off!; *siehe auch* **ab sein**. ◆ **ab und zu, ab und an** *adv* now and then.

ab|arbeiten *vt* to work off.

Ab|art *die* variety.

abartig *adj* deviant.

Abb. (*abk für* **Abbildung**) fig.

Abbau *der (ohne pl)* - **1.** [Demontage - von Bühne, Gerüst] taking down; [- von Maschine] dismantling - **2.** [Reduzierung] reduction - **3.** [beim Bergbau] mining - **4.** CHEM & BIOL breaking down.

ab|bauen ◇ *vt* - **1.** [abbrechen - Kulissen, Bühne, Zelt] to take down; [- Maschine] to dismantle - **2.** [reduzieren] to reduce - **3.** CHEM & BIOL to break down - **4.** [beim Bergbau] to mine. ◇ *vi* to go downhill.

ab|bekommen *vt (unreg)* - **1.** [Anteil, Partner, Prügel] to get; **Schaden abbekommen** to get damaged; **hast du etwas abbekommen?** [Verletzung] did you get hurt? - **2.** *fam* [Fleck] to get off.

ab|bestellen *vt* to cancel.

ab|bezahlen *vt* to pay off.

ab|biegen (*perf* **hat/ist abgebogen**) *(unreg)* ◇ *vi (ist)* to turn off; **nach links/rechts abbiegen** to turn left/right. ◇ *vt (hat)* [verhindern - Vorhaben] to avert; [- Thema] to change.

Ab|bild *das* picture.

ab|bilden *vt* to depict.

Ab|bildung *die* - **1.** [Bild] illustration - **2.** [Wiedergabe] depiction.

ab|binden *vt (unreg)* - **1.** [ausziehen] to undo - **2.** MED to ligature.

ab|blasen *vt (unreg) fam* to call off.

ab|blättern (*perf* **ist abgeblättert**) *vi* to flake off.

ab|blenden ◇ *vt* - **1.** [Lampe] to screen - **2.** [Scheinwerfer] to dip *UK*, to dim *US*. ◇ *vi* - **1.** FOTO to stop down - **2.** AUTO to dip *UK* ODER dim *US* one's headlights.

Abblend|licht *das* dipped *UK* ODER dimmed *US* headlights *Pl*.

ab|blitzen (*perf* **ist abgeblitzt**) *vi fam*: **bei jm abblitzen** to get short shrift from sb.

ab|blocken *vt* to block.

ab|brechen (*perf* **hat/ist abgebrochen**) *(unreg)* ◇ *vt (hat)* - **1.** [Stück, Ast] to break off; [Bleistift] to break - **2.** [Vorhaben, Beziehungen, Reise, Studium] to break off; [Streik] to call off. ◇ *vi* - **1.** *(hat)* [im Gespräch] to break off - **2.** *(ist)* [Geräusch] to stop.

ab|brennen (*perf* **hat/ist abgebrannt**) *(unreg)* ◇ *vt (hat)* - **1.** [Haus] to burn down - **2.** [Feuerwerk] to let off. ◇ *vi (ist)* to burn down.

ab|bringen *vt (unreg)*: **jn von seiner Meinung abbringen** to make sb change his/her mind; **jn davon abbringen, aus dem Fenster zu**

springen to stop sb from jumping out of the window; **das bringt uns vom Thema ab** we're getting off the subject.

ạb|bröckeln (*perf* **ist ạbgebröckelt**) *vi* to flake off.

Ạb|bruch *der* - **1.** [Ende] breaking off; **einer Sache** *(D)* **keinen Abbruch tun** *fig* not to harm sthg - **2.** [Zerstörung] demolition.

ạbbruchreif *adj* fit only for demolition.

ạb|buchen *vt* WIRTSCH: **abbuchen (von)** to debit (to).

Abc [a(:)be(:)'tse:] *das* ABC.

ạb|danken *vi* to abdicate.

ạb|decken *vt* - **1.** [gen] to cover - **2.** [abräumen - Tisch] to clear; [- Dach] to take off.

Ạbdeckung (*pl* **-en**) *die* - **1.** [zum Schutz] cover - **2.** WIRTSCH covering.

ạb|dichten *vt* [gegen kalte Luft] to insulate; [gegen Wasser] to waterproof; [Gefäß] to make airtight; [Fenster] to draughtproof.

Ạb|dichtung *die* [gegen kalte Luft] insulation; [gegen Wasser] waterproofing; [von Fenster] draughtproofing; [von Gefäß] making airtight.

ạb|drehen (*perf* **hat/ist ạbgedreht**) ◇ *vt (hat)* - **1.** [Wasser, Gas] to turn off - **2.** [Knopf, Schraube] to twist off - **3.** FILM [Szene] to shoot. ◇ *vi (hat, ist)* [den Kurs ändern] to turn away.

Ạbdruck (*pl* **-drücke**) *der* - **1.** [Spur] imprint - **2.** [Druck] printing.

ạb|drucken *vt* to print.

ạb|drücken ◇ *vt* [abquetschen] to constrict; **jm die Luft abdrücken** to squeeze the breath out of sb. ◇ *vi* [schießen] to pull the trigger. ◆ **sich abdrücken** *ref* to leave an impression.

Abend (*pl* **-e**) *der* evening; **am Abend** in the evening; **gestern/heute/morgen Abend** yesterday/this/tomorrow evening; **guten Abend!** good evening!; **zu Abend essen** to have one's dinner ODER evening meal; **bunter Abend** social evening.

Abend|brot *das* cold supper.

Abend|essen *das* dinner, evening meal.

Abend|kasse *die* box office *(where tickets may only be bought immediately before performance)*.

Abend|kurs *der* evening class.

abendlich *adj* evening *(vor Subst)*.

Abend|mahl *das* RELIG (Holy) Communion.

Abend|programm *das* evening programmes *Pl* ODER viewing *(U)*.

abends *adv* in the evening; **spätabends** late in the evening.

Abenteuer (*pl* -) *das* - **1.** [Erlebnis] adventure - **2.** [Wagnis] venture - **3.** [Liebesverhältnis] affair.

abenteuerlich *adj* - **1.** [waghalsig] adventurous - **2.** [fantastisch] fantastic.

Abenteurer, **in** (*mpl* -, *fpl* **-nen**) *der, die* adventurer.

aber ◇ *konj* but. ◇ *adv*: **das ist aber nett** how nice!; **aber gerne!** of course!; **aber immer!** *fam* sure!; **jetzt ist aber Schluss!** that' enough now!; **du kommst aber spät!** you're bit late, aren't you?

Aber|glaube, -n *der* superstition.

abergläubisch *adj* superstitious.

ạb|fahren (*perf* **hat/ist ạbgefahren**) *(unreg* ◇ *vi (ist)* [losfahren] to leave; [Zug] to depart to leave; **auf jn/etw abfahren** *fam fig* to b into sb/sthg. ◇ *vt (hat)* - **1.** [Ladung] to tak away - **2.** [Strecke] to go over - **3.** [Reifen] t wear down - **4.** [Fahrkarte] to get full use ou of.

Ạb|fahrt *die* - **1.** [Start] departure; **Vorsicht be der Abfahrt des Zuges!** stand clear of th doors, the train is about to depart! - **2.** [Auto bahnabfahrt] exit - **3.** [Skiabfahrt] descent.

Ạbfahrts|zeit *die* departure time.

Ạb|fall *der* - **1.** [Hausmüll] refuse; [industriel waste - **2.** *(ohne pl)* [Rückgang] drop, fall.

Ạbfall|beseitigung *die* waste disposal.

ạb|fallen (*perf* **ist ạbgefallen**) *vi (unreg* - **1.** [herunterfallen] to fall off - **2.** [übrig bleiber to be left over; **was fällt für mich ab?** what d I get out of it? - **3.** [schlechter sein]: **gegen jn etw abfallen** to suffer by comparison with sb sthg - **4.** [sich neigen] to slope (down) - **5.** [sic verringern] to drop, to fall.

ạbfällig ◇ *adj* disparaging. ◇ *adv* dispar agingly.

ạb|fangen *vt (unreg)* - **1.** [Brief, Anruf, Tran port] to intercept - **2.** [Person] to catc - **3.** [Schlag] to ward off - **4.** [Flugzeug] to regai control of.

ạb|färben *vi* to run; **auf jn/etw abfärben** *fi* to rub off on sb/sthg.

ạb|fassen *vt* to write.

ạb|fertigen *vt* - **1.** [Waren] to prepare for dis patch; [Gepäck] to check in; [Schiff, Flugzeug] t prepare for departure - **2.** [Passagier, Antragste ler] to attend to.

Ạb|fertigung *die* - **1.** [von Gepäck] check-i [von Waren] preparation for dispatch; [vc Schiff, Flugzeug] preparation for departur - **2.** [von Passagier, Antragssteller] attending to.

ạb|feuern *vt* [Gewehr, Schuss] to fire; [Raket to launch.

ạb|finden *vt (unreg)* [entschädigen]: **jn m etw abfinden** to give sb sthg in compens tion. ◆ **sich abfinden** *ref*: **sich mit etw al finden** to come to terms with sthg.

Ạbfindung (*pl* **-en**) *die* [für einen Verlust] com pensation; [für die vorzeitige Entlassung] seve ance pay.

ạb|fliegen (*perf* **ist ạbgeflogen**) *vi (unreg)* t take off.

ạb|fließen (*perf* **ist ạbgeflossen**) *vi (unreg)* [Spülwasser] to drain away; [Regenwasser] to run away.

Ạb|flug *der* - **1.** [von Flugzeug] take-off - **2.** [Flughafenbereich] departures *(U)*.

Ạbfluss (*pl* **-flüsse**) *der* - **1.** [Öffnung - von Waschbecken, Dusche] plughole - **2.** [von Kapital] flight - **3.** [von Spülwasser] draining away; [von Regenwasser] running away.

ạb|fragen *vt* to call up; **jn (etw) abfragen** to test sb (on sthg).

Ạbfuhr (*pl* **-en**) *die*: **jm eine Abfuhr erteilen** to rebuff sb.

ạb|führen ◇ *vt* - **1.** [festnehmen] to take away - **2.** [vom Thema] to lead away. ◇ *vi* MED to act as a laxative.

Ạbführ|mittel *das* laxative.

ạb|füllen *vt* - **1.** [Flüssigkeit]: **Wein in Flaschen abfüllen** to bottle wine - **2.** [Flaschen, Säcke] to fill - **3.** *fam* [betrunken machen]: **jn abfüllen** to get sb plastered.

Ạbgabe (*pl* **-n**) *die* - **1.** [Übergabe - von Gutachten] handing over; [- von Arbeit] handing in - **2.** [von Stimmen] casting - **3.** [Verkauf] sale - **4.** [von Ball] passing - **5.** [von Wärme, Sauerstoff] giving off. ◆ **Abgaben** *Pl* [Steuern] taxes.

ạbgabenfrei *adj* exempt from tax.

ạbgabenpflichtig *adj* taxable.

Ạbgangs|zeugnis *das* leaving certificate.

Ạbgase *Pl* exhaust fumes.

ạb|geben *vt (unreg)* - **1.** [abliefern - Brief, Geschenk] to hand over; [- Arbeit] to hand in; [- an der Garderobe] to leave - **2.** [verkaufen] to sell - **3.** [teilen]: **jm etw abgeben** to give sb sthg - **4.** [äußern - Erklärung] to make; [- Meinung] to give; [- Stimme] to cast - **5.** [abtreten] to give up - **6.** [darstellen - Figur] to cut; **einen guten Vater abgeben** to make a good father - **7.** SPORT [werfen] to pass - **8.** [ausströmen] to give off - **9.** [abfeuern] to fire. ◆ **sich abgeben** *ref*: **sich mit etw (nicht) abgeben** (not) to concern o.s. with sthg; **sie gibt sich mit ganz obskuren Typen ab** she mixes with some really dubious types.

ạbgebrüht *adj fam* hard-boiled, tough.

ạbgedroschen *adj* well-worn, hackneyed.

ạb|gehen (*perf* **ist ạbgegangen**) *(unreg)* ◇ *vi* - **1.** [sich lösen] to come off - **2.** [verlassen]: **von etw abgehen** to leave sthg - **3.** [abfahren] to leave, to depart - **4.** [abgeschickt werden] to go off - **5.** [abgerechnet werden] to be taken off ODER deducted - **6.** [abzweigen] to branch off - **7.** [abweichen]: **von seiner Meinung abgehen** to change one's mind; **von seinen Forderungen abgehen** to drop one's demands - **8.** [verlaufen] to go; **es ist gut abgegangen** it went well; **es geht ab** *salopp* things are really buzzing - **9.** [fehlen]: **ihm geht jedes Feingefühl ab** he lacks any sensitivity, he has no sensitivity. ◇ *vt* [Strecke, Straße] to walk along; [Grundstück] to walk over.

ạbgekämpft *adj* worn-out.

ạbgekartet *adj*: **ein abgekartetes Spiel** a put-up job.

ạbgelegen *adj* remote.

ạbgemacht *adj* settled; **abgemacht!** it's a deal!

ạbgemagert *adj* emaciated.

ạbgeneigt *adj*: **einer Sache** *(D)* **(nicht) abgeneigt sein** (not) to be opposed to sthg.

ạbgenutzt *adj* [Türgriff, Fußboden] worn; [Gerät] worn-out.

Ạbgeordnete (*pl* **-n**) *der, die* [im Bundestag] member of parliament; [im Landtag] representative.

Ạb|gesandte *der, die* envoy.

ạbgeschieden *adj* remote.

Ạbgeschiedenheit *die* remoteness.

ạbgesehen *adv*: **abgesehen von jm/etw** apart from sb/sthg. ◆ **abgesehen davon, dass** *konj* apart from the fact that.

ạbgespannt *adj* exhausted.

ạbgestanden *adj* [Bier] flat; [Luft] stale; [Wasser] stagnant.

ạbgestorben ◇ *pp* ▷ **absterben**. ◇ *adj* - **1.** [Baum, Ast] dead - **2.** [Fuß, Bein] numb.

ạbgestumpft *adj* - **1.** [gefühllos] hardened - **2.** [apathisch] apathetic.

ạbgetragen *adj* worn-out.

ạb|gewinnen *vt (unreg)*: **jm etw abgewinnen** to win sthg from sb; **einer Sache** *(D)* **Geschmack abgewinnen** to acquire a taste for sthg.

ạb|gewöhnen *vt*: **jm etw abgewöhnen** to get sb to give sthg up; **sich** *(D)* **etw abgewöhnen** to give sthg up.

ạb|grenzen *vt* - **1.** [abtrennen - mit Zaun] to fence off; [- mit Mauer] to wall off - **2.** [unterscheiden] to differentiate. ◆ **sich abgrenzen** *ref*: **sich von jm/etw abgrenzen** to distance o.s. from sb/sthg.

Ạbgrenzung (*pl* **-en**) *die* - **1.** [Grenze] boundary - **2.** [Definition] definition.

Ạb|grund *der* abyss; **vor dem Abgrund stehen** *fig* to be on the edge of the abyss.

ạbgrundtief ◇ *adj* profound, deep. ◇ *adv* profoundly, deeply.

ạb|gucken *vt fam* to copy; **etw von** ODER **bei jm abgucken** to copy sthg from sb.

ạb|hacken *vt* to chop off.

ạb|haken *vt* to check off.

ạb|halten *vt (unreg)* - **1.** [veranstalten] to hold - **2.** [fern halten]: **jn von etw abhalten** to keep sb from sthg.

abhạnden *adv*: **mir ist meine Brille abhanden gekommen** my glasses have gone missing.

Ạb|handlung *die* treatise.

Ạb|hang *der* slope.

ạb|hängen ◇ *vt (reg)* - **1.** [Bild] to take down - **2.** [Anhänger, Wagon] to uncouple - **3.** [Konkurrenten, Verfolger] to shake off. ◇ *vi (unreg)* - **1.**: **von jm/etw abhängen** to depend on sb/sthg - **2.** *fam* [sich entspannen] to chill (out).

ạbhängig *adj*: **von etw abhängig sein** [von Wetter, Geschmack, Zufall] to depend on sthg; [von Hilfe, Vormund] to be dependent on sthg; [von Drogen] to be addicted to sthg.

Ạbhängigkeit (*pl* **-en**) *die* - **1.** [gen] dependence; **Abhängigkeit von etw** dependence on sthg - **2.** [von Drogen] addiction.

ạb|härten ◇ *vt* to toughen up. ◇ *vi*: **dieses Wetter härtet ab** this weather toughens you up. ◆ **sich abhärten** *ref* to toughen (o.s.) up.

ạb|hauen (*perf* **ist ạbgehauen**) *vi fam* [verschwinden] to clear off.

ạb|heben *(unreg)* ◇ *vt* - **1.** [vom Konto] to withdraw - **2.** [am Telefon] to pick up - **3.** [beim Kartenspiel] to cut. ◇ *vi* [abfliegen] to take off. ◆ **sich abheben** *ref*: **sich von jm/etw** ODER **gegen jn/etw abheben** to stand out against sb/sthg.

ạb|heften *vt* to file away.

ạb|hetzen *vt* to drive hard. ◆ **sich abhetzen** *ref* to rush one's socks off.

Ạbhilfe *die*: **Abhilfe schaffen** to take remedial action.

ạb|holen *vt* [Paket, Ware] to collect; [Person] to pick up.

ạb|holzen *vt* [Wald, Allee] to clear; [Bäume] to cut down.

ạb|hören *vt* - **1.** [heimlich anhören - Gespräch] to listen in on; [- Telefon] to tap - **2.** [abfragen] to test; **jm etw abhören** to test sb on sthg - **3.** [abhorchen] to sound.

Ạbi (*pl* **-s**) *das abk für* **Abitur**.

Abitur (*pl* **-e**) *das* ≃ A levels *Pl UK*, ≃ SATs *US, final examination at a German "Gymnasium", qualifying pupils for university entrance.*

Abitur|feier *die party at end of school studies.*

Abituriẹnt, in [abituri̯'ɛnt, ɪn] (*mpl* **-en**, *fpl* **-nen**) *der, die pupil who is taking/has taken the "Abitur".*

Abitur|zeugnis *das certificate awarded to a pupil who has passed the "Abitur".*

ạb|kapseln ◆ **sich abkapseln** *ref* to cut o.s. off.

ạb|kaufen *vt* - **1.** [kaufen]: **jm etw abkaufen** to buy sthg from sb - **2.** *fam* [glauben]: **diese Geschichte kaufe ich dir nicht ab!** I'm not buying that story (of yours)!

ạb|klappern *vt fam*: **etw (nach etw) abklappern** to scour sthg (for sthg).

ạb|klingen (*perf* **ist ạbgeklungen**) *vi (unreg*[Fieber] to die down.

ạb|knöpfen *vt*: **jm etw abknöpfen** to ge sthg out of sb.

ạb|kochen *vt* to sterilize *(by boiling)*.

ạb|kommen (*perf* **ist ạbgekommen**) *vi (un reg)*: **von etw abkommen** [Kurs, Weg] to devi ate from sthg; [Thema] to get off sthg; [Ge wohnheit, Vorhaben] to give sthg up, t abandon sthg.

Ạbkommen (*pl* -) *das* agreement.

ạbkömmlich *adj* available.

ạb|können *vt (unreg) salopp*: **ich kann ihn/e nicht ab** I can't stand ODER stick *UK* him/it.

ạb|kriegen *vt fam* - **1.** [gen] to get; **das Aut hat was abgekriegt** the car got damaged; **ei nen/eine abkriegen** to get a man/woma - **2.** [Deckel, Schraube, Fleck] to get off.

ạb|kühlen (*perf* **hat/ist ạbgekühlt**) - **1.** [Temperatur] to cool down - **2.** [Stimmung Engagement] to cool. ◆ **sich abkühlen** *re* [Person] to cool down ODER off; [Verhältnis] t cool; **es hat sich abgekühlt** it has got cooler.

Ạbkühlung *die* cooling.

ạb|kürzen *vt* - **1.** [Weg]: **den Weg abkürze** to take a short cut - **2.** [Wort] to abbreviat - **3.** [Besuch, Reise] to cut short; [Verfahren] t shorten.

Ạb|kürzung *die* - **1.** [von Weg] short cu - **2.** [von Wörtern] abbreviation.

ạb|laden *vt (unreg)* - **1.** [abräumen] to unloa - **2.** [erzählen]: **seinen Kummer bei jm ablade** to unburden o.s. to sb.

Ạb|lage *die* - **1.** [für Papiere, Akten] filing cab inet - **2.** [Abheften] filing.

Ạb|lagerung *die* [Sediment] deposit.

ạb|lassen *(unreg)* ◇ *vt* - **1.** [Luft] to let ou - **2.** [Wasser] to drain off. ◇ *vi*: **von jm ablas sen** [in Ruhe lassen] to leave sb alone; **von etw ablassen** [aufgeben] to give sthg up.

Ạb|lauf *der* - **1.** [Verlauf] course; **um den fried lichen Ablauf der Veranstaltung zu gewäh leisten** to ensure that the event passes o peacefully - **2.** [Abfluss] drain; [Rinne] outle - **3.** [Ende] expiry.

ạb|legen ◇ *vt* - **1.** [Mantel] to take o - **2.** [sich abgewöhnen] to get rid of - **3.** [Eid, Prü fung] to take - **4.** [Akten] to file. ◇ *vi* - **1.** [Ga derobe] to take one's coat/hat/etc o - **2.** [Schiff] to cast off.

Ạbleger (*pl* -) *der* - **1.** [von Pflanzen] cuttin - **2.** [Filiale] subsidiary.

ạb|lehnen *vt* - **1.** [Angebot, Vorschlag] to re ject; [Einladung] to refuse, to turn dow - **2.** [Rauschgift, Schusswaffen] to disapprove o

Ạblehnung (*pl* **-en**) *die* - **1.** [von Angebot] re jection; [von Einladung] refusal; **auf Ablehnun stoßen** to be rejected - **2.** [Missbilligung] disap proval.

ạb|leisten *vt*: **den Wehrdienst ableisten** to do one's military service.

ạb|leiten *vt* - **1.** [Rauch, Gas] to draw off - **2.** [folgern, zurückführen]: **etw von** *ODER* **aus etw ableiten** [Wort, Recht] to derive sthg from sthg - **3.** [Gleichung] to differentiate.

Ạb|leitung *die* - **1.** [von Rauch, Gas] drawing off - **2.** [von Wort, Formel] derivation.

ạb|lenken *vt* - **1.** [zerstreuen] to distract; **jn von der Arbeit ablenken** to put sb off their work - **2.** [Aufmerksamkeit, Verdacht] to divert - **3.** [weglenken - Angriff] to ward off; [- Bewegung] to deflect.

Ạblenkung (*pl* **-en**) *die* - **1.** [Zerstreuung] distraction - **2.** [Richtungsänderung] deflection.

ạb|lesen *vt (unreg)* - **1.** [lesen] to read out - **2.** [den Stand feststellen] to read - **3.** [erraten]: **er liest ihr jeden Wunsch von den Augen ab** he can always tell what she wants from the look in her eyes.

ạb|liefern *vt* to deliver.

ạb|lösen *vt* - **1.** [ersetzen] to take over from - **2.** [abmachen] to take off. ◆ **sich ablösen** *ref* - **1.** [sich abwechseln] to take turns - **2.** [abgehen] to come off.

Ạblösung *die* - **1.** [Zahlung] paying off - **2.** [Ersatzperson] relief.

ạb|luchsen ['aplʊksn̩] *vt*: **jm etw abluchsen** to get sthg out of sb.

ABM [aːỹbeːˈɛm] (*pl* -) (*abk für* **Arbeitsbeschaffungsmaßnahme**) *die job creation scheme.*

ạb|machen *vt* - **1.** [entfernen] to take off - **2.** [verabreden] to agree on; **einen Termin abmachen** to make an appointment.

Ạbmachung (*pl* **-en**) *die* agreement.

ạb|magern (*perf* **ist ạbgemagert**) *vi* to get thinner.

Ạbmarsch *der* departure.

ạb|marschieren (*perf* **ist ạbmarschiert**) *vi* [bei Wandern] to set off; MIL to march off.

ạb|melden *vt* - **1.** [Personen]: **ein Kind von der Schule abmelden** to give notice of a child's removal from school; **sie ist bei mir abgemeldet** *fam fig* I've had it *ODER* I'm through with her - **2.** [Gegenstände - Telefon] to have disconnected; [- Auto] to take off the road. ◆ **sich abmelden** *ref*: **sich polizeilich abmelden** to notify the police that one is moving away; **sich bei einem Verein abmelden** to cancel one's membership of a club.

Ạb|meldung *die* - **1.** [beim Einwohnermeldeamt] *notification that one is moving away* - **2.** [von der Schule] *notification of a child's removal from school.*

ạb|messen *vt (unreg)* to measure.

ABṂ-|Stelle *die job created as part of a job creation scheme.*

ạb|mühen ◆ **sich abmühen** *ref* to struggle.

ạb|nehmen *(unreg)* ◇ *vt* - **1.** [herunternehmen - Vorhänge, Wäsche] to take down; [- Hut, Deckel] to take off; [- Hörer] to pick up - **2.** [wegnehmen]: **jm etw abnehmen** to take sthg (away) from sb - **3.** [entlasten]: **jm etw abnehmen** to relieve sb of sthg - **4.** [kontrollieren] to inspect - **5.** [kaufen]: **jm etw abnehmen** to buy sthg from sb - **6.** [glauben]: **das nimmt dir keiner ab!** nobody will buy that! - **7.** [entgegennehmen - Prüfung] to conduct; **jm ein Versprechen abnehmen** to make sb give a promise - **8.** [amputieren]: **jm einen Finger abnehmen** to take sb's finger off - **9.** [entnehmen]: **jm Blut abnehmen** to take sb's blood - **10.** [verlieren - Gewicht] to lose. ◇ *vi* - **1.** [leichter werden] to lose weight - **2.** [sich verringern - Temperatur, Luftdruck, Ressourcen] to decrease; [- Mond] to wane.

Ạbnehmer, in (*mpl* -, *fpl* **-nen**) *der, die* buyer.

Ạb|neigung *die* aversion.

ạb|nutzen, ạbnützen *vt* to wear out. ◆ **sich abnutzen, sich abnützen** *ref* to wear out.

Ạbo (*pl* **-s**) *das fam abk für* **Abonnement**.

Abonnement [abɔnəˈmɑ̃ː] (*pl* **-s**) *das* - **1.** [einer Zeitung] subscription - **2.** [im Theater] season ticket.

abonnieren *vt* to subscribe to.

ạb|packen *vt* to pre-pack.

ạb|passen *vt* - **1.** [Person] to catch - **2.** [Moment] to wait for.

ạb|pflücken *vt* to pick.

ạb|prallen (*perf* **ist ạbgeprallt**) *vi* - **1.** [zurückspringen - Ball] to bounce back, to rebound; [- Kugel] to ricochet - **2.** [Vorwurf, Worte]: **an jm** *ODER* **von jm abprallen** to make no impression on sb.

ạb|putzen *vt* to wipe.

ạb|quälen ◆ **sich abquälen** *ref* [sich plagen]: **sich mit etw abquälen** to struggle with sthg.

ạb|raten *vi (unreg)*: **(jm) von etw abraten** to advise (sb) against sthg.

ạb|räumen *vt* [Geschirr] to clear away; [Tisch] to clear.

ạb|reagieren *vt*: **etw an jm abreagieren** to take sthg out on sb. ◆ **sich abreagieren** *ref*: **sich an jm abreagieren** to take it out on sb.

ạb|rechnen ◇ *vi* [Kassiererin] to cash up; **mit jm abrechnen** [zahlen] to settle up with sb; [sich rächen] to get even with sb. ◇ *vt* [abziehen] to deduct.

Ạb|rechnung *die* - **1.** [Bilanz, Rechnung] accounts *Pl* - **2.** [Rache] reckoning.

ạb|reiben *vt (unreg)* - **1.** [Schmutz] to rub off - **2.** [Hände] to wipe - **3.** [Kind, Hund] to rub down.

Ạbreibung (*pl* **-en**) *die* thrashing.

Ạb|reise *die* departure.

ab|reisen (*perf* **ist abgereist**) *vi* to depart.

ab|reißen (*perf* **hat/ist abgerissen**) *(unreg)* ◇ *vt (hat)* - **1.** [Papier] to tear off - **2.** [Haus] to pull down. ◇ *vi (ist)* - **1.** [Teil, Knopf, Etikett] to come off; [Faden] to break off - **2.** [Kontakt] to break off.

ab|richten *vt* to train.

ab|riegeln *vt* - **1.** [verschließen] to bolt - **2.** [Gelände] to cordon off.

Abriss (*pl* **-e**) *der* - **1.** [Zerstörung] demolition - **2.** [Darstellung] outline.

ab|rollen (*perf* **hat/ist abgerollt**) ◇ *vt (hat)* [abspulen] to unwind. ◇ *vi (ist)* - **1.** [von einer Rolle] to unwind - **2.** [ablaufen] to go - **3.** SPORT to go into a roll.

ab|rücken (*perf* **hat/ist abgerückt**) ◇ *vt (hat)* to move away. ◇ *vi (ist)* [wegrücken]: **von jm/etw abrücken** [sich entfernen] to move away from sb/sthg; [sich distanzieren] to distance o.s. from sb/sthg.

Ab|ruf *der* EDV retrieval. ◆ **auf Abruf** *adv*: **auf Abruf bereitstehen** to be standing by.

ab|rufen *vt (unreg)* EDV to retrieve.

ab|runden *vt* - **1.** [Zahl, Summe] to round down - **2.** [Ecke, Küche, Programm] to round off.

abrupt ◇ *adj* abrupt. ◇ *adv* abruptly.

ab|rüsten ◇ *vi* to disarm. ◇ *vt* to get rid of.

Abrüstung *die* disarmament.

ab|rutschen (*perf* **ist abgerutscht**) *vi* - **1.** [wegrutschen] to slip - **2.** [Schüler]: **er ist in Mathematik abgerutscht** his marks in mathematics have gone down.

ab|sacken (*perf* **ist abgesackt**) *vi* - **1.** [sinken - Flugzeug, Druck] to drop; [- Gebäude] to subside - **2.** [Leistung]: **sie ist in Chemie abgesackt** her marks in chemistry have got worse.

Ab|sage *die* - **1.** [von Termin, Veranstaltung] cancellation - **2.** [Zurückweisung]: **jm/einer Sache eine Absage erteilen** to reject sb/sthg.

ab|sagen ◇ *vt* to cancel. ◇ *vi* to cancel.

ab|sägen *vt* - **1.** [sägen - Baum] to saw down; [- Brett] to saw off - **2.** *fam* [entlassen] to axe.

ab|sahnen *fam* ◇ *vt* to cream off. ◇ *vi* to make a killing.

Ab|satz *der* - **1.** [von Schuhen] heel - **2.** [Verkauf] sales *Pl* - **3.** [im Text] paragraph.

ab|saufen (*perf* **ist abgesoffen**) *vi (unreg)* - **1.** *salopp* [im Wasser - Schiff] to go to the bottom; [- Person] to go to a watery grave - **2.** *fam* [Motor] to flood.

ab|schaffen *vt* - **1.** [Regelung] to abolish - **2.** [aufheben] to do away with - **3.** [weggeben] to get rid of.

ab|schalten *vi* & *vt* [ausschalten] to switch off.

ab|schätzen *vt* - **1.** [Menge, Zahl] to estimate - **2.** [Menschen] to weigh up.

Abscheu *die* ODER *der* disgust, revulsion.

abscheulich ◇ *adj* disgusting. ◇ *adv* disgustingly.

ab|schicken *vt* to post *UK*, to mail *US*.

ab|schieben (*perf* **hat/ist abgeschoben**) *(unreg)* ◇ *vt (hat)* - **1.** [außer Landes] to deport - **2.** *fam abw* [versetzen] to shunt off. ◇ *vi (ist) salopp abw* [fortgehen] to push off.

Abschied (*pl* **-e**) *der* - **1.** [Trennung, Weggehen] parting; **von jm/etw Abschied nehmen** to say goodbye to sb/sthg - **2.** [Entlassung] resignation; **seinen Abschied nehmen** to resign.

ab|schießen *vt (unreg)* - **1.** [Flugzeug] to shoot down - **2.** [Kugel, Gewehr] to fire; [Pfeil] to shoot; [Rakete] to launch - **3.** [töten] to shoot - **4.** [Körperteil]: **ihm ist ein Bein abgeschossen worden** his leg has been shot off - **5.** *fam* [entlassen]: **jn abschießen** to give sb the boot, to kick sb out.

ab|schirmen *vt* to shield.

ab|schlachten *vt fam* to slaughter.

ab|schlagen *vt (unreg)* - **1.** [verweigern]: **jm etw abschlagen** to refuse sb sthg - **2.** [abtrennen - durch Schneiden] to chop off; [- durch Schlagen] to knock off.

abschlägig ◇ *adj* unfavourable. ◇ *adv* **etw abschlägig bescheiden** to refuse sthg.

Abschlepp|dienst *der* (vehicle) recovery service.

ab|schleppen *vt* - **1.** [Auto, Schiff] to tow away - **2.** *fam* [Person] to pick up.

Abschlepp|seil *das* towrope.

ab|schließen *(unreg)* ◇ *vt* - **1.** [Tür] to lock - **2.** [Tätigkeit] to finish - **3.** [Geschäft] to conclude; [Vertrag] to sign; [Versicherung] to take out - **4.** WIRTSCH to balance. ◇ *vi* [mit etw enden]: **mit etw abschließen** to finish with sthg; **mit der Vergangenheit abschließen** to draw a line under the past; **mit Verlust abschließen** to show a loss.

abschließend ◇ *adj* concluding. ◇ *adv* in conclusion.

Abschluss (*pl* **Abschlüsse**) *der* - **1.** [Ende] end; **zum Abschluss der Tagung spricht Professor Schulz** Professor Schulz will bring the conference to a close - **2.** [von Geschäft] conclusion; [von Vertrag] signing; [von Versicherung] taking out - **3.** [Abschlusszeugnis von Hochschule] degree.

Abschluss|zeugnis (*pl* **-zeugnisse**) *das* *school-leaving certificate*.

ab|schmecken *vt* - **1.** [würzen] to season - **2.** [kosten] to taste.

ab|schmieren ◇ *vt* - **1.** [Motor] to lubricate; [Fahrradkette] to grease - **2.** *fam* [abschreiben] to crib. ◇ *vi fam* [Flugzeug] to nosedive; [Computer, Programm] to crash.

ab|schminken *vt*: **jn abschminken** to remove sb's make-up. ◆ **sich abschminken** *ref*: **sich abschminken** to remove one's make-up.

ab|schnallen (*perf* **hat/ist abgeschnallt**) *vt* (*hat*) to unfasten. ◆ **sich abschnallen** *ref* to unfasten one's seatbelt.

ab|schneiden *(unreg)* ◇ *vt* - **1.** [Stück] to cut off - **2.** [Weg]: **jm den Weg abschneiden** to block sb's way - **3.** [Wort]: **jm das Wort abschneiden** to cut sb off. ◇ *vi*: **gut/schlecht abschneiden** to do well/badly.

Ab|schnitt *der* - **1.** [im Text, von Strecke] section - **2.** [von Formular, Karte] detachable portion; [von Scheck] counterfoil; [von Eintrittskarte] stub - **3.** [Zeitraum] period - **4.** MATH segment.

ab|schrauben *vt* to unscrew.

ab|schrecken *vt* - **1.** [abhalten] to deter - **2.** [mit kaltem Wasser - Eier] to put into cold water.

Abschreckung (*pl* **-en**) *die* deterrent.

ab|schreiben *vt (unreg)* - **1.** [kopieren] to copy - **2.** WIRTSCH [aufgeben] to write off.

Ab|schrift *die* copy.

Abschuss (*pl* **-schüsse**) *der* - **1.** [von Flugzeug] shooting down - **2.** [von Gewehr] firing; [von Rakete] launching - **3.** [von Wild] shooting.

abschüssig *adj* sloping.

ab|schütteln *vt eigtl* & *fig* to shake off.

ab|schwächen *vt* to lessen. ◆ **sich abschwächen** *ref* to grow weaker.

ab|schweifen (*perf* **ist abgeschweift**) *vi* [Gedanken, Blick] to wander; **vom Thema abschweifen** to digress.

ab|schwellen (*perf* **ist abgeschwollen**) *vi (unreg)* - **1.** [Schwellung] to go down - **2.** [Geräusch] to fade (away).

absehbar *adj* foreseeable; **in absehbarer Zeit** in the foreseeable future.

ab|sehen *(unreg)* ◇ *vt* [Folgen] to foresee; **das Ergebnis ist abzusehen** it's possible to tell what the result will be. ◇ *vi* - **1.** [verzichten]: **von etw absehen** to refrain from sthg - **2.** [ausnehmen]: **sieht man davon ab, dass er taub ist, ist er kerngesund** if you ignore the fact that he's deaf, he's perfectly healthy - **3.** [wollen]: **es auf etw** *(A)* **abgesehen haben** to be after sthg; **es darauf abgesehen haben, alle zu verärgern** to be intent on annoying everyone - **4.** [ärgern]: **es auf jn abgesehen haben** to have it in for sb.

ab|seifen *vt* [Kind] to soap down.

ab|seilen *vt* to lower down on a rope. ◆ **sich abseilen** *ref* - **1.** [mit einem Seil] to abseil - **2.** *fam* [verschwinden] to leg it.

ab sein (*perf* **ist ab gewesen**) *vi (unreg)* - **1.** [entfernt]: **dieses Dorf ist weit von allem ab** this village is far away from everything - **2.** [abgetrennt] to have come off.

abseits ◇ *präp*: **abseits eines Ortes** ODER **von einem Ort** away from a place. ◇ *adv* out of the way; **sich abseits halten** to keep oneself to oneself.

Abseits *das* - **1.** SPORT offside - **2.** [Isolation]: **ins Abseits geraten** to be left out in the cold.

ab|senden *vt* to send off.

Ab|sender *der* - **1.** [Person] sender - **2.** [Adresse] *sender's name and address.*

Absenderin (*pl* **-nen**) *die* sender.

ab|setzen *vt* - **1.** [herunternehmen - Hut, Brille] to take off - **2.** [hinstellen, hinlegen] to put down - **3.** [aussteigen lassen] to drop off - **4.** [Betrag]: **etw von der Steuer absetzen (können)** to (be able to) deduct sthg from one's tax - **5.** [Ware] to sell - **6.** [entmachten - König] to depose - **7.** [Aufführung] to drop, to take off - **8.** [Medikament] to come off - **9.** [Kleidung] to trim. ◆ **sich absetzen** *ref* - **1.** [fliehen] to take off - **2.** [sich ablagern] to be deposited - **3.** [sich entfernen]: **sich von etw absetzen** to pull away from sthg - **4.** [sich abheben]: **sich gegen etw absetzen** to stand out against sthg.

ab|sichern *vt* to make safe. ◆ **sich absichern** *ref* to cover o.s.; **sich gegen etw absichern** to protect o.s. against sthg.

Ab|sicht *die* intention; **es war nicht meine Absicht, dir zu schaden** I didn't mean to harm you.

absichtlich ◇ *adj* deliberate, intentional. ◇ *adv* deliberately, intentionally.

absolut ◇ *adj* absolute. ◇ *adv* absolutely; **das gefällt mir absolut nicht** I don't like that at all.

absolvieren [apzɔl'viːrən] *vt* [Kurs] to complete; [Prüfung] to pass.

ab|sondern *vt* - **1.** [Sekret] to secrete - **2.** [isolieren] to isolate. ◆ **sich absondern** *ref* to isolate o.s.

ab|spalten *vt* CHEM to separate. ◆ **sich abspalten** *ref*: **sich (von etw) abspalten** to break away (from sthg).

ab|speisen *vt*: **jn mit etw abspeisen** to fob sb off with sthg.

ab|sperren *vt* - **1.** [abriegeln] to seal off - **2.** [verschließen] to lock.

Ab|sperrung *die* - **1.** [Schranke, Sperre] barrier - **2.** [Absperren] sealing off.

ab|spielen *vt* to play. ◆ **sich abspielen** *ref* to take place.

Ab|sprache *die* arrangement; **nach vorheriger Absprache** after prior consultation.

ab|sprechen *vt (unreg)* - **1.** [vereinbaren] to agree on - **2.** [verweigern, aberkennen]: **jm etw absprechen** [Recht] to deny sb sthg; [Fähigkeit] to deny that sb has sthg. ◆ **sich absprechen** *ref*: **wir hatten keine Zeit, uns abzusprechen** we had no time to agree on what to say/do.

ab|springen (*perf* **ist abgesprungen**) *vi (unreg)* - **1.** SPORT to jump - **2.** [sich lösen] to come off - **3.** *fam* [zurücktreten]: **von etw abspringen** to back out of sthg.

ạb|spülen ◇ *vt* - **1.** [Geschirr] to wash - **2.** [Schmutz] to wash off. ◇ *vi* to wash up *UK*, to wash the dishes *US*.

ạb|stammen *vi*: **von jm/etw abstammen** to be descended from sb/sthg.

Ạbstammung *die* descent.

Ạb|stand *der* [räumlich] distance; [zeitlich] interval; **50 Meter Abstand** a distance of 50 metres; **von jm/etw Abstand halten** to keep one's distance from sb/sthg.

ạb|statten *vt*: **jm einen Besuch abstatten** to pay sb a visit.

ạb|stauben *vt* - **1.** [putzen] to dust - **2.** *fam* [mitnehmen]: **etw bei jm abstauben** to get sthg off sb.

Ạbstecher (*pl* -) *der* detour.

ạb|stehen (*perf* **hat/ist ạbgestanden**) *vi (unreg)*: **von etw abstehen** to stick out from sthg.

ạbstehend *adj*: **er hat abstehende Ohren** his ears stick out.

ạb|steigen (*perf* **ist ạbgestiegen**) *vi (unreg)* - **1.** [hinunterklettern] to get off - **2.** SPORT to be relegated - **3.** [übernachten] to stay.

ạb|stellen *vt* - **1.** [Gerät, Strom, Wasser] to turn off - **2.** [Last] to put down; [Möbel] to store, to put; [Auto, Fahrrad] to park - **3.** [Missstand] to put an end to - **4.** [freistellen]: **jn zu etw abstellen** to assign sb to sthg.

Ạbstell|raum *der* storage room.

ạb|stempeln *vt* - **1.** [stempeln - Dokument] to stamp; [- Briefmarke] to postmark - **2.** *abw* [anprangern]: **jn zu** ODER **als etw abstempeln** to label sb sthg.

ạb|sterben (*perf* **ist ạbgestorben**) *vi (unreg)* to die off.

Ạbstieg (*pl* **-e**) *der* - **1.** [vom Berg] descent - **2.** [sozial, finanziell] decline - **3.** SPORT relegation.

ạb|stimmen ◇ *vi* [wählen] to vote. ◇ *vt* - **1.** [einstellen]: **etw auf jn/etw abstimmen** to adapt sthg to sb/sthg; [Farben] to match sthg to sb/sthg - **2.** [absprechen]: **etw mit jm abstimmen** to agree on sthg with sb. ◆ **sich abstimmen** *ref*: **sich mit jm (über etw** *(A)***) abstimmen** to agree (on sthg) with sb.

Ạb|stimmung *die* - **1.** [Wahl] vote - **2.** [Koordinierung] coordination - **3.** [Absprache] agreement.

ạb|stoßen *vt (unreg)* - **1.** [wegdrücken] to push off - **2.** [verkaufen] to sell off - **3.** [anekeln] to repel - **4.** [abnützen - Farbe] to knock off.

ạbstoßend ◇ *adj* repulsive. ◇ *adv* repulsively.

abstrạkt ◇ *adj* abstract. ◇ *adv* in the abstract.

ạb|streiten *vt (unreg)* to deny.

Ạb|strich *der* - **1.** [Einschränkungen] reservation; **Abstriche machen** to make concessions - **2.** MED swab; [von Gebärmutter] smear.

ạb|stufen *vt* - **1.** [Löhne, Preise, Farben] t[o] grade - **2.** [Haare] to layer.

ạb|stumpfen (*perf* **hat/ist ạbgestumpf[t]**) ◇ *vt (hat)* - **1.** [Subj: Lärm, Monotonie] to du[ll] the senses of - **2.** [Subj: Leid, Schmerz] t[o] harden. ◇ *vi (ist)*: **gegen etw abstumpfen** t[o] become inured to sthg.

Ạb|sturz *der* crash.

ạb|stürzen (*perf* **ist ạbgestürzt**) *vi* [Flugzeug, EDV] to crash; [Bergsteiger] to fall.

ạb|suchen *vt*: **etw (nach jm/etw) absuchen** t[o] search sthg (for sb/sthg).

absụrd *adj* absurd.

Ạbt (*pl* **Ạ̈bte**) *der* abbot.

ạb|tasten *vt* to feel.

ạb|tauen (*perf* **hat/ist ạbgetaut**) ◇ *vt (ha[t])* to defrost. ◇ *vi (ist)* [Eis] to thaw; [Kühlschrank] to defrost.

Abtei (*pl* **-en**) *die* abbey.

Ab|teil (*pl* **-e**) *das* compartment.

ạb|teilen *vt* to divide off.

Abteilung[1] (*pl* **-en**) *die* - **1.** [einer Firma, i[m] Kaufhaus] department - **2.** MIL unit.

Ạb|teilung[2] *die* [Trennung] dividing off.

Äbtịssin (*pl* **-nen**) *die* abbess.

ạb|tragen *vt (unreg)* - **1.** [Erde, Steine - Sub[j]: Wind, Wasser] to erode; [Subj: Person] to re[-]move *(layer by layer)* - **2.** [Kleidung] to wear ou[t] - **3.** [Schulden] to pay off.

ạb|treiben (*perf* **hat/ist ạbgetrieben**) *(unreg)* ◇ *vt (hat)* [Kind]: **sie will das Kind abtreibe[n]** she wants to have an abortion. ◇ *vi* - **1.** *(ha[t])* MED [Abort vornehmen] to carry out an abor[-]tion; [Abort vornehmen lassen] to have an abor[-]tion - **2.** *(ist)* [Boot] to be driven off course.

Ạbtreibung (*pl* **-en**) *die* abortion.

ạb|trennen *vt* - **1.** [abschneiden - Coupon, Bla[tt]] to detach; [- Ärmel, Saum] to cut off - **2.** [abte[i]len] to divide off.

ạb|treten (*perf* **hat/ist ạbgetreten**) *(unreg)* ◇ *vt (hat)* - **1.** [Absätze] to wear dow[n] - **2.** [Rechte] to relinquish; **etw an jn abtreten** [,] **jm etw abtreten** to let sb have sthg. ◇ *vi (is[t])* [fortgehen] to make one's exit.

ạb|trocknen *vt* to dry; **sich die Hände ab[-]trocknen** to dry one's hands. ◆ **sich ab[-]trocknen** *ref* to dry o.s.

ạb|verlangen *vt*: **jm etw abverlangen** to de[-]mand sthg from sb.

ạb|wägen *vt* to weigh up; **zwei Dinge gegen[-]einander abwägen** to weigh up two thing[s] against each other.

ạb|wählen *vt* - **1.** [Politiker] to vote out (of o[f-]fice) - **2.** [Schulfach] to drop.

ạb|wälzen *vt*: **etw auf jn abwälzen** to shi[ft] sthg onto sb.

ạb|wandeln *vt* to vary.

ab|wandern (*perf* **ist abgewandert**) *vi* - **1.** [fortgehen] to migrate - **2.** [Kapital] to be removed.

Ab|wandlung *die* adaptation.

ab|warten <> *vt* to wait for; **ich kann es kaum abwarten, in Urlaub zu fahren** I can hardly wait to go on holiday. <> *vi* to wait and see.

abwärts *adv* downwards; **alle, vom Assistenten abwärts** everyone from the assistant down.

Abwasch *der (ohne pl)* washing-up *UK*, dishes *US Pl*.

ab|waschen *(unreg)* <> *vt* - **1.** [Geschirr] to wash - **2.** [Schmutz] to wash off. <> *vi* to wash up *UK*, to wash the dishes *US*.

Ab|wasser *das* [von Haushalt] sewage *(U)*; [von Industrie] effluent *(U)*.

ab|wechseln ['apvɛksln̩] ◆ **sich abwechseln** *ref* to alternate; **sich mit jm abwechseln** to take turns with sb.

abwechselnd ['apvɛkslnt] *adv* alternately.

Abwechselung ['apvɛksəlʊŋ], **Abwechslung** ['apvɛkslʊŋ] (*pl* **-en**) *die* change.

abwegig *adj* bizarre.

Abwehr *die* - **1.** [Widerstand] resistance - **2.** SPORT & MIL defence.

ab|wehren <> *vt* - **1.** [Schlag, Angriff] to ward off - **2.** [Störung] to deter. <> *vi* to refuse.

ab|weichen (*perf* **ist abgewichen**) *vi (unreg)*: **von etw abweichen** to deviate from sthg; **seine Ansichten weichen von meinen ab** his opinions differ from mine.

abweichend *adj* different.

ab|weisen *vt (unreg)* - **1.** [ablehnen] to reject - **2.** [Person] to turn away.

abweisend <> *adj* unfriendly. <> *adv* dismissively.

ab|wenden *vt (unreg)* - **1.** [wegdrehen]: **den Kopf abwenden** to turn away; **den Blick abwenden** to look away - **2.** [Unglück] to avert. ◆ **sich abwenden** *ref* to turn away; **sich von jm/etw abwenden** to turn one's back on sb/sthg.

ab|werfen *vt (unreg)* - **1.** [von Flugzeug] to drop - **2.** [Geld]: **Gewinn abwerfen** to yield a profit.

ab|werten *vt* to devalue.

ab|wertend *adj* pejorative.

abwesend <> *adj* - **1.** [nicht anwesend] absent - **2.** [unkonzentriert] absent, absent-minded. <> *adv* absently.

Abwesenheit *die* absence; **in js Abwesenheit** in sb's absence; **durch Abwesenheit glänzen** *iron* to be conspicuous by one's absence.

ab|wickeln *vt* - **1.** [Schnur] to unwind - **2.** [Geschäft] to complete - **3.** [Institution] to wind up, to close down.

Abwicklung (*pl* **-en**) *die* - **1.** [Abschluss] completion - **2.** [Auflösung] winding up, closing down.

ab|wiegen *vt (unreg)* to weigh out.

ab|wimmeln *vt fam* to get rid of.

ab|wischen *vt* - **1.** [Fläche] to wipe - **2.** [Dreck] to wipe off.

ab|würgen *vt fam* - **1.** [Motor] to stall - **2.** [beenden, unterdrücken] to stifle.

ab|zahlen *vt* to pay off.

ab|zählen <> *vt* to count. <> *vi* to use a counting-out rhyme.

Ab|zeichen *das* badge.

ab|zeichnen *vt* to draw. ◆ **sich abzeichnen** *ref* - **1.** [sich ankündigen] to emerge - **2.** [sich zeigen] to stand out.

ab|ziehen (*perf* **ist/hat abgezogen**) *(unreg)* <> *vt (hat)* - **1.** [Schürze, Mütze] to take off; [Schlüssel] to take out - **2.** [subtrahieren - Nummer] to subtract; [- Betrag] to deduct - **3.** [Bett] to strip - **4.** [Soldaten] to withdraw - **5.** [veranstalten]: **eine Schau** ODER **Show abziehen** *salopp* to make a fuss - **6.** [Haut]: **einem Kaninchen die Haut abziehen** to skin a rabbit. <> *vi (ist)* - **1.** [Gas] to clear - **2.** *fam* [Person] to clear off.

Ab|zug *der* - **1.** [von Kamin] flue; [Belüftung] vent - **2.** [Foto] print; [Druck] proof - **3.** [Subtraktion] deduction; **nach Abzug der Unkosten** after costs - **4.** [Fortgehen] withdrawal - **5.** [am Gewehr] trigger.

abzüglich *präp*: **abzüglich einer Sache** *(G)* less sthg.

ab|zweigen (*perf* **hat/ist abgezweigt**) <> *vi (ist)* to branch off. <> *vt (hat)* to put aside.

Abzweigung (*pl* **-en**) *die* turning.

Account (*pl* **-s**) *der* EDV account.

ach *interj* oh!

Achse ['aksə] (*pl* **-n**) *die* - **1.** [Linie & MATH] axis; **auf Achse sein** *fig* to be on the move - **2.** [von Auto] axle.

Achsel ['aksl] (*pl* **-n**) *die* shoulder; **mit den Achseln zucken** to shrug one's shoulders.

achselzuckend ['aksltsʊkn̩t] *adv* with a shrug.

acht *num* eight; *siehe auch* **sechs**.

Acht (*pl* **-en**) *die* eight; *siehe auch* **Sechs**.

Achte (*pl* **-n**) *der, die, das* eighth; *siehe auch* **Sechste**.

achte, r, s *adj* eighth; *siehe auch* **sechste**.

Achteck (*pl* **-e**) *das* octagon.

achtel *adj (unver)* eighth; *siehe auch* **sechstel**.

Achtel (*pl* -) *das* - **1.** [der achte Teil] eighth - **2.** MUS quaver *UK*, eighth note *US*; *siehe auch* **Sechstel**.

achten <> *vt* to respect. <> *vi*: **auf etw achten** to pay attention to sthg; **auf jn achten** to look after sb.

Achter|bahn *die* roller coaster.

achtfach <> *adj* eightfold. <> *adv* eight times.

Acht geben *vi* ▷ **Acht**.

achthundert *num* eight hundred.

achtlos <> *adj* careless. <> *adv* carelessly.

achtmal *adv* eight times.

achttausend *num* eight thousand.

Achtung *die* - **1.** [Respekt] respect - **2.** [Vorsicht]: **Achtung!** look out!; [formell] attention, please!; **Achtung, Stufe!** mind the step!; **Achtung, fertig, los!** SPORT on your marks, get set, go!

achtzehn *num* eighteen; *siehe auch* **sechs**.

Achtzehn (*pl* **-en**) *die* eighteen; *siehe auch* **Sechs**.

achtzig *num* eighty; **auf achtzig sein** *fam* to be livid; **jn auf achtzig bringen** *fam* to make sb livid; *siehe auch* **sechs**.

Achtzig *die* eighty; *siehe auch* **Sechs**.

Achtziger|jahre, achtziger Jahre *Pl*: **die Achtzigerjahre** the eighties.

ächzen *vi* to groan.

Acker (*pl* **Äcker**) *der* field.

Ackerbau *der* agriculture; **Ackerbau treiben** to farm.

ADAC [a:de:ǎa:'tse:] (*abk für* **Allgemeiner Deutscher Automobilklub**) *der* ≃ AA *UK*, ≃ AAA *US*.

addieren *vt* MATH to add up.

Adel *der* nobility.

adelig = **adlig**.

Ader (*pl* **-n**) *die* vein.

Adjektiv (*pl* **-e**) *das* adjective.

adjektivisch ['atjɛkti:vɪʃ] <> *adj* adjectival. <> *adv* GRAMM adjectivally.

Adler (*pl* **-**) *der* eagle.

adlig, adelig *adj* noble.

Admiral (*pl* **-e** ODER **Admiräle**) *der* MIL admiral.

adoptieren *vt* to adopt.

Adoption (*pl* **-en**) *die* adoption.

Adoptiveltern *Pl* adoptive parents.

Adoptiv|kind *das* adopted child.

Adressbuch (*pl* **-bücher**) *das* - **1.** [privat] address book - **2.** [von Stadt, Gemeinde] directory.

Adresse (*pl* **-n**) *die* address.

adressieren *vt* to address; **etw an jn adressieren** to address sthg to sb.

Adria *die*: **die Adria** the Adriatic.

Advent [at'vɛnt] *der* Advent; **erster/zweiter Advent** first/second Sunday in Advent.

Advents|kranz *der* Advent wreath.

Adverb [at'vɛrp] (*pl* **-ien**) *das* adverb.

adverbial [atvɛr'bi̯a:l] <> *adj* adverbial. <> *adv* adverbially.

Affäre (*pl* **-n**) *die* - **1.** [Skandal, Liebschaft] affair; **sich aus der Affäre ziehen** to get out of it - **2.** [Angelegenheit] matter.

Affe (*pl* **-n**) *der* - **1.** [Tier - klein] monkey; [- groß] ape - **2.** *salopp abw* [blöder Kerl] jerk, twit *UK*.

affektiert *abw* <> *adj* affected. <> *adv* affectedly.

affig *fam abw* <> *adj* stuck-up. <> *adv* in a stuck-up way.

Afrika *nt* Africa.

Afrikaner, in (*mpl* **-**, *fpl* **-nen**) *der, die* African.

afrikanisch *adj* African.

After (*pl* **-**) *der* anus.

AG [a:'ge:] (*pl* **-s**) (*abk für* **Aktiengesellschaft**) *die* ≃ plc *UK*, ≃ corp. *US*

Ägäis *die*: **die Ägäis** the Aegean.

Agent, in (*mpl* **-en**, *fpl* **-nen**) *der, die* - **1.** [Spion] secret agent - **2.** [Vermittler] agent.

Agentur (*pl* **-en**) *die* agency.

Aggression (*pl* **-en**) *die* aggression.

aggressiv <> *adj* aggressive. <> *adv* aggressively.

Agrar|politik *die* agricultural policy.

Ägypten [ɛ'gyptn̩] *nt* Egypt.

Ägypter, in (*mpl* **-**, *fpl* **-nen**) *der, die* Egyptian.

ägyptisch *adj* Egyptian.

ah *interj*: **ah!** [Ausdruck der Verwunderung] oh!; [Ausdruck plötzlichen Verstehens] ah!

aha *interj* aha!

Aha-|Erlebnis *das* revelation.

ähneln *vi*: **jm/einer Sache ähneln** to resemble sb/sthg.

ahnen *vt* - **1.** [im Voraus fühlen] to have a premonition of - **2.** [vermuten] to suspect.

ähnlich <> *adj* similar; **jm/etw ähnlich sein** to be similar to ODER like sb/sthg. <> *adv* similarly; **jm/etw ähnlich sehen** to look like sb/sthg; **das sieht dir/ihm ähnlich!** that's just like you/him!

Ähnlichkeit (*pl* **-en**) *die* similarity.

Ahnung (*pl* **-en**) *die* - **1.** [Vorgefühl] premonition; **ich habe so eine Ahnung, als ob** I have the feeling that - **2.** [Vorstellung, Vermutung] idea; **keine Ahnung!** I've no idea!; **keine/nicht die geringste Ahnung haben** to have no/not the faintest idea.

ahnungslos <> *adj* unsuspecting. <> *adv* unsuspectingly.

Ahnungslosigkeit *die* lack of suspicion.

ahoi *interj* SCHIFF ahoy!

Ahorn (*pl* **-e**) *der* maple.

Ähre (*pl* **-n**) *die* ear *(of corn)*.

Aids ['eidz] (*abk für* **Acquired Immune Deficiency Syndrome**) *nt* Aids.

Aids|kranke *der, die* Aids sufferer.

Aidstest (*pl* **-s**) *der* Aids test.

Akademie (*pl* **-n**) *die* academy.

Akademiker, in (*mpl* -, *fpl* **-nen**) *der, die* university graduate.

akademisch *adj* academic.

Akazie (*pl* **-n**) *die* acacia.

Akkord (*pl* **-e**) *der* chord. ◆ **im Akkord** *adv* WIRTSCH: **im Akkord arbeiten** to do piecework.

Akkordeon (*pl* **-s**) *das* accordion.

Akku (*pl* **-s**) *der* storage battery; [für Radio, Walkman] rechargeable battery.

Akkumulator (*pl* **-en**) *der* - **1.** ELEKTR storage battery - **2.** EDV accumulator.

Akkusativ (*pl* **-e**) *der* accusative.

Akne *die* acne.

Akrobat, in (*mpl* **-en**, *fpl* **-nen**) *der, die* acrobat.

akrobatisch ◇ *adj* acrobatic. ◇ *adv* acrobatically.

Akt (*pl* **-e**) *der* - **1.** [Handlung, Aufzug] act - **2.** [Bildnis] nude - **3.** [Zeremonie] ceremony.

Akte (*pl* **-n**) *die* file; **etw zu den Akten legen** to shelve sthg.

aktenkundig *adj*: **ein aktenkundiger Vorgang** an occurrence which is on record.

Akten|tasche *die* briefcase.

Aktie ['aktsiə] (*pl* **-n**) *die* share; **die Aktien steigen/fallen** share prices are rising/falling.

Aktien|gesellschaft *die* ≃ public limited company *UK*, ≃ corporation *US*.

Aktien|kurs *der* share price.

Aktion (*pl* **-en**) *die* - **1.** [Tätigkeit] action; **in Aktion sein/treten** to be in/go into action - **2.** [Verkauf] sale; [Werbung] promotion.

Aktionär, in [aktsio'nɛːɐ̯, rɪn] (*mpl* **-e**, *fpl* **-nen**) *der, die* shareholder.

aktiv ◇ *adj* active. ◇ *adv* actively.

Aktiv *das* GRAMM active.

aktivieren [akti'viːrən] *vt* - **1.** [System, Alarm] to activate - **2.** [Person] to mobilize.

Aktivität [aktivi'tɛːt] (*pl* **-en**) *die* activity.

Aktualität *die* relevance; **an Aktualität gewinnen** to become topical.

aktuell *adj* - **1.** [Theaterstück, Buch] topical; [Thema, Problem] current - **2.** [modisch] fashionable.

Akupunktur (*pl* **-en**) *die* acupuncture.

Akustik *(ohne pl) die* - **1.** PHYS acoustics *(U)* - **2.** [Schallverhältnisse] acoustics *Pl.*

akut ◇ *adj* - **1.** [vordringlich] urgent - **2.** MED acute. ◇ *adv* - **1.** [vordringlich] urgently - **2.** MED acutely.

AKW [aːkaː'veː] (*pl* **-s**) (*abk für* **Atomkraftwerk**) *das nuclear power station.*

Akzent (*pl* **-e**) *der* - **1.** GRAMM [Betonung] stress - **2.** [Tonfall] accent; **Akzente setzen** to set a new trend.

akzeptieren *vt* to accept.

Alarm (*pl* **-e**) *der* alarm; **Alarm schlagen** to raise the alarm; **es war blinder Alarm** it was a false alarm.

Alarm|anlage *die* [von Gebäude] burglar alarm; [von Auto] car alarm.

alarmieren *vt* - **1.** [aufschrecken] to alarm - **2.** [rufen] to alert.

Albaner, in (*mpl* -, *fpl* **-nen**) *der, die* Albanian.

Albanien *nt* Albania.

albanisch *adj* Albanian.

albern ◇ *adj* silly. ◇ *adv* in a silly way. ◇ *vi* to fool around.

Albino (*pl* **-s**) *der* albino.

Alb|traum (*pl* **-träume**) *der* nightmare.

Album (*pl* **Alben**) *das* album.

Alge (*pl* **-n**) *die* - **1.** [Seetang] piece of seaweed; **Algen** seaweed *(U)* - **2.** [Algenpest verursachend]: **Algen** algae.

Algebra *die* algebra.

Algerien *nt* Algeria.

Algerier, in [al'geːriɐ, rɪn] (*mpl* -, *fpl* **-nen**) *der, die* Algerian.

algerisch *adj* Algerian.

alias *adv* alias.

Alibi (*pl* **-s**) *das* - **1.** RECHT alibi - **2.** [Ausrede] excuse.

Alimente *Pl* maintenance *(U) UK*, child support *(U) US*.

alkalisch *adj* alkaline.

Alkohol (*pl* **-e** ODER **Alkoholika**) *der* - **1.** *(pl Alkohole)* CHEM alcohol - **2.** *(pl Alkoholika)* [Getränk] alcohol; **unter Alkohol stehen** *amt* to be under the influence (of alcohol).

alkoholabhängig *adj*: **alkoholabhängig sein** to be an alcoholic.

alkoholfrei *adj* alcohol-free.

Alkoholgehalt (*pl* **-e**) *der* alcohol content.

Alkoholiker, in (*mpl* -, *fpl* **-nen**) *der, die* alcoholic.

alkoholisch ◇ *adj* alcoholic. ◇ *adv* alcoholically.

Alkoholismus *der* alcoholism.

all *det* all (of); **all das Warten** all this waiting.

All *das*: **das All** space.

alle, s ◇ *det* - **1.** [sämtliche] all; **alle Kleider** all the clothes; **alle beide** both (of them); **alle fünf überlebten** all five survived; **wir alle** all of us - **2.** [verstärkend]: **in aller Ruhe** in peace and quiet; **in aller Öffentlichkeit** quite openly; **alle Welt** everyone - **3.** [allerlei]: **Getränke aller Art** all kinds of drinks; **alles Mögliche** all kinds of things - **4.** [im Abstand von] every; **alle 50 Meter/zwei Wochen** every 50 metres/two weeks. ◇ *pron* - **1.** [auf Personen bezogen] all, everyone; **alle sind gekommen** everyone came, they all came; **alles einsteigen!** all aboard! - **2.** [auf Sachen bezogen] all, everything; **das ist alles** that's all ODER everything. ◇ *adj fam*: **die Milch ist alle** we've run out of milk. ◆ **trotz allem** *adv* in spite of everything. ◆ **vor allem** *adv* above all.

Allee (*pl* **-n**) *die* [Straße] avenue.

allein ◇ *adj* - **1.** [für sich] alone; **heute Abend war ich allein zuhause** I was on my own at home this evening - **2.** [einsam] lonely. ◇ *adv* - **1.** [für sich] alone - **2.** [selbstständig] on one's own, by oneself - **3.** [einsam] alone; **allein zurückbleiben** to stay behind by oneself; **allein herumstehen** to stand around on one's own; **allein dastehen** to be all alone in the world - **4.** [nur] only; **allein das Handgepäck wiegt 10 kg** the hand luggage alone weighs 10 kg. ◇ *konj geh* however. ◆ **ganz allein** ◇ *adj* - **1.** [für sich] all alone - **2.** [einsam] all on one's own, all by oneself. ◇ *adv* - **1.** [für sich, einsam] all alone - **2.** [selbstständig] all on one's own, all by oneself. ◆ **von allein** *adv* by oneself/itself.

allein erziehend *adj*: **allein erziehende Mutter** single mother.

Allein|gang *der* single-handed effort. ◆ **im Alleingang** *adv* single-handedly.

alleinig *adj* sole.

allein stehend *adj* - **1.** [ledig] single - **2.** [allein wohnend]: **eine allein stehende Person** a person who lives alone.

Alleinstehende (*pl* **-n**) *der, die* - **1.** [ledig] single person - **2.** [allein wohnend] person who lives alone.

allemal *adv fam*: **dich schlage ich allemal** I could beat you no sweat; ▷ **Mal**.

allenfalls *adv* at most.

allerbeste, **r**, **s** *adj* very best.

allerdings *adv* - **1.** [als Antwort] certainly - **2.** [einschränkend] though.

allererste, **r**, **s** *adj* very first.

Allergie (*pl* **-n**) *die* allergy.

allergisch ◇ *adj* allergic; **gegen etw allergisch sein** MED to be allergic to sthg; [etw nicht ausstehen können] not to be able to stand sthg. ◇ *adv* - **1.** MED allergically; **auf etw allergisch reagieren** to have an allergic reaction to sthg - **2.** [ablehnend]: **auf Lügen reagiere ich wirklich allergisch** I really can't stand people lying.

allerhand ◇ *adj (unver)* all sorts of; **das ist ja allerhand!** [erbost] that really is the limit!; [anerkennend] that's not bad at all! ◇ *pron* all sorts of things.

Allerheiligen *nt* All Saints' Day.

allerhöchstens ['ale'hø:kstn̩s] *adv* at the very most.

allerlei *det* all sorts of.

allerletzte, **r**, **s** *adj* - **1.** [letzte] very last - **2.** [schlecht] most awful.

Allerletzte *das*: **das ist ja das Allerletzte!** that's the absolute limit!

Allerseelen *(ohne Artikel)* All Souls' Day.

allerseits *adv*: **guten Tag/Abend allerseit[s]** good afternoon/evening everyone.

alles ▷ **alle**.

allesamt *adv* all together.

Alles|kleber *der* all-purpose glue.

Allgäu *das*: **das Allgäu** the Allgäu.

allgemein ◇ *adj* - **1.** [gen] general - **2.** [Interesse, Sprachgebrauch] common; [Wehrpflicht, Wahlrecht] universal. ◇ *adv* generally. ◆ **im Allgemeinen** *adv* in general.

Allgemeinbildung *die* general education.

allgemein gültig ◇ *adj* universal. ◇ *ad[v]* universally.

Allgemeinheit (*pl* **-en**) *die* - **1.** [Öffentlichkeit] general public - **2.** [Undifferenziertheit] generality. ◆ **Allgemeinheiten** *Pl* [Floskel] generalities.

Allheil|mittel *das* cure-all, panacea.

Alligator (*pl* **-gatoren**) *der* alligator.

alliiert *adj* allied.

Alliierte *Pl* allies; **die Alliierten** HIST the Allies.

alljährlich ◇ *adj* annual. ◇ *adv* every year.

allmächtig *adj* almighty.

allmählich ◇ *adj* gradual. ◇ *adv* gradually.

allseits *adv* everywhere.

Alltag *der* everyday life.

alltäglich ◇ *adj* - **1.** [täglich] daily - **2.** [üblich] everyday. ◇ *adv* every day.

Alltagstrott *der* daily grind.

allwissend *adj* all-knowing, omniscient.

allzu *adv* far too. ◆ **allzu sehr** *adv* far too much. ◆ **allzu viel** *adv* far too much.

Alm (*pl* **-en**) *die* mountain pasture.

Almosen (*pl* **-**) *das* alms *Pl*.

Aloe ['ɑ:loe] (*pl* **-n**) *die* aloe.

Alpen *Pl*: **die Alpen** the Alps.

Alpen|veilchen *das* cyclamen.

Alpen|verein *der organization which promotes study of the Alps and organizes mountain hikes etc.*

Alpen|vorland *das (ohne pl)* foothills *Pl* o[f] the Alps.

Alpha (*pl* **-s**) *das* alpha.

Alphabet [alfa'be:t] (*pl* **-e**) *das* alphabet.

alphabetisch ◇ *adj* alphabetical. ◇ *ad[v]* alphabetically.

alpin *adj* alpine.

Alptraum *der* = **Albtraum**.

als *konj* - **1.** [zur Kennzeichnung eines Zeitpunkt[s]] when; **als es dunkel wurde** when it got dar[k]; **erst als** only when - **2.** [zur Kennzeichnung eine[r] Zeitspanne] as - **3.** [bei Vergleich]: **sie ist besse[r] als ihr Bruder** she is better than her brothe[r]; **der Wein ist besser, als ich dachte** the wine [is] better than I thought it would be; **mehr a[ls]** more than - **4.** [bei Vergleich vor Konjunktiv] as i[f] as though; **es sieht so aus, als würde es bald regnen** it looks like it's going to rain soon; **als ob** as if, as though - **5.** [zur Kennzeichnung einer Eigenschaft] as; **ich verstehe es als Kompliment** I take it as a compliment; **als Kind** as a child.

ạlso ◇ *interj* well; **also doch!** so I was right (after all)!; **also gut** ODER **schön!** oh, all right then!; **na also!** what did I tell you!, there you are!; **also dann!** *fam* right then!; **also bitte!** [Unmut ausdrückend] for heaven's sake!; [widerwillig nachgebend] if you must. ◇ *adv* - **1.** [das heißt] that is - **2.** [demnach] so; **da lag also der Fehler!** so that's where the mistake was - **3.** [endlich] so; **die Sache ist also erledigt** so the matter is settled.

ạlt (*kompar* **ạlter**, *superl* **ạlteste**) *adj* - **1.** [gen] old; **12 Jahre alt** 12 years old; **wie alt bist du?** how old are you?; **zwei Jahre älter** two years older; **dieser alte Schmarotzer!** *abw* the old sponger! - **2.** [antik] antique - **3.** [historisch] ancient; **alte Sprachen** classics, classical languages; **das alte Rom** ancient Rome; **alt aussehen** *salopp* to be up shit creek.

Ạlt (*pl* **-e** ODER **-**) ◇ *der (pl Alte)* MUS alto. ◇ *das (pl Alt)* [Bier] *type of dark German beer.*

Altar (*pl* **Altäre**) *der* altar.

Ạltbau (*pl* **-ten**) *der* old building.

ạltbekannt *adj* [Methode] well-known.

ạltbewährt *adj* proven.

Ạlt|bier *das type of dark German beer.*

Ạlte (*pl* **-n**) ◇ *der, die* - **1.** [alter Mensch] old man (old woman *die*) - **2.** *salopp abw* [Elternteil, Gatte] old man (old girl *die*) - **3.** *salopp abw* [Vorgesetzter] boss, guvnor *UK* - **4.** [Gleiche]: **ganz der/die Alte** exactly the same. ◇ *das (ohne pl)*: **alles beim Alten lassen** to leave everything just as it is.

alteingesessen *adj* long-established.

Ạlten|heim = Altersheim.

Ạltentages|stätte *die* old people's day centre.

Ạlter (*pl* -) *das* - **1.** [Lebensalter] age; **im Alter von 12 Jahren** at the age of 12; **eine Frau mittleren Alters** a middle-aged woman; **bis ins hohe Alter war er gesund** he remained healthy until a ripe old age - **2.** [Altsein] old age.

ạlter *adj* - **1.** ▷ **alt** - **2.** [ziemlich alt] elderly.

Ạltere (*pl* **-n**) *der*: **der Ältere** the Elder.

ạltern (*perf* **hat/ist geạltert**) *vi* - **1.** [Person] to age - **2.** [Cognac, Käse] to mature.

alternativ ◇ *adj* alternative. ◇ *adv* - **1.** [wahlweise] alternatively - **2.** [unkonventionell]: **alternativ leben** to have an alternative lifestyle.

Alternative [alterna'tiːvə] (*pl* **-n**) *die* alternative.

ạltersbedingt *adj* age-related.

Ạlters|genosse *der* contemporary.

Ạlters|genossin *die* contemporary.

Ạlters|grenze *die* - **1.** [Höchstalter, Mindestalter] age limit - **2.** [Rentenalter] retirement age.

Ạlters|gruppe *die* age group.

Ạlters|heim, Ạltenheim *das* old people's home.

ạltersschwach *adj* - **1.** [Person] old and infirm - **2.** [Gegenstände] decrepit.

Ạlters|versorgung *die* [privat] provision for one's old age; [vom Staat] provision for the elderly.

Ạltertum (*pl* **-tümer**) *das* [Antike] antiquity. ◆ **Altertümer** *Pl* [antike Objekte] antiquities.

Ạlteste (*pl* **-n**) *der, die* - **1.** [ältestes Kind] eldest - **2.** [älteste Person] eldest person.

althergebracht *adj* traditional.

ạltklug ◇ *adj* precocious. ◇ *adv* precociously.

ạltmodisch ◇ *adj* old-fashioned. ◇ *adv* in an old-fashioned way.

Ạlt|papier *das* paper for recycling; **aus Altpapier** made from recycled paper.

Ạltpapier|container *der* paper recycling bin.

ạltsprachlich *adj* ▷ **Gymnasium.**

Ạlt|stadt *die* old town.

Alu *das fam* aluminium *UK*, aluminum *US*.

Alu|folie *die* tinfoil *(U)*.

Aluminium *das* aluminium *UK*, aluminum *US*.

ạm *präp* - **1.** *(an + dem)* at the; **am Flughafen** at the airport; **das Schönste am Urlaub ist es, lange schlafen zu können** the nicest thing about holidays is being able to sleep in; **ich möchte am Ausflug teilnehmen** I would like to take part in the trip - **2.** *(nicht auflösbar)* [in geografischen Angaben]: **am Meer** by the sea - **3.** *(nicht auflösbar)* [im Datum] on the; **am Abend** in the evening; **am Montag** on Monday; **am 4. Oktober** on 4. October; **am Anfang des Jahres** at the start of the year - **4.** *(nicht auflösbar)* [in Superlativen]: **am schönsten** the most beautiful - **5.** *(nicht auflösbar) fam* [vor substantivierten Infinitiven]: **ich bin am Arbeiten** I am working; *siehe auch* **an.**

amateurhaft *abw* ◇ *adj* amateurish. ◇ *adv* amateurishly.

Ạmboss (*pl* **-e**) *der* - **1.** [Schmiedegerät] anvil - **2.** MED incus.

ambulạnt ◇ *adj* MED outpatient. ◇ *adv* MED [behandeln] as an outpatient.

Ambulạnz (*pl* **-en**) *die* MED outpatients' department.

Ameise (*pl* **-n**) *die* ant.

Ameisen|haufen *der* anthill.

amen *interj* amen!

Amen *das* [Zustimmung] blessing, approval.

Amerika *nt* America.

Amerikaner, in (*mpl* -, *fpl* **-nen**) *der, die* American.

amerikanisch *adj* American.
Ạmi (*pl* **-s**) *der fam* Yank.
Amino|säure *die* amino acid.
Ạmmoniak *das* ammonia.
Amnestie (*pl* **-n**) *die* amnesty.
Amöbe (*pl* **-n**) *die* amoeba.
Ạmok *der*: **Amok laufen** to run amok.
Ạmpel (*pl* **-n**) *die* traffic lights *Pl*; **rote Ampel** red light.
Ampere [am'pɛːɐ̯] (*pl* **Ampere**) *das* amp, ampere.
Amphi|theater *das* amphitheatre.
amputieren *vt* to amputate.
Ạmsel (*pl* **-n**) *die* blackbird.
Ạmt (*pl* **Ạ̈mter**) *das* - **1.** [Behörde] department; [Gebäude] office; **von Amts wegen** on official orders - **2.** [Stellung] position; [wichtige politische oder kirchliche Stellung] office - **3.** [Pflicht] duty; [Aufgabe] task.
amtierend *adj*: **der amtierende Bundeskanzler** the German chancellor in office.
ạmtlich ◇ *adj* official. ◇ *adv* officially.
Ạmts|geheimnis *das* official secret.
Ạmts|gericht *das* ≃ county court *UK*, ≃ district court *US*.
Ạmts|sitz *der* seat of office.
Ạmts|sprache *die* official language.
Ạmts|zeit *die* term of office.
Amulẹtt (*pl* **-e**) *das* amulet.
amüsieren *vt* to amuse. ◆ **sich amüsieren** *ref* to have fun; **sich über jn/etw amüsieren** [auslachen] to make fun of sb/sthg; [lustig finden] to find sb/sthg funny.
an ◇ *präp* - **1.** *(+ D)* [räumlich] at; **an einem Tisch sitzen** to be sitting at a table; **an der Wand** on the wall; **an der Hauptstraße** on the main road; **Lehrer an einem Gymnasium** teacher at a grammar school - **2.** *(+ A)* [räumlich] to; **sich an den Tisch setzen** to sit down at the table; **etw an die Wand lehnen** to lean sthg against the wall - **3.** *(+ D)* [zeitlich] on; **an diesem Tag** on that day; **an Fulda 15.09** arriving at Fulda at 15.09 - **4.** *(+ D)* [stellt Bezug her]: **an Krebs leiden** to have cancer; **an etw zweifeln** to doubt sthg - **5.** *(+ D)* [aus dieser Menge]: **genug an Beweisen haben** to have enough proof - **6.** *(+ D)* [mithilfe von] with; **am Stock gehen** to walk with a stick; **jn an der Stimme erkennen** to recognize sb by their voice - **7.** *(+ A) fam* [ungefähr]: **an die 30 Grad** about 30 degrees - **8.** *(+ A)* [stellt Bezug her]: **an jn denken** to think about sb; **sich an jn/etw erinnern** to remember sb/sthg; **an und für sich** generally; **an sich** in itself. ◇ *adv* - **1.** [elliptisch]: **Licht an!** turn the light on! - **2.** [zeitlich]: **von jetzt an** from now on.
Analogie (*pl* **-n**) *die geh* analogy.
Ạnalphabet, in (*mpl* **-en**, *fpl* **-nen**) *der, die* illiterate (person).
Analyse (*pl* **-n**) *die* analysis; [von Blut] test.
analysieren *vt* to analyse; [Blut] to test.
Ạnanas (*pl* - ODER **-se**) *die* pineapple.
Anarchie (*pl* **-n**) *die* anarchy.
Anarchịst, in (*mpl* **-en**, *fpl* **-nen**) *der, die* anarchist.
Anästhesie (*pl* **-n**) *die* anaesthesia.
Anatomie (*pl* **-n**) *die* anatomy.
ạn|bahnen *vt* [Geschäft, Treffen] to prepare; [Gespräch] to start. ◆ **sich anbahnen** *ref* to be on the way.
ạn|bändeln *vi fam*: **mit jm anbändeln** to start going out with sb.
Ạn|bau *der* - **1.** [Gebäudeteil] extension - **2.** [Bauen] building *(of extension)* - **3.** [von Pflanzen] growing.
ạn|bauen *vt* - **1.** [Gebäude] to add *(as an extension)* - **2.** [Pflanze] to grow.
ạn|behalten *vt (unreg)* to keep on.
anbei *adv amt* enclosed.
ạn|beißen *(unreg)* ◇ *vt* to take a bite of. ◇ *vi* - **1.** [Fisch] to bite - **2.** *fig* [Käufer] to take the bait.
ạn|belangen *vt*: **was jn/etw anbelangt** as far as sb/sthg is concerned.
ạn|beten *vt* to worship.
ạn|biedern ◆ **sich anbiedern** *ref abw* **sich bei jm anbiedern** to curry favour with sb.
ạn|bieten *vt (unreg)* to offer. ◆ **sich anbieten** *ref* - **1.** [Mensch] to offer one's services; **sie bot sich an, uns die Stadt zu zeigen** she offered to show us round the city - **2.** [Sache]: **der Montag bietet sich als Termin für das Treffen an** Monday would be the best day for the meeting - **3.** [geeignet erscheinen]: **folgende Möglichkeiten bieten sich an** we have the following possibilities.
Ạnbieter, in (*mpl* -, *fpl* **-nen**) *der, die* supplier.
ạn|binden *vt (unreg)* to tie (up).
Ạn|blick *der* sight.
ạn|blicken *vt* to look at.
ạn|braten *vt (unreg)* to brown.
ạn|brechen (*perf* **hat/ist ạngebrochen**) *(unreg)* ◇ *vt (hat)* - **1.** [Verpackung] to open - **2.** [Knochen] to crack - **3.** [Geldschein] to break into. ◇ *vi (ist) geh* [Tag] to dawn; [Morgen] to break; [Nacht] to fall.
ạn|brennen (*perf* **hat/ist ạngebrannt**) *(unreg)* ◇ *vt (hat)* [mit Feuer] to set fire to. ◇ *vi (ist)* [Essen] to burn; **nichts anbrennen lassen** *fam fig* never to let a single chance go by.
ạn|bringen *vt (unreg)* - **1.** [befestigen] to put up - **2.** [Kritik] to make - **3.** *fam abw* [mitbringen] to bring back.
Ạnbruch *der* [von Epoche] dawning; **bei Anbruch der Dunkelheit** when darkness falls/fell.

ạn|brüllen *vt fam* to bawl out; **gegen etw anbrüllen** to shout above sthg.

ạndächtig ◇ *adj* reverent. ◇ *adv* reverently.

ạn|dauern *vi* to continue.

ạndauernd ◇ *adj* continual. ◇ *adv* continually.

Ạndenken (*pl* -) *das* - **1.** [Erinnerung] memory; **zum Andenken an jn/etw** in memory of sb/sthg - **2.** [Gegenstand, Souvenir] souvenir.

ạndere, **r**, **s** ◇ *adj* - **1.** [unterschiedlich] different - **2.** [übrig, weitere] other. ◇ *pron*: **der/die/das andere** the other (one); **ein anderer/eine andere** [bei Dingen] a different one; [bei Personen] someone else; **ich habe noch zwei andere** I've got two others; **unter anderem** among other things.

ạnderenfalls = **andernfalls**.

ạndererseits, ạndrerseits *adv* on the other hand.

ạndermal ◆ **ein andermal** *adv* another time, some other time.

ạ̈ndern *vt* to change; [Kleid] to alter; **das lässt sich nicht ändern** there's nothing to be done about it. ◆ **sich ändern** *ref* to change.

ạndernfalls, ạnderenfalls *adv* otherwise.

ạnders ◇ *adv* - **1.** [andersartig, verschieden] differently; **sie sieht ganz anders aus als ihre Schwester** she doesn't look at all like her sister; **anders ausgedrückt** put another way; **so und nicht anders!** this way only! - **2.** [sonst] else; **jemand/irgendwo anders** somebody/somewhere else; **niemand anders als du kann uns jetzt noch helfen** only you can help us now. ◇ *adj* different; **das muss anders werden** this has got to change; **mir wird ganz anders** I feel weird.

ạndersherum *adv* the other way round.

ạnderswo *adv* elsewhere, somewhere else.

ạnderthalb *num* one and a half.

Ạ̈nderung (*pl* **-en**) *die* [gen] change; [an Kleid] alteration.

ạnderweitig ◇ *adj* other. ◇ *adv* - **1.** [anderswo] elsewhere - **2.** [auf andere Weise] otherwise.

ạn|deuten *vt* - **1.** [ansprechen] to hint at; **andeuten, dass ...** to hint that ... - **2.** [umreißen, skizzieren] to outline.

Ạn|deutung *die* hint; **eine Andeutung machen** to drop a hint.

Ạn|drang *der* crush; **es herrscht großer Andrang** there is a great crush.

ạn|drehen *vt fam* [verkaufen]: **jm etw andrehen** to flog sb sthg.

ạndrerseits = **andererseits**.

ạn|drohen *vt*: **jm etw androhen** to threaten sb with sthg.

Ạn|drohung *die*: **unter Androhung von etw** under threat of sthg.

ạn|ecken (*perf* **ist ạngeeckt**) *vi* - **1.** [stoßen]: **an etw anecken** to bang against sthg - **2.** [sich unbeliebt machen]: **bei jm/überall anecken** to rub sb/everybody up the wrong way.

ạn|eignen *vt*: **sich** *(D)* **etw aneignen** [lernen] to pick sthg up; *abw* [nehmen] to take sthg (for o.s.)

aneinạnder *adv* [drücken, befestigen] together; [reiben] against one another; [denken] about one another; **sich aneinander gewöhnen** to get used to one another.

aneinạnder fügen *vt* to put together. ◆ **sich aneinander fügen** *ref* to fit together.

aneinạnder geraten (*perf* **ist aneinạnder geraten**) *vi (unreg)* to clash.

aneinạnder grenzen *vi* [Länder] to border on one another; [Gärten, Wohnungen] to be adjacent.

aneinander hạ̈ngen *vi (unreg)* [einander lieben] to be attached to one another.

aneinạnder legen *vt* to lay down next to each other.

Anekdote (*pl* **-n**) *die* anecdote.

ạn|ekeln *vt* to make sick.

ạnerkannt *adj* recognized.

ạn|erkennen *vt (unreg)* - **1.** [Leistung, Begabung] to acknowledge - **2.** [Meinung, Person] to accept - **3.** [Autorität, Staat, Vaterschaft] to recognize.

Ạnerkennung (*pl* **-en**) *die* - **1.** [von Leistung, Begabung] acknowledgement - **2.** [von Meinung, Person] acceptance - **3.** [von Autorität, Staat, Vaterschaft] recognition.

ạn|fachen *vt* to fan.

ạn|fahren (*perf* **hat/ist ạngefahren**) *(unreg)* ◇ *vt (hat)* - **1.** [bei Unfall] to run into - **2.** [Ziel] to approach - **3.** [Last] to deliver - **4.** [tadeln] to scold. ◇ *vi (ist)* [losfahren] to start.

Ạn|fall *der* fit.

ạn|fallen (*perf* **hat/ist ạngefallen**) *(unreg)* ◇ *vi (ist)* [Kosten] to be incurred. ◇ *vt (hat)* [angreifen] to attack.

ạnfällig *adj*: **für etw anfällig sein** to be prone ODER susceptible to sthg.

Ạn|fang *der* beginning, start; **Anfang April** at the beginning of April; **von Anfang an** from the beginning ODER start; **von Anfang bis Ende** from start to finish.

ạn|fangen *(unreg)* ◇ *vi* - **1.** [gen] to begin, to start; **mit etw anfangen** to start sthg, to begin sthg; **wer fängt an?** who's first?; **er fängt schon wieder an!** there he goes again! - **2.** [machen]: **er weiß nichts mit sich anzufangen** he doesn't know what to do with himself; **mit etw nichts anfangen können** [verstehen] not to be able to get anywhere with sthg; [gebrauchen] not to be able to use sthg. ◇ *vt* [beginnen] to begin, to start.

Ạnfänger, in (*mpl* -, *fpl* **-nen**) *der, die* beginner; **ein blutiger Anfänger** a total beginner.

ạnfänglich ◇ *adj* initial. ◇ *adv* initially.

ạnfangs *adv* at first.

Ạnfangs|buchstabe *der* [von Wort] first letter; [von Name] initial.

Ạnfangs|stadium *das* initial stages *Pl*.

ạn|fassen ◇ *vt* - **1.** [berühren] to touch - **2.** [behandeln] to treat - **3.** [angehen] to handle. ◇ *vi* [helfen] to lend a hand; **mit anfassen** to lend a hand.

ạn|fechten *vt (unreg)* [anzweifeln - Testament] to contest; [- Urteil] to appeal against.

ạn|fertigen *vt* [Anzug, Schrank] to make; [Bericht] to write; [Protokoll] to take down; **ein Porträt anfertigen lassen** to have a portrait done.

Ạnfertigung *die (ohne pl)* [von Anzug, Möbeln] making; [von Bericht] writing; [von Protokoll] taking down.

ạn|feuchten *vt* [Lippen, Briefmarke] to moisten; [Haut] to moisturize; [Lappen] to wet.

ạn|feuern *vt* to spur on.

ạn|flehen *vt* to beg.

ạn|fliegen (*perf* **hat/ist ạngeflogen**) *(unreg)* ◇ *vt (hat)* [Subj: Flugzeug] to approach; [Subj: Fluggesellschaft] to serve, to fly to. ◇ *vi (ist)*: **angeflogen kommen** to come flying up.

Ạn|flug *der* - **1.** [von Flugzeug, Hubschrauber]: **im Anflug (auf etw** *(A)***) sein** to be approaching (sthg) - **2.** [Spur] hint.

ạn|fordern *vt* to ask for; [per Post] to send off for.

Ạn|forderung *die* - **1.** [Bestellung] request - **2.** [Anspruch] demand; **Anforderungen stellen** to make demands; **einer Anforderung genügen** to meet a requirement; **den Anforderungen einer Sache gewachsen sein** to be up to the demands of sthg.

Ạn|frage *die amt* enquiry.

ạnfreunden ◆ **sich anfreunden** *ref* to make friends; **sich mit jm anfreunden** to make friends with sb; **ich freunde mich langsam mit der Idee an** the idea is growing on me.

ạn|fühlen *vt* to feel. ◆ **sich anfühlen** *ref* to feel.

ạn|führen *vt* - **1.** [nennen] to quote - **2.** [täuschen] to take in - **3.** [führen] to lead.

Ạn|führer, in *der, die* leader.

Ạnführungs|zeichen *Pl* quotation marks, inverted commas.

Ạn|gabe *die* - **1.** [Hinweis] detail - **2.** [Aufschneiderei] showing off.

ạn|geben *(unreg)* ◇ *vt* - **1.** [nennen, zitieren - Personalien, Grund] to give; [- Zeuge] to name - **2.** [bestimmen - Richtung, Kurs] to set - **3.** [behaupten] to claim, to allege. ◇ *vi* [aufschneiden] to show off; **mit etw angeben** to show off about sthg.

Ạngeber (*pl* -) *der* show-off.

Ạngeberin (*pl* **-nen**) *die* show-off.

ạngeblich ◇ *adj* alleged. ◇ *adv* allegedly

ạngeboren *adj* [Krankheit] congenital; [Talent Abneigung] innate.

Ạn|gebot *das* - **1.** [Anbieten] offer; **Angebot und Nachfrage** supply and demand - **2.** [Sortiment] range; **etw im Angebot haben** to offer sthg.

ạngebracht ◇ *pp* ▷ **anbringen** ◇ *adj* appropriate.

ạngebunden ◇ *pp* ▷ **anbinden** ◇ *adj*: **kurz angebunden sein** to be brusque

ạngegriffen ◇ *pp* ▷ **angreifen** ◇ *adj* [Gesundheit, Position] weakened.

ạngeheitert *adj* merry.

ạn|gehen (*perf* **hat/ist ạngegangen**) *(unreg,* ◇ *vi (ist)* - **1.** [Licht] to go on; [Feuer] to catch - **2.** [akzeptabel sein]: **es geht nicht an, etw zu tun** it's not on to do sthg - **3.** [vorgehen]: **gegen jn/etw angehen** to fight sb/sthg. ◇ *vi* *(hat)* [betreffen] to concern; **jn etwas angehen** to concern sb; **das geht dich nichts an** it's none of your business.

ạngehend *adj* future.

ạn|gehören *vi*: **einer Sache** *(D)* **angehören** to belong to sthg.

Ạngehörige (*pl* **-n**) *der, die* - **1.** [Verwandte relative - **2.** [Mitglied] member.

Ạngeklagte (*pl* **-n**) *der, die* defendant.

Ạngel (*pl* **-n**) *die* - **1.** [zum Fischen] fishing roc - **2.** [Scharnier] hinge.

ạngelaufen ◇ *pp* ▷ **anlaufen**. ◇ *ad* [Silber, Messing] tarnished.

Ạn|gelegenheit *die* matter; **kümmere dich um deine eigenen Angelegenheiten!** minc your own business!

ạngeln ◇ *vi* - **1.** [fischen] to fish - **2.** [suchen]: **nach etw angeln** [suchen] to fish arounc for sthg. ◇ *vt* - **1.** [fischen] to fish for; [fangen to catch - **2.** [erobern]: **sich** *(D)* **jn angeln** to lanc o.s. sb.

ạngemessen ◇ *adj*: **(einer Sache** *(D)***) angemessen** appropriate (to sthg). ◇ *adv* appropriately.

ạngenehm ◇ *adj* pleasant. ◇ *adv* pleasantly.

ạngenommen ◇ *pp* ▷ **annehmen** ◇ *adj* [Kind] adopted; [Name] assumed ◆ **angenommen, dass** *adv* assuming (that).

ạngeregt ◇ *adj* lively. ◇ *adv*: **sich angeregt unterhalten** to have a lively conversation.

ạngeschlagen *adj* - **1.** [kaputt] chipped - **2.** [krank] groggy; **gesundheitlich angeschlagen sein** to be in poor health.

ạngesehen ◇ *pp* ▷ **ansehen**. ◇ *ad* respected.

Ạngesicht *das*: **im Angesicht einer Sache** *(G)* in the face of sthg; **von Angesicht zu Angesicht** face to face.

ạngesichts *präp*: **angesichts einer Sache** *(G)* in view of sthg.

ạngespannt ◇ *adj* tense. ◇ *adv* closely.

Ạngestellte (*pl* **-n**) *der, die* employee; [im Büro] white-collar worker.

ạngestrengt ◇ *adj* [Miene] strained; [Versuch] concerted. ◇ *adv* [arbeiten, rudern, zuhören] hard.

ạngetan ◇ *pp* ▷ **antun**. ◇ *adj*: **von jm/etw angetan sein** to be keen on sb/sthg.

ạngewiesen ◇ *pp* ▷ **anweisen**. ◇ *adj*: **auf jn/etw angewiesen sein** to be dependent on sb/sthg.

ạn|gewöhnen *vt*: **sich** *(D)* **angewöhnen, etw zu tun** to get into the habit of doing sthg; **jm etw angewöhnen** to get sb used to sthg.

Ạn|gewohnheit *die* habit.

ạngewurzelt *adv*: **wie angewurzelt stehen bleiben** to stand rooted to the spot.

Ạngler, in (*mpl* -, *fpl* **-nen**) *der, die* angler.

Anglịstik *die (ohne pl)* English language and literature.

ạn|greifen *(unreg)* ◇ *vt* - **1.** [gen] to attack - **2.** [Gesundheit] to affect - **3.** [Projekt] to tackle - **4.** [Vorrat] to draw on - **5.** *Süddt* [anfassen] to touch. ◇ *vi* to attack.

Ạngreifer, in (*mpl* -, *fpl* **-nen**) *der, die* attacker.

Ạn|griff *der* attack; **etw in Angriff nehmen** *fig* to set about sthg.

ạngriffslustig ◇ *adj* aggressive. ◇ *adv* aggressively.

ạngst *adj*: **mir wird angst und bange** I'm scared stiff.

Ạngst (*pl* **Ạngste**) *die* - **1.** [Furcht] fear; **vor jm/etw Angst haben** to be afraid of sb/sthg; **es mit der Angst zu tun bekommen** to get scared; **jm Angst machen** to frighten sb - **2.** [Sorge]: **Angst um jn/etw haben** to be anxious about sb/sthg.

Ạngst|hase *der fam abw* chicken.

ạ̈ngstigen *vt* to frighten. ◆ **sich ängstigen** *ref*: **sich vor jm/etw ängstigen** to be frightened of sb/sthg; **sich um jn/etw ängstigen** to be anxious about sb/sthg.

ạ̈ngstlich ◇ *adj* nervous. ◇ *adv* - **1.** [furchtsam] nervously - **2.** [genau] very carefully.

ạn|gucken *vt fam* to look at; [Fernsehsendung] to watch; **sich** *(D)* **etw angucken** to look at sthg; [Fernsehsendung] to watch sthg.

ạn|haben *vt (unreg)* - **1.** [Kleidung] to have on, to be wearing - **2.** [Schaden]: **jm/einer Sache nichts anhaben können** to be unable to harm sb/sthg.

ạn|halten *(unreg)* ◇ *vi* - **1.** [Fahrzeug] to stop - **2.** [Zustand] to last. ◇ *vt* [Bewegung] to stop; [Taxi] to hail; **den Atem anhalten** to hold one's breath.

ạnhaltend *adj* lasting.

Ạnhalter (*pl* -) *der* [Mitfahrer] hitchhiker; **per Anhalter fahren** to hitchhike.

Ạnhalterin (*pl* **-nen**) *die* [Mitfahrerin] hitchhiker.

Ạnhalts|punkt *der* clue.

anhạnd, an Hạnd *präp*: **anhand einer Sache** *(G)* with the aid of sthg.

Ạnhang *der (ohne pl)* - **1.** [Nachwort] appendix - **2.** *fam* [Familie] relatives *Pl*; **mit Anhang auf einem Fest erscheinen** to go to a party with someone.

ạn|hängen ◇ *vt (reg)* - **1.** [Wagen]: **etw an etw** *(A)* **anhängen** [Wagon] to couple sthg to sthg; [Anhänger] to hitch sthg to sthg - **2.** [Zeit]: **etw an etw** *(A)* **anhängen** to tag sthg onto sthg - **3.** [angebliche Schuld]: **jm etw anhängen** to pin sthg on sb. ◇ *vi (unreg)*: **einer Sache** *(D)* **anhängen** to be an adherent of sthg.

Ạnhänger (*pl* -) *der* - **1.** [von Fahrzeugen] trailer; [von Straßenbahn] carriage *(other than front carriage)* - **2.** [Person - von Kandidat, Mannschaft] supporter; [- von Sekte] member - **3.** [Schmuck] pendant.

Ạnhängerin (*pl* **-nen**) *die* [von Kandidat, Mannschaft] supporter; [von Sekte] member.

ạnhänglich *adj* [Hund, Partner] devoted.

ạn|hauchen *vt* to breathe on.

Ạnhäufung (*pl* **-en**) *die* accumulation.

ạn|heben *vt (unreg)* - **1.** [heben] to lift - **2.** [vergrößern] to raise.

ạn|heuern ◇ *vt* - **1.** [Matrosen] to sign on - **2.** [Arbeitskräfte] to take on. ◇ *vi* [auf einem Schiff] to sign on.

Ạnhieb ◆ **auf Anhieb** *adv* straight off.

Ạn|höhe *die* rise.

ạn|hören *vt* - **1.** [hören]: **sich** *(D)* **etw anhören** to listen to sthg; **etw mit anhören** to overhear sthg; **ich kann das nicht mehr mit anhören** I can't bear to listen to it any longer - **2.** [erraten]: **jm seine Freude/Wut anhören** to hear the joy/anger in sb's voice - **3.** *amt* [Zeugen] to give a hearing to. ◆ **sich anhören** *ref* to sound.

Anis *der* aniseed.

ạn|kämpfen *vi*: **gegen jn/etw ankämpfen** to fight against sb/sthg.

Ạn|kauf *der* purchase.

Ạnker (*pl* -) *der* anchor; **vor Anker gehen/liegen** to drop/be at anchor.

ạnkern *vi* to anchor; [Anker werfen] to drop anchor; [vor Anker liegen] to be at anchor.

ạn|ketten *vt* to chain.

Ạn|klage *die* - **1.** [vor Gericht] charge; **gegen jn Anklage erheben** to bring a charge against sb - **2.** [öffentlich] accusation - **3.** [Kläger] prosecution.

ạn|klagen *vt* - **1.** [vor Gericht]: **jn (wegen etw) anklagen** to charge sb (with sthg) - **2.** [öffentlich] to accuse.

Ạn|klang *der*: **(bei jm) Anklang finden** to meet with (sb's) approval.

ạn|kleben *vt* to stick.

ạn|klopfen *vi* to knock.

ạn|knüpfen ◇ *vt* - **1.** [Seil]: **etw an etw** *(A)* **anknüpfen** to tie sthg to sthg - **2.** [Gespräch] to strike up. ◇ *vi* [Worte, Vorlesung]: **an etw** *(A)* **anknüpfen** to take sthg up.

ạn|kommen (*perf* **ist ạngekommen**) *vi (unreg)* - **1.** [am Ziel] to arrive; **sie kommt mit dem Auto an** she's coming by car - **2.** [näher kommen] to approach - **3.** [mit Idee, Vorschlag]: **mit etw ankommen** to come up with sthg - **4.** *(RW)*: **bei jm gut/schlecht** ODER **nicht ankommen** to go down well/badly with sb - **5.** [sich durchsetzen]: **gegen jn/etw nicht ankommen** to be no match for sb/sthg - **6.** [wichtig sein]: **es kommt auf jn/etw an** it depends on sb/sthg; **es kommt darauf an** it depends; **es kommt mir vor allem auf die Qualität an** what matters to me is quality - **7.** [riskieren]: **es auf etw** *(A)* **ankommen lassen** to run the risk of sthg.

ạn|kreiden *vt*: **jm etw ankreiden** to hold sthg against sb.

ạn|kreuzen *vt* to mark with a cross.

ạn|kündigen *vt* to announce. ◆ **sich ankündigen** *ref*: **der Herbst kündigt sich an** autumn is on its way.

Ạnkunft *die* arrival.

ạn|kurbeln *vt* to boost.

ạn|lächeln *vt* to smile at.

ạn|lachen *vt* - **1.** [lachen] to look smilingly at - **2.** [erobern]: **sich** *(D)* **jn anlachen** to land o.s. sb.

Ạn|lage *die* - **1.** [Park - städtisch] park; [- von Schloss, Gebäude] grounds *Pl* - **2.** [Gelände - militärisch] installation; [- für Sport] facilities *Pl* - **3.** [Geldanlage] investment - **4.** [Bau] construction.

Ạnlass (*pl* **Ạnlässe**) *der* - **1.** [Grund] cause; **dazu gibt es keinen Anlass** there's no call for that - **2.** [Ereignis] occasion.

ạn|lassen *vt (unreg)* - **1.** [eingeschaltet lassen] to leave on - **2.** [starten] to start (up) - **3.** [anbehalten] to keep on.

Ạnlasser (*pl* -) *der* AUTO starter.

ạnlässlich *präp*: **anlässlich einer Sache** *(G)* on the occasion of sthg.

ạn|lasten *vt*: **jm etw anlasten** [verantwortlich machen für] to blame sb for sthg; [Verbrechen, Charakterfehler] to accuse sb of sthg.

Ạn|lauf *der* - **1.** [Schwung] run-up; **Anlauf nehmen** to take a run-up - **2.** [Versuch] attempt.

ạn|laufen (*perf* **hat/ist ạngelaufen**) *(unreg)* ◇ *vi (ist)* - **1.** [beginnen] to begin, to start; [Motor, Maschine] to start; FILM to open - **2.** [Körperteil]: **rot/blau anlaufen** to go red/blue - **3.** [Metall] to tarnish; [Fensterscheibe, Brille] to steam up - **4.** [sich nähern]: **angelaufen kommen** to come running up. ◇ *vt (hat)* [Hafen] to call at.

ạn|legen ◇ *vt* - **1.** [Garten, Park, Beet] to lay out; [Straße] to plan - **2.** [Kartei, Sammlung] to start - **3.** [Vorrat] to lay in - **4.** [beabsichtigen]: **es darauf anlegen, etw zu tun** to be determined to do sthg - **5.** [Geld] to invest - **6.** [anlehnen]: **etw (an etw** *(A)***) anlegen** to lay sthg (on sthg) - **7.** [umbinden] to put on - **8.** [Subj: Tier] to lay back; **die Ohren anlegen** to lay back its ears - **9.** [Waffe] to raise to one's shoulder - **10.** *geh* [anziehen - Geschmeide] to put on. ◇ *vi* - **1.** [Schiff] to dock - **2.** [mit Gewehr]: **auf jn/etw anlegen** to aim at sb/sthg. ◆ **sich anlegen** *ref*: **sich mit jm anlegen** to pick a fight with sb.

Ạnlege|stelle *die* mooring.

ạn|lehnen *vt* - **1.** [Tür, Fenster] to leave ajar - **2.** [an die Wand] to lean; **etw an etw** *(A)* **anlehnen** to lean sthg against sthg. ◆ **sich anlehnen** *ref*: **sich an etw** *(A)* **anlehnen** to lean against sthg; *fig* to draw upon sthg.

Ạnlehnung (*pl* **-en**) *die*: **in Anlehnung an einen Roman entstanden** based on a novel.

Ạn|leitung *die* - **1.** [Hinweis] instruction; **unter js Anleitung** under sb's guidance - **2.** [Text] instructions *Pl*.

ạn|lernen *vt* to train.

ạn|liegen *vi (unreg)* - **1.** [sitzen]: **eng anliegen** to be tight - **2.** *fam* [zu erledigen sein]: **was liegt heute an?** what do we have to do today?

Ạnlieger (*pl* -) *der* resident.

ạn|locken *vt* [Kunden] to attract; [mit Köder] to lure.

ạn|lügen *vt (unreg)* to lie to.

Anm. *abk für* **Anmerkung**.

ạn|machen *vt* - **1.** [Gerät] to turn on, to switch on - **2.** [Salat] to dress - **3.** *salopp* [ansprechen] to chat up *UK*, to hit on *US*.

ạn|malen *vt* [bemalen] to paint.

ạnmaßen *vt*: **sich** *(D)* **anmaßen, etw zu tun** to presume to do sthg.

ạnmaßend *adj* presumptuous.

Ạnmelde|formular *das* application form.

ạn|melden *vt* - **1.** [beim Amt - Auto, Wohnsitz, Gewerbe] to register; [- Fernseher] to get a licence for; [- Patent] to apply for - **2.** [in Schule, Kurs] to enrol - **3.** [zu Termin] to make an appointment for; **sind Sie für heute angemeldet?** do you have an appointment for today? - **4.** [Besuch] to announce. ◆ **sich anmelden** *ref* - **1.** [für Kurs] to enrol - **2.** [zu Termin] to make an appointment.

An|meldung *die* - **1.** [beim Amt] registration; [eines Patents] application - **2.** [in Schule, Kurs] enrolment - **3.** [zu Termin] making an appointment - **4.** [Rezeption] reception.

an|merken *vt* - **1.** [spüren]: **jm etw anmerken** to notice sthg in sb; **sich** *(D)* **nichts anmerken lassen** not to show one's feelings - **2.** [sagen] to comment.

Anmerkung (*pl* **-en**) *die* - **1.** [im Text] note - **2.** [gesprochen] comment.

an|nähern *vt* to bring closer. ◆ **sich annähern** *ref*: **sich einander annähern** to approach one another.

annähernd *adv* nearly.

Annäherung (*pl* **-en**) *die* approach; **die Annäherung von Wallonien an Flandern** the rapprochement between the Walloons and the Flemish.

Annahme (*pl* **-n**) *die* - **1.** [Meinung] assumption; **in der Annahme, dass...** on the assumption that... - **2.** [von Paket, Brief] receipt; [von Geschenk] acceptance.

annehmbar ◇ *adj* acceptable. ◇ *adv* reasonably (well).

an|nehmen *vt (unreg)* - **1.** [empfangen, zustimmen, akzeptieren, zulassen] to accept; [Anruf] to take - **2.** [vermuten] to assume - **3.** [Staatsangehörigkeit, Namen, Kind] to adopt; [Dialekt, Gewohnheit] to pick up - **4.** [Gestalt] to take on.

Annehmlichkeit (*pl* **-en**) *die*: **Annehmlichkeiten** [Vorteile] advantages; [Bequemlichkeiten] comforts.

Annonce [a'nɔŋsə] (*pl* **-n**) *die* advertisement.

annoncieren [anɔŋ'siːrən] ◇ *vi* to place an advertisement. ◇ *vt* to advertise.

annullieren *vt* [Ehe] to annul; [Vertrag] to cancel.

an|öden *vt fam* to bore to tears.

anonym ◇ *adj* anonymous. ◇ *adv* anonymously.

Anorak (*pl* **-s**) *der* anorak.

an|ordnen *vt* - **1.** [befehlen] to order - **2.** [Gegenstände] to arrange.

An|ordnung *die* - **1.** [Aufstellung] layout - **2.** [Befehl] order; **auf js Anordnung** *(A)* on sb's orders; **Anordnungen treffen** to make arrangements.

an|packen ◇ *vt* - **1.** [mit Händen] to grab - **2.** [behandeln]: **jn hart anpacken** to treat sb harshly - **3.** [lösen] to tackle. ◇ *vi* [helfen]: **mit anpacken** to lend a hand.

an|passen *vt*: **etw einer Sache** *(D)* **anpassen** to adapt sthg to sthg. ◆ **sich anpassen** *ref* to adapt.

Anpassung (*pl* **-en**) *die* adaptation.

An|pfiff *der* - **1.** [im Fußball] kick-off - **2.** *fam* [Tadel] ticking-off.

an|pflanzen *vt* to plant.

an|pöbeln *vt* to shout abuse at.

an|prangern *vt* to denounce.

an|preisen *vt (unreg)* [Waren] to tout.

An|probe *die* fitting.

an|probieren *vt* to try on.

an|rechnen *vt* - **1.** [einbeziehen] to take into account; **jm etw hoch anrechnen** to think highly of sb for sthg - **2.** [berechnen] to charge for.

An|recht *das* - **1.** [Recht]: **ein Anrecht auf etw** *(A)* **haben** ODER **besitzen** to have the right to sthg - **2.** [Abonnement] subscription.

An|rede *die* form of address.

an|reden *vt* - **1.** [ansprechen] to speak to - **2.** [mit Titel]: **den Chef mit "Herr Professor" anreden** to address the boss as "Professor"; **jn mit seinem Vornamen anreden** to call sb by their first name.

an|regen *vt* - **1.** [beleben] to stimulate - **2.** [empfehlen] to propose - **3.** [ermutigen]: **jn anregen, etw zu tun** to encourage sb to do sthg.

An|regung *die* - **1.** [Belebung] stimulation - **2.** [Anreiz] incentive.

An|reise *die* journey (there).

an|reisen (*perf* **ist angereist**) *vi* to travel (there).

An|reiz *der* incentive.

an|rempeln *vt* to barge into.

an|richten *vt* - **1.** [Abendessen] to prepare - **2.** [Schaden] to cause; **da hast du was Schönes angerichtet!** you've really gone and done it now!

an|rücken (*perf* **ist angerückt**) *vi* - **1.** [Truppen] to move in - **2.** *fam* [auftauchen] to show up.

An|ruf *der* call.

Anrufbeantworter (*pl* -) *der* answering machine.

an|rufen *(unreg)* ◇ *vt* [telefonieren] to call, to phone. ◇ *vi* to call, to phone; **bei jm anrufen** to call ODER phone sb.

an|rühren *vt* - **1.** [berühren - Person, Gegenstand] to touch; [- Thema] to touch on - **2.** [rühren] to mix.

ans *präp (an + das)*: **ans Fenster klopfen** to knock on the window; *siehe auch* **an**.

An|sage *die* announcement.

an|sagen *vt* to announce; **jm/etw den Kampf ansagen** to declare war on sb/sthg.

an|sammeln *vt* to collect. ◆ **sich ansammeln** *ref* - **1.** [anhäufen, anstauen] to pile up - **2.** [versammeln] to gather.

An|sammlung *die* - **1.** [Anhäufung] accumulation - **2.** [Versammlung] gathering.

An|satz *der* - **1.** [Anfang, Anzeichen] first sign; **im Ansatz stecken bleiben** to fall at the first hurdle; **gute Ansätze zeigen** to show promising signs - **2.** [von Körperteil] base - **3.** MATH formulation.

an|saugen *vt* to suck in.

an|schaffen *vt*: **sich** *(D)* **etw anschaffen** to get o.s. sthg.

Anschaffung (*pl* **-en**) *die* acquisition, purchase.

an|schalten *vt* to turn on.

an|schauen *vt* to look at; **sich** *(D)* **etw anschauen** to have a look at sthg.

anschaulich ◇ *adj* clear. ◇ *adv* clearly.

Anschein *der* appearance; **dem** ODER **allem Anschein nach** apparently; **es hat den Anschein, als ob** it looks like, it appears that.

anscheinend *adv* apparently.

an|schieben *vt (unreg)* to push-start.

Anschlag *der* - **1.** [Attentat - auf Person] assassination attempt; [- auf Botschaft] attack; **einen Anschlag auf jn verüben** to make an attempt on sb's life; **einen Anschlag auf etw** *(A)* **verüben** to attack sthg - **2.** [Zettel, Plakat] notice - **3.** [auf der Schreibmaschine] keystroke; **50 Anschläge pro Zeile** 50 characters per line - **4.** [am Klavier] touch.

an|schlagen (*perf* **hat/ist angeschlagen**) *(unreg)* ◇ *vt* - **1.** [Plakat] to put up - **2.** [Geschirr] to chip - **3.** [wählen] to adopt - **4.** [Taste] to strike - **5.** [beim Stricken] to cast on - **6.** [verletzen]: **sich** *(D)* **den Kopf an etw** *(D)* **anschlagen** to knock one's head against sthg. ◇ *vi* - **1.** [wirken] to work - **2.** [bellen] to start barking.

an|schließen *vt (unreg)* - **1.** [verbinden - Telefon, Wasserhahn] to connect; [- Elektrogerät] to plug in - **2.** [folgen lassen] to add - **3.** [festschließen]: **etw an etw** *(A)* **anschließen** to lock sthg to sthg. ◆ **sich anschließen** *ref* [mitmachen]: **sich jm/einer Sache anschließen** to join sb/sthg; **sich einer Meinung anschließen** to endorse an opinion.

anschließend ◇ *adv* afterwards. ◇ *adj* ensuing.

Anschluss (*pl* **-schlüsse**) *der* - **1.** [an Zug, Telefon] connection; **den Anschluss verpasst haben** *fig* to be left behind; **kein Anschluss unter dieser Nummer** the number you have dialled has not been recognized - **2.** [Telefonapparat] extension - **3.** [zu Freunden]: **Anschluss finden** to meet people - **4.** [Folge]: **im Anschluss an etw** *(A)* following sthg - **5.** POL Anschluss.

an|schmiegen ◆ **sich anschmiegen** *ref*: **sich an jn/etw anschmiegen** to snuggle up to sb/sthg.

an|schnallen *vt* [Skier, Rollschuhe] to put on; [Sicherheitsgurt] to fasten. ◆ **sich anschnallen** *ref* to fasten one's seat belt.

an|schneiden *vt (unreg)* - **1.** [schneiden] to cut into - **2.** *fig* [ansprechen] to broach.

an|schreiben *(unreg)* ◇ *vt* - **1.** [Schulden]: **sie ließ ihre Einkäufe anschreiben** she asked to pay for her purchases later - **2.** [per Brief] to write to. ◇ *vi*: **anschreiben lassen** to pay later.

an|schreien *vt (unreg)* to shout at.

An|schrift *die* address.

Anschuldigung (*pl* **-en**) *die* accusation.

an|schwellen (*perf* **ist angeschwollen**) *vi (unreg)* - **1.** [Körperteil] to swell - **2.** [Gewässer] to rise - **3.** [Geräusch] to grow louder.

an|schwemmen *vt* to wash up.

an|sehen *(unreg)* ◇ *vt* - **1.** [anblicken] to look at; **sich** *(D)* **etw ansehen** [zur Unterhaltung] to go and see sthg; **sich** *(D)* **jn/etw ansehen** [zur Prüfung] to look at sb/sthg - **2.** [erkennen]: **man sieht ihm sein Alter nicht an** he doesn't look his age; **man sieht ihr ihre Müdigkeit nicht an** her tiredness doesn't show - **3.** [erachten]: **jn/etw als etw ansehen** to regard sb/sthg as sthg - **4.** [ertragen]: **etw nicht (mit) ansehen können** not to be able to stand sthg. ◇ *vi*: **sieh mal an!** fancy that!

Ansehen *das* [Ruf] reputation.

ansehnlich *adj* - **1.** [groß] considerable - **2.** [schön] attractive.

an sein (*perf* **ist an gewesen**) *vi (unreg)* to be on.

an|setzen ◇ *vt* - **1.** [in Stellung bringen - Werkzeug] to place in position; [- Trinkgefäß, Blasinstrument] to raise to one's lips - **2.** [Termin] to arrange; [Preis] to fix - **3.** [Stück]: **etw an etw** *(A)* **ansetzen** to attach sthg to sthg - **4.** [Person]: **jn auf etw** *(A)* **ansetzen** to put sb on sthg - **5.** [zubereiten] to prepare - **6.** [anlagern]: **Rost ansetzen** to get rusty. ◇ *vi* [anfangen] to begin; **zum Sprung ansetzen** to get ready to jump; **das Flugzeug setzte zur Landung an** the plane was commencing its descent. ◆ **sich ansetzen** *ref* [sich ablagern - Rost, Schimmel] to form; [- Kalk] to accumulate, to build up.

Ansicht (*pl* **-en**) *die* - **1.** [Meinung] opinion, view; **der gleichen/anderer Ansicht sein** to be of the same/a different opinion; **meiner Ansicht nach** in my view ODER opinion - **2.** [Betrachtung]: **zur Ansicht** [zur Probe] on trial ODER approval - **3.** [Abbildung] view. ◆ **Ansichten** *Pl* opinions, views.

Ansichts|karte *die* postcard.

ansonsten *adv* otherwise.

an|spannen *vt* - **1.** [Muskel] to tense; [Seil] to tauten - **2.** [anstrengen] to put under strain - **3.** [Pferd] to harness.

An|spannung *die* strain; **nervöse Anspannung** nervous tension.

an|spielen ◇ *vi*: **auf jn/etw anspielen** to allude to sb/sthg. ◇ *vt* SPORT to play the ball to.

Anspielung (*pl* **-en**) *die* allusion.

an|spornen [ˈanʃpɔrnən] *vt* to spur on; **jn zu etw anspornen** to spur sb on to sthg.

Ansprache (*pl* **-n**) *die* speech.

ansprechbar *adj*: **nicht ansprechbar sein** [wegen Krankheit, Ohnmacht, Trunkenheit] to be in no fit state to talk to anybody; [beschäftigt sein] to be unavailable to talk to anybody.

ạn|springen (*perf* **hat/ist ạngesprungen**) *(unreg)* ◇ *vt (hat)* [angreifen] to pounce on. ◇ *vi (ist)* - **1.** [Auto, Motor] to start - **2.** *fam* [reagieren]: **auf etw** *(A)* **anspringen** to jump at sthg.

Ạn|spruch *der* - **1.** [Recht] claim; **auf etw Anspruch haben** to be entitled to sthg - **2.** [Forderung] demand; **hohe Ansprüche an jn stellen** to demand a lot of sb; **jn/etw in Anspruch nehmen** to make demands on sb/sthg; **viel Zeit in Anspruch nehmen** to take a lot of time; **ich nahm seine Hilfe gern in Anspruch** I was happy to accept his help.

ạnspruchslos ['anʃpruxslo:s] *adj* - **1.** [bescheiden] unpretentious; [Leben] simple - **2.** [Publikum, Person, Lektüre] undemanding - **3.** [Pflanze] easy to look after.

ạnspruchsvoll ['anʃpruxsfɔl] *adj* demanding; [Zeitung] quality *(vor Subst)*.

ạn|stacheln ['anʃtaxl̩n] *vt* [Ehrgeiz] to fire; **jn zu etw anstacheln** to goad sb into sthg.

Ạnstalt (*pl* **-en**) *die* - **1.** [Institution] institution - **2.** [Irrenanstalt] mental hospital, institution.

Ạnstand *der* [gutes Benehmen] decency.

ạnständig ◇ *adj* decent; **eine anständige Tracht Prügel** *fam* a real hiding. ◇ *adv* - **1.** [ordentlich, integer] decently - **2.** *fam* [kräftig]: **anständig bezahlen** to pay well; **anständig reinhauen** to stuff one's face.

ạnstandslos *adv* without hesitation.

ạn|starren *vt* to stare at.

anstạtt *präp*: **anstatt js/einer Sache** instead of sb/sthg. ◆ **anstatt dass** *konj*: **anstatt dass wir reden** instead of talking. ◆ **anstatt zu** *konj* instead of.

ạn|stecken ◇ *vt* - **1.** [infizieren, mitreißen] to infect; **jn mit etw anstecken** to infect sb with sthg, to give sthg to sb; **er hat uns alle mit seinem Lachen angesteckt** his laughter was infectious - **2.** [Zigarette, Kerze] to light; [Haus] to set fire to - **3.** [Orden, Brosche] to pin on; [einen Ring] to put on. ◇ *vi* to be infectious. ◆ **sich anstecken** *ref*: **sich (bei jm) mit etw anstecken** to catch sthg (from sb).

ạnsteckend *adj* infectious.

Ạnsteckung (*pl* **-en**) *die* infection.

ạn|stehen *vi (unreg)* - **1.** [in Schlange] to queue *UK*, to stand in line *US* - **2.** [Problem] to be on the agenda; [Termin] to be fixed.

ạn|steigen (*perf* **ist ạngestiegen**) *vi (unreg)* to rise.

anstẹlle *präp*: **anstelle js/einer Sache, anstelle von jm/etw** instead of sb/sthg.

ạn|stellen *vt* - **1.** [Gerät] to turn on - **2.** [Angestellte] to employ, to take on; **in einem Großbetrieb angestellt sein** to work in a big factory - **3.** [zustande bringen - Beobachtung, Vergleich] to make; [- Unfug] to get up to; [- Blödsinn] to talk; **sie hat alles Mögliche angestellt** she tried everything; **wie soll ich das anstellen?** how am I supposed to do that? ◆ **sich anstellen** *ref* - **1.** [Schlange stehen] to queue *UK*, to stand in line *US* - **2.** [sich benehmen] to act; **sie stellte sich sehr geschickt an** she got the hang of it very quickly.

Ạn|stellung *die* position.

Ạnstieg (*pl* **-e**) *der* - **1.** [Zunahme] rise - **2.** [Aufstieg] ascent.

ạn|stiften *vt*: **jn zu etw anstiften** to incite sb to sthg.

Ạn|stoß *der* - **1.** [Anlass] impetus *(U)*; **den Anstoß zu etw geben** to provide the impetus for sthg - **2.** [Ärger]: **an etw** *(D)* **Anstoß nehmen** to take offence at sthg - **3.** [im Fußball] kick-off.

ạn|stoßen (*perf* **hat/ist ạngestoßen**) *(unreg)* ◇ *vt (hat)* [mit dem Fuß] to kick; [mit dem Ellenbogen - mit Gewalt] to elbow; [- heimlich] to nudge; **sich das Knie am Tisch anstoßen** to bang one's knee on the table. ◇ *vi* - **1.** *(ist)* [anecken]: **mit der Schulter am Schrank anstoßen** to bang one's shoulder on the cupboard - **2.** *(hat)* [angrenzen]: **an etw** *(A)* **anstoßen** to adjoin sthg - **3.** *(hat)* [mit Gläsern]: **(mit jm) auf jn/etw anstoßen** to drink to sb/sthg (with sb).

ạn|strahlen *vt* - **1.** [beleuchten - Bauwerk] to floodlight; [- Schauspieler] to spotlight - **2.** [anlächeln] to beam at.

ạn|streichen *vt (unreg)* - **1.** [streichen] to paint - **2.** [kennzeichnen] to mark.

ạn|strengen ['anʃtrɛŋən] *vt* - **1.** [ermüden] to strain - **2.** [Kräfte, Fantasie, Kopf] to use - **3.** [Prozess] to start. ◆ **sich anstrengen** *ref* [sich bemühen] to make an effort, to try.

Ạnstrengung (*pl* **-en**) *die* effort.

Ạnstrich *der* - **1.** [Farbe] coat of paint - **2.** [Schein] air; **einer Sache** *(D)* **einen seriösen Anstrich geben** to lend authority to sthg.

Ạnsturm *der* - **1.** [Angriff] assault - **2.** [Andrang] rush.

ạn|stürmen (*perf* **ist ạngestürmt**) *vi*: **gegen etw anstürmen** [Festung] to storm sthg.

Antạrktis *die* Antarctic.

Ạnteil (*pl* **-e**) *der* - **1.** [Teil] share - **2.** [Teilnahme]: **an etw** *(D)* **Anteil haben** to participate in sthg; **an etw** *(D)* **Anteil nehmen** [bemitleiden] to share in sthg; [sich beteiligen] to participate in sthg.

Ạnteilnahme *die* - **1.** [Mitleid] sympathy - **2.** [Interesse] interest.

Antẹnne (*pl* **-n**) *die* - **1.** TECH aerial - **2.** [Gefühl]: **eine/keine Antenne für etw haben** to have a/no feel for sthg.

Ạnthrax (*pl* **Anthrax**) *das* anthrax.

Antialkoholiker, in [anti|alko'ho:likɐ, rɪn] (*mpl* **Antialkoholiker**, *fpl* **-nen**) *der, die* teetotaller.

ạntiautoritär [antiautori'tɛ:ɐ̯] ◇ *adj* permissive. ◇ *adv* permissively.

Antibiotikum [anti'bi̯o:tikum] (*pl* **-ka**) *das* antibiotic.

ạntifaschistisch *adj* antifascist.

antik [an'ti:k] *adj* - **1.** [klassisch] classical - **2.** [alt] antique.

Antike [an'ti:kə] *die*: **die Antike** (classical) antiquity.

Ạnti|körper *der* antibody.

ạn|tippen *vt* - **1.** [Gegenstand] to tap - **2.** [Thema] to touch on.

antiquarisch *adj* second-hand.

Antiquität [antikvi'tɛ:t] (*pl* **-en**) *die* antique.

Ạntrag ['antra:k] (*pl* **Ạnträge**) *der* - **1.** [Bitte] application; **einen Antrag auf etw** *(A)* **stellen** to apply for sthg - **2.** [im Parlament] motion - **3.** [Formular] application form.

Ạntrags|formular *das* application form.

ạn|treffen *vt (unreg)* to find.

ạn|treiben *vt (unreg)* - **1.** [Wagen] to drive; [Motor, Gerät] to power - **2.** [Person] to urge on; **jn zur Eile antreiben** to urge sb to hurry - **3.** [anschwemmen] to wash up.

ạn|treten (*perf* **hat/ist ạngetreten**) *(unreg)* ◇ *vt (hat)* - **1.** [beginnen] to start - **2.** [Erbschaft] to come into. ◇ *vi (ist)* - **1.** [sich aufstellen] to line up - **2.** [kämpfen]: **gegen jn antreten** [in Fußball, Tennis] to play sb; [im Boxen] to fight sb; [in Wahl] to stand against sb.

Ạntrieb *der* - **1.** [Kraft] drive; **mit elektrischem Antrieb** electrically-powered - **2.** [Motivation] impetus; **etw aus eigenem Antrieb tun** to do sthg on one's own initiative.

ạn|trinken *vt (unreg)*: **sich** *(D)* **Mut antrinken** to fill o.s. with Dutch courage.

Ạntritt *der (ohne pl)* - **1.** [Beginn] start - **2.** SPORT: **er hat einen schnellen Antritt** he has a good turn of pace.

ạn|tun *vt (unreg)* - **1.** [Unrecht] to do; **wie konntest du mir das antun?** how could you do that to me?; **sich** *(D)* **etwas antun** to take one's own life - **2.** [Gutes]: **jm zu viel Ehre antun** to do sb too much justice - **3.** [lieben]: **das Bild hat es mir angetan** I really like the picture.

Ạntwort ['antvɔrt] (*pl* **-en**) *die* - **1.** [Erwiderung] answer; [auf Brief] reply; **die Antwort auf etw** *(A)* the answer to sthg; **Antwort/keine Antwort geben** to reply/not to reply - **2.** [Reaktion] response; **als Antwort auf** *(+ A)* in response to.

ạntworten ◇ *vi* - **1.** [erwidern] to answer; **auf etw** *(A)* **antworten** to answer sthg, to reply to sthg - **2.** [reagieren] to respond. ◇ *vt* [auf Fragen] to answer, to reply.

ạn|vertrauen *vt*: **jm etw anvertrauen** to entrust sb with sthg. ◆ **sich anvertrauen** *ref*: **sich jm anvertrauen** to confide in sb.

ạn|wachsen ['anvaksn̩] (*perf* **ist ạngewachsen**) *vi (unreg)* - **1.** [festwachsen] to take root - **2.** [wachsen] to increase.

Ạnwalt ['anvalt] (*pl* **Ạnwälte**) *der* - **1.** [Rechtsanwalt] lawyer - **2.** *fig* [Fürsprecher] advocate.

Ạnwältin ['anvɛltɪn] (*pl* **-nen**) *die* - **1.** [Rechtsanwältin] lawyer - **2.** *fig* [Fürsprecherin] advocate.

Ạnwalts|büro *das* [Firma] firm of lawyers.

Ạnwärter, in (*mpl* -, *fpl* **-nen**) *der, die*: **ein Anwärter (auf etw** *(A)***)** a candidate (for sthg).

ạn|weisen *vt (unreg)* - **1.** [zeigen] to show; **jm etw anweisen** to show sthg to sb - **2.** [beauftragen]: **jn anweisen, etw zu tun** to instruct sb to do sthg.

Ạn|weisung *die* - **1.** [Befehl] instruction; **Anweisung haben, etw zu tun** to have instructions to do sthg - **2.** [Zahlung - per Bank] payment; [- per Post] postal order.

ạnwendbar *adj*: **(auf jn/etw) anwendbar sein** to be applicable (to sb/sthg).

ạn|wenden *vt* - **1.** [Hilfsmittel, Gewalt, List] to use - **2.** [Methode, Regel]: **etw auf jn/etw anwenden** to apply sthg to sb/sthg.

Ạn|wendung *die* - **1.** [Verwendung, Einsatz] use - **2.** [von Methode, Regel] application.

ạn|werben *vt (unreg)* to recruit.

ạnwesend *adj* present; **bei etw anwesend sein** to be present at sthg.

Ạnwesenheit *die* presence; **in js Anwesenheit** *(D)*, **in Anwesenheit von jm** in sb's presence.

ạn|widern ['anvi:dɐn] *vt* to fill with repulsion.

Ạnwohner, in (*mpl* -, *fpl* **-nen**) *der, die* resident.

Ạnzahl *die* number.

ạn|zahlen *vt* to pay a deposit on; **100 Euro anzahlen** to pay a deposit of 100 euros.

Ạn|zahlung *die* deposit, down payment.

Ạn|zeichen *das* sign.

Ạnzeige ['antsai̯gə] (*pl* **-n**) *die* - **1.** [in Zeitung] advertisement; [Brief] announcement - **2.** [Instrument] display - **3.** [Strafanzeige] charge; **gegen jn Anzeige erstatten** to bring a charge against sb.

ạn|zeigen *vt* - **1.** [melden] to report - **2.** [zeigen] to show.

Ạnzeigen|teil *der* advertisements section.

ạn|zetteln ['antsɛtl̩n] *vt* to instigate.

ạn|ziehen *(unreg)* ◇ *vt* - **1.** [Kleidung] to put on; **sich** *(D)* **etw anziehen** to put sthg on - **2.** [Person]: **jn anziehen** to dress sb - **3.** PHYS [anlocken] to attract - **4.** [Schraube, Tau] to tighten; [Bremse] to apply - **5.** [Körperteil] to draw up. ◇ *vi* - **1.** [steigen] to rise - **2.** [beschleunigen] to accelerate. ◆ **sich anziehen** *ref* [Person] to get dressed; **sich warm anziehen** to dress warmly.

ạnziehend *adj* attractive.

Ạnziehungs|kraft *die* - **1.** PHYS (gravitational) attraction - **2.** [Reiz] attractiveness, appeal.

Anlzug *der* - **1.** [Kleidungsstück] suit - **2.** [Nähern]: **im Anzug sein** to be approaching.

anzüglich ['antsy:klɪç] <> *adj* lewd. <> *adv* lewdly.

anlzünden *vt* [Streichholz, Kerze] to light; [Haus] to set fire to.

anlzweifeln *vt* to doubt.

Apartment = **Appartement**.

Aperitif [aperi'ti:f] (*pl* **-s**) *der* aperitif.

Apfel ['apfl] (*pl* **Äpfel**) *der* apple.

Apfellbaum *der* apple tree.

Apfellkuchen *der* apple cake.

Apfellmus *das* apple sauce *(usually eaten as dessert)*.

Apfellsaft *der* apple juice.

Apfelsine [apfl'zi:nə] (*pl* **-n**) *die* orange.

Apfellwein *der* cider.

Apostel [a'pɔstl] (*pl* -) *der* apostle.

Apostroph [apo'stro:f] (*pl* **-e**) *der* apostrophe.

Apotheke [apo'te:kə] (*pl* **-n**) *die* pharmacy, chemist's *UK*, drugstore *US*.

Apotheker, **in** (*mpl* -, *fpl* **-nen**) *der, die* pharmacist, chemist *UK*, druggist *US*.

Apparat [apa'ra:t] (*pl* **-e**) *der* - **1.** [Gerät] device - **2.** [Telefon]: **am Apparat!** speaking! - **3.** [von Partei, Staat] apparatus - **4.** *salopp* [Riesending] whopper.

Appartement [apartə'mɑ̃:], **Apartment** [a'partmənt] (*pl* **-s**) *das* [Wohnung] flat *UK*, apartment *US*.

Appell [a'pɛl] (*pl* **-e**) *der* - **1.** [Aufruf] appeal - **2.** MIL roll call.

appellieren *vi*: **an jn/etw appellieren** to appeal to sb/sthg.

Appetit [ape'ti:t] *der* appetite; **Appetit/keinen Appetit auf etw** *(A)* **haben** to feel/not to feel like sthg; **guten Appetit!** enjoy your meal!

appetitlich *adj* appetizing.

applaudieren [aplau'di:rən] *vi* to applaud.

Applaus [a'plaus] *der (ohne pl)* applause; **jm Applaus spenden** to applaud sb.

Aprikose [apri'ko:zə] (*pl* **-n**) *die* apricot.

April *der (ohne pl)* April; **April, April!** April fool!; *siehe auch* **September**.

Aprillscherz *der* April fool's trick.

apropos [apro'po:] *adv* by the way; **apropos Pizza, hast du Hunger?** talking of pizza, are you hungry?

Aquarell [akva'rɛl] (*pl* **-e**) *das* - **1.** [Bild] watercolour - **2.** [Farbe]: **in Aquarell malen** to paint in watercolours.

Aquarium [a'kva:rium] (*pl* **Aquarien**) *das* aquarium.

Äquator [ɛ'kva:tɔr] *der (ohne pl)* equator.

Ära ['ɛ:ra] (*pl* **Ären**) *die* era.

Araber, **in** ['arabɐ, rɪn] (*mpl* -, *fpl* **-nen**) *der, die* Arab.

Arabien *nt* Arabia.

arabisch *adj* [Kultur, Volk, Politik] Arab; [Sprache, Literatur] Arabic; [Halbinsel, Landschaft] Arabian.

Arabisch(e) *das (ohne pl)* Arabic; *siehe auch* **Englisch(e)**.

Arbeit ['arbait] (*pl* **-en**) *die* - **1.** [gen] work; **die Arbeiten am Tunnel** the work on the tunnel; **bei der Arbeit sein** to be working; **ihr Wagen ist in Arbeit** your car is being worked on; **zur Arbeit gehen** to go to work - **2.** [Arbeitsstelle] job; **keine Arbeit haben** to be out of work; **Arbeit suchen** to be looking for work ODER a job - **3.** [Leistung, Werk] work - **4.** [Klassenarbeit] test - **5.** [wissenschaftlich] paper.

arbeiten <> *vi* - **1.** [Person] to work; **bei der Post arbeiten** to work for the Post Office; **zu Hause arbeiten** to work from home; **an etw** *(D)* **arbeiten** to work on sthg; **an sich** *(D)* **arbeiten** to work hard - **2.** [funktionieren - Maschine] to operate; [- Herz] to function. <> *vt* to make; **sich** *(D)* **die Finger** ODER **Hände wund arbeiten** to work one's fingers to the bone. ◆ **sich arbeiten** *ref*: **sich nach oben arbeiten** to work one's way up.

Arbeiter (*pl* -) *der* worker.

Arbeiterin (*pl* **-nen**) *die* worker.

Arbeitgeber, **in** (*mpl* -, *fpl* **-nen**) *der, die* employer.

Arbeitnehmer, **in** (*mpl* -, *fpl* **-nen**) *der, die* employee.

Arbeitslamt *das* job centre *UK*, employment agency *US*.

Arbeitslaufwand *der*: **der Arbeitsaufwand ist zu hoch** it would take too much effort.

arbeitsfrei *adj*: **zwei arbeitsfreie Nachmittage in der Woche** two afternoons off a week.

Arbeitslkraft *die*: **sich** *(D)* **seine Arbeitskraft erhalten** to keep o.s. fit for work. ◆ **Arbeitskräfte** *Pl* workers.

Arbeitslkreis *der* [Lerngruppe] study group; [Ausschuss] working party.

arbeitslos *adj* unemployed.

Arbeitslose (*pl* **-n**) *der, die* unemployed person; **die Arbeitslosen** the unemployed.

Arbeitslosigkeit *die (ohne pl)* unemployment.

Arbeitslmarkt *der* labour market.

Arbeitslplatz *der* - **1.** [Stellung, Job] job - **2.** [Ort] workplace; **dort am Fenster ist mein Arbeitsplatz** I work over there by the window.

arbeitsscheu *adj* workshy.

Arbeitslspeicher *der* EDV RAM.

Arbeitslstelle *die* - **1.** [Stellung] job - **2.** [Ort, Abteilung] department.

Arbeits|suche *die*: **auf Arbeitssuche sein** to be looking for work *ODER* a job.

Arbeits|tag *der* working day.

Arbeits|teilung *die* division of labour.

Arbeits|unfall *der* industrial accident.

Arbeits|vermittlung *die* [private Agentur] employment agency.

Arbeits|weise *die* [von Person] way of working; [von Maschine] mode of operation.

Arbeits|zeit *die* working hours *Pl*.

Arbeits|zimmer *das* study.

Archäologe [arçeo'lo:gə] (*pl* **-n**) *der* archaeologist.

Archäologin [arçeo'lo:gɪn] (*pl* **-nen**) *die* archaeologist.

Arche ['arçə] (*pl* **-n**) *die*: **die Arche Noah** Noah's Ark.

Architekt, in [arçi'tɛkt, ɪn] (*mpl* **-en**, *fpl* **-nen**) *der, die* architect.

Architektur [arçitɛk'tu:ɐ̯] *die (ohne pl)* architecture.

Archiv [ar'çi:f] (*pl* **-e**) *das* archive.

archivieren [arçi'vi:rən] *vt* to (store in an) archive.

ARD [a:ɛr'de:] (*abk für* **Arbeitsgemeinschaft der öffentlich-rechtlichen Rundfunkanstalten der Bundesrepublik Deutschland**) *die German public broadcasting network, responsible for the Erstes Programm TV channel.*

Arena [a're:na] (*pl* **Arenen**) *die* arena.

arg [ark] (*kompar* **ärger**, *superl* **ärgste**) ◇ *adj* [schlimm] bad; [sehr schlimm] terrible; **js ärgster Feind** sb's arch enemy. ◇ *adv* [schlimm] badly; [sehr schlimm] terribly.

Argentinien *nt* Argentina.

Ärger ['ɛrgɐ] *der (ohne pl)* - **1.** [Verärgerung] annoyance; [Zorn] anger - **2.** [Problem] trouble; **(jm) Ärger machen** to cause (sb) trouble.

ärgerlich ◇ *adj* - **1.** [verärgert] annoyed; [zornig] angry; **auf jn/über etw** *(A)* **ärgerlich sein** [verärgert] to be annoyed with sb/at sthg; [zornig] to be angry with sb/at sthg - **2.** [unangenehm] annoying. ◇ *adv* [verärgert] angrily.

ärgern *vt* to annoy. ◆ **sich ärgern** *ref* to get annoyed; **sich über jn/etw ärgern** to get annoyed with sb/at sthg.

Ärgernis (*pl* **-se**) *das* - **1.** [Ärgerliches] nuisance - **2.** RECHT: **Erregung öffentlichen Ärgernisses** offence against public decency.

Argument (*pl* **-e**) *das* argument.

argumentieren *vi* to argue.

Argwohn *der (ohne pl)* suspicion.

argwöhnisch ◇ *adj* suspicious. ◇ *adv* suspiciously.

Arie ['a:ri̯ə] (*pl* **-n**) *die* aria.

aristokratisch *adj* aristocratic.

Arithmetik *die (ohne pl)* arithmetic.

Arkaden *Pl* ARCHIT arcade *sing*.

Arktis *die* Arctic.

arm (*kompar* **ärmer**, *superl* **ärmste**) ◇ *adj* poor; **um etw ärmer sein** to have lost sthg; **er ist nun um 50 Euro ärmer** he's now 50 euros worse off *ODER* the poorer; **arm dran sein** *fam* to be in a bad way. ◇ *adv* poorly; **jn arm essen** to eat sb out of house and home.

Arm (*pl* **-e**) *der* [gen] arm; **jn/etw im Arm halten** to hold sb/sthg in one's arms; **jn auf den Arm nehmen** to pull sb's leg; **jn mit offenen Armen aufnehmen** to welcome sb with open arms. ◆ **Arm in Arm** *adv* arm in arm.

Armatur (*pl* **-en**) *die* [von Maschine, Auto] instrument. ◆ **Armaturen** *Pl* [im Badezimmer] fittings.

Armaturen|brett *das* AUTO dashboard.

Arm|band (*pl* **-bänder**) *das* [Schmuck] bracelet; [von Uhr] strap.

Armband|uhr *die* wristwatch, watch.

Arm|binde *die* armband.

Arme (*pl* **-n**) *der, die* - **1.** [Bedauernswerte] poor thing; **du Armer!** you poor thing! - **2.** [Mittellose] poor man/woman; **die Armen** the poor.

Armee [ar'me:] (*pl* **-n**) *die* army.

Ärmel (*pl* -) *der* sleeve; **die Ärmel hochkrempeln** *eigtl* & *fig* to roll up one's sleeves.

Ärmelkanal *der*: **der Ärmelkanal** the (English) Channel.

Arm|lehne *die* arm, armrest.

ärmlich ◇ *adj* [Wohnung, Kleidung] shabby; [Verhältnisse] miserable. ◇ *adv* shabbily.

armselig *adj* - **1.** [ärmlich] shabby - **2.** [gering] meagre.

Armut *die (ohne pl)* poverty.

Aroma (*pl* **-s** *ODER* **Aromen**) *das* - **1.** [Geruch] aroma - **2.** [Würze] flavouring.

arrangieren [arɑ̃ŋ'ʒi:rən] *vt* [Treffen, Feier, Musik] to arrange. ◆ **sich arrangieren** *ref*: **sich mit jm arrangieren** [sich verständigen] to come to an understanding with sb.

arrogant ◇ *adj* arrogant. ◇ *adv* arrogantly.

Arroganz *die (ohne pl)* arrogance.

Arsch (*pl* **Ärsche**) *der salopp* - **1.** [Gesäß] arse *UK*, ass *US* - **2.** [Blödmann] arsehole *UK*, asshole *US*; **jm in den Arsch kriechen** *vulg* to lick sb's arse *UK ODER* ass *US*.

Arsen *das (ohne pl)* arsenic.

Art (*pl* **-en**) *die* - **1.** [Weise] way; **eine einfache Art, etw zuzubereiten** a simple way of preparing *ODER* to prepare sthg; **etw auf eine andere Art tun** to do sthg another way; **auf gesunde Art** healthily; **auf diese Art wird er nie gewinnen** he'll never win like this *ODER* this way; **die Art und Weise(, wie)** the way (that); **Bratkartoffeln nach Art des Hauses** the chef's special fried potatoes - **2.** *(ohne pl)* [Wesen] nature; [Verhalten] behaviour; **das entspricht nicht ihrer Art, sich zu beschweren** it's not like her to complain - **3.** [Sorte] sort, kind; **eine Art Grippe** a sort *ODER* kind of flu; **in dieser Art** in this form; **das Schloss ist in seiner Art einmalig** the castle is the only one of its kind - **4.** BIOL species.

Artensterben *das (ohne pl)* dying out of species.

Arterie (*pl* **-n**) *die* artery.

Arteriosklerose (*pl* **-n**) *die* arteriosclerosis *(U)*.

Arthritis *die* arthritis.

artig ◇ *adj* good. ◇ *adv*: **sie hat den Teller Spinat artig aufgegessen** she ate up all her spinach like a good girl.

Artikel (*pl* -) *der* - **1.** [in der Zeitung, im Gesetz] article; [im Wörterbuch] entry - **2.** [Ware] item, article - **3.** GRAMM: **der bestimmte/unbestimmte Artikel** the definite/indefinite article.

artikulieren *vt* to articulate.

Artillerie (*pl* **-n**) *die* MIL artillery.

Artischocke (*pl* **-n**) *die* artichoke.

Artist, in (*mpl* **-en**, *fpl* **-nen**) *der, die* [im Zirkus] (circus) performer.

artistisch *adj* acrobatic.

Arznei (*pl* **-en**) *die* medicine.

Arzt [aːɐ̯tst] (*pl* **Ärzte**) *der* doctor.

Arzt|helfer, in *der, die* doctor's receptionist.

Ärztin ['ɛːɐ̯tstɪn] (*pl* **-nen**) *die* doctor.

ärztlich *adj* medical.

Arzt|praxis *die* doctor's practice.

as (*pl* -), **As** (*pl* -) *das* MUS A flat.

As (*pl* **-se**) *das* = **Ass**.

Asbest (*pl* **-e**) *das* asbestos.

Asche (*pl* **-n**) *die* [von Feuer] ashes *Pl*; [von Zigarre, Vulkan] ash.

Aschen|becher *der* ashtray.

Aschen|puttel (*pl* **Aschenputtel**) *das* Cinderella.

Ascher|mittwoch *der* Ash Wednesday.

Asiat, in (*mpl* **-en**, *fpl* **-nen**) *der, die* Asian.

asiatisch *adj* Asian.

Asien *nt* Asia.

asozial ◇ *adj* antisocial. ◇ *adv* antisocially.

Aspekt (*pl* **-e**) *der* aspect.

Asphalt [as'falt] (*pl* **-e**) *der* asphalt.

asphaltieren *vt* to asphalt.

aß *prät* ▷ **essen**.

Ass (*pl* **-e**) *das* [Spielkarte, Person] ace.

Assistent, in (*mpl* **-en**, *fpl* **-nen**) *der, die* assistant.

assistieren *vi* to assist; **jm bei etw assistieren** to assist sb with sthg.

Ast (*pl* **Äste**) *der* branch; **sich** *(D)* **einen Ast lachen** *fam fig* to laugh o.s. silly.

AStA ['asta] (*pl* **ASten**) (*abk für* **Allgemeiner Studentenausschuss**) *der* students' union.

Aster (*pl* **-n**) *die* aster.

Ast|gabel *die* fork in a branch.

Ästhetik [ɛs'teːtɪk] (*pl* **-en**) *die* - **1.** *(ohne pl)* [das Schöne] aesthetic - **2.** [Wissenschaft] aesthetics *(U)*.

Asthma *das* asthma.

Astrologie *die (ohne pl)* astrology.

astrologisch *adj* astrological.

Astronaut, in (*mpl* **-en**, *fpl* **-nen**) *der, die* astronaut.

Astronomie *die (ohne pl)* astronomy.

Asyl (*pl* **-e**) *das* - **1.** *(ohne pl)* [Zuflucht] asylum - **2.** [Obdachlosenasyl] hostel.

Asylant (*pl* **-en**) *der* asylum seeker.

Asylantin (*pl* **-nen**) *die* asylum seeker.

Asyl|bewerber, in *der, die* asylum seeker.

Asylrecht *das (ohne pl)* right of asylum.

asymmetrisch *adj* asymmetrical.

Atem *der (ohne pl)* - **1.** [die Atmung] breathing - **2.** [die Atemluft] breath; **außer Atem sein** to be out of breath; **Atem holen** [einatmen] to breathe in; [sich ausruhen] to catch one's breath; **jn in Atem halten** [in Spannung versetzen] to keep sb on tenterhooks.

atemberaubend ◇ *adj* breathtaking. ◇ *adv* breathtakingly.

atemlos ◇ *adj* breathless. ◇ *adv* breathlessly.

Atem|not *die (ohne pl)* difficulty in breathing.

Atem|pause *die*: **eine Atempause einlegen** *ODER* **machen** to take a breather.

Atem|zug *der* breath.

Atheist, in (*mpl* **-en**, *fpl* **-nen**) *der, die* atheist.

Äther *der (ohne pl)* ether.

Äthiopien *nt* Ethiopia.

Athlet, in (*mpl* **-en**, *fpl* **-nen**) *der, die* athlete.

athletisch ◇ *adj* athletic. ◇ *adv* athletically.

Atlantik *der*: **der Atlantik** the Atlantic (Ocean).

Atlas (*pl* **-se** *ODER* **Atlanten**) *der* - **1.** [Buch] atlas - **2.** *(pl Atlasse)* [Satin] satin.

atmen *vt* & *vi* to breathe.

Atmosphäre (*pl* **-n**) *die eigtl* & *fig* atmosphere.

Atmung *die (ohne pl)* breathing.

Atoll (*pl* **-e**) *das* atoll.

Atom (*pl* **-e**) *das* atom.

atomar *adj* - **1.** [von Atomen] atomic - **2.** [mit Atomkraft] nuclear.

Atom|bombe *die* atom *ODER* atomic bomb.

Atom|kraft *die (ohne pl)* nuclear power.

Atom|kraftwerk *das* nuclear power station.

Atom|krieg *der* nuclear war.

Atom|macht *die* nuclear power *(country)*.

Atom|müll *der (ohne pl)* nuclear waste.

Atom|sprengkopf *der* nuclear warhead.

Atom|waffe *die* nuclear weapon.

Attentat (*pl* **-e**) *das* [erfolglos] assassination attempt; [erfolgreich] assassination.

Attentäter, in (*mpl* **-**, *fpl* **-nen**) *der, die* [erfolglos] would-be assassin; [erfolgreich] assassin.

Attest (*pl* **-e**) *das* doctor's certificate.

Attraktion (*pl* **-en**) *die* attraction.

attraktiv *adj* attractive.

Attrappe (*pl* **-n**) *die* dummy.

Attribut (*pl* **-e**) *das geh* [Merkmal & GRAMM] attribute.

au *interj* [Ausdruck von Schmerz] ouch!, ow!

Aubergine [obɛr'ʒiːnə] (*pl* **-n**) *die* aubergine *UK*, eggplant *US*.

auch *adv* - **1.** [ebenfalls] also, too; **ich auch** me too; **ich auch nicht** me neither; **auch das noch!** that's the last thing I need! - **2.** [sogar] even - **3.** [wirklich]: **sie war unkonzentriert, aber es war ja auch schon spät** she couldn't concentrate, but it **was** late - **4.** [verstärkend]: **dass du auch immer kleckern musst!** do you **have** to make such a mess!; **hast du die Tür auch wirklich zugemacht?** are you sure you closed the door? - **5.** [egal]: **wo auch (immer)** wherever; **was auch (immer)** whatever; **wer auch (immer)** whoever; **wie dem auch sei** be that as it may.

Audienz (*pl* **-en**) *die* audience.

audiovisuell [audiovi'zuɛl] *adj* audiovisual.

auf <> *präp* - **1.** *(+ D, A)* [räumlich] on; **auf dem/den Tisch** on the table; **auf dem Land** in the country; **aufs Land** to the country; **auf einen Berg steigen** to climb a mountain; **auf der Post** at the post office; **auf eine Feier gehen** to go to a party; **auf die Uni gehen** to go to university - **2.** *(+ D)* [zeitlich - während]: **auf der Reise** on the journey; **auf der Hochzeit/Feier** at the wedding/party - **3.** *(+ A)* [zur Angabe der Art und Weise]: **auf diese Art** in this way; **auf Deutsch** in German; **auf jeden Fall** in any case - **4.** [feste Verbindungen]: **auf Reisen gehen** to go on a tour; **von heute auf morgen** overnight - **5.** *(+ A)* [zur Angabe eines Wunsches]: **auf ihr Wohl!** your good health! - **6.** [zur Angabe eines Verhältnisses]: **auf ein Kilo Obst kommt ein Kilo Zucker** add a kilo of sugar for every kilo of fruit. <> *adv* - **1.** [offen] open; **Tür auf!** open the door! - **2.** [aufgestanden] up; **ich bin seit zehn Uhr auf** I've been up since ten o'clock - **3.** [feste Verbindungen]: **auf einmal knallte es** suddenly there was a bang; **er aß alle Süßigkeiten auf einmal** he ate all the sweets in one go. <> *interj* [los, weg]: **auf in die Kneipe!** (let's go) to the pub! ◆ **auf und ab** *adv* - **1.** [herauf und herunter] up and down - **2.** [hin und her] back and forth.

auf|atmen *vi* to breathe a sigh of relief.

Aufbau (*pl* **-ten**) *der* - **1.** *(ohne pl)* [Bauen - von Zelt, Gerüst] putting up; [- von Ruinen] rebuilding - **2.** *(ohne pl)* [Gründung] building up - **3.** *(ohne pl)* [Struktur] structure - **4.** [Anbau] superstructure.

auf|bauen *vt* - **1.** [bauen - Zelt, Gerüst] to put up; [- Ruinen] to rebuild - **2.** [gründen, schaffen] to build up - **3.** [zusammensetzen - Kulissen, Modelleisenbahn] to build; **aus etw aufgebaut sein** to be made up ODER composed of sthg - **4.** TELEKOM [Verbindung] to establish - **5.** [ordnen] to structure - **6.** [fördern]: **jn zu ODER als etw aufbauen** to make ODER turn sb into sthg - **7.** [trösten]: **jn aufbauen** to give sb strength - **8.** [begründen]: **etw auf etw *(D)* aufbauen** to base sthg on sthg. ◆ **sich aufbauen** *ref fam* [sich hinstellen] to plant o.s.

auf|bäumen ◆ **sich aufbäumen** *ref* - **1.** [Pferd] to rear (up) - **2.** [Person]: **sich gegen jn/etw aufbäumen** to rebel against sb/sthg.

auf|bauschen *vt* [übertreiben] to blow up.

auf|bekommen *vt (unreg)* - **1.** [öffnen] to get open - **2.** *fam* [aufessen] to manage (to eat) - **3.** [Schulaufgabe] to get for homework.

auf|bereiten *vt* to process; [Trinkwasser] to purify.

auf|bessern *vt* - **1.** [verbessern] to improve - **2.** [erhöhen] to increase.

auf|bewahren *vt* [in Tresor] to keep; **etw (für jn) aufbewahren** to look after sthg (for sb); **die Milch kühl aufbewahren** to store the milk in a cool place.

Aufbewahrung *die* storage.

auf|bieten *vt (unreg)* - **1.** [Kraft] to summon up; [Einfluss] to use - **2.** [Polizei, Militär] to call out.

auf|blasen *vt (unreg)* [Ballon, Luftmatratze] to blow up, to inflate; [Backen] to puff out.

auf|bleiben (*perf* **ist aufgeblieben**) *vi (unreg)* - **1.** [wach bleiben] to stay up - **2.** [offen bleiben] to stay open.

auf|blenden <> *vt* to turn on full beam *UK* ODER high beam *US*. <> *vi* to put one's headlights on full beam *UK* ODER high beam *US*.

auf|blicken *vi* - **1.** [hochsehen] to look up - **2.** [bewundern]: **zu jm aufblicken** to look up to sb.

auf|blitzen (*perf* **aufgeblitzt**) *vi* [Licht] to flash.

auf|blühen (*perf* **ist aufgeblüht**) *vi* - **1.** [blühen] to blossom - **2.** [aufleben] to blossom (out) - **3.** [wachsen] to flourish.

auf|brauchen *vt* to use up.

auf|brausen (*perf* **ist aufgebraust**) *vi* - **1.** [erklingen] to break out - **2.** [hochfahren] to flare up.

auf|brechen (*perf* **hat/ist aufgebrochen**) *(unreg)* ◇ *vt (hat)* [mit Gewalt öffnen - Tür] to force open; [- Schloss] to force; [- Deckel] to force off; [- Wohnung, Auto, Tresor] to break into. ◇ *vi (ist)* - **1.** [abreisen]: **aufbrechen (nach)** to set off (for) - **2.** [aufreißen] to open.

auf|bringen *vt (unreg)* - **1.** [beschaffen] to raise - **2.** [einsetzen] to summon up - **3.** [einführen - Gerücht] to start - **4.** [wütend machen] to make angry - **5.** [öffnen können] to get open.

Aufbruch *der (ohne pl)* departure.

auf|brummen *vt fam*: **jm etw aufbrummen** [Strafe] to slap sthg on sb.

auf|bürden *vt*: **jm/sich etw aufbürden** [Verantwortung] to burden sb/o.s. with sthg; [Last, Rucksack] to load sb/o.s. down with sthg.

auf|decken *vt* - **1.** [aufschlagen] to turn back - **2.** [entdecken] to uncover - **3.** [Spielkarten]: **seine Karten** *ODER* **sein Spiel aufdecken** to show one's hand - **4.** [im Bett]: **jn aufdecken** to pull the covers off sb.

auf|drängen *vt*: **jm etw aufdrängen** to force sthg onto sb. ◆ **sich aufdrängen** *ref* - **1.** [Person] to impose; **er hat sich uns vor der Reise aufgedrängt** he imposed himself on us before we set off - **2.** [Idee]: **dieser Gedanke/Verdacht drängte sich mir auf** I couldn't help thinking/suspecting that; **diese Idee drängt sich einem ja sofort auf, wenn man seinen Bericht hört** this idea comes immediately to mind on hearing his report.

auf|drehen ◇ *vt* - **1.** [Wasserhahn, Gas] to turn on; [Deckel] to unscrew; [Flasche, Dose] to open - **2.** *fam* [laut stellen] to turn up. ◇ *vi fam* - **1.** [schnell fahren] to put one's foot down - **2.** [in Stimmung kommen] to get going.

aufdringlich ◇ *adj* [Person] pushy; [Farbe] loud; [Parfüm] overpowering. ◇ *adv* insistently.

aufeinander *adv* - **1.** [einer auf dem anderen] one on top of the other; **sie liegen aufeinander** they are lying on top of each other - **2.** [gegenseitig] one another; **sie passen aufeinander auf** they look out for each other.

aufeinander folgen (*perf* **sind aufeinander gefolgt**) *vi* to come one after the other.

aufeinander prallen (*perf* **sind aufeinander geprallt**) *vi* - **1.** [zusammenstoßen] to crash into one another - **2.** [sich widersprechen] to clash.

aufeinander stoßen (*perf* **sind aufeinander gestoßen**) *vi (unreg)* - **1.** [Köpfe, Wagons] to bump into each other - **2.** [Meinungen] to clash.

Aufenthalt (*pl* **-e**) *der* - **1.** [Anwesenheit] stay; **der Aufenthalt im Bereich des Krans ist gefährlich** keep well clear of the crane - **2.** [Unterbrechung] stop; **in Köln haben wir eine Stunde Aufenthalt** we'll have an hour to wait in Cologne.

Aufenthalts|genehmigung *die* residence permit.

Aufenthalts|ort *der* place of residence.

Auferstehung *die (ohne pl)* resurrection.

auf|essen *vt (unreg)* to eat up.

auf|fädeln *vt* to string.

auf|fahren (*perf* **ist aufgefahren**) *(unreg)* ◇ *vi* - **1.** [im Auto]: **dicht auf den Vordermann auffahren** to sit right on the tail of the car in front; **auf jn/etw auffahren** to run into sb/sthg - **2.** [erschrecken] to start; **aus dem Schlaf auffahren** to awake with a start. ◇ *vt* - **1.** [heranfahren] to bring up - **2.** *fam* [anbieten] to lay on - **3.** [aufschütten] to put down.

Auffahrt (*pl* **-en**) *die* - **1.** [zur Autobahn] slip road *UK*, on-ramp *US* - **2.** [zu einem Gebäude] drive - **3.** [Aufstieg] climb - **4.** *Schweiz* [Himmelfahrt] Ascension Day.

Auffahr|unfall *der* rear-end collision.

auf|fallen (*perf* **ist aufgefallen**) *vi (unreg)* to stand out; **mir ist nichts Besonderes an ihm aufgefallen** nothing in particular struck me about him; **das ist mir aufgefallen** I've noticed that.

auffallend ◇ *adj* striking. ◇ *adv* strikingly.

auffällig ◇ *adj* [Kleidung, Auto] ostentatious; [Farbe] loud; [Verhalten] odd, unusual. ◇ *adv* [geschminkt] ostentatiously; [häufig] surprisingly.

auf|fangen *vt (unreg)* - **1.** [Ball] to catch - **2.** [Worte, Spruch, Signal] to pick up - **3.** [Stoß, Schlag] to cushion; [Inflation, Preissteigerung] to offset - **4.** [sammeln] to collect.

Auffang|lager *das* transit camp.

auf|fassen *vt* to understand; **etw als etw auffassen** to take sthg as sthg.

Auf|fassung *die* opinion; **zu der Auffassung kommen, dass ...** to come to the conclusion that ...; **nach js Auffassung** in sb's opinion.

Auffassungs|gabe *die (ohne pl)* intelligence; **eine schnelle Auffassungsgabe haben** to be quick on the uptake.

auf|flackern (*perf* **ist aufgeflackert**) *vi* [leuchten] to flicker into life.

auf|fliegen (*perf* **ist aufgeflogen**) *vi (unreg)* - **1.** [fliegen] to fly up - **2.** [sich öffnen] to fly open - **3.** *fam* [entdeckt werden - Vorhaben] to be uncovered; [- Bande] to be broken up.

auf|fordern *vt* - **1.** [bitten]: **jn zum Platznehmen auffordern** to ask *ODER* invite sb to be seated - **2.** [befehlen]: **jn dazu auffordern, etw zu tun** to require sb to do sthg - **3.** [zum Tanz] to ask to dance.

Auf|forderung *die* - **1.** [Bitte] request, invitation - **2.** [Befehl] demand.

auf|frischen ◇ *vt* - **1.** [erneuern - Bezug] to freshen up; [- Farbe] to brighten up; [- Möbel] to renovate - **2.** [erweitern - Kenntnisse] to brush up on; [- Erinnerung] to refresh. ◇ *vi* [Wind] to freshen.

auf|führen *vt* - **1.** [auf der Bühne] to perform - **2.** [nennen, auflisten] to give, to list. ◆ **sich aufführen** *ref abw* [sich benehmen] to behave.

Auf|führung *die* [Vorstellung] performance.

auf|füllen *vt* - **1.** [nachfüllen] to top up - **2.** [füllen] to fill up - **3.** [ergänzen] to replenish.

Auf|gabe *die* - **1.** [Pflicht] task; **das ist nicht meine Aufgabe** that's not my responsibility - **2.** [Kapitulation] surrender - **3.** *(ohne pl)* [von Geschäften]: **die Einzelhändler wurden zur Aufgabe genötigt** the retailers were forced to give up their businesses - **4.** [eines Pakets] posting *UK*, mailing *US*; [einer Anzeige] placing - **5.** [SCHULE - in Prüfung] question; [- in Mathematik] problem; [- Übung] exercise; [- Schulaufgabe] homework *(U)*.

Aufgaben|bereich *der* area of responsibility.

Aufgang (*pl* **Aufgänge**) *der* - **1.** [Treppe] stairs *Pl* - **2.** [Leuchten] rising.

auf|geben *(unreg)* ◇ *vt* - **1.** [Gewohnheit, Stelle, Geschäft] to give up; **das Rauchen aufgeben** to give up smoking - **2.** [Person] to give up on; [Plan, Idee, Hoffnung] to give up; [Wettkampf, Spiel] to pull out of; **ich gebe es auf!** I give up! - **3.** [auftragen] to set; **jm etw aufgeben** to set sb sthg - **4.** [Bestellung] to place; **eine Anzeige aufgeben** to place an advert in the paper - **5.** [verschicken] to send. ◇ *vi* [aufhören, kapitulieren] to give up.

aufgebläht *adj* [Ballon, Verwaltungsapparat] inflated; [Bauch] swollen; [Backen] puffed-out.

Auf|gebot *das* - **1.** [an Personen] contingent; [an Maschinen, Waren] array - **2.** [für Hochzeit] banns *Pl*; **das Aufgebot bestellen** to publish the banns.

aufgebracht ◇ *pp* ▷ **aufbringen**. ◇ *adj* [wütend] angry.

aufgedunsen *adj* bloated.

auf|gehen (*perf* **ist aufgegangen**) *vi (unreg)* - **1.** [Sonne, Mond] to rise - **2.** [Knoten, Knopf] to come undone - **3.** [sich öffnen] to open - **4.** [Rechnung] to work out - **5.** [verschwinden]: **in etw** *(D)* **aufgehen** to disappear into sthg; **in Flammen aufgehen** to go up in flames - **6.** [sich einsetzen]: **in etw** *(D)* **aufgehen** to be wrapped up in sthg - **7.** [deutlich werden]: **jm aufgehen** to dawn on sb - **8.** [Teig, Kuchen] to rise.

aufgehoben ◇ *pp* ▷ **aufheben**. ◇ *adj*: **(bei jm) gut/schlecht aufgehoben sein** to be/not to be in good hands (with sb).

aufgeklärt *adj* enlightened.

aufgelegt *adj*: **gut/schlecht aufgelegt sein** to be in a good/bad mood.

aufgeregt ◇ *adj* excited. ◇ *adv* excitedly.

aufgeschlossen ◇ *pp* ▷ **aufsch ließen**. ◇ *adj* open-minded; **etw gegenübe** ODER **für etw aufgeschlossen sein** to be open t sthg.

aufgeweckt *adj* bright.

auf|greifen *vt (unreg)* - **1.** [fangen] to pick u - **2.** [übernehmen] to take up.

aufgrund *präp*: **aufgrund einer Sache** *(G)* be cause of sthg.

auf|haben *(unreg)* ◇ *vt* - **1.** [Hausaufgaben to have for homework - **2.** [tragen] to have on to be wearing - **3.** [offen lassen - Mantel, Tür] t have open; [- Knopf] to have undone. ◇ v [geöffnet sein] to be open.

auf|halten *vt (unreg)* - **1.** [offen halten - Tü Tasche] to hold open; **die Hand aufhalten** t hold out one's hand; **die Augen aufhalten** t keep one's eyes open; **jm etw aufhalten** t hold sthg open for sb - **2.** [anhalten - Entwick lung, Inflation] to put a check on - **3.** [störe to hold up; **ich möchte Sie nicht aufhalten** don't want to keep you. ◆ **sich aufhalte** *ref* [sich befinden] to stay.

auf|hängen ◇ *vt* - **1.** [hinhängen - Mante Plakat] to hang up; [- Bild] to hang; [- Wäsche to hang out - **2.** [erhängen] to hang - **3.** [mit et begründen]: **etw an etw** *(D)* **aufhängen** to bas sthg on sthg. ◇ *vi* [am Telefon] to hang up ◆ **sich aufhängen** *ref fam* [sich erhängen] t hang o.s.

Aufhänger (*pl* -) *der* - **1.** [Halterung] loo - **2.** *fig* [Grund, Anstoß] pretext.

auf|häufen *vt* to pile up. ◆ **sich aufhäu fen** *ref* to pile up.

auf|heben *vt (unreg)* - **1.** [nehmen] to pick u - **2.** [aufbewahren] to keep; **etw gut aufhebe** to keep sthg safe - **3.** [Gesetz, Verordnung] t repeal; [Verbot, Embargo] to lift; [Visapflicht] t end - **4.** [ausgleichen]: **etw/einander aufhebe** to cancel sthg/each other out. ◆ **sich auf heben** *ref* to cancel each other out.

auf|heitern *vt* [Person] to cheer up. ◆ **sic aufheitern** *ref* - **1.** [fröhlich werden] to chee up - **2.** [sonnig werden] to clear up.

auf|hellen *vt* [heller machen] to lighten ◆ **sich aufhellen** *ref* - **1.** [Gesicht, Miene] t light up - **2.** [Wetter, Himmel] to clear up.

auf|hetzen *vt* to stir up; **jn gegen jn/etw auf hetzen** to stir sb up against sb/sthg.

auf|holen ◇ *vt* [Verspätung] to make up ◇ *vi* [Sportler, Wirtschaft] to catch up.

auf|horchen *vi* - **1.** [horchen] to prick u one's ears - **2.** [aufmerksam werden] to sit u and take notice.

auf|hören *vi* - **1.** [nicht weitermachen] to sto **aufhören, etw zu tun** to stop doing sthg; **mi etw aufhören** to stop sthg; **mit dem Rauche aufhören** to stop smoking - **2.** [kündigen] t finish - **3.** [zu Ende sein - Film, Straße, Weg] to end; [- Lärm, Regen] to stop; [- Nebel] to lift; **da hört sich doch alles auf!** *fig* that's the limit!

auf|klappen *vt* to open.

auf|klären *vt* - **1.** [Missverständnis] to clear up; [Mord] to solve - **2.** [informieren]**: jn über etw** *(A)* **aufklären** to tell sb about sthg - **3.** [über Sexualität informieren] to explain the facts of life to. ◆ **sich aufklären** *ref* - **1.** [sich auflösen] to be cleared up - **2.** [sonnig werden] to clear up.

Auf|klärung *die* - **1.** [von Irrtum] clearing up; [von Verbrechen] solving - **2.** [Information] informing - **3.** [Information über Sexualität] sex education - **4.** HIST Enlightenment.

Auf|kleber *der* sticker.

auf|knöpfen *vt* to unbutton.

auf|kommen (*perf* **ist aufgekommen**) *vi (unreg)* - **1.** [entstehen] to arise; [Sturm] to get up; **keine Zweifel aufkommen lassen** to leave no room for doubt - **2.** [übernehmen, zahlen]**: für jn/etw aufkommen** to pay for sb/sthg - **3.** [aufstehen können] to get up - **4.** [landen] to land.

auf|kriegen *vt fam* - **1.** [öffnen können - Tür, Paket] to get open; [- Knoten] to get undone - **2.** [aufessen]**: etw nicht aufkriegen** not to eat sthg up.

auf|laden *vt (unreg)* - **1.** [Lasten]**: etw auf etw** *(A)* **aufladen** to load sthg onto sthg - **2.** [aufbürden]**: jm/sich etw aufladen** to burden sb/o.s. with sthg - **3.** [Batterie] to charge.

Auf|lage *die* - **1.** [von Büchern] edition; [von Zeitung] circulation - **2.** [Bedingung] condition; **jm zur Auflage machen, dass...** to make it a condition for sb that...

auf|lassen *vt (unreg)* - **1.** [Tür, Jacke] to leave open; [Knopf] to leave undone - **2.** [Hut, Mütze] to keep on.

auf|lauern *vi*: **jm auflauern** to lie in wait for sb.

Auf|lauf *der* - **1.** [Speise] bake - **2.** [Menschenansammlung] crowd.

auf|laufen (*perf* **ist aufgelaufen**) *vi (unreg)* - **1.** [sich festfahren]**: auf etw** *(A)* **auflaufen** to run aground on sthg - **2.** [abblocken]**: jn auflaufen lassen** SPORT to bodycheck sb - **3.** [steigen]**: auf etw** *(A)* **auflaufen** to mount up to sthg.

auf|leben (*perf* **ist aufgelebt**) *vi* - **1.** [Person] to liven up - **2.** [Gespräch, Erinnerung] to revive.

auf|legen ◇ *vt* - **1.** [Tischtuch, Schallplatte, Schminke, Kohle] to put on; [Besteck] to put out - **2.** [Produkt, Buch] to bring out - **3.** [am Telefon] to hang up. ◇ *vi* [am Telefon] to hang up.

auf|lehnen ◆ **sich auflehnen** *ref*: **sich gegen jn/etw auflehnen** to rebel against sb/sthg.

auf|leuchten (*perf* **hat/ist aufgeleuchtet**) *vi* to light up.

auf|listen *vt* to list.

auf|lockern *vt* - **1.** [Erde, Boden] to break up; [Muskeln] to loosen up - **2.** [Stimmung, Rede] to liven up. ◆ **sich auflockern** *ref* - **1.** [Sportler] to limber up - **2.** [Bewölkung] to break up; [Knoten] to loosen.

auf|lösen *vt* - **1.** [in Flüssigkeit, in Bestandteile] to dissolve; **etw in etw** *(D)* **auflösen** to dissolve sthg in sthg - **2.** [Staatenverbund, Demonstration, Versammlung] to break up; [Vertrag] to cancel; [Verlobung] to break off; [Parlament] to dissolve - **3.** [Betrieb, Haushalt] to break up. ◆ **sich auflösen** *ref* - **1.** [Tablette, Kristalle] to dissolve; [Nebel] to lift; [Bewölkung] to break up; **sich in etw** *(D)* **auflösen** to dissolve in sthg; **er hat sich in Luft aufgelöst** he vanished into thin air - **2.** [Menge, Versammlung] to disperse.

Auf|lösung *die* - **1.** [in Flüssigkeit, in Bestandteile] dissolving; **ein Bildschirm mit hoher Auflösung** a high-resolution screen - **2.** [von Koalition, Demonstration, Versammlung] breaking up; [von Vertrag] cancellation; [von Verlobung] breaking off; [von Parlament] dissolving - **3.** [von Betrieb, Haushalt] breaking up.

auf|machen ◇ *vt* - **1.** [gen] to open; [Schnur, Knopf, Jacke] to undo - **2.** [gestalten] to make. ◇ *vi* - **1.** [öffnen] to open the door; **jm aufmachen** to let sb in - **2.** [Geschäft] to open. ◆ **sich aufmachen** *ref* [abreisen]**: sich aufmachen (nach)** to set off (for).

Aufmachung (*pl* **-en**) *die* - **1.** [Gestaltung] layout - **2.** [Kleidung] appearance.

aufmerksam ◇ *adj* - **1.** [konzentriert] attentive; **jn auf jn/etw aufmerksam machen** to draw sb's attention to sb/sthg - **2.** [höflich] thoughtful. ◇ *adv* attentively.

Aufmerksamkeit (*pl* **-en**) *die* - **1.** [Konzentration] attentiveness - **2.** [Mitbringsel] gift.

auf|muntern *vt* [aufheitern] to cheer up; [ermutigen] to encourage.

Aufnahme (*pl* **-n**) *die* - **1.** [Empfang] reception; **Aufnahme in etw** *(A)* [Verein, Intensivstation] admission into sthg - **2.** [Beginn - von Kontakt] establishment; [- von Arbeit, Gespräch, Verhandlungen] start - **3.** [Aufzeichnung] recording; [von Diktat] taking down - **4.** [Fotografie] photograph.

aufnahmefähig *adj* receptive.

Aufnahme|prüfung *die* entrance examination.

auf|nehmen *vt (unreg)* - **1.** [aufheben, ergreifen] to pick up - **2.** [empfangen - in Klub] to admit; [- Gast] to receive; [- Asylant] to take in; **Namen auf einer Liste aufnehmen** to include names on a list; **ein Wort im Wörterbuch aufnehmen** to include a word in the dictionary; **jn bei sich** *(D)* **aufnehmen** to take sb in - **3.** [essen]**: Nahrung aufnehmen** to eat - **4.** [Informationen] to take in; [Vorschlag] to take up - **5.** [reagieren auf]**: etw mit Begeisterung aufnehmen** to receive sthg enthusiastically - **6.** [beginnen - Gespräch, Arbeit, Verhandlungen] to start; [- Thema, Tätigkeit] to take up; **mit jm Kontakt auf-**

nehmen to contact sb - **7.** [konkurrieren]: **es mit jm/etw aufnehmen können** to be a match for sb/sthg - **8.** [sich leihen - Kredit, Hypothek] to get, to obtain; [- Geld, Summe] to borrow - **9.** [Foto] to take - **10.** [auf Tonband] to record.

auf|opfern ◆ **sich aufopfern** *ref*: **sich für jn/etw aufopfern** to sacrifice o.s. for sb/sthg.

auf|päppeln *vt* [nach Krankheit] to nurse back to health.

auf|passen *vi* to pay attention; **auf jn/etw aufpassen** [Kind, Tasche] to keep an eye on sb/sthg; **auf Fehler aufpassen** to watch out for mistakes; **pass bloß auf, wenn ich dich erwische!** just you wait until I catch you!

auf|platzen (*perf* **ist aufgeplatzt**) *vi* to burst (open).

Aufprall (*pl* **-e**) *der* impact.

auf|prallen (*perf* **ist aufgeprallt**) *vi*: **auf etw** *(A)* **aufprallen** to hit sthg.

Auf|preis *der* extra charge.

auf|pumpen *vt* to pump up.

Aufputsch|mittel *das* stimulant.

auf|quellen (*perf* **ist aufgequollen**) *vi (unreg)* to swell up.

auf|raffen ◆ **sich aufraffen** *ref* [sich entschließen]: **sich dazu aufraffen, etw zu tun** to face up to doing sthg.

auf|ragen *vi* to rise up.

auf|räumen ◇ *vt* - **1.** [ordnen] to tidy up - **2.** [forträumen] to tidy away. ◇ *vi* - **1.** [ordnen] to tidy up - **2.** [etw beenden]: **mit etw aufräumen** to put an end to sthg.

auf|rechnen *vt*: **etw gegen etw aufrechnen** to compare sthg with sthg.

aufrecht ◇ *adj* - **1.** [gerade] upright - **2.** [Demokrat, Haltung] upstanding. ◇ *adv* [gerade] upright.

aufrecht|erhalten *vt (unreg)* to maintain.

auf|regen *vt* [ärgern] to annoy; [beunruhigen] to upset. ◆ **sich aufregen** *ref* to get worked up; **sich über jn/etw aufregen** to get worked up about sb/sthg.

aufregend *adj* exciting.

Auf|regung *die* excitement; **das schlechte Wahlergebnis versetzte die Partei in Aufregung** the bad election result caused a great stir in the party.

aufreibend *adj* [anstrengend] exhausting.

auf|reißen (*perf* **hat/ist aufgerissen**) *(unreg)* ◇ *vt (hat)* - **1.** [öffnen - Brief, Verpackung] to tear open; [- Tür, Fenster] to fling open; [- Mund, Augen] to open wide - **2.** *salopp* [kennen lernen] to pick up. ◇ *vi (ist)* [Naht] to split; [Wolkendecke] to break up.

aufreizend ◇ *adj* provocative. ◇ *adv* provocatively.

auf|richten *vt* - **1.** [hochziehen - Kranken] to si[t] up; [- Rücken] to straighten (up) - **2.** [aufsteller] to erect - **3.** [trösten] to lift. ◆ **sich aufrichten** *ref* [sich hochziehen] to sit up.

aufrichtig ◇ *adj* sincere. ◇ *adv* sincerely

Auf|richtigkeit *die (ohne pl)* sincerity.

auf|rücken (*perf* **ist aufgerückt**) *vi* to mov[e] up; **zum Direktor aufrücken** to be promoted t[o] headmaster.

Auf|ruf *der* appeal.

auf|rufen *vt (unreg)* - **1.** [nennen, rufen] to cal[l] - **2.** [auffordern]: **jn zu etw aufrufen** to appea[l] to sb for sthg.

Aufruhr (*pl* **-e**) *der* - **1.** [Aufstand] uprisin[g] - **2.** [Unruhe] turmoil.

auf|runden *vt*: **aufrunden (auf** *(+ A)***)** t[o] round up (to).

auf|rüsten *vi* to rearm; **wieder aufrüsten** t[o] rearm.

Auf|rüstung *die* rearmament.

aufs *präp* = **auf + das**.

auf|sagen *vt* [Text] to recite.

auf|sammeln *vt* to pick up.

aufsässig *adj* rebellious.

Auf|satz *der* - **1.** [Schularbeit] essay *UK*, pape[r] *US* - **2.** [Abhandlung] paper - **3.** [Aufbau] uppe[r] section.

auf|saugen *vt* to soak up.

auf|schauen *vi* - **1.** [mit Bewunderung]: **zu jm aufschauen** to look up to sb - **2.** *Süddt* [aufblicken] to look up.

auf|scheuchen *vt* - **1.** [verscheuchen] t[o] startle - **2.** *fig* [stören] to disturb.

auf|schieben *vt (unreg)* - **1.** [verschieben] t[o] put off - **2.** [öffnen - Tür, Fenster] to slide open [- Riegel] to slide back.

Auf|schlag *der* - **1.** [Aufprall] impact - **2.** [au[f] den Preis] extra charge - **3.** [am Hosenbein] turn-up *UK*, cuff *US*; [am Ärmel] cuff - **4.** SPORT serve; **er hat Aufschlag** it's his serve.

auf|schlagen (*perf* **hat/ist aufgeschlagen**) *(unreg)* ◇ *vt (hat)* - **1.** [öffnen - Buch, Zeitung, Augen] to open - **2.** [Ei, Schale] to crack (open); [Eis] to break - **3.** [verletzen]: **sich das Knie aufschlagen** to cut one's knee - **4.** [aufbauen - Bett, Zelt] to put up; [- Lager] to pitch - **5.** [dazurechnen]: **etw auf etw** *(A)* **aufschlagen** to add sthg onto sthg. ◇ *vi* - **1.** *(ist)* [aufprallen]: **auf etw** *(A)* **aufschlagen** to hit sthg - **2.** *(hat)* SPORT t[o] serve.

auf|schließen *(unreg)* ◇ *vt* to unlock ◇ *vi* - **1.** [öffnen]: **jm aufschließen** to unlock the door for sb - **2.** [nachrücken] to move up.

Aufschluss *der (ohne pl)*: **über etw** *(A)* **Aufschluss geben** to provide information abou[t] sthg.

aufschlussreich *adj* informative.

auf|schneiden *(unreg)* ◇ *vt* to cut open. ◇ *vi* [angeben] to boast.

Auf|schnitt *der sliced cold meat and/or cheese.*

auf|schrauben *vt* [Deckel] to unscrew; [Glas] to screw the lid off.

auf|schrecken (*perf* **hat/ist aufgeschreckt**) ◇ *vt (hat)* to startle. ◇ *vi (ist)* to start.

Auf|schrei *der eigtl & fig* cry; **ein Aufschrei ging durchs Volk** there was a public outcry.

auf|schreiben *vt (unreg)* - **1.** [notieren] to write down - **2.** [Strafzettel geben] to book.

Auf|schrift *die* inscription.

Auf|schub *der* period of grace; **es duldet keinen Aufschub** it must not be delayed.

auf|schütten *vt* - **1.** [nachfüllen] to pour on - **2.** [anhäufen - Damm, Wall] to build up.

Auf|schwung *der* - **1.** [Auftrieb] upturn; **sein Optimismus gab uns Aufschwung** his optimism gave us a lift - **2.** SPORT swing-up.

auf|sehen *vi (unreg)* [hochschauen] to look up; **zu jm aufsehen** [bewundern] to look up to sb.

Aufsehen *das*: **Aufsehen erregen** to cause a stir; **Aufsehen erregend** sensational.

Aufseher, in (*mpl* -, *fpl* **-nen**) *der, die* [im Gefängnis] warder.

auf sein (*perf* **ist auf gewesen**) *vi (unreg) fam* - **1.** [offen sein] to be open - **2.** [wach sein] to be up.

auf|setzen ◇ *vt* - **1.** [gen] to put on - **2.** [schreiben] to draft. ◇ *vi* [landen] to touch down. ◆ **sich aufsetzen** *ref* [sich aufrichten] to sit up.

Auf|sicht *die (ohne pl)* - **1.** [Kontrolle] supervision; **die Aufsicht über jn/etw haben** to supervise sb/sthg - **2.** [Person] supervisor.

auf|sitzen (*perf* **hat/ist aufgessessen**) *vi (unreg)* - **1.** *(ist)* [aufsteigen - auf Motorrad] to get on; [- Pferd] to mount - **2.** *(ist)* [sich täuschen lassen]: **jm aufsitzen** to be taken in by sb - **3.** *(hat)* [wach bleiben] to sit up.

auf|spannen *vt* to put up.

auf|sparen *vt*: **sich** *(D)* **etw aufsparen** to save sthg.

auf|sperren *vt* - **1.** [aufschließen] to unlock - **2.** [offen halten] to open wide.

auf|spielen ◆ **sich aufspielen** *ref* [angeben] to give o.s. airs; **sich als Chef/Genie aufspielen** to play the boss/genius.

auf|springen (*perf* **ist aufgesprungen**) *vi (unreg)* - **1.** [aufstehen]: **aufspringen (vor (+ D))** to jump up (with) - **2.** [sich öffnen - Blüte, Tür] to burst open; [- Haut, Hände] to become chapped - **3.** [springen]: **auf etw** *(A)* **aufspringen** to jump onto sthg.

auf|stacheln *vt*: **jn (zu etw) aufstacheln** to spur sb on (to sthg).

auf|stampfen *vi*: **mit dem Fuß aufstampfen** to stamp one's foot.

Auf|stand *der* uprising, rebellion.

aufständisch *adj* rebellious.

auf|stauen *vt* to dam. ◆ **sich aufstauen** *ref* [Wasser] to collect; [Gefühle, Wut] to get bottled up.

auf|stecken *vt* - **1.** [hochstecken] to pin up - **2.** *fam* [aufgeben, abbrechen] to give up.

auf|stehen (*perf* **hat/ist aufgestanden**) *vi (unreg)* - **1.** *(ist)* [sich erheben] to get up - **2.** *(hat)* [offen stehen] to stand open.

auf|steigen (*perf* **ist aufgestiegen**) *vi (unreg)* - **1.** [auf Motorrad, Fahrrad, Pferd] to get on; **auf etw** *(A)* **aufsteigen** [Fahrrad, Pferd] to get on sthg - **2.** [Bergsteiger, Hubschrauber, Ballon] to climb; [Vogel] to soar; **auf einen Berg aufsteigen** to climb a mountain - **3.** [Rauch] to rise; [Nebel] to lift - **4.** [Erfolg haben] to be promoted.

auf|stellen *vt* - **1.** [hinstellen - Schachfiguren, Kegel, Lampe] to set up; [- Schild] to put up - **2.** [aufbauen - Gerüst, Gitter] to put up - **3.** [Liste, Plan] to draw up - **4.** [Theorie, Behauptung] to put forward - **5.** [auswählen] to select - **6.** [Ohren] to prick up; [Stacheln] to raise. ◆ **sich aufstellen** *ref* - **1.** [sich hinstellen] to take up one's position - **2.** [sich aufrichten - Haare] to stand on end.

Auf|stellung *die* - **1.** [Hinstellen - von Schachfiguren, Kegeln, Lampe] setting up; [- von Schild] putting up - **2.** [Aufbau - von Gerüst, Gitter] putting up - **3.** [von Liste, Plan] drawing up - **4.** [von Theorie, Behauptung] putting forward - **5.** [Wahl] selection.

Aufstieg (*pl* **-e**) *der* - **1.** [Aufsteigen] ascent - **2.** [Erfolg] promotion.

auf|stocken *vt* - **1.** [höher bauen] to raise the height of - **2.** [vergrößern] to increase.

auf|stoßen (*perf* **hat/ist aufgestoßen**) *(unreg)* ◇ *vt (hat)* [öffnen] to push open. ◇ *vi* - **1.** *(ist)* [stoßen]: **mit etw auf etw** *(D)* **aufstoßen** to hit sthg with sthg - **2.** *(hat)* [rülpsen] to belch - **3.** *(ist) fam* [unangenehm auffallen]: **sein Verhalten ist mir sauer** ODER **übel aufgestoßen** his behaviour left a nasty taste in my mouth.

aufstrebend *adj* up-and-coming.

auf|stützen *vt* to prop up. ◆ **sich aufstützen** *ref* to support o.s.

auf|suchen *vt* to go to.

Auf|takt *der* - **1.** [Anfang] start - **2.** MUS upbeat.

auf|tanken *vt* [Auto] to fill up; [Flugzeug] to refuel; **Benzin auftanken** to fill up with petrol *UK* ODER gas *US*.

auf|tauchen (*perf* **ist aufgetaucht**) *vi* - **1.** [aus dem Wasser] to surface - **2.** [sichtbar werden] to appear - **3.** [aufkommen] to arise - **4.** [gefunden werden, ankommen] to turn up.

auf|tauen ◇ *vt* (*perf* **hat aufgetaut**) [Lebensmittel] to defrost; [Boden, Eis] to thaw. ◇ *vi* (*perf* **ist aufgetaut**) [Lebensmittel] to defrost; [Boden, Eis] to thaw.

auf|teilen *vt* - **1.** [verteilen] to share out - **2.** [einteilen] to divide up; **etw in etw** *(A)* **aufteilen** to divide sthg up into sthg.

Auf|teilung *die* - **1.** [Verteilung]: **Aufteilung (unter** *(+D)*) sharing out (amongst) - **2.** [Einteilung]: **Aufteilung (in** *(+A)*) division (into).

auf|tischen *vt* - **1.** [servieren] to serve up - **2.** *fam fig* [erzählen] to come out with.

Auftrag (*pl* **Aufträge**) *der* - **1.** [Befehl, Aufgabe] task; **jm einen Auftrag geben** ODER **erteilen** to give sb a task - **2.** [Bestellung] order; **etw in Auftrag geben** [Untersuchung, Reparatur] to order sthg; [Studie, Gemälde] to commission sthg.

auf|tragen *(unreg)* ◇ *vt* - **1.** [aufstreichen] to apply - **2.** [bestellen]: **jm auftragen, etw zu tun** to tell sb to do sthg; **sie hat mir Grüße an dich aufgetragen** she asked me to pass on her regards to you - **3.** [abtragen] to wear out. ◇ *vi*: **dick auftragen** *fam* [übertreiben] to go over the top.

Auftraggeber, in (*mpl* **-**, *fpl* **-nen**) *der, die* [Kunde] client.

auf|treffen (*perf* **ist aufgetroffen**) *vi (unreg)* to land.

auf|treiben (*perf* **hat aufgetrieben**) *vt (unreg) (hat)* [finden] to find.

auf|treten (*perf* **ist aufgetreten**) *vi (unreg)* - **1.** [treten] to tread - **2.** [sich benehmen] to behave - **3.** [erscheinen - Person] to appear; [- Problem, Gefahr, Frage] to arise.

Auftreten *das* - **1.** [Benehmen] behaviour - **2.** [Erscheinen] occurrence.

Auf|trieb *der* buoyancy; **jm/einer Sache Auftrieb geben** *fig* to give sb/sthg a lift.

auf|tun *vt (unreg) fam* [finden] to come across. ◆ **sich auftun** *ref eigtl* & *fig* to open up.

auf|türmen *vt* to pile up. ◆ **sich auftürmen** *ref* [Masse, Probleme] to pile up; [Berge] to tower.

auf|wachen (*perf* **ist aufgewacht**) *vi* to wake up.

auf|wachsen ['aufvaksn̩] (*perf* **ist aufgewachsen**) *vi (unreg)* to grow up.

Aufwand *der* - **1.** [Einsatz - von Geld] expenditure; **es ist mit viel Aufwand verbunden** it takes a lot of time/effort/*etc* - **2.** [Luxus] extravagance.

aufwändig ◇ *adj* extravagant. ◇ *adv* extravagantly.

auf|wärmen *vt* - **1.** [warm machen] to warm up - **2.** *fam fig* [wieder erwähnen] to bring up again. ◆ **sich aufwärmen** *ref* to warm o.s. up.

aufwärts *adv* upwards; **von 50 cm³ aufwärts** from 50 cm³ up ODER upwards.

aufwärts gehen (*perf* **ist aufwärts gegangen**) *vi (unreg)*: **mit den Verkaufszahlen geht es aufwärts** the sales figures are looking up.

auf|wecken *vt* to wake up.

auf|weisen *vt (unreg)* [zeigen] to show; **d[er] Plan weist Mängel auf** the plan contain[s] flaws.

auf|wenden *vt* [Geld, Zeit] to spend; [Energi[e], Kraft] to use (up).

aufwendig *adj* & *adv* = **aufwändig**.

auf|werfen *vt (unreg)* - **1.** [anhäufen - Erd[e], Kies] to pile up - **2.** [ansprechen] to raise.

auf|werten *vt* [Währung] to revalue; [Ans[e]hen, Status] to enhance.

auf|wickeln *vt* to wind up.

auf|wiegeln *vt abw* to incite; **jn gegen j[n] aufwiegeln** to stir sb up against sb.

Auf|wind *der* upcurrent; **Aufwind bekommen** *fig* to get a boost; **Aufwind haben** to b[e] going strong.

auf|wirbeln *vt* & *vi* to swirl up.

auf|wischen *vt* to mop up.

auf|wühlen *vt* - **1.** [zerwühlen] to churn u[p] - **2.** [erregen] to stir up.

auf|zählen *vt* to list.

Auf|zählung *die* list.

auf|zeichnen *vt* - **1.** [zeichnen] to dra[w] - **2.** [aufnehmen] to record.

Auf|zeichnung *die* [Aufnahme] recordin[g]. ◆ **Aufzeichnungen** *Pl* [Notizen] notes; **sic[h]** *(D)* **Aufzeichnungen machen** to take notes.

auf|ziehen (*perf* **hat/ist aufgezogen**) *(unre[g])* ◇ *vt (hat)* - **1.** [Uhr, Spielzeugauto] to wind u[p] - **2.** [erziehen - Kind] to bring up; [- Tier] to rais[e] - **3.** [öffnen] to open - **4.** [necken] to tease; **jn m[it] etw aufziehen** to tease sb about sthg - **5.** *fa[m]* [organisieren - Geschäft, Arbeitsgruppe] to set u[p]; [- Fest, Kampagne] to organize. ◇ *vi (ist)* [G[e]witter] to brew; [Wolken] to mass.

Auf|zucht *die* rearing.

Auf|zug *der* - **1.** [Lift] lift *UK*, elevator *U[S]* - **2.** *abw* [Aufmachung] get-up - **3.** [Akt] act.

auf|zwingen *vt (unreg)*: **jm etw aufzwi[n]gen** to force sthg onto sb. ◆ **sich aufzwi[n]gen** *ref*: **der Gedanke zwingt sich regelrec[ht] auf** the thought is unavoidable.

Auge (*pl* **-n**) *das* - **1.** [Sehorgan] eye; **ein blaue[s] Auge** a black eye; **mit bloßem Auge** with th[e] naked eye; **etw mit eigenen Augen geseh[en] haben** to have seen sthg with one's ow[n] eyes; **ihm wurde schwarz vor Auge[n]** everything went black - **2.** [Würfelpunkt] do[t] **(große) Augen machen** to stare wide-eye[d] **seinen Augen nicht trauen** not to believ[e] one's eyes; **jn aus den Augen verlieren** to los[e] touch with sb; **ein Auge zudrücken** to turn [a] blind eye; **jn/etw im Auge behalten** to keep a[n] eye on sb/sthg; **in meinen/seinen/*etc* Auge[n]** as I see/he sees/*etc* it; **jn/etw mit anderen** OD[ER] **neuen Augen sehen** to see sb/sthg differentl[y] **jn/etw nicht aus den Augen lassen** not to tak[e] one's eyes off sb/sthg; **unter vier Augen** in private; **etw vor Augen haben** to have sthg in mind.

Augen|arzt, ärztin *der, die* eye specialist, ophthalmologist.

Augen|blick *der* moment; **im Augenblick** at the moment; **jeden Augenblick** at any moment, any time.

augenblicklich <> *adj* - **1.** [sofortig] immediate - **2.** [jetzig] current. <> *adv* - **1.** [umgehend] immediately - **2.** [jetzig] currently.

Augen|braue *die* eyebrow.

Augen|farbe *die*: **welche Augenfarbe hat sie?** what colour are her eyes?

Augen|höhe *die*: **in Augenhöhe** at eye level.

Augen|winkel *der*: **jn/etw aus den Augenwinkeln beobachten** to watch sb/sthg out of the corner of one's eye.

Augen|zeuge, zeugin *der, die* eyewitness.

augenzwinkernd *adv* with an air of complicity.

August *der* August; *siehe auch* **September**.

Auktion [auk'tsio:n] (*pl* **-en**) *die* auction.

Aula (*pl* **-s**) *die* hall.

Aupairmädchen, Au-pair-Mädchen [o'pɛ:rmɛ:tçən] (*pl* -) *das* au pair.

aus <> *präp (+ D)* - **1.** [heraus] out of; **aus dem Haus gehen** to go out of the house, to leave the house; **Rauch kam aus dem Fenster** smoke was coming out of the window - **2.** [zur Angabe der Herkunft] from; **aus Amerika** from America; **ein Lied aus den 70er Jahren** a song from the seventies - **3.** [zur Angabe des Materials]: **aus Plastik** made of plastic; **Möbel aus Eschenholz** ash furniture - **4.** [zur Angabe der Zugehörigkeit]: **einer aus der Gruppe** a member of the group - **5.** [zur Angabe der Entfernung] from; **aus 50 m Entfernung** from 50 m away - **6.** [zur Angabe des Grundes]: **aus welchem Grund?** for what reason?, why?; **aus Spaß** for fun; **aus Habgier** from greed, out of greed. <> *adv* - **1.** [elliptisch]: **Licht aus!** lights out! - **2.** [zu Ende] over; **aus und vorbei** all over.

Aus *das* end; **ins Aus gehen** SPORT to go out (of play).

aus|arbeiten *vt* [Plan, Liste, Vertrag] to draw up; [Methode, Vorschlag] to work out.

Ausarbeitung (*pl* **-en**) *die* [von Plan, Liste, Vertrag] drawing up; [von Methode, Vorschlag] working out.

aus|arten (*perf* **ist ausgeartet**) *vi* to degenerate; **in (+ A)** ODER **zu etw ausarten** to degenerate into sthg.

aus|atmen *vt* & *vi* to breathe out.

aus|baden *vt*: **etw ausbaden müssen** to pay (the price) for sthg.

Aus|bau *der* - **1.** [Beseitigung] removal - **2.** [Erweiterung - von Netz, Haus] extension; [- von Dachboden] conversion; [- von Kenntnissen] expansion.

aus|bauen *vt* - **1.** [beseitigen] to remove - **2.** [erweitern - Netz, Haus] to extend; [- Dachboden] to convert; [- Kenntnisse] to expand; [- Kontakte] to intensify, to strengthen.

aus|bessern *vt* [Schaden, Zaun] to repair; [Kleidungsstück] to mend.

aus|beulen *vt* - **1.** [glätten] to beat out - **2.** [verformen] to make baggy.

Aus|beute *die* gain.

aus|beuten *vt* to exploit.

aus|bilden *vt* - **1.** [schulen] to train; **sich zu etw ausbilden lassen** to train to be sthg - **2.** [hervorbringen] to develop.

Ausbilder, in (*mpl* -, *fpl* **-nen**) *der, die* instructor (instructress *die*).

Aus|bildung *die* [beruflich, fachlich] training; [schulisch] education; **in der Ausbildung sein** [beruflich, fachlich] to be a trainee; [schulisch] to be in education.

Ausbildungs|zeit *die* period of training, traineeship.

aus|bleiben (*perf* **ist ausgeblieben**) *vi (unreg)* - **1.** [Besserung, Katastrophe] to fail to materialize; [Gäste, Touristen] to fail to turn up; **das bleibt nicht aus** that's inevitable - **2.** [nicht nach Hause kommen] to stay out.

Aus|blick *der* view; **ein Ausblick auf etw** *(A) fig* a look ahead to sthg.

ausbooten *vt* to oust.

aus|brechen (*perf* **hat/ist ausgebrochen**) *(unreg)* <> *vi (ist)* - **1.** [Gefangene, Krieg, Panik, Epidemie] to break out; **aus etw ausbrechen** to break out of sthg - **2.** [verfallen]: **in Gelächter ausbrechen** to burst out laughing; **in Tränen ausbrechen** to burst into tears - **3.** [Auto] to spin out of control - **4.** [Vulkan] to erupt. <> *vt (hat)* [herausbrechen] to break off.

aus|breiten *vt* to spread out; **etw über jm/etw ausbreiten** to spread sthg out over sb/sthg. ◆ **sich ausbreiten** *ref* - **1.** [sich verbreiten] to spread - **2.** *fam* [sich breit machen] to spread o.s. out.

Aus|bruch *der* - **1.** [Flucht] break-out - **2.** [Beginn] outbreak; **nach einer Woche kam die Krankheit vollends zum Ausbruch** after a week the disease broke out fully - **3.** [von Vulkan] eruption - **4.** [Gefühlsäußerung] outburst.

aus|brüten *vt eigtl* & *fig* to hatch.

Aus|dauer *die* [Beharrungsvermögen] perseverance; SPORT stamina.

ausdauernd <> *adj* persevering; **ein ausdauernder Läufer** a runner with a lot of stamina. <> *adv* untiringly.

aus|dehnen *vt* - **1.** [Einzugsgebiet, Einfluss] to expand; [Gummiband] to extend; [Kleidungsstück] to lengthen - **2.** [zeitlich] to extend. ◆ **sich ausdehnen** *ref* [Metall, Handel] to expand; [Feuer] to spread; [Weite] to stretch out; **sich auf etw** *(A)* **ausdehnen** [Brand, Hysterie, Aktivitäten] to spread to sthg.

aus|denken *vt (unreg)*: **sich** *(D)* **etw ausdenken** [Geschichte, Plan] to think sthg up; [Geschenk] to think of sthg; **da musst du dir schon etwas anderes ausdenken!** *fam* you'll have to do better than that!

Aus|druck *(pl* **-drücke** ODER **-e)** *der* - **1.** *(pl Ausdrücke)* [Formulierung] expression - **2.** *(ohne pl)* [Zeichen] expression; **einer Sache** *(D)* **Ausdruck geben** ODER **verleihen** *geh* to express sthg - **3.** *(pl Ausdrucke)* EDV printout.

aus|drucken *vt* EDV to print (out).

aus|drücken *vt* - **1.** [Orange, Schwamm, Saft] to squeeze - **2.** [Zigarette] to stub out - **3.** [aussprechen] to express; **etw mit einfachen Worten ausdrücken** to put sthg simply - **4.** [zeigen - Gefühle, Dank] to express, to show. ◆ **sich ausdrücken** *ref* - **1.** [Person] to express o.s. - **2.** [Freude, Gier, Intoleranz] to reveal itself.

ausdrücklich ◇ *adj* explicit. ◇ *adv* explicitly.

Ausdrucks|weise *die* way of expressing o.s.

auseinander *adv* apart; **auseinander!** break it up!; **die Schwestern sind sechs Jahre auseinander** there's six years between the two sisters.

auseinander fallen *(perf* **ist auseinander gefallen)** *vi (unreg)* to fall apart.

auseinander gehen *(perf* **ist auseinander gegangen)** *vi (unreg)* - **1.** [sich trennen - Gruppe] to break up; [- Wege] to diverge; [- Personen] to part - **2.** [Vorhang] to open - **3.** [Meinungen] to differ - **4.** [Ehe] to break up.

auseinander halten *vt (unreg)* to distinguish.

auseinander laufen *(perf* **ist auseinander gelaufen)** *vi (unreg)* - **1.** [Gruppe] to disperse - **2.** [Eis, Käse] to melt; [Farbe] to run.

auseinander leben ◆ **sich auseinander leben** *ref* to drift apart.

auseinander nehmen *vt (unreg)* to dismantle.

auseinander setzen *vt*: **jm etw auseinander setzen** to explain sthg to sb. ◆ **sich auseinander setzen** *ref* - **1.** [sich beschäftigen]: **sich mit etw auseinander setzen** to examine sthg - **2.** [sich streiten]: **sich mit jm auseinander setzen** to argue with sb.

Auseinandersetzung *(pl* **-en)** *die* - **1.** [mit Thema]: **Auseinandersetzung (mit)** examination (of) - **2.** [Streit] argument; [Debatte] debate.

auserwählt *adj* chosen.

aus|fahren *(perf* **hat/ist ausgefahren)** *(unreg)* ◇ *vt (hat)* - **1.** [spazieren fahren - im Rollstuhl, Kinderwagen] to take out for a walk - **2.** [ausklappen - Antenne] to extend; [- Fahrwerk] to lower - **3.** [liefern] to deliver - **4.** [sehr schnell fahren] to drive flat out. ◇ *vi (ist)* - **1.** [spazieren fahren - im Rollstuhl, Kinderwagen] to go for a walk - **2.** [hinausfahren - Zug] to depart.

Aus|fahrt *die* - **1.** [Stelle] exit; **'Ausfahrt fre[i] halten!'** 'keep clear!' - **2.** [Auslaufen] departur[e]

aus|fallen *(perf* **ist ausgefallen)** *vi (unre[g])* - **1.** [Haare, Zahn] to fall out - **2.** [nicht stattfinde[n]] to be cancelled; [Fußballspiel] to be pos[t]poned - **3.** [Verdienst, Einnahme] to be los[t] - **4.** [Maschine] to break down; [Bremse, Signa[l]] to fail - **5.** [Mitarbeiter] to be absent; [Athlet] t[o] pull out - **6.** [sich erweisen]: **der Sieg fiel deu[t]lich aus** it was a clear victory; **gut/schlech[t] ausfallen** to turn out well/badly.

ausfallend *adj* abusive; **ausfallend werde[n]** to become abusive.

Ausfall|straße *die* arterial road.

aus|fegen ◇ *vt* to sweep out. ◇ *vi* t[o] sweep up.

aus|fertigen *vt amt* [Vertrag, Testament] t[o] draw up; [Pass, Zeugnis, Rechnung] to issue.

ausfindig *adv*: **jn/etw ausfindig machen** t[o] find sb/sthg.

aus|fließen *(perf* **ist ausgeflossen)** *vi (unreg)* to leak.

Ausflucht *(pl* **Ausflüchte)** *die* excuse; **Au[s]flüchte machen** to make excuses.

Aus|flug *der* trip; **einen Ausflug machen** ODE[R] **unternehmen** to go on a trip.

Ausflugs|lokal *das cafe or pub in the cour[n]tryside to which you can drive or walk out.*

Ausfluss *(pl* **-flüsse)** *der* - **1.** [im Waschbe[c]ken] plughole - **2.** [Ausfließen] leaking - **3.** ME[D] discharge.

aus|fragen *vt* to interrogate.

aus|fressen *vt (unreg)*: **er hat mal wieder e[t]was ausgefressen** *fam* he's been up to hi[s] tricks again.

Ausfuhr *(pl* **-en)** *die* - **1.** [Ware] export - **2.** [Tä]tigkeit] exporting.

aus|führen *vt* - **1.** [spazieren führen - Famili[e,] Hund] to take for a walk - **2.** [exportieren] to ex[]port - **3.** [realisieren - Reparatur, Befehl, Plan] t[o] carry out; [- Freistoß, Schritte] to take - **4.** [erkl[ä]ren] to explain.

ausführlich ◇ *adj* detailed. ◇ *adv* in de[]tail.

aus|füllen *vt* - **1.** [Formular, Antrag] to fill i[n] ODER out; [Kreuzworträtsel] to do; [Scheck] t[o] make out - **2.** [füllen] to fill (up) - **3.** [verbringen]: **seine Zeit mit etw ausfüllen** to spend one['s] time doing sthg - **4.** [zufrieden stellen] to fulfil.

Aus|gabe *die* - **1.** [Ausgeben] distributio[n]; [von Befehl, Banknoten] issuing; [von Esse[n]] serving - **2.** [von Geld] expenditure; **Ausgabe[n]** expenditure *(U)* - **3.** [Edition] edition.

Aus|gang *der* - **1.** [von Gebäude] exit; [vo[n]] Wald] edge; [von Ort] end - **2.** *(ohne pl)* [Ausge[h]erlaubnis] time off; [von Soldaten] pass - **3.** [End[e]] outcome.

Ausgangs|lage *die* starting position.

Ausgangs|punkt *der* starting point.

Ausgangs|sperre *die* curfew.

aus|geben *vt (unreg)* - **1.** [verteilen] [Lebensmittel, Decken] to hand out; [Befehl, Banknoten] to issue; [Essen] to serve - **2.** [Geld] to spend - **3.** *fam* [zu Drink einladen]: **jm einen ausgeben** *fam* to buy sb a drink - **4.** [bezeichnen]: **sich als jd/etw ausgeben** to pretend to be sb/sthg; **jn/etw als** ODER **für jn/etw ausgeben** to pass sb/sthg off as sb/sthg.

ausgebucht *adj* fully booked.

ausgedient *adj*: **dieser Sessel hat nun ausgedient** I/we/*etc* no longer have any use for this armchair.

ausgedörrt *adj* [Kehle, Erde] parched; [Pflanze] withered.

ausgefallen ◇ *adj* unusual. ◇ *adv* unusually.

ausgeflippt *adj fam* weird, freaky.

ausgeglichen *adj* [Mensch, Persönlichkeit] balanced; [Spiel] even; [Klima] stable; [Leistung] steady.

aus|gehen (*perf* **ist ausgegangen**) *vi (unreg)* - **1.** [ins Kino, in die Disko] to go out - **2.** [verlöschen - Kerze, Lampe] to go out; [- Motor] to stop; [- Heizung, Computer] to go off - **3.** [enden] to end - **4.** [hervorgebracht werden]: **von jm ausgehen** to come from sb - **5.** [zugrunde legen]: **von etw ausgehen** to assume sthg; **davon ausgehen,dass...** to assume (that...) - **6.** [ausfallen] to fall out - **7.** [zu Ende gehen] to run out; **mir gehen die Ideen aus** I'm running out of ideas.

ausgehungert *adj* starved.

ausgelassen ◇ *adj* exuberant. ◇ *adv* exuberantly.

ausgelaugt *adj* worn-out.

ausgemergelt *adj* [Körper, Mensch] emaciated.

ausgenommen *konj* - **1.** [es sei denn] unless - **2.** [außer] except.

ausgeprägt ◇ *adj* pronounced. ◇ *adv* particularly.

ausgerechnet *adv*: **ausgerechnet heute** today of all days; **ausgerechnet mir muss das passieren** it had to happen to me of all people.

ausgereift *adj* perfected.

ausgeschlossen *adj* out of the question.

ausgesprochen ◇ *adj* [Ähnlichkeit, Begabung] definite; [Abneigung, Vorliebe] marked; [Glück, Zufall] real. ◇ *adv* extremely, really.

ausgestorben *adj*: **wie ausgestorben** dead, deserted.

ausgewachsen ['ausgəvaksn̩] *adj* [erwachsen] fully-grown.

ausgewogen *adj* balanced.

ausgezeichnet ◇ *adj* excellent. ◇ *adv* excellently.

ausgiebig ◇ *adj* [Beratungen, Untersuchungen] extensive; [Frühstück] large; [Spaziergang] long. ◇ *adv* extensively; **ausgiebig frühstücken** to eat a large breakfast.

aus|gießen *vt (unreg)* to pour out.

Ausgleich (*pl* **-e**) *der* - **1.** [Gleichgewicht] balance; **er schafft sich einen Ausgleich zu seiner Arbeit, indem er sich sportlich betätigt** he balances out his work by doing sport - **2.** [Wiedergutmachung] compensation; **zum** ODER **als Ausgleich** in return - **3.** SPORT equalizer.

aus|gleichen *(unreg)* ◇ *vt* [Unterschiede, Unregelmäßigkeiten] to even out; [Mängel, Ungerechtigkeit] to make up for; [Gegensätze] to reconcile; [Konflikt] to settle; [Konto] to balance. ◇ *vi* SPORT to equalize. ◆ **sich ausgleichen** *ref* [Unterschiede] to even out; [Konto] to balance.

aus|graben *vt (unreg)* to dig up.

Aus|grabung *die* excavation, dig.

Ausguck (*pl* **-e**) *der* lookout (post).

Ausguss (*pl* **-güsse**) *der* drain.

aus|haken *vt* to unhook.

aus|halten *(unreg)* ◇ *vt* - **1.** [ertragen] to stand; **den Vergleich mit etw aushalten** to bear comparison with sthg; **mit ihr ist es nicht auszuhalten** she's unbearable - **2.** *abw* [bezahlen] to keep; **sich von jm aushalten lassen** to be kept by sb. ◇ *vi* [durchhalten] to hold out.

aus|handeln *vt* to negotiate.

aus|händigen *vt* to hand over.

Aus|hang *der* notice.

aus|hängen ◇ *vi (unreg)* [angeschlagen sein] to be up; **die Liste hängt am schwarzen Brett aus** the list is up on the noticeboard. ◇ *vt (reg)* - **1.** [anschlagen] to put up - **2.** [Tür] to take off its hinges.

Aushängeschild (*pl* **-er**) *das fig* advertisement.

aus|heben *vt (unreg)* - **1.** [ausschaufeln] to dig out - **2.** [aushängen] to take off its hinges - **3.** [Verbrechernest] to raid.

aus|hecken *vt* to think up.

aus|helfen *vi (unreg)* to help out.

Aus|hilfe *die* - **1.** [Aushelfen] assistance; **zur Aushilfe arbeiten** to help out - **2.** [Aushilfskraft] temporary worker; [im Büro] temp.

Aushilfs|kraft *die* temporary worker; [im Büro] temp.

aushilfsweise *adv* on a temporary basis.

aus|höhlen *vt* [Stamm] to hollow out.

aus|holen *vi* - **1.** [mit dem Arm] to move one's arm back - **2.** [beim Erzählen]: **weit ausholen** to go back a long way.

aus|horchen *vt* to sound out.

aus|kennen ◆ **sich auskennen** *ref* to know one's way around; **sich in einer Stadt**

auskennen to know one's way around a town; **sich mit Computern auskennen** to know a lot about computers.

aus|kippen *vt* to tip out.

aus|klammern *vt* [Thema] to leave aside.

aus|klappen *vt* to open out.

aus|klingen (*perf* **hat/ist ausgeklungen**) *vi (unreg) (hat, ist)* [Musik, Tag, Fest] to come to an end.

aus|klinken (*perf* **hat/ist ausgeklinkt**) ◇ *vt (hat)* to release. ◇ *vi (ist)* to come free. ◆ **sich ausklinken** *ref* to come free.

aus|klopfen *vt* [Teppich] to beat; [Pfeife] to knock out; [Kleidungsstück] to dust down.

aus|knipsen *vt fam* to switch off.

aus|knobeln *vt* - **1.** *fam* [auslosen - mit Würfeln] to throw dice to decide - **2.** [ausklügeln] to work out.

aus|kommen (*perf* **ist ausgekommen**) *vi (unreg)* - **1.** [genug haben] to get by, to manage; **mit etw auskommen** [Proviant] to make sthg last; [Gehalt] to get by on sthg; [Hilfe] to manage with sthg, to get by with sthg - **2.** [sich vertragen] to get on; **mit jm gut/schlecht auskommen** to get on well/badly with sb; **mit jm nicht auskommen** not to get on with sb.

aus|kosten *vt geh* to enjoy to the full.

aus|kratzen *vt* [Schüssel] to scrape out.

aus|kundschaften *vt* to spy out.

Auskunft (*pl* **Auskünfte**) *die* - **1.** [Information] information *(U)*; **eine Auskunft bekommen** to get some information - **2.** *(ohne pl)* [Auskunftsschalter] information desk; [Fernsprechauskunft] directory enquiries.

Auskunfts|schalter *der* information desk.

aus|kurieren *vt* to cure.

aus|lachen *vt* to laugh at.

aus|laden *vt (unreg)* - **1.** [entladen] to unload - **2.** [nach einer Einladung]: **jn ausladen** to tell sb not to come.

ausladend *adj* overhanging; [Hinterteil] protruding; [Bewegung] sweeping.

Aus|lage *die* display. ◆ **Auslagen** *Pl* expenses.

Ausland *das (ohne pl)*: **im Ausland** abroad; **ins Ausland** abroad.

Ausländer (*pl* -) *der* foreigner.

ausländerfeindlich ◇ *adj* xenophobic. ◇ *adv*: **ausländerfeindlich eingestellt sein** to be xenophobic.

Ausländerfeindlichkeit *die (ohne pl)* hostility to foreigners, xenophobia.

Ausländerin (*pl* **-nen**) *die* foreigner.

ausländisch *adj* foreign.

Auslands|gespräch *das* international call.

Auslands|korrespondent, in *der, die* foreign correspondent.

Auslands|reise *die* trip abroad.

aus|lassen *vt (unreg)* - **1.** [Absatz, Einzelheit] to leave out, to miss out; [Chance, Gelegenheit] to miss - **2.** [abreagieren]: **etw an jm auslassen** to take sthg out on sb. ◆ **sich auslassen** *ref fam* [sich äußern]: **sich über jn/etw auslassen** *abw* to bitch about sb/sthg.

aus|lasten *vt* - **1.** [Betrieb, Maschine] to run at full capacity - **2.** [beanspruchen] to keep fully occupied; **mit etw ausgelastet sein** to be kept fully occupied by sthg.

Auslauf *der (ohne pl)* room (to run about).

aus|laufen (*perf* **ist ausgelaufen**) *vi (unreg)* - **1.** [Tank, Fass] to leak - **2.** [Flüssigkeit] to leak out - **3.** [Schiff] to set sail - **4.** [Modell, Serie] to be discontinued - **5.** [Vertrag, Amtszeit] to expire.

aus|laugen *vt* - **1.** [Bestandteile entziehen]: **der Boden wurde völlig ausgelaugt** the soil was completely stripped of its nutrients - **2.** [erschöpfen] to wear out.

aus|lecken *vt* to lick out.

aus|leeren *vt* to empty; [Glas, Tasse, Flasche] to drain, to empty.

aus|legen *vt* - **1.** [Waren] to display; [Köder, Gift] to put down - **2.** [auskleiden]: **ein Zimmer mit Teppich auslegen** to carpet a room; **einen Schrank (mit Papier) auslegen** to line a cupboard (with paper) - **3.** [vorstrecken]: **jm etw auslegen** to lend sb sthg - **4.** [interpretieren] to interpret; **sein Zögern wurde ihm als Ängstlichkeit ausgelegt** his hesitation was interpreted as fear.

aus|leiern ◇ *vi* (*perf* **ist ausgeleiert**) [Kleidungsstück] to stretch. ◇ *vt* (*perf* **hat ausgeleiert**) [Kleidungsstück] to stretch.

Ausleihe (*pl* **-n**) *die* - **1.** *(ohne pl)* [Ausleihen] lending - **2.** [Ausleihstelle] issue desk.

aus|leihen *vt (unreg)*: **jm etw ausleihen** to lend sb sthg; **sich *(D)* etw ausleihen** to borrow sthg.

Auslese *die (ohne pl)* - **1.** [Selektion] selection - **2.** [Wein] *quality wine made from specially selected grapes.*

aus|liefern *vt* - **1.** [Verbrecher]: **jn jm ausliefern** to hand sb over to sb - **2.** [liefern] to deliver.

aus|liegen *vi (unreg)* to be on display; [Gift, Köder] to be down.

aus|loggen *vi* to log off, to log out. ◆ **sich ausloggen** *ref* EDV to log off, to log out.

aus|löschen *vt* - **1.** [löschen] to extinguish, to put out - **2.** [vernichten] to erase; [Spuren] to cover; [Bevölkerung] to annihilate.

aus|losen *vt* to draw lots for.

aus|lösen *vt* - **1.** [Alarm, Mechanismus] to set off, to trigger - **2.** [Krieg, Panik, Freude] to cause.

Auslöser (*pl* -) *der* - **1.** FOTO (shutter release) button - **2.** [Ursache] trigger.

aus|machen *vt* - **1.** [Radio, Licht, Motor] to turn off; [Zigarette] to put out - **2.** [vereinbaren - Tref fen] to arrange; [- Termin] to make; **wir haben ausgemacht, nichts zu verraten** we agreed not to say anything; **ich habe mit ihr ausgemacht, dass wir ins Kino gehen** I arranged to go to the cinema with her - **3.** [stören]: **macht es Ihnen etwas aus, wenn ich rauche?** do you mind if I smoke?; **das macht ihm nichts aus** it doesn't matter to him - **4.** [betragen] to come to; **der Umweg hat eine Stunde ausgemacht** the diversion took an hour - **5.** [bedeuten]: **viel ausmachen** to make a big difference; **wenig ausmachen** not to make much difference - **6.** *geh* [erkennen] to make out - **7.** [bilden - Reiz] to be, to constitute.

aus|malen *vt* - **1.** [ausfüllen] to colour in - **2.** [schildern] to describe vividly - **3.** [sich vorstellen]: **sich *(D)* etw ausmalen** to imagine sthg.

Aus|maß *das* extent.

aus|merzen *vt* to eradicate; [Erinnerungen] to obliterate.

aus|messen *vt (unreg)* to measure.

aus|mustern *vt* - **1.** MIL: **wegen seines Herzfehlers wurde er ausgemustert** the army rejected him because of his bad heart - **2.** [aussondern] to take out of service; [abgetragene Kleidung] to sort out.

Ausnahme (*pl* **-n**) *die* exception; **mit Ausnahme von** with the exception of; **eine Ausnahme machen** to make an exception.

Ausnahme|zustand *der*: **den Ausnahmezustand verhängen** to declare a state of emergency.

ausnahmslos *adv* without exception.

ausnahmsweise *adv*: **ausnahmsweise dürfen die Kinder aufbleiben** the children can stay up just this once.

aus|nutzen, ausnützen *vt* - **1.** [nutzen] to use, to make use of; [Gelegenheit, Vorteil] to use, to make the most of - **2.** [missbrauchen] to take advantage of, to exploit.

aus|packen ◇ *vt* to unpack; [Paket, Geschenk] to unwrap. ◇ *vi fam* to spill the beans.

aus|plaudern *vt* to give away.

aus|pressen *vt* - **1.** [Frucht] to squeeze - **2.** [ausbeuten] to squeeze dry.

aus|probieren *vt* to try out.

Auspuff (*pl* **-e**) *der* exhaust.

aus|pumpen *vt* to pump out; **jm den Magen auspumpen** to pump sb's stomach out.

aus|quetschen *vt* - **1.** [auspressen] to squeeze - **2.** *fam* [ausfragen] to grill; **jn über etw *(A)* ausquetschen** to grill sb about sthg.

aus|radieren *vt* - **1.** [durch Radieren] to rub out, to erase - **2.** *fig* [zerstören] to wipe out.

aus|rangieren *vt fam* [Kleidung, Möbel] to throw out; [Fahrzeug] to scrap.

aus|rauben *vt* [Person] to rob; [Geschäft] to loot.

aus|räumen *vt* - **1.** [entfernen, leeren] to clear out - **2.** *fam* [ausrauben] to clean out - **3.** [Missverständnis] to clear up; [Zweifel] to dispel.

aus|rechnen *vt* to calculate, to work out; **sich *(D)* etw ausrechnen** to work sthg out for o.s.; **sie hatte sich gute Chancen ausgerechnet** she had fancied her chances.

Aus|rede *die* excuse; **faule Ausrede** *fam* feeble excuse.

aus|reden ◇ *vi* to finish speaking. ◇ *vt*: **jm etw ausreden** to talk sb out of sthg.

aus|reichen *vi* to be enough; **es muss bis März ausreichen** it has to last until March.

ausreichend ◇ *adj* - **1.** [genügend] sufficient; **eine ausreichende Anzahl von Teilnehmern** enough participants - **2.** SCHULE *mark 4 on a scale of 1 to 6, indicating a pass, but only just.* ◇ *adv* sufficiently; **wir haben ausreichend für die Party eingekauft** we bought enough for the party.

Aus|reise *die*: **bei der Ausreise** on leaving the country.

Ausreise|genehmigung *die* exit visa.

aus|reisen (*perf* **ist ausgereist**) *vi*: **nach Deutschland ausreisen** to leave for Germany; **aus einem Land ausreisen** to leave a country.

aus|reißen (*perf* **hat/ist ausgerissen**) *(unreg)* ◇ *vi (ist) fam* to run away. ◇ *vt (hat)* [Unkraut] to pull up.

aus|renken *vt*: **jm/sich *(D)* den Arm ausrenken** to dislocate sb's/one's arm.

aus|richten *vt* - **1.** [übermitteln]: **jm etw ausrichten** to tell sb sthg; **ich soll Ihnen Grüße von meiner Tante ausrichten** my aunt sends her regards; **kann ich etwas ausrichten?** can I take a message? - **2.** [erreichen] to achieve; **ich habe bei der Behörde nichts ausrichten können** I didn't get anywhere with the authorities - **3.** [Text] to align - **4.** [anpassen]: **etw auf jn/etw ausrichten, etw nach jm/etw ausrichten** to gear sthg towards sb/sthg.

aus|rotten *vt* [Rasse, Ungeziefer] to exterminate; [Aberglauben] to eradicate.

aus|rücken (*perf* **ist ausgerückt**) *vi* - **1.** MIL to move out - **2.** *fam* [weglaufen] to run away.

aus|rufen *vt (unreg)* - **1.** [rufen] to cry, to exclaim - **2.** [öffentlich] to announce; **jn ausrufen lassen** to page sb - **3.** [verkünden]: **einen Streik ausrufen** to call a strike.

Ausrufe|zeichen, Ausrufungszeichen *das* exclamation mark.

aus|ruhen ◇ *vi* to rest. ◇ *vt* to rest; **die Beine/die Arme ausruhen** to rest one's legs/arms. ◆ **sich ausruhen** *ref* to rest, to have a rest.

aus|rüsten *vt* [Truppe] to equip; [Schiff] to fit out; **ein Auto mit einem Katalysator ausrüsten** to fit a car with a catalytic converter. ◆ **sich ausrüsten** *ref* to equip o.s.

Auslrüstung *die* - **1.** [das Ausstatten - von Truppe] equipping; [- von Schiff] fitting out - **2.** [Ausstattung] equipment *(U)*.

auslrutschen (*perf* **ist ausgerutscht**) *vi* to slip; **das Messer ist ihr ausgerutscht** the knife slipped out of her hand.

Ausrutscher (*pl* -) *der* slip.

Auslsage *die* - **1.** [Äußerung - vor Gericht] statement; **nach Aussage eines Fachmanns** according to an expert - **2.** [Inhalt] message.

Aussagekraft *die* expressiveness.

auslsagen ◇ *vt* - **1.** [ausdrücken]: **etw über jn/etw aussagen** to say sthg about sb/sthg, to reveal sthg about sb/sthg - **2.** [vor Gericht] to state. ◇ *vi* to testify, to give evidence.

auslschalten *vt* - **1.** [abstellen] to switch off, to turn off - **2.** [ausschließen] to eliminate.

Ausschau *die (ohne pl)*: **nach jm/etw Ausschau halten** to look out for sb/sthg.

auslschauen *vi* - **1.** [ausblicken]: **nach jm/etw ausschauen** to look out for sb/sthg, to be on the lookout for sb/sthg - **2.** *Süddt & Österr* [aussehen] to look; **er schaut gut aus** he looks well; **es schaut mit jm/etw gut/schlecht aus** things are looking good/bad for sb/sthg.

auslscheiden (*perf* **hat/ist ausgeschieden**) *(unreg)* ◇ *vi (ist)* - **1.** [aus Gruppe]: **aus etw ausscheiden** to leave sthg - **2.** [SPORT - verlieren] to get knocked out; [- wegen Verletzung] to pull out - **3.** [wegfallen] to be ruled out. ◇ *vt (hat)* [Giftstoff] to reject; [Eiter] to secrete.

auslschenken *vt* to serve.

auslschildern *vt* to signpost.

auslschlafen *vi (unreg)* to have a lie-in.

Auslschlag *der* - **1.** [auf Haut] rash - **2.** [das Entscheidende]: **den Ausschlag geben** to be the decisive factor.

auslschlagen (*perf* **hat/ist ausgeschlagen**) *(unreg)* ◇ *vt (hat)* - **1.** [entfernen]: **er hat ihm einen Zahn ausgeschlagen** he knocked out one of his teeth - **2.** [ablehnen] to turn down. ◇ *vi* - **1.** *(hat)* [treten] to kick out - **2.** *(hat, ist)* [Zeiger, Pendel] to swing - **3.** *(hat, ist)* [Pflanze, Baum] to produce leaves..

ausschlaggebend *adj* decisive.

auslschließen *vt (unreg)* - **1.** [Grund, Erklärung, Möglichkeit] to rule out; [Irrtum] to prevent; [Zweifel, Unsicherheit] to remove - **2.** [ausstoßen]: **jn von etw ausschließen** to expel sb from sthg - **3.** [aussperren] to lock out. ◆ **sich ausschließen** *ref* - **1.** [sich aussperren] to lock o.s. out - **2.** [sich fern halten - Person] to rule o.s. out; **diese beiden Möglichkeiten schließen sich gegenseitig aus** these two possibilities rule each other out.

ausschließlich ◇ *adj* exclusive. ◇ *adv* exclusively. ◇ *präp (+ G)* excluding.

Ausschluss (*pl* **-schlüsse**) *der* expulsion; **unter Ausschluss der Öffentlichkeit** RECHT in camera.

auslschmücken *vt* - **1.** [Raum] to decorat - **2.** [Geschichte] to embellish.

auslschneiden *vt (unreg)* to cut out.

Auslschnitt *der* - **1.** [Zeitungsausschnitt] cutting *UK*, clipping *US* - **2.** [Halsausschnitt] neckline; **ein Kleid mit tiefem Ausschnitt** a low-cu dress - **3.** [Auszug] excerpt; [eines Romans] excerpt, extract; [eines Films] clip, excerpt; [eine Bilds] detail.

auslschöpfen *vt* - **1.** [Schüssel] to scoop ou - **2.** *fig* [ausnutzen] to exhaust.

Auslschreibung *die* [von Stelle, Wettbewer advertisement; [von Projekt] call for tenders.

Ausschreitungen *Pl* violent clashes.

Ausschuss (*pl* **-schüsse**) *der* - **1.** [Gremiur committee - **2.** *(ohne pl)* [Ausschussware] re jects *Pl*.

auslschütteln *vt* to shake out.

auslschütten *vt* - **1.** [Gefäß] to empty; [Flü sigkeit] to pour out - **2.** [auszahlen] to pay ou to distribute.

ausschweifend *adj* [Fantasie] wild; [Lebe debauched.

auslsehen *vi (unreg)* to look; **sie sieht gu aus** she looks good; **es sieht nach Regen aus** looks like rain; **es sieht danach aus, als wü den wir gewinnen** it looks like we will wir it looks as if we will win; **mit dem Zuschus sieht es gut aus** things are looking good as fa as the grant is concerned; **wie siehts aus?** *fa* how's things?; **sehe ich danach aus, als würd ich stehlen?** do I look as if I would steal?; **s siehst du aus!** *fam fig* you can think again nothing doing!

aus sein (*perf* **ist aus gewesen**) *vi (unreg* - **1.** [zu Ende sein] to be over; **mit dem Trinke ist es aus** no more drinking for me; **es ist au mit ihm** he's had it; **es ist aus zwischen ihne** it is over between them - **2.** [nicht an sein] to b out - **3.** SPORT to be out - **4.** [erpicht sein]: **auf et** *(A)* **aus sein** *fam* to be after sthg; **sie ist darau aus, mir etw zu verkaufen** she is out to sell m sthg.

außen *adv* outside; **von außen** from (the outside; **nach außen** outwards.

Außenlhandel *der (ohne pl)* foreign trade.

Außenlminister, in *der, die* foreign minis ter.

Außenlpolitik *die (ohne pl)* foreign policy.

Außenlseite *die* outside.

Außenseiter, in (*mpl* -, *fpl* **-nen**) *der, d* outsider.

Außenstehende (*pl* **-n**) *der, die* outsider.

Außenlwelt *die (ohne pl)* outside world.

außer ◇ *präp (+ D)* - **1.** [außerhalb] out o **außer Haus sein** to be away from home; **auße Atem sein** to be out of breath; **außer Betrie** out of order; **außer sich sein (vor)** to be besid o.s. (with) - **2.** [abgesehen von] except (for apart from; **alle außer ihm** everyone excep (for) him; **nichts außer** nothing but - **3.** [zusätzlich] in addition to, as well as. ◇ *konj* except; **ich komme, außer es regnet** I'll come, unless it rains.

außerdem *adv* also; **es ist viel zu spät, außerdem regnet es** it's far too late and it's raining too.

äußere *adj* - **1.** [Wand, Umstände] external; [Ähnlichkeit, Schein] outward - **2.** [auswärtig] foreign.

Äußere *das (ohne pl)* (outward) appearance.

außergewöhnlich ◇ *adj* - **1.** [ungewöhnlich] unusual - **2.** [sehr gut] exceptional. ◇ *adv* exceptionally, remarkably.

außerhalb ◇ *präp (+ G)* outside; **außerhalb der Stadt** outside town; **außerhalb der Öffnungszeiten** outside opening hours. ◇ *adv* [nicht im Stadtgebiet] out of town.

außerirdisch *adj* extraterrestrial.

äußerlich ◇ *adj* - **1.** [an der Außenseite] external - **2.** [nach außen hin] outward; [oberflächlich] superficial. ◇ *adv*: **äußerlich war sie ruhig** she was outwardly calm; **die Salbe ist äußerlich anzuwenden** the ointment is for external application; **äußerlich betrachtet** on the face of it.

Äußerlichkeiten *Pl* - **1.** [Umgangsform und Aussehen] appearances - **2.** [Unwesentliches] trivialities.

äußern *vt* to express. ◆ **sich äußern** *ref* - **1.** [seine Meinung sagen]: **sich über jn/etw äußern** to give one's opinion on ODER about sb/sthg; **sich zu etw äußern** to comment on sthg - **2.** [sich zeigen]: **sich in etw *(D)* äußern** to reveal itself in sthg.

außerordentlich ◇ *adj* extraordinary. ◇ *adv* extremely, extraordinarily; **der Film hat mir außerordentlich gut gefallen** I thought the film was extremely good.

äußerst *adv* extremely.

außerstande, außer Stande *adj*: **zu etw außerstande sein** to be incapable of sthg.

äußerste *adj* - **1.** [Ende] furthest; [Rand] outermost - **2.** [größte] extreme; **von äußerster Dringlichkeit** of the utmost urgency, extremely urgent - **3.** [Termin] latest possible; [Preis, Angebot] final - **4.** [schlimmste] extreme.

Äußerung *(pl* **-en)** *die* [offizielle Aussage] statement; [Bemerkung] remark.

aus|setzen ◇ *vt* - **1.** [verlassen] to abandon - **2.** [versprechen] to offer - **3.** [ausliefern] to expose - **4.** [beanstanden]: **dieser Kunde fand an allem etwas auszusetzen** this customer found fault with everything. ◇ *vi* [Herz] to stop; [Motor] to cut out; **sein Atem setzte kurzzeitig aus** he stopped breathing momentarily; **beim Spiel aussetzen** to miss a go. ◆ **sich aussetzen** *ref*: **sich einer Sache *(D)* aussetzen** to expose o.s. to sthg.

Aussicht *(pl* **-en)** *die* - **1.** [Sicht] view - **2.** [Zukunftsperspektive] prospect; **sie hat eine Beförderung in Aussicht** she's in line for promotion; **jm etw in Aussicht stellen** to promise sb sthg.

aussichtslos *adj* hopeless.

aussichtsreich *adj* [Vorhaben] promising; **ein aussichtsreicher Kandidat** a candidate who stands a good chance of succeeding.

Aussichts|turm *der* lookout tower.

aus|söhnen *vt* to reconcile. ◆ **sich aussöhnen** *ref*: **sich mit jm/etw aussöhnen** to become reconciled with sb/to sthg.

aus|sortieren *vt* to sort out.

aus|spannen ◇ *vt* - **1.** [ausbreiten] to spread - **2.** *fam* [wegnehmen]: **jm die Freundin/den Freund ausspannen** to pinch sb's girlfriend/boyfriend. ◇ *vi* to relax.

aus|sperren *vt* to lock out.

aus|spielen *vt* - **1.** [einsetzen] to bring to bear - **2.** [im Sport] to outplay - **3.** [manipulieren]: **jn gegen jn ausspielen** to play sb off against sb.

aus|spionieren *vt* - **1.** [Geheimnis, Versteck] to uncover - **2.** [Person] to spy on.

Aus|sprache *die* - **1.** [Artikulation] pronunciation; **eine gute/schlechte Aussprache haben** to have a good/bad accent - **2.** [Gespräch] discussion *(to resolve a dispute)*.

aus|sprechen *vt (unreg)* - **1.** [artikulieren] to pronounce - **2.** [ausdrücken] to express; [Urteil, Strafe] to deliver. ◆ **sich aussprechen** *ref* - **1.** [sich äußern]: **sich über etw ausführlich aussprechen** to say what's on one's mind about sthg - **2.** [Stellung nehmen]: **sich gegen/für jn/etw aussprechen** to come out against/in favour of sb/sthg - **3.** [offen sprechen]: **sich mit jm aussprechen** to talk things through with sb.

aus|spucken ◇ *vi* to spit. ◇ *vt* - **1.** [spucken] to spit out - **2.** *fam* [ausgeben, bezahlen] to cough up - **3.** *fam* [erbrechen] to puke up.

aus|spülen *vt* to rinse out.

aus|statten *vt* [mit Geräten] to equip; [mit Lebensmitteln, Kleidung, Geld] to provide.

Ausstattung *(pl* **-en)** *die* - **1.** [mit Möbeln] furnishing; [mit Geräten] equipping; [mit Lebensmitteln, Kleidung, Geld] provision - **2.** [Ausrüstung] equipment; [von Küche, Auto] fittings *Pl* - **3.** [Einrichtung] furnishings *Pl*.

aus|stehen *(unreg)* ◇ *vt* to endure; **jn/etw nicht ausstehen können** *fam* not to be able to stand sb/sthg. ◇ *vi* [Zahlung] to be outstanding; **die Antwort steht noch aus** we're still waiting for an answer.

aus|steigen *(perf* **ist ausgestiegen)** *vi (unreg)* - **1.** [heraussteigen] to get out; **aus einem Bus/Zug aussteigen** to get off a bus/train - **2.** *fam* [ausscheiden]: **aus einem Geschäft aussteigen** to pull out of a deal - **3.** [aus Gesellschaft] to drop out (from society).

Aussteiger, in (*mpl* -, *fpl* **-nen**) *der, die* drop-out.

aus|stellen *vt* - **1.** [zeigen - Waren] to display; [- Kunstwerke] to exhibit - **2.** [ausfertigen - Scheck, Rezept] to make out; [- Visum] to issue; **einen Scheck auf jn ausstellen** to make out a cheque to sb - **3.** [ausschalten] to turn off.

Aus|stellung *die* exhibition.

aus|sterben (*perf* **ist ausgestorben**) *vi (unreg)* [Tierart] to become extinct; [Tradition] to die out.

Aus|steuer *die* dowry.

Ausstieg (*pl* **-e**) *der* - **1.** [Öffnung] exit - **2.** *(ohne pl)* [Rückzug]: **sie haben den Ausstieg aus der Kernenergie beschlossen** they have decided to abandon nuclear energy.

aus|stoßen *vt (unreg)* - **1.** [ausschließen] to expel - **2.** [hervorstoßen - Schrei] to give; [- Seufzer] to heave; [- Fluch] to utter - **3.** [produzieren] to emit.

aus|strahlen ◇ *vt* - **1.** [verbreiten] to radiate - **2.** [senden] to broadcast. ◇ *vi* [strahlen - Licht] to shine.

Aus|strahlung *die* - **1.** [Wirkung] charisma - **2.** [Senden] broadcasting.

aus|strecken *vt* [Zunge] to stick out; [Fühler] to put out; **die Beine/Arme ausstrecken** to stretch one's legs/arms. ◆ **sich ausstrecken** *ref* to stretch out.

aus|suchen *vt* to choose; **sich** *(D)* **etw aussuchen** to choose sthg.

Aus|tausch *der* exchange; [von Spielern] substitution.

austauschbar *adj* interchangeable.

aus|tauschen *vt* - **1.** [mitteilen] to exchange - **2.** [auswechseln] to replace; **einen Spieler (gegen einen anderen) austauschen** to substitute a player (with another).

aus|teilen *vt* [Prospekte] to hand out; [Karten] to deal (out); [Essen] to dish out.

Auster (*pl* **-n**) *die* oyster.

aus|toben *vt*: **seine Wut an jm austoben** to vent one's fury on sb. ◆ **sich austoben** *ref* to let off steam.

aus|tragen *vt (unreg)* - **1.** [Zeitung, Post] to deliver - **2.** [ausfechten]: **einen Streit mit jm austragen** to have it out with sb - **3.** [Wettkampf] to hold - **4.** [im Mutterleib] to carry to term. ◆ **sich austragen** *ref* to sign out.

Australien *nt* Australia.

Australier, in [aus'tra:liɐ, rɪn] (*mpl* -, *fpl* **-nen**) *der, die* Australian.

australisch *adj* Australian.

aus|treiben *vt (unreg)* - **1.** [verbannen] to exorcize - **2.** [abgewöhnen]: **jm etw austreiben** to cure sb of sthg.

aus|treten (*perf* **hat/ist ausgetreten**) *(unreg)* ◇ *vt (hat)* - **1.** [ersticken - Funken] to stamp out; [- Zigarette] to tread out - **2.** [abnutzen] to wear down - **3.** [weiten] to break in. ◇ *vi (ist* - **1.** [ausscheiden]: **aus etw austreten** to leav sthg - **2.** [zur Toilette gehen] to answer the cal of nature.

aus|trinken *(unreg)* ◇ *vt* [Kaffee, Bier] t drink up, to finish; [Glas] to drain, to finish ◇ *vi* to drink up.

Aus|tritt *der* [aus Partei] resignation; **die Ki che hat zahlreiche Austritte zu verzeichnen** lot of people have left the Church.

aus|trocknen ◇ *vi* (*perf* **ist ausgetrocknet** [Haut, Brot, Boden] to dry out; [See] to dry up ◇ *vt* (*perf* **hat ausgetrocknet**) [Haut, Brot, Bo den] to dry out; [See] to dry up.

aus|tüfteln *vt* to work out.

aus|üben *vt* [Beruf] to practise; [Amt] to hold [Einfluss, Druck] to exert; [Macht] to exercise, t wield.

aus|ufern (*perf* **ist ausgeufert**) *vi* to get ou of hand.

Aus|verkauf *der* sale.

ausverkauft *adj* sold out.

Aus|wahl *die* - **1.** *(ohne pl)* [Wahl] choic - **2.** [Auslese] selection - **3.** [Sortiment] range.

aus|wählen *vt* to choose, to select.

aus|walzen *vt* - **1.** [walzen] to roll out - **2.** *abv* [breittreten] to drag out.

aus|wandern (*perf* **ist ausgewandert**) *vi* t emigrate.

Auswanderung *die (ohne pl)* emigration.

auswärtig *adj* - **1.** [extern] external - **2.** [aus ei nem anderen Ort] from another town; [Mann schaft] away *(vor Subst)* - **3.** [außenpolitisch] for eign.

Auswärtige Amt *das* foreign ministry.

auswärts *adv* [spielen, übernachten] awa from home; **auswärts essen** to eat out.

aus|waschen *vt (unreg)* [Fleck] to wash ou [Kleidungsstück] to wash; [Pinsel] to rinse.

aus|wechseln ['ausvɛksln] *vt* [Reifen, Batte rien] to replace; [Spieler] to substitute; **wie aus gewechselt sein** to be a different person.

Aus|weg *der* way out.

ausweglos *adj* hopeless.

aus|weichen (*perf* **ist ausgewichen**) *vi (un reg)* - **1.** *(+ D)* [Fußgänger, Hindernis] to avoid [Schlag] to dodge; [Auto] to get out of the wa of - **2.** *(+ D)* [Frage, Entscheidung, Blick] to avoi - **3.** [zurückgreifen]: **auf etw** *(A)* **ausweichen** t switch to sthg.

ausweichend *adj* evasive.

aus|weinen ◆ **sich ausweinen** *ref*: **sic bei jm ausweinen** to cry on sb's shoulder.

Ausweis (*pl* **-e**) *der* [Personalausweis] identit card; [von Mitglied] membership card; [Zu gangsberechtigung] pass.

aus|weisen *vt (unreg)* - **1.** [verbannen] to deport, to expel - **2.** [erkennen lassen]: **jn als etw ausweisen** to identify sb as sthg. ◆ **sich ausweisen** *ref* to show one's identification.

Ausweis|kontrolle *die* identity card check.

Ausweispapiere *Pl* papers, identification *(U)*.

Ausweitung (*pl* **-en**) *die* - **1.** [Vergrößerung] expansion - **2.** [eines Streiks] spreading.

auswendig *adv* by heart; **etw auswendig wissen** ODER **können** to know sthg by heart.

Aus|wertung *die* evaluation.

Aus|wirkung *die* effect, impact; **die Auswirkung auf jn/etw** the effect ODER impact on sb/sthg.

aus|wringen (*prät* **wrang aus**, *perf* **ausgewrungen**) *vt (unreg)* to wring out.

Auswuchs ['ausvu:ks] ◆ **Auswüchse** *Pl* excesses.

aus|zahlen *vt* - **1.** [Gehalt, Lohn] to pay - **2.** [Teilhaber] to buy out; [Arbeiter] to pay off. ◆ **sich auszahlen** *ref* to pay off.

aus|zählen *vt* to count up.

aus|zeichnen *vt* - **1.** [mit Preisschild] to price - **2.** [ehren]: **jm mit einem Preis auszeichnen** to award a prize to sb - **3.** [charakterisieren]: **große Biegsamkeit zeichnet diesen Werkstoff aus** this material is characterized by its great flexibility. ◆ **sich auszeichnen** *ref* [Person] to distinguish o.s.; [Produkt] to stand out.

aus|ziehen (*perf* **hat/ist ausgezogen**) *(unreg)* ◇ *vt (hat)* - **1.** [ablegen] to take off; **die Jacke ausziehen** to take off one's jacket - **2.** [entkleiden] to undress - **3.** [vergrößern - Tisch, Antenne] to pull out - **4.** [herausziehen] to pull out. ◇ *vi (ist)* [umziehen] to move out. ◆ **sich ausziehen** *ref* to undress; **sich die Schuhe ausziehen** to take one's shoes off.

Auszubildende (*pl* **-n**) *der, die* trainee.

Aus|zug *der* - **1.** [Ausschnitt] excerpt - **2.** [Kontoauszug] statement - **3.** [Umzug] move.

auszugsweise *adv*: **ein Roman auszugsweise abdrucken** to publish a novel in instalments.

Auto (*pl* **-s**) *das* car; **mit dem Auto fahren** to go by car, to drive.

Auto|atlas *der* road atlas.

Auto|bahn *die* motorway *UK*, freeway *US*.

Autobahn|gebühr *die* toll.

Autobahn|kreuz *das* interchange.

Autobahn|meisterei (*pl* **-en**) *die* motorway *UK* ODER freeway *US* maintenance department.

Auto|bus *der* bus.

Auto|fahrer, in *der, die* (car) driver.

autogene Training *das* autogenics *(U)*, *relaxation technique based on self-hypnosis, developed by German neurologist J.H. Schultz.*

Autogramm (*pl* **-e**) *das* autograph.

Automat (*pl* **-en**) *der* [für Getränke, Zigaretten] vending machine.

Automatik (*pl* **-en**) *die* automatic mechanism.

Automatik|getriebe *das* automatic transmission.

automatisch ◇ *adj* automatic. ◇ *adv* automatically.

automatisieren *vt* to automate.

Autonomie (*pl* **-n**) *die* autonomy.

Autor (*pl* **-toren**) *der* author.

Auto|radio *das* car radio.

Auto|rennen *das* - **1.** [Sportart] motor racing - **2.** [Wettkampf] motor race.

Autorin (*pl* **-nen**) *die* author.

autoritär *adj* authoritarian.

Autorität (*pl* **-en**) *die* authority.

Auto|unfall *der* car accident.

Auto|verkehr *der* car traffic.

avantgardistisch [avɑ̃'gardɪstɪʃ] *adj* avant-garde.

Avocado [avo'kɑ:do] (*pl* **-s**) *die* avocado.

Axt (*pl* **Äxte**) *die* axe.

Azalee (*pl* **-n**) *die* azalea.

Azubi (*pl* **-s**) *der, die fam* trainee.

B

b, B (*pl* - ODER **-s**) [be:] *das* - **1.** [Buchstabe] B, b - **2.** [MUS - Note] B flat; [- Vorzeichen] flat. ◆ **B** (*pl* **B**) (*abk für* **Bundesstraße**) *die* ≃ A road *UK*, ≃ state highway *US*.

Baby ['be:bi] (*pl* **-s**) *das* baby.

Baby|sitter, in ['be:bisitɐ, rɪn] (*mpl* **Babysitter**, *fpl* **-nen**) *der, die* babysitter.

Bach (*pl* **Bäche**) *der* stream; **den Bach runtergehen** *fam* to go down the tubes.

Backbord *das (ohne pl)* SCHIFF port.

Backe (*pl* **-n**) *die* [Wange, von Po] cheek.

backen (*präs* **bäckt** ODER **backt**, *prät* **backte** ODER **buk**, *perf* **hat gebacken**) ◇ *vt* - **1.** [im Ofen] to bake - **2.** [braten] to fry. ◇ *vi* to bake.

Backen|zahn *der* molar.

Bäcker (*pl* -) *der* baker.

Bäckerei (*pl* **-en**) *die* bakery.

Bäckerin (*pl* **-nen**) *die* baker.

Back|form *die* baking tin.

Back|ofen *der* oven.

Back|pulver *das* baking powder.

Back|stein *der* brick; **ein Gebäude aus Backstein** a brick building.

bäckt *präs* ▷ **backen**.

Bad (*pl* **Bäder**) *das* - **1.** [Badezimmer] bathroom - **2.** [Baden - im Meer] bathing *(U)*; [- in der Wanne] bath; **ein Bad in der Menge nehmen** *fig* to press the flesh - **3.** [Schwimmbad] (swimming) pool - **4.** [Kurort] spa town.

Bade|anzug *der* swimming costume, swimsuit.

Bade|hose *die* swimming trunks *Pl*.

Bade|kappe *die* swimming cap.

Bade|mantel *der* bathrobe.

Bade|meister, in *der, die* [im Schwimmbad] pool attendant; [am Strand] lifeguard.

baden ◇ *vt* [Kind] to bath *UK*, to bathe *US*; [Wunde] to bathe. ◇ *vi* - **1.** [in der Wanne] to have a bath - **2.** [schwimmen] to swim; **baden gehen** to go for a swim; **wenn das passiert, werde ich bei** ODER **mit meinen Plänen baden gehen** *fam* if that happens, I can kiss my plans goodbye. ◆ **sich baden** *ref* to have a bath.

Bade|wanne *die* bath (tub).

Bade|zimmer *das* bathroom.

baff *adj*: **(ganz) baff sein** *fam* to be gobsmacked.

Bafög ['bɑ:fœk] (*abk für* **Bundesausbildungsförderungsgesetz**) *das* [Stipendium] *maintenance which is half grant and half loan awarded to students and trainees by the State*; **Bafög bekommen** to get a grant.

Bagel (*pl* **Bagel**) *der* bagel.

Bagger (*pl* -) *der* mechanical digger.

baggern ◇ *vt* [Graben] to dig; [Fahrrinne] to dredge. ◇ *vi fam* [Mädchen anmachen]: **er baggert schon wieder** he's on the pull again.

Bahn (*pl* **-en**) *die* - **1.** [Eisenbahn] train; **mit der Bahn fahren** to travel by train ODER rail - **2.** [Institution] railway *UK*, railroad *US*; **die Bahn** [Deutsche Bahn] *German rail company*; **bei der Bahn arbeiten** to work for the railways - **3.** [Weg] path; **wir haben freie Bahn** AUTO the road is clear, *fig* the way is clear - **4.** [von Rakete, Planet] path - **5.** SPORT [in Schwimmbad, Stadion] lane; **40 Bahnen schwimmen** to swim 40 lengths - **6.** [Straßenbahn] tram *UK*, streetcar *US* - **7.** [Streifen - von Stoff] length; [- von Tapete] strip; **auf die schiefe Bahn geraten** to fall into bad ways; **jn aus der Bahn werfen** to shatter sb.

bahnbrechend *adj* pioneering.

BahnCard® ['bɑ:nkɑ:d] (*pl* **-s**) *die card offering 50% discount on German rail fares*.

Bahn|damm *der* railway embankment.

bahnen *vt*: **jm/sich einen Weg bahnen** to clear a path for sb/o.s.

Bahn|hof *der* (railway) station.

Bahn|steig (*pl* **-e**) *der* platform.

Bahnsteig|kante *die* platform edge.

Bahnüber|gang *der* level crossing *UK*, grade crossing *US*.

Bahre (*pl* **-n**) *die* - **1.** [für Kranke] stretche[r] - **2.** [für Tote] bier.

Baiser [bɛ'ze:] (*pl* **-s**) *das* meringue.

Bakterien *Pl* bacteria, germs.

Balance [ba'laŋsə] *die* balance.

balancieren [balaŋ'si:rən] ◇ *vt* (*perf* **ha[t] balanciert**) to balance. ◇ *vi* (*perf* **ist balanciert**) to balance.

bald *adv* - **1.** [in Kürze, schnell] soon - **2.** *fam* [fast] almost, nearly - **3.** *fam* [endlich]: **hältst du jetzt bald den Mund?** just shut up, will you? ◆ **bis bald** *interj* see you soon ODER later!

Baldrian (*pl* **-e**) *der* valerian.

balgen *vi* to tussle. ◆ **sich balgen** *ref*: **sich (mit jm um etw) balgen** to tussle (with sb ove[r] sthg).

Balkan *der*: **der Balkan** the Balkans.

Balken (*pl* -) *der* beam.

Balkon [bal'kɔŋ, bal'ko:n] (*pl* **-s** ODER **-e**) *de[r]* balcony.

Ball (*pl* **Bälle**) *der* ball; **am Ball bleiben** [nicht aufhören] to stick at it; [auf dem Laufenden bleiben] to keep up to date.

Ballade (*pl* **-n**) *die* ballad.

Ballast *der* ballast.

Ballaststoffe *Pl* roughage *(U)*.

ballen *vt*: **die Faust ballen** to clench one's fist. ◆ **sich ballen** *ref* [Schnee, Lehm]: **sich zu etw ballen** to form into sthg.

Ballen (*pl* -) *der* - **1.** [Packen] bale - **2.** [von Hand] ball of the hand; [von Fuß] ball of the foot.

ballern *fam* ◇ *vi* - **1.** [schießen] to spray bullets - **2.** [schlagen]: **gegen** ODER **an etw (A) ballern** to hammer on sthg. ◇ *vt* - **1.** [ohrfeigen]: **jm eine/ein paar ballern** to sock sb one - **2.** [werfen]: **etw gegen etw ballern** to smash sthg against sthg.

Ballett (*pl* **-e**) *das* ballet; **ins Ballett gehen** to go to the ballet.

Ballon [ba'lɔŋ] (*pl* **-s** ODER **-e**) *der* balloon.

Ball|spiel *das* ball game.

Ballungs|gebiet *das* conurbation.

Balsam *der eigtl* & *fig* balm.

Balte (*pl* **-n**) *der* native/inhabitant of the Baltic.

Baltikum *das*: **das Baltikum** the Baltic.

Baltin (*pl* **-nen**) *die* native/inhabitant of the Baltic.

baltisch *adj* Baltic.

balzen *vi* to perform a courtship display.

Bambus (*pl* **-se**) *der* bamboo.

banal ◇ *adj* banal. ◇ *adv* banally.

Banane (*pl* **-n**) *die* banana.

Bananen|republik *die abw* banana republic.

Banause (*pl* **-n**) *der abw* philistine.

Banausin (*pl* **-nen**) *die abw* philistine.

Band[1] [bant] (*pl* **Bänder** ODER **Bände**) ◇ *das (pl Bänder)* - **1.** [aus Stoff] band; [als Zierde] ribbon - **2.** [Tonband] tape; **etw auf Band aufnehmen** to tape sthg - **3.** [Fließband] conveyor belt; **am laufenden Band** *fig* continuously - **4.** [aus Bindegewebe] ligament. ◇ *der (pl Bände)* [Buch] volume; **das spricht Bände** *fig* that speaks volumes.

Band[2] [bɛnt] (*pl* **-s**) *die* band.

Bandage [ban'dɑːʒə] (*pl* **-n**) *die* [Verband] bandage.

bandagieren [banda'ʒiːrən] *vt* to bandage.

Band|breite *die* - **1.** ELEKTR bandwidth - **2.** *fig* [Vielzahl] range.

Bande (*pl* **-n**) *die* - **1.** [von Verbrechern, Kindern] gang - **2.** [SPORT - von Bahn, Spielfeld] barrier; [- von Billardtisch] cushion.

bändigen *vt* [Tier] to tame; [Kind] to control.

Bandit (*pl* **-en**) *der* bandit.

Band|maß *das* tape measure.

Band|nudeln *Pl* tagliatelle *(U)*.

Band|scheibe *die* [Körperteil] disc.

Band|wurm *der* - **1.** [Wurm] tapeworm - **2.** *fig* [Gebilde]: **dieser Satz ist ein Bandwurm** this sentence is never-ending.

bange *adj* anxious; **mir ist/wird bange** I am/I'm getting worried.

Bange *die*: **keine Bange!** don't worry!

Bank (*pl* **Bänke** ODER **-en**) *die* - **1.** *(pl Bänke)* [in Park, Schule] bench; [in Kirche] pew; **etw auf die lange Bank schieben** *fig* to put sthg off - **2.** *(pl Banken)* [Geldinstitut] bank.

Bank|anweisung *die* banker's order.

Bankett (*pl* **-e**) *das* banquet.

Bank|geheimnis *das* banking confidentiality.

Bankier [baŋ'kjeː] (*pl* **-s**) *der* banker.

Bank|konto *das* bank account.

Bankleit|zahl *die* bank sort code.

Bank|note *die* banknote.

Bank|raub *der* bank robbery; **einen Bankraub verüben** to rob a bank.

Bank|räuber, in *der, die* bank robber.

bankrott *adj* bankrupt.

Bankrott (*pl* **-e**) *der* bankruptcy; **Bankrott gehen** to go bankrupt.

Bank|überfall *der* bank raid.

Bank|verbindung *die* account details *Pl*.

bannen *vt* - **1.** [fesseln] to hold spellbound - **2.** [Gefahr] to ward off; [bösen Geist] to exorcize.

Banner (*pl* **-**) *das* banner.

Baptist, in (*mpl* **-en**, *fpl* **-nen**) *der, die* Baptist.

bar ◇ *adj* - **1.** [mit Bargeld] cash; **bares Geld** cash - **2.** [pur - Zufall] pure; [- Unsinn] sheer. ◇ *adv* [in Bargeld] (in) cash. ◆ **gegen bar** *adv* [verkaufen] for cash. ◆ **in bar** *adv* in cash.

Bar (*pl* **-s**) *die* - **1.** [Nachtlokal] bar *(often also a brothel)* - **2.** [Theke] bar.

Bär (*pl* **-en**) *der* bear; **jm einen Bären aufbinden** *fig* to pull sb's leg.

Baracke (*pl* **-n**) *die* hut.

Barbar, in (*mpl* **-en**, *fpl* **-nen**) *der, die* barbarian.

barbarisch ◇ *adj* barbaric. ◇ *adv* barbarically.

barfuß *adv* barefoot.

barg *prät* ▷ **bergen**.

Bar|geld *das* cash.

bargeldlos ◇ *adj* cashless. ◇ *adv*: **bargeldlos zahlen** to use a cashless payment method.

Bariton (*pl* **-e**) *der* baritone.

Barkeeper ['bɑːɐ̯kiːpɐ] (*pl* **-**) *der* barman.

barock *adj* baroque.

Barock *der ODER das (ohne pl)* baroque period.

Barometer *das* barometer.

Baron [ba'roːn] (*pl* **-e**) *der* baron.

Baronesse [baro'nɛs(ə)] (*pl* **-n**) *die daughter of a baron*.

Baronin [ba'roːnɪn] (*pl* **-nen**) *die* baroness.

Barrel ['bɛrəl] (*pl* **-s** ODER **-**) *das* barrel.

Barren (*pl* **-**) *der* - **1.** [Block] bar - **2.** [Turngerät] parallel bars *Pl*.

Barriere [ba'ri̯eːrə] (*pl* **-n**) *die* barrier.

Barrikade (*pl* **-n**) *die* barricade; **sie ging auf die Barrikaden** *fig* she was up in arms.

barsch (*superl* **barsch(e)ste**) ◇ *adj* curt. ◇ *adv* curtly.

Barsch (*pl* **-e**) *der* [Fisch] perch.

Bar|scheck *der* uncrossed cheque.

Bart (*pl* **Bärte**) *der* - **1.** [Gesichtshaar] beard - **2.** [Schlüsselbart] bit; **jm um den Bart gehen** ODER **streichen** to butter sb up.

bärtig *adj* bearded.

Bar|zahlung *die* payment in cash.

Basar (*pl* **-e**)**, Bazar** (*pl* **-e**) *der* bazaar.

Basel *nt* Basel, Basle.

basieren *vi*: **auf etw** *(D)* **basieren** to be based on sthg.

Basilikum *das* basil.

Basis (*pl* **Basen**) *die* - **1.** [Grundlage] basis - **2.** MIL base - **3.** POL grass roots *Pl*; **an der Basis arbeiten** to work at grass-roots level.

Baske (*pl* **-n**) *der* Basque.

Baskenland *das*: **das Baskenland** the Basque Country.

Basket|ball ['bɑːskətbal] *der* basketball.

Baskin (*pl* **-nen**) *die* Basque.

baskisch *adj* Basque.

Bass (*pl* **Bässe**) *der* - **1.** [Stimme, Sänger] bass - **2.** [Kontrabass] double bass; [Bassgitarre] bass (guitar).

Bassist, in (*mpl* **-en**, *fpl* **-nen**) *der, die* - **1.** [im Orchester] double bass player; [in Rockgruppe] bass player, bass guitarist - **2.** [Sänger] bass.

Bassschlüssel (*pl* **--schlüssel**) *der* MUS bass clef.

Bast *der* raffia.

Bastelei (*pl* **-en**) *die* - **1.** [Basteln] handicrafts *Pl* - **2.** [Reparaturversuche]: **er hat genug von der ewigen Bastelei** he's had enough of tinkering around all the time.

basteln <> *vt* to make; **Weihnachtsgeschenke basteln** to make one's own Christmas presents. <> *vi* to do handicrafts; **sie bastelt gerne** she likes making things herself; **an etw** *(D)* **basteln** to tinker with sthg.

Bastler, in (*mpl* **-**, *fpl* **-nen**) *der, die* handicrafts enthusiast.

BAT [be'ːɑː'teː] (*abk für* **Bundesangestelltentarif**) *der statutory salary scale for public employees.*

Batterie (*pl* **-n**) *die* - **1.** [Stromspeicher] battery - **2.** [große Menge] array.

batteriebetrieben *adj* battery-powered.

Batzen (*pl* **-**) *der fam*: **das hat mich einen Batzen Geld gekostet** that cost me a packet.

Bau (*pl* **-ten** ODER **-e**) *der* - **1.** [das Bauen] construction; **in** ODER **im Bau sein** to be under construction - **2.** *(ohne pl)* [Baustelle] building site - **3.** *(pl Bauten)* [Gebäude] building - **4.** *(pl Baue)* [von Kaninchen] burrow; [von Fuchs] den; [von Dachs] set.

Bau|arbeiten *Pl* construction work *(U).*

Bau|arbeiter, in *der, die* construction worker.

Bauch (*pl* **Bäuche**) *der* stomach; **sich** *(D)* **den Bauch voll schlagen** *fam* to stuff o.s. ODER one's face; **mit etw auf den Bauch fallen** *fig* to make a botch ODER mess of sthg.

bauchig *adj* bulbous.

Bauch|nabel *der* navel.

Bauch|schmerzen ['bauxʃmɛrtsn̩] *Pl* stomachache *(U).*

Bau|denkmal *das* listed building.

bauen <> *vt* - **1.** [anlegen, errichten] to build - **2.** [herstellen] to make; [Auto, Flugzeug] to build, to make - **3.** *fam* [verursachen - Unfall] to cause; **Mist bauen** to mess up. <> *vi* - **1.** [arbeiten, bauen lassen] to build; **an etw** *(D)* **bauen** to be building sthg - **2.** [vertrauen]: **auf jn/etw bauen** to rely on sb/sthg.

Bauer (*pl* **-n** ODER **-**) <> *der* (*pl Bauern*) - **1.** [Landwirt] farmer; HIST peasant - **2.** [Schachfigur] pawn - **3.** [Spielkarte] jack. <> *das & der (pl Bauer)* [Vogelkäfig] (bird) cage.

Bäuerin (*pl* **-nen**) *die* [Frau des Bauern] farmer's wife; [Landwirtin] farmer.

bäuerlich <> *adj* rural. <> *adv*: **sich bäuerlich kleiden** to wear rustic clothes.

Bauern|frühstück *das fried potatoes with scrambled egg and pieces of bacon.*

Bauern|hof *der* farm.

baufällig *adj* dilapidated.

Bau|firma *die* construction firm, building contractor.

Bau|genehmigung *die* planning permission *(U).*

Bau|land *das (ohne pl)* development site.

Baum (*pl* **Bäume**) *der* tree.

baumeln *vi* to dangle; **die Beine baumeln lassen** to dangle one's legs.

Baum|schule *die* (tree) nursery.

Baum|stamm *der* tree trunk.

Baum|sterben *das* forest dieback.

Baum|stumpf *der* tree stump.

Baum|wolle *die* cotton.

Bau|satz *der* kit.

Bausch (*pl* **-e** ODER **Bäusche**) *der* ball.

bauschen *vt* [Kleidungsstück] to puff out; [Segel] to fill. <> **sich bauschen** *ref* [Vorhänge, Segel] to billow; [Ärmel] to puff out.

Bau|sparkasse *die* building society *UK*, savings and loan association *US*.

Bau|stein *der* - **1.** [zum Bauen] brick - **2.** [zum Spielen] building block - **3.** [Bestandteil] constituent part, component.

Bau|stelle *die* building site; [auf einer Straße] roadworks *Pl*.

Bauten *Pl* ▷ **Bau**.

Bau|unternehmer, in *der, die* building contractor.

Bau|werk *das* building.

Bayer, in (*mpl* **-n**, *fpl* **-nen**) *der, die* Bavarian.

bayerisch = **bayrisch**.

Bayerisch = **Bayrisch**.

Bayerische = **Bayrische**.

Bayern *nt* Bavaria.

bayrisch, bayerisch <> *adj* Bavarian. <> *adv* like a Bavarian.

Bayrisch, Bayerisch *das (ohne Pl)* Bavarian (dialect).

Bazille (*pl* **-n**) *die* MED bacillus; **Bazillen** germs.

Bd. (*abk für* **Band**) vol.

beabsichtigen *vt* to intend.

beachten *vt* - **1.** [befolgen - Vorschriften, Verbot] to observe; [- Ratschläge, Anweisungen] to follow - **2.** [berücksichtigen - Umstände, Gefahr] to take into consideration; **jn nicht beachten** to take no notice of sb.

beachtlich <> *adj* [Leistung, Verbesserung, Erfolg] considerable; [Position] important. <> *adv* considerably.

Beạchtung *die* - **1.** [Befolgung - von Regeln] observing - **2.** [Berücksichtigung] consideration; **unter Beachtung aller Umstände** taking everything into consideration; **einer Sache** *(D)* **Beachtung schenken** to take sthg into consideration; **jm keine Beachtung schenken** to take no notice of sb; **Beachtung finden** to be taken into consideration.

Beạmte (*pl* **-n**) *der* State employee *(e.g. teacher, policeman, civil servant).*

Beạmtenschaft *die (ohne pl)* State employees *Pl.*

Beạmtin (*pl* **-nen**) *die* State employee *(e.g. teacher, policewoman, civil servant).*

beạ̈ngstigend ◇ *adj* frightening. ◇ *adv* frighteningly.

beạnspruchen *vt* - **1.** [fordern] to claim - **2.** [Material, Bremsen] to wear out - **3.** [strapazieren - Geduld, Person] to tax; **wir möchten Ihre Gastfreundschaft nicht länger beanspruchen** we don't want to impose on you any longer - **4.** [Raum, Zeit, Energie] to take up.

Beạnspruchung (*pl* **-en**) *die* - **1.** [von Material, Nerven] strain - **2.** [im Beruf] demands *Pl.*

beạnstanden *vt* to complain about.

Beạnstandung (*pl* **-en**) *die* complaint.

beạntragen *vt* - **1.** [verlangen] to apply for - **2.** [vorschlagen] to propose.

beạntworten *vt* to answer.

Beạntwortung (*pl* **-en**) *die*: **die Beantwortung der Frage** the answer to the question.

beạrbeiten *vt* - **1.** [mit Werkzeug] to work - **2.** [Text] to edit; [Musikstück] to arrange; **ein Buch für den Film bearbeiten** to adapt a book for the screen - **3.** [betreuen] to deal with - **4.** *fam* [misshandeln - Schlagzeug] to bang away at; **jn mit den Fäusten bearbeiten** to do sb over - **5.** *fam* [beeinflussen] to work on.

Beạrbeitung (*pl* **-en**) *die* - **1.** [von Werkstück, Metall] working - **2.** [von Text] editing; [von Musikstück] arranging; [für Film, Fernsehen] adaptation - **3.** [von Antrag] processing.

beatmen *vt*: **jn künstlich beatmen** to give sb artificial respiration.

Beatmung (*pl* **-en**) *die*: **künstliche Beatmung** artificial respiration.

beaufsichtigen *vt* to supervise.

beauftragen *vt*: **jn beauftragen, etw zu tun** [bitten] to tell sb to do sthg; [Auftrag erteilen] to commission sb to do sthg; **beauftragt sein, etw zu tun** to be charged with doing sthg.

Beauftragte (*pl* **-n**) *der, die* representative.

bebauen *vt* [mit Gebäuden] to build on, to develop; **ein Gelände mit Häusern bebauen** to build houses on a site.

beben *vi* - **1.** [durch Explosion] to shake - **2.** [Hände, Person, Stimme] to tremble.

Beben (*pl* -) *das* - **1.** [von Händen, Person, Stimme] trembling - **2.** [Erdbeben] earthquake.

Bẹcher (*pl* -) *der* - **1.** [Kaffeebecher - ohne Henkel, aus Pappe, Styropor] **cup**; [- ohne Henkel, aus hartem Kunststoff] beaker; [- mit Henkel, aus Porzellan] mug - **2.** [Pokal] goblet - **3.** [für Jogurt] pot; [für Eis] tub.

Bẹcken (*pl* -) *das* - **1.** [Waschbecken] basin; [Spülbecken] sink; [Schwimmbecken] pool - **2.** [Körperteil] pelvis - **3.** [Instrument] cymbal.

bedạcht ◇ *pp* ▷ **bedenken**. ◇ *adj* - **1.** [vorsichtig] careful - **2.** [bemüht]: **auf etw** *(A)* **bedacht sein** to be concerned about sthg. ◇ *adv* [vorsichtig] carefully.

bedạ̈chtig ◇ *adj* - **1.** [langsam] deliberate - **2.** [nachdenklich - Person, Miene] thoughtful; [- Worte] well-considered. ◇ *adv* - **1.** [langsam] deliberately - **2.** [überlegt - sprechen] with well-considered words.

bedạnken ◆ **sich bedanken** *ref* to say thank you; **ich möchte mich herzlich bedanken** thank you very much; **sich bei jm für etw bedanken** to thank sb for sthg.

Bedạrf *der* need; **Bedarf an etw** *(D)* **haben** to be in need of sthg. ◆ **bei Bedarf** *adv* should the need arise.

bedauerlich *adj* regrettable.

bedauern *vt* - **1.** [Irrtum, Unüberlegtheit] to regret - **2.** [Person] to feel sorry for; **bedaure!** I'm sorry!

Bedauern *das* - **1.** [Mitleid] sympathy - **2.** [Reue] regret.

bedauernswert *adj* - **1.** [Irrtum] regrettable - **2.** [Person] pitiable.

bedẹcken *vt* to cover. ◆ **sich bedecken** *ref* [Himmel] to cloud over.

bedẹckt ◇ *pp* ▷ **bedecken**. ◇ *adj* [Himmel] overcast.

bedẹnken (*prät* **bedạchte**, *perf* **hat bedạcht**) *vt* - **1.** [überlegen] to consider - **2.** *geh* [beschenken - im Testament] to remember.

Bedẹnken (*pl* -) *das* - **1.** [Nachdenken] consideration - **2.** [Zweifel] doubt.

bedẹnklich *adj* - **1.** [prekär] serious - **2.** [besorgt] anxious - **3.** [fragwürdig] dubious.

Bedẹnkzeit *die*: **jm Bedenkzeit geben** to give sb some time to think it over.

bedeuten *vt* - **1.** [gen] to mean; **viel/nichts bedeuten** to mean a lot/nothing; **jm viel/wenig/nichts bedeuten** to mean a lot/not to mean much/to mean nothing to sb; **das hat nichts zu bedeuten** that doesn't matter - **2.** *geh* [zu verstehen geben]: **jm etw bedeuten** to indicate sthg to sb.

bedeutend ◇ *adj* - **1.** [wichtig] important - **2.** [groß] considerable. ◇ *adv* [sehr] considerably.

Bedeutung (*pl* **-en**) *die* - **1.** [Sinn] meaning - **2.** [Wichtigkeit] importance; **einer Sache** *(D)* **große/keine Bedeutung beimessen** to attach great/no importance to sthg.

bedienen <> *vt* - **1.** [Person] to serve; **mit diesem Produkt sind Sie gut bedient** this product is a good deal - **2.** [Maschine] to operate. <> *vi* to serve. ◆ **sich bedienen** *ref* to help o.s.; **bedienen Sie sich!** help yourself!

Bedienung (*pl* **-en**) *die* - **1.** [Versorgung] service - **2.** [Steuerung, Anwendung] operation - **3.** [Kellner] waiter; [Kellnerin] waitress.

Bedienungs|anleitung *die* operating instructions *Pl*.

bedingen *vt* [verursachen] to bring about.

Bedingung (*pl* **-en**) *die* [Voraussetzung] condition; **eine Bedingung stellen** to stipulate a condition; **unter einer Bedingung** on one condition. ◆ **Bedingungen** *Pl* [Umstände] conditions.

bedingungslos <> *adj* unconditional. <> *adv* unconditionally.

bedrängen *vt* [unter Druck setzen] to pressurize; [mit Truppen] to advance on; **jn mit Fragen bedrängen** to badger sb with questions.

bedrohen *vt* to threaten.

bedrohlich <> *adj* [Situation, Aussehen] threatening; [Nähe, Intensität] dangerous. <> *adv* [ansehen] threateningly; [nah, schnell] dangerously.

Bedrohung (*pl* **-en**) *die* threat.

bedrücken *vt* to depress.

bedrückt *adj* - **1.** [Person] depressed - **2.** [Schweigen, Stimmung] oppressive.

Bedürfnis (*pl* **-se**) *das* need.

bedürftig *adj* needy.

beeilen [bə'ailən] ◆ **sich beeilen** *ref* to hurry; **beeile dich!** hurry up!

beeindrucken [bə'aindrʊkn̩] <> *vt* to impress. <> *vi* to make an impression.

beeinflussen [bə'ainflʊsn̩] *vt* to influence.

beeinträchtigen [bə'aintrɛçtɪgn̩] *vt* [Bewegungsfähigkeit, Sicht] to impair; [Produktion, Stimmung] to affect adversely; [Wert, Qualität] to reduce; [Gesundheit] to damage; [Konzentration] to hamper.

Beeinträchtigung [bə'aintrɛçtɪgʊŋ] (*pl* **-en**) *die* [von Bewegungsfähigkeit, Sicht] impairment; [von Produktion, Stimmung] adverse effect; [von Wert, Qualität] reduction; [von Gesundheit] damaging; [von Konzentration] hampering.

beenden [bə'ɛndn̩] *vt* to end.

beengt [bə'ɛŋt] *adv*: **beengt wohnen** to live in cramped conditions.

beerben [bə'ɛrbn̩] *vt*: **jn beerben** to inherit sb's estate.

beerdigen [bə'eːɐ̯dɪgn̩] *vt* to bury.

Beerdigung [bə' eːɐ̯dɪgʊŋ] (*pl* **-en**) *die* funeral.

Beerdigungs|institut *das* funeral directors *Pl*.

Beere (*pl* **-n**) *die* berry.

Beet (*pl* **-e**) *das* [mit Blumen] flowerbed; [mit Gemüse] vegetable patch.

Beete *die* = **Bete**.

befahl *prät* ▷ **befehlen**.

befahrbar *adj* [Straße, Weg] passable; [Fluss] navigable.

befahren (*präs* **befährt**, *prät* **befuhr**, *perf* **hat befahren**) <> *vt* to use. <> *adj*: **eine stark befahrene Straße** a busy street.

befangen <> *adj* - **1.** [schüchtern] shy - **2.** RECHT partial - **3.** *geh* [gefangen]: **in dem Glauben befangen sein, dass...** to labour under the misconception that... <> *adv* shyly.

Befangenheit *die* - **1.** [Schüchternheit] shyness - **2.** RECHT partiality.

befassen (*präs* **befasst**, *prät* **befasste**, *perf* **hat befasst**) *vt*: **jn mit etw befassen** *geh* to assign sthg to sb. ◆ **sich befassen** *ref*: **sich mit einer Frage befassen** to look into a question; **sich intensiv mit einem Thema befassen** to study ODER look at a matter in great detail.

Befehl (*pl* **-e**) *der* - **1.** [Aufforderung] order - **2.** EDV command.

befehlen (*präs* **befiehlt**, *prät* **befahl**, *perf* **hat befohlen**) <> *vt* to order; **jm befehlen, etw zu tun** to order sb to do sthg; **du hast mir gar nichts zu befehlen** I don't take orders from you. <> *vi*: **über jn/etw befehlen** to command sb/sthg.

Befehls|form *die* GRAMM imperative.

befestigen *vt* - **1.** [anbringen]: **etw an etw (D) befestigen** to attach sthg to sthg; **etw mit Schrauben an der Wand befestigen** to screw sthg to the wall - **2.** [verstärken - Stadt] to fortify; [- Ufer, Damm] to reinforce; [- Straße] to make up.

Befestigung (*pl* **-en**) *die* - **1.** [das Anbringen] attaching - **2.** [die Verstärkung - von Stadt] fortification; [- von Ufer, Damm] reinforcement; [- von Straße] making up.

befiehlt *präs* ▷ **befehlen**.

befinden (*prät* **befand**, *perf* **hat befunden**) *vt*: **etw für gut/richtig befinden** *geh* to deem sthg good/right. ◆ **sich befinden** *ref* to be; **sein Büro befindet sich im ersten Stock** his office is on the first floor.

Befinden *das* (state of) health.

beflecken *vt* to stain.

befohlen *pp* ▷ **befehlen**.

befolgen *vt* [Rat] to follow; [Befehl, Vorschrift] to obey.

befördern *vt* - **1.** [transportieren] to transport - **2.** [im Beruf] to promote.

Beförderung (*pl* **-en**) *die* - **1.** [Transport] transportation - **2.** [im Beruf] promotion.

Beförderungs|mittel *das* means of transport.

befragen *vt* - **1.** [Person, Zeugen] to question - **2.** [Karten, Wahrsagerin] to consult.

Befragung (*pl* **-en**) *die* questioning.

befreien *vt* [Gefangenen] to free; [Land, Volk] to liberate; [Tier] to set free; **jn von etw befreien** [von Diktatur, Schmerzen] to free sb from sthg; [vom Unterricht] to excuse sb from sthg.

Befreiung *die* [von Gefangenen, Tier] freeing; [von Land, Volk] liberation; [der Frau] emancipation; **eine Befreiung vom Unterricht kommt nicht infrage** there's no question of you being excused from classes.

befreundet *adj* [Länder] friendly; **mit jm befreundet sein** to be friends with sb.

befriedigen *vt* to satisfy.

befriedigend *adj* **- 1.** [zufrieden stellend] satisfactory **- 2.** SCHULE ≃ C, *mark equivalent to 3 on scale of 1 to 6.*

Befriedigung *die* **- 1.** [Zufriedenheit] satisfaction **- 2.** [Zufriedenstellung] satisfying.

befristen *vt* to put a time limit on; **ihre Tätigkeit ist auf ein Jahr befristet** her contract only runs for one year.

befristet *adj* [Vertrag] fixed-term, temporary.

befruchten *vt* to fertilize.

Befruchtung (*pl* **-en**) *die* fertilization; **künstliche Befruchtung** artificial insemination.

befugt *adj*: **zur Unterschrift befugt sein** to be authorized to sign.

Befund (*pl* **-e**) *der* [ärztlich] results *Pl*; [von Fachmann] findings *Pl*; **'ohne Befund'** MED 'negative'.

befürchten *vt* to fear.

Befürchtung (*pl* **-en**) *die* fear.

befürworten *vt* to support.

Befürworter, in (*mpl* **-**, *fpl* **-nen**) *der, die* supporter.

begabt *adj* talented.

Begabung (*pl* **-en**) *die* talent.

begann *prät* ▷ **beginnen**.

Begebenheit (*pl* **-en**) *die* occurrence; **eine wahre Begebenheit** something that really happened.

begegnen *vi* [entgegenkommen, treffen]: **jm begegnen** to meet sb; **etw *(D)* begegnen** [Gefahr] to face sthg; **einer Person mit Freundlichkeit begegnen** to treat sb in a friendly manner. ◆ **sich begegnen** *ref* [treffen] to meet.

Begegnung (*pl* **-en**) *die* meeting.

begehen (*prät* **beging**, *perf* **hat begangen**) *vt* **- 1.** [verüben - Mord, Verbrechen] to commit; [- Fehler] to make; **eine Dummheit begehen** to do something stupid **- 2.** *geh* [feiern] to celebrate **- 3.** [benützen] to use.

begehren *vt* to desire; **sehr begehrt sein** to be much sought after.

begeistern *vt*: **sie begeisterte das Publikum** she delighted the audience; **man kann ihn für nichts begeistern** you can't make him enthusiastic about anything. ◆ **sich begeistern** *ref*: **sich für etw begeistern** [Idee] to be enthusiastic about sthg; FILM [Hobby] really to like sthg.

begeistert ◇ *adj* [Reiter, Schwimmer] enthusiastic, keen; [Publikum] delighted; **von dieser Idee bin ich gar nicht begeistert** I'm not very enthusiastic about *ODER* keen on that idea. ◇ *adv* enthusiastically.

Begeisterung *die* [über Idee, Beschluss, für Hobby] enthusiasm; [über Leistung] delight.

begierig ◇ *adj* [Blicke] longing; [Lippen, Hände] eager; **nach etw** *ODER* **auf etw *(A)* begierig sein** to be eager for sthg; **darauf begierig sein, etw zu tun** to be eager to do sthg. ◇ *adv* eagerly.

begießen (*prät* **begoss**, *perf* **hat begossen**) *vt* **- 1.** [mit Wasser] to water **- 2.** [feiern] to celebrate with a drink.

Beginn *der* beginning, start. ◆ **zu Beginn** *adv* at the beginning *ODER* start.

beginnen (*prät* **begann**, *perf* **hat begonnen**) ◇ *vt* to begin, to start. ◇ *vi* to begin, to start; **mit etw beginnen** to begin sthg, to start sthg.

beglaubigen *vt* to certify.

Beglaubigung (*pl* **-en**) *die* [Bescheinigung] certificate.

begleiten *vt* to accompany.

Begleiter, in (*mpl* **-**, *fpl* **-nen**) *der, die* companion; [beim Musizieren] accompanist.

Begleit|erscheinung *die* side effect.

Begleitung (*pl* **-en**) *die* **- 1.** [Begleiten]: **sie kam in Begleitung** she came with someone; **in Begleitung einer Freundin** accompanied by a friend **- 2.** MUS accompaniment **- 3.** [Begleitperson] escort; [Freund] companion.

beglückwünschen *vt*: **jn zu etw beglückwünschen** to congratulate sb on sthg.

begnadigen *vt* to pardon.

Begnadigung (*pl* **-en**) *die* pardon.

begnügen ◆ **sich begnügen** *ref*: **sich mit etw begnügen** to make do with sthg.

begonnen *pp* ▷ **beginnen**.

begraben (*präs* **begräbt**, *prät* **begrub**, *perf* **hat begraben**) *vt* **- 1.** [beerdigen] to bury **- 2.** [beenden, vergessen - Streit] to bury; [- Hoffnung, Vorhaben] to abandon.

Begräbnis (*pl* **-se**) *das* funeral.

begreifen (*prät* **begriff**, *perf* **hat begriffen**) *vt* & *vi* to understand.

begrenzen *vt* **- 1.** [Zeit, Geschwindigkeit] to limit, to restrict **- 2.** [Fläche, Raum]: **der Park wird vom Fluss begrenzt** the river forms the park's boundary.

Begrenzung (*pl* **-en**) *die* **- 1.** [von Zeit, Geschwindigkeit] restriction, limit **- 2.** [von Fläche, Raum] boundary.

Begriff (*pl* **-e**) *der* **- 1.** [Wort] term **- 2.** [Vorstellung] idea, concept; **im Begriff sein** *ODER* **ste-**

hen, etw zu tun to be about to do sthg; **jm ein Begriff sein** to mean something to sb; **sich** *(D)* **einen Begriff von etw machen** to get an idea of sthg.

begriffsstutzig *adj abw* slow.

begründen *vt* - **1.** [erklären] to justify; **sie begründete ihr Verhalten mit persönlichen Problemen** she gave personal problems as the reason for her behaviour - **2.** [gründen - Firma, Stadt, Religion] to found; [- Theorie] to originate.

Begründer, in (*mpl* **-**, *fpl* **-nen**) *der, die* [von Religion, Stadt, Firma] founder; [von Theorie] originator.

Begründung (*pl* **-en**) *die* - **1.** [Angabe von Gründen] reason - **2.** [Gründung - von Firma, Stadt, Religion] founding; [- von Stil] establishment.

begrüßen *vt* - **1.** [grüßen] to greet - **2.** [gut finden] to welcome.

Begrüßung (*pl* **-en**) *die* greeting; [von Gästen] welcome.

begünstigen *vt* to favour.

begutachten *vt* - **1.** [Subj: Fachmann] to examine and report on - **2.** [betrachten] to have a look at.

begütert *adj* well-to-do.

behaart *adj* hairy.

behäbig *adj* [Mensch] portly; [Ausdrucksweise, Schritte] ponderous.

behaglich ◇ *adj* [Sessel] comfortable; [Wärme] cosy. ◇ *adv* comfortably.

behalten (*präs* **behält**, *prät* **behielt**, *perf* **hat behalten**) *vt* - **1.** [nicht abgeben] to keep - **2.** [sich merken] to remember.

Behälter (*pl* -) *der* container.

behandeln *vt* - **1.** [gen] to treat; **jn gut/schlecht behandeln** to treat sb well/badly - **2.** [Problem, Thema] to deal with.

Behandlung (*pl* **-en**) *die* treatment.

beharren *vi* to insist; **auf etw** *(D)* **beharren** to insist on sthg.

beharrlich ◇ *adj* persistent. ◇ *adv* persistently.

behaupten *vt* - **1.** [versichern] to claim - **2.** [verteidigen - Vorteil, Position] to maintain. ◆ **sich behaupten** *ref* - **1.** [sich durchsetzen] to assert o.s. - **2.** [gewinnen]: **sich gegen jn behaupten** to overcome sb.

Behauptung (*pl* **-en**) *die* - **1.** [Aussage] claim - **2.** [Verteidigung] maintenance.

beheben (*prät* **behob**, *perf* **hat behoben**) *vt* to rectify.

beheimatet *adj*: **beheimatet in** *(+ D)* [Pflanze, Tierart] native to; [Person] from.

beheizen *vt* to heat.

behelfen (*präs* **behilft**, *prät* **behalf**, *perf* **hat beholfen**) *vi*: **sich** *(D)* **mit/ohne etw behelfen** to make do with/without sthg.

behelfsmäßig *adj* [Unterkunft, Konstruktion] makeshift; [Ersatz] temporary.

beherbergen *vt* to put up.

beherrschen *vt* - **1.** [Land, Stadt] to rule - **2.** [Leidenschaft, Markt] to control - **3.** [dominieren] to dominate - **4.** [meistern - Pferd, Wagen] to have control of; [- Arbeit, Sport, Instrument] to have mastered; [- Sprache] to have a command of. ◆ **sich beherrschen** *ref* to control o.s.

beherrscht ◇ *adj* self-controlled. ◇ *adv* with self-control.

Beherrschung *die* - **1.** [von Leidenschaft] control; **die Beherrschung verlieren** to lose control - **2.** [von Pferd, Wagen] control; [von Instrument] mastery; [von Sprache] command.

beherzigen *vt* to take to heart.

behilflich *adj*: **jm bei etw behilflich sein** to help sb with sthg.

behindern *vt* - **1.** [Verkehr, Sicht] to obstruct - **2.** [Person]: **jn bei etw behindern** to hinder sb in sthg.

behindert *adj* disabled.

Behinderte (*pl* **-n**) *der, die* disabled person; **die Behinderten** the disabled.

behindertengerecht *adj suitable for people with disabilities.*

Behinderung (*pl* **-en**) *die* - **1.** [Behindern] obstruction - **2.** [Handicap] disability.

Behörde (*pl* **-n**) *die* authority. ◆ **Behörden** *Pl* authorities.

behutsam ◇ *adj* careful. ◇ *adv* carefully.

bei *präp (+ D)* - **1.** [räumlich - nahe] near; [- innen] at; **das Hotel ist gleich beim Bahnhof** the hotel is right next to the station; **Bernau bei Berlin** Bernau near Berlin; **beim Arzt** at the doctor's; **sie arbeitet bei einem Verlag** she works for a publishing company; **bei meiner Tante** at my aunt's; **bei mir** at my house; **die Schuld liegt allein bei mir** *fig* I alone am to blame; **ein Kind bei der Hand nehmen** to take a child's hand, to take a child by the hand - **2.** [zusammen mit einer Person] with; **ich bleibe bei dir** I'm staying with you - **3.** [zeitlich] at; **bei Beginn** at the beginning; **bei der Arbeit** at work; **bei seiner Beerdigung** at his funeral; **Vorsicht beim Ein- und Aussteigen** be careful when getting on and off; **beim Sport brach er sich den Arm** he broke his arm (while) playing sports - **4.** [als Teil einer Menge] among; **einige dieser Stilelemente finden sich auch bei Picasso** some of these stylistic touches are also found in Picasso's work - **5.** [zur Angabe von Umständen]: **bei Tag/Nacht** by day/night; **bei Gelegenheit** some time - **6.** [zur Angabe der Ursache]: **bei Regen fällt der Ausflug aus** if it rains the trip will be cancelled; **bei deinem Talent solltest du Maler werden** with your talent you should be an artist. ◆ **bei sich** *adv*: **hast du Geld bei dir?** have you got any money on you?; **bei sich** *(D)* **sein** *fig* to be (feeling) o.s.

bei|behalten *vt (unreg)* [Methode] to keep to; [Gegenstände] to keep.

bei|bringen *vt (unreg)* - **1.** [lehren]: **jm etw beibringen** to teach sb sthg - **2.** [mitteilen]: **jm etw (schonend) beibringen** to break sthg (gently) to sb - **3.** *amt* [bringen] to produce.

Beichte (*pl* **-n**) *die* confession.

beichten ◇ *vt* to confess; **jm etw beichten** to confess sthg to sb. ◇ *vi* to confess.

beide ◇ *pron* [zwei] both; **die beiden** both of them; **diese beiden** these two; **ihr beiden** you two. ◇ *adj* - **1.** [zwei]: **die beiden Pferde** both (of) the horses, the two horses; **diese beiden Exemplare** both (of) these copies, these two copies - **2.** [alle zwei] both. ◆ **beides** *pron* both.

beiderlei *det* both.

beiderseitig *adj* mutual.

beiderseits *präp (+ G)* on both sides of.

beidseitig ◇ *adj* mutual. ◇ *adv* on both sides.

beieinander *adv* together.

Beifahrer, in (*mpl* **-**, *fpl* **-nen**) *der, die* front-seat passenger.

Beifahrer|sitz *der* passenger seat.

Beifall *der* applause; **Beifall spenden** ODER **klatschen** to applaud.

beifällig ◇ *adj* approving. ◇ *adv* approvingly.

bei|fügen *vt*: **einer Sache** *(D)* **etw beifügen** to enclose sthg with sthg.

beige [beːʃ] *adj* beige.

Beigeschmack *der* - **1.** [von Esswaren]: **das Bier hat einen bitteren Beigeschmack** the beer tastes slightly bitter - **2.** [von Begriff] connotation; **die ganze Affäre hatte einen bitteren Beigeschmack** the whole affair left a bitter taste in the mouth.

Bei|hilfe *die* - **1.** [finanziell] financial aid - **2.** [kriminell] aiding and abetting; **jm Beihilfe leisten** to aid and abet sb.

bei|kommen (*perf* **ist beigekommen**) *vi (unreg)*: **jm beikommen** [fertig werden mit] to get the better of sb.

Beil (*pl* **-e**) *das* axe.

Bei|lage *die* - **1.** [Speise] side dish; **mit Reis als Beilage** served with rice - **2.** [zu Zeitung] supplement - **3.** *amt* [Beilegen] enclosure.

beiläufig ◇ *adj* casual. ◇ *adv* casually, in passing.

bei|legen *vt* - **1.** [beifügen]: **einer Sache** *(D)* **etw beilegen** to enclose sthg with sthg - **2.** [schlichten] to resolve.

Beileid *das (ohne pl)* condolences *Pl*; **herzliches** ODER **aufrichtiges Beileid!** my sincere condolences!

beiliegend *adj amt* enclosed; **beiliegend übersenden wir Ihnen** please find enclosed.

beim *präp (bei + dem)*: **ich bin beim Essen** I'm eating at the moment; **beim letzten Test** in the last test; **sie war beim Arzt** she was at the doctor's; **sie traf ihn beim Einkaufen** she met him while she was shopping; **beim Rasenmähen helfen** to help with mowing the lawn; *siehe auch* **bei**.

bei|messen *vt (unreg)*: **einer Sache** *(D)* **große/keine Bedeutung beimessen** to attach great/no importance to sthg.

Bein (*pl* **-e**) *das* leg.

beinah, beinahe *adv* almost, nearly.

Bei|name *der* epithet.

beinhalten [bəˈɪnhaltn̩] *vt* to contain.

Beipack|zettel *der* instruction leaflet.

bei|pflichten *vi*: **jm/einer Sache beipflichten** to agree with sb/sthg.

beisammen *adv* together.

Beisammensein *das* get-together.

Beisein *das*: **im Beisein von jm, in js Beisein** in the presence of sb, in sb's presence.

beiseite *adv* aside, to one side; **beiseite lassen** to leave aside ODER to one side; **beiseite legen** to put aside.

Beisetzung (*pl* **-en**) *die* funeral.

Bei|spiel *das* example; **sich** *(D)* **an jm ein Beispiel nehmen** to follow sb's example; **sich** *(D)* **ein Beispiel an etw** *(D)* **nehmen** to take sthg as one's example. ◆ **zum Beispiel** *adv* for example.

beispielhaft ◇ *adj* exemplary. ◇ *adv* in exemplary fashion.

beispiellos ◇ *adj* unprecedented; [Unverschämtheit] unbelievable. ◇ *adv* unprecedentedly.

beispielsweise *adv* for example.

beißen (*prät* **biss**, *perf* **hat gebissen**) ◇ *vt* to bite. ◇ *vi* - **1.** [mit den Zähnen] to bite; **in etw** *(A)* **beißen** to bite into sthg - **2.** [brennen] to sting; **Qualm beißt in den Augen** smoke makes your eyes sting. ◆ **sich beißen** *ref* - **1.** [mit den Zähnen] to bite each other - **2.** [Farben] to clash.

bei|stehen *vi (unreg)*: **jm beistehen** to stand by sb.

bei|steuern *vt*: **etw (zu etw) beisteuern** to contribute sthg (to sthg).

Beitrag (*pl* **Beiträge**) *der* - **1.** [Geld, Mitarbeit] contribution; [als Vereinsmitglied] subscription - **2.** [Artikel] article.

bei|tragen *(unreg)* ◇ *vt* to contribute. ◇ *vi*: **zu etw beitragen** to contribute to sthg.

bei|treten (*perf* **ist beigetreten**) *vi (unreg)*: **etw** *(D)* **beitreten** to join sthg.

Bei|tritt *der* [zur EU] entry; [zu Verein] joining.

beizeiten *adv* in good time.

bejahen *vt* [Frage] to say yes to; [Standpunkt] to approve of.

bekämpfen *vt* [Feind, Kriminalität] to fight; [Schädlinge] to control.

Bekämpfung *die*: **die Bekämpfung von etw** the fight against sthg; [von Schädlingen] the control of sthg.

bekannt *adj* well-known.

Bekannte (*pl* **-n**) *der, die* acquaintance.

Bekannten|kreis *der* circle of acquaintances.

Bekannt|gabe *die* announcement.

bekannt geben *vt (unreg)* to announce.

bekanntlich *adv* as is well known.

bekannt machen *vt* [Beschluss, Plan] to announce; [Fremde, Gäste] to introduce; **jn mit jm bekannt machen** to introduce sb to sb; **jn/sich mit etw bekannt machen** to familiarize sb/o.s. with sthg.

Bekanntschaft (*pl* **-en**) *die* - **1.** [Kennen, Bekannte] acquaintance; **mit jm Bekanntschaft schließen** to make sb's acquaintance - **2.** [Bekanntenkreis] acquaintances *Pl*.

bekehren *vt* to convert. ◆ **sich bekehren** *ref*: **sich (zu etw) bekehren** to convert (to sthg).

bekennen (*prät* **bekannte**, *perf* **hat bekannt**) *vt* [Sünde] to confess; [Fehler] to admit. ◆ **sich bekennen** *ref*: **sich zu etw bekennen** [Glauben] to profess sthg; [Überzeugung] to declare one's support for sthg; [Attentat] to claim responsibility for sthg.

beklagen *vt* to mourn. ◆ **sich beklagen** *ref*: **sich (bei jm über jn/etw) beklagen** to complain (about sb/sthg to sb).

bekleckern *vt*: **etw mit etw bekleckern** to spill sthg on sthg. ◆ **sich bekleckern** *ref*: **sich mit etw bekleckern** to spill sthg on o.s.

bekleidet *adj*: **mit etw bekleidet sein** to be wearing sthg.

Bekleidung *die (ohne pl)* - **1.** [Kleidung] clothes *Pl* - **2.** *geh* [von Posten, Amt] tenure.

beklemmend ◇ *adj* oppressive. ◇ *adv* oppressively.

Beklemmung (*pl* **-en**) *die* anxiety.

beklommen ◇ *adj* anxious. ◇ *adv* anxiously.

bekommen (*prät* **bekam**, *perf* **hat/ist bekommen**) ◇ *vt (hat)* to get; [Zug, Bus, Krankheit] to catch; **ich bekomme noch 100 Euro von dir** you owe me 100 euros; **was bekommen Sie?** what would you like?; **was bekommen Sie dafür?** how much is it?; **es sind keine Karten mehr zu bekommen** there are no more tickets available ODER to be had; **Prügel/eine Strafe bekommen** to be beaten/punished; **sie bekommt ein Kind** she's expecting (a baby); **Besuch bekommen** to have visitors; **etw geschenkt/geliehen bekommen** to be given/lent sthg; **Angst/Hunger bekommen** to get frightened/hungry; **seine Stimme bekam einen zärtlichen Ton** his voice took on a gentle tone. ◇ *vi (ist)*: **jm gut bekommen** [Essen] t agree with sb; **der Wein ist mir nicht bekommen** the wine disagreed with me.

bekräftigen *vt* [Meinung, Kritik] to confirm to reinforce; **jn in etw** *(D)* **bekräftigen** to confirm sb in sthg.

bekreuzigen ◆ **sich bekreuzigen** *ref* t cross o.s.

bekritzeln *vt* to scribble on.

bekümmert ◇ *adj* worried. ◇ *ad* worriedly.

belächeln *vt abw* to laugh at.

beladen (*präs* **belädt**, *prät* **belud**, *perf* **hat beladen**) *vt*: **etw (mit etw) beladen** to load sth (with sthg).

Belag (*pl* **Beläge**) *der* - **1.** [von Bremser lining; [von Straße] surface; [von Fußboden] covering - **2.** [auf Brot] topping - **3.** [auf der Zunge fur; [auf den Zähnen] film.

belagern *vt* to besiege.

Belagerung (*pl* **-en**) *die* siege.

Belang (*pl* **-e**) *der* [Bedeutung]: **von/ohne Belang sein (für jn)** to be important/of no importance (to sb). ◆ **Belange** *Pl* [Interessen interests.

belangen *vt* RECHT: **jn (für etw) belangen** to prosecute sb (for sthg).

belasten *vt* - **1.** [mit Gewicht] to put a load on **etw mit etw belasten** to weight sthg down with sthg - **2.** [Umwelt] to pollute; [Leber] to pu a strain on - **3.** [beanspruchen] to weigh heavily on; **jn mit etw belasten** to burden sb with sthg - **4.** [besorgen]: **jn belasten** to weigh on sb's mind - **5.** RECHT to incriminate - **6.** [finanzie - Konto] to debit; **ein Haus mit einer Hypothek belasten** to mortgage a house.

belästigen *vt* to bother; [sexuell] to harass.

Belästigung (*pl* **-en**) *die* annoyance; [sexuell harassment.

Belastung (*pl* **-en**) *die* - **1.** [mit Gewicht] load - **2.** [von Umwelt] pollution - **3.** [psychisch] strain - **4.** [von Konto] debiting.

belauern *vt* [Person] to spy on; [Verhalten] to observe secretly.

belaufen (*präs* **beläuft**, *prät* **belief**, *perf* **hat belaufen**) ◆ **sich belaufen** *ref*: **sich auf etw** *(A)* **belaufen** to amount to sthg.

belauschen *vt* to eavesdrop on.

belebt *adj* busy.

Beleg (*pl* **-e**) *der* - **1.** [Quittung] receipt - **2.** [Nachweis] proof.

belegen *vt* - **1.** [mit Belag]: **etw mit etw belegen** [Brot] to top sthg with sthg; [Boden] to cover sthg with sthg - **2.** [besuchen] to enrol for - **3.** [okkupieren] to occupy - **4.** [einnehmen] **den ersten/zweiten Platz belegen** to come first/second - **5.** [nachweisen - Zahlung] to provide proof of; [- Behauptung, Argument] to back up; [- Zitat] to reference.

Belegschaft (*pl* **-en**) *die* workforce.

belegt *adj* - **1.** [mit Aufschnitt]: **belegtes Brot/Brötchen** open sandwich/roll; **ein belegtes Brot mit Käse** a slice of bread with cheese on it - **2.** [Zunge] furred - **3.** [besetzt - Zimmer] occupied; [- Hotel, Kurs] full - **4.** [Stimme] hoarse.

belehren *vt* to instruct; **jn über etw** *(A)* **belehren** to instruct sb about sthg; [Rechte] to inform sb of sthg; **jn eines Besseren/anderen belehren** to teach sb better/otherwise.

beleibt *adj* corpulent.

beleidigen *vt* [Person] to insult; [Empfinden] to offend.

Beleidigung (*pl* **-en**) *die* insult; **Beleidigung des guten Geschmacks** offence against good taste.

beleuchten *vt* - **1.** [Denkmal, Brunnen] to illuminate; [Straße, Raum] to light - **2.** [Thema] to examine.

Beleuchtung (*pl* **-en**) *die* - **1.** [mit Licht] lighting - **2.** [Lampen, Scheinwerfer] lights *Pl* - **3.** *(ohne pl)* [von Thema, Theorie] examination.

Belgien *nt* Belgium.

Belgier, in ['bɛlgiɐ, rɪn] (*mpl* **-**, *fpl* **-nen**) *der, die* Belgian.

belgisch *adj* Belgian.

belichten *vt* to expose.

Belich|tung (*pl* **-en**) *die* FOTO exposure.

Belieben *das*: **nach Belieben** as you like; **das steht** ODER **liegt in deinem Belieben** that is up to you.

beliebig ◇ *adj* any; **eine beliebige Summe** any amount. ◇ *adv*: **beliebig viel/viele** as much/many as you like; **beliebig lange** as long as you like.

beliebt *adj* popular; **bei jm beliebt sein** to be popular with sb; **sich bei jm beliebt machen** to make o.s. popular with sb.

Beliebtheit *die* popularity.

beliefern *vt*: **jn (mit etw) beliefern** to supply sb (with sthg).

bellen *vi* to bark.

belohnen *vt* to reward.

Belohnung (*pl* **-en**) *die* - **1.** [Belohnen] rewarding - **2.** [Lohn, Entgelt] reward.

Belüftung *die* ventilation.

belügen (*prät* **belog**, *perf* **hat belogen**) *vt* to lie to.

bemalen *vt* [anmalen] to paint.

bemängeln *vt* to criticize.

bemerkbar *adj* noticeable; **sich bemerkbar machen** [Person] to attract attention; [Sache] to become apparent.

bemerken *vt* - **1.** [wahrnehmen] to notice - **2.** [sagen] to remark.

bemerkenswert ◇ *adj* remarkable. ◇ *adv* remarkably.

Bemerkung (*pl* **-en**) *die* remark.

bemitleiden *vt* to feel sorry for.

bemühen *vt geh* [Anwalt, Gutachter] to call on. ◆ **sich bemühen** *ref* - **1.** [sich anstrengen] to try; **sich bemühen, etw zu tun** to try to do sthg - **2.** [sich kümmern]: **sich um jn bemühen** to take care of sb.

Bemühung (*pl* **-en**) *die*: **Bemühungen** efforts.

benachbart *adj* [Personen, Dörfer] neighbouring; [Disziplinen] related.

benachrichtigen *vt* to inform.

benachteiligen *vt* to disadvantage; [Minderheiten] to discriminate against.

benehmen (*präs* **benimmt**, *prät* **benahm**, *perf* **hat benommen**) ◆ **sich benehmen** *ref* to behave; **sich gut/schlecht benehmen** to behave well/badly.

Benehmen *das* behaviour.

beneiden *vt*: **jn (um etw) beneiden** to envy sb (sthg).

beneidenswert ◇ *adj* enviable. ◇ *adv* enviably.

Benelux-Länder *Pl* Benelux countries.

benennen (*prät* **benannte**, *perf* **hat benannt**) *vt* to name; RECHT to call.

Bengel (*pl* -) *der* little rascal.

benommen ◇ *adj* groggy. ◇ *adv* groggily.

benoten *vt* to mark.

benötigen *vt* to need.

benutzen, benützen *vt* to use.

Benutzer, in (*mpl* **-**, *fpl* **-nen**) *der, die* user.

Benutzung *die* use.

Benzin (*pl* **-e**) *das* petrol *UK*, gas *US*; **bleifreies/verbleites Benzin** unleaded/leaded petrol *UK* ODER gas *US*; **Benzin tanken** to fill up with petrol *UK* ODER gas *US*.

Benzin|kanister *der* petrol can *UK*, gas can *US*.

beobachten *vt* - **1.** [observieren] to observe - **2.** [überwachen] to watch - **3.** [bemerken] to notice.

Beobachter, in (*mpl* **-**, *fpl* **-nen**) *der, die* observer.

Beobachtung (*pl* **-en**) *die* observation.

bepackt *adj* loaded up.

bequem ◇ *adj* - **1.** [gemütlich] comfortable; **es sich** *(D)* **bequem machen** to make o.s. comfortable - **2.** [faul] lazy - **3.** [Lösung, Weg] easy. ◇ *adv* - **1.** [liegen, sitzen] comfortably - **2.** [leicht] easily.

Bequemlichkeit (*pl* **-en**) *die* - **1.** [Gemütlichkeit] comfort - **2.** [Faulheit] laziness.

beraten (*präs* **berät**, *prät* **beriet**, *perf* **hat beraten**) ◇ *vt* - **1.** [Rat geben] to advise; **jn bei etw beraten** to advise sb on sthg - **2.** [besprechen] to discuss. ◇ *vi*: **über etw** *(A)* **beraten** to discuss sthg. ◆ **sich beraten** *ref*: **sich mit jm über etw** *(A)* **beraten** to discuss sthg with sb.

Berater, **in** (*mpl* -, *fpl* **-nen**) *der, die* adviser.

beratschlagen *vi* to discuss; **über etw** *(A)* **beratschlagen** to discuss sthg.

Beratung (*pl* **-en**) *die* - **1.** [Ratgeben] advice - **2.** [Besprechung] discussion.

Beratungs|stelle *die* advice centre.

berauben *vt*: **jn einer Sache** *(G)* **berauben** to rob sb of sthg.

berauschend <> *adj* intoxicating. <> *adv*: **berauschend wirken** to have an intoxicating effect.

berechenbar <> *adj* - **1.** [Summe, Größe] calculable - **2.** [Person, Reaktion] predictable. <> *adv* predictably.

berechnen *vt* - **1.** [ausrechnen] to calculate - **2.** [anrechnen] to charge.

berechnend <> *adj* calculating. <> *adv* calculatingly.

Berechnung (*pl* **-en**) *die* calculation; **aus Berechnung handeln** to act in a calculating manner.

berechtigen *vt*: **jn zu etw berechtigen** to entitle sb to sthg.

berechtigt *adj* justified.

Berechtigung (*pl* **-en**) *die* - **1.** [Genehmigung] right - **2.** [Korrektheit] legitimacy.

bereden *vt* [besprechen]: **etw (mit jm) bereden** to discuss sthg (with sb).

Bereich (*pl* **-e**) *der* - **1.** [Gebiet] area - **2.** [Aufgabe, Thema] field.

bereichern *vt* to enrich. ◆ **sich bereichern** *ref*: **sich (an jm/etw) bereichern** to make money (at sb's expense/from sthg).

Bereicherung (*pl* **-en**) *die* enrichment.

bereisen *vt* to travel around.

bereit *adj* - **1.** [fertig]: **bereit sein** to be ready - **2.** [gewillt]: **bereit sein, etw zu tun** to be willing to do sthg; **sich bereit erklären, etw zu tun** to agree to do sthg.

bereit|haben *vt* to have ready.

bereit|halten *vt (unreg)* to have ready. ◆ **sich bereithalten** *ref*: **sich zu** ODER **für etw bereithalten** to be ready for sthg.

bereit|machen *vt* to get ready. ◆ **sich bereitmachen** *ref* to get ready.

bereits *adv* already; **bereits um sechs Uhr** as early as six o'clock.

Bereitschaft *die* - **1.** [Wille] willingness - **2.** [Bereitschaftsdienst] emergency service; **Bereitschaft haben** [Polizei, Feuerwehr] to be on standby; [Arzt] to be on call.

bereit|stehen *vi (unreg)* [Fahrzeug, Koffer] to be ready; [Sanitäter, Polizei] to be on standby.

Bereit|stellung *die* provision.

bereitwillig <> *adj* willing. <> *adv* willingly.

bereuen *vt* [Fehler, Worte, Verhalten] to regret; [Sünde] to repent of.

Berg (*pl* **-e**) *der* [Erhöhung, große Menge] mountain; [kleiner] hill. ◆ **Berge** *Pl* mountains; **in die Berge fahren** to go to the mountains.

bergab *adv* downhill; **mit jm/etw geht es bergab** sb/sthg is going downhill.

bergan = **bergauf**.

bergauf, bergan *adv* uphill; **mit jm/etw geht es bergauf** things are looking up for sb/sthg.

Bergbau *der* mining.

bergen (*präs* **birgt**, *prät* **barg**, *perf* **hat geborgen**) *vt* - **1.** [Verunglückte] to rescue; [Leiche, Unfallwagen] to recover; [Boot] to salvage - **2.** *geh* [enthalten]: **etw in sich** *(D)* **bergen** to involve sthg.

Berg|führer, **in** *der, die* mountain guide.

Berg|hütte *die* mountain hut.

bergig *adj* mountainous.

Berg|mann (*pl* **-leute**) *der* miner.

Berg|steigen *das* (mountain) climbing.

Berg|steiger, **in** *der, die* (mountain) climber; [professionell] mountaineer.

Bergung (*pl* **-en**) *die* [von Verletzten] rescue; [von Leiche, Unfallwagen] recovery; [von Boot] salvage.

Berg|wacht *die (ohne pl)* mountain rescue service.

Berg|wandern *das* hill walking.

Berg|werk *das* mine.

Bericht (*pl* **-e**) *der* report; **über etw** *(A)* **Bericht erstatten** to report on sthg.

berichten <> *vt* to report. <> *vi* to report; **von jm/etw** ODER **über jn/etw berichten** to report on sb/sthg.

Bericht|erstattung *die* reporting.

berichtigen *vt* to correct.

Berichtigung (*pl* **-en**) *die* correction.

Berlin *nt* Berlin.

Berliner (*pl* -) <> *der* - **1.** [Person] Berliner - **2.** [Gebäck] doughnut *(filled with jam)*. <> *adj (unver)* Berlin *(vor Subst)*.

Berlinerin (*pl* **-nen**) *die* Berliner.

berlinerisch *adj* Berlin *(vor Subst)*.

Berliner Mauer *die* Berlin Wall.

Berliner Philharmoniker *Pl* Berlin Philharmonic *(sg)*.

Bern *nt* Bern, Berne.

Bernstein *der* amber.

bersten (*präs* **birst**, *prät* **barst**, *perf* **ist geborsten**) *vi* [Schiff, Gebäude] to break up; [Glas, Eis] to shatter.

berüchtigt *adj* notorious; **für** ODER **wegen etw berüchtigt sein** to be notorious for sthg.

berücksichtigen *vt* - **1.** [Vorschlag, Wunsch] to take into consideration; **wenn man berücksichtigt, dass...** considering (that...) - **2.** [Bewerber, Antrag] to consider.

Beruf (*pl* -e) *der* profession; **was sind Sie von Beruf?** what do you do (for a living)?

berufen[1] *adj* - **1.** [fähig] competent - **2.** [bestimmt]: **zu etw berufen sein** to have a vocation as sthg.

berufen[2] (*prät* **berief**, *perf* **hat berufen**) *vt* to appoint; **jn ins Ausland berufen** to post sb abroad. ◆ **sich berufen** *ref*: **sich auf jn/etw berufen** to quote sb/sthg as one's authority.

beruflich ◇ *adj* professional. ◇ *adv* [reisen] on business.

Berufs|ausbildung *die* vocational training.

Berufs|beratung *die* career guidance.

Berufs|leben *das* working life.

Berufs|schule *die* vocational school *(attended part-time by apprentices)*.

Berufs|soldat *der* professional soldier.

berufstätig *adj*: **berufstätig sein** to have a job, to work; **sie ist nicht berufstätig** she doesn't work.

Berufstätige (*pl* -n) *der, die* working person; **die Berufstätigen** the working population.

Berufsverkehr *der* rush-hour traffic.

Berufung (*pl* -en) *die* - **1.** [Ruf] appointment; [ins Ausland] posting - **2.** RECHT appeal; **Berufung einlegen** to appeal - **3.** [Begabung] vocation - **4.** [Bezug] reference; **unter Berufung auf jn/etw** with reference to sb/sthg.

beruhen *vi*: **auf etw *(D)* beruhen** to be based on sthg; **etw auf sich *(D)* beruhen lassen** to let sthg rest.

beruhigen *vt* to calm (down). ◆ **sich beruhigen** *ref* [Person] to calm down; [Lage] to settle down; [Meer] to become calm.

Beruhigung (*pl* -en) *die* [von Person, Meer] calming; [von Lage] settling down.

Beruhigungs|mittel *das* sedative.

berühmt *adj* famous; **wegen** ODER **für etw berühmt sein** to be famous for sthg.

Berühmtheit (*pl* -en) *die* - **1.** [Berühmtsein] fame - **2.** [Person] celebrity.

berühren *vt* - **1.** [anfassen] to touch - **2.** [beeindrucken] to move.

Berührung (*pl* -en) *die* - **1.** [Anfassen] touch - **2.** [Kontakt]: **mit jm/etw in Berührung kommen** to come into contact with sb/sthg.

besänftigen *vt* to soothe.

Besatzung (*pl* -en) *die* - **1.** [Personal] crew - **2.** MIL occupying forces *Pl*.

beschädigen *vt* to damage.

Beschädigung (*pl* -en) *die* - **1.** [Beschädigen] damaging - **2.** [Schaden] damage *(U)*.

beschaffen ◇ *vt* to obtain; **jm etw beschaffen** to get sb sthg; **sich *(D)* etw beschaffen** to get sthg. ◇ *adj*: **das Material ist so beschaffen, dass es große Belastungen aushält** the nature of the material is such that it can withstand heavy loads.

Beschaffenheit *die* - **1.** [Art] nature - **2.** [Zustand] condition.

beschäftigen *vt* - **1.** [anstellen] to employ; **er ist bei Siemens beschäftigt** he works for Siemens - **2.** [ablenken] to keep busy - **3.** [beanspruchen - Frage] to preoccupy; **sie ist im Moment sehr beschäftigt** she is very busy at present. ◆ **sich beschäftigen** *ref*: **sie beschäftigt sich intensiv mit Religion** she's heavily involved in religion; **wir beschäftigen uns gegenwärtig mit der Frage, wie** we are currently considering ODER looking at the issue of how to.

Beschäftigte (*pl* -n) *der, die* employee.

Beschäftigung (*pl* -en) *die* - **1.** [Tätigkeit - Arbeit] occupation; [- Hobby] activity - **2.** [Arbeitsstelle] job; **eine Beschäftigung suchen** to be looking for work; **ohne Beschäftigung sein** to be out of work - **3.** [Anstellen] employment - **4.** [Auseinandersetzung]: **Beschäftigung mit etw** [Thema, Problem] consideration of sthg.

Bescheid (*pl* -e) *der* [Entscheidung] decision; **den Bescheid vom Finanzamt erwarten** to be waiting for an answer from the tax office; **Bescheid wissen** to know; **jm Bescheid sagen** ODER **geben** [benachrichtigen] to let sb know; *fam* [jm die Meinung sagen] to give sb a piece of one's mind.

bescheiden ◇ *adj* - **1.** [anspruchslos, einfach] modest; [Benehmen] unassuming - **2.** [Essen] frugal; [Ergebnis, Leistung] mediocre. ◇ *adv* [sich kleiden, leben] simply.

bescheinigen *vt* [mit Zeugnis] to certify; **den Empfang von etw bescheinigen** to sign for sthg; **sich etw bescheinigen lassen** to get sthg confirmed in writing.

Bescheinigung (*pl* -en) *die* - **1.** [bescheinigen] certification - **2.** [Schein] certificate.

bescheißen (*prät* **beschiss**, *perf* **hat beschissen**) *vt salopp*: **jn (um etw) bescheißen** to con sb (out of sthg).

Bescherung (*pl* -en) *die* giving of Christmas presents.

beschießen (*prät* **beschoss**, *perf* **hat beschossen**) *vt* to fire on.

beschimpfen *vt* to insult; [mit groben Worten] to swear at.

Beschimpfung (*pl* -en) *die* insult; **Beschimpfungen** abuse *(U)*.

beschissen *vulg* ◇ *pp* ▷ **bescheißen**. ◇ *adj* shitty. ◇ *adv* [sich benehmen] shittily; **es geht mir beschissen** things are going like shit for me.

beschlagen (*präs* **beschlägt**, *prät* **beschlug**, *perf* **hat/ist beschlagen**) ◇ *vt (hat)* [Pferd] to shoe; [Schuhsohlen] to stud. ◇ *vi (ist)* to mist ODER steam up. ◇ *adj* well-informed; **in etw *(D)* beschlagen sein** to be well up on sthg.

beschlagnahmen *vt* to confiscate.

beschleunigen ◇ *vt* [Tempo, Schritte] to quicken; [Abreise] to hasten; [Arbeitsprozess] to speed up. ◇ *vi* to accelerate.

Beschleunigung (*pl* **-en**) *die* [von Verfahren, Entwicklung] speeding up; [von Auto] acceleration.

beschließen (*prät* **beschloss**, *perf* **hat beschlossen**) ◇ *vt* - **1.** [entscheiden] to decide on; **beschließen, etw zu tun** to decide to do sthg; [Gesetz] to pass; [Vorhaben] to approve - **2.** *geh* [beenden] to end. ◇ *vi* [beraten]: **über etw** *(A)* **beschließen** to decide on sthg.

Beschluss (*pl* **-schlüsse**) *der* decision; **einen Beschluss fassen** to take a decision.

beschmutzen *vt* [Teppich, Kleidung] to soil; [Wand] to stain; **jm/sich das Kleid beschmutzen** to get sb's/one's dress dirty.

beschränken *vt* to limit, to restrict. ◆ **sich beschränken** *ref*: **sich auf etw** *(A)* **beschränken** [Sache] to be confined to sthg; [Person] to confine o.s. to sthg.

beschränkt *adj* - **1.** *abw* [engstirnig] narrow-minded - **2.** [dürftig] limited; **in beschränkten Verhältnissen leben** to live in straitened circumstances - **3.** *abw* [dumm] slow, dim.

beschreiben (*prät* **beschrieb**, *perf* **hat beschrieben**) *vt* - **1.** [darstellen, formen] to describe; [Weg] to tell - **2.** [voll schreiben] to write on.

Beschreibung (*pl* **-en**) *die* description.

beschriften *vt* to label; [Brief] to address; [Etikett] to write on.

beschuldigen *vt* to accuse; **jn einer Sache** *(G)* **beschuldigen** to accuse sb of sthg.

Beschuldigung (*pl* **-en**) *die* accusation.

beschützen *vt* to protect; **jn vor etw** *(D)* **beschützen** to protect sb from sthg.

Beschützer, in (*mpl* **-**, *fpl* **-nen**) *der* protector.

Beschwerde (*pl* **-n**) *die* [Klage] complaint. ◆ **Beschwerden** *Pl* [Schmerzen] trouble *(U)*; **Beschwerden im Kreuz haben** to have back problems ODER trouble with one's back.

beschweren *vt* [belasten] to weight down. ◆ **sich beschweren** *ref*: **sich (über jn/etw) beschweren** to complain (about sb/sthg).

beschwichtigen *vt* [Person] to placate; [Zorn] to calm.

beschwindeln *vt* to dupe.

beschwingt *adj* [Stimmung] lively; [Melodie] lilting.

beschwipst *adj* tipsy.

beschwören (*prät* **beschwor**, *perf* **hat beschworen**) *vt* - **1.** [beeiden] to swear to - **2.** [erscheinen lassen - Geister] to invoke; [- Bilder] to conjure up; [- Erinnerungen] to evoke - **3.** [bitten] to entreat, to implore.

beseitigen *vt* - **1.** [entfernen - Fleck] to remove; [- Abfall] to get rid of, to dispose of; [- Schwierigkeiten, Missbrauch] to eliminate [- Schnee] to clear away - **2.** [ermorden] to eliminate.

Beseitigung (*pl* **-en**) *die* - **1.** [Entfernung - von Fleck] removal; [- von Abfall] disposal; [- von Schwierigkeiten, Missbrauch] elimination - **2.** [Ermordung] elimination.

Besen (*pl* **-**) *der* broom.

besessen *adj* - **1.** [verrückt]: **wie besessen** lik… someone possessed - **2.** [begeistert]: **von etw besessen sein** to be obsessed with sthg.

besetzen *vt* - **1.** [Stelle, Rolle] to fill - **2.** [Sitzplatz, Haus, Gebiet, Land] to occupy - **3.** [verzieren]: **etw mit etw besetzen** to trim sthg with sthg.

besetzt *adj* occupied; [Telefon] engaged; [Sitz] taken; **nicht besetzt** [Büro] closed.

Besetzung (*pl* **-en**) *die* - **1.** [von Posten] fillin… - **2.** [Team - von Schauspielern] cast; [- von Sportlern] team - **3.** [von Land, Gebiet, Haus] occupation.

besichtigen *vt* [Museum] to visit; [Wohnung] to view; [Stadt] to go sightseeing in.

Besichtigung (*pl* **-en**) *die* [von Museum] visit; [von einer Wohnung] viewing; [von einer Stadt] sightseeing; [Führung] tour.

besiegen *vt* - **1.** [Feind] to defeat; [Mannschaft] to beat - **2.** [Zweifel, Neugier] to overcome.

Besiegte (*pl* **-n**) *der, die* loser.

Besinnung *die*: **die Besinnung verlieren** t… lose consciousness.

Besitz *der* - **1.** [Eigentum] property - **2.** [Besitzen] possession - **3.** [Landgut] estate.

besitzen (*prät* **besaß**, *perf* **hat besessen**) *vt* t… possess, to own; [Recht, Qualität] to have.

Besitzer, in (*mpl* **-**, *fpl* **-nen**) *der, die* owne…

besondere, r, s *adj* [speziell] special; [außergewöhnlich] particular; **besondere Kennzeichen** distinguishing features; **im Besonderen** in particular, especially.

Besonderheit (*pl* **-en**) *die* special feature, peculiarity.

besonders ◇ *adv* - **1.** [vor allem, sehr] especially, particularly - **2.** [gut]: **nicht besonders** not very well. ◇ *adj*: **nicht besonders sein** to be not very good; **der Film ist nicht besonders** the film isn't up to much.

besorgen *vt* - **1.** [beschaffen] to get (hold of); **jm/sich etw besorgen** to get sb/o.s. sth… - **2.** [sich um etw kümmern] to see to.

besorgt ◇ *adj* worried; **um jn besorgt sein** to be worried about sb; **rührend um jn besorgt sein** to be concerned for sb's wellbeing. ◇ *adv* anxiously; **besorgt aussehen** to look worried.

Besorgung (*pl* **-en**) *die* [Einkäufe] purchase; **Besorgungen** shopping *(U)*.

bespielen *vt* to record on.

bespitzeln *vt* to spy on.

besprechen (*präs* **bespricht**, *prät* **besprach**, *perf* **hat besprochen**) *vt* - **1.** [erötern]: **etw (mit jm) besprechen** to discuss sthg (with sb) - **2.** [rezensieren] to review - **3.** [aufnehmen] to record (one's voice) on. ◆ **sich besprechen** *ref*: **sich (mit jm über etw) besprechen** to confer (with sb about sthg).

Besprechung (*pl* **-en**) *die* - **1.** [Beratung] discussion; **in einer Besprechung sein** to be in a meeting - **2.** [Rezension] review.

bespritzen *vt* - **1.** [nass machen] to splash - **2.** [beschmutzen] to spatter.

besser ◇ *adj* - **1.** [als Komparativ von gut] better; [ziemlich gut] good; **das hier ist schon ein besseres Gerät** this is a pretty good machine; **das Hotel ist eine bessere Absteige** the hotel is just a glorified dosshouse; **besser ist besser** better safe than sorry - **2.** [gesellschaftlich gehoben] superior. ◇ *adv* better.

Bessere (*pl* **-n**) *der, die, das* better; **Besseres zu tun haben** to have better things to do.

bessern *vt* to improve; [Verbrecher] to reform. ◆ **sich bessern** *ref* [Wetter, Zustand] to improve; [Mensch] to mend one's ways.

Besserung *die* improvement. ◆ **gute Besserung** *interj* get well soon!

Bestand (*pl* **-stände**) *der* - **1.** [Bestehen] continued existence; **Bestand haben** to last - **2.** [Vorrat] stock.

bestanden *pp* ▷ **bestehen**.

beständig ◇ *adj* - **1.** [dauernd] constant - **2.** [gleich bleibend - Wetter] settled; [- Freund] faithful; [- Mitarbeiter] reliable - **3.** [widerstandsfähig]: **gegen etw beständig sein** to be resistant to sthg. ◇ *adv* - **1.** [dauernd] constantly - **2.** [zuverlässig] steadily, reliably.

Bestandsaufnahme *die* stocktaking.

Bestandteil *der* component.

bestätigen *vt* to confirm; [Urteil] to uphold. ◆ **sich bestätigen** *ref* to be confirmed, to prove true.

Bestätigung (*pl* **-en**) *die* confirmation; [von Urteil] upholding.

beste, r, s ◇ *adj* best; **sich bester Gesundheit erfreuen** to enjoy the best of health. ◇ *adv*: **am besten gehe ich jetzt** I'd better go now.

Beste (*pl* **-n**) *der, die, das* best (one); **das Beste aus etw (D) machen** *fig* to make the best of sthg; **es steht nicht zum Besten mit jm/etw** things are not looking good for sb/sthg; **eine Anekdote zum Besten geben** to tell a story; **jn zum Besten halten** *fig* to pull sb's leg.

bestechen (*präs* **besticht**, *prät* **bestach**, *perf* **hat bestochen**) ◇ *vt* to bribe. ◇ *vi*: **sie besticht durch ihre Schlagfertigkeit** she makes an impression with her quick-wittedness.

bestechlich *adj* open to bribery.

Besteck (*pl* **-e**) *das* [Essbesteck] cutlery *(U)*; **ein Besteck** a place setting.

bestehen (*prät* **bestand**, *perf* **hat bestanden**) ◇ *vi* - **1.** [existieren] to exist; **es besteht** there is - **2.** [sich zusammensetzen]: **das Buch besteht aus zehn Kapiteln** the book consists of ten chapters; **der Rahmen besteht aus Kunststoff** the frame is made of plastic - **3.** [beinhalten]: **ihre Aufgabe besteht in der Planung des Projekts** her job consists of ODER involves planning the project; **das Problem besteht darin, dass...** the problem is that... - **4.** [beharren]: **auf etw *(D)* bestehen** to insist on sthg - **5.** [standhalten]: **vor jm/etw bestehen** to stand up to sb/sthg. ◇ *vt* to pass.

bestehen bleiben (*perf* **ist bestehen geblieben**) *vi (unreg)* - **1.** [übrig bleiben] to remain - **2.** [Vorschrift] to be upheld.

bestellen ◇ *vt* - **1.** [anfordern] to order; **sich *(D)* etw bestellen** to order sthg (for o.s.) - **2.** [reservieren] to book, to reserve - **3.** [kommen lassen] to summon - **4.** [ausrichten]: **jm Grüße bestellen** to give ODER send one's regards to sb; **kann ich ihm etwas (von dir) bestellen?** can I give him a message (from you)? - **5.** [bearbeiten] to cultivate; **es ist um jn/etw schlecht bestellt** sb/sthg is in a bad way. ◇ *vi* to order.

Bestellung (*pl* **-en**) *die* - **1.** [Anforderung, Waren] order - **2.** [Reservierung] booking, reservation - **3.** [Bearbeitung] cultivation. ◆ **auf Bestellung** *adv* to order; **wie auf Bestellung** as if by command.

bestenfalls *adv* at best.

bestens *adv* very well.

bestialisch ◇ *adj abw* [Mord, Tat] brutal. ◇ *adv* - **1.** *abw* [grausam] brutally - **2.** *fam* [unerträglich] dreadfully.

Bestie (*pl* **-n**) *die* - **1.** [Raubtier] beast - **2.** *abw* [Unmensch] brute.

bestimmen ◇ *vt* - **1.** [Preis, Termin] to fix; **jn zum Nachfolger bestimmen** to designate sb as one's successor - **2.** [vorsehen]: **für jn/etw bestimmt sein** to be intended for sb/sthg - **3.** [ermitteln] to determine; [Pflanze] to classify; [Bedeutung] to define - **4.** [Charakter] to determine; [Stadtbild, Atmosphäre] to characterize. ◇ *vi* - **1.** [entscheiden] to decide; **sie bestimmt in dieser Firma** she makes the decisions in this firm - **2.** [verfügen]: **über etw (frei) bestimmen können** to be able to do what one likes with sthg.

bestimmt ◇ *adj* - **1.** [gewiss] certain; [genau] particular - **2.** [festgelegt] fixed - **3.** GRAMM definite; **der bestimmte Artikel** the definite article - **4.** [entschieden] definite, firm. ◇ *adv* - **1.** [entschieden] firmly, decisively - **2.** [sehr wahrscheinlich] no doubt; [sicher] certainly; **das ist bestimmt kein Problem** I'm sure that won't be a problem; **etw bestimmt wissen** to know sthg for sure ODER certain; **ganz bestimmt** definitely.

Bestimmtheit *die* firmness, decisiveness; **mit Bestimmtheit** [entschlossen] decisively.

Bestimmung *die* - **1.** *(ohne pl)* [von Preis, Frist] fixing - **2.** (*pl* **-en**) [Vorschrift] regulation; **eine gesetzliche Bestimmung** a legal provision - **3.** *(ohne pl)* [Zweck] (intended) purpose; **ein Schiff seiner Bestimmung übergeben** to launch a ship - **4.** (*pl* **-en**) [Ermitteln] determining; [von Pflanze] classification; [von Begriff, Bedeutung] definition - **5.** (*pl* **-en**) GRAMM modifier.

Bestleistung *die* SPORT best performance; **ihre persönliche Bestleistung** her personal best.

Best.Nr. (*abk für* **Bestellnummer**) order no.

bestrafen *vt*: **jn (für etw) bestrafen** to punish sb (for sthg); **jn mit Gefängnis bestrafen** to sentence sb to imprisonment.

Bestrafung (*pl* **-en**) *die* punishment; [gerichtlich] sentence.

bestreiten (*prät* **bestritt**, *perf* **hat bestritten**) *vt* - **1.** [leugnen - Meinung, Aussage] to contest; [- Beschuldigung] to deny; **es lässt sich nicht bestreiten** it is indispensable - **2.** [finanzieren] to pay for - **3.** [gestalten] to carry.

bestürmen *vt* - **1.** MIL to storm - **2.** [bedrängen]: **jn mit Fragen bestürmen** to bombard sb with questions.

bestürzt ◇ *adj*: **über etw** *(A)* **bestürzt sein** to be dismayed about sthg. ◇ *adv* in dismay.

Bestzeit *die* SPORT fastest time.

Besuch (*pl* **-e**) *der* - **1.** [Besuchen] visit; [von Schule, Kirche] attendance; **bei jm zu Besuch sein** to be staying with ODER visiting sb - **2.** *(ohne pl)* [Gast] visitor, guest; [Gäste] visitors *Pl*, guests *Pl*; **wir haben Besuch** we have a visitor/visitors.

besuchen *vt* to visit; [Kirche, Schule, Vorlesung] to attend.

Besucher, in (*mpl* **-**, *fpl* **-nen**) *der, die* visitor.

besucht *adj*: **gut/schlecht besucht** well/poorly attended.

betätigen *vt* [Hebel] to operate; [Bremse] to apply. ◆ **sich betätigen** *ref*: **sich politisch/sportlich betätigen** to engage in politics/sport.

betäuben *vt* - **1.** MED to anaesthetize - **2.** [Trauer, Schmerz] to deaden, to dull.

Bete ◆ **Rote Bete** *die* beetroot.

beteiligen *vt*: **jn an etw** *(D)* **beteiligen** to give sb a share in sthg. ◆ **sich beteiligen** *ref*: **sich an etw** *(D)* **beteiligen** to participate in sthg; [Kosten] to contribute to sthg.

Beteiligung (*pl* **-en**) *die* - **1.** [Mitwirkung]: **Beteiligung (an etw** *(D)***)** participation (in sthg); [an Verbrechen] involvement (in sthg) - **2.** [an Gewinn] share.

beten ◇ *vi* to pray; **um** ODER **für etw beten** to pray for sthg; **für jn beten** to pray for sb. ◇ *vt* to say.

beteuern *vt* to declare.

Beton [be'tɔŋ] (*pl* **-s**) *der* concrete.

betonen *vt* - **1.** [aussprechen] to stress - **2.** [he vorheben] to emphasize, to stress.

Betonung (*pl* **-en**) *die* - **1.** [Betonen] stre - **2.** [Hervorhebung] emphasis.

Betracht *(ohne Artikel)* ◆ **in Betracht** *ad* **jn/etw in Betracht ziehen** [erwägen] to co sider sb/sthg; [berücksichtigen] to take sb/st into account; **(nicht) in Betracht kommen** (nc to be worth considering. ◆ **außer B tracht** *adv*: **etw außer Betracht lassen** to di regard sthg.

betrachten *vt* - **1.** [ansehen] to look at; **si** *(D)* **etw (näher) betrachten** to have a (close look at sthg - **2.** [beurteilen] to regard - **3.** [übe prüfen] to examine, to consider. ◆ **sich b trachten** *ref* to look at o.s.

Betrachter, in (*mpl* **-**, *fpl* **-nen**) *der, die* o server.

beträchtlich ◇ *adj* considerable. ◇ *a* considerably.

Betrachtung (*pl* **-en**) *die* - **1.** [Betrachten] co templation - **2.** [Überlegung] reflection.

Betrag (*pl* **Beträge**) *der* amount *(of money*

betragen (*präs* **beträgt**, *prät* **betrug**, *perf* **h betragen**) *vt* [Preis, Rechnung] to amount OD come to; **die Entfernung von A zu B beträgt Kilometer** A is 10 kilometres away from ◆ **sich betragen** *ref*: **sich gut/schlecht b tragen** to behave well/badly.

betreffen (*präs* **betrifft**, *prät* **betraf**, *perf* **h betroffen**) *vt* [angehen] to concern; [Auswirku gen haben auf] to affect; **was mich/diese Ang legenheit betrifft** as far as I am/this matter concerned.

Betreffende (*pl* **-n**) *der, die* person co cerned.

betreiben (*prät* **betrieb**, *perf* **hat betriebe** *vt* - **1.** [vorantreiben] to pursue - **2.** [führen - G werbe] to carry on; [- Laden] to run - **3.** [antr ben]: **mit etw betrieben werden** to be driv by sthg; **diese Anlage wird mit Solarenerg betrieben** this system is solar-powered.

betreten[1] ◇ *adj* embarrassed. ◇ *a* sheepishly.

betreten[2] (*präs* **betritt**, *prät* **betrat**, *perf* **h betreten**) *vt* to enter; [Rasen] to walk on; [Bü ne] to walk onto.

betreuen *vt* to look after, to take care [Sportler] to coach.

Betreuer, in (*mpl* **-**, *fpl* **-nen**) *der, die* [v Kindern] child-minder; [von Sportlern] coac [von Touristen] guide; [von Alten] care worker

Betreuung *die* care; [von Sportler] coaching

Betrieb (*pl* **-e**) *der* - **1.** [Unternehmen] co pany, firm; [Produktionsstätte] plant; **heute er nicht im Betrieb** he is not at work tod - **2.** [Tätigkeit] operation - **3.** [Treiben, Verke **es ist** ODER **herrscht viel Betrieb** it is very bus

◆ **in Betrieb** *adv* in operation; **etw in Betrieb setzen** [Maschine] to start (up) sthg; [Fabrik] to commission sthg. ◆ **außer Betrieb** *adv* out of order; **etw außer Betrieb setzen** [Maschine] to stop sthg, to shut down sthg; [Fabrik] to decommission sthg.

betriebsam *adj* busy.

Betriebs|rat *der* - **1.** [Gremium] works council - **2.** [Mensch] works council member.

Betriebs|system *das* EDV operating system.

Betriebs|wirtschaft *die* business administration.

betrinken (*prät* **betrank**, *perf* **hat betrunken**) ◆ **sich betrinken** *ref* to get drunk.

betroffen ◇ *pp* ▷ **betreffen**. ◇ *adj* - **1.** [bestürzt] shaken, upset; [Schweigen] stunned - **2.** [nicht verschont]: **von etw betroffen sein** to be affected by sthg. ◇ *adv*: **jn betroffen ansehen** to look at sb in consternation.

betrübt *adj* [Gesicht] sad; [Stimmung] gloomy; **über etw** *(A)* **betrübt sein** to be sad about sthg.

Betrug *der* fraud; **das ist ja Betrug!** that is daylight robbery!

betrügen (*prät* **betrog**, *perf* **hat betrogen**) ◇ *vt* to cheat; [Ehepartner] to cheat on; **jn um etw betrügen** to cheat sb out of sthg. ◇ *vi* to cheat.

Betrüger (*pl* -) *der* conman, con artist.

Betrügerei (*pl* **-en**) *die* swindling.

Betrügerin (*pl* **-nen**) *die* con artist.

betrunken ◇ *pp* ▷ **betrinken**. ◇ *adj* drunk.

Bett (*pl* **-en**) *das* - **1.** [gen] bed; **ins** ODER **zu Bett gehen** to go to bed; **das Bett machen** to make the bed - **2.** [Federbett] duvet, quilt.

Bett|decke *die* [aus Wolle] blanket; [gesteppt] quilt, duvet.

betteln *vi* to beg; **um etw betteln** to beg for sthg.

betten *vt*: **jn auf etw** *(A)* **betten** to lay sb (down) on sthg.

Bettler, in (*mpl* -, *fpl* **-nen**) *der, die* beggar.

Betttuch (*pl* **-tücher**) *das* sheet.

Bett|wäsche *die* bed linen.

Bett|zeug *das (ohne pl)* bedding, bedclothes *Pl*.

beugen *vt* - **1.** [Körper, Finger, Gesetz] to bend - **2.** [Substantiv, Adjectiv] to inflect; [Verb] to conjugate. ◆ **sich beugen** *ref* - **1.** [sich lehnen] to lean - **2.** [sich unterwerfen]: **sich einer Sache** *(D)* **beugen** to submit ODER bow to sthg.

Beule (*pl* **-n**) *die* [am Kopf] lump; [am Auto] dent.

beunruhigen [bə'ʊnruːɪgn̩] *vt* to worry; **über etw** *(A)* **beunruhigt sein** to be worried about sthg.

beurlauben [bə'luːɐ̯laubn̩] *vt* [suspendieren] to suspend.

beurteilen [bə'luːɐ̯tailn̩] *vt* to judge; [Größe, Qualität] to assess; **jn falsch beurteilen** to misjudge sb.

Beurteilung [bə'luːɐ̯tailʊŋ] (*pl* **-en**) *die* judgement; [von Größe, Qualität] assessment.

Beute *die* - **1.** [von Einbrecher] loot - **2.** [von Raubtier] prey.

Beutel (*pl* -) *der* [Sack] bag.

bevölkern *vt* - **1.** [bewohnen] to inhabit - **2.** [füllen] to fill.

Bevölkerung (*pl* **-en**) *die* population.

bevollmächtigen *vt* to authorize.

bevor *konj* before.

bevor|stehen *vi (unreg)* to be imminent.

bevorzugen *vt* - **1.** [vorziehen] to prefer - **2.** [protegieren] to give preferential treatment to.

bewachen *vt* to guard.

Bewacher, in (*mpl* -, *fpl* **-nen**) *der, die* guard.

bewaffnen *vt* to arm. ◆ **sich bewaffnen** *ref* to arm o.s.

Bewaffnung (*pl* **-en**) *die* - **1.** [Ausrüstung] armament, arming - **2.** [Waffen] arms *Pl*.

bewahren *vt* - **1.** [Person]: **jn vor etw** *(D)* **bewahren** to protect sb from sthg - **2.** [Nerven, Ruhe] to keep.

bewähren ◆ **sich bewähren** *ref* to prove one's/its worth.

bewahrheiten ◆ **sich bewahrheiten** *ref* to prove (to be) true.

Bewährung *die* - **1.** [Profilierung] test, trial - **2.** RECHT probation; **auf** ODER **mit Bewährung** on probation.

bewaldet *adj* wooded.

bewältigen *vt* [Arbeit, Problem] to cope with; [js Tod, die Vergangenheit] to come to terms with; [Papierberge] to get through.

bewässern *vt* to irrigate.

bewegen[1] (*prät* **bewegte**, *perf* **hat bewegt**) *vt (reg)* - **1.** [gen] to move - **2.** [beschäftigen] to concern, to preoccupy. ◆ **sich bewegen** *ref* - **1.** [körperlich] to move; [im Freien] to take ODER get some exercise - **2.** [sich verhalten] to act.

bewegen[2] (*prät* **bewog**, *perf* **hat bewogen**) *vt (unreg) geh*: **jn zu etw bewegen** [veranlassen] to induce sb to do sthg; [überreden] to prevail upon sb to do sthg.

beweglich *adj* agile; [Hebel] movable.

bewegt *adj* - **1.** [unruhig - Leben] eventful; [- See, Meer] choppy - **2.** [Stimme, Worte] emotional.

Bewegung (*pl* **-en**) *die* - **1.** [körperlich, politisch] movement; **etw in Bewegung setzen** to set sthg in motion; **sich in Bewegung setzen** *fam* [Person] to get moving; [Zug] to start to move - **2.** [körperlich] exercise.

Bewegungsfreiheit *die* freedom of movement; [Handlungsspielraum] room for manoeuvre.

bewegungslos ◇ *adj* motionless. ◇ *adv*: **bewegungslos dastehen** to stand there motionless.

Beweis (*pl* **-e**) *der*: **ein Beweis** a piece of evidence; **Beweise** evidence, proof.

beweisen (*prät* **bewies**, *perf* **hat bewiesen**) *vt* - **1.** [gen] to prove; [Unschuld] to establish - **2.** [Mut] to show.

bewẹrben (*präs* **bewịrbt**, *prät* **bewạrb**, *perf* **hat bewọrben**) ◆ **sich bewerben** *ref* to apply; **sich bei einer Firma bewerben** to apply for a job with a firm; **sich um etw bewerben** to apply for sthg.

Bewẹrber, in (*mpl* **-**, *fpl* **-nen**) *der, die* applicant.

Bewẹrbung (*pl* **-en**) *die* application.

bewẹrfen (*präs* **bewịrft**, *prät* **bewạrf**, *perf* **hat bewọrfen**) *vt*: **jn/etw mit etw bewerfen** to pelt sb/sthg with sthg.

bewerten *vt* to assess, to evaluate; [Klassenarbeit] to mark; **etw zu hoch/niedrig bewerten** to overrate/underrate sthg.

bewịlligen *vt* [Antrag] to approve; [Hilfe, Kredit] to grant.

bewịrken *vt* to cause; **es bewirkte das Gegenteil** it had the opposite effect; **wir haben bewirkt, dass jetzt Nachtbusse eingesetzt werden** we have managed to get them to lay on a night bus service.

bewohnen *vt* to inhabit.

Bewohner, in (*mpl* **-**, *fpl* **-nen**) *der, die* inhabitant.

bewọ̈lkt *adj* cloudy, overcast.

Bewọ̈lkung *die (ohne pl)* - **1.** clouding over - **2.** [Wolken] clouds *Pl*.

bewụndern *vt* to admire.

Bewụnderung *die* admiration.

bewụsst ◇ *adj* - **1.** [absichtlich] deliberate - **2.** [bedacht] conscious; **ihre Absichten sind mir bewusst** I am aware of her motives; **ihre Absichten wurden mir bewusst** I realized what her motives were; **sich** *(D)* **einer Sache** *(G)* **bewusst sein** to be aware of sthg. ◇ *adv* - **1.** [absichtlich] deliberately - **2.** [bedacht] consciously.

bewụsstlos *adj* unconscious.

Bewụsstlosigkeit *die* (state of) unconsciousness.

Bewụsstsein *das* - **1.** [Wissen] awareness - **2.** [geistige Klarheit] consciousness; **bei Bewusstsein sein** to be conscious; **das Bewusstsein verlieren** to lose consciousness.

bezahlen ◇ *vt* [Ware, Leistung] to pay for [Person, Miete, Rechnung] to pay. ◇ *vi* to pay **wir möchten bitte bezahlen!** may we have the bill please?

bezahlt *adj* paid.

Bezahlung *die* - **1.** [von Ware, Rechnung] payment - **2.** [Entgelt] pay.

bezeichnen *vt* - **1.** [nennen] to call; **jn/etw al etw bezeichnen** to describe sb/sthg as sthg - **2.** [markieren] to mark, to indicate.

bezeichnend *adj* characteristic; **bezeichnend für etw sein** to be characteristic of sthg

Bezeichnung *die* - **1.** (*pl* **-en**) [Benennung name; [Beschreibung] description - **2.** *(ohne Pl* [Markierung] marking.

beziehen (*prät* **bezog**, *perf* **hat bezogen**) *v* - **1.** [Kissen, Sofa] to cover; **das Bett frisch beziehen** to change the bedclothes - **2.** [Haus, Wohnung] to move into - **3.** [Ware, Zeitung, Einkünfte] to get; [Arbeitslosenhilfe] to receive - **4.** [anwenden]: **etw auf sich** *(A)***/jn beziehen** to understand sthg to refer to o.s./to sb; **eine Aussage auf sich** *(A)* **beziehen** to take a remark personally. ◆ **sich beziehen** *re* - **1.** [angewendet werden]: **sich auf jn/etw beziehen** to refer to sb/sthg; **meine Kritik bezog sich nicht auf Sie** my criticism wasn't aimed a you - **2.** [sich berufen]: **sich auf etw** *(A)* **beziehen** to refer to sthg - **3.** [sich bewölken]: **der Himmel bezieht sich** the sky is clouding over.

Beziehung (*pl* **-en**) *die* - **1.** [Kontakt - zu Person relationship; **Beziehungen** [politisch] relations; **gute/schlechte Beziehungen zu jn haben** to be on good/bad terms with sb; **er verfügt über gute Beziehungen** he has lots c contacts - **2.** [Verhältnis] connection - **3.** [Hinsicht] respect.

beziehungsweise *konj* - **1.** [genauer gesag or rather, that is - **2.** [oder] or; **die Kinder sind ins Kino beziehungsweise ins Schwimmbad gegangen** the children have either gone to the cinema or gone swimming - **3.** [jeweils and respectively; **die Uhren kosten 300 beziehungsweise 400 Euro** the watches cost 300 and 400 euros respectively.

Bezirk (*pl* **-e**) *der* district; [von Kirche] diocese

Bezug (*pl* **Bezüge**) *der* - **1.** [Überzug] cove - **2.** [Beziehung]: **auf etw** *(A)* **Bezug nehmen** *am* to refer to sthg; **in Bezug auf etw** *(A)* with regard to sthg. ◆ **Bezüge** *Pl* income *(U)*.

Bezugs|person *die person to whom on looks for guidance, support etc.*

bezwẹcken *vt*: **etw mit etw bezwecken** t aim to achieve sthg by sthg.

bezweifeln *vt* to doubt.

BGB [beːgeːˈbeː] (*abk für* **Bürgerliches Gesetzbuch**) *das German civil code.*

BH [beːˈhaː] (*pl* **-s**) (*abk für* **Büstenhalter**) *de* bra.

Bhf. *abk für* **Bahnhof**.

Bibel (*pl* **-n**) *die* bible.

Biber (*pl* -) *der* [Tier] beaver.

Bibliothek (*pl* **-en**) *die* library.

biegen (*prät* **bog**, *perf* **hat/ist gebogen**) <> *vt (hat)* to bend. <> *vi (ist)* [Auto, Fahrer]: **um die Ecke biegen** to go round the corner. ◆ **sich biegen** *ref* to bend.

Biegung (*pl* **-en**) *die* bend.

Biene (*pl* **-n**) *die* bee.

Bier (*pl* **-e**) *das* beer; **ein großes/kleines Bier** a half-litre/30 cl glass of beer.

Bier|dose *die* beer can.

Bier|garten *der* beer garden.

Bier|glas *das* beer glass.

bieten (*prät* **bot**, *perf* **hat geboten**) *vt* - **1.** [anbieten] to offer; [Schutz, Chance] to provide; **jm etw bieten** to offer sb sthg; [Gelegenheit, Schutz] to provide sb with sthg - **2.** [zeigen] to present; **einen schrecklichen Anblick bieten** to look terrible - **3.** [gefallen]: **sich** *(D)* **etw nicht bieten lassen** not to stand for sthg. ◆ **sich bieten** *ref*: **es bot sich eine Gelegenheit** an opportunity came up.

Bikini (*pl* **-s**) *der* bikini.

Bilanz (*pl* **-en**) *die* - **1.** WIRTSCH balance; [schriftlich] balance sheet - **2.** [Ergebnis] outcome.

Bild (*pl* **-er**) *das* - **1.** [gen & TV] picture; [Gemälde] painting; [Zeichnung] drawing; [Foto] photograph - **2.** [Anblick] sight - **3.** [Vorstellung] idea, impression; **sich** *(D)* **ein Bild von jm/etw machen** to get an idea of sb/sthg - **4.** [Metapher] image; **(über etw** *(A)***) im Bilde sein** to be in the picture (about sthg).

bilden <> *vt* [gen] to form. <> *vi*: **Lesen bildet** reading improves your mind. ◆ **sich bilden** *ref* - **1.** [sich formen] to form - **2.** [sich informieren] to educate o.s.

Bilder|buch *das* picture book.

Bild|hauer, in (*mpl* -, *fpl* **-nen**) *der, die* sculptor (sculptress *die*).

bildlich <> *adj* - **1.** [Darstellung] pictorial - **2.** [Wendung, Ausdruck] figurative. <> *adv* - **1.** [darstellen] pictorially - **2.** [gesprochen] figuratively.

Bild|schirm *der* screen.

Bildschirmschoner (*pl* -) *der* EDV screen saver.

Bildung (*pl* **-en**) *die* - **1.** [Ausbildung] education; **eine umfassende Bildung besitzen** to be well-educated *ODER* cultured - **2.** [Formung] formation.

Bildungs|politik *die* education policy.

Bildungs|weg *der*: **der zweite Bildungsweg** *second chance for people outside the education system to obtain educational qualifications.*

Billard ['bɪljart] *das* billiards *(U)*.

billig <> *adj* - **1.** [preiswert] cheap - **2.** *abw* [schlecht - Anzug, Papier, Scherz, Trick] cheap; [- Ausrede] feeble. <> *adv* cheaply; **die Vase habe ich billig gekauft** I got the vase cheap.

Billig|angebot *das* special offer.

Billiglohn|land *das*: **Arbeiter aus Billiglohnländer wie Indonesien** cheap labour from countries like Indonesia.

bimmeln *vi* to ring.

bin *präs* ▷ **sein**.

Binde (*pl* **-n**) *die* - **1.** [Verband] bandage - **2.** [über den Augen] blindfold; [um den Arm] armband - **3.** [Damenbinde] sanitary towel.

Binde|mittel *das* binding agent.

binden (*prät* **band**, *perf* **hat gebunden**) <> *vt* - **1.** [zusammenbinden] to tie together - **2.** [festbinden]: **etw an etw** *(A)* **binden** to tie sthg to sthg - **3.** [Krawatte] to knot; [Schleife, Knoten] to tie - **4.** [Soße, Buch, durch Vertrag] to bind. <> *vi* to bind. ◆ **sich binden** *ref* [heiraten] to get married.

Binde|strich *der* hyphen.

Bind|faden *der* string.

Bindung (*pl* **-en**) *die* - **1.** [Verbundenheit] bond; [Verpflichtung] commitment - **2.** [Skibindung] binding.

Binnen|markt *der* internal market; [von EU] single market; **der europäische Binnenmarkt** the European single market.

Biochemie *die* biochemistry.

Biokost *die* health food.

Biologe (*pl* **-n**) *der* biologist.

Biologie *die* biology.

Biologin (*pl* **-nen**) *die* biologist.

biologisch *adj* - **1.** [der Biologie] biological - **2.** [natürlich - Farben] natural; [- Brot] organic.

Bio|müll *der* organic waste.

birgt *präs* ▷ **bergen**.

Birke (*pl* **-n**) *die* birch.

Birn|baum *der* pear tree.

Birne (*pl* **-n**) *die* - **1.** [Frucht] pear - **2.** [Glühbirne] light bulb - **3.** *fam* [Kopf] nut.

birst *präs* ▷ **bersten**.

bis <> *präp (+ A)* - **1.** [zeitlich] until; **wir bleiben bis morgen** we're staying until tomorrow; **von Montag bis Freitag** from Monday to Friday, Monday through Friday *US*; **bis auf Weiteres** until further notice; **bis bald!** see you soon!; **bis dann!** see you then!; **bis morgen!/später!** see you tomorrow/later! - **2.** [spätestens] by; **das muss bis Mittwoch fertig sein** it must be ready by Wednesday - **3.** [räumlich] to; **es sind noch 200 km bis Berlin** there are still 200 km to go to Berlin; **bis auf die Haut durchnässt** soaked to the skin. <> *konj* until; **warte, bis ich komme** wait until I'm there. ◆ **bis auf** *präp (+ A)* except for, apart from. ◆ **bis zu** *präp* up to; **bis zu 20 Personen** up to 20 people.

Bischof (*pl* **Bischöfe**) *der* bishop.

bischöflich *adj* episcopal.

bisher *adv*: **bisher hat sie nicht angerufen** she hasn't called so far; **wir haben das bisher immer so gemacht** until now we've always done it this way.

bisherig *adj* [ehemalig] former; **sein bisheriges Verhalten** his behaviour up to now.

bislang *adv*: **bislang hat sie nicht angerufen** she hasn't called so far; **wir haben das bislang immer so gemacht** until now we've always done it this way.

Bison (*pl* **-s**) *der* bison.

biss *prät* ⊳ **beißen**.

Biss (*pl* **-e**) *der eigtl* & *fig* bite.

bisschen *adj* [wenig]: **das bisschen Regen macht doch nichts** that little bit of rain won't do any harm. ◆ **das bisschen** *pron*: **das bisschen kannst du jetzt auch noch essen** you can eat that little bit up. ◆ **ein bisschen** ◇ *adj* [etwas] a bit of, a little; **ein bisschen Kaffee** a drop of coffee. ◇ *adv* [ein wenig] a bit; **ein bisschen bleiben** to stay a while. ◆ **kein bisschen** ◇ *adj*: **wir haben kein bisschen Brot** we have no bread at all. ◇ *adv* [nicht] not at all. ◆ **ach du liebes bisschen** *interj* oh, dear!

Bissen (*pl* -) *der* [Stück] bite.

bissig *adj eigtl* & *fig* vicious; **'Vorsicht, bissiger Hund'** 'beware of the dog'.

bist *präs* ⊳ **sein**.

Bistum (*pl* **-tümer**) *das* diocese.

bitte ◇ *adv* please. ◇ *interj* - **1.** [als Bitte, Aufforderung] please; **bedient euch, bitte!** please help yourselves!; **bitte! hier ist Ihr Kaffee!** here's your coffee for you; **bitte sehr! kommen Sie herein!** (do) come in!; **bitte schön! was möchten Sie kaufen?** yes Sir/ Madam, how can I help you? - **2.** [als Antwort]: **danke! - bitte!** thanks! - don't mention it!; **Entschuldigung! - bitte!** sorry! - that's all right!; **kann ich nur einen Apfel nehmen? - bitte!** may I have an apple? - of course!; **bitte sehr** ODER **schön!** [Antwort auf einen Dank] don't mention it!, you're welcome! - **3.** [als Nachfrage] pardon?, sorry?; **wie bitte?** pardon?, sorry? - **4.** [am Telefon]: **ja bitte?** hello? - **5.** [zur Selbstbestätigung]: **na bitte!** there you are, you see!

Bitte (*pl* **-n**) *die* [Anliegen] request; **eine Bitte um etw** a request for sthg.

bitten (*prät* **bat**, *perf* **hat gebeten**) ◇ *vt* - **1.** [höflich auffordern]: **jn bitten, etw zu tun** to ask sb to do sthg; **ich bitte Sie, etwas leiser zu sein!** please be a little quieter!; **jn um etw bitten** to ask sb for sthg; **ich bitte Sie um Aufmerksamkeit!** may I have your attention, please! - **2.** [einladen]: **jn zu sich bitten** to ask sb to come round to one's house. ◇ *vi* [Bitte aussprechen]: **um etw bitten** to ask for sthg; **ich bitte um Ruhe!** silence, please!

bitter ◇ *adj* - **1.** [gen] bitter - **2.** [Ironie] biting - **3.** [Not] desperate; [Armut] abject ◇ *adv* - **1.** [gen] bitterly; **bitter schmecken** to taste bitter - **2.** [benötigen] desperately.

Bitterkeit *die eigtl* & *fig* bitterness.

Bizeps (*pl* **-e**) *der* biceps *(sg)*.

BKA [beːkaːˈaː] (*abk für* **Bundeskriminalamt**) *das Federal Office for criminal investigation*.

Blähungen *Pl* wind *(U)*.

Blamage [blaˈmaːʒə] (*pl* **-n**) *die* disgrace.

blamieren *vt* [kompromittieren] to disgrace ◆ **sich blamieren** *ref* [sich bloßstellen] to disgrace o.s.

blank *adj* - **1.** [glänzend] shiny - **2.** [pur] sheer pure - **3.** [unbedeckt] bare; **blank sein** *fam* to be broke.

Blase (*pl* **-n**) *die* - **1.** [auf der Haut] blister - **2.** [Luftblase] bubble - **3.** [Harnblase] bladder.

Blasebalg (*pl* **-bälge**) *der* bellows *Pl*.

blasen (*präs* **bläst**, *prät* **blies**, *perf* **hat geblasen**) ◇ *vt* - **1.** [gen] to blow - **2.** [Trompete, Horn] to play - **3.** *vulg*: **jm einen blasen** to give sb a blow job. ◇ *vi* - **1.** [gen] to blow - **2.** [auf Trompete, Horn] to play.

Blas|instrument *das* wind instrument.

Blas|kapelle *die* brass band.

blass (*kompar* **blasser** ODER **blässer**, *superl* **blasseste** ODER **blässeste**) *adj* - **1.** [Haut] pale - **2.** [Erinnerung, Ahnung] vague; [Hoffnung] faint.

Blässe *die* paleness.

bläst *präs* ⊳ **blasen**.

Blatt (*pl* **Blätter**) *das* - **1.** [von Pflanzen] leaf - **2.** [Papier] sheet - **3.** [Seite] page - **4.** [Zeitung] paper; **ein unbeschriebenes Blatt sein** [unbekannt] to be an unknown quantity; [unerfahren] to be inexperienced; **kein Blatt vor den Mund nehmen** not to mince one's words; **das Blatt hat sich gewendet** the tide has turned.

blättern (*perf* **hat/ist geblättert**) ◇ *vi* - **1.** *(hat)* [umschlagen]: **in etw** *(D)* **blättern** to leaf through sthg - **2.** *(ist)* [abblättern] to flake (off). ◇ *vt (hat)* [Geldscheine] to count out.

Blätter|teig *der* puff pastry.

blau (*kompar* **blauer**, *superl* **blau(e)ste**) *adj* - **1.** [Farbe] blue - **2.** [geprellt]: **ein blaues Auge** a black eye; **ein blauer Fleck** a bruise - **3.** [betrunken]: **blau sein** *fam* to be sloshed - **4.** *fam* [geschwänzt]: **einen blauen Montag machen** to skip ODER skive off *UK* work on Monday.

Blau *das* [Farbe] blue.

blauäugig *adj* - **1.** [Augen] blue-eyed - **2.** [naiv] naïve.

Blau|beere *die* bilberry, blueberry.

Blaue (*pl* **-n**) *das* - **1.** [Farbe] blue - **2.** [Unbekannte]: **ins Blaue** [fahren] with no particular place to go; [reden] aimlessly.

Blau|helm *der* blue beret.

bläulich *adj* bluish.

Blau|licht *das* [Signal] flashing blue light *(on ambulance etc.)*

blau|machen *vi fam* [schwänzen] to skip ODER skive off *UK* school/work.

Blazer ['ble:zɐ] (*pl* -) *der* blazer.

Blech (*pl* **-e**) *das* - **1.** [Metall] sheet metal - **2.** [Backblech] baking sheet *UK*, cookie sheet *US* - **3.** *fam* [Unsinn] rubbish.

blechen *fam vt* & *vi* to fork out.

Blech|instrument *das* brass instrument.

Blech|schaden *der* bodywork damage *(U)*.

Blei *das* [Metall] lead.

Bleibe (*pl* **-n**) *die* place to stay.

bleiben (*prät* **blieb**, *perf* **ist geblieben**) *vi* - **1.** [an einem Ort] to stay; **wo bleibst du denn so lange?** [bei Eintreffen] what kept you? - **2.** [in einem Zustand] to remain; **sie ist ganz die Alte geblieben** she hasn't changed a bit; **wir bleiben in Kontakt** we keep in touch; **bei etw bleiben** to stick to sthg; **es bleibt also dabei, morgen um zehn Uhr** ten o'clock tomorrow morning, like we said, then?; **das bleibt unter uns** it's strictly between ourselves - **3.** [als Übriges] to be left; **uns bleiben nur noch wenige Tage** we only have a few days left.

bleibend *adj* lasting.

bleiben lassen *vt (unreg)* - **1.** [unterlassen] to leave be - **2.** [aufgeben] to give up.

bleich *adj* pale.

bleifrei *adj* unleaded.

Blei|stift *der* pencil.

Bleistiftspitzer (*pl* -) *der* pencil sharpener.

Blende (*pl* **-n**) *die* - **1.** [vor Fenster] blind, screen; AUTO visor - **2.** [FOTO - Objektivöffnung] diaphragm; [- Blendenzahl] aperture.

blenden <> *vt eigtl* & *fig* to dazzle. <> *vi* [Licht] to be dazzling.

blendend <> *adj* dazzling. <> *adv* marvellously; **du siehst blendend aus!** you look dazzling!

Blick (*pl* **-e**) *der* - **1.** [der Augen] look; [kurz] glance; **den Blick heben/senken** to raise/lower one's eyes; **einen Blick auf etw** *(A)* **werfen** to glance at sthg; **sie würdigte mich/es keines Blickes** she did not deign to look at me/it - **2.** [Ausblick] view - **3.** [Urteil] eye; **keinen Blick für etw haben** not to appreciate sthg.

blicken *vi* to look; **sich (nicht) blicken lassen** (not) to show one's face; **das lässt tief blicken** that explains a lot.

Blick|punkt *der*: **im Blickpunkt der Öffentlichkeit** in the public eye.

blieb *prät* ▷ **bleiben**.

blies *prät* ▷ **blasen**.

blind <> *adj* - **1.** [gen] blind; **blind für etw sein** to be blind to sthg - **2.** [versteckt] ▷ **Passagier** - **3.** [falsch] ▷ **Alarm**. <> *adv* blindly.

Blinddarm|entzündung *die* appendicitis *(U)*.

Blinde (*pl* **-n**) *der, die* blind man (blind woman *die*).

Blinden|schrift *die* braille.

Blindheit *die eigtl* & *fig* blindness.

blinken *vi* - **1.** [funkeln - Metall] to gleam; [- Sterne] to twinkle; [- Wasser, Edelstein] to sparkle - **2.** [signalisieren - Verkehr] to indicate; [Signal geben] to signal.

Blinker (*pl* -) *der* indicator *UK*, turn signal *US*.

Blink|licht *das* flashing light.

blinzeln *vi* [mit einem Auge, als Zeichen] to wink; [mit beiden Augen] to blink.

Blitz (*pl* **-e**) *der* - **1.** [am Himmel] lightning *(U)*; **ein Blitz** a flash of lightning; **wie der Blitz** like lightning - **2.** [Blitzlicht] flash.

Blitzableiter (*pl* -) *der* lightning conductor.

blitzblank *adj* [Geschirr] sparkling clean; [Wohnung] spotless.

blitzen <> *vi* - **1.** [am Himmel]: **es blitzt** there is lightning - **2.** [funkeln - Schmuck, Wohnung] to sparkle; [- Metall] to gleam. <> *vt fam* [fotografieren] to take a flash photo of; **geblitzt werden** to be caught by a speed camera.

Blitz|licht *das* flash.

Blitz|schlag *der* flash of lightning; **vom Blitzschlag getroffen werden** to be struck by lightning.

blitzschnell <> *adj* lightning. <> *adv* like lightning.

Block (*pl* **Blöcke** ODER **-s**) *der* - **1.** *(pl Blöcke)* [Stück] block - **2.** *(pl Blöcke)* [aus Papier] pad - **3.** *(pl Blöcke, Blocks)* [Häuserblock] block - **4.** *(pl Blocks)* [Gruppe - von Staaten] bloc; [Fraktion] faction.

Blockade (*pl* **-n**) *die* blockade.

Block|flöte *die* recorder.

Block|haus *das* log cabin.

blockieren <> *vt* - **1.** EDV [versperren] to block - **2.** [zum Stillstand bringen] to obstruct. <> *vi* [Motor] to jam; [Räder] to lock.

Block|schrift *die* block capitals *Pl*.

blöd, blöde *fam* <> *adj* stupid. <> *adv* stupidly.

Blödsinn *der fam* rubbish.

blond *adj* blond (blonde *die*).

Blondine (*pl* **-n**) *die* blonde.

bloß <> *adv* - **1.** *fam* [lediglich] only, just; **jetzt bloß noch etwas drehen** now just turn it some more - **2.** [zum Ausdruck von Ratlosigkeit]: **was sollen wir bloß machen?** what on earth shall we do? - **3.** [zum Ausdruck von Ärger]: **warum musstest du bloß den Schlüssel stecken lassen?** why did you have to go and leave the key in the lock? - **4.** [zum Ausdruck einer Drohung]: **hau bloß ab!** just push off, all right?; **unterschreib das bloß nicht!** don't you dare sign that! - **5.** [zum Ausdruck einer Aufforderung]: **bloß keine Panik!** just don't panic! - **6.** [zum Ausdruck eines Wunsches]: **hätte ich bloß nichts gesagt!** if only I hadn't said anything! ◇ *adj* - **1.** [nackt] bare; **mit bloßen Füßen** barefoot; **mit bloßem Auge** with the naked eye - **2.** [rein] sheer.

bloß|stellen *vt* to show up; [Betrüger] to unmask.

bluffen [blœfn̩] *abw vt* & *vi* to bluff.

blühen *vi* - **1.** [Pflanze] to bloom, to flower; [Baum] to blossom - **2.** [florieren] to flourish - **3.** *fam* [drohen]: **das kann dir auch noch blühen!** you're not out of the woods yet!

blühend *adj* - **1.** [Pflanze] blooming, flowering; [tree] blossoming - **2.** [frisch] radiant - **3.** [ausufernd]: **eine blühende Fantasie** a vivid imagination.

Blume (*pl* **-n**) *die* [Pflanze] flower.

Blumen|kohl *der* cauliflower.

Blumen|strauß *der* bunch of flowers.

Blumen|topf *der* flowerpot.

Bluse (*pl* **-n**) *die* blouse.

Blut *das* blood; **Blut spenden** to give blood; **Blut stillend** styptic.

Blut|abnahme *die* blood test.

Blut|bad *das* bloodbath.

Blut|druck *der* blood pressure.

Blüte (*pl* **-n**) *die* - **1.** [Pflanzenteil] flower, bloom; [von Baum] blossom - **2.** [das Blühen] flowering, blooming; [von Baum] blossoming; **in voller Blüte** in full flower; [Baum] in full blossom - **3.** [Aufschwung] flowering.

Blutegel (*pl* **-**) *der* leech.

bluten *vi* to bleed; **aus der Nase bluten** to have a nosebleed.

Bluter, in (*mpl* **-**, *fpl* **-nen**) *der, die* haemophiliac.

Blut|erguss *der* MED haematoma; [blauer Fleck] bruise.

Blüte|zeit *die* - **1.** [von Pflanze] flowering period - **2.** [von Kultur, Reich] heyday.

Blut|gefäß *das* blood vessel.

Blut|gruppe *die* blood group.

blutig ◇ *adj* bloody. ◇ *adv* - **1.** [befleckt]: **jn blutig schlagen** to beat sb to a pulp - **2.** [niederschlagen] bloodily.

Blut|konserve *die* unit of stored blood *(for transfusions etc.)*

Blut|körperchen (*pl* **Blutkörperchen**) *das* corpuscle; **weiße/rote Blutkörperchen** white/red blood cells.

Blut|kreislauf *der* blood circulation.

Blut|probe *die* - **1.** [Untersuchung] blood test - **2.** [entnommenes Blut] blood sample.

Blut|spender, in *der, die* blood donor.

Blut|übertragung *die* blood transfusion.

Blutung (*pl* **-en**) *die* bleeding; MED haemorrhage; [Monatsblutung] period.

blutunterlaufen *adj* bloodshot.

Blut|wurst *die* black pudding *UK*, blood sausage *US*.

BLZ *abk für* **Bankleitzahl**.

Bö = **Böe**.

Bock (*pl* **Böcke**) *der* - **1.** [Kaninchen, Reh] buck; [Ziege] billy-goat; [Schaf] ram; **stur wie ein Bock** as stubborn as a mule; **ein geiler Bock** *salopp* a randy old goat - **2.** SPORT (vaulting) horse - **3.** [Gerüst] trestle; **darauf hab ich keinen Bock** *fam* I can't be fagged.

Bock|bier *das* bock, *strong dark beer*.

bockig *adj* [trotzig] contrary.

Bockspringen *das* - **1.** SPORT vaulting - **2.** [Spiel] leapfrog.

Bock|wurst *die type of pork sausage, usually boiled and eaten in a bread roll with mustard*

Boden (*pl* **Böden**) *der* - **1.** [Grund] ground; [Erdreich] soil; **auf deutschem Boden** on German soil; **er hat den Boden unter den Füßen verloren** [beim Klettern] he lost his footing; [im Leben] his world has fallen apart - **2.** [Fußboden] floor; **zu Boden gehen** [im Boxsport] to go down - **3.** [von Gefäß, Koffer, Meer] bottom - **4.** [Speicher] loft; **am Boden zerstört** absolutely shattered; **an Boden gewinnen/verlieren** to gain/lose ground.

bodenlos *adj* - **1.** [tief] bottomless - **2.** [unglaublich] incredible.

Bodenpersonal *das* ground staff.

Bodenschätze *Pl* mineral resources.

Bodenturnen *das* floor exercises *Pl*.

Böe (*pl* **-n**), **Bö** (*pl* **-en**) *die* gust.

bog *prät* ▷ **biegen**.

Bogen (*pl* - ODER **Bögen**) *der* - **1.** [Biegung] curve; **dort macht die Straße einen Bogen nach links** the road curves to the left there; **einen Bogen um jn/etw machen** to steer clear of sb/sthg; **in hohem Bogen** [Wasser] in a great arc; **in hohem Bogen hinausgeworfen werden** ODER **hinausfliegen** to be thrown out on one's ear - **2.** [Bauwerk] arch - **3.** [Schusswaffe & MUS] bow - **4.** [Blatt] sheet.

Bogenschießen *das* archery.

Bohle (*pl* **-n**) *die* thick plank.

Böhmen *nt* Bohemia.

Böhmerwald *der* Bohemian Forest.

Bohne (*pl* **-n**) *die* bean; **dicke/grüne Bohnen** broad/green beans; **das interessiert mich nicht die Bohne** *fam* I'm not in the slightest bit interested in that.

bohnern *vt* to polish.

bohren ◇ *vt* - **1.** [Loch] to drill; [Brunnen, Schacht] to sink - **2.** [hineinstoßen] to stick, to thrust. ◇ *vi* - **1.** [mit einem Bohrer] to drill; **nach Öl/Wasser bohren** to drill for oil/water in *ODER* an einem Zahn bohren to drill a tooth; **in der Nase bohren** to pick one's nose - 2. *fam* [drängen] to keep on. ◆ **sich bohren** *ref* [eindringen]: **sich in etw (A) bohren** to bore one's way into sthg.

bohrend *adj* [Blick] piercing; [Schmerz] gnawing; [Fragen] probing.

Bohrer (*pl* -) *der* [Gerät] drill.

Bohr|maschine *die* drill.

Bohrung (*pl* **-en**) *die* drilling.

böig *adj* gusty.

Boiler [bɔylɐ] (*pl* -) *der* boiler.

Boje (*pl* **-n**) *die* buoy.

Bolzen (*pl* -) *der* bolt.

bombardieren *vt* to bombard; **jn mit etw bombardieren** *eigtl* & *fig* to bombard sb with sthg.

Bombe (*pl* **-n**) *die* bomb.

Bomben|anschlag *der* bombing, bomb attack.

Bombenerfolg (*pl* **-e**) *der fam* smash hit.

Bomben|stimmung *die fam* wild atmosphere.

Bon [bɔŋ] (*pl* **-s**) *der* - **1.** [Beleg] receipt - **2.** [für Speisen und Getränke] voucher.

Bonbon [bɔŋ'bɔŋ] (*pl* **-s**) *der ODER das* sweet.

Bonn *nt* Bonn.

Bonze (*pl* **-n**) *der abw* bigwig.

Boom [buːm] (*pl* **-s**) *der* boom.

Boot (*pl* **-e**) *das* boat; **mit** *ODER* **in einem Boot fahren** to go by boat; **Boot fahren** to go boating; **wir sitzen alle in einem** *ODER* **im selben Boot** *fig* we are all in the same boat.

Bord (*pl* **-e**) ◇ *das* [Brett] shelf. ◇ *der* SCHIFF & FLUG side; **von Bord gehen** to disembark; **alle Vorsicht über Bord werfen** to throw caution to the winds. ◆ **an Bord** ◇ *adv* on board; **alle Mann an Bord!** all aboard! ◇ *präp (+ G)* on board.

Bordell (*pl* **-e**) *das* brothel.

Bord|karte *die* boarding card.

Bordstein|kante *die* kerb.

borgen *vt* - **1.** [entleihen] to borrow; **etw von** *ODER* **bei jm borgen** to borrow sthg from sb; **sich (D) etw borgen** to borrow sthg - **2.** [verleihen]: **jm etw borgen** to lend sb sthg.

Borke (*pl* **-n**) *die* bark.

Börse (*pl* **-n**) *die* - **1.** [Geldbeutel] purse - **2.** WIRTSCH stock market; [Gebäude] stock exchange; **das Unternehmen geht an die Börse** the company is being floated (on the stock market).

bösartig *adj* - **1.** [Verhalten, Mensch, Bemerkung] malicious; [Hund] vicious - **2.** [Krankheit] malignant.

Böschung (*pl* **-en**) *die* bank.

böse ◇ *adj* - **1.** [schlecht] bad; [verwerflich] wicked, evil - **2.** [wütend]: **(über etw (A)) böse sein/werden** to be/get angry (about sthg); **auf jn böse sein, jm böse sein** to be angry with sb - **3.** *fam* [schlimm] bad; [Entzündung] nasty - **4.** [frech, ungezogen] naughty. ◇ *adv* - **1.** [schlimm] badly; **sich böse erkälten** to catch a nasty cold - **2.** [bösartig]: **es war nicht böse gemeint** I didn't mean it nastily - **3.** [wütend] angrily.

Böse (*pl* **-n**) ◇ *der, die* villain. ◇ *das*: **nichts Böses tun/vorhaben** not to do/mean any harm; **etw Böses sagen** to say sthg nasty; **nichts Böses ahnen** to be unsuspecting.

Bösewicht (*pl* **-er** *ODER* **-e**) *der* - **1.** [Schuft] villain - **2.** [Schlingel] rascal.

boshaft ◇ *adj* - **1.** [böse] wicked, evil - **2.** [höhnisch] malicious. ◇ *adv* [höhnisch] maliciously.

Bosheit (*pl* **-en**) *die* - **1.** [Gesinnung] malice - **2.** [Handlung] malicious thing.

Bosnien-Herzegowina *nt* Bosnia-Herzegovina.

bosnisch *adj* Bosnian.

Boss (*pl* **-e**) *der* boss; [von Bande] leader.

böswillig ◇ *adj* malicious. ◇ *adv* [handeln] maliciously.

bot *prät* ▷ **bieten**.

Botanik *die* botany.

botanisch *adj* botanical ▷ **Garten**.

Bote (*pl* **-n**) *der* - **1.** [gen] messenger; [von Kurierdienst] courier - **2.** [Vorbote] herald.

Botin (*pl* **-nen**) *die* - **1.** [gen] messenger; [von Kurierdienst] courier - **2.** [Vorbotin] herald.

Botschaft (*pl* **-en**) *die* - **1.** [Mitteilung] message - **2.** [diplomatische Vertretung] embassy.

Botschafter, in (*mpl* -, *fpl* **-nen**) *der, die* ambassador.

Bouillon [bʊl'jɔŋ] (*pl* **-s**) *die* bouillon.

Boulette = **Bulette**.

Boulevard [bul(ə)'vaːɐ̯] (*pl* **-s**) *der* boulevard.

Boulevard|presse *die* tabloid press, sensationalist press.

Boulevard|theater *das* light theatre.

Boutique (*pl* **-n**), **Butike** (*pl* **-n**) [bu'tiːk] *die* boutique.

Bowle ['boːlə] (*pl* **-n**) *die* punch.

Bowling ['boʊːlɪŋ] (*pl* **-s**) *das* bowling.

Box (*pl* **-en**) *die* - **1.** [Lautsprecherbox] speaker - **2.** [Kasten] box - **3.** [an Rennstrecke] pit; [in Pferdestall] box; [in Garage] space.

boxen ◇ *vi* to box. ◇ *vt* - **1.** SPORT to fight - **2.** [schlagen] to punch. ◆ **sich boxen** *ref* [kämpfen] to fight.

Boxer (*pl* -) *der* [Hund & SPORT] boxer.

Box|kampf *der* boxing match.

boykottieren [bɔykɔ'tiːrən] *vt* to boycott.

brach *prät* ▷ **brechen**.

brachte *prät* ▷ **bringen**.

Branche ['brɑ̃:ʃə] (*pl* **-n**) *die* (branch of) industry; [Gewerbe] trade.

Brand (*pl* **Brände**) *der* [großes Feuer] fire, blaze; **etw gerät in Brand** sthg catches fire; **etw in Brand setzen** ODER **stecken** to set fire to sthg, to set sthg on fire; **einen Brand haben** *fam* to be dying of thirst.

Brandenburg *nt* Brandenburg.

Brandenburger Tor *das* Brandenburg Gate.

brandneu *adj* brand-new.

Brand|stifter, in *der, die* arsonist.

Brand|stiftung *die* arson.

Brandung (*pl* **-en**) *die* surf.

Brand|wunde *die* burn.

brannte *prät* ▷ **brennen**.

Brannt|wein *der* spirits *Pl*; **Whisky ist ein Branntwein** whisky is a type of spirit.

Brasilianer, in (*mpl* **-**, *fpl* **-nen**) *der, die* Brazilian.

brasilianisch *adj* Brazilian.

Brasilien *nt* Brazil.

brät *präs* ▷ **braten**.

braten (*präs* **brät**, *prät* **briet**, *perf* **hat gebraten**) *vt* & *vi* [in der Pfanne] to fry; [im Ofen mit Fett] to roast; [im Ofen ohne Fett] to bake.

Braten (*pl* -) *der* roast.

Brat|hähnchen *das* roast chicken.

Bratkartoffeln *Pl* fried potatoes.

Brat|pfanne *die* frying pan.

Bratsche (*pl* **-n**) *die* MUS viola.

Brat|wurst *die* (fried) sausage.

Brauch (*pl* **Bräuche**) *der* custom.

brauchbar ◇ *adj* [Vorschlag] useful; [Material, Kleidung] usable. ◇ *adv* usefully; **brauchbar arbeiten** to do acceptable work.

brauchen ◇ *vt* - **1.** [benötigen] to need; **jn/etw für** ODER **zu etw brauchen** to need sb/sthg for sthg - **2.** [verbrauchen] to use (up) - **3.** [verwenden]: **jn/etw (nicht) brauchen können** (not) to be able to use sb/sthg. ◇ *aux* [müssen] to need; **ihr braucht nicht zu grinsen** there's no need for you to grin.

Braue (*pl* **-n**) *die* brow, eyebrow.

brauen *vt* [Bier, Tee] to brew; [Trank] to make.

Brauerei (*pl* **-en**) *die* brewery.

braun ◇ *adj* - **1.** [Farbe] brown; **braune Butter** *butter melted in frying pan until brown* - **2.** [nationalsozialistisch] Nazi. ◇ *adv* [farbig] brown; [braten] until brown; *siehe auch* **braun gebrannt**.

Braun *das* brown.

Bräune *die* suntan.

bräunen (*perf* **hat/ist gebräunt**) ◇ *vt (hat)* - **1.** [Körper, Gesicht] to tan - **2.** [Zwiebeln] to brown; [Zucker] to caramelize. ◇ *vi* - **1.** *(hat)* [durch Sonne] to tan - **2.** *(ist)* [Braten] to turn brown. ◆ **sich bräunen** *ref* [durch Sonne Person] to get a tan; [- Haut] to go brown; [sonnenbaden] to sunbathe.

braun gebrannt *adj* tanned.

Braunkohle *die* brown coal, lignite.

Brause (*pl* **-n**) *die* - **1.** [Getränk, Pulver] sherbe - **2.** [Dusche] shower.

brausen (*perf* **hat/ist gebraust**) *vi* - **1.** *(hat* [Meer, Wind] to roar; [Beifall] to thunder - **2.** *(ist* [sich fortbewegen] to race.

Braut (*pl* **Bräute**) *die* - **1.** [am Hochzeitstag bride - **2.** [Verlobte] fiancée - **3.** *salopp* [Mädchen] bird *UK*, chick *US*.

Bräutigam (*pl* **-e**) *der* - **1.** [am Hochzeitstag bridegroom - **2.** [Verlobter] fiancé.

Braut|paar *das* bride and groom *Pl*.

brav *adj* - **1.** [artig] good - **2.** [bieder] plain.

bravo ['brɑːvo] *interj* bravo!

BRD [beːɛr'deː] (*abk für* **Bundesrepublik Deutschland**) *die* FRG.

brechen (*präs* **bricht**, *prät* **brach**, *perf* **hat/ist gebrochen**) ◇ *vt* - **1.** *(hat)* [gen] to break; [Ast to break off; [Rose, Blume] to pluck; [Trotz, Hartnäckigkeit] to overcome; [Ehe] to break up; **jm sich den Arm brechen** to break sb's/one's arm - **2.** *(hat)* [erbrechen] to vomit (up). ◇ *v* - **1.** *(ist)* [durchbrechen] to break - **2.** *(hat)* [erbrechen] to vomit, to be sick - **3.** *(hat)* [Kontakt abbrechen]: **mit jm brechen** to break off contact with sb - **4.** *(hat)* [Brauch aufgeben]: **mit einer Tradition brechen** to break with a tradition - **5.** *(ist)* [durchkommen] to burst out ◆ **sich brechen** *ref* [Schall] to echo; [Licht] to be refracted; [Wellen] to break.

brechend *adv*: **brechend voll** full to bursting

Brech|reiz *der* nausea *(U)*.

Brei (*pl* **-e**) *der* purée; [aus Haferflocken porridge; [aus Kartoffeln] mashed potatoes *Pl* [aus Gries] semolina.

breit ◇ *adj* - **1.** [gen] wide; [Schultern, Gesicht Hüften, Aussprache] broad; **ein breites Lachen** a guffaw - **2.** [allgemein] general. ◇ *ad* - **1.** [seitlich ausgedehnt]: **breit gebaut** sturdily built - **2.** [ausgedehnt - darstellen] in great detail [- lächeln] broadly; **breit lachen** to guffaw.

breitbeinig *adv* [dastehen] with one's leg apart; **breitbeinig gehen** to walk with a rolling gait.

Breite (*pl* **-n**) *die* - **1.** [Ausdehnung] width - **2.** [geografische Lage] latitude.

Breiten|grad *der* (degree of) latitude.

breit machen *vt*: **die Beine breit machen** *fam* to spread one's legs. ◆ **sich breit machen** *ref fam* - **1.** [Raum beanspruchen] to take up a lot of room - **2.** [sich einquartieren] to make o.s at home - **3.** [sich verbreiten] to spread.

breit|schlagen *vt (unreg) fam* [überreden] to talk round; **sich zu etw breitschlagen lassen** to let o.s. be talked into sthg.

breitschultrig, breitschulterig *adj* broad-shouldered.

Brems|belag *der* brake lining.

Bremse (*pl* **-n**) *die* - **1.** [Bremsvorrichtung] brake - **2.** [Insekt] horsefly.

bremsen ◇ *vi* [halten] to brake. ◇ *vt* - **1.** [Fahrzeug] to brake - **2.** [Entwicklung, Person] to slow down.

Brems|licht *das* brake light.

Brems|pedal *das* brake pedal.

Brems|weg *der* braking distance.

brennbar *adj* flammable.

brennen (*prät* **brannte**, *perf* **hat gebrannt**) ◇ *vi* - **1.** [gen] to burn; [Haus, Wald, Gardine] to be on fire, to burn; **es brennt!** fire! - **2.** [Lampe, Birne] to be on - **3.** [Wunde, Augen] to smart; [Füße] to be sore - **4.** [erregt sein]: **auf etw** *(A)* **brennen** to be dying for sthg. ◇ *vt* - **1.** [Loch] to burn - **2.** [Ziegel, Ton] to fire; [Schnaps] to distil; [Mandeln] to roast - **3.** *fam* [CD-Rom] to burn.

Brenner *der*: **der Brenner** the Brenner Pass.

Brennholz *das* firewood.

Brenn|nessel, Brenn-Nessel *die* stinging nettle.

brenzlig *adj* - **1.** [Geschmack] burnt; **ein brenzliger Geruch** a smell of burning - **2.** *fam* [heikel] dicey.

Brett (*pl* **-er**) *das* - **1.** [aus Holz] plank; **schwarzes Brett** noticeboard - **2.** [zum Spielen] board.

Brett|spiel *das* board game.

Brezel (*pl* **-n**) *die* pretzel.

bricht *präs* ▷ **brechen.**

Brief (*pl* **-e**) *der* letter.

Brief|freund, in *der, die* pen pal.

Brief|kasten *der* - **1.** [bei der Post] postbox *UK*, mailbox *US* - **2.** [am Hauseingang] letterbox *UK*, mailbox *US*.

Brief|kopf *der* letterhead.

Brief|marke *die* stamp.

Brief|tasche *die* wallet.

Brief|träger, in *der, die* postman (postwoman *die*).

Brief|umschlag *der* envelope.

briet *prät* ▷ **braten.**

Brillant [brɪl'jant] (*pl* **-en**) *der* brilliant.

Brille (*pl* **-n**) *die* - **1.** [Sehhilfe, Augengläser] glasses *Pl*; **eine Brille tragen** to wear glasses - **2.** *fam* [Klosettbrille] toilet seat.

bringen (*prät* **brachte**, *perf* **hat gebracht**) *vt* - **1.** [herbringen] to bring; **jm etw bringen** to bring sb sthg - **2.** [holen] to get, to fetch; **jm etw bringen** to get ODER fetch sb sthg - **3.** [befördern] to take, to give a lift to; **ich bringe Sie zum Bahnhof** I'll take you ODER give you a lift to the station - **4.** [begleiten] to see; **jn zur Tür bringen** to see sb to the door - **5.** *fig* [lenken]: **die Rede auf etw bringen** to bring the conversation round to sthg; **jn auf die Idee bringen, etw zu tun** to give sb the idea of doing sthg; **jn in Gefahr bringen** to put sb in danger - **6.** [Ergebnis]: **das bringt nur Ärger** that'll cause nothing but trouble; **jn dazu bringen, dass er etw tut** to make sb do sthg, to get sb to do sthg; **Gewinn bringen** to yield a profit; **das bringt nichts** *fam* that won't achieve anything - **7.** [leisten]: **es weit bringen** to go far ODER a long way; **er brachte es bis zum Minister** he made it to minister - **8.** [veröffentlichen - in einer Zeitung] to publish; [- im Fernsehen, Radio] to broadcast; FILM to screen; **etw hinter sich** *(A)* **bringen** to get sthg over and done with; **ich kann es nicht über mich bringen, so etwas zu tun** I can't bring myself to do such a thing; **jn um etw bringen** to do sb out of sthg; **du bringst mich noch mal um den Verstand!** you're driving me mad!

brisant *adj* [heikel] explosive.

Brise (*pl* **-n**) *die* breeze.

Brite (*pl* **-n**) *der* Briton, British person; **die Briten** the British; **ich bin Brite** I'm British.

Britin (*pl* **-nen**) *die* Briton, British person.

britisch *adj* British.

Britische Inseln *Pl* British Isles.

Broccoli, Brokkoli ['brɔkoli] *der* broccoli.

bröckeln (*perf* **hat/ist gebröckelt**) *vi* - **1.** *(hat)* [zerfallen] to crumble - **2.** *(ist)* [sich lösen]: **der Putz bröckelt von den Wänden** the plaster is flaking off the walls.

Brocken (*pl* -) *der* - **1.** [von Brot, Fleisch] bit, chunk; [von Lehm] lump - **2.** *fam* [dicker Mensch] hefty fellow; **ein paar Brocken einer Sprache sprechen** to speak a few words of a language.

brodeln *vi* [Wasser, Suppe, Lava] to bubble.

Brokkoli = **Broccoli.**

Brom|beere *die* blackberry.

Bronchien ['brɔnçi̯ən] *Pl* bronchial tubes.

Bronchitis [brɔn'çiːtɪs] *die* bronchitis *(U)*.

Bronze ['brɔŋsə] *die* bronze.

Brosche (*pl* **-n**) *die* brooch.

Broschüre (*pl* **-n**) *die* brochure.

Brot (*pl* **-e**) *das* - **1.** [als Laib] bread; **ein Laib Brot** a loaf of bread - **2.** [als Scheibe] slice of bread; **ein belegtes Brot** an open sandwich; **ein Brot mit Schinken** a slice of bread with ham on it - **3.** [Lebensunterhalt]: **sich sein Brot verdienen** to earn a living.

Brötchen (*pl* -) *das* (bread) roll.

Browser ['brauzəʳ] (*pl* -) *der* EDV browser.

Bruch (*pl* **Brüche**) *der* - **1.** *(ohne pl)* [Brechen] breaking; [von Damm] bursting; **zu Bruch gehen** [Glas] to smash, to shatter - **2.** [von Versprechen, Wort] breaking; [von Vertrag] breach - **3.** [Trennung]: **ein Bruch mit der Tradition** a break with tradition; **es kam zum Bruch mit seiner Familie** he broke off contact with his family - **4.** [MED - von Knochen] fracture; [- von Eingeweide] hernia; **sich einen Bruch heben** to have ODER suffer a hernia - **5.** MATH fraction.

brüchig *adj* [Material] brittle; [Teig] crumbly; [Beziehung] fragile; [Stimme] cracked.

Bruch|landung *die* crash landing.

Bruch|rechnung *die (ohne pl)* fractions *Pl.*

Bruch|strich *der* line *(of a fraction).*

Bruch|stück *das* [von Vase, Werk] fragment.

bruchstückhaft ['brʊxʃtykhaft] ◇ *adj* fragmentary. ◇ *adv* in fragments.

Bruch|teil *der* fraction.

Brücke (*pl* **-n**) *die* - **1.** [gen] bridge; **eine Brücke schlagen** [Turnübung] to make a bridge - **2.** [Teppich] rug.

Bruder (*pl* **Brüder**) *der* - **1.** [Geschwister, Mönch] brother - **2.** *fam* [Kerl] guy.

brüderlich ◇ *adj* brotherly. ◇ *adv* like brothers.

Brühe (*pl* **-n**) *die* - **1.** [Suppe] broth; [zum Kochen] stock - **2.** [Wasser] dirty water - **3.** *abw* [Tee, Kaffee] dishwater.

Brüh|würfel *der* stock cube.

brüllen ◇ *vt* to roar. ◇ *vi* [Löwe, Person] to roar; [Stier] to bellow; [Baby, Affe] to screech; **vor Schmerz brüllen** to howl with pain.

brummen *vi* - **1.** [Hummel] to buzz; [Bär] to growl - **2.** [Person, Motor] to drone.

brummig ◇ *adj* [Person] grumpy; [Antwort] bad-tempered, surly. ◇ *adv* grumpily.

brünett *adj*: **eine brünette Frau** a brunette.

Brunnen (*pl* -) *der* - **1.** [zum Wasserholen] well - **2.** [Springbrunnen] fountain - **3.** [Wasser] mineral water.

Brunst (*pl* **Brünste**) *die* [von Reh] heat; [von Hirsch] rut.

brüsk ◇ *adj* brusque. ◇ *adv* brusquely.

Brüssel *nt* Brussels.

Brust (*pl* **Brüste**) *die* - **1.** *(ohne pl)* [Thorax] chest - **2.** [Busen] breast.

brüsten ◆ **sich brüsten** *ref abw*: **sich mit etw brüsten** to boast about sthg.

Brust|korb *der* thorax.

Brust|schwimmen *das* breaststroke.

Brüstung (*pl* **-en**) *die* parapet.

Brust|warze *die* nipple.

brutal ◇ *adj* brutal. ◇ *adv* brutally.

Brutalität (*pl* **-en**) *die* brutality.

brüten *vi* - **1.** [Vögel] to brood - **2.** [nachdenken]: **über etw** *(D)* **brüten** to ponder sthg.

brutto *adv* gross.

Bruttosozial|produkt *das* gross national product, GNP.

brutzeln ◇ *vi* to sizzle. ◇ *vt fam* to fry (up).

BSE (*abk für* **Bovine Spongiforme Enzephalopathie**) *die* BSE.

Bube (*pl* **-n**) *der* - **1.** [Junge] boy - **2.** [Spielkarte] jack.

Buch (*pl* **Bücher**) *das* book; **die Bücher führen** to keep the books; **über etw** *(A)* **Buch führen** to keep a record of sthg.

Buchbinder, in (*mpl* -, *fpl* **-nen**) *der, die* bookbinder.

Buche (*pl* **-n**) *die* beech.

buchen *vt* - **1.** [verbuchen] to enter - **2.** [reservieren] to book.

Bücherei (*pl* **-en**) *die* library.

Bücher|regal *das* bookshelves *Pl.*

Bücher|schrank *der* bookcase.

Buch|führung *die* bookkeeping.

Buchhalter, in (*mpl* -, *fpl* **-nen**) *der, die* accountant, bookkeeper.

Buch|haltung *die* accountancy, bookkeeping.

Buch|händler, in *der, die* bookseller.

Buch|handlung (*pl* **-en**) *die* bookshop.

Buchladen (*pl* **-läden**) *der* bookshop.

Buchse ['bʊksə] (*pl* **-n**) *die* socket.

Büchse ['byksə] (*pl* **-n**) *die* - **1.** [Dose] can, tin *UK* - **2.** [Gewehr] shotgun.

Büchsen|milch *die* tinned milk *UK*, canned milk *US*.

Büchsen|öffner *der* can opener, tin opener *UK*.

Buchstabe ['bu:xʃtɑ:bə] (*pl* **-n**) *der* letter; **grosser Buchstabe** capital (letter); **kleiner Buchstabe** lower-case letter; **in fetten Buchstaben** in bold.

buchstabieren [bu:xʃta'bi:rən] *vt* to spell.

buchstäblich ['bu:xʃtɛ:plɪ] *adv* literally.

Bucht (*pl* **-en**) *die* bay.

Buchung (*pl* **-en**) *die* - **1.** [Verbuchung] entry - **2.** [Reservierung] booking.

Buchweizen *der* buckwheat.

Buckel (*pl* -) *der* [Rücken] hump; **einen Buckel haben** to be a hunchback; **rutsch mir den Buckel runter!** *fam abw* get lost ODER stuffed!

bucklig *adj* [Person] hunchbacked; [Oberfläche, Straße] bumpy.

Bückling (*pl* **-e**) *der* - **1.** *hum* [Verbeugung] bow - **2.** [Hering] smoked herring.

Budapest *nt* Budapest.

buddeln *vt* & *vi* to dig.

buddhistisch *adj* Buddhist.

Bude (*pl* **-n**) *die* - **1.** [Verkaufsstand] stall - **2.** *fam* [kleine Wohnung, möbliertes Zimmer] pad; **die Leute rennen ihr die Bude ein** *fam* she has people queuing on her doorstep - **3.** *fam abw* [Wohnung] dump.

Budget [by'dʒe:] (*pl* **-s**) *das* budget.

Büfett [by'fɛt] (*pl* **-s**), **Buffet** [by'fe:] (*pl* **-s**) *das* - **1.** [Verkaufstisch] counter - **2.** [Speisen]: **kaltes Büfett** cold buffet - **3.** [Geschirrschrank] sideboard.

Büffel (*pl* -) *der* buffalo.

Buffet [by'feː] (*pl* **-s**) *das Österr & Schweiz* = **Büfett**.

Bug (*pl* **-e**) *der* [von Schiff] bow; [von Flugzeug] nose.

Bügel (*pl* -) *der* - **1.** [Kleiderbügel] (coat) hanger - **2.** [Griff] handle - **3.** [Steigbügel] stirrup - **4.** [Brillenbügel] side-piece.

Bügel|brett *das* ironing board.

Bügel|eisen *das* iron.

Bügel|falte *die* crease.

bügeln *vt* & *vi* to iron.

Buggy (*pl* **-s**) *der* buggy.

Bühne (*pl* **-n**) *die* - **1.** [Theaterraum] stage - **2.** [Theater] theatre.

Bühnen|bild *das* set.

buk *prät* ▻ **backen**.

Bukarest *nt* Bucharest.

Bulette (*pl* **-n**), **Boulette** (*pl* **-n**) *die* rissole.

Bulgarien *nt* Bulgaria.

bulgarisch *adj* Bulgarian.

Bull|auge *das* porthole.

Bull|dogge *die* bulldog.

Bulldozer ['bʊldoːzɐ] (*pl* **Bulldozer**) *der* bulldozer.

Bulle (*pl* **-n**) *der* - **1.** [Tier] bull - **2.** *salopp abw* [Polizist] pig, cop.

Bummel (*pl* -) *der* stroll; **einen Bummel machen** to go for a stroll.

bummeln (*perf* **hat/ist gebummelt**) *vi* - **1.** *(ist)* [spazieren] to stroll - **2.** *(hat)* [langsam sein] to dawdle.

Bummel|zug *der* slow train.

bumsen (*perf* **hat/ist gebumst**) ◇ *vi* - **1.** *(hat) fam* [knallen] to bang; **es hat gebumst** [Lärm] there was a bang; [bei Unfall] there was a crash - **2.** *(ist) fam* [prallen]: **gegen** ODER **an etw** *(A)* **bumsen** to bang into sthg - **3.** *(hat) fam* [koitieren] to get laid, to have it off *UK*. ◇ *vt (hat) fam* to lay, to have it off with *UK*.

Bund (*pl* **Bünde** ODER **-e**) ◇ *der* - **1.** *(pl Bünde)* [Zusammenschluss] association - **2.** [Bundesrepublik] central government - **3.** *fam* [Bundeswehr]: **der Bund** the army - **4.** *(pl Bünde)* [an Kleidung] waistband. ◇ *das (pl Bunde)* [von Gemüse] bunch.

Bündel (*pl* -) *das* - **1.** [von Wäsche, Anträgen] bundle; [von Geldscheinen] wad - **2.** [aus Stroh] bale.

bündeln *vt* - **1.** [Heu, Stroh] to bale - **2.** [Kleidung, Papier, Banknoten] to tie into bundles - **3.** [Produkte] to combine.

Bundes|bahn ▻ **Deutsche Bahn**.

Bundes|bürger, **in** *der, die* German citizen.

Bundesgrenz|schutz *der (ohne pl) German border police.*

Bundes|kanzler, **in** *der, die* German chancellor.

Bundes|land *das* federal state; **die alten/neuen Bundesländer** the old/new federal states.

Bundes|liga *die German national league for football, ice hockey etc.*

Bundes|post ▻ **Deutsche Bundespost**.

Bundes|präsident, **in** *der, die* - **1.** [in Deutschland, Österreich] president - **2.** [in der Schweiz] chair of the "Bundesrat".

Bundes|rat *der (ohne pl)* [Parlament] Bundesrat, *upper chamber of the German Parliament, made up of representatives from each of the German states.*

Bundes|regierung *die* German ODER federal government.

Bundes|republik *die* - **1.** [Föderation] federal republic - **2.** ▻ **Bundesrepublik Deutschland**.

Bundesrepublik Deutschland *die* Federal Republic of Germany.

Bundes|staat *der* federal state.

Bundes|straße *die* ≃ A road *UK*, ≃ state highway *US*.

Bundes|tag ▻ **Deutsche Bundestag**.

Bundes|wehr *die* German army.

bundesweit *adj* & *adv* nationwide *(in Germany, Austria).*

bündig ◇ *adj* [kurz] concise. ◇ *adv* [kurz] concisely.

Bündnis (*pl* **-se**) *das* alliance.

Bungalow ['bʊŋgalo] (*pl* **-s**) *der* bungalow.

Bunker (*pl* -) *der* [Schutzraum] bunker.

bunt ◇ *adj* - **1.** [vielfarbig] colourful - **2.** [abwechslungsreich] [Programm] varied; **eine bunte Mischung** a motley assortment; **ein bunter Abend** a social evening - **3.** [durcheinander] mixed-up; **jetzt wirds mir zu bunt** I've had enough. ◇ *adv* - **1.** [vielfarbig] colourfully - **2.** [abwechslungsreich]: **bunt gemischt** assorted; **es zu bunt treiben** to overdo it.

Bunt|stift *der* coloured pencil.

Burg (*pl* **-en**) *die* - **1.** [Gebäude] castle - **2.** [Sandburg] *circular wall of sand built on beach by holidaymakers to mark off the area where they are sitting.*

Bürge (*pl* **-n**) *der* guarantee.

bürgen *vi*: **für jn/etw bürgen** *fig* to vouch for sb/sthg; **für jn bürgen** WIRTSCH to stand surety for sb.

Bürger, **in** (*mpl* -, *fpl* **-nen**) *der, die* - **1.** [Einwohner] citizen - **2.** [Mittelständler] middle-class person.

Bürger|initiative *die* [Gruppe] grass-roots pressure group.

Bürger|krieg *der* civil war.

bürgerlich ◇ *adj* - **1.** [staatlich] civil - **2.** [des Bürgertums - Partei, Familie] middle-class; [- Küche] traditional - **3.** HIST & POL [spießig] bourgeois. <> *adv* [wie das Bürgertum]: **Ulm ist eine bürgerlich geprägte Stadt** Ulm is a middle-class city.

Bürgerlmeister, in *der, die* mayor. ◆ **Regierende Bürgermeister** *der mayor and leader of local government.*

Bürgersteig (*pl* **-e**) *der* pavement *UK*, sidewalk *US*.

Bürgertum *das* bourgeoisie.

Bürgschaft (*pl* **-en**) *die* surety.

Büro [by'ro:] (*pl* **-s**) *das* office.

Bürolklammer *die* paper clip.

bürokratisch <> *adj* bureaucratic. <> *adv* bureaucratically.

Bursche (*pl* **-n**) *der* - **1.** [Junge] lad - **2.** [Prachtexemplar]: **ein prächtiger Bursche** a magnificent specimen.

burschikos *adj* [Frau] mannish; [Mädchen] boyish.

Bürste (*pl* **-n**) *die* [Gerät] brush.

bürsten *vt* to brush; **sich** *(D)* **die Haare bürsten** to brush one's hair.

Bus (*pl* **-se**) *der* - **1.** [Omnibus] bus - **2.** [Reisebus] bus, coach *UK*.

Busch (*pl* **Büsche**) *der* [Strauch, Zone] bush.

Büschel (*pl* **-**) *das* [von Gras, Haaren] tuft; [von Stroh] bundle.

buschig *adj* bushy.

Busen (*pl* **-**) *der* bosom.

Buslfahrer, in *der, die* - **1.** [von Omnibus] bus driver - **2.** [von Reisebus] bus driver, coach driver *UK*.

Bushaltelstelle *die* bus stop.

Business Class *die (ohne pl)* business class.

Bussard (*pl* **-e**) *der* buzzard.

büßen <> *vt* - **1.** [Sünden] to atone for - **2.** [Untat] to pay for. <> *vi* - **1.** RELIG: **für etw büßen** to atone for sthg - **2.** [bestraft werden]: **für etw büßen** to pay for sthg.

Bußlgeld *das* fine.

Buß- und Betltag *der* Day of Prayer and Repentance, *German public holiday in November.*

Büste (*pl* **-n**) *die* bust.

Büstenlhalter *der* bra.

Butike = **Boutique**.

Butter *die* butter.

Butterlbrot *das* slice of bread and butter.

Butterldose *die* butter dish.

Butterlmilch *die* buttermilk.

BWL [be:ve:'ɛl] (*abk für* **Betriebswirtschaftslehre**) *die business studies.*

Byzanz *nt* HIST Byzantium.

bzg. (*abk für* **bezüglich**) re.

bzw. *abk für* **beziehungsweise**.

C

c (*pl* - ODER **-s**), **C** (*pl* - ODER **-s**) [tse:] *das* - **1.** [Buchstabe] c, C - **2.** MUS C. ◆ **C** (*abk für* **Celsius**) C.

ca. (*abk für* **circa**) approx.

Cabaret [kaba're:] (*pl* **-s**) *das* cabaret.

Cabrio ['ka:brio] (*pl* **-s**) *das* = **Kabrio**.

Café [ka'fe:] (*pl* **-s**) *das* cafe.

Cafeteria [kafetə'ri:a] (*pl* **-s**) *die* cafeteria.

Callcenter ['kɔ:lsɛntɐ] (*pl* **-s**) *das* TELEKOM call centre.

Calzium ['kaltsi̯ʊm] *das* = **Kalzium**.

campen ['kɛmpn̩] *vi* to camp.

Camping ['kɛmpɪŋ] *das* camping; **zum Camping fahren** to go camping.

Campus *der (ohne Pl)* campus.

canceln ['kɛnsəln̩] (*präs* **cancelt**, *prät* **cancelte**, *perf* **hat gecancelt**) *vt* to cancel.

Cape [ke:p] (*pl* **-s**) *das* cape.

Carsharing *das* car sharing.

CB-lFunker [tse:'be:fuŋkɐ] *der* CB ham.

CD [tse:'de:] (*pl* **-s**) (*abk für* **Compactdisc**) *die* CD.

CD-Brenner (*pl* **-**) *der* CD burner.

CD-ROM [tse:de:'rɔm] (*pl* **-**) (*abk für* **Compact Disk read only memory**) *die* EDV CD-ROM.

CD-Spieler [tse:'de:ʃpi:lɐ] (*pl* **-**) *der* CD player.

CDU [tse:de:'u:] (*abk für* **Christlich-Demokratische Union**) *die* Christian Democratic Union, *major German political party to the right of the political spectrum.*

C-Dur ['tse:du:ɐ̯] *das* C major.

Cello ['tʃɛlo] (*pl* **-s**) *das* cello.

Celsius ['tsɛlzi̯ʊs] Celsius, centigrade; **10 Grad Celsius** 10 degrees Celsius ODER centigrade.

Cent [(t)sɛnt] (*pl* **-s** ODER **-**) *der* - **1.** [in EU] (euro)cent - **2.** *(pl Cents)* [in USA] cent.

Chamäleon [ka'mɛ:leɔn] (*pl* **-s**) *das* chameleon.

Champagner [ʃam'panjɐ] (*pl* **-**) *der* champagne.

Champignon ['ʃampɪnjɔŋ] (*pl* **-s**) *der* mushroom.

Chance ['ʃã:s(ə)] (*pl* **-n**) *die* [Möglichkeit] chance; **jm eine Chance geben** to give sb a chance.

Chaos ['ka:ɔs] *das* chaos.

chaotisch [ka'o:tɪʃ] <> *adj* chaotic. <> *adv* chaotically.

Charakter [ka'raktɐ] (*pl* **-tere**) *der* character.

charakterisieren [karakteri'ziːrən] *vt* to characterize.

Charakteristik [karakte'rɪstɪk] (*pl* **-en**) *die* characteristic.

charakteristisch [karakte'rɪstɪʃ] <> *adj* characteristic; **für jn/etw charakteristisch sein** to be characteristic of sb/sthg. <> *adv* characteristically.

charakterlich [ka'raktɐlɪç] *adj*: **charakterliche Schwäche** weakness of character.

charakterlos [ka'raktɐloːs] <> *adj* unprincipled. <> *adv* without principle.

charmant, scharmant [ʃar'mant] <> *adj* charming. <> *adv* charmingly.

Charme, Scharm [ʃarm] *der* charm.

Charter|flug ['tʃartɐfluːk] *der* charter flight.

Charter|maschine *die* charter plane.

chartern ['tʃartɐn] *vt* to charter.

Chat [tʃɛt] (*pl* **-s**) *der* EDV chat.

Chatroom ['tʃɛtˌruːm] (*pl* **-s**) *der* EDV chatroom.

Chauvinismus [ʃovi'nɪsmʊs] *der abw* chauvinism.

chauvinistisch [ʃovi'nistɪʃ] *abw* <> *adj* chauvinist. <> *adv* chauvinistically.

checken ['tʃɛkn̩] *vt* - **1.** [untersuchen] to check - **2.** *salopp* [verstehen]: **sie checkt es einfach nicht!** she just doesn't get it!

Chef [ʃɛf] (*pl* **-s**) *der* [von Firma, Mafiosi] boss; [von Organisation] head.

Chef|arzt *der* senior consultant *UK*, specialist *US*.

Chef|ärztin *die* senior consultant *UK*, specialist *US*.

Chefin (*pl* **-nen**) *die* [von Firma] boss; [von Organisation] head.

Chef|redakteur, in *der, die* editor-in-chief.

Chemie [çe'miː] *die (ohne pl)* - **1.** [Wissenschaft] chemistry - **2.** *fam* [Chemikalien] chemicals *Pl*.

Chemikalie [çemi'kaːli̯ə] (*pl* **-n**) *die* chemical.

Chemiker, in ['çeːmikɐ, rɪn] (*mpl* **-**, *fpl* **-nen**) *der, die* chemist.

chemisch ['çeːmiʃ] <> *adj* [Reaktion, Zusammensetzung] chemical; **chemisches Labor** chemistry lab; **chemische Reinigung** dry-cleaning. <> *adv* chemically; **chemisch reinigen** to dry-clean.

Chemotherapie [çemotera'piː] (*pl* **-n**) *die* chemotherapy.

Chicorée, Schikoree ['ʃikore] *die ODER der* chicory.

Chiffre ['ʃifrə] (*pl* **-n**) *die* - **1.** [Zeichen] (code) symbol - **2.** [von Anzeigen] box number.

chiffrieren [ʃɪ'friːrən] *vt* to encode.

Chile ['tʃiːle] *nt* Chile.

Chili ['tʃiːli] (*pl* **-s**) *der* - **1.** [Schote] chilli (pepper) - **2.** [Gewürz] chilli (powder).

China ['çiːna] *nt* China.

Chinakohl *der (ohne pl)* Chinese leaves *Pl UK*, bok choy *US*.

Chinese [çi'neːzə] (*pl* **-n**) *der* Chinese (man).

Chinesin [çi'neːzin] (*pl* **-nen**) *die* Chinese (woman).

chinesisch [çi'neːzɪʃ] *adj* Chinese.

Chinin [çi'niːn] *das* quinine.

Chip [tʃɪp] (*pl* **-s**) *der* [beim Spiel, ELEKTR & EDV] chip.

Chips [tʃɪps] *Pl* crisps *UK*, chips *US*.

Chirurg [çi'rʊrk] (*pl* **-en**) *der* surgeon.

Chirurgie [çirʊr'giː] (*pl* **-n**) *die* - **1.** [Wissenschaft] surgery - **2.** [Krankenhausabteilung] surgical unit; **auf der Chirurgie liegen** to be in surgery.

Chirurgin [çi'rʊrgɪn] (*pl* **-nen**) *die* surgeon.

chirurgisch [çi'rʊrgɪʃ] <> *adj* surgical. <> *adv* surgically.

Chlor [kloːɐ̯] *das* chlorine.

Cholesterin [kolɛste'riːn] *das* cholesterol.

Chor [koːɐ̯] (*pl* **Chöre**) *der* MUS & ARCHIT choir; **im Chor** in chorus.

Choreografie (*pl* **-n**), **Choreographie** (*pl* **-n**) [koreogra'fiː] *die* choreography.

Christ ['krɪst] (*pl* **-en**) *der* Christian.

Christ|baum *der* Christmas tree.

Christ|demokrat, in *der, die* Christian Democrat.

Christentum ['krɪstn̩tuːm] *das* Christianity.

Christi Himmelfahrt *(ohne Artikel)* [Feiertag] Ascension Day.

Christin ['krɪstɪn] (*pl* **-nen**) *die* Christian.

Christkind *das* - **1.** [Jesuskind] baby Jesus, Christ Child - **2.** [zu Weihnachten] ≃ Santa Claus.

christlich ['krɪstlɪç] <> *adj* Christian. <> *adv*: **christlich handeln** to act like a Christian.

Christus ['krɪstʊs] *der* Christ.

Chrom [kroːm] *das* [als Überzug] chrome; CHEM chromium.

Chromosom [kromo'zoːm] (*pl* **-en**) *das* chromosome.

Chronik ['kroːnɪk] (*pl* **-en**) *die* chronicle.

chronisch ['kroːnɪʃ] *adj* chronic.

chronologisch [krono'loːgɪʃ] <> *adj* chronological. <> *adv* chronologically.

circa ['tsɪrka] *adv* = **zirka**.

clever ['klɛvɐ] <> *adj* clever, smart. <> *adv* cleverly, smartly.

Clique ['klɪkə] (*pl* **-n**) *die* - **1.** [Gruppe] group of friends - **2.** *abw* [Interessengemeinschaft] clique; [von Verbrechern] gang.

Clown, in [klau̯n, ɪn] (*mpl* **-s**, *fpl* **-nen**) *der, die* clown.

Club = **Klub**.

cm (*abk für* **Zentimeter**) cm.

c-Moll ['tseːmɔl] *das* MUS C minor.

Cocktail ['kɔkteːl] (*pl* **-s**) *der* cocktail.

Code ['koːt] (*pl* **-s**) *der* = **Kode**.

Cognac® ['kɔnjak] (*pl* **-s**) *der* cognac.

Cola ['koːla] (*pl* **-s**) *die ODER das* Coke®.

Comer See ['koːmɐ 'zeː] *der* Lake Como.

Comic ['kɔmɪk] (*pl* **-s**) *der* - **1.** [Geschichte] cartoon - **2.** [Heft] comic.

Computer [kɔm'pjuːtɐ] (*pl* -) *der* computer.

Computer|spiel *das* computer game.

Container [kɔn'teːnɐ] (*pl* -) *der* [gen] container; [für Altglas, Papier] bank.

contra ['kɔntra] *präp* = **kontra**.

Cord [kɔrt] *der* = **Kord**.

Couch [kautʃ] (*pl* **-s** ODER **-en**) *die* couch.

Count-down ['kaunt'daun] (*pl* **-s**) *das* & *der* countdown.

Cousin [ku'zɛ̃] (*pl* **-s**) *der* cousin.

Cousine (*pl* **-n**), **Kusine** (*pl* **-n**) [ku'ziːnə] *die* cousin.

Cowboy ['kaubɔy] (*pl* **-s**) *der* cowboy.

Creme [krɛːm] (*pl* **-s** ODER **-n**), **Krem** [kreːm] (*pl* **-s**) *die* - **1.** [Hautcreme] cream - **2.** [Speise] confectioner's custard.

cremig, kremig ['kreːmɪç] ◇ *adj* creamy. ◇ *adv*: **etw cremig schlagen** to cream sthg.

Crew [kruː] (*pl* **-s**) *die* [Besatzung] crew.

CSU [tseːɛs'uː] (*abk für* **Christlich-Soziale Union**) *die* Christian Social Union, *Bavarian political party to the right of the political spectrum, long-time alliance partners of the CDU.*

Cup [kap] (*pl* **-s**) *der* SPORT cup.

Curry ['kœri] (*pl* **-s**) *das* - **1.** [Gewürz] curry powder - **2.** [Gericht] curry.

Curry|wurst *die sausage with curry sauce.*

CVP [tseːfaupeː] (*abk für* **Christliche Volkspartei (der Schweiz)**) *die* Popular Christian Democratic Party, *right-wing political party in Switzerland.*

Cyberspace ['saibɐspeɪs] *der (ohne pl)* cyberspace.

D

d (*pl* - ODER **-s**), **D** (*pl* - ODER **-s**) [deː] *das* - **1.** [Buchstabe] d, D - **2.** MUS D.

da ◇ *adv* - **1.** [dort] there; **guck mal da!** look over there!; **da kommt der Bus!** here comes the bus!; **das da gefällt mir am besten** I like that one best; **da drüben** over there - **2.** [hier] here; **da bin ich!** here I am!; **ist noch etwas Brot da?** is there any bread left?; **ich bin gleich wieder da** I'll be back in a minute - **3.** [in diesem Zusammenhang]: **da fällt mir ein** I've just thought - **4.** [in dieser Beziehung] there; **da irren Sie sich** you're wrong there - **5.** [unter dieser Bedingung] in that case; **da gehe ich lieber gleich** in that case I'd rather go straight away. ◇ *konj* [weil] as, since; **da ihr Vater krank war, musste sie zu Hause bleiben** as her father was ill, she had to stay at home.

DAAD [deːaːaː'deː] (*abk für* **Deutscher Akademischer Austauschdienst**) *der* German Academic Exchange Service, *cultural body which organizes academic exchanges for students and staff.*

da|behalten *vt (unreg)* to keep (in ODER back).

dabei, dabei *adv* - **1.** [räumlich]: **waren Sie bei der Auktion dabei?** were you at the auction?; **hast du zufällig eine Briefmarke dabei?** do you happen to have a stamp on you?; **nicht dabei sein** to be missing; **ich bin dabei!** *fig* count me in! - **2.** [zeitlich] at the same time; **sie waren gerade dabei, das Haus zu verlassen** they were just leaving the house - **3.** [bei dieser Sache]: **dabei kam heraus, dass...** in the process it came out that...; **mir ist nicht ganz wohl dabei (zumute)** I don't really feel happy about it; **und dabei bleibts!** and that's the end of it!; **es ist nichts dabei** *fam fig* there's nothing wrong with it - **4.** [obwohl] although - **5.** [überdies]: **und dabei ist sie auch noch intelligent** and (what is more) she's clever too; *siehe auch* **dabei sein**.

dabei|haben *vt (unreg)* [Person] to have with one; [Gegenstand] to have on one; **sie wollten ihn nicht dabeihaben** they didn't want him there.

dabei sein (*perf* **ist dabei gewesen**) *vi (unreg)* - **1.** [anwesend sein] to be present ODER there - **2.** [im Begriff sein]: **dabei sein, etw zu tun** to be just doing sthg.

da|bleiben (*perf* **ist dageblieben**) *vi (unreg)* to stay.

Dach (*pl* **Dächer**) *das* roof; **das Dach decken** to roof the house; **unterm Dach wohnen** to live in the attic.

Dach|boden *der* attic; **auf dem Dachboden** in the attic.

Dach|luke *die* skylight.

Dach|rinne *die* gutter.

Dachs [daks] (*pl* **-e**) *der* badger.

dachte *prät* ▷ **denken**.

Dach|ziegel *der* roof tile.

Dackel (*pl* -) *der* dachshund.

Dadaismus [dada'ɪsmʊs] *der* Dadaism.

dadurch, dadurch *adv* - **1.** [auf diese Art] because of this; **dadurch, dass...** because...; **dadurch, dass wir uns viel Mühe gaben** because we tried very hard; **dadurch kam es, dass...** that was why... - **2.** [räumlich] through it.

dafür, dafür *adv* - **1.** [für etwas] for it; **30 Euro dafür bezahlen** to pay 30 euros for it; **er kann nichts dafür** it's not his fault; **er hat kein Ver-**

ständnis **dafür** he has no feeling for that - **2.** [bejahend] for it, in favour of it; **dafür spricht, dass** this is confirmed by the fact that - **3.** [als Ausgleich]: **er arbeitet langsam, dafür aber gründlich** he works slowly yet thoroughly - **4.** [im Tausch] in exchange.

dafür|können *vt (unreg)*: **nichts dafürkönnen** not to be able to help it; **ich kann doch nichts dafür, dass der Zug zu spät kommt!** it's not my fault if the train is late!

DAG [deːɑːˈgeː] (*abk für* **Deutsche Angestellten Gewerkschaft**) *die German white-collar union.*

dagegen, dagegen *adv* - **1.** [räumlich] against it; **das Auto fuhr dagegen** the car drove into it - **2.** [ablehnend] against it; **etwas dagegen haben** to object; **hast du etwas dagegen, wenn ich rauche?** do you mind if I smoke?; **dagegen lässt sich nichts machen** nothing can be done about it - **3.** [im Gegensatz] in comparison; **sie ist groß, er dagegen ist klein** she's tall, whereas he is short; **dieser ist nichts dagegen!** this is nothing in comparison!

da gewesen ◇ *pp* ▷ **da sein**. ◇ *adj*: **noch nie da gewesen** unheard of.

Daheim *das Süddt, Österr & Schweiz* home.

daher, daher *adv* - **1.** [aus dieser Richtung] from there; **ach, daher weht (also) der Wind!** *fig* so that's the way the wind is blowing! - **2.** [deswegen] that is why; **daher (auch) der Name** hence the name; **daher der ganze Ärger** that's the reason for all the hassle; **daher kommt es, dass...** that is why/how...

dahin, dahin ◇ *adv* - **1.** [räumlich] there - **2.** [zeitlich]: **bis dahin** until then; **bis dahin sind wir fertig** we'll be ready by then - **3.** [als Ziel]: **seine Bemühungen gehen dahin, sich selbstständig zu machen** he's trying to set up his own business. ◇ *adj fam* [kaputt, beendet, weg]: **das Kleid ist dahin!** the dress has had it!; **meine Träume sind dahin** my dreams have been shattered.

dahingestellt *pp*: **es bleibt** ODER **sei dahingestellt** it remains to be seen.

dahinten *adv* back there, over there.

dahinter *adv eigtl & fig* behind it.

dahinter kommen (*perf* **ist dahinter gekommen**) *vi (unreg) fam* to find out.

dahinter stecken *vi* to be behind it.

dahinter stehen *vi (unreg)* to be behind it.

damalig *adj* [Bedingungen, Zustände] at that time; **der damalige President** the then president.

damals *adv* then, in those days; **als ich damals krank wurde** when I got ill; **seit damals** since then.

Damast (*pl* **-e**) *der* damask.

Dame (*pl* **-n**) *die* - **1.** [Frau] lady; **der Wettbewerb der Damen** the women's competition; **meine (sehr verehrten) Damen und Herren** ladies and gentlemen - **2.** [Spielkarte] queen - **3.** [Spiel] draughts *(U)*. ◆ **Damen** *Pl* [Toilette] ladies *(sg)*.

Damen|binde *die* sanitary towel *UK*, sanitary napkin *US*.

damenhaft ◇ *adj* ladylike. ◇ *adv* like a lady.

Damen|toilette *die* ladies (toilet).

damit, damit ◇ *konj* so that. ◇ *adv* - **1.** [mit dieser Sache]: **was soll ich damit?** what am I supposed to do with this?; **sie war damit einverstanden** she agreed to it; **was meinst du damit?** what do you mean by that?; **her damit!** *fam* hand it over!; **hör auf damit!** *fam* stop it! - **2.** [somit] because of that.

dämlich *fam abw* ◇ *adj* stupid. ◇ *adv* stupidly.

Damm (*pl* **Dämme**) *der* [Deich] dam; **wieder auf dem Damm sein** *fam fig* to be up and about again.

dämmern *vi* - **1.** [einsetzen]: **es dämmert** [am Morgen] it's getting light, day is breaking; [am Abend] it's getting dark, night is falling - **2.** [halb schlafen]: **(vor sich hin) dämmern** to doze - **3.** *fam* [bewusst werden]: **eine Ahnung dämmerte ihm** a suspicion dawned on him.

Dämmerung (*pl* **-en**) *die* [am Morgen] dawn; [am Abend] dusk.

dämmrig, dämmerig *adj* [Licht] dim; [Tag] gloomy, dull.

Dämon (*pl* **Dämonen**) *der* demon.

dämonisch *adj* demonic.

Dampf (*pl* **Dämpfe**) *der* [Dunst] steam; **giftige Dämpfe** poisonous fumes; **jm Dampf machen** *fam* to make sb get a move on.

Dampf|bad *das* steam bath, Turkish bath.

dampfen *vi* to steam.

dämpfen *vt* - **1.** [dünsten] to steam - **2.** [Geräusch, Schritte] to muffle; [Instrument, Farbton] to mute; [Licht] to dim; [Stoß] to cushion; [Stimme] to lower - **3.** [Wut, Aufregung] to calm; [Begeisterung] to dampen - **4.** [verringern] to curb.

Dampfer (*pl* -) *der* steamship, steamer.

Dämpfer (*pl* -) *der*: **jm einen Dämpfer aufsetzen** ODER **verpassen** to dampen sb's spirits.

Dampf|maschine *die* steam engine.

Dampf|walze *die* steamroller.

danach, danach *adv* - **1.** [zeitlich] after, afterwards; **zwei Stunden danach** two hours later; **wir können doch erst ins Theater gehen und danach etwas essen** why don't we go to the theatre first and eat afterwards? - **2.** [nach etwas]: **danach schnappen/greifen** to snap/grab at it; **sich danach sehnen** to long for it; **ich habe danach gefragt** I asked about it - **3.** [entsprechend]: **es sieht ganz danach aus** it looks like it; **mir ist jetzt nicht danach (zumute)** I don't feel like it at the moment.

Däne (*pl* **-n**) *der* Dane.

daneben *adv* - **1.** [räumlich] next to it/him/*etc*, beside it/him/*etc*; **gleich daneben** right next to it - **2.** [vergleichend] in comparison - **3.** [außerdem] in addition (to that).

daneben|benehmen *(unreg)* ◆ **sich danebenbenehmen** *ref* to make an exhibition of o.s.

daneben|gehen (*perf* **ist danebengegangen**) *vi (unreg)* - **1.** [danebenzielen] to miss (the target) - **2.** *fam* [misslingen] to fail.

Dänemark *nt* Denmark.

Dänin (*pl* **-nen**) *die* Dane.

dänisch *adj* Danish.

dank *präp*: **dank einer Sache** *(G)* thanks to sthg.

Dank *der (ohne pl)* thanks *Pl*; **zum Dank dafür** as a reward, by way of saying thank you; **vielen Dank!** thank you (very much)!; **schönen** *ODER* **besten Dank auch!** thank you (very much)!

dankbar ◇ *adj* - **1.** [voller Dank] grateful; **jm (für etw) dankbar sein** to be grateful to sb (for sthg) - **2.** [lohnend] rewarding. ◇ *adv* [voller Dank] gratefully.

Dankbarkeit *die* gratitude.

danke *interj* thanks!, thank you!; **danke, dass du gekommen bist!** thanks *ODER* thank you for coming!; **noch einen Kaffee? - danke, gern/im Moment nicht** would you like another coffee? - yes, please/no thanks *ODER* no thank you, not just now; **danke gleichfalls!** thanks, you too!; **danke sehr** *ODER* **schön!** thanks (very much)!, thank you (very much)!

danken *vi*: **jm (für etw) danken** to thank sb (for sthg); **na, ich danke!** *fam* no thanks!, no thank you!; **nichts zu danken!** don't mention it!

Dankeschön *das* thank you.

Dank|schreiben *das* letter of thanks.

dann *adv* - **1.** [gen] then; **bis dann** see you (then) - **2.** [außerdem] then; **und dann (noch)** and, on top of that - **3.** [konditional] in that case, then. ◆ **also dann** *interj* all right then. ◆ **dann und dann** *adv* at such and such time. ◆ **dann und wann** *adv* now and then.

daran, daran *adv* - **1.** [an diese Sache]: **ich denke gerade daran** I'm just thinking about it; **er arbeitete lange daran** he worked at *ODER* on it for a long time; **es ist nichts Wahres daran** there is no truth in it; **mir liegt viel daran** it is very important to me; **er war schuld daran** it was his fault - **2.** [räumlich]: **er klebte Papier daran** he stuck paper (on)to it; **wir gingen daran vorbei** we went past it; **nahe daran** close to it - **3.** [deshalb]: **sie ist daran gestorben** she died of it; **es liegt daran, dass...** it is because...

daran|setzen *vt* [Energie, Kraft] to use; **alles daransetzen** to do one's utmost.

darauf, darauf *adv* - **1.** [räumlich] on it - **2.** [Richtung]: **darauf zielen** to aim at it; **das deutet darauf hin, dass...** *fig* this implies that... - **3.** [zeitlich] after that; **am Tag darauf** the day after, the next day; **bald darauf** soon after(wards) - **4.** [als Reaktion] to that; **darauf steht die Todesstrafe** the penalty for that is death - **5.** [zum Ausdruck einer Intention]: **sie ist darauf aus, einen Mann zu bekommen** she's out to get a husband; **sie bestand darauf** she was most particular about it; **besonders darauf achten, dass...** to take particular care to...

daraufhin *adv* - **1.** [aus einem Grund] as a result - **2.** [zu einem Zweck]: **das Produkt daraufhin prüfen, ob es den Normen entspricht** to test the product (in order) to see if it meets the standards.

daraus, daraus *adv* - **1.** [räumlich] from it, out of it - **2.** [aus dieser Sache] from it; **daraus folgt, dass...** from this it follows that...; **mach dir nichts daraus!** don't let it bother you!; **ich mache mir nichts daraus** I'm not very keen on it; **daraus wird nichts!** *fam* nothing doing! - **3.** [aus einem Material] from it, out of it.

darf *präs* ▷ **dürfen**.

darin, darin *adv* - **1.** [in etwas] in it, inside - **2.** [in diesem Sachverhalt] there.

dar|legen *vt* to explain.

Darlehen (*pl* -) *das* loan.

Darm (*pl* **Därme**) *der* - **1.** [Organ] intestine - **2.** [Material] gut.

Darm|infektion *die* bowel infection.

dar|stellen *vt* - **1.** [Subj: Bild] to portray, to depict - **2.** [beschreiben] to describe - **3.** [Subj Schauspieler] to play - **4.** [sein] to represent, to constitute; **als Wissenschaftler stellt er etwas dar** he is an impressive scientist.

Darsteller, in (*mpl* -, *fpl* **-nen**) *der, die* actor (actress *die*); **der Darsteller des Hamlet** the actor playing Hamlet.

Dar|stellung *die* - **1.** [als Bild] depiction, portrayal; **eine grafische Darstellung** a graphic representation - **2.** [Bericht] account.

darüber, darüber *adv* - **1.** [räumlich - über etw] above it, over it; [- über etw hinweg] across it, over it; **darüber hinaus** *fig* in addition; **darüber sind wir schon hinaus** we have already passed that stage - **2.** [über diese Sache] about it; **hast du darüber nachgedacht?** did you think about it?; **ich komme nicht darüber hinweg** I can't get over it; **darüber hinwegsehen** to ignore it - **3.** [mehr] above that over that; **nichts geht darüber!** *fig* there is nothing to beat it.

darum, darum *adv* - **1.** [räumlich] round it - **2.** [um diese Sache] about it; **jn darum bitten, etw zu tun** to ask sb to do sthg; **darum geht es nicht** that's not the point; **es geht darum, dass...** the thing is that... - **3.** [deswegen] that's why; **ach darum!** so that's why!; **eben darum** for that very reason; **warum? darum!** *fam* why? because!

darunter, darunter *adv* - **1.** [räumlich] under it; **sie hob das Kissen und fand ihre Kette darunter** she lifted the cushion and found her necklace underneath - **2.** [unter dieser Sache]: **er leidet darunter** he suffers from it; **was verstehst du darunter?** what do you understand by that?; **darunter kann ich mir nichts vorstellen** that doesn't mean anything to me - **3.** [weniger]: **30 Meter oder etwas darunter** 30 metres or a little less - **4.** [in dieser Menge] among(st) them; **viele Besucher, darunter auch einige aus dem Ausland** many visitors, including some foreigners.

das ◇ *det* the; **das Rauchen** smoking. ◇ *pron* - **1.** [Demonstrativpronomen] that; **das da** that one there; **unser Haus? das haben wir verkauft** our house? we've sold it; **das regnet heute wieder wie verrückt** it's raining like mad again today - **2.** [Relativpronomen - Person] who, that; [- Sache] which, that.

da sein (*perf* **ist da gewesen**) *vi (unreg)* - **1.** [vorhanden sein, anwesend sein] to be there; **es ist keine Milch mehr da** there's no more milk, there's no milk left; **ich bin gleich wieder da** I'll be back in a second - **2.** [eingetreten sein - Situation] to arise; [- Augenblick] to arrive; **er überbot alles, was bisher da gewesen war** he surpassed everything which had gone before - **3.** [leben] to live - **4.** *fam* [wach sein] to be with it; **geistig voll da sein** to be all there.

da|sitzen *vi (unreg)* - **1.** [an einer Stelle] to sit (there) - **2.** *fam* [in einer Situation] to be left (there).

dasjenige ◇ *det* the; **dasjenige Kind, das hingefallen ist** the child who fell. ◇ *pron*: **dasjenige, was sie am liebsten tut** the thing she likes to do most; **dasjenige, das** the one which.

dass *konj* - **1.** [im Objektsatz] that; **ich weiß, dass du gern angelst** I know (that) you like fishing - **2.** [im Subjektsatz] the fact that; **du musst bedenken, dass er nicht mehr klein ist** you must remember (that) he's not young anymore - **3.** [im Attributsatz] that; **unter der Bedingung, dass...** on (the) condition that...; **es war eine Dummheit, dass er das gesagt hat** it was stupid of him to say that - **4.** [in festen Verbindungen]: **anstatt, dass er selbst kam** instead of coming himself; **ohne dass sie etwas gemerkt hat** without her noticing anything.

dasselbe ◇ *det* the same. ◇ *pron* the same one; **genau dasselbe hast du gestern gesagt** you said exactly the same thing yesterday.

da|stehen *vi (unreg)* - **1.** [an Stelle] to stand (there) - **2.** [in Situation] to find o.s.; **mit leeren Händen dastehen** to be left empty-handed; **gut** ODER **glänzend dastehen** to be in a good ODER splendid position.

Datei (*pl* **-en**) *die* EDV file.

Daten *Pl* - **1.** [Zeiten] ▷ **Datum** - **2.** [Informationen] data; **Daten verarbeitend** data-processing.

Datenauto|bahn *die* EDV information superhighway.

Datenbank (*pl* **-en**) *die* databank.

Daten|netz *das*: **das Datennetz** the Net; **im Datennetz** on the Net.

Datenschutz|gesetz *das* data protection law.

Datentypist, in (*mpl* **-en**, *fpl* **-nen**) *der, die* data inputter.

Daten|verarbeitung *die* data processing.

datieren *vt* to date.

Dativ (*pl* **-e**) *der* dative.

Datum (*pl* **Daten**) *das* date; **welches Datum haben wir heute?** what's today's date?

Dauer *die* length; **dieses Glück hatte keine Dauer** this happiness did not last; **auf (die) Dauer** in the long term; **seine Ehe war nicht von Dauer** his marriage was short-lived.

dauerhaft ◇ *adj* [Friede, Freundschaft] lasting; [Material] durable. ◇ *adv*: **das Problem dauerhaft lösen** to find a lasting solution to the problem.

Dauer|karte *die* season ticket.

Dauer|lauf *der* jog.

dauern *vi* to last; **es dauert zu lange** it's taking too long; **eine Weile wird es schon noch dauern, bis ich fertig bin** it will still be a while before I'm finished.

dauernd ◇ *adj* constant. ◇ *adv* constantly.

Dauer|welle *die* perm.

Dauer|zustand *der* permanent state.

Däumchen (*pl* -) *das*: **Däumchen drehen** *fam* to twiddle one's thumbs.

Daumen (*pl* -) *der* thumb; **am Daumen lutschen** to suck one's thumb; **jm die Daumen drücken** ODER **halten** *fig* to keep one's fingers crossed for sb.

Daune (*pl* **-n**) *die*: **Daunen** down *(U)*.

Daunen|decke *die* eiderdown.

davon, davon *adv* - **1.** [räumlich] from it - **2.** [von diesem Gegenstand, aus dieser Menge] of it - **3.** [von dieser Sache] about it - **4.** [dadurch]: **er ist nicht davon betroffen** he is not affected by it; **sie ist davon krank geworden** it made her ill; **das kommt davon!** that's what happens!

davon|kommen (*perf* **ist davongekommen**) *vi (unreg)* to escape.

davon|laufen (*perf* **ist davongelaufen**) *vi (unreg)* to run away; **jm davonlaufen** [Ehepartner, Hausmädchen] to walk out on sb; [Verfolger] to shake sb off.

davor, davor *adv* - **1.** [räumlich] in front of it - **2.** [zeitlich] beforehand; **kurz davor sein, etw zu tun** to be on the point of doing sthg - **3.** [vor dieser Sache]: **jn davor warnen** to warn sb of it; **ich habe Angst davor** I'm scared of it.

dazu, dazu *adv* - **1.** [außerdem] in addition, into the bargain; **es schneit und es ist noch kalt dazu** it's snowing, and it's cold too - **2.** [zu dieser Sache]: **er hat nicht die Zeit dazu** he hasn't got time for it; **ich habe keine Lust dazu** I don't feel like it; **ich bin nicht dazu gekommen** I didn't get round to it.

dazu|geben *vt (unreg)* to add.

dazu|gehören *vi* - **1.** [zu etwas gehören] to belong; **gehört der Drucker dazu?** is the printer included? - **2.** [nötig sein]: **es gehört Mut dazu, das zu tun** it takes courage to do that.

dazu|kommen (*perf* **ist dazugekommen**) *vi (unreg)* - **1.** [ankommen] to arrive - **2.** [hinzukommen]: **sie ist neu dazugekommen** she's a recent arrival; **kommt noch etwas dazu?** would you like anything else?

dazu|tun *vt (unreg)* to add.

dazwischen *adv* - **1.** [örtlich, zeitlich] in between - **2.** [dabei] among them.

dazwischen|kommen (*perf* **ist dazwischengekommen**) *vi (unreg)* - **1.** [dazwischengeraten]: **er kam mit dem Finger dazwischen** he got his finger caught in it - **2.** [ungeplant passieren]: **mir ist etw dazwischengekommen** sthg has cropped up.

dazwischen|rufen *(unreg)* ◇ *vt*: **etw dazwischenrufen** to interrupt by shouting sthg. ◇ *vi* to interrupt by shouting.

DB (*abk für* **Deutsche Bahn**) *German railway company*.

DDR [de:de:'ɛr] (*abk für* **Deutsche Demokratische Republik**) *die* GDR.

Dealer, in ['di:lɐ, rɪn] (*mpl* -, *fpl* **-nen**) *der, die fam* pusher.

Debatte (*pl* **-n**) *die* debate; **zur Debatte stehen** to be on the agenda.

debattieren ◇ *vt* to debate. ◇ *vi*: **über etw** *(A)* **debattieren** to debate sthg.

Deck (*pl* **-s**) *das* deck; **unter Deck gehen** to go below. ◆ **an Deck** *adv* on deck.

Deck|blatt *das* title page.

Decke (*pl* **-n**) *die* - **1.** [Tischdecke] tablecloth - **2.** [zum Zudecken - Wolldecke] blanket; [- Steppdecke] quilt, duvet - **3.** [Zimmerdecke] ceiling; **(mit jm) unter einer Decke stecken** to be in cahoots (with sb).

Deckel (*pl* -) *der* - **1.** [von Gefäßen] lid - **2.** [von Büchern] cover.

decken ◇ *vt* - **1.** [bedecken - Haus] to roof; **das Dach decken** [- mit Ziegeln] to tile the roof; [- mit Stroh] to thatch the roof - **2.** [Tisch] to lay, to set - **3.** [legen]: **die Hand über die Augen decken** to cover one's eyes with one's hand - **4.** [schützen - Kind, Körperteil, Rückzug] to cover; [- Komplizen] to cover up for - **5.** SPORT to mark - **6.** [Bedarf] to meet - **7.** WIRTSCH [Zoologie] to cover. ◇ *vi* - **1.** [den Tisch decken] to lay ODER set the table - **2.** [Farbe] to cover. ◆ **sich decken** *ref* [Dreiecke] to be congruent; [Meinungen] to coincide; [Aussagen] to tally.

Deck|name *der* assumed name.

Deckung (*pl* **-en**) *die* - **1.** [Schutz] cover; **in Deckung gehen** to take cover - **2.** SPORT [beim Boxen] guard; [Manndeckung] marking; [Verteidigung] defence - **3.** [Befriedigung - von Bedarf] covering; **zur Deckung der Nachfrage** in order to meet demand - **4.** [Versicherungsschutz, von Scheck] cover - **5.** MATH congruence.

deckungsgleich *adj* [Dreiecke] congruent; [Ansichten, Theorien] matching.

Decoder [de'ko:dɐ] (*pl* -) *der* ELEKTR decoder.

decodieren = **dekodieren**.

defekt *adj* faulty, defective.

Defekt (*pl* **-e**) *der* fault, defect.

defensiv [defen'zi:f] ◇ *adj* defensive; [Fahrweise] safe, careful. ◇ *adv* defensively; [fahren] safely, carefully.

definieren *vt* to define. ◆ **sich definieren** *ref* to be defined.

Definition (*pl* **-en**) *die* definition.

definitiv ◇ *adj* final. ◇ *adv*: **sich definitiv entscheiden** to make a final decision; **kannst du mir definitiv sagen, ob du kommst?** can you let me know for sure whether you're coming?

Defizit (*pl* **-e**) *das* - **1.** [Fehlbetrag] deficit - **2.** [Fehlen] shortage.

deformieren *vt* to deform.

deftig *adj* - **1.** [nahrhaft] substantial, hearty - **2.** [derb] coarse.

Degen (*pl* -) *der* rapier.

dehnbar *adj* [Stoff, Gummi, Begriff] elastic; [Metall] ductile.

dehnen *vt* - **1.** [Substanz, Glieder] to stretch - **2.** [Laut] to draw out. ◆ **sich dehnen** *ref* - **1.** [gen] to stretch - **2.** [Gespräch, Warten] to drag on.

Deich (*pl* **-e**) *der* dyke.

Deichsel ['daiksl̩] (*pl* **-n**) *die* shafts *Pl*.

dein, e *det* your.

deine, r, s ODER **deins** *pron* yours.

deiner *pron (Genitiv von du)* of you; **ich erinnere mich deiner** I remember you.

deinerseits *adv* - **1.** [du selbst] for your part - **2.** [von dir] on your part.

deinesgleichen *pron* people like you; **du und deinesgleichen** you and your like.

deinetwegen *adv* - **1.** [dir zuliebe] for your sake - **2.** [wegen dir] because of you.

deinetwillen ◆ **um deinetwillen** *adv* for your sake.

dekadent *adj* decadent.

Deklination (*pl* **-en**) *die* declension.

deklinieren *vt* to decline.

dekodieren, decodieren [deko'di:rən] *vt* to decode.

Dekolletee (*pl* -s), **Dekolletté** (*pl* -s) [dekɔl'te:] *das* décolleté.

Dekor (*pl* -s ODER -e) <> *das* & *der* [Verzierung] pattern. <> *das* [im Theater, Film] décor.

Dekoration (*pl* -en) *die* - 1. [Ausschmückung, Auszeichnung] decoration; [von Schaufenster] window-dressing - 2. [Kulisse] set.

dekorativ *adj* decorative.

dekorieren *vt* [schmücken, auszeichnen] to decorate; [Schaufenster] to dress.

Delegation (*pl* -en) *die* delegation.

Delegierte (*pl* -n) *der, die* delegate.

Delfin (*pl* -e) *der* = **Delphin**.

delikat <> *adj* - 1. [Speise] delicious - 2. [Person, Angelegenheit, Lage] delicate. <> *adv* [behutsam] delicately.

Delikatesse (*pl* -n) *die* [Leckerbissen] delicacy.

Delikt (*pl* -e) *das* offence; **ein Delikt begehen** to commit an offence.

Delle (*pl* -n) *die* dent.

Delphin (*pl* -e), **Delfin** (*pl* -e) <> *der* [Säugetier] dolphin. <> *das (ohne Pl)* [Sportart] butterfly.

Delta (*pl* -s) *das* delta.

dem <> *det (Dativ Singular von der, das)*: **mit dem Kind** with the child. <> *pron (Dativ Singular)* - 1. [Demonstrativ von der, das - Person] to him; [- Sache] to that one; **mit dem** [- Person] with him; [- Sache] with that one - 2. [Relativpronomen von der, das - Person] to whom; [- Sache] to which; **mit dem** [- Person] with whom; [- Sache] with which.

demaskieren *vt* [entlarven] to unmask.

dementsprechend <> *adj* appropriate. <> *adv* accordingly.

demgegenüber *adv* on the other hand.

demgemäß *adv* accordingly.

demnach *adv* so.

demnächst [de:m'nɛ:st] *adv* soon.

Demokrat (*pl* -en) *der* democrat.

Demokratie (*pl* -n) *die* democracy.

Demokratin (*pl* -nen) *die* democrat.

demokratisch <> *adj* democratic. <> *adv* democratically.

demolieren *vt* to wreck.

Demonstrant, in (*mpl* -en, *fpl* -nen) *der, die* demonstrator.

Demonstration (*pl* -en) *die* demonstration.

demonstrativ *adj* - 1. [betont auffällig] pointed - 2. [anschaulich] revealing.

Demonstrativ|pronomen *das* GRAMM demonstrative pronoun.

demonstrieren <> *vi* to demonstrate; **gegen/für etw demonstrieren** to demonstrate against/in support of sthg. <> *vt* to demonstrate.

demoskopisch <> *adj* opinion poll *(vor Subst)*; **demoskopische Untersuchung** opinion poll. <> *adv* through opinion polls.

demütig *adj* - 1. [ergeben] humble - 2. [unterwürfig] submissive.

demütigen *vt* to humiliate. ◆ **sich demütigen** *ref* to humiliate o.s.

Demütigung (*pl* -en) *die* humiliation.

demzufolge *adv* consequently.

den <> *det* - 1. *(Akkusativ Singular von der)* the - 2. *(Dativ Plural von der, die, das)* to the; **mit den Kindern** with the children. <> *pron (Akkusativ Singular)* - 1. [Demonstrativ von der - Person] him; [- Sache] that one - 2. [Relativpronomen von der - Person] whom; [- Sache] which.

denen *pron (Dativ Plural)* - 1. [Demonstrativ von der, die, das] to them; **mit denen** with them - 2. [Relativpronomen von der, die, das - Personen] to whom; [- Sachen] to which; **mit denen** [- Personen] with whom; [- Sachen] with which.

Denglisch *das language made up of a mixture of German and English.*

Den Haag *nt* The Hague.

denkbar <> *adj* [vorstellbar] conceivable; **nicht denkbar** unthinkable. <> *adv* [äußerst] extremely; **die denkbar besten/schlechtesten Bedingungen** the best/worst conditions imaginable.

denken (*prät* **dachte**, *perf* **hat gedacht**) <> *vi* - 1. [gen] to think; **es gab mir zu denken** it made me think; **ich denke nicht** I don't think so; **denkst du, er schafft das?** do you think he'll manage?; **an jn/etw denken** to think of sb/sthg; **denk an den Kaffee!** don't forget the coffee!; **er denkt immer nur an sich** he always thinks about himself - 2. [planen]: **an etw** *(A)* **denken** to think about sthg; **ich denke nicht daran, das zu tun** I have no intention of doing it. <> *vt* - 1. [gen] to think; **wer hätte das gedacht!** who would have thought it! - 2. [sich vorstellen]: **das hätte ich mir denken können** I might have known; **das habe ich mir schon gedacht!** I thought as much!

denkfaul *adj* mentally lazy; **sei nicht so denkfaul** use your brain.

Denk|fehler *der* mistake in one's reasoning; **einen Denkfehler machen** to make a mistake in one's reasoning.

Denkmal (*pl* -mäler ODER -e) *das* [Monument] monument; **sich** *(D)* **ein Denkmal setzen** to ensure one's place in history.

denkmalgeschützt *adj* listed.

Denkmalspflege, Denkmalpflege *die* preservation of historical monuments.

Denkmalsschutz, Denkmalschutz *der* protection of historical monuments.

Denkweise *die* way of thinking.

denkwürdig *adj* memorable.

Denkzettel *der* lesson; **jm einen Denkzettel geben** ODER **verpassen** to teach sb a lesson.

denn ◇ *konj* [weil] because. ◇ *adv* - **1.** [verstärkend] then; **was hast du denn?** so what's wrong?; **warum denn nicht?** why not?; **was ist denn eigentlich passiert?** so what **actually** happened? - **2.** [dann] then.

dennoch *adv* nevertheless.

Deo (*pl* **-s**) *das* deodorant.

Deodorant (*pl* **-s** ODER **-e**) *das* deodorant.

Deponie (*pl* **-n**) *die* dump.

deponieren *vt* to deposit.

Depp [dɛp] (*pl* **-en**) *der Österr, Schweiz & Süddt fam* twit.

Depression (*pl* **-en**) *die* depression; **an** ODER **unter Depressionen** *(D)* **leiden** to suffer from depression.

depressiv *adj* - **1.** MED depressive - **2.** [Situation, Stimmung] depressing.

der ◇ *det* - **1.** [Nominativ] the; **der Tod** death - **2.** [Genitiv] of the; **der Hut der Frau** the woman's hat; **der Duft der Rosen** the fragrance of the roses - **3.** [Dativ] the. ◇ *pron* - **1.** [Demonstrativpronomen - Person] he; **der war es** it was him; **der hat es getan** he did it; **unser Sohn? der geht schon längst in die Schule** our son? he's been at school for a long time - **2.** [Demonstrativpronomen - Sache] that one; **der Wein? der war fantastisch** the wine? it was great; **der und der** so-and-so - **3.** [Relativpronomen - Person] who, that; [- Sache] which, that; **die Frau, der ich das Buch gab** the woman I gave the book to, the woman to whom I gave the book.

derart *adv* so; **es hat lange nicht mehr derart geregnet** it's a long time since it rained so much; **ein derart teures Auto kann ich mir nicht leisten** I can't afford such an expensive car. ◆ **derart, dass** *konj* so that.

derartig *adj* such; **eine derartige Frechheit** such (a) cheek.

derb ◇ *adj* - **1.** [kräftig - Stoß, Schlag] hefty; [- Leder] tough - **2.** [grob] coarse, crude. ◇ *adv* - **1.** [fest] roughly - **2.** [grob] crudely.

deren *det* - **1.** [Genitiv Singular von die - Person] her; [- Sache] its - **2.** [Genitiv Plural von der, die, das] their - **3.** [Relativpronomen - Person] whose; [- Sache] of which.

derentwegen ◇ *adv* - **1.** [ihr zuliebe] for her sake; [ihnen zuliebe] for their sake - **2.** [wegen ihr] because of her; [wegen ihnen] because of them. ◇ *pron* - **1.** [der, denen zuliebe - Person] for whose sake; [- Sache] for the sake of which - **2.** [wegen der, denen - Person] because of whom; [- Sache] because of which.

dergleichen *pron* that sort of thing.

derjenige ◇ *det*: **derjenige Mensch, der** th[e] person who. ◇ *pron*: **derjenige, der das ge[...]tan hat** whoever did this; **von allen Posten er[...]fordert derjenige des Vorsitzenden besonde[rs] viel Einsatz** of all the jobs, the chairman's i[s] the one which requires the most effort; **vo[n] allen Teilnehmern erhält derjenige den Preis der** the prize goes to the contestant who.

dermaßen ◆ **dermaßen, dass** *konj* s[o] that.

derselbe ◇ *det* the same. ◇ *pron* th[e] same one.

derzeit *adv* at the moment, at present.

derzeitig *adj* current.

des *det (Genitiv Singular von der, das)* of the; **der Schwanz des Hundes** the dog's tail.

desertieren (*perf* **ist desertiert**) *vi* to desert.

desgleichen *adv* likewise.

deshalb *adv* therefore. ◆ **deshalb, wei[l]** *konj* because.

Desinfektionsmittel *das* disinfectant.

desinfizieren *vt* to disinfect.

Desktop-Publishing ['dɛsktɔppʌbliʃiŋ] *das (ohne pl)* EDV desktop publishing.

dessen *pron* - **1.** [Genitiv Singular von der, das Person] his; [- Sache] its - **2.** [Relativpronomen vo[n] der, das - Person] whose; [- Sache] of which.

Dessert [dɛ'seːɐ̯] (*pl* **-s**) *das* dessert; **zum Dessert** for dessert.

destillieren *vt* to distil.

desto *konj*: **je eher, desto besser!** the sooner the better!

deswegen *adv* therefore; **er ist krank und kann deswegen nicht kommen** he's ill, which is why he can't come; **er ist gerade deswegen nicht gekommen** that's precisely the reason he didn't come; **ach, deswegen!** oh, that's why! ODER the reason!; **deswegen, weil** because.

Detail [de'tai] (*pl* **-s**) *das* detail. ◆ **im Detail** *adv* [detailliert] in detail.

detailliert ◇ *adj* detailed. ◇ *adv* in detail.

Detektiv, in (*mpl* **-e**, *fpl* **-nen**) *der, die* detective.

deuten ◇ *vt* [auslegen] to interpret; [Sterne] to read. ◇ *vi* - **1.** [zeigen]: **auf jn/etw deuten** to point at sb/sthg - **2.** [schließen lassen]: **auf etw** *(A)* **deuten** to point to sthg, to indicate sthg.

deutlich ◇ *adj* - **1.** [klar erkennbar, leicht verständlich] clear; **jm etw deutlich machen** to make sthg clear to sb - **2.** [rücksichtslos offen] blunt; **deutlich werden** to speak one's mind. ◇ *adv* - **1.** [klar, verständlich] clearly - **2.** [rücksichtslos offen] bluntly.

Deutlichkeit *die* - **1.** [Klarheit] clarity - **2.** [Offenheit] bluntness. ◆ **mit aller Deutlichkeit** *adv* [nachdrücklich] quite clearly.

deutsch <> *adj* German. <> *adv* [in deutscher Sprache] in German; *siehe auch* **englisch**.

Deutsch *das* German.

Deutsche (*pl* **-n**) <> *der, die* [Person] German; **die Deutschen** the Germans. <> *das* - **1.** [deutsche Sprache] German - **2.** [deutsche Wesensart]: **das ist das typisch Deutsche an ihm** that is what is typically German about him; *siehe auch* **Englische**.

Deutsche Bahn *die (ohne pl) German railway company*.

Deutsche Bundesbahn *die (ohne pl)* = **Deutsche Bahn**.

Deutsche Bundesbank *die* Bundesbank.

Deutsche Bundespost *die (ohne pl)* = **Deutsche Post**.

Deutsche Bundestag *der (ohne pl)* Bundestag, *lower house of the German Parliament*.

Deutsche Demokratische Republik *die* German Democratic Republic.

Deutsche Gewerkschaftsbund *der* German Trade Union Federation.

Deutsche Mark *die (pl -)* German mark, Deutschmark.

Deutsche Post *die German postal service*.

Deutsche Reich *das* German Reich.

Deutschland *nt* Germany.

Deutschlandlied *das German national anthem*.

deutschsprachig [ˈdɔytʃʃpraːxɪç] *adj* - **1.** [Bevölkerung] German-speaking - **2.** [Unterricht]: **deutschsprachigen Unterricht erteilen** to teach in German.

Deutschunterricht *der (ohne pl)* German lessons *Pl*; **Deutschunterricht geben** to teach German.

Devise [deˈviːzə] (*pl* **-n**) *die* motto. ◆ **Devisen** *Pl* foreign currency *(U)*.

Devisen|kurs *der* exchange rate.

Dezember *der* December; *siehe auch* **September**.

dezent <> *adj* - **1.** [taktvoll] discreet - **2.** [unaufdringlich] tasteful. <> *adv* - **1.** [taktvoll] discreetly - **2.** [unaufdringlich] tastefully.

dezimal *adj* decimal.

Dezimal|system *das* decimal system.

Dezimal|zahl *die* decimal.

DGB [deːgeːˈbeː] (*abk für* **Deutscher Gewerkschaftsbund**) *der Federation of German Trade Unions*.

dgl. *abk für* **dergleichen**.

d. h. (*abk für* **das heißt**) i.e.

Dia (*pl* **-s**) *das* slide.

Diabetes *der* diabetes *(U)*.

Diabetiker, in (*mpl* -, *pl* **-nen**) *der, die* diabetic.

Diagnose (*pl* **-n**) *die fig* & MED diagnosis; **die Diagnose auf etw *(A)* stellen** to diagnose sthg.

diagonal <> *adj* diagonal. <> *adv*: **etw diagonal lesen** to skim-read sthg.

Diagonale (*pl* **-n**) *die* diagonal; **eine Diagonale zeichnen** to draw a diagonal line.

Diakon (*pl* **-e** *ODER* **-en**) *der* - **1.** [evangelisch] Church welfare worker - **2.** [katholisch] deacon.

Diakonisse (*pl* **-n**) *die* - **1.** [evangelisch] community nurse *(working for the Church)* - **2.** [katholisch] deaconess.

Dialekt (*pl* **-e**) *der* dialect.

Dialog (*pl* **-e**) *der* dialogue.

Diamant (*pl* **-en**) *der* diamond.

Dia|projektor *der* slide projector.

Diät (*pl* **-en**) *die* diet; **Diät halten** to be on a diet; **eine Diät machen** to go on a diet; **Diät kochen** to cook dietary meals; **(nach einer) Diät leben** to follow a diet.

Diäten *Pl* [in der Politik] allowance *(sg)*.

dich *pron (Akkusativ von du)* - **1.** [Personalpronomen] you - **2.** [Reflexivpronomen] yourself; **hast du dich umgezogen?** have you changed?; **beeil dich!** hurry up!

dicht <> *adj* - **1.** [gegen Luft] airtight; [gegen Wasser] watertight; [Schuhe, Stoff] waterproof; **nicht dicht sein** [Dach] to be leaking; [Schuh] to be letting water in; **nicht** *ODER* **nicht mehr ganz dicht sein** *fam fig* & *abw* to be funny in the head - **2.** [Wald, Nebel] dense - **3.** [Haar, Gefieder] thick; [Verkehr] heavy. <> *adv* - **1.** [undurchlässig]: **dicht schließen** to close tight - **2.** [gedrängt] tightly; [bevölkert] densely; **er ist dicht behaart** he is very hairy - **3.** [ganz nahe]: **dicht dahinter/daneben** right behind/next to it.

Dichte *die* - **1.** [Undurchlässigkeit] impermeability - **2.** [von Wald, Nebel] denseness - **3.** [von Bevölkerung & PHYS] density; [von Verkehr] heaviness.

dichten <> *vt* - **1.** [in Verse fassen] to write - **2.** [gegen Wasser] to make watertight; [gegen Luft] to make airtight; [Fugen] to seal; [Leck] to stop. <> *vi* - **1.** [dicht machen] to seal - **2.** [Verse schreiben] to write (poetry).

Dichter, in (*mpl* -, *fpl* **-nen**) *der, die* poet; [von Dramen] writer.

dichterisch <> *adj* poetic. <> *adv* poetically.

Dichtung (*pl* **-en**) *die* - **1.** [Kunstwerk] poem - **2.** [Literatur] literature - **3.** [für Wasserhahn] washer; [im Maschinenbau] gasket.

dick <> *adj* - **1.** [gen] thick; [Person, Bauch] fat - **2.** [geschwollen] swollen - **3.** *fam* [groß, bedeutend - Auto, Gehalt, Fehler] whacking great; **ein dickes Lob** a big pat on the back; **sie sind dicke Freunde** they're as thick as thieves. <> *adv* - **1.** [stark] thickly - **2.** *fam* [sehr] really; **mit jm dick befreundet sein** to be as thick as thieves with sb; **jn/etw dick(e) haben** *fam* to have had one's fill of sb/sthg; **mit jm durch dick und dünn gehen** to go through thick and thin with sb.

Dicke (*pl* **-n**) ◇ *die* [gen] thickness; [von Person, Bauch] fatness; **die Wand hat eine Dicke von 20 cm** the wall is 20 cm thick. ◇ *der, die* [Person] fatty.

dickflüssig *adj* thick.

Dickicht (*pl* **-e**) *das* thicket.

Dick|kopf *der* - **1.** [Person] pig-headed person - **2.** [Haltung]: **einen Dickkopf haben** to be pig-headed.

dickköpfig *adj* pig-headed.

Dickmilch *die* sour milk.

die ◇ *det* the; **sich** *(D)* **die Hände waschen** to wash one's hands; **die Natur** nature. ◇ *pron* - **1.** [Demonstrativpronomen - Person] she, they *Pl*; **die war es** it was her; **die hat es getan** she did it; **meine Tochter? die geht schon längst in die Schule** my daughter? she's been at school for a long time - **2.** [Demonstrativpronomen - Sache] that one, those ones *Pl*; **meine Lehre? die habe ich abgebrochen** my training? I've given it up - **3.** [Relativpronomen - Person] who, that; [- Sache] which, that.

Dieb (*pl* **-e**) *der* thief.

Diebin (*pl* **-nen**) *die* thief.

diebisch ◇ *adj* - **1.** [schadenfroh] gloating - **2.** [stehlend] thieving. ◇ *adv*: **sich diebisch freuen** to gloat.

Diebstahl (*pl* **-stähle**) *der* theft.

diejenige ◇ *det*: **diejenige Frau, die** the woman who. ◇ *pron*: **unter allen Bewerbungen wurde diejenige ausgewählt, die am originellsten war** the application that was chosen was the most original one.

Diele (*pl* **-n**) *die* - **1.** [Flur] hall - **2.** [Brett] floorboard.

dienen *vi* - **1.** [nützen]: **einer Sache** *(D)* **dienen** to help with sthg; **jm dienen** to be of use to sb; **als etw dienen** to serve as sthg; **der Teppich dient nur zur Zierde** the carpet is only for decoration - **2.** [behilflich sein] to be of help - **3.** [für etw wirken]: **jm/einer Sache dienen** to serve sb/sthg - **4.** [Subj: Butler]: **jm dienen** to serve sb - **5.** [Soldat sein] to serve.

Diener, in (*mpl* **-**, *fpl* **-nen**) *der, die eigtl & fig* servant.

Dienst (*pl* **-e**) *der* - **1.** [gen] service; **der öffentliche Dienst** the civil service; **jm seine Dienste anbieten** to offer sb one's services; **jm einen (guten) Dienst erweisen** to serve sb well - **2.** [Arbeit, Pflicht] work; [von Arzt, Soldat] duty; **zum Dienst gehen** to go to work; [Arzt, Soldat] to go on duty; **Dienst haben** to be working; [Arzt, Soldat] to be on duty; **Dienst habend** on duty; **Dienst nach Vorschrift** work-to-rule - **3.** [Arbeitsverhältnis] post.

Dienstag (*pl* **-e**) *der* Tuesday; *siehe auch* **Samstag**.

dienstags *adv* on Tuesdays; *siehe auch* **samstags**.

Dienst|geheimnis *das* official secret.

Dienst|grad *der* rank.

diensthabend *adj* = **Dienst habend**.

Dienst|leistung *die* service.

dienstlich ◇ *adj* - **1.** *amt* [den Dienst betreffend] business *(vor Subst)*; [Befehl] official - **2.** [unpersönlich] impersonal. ◇ *adv amt* [verreisen] on business.

Dienst|reise *die* business trip; **auf Dienstreise sein** [geschäftlich] to be away on business; [Politiker] to be away on official business.

Dienst|stelle *die*: **die oberste Dienststelle** the highest authority.

Dienst|wagen *der* company car.

Dienst|weg *der*: **den Dienstweg einhalten** to go through the proper channels.

Dienst|zeit *die* - **1.** [Dienststunden] working hours *Pl* - **2.** [Soldatenzeit] term of service.

dies *pron* this, these *Pl*; **dies und das** ODER **jenes** *fig* this and that.

diesbezüglich ◇ *adj* related (to this). ◇ *adv* regarding this (matter).

diese, r, s ODER **dies** ◇ *det* this, these *Pl* [jene] that, those *Pl*; **am 9. dieses Monats** on the 9th of this month. ◇ *pron* this one, these ones *Pl*; [jene] that one, those ones *Pl*.

Diesel (*pl* **-**) *der* diesel.

dieselbe ◇ *det* the same. ◇ *pron* the same one.

diesig *adj* misty.

diesjährig *adj*: **die diesjährige Ernte** this year's harvest.

diesmal *adv* this time.

diesseits *präp* [auf dieser Seite]: **diesseits eines Ortes** *(G)* on this side of a place.

Dietrich (*pl* **-e**) *der* skeleton key.

Differenz (*pl* **-en**) *die* - **1.** [gen] difference - **2.** [Fehlbetrag] deficit. ◆ **Differenzen** *Pl* [Meinungsverschiedenheiten] differences.

differenzieren ◇ *vt* to differentiate between. ◇ *vi* to make distinctions.

digital *adj* digital.

Digital|anzeige *die* digital display.

Digitalkamera (*pl* **-s**) *die* digital camera.

Diktat (*pl* **-e**) *das* - **1.** [Nachschrift] dictation - **2.** *geh* [Zwang] dictate.

Diktator (*pl* **-toren**) *der* dictator.

Diktatorin (*pl* **-nen**) *die* dictator.

Diktatur (*pl* **-en**) *die abw* dictatorship.

diktieren *vt* to dictate; **jm etw diktieren** to dictate sthg to sb.

Dill *der* dill.

Dimension (*pl* **-en**) *die eigtl & fig* dimension; **ungeahnte Dimensionen annehmen** to take on unprecedented proportions.

DIN [diːn] (*abk für* **Deutsche Industrienorm**) *die* DIN.

Ding (*pl* **-e** ODER **-er**) *das* - **1.** (*pl Dinge*) [Gegenstand, Angelegenheit] thing; **vor allen Dingen** above all; **über den Dingen stehen** to be above it all; **den Dingen ihren Lauf lassen** to let things take their course; **es ist nicht mit rechten Dingen zugegangen** there was something odd about it; **wie die Dinge liegen** as things stand - **2.** (*pl Dinger*) *fam* [Sache] thing - **3.** (*pl Dinger*) [Mädchen]: **ein junges/dummes Ding** a young/stupid thing; **das is (ja) 'n Ding!** *fam* would you believe it!, there's a thing!; **ein Ding drehen** *fam* to do a job.

Dings *fam* <> *der, die* [Person] thingy, thingummy. <> *das* [Gegenstand, Ort] thingy, thingummy.

Dinosaurier (*pl* -) *der* dinosaur.

Diözese (*pl* **-n**) *die* diocese.

Diplom (*pl* **-e**) *das* - **1.** [akademischer Grad] degree *(in science or technology)* - **2.** [Urkunde] diploma.

Diplom|arbeit *die* dissertation *(submitted for a degree)*.

Diplomat (*pl* **-en**) *der* diplomat.

Diplomatie *die* diplomacy.

Diplomatin (*pl* **-nen**) *die* diplomat.

diplomatisch <> *adj* diplomatic. <> *adv* diplomatically.

Diplom|ingenieur, in *der, die* qualified engineer.

dir *pron (Dativ von du)* (to) you; **das gehört dir** it belongs to you, it's yours; **ich komme mit dir** I'm coming with you; **tun dir die Füße weh?** do your feet hurt?

direkt <> *adj* direct. <> *adv* - **1.** [sofort] straight; TV live - **2.** [nahe] right; **direkt neben** right next to - **3.** [unmittelbar]: **sie kaufen ihre Milch direkt beim Bauern** they buy their milk direct from the farmer - **4.** [unverblümt] directly.

Direktor (*pl* **-toren**) *der* [von Schule] headmaster *UK*, principal *US*; [von Museum] director; [von Strafanstalt] governor *UK*, warden *US*; [von Abteilung] manager.

Direktorin (*pl* **-nen**) *die* [von Schule] headmistress *UK*, principal *US*; [von Museum] director; [von Strafanstalt] governor *UK*, warden *US*; [von Abteilung] manager.

Direkt|übertragung *die* live broadcast.

Dirigent, in (*mpl* **-en**, *fpl* **-nen**) *der, die* conductor.

dirigieren <> *vt* - **1.** MUS to conduct - **2.** [Unternehmen] to manage, to run; [Verkehr] to direct. <> *vi* to conduct.

Disketten|lauf|werk *das* EDV disk drive.

Disko (*pl* **-s**) *die fam* disco.

Diskont|satz *der* WIRTSCH discount rate.

Diskothek (*pl* **-en**) *die* discotheque.

Diskretion *die* discretion; **in Bezug auf etw Diskretion wahren** to treat sthg in confidence.

diskriminieren *vt* - **1.** [benachteiligen] to discriminate against - **2.** [herabwürdigen] to disparage.

Diskussion (*pl* **-en**) *die* discussion.

Diskuswerfen *das* SPORT discus.

diskutieren <> *vi* to discuss; **über jn/etw diskutieren** to discuss sb/sthg. <> *vt* to discuss.

disqualifizieren *vt* to disqualify.

Dissertation (*pl* **-en**) *die* (doctoral) thesis.

Distanz (*pl* **-en**) *die* - **1.** [Entfernung] distance - **2.** [persönlicher Abstand] detachment; **etw aus der Distanz heraus beurteilen** to judge sthg from a distance; **jm gegenüber auf Distanz gehen/bleiben** to distance o.s./keep one's distance from sb.

distanziert <> *adj* detached. <> *adv*: **distanziert wirken** to seem distant.

Distel (*pl* **-n**) *die* thistle.

Disziplin (*pl* **-en**) *die* discipline.

disziplinarisch <> *adj* disciplinary. <> *adv*: **gegen jn disziplinarisch vorgehen** to take disciplinary action against sb.

diszipliniert <> *adj* disciplined. <> *adv* in a disciplined way.

diverse [di'vɛrzə] *adj Pl* various.

Dividende [divi'dɛndə] (*pl* **-n**) *die* dividend.

dividieren [divi'diːrən] *vt*: **etw (durch etw) dividieren** to divide sthg (by sthg).

Division [divi'zioːn] (*pl* **-en**) *die* MATH & MIL division.

Diwan (*pl* **-e**) *der* divan.

DM (*abk für* **Deutsche Mark**) DM.

D-Mark ['deːmark] (*pl* -) (*abk für* **Deutsche Mark**) *die* German mark, Deutschmark.

d-Moll *das* D minor.

DNA [deːɛn'ɛa] (*abk für* **desoxyribonucleic acid**) *die* = **DNA**.

DNS [deːɛn'ɛs] (*abk für* **Desoxyribonukleinsäure**) *die* = **DNA**.

doch <> *konj* [aber] yet, but. <> *adv* - **1.** [trotzdem] anyway; **er wollte erst nicht, aber dann hat er es doch gemacht** at first he didn't want to, but then he did it anyway; **willst du nicht? - doch** don't you want to? - yes, I do; **doch noch** after all - **2.** [verstärkend]: **setzen Sie sich doch!** do sit down!; **das kann doch nicht wahr sein!** I don't believe it!; **aber das konnte ich doch nicht wissen!** but how could I have known! ◆ **nicht doch** *interj* don't do that!

Docht (*pl* **-e**) *der* wick.

Dock (*pl* **-s**) *das* dock.

Dogge (*pl* **-n**) *die* mastiff.

Doktor (*pl* **-toren**) *der* - **1.** [Titel] doctorate; **seinen Doktor machen** to do one's doctorate - **2.** [Träger des Doktortitels, Arzt] doctor.

Doktorand, in (*mpl* **-en**, *fpl* **-nen**) *der, die* PhD student.
Doktor|arbeit *die* doctoral thesis.
Doktorin (*pl* **-nen**) *die* doctor.
Doktrin (*pl* **-en**) *die* doctrine.
Dokument (*pl* **-e**) *das* document.
Dokumentar|film *der* documentary.
Dokumentation (*pl* **-en**) *die* - **1.** [Informationsmaterial] documentation *(U)* - **2.** [Darstellung]: **eine Dokumentation über etw** *(A)* **machen** to document sthg.
Dolch (*pl* **-e**) *der* dagger.
Dollar (*pl* **-s** ODER **-**) *der* dollar.
dolmetschen *vt* & *vi* to interpret.
Dolmetscher, in (*mpl* **-**, *fpl* **-nen**) *der, die* interpreter.
Dolomiten *Pl* Dolomites.
Dom (*pl* **-e**) *der* cathedral.
dominant *adj* dominant.
Dominanz (*pl* **-en**) *die* dominance.
dominieren ◇ *vi* to predominate. ◇ *vt* to dominate.
Dominikaner, in (*mpl* **-**, *fpl* **-nen**) *der, die* GEOGR & RELIG Dominican.
Dominikanische Republik *die* Dominican Republic.
Donau *die*: **die Donau** the Danube.
Donner *der* thunder.
donnern (*perf* **hat/ist gedonnert**) ◇ *vi* - **1.** *(hat)* [beim Gewitter]: **es donnert** it is thundering - **2.** *(ist)* [sich bewegen] to thunder - **3.** *(hat) fam* [schlagen] to hammer - **4.** *(ist) fam* [prallen]: **gegen etw donnern** to slam into sthg. ◇ *vt (hat) fam* to hurl.
Donnerstag (*pl* **-e**) *der* Thursday; *siehe auch* **Samstag**.
donnerstags *adv* on Thursdays; *siehe auch* **samstags**.
Donnerwetter *das (ohne pl) fam* almighty row; **Donnerwetter!** my goodness!
doof *fam* ◇ *adj* stupid. ◇ *adv* stupidly.
dopen ['do:pn̩] *vt* [Pferd] to dope. ◆ **sich dopen** *ref* [Sportler] to take drugs.
Doping ['do:pɪŋ] (*pl* **-s**) *das* drug-taking.
Doppel (*pl* **-**) *das* - **1.** [Kopie] duplicate - **2.** SPORT doubles *(U)*.
Doppel|bett *das* double bed.
Doppel|decker (*pl* **-**) *der* - **1.** FLUG biplane - **2.** [Omnibus] double-decker (bus).
doppeldeutig *adj* ambiguous; **doppeldeutiger Witz** double entendre.
Doppel|gänger, in (*mpl* **-**, *fpl* **-nen**) *der, die* double.
Doppel|haus *das* pair of semi-detached houses.
Doppel|kinn *das* double chin.
Doppelklick (*pl* **-s**) *der* EDV double click.
Doppel|name *der* double-barrelled name.
Doppel|punkt *der* colon.
doppelseitig *adj* - **1.** [Lungenentzündun double - **2.** [zwei Seiten umfassend] two-page.
doppelt ◇ *adj* - **1.** [zweifach] double - **2.** [ge steigert] twice as much. ◇ *adv* twice; **doppe so viel** twice as much.
Doppel|zimmer *das* double room.
Dorf (*pl* **Dörfer**) *das* [Ort] village; **auf dem Do** in the country.
Dorf|bewohner, in *der, die* villager.
dörflich *adj* village *(vor Subst)*; [Gegend] ru al.
Dorn (*pl* **-en**) *der* [von Rose] thorn; [von Schna le] prong.
Dornröschen *das* Sleeping Beauty.
Dörrobst *das* dried fruit.
Dorsch (*pl* **-e**) *der* cod.
dort *adv* there; **dort drüben** over there; **dor wo wir Fußball spielen** where we play foo ball.
dorther *adv* from there.
dorthin *adv* there.
dortig *adj* local.
Dose (*pl* **-n**) *die* - **1.** [Behälter] box; [für Zucke bowl; [für Butter] dish - **2.** [Konservendose] ca tin *UK*; [Bierdose] can; **Erbsen aus der Dos** tinned *UK* ODER canned peas.
dösen *vi* to doze.
Dosen|milch *die* condensed ODER evaporate milk.
Dosen|öffner *der* can ODER tin *UK* opener.
dosieren *vt* to measure out.
Dosierung (*pl* **-en**) *die* dosage.
Dosis (*pl* **Dosen**) *die* dose.
Dotter (*pl* **-**) *das* & *der* yolk.
Double ['du:bl̩] (*pl* **-s**) *das* double.
down [daʊn] *adj fam*: **down sein** to be dow
down|loaden (*präs* **loadet down**, *prät* **lo dete down**, *perf* **hat downgeloadet**) *vt* EDV download.
Dozent, in (*mpl* **-en**, *fpl* **-nen**) *der, die* le turer *UK*, assistant professor *US*.
dpa [de:pe'ɑ:] (*abk für* **Deutsche Presseage tur**) *die* German Press Agency.
Dr. (*abk für* **Doktor**) Dr.
Drache (*pl* **-n**) *der* dragon.
Drachen (*pl* **-**) *der* - **1.** [Spielzeug] kite - **2.** *ab* [Frau] dragon.
Draht (*pl* **Drähte**) *der* wire; **auf Draht se** *fam* to be on the ball; **einen guten Draht zu j haben** to be well in with sb.
Drahtseil|bahn *die* cable railway.
Drahtzieher, in (*mpl* **-**, *fpl* **-nen**) *der, d* [Hintermann] person pulling the strings.
Drama (*pl* **Dramen**) *das* drama.
dramatisch *adj* dramatic.
dramatisieren *vt* [hochspielen] to play up, make a big thing of.

Dramaturg, in (*mpl* **-en**, *fpl* **-nen**) *der, die person who selects and adapts plays for the stage.*

dran *adv* - **1.** *fam* = **daran** - **2.** [an der Reihe]: **ich bin jetzt dran** it's my turn; **wer ist als Nächster dran?** who's next?, whose turn is it?; **dran sein** to be for it.

drang *prät* ▷ **dringen**.

Drängelei (*pl* **-en**) *die* - **1.** *abw* [durch Schieben] pushing (and shoving) - **2.** [durch Reden] pestering.

drängeln ◇ *vi* - **1.** [durch Schieben] to push - **2.** [durch Reden] to go on (and on). ◇ *vt* - **1.** [durch Schieben] to push - **2.** [durch Reden] to pester. ◆ **sich drängeln** *ref*: **sich nach vorn drängeln** to push one's way to the front.

drängen ◇ *vi* - **1.** [schieben] to push - **2.** [nicht warten]: **zum Aufbruch drängen** to insist on leaving; **zur Eile drängen** to urge haste; **auf etw** *(A)* **drängen** to push ODER press for sthg. ◇ *vt* - **1.** [schieben] to push - **2.** [antreiben] to urge.

dran|halten ◆ **sich dranhalten** *ref (unreg) fam* to get a move on.

dran|kommen (*perf* **ist drangekommen**) *vi (unreg)* - **1.** [an die Reihe kommen] to have one's turn; **ich bin als Letzter drangekommen** I was last - **2.** [heranreichen] to reach.

drastisch ◇ *adj* - **1.** [einschneidend] drastic - **2.** [sehr deutlich] graphic. ◇ *adv* - **1.** [stark] drastically - **2.** [sehr deutlich] graphically.

drauf *adv fam* = **darauf; es kommt drauf an** it depends; **etw drauf haben** [Fähigkeit] to be really good at sthg; **er hatte hundert Sachen drauf** AUTO he was doing a hundred; **gut drauf sein** to be in a good mood; **drauf und dran sein, etw zu tun** to be on the point of doing sthg.

Draufgänger, in (*mpl* **-**, *fpl* **-nen**) *der, die* daredevil.

drauf|gehen (*perf* **ist draufgegangen**) *vi (unreg) fam* - **1.** [umkommen] to buy it - **2.** [verbraucht werden] to be used up.

draußen *adv* outside. ◆ **nach draußen** *adv* outside. ◆ **von draußen** *adv* from outside.

Dreck *der fam* [Schmutz] muck, dirt; **Dreck machen** to make a mess; **das geht dich einen Dreck an** it's none of your damn business; **jn/etw in den Dreck ziehen** to drag sb/sthg through the mud.

Dreck|arbeit *die fam* - **1.** [schmutzige Arbeit] dirty work - **2.** [niedere Arbeit] menial jobs *Pl.*

dreckig ◇ *adj* - **1.** [schmutzig, unverschämt] dirty; **sich dreckig machen** to get dirty - **2.** *fam abw* [gemein]: **du dreckiges Schwein!** you filthy swine! ◇ *adv fam* - **1.** *abw* [unverschämt] dirtily - **2.** [schlecht]: **ihr geht es dreckig** she is in a bad way.

Dreck|spatz *der fam* mucky pup.

Dreh|buch *das* screenplay.

drehen ◇ *vt* - **1.** [im Kreis bewegen] to turn - **2.** [einstellen]: **das Radio laut/leise drehen** to turn the radio up/down - **3.** [formen - Seil] to twist; [- Zigarette, Pillen] to roll - **4.** TV to film, to shoot. ◇ *vi* - **1.** [wenden] to turn - **2.** [am Knopf, Schalter]: **an etw** *(D)* **drehen** to turn sthg; **am Radio drehen** to turn the knob on the radio. ◆ **sich drehen** *ref* [sich wenden] to turn; **mir dreht sich alles** *fam* my head is spinning; **sich um jn/etw drehen** to be about sb/sthg; **es dreht sich darum, dass...** the thing is...

Dreh|orgel *die* barrel organ.

Dreh|scheibe *die* [Knotenpunkt] hub.

Dreh|stuhl *der* swivel chair.

Dreh|tür *die* revolving door.

Drehung (*pl* **-en**) *die* turn.

Dreh|zahl *die* revs *Pl.*

drei *num* [Zahl] three; **für drei essen** to eat like a horse; *siehe auch* **sechs**.

Drei (*pl* **-en**) *die* - **1.** [Zahl] three - **2.** [Schulnote] ≃ C, *mark of 3 on a scale from 1 to 6; siehe auch* **Sechs**.

dreidimensional ◇ *adj* three-dimensional. ◇ *adv* three-dimensionally.

Dreieck (*pl* **-e**) *das* triangle.

dreieckig *adj* triangular.

Dreier (*pl* **-**) *der* - **1.** [Drei] three - **2.** [beim Lotto] three correct numbers *Pl* - **3.** *fam* [Sprungbrett] three-metre board.

dreierlei *adj (unver)* three different; **auf dreierlei Weise** in three different ways.

dreifach ◇ *adj* triple; **die dreifache Menge** three times as much; **in dreifacher Größe** three times as big; **in dreifacher Ausfertigung** in triplicate; **der dreifache Gewinner** the three times ODER triple winner. ◇ *adv* three times.

dreihundert *num* three hundred.

Dreikönigs|fest *das* Epiphany.

dreimal *adv* three times.

Drei|satz *der* rule of three.

dreißig *num* thirty; *siehe auch* **sechs**.

Dreißig *die* thirty; *siehe auch* **Sechs**.

Dreißigerjahre, dreißiger Jahre *Pl*: **die Dreißigerjahre** the thirties.

dreist ◇ *adj* impudent. ◇ *adv* impudently.

Dreistigkeit (*pl* **-en**) *die* [Wesen, Verhalten] impudence.

dreistöckig *adj* - **1.** [Haus] three-storeyed - **2.** [Torte] three-tiered.

dreitausend *num* three thousand.

dreiteilig *adj* three-part; [Kostüm, Anzug] three-piece.

drei viertel *num* three quarters; **drei viertel Liter** three-quarters of a litre; **drei viertel acht** a quarter to *UK* ODER of *US* eight.

Dreivierteltakt *der* three-four time.

dreizehn *num* thirteen; *siehe auch* **sechs**.

Dreizimmer|wohnung *die* three-roomed flat *UK* ODER apartment *US*.

dreschen (*präs* **drischt**, *prät* **drosch**, *perf* **hat gedroschen**) ◇ *vt* - **1.** [Getreide] to thresh - **2.** *fam* [prügeln] to thrash. ◇ *vi fam* [schlagen] to bang.

Dresden *nt* Dresden.

Dress (*pl* **-e**) *der* - **1.** SPORT kit - **2.** *fam* [Kleidung] outfit.

dressieren *vt* to train.

Dressing (*pl* **-s**) *das* dressing.

Dressur (*pl* **-en**) *die* - **1.** [Dressieren] training - **2.** [Pferdedressur] dressage.

drillen *vt* to drill.

drin *adv fam* - **1.** = **darin** - **2.** [möglich]: **drin sein** to be on the cards; **bei diesem Spiel ist noch alles drin** there is still everything to play for in this game - **3.** [gewöhnt]: **drin sein** to have got into the swing of things.

dringen (*prät* **drang**, *perf* **hat/ist gedrungen**) *vi* - **1.** *(ist)* [eindringen]: **durch** ODER **in etw** *(A)* **dringen** to penetrate sthg; **Wasser dringt durch die Decke** water is leaking through the ceiling; **Gas drang in den Raum** gas seeped into the room - **2.** *(hat)* [drängen]: **auf etw** *(A)* **dringen** to insist on sthg.

dringend ◇ *adj* urgent. ◇ *adv* urgently.

Dringlichkeit *die* urgency.

drinnen *adv* inside; **nach drinnen gehen** to go inside.

drischt *präs* ▷ **dreschen**.

dritt ◆ **zu dritt** *num*: **wir sind zu dritt** there are three of us; **wir sind zu dritt ins Kino gegangen** three of us went to the cinema.

dritte, **r**, **s** *adj* third; *siehe auch* **sechste**.

Dritte *der, die, das* third; [außenstehende Person] third party; *siehe auch* **Sechste**.

drittel *adj (unver)* third of a; *siehe auch* **sechstel**.

Drittel (*pl* -) *das* third; *siehe auch* **Sechstel**.

dritteln *vt* to divide into three.

drittens *adv* thirdly.

Dritte Reich *das*: **das Dritte Reich** the Third Reich.

Droge (*pl* **-n**) *die* drug.

drogenabhängig *adj*: **drogenabhängig sein** to be a drug addict.

Drogen|abhängige (*pl* **-n**) *der, die* drug addict.

Drogen|händler, **in** *der, die* drug dealer.

Drogerie (*pl* **-n**) *die* chemist's (shop) *(non-dispensing) UK*, drugstore *US*.

drohen *vi* to threaten; **drohen, etw zu tun** to threaten to do sthg; **jm (mit etw) drohen** to threaten sb (with sthg).

dröhnen *vi* - **1.** [hallen] to boom - **2.** *salopp* [berauschen] to give you a high.

Drohung (*pl* **-en**) *die* threat.

Dromedar (*pl* **-e**) *das* dromedary.

drosch *prät* ▷ **dreschen**.

Drossel (*pl* **-n**) *die* thrush.

drosseln *vt* [Geschwindigkeit, Leistung] to reduce; [Heizung] to turn down.

drüben *adv* [nebenan] over there.

drüber = **darüber**.

Druck (*pl* **-e**) *der* - **1.** [Kraft, Zwang] pressure; **Druck hinter etw** *(A)* **machen** *fam fig* to pu[t] pressure on regarding sthg; **Druck auf jn aus[-] üben, jn unter Druck setzen** to put pressure o[n] sb; **Druck machen** to put pressure on; **unte[r] Druck stehen** to be under pressure - **2.** [Dru[-] cken] printing - **3.** [Gravur] print.

Druck|buchstabe *der* printed letter; **i[n] Druckbuchstaben schreiben** to print.

Drückeberger, **in** (*mpl* -, *fpl* **-nen**) *der, di[e] abw* shirker.

druckempfindlich *adj* [Körperstelle] sensit[-] ive to pressure; **Pfirsiche sind druckempfind[-] lich** peaches bruise easily.

drucken *vt* to print.

drücken ◇ *vt* - **1.** [pressen] to press; **jn/etw an sich** *(A)* **drücken** to hold sb/sthg to on[e] - **2.** *fam* [umarmen] to hug, to squeeze - **3.** [mir[-] dern] to lower. ◇ *vi* - **1.** [pressen]: **auf etw** *(A)* **drücken** to press sthg; **es drückt auf die Lau[-] ne** it gets you down - **2.** [Schuhe] to pinc[h] - **3.** *salopp* [fixen] to shoot up. ◆ **sich drü[-] cken** *ref* - **1.** [sich pressen]: **sich an etw** *(A)* **drü[-] cken** to flatten o.s. against sthg - **2.** [sich ent[-] ziehen]: **sich vor etw** *(D)* **drücken** *abw* to ge[t] out of sthg.

drückend *adj* - **1.** [Probleme, Sorgen] seriou[s]; [Verantwortung, Schulden] heavy; [Armut] grind[-] ing - **2.** [Hitze] oppressive.

Drucker (*pl* -) *der* printer.

Drücker (*pl* -) *der* - **1.** [Türdrücker] hand[le] - **2.** [Hausierer] door-to-door salesman; **am Drü[-] cker sitzen** *fam* to call the shots.

Druckerei (*pl* **-en**) *die* printing works, print[-] er's.

Druck|fehler *der* misprint.

Druck|knopf *der* press stud *UK*, snap fasten[-] er *US*.

Druck|sache *die* printed matter *(U)*.

Druck|schrift *die* block capitals *Pl*.

drum *fam* = **darum**.

drunter *adv fam* = **darunter**; **alles** ODER **e[s] geht drunter und drüber** everything is goin[g] haywire.

Drüse (*pl* **-n**) *die* gland.

Dschungel (*pl* -) *der* jungle.

dt. (*abk für* **deutsch**) Ger.

DTP (*abk für* **Desktop-Publishing**) *das (ohn[e] pl)* EDV DTP.

du *pron* du; **ach, du bists!** oh, it's you!; **du sagen** to use the du form of address; **mit jm per du sein** ≃ to be on first name terms with sb.

Duale System *das privately run waste disposal and recycling system.*

Dübel (*pl* -) *der* Rawlplug®.

Dụblin ['dablin] *nt* Dublin.

dụcken ◆ **sich ducken** *ref* to duck.

dudeln *fam abw* ◇ *vi* [Plattenspieler, Radio] to drone; [auf Instrument] to tootle. ◇ *vt* [auf Blasinstrument] to tootle on.

Dudel|sack *der* bagpipes *Pl.*

Duẹll [du'ɛl] (*pl* **-e**) *das* duel.

Duẹtt [du'ɛt] (*pl* **-e**) *das* duet.

Dụft (*pl* **Dụ̈fte**) *der* scent.

dụften *vi* to smell nice; **nach etw duften** to smell of sthg.

dụlden *vt geh* to tolerate.

dụmm (*kompar* **dụ̈mmer**, *superl* **dụ̈mmste**) ◇ *adj* - **1.** [gen] stupid; **dummes Zeug** rubbish, nonsense; **es ist** ODER **wird mir zu dumm** I've had enough of it - **2.** [unangenehm - Fehler, Zufall] annoying. ◇ *adv* stupidly.

Dụmme (*pl* **-n**) *der, die*: **der Dumme sein** to be the one who loses out.

dụmmerweise *adv* - **1.** [ärgerlicherweise] unfortunately - **2.** [aus Dummheit] stupidly.

Dụmmheit (*pl* **-en**) *die* - **1.** [fehlende Klugheit] stupidity - **2.** [Handlung] stupid thing; **mach keine Dummheiten** don't do anything stupid.

Dụmm|kopf *der* idiot.

dụ̈mmlich ◇ *adj* stupid. ◇ *adv* stupidly.

dụmpf ◇ *adj* - **1.** [Klang] dull, muffled - **2.** [Schmerz] dull; [Befürchtung, Verdacht] vague - **3.** [stumpfsinnig] apathetic. ◇ *adv* - **1.** [dunkel] dully - **2.** [stumpfsinnig] apathetically.

Düne (*pl* **-n**) *die* dune.

düngen ◇ *vt* to fertilize. ◇ *vi* - **1.** [Dung] to act as a fertilizer - **2.** [Person] to fertilize one's land/garden/*etc.*

Dünger (*pl* -) *der* fertilizer.

dụnkel ◇ *adj* - **1.** [gen] dark; **im Dunkeln tappen** *fig* to grope around in the dark - **2.** [Ton, Stimme] deep - **3.** [vage] vague; **jn über etw (A) im Dunkeln lassen** to keep sb in the dark about sthg - **4.** [dubios] shady. ◇ *adv* - **1.** [streichen, färben] in dark colours/a dark colour - **2.** [klingen] deep - **3.** [unklar] vaguely.

dụnkelblau *adj* & *adv* dark blue.

dụnkelblond ◇ *adj* light brown; [Person] with light brown hair. ◇ *adv* light brown.

dụnkelhaarig *adj* dark-haired.

Dụnkelheit *die* darkness.

Dụnkel|ziffer *die* number of unreported incidents.

dụ̈nn ◇ *adj* - **1.** [gen] thin; **sich dünn machen** [wenig Platz brauchen] to squeeze up - **2.** [Getränk, Stimme] weak - **3.** [Haare, Bewuchs] sparse. ◇ *adv* [bevölkert, bewachsen] sparsely; [auftragen] thinly.

dụ̈nnflüssig *adj* thin.

Dụnst (*pl* **Dụ̈nste**) *der* - **1.** [Nebel] haze, mist - **2.** [von Zigaretten] smoke; [in der Küche] steam; **keinen (blassen) Dunst von etw haben** *fam* not to have the foggiest (idea) about sthg.

dụ̈nsten *vt* to steam.

dụnstig *adj* [neblig] hazy, misty.

Duo (*pl* **-s**) *das* duo.

Dur *das* major; **eine Sonate in Dur** a sonata in a major key.

dụrch ◇ *präp* (+ *A*) - **1.** [räumlich, zeitlich] through; **darf ich mal bitte durch?** excuse me, please!; **durch die Schweiz reisen** to travel across Switzerland; **die ganze Nacht durch** throughout the night - **2.** [mittels] by; **durch eigene Schuld** through one's own fault; **durch Ihre Hilfe** with your help; **das Haus wurde durch ein Erdbeben zerstört** the house was destroyed by an earthquake - **3.** MATH divided by; **sechs durch drei** six divided by three. ◇ *adv* - **1.** *fam* [später als]: **es ist schon zwölf durch** it's gone ODER past twelve - **2.** *fam* [durchgebraten] well done - **3.** *fam* [beendet]: **bis morgen muss ich mit dem Buch durch sein** I have to finish the book by tomorrow; **durch und durch** through and through; **durch und durch nass** wet through.

dụrch|arbeiten ◇ *vt* to work through. ◇ *vi* to work without a break. ◆ **sich durcharbeiten** *ref*: **sich durch etw durcharbeiten** [Menschenmenge, Text] to work one's way through sthg.

dụrch|atmen *vi* to breathe deeply.

durchaus, dụrchaus *adv* - **1.** [gut, ohne weiteres] perfectly; **es kann durchaus sein** it is perfectly possible - **2.** [unbedingt] absolutely - **3.** [absolut, überhaupt]: **durchaus nicht** definitely not, not at all.

dụrch|blättern *vt* to flick through.

Dụrch|blick *der fam* overview; **den Durchblick verlieren** to lose track of things.

durchblịcken *vt* to see through.

Durchblutung *die* circulation.

dụrch|bohren[1] ◇ *vt* [Brett] to drill through; [Loch] to drill. ◇ *vi* to drill through.

durchbohren[2] *vt* [Subj: Kugel] to go through; **jn mit Blicken durchbohren** to fix sb with a piercing gaze.

dụrch|braten *vt (unreg)* to cook well ODER through.

dụrch|brechen[1] (*perf* **hat/ist dụrchgebrochen**) *(unreg)* ◇ *vt (hat)* - **1.** [zerbrechen] to break in two - **2.** [einreißen - Wand] to knock in. ◇ *vi (ist)* - **1.** [zerbrechen] to break in two; [Boden] to give way - **2.** [durchdringen] to break through; [Geschwür, Abszess] to perforate.

durchbrechen[2] (*präs* **durchbricht**, *prät* **durchbrach**, *perf* **hat durchbrochen**) *vt* to break through.

durch|brennen (*perf* **ist durchgebrannt**) *vi (unreg)* - **1.** [Draht] to blow, to go - **2.** *fam* [weglaufen] to run away.

Durch|bruch *der* - **1.** [Erfolg] breakthrough - **2.** [Öffnung] opening.

durch|checken ['durçtʃɛkn̩] *vt* to check over.

durchdacht *adj* well thought out; **gut/schlecht durchdacht** well/badly thought out.

durch|denken[1] *vt (unreg)* to think through.

durchdenken[2] (*prät* **durchdachte**, *perf* **hat durchdacht**) *vt* to think out.

durch|diskutieren *vt* to talk through.

durch|drehen (*perf* **hat/ist durchgedreht**) ◇ *vi* - **1.** *(ist) fam* [verrückt werden] to crack up - **2.** *(hat)* [Räder] to spin. ◇ *vt (hat)* to mince.

durch|dringen (*perf* **ist durchgedrungen**) *vi (unreg)* [Geräusch, Licht, Nachricht] to get through; [Wasser] to seep through.

durch|drücken *vt* - **1.** *fam* [durchsetzen] to push through - **2.** [Gelenk] to straighten - **3.** [passieren] to press through.

Durcheinander *das* [von Menschen] confusion; [von Dingen] chaos.

durcheinander bringen *vt (unreg)* - **1.** [Person] to confuse - **2.** [Dinge] to muddle up - **3.** [verwechseln] to mix up.

durch|exerzieren *vt* to go through.

durch|fahren (*perf* **ist durchgefahren**) *vi (unreg)* - **1.** [durchqueren] to go ODER drive through - **2.** [durchgehend fahren] to go ODER drive non-stop.

Durch|fahrt *die* - **1.** [Durchfahren]: **die Durchfahrt freigeben** to open the road (again) - **2.** [Durchreise] way through; **auf der Durchfahrt sein** to be travelling through - **3.** [Weg] access road.

Durchfall *der* - **1.** [Diarrhöe] diarrhoea - **2.** *fam* [Misserfolg] flop; [bei einer Prüfung] failure.

durch|fallen (*perf* **ist durchgefallen**) *vi (unreg)* - **1.** *fam* [versagen] to flop; [bei einer Prüfung] to fail - **2.** [durch eine Öffnung] to fall through.

durchforsten *vt* - **1.** [durchsuchen - Gegend] to search; [- Textmaterial] to search through - **2.** [ausdünnen - Wald] to thin out.

durch|fragen ◆ **sich durchfragen** *ref* to ask one's way.

durchführbar *adj* practicable.

durch|führen ◇ *vt* to carry out; [Veranstaltung] to hold. ◇ *vi* to go through.

Durch|gang *der* - **1.** [Durchgehen]: **'Durchgang verboten'** 'no right of way' - **2.** [Weg] passage - **3.** [Phase] stage; [von Wahl] round.

durchgängig ◇ *adj* [Auffassung] general; **ein durchgängiges Motiv in seinen Werken** a motif that runs through his works. ◇ *ad*[v] universally; **durchgängig gute Leistunge[n] bringen** to achieve consistently good results

Durchgangsverkehr *der* through traffic.

durch|geben *vt (unreg)* to pass on; TV & RADI[O] to broadcast.

durchgebraten ◇ *pp* ▷ **durchbraten** ◇ *adj*: **gut durchgebraten** well done.

durchgefroren *adj* frozen through.

durch|gehen (*perf* **ist durchgegangen**) *(un-reg)* ◇ *vi* - **1.** [gen] to go through; **bitte durch gehen!** [im Bus] please move to the back o[f] the bus! - **2.** [durchdringen] to get throug[h] - **3.** [Pferd] to bolt; **mit jm durchgehen** [Gefühle] to run away with sb - **4.** [andauern - Sitzung, Veranstaltung] to go on non-stop - **5.** [akzeptier[t] werden - Fehler, Gesetzesvorlage] to get through; **jm etw durchgehen lassen** to let sb get awa[y] with sthg. ◇ *vt* to go through.

durch|greifen *vi (unreg)* - **1.** [einschreiten] t[o] take action - **2.** [durch eine Öffnung]: **durch etw durchgreifen** to reach through sthg.

durch|halten *(unreg)* ◇ *vi* to hold out ◇ *vt* [Belastung] to withstand; [Strecke, Wett kampf] to make it to the end of.

Durchhaltevermögen *das* stamina.

durchkämmen *vt* to comb.

durch|kommen (*perf* **ist durchgekommen**) *vi (unreg)* - **1.** [durch etw gelangen]: **durch etw durchkommen** to get through sthg - **2.** [am Te lefon, bei Prüfung] to get through - **3.** [Nach richt] to be announced - **4.** [durchfahren] to pas[s] through - **5.** [durchdringen - Wasser, Sonne] t[o] come through - **6.** [überleben] to pull throug[h] - **7.** [erfolgreich sein]: **mit dieser Idee wirst d[u] beim Chef kaum durchkommen** you won't ge[t] anywhere with the boss with that idea.

durch|lassen *vt (unreg)* to let through.

durchlässig *adj* [Boden] porous; [Materia[l]] permeable; [Grenze] open.

durch|lesen *vt (unreg)* to read through.

durchleuchten *vt* - **1.** [röntgen] to X-ra[y] - **2.** [untersuchen] to examine, to investigate.

durch|machen ◇ *vt* - **1.** [Schwierigkeiten, schwere Zeiten] to go through; **sie hat vie[l] durchgemacht** she's been through a lo[t] - **2.** *fam* [feiern]: **eine Nacht durchmachen** t[o] party all night. ◇ *vi fam* to stay up.

Durch|messer *der* diameter.

durch|nehmen *vt (unreg)* to do.

durchqueren *vt* [Zimmer, Fluss] to cross [Land] to go across; [Gegend] to go through.

durch|rechnen *vt* to calculate.

Durch|reise *die*: **Durchreise (durch)** journe[y] through; **auf der Durchreise** passing through

durch|reißen (*perf* **hat/ist durchgerissen**) *(unreg)* ◇ *vt (hat)* [Papier, Stoff] to tear in two [Faden] to break in two. ◇ *vi (ist)* [Stoff] t[o] tear in two; [Faden, Draht] to break in two.

durch|ringen ◆ **sich durchringen** *ref (unreg)*: **sich zu etw durchringen** to make up one's mind finally to do sthg.

durch|rosten (*perf* **ist durchgerostet**) *vi* to rust through.

durch|sagen *vt* to announce.

durch|schauen[1] *vt* to look through.

durchschauen[2] *vt* to see through.

Durch|schlag *der* - **1.** [Kopie] carbon copy - **2.** [Sieb] strainer.

durch|schlagen (*perf* **hat/ist durchgeschlagen**) *(unreg)* ◇ *vt (hat)* [Glas] to smash through; [Stein, Holz] to split; [Wand] to knock through; **etw durch etw durchschlagen** to knock sthg through sthg. ◇ *vi (ist)* to show through. ◆ **sich durchschlagen** *ref* - **1.** [durch Gegend] to make it - **2.** [durch Zeit] to struggle through.

durch|schneiden *vt (unreg)* [Faden, Stoff] to cut through; [Brot, Blatt Papier] to cut in half; [Kehle] to cut.

Durch|schnitt *der* average.

durchschnittlich ◇ *adj* average. ◇ *adv* [im Durchschnitt] on average; *abw* [mittelmäßig] averagely.

durch|schütteln *vt* to shake well; **im Bus durchgeschüttelt werden** to be shaken about on the bus.

durch|schwitzen *vt* to soak with sweat.

durch|sehen *(unreg)* ◇ *vt* to look through. ◇ *vi*: **durch etw durchsehen** to see through sthg.

durch sein (*perf* **ist durch gewesen**) *vi (unreg) fam* - **1.** [Zug, Kontrolleur] to have come through; **bei jm unten durch sein** *fig & abw* to be in sb's bad books - **2.** [mit Buch, Arbeit] to have finished - **3.** [Braten, Kartoffeln] to be done - **4.** [Sohle, Ärmel] to be worn out - **5.** [Gesetz] to have gone through.

durch|setzen *vt* [Plan, Vorhaben, Reform] to push through; [Anspruch] to assert. ◆ **sich durchsetzen** *ref* to assert o.s.; [Erfindung] to gain acceptance.

durchsichtig *adj* [Stoff, Folie] transparent.

durch|sprechen *vt (unreg)* to talk over.

durch|stehen *vt (unreg)* to come through.

durch|stellen *vt* to put through.

durchstöbern *vt* to rummage through.

durch|stoßen[1] *vt (unreg)*: **etw durch etw durchstoßen** to push sthg through sthg.

durchstoßen[2] (*präs* **durchstößt**, *prät* **durchstieß**, *perf* **hat durchstoßen**) *vt* to break through.

durch|streichen *vt (unreg)* to cross out.

durchsuchen *vt* to search.

durchtrainiert ['dʊrçtrɛniːɐ̯t] *adj* in peak condition.

durch|trennen[1] *vt* to sever.

durchtrennen[2] *vt* to sever.

durchtrieben ◇ *adj* cunning. ◇ *adv* cunningly.

Durchwahl *die (ohne pl)* extension.

durchweg *adv* without exception.

durchwühlen[1] *vt* [Schublade] to rummage through; [Zimmer] to ransack.

durch|wühlen[2] *vt* [Schublade] to rummage through; [Zimmer] to ransack.

durch|zählen *vt* to count.

durch|ziehen[1] (*perf* **hat/ist durchgezogen**) *(unreg)* ◇ *vt (hat)* - **1.** [durch Öffnung] to pull through; **etw durch etw durchziehen** to pull sthg through sthg - **2.** *fam* [Plan] to see through. ◇ *vi (ist)* - **1.** [durch Gegend] to pass through - **2.** [in Marinade - Fleisch] to marinate; [- Gemüse] to steep.

durchziehen[2] *vt (unreg)* to pass through.

Durch|zug *der* - **1.** [von Wetter] passage - **2.** *(ohne pl)* [Zugluft] draught.

dürfen (*präs* **darf**, *prät* **durfte**, *perf* **hat gedurft** ODER **dürfen**) ◇ *aux (perf hat dürfen)* - **1.** [als Erlaubnis]: **etw tun dürfen** to be allowed to do sthg; **darf ich mich setzen?** may I sit down?; **darf ich fragen?** may I ask?; **darf ich Ihnen behilflich sein?** *geh* can I be of help? - **2.** [als Überzeugung, Wunsch]: **das dürfen wir nicht vergessen** we mustn't forget that; **so etwas darf einfach nicht passieren** such a thing simply should not happen; **du darfst nicht traurig sein!** don't be sad! - **3.** [Veranlassung haben]: **man darf davon ausgehen, dass...** we can assume that... - **4.** [als Annahme]: **das dürfte genügen** that should be enough. ◇ *vi (perf hat gedurft)*: **sie darf nicht ins Schwimmbad** she's not allowed to go swimming. ◇ *vt (perf hat gedurft) fam*: **das darf man nicht!** you're not allowed to do that!; **was darf es sein?** what can I get you?

dürftig ◇ *adj* - **1.** [Einkünfte, Bezahlung] meagre - **2.** *abw* [Ergebnis] poor; [Bearbeitung] sketchy; [Bewuchs] sparse. ◇ *adv* - **1.** [entlohnt] meagrely; [bekleidet] scantily - **2.** *abw* [unzureichend] poorly; [sich entschuldigen] lamely.

dürr *adj* - **1.** [Person] scrawny - **2.** [Blatt] dry - **3.** [Worte] blunt.

Dürre (*pl* **-n**) *die* drought.

Durst *der* [Gefühl] thirst; **Durst haben** to be thirsty.

durstig ◇ *adj* thirsty. ◇ *adv* thirstily.

Durst|strecke *die* lean period.

Dusche (*pl* **-n**) *die* shower.

duschen ◇ *vi* to have a shower. ◇ *vt* to shower. ◆ **sich duschen** *ref* to have a shower.

Dusch|raum *der* shower room.

Düse (*pl* **-n**) *die* nozzle.

düsen (*perf* **ist gedüst**) *vi fam* to rush.

Düsen|flugzeug *das* jet aircraft.

Dussel (*pl* -) *der fam* dope.
düster ◇ *adj* gloomy. ◇ *adv* gloomily.
Dutzend (*pl* -) *das* [zwölf] dozen; **im Dutzend** by the dozen. ◆ **Dutzende** *Pl* [viele] dozens; **zu Dutzenden** in their dozens.
dutzendmal *adv* a dozen times.
dutzendweise *adv* by the dozen.
duzen *vt to address someone using the familiar "du" form.* ◆ **sich duzen** *ref to address each other using the familiar "du" form*; **sich mit jm duzen** to use the "du" form with sb.
DVD (*pl* -s) (*abk für* **Digital Versatile Disc**) *die* EDV DVD.
Dynamit *das* dynamite.
DZ *abk für* **Doppelzimmer**.

E

e (*pl* - ODER -s), **E** (*pl* - ODER -s) [eː] *das* - **1.** [Buchstabe] e, E - **2.** MUS E. ◆ **E** *der abk für* **Eilzug**.
Ebbe (*pl* -n) *die* tide *(outgoing)*; **es ist Ebbe** it is low tide; **bei Eintritt der Ebbe** when the tide is going out.
eben ◇ *adj* [flach - Gegend, Weg] flat; [glatt - Brett, Boden] smooth. ◇ *adv* - **1.** just; **kannst du mal eben vorbeikommen?** can you just come round for a minute? - **2.** [knapp]: **er hat ihn nur so eben berührt** he just touched him; **ich mache das eben zu Ende** I'll just finish it off - **3.** [genau]: **eben den Anwalt meine ich** he's the very lawyer I mean; **eben das war es, was ich sagen wollte!** that was exactly what I wanted to say! ◇ *interj* - **1.** [zum Ausdruck von Einverständnis] exactly - **2.** [zum Ausdruck von Widerspruch]: **aber du hast doch dein Geld! - eben nicht!** but you've got your money, haven't you! - no I haven't!
Eben|bild *das* image.
ebenbürtig *adj* equal; **jm ebenbürtig sein** to be sb's equal; **einer Sache ebenbürtig sein** to be equal to sthg.
Ebene (*pl* -n) *die* - **1.** [Flachland] plain - **2.** PHYS & MATH plane - **3.** [Niveau] level; **auf gleicher** ODER **der gleichen Ebene** on the same level; **auf höchster Ebene** at the highest level.
ebenfalls *adv* as well; **danke, ebenfalls** thanks, same to you.
ebenso *adv* just as.
ebenso gut *adv* just as well.
Eber (*pl* -) *der* boar.
ebnen *vt* to level; **jm den Weg ebnen** to smooth sb's path.
ec *abk für* **Eurocheque**.
Echo (*pl* -s) *das* echo.
Echse ['ɛksə] (*pl* -n) *die* lizard.
echt ◇ *adj* - **1.** [unverfälscht] genuin - **2.** [wahr, typisch] real. ◇ *adv* - **1.** [rein] real **echt italienisch essen** to eat real Italian foo - **2.** *fam* [wirklich] really.
Echtheit *die* genuineness.
Ecke (*pl* -n) *die* - **1.** [gen] corner - **2.** *fam* [Gegend] area; **eine hübsche Ecke!** a pretty spot! **das ist noch eine ganze Ecke!** it's still quite way!; **um die Ecke** *fam* round the corner; **es fehlt (bei uns) an allen Ecken und Enden** we are short of everything.
eckig ◇ *adj* - **1.** [Form] square - **2.** [Bewegung] awkward. ◇ *adv* [ungelenk] awkwardly.
Eck|zahn *der* canine tooth.
edel *adj* - **1.** *geh* [Person, Geste] noble - **2.** *geh* [Form] well-formed - **3.** [Holz, Wein] fine.
Edel|metall *das* precious metal.
Edel|stahl *der* stainless steel.
Edel|stein *der* precious stone.
EDV [eːdeː'fau] (*abk für* **elektronische Datenverarbeitung**) *die* data-processing.
Efeu *der (ohne pl)* ivy.
Effeff *das*: **etw aus dem Effeff beherrschen** *fam* to know sthg inside out.
Effekt (*pl* -e) *der* effect.
effektiv ◇ *adj* effective; [Gewinn, Leistung] net. ◇ *adv* effectively.
Effektivität [ɛfɛktivi'tɛːt] *die* effectiveness.
effektvoll ◇ *adj* effective. ◇ *adv* effectively.
egal *adj*: **es ist mir egal** it's all the same to me **das kann dir doch egal sein** that's no concern of yours; **das ist egal** it doesn't matter ◆ **egal ob** *adv* no matter whether.
Egoismus *der* egoism.
eh ◇ *interj fam* hey. ◇ *adv* - **1.** [immer]: **wie eh und je** as always - **2.** *Süddt & Österr fam* [sowieso] anyway.
Ehe (*pl* -n) *die* marriage.
Ehe|bett *das* double bed.
Ehe|bruch *der* adultery *(U)*.
Ehe|frau *die* wife.
Ehe|leute *Pl* married couple.
ehelich *adj* marital; [Recht] conjugal.
ehemalig *adj* former.
ehemals *adv* formerly.
Ehe|mann (*pl* -männer) *der* husband.
Ehe|paar *das* married couple.
Ehe|partner *der* marriage partner.
eher *adv* - **1.** [vorher] earlier, sooner - **2.** [lieber] rather - **3.**: **das ist schon eher möglich** that is more likely - **4.** [vielmehr] more.
Ehe|ring *der* wedding ring.
Ehe|schließung *die* marriage ceremony.

Ehre *die* honour; **jm zu Ehren** in sb's honour.

ehren *vt* [Achtung erweisen] to honour; **deine Großmut ehrt dich** your generosity does you credit; **dieses Angebot ehrt mich** I am honoured by this offer.

ehrenamtlich ◇ *adj* honorary. ◇ *adv* in an honorary capacity.

Ehren|bürger, **in** *der, die* honorary citizen.

Ehren|gast *der* guest of honour.

ehrenhaft ◇ *adj* honourable. ◇ *adv* honourably.

Ehren|mann (*pl* **-männer**) *der* man of honour.

Ehren|mitglied *das* honorary member.

Ehren|sache *die* point of honour; **das ist doch Ehrensache, dass ich bald wieder zurück bin** you can count on me to be back soon.

Ehrenwort (*pl* **-e**) *das* word of honour; **(großes) Ehrenwort!** *fam* I/we promise!

Ehrfurcht *die* [Verehrung] reverence; [Scheu] awe.

ehrfürchtig ◇ *adj* reverent. ◇ *adv* reverently.

Ehrgeiz *der* ambition.

ehrgeizig ◇ *adj* ambitious. ◇ *adv* ambitiously.

ehrlich ◇ *adj* honest. ◇ *adv* fairly; **ehrlich gesagt** to be honest.

Ehrlichkeit *die* honesty.

Ehrung (*pl* **-en**) *die* [das Ehren] honouring *(U)*; [Ehre] honour.

ehrwürdig *adj* venerable.

Ei (*pl* **-er**) *das* - **1.** [gen] egg; **jn/etw wie ein rohes Ei behandeln** to treat sb/sthg with kid gloves - **2.** *vulg* [Hoden] ball.

Eiche (*pl* **-n**) *die* oak.

Eichel (*pl* **-n**) *die* - **1.** [Frucht] acorn - **2.** [des männlichen Gliedes] glans (penis).

Eichhörnchen (*pl* **-**) *das* squirrel.

Eid (*pl* **-e**) *der* oath. ◆ **unter Eid** *adv* under oath.

Eidechse ['aidɛksə] (*pl* **-n**) *die* lizard.

eidesstattlich ◇ *adj* sworn. ◇ *adv* solemnly.

Eid|genosse *der* Swiss citizen.

Eid|genossin *die* Swiss citizen.

Ei|dotter *das* & *der* egg yolk.

Eier|becher *der* egg cup.

Eier|kuchen *der* pancake.

Eier|schale *die* eggshell.

Eier|stock *der* ovary.

Eifer *der* eagerness.

Eifersucht *die* jealousy.

eifersüchtig ◇ *adj* jealous; **auf jn eifersüchtig sein** to be jealous of sb. ◇ *adv* jealously.

eifrig ◇ *adj* eager. ◇ *adv* eagerly.

Eigelb (*pl* **-** ODER **-e**) *das* egg yolk.

eigen *adj* - **1.** [jm gehörend] own - **2.** [typisch] typical. ◆ **Eigen** *das*: **sich** *(D)* **etw zu Eigen machen** to make sthg one's own.

Eigen|art *die* characteristic.

eigenartig ◇ *adj* strange. ◇ *adv* strangely.

Eigenbedarf *der (ohne pl)* personal requirements *Pl*; **für den Eigenbedarf** for one's own use.

eigenbrötlerisch ◇ *adj* reclusive. ◇ *adv* like a recluse.

eigenhändig ◇ *adj* own. ◇ *adv* with one's own hands.

eigenmächtig ◇ *adj* unauthorized. ◇ *adv* on one's own authority.

Eigen|name *der* proper name.

eigennützig ◇ *adj* selfish. ◇ *adv* selfishly.

eigens *adv* specially.

Eigenschaft (*pl* **-en**) *die* characteristic; [von Auto] feature; **in seiner Eigenschaft als etw** in one's capacity as sthg.

Eigenschaftswort (*pl* **-wörter**) *das* adjective.

eigensinnig ◇ *adj* stubborn. ◇ *adv* stubbornly.

eigenständig ◇ *adj* independent. ◇ *adv* independently.

eigentlich ◇ *adv* - **1.** [im Grunde, wirklich] really - **2.** [übrigens] by the way; **wer ist eigentlich Petra?** who is Petra(, by the way)? - **3.** [zum Ausdruck von Ärger]: **was erlauben Sie sich eigentlich?** what do you think you're doing? ◇ *adj* [wirklich] real.

Eigen|tor *das* own goal.

Eigentum *das* - **1.** [Besitz] property - **2.** [Besitzerrecht] ownership.

Eigentümer, **in** (*mpl* **-**, *fpl* **-nen**) *der, die* owner.

eigentümlich *adj* peculiar.

eigenwillig *adj* - **1.** [eigen] original - **2.** [starrsinnig] obstinate.

eignen ◆ **sich eignen** *ref* to be suitable; **sich zu** ODER **für etw eignen** to be suitable for sthg.

Eignungs|prüfung *die* aptitude test.

Eil|brief *der* express letter.

Eile *die* hurry; **in Eile sein** to be in a hurry; **etw hat Eile/keine Eile** sthg is/is not urgent.

eilen (*perf* **hat/ist geeilt**) *vi* - **1.** *(ist)* [Person] to hurry - **2.** *(hat)* [Angelegenheit] to be urgent; **eilt!** urgent!; **mit etw eilt es/eilt es nicht** sthg is/is not urgent.

eilig ◇ *adj* - **1.** [Bewegung] hurried; **es eilig haben** to be in a hurry - **2.** [Angelegenheit, Brief] urgent. ◇ *adv* hurriedly.

Eimer (*pl* **-**) *der* bucket.

ein, **e** ◇ *num* one; **eine einzelne Rose** a single rose; **ein Uhr** one o'clock; **einer Mei-**

nung sein to have the same opinion; **für alle Mal** *fam fig* once and for all; **in einem fort** *fig* non-stop; **js Ein und Alles sein** *fig* to mean everything to sb. ◇ *det* a, an *(vor Vokal)*; **ein Hund** a dog; **eine Idee** an idea; **ein Mädchen** a girl; **eines Tages** one day; **da ist eine Frau Schmidt am Apparat** there's a Mrs Schmidt on the phone. ◇ *pron* - **1.** [als Teil einer Menge] one; **hier ist noch eins/eine** here's another one; **ein und dasselbe** one and the same - **2.** *fam* [jemand] someone, somebody; **sieh mal einer an!** well I never!; **das kann einem schon mal passieren** these things can happen to you. ◇ *adv*: **ein-aus** on-off; **ein und aus gehen** *fig* to come and go; **nicht ein noch aus wissen** *fig* not to know whether one is coming or going.

ein|arbeiten *vt* [an die Arbeit gewöhnen] to train. ◆ **sich einarbeiten** *ref* to settle in.

ein|atmen *vt* & *vi* to breathe in.

Einbahn|straße *die* one-way street.

Einband (*pl* **-bände**) *der* book cover.

ein|bauen *vt* - **1.** [Schrank, Bad] to fit; [Motor] to install - **2.** [in Text] to incorporate.

Einbau|küche *die* fitted kitchen.

ein|berufen *vt (unreg)* - **1.** [Sitzung] to summon - **2.** [Wehrpflichtige] to call up *UK*, to draft *US*.

Ein|berufung *die* - **1.** [einer Sitzung] summoning *(U)* - **2.** [von Wehrpflichtigen] call-up *UK*, draft *US*.

ein|betten *vt* to wrap.

ein|beziehen *vt (unreg)*: **jn/etw in etw** *(A)* **einbeziehen** to include sb/sthg in sthg.

ein|biegen (*perf* **hat/ist eingebogen**) *(unreg)* ◇ *vi (ist)* [abbiegen] to turn; **nach rechts/links einbiegen** to turn right/left. ◇ *vt (hat)* [verbiegen] to bend.

ein|bilden *vt* - **1.** [sich einreden]: **sich** *(D)* **etw einbilden** to imagine sthg; **was bildest du dir eigentlich ein, wer du bist?** who do you think you are? - **2.** [stolz sein]: **er bildet sich ganz schön viel ein** he is really full of himself; **sich** *(D)* **viel auf etw** *(A)* **einbilden** to be conceited about sthg; **darauf brauchst du dir nichts einzubilden** that's nothing to be proud of.

Einbildung (*pl* **-en**) *die* - **1.** [Fantasie] imagination - **2.** [Hochmut] conceit.

Einbildungskraft *die* imagination.

ein|binden *vt (unreg)* - **1.** [einschlagen] to bind - **2.** [einbeziehen]: **jn/etw in etw** *(A)* **einbinden** to integrate sb/sthg into sthg.

ein|bläuen *vt*: **jm etw einbläuen** to drum sthg into sb.

einbleuen = **einbläuen**.

Ein|blick *der* - **1.** [Blick]: **Einblick in die Dokumente bekommen** to get a look at the documents; **Einblick in etw** *(A)* **nehmen** to examine sthg; **jm Einblick in etw** *(A)* **gewähren** to allow sb to examine sthg - **2.** [Einsicht] insight.

ein|brechen (*perf* **hat/ist eingebrochen**) *v (unreg)* - **1.** *(hat)* [gewaltsam eindringen] t break in; **bei jm einbrechen** to burgle s - **2.** *(ist)* [einstürzen] to fall in - **3.** *(ist)* [Parte Mannschaft] to come unstuck - **4.** *(ist)* [durch brechen] to fall through - **5.** *(ist)* [eindringen **(in ein Land) einbrechen** to invade (a country - **6.** *(ist)* *geh* [Nacht, Dunkelheit] to fall; [Winte to set in.

Einbrecher, in (*mpl* -, *fpl* **-nen**) *der* burglar

ein|bringen *vt (unreg)* - **1.** [Ernte] to bring i - **2.** [Gewinn] to bring in; [Anerkennung] t bring; [Erfahrung] to give; **das bringt nichts ei** that's not worth it - **3.** [vorlegen] to introduc - **4.** *amt* [einsetzen - Geld, Vermögen] to invest [- in eine Ehe] to put in.

ein|brocken *vt fam*: **jm/sich etwas einbrocken** to land sb/o.s. in it; **dieses Problem has du dir selbst eingebrockt!** you brought thi problem on yourself!

Ein|bruch *der* - **1.** [Straftat] break-in; **eine Einbruch begehen** to commit a burglar - **2.** [Zusammenbruch] collapse - **3.** [Eindringer penetration - **4.** *fam* [bei Wahl] drubbin - **5.** [Beginn - von Winter] onset; **vor Einbruch de Nacht** before nightfall.

einbürgern *vt* [eine Staatsangehörigkeit verle hen] to naturalize. ◆ **sich einbürgern** *re* [üblich werden] to become established.

Ein|buße *die* loss.

ein|büßen ◇ *vt* to lose. ◇ *vi*: **an etw** *(D* **einbüßen** to lose sthg.

ein|checken ['aintʃɛkn̩] *vt* & *vi* to check in

ein|cremen, einkremen *vt* to put crean on. ◆ **sich eincremen** *ref* to put cream or

ein|dämmen *vt* - **1.** [stauen] to dam - **2.** [zu rückhalten] to contain.

ein|decken *vt fam* [überhäufen]: **jn mit et eindecken** to swamp sb with sthg.

eindeutig ◇ *adj* clear. ◇ *adv* clearly.

ein|dringen (*perf* **ist eingedrungen**) *vi (ur reg)* - **1.** [hineingelangen]: **in etw** *(A)* **eindringe** [Wasser] to get into sthg; [Messer] to enter sth - **2.** [einbrechen]: **in etw** *(A)* **eindringen** [Gebäu de] to break into sthg; [Land] to invade sthg.

eindringlich ◇ *adj* insistent. ◇ *adv* in sistently.

Eindringling (*pl* **-e**) *der* intruder.

Eindruck (*pl* **-drücke**) *der* impression; **Ei druck auf jn machen** to make an impressio on sb; **einen Eindruck von etw bekomme** ODER **erhalten** to get an impression of sthg; **e nen guten/schlechten Eindruck (auf jn) ma chen** to make a good/bad impression (on sb

ein|drücken *vt* - **1.** [beschädigen - Kotflüge Fensterscheibe] to smash in; [- Nase, Kissen] t flatten - **2.** [in etw hineindrücken] to press.

eindrucksvoll ◇ *adj* impressive. ◇ *ad* impressively.

ein|ebnen *vt* to level.

eineiig ['ain aiiç] *adj*: **eineiige Zwillinge** identical twins.

eineinhalb *num* one and a half.

ein|engen *vt* - **1.** [beschränken] to constrict - **2.** [einschränken] to restrict; **jn in seiner Freiheit einengen** to curb sb's freedom.

einerlei *adj* immaterial; **das ist mir einerlei** that's all the same to me.

einerseits *adv*: **einerseits... andererseits...** on the one hand... on the other (hand)...

einfach ◇ *adj* - **1.** [leicht, schlicht] simple - **2.** [Fahrkarte, Knoten] single. ◇ *adv* - **1.** [leicht, schlicht] simply; **ich komme einfach mit** I'll just come with you; **es sich einfach machen** to make it easy for o.s. - **2.** [nicht mehrfach]: **etw einfach falten** to fold sthg once.

Einfachheit *die* simplicity.

ein|fädeln *vt* - **1.** [Faden, Nadel] to thread - **2.** [bewerkstelligen]: **sie hat die Sache schlau eingefädelt** she worked things very cleverly.

ein|fahren (*perf* **hat/ist eingefahren**) *(unreg)* ◇ *vi (ist)* [Zug] to arrive. ◇ *vt (hat)* - **1.** [hineinschaffen - Ernte] to bring in - **2.** [beschädigen - Tor, Mauer] to knock down; [- Kotflügel] to smash in - **3.** AUTO to run in *UK*, to break in *US* - **4.** [einziehen - Fahrwerk] to retract.

Ein|fahrt *die* - **1.** [Einfahren] arrival; **der Zug hat noch keine Einfahrt** the train still hasn't arrived - **2.** [Stelle zum Hineinfahren] entrance.

Ein|fall *der* - **1.** [Idee] idea; **ihm kam ein Einfall** he had an idea - **2.** [Einfallen]: **der Einfall von Sonnenstrahlen** the sun's rays shining in - **3.** [Eindringen] invasion; **der Einfall der Römer in Gallien** the invasion of Gaul by the Romans.

ein|fallen (*perf* **ist eingefallen**) *vi (unreg)* - **1.** [in den Sinn kommen]: **ihm fiel nichts Besseres ein** no better idea occurred to him; **ihm fällt immer eine passende Ausrede ein** he always thinks of a suitable excuse; **mir fällt nichts ein, was ich kochen könnte** I can't think of anything that I could cook; **sich** *(D)* **etwas einfallen lassen** to think of something; **was fällt dir/Ihnen ein!** what(ever) are you thinking of! - **2.** [wieder in den Sinn kommen] to remember; **da fällt mir ein** that reminds me - **3.** [hereinkommen] to shine in - **4.** MIL: **in etw** *(A)* **einfallen** to invade sthg - **5.** [einstimmen] to join in - **6.** [einstürzen] to collapse.

einfallslos *adj* unimaginative.

einfallsreich *adj* imaginative.

einfältig *adj* - **1.** [arglos] naive; [Lächeln] innocent - **2.** [beschränkt] simple-minded.

Einfamilien|haus *das house designed for one family.*

ein|fangen *vt (unreg)* - **1.** [fangen und fest halten] to capture - **2.** *fam* [bekommen]: **sich** *(D)* **etw einfangen** to get sthg.

einfarbig *adj* all one colour.

ein|fassen *vt* - **1.** [Stoff] to edge - **2.** [mit Mauer] to enclose - **3.** [Edelstein] to set.

ein|fliegen *vt (unreg)* to fly in; **jn/etw einfliegen lassen** to fly sb/sthg in.

ein|fließen (*perf* **ist eingeflossen**) *vi (unreg)* [Wasser, Luft] to flow in; **eine Kritik einfließen lassen** to slip in a criticism.

ein|flößen *vt* - **1.** [zu trinken geben] to help to drink - **2.** [erregen]: **jm etw einflößen** [Ehrfurcht, Vertrauen, Angst] to inspire sthg in sb.

Einfluss (*pl* **-flüsse**) *der* influence; **unter Einfluss von Alkohol** under the influence of alcohol; **auf jn/etw Einfluss haben** [Macht] to have influence over sb/sthg; [Effekt] to influence sb/sthg; **auf jn/etw Einfluss nehmen** to influence sb/sthg.

einflussreich *adj* influential.

einförmig *adj* monotonous.

ein|frieren (*perf* **hat/ist eingefroren**) *(unreg)* ◇ *vt (hat)* to freeze; [Beziehungen] to suspend. ◇ *vi (ist)* [Wasserleitung] to freeze; [Teich] to freeze over.

ein|fügen *vt* [gen & EDV] to insert. ◆ **sich einfügen** *ref* [sich anpassen] to fit in.

einfühlsam *adj* sensitive.

Einfuhr (*pl* **-en**) *die* - **1.** [Einführen] importation - **2.** [Ware] import.

ein|führen *vt* - **1.** [gen] to introduce; **jn in etw** *(A)* **einführen** to introduce sb to sthg - **2.** [importieren] to import - **3.** [hineinschieben] to insert, to introduce.

Ein|führung *die* introduction.

ein|füllen *vt* to pour in; **etw in etw** *(A)* **einfüllen** to pour sthg into sthg.

Ein|gang *der* - **1.** [Eingangstür] entrance - **2.** [von Geld, Post] receipt.

eingangs *adv* at the beginning.

Eingangs|halle *die* entrance hall.

ein|geben *vt (unreg)* EDV to enter.

eingebildet *adj* - **1.** [nicht wirklich] imaginary - **2.** [hochmütig] arrogant.

Eingeborene (*pl* **-n**), **Eingeborne** (*pl* **-n**) *der, die* native.

eingefleischt *adj* ▷ **Junggeselle**.

ein|gehen (*perf* **ist eingegangen**) *(unreg)* ◇ *vi* - **1.** [ankommen] to arrive; **bei uns ist noch keine Antwort eingegangen** we have not yet received a reply - **2.** [Tier, Pflanze] to perish - **3.** [Firma] to close down - **4.** [beachten]: **auf jn/etw eingehen** to respond to sb/sthg; **auf etw** *(A)* **eingehen** [Angebot, Vorschlag] to agree to sthg - **5.** [Kleidung] to shrink - **6.** *geh* [Einzug halten]: **in die Geschichte eingehen** to go down in history. ◇ *vt* [Bündnis, Ehe, Verpflichtung] to enter into; [Risiko] to take; [Wette] to make.

eingehend ◇ *adj* detailed. ◇ *adv* in detail.

eingenommen ◇ *pp* ▷ **einnehmen**. ◇ *adj*: **von sich eingenommen sein** to have a high opinion of o.s.; **für/gegen etw eingenommen sein** to be taken with/biased against sthg; **von jm/etw eingenommen sein** to be taken with sb/sthg.

eingeschlossen *pp* ▷ **einschließen**.

eingetragen ◇ *pp* ▷ **eintragen**. ◇ *adj* registered, ▷ **Verein**; *siehe auch* **Warenzeichen**.

Eingeweide *Pl* entrails.

ein|gewöhnen ◆ **sich eingewöhnen** *ref* to settle in.

ein|gießen *vt (unreg)* [Tasse, Glas] to pour; **jm etw eingießen** to pour sb sthg.

ein|gliedern *vt*: **jn/etw in etw** *(A)* **eingliedern** to integrate sb/sthg into sthg. ◆ **sich eingliedern** *ref*: **sich in etw** *(A)* **eingliedern** to integrate into sthg.

ein|graben *vt (unreg)* - **1.** [in den Boden] to bury - **2.** [eindrücken - Spuren] to carve. ◆ **sich eingraben** *ref*: **sich in etw** *(A)* **eingraben** [Tier] to burrow into sthg; [Fluss] to carve (itself) a channel into sthg.

ein|greifen *vi (unreg)*: **(in etw** *(A)*) **eingreifen** to intervene (in sthg).

Ein|griff *der* - **1.** [Intervention] intervention - **2.** MED operation.

ein|haken ◇ *vt* to fasten. ◇ *vi* to interrupt.

ein|halten *(unreg)* ◇ *vt* [befolgen, erfüllen - Termin] to keep; [- Plan] to keep to; [- Vorschrift] to observe. ◇ *vi* [innehalten]: **in** *ODER* **mit seinem Tun einhalten** to interrupt what one is doing.

einhändig *adv* one-handed.

ein|hängen ◇ *vt* - **1.** [in ein Scharnier - Tür] to hang; [- Fenster] to put in - **2.** [auflegen - Telefonhörer] to put down. ◇ *vi* to hang up.

einheimisch *adj* local.

Einheit *(pl* **-en**) *die* - **1.** [Geschlossenheit] unity - **2.** MIL [Maßeinheit] unit.

einheitlich ◇ *adj* - **1.** [geschlossen] unified - **2.** [gleich] uniform; [Standard] standardized. ◇ *adv* uniformly; [sich kleiden] in the same way.

einhellig ◇ *adj* unanimous. ◇ *adv* unanimously.

ein|holen ◇ *vt* - **1.** [Person, Wagen] to catch up with; [verlorene Zeit] to make up for - **2.** [holen] to obtain - **3.** [einziehen - Netz] to haul in; [- Leine] to reel in - **4.** [einkaufen] to get. ◇ *vi*: **einholen gehen** to go shopping.

einig *adj* [einer Meinung]: **(sich) über jn/etw einig sein** to agree about sb/sthg; [vereint] united.

einige ◇ *det* - **1.** [eine gewisse Menge] a few, some; **nach einiger Zeit** after some time; **einige Probleme** a few problems; **nur einige waren da** there were only a few people there - **2.** [beträchtlich] quite a few; **das brachte so einige Probleme mit sich** this caused quite a lo[t] of problems; **so einige waren da** there wer[e] quite a lot of people there. ◇ *pron* a few, some. ◆ **einiges** *pron* something; **das ha[t] einiges für sich** there is something to be sai[d] for it; **ich könnte dir einiges erzählen** I coul[d] tell you a thing or two.

einigen *vt* to unite. ◆ **sich einigen** *ref*: **sich (mit jm) einigen** to reach an agreemen[t] (with sb); **sich auf etw** *(A)* **einigen** to agree o[n] sthg.

einigermaßen *adv* fairly.

Einigkeit *die* - **1.** [Eintracht] unity - **2.** [Übereinstimmung] agreement.

Einigung *(pl* **-en**) *die* - **1.** [Übereinkunft] agreement - **2.** [Vereinigung] unification.

Ein|kauf *der* - **1.** [Einkaufen] shopping - **2.** [eingekaufte Ware] purchase; **die Einkäufe aus dem Wagen holen** to get the shopping out of the car - **3.** WIRTSCH purchasing.

ein|kaufen ◇ *vt* to buy. ◇ *vi*: **einkaufen gehen** to go shopping.

Einkaufs|bummel *der* shopping expedition; **einen Einkaufsbummel machen** to go o[n] a shopping expedition.

Einkaufs|tasche *die* shopping bag.

ein|kehren *(perf* **ist eingekehrt**) *vi* to sto[p] off.

ein|klammern *vt* to put in brackets, t[o] bracket.

Einklang *der* harmony.

ein|kleiden *vt* to kit out. ◆ **sich einkleiden** *ref*: **sich neu einkleiden** to buy o.s. a new wardrobe.

Einkommen *(pl* **-**) *das* income.

Einkommens|steuer *die* income tax.

ein|kreisen *vt* - **1.** [umzingeln] to surroun[d] - **2.** [eingrenzen] to pin down - **3.** [mit Stift] to circle.

ein|kremen = **eincremen**.

Einkünfte *Pl* income *(U)*.

ein|laden *vt (unreg)* - **1.** [Gast] to invite; **j[n] zu etw einladen** [Hochzeit, Party] to invite sb t[o] sthg; **darf ich Sie zu einem Kaffee einladen** can I buy you a coffee?; **jn in ein Restauran[t] einladen** to take sb out for a meal - **2.** [Last] t[o] load.

einladend ◇ *adj* inviting. ◇ *adv* invitingly.

Ein|ladung *die* invitation.

Ein|lage *die* - **1.** [im Schuh] insole - **2.** KÜCH *vegetables, noodles, meat etc added to a clea[r] soup* - **3.** [im Programm] interlude - **4.** WIRTSC[H] [bei Bank] deposit; [bei Firma] investment.

Einlass *der* admission.

ein|lassen *vt (unreg)* - **1.** [hereinlassen] to admit - **2.** [Wasser] to run - **3.** [einsetzen] to set. ◆ **sich einlassen** *ref*: **sich mit jm/auf etw** *(A)* **einlassen** to get involved with sb/in sthg.

ein|laufen (*perf* **hat/ist eingelaufen**) *(unreg)* ◇ *vi (ist)* - **1.** SPORT: **ins Stadion einlaufen** to enter the stadium; **ins Ziel einlaufen** to cross the finishing line - **2.** [Wasser] to run in - **3.** [einfahren] to come in - **4.** [Stoff] to shrink. ◇ *vt (hat)* [Schuhe] to wear in. ◆ **sich einlaufen** *ref* to warm up.

ein|leben ◆ **sich einleben** *ref* to settle in.

ein|legen *vt* - **1.** [hineintun] to put in; **den ersten Gang einlegen** to go into first gear - **2.** KÜCHE to preserve; [in Essig] to pickle - **3.** [Pause] to have, to take - **4.** [Berufung, Bitte] to lodge; **ein gutes Wort für jn einlegen** to put in a good word for sb.

ein|leiten *vt* - **1.** [beginnen - Untersuchung, Verfahren] to start; [- Schritte] to take; [- Geburt] to induce - **2.** [einführen] to open - **3.** [einlassen]: **Abwässer in den Fluss einleiten** to let effluent into the river.

einleitend ◇ *adj* introductory. ◇ *adv* by way of introduction.

Ein|leitung *die* - **1.** [Einführung] introduction - **2.** [Beginn - von Untersuchung] start.

ein|lenken *vi* to give way.

ein|leuchten *vi*: **es leuchtet mir ein, dass...** I can see that...

einleuchtend ◇ *adj* convincing. ◇ *adv* convincingly.

ein|liefern *vt* [bringen - in psychiatrische Anstalt] to commit; **jn in ein Krankenhaus einliefern** to take sb to hospital.

sich ein|loggen *ref* EDV to log on; **sich ins Internet einloggen** to log on to the Internet.

ein|lösen *vt* - **1.** [Scheck] to cash; [Gutschein] to redeem - **2.** [Versprechen] to keep.

Ein|lösung *die* [von Scheck] cashing; [von Gutschein] redemption.

ein|machen *vt* to preserve.

einmal *adv* - **1.** [ein einzelnes Mal] once; **noch einmal** (once) again - **2.** [irgendwann - zuvor] before; [- in Zukunft] sometime; **haben wir uns nicht schon einmal gesehen?** haven't we met before?; **irgendwann einmal möchte sie nach England ziehen** she'd like to move to England someday - **3.** [mal, bitte]: **komm einmal her!** come here, will you!; **hör mir einmal gut zu!** now listen to me carefully! ◆ **auf einmal** *adv* - **1.** [plötzlich] suddenly - **2.** [zusammen, gleichzeitig] at once. ◆ **nicht einmal** *adv* not even.

Einmaleins *das (ohne pl)* - **1.** [Zahlenreihe] multiplication tables *Pl* - **2.** [Grundwissen] ABC.

einmalig *adj* - **1.** [einzeln - Zahlung] one-off - **2.** [außergewöhnlich] unique - **3.** [wunderbar] fantastic.

ein|marschieren (*perf* **ist einmarschiert**) *vi* to invade.

ein|mischen ◆ **sich einmischen** *ref*: **sich (in etw** *(A)***) einmischen** to interfere (in sthg).

Ein|mischung *die* interference.

ein|münden (*perf* **hat/ist eingemündet**) *vi*: **in etw** *(A)* **einmünden** [Fluss] to flow into sthg; [Straße] to lead into sthg.

einmütig ◇ *adj* unanimous. ◇ *adv* unanimously.

Einnahme (*pl* **-n**) *die* - **1.** [Einkommen] income; [an einer Kasse] takings *Pl*; [vom Staat] revenue - **2.** [von Medikament] taking - **3.** [Eroberung] capture.

ein|nehmen *vt (unreg)* - **1.** [Geld, Medikament, Platz] to take; **viel Raum einnehmen** to take up a lot of room - **2.** [erobern] to capture; **jn für sich einnehmen** *fig* to win sb over.

einnehmend *adj* captivating.

ein|ordnen *vt* to put in its place; [Akten] to file; [Dichter, Politiker] to categorize. ◆ **sich einordnen** *ref* [Auto] to get into the correct lane; [Person] to fit in.

ein|packen *vt* - **1.** [verpacken - Kleidung] to pack; [- Geschenk] to wrap - **2.** *fam* [anziehen] to wrap up.

ein|parken ◇ *vt* to park. ◇ *vi* to park.

ein|passen *vt* to fit.

ein|pflanzen *vt* - **1.** [pflanzen] to plant - **2.** MED to implant.

ein|planen *vt* [Verlust, Verzögerung] to allow for; [Person] to count in.

ein|prägen *vt* - **1.** [eingravieren] to imprint - **2.** [einschärfen]: **sich** *(D)* **etw einprägen** to memorize sthg; **jm etw einprägen** to impress sthg on sb.

einprägsam *adj* easily remembered; [Melodie] catchy.

ein|rahmen *vt* to frame.

ein|räumen *vt* - **1.** [einordnen, ordnen - Kleidung, Geschirr] to put away; **den Schrank einräumen** to put things away in the cupboard - **2.** [Frist, Kredit] to grant - **3.** [zugeben] to admit.

ein|reden ◇ *vi*: **auf jn einreden** to keep on at sb. ◇ *vt*: **jm etw einreden** to talk sb into sthg.

ein|reiben *vt (unreg)* to rub in.

ein|reichen *vt* [Antrag] to submit; [Beschwerde] to lodge.

Ein|reise *die* entry.

ein|reisen (*perf* **ist eingereist**) *vi* to enter; **nach Deutschland einreisen** to enter Germany.

Einreise|visum *das* entry visa.

ein|reißen (*perf* **hat/ist eingerissen**) *(unreg)* ◇ *vt (hat)* - **1.** [Gebäude] to pull down - **2.** [Papier, Stoff] to tear. ◇ *vi (ist)* - **1.** [Papier, Stoff] to tear - **2.** *abw* [Unsitte] to become a habit.

ein|renken *vt* - **1.** MED to put back in its socket - **2.** [bereinigen] to sort out. ◆ **sich einrenken** *ref* to sort itself out.

ein|richten *vt* - **1.** [möblieren] to furnish - **2.** [organisieren]: **etw so einrichten, dass...** to organize sthg in such a way that... - **3.** [Stelle, Institution] to set up. ◆ **sich einrichten** *ref* - **1.** [mit Möbeln] to furnish one's home - **2.** [sich einstellen]: **sich auf etw** *(A)* **einrichten** to prepare for sthg.

Ein|richtung *die* - **1.** [Möbel] furnishings *Pl* - **2.** [Einrichten] furnishing - **3.** [Schaffung] setting up - **4.** [Institution] institution.

ein|rücken (*perf* **hat/ist eingerückt**) ◇ *vi* *(ist)* to enter. ◇ *vt (hat)* to indent.

eins ◇ *num* [als Zahl] one; **eins A** top-quality, A-1. ◇ *pron* one; *siehe auch* **sechs**.

Eins (*pl* **-en**) *die* - **1.** [Zahl] one - **2.** [Schulnote] ≃ A, *mark of 1 on a scale from 1 to 6*; *siehe auch* **Sechs**.

einsam *adj* - **1.** [Person] lonely - **2.** [Haus, Gegend] isolated.

Einsamkeit *die* - **1.** [von Person] loneliness - **2.** [von Haus, Gegend] isolation.

ein|sammeln *vt* [Werkzeug, Spielzeug] to gather up; [Kinder] to pick up; [Klassenarbeiten] to collect in; [Geld] to collect.

Ein|satz *der* - **1.** [Geld] stake - **2.** [Einsetzen] use; **unter Einsatz aller Kräfte** with a huge effort; **zum Einsatz kommen** to be used - **3.** [Engagement] commitment - **4.** MIL mission; **im Einsatz sein** to be in action - **5.** [Fach] compartment - **6.** MUS entry.

einsatzbereit *adj* [Truppe] ready for action; [Maschine] ready for use.

ein|schalten *vt* - **1.** [anstellen] to switch on - **2.** [hinzuziehen] to call in. ◆ **sich einschalten** *ref* - **1.** [von selbst angehen] to switch on - **2.** [eingreifen] to intervene.

ein|schärfen *vt*: **jm etw einschärfen** to impress sthg upon sb.

ein|schätzen *vt* [Gefahr, Lage] to assess; [Vermögen, Umsatz] to estimate; [Person] to judge; **jn/etw falsch einschätzen** to misjudge sb/sthg.

Ein|schätzung *die* [von Gefahr, Lage] assessment; [von Vermögen, Umsatz] estimation; [von Person] judgement.

ein|schenken *vt*: **jm etw einschenken** to pour sb sthg.

ein|schicken *vt* to send in.

ein|schieben *vt (unreg)* - **1.** [hineinschieben] to insert - **2.** [einfügen] to fit in.

ein|schlafen (*perf* **ist eingeschlafen**) *vi (unreg)* - **1.** [aus Müdigkeit] to fall asleep - **2.** [Körperteil] to go to sleep - **3.** [aufhören] to peter out - **4.** [sterben] to pass away.

ein|schläfern *vt* - **1.** [töten] to put to sleep - **2.** [in Schlaf versetzen] to send to sleep.

einschläfernd *adj* soporific.

ein|schlagen (*perf* **hat/ist eingeschlagen**) *(unreg)* ◇ *vi* - **1.** *(ist)* [treffen] to strike - **2.** *(hat)* [zustimmen] to agree; [mit Händedruck] to shake on it - **3.** *(hat)* [lenken] to steer; **nach rechts einschlagen** to turn right - **4.** *(hat)* [Furore machen - Schallplatte] to be a hit; [- Erfindung] to be a success; [- Enthüllungen] to cause a furore - **5.** *(hat)* [schlagen]: **auf jn einschlagen** to beat sb. ◇ *vt (hat)* - **1.** [Nagel] to knock in - **2.** [Glas, Tür] to smash in - **3.** [Buch, Geschenk] to wrap (up) - **4.** [Weg] to take.

einschlägig ◇ *adj* [Literatur] relevant; [Methode] appropriate. ◇ *adv*: **einschlägig vorbestraft sein** to have a previous conviction for a similar offence.

ein|schleichen ◆ **sich einschleichen** *ref (unreg) eigtl* & *fig* to creep in.

ein|schleusen *vt* [Waffen] to smuggle in; [V-Leute] to infiltrate.

ein|schließen *vt (unreg)* - **1.** [einsperren] to lock up - **2.** [aufbewahren] to lock away - **3.** [umzingeln] to surround - **4.** [beinhalten] to include.

einschließlich ◇ *präp (+ G)* including; **von 1,3 bis einschließlich 5,5** from 1.3 to 5.5 inclusive. ◇ *adv*: **bis Montag einschließlich** up to and including Monday.

ein|schmeicheln ◆ **sich einschmeicheln** *ref*: **sich bei jm einschmeicheln** *abw* to curry favour with sb.

einschneidend ◇ *adj* drastic. ◇ *adv* drastically.

ein|schneien (*perf* **ist eingeschneit**) *vi* to get snowed in.

Ein|schnitt *der* - **1.** [Schnitt] cut; [bei Operation] incision - **2.** [Zäsur] turning point.

ein|schränken *vt* to limit; [Rauchen, Trinken] to cut down on; [Menge, Anzahl] to reduce. ◆ **sich einschränken** *ref* to economize.

Einschränkung (*pl* **-en**) *die* - **1.** [Einschränken] limitation; [von Kosten] reduction - **2.** [Vorbehalt] reservation.

ein|schreiben *vt (unreg)* - **1.** [hineinschreiben]: **eingeschrieben sein** to be registered - **2.** [Brief]: **etw einschreiben lassen** ODER **eingeschrieben schicken** to send sthg recorded delivery. ◆ **sich einschreiben** *ref* [sich anmelden] to register.

Ein|schreiben *das*: **etw per Einschreiben schicken** to send sthg recorded delivery.

ein|schreiten (*perf* **ist eingeschritten**) *vi (unreg)* to intervene.

ein|schüchtern *vt* to intimidate.

Einschüchterung (*pl* **-en**) *die* intimidation.

ein|schulen *vt*: **eingeschult werden** to start school.

Ein|schulung *die* [Tag] first day at school.

ein|sehen *vt (unreg)* - **1.** [Fehler, Schuld] to recognize, to admit - **2.** [Papiere] to examine.

einseitig ◇ *adj* - **1.** [subjektiv] one-sided - **2.** [auf einer Seite] on one side - **3.** [Beziehung] unilateral. ◇ *adv* - **1.** [subjektiv] one-sidedly - **2.** [auf einer Seite] on one side - **3.** [unausgewogen]: **sich einseitig ernähren** to eat an unbalanced diet.

ein|senden (*prät* **sẹndete ein** *ODER* **sạndte ein**, *perf* **hat eingesendet** *ODER* **eingesạndt**) *vt* to send in.

ein|setzen ◇ *vt* - **1.** [hineinsetzen] to put in - **2.** [gebrauchen] to use; **die Polizei/das Militär einsetzen** to bring in the police/army - **3.** [in Amt] to appoint - **4.** [Leben] to risk; [Geld] to stake. ◇ *vi* to begin; [Sturm] to break. ◆ **sich einsetzen** *ref* to be committed; **sich für jn einsetzen** to stand up for sb; **sich für etw einsetzen** to support sthg.

Ein|sicht *die* - **1.** [Erkenntnis] insight; **zu der Einsicht kommen, dass...** to come to realize that... - **2.** [Einblick]: **in etw** *(A)* **Einsicht bekommen** to get a look at sthg.

einsichtig ◇ *adj* - **1.** [vernünftig] sensible - **2.** [verständlich] clear. ◇ *adv* - **1.** [vernünftig] sensibly - **2.** [verständlich] clearly.

Ein|siedler, in *der, die* hermit.

einsilbig ◇ *adj* - **1.** [Person] taciturn - **2.** [Wort, Antwort] monosyllabic. ◇ *adv* [antworten] in monosyllables.

ein|sinken (*perf* **ist eingesunken**) *vi (unreg)* to sink (in).

ein|spannen *vt* - **1.** [Pferd] to harness - **2.** [zur Arbeit] to rope in - **3.** [in Schreibmaschine] to insert.

ein|sparen *vt* to save; [Personal] to cut back on.

ein|sperren *vt* to lock up.

ein|spielen *vt* - **1.** [Geld] to bring in; [Unkosten] to cover - **2.** [Instrument] to play in - **3.** [einfügen] to fit in. ◆ **sich einspielen** *ref* - **1.** [sich aufwärmen] to warm up - **2.** [sich abstimmen] to settle down; **die Kollegen haben sich aufeinander eingespielt** the colleagues are now working well together.

ein|springen (*perf* **ist eingesprungen**) *vi (unreg)*: **(für jn) einspringen** to stand in (for sb).

Ein|spruch *der* objection; **Einspruch (gegen etw) erheben** to object (to sthg).

einspurig ◇ *adj* single-lane. ◇ *adv*: **'nur einspurig befahrbar'** 'single-lane traffic only'.

ein|stecken *vt* - **1.** [in Tasche] to put in one's pocket; **vergiss nicht, Geld einzustecken!** don't forget to take some money with you! - **2.** [Kritik, Niederlage, Verlust] to take - **3.** [Stecker] to plug in - **4.** [Brief] to post *UK*, to mail *US* - **5.** [stehlen] to pocket.

ein|steigen (*perf* **ist eingestiegen**) *vi (unreg)* - **1.** [in Auto] to get in; [in Bus, Zug] to get on; **ins Auto/in den Zug einsteigen** to get in the car/on the train - **2.** [anfangen]: **in etw** *(A)* **einsteigen** [Beruf, Politik] to go into sthg - **3.** [sich einkaufen]: **bei RTL/in eine Firma einsteigen** to buy a share in RTL/a company.

einstellbar *adj* adjustable.

ein|stellen *vt* - **1.** [Angestellte] to take on - **2.** [Gerät, Lautstärke - zum ersten Mal] to set; [- genauer] to adjust; [Sender] to tune into - **3.** [anmachen] to switch on - **4.** [beenden] to stop. ◆ **sich einstellen** *ref* - **1.** [sich vorbereiten]: **sich auf jn/etw einstellen** to prepare for sb/sthg; [sich anpassen] to get used to sb/sthg - **2.** *geh* [anfangen] to begin.

Ein|stellung *die* - **1.** [von Angestellten] appointment - **2.** [von Gerät, Lautstärke - zum ersten Mal] setting; [- genauer] adjustment; [von Sender] tuning - **3.** [Beendigung - von Verfahren, Zahlungen] termination, stopping - **4.** [Meinung, Haltung] attitude - **5.** [Szene] take.

Einstellungs|gespräch *das* interview.

Einstieg (*pl* **-e**) *der* - **1.** [Beginn] entry - **2.** [in Bus, Zug] boarding.

ein|stimmen *vi* - **1.** [mitsingen, mitspielen]: **(in etw** *(A)***) einstimmen** to join in (sthg) - **2.** [vorbereiten]: **jn auf etw** *(A)* **einstimmen** to get sb in the right mood for sthg.

einstimmig ◇ *adj* - **1.** MUS for one voice - **2.** [übereinstimmend] unanimous. ◇ *adv* - **1.** MUS in unison - **2.** [übereinstimmend] unanimously.

einstöckig *adj* single-storey.

ein|studieren *vt* to rehearse.

ein|stufen *vt* to categorize; **jn in eine Gehaltsgruppe einstufen** to put sb in an income bracket.

einstündig *adj* one-hour.

Ein|sturz *der* collapse.

ein|stürzen (*perf* **ist eingestürzt**) *vi* - **1.** [Haus, Mauer] to collapse - **2.** [hereinbrechen]: **neue Eindrücke stürzten auf sie ein** she was overwhelmed by new impressions.

Einsturz|gefahr *die*: **'Vorsicht, Einsturzgefahr!'** 'danger, building unsafe!'

einstweilig *amt* ◇ *adj* temporary. ◇ *adv* temporarily.

eintägig *adj* one-day.

ein|tauchen (*perf* **hat/ist eingetaucht**) ◇ *vt (hat)* to dip; [völlig] to immerse; [Keks] to dunk. ◇ *vi (ist)* to dive in.

ein|tauschen *vt*: **etw gegen etw eintauschen** to exchange sthg for sthg.

eintausend *num* a *ODER* one thousand.

ein|teilen *vt* - **1.** [klassifizieren] to classify - **2.** [unterteilen] to divide up - **3.** [Arbeit, Zeit] to organize - **4.** [einplanen]: **jn für** *ODER* **zu etw einteilen** to assign sb to sthg.

einteilig *adj* one-piece.

Ein|teilung *die* - **1.** [Klassifizierung] classification - **2.** [Unterteilung] division - **3.** [von Arbeit, Zeit] organization.

eintönig ◇ *adj* monotonous. ◇ *adv* monotonously.

Ein|topf *der* stew.

einträchtig *adv* harmoniously.

Eintrag (*pl* **-träge**) *der* [Notiz] entry.

ein|tragen *vt (unreg)* - **1.** [notieren] to write down - **2.** *amt* [registrieren] to register - **3.** [Geld] to bring in; [Ärger, Sympathie] to bring. ◆ **sich eintragen** *ref* to put one's name down.

einträglich *adj* lucrative.

ein|treffen (*perf* **ist eingetroffen**) *vi (unreg)* - **1.** [ankommen] to arrive - **2.** [wahr werden] to come true.

ein|treiben *vt (unreg)* to collect.

ein|treten (*perf* **hat/ist eingetreten**) *(unreg)* ◇ *vi (ist)* - **1.** [in Raum, Phase] to enter; **in etw** *(A)* **eintreten** to enter sthg - **2.** [in Gruppe, Verein]: **in etw** *(A)* **eintreten** to join sthg - **3.** [sich einsetzen]: **für jn/etw eintreten** to stand up for sb/sthg - **4.** [Tod] to occur; [Fall, Umstände] to arise. ◇ *vt (hat)* to kick in.

Ein|tritt *der* - **1.** [in Raum, Phase] entry; **'Eintritt frei'** 'admission free'; **'Eintritt verboten'** 'no entry' - **2.** [Eintrittspreis] admission - **3.** [in Gruppe, Verein] joining - **4.** [Anfang]: **bei Eintritt der Dämmerung** at dawn.

Eintritts|geld *das* admission fee.

Eintritts|karte *die* ticket.

ein|trüben ◆ **sich eintrüben** *ref* to cloud over; **es trübt sich ein** it's clouding over.

ein|üben *vt* to rehearse.

einverstanden ◇ *adj*: **mit jm/etw einverstanden sein** to agree with sb/sthg; **sich mit etw einverstanden erklären** to agree to sthg. ◇ *interj* OK!

Ein|verständnis *das* - **1.** [Übereinstimmung] agreement - **2.** [Billigung] consent.

Ein|wand *der* objection; **Einwand (gegen etw) erheben** to object (to sthg).

ein|wandern (*perf* **ist eingewandert**) *vi* to immigrate.

Ein|wanderung *die* immigration.

einwandfrei ◇ *adj* perfect; [Material] flawless; [Nachweis] irrefutable. ◇ *adv* perfectly.

einwärts *adv* inwards.

Einweg|flasche *die* non-returnable bottle.

ein|weichen *vt* to soak.

ein|weihen *vt* - **1.** [Gebäude] to open - **2.** [Wagen, Sofa] to christen, to use for the first time.

Ein|weihung *die* [von Gebäude] opening; [von Wohnung] housewarming party.

ein|weisen *vt (unreg)* - **1.** [Patienten] to admit - **2.** [Anfänger]: **jn in etw** *(A)* **einweisen** to introduce sb to sthg.

Ein|weisung *die* - **1.** [von Patienten] admission - **2.** [von Anfänger] introduction.

ein|wenden *vt*: **einwenden, dass...** to object that...; **dagegen ist nichts einzuwenden** there's no reason why not.

ein|werfen *vt (unreg)* - **1.** [Münze] to insert; [Brief] to post *UK*, to mail *US* - **2.** [Ball, Frage, Bemerkung] to throw in - **3.** [kaputtwerfen] to smash.

ein|wickeln *vt* - **1.** [einpacken] to wrap up - **2.** *fam abw* [überreden] to take in.

ein|willigen *vi*: **(in etw** *(A)***) einwilligen** to agree (to sthg).

Einwilligung (*pl* **-en**) *die* consent.

ein|wirken *vi* - **1.** [Salbe] to take effect - **2.** [Person]: **auf jn beruhigend einwirken** to have a calming influence on sb.

Einwohner, in (*mpl* **-**, *fpl* **-nen**) *der, die* inhabitant.

Einwohnermelde|amt *das local government office at which inhabitants of a town must register at the beginning and end of their residency.*

Ein|wurf *der* - **1.** [Ausspruch] comment - **2.** [von Ball] throw-in - **3.** [von Münze] insertion; [von Brief] posting *UK*, mailing *US* - **4.** [Schlitz] slot.

Einzahl *die* singular.

ein|zahlen *vt* to pay in.

Ein|zahlung *die* deposit.

ein|zeichnen *vt* to mark.

Einzel (*pl* **-**) *das* singles *Pl*.

Einzel|fall *der* isolated case.

Einzel|gänger, in (*mpl* **-**, *fpl* **-nen**) *der, die* loner.

Einzel|handel *der* retail trade.

Einzelheit (*pl* **-en**) *die* detail; **in allen Einzelheiten** down to the last detail.

Einzel|kind *das* only child.

einzeln ◇ *adj* - **1.** [speziell] individual - **2.** [isoliert] single; **jedes einzelne Exemplar** every single copy - **3.** [Schuh, Socke] odd. ◇ *adv* individually; [ankommen, abholen] separately; **einzeln stehend** solitary. ◇ *det (nur pl)* a few.

Einzelne ◇ *pron sing* - **1.** [Person]: **jede/jeder Einzelne** (each and) every one - **2.** [Sache]: **jede/jeder/jedes Einzelne** every single one. ◇ *pron Pl* - **1.** [Personen] some (people) - **2.** [Sachen] some. ◇ *der, die* [Mensch] individual. ◇ *das*: **ins Einzelne gehen** to go into detail; **im Einzelnen** in detail. ◆ **Einzelnes** *pron* some things *Pl*.

Einzel|person *die* single person.

Einzel|stück *das* [Kunstgegenstand] piece.

Einzel|zimmer *das* single room.

ein|ziehen (*perf* **hat/ist eingezogen**) *(unreg)* ◇ *vt (hat)* - **1.** [Bauch, Netz] to pull in; [Krallen, Fahrgestell] to retract - **2.** [Faden, Band] to thread in - **3.** [Wand] to put in - **4.** [zur Armee] to call up - **5.** [Geld, Steuern] to collect - **6.** [beschlagnahmen] to confiscate - **7.** [Banknoten, Münzen] to withdraw (from circulation) - **8.** *amt* [Informationen] to gather. ◇ *vi (ist)* - **1.** [in Wohnung] to move in - **2.** [Einzug halten] to enter - **3.** [Fett, Creme, Flüssigkeit] to be absorbed.

einzig ◇ *adj (ohne Kompar)* - **1.** [alleinig] only; **nur noch ein einziges Mal** just one more time; **ein einziger Besucher** a single visitor - **2.** *geh* [einzigartig] unique - **3.** [total] complete. ◇ *adv* only; **einzig und allein** entirely.

einzigartig *adj* unique.

Einzige *der, die, das*: **der/die/das Einzige** [Person] the only one; [Sache] the only thing; **das Einzige, was** the only thing that; **nur ein Einziger erhob sich** only one person stood up.

Einzịmmer|wohnung *die* one-room flat *UK* ODER apartment *US*.

Ein|zug *der* - **1.** [von Jahreszeit] arrival - **2.** [von Sportler, Sieger] entrance - **3.** MIL entry - **4.** [in Wohnung] move - **5.** [von Geld, Steuern] collection.

Eis *(pl -) das* - **1.** [Gefrorenes] ice; **etw ạuf Eis legen** *eigtl* & *fig* to put sthg on ice - **2.** [Eiscreme] ice cream.

Eis|bahn *die* ice rink.

Eis|bär *der* polar bear.

Eis|becher *der* (ice-cream) sundae.

Eis|bein *das* knuckle of pork.

Eis|berg *der* iceberg.

Eis|café ['aiskafe:] *das* ice-cream parlour.

Eischnee *der*: **das Eiweiß zu Eischnee schlagen** to beat the egg white until stiff.

Eiscreme, Eiskrem ['aiskre:m] *die* ice cream.

Eis|diele *die* ice-cream parlour.

Eisen *(pl -) das* [gen] iron.

Eisen|bahn *die* - **1.** [Zug] train; **mit der Eisenbahn fahren** to travel by train - **2.** [Institution] railway *UK*, railroad *US* - **3.** [Modelleisenbahn] train set.

Eisenbahn|netz *das* rail network.

Eisen|erz *das* iron ore.

eisenhaltig *adj* [Erz] iron-bearing, ferrous; [Nahrung] containing iron.

eisern ◇ *adj eigtl* & *fig* iron; **eisern bleiben** to remain resolute. ◇ *adv* [unnachgiebig] resolutely.

eisgekühlt *adj* chilled.

Eis|hockey *das* ice hockey.

eisig ◇ *adj* - **1.** [eiskalt] freezing - **2.** [abweisend] icy, frosty. ◇ *adv* - **1.** [eiskalt]: **eisig kalt** freezing cold - **2.** [abweisend]: **eisig lächeln** to give a frosty smile.

eiskalt ◇ *adj* - **1.** [Körperteil, Getränk, Wind] ice-cold - **2.** [Mensch, Mord] cold-blooded; [Blick] frosty. ◇ *adv* - **1.** [sehr kalt] ice-cold - **2.** [herzlos] in cold blood.

Eiskrem = **Eiscreme**.

Eiskunstlauf *der* figure skating.

Eis|zapfen *der* icicle.

Eis|zeit *die* Ice Age.

eitel *adj abw* vain.

Eitelkeit *(pl -en) die abw* vanity.

Eiter *der* pus.

eitern *vi* to fester.

eitrig, eiterig *adj* [Wunde] festering; [Geschwür] suppurating.

Eiweiß *(pl -e) das* - **1.** [im Hühnerei] egg white - **2.** BIOL & CHEM protein.

Ei|zelle *die* ovum.

EKD [e:ǩa:'de:] (*abk für* **Evangelische Kirche in Deutschland**) *die Protestant Church in Germany*.

Ekel *(pl -)* ◇ *der* [Abscheu] disgust; **Ekel vor etw** *(D)* **empfinden** to find sthg disgusting. ◇ *das fam abw* [Person] horror.

ekelhaft ◇ *adj* - **1.** [Ekel erregend] disgusting - **2.** [Arbeit, Chef] nasty. ◇ *adv* [Ekel erregend] disgustingly.

ekeln *vt*: **das ekelt mich** I find that disgusting. ◆ **sich ekeln** *ref*: **sich (vor jm/etw) ekeln** to be disgusted (by sb/sthg).

eklig, ekelig *adj* - **1.** [Ekel erregend] disgusting - **2.** *fam* [gemein] nasty.

Ekzem *(pl -e) das* eczema *(U)*.

elạstisch *adj* - **1.** [Gummi] elastic - **2.** [Körper] supple; [Gang] springy.

Ẹlbe *die*: **die Elbe** the (River) Elbe.

Ẹlch *(pl -e) der* elk.

Elefạnt *(pl -en) der* elephant; **wie ein Elefant im Porzellanladen** *fam* like a bull in a china shop.

elegạnt ◇ *adj* elegant. ◇ *adv* elegantly.

Elegạnz *die* elegance.

Elẹktriker, in *(mpl -, fpl -nen) der, die* electrician.

elẹktrisch ◇ *adj* - **1.** [elektrisch betrieben - Licht, Rasierapparat, *etc*] electric; **elektrisches Gerät** electrical appliance - **2.** [mit Elektrizität zusammenhängend - Widerstand, Ladung] electrical. ◇ *adv* electrically.

Elektrizitäts|werk *das* power station.

Elektrode *(pl -n) die* electrode.

Elẹktro|gerät *das* electrical appliance.

Elẹktro|geschäft *das* electrical goods store.

Elẹktro|herd *der* electric oven.

Elẹktro|motor *der* electric motor.

Elektronik *die (ohne pl)* - **1.** [Wissenschaft] electronics *(U)* - **2.** [Teile] electronics *Pl*.

elektronisch ◇ *adj* electronic. ◇ *adv* electronically.

Elẹktrotechnik *die* electrical engineering.

Elemẹnt *(pl -e) das* element; **in seinem Element sein** to be in one's element; **dunkle** ODER **zwielichtige Elemente** shady characters.

elend ◇ *adj* - **1.** [erbärmlich] miserable - **2.** [krank] wretched. ◇ *adv* - **1.** [erbärmlich] miserably - **2.** [schlecht] wretchedly; **sich elend fühlen** to feel wretched.

Elend *das* - **1.** [Unglück] misery - **2.** [Ärmlichkeit] poverty.

Elends|viertel *das* slum.

ẹlf *num* eleven; *siehe auch* **sechs**.

Ẹlf (*pl* **-en**) ◇ *die* [Zahl & SPORT] eleven. ◇ *der* elf; *siehe auch* **Sechs**.

Ẹlfenbein *das* ivory.

ẹlfhundert *num* one thousand one hundred.

Elfmeter (*pl* -) *der* penalty.

ẹlfte, **r**, **s** *adj* eleventh; *siehe auch* **sechste**.

Ẹlfte (*pl* **-n**) *der, die, das* eleventh; *siehe auch* **Sechste**.

ẹlftel *adj (unver)* eleventh; *siehe auch* **sechstel**.

Ẹlftel (*pl* -) *das* eleventh; *siehe auch* **Sechstel**.

Elite (*pl* **-n**) *die* elite.

Elite|schule *die* prestigious school.

Ẹllbogen (*pl* -), **Ẹllenbogen** (*pl* -) *der* elbow.

Ẹlle (*pl* **-n**) *die* - **1.** [Knochen] ulna - **2.** [Maßeinheit] cubit.

Ẹllenbogen = **Ellbogen**.

Ẹlsass *das* Alsace.

ẹlsässisch *adj* Alsatian.

Ẹlster (*pl* **-n**) *die* magpie.

ẹlterlich *adj* parental.

Ẹltern *Pl* parents.

Ẹltern|abend *der* SCHULE parents' evening.

Ẹltern|haus *das* home.

Ẹltern|teil *der* parent.

Email [e'mai̯] *das* enamel.

E-Mail ['iːmɛi̯l] (*pl* **-s**) *die* EDV e-mail; **jm eine E-Mail schicken** to send sb an e-mail, to e-mail sb.

E-Mail-|Adresse *die* e-mail address.

Emanzipation (*pl* **-en**) *die* emancipation.

emanzipieren ◆ **sich emanzipieren** *ref* to become emancipated.

Embargo (*pl* **-s**) *das* embargo.

Ẹmbryo (*pl* **-s** ODER **-onen**) *der* embryo.

Emigrạnt, **in** (*mpl* **-en**, *fpl* **-nen**) *der, die* émigré.

emigrieren (*perf* **ist emigriert**) *vi* to go into (voluntary) exile, to leave the country.

Emission (*pl* **-en**) *die* emission.

emotional ◇ *adj* emotional. ◇ *adv* emotionally.

empfahl *prät* ▷ **empfehlen**.

empfạnd *prät* ▷ **empfinden**.

Empfạng (*pl* **Empfạ̈nge**) *der* - **1.** [Erhalt - von Brief, Ware] receipt; **etw in Empfang nehmen** to receive sthg; **ein Paket für die Nachbarn in Empfang nehmen** to take a parcel for the neighbours - **2.** [Begrüßung] welcome - **3.** [Veranstaltung, Rezeption & TV] reception.

empfạngen (*präs* **empfạ̈ngt**, *prät* **empfịng**, *perf* **hat empfạngen**) *vt* - **1.** [gen] to receive - **2.** [begrüßen] to greet; **Gäste empfangen** to receive visitors.

Empfạ̈nger (*pl* -) *der* - **1.** [Gerät] receiver - **2.** [Adressat] addressee; [von Arbeitslosengeld] recipient.

Empfạ̈ngerin (*pl* **-nen**) *die* [Adressat] addressee; [von Arbeitslosengeld] recipient.

empfạ̈nglich *adj*: **(für etw) empfänglich sein** to be susceptible (to sthg).

Empfạ̈ngnis *die* conception.

Empfạ̈ngnisverhütung *die* contraception.

Empfạngs|bescheinigung *die* acknowledgement of receipt.

empfạ̈ngt *präs* ▷ **empfangen**.

empfehlen (*präs* **empfiehlt**, *prät* **empfahl**, *perf* **hat empfohlen**) *vt* to recommend; **jm empfehlen, etw zu tun** to recommend that sb do sthg. ◆ **sich empfehlen** *ref* - **1.** [sich anbieten] to be recommended; **es empfiehlt sich, etw zu tun** it is advisable to do sthg - **2.** *geh* [sich verabschieden] to take one's leave.

empfehlenswert *adj* - **1.** [gut] recommendable - **2.** [ratsam] advisable.

Empfehlung (*pl* **-en**) *die* - **1.** [Ratschlag] recommendation; **auf js Empfehlung hin, auf Empfehlung von jm** on sb's recommendation - **2.** [Beurteilung] reference - **3.** *geh* [Gruß] regards *Pl*.

Empfehlungs|schreiben *das* reference.

empfiehlt *präs* ▷ **empfehlen**.

empfịnden (*prät* **empfạnd**, *perf* **hat empfụnden**) *vt* to feel; **etw als Kränkung empfinden** to take offence at sthg.

Empfịnden *das* feeling; **das Empfinden für Gut und Böse** the sense of good and evil; **für** ODER **nach meinem Empfinden** if you ask me.

empfịndlich ◇ *adj* - **1.** [Haut, Film, Gemüt] sensitive - **2.** [Gesundheit, Person] delicate - **3.** [Strafe, Verlust] severe. ◇ *adv* - **1.** [verletzlich] sensitively - **2.** [merklich] severely; **jn empfindlich treffen** to hurt sb badly - **3.** [sehr - kalt] bitterly.

Empfịndlichkeit *die* - **1.** [von Haut, Film, Gemüt] sensitivity - **2.** [von Person] susceptibility - **3.** [von Material, Gemüt] delicacy.

Empfịndung (*pl* **-en**) *die* - **1.** [Wahrnehmung] sensation - **2.** [Emotion] feeling.

empfịng *prät* ▷ **empfangen**.

empfohlen *pp* ▷ **empfehlen**.

empfụnden *pp* ▷ **empfinden**.

empören *vt* to outrage. ◆ **sich empören** *ref*: **sich über etw** *(A)* **empören** to be outraged by sthg.

empört *adj* outraged.

Empörung *die* outrage.

ẹmsig ◇ *adj* industrious; [Biene] busy; [Treiben] bustling. ◇ *adv* industriously.

Ẹnde (*pl* **-n**) *das* - **1.** [gen] end; **Ende März** at the end of March; **zu Ende sein** to be over; **zu Ende gehen** to come to an end; **ein Ende nehmen** to be over; **kein Ende nehmen** to go on and on - **2.** *fam* [Wegstrecke]: **es ist noch ein ganzes Ende** it's still quite a way; **am Ende sein** [körperlich] to be completely exhausted; [nervlich] to be at the end of one's tether *UK* ODER rope *US*; **mit seiner Geduld am Ende sein** to have run out of patience; **mit seiner Weisheit am Ende sein** to be at one's wit's end. ◆ **am Ende** *adv* in the end. ◆ **letzten Endes** *adv* - **1.** [am Schluss] in the end - **2.** [im Grunde genommen] ultimately, in the final analysis.

Ẹndeffekt *der*: **im Endeffekt** in the end.

ẹnden (*perf* **hat/ist geẹndet**) *vi* - **1.** *(hat)* [zu Ende gehen] to end; **der Zug endet in Köln** the train terminates in Cologne; **gut/schlecht enden** to have a happy/an unhappy ending; **nicht enden wollend** unending - **2.** *(hat, ist)* [sterben] to meet one's end; [schließlich landen]: **im Gefängnis enden** to end up in prison.

Ẹnd|ergebnis *das* end result.

ẹndgültig ◇ *adj* final; [Antwort] definitive; [Beweis] conclusive. ◇ *adv* finally; [erklären] definitively.

Endivie [ɛnˈdiːvi̯ə] (*pl* **-n**) *die* endive.

ẹndlich ◇ *adv* - **1.** [nach langem Warten] at last; **wann kommst du denn endlich?** so when are you finally going to come? - **2.** [am Ende] finally; **um neun erreichten wir endlich das Ziel** we eventually got there at nine. ◇ *adj* finite.

ẹndlos ◇ *adj* endless. ◇ *adv* interminably; [dauern] for ages.

Ẹnd|spurt *der* final spurt.

Ẹnd|station *die* terminus.

Ẹndung (*pl* **-en**) *die* ending.

Energie (*pl* **-n**) *die* energy.

Energiebedarf *der (ohne pl)* energy requirements *Pl*.

Energie|krise *die* energy crisis.

Energie|verbrauch *der* energy consumption.

enẹrgisch ◇ *adj* forceful. ◇ *adv* forcefully.

ẹng ◇ *adj* - **1.** [Raum] narrow; **im Auto ist es eng** it's cramped in the car - **2.** [Kleidung] tight - **3.** [Auslegung, Interpretation] narrow; **im engeren Sinn (des Wortes)** in the narrowest sense (of the word) - **4.** [Beziehung, Freund, Verwandte] close. ◇ *adv* - **1.** [dicht gedrängt] close together - **2.** [anliegen] tightly - **3.** [auslegen, interpretieren] narrowly - **4.** [nah] close; **eng mit jm befreundet sein** to be close friends with sb.

engagieren [ɑ̃gaˈʒiːrən] *vt* to engage. ◆ **sich engagieren** *ref*: **sie engagiert sich politisch** she's very involved in politics; **sich für jn/etw engagieren** to show commitment to sb/sthg.

Ẹnge *die* - **1.** [Schmalheit] narrowness - **2.** [Platzmangel] crampedness.

Ẹngel (*pl* -) *der* angel.

Ẹngland *nt* England.

Ẹngländer, in (*mpl* -, *fpl* **-nen**) *der, die* Englishman (Englishwoman *die*); **die Engländer** the English.

ẹnglisch ◇ *adj* English. ◇ *adv* [sprechen] in English.

Ẹnglisch(e) *das* English; **auf/in Englisch** in English.

ẹngstirnig *abw* ◇ *adj* narrow-minded. ◇ *adv* narrow-mindedly.

Ẹnkel, in (*mpl* -, *fpl* **-nen**) *der, die* grandson (granddaughter *die*); **unsere Enkel** our grandchildren.

Ẹnkel|kind *das* grandchild.

enọrm ◇ *adj* enormous, immense. ◇ *adv* tremendously, terribly; **sich enorm anstrengen** to make a tremendous effort.

entarten (*perf* **ist entartet**) *vi* to degenerate.

entbehren ◇ *vt* - **1.** [verzichten auf] to do without - **2.** *geh* [vermissen] to miss. ◇ *vi*: **einer Sache** *(G)* **entbehren** *geh* to lack sthg.

entbehrlich *adj* dispensable.

Entbehrung (*pl* **-en**) *die* privation.

Entbịndung (*pl* **-en**) *die* - **1.** [Befreiung] discharge - **2.** [Gebären] delivery.

entblößen *vt* - **1.** [Körper] to bare, to expose - **2.** [Mensch] to expose; [Gedanken, Gefühle] to reveal. ◆ **sich entblößen** *ref* [sich ausziehen] to undress; [Exhibitionist] to expose o.s.

entdẹcken *vt* - **1.** [gen] to discover - **2.** [Fehler] to detect; [Urheber] to identify; **kannst du ihn entdecken?** can you make him out?

Entdẹcker, in (*mpl* -, *fpl* **-nen**) *der, die* discoverer.

Entdẹckung (*pl* **-en**) *die* discovery.

Ẹnte (*pl* **-n**) *die* - **1.** [Tier] duck - **2.** [Zeitungsmeldung] hoax - **3.** *fam* [Auto] *Citroën 2 CV*.

enteignen *vt* [Mensch] to dispossess; [Vermögen] to expropriate.

entẹrben *vt* to disinherit.

entfạllen (*präs* **entfạllt**, *prät* **entfiel**, *perf* **ist entfạllen**) *vi* - **1.** [vergessen]: **ihr Name ist mir entfallen** her name has slipped my mind - **2.** [sich verteilen]: **auf jn entfallen** to fall ODER go to sb.

entfạlten *vt* - **1.** [öffnen] to unfold - **2.** [entwickeln] to develop - **3.** [zeigen] to display, to show; [Aktivität] to launch into - **4.** [erläutern] to set out. ◆ **sich entfalten** *ref* - **1.** [Blüte, Fallschirm] to open; [Segel] to unfurl - **2.** [sich verwirklichen] to develop.

Entfạltung (*pl* **-en**) *die* - **1.** [von Persönlichkeit] development; [von Aktivität] launching into; **etw zur Entfaltung bringen** to develop sthg to its full potential - **2.** [von Blüte] opening.

entfẹrnen *vt* [beseitigen] to remove; **ein Kind von seiner Mutter entfernen** to take a child away from its mother. ◆ **sich entfernen** *ref* [sich wegbegeben] to leave; **sich von etw entfernen** [weggehen] to leave sthg; [von Pfad, Thema] to stray from sthg.

entfẹrnt ◇ *adj* - **1.** [fort]: **wenige Kilometer von hier entfernt** a few kilometres away ODER from here; **weit entfernt** a long way away - **2.** [abgelegen] remote; **weit davon entfernt sein, etw zu tun** not to have the slightest intention of doing sthg - **3.** [Verwandte] distant; [Ähnlichkeit] vague - **4.** [Ahnung] faint, vague. ◇ *adv* - **1.** [weitläufig] distantly, remotely - **2.** [blass, gering] vaguely, faintly. ◆ **Entfernteste** *das*: **nicht im Entferntesten hatte ich daran gedacht** I didn't have the slightest intention of doing it.

Entfẹrnung (*pl* **-en**) *die* - **1.** [Distanz] distance; **in einer Entfernung von 2 km** at a distance of 2 km; **aus der Entfernung zugucken** to look on from afar - **2.** [Beseitigung] removal - **3.** [Weggehen] departure.

entfrẹmden *vt* [Person] to alienate; **jn jm/einer Sache entfremden** to alienate ODER estrange sb from sb/sthg.

entführen *vt* [Mensch] to kidnap; [Flugzeug] to hijack.

Entführer, in (*mpl* -, *fpl* **-nen**) *der, die* [von Menschen] kidnapper; [von Flugzeug] hijacker.

Entführung (*pl* **-en**) *die* [von Menschen] kidnapping; [von Flugzeug] hijacking.

entgegen *präp (+ D)* contrary to; **sie kam ihm entgegen** she was coming towards him.

entgegen|gehen (*perf* **ist entgegengegangen**) *vi (unreg)*: **jm/einer Sache entgegengehen** to approach sb/sthg; **dem Ende entgegengehen** to draw to a close.

entgegengesetzt *adj* [Richtung, Seite, Meinung] opposite; **entgegengesetzte Ansichten** conflicting ODER opposing opinions.

entgegen|kommen (*perf* **ist entgegengekommen**) *vi (unreg)* - **1.** [herankommen]: **jm entgegenkommen** to approach sb - **2.** [auf Wünsche eingehen]: **js Wünschen/Erwartungen entgegenkommen** to meet sb's wishes/expectations.

Entgegenkommen *das* goodwill; **zu großem Entgegenkommen bereit sein** to be ready to make major concessions.

entgegenkommend ◇ *adj* [Mensch, Verhalten] accommodating, obliging. ◇ *adv* accommodatingly, obligingly.

entgegen|nehmen *vt (unreg)* to accept.

entgegen|setzen *vt*: **jm/etw Widerstand entgegensetzen** to resist sb/sthg; **einer Behauptung Beweise entgegensetzen** to produce evidence that contradicts a statement; **diesen Vorwürfen habe ich nichts entgegenzusetzen** I have no answer to these reproaches.

entgegen|stehen *vi (unreg)*: **einer Sache (D) entgegenstehen** to stand in sthg's way; **dem steht nichts entgegen** there is no objection to that.

entgegnen *vt* [antworten] to reply; [barsch] to retort.

entgehen (*prät* **entgịng**, *perf* **ist entgạngen**) *vi* - **1.** [entkommen]: **einer Sache (D) entgehen** to escape sthg - **2.** [unbemerkt bleiben]: **dieser Fehler ist mir entgangen** this mistake escaped my notice.

entgleisen (*perf* **ist entgleist**) *vi* - **1.** [Zug] to be derailed - **2.** [taktlos sein] to commit a faux pas.

entgleiten (*prät* **entglịtt**, *perf* **ist entglịtten**) *vi*: **jm** ODER **js Händen entgleiten** to slip from sb's hands.

enthạlten (*präs* **enthạ̈lt**, *prät* **enthielt**, *perf* **hat enthạlten**) *vt* to contain. ◆ **sich enthalten** *ref* - **1.** [nicht abstimmen]: **sich der Stimme enthalten** to abstain - **2.** *geh* [auf etw verzichten] to abstain; **sich einer Sache (G) enthalten** to abstain from sthg.

enthạltsam *adj* abstemious; **sexuell enthaltsam sein** to abstain from sex.

Enthạltsamkeit *die* abstinence.

Enthạltung (*pl* **-en**) *die* abstention.

enthüllen *vt* - **1.** [Denkmal, Gemälde] to unveil - **2.** [Wahrheit, Geheimnis] to reveal.

entkọmmen (*prät* **entkam**, *perf* **ist entkọmmen**) *vi* to escape; **jm entkommen** to elude sb.

entkrạ̈ftet *adj* [kraftlos] exhausted.

entladen (*präs* **entlädt**, *prät* **entlud**, *perf* **hat entlạden**) *vt* [Lkw, Waffe] to unload. ◆ **sich entladen** *ref* - **1.** [Gewitter] to break - **2.** [Wut, Aggressionen] to erupt - **3.** [Batterie] to discharge.

entlạng ◇ *präp* along; **die Straße entlang entlang der Straße** along the road. ◇ *adv* **am Fluss entlang** along the river.

entlạng|gehen (*perf* **ist entlạnggegangen**) *vi & vt (unreg)*: **etw (A)** ODER **an etw (D) entlanggehen** to go along sthg.

entlạrven [ɛnt'larfn̩] *vt* to expose.

entlạssen (*präs* **entlạ̈sst**, *prät* **entließ**, *perf* **hat entlạssen**) *vt* - **1.** [Kranken, Soldat] to discharge; [Gefangenen] to release - **2.** [kündigen] to sack.

Entlạssung (*pl* **-en**) *die* - **1.** [aus dem Krankenhaus, aus der Armee] discharge; [aus dem Gefängnis] release - **2.** [Kündigung] redundancy; [Aktion] sacking.

entlasten *vt* - **1.** [von einer Belastung befreien] to relieve the strain on; [Gewissen] to ease - **2.** RECHT to exonerate - **3.** WIRTSCH: **sein Konto entlasten** to reduce one's overdraft.

entleeren *vt* to empty. ◆ **sich entleeren** *ref* to empty.

entlegen *adj* remote.

entleihen (*prät* **entlieh**, *perf* **hat entliehen**) *vt* to borrow; **etw von jm entleihen** to borrow sthg from sb.

entlocken *vt*: **jm etw entlocken** to coax sthg out of sb.

entlüften *vt* to ventilate.

Entmachtung (*pl* **-en**) *die* removal from power.

entmilitarisieren *vt* to demilitarize.

entmündigen *vt*: **jn entmündigen** to declare sb unfit to manage his/her own affairs.

entmutigen *vt* to discourage, to dishearten.

entnervt *adj*: **entnervt sein** to have reached the end of one's tether *UK* ODER rope *US*.

entreißen (*prät* **entriss**, *perf* **hat entrissen**) *vt* [wegnehmen] to snatch away.

entrüsten *vt* to incense. ◆ **sich entrüsten** *ref*: **sich über jn/etw entrüsten** to be incensed by sb/sthg.

Entrüstung *die* indignation.

entschädigen *vt* to compensate; **jn für etw entschädigen** to compensate sb for sthg.

Entschädigung (*pl* **-en**) *die* compensation.

entschärfen *vt* - **1.** [Bombe, Debatte] to defuse - **2.** [Kritik] to take the sting out of.

entscheiden (*prät* **entschied**, *perf* **hat entschieden**) ◇ *vi*: **über etw** *(A)* **entscheiden** to decide on sthg. ◇ *vt* [Streit] to settle; [Fußballspiel] to decide. ◆ **sich entscheiden** *ref* [sich entschließen] to decide; **sich für/gegen jn/etw entscheiden** to decide on/against sb/sthg.

entscheidend ◇ *adj* [Problem, Frage] decisive; [Stimme, Tor] deciding. ◇ *adv* decisively.

Entscheidung (*pl* **-en**) *die* decision; [von Jury] verdict; [von Gericht, Ausschuss] ruling; **eine Entscheidung treffen** to make ODER take a decision.

entschieden ◇ *pp* ▷ **entscheiden**. ◇ *adj* [Verteidiger] staunch, steadfast; [Gegner] firm, strong. ◇ *adv* firmly, emphatically; **das geht entschieden zu weit!** that's going far too far!

entschließen (*prät* **entschloss**, *perf* **hat entschlossen**) ◆ **sich entschließen** *ref* to decide; **sich zur Annahme des Angebots entschließen** to decide to accept the offer.

entschlossen ◇ *pp* ▷ **entschließen**. ◇ *adj* determined, resolute. ◇ *adv* without hesitation.

Entschlossenheit *die* determination, resolution.

Entschluss (*pl* **-üsse**) *der* decision; **einen Entschluss fassen** to make ODER take a decision.

entschlüsseln *vt* to decipher.

entschuldigen *vt* to excuse; **entschuldige bitte!** (I'm) sorry!; **entschuldigen Sie bitte!** [vor Frage, Bitte] excuse me!; [tut mir Leid!] (I'm) sorry!

Entschuldigung (*pl* **-en**) ◇ *die* - **1.** [Rechtfertigung] excuse - **2.** SCHULE note *(from one's parents or a doctor)* - **3.** [Bitte um Verzeihung] apology - **4.** [Nachsicht]: **jn um Entschuldigung bitten** to beg sb's pardon. ◇ *interj* [vor Frage, Bitte] excuse me!; [tut mir Leid!] (I'm) sorry!

Entsetzen *das* horror; **zu js Entsetzen** to sb's horror.

entsetzlich ◇ *adj* - **1.** [schrecklich] horrible - **2.** [stark] terrible. ◇ *adv* [sehr] terribly.

entsetzt ◇ *adj* horrified; **über etw** *(A)* **entsetzt sein** to be horrified at sthg. ◇ *adv* in horror, aghast.

entsichern *vt* to release the safety catch of.

Entsorgung (*pl* **-en**) *die* waste disposal.

entspannen *vt* to relax. ◆ **sich entspannen** *ref* - **1.** [Person] to relax - **2.** [Situation] to ease.

Entspannung *die* - **1.** [Erholung] relaxation - **2.** [von Situationen] reduction of tension.

Entspannungs|politik *die* policy of détente.

entsprechen (*präs* **entspricht**, *prät* **entsprach**, *perf* **hat entsprochen**) *vi* - **1.** [genügen]: **einer Sache** *(D)* **entsprechen** [Tatsachen] to correspond to sthg; [Erwartungen, Anforderungen] to meet sthg; **100° Celsius entsprechen 212° Fahrenheit** 100° Celsius is equivalent to 212° Fahrenheit; **einem Zweck entsprechen** to fulfil a purpose - **2.** [nachkommen]: **einer Sache** *(D)* **entsprechen** to comply with sthg.

entsprechend ◇ *adj* - **1.** [angemessen, zuständig] appropriate - **2.** [dementsprechend] corresponding. ◇ *adv* [angemessen] appropriately; [dementsprechend] correspondingly. ◇ *präp*: **einer Sache** *(D)* **entsprechend, entsprechend einer Sache** *(D)* in accordance with sthg.

entspringen (*prät* **entsprang**, *perf* **ist entsprungen**) *vi* - **1.** [Fluss] to rise - **2.** [entstehen aus]: **einer Sache** *(D)* **entspringen** to arise from sthg.

entstehen (*prät* **entstand**, *perf* **ist entstanden**) *vi* - **1.** [geschaffen werden] to come into being; [Gebäude] to be built; [Kunstwerk] to be created; [Beziehung] to develop; [Roman] to be written; [Streit] to arise; **aus etw** ODER **durch etw entstehen** to come about as a result of sthg - **2.** [Schaden, Kosten] to be incurred.

Entstehung (*pl* **-en**) *die* - **1.** [eines Gebäudes] building; [eines Kunstwerkes] creation; [des Lebens] origins *Pl* - **2.** [von Kosten, Schaden] incurring.

entstẹllen *vt* - **1.** [Person] to disfigure - **2.** [Sachverhalt] to distort.

enttäuschen <> *vt* to disappoint; [Hoffnungen] to dash. <> *vi* to be disappointing.

enttäuscht <> *adj* disappointed; [Hoffnungen] dashed; **von jm enttäuscht sein** to be disappointed in ODER with sb. <> *adv* disappointed.

Enttäuschung (*pl* **-en**) *die* disappointment.

entwạffnen *vt eigtl* & *fig* to disarm.

Entwạrnung (*pl* **-en**) *die* all-clear (signal).

entwạ̈ssern *vt* to drain; MED to dehydrate.

entweder ◆ **entweder... oder...** *konj* either... or...

entweichen (*prät* **entwịch**, *perf* **ist entwịchen**) *vi* to escape.

entwẹrfen (*präs* **entwịrft**, *prät* **entwạrf**, *perf* **hat entwọrfen**) *vt* [Möbelstück, Kleidungsstück] to design; [Text] to draft; [Programm] to plan.

entwerten *vt* - **1.** [Fahrkarte] to cancel, to validate - **2.** [Geld] to devalue.

entwịckeln *vt* to develop; [Gase] to produce. ◆ **sich entwickeln** *ref* to develop; [Gase] to be produced; **sich aus etw entwickeln** to develop out of sthg; **sich zu etw entwickeln** to develop into sthg, to become sthg.

Entwịcklung (*pl* **-en**) *die* - **1.** [Entfaltung, Ausarbeitung] development; **in der Entwicklung (sein)** (to be) at the development stage - **2.** FOTO developing - **3.** [von Gasen] production.

Entwịcklungs|helfer, in *der, die* overseas aid worker.

Entwịcklungs|hilfe *die* development aid.

Entwịcklungs|land *das* developing country.

entwịrren *vt eigtl* & *fig* to unravel.

entwịschen (*perf* **ist entwịscht**) *vi fam* to make off; **jm entwischen** to give sb the slip.

entwöhnen *vt* to wean.

entwürdigend <> *adj* degrading. <> *adv* degradingly.

Entwụrf (*pl* **-ụ̈rfe**) *der* - **1.** [Zeichnung] blueprint - **2.** [Konzept] draft.

entwụrzeln *vt eigtl* & *fig* to uproot.

entziehen (*prät* **entzog**, *perf* **hat entzogen**) *vt*: **jm etw entziehen** to withdraw sthg from sb; **einer Sache** *(D)* **etw entziehen** to draw ODER extract sthg from sthg. ◆ **sich entziehen** *ref*: **sich jm/einer Sache entziehen** to escape sb/sthg; **sich der Verantwortung entziehen** to evade responsibility; **das entzieht sich meiner Kenntnis** I don't know anything about that.

Entziehungs|kur *die* detox.

entzịffern *vt* to decipher.

entzụ̈cken *vt* to delight; **sie war von dem Gemälde entzückt** she thought the painting was delightful.

entzụ̈ckend *adj* delightful, charming.

Entzug *der* withdrawal; **im Entzug sein** to be in detox.

Entzugs|erscheinung *die* withdrawal symptom.

ent|zụ̈nden *vt* to light. ◆ **sich entzünden** *ref* - **1.** [brennen] to catch fire; TECH to ignite - **2.** MED to become inflamed - **3.** [entstehen]: **sich an etw** *(D)* **entzünden** to be ignited by sthg.

Entzündung (*pl* **-en**) *die* inflammation.

Ẹnzian (*pl* **-e**) *der* [Pflanze] gentian.

Enzyklopädie (*pl* **-n**) *die* encyclopedia.

Enzym (*pl* **-e**) *das* enzyme.

Epidemie (*pl* **-n**) *die* epidemic.

Epik *die* [Gattung] epic poetry.

Epilepsie (*pl* **-n**) *die* epilepsy.

Episode (*pl* **-n**) *die* episode.

Epọche (*pl* **-n**) *die* period, era.

Epos (*pl* **Epen**) *das* epic.

er *pron* he; [bei Sachen, Tieren] it; **er wars!** it was him!

erạchten *vt*: **jn/etw als** ODER **für etw erachten** to consider sb/sthg (to be) sthg.

Erạchten *das*: **meines Erachtens** in my opinion.

erahnen *vt* [im Dämmerlicht] to barely make out; [Absicht] to get an inkling of.

erạrbeiten *vt* - **1.** [Stellung, Wissen] to acquire *(through one's own efforts)* - **2.** [Bericht, Programm] to draw up.

Erbạrmen *das* mercy, compassion; **mit jm/etw Erbarmen haben** to take pity on sb/sthg.

erbạ̈rmlich <> *adj* - **1.** [armselig, unzureichend] wretched, terrible - **2.** *abw* [gemein] despicable - **3.** [sehr groß] terrible. <> *adv* [sehr] terribly.

erbạrmungslos <> *adj* merciless. <> *adv* mercilessly.

erbauen *vt* - **1.** [errichten] to build - **2.** *geh* [erheben] to uplift.

Erbauer, in (*mpl* **-**, *fpl* **-nen**) *der, die* builder.

Ẹrbe (*pl* **-n**) <> *das* - **1.** [Vermögen] inheritance - **2.** [geistiges Vermächtnis] legacy. <> *der* heir.

ẹrben <> *vt* to inherit. <> *vi* to come into an inheritance.

erbeuten *vt* to capture *(as booty)*.

Ẹrb|folge *die* succession.

Ẹrbgut *das* BIOL genetic make-up.

Ẹrbin (*pl* **-nen**) *die* heiress.

erbịttert <> *adj* [Kampf] fierce; [Feind] bitter. <> *adv* fiercely.

Ẹrb|krankheit *die* hereditary disease.

ẹrblich <> *adj* hereditary. <> *adv*: **erblich belastet sein** to have a hereditary condition.

erblịnden (*perf* **ist erblịndet**) *vi* to go blind.

erbrẹchen (*präs* **erbrịcht**, *prät* **erbrach**, *perf* **hat erbrọchen**) *vt* to vomit (up). ◆ **sich erbrechen** *ref* to vomit.

Erbrechen *das* vomiting.

erbringen (*prät* **erbrachte**, *perf* **hat erbracht**) *vt* - **1.** [ergeben] to result in; [Geldsumme] to bring in; **Leistung erbringen** to produce; **eine notwendige Leistung erbringen** to do some necessary work - **2.** [Nachweis] to produce.

Erbschaft (*pl* **-en**) *die* inheritance.

Erbse (*pl* **-n**) *die* pea.

Erb|stück *das* heirloom.

Erd|ball *der* globe.

Erd|beben *das* earthquake.

Erd|beere *die* strawberry.

Erd|boden *der* [Boden] ground, earth; **etw dem Erdboden gleichmachen** to raze sthg to the ground; **wie vom Erdboden verschluckt sein** to seem to have vanished from the face of the earth.

Erde *die* - **1.** [Erdreich] soil, earth - **2.** [fester Boden] ground; **etw aus der Erde stampfen** *fam* [Gebäude] to build sthg overnight; **jn unter die Erde bringen** *fam* [begraben] to bury sb; **du bringst mich noch unter die Erde!** you'll be the death of me! - **3.** [Welt] world; **auf der ganzen Erde** in the whole world - **4.** [Planet] Earth.

erden *vt* ELEKTR to earth.

erdenklich *adj* conceivable, imaginable. ◆ **alles Erdenkliche** *adv*: **alles Erdenkliche tun** to do one's utmost.

Erd|gas *das* natural gas.

Erdgeschoss (*pl* **-e**) *das* ground floor *UK*, first floor *US*.

Erd|kugel *die* globe.

Erd|kunde *die* geography.

Erdnuss (*pl* **-nüsse**) *die* peanut.

Erd|öl *das* (mineral) oil.

erdrosseln *vt* to strangle.

erdrücken *vt* - **1.** [zu Tode drücken] to crush to death - **2.** [belasten] to overwhelm.

Erd|rutsch *der* landslide.

Erd|teil *der* continent.

erdulden *vt* to endure.

ereifern ◆ **sich ereifern** *ref* to get worked up.

ereignen ◆ **sich ereignen** *ref* to happen; [Unfall] to occur.

Ereignis (*pl* **-se**) *das* event.

ereignisreich *adj* eventful.

erfahren (*präs* **erfährt**, *prät* **erfuhr**, *perf* **hat erfahren**) ◇ *vt* - **1.** [Kenntnis erhalten von] to learn; [hören] to hear; **etw von jm erfahren** to hear sthg from sb; **etw über jn/etw erfahren** to find out sthg about sb/sthg; **etw durch jn/etw erfahren** to find out about sthg from sb/sthg - **2.** *geh* [erleben - Glück, Leid] to experience; [- Veränderung] to undergo. ◇ *adj* experienced.

Erfahrung (*pl* **-en**) *die* - **1.** [Kenntnis] experience *(U)* - **2.** [durch Nachforschen]: **etw in Erfahrung bringen** to find sthg out.

erfahrungsgemäß *adv* judging from experience.

erfassen *vt* - **1.** [Bedeutung] to grasp, to understand - **2.** [Daten, Zahlen] to record - **3.** [mitreißen - von Fahrzeug] to drag along; [- Wasser] to sweep along - **4.** [überkommen]: **Angst erfasste sie** she was overcome with fear.

erfinden (*prät* **erfand**, *perf* **hat erfunden**) *vt* to invent.

Erfinder, in (*mpl* **-**, *fpl* **-nen**) *der, die* inventor.

Erfindung (*pl* **-en**) *die* - **1.** [Entwicklung] invention; **eine Erfindung machen** to invent something - **2.** [Ausgedachtes] fabrication.

Erfolg (*pl* **-e**) *der* success; **Erfolg haben** to be successful; **mit Erfolg** successfully. ◆ **Erfolg versprechend** *adj* promising. ◆ **viel Erfolg** *interj* good luck!

erfolglos ◇ *adj* unsuccessful. ◇ *adv* unsuccessfully.

erfolgreich ◇ *adj* successful. ◇ *adv* successfully.

Erfolgs|erlebnis *das* feeling of success.

erforderlich *adj* required; **für** ODER **zu etw erforderlich sein** to be required for sthg.

erfordern *vt* to require.

Erfordernis (*pl* **-se**) *das* requirement.

erforschen *vt* [Wissensgebiet] to study; [Land, Gelände] to explore; [Möglichkeiten] to investigate.

Erforschung (*pl* **-en**) *die* [von Wissensgebiet] study; [von Land, Gelände] exploration; [von Möglichkeiten] investigation.

erfreuen *vt* to please. ◆ **sich erfreuen** *ref*: **sich an etw** *(D)* **erfreuen** to take pleasure in sthg. ◆ **sehr erfreut** *interj* pleased to meet you!

erfreulich *adj* pleasing.

erfreulicherweise *adv* luckily.

erfrieren (*prät* **erfror**, *perf* **ist erfroren**) *vi* to freeze to death; [Blüten] to be killed by frost; **sich die Hände/Füße erfrieren** to suffer frostbite in one's hands/feet.

erfrischen *vt* to refresh; [geistig] to stimulate. ◆ **sich erfrischen** *ref* to refresh o.s.

erfrischend *adj* refreshing; [Gespräch] stimulating.

Erfrischung (*pl* **-en**) *die* refreshment.

erfüllen *vt* - **1.** [Wunsch, Vertrag, Pflicht, Bedingungen] to fulfil - **2.** [füllen, ausfüllen] to fill. ◆ **sich erfüllen** *ref* [Wunsch] to come true.

ergänzen *vt* - **1.** [vervollständigen] to complete - **2.** [hinzufügen] to add. ◆ **sich ergänzen** *ref* to complement one another.

Ergänzung (*pl* **-en**) *die* - **1.** [Vervollständigung] completion *(U)* - **2.** [Zusatz] supplement; [zu Gesetz] amendment.

ergeben (*präs* **ergibt**, *prät* **ergab**, *perf* **hat ergeben**) *vt* [Ertrag] to produce; [herausfinden] to show; **eins mal eins ergibt eins** one times one is ODER makes one; **das ergibt keinen Sinn** that doesn't make any sense. ◆ **sich ergeben** *ref* - **1.** [erfolgen] to arise; **sich aus etw ergeben** to result from ODER be the result of sthg - **2.** [kapitulieren] to surrender.

Ergebenheit *die* devotion.

Ergebnis (*pl* **-se**) *das* result.

ergebnislos *adj* unsuccessful.

ergiebig *adj* [Quelle] rich; [Thema] fertile; [Gespräch] productive.

ergießen (*prät* **ergoss**, *perf* **hat ergossen**) ◆ **sich ergießen** *ref* to pour.

ergreifen (*prät* **ergriff**, *perf* **hat ergriffen**) *vt* - **1.** [packen, Macht] to seize - **2.** [festnehmen] to capture - **3.** [Initiative, Gelegenheit] to take; [Beruf] to take up; [Maßnahmen] to adopt - **4.** [erfassen] to overcome.

ergreifend ◇ *adj* moving. ◇ *adv* movingly.

ergriffen ◇ *pp* ▷ **ergreifen**. ◇ *adj*: **ergriffen sein** to be (deeply) moved.

ergründen *vt* to discover.

erhalten (*präs* **erhält**, *prät* **erhielt**, *perf* **hat erhalten**) *vt* - **1.** [bekommen] to receive, to get - **2.** [bewahren] to preserve; **gut erhalten** in good condition.

erhältlich *adj* available.

Erhaltung *die* preservation; [von Tierarten] conservation.

erhängen *vt* to hang. ◆ **sich erhängen** *ref* to hang o.s.

erheben (*prät* **erhob**, *perf* **hat erhoben**) *vt* - **1.** [Arm, Stimme, Glas] to raise - **2.** [Gebühren] to charge; [Steuern] to levy - **3.** [Daten] to gather - **4.** [vorbringen]: **Anklage erheben** to bring charges; **auf etw** *(A)* **Anspruch erheben** to make a claim for sthg; **Einspruch erheben** to raise an objection; **etw zum Prinzip erheben** to make sthg a principle. ◆ **sich erheben** *ref* - **1.** [aufstehen] to rise, to get up - **2.** [losfliegen] to rise - **3.** [rebellieren]: **sich gegen jn/etw erheben** to rise up against sb/sthg - **4.** [überragen]: **sich über jn/etw erheben** to rise above sb/sthg.

erheblich ◇ *adj* considerable. ◇ *adv* considerably.

Erhebung (*pl* **-en**) *die* - **1.** [Hügel] rise - **2.** [Aufstand] uprising - **3.** [Untersuchung] survey.

erhitzen *vt* - **1.** [heiß machen] to heat - **2.** [erregen] to excite.

erhoffen *vt* to anticipate; **sich** *(D)* **etw von jm erhoffen** to expect sthg from sb.

erhöhen *vt* - **1.** [Preis, Einsatz, Geschwindigkeit] to increase - **2.** [Mauer] to raise. ◆ **sich erhöhen** *ref* [steigen] to increase.

Erhöhung (*pl* **-en**) *die* increase.

erholen ◆ **sich erholen** *ref*: **sich (von etw) erholen** to recover (from sthg).

erholsam *adj* relaxing.

Erholung *die* [von Krankheit] recovery; [von Anstrengung] rest.

erinnern ◇ *vt* - **1.** [an Aufgabe, Termin]: **jn an etw** *(A)* **erinnern** to remind sb about ODER of sthg - **2.** [an Vergangenheit]: **jn an jn/etw erinnern** to remind sb of sb/sthg. ◇ *vi* - **1.** [an Aufgabe, Termin]: **ich muss daran erinnern, dass...** I must remind you that... - **2.** [an Vergangenes]: **an jn/etw erinnern** to be reminiscent of sb/sthg. ◆ **sich erinnern** *ref* to remember; **sich an jn/etw erinnern** to remember sb/sthg.

Erinnerung (*pl* **-en**) *die* - **1.** [Eindruck] memory; **Erinnerung an etw** *(A)* memory of sthg - **2.** [Gedenken]: **zur Erinnerung an jn** in memory of sb; **jn/etw in guter/schlechter Erinnerung behalten** to have fond/bad memories of sb/sthg - **3.** [Gedächtnis] memory - **4.** [Andenken] memento.

erkälten ◆ **sich erkälten** *ref* to catch (a) cold.

Erkältung (*pl* **-en**) *die* cold.

erkennbar *adj* recognizable.

erkennen (*prät* **erkannte**, *perf* **hat erkannt**) *vt* - **1.** [sehen können] to make out - **2.** [Person, Fehler] to recognize; **etw zu erkennen geben** to reveal sthg - **3.** [Irrtum] to acknowledge.

erkenntlich *adj*: **sich erkenntlich zeigen** to show one's gratitude.

Erkenntnis (*pl* **-se**) *die* - **1.** [Entdeckung, Einsicht] realization; **wissenschaftliche Erkenntnisse** scientific discoveries; **zu der Erkenntnis kommen, dass...** to realize that... - **2.** [Erkennen] knowledge.

Erker (*pl* -) *der* bay window.

erklärbar *adj* explicable; **nicht erklärbar** inexplicable; **leicht erklärbar** easily explained.

erklären *vt* - **1.** [erläutern] to explain; **ich kann es mir nicht erklären** I can't explain it - **2.** [bezeichnen] to declare; [Absicht] to state; [Rücktritt] to announce; **etw für ungültig erklären** to declare sthg invalid; **jn für vermisst erklären** to declare sb missing. ◆ **sich erklären** *ref* [sich äußern]: **sich (mit etw) einverstanden erklären** to declare that one is in agreement (with sthg); **er erklärte sich bereit, es zu tun** he said he was willing to do it.

Erklärung (*pl* **-en**) *die* - **1.** [Erläuterung] explanation - **2.** [Mitteilung] statement.

erklingen (*prät* **erklang**, *perf* **ist erklungen**) *vi* [Ton, Instrument] to sound; **am Schluss erklang die Nationalhymne** at the end the national anthem was played.

erkranken (*perf* **ist erkrankt**) *vi* to fall ill.

Erkrankung (*pl* **-en**) *die* illness.

erkundigen ◆ **sich erkundigen** *ref* to enquire; **sich nach jm erkundigen** to ask after sb; **sich nach etw erkundigen** to ask about sthg.

Erkundigung (*pl* **-en**) *die* enquiry; **Erkundigungen über jn/etw einziehen** ODER **einholen** to make enquiries about sb/sthg.

erlangen *vt* to obtain.

Erlass (*pl* **-e** ODER **Erlässe**) *der* - **1.** [von Befehl] decree - **2.** [von Schulden] remission.

erlassen (*präs* **erlässt**, *prät* **erließ**, *perf* **hat erlassen**) *vt* - **1.** [Befehl] to issue; [Gesetz] to enact - **2.** [Strafe, Schulden]: **jm etw erlassen** to let sb off sthg.

erlauben *vt* to allow; **jm etw erlauben** to allow sb sthg; **sich** *(D)* **etw erlauben** [sich herausnehmen] to take the liberty of doing sthg; [sich gönnen] to allow o.s. sthg. ◆ **erlaube mal** *interj* how dare you!

Erlaubnis *die* permission.

erläutern *vt* to explain.

Erläuterung (*pl* **-en**) *die* explanation.

Erle (*pl* **-n**) *die* alder.

erleben *vt* - **1.** [erfahren, kennen lernen] to experience; [Abenteuer] to have - **2.** [Geburtstag, Jubiläum] to live to see.

Erlebnis (*pl* **-se**) *das* experience.

erledigen *vt* - **1.** [Frage, Angelegenheit, Auftrag] to deal with; [Arbeit] to get through; [Einkäufe, Hausaufgaben] to do - **2.** *fam* [töten] to bump off - **3.** *fam* [besiegen] to wipe out. ◆ **sich erledigen** *ref* [sich erübrigen]: **etw erledigt sich (von selbst)** sthg takes care of itself.

erledigt *adj* - **1.** [ausgeführt, beendet - Angelegenheit] settled; [- Auftrag] carried out; [- Arbeit] done - **2.** *fam* [erschöpft]: **erledigt sein** to be worn out.

erleichtern *vt* - **1.** [leichter machen - Arbeit, Situation] to make easier; [- Gepäck] to make lighter; **jm das Verständnis erleichtern** to make it easier for sb to understand - **2.** [Gewissen] to ease.

erleichtert ◇ *adj*: **erleichtert sein** to be relieved. ◇ *adv*: **erleichtert aufatmen** to breathe a sigh of relief.

Erleichterung (*pl* **-en**) *die* - **1.** [Befreiung] relief - **2.** [von Aufgabe] facilitation *(U)*; [von Last] easing *(U)*.

erleiden (*prät* **erlitt**, *perf* **hat erlitten**) *vt* to suffer.

erlernen *vt* to learn.

erlesen *adj geh* [Gemälde, Porzellan, Wein] fine; [Mahl] choice.

erleuchten *vt* - **1.** [erhellen] to light up - **2.** *geh* [inspirieren] to inspire.

erlischt *präs* ▷ **erlöschen**.

Erlös (*pl* **-e**) *der* proceeds *Pl*.

erlöschen (*präs* **erlischt**, *prät* **erlosch**, *perf* **ist erloschen**) *vi* - **1.** [Feuer, Licht] to go out; [Vulkan] to become extinct - **2.** [Gefühle] to die; [Anspruch, Mitgliedschaft] to lapse.

erlösen *vt* to rescue; **jn von etw erlösen** [Leid, Schmerz] to release sb from sthg; RELIG to deliver sb from sthg.

ermächtigen *vt*: **jn zu etw ermächtigen** to authorize sb to do sthg.

ermahnen *vt* to remind; **jn zu mehr Vorsicht ermahnen** to remind sb to be more careful.

Ermahnung (*pl* **-en**) *die* reminder.

ermäßigt *adj* reduced.

Ermäßigung (*pl* **-en**) *die* reduction.

Ermessen *das* judgement; **das liegt ganz in Ihrem Ermessen** that is entirely up to you.

ermitteln ◇ *vt* to determine; [Schuldige, Täter] to identify; [Sieger] to decide. ◇ *vi* to investigate.

Ermittlung (*pl* **-en**) *die* [Erkundigung] enquiries *Pl*; [Entdeckung] identification *(U)*.

ermöglichen *vt* to make possible.

ermorden *vt* to murder.

Ermordung (*pl* **-en**) *die* murder; [von Politiker] assassination.

ermüden ◇ *vi* (*perf* **ist ermüdet**) to tire. ◇ *vt* (*perf* **hat ermüdet**) to tire.

Ermüdung *die* tiredness.

ermuntern *vt* to encourage.

ermutigen *vt* to encourage.

ernähren *vt* - **1.** [beköstigen] to feed - **2.** [unterhalten] to support. ◆ **sich ernähren** *ref* to eat; **sich vegetarisch ernähren** to eat a vegetarian diet; **sich mit** ODER **von etw ernähren** [Person] to live on sthg; [Tier] to feed on sthg.

Ernährung *die* - **1.** [Ernähren] feeding - **2.** [Mahlzeit] diet; **gesunde Ernährung** a healthy diet.

ernennen (*prät* **ernannte**, *perf* **hat ernannt**) *vt* to appoint; **jn zu etw ernennen** to appoint sb (as) sthg.

erneuern [ɛɐ̯'nɔyɐn] *vt* - **1.** [ersetzen] to replace - **2.** [ausbessern - Gebäude] to renovate; [- Gemälde] to restore; [- kaputten Zaun] to repair - **3.** [Vertrag, Angebot] to renew.

Erneuerung [ɛɐ̯'nɔyərʊŋ] (*pl* **-en**) *die* - **1.** [Ersatz] replacement *(U)* - **2.** [Ausbesserung - von Gebäude] renovation *(U)*; [- von Gemälde] restoration *(U)* - **3.** [von Vertrag, Angebot] renewal.

erneut ◇ *adj* [Angebot, Vorschlag] new; [Kraft] renewed; [Weigerung] further. ◇ *adv* again.

erniedrigen *vt* to humiliate. ◆ **sich erniedrigen** *ref* [sich demütigen] to lower o.s.

Erniedrigung (*pl* **-en**) *die* humiliation *(U)*.

ernst ◇ *adj* - **1.** [gen] serious; [Verhalten] solemn - **2.** [Absicht, Vorschlag] sincere. ◇ *adv* - **1.** [gen] seriously - **2.** [Absicht, Vorschlag] sincerely; **es mit etw ernst meinen** to be serious about sthg; **jn/etw ernst nehmen** to take sb/sthg seriously.

Ẹrnst *der* seriousness; **mit etw Ernst machen** to be serious about sthg; **im Ernst?** really?

Ẹrnst|fall *der* (case of) emergency.

ẹrnsthaft ◇ *adj* serious; [Verhalten] solemn. ◇ *adv* - **1.** [gen] seriously - **2.** [aufrichtig] sincerely.

ẹrnstlich *adv* - **1.** [gen] seriously - **2.** [beabsichtigen, bereuen] sincerely.

Ẹrnte (*pl* **-n**) *die* harvest.

ẹrnten *vt* - **1.** [Früchte] to harvest; [Obst] to pick - **2.** [Beifall] to earn; [Undank] to receive.

ernụ̈chtern *vt* [desillusionieren] to bring down to earth.

Ernụ̈chterung (*pl* **-en**) *die* [Desillusion] disillusionment *(U)*.

erobern *vt* - **1.** [erkämpfen] to conquer - **2.** [gewinnen] to capture.

Eroberung (*pl* **-en**) *die* conquest.

erọ̈ffnen *vt* - **1.** [gen] to open - **2.** [bekannt geben]: **jm etw eröffnen** to reveal sthg to sb - **3.** [Gerichtsverfahren] to institute - **4.** [von Möglichkeit] to open up. ◆ **sich eröffnen** *ref*: **sich jm eröffnen** to open up to sb.

Erọ̈ffnung (*pl* **-en**) *die* - **1.** [gen] opening *(U)* - **2.** [Bekanntgabe - unerwartet] revelation *(U)*; [- von Plan] disclosure *(U)* - **3.** [von Gerichtsverfahren] institution - **4.** [Möglichkeit] opening up *(U)*.

erọ̈rtern *vt* to discuss.

Erọ̈rterung (*pl* **-en**) *die* discussion.

Erotik *die* eroticism.

erotisch *adj* erotic.

erprẹssen *vt*: **jn (mit etw) erpressen** to blackmail sb (with sthg).

Erprẹsser, in (*mpl* **-**, *fpl* **-nen**) *der, die* blackmailer.

Erprẹssung (*pl* **-en**) *die* blackmail *(U)*.

erproben *vt* [Maschine, Mittel] to test; [Ausdauer, Zuverlässigkeit] to put to the test; [Methode] to try out.

erraten (*präs* **errät**, *prät* **erriet**, *perf* **hat erraten**) *vt* to guess.

erregen *vt* - **1.** [aufregen - Person] to excite; [- Gemüt, sexuell] to arouse - **2.** [anregen] to stimulate - **3.** [verursachen - Aufmerksamkeit, Aufsehen] to attract; [- Widerspruch] to give rise to; [- Mitleid, Neid] to arouse.

Erreger (*pl* **-**) *der* MED pathogene.

Erregung (*pl* **-en**) *die* - **1.** [von Person] excitement *(U)*; [sexuelle] arousal *(U)* - **2.** [von Nerven] stimulation *(U)* - **3.** [Verursachen - von Mitleid, Neid] arousing *(U)*; [- von Aufmerksamkeit] attracting *(U)*.

erreichbar *adj* [Person] available; [Ort] within reach.

erreichen *vt* - **1.** [Ort, Person, Geschwindigke… to reach; [Ziel] to achieve; [Bahn] to catc… - **2.** [telefonisch] to contact; **wo/wạnn sind Si… zu erreichen?** where/when can you be co… tacted? - **3.** [durchsetzen] to achieve; **bei ih… kann man nichts erreichen** you'll not get any… where with him.

errịchten *vt* - **1.** [bauen, aufbauen] to ere… - **2.** [Herrschaft] to establish.

Errịchtung *die* - **1.** [Bau, Aufbau] erectio… - **2.** [von Herrschaft] establishment.

errịngen (*prät* **errạng**, *perf* **hat errụngen**) … [Sieg, Freundschaft] to win; [Vorteil, Mehrheit] t… gain.

erröten (*perf* **ist errötet**) *vi* to blush; **vor W… erröten** to flush with anger.

Errụngenschaft (*pl* **-en**) *die* achievemen… **technische Errungenschaften** technical a… vances; **meine neueste Errungenschaft** m… latest acquisition.

Ersạtz *der* - **1.** [Ausgleich] substitute - **2.** [En… schädigung] compensation.

Ersạtz|dienst *der community work done b… conscientious objectors instead of military se… vice.*

ersạtzlos *adv* without substitution; **ersat… los gestrichen** abolished.

Ersạtz|mann (*pl* **-männer** ODER **-leute**) *d…* [beim Fußball] substitute; [bei der Arbeit] re… placement.

Ersạtz|rad *das* spare wheel.

Ersạtz|teil *das* spare part.

erscheinen (*prät* **erschien**, *perf* **ist erschi… nen**) *vi* - **1.** [kommen, sich zeigen] to appe… - **2.** [Buch, Zeitung] to come out - **3.** [wirken] t… seem.

Erscheinung (*pl* **-en**) *die* - **1.** [Ereignis] ph… nomenon - **2.** [Gestalt] appearance - **3.** [Visio… apparition.

erschießen (*prät* **erschọss**, *perf* **hat e… schọssen**) *vt* to shoot. ◆ **sich erschieße…** *ref* to shoot o.s.

erschlagen (*präs* **erschlägt**, *prät* **erschlu…** *perf* **hat erschlagen**) *vt* to kill; **vom Blitz e… schlagen werden** to be struck by lightning.

erschọ̈pft ◇ *adj* exhausted. ◇ *adv* [müd… wearily.

Erschọ̈pfung *die* exhaustion.

erschrak *prät* ▷ **erschrecken**.

erschrẹcken (*präs* **erschrẹckt** ODER **erschrịck…** *prät* **erschreckte** ODER **erschrak**, *perf* **hat ersc… rẹckt** ODER **ist erschrọcken**) ◇ *vt (hat) (re…* [überraschen] to startle; [ängstigen] to frighte… ◇ *vi (ist) (unreg)* [überrascht sein] to b… startled; [Angst haben] to be frightened; **üb… etw** *(A)* **erschrecken** to be alarmed by sth… ◆ **sich erschrecken** *ref (unreg)* to get … fright.

erschrẹckend ◇ *adj* alarming. ◇ *a…* alarmingly.

erschrickt *präs* ▷ **erschrecken.**

erschrocken *pp* ▷ **erschrecken.**

erschüttern *vt* - **1.** [Haus, Person] to shake; **er lässt sich durch nichts erschüttern** he's unflappable - **2.** [Vertrauen, Ruf] to shatter.

erschütternd *adj* distressing.

Erschütterung (*pl* **-en**) *die* - **1.** [von Haus] shaking *(U)* - **2.** [von Person] (state of) shock - **3.** [von Vertrauen, Ruf] shattering.

erschweren *vt* to make (more) difficult.

erschwinglich *adj* affordable.

ersetzbar *adj* replaceable.

ersetzen *vt* - **1.** [auswechseln, ausgleichen] to replace - **2.** [erstatten - Auslagen] to reimburse; [- Schaden] to make good.

ersichtlich *adj* obvious.

ersparen *vt* to save.

Ersparnis (*pl* **-se**) *die* saving. ◆ **Ersparnisse** *Pl* savings.

erst *adv* - **1.** [nicht eher] not until; **er fährt erst morgen los** he's not going until tomorrow; **erst als** only when - **2.** [vor kurzem] (only) just; **sie war erst gestern hier** she was here only yesterday - **3.** [zuerst] first; [anfänglich] at first - **4.** [emphatisierend]: **sie ist ja schon groß, aber ihr Bruder erst!** she is tall but her brother is even taller; **jetzt werde ich es erst recht/recht nicht tun!** now I'm definitely going/not going to do it! ◆ **erst einmal** *adv* - **1.** [nur einmal] only once - **2.** [zuerst] at first.

erstarren (*perf* **ist erstarrt**) *vi* [vor Kälte] to go numb; [vor Schreck] to become paralysed; [Gips] to harden.

erstatten *vt* - **1.** [Betrag] to reimburse - **2.** [vorbringen]: **gegen jn Anzeige erstatten** to report sb (to the authorities); **Bericht erstatten** to (make a) report.

Erstauf|führung *die* première.

erstaunen (*perf* **hat/ist erstaunt**) ◇ *vt (hat)* to astonish, to amaze. ◇ *vi (ist)*: **über etw** *(A)* **erstaunen** to be astonished ODER amazed at sthg.

Erstaunen *das* astonishment; **jn in Erstaunen (ver)setzen** to astonish ODER amaze sb.

erstaunlich *adj* astonishing, amazing.

erstaunt *adj* [Person] astonished, amazed; [Gesicht, Miene] surprised; **über etw** *(A)* **erstaunt sein** to be astonished by sthg.

erstbeste, r, s *adj*: **kaufe nicht gleich den erstbesten Wagen!** don't just buy the first car you look at! ◆ **Erstbeste** *der, die, das* first thing to come along.

erste, r, s *adj* - **1.** [anfänglich] first - **2.** [beste - Qualität, Wahl] top; [- Liga, Geige] first - **3.** [Ergebnis, Erfolg] initial.

Erste *der, die, das* first; *siehe auch* **Sechste.** ◆ **als Erstes** *adv* first (of all). ◆ **fürs Erste** *adv* for the time being.

erstechen (*präs* **ersticht**, *prät* **erstach**, *perf* **hat erstochen**) *vt* to stab to death.

erste Hilfe *die* first aid.

erstens *adv* firstly, in the first place.

ersticken (*perf* **hat/ist erstickt**) ◇ *vi (ist)* to suffocate; **wir ersticken zurzeit in Arbeit** we're up to our eyes in work at the moment. ◇ *vt (hat)* [Person, Tier] to suffocate; [Feuer] to put out; **etw im Keim ersticken** to nip sthg in the bud.

erstklassig ◇ *adj* first-class. ◇ *adv* excellently.

erstmalig ◇ *adj* first. ◇ *adv* for the first time.

erstmals *adv* for the first time.

erstrangig ◇ *adj* - **1.** [vorrangig] of prime importance - **2.** [erstklassig] first-rate. ◇ *adv* as a matter of priority.

erstrebenswert *adj* worthwhile.

erstrecken ◆ **sich erstrecken** *ref* - **1.** [jn/etw betreffen]: **sich auf jn/etw erstrecken** to apply to sb/sthg - **2.** [sich ausdehnen]: **sich erstrecken bis** [räumlich] to extend as far as; **sich über etw** *(A)* **erstrecken** [zeitlich] to last for sthg; [räumlich] to extend over sthg.

ertappen *vt* to catch; **jn bei etw ertappen** to catch sb doing sthg; **jn auf frischer Tat ertappen** to catch sb red-handed.

erteilen *vt*: **jm etw erteilen** to give sb sthg.

ertönen (*perf* **ist ertönt**) *vi* [Instrument] to sound; [Stimme] to ring out; [Geräusch] to be heard.

Ertrag (*pl* **-träge**) *der* [an Gemüse, Getreide] yield; [finanziell] profits *Pl*.

ertragen (*präs* **erträgt**, *prät* **ertrug**, *perf* **hat ertragen**) *vt* to bear.

erträglich *adj* [Zustände] tolerable; [Schmerz] bearable.

ertränken *vt* to drown.

ertrinken (*prät* **ertrank**, *perf* **ist ertrunken**) *vi* to drown.

erübrigen *vt* to spare. ◆ **sich erübrigen** *ref* to be unnecessary.

Erw. (*abk für* **Erwachsene**) adult.

Erwachen *das* awakening; **das gab ein böses Erwachen** *fig* it was a rude awakening.

Erwachsene [ɛɐ̯'vaksn̩ə] (*pl* **-n**) *der, die* adult.

Erwachsenenbildung *die* adult education.

erwägen (*prät* **erwog**, *perf* **hat erwogen**) *vt* to consider.

erwähnen *vt* to mention.

erwähnenswert *adj* worth mentioning.

Erwähnung (*pl* **-en**) *die* mention *(U)*.

erwärmen *vt* [wärmen] to warm. ◆ **sich erwärmen** *ref* - **1.** [sich aufwärmen] to warm up - **2.** [sich begeistern]: **ich kann mich für deine Idee nicht erwärmen** I can't generate any enthusiasm for your idea.

erwạrten *vt* - **1.** [warten auf] to wait for; **ich kann es kaum erwarten!** I can hardly wait! - **2.** [mit etw rechnen, erhoffen] to expect.

Erwạrtung (*pl* **-en**) *die* expectation. ◆ **Erwartungen** *Pl* expectations; [Anforderung] requirements.

erwạrtungsvoll ◇ *adj* expectant. ◇ *adv* expectantly.

erwẹcken *vt* - **1.** [Ehrgeiz, Misstrauen] to arouse; [Hoffnungen] to raise - **2.** [Tote] to awaken.

erweisen (*prät* **erwies**, *perf* **hat erwiesen**) *vt* [Schuld] to prove; **jm einen Dienst** ODER **Gefallen erweisen** to do sb a favour; **es ist erwiesen, dass...** it has been proved that... ◆ **sich erweisen** *ref* [sich zeigen]: **sich als etw erweisen** to prove to be sthg.

erweitern *vt* [Raum, Angebot, Umfang] to extend; [Bekanntenkreis, Wissen] to expand. ◆ **sich erweitern** *ref* [Straße, Angebot] to extend; [Bekanntenkreis, Produktion] to expand; [Pupillen] to dilate.

Erweiterung (*pl* **-en**) *die* [von Raum, Angebot] extension *(U)*; [von Bekanntenkreis, Wissen] expansion *(U)*; [von Pupillen] dilation *(U)*.

Erwẹrb *der* - **1.** [von Haus, Grundstück] purchase - **2.** [von Kenntnissen] acquisition - **3.** [aus Geschäft] earnings *Pl*.

erwẹrben (*präs* **erwịrbt**, *prät* **erwạrb**, *perf* **hat erwọrben**) *vt* - **1.** [kaufen] to purchase - **2.** [erlangen] to acquire.

erwẹrbslos *adj* unemployed.

erwẹrbstätig *adj* employed; **die erwerbstätige Bevölkerung** the working population.

erwidern *vt* - **1.** [antworten] to reply - **2.** [Besuch, Gruß, Gefälligkeit] to return.

erwiesen ◇ *pp* ▷ **erweisen**. ◇ *adj* proven.

erwịschen *vt* - **1.** [ertappen]: **jn (bei etw) erwischen** to catch sb (doing sthg) - **2.** [rechtzeitig erreichen] to catch - **3.** [bekommen] to get; **ihn hat es erwischt** *fam* [krank sein] he's got it; [verletzt sein] he's hurt; [verliebt sein] he's got it bad; [tot sein] he's dead.

erwog *prät* ▷ **erwägen**.

erwogen *pp* ▷ **erwägen**.

erwụ̈nscht *adj* [Gäste, Entwicklung] welcome; [Ergebnis] desired; **nicht erwünscht sein** not to be welcome.

erwụ̈rgen *vt* to strangle.

Erz (*pl* **-e**) *das* ore.

erzählen *vt* [Geschichte, Witz] to tell; **dem werde ich was erzählen!** *fam* I'll give him a piece of my mind!

Erzählung (*pl* **-en**) *die* - **1.** [Bericht] account - **2.** [Dichtung] story.

Ẹrz|bischof *der* archbishop.

Ẹrz|engel *der* archangel.

erzeugen *vt* [Produkt] to produce; [Energie Angst, Druck] to generate.

Erzeugnis (*pl* **-se**) *das* product.

Erzeugung *die* [von Produkten] productior [von Energie, Druck] generation.

erziehen (*prät* **erzog**, *perf* **hat erzogen**) *v* [Kinder - in der Familie] to bring up; [- in der Schu le] to educate; [Tier] to train; **jn zu jm/etw er ziehen** to bring sb up to be sb/sthg.

Erzieher, in (*mpl* -, *fpl* **-nen**) *der, die* - **1.** [Be rufsbezeichnung] teacher - **2.** [Eltern, Lehrer] edu cator.

erzieherisch ◇ *adj* educational. ◇ *ad* educationally.

Erziehung *die* [in der Familie] upbringing; [i der Schule] education.

Erziehungs|berechtigte *der, die* *an* parent ODER guardian.

erzielen *vt* [Kompromiss] to reach; [Ertrag, Ge winn] to make.

erzogen ◇ *pp* ▷ **erziehen**. ◇ *adj*: **gu schlecht erzogen** well/badly brought up.

erzwịngen (*prät* **erzwạng**, *perf* **hat er zwụngen**) *vt* to force.

ẹs *pron* - **1.** [Personalpronomen im Nominativ bei Sachen] it; [- bei Personen] he (she *die* - **2.** [Personalpronomen im Akkusativ - bei Sachen it; [- bei Personen] him (her *die*); **ich hoffe es** hope so; **ich weiß es** I know - **3.** [unpersönl ches Pronomen] it; **es ist drei Uhr** it's thre o'clock; **es regnet/schneit** it's raining/snow ing; **es freut mich, dass...** I'm pleased that.. **gestern gab es Nudeln** yesterday we ha pasta; **es ist sehr interessant, sich mit Jill z unterhalten** Jill is very interesting to talk t **es geht mir gut** I'm fine; **wer war es?** who wa it?

Ẹs (*pl* -) *das* - **1.** MUS E flat - **2.** [Psychologie] id.

Ẹsche (*pl* **-n**) *die* ash.

Esel (*pl* -) *der* - **1.** [Tier] donkey - **2.** *fa* [Schimpfwort] ass; **ich Esel!** stupid me!

Eselin (*pl* **-nen**) *die* she-ass.

Ẹskimo (*pl* **-s**) *der* Eskimo.

Ẹspe (*pl* **-n**) *die* aspen.

Esprẹsso [ɛsˈprɛso] (*pl* - ODER **-s**) ◇ *der* e presso. ◇ *das* [Lokal] coffee bar.

Essay [ˈɛse] (*pl* **-s**) *das* & *der* essay.

ẹssbar *adj* edible.

ẹssen (*präs* **ịsst**, *prät* **aß**, *perf* **hat gegẹsse** ◇ *vi* to eat; **essen gehen** to go out for a mea **warm/kalt essen** to have a hot/cold mea ◇ *vt* to eat; **seinen Teller leer essen** to e everything on one's plate.

Ẹssen (*pl* -) *das* meal; **Essen machen** ODER **k chen** to make ODER cook a meal.

Ẹssig (*pl* **-e**) *der* vinegar.

Ẹss|löffel (*pl* -) *der* dessertspoon.

Ẹss|zimmer (*pl* -) *das* dining room.

Ẹstland *nt* Estonia.

estnisch *adj* Estonian.

Estragon *der* tarragon.

Etage [e'ta:ʒə] (*pl* **-n**) *die* floor.

Etagen|wohnung *die* flat *UK*, apartment *US* *(in a block)*.

Etappe (*pl* **-n**) *die* stage.

Etat [e'ta:] (*pl* **-s**) *der* budget.

Ethik (*pl* **-en**) *die* - **1.** [Lehre] ethics *(U)* - **2.** *(ohne pl)* [Moral] ethics *Pl.*

ethnisch *adj* ethnic.

Etikett (*pl* **-e(n)** ODER **-s**) *das* label.

etliche, r, s *det* several, quite a few; **etliche Male** several times. ◆ **etliches** *pron*: **etliches zahlen** to pay quite a lot; **es gibt etliches zu erwähnen** there are quite a few things to mention.

Etui [ɛt'vi:] (*pl* **-s**) *das* case.

etwa *adv* - **1.** [zirka, ungefähr] about; **es funktioniert etwa so** it works roughly like this - **2.** [zum Beispiel] for example - **3.** [zum Ausdruck der Beunruhigung, eines Vorwurfs in Fragen]: **ist es etwa schon 24 Uhr?** don't tell me it's 12 o'clock already - **4.** [zur Bekräftigung]: **Edinburgh ist nicht etwa groß, aber schön** Edinburgh is certainly not big but it is beautiful.

etwaig *adj* possible; **etwaige Fragen** any questions that might arise.

etwas ◇ *det* - **1.** [gen] something; [in Fragen] anything; **etwas Anderes/Schönes** something else/nice - **2.** [ein wenig] some; **möchten Sie noch etwas Kaffee?** would you like some more coffee? ◇ *pron* something; [in Fragen] anything; **hast du etwas für mich?** have you got anything for me?; **das ist doch wenigstens etwas!** that's something at least!; **so etwas** such a thing. ◇ *adv* a little; **etwas spät** rather late.

EU (*abk für* **Europäische Union**) *die* EU.

euch *pron (Akkusativ und Dativ von ihr)* - **1.** [Personalpronomen] you; **wir haben es euch gesagt** we told you; **das gehört euch** this is yours, this belongs to you; **mit euch** with you - **2.** [Reflexivpronomen] yourselves; **könnt ihr euch das vorstellen?** can you imagine that? - **3.** [einander] each other.

euer, e ODER **eure** *det* your; **alles Gute, Euer Thomas** yours, Thomas.

eure, r, s *pron* yours.

eurer *pron (Genitiv von ihr)* you.

eurerseits *adv* - **1.** [Ihr selbst] for your part - **2.** [von Euch] on your part.

euretwegen *adv* - **1.** [euch zuliebe] for your sake - **2.** [wegen euch] because of you.

eurige (*pl* **-n**) *pron (mit Artikel) geh* yours.

Euro ['ɔyro] (*pl* **-**) *der* euro.

Eurocent ['ɔyrosɛnt] (*pl* **-s**) *der* eurocent.

Eurocheque (*pl* **-s**), **Euro|scheck** (*pl* **-s**) ['ɔyroʃɛk] *der* Eurocheque.

Eurocheque-|Karte, Euroscheckkarte *die* Eurocheque card.

Eurocity ['ɔyrosɪti] (*pl* **-s**) *der international train linking two or more major European cities.*

Euro|land *das* Euroland.

Europa *nt* Europe.

Europäer, in (*mpl* **-**, *fpl* **-nen**) *der, die* European.

europäisch *adj* European.

Europa|parlament *das* European Parliament.

Europa|rat *der* Council of Europe.

Euro|scheck = **Eurocheque**.

Euro|zone *die* euro zone.

ev. *abk für* **evangelisch**.

e. V. (*abk für* **eingetragener Verein**), *registered society.*

evakuieren [evaku'i:rən] *vt* to evacuate.

evangelisch [evaŋ'ge:lɪʃ] *adj* Protestant.

Evangelium [evaŋ'ge:li̯ʊm] (*pl* **-ien**) *das* gospel.

eventuell [evɛn'tu̯ɛl] ◇ *adj* possible. ◇ *adv* maybe, perhaps.

ewig ◇ *adj* - **1.** [nie endend] eternal - **2.** *fam abw* [andauernd] constant. ◇ *adv* - **1.** [endlos] eternally - **2.** *fam abw* [zu lange] constantly. ◆ **auf ewig** *adv* [für immer] forever.

Ewigkeit (*pl* **-en**) *die* eternity.

EWS [e:ÿve:'ɛs] (*abk für* **Europäisches Währungssystem**) *das* EMS.

exakt ◇ *adj* exact; [Arbeit] precise. ◇ *adv* exactly; [arbeiten] with precision.

Exaktheit *die* precision.

Examen (*pl* **-**) *das* examination; **Examen machen** to take one's examinations.

Exekutive [ɛkseku'ti:və] *die (ohne pl)* executive.

Exempel (*pl* **-**) *das* example; **an jm ein Exempel statuieren** to make an example of sb.

Exemplar (*pl* **-e**) *das* example; [von Buch] copy.

Exil (*pl* **-e**) *das* exile *(U)*.

existent *adj* existing.

Existenz (*pl* **-en**) *die* - **1.** [Bestehen] existence - **2.** [Existenzgrundlage] livelihood - **3.** *abw* [Person] character.

Existenz|minimum *das (ohne pl)* subsistence level.

existieren *vi* - **1.** [bestehen] to exist - **2.** [auskommen] to live.

exklusiv ◇ *adj* exclusive. ◇ *adv* - **1.** [vornehm, abgesondert]: **exklusiv leben** to live an exclusive lifestyle - **2.** [ausschließlich] exclusively.

Exkursion (*pl* **-en**) *die* study trip.

Exmatrikulation (*pl* **-en**) *die* UNI *removal of someone's name from a university register.*

Exot (*pl* **-en**), **Exote** (*pl* **-n**) *der* [Mensch] exotic person; [Tier] exotic animal.

exotisch <> *adj* exotic. <> *adv* exotically.

Expedition (*pl* **-en**) *die* expedition.

Experiment (*pl* **-e**) *das* - **1.** [Versuch] experiment - **2.** [Wagnis] experimentation.

experimentell <> *adj* experimental. <> *adv* experimentally.

experimentieren *vi* to experiment; **mit etw experimentieren** to experiment on sthg.

Experte (*pl* **-n**) *der* expert.

Expertin (*pl* **-nen**) *die* expert.

explodieren (*perf* **ist explodiert**) *vi* to explode.

Explosion (*pl* **-en**) *die* explosion.

explosiv *adj* explosive.

Export (*pl* **-e**) *der* export.

Exporteur [ɛkspɔr'tøːɐ̯] (*pl* **-e**) *der* exporter.

Expressionismus *der* expressionism.

extra <> *adv* - **1.** [separat] separately - **2.** [zusätzlich] extra - **3.** [speziell] specially. <> *adj (unver)* extra.

Extrakt (*pl* **-e**) *der* extract.

extrem <> *adj* extreme. <> *adv* [billig, auffällig] extremely; [reagieren, denken] in an extreme way; **extrem rechts stehen** to be on the extreme right.

Extrem|fall *der* extreme case.

Extremist, in (*mpl* **-en**, *fpl* **-nen**) *der, die* extremist.

Extrem|sport *der* extreme sports *Pl*.

exzellent <> *adj* excellent. <> *adv* excellently.

Exzess (*pl* **-e**) *der* excess.

EZ *abk für* **Einzelzimmer**.

EZB (*abk für* **Europäische Zentralbank**) *die European Central Bank*.

F

f (*pl* - ODER **-s**), **F** (*pl* - ODER **-s**) [ɛf] *das* - **1.** [Buchstabe] f, F - **2.** MUS F. ◆ **F** (*abk für* **Fahrenheit**) F.

Fa. (*abk für* **Firma**) Co.

fabelhaft <> *adj* fantastic. <> *adv* fantastically.

Fabrik (*pl* **-en**) *die* factory.

Fabrikant, in (*mpl* **-en**, *fpl* **-nen**) *der, die* factory owner.

Fabrik|arbeiter, in *der, die* factory worker.

fabrikneu *adj* brand new.

fabrizieren *vt fam abw* [machen] to throw together.

Facette (*pl* **-n**), **Fassette** (*pl* **-n**) [fa'sɛtə] *die* facet.

Fach (*pl* **Fächer**) *das* - **1.** [in Möbel, Behälter] compartment; [für Brief, Schlüssel] pigeonhole - **2.** [in Schule, Studium] subject; **vom Fach sein** to be an expert.

Fach|abitur *das exam taken at the end of a secondary vocational school which enables students to enter a "Fachhochschule" but not university.*

Fach|arbeiter, in *der, die* skilled worker.

Fach|arzt, ärztin *der, die* specialist.

Fach|ausdruck *der* technical term.

Fächer (*pl* -) *der* fan.

Fach|geschäft *das* specialist shop *UK* ODER store *US*.

Fachhoch|schule *die college offering primarily vocational courses to the equivalent of bachelor level.*

Fach|kenntnis *die* specialist knowledge *(U)*

Fach|kraft *die* skilled worker.

fachkundig <> *adj* expert. <> *adv* expertly

fachlich <> *adj* [Problem] technical; [beruflich] professional. <> *adv* technically; [beruflich] professionally; **sich fachlich weiterbilden** to gain professional qualifications.

Fachmann (*pl* **-leute**) *der* expert.

fachmännisch <> *adj* expert. <> *adv* expertly.

fachsimpeln ['faxzɪmpl̩n] *vi fam* to talk shop.

Fach|wissen *das* specialist knowledge.

Fackel (*pl* **-n**) *die* torch.

Faden (*pl* **Fäden**) *der* - **1.** [Faser] thread - **2.** MED stitch; **den Faden verlieren** to lose the thread

fähig *adj* capable; **zu etw fähig sein** to be capable of sthg.

Fähigkeit (*pl* **-en**) *die* - **1.** [Begabung] talent - **2.** [Können] ability.

fahnden *vi*: **nach jm/etw fahnden** to search for sb/sthg.

Fahndung (*pl* **-en**) *die* search.

Fahne (*pl* **-n**) *die* flag; **eine Fahne haben** *fam fig* to smell of drink.

Fahnen|flucht *die* MIL desertion.

Fahr|ausweis *der* - **1.** [Fahrschein] ticket - **2.** *Schweiz* [Führerschein] driving licence *UK* driver's license *US*.

Fahr|bahn *die* road.

Fähre (*pl* **-n**) *die* ferry.

fahren (*präs* **fährt**, *prät* **fuhr**, *perf* **hat/ist gefahren**) <> *vi (ist)* - **1.** [Person - gen] to go; [- mit Auto] to drive; [- mit Fahrrad] to ride; **mit dem Zug/Bus fahren** to go by train/bus; **ins Gebirge fahren** to go to the mountains; **wir fahre**

nach England we're going to England; **durch Wien fahren** to drive through Vienna; **langsam/zu schnell fahren** to drive slowly/too fast; **120 km/h fahren** to drive at 120 km/h; **ein Gedanke fuhr ihm durch den Kopf** a thought flashed through his mind; **was ist denn in dich gefahren?** *fig* what's got into you? - **2.** [Fahrzeug] to go; [Schiff] to sail - **3.** [abfahren] to leave; **wann fährst du?** when are you leaving ODER going?; **der Bus fährt alle 30 Minuten** the bus leaves ODER runs every half hour; **einen fahren lassen** *fam* to fart. ◇ *vt* - **1.** *(hat)* [Fahrzeug] to drive; [Fahrrad] to ride - **2.** *(ist)* [Entfernung, Strecke] to drive; **ich fahre diese Strecke jeden Tag** I drive ODER come this way every day - **3.** *(ist)* SPORT: **Rollschuh fahren** to rollerskate; **Ski fahren** to ski; **Schlitten fahren** to go sledging.

Fahrenheit *nt* Fahrenheit.

Fahrer (*pl* -) *der* driver.

Fahrerflucht *die* failure to stop after an accident.

Fahrerin (*pl* **-nen**) *die* driver.

Fahr|gast *der* passenger.

Fahr|geld *das* fare.

Fahr|karte *die* ticket.

Fahrkarten|schalter *der* ticket desk.

fahrlässig ◇ *adj* negligent; **fahrlässige Tötung** manslaughter *UK*, murder in the second degree *US*. ◇ *adv* negligently.

Fahrlässigkeit *die* negligence.

Fahr|plan *der* timetable.

fahrplanmäßig ◇ *adj* scheduled. ◇ *adv* on schedule.

Fahr|preis *der* fare.

Fahr|prüfung *die* driving test.

Fahr|rad *das* bicycle; **mit dem Fahrrad fahren** to cycle.

Fahr|schein *der* ticket.

Fahr|schule *die* driving school.

Fahr|stuhl *der* lift *UK*, elevator *US*.

Fahrt (*pl* **-en**) *die* - **1.** [gen] journey; [kurzer Ausflug] trip; **auf der Fahrt nach Berlin** on the way to Berlin; **freie Fahrt haben** to have a clear run - **2.** *(ohne pl)* [Geschwindigkeit] speed; **in Fahrt kommen** ODER **geraten** [in Schwung kommen] to get going; *fam* [wütend werden] to flare up. ◆ **gute Fahrt** *interj* have a good journey!

fährt *präs* ▷ **fahren**.

Fährte (*pl* **-n**) *die* trail.

Fahrtkosten, Fahrkosten *Pl* travelling expenses.

Fahrt|richtung *die* [im Verkehr] direction; [im Zug] direction of travel; **die A9 in Fahrtrichtung Berlin/München** the northbound/southbound section of the A9.

fahrtüchtig *adj* [Person] fit to drive; [Fahrzeug] roadworthy.

Fahr|verbot *das* driving ban.

Fahr|zeug (*pl* **-e**) *das* vehicle.

Fahr|zeughalter, in (*mpl* **Fahrzeughalter**, *fpl* **-nen**) *der, die* registered owner.

fair [fɛːɐ̯] ◇ *adj* fair. ◇ *adv* fairly.

Fairness ['fɛːɐ̯nɛs] *die* fairness.

Faktor (*pl* **-toren**) *der* factor.

Fakultät (*pl* **-en**) *die* UNI faculty.

Falke (*pl* **-n**) *der* falcon.

Fall (*pl* **Fälle**) *der* - **1.** [gen] case; **für alle Fälle** for all eventualities; **klarer Fall!** sure thing!; **jd/etw ist ganz sein Fall** *fam fig* one is very keen on sb/sthg - **2.** *(ohne pl)* [Sturz] fall; **zu Fall kommen** to fall; **jn zu Fall bringen** *fig* to bring sb down; **etw zu Fall bringen** *fig* to thwart sthg. ◆ **auf alle Fälle** *adv* - **1.** [unbedingt] definitely - **2.** [vorsichtshalber] in any case. ◆ **auf jeden Fall** *adv* in any case. ◆ **auf keinen Fall** *adv* under no circumstances. ◆ **für den Fall, dass** *konj* in case.

Falle (*pl* **-n**) *die* - **1.** [zum Fangen] trap; **(jm) eine Falle stellen** to set a trap (for sb); **in eine Falle geraten** *fig* to fall into a trap - **2.** *fam* [Bett] bed.

fallen (*präs* **fällt**, *prät* **fiel**, *perf* **ist gefallen**) *vi* - **1.** [gen] to fall; [Preise, Niveau, Temperatur] to drop; [Haare, Stoff] to hang - **2.** [Urteil] to be passed; [Entscheidung] to be made; [Wort] to be spoken; [Schuss] to be fired; **die Würfel sind gefallen** the die is cast; **in Ungnade fallen** to fall out of favour; **durch eine Prüfung fallen** to fail an exam.

fällen *vt* - **1.** [Baum] to fell - **2.** [Urteil] to pass; [Entscheidung] to make.

fällig *adj* due.

Fallobst *das (ohne pl)* windfalls *Pl*.

falls *konj* if; **falls es dir nicht gefällt** in case ODER if you don't like it.

Fall|schirm *der* parachute.

Fallschirm|springer, in *der, die* parachutist.

fällt *präs* ▷ **fallen**.

Fall|tür *die* trapdoor.

falsch ◇ *adj* - **1.** [nicht korrekt, nicht passend] wrong - **2.** [imitiert, gefälscht, irreführend - Gebiss, Stolz, Angaben] false; [- Pass, Geldschein] forged. ◇ *adv* - **1.** [nicht korrekt] wrongly; **etw falsch verstehen** to misunderstand sthg; **falsch singen** to sing out of tune; **falsch abbiegen** to take the wrong turning - **2.** [hinterhältig] falsely.

Falsche (*pl* **-n**) *der, die, das* [Person] wrong person; [Sache] wrong thing; **an den Falschen** ODER **die Falsche geraten** *fam* to come to the wrong person.

fälschen *vt* to forge.

Fälscher, in (*mpl* -, *fpl* **-nen**) *der, die* forger.

Falsch|fahrer, in *der, die person who drives into oncoming traffic on a motorway.*

Falschgeld *das* counterfeit money.
fälschlich ◇ *adj* false. ◇ *adv* falsely.
Fälschung (*pl* **-en**) *die* - **1.** [Fälschen] forging - **2.** [Gefälschtes] forgery.
Falte (*pl* **-n**) *die* [in Stoff, Papier] fold; [in Hose, Hemd] crease; [in Haut] wrinkle.
falten *vt* [Stoff, Papier, Hände] to fold.
Falter (*pl* -) *der* butterfly.
faltig *adj* [Haut, Hände] wrinkled; [Hemd, Tischtuch] creased.
familiär ◇ *adj* [die Familie betreffend] family *(vor Subst).* ◇ *adv* [zwanglos] informally.
Familie [fa'mi:li̯ə] (*pl* **-n**) *die* family; **Familie haben** to have a family.
Familien|betrieb *der* family business.
Familien|feier *die* family celebration.
Familien|kreis *der (ohne pl)* family circle.
Familien|name *der* surname.
Familien|stand *der* marital status.
famos [fa'mo:s] *fam adj* marvellous.
Fan (*pl* **-s**) *der* fan.
Fanatiker, in (*mpl* -, *fpl* **-nen**) *der, die* fanatic.
fand *prät* ▷ **finden**.
Fanfare (*pl* **-n**) *die* fanfare.
Fang *der* - **1.** [Fangen] catching - **2.** [Beute] catch.
fangen (*präs* **fängt**, *prät* **fing**, *perf* **hat gefangen**) *vt* to catch. ◆ **sich fangen** *ref* - **1.** [in Falle, Netz] to get caught - **2.** [nach Schwierigkeiten] to regain one's composure.
fängt *präs* ▷ **fangen**.
Fantasie (*pl* **-n**), **Phantasie** (*pl* **-n**) [fanta'zi:] *die* - **1.** *(ohne pl)* [Vorstellungskraft] imagination - **2.** [Vorstellung] fantasy.
fantasielos, phantasielos ◇ *adj* unimaginative. ◇ *adv* unimaginatively.
fantasieren, phantasieren *vi* - **1.** [irrereden] to be delirious - **2.** [träumen] to fantasize.
fantasievoll, phantasievoll ◇ *adj* imaginative. ◇ *adv* imaginatively.
fantastisch, phantastisch ◇ *adj* fantastic. ◇ *adv* fantastically.
Farb|aufnahme *die* colour photograph.
Farbband (*pl* **-bänder**) *das* (typewriter) ribbon.
Farb|drucker *der* EDV colour printer.
Farbe (*pl* **-n**) *die* - **1.** [Licht, Buntheit] colour; **Farbe bekommen** *fig* to get some colour - **2.** [Material] paint - **3.** [in Kartenspiel] suit.
farbecht *adj* colourfast.
färben ◇ *vt* to dye. ◇ *vi* to run. ◆ **sich färben** *ref* to change colour; **sich rosa färben** to turn pink.
farbenblind *adj* colour-blind.
Farb|fernsehen *das* colour television.
Farb|fernseher *der* colour television.
Farb|film *der* colour film.
Farb|foto *das* colour photo.
farbig ◇ *adj* - **1.** [Druck, Fernsehen] colour - **2.** [bunt, lebhaft] colourful - **3.** [Person, Papier] coloured. ◇ *adv* colourfully.
Farbige (*pl* **-n**) *der, die* coloured person.
farblich *adv* as regards colour.
farblos *adj* colourless.
Farb|stoff *der* colouring.
Färbung (*pl* **-en**) *die* - **1.** [Farbgebung] tinge - **2.** [Tendenz] slant.
Farn (*pl* **-e**) *der* fern.
Fasan (*pl* **-e** ODER **-en**) *der* pheasant.
Fasching (*pl* **-e** ODER **-s**) *der carnival before Lent.*
Faschismus *der* fascism.
Faschist, in (*mpl* **-en**, *fpl* **-nen**) *der, die* fascist.
Faser (*pl* **-n**) *die* fibre.
faserig *adj* [Fleisch] stringy; [Holz] coarse.
Fass (*pl* **Fässer**) *das* barrel. ◆ **vom Fass** *adj* & *adv* draught.
Fassade (*pl* **-n**) *die* facade.
fassen (*präs* **fasst**, *prät* **fasste**, *perf* **hat gefasst**) ◇ *vt* - **1.** [anfassen] to take hold of; **jn etw zu fassen bekommen** to catch hold of sb/sthg - **2.** [Dieb] to catch - **3.** [Entschluss] to make - **4.** [begreifen]: **ich kann es nicht fassen** I can't take it in - **5.** [als Inhalt] to hold. ◇ *vi*: **an** ODER **in etw** *(A)* **fassen** [kurz] to touch sthg; [lang] to feel sthg. ◆ **sich fassen** *ref* to pull o.s. together; **sich auf etw** *(A)* **gefasst machen** *fig* to prepare o.s. for sthg; **sich kurz fassen** to keep it short.
Fassette *die* = **Facette**.
Fassung (*pl* **-en**) *die* - **1.** [von Glühbirne] socket; [von Perle] setting - **2.** [von Text] version - **3.** [Selbstbeherrschung]: **jn aus der Fassung bringen** to put sb out.
fassungslos ◇ *adj* [Person] speechless; [Gesicht] astounded. ◇ *adv* speechlessly.
Fassungsvermögen *das* capacity.
fast *adv* nearly, almost.
fasten *vi* to fast.
Fasten|zeit *die* - **1.** [Zeit religiösen Fastens] fasting period - **2.** [vor Ostern] Lent.
Fastnacht *die carnival before Lent.*
fatal *adj* [verhängnisvoll] fatal.
fauchen *vi* to hiss.
faul ◇ *adj* - **1.** [Lebensmittel, Holz] rotten - **2.** [Person] lazy - **3.** *fam* [Witz, Ausrede] dubious. ◇ *adv* [träge] lazily.
faulen (*perf* **hat/ist gefault**) *vi* [Holz, Fleisch] to rot; [Zahn] to decay.
faulenzen *vi* to laze around.
Faulheit *die* laziness.
faulig *adj* [Obst] rotten; [Wasser] stagnant.
Fäulnis *die* rot.
Fauna *die* BIOL fauna.

Faust (*pl* **Fäuste**) *die* fist; **auf eigene Faust** *fig* off one's own bat.

Faust|regel *die* rule of thumb.

Faust|schlag *der* punch.

Fạx (*pl* - ODER **-e**) *das* fax.

fạxen *vt* to fax.

Fạxen *Pl fam*: **die Faxen dick** ODER **satt haben** to have had enough.

FAZ ['ɛfɑːtsɛt] (*abk für* **Frankfurter Allgemeine Zeitung**) *die German newspaper, renowned for its business and financial news.*

Fazit (*pl* **-s** ODER **-e**) *das* result.

FCKW [ɛfỹtseːkɑː'veː] (*abk für* **Fluorchlorkohlenwasserstoff**) *der (ohne pl)* CFC.

F.D.P. [ɛfỹdeː'peː] (*abk für* **Freie Demokratische Partei**) *die German liberal party.*

Februar *der* February; *siehe auch* **September**.

fẹchten (*präs* **fịcht**, *prät* **fọcht**, *perf* **hat gefọchten**) *vi* to fence.

Fẹchter, in (*mpl* -, *fpl* **-nen**) *der, die* fencer.

Feder (*pl* **-n**) *die* - **1.** [von Vogel] feather - **2.** [zum Schreiben] nib; **zur Feder greifen** to take up one's pen - **3.** [in Maschine, Matratze] spring. ◆ **Federn** *Pl*: **(noch) in den Federn liegen** *fam* to be (still) in bed.

Feder|ball *der* - **1.** [Spiel] badminton - **2.** [Ball] shuttlecock.

Feder|bett *das* quilt.

federn ◇ *vi* [elastisch sein] to be springy; [bei Sprung, Druck] to spring back; **in den Knien federn** to give at the knees. ◇ *vt* [Fahrzeug]: **gut gefedert sein** [Auto] to have good suspension; [Matratze] to be well sprung.

Federung (*pl* **-en**) *die* [von Wagen] suspension *(U)*; [von Bett] springs *Pl*.

Fee (*pl* **-n**) *die* fairy.

fegen (*perf* **hat/ist gefegt**) ◇ *vt (hat)* to sweep. ◇ *vi* - **1.** *(hat) Norddt* [säubern] to sweep up - **2.** *(ist)* [rasen] to sweep.

fehl *adv*: **fehl am Platz sein** to be out of place.

Fehl|betrag *der* shortfall.

fehlen *vi* - **1.** [nicht vorhanden sein] to be missing; **für ein Hobby fehlt ihr die Zeit** she doesn't have time for a hobby; **(in der Schule) fehlen** to miss school; **es fehlt an etw** *(D)* there is a lack of sthg; **es fehlt ihm einiges an Erfahrung** he is somewhat lacking in experience - **2.** [vermisst werden]: **sie fehlt mir** I miss her - **3.** [irren]: **weit gefehlt!** far from it! - **4.** [erkrankt sein]: **was fehlt dir/Ihnen?** what is the matter with you?

Fehl|entscheidung *die* wrong decision.

Fehler (*pl* -) *der* - **1.** [Unrichtigkeit] mistake - **2.** [Schwäche] fault; **ist es mein Fehler, dass er geht?** is it my fault that he's leaving? - **3.** [Mangel] defect.

fehlerfrei ◇ *adj* perfect. ◇ *adv* perfectly.

fehlerhaft ◇ *adj* [Maschine] defective; [Aussprache] poor. ◇ *adv* [schreiben, arbeiten] poorly; [verarbeitet] defectively.

Fehl|geburt *die* miscarriage.

Fehl|griff *der* mistake.

fehl|schlagen (*perf* **ist fehlgeschlagen**) *vi (unreg)* to fail.

Fehl|start *der* - **1.** [von Sportlern] false start - **2.** [von Rakete] abortive launch.

Fehl|urteil *das* - **1.** [Rechtspruch - von Richter] wrong judgement; [- von Geschworenen] wrong verdict - **2.** [Beurteilung] misjudgement.

Feier (*pl* **-n**) *die* party.

Feier|abend *der evening after work*; **Feierabend machen** to finish work; **nach Feierabend** after work; **mit etw ist Feierabend** *fam fig* it's all over with sthg.

feierlich ◇ *adj* - **1.** [Akt, Handlung, Stille] dignified - **2.** [Erklärung] solemn; **das ist schon nicht mehr feierlich** *fam* that really is too much. ◇ *adv* - **1.** [verabschieden, begehen] in a dignified manner - **2.** [erklären] solemnly.

Feierlichkeit (*pl* **-en**) *die* [Würde] solemnity. ◆ **Feierlichkeiten** *Pl* celebrations.

feiern ◇ *vt* - **1.** [Fest, Feiertag] to celebrate - **2.** [Person] to fête. ◇ *vi* to celebrate.

Feier|tag *der* holiday; **kirchlicher Feiertag** feast day.

feige *adj* cowardly.

Feige (*pl* **-n**) *die* fig.

Feigheit *die* cowardice.

Feigling (*pl* **-e**) *der* coward.

Feile (*pl* **-n**) *die* file.

feilen ◇ *vt* to file. ◇ *vi*: **an etw** *(D)* **feilen** *fig* to polish sthg up.

feilschen *vi*: **um etw feilschen** to haggle over sthg.

fein ◇ *adj* - **1.** [Haar, Spitze, Pulver] fine - **2.** *fam* [erfreulich, sympathisch] great - **3.** [Gesicht] delicate - **4.** [Material, Zutat, Küche] top-quality - **5.** [Sinne] keen - **6.** [Spott, Nuance] subtle - **7.** [Leute] refined; **sich fein machen** to make o.s. smart. ◇ *adv* - **1.** [gemahlen, gezeichnet] finely - **2.** *fam* [schön, erfreulich]: **fein gemacht!** well done!; **fein heraus sein** *fig* to have done well for o.s. - **3.** [sich verhalten] nicely - **4.** [vornehm, elegant] elegantly. ◆ **vom Feinsten** *adj* top-quality.

Feind (*pl* **-e**) *der* enemy; **sich** *(D)* **Feinde machen** to make enemies.

Feindin (*pl* **-nen**) *die* enemy.

feindlich ◇ *adj* - **1.** [Haltung, Nachbarn] hostile - **2.** [Soldaten] enemy *(vor Subst)*. ◇ *adv* hostilely.

Feindlichkeit *die* [Gesinnung] hostility.

Feindschaft (*pl* **-en**) *die* enmity *(U)*.

feindselig ◇ *adj* hostile. ◇ *adv* hostilely.

Feindseligkeit (*pl* **-en**) *die* hostility. ◆ **Feindseligkeiten** *Pl* hostilities.

feinfühlig *adj* sensitive.

Feinheit (*pl* **-en**) *die* - **1.** [Beschaffenheit] fineness - **2.** [Vornehmheit] refinement. ◆ **Feinheiten** *Pl* subtleties.

Feinkost|geschäft *das* delicatessen.

Fein|schmecker, in (*mpl* **Feinschmecker**, *fpl* **-nen**) *der, die* gourmet.

Feld (*pl* **-er**) *das* - **1.** [gen] field - **2.** [Teil - von Formular] box; [- von Brettspiel] square; **das Feld räumen** to bow out; **jm das Feld überlassen** to make way for sb.

Feld|bett *das* camp bed *UK*, cot *US*.

Feld|flasche *die* water bottle.

Feld|salat *der (ohne pl)* lamb's lettuce.

Feld|weg *der* footpath *(between fields)*.

Feld|zug *der* campaign.

Felge (*pl* **-n**) *die* - **1.** [Teil des Rades] (wheel) rim - **2.** [Turnübung] circle.

Fell (*pl* **-e**) *das* [Haarkleid] fur; [von Hund, Pferd] coat; [von Schaf] fleece.

Fels (*pl* **-en**) *der* - **1.** *(ohne pl)* [Gestein] rock - **2.** *geh* [Felsen] cliff.

Felsen (*pl* -) *der* cliff.

felsenfest ◇ *adj* firm. ◇ *adv* firmly.

felsig *adj* rocky.

feminin ◇ *adj* - **1.** [gen] feminine - **2.** *abw* [unmännlich] effeminate. ◇ *adv* - **1.** [weiblich] femininely - **2.** *abw* [unmännlich] effeminately.

Femininum (*pl* **-nina**) *das* GRAMM feminine noun.

Feminismus *der* [Frauenbewegung] feminism.

Feminist, in (*mpl* **-en**, *fpl* **-nen**) *der, die* feminist.

feministisch ◇ *adj* feminist. ◇ *adv* in a feminist way.

Fenchel *der* fennel.

Fenster (*pl* -) *das* window; **weg vom Fenster sein** *fam fig* to be out of it.

Fenster|laden *der* shutter.

Fenster|platz *der* window seat.

Fenster|scheibe *die* window pane.

Ferien *Pl* holiday *sing UK*, vacation *sing US*; **die großen Ferien** the summer holidays *UK*, the summer vacation *US*; **in die Ferien fahren, Ferien machen** to go on holiday *UK*, to go on vacation *US*.

Ferien|lager *das* summer camp.

Ferien|ort *der* resort.

Ferkel (*pl* -) *das* - **1.** [Tier] piglet - **2.** *fam* [dreckiger Mensch] mucky pup - **3.** *fam* [unanständiger Mensch] filthy swine.

fern ◇ *adj* - **1.** [räumlich] far-off - **2.** [zeitlich] distant. ◇ *adv* far; **von fern** from a distance. ◇ *präp geh*: **fern einer Sache** *(D)* far from sthg.

Fern|bedienung *die* remote control.

Ferne *die (ohne pl)* [räumlich]: **ihr Blick schweifte in die Ferne** she stared off into the distance; **in der Ferne** in the distance; **aus der Ferne** [betrachten] from a distance; [Gruß] from far-off lands.

Ferne Osten *der* Far East.

ferner ◇ *konj* in addition. ◇ *adv geh* in future. ◇ *adj (Kompar)* ▷ **fern**.

Fern|gespräch *das* long-distance call.

ferngesteuert *adj* remote-controlled.

Fern|glas *das* binoculars *Pl*.

fern halten *vt (unreg)*: **jn/etw von jm/etw fern halten** to keep sb/sthg away from sb/sthg. ◆ **sich fern halten** *ref*: **sich von jm/etw fern halten** to keep away from sb/sthg.

Fernlicht *das* full beam *UK*, high beam *US*.

Fern|rohr *das* telescope.

Fernseh|apparat *der* television set.

fern|sehen *vi (unreg)* to watch television.

Fernsehen *das* television; **im Fernsehen** on television, on TV.

Fernseher (*pl* -) *der* - **1.** [Gerät] television, TV - **2.** [Fernsehzuschauer] viewer.

Fernseh|film *der* television ODER TV film.

Fernseh|programm *das* - **1.** [Sendungen] television ODER TV programmes *Pl* - **2.** [Programmheft] television ODER TV guide.

Fern|steuerung *die* remote control.

Fern|straße *die* trunk road *UK*, highway *US*.

Fern|verkehr *der* long-distance traffic.

Ferse (*pl* **-n**) *die* heel; **jm auf den Fersen sein/bleiben** *fig* to be/stay on sb's heels.

fertig *adj* - **1.** [vollendet - gen] finished; [- Essen] ready - **2.** [bereit]: **fertig sein** to be ready - **3.** [am/zu Ende]: **(mit etw) fertig sein** to have finished (sthg) - **4.** [müde]: **fertig sein** *fam* [körperlich] to be worn out; [psychisch] to be shattered; **mit den Nerven fertig sein** to be at the end of one's tether *UK* ODER rope *US*; **mit jm fertig sein** *fam* to be finished ODER through with sb; **mit etw fertig/nicht fertig werden** to cope/not cope with sthg; **mit jm schon/nicht fertig werden** *fam* to cope/not cope with sb.

fertig bringen *vt (unreg)* [zustande bringen]: **er hat es fertig gebracht, dass die Familien wieder miteinander reden** he has managed to get the families talking to each other again.

Fertig|haus *das* prefabricated house.

Fertigkeit (*pl* **-en**) *die* skill. ◆ **Fertigkeiten** *Pl* skills.

fertig|machen *vt* - **1.** *fam* [zurechtweisen] to lay into - **2.** *fam* [zur Verzweiflung bringen]: **der macht mich fertig** he does my head in - **3.** *fam* [erschöpfen] to wear out.

fertig machen *vt* - **1.** [abschließen] to finish - **2.** [bereitmachen] to get ready - **3.** *fam* [erledigen] to sort out; [zusammenschlagen] to do in. ◆ **sich fertig machen** *ref* [sich bereitmachen] to get ready.

fẹrtig stellen *vt* to complete.

Fẹssel (*pl* **-n**) *die* - **1.** [Strick, Zwang] bond - **2.** [Körperteil - bei Tieren] pastern; [- bei Menschen] ankle.

fẹsseln *vt* - **1.** [anketten, binden] to tie up; **jm die Hände fesseln** to tie sb's hands up - **2.** [faszinieren] to grip.

fẹsselnd ◇ *adj* gripping. ◇ *adv* grippingly.

fẹst ◇ *adj* - **1.** [gut befestigt - Knoten, Verband] tight - **2.** [Griff, Druck, Meinung] firm - **3.** [Wohnsitz, Angestellte] permanent; [Arbeitszeiten, Gehalt, Termin] fixed - **4.** [Stoff, Schuhe] strong - **5.** [verbindlich - Vereinbarung, Vorgaben] binding; [- Zusage] definite - **6.** [Nahrung] solid - **7.** [entschlossen - Blick, Stimme] steady. ◇ *adv* - **1.** [haltbar, straff] tightly - **2.** [drücken, ziehen] hard - **3.** [überzeugt - glauben] firmly - **4.** [verbindlich - zusagen, vereinbaren] definitely - **5.** [angestellt] permanently - **6.** [schlafen] soundly - **7.** *fam* [tüchtig - zugreifen] with a will.

Fẹst (*pl* **-e**) *das* - **1.** [Veranstaltung] party - **2.** [Feiertag] festival. ◆ **frohes Fest** *interj* happy Christmas!

fẹstangestellt ▷ **fest**.

Fẹst|betrag *der* fixed amount.

fẹst|binden *vt (unreg)* to tie up.

Fẹst|essen *das* banquet.

fẹst|halten *(unreg)* ◇ *vt* - **1.** [aufzeichnen] to record - **2.** [feststellen]: **wir können festhalten, dass...** it is clear that... ◇ *vi*: **an jm festhalten** to stand by sb; **an etw festhalten** to stick to sthg.

fẹst halten *(unreg) vt* [halten] to hold on to. ◆ **sich fest halten** *ref*: **sich an jm/etw fest halten** to hold on to sb/sthg.

fẹstigen *vt* to strengthen. ◆ **sich festigen** *ref* to become stronger.

Fẹstiger (*pl* -) *der* [Schaum] styling mousse; [Spray] hairspray.

Fẹstigkeit *die* - **1.** [Widerstandsfähigkeit] strength - **2.** [Standhaftigkeit] steadfastness.

Fẹstival ['fɛstivəl] (*pl* **-s**) *das* festival.

Fẹstland *das* mainland.

fẹst|legen *vt* - **1.** [bestimmen] to fix - **2.** [verpflichten]: **jn auf etw** *(A)* **festlegen** to pin sb down to sthg. ◆ **sich festlegen** *ref* [sich binden] to commit o.s.; **sich auf etw** *(A)* **festlegen** to commit o.s. to sthg.

fẹstlich ◇ *adj* [Essen, Veranstaltung] festive; [Kleidung] formal. ◇ *adv* festively.

Fẹstlichkeit (*pl* **-en**) *die* [Atmosphäre] festiveness. ◆ **Festlichkeiten** *Pl* festivities.

fẹst|machen *vt* - **1.** [befestigen] to fix; [Boot] to moor - **2.** [vereinbaren - Termin] to fix; [- Geschäft] to secure.

Fẹstnahme (*pl* **-n**) *die* arrest.

fẹst|nehmen *vt (unreg)* to arrest.

Fẹst|netz *das* TELEKOM land-line telephone network *(as opposed to mobile phones)*.

Fẹst|platte *die* EDV hard disk.

fẹst|setzen *vt* - **1.** [bestimmen] to fix - **2.** [verhaften] to arrest. ◆ **sich festsetzen** *ref* [Dreck] to collect.

fẹst sitzen *vi (unreg)*: **es sitzt fest** [Dübel] it won't come out; [Farbe] it won't come off.

Fẹstspiele *Pl* festival *sing*.

fẹst|stehen *vi (unreg)* - **1.** [bestimmt sein] to have been fixed - **2.** [sicher sein] to be definite.

fẹst|stellen *vt* - **1.** [in Erfahrung bringen] to find out; [diagnostizieren] to establish - **2.** [beobachten] to notice; **sie stellte fest, dass er Recht hatte** she realized that he was right - **3.** [anmerken] to state.

Fẹst|stellung *die* - **1.** [Ermittlung] establishing - **2.** [Wahrnehmung] realization; **ich machte die Feststellung, dass...** I realized that... - **3.** [Erklärung] remark.

Fẹstung (*pl* **-en**) *die* fortress.

Fete ['feːtə] (*pl* **-n**) *die fam* party.

fẹtt ◇ *adj* - **1.** [Fleisch, Gericht] fatty - **2.** [Person, Tier, Erbe, Beute] fat. ◇ *adv* [mit viel Fett]: **fett essen** to eat fatty food.

Fẹtt (*pl* **-e**) *das* fat; **er hat sein Fett weg** *fam fig* he got what was coming to him.

fẹttarm *adj* low-fat.

fẹtten ◇ *vt* to grease. ◇ *vi* to be greasy.

fẹtt gedruckt *adj* in bold (type).

fẹttig *adj* greasy.

Fẹttnäpfchen *das*: **ins Fettnäpfchen treten** *fam* to put one's foot in it.

Fẹtzen (*pl* -) *der* scrap; **etw in Fetzen zerreißen** to tear sthg to pieces; **das Kleid ist ein billiger Fetzen!** that dress is just cheap rubbish!

fẹtzig *adj fam* [toll] cool.

feucht ◇ *adj* [Wand, Tuch, Haar] damp; [Hände, Augen] moist; [Klima] humid. ◇ *adv* [wischen] with a damp cloth.

Feuchtigkeit *die* - **1.** [leichte Nässe] moisture - **2.** [Feuchtsein - von Wand, Tuch, Haar] dampness; [- von Händen, Augen] moistness; [- von Klima] humidity.

feudal ◇ *adj* - **1.** [den Feudalismus betreffend] feudal - **2.** [aristokratisch] aristocratic - **3.** *fam* [vornehm] grand. ◇ *adv fam* [vornehm] grandly.

Feuer (*pl* -) ◇ *das* - **1.** [gen] fire; **auf offenem Feuer kochen** to cook over an open fire; **Feuer machen** to light a fire; **im Ofen Feuer machen** to light the oven; **jm Feuer geben** to give sb a light; **Feuer legen** to start a fire; **das Feuer einstellen/eröffnen** to cease/open fire - **2.** *(ohne pl)* [Schwung, Temperament - von Person] passion; [- von Begeisterung, Leidenschaft] fervour;

Feuer fangen *fam* [sich verlieben] to be smitten; **(für jn/etw) Feuer und Flamme sein** *fam* to be really keen (on sb/sthg). ◇ *interj* fire!

Feueralarm *der* fire alarm.

feuerfest *adj* fireproof; [Backform] ovenproof.

feuergefährlich *adj* flammable.

Feuer|löscher (*pl* **Feuerlöscher**) *der* fire extinguisher.

feuern ◇ *vt fam* - **1.** [entlassen, heizen] to fire - **2.** [schleudern] to fling. ◇ *vi* [schießen]: **auf jn/etw feuern** to fire at sb/sthg.

Feuer|wehr (*pl* **-en**) *die* fire brigade.

Feuer|wehrmann (*pl* **-männer** ODER **-leute**) *der* fireman.

Feuer|werk *das* - **1.** [Veranstaltung] firework display - **2.** [Raketen] fireworks *Pl*.

Feuer|zeug *das* lighter.

Feuilleton [fœjə'tõ] (*pl* **-s**) *das* - **1.** [literarischer Teil einer Zeitung] arts section - **2.** [literarischer Beitrag] arts feature.

ff. (*abk für* **folgende Seiten**) ff.

FH [ɛf'hɑ:] (*pl* **-s**) *die* ▷ **Fachhochschule**.

ficht *präs* ▷ **fechten**.

Fichte (*pl* **-n**) *die* spruce.

Fieber *das* - **1.** [hohe Körpertemperatur] temperature; **Fieber haben** to have a temperature; **bei jm Fieber messen** to take sb's temperature - **2.** *geh* [Besessenheit] fever.

fieberhaft ◇ *adj* feverish. ◇ *adv* feverishly.

fiebern *vi* - **1.** [Fieber haben] to have a temperature - **2.** [angespannt warten]: **vor Erregung fiebern** to be in a fever of excitement; **nach etw fiebern** to yearn for sthg.

Fieber|thermometer *das* thermometer.

fiel *prät* ▷ **fallen**.

fies *fam abw* ◇ *adj* nasty. ◇ *adv* - **1.** [gemein] nastily - **2.** [ekelhaft]: **fies schmecken** to taste horrible.

Figur (*pl* **-en**) *die* - **1.** [gen] figure; [männlich] physique - **2.** [literarische Darstellung] character - **3.** [Spielstein] piece; **eine gute/schlechte Figur abgeben** ODER **machen** to cut a good/poor figure.

Filet [fi'le:] (*pl* **-s**) *das* fillet.

Filiale (*pl* **-n**) *die* branch.

Film (*pl* **-e**) *der* film; **beim Film sein** ODER **arbeiten** to be in the movies.

filmen *vt* & *vi* to film.

Film|kamera *die* film camera, movie camera *US*.

Film|star ['fɪlmʃtɑ:ɐ̯] *der* film star, movie star.

Filter (*pl* -) *das* & *der* filter.

filtern *vt* to filter.

Filter|tüte *die* filter (paper).

Filter|zigarette *die* filter cigarette.

Filz (*pl* **-e**) *der* - **1.** [Stoff] felt - **2.** *abw* [Vetternwirtschaft] jobs *Pl* for the boys.

filzen *vt fam* [Person] to frisk; [Haus, Koffer] to search.

Filz|stift *der* felt-tip (pen).

Finale (*pl* -) *das* - **1.** [Endkampf, Endspiel] final - **2.** MUS finale.

Finanz|amt *das* tax office.

Finanz|beamte *der* tax inspector.

Finanz|beamtin *die* tax inspector.

Finanz|bedarf *der* (*ohne pl*) financial needs *Pl*.

Finanzen *Pl* finances.

finanziell [finan'tsi̯ɛl] ◇ *adj* financial. ◇ *adv* financially.

finanzieren *vt* to finance.

Finanzierung (*pl* **-en**) *die* financing.

Finanz|ministerium *das* finance ministry, ≃ Treasury *UK*, ≃ Department of the Treasury *US*.

finden (*prät* **fand**, *perf* **hat gefunden**) ◇ *vt* - **1.** [gen] to find; **wo finde ich die Post?** where is the post office?; **er fand die Kinder schlafend** he found the children sleeping; **an etw Gefallen finden** to get ODER come to like sthg - **2.** [erhalten]: **Verwendung finden** to be used; **Anerkennung finden** to receive recognition - **3.** [beurteilen]: **ich finde sie nett** I think she's nice; **wie findest du...?** what do you think of...? ◇ *vi* - **1.** [erfolgreich suchen]: **er hat nicht zu uns gefunden** he couldn't find his way to our place - **2.** [beurteilen]: **ich finde, dass...** I think (that...); **ich finde nichts dabei** I don't see anything wrong with it. ◆ **sich finden** *ref* [wieder auftauchen]: **der Schlüssel hat sich gefunden** I/we found the key; **das wird sich (schon) alles finden!** everything will be all right.

Finder, in (*mpl* -, *fpl* **-nen**) *der* finder.

Finder|lohn *der* reward (*for finding something*).

fing *prät* ▷ **fangen**.

Finger (*pl* -) *der* [Glied] finger; **jn in die Finger kriegen** ODER **bekommen** *fam* to get one's hands on sb; **etw in die Finger kriegen** ODER **bekommen** *fam* to get hold of sthg; **lange Finger machen** *fam abw* to be light-fingered.

Finger|abdruck *der* fingerprint.

Finger|hut *der* - **1.** [zum Nähen] thimble - **2.** [Blume] foxglove.

Finger|nagel *der* fingernail.

Finger|spitze *die* fingertip.

Finger|spitzengefühl *das* sensitivity; **Fingerspitzengefühl haben** ODER **besitzen** ODER **beweisen** to show sensitivity.

Fink (*pl* **-en**) *der* finch.

finnisch *adj* Finnish; *siehe auch* **englisch**.

Finnisch(e) *das* Finnish; *siehe auch* **Englisch(e)**.

Finnland *nt* Finland.

finster <> *adj* - **1.** [Nacht, Straße, Zimmer, Zeiten] dark - **2.** [Person, Miene] grim, sombre - **3.** [Gegend, Gestalt] sinister. <> *adv* [unfreundlich] grimly.

Finsternis (*pl* **-se**) *die* darkness.

Finte (*pl* **-n**) *die* ruse.

Firma (*pl* **Firmen**) *die* firm, company.

Firmen|name *der* company name.

Firmen|wagen *der* company car.

Firmung (*pl* **-en**) *die* RELIG confirmation.

First Class *die* first class.

Fisch (*pl* **-e**) *der* - **1.** [Tier, Gericht] fish - **2.** ASTROL Pisces; **Fisch sein** to be a Pisces. ◆ **Fische** *Pl* ASTROL Pisces *(U)*.

Fisch|besteck *das* fish knives and forks *Pl*.

fischen <> *vt* - **1.** [fangen] to catch - **2.** [angeln] to fish for - **3.** [holen] to fish out. <> *vi* - **1.** [Fische fangen] to fish; **fischen gehen** to go fishing - **2.** *fam* [greifen]: **nach etw fischen** to fish for sthg.

Fischer, in (*mpl* **-**, *fpl* **-nen**) *der, die* fisherman (fisherwoman *die*).

Fischer|boot *das* fishing boat.

Fischerei *die* fishing.

Fischfang *der* fishing.

Fisch|händler, in *der, die* fishmonger *UK*, fish seller *US*.

Fisch|stäbchen [ˈfɪʃʃtɛːpçən] *das* fish finger *UK*, fish stick *US*.

Fiskus *der* treasury.

fit *adj* [körperlich] fit; [geistig] sharp, mentally alert; **fit in Chemie sein** *fam* to be good at chemistry.

Fitness [ˈfɪtnɛs] *die* [körperliche] fitness; [geistige] sharpness, mental alertness.

Fitnesscenter (*pl* **-**) *das* fitness centre.

fix <> *adj* - **1.** *fam* [schnell] quick - **2.** [Kosten] fixed - **3.** [erschöpft]: **fix und fertig sein** *fam* to be beat ODER knackered *UK*. <> *adv fam* [schnell] quickly.

Fixer, in (*mpl* **-**, *fpl* **-nen**) *der, die fam* junkie.

fixieren *vt* - **1.** [anstarren] to stare fixedly at - **2.** [befestigen, konservieren] to fix - **3.** *geh* [festhalten] to record.

FKK [ɛfˈkaːˈkaː] (*abk für* **Freikörperkultur**) *das* nudism; **am Strand FKK machen** to sunbathe on the beach in the nude.

flach <> *adj* - **1.** [eben] flat - **2.** [niedrig, dünn - Gebäude, Absätze] low; [- Stein, Schuhe] flat; [- Teller] shallow - **3.** [seicht, oberflächlich] shallow. <> *adv*: **flach atmen** to take shallow breaths.

Fläche (*pl* **-n**) *die* - **1.** [Gebiet] area - **2.** [geometrisch] plane - **3.** [Seite] surface.

flach|fallen (*perf* **ist flachgefallen**) *vi (unreg) fam*: **die Party fällt flach** the party's off; **23 Stellen fallen flach** 23 people are getting the boot.

Flachland *das (ohne pl)* lowlands *Pl*.

flackern *vi* to flicker.

Fladen (*pl* **-**) *der* - **1.** [Brotfladen] *flat, round loaf* - **2.** [Kuchen] pancake - **3.** [Kuhfladen] cowpat.

Flagge (*pl* **-n**) *die* flag.

flambieren *vt* to flambé.

Flamingo (*pl* **-s**) *der* flamingo.

flämisch *adj* Flemish.

Flamme (*pl* **-n**) *die* - **1.** [Feuer] flame - **2.** [zum Kochen] burner.

Flandern *nt* Flanders *sing*.

Flanell (*pl* **-e**) *der* flannel.

Flanke (*pl* **-n**) *die* flank.

Flasche (*pl* **-n**) *die* - **1.** [Gefäß] bottle; **eine Flasche Sekt** a bottle of champagne - **2.** *salopp abw* [Versager] drip.

Flaschen|bier *das* bottled beer.

Flaschen|öffner *der* bottle opener.

Flaschen|zug *der* block and tackle.

flattern (*perf* **ist/hat geflattert**) *vi* - **1.** [gen] to flutter - **2.** [schlagen]: **mit den Flügeln flattern** to flutter its wings.

Flaum *der* down.

flauschig *adj* fleecy.

Flausen *Pl*: **Flausen im Kopf haben** always to be up to some trick or other.

Flaute (*pl* **-n**) *die* - **1.** [wirtschaftlich] slack period - **2.** [Windstille] calm.

Flechte (*pl* **-n**) *die* - **1.** [Pflanze] lichen - **2.** [Hautausschlag] eczema.

flechten (*präs* **flicht**, *prät* **flocht**, *perf* **hat geflochten**) *vt* [Haare, Zopf] to plait *UK*, to braid *US*; [Korb] to weave.

Fleck (*pl* **-e** ODER **-en**) *der* - **1.** [Klecks] stain - **2.** [Stelle] patch; **blauer Fleck** bruise - **3.** [Ort] spot.

fleckenlos <> *adj* spotless. <> *adv* spotlessly.

Fleck|entferner *der* stain remover.

fleckig *adj* - **1.** [schmutzig] stained - **2.** [gefleckt - Haut] blotchy; [- Obst] blemished.

Floder|maus *die* bat.

Flegel (*pl* **-**) *der* lout.

flegelhaft <> *adj* loutish. <> *adv* loutishly.

flehen *vi*: **(um etw) flehen** to plead (for sthg).

Fleisch *das* - **1.** [Nahrungsmittel] meat - **2.** [Muskelgewebe, Fruchtfleisch] flesh; **Fleisch fressend** carnivorous.

Fleisch|brühe *die* meat stock.

Fleischer (*pl* **-**) *der* butcher.

Fleischerei (*pl* **-en**) *die* butcher's (shop).

Fleischerin (*pl* **-nen**) *die* butcher.

fleischfressend = **Fleisch**.

fleischig *adj* fleshy.

Fleisch|wolf *der* mincer *UK*, meat grinder *US*.

Fleisch|wurst *die type of cold pork sausage similar to mortadella.*

Fleiß *der* diligence; **viel Fleiß auf etw** *(A)* **verwenden** to put a lot of work into sthg.

fleißig ◇ *adj* [eifrig, arbeitsam] hard-working. ◇ *adv* - **1.** [eifrig, arbeitsam] hard - **2.** *fam* [oft, viel] a lot; **fleißig bezahlen** to fork out money.

flẹtschen *vt*: **die Zähne fletschen** to bare one's teeth.

flịcht *präs* ▷ **flechten.**

flịcken *vt* to mend.

Flịcken (*pl* -) *der* patch.

Flịckzeug *das (ohne pl)* [für Reifen] repair kit; [für Kleidung] sewing kit.

Flieder (*pl* -) *der* lilac.

Fliege (*pl* **-n**) *die* - **1.** [Insekt] fly - **2.** [Schleife] bow tie.

fliegen (*prät* **flog**, *perf* **hat/ist geflogen**) ◇ *vi (ist)* - **1.** [gen] to fly - **2.** *fam* [stürzen] to fall - **3.** *fam* [entlassen werden] to get fired, to get the sack *UK* - **4.** [attraktiv finden]: **auf jn/etw fliegen** to be crazy about sb/sthg. ◇ *vt (hat)* to fly.

Fliegen|pilz *der* fly agaric.

Flieger (*pl* -) *der* - **1.** [Pilot] pilot - **2.** *fam* [Flugzeug] plane.

Fliegerin (*pl* **-nen**) *die* pilot.

fliehen (*prät* **floh**, *perf* **hat/ist geflohen**) ◇ *vi (ist)*: **aus dem Gefängnis fliehen** to escape from jail; **vor jm/etw fliehen** to flee from sb/sthg. ◇ *vt (hat)* to shun.

Fliese (*pl* **-n**) *die* tile.

Fließband (*pl* **-bänder**) *das* conveyor belt; **am Fließband arbeiten** to be an assembly-line ODER a production-line worker.

fließen (*prät* **flọss**, *perf* **ist geflọssen**) *vi* to flow; **das Blut fließt aus der Wunde** the blood is flowing from the wound.

fließend ◇ *adj* - **1.** [perfekt] fluent - **2.** [ungenau, unscharf - Grenzen, Übergang] fluid - **3.** [Verkehr, Material] flowing; [Wasser] running. ◇ *adv* [sprechen] fluently.

flịmmern *vi* - **1.** [Luft, Wasser, Oberflächen] to shimmer - **2.** [Fernsehbild] to flicker.

flịnk ◇ *adj* - **1.** [geschickt] nimble - **2.** [schnell] quick. ◇ *adv* - **1.** [geschickt] nimbly - **2.** [schnell] quickly.

Flịnte (*pl* **-n**) *die* shotgun.

flịrten ['flœrtn̩] *vi*: **(mit jm) flirten** to flirt (with sb).

Flịtterwochen *Pl* honeymoon *sing*; **in die Flitterwochen fahren** to go on honeymoon.

flịtzen (*perf* **ist geflịtzt**) *vi fam* [Person, Wagen] to whizz.

flọcht *prät* ▷ **flechten.**

Flọcke (*pl* **-n**) *die* [von Schnee, Getreide] flake; [von Staub] ball; [von Schaum] blob.

flog *prät* ▷ **fliegen.**

floh *prät* ▷ **fliehen.**

Floh (*pl* **Flöhe**) *der* flea.

Floh|markt *der* flea market.

Flora *die* flora.

florieren *vi* to flourish.

Flọskel (*pl* **-n**) *die* cliché.

flọss *prät* ▷ **fließen.**

Floß (*pl* **Flöße**) *das* raft.

Flọsse (*pl* **-n**) *die* - **1.** [von Fisch, Rückenflosse von Delfin] fin; [Bauchflosse von Delfin und Robbe] flipper - **2.** [Schwimmflosse] flipper - **3.** *salopp abw* [Hand] paw.

Flöte (*pl* **-n**) *die* [Querflöte] flute; [Blockflöte] recorder.

flöten ◇ *vi* - **1.** [Flöte spielen] to play the flute/recorder - **2.** [pfeifen - Person] to whistle - **3.** *fam abw* [einschmeichelnd sprechen] to speak in honeyed tones. ◇ *vt* - **1.** [spielen] to play on the flute/recorder - **2.** [pfeifen] to whistle - **3.** *fam abw* [einschmeichelnd sagen]: **sie flötete mir Schmeicheleien ins Ohr** she murmured flattering remarks into my ear.

flọtt ◇ *adj* - **1.** [schick] smart, stylish - **2.** [lebhaft, schnell - Musik, Person] lively; [- Service] speedy; [- Auto] fast - **3.** [fahrtüchtig - Wagen] roadworthy; [- Kahn] seaworthy. ◇ *adv* - **1.** [schnell, lebhaft - arbeiten, laufen] quickly; [- tanzen, spielen] in a lively manner; **mach flott!** make it snappy! - **2.** [schick] smartly.

Flọtte (*pl* **-n**) *die* fleet.

Fluch (*pl* **Flüche**) *der* - **1.** [Schimpfwort] curse - **2.** *(ohne pl)* [Verwünschung] curse.

fluchen *vi* to swear.

Flụcht *die* [aus dem Gefängnis] escape; **sie sind auf der Flucht** they are fleeing; **die Flucht ergreifen** to take flight.

flụchtartig ◇ *adj* hurried. ◇ *adv* hurriedly.

flụ̈chten (*perf* **hat/ist geflụ̈chtet**) *vi (ist)* to flee; **vor jm/etw flüchten** to flee from sb/sthg. ◆ **sich flüchten** *ref (hat)*: **sich in etw** *(A)* **flüchten** to take refuge in sthg.

flụ̈chtig ◇ *adj* - **1.** [kurz] fleeting; [Gruß, Abschied] brief - **2.** [ungenau - Eindruck] superficial; [- Arbeit] hurried - **3.** [flüchtend - Gefangene] escaped; [- Mörder] wanted. ◇ *adv* - **1.** [ungenau] superficially; [arbeiten] hurriedly - **2.** [kurz] briefly.

Flụ̈chtigkeits|fehler *der* careless mistake.

Flụ̈chtling (*pl* **-e**) *der* refugee.

Flụcht|weg *der* escape route.

Flug (*pl* **Flüge**) *der* flight.

Flug|bahn *die* [von Rakete] trajectory.

Flug|blatt *das* leaflet.

Flügel (*pl* -) *der* - **1.** [gen] wing - **2.** [Musikinstrument] grand piano.

Flug|gast *der* passenger *(on plane).*

flụ̈gge *adj* [Vogeljunge] fully-fledged; **flügge werden** [Kind] to be ready to leave the nest.

Flug|gesellschaft *die* airline.
Flug|hafen *der* airport.
Flug|lotse *der* air traffic controller.
Flug|platz *der* airfield.
Flug|verkehr *der* air traffic.
Flug|zeug *das* plane, aeroplane *UK*, airplane *US*; **mit dem Flugzeug fliegen** to fly.
Flugzeug|träger *der* aircraft carrier.
Flunder (*pl* **-n**) *die* flounder.
flunkern *vi* to tell stories.
Fluor *das* fluorine.
Flur (*pl* **-e** ODER **-en**) ◇ *der (pl Flure)* [Korridor] corridor; [am Eingang] hallway. ◇ *die (pl Fluren)* [Gelände] fields *Pl*.
Fluss (*pl* **Flüsse**) *der* - **1.** [Wasserlauf] river - **2.** [Bewegung] flow.
flussabwärts *adv* downstream.
flussaufwärts *adv* upstream.
Flussbett (*pl* **-en**) *das* river bed.
flüssig ◇ *adj* - **1.** [nicht fest] liquid; [Metall] molten; [Butter] melted - **2.** [Stil, Verkehr] flowing; [Ausdruck] fluent - **3.** [zahlungsfähig, verfügbar]: **flüssig sein** to be solvent; **nicht flüssig sein** to be short of money. ◇ *adv* [sprechen] fluently.
Flüssigkeit (*pl* **-en**) *die* liquid.
Flusslauf (*pl* **-läufe**) *der* course *(of a river)*.
Flusspferd (*pl* **-e**) *das* hippopotamus.
flüstern ◇ *vi* to whisper. ◇ *vt* to whisper; **jm etw ins Ohr flüstern** to whisper sthg into sb's ear; **jm was flüstern** *fam fig* to tell sb a thing or two.
Flut (*pl* **-en**) *die* - **1.** *(ohne pl)* [Ansteigen des Wasserstandes] tide *(incoming)*; **die Flut kommt** the tide is coming in; **bei Flut** at high tide; **eine Flut von etw** *fig* a flood of sthg - **2.** *geh* [Wassermasse] waters *Pl*.
Flutlicht *das (ohne pl)*: **bei Flutlicht spielen** to play under floodlights.
focht *prät* ▻ **fechten**.
Fohlen (*pl* -) *das* foal.
Föhn (*pl* **-e**) *der* - **1.** [Wind] *hot, dry wind typical of the Alps* - **2.** [Haartrockner] hairdryer.
föhnen *vt*: **jm/sich die Haare föhnen** [zum Trocknen] to dry sb's/one's hair; **jm die Haare föhnen** [zum Frisieren] to blow-dry sb's hair.
Folge (*pl* **-n**) *die* - **1.** [Konsequenz] consequence; **etw zur Folge haben** to result in sthg - **2.** [Fortsetzung] episode - **3.** [Serie] succession - **4.** *amt* [Befolgung]: **jm/einem Befehl Folge leisten** to obey sb/an order; **einer Einladung Folge leisten** to accept an invitation.
folgen (*perf* **ist gefolgt**) *vi* - **1.** [nachfolgen, verstehen, sich richten nach]: **jm/einer Sache folgen** to follow sb/sthg - **2.** [sich anschließen]: **auf etw** *(A)* **folgen** to follow sthg; **wie folgt** as follows - **3.** [gehorchen]: **(jm/einer Sache) folgen** to obey (sb/sthg) - **4.** [sich logisch ergeben]: **aus etw folgen** to follow from sthg.
folgend *adj* following. ◆ **Folgende** *das*: **das Folgende** the following. ◆ **Folgendes** *nt* the following.
folgendermaßen *adv* as follows.
folgern *vt*: **aus etw folgern, dass...** to conclude from sthg that...
Folgerung (*pl* **-en**) *die* conclusion.
folglich *adv* consequently.
folgsam ◇ *adj* obedient. ◇ *adv* obediently.
Folie ['fo:li̯ə] (*pl* **-n**) *die* - **1.** [Verpackung - aus Plastik] film; [- aus Metall] foil - **2.** [für Overheadprojektor] transparency.
Folklore *die* - **1.** [Musik] folk music - **2.** [Brauchtum] folklore.
folkloristisch *adj* folkloric; [Musik] folk.
Folter (*pl* **-n**) *die* torture; **jn auf die Folter spannen** *fig* to keep sb on tenterhooks.
foltern *vt* to torture.
Fön® (*pl* **-e**) *der* = **Föhn**.
fönen = **föhnen**.
Fonetik, Phonetik *die (ohne pl)* phonetics.
fonetisch, phonetisch ◇ *adj* phonetic. ◇ *adv* phonetically.
Fontäne (*pl* **-n**) *die* - **1.** [von Wasser] jet - **2.** [Springbrunnen] fountain.
Förder|kurs *der* SCHULE extra classes *Pl*.
fordern *vt* - **1.** [verlangen] to demand - **2.** [beanspruchen] to make demands on.
fördern *vt* - **1.** [unterstützen] to support; [Handel, Frieden] to promote; [Begabung] to foster - **2.** [Bodenschätze] to mine.
Forderung (*pl* **-en**) *die* - **1.** [Verlangen] demand - **2.** [finanzieller Anspruch] claim.
Förderung (*pl* **-en**) *die* - **1.** [Unterstützung] support; [von Handel, Frieden] promotion; [von Begabung] fostering - **2.** [von Bodenschätzen] mining.
Forelle (*pl* **-n**) *die* trout.
Form (*pl* **-en**) *die* - **1.** [gen] form; **in Form einer Sache** in the form of sthg; **in Form sein** to be in good form; **sich/jn in Form bringen** to get o.s./sb into shape; **die Form wahren** to observe the proprieties - **2.** [Gestalt] shape - **3.** [für Kuchen] baking tin.
formal ◇ *adj* formal. ◇ *adv* formally.
Formalität (*pl* **-en**) *die* formality.
Format (*pl* **-e**) *das* - **1.** [Größe] size; **im Format DIN A 3** in A3 format - **2.** [Niveau - von Person] stature; **die Frau hat Format** she's a woman of stature.
formatieren *vt* EDV to format.
Formation (*pl* **-en**) *die* - **1.** [gen] formation - **2.** [Gruppe] group.
Formel (*pl* **-n**) *die* formula; **Formel 1** SPORT Formula One.
formell ◇ *adj* formal. ◇ *adv* formally.

formen *vt* - **1.** [Material] to shape - **2.** [Person] to mould. ◆ **sich formen** *ref* [sich bilden] to take shape.

formieren *vt* to form. ◆ **sich formieren** *ref* [sich aufstellen] to get into formation; [Organisation] to form.

förmlich ◇ *adj* formal. ◇ *adv* - **1.** [gen] formally - **2.** [regelrecht] really.

formlos ◇ *adj* - **1.** [nicht formal] informal - **2.** [amorph] shapeless - **3.** [ungezwungen] casual. ◇ *adv* - **1.** [nicht formal] informally - **2.** [ungezwungen] casually.

Formular (*pl* **-e**) *das* form.

formulieren *vt* to formulate.

Formulierung (*pl* **-en**) *die* - **1.** [Formulieren] formulation - **2.** [Textstelle] wording.

forsch ◇ *adj* self-confident. ◇ *adv* self-confidently.

forschen *vi* - **1.** [wissenschaftlich untersuchen] to do research - **2.** [ermitteln]: **in js Augen forschen** to search sb's eyes; **nach jm/etw forschen** to search for sb/sthg.

Forscher, in (*mpl* **-**, *fpl* **-nen**) *der, die* researcher.

Forschung (*pl* **-en**) *die* research; **Forschungen** research.

Förster, in (*mpl* **-**, *fpl* **-nen**) *der, die* forest ranger.

fort *adv* [weg] away; **fort sein** to be gone. ◆ **und so fort** *adv* and so forth.

fort|bestehen *vi (unreg)* to continue; [trotz Bedrohung] to continue to exist.

fort|bewegen *vt* to move. ◆ **sich fortbewegen** *ref* to move.

Fortbildung (*pl* **-en**) *die* - **1.** [Weiterbildung] training; **Fortbildung zur Bekämpfung der Arbeitslosigkeit** lifelong learning as a means of combatting unemployment - **2.** [Kurs] training course.

fort|fahren (*perf* **hat/ist fortgefahren**) *(unreg)* ◇ *vi* - **1.** *(ist)* [wegfahren] to leave - **2.** [nicht aufhören] to continue. ◇ *vt (hat)* [wegfahren] to take away.

fort|führen *vt* - **1.** [weitermachen] to carry on - **2.** [fortbringen] to take away.

fort|gehen (*perf* **ist fortgegangen**) *vi (unreg)* - **1.** [weggehen] to leave - **2.** [weitergehen] to continue.

fortgeschritten ◇ *pp* ▷ **fortschreiten**. ◇ *adj* advanced; **zu fortgeschrittener Stunde** at a late hour.

Fortgeschrittene (*pl* **-n**) *der, die* advanced student.

fort|kommen (*perf* **ist fortgekommen**) *vi (unreg)* - **1.** [wegkommen] to get away - **2.** [fortgebracht werden] to be taken away - **3.** [abhanden kommen] to disappear.

fortlaufend *adv* [ständig] continually; [nummerieren] consecutively.

fort|pflanzen ◆ **sich fortpflanzen** *ref* - **1.** [sich reproduzieren] to reproduce - **2.** [sich ausbreiten] to spread.

Fortpflanzung *die* reproduction.

fort|schreiten (*perf* **ist fortgeschritten**) *vi (unreg)* to progress; [Zeit] to move on; [Krankheit, Prozess] to advance.

Fort|schritt *der* progress *(U)*; **Fortschritte** progress; **Fortschritte machen** to make progress.

fortschrittlich ◇ *adj* progressive. ◇ *adv* progressively.

fort|setzen *vt* to continue.

Fortsetzung (*pl* **-en**) *die* continuation; [von Film] sequel.

Fossil (*pl* **-ien**) *das* fossil.

Foto (*pl* **-s**), **Photo** (*pl* **-s**) *das* photo; **ein Foto machen** to take a photo.

Foto|apparat *der* camera.

Fotograf (*pl* **-en**) *der* photographer.

Fotografie (*pl* **-n**) *die* - **1.** [Fotografieren] photography - **2.** [Foto] photograph.

fotografieren ◇ *vt* to photograph. ◇ *vi* to take photographs.

Fotografin (*pl* **-nen**) *die* photographer.

Fotokopie (*pl* **-n**) *die* photocopy.

fotokopieren ◇ *vt* to photocopy. ◇ *vi* to make photocopies.

Foto|modell *das* (photographic) model.

Fotozelle (*pl* **-n**), **Photozelle** *die* photoelectric cell, photocell.

Fötus (*pl* **-se** ODER **-ten**) *der* foetus.

foulen ['faulən] ◇ *vt* SPORT to foul. ◇ *vi* SPORT to commit a foul.

FPÖ [ɛfÿpeː'ø] (*abk für* **Freiheitliche Partei Österreichs**) *die* Austrian Freedom Party.

Fr. - **1.** [verheiratet] (*abk für* **Frau**) Mrs; [unverheiratet] Ms, Miss - **2.** (*abk für* **Freitag**) Fri.

Fracht (*pl* **-en**) *die* freight; [mit Schiff] cargo.

Frachter (*pl* **-**) *der* freighter.

Fracht|gut *das* freight.

Frack (*pl* **Fräcke**) *der* tails *Pl*; **im Frack** in tails.

Frage (*pl* **-n**) *die* question; **eine rhetorische Frage** a rhetorical question; **jm Fragen stellen** to ask sb questions; **in diesen Fragen weiß er am besten Bescheid** he knows most about these issues ODER matters; **das kommt nicht in Frage** that's out of the question; **etw in Frage stellen** [bezweifeln] to question sthg; [gefährden] to jeopardize sthg.

Frage|bogen *der* questionnaire.

fragen ◇ *vt* to ask; **jn um Rat fragen** to ask sb for advice; **jn nach jm/etw fragen** to ask sb about sb/sthg; **jn nach seinem Namen/der Uhrzeit fragen** to ask sb his name/the time. ◇ *vi* to ask; **nach jm fragen** [sich erkundigen] to ask about sb; [Treffen] to ask to see sb; **der Polizist fragte nach dem genauen Hergang** the policeman asked for a precise description of events; **da fragst du noch!** you need to ask? ◆ **sich fragen** *ref* to wonder; **ich frage mich, ob** I wonder if ODER whether; **es fragt sich noch, ob** it is debatable whether.

Frage|wort (*pl* **-wörter**) *das* interrogative pronoun.

Frage|zeichen *das* question mark.

fraglich *adj* - **1.** [zweifelhaft]: **es ist fraglich, ob** it is doubtful whether - **2.** [infrage kommend] in question.

fragwürdig *adj* dubious.

Fraktion [frak'tsio:n] (*pl* **-en**) *die* - **1.** [im Parlament] (parliamentary) party - **2.** [innerhalb einer Partei] faction.

Franc [frã:] (*pl* **-s** ODER **-**) *der* franc.

Franken (*pl* **-**) ◇ *nt* Franconia. ◇ *der* Swiss franc.

Frankfurt *nt*: **Frankfurt am Main/an der Oder** Frankfurt (am Main)/an der Oder.

frankieren *vt* to stamp.

fränkisch *adj* - **1.** [aus Franken] Franconian - **2.** HIST [westgermanisch] Frankish.

Frankreich *nt* France.

Franse (*pl* **-n**) *die* strand; **ein Schal mit Fransen** a scarf with a fringe.

Franziskaner, in (*mpl* **-**, *fpl* **-nen**) *der, die* Franciscan.

Franzose (*pl* **-n**) *der* Frenchman; **die Franzosen** the French.

Französin (*pl* **-nen**) *die* Frenchwoman.

französisch *adj* French; *siehe auch* **englisch**.

Französisch(e) *das* French; *siehe auch* **Englisch(e)**.

fraß *prät* ▷ **fressen**.

Fratze (*pl* **-n**) *die* [Grimasse] grotesque face; [aus Schmerz, Widerwille] grimace.

Frau (*pl* **-en**) *die* - **1.** [Erwachsene] woman - **2.** [Gattin] wife - **3.** [als Anrede - verheiratet] Mrs; [- neutral] Ms; **Frau Doktor** Doctor.

Frauen|arzt, ärztin *der, die* gynaecologist.

frauenfeindlich ◇ *adj* misogynistic. ◇ *adv* in a misogynistic way.

fraulich ◇ *adj* feminine. ◇ *adv* in a feminine way.

frdl. ▷ **freundlich**.

frech ◇ *adj* - **1.** [gen] cheeky; [unartig] naughty; [Lüge] barefaced - **2.** [Minirock] daring. ◇ *adv* [gen] cheekily; [unartig] naughtily.

Frechheit (*pl* **-en**) *die* - **1.** *(ohne pl)* [freches Verhalten] cheek - **2.** [freche Bemerkung] cheeky remark.

frei ◇ *adj* - **1.** [gen] free; **frei von etw** free of sthg; **ist dieser Stuhl frei?** is this seat free?; **drei Wochen frei haben** to have three weeks off; **bei der Reaktion wird Energie frei** energy is released during the reaction - **2.** [Mitarbeiter] freelance - **3.** [nackt] bare; **machen Sie sich bitte frei** would you mind undressing? ◇ *adv* - **1.** [gen] freely; **frei lebende Tiere** animals living in the wild; **frei sprechen** to speak without notes - **2.** [gratis] for free; **etw frei Haus liefern** to deliver sthg free. ◆ **im Freien** *adv* in the open (air).

Frei|bad *das* open-air swimming pool.

Freiberufler, in (*mpl* **-**, *fpl* **-nen**) *der, die* - **1.** [Mitarbeiter] freelancer - **2.** [Arzt, Anwalt] doctor/lawyer in private practice.

freiberuflich ◇ *adj* [Journalist, Übersetzer, Fotograf] freelance; **freiberuflicher Mitarbeiter** freelancer. ◇ *adv*: **freiberuflich tätig sein** to be self-employed.

Frei|bier *das* free beer.

frei|geben *(unreg)* ◇ *vt* - **1.** [gen] to release - **2.** [genehmigen - FILM] to pass as fit for public viewing; [- Straße, Brücke] to open; **jm einen Tag freigeben** to give sb a day off. ◇ *vi* [Freizeit genehmigen]: **jm freigeben** to give sb time off.

freigebig *adj* generous.

Freiheit (*pl* **-en**) *die* - **1.** [Ungebundenheit] freedom; **ein Tier in die Freiheit entlassen** to set an animal free - **2.** [Privileg] liberty.

Freiheits|strafe *die* prison sentence.

freiheraus *adv* freely.

Frei|karte *die* free ticket.

Freikörperkultur *die* naturism.

Freiland|ei *das* free-range egg.

frei|lassen *vt (unreg)* [Gefangene] to release; [Tier] to set free.

freilich *adv* - **1.** [jedoch] admittedly - **2.** *Süddt* [sicher] of course.

Freilicht|bühne *die* open-air theatre.

frei|machen ◇ *vt* - **1.** [Brief] to stamp - **2.** [ausziehen]: **den Oberkörper freimachen** to take one's top off, to strip to the waist. ◇ *vi* to take time off. ◆ **sich freimachen** *ref* - **1.** *fam* [als Urlaub] to take time off - **2.** [sich ausziehen] to take one's clothes off.

freimütig ◇ *adj* frank. ◇ *adv* frankly.

frei|sprechen *vt (unreg)* to acquit.

frei|stehen *vi (unreg)* - **1.** [Wohnung] to stand ODER be empty - **2.** [Entscheidung]: **es steht ihm frei, zu gehen oder zu bleiben** it's up to him whether he stays or goes.

frei|stellen *vt* - **1.** [entbinden]: **jn von etw freistellen** to exempt sb from sthg - **2.** [überlassen]: **jm etw freistellen** to leave sthg up to sb.

Frei|stoß *der* SPORT free kick.

Frei|stunde *die* free period.

Freitag (*pl* **-e**) *der* Friday; *siehe auch* **Samstag**.

freitags *adv* on Fridays; *siehe auch* **samstags**.

freiwillig ◇ *adj* voluntary. ◇ *adv* voluntarily.

Freiwillige (*pl* **-n**) *der, die* volunteer.

Freilzeichen *das* dial tone.

Freilzeit *die* - 1. *(ohne pl)* [Mußezeit] free time - 2. [Gruppenreise - für Kinder] holiday camp.

freizügig ◇ *adj* - 1. [gewagt] daring - 2. [großzügig] generous - 3. [frei] liberal. ◇ *adv* - 1. [gewagt] daringly - 2. [großzügig] generously - 3. [frei] liberally.

fremd *adj* - 1. [ausländisch] foreign - 2. [nicht einem selbst gehörend]: **fremde Angelegenheiten** other people's business; **in einer fremden Wohnung übernachten** to spend the night in someone else's flat - 3. [unvertraut] strange; **er ist fremd in dieser Stadt** he is a stranger to this town.

fremdartig *adj* strange.

Fremde (*pl* **-n**) ◇ *der, die* stranger. ◇ *die (ohne plural)* foreign parts *Pl*.

Fremdenlführer, in *der, die* tourist guide.

Fremdenhass *der (ohne pl)* xenophobia.

Fremdenlverkehr *der* tourism.

Fremdenverkehrslbüro *das* tourist information office.

Fremdenlzimmer *das* (guest) room.

Fremdlkörper *der* foreign body.

Fremdlsprache *die* foreign language.

fremdsprachig *adj* in a foreign language.

Fremdwort (*pl* **-wörter**) *das* foreign word.

Frequenz (*pl* **-en**) *die* - 1. PHYS frequency - 2. MED rate.

fressen (*präs* **frisst**, *prät* **fraß**, *perf* **hat gefressen**) ◇ *vt* - 1. [beim Tier] to eat - 2. *fam abw* [essen] to guzzle, to scoff *UK* - 3. *fam* [Strom, Geld] to eat up; **jn gefressen haben** *fam* not to be able to stand sb, to hate sb's guts. ◇ *vi* - 1. [Tier] to feed; **der Vogel frisst einem aus der Hand** the bird will eat out of your hand - 2. *salopp abw* [Mensch] to stuff one's face - 3. [zehren, nagen]: **an etw *(D)* fressen** to eat away at sthg.

Freude (*pl* **-n**) *die* joy; **es ist mir eine Freude zu kommen** it would be a pleasure for me to come; **jm die Freude an etw verderben** to spoil sb's enjoyment of sthg; **an etw Freude haben** to take pleasure in sthg; **jm eine Freude machen** to make sb happy.

freudig ◇ *adj* - 1. [Begrüßung] joyful - 2. [Überraschung] pleasant. ◇ *adv* - 1. [begrüßen] joyfully - 2. [überrascht] pleasantly.

freuen *vt* to please. ◆ **sich freuen** *ref* to be pleased; **es freut mich, dass...** I'm pleased that...; **freut mich sehr!** pleased to meet you!; **sich an etw *(D)* freuen** to get a lot of pleasure from sthg; **sich über etw *(A)* freuen** to be pleased about sthg; **sich auf etw *(A)* freuen** to be looking forward to sthg.

Freund (*pl* **-e**) *der* - 1. [guter Bekannter] friend - 2. [Liebhaber] boyfriend - 3. [Anhänger] lover; **ein Freund klassischer Musik** a classical music lover.

Freundin (*pl* **-nen**) *die* - 1. [gute Bekannte] friend - 2. [Geliebte] girlfriend.

freundlich ◇ *adj* - 1. [Mensch, Geste, Rat] friendly; **danke für die freundliche Begrüßung** thank you for your kind welcome; **bist du so freundlich und begleitest mich?** would you be so kind as to accompany me? - 2. [Umgebung, Stimmung] nice. ◇ *adv* [nett] in a friendly way; **jm freundlich gesinnt sein** to be well-disposed towards sb.

Freundlichkeit (*pl* **-en**) *die* - 1. *(ohne pl)* [nette Art] friendliness - 2. [Gefälligkeit] favour.

Freundschaft (*pl* **-en**) *die* friendship; **mit jm Freundschaft schließen** to make friends with sb.

freundschaftlich ◇ *adj* friendly. ◇ *adv* in a friendly way; **jm freundschaftlich verbunden sein** to be friends with sb.

Frieden, Friede *der* peace; **jn in Frieden lassen** to leave sb in peace; **mit jm Frieden schließen** to make peace with sb.

Friedenslbewegung *die* peace movement.

Friedenslvertrag *der* peace treaty.

Friedlhof *der* cemetery.

friedlich ◇ *adj* peaceful. ◇ *adv* peacefully.

frieren (*prät* **fror**, *perf* **hat/ist gefroren**) *vi* - 1. *(hat)* [an Kälte leiden] to be cold; **es friert ihn** he is cold; **an den Füßen frieren** to have cold feet; **es friert mich an den Händen** my hands are cold - 2. *(hat)* [sehr kalt sein]: **es friert** it is freezing - 3. *(ist)* [gefrieren] to freeze.

Frikadelle (*pl* **-n**) *die* rissole.

frisch ◇ *adj* - 1. [gen] fresh; [Verletzung] recent; [Farbe] wet; [Kraft] renewed; **diese Erinnerung ist noch frisch** it's still fresh in my memory - 2. [sauber] clean; **sich frisch machen** to freshen up; **du bist wohl nicht ganz frisch!** *salopp* are you crazy? - 3. [kühl - unangenehm] chilly; [- angenehm] cool - 4. [in Form] refreshed; **frisch und munter sein** to be bright and cheery. ◇ *adv* [gewaschen, zubereitet] freshly; [renoviert] newly; **das Brot kommt frisch vom Bäcker** the bread is fresh from the baker's; **'frisch gestrichen'** "wet paint".

Frische *die* - 1. [gen] freshness; **in alter Frische** as fresh as ever - 2. [Kühle - unangenehm] chilliness; [- angenehm] coolness.

Frischlkäse *der* soft cream cheese.

Friseur, in (*mpl* **-e**, *fpl* **-nen**), **Frisör, in** (*mpl* **-e**, *fpl* **-nen**) [fri'zøːɐ̯, rɪn] *der, die* hairdresser.

Friseuse (*pl* **-n**), **Frisöse** (*pl* **-n**) [fri'zøːzə] *die* hairdresser.

frisieren *vt* - 1. [Person]: **jn frisieren** to do sb's hair; **sie ist schick frisiert** she has a trendy hairstyle - 2. *fam* [Zahlen] to fiddle; **die Bilanzen frisieren** to cook the books - 3. *fam* AUTO to soup up. ◆ **sich frisieren** *ref* [sich kämmen] to do one's hair.

Frisör, in = **Friseur**.
Frisöse = **Friseuse**.
frisst *präs* ▷ **fressen**.
Frist (*pl* **-en**) *die*: **jm eine Frist von einer Woche geben** to give sb a week; **bis zur Prüfung bleibt dir noch eine Frist von drei Tagen** you still have three days to go until the exam; **die Frist wird nicht verlängert** the deadline is not being extended; **eine Frist einhalten** to meet a deadline; **innerhalb kürzester Frist** in a very short space of time.
fristlos ◇ *adj* immediate. ◇ *adv* without notice, with immediate effect.
Frisur (*pl* **-en**) *die* hairstyle.
froh *adj* - **1.** [vergnügt] happy - **2.** [erleichtert] glad; **über etw** *(A)* **froh sein** to be pleased ODER glad about sthg - **3.** [Nachricht] good.
fröhlich ◇ *adj* - **1.** [Mensch, Lachen] cheerful - **2.** [Fest] jolly. ◇ *adv* [vergnügt] cheerfully.
Fröhlichkeit *die* cheerfulness.
fromm (*kompar* **frommer** ODER **frömmer**, *superl* **frommste** ODER **frömmste**) *adj* - **1.** [Mensch, Christ] devout; [Worte, Einstellung] pious - **2.** [heuchlerisch] sanctimonious, pious.
Fronleichnam *(ohne Artikel)* Corpus Christi.
Front (*pl* **-en**) *die* front.
frontal ◇ *adj* - **1.** [Zusammenstoß] head-on - **2.** [Angriff, Darstellung] frontal. ◇ *adv* - **1.** [von vorn] head-on - **2.** [angreifen] from the front.
fror *prät* ▷ **frieren**.
Frosch (*pl* **Frösche**) *der* frog.
Frost (*pl* **Fröste**) *der* frost.
frösteln *vi* to shiver.
frostig ◇ *adj eigtl & fig* frosty. ◇ *adv* frostily.
Frottee [frɔ'teː] (*pl* **-s**) *der ODER das* towelling.
Frucht (*pl* **Früchte**) *die* fruit; **Früchte** fruit *(U)*.
fruchtbar *adj* - **1.** [Erde, Lebewesen] fertile - **2.** [Gespräch, Idee] fruitful.
Fruchtbarkeit *die* fertility.
fruchtig *adj* fruity.
Frucht|saft *der* fruit juice.
früh ◇ *adj* early; **am frühen Morgen/Abend** early in the morning/evening; [Tat] premature. ◇ *adv* early; **früh am Abend/Morgen** early in the evening/morning; **er ist früh gestorben** he died young; **gestern/heute/morgen Früh** yesterday/this/tomorrow morning; **etw zu früh verkaufen** to sell sthg too soon.
früher ◇ *adv* formerly. ◇ *adj* former; **in früheren Zeiten** in the past.
frühestens *adv* at the earliest.
Früh|geburt *die* - **1.** [Geburt] premature birth; **eine Frühgeburt haben** to give birth prematurely - **2.** [Baby] premature baby.
Früh|jahr *das* spring; **im Frühjahr** in spring.
Frühling (*pl* **-e**) *der* spring; **im Frühling** in spring.
frühreif *adj* [Kind] precocious.
Früh|rentner, in *der, die* person who has taken early retirement.
Früh|stück *das* breakfast; **nach dem Frühstück** after breakfast; **zum Frühstück** for breakfast.
frühstücken ◇ *vi* to have breakfast. ◇ *vt* to have for breakfast.
frustrieren *vt* to frustrate.
Fuchs [fʊks] (*pl* **Füchse**) *der* - **1.** [Tier] fox - **2.** [Pelz] fox fur - **3.** *fam* [Mensch]: **ein schlauer Fuchs** a cunning devil.
Fuchsie ['fʊksi̯ə] (*pl* **-n**) *die* fuchsia.
Füchsin ['fʏksɪn] (*pl* **-nen**) *die* vixen.
fuchteln *vi*: **mit etw fuchteln** to wave sthg around.
Fuge (*pl* **-n**) *die* - **1.** [Ritze] gap - **2.** MUS fugue.
fügen *vt* [einfügen]: **etw an etw** *(A)* **fügen** to join sthg to sthg; **etw in etw** *(A)* **fügen** to fit sthg into sthg; **fest gefügt** firmly established. ◆ **sich fügen** *ref* - **1.** [hineinpassen] to fit - **2.** [sich unterordnen]: **sich einer Sache** *(D)* **fügen** to obey sthg.
fühlbar ◇ *adj* noticeable. ◇ *adv* noticeably.
fühlen ◇ *vt* to feel. ◇ *vi* to feel; **nach etw fühlen** to feel for sthg. ◆ **sich fühlen** *ref* to feel; **sich krank fühlen** to feel ill.
Fühler (*pl* -) *der* feeler, antenna.
fuhr *prät* ▷ **fahren**.
Fuhre (*pl* **-n**) *die* load; [von Taxi] fare.
führen ◇ *vt* - **1.** [Person, Tier] to lead; **jn zu einem Versteck führen** to show ODER lead sb to a hiding-place - **2.** [leiten - Firma, Hotel] to run, to manage; [- Partei] to lead; [- Haushalt] to run; [- Truppen] to command; [- Krieg, Kampf] to wage; **den Vorsitz führen** to be the chairperson - **3.** [durchführen - Gespräch] to hold; **ein Ferngespräch führen** to make a long-distance call; **das Protokoll führen** to take the minutes; **ein langes Gespräch geführt haben** to have had a long conversation; **einen Prozess gegen jn führen** to take legal action against sb - **4.** [Gegenstand]: **etw mit sich** ODER **bei sich führen** to carry sthg - **5.** [Ware] to stock - **6.** [Liste] to keep; **sie wird als Mitglied geführt** she's listed as a member - **7.** [Touristen] to show around - **8.** [Name, Titel] to have - **9.** [bewegen] to handle. ◇ *vi* - **1.** SPORT to lead; **knapp führen** to be just in the lead; **mit 1:0 führen** to be leading 1-0, to be 1-0 up - **2.** [Straße] to lead - **3.** [zu einem Ergebnis]: **zu etw führen** to lead to sthg; **zum Erfolg führen** to bring success; **das führt zu nichts** that won't get us anywhere. ◆ **sich führen** *ref* to behave.
führend *adj* leading.

Führer, **in** (*mpl* -, *fpl* **-nen**) *der, die* - **1.** [Anführer] leader; **der Führer** [Hitler] the Führer - **2.** [Fremdenführer, Buch] guide.

Führer|schein *der* driving licence *UK*, driver's license *US*.

Führung (*pl* **-en**) *die* - **1.** [das Führen - von Firma, Hotel] running, management; [- von Truppen] command; [- von Partei] leadership; [- von Haushalt] running; **unter (der) Führung von** under the direction of - **2.** [Personen - von Firma] management; [- von Partei] leadership - **3.** [führende Stellung] lead; **in Führung liegen** to be in the lead ODER ahead; **in Führung gehen** to take the lead - **4.** [Besichtigung] guided tour - **5.** [Verhalten]: **wegen guter Führung** on the grounds of good conduct - **6.** [Handhabung, Steuerung] operation.

Führungs|zeugnis *das*: **polizeiliches Führungszeugnis** *police certificate stating that holder has no criminal record.*

Fülle *die (ohne pl)* [Menge, Übermaß] abundance.

füllen *vt* - **1.** [gen] to fill; [Geflügel, Tomate] to stuff - **2.** [hineingeben]: **etw in etw** *(A)* **füllen** to put sthg into sthg; **den Saft in Flaschen füllen** to fill the bottles with juice. ◆ **sich füllen** *ref* [voll werden]: **sich mit etw füllen** to fill up with sthg.

Füller (*pl* -) *der* fountain pen.

Füllfeder|halter *der* fountain pen.

füllig *adj* plump.

Füllung (*pl* **-en**) *die* [von Geflügel, Tomate] stuffing; [von Gebäck, in Zahn] filling.

fummeln *vi* - **1.** *fam* [tasten]: **nach etw fummeln** to fumble about for sthg; **an etw** *(D)* **fummeln** to fumble around with sthg - **2.** *salopp* [sexuell berühren] to make out.

Fund (*pl* **-e**) *der* - **1.** [Objekt] find - **2.** [Handlung] discovery.

Fundament (*pl* **-e**) *das* - **1.** [Grundmauer] foundations *Pl*; **bis auf die Fundamente abgerissen** to be razed to the ground - **2.** [Grundlage] basis.

Fund|büro *das* lost property office *UK*, lost-and-found office *US*.

Fund|grube *die* treasure trove.

fundiert *adj* [Wissen, Firma] sound; [Kritik, Überlegungen] well-founded; [Vortrag, Bericht] well-reasoned.

fündig *adj*: **fündig werden** to make a find.

Fund|sache *die*: **Fundsachen** lost property *(U)*.

fünf *num* five; *siehe auch* **sechs**.

Fünf (*pl* **-en**) *die* - **1.** [Zahl] five - **2.** [Schulnote] ≃ E, *mark of 5 on a scale from 1 to 6; siehe auch* **Sechs**.

fünffach ◇ *adj*: **die fünffache Menge** five times as much; **in fünffacher Größe** five times as big; **der fünffache Gewinner** the five-times winner. ◇ *adv* [auffordern] five times; **fünffach gelagert** with five bearings.

fünfhundert *num* five hundred.

Fünf|kampf *der* pentathlon.

fünfmal *adv* five times.

fünftausend *num* five thousand.

fünfte *num* fifth; *siehe auch* **sechste**.

Fünfte (*pl* **-n**) *der, die, das* fifth; *siehe auch* **Sechste**.

fünftel *adj (unver)* fifth; *siehe auch* **sechstel**.

Fünftel (*pl* -) *das* fifth; *siehe auch* **Sechstel**.

fünfzehn *num* fifteen; *siehe auch* **sechs**.

Fünfzehn (*pl* **-en**) *die* fifteen; *siehe auch* **Sechs**.

fünfzig *num* fifty; *siehe auch* **sechs**.

Fünfzig *die* fifty; *siehe auch* **Sechs**.

Fünfzigerjahre, fünfziger Jahre *Pl*: **die Fünfzigerjahre** the fifties.

Funk *der* [Übermittlung] radio.

Funke (*pl* **-n**), **Funken** (*pl* -) *der* spark; **keinen Funken von etw haben** ODER **besitzen** not to have a scrap of sthg.

funkeln *vi* [Licht] to sparkle; [Stern] to twinkle; [Gold] to glitter.

funken ◇ *vt* to radio. ◇ *vi*: **bei ihm hat es endlich gefunkt** *fam* [er versteht] he finally got it; **bei den beiden hat es gefunkt** *fam* [sie sind verliebt] they've fallen for each other.

Funken = **Funke**.

Funk|gerät *das* radio set; [tragbar] walkie-talkie.

Funk|haus *das* broadcasting centre.

Funktion [fʊnk'tsi̯oːn] (*pl* **-en**) *die* - **1.** MATH [Aufgabe] function; [Tätigkeit] functioning - **2.** [Position] position.

Funktionär, **in** (*mpl* **-e**, *fpl* **-nen**) *der, die* official.

funktionieren *vi* to work.

für *präp (+ A)* - **1.** [gen] for; **sich für etw entschuldigen** to apologize for sthg; **sich für Geschichte interessieren** to be interested in history; **für jn einspringen** to stand in for sb; **jn für dumm halten** to think sb is stupid; **einen Mantel für 700 Euro kaufen** to buy a coat for 700 euros; **für ein halbes Jahr** for half a year; **für immer** for ever, for good; **für sein Alter ist er noch recht munter** he's still very sprightly for his age - **2.** [Unterstützung - ausdrückend] in favour of; **für die Abschaffung der Todesstrafe sein** to be in favour of abolishing the death penalty; **früh aufstehen hat etwas für sich** there is something to be said for getting up early - **3.** [zur Angabe der Folge]: **Wort für Wort** word by word; **Tag für Tag** day after day.

Furcht *die* fear; **Furcht haben (vor jm/etw)** to be afraid (of sb/sthg); **aus Furcht vor jm/etw** for fear of sb/sthg. ◆ **Furcht erregend** ◇ *adj* frightening. ◇ *adv* frighteningly.

furchtbar ◇ *adj* terrible. ◇ *adv* [sehr] terribly; **sich furchtbar anstrengen** to make an enormous effort.

fürchten ◇ *vt* to fear; **ich fürchte, dass der Wagen kaputt ist** I'm afraid the car is out of action; **er fürchtet, zu spät zu kommen** he's afraid of arriving late. ◇ *vi*: **um etw fürchten** to fear for sthg. ◆ **sich fürchten** *ref*: **sich (vor jm/etw) fürchten** to be afraid (of sb/sthg).

fürchterlich ◇ *adj* terrible. ◇ *adv* [sehr] terribly; **sich fürchterlich anstrengen** to make an enormous effort.

furchtsam *adj* [Person, Tier] easily frightened; [Blick] fearful.

füreinander *adv* for each other.

Furnier (*pl* **-e**) *das* veneer.

fürs *präp (für + das)* ▷ **für**.

Fürsorge *die* **- 1.** [menschliche Unterstützung] care **- 2.** [Sozialhilfe] social security *UK*, welfare *US* **- 3.** [Sozialamt] social services *Pl UK*, welfare services *Pl US*.

fürsorglich ◇ *adj* attentive. ◇ *adv* attentively.

Für|sprecher, in *der, die* advocate.

Fürst (*pl* **-en**) *der* prince.

Fürstentum (*pl* **-tümer**) *das* principality.

Fürstin (*pl* **-nen**) *die* princess.

fürstlich ◇ *adj* **- 1.** [von einem Fürsten]: **das fürstliche Schloss** the prince's castle **- 2.** [Bezahlung] handsome. ◇ *adv* [bezahlen] handsomely; **fürstlich leben** to live like a prince.

Fuß (*pl* **Füße**) *der* **- 1.** [Körperteil, von Berg] foot **- 2.** [tragender Teil - von Lampe, Gefäß] base; [- von Möbeln] leg; **auf eigenen Füßen stehen** to stand on one's own two feet; **(festen) Fuß fassen** to find one's feet. ◆ **zu Fuß** *adv* on foot; **ich gehe oft zu Fuß zur Arbeit** I often walk to work.

Fuß|ball *der* **- 1.** SPORT football *UK*, soccer *US* **- 2.** [Ball] football *UK*, soccer ball *US*.

Fußballer, in (*mpl* **-**, *fpl* **-nen**) *der, die* footballer *UK*, soccer player *US*.

Fußball|mannschaft *die* football team *UK*, soccer team *US*.

Fußball|platz *der* football ground *UK*, soccer ground *US*.

Fußball|spiel *das* football match *UK*, soccer game *US*.

Fußball|spieler, in *der, die* football player *UK*, soccer player *US*.

Fuß|boden *der* floor.

Fussel (*pl* **-** *ODER* **-n**) *die ODER der* fluff *(U)*; **Fusseln** fluff.

fusseln *vi* to go bobbly.

Fußgänger (*pl* **-**) *der* pedestrian.

Fußgängerin (*pl* **-nen**) *die* pedestrian.

Fußgängerüber|weg *der* pedestrian crossing *UK*, crosswalk *US*.

Fußgänger|zone *die* pedestrian precinct *UK* *ODER* zone *US*.

Fuß|gelenk *das* ankle.

Fuß|note *die* footnote.

Fuß|sohle *die* sole *(of the foot)*.

Fuß|spur *die* footprint.

Fuß|tritt *der* kick.

Fuß|weg *der* footpath.

futsch *adj fam*: **futsch sein** [fort] to have all gone; [kaputt] to be bust.

Futter (*pl* **-**) *das* **- 1.** [für Haustiere] food; [für Vieh] feed; [Heu] fodder **- 2.** [Stoff] lining.

futtern *fam* ◇ *vt* to feed. ◇ *vi*: **sie kann viel futtern** she can put away a lot of food.

füttern *vt* **- 1.** [gen] to feed **- 2.** [Kleidung] to line.

Futur (*pl* **-e**) *das* GRAMM future (tense).

G

g (*pl* **-** *ODER* **-s**), **G** (*pl* **-** *ODER* **-s**) [geː] *das* **- 1.** [Buchstabe] g, G **- 2.** MUS G. ◆ **g** *(abk für* Gramm) g.

gab *prät* ▷ **geben**.

Gabe (*pl* **-n**) *die* [Geschenk, Talent] gift.

Gabel (*pl* **-n**) *die* **- 1.** [Besteckteil, beim Fahrrad] fork **- 2.** [in der Landwirtschaft] pitchfork **- 3.** [vom Telefon] cradle; **den Hörer auf die Gabel legen** to hang up.

Gabelung (*pl* **-en**), **Gablung** (*pl* **-en**) *die* fork.

gackern *vi eigtl & fig* to cackle.

gaffen *vi fam abw* to gawp.

Gag [gɛ(ː)k] (*pl* **-s**) *der* **- 1.** *fam* [Witz] gag **- 2.** [Besonderheit] gimmick.

Gage ['gaːʒə] (*pl* **-n**) *die* fee.

gähnen *vi eigtl & fig* to yawn.

Gala (*pl* **-s**) *die* **- 1.** [Galavorstellung] gala **- 2.** [Kleidung] formal dress.

Galaxis (*pl* **-xien**) *die* **- 1.** [Milchstraße]: **die Galaxis** the Galaxy **- 2.** [Sternsystem] galaxy.

Galerie (*pl* **-n**) *die* gallery.

Galgen (*pl* **-**) *der* gallows *(sg)*.

Galgenfrist *die* grace.

Galle (*pl* **-n**) *die* **- 1.** [Organ] gall bladder **- 2.** [Flüssigkeit] bile; **mir kommt die Galle hoch** *fam* it makes my blood boil.

Galopp (*pl* **-s** *ODER* **-e**) *der* gallop; **im Galopp** [beim Pferd] at a gallop; *fam* [schnell] at top speed.

galoppieren (*perf* **hat/ist galoppiert**) *vi* to gallop.

galt *prät* ▷ **gelten**.

gammeln *vi fam* - **1.** *abw* [nichts tun] to loaf around - **2.** [verderben] to go off.

Gämse (*pl* **-n**) *die* chamois.

Gang[1] [gaŋ] (*pl* **Gänge**) *der* - **1.** [Gangart] gait; **er hat einen Gang wie John Wayne** he walks like John Wayne - **2.** [Spaziergang, Ausgang] walk - **3.** [Flur, Weg] corridor; [in Flugzeug] aisle; **unterirdischer Gang** underground passage - **4.** [beim Kfz] gear; **im ersten Gang** in first gear - **5.** [Bewegung]: **etw in Gang bringen** ODER **setzen** [gen] to get sthg going; [Maschine] to start sthg up; **der Motor ist/kam in Gang** the engine is running/started up; **die Diskussion kam erst nach einer Stunde in Gang** it was an hour before the discussion got going - **6.** [Ablauf] course; **im Gange sein** to be going on - **7.** [Speisegang] course.

Gang[2] [gɛŋ] (*pl* **-s**) *die* gang.

gängig *adj* - **1.** [üblich] common - **2.** [aktuell] current - **3.** [handelsüblich] popular.

Gangway ['gɛŋweː] (*pl* **-s**) *die* [von Schiff] gangway; [von Flugzeug] steps *Pl*.

Ganove [ga'noːvə] (*pl* **-n**) *der* crook.

Gans (*pl* **Gänse**) *die* goose; **dumme Gans!** *fam* silly goose!

Gänse|blümchen *das* daisy.

Gänse|braten *der* roast goose.

Gänse|füßchen *Pl fam* quotation marks.

Gänse|haut *die (ohne pl)* goose-pimples *Pl UK*, goosebumps *US*.

Gänse|marsch *der*: **im Gänsemarsch** in single file.

Gänserich (*pl* **-e**) *der* gander.

ganz ◇ *adj* - **1.** [komplett] whole, entire; **den ganzen Tag** all day, the whole day; **eine ganze Zahl** a whole number; **ganze Note** MUS semibreve *UK*, whole note *US* - **2.** [alle] all; **der ganze Kaffee** all the coffee; **ganz Paris** the whole of Paris - **3.** *fam* [heil] whole, intact; **die Tasse ist noch ganz** the cup is still intact ODER in one piece - **4.** [nur]: **wir haben ganze zehn Minuten dafür gebraucht** it took us no more than ten minutes - **5.** [verstärkend]: **eine ganze Menge** quite a lot; **was soll der ganze Quatsch!** what's all this nonsense about? ◇ *adv* - **1.** [sehr] really; **er ist ein ganz seltsamer Mensch** he's a very strange person; **ganz viel/wenig** very much/little - **2.** [völlig] completely; **er kommt ganz bestimmt** he is sure to come; **ganz und gar** completely; **ganz und gar nicht** not at all - **3.** [einschränkend] quite; **der Film war ganz gut** the film was quite good.

Ganze *das* - **1.** [Einheit] whole; **eine Sache als Ganzes beurteilen** to judge sthg as a whole - **2.** [alles] whole thing; **das Ganze war eine Farce** the whole thing was a farce; **aufs Ganze gehen** to go for it; **es geht ums Ganze** it's all or nothing.

gänzlich ◇ *adj* complete. ◇ *adv* completely.

ganztägig ◇ *adj* all-day; **ein ganztägiger Ausflug** a day trip. ◇ *adv* [geöffnet] all day; [arbeiten] full-time.

ganztags *adv*: **ganztags arbeiten** to work full-time.

Ganztags|schule *die school attended in the morning and afternoon, rather than just in the morning as with most German schools.*

gar ◇ *adv*: **gar kein** no/not at all; **es war gar keiner da** there was no one there at all; **auf gar keinen Fall** under no circumstances at all; **gar nicht** not at all; **aber du hast doch gar nicht gefragt!** but you didn't even ask!; **gar nichts** nothing at all. ◇ *adj* [Speise] done.

Garage (*pl* **-n**) *die* garage.

Garantie (*pl* **-n**) *die* guarantee.

garantieren ◇ *vt* to guarantee. ◇ *vi*: **für etw garantieren** to guarantee sthg.

garantiert ◇ *adv fam*: **er hat garantiert verschlafen** I bet he's overslept; **wir werden garantiert gewinnen** we're bound to win. ◇ *adj* guaranteed.

Garderobe (*pl* **-n**) *die* - **1.** [in der Wohnung] hallstand - **2.** [in öffentlichen Räumen] cloakroom *UK*, coatroom *US* - **3.** *(ohne pl)* [Kleidung] clothes *Pl (except underwear)*; **eine neue Garderobe kaufen** to buy a new wardrobe - **4.** [für Künstler] dressing room.

Garderoben|ständer *der* coatstand.

Gardine (*pl* **-n**) *die* net curtain; **hinter schwedischen Gardinen** *fam* behind bars.

garen *vt* to cook.

gären (*prät* **gor** ODER **gärte**, *perf* **hat/ist gegoren** ODER **gegärt**) *vi* - **1.** *(ist) (unreg)* [in Gärung sein] to ferment - **2.** *(hat) (reg)* [Unzufriedenheit, Ärger]: **es gärte im Volk** the people were growing restless.

Garn (*pl* **-e**) *das* [zum Nähen] thread; [zum Weben] yarn.

Garnele (*pl* **-n**) *die* shrimp.

garnieren *vt* to garnish.

Garnitur (*pl* **-en**) *die* - **1.** [Satz] set; **eine Polstermöbelgarnitur** a three-piece suite - **2.** [Garnierung] garnish.

Garten (*pl* **Gärten**) *der* garden. ◆ **botanische Garten** *der* botanical gardens *Pl*, botanical garden. ◆ **zoologische Garten** *der* zoo.

Garten|arbeit *die* gardening.

Garten|bau *der* horticulture.

Garten|schere *die* [klein] secateurs *Pl*; [Heckenschere] shears *Pl*.

Gärtner (*pl* **-**) *der* gardener.

Gärtnerei (*pl* **-en**) *die* - **1.** [Betrieb] nursery - **2.** [Gartenarbeit] gardening.

Gärtnerin (*pl* **-nen**) *die* gardener.

Gar|zeit *die* cooking time.

Gas (*pl* **-e**) *das* - **1.** [gen] gas - **2.** [Gaspedal] accelerator *UK*, gas pedal *US*; [Treibstoff] petrol *UK*, gas *US*; **(das) Gas wegnehmen** to take one's foot off the accelerator *UK* ODER gas *US*; **Gas geben** to accelerate.

Gas|flasche *die* gas cylinder.

gasförmig *adj* gaseous.

Gas|hahn *der* gas tap.

Gas|heizung *die* gas heating.

Gas|herd *der* gas cooker *UK*, gas stove *US*.

Gas|kocher *der* camping stove, Primus stove®.

Gas|maske *die* gas mask.

Gas|pedal *das* accelerator *UK*, gas pedal *US*.

Gas|pistole *die pistol that fires gas cartridges.*

Gasse (*pl* **-n**) *die* alley; **die Menschenmenge bildete eine Gasse für das Fahrzeug** the crowd parted to let the vehicle through.

Gast (*pl* **Gäste**) *der* - **1.** [Eingeladene] guest; **bei jm zu Gast sein** to be sb's guest; **Gäste haben** to have guests; **wir haben heute Abend Freunde zu Gast** we are having some friends round ODER over this evening - **2.** [im Hotel] guest; [im Lokal] customer - **3.** [Tourist] visitor.

Gast|arbeiter, in *der, die* foreign worker.

Gäste|buch *das* visitors' book.

Gäste|zimmer *das* guest room.

gastfreundlich *adj* hospitable.

Gast|geber, in (*mpl* **-**, *fpl* **-nen**) *der, die* - **1.** [Einladende] host - **2.** [heimische Mannschaft] home team.

Gast|haus *das* inn.

Gast|hof *der* inn.

Gast|hörer, in *der, die* UNI auditor *US*, *person permitted to attend university lectures without being registered as a student.*

gastieren *vi* to give a guest performance.

Gast|land *das* [für Veranstaltung] host country.

Gast|mannschaft *die* away team.

Gastronomie *die* - **1.** [Gewerbe] catering - **2.** [Kochkunst] gastronomy.

Gast|spiel *das* guest performance.

Gast|stätte *die rustic restaurant with pub attached.*

Gatter (*pl* **-**) *das* - **1.** [Tor] gate - **2.** [Zaun] fence.

Gattung (*pl* **-en**) *die* - **1.** BIOL genus - **2.** [Art, Untergruppe] kind, type; [von Literatur, Kunst, Musik] genre.

GAU [gau] (*pl* **-s**) (*abk für* **größter anzunehmender Unfall**) *der* MCA, *maximum credible accident.*

Gaumen (*pl* **-**) *der* palate.

Gauner (*pl* **-**) *der* - **1.** [Betrüger] crook - **2.** *fam* [Spitzbube] cunning devil.

Gaunerin (*pl* **-nen**) *die* crook.

Gazelle (*pl* **-n**) *die* gazelle.

geb. - **1.** (*abk für* **geborene**) née - **2.** (*abk für* **geboren**) b.

Gebäck (*pl* **-e**) *das* pastries *Pl*.

gebacken ◇ *pp* ▷ **backen**. ◇ *adj* baked.

gebar *prät* ▷ **gebären**.

gebären (*präs* **gebärt** ODER **gebiert**, *prät* **gebar**, *perf* **hat geboren**) *vt* to give birth to.

Gebär|mutter *die* womb.

Gebäude (*pl* **-**) *das* - **1.** [Bauwerk] building - **2.** [gedanklich] structure; [aus Lügen] web.

geben (*präs* **gibt**, *prät* **gab**, *perf* **hat gegeben**) ◇ *vt* - **1.** [gen]: **jm etw geben** to give sb sthg, to give sthg to sb; **jm einen Kuss geben** to give sb a kiss, to kiss sb; **Unterricht geben** to teach; **eine Party geben** to have a party; **sein Einverständnis geben** to agree, to give one's consent - **2.** [platzieren]: **den Teig in die Kuchenform geben** to put the dough in the baking tin - **3.** [vorhanden sein]: **es gibt** there is/are; **hier gibt es viele Studenten** there are a lot of students here; **die schönsten Fresken gibt es in Italien** the most beautiful frescoes can be found in Italy; **was gibt es heute zum Mittagessen?** what's for lunch today?; **was gibts?** *fam* what's up?; **das gibts doch nicht!** *fam fig* I don't believe it! - **4.** [eine Bedeutung beimessen]: **viel/wenig auf etw** *(A)* **geben** *fam* to set a lot of/little store by sthg - **5.** [telefonisch]: **geben Sie mir bitte die Personalabteilung!** can you put me through to the personnel department, please? - **6.** [kausal]: **die Kuh gibt Milch** the cow produces milk; **das gibt doch nie etwas** nothing will ever come of that; **das Buch gibt mir nichts** *fam* I didn't get much out of the book. ◇ *vi* [beim Kartenspielen] to deal; **du gibst!** it's your deal.

Gebet (*pl* **-e**) *das* prayer; **ein Gebet sprechen** to say a prayer.

gebeten *pp* ▷ **bitten**.

Gebiet (*pl* **-e**) *das* - **1.** [Region, Gegend] area - **2.** [Bereich] field, area.

gebieten (*prät* **gebot**, *perf* **hat geboten**) *vt* - **1.** [befehlen]: **jm gebieten, etw zu tun** to command sb to do sthg - **2.** [verlangen] to call for; **Vorsicht ist geboten** caution is called for.

gebieterisch ◇ *adj* imperious. ◇ *adv* imperiously.

Gebilde (*pl* **-**) *das* structure.

gebildet ◇ *adj* educated. ◇ *adv* eruditely.

Gebirge (*pl* **-**) *das* mountains *Pl*; [Bergkette] mountain range; **im Gebirge** in the mountains.

gebirgig *adj* mountainous.

Gebirgspass (*pl* **-pässe**) *der* mountain pass.

Gebiss (*pl* -e) *das* - **1.** [Zähne] teeth *Pl* - **2.** [Zahnersatz] dentures *Pl*.

gebissen *pp* ▷ **beißen**.

Gebläse (*pl* -) *das* fan.

geblasen *pp* ▷ **blasen**.

geblieben *pp* ▷ **bleiben**.

geblümt *adj* [Kleid, Stil] flowery.

gebogen ◇ *pp* ▷ **biegen**. ◇ *adj* curved.

geboren ◇ *pp* ▷ **gebären**. ◇ *adj* born; **Frau Maier, geborene Müller** Mrs. Maier, née Müller; **dazu geboren sein, etw zu tun** *fig* to be born to do sthg.

geborgen ◇ *pp* ▷ **bergen**. ◇ *adj* safe; **sich (bei jm) geborgen fühlen** to feel secure ODER safe with sb.

Geborgenheit *die* security.

geborsten *pp* ▷ **bersten**.

Gebot (*pl* -e) *das* - **1.** [Befehl] directive; [moralisch] precept; [göttlich] commandment - **2.** [Erfordernis] requirement; **das Gebot der Stunde** the needs of the moment - **3.** [Angebot] bid.

geboten ◇ *pp* ▷ **bieten**, **gebieten**; *(RW)*: **etw für sein Geld geboten bekommen** to get sthg for one's money. ◇ *adj* necessary, requisite.

gebracht *pp* ▷ **bringen**.

gebrannt ◇ *pp* ▷ **brennen**. ◇ *adj* burnt; **gebrannte Mandeln** toasted almonds.

gebraten ◇ *pp* ▷ **braten**. ◇ *adj* [in der Pfanne] fried; [im Backofen] roast.

Gebrauch [gə'braux] (*pl* **-bräuche**) *der* use; **etw in Gebrauch nehmen** to start using sthg.

gebrauchen *vt* to use; **ich könnte etwas zu essen gebrauchen** I could use something to eat.

gebräuchlich *adj* - **1.** [verbreitet] common - **2.** [üblich] usual.

Gebrauchs|anweisung [gə'brauxsanvaizʊŋ] *die* instructions *Pl*.

gebrauchsfertig [gə'brauxsfertɪç] *adj* ready-to-use.

Gebrauchs|gegenstand [gə'brauxsgeːgn̩ʃtant] *der* everyday object.

gebraucht *adj* second-hand.

Gebraucht|wagen *der* used ODER second-hand car.

gebrochen ◇ *pp* ▷ **brechen**. ◇ *adj* broken. ◇ *adv* [unvollkommen]: **er spricht gebrochen Italienisch** he speaks broken Italian.

Gebrüll *das (ohne pl)* [von Löwe, Menschenmenge] roaring; [von Stier] bellowing; [von Kind, Affe] screeching.

Gebühr (*pl* -en) *die* charge; [für Arzt, Anwalt] fee; [für Autobahn] toll; [für Post] postage.

gebührend ◇ *adj* [Strafe, Belohnung] suitable; [Sorgfalt] due. ◇ *adv* [strafen, belohnen] suitably; **etw gebührend sorgfältig machen** to do sthg with due care.

Gebühren|einheit *die* TELEKOM unit.

gebührenfrei *adj* & *adv* free of charge.

gebührenpflichtig *adj* subject to a charge

Geburt (*pl* -en) *die* birth; **er ist von Geburt kein Deutscher** he is not German by birth.

gebürtig *adj*: **sie ist gebürtige Bayerin, sie ist aus Bayern gebürtig** she's Bavarian by birth.

Geburts|datum *das* date of birth.

Geburts|ort *der* place of birth.

Geburts|tag *der* - **1.** [Jahrestag] birthday; **wann hast du Geburtstag?** when is your birthday?; **jm zum Geburtstag gratulieren** to wish sb a happy birthday; **alles Gute zum Geburtstag!** happy birthday! - **2.** *amt* [Geburtsdatum] date of birth.

Geburtstags|feier *die* birthday party.

Geburtstags|kind *das* birthday boy/girl.

Geburts|urkunde *die* birth certificate.

Gebüsch (*pl* -e) *das* bushes *Pl*.

gedacht ◇ *pp* ▷ **denken**. ◇ *adj*: **das Geschenk ist als Trost gedacht** the present is meant to be a consolation; **eigentlich war das anders gedacht** actually that's not what was intended.

Gedächtnis (*pl* -se) *das* memory; **kein Gedächtnis für Zahlen haben** to have no head for numbers; **zum Gedächtnis an jn** in memory of sb.

Gedächtnis|feier *die* commemoration.

gedämpft *adj* [Licht, Musik, Stimmung] subdued; [Geräusch, Schritte] muffled; [Farbton, Musikinstrument] muted; [Stimme] low.

Gedanke (*pl* -n) *der* - **1.** [Gedachte, Überlegung] thought; **sich (D) Gedanken über etw (A) machen** to think about sthg; **js Gedanken lesen können** to be able to read sb's mind; **er hat sich entschlossen, keinen Gedanken daran zu verschwenden** he decided not to waste any time thinking about it; **der bloße Gedanke, dass...** the very idea that... - **2.** [Vorstellung, Vorhaben] idea; **mit dem Gedanken spielen, etw zu tun** to toy with the idea of doing sthg - **3.** [Sorge]: **sich (D) Gedanken über jn/etw machen** to be worried about sb/sthg.

gedankenlos ◇ *adj* [ohne nachzudenken] thoughtless; [unaufmerksam] absent-minded. ◇ *adv* [ohne nachzudenken] without thinking; [unaufmerksam] absent-mindedly.

Gedanken|strich *der* dash.

gedankenverloren *adv* lost in thought.

Gedeck (*pl* -e) *das* - **1.** [Geschirr und Besteck] place setting - **2.** [Speisenfolge] set meal.

Gedenk|minute *die* minute's silence.

Gedenk|stätte *die* memorial.

Gedenk|tafel *die* plaque.

Gedicht (*pl* -e) *das* poem.

Gedränge *das* crush.

gedrängt ◇ *adj* [Bericht, Beschreibung] succinct; [Zeitplan] busy. ◇ *adv* succinctly.

gedroschen *pp* ▷ **dreschen**.

gedrückt *adj* depressed.

gedrungen ◇ *pp* ▷ **dringen**. ◇ *adj* stocky.

Geduld *die* patience; **mit jm Geduld haben** to be patient with sb; **die Geduld verlieren** to lose one's patience.

geduldig ◇ *adj* patient. ◇ *adv* patiently.

Geduldsfaden *der*: **ihm reißt (gleich) der Geduldsfaden** he's losing his patience.

gedurft *pp* ▷ **dürfen**.

geeignet *adj* suitable; **für etw geeignet sein** to be suitable for sthg; **nicht geeignet** unsuitable; **er ist zum Lehrer geeignet** he'd make a good teacher.

Gefahr (*pl* **-en**) *die* danger; **es besteht die Gefahr eines Unfalls** there's the risk of an accident; **außer Gefahr sein** no longer to be in danger; **Gefahr laufen, etw zu tun** to be in danger of doing sthg.

gefährden *vt* [Gesundheit, Leben, Mensch] to endanger; [Unternehmen, Projekt] to jeopardize.

gefahren *pp* ▷ **fahren**.

gefährlich ◇ *adj* dangerous. ◇ *adv* dangerously.

gefahrlos ◇ *adj* safe. ◇ *adv* safely.

Gefälle (*pl* -) *das* - **1.** [von Straße, Dach] slope - **2.** [Unterschied] difference.

gefallen (*präs* **gefällt**, *prät* **gefiel**, *perf* **hat gefallen**) *vi* - **1.** [gut finden]: **er/es gefällt mir** I like him/it - **2.** [ertragen]: **sich *(D)* etw gefallen lassen** to put up with sthg; **sich *(D)* nichts gefallen lassen** not to put up with any nonsense; **das lasse ich mir gefallen!** *fam* I can handle this!

Gefallen (*pl* -) *der* favour; **jm einen Gefallen tun** to do sb a favour; **jn um einen Gefallen bitten** to ask sb a favour.

gefällig *adj* - **1.** [entkommend] helpful; **jm gefällig sein** to be of help to sb - **2.** [angenehm] pleasant - **3.** [genehm]: **noch ein Bier gefällig?** would you like another beer?

Gefälligkeit (*pl* **-en**) *die* [Gefallen] favour.

gefälligst *adv* kindly.

Gefangene (*pl* **-n**) *der, die* prisoner.

gefangen nehmen *vt (unreg)* - **1.** [festnehmen] to capture - **2.** [in Bann ziehen] to captivate.

Gefangenschaft *die* captivity.

Gefängnis (*pl* **-se**) *das* - **1.** [Haftanstalt] prison - **2.** [Haftstrafe] imprisonment.

Gefängnis|strafe *die* prison sentence.

gefärbt *adj* dyed.

Gefäß (*pl* **-e**) *das* - **1.** [Behältnis] container - **2.** [von Lebewesen] blood vessel.

gefasst ◇ *adj* - **1.** [gelassen] composed - **2.** [vorbereitet]: **auf etw *(A)* gefasst sein** to be prepared for sthg; **du kannst dich darauf gefasst machen, dass...** *fam* you'd better start getting used to the idea that...; **sonst kannst du dich auf was gefasst machen** *fam* otherwise you're in for it. ◇ *adv* [gelassen] calmly.

Gefecht (*pl* **-e**) *das* skirmish.

Gefieder (*pl* -) *das* feathers *Pl*.

geflogen *pp* ▷ **fliegen**.

geflohen *pp* ▷ **fliehen**.

geflossen *pp* ▷ **fließen**.

Geflügel *das* poultry.

Geflüster *das* whispering.

gefochten *pp* ▷ **fechten**.

Gefolge *das* entourage; [bei Beerdigung] cortege.

Gefolgschaft (*pl* **-en**) *die* - **1.** *(ohne pl)* [Loyalität] allegiance; **jm die Gefolgschaft verweigern** to stop supporting sb - **2.** [Anhängerschaft] followers *Pl*.

gefragt *adj* popular; **sehr gefragt sein** to be very much in demand.

gefräßig *adj abw* greedy.

Gefreite (*pl* **-n**) *der* lance corporal *UK*, private first class *US*.

gefressen *pp* ▷ **fressen**.

gefrieren (*prät* **gefror**, *perf* **hat/ist gefroren**) *vi (ist)* to freeze; **es hat gefroren** there has been a frost.

Gefrier|fach *das* freezer (compartment).

Gefrier|truhe *die* (chest) freezer.

gefroren ◇ *pp* ▷ **frieren**, **gefrieren**. ◇ *adj* frozen.

Gefühl (*pl* **-e**) *das* - **1.** [gen] feeling; **seine Beine sind ohne Gefühl** he's got no feeling in his legs; **er kennt keine Gefühle** he doesn't have any feelings; **etw im Gefühl haben** to know sthg instinctively - **2.** [Gespür] sense; **ein Gefühl für etw** a sense of sthg.

gefühllos ◇ *adj* - **1.** [taub] numb - **2.** [herzlos] callous. ◇ *adv* [herzlos] callously.

Gefühlsleben *das* emotional life.

gefühlsmäßig ◇ *adj* emotional. ◇ *adv* emotionally.

gefunden *pp* ▷ **finden**.

gegangen *pp* ▷ **gehen**.

gegebenenfalls *adv* if necessary.

Gegebenheit (*pl* **-en**) *die* condition, circumstance.

gegen *präp (+ A)* - **1.** [gen] against; **gegen die Tür hämmern** to bang on the door; **das Schiff fährt gegen die Strömung** the ship is sailing upstream; **gegen etw sein** to be opposed to ODER against sthg; **heute spielt Leipzig gegen Bremen** Leipzig are playing Bremen today; **ein Mittel gegen Grippe** a flu remedy, a medicine for flu - **2.** [zeitlich]: **gegen fünf Uhr** at about five o'clock; **gegen Abend wurde es kühler** it cooled down towards evening

- **3.** [im Austausch für] for; **gegen bar** for cash - **4.** [im Vergleich zu] in comparison to, compared with.

Gegen|argument *das* counterargument.

Gegend (*pl* **-en**) *die* - **1.** [Gebiet, Bereich] area; **in der Gegend** nearby; **in der Gegend von** near; **in der Nierengegend** in the region of the kidneys; **hier in der Gegend** round here - **2.** [Nachbarschaft] neighbourhood; **so in der Gegend** *fam* thereabouts.

Gegen|darstellung *die* conflicting account.

gegeneinander *adv* against one another ODER each other.

Gegenfahr|bahn *die* opposite side of the road.

Gegen|gewicht *das* counterbalance; **ein** ODER **das Gegengewicht zu etw bilden** to counterbalance sthg.

Gegen|gift *das* antidote.

gegenläufig ◇ *adj* opposite. ◇ *adv* in the opposite direction.

Gegen|leistung *die*: **als Gegenleistung (für etw)** in return (for sthg).

Gegen|maßnahme *die* countermeasure.

Gegen|mittel *das* antidote.

Gegen|richtung *die* opposite direction.

Gegen|satz *der* contrast; **im Gegensatz zu** in contrast to; **im Gegensatz zu etw stehen** to contrast with sthg.

gegensätzlich ◇ *adj* conflicting. ◇ *adv* completely differently.

Gegen|seite *die* - **1.** [Gegenpartei] opposing side; [vor Gericht] opposing party; SPORT opposition - **2.** [andere Seite] other side.

gegenseitig ◇ *adj* mutual. ◇ *adv* each other, one another; **sich gegenseitig helfen** to help each other ODER one another.

Gegen|spieler, in *der, die* - **1.** [Gegner] opponent - **2.** [im Theater] antagonist.

Gegensprechan|lage *die* intercom.

Gegen|stand *der* - **1.** [Ding, Objekt] object - **2.** [Thema] subject.

gegenständlich *adj* [Kunst] representational.

Gegen|stimme *die* - **1.** [Stimme dagegen] vote against - **2.** [abweichende Meinung] dissenting voice.

Gegen|teil *das* opposite; **das Gegenteil von jm/etw sein** to be the opposite of sb/sthg.
◆ **im Gegenteil** *adv* on the contrary; **ganz im Gegenteil** quite the reverse ODER opposite.

gegenteilig *adj* opposite.

gegenüber ◇ *präp (+ D)* - **1.** [räumlich] opposite; **gegenüber der Kirche** opposite the church; **mir gegenüber** opposite me - **2.** [zur Angabe einer Beziehung] towards; **so kannst du dich den Schülern gegenüber nicht verhalten** you can't behave like that towards the pupils - **3.** [zur Angabe eines Vergleichs] compared with; **gegenüber der alten Wohnun**[g] compared with the old flat *UK* ODER apartment *US*. ◇ *adv* opposite; **der Garten gegenüber** the garden over ODER across the road.

Gegenüber *das* person sitting opposite.

gegenüber|liegen *vi (unreg)* to be opposite; **das gegenüberliegende Gebäude** th[e] building opposite; **einander gegenüberliegen** to face one another ODER each othe[r].
◆ **sich gegenüberliegen** *ref* to face on[e] another ODER each other.

gegenüber|stehen *vi (unreg)* - **1.** [zugewandt stehen]: **jm/einer Sache gegenüberstehen** to be facing sb/sthg - **2.** [gegenübergestellt sein]: **einer Sache** *(D)* **gegenüberstehen** t[o] be faced with sthg; **jm feindlich gegenübe[r]stehen** to have a hostile attitude towards s[b].
◆ **sich gegenüberstehen** *ref* - **1.** [sich zugewandt stehen, gegeneinander spielen] to face on[e] another ODER each other - **2.** [in Konflikt stehe[n]] to clash.

gegenüber|stellen *vt* - **1.** [mit jm konfronti[e]ren]: **dem Zeugen die Verdächtigen gegenüberstellen** to line the suspects up in front o[f] the witness - **2.** [nebeneinander halten]: **das A[l]terswerk eines Autors seinen frühen Romane[n] gegenüberstellen** to compare the late work of an author with his early novels.

gegenüber|treten (*perf* **ist gegenübergetreten**) *vi (unreg)*: **jm gegenübertreten** to fac[e] sb.

Gegenverkehr *der* oncoming traffic.

Gegenwart *die* - **1.** [Zeitpunkt] present; **di[e] Kunst der Gegenwart** contemporary art; **bis i[n] die Gegenwart** up to the present day - **2.** [Präsenz] presence; **in js Gegenwart** in sb's presence - **3.** GRAMM present (tense).

Gegen|wert *der* equivalent amount.

Gegen|wind *der* headwind.

gegessen *pp* ▷ **essen**.

geglichen *pp* ▷ **gleichen**.

geglitten *pp* ▷ **gleiten**.

geglommen *pp* ▷ **glimmen**.

Gegner, in (*mpl* **-**, *fpl* **-nen**) *der, die* - **1.** [W[i]dersacher, im Sport] opponent - **2.** [Feind] enemy.

gegnerisch *adj* opposing.

gegolten *pp* ▷ **gelten**.

gegoren ◇ *pp* ▷ **gären**. ◇ *adj* fe[r]mented.

gegossen *pp* ▷ **gießen**.

gegraben *pp* ▷ **graben**.

gegriffen *pp* ▷ **greifen**.

Gehabe *das abw* affected behaviour.

gehabt *pp* ▷ **haben**.

Gehackte *das* mince *UK*, mincemeat *US*.

Gehalt (*pl* **Gehälter**) ◇ *das* salary. ◇ *d[er]* - **1.** [Inhalt] content - **2.** [Anteil]: **ein geringer G[e]halt an Gold** a low gold content.

gehalten *pp* ▷ **halten**.

Gehalts|abrechnung *die* salary statement.

gehandikapt [gə'hɛndikɛpt] *adj* handicapped.

gehangen *pp* ▷ **hängen**.

gehässig ◇ *adj* spiteful. ◇ *adv* spitefully.

Gehäuse (*pl* -) *das* - **1.** [von Uhr, Fotoapparat, Radio] casing; [von Schnecke] shell - **2.** [von Apfel, Birne] core.

gehbehindert *adj* disabled *(used of people who have difficulty walking)*.

Gehege (*pl* -) *das* reserve; [im Zoo] enclosure.

geheim ◇ *adj* - **1.** [heimlich] secret - **2.** [geheimnisvoll] mysterious. ◇ *adv* [nicht offen] in secret; **geheim abstimmen** to vote by secret ballot. ◆ **im Geheimen** *adv* secretly.

Geheim|dienst *der* secret service.

geheim halten *vt (unreg)* to keep secret.

Geheimnis (*pl* **-se**) *das* - **1.** [Geheimgehaltenes] secret - **2.** [Unbekanntes] mystery.

geheimnisvoll ◇ *adj* mysterious. ◇ *adv* mysteriously.

Geheim|nummer *die* [von Telefon] ex-directory number *UK*, unlisted number *US*; [von Scheckkarte] PIN (number); [von Tresor] combination.

Geheim|polizei *die* secret police.

geheißen *pp* ▷ **heißen**.

gehen (*prät* **ging**, *perf* **ist gegangen**) ◇ *vi* - **1.** [Fortbewegung] to go; **einkaufen gehen** to go shopping; **in die Stadt gehen** to go into town; **zur Armee gehen** to join the army; **in Serienproduktion gehen** to go into mass production - **2.** [weggehen, abfahren] to go; **ich gehe jetzt** I'm off now; **mein Zug geht um acht Uhr** my train leaves ODER goes at eight o'clock - **3.** [zu Fuß gehen] to walk; **mit jm gehen** *fam* [eine Beziehung haben] to go out with sb - **4.** [verkehren] to go; **der Bus geht drei Mal täglich** the bus goes ODER runs three times a day - **5.** [ergehen]: **wie geht es dir/Ihnen?** how are you?; **es geht mir gut/schlecht** I'm well/not very well; **der Firma geht es gut/schlecht** the company is doing well/badly - **6.** [sich handeln um]: **es geht um deine Mutter** it's about your mother; **worum geht es in diesem Buch?** what's this book about?; **es geht darum, alle Karten loszuwerden** the idea is to get rid of all your cards; **darum geht es nicht** that's not the point - **7.** [annehmbar sein]: **wie gefällt es dir? - es geht** how do you like it? - it's OK - **8.** [funktionieren - gen] to work; [- Uhr, Auto] to go; **das Geschäft geht gut** business is going well - **9.** [zur Beschreibung von Vorgängen]: **wie geht das mit der Anmeldung?** how's the application going?; **das geht doch ganz einfach** it's quite simple; **was geht denn hier vor sich?** what's going on here, then? - **10.** [möglich, erlaubt sein] to be OK; **aber das geht doch nicht!** you can't do that!; **ginge es vielleicht, dass wir...?** do you think we could possibly...? - **11.** [sich erstrecken]: **das Wasser ging ihm bis zu den Knien** the water came up to his knees; **die Straße geht bis zum Rathaus** the street goes as far as the town hall; **das geht über unsere Mittel** that's beyond our means - **12.** [passen]: **in/durch etw gehen** to go in/through sthg - **13.** [sich richten]: **es kann nicht immer nur nach dir gehen** you can't always have things your own way; **wenn es nach mir ginge** if I had my way - **14.** [ein Arbeitsverhältnis beenden] to leave - **15.** [Teig] to rise. ◇ *vt* to walk. ◆ **sich gehen** *ref*: **sich gehen lassen** to let o.s. go.

geheuer *adj*: **das ist mir nicht (ganz) geheuer** [Furcht einflößend] I find that (rather) eerie; [unwohl] I'm not (too) sure about that; [verdächtig] I find that (rather) odd ODER suspicious.

Geheul, Geheule *das* - **1.** [Heulen] howling - **2.** *fam abw* [Heulerei] wailing.

Gehilfe (*pl* **-n**) *der* - **1.** [Ausgebildeter] qualified assistant *(who has successfully completed an apprenticeship)* - **2.** [Helfer] assistant.

Gehilfin (*pl* **-nen**) *die* - **1.** [Ausgebildete] qualified assistant *(who has successfully completed an apprenticeship)* - **2.** [Helferin] assistant.

Gehirn (*pl* **-e**) *das* - **1.** [Hirn] brain - **2.** *(ohne pl) fam* [Verstand] brain, brains *Pl*; **sich das Gehirn zermartern** to rack one's brain ODER brains.

Gehirn|erschütterung *die* concussion *(U)*.

gehoben ◇ *pp* ▷ **heben**. ◇ *adj* - **1.** [höher - Position, Stellung] senior; [- Einkommen, Erwartung] higher - **2.** [exklusiv] sophisticated - **3.**: **in gehobener Stimmung** in high spirits.

geholfen *pp* ▷ **helfen**.

Gehör (*pl* **-e**) *das* hearing; **ein schlechtes Gehör haben** to be hard of hearing; **nach dem Gehör** by ear; **jm/einer Sache Gehör/kein Gehör schenken** to listen/not to listen to sb/sthg.

gehorchen *vi* to obey; **jm gehorchen** to obey sb; **der Vernunft gehorchen** to listen to reason.

gehören *vi* - **1.** [einer Person]: **jm gehören** to belong to sb - **2.** [an Ort] to belong; **wohin gehört das Werkzeug?** where does this tool belong? - **3.** [als Bestandteil]: **zu etw gehören** to be part of sthg; **sie gehört zum Krankenhauspersonal** she's a member of the hospital staff - **4.** [als Notwendigkeit]: **zum Reiten gehört viel Geschick** riding requires a lot of skill; **es gehört Mut dazu, dies zu tun** it takes a lot of courage to do it - **5.** [müssen]: **solche Leute gehören eingesperrt** such people ought to be locked up. ◆ **sich gehören** *ref*: **es** ODER **das gehört sich nicht** it's not the done thing.

gehörig ◇ *adj* - **1.** [gebührend] proper - **2.** [beachtlich] considerable; **mit einer gehörigen Portion Mut** with a good deal of courage.

◇ *adv* - **1.** [gebührend] properly - **2.** [beachtlich - steigen, erhöhen] considerably; **jn gehörig durchprügeln** to give sb a good thrashing.

Gehörlose (*pl* **-n**) *der, die* deaf person; **die Gehörlosen** the deaf.

gehorsam *adj* obedient.

Gehorsam *der* obedience; **jm den Gehorsam verweigern** to refuse to obey sb.

Gehorsamkeit *die* obedience.

Gehlweg *der* - **1.** [Gehsteig] pavement *UK*, sidewalk *US* - **2.** [Weg] footpath.

Geige (*pl* **-n**) *die* [im Orchester] violin; [in Folk] fiddle.

geil *adj* - **1.** *fam* [begierig auf Sex] horny; **er war geil auf sie** he wanted to get into her knickers - **2.** *abw* [lüstern - Mann] lecherous; [- Blick, Gedanke] lewd - **3.** *fam* [toll] wicked.

Geisel (*pl* **-n**) *die* hostage.

Geisellnahme (*pl* **-n**) *die* hostage-taking.

Geist (*pl* **-e** ODER **-er**) *der* - **1.** [Verstandeskraft] mind; **den Geist aufgeben** *fam* to give up the ghost; **jm auf den Geist gehen** *fam* to get on sb's nerves - **2.** [Intellekt] intellect - **3.** [Gesinnung] spirit - **4.** *(pl Geiste)* [Spirituose] *schnapps distilled from fruit, especially berries* - **5.** *(pl Geister)* [Person, Genie] mind - **6.** *(pl Geister)* [überirdische Wesenheit]: **der Heilige Geist** the Holy Ghost - **7.** *(pl Geister)* [Gespenst] ghost.

Geisterlfahrer, in *der, die person who drives into oncoming traffic on a motorway.*

geistesabwesend ◇ *adj* absent-minded. ◇ *adv* absent-mindedly.

Geisteslblitz *der* flash of inspiration.

geistesgegenwärtig ◇ *adj* quick-witted. ◇ *adv* with great presence of mind.

geistesgestört *adj* mentally disturbed ODER unbalanced.

geisteskrank *adj* mentally ill.

Geisteslkranke *der, die* mentally ill person; [im Krankenhaus] mental patient.

Geisteslwissenschaft *die* arts subject; **die Geisteswissenschaften** the arts.

geistig ◇ *adj* - **1.** [intellektuell - Mensch, Freiheit, Vermächtnis] intellectual; [- Anstrengung, Kraft, Fähigkeit] mental - **2.** [alkoholisch] alcoholic. ◇ *adv* [intellektuell - frei, überlegen] intellectually; [- fit, frisch, behindert] mentally; **sich geistig anstrengen** to make a mental effort.

geistlich ◇ *adj* [gen] religious; [Beistand] spiritual. ◇ *adv*: **jm geistlich beistehen** to lend sb spiritual guidance.

Geistliche (*pl* **-n**) *der* clergyman.

geistlos ◇ *adj* inane. ◇ *adv* inanely.

geistreich ◇ *adj* intelligent. ◇ *adv* intelligently.

Geiz *der* meanness.

geizen *vi*: **mit etw geizen** [Geld] to be mean with sthg; [Lob] to be sparing with sthg.

Geizlhals *der fam abw* skinflint.

geizig ◇ *adj* mean. ◇ *adv* meanly.

Geizlkragen *der fam abw* skinflint.

Gejammer *das fam abw* moaning.

gekannt *pp* ▷ **kennen**.

Gekicher *das* giggling.

geklungen *pp* ▷ **klingen**.

gekniffen *pp* ▷ **kneifen**.

gekommen *pp* ▷ **kommen**.

gekonnt ◇ *pp* ▷ **können**. ◇ *adj* masterful. ◇ *adv* masterfully.

gekrochen *pp* ▷ **kriechen**.

gekünstelt *abw* ◇ *adj* artificial. ◇ *adv* artificially.

Gel (*pl* **-e**) *das* gel.

Gelächter (*pl* -) *das* laughter.

geladen ◇ *pp* ▷ **laden**. ◇ *adj* loaded, **geladen sein** *fam fig* to be fuming.

gelähmt *adj* paralysed.

Gelähmte (*pl* **-n**) *der, die* paralysed man (-woman *die*).

Gelände (*pl* -) *das* - **1.** [Land] country; **ein bergiges Gelände** mountainous terrain; **auf freiem Gelände** in the open country - **2.** [Gebiet] area - **3.** [Grundstück - zum Bau] site; [- um Haus] grounds *Pl*.

Geländellauf *der* - **1.** SPORT cross-country (running) - **2.** [Wettkampf] cross-country run.

Geländer (*pl* -) *das* [von Treppe] banister; [von Brücke] parapet; [von Balkon] railing.

gelang *prät* ▷ **gelingen**.

gelangen (*perf* **ist gelangt**) *vi*: **an etw** *(A)* **gelangen** to arrive at sthg; **an die Öffentlichkeit gelangen** to become public; **in js Besitz gelangen** to come into sb's possession; **zu etw gelangen** [Ruhm, Ansehen] to gain sthg; [Verständigung] to come to sthg; **zu Geld gelangen** [durch Erbe] to come into money; [durch Arbeit] to make money.

gelassen ◇ *pp* ▷ **lassen**. ◇ *adj* calm. ◇ *adv* calmly.

Gelassenheit *die* composure.

gelaufen *pp* ▷ **laufen**.

geläufig *adj* [vertraut] common; **es ist mir geläufig** it is familiar to me.

gelb *adj* & *adv* yellow.

Gelb *das* yellow. ◆ **bei Gelb** *adv* on amber *UK*, on yellow *US*.

Gelbe Sack *der yellow refuse bag used for recyclable packaging*.

gelblich *adj* [Tapete, Papier] yellowish; [Haut] sallow.

Gelbsucht *die* jaundice.

Geld (*pl* **-er**) *das* money; **großes Geld** notes *Pl*; **kleines Geld** change, coins *Pl*; **ins Geld gehen** to be expensive; **es ist sein Geld wert** it is worth every penny. ◆ **Gelder** *Pl* funds.

Geldlautomat *der* cash machine ODER dispenser.

Gẹld|börse *die* [Brieftasche] wallet; [für Münzen] purse.

Gẹld|geber, in *der, die* financial backer.

gẹldgierig *adj* greedy *(for money)*.

Gẹld|karte *die* Switch card® *UK, smart card which charges payments straight to one's bank account*.

Gẹld|mittel *Pl* funds.

Gẹld|schein *der* banknote *UK*, bill *US*.

Gẹld|schrank *der* safe.

Gẹld|strafe *die* fine.

Gẹld|stück *das* coin.

Gelee [ʒəˈleː] (*pl* **-s**) *das* & *der* jelly.

gelegen ◇ *pp* ▷ **liegen**. ◇ *adj* **- 1.** [befindlich] situated **- 2.** [bedeutsam]: **mir ist an deinem Besuch viel gelegen** *geh* your visit means a great deal to me.

Gelegenheit (*pl* **-en**) *die* **- 1.** [geeignete Möglichkeit] opportunity **- 2.** [Anlass] occasion **- 3.** [Angebot] bargain. ◆ **bei Gelegenheit** *adv* when the opportunity arises.

gelegentlich ◇ *adj* occasional. ◇ *adv* **- 1.** [manchmal] occasionally **- 2.** [bei Gelegenheit] some time.

gelehrt ◇ *adj* learned. ◇ *adv* learnedly.

Gelehrte (*pl* **-n**) *der, die* scholar.

Gelẹnk (*pl* **-e**) *das* [beim Menschen] joint.

gelẹnkig *adj* supple.

gelẹrnt *adj* trained.

gelesen *pp* ▷ **lesen**.

Geliebte (*pl* **-n**) *der, die* lover.

geliehen *pp* ▷ **leihen**.

gelịngen (*prät* **gelang**, *perf* **ist gelụngen**) *vi*: **die Zeichnung ist mir gut gelungen** my drawing turned out well; **es gelang mir, den Brief zu schreiben** I managed to write the letter; **es gelang ihm, das Buch zu finden** he succeeded in finding the book.

gelịtten *pp* ▷ **leiden**.

gelọckt *adj*: **gelocktes Haar** curly hair.

gelogen *pp* ▷ **lügen**.

gelöst *adj* relaxed.

gẹlten (*präs* **gịlt**, *prät* **gạlt**, *perf* **hat gegọlten**) *vi* **- 1.** [gültig sein] to be valid; **für jn/etw gelten** to apply to sb/sthg **- 2.** SPORT to count **- 3.** [anerkannt sein]: **als etw gelten** to be considered to be sthg **- 4.** [korrekt sein]: **das gilt nicht!** *fam* [gen] that doesn't count!; [schummeln] that's cheating! **- 5.** [akzeptieren]: **etw gelten lassen** to accept sthg **- 6.** [wert sein] to count; **Kreativität gilt hier nichts** creativity counts for nothing here **- 7.** [adressiert sein an]: **seine Bemerkung galt nicht allein dir** his remark was not only directed at you, his remark didn't only apply to you **- 8.** [müssen]: **in dieser Lage gilt es, einen kühlen Kopf zu bewahren** in this situation you need to *ODER* it is necessary to keep a cool head.

gẹltend *adj* current; **etw geltend machen** [Forderung] to make sthg; [Einwand] to raise/put forward sthg.

Gẹltung *die* **- 1.** [Gültigkeit] validity; **dieses Gesetz hat keine Geltung mehr** this law is no longer valid **- 2.** [Wirkung] prominence; **zur Geltung kommen** to be shown to its best advantage.

gelụngen ◇ *pp* ▷ **gelingen**. ◇ *adj* successful.

gemächlich ◇ *adj* leisurely. ◇ *adv*: **gemächlich im Wald spazieren gehen** to go for a leisurely walk in the woods.

Gemälde (*pl* **-**) *das* painting.

gemäß *präp*: **gemäß einer Sache** *(D)*, **einer Sache** *(D)* **gemäß** in accordance with sthg.

gemäßigt *adj* [Politiker] moderate; [Klima] temperate.

Gemẹcker, Gemẹckere *das* **- 1.** [von Ziegen] bleating **- 2.** *fam abw* [Nörgelei] moaning.

gemein ◇ *adj* **- 1.** [niederträchtig - Person, Verhalten] mean; [- Trick, Lüge] nasty; [- Witz] dirty **- 2.** *fam* [unfair]: **das ist gemein!** that's not fair! ◇ *adv* **- 1.** [gemeinsam]: **etw mit jm/etw gemein haben** to have sthg in common with sb/sthg **- 2.** [niederträchtig] meanly **- 3.** *fam* [sehr]: **die Verletzung hat gemein wehgetan** the injury hurt like hell.

Gemeinde|zentrum *das* community centre.

gemeingefährlich ◇ *adj* dangerous. ◇ *adv* dangerously.

Gemeinheit (*pl* **-en**) *die* **- 1.** [verwerfliche Art] meanness **- 2.** [Handlung] mean trick **- 3.** *fam* [Ärgernis]: **so eine Gemeinheit!** it's not fair!

gemeinnützig ◇ *adj* for the benefit of the community; [Verein] charitable, non-profit-making. ◇ *adv* for the benefit of the community.

gemeinsam ◇ *adv* **- 1.** [zusammen] together; **gemeinsam verantwortlich** jointly responsible **- 2.** [gleich]: **etw gemeinsam haben** to have sthg in common. ◇ *adj* [Weg, Interessen] common; [Verantwortung] joint; **ein gemeinsamer Urlaub/Spaziergang** a holiday/walk together.

Gemeinsamkeit (*pl* **-en**) *die* **- 1.** [gleiche Eigenschaft] common feature; **sie haben viele Gemeinsamkeiten** they have a lot in common **- 2.** *(ohne pl)* [Zusammengehörigkeit]: **Gefühl der Gemeinsamkeit** sense of community.

Gemeinschaft (*pl* **-en**) *die* **- 1.** [Gruppe] community **- 2.** [Verbundenheit] company; **in unserer Klasse haben wir eine gute Gemeinschaft** in our class we have a good sense of community; **in js Gemeinschaft** in sb's company.

gemeinschaftlich ◇ *adj* joint; [Interessen] common. ◇ *adv* jointly.

Gemeinschafts|kunde *die (ohne pl)* SCHULE social studies *Pl*.

Gemeinschafts|raum *der* common room.

gemeint *adj* meant; **das war nicht so gemeint!** I didn't mean it like that!; **mein Rat war gut gemeint** my advice was well-intentioned.

Gemetzel (*pl* -) *das* bloodbath.

Gemisch (*pl* -e) *das* mixture.

gemischt *adj* mixed.

gemocht *pp* ▷ **mögen**.

gemolken *pp* ▷ **melken**.

Gemurmel *das* murmuring.

Gemüse (*pl* -) *das* vegetables *Pl*.

Gemüse|eintopf *der* vegetable stew.

Gemüse|händler, in *der, die* greengrocer.

gemusst *pp* ▷ **müssen**.

Gemüt (*pl* -er) *das* - **1.** [Wesen] disposition - **2.** *(ohne pl)* [Empfindungsvermögen] heart; **dieses Buch ist etwas fürs Gemüt** this is a moving book; **der Film ist ihr aufs Gemüt geschlagen** the film really got her down; [Text] to study sthg. ◆ **Gemüter** *Pl* feelings; **der Skandal hat die Gemüter erregt** the scandal has caused feelings to run high.

gemütlich ◇ *adj* - **1.** [behaglich] cosy; **es sich** *(D)* **gemütlich machen** to make o.s. at home - **2.** [Beisammensein] informal; [Abend] pleasant; [Fahrt] leisurely - **3.** [Person] friendly. ◇ *adv* - **1.** [behaglich] cosily - **2.** [zusammensitzen, sich unterhalten] pleasantly; [arbeiten] at a leisurely pace.

Gemütlichkeit *die* - **1.** [Behaglichkeit] cosiness - **2.** [Zwanglosigkeit, Ruhe] pleasant atmosphere; **in aller Gemütlichkeit** at one's leisure.

Gen (*pl* -e) *das* gene.

genannt *pp* ▷ **nennen**.

genau ◇ *adj* - **1.** [exakt] exact; [Waage, Voraussage, Arbeit] accurate - **2.** [gründlich] thorough. ◇ *adv* - **1.** [exakt] precisely, exactly; **genau!** precisely!, exactly!; **genau um zehn Uhr** at exactly ten o'clock; **auf die Minute/Sekunde** to the very minute/second; **die Uhr geht genau** the clock keeps perfect time - **2.** [zuhören, hinsehen] carefully; **ich kenne ihn genau** I know exactly what he's like.

genau genommen *adv* strictly speaking.

Genauigkeit *die* - **1.** [Exaktheit] exactness; [von Waage, Voraussage, Arbeit] accuracy - **2.** [Gründlichkeit] thoroughness.

genauso *adv* just as; **er sieht genauso aus** he looks just the same.

Gen|datei *die* DNA database.

genehmigen *vt* [Antrag, Plan] to approve; [Demonstration, Aufenthalt] to authorize; **sich** *(D)* **etw genehmigen** *fam* to treat o.s. to ODER allow o.s. sthg.

Genehmigung (*pl* -en) *die* - **1.** [von Antrag, Plan] approval; [von Demonstration, Aufenthalt] authorization - **2.** [Dokument] permit.

General (*pl* -rale ODER -räle) *der* general.

General|probe *die eigtl* & *fig* dress rehearsal.

generalüberholen *vt* to give a complete overhaul.

Generalver|sammlung *die* annual general meeting.

Generation (*pl* -en) *die* generation.

Generations|konflikt *der* conflict between the generations.

Generator (*pl* -toren) *der* generator.

generell ◇ *adj* general. ◇ *adv* generally.

Genetik *die* genetics *(U)*.

Genf *nt* Geneva.

Genfer See *der* Lake Geneva.

genial ◇ *adj* brilliant. ◇ *adv* brilliantly.

Genick (*pl* -e) *das* (back of the) neck.

Genie [ʒe'ni:] (*pl* -s) *das* genius.

genieren [ʒe'ni:rən] *vt* to bother. ◆ **sich genieren** *ref* to be embarrassed; **sich vor jm genieren** to be shy of sb, to get embarrassed in sb's presence.

genießbar *adj* [essbar] edible; [trinkbar] drinkable.

genießen (*prät* **genoss**, *perf* **hat genossen**) *vt* - **1.** [gen] to enjoy - **2.** [essen] to eat; [trinken] to drink.

Genießer, in (*mpl* -, *fpl* -nen) *der, die* pleasure lover, bon vivant; [beim Essen] gourmet.

genießerisch ◇ *adj* [Mensch] appreciative; [Leben] pleasurable. ◇ *adv* with relish.

Genitalien *Pl* genitals.

Genitiv (*pl* -e) *der* GRAMM genitive.

genommen *pp* ▷ **nehmen**.

genormt *adj* standardized.

genoss *prät* ▷ **genießen**.

genossen *pp* ▷ **genießen**.

Genossenschaft (*pl* -en) *die* cooperative.

gentechnisch ◇ *adj*: **gentechnische Änderungen** genetic modifications. ◇ *adv*: **gentechnisch veränderte Lebensmittel** genetically modified foods, GM foods.

genug *adv* enough; **genug (von etw) haben** to have had enough (of sthg).

Genüge *die*: **einer Sache** *(D)* **Genüge tun** *geh* to satisfy sthg; **zur Genüge** *abw* only too well.

genügen *vi* - **1.** [ausreichen] to be enough; **ein Glas Wein genügt mir** a glass of wine is enough for me; **das genügt!** that's enough - **2.** [entsprechen]: **einer Sache** *(D)* **genügen** [Anforderungen] to meet sthg; [Vorschriften] to comply with sthg.

genügend *adj* & *adv* enough.

genügsam ◇ *adj* [Mensch] modest. ◇ *adv* modestly.

Genugtuung *die* satisfaction; **Genugtuung für etw** satisfaction for sthg; **mit Genugtuung** with satisfaction.

Genus (*pl* **Genera**) *das* GRAMM gender.

Genuss (*pl* **Genüsse**) *der* - **1.** [Konsum] consumption; **in den Genuss von etw kommen** *fig* to receive sthg - **2.** [Befriedigung] pleasure; **das Konzert war ein Genuss** the concert was a delight.

Geografie, Geographie *die* geography.

geografisch, geographisch ◇ *adj* geographical. ◇ *adv* geographically.

Geologie *die* geology.

geologisch ◇ *adj* geological. ◇ *adv* geologically.

Geometrie *die* geometry.

geordnet *adj* orderly.

Gepäck *das* luggage.

Gepäck|abfertigung *die* - **1.** [Handlung] luggage check-in - **2.** [Schalter - am Flughafen] (baggage) check-in; [- am Bahnhof] luggage office.

Gepäckab|lage *die* luggage rack.

Gepäck|annahme *die* [am Flughafen] (baggage) check-in.

Gepäck|aufbewahrung *die* [Schalter] left-luggage office *UK*, baggage room *US*.

Gepäckaus|gabe *die* [am Flughafen] baggage reclaim.

Gepäck|schein *der* luggage ticket.

Gepäck|stück *das* item of luggage.

Gepäck|träger *der* - **1.** [von Fahrrad] carrier; [von Auto] luggage rack - **2.** [Person] porter.

Gepäck|wagen *der* luggage van *UK*, baggage car *US*.

gepfiffen *pp* ▷ **pfeifen**.

gepflegt ◇ *adj* - **1.** [Äußeres] well-groomed; [Hände] well-cared-for; [Haare, Kleidung] neat; [Garten, Haus] well-kept - **2.** [von Qualität] quality *(vor Subst)* - **3.** [Stil, Ausdruck] refined. ◇ *adv* - **1.** [essen] well - **2.** [gewählt]: **sie drückt sich sehr gepflegt aus** she has a very refined way of speaking.

gepriesen *pp* ▷ **preisen**.

gequollen *pp* ▷ **quellen**.

gerade ◇ *adv* - **1.** [vor kurzem] just; **ich bin gerade gekommen** I've just arrived; **gerade erst** only just - **2.** [jetzt] at the moment; **ich bin gerade beim Saubermachen** I'm just tidying up at the moment - **3.** [in jenem Moment] just; **er wollte gerade gehen** he was just about to go - **4.** [nicht schief oder gekrümmt] straight - **5.** [besonders] exactly; **gerade deshalb** precisely for that reason; **er war nicht gerade erfreut** he wasn't exactly pleased - **6.** [ausgerechnet]: **warum gerade ich?** why me of all people?; **dass das gerade jetzt passieren musste!** why did it have to happen now of all times?; **das hat mir gerade noch gefehlt!** that's all I needed! - **7.** [knapp]: **gerade noch** only just. ◇ *adj* - **1.** [nicht gekrümmt] straight - **2.** [Haltung] upright.

Gerade (*pl* **-n**) *die* - **1.** MATH straight line - **2.** SPORT straight.

geradeaus *adv* straight ahead.

gerade|biegen *vt (unreg) fam* [bereinigen] to straighten out.

geradeheraus ◇ *adj*: **geradeheraus sein** to be frank. ◇ *adv* frankly.

gerade|stehen *vi (unreg)* [einstehen]: **für jn/etw geradestehen** to take responsibility for sb/sthg.

gerade stehen *vi (unreg)* [aufrecht stehen] to stand up straight.

geradewegs *adv* - **1.** [ohne Umweg] directly - **2.** [unmittelbar] immediately.

geradezu *adv* downright; **es wäre geradezu ein Wunder, wenn** it would be downright incredible if.

geradlinig ◇ *adj* straight. ◇ *adv* in a straight line.

Gerangel *das* - **1.** [Rauferei] scrapping - **2.** *abw* [Kampf] scramble.

Geranie (*pl* **-n**) *die* geranium.

gerannt *pp* ▷ **rennen**.

gerät *präs* ▷ **geraten**.

Gerät (*pl* **-e**) *das* [Apparat] device; [Werkzeug] tool; [in der Küche] utensil; **elektrisches Gerät** (electrical) appliance; **schalt das Gerät ab!** switch off the set!

geraten (*präs* **gerät**, *prät* **geriet**, *perf* **ist geraten**) ◇ *vi* - **1.** [gelangen]: **an eine unfreundliche Verkäuferin geraten** to get an unfriendly shop assistant; **in etw** *(A)* **geraten** [Schwierigkeiten, Not] to get into sthg; [Verdacht] to come under sthg; [Sturm] to be caught in sthg; **in Vergessenheit geraten** to be forgotten - **2.** [gelingen] to turn out; **das Bild ist mir gut geraten** my picture turned out well - **3.** [ähneln]: **nach jm geraten** to take after sb. ◇ *pp* ▷ **raten**.

Geräteturnen *das*: **im Geräteturnen** on the apparatus.

Geratewohl *das*: **sie bewarb sich aufs Geratewohl** she applied on the off-chance; **er nahm aufs Geratewohl ein Buch aus dem Regal** he randomly selected a book from the shelf.

geräumig *adj* roomy.

Geräusch (*pl* **-e**) *das* noise.

geräuschempfindlich *adj* sensitive to noise.

geräuschlos ◇ *adj* silent. ◇ *adv* silently.

gerecht ◇ *adj* fair; [Belohnung] just; **jm/einer Sache gerecht werden** to do sb/sthg justice; **er konnte den Ansprüchen des Chefs nicht gerecht werden** he couldn't match up to the boss's expectations. ◇ *adv* fairly.

Gerechtigkeit *die* justice.

Gerede *das abw* - **1.** [Geschwätz] chatter - **2.** [Klatsch]: **ins Gerede kommen** to get o.s. talked about.

geregelt *adj* [Arbeit] steady; [Leben] orderly.

gereizt ◇ *adj* [Person] irritable; [Stimmung] strained. ◇ *adv* irritably.

Gerịcht (*pl* **-e**) *das* - **1.** [Speise] dish - **2.** [Institution] court; **vor Gericht gehen** to go to court; **vor Gericht stehen** to stand trial - **3.** [Richter]: **das Gericht** the bench - **4.** [Gebäude] court *UK*, courthouse *US* - **5.** *(ohne pl)* [Richten] judgement; **über jn Gericht halten** to sit in judgement on sb.

gerịchtlich ◇ *adj* [Verfahren, Akte] legal; [Untersuchung] judicial. ◇ *adv*: **gegen jn gerichtlich vorgehen** to start legal proceedings against sb.

Gerịchts|hof *der* Court of Justice.

Gerịchts|verhandlung *die* hearing.

Gerịchtsvollzieher, in (*mpl* **-**, *fpl* **-nen**) *der, die* bailiff.

gerieben *pp* ▷ **reiben.**

geriet *prät* ▷ **geraten.**

gerịng *adj* [Gewicht, Preis, Temperatur] low; [Menge] small; [Problem, Chance] slight; [Bedeutung, Rolle] minor; [Dauer] short. ◆ **nicht im Geringsten** *adv* not in the least.

gerịngfügig ◇ *adj* slight, minor. ◇ *adv* slightly.

gerịng schätzen *vt* to have a low opinion of.

gerịnnen (*prät* **gerạnn**, *perf* **ist gerọnnen**) *vi* [Milch] to curdle; [Blut] to coagulate.

Gerịppe (*pl* **-**) *das* skeleton.

gerịssen ◇ *pp* ▷ **reißen.** ◇ *adj* crafty. ◇ *adv* craftily.

gerịtten *pp* ▷ **reiten.**

Germane (*pl* **-n**) *der* Germanic man.

Germanin (*pl* **-nen**) *die* Germanic woman.

germanisch *adj* Germanic.

Germanịstik *die (ohne pl)* German language and literature.

gẹrn (*kompar* **lieber**, *superl* **am liebsten**), **gẹrne** (*kompar* **lieber**, *superl* **am liebsten**) *adv* - **1.** [gen] with pleasure; **jn/etw gern haben** to like sb/sthg; **etw gern tun** to like doing sthg; **das kann ich gern machen** I'll gladly do it; **aber gern!, ja gern!** I'd love to!; **gern geschehen!** don't mention it!; **ich möchte gern wissen** I'd like to know - **2.** [oft]: **der Computer stürzt gern ab** the computer tends to crash.

gerọchen *pp* ▷ **riechen.**

Gerọ̈ll *das (ohne pl)* [im Gebirge] scree; [im Bach] (loose) pebbles *Pl.*

gerọnnen *pp* ▷ **rinnen.**

Gẹrste *die* barley.

Gẹrte (*pl* **-n**) *die* switch.

Gerụch (*pl* **Gerụ̈che**) *der* smell.

gerụchlos *adj* odourless.

Gerụchs|sinn [gəˈrʊxszɪn] *der* sense of smell.

Gerụ̈cht (*pl* **-e**) *das* rumour.

gerufen *pp* ▷ **rufen.**

geruhsam ◇ *adj* leisurely. ◇ *adv*: **geruhsam durch den Garten gehen** to go for a leisurely walk round the garden.

Gerụ̈mpel *das abw* junk.

Gerụndium (*pl* **-dien**) *das* GRAMM gerund.

gerụngen *pp* ▷ **ringen.**

Gerụ̈st (*pl* **-e**) *das* - **1.** [beim Bauen] scaffolding - **2.** [von Text] framework.

gesạlzen ◇ *pp* ▷ **salzen.** ◇ *adj fam* [Preis, Miete] steep; [Beschwerde] harsh.

gesạmt ◇ *adj* whole, entire; [Einkommen, Kosten] total. ◇ *adv* entirely.

Gesạmtaus|gabe *die* complete edition.

gesạmtdeutsch *adj relating to both eastern and western Germany.*

Gesạmt|eindruck *der* overall impression.

Gesạmt|schule *die* ≃ comprehensive school.

gesạndt *pp* ▷ **senden.**

Gesạndte, tin (*mpl* **-n**, *fpl* **-nen**) *der, die* envoy.

Gesạng (*pl* **Gesạ̈nge**) *der* - **1.** [Singen] singing - **2.** [Lied, von Vogel] song.

Gesäß (*pl* **-e**) *das geh* buttocks *Pl.*

Geschädigte (*pl* **-n**) *der, die* injured party.

geschạffen *pp* ▷ **schaffen.**

Geschạ̈ft (*pl* **-e**) *das* - **1.** [Handel] business; **die Geschäfte gehen schlecht** business is slack; **ein Geschäft abschließen** to close a deal; **du hast damit ein gutes/schlechtes Geschäft gemacht** that was a good/bad deal (for you); **mit jm Geschäfte machen** to do business with sb - **2.** [Laden] shop, store; [Firma] business - **3.** [Gewinn] profit - **4.** [Angelegenheit] task; **sich um seine Geschäfte kümmern** to go about one's business.

geschạ̈ftig ◇ *adj* [Treiben] bustling; [Person] busy. ◇ *adv* busily.

geschạ̈ftlich ◇ *adj* - **1.** [beruflich] business *(vor Subst)* - **2.** [unpersönlich] businesslike. ◇ *adv* - **1.** [verreisen, fliegen] on business - **2.** [unpersönlich] in a businesslike manner.

Geschạ̈fts|bedingungen *Pl* terms (and conditions).

Geschạ̈fts|beziehungen *Pl* business contacts.

Geschạ̈fts|frau *die* businesswoman.

Geschạ̈fts|führer, in *der, die* - **1.** [von Unternehmen] manager; [von GmbH] managing director - **2.** [von Organisation] secretary.

Geschạ̈fts|führung *die* management.

Geschạ̈fts|lage *die* - **1.** [wirtschaftlich] commercial situation - **2.** [örtlich] business location.

Geschạ̈fts|leute *Pl* businessmen.

Geschạ̈fts|mann (*pl* **-leute** ODER **-männer**) *der* businessman.

Geschạ̈fts|reise *die* business trip.

Geschäftsschluss *der (ohne pl)* closing time.

Geschäfts|stelle *die* office; [von Bank] branch.

Geschäfts|straße *die* high street *UK*, main (shopping) street *US*.

geschäftstüchtig *adj* with good business acumen.

Geschäfts|zeit *die* [von Laden] opening hours *Pl*; [von Firma] office hours *Pl*.

geschah *prät* ▷ **geschehen**.

gescheckt *adj* [Hund, Katze, Stoff] spotted; [Pferd - braunweiß] skewbald; [- schwarzweiß] piebald.

geschehen (*präs* **geschieht**, *prät* **geschah**, *perf* **ist geschehen**) *vi* - **1.** [sich ereignen] to happen - **2.** [widerfahren]: **es kann dir nichts geschehen** nothing can happen to you; **ihm ist ein Unrecht geschehen** he has been wronged; **das geschieht dir/ihm (ganz) recht!** *abw* that serves you/him right! - **3.** [verloren sein]: **es ist um seine Zukunft geschehen** he has no future.

gescheit ◇ *adj* - **1.** [klug] clever - **2.** [vernünftig] sensible. ◇ *adv* - **1.** [klug] cleverly - **2.** [vernünftig] sensibly.

Geschenk (*pl* **-e**) *das* present.

Geschichte (*pl* **-n**) *die* - **1.** [geschichtliche Entwicklung, Fach] history; **Geschichte machen** to make history - **2.** [Erzählung, Bericht] story - **3.** [Begebenheit]: **es ist wieder die alte Geschichte** it's the same old story; **mir ist heute eine seltsame Geschichte passiert** a strange thing happened to me today; **du machst ja Geschichten!** *hum* you are a one!

geschichtlich ◇ *adj* historical. ◇ *adv* historically.

Geschichts|unterricht *der (ohne pl)* [Schulstunden] history lessons *Pl*.

Geschick (*pl* **-e**) *das (ohne pl)* [Talent, Können] skill.

Geschicklichkeit *die* skilfulness.

geschickt ◇ *adj* - **1.** [fingerfertig] skilful - **2.** [raffiniert, gewandt] clever. ◇ *adv* - **1.** [fingerfertig] skilfully - **2.** [raffiniert, gewandt] cleverly.

geschieden ◇ *pp* ▷ **scheiden**. ◇ *adj* divorced.

geschieht *präs* ▷ **geschehen**.

geschienen *pp* ▷ **scheinen**.

Geschirr (*pl* **-e**) *das* - **1.** *(ohne pl)* [Gefäße, Service] crockery; [benutzt] dishes *Pl*; **ein Geschirr für sechs Personen** a dinner/tea service for six people; **Geschirr spülen** ODER **abwaschen** to do the dishes, to wash up *UK* - **2.** [für Zugtiere] harness.

Geschirrspül|maschine *die* dishwasher.

Geschirr|tuch *das* tea towel *UK*, dish towel *US*.

geschissen *pp* ▷ **scheißen**.

geschlafen *pp* ▷ **schlafen**.

Geschlecht (*pl* **-er**) *das* - **1.** [biologische Einteilung] sex - **2.** *(ohne pl)* [Geschlechtsteil] genitals *Pl* - **3.** [Familie] lineage - **4.** [Genus] gender.

Geschlechts|krankheit *die* sexually transmitted disease.

Geschlechts|organ *das* sexual organ.

geschlechtsreif *adj* sexually mature.

Geschlechtsverkehr *der* sexual intercourse.

geschlichen *pp* ▷ **schleichen**.

geschlungen *pp* ▷ **schlingen**.

Geschmack (*pl* **Geschmäcke** ODER **Geschmäcker**) *der* - **1.** [gen] taste; **Geschmack haben** to have taste; **guten/schlechten Geschmack haben** to have good/bad taste; **an etw** *(D)* **Geschmack finden** to acquire a taste for sthg - **2.** [Geschmackssinn] sense of taste.

geschmacklos ◇ *adj* tasteless. ◇ *adv* tastelessly.

Geschmack|sache = **Geschmackssache**.

Geschmacks|richtung *die* - **1.** [von Nahrungsmitteln] flavour - **2.** [Stilrichtung, Vorliebe] taste.

Geschmackssache, Geschmacksache *die*: **das ist Geschmackssache** that is a matter of taste.

Geschmackssinn *der* sense of taste.

geschmackvoll ◇ *adj* tasteful. ◇ *adv* tastefully.

geschmeidig ◇ *adj* [Material, Bewegung] supple. ◇ *adv* [gewandt] supplely.

geschmissen *pp* ▷ **schmeißen**.

geschmolzen *pp* ▷ **schmelzen**.

Geschnetzelte *das (ohne pl) small, thin strips of meat cooked in a sauce.*

geschnitten ◇ *pp* ▷ **schneiden**. ◇ *adj* - **1.** [Fleisch] sliced - **2.** [Kleid] cut; **ihr Gesicht ist hübsch geschnitten** she has pretty features.

geschoben *pp* ▷ **schieben**.

Geschöpf (*pl* **-e**) *das* - **1.** [Lebewesen, Person] creature - **2.** [Erfindung] creation.

geschoren *pp* ▷ **scheren**.

Geschoss (*pl* **-e**) *das* - **1.** [Kugel] bullet; [Granate] shell - **2.** [Stockwerk] floor.

geschossen *pp* ▷ **schießen**.

Geschrei *das abw* - **1.** [Schreien] shouting - **2.** [Gezeter] fuss.

geschrieben *pp* ▷ **schreiben**.

geschrien *pp* ▷ **schreien**.

Geschütz (*pl* **-e**) *das* (big) gun; **Geschütze** artillery *(U)*.

Geschwätz *das abw* - **1.** [Gerede] prattle - **2.** [Tratsch] gossip.

geschwätzig *adj abw* prattling; [tratschend] gossipy.

geschweige *konj*: **geschweige denn** let alone.

geschwiegen *pp* ▷ **schweigen**.

geschwind *Süddt* ◇ *adj* quick. ◇ *adv* quickly.

Geschwindigkeit (*pl* **-en**) *die* speed.

Geschwister *Pl* brothers and sisters.

geschwollen ◇ *pp* ▷ **schwellen**. ◇ *adj* - **1.** [Finger, Gesicht] swollen - **2.** *abw* [Sätze, Ausdruck] pompous. ◇ *adv abw* [pompös] pompously.

geschwommen *pp* ▷ **schwimmen**.

geschworen *pp* ▷ **schwören**.

Geschworene (*pl* **-n**) *der, die* juror.

Geschwulst (*pl* **Geschwülste**) *die* tumour.

Geschwür (*pl* **-e**) *das* ulcer.

gesehen *pp* ▷ **sehen**.

Geselle (*pl* **-n**) *der* - **1.** [Handwerker] qualified craftsman - **2.** [Kerl] fellow.

gesellig *adj* - **1.** [kontaktfreudig - Person] sociable; [- Tier] gregarious - **2.** [anregend] convivial.

Geselligkeit *die* conviviality; **Geselligkeit brauchen** to need company.

Gesellin (*pl* **-nen**) *die* qualified craftswoman.

Gesellschaft (*pl* **-en**) *die* - **1.** [Gemeinschaft] society - **2.** [Anwesenheit, Umgang] company; **jm Gesellschaft leisten** to keep sb company - **3.** [Fest] party; **geschlossene Gesellschaft** private party - **4.** [Gruppe] group (of people) - **5.** [Wirtschaftsunternehmen] company.

gesessen *pp* ▷ **sitzen**.

Gesetz (*pl* **-e**) *das* [staatliche Vorschrift, Regel] law.

Gesetz|buch *das* statute book.

gesetzgebend *adj* legislative.

Gesetz|geber *der* legislature.

Gesetzgebung *die* legislation.

gesetzlich ◇ *adj* legal; **gesetzlicher Feiertag** public holiday; **ein gesetzlicher Anspruch** a legitimate claim. ◇ *adv* legally; **gesetzlich verankert** established in law.

gesetzmäßig *adj* - **1.**: **ein gesetzmäßiger Prozess** a process governed by a natural law - **2.** [Macht] legal; [Inhaber] lawful.

gesetzt *adj* sedate; **gesetzt den Fall, dass...** assuming that...

Gesicht (*pl* **-er** ODER **-e**) *das* face; **jm etw ins Gesicht sagen** *fig* to say sthg to sb's face.

Gesichts|punkt *der* point of view.

Gesichts|züge *Pl* features.

Gesinnung (*pl* **-en**) *die* [Überzeugungen] convictions *Pl*; [Einstellung] outlook *(U)*.

gesittet ◇ *adj* civilized. ◇ *adv* in a civilized manner.

gesoffen *pp* ▷ **saufen**.

gesogen *pp* ▷ **saugen**.

gesondert ◇ *adj* separate. ◇ *adv* separately.

gespannt ◇ *adj* - **1.** [Stoff, Saite] taut - **2.** [Person] eager; **ich bin gespannt auf seine neue Freundin** I can't wait to see his new girlfriend - **3.** [Situation] tense. ◇ *adv* [erwartungsvoll, aufgeregt] eagerly.

Gespenst (*pl* **-er**) *das* ghost; [Bedrohung] spectre.

gespien *pp* ▷ **speien**.

gesponnen *pp* ▷ **spinnen**.

Gespött *das* mockery; **jn/sich zum Gespött der Leute machen** to make sb/o.s. a laughing stock.

Gespräch (*pl* **-e**) *das* - **1.** [Konversation] conversation, talk; **etw ist im Gespräch** *fig* sthg is under discussion - **2.** [Telefonanruf] call.

gesprächig *adj* talkative.

Gesprächs|partner, in [gəˈʃprɛːçspartnɐ] *der, die*: **mein Gesprächspartner** the person I am/was talking to; **seine Gesprächspartner bei den Verhandlungen** his partners in the negotiations.

Gesprächs|thema [gəˈʃprɛːçsteːma] *das* topic of conversation.

gesprochen *pp* ▷ **sprechen**.

gesprossen *pp* ▷ **sprießen**.

gesprungen *pp* ▷ **springen**.

Gespür *das* feel; **ein/kein Gespür für etw haben** to have a/no feel for sthg.

Gestalt (*pl* **-en**) *die* - **1.** [Person] figure - **2.** *(ohne pl)* [Körperform] build - **3.** [in Literatur] character - **4.** *(ohne pl)* [Form] shape; **unser Plan nimmt Gestalt an** our plan is taking shape. ◆ **in Gestalt** *präp*: **in Gestalt einer Sache** *(G)* in the shape of sthg.

gestalten *vt* [Fest] to organize; [Schaufenster, Garten] to design. ◆ **sich gestalten** *ref* to turn out.

Gestaltung *die* [von Fest] organizing; [von Schaufenster, Garten] designing.

Geständnis (*pl* **-se**) *das* confession; **ein Geständnis ablegen** to make a confession.

Gestank *der (ohne pl) abw* stench.

gestatten *vt*: **jm etw gestatten** to allow sb sthg. ◆ **gestatten Sie** *interj*: **gestatten Sie?** may I?; **gestatten Sie, dass ich rauche?** do you mind if I smoke?

Geste (*pl* **-n**) *die* gesture.

gestehen (*prät* **gestand**, *perf* **hat gestanden**) ◇ *vt*: **ein Verbrechen/einen Mord gestehen** to confess to a crime/murder; **jm die Wahrheit gestehen** to confess the truth to sb. ◇ *vi* [aussagen] to confess.

Gestein (*pl* **-e**) *das* rock.

Gestell (*pl* **-e**) *das* stand.

gestern *adv* yesterday; **gestern Früh** first thing yesterday; **gestern Morgen/Mittag/**

Abend yesterday morning/lunchtime/evening; **von gestern sein** *fig* to be behind the times.

gestiegen *pp* ▷ **steigen**.

gestochen *pp* ▷ **stechen**.

gestohlen *pp* ▷ **stehlen**.

gestorben *pp* ▷ **sterben**.

gestoßen *pp* ▷ **stoßen**.

gestreift *adj* striped.

gestrig *adj* yesterday's; **am gestrigen Abend** yesterday evening.

gestritten *pp* ▷ **streiten**.

Gestrüpp *das* undergrowth.

gestunken *pp* ▷ **stinken**.

Gestüt (*pl* **-e**) *das* stud.

Gesuch (*pl* **-e**) *das* request.

gesund (*kompar* **gesünder** ODER **gesunder**, *superl* **gesündeste** ODER **gesundeste**) ◇ *adj* healthy; **gesunder Menschenverstand** common sense. ◇ *adv* healthily; **jn gesund schreiben** to certify sb fit; **jn gesund pflegen** to nurse sb back to health.

Gesundheit *die* health.

gesundheitlich ◇ *adj* health; **ihr gesundheitlicher Zustand** the state of her health. ◇ *adv* health-wise.

Gesundheits|amt *das* public health department.

gesundheitsschädlich *adj* damaging to one's health.

Gesundheitszu|stand *der* state of health.

gesungen *pp* ▷ **singen**.

gesunken *pp* ▷ **sinken**.

getan *pp* ▷ **tun**.

Getöse *das* roar.

getragen *pp* ▷ **tragen**.

Getränk (*pl* **-e**) *das* drink.

Getreide *das* cereals *Pl*, grain.

Getreidean|bau *der* cereal growing.

getrennt ◇ *adj* separate. ◇ *adv* separately; **(von jm) getrennt leben** to be separated (from sb).

getreten *pp* ▷ **treten**.

Getriebe (*pl* **-**) *das* gearbox.

getrieben *pp* ▷ **treiben**.

getrogen *pp* ▷ **trügen**.

getrost *adv* without any problem.

getrunken *pp* ▷ **trinken**.

Getto (*pl* **-s**), **Ghetto** (*pl* **-s**) *das* ghetto.

Getue [gə'tuːə] *das abw* fuss.

Getümmel *das*: **sich ins Getümmel stürzen** to throw o.s. into the fray.

Gewächs [gə'vɛks] (*pl* **-e**) *das* plant.

gewachsen [gə'vaksn̩] ◇ *pp* ▷ **wachsen**. ◇ *adj*: **jm gewachsen sein** to be a match for sb; **etw gewachsen sein** to be up to sthg.

Gewächs|haus *das* greenhouse.

gewagt ◇ *adj* daring. ◇ *adv* [freizügig] daringly.

gewählt ◇ *adj* - **1.** [durch Abstimmung bestimmt] elected - **2.** [gehoben] refined. ◇ *adv* [gehoben] in a refined manner.

Gewähr *die (ohne pl)* guarantee; **Gewähr leisten** to guarantee. ◆ **ohne Gewähr** *adv* subject to alteration.

gewähren *vt* to give; **jm etw gewähren** to grant sb sthg; **jn gewähren lassen** to let sb do as he/she likes.

gewährleisten *vt* ▷ **Gewähr**.

Gewalt (*pl* **-en**) *die* - **1.** [Brutalität, Willkür] violence; **etw mit Gewalt öffnen** to force sthg open; **jn mit Gewalt zu etw zwingen** to compel sb to do sthg by (using) force; **etw mit aller Gewalt machen** to do sthg with all one's might - **2.** [Macht, Beherrschung] power; **jn/sich/etw in der Gewalt haben** to be in control of sb/o.s./sthg - **3.** [Naturgewalt] force, power.

Gewalt|herrschaft *die* tyranny.

gewaltig ◇ *adj* [Kraft, Größe] enormous, huge; [Schönheit] tremendous. ◇ *adv* enormously.

gewaltsam ◇ *adj* violent; **gewaltsame Vertreibung** forcible expulsion. ◇ *adv* forcibly; [schließen] by force; **jn gewaltsam an etw hindern** to prevent sb forcibly from doing sthg.

gewalttätig ◇ *adj* violent. ◇ *adv* violently.

Gewalt|verbrechen *das* violent crime.

gewandt ◇ *pp* ▷ **wenden**. ◇ *adj* - **1.** [Ausdrucksweise, Redner] skilful - **2.** [Auftreten] confident - **3.** [Bewegung] agile. ◇ *adv* - **1.** [sich ausdrücken] skilfully - **2.** [auftreten] confidently - **3.** [sich bewegen] agilely.

Gewandtheit *die* - **1.** [von Redner] skilfulness - **2.** [von Umgangsformen] confidence - **3.** [von Bewegungen] agility.

gewann *prät* ▷ **gewinnen**.

gewaschen *pp* ▷ **waschen**.

Gewässer (*pl* **-**) *das* stretch of water. ◆ **Gewässer** *Pl* waters.

Gewebe (*pl* **-**) *das* - **1.** [Stoff] fabric - **2.** [im Körper] tissue.

Gewehr (*pl* **-e**) *das* rifle.

Geweih (*pl* **-e**) *das* antlers *Pl*; [Trophäe] set of antlers.

Gewerbe (*pl* **-**) *das* - **1.** [Beruf] trade - **2.** *(ohne pl)* [Bereich] trade.

Gewerbe|schein *der* trading licence.

gewerblich ◇ *adj* commercial. ◇ *adv* commercially.

Gewerkschaft (*pl* **-en**) *die* trade union *UK*, labor union *US*.

Gewerkschaft(l)er, in (*mpl* **-**, *fpl* **-nen**) *der, die* trade *UK* ODER labor *US* unionist.

Gewẹrkschaftsbund *der* trade union federation.

gewẹsen *pp* ▷ **sein**.

Gewịcht (*pl* **-e**) *das* weight; **etw fällt ins Gewicht** *fig* sthg is of consequence.

Gewịchtheben *das* weightlifting.

Gewịnde (*pl* -) *das* thread.

Gewịnn (*pl* **-e**) *der* - **1.** [Profit] profit - **2.** *(ohne pl)* [Nutzen] benefit - **3.** [Preis] prize. ◆ **Gewinn bringend** ◇ *adj* profitable. ◇ *adv* profitably.

gewịnnen (*prät* **gewạnn**, *perf* **hat gewọnnen**) ◇ *vi* - **1.** [siegen] to win - **2.** [wachsen]: **an etw** *(D)* **gewinnen** to gain in sthg - **3.** [besser werden]: **durch etw gewinnen** to benefit from sthg. ◇ *vt* - **1.** [Wettkampf, Preis] to win - **2.** [Ansehen] to gain; **jn für etw gewinnen** to win sb over to sthg - **3.** [Produkt] to produce.

gewịnnend *adj* winning.

Gewịnner, in (*mpl* **-**, *fpl* **-nen**) *der, die* winner.

Gewịnnung *die* extraction.

Gewịrr, Gewịrre *das* [von Kabeln] tangle; [von Stimmen] confusion.

gewịss ◇ *adj* certain; **sich** *(D)* **einer Sache** *(G)* **gewiss sein** to be certain of sthg; **der Sieg ist uns gewiss** we are certain of victory. ◇ *adv* [sicherlich] certainly.

Gewịssen *das (ohne pl)* [seelische Instanz] conscience; **gutes/schlechtes Gewissen** clear/bad conscience.

gewịssenhaft ◇ *adj* conscientious. ◇ *adv* conscientiously.

Gewịssens|bisse *Pl* pangs of conscience.

Gewịssens|konflikt *der* moral dilemma; **in einen Gewissenskonflikt geraten** to be faced with a moral dilemma.

gewịssermaßen *adv* as it were.

Gewịssheit *die (ohne pl)* certainty; **Gewissheit erlangen** to find out for certain; **etw mit Gewissheit sagen/wissen** to say/know sthg for certain.

Gewịtter (*pl* -) *das* thunderstorm.

gewịttrig *adj* thundery.

gewịtzt ◇ *adj* shrewd. ◇ *adv* shrewdly.

gewogen *pp* ▷ **wiegen**.

gewöhnen *vt*: **jn an jn/etw gewöhnen** to accustom sb to sb/sthg. ◆ **sich gewöhnen** *ref*: **sich an jn/etw gewöhnen** to get used to sb/sthg; **sich daran gewöhnen, etw zu tun** to get used to doing sthg.

Gewohnheit (*pl* **-en**) *die* habit; **jm zur Gewohnheit werden** to become a habit with sb.

gewöhnlich ◇ *adj* - **1.** [normal] normal, ordinary - **2.** [gewohnt] usual - **3.** *abw* [primitiv] common. ◇ *adv* - **1.** [normalerweise] normally, usually - **2.** *abw* [primitiv] in a common way. ◆ **wie gewöhnlich** *adv* as usual.

gewohnt *adj* usual; **etw gewohnt sein** to be used to sthg.

gewöhnt *adj*: **an etw** *(A)* **gewöhnt sein** to be used to sthg.

Gewö̩lbe (*pl* -) *das* vault.

gewọnnen *pp* ▷ **gewinnen**.

gewọrben *pp* ▷ **werben**.

gewọrden *pp* ▷ **werden**.

gewọrfen *pp* ▷ **werfen**.

Gewühl *das* - **1.** [Menschenmenge] crush - **2.** [Wühlen] rummaging.

gewụnden ◇ *pp* ▷ **winden**. ◇ *adj* - **1.** [Weg] winding - **2.** [Sätze] tortuous.

Gewü̩rz (*pl* **-e**) *das* spice.

Gewü̩rz|gurke *die* pickled gherkin.

gewụsst *pp* ▷ **wissen**.

Gezeiten *Pl* tides.

Gezeter *das abw* scolding.

gezielt ◇ *adj* specific; **eine gezielte Frage/Antwort** a specific question/answer. ◇ *adv*: **gezielt vorgehen** to take specific action; **jn gezielt auf etw ansprechen** to ask sb specifically about sthg.

geziert *abw* ◇ *adj* affected. ◇ *adv* affectedly.

gezọgen *pp* ▷ **ziehen**.

gezwụngen ◇ *pp* ▷ **zwingen**. ◇ *adj* forced. ◇ *adv* in a forced way.

gezwungenermaßen *adv*: **etw gezwungenermaßen machen** to be forced to do sthg.

ggf. *abk für* **gegebenenfalls**.

Ghẹtto *das* = **Getto**.

gịbt *präs* ▷ **geben**.

Gịcht *die* gout.

Giebel (*pl* -) *der* - **1.** [auf Dach] gable - **2.** [über Tor] pediment.

Gier *die* greed; **Gier nach etw** craving for sthg.

gierig ◇ *adj* greedy; **gierig nach** ODER **auf etw** *(A)* **sein** to have a craving for sthg. ◇ *adv* greedily.

gießen (*prät* **gọss**, *perf* **hat gegọssen**) ◇ *vt* - **1.** [schütten] to pour - **2.** [verschütten] to spill - **3.** [Blumen] to water - **4.** [Glocke, Blei] to cast; [Kerzen] to mould. ◇ *vi* [regnen]: **es gießt** it's pouring.

Gịft (*pl* **-e**) *das* [schädliche Substanz] poison.

gịftgrün *adj* lurid green.

gịftig ◇ *adj* - **1.** [Gift enthaltend, gesundheitsschädlich] poisonous - **2.** *fam abw* [gehässig] venomous - **3.** [grell] lurid. ◇ *adv fam abw* [gehässig] venomously.

Gịft|müll *der* toxic waste.

Gigạnt, in (*mpl* **-en**, *fpl* **-nen**) *der, die* giant.

gịlt *präs* ▷ **gelten**.

Gin [dʒɪn] *der* gin.

gịng *prät* ▷ **gehen**.

Ginster (*pl* -) *der* broom *(U)*; [Stechginster] gorse *(U)*.

Gipfel (*pl* -) *der* - **1.** [von Bergen] summit, peak - **2.** [Höhepunkt] height - **3.** [Gipfeltreffen] summit.

Gipfel|treffen *das* summit meeting.

Gips *der* - **1.** [Material] plaster - **2.** [Gipsverband] plaster cast.

Gips|bein *das*: **ein Gipsbein haben** to have a leg in plaster.

Gips|verband *der* plaster cast.

Giraffe (*pl* **-n**) *die* giraffe.

Girlande (*pl* **-n**) *die* garland.

Giro|konto ['ʒiːro|kɔnto] *das* current account *UK*, checking account *US*.

Gischt *die ODER der* spray.

Gitarre (*pl* **-n**) *die* guitar.

Gitarrist, in (*mpl* **-en**, *fpl* **-nen**) *der, die* guitarist.

Gitter (*pl* -) *das* [aus Eisen] bars *Pl*; [gekreuzt] grille; [aus Holz] trellis; [Geländer] railings *Pl*. ◆ **hinter Gittern** *adv fam* behind bars.

Glanz *der* - **1.** [von Stern] brightness - **2.** [von Perl] gleam - **3.** [von Augen] sparkle.

glänzen *vi* - **1.** [gen] to shine, to gleam; [Augen, Edelsteine] to sparkle; [Farbe] to be shiny - **2.** [herausragen] to shine.

glänzend ◇ *adj* - **1.** [mit Glanz] shiny; [Lack] gloss - **2.** [sehr gut] brilliant. ◇ *adv* [sehr gut] brilliantly.

Glas (*pl* **Gläser**) *das* - **1.** [Material, Trinkglas] glass; **eine Kanne aus Glas** a glass pot; **ein Glas Saft** a glass of juice; **ein Glas über den Durst trinken** *fig* to have one too many - **2.** [für Marmelade] jar - **3.** [Brillenglas] lens.

Glaser, in (*mpl* -, *fpl* **-nen**) *der, die* glazier.

glasig *adj* - **1.** [Blick, Ausdruck] glazed - **2.** [beim Braten] transparent.

glasklar *adj* crystal clear.

Glas|scheibe *die* pane (of glass).

Glasur (*pl* **-en**) *die* - **1.** [für Keramik] glaze - **2.** [für Speisen] icing *UK*, frosting *US*.

glatt ◇ *adj* - **1.** [Oberfläche] smooth; **glatte Haare** straight hair - **2.** [rutschig] slippery - **3.** [reibungslos] smooth - **4.** *fam* [eindeutig]: **eine glatte Lüge** a downright lie; **eine glatte Ablehnung** a flat refusal; **das ist glatter Wahnsinn!** that's utter madness! ◇ *adv* - **1.**: **etw glatt streichen** to smooth sthg - **2.** [verlaufen] smoothly - **3.** *fam* [eindeutig]: **das haute ihn glatt um** that completely floored him.

Glätte *die* - **1.** [Ebenheit] smoothness - **2.** [Schlüpfrigkeit] slipperiness.

Glatteis *das (ohne pl)* black ice.

glätten *vt* [Decke] to smooth; [Falte] to smooth out. ◆ **sich glätten** *ref* [Meer] to become calm.

Glatze (*pl* **-n**) *die* - **1.** [kahler Kopf] bald head; **eine Glatze haben** to be bald - **2.** [kahle Stelle] bald patch; **eine Glatze haben** to be going bald.

Glaube *der* - **1.** [Annahme] belief; **Glaube an etw** *(A)* belief in sthg; **in gutem** ODER **im guten Glauben** in good faith; **jm/einer Sache Glauben/keinen Glauben schenken** to/not to believe sb/sthg - **2.** [Religion] faith.

glauben ◇ *vt* - **1.** [denken] to think - **2.** [für richtig halten] to believe; **jm glauben** to believe sb; **ich glaube ihm nichts mehr** I don't believe anything he says any more. ◇ *vi* - **1.** [für wahr halten]: **an jn/etw glauben** to believe in sb/sthg; **jm glauben** to believe sb - **2.** [gläubig sein] to believe; **dran glauben müssen** [umkommen] to bite the dust.

Glaubens|bekenntnis *das (ohne pl)* RELIG creed.

glaubhaft ◇ *adj* credible. ◇ *adv* convincingly.

gläubig ◇ *adj* - **1.** [fromm] devout - **2.** [vertrauensselig] trusting. ◇ *adv* - **1.** [fromm] devoutly - **2.** [vertrauensselig] trustingly.

Gläubige (*pl* **-n**) *der, die* believer.

Gläubiger, in (*mpl* -, *fpl* **-nen**) *der, die* creditor.

glaubwürdig ◇ *adj* credible. ◇ *adv* convincingly.

gleich ◇ *adj* - **1.** [übereinstimmend] same; **den gleichen Namen haben** to have the same name; **zwei gleiche Tassen** two identical cups - **2.** [egal]: **das ist mir gleich** it's all the same to me. ◇ *adv* - **1.** [ebenso] equally; **gleich groß/alt sein** to be the same size/age - **2.** [auf gleiche Weise] the same; **die beiden Wörter werden gleich ausgesprochen** the two words are pronounced the same - **3.** [egal]: **das bleibt sich gleich, ob du nun...** it makes no difference whether you... - **4.** [zeitlich] straight away, immediately; **ich komme gleich** I'm just coming; **ich komme gleich wieder** I'll be right back; **bis gleich!** see you soon! - **5.** [räumlich] right; **gleich daneben** right next to it - **6.** [in Fragesätzen] again; **wie hieß er doch gleich?** what's his name again? - **7.** [ebensogut] just as well; **bei dem Reparaturpreis können wir doch gleich ein neues kaufen** if it's going to cost that much to repair it, we might as well buy a new one. ◇ *präp (+ D) geh* like.

gleichaltrig, gleichalterig *adj* of the same age; **gleichaltrig sein** to be the same age.

gleichberechtigt *adj* with equal rights; **gleichberechtigt sein** to have equal rights.

Gleichberechtigung *die (ohne pl)* equality, equal rights *Pl*.

gleichen (*prät* **glich**, *perf* **hat geglichen**) *vi*: **jm/einer Sache gleichen** to be like ODER resemble sb/sthg; **sich** *(D)* **gleichen** to resemble each other.

gleichfalls *adv* also, as well; **danke gleichfalls!** you too!

Gleichgewicht *das* - **1.** [Balance] balance; **im Gleichgewicht** balanced; **das Gleichgewicht halten/verlieren** to keep/lose one's balance - **2.** [Harmonie] equilibrium; **die Veränderungen brachten sie völlig aus dem Gleichgewicht** the changes threw her completely off balance.

gleichgültig <> *adj* - **1.** [desinteressiert] indifferent - **2.** [einerlei - Themen] trivial; **es ist gleichgültig, ob er kommt oder nicht** it's all the same whether he comes or not; **sie ist mir gleichgültig** she means nothing to me; **Politik ist ihm völlig gleichgültig** he's completely indifferent about politics. <> *adv* [desinteressiert] indifferently; **gleichgültig was er macht** no matter what he does.

Gleichheit *die* - **1.** [Übereinstimmung] similarity - **2.** [Gleichberechtigung] equality.

gleich|kommen (*perf* **ist gleichgekommen**) *vi (unreg)*: **jm an etw** *(D)* **gleichkommen** to match sb for sthg.

gleich lautend *adj* identical.

gleichmäßig <> *adj* - **1.** [Atmung, Schritte, Schichten] even - **2.** [Geschwindigkeit, Rhythmus] steady - **3.** [Abstände] regular. <> *adv* - **1.** [atmen, anordnen, verteilen] evenly - **2.** [sich vorwärts bewegen] steadily - **3.** [wiederkehrend]: **gleichmäßig hohe Punktzahlen** consistently high scores.

Gleichnis (*pl* **-se**) *das* parable.

gleichschenklig, gleichschenkelig ['glaiçʃɛŋk(ə)lɪç] *adj* MATH: **gleichschenkliges Dreieck** isosceles triangle.

Gleichschritt *der*: **im Gleichschritt** in step.

gleich|stellen ['glaiçʃtɛlən] *vt* to treat equally.

Gleichstrom *der* direct current.

Gleichung (*pl* **-en**) *die* equation.

gleichzeitig <> *adj* simultaneous. <> *adv* at the same time.

gleich|ziehen *vi (unreg)*: **mit jm gleichziehen** to draw level with sb, to catch up with sb.

Gleis (*pl* **-e**) *das* [Schienen] track; [Bahnsteig] platform.

gleiten (*prät* **glitt**, *perf* **hat/ist geglitten**) *vi* - **1.** *(ist)* [sich bewegen] to glide; [rutschen] to slip - **2.** *(hat) fam* [Arbeitnehmer] to work flexitime *UK* ODER flextime *US*.

Gleit|zeit *die* flexitime *UK*, flextime *US*.

Gletscher (*pl* -) *der* glacier.

glich *prät* ▷ **gleichen**.

Glied (*pl* **-er**) *das* - **1.** [Gelenk] joint - **2.** [Körperteil] limb - **3.** [Penis] (male) member - **4.** [Bindeglied - von Kette] link - **5.** [Einzelteil] part; [von Satz] clause.

gliedern *vt* to organize, to structure. ◆ **sich gliedern** *ref*: **sich in etw** *(A)* **gliedern** to be divided into sthg.

Gliederung (*pl* **-en**) *die* - **1.** [Gliedern] organization, structuring - **2.** [Struktur] structure.

Gliedmaßen *Pl* limbs.

glimmen (*prät* **glimmte** ODER **glomm**, *perf* **hat geglimmt** ODER **geglommen**) *vi* to glow.

glimpflich <> *adj* [ohne Schaden]: **die Entführung nahm ein glimpfliches Ende** the kidnapping was resolved without anyone being seriously hurt. <> *adv* [ohne Schaden]: **glimpflich davonkommen** to get off lightly.

glitschig *adj* slippery.

glitt *prät* ▷ **gleiten**.

glitzern *vi* [Sterne] to twinkle; [Schmuck, Augen] to sparkle; [Schnee, Tränen] to glisten; [Silber, Gold] to glitter.

global <> *adj* - **1.** [weltumfassend] global; [Frieden] world *(vor Subst)* - **2.** [vielseitig, allgemein] general. <> *adv* - **1.** [weltumfassend] globally - **2.** [vielseitig, allgemein] generally.

Globalisierung *die* globalization.

Globus (*pl* **-se** ODER **Globen**) *der* globe.

Glocke (*pl* **-n**) *die* bell.

Glocken|spiel *das* - **1.** [von Türmen] carillon - **2.** [Musikinstrument] glockenspiel.

Glocken|turm *der* belfry, bell tower.

glomm *prät* ▷ **glimmen**.

glorreich <> *adj* [Sieg, Geschichte, Ergebnis] glorious; [Einfall] brilliant. <> *adv* triumphantly.

Glossar (*pl* **-e**) *das* glossary.

glotzen *vi fam abw* to gawk, to gawp *UK*.

Glück *das* - **1.** [Glücksfall] luck; **ein Glück, dass...** it's lucky that...; **Glück bringen** to bring luck, to be lucky; **Glück haben** to be lucky; **bei jm (mit etw** *(D)***) kein Glück haben** to have no joy with sb (sthg); **er hatte mit dem Auto kein Glück** he had no luck with the car - **2.** [Fortuna] fortune; **das Glück verließ ihn** *geh* fortune ODER luck abandoned him - **3.** [Segen] happiness; **das Kind war ihr ganzes Glück** the child meant everything to her. ◆ **auf gut Glück** *adv* on the off chance. ◆ **viel Glück** *interj* good luck! ◆ **zum Glück** *adv* luckily, fortunately.

glücken (*perf* **ist geglückt**) *vi* to be successful; **ihm glückt alles, was er in Angriff nimmt** he succeeds at everything he does.

gluckern *vi* [Wasser, Flüssigkeit] to gurgle; [Wein] to glug.

glücklich <> *adj* - **1.** [Person, Ehe, Ende] happy - **2.** [Zufall] happy, lucky; [Zeitpunkt, Reise] good - **3.** [Sieger, Sieg] lucky. <> *adv* - **1.** [verheiratet, enden] happily - **2.** [letztendlich] eventually.

glücklicherweise *adv* luckily, fortunately.

Glücksbringer (*pl* -) *der* [Sache] lucky charm; [Person] lucky mascot.

Glücks|fall *der* stroke of luck.

Glücks|spiel *das* - **1.** [um Geld] game of chance - **2.** [Glückssache] lottery.

Glücks|strähne *die* lucky streak.

Glück|wunsch *der* congratulations *Pl*; **jm seine Glückwünsche aussprechen** to congratulate sb, to offer sb one's congratulations; **herzlichen Glückwunsch zum Geburtstag!** happy birthday!; **herzliche Glückwünsche!** congratulations!

Glucose = **Glukose**.

Glüh|birne *die* light bulb.

glühen *vi* - **1.** [brennen] to glow - **2.** *geh* [bewegt sein] to burn.

glühend <> *adj* - **1.** [brennend] glowing; [Metall, Nadel] red-hot; [Hitze] scorching - **2.** [leidenschaftlich] passionate; [Neid] deep. <> *adv* [leidenschaftlich] passionately.

Glüh|wein *der* mulled wine.

Glukose, Glucose *die* glucose.

Glut (*pl* **-en**) *die* - **1.** [in Feuer] embers *Pl* - **2.** *geh* [Inbrunst] ardour.

GmbH [ge:ɛmbe:'ha:] (*pl* **-s**) (*abk für* **Gesellschaft mit beschränkter Haftung**) *die* ≃ Ltd *UK*, ≃ Inc *US*.

Gnade *die* - **1.** [Gunst] favour - **2.** [Erbarmen - menschlich] mercy; [- göttlich] grace.

gnadenlos <> *adj* merciless; [Hitze, Druck, Stress] unrelenting. <> *adv* mercilessly; [heiß] mercilessly, unrelentingly.

gnädig <> *adj* - **1.** [wohlmeinend] kind - **2.** [nachsichtig] lenient - **3.** [barmherzig] merciful. <> *adv* - **1.** [wohlmeinend] kindly - **2.** [nachsichtig] leniently. ◆ **gnädige Frau** *interj* Madam!

Gold *das* gold; **eine Uhr aus Gold** a gold watch.

Gold|barren *der* gold bar ODER ingot.

golden <> *adj* - **1.** [aus Gold] gold - **2.** [goldfarben] golden - **3.** [großartig - Jahre, Zeit] golden; [- Freiheit, Moment] glorious. <> *adv* [glänzen] like gold.

Gold|fisch *der* goldfish.

goldgelb *adj* & *adv* golden yellow.

Gold|medaille *die* gold medal.

Gold|schmied, in *der, die* goldsmith.

Golf (*pl* **-e**) <> *der* gulf. <> *das* golf.

Golf|platz *der* golf course.

Golf|strom *der* Gulf Stream.

gönnen *vt*: **jm etw gönnen** not to begrudge sb sthg; **sich** *(D)* **etw gönnen** to allow o.s. sthg.

Gönner (*pl* -) *der* patron.

gönnerhaft *abw* <> *adj* patronizing. <> *adv* patronizingly.

Gönnerin (*pl* **-nen**) *die* patron, patroness.

Gorilla (*pl* **-s**) *der eigtl* & *fig* gorilla.

goss *prät* ▷ **gießen**.

Gosse (*pl* **-n**) *die* gutter.

Gotik *die (ohne pl)* [Stil] Gothic (style); [Epoche] Gothic period.

gotisch *adj* Gothic.

Gott (*pl* **Götter**) *der* - **1.** [christlich] God; **um Gottes Willen!** [Schrecken ausdrückend] oh my God!; [flehend] for heaven's sake! - **2.** [Gottheit] god. ◆ **Gott sei Dank** *adv* thank goodness. ◆ **grüß Gott** *interj Süddt & Österr* hello!

Gottes|dienst *der* service; **zum Gottesdienst gehen** to go to church.

Göttin (*pl* **-nen**) *die* goddess.

göttlich <> *adj eigtl* & *fig* divine. <> *adv* [wunderbar] divinely.

gottlos <> *adj* - **1.** [respektlos, gottvergessen] ungodly - **2.** [ungläubig] godless. <> *adv* [respektlos, gottvergessen] in an ungodly manner.

Gouverneur, in [guvɛr'nø:ɐ̯, rɪn] (*mpl* **-e**, *fpl* **-nen**) *der, die* governor.

GPS [ge:pe:'ɛs] (*abk für* **Grüne Partei der Schweiz**) *die Swiss Green Party*.

Grab (*pl* **Gräber**) *das* grave.

graben (*präs* **gräbt**, *prät* **grub**, *perf* **hat gegraben**) *vt* & *vi* to dig.

Graben (*pl* **Gräben**) *der* ditch; [um eine Festung] moat; [Schützengraben] trench.

Grab|stein *der* gravestone, tombstone.

gräbt *präs* ▷ **graben**.

Grabung (*pl* **-en**) *die* excavation.

Grad (*pl* **-e**) *der* - **1.** [gen] degree; **es hängt in hohem Grad davon ab, ob...** it depends to a large extent on whether...; **die Temperatur beträgt 25 Grad** the temperature is 25 degrees; **in hohem Grad verschmutzt** highly polluted - **2.** MIL rank.

gradweise *adv* gradually.

Graf (*pl* **-en**) *der* count.

Grafik (*pl* **-en**), **Graphik** (*pl* **-en**) *die* - **1.** [Kunst] graphic art; [Technik] graphics *(U)* - **2.** [Kunstwerk] graphic artwork - **3.** [Schema] diagram.

Gräfin (*pl* **-nen**) *die* countess.

grafisch, graphisch <> *adj* - **1.** [die Kunst betreffend] graphic - **2.** [schematisch] diagrammatic. <> *adv* - **1.** [künstlerisch] graphically - **2.** [schematisch] diagrammatically.

Grafschaft (*pl* **-en**) *die* - **1.** [von Graf] count's lands *Pl* - **2.** [Verwaltungsbezirk] county.

Gramm (*pl* **-e** ODER **-**) *das* gram; **500 Gramm** 500 grams.

Grammatik (*pl* **-en**) *die* grammar.

grammatikalisch, grammatisch <> *adj* grammatical. <> *adv* grammatically.

Granate (*pl* **-n**) *die* shell; [Handgranate] grenade.

grandios <> *adj* superb. <> *adv* superbly.

Granit *der* granite.

Grapefruit ['gre:pfru:t] (*pl* **-s**) *die* grapefruit.

Graphik = **Grafik**.

graphisch = **grafisch**.

Gras (*pl* Gräser) *das* grass; **wir sollten warten bis Gras über die Sache gewachsen ist** we should wait until the dust has settled.

grasen *vi* to graze; **Kühe grasen lassen** to graze cattle.

Gras|halm *der* blade of grass.

grassieren *vi* [Krankheit, Pest] to rage; [Mode] to be all the rage.

grässlich ◇ *adj* terrible. ◇ *adv* terribly.

Grat (*pl* -e) *der* ridge.

Gräte (*pl* -n) *die* (fish) bone.

gratis *adj* & *adv* free (of charge).

Grätsche (*pl* -n) *die*: **eine Grätsche über etw** *(A)* **machen** to hurdle sthg; **in der Grätsche stehen** to stand with one's legs astride.

gratulieren *vi* to offer one's congratulations; **jm (zu etw) gratulieren** to congratulate sb (on sthg); **jm zum Geburtstag gratulieren** to wish sb a happy birthday.

grau *adj* grey; **grau meliert** [Haar] greying; [Wolle, Stoff] flecked with grey.

Grau *das* - **1.** [graue Farbe] grey - **2.** [Tristheit] greyness.

Grau|brot *das bread made from mixed wholemeal, rye and wheat flour.*

Graubünden *nt* Graubünden.

grauhaarig *adj* grey-haired.

grausam ◇ *adj* - **1.** [brutal] cruel - **2.** [fürchterlich, schlimm] terrible. ◇ *adv* - **1.** [brutal] cruelly - **2.** [fürchterlich, äußerst] terribly.

Grausamkeit (*pl* -en) *die* - **1.** *(ohne pl)* [grausames Wesen] cruelty - **2.** [grausame Tat] atrocity.

grausig ◇ *adj* terrible. ◇ *adv* terribly.

Gravur [gra'vu:ɐ̯] (*pl* -en) *die* engraving.

Graz *nt* Graz.

Grazie (*pl* -n) *die* grace; **mit Grazie** gracefully.
◆ **Grazien** *Pl* [Mythologie] Graces.

graziös ◇ *adj* graceful. ◇ *adv* gracefully.

greifbar ◇ *adj* - **1.** [in Reichweite] to hand, handy - **2.** [parat] available - **3.** [absehbar] tangible. ◇ *adv* [sehr]: **greifbar nahe** within reach.

greifen (*prät* **griff**, *perf* **hat gegriffen**) ◇ *vt* - **1.** [fassen] to take hold of - **2.** [erwischen] to catch - **3.** [Akkord] to play. ◇ *vi* - **1.** [fassen]: **zur Flasche/Zigarette greifen** *fig* to reach for the bottle/cigarettes; **nach etw greifen** to reach for sthg; [Macht] to strive for sthg - **2.** [langen] to reach; **in etw** *(A)* **greifen** to reach into sthg - **3.** [Halt finden] to grip; [Zahnrad] to catch - **4.** [funktionieren] to work; **um sich greifen** to spread; **die Zahl ist zu hoch/niedrig gegriffen** the number is an overestimate/underestimate; **ihre Erwartungen sind zu hoch/niedrig gegriffen** she has set her sights too high/low.

Greif|vogel *der* bird of prey.

Greis, in (*mpl* -e, *fpl* -nen) *der, die* old man (old woman *die*).

grell ◇ *adj* - **1.** [Licht, Sonne, Lampe] glaring; [Farbe, Muster] garish - **2.** [Geräusch] shrill. ◇ *adv* - **1.** [scheinen, leuchten] glaringly; [bunt, gefärbt] garishly - **2.** [klingen, rufen] shrilly.

Grenz|bereich *der* - **1.** *(ohne pl)* [von Ländern] border area - **2.** [Begrenzung] limits *Pl*.

Grenze (*pl* -n) *die* - **1.** [Staatsgrenze] border - **2.** [Gebietsgrenze] boundary - **3.** [Trennlinie] dividing line, boundary - **4.** [Beschränkung] limit.
◆ **grüne Grenze** *die*: **über die grüne Grenze gehen** *to cross the border at a point in the countryside where there is no border control.*

grenzen *vi*: **an etw** *(A)* **grenzen** [Gebiet, Land] to border sthg; [Betrug, Tollkühnheit] to border ODER verge on sthg; **aneinander grenzen** to have a common border.

grenzenlos ◇ *adj* [Landschaft, Vertrauen, Liebe] boundless; [Verlegenheit, Sorge, Ekel] extreme. ◇ *adv* [weit, lieben, begeistert] boundlessly; [verlegen, erstaunt, traurig] extremely.

Grenz|fall *der* borderline case.

Grenz|kontrolle *die* border check.

Grenz|posten *der* border guard.

Grenz|schutz *der (ohne pl)* border police; [in Deutschland] ▷ **Bundesgrenzschutz**.

Grenzüber|gang *der* [Grenzkontrollstelle] border crossing.

grenzüberschreitend ◇ *adj* cross-border. ◇ *adv* at a cross-border level.

Grenzverkehr *der* cross-border traffic.

Grenz|wert *der* limit.

Grieche (*pl* -n) *der* Greek.

Griechenland *nt* Greece.

Griechin (*pl* -nen) *die* Greek.

griechisch *adj* Greek.

griesgrämig ◇ *adj* grumpy. ◇ *adv* grumpily.

Grieß *der* semolina.

griff *prät* ▷ **greifen**.

Griff (*pl* -e) *der* - **1.** [Greifen] grip; [von Ringer] hold; **beim Griff in die Tasche** on reaching into the pocket; **der Griff nach der Flasche** reaching for the bottle; **etw mit einem Griff tun** to do sthg in next to no time; **etw im Griff haben/bekommen** *fig* to be/get on top of sthg; **jn in den Griff bekommen** ODER **kriegen** *fig* to gain control of sb - **2.** [Teil, Henkel] handle.

griffbereit *adj* & *adv* ready to hand.

griffig *adj* - **1.** [handlich] easy to use - **2.** [gut greifend] with a good grip.

Grill (*pl* -s) *der* grill.

Grille (*pl* -n) *die* - **1.** [Insekt] cricket - **2.** [verrückte Idee] whim.

grillen ◇ *vt* to grill. ◇ *vi* to have a barbecue.

Grimasse (*pl* -n) *die* grimace.

grịmmig ◇ *adj* - **1.** [Gesicht, Ausdruck] grim; [Feind] fierce - **2.** [Kälte, Hunger] terrible. ◇ *adv* [lachen] grimly.

grịnsen *vi* to grin.

Grịppe (*pl* **-n**) *die* flu.

Grịps *der (ohne pl) fam* brains *Pl*.

grob (*kompar* **gröber**, *superl* **gröbste**) ◇ *adj* - **1.** [Sand, Salz, Züge] coarse - **2.** [Leinen, Haut, Papier, Übersicht, Skizze] rough - **3.** [unhöflich] crude - **4.** [schlimm] serious; **aus dem Gröbsten heraus sein** [Kind] to be old enough to look after oneself. ◇ *adv* - **1.** [mahlen, hacken] coarsely - **2.** [planen, schätzen] roughly - **3.** [schwer wiegend]: **grob fahrlässig handeln** to be grossly negligent - **4.** [unhöflich] crudely.

Grobheit (*pl* **-en**) *die* - **1.** [grobe Wesensart] crudeness - **2.** [Äußerung] crude remark.

grölen *abw vi* & *vt* to bawl.

Grönland *nt* Greenland.

Grọschen (*pl* **-**) *der* - **1.** [10 deutsche Pfennig] ten-pfennig coin; **bei ihm ist der Groschen gefallen** *fam fig* the penny dropped *UK*, he got it - **2.** [österreichische Münze] groschen.

groß (*kompar* **größer**, *superl* **größte**) ◇ *adj* - **1.** [räumlich] big, large; [Person] tall; **sie ist 1,80 groß** she's 1.80 m (tall) - **2.** [Angebot] wide; **eine große Vielfalt** a wide variety - **3.** [intensiv] great; **eine große Enttäuschung** a great disappointment; **sich große Mühe geben** to try hard - **4.** [älter] big; **mein großer Bruder** my big brother - **5.** [erwachsen] grown-up - **6.** [Buchstabe] capital - **7.** [bedeutend] great; **ein großer Dichter** a great poet; **heute kommt meine große Stunde** it's my big moment today. ◇ *adv (kompar größer; superl am größten)* - **1.** [räumlich]: **ein groß angelegtes Projekt** a large-scale project - **2.** [sehr] a lot; **wir haben dann nicht mehr groß gearbeitet** we didn't do a lot of work afterwards; **groß und breit** *fam* at great length - **3.** [im großen Stil] in style; **der Sänger ist groß herausgekommen** the singer became a big success - **4.** [erstaunt]: **jn groß ansehen** to stare at sb wide-eyed - **5.** [Buchstabe]: **es wird groß geschrieben** it's written with a capital letter. ◆ **Groß und Klein** *pron*: **ein Buch für Groß und Klein** a book for young and old. ◆ **im Großen und Ganzen** *pron*: **im Großen und Ganzen** on the whole, by and large.

großartig ◇ *adj* - **1.** [gut] marvellous - **2.** [angeberisch] showy. ◇ *adv* - **1.** [gut] marvellously - **2.** [angeberisch] showily.

Groß|aufnahme *die* close-up.

Großbritạnnien *nt* Great Britain.

Groß|buchstabe *der* capital (letter).

Größe (*pl* **-n**) *die* - **1.** [von Gegenständen, Baby, Kleidern] size - **2.** [von Personen] height - **3.** [Wichtigkeit] greatness - **4.** [Person] leading figure.

großenteils *adv* largely.

Größenwahn *der abw* megalomania.

größenwahnsinnig *adj* megalomaniac.

größer *adj* bigger, larger; **eine größere Summe** quite a large sum; **ohne größere Schwierigkeiten** without any great difficulty.

Groß|familie *die* extended family.

Groß|handel *der* wholesale trade; **etw im Großhandel beziehen** to get sthg wholesale.

Groß|händler, in *der, die* wholesaler.

Groß|macht *die* great power.

Groß|maul *das fam abw* big mouth.

großmütig ◇ *adj* generous. ◇ *adv* generously.

Groß|mutter *die* grandmother.

Großraum (*pl* **-räume**) *der* area; **im Großraum Berlin** in the Greater Berlin area.

Groß|rechner *der* EDV mainframe.

groß|schreiben *vt (unreg)* [mit großem Anfangsbuchstaben] to write with a capital letter, to capitalize.

Großschreibung *die* capitalization.

großspurig *abw* ◇ *adj* pretentious. ◇ *adv* pretentiously.

Groß|stadt *die* city *(vor Subst)*.

größtenteils *adv* for the most part.

größtmöglich *adj* greatest possible.

groß|tun *vi (unreg) abw* to boast.

Groß|vater *der* grandfather.

Groß|verdiener, in (*mpl* **Großverdiener**, *fpl* **-nen**) *der, die* high earner.

groß|ziehen *vt (unreg)* [Kind] to bring up; [Tier] to rear.

großzügig ◇ *adj* - **1.** [Person, Geste] generous - **2.** [Raum] spacious. ◇ *adv* - **1.** [freigebig, großmütig] generously - **2.** [weiträumig] spaciously.

Grọtte (*pl* **-n**) *die* grotto.

grub *prät* ▷ **graben**.

Grübchen (*pl* **-**) *das* dimple.

Grube (*pl* **-n**) *die* pit.

grübeln *vi* to ponder.

Grübeln *das*: **ins Grübeln kommen** to start to ponder.

Grụft (*pl* **Grụ̈fte**) *die* crypt.

grün ◇ *adj* [farbig, unreif, ökologisch] green. ◇ *adv* [ökologisch]: **grün wählen** to vote Green.

Grün (*pl* **-** ODER **-s**) *das* - **1.** green - **2.** *(ohne pl)* [Pflanzen] greenery. ◆ **bei Grün** *adv* on green.

Grün|anlage *die* park.

Grụnd (*pl* **Grụ̈nde**) *der* - **1.** [Ursache] reason - **2.** *(ohne pl)* [Boden] ground; [von Meer, Bach, Glas] bottom; **auf Grund laufen** to run aground; **einer Sache** *(D)* **auf den Grund gehen** to try to get to the bottom of sthg; **jn in Grund und Boden reden** not to let sb get a word in edgeways. ◆ **im Grunde** *adv* basically. ◆ **von Grund auf** *adv* thoroughly. ◆ **zu Grunde** *adv* = **zugrunde**.

Grụnd|ausstattung *die* basic equipment.

Grụnd|bedürfnis *das* basic need.

Grụnd|begriff *der* basic principle.

Grụnd|besitz *der* land.

grụ̈nden ◇ *vt* [Partei, Unternehmen] to found; [Familie] to start; [Stiftung] to set up. ◇ *vi* [basieren auf]: **auf etw** *(D)* **gründen** to be based on sthg. ◆ **sich gründen** *ref*: **sich auf etw** *(A)* **gründen** to be based on sthg.

Grụ̈nder, in (*mpl* -, *fpl* **-nen**) *der, die* founder.

Grụnd|gebühr *die* standing charge.

Grụnd|gedanke *der* basic idea.

Grụnd|gesetz *das* Basic Law.

Grụnd|kurs *der* basic course.

Grụnd|lage *die* basis.

grụndlegend ◇ *adj* fundamental. ◇ *adv* fundamentally.

grụ̈ndlich ◇ *adj* thorough. ◇ *adv* thoroughly; **sich gründlich blamieren** to make a complete fool of o.s.

Grụnd|lohn *der* basic wage.

grụndlos ◇ *adj* unfounded. ◇ *adv* without reason; **grundlos lachen** to laugh for no reason.

Grụndnahrungs|mittel *das* basic foodstuff.

Gründọnnerstag *der* Maundy Thursday.

Grụnd|recht *das* basic right.

Grụndriss (*pl* **-se**) *der* [von Gebäude] ground plan; [Schema] outline.

Grụnd|satz *der* principle.

grụndsätzlich ◇ *adj* - **1.** [wichtig] fundamental - **2.** [allgemein] basic - **3.** [bedingungslos] on principle. ◇ *adv* - **1.** [allgemein] basically - **2.** [bedingungslos] on principle - **3.** [grundlegend] fundamentally; **sich grundsätzlich äußern** to state one's principles.

Grụnd|schule *die* primary school *UK*, elementary school *US (for pupils aged 6 to 10)*.

Grụnd|stück *das* plot of land.

Grụ̈ndung (*pl* **-en**) *die* [von Partei, Verein] foundation *(sg)*; [von Familie] starting *(U)*; [von Stiftung] setting up *(U)*.

grụndverschieden *adj* completely different.

Grụnd|wasser *das* ground water.

Grụ̈ne (*pl* **-n**) *das* - **1.** [Farbe] green - **2.** [Natur]: **im Grünen/ins Grüne** in/into the country.

Grụ̈nen *Pl*: **die Grünen** the Greens.

Grụ̈ne Pụnkt *der (ohne pl) symbol on product packaging indicating that it is suitable for recycling*.

Grụ̈n|fläche *die* green area.

Grụ̈n|kohl *der* kale.

grụ̈nlich ◇ *adj* greenish. ◇ *adv* with a greenish colour.

grụnzen *vi* to grunt.

Grụppe (*pl* **-n**) *die* group.

Grụppen|arbeit *die* [im Unterricht] group work.

Grụppen|reise *die* group tour.

gruppieren *vt* to arrange. ◆ **sich gruppieren** *ref* to form a group/groups.

gruselig *adj* [von Film] spine-chilling; [von Erscheinung] eerie.

gruseln *vt*: **es gruselt jm** ODER **jn vor jm/etw** sb/sthg makes sb's flesh creep. ◆ **sich gruseln** *ref* to be frightened; **sich vor jm/etw gruseln** sb/sthg makes one's flesh creep.

Gruß (*pl* **Grüße**) *der* greeting; **jm Grüße von jm bestellen** ODER **ausrichten** to give sb sb's regards ODER best wishes; **herzliche Grüße!** greetings!; **viele Grüße!** best wishes!; **mit freundlichen Grüßen** yours sincerely.

grüßen ◇ *vt* - **1.** [begrüßen] to greet - **2.** [Gruß senden]: **jn von jm grüßen** to give sb sb's regards ODER best wishes. ◇ *vi* [begrüßen] to say hello. ◆ **grüß dich** *interj* hello! ◆ **grüß Gott** *interj Süddt* hello!

Grụ̈tze (*pl* **-n**) *die* gruel; **rote Grütze** *jelly-like dessert made of red berries, fruit juice and sugar*.

gụcken *fam* ◇ *vi* to look. ◇ *vt* [Fotos, Zeitschriften] to look at; [Fernsehen] to watch.

Guillotine [gijo'tiːnə] (*pl* **-n**) *die* guillotine.

Gụlasch (*pl* **-e** ODER **-s**) *das* & *der* goulash.

Gụlasch|kanone *die large tureen used to serve hot food at outdoor public events*.

Gụlden (*pl* -) *der* guilder.

Gụlly (*pl* **-s**) *der* drain.

gụ̈ltig *adj* valid; **nicht mehr gültig sein** [Kreditkarte, Reisepass] to be no longer valid.

Gụ̈ltigkeit *die* validity; **seine Gültigkeit verlieren** [Kreditkarte, Reisepass] to become invalid.

Gụmmi (*pl* **-s**) ◇ *das* & *der* - **1.** [Material] rubber - **2.** *fam* [Band] rubber band. ◇ *der* rubber.

Gụmmi|band (*pl* **-bänder**) *das* (piece of) elastic.

Gụmmi|knüppel *der* rubber truncheon.

Gụmmi|stiefel *der* rubber boot, wellington *UK*.

Gụnst *die* favour; **die Gunst der Stunde nutzen** to seize the moment; *siehe auch* **zugunsten**.

gụ̈nstig ◇ *adj* - **1.** [Gelegenheit, Umstände] favourable - **2.** [Preis] good. ◇ *adv* - **1.** [beeinflussen] favourably - **2.** [kaufen] for a good price.

Gụrgel (*pl* **-n**) *die* throat.

gụrgeln *vi* to gurgle; [mit Mundwasser] to gargle.

Gurke (*pl* **-n**) *die* - **1.** [Salatgurke] cucumber - **2.** [Gewürzgurke] gherkin.

Gurt (*pl* **-e**) *der* - **1.** [Sicherheitsgurt] belt - **2.** [Band] strap.

Gürtel (*pl* -) *der* belt.

Gürtel|linie *die*: **unter der Gürtellinie** [unfair] below the belt; [anzüglich] near the bone.

Gurtpflicht *die* obligatory use of seat belts.

Guss (*pl* **Güsse**) *der* - **1.** [Gießen] casting *(U)* - **2.** [Wasserstrahl] stream - **3.** [Regen] downpour - **4.** [Zuckerguss] icing *(U) UK*, frosting *(U) US*.

Gusseisen *das* cast iron.

gut (*kompar* **besser**, *superl* **beste**) <> *adj* [gen] good; **in etw gut sein** [fähig] to be good at sthg; **für etw gut sein** [günstig] to be good for sthg; **das Mittel ist gut gegen Magendrücken** this medicine is good for stomach ache; **du hast es gut!** you've got it easy!; **etw gut sein lassen** *fig* to leave ODER drop sthg. <> *adv (kompar besser; superl am besten)* - **1.** [gen] well; **gut kochen können** to be able to cook well, to be a good cook; **gut befreundet sein mit jm** to be good friends with sb - **2.** [schön, erfreulich]: **gut schmecken/aussehen** to taste/look good; **gut gelaunt sein** to be in a good mood; **ihr ist nicht gut** she's not well - **3.** [leicht] easily; **du hast gut reden!** it's easy for you to talk!; **so gut wie** as good as.

Gut (*pl* **Güter**) *das* - **1.** [Bauernhof] estate - **2.** [Ware] goods *Pl*.

Gutachten (*pl* -) *das* report.

Gutachter, **in** (*mpl* -, *fpl* **-nen**) *der, die* expert.

gutartig *adj* - **1.** [Hund, Charakter] good-natured - **2.** [Geschwulst, Tumor] benign.

gutbürgerlich *adj*: **gutbürgerliche Küche** traditional cooking.

Gute *das* good. ◆ **alles Gute** *interj* all the best! ◆ **im Guten** *adv* [versuchen] amicably; [sagen] nicely.

Güte *die* - **1.** [Milde] goodness; **(ach) du meine** ODER **liebe Güte!** (oh) my goodness! - **2.** [Qualität] quality.

Güte|klasse *die* grade.

Güter|bahnhof *der* freight depot.

Güter|verkehr *der* freight traffic.

Güter|zug *der* freight train.

Güte|zeichen *das* quality mark.

gut gehen (*perf* **ist gut gegangen**) *vi (unreg)* - **1.** [gesundheitlich]: **es geht ihr gut** she is doing well - **2.** [glücken] to turn out well - **3.** [Geschäft] to do well - **4.** [Ware] to go well.

gut gelaunt *adj* cheerful.

gut gemeint *adj* well-meant.

gutgläubig *adj* trusting.

Guthaben (*pl* -) *das* (credit) balance.

gütig <> *adj* kind. <> *adv* kindly.

gütlich *adj* amicable.

gutmütig *adj* good-natured.

Gutmütigkeit *die (ohne pl)* good nature.

Gut|schein *der* voucher.

gut|schreiben *vt (unreg)*: **jm etw gutschreiben** to credit sthg to sb.

Gut|schrift *die* - **1.** [Handlung] crediting - **2.** [Quittung] credit slip.

gut tun *vi (unreg)*: **ein heißes Bad wird dir gut tun** a hot bath will do you good.

gutwillig *adj* willing.

Gymnasial|lehrer, **in** *der, die* ≃ grammar-school teacher *UK*.

Gymnasiast, **in** (*mpl* **-en**, *fpl* **-nen**) *der, die* ≃ grammar-school pupil *UK*.

Gymnasium (*pl* **Gymnasien**) *das* ≃ grammar school *UK*, *selective secondary school attended by 10- to 19-year-olds*; **altsprachliches/neusprachliches Gymnasium** *"Gymnasium" with focus on classical/modern languages.*

Gymnastik *die* keep-fit.

Gynäkologe (*pl* **-n**) *der* gynaecologist.

Gynäkologin (*pl* **-nen**) *die* gynaecologist.

h (*pl* - ODER **-s**), **H** (*pl* - ODER **-s**) [haː] *das* - **1.** [Buchstabe] h, H - **2.** MUS B. ◆ **h** (*abk für* **Stunde, Uhr**) h, hr.

ha[1] (*abk für* **Hektar**) ha.

ha[2] *interj* ha!

Haar (*pl* **-e**) *das*: **graues Haar** ODER **graue Haare haben** to have grey hair; **ein paar graue Haare haben** to have a few grey hairs; **sich** *(D)* **die Haare schneiden lassen** to have one's hair cut; **jm aufs Haar gleichen** to be the spitting image of sb; **etw aufs Haar gleichen** to be an exact copy of sthg; **der Hund hat ihm kein Haar gekrümmt** the dog didn't touch a hair on his head; **sich in die Haare kriegen** ODER **geraten** *fam* to start squabbling.

Haar|bürste *die* hairbrush.

haaren *vi* to moult.

Haaresbreite *die*: **um Haaresbreite** by a hair's breadth; **um Haaresbreite hätte es einen Unfall gegeben** there was very nearly an accident.

Haar|festiger *der* setting lotion.

haargenau <> *adj* exact. <> *adv* exactly.

haarig *adj* hairy.

haarklein *adv* in minute detail.

haarscharf <> *adj* precise; [Beobachtung] very close. <> *adv* - **1.** [knapp]: **das Auto fuhr**

haarscharf an ihr vorbei the car only just missed her - 2. [sehr genau] precisely; [beobachten] very closely.

Haar|schnitt *der* haircut.

Haar|spange *die* hairclip.

Haar|spray *das* & *der* hairspray.

haarsträubend *adj* - 1. [empörend] shocking - 2. [grauenhaft] horrifying.

Haarwasch|mittel *das* shampoo.

haben (*präs* **hat**, *prät* **hatte**, *perf* **hat gehabt**) <> *aux* to have; **sie hat gegessen** she has eaten. <> *vt* - 1. [besitzen] to have; **ich hätte gerne** [im Restaurant, Geschäft] I'd like; **er hat zwei kleine Schwestern** he's got ODER he has two younger sisters; **das Buch hat 600 Seiten** the book has (got) 600 pages; **sie hat blaue Augen** she has (got) blue eyes - 2. [zur Verfügung haben] to have; **hast du Geld dabei?** have you got any money on you?; **das Haus ist noch zu haben** the house is still available - 3. [erleben] to have; **Angst/Durst/Hunger haben** to be afraid/thirsty/hungry; **sie hatte es schwer im Leben** she's had a hard life - 4. [an etw leiden] to have; **Kopfschmerzen haben** to have a headache; **was hast du denn?** what's wrong? - 5. [mit Zeitangaben]: **wie spät haben wir (es)?** *fam* what's the time?; **wir haben (jetzt) zehn Uhr** *fam* it's ten o'clock; **wir haben heute Dienstag** *fam* it's Tuesday today; **und damit hat es sich!** and that's that!; **was hast du davon?** what do you get out of it?; **der hat sie wohl nicht mehr alle!** *fam* he's not all there!; **haben Sie etwas dagegen, wenn ...?** do ODER would you mind if ...?; **sie scheint was gegen dich zu haben** she seems to have something against you; **sie haben hier nichts zu suchen!** they've no business here; **ich habe zu tun** I'm busy. ◆ **sich haben** *ref fam* to make a fuss.

Habenichts (*pl* -e) *der abw* pauper.

Habseligkeiten *Pl* belongings.

habsüchtig *adj* greedy.

Hack|braten *der* meat loaf.

Hacke (*pl* -n) *die* - 1. [Ferse, Absatz] heel - 2. [Gartengerät] hoe.

hacken ['hakən] <> *vt* - 1. [zerkleinern] to chop - 2. [schlagen] to hack - 3. [bearbeiten] to hoe. <> *vi* [mit dem Schnabel]: **nach jm/etw hacken** to peck at sb/sthg.

Hackfleisch *das* mince *UK*, mincemeat *US*.

Hafen (*pl* **Häfen**) *der* [klein] harbour; [groß] port.

Hafen|arbeiter, in *der, die* docker, dock worker.

Hafen|stadt *die* port.

Hafer *der (ohne pl)* oats *Pl*.

Hafer|flocken *Pl* rolled oats.

Haft *die* [Gewahrsam] custody; [Strafe] imprisonment.

Haft|anstalt *die* prison.

haftbar *adj*: **für etw haftbar sein** to be liable for sthg.

Haft|befehl *der* warrant.

haften *vi* - 1. [kleben] to stick - 2. [bürgen]: **für jn haften** to be responsible for sb.

Häftling (*pl* -e) *der* prisoner.

Haftpflicht|versicherung *die* third party insurance.

Haft|strafe *die* prison sentence.

Haftung *die* [Verantwortung] liability; **Gesellschaft mit beschränkter Haftung** limited company.

Hagebutte (*pl* -n) *die* - 1. [Frucht] rose hip - 2. [Strauch] dog rose.

Hagel *der* hail.

Hagel|korn *das* hailstone.

hageln <> *vi*: **es hagelt** it is hailing. <> *vt*: **es hagelte Beschwerden** *fig* there was a stream of complaints.

Hahn (*pl* **Hähne**) *der* - 1. [Vogel] cock - 2. [an der Leitung] tap *UK*, faucet *US*.

Hähnchen (*pl* -) *das* - 1. [Brathähnchen] chicken - 2. [kleiner Hahn] cockerel.

Hai (*pl* -e) *der* shark.

Hai|fisch *der* shark.

häkeln *vt* & *vi* to crochet.

Häkel|nadel *die* crochet hook.

Haken (*pl* -) *der* - 1. [Aufhänger] hook - 2. [Zeichen] tick - 3. [Problem] catch, snag.

halb <> *adj (ohne Kompar)* half; **ein halber Liter** half a litre; **der halbe Tag** half the day; **halb und halb** *fam* half and half; **es ist halb drei** it is half past two; **keine halben Sachen machen** not to do things by halves; **halb Düsseldorf** half of Düsseldorf. <> *adv* half; **ihre Haare sind halb lang** she has shoulder-length hair.

Halb|bruder *der* half-brother.

Halbdunkel *das* semi-darkness.

Halbe (*pl* -n) *das* & *der* half litre; **ein Halbes** [Bier] a half litre.

Halb|finale *das* semi-final.

halbherzig <> *adj* half-hearted. <> *adv* half-heartedly.

halbieren *vt* - 1. [Kuchen, Apfel] to cut in half, to halve - 2. [Linie] to bisect - 3. [Geldsumme, Zahl] to halve. ◆ **sich halbieren** *ref* to halve.

Halb|insel *die* peninsula.

Halb|jahr *das* six months *Pl*; [Schule] ≃ term.

halbjährlich <> *adj* six-monthly, half yearly. <> *adv* every six months, twice a year.

Halb|kreis *der* semi-circle.

Halb|kugel *die* hemisphere.

halblaut <> *adj* low. <> *adv* in a low voice.

halbmast *adv*: **auf halbmast** at half-mast.

Halbmond *der* [Mondsichel] half-moon.

halb offen *adj* half-open.

Halbpension ['halppaŋzio:n] *die* half board.

Halb|schuh *der* shoe.

Halbtags|arbeit *die* part-time work.

Halbton (*pl* **-töne**) *der* MUS semitone.

halbtrocken *adj* medium-dry.

halb voll *adj* half-full.

Halb|wahrheit *die* half-truth.

Halb|waise *die child with only one living parent.*

halbwegs *adv* reasonably, fairly.

Halb|zeit *die* - **1.** [Hälfte] half - **2.** [Pause] half-time.

Halde (*pl* **-n**) *die* [Kohlenhalde] slag heap.

half *prät* ▷ **helfen**.

Hälfte (*pl* **-n**) *die* half; **die Hälfte der Angestellten** half (of) the employees. ◆ **zur Hälfte** *adv*: **zur Hälfte gefüllt** half-full; **etw zur Hälfte tun** to half-do sthg; **der Erlös ging zur Hälfte ans Rote Kreuz** half the proceeds went to the Red Cross.

Halfter (*pl* -) ◇ *das* & *der* [für Pferde] halter. ◇ *das* [für Pistole] holster.

Halle (*pl* **-n**) *die* [gen] hall; [von Hotel] lobby; [zum Reiten] arena; [zum Turnen] gym; [zum Tennisspielen] covered court.

hallen *vi* to resound, to ring out.

Hallen|bad *das* indoor swimming pool.

hallo *interj* hello.

Halm (*pl* **-e**) *der* [von Gras] blade; [von Getreide] stalk.

Halogen|lampe *die* halogen lamp.

Hals (*pl* **Hälse**) *der* - **1.** [Körperteil - außen] neck; [- innen] throat - **2.** [von Flasche, Instrument] neck; **aus vollem Hals** at the top of one's voice; **es hängt mir zum Hals heraus** *fam abw* I'm sick of it; **etw in den falschen Hals bekommen** *fam* to take sthg the wrong way; **Hals über Kopf** in a rush ODER hurry; **jm um den Hals fallen** to fling one's arms around sb's neck.

Halsaus|schnitt *der* neckline.

Hals|band (*pl* **-bänder**) *das* - **1.** [für Tiere] collar - **2.** [Samtband] choker.

halsbrecherisch ◇ *adj* [Geschwindigkeit] breakneck; [Fahrt] madcap. ◇ *adv* [fahren] at breakneck speed.

Hals|entzündung *die* sore throat.

Hals|kette *die* necklace.

Hals-Nasen-Ohren-|Arzt, Ärztin *der, die* ear, nose and throat specialist.

Halsschlag|ader *die* carotid artery.

Hals|schmerzen *Pl* sore throat *(sg)*; **Halsschmerzen haben** to have a sore throat.

Hals|tuch *das* scarf.

halt ◇ *interj* stop!; MIL halt!; **sag halt, wenn ich aufhören soll!** tell me when to stop. ◇ *adv Süddt, Österr & Schweiz* just, simply.

Halt (*pl* **-e** ODER **-s**) *der* - **1.** [Stütze] hold, grip; **die Leiter hat keinen Halt** the ladder is unstable; **den Halt verlieren** to lose one's hold - **2.** [Haltestelle] stop - **3.** [Stopp]: **Halt machen** to stop; **vor jm/etw nicht Halt machen** *fig* to spare no one/nothing.

haltbar *adj* - **1.** [konserviert]: **haltbar sein** to keep well - **2.** [strapazierfähig] hard-wearing, durable - **3.** [glaubhaft] tenable.

Haltbarkeit *die* [von Lebensmitteln] life; [von Material] durability.

Haltbarkeits|datum *das* best-before date.

halten (*präs* **hält**, *prät* **hielt**, *perf* **hat gehalten**) ◇ *vt* - **1.** [fest halten] to hold - **2.** [beibehalten] to keep; **die dicken Wände halten die Wärme** the thick walls keep the heat in; **Kontakt halten** to keep in touch - **3.** [binden] to keep - **4.** SPORT to save - **5.** [behalten] to hold on to - **6.** [Rede] to make; [Vortrag, Predigt] to give; [Plädoyer] to present - **7.** [einhalten - Versprechen] to keep - **8.** [Tier] to keep - **9.** [verteidigen] to hold - **10.** [ausführen, komponieren]: **die Wohnung ist ganz in Blau gehalten** the flat is decorated entirely in blue; **das Kleid ist sehr schlicht gehalten** the dress is very simple in style; **jeder, der etw auf sich hält** any self-respecting person; **jn/etw für jn/etw halten** to take sb/sthg to be sb/sthg; **ich habe ihn für klüger gehalten** I thought he was cleverer than that; **er war nicht zu halten** there was no holding him; **viel/wenig von jm/etw halten** to have a high/low opinion of sb/sthg; **was hältst du von ihr?** what do you think of her? ◇ *vi* - **1.** [anhalten, stoppen] to stop - **2.** [ganz bleiben - Gegenstand] to hold; [- Freundschaft] to last; **zu jm halten** to stand by sb. ◆ **sich halten** *ref* - **1.** [in einem Zustand - Lebensmittel] to keep; **für sein Alter hält er sich gut** he's keeping well for his age; **sich fit halten** to keep fit - **2.** [in einer Position] to stay, to remain - **3.** [an einem Ort - sich fest halten] to hold on; [- bleiben] to stay; **sich rechts/links halten** to keep (to the) right/left - **4.** [in einer Körperhaltung]: **sich gerade halten** to stand up straight - **5.** [bei einer Herausforderung] to hold one's own.

Halterung (*pl* **-en**) *die* holder.

Halte|stelle *die* stop.

Halteverbot *das* [Stelle] no waiting zone, clearway *UK*; **'hier herrscht Halteverbot'** 'this is a no waiting zone'.

haltlos ◇ *adj* [grundlos] unfounded. ◇ *adv* [unbeherrscht] uncontrollably.

halt|machen *vi* ▷ **Halt**.

Haltung (*pl* **-en**) *die* - **1.** [Körperhaltung] posture - **2.** [Meinung, Einstellung] attitude - **3.** [Beherrschung] composure; **Haltung bewahren/verlieren** to keep/lose one's composure - **4.** [von Tieren] keeping.

Halunke (*pl* **-n**) *der* - **1.** [Gauner] scoundrel - **2.** *hum* [Lausejunge] young rascal.

Hamburg *nt* Hamburg.

hämisch ◇ *adj* gloating; [Grinsen, Lachen] malicious. ◇ *adv* gloatingly; [grinsen, lachen] maliciously.

Hammel (*pl* -) *der* - **1.** [Tier] castrated ram - **2.** [Fleisch] mutton - **3.** *fam abw* [Schimpfwort] ass, twit *UK*.

Hammer (*pl* **Hämmer**) *der* [Werkzeug & SPORT] hammer.

hämmern ◇ *vi* - **1.** [mit Hammer, Faust] to hammer - **2.** [schlagen - Herz, Puls] to pound, to throb. ◇ *vt* - **1.** [mit Hammer] to hammer - **2.**: **auf dem Klavier hämmern** to pound away at the piano.

Hampelmann (*pl* **-männer**) *der* - **1.** [Spielzeug] jumping jack - **2.** *salopp abw* [Person] spineless person.

Hamster (*pl* -) *der* hamster.

hamstern *vt* to hoard.

Hand (*pl* **Hände**) *die* - **1.** [Körperteil] hand; **per Hand** manually; **Hände hoch!** hands up!; **jn an die Hand nehmen** to take sb by the hand; **etw in die Hand nehmen** [ergreifen] to take sthg in one's hand; [initiativ werden] to take sthg in hand - **2.** SPORT handball; **alle Hände voll zu tun haben** to have one's hands full; **eine Hand voll** a handful; **aus erster Hand** second-hand *(with one previous owner)*; **aus zweiter Hand** second-hand *(with two previous owners)*; **von der öffentlichen Hand bezahlt** paid for out of public funds; **etw aus der Hand geben** to give sthg up; **freie Hand haben** to have a free hand; **in festen Händen sein** to be spoken for; **in js Hand sein** to be at sb's mercy; **er ist die rechte Hand des Chefs** he's the boss's right-hand man; **linker/rechter Hand** on the left/right, on the left-hand/right-hand side; **unter der Hand** secretly. ◆ **an Hand** *präp* = **anhand**.

Hand|arbeit *die* - **1.** [Herstellung]: **in Handarbeit hergestellte Töpferwaren** handmade pottery - **2.** [Artikel] handmade article - **3.** [Textilien]: **Handarbeiten** needlework *(U)*; **eine Handarbeit** a piece of needlework - **4.** *fam* [Unterricht] needlework.

Hand|ball *der* handball.

Hand|bewegung *die* gesture.

handbreit ◇ *adj* about 10 cm, *distance of a hand's breadth*. ◇ *adv*: **handbreit offen stehen** to be ajar.

Hand|bremse *die* handbrake *UK*, parking brake *US*.

Hand|buch *das* [Lehrbuch] handbook.

Hände|druck *der* handshake.

Handel *der* - **1.** [Handeln] trade; **mit jm Handel treiben** to do business with sb; **mit etw Handel treiben** to deal in sthg - **2.** [Geschäftsleben, Laden] business.

handeln ◇ *vi* - **1.** [Handel treiben]: **mit etw handeln** to trade ODER deal in sthg; **mit jm handeln** to do business with sb - **2.** [feilschen] to bargain, to haggle; **mit jm um etw handeln** to bargain ODER haggle with sb over sthg - **3.** [agieren] to act - **4.** [behandeln]: **von etw handeln** to be about sthg. ◇ *vt* [verkaufen] to trade. ◆ **sich handeln** *ref*: **worum handelt es sich?** what is it about?; **bei diesem Buch handelt es sich um einen Roman** this book is a novel.

Handels|beziehungen *Pl* trade relations.

Handels|kammer *die* chamber of commerce.

Handels|partner *der* trading partner.

Handels|schule *die college attended by people who left school at 16 and wish to obtain a commercial qualification*.

handelsüblich *adj* standard, customary.

Handels|vertreter, in *der, die* commercial representative, rep.

händeringend *adv* desperately.

Hand|feger *der* brush.

handfest *adj* - **1.** [bodenständig] sturdy - **2.** [klar, stark] solid, firm.

Hand|fläche *die* palm.

Hand|gelenk *das* wrist.

Hand|gemenge *das* scuffle.

Hand|gepäck *das* hand luggage.

handgeschrieben *adj* handwritten.

Hand|granate *die* hand grenade.

handgreiflich *adj*: **handgreiflich werden** to become violent.

Handgreiflichkeit (*pl* **-en**) *die* violence; **es kam zu Handgreiflichkeiten** they came to blows.

Hand|griff *der* - **1.** [Handbewegung] movement (of the hand); **mit ein paar Handgriffen** in no time - **2.** [Haltegriff] handle.

Hand|habe *die*: **keine Handhabe gegen jn haben** RECHT to have no evidence against sb.

handhaben *vt* - **1.** [Werkzeug] to use; [Maschine] to operate; [Gesetze, Vorschriften] to apply - **2.** [Fall] to handle.

Handicap (*pl* **-s**), **Handikap** (*pl* **-s**) ['hɛndikɛp] *das* handicap.

Hand|langer (*pl* **Handlanger**) *der* - **1.** [Hilfsarbeiter] labourer - **2.** *abw* [Zuarbeiter] dogsbody; [von Geheimpolizei] henchman.

Händler, in (*mpl* -, *fpl* **-nen**) *der, die* dealer.

handlich *adj* handy.

Handlung (*pl* **-en**) *die* - **1.** [Tat] act - **2.** [in Texten] plot - **3.** [Laden] shop, business.

Handlungsfreiheit *die* freedom of action.

Handlungs|weise *die* conduct.

Hand|schellen *Pl* handcuffs; **jm Handschellen anlegen** to handcuff sb.

Hand|schrift *die* - **1.** [Schrift] handwriting - **2.** [Text] manuscript.

handschriftlich *adj* handwritten.

Hand|schuh *der* glove.

Handschuh|fach *das* glove compartment.

Hand|stand *der* handstand.

Hand|tasche *die* handbag.

Hand|tuch *das* towel.

Hand|umdrehen *das*: **im Handumdrehen** in (next to) no time.

Hand|werk *das* - **1.** [Beruf] trade; [künstlerisch] craft; **jm das Handwerk legen** to put an end to sb's misdemeanours - **2.** *(ohne pl)* [Berufsstand] trade and crafts sector.

Hand|werker, in (*mpl* **Handwerker**, *fpl* **-nen**) *der, die* tradesman (tradeswoman *die*).

handwerklich <> *adj* [Beruf] skilled; [künstlerisch] as a craftsman/craftswoman. <> *adv*: **handwerklich gut gearbeitet** well-crafted; **handwerklich geschickt sein** to be good with one's hands.

Handwerkszeug *das (ohne pl)* tools *Pl* of the trade.

Handy ['hɛndi] (*pl* **-s**) *das* mobile (phone); **er nahm sein Handy mit** he took his mobile with him.

Hand|zeichen *das* signal (with one's hand); **durch Handzeichen abstimmen** to decide by a show of hands.

Hanf *der* hemp.

Hang (*pl* **Hänge**) *der* - **1.** [Abhang] slope - **2.** [Vorliebe]: **einen Hang zum Selbstmitleid haben** to be inclined to be self-pitying.

Hänge|brücke *die* suspension bridge.

hangeln (*perf* **hat/ist gehangelt**) *vi (ist)*: **an etw** *(D)* **hangeln** to move along sthg hand over hand. ◆ **sich hangeln** *ref (hat)*: **sich nach unten/oben hangeln** to let o.s. down/ pull o.s. up hand over hand.

Hänge|matte *die* hammock.

hängen (*prät* **hing** ODER **hängte**, *perf* **hat gehangen** ODER **hat gehängt**) <> *vt (reg)* - **1.** [anbringen] to hang; **etw an etw** *(A)* **hängen** to hang sthg on sthg; **sich einen Pullover um die Schultern hängen** to drape a pullover over one's shoulders - **2.** [Körperteil] to dangle - **3.** [töten] to hang. <> *vi (unreg)* - **1.** [gen] to hang - **2.** [emotional]: **an jm/etw hängen** to be attached to sb/sthg - **3.** [haften] to be stuck. ◆ **sich hängen** *ref (reg)*: **sich an etw** *(A)* **hängen** to hang onto sthg.

hängen bleiben (*perf* **ist hängen geblieben**) *vi (unreg)* - **1.** [festhängen]: **mit dem Ärmel an der Türklinke hängen bleiben** to catch one's sleeve on the doorhandle - **2.** [bleiben] to stay longer than one intended - **3.** [übrig bleiben]: **von dem Gelernten blieb nichts hängen** she didn't remember any of what she'd learned; **diese Arbeit bleibt immer an mir hängen** it is always me who ends up having to do this job - **4.** *fam* [sitzen bleiben] to have to repeat the year.

hängen lassen *vt (unreg)* - **1.** [vergessen] to leave (behind) - **2.** [Person] to let down, to leave in the lurch - **3.** [Körperteil]: **die Schultern hängen lassen** to let one's shoulders droop. ◆ **sich hängen lassen** *ref* [vernachlässigen] to let o.s. go.

Hannover *nt* Hanover.

Hanse *die* Hanseatic League.

hänseln *vt*: **jn (wegen etw) hänseln** to tease sb (about sthg).

Hanse|stadt *die* Hanseatic town.

Hantel (*pl* **-n**) *die* dumbbell.

Häppchen (*pl* **-**) *das* canapé.

happig *fam* <> *adj* [Preis] steep. <> *adv* greedily.

Hardware ['hɑ:(r)dwɛə] *die* EDV hardware.

Harfe (*pl* **-n**) *die* harp.

Harke (*pl* **-n**) *die* rake.

harken *vt* to rake.

harmlos <> *adj* [Tier, Person, Bemerkung] harmless; [Eingriff, Verletzung] minor; [Vergnügen] innocent. <> *adv* [lachen, tun] innocently.

Harmlosigkeit (*pl* **-en**) *die* [von Tier, Person, Bemerkung] harmlessness; [von Krankheit] mildness; [von Verletzung] minor nature; [von Vergnügen] innocence.

Harmonie (*pl* **-n**) *die* harmony.

harmonieren *vi*: **miteinander harmonieren** [Farben] to go (well) together; [Töne] to be in harmony; [Menschen] to get on (well) with one another.

harmonisch <> *adj* harmonious. <> *adv* - **1.** [passend] harmoniously - **2.** MUS: **harmonisch klingen** to be harmonious.

Harn (*pl* **-e**) *der* urine.

Harn|blase *die* bladder.

Harpune (*pl* **-n**) *die* harpoon.

hart (*kompar* **härter**, *superl* **härteste**) <> *adj* - **1.** [nicht weich - gen] hard; [- Ei] hard-boiled; **harte Währung** hard currency - **2.** [widerstandsfähig] tough; **hart im Nehmen sein** to be tough - **3.** [streng - Urteil, Strafe, Winter] harsh; [- Drogen] hard; [- Aufprall] violent - **4.**: **es geht hart auf hart** *fig* it's a pitched battle. <> *adv (kompar härter; superl am härtesten)* - **1.** [nicht weich] hard; **das Ei hart kochen** to hard-boil the egg - **2.** [streng - bestrafen, urteilen] harshly; [- arbeiten, aufschlagen] hard - **3.** [räumlich]: **hart an** *(+ D)* close to; **das war hart an der Grenze des Erlaubten** *fig* it was right on the limit of what is allowed.

Härte (*pl* **-n**) *die* - **1.** [gen] hardness - **2.** [Belastung] hardship - **3.** [von Urteil, Person, Worte, Farbe, Aussprache] harshness - **4.** *fam abw* [Zumutung]: **das ist die Härte!** that's a bit much!

hart gekocht *adj* hard-boiled.

hartherzig *adj* hard-hearted.

hartnäckig ◇ *adj* [Person] stubborn; [Verfolger, Krankheit] persistent. ◇ *adv* [schweigen, sich weigern] stubbornly; [verfolgen, nachfragen] persistently.

haschen *vi* - **1.** [fangen wollen]: **nach jm/etw haschen** to snatch at sb/sthg - **2.** *fam* [Haschisch rauchen] to smoke hash.

Haschisch *das* & *der* hashish.

Hase (*pl* **-n**) *der* hare; [Kaninchen] rabbit.

Haselnuss (*pl* **-nüsse**) *die* hazelnut.

Hass *der*: **Hass (auf jn/etw)** hatred (of sb/sthg).

hassen *vt* to hate.

hässlich ◇ *adj* - **1.** [unattraktiv] ugly - **2.** [gemein] nasty. ◇ *adv* - **1.** [unattraktiv] tastelessly; **sich hässlich kleiden** to wear ugly clothes - **2.** [gemein] nastily.

Hässlichkeit *die* [von Person, Einrichtung] ugliness.

hast *präs* ▷ **haben**.

Hast *die* haste; **etw in Hast tun** to do sthg hastily.

hasten (*perf* **ist gehastet**) *vi* to hurry.

hastig ◇ *adv* hastily, hurriedly; **hastig laufen** to rush. ◇ *adj* hasty.

hat *präs* ▷ **haben**.

hätscheln *vt* to pet.

hatschi *interj fam* atishoo!

hatte *prät* ▷ **haben**.

Haube (*pl* **-n**) *die* - **1.** [von Krankenschwester] cap; [von Nonne] veil - **2.** [Motorhaube] bonnet *UK*, hood *US* - **3.** [Trockenhaube] hairdryer.

Hauch *der* - **1.** [leichter Wind] gentle breeze - **2.** [Spur]: **ein Hauch von etw** a hint of sthg.

hauchdünn ◇ *adj* wafer-thin. ◇ *adv* [auftragen] very sparingly; [schneiden] into very thin slices.

hauchen *vt* & *vi* to breathe.

hauen (*prät* **haute** ODER **hieb**, *perf* **hat gehauen**) ◇ *vt* - **1.** *(prät haute) fam* [Person] to hit - **2.** [Gegenstand]: **einen Pfahl in den Boden hauen** to bang a post into the ground - **3.** *(prät haute) salopp* [werfen] to chuck, to bung *UK*. ◇ *vi fam* [auf Tisch, gegen Wand] to bang; **jm ins Gesicht hauen** to smack sb in the mouth.

Haufen (*pl* **-**) *der* - **1.** [Anhäufung]: **alles auf einen Haufen legen** to pile everything up - **2.** *fam* [Menge]: **ein Haufen Freunde/Geld** loads of friends/money.

häufen *vt* to pile up. ◆ **sich häufen** *ref* [Briefe, Abfälle] to pile up; [Beweise] to accumulate; [Vorfall] to be on the increase.

haufenweise *adv fam*: **haufenweise Geld verdienen** to earn heaps ODER loads of money.

häufig ◇ *adj* [gen] frequent; [Fehler] common. ◇ *adv* often.

Häufigkeit (*pl* **-en**) *die* frequency.

Häufung (*pl* **-en**) *die* [von Gegenständen] accumulation; [von Vorfällen] mounting frequency.

Haupt|bahnhof *der* main station; **Leipzig Hauptbahnhof** Leipzig central (station).

hauptberuflich ◇ *adj*: **hauptberufliche Tätigkeit** main job. ◇ *adv*: **hauptberuflich ist er Landwirt** farming is his principal occupation

Haupt|beschäftigung *die* main occupation

Haupt|bestandteil *der* main component.

Haupt|darsteller, in *der, die* leading man (leading lady *die*).

Haupt|eingang *der* main entrance.

Haupt|fach *das* main subject; **etw im Hauptfach studieren** to study sthg as one's main subject.

Haupt|figur *die* central figure.

Haupt|gericht *das* main course.

Haupt|gewinn *der* first prize.

Haupt|grund *der* main reason.

Häuptling (*pl* **-e**) *der* chief.

Haupt|person *die* - **1.** [von Buch, Film] main character - **2.** [wichtigste Person]: **die Hauptperson sein** to be the star of the show.

Haupt|post *die* main post office.

Haupt|quartier *das* headquarters *Pl*.

Haupt|rolle *die* [in Film] starring role; **Tennis spielt in ihrem Leben die Hauptrolle** tennis is the most important thing in her life.

Haupt|sache *die* main ODER most important thing; **Hauptsache, ich bestehe** the main thing is for me to pass. ◆ **in der Hauptsache** *adv* mainly, in the main.

hauptsächlich ◇ *adv* principally, mainly ◇ *adj* main, chief.

Haupt|saison ['hauptzezõ] *die* high season.

Haupt|satz *der* main clause.

Haupt|schule *die secondary school attended by less academically gifted pupils aged between 10 and 15.*

Haupt|stadt *die* capital.

Haupt|straße *die* main road ODER street.

Haupt|teil *der* [von Text, Rede] main body; **der Hauptteil der Fracht war beschädigt** most of the cargo was damaged.

Hauptverkehrs|straße *die* main thoroughfare.

Hauptverkehrs|zeit *die* rush hour.

Haupt|wohnsitz *der* main place of residence.

Haupt|wort (*pl* **-wörter**) *das* noun.

Haus (*pl* **Häuser**) *das* - **1.** [Wohnhaus] house - **2.** [Betrieb] firm; **er ist zurzeit nicht im Haus** he is not on the premises just now; **mit den besten Empfehlungen des Hauses** with the compliments of the house - **3.** [Familie] family - **4.** [Theater] auditorium; **volles Haus haben** to have a full house; **Haus halten** [sparen] to budget; **mit etw Haus halten** to be careful with sthg; **mit seinen Kräften Haus halten** to conserve one's energy; **die Kinder sind von Haus aus gewöhnt mitzuhelfen** the children have been brought up to be helpful.

Hauslapotheke *die* - **1.** [Medikamente] first-aid kit - **2.** [Schränkchen] medicine cabinet.

Hauslarbeit *die* - **1.** [im Haushalt] housework - **2.** [für die Schule, für die Universität] homework.

Hauslarzt, **ärztin** *der, die* family doctor.

Hauslaufgabe *die*: **als Hausaufgabe für morgen** for tomorrow's homework; **Hausaufgaben** homework *(U)*.

Hausbesetzer, **in** (*mpl* -, *fpl* **-nen**) *der, die* squatter.

Hauslbewohner, **in** *der, die* occupant.

Häuschen ['hɔyzçən] (*pl* -) *das* [Haus] cottage; **vor Freude ganz aus dem Häuschen sein** *fam* to be beside o.s. with joy.

Hausleigentümer, **in** *der, die* homeowner; [Vermieter] landlord (landlady *die*).

hausen *vi* - **1.** [wohnen] to live - **2.** *fam* [toben - Sturm, Krieg] to rage; [- Eroberer, Besatzer] to rampage.

Häuserblock (*pl* **-blöcke**) *der* block.

Hauslflur *der* (entrance) hall, hallway.

Hauslfrau *die* housewife.

hausgemacht *adj* home-made.

Haushalt (*pl* **-e**) *der* - **1.** [Hausarbeit] housework; **im Haushalt helfen** to help around the house - **2.** [Hausstand] estate - **3.** [Familie] household; **einen Haushalt gründen** to set up home - **4.** WIRTSCH budget.

hauslhalten *vi (unreg)* ▷ **Haus**.

Haushälter, **in** (*mpl* -, *fpl* **-nen**) *der, die* housekeeper.

Haushaltslartikel *der* household article.

Hauslherr, **in** *der, die* host (hostess *die*).

haushoch ◇ *adj* [Flammen, Wellen] towering; [Favorit, Sieg, Überlegenheit] overwhelming. ◇ *adv* [wachsen] as high as a house; [gewinnen] by a mile; **jm haushoch überlegen sein** to be head and shoulders above sb; **haushoch verlieren** to be hammered.

hausieren *vi*: **mit etw hausieren (gehen)** [verkaufen] to sell sthg from door to door; *fam* [sprechen über] to go on about sthg.

häuslich ◇ *adj* - **1.** [im Haus - Arbeiten, Probleme, Frieden] domestic; [- Angelegenheit] family *(vor Subst)*; [- Pflege] home *(vor Subst)* - **2.** [Person]: **sie ist sehr häuslich** she's a real home bird. ◇ *adv*: **sich häuslich niederlassen** *fam* to make o.s. at home; **sich häuslich einrichten** *fam* to settle in.

Hauslmann *der* house husband.

Hausmannskost *die* traditional, simple fare.

Hauslmarke *die* - **1.** [Wein] house wine - **2.** [von Geschäft] own-brand product - **3.** [Lieblingsmarke] favourite brand.

Hauslmeister, **in** *der, die* caretaker *UK*, janitor *US*.

Hauslmittel *das* home remedy.

Hauslnummer *die* house number.

Hauslordnung *die* house rules *Pl*.

Hauslrat *der (ohne pl)* household contents *Pl*.

Hauslschuh *der* slipper.

Hausltier *das* pet.

Hausltür *die* front door.

Hauslverwaltung *die* property managers *Pl*.

Hauslwirt, **in** *der, die* landlord (landlady *die*).

Haut (*pl* **Häute**) *die* [gen] skin; [von Tier] hide; **es ging mir unter die Haut** it got under my skin; **ihm war nicht wohl in seiner Haut** he felt uncomfortable.

Hautlabschürfung (*pl* **-en**) *die* graze.

Hautlarzt, **ärztin** *der, die* dermatologist.

Hautlausschlag *der* (skin) rash.

Hautlcreme ['hautkreːm] *die* skin cream.

häuten *vt* [Früchte] to peel; [Tier] to skin. ◆ **sich häuten** *ref* to shed its skin.

hauteng *adj* skintight.

Hautlfarbe *die* skin colour.

hautnah ◇ *adj* [Bild, Darstellung] graphic. ◇ *adv* [tanzen] very closely; **hautnah mit etw in Kontakt kommen** to come into close contact with sthg; **hautnah an etw** *(D)* **teilnehmen** to be closely involved in sthg.

Hbf. *abk für* **Hauptbahnhof**.

Headhunter (*pl* -) *der* headhunter.

Hebamme (*pl* **-n**) *die* midwife.

Hebel (*pl* -) *der* lever.

heben (*prät* **hob**, *perf* **hat gehoben**) *vt* - **1.** [hochnehmen] to lift; [Arm, Glas] to raise; **einen heben** *fam* to have a drink - **2.** [Niveau] to raise; [Umsatz, Selbstsicherheit] to boost, to improve; [Stimmung, Laune] to improve - **3.** [Wrack] to hoist, to salvage. ◆ **sich heben** *ref* - **1.** [hochgehen - Vorhang, Flugzeug, Ballon] to rise; [- Nebel] to lift - **2.** [Niveau] to rise; [Umsatz, Laune] to improve.

hebräisch *adj* Hebrew.

hecheln *vi* [atmen] to pant.

Hecht (*pl* **-e**) *der* pike.

Heck (*pl* **-e** ODER **-s**) *das* [von Auto, Flugzeug] rear; [von Schiff] stern.

Hecke (*pl* **-n**) *die* hedge.

Heckenlschütze *der* sniper.

Hecklklappe *die* tailgate.

Hecklscheibe *die* rear windscreen *UK* ODER windshield *US*.

Heer (*pl* **-e**) *das* army.

Hefe (*pl* **-n**) *die* yeast.

Hefelteig *der* leavened dough *(U)*.

Heft (*pl* **-e**) *das* - **1.** [Schulheft] exercise book - **2.** [geheftetes Büchlein] booklet - **3.** [von Zeitschriften] issue.

heften *vt* - **1.** [befestigen]: **etw an etw** *(A)* **heften** [gen] to attach sthg to sthg; [mit Heftmaschine] to staple sthg to sthg - **2.** [nähen] to tack - **3.** [richten]: **die Augen auf etw** *(A)* **heften** to fix one's eyes on sthg. ◆ **sich heften** *ref* [sich richten]: **sich auf etw** *(A)* **heften** to fix onto sthg.

Hefter (*pl* -) *der* folder.

heftig ◇ *adj* violent. ◇ *adv* violently.

Heft|klammer *die* staple.

Heft|pflaster *das* (sticking) plaster *UK*, Band-Aid® *US*.

Heft|zwecke (*pl* **-n**) *die* drawing pin *UK*, thumbtack *US*.

hegen *vt* - **1.** [Verdacht, Gefühle, Hoffnung] to harbour; [Abneigung, Misstrauen, Achtung] to feel - **2.** [Wald, Wild, Garten] to tend; **jn/etw hegen und pflegen** to lavish care on sb/sthg.

Hehl *das* & *der*: **kein** ODER **keinen Hehl aus etw machen** to make no secret of sthg.

Hehlerei (*pl* **-en**) *die* receiving (stolen goods).

Heide (*pl* **-n**) ◇ *die* heath. ◇ *der* heathen, pagan.

Heidekraut *das* heather.

Heidel|beere *die* bilberry.

Heiden|angst *die fam*: **eine Heidenangst haben** to be scared stiff.

Heiden|geld *das fam* fortune.

Heiden|spaß *der fam* great fun.

Heidin (*pl* **-nen**) *die* heathen, pagan.

heidnisch *adj* heathen, pagan.

heikel (*kompar* **heikler**, *superl* **heikelste**) *adj* - **1.** [kompliziert] awkward, tricky - **2.** [anspruchsvoll] fussy.

heil *adj* - **1.** [unzerstört] intact; [Welt] perfect - **2.** [geheilt] healed.

Heiland *der* Saviour.

Heil|bad *das* - **1.** [Kurort] spa - **2.** [Baden] medicinal bath.

heilbar *adj* [Krankheit, Patient] curable; [Wunde] healable.

heilen (*perf* **hat/ist geheilt**) ◇ *vt (hat)* to cure; **jn von etw heilen** [Idee] to cure sb of sthg; **jn von seinen Zweifeln heilen** to allay sb's doubts. ◇ *vi (ist)* to heal.

heilfroh *adj* relieved; **heilfroh über etw** *(A)* **sein** to be relieved about sthg.

heilig *adj* - **1.** [geheiligt] holy; **der heilige Christopherus** Saint Christopher; **denen ist nichts heilig** nothing is sacred to them - **2.** [Schrecken] almighty.

Heiligabend (*pl* **-s**) *der* Christmas Eve.

Heilige (*pl* **-n**) *der, die* saint.

Heiligen|schein *der* halo.

Heiligtum (*pl* **-tümer**) *das* - **1.** [Ort] shrine - **2.** [Gegenstand] relic.

Heil|kraft *die* healing power.

Heil|kraut *das* medicinal herb.

heillos ◇ *adj* terrible. ◇ *adv* terribly.

Heil|mittel *das* remedy, cure.

Heil|pflanze *die* medicinal plant.

Heil|praktiker, in *der, die* alternative therapist.

heilsam *adj* salutary.

Heilsarmee *die* Salvation Army.

Heilung (*pl* **-en**) *die* [von Patient, Krankheit] curing; [von Wunde] healing.

heim *adv* home.

Heim (*pl* **-e**) *das* home.

Heimarbeit *die*: **etw in Heimarbeit anfertigen** to make sthg at home; **Heimarbeit machen** to work from home.

Heimat *die* [von Person] home, native country/region; [von Tier] original habitat.

Heimat|anschrift *die* home address.

Heimat|hafen *der* home port, port of registration.

Heimat|kunde *die primary school subject covering local history, natural history and geography.*

Heimat|land *das* native country.

heimatlich *adj* of/from one's native country/region; **jm ein heimatliches Gefühl geben** to remind sb of home.

heimatlos *adj* [Mensch] homeless; [Tier] stray.

Heimat|museum *das* local history museum.

Heim|computer *der* home computer.

Heim|fahrt *die* journey home.

heimisch *adj* - **1.** [Bevölkerung, Industrie, Sitte] local; [Pflanze, Tier] indigenous - **2.** [zu Hause]: **heimisch werden** to become acclimatized; **sich heimisch fühlen** to feel at home.

Heimkehr *die* return journey.

heim|kehren (*perf* **ist heimgekehrt**) *vi* to return home.

heim|kommen (*perf* **ist heimgekommen**) *vi* *(unreg)* to come home.

heimlich ◇ *adj* secret. ◇ *adv* secretly.

Heimlichkeit (*pl* **-en**) *die* secrecy. ◆ **Heimlichkeiten** *Pl* secrets.

Heim|reise *die* journey home.

Heim|spiel *das* home game.

heim|suchen *vt* - **1.** [Pest, Alptraum, Krankheit] to afflict; [Erdbeben] to hit - **2.** *hum* [belästigen] to descend on.

Heim|trainer [haim'trɛ:nɐ] *der* exercise bike.

heimtückisch ◇ *adj* [Mensch, Verbrecher] malicious; [Krankheit] insidious. ◇ *adv* maliciously.

Heim|weg *der* way home.

Heimweh *das* homesickness; **(nach jm/etw) Heimweh haben** to be homesick (for sb/sthg).

heim|zahlen *vt*: **jm etw heimzahlen** to pay sb back for sthg.

Heirat (*pl* **-en**) *die* marriage.

heiraten ◇ *vi* to marry, to get married; **kirchlich heiraten** to have a church wedding. ◇ *vt* to marry.

Heirats|annonce *die advertisement seeking a marriage partner.*

Heirats|antrag *der* proposal (of marriage).

Heirats|vermittlung *die* [Ort] marriage bureau.

heiser ◇ *adj* hoarse. ◇ *adv* hoarsely; **sie hat sich heiser geschrien** she shouted until she was hoarse.

Heiserkeit (*pl* **-en**) *die* hoarseness.

heiß ◇ *adj* **- 1.** [warm] [gen] hot; **mir ist heiß** I'm hot; **es überläuft mich heiß und kalt** I feel hot and cold all over; **heiß auf jn sein** *fam* to have the hots for sb **- 2.** [heftig - Diskussion, Auseinandersetzung] heated; [- Liebe, Wunsch] ardent, burning **- 3.** *fam* [gut] brilliant. ◇ *adv* **- 1.** [warm]**: heiß baden** to have a hot bath **- 2.** [heftig]**: heiß umstritten** hotly contested; **jn heiß lieben** to love sb passionately; **es ging heiß her** things got a bit heated.

heißblütig *adj* hot-blooded.

heißen (*prät* **hieß**, *perf* **hat geheißen**) *vi* **- 1.** [mit Namen] to be called; **er heißt Tom** he's called Tom, his name is Tom; **wie heißt du?** what's your name? **- 2.** [bedeuten] to mean; **was heißt das auf Deutsch?** how do you say that in German?; **das will was heißen!** that's quite something!; **das heißt, wenn du willst** if you want, that is **- 3.** [lauten] to be; **wie heißt der Titel?** what's the title?

Heißhunger *der* voracious appetite.

heiß laufen (*perf* **hat/ist heiß gelaufen**) *vi (unreg) (ist)* [Motor] to overheat; [Telefon] to buzz.

Heißluft|ballon *der* hot-air balloon.

heiter *adj* **- 1.** [fröhlich] cheerful **- 2.** [sonnig] fine.

Heiterkeit *die* **- 1.** [Fröhlichkeit] cheerfulness **- 2.** [vom Wetter] fineness.

heizen ◇ *vi* to turn on the heating; **wir heizen mit Gas/elektrisch** we have gas/electric heating. ◇ *vt* to heat.

Heiz|kessel *der* boiler.

Heiz|kissen *das* heated pad *(for back pain etc).*

Heiz|körper *der* radiator.

Heiz|öl *das* fuel oil.

Heizung (*pl* **-en**) *die* **- 1.** [System] heating **- 2.** [Heizkörper] radiator.

Heizungs|keller *der* boiler room.

Hẹktar (*pl* **-e** ODER **-**) *das* & *der* hectare.

Hẹktik *die* hectic pace; **bloß keine Hektik!** *fam* don't panic!

hẹktisch ◇ *adj* **- 1.** [Person, Bewegung] frantic; **hektisch werden** to panic **- 2.** [Ort] hectic. ◇ *adv* frantically.

Hẹkto|liter *das* & *der* hectolitre.

Hẹld (*pl* **-en**) *der* hero.

hẹldenhaft ◇ *adj* heroic. ◇ *adv* heroically.

Hẹlden|tat *die* heroic deed.

Hẹldin (*pl* **-nen**) *die* heroine.

hẹlfen (*präs* **hịlft**, *prät* **hạlf**, *perf* **hat gehọlfen**) *vi* **- 1.** [Hilfe leisten] to help; **jm (bei etw) helfen** to help sb (with sthg); **sich *(D)* zu helfen wissen** to know what to do **- 2.** [nützlich sein] to help; **es hilft nichts** it's no use ODER good; **das hilft gegen Zahnschmerzen** it's good for toothache; **es hilft kein Weinen** it's no good crying.

Hẹlfer, in (*mpl* **-**, *fpl* **-nen**) *der, die* helper.

Helium *das* helium.

hẹll ◇ *adj* **- 1.** [Zimmer, Licht, Tag] bright; **es wird hell** it's getting light **- 2.** [Farbe] light; [Haar, Haut] fair **- 3.** [Stimme] high *(esp. of child's voice)* **- 4.** [schlau] lucid **- 5.** [groß, intensiv - Freude, Begeisterung] sheer; [- Empörung, Wahnsinn] utter. ◇ *adv* **- 1.** [leuchtend] brightly **- 2.** [hoch]**: hell klingen** to ring out clearly **- 3.** [sehr] totally.

hẹllblau *adj* light blue.

hẹllblond *adj* very fair.

hẹllhörig *adj* **- 1.** [misstrauisch]**: sie wurde hellhörig** her suspicions were aroused; **jn hellhörig machen** to arouse sb's suspicions **- 2.** [Raum]**: die Wohnung ist sehr hellhörig** you can hear everything through the walls in this flat.

Hẹlligkeit (*pl* **-en**) *die* [von Licht] brightness.

hẹll|sehen *vi (unreg)* to see into the future.

Hẹllseher, in (*mpl* **-**, *fpl* **-nen**) *der, die* clairvoyant.

hẹllwach *adj* **- 1.** [wach] wide awake **- 2.** *fam* [rege] on the ball.

Hẹlm (*pl* **-e**) *der* helmet.

Hẹmd (*pl* **-en**) *das* **- 1.** [Oberhemd] shirt **- 2.** [Unterhemd] vest *UK*, undershirt *US*; **jn bis aufs Hemd ausziehen** *fam* to have the shirt off sb's back.

hẹmdsärmelig *adj* casual.

hẹmmen *vt* **- 1.** [bremsen - Bewegung, Geschwindigkeit] to slow down; [Fluss] to stem **- 2.** [behindern] to impede, to hinder.

Hẹmm|schwelle *die* mental block.

Hẹmmung (*pl* **-en**) *die* [Behinderung] hindrance. ◆ **Hemmungen** *Pl* inhibitions; **Hemmungen haben** to feel inhibited.

hẹmmungslos ◇ *adj* uninhibited. ◇ *adv* uninhibitedly.

Hẹngst (*pl* **-e**) *der* [Pferd] stallion.

Henkel (*pl* -) *der* handle.

Henker (*pl* -) *der* [gen] executioner; [beim Erhängen] hangman.

Henne (*pl* -**n**) *die* hen.

her *adv* - **1.** [räumlich]: **komm her!** come here!; **her damit!** give me that!; **von Norden her** from the north; **von weit her** from a long way away - **2.** [zeitlich]: **das ist zehn Jahre her** that was ten years ago; **ich kenne sie von früher her** I know her from before - **3.** [unter dem Aspekt]: **von der Größe her** as far as size is concerned; *siehe auch* **her sein**.

herab|lassen *vt (unreg)* to lower. ◆ **sich herablassen** *ref*: **sich herablassen, etw zu tun** to condescend to do sthg.

herablassend <> *adj* condescending, patronizing. <> *adv* condescendingly, patronizingly.

herab|setzen *vt* - **1.** [Betrag] to reduce - **2.** [Person] to put down.

heran, ran *adv*: **nur heran!** come closer!

heran|kommen (*perf* **ist herangekommen**) *vi (unreg)* - **1.** [kommen] to approach; **sie lässt nichts an sich** *(A)* **herankommen** she doesn't let anything bother her; **an jn herankommen** [erreichen] to get hold of sb; [entsprechen] to match up to sb; **an etw** *(A)* **herankommen** to be able to reach sthg - **2.** [bekommen]: **an etw** *(A)* **herankommen** to get hold of sthg.

heran|machen ◆ **sich heranmachen** *ref*: **sich an etw** *(A)* **heranmachen** to get down to sthg.

heran|treten (*perf* **ist herangetreten**) *vi (unreg)*: **an jn herantreten** to approach sb.

heran|wachsen [hɛ'ranvaksn̩] (*perf* **ist herangewachsen**) *vi (unreg)* to grow up.

Heranwachsende [hɛ'ranvaksn̩də] (*pl* -**n**) *der, die* adolescent.

heran|ziehen (*perf* **hat/ist herangezogen**) *(unreg)* <> *vt (hat)* - **1.** [ziehen]: **etw an etw** *(A)* **heranziehen** to pull sthg up to sthg - **2.** [befragen] to consult - **3.** [erziehen] to teach. <> *vi (ist)* [kommen] to draw near.

herauf, rauf *adv* up; **die Treppe herauf** up the stairs; **vom Tal herauf** up from the valley.

herauf|beschwören *vt (unreg)* - **1.** [verursachen] to cause - **2.** [Vergangenes] to evoke.

herauf|kommen (*perf* **ist heraufgekommen**) *vi (unreg)* to come up/upstairs.

heraus, raus *adv* out; **heraus aus dem Bett** (get) out of bed!; **heraus mit der Sprache!** spit it out!, out with it!; **aus dieser Überlegung heraus** as a result of these reflections; **es ist noch nicht heraus, wer das Rennen gewonnen hat** it's still unclear who won the race; *siehe auch* **heraus sein**.

heraus|bekommen *vt (unreg)* - **1.** [Geheimnis] to find out; [Lösung] to work out - **2.** [entfernen] to get out - **3.** [Wechselgeld] to get back.

heraus|bringen *vt (unreg)* - **1.** [bringen] to bring/take out - **2.** [veröffentlichen, verkaufen] to bring out; **etw (ganz) groß herausbringen** to launch sthg amid a fanfare of publicity - **3.** *fam* [entlocken]: **etw aus jm herausbringen** to get sthg out of sb - **4.** [aussprechen, artikulieren] to utter.

heraus|finden *(unreg)* <> *vt* [entdecken] to find out. <> *vi* [herauskommen]: **aus etw herausfinden** to find a way out of sthg.

heraus|fliegen (*perf* **hat/ist herausgeflogen**) *(unreg)* <> *vt (hat)* [fliegen] to fly out. <> *vi (ist)* - **1.** [fliegen - Tier, Gegenstand]: **aus etw herausfliegen** to fly out of sthg - **2.** *fam* [zur Strafe] to be thrown out - **3.** *fam* [herausfallen]: **aus etw herausfliegen** to fall out of sthg.

heraus|fordern *vt* - **1.** SPORT [Feind] to challenge; **jn herausfordern, etw zu tun** to challenge sb to do sthg - **2.** [provozieren] to provoke; **das Schicksal herausfordern** to tempt fate.

herausfordernd <> *adj* provocative; [Frage] challenging. <> *adv* provocatively.

Heraus|forderung *die* - **1.** SPORT [Aufgabe] challenge - **2.** [Provokation] provocation; [von Schicksal] tempting.

heraus|geben *vt (unreg)* - **1.** [veröffentlichen] to publish - **2.** [geben]: **jm etw herausgeben** to pass ODER hand sthg out to sb - **3.** [freilassen] to return - **4.** [Wechselgeld] to give back; **auf 100 Euro herausgeben** to give change from 100 euros.

Herausgeber, in (*mpl* -, *fpl* -**nen**) *der, die* - **1.** [Redakteur] editor - **2.** [Verleger] publisher.

heraus|gehen (*perf* **ist herausgegangen**) *vi (unreg)* - **1.** [nach draußen] to go out; **aus sich herausgehen** *fig* to come out of one's shell - **2.** [Fleck, Schraube] to come out.

heraus|halten *(unreg) vt* - **1.** [nach draußen] to hold out - **2.** *fam* [fern halten]: **jn aus etw heraushalten** to keep sb out of sthg. ◆ **sich heraushalten** *ref*: **sich aus etw heraushalten** to keep out of sthg.

heraus|holen *vt* - **1.** [holen]: **jn/etw aus etw herausholen** to get sb/sthg out of sthg - **2.** [Information]: **etw aus jm herausholen** to get sthg out of sb - **3.** [Leistung] to get ODER squeeze out - **4.** [Geld, Gewinn] to make - **5.** SPORT to make up.

heraus|hören *vt*: **etw aus etw heraushören** [erahnen] to detect sthg from sthg; [hören] to make out sthg amid sthg.

heraus|kommen (*perf* **ist herausgekommen**) *vi (unreg)* - **1.** [nach draußen]: **(aus etw) herauskommen** to come out (from sthg) - **2.** [Resultat]: **was kommt dabei heraus** what's that going to achieve?; **das kommt auf dasselbe heraus** it amounts to the same thing, it makes no difference - **3.** [auf den Markt kommen] to come out; **(ganz) groß herauskommen** *fig* to make a real splash - **4.** [Verbrechen] t come to light - **5.** [entkommen]: **aus etw herauskommen** to come out ODER emerge from sthg - **6.** [deutlich werden] to stand out - **7.** [aus dem Takt kommen] to get out of time - **8.** [beim Kartenspiel] to lead - **9.** *fam* [sagen]: **mit etw herauskommen** to come out with sthg.

heraus|nehmen *vt (unreg)* - **1.** [entfernen]: **etw (aus etw) herausnehmen** to take sthg out (of sthg) - **2.** [wagen]: **sich** *(D)* **Freiheiten herausnehmen** to take liberties.

heraus|ragen *vi* - **1.** [hervorstechen] to stand out - **2.** [herausstehen] to jut out.

heraus|reden ◆ **sich herausreden** *ref*: **sich damit herausreden, dass...** to make excuses for o.s. by saying that...

heraus|rücken (*perf* **hat/ist herausgerückt**) ◇ *vt (hat) fam* [Geld] to cough up. ◇ *vi (ist)* [sagen]: **mit etw herausrücken** to come out with sthg.

heraus|schlagen (*perf* **hat/ist herausgeschlagen**) *(unreg)* ◇ *vt (hat)* - **1.** [schlagen] to knock out - **2.** [Gewinn] to make. ◇ *vi (ist)* [Feuer]: **aus etw herausschlagen** to leap out of sthg.

heraus sein (*perf* **ist heraus gewesen**) *vi (unreg)* - **1.** [entlassen sein]: **aus etw heraus sein** to be out of sthg, to have left sthg - **2.** [entkommen sein]: **fein heraus sein** to be sitting pretty - **3.** [Produkt] to be out - **4.** [herausgegangen sein]: **aus einer Phase heraus sein** to be past a phase - **5.** [entfernt sein] to be out - **6.** [klar sein] to be known.

heraus|stellen *vt* - **1.** [nach draußen] to put out - **2.** [hervorheben] to highlight. ◆ **sich herausstellen** *ref* [klar werden] to become clear; **wer gelogen hat, wird sich noch herausstellen** we'll soon see who has been lying; **sich als falsch/richtig herausstellen** to turn out to be wrong/right.

heraus|strecken *vt* to stick out.

heraus|suchen *vt* to pick out; **jm etw heraussuchen** to find sthg for sb.

herbei *adv* here; **komm herbei!** come here!

her|bitten *vt (unreg)* to ask to come.

her|bringen *vt (unreg)* to bring here.

Herbst (*pl* **-e**) *der* autumn *UK*, fall *US*; **im Herbst** in the autumn *UK*, in the fall *US*.

herbstlich *adj* autumnal.

Herd (*pl* **-e**) *der* - **1.** [Ofen] cooker *UK*, stove *US* - **2.** [von Revolte] seat; [von Krankheit] focus.

Herde (*pl* **-n**) *die* - **1.** [von Rindern, Elefanten] herd; [von Schafen] flock - **2.** *abw* [von Menschen] gang.

Herd|platte *die* hotplate.

herein, rein *adv* in; **herein!** come in!

herein|brechen (*perf* **ist hereingebrochen**) *vi (unreg) geh* - **1.** [Nacht] to fall - **2.** [Unglück]: **über jn hereinbrechen** to befall sb.

herein|fallen (*perf* **ist hereingefallen**) *vi (unreg)* - **1.** [getäuscht werden] to be conned; **auf jn/etw hereinfallen** to be taken in by sb/sthg - **2.** [fallen] to fall in - **3.** [Licht] to come in, to enter.

herein|kommen (*perf* **ist hereingekommen**) *vi (unreg)* to come in.

herein|lassen *vt (unreg)* to let in.

herein|legen *vt* [täuschen] to take for a ride.

Her|fahrt *die* journey here.

her|fallen (*perf* **ist hergefallen**) *vi (unreg)*: **über jn herfallen** [angreifen] to attack sb; **über etw** *(A)* **herfallen** [essen] to attack sthg.

Her|gang *der*: **der Hergang der Tat** the course of events leading to the crime.

her|geben *vt (unreg)* - **1.** [geben] to give; [überreichen] to hand over - **2.** [verschenken] to give away - **3.** [verzichten auf] to give up - **4.** [erbringen]: **der Text gibt für unser Thema nichts her** the text is of no use for our topic. ◆ **sich hergeben** *ref*: **sich zu etw hergeben** *abw* to allow o.s. to get involved in sthg.

hergeholt *adj*: **weit hergeholt** far-fetched.

her|haben *vt (unreg) fam*: **wo hast du das her?** where did you get this?

her|halten *(unreg) vi abw* [dienen]: **als etw herhalten** to be used as sthg; **für jn herhalten** to have to take the blame for sb.

her|hören *vi* to listen.

Hering (*pl* **-e**) *der* - **1.** [Fisch] herring - **2.** [am Zelt] tent peg.

her|kommen (*perf* **ist hergekommen**) *vi (unreg)* - **1.** [kommen] to come here; **wo kommst du denn jetzt her?** where have you just been? - **2.** [entstehen, stammen] to come from; **wo kommen Sie her?** where do you come from?

herkömmlich *adj* conventional.

Herkunft *die (ohne pl)* [von Person] origins *Pl*; [von Sache] origin.

Herkunfts|land *das* country of origin.

her|machen *vi*: **viel hermachen** to look impressive; **wenig hermachen** not to look very impressive; **nichts hermachen** not to be up to much. ◆ **sich hermachen** *ref fam*: **sich über etw** *(A)* **hermachen** to set about sthg.

her|nehmen *vt (unreg)* [nehmen, bekommen] to get.

Heroin *das* heroin.

Herr (*pl* **-en**) *der* - **1.** [Mann] gentleman; **meine Herren!** gentlemen!; **'Herren'** [WC] 'gents' - **2.** [Anrede] Mr; **an Herrn Müller** to Mr Müller; **Herr Doktor** Doctor - **3.** [Gott] Lord - **4.** [Oberhaupt, Gebieter] lord; **der Herr des Hauses** the master of the house.

herrenlos *adj* [Tier] stray; [Koffer] abandoned.

her|richten *vt* - **1.** [vorbereiten] to get ready - **2.** [reparieren] to renovate.

Herrin (*pl* **-nen**) *die* mistress.

herrisch ◇ *adj* [Person, Worte] overbearing; [Blick] imperious. ◇ *adv* in an overbearing manner.

herrlich *adj* wonderful.

Herrschaft (*pl* **-en**) *die* [über Staat, Volk] rule. ◆ **Herrschaften** *Pl* people; **meine Herrschaften!** ladies and gentlemen!

herrschen *vi* - **1.** [regieren]: **(über jn/etw) herrschen** to rule (over sb/sthg) - **2.** [bestehen] to prevail; **es herrschte allgemeine Unruhe** there was general unrest.

Herrscher, in (*mpl* **-**, *fpl* **-nen**) *der, die* ruler.

her|schieben *vt (unreg)* to push here; **etw vor sich** *(D)* **herschieben** [schieben] to push sthg along ahead of one; [vertagen] to put sthg off.

her sein (*perf* **ist her gewesen**) *vi (unreg)* - **1.** [vergangen sein]: **es ist drei Tage her, dass wir telefoniert haben** it is three days since we phoned - **2.** [herkommen] to come from; **hinter jm/etw her sein** to be after sb/sthg.

her|stellen *vt* - **1.** [produzieren] to produce, to make; [industriell] to manufacture - **2.** [Ruhe, Ordnung] to establish; **ihre Gesundheit ist wieder hergestellt** she has recovered, her health has been restored - **3.** [näher rücken] to put (over) here.

Hersteller, in (*mpl* **-**, *fpl* **-nen**) *der, die* manufacturer.

Her|stellung *die* [Produktion] production; [industriell] manufacture.

herüber, rüber *adv* over.

herum *adv* - **1.** [räumlich] round; **um etw herum** around sthg; **um den Tisch herum** around the table; **das Gerücht ist schon in der ganzen Nachbarschaft herum** the rumour has already got around the whole neighbourhood; **du trägst den Pullover verkehrt herum** your pullover is on the wrong way round; **was um sie herum geschieht** what's going on around her - **2.** [ungefähr] around, about; **um die 50 Euro herum** around ODER about 50 euros.

herum|drehen ◇ *vt* [Blatt, Decke] to turn over; [Schlüssel] to turn; [Pfannkuchen] to toss. ◇ *vi* [drehen]: **an etw** *(D)* **herumdrehen** to turn sthg. ◆ **sich herumdrehen** *ref* [sich umdrehen] to turn round.

herum|fahren (*perf* **hat/ist herumgefahren**) *(unreg)* ◇ *vi (ist)* - **1.** [im Kreis]: **um etw herumfahren** to go round sthg - **2.** [umherfahren] to drive around - **3.** [sich umdrehen] to turn round - **4.** [wischen] to wipe around. ◇ *vt (hat)* to drive around.

herum|geben *vt (unreg)* to pass round.

herum|gehen (*perf* **ist herumgegangen**) *vi (unreg)* - **1.** [spazieren] to walk around - **2.** [zwischen Personen] to go around - **3.** [im Kreis]: **um etw herumgehen** to go round sthg - **4.** [Gerücht] to go around - **5.** [Zeit] to pass.

herum|kommen (*perf* **ist herumgekommen**) *vi (unreg) fam* - **1.** [reisen] to get around - **2.** [gehen, fahren]: **um etw herumkommen** to get round sthg - **3.** [vermeiden]: **um etw herumkommen/nicht herumkommen** to get out of/not to get out of sthg.

herum|kriegen *vt fam* - **1.** [überreden]: **sie hat mich doch noch herumgekriegt** she talked me into it in the end - **2.** [verbringen]: **die Zeit herumkriegen** to kill time - **3.** [räumlich]: **etw um etw herumkriegen** to get sthg round sthg.

herum|liegen *vi (unreg)* to lie around.

herum|lungern (*perf* **hat/ist herumgelungert**) *vi fam* [in der Stadt] to hang around; [auf dem Sofa] to lounge around.

herum|sprechen ◆ **sich herumsprechen** *ref (unreg)* to get around.

herum|treiben ◆ **sich herumtreiben** *ref (unreg) fam* to hang around.

herum|zeigen *vt* to show round.

herum|ziehen (*perf* **hat/ist herumgezogen**) *(unreg)* ◇ *vi (ist)* - **1.** [herumfahren] to wander about; **in der Welt herumziehen** to roam the world - **2.** [im Kreis]: **um etw herumziehen** to go round sthg. ◇ *vt (hat)*: **etw um etw herumziehen** to put sthg round sthg.

herunter, runter *adv* down; **herunter vom Dach!** get down from the roof!; **auf der Fahrt von Hamburg herunter** on the journey down from Hamburg.

herunter|bekommen *vt (unreg) fam* - **1.** [schlucken können, nach unten bekommen] to get down - **2.** [entfernen können] to get off; **den Schmutz vom Teppich herunterbekommen** to get the dirt out of the carpet.

herunter|fahren *vt (unreg)* - **1.** [reduzieren Produktion] to scale down; [- Temperatur] to reduce - **2.** EDV to shut down.

heruntergekommen *adj* - **1.** [Haus] dilapidated - **2.** [Person] down-at-heel.

herunter|holen *vt* to bring down.

herunter|laden *vt (unreg)* EDV to download.

herunter|lassen *vt (unreg)* - **1.** [senken] to lower - **2.** [gehen lassen] to let down.

herunter|machen *vt*: **jn/etw heruntermachen** *fam* to pull sb/sthg to pieces, to knock sb/sthg.

herunter|schlucken *vt* to swallow.

hervor *adv*: **hervor mit euch!** out you come!

hervor|bringen *vt (unreg)* - **1.** [Ton] to utter - **2.** [entwickeln] to produce.

hervor|gehen (*perf* **ist hervorgegangen**) *vi (unreg)*: **aus etw hervorgehen** [zu entnehmen sein] to be clear from sthg; **aus dieser Familie sind mehrere Künstler hervorgegangen** this family has produced several artists; **aus etw als Sieger hervorgehen** to emerge victorious from sthg.

hervor|heben *vt (unreg)* to emphasize; **js Leistung hervorheben** to single out sb's performance.

hervor|holen *vt* to bring out.

hervorragend ◇ *adj* excellent. ◇ *adv* excellently; **hervorragend angezogen sein** to be extremely well-dressed; **hervorragend schmecken** to taste excellent.

hervor|rufen *vt (unreg)* - **1.** [verursachen] to cause - **2.** [rufen] to call out.

hervor|stechen *vi (unreg)* to stand out.

hervor|tun ◆ **sich hervortun** *ref (unreg)* - **1.** [auffallen] to distinguish o.s. - **2.** *abw* [angeben] to show off.

Herz (*pl* **-en** ODER **-**) *das* - **1.** [gen] heart - **2.** *(ohne Artikel) (ohne pl)* [Spielkartenfarbe] hearts *Pl*; **die Herzsechs** the six of hearts; **ein Herz für jn/etw haben** to be fond of sb/sthg; **es nicht übers Herz bringen, etw zu tun** not to have the heart to do sthg; **etwas auf dem Herzen haben** to have sthg on one's mind; **jm das Herz brechen** to break sb's heart; **ich möchte dir etwas ans Herz legen** allow me to give you a piece of advice; **sie/es liegt ihm am Herzen** she/it matters to him; **kein Herz haben** to be heartless. ◆ **von ganzem Herzen** *adv* wholeheartedly.

Herzenslust *die*: **nach Herzenslust** to one's heart's content.

herzerfrischend ◇ *adj* refreshing. ◇ *adv* refreshingly.

herzergreifend ◇ *adj* heartrending. ◇ *adv* heartrendingly.

herzhaft ◇ *adj* - **1.** [fest] hearty - **2.** [nahrhaft] hearty and tasty. ◇ *adv* - **1.** [fest] heartily - **2.** [nahrhaft]: **herzhaft schmecken** to be hearty and tasty.

her|ziehen (*perf* **hat/ist hergezogen**) *(unreg)* ◇ *vt (hat)* [heranziehen] to pull up; **jn/etw hinter sich** *(D)* **herziehen** to drag sb/sthg along behind one. ◇ *vi* - **1.** *abw* [lästern]: **über jn herziehen** to pull sb to pieces - **2.** *(ist)* [umziehen] to move here - **3.** *(ist)* [gehen] to walk along.

Herz|infarkt *der* heart attack.

Herz|klopfen *das*: **ich habe Herzklopfen** my heart is pounding.

herzlich ◇ *adj* - **1.** [freundlich] warm - **2.** [aufrichtig] sincere. ◇ *adv* - **1.** [freundlich] warmly - **2.** [aufrichtig] sincerely - **3.** [sehr] really; **herzlich wenig** very little.

Herzog, in (*mpl* **Herzöge**, *fpl* **-nen**) *der, die* duke (duchess *die*).

Herz|schlag *der* - **1.** [Herzrhythmus] heartbeat - **2.** [Herzstillstand] heart failure *(U)*.

Herz|schrittmacher (*pl* **-**) *der* pacemaker.

Herz|stillstand *der* cardiac arrest.

herzzerreißend ◇ *adj* heartrending. ◇ *adv* heartrendingly.

Hessen *nt* Hesse.

hessisch *adj* Hessian.

Hetze *die* - **1.** [Hast] (mad) rush - **2.** [Lästern] hate campaign.

hetzen (*perf* **hat/ist gehetzt**) ◇ *vi* - **1.** *(ist)* [rennen] to rush - **2.** *(hat)* [lästern]: **gegen jn hetzen** to stir up hatred against sb. ◇ *vt (hat)*: **jn/etw auf jn hetzen** to set sb/sthg on sb.

Heu *das* - **1.** [getrocknetes Gras] hay - **2.** *fam* [Geld] dough, dosh *UK*.

Heuchelei (*pl* **-en**) *die abw* - **1.** [Vortäuschen] hypocrisy - **2.** [Tat] piece of hypocrisy; [Äußerung] hypocritical remark.

heucheln ◇ *vt* to feign. ◇ *vi* to be a hypocrite.

Heuchler, in (*mpl* **-**, *fpl* **-nen**) *der, die* hypocrite.

heulen *vi* - **1.** [Person, Tier] to howl - **2.** [Sirene] to wail.

Heuschnupfen *der* hay fever.

heute *adv* - **1.** [als ein Tag] today; **heute Früh** early this morning; **heute Morgen/Mittag/Abend** this morning/lunchtime/evening; **heute in vierzehn Tagen/einer Woche** a fortnight/a week today; **lieber heute als morgen** sooner rather than later; **von heute auf morgen** from one day to the next, overnight - **2.** [gegenwärtig] nowadays.

heutig *adj* today's; **der heutige Tag** today.

heutzutage *adv* nowadays.

Hexe (*pl* **-n**) *die* witch.

Hexenschuss *der*: **einen Hexenschuss haben** to have lumbago.

Hexerei (*pl* **-en**) *die* witchcraft.

Hieb (*pl* **-e**) *der* [Schlag] blow. ◆ **Hiebe** *Pl fam* [Prügel]: **Hiebe bekommen** to get a beating.

hiebfest *adj*: **hieb- und stichfest** watertight.

hielt *prät* ▷ **halten**.

hier *adv* - **1.** [räumlich] here; [in der Schule]: **hier!** here!, present!; **der/die/das hier** this one here; **ab hier** from here; **von hier aus** from here; **hier und da** here and there; **"hier spricht Stefan"** [beim Telefon] "Stefan speaking"; **ich bin nicht von hier** I'm not from around here; **hier, nimm schon!** here, take it! - **2.** [zeitlich] now; **hier brach sie in Tränen aus** then she burst into tears; **von hier an** from now on; **hier und da** now and then - **3.** [in dieser Sache]: **hier täuschst du dich aber!** but that's where you're wrong.

hieran *adv* - **1.** [an dieser/diese Sache]: **die Erinnerung hieran fällt ihm schwer** he has difficulty remembering this - **2.** [an diesem/diesen Platz]: **hieran sind wir schon vorbeigekommen** we've already come past here.

Hierarchie (*pl* **-n**) *die* hierarchy.

hierauf *adv* - **1.** [auf dieser/diese Sache]: **hierauf beharren** to insist on this; **hierauf keine Antwort finden** to find no answer to this - **2.** [auf diesem/diesen Platz] on here - **3.** [daraufhin] hereupon.

hieraus *adv* out of this.

hier behalten *vt (unreg)* to keep here.

hierbei *adv* - **1.** [zeitlich] on this occasion - **2.** [bei dieser Sache]: **hierbei ist Konzentration nötig** you need to concentrate whilst doing this.

hier bleiben (*perf* **ist hier geblieben**) *vi (unreg)* to stay here.

hierdurch *adv* - **1.** [örtlich] through here - **2.** [ursächlich] as a result of this - **3.** [hiermit] hereby.

hierfür *adv* for this.

hierher *adv* here.

hierhin *adv* here.

hierin *adv* - **1.** [örtlich] in here - **2.** [in dieser Angelegenheit] in this.

hiermit *adv* - **1.** [mit diesem Gegenstand, mit dieser Angelegenheit] with this - **2.** [mit dieser Handlung] hereby.

hiernach *adv* - **1.** [zeitlich] after this - **2.** [dieser Aussage folgend] according to this.

hier sein (*perf* **ist hier gewesen**) *vi (unreg)* to be here.

hierüber *adv* - **1.** [räumlich] over here - **2.** [über diese Angelegenheit] about this - **3.** *geh* [zeitlich]: **hierüber vergingen mehrere Monate** this took several months.

hierum *adv* - **1.** [örtlich] around here - **2.** [um diese Sache] about this.

hierunter *adv* - **1.** [räumlich] under here - **2.** [unter dieser Sache] by this - **3.** [bei Menge] among these.

hiervon *adv* - **1.** [von diesem Gegenstand] of this - **2.** [von dieser Angelegenheit]: **hiervon hängt es ab** it depends on this; **hiervon halte ich viel** I think very highly of this - **3.** [örtlich] from here - **4.** [ursächlich] from this - **5.** [von dieser Menge] of these.

hierzu *adv* - **1.** [zu dieser Angelegenheit] to this; **ich rate dir dringend hierzu** I urge you to do this - **2.** [zu diesem Gegenstand] with this - **3.** [zu dieser Menge]: **stellen Sie sich bitte hierzu** please stand with these people here; **legen Sie die Zeitungen bitte hierzu** please add your newspapers to these.

hierzulande *adv* in this country.

hiesig *adj* local.

hieß *prät* ▷ **heißen**.

Hilfe (*pl* -n) ◇ *die* - **1.** [Helfen] help; **mit js Hilfe** with sb's help; **jn/etw zu Hilfe nehmen** to use sb/sthg - **2.** [Geld - freiwillig] aid; [- rechtlicht garantiert] benefit - **3.** [Haushaltshilfe] cleaner. ◇ *interj* help! ◆ **Hilfe suchend** ◇ *adj* [Blick] beseeching. ◇ *adv* beseechingly. ◆ **mit Hilfe** *adv* = **mithilfe**.

Hilfe|leistung *die* aid *(U)*.

Hilfe|ruf *der* call for help.

hilflos ◇ *adj* - **1.** [hilfsbedürftig] helpless - **2.** [ratlos] clueless - **3.** [unbeholfen] awkward. ◇ *adv* - **1.** [hilfsbedürftig] helplessly - **2.** [ratlos] cluelessly - **3.** [unbeholfen] awkwardly.

hilfreich ◇ *adj* helpful; **eine hilfreiche Hand** a helping hand. ◇ *adv*: **jm hilfreich zur Seite stehen** to be a big help to sb.

Hilfs|arbeiter, in *der, die* [in der Fabrik] unskilled worker; [beim Bau] labourer.

hilfsbedürftig *adj* in need (of help).

hilfsbereit *adj* helpful.

Hilfs|kraft *die* assistant.

Hilfs|mittel *das* aid.

Hilfs|verb *das* GRAMM auxiliary verb.

hilft *präs* ▷ **helfen**.

Himalaya *der*: **der Himalaya** the Himalayas.

Him|beere *die* raspberry.

Himmel (*pl* -) *der* - **1.** [Firmament] sky; **am Himmel** in the sky; **unter freiem Himmel** in the open, out of doors - **2.** [Jenseits] heaven - **3.** [Vorsehung]: **der Himmel weiß, wann er endlich zurückkommt** heaven (only) knows when he will finally come back - **4.** [Baldachin] canopy; **aus heiterem Himmel** out of the blue; **im siebenten Himmel sein** to be in seventh heaven.

himmelblau *adj* sky-blue.

Himmel|fahrt *die* Ascension Day.

Himmels|richtung *die* direction; **die vier Himmelsrichtungen** the four points of the compass.

himmlisch ◇ *adj* heavenly; **eine himmlische Fügung** divine providence. ◇ *adv* [leicht, bequem, schön] wonderfully; **himmlisch schmecken/aussehen** to taste/look divine.

hin *adv* - **1.** [räumlich]: **bis zum Baum hin** up to the tree; **zur Straße hin** towards the street; **zum Norden hin** (towards the) north; **wo ist er hin?** where has he gone?; **hin und her** back and forth; **der Weg hin** the way there; **zweimal London hin und zurück** two returns *UK* ODER round-trip tickets *US* to London; **einmal London nur hin, bitte!** one for London, just a single please - **2.** [zeitlich]: **zum Abend hin** towards evening; **über viele Jahre hin** for many years; **hin und wieder** now and then - **3.** *fig*: **er brabbelte da was vor sich hin** he was mumbling something to himself; **nach außen hin** outwardly; **auf deinen Rat hin** on your advice; **auf den Verdacht hin, dass...** on the suspicion that...; **ihr Kleid/Ruf ist hin** her dress/reputation is ruined; **er war von dem Mädchen ganz hin (und weg)** he was completely taken with the girl.

hinab *adv* = **hinunter**.

hinab|gehen (*perf* **ist hinabgegangen**) *(unreg) vt & vi geh* to go down.

hin|arbeiten *vi*: **auf etw** *(A)* **hinarbeiten** to work towards sthg.

hinauf *adv* up; **den Berg hinauf** up the mountain; **von den Alpen bis an die Ostsee hinauf** from the Alps right up to the Baltic.

hinauf|gehen (*perf* **ist hinaufgegangen**) *(unreg)* ◇ *vi* to go up; **es geht hinauf** the road climbs. ◇ *vt* to go up.

hinauf|sehen *vi (unreg)*: **zu jm/etw hinaufsehen** to look up at sb/sthg.

hinauf|steigen (*perf* **ist hinaufgestiegen**) *vi* & *vt (unreg)* to climb.

hinaus *adv* - **1.** [räumlich] out; **das Fenster geht zur Straße hinaus** the window looks (out) onto the street; **hinaus mit dir!** get out!; **über unsere Grenzen hinaus bekannt** known beyond our borders - **2.** [zeitlich]: **über das Abendbrot hinaus bleiben** to stay over dinner; **auf Monate hinaus** for months to come.

hinaus|begleiten *vt* to see out.

hinaus|gehen (*perf* **ist hinausgegangen**) *vi (unreg)* - **1.** [nach draußen] to go out - **2.**: **auf etw** *(A)* **hinausgehen** [gerichtet sein Zimmer, Fenster] to look onto sthg; [Tür, Gang] to lead into sthg; [in eine Richtung] to face sthg - **3.** [überschreiten]: **über etw** *(A)* **hinausgehen** to go beyond sthg.

hinaus|laufen (*perf* **ist hinausgelaufen**) *vi (unreg)* - **1.** [nach draußen] to run outside - **2.** [abzielen]: **auf etw** *(A)* **hinauslaufen** to amount to sthg; **das läuft auf dasselbe hinaus** it amounts to the same thing.

hinaus|schieben *vt (unreg)* - **1.** [nach draußen] to push outside - **2.** [zeitlich] to put off, to postpone. ◆ **sich hinausschieben** *ref* [örtlich] to push one's way out.

hinaus|werfen *vt (unreg)* to throw out.

hinaus|zögern *vt* to put off. ◆ **sich hinauszögern** *ref* to be delayed.

hin|bekommen *vt (unreg)*: **wie willst du denn das hinbekommen?** how do you intend to do ODER manage that?; **etw wieder hinbekommen** to mend sthg.

hin|bestellen *vt* to tell to come/go.

Hinblick *der*: **in** ODER **im Hinblick auf jn/etw** [in Bezug auf] with regard to sb/sthg; **in** ODER **im Hinblick auf etw** *(A)* [wegen] in view of sthg.

hinderlich *adj*: **jm/einer Sache hinderlich sein** to get in sb's/sthg's way.

hindern *vt* to prevent; **was hindert dich zu bleiben?** what is preventing you from staying?

Hindernis (*pl* **-se**) *das* obstacle; [in Leichtathletik] hurdle; [in Springreiten] jump.

hin|deuten *vi* to point; **auf jn/etw hindeuten** [zeigen] to point at sb/sthg; [in einer Menge] to point sb/sthg out; [erkennen lassen] to point to sb/sthg.

Hindi *das* Hindi; *siehe auch* **Englisch(e)**.

Hindu (*pl* **-s**) *der* Hindu.

hindurch *adv* - **1.** [zeitlich]: **den ganzen Tag hindurch** throughout the whole day - **2.** [örtlich]: **durch den Berg hindurch** through the mountain.

hinein *adv* - **1.** [räumlich] in; **hinein ins Bett!** get into bed! - **2.** [zeitlich]: **bis tief in die Nacht hinein arbeiten** to work late into the night.

hinein|denken ◆ **sich hineindenken** *ref (unreg)*: **sich in jn/etw hineindenken** to put o.s. in sb's/sthg's position.

hinein|fressen *vt (unreg)*: **etw in sich** *(A)* **hineinfressen** to gobble sthg up; *fam* [Sorgen] to bottle sthg up.

hinein|gehen (*perf* **ist hineingegangen**) *vi (unreg)* - **1.** [nach drinnen] to go inside - **2.** [hineinpassen]: **in diese Flasche geht nicht mehr als ein Liter hinein** this bottle won't hold more than a litre.

hinein|geraten (*perf* **ist hineingeraten**) *vi (unreg)*: **in etw** *(A)* **hineingeraten** to get into sthg; **in einen einsamen Wald hineingeraten** to find o.s. in a lonely wood.

hinein|steigern ◆ **sich hineinsteigern** *ref*: **sie hat sich in diese Sache hineingesteigert** she has become completely caught up in this affair.

hinein|versetzen ◆ **sich hineinversetzen** *ref*: **sich in jn** ODER **in js Lage hineinversetzen** to put o.s. in sb's position.

hinein|ziehen (*perf* **hat/ist hineingezogen**) *(unreg)* ◇ *vt (hat)* - **1.** [nach drinnen] to pull in - **2.** [verwickeln]: **jn in etw** *(A)* **hineinziehen** to draw sb into sthg. ◇ *vi (ist)* - **1.** [umziehen] to move in - **2.** [gehen] to go in.

hin|fahren (*perf* **hat/ist hingefahren**) *(unreg)* ◇ *vi (ist)* to go there; [mit Auto] to drive there; **wo ist er hingefahren?** where did he go (to)? ◇ *vt (hat)* to take there.

Hin|fahrt *die* [mit dem Auto] journey there; [mit dem Zug] outward journey.

hin|fallen (*perf* **ist hingefallen**) *vi (unreg)* to fall (down); **sie hat die Vase hinfallen lassen** she dropped the vase.

hinfällig *adj* - **1.** [altersschwach] frail - **2.** [ungültig] invalid.

Hin|flug *der* outward flight.

hin|führen ◇ *vt* to lead there. ◇ *vi* to lead there; **zu etw hinführen** to lead to sthg.

hing *prät* ▷ **hängen**.

hin|geben *vt (unreg) geh* to give up. ◆ **sich hingeben** *ref*: **sich einer Sache** *(D)* **hingeben** to devote o.s. to sthg; **sich einer Illusion hingeben** to cherish an illusion; **sich jm hingeben** to give o.s. to sb.

hingegen *konj* on the other hand.

hin|gehen (*perf* **ist hingegangen**) *vi (unreg)* [gehen] to go there; **zu etw hingehen** to go to sthg.

hin|halten *vt (unreg)* - **1.** [reichen] to hold out - **2.** [vertrösten] to keep waiting.

hin|hocken ◆ **sich hinhocken** *ref* to crouch down.

hịnken (*perf* **hat/ist gehịnkt**) *vi* - **1.** *(hat)* [humpeln] to (have a) limp - **2.** *(ist)* [an einen Ort] to limp, to hobble.

hịn|knien ◆ **sich hinknien** *ref* to kneel down.

hịn|kommen (*perf* **ist hịngekommen**) *vi (unreg)* - **1.** [ankommen] to get there; **zu etw hinkommen** to get to sthg - **2.** [hingehören] to belong, to go - **3.** [hingeraten]: **wenn ich wüsste, wo meine Brille hingekommen ist** if I knew where my glasses had gone - **4.** [auskommen]: **mit etw hinkommen** to manage with sthg - **5.** [zutreffen] to work out; **das kommt hin/nicht hin!** that is right/wrong!

hịn|kriegen *vt fam* to manage; **sie hat das gut hingekriegt** she made a good job of that; **etw wieder hinkriegen** to fix sthg.

hịnlänglich ◇ *adj* sufficient. ◇ *adv* sufficiently.

hịn|legen *vt* - **1.** [Gegenstand] to put down; [Zettel] to leave - **2.** [ins Bett] to put to bed - **3.** *fam* [bezahlen] to fork out - **4.** *fam* [Darbietung] to turn in; [Prüfung] to do. ◆ **sich hinlegen** *ref* - **1.** [sich legen] to lie down - **2.** *fam* [stürzen] to come a cropper.

hịn|nehmen *vt (unreg)* - **1.** [ertragen] to take - **2.** *fam* [mitnehmen]: **jn/etw (zu jm) mit hinnehmen** to take sb/sthg (to sb).

hịn|pflanzen ◆ **sich hinpflanzen** *ref fam* [sich hinstellen]: **sich (vor jn) hinpflanzen** to plant o.s. (in front of sb).

hịn|reichen ◇ *vt* [zureichen]: **jm etw hinreichen** to hand sb sthg. ◇ *vi* - **1.** [sich erstrecken] to reach - **2.** [ausreichen] to be enough.

Hịnreise *die* journey there.

hịn|reißen *vt (unreg)* - **1.** [ziehen] to pull - **2.** [begeistern] to captivate - **3.** [verleiten]: **sich zu etw hinreißen lassen** [überzeugen] to let o.s. be carried away into doing sthg; [provozieren] to be driven to do sthg.

hịnreißend *adj* captivating.

hịn|richten *vt* to execute.

Hịn|richtung *die* execution.

hịn|schauen *vi* to look; **genau hinschauen** to look closely.

hịn sein (*perf* **ist hịn gewesen**) *vi (unreg) fam* [kaputt] to have had it; [ruiniert] to be shattered; [vor Glück] to be overjoyed.

hịn|setzen *vt* [Gegenstand] to put down; [Baby] to sit down. ◆ **sich hinsetzen** *ref* - **1.** [sich setzen] to sit down - **2.** *fam* [stürzen] to land on one's backside.

Hịnsicht *die (ohne pl)*: **in dieser/jeder Hinsicht** in this/every respect; **in doppelter Hinsicht** in two respects.

hịn|stellen *vt* - **1.** [stellen] to put - **2.** [absetzen] to put down - **3.** [darstellen]: **jn/etw als etw hinstellen** to describe sb/sthg as sthg. ◆ **sich hinstellen** *ref* - **1.** [sich stellen] to stand - **2.** [darstellen]: **sich als jn/etw hinstellen** to pretend to be sb/sthg.

hịnten *adv* - **1.** [am Ende] at the back; **da** ODER **dort hinten** back there; **sie ist hinten im Garten** she's out the back (in the garden); **im Auto hinten sitzen** to sit in the back of the car; **das dritte Haus von hinten** the third house from the end - **2.** [weit entfernt]: **weit hinten** a long way behind - **3.** [an der Rückseite] on the back; **das Haus hat hinten einen Balkon** the house has a balcony at the back - **4.** [als Richtungsangabe] back; **von hinten** from behind.

hịntenherum *adv fam* - **1.** [um etw herum] round the back - **2.** [indirekt] indirectly.

hịnter *präp* - **1.** *(+ D, A)* [räumlich] behind; **hinter dem Haus** behind the house, in back of the house *US*; **hinter jm herlaufen** to run after sb; **3 km hinter Köln** 3 km after Cologne - **2.** [zeitlich]: **etw hinter sich** *(A)* **bringen** to put sthg behind one; **das hätten wir endlich hinter uns!** thank God that's behind us!

Hịnter|ausgang *der* rear exit.

Hinterbliebene (*pl* **-n**) *der, die* surviving dependant.

hịntere, r, s *adj* back.

Hịntere (*pl* **-n**) *der, die, das*: **der/die/das Hintere** the one at the back.

hintereinạnder *adv* - **1.** [räumlich] behind each other - **2.** [zeitlich] in a row.

Hịnter|eingang *der* rear entrance.

Hịnter|gedanke *der* ulterior motive.

hintergehen (*prät* **hinterging**, *perf* **hat hintergangen**) *vt* to deceive.

Hịnter|grund *der* background; **im Hintergrund bleiben** to remain in the background; **jn/etw in den Hintergrund drängen** to push sb/sthg into the background.

Hịnterhalt (*pl* **-e**) *der* ambush; **im Hinterhalt liegen** to lie in ambush; **in einen Hinterhalt geraten** ODER **fallen** to be ambushed.

hịnterhältig ◇ *adj* devious. ◇ *adv* deviously.

hinterher[1] *adv* [räumlich] behind.

hịnterher[2] *adv* [zeitlich] afterwards.

hinterher|fahren (*perf* **ist hinterhergefahren**) *vi (unreg)*: **jm/etw hinterherfahren** to drive behind sb/sthg; [verfolgen] to drive after sb/sthg.

hinterher|gehen (*perf* **ist hinterhergegangen**) *vi (unreg)*: **jm hinterhergehen** to follow sb.

Hịnter|kopf *der* back of the head; **etw im Hinterkopf haben/behalten** *fig* to have/keep sthg at the back of one's mind.

hinterlạssen (*präs* **hinterlạ̈sst**, *prät* **hinterließ**, *perf* **hat hinterlạssen**) *vt* to leave; **jm etw hinterlassen** to leave sb sthg.

hinterlegen *vt*: **etw bei jm hinterlegen** to leave sthg with sb.

Hịnterlist *die* cunning.

hịnterlistig ◇ *adj* cunning. ◇ *adv* cunningly.

Hịntern (*pl* -) *der fam* backside.

Hịnter|rad *das* back wheel.

Hịnter|seite *die* back.

Hịnter|teil *das fam* backside.

Hịntertreffen *das (ohne pl)*: **ins Hintertreffen geraten** to fall behind.

hintertreiben (*prät* **hintertrieb**, *perf* **hat hintertrieben**) *vt* [Plan] to thwart; [Heirat] to prevent; [Gesetz, Reform] to block.

Hịnter|tür *die* back door.

hinterziehen (*prät* **hinterzog**, *perf* **hat hinterzogen**) *vt*: **Steuern hinterziehen** to evade tax.

hịn|treten (*perf* **hat/ist hịngetreten**) *vi (unreg)* - **1.** *(ist)* [an einen Ort]: **zu jm/etw hintreten** to step over to sb/sthg; **vor jn hintreten** to go up to sb - **2.** *(hat)* [mit Fuß] to kick.

hinüber *adv* over, across; **da hinüber** over there; **gehen Sie links/rechts hinüber** go left/right; *siehe auch* **hinüber sein**.

hinüber sein (*perf* **ist hinüber gewesen**) *vi (unreg) fam* - **1.** [kaputt] to have had it; [erschöpft] to be done in; [betrunken] to be well away - **2.** [gehen] to have gone over.

hinụnter *adv* down; **die Treppe hinunter** down the stairs; **vom General bis hinunter zum einfachen Soldat** from the general down to the private.

hinụnter|blicken *vi*: **in etw** *(A)* **hinunterblicken** to look down into sthg; **an sich** *(D)* **hinunterblicken** to look down at o.s.

hinụnter|schlucken *vt eigtl* & *fig* to swallow.

hinụnter|stürzen (*perf* **hat/ist hinụntergestürzt**) *vt* - **1.** *(ist)* [hinunterfallen] to fall down - **2.** *(hat)* [werfen] to throw down - **3.** *(hat) fam* [schnell trinken] to gulp down. ◆ **sich hinunterstürzen** *ref* [sich hinunterwerfen]: **sich (von etw) hinunterstürzen** to throw o.s. off (sthg).

hinwẹg *adv geh* away; **über jn/etw hinweg** over sb/sthg; **über Jahre hinweg** for many years.

Hịnweg *der* way there; **auf dem Hinweg** on the way there.

hinwẹg|gehen (*perf* **ist hinwẹggegangen**) *vi (unreg)*: **über etw** *(A)* **hinweggehen** to pass over sthg.

hinwẹg|kommen (*perf* **ist hinwẹggekommen**) *vi (unreg)*: **über etw** *(A)* **hinwegkommen** to get over sthg.

hinwẹg|sehen *vi (unreg)*: **über jn/etw hinwegsehen** to see over sb/sthg; **über etw** *(A)* **hinwegsehen** *fig* to overlook sthg.

hinwẹg|setzen ◆ **sich hinwegsetzen** *ref*: **sich über etw** *(A)* **hinwegsetzen** to disregard sthg.

Hịnweis (*pl* **-e**) *der* [Tip, Fingerzeig] tip; [Anleitung] instruction; [Indiz] sign.

hịn|weisen *(unreg)* ◇ *vi* - **1.** [auf etw schließen lassen]: **auf etw** *(A)* **hinweisen** to point to sthg - **2.** [zeigen]: **auf jn/etw hinweisen** to point to sb/sthg. ◇ *vt*: **jn auf etw** *(A)* **hinweisen** to point sthg out to sb.

hịn|wenden *vt* to turn. ◆ **sich hinwenden** *ref* to turn.

hịn|werfen *vt (unreg)* - **1.** [werfen] to throw down - **2.** *fam* [Arbeit, Projekt] to chuck in - **3.** [Skizze] to dash off - **4.** [Bemerkung] to drop casually; [Frage] to ask casually - **5.** *fam* [fallen lassen] to drop. ◆ **sich hinwerfen** *ref* to throw o.s. down.

hịn|ziehen (*perf* **hat/ist hịngezogen**) *(unreg)* ◇ *vt (hat)* - **1.** [anziehen]: **jn/etw zu sich hinziehen** to attract sb/sthg - **2.** [zeitlich] to draw out. ◇ *vi (ist)* [umziehen] to move. ◆ **sich hinziehen** *ref* [lange dauern] to drag on.

hinzu *adv* in addition; **hinzu kommt noch** (and) what is more.

hinzu|fügen *vt* to add; **etw zu etw hinzufügen** to add sthg to sthg.

hinzu|kommen (*perf* **ist hinzugekommen**) *vi (unreg)* - **1.** [ankommen]: **zu jm/etw hinzukommen** to join sb/sthg - **2.** [sich ergeben] to be added on.

hinzu|ziehen *vt (unreg)* to call in.

Hịrn (*pl* **-e**) *das* - **1.** [Gehirn] brain - **2.** *fam* [Denkvermögen] brains *Pl*.

Hịrngespinst (*pl* **-e**) *das abw* figment of one's imagination.

Hịrsch (*pl* **-e**) *der* [Tier] deer; [männlich] stag; [Fleisch] venison.

Hịrse *die* millet.

Hịrte (*pl* **-n**), **Hịrt** (*pl* **-en**) *der* shepherd.

Hịrtin (*pl* **-nen**) *die* shepherdess.

hịssen *vt* to hoist.

Historiker, **in** (*mpl* -, *fpl* **-nen**) *der, die* historian.

historisch ◇ *adj* - **1.** [geschichtlich] historical - **2.** [entscheidend] historic. ◇ *adv* [geschichtlich] historically; **etw historisch betrachten** to look at sthg in historical terms.

Hịt (*pl* **-s**) *der* hit.

Hịt|parade *die* charts *Pl*.

Hịtze *die* heat.

hịtzebeständig *adj* heat-resistant.

hịtzefrei *adj*: **hitzefrei haben** *to have the day off school because of hot weather.*

Hịtze|welle *die* heatwave.

hịtzig ◇ *adj* - **1.** [Person] hot-blooded; [Temperament] fiery - **2.** [Diskussion, Streit] heated. ◇ *adv* [lebhaft] heatedly.

hịtzköpfig *adj* [Person] hot-tempered.

Hịtz|schlag *der* heat stroke.

HIV-positiv *adj* MED HIV-positive.

H-Milch *die* long-life milk.

hob *prät* ▻ **heben**.

Hobby ['hɔbi] (*pl* **-s**) *das* hobby.

Hobby|koch *der* amateur cook.

Hobby|köchin *die* amateur cook.

Hobel (*pl* -) *der* - **1.** [Werkzeug] plane - **2.** [Küchengerät] slicer.

Hobelbank (*pl* **-bänke**) *die* carpenter's bench.

hobeln ◇ *vt* [Holz] to plane; [Gemüse] to slice. ◇ *vi* to plane; **an etw** *(D)* **hobeln** to plane sthg.

hoch (*kompar* **höher**, *superl* **höchste**) ◇ *adj* - **1.** [räumlich] high; [Baum, Gebäude] tall; [Schnee] deep; **drei Meter hoch** three metres high/tall/deep; **im hohen Norden** in the far north - **2.** [bezeichnet Ausmass - Blutdruck, Tempo, Mieten, Preis *etc*] high; [- Gewicht, Strafe] heavy; [- Anzahl, Summe] large; **in hohem Grade** to a large extent; **wenn es hoch kommt** at the most - **3.** [bezeichnet Qualität - Position, Ansprüche] high; [- Ehre, Begabung] great; **das ist mir zu hoch** *fam fig* that's beyond me - **4.** [gesellschaftlich gehoben]: **von hoher Geburt** of high birth; **von hohem Ansehen** highly regarded; **ein hoher Beamter** a high-ranking official - **5.** MUS high; **jn in den höchsten Tönen loben** *fig* to praise sb to the skies. ◇ *adv* *(kompar höher; superl am höchsten)* - **1.** [räumlich]: **das Dorf ist hoch gelegen** the village is situated high up; **zwei Treppen hoch** two floors up; **das Flugzeug fliegt 3000 Meter hoch** the plane is flying at (a height of) 3,000 metres; **ein hoch aufgeschossener Junge** a tall boy - **2.** [bezeichnet Ausmass, Qualität] highly; **hoch verlieren** to lose heavily; **hoch zufrieden** very content; **hoch und heilig versprechen** to promise solemnly - **3.** MUS high; **du singst zu hoch!** you're singing sharp!

Hoch (*pl* **-s**) *das* - **1.** [Jubelruf] cheer; **jm ein dreifaches Hoch ausbringen** to give three cheers for sb - **2.** [Hochdruckgebiet] high.

Hochachtung *die* great respect.

hochachtungsvoll *adv* Yours faithfully *(nach Dear Sir/Madam)*; Yours sincerely *(nach Dear Mr/Mrs X)*.

hoch|arbeiten ◆ **sich hocharbeiten** *ref* to work one's way up.

hoch begabt *adj* highly talented.

Hochbetrieb *der*: **im Büro herrscht Hochbetrieb** it's very busy in the office.

hoch bezahlt *adj* highly-paid.

Hoch|burg *die* stronghold.

hochdeutsch ◇ *adj* standard German. ◇ *adv* in standard German.

Hochdruck *der* - **1.** [technisch, meteorologisch] high pressure; **unter Hochdruck stehen** to be under high pressure - **2.** *fam fig* [Hochbetrieb]: **unter Hochdruck stehen** to be at full stretch.

Hochdruck|gebiet *das* high-pressure area.

hoch empfindlich *adj* highly sensitive.

hocherfreut ◇ *adj* highly delighted. ◇ *adv* with great delight.

hoch|fahren (*perf* **hat/ist hochgefahren**) *(unreg)* ◇ *vi (ist)* - **1.** [nach oben] to go up; [in Auto] to drive up - **2.** [erschrecken] to start; **aus dem Schlaf hochfahren** to wake up with a start - **3.** [zornig] to flare up. ◇ *vt (hat) fam* [nach oben] to take up.

hoch|fliegen (*perf* **ist hochgeflogen**) *vi (unreg)* [Vogel, Flugzeug] to fly up.

Hoch|form *die*: **in Hochform sein** to be on top form.

Hoch|frequenz *die* PHYS high frequency.

Hoch|gebirge *das* high mountains *Pl*.

Hoch|gefühl *das*: **im Hochgefühl einer Sache** *(G)* elated by sthg.

hoch|gehen (*perf* **ist hochgegangen**) *vi (unreg)* - **1.** [gehen, sich heben] to go up - **2.** [Mine, Bombe] to go off; [Gebäude] to blow up; **etw hochgehen lassen** to blow sthg up - **3.** *fam* [wütend werden] to hit the roof - **4.** [aufgedeckt werden] to be uncovered; **jn hochgehen lassen** *fam* to squeal on sb.

hochgestellt *adj* [Zahl] superscript.

Hochglanz *der*: **ein Fotoabzug in Hochglanz** a gloss print; **auf Hochglanz poliert** polished until it shines; **etw auf Hochglanz bringen** *fig* to make sthg spick-and-span.

hochgradig ◇ *adj* extreme. ◇ *adv* extremely.

hoch|halten *vt (unreg)* [bewahren] to uphold.

hoch halten *vt (unreg)* [nach oben] to hold up.

Hoch|haus *das* high-rise building.

hoch|heben *vt (unreg)*: **jn/etw hochheben** to lift sb/sthg (up).

hochkant *adv* on end.

hoch|klappen (*perf* **hat/ist hochgeklappt**) ◇ *vt (hat)* [Klapptisch] to fold up; [Verdeck, Armlehne] to fold back; [Kragen] to turn up; [Sitz] to tip up. ◇ *vi (ist)* [Kragen, Hutkrempe] to turn up; [Sitz] to tip up.

hoch|klettern (*perf* **ist hochgeklettert**) *vi*: **an etw** *(D)* **hochklettern** to climb (up) sthg.

hoch|kommen (*perf* **ist hochgekommen**) *vi (unreg)* - **1.** [nach oben] to come up - **2.** [aufstehen] to get up - **3.** [beruflich] to get on - **4.** [erbrechen]: **es kommt ihr bei dem Gedanken daran heute noch hoch** the thought of it still makes her feel sick today.

Hoch|konjunktur *die* boom.

hoch|krempeln *vt* to roll up.

Hoch|land *das* uplands *Pl*.

hoch|leben *vi*: **jn/etw hochleben lassen** to give three cheers for sb/sthg.

Hochleistungssport *der* top-level sport.

Hochmut *der* arrogance.

hochmütig ◇ *adj* arrogant. ◇ *adv* arrogantly.

hochnäsig *abw adj* conceited.

hoch nehmen *vt (unreg)* [Teppich] to lift up; [Baby] to pick up.

Hoch|ofen *der* blast furnace.

hochprozentig *adj* [Getränk, Spirituose] high-proof; [Lösung] highly concentrated.

Hoch|rechnung *die* projection.

hochrot *adj* bright red.

Hoch|saison *die* high season.

hoch|schlagen ['hoːxʃlaːgn̩] (*perf* **hat/ist hochgeschlagen**) *(unreg)* ◇ *vt (hat)* to turn up. ◇ *vi (ist)* to leap up.

hoch|schrecken ['hoːxʃrɛkn̩] (*prät* **schreckte** ODER **schrak hoch**, *perf* **hat/ist hochgeschreckt**) ◇ *vt (hat) (reg)* to startle. ◇ *vi (ist)* to start; **er ist aus dem Schlaf hochgeschreckt** he was startled out of sleep.

Hochschulabschluss (*pl* **-schlüsse**) *der* (university) degree.

Hoch|schule *die* college; [Universität] university.

Hochschul|lehrer, in *der, die* college lecturer; [an der Universität] university lecturer.

Hochschul|reife *die qualification required by school-leavers for university entrance.*

hochschwanger ['hoːxʃvaŋɐ] *adj* heavily pregnant.

Hoch|sommer *der* midsummer.

Hoch|spannung *die* - **1.** [Strom] high voltage - **2.** [Stimmung] great tension.

hoch|spielen ['hoːxʃpiːlən] *vt* to blow up.

Hoch|springer, in *der, die* SPORT high jumper.

Hochsprung *der* SPORT high jump.

höchst ['høːçst] *adv* highly.

Hochstapler, in ['hoːxʃtaːplɐ, ərɪn] (*mpl* -, *fpl* **-nen**) *der, die* con artist.

Höchst|belastung *die* extreme pressure; [eines Materials, einer Konstruktion] maximum load.

höchstens ['høːçstn̩s] *adv* - **1.** [im äußersten Fall] at best - **2.** [außer] except.

Höchstfall *der (ohne pl)*: **im Höchstfall** at (the) most.

Höchstform *die*: **in Höchstform sein** to be on top form.

Höchst|geschwindigkeit *die* speed limit.

Höchst|grenze *die* upper limit.

Hochstimmung *die* festive mood.

höchstmöglich ['høːçstmøːklɪç] *adj* highest possible.

höchstwahrscheinlich ['høːçstvaːɐ̯ʃaɪ̯nlɪç] *adv* most probably.

Hoch|tour *die*: **auf Hochtouren laufen** [Maschine] to run at top speed; [Vorbereitungen] to be in full swing.

hochtrabend *abw* ◇ *adj* pompous. ◇ *adv* pompously.

Hochwasser *das* high water; **Hochwasser haben** to be in spate; *fam fig* to be at half-mast.

hochwertig *adj* [Produkte] high-quality; [Eiweiß] highly nutritious.

Hoch|zeit *die* wedding; **silberne/goldene Hochzeit** silver/golden wedding.

Hochzeits|kleid *das* wedding dress.

Hochzeits|nacht *die* wedding night.

Hochzeits|paar *das* bride and groom.

Hochzeits|reise *die* honeymoon.

Hochzeits|tag *der* [Tag der Hochzeit] wedding day; [Jubiläum] wedding anniversary.

hoch|ziehen *vt (unreg)* - **1.** [Rollladen, Hose] to pull up; [Segel, Flagge] to hoist - **2.** [heben] to raise; **die Nase hochziehen** to sniff - **3.** [bauen] to put up. ◆ **sich hochziehen** *ref*: **sich an etw** *(D)* **hochziehen** to pull o.s. up by holding on to sthg; *fig* to take pleasure in sthg.

Hocke (*pl* **-n**) *die* - **1.** [Haltung]: **in die Hocke gehen** to crouch down - **2.** [Sprung] squat vault.

hocken *vi* - **1.** [kauern] to crouch - **2.** *fam* [sitzen] to sit. ◆ **sich hocken** *ref* - **1.** [sich kauern] to crouch - **2.** *fam* [sich setzen] to sit o.s. down.

Hocker (*pl* -) *der* stool.

Höcker (*pl* -) *der* - **1.** [Ausbuchtung] bump - **2.** [von Kamel] hump.

Hockey *das* hockey.

Hoden (*pl* -) *der* testicle.

Hof (*pl* **Höfe**) *der* - **1.** [von Häusern] courtyard - **2.** [Bauernhof] farm - **3.** [Schulhof] playground - **4.** [von Gefängnissen] yard - **5.** [von Königen] court; **jm den Hof machen** *fig* to court sb.

Hofbräuhaus *das large beer hall in Munich.*

hoffen ◇ *vt* to hope; **hoffen wir das Beste!** let's hope for the best! ◇ *vi*: **auf etw hoffen** to hope for sthg; **auf jn hoffen** to pin one's hopes on sb; **auf Gott hoffen** to trust in God.

hoffentlich *adv* hopefully; **kommt er? - ja, hoffentlich!** is he coming? - I hope so!

Hoffnung (*pl* **-en**) *die* hope; **die Hoffnung aufgeben/nicht aufgeben** to give up/not to give up hope; **seine Hoffnungen auf jn/etw setzen** to pin one's hopes on sb/sthg.

hoffnungslos ◇ *adj* hopeless. ◇ *adv* hopelessly.

Hoffnungslosigkeit *die* hopelessness.

hoffnungsvoll ◇ *adj* - **1.** [optimistisch] hopeful - **2.** [Erfolg versprechend] promising. ◇ *adv* - **1.** [optimistisch] hopefully - **2.** [Erfolg versprechend] promisingly.

höflich ◇ *adj* polite. ◇ *adv* politely.

Höflichkeit (*pl* **-en**) *die* - **1.** [im Auftreten] politeness - **2.** [Floskel] polite remark.

Höhe (*pl* **-n**) *die* - **1.** [von Schrank, Berg] height; [von Dreieck] altitude - **2.** [von Preis, Temperatur] level; **ein Bußgeld in Höhe von 50 Euro** a fine of 50 euros - **3.** [Richtung]: **in die Höhe** up

- **4.** [Linie]: **auf der** ODER **in Höhe von etw** level with sthg; **auf gleicher Höhe** level; **das ist die Höhe!** *fam* that's the limit!

Hoheit (*pl* **-en**) *die* **- 1.** [Herrschaft] sovereignty **- 2.** [als Anrede] Your Highness.

Hoheits|gebiet *das* sovereign territory.

Höhen|lage *die* altitude; **in Höhenlage** at high altitude.

Höhen|sonne *die* sun lamp.

Höhe|punkt *der* high point.

hohl ◇ *adj* **- 1.** [gen] hollow; [Augen] sunken; **in der hohlen Hand** in the hollow of one's hand **- 2.** *fam abw* [dumm - Phrase] empty; [- Person] empty-headed. ◇ *adv* **- 1.** [dumpf] hollowly **- 2.** *fam abw* [geistlos] emptily.

Höhle (*pl* **-n**) *die* **- 1.** [Grotte] cave **- 2.** [von Dachs] sett; [von Löwe] den; [von Fuchs] lair.

Hohl|kreuz *das (ohne pl)* hollow back.

Hohl|raum *der* cavity.

höhnisch ◇ *adj* scornful. ◇ *adv* scornfully.

holen *vt* **- 1.** [herbeischaffen] to fetch, to get; **sich** *(D)* **bei jm Rat holen** to ask sb for advice; **etw holen kommen** to come for sthg; **sich** *(D)* **etw holen** [gen] to get sthg; [Krankheit] to catch sthg **- 2.** [kaufen] to get **- 3.** [herausnehmen]: **etw aus etw holen** to take sthg out of sthg **- 4.** [Arzt, Polizei, Handwerker] to call.

Holland *nt* Holland.

Holländer (*pl* -) ◇ *der* Dutchman; **die Holländer** the Dutch. ◇ *adj (unver)* Dutch.

Holländerin (*pl* **-nen**) *die* Dutchwoman.

holländisch *adj* Dutch.

Hölle *die* hell; **die Hölle ist los!** *fam fig* all hell has broken loose!; **jm die Hölle heiß machen** *fam fig* to give sb hell.

höllisch ◇ *adj* **- 1.** [schrecklich] appalling **- 2.** *fam* [intensiv] infernal. ◇ *adv fam* [sehr]: **die Wunde tut höllisch weh** the wound hurts like hell; **höllisch aufpassen** to be incredibly careful.

Holm (*pl* **-e**) *der* SPORT bar.

holpern (*perf* **hat/ist geholpert**) *vi* **- 1.** *(ist)* [beim Fahren] to jolt **- 2.** *(hat)* [beim Sprechen] to stumble.

holprig ◇ *adj* **- 1.** [Weg] bumpy **- 2.** [Fremdsprache] halting **- 3.** [Stil] clumsy. ◇ *adv* [sprechen, lesen] haltingly.

Holunder (*pl* -) *der* **- 1.** [Baum] elder **- 2.** [Beere] elderberry.

Holz (*pl* **Hölzer**) *das* wood; [Bauholz] timber *UK*, lumber *US*; **aus dem gleichen** ODER **demselben Holz (geschnitzt) sein** *fig* to be cast from the same mould. ◆ **Holz verarbeitend** *adj* timber-processing.

Holzfäller, in (*mpl* -, *fpl* **-nen**) *der, die* woodcutter *UK*, lumberjack *US*.

holzig *adj* woody.

Holz|kohle *die* charcoal.

Holz|schuh *der* clog.

Holz|weg *der*: **auf dem Holzweg sein** to be barking up the wrong tree.

Homebanking ['ho:mbɛŋkɪŋ] *das* home banking.

Homepage ['ho:mpe:dʒ] (*pl* **-s**) *die* EDV home page.

Homeshopping *das (ohne pl)* home shopping.

Homöopathie *die* homeopathy.

Homosexualität *die* homosexuality.

homosexuell *adj* homosexual.

Honig *der* honey.

Honorar (*pl* **-e**) *das* fee.

Hopfen (*pl* -) *der* hops *Pl*; **bei ihm ist Hopfen und Malz verloren** he's a hopeless case.

hörbar ◇ *adj* audible. ◇ *adv* audibly.

hörbehindert *adj* hard of hearing.

horchen *vi* to listen.

Horde (*pl* **-n**) *die* horde.

hören ◇ *vt* **- 1.** [wahrnehmen, erfahren] to hear; **er hat lange nichts von sich hören lassen** we haven't heard from him for ages; **von ihm hört man nur Gutes** you only hear good things about him **- 2.** [willkürlich] to listen to. ◇ *vi* **- 1.** [unwillkürlich, erfahren] to hear; **schwer hören** to be hard of hearing; **Sie werden noch von mir hören!** you haven't heard the last of this! **- 2.** [zuhören, gehorchen] to listen; **hör mal!** listen!; **hören auf** *(+ A)* to listen to; **hätte ich doch auf ihren Rat gehört!** if only I'd listened to her advice!

Hörensagen *das*: **etw vom Hörensagen kennen** to know sthg from hearsay.

Hörer (*pl* -) *der* **- 1.** [Zuhörer] listener **- 2.** [Telefonhörer] receiver.

Hörerin (*pl* **-nen**) *die* listener.

Hörerschaft *die* listeners *Pl*.

Hör|fehler *der* hearing defect.

Hör|funk *der* radio.

Hör|gerät *das* hearing aid.

hörgeschädigt *adj* hard of hearing.

Horizont (*pl* **-e**) *der* horizon; **das geht über meinen Horizont** *fig* that's beyond me; **seinen Horizont erweitern** *fig* to broaden one's horizons.

horizontal ◇ *adj* horizontal. ◇ *adv* horizontally.

Hormon (*pl* **-e**) *das* hormone.

Horn (*pl* **Hörner** ODER **-e**) *das* horn.

Hörnchen (*pl* -) *das* **- 1.** [Gebäck] croissant **- 2.** [Horn] small horn.

Horn|haut *die* **- 1.** [Hautschicht] patch of hard skin, callus **- 2.** [des Auges] cornea.

Hornisse (*pl* **-n**) *die* hornet.

Horoskop (*pl* **-e**) *das* horoscope.

horrend *adj* horrendous.

Horror *der* - **1.** [Entsetzen] horror; **einen Horror vor jm/etw haben** to be terrified of sb/sthg - **2.** *fam* [Unangenehmes]: **das war der (reine) Horror** it was a (total) nightmare.
Hör|saal *der* lecture hall.
Hör|spiel *das* radio play.
Hort (*pl* **-e**) *der* - **1.** [Kinderhort] *day-centre where children can spend the afternoon after lessons have finished* - **2.** *geh* [Schutz] refuge.
horten *vt* to hoard.
Hörweite *die*: **in/außer Hörweite** in/out of earshot.
Hose (*pl* **-n**) *die* trousers *Pl UK*, pants *Pl US*; [Unterhose - von Männern] pants *Pl UK*, shorts *Pl US*; [- von Frauen] knickers *Pl UK*, panties *Pl US*; **eine neue Hose kaufen** to buy a new pair of trousers *UK* ODER pants *US*, to buy some new trousers *UK* ODER pants *US*; **sich** *(D)* **die Hose anziehen** to put one's trousers on; **kurze Hose** shorts *Pl*; **die Hosen anhaben** *fam fig* to wear the trousers; **die Hosen voll haben** *fam fig* to be crapping o.s.; **in die Hose gehen** *fam* to be a flop; **da ist tote Hose** *fam* it's totally dead there.
Hosen|bein *das* trouser leg.
Hosen|schlitz *der* fly, flies *Pl UK*.
Hosen|träger *der* braces *Pl UK*, suspenders *Pl US*.
Hospital (*pl* **-e** ODER **-täler**) *das* hospital.
Hostess (*pl* **-en**) *die* hostess.
Hostie (*pl* **-n**) *die* RELIG host.
Hotdog ['hɔt'dɔk] (*pl* **-s**) *das* & *der* hot dog.
Hotel (*pl* **-s**) *das* hotel; **Hotel garni** ≃ bed and breakfast.
Hotel|zimmer *das* hotel room.
Hotline ['hotlain] (*pl* **-s**) *die* hotline.
Hr. (*abk für* **Herr**) Mr.
hrsg. (*abk für* **herausgegeben**) ed.
Hubraum *der* cubic capacity.
hübsch ◇ *adj* - **1.** [Person, Anblick, Kleid, Blumen] pretty - **2.** [Idee, Umgebung] nice - **3.** *fam* [groß - Summe] tidy - **4.** *fam iron* [unangenehm]: **das ist ja eine hübsche Überraschung!** what a pleasant surprise! ◇ *adv* - **1.** [schön] prettily - **2.** *fam* [sehr] jolly; **sei hübsch brav!** be really good!
Hubschrauber (*pl* -) *der* helicopter.
huckepack *adv*: **jn huckepack nehmen** ODER **tragen** *fam* to give sb a piggyback.
Huf (*pl* **-e**) *der* hoof.
Huf|eisen *das* horseshoe.
Hüfte (*pl* **-n**) *die* hip.
Huf|tier *das* hoofed animal.
Hügel (*pl* -) *der* - **1.** [Berg] hill - **2.** [Haufen] mound.
hügelig *adj* hilly.
Huhn (*pl* **Hühner**) *das* - **1.** [Vogel] chicken - **2.** *fam* [Mädchen, Frau]: **ein dummes Huhn** a silly cow; **ein verrücktes Huhn** a queer fish.
Hühnchen (*pl* -) *das* chicken.
Hühner|auge *das* corn.
Hühner|brühe *die* chicken broth.
Hühner|ei *das* hen's egg.
Hülle (*pl* **-n**) *die* cover; [Verpackung] wrapping; [von Schallplatte] sleeve; **etw in Hülle und Fülle haben** to have plenty of sthg.
hüllen *vt*: **jn/sich/etw in etw** *(A)* **hüllen** to wrap sb/o.s./sthg in sthg.
Hülse (*pl* **-n**) *die* - **1.** [Hülle] case; [von Film, Zigarre] tube - **2.** [bei Pflanzen] pod.
Hülsen|frucht *die* pulse.
Hummel (*pl* **-n**) *die* bumblebee.
Hummer (*pl* -) *der* lobster.
Humor *der* humour; **viel Humor haben** to have a great sense of humour; **etw mit Humor nehmen** ODER **tragen** to bear sthg with great humour.
humoristisch ◇ *adj* humorous. ◇ *adv* humorously.
humorvoll ◇ *adj* humorous. ◇ *adv* humorously.
humpeln (*perf* **hat/ist gehumpelt**) *vi* - **1.** *(hat, ist)* [hinken] to walk with ODER have a limp - **2.** *(ist)* [in eine Richtung] to limp.
Hund (*pl* **-e**) *der* - **1.** [Tier] dog; **'Vorsicht, bissiger Hund!'** 'beware of the dog' - **2.** *salopp* [Mann]: **er ist ein blöder Hund** he's a stupid git; **vor die Hunde gehen** *fam* to go to the dogs.
Hunde|hütte *die* kennel.
Hunde|leine *die* lead *UK*, leash *US*.
hundemüde *adj* dog-tired.
hundert *num* - **1.** [Zahl] a ODER one hundred; **auf hundert kommen** *fam* to hit the roof - **2.** *fam* [sehr viele] hundreds of; *siehe auch* **sechs**.
Hundert (*pl* **-e**) *die ODER das* hundred. ◆ **Hunderte** *Pl* [große Anzahl]: **Hunderte von** hundreds of. ◆ **zu Hunderten** *adv*: **zu Hunderten kommen** to come in their hundreds; *siehe auch* **Sechs**.
Hunderteuro|schein *der* hundred euro note *UK* ODER bill *US*.
hundertfach *adv* a hundred times.
Hundertjahr|feier *die* centenary.
hundertjährig *adj* hundred-year-old.
hundertprozentig ◇ *adj* - **1.** [von hundert Prozent] one hundred percent - **2.** [vollkommen] complete; **er ist ein hundertprozentiger Bayer** he's a Bavarian through and through. ◇ *adv fam* [völlig] completely; **etw hundertprozentig wissen** to know sthg for certain.
hundertste, r, s *adj* hundredth; *siehe auch* **sechste**.
Hundertste (*pl* **-n**) *der, die, das* hundredth; *siehe auch* **Sechste**.
hundertstel *adj (unver)* hundredth; **eine hundertstel Sekunde** a hundredth of a second; *siehe auch* **sechstel**.

Hụndertstel (*pl* -) *das* hundredth; *siehe auch* **Sechstel**.
hụnderttausend *num* a ODER one hundred thousand.
Hụnde|steuer *die* dog licence fee.
Hụnde|zwinger *der* dog cage.
Hụ̈ndin (*pl* **-nen**) *die* bitch.
Hụnger *der eigtl* & *fig* hunger; **auf etw** *(A)* **Hunger haben** to feel like eating sthg.
Hụnger|lohn *der abw* starvation wage, pittance.
hụngern *vi* - **1.** [nach Nahrung] to go hungry - **2.** *geh* [verlangen]: **nach etw hungern** to be hungry for sthg, to crave sthg.
Hụngers|not *die* famine.
Hụnger|streik *der* hunger strike.
hụngrig ◇ *adj* hungry. ◇ *adv* hungrily.
Hupe (*pl* **-n**) *die* horn.
hupen *vi* to sound one's horn.
hụ̈pfen (*perf* **ist gehụ̈pft**) *vi* to hop.
Hụ̈rde (*pl* **-n**) *die* hurdle.
Hürden|lauf *der*: **der Hürdenlauf** the hurdles.
Hure (*pl* **-n**) *die abw* whore.
hurra *interj* hurray!
hụschen (*perf* **ist gehụscht**) *vi* to dart; [Lächeln] to flit.
hüsteln *vi* to give a slight cough.
husten ◇ *vi* to cough; **auf dieses Angebot huste ich!** *fam* you can keep your offer! ◇ *vt* [Blut, Schleim] to cough up; **jm eins** ODER **was husten** *fam* to tell sb to get lost.
Husten *der (ohne pl)* cough; **Husten haben** to have a cough.
Husten|saft *der* cough mixture.
Hụt (*pl* **Hüte**) ◇ *der* [Kleidungsstück] hat; **das ist ein alter Hut** *fam* that's old hat; **mit jm/etw nichts am Hut haben** *fam* to have no time for sb/sthg; **seinen Hut nehmen** to pack one's bags; **dein Geld kannst du dir an den Hut stecken!** *fam* you can keep your money!; **verschiedene Interessen unter einen Hut bringen** to reconcile different interests. ◇ *die*: **(vor jm) auf der Hut sein** to be on one's guard (with sb); **beim Autofahren bin ich auf der Hut** I'm on the alert when I'm driving. ◆ **Hut ab** *interj*: **das hätte ich dir gar nicht zugetraut - Hut ab!** I wouldn't have thought you capable of that - hats off to you!
hüten *vt* [Kinder] to look after; [Geheimnis] to keep; [Tiere] to watch over. ◆ **sich hüten** *ref*: **sich vor jm/etw hüten** to be on one's guard against sb/sthg; **sich hüten, etw zu tun** to take care not to do sthg.
Hụ̈tte (*pl* **-n**) *die* - **1.** [Haus] hut; [bewirtschaftete Berghütte] mountain lodge - **2.** [Eisenhütte] iron and steel works *(sg)*.
Hụ̈tten|käse *der* cottage cheese.
Hyäne (*pl* **-n**) *die* hyena.
Hyazịnthe (*pl* **-n**) *die* hyacinth.
Hydrạnt (*pl* **-en**) *der* hydrant.
Hydraulik *die* hydraulics *Pl*.
hydraulisch ◇ *adj* hydraulic. ◇ *adv* hydraulically.
Hydrokultur *die* hydroponics *(U)*.
Hygiene [hy'gi̯e:nə] *die* hygiene.
hygienisch [hy'gi̯e:nɪʃ] ◇ *adj* hygienic. ◇ *adv* hygienically.
Hymne (*pl* **-n**) *die* hymn.
hypnotisieren *vt* to hypnotize.
Hypothek (*pl* **-en**) *die* mortgage.
Hypothese (*pl* **-n**) *die* hypothesis.
Hysterie [hyste'ri:] (*pl* **-n**) *die* hysteria.
hysterisch ◇ *adj* hysterical; **hysterischer Anfall** (fit of) hysterics. ◇ *adv* hysterically.

I

i (*pl* - ODER **-s**), **I** (*pl* - ODER **-s**) [i:] *das* i, I.
i.A. (*abk für* **im Auftrag**) pp.
IC [i:'tse:] (*pl* **-s**) (*abk für* **Intercity**) *der intercity train*.
ICE [i:tse:'e:] (*pl* **-s**) (*abk für* **Intercity Express**) *der intercity express train*.
ịch *pron* I; **ich bins** it's me.
ideal ◇ *adj* ideal. ◇ *adv* ideally.
Ideal (*pl* **-e**) *das* ideal.
Ideal|fall *der* ideal case.
Idealịsmus *der* idealism.
Idee (*pl* **-n**) *die* - **1.** [gen] idea; **eine fixe Idee** an obsession - **2.** [Kleinigkeit] bit.
identifizieren *vt* to identify; **jn/etw mit etw identifizieren** to identify sb/sthg with sthg. ◆ **sich identifizieren** *ref*: **sich mit jm/etw identifizieren** to identify with sb/sthg.
Identifizierung (*pl* **-en**) *die* identification.
idẹntisch *adj* identical.
Identität *die* identity.
Ideologie (*pl* **-n**) *die* ideology.
Idiot (*pl* **-en**) *der fam abw* [Dummkopf] idiot.
Idiotin (*pl* **-nen**) *die* idiot.
idiotisch *fam abw* ◇ *adj* [dumm, unsinnig] idiotic. ◇ *adv* [unsinnig] idiotically.
Idol (*pl* **-e**) *das* idol.
Idylle (*pl* **-n**) *die* idyll.
idyllisch ◇ *adj* idyllic. ◇ *adv* idyllically.
Igel (*pl* -) *der* hedgehog.
ignorieren *vt* to ignore.

IHK [iːhaːˈkaː] (*abk für* **Industrie- und Handelskammer**) *die chamber of commerce and industry.*

ihm *pron (Dativ von er)* - **1.** [Person] (to) him; **sie sagte es ihm** she told him; **das gehört ihm** this is his, this belongs to him - **2.** [Sache] (to) it.

ihn *pron (Akkusativ von er)* - **1.** [Person] him - **2.** [Sache] it.

ihnen *pron (Dativ Plural von er/sie)* (to) them; **er ist von ihnen** it's theirs, it belongs to them; **gib ihnen den Schlüssel** give them the key.

Ihnen *pron (Dativ von Sie)* (to) you; **gehört das Ihnen?** is this yours?, does this belong to you?; **wer hat es Ihnen gegeben?** who gave you it?, who gave it to you?; **entschuldigen Sie, meine Herren, ist der Platz neben Ihnen frei?** excuse me, gentlemen, is the seat next to you free?

ihr, **e** *det* - **1.** *(Singular)* her - **2.** *(Plural)* their.

ihr *pron* - **1.** [Nominativ Plural] you - **2.** [Dativ von sie - Person] (to) her; [- Sache] (to) it; **er sagte es ihr** he told her; **das gehört ihr** this is hers, this belongs to her; **mit ihr** with her.

Ihr, **e** *det* your.

ihre, **r**, **s** *pron* - **1.** [Singular - von Person] hers; [- von Ding] its - **2.** [Plural] theirs.

Ihre, **r**, **s** *pron* yours.

ihrer *pron (Genitiv von sie)* [Singular von Person] (of) her; [Plural] (of) them; [Singular von Ding] (of) it.

ihrerseits *adv* - **1.** [sie selbst - Singular] for her part; [- Plural] for their part - **2.** [von ihr - Person] on her part; [- Tier, Sache] on its part; [- Plural] on their part.

Ihrerseits *adv* on your part.

ihretwegen *adv* - **1.** [ihr zuliebe - von Person] for her sake; [- von Ding] for its sake; [ihnen zuliebe] for their sake - **2.** [wegen ihr - Person] because of her; [- Ding] because of it; [wegen ihnen] because of them.

Ihretwegen *adv* - **1.** [Ihnen zuliebe] for your sake - **2.** [wegen Ihnen] because of you.

ihretwillen ◆ **um ihretwillen** *adv* [Singular - Person] for her sake; [- Ding] for its sake; [Plural] for their sake.

Ihretwillen ◆ **um Ihretwillen** *adv* for your sake.

ihrige (*pl* **-n**) *pron geh*: **der/die/das ihrige** [Singular - von Person] hers; [- von Ding] its; [Plural] theirs.

illegal ◇ *adj* illegal. ◇ *adv* illegally.

Illusion (*pl* **-en**) *die* illusion.

Illustration (*pl* **-en**) *die* illustration.

illustrieren *vt* to illustrate.

Illustrierte (*pl* **-n**) *die* magazine.

im *präp (in + dem)* ▷ **in.**

Image [ˈɪmɪtʃ] (*pl* **-s**) *das* image.

Imbiss (*pl* **-e**) *der* - **1.** [Mahlzeit] snack - **2.** [Imbissbude] snack bar.

Imbissbude (*pl* **-n**) *die fam* snack bar.

Imitation (*pl* **-en**) *die* imitation.

imitieren *vt* to imitate.

Immatrikulation (*pl* **-en**) *die* - **1.** UNI matriculation - **2.** *Schweiz* [Kfz-Zulassung] registration.

immatrikulieren *vt* - **1.** UNI to enrol - **2.** *Schweiz* [zulassen] to register. ◆ **sich immatrikulieren** *ref* UNI to matriculate.

immens ◇ *adj* immense. ◇ *adv* immensely; **immens viel** an immense amount.

immer *adv* - **1.** [zeitlich] always; **für immer und ewig** for ever and ever; **immer wieder** again and again, time and again; **immer wenn** whenever; **immer geradeaus!** keep going straight ahead!; **immer mit der Ruhe!** take it easy!; **immer noch** still - **2.** [mit Komparativ]: **immer schwieriger** more and more difficult; **immer stärker** stronger and stronger - **3.** [egal]: **was (auch) immer** whatever; **wer (auch) immer** whoever; **wie (auch) immer** however; **wo (auch) immer** wherever.

immerfort *adv* constantly.

immerhin *adv* - **1.** [wenigstens] at least - **2.** [schließlich] after all - **3.** [trotzdem] nevertheless.

immerzu *adv* constantly.

Immigrant, **in** (*mpl* **-en**, *fpl* **-nen**) *der, die* immigrant.

Immigration (*pl* **-en**) *die* immigration.

Immobilien [ɪmoˈbiːli̯ən] *Pl* property *(U).*

immun *adj*: **gegen etw immun sein** to be immune to sthg.

Immunität *die* immunity.

Imperativ (*pl* **-e**) *der* GRAMM imperative.

Imperfekt (*pl* **-e**) *das* GRAMM imperfect.

impfen *vt* to vaccinate; **jn gegen etw impfen** to vaccinate sb against sthg.

Impfstoff *der* vaccine.

Impfung (*pl* **-en**) *die* vaccination.

imponieren *vi* to impress; **jm (durch etw) imponieren** to impress sb (with sthg).

imponierend ◇ *adj* impressive. ◇ *adv* impressively.

Import (*pl* **-e**) *der* - **1.** [Ware] import - **2.** [Einfuhr] importation.

importieren *vt* to import.

impotent *adj* impotent.

Impotenz *die* impotence.

imprägnieren *vt* to impregnate; [gegen Wasser] to waterproof.

improvisieren [ɪmproviˈziːrən] *vt* & *vi* to improvise.

Impuls (*pl* **-e**) *der* - **1.** [Anregung] stimulus; [innere Regung] impulse; **einer Sache** *(D)* **neue Impulse geben** to breathe new life into sthg - **2.** [Stoß] impulse.

impulsiv <> *adj* impulsive. <> *adv* impulsively.

imstande, im Stande *adj*: **zu etw imstande sein** to be capable of sthg.

in <> *präp* - **1.** *(+ D)* [räumlich] in; **im Bett liegen** to be in bed; **in der Schule** at school - **2.** *(+ A)* [räumlich] into; **in den Fluss fallen** to fall into the river; **in die Stadt fahren** to go to ODER into town; **in die Schule gehen** to go to school; **sich in jn verlieben** to fall in love with sb - **3.** *(+ D)* [zeitlich] in; **in dieser Woche** this week; **im Moment** at the moment; **wir fahren in einer Stunde** we're going in an hour - **4.** *(+ A)* [zeitlich] into; **wir arbeiteten bis spät in die Nacht** we worked late into the night - **5.** *(+ D)* [modal]: **in aller Eile** hurriedly; **in Betrieb sein** to be working; **ich habe mich in der Zeit geirrt** I got the time wrong - **6.** *(+ A)* [modal]: **etw in seine Einzelteile zerlegen** to take sthg to pieces - **7.** *(+ D)* [mit Maß- oder Mengenangaben] in; **in Millimetern** in millimetres. <> *adj*: **in sein** *fam* to be in.

Inbegriff *der* embodiment, epitome.

inbegriffen <> *adj*: **in etw** *(D)* **inbegriffen sein** to be included in sthg. <> *adv*: **Steuern inbegriffen** including tax.

Inbetriebnahme *(pl* **-n)** *die* - **1.** [von Maschine, Kraftwerk] commissioning; **vor Inbetriebnahme des Gerätes die Gebrauchsanweisung lesen** read the instructions before switching the appliance on for the first time - **2.** [von Flughafen, Schwimmbad] opening.

Indefinit|pronomen *das* GRAMM indefinite pronoun.

indem *konj* - **1.** [instrumental] by; **er vernichtete die Unterlagen, indem er sie in den Reißwolf steckte** he destroyed the documents by putting them through the shredder - **2.** [während] while.

Inder, in *(mpl* **-**, *fpl* **-nen)** *der, die* Indian.

Indianer, in *(mpl* **-**, *fpl* **-nen)** *der, die abw* (Red) Indian.

indianisch *adj* (Red) Indian.

Indien *nt* India.

Indikativ *(pl* **-e)** *der* GRAMM indicative (mood).

indirekt <> *adj* indirect. <> *adv* indirectly.

indisch *adj* Indian.

Indischer Ozean *der* Indian Ocean.

indiskret <> *adj* indiscreet. <> *adv* indiscreetly.

indiskutabel *adj abw* out of the question.

Individualist, in [ɪndividu̯a'lɪst, ɪn] *(mpl* **-en**, *fpl* **-nen)** *der, die* individualist.

individuell [ɪndividu̯'ɛl] <> *adj* individual. <> *adv* individually; **individuell verschieden sein** to vary from case to case.

Individuum [ɪndi'viːduʊm] *(pl* **-viduen)** *das* individual.

Indiz [ɪn'diːts] *(pl* **-ien)** *das* - **1.** RECHT piece of circumstantial evidence; **Indizien** circumstantial evidence - **2.** [Anzeichen] indication.

Indonesien *nt* Indonesia.

Industrie *(pl* **-n)** *die* industry.

Industrie|gebiet *das* industrial area.

industriell <> *adj* industrial. <> *adv* industrially.

ineinander *adv* in/into one another; **ineinander verliebt sein** to be in love (with one another); **ineinander verwickelt** tangled up (in each other).

ineinander fügen *vt* to fit together. ◆ **sich ineinander fügen** *ref* to fit together.

Infanterie ['ɪnfantəriː] *die* infantry.

Infarkt *(pl* **-e)** *der* heart attack.

Infekt *(pl* **-e)** *der* MED infection.

Infektion *(pl* **-en)** *die* infection.

Infektions|krankheit *die* infectious disease.

Infinitiv *(pl* **-e)** *der* GRAMM infinitive.

infizieren *vt*: **jn (mit etw) infizieren** to infect sb (with sthg). ◆ **sich infizieren** *ref*: **sich (mit etw) infizieren** to become infected (with sthg).

Inflation *(pl* **-en)** *die* inflation.

Inflations|rate *die* rate of inflation.

infolge *präp*: **infolge einer Sache** *(G)* ODER **von etw** as a result of sthg.

infolgedessen *adv* consequently.

Informatik *die* computer science.

Informatiker, in *(mpl* **-**, *fpl* **-nen)** *der, die* computer scientist.

Information *(pl* **-en)** *die* - **1.** information *(U)*; **Informationen** information; **eine Information über jn/etw** (a piece of) information about sb/sthg - **2.** *(ohne pl)* [in Kaufhaus, Bahnhof] information desk.

Informations|material *das* information.

Informations|stand *der* information stand.

informativ *adj* informative.

informieren *vt*: **jn über jn/etw informieren** to inform sb about sb/sthg. ◆ **sich informieren** *ref*: **sich (über jn/etw) informieren** to find out (about sb/sthg).

Infrarot *das* infra-red.

Infra|struktur *die* infrastructure.

Infusion *(pl* **-en)** *die* MED infusion.

Ingenieur, in [ɪnʒe'ni̯øːɐ̯, rɪn] *(mpl* **-e**, *fpl* **-nen)** *der, die* engineer.

Ingwer *der* ginger.

Inh. *(abk für* **Inhaber)** prop.

Inhaber, in *(mpl* **-**, *fpl* **-nen)** *der, die* - **1.** [von Geschäft] owner - **2.** [von Amt, Titel] holder.

inhaftieren *vt* to take into custody.

inhalieren ◇ *vt* to inhale. ◇ *vi* - **1.** MED to use an inhalant - **2.** *fam* [einen Lungenzug machen] to inhale.

Ịnhalt (*pl* **-e**) *der* - **1.** [von Gefäß, Behälter] contents *Pl* - **2.** [von Text, Gespräch] content; **Form und Inhalt** form and content - **3.** [Größe - von Fläche] area; [- von Raum] volume - **4.** [Sinn] meaning.

ịnhaltlich ◇ *adj*: **der inhaltliche Aufbau eines Textes** the way the content of a text is structured. ◇ *adv* as far as content is concerned.

Ịnhalts|angabe *die* - **1.** [von Text] summary - **2.** [von Paket] description of contents.

Ịnhalts|verzeichnis *das* [von Buch] table of contents; [von Paket] list of contents.

Initiative [initsi̯aˈtiːvə] (*pl* **-n**) *die* - **1.** [gen] initiative; **die Initiative ergreifen** to take the initiative; **aus eigener Initiative** on one's own initiative - **2.** [Gruppe] local action group.

Injektion (*pl* **-en**) *die* injection.

inkl. (*abk für* **inklusive**) incl.

inklusive [ɪnkluˈziːvə] ◇ *präp*: **inklusive einer Sache** *(G)* including sthg. ◇ *adv*: **bis zum 10. August inklusive** until 10 August inclusive.

ịnkompatibel *adj* incompatible.

ịnkompetent ◇ *adj* incompetent. ◇ *adv* incompetently.

ịnkonsequent ◇ *adj* inconsistent. ◇ *adv* inconsistently.

Ịnland *das*: **im Inland** at home; **die Waren sind für das Inland bestimmt** the goods are for the domestic market; **die Reaktionen des In- und Auslandes** the reactions at home and abroad.

ịnländisch *adj* - **1.** [Waren, Produkte] domestic - **2.** [Presse] national.

Ịnlineskates [ˈɪnlai̯nskei̯ts] *Pl* roller-blades, inline skates; **auf/mit Inlineskates fahren** to go rollerblading.

inmịtten ◇ *präp*: **inmitten einer Sache/Gruppe** *(G)* in the midst of sthg/a group. ◇ *adv*: **inmitten von jm/etw** amidst sb/sthg.

ịnnen *adv* inside; **die Schale ist innen versilbert** the bowl is silver-plated on the inside. ◆ **nach innen** *adv* inwards. ◆ **von innen** *adv* from inside; **etw von innen nach außen kehren** to turn sthg inside out.

Ịnnen|leben *das (ohne pl)* - **1.** [Seele]: **sein Innenleben vor jm ausbreiten** to tell sb one's innermost thoughts - **2.** [von Gerät] insides *Pl*.

Ịnnen|minister, in *der, die* Minister of the Interior, ≃ Home Secretary *UK*, ≃ Secretary of the Interior *US*.

Ịnnen|politik *die (ohne pl)* - **1.** [Handeln] domestic policy - **2.** [Bereich der Politik] home affairs *Pl*.

Ịnnen|seite *die* inside.

Ịnnen|stadt *die* town centre; [in Großstadt] city centre.

ịnnere, r, s *adj* - **1.** [innen befindlich, persönlich] inner - **2.** [Struktur, Angelegenheit & MED] internal.

Ịnnere *das (ohne pl)* - **1.** [Inhalt] inside - **2.** [von Raum] inside, interior; [von Land] interior; **Ministerium des Inneren** Ministry of the Interior - **3.** [Geist, Seele, Basis] heart; **im tiefsten Inneren** deep down (inside).

ịnnerhalb ◇ *präp*: **innerhalb einer Sache** *(G)* within sthg. ◇ *adv*: **innerhalb von** within.

ịnnerlich ◇ *adj* [Erregung] inner. ◇ *adv* inwardly.

ịnnig ◇ *adj* - **1.** [Verehrung, Wunsch, Beileid] heartfelt - **2.** [Dank] sincere - **3.** [Freundschaft] intimate. ◇ *adv* [verbunden] closely.

ịnoffiziell ◇ *adj* unofficial. ◇ *adv* unofficially.

Ịnput (*pl* **-s**) *das* & *der* EDV & WIRTSCH input.

ịns *präp (in + das)* [räumlich]: **ins Wohnzimmer gehen** to go into the living room; **ins Kino gehen** to go to the cinema; *siehe auch* **in**.

Ịnsasse (*pl* **-n**) *der* - **1.** [im Fahrzeug] passenger - **2.** [von Gefängnis, psychiatrischer Anstalt] inmate.

Ịnsassin (*pl* **-nen**) *die* - **1.** [im Fahrzeug] passenger - **2.** [von Gefängnis, psychiatrischer Anstalt] inmate.

insbes. (*abk für* **insbesondere**) esp.

insbesọndere, insbesọndre *adv* especially, particularly.

Ịn|schrift *die* inscription.

Insẹkt (*pl* **-en**) *das* insect.

Insẹktenschutz|mittel *das* insect repellent.

Insẹkten|stich *der* [von Wespe] insect sting; [von Mücke] insect bite.

Ịnsel (*pl* **-n**) *die* island; **die Insel Sylt** the island of Sylt.

Inserat (*pl* **-e**) *das* advertisement; **ein Inserat aufgeben** to put an advertisement in the paper.

insgeheim *adv* secretly.

insgesamt *adv* - **1.** [in der Summe] in total - **2.** [im Großen und Ganzen] overall; **sie hat insgesamt einen guten Eindruck hinterlassen** she made a good overall impression.

insofern[1] *adv* in this respect.

insofẹrn[2] *konj* provided that, so long as. ◆ **insofern als** *konj* insofar as.

in spe [ɪnˈspeː] *adj* to be; **der Bürgermeister in spe** the mayor-elect.

Inspektion (*pl* **-en**) *die* - **1.** [von Anlage, Schule] inspection - **2.** [von Auto] service.

inspizieren *vt* to inspect.

installieren *vt* [gen & EDV] to install.

ịnständig ◇ *adv* urgently. ◇ *adj* urgent.

Instanz (*pl* **-en**) *die* **- 1.** [im Gerichtsverfahren] court **- 2.** [Dienststelle] authority.
Instinkt (*pl* **-e**) *der* instinct.
instinktiv <> *adj* instinctive. <> *adv* instinctively.
Institut (*pl* **-e**) *das* institute.
Institution (*pl* **-en**) *die* institution.
Instrument (*pl* **-e**) *das* instrument.
inszenieren *vt* **- 1.** [Theaterstück] to direct; TV & RADIO to produce **- 2.** [Skandal] to engineer; [Kampagne] to stage **- 3.** *abw* [vortäuschen - Protest] to stage-manage.
Inszenierung (*pl* **-en**) *die* **- 1.** [Aufführung] production **- 2.** [Aufführen - von Theaterstück] direction; TV & RADIO production **- 3.** [von Skandal] engineering; [von Kampagne] staging **- 4.** *abw* [Vortäuschung - von Protest] stage-managing.
intakt *adj* [Gerät, Organ] intact; [Beziehung] healthy.
Integral|rechnung *die* integral calculus.
integrieren *vt* to integrate.
intellektuell [ɪntɛlɛk'tu̯ɛl] <> *adj* intellectual. <> *adv* intellectually.
Intellektuelle [ɪntɛlɛk'tu̯ɛlə] (*pl* **-n**) *der, die* intellectual.
intelligent <> *adj* intelligent. <> *adv* intelligently.
Intelligenz *die* **- 1.** [Verstand, Klugheit] intelligence **- 2.** [Intellektuelle] intelligentsia.
Intendant, in (*mpl* **-en**, *fpl* **-nen**) *der, die* **- 1.** [von Theater] *artistic director and theatre manager* **- 2.** [von Fernsehanstalt] director general.
intensiv <> *adj* **- 1.** [Gefühl, Farbe] strong **- 2.** [Licht] intense **- 3.** [Arbeit] intensive. <> *adv* **- 1.** [fühlen] strongly **- 2.** [leuchten] intensely **- 3.** [arbeiten] intensively.
Intensiv|kurs *der* crash course.
Intensiv|station *die* intensive care unit.
interaktiv *adj* EDV interactive.
InterCity (*pl* **-s**) *der* intercity train.
interessant <> *adj* interesting. <> *adv* interestingly; **sich interessant machen** *abw* to attract attention (to o.s.)
Interesse (*pl* **-n**) *das* interest; **an jm/etw Interesse haben** to be interested in sb/sthg; **Interesse für jn/etw zeigen** to show an interest in sb/sthg; **in js eigenen Interesse** in sb's own interest. ◆ **Interessen** *Pl* [Neigung] interests.
Interessent, in (*mpl* **-en**, *fpl* **-nen**) *der, die* **- 1.** [Interessierte] interested person **- 2.** [Kunde] prospective customer.
interessieren *vt* to interest. ◆ **sich interessieren** *ref*: **sich für jn/etw interessieren** to be interested in sb/sthg.
interessiert <> *adj* interested; **an jm/etw interessiert sein** to be interested in sb/sthg. <> *adv* with interest.
intern <> *adj* internal. <> *adv* internally.
Internat (*pl* **-e**) *das* boarding school.
international <> *adj* international. <> *adv* internationally.
Internet ['ɪnte(r)nɛt] *das* Internet; **im Internet** on the Internet; **im Internet surfen** to surf the Net; **etw über das Internet verkaufen** to sell sthg on ODER over the Internet.
Internetadresse (*pl* **-n**) *die* Internet address.
Internet|café *das* Internet cafe, cybercafe.
Internetzugang (*pl* **- zugänge**) *der* Internet access.
Interpretation (*pl* **-en**) *die* **- 1.** [Deutung] interpretation **- 2.** MUS performance.
interpretieren *vt* **- 1.** [deuten] to interpret **- 2.** MUS to perform.
Interpunktion *die* punctuation.
InterRegio (*pl* **-s**) *der train which covers medium distances and makes frequent stops.*
Intervall [ɪntɐ'val] (*pl* **-e**) *das* [gen & MUS] interval.
Interview [ɪntɐ'vju:] (*pl* **-s**) *das* interview.
interviewen [ɪntɐ'vju:ən] *vt* to interview.
intim *adj* intimate; **mit jm intim werden** *amt* to become intimate with sb.
Intimität (*pl* **-en**) *die* intimacy.
intolerant *adj* intolerant; **jm/etw gegenüber intolerant sein** to be intolerant of sb/sthg.
Intrige (*pl* **-n**) *die* intrigue, plot.
Intuition (*pl* **-en**) *die* intuition.
intuitiv <> *adj* intuitive. <> *adv* intuitively
Invalide [ɪnva'li:də] (*pl* **-n**) *der, die* invalid.
Invasion [ɪnva'zi̯o:n] (*pl* **-en**) *die eigtl & fig* invasion.
Inventar [ɪnvɛn'tɑ:ɐ̯] (*pl* **-e**) *das* **- 1.** [von Geschäft] fittings *Pl* and equipment; [von Haus fixtures and fittings *Pl* **- 2.** [von Betrieb] machinery and equipment **- 3.** [Verzeichnis] inventory.
Inventur [ɪnvɛn'tu:ɐ̯] (*pl* **-en**) *die* stocktaking; **Inventur machen** to stocktake.
investieren [ɪnvɛs'ti:rən] *vt*: **(in etw (*A*)) investieren** to invest (in sthg).
Investition [ɪnvɛsti'tsi̯o:n] (*pl* **-en**) *die* investment.
inwiefern *adv & konj* [in welcher Hinsicht] in what way; [bis zu welchem Grad] to what extent.
inwieweit *adv & konj* to what extent.
Inzest (*pl* **-e**) *der* incest.
inzwischen *adv* **- 1.** [gleichzeitig] in the meantime **- 2.** [mittlerweile, jetzt] now; **inzwischen war es Winter geworden** by now winter had arrived.
Ion [i̯o:n] (*pl* **-en**) *das* ion.
IQ [i:'ku:, ai'kju:] (*pl* **-s**) (*abk für* **Intelligenzquotient**) *der* IQ.

i.R. (*abk für* **im Ruhestand**) retd.

Irak *der* Iraq.

Iran *der* Iran.

irdisch *adj* earthly, worldly.

Ire (*pl* **-n**) *der* Irishman.

irgend *adv* [irgendwie]: **wenn es irgend möglich ist** if (it's) at all possible; **wenn ich es irgend schaffe, komme ich** I'll come if I possibly can. ◆ **irgend so ein** *det fam* some.

irgendein, e *det* - **1.** [unbekannt] some - **2.** [beliebig] any.

irgendeine, r, s *pron* - **1.** [Person] someone, somebody; [in Fragen] anyone, anybody; **irgendeiner von uns muss es tun** one of us has to do it - **2.** [Sache] any (one); **irgendeins von den Büchern** one or other of the books.

irgendetwas *pron* [unbekannte Sache] something; [beliebige Sache, in Fragen] anything.

irgendjemand *pron* [unbekannte Person] someone, somebody; [beliebige Person, in Fragen] anyone, anybody.

irgendwann *adv* [zu unbekannter Zeit] sometime; [zu beliebiger Zeit] any time.

irgendwas *adv* [unbekannte Sache] something; [beliebige Sache, in Fragen] anything.

irgendwer *pron fam* - **1.** [unbekannte Person] someone, somebody - **2.** [beliebige Person, in Fragen] anyone, anybody.

irgendwie *adv* [auf unbekannte Weise] somehow; [auf beliebige Weise] anyhow.

irgendwo *adv* [an unbekanntem Ort] somewhere; [an beliebigem Ort] anywhere.

Irin (*pl* **-nen**) *die* Irishwoman.

Iris (*pl* -) *die* iris.

irisch *adj* Irish.

Irland *nt* Ireland.

Ironie *die* irony.

ironisch ◇ *adj* ironic. ◇ *adv* ironically.

Irre (*pl* **-n**) ◇ *der, die (pl Irren)* [Person] lunatic. ◇ *die (ohne pl)* [Ungewissheit]: **in die Irre führen** to be misleading.

irre|führen *vt* - **1.** [belügen] to mislead - **2.** [auf einem Weg] to cause to get lost.

irren (*perf* **hat/ist geirrt**) *vi (ist)* to wander. ◆ **sich irren** *ref (hat)*: **sich (in jm/etw** *(D)***) irren** to be wrong (about sb/sthg); **wenn ich mich nicht irre** if I am not mistaken.

irritieren *vt* [stören] to annoy; **ihr Verhalten irritiert mich** I find her behaviour disconcerting ODER confusing.

Irrtum (*pl* **-tümer**) *der* mistake.

irrtümlich ◇ *adj* mistaken. ◇ *adv* [verwechseln, mitnehmen] by mistake.

ISDN-Anschluss (*pl* **-Anschlüsse**) *der* TELEKOM ISDN link.

Islam *der* Islam.

islamisch *adj* Islamic.

Island *nt* Iceland.

Isländer, in (*mpl* -, *fpl* **-nen**) *der, die* Icelander.

isländisch *adj* Icelandic.

Isolation (*pl* **-en**) *die* - **1.** [von Person] isolation - **2.** [Material, Abdichtung] insulation; [von Rohr, Boiler] lagging.

Isolierband (*pl* **-bänder**) *das* insulating tape.

isolieren *vt* - **1.** [Person & CHEM] to isolate - **2.** [Leitung, Wand] to insulate.

Israel *nt* Israel.

Israeli (*pl* - ODER **-s**) *der, die* Israeli.

israelisch *adj* Israeli.

isst *präs* ▷ **essen**.

ist *präs* ▷ **sein**.

Istanbul *nt* Istanbul.

Italien *nt* Italy.

Italiener, in [ita'li̯eːnɐ, rɪn] (*mpl* -, *fpl* **-nen**) *der, die* Italian.

italienisch [ita'li̯eːnɪʃ] *adj* Italian.

Italienisch(e) *das* Italian; *siehe auch* **Englisch(e)**.

J

j (*pl* - ODER **-s**), **J** (*pl* - ODER **-s**) [jɔt] *das* j, J.

ja *interj* - **1.** [zum Ausdruck der Zustimmung] yes - **2.** [einschränkend]: **ich würde ja gerne, aber** I'd love to, but; **ich kann es ja versuchen, aber** I can always try, but - **3.** [emphatisierend]: **da bist du ja!** there you are!; **das ist ja großartig!** that's really great!; **ich habe es dir ja gesagt!** I told you so!; **das ist es ja (eben)!** that's just it! - **4.** [als rhetorisches Element] well; **ja, wenn das so ist** well, if that's the case - **5.** [zum Ausdruck einer Drohung]: **sag ja nichts!** don't you dare say anything!; **dass du mir ja pünktlich kommst!** you'd better be on time! - **6.** [zum Ausdruck einer Bitte]: **du bleibst doch, ja?** you will stay, won't you? - **7.** [drückt Überraschung aus]: **(ach) ja?** really?

Jacht (*pl* **-en**), **Yacht** (*pl* **-en**) [jaxt] *die* yacht.

Jacke (*pl* **-n**) *die* - **1.** [Mantel, Jackett] jacket - **2.** [Strickjacke] cardigan.

Jackett [ʒa'kɛt] (*pl* **-s**) *das* jacket.

Jagd (*pl* **-en**) *die* - **1.** [auf Tiere] hunting; **auf die Jagd gehen** to go hunting - **2.** [auf Personen, Dinge]: **Jagd nach jm/etw** hunt for sb/sthg.

jagen (*perf* **hat/ist gejagt**) ◇ *vt (hat)* to hunt; **der Dieb wurde aus der Stadt gejagt** the thief was driven out of town; **sich** *(D)* **eine**

Kugel in den Kopf jagen to shoot o.s. in the head. <> *vi* - **1.** *(hat)* [als Sport] to hunt - **2.** *(ist)* [hetzen] to race.

Jäger (*pl* -) *der* - **1.** [von Tieren] hunter - **2.** [Flugzeug] fighter (plane).

Jägerin (*pl* **-nen**) *die* hunter.

Jägerschnitzel (*pl* -) *das escalope of pork or beef with mushroom sauce.*

jäh <> *adj* sudden. <> *adv* suddenly.

Jahr (*pl* **-e**) *das* year; **im Jahr(e) 1992** in 1992; **die 90er Jahre** the nineties; **seit Jahren** for years; **(ein) gutes neues Jahr!** Happy New Year!; **Jahr für Jahr** year after year; **in jungen Jahren** at an early age.

jahrelang <> *adj*: **jahrelange Arbeit** years of work. <> *adv* for years.

Jahresltag *der* anniversary.

Jahreslzeit *die* season.

Jahrlgang *der* - **1.** [Geburtsjahr]: **der Jahrgang 1967** the people who were born in 1967; **er ist mein Jahrgang** he was born in the same year as me - **2.** [an der Schule] year - **3.** [von Wein] vintage, year - **4.** [von Zeitschrift] year's issues *Pl.*

Jahrhundert (*pl* **-e**) *das* century; **im 19. Jahrhundert** in the 19th century.

Jahrhundertlwende *die* turn of the century; **um die Jahrhundertwende** at the turn of the century.

jährlich <> *adj* annual. <> *adv* annually; **dreimal jährlich** three times a year.

Jahrlmarkt *der* fair.

Jahrtausend (*pl* **-e**) *das* millennium.

Jahrzehnt (*pl* **-e**) *das* decade.

jähzornig <> *adj* irascible. <> *adv* in a violent temper.

Jalousie [ʒalu'zi:] (*pl* **-n**) *die* Venetian blind.

Jammer *der* misery; **es ist ein Jammer** it's a crying shame.

jämmerlich <> *adj* - **1.** [traurig] miserable - **2.** *abw* [würdelos, schlecht] pathetic. <> *adv* - **1.** [traurig] miserably - **2.** *abw* [würdelos, schlecht] pathetically - **3.** [sehr]: **jämmerlich frieren** to be frozen stiff.

jammern *vi* to moan.

Januar *der* January; *siehe auch* **September**.

Japan *nt* Japan.

Japaner, in (*mpl* -, *fpl* **-nen**) *der, die* Japanese.

japanisch *adj* Japanese.

Japanisch(e) *das* Japanese; *siehe auch* **Englisch(e)**.

Jargon [ʒar'gõ] (*pl* **-s**) *der* jargon.

jäten *vt* [Garten] to weed; [Unkraut] to pull up.

jaulen *vi* to howl.

jawohl *interj* certainly!

Jalwort *das*: **jm sein Jawort geben** to tie the knot with sb.

Jazz [dʒɛs] *der* jazz.

je <> *adv* - **1.** [jeweils] each; **drei Gruppen mit je fünf Personen** three groups, each of five people; **die drei Tore sind mit je zwei Schlössern gesichert** the three gates each have two locks - **2.** [jemals] ever; **seit eh und je** since time immemorial; **sie ist schöner denn je** she is more beautiful than ever. <> *präp* [pro] per; **je nach** depending on. <> *konj*: **je schneller, desto besser** the quicker the better; **je nachdem** it depends; **je nachdem, ob** depending on whether. <> *interj*: **oh je!** oh no!, oh dear!

Jeans [dʒi:nz] (*pl* -) *die* jeans *Pl*; **eine Jeans** a pair of jeans.

jede, r, s <> *det* every, each; [in negativen Konstruktionen] any; **ohne jeden Zweifel** without any doubt; **jeden zweiten Tag** every second day. <> *pron* - **1.** [Person] everyone, everybody; **jede von ihnen** each of them; **jeder Zweite** every second ODER other one; **jeder kann teilnehmen** anyone can take part - **2.** [Sache] each (one).

jedenfalls *adv* - **1.** [wenigstens] at least; **ich jedenfalls habe keine Lust** I at any rate don't want to - **2.** [auf jeden Fall] in any case.

jedermann *pron* everybody, everyone.

jederzeit *adv* at any time.

jedesmal *adv* ▷ **Mal**.

jedoch *adv* & *konj* however.

jegliche, r, s *pron*: **hier kommt jegliche Hilfe zu spät** any help will come too late; **ohne jegliches Risiko** with no risk.

jeher *adv*: **von jeher** always.

jemals *adv* ever.

jemand *pron* someone, somebody; [in Fragen] anyone, anybody.

jene, r, s *geh* <> *det* that, those *Pl.* <> *pron* that one, those ones *Pl.*

jenseits *präp*: **jenseits einer Sache** *(G)* ODER **von etw** [räumlich] on the other side of sthg; [ideell] beyond sthg.

Jerusalem *nt* Jerusalem.

Jetlag ['dʒɛtlɛg] (*pl* **-s**) *der* jet lag.

jetzig *adj* current.

jetzt *adv* - **1.** [momentan, mittlerweile] now; **bis jetzt** so far; **von jetzt an** from now on; **erst jetzt** only just; **schon jetzt** already - **2.** [gegenwärtig, heute] nowadays; **das gibt es jetzt nicht mehr** you don't get that any more (nowadays) - **3.** [gleich, sofort] in a moment **jetzt gleich** right away; **von jetzt auf gleich** on the spur of the moment - **4.** [damals] then - **5.** [zum Ausdruck des Ärgers]: **das ist doch jetzt kein Argument!** that's no argument!; **jetzt mach endlich voran!** get a move on, will you

jeweilig *adj* - **1.** [zeitlich]: **nach der jeweiligen Mode angezogen sein** to be dressed in the fashion of the day; **die Stimmung ändert sich mit der jeweiligen Laune des Chefs** the at mosphere changes depending on what mood the boss happens to be in - **2.** [zugehörig] respective.

jeweils *adv* - **1.** [jedes Mal] each time - **2.** [jeder] each; **jeweils drei Karten** three cards each - **3.** [momentan] at the time.

Jh. (*abk für* **Jahrhundert**) C.

Jiddisch(e) *das* Yiddish; *siehe auch* **Englisch(e)**.

Job [dʒɔp] (*pl* **-s**) *der* - **1.** [als Aushilfe] (temporary) job - **2.** [Arbeit] job.

jobben [dʒɔbn̩] *vi* to work.

Jockey ['dʒɔke, 'dʒɔki] (*pl* **-s**) *der* jockey.

Jod *das* iodine.

jodeln *vi* to yodel.

Joga, Yoga ['joːga] = **Yoga**.

Jogging ['dʒɔgɪŋ] *das* jogging.

Joghurt, Yoghurt, Jogurt (*pl* - ODER **-s**) *das* & *der* yoghurt.

Johannis|beere *die*: **Rote Johannisbeere** redcurrant; **Schwarze Johannisbeere** blackcurrant.

Joker ['dʒoːkɐ] (*pl* -) *der* joker.

jonglieren [ʒɔŋ'liːrən] ◇ *vi* to juggle; **mit etw jonglieren** *eigtl* & *fig* to juggle sthg. ◇ *vt* [balancieren] to juggle.

Journalist, in [ʒʊrna'lɪst, ɪn] (*mpl* **-en**, *fpl* **-nen**) *der, die* journalist.

Jubel *der* - **1.** [Freude] jubilation - **2.** [Rufen] cheering.

jubeln *vi* - **1.** [sich freuen] to rejoice - **2.** [rufen] to cheer.

Jubiläum [jubi'lɛːʊm] (*pl* **Jubiläen**) *das* anniversary; **ein Jubiläum feiern** to celebrate an anniversary.

jucken ◇ *vi* - **1.** [Haut] to itch - **2.** [Material] to be itchy. ◇ *vt* - **1.** [kratzen]: **die Narbe juckt ihn** his scar is itchy - **2.** *fam* [beeinflussen]: **es juckt mich, es zu versuchen** I'm itching to try; **das juckt mich nicht** I don't care.

Juck|reiz *der* itching; **Juckreiz verspüren** to have an itch.

Jude (*pl* **-n**) *der* Jew.

Jüdin (*pl* **-nen**) *die* Jew.

jüdisch *adj* Jewish.

Judo *das* judo.

Jugend *die (ohne pl)* - **1.** [junges Alter] youth - **2.** [junge Personen] young people *Pl*; **die Jugend von heute** today's youth, young people today.

Jugend|amt *das local authority service responsible for the welfare of young people.*

Jugendarbeit *die* youth work.

jugendfrei *adj*: **'nicht jugendfrei'** 'not suitable for persons under 18'.

Jugend|herberge *die* youth hostel.

jugendlich ◇ *adj* - **1.** [jung] young - **2.** [jung wirkend] youthful. ◇ *adv*: **sich jugendlich geben/kleiden** to act/dress young.

Jugendliche (*pl* **-n**) *der, die* young person.

Jugendstil *der* art nouveau.

Jugoslawien *nt* Yugoslavia.

Juli *der* July; *siehe auch* **September**.

jung (*kompar* **jünger**, *superl* **jüngste**) ◇ *adj* - **1.** [gen] young; [Aussehen, Stil] young, youthful; **meine jüngere Schwester** my younger sister - **2.** [nicht lange zurückliegend]: **die jüngsten Ereignisse** recent events. ◇ *adv (kompar jünger; superl am jüngsten)*: **jung sterben** to die young.

Junge (*pl* **-n** ODER **Jungs**) ◇ *der (pl Jungen, Jungs)* [Knabe, Mann] boy; **hallo, alter Junge** hello, my old pal; **ein schwerer Junge** *fam fig* a thug. ◇ *das (pl Jungen)* [Tier] young animal; **die Jungen** the young; **Junge kriegen** ODER **werfen** to give birth to young.

Jünger, in (*mpl* -, *fpl* **-nen**) *der, die* disciple.

Jungfer (*pl* **-n**) *die*: **alte Jungfer** *abw* old maid.

Jung|frau *die* - **1.** [Frau] virgin - **2.** ASTROL Virgo; **Jungfrau sein** to be a Virgo.

Jung|geselle *der* bachelor; **ein eingefleischter Junggeselle** a confirmed bachelor.

jüngste *adj* ▷ **jung**.

Jüngste (*pl* **-n**) *der, die, das* youngest; **er ist nicht mehr der Jüngste** he's not as young as he used to be.

Juni *der* June; *siehe auch* **September**.

Junior (*pl* **Junioren**) *der* - **1.** [gen] junior - **2.** [im Geschäft] junior partner.

Juniorin (*pl* **-nen**) *die* - **1.** [Tochter] daughter - **2.** [im Geschäft] junior partner - **3.** SPORT junior.

Jura *der* - **1.** *(ohne Artikel)* [Studienfach] law - **2.** [Gebirge]: **der Jura** the Jura - **3.** [Erdzeitalter] Jurassic period.

Jurist, in (*mpl* **-en**, *fpl* **-nen**) *der, die* lawyer.

juristisch ◇ *adj* legal. ◇ *adv* legally.

Jury [ʒy'riː] (*pl* **-s**) *die* jury.

Justiz *die* - **1.** [Behörde]: **jn der deutschen Justiz ausliefern** to hand sb over to the German courts; **unabhängige Justiz** independent judiciary - **2.** [Rechtsprechung]: **nach irischer Justiz** under Irish law.

Justiz|ministerium *das* Ministry of Justice.

Justizvollzugs|anstalt *die amt* penal institution, penitentiary *US*.

Juwel (*pl* **-en**) *das* & *der* - **1.** *(der)* [Schmuck] piece of jewellery - **2.** [Edelstein, Prachtstück] jewel; **sie ist ein Juwel** she is a gem.

Juwelier (*pl* **-e**) *der* jeweller.

Juwelierin (*pl* **-nen**) *die* jeweller.

K

k (*pl* - *ODER* **-s**), **K** (*pl* - *ODER* **-s**) [kɑː] *das* k, K.

Kabarett [kaba'rɛt] (*pl* **-s** *ODER* **-e**), **Cabaret** [kaba'reː] (*pl* **-s** *ODER* **-e**) *das* - **1.** [Aufführung] satirical revue - **2.** [Institution] *theatre where satirical revues are performed.*

Kabarettist, in (*mpl* **-en**, *fpl* **-nen**) *der, die* satirical revue artist.

Kabel (*pl* -) *das* cable.

Kabelanschluss (*pl* **-es**) *der*: **Kabelanschluss haben** to have cable television.

Kabelfernsehen *das* cable television.

Kabeljau (*pl* **-s**) *der* cod.

Kabine (*pl* **-n**) *die* - **1.** [von Schiff, Flugzeug] cabin - **2.** [in Schwimmbad] cubicle; [in Kleidergeschäft] fitting room.

Kabinett (*pl* **-e**) *das* - **1.** [aus Ministern] cabinet - **2.** [Wein] *term designating a high-quality German wine.*

Kabrio (*pl* **-s**), **Cabrio** (*pl* **-s**) *das* convertible.

Kachel (*pl* **-n**) *die* tile.

kacheln (*perf* **hat/ist gekachelt**) ◇ *vt (hat)* [auslegen] to tile. ◇ *vi (ist) fam* [rasen] to zoom along.

Kadaver [ka'dɑːvɐ] (*pl* -) *der* carcass.

Käfer (*pl* -) *der* [Insekt, Auto] beetle.

Kaff (*pl* **-s** *ODER* **-e**) *das fam* dump.

Kaffee ['kafe] (*pl* **-s**), **Kaffee** [ka'feː] (*pl* **-s**) *der* - **1.** [gen] coffee; **eine Tasse Kaffee** a cup of coffee; **Kaffee mit Milch** white coffee; **schwarzer Kaffee** black coffee - **2.** [Mahlzeit] afternoon coffee and cake; **Kaffee trinken** [am Nachmittag] to have afternoon coffee; [in der Pause] to have a coffee break.

Kaffee|filter *der* filter (paper).

Kaffee|kanne *die* coffeepot.

Kaffee|klatsch (*pl* **-e**) *der*: **sich zum Kaffeeklatsch treffen** to meet for a chat over a cup of coffee.

Kaffee|löffel *der* coffee spoon.

Kaffee|maschine *die* coffee machine.

Kaffee|tasse *die* coffee cup.

Käfig (*pl* **-e**) *der* cage.

kahl *adj* - **1.** [ohne Haare] bald; **kahl werden** to go bald - **2.** [Berg, Baum] bare.

Kahn (*pl* **Kähne**) *der* - **1.** [Ruderboot] rowing boat *UK*, rowboat *US* - **2.** [Stechkahn] punt - **3.** [Lastkahn] barge.

Kai (*pl* **-s** *ODER* **-e**) *der* quay.

Kairo *nt* Cairo.

Kaiser (*pl* -) *der* emperor.

Kaiserin (*pl* **-nen**) *die* empress.

kaiserlich *adj* imperial.

Kaiser|reich *das* empire.

Kaiser|schmarrn (*pl* **Kaiserschmarrn**) *der pancake torn into thin strips.*

Kaiser|schnitt *der* MED caesarean (section).

Kajak (*pl* **-s**) *das* & *der* kayak.

Kajüte (*pl* **-n**) *die* cabin.

Kakao [ka'kau] *der* cocoa; **jn/etw durch den Kakao ziehen** *fam* to take the mickey out of sb/sthg.

Kakerlake (*pl* **-n**) *die* cockroach.

Kaktee = **Kaktus**.

Kaktus (*pl* **Kakteen** *ODER* **-se**) *der* cactus.

Kalb (*pl* **Kälber**) *das* - **1.** [Tier] calf - **2.** [Fleisch] veal.

Kalbfleisch *das* veal.

Kalender (*pl* -) *der* - **1.** [Wandkalender] calendar - **2.** [Taschenkalender] diary; **sich** *(D)* **etw im Kalender rot anstreichen** *fig* to make sthg a red-letter day.

Kaliber (*pl* -) *das* - **1.** [von einem Geschütz] calibre - **2.** [Art, Sorte] kind, ilk.

Kalium *das* potassium.

Kalk *der (ohne pl)* - **1.** [Kalkstein] limestone - **2.** [in Wasserkessel] lime - **3.** [zum Tünchen] whitewash.

Kalk|stein *der* limestone.

kalkulieren ◇ *vt* [berechnen] to calculate. ◇ *vi* to calculate; **genau/scharf kalkulieren** to make precise calculations.

Kalorie [kalo'riː] (*pl* **-n**) *die* calorie.

kalorienarm [kalo'riːənarm] ◇ *adj* low-calorie. ◇ *adv*: **kalorienarm essen** to eat low-calorie food.

kalt (*kompar* **kälter**, *superl* **kälteste**) ◇ *adj* cold; **es ist kalt** it's cold; **mir ist kalt** I'm cold; **kalte Füße kriegen** *fig* to get cold feet. ◇ *adv (kompar kälter; superl am kältesten)*: **kalt duschen** to have a cold shower; **das Bier kaltstellen** to chill the beer; **kalt lächeln** to smile coldly.

kaltblütig ◇ *adj* cold-blooded. ◇ *adv* in cold blood.

Kälte *die (ohne pl)* - **1.** [gen] coldness - **2.** [Wetter] cold; **bei Kälte** in cold weather.

Kälte|einbruch *der* cold snap.

Kalte Krieg *der* cold war.

Kalt|miete *die* rent not including bills.

Kalzium *das* calcium.

kam *prät* ▷ **kommen**.

Kambodscha *nt* Cambodia.

Kamel (*pl* **-e**) *das* - **1.** [Tier] camel - **2.** *fig* [Trottel] idiot.

Kamera (*pl* **-s**) *die* camera.

Kamerad, in (*mpl* **-en**, *fpl* **-nen**) *der, die* friend.

kameradschaftlich ◇ *adj* friendly. ◇ *adv* in a friendly way.

Kamerun *nt* Cameroon.

Kamille (*pl* -n) *die* camomile.

Kamillen|tee *der* camomile tea.

Kamin (*pl* -e) *der* - 1. [Schornstein] chimney - 2. [Feuerstelle] fireplace; **offener Kamin** open fireplace.

Kamm (*pl* **Kämme**) *der* - 1. [Haarkamm, Hahnenkamm] comb; **alles über einen Kamm scheren** *fig* [keinen Unterschied machen] to lump everything together - 2. [Bergkamm] ridge.

kämmen *vt* to comb.

Kammer (*pl* -n) *die* - 1. [kleines Zimmer] cubbyhole - 2. POL chamber.

Kammer|musik *die* chamber music.

Kampagne (*pl* -n) *die* campaign.

Kampf (*pl* **Kämpfe**) *der* - 1. [Streit] fight; [politisch, sozial] struggle, fight; [in Sport] contest; [in Krieg] battle; **Kampf um etw** fight for sthg; **Kampf gegen jn/etw** fight against sb/sthg; **jm/einer Sache den Kampf ansagen** to declare war on sb/sthg - 2. MIL fighting *(U)*.

kämpfen *vi* to fight; **gegen jn/etw kämpfen** to fight against sb/sthg; **für jn/etw kämpfen** to fight for sb/sthg; **um jn/etw kämpfen** to fight for sb/sthg; **mit etw kämpfen** *fig* [Schlaf, Tod] to fight sthg off; [Tränen] to fight sthg back.

Kampf|gebiet *das* combat zone.

kampflos ◇ *adj* MIL peaceful. ◇ *adv* without a fight.

Kampf|richter, in *der, die* SPORT referee.

Kanada *nt* Canada.

Kanadier [ka'nɑːdi̯ɐ] (*pl* -) *der* - 1. [Einwohner Kanadas] Canadian - 2. [Sportboot] Canadian canoe.

Kanadierin [ka'nɑːdi̯ərɪn] (*pl* -nen) *die* Canadian.

kanadisch *adj* Canadian.

Kanal (*pl* **Kanäle**) *der* - 1. [Wasserweg] canal - 2. TELEKOM channel; **den Kanal voll haben** *fam* [betrunken sein] to be plastered; *fam* [es satt haben] to be fed up to the back teeth.

Kanalisation (*pl* -en) *die* - 1. [für Abwässer] sewers *Pl* - 2. [Ausbau eines natürlichen Wasserweges] canalization *(U)*.

Kanal|tunnel *der* Channel Tunnel.

Kanarien|vogel *der* canary.

Kanarische Inseln *Pl* Canary Islands.

Kandidat, in (*mpl* -en, *fpl* -nen) *der, die* candidate; **jn als Kandidaten aufstellen** ODER **nominieren** to put sb forward as a candidate.

Kandis|zucker *der* sugar candy.

Känguru (*pl* -s) *das* kangaroo.

Kaninchen (*pl* -) *das* rabbit.

Kanister (*pl* -) *der* can.

kann *präs* ▷ **können**.

Kanne (*pl* -n) *die* pot.

Kannibale (*pl* -n) *der* cannibal.

Kannibalin (*pl* -nen) *die* cannibal.

kannte *prät* ▷ **kennen**.

Kanon (*pl* -s) *der* MUS canon.

Kanone (*pl* -n) *die* [Geschütz] cannon; **unter aller Kanone sein** *fam* [miserabel] to be the pits.

Kante (*pl* -n) *die* edge.

Kantine (*pl* -n) *die* canteen.

Kanton (*pl* -e) *der* canton.

Kantor (*pl* -toren) *der* choirmaster and organist.

Kantorin (*pl* -nen) *die* choirmistress and organist.

Kanu (*pl* -s) *das* canoe.

Kanzel (*pl* -n) *die* - 1. [von Kirchen] pulpit - 2. [von Flugzeugen] cockpit.

Kanzlei (*pl* -en) *die* office.

Kanzler (*pl* -) *der* - 1. [Bundeskanzler] chancellor - 2. UNI vice-chancellor *UK*, chancellor *US*.

Kanzler|amt *das* [Amtssitz des Bundeskanzlers] chancellery.

Kap (*pl* -s) *das* cape.

Kapazität (*pl* -en) *die* - 1. [gen] capacity - 2. [Experte] authority.

Kapelle (*pl* -n) *die* - 1. [kleine Kirche] chapel - 2. MUS band.

Kapell|meister, in *der, die* [Leiter - einer Musikkapelle] bandmaster; [- eines Orchesters] conductor.

Kaper (*pl* -n) *die* caper.

kapieren *vt fam* to get.

kapital [kapi'tɑːl] *adj* - 1. [Irrtum] serious - 2. [Hirsch] magnificent.

Kapital (*pl* -ien ODER -e) *das* [gen] capital; **aus etw Kapital schlagen** to make capital out of sthg; **geistiges Kapital** intellectual assets *Pl*; **totes Kapital** unused skills *Pl*.

Kapital|anlage *die* capital investment.

Kapitalismus *der* capitalism.

Kapitalist, in (*mpl* -en, *fpl* -nen) *der, die* capitalist.

kapitalistisch *adj* capitalist.

Kapitän (*pl* -e) *der* captain.

Kapitel (*pl* -) *das* chapter; **ein Kapitel für sich sein** *fig* to be an awkward business; **das ist ein anderes Kapitel** that's another story.

Kapitulation (*pl* -en) *die* [Aufgabe] surrender *(U)*; **bedingungslose Kapitulation** unconditional surrender *(U)*.

kapitulieren *vi* to surrender; **vor etw** *(D)* **kapitulieren** to give up in the face of sthg.

Kaplan (*pl* **Kapläne**) *der* curate.

Kappe (*pl* -n) *die* cap.

kappen *vt* - 1. [beschneiden] to cut back - 2. [durchschneiden] to cut through.

Kapsel (*pl* -n) *die* - 1. [kleiner Behälter] box - 2. [von Medikament, von Blüten] capsule.

kaputt *adj fam* - **1.** [Vase, Gerät] broken; [Beziehung, Gesundheit] ruined - **2.** *fig* [erschöpft]: **kaputt sein** to be done in.

kaputt|gehen (*perf* **ist kaputtgegangen**) *vi (unreg) fam* - **1.** [Gerät, Gegenstand] to break; [Beziehungen, Geschäfte] to be ruined - **2.** [eingehen] to die.

kaputt|lachen ◆ **sich kaputtlachen** *ref fam* to kill o.s. laughing; **sich über jn/etw kaputtlachen** to kill o.s. laughing at sb/sthg.

Kapuze (*pl* **-n**) *die* hood.

Karaffe (*pl* **-n**) *die* - **1.** [mit Stöpsel] decanter - **2.** [ohne Stöpsel] carafe.

Karamell *der* caramel.

Karamellbonbon (*pl* **-s**) *das* & *der* toffee.

Karat (*pl* **-e** ODER **-**) *das* - **1.** [Edelsteingewicht] carat - **2.** [Einheit]: **dieser Ring hat 20 Karat** this ring is 20 carats.

Karate *das* karate.

Karawane (*pl* **-n**) *die* caravan.

Kardinal (*pl* **Kardinäle**) *der* cardinal.

Karfreitag (*pl* **-e**) *der* Good Friday.

karg *adj* - **1.** [Mahlzeit, Lohn] meagre - **2.** [Raum] bare - **3.** [Boden] barren.

Karibik *die* Caribbean.

karibisch *adj* Caribbean.

kariert ◇ *adj* - **1.** [Stoff] checked - **2.** [Papier] squared. ◇ *adv fam* [verwirrt]: **kariert schauen** to look bewildered.

Karies ['kaːriɛs] *die* MED tooth decay.

Karikatur (*pl* **-en**) *die* cartoon; [Porträt] caricature.

kariös *adj* decayed.

Karlsruhe *nt* - **1.** [Stadt] Karlsruhe - **2.** [Gericht] the Federal Constitutional Court.

Karneval ['karnəval] (*pl* **-e** ODER **-s**) *der* carnival.

karnevalistisch [karnəva'lɪstɪʃ] *adj* carnival *(vor Subst)*.

Karnevals|zug *der* carnival procession.

Kärnten *nt* Carinthia.

Karo (*pl* **-s**) *das* - **1.** [Raute] diamond - **2.** *(ohne Artikel, ohne pl)* [Spielfarbe] diamonds *Pl* - **3.** [Spielkarte] diamond; **die Karosechs** the six of diamonds.

Karosserie (*pl* **-n**) *die* bodywork *(U)*.

Karotte (*pl* **-n**) *die* carrot.

Karpfen (*pl* **-**) *der* carp.

Karre (*pl* **-n**) *die* - **1.** [Handkarre] cart - **2.** *fam* [Auto] jalopy, banger *UK*.

Karren (*pl* **-**) *der* [kleiner Wagen] cart.

Karriere [ka'rieːrə] (*pl* **-n**) *die* career; **Karriere machen** to make a career for o.s.

Karte (*pl* **-n**) *die* - **1.** [Postkarte, Spielkarte] card - **2.** [Landkarte] map; **jm die gelbe/rote Karte zeigen** to show sb the yellow/red card; **mit offenen Karten spielen** to put one's cards on the table; **alles auf eine Karte setzen** to stake everything on one chance; **schlechte Karten haben** to have been dealt a bad hand.

Kartei (*pl* **-en**) *die* card index.

Kartei|karte *die* index card.

Kartei|kasten *der* index-card box.

Kartell (*pl* **-e**) *das* WIRTSCH cartel.

Karten|spiel *das* - **1.** [Gesellschaftsspiel] card game - **2.** [Spielkarten] pack *UK* ODER deck *US* of cards.

Karten|telefon *das* cardphone.

Karten|vorverkauf *der* advance booking.

Kartoffel (*pl* **-n**) *die* potato.

Kartoffel|brei *der* KÜCHE mashed potatoes *Pl*.

Kartoffel|chips *Pl* crisps *UK*, chips *US*.

Kartoffel|puffer *der* KÜCHE potato pancake *(made from grated potatoes)*.

Kartoffel|püree *das* KÜCHE mashed potatoes *Pl*.

Kartoffel|salat *der* KÜCHE potato salad.

Karton (*pl* **-s**) *der* - **1.** [Pappe] card - **2.** [Kiste] (cardboard) box.

Karussell (*pl* **-s**) *das* merry-go-round; **Karussell fahren** to go on the merry-go-round.

Kar|woche *die* Holy Week.

Käse (*pl* **-**) *der* cheese; **das ist Käse!** *abw* & *fig* that's rubbish!

Käse|fondue *das* KÜCHE cheese fondue.

Käse|kuchen *der* KÜCHE cheesecake.

Kaserne (*pl* **-n**) *die* MIL barracks *Pl*.

käsig *adj* pale.

Kasino (*pl* **-s**) *das* - **1.** [Spielkasino] casino - **2.** MIL (officers') mess.

Kasperle|theater *das* [Vorstellung] Punch and Judy show; [Gebäude] Punch and Judy theatre.

Kasse (*pl* **-n**) *die* - **1.** [Kassette] cashbox - **2.** [im Laden] till - **3.** [im Supermarkt] checkout - **4.** [im Theater, Kino] box office - **5.** *fam* [Krankenkasse] (health) insurance *(U)*; **Kasse machen** to cash up; **knapp bei Kasse sein** *fam* to be short of cash.

Kassen|arzt, **ärztin** *der, die doctor who treats patients with health insurance*.

Kassen|bon *der* receipt.

Kassen|patient, **in** *der, die patient with health insurance*.

Kassen|zettel *der* receipt.

Kassette (*pl* **-n**) *die* - **1.** [Musik- und Videokassette] cassette, tape; **etw auf Kassette aufnehmen** to record sthg on cassette ODER tape - **2.** [für Schmuck, Schallplatten, Bücher] box.

Kassetten|rekorder *der* cassette recorder.

kassieren *vt* - **1.** [einziehen] to collect - **2.** *fam* [einnehmen] to pocket - **3.** *fam* [einheimsen Lob, Kritik] to get; [- Niederlage] to suffer - **4.** *fam* [Führerschein] to take away.

Kassierer, in (*mpl* -, *fpl* **-nen**) *der, die* - **1.** [von Geschäft, Bank] cashier - **2.** [von Verein] treasurer.

Kastanie [kas'tɑːni̯ə] (*pl* **-n**) *die* chestnut.

Kasten (*pl* **Kästen**) *der* - **1.** [Kiste] box - **2.** [für Flaschen] crate - **3.** [Briefkasten] postbox *UK*, mailbox *US* - **4.** *fam* [Gebäude] great box of a building - **5.** SPORT box - **6.** *fam* [Kopf]: **etwas/viel auf dem Kasten haben** [intelligent sein] to be brainy/very brainy.

kastrieren *vt* MED to castrate.

Kasus (*pl* **Kasus**) *der* GRAMM case.

Kat [kat] (*pl* **-s**) (*abk für* **Katalysator**) *der* AUTO cat.

Katalanisch(e) *das* Catalan; *siehe auch* **Englisch(e)**.

Katalog (*pl* **-e**) *der* catalogue.

Katalysator (*pl* **-toren**) *der* [am Auto] catalytic converter; [in Chemie] catalyst.

Katamaran (*pl* **-e**) *der* catamaran.

katastrophal [katastro'fɑːl] ◇ *adj* disastrous. ◇ *adv* disastrously.

Katastrophe [katas'troːfə] (*pl* **-n**) *die* disaster; **eine Katastrophe sein** *fam* to be a disaster.

Katastrophen|gebiet [katas'troːfəngəbiːt] *das* disaster area.

Katechismus (*pl* **-men**) *der* catechism.

Kategorie (*pl* **-n**) *die* category.

kategorisch ◇ *adj* categorical. ◇ *adv* categorically.

Kater (*pl* -) *der* - **1.** [Tier] tomcat - **2.** *fam* [von Alkohol] hangover; **einen Kater haben** to have a hangover.

kath. (*abk für* **katholisch**) Cath.

Kathedrale (*pl* **-n**) *die* cathedral.

Kathode (*pl* **-n**) *die* PHYS cathode.

Katholik (*pl* **-en**) *der* Catholic.

Katholiken|tag *der biannual congress of German Catholics*.

Katholikin (*pl* **-nen**) *die* Catholic.

katholisch *adj* Catholic.

Katholizismus *der* Catholicism.

Katz *die*: **Katz und Maus spielen** to play cat and mouse; **für die Katz sein** *fam* to be a waste of time.

Katze (*pl* **-n**) *die* - **1.** [Tier] cat - **2.** [weibliches Tier] she-cat.

Katzen|sprung *der*: **etw ist nur ein Katzensprung von etw entfernt** sthg is only a stone's throw away from sthg.

Kauderwelsch *das* gibberish.

kauen ◇ *vi* to chew; **an etw** *(D)* **kauen** [herumkauen] to chew sthg; [bewältigen] to grapple with sthg. ◇ *vt* to chew.

kauern *vi* to crouch.

Kauf (*pl* **Käufe**) *der* purchase; **einen Kauf abschließen** to complete a purchase; **etw in Kauf nehmen** *fig* to accept sthg.

kaufen *vt* to buy; **jm/sich etw kaufen** to buy sb/o.s. sthg.

Käufer, in (*mpl* -, *fpl* **-nen**) *der, die* buyer.

Kauf|frau *die* businesswoman.

Kauf|haus *das* department store.

Kauf|kraft *die* purchasing power.

Kauf|leute *Pl* business people.

käuflich *adj* - **1.** [zu erwerben]: **etw käuflich erwerben** *amt* to purchase sthg; **käuflich sein** [Ware] to be for sale; [Person] to be easily bought; **nicht käuflich sein** [Ware] not to be for sale; [Person] not to be easily bought - **2.** [prostituiert]: **käufliches Mädchen** prostitute; **käufliche Liebe** prostitution.

Kaufmann (*pl* **-leute**) *der* businessman.

kaufmännisch *adj* commercial.

Kauf|preis *der* purchase price.

Kau|gummi *das & der* chewing gum.

kaum *adv* - **1.** [gen] hardly; **das ist kaum zu glauben** that's hard to believe; **kaum dass ich angerufen hatte, standen sie schon vor der Tür** no sooner had I rung than they were at the door - **2.** [höchstens] barely.

Kaution (*pl* **-en**) *die* - **1.** [für Wohnung] deposit - **2.** [für Häftling] bail; **gegen Kaution freikommen** to be released on bail.

Kautschuk *der* (India) rubber.

Kauz (*pl* **Käuze**) *der*: **ein komischer Kauz** *fig* an odd bird.

Kavalier [kava'liːɐ̯] (*pl* **-e**) *der* gentleman.

Kaviar [kɑːvi̯ar] (*pl* **-e**) *der* caviar.

Kegel (*pl* -) *der* - **1.** MATH cone - **2.** [zum Spielen] skittle.

Kegel|klub *der* bowling club.

kegeln *vi* to bowl.

Kehle (*pl* **-n**) *die* [gen] throat; **etw in die falsche Kehle bekommen** *fam* to take sthg the wrong way; **aus voller Kehle singen/schreien** to sing/shout at the top of one's voice.

Kehl|kopf *der* larynx.

kehren *vt* - **1.** [fegen] to sweep - **2.** [wenden] to turn; **den starken Mann nach außen kehren** to act the tough guy; **in sich gekehrt** lost in one's own world. ◆ **sich kehren** *ref* - **1.** [sich kümmern]: **sich nicht an** *ODER* **um etw kehren** not to care about sthg - **2.** [sich richten]: **sich gegen jn kehren** to turn against sb.

Kehr|reim *der* refrain.

Kehr|seite *die* drawback, downside; **die Kehrseite der Medaille** the downside.

kehrt|machen *vi* to turn round.

Kehrt|wendung *die*: **eine Kehrtwendung machen** to turn round; [politisch] to do a U-turn.

keifen *vi abw* to nag.

Keil (*pl* **-e**) *der* wedge.

Keil|riemen *der* fan belt.

Keim (*pl* **-e**) *der* - **1.** [Pflanzentrieb] shoot; **etw im Keim ersticken** *fig* to nip sthg in the bud - **2.** [Bakterie] germ.

keimen *vi* [Saat] to germinate; [Kartoffeln, Zwiebeln] to sprout.

keimfrei ◇ *adj* [Instrumente, Milch] sterilized; [Bedingungen] sterile. ◇ *adv* [arbeiten] in a sterile environment.

keimtötend *adj* germicidal, antiseptic.

Keim|zelle *die* - **1.** BIOL sex cell - **2.** [Ausgangspunkt] germ.

kein, e *det* no, not any; **kein Mensch** no one; **es gibt keine Bananen** there are no bananas, there aren't any bananas; **ich habe kein Geld/keine Zeit** I haven't got any money/time; **das ist doch keine Schande** it's no disgrace; **kein Wunder, dass...** it's no wonder (that...)

keine, r, s *pron* - **1.** [Person] no one, nobody; **keiner weiß, dass...** no one ODER nobody knows that...; **keiner der Schüler** ODER **von den Schülern** none of the pupils - **2.** [Gegenstand] none; **welchen nehmen Sie? - keinen** which do you want? - neither.

keinerlei *adj (unver)* no... at all; **keinerlei Bedenken haben** to have no scruples at all.

keinesfalls *adv* on no account; **das ist keinesfalls schwer** that's not at all difficult.

keineswegs *adv* not at all; **keineswegs besser** in no way better.

Keks (*pl* **-e**) *der* biscuit *UK*, cookie *US*.

Kẹlle (*pl* **-n**) *die* [Schöpflöffel] ladle.

Kẹller (*pl* -) *der* cellar.

Kẹllner, in (*mpl* -, *fpl* **-nen**) *der, die* waiter (waitress *die*).

Kẹlte (*pl* **-n**) *der* Celt.

kẹltern *vt* to press.

Kẹltin (*pl* **-nen**) *die* Celt.

kẹltisch *adj* Celtic.

Kenia *nt* Kenya.

kẹnnen (*prät* **kạnnte**, *perf* **hat gekạnnt**) *vt* to know; **jn/etw gut kennen** to know sb/sthg well; **ich kenne mich** I know what I'm like; **kennen wir uns nicht?** haven't we met somewhere before?; **da kennst du ihn aber schlecht!** you don't know what he's like!

kẹnnen lernen *vt* - **1.** [Person] to get to know, to meet; **freut mich, Sie kennen zu lernen!** pleased to meet you! - **2.** [Sache] to get to know, to familiarize o.s. with. ◆ **sich kennen lernen** *ref* [sich begegnen] to meet.

Kẹnntnis (*pl* **-nisse**) *die* knowledge; **etw zur Kenntnis nehmen** to take note of sthg, to note sthg; **jn von etw in Kenntnis setzen** to inform sb of sthg; **dieser Vorfall entzieht sich meiner Kenntnis** *geh* I don't know anything about this incident. ◆ **Kenntnisse** *Pl* knowledge *(U)*.

Kẹnnwort (*pl* **-wörter**) *das* password.

Kẹnn|zahl *die* code number.

Kẹnn|zeichen *das* - **1.** [Merkmal] symbol, sign; **besondere Kennzeichen** distinguishing features - **2.** [an Kfz]: **amtliches Kennzeichen** registration number *UK*, license number *US*.

kẹnnzeichnen *vt* [markieren]: **etw (mit** ODER **durch etw) kennzeichnen** to mark sthg (with sthg); **etw als etw kennzeichnen** [Produkt, Ware] to label sthg as sthg; **jn als etw kennzeichnen** to describe sb as sthg.

kẹnnzeichnend *adj*: **für jn/etw kennzeichnend sein** to be typical ODER characteristic of sb/sthg.

Kẹnn|zeichnung *die* labelling.

Kẹnn|ziffer *die* reference number.

kẹntern (*perf* **ist gekẹntert**) *vi* to capsize.

Keramik (*pl* **-en**) *die* - **1.** [Gefäß]: **eine Keramik** a piece of pottery - **2.** *(ohne pl)* [Ton] pottery, ceramics *Pl*.

Kẹrbe (*pl* **-n**) *die* notch.

Kẹrbel *der* chervil.

Kẹrker (*pl* -) *der* dungeon.

Kẹrl (*pl* **-e**) *der fam* guy, bloke *UK*; **ein netter Kerl** a nice guy; **ein gemeiner Kerl** a swine.

Kẹrn (*pl* **-e**) *der* - **1.** [von Apfel, Birne, Zitrusfrucht] pip; [von Pfirsich, Kirsche] stone, pit *US*; [von Nuß] kernel - **2.** [Wichtigstes] core, crux - **3.** PHYS nucleus.

Kẹrn|energie *die* nuclear power.

kẹrngesund *adj* as fit as a fiddle.

Kẹrnkraft|gegner, in *der, die* opponent of nuclear power.

Kẹrnkraft|werk *das* nuclear power station.

Kẹrn|punkt *der* [eines Vortrags] central point; [eines Problems] crux.

Kẹrn|stück *das* centrepiece.

Kẹrn|waffe *die* nuclear weapon.

Kẹrze (*pl* **-n**) *die* - **1.** [zur Beleuchtung] candle - **2.** [Turnübung] shoulder stand.

kẹrzengerade *adj* & *adv* bolt upright.

Kẹrzenlicht *das* candlelight.

kẹss (*kompar* **kẹsser**, *superl* **kesseste**) ◇ *adj* - **1.** [Person, Verhalten] cheeky - **2.** [Kleidung] jaunty. ◇ *adv* [frech] cheekily.

Kẹssel (*pl* -) *der* - **1.** [Topf] kettle; [groß] cauldron - **2.** [Tal] basin, basin-shaped valley.

Kẹtchup, Kẹtschup ['kɛtʃap] *das* & *der* ketchup.

Kẹtte (*pl* **-n**) *die* chain; [aus Perlen] string; [von Polizisten] cordon; [von Unfällen, Ereignissen] string, series.

kẹtten *vt*: **jn/etw an etw *(A)* ketten** to chain sb/sthg to sthg.

Kẹtten|fahrzeug *das* tracked vehicle.

Kẹtten|reaktion *die* chain reaction.

Kẹtten|säge *die* chain saw.

Kẹtzer (*pl* -) *der* heretic.

Kẹtzerin (*pl* **-nen**) *die* heretic.

keuchen (*perf* **hat/ist gekeucht**) *vi* to pant.

Keuchhusten *der* whooping cough.

Keule (*pl* **-n**) *die* - **1.** KÜCHE leg - **2.** [Waffe & SPORT] club.

keusch ◇ *adj* chaste. ◇ *adv* chastely.

Keuschheit *die* chastity.

Keyboard ['ki:bɔ:d] (*pl* **-s**) *das* [Musikinstrument & EDV] keyboard.

Kfz [kɑ:ɛf'tsɛt] (*pl* -) *das abk für* **Kraftfahrzeug**.

Kfz-Steuer *die* road tax.

kg (*abk für* **Kilogramm**) kg.

kichern *vi* to giggle.

kicken ◇ *vi* to play (football). ◇ *vt* to kick.

kidnappen ['kɪtnɛpn̩] *vt* to kidnap.

Kidnapper, in ['kɪtnɛpɐ, rɪn] (*mpl* -, *fpl* **-nen**) *der, die* kidnapper.

Kiefer (*pl* - ODER **-n**) ◇ *der (pl Kiefer)* jaw. ◇ *die (pl Kiefern)* pine.

Kiel (*pl* **-e**) *der* - **1.** [von Schiff] keel - **2.** [von Federn] quill.

Kieme (*pl* **-n**) *die* gill.

Kies *der* - **1.** [auf Weg] gravel; [am Ufer] shingle - **2.** *salopp* [Geld] cash, dosh *UK*.

Kiesel|stein *der* pebble.

Kies|grube *die* gravel pit.

Kiew ['ki:ɛf] *nt* Kiev.

kikeriki *interj* cock-a-doodle-doo!

Killer, in (*mpl* -, *fpl* **-nen**) *der, die* killer.

Kilo (*pl* - ODER **-s**) *das* kilo.

Kilogramm (*pl* **-e**) *das* kilogram.

Kilohertz (*pl* **Kilohertz**) *das* kilohertz.

Kilokalorie (*pl* **-n**) *die* kilocalorie.

Kilometer (*pl* -) *der* kilometre; **Kilometer pro Stunde** kilometres per hour.

kilometerlang *adj* ≃ miles long; **kilometerlange Strände** miles and miles of beaches.

Kilometer|stand *der* ≃ mileage; **bei Kilometerstand 10.000** when there are 10,000 km on the clock.

Kilometer|zähler *der* ≃ mileometer.

Kilowatt (*pl* -) *das* kilowatt.

Kilowattstunde (*pl* **-n**) *die* kilowatt hour.

Kind (*pl* **-er**) *das* child; **von Kind auf** ODER **an** from childhood; **ein Kind erwarten** to be expecting (a baby); **ein Kind bekommen** ODER **kriegen** to have a baby; **mit Kind und Kegel** with the whole tribe.

Kinder|arzt, ärztin *der, die* paediatrician.

Kinder|buch *das* children's book.

Kinder|garten *der* nursery school.

Kinder|gärtner, in *der, die* = **Erzieher**.

Kindergeld *das (ohne Pl)* child benefit *UK*, child allowance *US*.

Kinder|heim *das* children's home.

Kinder|hort *der day centre where children can spend the afternoon after lessons have finished.*

Kinder|krankheit *die* illness affecting children.

Kinder|krippe *die* crèche.

Kinder|lähmung *die* polio.

kinderleicht *adj fam* dead easy; **es war kinderleicht** it was child's play.

kinderlieb *adj* fond of children.

Kinder|lied *das* nursery rhyme.

Kinder|mädchen *das* nursemaid.

kinderreich *adj*: **eine kinderreiche Familie** a large family, a family with lots of children.

Kinderschutz|bund *der* child protection league.

Kinder|sicherung *die* [an Auto] childproof lock.

Kinder|sitz *der* child seat.

Kinder|spiel *das* children's game; **ein Kinderspiel sein** to be child's play.

Kinder|stube *die*: **eine gute/schlechte Kinderstube haben** to have been well/badly brought up.

Kindertages|stätte *die* day nursery.

Kinder|wagen *der* pram *UK*, baby carriage *US*.

Kinder|zimmer *das* children's bedroom.

Kindes|alter *das* childhood; **im Kindesalter** as a child, at an early age.

Kindesmisshandlung (*pl* **-en**) *die* child abuse.

Kindheit *die* childhood; **von Kindheit an** from an early age.

kindisch *abw* ◇ *adj* childish. ◇ *adv* childishly.

kindlich ◇ *adj* childlike. ◇ *adv* like a child.

Kinn (*pl* **-e**) *das* chin.

Kinn|haken *der* hook (to the chin).

Kino (*pl* **-s**) *das* cinema, movie theater *US*; **ins Kino gehen** to go to the movies, to go to the cinema.

Kino|besucher, in *der, die* moviegoer, cinemagoer.

Kino|programm *das* movie guide, cinema guide.

Kiosk (*pl* **-e**) *der* kiosk.

Kippe (*pl* **-n**) *die* - **1.** *fam* [Zigarette] ciggy, fag *UK* - **2.** *fam* [Zigarettenstummel] cigarette butt, fag end *UK*; **auf der Kippe stehen** [zu fallen drohen] to be precariously balanced; [gefährdet oder unsicher sein] to be in the balance; [Schüler] to be in danger of staying down a year.

kippen (*perf* **hat/ist gekippt**) ◇ *vi (ist)* to topple. ◇ *vt (hat)* - **1.** [Fenster, Möbel] to tilt - **2.** [Flüssigkeit] to tip - **3.** *fam* [Schnaps] to knock back.

Kirche (*pl* **-n**) *die* church; **in die Kirche gehen** to go to church.

Kirchen|chor *der* church choir.

Kirchen|gemeinde *die* [Bezirk] parish; [Gottesdienstteilnehmer] congregation.

Kirchen|musik *die* church music.

Kirchen|schiff *das* ARCHIT nave.

Kirchen|steuer *die* church tax.

kirchlich ◇ *adj* church *(vor Subst)*. ◇ *adv*: **sich kirchlich trauen lassen** to have a church wedding.

Kirch|turm *der* [mit Spitze] steeple; [ohne Spitze] church tower.

Kirmes *die* fair.

Kirsch|baum *der* cherry tree.

Kirsche (*pl* **-n**) *die* cherry.

Kirsch|torte *die*: **Schwarzwälder Kirschtorte** Black Forest gâteau.

Kissen (*pl* -) *das* [auf Stuhl, Sofa] cushion; [für Bett] pillow.

Kiste (*pl* **-n**) *die* - **1.** [Behälter] crate, box - **2.** *fam* [Auto] jalopy, banger *UK*.

kitschig *adj* kitschy.

Kitt *der* putty.

Kittchen (*pl* -) *das fam* nick *UK*, can *US*; **im Kittchen sein** ODER **sitzen** *fam* to be in the nick *UK* ODER can *US*.

Kittel (*pl* -) *der* [für Werkstatt] overalls *Pl*; [für Arzt] white coat; [für Labor] lab coat.

Kittel|schürze (*pl* **-n**) *die* housecoat.

kitten *vt* - **1.** [kleben] to glue together - **2.** [Ehe] to patch up.

Kitzel (*pl* -) *der* thrill.

kitzelig = **kitzlig**.

kitzeln *vt* - **1.** [krabbeln] to tickle; **jn an den Füßen kitzeln** to tickle sb's feet - **2.** *fam* [reizen - Ehrgeiz] to arouse.

kitzlig, kitzelig *adj* - **1.** [empfindlich] ticklish - **2.** [heikel] tricky.

Kiwi (*pl* **-s**) *die* kiwi fruit.

klaffen *vi* to gape.

kläffen *vi abw* to yap.

Klage (*pl* **-n**) *die* - **1.** [Beschwerde] complaint - **2.** RECHT action, suit; **gegen jn Klage einreichen** to bring an action against sb.

klagen ◇ *vi* - **1.** [jammern] to complain; **über jn/etw klagen** to complain about sb/sthg; **über Rückenschmerzen klagen** to complain of backache - **2.** [vor Gericht]: **gegen jn klagen** to take legal action against sb; **auf Schadenersatz klagen** to sue for damages. ◇ *vt*: **jm seine Not klagen** to pour out one's troubles to sb.

Kläger, in (*mpl* -, *fpl* **-nen**) *der, die* RECHT plaintiff.

klaglos *adv* uncomplainingly.

Klammer (*pl* **-n**) *die* - **1.** [für Blätter] paper clip; [für Wäsche] (clothes) peg *UK*, clothespin *US*; [für Wunde, von Heftmaschine] staple; [für Zähne] brace - **2.** [Symbol] bracket; **etw in Klammern setzen** to bracket sthg; **in Klammern stehen** to be in brackets.

Klammer|affe *der fam* EDV at-sign.

klammern *vt*: **etw an etw** *(A)* **klammern** to attach sthg to sthg. ◆ **sich klammern** *ref*: **sich an jn/etw klammern** *eigtl* & *fig* to cling to sb/sthg.

Klamotten *Pl fam* gear *(U)*, clothes.

klang *prät* ▷ **klingen**.

Klang (*pl* **Klänge**) *der* sound.

Klapp|bett *das* folding bed.

Klappe (*pl* **-n**) *die* - **1.** [Gegenstand] flap; [bei Blasinstrument, Motor] valve; [bei Film] clapperboard; **"Klappe die Fünfte"** "take five" - **2.** *fam* [Mund] trap.

klappen ◇ *vt*: **etw nach oben/unten klappen** [Sitz] to tip sthg forward/back. ◇ *vi* [gelingen] to work, to come off; **hat alles geklappt?** did everything go OK?; **es klappt (gut)** it works; **es klappt nicht** it doesn't work.

klapperig = **klapprig**.

klappern *vi* [Tür, Fensterladen] to rattle; [Kastagnette] to clack (together); **ich klappere mit den Zähnen** my teeth are chattering.

Klapp|rad, Klappfahrrad *das* folding bicycle.

klapprig, klapperig *adj* - **1.** [Gegenstand] rickety - **2.** [Person] doddery.

Klapp|sitz *der* folding seat.

Klaps (*pl* **-e**) *der* [leichter Schlag] pat.

klar ◇ *adj* - **1.** [gen] clear; **mir ist nicht klar, wie das funktioniert** I'm not clear how it works; **ist dir das jetzt klar?** do you understand now?; **na klar!** of course! - **2.** [bewusst]: **sich** *(D)* **über etw im Klaren sein** to be aware of sthg. ◇ *adv* - **1.** [deutlich] clearly - **2.** [fertig]: **klar zu etw** ready for sthg. ◆ **alles klar** *interj*: **alles klar?** OK?; **alles klar!** OK! ◆ **klar und deutlich** ◇ *adj* perfectly clear. ◇ *adv* quite clearly.

Klär|anlage *die* sewage works *(sg)*.

Klare (*pl* **-n**) *der* schnapps.

klären *vt* [Problem, Angelegenheit] to clear up

klar|gehen (*perf* **ist klargegangen**) *vi (unreg)* *fam* to go OK.

Klarheit *die* [Gewissheit, Deutlichkeit] clarity; **über etw** *(A)* **Klarheit gewinnen** ODER **bekommen** to clarify sthg; **sich** *(D)* **Klarheit verschaffen** to get sthg clear.

Klarinette (*pl* **-n**) *die* clarinet.

klar|kommen (*perf* **ist klargekommen**) *vi (unreg)*: **mit jm/etw klarkommen** to be able to cope with sb/sthg.

klar machen *vt*: **jm etw klar machen** to explain sthg to sb, to make sthg clear to sb.

Klarsicht|folie *die* transparent film, clingfilm *UK*.

Klarsicht|hülle *die* plastic cover.

klar|stellen *vt* [Problem, Frage] to clear up; **klarstellen, dass...** to make it clear that...

Klärung (*pl* **-en**) *die* clearing up.

klar werden (*perf* **ist klar geworden**) *vi (unreg)*: **jm klar werden** to become clear to sb; **sich** *(D)* **über etw klar werden** to be able to understand sthg.

klasse *adj fam* great, neat *US*.

Klasse (*pl* **-n**) *die* - **1.** [gen] class; **erster/zweiter Klasse** first/second class - **2.** [Zimmer] classroom - **3.** [Schuljahr] form *UK*, grade *US*; **eine Klasse wiederholen** to repeat a year.

Klassen|arbeit *die* class test.

Klassen|kamerad, in *der, die* classmate.

Klassen|lehrer, in *der, die* class teacher.

Klassen|zimmer *das* classroom.

Klassik *die (ohne pl)* - **1.** [Epoche] classical period - **2.** [Antike]: **die Klassik** classical antiquity - **3.** [Musik] classical music - **4.** [Literatur] classical literature.

Klassiker, in (*mpl* **-**, *fpl* **-nen**) *der, die* - **1.** [Dichter] classical author; **die Klassiker lesen** to read the classics - **2.** [Referenz] classic.

klassisch *adj* - **1.** [Kunst, Kultur] classical - **2.** [Fehler] classic.

Klatsch *der fam* [Gerede] gossip.

klatschen (*perf* **hat/ist geklatscht**) ◇ *vi* - **1.** *(hat)* [schlagen] to slap; **in die Hände klatschen** to clap (one's hands) - **2.** *(hat)* [Publikum] to clap - **3.** *(ist)* [Regen] to drum; [Wellen] to slap - **4.** *(hat) fam* [tratschen]: **über jn/etw klatschen** to gossip about sb/sthg. ◇ *vt*: **Beifall klatschen** to applaud; **jm eine klatschen** *fam* to give sb a slap.

Klaue (*pl* **-n**) *die* - **1.** [von Adler, Löwen] claw - **2.** *fam* [Schrift] scrawl.

klauen *fam* ◇ *vt* to pinch, to nick *UK*; **jm etw klauen** to pinch sthg from sb, to nick sthg off sb *UK*. ◇ *vi* [stehlen]: **hier wird viel geklaut** a lot of stuff gets pinched ODER nicked *UK* round here.

Klausel (*pl* **-n**) *die* clause.

Klausur (*pl* **-en**) *die* UNI exam.

Klavier [kla'viːɐ̯] (*pl* **-e**) *das* piano; **Klavier spielen** to play the piano.

Klavier|konzert *das* - **1.** [Musikstück] piano concerto - **2.** [Konzert] piano recital.

kleben ◇ *vt* [ankleben] to stick, to glue; [reparieren] to stick ODER glue together. ◇ *vi* [halten]: **an etw** *(D)* **kleben** *eigtl* & *fig* to stick to sthg.

Kleber (*pl* -) *der* adhesive.

Klebe|streifen *der* adhesive tape.

klebrig *adj* sticky.

Kleb|stoff *der* adhesive, glue.

kleckern ◇ *vi* [verschütten] to make a mess; **du hast gekleckert** [beim Essen] you've spilt your food. ◇ *vt* [verschütten] to spill.

Klecks (*pl* **-e**) *der* [von Farbe, Senf] blob; [von Tinte] blot.

Klee *der* clover.

Klee|blatt *das* clover leaf.

Kleid (*pl* **-er**) *das* [Frauenkleid] dress. ◆ **Kleider** *Pl* [Kleidungsstücke] clothes.

Kleider|bügel *der* coathanger.

Kleider|schrank *der* - **1.** [Möbelstück] wardrobe, closet *US* - **2.** *fam* [Mann] man mountain.

Kleidung (*pl* **-en**) *die* clothes *Pl*, clothing.

Kleie (*pl* **-n**) *die* bran.

klein ◇ *adj* - **1.** [gen] small, little; **mein kleiner Finger** my little finger - **2.** [temporal] short; **eine kleine Pause** a short break - **3.** [unerheblich] little; **meine kleinste Sorge** the least of my worries; **kleine Leute** ordinary people; **aus kleinen Verhältnissen stammen** to come from a humble background. ◇ *adv*: **ein klein wenig** a little bit; **haben Sie es nicht kleiner?** don't you have anything smaller?

Klein|anzeige *die* small ad *UK*, want ad *US*.

kleinbürgerlich *abw* ◇ *adj* petty bourgeois. ◇ *adv* in a petty bourgeois way.

Kleine (*pl* **-n**) ◇ *der, die* - **1.** [Kind] little one - **2.** [als Anrede - nett] little one; [- beleidigend] shorty. ◇ *das* [Baby] little one.

klein gedruckt *adj* in small print.

Kleingeld *das* change.

Kleinigkeit (*pl* **-en**) *die* - **1.** [unwichtig] trifle; **für jn eine/keine Kleinigkeit sein** to be an/no easy matter for sb - **2.** [klein, wenig]: **ein paar Kleinigkeiten einkaufen** to buy a few little things - **3.** [zu essen] snack.

Klein|kind *das* small child.

Kleinkram *der (ohne pl) fam* - **1.** [Gegenstände] bits and pieces *Pl* - **2.** [Angelegenheiten] trifling things *Pl*.

klein|kriegen *vt* - **1.** [Person]: **jn kleinkriegen** to bring sb into line; **lass dich davon nicht kleinkriegen** don't let that get you down - **2.** [Gegenstand]: **etw ist nicht kleinzukriegen** sthg will last forever - **3.** [zerkleinern mit Messer] to chop up.

kleinlaut ◇ *adj* subdued. ◇ *adv* in a subdued manner.

kleinlich *adj abw* petty.

klein machen *vt* - **1.** [Holz, Pappe] to chop up - **2.** *fam* [Geldschein] to change.

klein schneiden *vt (unreg)* to chop into small pieces.

klein|schreiben *vt (unreg)* [mit kleinem Anfangsbuchstaben] to write with a small initial letter.

Kleinschreibung *die* use of small initial letters.

Klein|stadt *die* small town.

Kleister (*pl* -) *der* paste.

Klemme (*pl* **-n**) *die* - **1.** *(ohne pl) fam* [Bedrängnis] tight spot; **jm aus der Klemme helfen**

to help sb out of a tight spot; **in der Klemme stecken** *ODER* **sitzen** *ODER* **sein** to be in a tight spot - **2.** ELEKTR terminal.

klẹmmen ◇ *vt* - **1.** [feststecken] to jam - **2.** [Finger]**: sich** *(D)* **etw klemmen** to get sthg caught. ◇ *vi* [Tür, Schublade] to jam. ◆ **sich klemmen** *ref fam*: **sich dahinter klemmen** to get stuck in.

Klẹmpner, in (*mpl* -, *fpl* **-nen**) *der, die* plumber.

Klerus *der (ohne pl)* clergy *Pl*.

Klẹtte (*pl* **-n**) *die* - **1.** *fam* [Mensch] limpet - **2.** [Pflanze] burdock.

klẹttern (*perf* **hat/ist geklettert**) *vi* - **1.** *(ist)* [gen] to climb - **2.** *(hat)* SPORT to climb.

klịcken *vi* to click.

Kliẹnt (*pl* **-en**) *der* client.

Kliẹntin (*pl* **-nen**) *die* client.

Klịff (*pl* **-e**) *das* cliff.

Klima (*pl* **-s**) *das* climate.

Klima|anlage *die* air conditioning *(U)*.

Klimaschutz *(ohne Pl) der* climate protection.

klịmpern *vi* [spielen - auf Klavier] to tinkle away; [- auf Gitarre] to strum.

Klịnge (*pl* **-n**) *die* blade.

Klịngel (*pl* **-n**) *die* bell.

klịngeln *vi* to ring (the bell); **es hat geklingelt** [an der Tür] there's someone at the door; [in der Schule] the bell has gone; **bei jm klingeln** to ring sb's bell; **nach jm klingeln** to ring for sb.

klịngen (*prät* **klang**, *perf* **hat geklungen**) *vi* - **1.** [gen] to sound - **2.** [Glocken, Gläser] to ring.

Klinik (*pl* **-en**) *die* clinic.

klinisch ◇ *adj* clinical. ◇ *adv* clinically.

Klịnke (*pl* **-n**) *die* (door) handle.

Klịpp (*pl* **-s**)**, Clip** (*pl* **-s**) *der* clip.

Klịppe (*pl* **-n**) *die* rock; **alle Klippen umfahren** to negotiate all obstacles.

klịrren *vi* [Scheiben] to rattle; [Gläser] to clink.

klịrrend *adj*: **klirrende Kälte** freezing cold.

Klischee (*pl* **-s**) *das* cliché.

Klo (*pl* **-s**) *das fam* loo *UK*, john *US*; **aufs Klo gehen** to go to the loo *UK* *ODER* john *US*.

klobig *adj* - **1.** [ungeschliffen] clumsy - **2.** [massig - Hände] massive; [- Stuhl, Bau, Schuhe] clunky.

Klo|frau *die fam* toilet attendant.

Klo|papier *das fam* toilet paper.

klọpfen ◇ *vi* - **1.** [Person - an die Tür] to knock; [- auf den Tisch] to rap; **es hat geklopft** there's someone at the door - **2.** [Herz] to beat. ◇ *vt* [Teppich, Kissen] to beat.

Klọps (*pl* **-e**) *der* meatball.

Closẹtt (*pl* **-e**) *das* toilet.

Kloß (*pl* **Klöße**) *der* dumpling; **einen Kloß im Hals haben** *fig* to have a lump in one's throat.

Kloster (*pl* **Klöster**) *das* [für Nonnen] convent; [für Mönche] monastery.

Klọtz (*pl* **Klọ̈tze**) *der* - **1.** block - **2.** [Scheit] log - **3.** *abw* [Gebäude] concrete block; **einen Klotz am Bein haben** to have a millstone round one's neck.

klọtzig *fam* ◇ *adj* [groß] clunky. ◇ *adv*: **klotzig verdienen** to earn a packet.

Klụb (*pl* **-s**)**, Clụb** (*pl* **-s**) *der* club.

Klụft (*pl* **-en** *ODER* **Klụ̈fte**) *die* - **1.** *(pl Klüfte)* [zwischen Gegensätzen] gulf - **2.** *(pl Klüfte)* [im Fels] cleft - **3.** *(pl Kluften)* [Kleidung] outfit.

klug (*kompar* **klüger**, *superl* **klügste**) ◇ *adj* - **1.** [schlau] clever - **2.** [weise] wise; **jd wird aus jm/etw nicht klug** sb can't make sb/sthg out; **der Klügere gibt nach** discretion is the better part of valour. ◇ *adv* [umsichtig] wisely.

Klugheit (*pl* **-en**) *die* - **1.** [Schläue] cleverness - **2.** [Weisheit] wisdom.

Klụmpen (*pl* **-**) *der* lump.

km (*abk für* **Kilometer**) km.

km/h (*abk für* **Stundenkilometer**) kph.

knạbbern ◇ *vt* to nibble. ◇ *vi*: **an etw** *(D)* **knabbern** to nibble sthg.

Knabe (*pl* **-n**) *der* - **1.** *geh* [Junge] boy - **2.** *fam* [Mann] chap.

Knạ̈cke|brot *das* crispbread.

knạcken ◇ *vt* - **1.** [Nüsse, Finger] to crack - **2.** [mit Gewalt - Schloss] to force; [- Bank] to break into - **3.** [Code] to crack. ◇ *vi* - **1.** [Holz, Finger] to crack; [Feuer, im Radio, Telefon] to crackle - **2.** *salopp* [schlafen] to crash out - **3.** [an Problemen]: **an etw** *(D)* **zu knacken haben** *fig* [sich bemühen] to have one's work cut out with sthg; [die Folgen spüren] to have a hard time getting over sthg.

knạckig *adj* - **1.** [Salat] crisp - **2.** *salopp* [Po] sexy.

Knạcks (*pl* **-e**) *der fam* [psychischer Schaden]: **einen Knacks haben/bekommen** to be/get screwed up.

Knạll (*pl* **-e**) *der* [von Schuss, Tür] bang; [von Korken] pop.

knạllen (*perf* **hat/ist geknallt**) ◇ *vi* - **1.** *(hat)* [Schuss] to ring out; [Peitsche] to crack; [Korken] to pop - **2.** *(ist) fam* [aufprallen] to crash; **mit dem Kopf auf den Boden knallen** to bang one's head on the floor - **3.** *(hat)* [Sonne] to beat down. ◇ *vt* - **1.** [werfen] to fling; **die Tür ins Schloss knallen** to slam the door - **2.** [ohrfeigen]: **jm eine knallen** *fam* to clout sb.

knạpp ◇ *adj* - **1.** [Ergebnis, Rennen] close; [Vorsprung, Stimmenmehrheit] narrow - **2.** [Kleid, Schuhe] tight - **3.** [fast ganz]: **eine knappe Stunde** just under an hour; **das war knapp** that was close - **4.** [wenig]: **knapp bei Kasse sein** to be short of money; **knapp werden** to be running short. ◇ *adv* - **1.** [um weniges] narrowly - **2.** [eng] tightly.

knạrren *vi* to creak.

Knast (*pl* **Knäste**) *der fam* clink.
Knatsch *der (ohne pl) fam* row.
knattern *vi* [Motor] to roar; [Maschinengewehr] to rattle; [Fahne] to flap.
Knäuel (*pl* -) *das* ball.
Knauf (*pl* **Knäufe**) *der* knob.
knauserig *adj* stingy.
knausern *vi*: **mit etw knausern** to be stingy with sthg.
knautschen *vt* & *vi* to crumple.
Knebel (*pl* -) *der* gag.
knebeln *vt* to gag.
Knecht (*pl* **-e**) *der* [auf Bauernhof] farmhand; [Diener] servant.
kneifen (*prät* **kniff**, *perf* **hat gekniffen**) ◇ *vi* - **1.** [Kleidung] to pinch - **2.** *fam abw* [sich drücken]: **(vor etw** *(D)***) kneifen** to duck out (of sthg). ◇ *vt* to pinch.
Kneif|zange *die* pincers *Pl*.
Kneipe (*pl* **-n**) *die fam* bar, pub *UK*.
kneten *vt* [Teig, Muskeln] to knead; [Figur] to model.
Knick (*pl* **-e** ODER **-s**) *der* - **1.** *(pl Knicke)* [Falte] crease - **2.** *(pl Knicke)* [in Straße] sharp bend.
knicken *vt* - **1.** [falten] to fold - **2.** [Äste, Blumen] to bend.
Knicks (*pl* **-e**) *der* curtsey.
Knie (*pl* -) *das* [Körperteil] knee; **etw übers Knie brechen** to rush sthg.
Knie|beuge (*pl* **-n**) *die* knee-bend.
Knie|gelenk *das* knee joint.
Knie|kehle *die* hollow of the knee.
knien *vi* to kneel. ◆ **sich knien** *ref* to kneel; **sich in etw** *(A)* **knien** *fig* to buckle down to sthg.
Knie|scheibe *die* kneecap.
Knie|strumpf *der* knee-length sock.
kniff *prät* ▷ **kneifen**.
Kniff (*pl* **-e**) *der* [Trick] trick.
knifflig *adj* tricky.
knipsen *fam* ◇ *vi* [fotografieren] to take snaps. ◇ *vt* - **1.** [Fahrkarte] to punch - **2.** [fotografieren]: **jn/etw knipsen** to snap sb/sthg.
Knirps (*pl* **-e**) *der* [Kind] little lad.
knirschen *vi* - **1.**: **mit den Zähnen knirschen** to grind one's teeth - **2.** [Schnee, Sand] to crunch.
knistern *vi* [Feuer, brennendes Holz] to crackle; [Papier] to rustle; **mit etw knistern** to rustle sthg.
knitterfrei *adj* crease-resistant.
knittern *vi* to crease.
knobeln *vi* - **1.** [losen] to toss - **2.** [spielen] to play dice - **3.** [tüfteln]: **an etw** *(D)* **knobeln** to puzzle over sthg.
Knoblauch *der* garlic.
Knöchel (*pl* -) *der* ankle.
Knochen (*pl* -) *der* bone.
Knochen|bruch *der* fracture.
Knochenmark *das* bone marrow.
knochig *adj* bony.
Knödel (*pl* -) *der* dumpling.
Knolle (*pl* **-n**) *die* BIOL tuber.
Knopf (*pl* **Knöpfe**) *der* button.
Knopfdruck *der*: **auf Knopfdruck** at the push of a button.
knöpfen *vt* to button.
Knopf|loch *das* buttonhole.
Knorpel (*pl* -) *der* cartilage.
Knospe (*pl* **-n**) *die* bud.
knoten *vt* to tie.
Knoten (*pl* -) *der* - **1.** [gen] knot - **2.** MED lump.
Knoten|punkt *der* - **1.** [von Straßen] junction - **2.** [wichtiger Ort] centre.
Know-how ['noʊhaʊ̯] (*pl* **-s**) *das* know-how *(U)*.
knüllen *vt* to crumple.
Knüller (*pl* -) *der fam* sensation.
knüpfen *vt* to knot; [Netz] to make; **etw an etw** *(A)* **knüpfen** [mit Faden] to tie sthg to sthg; *fig* [Erwartungen, Bedingungen] to attach sthg to sthg.
Knüppel (*pl* -) *der* club; **jm einen Knüppel zwischen die Beine werfen** *fig* to put a spoke in sb's wheel.
knurren *vi* - **1.** [Magen] to rumble - **2.** [Hund] to growl - **3.** [Person] to grumble.
knusprig, knusperig ◇ *adj* crisp. ◇ *adv*: **knusprig braun** crisp and brown.
knutschen *fam* ◇ *vt* to smooch with. ◇ *vi* to smooch.
K. o. (*pl* -) *der* knockout.
Kobalt *das* CHEM cobalt.
Koch [kɔx] (*pl* **Köche** ['kœçə]) *der* cook.
Koch|buch *das* cookbook.
kochen ◇ *vt* - **1.** [Essen] to cook; [Kaffee] to make; **jm/sich etw kochen** to cook sb/o.s. sthg - **2.** [Wäsche] to boil. ◇ *vi* - **1.** [Wasser, Person] to boil - **2.** [Koch]: **gut/schlecht kochen** to be a good/bad cook.
Koch|gelegenheit *die* cooking facilities *Pl*.
Köchin [kœçɪn] (*pl* **-nen**) *die* cook.
Koch|löffel *der* wooden spoon.
Koch|rezept *das* recipe.
Koch|salz *das* cooking salt.
Koch|topf *der* saucepan.
Koch|wäsche *die washing that needs to be boiled*.
Kode (*pl* **-s**), **Code** (*pl* **-s**) ['koːt] *der* code.
Köder (*pl* -) *der* bait.
ködern *vt* to lure.
kodieren, codieren [ko'diːrən] *vt* to encode.
Koffein *das* caffeine.
koffeinfrei *adj* decaffeinated.

Koffer (*pl* -) *der* suitcase; **die Koffer packen** to pack one's bags.

Koffer|raum *der* boot *UK*, trunk *US*.

Kognak ['kɔnjak] (*pl* **-s**) *der* brandy.

Kohl *der* cabbage.

Kohle (*pl* **-n**) *die* - **1.** [Brennstoff] coal *(U)*; **wie auf glühenden Kohlen sitzen** *fig* to be like a cat on hot bricks - **2.** *fam* [Geld] cash.

Kohlenhydrat (*pl* **-e**) *das* carbohydrate.

Kohlen|säure *die*: **Mineralwasser mit/ohne Kohlensäure** sparkling/still mineral water.

Kohle|zeichnung *die* KUNST charcoal drawing.

Kohlrabi (*pl* - ODER **-s**) *der* kohlrabi.

Kohl|roulade *die* stuffed cabbage leaves *Pl*.

Koje (*pl* **-n**) *die* - **1.** *fam* [Bett] bed - **2.** [Schiffsbett] bunk.

Kokain *das* cocaine.

Kokosnuss (*pl* **-nüsse**) *die* coconut.

Koks *der* coke.

Kolben (*pl* -) *der* - **1.** TECH piston - **2.** CHEM flask.

Kolik (*pl* **-en**), **Kolik** (*pl* **-en**) *die* colic *(U)*.

Kollaps (*pl* **-e**), **Kollaps** (*pl* **-e**) *der* collapse *(sg)*.

Kollege (*pl* **-n**) *der* colleague.

Kollegin (*pl* **-nen**) *die* colleague.

Kollegium [kɔ'le:gi̯ʊm] (*pl* **-gien**) *das* [in Schule] teaching staff.

Kollektion (*pl* **-en**) *die* collection.

kollidieren (*perf* **ist kollidiert**) *vi* - **1.** [Fahrzeuge] to collide - **2.** [Interessen] to clash.

Kollision (*pl* **-en**) *die* collision.

Köln *nt* Cologne.

Kolonie [kolo'ni:] (*pl* **-n**) *die* colony.

Kolonne (*pl* **-n**) *die* column; **(in) Kolonne fahren** to drive in convoy.

kolossal *adj* colossal; **ein kolossaler Irrtum** a huge mistake.

Kolumbien *nt* Colombia.

Koma (*pl* **-s**) *das* coma.

Kombination (*pl* **-en**) *die* - **1.** [Zusammenfügung] combination - **2.** [Schlussfolgerung] deduction - **3.** [Arbeitsanzug] overalls *Pl*.

kombinieren ◇ *vi* to reason. ◇ *vt* to combine; **etw mit etw kombinieren** to combine sthg with sthg.

Komet (*pl* **-en**) *der* ASTRON comet.

Komfort [kɔm'fo:ɐ̯] *der*: **mit allem Komfort** with all mod cons.

komfortabel ◇ *adj* comfortable. ◇ *adv* [bequem] comfortably.

Komik *die* comic effect.

Komiker, in (*mpl* -, *fpl* **-nen**) *der, die* comedian.

komisch *adj* funny.

Komitee (*pl* **-s**) *das* committee.

Komma (*pl* **-s** ODER **-ta**) *das* - **1.** [Satzzeichen] comma - **2.** [mathematisches Zeichen] decimal point.

Kommandeur, in [kɔman'dø:ɐ̯, rɪn] (*mpl* **-e**, *fpl* **-nen**) *der, die* commander.

kommandieren *vt* [Soldaten] to command.

Kommando (*pl* **-s**) *das* - **1.** [gen] command; **auf Kommando** on command; **das Kommando haben/übernehmen** to be in/take command - **2.** [kleine Einheit] detachment.

kommen (*prät* **kam**, *perf* **ist gekommen**) ◇ *vi* - **1.** [herkommen] to come; **den Arzt kommen lassen** to call the doctor - **2.** [ein Ziel erreichen] to get; **wie komme ich zum Markt?** how do I get to the market?; **nach Hause kommen** to get home; **an die Macht kommen** to come to power - **3.** [mit Institutionen] to go; **ins/aus dem Krankenhaus kommen** to go to/leave hospital; **in die Schule kommen** to start school - **4.** [stammen] to come; **aus Deutschland kommen** to come from Germany - **5.** [folgen] to come; **rechts kommt der Bahnhof** the station's coming up on the right - **6.** [resultieren]: **von etw kommen** to result from sthg; **das kommt daher, dass...** it's because...; **das kommt davon!** see what happens!; **wie kommt es, dass...?** how is it that...? - **7.** [passieren] to happen; **das musste ja so kommen!** it had to happen!; **überraschend kommen** to come as a surprise - **8.** [Programm, Film]: **im Fernsehen kommen** to be on (the) television; **im Kino kommen** to be on at the cinema *UK* ODER the movies *US* - **9.** *fam* [einen Orgasmus haben] to come - **10.** [hingehören] to go, to belong; **die Kisten kommen in den Keller** the crates go ODER belong in the cellar - **11.** [anfangen]: **ins Schleudern kommen** to skid; **auf etw *(A)* zu sprechen kommen** to get around to talking about sthg - **12.** [mit Dativ]: **mir kam eine Idee** an idea came to me; **jm frech kommen** *fam* to be cheeky to sb - **13.** [figurative Verwendungen mit Präposition]: **auf eine Idee kommen** to think of an idea; **hinter etw *(A)* kommen** to get to the bottom of sthg; **ums Leben kommen** to lose one's life, to die; **zu sich kommen** to come round; **dazu kommen, etw zu tun** to get round to doing sthg. ◇ *vt fam*: **welchen Weg bist du gekommen?** which way did you come?

kommend *adj* - **1.** [Woche] coming - **2.** [Generation, Mode] future.

Kommentar (*pl* **-e**) *der* - **1.** [in Zeitung, Buch, Radio] commentary - **2.** *fam* [Bemerkung] comment; **kein Kommentar** no comment.

kommentieren *vt* - **1.** [Ereignis] to comment on - **2.** [Text, Buch] to provide a commentary on.

kommerziell ◇ *adj* commercial. ◇ *adv* commercially.

Kommilitone (*pl* **-n**) *der* UNI fellow student.

Kommilitonin (*pl* **-nen**) *die* UNI fellow student.
Kommissar, in (*mpl* **-e**, *fpl* **-nen**) *der, die* [bei der Polizei] superintendent *UK*, captain *US*.
kommunal *adj* local.
Kommune (*pl* **-n**) *die* - **1.** [Gemeinde] local authority - **2.** [Wohngemeinschaft] commune.
Kommunikation (*pl* **-en**) *die* communication.
Kommunion (*pl* **-en**) *die* RELIG Communion *(U)*.
Kommunismus *der* Communism.
Kommunist, in (*mpl* **-en**, *fpl* **-nen**) *der, die* Communist.
kommunistisch *adj* Communist.
Komödie [ko'møːdi̯ə] (*pl* **-n**) *die* comedy; **jm eine Komödie vorspielen** to put on an act for sb.
kompakt ◇ *adj* compact. ◇ *adv* compactly.
Kompanie [kɔmpa'niː] (*pl* **-n**) *die* MIL company.
Komparativ (*pl* **-e**) *der* GRAMM comparative.
Kompass (*pl* **-e**) *der* compass.
kompatibel *adj* EDV compatible; **mit etw kompatibel sein** to be compatible with sthg.
kompetent ◇ *adj* competent. ◇ *adv* competently.
Kompetenz (*pl* **-en**) *die* competence *(U)*.
komplett ◇ *adj* complete. ◇ *adv* - **1.** [vollständig] fully - **2.** *fam* [völlig] completely.
Komplex (*pl* **-e**) *der* [gen] [Psychologie] complex; **Komplexe haben** to have a complex.
Kompliment (*pl* **-e**) *das* compliment; **mein Kompliment!** my compliments!; **jm ein Kompliment machen** to pay sb a compliment.
Komplize (*pl* **-n**) *der* accomplice.
kompliziert ◇ *adj* complicated. ◇ *adv* in a complicated way.
Komplizin (*pl* **-nen**) *die* accomplice.
Komplott (*pl* **-e**) *das* plot.
komponieren *vt* [zusammenstellen & MUS] to compose.
Komponist, in (*mpl* **-en**, *fpl* **-nen**) *der, die* composer.
Komposition (*pl* **-en**) *die* [Zusammenstellung & MUS] composition.
Kompost (*pl* **-e**)**, Kompost** (*pl* **-e**) *der* compost *(U)*.
Kompott (*pl* **-e**) *das* stewed fruit.
Kompromiss (*pl* **-e**) *der* compromise.
kompromissbereit *adj* ready to compromise.
kondensieren *vt* & *vi* to condense.
Kondensmilch *die* condensed milk.
Kondenswasser *das* condensation.
Konditional (*pl* **-e**) *der* GRAMM conditional.
Konditions|training *das* fitness training.
Konditorei (*pl* **-en**) *die* cake shop.
Kondom (*pl* **-e**) *das* condom.
Konfekt (*pl* **-e**) *das* confectionery *(U)*.
Konfektion (*pl* **-en**) *die* - **1.** [Kleidung] ready-to-wear clothes *Pl* - **2.** [Herstellung] manufacture of ready-to-wear clothes.
Konferenz (*pl* **-en**) *die* - **1.** [Tagung] conference - **2.** [Besprechung] meeting.
Konfession (*pl* **-en**) *die* RELIG denomination.
Konfirmation (*pl* **-en**) *die* RELIG confirmation.
konfirmieren *vt* RELIG to confirm.
Konfitüre (*pl* **-n**) *die geh* jam.
Konflikt (*pl* **-e**) *der* conflict; **mit etw in Konflikt geraten** ODER **kommen** to come into conflict with sthg.
konform ◇ *adj* concurrent; **mit jm/etw konform gehen** *geh* to concur with sb/sthg. ◇ *adv*: **sich konform verhalten** to behave like everyone else.
Konfrontation (*pl* **-en**) *die* confrontation.
konfrontieren *vt*: **jn mit jm/etw konfrontieren** to confront sb with sb/sthg.
konfus ◇ *adj* confused. ◇ *adv* confusedly.
Kongo *der*: **der Kongo** the Congo.
Kongress (*pl* **-e**) *der* - **1.** [Tagung] conference - **2.** POL Congress.
König (*pl* **-e**) *der* - **1.** [gen] king; **die Heiligen Drei Könige** the Three Wise Men - **2.** [Feiertag]: **Heilige Drei Könige** Epiphany.
Königin (*pl* **-nen**) *die* queen.
königlich ◇ *adj* - **1.** [des Monarchen] royal - **2.** [reichlich - Mahl] lavish; [- Trinkgeld, Geschenk] handsome; [- Vergnügen] tremendous. ◇ *adv* - **1.** [riesig] tremendously - **2.** [bewirten] lavishly.
König|reich *das* kingdom.
Konjugation (*pl* **-en**) *die* GRAMM conjugation.
konjugieren *vt* GRAMM to conjugate.
Konjunktiv (*pl* **-e**) *der* GRAMM subjunctive.
Konjunktur (*pl* **-en**) *die* economic situation; **rückläufige Konjunktur** declining economic activity; **Konjunktur haben** to be in demand.
konkret ◇ *adj* concrete. ◇ *adv* concretely.
Konkurrent, in (*mpl* **-en**, *fpl* **-nen**) *der, die* competitor.
Konkurrenz (*pl* **-en**) *die* competition; **jm Konkurrenz machen** to compete with sb. ◆ **außer Konkurrenz** *adv* as an unofficial competitor.
konkurrenzfähig ◇ *adj* competitive. ◇ *adv* competitively.
Konkurrenz|kampf *der* competition.
Konkurs (*pl* **-e**) *der* - **1.** [Zahlungsunfähigkeit] bankruptcy - **2.** [Verfahren] bankruptcy proceedings *Pl*.

kọnnen (*präs* **kạnn**, *prät* **kọnnte**, *perf* **hat kọnnen** ODER **hat gekọnnt**) <> *aux* - **1.** [vermögen, dürfen] can; **er kann Klavier spielen** he can play the piano; **kann ich noch ein Eis haben?** can I have another ice cream?; **könnte ich mal telefonieren?** could I use the telephone? - **2.** [zum Ausdruck der Möglichkeit] can; **es könnte verloren gegangen sein** it could ODER might have got lost; **sie kann nicht kommen** she can't come; **wir können es versuchen** we can try; **das kann schon sein** that's quite possible; **man kann nie wissen** you never know. <> *vi*: **fahren, so schnell man kann** to drive as fast as you can; **kann ich ins Kino?** can I go to the cinema?; **ich kann nicht mehr** *fam* I've had it, I'm exhausted. <> *vt (perf hat gekonnt)* [vermögen]: **kannst du Deutsch?** can ODER do you speak German?; **etw auswendig können** to know sthg by heart; **der kann nichts** he's useless; **du kannst mich mal!** *vulg* piss off!

Kọnnen *das (ohne pl)* ability; **sein Können unter Beweis stellen** to prove one's ability.

Kọnner, in (*mpl* -, *fpl* **-nen**) *der, die* expert.

kọnnte *prät* ▷ **können**.

konsequẹnt <> *adj* - **1.** [folgerichtig] consistent - **2.** [Gegner] resolute; [Nichtraucher, Christ] strict. <> *adv* - **1.** [folgerichtig] consistently - **2.** [bekämpfen] resolutely.

Konsequẹnz (*pl* **-en**) *die* - **1.** [Folge] consequence; **aus etw die Konsequenzen ziehen** to draw the obvious conclusion from sthg - **2.** [Unbeirrbarkeit] resolution.

konservativ [kɔnzɛrva'tiːf] <> *adj* conservative. <> *adv* conservatively.

Konservative [kɔnzɛrva'tiːvə] (*pl* **-n**) *der, die* Conservative.

Konsẹrve [kɔn'zɛrvə] (*pl* **-n**) *die* [Dose] can, tin *UK*; **sich nur von Konserven ernähren** to live only on tinned *UK* ODER canned *US* food.

Konsẹrven|dose *die* can, tin *UK*.

konservieren [kɔnzɛr'viːrən] *vt* to preserve.

Konservierungsstoffe [kɔnzɛr'viːrʊŋsʃtɔfə] *Pl* preservatives.

Konsonạnt (*pl* **-en**) *der* consonant.

konstạnt <> *adj* constant. <> *adv* constantly.

konstruieren [kɔnstru'iːrən] *vt* - **1.** [bauen] to construct - **2.** *abw* [erfinden] to fabricate.

Konstrukteur, in [kɔnstrʊk'tøːɐ̯, rɪn] (*mpl* **-e**, *fpl* **-nen**) *der, die* designer.

Konstruktion (*pl* **-en**) *die* construction.

Konsulat (*pl* **-e**) *das* POL consulate.

Konsum *der* [Verbrauch] consumption.

Konsumẹnt, in (*mpl* **-en**, *fpl* **-nen**) *der, die* consumer.

konsumieren *vt* to consume.

Kontạkt (*pl* **-e**) *der* contact; **mit jm Kontakt aufnehmen** to get in touch with sb; **zu** ODER **mit jm/etw Kontakt haben** to be in contact with sb/sthg.

kontạktarm *adj*: **er ist kontaktarm** he finds it difficult to make friends.

kontạktfreudig *adj* sociable.

Kontạkt|linse *die* contact lens.

Kontinẹnt (*pl* **-e**), **Kọntinent** (*pl* **-e**) *der* continent.

Kọnto (*pl* **Kọnten**) *das* [Bankkonto] account; **ein Konto eröffnen/auflösen** to open/close an account; **etw geht auf js Konto** sb is to blame for sthg.

Kọnto|auszug *der* bank statement.

Kọnto|stand *der* bank balance.

kọntra, cọntra <> *präp* versus. <> *adv*: **kontra eingestellt sein** to be against.

Kọntra (*pl* **-s**) *das* double; **jm Kontra geben** *fam* to contradict sb.

Kọntrabass (*pl* **-bässe**) *der* double bass.

Kontrạst (*pl* **-e**) *der* contrast; **einen Kontrast zu etw bilden** to contrast with sthg.

Kontrọlle (*pl* **-n**) *die* - **1.** [Überwachung] check; **jn/etw unter Kontrolle haben** to keep a check on sb/sthg - **2.** [Beherrschung] control; **jn/etw unter Kontrolle bekommen/haben** to get/have sb/sthg under control; **die Kontrolle über sich verlieren** to lose control.

kontrollieren *vt* - **1.** [überprüfen] to check - **2.** [überwachen] to keep a check on - **3.** [beherrschen] to control.

Kontur (*pl* **-en**) *die* contour; [von Politiker] profile; **Kontur gewinnen/verlieren** to take/lose shape.

konventionẹll [kɔnvɛntsio'nɛl] <> *adj* conventional. <> *adv* conventionally.

Konversation [kɔnvɛrza'tsioːn] (*pl* **-en**) *die* *geh* conversation.

Konzentrat (*pl* **-e**) *das* concentrate.

Konzentration (*pl* **-en**) *die* concentration.

Konzentrations|lager *das* concentration camp.

konzentrieren *vt* - **1.** [richten]: **etw auf etw (A) konzentrieren** to concentrate sthg on sthg - **2.** [vereinigen] to concentrate. ◆ **sich konzentrieren** *ref* to concentrate; **sich auf etw (A) konzentrieren** to concentrate on sthg.

konzentriert <> *adj* concentrated. <> *adv* with concentration; **konzentriert nachdenken** to concentrate.

Konzẹpt (*pl* **-e**) *das* - **1.** [Entwurf] draft - **2.** [Plan] plan; **jn aus dem Konzept bringen** to put sb off his/her stride.

Konzẹrn (*pl* **-e**) *der* group (of companies).

Konzẹrt (*pl* **-e**) *das* [Veranstaltung] concert; [Musikstück] concerto.

Konzẹrthaus (*pl* **-häuser**) *das* concert hall.

Konzession (*pl* **-en**) *die* - **1.** WIRTSCH licence - **2.** [Zugeständnis] concession.

Koordinate (*pl* **-n**) *die* coordinate.

koordinieren *vt* to coordinate.

Kopenhagen *nt* Copenhagen.

Kopf (*pl* **Köpfe**) *der* - **1.** [gen] head; **mit dem** ODER **den Kopf schütteln** to shake one's head; **jm etw an den Kopf werfen** *eigtl* & *fig* to hurl sthg at sb - **2.** [Anführer] leader; **den Kopf hängen lassen** to be downhearted; **jm über den Kopf wachsen** to overwhelm sb; **jm zu Kopf steigen** to go to sb's head; **etw auf den Kopf stellen** *fam* to turn sthg upside down; **und wenn du dich auf den Kopf stellst** you're wasting your breath; **sich** *(D)* **etw durch den Kopf gehen lassen** to think sthg over; **sich** *(D)* **(über etw** *(A)***) den Kopf zerbrechen** to rack one's brains (over sthg). ◆ **aus dem Kopf** *adv* off the top of one's head. ◆ **Kopf an Kopf** *adv* neck and neck. ◆ **pro Kopf** *adv* per head. ◆ **von Kopf bis Fuß** *adv* from head to toe.

Köpfchen (*pl* -) *das* little head; **Köpfchen haben** *fam fig* to have brains.

köpfen ◇ *vt* - **1.** SPORT to head - **2.** [hinrichten] to behead - **3.** *fam* [öffnen - Flasche] to crack open; [- Ei] to slice the top off. ◇ *vi* SPORT to head.

Kopf|haut *die* scalp.

Kopf|hörer *der* headphones *Pl.*

Kopf|kissen *das* pillow.

kopflos ◇ *adj* - **1.** [ohne Kopf] headless - **2.** [wirr] panicky. ◇ *adv* in a state of panic.

Kopf|rechnen *das* mental arithmetic.

Kopf|salat *der* lettuce.

Kopf|schmerzen *Pl* headache *(sg)*; **Kopfschmerzen haben** to have a headache.

Kopf|sprung *der* dive.

Kopf|stand *der* headstand.

Kopf|stütze *die* headrest.

Kopf|tuch *das* headscarf.

Kopfzerbrechen *das*: **jm Kopfzerbrechen machen** ODER **bereiten** to be a real headache for sb.

Kopie [ko'pi:] (*pl* **-n**) *die* copy.

kopieren *vt* to copy.

Kopierer (*pl* -) *der* photocopier.

Kopier|gerät *das* photocopier.

Ko|pilot, in ['ko:pilo:t, ɪn] *der, die* co-pilot.

koppeln *vt* - **1.** [knüpfen] to attach - **2.** [anschließen] to couple.

Koppelung (*pl* **-en**), **Kopplung** (*pl* **-en**) *die* coupling.

Koralle (*pl* **-n**) *die* coral.

Koran (*pl* **-e**) *der* Koran.

Korb (*pl* **Körbe**) *der* - **1.** [Behälter & SPORT] basket - **2.** [Abfuhr] rebuff; **jm einen Korb geben** to turn sb down.

Korb|stuhl *der* wicker chair.

Kord, Cord [kɔrt] *der* corduroy.

Kordel (*pl* **-n**) *die* cord.

Kork *der* cork.

Korken (*pl* -) *der* cork.

Korkenzieher (*pl* -) *der* corkscrew.

Korn (*pl* **Körner** ODER -) ◇ *das* - **1.** [Getreide] grain, corn *UK* - **2.** *(pl Körner)* [Pflanzenfrucht, kleines Partikel] grain; **jn/etw aufs Korn nehmen** *fam fig* to hit out at sb/sthg. ◇ *der (pl Korn)* [Schnaps] schnapps.

Korn|blume *die* cornflower.

Körper (*pl* -) *der* body.

Körperbau *der* build.

körperbehindert *adj* disabled.

Körper|gewicht *das amt* weight.

Körper|größe *die amt* height.

körperlich ◇ *adj* physical. ◇ *adv* physically.

Körperpflege *die* personal hygiene.

Körperschaft (*pl* **-en**) *die* RECHT corporation.

Körper|teil *der* part of the body.

Körper|verletzung *die* bodily harm.

korpulent *adj* corpulent.

korrekt ◇ *adj* correct. ◇ *adv* correctly.

Korrektur (*pl* **-en**) *die* correction; **Korrektur lesen** to read the proofs.

Korrespondent, in (*mpl* **-en**, *fpl* **-nen**) *der, die* [Berichterstatter] correspondent.

Korrespondenz *die* correspondence.

Korridor (*pl* **-e**) *der* corridor.

korrigieren *vt* to correct.

korrupt *adj* corrupt.

Korruption (*pl* **-en**) *die* corruption *(U)*.

Kosmetik (*pl* **-ka**) *die* [Pflege] beauty care.

Kosmetiker, in (*mpl* -, *fpl* **-nen**) *der, die* beautician.

kosmetisch ◇ *adj* cosmetic. ◇ *adv* cosmetically.

Kosmos *der* cosmos.

Kost *die* food.

kostbar *adj* - **1.** [wertvoll, erlesen] valuable - **2.** [wichtig] precious.

Kostbarkeit (*pl* **-en**) *die* - **1.** [Wert] value - **2.** [Gegenstand] treasure.

kosten ◇ *vi* [probieren] to have a taste; **von der Suppe kosten** to taste the soup. ◇ *vt* - **1.** [gen] to cost; **was** ODER **wie viel kostet das?** how much is it?, how much does it cost?; **Fragen kostet nichts** there's no harm in asking - **2.** [probieren] to taste, to try.

Kosten *Pl* costs; **auf js Kosten** *(A)* at sb's expense; **auf js Kosten gehen** to be at sb's expense; **auf Kosten einer Sache** *(G)* **gehen** to be at the expense of sthg; **auf seine Kosten kommen** to get one's money's worth; [bei einer Party] to have a good time.

kostenlos <> *adj* free. <> *adv* free of charge.

Kostenlvoranschlag *der* estimate.

köstlich <> *adj* - **1.** [im Geschmack] delicious - **2.** [amüsant] delightful. <> *adv* - **1.: köstlich speisen** to have a delicious meal - **2.: sich köstlich amüsieren** to enjoy o.s. enormously.

Kostlprobe *die* [von Speise] taste; [von js Können] sample.

kostspielig *adj* costly.

Kostüm (*pl* **-e**) *das* - **1.** [Rock und Jacke] suit - **2.** [im Theater, zu Fasching] costume.

kostümieren ◆ **sich kostümieren** *ref* to dress up *(in fancy dress)*.

Kot *der* excrement.

Kotelett (*pl* **-s**) *das* chop, cutlet.

Koteletten *Pl* sideboards *UK*, sideburns *US*.

Kotlflügel *der* wing.

kotzen *vi salopp* to puke.

Krabbe (*pl* **-n**) *die* [Krebs] crab; [Garnele] shrimp.

krabbeln (*perf* **hat/ist gekrabbelt**) <> *vi (ist)* to crawl. <> *vt (hat) fam* [kratzen] to scratch; [kitzeln] to tickle.

Krach (*pl* **Kräche**) *der* - **1.** [Lärm] racket; **Krach machen** to make a racket - **2.** *fam* [Ärger] row; **er hat Krach mit seiner Freundin** he's rowing with his girlfriend - **3.** [Zusammenbruch] crash.

krachen (*perf* **hat/ist gekracht**) <> *vi* - **1.** *(hat)* [lärmen - Donner] to crash; [- Schuss] to ring out; [- Gewehr] to bang; **dann krachts!** there'll be trouble!; **an der Ecke hat es gekracht** there's been a crash on the corner - **2.** *(ist) fam* [kaputtgehen - Bett, Stuhl] to collapse; [- Reißverschluss, Brett] to split; [- Eis] to crack. <> *vt (hat) fam* to bang.

krächzen <> *vi* [Rabe] to caw; [Person] to croak. <> *vt* to croak out.

Kraft (*pl* **Kräfte**) *die* - **1.** [Körperkraft] strength *(U)*; **am Ende seiner Kräfte sein** to be completely exhausted; **Kraft/keine Kraft haben** to be strong/weak - **2.** [Fähigkeit, Wirksamkeit] power; **aus eigener Kraft** by oneself; **mit vereinten Kräften** by joining forces - **3.** [Hilfskraft] helper. ◆ **Kräfte** *Pl* [politisch] forces. ◆ **außer Kraft** *adv*: **außer Kraft treten/sein** to cease to be/be no longer in force. ◆ **in Kraft** *adv*: **in Kraft treten/setzen/sein** to come into/put into/be in force.

Kraftlfahrzeug *das amt* motor vehicle.

Kraftfahrzeuglsteuer *die amt* road tax *UK*, vehicle tax *US*.

kräftig <> *adj* - **1.** [stark - Person] strong; [- Schlag] powerful; [- Körperbau, Stimme] powerful, strong - **2.** [Hunger, Farben] intense - **3.** [Mahlzeit] nourishing - **4.** [Fluch] coarse. <> *adv* - **1.** [stark] hard - **2.** [fluchen] violently.

kräftigen *vt* to strengthen.

kraftlos <> *adj* weak. <> *adv* [wanken] weakly; [herabhängen] limply.

Kraftlprobe *die* trial of strength.

Kraftlstoff *der* fuel.

kraftvoll <> *adj* powerful. <> *adv* powerfully.

Kraftlwerk *das* power station.

Kragen (*pl* - ODER **Krägen**) *der* collar; **es geht jm an den Kragen** *fam fig* sb is in for it; **ihr platzte der Kragen** *fam fig* she blew her top.

Krähe (*pl* **-n**) *die* crow.

krähen *vi* to crow.

Kralle (*pl* **-n**) *die* claw.

Kram *der fam* - **1.** [Zeug] stuff; **jm nicht in den Kram passen** *fam fig* not to fit in with sb's plans - **2.** [Arbeit] business.

kramen *vi* to rummage about.

Krampf (*pl* **Krämpfe**) *der* cramp; **einen Krampf bekommen/haben** to get/have cramp.

Krampflader *die* varicose vein.

krampfhaft <> *adj* [Husten, Verrenkungen] convulsive; [Anstrengungen] strenuous. <> *adv* [zucken] convulsively; [lächeln] in a strained way; **sich krampfhaft bemühen** to make strenuous efforts; **krampfhaft nachdenken** to rack one's brains.

Kran (*pl* **Kräne**) *der* crane.

krank (*kompar* **kränker**, *superl* **am kränksten**) *adj* sick, ill; **er ist krank** he is ill ODER sick; **krank werden** to be taken ill; **diese ständigen Streitereien machen mich krank** these constant arguments are getting on my nerves.

Kranke (*pl* **-n**) *der, die* sick person; [im Krankenhaus] patient.

kranken *vi*: **an etw** *(D)* **kranken** to suffer from sthg.

kränken *vt* to hurt.

Krankenlgeld *das (ohne pl)* sickness benefit.

Krankenlgymnastik *die* physiotherapy.

Krankenlhaus *das* hospital.

Krankenlkasse *die* health insurance association.

Krankenlpfleger *der* (male) nurse.

Krankenlschwester *die* nurse.

Krankenlversicherung *die* health insurance.

Krankenlwagen *der* ambulance.

krankhaft <> *adj* pathological. <> *adv* [übertrieben] pathologically.

Krankheit (*pl* **-en**) *die* - **1.** [Zustand] illness - **2.** [bestimmte Krankheit] disease.

kränklich *adj* sickly.

krank|melden ◆ **sich krankmelden** *ref* to report sick.

Kränkung (*pl* **-en**) *die* hurt.

Kranz (*pl* **Kränze**) *der* - **1.** [Schmuck] wreath - **2.** [Kuchen] ring.

krass ◇ *adj* [Gegensatz] stark; [Verstoß, Fall] blatant. ◇ *adv* [ausdrücken] bluntly.

Krater (*pl* -) *der* crater.

kratzen ◇ *vi* - **1.** [verletzen] to scratch - **2.** [schaben] to scrape - **3.** [jucken] to itch; **es kratzt im Hals** I've got a tickle in my throat. ◇ *vt* - **1.** [verletzen] to scratch - **2.** [schaben] to scrape - **3.** [jucken]: **jn kratzen** to make sb itch. ◆ **sich kratzen** *ref* to scratch o.s.

Kratzer (*pl* -) *der* scratch.

kratzig *adj* - **1.** [rau] scratchy - **2.** [heiser] rough.

Kraul *das* SPORT crawl.

kraulen (*perf* **hat/ist gekrault**) ◇ *vi (ist)* SPORT to do the crawl. ◇ *vt (hat)* [streicheln] to tickle.

kraus *adj* - **1.** [lockig] frizzy - **2.** [gerunzelt] wrinkled - **3.** [wirr] confused.

kräuseln *vt* - **1.** [in Locken] to frizz - **2.** [in Wellen] to ripple. ◆ **sich kräuseln** *ref* [in Locken] to go frizzy.

Kraut (*pl* **Kräuter**) *das* - **1.** *(ohne pl)* [Kohl] cabbage - **2.** *(ohne pl)* [Grünes] leaves *Pl* - **3.** *fam* [Tabak] weed; **dagegen ist kein Kraut gewachsen** there is no cure for it. ◆ **Kräuter** *Pl* herbs.

Kräuter|tee *der* herbal tea.

Krawall (*pl* **-e**) *der* [Krach, Lärm] row; **Krawall machen** to make a row. ◆ **Krawalle** *Pl* [Unruhen] riots.

Krawatte (*pl* **-n**) *die* tie.

kreativ *adj* creative.

Kreativität [kreativi'tɛ:t] *die* creativity.

Kreatur (*pl* **-en**) *die* creature.

Krebs (*pl* **-e**) *der* - **1.** [Tier] crab - **2.** *(ohne pl)* [Tumor] cancer; **Krebs haben** to have cancer - **3.** ASTROL Cancer; **Krebs sein** to be a Cancer.

Kredit (*pl* **-e**) *der* [Darlehen] credit *(U)*; **einen Kredit aufnehmen/gewähren** to take out/ grant credit.

Kredit|karte *die* credit card.

Kreide (*pl* **-n**) *die* chalk; **bei jm in der Kreide stehen** *fig* to be in debt to sb.

kreideweiß *adj* as white as a sheet.

kreieren [kre'i:rən] *vt* to create.

Kreis (*pl* **-e**) *der* - **1.** [Form, Personenkreis] circle; **im Kreis** in a circle - **2.** [Verwaltungsbezirk] district; **Kreise ziehen** to have repercussions; **sich im Kreis drehen** to go round in circles.

kreischen *vi* [Person] to shriek; [Tier, Säge, Bremsen] to screech.

kreisen (*perf* **hat/ist gekreist**) *vi* - **1.** [sich drehen] to circle; **die Erde kreist um die Sonne** the earth goes round the sun - **2.** [Gedanken]: **um etw kreisen** to revolve aroung sthg.

Kreis|lauf *der* - **1.** [Zyklus] cycle - **2.** [Blutkreislauf] circulation.

Kreis|laufstörungen *Pl* circulatory trouble *(U)*.

Kreis|säge *die* - **1.** [Säge] circular saw - **2.** [Hut] boater.

Kreis|stadt *die* chief town of a district.

Kreis|verkehr *der* roundabout *UK*, traffic circle *US*.

Krem (*pl* **-s**) *die* = **Creme**.

Kreme (*pl* **-s** ODER **-n**) *die* = **Creme**.

kremig *adj* = **cremig**.

Krempe (*pl* **-n**) *die* brim.

Krempel *der fam* junk.

Kreppapier *das* crepe paper.

Kresse (*pl* **-n**) *die* cress *(U)*.

Kreta *nt* Crete.

Kreuz (*pl* **-e**) *das* - **1.** [Zeichen & RELIG] cross; **über Kreuz** crosswise - **2.** [Rücken] small of the back; **mir tut das Kreuz weh** my back aches; **jn aufs Kreuz legen** *fam fig* to take sb for a ride - **3.** [Autobahnkreuz] intersection - **4.** *(ohne pl)* [Qual] burden - **5.** *(ohne Artikel, ohne pl)* [Spielfarbe] clubs *Pl* - **6.** [Spielkarte] club; **die Kreuzsechs** the six of clubs.

kreuzen (*perf* **hat/ist gekreuzt**) ◇ *vt (hat)* to cross. ◇ *vi (hat, ist)* - **1.** [Boot - hin und her fahren] to cruise - **2.** [gegen den Wind segeln] to tack. ◆ **sich kreuzen** *ref* - **1.** [Weg, Brief, Linie] to cross - **2.** [Ansichten] to clash.

Kreuz|fahrt *die* cruise.

Kreuz|gang *der* cloister.

kreuzigen *vt* to crucify.

Kreuzigung (*pl* **-en**) *die* crucifixion.

Kreuzung (*pl* **-en**) *die* - **1.** [Straßenkreuzung] crossroads *(sg)* - **2.** [Züchtung] cross.

Kreuzwort|rätsel *das* crossword (puzzle).

kriechen (*prät* **kroch**, *perf* **ist gekrochen**) *vi* - **1.** [Wurm, Verkehr, Kind] to crawl - **2.** [Zeit] to creep by - **3.** *abw* [unterwürfig sein]: **vor jm kriechen** to crawl to sb.

Kriech|spur *die* crawler lane.

Krieg (*pl* **-e**) *der* war; **jm/einer Sache den Krieg erklären** to declare war on sb/sthg.

kriegen *vt fam* [bekommen] to get; [Zug, Bus, Straßenbahn] to catch; [gebären - Kind] to have; **wenn wir den kriegen!** just wait till we get hold of him!

Kriegs|dienstverweigerer (*pl* **Kriegsdienstverweigerer**) *der* conscientious objector.

Kriegs|gefangene *der, die* prisoner of war.

Krimi (*pl* **-s**) *der fam* thriller.

Kriminal|beamte *der* detective.

Kriminal|beamtin *die* detective.

Kriminalität *die* crime.

Kriminalpolizei *die* ≃ Criminal Investigation Department *UK*, ≃ Federal Bureau of Investigation *US*.

kriminell *adj* criminal; **kriminell werden** to turn to crime.

Kripo (*abk für* **Kriminalpolizei**) *die* ≃ CID *UK*, ≃ FBI *US*.

Krippe (*pl* **-n**) *die* - **1.** [Kinderkrippe] crèche *UK*, day nursery *US* - **2.** [Futterkrippe] manger - **3.** [Weihnachtskrippe] crib.

Krise (*pl* **-n**) *die* crisis; **in einer Krise stecken** to be in (a) crisis.

Krisen|herd *der* trouble spot.

Kristall (*pl* **-e**) *das* & *der* crystal.

Kriterium (*pl* **Kriterien**) *das* criterion.

Kritik (*pl* **-en**) *die* - **1.** [Beurteilung] criticism; **an jm/etw Kritik üben** to criticize sb/sthg - **2.** [Rezension] review.

Kritiker, in (*mpl* **-**, *fpl* **-nen**) *der, die* critic.

kritisch ◇ *adj* critical. ◇ *adv* - **1.** [prüfend, negativ] critically - **2.** [gefährlich]: **es steht kritisch um den Kranken** the patient is critical.

kritisieren *vt* to criticize.

kritzeln *vt* to scribble.

Kroatien [kro'aːtsi̯ən] *nt* Croatia.

kroatisch [kro'aːtɪʃ] *adj* Croatian.

kroch *prät* ▷ **kriechen**.

Krokant *der (ohne pl)* praline.

Krokodil (*pl* **-e**) *das* crocodile.

Krokus (*pl* **-se**) *der* crocus.

Krone (*pl* **-n**) *die* - **1.** [gen] crown - **2.** [Herrschaft] Crown - **3.** [Währung - dänische] krone; [- schwedische] krona; **einer Sache** *(D)* **die Krone aufsetzen** to cap sthg.

krönen *vt* to crown; **jn zum König krönen** to crown sb king.

Kron|leuchter *der* chandelier.

Krönung (*pl* **-en**) *die* - **1.** [das Krönen] coronation - **2.** [Höhepunkt] culmination.

Kropf (*pl* **Kröpfe**) *der* goitre.

Kröte (*pl* **-n**) *die* toad.

Krücke (*pl* **-n**) *die* - **1.** [Stock] crutch - **2.** *fam abw* [Person] clown.

Krug (*pl* **Krüge**) *der* [für Milch, Wein] jug; [für Bier] mug.

Krümel (*pl* **-**) *der* crumb.

krumm ◇ *adj* - **1.** [Linie] curved; [Nagel, Rücken] bent; [Nase] hooked; [Finger, Beine] crooked - **2.** *fam* [unehrlich] crooked; **auf eine krumme Tour** by crooked means. ◇ *adv* [gehen, stehen] with a stoop; [sitzen] bent over.

krümmen *vt* to bend. ◆ **sich krümmen** *ref* to bend; [vor Schmerzen] to double up.

krumm nehmen *vt (unreg) fam* to take offence at; **jm etw krumm nehmen** to hold sthg against sb.

Krümmung (*pl* **-en**) *die* [von Horizont, Rücken] curve; [von Straße, Fluss] bend.

Krüppel (*pl* **-**) *der* cripple.

Kruste (*pl* **-n**) *die* - **1.** [Rinde] crust - **2.** [Schicht] scab.

Kruzifix (*pl* **-e**) *das* crucifix.

Kto. (*abk für* **Konto**) a/c.

Kuba *nt* Cuba; **auf Kuba** in Cuba.

Kübel (*pl* **-**) *der* [für Abfälle] bin; [für Pflanzen] tub.

Kubik|meter *der* cubic metre.

Küche (*pl* **-n**) *die* - **1.** [Raum] kitchen - **2.** [Kochen] cooking; **kalte/warme Küche** cold/hot food.

Kuchen (*pl* **-**) *der* cake.

Kuchen|blech *das* baking sheet.

Kuchen|form *die* cake tin *UK* ODER pan *US*.

Kuchen|gabel *die* cake fork.

Küchen|schabe *die* cockroach.

Kuckuck (*pl* **-e**) *der* cuckoo.

Kufe (*pl* **-n**) *die* runner.

Kugel (*pl* **-n**) *die* - **1.** [gen & SPORT] ball; [am Weihnachtsbaum] bauble; [beim Kugelstoßen] shot - **2.** [Form] sphere - **3.** [Geschoss] bullet; **eine ruhige Kugel schieben** *fam fig* to have it easy.

Kugel|lager *das* ball bearing.

Kugelschreiber (*pl* **-**) *der* ballpoint (pen), Biro®.

kugelsicher *adj* bullet-proof.

Kugelstoßen *das* SPORT shot put.

Kuh (*pl* **Kühe**) *die* cow.

kühl ◇ *adj* cool. ◇ *adv* coolly; **kühl servieren** serve chilled; **kühl und trocken lagern** keep in a cool, dry place.

kühlen *vt* to cool.

Kühler (*pl* **-**) *der* - **1.** AUTO radiator - **2.** [für Getränke] cooler.

Kühler|haube *die* bonnet *UK*, hood *US*.

Kühl|schrank *der* fridge.

Kühl|truhe *die* freezer.

Kühlung (*pl* **-en**) *die* - **1.** [Erfrischung] coolness - **2.** TECH cooling.

kühn *adj* bold.

Küken (*pl* **-**) *das* - **1.** [Tier] chick - **2.** *fam fig* [Nesthäkchen] baby; [Mädchen] little girl.

kulant *adj* [Verkäufer, Geschäftspartner] obliging; [Preis] reasonable.

Kuli (*pl* **-s**) *der* - **1.** [Mensch] coolie - **2.** *fam* [Schreiber] Biro®.

Kulisse (*pl* **-n**) *die* - **1.** [Bühnenbild] scenery *(U)* - **2.** [Hintergrund] background.

kullern (*perf* **ist gekullert**) *vi* to roll.

Kult (*pl* **-e**) *der* cult.

kultivieren [kʊlti'viːrən] *vt* to cultivate.

kultiviert [kʊlti'viːɐt] ◇ *adj* refined. ◇ *adv* in a refined manner.

Kultur (*pl* **-en**) *die* culture.

Kultur|beutel *der* toilet bag.

kulturẹll ◇ *adj* cultural. ◇ *adv* culturally.

Kulturhaus (*pl* **-häuser**) *das* arts centre *UK* ODER center *US*.

Kụltus|minister, in *der, die minister of a German Federal state responsible for education and cultural affairs.*

Kụ̈mmel (*pl* -) *der* - **1.** *(ohne pl)* [Gewürzpflanze] caraway - **2.** [Schnaps] kümmel.

Kụmmer *der* worries *Pl*; **Kummer mit jm haben** to worry about sb; **jm Kummer machen** to worry sb.

kụ̈mmerlich *adj* miserable.

kụ̈mmern *vt* to concern; **das kümmert sie nicht** she doesn't care about that; **was kümmert es ihn?** what is it to him? ◆ **sich kümmern** *ref*: **sich um jn kümmern** [helfen] to look after sb; **sich um etw kümmern** [organisieren, zubereiten] to see to sthg; [beachten] to worry about sthg; **kümmere dich um deine eigenen Angelegenheiten!** mind your own business!

Kụmpel (*pl* -) *der* - **1.** [Bergarbeiter] miner - **2.** *fam* [Kamerad] pal.

kụ̈ndbar *adj* [Stellung, Vertrag] terminable; [Mitarbeiter] dismissible.

Kụnde (*pl* **-n**) *der* customer.

Kụnden|dienst *der* - **1.** [Service] customer service - **2.** [Servicestelle] customer service department.

Kụndgebung (*pl* **-en**) *die* rally.

kụ̈ndigen ◇ *vi* [Arbeitnehmer] to hand in one's notice; [Mieter] to give notice that one is leaving; **jm kündigen** [Firma] to give sb his/her notice; [Vermieter] to give sb notice to quit. ◇ *vt* [Vertrag, Kredit] to terminate; **seine Arbeitsstelle kündigen** to hand in one's notice; **seine Wohnung kündigen** to give notice that one is leaving; **jm die Freundschaft kündigen** to break off one's friendship with sb.

Kụ̈ndigung (*pl* **-en**) *die* [von Vertrag] termination; [von Arbeitsstelle] notice; [von Wohnung] notice to quit; **jm die Kündigung aussprechen** to give sb his/her notice.

Kụ̈ndigungs|frist *die* period of notice.

Kụ̈ndigungsschutz *der* [für Mieter] protection against wrongful eviction; [für Arbeitnehmer] protection against wrongful dismissal.

Kụndin (*pl* **-nen**) *die* customer.

Kụndschaft *die (ohne pl)* customers *Pl*.

kụ̈nftig ◇ *adj* future. ◇ *adv* in future.

Kụnst (*pl* **Kụ̈nste**) *die* art; **das ist keine Kunst!** there is nothing to it!

Kụnst|dünger *der* artificial fertilizer.

Kụnst|erziehung *die (ohne pl)* art lessons *Pl*.

Kụnst|faser *die* synthetic fibre.

Kụnst|fehler *der* professional error.

kụnstfertig ◇ *adj* skilful. ◇ *adv* skilfully.

Kụnstgegen|stand *der* objet d'art.

Kụnst|geschichte *die* history of art.

Kụnst|gewerbe *das (ohne pl)* arts and crafts *Pl*.

Kụnsthand|werk *das* craft.

Kụ̈nstler, in (*mpl* -, *fpl* **-nen**) *der, die* - **1.** [Kunstschaffende] artist - **2.** [Könner] master.

kụ̈nstlerisch ◇ *adj* artistic. ◇ *adv* artistically.

Kụ̈nstler|name *der* pseudonym.

kụ̈nstlich ◇ *adj* - **1.** [nicht natürlich] artificial - **2.** [übertrieben] forced. ◇ *adv* - **1.** [nicht natürlich] artificially - **2.** [übertrieben] in a forced way.

Kụnst|stoff *der* plastic.

Kụnst|stück *das* - **1.** [Trick] trick - **2.** [Leistung] feat.

Kụnst|werk *das* work of art.

kụnterbunt ◇ *adj* varied. ◇ *adv* in a jumble.

Kụpfer *das* copper.

Kụppe (*pl* **-n**) *die* - **1.** [landschaftlich] (hill)top - **2.** [von Fingern] tip.

Kụppel (*pl* **-n**) *die* dome.

Kụpplung (*pl* **-en**) *die* - **1.** [in Auto] clutch - **2.** [für Anhänger] coupling.

Kur (*pl* **-en**) *die* health cure; **auf** ODER **zur Kur sein/gehen** to be/go on a health cure.

Kür (*pl* **-en**) *die* free programme.

Kụrbel (*pl* **-n**) *die* [von Fenster, Rollo] winder; [von Drehorgel, Spieluhr] handle; [von Maschine, zum Aufziehen] crank.

Kụ̈rbis (*pl* **-se**) *der* pumpkin.

Kụrdistan *nt* Kurdistan.

Kur|gast *der visitor to a health resort.*

Kurier (*pl* **-e**) *der* courier.

kurieren *vt* to cure; **von etw kuriert sein** *fam fig* to be cured of sthg.

kurios *adj* curious.

Kuriosität (*pl* **-en**) *die* curiosity.

Kur|ort *der* health resort.

Kụrs (*pl* **-e**) *der* - **1.** [Fahrtrichtung, Lehrgang] course - **2.** [Teilnehmer] course members *Pl* - **3.** [Marktpreis - von Aktien] price; [- von Währung] exchange rate; **hoch im Kurs stehen** to be very popular.

Kụrs|buch *das* timetable.

kursieren *vi* to circulate.

Kụrsus (*pl* **Kụrse**) *der* course.

Kur|taxe *die tax paid by visitors to health resorts.*

Kụrve ['kʊrvə] (*pl* **-n**) *die* - **1.** [Straßenkrümmung] bend; **die Straße macht eine Kurve** the road bends - **2.** [Bogenlinie] curve.

kụrvenreich *adj* [Straße] winding; [Frau] curvaceous.

kurz (*kompar* **kürzer**, *superl* **kürzeste**) <> *adj* - **1.** [räumlich] short; **was ist der kürzeste Weg zum Bahnhof?** what's the quickest way to the station? - **2.** [zeitlich] short, brief; **innerhalb kurzer Zeit** within a short space of time; **vor kurzem** recently; **über kurz oder lang** sooner or later. <> *adv* - **1.** [räumlich]: **kurz vor/hinter** just in front of/behind; **alles kurz und klein schlagen** *fam* to smash everything to pieces - **2.** [zeitlich] briefly; **ich gehe mal kurz in das Geschäft dort** I'm just popping into that shop; **kurz vor dem Konzert** shortly before the concert.

kurzärmelig, kurzärmlig <> *adj* short-sleeved. <> *adv* in short sleeves.

Kürze *die* shortness. ◆ **in Kürze** *adv* shortly.

kürzen *vt* - **1.** [Haare, Nägel, Film, Text] to cut; [Rock, Kabel] to shorten - **2.** [finanziell] to cut - **3.** MATH to cancel.

kurzerhand *adv* without further ado.

kurzfristig <> *adj* - **1.** [unangemeldet] sudden - **2.** [kurz dauernd] short-term - **3.** [rasch] quick. <> *adv* - **1.** [unangemeldet] at short notice - **2.** [kurz dauernd] for a short time - **3.** [rasch] quickly.

Kurz|geschichte *die* short story.

kurzhaarig *adj* short-haired.

kürzlich *adv* recently.

kurz|schließen *vt (unreg)* to short-circuit. ◆ **sich kurzschließen** *ref* to get in touch.

Kurzschluss (*pl* **-schlüsse**) *der* - **1.** [elektrisch] short-circuit - **2.** [seelisch]: **er muss es aus einem Kurzschluss heraus getan haben** something must have snapped to make him do that.

kurzsichtig <> *adj eigtl* & *fig* short-sighted. <> *adv* short-sightedly.

Kürzung (*pl* **-en**) *die* cut.

Kurzwahl|taste *die* EDV speed-dial button.

Kurzwelle *die* short wave.

kuschelig *adj* cosy.

kuscheln *vi* to cuddle up; **mit jm kuscheln** to cuddle sb. ◆ **sich kuscheln** *ref* to cuddle up; **sich an jn kuscheln** to cuddle up to sb.

Kusine (*pl* **-n**) *die* cousin.

Kuss (*pl* **Küsse**) *der* kiss.

küssen *vt* & *vi* to kiss. ◆ **sich küssen** *ref* to kiss.

Küste (*pl* **-n**) *die* coast.

Küster, in (*mpl* **-**, *fpl* **-nen**) *der, die* verger.

Kutsche (*pl* **-n**) *die* - **1.** [Pferdewagen] coach - **2.** *fam* [Auto] jalopy, motor *UK*.

Kuvert [ku'vɛːɐ̯] (*pl* **-e**) *das* envelope.

KZ [kaːʏ̆tsɛt] (*pl* **-s**) *das abk für* **Konzentrationslager**.

L

l (*pl* - ODER **-s**), **L** (*pl* - ODER **-s**) [ɛl] *das* l, L. ◆ **l** (*abk für* **Liter**) l.

labil *adj* unstable; [Kreislauf] bad; [Konstitution, Gleichgewicht] delicate.

Labor (*pl* **-s** ODER **-e**) *das* laboratory.

Laborant, in (*mpl* **-en**, *fpl* **-nen**) *der, die* laboratory technician.

Labyrinth (*pl* **-e**) *das* maze.

Lache (*pl* **-n**) *die* [von Wasser] puddle; [von Blut, Öl] pool.

lächeln *vi* to smile; **über jn/etw lächeln** to smile about sb/at sthg.

Lächeln *das (ohne pl)* smile.

lachen *vi* to laugh; **über jn/etw lachen** to laugh at sb/sthg; **es** ODER **das wäre doch gelacht, wenn** *fig* it would be ridiculous if; **du hast gut lachen!** *fig* it's all right for you!

Lachen *das* laughter; **ein leises Lachen** a quiet laugh; **jn zum Lachen bringen** to make sb laugh; **etw ist zum Lachen** *fam fig* sthg is laughable; **ihm wird das Lachen schon noch vergehen** he'll soon be laughing on the other side of his face.

lächerlich *adj* [komisch] ridiculous; **jn/sich lächerlich machen** to make a fool of sb/o.s.

Lächerliche *das*: **etw ins Lächerliche ziehen** to make a joke out of sthg.

lachhaft *adj* ludicrous.

Lachs [laks] (*pl* **-e**) *der* salmon.

Lack (*pl* **-e**) *der* [farblos] varnish; [farbig] paint; [Nagellack] varnish *UK*, polish *US*.

lackieren *vt* - **1.** [Holz] to varnish; [Auto] to spray - **2.** [mit Nagellack] to paint.

Lackierung (*pl* **-en**) *die* - **1.** [Lackieren - von Holz] varnishing; [- von Auto] spraying - **2.** [Lack - farblos] varnish; [- farbig] paint.

Lade|fläche *die* load area.

laden (*präs* **lädt**, *prät* **lud**, *perf* **hat geladen**) <> *vt* - **1.** [Fracht, Waffe & EDV] to load; **der Lkw hat Kies geladen** the lorry has loaded up with gravel; **etw auf/in etw** *(A)* **laden** to load sthg onto/into sthg - **2.** [mit Elektrizität] to charge - **3.** *geh* [vorladen] to summon. <> *vi* [mit einer Last] to load up; **der Laster hat schwer geladen** the truck is heavily laden.

Laden (*pl* **Läden**) *der* - **1.** [Geschäft] shop *UK*, store *US* - **2.** *fam* [Angelegenheit] business - **3.** *fam* [Betrieb] outfit.

Laden|dieb, in *der, die* shoplifter.

Ladenschluss *der (ohne pl)* closing time.

Laden|tisch *der* counter.

Lade|rampe *die* loading platform.

lädieren *vt* to damage.

lädt *präs* ▷ **laden**.

Ladung (*pl* **-en**) *die* - **1.** [gen] load - **2.** [zum Schießen] charge - **3.** PHYS: **positive/negative Ladung** positive/negative charge.

lag *prät* ▷ **liegen**.

Lage (*pl* **-n**) *die* - **1.** [Stelle, Stellung] position - **2.** [Situation] situation; **zu etw in der Lage sein** to be able to do sthg; **in der Lage sein, etw zu tun** to be able to do sthg; **sich in js Lage** *(A)* **versetzen** to put o.s. in sb's position - **3.** [Schicht] layer.

Lager (*pl* -) *das* - **1.** *eigtl* & *fig* [Feldlager, Gesinnung] camp - **2.** [für Waren] store; **etw auf Lager haben** [als Ware] to have sthg in stock; [zur Unterhaltung] to be ready with sthg - **3.** TECH bearing.

Lagerbe|stand *der* stock.

Lager|feuer *das* camp fire.

Lager|haus *das* warehouse.

lagern ◇ *vt* - **1.** [aufbewahren] to store - **2.**: **einen Kranken bequem lagern** to make an ill person comfortable; **den Arm hoch lagern** to put one's arm in a raised position. ◇ *vi* [kampieren] to camp.

Lagerung (*pl* **-en**) *die* storage *(U)*.

lahm ◇ *adj* - **1.** [gelähmt, Ausrede] lame - **2.** [ermüdet] stiff - **3.** [matt - Mensch] dull; [- Bewegung] sluggish. ◇ *adv fam* [sich bewegen] sluggishly; [sich entschuldigen] lamely.

lähmen *vt eigtl* & *fig* to paralyse.

lahm legen *vt* to bring to a standstill.

Lähmung (*pl* **-en**) *die eigtl* & *fig* paralysis.

Laib (*pl* **-e**) *der*: **ein Laib Brot** a loaf of bread; **ein Laib Käse** a cheese.

Laie ['laiə] (*pl* **-n**) *der* layman (laywoman *die*); **ein medizinischer Laie** a layman when it comes to medicine.

laienhaft ['laiənhaft] ◇ *adj* inexpert. ◇ *adv* inexpertly.

Laken (*pl* -) *das* sheet.

Lakritz (*pl* **-e**) *das* & *der* liquorice.

lallen *vt* & *vi* to babble.

Lama (*pl* **-s**) *das* llama.

Lamelle (*pl* **-n**) *die* - **1.** [von Jalousie] slat - **2.** [von Heizkörper] fin - **3.** [von Pilzen] gill.

Lamm (*pl* **Lämmer**) *das* lamb.

Lampe (*pl* **-n**) *die* light; [Bürolampe, Stehlampe] lamp.

Lampenfieber *das* stage fright.

Lampen|schirm *der* lampshade.

Land (*pl* **Länder**) *das* - **1.** [Staatsgebiet, ländliche Gegend] country; **jn des Landes verweisen** to deport sb; **auf dem Land** in the country - **2.** [Gelände, Festland] land; **an Land gehen** to go ashore - **3.** [Bundesland - in Deutschland] state; [- in Österreich] province; **wieder im Land(e) sein** to be back. ◆ **hier zu Lande** *adv* = **hierzulande**.

Land|bevölkerung *die* rural population.

Lande|bahn *die* runway.

landen (*perf* **hat/ist gelandet**) ◇ *vi (ist)* - **1.** [nach einem Flug] to land - **2.** *fam* [ankommen] to land up; **bei jm (mit etw) nicht landen können** *fam* not to be able to get anywhere with sb (sthg). ◇ *vt (hat) eigtl* & *fig* to land.

Lande|platz *der* landing strip.

Länder|spiel *das* international match.

Landes|ebene *die*: **auf Landesebene** at state level.

Landeshaupt|mann *der Österr head of a regional government in Austria*.

Landes|innere *das* interior *(of the country)*.

Landes|kunde *die study of a country and its culture*.

Landes|regierung *die* state government.

Landes|sprache *die* national language.

Landesverrat *der* treason.

Landes|währung *die* national currency.

Land|haus *das* country house.

Land|karte *die* map.

Land|kreis *der* district.

landläufig *adj* popular.

Landleben *das* country life.

ländlich *adj* rural.

Landschaft (*pl* **-en**) *die* [Gelände] countryside; [Abbildung] landscape.

landschaftlich ◇ *adj* [Schönheit, Besonderheit] of the countryside; [Sitte] regional. ◇ *adv*: **der Schwarzwald ist landschaftlich schön** the countryside of the Black Forest is beautiful.

Lands|leute *Pl* compatriots.

Land|straße *die* country road.

Land|streicher, in (*mpl* **Landstreicher**, *fpl* **-nen**) *der, die* tramp.

Land|strich *der* area.

Land|tag *der* - **1.** [Volksvertretung] state parliament - **2.** [Gebäude] state parliament building.

Landung (*pl* **-en**) *die* landing.

Land|weg *der* overland route.

Land|wirt, in *der, die* farmer.

Land|wirtschaft *die* [Agrarwesen] agriculture.

lang (*kompar* **länger**, *superl* **längste**) ◇ *adj* long; [Person] tall; **drei Meter lang** three metres long; **vor langer Zeit** a long time ago; **vor nicht zu langer Zeit** not (so) long ago; **drei lange Jahre** three long years. ◇ *adv fam* - **1.** [entlang] along; **hier/dort lang** this/that way - **2.** [zeitlich]: **drei Jahre lang** for three years; **den ganzen Tag lang** all day.

langärmelig, langärmlig *adj* long-sleeved.

langatmig ◇ *adj* long-winded. ◇ *adv* long-windedly.

lange (*kompar* **länger**, *superl* **am längsten**) *adv* [während langer Zeit] a long time; [seit langer Zeit] for a long time; **es dauert nicht mehr lange** it won't be long; **das mache ich nicht mehr länger** I won't be doing this for much longer; **das ist noch lange nicht alles** that's not all by any means; **ich war schon lange nicht mehr zu Hause** I haven't been home for a long time; **etw ist lange her** sthg was a long time ago.

Länge (*pl* **-n**) *die* - **1.** [von Brett, Brief] length; **ein Stau von 5 km Länge** a 5 km-long traffic jam; **der Länge nach** [teilen] lengthways; [hinstürzen] flat on one's face - **2.** *(ohne pl)* [Körpergröße] height - **3.** GEOGR longitude - **4.** *(ohne pl)* [Dauer] length; **in die Länge ziehen** to drag out. ◆ **Längen** *Pl* [von Film] tedious scenes; [von Buch] tedious passages.

langen *vi fam* - **1.** [ausreichen] to be enough; **mir langt es!** *fam* that's enough! - **2.** [greifen] to reach.

Längen|grad *der* degree of longitude.

Längen|maß *das* unit of length.

längerfristig ◇ *adj* longer-term. ◇ *adv* on a longer-term basis.

Langeweile, Langeweile *die* boredom; **aus Langeweile** out of boredom.

langfristig ◇ *adj* long-term. ◇ *adv* on a long-term basis.

Langlauf *der* SPORT cross-country skiing.

langlebig *adj* - **1.** [lange lebend] long-lived - **2.** [lange gebrauchsfähig] durable.

länglich *adj* oblong.

längs ◇ *präp*: **längs einer Sache** *(G)* along sthg. ◇ *adv* lengthways.

Längs|achse ['lɛŋsaksə] *die* longitudinal axis.

langsam ◇ *adj* - **1.** [nicht schnell] slow - **2.** [allmählich] gradual. ◇ *adv* - **1.** [nicht schnell] slowly - **2.** [nach und nach] gradually; **das wird ja langsam Zeit!** it's about time!

Langschläfer, in (*mpl* -, *fpl* **-nen**) *der, die* late riser.

Längs|richtung *die*: **in Längsrichtung** lengthways.

Längs|seite *die* long side.

längst *adv* for a long time; **sie war längst tot** she was long since dead, she had died a long time ago; **längst nicht** nowhere near.

längstens *adv fam* - **1.** [höchstens] at (the) most - **2.** [seit langem] for a long time; **es war längstens entschieden** it was long since agreed, it had been agreed a long time ago.

Langstrecken|lauf *der* [Wettbewerb] long-distance race; [Sportart] long-distance running *(U)*.

Languste [laŋ'gʊstə] (*pl* **-n**) *die* crayfish.

langweilen *vt* to bore. ◆ **sich langweilen** *ref* to be bored.

langweilig ◇ *adj* - **1.** [uninteressant] boring - **2.** *fam* [Zeit raubend] slow. ◇ *adv* boringly.

Langwelle *die* long wave.

langwierig *adj* lengthy.

Lanze (*pl* **-n**) *die* spear.

Lappalie [la'pɑːli̯ə] (*pl* **-n**) *die* trifle.

Lappen (*pl* -) *der* cloth; **etw geht jm durch die Lappen** *fam fig* sthg slips through sb's fingers.

läppern ◆ **sich läppern** *ref*: **das** ODER **es läppert sich** it mounts up.

läppisch *adj abw* - **1.** [albern] silly - **2.** [lächerlich] ridiculous.

Laptop ['lɛptɔp] (*pl* **-s**) *der* EDV laptop.

Lärche (*pl* **-n**) *die* larch.

Lärm *der* noise; **Lärm schlagen** *fam fig* to kick up a fuss.

lärmen *vi* to make a noise; [Radio] to blare.

Larve ['larfə] (*pl* **-n**) *die* larva.

las *prät* ▭▷ **lesen**.

lasch ◇ *adj* - **1.** [Bewegung, Spiel] listless; [Händedruck] limp - **2.** [fade] insipid - **3.** [nachlässig] lax. ◇ *adv* - **1.** [schlaff] listlessly - **2.** [fade] insipidly - **3.** [nachlässig] laxly.

Lasche (*pl* **-n**) *die* [von Umschlag] flap; [von Schuh] tongue.

Laser ['leːzɐ] (*pl* -) *der* laser.

Laser|drucker *der* EDV laser printer.

lassen (*präs* **lässt**, *prät* **ließ**, *perf* **hat gelassen** ODER **lassen**) ◇ *vt* - **1.** [geschehen lassen] to let; **jn nicht ins Haus lassen** not to let sb in the house; **Wasser in die Badewanne lassen** to run a bath - **2.** [unterlassen] to stop; **das Rauchen lassen** to stop smoking; **lass das!** stop it! - **3.** [überlassen]: **jm etw lassen** to let sb have sthg; **eines muss man dir ja lassen** *fig* I'll say this much for you - **4.** [belassen, zurücklassen] to leave; **lass mich!** let me go!; **lass alles so, wie es ist** leave everything as it is. ◇ *vi (perf hat gelassen)* - **1.** [belassen]: **von jm/etw lassen** *geh* to abandon sb/sthg - **2.** [geschehen lassen]: **lass mal, ich mach das schon!** leave it, I'll do it. ◇ *aux* - **1.** [veranlassen]: **etw machen** ODER **tun lassen** to have sthg done; **jn etw tun lassen** to have sb do sthg; **sich** *(D)* **die Haare schneiden lassen** to get ODER have one's hair cut; **sich** *(D)* **einen Anzug machen lassen** to have a suit made - **2.** [belassen] leave; **lass die Vase auf dem Tisch stehen** leave the vase on the table - **3.** [geschehen lassen]: **jn etw tun lassen** to let sb do sthg; **ich lasse mich überraschen** I want it to be a surprise; **etw mit sich/nicht mit sich machen lassen** to put up/not to put up with sthg; **die Vase fallen lassen** to drop the vase; **jn warten lassen** to keep sb waiting. ◆ **sich lassen** *ref (perf hat lassen)*: **das lässt sich machen** it can be done; **die Fenster lassen sich nicht öffnen** the windows don't open.

lässig ◇ *adj* casual. ◇ *adv* - **1.** [salopp] casually - **2.** *fam* [leicht] easily.

Lässigkeit *die* [Lockerheit] casualness; [Leichtigkeit] ease.

lässt *präs* ▷ **lassen**.

Last (*pl* **-en**) *die* - **1.** [Gewicht] load - **2.** *geh* [Bürde] burden; **jm zur Last fallen** to be a burden on sb; **jm etw zur Last legen** to accuse sb of sthg. ◆ **Lasten** *Pl* [Kosten] costs; **zu js Lasten** chargeable to sb.

lasten *vi* - **1.** [Gewicht]: **auf jm lasten** to weigh sb down; **auf etw** *(D)* **lasten** [auf Schultern] to weigh down on sthg; [auf Pfeilern] to bear down on sthg - **2.** [Verantwortung]: **auf jm lasten** to weigh on sb - **3.** [finanziell]: **auf jm/etw lasten** to be a burden on sb/sthg.

Laster (*pl* -) ◇ *das* [Untugend] vice. ◇ *der fam* [Lastwagen] truck, lorry *UK*.

lästern *vi*: **über jn/etw lästern** to make nasty remarks about sb/sthg.

lästig *adj* annoying; **jm lästig werden/sein** to become/be a nuisance to sb.

Lastkraft|wagen *der amt* heavy goods vehicle.

Last-Minute-|Flug [lɑːstˈmɪnɪt|fluːk] *der* last-minute flight.

Last|schrift *die* [Abbuchung] debit; [Mitteilung] debit advice.

Last|wagen *der* truck, lorry *UK*.

Latein *das* Latin; *siehe auch* **Englisch(e)**.

Lateinamerika *nt* Latin America.

lateinisch *adj* Latin.

latent ◇ *adj* latent. ◇ *adv* latently.

Laterne (*pl* **-n**) *die* - **1.** [Lampion] Chinese lantern - **2.** [Straßenlaterne] streetlamp.

Latinum *das*: **großes/kleines Latinum** *school examination in Latin taken after at least six/three years.*

latschen (*perf* **hat/ist gelatscht**) *fam* ◇ *vi (ist)* to traipse. ◇ *vt (hat)*: **jm eine** ODER **ein paar latschen** to give sb a clout.

Latschen (*pl* -) *der fam* [Schuh] worn-out shoe; [Hausschuh] worn-out slipper.

Latte (*pl* **-n**) *die* [Brett] slat; [bei Hochsprung] bar; [von Tor] crossbar; **lange Latte** *fam* beanpole.

Latten|rost *der* slatted base.

Latz (*pl* **Lätze**) *der* bib.

Latz|hose *die* dungarees *Pl*.

lau ◇ *adj* - **1.** [mäßig warm, zurückhaltend] lukewarm - **2.** [mild] mild - **3.** [mäßig] moderate. ◇ *adv* - **1.** [zurückhaltend] lukewarmly - **2.** [mäßig] moderately well.

Laub *das (ohne pl)* leaves *Pl*.

Laub|baum *der* deciduous tree.

Laub|frosch *der* tree frog.

Laub|säge *die* fretsaw.

Laub|wald *der* deciduous forest.

Lauch *der* leek.

Lauer *die*: **auf der Lauer sitzen** ODER **liegen** *fam* to be on the lookout.

lauern *vi*: **auf jn/etw lauern** [warten] to lie in wait for sb/sthg.

Lauf (*pl* **Läufe**) *der* - **1.** *(ohne pl)* [Laufen] run - **2.** [Betrieb] running - **3.** *(ohne pl)* [Verlauf, von Fluss] course; **im Laufe des Tages** during the day; **etw nimmt seinen Lauf** sthg takes its course; **im Lauf(e) der Zeit** in the course of time; **einer Sache** *(D)* **freien** ODER **ihren Lauf lassen** [Tränen, Gefühlen] to give free rein to sthg; [Angelegenheit] to let sthg take its course - **4.** [von Gewehren] barrel.

Lauf|bahn *die* career.

laufen (*präs* **läuft**, *prät* **lief**, *perf* **hat/ist gelaufen**) ◇ *vi (ist)* - **1.** [schnell] to run - **2.** *fam* [gehen] to walk; **jn laufen lassen** to let sb go; **er läuft dauernd zum Arzt** he's always going to the doctor's - **3.** [zugange sein] to go on; **die Verhandlungen laufen noch** negotiations are still going on; **was läuft im Kino?** what's on at the cinema ODER movies? - **4.** [einen bestimmten Verlauf nehmen] to go; **es läuft gut** it's going well - **5.** [Motor, Maschine] to run, to be on; **ihr Radio läuft schon stundenlang** their radio has been on for hours; **bei laufender Maschine** when the machine is running ODER on - **6.** [funktionieren] to work - **7.** [fließen] to run; **mir läuft die Nase** my nose is running - **8.** [amtlich geführt werden]: **das Konto läuft auf ihren Namen** the account is in her name - **9.** [juristisch gültig sein] to run; **der Vertrag läuft bis zum 31.12.** the contract runs ODER is valid until 31 December. ◇ *vt* - **1.** *(hat, ist)* SPORT to run; **er ist eine neue Bestzeit gelaufen** he set a new record; **Marathon laufen** to run the marathon - **2.** *(ist)* [gehen] to walk - **3.** *(ist)* [mit Sportgerät]: **Ski laufen** to ski; **Schlittschuh laufen** to skate. ◆ **sich laufen** *ref*: **sich warm laufen** to warm up.

laufend ◇ *adj* - **1.** [Kosten] regular; [Beschwerden, Störungen] continual - **2.** [gerade ablaufend] current - **3.** [in Betrieb] running; **auf dem Laufenden sein/bleiben** to be/keep up-to-date. ◇ *adv* [ständig] continually.

Läufer (*pl* -) *der* - **1.** SPORT runner - **2.** [Schachfigur] bishop.

Läuferin (*pl* **-nen**) *die* runner.

läufig *adj* on heat.

Lauf|masche *die* ladder *UK*, run *US*.

Lauf|schritt *der* running step; **im Laufschritt** at a run.

läuft *präs* ▷ **laufen**.

Lauf|werk *das* EDV drive.

Lauge (*pl* **-n**) *die* - **1.** CHEM alkaline solution - **2.** [Waschlauge] soapy water *(U)*.

Laugen|brezel *die* pretzel.

Laune (*pl* **-n**) *die* - **1.** *(ohne pl)* [Stimmung] mood; **gute/schlechte Laune haben** to be in a good/bad mood - **2.** [Einfall] whim; **etw aus ei-**

ner Laune heraus tun to do sthg on a whim. ◈ **Launen** *Pl* [von Person] moods; [von Wetter] vagaries.

launisch *adj* moody.

Laus (*pl* **Läuse**) *die* louse.

Lausbub (*pl* **-en**), **Lausbube** (*pl* **-n**) *der* little rascal.

lauschen *vi* [horchen] to listen; [heimlich] to eavesdrop.

lausig *fam* ◇ *adj* - **1.** [schlecht, Geld] lousy - **2.** [groß] terrible. ◇ *adv* lousily; **lausig kalt** *fam* freezing (cold).

laut ◇ *adj* loud; [lärmend] noisy; **es wurden Zweifel laut** doubts were voiced; **lauter sprechen** to speak up, to speak louder. ◇ *adv* loudly; [lärmend] noisily. ◇ *präp (+ G or D) amt* according to.

Laut (*pl* **-e**) *der* sound.

lauten *vi*: **die Anweisung lautet folgendermaßen** the instructions are as follows; **auf etw** *(A)* **lauten: die Anklage lautet auf versuchten Mord** the charge is attempted murder.

läuten *vi* to ring; **bei jm läuten** to ring sb's bell; **es läutet** there is someone at the door; **von etw läuten hören** to hear something about sthg.

lauter *adv* nothing but; **vor lauter Lärm** because of all the noise.

lauthals *adv* at the top of one's voice.

lautlos ◇ *adj* silent; [Stille] complete. ◇ *adv* silently.

Laut|schrift *die* phonetic alphabet.

Laut|sprecher *der* - **1.** [Tonverstärker] (loud)speaker - **2.** [Megafon] loudspeaker.

lautstark ◇ *adj* loud. ◇ *adv* loudly.

Laut|stärke *die* volume.

lauwarm ◇ *adj* lukewarm. ◇ *adv* [baden] in lukewarm water; **etw lauwarm essen/trinken** to eat/drink sthg lukewarm.

Lava ['lɑːva] (*pl* **Laven**) *die* lava.

Lavendel [la'vɛndl̩] *der* lavender.

Lawine (*pl* **-n**) *die eigtl & fig* avalanche.

lax ◇ *adj* lax. ◇ *adv* laxly.

Leasing ['liːzɪŋ] *das* leasing *(U)*.

leben ◇ *vi* to live; **seine Mutter lebt noch** his mother is still alive; **von etw leben** to live off ODER on sthg; **vom Schreiben leben** to make one's living by ODER from writing; **es lebe der Präsident!** long live the president!; **damit kann ich leben** I can live with that. ◇ *vt* to live; **sie lebte ein erfülltes Leben** she lived a full life.

Leben (*pl* -) *das* - **1.** [gen] life; **jm das Leben schwer machen** to make life difficult for sb; **sich** *(D)* **das Leben nehmen** to take one's (own) life; **ums Leben kommen** to die - **2.** [Treiben] activity; **etw ins Leben rufen** to bring sthg into being.

lebendig ◇ *adj* - **1.** [lebend, fortwirkend] living - **2.** [lebhaft] lively. ◇ *adv* [lebhaft] in a lively manner.

lebensfähig *adj* capable of survival.

Lebens|gefahr *die* mortal danger; **außer Lebensgefahr sein** to be out of danger; **Vorsicht, Lebensgefahr!** danger of death!

lebensgefährlich ◇ *adj* [Situation, Handlung] extremely dangerous; [Verletzung] critical. ◇ *adv* [handeln] extremely dangerously; [sich verletzen] critically.

Lebens|gefährte *der* partner.

Lebens|gefährtin *die* partner.

Lebens|haltungskosten *Pl* cost of living *(U)*.

lebenslänglich *adj & adv* for life.

Lebens|lauf *der* curriculum vitae *UK*, resumé *US*.

lebens|lustig *adj* full of life.

Lebens|mittel *das* food.

Lebensmittel|geschäft *das* grocer's (shop).

lebensmüde *adj* - **1.** [den Tod herbeisehnend] tired of life - **2.** *fam* [leichtsinnig]: **du bist wohl lebensmüde** you're out of your mind.

Lebens|standard *der* standard of living.

Lebens|unterhalt *der* maintenance; **seinen Lebensunterhalt verdienen** to earn one's living.

Lebens|versicherung *die* life insurance *(U)*.

Lebens|wandel *der (ohne pl)* lifestyle.

Lebens|weise *die* way of life.

lebenswichtig *adj* essential.

Lebens|zeichen *das eigtl & fig* sign of life.

Leber (*pl* **-n**) *die* liver.

Leber|fleck *der* mole.

Leber|käse *der spiced meat loaf, sliced and often fried.*

Leber|tran *der* cod-liver oil.

Leber|wurst *die* liver sausage.

Lebe|wesen *das* living being; [tierisch, pflanzlich] living thing.

lebhaft ◇ *adj* - **1.** [gen] lively - **2.** [Auseinandersetzung] vigorous; [Interesse] keen; [Bedauern] deep. ◇ *adv* - **1.** [angeregt] in a lively manner - **2.** [sich widersetzen] vigorously; [sich interessieren] keenly; [bedauern] deeply - **3.** [gut] well.

Leb|kuchen *der* gingerbread *(U)*.

leblos ◇ *adj* lifeless. ◇ *adv* lifelessly.

leck *adj* leaky.

Leck (*pl* **-s**) *das* leak.

lecken ◇ *vt* to lick; **sich die Lippen lecken** to lick one's lips; **die Katze leckte sich das Fell** the cat licked its coat. ◇ *vi* - **1.** [schlecken]: **an etw** *(D)* **lecken** to lick sthg - **2.** [undicht sein] to leak. ◈ **sich lecken** *ref* to lick o.s.

lecker *adj* delicious.

Lecker|bissen *der* - **1.** [essbar] delicacy - **2.** [Genuss] treat.

Leder (*pl* -) *das* leather *(U)*; **jm ans Leder gehen/wollen** *fam fig* to go for/want to go for sb.

Leder|hose *die* lederhosen *Pl*.

Leder|waren *Pl* leather goods.

ledig *adj* single.

lediglich *adv* only.

leer *adj* - **1.** [gen] empty; **leer ausgehen** to come away empty-handed - **2.** [unbeschrieben] blank.

Leere *die* emptiness; **sein Schlag ging ins Leere** his punch missed; **ins Leere starren** to stare into space.

leeren *vt* to empty. ◆ **sich leeren** *ref* to empty.

Leer|gut *das (ohne pl)* empties *Pl*.

Leer|lauf *der* - **1.** TECH neutral; **im Leerlauf** in neutral - **2.** [unproduktive Phase] slack period.

leer stehend *adj* empty.

Leerung (*pl* **-en**) *die* emptying *(U)*; [von Briefkasten] collection.

legal ◇ *adj* legal. ◇ *adv* legally.

legalisieren *vt* - **1.** [legal machen] to legalize - **2.** RECHT to authenticate.

Legalität *die* legality.

legen *vt* - **1.** [ablegen] to put; **leg den Schlüssel auf den Tisch** put the key on the table - **2.** [in horizontale Position bringen] to lay; **du musst die Flaschen ins Regal legen, nicht stellen** you should lay the bottles flat in the rack, not put them upright - **3.** [Termin] to arrange; **den Urlaub auf Juli legen** to arrange one's holidays for July - **4.** [installieren - Rohre, Kabel] to lay; **Minen legen** to lay mines; **Feuer legen** to lay a fire - **5.** [Ei] to lay. ◆ **sich legen** *ref* - **1.** [sich hinlegen] to lie down; **sich schlafen legen** to lie down to sleep - **2.** [Staub, Nebel] to settle - **3.** [Aufregung, Sturm] to die down.

Legende (*pl* **-n**) *die* - **1.** [gen] legend - **2.** [Irrglaube] myth.

leger [le'ʒɛːɐ̯] ◇ *adj* casual. ◇ *adv* casually.

Legierung (*pl* **-en**) *die* alloy.

Legislative [legɪsla'tiːvə] (*pl* **-n**) *die* legislature.

legitim *adj* legitimate.

Lehm *der* clay.

lehmig *adj* clayey.

Lehne (*pl* **-n**) *die* [Rückenlehne] back; [Armlehne] arm.

lehnen ◇ *vt*: **etw gegen** ODER **an etw** *(A)* **lehnen** to lean sthg against sthg. ◇ *vi*: **an etw** *(D)* **lehnen** to lean against sthg. ◆ **sich lehnen** *ref* - **1.** [stützen]: **sich gegen** ODER **an jn/etw lehnen** to lean against sb/sthg - **2.** [sich beugen] to lean.

Lehr|amt *das amt* teaching *(U)*.

Lehr|buch *das* textbook.

Lehre (*pl* **-n**) *die* - **1.** [Ausbildung] apprenticeship; **in der Lehre sein** to be serving one's apprenticeship - **2.** [lehrreiche Erfahrung] lesson - **3.** [Ideologie - von Propheten, Philosophen] teachings *Pl*; [- katholisch, marxistisch] doctrine.

lehren ◇ *vi* to teach. ◇ *vt* to teach; **jn etw lehren** to teach sb sthg.

Lehrer, in (*mpl* -, *fpl* **-nen**) *der, die* [in Schule] teacher; [in Sportverein] instructor.

Lehr|gang *der* course.

Lehrling (*pl* **-e**) *der* apprentice.

Lehr|plan *der* syllabus.

lehrreich *adj* instructive.

Lehr|stelle *die* apprenticeship.

Lehr|stuhl *der amt* chair.

Lehr|zeit *die* apprenticeship.

Leib (*pl* **-er**) *der geh* [Körper] body; **sie ist mit Leib und Seele Krankenschwester** she is a dedicated nurse; **mit Leib und Seele dabei sein** to put one's whole heart into it; **jm jn/etw vom Leib halten** *fam* to keep sb/sthg away from sb; **sich** *(D)* **jn/etw vom Leib halten** *fam* to keep sb/sthg at bay.

Leibeskräfte *Pl*: **aus Leibeskräften** with all one's might.

Leib|gericht *das* favourite dish.

leiblich *adj* - **1.** [körperlich] physical - **2.** [blutsverwandt] natural.

Leiche (*pl* **-n**) *die* corpse; **über Leichen gehen** *fam fig* to stop at nothing.

Leichen|halle *die* mortuary.

Leichnam (*pl* **-e**) *der geh* body.

leicht ◇ *adj* - **1.** [an Gewicht] light - **2.** [geringfügig] slight; **leichte Kopfschmerzen** a slight headache; **eine leichte Grippe** a mild attack of flu - **3.** [einfach] easy; **es leicht haben** to have it easy; **er hat es nicht leicht** he is having a hard time - **4.** [kalorienarm] diet, low-fat; [Mahlzeit] light; [Zigarette] mild. ◇ *adv* - **1.** [einfach, schnell] easily; **das ist sehr leicht möglich** that's perfectly possible; **er ist leicht beleidigt** he is quick to take offence - **2.** [geringfügig] slightly; **leicht nicken** to give a little nod; **es riecht leicht angebrannt** there's a slight smell of burning; **leicht bekleidet** scantily clad - **3.** [unbeschwert] lightly.

Leicht|athletik *die* athletics *(U)*.

leicht fallen (*perf* **ist leicht gefallen**) *vi (unreg)*: **es fällt ihm leicht/nicht leicht** it comes/doesn't come easy to him.

leichtfertig *abw* ◇ *adj* rash. ◇ *adv* rashly.

leichtgläubig *adj* credulous.

Leichtigkeit *die* - **1.** [geringes Gewicht] lightness - **2.** [Mühelosigkeit] ease.

leicht machen *vt* to make easy; **jm etw leicht machen** to make sthg easy for sb.

Leicht|metall *das* light metal.

leicht nehmen *vt (unreg)* not to take seriously.

Leichtsinn *der* recklessness.

leichtsinnig ◇ *adj* reckless. ◇ *adv* recklessly.

leid *adj*: **jn/etw leid sein** ODER **haben** to be tired of sb/sthg.

Leid *das* sorrow; **sie tut mir Leid** I feel sorry for her; **es tut mir Leid** I'm sorry.

leiden (*prät* **litt**, *perf* **hat gelitten**) ◇ *vi* to suffer; **an/unter etw** *(D)* **leiden** to suffer from sthg. ◇ *vt* - **1.** [erdulden] to suffer - **2.** [mögen]: **jn gut/nicht leiden können** to like/not to like sb.

Leiden (*pl* -) *das* illness.

Leidenschaft (*pl* **-en**) *die* passion.

leidenschaftlich ◇ *adj* passionate. ◇ *adv* passionately; **leidenschaftlich gern tanzen** to adore dancing.

leider *adv* unfortunately.

Leidtragende (*pl* **-n**) *der, die*: **die Kinder sind immer die Leidtragenden** the children are always the ones to suffer.

Leih|bücherei *die* lending library.

leihen (*prät* **lieh**, *perf* **hat geliehen**) *vt* - **1.** [leihweise geben]: **jm etw leihen** to lend sb sthg - **2.** [ausleihen]: **sich** *(D)* **etw (von jm) leihen** to borrow sthg (from sb); [mieten] to hire *UK* ODER rent *US* sthg (from sb).

Leih|gebühr *die* [für Auto] hire *UK* ODER rental *US* charge; [für Buch] lending charge.

Leih|wagen *der* hire *UK* ODER rental *US* car.

Leim (*pl* **-e**) *der* glue; **aus dem Leim gehen** *fam* [kaputtgehen] to fall to pieces; [an Gewicht zunehmen] to put on weight.

leimen *vt* - **1.** [zusammenfügen] to glue together - **2.** [ankleben] to glue.

Leine (*pl* **-n**) *die* - **1.** [Seil] cord; **Leine ziehen** *salopp fig* to scram - **2.** [Wäscheleine] line - **3.** [Hundeleine] lead *UK*, leash *US*.

Leinen *das* linen.

Lein|samen *der* linseed.

Lein|wand *die* [Projektionswand] screen.

leise ◇ *adj* - **1.** [nicht laut] quiet - **2.** [schwach] slight. ◇ *adv* quietly.

Leiste (*pl* **-n**) *die* - **1.** [Latte] edging strip - **2.** [Körperteil] groin.

leisten *vt* - **1.** [vollbringen] to achieve - **2.** [machen] to do - **3.** [Beitrag, Anzahlung] to make.

Leistung (*pl* **-en**) *die* - **1.** TECH [das Geleistete] performance - **2.** [Ergebnis] achievement - **3.** [Bezahlung] payment.

Leistungsdruck *der* pressure to do well.

Leistungs|kurs *der one of two specialist subjects chosen by pupils for their "Abitur".*

Leistungs|sport *der* competitive sport.

Leit|artikel *der* editorial.

leiten ◇ *vt* - **1.** [anführen - Unternehmen, Projekt] to run; [- Gruppe, Diskussion] to lead - **2.** PHYS to conduct - **3.** [lenken - Bach, Verkehr] to divert; [- Antrag] to forward; **sich von etw leiten lassen** *fig* to let o.s. be guided by sthg. ◇ *vi* to conduct.

leitend *adj* - **1.** [Stellung] managerial; [Direktor] managing; [Architekt] chief; **leitender Angestellter** manager - **2.** [führend] guiding - **3.** [weiterleitend] conductive.

Leiter (*pl* **-n** ODER **-**) ◇ *die (pl Leitern)* ladder. ◇ *der (pl Leiter)* [von Firma, Abteilung] manager; [von Gruppe, Projekt] leader.

Leiterin (*pl* **-nen**) *die* [von Firma, Abteilung] manager; [von Gruppe, Projekt] leader.

Leit|faden *der* introductory guide.

Leit|planke *die* crash barrier *UK*, guardrail *US*.

Leitung (*pl* **-en**) *die* - **1.** [Führung] running; **unter der Leitung von jm** conducted by sb - **2.** [Führungsgruppe] management *(U)* - **3.** [Rohr] pipe - **4.** [Draht] wire; [Kabel] cable - **5.** [Telefonleitung] line; **eine lange Leitung haben** *fam fig* to be slow on the uptake.

Leitungs|rohr *das* pipe.

Leitungs|wasser *das* tap water.

Lektion (*pl* **-en**) *die eigtl* & *fig* lesson.

Lektor, in (*mpl* **-toren**, *fpl* **-nen**) *der, die* - **1.** [bei Verlag] editor - **2.** [an Hochschulen] language assistant.

Lektüre (*pl* **-n**) *die* - **1.** [das Lesen] reading - **2.** [Lesestoff] reading matter.

Lende (*pl* **-n**) *die* loin.

lenken *vt* - **1.** [Fahrzeug, Gespräch] to steer - **2.** [richten]: **die Aufmerksamkeit auf jn/etw lenken** to draw attention to sb/sthg; **er lenkte den Verdacht auf sich** he attracted suspicion - **3.** [führen] to control.

Lenker (*pl* -) *der* - **1.** [Lenkstange] handlebars *Pl* - **2.** [Person] driver.

Lenkerin (*pl* **-nen**) *die* driver.

Lenk|rad *das* steering wheel.

Lenkung (*pl* **-en**) *die* - **1.** [Steuerung] steering *(U)* - **2.** [Beeinflussung] control.

Leopard (*pl* **-en**) *der* leopard.

Lepra *die* leprosy.

Lerche (*pl* **-n**) *die* lark.

lernen ◇ *vt* to learn; **Klavier spielen lernen** to learn to play the piano; **Bäcker lernen** to train to be a baker. ◇ *vi* - **1.** [gen] to learn; **aus der Geschichte lernen** to learn from history - **2.** [für Prüfung] to study, to revise.

Lesbierin ['lɛsbjərɪn] (*pl* **-nen**) *die* lesbian.

lesbisch *adj* lesbian.

lesen (*präs* **liest**, *prät* **las**, *perf* **hat gelesen**) ◇ *vt* - **1.** [gen] to read - **2.** [Früchte, Trauben] to pick. ◇ *vi* - **1.** [gen] to read; **in seiner Miene war die Verzweiflung zu lesen** despair was written all over his face - **2.** [einen Vortrag halten] to lecture.

Leser (*pl* -) *der* reader.

Leser|brief *der* reader's letter, letter to the editor.

Leserin (*pl* **-nen**) *die* reader.

leserlich <> *adj* legible. <> *adv* legibly.

Lese|zeichen *das* bookmark.

Lettland *nt* Latvia.

Letzt ◆ **zu guter Letzt** *adv* in the end.

letzte, **r**, **s** *adj* last; **das ist mein letztes Geld** that's the last of my money; **letztes Jahr** last year.

Letzte (*pl* **-n**) <> *der, die* [Person] last; **Letzter werden** to come last; **sie kam als Letzte an die Reihe** she had her turn last. <> *der* [Tag] last day. <> *das* **- 1.: er ist das Letzte** *fam* he's scum; **der Film ist das Letzte** *fam* the film is the pits **- 2.: bis ins Letzte** down to the last detail.

letztemal *adv* ▷ **Mal**.

letztendlich *adv* **- 1.** [am Schluss] in the end **- 2.** [im Grunde genommen] ultimately, in the final analysis.

letztenmal *adv* ▷ **Mal**.

letztens *adv* **- 1.** [an letzter Stelle] lastly **- 2.** [vor kurzem] recently.

letztere, **r**, **s** <> *adj* the latter; **in letzterem Fall** in the latter case. <> *pron* the latter.

Letztere *der*: **der/die/das Letztere** the latter.

letztgenannte, **r**, **s** *adj*: **die letztgenannte Alternative** the last alternative mentioned.

letztlich *adv* **- 1.** [am Schluss] in the end **- 2.** [im Grunde genommen] ultimately, in the final analysis.

leuchten *vi* to shine; [Feuer, Himmel] to glow.

leuchtend <> *adj* **- 1.** [Farbe] bright; **sie bekam leuchtende Augen** her eyes lit up **- 2.** [Vorbild, Beispiel] shining. <> *adv*: **leuchtend blau/rot** bright blue/red.

Leuchter (*pl* **-**) *der* candelabrum; [für eine Kerze] candlestick.

Leucht|farbe *die* luminous paint.

Leuchtstoff|röhre *die* fluorescent tube.

Leucht|turm *der* lighthouse.

leugnen <> *vt* to deny. <> *vi* to deny everything.

Leukämie *die* leukaemia.

Leute *Pl* [Menschen] people; **die jungen Leute** young people; **was die Leute sagen** what people say; **etw unter die Leute bringen** *fam* to spread sthg around; **unter (die) Leute gehen** *fam* to get out and meet people.

Leutnant (*pl* **-s**) *der* second lieutenant.

Lexikon (*pl* **-ka** ODER **-ken**) *das* [Enzyklopädie] encyclopaedia.

Libanon *der*: **(der) Libanon** (the) Lebanon.

Libelle (*pl* **-n**) *die* [Insekt] dragonfly.

liberal <> *adj* liberal. <> *adv* **- 1.** [tolerant]: **liberal eingestellt sein** to be liberal-minded **- 2.** POL: **liberal wählen** to vote Liberal.

Libyen *nt* Libya.

Licht (*pl* **-er**) *das* **- 1.** [Helligkeit, Lampe] light; **Licht machen** to put the light on **- 2.** [Kerze] candle; **ans Licht kommen** to come to light; **grünes Licht geben** to give the green light; **jetzt geht mir ein Licht auf** now I see; **jn hinters Licht führen** to pull the wool over sb's eyes.

Licht|blick *der* bright spot.

lichten *vt* to thin out. ◆ **sich lichten** *ref* to thin out.

lichterloh *adv*: **lichterloh brennen** to blaze fiercely.

Licht|hupe *die* AUTO: **die Lichthupe betätigen** to flash one's headlights.

Licht|maschine *die* AUTO alternator.

Licht|schalter *der* light switch.

Licht|schranke *die* photoelectric beam.

Lichtschutz|faktor *der* (protection) factor; **Lichtschutzfaktor 10** factor 10.

Licht|strahl *der* beam (of light).

Lichtung (*pl* **-en**) *die* clearing.

Lid (*pl* **-er**) *das* eyelid.

Lid|schatten *der* eye shadow.

lieb <> *adj* **- 1.** [nett] kind, nice; **wie lieb von Ihnen, dass Sie daran gedacht haben!** how kind ODER nice of you to remember! **- 2.** [als Anrede] dear; **Liebe Sue!** Dear Sue; **Liebe Kollegen!** colleagues! **- 3.** [brav] good; **sei schön lieb!** be a good boy/girl! <> *adv* nicely; *siehe auch* **lieb gewinnen**., **lieb haben**

liebäugeln *vi*: **mit etw liebäugeln** [Gegenstand, Kauf, Arbeitsstelle] to have one's eye on sthg; [Idee, Plan] to be thinking about sthg.

Liebe *die* **- 1.** [gen] love; **die Liebe zur Kunst** love of art; **sie war seine erste Liebe** she was his first love **- 2.** [Sex] sex; **käufliche Liebe** prostitution; **Liebe machen** to make love; **Liebe auf den ersten Blick** love at first sight.

lieben *vt* to love. ◆ **sich lieben** *ref* **- 1.** [lieb haben] to be in love **- 2.** [sexuell] to make love.

liebenswert *adj* [Art, Geste] endearing; [Person] likable.

liebenswürdig *adj* kind.

lieber <> ▷ **gern**. <> *adv* better; **das hättest du lieber nicht sagen sollen** it would have been better if you hadn't said that; **lieber nicht** maybe we shouldn't, maybe not. <> *adj*: **das wäre mir lieber** I'd prefer that.

Liebes|brief *der* love letter.

Liebes|kummer *der*: **Liebeskummer haben** to be lovesick.

Liebes|paar *das* lovers *Pl*.

liebevoll <> *adj* loving. <> *adv* lovingly.

lieb gewinnen *vt (unreg)*: **jn/etw lieb gewinnen** to grow fond of sb/sthg.

lieb haben *vt (unreg)* to love; [gern haben] to be fond of. ◆ **sich lieb haben** *ref* to be in love.

Liebhaber (*pl* -) *der* - **1.** [gen] lover - **2.** [Sammler] collector.

Liebhaberin (*pl* -nen) *die* - **1.** [gen] lover - **2.** [Sammlerin] collector.

Liebling (*pl* -e) *der* - **1.** [als Anrede, der Oma] darling - **2.** [Bevorzugte] favourite.

Lieblings|gericht *das* favourite dish.

lieblos ◇ *adj* unaffectionate. ◇ *adv* - **1.** [ohne Liebe] unaffectionately - **2.** [nachlässig]: **sie hat das Essen lieblos zubereitet** she carelessly threw the meal together.

Liebschaft (*pl* -en) *die abw* casual affair.

liebsten ▷ **gern**. ◆ **am liebsten** *adv*: **am liebsten würde ich jetzt nach Hause gehen** what I'd really like to do now would be to go home; **das ist mir am liebsten** I like it best of all.

Liechtenstein *nt* Liechtenstein.

Lied (*pl* -er) *das* song; RELIG hymn.

liederlich *adj* [Person] slovenly; [Arbeit] sloppy; [Lebenswandel] dissolute.

lief *prät* ▷ **laufen**.

Lieferant, in (*mpl* -en, *fpl* -nen) *der, die* supplier.

lieferbar *adj* available.

liefern ◇ *vt* - **1.** [Ware - zustellen] to deliver; [- verkaufen] to supply; **jetzt bin ich geliefert** *fam* I've had it now - **2.** [Ernte, Eier] to produce - **3.** [Beispiel, Beweis] to provide; **sie lieferten sich ein spannendes Match** they provided an exciting match. ◇ *vi* to deliver.

Lieferung (*pl* -en) *die* [Versand] delivery; [Versorgung] supply.

Liefer|wagen *der* van.

Liege (*pl* -n) *die* [für Garten] sun lounger; [zum Übernachten] camp bed *UK*, cot *US*.

liegen (*prät* **lag**, *perf* **hat gelegen**) *vi* - **1.** [gen] to lie; **das Schiff liegt im Hafen** the ship is docked; **in den Bergen liegt viel Schnee** there's a lot of snow on the hills - **2.** [angelehnt sein]: **an** ODER **auf etw** *(A)* **liegen** to rest on sthg - **3.** [sich befinden] to be; **Dresden liegt an der Elbe** Dresden is on the Elbe - **4.** [in Reihenfolge] to lie; **sie liegt auf dem vierten Platz** she's (lying) in fourth place; **an der Spitze liegen** to be in the lead - **5.** [mit Dativ]: **Physik liegt mir nicht** physics isn't my thing; **es liegt mir viel daran** it matters a lot to me - **6.** [mit Präpositionen]: **an mir soll es nicht liegen!** don't let me stop you!; **es liegt nicht an dir** it's not your fault; **die Entscheidung liegt bei Ihnen** it's your decision; **das liegt daran, dass...** this is because...

liegen bleiben (*perf* **ist liegen geblieben**) *vi (unreg)* - **1.** [nicht aufstehen] to remain lying down; **(im Bett) liegen bleiben** to stay in bed - **2.** [Schnee, Laub] to lie - **3.** [vergessen werden] to be left behind - **4.** [unerledigt bleiben] to be left undone - **5.** [eine Panne haben] to break down.

liegen lassen (*perf* **hat liegen gelassen** ODER **liegen lassen**) *vt (unreg)* to leave; **jn/etw links liegen lassen** *fam fig* to ignore sb/sthg.

Liege|sitz *der* reclining seat.

Liege|stuhl *der* [am Strand] deckchair; [im Garten] sun lounger.

Liege|stütz (*pl* -e) *der* press-up.

Liege|wagen *der* couchette car.

lieh *prät* ▷ **leihen**.

ließ *prät* ▷ **lassen**.

liest *präs* ▷ **lesen**.

Lifestyle ['laɪfstaɪl] *der (ohne pl)* lifestyle.

Lift (*pl* -e ODER -s) *der* - **1.** [Aufzug] lift *UK*, elevator *US* - **2.** *(pl Lifte)* [Skilift] ski lift.

Likör (*pl* -e) *der* liqueur.

lila *adj (unver)* lavender; [dunkler] mauve.

Lila *das* purple; [Zartlila] lilac; [Tieflila] mauve.

Lilie ['liːli̯ə] (*pl* -n) *die* lily.

Limit (*pl* -s) *das* limit.

Limonade (*pl* -n) *die* fizzy drink *UK*, soda *US*; [mit Zitronengeschmack] lemonade; [mit Orangengeschmack] orangeade.

Linde (*pl* -n) *die* lime tree.

lindern *vt* [Schmerzen] to relieve; [Not] to alleviate.

Lineal (*pl* -e) *das* ruler.

Linguistik *die* linguistics *(U)*.

Linie ['liːni̯ə] (*pl* -n) *die* - **1.** [Strich, Verwandtschaftslinie] line; **sie stammt in direkter Linie vom Kaiser Karl ab** she is directly descended from Emperor Charles - **2.** [Denkrichtung] policy - **3.** [von Verkehrsmittel] number; **die Linie 3** the number 3 - **4.** [Figur]: **auf die schlanke Linie achten** to watch one's figure; **in erster Linie** first and foremost.

Linien|bus *der* bus *(forming part of public transport network)*.

Linien|flug *der* scheduled flight.

Linienverkehr *der (ohne pl)* [Flugverkehr] scheduled flights *Pl*; [Omnibusverkehr] buses *(forming part of public transport network)*.

linieren, liniieren *vt* to rule (lines on).

link *adj fam abw* shady.

linke, r, s *adj* - **1.** [Seitenangabe] left - **2.** [linkspolitisch] left-wing.

Linke (*pl* -n) ◇ *die* - **1.** [Hand] left hand; **zu Linken** to the left - **2.** POL: **die Linke** the Left - **3.** [Schlag] left. ◇ *der, die* [Person] left-winger.

links ◇ *adv* - **1.** [Angabe der Seite] on the left; [Angabe der Richtung] left; **links von jm/etw** on sb's/sthg's left; **nach links fahren** to turn left; **von links** from the left; **etw mit links machen** *fam fig* to do sthg easily - **2.** [verkehrt herum] inside out; **etw von links bügeln** to iron sthg on the wrong side - **3.** [linkspolitisch] left-wing; **links wählen** to vote for the Left. ◇ *präp (+ G)* - **1.** [Angabe der Seite] on the left-hand side of - **2.** [politisch] to the left of.

Lịnks|abbieger *der* car turning left.

Linksaußen (*pl* **Linksaußen**) *der* outside left.

lịnksextrem *adj* extreme left-wing.

Lịnks|extremist, in *der, die* left-wing extremist.

lịnksgerichtet *adj* left-wing.

Lịnkshänder, in (*mpl* -, *fpl* **-nen**) *der, die* left-hander.

lịnksherum *adv* - **1.** [nach links] round to the left - **2.** [falsch herum] inside out.

Lịnks|kurve *die* left-hand bend.

lịnksradikal *adj* radical left-wing.

Lịnksverkehr *der*: **in Großbritannien herrscht Linksverkehr** people drive on the left in Great Britain.

Lịnse (*pl* **-n**) *die* - **1.** [Nahrungsmittel] lentil - **2.** [optisch] lens.

Lịppe (*pl* **-n**) *die* lip; **keine Klage kam über ihre Lippen** she didn't utter a word of complaint.

Lịppen|stift *der* lipstick.

lịspeln *vi* to lisp.

Lịssabon *nt* Lisbon.

Lịst (*pl* **-en**) *die* - **1.** [listiges Verhalten] cunning - **2.** [listige Handlung] cunning trick.

Lịste (*pl* **-n**) *die* list; **auf der schwarzen Liste stehen** to be on the blacklist.

lịstig ◇ *adj* cunning. ◇ *adv* cunningly.

Litauen *nt* Lithuania.

litauisch *adj* Lithuanian.

Liter (*pl* -) *der ODER das* litre; **ein Liter Milch** a litre of milk.

literarisch ◇ *adj* literary. ◇ *adv* - **1.** [Literatur betreffend]: **literarisch interessiert sein** to be interested in literature; **literarisch gebildet sein** to have studied literature - **2.** [gewählt] in a literary manner.

Literatur (*pl* **-en**) *die* literature.

Literatur|wissenschaft *die* literary studies *Pl*.

Liter|flasche *die* litre bottle.

Lịtfaß|säule *die* advertising column.

lịtt *prät* ▷ **leiden**.

Lizẹnz (*pl* **-en**) *die* licence.

Lkw (*pl* **-s**), **LKW** (*pl* **-s**) [ɛlkaː'veː] (*abk für* **Lastkraftwagen**) *der* truck, HGV *UK*, lorry *UK*.

Lob *das* praise; **ein hohes Lob** high praise.

loben *vt* to praise; **das lobe ich mir!** [sehr gut] that's what I like (to see)!; **da lobe ich mir doch meine alte Schreibmaschine!** give me my old typewriter any day!

lobenswert *adj* commendable, praiseworthy.

Lọch (*pl* **Lọ̈cher**) *das* hole; [im Zahn] cavity.

lọchen *vt* to punch a hole/holes in.

Lọcher (*pl* -) *der* hole punch.

lọ̈chern *vt fam* to pester.

lọ̈chrig *adj* full of holes.

Lọcke (*pl* **-n**) *die* curl; **Locken haben** to have curly hair.

lọcken *vt* - **1.** [anlocken] to entice; **jn in eine Falle locken** to lure sb into a trap - **2.** [wellen] to curl.

Lọckenwickler (*pl* -) *der* curler.

lọcker ◇ *adj* - **1.** [gen] loose; **ein lockeres Mundwerk haben** to have a loose tongue - **2.** [Beziehung] casual; [Haltung] laid-back. ◇ *adv* - **1.** [nicht fest] loosely - **2.** [zwanglos] casually - **3.** *fam* [mit Leichtigkeit] no sweat.

lọcker|lassen *vi (unreg)*: **nicht lockerlassen** not to give up.

lọckern *vt* - **1.** [Schraube, Griff, Erde, Krawatte] to loosen; **die Muskeln lockern** to limber up - **2.** [Gesetze, Vorschriften] to relax. ◆ **sich lockern** *ref* - **1.** [Schraube, Zahn] to work itself loose - **2.** [Stimmung] to become more relaxed; [Muskeln, Griff] to relax.

lọckig *adj* [Haare] curly; [Mensch] curly-haired.

Lọck|vogel *der* decoy.

lodern *vi* [Feuer] to blaze.

Lọ̈ffel (*pl* -) *der* spoon.

lọ̈ffeln *vt* to spoon.

log *prät* ▷ **lügen**.

Logarịthmus (*pl* **--men**) *der* logarithm.

Loge ['loːʒə] (*pl* **-n**) *die* - **1.** [im Theater] box - **2.** [von Freimaurern, Portier] lodge.

Logik *die* logic.

logisch ◇ *adj* logical. ◇ *adv* logically.

Lohn (*pl* **Löhne**) *der* - **1.** [Bezahlung] wages *Pl*, pay - **2.** [Belohnung] reward.

lohnen *vt* - **1.** [rechtfertigen] to be worth; **es lohnt eine Renovierung nicht mehr** it's no longer worth repairing - **2.** *geh* [vergelten]: **jm etw lohnen** to repay sb for sthg. ◆ **sich lohnen** *ref* to be worth it; **es lohnt sich, etw zu tun** it's worth doing sthg.

lohnend *adj* worthwhile.

Lohn|steuer *die* income tax *(paid by employees)*, ≃ PAYE *UK*.

Lohnsteuerjahres|ausgleich *der* annual adjustment of income tax.

Lohnsteuer|karte *die form filled in by employer stating employee's annual income and tax paid*.

Lọk (*pl* **-s**) *die* (railway) engine.

lokal *adj* local.

Lokal (*pl* **-e**) *das* bar, pub *UK*; [Restaurant] restaurant.

Lokal|nachrichten *Pl* local news *(U)*.

Lokomotive [lokomo'tiːvə] (*pl* **-n**) *die* (railway) engine.

Lọndon *nt* London.

Lọrbeer (*pl* **-en**) *der* [Gewürz] bay leaf.

Lọrbeer|blatt *das* bay leaf.

los <> *adj* [lose] loose; **jn/etw los sein** *fam* to have got rid of sb/sthg; **es ist viel/wenig/ nichts los** *fam* there is a lot/not much/nothing going on; **was ist los?** *fam* what's the matter?, what's wrong?; **was ist hier los?** *fam* what's going on here? <> *interj* come on!

Los (*pl* -e) *das* - **1.** [Losentscheid]: **durch das Los bestimmen** to decide by drawing lots - **2.** [in der Lotterie] ticket; **das große Los** the jackpot - **3.** *geh* [Schicksal] lot.

lösbar *adj* solvable.

los|binden *vt (unreg)* to untie.

löschen *vt* - **1.** [Kerze, Feuer] to extinguish, to put out - **2.** [Konto] to close; [Schuld, Hypothek] to pay off - **3.** [Tonträger] to erase - **4.** [Schiff, Ladung] to unload - **5.** EDV to delete.

Löschen *das* - **1.** [von Feuer] extinguishing - **2.** [von Konto] closing; [von Schuld, Hypothek] paying off - **3.** [von Tonträger] erasure - **4.** [von Schiff, Ladung] unloading - **5.** EDV deletion.

Löschpapier *das* blotting paper.

lose <> *adj* loose; **ein loses Mundwerk haben** to have a loose tongue. <> *adv* [locker] loosely.

Löse|geld *das* ransom.

losen *vi* [mit einem Los] to draw lots; **darum losen, wer/wann/was** to draw lots to see who/ when/what.

lösen *vt* - **1.** [trennen - Knoten] to undo; [- Bremse] to release; [- Schraube] to unscrew; [- Haare] to let down - **2.** [locker machen] to loosen - **3.** [abmachen]: **etw von etw lösen** to remove sthg from sthg - **4.** [rechnen] to work out - **5.** [klären - Aufgabe, Rätsel] to solve - **6.** [Vertrag] to cancel; [Verlobung] to break off; [Ehe] to dissolve - **7.** [Fahrkarte] to buy - **8.** [auflösen] to dissolve - **9.** [Husten, Schleim] to loosen; [Krampf] to ease. ◆ **sich lösen** *ref* - **1.** [aus Versehen] to break free; [Schuss] to go off; [Lawine] to start; **sich aus etw lösen** to break away from sthg - **2.** [Tapete, Briefmarke] to come off; [Knoten] to come undone; [Schraube] to work loose - **3.** [sich auflösen] to dissolve; [Schleim] to loosen - **4.** [umdenken]: **sich von etw lösen** [von Vorurteilen, Vorstellung] to rid o.s. of sthg - **5.** [sich trennen]: **sich von jm lösen** to break away from sb - **6.** [Muskeln] to relax; [Verkrampfung, Spannung] to ease - **7.** [Problem, Rätsel] to be solved.

los|fahren (*perf* **ist losgefahren**) *vi (unreg)* to set off.

los|gehen (*perf* **ist losgegangen**) *vi (unreg)* - **1.** [weggehen] to set off; **auf jn losgehen** *fig* to go for sb; **auf ein Ziel losgehen** to pursue a goal - **2.** [anfangen] to start; **gleich gehts los** it's just about to start; **jetzt geht das schon wieder los!** here we go again!; **los gehts!** off we go!

los|kommen (*perf* **ist losgekommen**) *vi (unreg)* to get away; **(nicht) von jm/etw loskommen** (not) to get away from sb/sthg.

los|lassen *vt (unreg)* - **1.** [Person, Gegenstand] to let go of; **lass mich los!** let go of me!, let me go! - **2.** [Tier]: **einen Hund auf jn loslassen** to set a dog on sb; **den Hund loslassen** to let the dog off the lead *UK* ODER leash *US* - **3.** [Schrei, Fluch] to let out - **4.** [Subj: Gedanke, Problem]: **der Gedanke lässt mich nicht los** I can't get the thought out of my head.

los|legen *vi fam* to get started; **mit Fragen loslegen** to start firing questions; **na, denn leg mal los!** fire away, then!

löslich *adj* soluble; [Kaffeepulver, Milchpulver] instant.

los|machen *vt* to undo; [Hund] to let off the lead *UK* ODER leash *US*. ◆ **sich losmachen** *ref* to free o.s.

Losung (*pl* **-en**) *die* - **1.** [Motto] motto; [Spruch] slogan - **2.** [Kennwort] password.

Lösung (*pl* **-en**) *die* - **1.** [gen] solution; [von Konflikt] resolution - **2.** [von Eltern, Tradition] breaking away - **3.** [von Ehe, Bündnis] breakup; [von Arbeitsverhältnis] termination.

los|werden (*perf* **ist losgeworden**) *vt (unreg) fam* - **1.** [gen] to get rid of; **ich werde das Gefühl nicht los, dass...** I can't escape the feeling that... - **2.** [Vermögen] to lose.

Lot (*pl* -e) *das* - **1.** [Senkblei] plumb line; **etw wieder ins Lot bringen** *fig* to put sthg right - **2.** SCHIFF sounding line - **3.** MATH perpendicular.

löten *vt* to solder.

Lothringen *nt* Lorraine.

Lotion [lo'tsi̯o:n] (*pl* **-en**) *die* lotion.

Lotse (*pl* **-n**) *der* - **1.** [von Schiff] pilot - **2.** [Fluglotse] air traffic controller.

lotsen *vt* to guide.

Lotterie [lɔtə'ri:] (*pl* **-n**) *die* lottery.

Lotto *das* - **1.** [Glücksspiel] (national) lottery; **im Lotto gewinnen** to win the (national) lottery - **2.** [Gesellschaftsspiel] lotto.

Lotto|schein *der* (national) lottery ticket.

Loveparade ['lavpəreid] *die* Love Parade, *annual open-air mass rave and procession in the centre of Berlin.*

Löwe (*pl* **-n**) *der* - **1.** [Tier] lion - **2.** [Sternzeichen, Person] Leo; **Löwe sein** to be a Leo.

Löwenzahn *der* dandelion.

Löwin (*pl* **-nen**) *die* lioness.

Luchs [lʊks] (*pl* **-e**) *der* lynx; **Augen wie ein Luchs haben** to have eyes like a hawk.

Lücke (*pl* **-n**) *die* - **1.** [gen] gap; [zum Parken] space - **2.** [in Gesetz] loophole.

lückenhaft <> *adj* [Erinnerung, Beweisführung, Wissen] sketchy; **sein Lebenslauf ist lückenhaft** he has gaps in his CV *UK* ODER resumé *US*. <> *adv* [sich erinnern] sketchily.

lud *prät* ▷ **laden**.

Luft (*pl* **Lüfte**) *die* - **1.** [gen] air; **freie Luft** open air; **die Luft anhalten** to hold one's breath;

Luft holen [atmen] to take a breath; [eine Pause machen] to catch one's breath; **frische Luft schöpfen** to get some fresh air; **nach Luft schnappen** to gasp - **2.** [Platz] room; **die Luft ist rein** *fam* the coast is clear; **in der Luft liegen** to be in the air; **jn in der Luft hängen lassen** to leave sb hanging; **in die Luft gehen** *fam* to blow one's top; **mir blieb die Luft weg** *fam* I was gobsmacked.

Luftan|griff *der* air raid.

Luft|ballon *der* balloon.

Luft|brücke *die* airlift.

luftdicht ◇ *adj* airtight. ◇ *adv* [verschließen] hermetically.

Luftdruck *der* air pressure.

lüften ◇ *vt* - **1.** [Zimmer, Wäsche] to air - **2.** [Geheimnis] to reveal. ◇ *vi* to let some air in.

Luft|fahrt *die* aviation.

luftig ◇ *adj* - **1.** [Kleidung] light - **2.** [hochgelegen]: **in luftiger Höhe** high up - **3.** [Raum] airy. ◇ *adv* [leicht] lightly.

Luft|linie *die*: **600 km Luftlinie** 600 km as the crow flies.

Luft|matratze *die* airbed.

Luft|pirat, in *der, die* (aircraft) hijacker.

Luft|post *die* airmail; **mit** ODER **per Luftpost** (by) airmail.

Luft|pumpe *die* air pump.

Luft|röhre *die* windpipe.

Luft|schlange *die* streamer.

Lüftung (*pl* **-en**) *die* - **1.** [Gerät] ventilation (system) - **2.** [Lüften] ventilation.

Luft|verkehr *der* air traffic.

Luft|verschmutzung *die* air pollution.

Luft|waffe *die* airforce; HIST Luftwaffe.

Luft|zug *der* [in Gebäude] draught; [im Freien] breath of wind.

Lüge (*pl* **-n**) *die* lie.

lügen (*prät* **log**, *perf* **hat gelogen**) *vi* to lie; **das ist gelogen!** that's a lie!

Lügner, in (*mpl* **-**, *fpl* **-nen**) *der, die* liar.

Lümmel (*pl* **-**) *der fam* - **1.** [Kind] rascal - **2.** *abw* [Rüpel] lout.

lümmeln ◆ **sich lümmeln** *ref fam abw* to sprawl.

Lump (*pl* **-en**) *der abw* scoundrel.

Lumpen (*pl* **-**) *der* rag.

Lunge (*pl* **-n**) *die* lungs *Pl*.

Lungenent|zündung *die* pneumonia.

Lunte (*pl* **-n**) *die* fuse.

Lupe (*pl* **-n**) *die* magnifying glass; **jn/etw unter die Lupe nehmen** *fam fig* to examine sb/sthg very closely.

Lust (*pl* **Lüste**) *die* - **1.** [Bedürfnis] desire; **die Lust am Reisen ist mir vergangen** I don't feel like travelling any more; **Lust bekommen/haben, etw zu tun** to feel like doing sthg; **ich habe keine Lust zum Spazierengehen** I don't feel like going for a walk; **Lust/keine Lust auf etw** *(A)* **haben** to feel/not to feel like sthg; **ich hätte jetzt Lust auf ein Eis** I fancy an ice cream; **er arbeitet ganz nach Lust und Laune** he works as and when he feels like it - **2.** [Freude] pleasure; **die Lust an etw** *(D)* **verlieren** no longer to take any pleasure in sthg - **3.** [Begierde] desires *Pl*, lust.

lüstern ◇ *adj* lascivious. ◇ *adv*: **lüstern blicken** to leer.

lustig ◇ *adj* - **1.** [komisch] funny; [unterhaltsam] entertaining; **sich über jn/etw lustig machen** to make fun of sb/sthg - **2.** [fröhlich - Person, Augen] merry; [- Abend] fun, enjoyable. ◇ *adv* - **1.** [komisch] funnily; [unterhaltsam] entertainingly - **2.** [unbekümmert] merrily.

lustlos ◇ *adj* unenthusiastic. ◇ *adv* unenthusiastically.

lutschen ◇ *vt* to suck. ◇ *vi*: **an etw** *(D)* **lutschen** to suck sthg.

Lutscher (*pl* **-**) *der* [Süßigkeit] lollipop.

Luxemburg *nt* Luxembourg.

luxemburgisch *adj* of/from Luxembourg.

luxuriös ◇ *adj* luxurious. ◇ *adv* luxuriously.

Luxus *der* luxury.

Luzern *nt* Lucerne.

Lyrik *die* lyric poetry.

lyrisch ◇ *adj* [Dichtung] lyric; [Stil] lyrical. ◇ *adv* lyrically.

m (*pl* - ODER **-s**), **M** (*pl* - ODER **-s**) [ɛm] *das* m, M.

m. *abk für* **mit**.

MA *abk für* **Mittelalter**.

machbar *adj* feasible.

machen ◇ *vt* - **1.** [tun] to do; **so was macht man nicht!** you can't ODER mustn't do that! - **2.** [herstellen] to make; **ein Foto machen** to take a photo; **etw aus etw machen** to make sthg out of sthg; **sich** *(D)* **etw machen lassen** to have sthg made - **3.** [Summe, Ergebnis] to be; **zwei mal drei macht sechs** two times three is six; **das macht fünf Euro** that comes to five euros - **4.** [mit Substantiv]: **das Abendessen machen** to make dinner; **mach bloß keine Dummheiten!** don't do anything silly!; **eine Prüfung machen** to take an exam; **den Doktor machen** to do a doctorate; **einen Handstand machen** to do a handstand; **täglich 1000 Euro Umsatz ma-**

chen to turn over 1000 euros a day - **5.** [erledigen] to do; **Einkäufe machen** to go shopping; **(seine) Hausaufgaben machen** to do one's homework; **sich** *(D)* **die Haare machen** to do one's hair; **da ist nichts zu machen** there's nothing we can do about it - **6.** [durchführen]: **eine Party machen** to have a party; **eine Reise/ einen Spaziergang machen** to go on a journey/for a walk; **eine Pause machen** to have a break - **7.** [verursachen]: **Licht machen** to switch on the light; **was macht das schon!** so what!; **jm Angst/Freude machen** to make sb afraid/ happy; **jm Hoffnung machen** to raise sb's hopes - **8.** [mit Adjektiv] to make; **sich bemerkbar machen** to become noticeable; **mach die Musik leiser** turn the music down; **jn krank/ glücklich machen** to make sb ill/happy; **machs gut!** take care! - **9.** [mit Präposition]: **sie haben aus dem alten Häuschen etwas gemacht** they've really made something out of that old cottage; **sie lässt alles mit sich machen** she is very long-suffering. ◇ *vi* - **1.** [verursachen]: **macht, dass ihr bald zurück seid!** make sure you're back soon; **mach schon** ODER **doch!** *fam* get a move on! - **2.** *fam* [Toilette verrichten]: **der Hund hat vor die Haustür gemacht** the dog made a mess outside the front door; **in die Hosen machen** to wet/dirty one's pants - **3.** [mit Adjektiv]: **Joggen macht schlank** jogging helps you lose weight; **mach schnell!** hurry up! ◆ **sich machen** *ref* - **1.** *fam* [sich entwickeln] to come on; **du machst dich!** you're coming on very well - **2.** [mit Adjektiv]: **sich beliebt/verständlich machen** to make o.s. popular/understood; **der Hut macht sich gut zu Ihrem Kleid** the hat goes well with your dress - **3.** [mit Präposition]: **sich an die Arbeit machen** to get down to work; **sich auf den Weg machen** to set off; **sich** *(D)* **aus etw nichts machen** not to be keen on sthg; **mach dir nichts draus!** don't let it bother you!

Mạchenschaft (*pl* **-en**) *die abw* intrigue.

Mạcht (*pl* **Mạ̈chte**) *die* power; **an die Macht kommen** to come to power; **an der Macht sein** to be in power; **die Macht der Gewohnheit** force of habit; **Macht über jn haben** to have a hold on sb; **mit aller Macht** with all one's might.

Mạchthaber, in (*mpl* **-**, *fpl* **-nen**) *der, die*: **die Machthaber** those in power.

mạ̈chtig ◇ *adj* - **1.** [einflussreich] powerful - **2.** [Stimme, Hieb, Stamm] mighty; [Hunger, Angst] terrible; [Gebäude] enormous. ◇ *adv* [enorm] terribly.

mạchtlos *adj* powerless; **gegen etw machtlos sein** to be powerless in the face of sthg.

Mạcht|probe *die* trial of strength.

Mạchtwort (*pl* **-e**) *das*: **ein Machtwort sprechen** to put one's foot down, to exercise one's authority.

Mạcke (*pl* **-n**) *die fam* - **1.** [Tick] quirk - **2.** [Fehler]: **mein Auto hat eine Macke** there's something up ODER wrong with my car.

Madagạskar *nt* Madagascar.

Mädchen (*pl* **-**) *das* - **1.** [gen] girl - **2.** [Hausangestellte] maid.

Mädchen|name *der* maiden name.

Made (*pl* **-n**) *die* maggot.

madig *adj* maggoty, full of maggots; **jm etw madig machen** *fam fig* to spoil sthg for sb.

Madọnna (*pl* **Madọnnen**) *die* - **1.** [Muttergottes] Madonna - **2.** [Bild, Plastik] madonna.

mag *präs* ▷ **mögen**.

Magazin (*pl* **-e**) *das* - **1.** [Illustrierte, Behälter für Patronen] magazine - **2.** [Lager] storeroom - **3.** [Fernsehsendung] magazine (programme).

Magd (*pl* **Mägde**) *die* - **1.** [Dienstmagd] maid - **2.** [Landarbeiterin] farmhand.

Magen (*pl* **Mägen** ODER **-**) *der* stomach; **jm auf den Magen schlagen** *fam* to upset sb; **sich** *(D)* **den Magen verderben** to get an upset stomach; **mir knurrt der Magen** *fam* my stomach is rumbling.

Magen|beschwerden *Pl* stomach trouble *(U)*.

Magen|geschwür *das* stomach ulcer.

Magen|schmerzen *Pl* stomachache *(U)*.

mager ◇ *adj* - **1.** [Person, Tier, Gesicht] thin - **2.** [Fleisch] lean; [Quark] low-fat - **3.** [Ergebnis, Ernte] meagre. ◇ *adv* [fettarm]: **mager essen** to eat a low-fat diet.

Magermilch *die* skimmed milk.

magersüchtig *adj* anorexic.

Magie [ma'giː] *die* magic.

magisch ◇ *adj* magical; [Kräfte] magic. ◇ *adv* magically.

Magịster (*pl* **-**) *der* [Titel] ≃ Master's degree.

Magnesium *das* magnesium.

Magnet (*pl* **-e** ODER **-en**) *der* magnet.

magnetisch ◇ *adj* magnetic. ◇ *adv* magnetically.

Mahagoni *das* mahogany.

mähen ◇ *vt* [Rasen] to mow; [Getreide] to reap. ◇ *vi* - **1.** [mit Mäher] to mow; [mit Sense] to reap - **2.** [blöken] to bleat.

mahlen *vt* & *vi* to grind.

Mahl|zeit ◇ *die* meal. ◇ *interj* hello! *(said around lunchtime to work colleagues)*.

Mähne (*pl* **-n**) *die* mane.

mahnen ◇ *vt* - **1.** [ermahnen] to urge; **jn mahnen, etw zu tun** to urge sb to do sthg - **2.** [erinnern]: **jn an etw** *(A)* **mahnen** to remind sb of sthg. ◇ *vi* [ermahnen]: **das Ozonloch mahnt zur Vorsicht beim Sonnen** because of the hole in the ozone layer it is advisable to take care whilst sunbathing.

Mahn|mal *das* memorial.

Mahnung (*pl* **-en**) *die* - **1.** [Ermahnung] exhortation - **2.** [Schreiben] reminder.

Mai *der* May; **der Erste Mai** May Day; *siehe auch* **September**.

Mai|glöckchen (*pl* **Maiglöckchen**) *das* lily of the valley.

Mai|käfer *der* cockchafer.

Mailand *nt* Milan.

Mailbox ['meilbɔks] (*pl* **-en**) *die* EDV mailbox.

mailen ◇ *vi* EDV to send an e-mail. ◇ *vt* EDV to e-mail.

Main *der*: **der Main** the (River) Main.

Mainz *nt* Mainz.

Mais *der* [als Konserve] sweetcorn; [Pflanze] maize.

Mais|kolben *der* corn on the cob.

Majestät (*pl* **-en**) *die* Majesty.

majestätisch ◇ *adj* majestic. ◇ *adv* majestically.

Majonäse (*pl* **-n**), **Mayonnaise** (*pl* **-n**) [majɔ'nɛːzə] *die* mayonnaise.

Major (*pl* **-e**) *der* major.

Majoran *der* marjoram.

makaber *adj* macabre.

makellos ◇ *adj* - **1.** [tadellos] impeccable; [Figur] perfect - **2.** [fehlerlos] flawless. ◇ *adv* - **1.** [tadellos] impeccably - **2.** [sauber] spotlessly.

Make-up [meːk'ap] (*pl* **-s**) *das* - **1.** [Schminken] make-up - **2.** [Creme] foundation.

Makler, in (*mpl* **-**, *fpl* **-nen**) *der, die* [für Immobilien] estate agent *UK*, realtor *US*; [an Börse] broker.

Makrele (*pl* **-n**) *die* mackerel.

mal ◇ *adv fam* - **1.** [irgendwann - in Zukunft] sometime, someday; [- in Vergangenheit] once; **hier stand mal ein Gebäude** there was a building here once; **aus ihr wird mal was werden** she'll be someone some ODER one day - **2.** [zum Ausdruck der Verbindlichkeit]: **ich komme um neun Uhr mal vorbei** I'll drop by at nine o'clock; **wir müssen das am Sonntag mal besprechen** we ought to discuss this on Sunday - **3.** [als Aufforderung]: **hör mir mal gut zu!** now listen to me carefully!; **gib mir mal bitte den Schlüssel!** would you give me the key?; **beruhige dich mal!** calm down, will you!; **sag mal!** tell me!; **hör mal!** listen! - **4.** [zur Verstärkung eines Adverbs]: **nimm schon mal Platz, ich komme gleich** just take a seat, I'll be there in a minute; **vielleicht mal** maybe; **höchstens mal** at the very most - **5.** [einmal]: **er redet mal so, mal so** he says one thing one minute and another thing the next. ◇ *konj* [zur Multiplikation] times.

Mal (*pl* **-e** ODER **Mäler**) *das* - **1.** *(pl Male)* [Zeitpunkt] time; **letztes/nächstes Mal** last/next time; **jedes Mal** every time; **mit einem Mal(e)** all of a sudden; **von Mal zu Mal** [immer mehr] more and more; [jedes Mal] every time; **beim ersten Mal** the first time; **beim letzten Mal** last time; **zum ersten/letzten Mal** for the first/last time - **2.** *(pl Male, Mäler)* [Fleck] mark; [Muttermal] birthmark; [Pigmentmal] mole.

Mal|buch *das* colouring book.

malen *vt* & *vi* to paint.

Maler (*pl* **-**) *der* - **1.** [Künstler] painter, artist - **2.** [Handwerker] painter.

Malerei (*pl* **-en**) *die* painting.

Malerin (*pl* **-nen**) *die* - **1.** [Künstlerin] painter, artist - **2.** [Handwerkerin] painter.

malerisch ◇ *adj* [idyllisch] picturesque. ◇ *adv* [schön] picturesquely.

mal|nehmen *vt (unreg)*: **etw mit etw malnehmen** to multiply sthg by sthg.

Malta *nt* Malta.

Malz *das* malt.

Malz|bier *das* malt beer.

Mama (*pl* **-s**) *die fam* mummy *UK*, mommy *US*.

man *pron* - **1.** [jemand]: **man sagte mir** I was told; **man hat ihm eine Stelle angeboten** he was offered a job - **2.** [generalisierend] you; **wie sagt man das auf Deutsch?** how do you say that in German?; **das sagt man nicht** you don't say that; **man sagt, dass...** people say that...

manche, r, s ◇ *pron* - **1.** [bei Dingen - einige] some; [- viele] many (things) - **2.** [bei Personen - einige] some people; [- viele] many (people); **manch einer** many a person. ◇ *det* - **1.** [einige] some - **2.** [viele] many. ◆ **so manche, r, s** *pron* & *det* quite a few.

manchmal *adv* sometimes.

Mandarine (*pl* **-n**) *die* mandarin.

Mandat (*pl* **-e**) *das* - **1.** [gen] mandate; [von Anwalt] brief - **2.** [POL - Amt] seat.

Mandel (*pl* **-n**) *die* almond. ◆ **Mandeln** *Pl* [im Hals] tonsils.

Mandelent|zündung *die* tonsillitis *(U)*.

Manege [ma'neːʒə] (*pl* **-n**) *die* (circus) ring.

Mangel (*pl* **Mängel** ODER **-n**) ◇ *der (pl Mängel)* - **1.** [an Verantwortungsbewusstsein, Geistesgegenwart] lack; [an Lebensmitteln, Medikamenten] shortage; **aus Mangel an etw** *(D)* for lack of sthg; **es herrscht Mangel an etw** *(D)* there is a shortage of sthg - **2.** [Fehler] fault; **Mängel beheben** ODER **beseitigen** to rectify faults - **3.** [Not] hardship. ◇ *die (pl Mangeln)* mangle.

Mangel|erscheinung *die* deficiency symptom.

mangelhaft ◇ *adj* [unzureichend - Schulnote] poor. ◇ *adv* poorly.

mangeln ◇ *vi*: **es mangelt jm an etw** *(D)* sb lacks sthg; **es mangelt an etw** *(D)* [nicht genug sein] there is a shortage of sthg; [fehlen] there is a lack of sthg. ◇ *vt* to mangle.

mangelnd *adj* inadequate.

mangels *präp*: **mangels einer Sache** *(G)* for lack of sthg.

Mangelware *die*: **Mangelware sein** to be a scarce commodity; *fam fig* to be thin on the ground.

Mango (*pl* **-s**) *die* mango.

Manie (*pl* **-n**) *die* - **1.** [Tick] obsession - **2.** MED mania.

Manier (*pl* **-en**) *die* manner. ◆ **Manieren** *Pl* manners.

manisch ◇ *adj* manic. ◇ *adv* [krankhaft] manically.

Manko (*pl* **-s**) *das* - **1.** [Fehler] drawback - **2.** [Geldsumme] deficit.

Mann (*pl* **Männer, Leute** ODER **-en**) *der* - **1.** [gen] man; **von Mann zu Mann** man to man - **2.** [Ehemann] husband; **seinen Mann stehen** to hold one's own. ◆ **alle Mann** *pron fam* everyone; **alle Mann an Deck!** all hands on deck! ◆ **kleine Mann** *der fam*: **der kleine Mann** the ordinary man.

Männchen (*pl* -) *das* - **1.** [Tier] male - **2.** *fam* [kleiner Mann] little man.

männlich ◇ *adj* - **1.** [Lebewesen] male - **2.** [viril] manly - **3.** [zum Mann gehörig] man's - **4.** GRAMM [Substantiv] masculine. ◇ *adv* [viril] in a manly way.

Mannschaft (*pl* **-en**) *die* - **1.** [im Sport, Team] team; **vor versammelter Mannschaft** *fam* in front of everybody - **2.** [Besatzung] crew - **3.** [Soldaten] men *Pl*.

Mannschafts|geist *der* team spirit.

Mannschafts|sport *der* team sport.

Manöver [ma'nøːvɐ] (*pl* -) *das* manoeuvre.

manövrieren [manøː'vriːrən] *vt* & *vi eigtl* & *fig* to manoeuvre. ◆ **sich manövrieren** *ref* [sich bringen] to manoeuvre o.s.

Manschetten|knopf *der* cufflink.

Mantel (*pl* **Mäntel**) *der* - **1.** [Kleidungsstück] coat - **2.** *fig* [Deckmantel] cloak - **3.** TECH casing; [von Kabel] sheath.

manuell ◇ *adj* manual. ◇ *adv* manually.

Manuskript (*pl* **-e**) *das* - **1.** [Entwurf] notes *Pl* - **2.** [Handschrift, Satzvorlage] manuscript.

Mappe (*pl* **-n**) *die* - **1.** [Hülle] folder - **2.** [Tasche] briefcase.

Marathon (*pl* **-s**) *der* ODER *das* marathon.

Marathon|läufer, in *der, die* marathon runner.

Märchen (*pl* -) *das* - **1.** [Erzählung] fairy tale - **2.** [Lüge] tall story.

märchenhaft ◇ *adj* - **1.** [sagenhaft] fairy-tale - **2.** [wunderschön] wonderful - **3.** [unglaublich] fantastic. ◇ *adv* - **1.** [wunderbar] wonderfully - **2.** [unglaublich] fantastically.

Marder (*pl* -) *der* marten.

Margarine *die* margarine.

Margerite (*pl* **-n**) *die* daisy.

Mariä Himmelfahrt *(ohne Artikel)* Assumption.

Marien|käfer *der* ladybird *UK*, ladybug *US*.

Marihuana *das* marijuana.

Marine *die (ohne pl)* MIL navy.

marineblau *adj* navy blue.

Marionette (*pl* **-n**) *die* - **1.** [Puppe] marionette, puppet - **2.** *fig* [Person] puppet.

Mark (*pl* **Mark**) ◇ *die* mark. ◇ *das (ohne pl)* - **1.** [im Knochen] marrow; **es geht mir durch Mark und Bein** *fig* it goes right through me - **2.** [Konzentrat] purée.

markant *adj* striking; [Kinn, Nase] prominent.

Marke (*pl* **-n**) *die* - **1.** [Lebensmittel, Verbrauchsgüter] brand; [Auto, Gebrauchsgegenstände] make - **2.** [Briefmarke] stamp - **3.** [Erkennungszeichen - von Hund] identity disc; [- von Polizist] badge - **4.** [Wertzeichen - für Lebensmittel] coupon; [- für Garderobe] ticket *UK*, check *US* - **5.** *fam* [Person] character.

Marken|artikel *der* branded item.

Marken|zeichen *das* trademark.

markieren ◇ *vt* - **1.** [kennzeichnen] to mark - **2.** [hervorheben] to highlight - **3.** *fam* [vortäuschen] to play. ◇ *vi fam* [vortäuschen] to fake.

Markise (*pl* **-n**) *die* awning.

Markt (*pl* **Märkte**) *der* - **1.** [gen] market; **auf den** ODER **zum Markt gehen** to go to the market; **auf den Markt bringen** to put on the market - **2.** [Platz] marketplace.

Markt|forschung *die* market research.

Markt|halle *die* covered market.

Markt|lücke *die* gap in the market.

Markt|platz *der* marketplace.

Markt|preis *der* market price.

Markt|wert *der* market value.

Markt|wirtschaft *die* market economy.

Marmelade (*pl* **-n**) *die* jam.

Marmor *der* marble.

Marokkaner, in (*mpl* -, *fpl* **-nen**) *der, die* Moroccan.

marokkanisch *adj* Moroccan.

Marokko *nt* Morocco.

Marone (*pl* **-n**) *die* (sweet) chestnut.

marsch *interj*: **marsch, an die Arbeit/ins Bett** off to work/to bed!; **vorwärts marsch!** forward march!

Marsch (*pl* **Märsche**) *der* - **1.** [Gehen] walk **sich in Marsch setzen** to set off - **2.** [beim Militär Musikstück] march.

marschieren (*perf* **ist marschiert**) *vi* - **1.** [Soldaten] to march - **2.** [gehen] to walk.

Marschmusik *die* marching music.

Märtyrer, in (*mpl* -, *fpl* **-nen**) *der, die* martyr.

marxistisch ◇ *adj* Marxist. ◇ *adv* in a Marxist way.

März *der* March; *siehe auch* **September**.

Marzipan (*pl* -e), **Marzipan** (*pl* -e) *das* marzipan *(U)*.

Masche (*pl* -n) *die* - **1.** [beim Stricken, Häkeln] stitch - **2.** [Art und Weise] trick; **die neueste Masche** *fam* [Marotte] the latest fad; *fam* [Mode] the latest thing.

Maschine (*pl* -n) *die* - **1.** [Gerät, Motorrad] machine - **2.** *fam* [Motor] engine - **3.** [Flugzeug] plane - **4.** [Schreibmaschine]: **Maschine schreiben** to type.

maschinell ◇ *adj* [Herstellung, Bearbeitung] machine *(vor Subst)*; [Vorgang] mechanical. ◇ *adv* by machine.

Maschinenbau *der* mechanical engineering.

Maschinen|gewehr *das* machine gun.

Maschinen|pistole *die* submachine gun.

Maschinen|schaden *der* engine trouble *(U)*.

maschineschreiben, maschinenschreiben *vi (unreg)* ▷ **Maschine**.

Masern *Pl* measles *(U)*.

Maske (*pl* -n) *die* - **1.** [zum Verkleiden & EDV] mask - **2.** [beim Theater] make-up.

Masken|ball *der* masked ball.

maskieren *vt eigtl* & *fig* to mask. ◆ **sich maskieren** *ref* - **1.** [sich verdecken] to disguise o.s. - **2.** [sich verkleiden] to dress up.

Maskottchen (*pl* -) *das* mascot.

maskulin, maskulin *adj* masculine.

Maskulinum (*pl* **Maskulina**) *das* GRAMM masculine noun.

maß *prät* ▷ **messen**.

Maß (*pl* -e ODER -) ◇ *das* (*pl Maße)* - **1.** [Maßeinheit] measure - **2.** [Messgerät] (tape) measure - **3.** [Körpermaß]: **Maß nehmen** to take measurements - **4.** [Umfang, Verhältnis] degree; **in demselben/höherem Maß als** to the same/a greater degree as/than; **Maß halten** to be moderate. ◇ *die (pl Maß) Süddt & Österr* [Krug] litre (of beer). ◆ **in Maßen** *adv* in moderation. ◆ **nach Maß** *adv* [Anzug] made-to-measure; [Urlaub] tailor-made. ◆ **Maße** *Pl* - **1.** [von Räumen] dimensions - **2.** [von Personen] measurements.

Massage [ma'sɑːʒə] (*pl* -n) *die* massage.

Massaker (*pl* -) *das* massacre.

Maßarbeit *die*: **Maßarbeit sein** to be made-to-measure.

Masse (*pl* -n) *die* mass; **die breite Masse** *abw* the masses *Pl*. ◆ **in Massen** *adv* [einkaufen] in bulk; **die Leute kamen in Massen** masses of people came.

Maß|einheit *die* unit of measurement.

massenhaft ◇ *adj* in great numbers; **die massenhaften Hinrichtungen** the great number of executions. ◇ *adv* in great numbers.

Massen|medien *Pl* mass media.

Massen|mord *der* mass murder.

maßgebend, maßgeblich ◇ *adj* [Person] influential; [Meinung] authoritative; [Urteil, Argument] decisive. ◇ *adv*: **an etw** *(D)* **maßgebend beteiligt sein** to play a decisive role in sthg.

maßgeschneidert *adj* made-to-measure.

massieren *vt* to massage.

massig ◇ *adj* massive. ◇ *adv fam*: **massig zu essen** loads to eat; **massig Arbeit** loads of work.

mäßig ◇ *adj* - **1.** [gen] moderate - **2.** [mittelmäßig - Leistung, Wetter, Schüler] average. ◇ *adv* - **1.** [maßvoll] in moderation - **2.** [wenig] moderately.

mäßigen *vt* [Wut] to curb; [Worte] to moderate. ◆ **sich mäßigen** *ref* [Person] to restrain o.s.; [Unwetter] to die down.

massiv ◇ *adj* - **1.** [Holz, Metall] solid - **2.** [wuchtig] massive - **3.** [heftig] strong. ◇ *adv* - **1.** [wuchtig] massively - **2.** [heftig] strongly.

Massiv (*pl* -e) *das* massif.

Maß|krug *der Süddt & Österr* litre beer mug.

maßlos ◇ *adj* extreme. ◇ *adv* extremely.

Maßnahme (*pl* -n) *die* measure; **Maßnahmen einleiten** to introduce measures; **Maßnahmen ergreifen** ODER **treffen** to take measures.

Maß|stab *der* - **1.** [auf Landkarten] scale - **2.** [Richtlinie] standard. ◆ **im Maßstab** *adv*: **im Maßstab 1:25000** to a scale of 1:25,000.

maßstabgetreu, maßstabsgetreu *adj* & *adv* to scale.

Mast (*pl* -en ODER -e) ◇ *der (pl Maste, Masten)* - **1.** [auf Schiffen, für Antenne] mast - **2.** [Stange - für Fahne, Leitungen] pole; [- für Hochspannungsleitungen] pylon. ◇ *die (pl Masten)* [Mästen] fattening *(U)*.

mästen *vt* to fatten.

masturbieren *vi* & *vt* to masturbate.

Material [mate'ri̯ɑːl] (*pl* -ien) *das* - **1.** [Werkstoff, Unterlagen] material - **2.** [Gerät] equipment.

materialistisch *adj* materialistic.

Materie [ma'teːri̯ə] (*pl* -n) *die* - **1.** matter - **2.** *geh* [Themenbereich] subject matter.

materiell ◇ *adj* - **1.** [wirtschaftlich] financial - **2.** [materialistisch] materialistic - **3.** [stofflich] material. ◇ *adv* - **1.** [materialistisch] materialistically - **2.** [wirtschaftlich] financially.

Mathematik, Mathematik *die* mathematics *(U)*.

Mathematiker, in (*mpl* -, *fpl* -nen) *der, die* mathematician.

mathematisch ◇ *adj* mathematical. ◇ *adv* mathematically.

Matjes|hering *der* salted herring.

Matratze (*pl* -n) *die* mattress.

Matrose (*pl* -n) *der* sailor.

Matsch *der* - **1.** [Schlamm] mud; [von Schnee] slush - **2.** *fam* [Brei] mush.

matschen *vi fam* [in Pfütze] to splash around; [in Schlamm] to squelch around; **mit etw matschen** [beim Essen] to make a mush of sthg.

matt ◇ *adj* - **1.** [kraftlos] weak; [Händedruck, Reaktion] feeble - **2.** [nicht glänzend] matt - **3.** [trübe - Licht] dim; [- Augen, Farbe, Glanz] dull; [- Glühbirne] pearl; [- Glas] frosted - **4.** [im Schach]: **matt sein** to be checkmated. ◇ *adv* - **1.** [im Schach]: **jn matt setzen** to checkmate sb - **2.** [trübe] dimly - **3.** [kraftlos] weakly; [reagieren] feebly.

Matte (*pl* **-n**) *die* mat.

Mauer (*pl* **-n**) *die* wall.

mauern ◇ *vi* - **1.** [bauen] to build - **2.** SPORT to play defensively. ◇ *vt* [bauen] to build.

Mauerwerk *das* masonry.

Maul (*pl* **Mäuler**) *das* - **1.** [bei Tieren] mouth - **2.** *salopp* [Mundwerk] trap; **halts Maul!** shut your trap!; **böses Maul** malicious tongue.

maulen *vi fam abw* to moan.

Maul|korb *der* muzzle.

Maul|wurf *der* mole.

Maulwurfs|hügel *der* molehill.

Maurer, in (*mpl* -, *fpl* **-nen**) *der, die* bricklayer.

Mauritius *nt* Mauritius.

Maus (*pl* **Mäuse**) *die* - **1.** EDV [Tier] mouse - **2.** *fam* [Mädchen] cutie; **eine graue Maus** *fam abw* a nondescript kind of woman.

Mause|falle *die* mousetrap.

mausern ◆ **sich mausern** *ref* - **1.** [Vögel] to moult - **2.** [Person] to blossom.

mausetot *adj fam* as dead as a doornail.

Mausklick (*pl* **-s**) *der* EDV mouse click; **per Mausklick die Adresse einfügen** to add the address by clicking the mouse.

Mauspad (*pl* **-s**) *das* mouse mat.

Maut|gebühr *die Österr* toll.

Maut|stelle *die Österr* tollgate.

max. (*abk für* **maximal**) max.

maximal ◇ *adj* maximum. ◇ *adv*: **das maximal zulässige Gewicht** the maximum permitted weight; **maximal 30 Personen** a maximum of 30 people.

Maximum (*pl* **Maxima**) *das* maximum.

Mayonnaise *die* = **Majonäse**.

Mazedonien [maze'do:ni̯ən] *nt* Macedonia.

MB (*abk für* **Megabyte**) MB, Mb.

MdB (*abk für* **Mitglied des Bundestags**) Member of the "Bundestag".

Mechanik (*pl* **-en**) *die* - **1.** [Fach] mechanics *(U)* - **2.** [Mechanismus] mechanism.

Mechaniker, in (*mpl* -, *fpl* **-nen**) *der, die* mechanic.

mechanisch ◇ *adj* mechanical. ◇ *adv* mechanically.

Mechanismus (*pl* **Mechanismen**) *der* mechanism.

meckern *vi* - **1.** [Ziege] to bleat - **2.** *fam* [nörgeln]: **über jn/etw meckern** to moan about sb/sthg.

Mecklenburg-Vorpommern *nt* Mecklenburg-West Pomerania.

Medaille [me'daljə] (*pl* **-n**) *die* medal.

Medaillon [medalj'ɔŋ] (*pl* **-s**) *das* - **1.** [Schmuck] locket - **2.** [Fleisch, Fisch] medallion.

Medien *Pl* media.

Medikament (*pl* **-e**) *das* medicine; **ein Medikament gegen etw** a medicine for sthg.

Meditation (*pl* **-en**) *die* meditation.

meditieren *vi* - **1.** [versunken sein] to meditate - **2.** [nachdenken]: **über etw** *(A)* **meditieren** to meditate on sthg.

Medium ['me:di̯ʊm] (*pl* **Medien**) *das* medium.

Medizin (*pl* **-en**) *die* medicine.

Mediziner, in (*mpl* -, *fpl* **-nen**) *der, die* [Arzt] doctor; [Student] medical student.

medizinisch ◇ *adj* - **1.** [heilkundlich, ärztlich] medical - **2.** [heilend] medicinal. ◇ *adv* medically.

Meer (*pl* **-e**) *das eigtl* & *fig* sea; **ans Meer fahren** to go to the seaside.

Meer|enge *die* strait.

Meeres|früchte *Pl* seafood *(U)*.

Meeres|grund *der* seabed.

Meeres|spiegel *der* sea level.

Meer|rettich *der* horseradish.

Meer|schweinchen (*pl* -) *das* guinea pig.

Meer|wasser *das* seawater.

Megafon (*pl* **-e**), **Megaphon** (*pl* **-e**) [mega'fo:n] *das* megaphone.

Mehl *das* - **1.** [zum Backen] flour - **2.** [Pulver - von Holz] sawdust; [- von Knochen] meal; [- von Gestein] powder.

Mehl|schwitze (*pl* **-n**) *die* roux.

mehr ◇ *pron* [komparativ von viel] more. ◇ *adv* - **1.** [komparativ von viel] more; **50 Euro, mehr nicht?** 50 euros, no more than that?; **er ist mehr Gelehrter als Künstler** he is more of a scholar than an artist - **2.** [übrig] more; **mehr denn je** more than ever; **es ist keiner mehr da** there is no one left; **nichts mehr** nothing more - **3.** [zeitlich]: **nicht mehr** not any longer; **du bist doch kein Kind mehr!** you are not a child any more; **immer mehr, mehr und mehr** more and more; **mehr oder weniger** more or less.

Mehr|aufwand *der* extra expenditure.

mehrdeutig *adj* ambiguous.

mehrere *det* & *pron* several. ◆ **mehreres** *pron* several things. ◆ **zu mehreren** *adv*: **sie kommen zu mehreren** several (of them) are coming.

mehrfach <> *adj* multiple; [Olympiasieger] several times over; **ein Bericht in mehrfacher Ausfertigung** several copies of a report; **in mehrfacher Hinsicht** in more than one respect. <> *adv* several times.

mehrfarbig <> *adj* multicoloured. <> *adv* in many colours.

Mehrheit (*pl* **-en**) *die* majority; **mit großer/knapper Mehrheit** by a large/narrow majority; **die absolute Mehrheit** an absolute majority.

mehrheitlich <> *adj* majority. <> *adv* by a majority.

mehrmalig *adj* repeated.

mehrmals *adv* several times.

mehrsprachig <> *adj* [Wörterbuch, Ausgabe, Person] multilingual; [Unterhaltung] in several languages. <> *adv*: **mehrsprachig aufwachsen** to grow up multilingual.

mehrstimmig <> *adj* for several voices. <> *adv* in harmony.

Mehrwertsteuer *die* VAT *UK*, sales tax *US*.

Mehrzahl *die* - **1.** [größerer Anteil] majority - **2.** [Plural] plural.

Mehrzweck|halle *die* multipurpose hall.

Meile (*pl* **-n**) *die* mile.

meilenweit *adv* for miles; **meilenweit entfernt** miles away.

mein, **e** <> *det* my; **meine Damen und Herren** ladies and gentlemen. <> *pron* mine.

meine, **r**, **s** ODER **meins** *pron* mine.

Mein|eid *der* perjury *(U)*.

meinen <> *vt* - **1.** [denken, glauben] to think; **was meinst du dazu?** what do you think? - **2.** [sagen] to say; **was meint er?** *fam* what did he say? - **3.** [zum Ausdruck einer Intention] to mean; **etw ironisch meinen** to mean sthg ironically; **wie meinen Sie das?** what do you mean by that?; **das war nicht so gemeint** it wasn't meant like that; **gut gemeint** well-intentioned. <> *vi* to think; **ich meine ja nur!** it was just a suggestion; **meinen Sie?** do you think so?; **wie meinen Sie?** what did you say?; **wie Sie meinen!** as you wish!

meiner *pron (Genitiv von ich)* of me; **er erinnert sich meiner** he remembers me.

meinetwegen *adv* - **1.** [mir zuliebe] for my sake - **2.** [wegen mir] because of me - **3.** [von mir aus] as far as I'm concerned; **(also) meinetwegen!** if you like.

meinetwillen ◆ **um meinetwillen** *adv* for my sake.

Meinung (*pl* **-en**) *die* opinion; **eine vorgefasste Meinung** a preconceived idea; **anderer Meinung sein** to be of a different opinion; **der Meinung sein, dass...** to be of the opinion that...; **einer** ODER **derselben Meinung sein** to agree; **jm die Meinung sagen** *fam fig* to give sb a piece of one's mind; **meiner Meinung nach** in my opinion.

Meinungs|austausch *der* exchange of views.

Meinungs|freiheit *die* freedom of expression.

Meinungsum|frage *die* opinion poll.

Meinungs|verschiedenheit *die* difference of opinion.

Meise (*pl* **-n**) *die* tit.

Meißel (*pl* **-**) *der* chisel.

meißeln *vi* & *vt* to chisel.

meist *adv* usually, mostly. ◆ **am meisten** *adv* most; **die am meisten besuchte Ausstellung** the most visited exhibition.

meiste <> *adj* (the) most; **die meisten Leute** most people; **er hat das meiste Geld** he has the most money. <> *pron*: **das/die meiste** (the) most. ◆ **die meisten** *pron* most people.

meistens *adv* usually, mostly.

Meister (*pl* -) *der* - **1.** [Handwerker] master craftsman; **seinen Meister machen** *fam* to get one's master craftsman's certificate - **2.** [Experte, Künstler] master - **3.** [im Sport] champion.

Meisterin (*pl* **-nen**) *die* [Handwerkerin] master craftswoman; [Expertin, Künstlerin] master; [im Sport] champion.

meistern *vt* - **1.** [bewältigen] to master - **2.** *geh* [zügeln] to control.

Meisterschaft (*pl* **-en**) *die* - **1.** SPORT championship - **2.** [Können] mastery.

Meister|werk *das* masterpiece.

Mekka *nt* Mecca.

melancholisch [melaŋ'ko:lɪʃ] <> *adj* melancholy. <> *adv* in a melancholy way.

melden *vt* - **1.** [anzeigen, berichten] to report; [Geburt] to register; **(bei jm) nichts/nicht viel zu melden haben** *fam fig* to have no/little say (with sb) - **2.** [anmelden] to announce. ◆ **sich melden** *ref* - **1.** [sich bemerkbar machen - im Unterricht] to put one's hand up; [- Finder] to make o.s. known - **2.** [Nachricht geben]: **melde dich mal wieder!** keep in touch!; **sich bei jm melden** [bei Freunden] to get in touch with sb; [bei Polizei] to report to sb - **3.** [am Telefon] to answer; **es meldet sich niemand** there's no answer - **4.** [sich anmelden] to register; **sich freiwillig zu etw melden** to volunteer for sthg.

Meldung (*pl* **-en**) *die* - **1.** [Nachricht, Anzeige] report - **2.** [Mitteilung] announcement - **3.** [Anmeldung] entry.

melken (*prät* **melkte** ODER **molk**, *perf* **hat gemolken**) *vt* & *vi* to milk.

Melodie [melo'di:] (*pl* **-n**) *die* tune.

melodisch <> *adj* melodic. <> *adv* melodically.

Melone (*pl* **-n**) *die* - **1.** [Frucht] melon - **2.** [Hut] bowler (hat).

Membran (*pl* **-en**) *die* - **1.** TECH diaphragm - **2.** BIOL, CHEM & PHYS membrane.

Memoiren [me'mo̯aːrən] *Pl* memoirs.

Mẹnge (*pl* **-n**) *die* - **1.** [Anzahl] amount; **die doppelte/dreifache Menge** twice/three times the amount; **in rauen Mengen** *fam*: **die Leute kamen in rauen Mengen** loads of people came - **2.** [Vielzahl] a lot ODER lots; **eine Menge Bücher** a lot ODER lots of books - **3.** *(ohne pl)* [Menschenmasse] crowd - **4.** MATH set. ◆ **eine ganze Menge** *adv* quite a lot; **eine ganze Menge Geld** quite a lot of money. ◆ **jede Menge** *adv fam* loads; **jede Menge Arbeit** loads of work.

Mẹngenlehre *die* MATH set theory.

mẹngenmäßig ◇ *adj* quantitative. ◇ *adv* quantitatively.

Mẹngen|rabatt *der* bulk discount.

Mẹnsa (*pl* **Mẹnsen**) *die* UNI university canteen.

Mẹnsch (*pl* **-en**) ◇ *der* - **1.** [Art, Lebewesen] human (being); **der Mensch ist ein vernunftbegabtes Tier** man is a rational animal - **2.** [Person] person. ◇ *interj* [wütend] for heaven's sake!; [begeistert] wow! ◆ **kein Mensch** *pron* no one.

Mẹnschen|kenntnis *die* knowledge of human nature.

mẹnschenleer *adj* deserted.

Mẹnschen|menge *die* crowd.

Mẹnschenrechte *Pl* human rights.

Mẹnschen|seele *die*: **keine Menschenseele** not a soul.

menschenụnwürdig *adj* inhumane.

Mẹnschenverstand *der*: **der gesunde Menschenverstand** common sense.

Mẹnschenwürde *die* human dignity.

Mẹnschheit *die* humanity, mankind.

mẹnschlich ◇ *adj* - **1.** [des Menschen] human - **2.** [human] humane. ◇ *adv* [hụman] humanely.

Menstruation (*pl* **-en**) *die* MED menstruation.

Mentalität (*pl* **-en**) *die* mentality.

Menthol *das* menthol.

Menü (*pl* **-s**) *das* - **1.** [Speisenfolge] set menu - **2.** EDV menu.

mẹrken *vt* to notice; **sich** *(D)* **etw merken** to remember sthg; **du merkst aber auch alles!** *fam iron* how observant of you!

Mẹrkmal (*pl* **-e**) *das* feature.

Mẹrk|satz *der* mnemonic.

mẹrkwürdig ◇ *adj* strange. ◇ *adv* strangely.

Mẹsse (*pl* **-n**) *die* - **1.** [Gottesdienst] mass - **2.** [Ausstellung] (trade) fair.

mẹssen (*präs* **mịsst**, *prät* **maß**, *perf* **hat gemẹssen**) ◇ *vt* to measure; [Temperatur] to take. ◇ *vi* [eine bestimmte Größe haben] to measure; **er misst 1,76 m** he is 1.76m tall.

Mẹsser (*pl* -) *das* [zum Schneiden] knife; [zum Rasieren] razor. ◆ **bis aufs Messer** *adv* to the bitter end.

mẹsserscharf ◇ *adj* razor-sharp. ◇ *adv* [scharfsinnig] incisively.

Mẹsse|stand *der* stand at a (trade) fair.

Mẹssing *das* brass.

Mẹssung (*pl* **-en**) *die* measurement.

Metạll (*pl* **-e**) *das* metal.

Metạll|arbeiter, in *der, die* metalworker.

Metạll|industrie *die* metalworking industry.

metạllisch ◇ *adj* metallic. ◇ *adv*: **metallisch schimmern** to have a metallic gleam.

Metạpher [me'tafɐ] (*pl* **-n**) *die* metaphor.

Meteor (*pl* **-e**) *der* meteor.

Meteorologe (*pl* **-n**) *der* weather forecaster.

Meteorologin (*pl* **-nen**) *die* weather forecaster.

Meter (*pl* -) *das* & *der* metre; **zwei Meter breit/hoch/lang/tief sein** to be two metres wide/high/long/deep.

Meter|maß *das* tape measure.

Methan *das* methane.

Methode (*pl* **-n**) *die* method.

methodisch ◇ *adj* methodical. ◇ *adv* methodically.

Mẹtt|wurst *die soft, smoked pork or beef sausage, usually spread on bread.*

Mẹtzger (*pl* -) *der* butcher.

Metzgerei (*pl* **-en**) *die* butcher's.

Mẹtzgerin (*pl* **-nen**) *die* butcher.

Meute (*pl* **-n**) *die* - **1.** [Hunde] pack - **2.** *fam* [Menschen] mob.

Meuterei (*pl* **-en**) *die* [auf Schiff] mutiny; [in Gefängnis] revolt.

meutern *vi* - **1.** [sich auflehnen - Besatzung] to mutiny; [- Strafgefangene] to revolt - **2.** *fam* [sich weigern] to protest.

Mẹxiko *nt* Mexico.

MEZ [ɛmɟeː'tsɛt] (*abk für* **mitteleuropäische Zeit**) *die* CET.

MFG [ɛmɟɛfɟeː] (*pl* **-s**) *die abk für* **Mitfahrgelegenheit**.

mg (*abk für* **Milligramm**) mg.

miauen *vi* to miaow.

mịch *pron (Akkusativ von ich)* - **1.** [Personalpronomen] me - **2.** [Reflexivpronomen] myself; **ich entschied mich zu kündigen** I decided to hand in my notice.

Miene (*pl* **-n**) *die* expression; **keine Miene verziehen** not to bat an eyelid.

mies *fam abw* ◇ *adj* lousy. ◇ *adv*: **mies gelaunt sein** to be in a foul mood.

Miese *Pl fam*: **in den Miesen sein, Miese haben** to be in the red; **Miese machen** to make a loss.

Mies|muschel *die* mussel.

Miete (*pl* **-n**) *die* [für Wohnung, Geschäftsfläche, Garage] rent; [für Fahrzeug] hire charge *UK*, rental *US*; **zur Miete wohnen** to live in rented accommodation.

mieten *vt*: **(sich** *(D)***) etw mieten** [Wohnung, Geschäftsfläche, Garage] to rent; [Fahrzeug] to hire *UK*, to rent *US*.

Mieter, in (*mpl* **-**, *fpl* **-nen**) *der, die* tenant.

Miet|preis *der* rent.

Miets|haus *das* block of flats *UK*, apartment building *US*.

Miet|vertrag *der* [für Wohnung, Geschäftsfläche] lease; [für Fahrzeug] hire *UK* ODER rental *US* agreement.

Migräne *die* migraine.

Mikro|chip *der* microchip.

Mikrofon (*pl* **-e**), **Mikrophon** (*pl* **-e**) *das* microphone.

Mikroskop (*pl* **-e**) *das* microscope.

mikroskopisch ◇ *adj* microscopic. ◇ *adv* **- 1.** [mit einem Mikroskop] under the microscope **- 2.** [winzig] microscopically.

Mikrowellen|herd *der* microwave (oven).

Milch *die* milk.

Milch|flasche *die* [für Säugling] feeding bottle; [von Molkerei] milk bottle.

milchig ◇ *adj* milky. ◇ *adv*: **milchig trüb** milky and cloudy.

Milch|produkt *das* dairy product.

Milch|pulver *das* powdered milk.

Milch|reis *der (ohne pl)* rice pudding.

Milch|straße *die* ASTRON Milky Way.

Milch|zahn *der* milk tooth.

mild, milde ◇ *adj* **- 1.** [gen] mild **- 2.** [Licht, Worte, Lächeln] gentle **- 3.** [Strafe, Urteil] lenient; [Herrscher] benevolent. ◇ *adv* **- 1.** [urteilen, strafen] leniently **- 2.** [scheinen, wehen, lächeln] gently **- 3.** [nicht scharf - würzen] lightly.

Milde *die* **- 1.** [von Urteil] leniency **- 2.** [von Licht] gentleness; [von Abend, Klima, Aroma] mildness.

mildern *vt* **- 1.** [abschwächen - Wut, Worte, Urteil] to moderate; [- Schärfe] to reduce; [- Aufprall] to soften **- 2.** [lindern] to alleviate, to relieve. ◆ **sich mildern** *ref* **- 1.** [Wut, Zorn] to abate **- 2.** [Klima] to become milder.

Milieu [miˈli̯øː] (*pl* **-s**) *das* **- 1.** [Umfeld, Umwelt] environment **- 2.** [Unterwelt] world of prostitution.

militant ◇ *adj* militant. ◇ *adv* militantly.

Militär (*pl* **-s**) ◇ *das*: **das Militär** the military. ◇ *der* army officer.

Militärdienst *der* military service.

militärisch ◇ *adj* military. ◇ *adv* militarily.

Militär|regierung *die* military government.

Milliardär, in (*mpl* **-e**, *fpl* **-nen**) *der, die* billionaire.

Milliarde (*pl* **-n**) *die* billion.

Milligramm (*pl* **-**) *das* milligram.

Milliliter (*pl* **-**) *der* millilitre.

Millimeter (*pl* **-**) *der* millimetre.

Millimeterpapier *das* graph paper.

Million (*pl* **-en**) *die* million.

Millionär, in (*mpl* **-e**, *fpl* **-nen**) *der, die* millionaire.

Millionen|stadt *die* city with a population of over one million.

Milz (*pl* **-en**) *die* spleen.

Milzbrand *der (ohne Pl)* foot and mouth disease.

Mimik *die (ohne pl)* facial expressions and gestures.

Minderheit (*pl* **-en**) *die* minority; **in der Minderheit sein** to be in a/the minority.

minderjährig *adj* underage.

Minderjährige (*pl* **-n**) *der, die* minor.

mindern *vt* [Strafmaß, Preis, Wert] to reduce; [Ansehen] to diminish.

minderwertig ◇ *adj* inferior. ◇ *adv* [herstellen] poorly.

Mindestalter *das* minimum age.

mindeste *adj* slightest; **das ist das Mindeste, was man erwarten kann** that is the least you can expect. ◆ **nicht im Mindesten** *adv* not in the slightest.

mindestens *adv* at least.

Mindest|lohn *der* minimum wage.

Mine (*pl* **-n**) *die* **- 1.** [Schreibutensil - von Kugelschreiber] refill; [- von Bleistift] lead **- 2.** [Bergwerk, Sprengsatz] mine; [Stollen] tunnel.

Mineral (*pl* **-e** ODER **-ien**) *das* mineral.

Mineral|öl *das* mineral oil.

Mineralöl|steuer *die tax on oil.*

Mineral|wasser *das* mineral water.

mini *adv*: **mini tragen** to wear a mini.

Mini (*pl* **-s**) ◇ *das* **- 1.** *(ohne pl, ohne Artikel)* [Mode] miniskirts *Pl* **- 2.** *fam* [Kleid] mini. ◇ *der fam* [Rock] mini.

minimal ◇ *adj* minimal. ◇ *adv* minimally.

Minimum (*pl* **Minima**) *das* minimum *(U)*.

Minister (*pl* **-**) *der* minister.

ministeriell ◇ *adj* ministerial. ◇ *adv* ministerially.

Ministerin (*pl* **-nen**) *die* minister.

Ministerium [minɪsˈteːri̯ʊm] (*pl* **Ministerien**) *das* ministry; **Ministerium des Inneren/der Finanzen** interior/finance ministry.

Minister|präsident, in *der, die* **- 1.** [von Bundesländern] minister president, *title given to leader of government in the German federal states* **- 2.** [Premierminister] prime minister.

Minister|rat *der* Council of Ministers.

minus ◇ *präp* minus. ◇ *adv*: **minus dreizehn Grad** minus thirteen degrees. ◇ *konj*: **zehn minus drei** ten minus three.

Minus *das (ohne pl)* - **1.** [Fehlbetrag] deficit; **im Minus stehen** to be in the red - **2.** [Zeichen] minus (sign).

Minute (*pl* **-n**) *die* minute; **auf die Minute pünktlich** on the dot.

Mịnze (*pl* **-n**) *die* mint.

Mio. (*abk für* **Million**) m.

mir *pron (Dativ von ich)* - **1.** (to) me; **er sagte es mir** he told me; **das gehört mir** this is mine, this belongs to me; **mit mir** with me - **2.** [Reflexivpronomen] myself.

Mịsch|brot *das bread made from a mixture of rye and wheat flour.*

mịschen *vt* [Farben, Zutaten] to mix; [Karten] to shuffle; **etw mit etw mischen** to mix sthg with sthg. ◆ **sich mischen** *ref*: **sich unter etw** *(A)* **mischen** to mix with sthg.

Mịschling (*pl* **-e**) *der* [Tier] half-breed.

Mịschung (*pl* **-en**) *die* mixture.

missachten *vt* - **1.** [nicht befolgen] to disregard - **2.** [verachten] to despise.

missbịlligen *vt* to disapprove of.

Mịss|brauch *der* - **1.** [sexuell, von Medikamenten, von Drogen] abuse - **2.** [schlechter Gebrauch] misuse.

missbrauchen *vt* - **1.** [ausnutzen - Macht, Mittel] to misuse; [- Vertrauen] to abuse; [- Gutmütigkeit] to take advantage of - **2.** [übermäßig nutzen, sexuell] to abuse.

mịssen *vt* to do without; **etw nicht (mehr) missen wollen** not to want to be without sthg.

Mịsserfolg (*pl* **-e**) *der* failure.

missfạllen (*präs* **missfạ̈llt**, *prät* **missfiel**, *perf* **hat missfạllen**) *vi*: **es missfällt mir, wie sie...** I dislike the way she...; **der Plan missfiel ihm** he disliked the plan.

Missfạllen *das* displeasure.

mịssgebildet *adj* deformed.

Mịssgeschick (*pl* **-e**) *das* mishap; **jm passiert ein Missgeschick** sb has a mishap.

missglụ̈cken (*perf* **ist missglụ̈ckt**) *vi* to be unsuccessful; **der Versuch ist mir missglückt** my attempt was unsuccessful.

missgọ̈nnen *vt*: **jm etw missgönnen** to begrudge sb sthg.

Mịssgunst *die* resentment.

misshạndeln *vt* to ill-treat.

Misshạndlung (*pl* **-en**) *die* ill-treatment *(U)*.

Mission (*pl* **-en**) *die* mission.

Mịsskredit *der*: **jn in Misskredit bringen** to discredit sb; **in Misskredit geraten** ODER **kommen** to be discredited.

misslạng *prät* ▷ **misslingen**.

misslịngen (*prät* **misslạng**, *perf* **ist misslụngen**) *vi* to fail; **das Experiment ist mir misslungen** my experiment was a failure; **ein misslungener Versuch** an unsuccessful attempt.

misslụngen *pp* ▷ **misslingen**.

mịssmutig ◇ *adj* [Person, Charakter] bad-tempered; [Gesicht, Laune] sullen; **missmutig sein** to be in a bad mood. ◇ *adv* bad-temperedly; [ansehen] sullenly.

missraten (*präs* **missrät**, *prät* **missriet**, *perf* **ist missraten**) ◇ *vi*: **der Braten war ihr missraten** her roast had turned out badly. ◇ *adj* which/who turned out badly.

mịsst *präs* ▷ **messen**.

misstrauen *vi*: **jm/etw misstrauen** to mistrust sb/sthg.

Mịsstrauen *das* mistrust.

mịsstrauisch ◇ *adj* mistrustful; **jm gegenüber misstrauisch sein** to be mistrustful of sb. ◇ *adv* mistrustfully.

Mịssverhältnis (*pl* **-se**) *das* discrepancy.

Mịssverständnis (*pl* **-nisse**) *das* misunderstanding.

mịssverstehen (*prät* **mịssverstand**, *perf* **hat mịssverstanden**) *vt* to misunderstand.

Mịsswirtschaft *die* mismanagement.

Mịst *der* - **1.** [Dung] dung; [Düngemittel] manure - **2.** *fam fig & abw* [Plunder, Blödsinn] rubbish; **Mist machen** ODER **bauen** to make a mess of things - **3.** *fam* [als Ausruf]: **(so ein) Mist!** damn it!

mịt ◇ *präp (+ D)* - **1.** [zusammen mit] with; **er kommt mit seiner Frau** he's coming with his wife; **Kaffee mit Zucker** coffee with sugar; **ein Haus mit Garten** a house with a garden; **eine Scheibe Brot mit Butter** a slice of bread and butter; **sich mit jm unterhalten** to talk to sb - **2.** [modal]: **mit lauter Stimme** in a loud voice; **mit Nachdruck** emphatically; **mit 100 Stundenkilometern** at 100 kilometres per hour; **mit Verspätung eintreffen** to arrive late - **3.** [mittels] with; **mit dem Hammer** with a hammer; **mit dem Zug** by train; **mit der Post** by post; **mit Scheck bezahlen** to pay by cheque - **4.** [stellt Bezug her]: **wie weit bist du mit deiner Arbeit?** how far have you got with your work?; **wie wäre es mit einer Tasse Kaffee?** how about a cup of coffee?; **er hat es mit dem Magen** he has stomach trouble - **5.** [temporal] at; **mit jedem Tag** every day; **mit 16 Jahren** at (the age of) 16; **mit der Zeit** in (the course of) time. ◇ *adv* - **1.** [auch] too; **sie war nicht mit dabei** she wasn't there - **2.** [unter anderen]: **er ist mit der beste Schüler seiner Klasse** he is one of the best pupils in his class.

Mịtarbeit *die* [an Projekt] collaboration; [von Schülern, Bevölkerung] participation.

mitlarbeiten *vi* **- 1.** [in Projekt] to collaborate; [im Haushalt] to help out; **bei/an etw** *(D)* **mitarbeiten** to collaborate on sthg **- 2.** [in der Schule] to participate.

Mitlarbeiter, in *der, die* [Betriebsangehörige] colleague, co-worker *US*.

mitlbekommen *vt (unreg)* **- 1.** [verstehen] to follow **- 2.** [aufschnappen]: **etw von etw mitbekommen** to hear sthg about sthg; **(von etw) nicht viel mitbekommen** not to take much (of sthg) in **- 3.** [bekommen]: **etw mitbekommen** to get sthg to take with one.

Mitbestimmung *die* codetermination.

Mitlbewohner, in *der, die* [in Haus] other occupant; [in Wohnung] flatmate *UK*, roommate *US*.

mitlbringen *vt (unreg)* **- 1.** [Geschenk, Personen] to bring (with one); [von Reise] to bring back; **jm etw mitbringen** to bring sthg for sb **- 2.** [Fähigkeiten] to have.

Mitlbürger, in *der, die* fellow citizen.

miteinander *adv* [auskommen, streiten, flirten] with each other; [reden, verbinden] to each other; [gemeinsam] together. ◆ **alle miteinander** *pron* all (together).

mitlerleben *vt* to witness.

Mitesser *(pl -) der* blackhead.

mitlfahren *(perf* **ist mitgefahren**) *vi (unreg)* to go/come along; **mit** *ODER* **bei jm mitfahren** to get a lift *UK ODER* ride *US* with sb.

Mitfahrlgelegenheit *die* lift *UK*, ride *US*.

Mitfahrlzentrale, Mitfahrerzentrale *die agency which organizes lifts, with passengers contributing to costs.*

mitlfühlen ◇ *vi*: **mit jm mitfühlen** to sympathize with sb. ◇ *vt* to share.

mitlgeben *vt (unreg)*: **jm etw mitgeben** to give sb sthg.

Mitgefühl *das* sympathy.

mitlgehen *(perf* **ist mitgegangen**) *vi (unreg)* **- 1.** [mitkommen] to go/come along; **mit jm mitgehen** to go/come with sb **- 2.** [teilhaben] to be carried along **- 3.** *fam* [stehlen]: **etw mitgehen lassen** to pinch sthg.

mitgenommen ◇ *pp* ▷ **mitnehmen**. ◇ *adj* worn out; **mitgenommen aussehen** to look worn out.

Mitgift *(pl* **-en**) *die* dowry.

Mitlglied *das* member.

Mitgliedslbeitrag *der* membership fee.

Mitgliedschaft *(pl* **-en**) *die* membership *(U)*.

mitlhalten *vi (unreg)*: **bei etw (nicht) mithalten können** (not) to be able to keep up in sthg; **mit jm/etw (nicht) mithalten können** (not) to be able to keep up with sb/sthg.

mithilfe ◇ *adv*: **mithilfe von etw/** with the help of sthg/sb. ◇ *präp*: **mithilfe js/einer Sache** with the help of sb/sthg.

mitlhören ◇ *vi* [zufällig] to overhear; [heimlich] to listen in. ◇ *vt* [zufällig] to overhear; [heimlich] to listen in on.

mitlkommen *(perf* **ist mitgekommen**) *vi (unreg)* **- 1.** [auch kommen] to come along; **kommst du mit?** are you coming? **- 2.** [folgen können] to keep up; **da komme ich nicht (mehr) mit!** *fam* it's beyond me! **- 3.** [eintreffen] to arrive.

Mitleid *das* pity; **mit jm Mitleid haben** *ODER* **empfinden** to feel pity for sb.

Mitleidenschaft *die*: **jn/etw in Mitleidenschaft ziehen** to affect sb/sthg.

mitleidig ◇ *adj* pitying. ◇ *adv* pityingly.

mitlmachen ◇ *vt* **- 1.** [Spiel, Kurs] to take part in; [Mode] to follow; **das mache ich nicht mehr länger mit** I'm not going to put up with this any longer **- 2.** [erledigen]: **etw für jn mitmachen** to do sthg for sb **- 3.** [aushalten] to put up with; **sie hat schon viel mitgemacht** she has been through a lot. ◇ *vi* [sich beteiligen] to take part; **bei etw (nicht) mitmachen** (not) to take part in sthg.

Mitmenschen *Pl* fellow human beings *ODER* men.

mitlmischen *vi fam*: **bei etw mitmischen** [sich einmischen] to interfere in sthg; [teilnehmen] to get involved in sthg.

mitlnehmen *vt (unreg)* **- 1.** [mit sich nehmen] to take (with one); **ich kann dich bis zum Bahnhof mitnehmen** I can give you a lift *UK ODER* ride *US* to the station; **sich** *(D)* **etw mitnehmen** to take sthg (with one) **- 2.** [strapazieren] to take it out of **- 3.** [kaufen] to buy **- 4.** [stehlen] to make off with **- 5.** *fam* [wahrnehmen, besuchen] to take in.

Mitlreisende *der, die* fellow passenger.

mitlreißen *vt (unreg)* **- 1.** [begeistern] to carry away **- 2.** [fortreißen - bei Sturz] to pull down; [- bei Lawine] to sweep away.

mitsamt *präp*: **mitsamt einer Sache** *(D)* together with sthg.

mitlschreiben *(unreg)* ◇ *vt* **- 1.** [festhalten] to take down **- 2.** [Klassenarbeit, Prüfung] to do. ◇ *vi* [festhalten] to take notes.

Mitschuld *die* share of the blame.

mitschuldig *adj*: **(an etw** *(D)***) mitschuldig sein** to be partly to blame (for sthg).

Mitlschüler, in *der, die* schoolmate.

mitlspielen ◇ *vi* **- 1.** [auch spielen]: **bei/in etw** *(D)* **mitspielen** [Spiel] to join in sthg; [Mannschaft, Orchester] to play in sthg; [Theatergruppe, Film] to act in sthg **- 2.** [wichtig sein]: **bei etw mitspielen** to play a part in sthg **- 3.** [mitmachen] to play along; **bei etw mitspielen** to go along with sthg **- 4.** [schaden]: **jm übel mitspielen** to give sb a hard time. ◇ *vt* [Spiel] to play.

Mitlspieler, in *der, die* [bei Spiel, in Mannschaft] other player.

Mittag (*pl* **-e**) *der* midday; **am Mittag** at midday; **über Mittag** at lunchtime; **zu Mittag essen** to have lunch; **gestern/heute/morgen Mittag** at midday yesterday/today/tomorrow.

Mittag|essen *das* lunch.

mittags *adv* at midday.

Mittags|pause *die* lunch break.

Mittags|schlaf *der (ohne pl)* afternoon nap.

Mitte (*pl* **-n**) *die* middle; **in der Mitte** in the middle; **Mitte vierzig** in one's mid-forties; **Mitte nächster Woche** in the middle of next week.

mit|teilen *vt*: **jm etw mitteilen** to tell sb sthg.

Mit|teilung *die* communication; [an Presse] statement; **jm eine Mitteilung machen** to inform sb; **eine schriftliche Mitteilung** a written communication.

Mittel (*pl* -) *das* - **1.** [Hilfsmittel] means *(sg)*; **mit allen Mitteln** by every means - **2.** [Medikament] medicine; **ein Mittel gegen etw** a remedy for sthg - **3.** [zur Reinigung] cleaning agent. ◆ **Mittel** *Pl* [Geldmittel] means; **öffentliche Mittel** public funds.

Mittelalter *das (ohne pl)* Middle Ages *Pl*.

mittelalterlich <> *adj* medieval. <> *adv* like in medieval times.

Mittelamerika *nt* Central America.

Mittel|europa *nt* Central Europe.

Mittel|finger *der* middle finger.

Mittel|gebirge *das* low-lying mountain range.

mittelgroß *adj* medium-sized; [Person] of medium height.

mittellos *adj* penniless.

mittelmäßig *abw* <> *adj* average. <> *adv* averagely.

Mittelmeer *das*: **das Mittelmeer** the Mediterranean (Sea).

Mittel|punkt *der* centre; **im Mittelpunkt stehen** to be the centre of attention.

Mittel|streifen *der* central reservation *UK*, median *US*.

Mittel|weg *der* middle way.

Mittel|wert *der* mean.

mitten *adv*: **mitten auf** in the middle of; **mitten durch** through the middle of; **mitten in etw** *(D)* in the middle of sthg; **mitten in etw** *(A)* into the middle of sthg; **mitten unter** among; **mitten am Tag/in der Nacht** in the middle of the day/night.

mittendrin *adv* in the middle.

mittendurch *adv* through the middle.

Mitternacht *die* midnight.

mittlere, r, s *adj* - **1.** [zwischen den Extremen] average; **im mittleren Alter** middle-aged - **2.** [in der Mitte liegend] middle.

Mittlere Osten *der*: **der Mittlere Osten** the Middle East.

mittlerweile *adv* [inzwischen] in the meantime; [jetzt] now.

Mittwoch (*pl* **-e**) *der* Wednesday; *siehe auch* **Samstag**.

mittwochs ['mɪtvɔxs] *adv* on Wednesdays; *siehe auch* **samstags**.

mitunter *adv* occasionally.

mitverantwortlich *adj* jointly responsible.

mit|verdienen *vi* to earn money as well.

mit|wirken *vi*: **(bei etw) mitwirken** [mitarbeiten] to contribute (to sthg); [mitspielen] to take part (in sthg).

mixen *vt* to mix.

MKS (*abk für* **Maul- und Klauenseuche**) *die (ohne pl)* foot-and-mouth (disease).

mobben *vt*: **jdn mobben** to bully sb at work.

Mobbing *das* workplace bullying.

Möbel (*pl* -) *das* piece of furniture; **die Möbel** the furniture.

Möbel|wagen *der* removal *UK* ODER moving *US* van.

mobil *adj* - **1.** [beweglich] mobile - **2.** [munter] lively; **mobil machen** MIL to mobilize; **jn mobil machen** [munter machen] to liven sb up.

Mobil|funk *der (ohne pl)* TELEKOM mobile phone network *UK*, cellphone network *US*.

Mobil|telefon *das* mobile phone *UK*, cellphone *US*.

möblieren *vt* to furnish.

möbliert <> *adj* furnished. <> *adv*: **möbliert wohnen** to live in furnished accommodation.

mochte *prät* ▷ **mögen**.

Mode (*pl* **-n**) *die* [Kleidungsstil, Zeitgeschmack] fashion; **es ist jetzt groß in Mode** it is very fashionable now; **mit der Mode gehen** to follow the fashion.

Mode|haus *das* - **1.** [Einzelgeschäft] fashion store - **2.** [Unternehmen] fashion house.

Modell (*pl* **-e**) *das* model; **Modell stehen** [für Maler] to model.

modellieren *vt* to model.

Modem (*pl* **-s**) *das* EDV modem.

Moden|schau *die* fashion show.

Moderator (*pl* **-en**) *der* presenter.

Moderatorin (*pl* **-nen**) *die* presenter.

moderig = **modrig**.

modern[1] (*perf* **hat/ist gemodert**) *vi* to moulder.

modern[2] <> *adj* modern; [modisch] fashionable. <> *adv* - **1.** [zeitgemäß] in a modern way; **modern denken** to have modern ideas - **2.** [zeitgenössisch] in a modern style.

modernisieren *vt* to modernize.

Mode|schmuck *der* costume jewellery.

modisch <> *adj* fashionable. <> *adv* fashionably.

modrig, moderig *adj* & *adv* musty.

Mofa (*pl* **-s**) *das* moped.

mogeln *vi* to cheat.

mögen (*präs* **mag**, *prät* **mochte**, *perf* **hat gemocht** ODER **mögen**) ◇ *vt (perf hat gemocht)* - **1.** [gern haben] to like; **jn/etw (nicht) mögen** (not) to like sb/sthg - **2.** [wollen]: **ich möchte bitte ein Eis** I'd like an ice-cream please; **was möchten Sie?** what would you like? ◇ *vi (perf hat gemocht)* [wollen]: **er möchte nach Hause** he wants to go home. ◇ *aux (perf hat mögen)*: **ich möchte etwas trinken** I'd like something to drink; **möchtest du mitkommen?** would you like to come?; **mag sein** that may well be.

möglich *adj* & *adv* possible; **ich habe es so gut wie möglich gemacht** I did it as well as I could; **jm ist es (nicht) möglich, etw zu tun** it is (not) possible for sb to do sthg. ◆ **alles Mögliche** *pron* absolutely everything.

möglicherweise *adv* possibly.

Möglichkeit (*pl* **-en**) *die* - **1.** [das Mögliche] possibility; **es besteht die Möglichkeit, dass...** it is possible that...; **nach Möglichkeit** if possible - **2.** [Chance] opportunity. ◆ **Möglichkeiten** *Pl* [Fähigkeiten] capabilities.

möglichst ['mø:klɪçst] *adv* - **1.** [wenn möglich] if possible - **2.** [so viel wie möglich]: **möglichst groß/stark/viel** as big/strong/much as possible.

Mohammedaner, in (*mpl* -, *fpl* **-nen**) *der, die* Muslim.

mohammedanisch *adj* Muslim.

Mohn (*pl* **-e**) *der* - **1.** [Pflanze] poppy - **2.** [Samen] poppy seeds *Pl*.

Mohn|blume *die* poppy.

Möhre (*pl* **-n**) *die* carrot.

Mokka (*pl* **-s**) *der* mocha.

Molekül (*pl* **-e**) *das* molecule.

molk *prät* ▷ **melken**.

Molke *die* whey.

Molkerei (*pl* **-en**) *die* dairy.

Moll *das* minor (key).

mollig *adj* plump.

Moment (*pl* **-e**) ◇ *der* moment; **im Moment** at the moment; **jeden Moment** (at) any moment; **(einen) Moment, bitte!** just a moment, please!; **Moment mal!** *fam* wait a moment! ◇ *das* element.

momentan ◇ *adj* present. ◇ *adv* at the moment.

Monaco *nt* Monaco.

Monarchie (*pl* **-n**) *die* monarchy.

Monat (*pl* **-e**) *der* month; **diesen/nächsten/vorigen Monat** this/next/last month; **sie ist im fünften Monat (schwanger)** she is over four months pregnant.

monatelang ◇ *adj* lasting for months. ◇ *adv* for months.

monatlich *adj* & *adv* monthly.

Monats|karte *die* monthly season ticket.

Mönch (*pl* **-e**) *der* monk.

Mond (*pl* **-e**) *der* moon.

Mond|finsternis *die* eclipse of the moon.

Mond|landung *die* moon landing.

Mond|schein *der* moonlight.

Monitor (*pl* **-en** ODER **-e**) *der* monitor.

Monogramm (*pl* **-e**) *das* monogram.

Monolog (*pl* **-e**) *der* monologue.

Monopol (*pl* **-e**) *das* monopoly; **das Monopol auf etw** *(A)* **haben** to have a monopoly on sthg.

monoton ◇ *adj* monotonous. ◇ *adv* monotonously.

Monster (*pl* -) *das* monster.

Monsun (*pl* **-e**) *der* monsoon.

Montag (*pl* **-e**) *der* Monday; *siehe auch* **Samstag**.

Montage [mɔn'tɑ:ʒə] (*pl* **-n**) *die* - **1.** TECH [Zusammenbau] assembly *(U)*; [Einbau] installation *(U)*; **auf Montage sein** to be away on assembly/installation work - **2.** [Schnitt] editing *(U)* - **3.** KUNST montage.

montags *adv* on Mondays; *siehe auch* **samstags**.

Montblanc [mɔ̃'blɑ̃:] *der* Mont Blanc.

montieren *vt* - **1.** TECH [zusammenbauen] to assemble; [einbauen] to install; [festmachen] to fix - **2.** [schneiden] to edit.

Monument (*pl* **-e**) *das* monument.

monumental ◇ *adj* monumental. ◇ *adv* on a monumental scale.

Moor (*pl* **-e**) *das* bog.

Moos (*pl* **-e**) *das* - **1.** [Pflanze, Pflanzengattung] moss - **2.** *fam* [Geld] dough.

Moped (*pl* **-s**) *das* moped.

Mops (*pl* **Möpse**) *der* - **1.** [Hund] pug (dog) - **2.** *fam fig* [Mensch] roly-poly.

Moral *die* - **1.** [Normen] morals *Pl* - **2.** [Stimmung] morale - **3.** [das Lehrreiche] moral - **4.** [Ethik] morality.

moralisch ◇ *adj* moral. ◇ *adv* morally.

Morast (*pl* **-e**) *der* quagmire.

Morchel (*pl* **-n**) *die* morel.

Mord (*pl* **-e**) *der* murder, homicide *US*; [durch Attentat] assassination; **einen Mord begehen** to commit murder.

Mörder, in (*mpl* -, *fpl* **-nen**) *der, die* murderer; [durch Attentat] assassin.

mörderisch ◇ *adj* - **1.** [lebensgefährlich] deadly; [Tempo] breakneck - **2.** [Verbrechen, Absicht] murderous - **3.** *fam* [groß] terrible. ◇ *adv* - **1.** [steil, schnell] murderously - **2.** *fam* [sehr] terribly.

morgen *adv* - **1.** [am Tag nach heute, zukünftig] tomorrow; **bis morgen!** see you tomorrow!; **morgen früh** tomorrow morning - **2.** [vormittag] morning.

Mọrgen (*pl* -) *der* morning; **am Morgen** in the morning; **gestern/heute Morgen** yesterday/this morning. ◆ **guten Morgen** *interj* good morning!

Mọrgen|grauen *das* dawn.

Mọrgen|rot *das* red dawn sky.

mọrgens *adv* in the morning; [jeden Morgen] every morning; **von morgens bis abends** from dawn till dusk.

mọrgig *adj* [Treffen] tomorrow's; **der morgige Tag** tomorrow.

Mọrphium *das* morphine.

mọrsch *adj* rotten.

mọrsen ◇ *vt* to send in Morse (code). ◇ *vi* to use Morse (code).

Mọ̈rtel (*pl* -) *der* mortar.

Mosaik (*pl* **-e** *ODER* **-en**) *das* mosaic.

Moschee [mɔ'ʃeː] (*pl* **-n**) *die* mosque.

Mosel *die* Moselle.

Mọskau *nt* Moscow.

Mọskauer (*pl* -) ◇ *der* Muscovite. ◇ *adj (unver)* of/from Moscow.

Mọskauerin (*pl* **-nen**) *die* Muscovite.

Moskito (*pl* **-s**) *der* mosquito.

Mọslem (*pl* **-s**) *der* Muslim.

Moslemin (*pl* **-nen**) *die* Muslim.

Mọst (*pl* **-e**) *der* - **1.** [Fruchtsaft] (cloudy) fruit juice - **2.** *Süddt* [Apfelwein] cider.

Motiv (*pl* **-e**) *das* - **1.** [von Handlung] motive - **2.** [von Bild] subject - **3.** [Thema] motif.

motivieren [moti'viːrən] *vt* to motivate; **jn motivieren, etw zu tun** to motivate sb to do sthg.

Motor (*pl* **-toren**), **Motor** (*pl* **-toren**) *der* - **1.** [von Fahrzeug] engine; [von Gerät] motor - **2.** *fig* [Triebfeder] driving force.

Motor|rad *das* motorcycle, motorbike.

Motor|schaden *der* engine trouble *(U)*.

Mọtte (*pl* **-n**) *die* moth.

Mọtto (*pl* **-s**) *das* motto; **unter dem Motto "keine Steuererhöhung" stehen** to have "no tax increases" as its motto.

Möwe (*pl* **-n**) *die* seagull.

Mrd. *abk für* **Milliarde**.

Mụcke (*pl* **-n**) *die* [in Tropen] mosquito; [kleiner] midge, gnat.

Mụcken|stich *der* mosquito bite.

müde ◇ *adj* tired; **einer Sache** *(G)* **müde sein** *geh* to be tired of sthg; **nicht müde werden, etw zu tun** never to tire of doing sthg. ◇ *adv* wearily.

Müdigkeit *die* tiredness.

muffig ◇ *adj* - **1.** [modrig] musty - **2.** *fam* [schlecht gelaunt] grumpy. ◇ *adv*: **muffig riechen** to smell musty.

Mühe (*pl* **-n**) *die* effort; **es macht mir keine Mühe** it's no trouble; **sich** *(D)* **Mühe machen (mit etw)** to go to some trouble (over sthg); **sich** *(D)* **Mühe geben** to make an effort; **gib dir keine Mühe** don't bother; **mit Müh und Not** by the skin of one's teeth.

mühelos ◇ *adj* effortless. ◇ *adv* effortlessly.

mühevoll ◇ *adj* laborious, painstaking. ◇ *adv* laboriously, painstakingly.

Mühle (*pl* **-n**) *die* - **1.** [Mahlwerk - für Getreide] mill; [- für Kaffee] grinder - **2.** [Gebäude] mill - **3.** [Spiel] nine men's morris - **4.** *fam* [Fahrzeug] jalopy, banger *UK*.

mühsam ◇ *adj* laborious. ◇ *adv* laboriously.

mühselig ◇ *adj* [Arbeit, Tun] laborious; [Leben] arduous. ◇ *adv* laboriously.

Mụlde (*pl* **-n**) *die* GEOGR hollow; [Griffmulde] grip.

Mụll (*pl* **-e**) *der* [Material] muslin; [für Verband] gauze.

Mụ̈ll *der* rubbish *UK*, garbage *US*; [radioaktiv] waste; **etw in den Müll werfen** *ODER* **tun** to throw sthg out *ODER* away.

Mụ̈ll|abfuhr *die* - **1.** [Transport] refuse *UK ODER* garbage *US* collection - **2.** [Unternehmen] refuse *UK ODER* garbage *US* collection service.

Mụll|binde *die* gauze dressing.

Mụ̈ll|deponie *die* refuse disposal site.

Mụ̈ll|eimer *der* dustbin *UK*, garbage *ODER* trash can *US*.

Mụ̈ller, in (*mpl* -, *fpl* **-nen**) *der, die* miller.

Mụ̈ll|schlucker *der* rubbish *UK ODER* garbage *US* chute.

Mụ̈ll|tonne *die* dustbin *UK*, garbage *ODER* trash can *US*.

Mụ̈ll|trennung *die separation of household waste for recycling purposes.*

Mụ̈ll|wagen *der* dustbin lorry *UK*, garbage truck *US*.

mụlmig *adj* uncomfortable; **mir wird mulmig** [körperlich] I feel queasy.

mụltikulturell *adj* multicultural.

mụltinational *adj* multinational.

Mụltiplex|kino *das* multiplex (cinema).

multiplizieren *vt*: **etw mit etw multiplizieren** to multiply sthg by sthg.

Mumie ['muːmi̯ə] (*pl* **-n**) *die* mummy.

Mụmm *der (ohne pl) fam* guts *Pl*; **(keinen) Mumm haben** to have (no) guts.

Mụmps *der* MED mumps *(U)*.

Mụ̈nchen *nt* Munich.

Mụnd (*pl* **Mụ̈nder**) *der* mouth; **jn von Mund zu Mund beatmen** to give sb mouth-to-mouth resuscitation; **halt den Mund!** *fam* shut up!

Mụnd|art *die amt* dialect.

mụ̈nden (*perf* **hat/ist gemụ̈ndet**) *vi* - **1.** [einmünden]: **(in etw** *(A)***) münden** [Fluss] to flow (into sthg); [Straße] to lead (to sthg) - **2.** *geh* [enden]: **in etw** *(D)* **münden** [Vorgang] to end in sthg.

Mundlharmonika *die* harmonica, mouth-organ.

mündig *adj* - **1.** [volljährig] of age; **mündig werden** to come of age - **2.** [urteilsfähig] responsible.

mündlich <> *adj* [Vereinbarung, Versprechung] verbal; [Prüfung] oral. <> *adv* verbally.

mundtot *adj*: **jn mundtot machen** to silence sb.

Mündung (*pl* **-en**) *die* - **1.** [von Fluss] mouth; GEOGR estuary - **2.** [von Straße] end - **3.** [von Gewehr] muzzle.

Mundwerk *das fam*: **ein großes Mundwerk haben** to be a bigmouth; **ein loses Mundwerk haben** to be cheeky.

Munition (*pl* **-en**) *die* ammunition.

munkeln <> *vi*: **es wurde schon lange darüber gemunkelt** there had already been rumours about it for some time. <> *vt*: **man munkelt, dass...** it is rumoured that...

Münster (*pl* -) *das* cathedral, minster.

munter <> *adj* - **1.** [wach]: **munter sein** to be (wide) awake - **2.** [lebhaft - Mensch, Tier, Spiel] lively - **3.** [fröhlich] cheerful. <> *adv* cheerfully.

Münze (*pl* **-n**) *die* coin.

münzen *vt* [Geld] to mint; **auf jn/etw gemünzt sein** *fig* to refer to sb/sthg.

Münzfernlsprecher *der amt* pay phone *UK*, pay station *US*.

mürbe *adj* - **1.** [Kuchen, Teig] crumbly; [Fleisch] tender; [Obst] soft - **2.** [Material] rotten, crumbling - **3.** [zermürbt]: **jn mürbe machen** to wear sb down.

Mürbelteig *der* shortcrust pastry.

murmeln *vt* & *vi* to murmur.

murren *vi*: **(über etw** *(A)***) murren** to grumble (about sthg).

mürrisch <> *adj* sullen, surly. <> *adv* in a sullen ODER surly manner.

Mus (*pl* **-e**) *das* puree.

Muschel (*pl* **-n**) *die* - **1.** [Tier] mussel - **2.** [Schale] shell.

Museum [mu'ze:ʊm] (*pl* **Museen**) *das* museum.

Musical ['mju:zik(ə)l] (*pl* **-s**) *das* musical.

Musik (*pl* **-en**) *die* music.

musikalisch <> *adj* musical. <> *adv* musically.

Musiker, in (*mpl* -, *fpl* **-nen**) *der, die* musician.

Musiklunterricht *der (ohne pl)* [Schulfach] music; [Musikstunden] music lessons *Pl*.

musizieren *vi* to make music.

Muskatnuss (*pl* **-nüsse**) *die* nutmeg.

Muskel (*pl* **-n**) *der* muscle.

Muskelkater *der*: **(einen) Muskelkater haben** to be stiff.

Muskulatur (*pl* **-en**) *die* muscles *Pl*.

muskulös *adj* muscular.

Müsli (*pl* -) *das* muesli.

muss *präs* ▷ **müssen**.

Muss *das (ohne pl)* necessity, must.

Muße *die* leisure; **Zeit und Muße haben, etw zu tun** to have enough time to do sthg at one's leisure.

müssen (*präs* **muss**, *prät* **musste**, *perf* **hat gemusst** ODER **müssen**) <> *aux (perf hat müssen)* - **1.** [gezwungen sein] must; **etw tun müssen** to have to do sthg; **du musst aufstehen** you must get up; **sie musste lachen/niesen** she had to laugh/sneeze; **etw nicht tun müssen** not to need to do sthg - **2.** [nötig sein]: **der Brief muss noch heute weg** the letter has to go today; **muss das sein?** is that really necessary? - **3.** [wahrscheinlich sein]: **du musst Hunger haben nach der langen Reise** you must be hungry after your long journey; **das müsste alles sein** that should be all. <> *vi (perf hat gemusst)* to have to; **ich muss ins Büro (gehen)** I have to go to the office; **ich muss mal** *fam* I need the toilet.

musste *prät* ▷ **müssen**.

Muster (*pl* -) *das* - **1.** [Vorlage, Beispiel] model; **ein Muster an etw** *(D)* a model of sthg - **2.** [Musterung] pattern - **3.** [Warenprobe] sample.

mustern *vt* - **1.** [betrachten] to study, to scrutinize - **2.** [Wehrpflichtigen] to inspect.

Musterung (*pl* **-en**) *die* - **1.** [von Wehrpflichtigen] inspection - **2.** [Betrachtung] scrutiny.

Mut *der* courage; **jm Mut machen** to encourage sb. ◆ **nur Mut** *interj* chin up!

mutig <> *adj* brave, courageous. <> *adv* bravely, courageously.

mutmaßlich *adj* suspected.

Mutter (*pl* **Mütter** ODER **-n**) *die* - **1.** *(pl Mütter)* [gen] mother - **2.** *(pl Muttern)* [von Schraube] nut.

mütterlich <> *adj* [Liebe, Frau] motherly; [Eigenschaft, Erbe] maternal. <> *adv* [fürsorgend] in a motherly fashion.

mütterlicherseits *adv* on one's mother's side.

Mutterlmal *das* mole.

Mutterlsprache *die* mother tongue, native language.

Mutterltag *der* Mother's Day.

mutwillig <> *adj* wilful. <> *adv* wilfully.

Mütze (*pl* **-n**) *die* cap; [aus Wolle] hat.

MwSt. (*abk für* **Mehrwertsteuer**) VAT *UK*, sales tax *US*.

Mythos (*pl* **Mythen**) *der* myth; **er ist schon jetzt ein Mythos** he is already a legend.

N

n (*pl* - ODER **-s**), **N** (*pl* - ODER **-s**) [ɛn] *das* n, N. ◆ **N** (*abk für* **Nord**) N.

nạ *interj* well?; **na, wie gehts?** so how's it going, then?; **na los, mach schon!** well go on then, do it!; **na, lass das sein!** hey, leave that alone! ◆ **na also** *interj* there you are! ◆ **na gut** *interj* all right, then! ◆ **na ja** *interj* well! ◆ **na und** *interj*: **na und?** so (what)?

Nabel (*pl* -) *der* navel.

Nabel|schnur *die* umbilical cord.

nach *präp (+ D)* - **1.** [zeitlich, zur Angabe einer Reihenfolge] after; **nach dem Essen** after the meal; **fünf (Minuten) nach drei** five (minutes) past three *UK*, five (minutes) after three *US*; **nach Ihnen!** after you! - **2.** [räumlich] to; **nach Frankfurt** to Frankfurt; **nach Hause gehen** to go home; **nach Süden** south, southwards; **nach links/rechts abbiegen** to turn left/right - **3.** [gemäß] according to; **nach Angaben der Polizei** according to the police - **4.** [stellt Bezug her]: **seinem Akzent nach ist er kein Deutscher** judging by his accent, he is not German; **meiner Meinung nach** in my opinion. ◆ **nach und nach** *adv* little by little. ◆ **nach wie vor** *adv* as before.

nach|ahmen *vt* to imitate, to copy.

Nạchbar, in (*mpl* **-n**, *fpl* **-nen**) *der, die* neighbour.

Nạchbarschaft *die* neighbourhood.

nach|bessern *vt* [Vorschlag, Entwurf] to amend; [Preisangebot] to raise; **sie musste ihre Arbeit nachbessern** she had to redo the bits she had got wrong.

nachdem *konj* after. ◆ **je nachdem** *konj* depending on.

nach|denken *vi (unreg)*: **(über jn/etw) nachdenken** to think (about sb/sthg).

nachdenklich ◇ *adj* thoughtful, pensive; **jn nachdenklich machen** to set sb thinking. ◇ *adv* thoughtfully, pensively.

Nachdruck (*pl* **-e**) *der* - **1.** [Eindringlichkeit] emphasis; **einer Sache** *(D)* **Nachdruck verleihen** to reinforce sthg; **mit Nachdruck** emphatically - **2.** [Nachdrucken - von Buch] reprinting; [- von Druck] reproduction - **3.** [Ausgabe] reprint.

nachdrücklich ◇ *adj* emphatic, forceful. ◇ *adv* emphatically.

nach|eifern *vi*: **jm (in etw** *(D)***) nacheifern** to seek to emulate sb (in sthg).

nacheinạnder *adv* - **1.** [der Reihe nach] one after the other - **2.** [gegenseitig] one another.

nach|empfinden *vt (unreg)* [nachfühlen]: **js Schmerz nachempfinden** to share sb's pain; **ich kann dir nachempfinden, wie du dich jetzt fühlst** I can understand how you feel.

Nacher|zählung *die* retelling *(in one's own words)*.

Nachfolge *die* succession.

nach|folgen (*perf* **ist nachgefolgt**) *vi* - **1.** [Nachfolge antreten]: **jm (in einem Amt) nachfolgen** to succeed sb (in an office) - **2.** [nachkommen] to follow; **das nachfolgende Fahrzeug** the vehicle behind.

Nachfolger, in (*mpl* -, *fpl* **-nen**) *der, die* successor.

nach|forschen *vi* to make enquiries; **jm/einer Sache nachforschen** *geh* to investigate sb/sthg.

Nachfrage *die* WIRTSCH demand.

nach|fragen *vi* - **1.** [nachhaken] to ask repeatedly - **2.** [fragen] to enquire.

nach|füllen *vt* - **1.** [füllen] to refill - **2.** [nachgießen] to top up with.

nach|geben *vi (unreg)* - **1.** [bei Streit] to give in - **2.** [Brücke, Boden] to give way; [Preise, Kurse] to fall.

nach|gehen (*perf* **ist nachgegangen**) *vi (unreg)* - **1.** [folgen]: **jm/einer Sache nachgehen** to follow sb/sthg - **2.** [etw prüfen]: **einer Sache** *(D)* **nachgehen** to look into sthg - **3.** [Uhr] to be slow; **meine Uhr geht zehn Minuten nach** my watch is ten minutes slow - **4.** [nachwirken]: **jm nachgehen** to stick in sb's mind - **5.** [sich widmen]: **einer Sache** *(D)* **nachgehen** to pursue sthg.

Nachgeschmack *der* aftertaste.

nachgiebig *adj* compliant; [Eltern] indulgent.

nach|haken *vi* to return to the same question.

nachhaltig ◇ *adj* lasting. ◇ *adv*: **nachhaltig wirken** to have a lasting effect.

nach|hängen *vi (unreg)* - **1.** [sich erinnern]: **einer Sache** *(D)* **nachhängen** to dwell on sthg - **2.** *fam* [zurückliegen]: **in etw** *(D)* **nachhängen** to lag behind in sthg.

Nachhause|weg *der* way home.

nach|helfen *vi (unreg)* - **1.** [antreiben]: **bei jm nachhelfen müssen** to have to chivvy sb along - **2.** [helfen]: **(jm) nachhelfen** to lend (sb) a hand.

nachher, nachher *adv* - **1.** [später] later (on) - **2.** [anschließend] afterwards. ◆ **bis nachher** *interj* see you later!

Nachhilfe *die* extra tuition.

Nachhinein *adv*: **im Nachhinein** with hindsight; **im Nachhinein zeigte sich, dass er gelogen hatte** it later turned out that he had lied.

nach|holen *vt* - **1.** [nachträglich machen]: **etw nachholen** [Versäumtes] to catch up on sthg;

[Prüfung] to do sthg later - **2.** [nachziehen lassen]: **er holte seine Familie nach** his family joined him later.

nach|jagen (*perf* **ist nachgejagt**) *vi*: **jm/einer Sache nachjagen** to chase after sb/sthg.

Nachkomme (*pl* **-n**) *der* descendant.

nach|kommen (*perf* **ist nachgekommen**) *vi (unreg)* - **1.** [später kommen] to come (along) later - **2.** *geh* [entsprechen]: **einer Sache** *(D)* **nachkommen** to comply with sthg.

Nachkriegs|zeit *die* post-war period.

nach|lassen *(unreg)* ◇ *vi* [Schmerz, Spannung] to ease; [Regen] to ease off; [Augen, Gehör] to fail; [Geschäft, Anstrengung] to slacken; [Qualität] to drop off. ◇ *vt* [Preis]: **jm 10% nachlassen** to give sb a 10% discount.

nachlässig ◇ *adj* careless. ◇ *adv* carelessly.

nach|laufen (*perf* **ist nachgelaufen**) *vi (unreg)*: **jm/einer Sache nachlaufen** [laufen nach] to run after sb/sthg; [folgen] to follow sb/sthg; *fam* [sich bemühen um] to pursue sb/sthg.

nach|machen *vt* - **1.** [nachahmen, kopieren] to copy; [nachäffen] to mimic; [fälschen] to forge; **jm etw nachmachen** to copy sthg off sb; **etw nachmachen lassen** to have sthg copied - **2.** [nachholen]: **etw** *(A)* **nachmachen** to catch up on sthg later.

Nach|mittag *der* afternoon; **am Nachmittag** in the afternoon; **gestern/heute/morgen Nachmittag** yesterday/this/tomorrow afternoon; **Dienstag Nachmittag** on Tuesday afternoon.

nachmittags *adv* in the afternoon.

Nachnahme (*pl* **-n**) *die*: **etw als Nachnahme versenden** to send sthg cash on delivery; **per** ODER **gegen Nachnahme** cash on delivery.

Nach|name *der* surname.

nach|prüfen *vt* - **1.** [kontrollieren] to check - **2.** [erneut prüfen] to re-examine.

nach|rechnen ◇ *vt* - **1.** [nochmals rechnen] to check - **2.** [nachzählen] to work out. ◇ *vi* - **1.** [nochmals rechnen] to check - **2.** [nachzählen] to work it out.

Nach|rede *die*: **üble Nachrede** slander.

Nachricht (*pl* **-en**) *die* [Neuigkeit] piece of news; [Mitteilung] message; **eine gute Nachricht haben** to have (some) good news; **die Nachricht, dass...** the news that...; **eine Nachricht von jm** [Neuigkeiten] news of sb; [Mitteilung] a message from sb. ◆ **Nachrichten** *Pl*: **die Nachrichten** the news *(sg)*.

Nachrichten|agentur *die* news agency.

Nachrichten|sprecher, **in** *der, die* newsreader.

nach|rücken (*perf* **ist nachgerückt**) *vi* to move up.

Nach|ruf *der* obituary.

nach|rüsten ◇ *vt* EDV to upgrade. ◇ *vi* MIL to rearm.

nach|sagen *vt* [behaupten]: **jm etw nachsagen** to say sthg of sb.

Nachsaison *die* low season.

nach|schicken *vt* to forward.

Nach|schlag *der* second helping.

nach|schlagen (*perf* **hat/ist nachgeschlagen**) *(unreg)* ◇ *vi* - **1.** *(hat)* [nachlesen]: **in einem Wörterbuch nachschlagen** to consult a dictionary - **2.** *(ist)* [ähneln]: **jm nachschlagen** to take after sb. ◇ *vt (hat)* [nachlesen] to look up.

Nachschlage|werk *das* reference work.

Nach|schlüssel *der* duplicate key.

Nachschub *der (ohne pl)* supplies *Pl*.

nach|sehen *(unreg)* ◇ *vi* - **1.** [hinterhersehen]: **jm/einer Sache nachsehen** to gaze after sb/sthg - **2.** [suchen] to look - **3.** [prüfen] to check - **4.** [nachschlagen]: **in etw** *(D)* **nachsehen** to consult sthg. ◇ *vt* - **1.** [nachschlagen]: **etw in etw** *(D)* **nachsehen** to look sthg up in sthg - **2.** [prüfen] to check - **3.** [verzeihen]: **jm seine Fehler nachsehen** to overlook sb's mistakes.

Nachsehen *das*: **das Nachsehen haben** [unterlegen sein] to come off badly; [etw nicht bekommen] to be left empty-handed.

nach|senden *vt (unreg)* to forward.

nach|sitzen *vi (unreg)*: **nachsitzen müssen** to get detention.

Nach|speise *die* dessert.

Nach|spiel *das* [Folgen] consequences *Pl*; [Theaterstück] epilogue; **es wird ein Nachspiel haben** it will have consequences.

nach|sprechen *vt* & *vi (unreg)* to repeat.

nächstbeste, **r**, **s** *adj*: **bei der nächstbesten Gelegenheit** at the first available opportunity. ◆ **Nächstbeste** *der, die, das*: **der/die/das Nächstbeste** *fig* the first available one.

nächste, **r**, **s** ['nɛːçstə, ɐ, əs] *adj* - **1.** [nah] nearest, closest - **2.** [folgend] next; **der Nächste bitte!** next, please!; **wie heißt die nächste Haltestelle?** what's the next stop?; **die nächste Straße links** the next road on the left.

Nächsten|liebe ['nɛːçstənliːbə] *die* charity.

nächstens ['nɛːçstn̩s] *adv* shortly, soon.

nächstliegend ['nɛːçstliːgn̩t] *adj* most obvious.

nächstmöglich ['nɛːçstmøːklɪç] *adj* next possible.

Nacht (*pl* **Nächte**) *die* night; **gestern/morgen Nacht** last/tomorrow night; **heute Nacht** tonight. ◆ **gute Nacht** *interj* good night!

Nach|teil *der* disadvantage; **zu js Nachteil** to sb's disadvantage.

nächtelang ◇ *adj* lasting several nights. ◇ *adv* night after night.

Nacht|frost *der* night frost.

Nacht|hemd *das* [für Frauen] nightdress; [für Männer] nightshirt.

Nachtigall (*pl* **-en**) *die* nightingale.

Nachtisch *der (ohne pl)* dessert.

nạchtlich *adj* nocturnal; [Stille] of the night.

nach|tragen *vt (unreg)* - **1.** [übel nehmen]: **jm etw nachtragen** to hold sthg against sb - **2.** [ergänzen] to add - **3.** [hinterhertragen]: **jm etw nachtragen** to follow behind sb carrying sthg.

nachträglich ◇ *adj* [Glückwunsch] belated; [Beweis] subsequent. ◇ *adv* [beglückwünschen] belatedly; [beweisen] subsequently.

nach|trauern *vi*: **jm/einer Sache nachtrauern** to miss sb/sthg.

Nạcht|ruhe *die* night's sleep.

nachts *adv* at night; **um vier Uhr nachts** at four in the morning.

Nạcht|schicht *die* night shift.

Nạcht|wache *die* - **1.** [Dienst] night watch - **2.** [Person] person on night watch.

Nạcht|wächter, in *der, die* night watchman (-woman *die*).

nach|vollziehen *vt (unreg)* to comprehend.

nach|wachsen ['na:xvaksn̩] (*perf* **ist nachgewachsen**) *vi (unreg)* to grow again.

Nachweis (*pl* **-e**) *der* proof *(U)*.

nach|weisen *vt (unreg)* - **1.** [Fehler] to prove - **2.** [Substanz] to detect.

Nach|welt *die* posterity.

Nach|wirkung *die* aftereffect.

Nach|wuchs ['na:xvu:ks] *der* - **1.** [Kinder] offspring - **2.** [im Beruf]: **künstlerischer/wissenschaftlicher Nachwuchs** rising generation of artists/scientists; **es fehlt an Nachwuchs** there is a lack of new blood.

nach|zahlen ◇ *vi* to pay the extra. ◇ *vt*: **drei Euro nachzahlen** to pay three euros extra.

nach|zählen *vt* to check.

Nạcken (*pl* -) *der* back ODER nape of the neck; **ihm sitzt die Angst im Nacken** he is afraid.

nạckt ◇ *adj* - **1.** [ohne Kleider/Fell] naked; [Körperteil] bare - **2.** [bloß] bare; **die nackte Wahrheit** the plain truth; **nackte Tatsachen** hard facts. ◇ *adv* naked.

Nadel (*pl* **-n**) *die* [gen] needle; [Stecknadel] pin.

Nadel|baum *der* conifer.

Nadel|öhr *das* - **1.** [von Nadeln] eye - **2.** *fig* [enge Stelle] bottleneck.

Nadel|wald *der* coniferous forest.

Nagel (*pl* **Nägel**) *der* nail; **den Nagel auf den Kopf treffen** to hit the nail on the head; **etw an den Nagel hängen** to give sthg up; **sich *(D)* etw unter den Nagel reißen** *fam abw* to pinch sthg for o.s.

Nagel|feile *die* nail file.

Nagel|lack *der* nail varnish.

nageln *vt* to nail; [Knochen] to pin.

nagelneu *adj* brand-new.

nagen ◇ *vi* - **1.** [knabbern]: **an etw *(D)* nagen** to gnaw at sthg - **2.** [jn beunruhigen]: **an jm nagen** [Zweifel] to prey on sb; [Hunger] to gnaw at sb. ◇ *vt* to gnaw.

Nage|tier *das* rodent.

nah (*kompar* **näher**, *superl* **nächste**), **nahe** (*kompar* **näher**, *superl* **nächste**) ◇ *adj* near; **nah an/bei jm/etw** close to ODER near sb/sthg; **zu nah** too close; **in naher Zukunft** in the near future; **den Tränen/dem Wahnsinn nah sein** to be on the verge of tears/madness; **nah daran sein, etw zu tun** to be on the point ODER verge of doing sthg. ◇ *adv* - **1.** [räumlich]: **eine nahe gelegene Stadt** a nearby town; **komm mir nicht zu nahe!** keep your distance!; **von nahem** from close up; **von nah und fern** from near and far - **2.** [vertraut] closely; **nahe verwandt** closely related; **jm zu nah treten** *fig* to offend sb.

Nah|aufnahme *die* close-up.

Nähe *die* - **1.** [räumlich, zeitlich] closeness; **in meiner Nähe** near me; **aus der Nähe** from close-up; **in der Nähe** nearby; **in greifbarer Nähe** within reach - **2.** [emotional] closeness, intimacy; **js Nähe suchen** to seek sb's company.

nahe gehen (*perf* **ist nahe gegangen**) *vi (unreg)*: **jm nahe gehen** to affect sb deeply.

nahe legen *vt* - **1.** [Verdacht, Vermutung] to give rise to - **2.** [jn auffordern]: **jm nahe legen, etw zu tun** to advise sb to do sthg.

nahe liegen *vi (unreg)* [Idee, Plan] to suggest itself; **der Verdacht/die Vermutung liegt nahe, dass...** it seems reasonable to suspect/suppose that...

nähen ◇ *vt* - **1.** [Kleid, Hose] to make - **2.** [Riss] to mend - **3.** [Wunde] to stitch. ◇ *vi* [schneidern] to sew.

Nahe Ọsten *der*: **der Nahe Osten** the Middle East.

näher ◇ *adj* - **1.** [Komparativ von nahe] closer, nearer - **2.** [Umstände, Angaben] more precise. ◇ *adv* - **1.** [Komparativ von nahe] closer, nearer - **2.** [betrachten] more closely; [erklären] more precisely.

Naherholungs|gebiet *das amt area close to a town, offering recreational facilities.*

näher kommen (*perf* **ist näher gekommen**) *vi (unreg)* - **1.** [nahe kommen]: **jm näher kommen** to get to know sb better - **2.** [entsprechen]: **einer Sache *(D)* näher kommen** to get closer to sthg. ◆ **sich näher kommen** *ref* [sich nahe kommen] to get to know one another better.

nähern ◆ **sich nähern** *ref* to approach.

nahe stehen *vi (unreg)*: **sich/jm nahe stehen** to be close to one another/sb.

nahe stehend *adj* - **1.**: **jm nahe stehend** [persönlich] close to sb; **einer Sache *(D)* nahe stehend** [politisch] sympathetic to sthg - **2.** [in der Nähe] nearby.

nahezu *adv* nearly, almost.

nahm *prät* ▷ **nehmen**.

Näh|maschine *die* sewing machine.

Näh|nadel *die* (sewing) needle.

Nahost *(ohne Artikel)* the Middle East.

nahrhaft *adj* nourishing, nutritious.

Nähr|stoff *der* nutrient.

Nahrung *die* food; **feste Nahrung** solids *Pl*.

Nahrungs|mittel *das* food.

Naht (*pl* **Nähte**) *die* - **1.** [an Kleidung] seam; **aus allen Nähten platzen** *fig* to burst at the seams - **2.** [in der Medizin] suture - **3.** [in der Technik] join.

nahtlos ◇ *adj* seamless; **nahtlose Bräune** all-over tan. ◇ *adv* [ununterbrochen] seamlessly.

Nahverkehr *der* local traffic.

Nähzeug *das (ohne pl)* sewing things *Pl*.

naiv [na'i:f] ◇ *adj* naive. ◇ *adv* naively.

Naivität [naivi'tɛ:t] *die* naivety.

Name (*pl* **-n**) *der* name; **im Namen von jm** in the name of sb; **jn/etw (nur) dem Namen nach kennen** to know sb/sthg (only) by name.

namhaft *adj* renowned.

Namibia *nt* Namibia.

nämlich *adv* because; **zwei von ihnen, nämlich Anna und Berthold** two of them, namely Anna and Berthold; **übermorgen, nämlich am Donnerstag** the day after tomorrow, that is, on Thursday; **wir treffen uns jetzt nämlich am Freitag** we'll now actually be meeting on Friday.

nanu *interj* well (I never)!

Napf (*pl* **Näpfe**) *der* dish, bowl.

Narbe (*pl* **-n**) *die* scar.

narbig *adj* scarred.

Narkose (*pl* **-n**) *die* anaesthetic.

närrisch ◇ *adj* - **1.** [verrückt] mad, crazy; **das närrische Treiben** [im Karneval] carnival festivities - **2.** *fam* [unglaublich] terrific. ◇ *adv* - **1.** [verrückt]: **sich närrisch gebärden** to act crazy - **2.** *fam* [unglaublich] terribly.

Narzisse (*pl* **-n**) *die* narcissus.

naschen *vt* & *vi* to nibble.

Nase (*pl* **-n**) *die* nose; **sich** *(D)* **die Nase putzen** to blow one's nose; **jm läuft die Nase** sb's nose is running; **über etw die Nase rümpfen** to turn one's nose up at sthg; **jn an der Nase herumführen** to pull the wool over sb's eyes.

Nasen|bluten *das (ohne pl)* nosebleed.

Nasen|loch *das* nostril.

Nashorn (*pl* **-hörner**) *das* rhinoceros.

nass ◇ *adj* wet. ◇ *adv*: **nass machen** to wet.

Nässe *die* wet; **vor Nässe triefen** to be dripping wet.

Nation (*pl* **-en**) *die* nation.

national ◇ *adj* national. ◇ *adv*: **national denken** to think in national terms.

National|feier|tag *der* national day.

National|hymne *die* national anthem.

Nationalismus *der* nationalism.

nationalistisch ◇ *adj* nationalistic. ◇ *adv*: **nationalistisch orientiert** with nationalistic leanings.

Nationalität (*pl* **-en**) *die* nationality.

Nationalsozialismus *der* National Socialism, Nazism.

NATO ['na:to:] (*abk für* **North Atlantic Treaty Organization**) *die* NATO.

Natron *das* CHEM soda.

Natur (*pl* **-en**) *die* nature; **Tiere in der freien Natur** animals in the wild; **hinaus in die Natur fahren** to go out into the countryside. ◆ **von Natur aus** *adv* by nature.

Naturalien [natu'ra:li̯ən] *Pl*: **in Naturalien bezahlen** to pay in kind.

Naturalismus *der* naturalism.

naturbelassen *adj* natural; [Obst, Gemüse] organic.

Natur|ereignis *das* natural phenomenon.

naturgemäß ◇ *adj* natural. ◇ *adv* - **1.** [gemäß der Natur] in accordance with natural laws - **2.** [grundsätzlich] by its very nature.

naturgetreu ◇ *adj* [Abbildung] lifelike. ◇ *adv* in a lifelike manner.

Naturheilkunde *die* naturopathy.

natürlich ◇ *adj* natural. ◇ *adv* - **1.** [nicht künstlich] naturally - **2.** [selbstverständlich] of course, naturally; **natürlich war er wieder zu spät** naturally he was late again; **natürlich stimmt das, aber...** of course that's correct but... ◇ *interj* (but) of course!

naturrein *adj* pure.

Natur|schutz *der* nature conservation; **unter Naturschutz stehen** to be protected.

Naturschutz|gebiet *das* nature reserve.

Natur|wissenschaft *die* natural science.

Natur|wissenschaftler, in *der, die* scientist.

Nazi (*pl* **-s**) *der abw* Nazi.

n. Chr. (*abk für* **nach Christus**) AD.

NDR [ɛnýde:'ɛr] (*abk für* **Norddeutscher Rundfunk**) *der North German Radio.*

Neapel *nt* Naples.

Nebel (*pl* -) *der* fog; **leichter Nebel** mist.

nebelig = **neblig**.

Nebel|scheinwerfer *der* fog lamp.

Nebel|schwaden *Pl* swathes of mist.

neben *präp* - **1.** *(+ D)* [lokal] beside, next to - **2.** *(+ D)* [außer] apart from, as well as - **3.** *(+ D)* [verglichen mit] compared to ODER with - **4.** *(+ A)* beside, next to.

nebenan *adv* next door.

nebenbei *adv* - **1.** [außerdem] in addition, as well; **etw nebenbei erledigen** to do sthg on the side - **2.** [beiläufig] in passing; **nebenbei bemerkt** by the way.

nebenberuflich ◇ *adj*: **nebenberufliche Tätigkeit** second job. ◇ *adv*: **nebenberuflich tätig sein** to have a second job.

nebeneinander *adv* - **1.** [neben jm/etw] next to each other - **2.** [gleichzeitig] simultaneously.

Neben|fach *das* SCHULE subsidiary subject.

Nebenfluss (*pl* **-flüsse**) *der* tributary.

Neben|geräusch *das* background noise.

nebenher *adv* in addition, as well; **nebenher arbeiten** to work on the side.

Neben|job *der* second job.

Neben|kosten *Pl* - **1.** [bei Miete] additional charges - **2.** [zusätzliche Auslagen] additional costs.

Neben|rolle *die* minor part.

Neben|sache *die* minor issue.

nebensächlich *adj* of secondary importance.

Neben|satz *der* GRAMM subordinate clause.

Neben|straße *die* side street.

neblig, nebelig *adj* foggy; **leicht neblig** misty.

necken *vt* to tease; **jn mit jm/etw necken** to tease sb about sb/sthg. ◆ **sich necken** *ref* to tease each other.

neckisch *adj* - **1.** [verschmitzt] teasing - **2.** [frech] coquettish.

Neffe (*pl* **-n**) *der* nephew.

negativ ◇ *adj* negative. ◇ *adv* negatively; **jm/etw negativ beeinflussen** to have a negative influence on sb/sthg.

Negativ (*pl* **-e**) *das* negative.

Neger, in (*mpl* **-**, *fpl* **-nen**) *der, die abw* negro (negress *die*).

nehmen (*präs* **nimmt**, *prät* **nahm**, *perf* **hat genommen**) *vt* - **1.** [gen] to take; **für etw fünf Euro nehmen** to charge five euros for sthg; **ich nehme ein Omelett** I'll have an omelette; **sich** *(D)* **etw nehmen** to help o.s. to sthg; **jn/etw für voll nehmen** to take sb/sthg seriously; **es leicht/schwer nehmen** to take it lightly/hard; **wie mans nimmt** it depends (how you look at it); **etw zu sich nehmen** [Nahrung] to take sthg, to eat sthg; **etw an sich** *(A)* **nehmen** to look after sthg; **etw auf sich** *(A)* **nehmen** to take sthg on - **2.** [wegnehmen] to take away; **jm den Glauben/die Illusionen nehmen** to destroy sb's faith/illusions; **jm seine/ihre Freiheit nehmen** to deprive sb of his/her freedom - **3.** [einstellen] to take on - **4.** [verwenden] to use; **den Zug nehmen** to take the train; **sich** *(D)* **einen Anwalt nehmen** to get o.s. a lawyer.

Neid *der* envy.

neidisch ◇ *adj* envious. ◇ *adv* enviously.

neigen ◇ *vi*: **zu etw neigen** [tendieren] to have a tendency ODER be inclined to sthg; [anfällig sein] to be prone to sthg. ◇ *vt* [beugen - Körper] to bend; [- Kopf] to bow. ◆ **sich neigen** *ref* [sich beugen - Gegenstand] to bend; [- Mensch] to lean.

Neigung (*pl* **-en**) *die* - **1.** [Veranlagung] inclination; **künstlerische Neigungen** artistic leanings - **2.** *(ohne pl)* [Anfälligsein] susceptibility - **3.** *(ohne pl)* [Tendenz] tendency - **4.** [von Linie, Fläche] inclination.

nein *adv* no; **nein, danke!** no thank you!; **regnet es? - ich glaube nein** is it raining? - I don't think so; **aber nein!** certainly not!; **zu etw nein sagen** to say no to sthg; **nein so was!** well I never!

Nektar (*pl* **-e**) *der* - **1.** [Pflanzensaft] nectar *(U)* - **2.** [Getränk] fruit drink.

Nelke (*pl* **-n**) *die* - **1.** [Blume] carnation - **2.** [Gewürz] clove.

nennen (*prät* **nannte**, *perf* **hat genannt**) *vt* - **1.** [benennen, bezeichnen] to call - **2.** [anführen] to name; [Adresse, Name] to give. ◆ **sich nennen** *ref* - **1.** [heißen] to be called - **2.** [sich bezeichnen] to call o.s.

nennenswert ◇ *adj* significant. ◇ *adv* significantly.

Nenner (*pl* **-**) *der* MATH denominator.

Neon *das* CHEM neon.

Neon|licht (*pl* **-er**) *das* neon light.

Nerv (*pl* **-en**) *der* nerve. ◆ **Nerven** *Pl* nerves; **die Nerven verlieren/behalten** to lose/keep one's cool; **jm auf die Nerven gehen** ODER **fallen** to get on sb's nerves.

Nervenzusammen|bruch *der* nervous breakdown.

nervlich ◇ *adj* nervous. ◇ *adv*: **nervlich völlig am Ende sein** to be a nervous wreck.

nervös ◇ *adj* nervous; **jn nervös machen** to make sb nervous. ◇ *adv* nervously.

Nervosität *die* nervousness.

Nerz (*pl* **-e**) *der* - **1.** [Pelz] mink coat - **2.** [Tier] mink.

Nest (*pl* **-er**) *das* - **1.** [von Vögeln] nest - **2.** *fam abw* [Ortschaft] little place; **ein trostloses Nest** a miserable hole - **3.** *fam* [Bett] bed.

nett ◇ *adj* nice; **wären Sie so nett mir zu helfen?** would you mind helping me?; **eine nette Summe** a tidy sum; **das ist ja eine nette Bescherung!** what a nice mess! ◇ *adv* - **1.** [ansprechend] nicely; **sich nett unterhalten** to have a nice chat - **2.** *fam* [ziemlich]: **ganz nett verdienen** to earn pretty well.

netterweise *adv* kindly.

netto *adv* net.

Netz (*pl* **-e**) *das* - **1.** [zum Fischen, für Haare, im Sport] net; **jm ins Netz gehen** *fig* [gefasst werden] to fall into sb's trap - **2.** [System] network; [Strom] grid; [Internet] Web, Net; **ins Netz ge-**

hen to go on the Web - **3.** [für Akrobaten] safety net - **4.** [von Spinnen] web - **5.** [Einkaufstasche] string bag.

Netz|haut *die* retina.

neu <> *adj* - **1.** [gen] new; **das ist mir neu** that's news to me; **ich bin hier neu** I'm new here - **2.** [erneuert] fresh; **eine neue Flasche holen** to fetch another bottle - **3.** [aktuell]: **die neuesten Nachrichten** the latest news; **was gibts Neues?** what's new?; **seit neuestem** just lately *ODER* recently. <> *adv* newly; **sie sind neu eingezogen** they have just (recently) moved in; **neu anfangen** to start (all over) again; **etw noch mal neu machen** to redo sthg; **neu streichen** to repaint. ◆ **aufs Neue** *adv* again. ◆ **von neuem** *adv* again.

neuartig *adj* new; **ein neuartiges Produkt** a new kind of product.

Neubau (*pl* **-ten**) *der* new building.

neuerdings *adv* recently, lately.

Neuerung (*pl* **-en**) *die* innovation; **Neuerungen einführen** to make changes.

Neugier, Neugierde *die* curiosity.

neugierig <> *adj* inquisitive; **sie ist neugierig, ob...** she is curious to see whether... <> *adv* inquisitively.

Neuheit (*pl* **-en**) *die* - **1.** [Produkt] innovation - **2.** [Originalität] innovativeness - **3.** [Neusein] newness.

Neuigkeit (*pl* **-en**) *die* news *(U)*; **Neuigkeiten** news; **ich habe gute Neuigkeiten** I have some good news.

Neu|jahr *(ohne Artikel)* New Year. ◆ **prost Neujahr** *interj* Happy New Year!

neulich *adv* recently.

Neuling (*pl* **-e**) *der* novice.

Neu|mond *der* new moon.

neun *num* nine; *siehe auch* **sechs**.

Neun (*pl* **-en**) *die* nine; *siehe auch* **Sechs**.

neunfach <> *adj* ninefold. <> *adv* nine times.

neunhundert *num* nine hundred.

neunmal *adv* nine times.

neuntausend *num* nine thousand.

neunte, r, s *adj* ninth; *siehe auch* **sechste**.

Neunte (*pl* **-n**) *der, die, das* ninth; *siehe auch* **Sechste**.

neuntel *adj (unver)* ninth; *siehe auch* **sechstel**.

Neuntel (*pl* -) *das* ninth; *siehe auch* **Sechstel**.

neunzehn *num* nineteen; *siehe auch* **sechs**.

Neunzehn (*pl* **-en**) *die* nineteen; *siehe auch* **Sechs**.

neunzig *num* ninety; *siehe auch* **sechs**.

Neunzig *die* ninety; *siehe auch* **Sechs**.

Neunzigerjahre, neunziger Jahre *Pl*: **die Neunzigerjahre** the nineties.

neureich *adj abw* nouveau riche.

Neurose (*pl* **-n**) *die* neurosis.

neurotisch *adj* neurotic.

Neuseeland *nt* New Zealand.

neusprachlich *adj* ▷ **Gymnasium**.

neutral <> *adj* neutral. <> *adv* neutrally.

Neutralität *die* neutrality.

Neutron (*pl* **-en**) *das* neutron.

Neutrum (*pl* **Neutra** *ODER* **Neutren**) *das* - **1.** GRAMM neuter - **2.** *abw* [Mensch] asexual creature.

neuwertig *adj* nearly new.

Neu|zeit *die (ohne pl)* modern times *Pl*.

Newsgroup (*pl* **-s**) *die* EDV newsgroup.

Nicaragua *nt* Nicaragua.

nicht <> *adv* - **1.** [gen] not; **sie raucht nicht** she doesn't smoke; **sie mag kein Marzipan - ich auch nicht** she doesn't like marzipan - neither do I; **warum nicht?** why not? - **2.** [als Bestätigungsfrage]: **der Film war großartig, nicht wahr?** the film was great, wasn't it?; **du wusstest es schon länger, nicht (wahr)?** you've known for a while, haven't you?; **ist das nicht schön?** isn't that nice? - **3.** [verstärkend]: **was habe ich nicht alles für dich getan!** all the things I've done for you! <> *konj*: **nicht dass ich...** it's not that I...; **nicht nur..., sondern auch...** not only..., but also... ◆ **nicht einmal** *adv* not even; **er kann nicht einmal Englisch** he can't even speak English.

Nichte (*pl* **-n**) *die* niece.

Nicht|raucher *der* - **1.** [Person] non-smoker - **2.** [Abteil] no-smoking compartment.

Nicht|raucherin *die* non-smoker.

nichts *pron* nothing; **ich weiß nichts darüber** I don't know anything about it; **das macht nichts** *fig* it doesn't matter; **nichts zu danken** don't mention it; **das ist nichts für dich** it's not your kind of thing. ◆ **nichts als** *pron* nothing but. ◆ **nichts anderes** *pron* nothing else. ◆ **nichts da** *interj fam* no way!

nichts ahnend <> *adj* unsuspecting. <> *adv* unsuspectingly.

Nicht|schwimmer, in *der, die* non-swimmer.

nichts sagend *adj* [Worte, Geschwätz] empty.

Nichtstun *das* inactivity; **ich hasse dieses Nichtstun** I hate all this sitting around doing nothing.

Nickel *das* nickel.

nicken *vi* - **1.** [zustimmen] to nod; **mit dem Kopf nicken** to nod (one's head) - **2.** [dösen] to doze.

Nickerchen (*pl* -) *das*: **ein Nickerchen machen** to have a nap.

nie *adv* never; **nie im Leben!** not on your life! ◆ **nie mehr** *adv* never again. ◆ **nie und nimmer** *adv* not on your life.

nieder *adv*: **nieder mit...!** down with...!

niedere, **r**, **s** *adj* [Einkommen, Lohn, Steuerklasse] low; [Arbeit] lowly; [Motive, Triebe] base; [Adel] lesser.

Niedergang *der* decline.

niedergeschlagen ◇ *pp* ▷ **niederschlagen**. ◇ *adj* dejected. ◇ *adv* dejectedly.

Nieder|lage *die* defeat.

Niederlande *Pl*: **die Niederlande** the Netherlands.

Niederländer, **in** (*mpl* -, *fpl* **-nen**) *der, die* Dutchman (Dutchwoman *die*).

niederländisch *adj* Dutch.

Niederländisch(e) *das* Dutch; *siehe auch* **Englisch(e)**.

nieder|lassen ◆ **sich niederlassen** *ref (unreg)* - **1.** [sich setzen] to sit down - **2.** [beruflich]: **sich als etw niederlassen** to set up as sthg - **3.** [sich ansiedeln] to settle.

Niederlassung (*pl* -en) *die* - **1.** [Unternehmen] branch - **2.** [als Arzt, Rechtsanwalt] setting up in practice.

nieder|legen *vt* - **1.** [Amt, Mandat] to resign from - **2.** *geh* [aufzeichnen] to put down - **3.** *geh* [hinlegen] to lay.

Nieder|österreich *nt* Lower Austria.

Nieder|sachsen ['niːdɐzaksn̩] *nt* Lower Saxony.

niedersächsisch ['niːdɐ'zɛksɪʃ] *adj* of/from Lower Saxony.

Nieder|schlag *der* precipitation.

nieder|schlagen *vt (unreg)* - **1.** [zusammenschlagen] to knock down - **2.** [Blick, Augen] to lower - **3.** [Revolution] to put down. ◆ **sich niederschlagen** *ref* - **1.** [sich auswirken]: **sich in etw** *(D)* ODER **auf etw** *(A)* **niederschlagen** to be reflected in sthg - **2.** [sich ablagern] to condense.

niederträchtig ◇ *adj* malicious. ◇ *adv* maliciously.

niedlich ◇ *adj* cute. ◇ *adv* cutely.

niedrig ◇ *adj* low; [Arbeit] lowly. ◇ *adv*: **niedrig fliegen** to fly low; **die Preise niedrig halten** to keep prices low.

niemals ◇ *adv* never. ◇ *interj* never!

niemand *pron* nobody, no one; **ich habe niemanden gesehen** I didn't see anybody; **niemand von uns spricht Französisch** none of us speaks French; **niemand anders, sonst niemand** nobody else.

Niere (*pl* -n) *die* kidney.

nieseln *vi*: **es nieselt** it's drizzling.

Niesel|regen *der* drizzle.

niesen *vi* to sneeze.

Niete (*pl* -n) *die* - **1.** [Los] losing ticket - **2.** [Bolzen, Knopf] stud - **3.** *fam* [Mensch] dead loss.

niet- und nagelfest *adj*: **sie haben alles, was nicht niet- und nagelfest war, mitgenommen** they took everything that wasn't nailed down.

Nigeria *nt* Nigeria.

Nikolaus (*pl* -läuse) *der* - **1.** [Person]: **der Nikolaus** St Nicholas *(who brings children presents on 6 December)*, ≃ Santa Claus - **2.** [aus Schokolade] chocolate Santa Claus.

Nikolaus|tag *der* St Nicholas' Day *(6 December)*.

Nikotin *das* nicotine.

Nil *der*: **der Nil** the (River) Nile.

Nil|pferd *das* hippopotamus.

nimmt *präs* ▷ **nehmen**.

nirgends, nirgendwo *adv* nowhere.

Nische (*pl* -n) *die* - **1.** [in der Wand - klein] niche; [- groß] recess - **2.** [für Produkt, Lebewesen] niche.

nisten *vi* to nest.

Niveau [ni'voː] (*pl* -s) *das* level; **Niveau haben** [Person] to be cultured; **der Krimi hat Niveau** the detective story is quality literature.

Nixe (*pl* -n) *die* water nymph.

nobel ◇ *adj* - **1.** [kostspielig] luxurious - **2.** *hum* [vornehm] posh - **3.** *geh* [großzügig] noble. ◇ *adv* - **1.** [kostspielig] luxuriously - **2.** *geh* [großzügig] nobly - **3.** *hum* [vornehm]: **sich nobel kleiden** to dress posh.

noch ◇ *adv* - **1.** [immer noch] still; **wir haben noch Zeit** we still have time; **er hat noch nichts gesagt** he still hasn't said anything; **hast du noch Geld?** have you got any money left? - **2.** [nicht später] only; **das muss noch heute gemacht werden** it has to be done today; **schafft ihr das noch bis Freitag?** do you think you'll manage it by Friday? - **3.** [zur Warnung]: **du wirst noch an meine Worte denken!** mark my words! - **4.** [zusätzlich]: **noch einen Kaffee, bitte!** another coffee, please!; **ich muss noch ein paar Einkäufe machen** I have to buy a few more things; **wer noch?** who else? - **5.** *(+ kompar)* even; **noch schneller** even quicker; **noch komplizierter** even more complicated - **6.** [rhetorisch]: **wie war noch sein Name?** what was his name again?; **man wird ja wohl noch fragen dürfen** I was only asking. ◇ *konj*: **weder... noch...** neither... nor... ◆ **noch einmal, noch mal** *adv* again. ◆ **noch immer, immer noch** *adv* still. ◆ **noch mehr** *adv* even more. ◆ **noch nicht** *adv* not yet. ◆ **noch und noch** *adv*: **Leute noch und noch** lots and lots of people; **es regnete noch und noch** it rained for hours on end. ◆ **noch so** *adv*: **sei es auch noch so klein** however small it may be; **es kann noch so regnen** however much it rains.

nochmals *adv* again.

Nomade (*pl* -n) *der* nomad.

Nomadin (*pl* -nen) *die* nomad.

Nominativ (*pl* -e) *der* nominative.

Nonne (*pl* -n) *die* nun.

Nord|amerika *nt* North America.

norddeutsch *adj* Northern German.

Norden *der* north; **nach Norden** north; **im Norden** in the north.

Nord|europa *nt* Northern Europe.

Nord|irland *nt* Northern Ireland.

nordisch *adj* Nordic.

Nord|kap *das* North Cape.

Nord|korea *nt* North Korea.

nördlich ◇ *adj* northern; [Wind] northerly. ◇ *präp*: **nördlich einer Sache** *(G)* ODER **von etw** to the north of sthg.

Nord|osten *der* northeast.

Nord|pol *der* - **1.** GEOGR North Pole - **2.** PHYS north pole.

Nordrhein-Westfalen *nt* North Rhine-Westphalia.

Nord|see *die* North Sea.

Nord|westen *der* northwest.

nörgeln *vi*: **(über jn/etw) nörgeln** to moan (about sb/sthg).

Norm (*pl* **-en**) *die* - **1.** TECH [Regel] norm - **2.** [Leistung] standard.

normal ◇ *adj* normal. ◇ *adv* normally.

Normal|benzin *das* regular petrol *UK*, regular gas *US*.

normalerweise *adv* normally, usually.

normalisieren *vt* to normalize. ◆ **sich normalisieren** *ref* to return to normal.

normen *vt* to standardize.

Norwegen *nt* Norway.

Norweger, in (*mpl* -, *fpl* **-nen**) *der, die* Norwegian.

norwegisch *adj* Norwegian.

Norwegisch(e) *das* Norwegian; *siehe auch* **Englisch(e)**.

Not (*pl* **Nöte**) *die* - **1.** [Notlage, Armut] need; **in Not sein** to be in need; **Not leidend** needy - **2.** [Verzweiflung] despair; **Nöte** [Sorgen] troubles; **Not tun** to be needed; **zur Not** *fam* if needs be.

Notar (*pl* **-e**) *der* notary.

notariell ◇ *adj* notarial, notary's. ◇ *adv* by a notary.

Notarin (*pl* **-nen**) *die* notary.

Not|arzt, ärztin *der, die* emergency doctor.

Not|ausgang *der* emergency exit.

Not|bremse *die* emergency brake.

notdürftig ◇ *adj* makeshift. ◇ *adv* provisionally; [bekleidet] scantily.

Note (*pl* **-n**) *die* - **1.** [Beurteilung] mark *UK*, grade *US* - **2.** MUS note; **nach Noten** with music ODER a score - **3.** [Eigenschaft] touch.

Not|fall *der* emergency. ◆ **im Notfall** *adv* in an emergency.

notfalls *adv* if necessary.

notgedrungen *adv* out of necessity.

notieren ◇ *vt* - **1.** [aufschreiben] to note down; **sich** *(D)* **etw notieren** to make a note of sthg - **2.** [Aktie] to quote. ◇ *vi* WIRTSCH: **höher/niedriger notieren** to rise/fall.

nötig ◇ *adj* necessary; **etw nötig haben** to need sthg; **du hast es gerade nötig!** *iron* you can talk!; **sie hat es nicht nötig zu putzen** ha, she doesn't have ODER need to do the cleaning! ◇ *adv fam* urgently.

Notiz (*pl* **-en**) *die* note; [in der Zeitung] notice; **keine Notiz von jm/etw nehmen** to take no notice of sb/sthg. ◆ **Notizen** *Pl* notes.

Notiz|buch *das* notebook.

Not|lage *die* crisis.

Not|lösung *die* temporary solution.

Not|ruf *der* emergency call; [Nummer] emergency number.

Notruf|säule *die* emergency phone.

notwendig, notwendig ◇ *adj* - **1.** [nötig] necessary - **2.** [logisch] inevitable. ◇ *adv* necessarily.

Novelle [no'vɛlə] (*pl* **-n**) *die* - **1.** [Literatur] novella - **2.** RECHT amendment.

November [no'vɛmbɐ] *der* November; *siehe auch* **September**.

Nr. (*abk für* **Nummer**) no.

NRW *abk für* **Nordrhein-Westfalen**.

nüchtern ◇ *adj* - **1.** [nicht betrunken] sober - **2.** [sachlich] matter-of-fact - **3.** [mit leerem Magen]: **nüchtern sein** to have an empty stomach; **auf nüchternen Magen** on an empty stomach. ◇ *adv* - **1.** [nicht betrunken] soberly - **2.** [sachlich] matter-of-factly - **3.** [mit leerem Magen] on an empty stomach.

Nudel (*pl* **-n**) *die* noodle; **Nudeln** [italienisch] pasta; [chinesisch, in Suppe] noodles.

null ◇ *num* zero; **null Komma fünf** zero ODER nought *UK* point five; **eins zu null** one-zero, one-nil *UK*; **null und nichtig** *fig* null and void. ◇ *adj (unver) fam* no; *siehe auch* **sechs**.

Null (*pl* **-en**) *die* - **1.** [Zahl] zero - **2.** *fam abw* [Mensch] dead loss.

Null|punkt *der* - **1.** [Tiefpunkt]: **auf den Nullpunkt sinken** to hit rock-bottom - **2.** PHYS zero.

numerieren = nummerieren.

Nummer (*pl* **-n**) *die* - **1.** [Zahl] number - **2.** [Größe] size - **3.** [im Zirkus] act - **4.** *fam* [Mensch] character - **5.** *salopp* [Geschlechtsakt] shag.

nummerieren *vt* to number.

Nummern|schild *das* numberplate *UK*, license plate *US*.

nun ◇ *adv* - **1.** [gen] now; **von nun an** from now on - **2.** [Ausdruck der Ungeduld]: **bist du nun zufrieden?** are you happy now?; **was denn nun?** so what happens now? ◇ *interj* now; **nun denn** right ODER well then; **nun gut** oh well. ◆ **nun mal** *adv* now; **das ist nun mal so!** that's just the way it is!

nur *adv* - **1.** [lediglich] only, just; **ich bin nicht krank, nur müde** I'm not ill, just tired - **2.** [jedoch] but, yet - **3.** [verstärkend]: **was meint er nur?** what does he mean?; **wenn sie nur käme!** if only she would come!; **kommen Sie nur**

herein! do come in!; **nur keine Panik!** don't panic!; **hätte ich nur auf dich gehört!** if only I'd listened to you! ◆ **nur noch** *adv*: **ich habe nur noch 10 Euro** I've only got 10 euros left. ◆ **nur so** *adv*: **das sagt er nur so** *fam* he's just saying that; **der Putz bröckelt nur so** the plaster is crumbling really badly. ◆ **nur zu** *interj* go on!

nụscheln *vi* to mumble.

Nụss (*pl* **Nüsse**) *die* - **1.** [Frucht] nut - **2.** *fam abw* [Mensch]: **du dumme Nuss!** you stupid idiot!

Nụssbaum (*pl* **-bäume**) *der* - **1.** [Baum] walnut tree - **2.** [Holz] walnut.

Nụssknacker (*pl* -) *der* [Gerät] nut-cracker.

Nụtte (*pl* **-n**) *die salopp* - **1.** [Prostituierte] tart, hooker *US* - **2.** *abw* [Frau] slut.

nụtzbar *adj* usable; **(sich** *(D)***) etw nutzbar machen** [Energiequelle] to harness sthg; [Boden, Land] to cultivate sthg.

nụ̈tze *adj (unver)*: **zu etwas/nichts nütze sein** to be of some/no use.

nụtzen, nụ̈tzen ◇ *vt* to use; **das nützt nichts/nicht viel** that's no/not much use. ◇ *vi*: **jm nutzen** to be of use to sb.

Nụtzen *der* benefit.

nụ̈tzlich *adj* useful; **sich nützlich machen** to make o.s. useful.

nụtzlos ◇ *adj* useless. ◇ *adv* uselessly.

Nụtzung (*pl* **-en**) *die* [von Bodenschätzen] exploitation; [von Energiequelle] harnessing.

NW (*abk für* **Nordwest**) NW.

Nylon® ['nailɔn] *das* nylon.

O

o (*pl* **o** ODER **-s**), **O** (*pl* **O** ODER **-s**) [oː] *das* o, O. ◆ **O** (*abk für* **Ost**) E.

Oase (*pl* **-n**) *die* oasis.

ọb *konj* whether; **ich weiß nicht, ob er kommt** I don't know whether ODER if he'll come; **ob er wohl kommt?** I wonder if he'll come?; **und ob!** you bet! ◆ **als ob** *konj* as if, as though; **(so) tun als ob** to pretend (that); **er tat, als ob er sie nicht gesehen hätte** he pretended not to have seen her.

ÖBB (*abk für* **Österreichische Bundesbahn**), *Austrian Railways.*

Obelịsk (*pl* **-en**) *der* obelisk.

oben *adv* - **1.** [räumlich] up; [obenauf] at the top; **hier/dort oben** up here/there; **links/rechts oben im Bild** in the top left-hand/right-hand corner of the picture; **bis oben hin** up to the top; **nach oben** up; [im Haus] upstairs; **mit dem Gesicht nach oben** face up; **von oben** down; **von oben bis unten** from top to bottom; **von oben herab** *fig* condescendingly; **weiter oben** further up; **oben ohne** *fig* topless - **2.** [im Text] above; **siehe oben** see above; **oben erwähnt** above-mentioned.

Ober (*pl* -) *der* waiter; **Herr Ober!** waiter!

Ober|arm *der* upper arm.

obere, **r**, **s** *adj* upper.

Ober|fläche *die* - **1.** [Außenfläche] surface - **2.** MATH (surface) area.

oberflächlich ◇ *adj* superficial. ◇ *adv* superficially.

Obergeschoss (*pl* **-e**) *das* top floor; **im dritten Obergeschoss** on the third *UK* ODER fourth *US* floor.

Ober|haupt *das* head.

Ober|hemd *das* shirt.

Ober|körper *der* upper body; **den Oberkörper freimachen** to strip to the waist, to take one's top off.

Ober|lippe *die* upper lip.

Ober|österreich *nt* Upper Austria.

Ober|schenkel *der* thigh.

Ober|schicht *die*: **die Oberschicht** the upper classes *Pl*.

Oberst (*pl* **-en** ODER **-e**) *der* colonel.

oberste, **r**, **s** *adj* top; [Gericht] supreme; **die oberste Heeresleitung** the military high command.

Ober|stufe *die* SCHULE *final three years of secondary education.*

Ober|teil *das* top.

Ober|weite *die* bust (measurement).

Objẹkt (*pl* **-e**) *das* - **1.** [Gegenstand, KUNST & GRAMM] object - **2.** [Immobilie] property.

objektiv [ɔpjɛk'tiːf] ◇ *adj* objective. ◇ *adv* objectively.

Objektiv (*pl* **-e**) *das* FOTO lens.

Oboe (*pl* **-n**) *die* oboe.

Obst *das* fruit.

Obst|baum *der* fruit tree.

obszön ◇ *adj* obscene. ◇ *adv* obscenely.

obwohl *konj* although.

Ọchse ['ɔksə] (*pl* **-n**) *der* [Rind] ox.

öde *adj* - **1.** [trostlos] desolate - **2.** *fam* [langweilig] dreary.

oder *konj* - **1.** [gen] or - **2.** *fam* [als Bestätigungsfrage]: **du kommst doch mit, oder?** you're going to come, aren't you?; **du hast doch kein Auto, oder?** you haven't got a car, have you? ◆ **oder aber** *konj* or (else). ◆ **oder auch** *konj* or. ◆ **oder so** *adv* or something like that.

Oder *die*: **die Oder** the (River) Oder.

Ofen (*pl* **Öfen**) *der* - **1.** [Wärmespender] stove; **elektrischer Ofen** (electric) heater - **2.** [Backofen] oven - **3.** *fam* [Motorrad] bike.

offen <> *adj* - **1.** [gen] open; **das Geschäft hat bis 6 Uhr offen** the shop is open until 6 o'clock; **sperrangelweit offen** wide open; **mit offenen Augen** with one's eyes open; **auf offenem Meer** on the open sea; **für etw offen sein** to have an open mind about sthg; **offen zu jm sein, jm gegenüber offen sein** to be frank ODER open with sb - **2.** [unverpackt] loose, unpacked; **offene Weine** wine by the glass/carafe - **3.** [lose] undone; **der Knopf ist offen** the button has come undone; **mit offenen Haaren** with one's hair down - **4.** [Rechnung] outstanding. <> *adv* openly; **etw offen zugeben** to admit sthg openly; **offen gesagt** quite honestly.

offenbar *adv* obviously, clearly.

offen bleiben (*perf* **ist offen geblieben**) *vi (unreg)* - **1.** [Tür, Geschäft] to stay open - **2.** [Frage, Problem] to remain unresolved.

Offenheit (*pl* **-en**) *die* - **1.** [Ehrlichkeit] frankness; **in aller Offenheit** in all honesty - **2.** [Aufgeschlossenheit] openness.

offenherzig *adj* - **1.** [Mensch] open-hearted - **2.** *fam hum* [Kleidung] revealing.

offen lassen *vt (unreg) eigtl* & *fig* to leave open.

offensichtlich <> *adj* [Lüge, Betrug, Bevorzugung] blatant; [Wohlstand, Begabung] obvious; **es ist offensichtlich, dass...** [eindeutig] it is clear that... <> *adv* obviously, clearly; [lügen] blatantly.

offen stehen *vi (unreg)* - **1.** [Tür, Fenster] to be open - **2.** [zugänglich sein]: **jm offen stehen** to be open to sb - **3.** [Rechnung] to be outstanding.

öffentlich <> *adj* public. <> *adv* publicly; [auftreten] in public.

Öffentlichkeit *die* public; **etw an die Öffentlichkeit bringen** to make sthg public; **in aller Öffentlichkeit** in front of everyone.

offiziell <> *adj* official. <> *adv* officially.

Offizier (*pl* **-e**) *der* officer.

offline ['ɔflain] *adv* EDV offline; **offline gehen** to go offline.

öffnen <> *vt* - **1.** [gen] to open - **2.** [lösen] to undo. <> *vi* to open; **jm öffnen** to open the door to sb. ◆ **sich öffnen** *ref* to open; [neue Märkte *etc*] to open up.

Öffnung (*pl* **-en**) *die* opening; [von Körper] orifice; [von Flasche] mouth; [in Mauer] gap.

Öffnungszeiten *Pl* opening hours.

oft (*kompar* **öfter**, *superl* **am öftesten**) *adv* often; **wie oft?** how often?, how many times?

öfter, öfters *adv* quite often; **warst du schon öfter hier?** have you been here often?; **öfter als mir lieb ist** more often than I'd like.

ohne <> *präp (+ A)* without; **ein Ehepaar ohne Kinder** a couple with no children; **das ist ohne Weiteres möglich** it's perfectly possible. <> *konj* without; **sie tat es, ohne dass er es merkte** she did it without him noticing; **ohne zu fragen** without asking. ◆ **ohne mich** *interj* count me out!

ohnehin *adv* anyway.

Ohnmacht (*pl* **-en**) *die* - **1.** [Bewusstlosigkeit] unconsciousness; **in Ohnmacht fallen** to faint - **2.** [Machtlosigkeit] impotence.

ohnmächtig <> *adj* - **1.** [bewusstlos] unconscious; **ohnmächtig werden** to faint - **2.** [machtlos] impotent. <> *adv* - **1.** [bewusstlos]: **ohnmächtig daliegen** to lie there unconscious - **2.** [zusehen, ausgeliefert] helplessly.

Ohr (*pl* **-en**) *das* [von Person, Tier] ear; **halt die Ohren steif!** *fam* chin up!; **jn übers Ohr hauen** *fam* to take sb for a ride.

ohrenbetäubend <> *adj* deafening. <> *adv* deafeningly.

Ohr|feige *die* slap (in the face).

ohrfeigen *vt* to slap (in the face).

Ohr|läppchen (*pl* **Ohrläppchen**) *das* earlobe.

Ohr|ring *der* earring.

Ohr|wurm *der* catchy tune; **ein Ohrwurm sein** to be catchy.

Öko|laden *der* wholefood store.

ökologisch <> *adj* ecological. <> *adv* ecologically.

ökonomisch <> *adj* - **1.** WIRTSCH economic - **2.** [sparsam] economical. <> *adv* economically.

Öko|steuer *die* ecotax.

Öko|system *das* ecosystem.

Oktan (*pl* **-e**) *das* octane.

Oktave [ɔk'taːvə] (*pl* **-n**) *die* octave.

Oktober *der* October; **der 3. Oktober** *German national holiday commemorating reunification on 3 October 1990*; *siehe auch* **September**.

Oktober|fest *das* Munich beer festival.

Öl (*pl* **-e**) *das* - **1.** [gen] oil - **2.** KUNST oils *Pl*.

ölen *vt* to oil.

Öl|farbe *die* - **1.** KUNST oil paint; **mit Ölfarben malen** to paint in oils - **2.** [Streichmittel] oil-based paint.

Öl|gemälde *das* oil painting.

Öl|heizung *die* oil-fired central heating.

ölig <> *adj* oily. <> *adv*: **ölig glänzen** to have an oily sheen.

Olive [o'liːvə] (*pl* **-n**) *die* olive.

Öl|pest *die* oil slick.

Öl|quelle *die* oil well.

olympisch *adj* SPORT Olympic.

Olympische Spiele *Pl* Olympic Games.

Oma (*pl* **-s**) *die* - **1.** [Großmutter] grandma, granny - **2.** *fam abw* [Frau] grandma; **die Oma vor mir** the old dear in front of me.

Omelẹtt [ɔm(ə)'lɛt] (*pl* **-e** *ODER* **-s**) *das* omelette.

Ọmni|bus *der* [Linienbus] bus; [Reisebus] bus, coach *UK*.

Ọnkel (*pl* -) *der* - **1.** [Verwandter, Freund] uncle - **2.** *fam* [Mann]: **gib dem Onkel die Hand** give the nice man your hand.

ọnline ['ɔnlain] ◇ *adj* EDV [angeschlossen] online; **online sein** to be online. ◇ *adv* online.

Ọnline-Banking ['ɔnlainbɛŋkiŋ] *das* online *ODER* Internet banking.

Ọnline-|Dienst ['ɔnlaindiːnst] *der* EDV online service.

OP [oː'peː] (*pl* **-s**) (*abk für* **Operationssaal**) *der* OR *US*, operating theatre *UK*.

Opa (*pl* **-s**) *der* - **1.** [Großvater] grandpa, grandad - **2.** *fam abw* [Mann] grandpa, grandad.

Open-Air-|Konzert *das* open-air concert.

Oper (*pl* **-n**) *die* - **1.** MUS opera - **2.** [Opernhaus] opera house; **in die Oper gehen** to go to the opera.

Operation (*pl* **-en**) *die* operation.

Operẹtte (*pl* **-n**) *die* operetta.

operieren ◇ *vt* to operate on; **jn am Blinddarm operieren** to operate on sb's appendix; **sich operieren lassen** to have an operation. ◇ *vi* to operate; **behutsam operieren** to proceed carefully.

Ọpfer (*pl* -) *das* - **1.** [Mensch - von Unglück, Leidenschaften] victim - **2.** [Verzicht & RELIG] sacrifice; **jm/einer Sache zum Opfer fallen** to fall victim to sb/sthg.

ọpfern *vt* to sacrifice; **jm etw opfern** to sacrifice sthg for sb; **jetzt habe ich dir so viel Zeit geopfert** now I've given up so much time for you. ◆ **sich opfern** *ref* - **1.** [sich aufopfern] to sacrifice o.s. - **2.** *fam hum* [sich bereit erklären]: **wer opfert sich freiwillig und geht zum Chef?** who's going to volunteer to go to the boss?

Opium *das* opium.

Opposition (*pl* **-en**) *die* opposition; **in Opposition zu etw stehen** to be opposed to sthg.

Ọptik *die* - **1.** PHYS optics *(U)* - **2.** [Sichtweise] point of view - **3.** [Erscheinungsbild] appearance.

Ọptiker, in (*mpl* -, *fpl* **-nen**) *der, die* optician.

optimal ◇ *adj* optimal. ◇ *adv* optimally.

Optimịsmus *der* optimism.

optimịstisch ◇ *adj* optimistic. ◇ *adv* optimistically.

ọptisch ◇ *adj* - **1.** PHYS optical - **2.** [visuell] visual. ◇ *adv* [visuell] visually.

orange [o'rɑ̃ːʒe] *adj* orange.

Orạnge[1] [o'raŋːʒə] (*pl* **-n**) *die* [Frucht] orange.

Orạnge[2] [o'rɑ̃ːʒ] (*pl* **Orange**) *das* [Farbe] orange.

Orạngen|saft *der* orange juice.

Orchẹster [ɔr'kɛstɐ] (*pl* -) *das* orchestra.

Orchidee [ɔrçi'deːə] (*pl* **-n**) *die* orchid.

Ọrden (*pl* -) *der* - **1.** [Auszeichnung] decoration; [Medaille] medal; **jm einen Orden verleihen** to decorate sb - **2.** RELIG order.

ọrdentlich ◇ *adj* - **1.** [Person, Schreibtisch, Wohnung] tidy; [Schrift, Hausaufgabe] neat; [Leben] orderly - **2.** [regelgerecht - Mitglied] full; **ordentliches Gericht** *court for civil and criminal cases* - **3.** [Note, Ergebnis] respectable - **4.** [Verdienst, Schluck] good; [Portion] good-sized; **einen ordentlichen Schreck kriegen** to get a real fright - **5.** [anständig] proper. ◇ *adv* - **1.** [sauber] tidily; [schreiben, gekleidet] neatly - **2.** [nach Regeln] correctly, in accordance with correct procedures - **3.** [viel] really well; **ordentlich verdienen** to earn good money; **sie hat mit mir ordentlich geschimpft** she gave me a real telling-off.

ordinär ◇ *adj* - **1.** *abw* [vulgär - Person, Witz] crude; [- Benehmen, Kleidung] vulgar, common - **2.** [normal] ordinary. ◇ *adv abw* [vulgär - lachen, fluchen] crudely; [- sich verhalten, sich kleiden] vulgarly, commonly.

ọrdnen *vt* - **1.** [sortieren] to sort out; [Gedanken] to organize; **etw nach Datum ordnen** to arrange sthg according to date - **2.** [aufräumen] to tidy up - **3.** [regeln - Finanzen, Affären, Privatleben] to put in order. ◆ **sich ordnen** *ref*: **sich zu etw ordnen** to form sthg.

Ọrdner (*pl* -) *der* - **1.** [Hefter] file - **2.** [Person] steward.

Ọrdnerin (*pl* **-nen**) *die* steward.

Ọrdnung (*pl* **-en**) *die* - **1.** [geordneter Zustand] tidiness; **Ordnung schaffen** to tidy up - **2.** [Disziplin, Gesetzmäßigkeit] order; **für Ordnung sorgen** to keep order - **3.** [Anordnung] order; **in alphabetischer Ordnung** in alphabetical order - **4.** [Grad]: **eine Dummheit erster Ordnung** an extremely stupid thing to do; **etw in Ordnung bringen** [ordnen, erledigen] to sort sthg out; **in Ordnung sein** *fam* to be okay; **sie lässt ihre Tochter allein zu Hause? das ist nicht in Ordnung** she leaves her daughter alone at home? that's not right; **der Computer ist nicht in Ordnung** there's something wrong with the computer. ◆ **in Ordnung** *interj* okay!

ọrdnungsgemäß *adj* & *adv* in accordance with the regulations.

ọrdnungswidrig *amt* ◇ *adj* [Parken] illegal; **ordnungswidriges Verhalten im**

Straßenverkehr minor traffic offence. <> *adv* [parken] illegally; **sich ordnungswidrig verhalten** to contravene the regulations.

Oregano *der* oregano.

ORF (*abk für* **Österreichischer Rundfunk**) *Austrian radio and television corporation.*

Organ (*pl* **-e**) *das* - **1.** [gen] organ - **2.** [Stimme] voice.

Organisation (*pl* **-en**) *die* organization.

organisatorisch <> *adj* organizational. <> *adv* organizationally.

organisch *adj* - **1.** [eines Körperteils] physical - **2.** [natürlich & CHEM] organic.

organisieren *vt* - **1.** [veranstalten, ordnen] to organize - **2.** [gründen] to form - **3.** *fam* [beschaffen] to get hold of - **4.** *fam* [stehlen] to pinch. ◆ **sich organisieren** *ref* - **1.** [sich zusammenschließen] to organize - **2.** [sich bilden] to develop.

Organismus (*pl* **-men**) *der* organism.

Organizer *der* (electronic) organizer.

Organ|spende *die* organ donation.

Orgasmus (*pl* **-men**) *der* orgasm.

Orgel (*pl* **-n**) *die* organ.

Orient ['o:ri̯ɛnt] *der* - **1.** [der Nahe Osten] Middle East - **2.** [Asien] Orient.

orientalisch *adj* - **1.** [vom Nahen Osten] Middle Eastern - **2.** [vom Morgenland] oriental.

orientieren [ori̯ɛn'ti:rən] *vt* - **1.** [ausrichten]: **etw nach** *ODER* **an etw** *(D)* **orientieren** to base sthg on sthg - **2.** [informieren]: **jn über etw** *(A)* **orientieren** to inform sb about sthg. ◆ **sich orientieren** *ref* - **1.** [sich zurechtfinden] to orientate o.s., to get one's bearings - **2.** [sich informieren]: **sich über etw** *(A)* **orientieren** to inform o.s. about sthg - **3.** [sich ausrichten]: **sich nach** *ODER* **an etw** *(D)* **orientieren** to be orientated towards sthg; **sich nach der Mutter orientieren** to follow the example of one's mother.

Orientierung *die (ohne pl)* - **1.** [Zurechtfinden]: **die Orientierung in der Wüste ist nicht einfach** it's not easy to get one's bearings in the desert; **dieser Stadtplan ist zu Ihrer Orientierung** this city map is to help you find your way around; **die Orientierung verlieren** to lose one's bearings - **2.** [Information] information - **3.** [Ausrichtung]: **Orientierung nach** *ODER* **an etw** *(D)* orientation towards sthg; [nach Vorgaben, Richtlinien] conformance to sthg; **vielen Jugendlichen fehlt die Orientierung an religiösen Werten** many young people are not guided by religious values.

Orientierungs|sinn *der* sense of direction.

original <> *adj* - **1.** [ursprünglich] original - **2.** [unverfälscht] genuine. <> *adv* - **1.** [echt]: **eine original chinesische Tasse** a genuine Chinese tea cup - **2.** [direkt] live.

Original (*pl* **-e**) *das* - **1.** [Urform] original - **2.** [Person] character.

Orkan (*pl* **-e**) *der* hurricane.

Ort (*pl* **-e**) *der* - **1.** [gen] place; [von Verbrechen] scene; **an Ort und Stelle** on the spot - **2.** [Ortschaft - Dorf] village; [- Stadt] small town. ◆ **vor Ort** *adv* on the spot.

Orthografie (*pl* **-n**), **Orthographie** (*pl* **-n**) [ɔrtogra'fi:] *die* spelling, orthography.

Orthopädie *die* orthopaedics *(U)*.

orthopädisch <> *adj* orthopaedic. <> *adv* orthopaedically.

ortsansässig *adj* local.

Ortschaft (*pl* **-en**) *die* village.

Orts|gespräch *das* TELEKOM local call.

ortskundig *adj*: **ich bin hier ortskundig** I'm familiar with this area.

Orts|netz *das* - **1.** TELEKOM local (telephone) exchange - **2.** ELEKTR local grid.

öS (*abk für* **österreichischer Schilling**) Sch.

Öse (*pl* **-n**) *die* eye; [von Schuh] eyelet.

Oslo *nt* Oslo.

Ossi (*pl* **-s**) *der fam term used to describe citizen of the former GDR.*

Ost|block *der* Eastern bloc.

ostdeutsch *adj* [Gebiet] Eastern German; POL East German.

Ost|deutschland *nt* [Gebiet] Eastern Germany; [DDR] East Germany.

Osten *der* - **1.** [Richtung] east; **nach Osten** east - **2.** [Gegend] East; **im Osten** in the East - **3.** POL: **der Osten** the East.

Oster|ei *das* Easter egg.

Oster|hase *der* Easter Bunny.

Ostern *nt* Easter; **an** *ODER* **zu Ostern** at Easter. ◆ **frohe Ostern** *interj* Happy Easter!

Österreich *nt* Austria.

Österreicher, in (*mpl* -, *fpl* **-nen**) *der, die* Austrian.

österreichisch *adj* Austrian.

Oster|sonntag (*pl* **-e**) *der* Easter Sunday.

Ost|europa *nt* Eastern Europe.

Ost|friesland *nt* East Frisia.

Ost|küste *die* east coast.

östlich <> *adj* eastern; [Wind] east. <> *adv*: **östlich einer Sache** *(G)* *ODER* **von etw** to the east of sthg.

Ost|politik *die* Ostpolitik.

Ost|preußen *nt* East Prussia.

Ost|see *die*: **die Ostsee** the Baltic (Sea).

Otter (*pl* - *ODER* **-n**) <> *der (pl Otter)* otter. <> *die (pl Ottern)* viper.

ÖTV [øy:te:'fau̯] (*abk für* **Gewerkschaft Öffentliche Dienste, Transport und Verkehr**) *die German public services and transport workers' union.*

Outdoor-Aktivitäten *Pl* outdoor pursuits.

outen *vt* to out. ◆ **sich outen** *ref* to come out.

outsourcen *vt* to outsource.

Outsourcing ['au̯tsoː(r)sɪŋ] *das* outsourcing.

oval [o'vɑːl] ◇ *adj* oval. ◇ *adv* in/into an oval.

ÖVP [øỹːfau̯'peː] (*abk für* **Österreichische Volkspartei**) *die* Austrian People's Party, *Christian Democratic political party in Austria*.

oxidieren, oxydieren ◇ *vi* (*perf* **hat/ist oxidiert** ODER **oxydiert**) to oxidize. ◇ *vt* (*perf* **hat oxidiert** ODER **oxydiert**) to oxidize.

Ozean (*pl* **-e**) *der* ocean.

Ozon *der ODER das* ozone.

P

p (*pl* **-** ODER **-s**), **P** (*pl* **-** ODER **-s**) [peː] *das* p, P.

paar *adj* few. ◆ **ein paar** *det* a few; **kannst du mal ein paar Minuten rüberkommen?** can you come over here for a couple of minutes?

Paar (*pl* **-e** ODER **-**) *das* **- 1.** *(pl Paare)* [zwei Personen] couple **- 2.** *(pl Paar)* [zwei Dinge] pair; **ein Paar Strümpfe** a pair of socks.

paaren *vt* **- 1.** [Tiere] to mate **- 2.** [kombinieren] to combine. ◆ **sich paaren** *ref* [kopulieren] to mate.

paarmal ◆ **ein paarmal** *adv* a few times; **den Film habe ich ein paarmal gesehen** I've seen the film a couple of times.

Paarung (*pl* **-en**) *die* **- 1.** [von Tieren] mating **- 2.** [von Spielern, Mannschaften] pairing.

paarweise *adv* in pairs.

Pacht (*pl* **-en**) *die* **- 1.** [das Pachten, Vertrag] lease; **etw in Pacht haben** to lease sthg **- 2.** [Geld] rent.

Pächter, in (*mpl* **-**, *fpl* **-nen**) *der, die* **- 1.** [von Geschäft] leaseholder **- 2.** [von Grundstück] tenant.

Pack *das abw* rabble.

Päckchen (*pl* **-**) *das* **- 1.** [Paket] small parcel **- 2.** [Packung] packet.

packen ◇ *vt* **- 1.** [voll packen] to pack; **seine Sachen packen** to pack one's things **- 2.** [legen, stellen]: **etw auf/unter etw** *(A)* **packen** to put sthg on/under sthg; **etw aus etw packen** to take sthg out of sthg **- 3.** [fassen] to seize **- 4.** [überkommen]: **mich packt das Grauen** I am filled with horror **- 5.** [emotional bewegen] to grip **- 6.** *fam* [schaffen - Studium, Prüfung] to get through; **glaubst du, du packst es?** do you think you can manage?; **sie hat den Bus noch gepackt** she managed to catch the bus **- 7.** *salopp* [begreifen] to get. ◇ *vi* [vor Reisen] to pack.

Packen (*pl* **-**) ◇ *der* pile; [zusammengeschnürt] bundle. ◇ *das* packing.

packend ◇ *adj* gripping. ◇ *adv* grippingly.

Pack|papier *das* brown paper.

Packung (*pl* **-en**) *die* **- 1.** [für Waren] packet **- 2.** MED compress; [aus Eis] ice pack **- 3.** [Gesichtspackung] face pack.

Pädagogik *die* education.

pädagogisch ◇ *adj* educational; **ihre pädagogischen Fähigkeiten** her teaching ability; **meine pädagogische Ausbildung** my training in education. ◇ *adv* educationally.

Paddel (*pl* **-**) *das* paddle.

Paddel|boot *das* canoe.

paddeln (*perf* **hat/ist gepaddelt**) *vi* **- 1.** *(hat)* [rudern] to paddle **- 2.** *(ist)* [Boot fahren] to canoe.

paffen *fam* ◇ *vt* [rauchen] to puff at. ◇ *vi* **- 1.** *abw* [rauchen] to puff away **- 2.** [nicht Lunge rauchen]: **du paffst ja nur!** you're not inhaling!

Page ['pɑːʒə] (*pl* **-n**) *der* [im Hotel] bellboy *UK*, bellhop *US*.

Paket (*pl* **-e**) *das* **- 1.** [Postsendung] parcel **- 2.** [Packung] packet **- 3.** [Packen] bundle **- 4.** [Zusammenstellung] package.

Pakistan *nt* Pakistan.

Pakt (*pl* **-e**) *der* pact; **einen Pakt schließen** to make a pact.

Palast (*pl* **Paläste**) *der* palace.

Palästina *nt* Palestine.

Palästinenser, in (*mpl* **-**, *fpl* **-nen**) *der, die* Palestinian.

palästinensisch *adj* Palestinian.

Palette (*pl* **-n**) *die* **- 1.** [für Farben] palette **- 2.** [zum Transport] pallet **- 3.** [Vielfalt] range.

Palme (*pl* **-n**) *die* palm (tree).

Palm|sonntag (*pl* **-e**) *der* Palm Sunday.

Pampelmuse (*pl* **-n**) *die* grapefruit.

pampig *fam* ◇ *adj* **- 1.** [frech] insolent **- 2.** [breiig] mushy. ◇ *adv* [frech] insolently.

Panama|kanal *der* Panama Canal.

panieren *vt* to coat with breadcrumbs; **paniertes Schnitzel** breaded escalope of pork.

Panier|mehl *das (ohne pl)* breadcrumbs *Pl*.

Panik *die* panic; **in Panik geraten** to panic.

panisch ◇ *adj* [Reaktion] panic-stricken; **eine panische Angst vor etw** *(D)* **haben** to be terrified of sthg. ◇ *adv* [reagieren] with panic; **sich panisch fürchten** to be terrified.

Panne (*pl* **-n**) *die* **- 1.** [mit Auto, Maschine] breakdown; **eine Panne haben** to break down **- 2.** [Fehler] slip-up; [Versprecher] slip; **die Veranstaltung verlief ohne jede Panne** the event went off without a hitch.

Pannen|dienst *der* breakdown service.

panschen ◇ *vt* [mit Chemikalien] to adulterate; [mit Wasser] to water down. ◇ *vi* [mit Chemikalien] to adulterate the drinks; [mit Wasser] to water down the drinks.

Panther (*pl* -), **Panter** (*pl* -) *der* panther.

Pantoffel (*pl* -n) *der* slipper.

Pantomime (*pl* -n) ◇ *die* mime. ◇ *der* mime artist.

Panzer (*pl* -) *der* - **1.** [Fahrzeug] tank - **2.** [von Insekt, Schildkröte] shell; [von Krokodil] armour - **3.** [Schutzplatte] armour plating.

Papa (*pl* -s) *der fam* dad, daddy.

Papagei (*pl* -en) *der* parrot.

Papier (*pl* -e) *das* - **1.** [gen] paper - **2.** [Wertpapier] security. ◆ **Papiere** *Pl* [Ausweis, persönliches Dokument] documents; **Ihre Papiere bitte** your papers, please; **seine Papiere bekommen** ODER **kriegen** *fam fig* to be fired, to get the sack *UK*.

Papier|geld *das* paper money.

Papier|korb *der* wastepaper basket *UK*, wastebasket *US*.

Papier|kram *der fam abw* paperwork.

Papierwaren|geschäft *das* stationer's.

Papp|becher *der* paper cup.

Pappe (*pl* -n) *die* cardboard.

Papp|karton *der* cardboard box.

Paprika (*pl* - ODER -s) *der* - **1.** [Gemüse] pepper - **2.** [Gewürz] paprika.

Paprika|schote *die* pepper.

Papst (*pl* **Päpste**) *der* pope.

Parabel (*pl* -n) *die* - **1.** MATH parabola - **2.** [Gleichnis] parable.

Parade (*pl* -n) *die* - **1.** [Aufmarsch] parade - **2.** [bei Fechten] parry; [bei Ballspiel] save.

Paradies (*pl* -e) *das* paradise.

paradiesisch *adj* heavenly.

Paragraf (*pl* -en), **Paragraph** (*pl* -en) *der* - **1.** [in Vertrag, Gesetz] section; [in Verfassung] article - **2.** [typografisches Zeichen] paragraph.

parallel ◇ *adj* parallel. ◇ *adv* - **1.** [gleichzeitig]: **parallel zu etw** at the same time as sthg - **2.** [in gleichem Abstand]: **parallel zu etw verlaufen** to run parallel to sthg.

Parallele (*pl* -n) *die* - **1.** MATH parallel line - **2.** [Entsprechung] parallel; **Parallelen zu etw ziehen** to draw parallels with sthg.

Parallelogramm (*pl* -e) *das* parallelogram.

Paranuss (*pl* -**nüsse**) *die* brazil nut.

Parasit (*pl* -en) *der eigtl* & *fig* parasite.

parat ◇ *adv*: **etw parat haben/halten** to have/keep sthg ready; **auf diese Frage habe ich keine passende Antwort parat** I don't have a ready answer to this question. ◇ *adj (unver)*: **parat sein** to be ready.

Pärchen (*pl* -) *das* couple.

Parfüm (*pl* -e ODER -s) *das* perfume.

Parfümerie [parfymə'ri:] (*pl* -n) *die* perfumery.

parfümieren *vt* to perfume. ◆ **sich parfümieren** *ref*: **sich stark parfümieren** [Frau] to wear a lot of perfume; [Mann] to wear a lot of aftershave.

Pariser (*pl* -) *der fam* [Kondom] rubber.

Park (*pl* -s) *der* park.

Parka (*pl* -s) *der* parka.

Parkan|lage *die* [von Stadt] park; [von Schloss] grounds *Pl*.

parken ◇ *vt* to park. ◇ *vi* - **1.** [Person] to park; **falsch parken** to park illegally - **2.** [Fahrzeug]: **ein parkendes Auto** a parked car.

Parken *das* parking.

Parkett (*pl* -e ODER -s) *das* - **1.** [Fußbodenbelag] parquet - **2.** [im Kino, Theater] stalls *Pl UK*, parquet *US*.

Park|gebühr *die* parking fee.

Park|haus *das* multi-storey car park *UK*, parking garage *US*.

Park|lücke *die* parking space.

Park|platz *der* - **1.** [Platz] car park *UK*, parking lot *US* - **2.** [Parklücke] parking space.

Park|scheibe *die* parking disc.

Park|schein *der* car park ticket *UK*, parking lot ticket *US*.

Park|uhr *die* parking meter.

Park|verbot *das*: **im Parkverbot stehen** to be in a no-parking zone.

Parlament (*pl* -e) *das* parliament.

Parlamentarier, in [parlamen'ta:riə, rın] (*mpl* -, *fpl* -nen) *der, die* Member of Parliament.

parlamentarisch ◇ *adj* parliamentary. ◇ *adv* in parliament.

Parmesan *der* Parmesan.

Parodie [paro'di:] (*pl* -n) *die* parody; **eine Parodie auf etw** a parody of sthg; **eine Parodie auf jn** a take-off of sb.

Parole (*pl* -n) *die* - **1.** [Kennwort] password - **2.** [Leitspruch] slogan - **3.** *abw* [Behauptung]: **eine ausländerfeindliche Parole** a racial stereotype.

Partei (*pl* -en) *die* - **1.** [gen] party; **für jn Partei ergreifen** *fig* to side with sb - **2.** [bei Streit] side.

parteiisch ◇ *adj* biased. ◇ *adv*: **parteiisch urteilen** to make a biased judgement.

Parterre [par'tɛr] (*pl* -s) *das* ground floor *UK*, first floor *US*. ◆ **im Parterre** *adv* on the ground floor *UK* ODER first floor *US*.

Partie [par'ti:] (*pl* -n) *die* - **1.** [Teil] part - **2.** [Spiel] game; **eine Partie Schach/Tennis spielen** to play a game of chess/tennis; **da bin ich mit von der Partie!** count me in!

Partitur (*pl* -en) *die* score.

Partizip (*pl* -ien) *das* participle. ◆ **Partizip Perfekt** *das* past participle. ◆ **Partizip Präsens** *das* present participle.

Pạrtner, in (*mpl* -, *fpl* **-nen**) *der, die* partner; [in Film] co-star.

Pạrtnerschaft (*pl* **-en**) *die* - **1.** [zwischen Personen] partnership - **2.** [zwischen Städten] twinning.

pạrtnerschaftlich ◇ *adj* [Verhältnis] based on partnership; **partnerschaftliche Beziehung** partnership; **partnerschaftliche Zusammenarbeit** cooperation. ◇ *adv* - **1.** [freundschaftlich] in a spirit of partnership; [zusammenleben] as partners - **2.** [kollegial] in partnership.

Pạrtner|stadt *die* twin town.

partout [par'tu:] *adv fam* at all costs; **sie will partout nicht gehorchen!** she simply refuses to obey!

Party ['pɑ:ɐ̯ti] (*pl* **-s**) *die* party.

Pạss (*pl* **Pässe**) *der* - **1.** [Dokument] passport - **2.** [Gebirgspass, beim Fußball] pass.

Passage [pa'sɑ:ʒə] (*pl* **-n**) *die* - **1.** [gen] passage - **2.** [Geschäftsstraße] arcade.

Passagier [pasa'ʒi:ɐ̯] (*pl* **-e**) *der* passenger; **blinder Passagier** [auf Schiff] stowaway; [im Zug] fare dodger.

Passagierin [pasa'ʒi:rɪn] (*pl* **-nen**) *die* passenger.

Passạnt, in (*mpl* **-en**, *fpl* **-nen**) *der, die* passerby.

Pạssbild (*pl* **-er**) *das* passport photo.

pạssen *vi* - **1.** [die richtige Größe haben] to fit; **die Schuhe passen mir nicht** these shoes don't fit; **in etw** *(A)* **passen** to fit in sthg - **2.** [angenehm sein]: **passt es (dir) morgen besser?** does tomorrow suit you better?; **das passt mir nicht** that doesn't suit me; **das könnte dir so passen!** no way!; **das könnte ihm so passen!** he should be so lucky! - **3.** [zusammenpassen - Farben] to match; **zu jm passen** to suit sb; **sie passt in keinster Weise zu ihm** she isn't at all suited to him; **diese Schuhe passen nicht zu dem Rock** these shoes don't go with the skirt - **4.** [nicht können] to pass; **da muss ich passen!** pass!

pạssend ◇ *adj* - **1.** [Gelegenheit, Methode, Kleidung] suitable; [Worte] right; **der passende Schlüssel** the right key - **2.** [Farbe] matching. ◇ *adv* suitably; **passend antworten** to give a fitting reply; **haben Sie es passend?** do you have the exact amount?

Pạss|foto (*pl* **-s**) *das* passport photo.

passieren (*perf* **hat/ist passiert**) ◇ *vt (hat)* - **1.** [überschreiten, durchschreiten] to cross - **2.** [Zollkontrolle] to go through - **3.** SPORT to pass - **4.** KÜCHE to pass through a sieve. ◇ *vi (ist)* to happen; **es ist ein Unglück passiert** there's been an accident; **mir ist etwas Unglaubliches passiert** something incredible happened to me; **bei dem Unfall ist zum Glück nichts passiert** fortunately, nobody was hurt in the accident.

pạssiv, passiv ◇ *adj* - **1.** [untätig] passive - **2.** [Mitglied] non-active. ◇ *adv* passively.

Pạssiv ['pasif] (*pl* **-e**) *das* GRAMM passive (voice).

Pạsskontrolle (*pl* **-n**) *die* - **1.** [Kontrollieren] passport check - **2.** [Kontrollstelle] passport control.

Pạste (*pl* **-n**) *die* paste.

Pastẹll|farbe *die* pastel colour.

Pastete (*pl* **-n**) *die* - **1.** [mit Blätterteig] vol-au-vent - **2.** [ohne Blätterteig] pâté.

Pạstor (*pl* **-toren**) *der* [katholisch] priest; [evangelisch] vicar.

Pastorin (*pl* **-nen**) *die* - **1.** [Pfarrerin] vicar - **2.** [Ehefrau des Pastors] vicar's wife.

Pate (*pl* **-n**) *der* godfather; **bei etw Pate stehen** to be the influence behind sthg.

Paten|kind *das* godchild.

Paten|onkel *der* godfather.

Patenschaft (*pl* **-en**) *die*: **die Patenschaft für etw übernehmen** to sponsor sthg; **die Patenschaft für jn übernehmen** to become sb's godparent.

patẹnt ◇ *adj* - **1.** [lebenstüchtig] capable - **2.** [praktisch] neat - **3.** *fam* [nett] great. ◇ *adv* [tüchtig] capably.

Patẹnt (*pl* **-e**) *das* patent; **auf etw** *(A)* **ein Patent anmelden** to apply for a patent for sthg.

Paten|tante *die* godmother.

patentieren *vt* to patent; **sich** *(D)* **etw patentieren lassen** to take out a patent on sthg.

Pater (*pl* -) *der* father *(priest)*.

Patiẹnt, in (*mpl* **-en**, *fpl* **-nen**) *der, die* patient.

Patin (*pl* **-nen**) *die* godmother.

Patina *die* patina.

Patriot, in (*mpl* **-en**, *fpl* **-nen**) *der, die* patriot.

patriotisch ◇ *adj* patriotic. ◇ *adv* patriotically.

Patron, in (*mpl* **-e**, *fpl* **-nen**) *der, die* patron saint.

Patrone (*pl* **-n**) *die* cartridge.

patrouillieren [patrʊl'(j)i:rən] (*perf* **hat/ist patrouilliert**) *vi* to patrol.

Pạtsche (*pl* **-n**) *die fam* - **1.** [Not]: **in der Patsche sitzen** to be in a fix; **jm aus der Patsche helfen** to help sb out of a tight spot - **2.** [Hand] paw.

pạtschnạss *adj fam* soaking wet.

pạtzig ◇ *adj* nasty. ◇ *adv* nastily.

Pauke (*pl* **-n**) *die* kettledrum; **auf die Pauke hauen** *fam fig* to paint the town red.

pauken *fam* ◇ *vi* to swot *UK*, to grind *US*. ◇ *vt* to swot up on *UK*, to bone up on *US*.

pauschal ◇ *adj* - **1.** [Preis, Versicherung] all-inclusive - **2.** [Urteil] sweeping. ◇ *adv* - **1.** [beurteilen] sweepingly - **2.** [abrechnen] altogether.

Pauschale (*pl* **-n**) *die* flat rate.

Pauschal|reise *die* package tour.

Pauschal|urteil *das* sweeping judgement.

Päuschen ['pɔyscən] (*pl* -) *das fam* breather.

Pause (*pl* **-n**) *die* - **1.** [Unterbrechung] break; [im Theater, Konzert] interval - **2.** MUS rest.

Pausen|brot *das* snack (for the break).

pausenlos *adj* & *adv* non-stop.

Pavian ['pɑːvi̯ɑːn] (*pl* **-e**) *der* baboon.

Pazifik *der*: **der Pazifik** the Pacific.

Pazifische Ozean *der* Pacific Ocean.

Pazifist, in (*mpl* **-en**, *fpl* **-nen**) *der, die* pacifist.

pazifistisch ◇ *adj* pacifist. ◇ *adv* in a pacifist way.

PC [peː'tseː] (*pl* - ODER **-s**) (*abk für* **Personal Computer**) *der* PC.

PDS [peːdeː'ɛs] (*abk für* **Partei des Demokratischen Sozialismus**) *die Democratic Socialist Party*.

Pech (*pl* **-e**) *das* - **1.** [Unglück] bad luck; **Pech haben** to be unlucky - **2.** [Erdölprodukt] pitch.

Pech|strähne *die* run of bad luck.

Pech|vogel *der* unlucky person.

Pedal (*pl* **-e**) *das* pedal.

pedantisch *abw* ◇ *adj* fastidious. ◇ *adv* fastidiously.

Pegel (*pl* -) *der* [von Fluss] water level; [von Lärm] level.

peilen ◇ *vt* to take a bearing on; **die Lage peilen** to see how the land lies. ◇ *vi fam*: **über den Daumen peilen** to make a rough guess.

peinlich ◇ *adj* - **1.** [unangenehm] embarrassing; **das ist mir sehr peinlich** I feel very embarrassed about it - **2.** [sorgfältig] scrupulous. ◇ *adv* - **1.** [unangenehm] embarrassingly - **2.** [sorgfältig] scrupulously.

Peitsche (*pl* **-n**) *die* whip.

peitschen (*perf* **hat/ist gepeitscht**) ◇ *vt (hat)* to whip. ◇ *vi (ist)* [Wind, Regen] to lash; [Schuss] to ring out.

Peking *nt* Peking.

Pelikan (*pl* **-e**) *der* pelican.

Pelle (*pl* **-n**) *die Norddt* [von Kartoffel] peel; [von Wurst] skin.

pellen *vt Norddt* [Kartoffel] to peel; [Wurst] to skin. ◆ **sich pellen** *ref* to peel.

Pell|kartoffel *die* unpeeled boiled potato.

Pelz (*pl* **-e**) *der* - **1.** [Fell] fur *(U)*; **jm auf den Pelz rücken** *fam fig* to pester sb - **2.** [Pelzmantel] fur (coat).

pelzig *adj* - **1.** [taub] numb - **2.** [pelzartig] furry.

Pelz|mantel *der* fur coat.

Pendel (*pl* -) *das* pendulum.

pendeln (*perf* **ist/hat gependelt**) *vi* - **1.** *(ist)* [fahren] to commute - **2.** *(hat)* [schwingen - Glocken] to swing; [- Beine] to dangle.

Pendel|verkehr *der* [für Pendler] commuter traffic; [Hin- und Herfahren] shuttle service.

Pendler, in (*mpl* -, *fpl* **-nen**) *der, die* commuter.

penetrant *abw* ◇ *adj* [Mensch, Fragerei] obtrusive; [Geruch, Geklingel] penetrating. ◇ *adv* [nach etw riechen] penetratingly; [auf jn einreden] obtrusively.

Penis (*pl* **-se**) *der* penis.

Penizillin *das* penicillin.

pennen *vi fam* - **1.** [schlafen] to sleep, to kip *UK* - **2.** [nicht aufpassen] to be half-asleep - **3.** [mit jm schlafen]: **mit jm pennen** *salopp* to do it with sb.

Penner, in (*mpl* -, *fpl* **-nen**) *der, die fam* - **1.** [Stadtstreicher] tramp, bum *US* - **2.** [Schlafmütze] sleepyhead.

Pension [paŋ'zi̯oːn] (*pl* **-en**) *die* - **1.** [Hotel] guesthouse - **2.** [Ruhestand]: **in Pension gehen** to retire; **in Pension sein** to be retired - **3.** *(ohne pl)* [Bezüge] pension.

Pensionär, in [paŋzi̯o'nɛːɐ̯, rɪn] (*mpl* **-e**, *fpl* **-nen**) *der, die* pensioner *(retired civil servant)*.

pensionieren [paŋzi̯o'niːrən] *vt* to pension off.

Pensum (*pl* **Pensen**) *das* quota.

Peperoni (*pl* -) *die* chilli (pepper).

per *präp (+A)* by.

perfekt ◇ *adj* - **1.** [vollkommen] perfect - **2.** [abgeschlossen]: **perfekt sein** [Vertrag, Kauf] to be finalized; [Niederlage, Sieg] to be complete; **perfekt machen** to finalize. ◇ *adv* [vollkommen] perfectly.

Perfekt (*pl* **-e**) *das* GRAMM perfect.

Perfektion *die* perfection.

Pergament (*pl* **-e**) *das* parchment.

Pergament|papier *das* greaseproof paper.

Periode (*pl* **-n**) *die* - **1.** [Epoche, Menstruation] period - **2.** MATH repetend; **1,6 Periode** 1.6 recurring.

periodisch ◇ *adj* periodic. ◇ *adv* periodically.

Perle (*pl* **-n**) *die* - **1.** [Schmuck - aus Muschel] pearl; [- aus Holz, Glas] bead - **2.** *geh* [Kostbarkeit] gem.

perlen (*perf* **hat/ist geperlt**) *vi* - **1.** *(hat)* [sprudeln] to bubble - **2.** *(ist) geh* [abperlen]: **Schweiß perlt ihm auf der Stirn** beads of sweat are forming on his brow.

Perlen|kette *die* pearl necklace.

Perlmutt, Perlmutt *das* mother of pearl.

Perlon® *das* ≃ nylon.

permanent ◇ *adj* permanent. ◇ *adv* permanently.

perplex *adj*: **(ganz) perplex sein** to be stunned.

Persien *nt* Persia.

Person (*pl* **-en**) *die* - **1.** [Mensch & GRAMM] person; **sie ist Köchin und Inhaberin in einer Person** she is chef and owner rolled into one; **etw in Person sein** *fig* to be sthg personified - **2.** [Figur] character.

Personal *das* staff.

Personal|abteilung *die* personnel department.

Personal|ausweis *der* identity card.

Personal|chef, in *der, die* personnel manager.

Personal|computer *der* EDV personal computer.

Personalien [pɛrzo'nɑːli̯ən] *Pl* personal details.

Personal|pronomen *das* GRAMM personal pronoun.

Personal|rat *der* - **1.** [Gremium] staff council *(for civil servants)* - **2.** [Vertreter] staff council representative *(for civil servants)*.

Personal|rätin *die* staff council representative *(for civil servants)*.

personell ◇ *adj* staff *(vor Subst)*. ◇ *adv* with regard to staff; **personell unterbesetzt** understaffed.

Personen|wagen *der* car.

persönlich ◇ *adj* personal; **persönlich werden** to get personal. ◇ *adv* personally; **etw persönlich nehmen** to take sthg personally.

Persönlichkeit (*pl* **-en**) *die* personality.

Perspektive [pɛrspɛk'tiːvə] (*pl* **-n**) *die* - **1.** [Bildaufbau, Sichtweise] perspective; **aus js Perspektive** from sb's perspective - **2.** [Aussicht] prospect.

Peru *nt* Peru.

Perücke (*pl* **-n**) *die* wig.

Pessimismus *der* pessimism.

pessimistisch ◇ *adj* pessimistic. ◇ *adv* pessimistically.

Pest *die (ohne pl)* [Seuche] plague; **jn/etw meiden wie die Pest** *fam fig* to avoid sb/sthg like the plague; **stinken wie die Pest** *fam fig* to stink to high heaven.

Petersilie [petɐ'ziːli̯ə] *die* parsley.

Petroleum [pe'troːleum] *das* paraffin *UK*, kerosene *US*.

petzen *vi fam* to tell tales.

Pf. (*abk für* **Pfennig**) pf.

Pfad (*pl* **-e**) *der* [gen & EDV] path.

Pfadfinder, in (*mpl* **-**, *fpl* **-nen**) *der, die* boy scout, girl guide *UK*, girl scout *US*.

Pfahl (*pl* **Pfähle**) *der* post.

Pfalz *die*: **die Pfalz** the Palatinate.

pfälzisch *adj* of/from the Palatinate.

Pfand (*pl* **Pfänder**) *das* [von Flasche] deposit; [als Sicherheit] security; [beim Pfänderspiel] token; **etw als Pfand nehmen** to take sthg as security.

pfänden *vt* to seize.

Pfand|flasche *die* returnable bottle.

Pfand|haus *das* pawnshop.

Pfändung (*pl* **-en**) *die* seizure *(U)*.

Pfanne (*pl* **-n**) *die* (frying) pan.

Pfann|kuchen *der* pancake.

Pfarrei (*pl* **-en**) *die* parish.

Pfarrer (*pl* **-**) *der* [katholisch] priest; [evangelisch] minister.

Pfarrerin (*pl* **-nen**) *die* minister.

Pfau (*pl* **-en**) *der* peacock.

Pfeffer *der* pepper.

Pfefferminze, Pfefferminze *die* peppermint.

pfeffern *vt* - **1.** [würzen] to put pepper on/in - **2.** *fam* [werfen] to chuck - **3.** *fam* [ohrfeigen]: **jm eine pfeffern** to give sb a clout.

Pfeife (*pl* **-n**) *die* - **1.** [zum Rauchen, Musikinstrument] pipe; **nach js Pfeife tanzen** *fam fig* to dance to sb's tune; **Pfeife rauchen** to smoke a pipe - **2.** [zum Pfeifen] whistle - **3.** *fam abw* [Mensch] dead loss.

pfeifen (*prät* **pfiff**, *perf* **hat gepfiffen**) ◇ *vi* to whistle; **auf jn/etw pfeifen** *fam fig* not to give a damn about sb/sthg. ◇ *vt* - **1.** [Lied] to whistle - **2.** [Spiel] to referee.

Pfeil (*pl* **-e**) *der* - **1.** [Waffe, Hinweiszeichen] arrow; **grüner Pfeil** filter arrow - **2.** *fam* [Stichelei] barb.

Pfeiler (*pl* **-**) *der* pillar.

Pfennig (*pl* **-e** ODER **-**) *der* pfennig; **keinen Pfennig haben** *fam* not to have a penny.

Pferd (*pl* **-e**) *das* horse; **aufs falsche/richtige Pferd setzen** to back the wrong/right horse.

Pferde|äpfel *Pl* horse droppings.

Pferde|rennen *das* horse race.

Pferde|schwanz *der* [Frisur] ponytail.

Pferde|sport *der (ohne pl)* equestrian sports *Pl*.

Pferde|stall *der* stable.

Pferde|stärke *die* horsepower *(U)*.

pfiff *prät* ▷ **pfeifen**.

Pfiff (*pl* **-e**) *der* - **1.** [Ton] whistle - **2.** *fig* [Reiz] style; **mit Pfiff** stylish.

Pfifferling (*pl* **-e**) *der* chanterelle; **nicht einen** ODER **keinen Pfifferling** *fam fig* not a thing.

pfiffig ◇ *adj* [Mensch, Idee] smart; [Gesicht] knowing. ◇ *adv* cleverly.

Pfingsten *(ohne Artikel)* Whitsun.

Pfirsich (*pl* **-e**) *der* peach.

Pflanze (*pl* **-n**) *die* plant.

pflanzen *vt* to plant.

pflanzlich ◇ *adj* [Nährstoffe, Fasern] plant *(vor Subst)*; [Öl] vegetable *(vor Subst)*; **pflanzliche Ernährung** [von Person] vegetarian diet; [von Tier] herbivorous diet. ◇ *adv*: **sich pflanzlich ernähren** [Person] to be a vegetarian; [Tier] to be a herbivore.

Pflaster (*pl* -) *das* - **1.** [Verband] plaster - **2.** *(ohne pl)* [Straßenbelag] (road) surface; **ein teures Pflaster sein** *fig* to be an expensive place.

Pflaume (*pl* -n) *die* - **1.** [Frucht] plum - **2.** *fam* [Mensch] drip.

Pflaumen|baum *der* plum tree.

Pflaumen|mus *das thick plum purée, used like jam.*

Pflege *die* - **1.** [von Lebewesen] care; **bei jm in Pflege sein** to be looked after by sb; **jn in Pflege nehmen/haben** to look after sb; **ein Kind in Pflege nehmen** to foster a child - **2.** [von Sprache, Beziehung] cultivation; [von Garten, Tradition] maintenance.

Pflege|eltern *Pl* foster parents.

Pflege|heim *das* nursing home.

Pflege|kind *das* foster child.

pflegeleicht *adj* - **1.** [Material] easy-care - **2.** *fam* [Person] easy to deal with.

pflegen *vt* - **1.** [versorgen] to look after; **jn gesund pflegen** to nurse sb back to health - **2.** [schonen] to take care of - **3.** [gewohnt sein]: **etw zu tun pflegen** *geh* to be in the habit of doing sthg.

Pflege|personal *das* nursing staff.

Pfleger, in (*mpl* -, *fpl* -nen) *der, die* nurse.

Pflicht (*pl* -en) *die* - **1.** [Aufgabe] duty; **etw ist Pflicht** sthg is compulsory - **2.** *(ohne pl)* SPORT compulsories *Pl*.

pflichtbewusst <> *adj* conscientious. <> *adv* conscientiously.

Pflicht|fach *das* compulsory subject.

Pflicht|gefühl *das* sense of duty.

Pflicht|versicherung *die* compulsory insurance.

Pflock (*pl* **Pflöcke**) *der* [für Tier] stake; [für Zelt] peg.

pflücken *vt* to pick.

Pflug (*pl* **Pflüge**) *der* plough.

pflügen *vt* & *vi* to plough.

Pforte (*pl* -n) *die* - **1.** [von Krankenhaus, Firma - Tor] gate; [- Eingang] entrance - **2.** *geh* [kleine Tür] door.

Pförtner, in (*mpl* -, *fpl* -nen) *der, die* porter.

Pfosten (*pl* -) *der* post.

Pfote (*pl* -n) *die* paw.

Pfropf (*pl* -e) *der* blockage; [in Ader] clot.

Pfropfen (*pl* -) *der* stopper.

pfui *interj* ugh!

Pfund (*pl* -e) *das* - **1.** [Gewicht] 500 grams, ≃ pound - **2.** [Währung] pound.

Pfusch *der (ohne pl) fam abw* botched job.

Pfuscher, in (*mpl* -, *fpl* -nen) *der, die fam abw* bungler.

Pfütze (*pl* -n) *die* puddle.

Phantasie = **Fantasie**.

phantasieren = **fantasieren**.

phantastisch = **fantastisch**.

Pharao (*pl* -s ODER -aonen) *der* Pharaoh.

Phase (*pl* -n) *die* phase.

Philharmoniker *Pl* Philharmonic (Orchestra) *(sg)*.

Philippinen *Pl*: **die Philippinen** the Philippines.

Philosoph, in (*mpl* -en, *fpl* -nen) *der, die* philosopher.

Philosophie [fılozo'fiː] (*pl* -n) *die* philosophy.

philosophisch <> *adj* philosophical. <> *adv* philosophically.

Phonetik = **Fonetik**.

Phosphat (*pl* -e) *das* phosphate.

Phosphor *der* phosphorus.

phosphoreszieren *vi* to phosphoresce.

Phrase (*pl* -n) *die* cliché; **leere Phrasen** empty phrases; **Phrasen dreschen** *fam fig* to spout clichés.

pH-|Wert [peː'haːveːɐ̯t] *der* pH-value.

Physik *die* physics *(U)*.

physikalisch <> *adj* - **1.** [gen] physical - **2.** [Forschung, Institut] physics *(vor Subst)*. <> *adv* in terms of physics.

Physiker, in (*mpl* -, *fpl* -nen) *der, die* physicist.

physisch <> *adj* physical. <> *adv* physically.

Pianist, in (*mpl* -en, *fpl* -nen) *der, die* pianist.

Pickel (*pl* -) *der* - **1.** [Entzündung] spot - **2.** [Gerät] pickaxe; [für Eis] ice-pick.

pickelig, picklig *adj* spotty.

picken *vt* & *vi* to peck.

Picknick (*pl* -s ODER -e) *das* picnic; **ein Picknick machen** to have a picnic.

pieken *vi* to prick.

piepen *vi* [Vogel] to cheep; [Maus] to squeak; [Piepser] to bleep; **bei dir piepts wohl!** *fam fig* you're off your head!

piercen ◆ **sich piercen** *ref*: **sich die Nase piercen** to have one's nose pierced.

Piercing ['piːrsıŋ] (*pl* -s) *das* body piercing; **ein Piercing in der Zunge/Augenbraue haben** to have a pierced tongue/eyebrow.

piesacken *vt fam* to torment.

Pigment (*pl* -e) *das* pigment.

Pik (*pl* -) *das* - **1.** *(ohne Artikel, ohne pl)* [Spielfarbe] spades *Pl* - **2.** *(pl Pik)* [Spielkarte] spade; **die Piksechs** the six of spades.

pikant <> *adj* spicy. <> *adv* - **1.** [scharf]: **etw pikant würzen** to spice sthg well - **2.** [frivol] spicily.

Pike (*pl* -n) *die*: **etw von der Pike auf lernen** *fam fig* to learn sthg by working one's way up from the bottom.

Pilger (*pl* -) *der* pilgrim.

Pilger|fahrt *die* pilgrimage.

Pilgerin (*pl* **-nen**) *die* pilgrim.

pilgern (*perf* **ist gepilgert**) *vi* - **1.** [wallfahren] to go on a pilgrimage - **2.** *fam* [laufen] to trek.

Pille (*pl* **-n**) *die* - **1.** [Verhütungsmittel]: **die Pille** the pill; **die Pille nehmen** to be on the pill - **2.** *fam* [Tablette] pill.

Pilot (*pl* **-en**) *der* [von Flugzeug] pilot; [von Rennwagen] driver.

Pilotin (*pl* **-nen**) *die* [von Flugzeug] pilot; [von Rennwagen] driver.

Pils (*pl* **-**) *das* Pilsner.

Pilz (*pl* **-e**) *der* - **1.** [Pflanze - essbar] mushroom; [- giftig] toadstool - **2.** *(ohne pl)* [Hautpilz] fungal infection.

PIN (*pl* **-s**) (*abk für* **persönliche Identifikationsnummer**) *die* PIN (number).

pingelig *fam* ◇ *adj* fussy. ◇ *adv* fussily.

Pinguin ['pɪŋguiːn] (*pl* **-e**) *der* penguin.

Pinie ['piːnjə] (*pl* **-n**) *die* stone pine.

pink *adj (unver)* bright pink.

Pink *das* bright pink.

pinkeln *vi fam* to pee.

Pinsel (*pl* **-**) *der* brush.

pinseln *vt* & *vi* to paint.

Pinzette (*pl* **-n**) *die* tweezers *Pl*.

Pionier (*pl* **-e**) *der* - **1.** [Vorkämpfer] pioneer - **2.** [Soldat] engineer.

Pionierin (*pl* **-nen**) *die* pioneer.

Pipi *das fam*: **Pipi machen** to do a wee-wee.

Pirat (*pl* **-en**) *der* pirate.

Piraten|sender *der* pirate radio station.

Piratin (*pl* **-nen**) *die* pirate.

Pirsch *die*: **auf die Pirsch gehen** to go stalking.

Pistazie [pɪs'tɑːtsi̯ə] (*pl* **-n**) *die* pistachio.

Piste (*pl* **-n**) *die* - **1.** [für Flugzeuge] runway - **2.** [Skipiste] piste - **3.** [für Fahrzeuge] track.

Pistole (*pl* **-n**) *die* pistol; **wie aus der Pistole geschossen** *fam fig* like a shot.

Pizza ['pɪtsa] (*pl* **-s**) *die* pizza.

Pizzeria [pɪtse'riːa] (*pl* **Pizzerien** ODER **-s**) *die* pizzeria.

Pkw ['peːkɑːveː] (*pl* **-s**) (*abk für* **Personenkraftwagen**) *der* car, automobile *US*.

plädieren *vi* - **1.** *geh* [stimmen]: **für etw plädieren** to argue for sthg - **2.** RECHT: **für** ODER **auf etw** *(A)* **plädieren** to plead for sthg.

Plage (*pl* **-n**) *die* nuisance.

plagen *vt* to torment; **von etw geplagt sein** to be tormented by sthg. ◆ **sich plagen** *ref* to slave away; **sich mit etw plagen** to slave away at sthg.

Plakat (*pl* **-e**) *das* poster.

Plakette (*pl* **-n**) *die* [Tafel] plaque; [Abzeichen] badge.

Plan (*pl* **Pläne**) *der* - **1.** [Vorgehensweise, Vorhaben] plan; **Pläne schmieden** to make plans - **2.** [Karte] map. ◆ **nach Plan** *adv* according to plan.

Plane (*pl* **-n**) *die* tarpaulin.

planen *vt* to plan.

Planet (*pl* **-en**) *der* planet.

planieren *vt* to level.

Planke (*pl* **-n**) *die* plank.

planlos ◇ *adj* unsystematic. ◇ *adv* unsystematically.

planmäßig ◇ *adj* - **1.** [nach Plan] scheduled - **2.** [systematisch] systematic. ◇ *adv* - **1.** [nach Plan] on time - **2.** [systematisch] systematically.

planschen, plantschen *vi* to splash about.

Plantage [plan'tɑːʒə] (*pl* **-n**) *die* plantation.

Planung (*pl* **-en**) *die* - **1.** [Vorbereitung] planning *(U)* - **2.** [Ergebnis] plan.

plappern *vi* to prattle.

plärren *vi abw* - **1.** [weinen] to wail - **2.** [rufen] to yell - **3.** [Krach machen] to blare.

Plastik (*pl* **-en**) ◇ *das (ohne pl)* plastic. ◇ *die* sculpture.

Plastik|tüte *die* plastic bag.

plastisch ◇ *adj* [dreidimensional] three-dimensional; **eine plastische Darstellung** a vivid description. ◇ *adv* - **1.** [dreidimensional] three-dimensionally - **2.** [lebendig] vividly.

Platane (*pl* **-n**) *die* plane tree.

Platin *das* platinum.

platonisch *adj* platonic.

plätschern (*perf* **hat/ist geplätschert**) *vi* - **1.** *(ist)* [fließen] to splash; [Bach] to babble - **2.** *(hat)* [Geräusch machen] to splash.

platt ◇ *adj* - **1.** [flach] flat (tyre); **einen Platten haben** *fam* to have a flat; **platt sein** *fam fig* to be flabbergasted - **2.** [nichts sagend] trite. ◇ *adv* - **1.** [flach] flat - **2.** [nichts sagend] tritely.

Platt *das* Low German, *dialect spoken in northern Germany*; **Platt sprechen** to speak Low German.

Plattdeutsch(e) *das* Low German, *dialect spoken in northern Germany*; *siehe auch* **Englisch(e)**.

Platte (*pl* **-n**) *die* - **1.** [Bauelement - aus Metall, Glas] sheet; [- aus Stein, Beton] slab; [- aus Holz] board - **2.** [Servierplatte] plate - **3.** [Schallplatte] record; **eine Platte auflegen** ODER **spielen** to put on ODER play a record - **4.** [Herdplatte] ring - **5.** *fam* [Glatze] bald patch. ◆ **kalte Platte** *die meal of cold meats, cheese, salad etc.*

Platten ▷ **platt**.

plätten *vt Norddt* [bügeln] to iron.

Platten|spieler *der* record player.

Platt|fuß *der (ohne pl) fam* flat. ◆ **Plattfüße** *Pl*: **Plattfüße haben** to have flat feet.

Platz (*pl* **Plätze**) *der* - **1.** [Sitzplatz] seat; **Platz nehmen** *geh* to take a seat - **2.** [Freiraum] room, space; **jm/etw Platz machen** [zur Seite gehen] to make room for sb/sthg; [weichen] to make way for sb/sthg; **keinen/genug Platz haben** to have no/enough room - **3.** [Stelle, Rang] place; **auf die Plätze, fertig, los!** on your marks, get set, go! - **4.** [in Stadt] square - **5.** [bei Fußball, Hockey] pitch; [bei Tennis, Volleyball] court. ◆ **fehl am Platz** *adj* out of place. ◆ **Platz sparend** ◇ *adj* space-saving. ◇ *adv* in order to save space.

Platz|anweiser, in (*mpl* -, *fpl* **-nen**) *der, die* usher (usherette *die*).

Plätzchen (*pl* -) *das* - **1.** [Platz] spot - **2.** [Gebäck] biscuit *UK*, cookie *US*.

platzen (*perf* **ist geplatzt**) *vi* - **1.** [bersten] to burst - **2.** *fam* [ausfallen, scheitern - Termin, Vorstellung] to be cancelled; [- Projekt, Vertrag] to fall through; **etw platzen lassen** to cancel sthg; **vor etw** *(D)* **platzen** to be seething with sthg.

platzieren *vt* to place. ◆ **sich platzieren** *ref* [Platz belegen] to be placed.

Platz|karte *die* seat reservation.

Platz|mangel *der* lack of space.

platzsparend *adj* ▷ **Platz**.

Platz|wunde *die* laceration.

plaudern *vi* to chat.

plausibel ◇ *adj* plausible; **jm etw plausibel machen** to make sthg clear to sb. ◇ *adv* plausibly.

plazieren *vt* = **platzieren**.

pleite *adj fam*: **pleite sein** to be broke.

Pleite (*pl* **-n**) *die fam* - **1.** [Ruin] bankruptcy; **Pleite gehen/machen** to go bust; **vor der Pleite stehen** *fam* to be faced with bankruptcy - **2.** [Reinfall] flop.

Plombe (*pl* **-n**) *die* - **1.** [Zahnfüllung] filling - **2.** [Siegel] lead seal.

plombieren *vt* - **1.** [füllen] to fill - **2.** [versiegeln] to put a lead seal on.

plötzlich ◇ *adj* sudden; **ganz plötzlich** all of a sudden. ◇ *adv* suddenly; **aber ein bisschen plötzlich!** *fam* get a move on!

plump *abw* ◇ *adj* clumsy. ◇ *adv* clumsily.

plumpsen (*perf* **ist geplumpst**) *vi* to crash; [ins Wasser] to splash.

Plunder *der fam abw* junk.

plündern ◇ *vt* - **1.** [ausrauben] to loot - **2.** [leeren] to raid. ◇ *vi* to loot.

Plural (*pl* **-e**) *der* GRAMM plural; **im Plural** in the plural.

plus *adv, präp & konj* plus.

Plus *das (ohne pl)* - **1.** [Mehrbetrag]: **(ein) Plus (von 100 Euro) machen** to make a profit (of 100 euros); **im Plus stehen** to be in credit - **2.** [Vorteil] advantage.

Plüsch *der* plush.

Plus|pol *der* positive pole.

Plus|punkt *der* - **1.** [Vorteil] plus point - **2.** [Punkt] point.

Plusquam|perfekt *das* GRAMM pluperfect.

Plutonium *das* CHEM plutonium.

PLZ *abk für* **Postleitzahl**.

Po (*pl* **-s**) *der* bottom.

pochen *vi* - **1.** [klopfen] to knock; **auf etw** *(A)* **pochen** *fig* to insist on sthg - **2.** [pulsieren - Herz] to pound; [- Blut] to throb.

Pocken *Pl* MED smallpox *(U)*.

Podest (*pl* **-e**) *das* [für Redner] rostrum; [für Orchester, Chor] platform.

Podium ['po:di̯ʊm] (*pl* **Podien**) *das* podium.

Podiums|diskussion *die* panel discussion.

Poesie *die geh* poetry.

poetisch ◇ *adj* poetic. ◇ *adv* poetically.

Pointe ['po̯ɛ̃:tə] (*pl* **-n**) *die* punchline.

Pokal (*pl* **-e**) *der* - **1.** [Trophäe] cup - **2.** [Gefäß] goblet.

Poker *der ODER das* poker.

pokern *vi* to play poker.

Pol (*pl* **-e**) *der* pole; **er ist in der Familie der ruhende Pol** he is the calming influence in the family.

polar *adj* polar.

Polar|kreis *der* polar circle.

Pole (*pl* **-n**) *der* Pole.

polemisch ◇ *adj* polemical. ◇ *adv* polemically.

Polen *nt* Poland.

polieren *vt* to polish.

Polin (*pl* **-nen**) *die* Pole.

Politesse (*pl* **-n**) *die* traffic warden.

Politik *die (ohne pl)* - **1.** [des Staates] politics *(U)* - **2.** [Vorgehensweise] policy.

Politiker, in (*mpl* -, *fpl* **-nen**) *der, die* politician.

politisch ◇ *adj* political. ◇ *adv* politically.

Politur (*pl* **-en**) *die* polish.

Polizei *die (ohne pl)* police *Pl*.

Polizei|beamte *der* police officer.

Polizei|beamtin *die* police officer.

polizeilich ◇ *adj* police *(vor Subst)*; **polizeiliches Kennzeichen** registration *UK* ODER license *US* number. ◇ *adv* by the police.

Polizei|revier *das* - **1.** [Polizeiwache] police station - **2.** [Bereich] police district.

Polizei|stunde *die (ohne pl)* closing time.

Polizei|wache *die* police station.

Polizist, in (*mpl* **-en**, *fpl* **-nen**) *der, die* policeman (policewoman *die*).

Pollen (*pl* -) *der* pollen *(U)*.

polnisch *adj* Polish.

Polnisch(e) *das* Polish; *siehe auch* **Englisch(e)**.

Polo *das* polo.

Polster (*pl* -) *das* - **1.** [zum Sitzen, finanziell] cushion - **2.** [Schulterpolster] shoulder pad - **3.** *fam* [Fettpolster] wad of fat.

Polster|möbel *Pl* upholstered furniture *(U)*.

polstern *vt* - **1.** [Möbel] to upholster - **2.** [Kleidung] to pad.

Polsterung (*pl* **-en**) *die* - **1.** [Polstern] upholstering - **2.** [Polster] upholstery *(U)*.

Polter|abend *der celebration usually held on the evening before a wedding, when crockery is broken to bring good luck.*

poltern (*perf* **hat/ist gepoltert**) *vi* - **1.** *(ist)* [sich laut bewegen] to crash - **2.** *(hat)* [Krach machen] to make a racket; **draußen hat etwas gepoltert** there was a crash outside - **3.** *(hat)* [am Polterabend] *to celebrate a "Polterabend"*.

Polyester [poli'ɛstɐ] *das* polyester.

Pommes frites [pɔm'frits] *Pl* chips *UK*, French fries *US*.

Pomp *der* pomp.

pompös <> *adj* lavish. <> *adv* lavishly.

Pony ['pɔni] (*pl* **-s**) <> *das* pony. <> *der* fringe *UK*, bangs *US*.

popelig, poplig *fam abw* <> *adj* - **1.** [minderwertig] lousy - **2.** [geizig] stingy - **3.** [gewöhnlich] ordinary. <> *adv* - **1.** [geizig] stingily - **2.** [billig] cheaply.

poplig = **popelig**.

Pop|musik *die* pop music.

Popo (*pl* **-s**) *der fam* bottom.

populär <> *adj* popular. <> *adv*: **populär schreiben** to write in an accessible way.

Popularität *die* popularity.

Pore (*pl* **-n**) *die* pore.

Porno (*pl* **-s**) *der fam* FILM porn film; [Pornoheft] porn mag.

Pornografie, Pornographie *die* pornography.

porös *adj* porous.

Porree *der (ohne pl)* leek.

Portal (*pl* **-e**) *das* portal.

Portier [pɔr'tje:] (*pl* **-s**) *der* porter.

Portion (*pl* **-en**) *die* - **1.** [von Essen] portion - **2.** [viel] amount.

Portmonee (*pl* **-s**), **Portemonnaie** (*pl* **-s**) [pɔrtmɔ'ne:] *das* purse.

Porto (*pl* **-s**) *das* postage *(U)*.

portofrei *adj* & *adv* post-free *UK*, postpaid *US*.

Porträt [pɔr'trɛ:] (*pl* **-s**) *das* portrait.

porträtieren *vt* to do a portrait of.

Portugal *nt* Portugal.

Portugiese (*pl* **-n**) *der* Portuguese.

Portugiesin (*pl* **-nen**) *die* Portuguese.

portugiesisch *adj* Portuguese.

Portugiesisch(e) *das* Portuguese; *siehe auch* **Englisch(e)**.

Port|wein *der* port.

Porzellan (*pl* **-e**) *das* - **1.** [Material] porcelain - **2.** [Geschirr] china.

Posaune (*pl* **-n**) *die* trombone.

posieren *vi* to pose.

Position (*pl* **-en**) *die* position.

positiv <> *adj* positive. <> *adv* positively.

Possessiv|pronomen *das* GRAMM possessive pronoun.

Post *die (ohne pl)* - **1.** [Institution, Amt] post office; **etw mit der Post schicken** to send sthg by post *UK* ODER mail *US*; **auf die** ODER **zur Post gehen** to go to the post office - **2.** [Postsendung] post *UK*, mail *US*.

Post|amt *das* post office.

Post|anweisung *die* ≃ postal order *UK*, ≃ money order *US*.

Post|bote *der* postman *UK*, mailman *US*.

Post|botin *die* postwoman *UK*, mailwoman *US*.

Posten (*pl* -) *der* - **1.** [Ware] item - **2.** [Arbeitsstelle, Wachposten] post; **auf dem Posten sein** *fam* to be fit; **nicht auf dem Posten sein** *fam* to be under the weather.

Poster (*pl* -) *der ODER das* poster.

Postf. *abk für* **Postfach**.

Post|fach *das* PO box.

Post|karte *die* postcard.

postlagernd *adj* & *adv* poste restante *UK*, general delivery *US*.

Postleit|zahl *die* postcode *UK*, zip code *US*.

Postspar|buch *das* post office savings book.

Postspar|kasse *die* post office savings bank.

Post|stempel *der* postmark.

Post|weg *der*: **auf dem Postweg verloren gehen** to get lost in the post *UK* ODER mail *US*.

postwendend *adv* by return (of post) *UK*, by return mail *US*.

potent *adj* - **1.** [Mann] potent - **2.** *geh* [solvent] financially strong - **3.** *geh* [mächtig] powerful.

Potenz (*pl* **-en**) *die* - **1.** [sexuelle] potency - **2.** [Kraft & MATH] power; **die zweite/dritte Potenz von fünf** the square/cube of five.

Potenzial (*pl* **-e**), **Potential** (*pl* **-e**) [potɛn'tsi̯a:l] *das* potential.

Pott (*pl* **Pötte**) *der Norddt fam* pot.

Pracht *die* magnificence; **eine wahre Pracht sein** *fam* to be magnificent.

Pracht|exemplar *das* [Gegenstand] magnificent example; [Person] magnificent specimen.

prächtig <> *adj* - **1.** [wunderschön] magnificent - **2.** [hervorragend] marvellous. <> *adv* - **1.** [wunderschön] magnificently - **2.** [hervorragend] marvellously.

prachtvoll <> *adj* magnificent. <> *adv* magnificently.

Prädikat (*pl* **-e**) *das* - **1.** [Gütezeichen] rating - **2.** GRAMM predicate.

Prag *nt* Prague.

prägen *vt* - **1.** [in der Entwicklung] to influence; **von etw geprägt sein** to be influenced by sthg - **2.** [von Anfang an] to shape - **3.** [Wort] to coin - **4.** [Münzen] to mint; [Metall, Leder] to emboss.

prägnant ◇ *adj* concise. ◇ *adv* concisely.

Prägung (*pl* **-en**) *die* - **1.** [Muster] impression - **2.** [in der Entwicklung] influence; **gesellschaftliche Prägung** social influence - **3.** [von Anfang an] shaping - **4.** [von Worten] coining *(U)*.

prahlen *vi* to boast; **mit etw prahlen** to boast about sthg.

Praktik (*pl* **-en**) *die* practice. ◆ **Praktiken** *Pl abw* practices.

praktikabel ◇ *adj* practicable. ◇ *adv* practicably.

Praktikant, in (*mpl* **-en**, *fpl* **-nen**) *der, die* trainee.

Praktikum (*pl* **Praktika**) *das* work placement; **ein Praktikum machen** ODER **absolvieren** to be on a work placement.

praktisch ◇ *adj* practical. ◇ *adv* - **1.** [gen] practically; **praktisch alles** practically everything - **2.** [nicht theoretisch] in practice.

praktizieren *vt* & *vi* to practise.

Praline (*pl* **-n**) *die* chocolate.

prall ◇ *adj* [Po, Busen] well-rounded; [Sack] bulging; [Tomate] firm; **in der prallen Sonne** under the blazing sun. ◇ *adv*: **prall gefüllt** filled to bursting.

prallen (*perf* **hat/ist geprallt**) *vi* - **1.** *(ist)* [stoßen]: **gegen/auf etw** *(A)* **prallen** to crash into sthg; **er ist mit dem Kopf auf den Boden geprallt** he banged his head on the floor - **2.** *(hat)* [Sonne] to blaze down.

Prämie ['prɛːmi̯ə] (*pl* **-n**) *die* - **1.** [Beitrag] premium - **2.** [Belohnung] reward - **3.** [Sonderzahlung] bonus.

prämieren *vt* to give an award to.

Pranger (*pl* -) *der*: **jn/etw an den Pranger stellen** *fig* to pillory sb/sthg.

Pranke (*pl* **-n**) *die* paw.

Präparat (*pl* **-e**) *das geh* preparation.

Präposition (*pl* **-en**) *die* GRAMM preposition.

Prärie [prɛ'riː] (*pl* **-n**) *die* prairie.

Präsens ['prɛːzɛns] *das* GRAMM present (tense).

Präservativ [prezɛrva'tiːf] (*pl* **-e**) *das* condom.

Präsident, in (*mpl* **-en**, *fpl* **-nen**) *der, die* president.

Präsidentschaft (*pl* **-en**) *die* presidency.

Präsidium [prɛ'ziːdi̯ʊm] (*pl* **-dien**) *das* - **1.** [von Verein] committee - **2.** [Polizeipräsidium] headquarters *Pl*.

prasseln (*perf* **hat/ist geprasselt**) *vi* - **1.** *(ist)* [Regen] to drum - **2.** *(hat)* [Feuer] to crackle.

Präteritum *das* GRAMM preterite.

Praxis (*pl* **Praxen**) *die* - **1.** [Wirklichkeit] practice; **etw in die Praxis umsetzen** to put sthg into practice - **2.** [Erfahrung] experience - **3.** [Räumlichkeit - von Anwalt] office; [- von Arzt] surgery *UK*, office *US*. ◆ **in der Praxis** *adv* in practice.

präzis, präzise ◇ *adj* precise. ◇ *adv* precisely.

predigen *vt* & *vi* to preach.

Prediger, in (*mpl* -, *fpl* **-nen**) *der, die* preacher.

Predigt (*pl* **-en**) *die* sermon; **(jm) eine Predigt halten** to give (sb) a sermon.

Preis (*pl* **-e**) *der* - **1.** [Geldbetrag] price - **2.** [ausgesetzte Prämie] prize; **der Preis für etw** the price of sthg; **um jeden/keinen Preis** at any/not at any price. ◆ **zum halben Preis** *adv* at half-price.

Preisaus|schreiben *das* competition.

preisbewusst ◇ *adj* price-conscious. ◇ *adv* price-consciously.

Preisel|beere *die* cranberry.

preisen (*prät* **pries**, *perf* **hat gepriesen**) *vt geh* to praise; **sich glücklich preisen** to count o.s. lucky.

preisgünstig ◇ *adj* cheap. ◇ *adv* cheaply.

preislich ◇ *adj* price *(vor Subst)*. ◇ *adv* with regard to price.

Preis|richter, in *der, die* judge.

Preis|schild (*pl* **-er**) *das* price tag.

Preis|träger, in *der, die* prizewinner.

Preis|verleihung *die* prize ceremony.

preiswert ◇ *adj* cheap. ◇ *adv* cheaply.

prellen *vt* - **1.** [betrügen] to cheat - **2.** [stoßen]: **sich** *(D)* **den Schenkel/Arm prellen** to bruise one's thigh/arm - **3.** [Ball] to bounce.

Prellung (*pl* **-en**) *die* bruise.

Premiere [prə'mi̯eːrə] (*pl* **-n**) *die* premiere.

Premier|minister, in [prə'mi̯eːminɪstɐ, rɪn] *der, die* prime minister.

Presse (*pl* **-n**) *die* press.

Presse|agentur *die* press agency.

Presse|bericht *der* press report.

Presse|freiheit *die* freedom of the press.

Presse|konferenz *die* press conference.

Presse|meldung *die* press report.

pressen ◇ *vt* to press. ◇ *vi* [Schwangere] to push.

Presse|sprecher, in *der, die* press officer.

Presse|stelle *die* press office.

Preuße (*pl* **-n**) *der* HIST Prussian.

Preußin (*pl* **-nen**) *die* HIST Prussian.

preußisch *adj* HIST Prussian.

prickeln *vi* - **1.** [kitzeln] to tingle - **2.** [perlen] to sparkle.

prickelnd *adj* [Gefühl] thrilling; [Wein, Wasser] sparkling.

pries *prät* ▷ **preisen**.

Priester, **in** (*mpl* -, *fpl* **-nen**) *der, die* - **1.** [katholischer] priest - **2.** [heidnischer] priest (priestess *die*).

prima *fam* <> *adj (unver)* fantastic. <> *adv* fantastically.

Primel (*pl* **-n**) *die* primula.

primitiv <> *adj* - **1.** [gen] primitive - **2.** [Regeln, Bedürfnisse] basic. <> *adv* primitively.

Prinz (*pl* **-en**) *der* prince.

Prinzessin (*pl* **-nen**) *die* princess.

Prinzip (*pl* **-ien**) *das* principle. ◆ **aus Prinzip** *adv* on principle. ◆ **im Prinzip** *adv* in principle.

prinzipiell <> *adj* basic. <> *adv* - **1.** [aus Prinzip] on principle; [im Prinzip] in principle - **2.** [grundsätzlich] basically.

Priorität (*pl* **-en**) *die* priority. ◆ **Prioritäten** *Pl* priorities.

Prise (*pl* **-n**) *die*: **eine Prise Salz/Pfeffer** a pinch of salt/pepper.

pritschen *vt* SPORT to flick.

privat [pri'vaːt] <> *adj* private. <> *adv* privately.

Privat|adresse *die* home address.

Privatan|gelegenheit *die* private matter; **das ist meine Privatangelegenheit** that is a private matter.

Privat|eigentum *das* private property.

Privat|initiative *die* private initiative.

Privat|leben *das (ohne pl)* private life.

Privat|person *die* private person.

Privat|unterricht *der* private tuition.

Privileg [privi'leːk] (*pl* **-ien**) *das* privilege.

pro <> *präp* per; **einmal pro Tag** once a day. <> *adv*: **pro und kontra argumentieren** to argue for and against.

Pro (*pl* **-s**) *das*: **das Pro und Kontra** the pros and cons *Pl*.

Probe (*pl* **-n**) *die* - **1.** [Test] test; **jn/etw auf die Probe stellen** to put sb/sthg to the test - **2.** [Stichprobe, Warenprobe] sample - **3.** [Übung] rehearsal. ◆ **auf Probe** *adv* on a trial basis.

Probe|exemplar *das* specimen copy.

proben *vt* & *vi* to rehearse.

probeweise *adv* on a trial basis.

probieren *vt* to try.

Problem (*pl* **-e**) *das* problem; **Probleme mit jm/etw haben** to have problems with sb/sthg. ◆ **kein Problem** *interj* no problem!

problematisch *adj* problematic.

problemlos <> *adj* problem-free. <> *adv* without any problems.

Produkt (*pl* **-e**) *das* product.

Produktion (*pl* **-en**) *die* - **1.** [Herstellung] production - **2.** [Erzeugnis] product; FILM [Sendung] production.

produktiv <> *adj* productive. <> *adv* productively.

Produktivität [produktivi'tɛːt] *die* productivity.

Produzent, **in** (*mpl* **-en**, *fpl* **-nen**) *der, die* producer.

produzieren *vt* - **1.** [Ware, Film] to produce - **2.** *fam abw* [machen] to make.

professionell <> *adj* professional. <> *adv* professionally.

Professor (*pl* **--en**) *der* professor.

Professorin (*pl* **-nen**) *die* professor.

Profi (*pl* **-s**) *der* professional.

Profil (*pl* **-e**) *das* - **1.** [Persönlichkeit] image - **2.** [Seitenansicht] profile - **3.** [von Reifen, Sohle] tread.

Profit (*pl* **-e**) *der* profit; **aus etw Profit schlagen** ODER **ziehen** *fig* to profit from sthg; *eigtl* to make a profit out of sthg; **Profit machen** to make a profit.

profitieren *vi*: **von etw profitieren** to profit from sthg.

pro forma *adv* for form's sake.

Prognose (*pl* **-n**) *die* prognosis.

Programm (*pl* **-e**) *das* - **1.** [Programmvorschau] listings *Pl* - **2.** [Sendungen] programmes *Pl* - **3.** [Sender] channel - **4.** [Programmheft, Veranstaltungsablauf, Konzeption] programme; **auf dem Programm stehen** to be on the programme - **5.** [Tagesablauf] schedule; **auf dem Programm stehen** to be on the agenda - **6.** EDV program.

Programm|heft *das* programme.

Programm|hinweis *der* programme announcement.

programmieren *vt* - **1.** [Computer] to program - **2.** [Videorecorder] to programme.

Programmierer, **in** (*mpl* -, *fpl* **-nen**) *der, die* EDV programmer.

Programm|punkt *der* item *(on programme/agenda)*.

progressiv <> *adj* progressive. <> *adv* progressively.

Projekt (*pl* **-e**) *das* project.

Projektor (*pl* **-toren**) *der* projector.

projizieren *vt* to project.

Prolet (*pl* **-en**) *der abw* peasant.

Promenade (*pl* **-n**) *die* promenade.

Promille (*pl* -) *das* - **1.** MATH thousandth - **2.** [Alkoholgehalt] alcohol level; **er hatte 1,5 Promille** he had a blood alcohol level of 1.5 parts per thousand.

prominent *adj* prominent.

Prominenz *die (ohne pl)* prominent figures *Pl*.

Promotion [promo'tsjoːn] (*pl* **-en**) *die* UNI doctorate.

promovieren [promo'viːrən] *vi* to gain a doctorate.

prompt <> *adj* prompt. <> *adv* [erwartungsgemäß] of course; [sofort] promptly.

Pronomen (*pl* - ODER **Pronomina**) *das* GRAMM pronoun.

Propaganda *die* - **1.** [Verbreitung] propaganda - **2.** [Werbung]: **für jn/etw Propaganda machen** to publicize sb/sthg.

Propan|gas *das* propane (gas).

Propeller (*pl* -) *der* propeller.

Prophet, in (*mpl* **-en**, *fpl* **-nen**) *der, die* prophet (prophetess *die*).

prophezeien *vt* to predict; [Subj: prophet] to prophesy; **jm etw prophezeien** to predict sthg for sb.

Proportion (*pl* **-en**) *die* proportion.

proportional <> *adj* proportional. <> *adv* proportionally.

Prosa *die* prose.

prosit, prost *interj* cheers! ◆ **prost Neujahr** *interj* Happy New Year!

Prospekt (*pl* **-e**) *der* brochure.

Prostituierte (*pl* **-n**) *die* prostitute.

Prostitution *die* prostitution.

Protest (*pl* **-e**) *der* protest; **gegen etw Protest einlegen** ODER **erheben** to make a protest against sthg.

Protestant, in (*mpl* **-en**, *fpl* **-nen**) *der, die* Protestant.

protestantisch *adj* Protestant.

protestieren *vi* to protest; **gegen etw protestieren** to protest against ODER about sthg.

Protest|kundgebung *die* protest rally.

Prothese (*pl* **-n**) *die* [für Arm, Bein] artificial limb; [für Zähne] dentures *Pl*.

Protokoll (*pl* **-e**) *das* - **1.** [gen] record; [Aufzeichnung - wortgetreu] transcript; [- von Sitzung] minutes *Pl*; [- polizeilich] statement; **etw zu Protokoll geben** to put sthg on the record; [- polizeilich] to say sthg in one's statement; **eine Aussage zu Protokoll nehmen** to take down a statement; **Protokoll führen** to take the minutes; [- wortgetreu] to make a transcript - **2.** [Zeremoniell] protocol.

Protokoll|führer, in *der, die* [von Sitzung] minute-taker; [im Gericht] clerk.

protokollieren <> *vt* to take down; [Sitzung] to minute. <> *vi* to keep a record; [bei Sitzung] to take the minutes.

protzig *abw adj fam* showy.

Proviant [pro'vi̯ant] *der (ohne pl)* provisions *Pl*.

Provider [pro'vaidɐ] (*pl* -) *der* EDV Internet Service Provider.

Provinz [pro'vɪnts̯] (*pl* **-en**) *die* - **1.** [Verwaltungsbezirk] province - **2.** *(ohne pl) abw* [Gegend] provinces *Pl*.

provinziell [provɪn'tsi̯ɛl] *abw* <> *adj* provincial. <> *adv* provincially.

Provision [provi'zi̯oːn] (*pl* **-en**) *die* commission.

provisorisch [provi'zoːrɪʃ] <> *adj* temporary. <> *adv* temporarily.

Provokation [provoka'ts̯i̯oːn] (*pl* **-en**) *die* provocation.

provozieren [provo'ts̯iːrən] <> *vt* to provoke. <> *vi* to be provocative.

Prozent (*pl* - ODER **-e**) *das* percent; **Prozente bekommen** to get a discount.

Prozent|satz *der* percentage.

prozentual <> *adj* percentage *(vor Subst)*. <> *adv* in percentage terms.

Prozess (*pl* **-e**) *der* - **1.** [Rechtsstreit] trial; **jm den Prozess machen** to put sb on trial - **2.** [Vorgang] process.

prozessieren *vi* to go to court; **gegen jn prozessieren** to take sb to court.

Prozession (*pl* **-en**) *die* - **1.** [kirchliche] procession - **2.** *fam* [Schlange] line.

prüde <> *adj* prudish. <> *adv* prudishly.

prüfen <> *vt* - **1.** [Gerät, Material] to test; [bei Examen] to examine; **jn auf etw** *(A)* **prüfen** to examine sb on sthg; **jn in etw** *(D)* **prüfen** to examine sb in sthg; **etw auf etw** *(A)* **prüfen** to test sthg for sthg - **2.** [Rechnung, Aussage, Unterschrift] to check - **3.** [Angebot] to consider. <> *vi* [examinieren] to be an/the examiner.

Prüfer, in (*mpl* -, *fpl* **-nen**) *der, die* - **1.** [Lehrer] examiner - **2.** [Tester] tester.

Prüfling (*pl* **-e**) *der* candidate.

Prüfung (*pl* **-en**) *die* - **1.** [Kontrolle] check - **2.** [Examen] exam, examination; **eine Prüfung machen** ODER **haben** to take an exam; **eine mündliche/schriftliche Prüfung** an oral/a written exam; **eine Prüfung bestehen** to pass an exam - **3.** *geh* [Belastung] trial - **4.** [im Sport] test.

Prügel (*pl* -) *der* club. ◆ **Prügel** *Pl* thrashing *(U)*.

Prügelei (*pl* **-en**) *die* fight.

prügeln *vt* to beat. ◆ **sich prügeln** *ref* to fight.

Prunk *der abw* splendour.

prunkvoll <> *adj* magnificent. <> *adv* magnificently.

Psalm (*pl* **-en**) *der* psalm.

Psychiater, in (*mpl* -, *fpl* **-nen**) *der, die* psychiatrist.

psychisch <> *adj* [Wohlbefinden, Probleme] psychological; [Krankheit] mental. <> *adv* mentally.

Psycho|analyse *die* psychoanalysis.

Psychologe (*pl* **-n**) *der* psychologist.

Psychologie *die* psychology.

Psychologin (*pl* **-nen**) *die* psychologist.

psychologisch <> *adj* psychological. <> *adv* - **1.** [als Psychologe]: **jn psychologisch begutachten** to give sb a psychological examination - **2.** [mit Menschenkenntnis] psychologically.

Psycho|therapie (*pl* -n) *die* psychotherapy.
Pubertät *die* puberty.
publik *adj*: **etw publik machen** to make sthg public.
Publikation [publika'tsio:n] (*pl* -en) *die* publication.
Publikum *das (ohne pl)* - **1.** [Zuhörer, Zuschauer] audience - **2.** [Gäste] clientele - **3.** [Anhänger] public; [von Schriftsteller] readership.
Pudding (*pl* -e ODER -s) *der* blancmange.
Pudel (*pl* -) *der* poodle.
Puder (*pl* -) *der ODER das* powder.
Puder|dose *die* (powder) compact.
pudern *vt* to powder. ◆ **sich pudern** *ref* to powder o.s.
Puder|zucker *der* icing sugar.
Puff (*pl* -s) *der ODER das fam* brothel.
Puffer (*pl* -) *der* - **1.** [von Bahnen] buffer - **2.** [Kartoffelpuffer] potato pancake.
Pulli (*pl* -s) *der fam* sweater, jumper *UK*.
Pullover [pu'lo:vɐ] (*pl* -) *der* sweater, jumper *UK*.
Puls (*pl* -e) *der* pulse; **am Puls von etw sein** to have one's finger on the pulse of sthg.
Puls|ader *die* artery; **sich** *(D)* **die Pulsadern aufschneiden** to slit one's wrists.
pulsieren *vi* to pulsate; [Blut] to pulse.
Pult (*pl* -e) *das* desk; [Stehpult] lectern.
Pulver ['pulfɐ, 'pulvɐ] (*pl* -) *das* - **1.** [Stoff] powder - **2.** [Schießpulver] gunpowder *(U)*.
Pulver|kaffee *der* instant coffee.
Pulver|schnee *der* powder snow.
Puma (*pl* -s) *der* puma.
pummelig *adj* chubby.
Pumpe (*pl* -n) *die* - **1.** [Gerät] pump - **2.** *salopp* [Herz] ticker.
pumpen ◇ *vt* - **1.** [saugen] to pump - **2.** *fam* [leihen]: **jm etw pumpen** to lend sb sthg; **(sich** *(D)***) etw von jm pumpen** to borrow sthg from sb - **3.** [investieren]: **Geld in etw pumpen** to pump money into sthg. ◇ *vi* [saugen] to pump.
Pumps [pœmps] (*pl* -) *der* court shoe *UK*, pump *US*.
Punker, in ['paŋkɐ, rın] (*mpl* -, *fpl* -nen) *der, die* punk.
Punkt (*pl* -e) *der* - **1.** [gen] point - **2.** [Fleck, typografisches Zeichen] dot; [am Satzende] full stop *UK*, period *US* - **3.** [Zeitpunkt]: **Punkt ein Uhr** one o'clock on the dot; **der springende Punkt** the crux of the matter; **an einem toten Punkt angelangt sein** [Verhandlungen] to have reached deadlock; **ein wunder** ODER **schwacher Punkt** [Schwäche] a weak point; [heikles Thema] a sore point.
pünktlich ◇ *adj* punctual. ◇ *adv* punctually, on time.
Pünktlichkeit *die* punctuality.
Pupille (*pl* -n) *die* pupil.
Puppe (*pl* -n) *die* - **1.** [Figur] doll - **2.** *salopp* [Frau, Mädchen] bird *UK*, doll *US*; [als Anrede] baby.
pur *adj* - **1.** [rein] pure - **2.** [Whisky] neat.
Püree (*pl* -s) *das* puree.
Purzel|baum *der*: **einen Purzelbaum machen** ODER **schlagen** to do a somersault.
Puste *die fam* puff; **aus der** ODER **außer Puste sein** to be out of puff.
pusten *vt* & *vi* to blow.
Pute (*pl* -n) *die* - **1.** [Tier] turkey (hen) - **2.** *salopp abw* [Frau] cow.
Puter (*pl* -) *der* turkey (cock).
Putsch (*pl* -e) *der* putsch.
Putz *der* plaster.
putzen ◇ *vt* to clean; [Gemüse] to wash; **jm die Nase putzen** to wipe sb's nose; **sich** *(D)* **die Zähne putzen** to clean ODER brush one's teeth; **sich** *(D)* **die Nase putzen** to blow one's nose. ◇ *vi* to clean. ◆ **sich putzen** *ref* to wash o.s.; [Vogel] to preen o.s.
Putz|frau *die* cleaner.
Putz|lappen *der* cloth.
Putz|mittel *das* cleaning fluid.
Puzzle ['pazl̩] (*pl* -s) *das* jigsaw (puzzle).
Pyramide (*pl* -n) *die* pyramid.
Pyrenäen *Pl*: **die Pyrenäen** the Pyrenees.

Q

q (*pl* - ODER -s), **Q** (*pl* - ODER -s) [ku:] *das* q, Q.
qm (*abk für* **Quadratmeter**) m^2.
Quader (*pl* -) *der* - **1.** MATH rectangular solid - **2.** [Block] stone block.
Quadrat (*pl* -e) *das* square.
quadratisch ◇ *adj* square. ◇ *adv* in squares.
Quadrat|meter *der* square metre.
quaken *vi* - **1.** [Frosch] to croak; [Ente] to quack - **2.** *fam abw* [reden] to squawk.
Qual (*pl* -en) *die* agony; [seelisch] torment; **jm das Leben zur Qual machen** to make sb's life a misery. ◆ **Qualen** *Pl* suffering *(sg)*, agony *(sg)*; [seelisch] torment *(sg)*; **jn von seinen/ihren Qualen erlösen** to put sb out of his/her misery.
quälen *vt* - **1.** [gen] to torment; [foltern] to torture - **2.** *fam* [bedrängen] to pester; **jn mit etw**

quälen to plague sb with sthg. ◆ **sich quälen** *ref* - **1.** [leiden] to suffer - **2.** [sich abmühen] to struggle.

Quälerei (*pl* **-en**) *die* - **1.** [Peinigung] torment; [Folter] torture; [Grausamkeit] cruelty; **Quälerei der Tiere** cruelty to animals - **2.** *(ohne pl)* [Anstrengung] struggle.

qualifizieren *vt* - **1.** [befähigen] to qualify - **2.** [beurteilen] to classify. ◆ **sich qualifizieren** *ref* [sich befähigen] to obtain qualifications; [für Wettbewerb] to qualify.

Qualität (*pl* **-en**) *die* quality.

Qualle (*pl* **-n**) *die* jellyfish.

Qualm *der* - **1.** [von Feuer] thick smoke - **2.** *fam abw* [von Zigaretten] fug.

qualmen ◇ *vi* to smoke. ◇ *vt salopp* [Zigaretten] to puff away at.

qualvoll ◇ *adj* agonizing. ◇ *adv* in agony.

Quantität *die (ohne pl)* quantity.

Quarantäne [karan'tɛːnə] (*pl* **-n**) *die* quarantine *(U)*.

Quark *der* quark, *type of soft cheese*.

Quartal (*pl* **-e**) *das* quarter.

Quartett (*pl* **-e**) *das* - **1.** MUS quartet - **2.** *(ohne pl)* [Kartenspiel] *children's card game where players have to collect four of a kind*.

Quartier (*pl* **-e**) *das* accommodation *(U)*.

Quarz|uhr *die* quartz watch.

quasi *adv* virtually.

Quatsch *der fam* rubbish.

quatschen *fam* ◇ *vi* - **1.** [reden] to chat - **2.** *abw* [quasseln] to chatter. ◇ *vt* [reden] to talk.

Queck|silber *das* CHEM mercury.

Quelle (*pl* **-n**) *die* - **1.** [Wasserquelle] spring - **2.** [Informant(en), Fundstelle] source.

quellen (*präs* **quillt**, *prät* **quoll**, *perf* **ist gequollen**) *vi* - **1.** [austreten - Flüssigkeit] to stream; [- Rauch] to billow - **2.** [hervortreten] to swell; [Augen] to bulge - **3.** [Feuchtigkeit aufnehmen] to soak.

quengeln *vi fam* to whine.

quer *adv* diagonally; **quer durch etw** straight through sthg; **quer über etw** *(A)*, **quer auf etw** *(D)* across sthg; **quer zu etw** at right angles to sthg.

Quere *die*: **jm in die Quere kommen** *fig* [behindern] to get in sb's way; [Weg abschneiden] to block sb's path; [treffen] to bump into sb.

querfeldein *adv* cross-country.

Quer|flöte *die* flute.

Quer|schnitt *der* - **1.** [Auswahl, Abbildung] cross-section - **2.** [Schnitt] cut.

querschnittsgelähmt *adj* paraplegic.

Quer|straße *die*: **die nächste Querstraße rechts** the next turning on the right.

quetschen *vt* - **1.** [unterbringen, drängen] to squeeze - **2.** [zerdrücken] to crush - **3.** [verletzen]: **der Baum hat mir das Bein gequetscht** the tree crushed my leg. ◆ **sich quetschen** *ref* [sich zwängen] to squeeze.

Quetschung (*pl* **-en**) *die* bruise.

quieken *vi* [Ferkel] to squeal; [Maus] to squeak.

quietschen *vi* - **1.** [Tür, Bremse] to squeak - **2.** *fam* [juchzen] to squeal.

quillt *präs* ▷ **quellen**.

Quirl (*pl* **-e**) *der* whisk.

quitt *adj (unver)*: **mit jm quitt sein** *fam* to be quits with sb.

quittieren ◇ *vt* - **1.** [bestätigen] to sign for; **etw quittieren lassen** to get a receipt for sthg - **2.** [erwidern] to respond to - **3.** [kündigen]: **den Dienst quittieren** to resign. ◇ *vi* [Empfang bestätigen] to sign.

Quittung (*pl* **-en**) *die* - **1.** [Beleg] receipt - **2.** *fig* [Konsequenz]: **da hast du die Quittung!** that's the price you pay!

Quiz [kvis] (*pl* **-**) *das* quiz.

quoll *prät* ▷ **quellen**.

Quote (*pl* **-n**) *die* [Anteil] proportion; [festgeschriebene Zielmenge] quota; [Einschaltquote] viewing figures *Pl*.

R

r (*pl* - ODER **-s**), **R** (*pl* - ODER **-s**) [ɛr] *das* r, R.

Rabatt (*pl* **-e**) *der* discount.

Rabbi (*pl* **-s**) *der* rabbi.

Rabe (*pl* **-n**) *der* raven.

rabiat ◇ *adj* [gewalttätig] brutal; [wütend] furious. ◇ *adv* [gewalttätig] brutally; [wütend] furiously.

Rache *die* revenge.

Rachen (*pl* **-**) *der* throat.

rächen *vt* to avenge. ◆ **sich rächen** *ref* - **1.** [Rache nehmen] to get one's revenge; **sich an jm (für** ODER **wegen etw) rächen** to take revenge on sb (for sthg) - **2.** [Konsequenzen haben]: **seine Faulheit wird sich rächen** he'll pay for his laziness.

Rad (*pl* **Räder**) *das* - **1.** [von Fahrzeug] wheel - **2.** [Fahrrad] bike; **Rad fahren** to cycle - **3.** [von Maschine] cog.

Radar *der* ODER *das* radar.

Radar|kontrolle *die* radar speed check.

Radau *der* racket.

radebrechen ◇ *vt*: **Englisch/Deutsch radebrechen** to speak broken English/German. ◇ *vi*: **er radebrechte in Englisch** he spoke broken English.

radeln (*perf* **ist geradelt**) *vi* to cycle.

rad|fahren *vi (unreg)* ▷ **Rad**.

Rad|fahrer, in *der, die* cyclist.

Radfahr|weg *der* cycle track.

radieren *vt* & *vi* [mit Radiergummi] to erase.

Radier|gummi *der* rubber *UK*, eraser *US*.

Radieschen [ra'di:sçən] (*pl* -) *das* radish.

radikal ◇ *adj* radical. ◇ *adv* radically.

Radio (*pl* **-s**) *das* - **1.** [gen] radio; **Radio hören** to listen to the radio - **2.** *(ohne pl)* [Anstalt] radio station.

Radioaktivität *(ohne Pl) die* radioactivity.

Radio|rekorder (*pl* -) *der* radio cassette recorder.

Radio|sendung *die* radio programme.

Radio|wecker *der* radio alarm.

Radius (*pl* **Radien**) *der* radius.

Rad|rennen *das* cycle race.

Rad|sport *der* cycling.

Rad|tour *die* cycling tour.

Rad|weg *der* cycle path.

rạffen *vt* - **1.** *abw* [nehmen] to stuff; **etw an sich** *(A)* **raffen** to grab sthg - **2.** [Stoff] to gather - **3.** *salopp* [begreifen] to get.

Raffinerie [rafinə'ri:] (*pl* **-n**) *die* refinery.

raffiniert ◇ *adj* - **1.** [Person, Plan, System] ingenious; [Geschmack, Farbe] subtle; [Kleiderschnitt] sophisticated - **2.** [gerissen] cunning. ◇ *adv* - **1.** [planen, arrangieren] ingeniously; [würzen] subtly; **raffiniert kochen** to be a sophisticated cook - **2.** [gerissen] cunningly.

ragen (*perf* **hat/ist geragt**) *vi*: **aus etw ragen** to stick out of sthg; [Berg, Baum, Gebäude] to rise up out of sthg.

Ragout [ra'gu:] (*pl* **-s**) *das* stew.

Rahm *der* cream.

rahmen *vt* to frame.

Rahmen (*pl* -) *der* - **1.** [von Bild, Fenster, Fahrrad] frame - **2.** [von Fahrzeugen] chassis - **3.** *(ohne pl)* [Umgebung] setting; [Kontext] context; **aus dem Rahmen fallen** to be out of place. ◆ **im Rahmen** *adv*: **im Rahmen einer Sache** *(G)* [Zusammenhang] in the context of sthg; [Verlauf] in the course of sthg; [innerhalb der Grenzen] within the bounds of sthg; [als Teil] as part of sthg.

räkeln, rekeln ◆ **sich räkeln, sich rekeln** *ref* to stretch out.

Rakete (*pl* **-n**) *die* rocket; MIL missile.

rạmmen *vt* to ram.

Rạmpe (*pl* **-n**) *die* - **1.** [Laderampe, Auffahrt] ramp - **2.** [in Theater] apron.

Rạmpen|licht *das (ohne pl)* footlights *Pl*; **im Rampenlicht stehen** *fig* to be in the limelight.

ramponiert *adj fam* battered.

Rạmsch *der fam abw* junk.

rạn *fam* = **heran**.

Rạnd (*pl* **Rạ̈nder**) *der* - **1.** [von Stadt, Tisch, Teich] edge - **2.** [von Gefäßen] rim - **3.** [von Buchseite] margin - **4.** [Umrandung] edging *(U)*; **(dunkle) Ränder um die Augen haben** to have dark rings around one's eyes; **mit jm/etw (nicht) zu Rande kommen** *fam* (not) to be able to cope with sb/sthg. ◆ **am Rande** *adv* - **1.** [nebenbei] in passing; **sich am Rande abspielen** to take place on the sidelines - **2.** [nahe]: **am Rande der Verzweiflung sein** to be close to despair.

randalieren *vi* to rampage.

Rạnd|bezirk *der* suburb.

Rạnd|gruppe *die* marginal group.

rạndvoll ◇ *adj* full to the brim. ◇ *adv* to the brim.

rạng *prät* ▷ **ringen**.

Rạng (*pl* **Rạ̈nge**) *der* - **1.** [Position] rank - **2.** [Ansehen] class; **ein Wissenschaftler von Rang** a renowned scientist - **3.** [in Theater, Stadion] circle; **der erste/zweite Rang** [in Theater] the dress/upper circle; [im Wettbewerb] first/second place.

rangieren [raŋ'ʒi:rən] ◇ *vt* to shunt. ◇ *vi* to be ranked.

Rạng|liste *die* (army/navy/civil service) list.

Rạng|ordnung *die* order of precedence.

rạn|halten ◆ **sich ranhalten** *ref (unreg) fam* to get on with it.

Rạnke (*pl* **-n**) *die* tendril.

rạnken (*perf* **hat/ist gerạnkt**) *vi (ist)* to climb. ◆ **sich ranken** *ref* to climb; **sich um etw ranken** [wachsen] to entwine itself around sthg; *fig* & *geh* [spinnen] to grow up around sthg.

rạnn *prät* ▷ **rinnen**.

rạnnte *prät* ▷ **rennen**.

rạnzig *adj* rancid.

Rạps *der* rape.

rar *adj* rare.

Rarität (*pl* **-en**) *die* rarity.

rasạnt ◇ *adj* - **1.** [schnell] rapid - **2.** *fam* [imponierend] stunning. ◇ *adv* [schnell] rapidly.

rạsch ◇ *adj* quick. ◇ *adv* quickly.

rạscheln *vi* to rustle.

rasen (*perf* **hat/ist gerast**) *vi* - **1.** *(ist)* [fahren] to race; **gegen etw rasen** to crash into sthg - **2.** *(hat)* [toben] to rage; **das Publikum raste vor Begeisterung** the audience went wild with enthusiasm.

Rasen (*pl* -) *der* [Rasenfläche] lawn; [Gras] grass.

rasend ◇ *adj* - **1.** [Entwicklung] rapid; [Geschwindigkeit] lightning *(vor Subst)*; [Eile] great - **2.** [gewaltig] raging - **3.** [wütend]: **jn rasend ma-**

chen *fam* to drive sb mad. ◇ *adv* - **1.**: **rasend schnell** incredibly quickly - **2.** [enorm] terribly; **rasend verliebt sein** to be madly in love.

Rasen|mäher *der* lawnmower.

Raserei *die (ohne pl)* - **1.** [Toben] rage; **jn zur Raserei bringen** to drive sb mad - **2.** *abw* [Schnelligkeit] speeding.

Rasier|apparat *der* shaver.

rasieren *vt* to shave. ◆ **sich rasieren** *ref* to shave; **sich nass/trocken rasieren** to have a wet/dry shave.

Rasierer (*pl* -) *der fam* shaver.

Rasier|klinge *die* razor blade.

Rasier|schaum *der* shaving foam.

Rasier|wasser *das* aftershave.

raspeln *vt* [reiben] to grate.

Rasse (*pl* **-n**) *die* - **1.** [bei Tieren] breed - **2.** [bei Menschen] race.

Rassel (*pl* **-n**) *die* rattle.

rasseln (*perf* **hat/ist gerasselt**) *vi* - **1.** *(hat)* [Geräusch erzeugen] to rattle - **2.** *(ist) fam* [durchfallen]: **durch eine Prüfung rasseln** to flunk an exam.

Rassismus *der* racism.

rassistisch *adj* racist.

Rast (*pl* **-en**) *die* rest; **Rast machen** [beim Fahren] to stop for a break; [beim Gehen] to stop for a rest.

rasten *vi* [beim Fahren] to stop for a break; [beim Gehen] to stop for a rest.

Raster (*pl* -) *das* TECH screen; [System] framework.

Rast|hof *der* [an Autobahnen] services *Pl*.

rastlos ◇ *adj* tireless. ◇ *adv* tirelessly.

Rast|platz *der* picnic area *(with toilet facilities)*.

Rast|stätte *die* [auf Autobahnen] services *Pl*.

Rasur (*pl* **-en**) *die* shave.

Rat (*pl* **Räte**) *der* - **1.** [Ratschlag] advice *(U)*; **jm einen Rat geben** to give sb a piece of advice; **jn/etw zu Rate ziehen** to consult sb/sthg; **jn um Rat fragen** ODER **bitten** to ask sb for advice; **sich** *(D)* **keinen Rat (mehr) wissen** to be at one's wits' end - **2.** [Versammlung] council - **3.** [Person] councillor.

rät *präs* ▷ **raten**.

Rate (*pl* **-n**) *die* - **1.** [Teilzahlung] instalment; **etw auf Raten kaufen** to buy sthg on hire purchase - **2.** [statistische] rate.

raten (*präs* **rät**, *prät* **riet**, *perf* **hat geraten**) ◇ *vt* - **1.** [erraten] to guess - **2.** [empfehlen]: **jm raten, etw zu tun** to advise sb to do sthg. ◇ *vi* - **1.** [erraten] to guess - **2.** [Rat geben]: **jm zu etw raten** to advise sb to do sthg.

Raten|zahlung *die* payment by instalments.

Ratgeber (*pl* -) *der* - **1.** [Mensch] adviser - **2.** [Buch] guide.

Ratgeberin (*pl* **-nen**) *die* adviser.

Rat|haus *das* town hall.

Ration (*pl* **-en**) *die* ration.

rational ◇ *adj* rational. ◇ *adv* rationally.

rationalisieren *vt* to rationalize.

rationell ◇ *adj* efficient. ◇ *adv* efficiently.

rationieren *vt* to ration.

ratlos ◇ *adj* helpless. ◇ *adv* helplessly.

Rätoromanisch(e) *das* Rhaeto-Romanic; *siehe auch* **Englisch(e)**.

ratsam *adj* advisable.

Rat|schlag *der* piece of advice.

Rätsel (*pl* -) *das* - **1.** [Aufgabe] puzzle; **jm ein Rätsel aufgeben** to ask sb a riddle - **2.** [Geheimnis] mystery; **etw ist jm ein Rätsel** sthg is a mystery to sb; **vor einem Rätsel stehen** to be faced with a mystery.

rätselhaft *adj* mysterious; **es ist mir rätselhaft** it's a mystery to me.

rätseln *vi*: **über etw** *(A)* **rätseln** to puzzle over sthg.

Ratte (*pl* **-n**) *die* rat.

rau *adj* - **1.** [Oberfläche, Person, Sitten] rough - **2.** [Klima, Leben] harsh - **3.** [angegriffen - Stimme] hoarse; [- Hals] sore.

Raub *der* robbery.

Raub|bau *der* overexploitation.

rauben *vt* - **1.** [stehlen] to steal - **2.** [kosten]: **jm etw rauben** to rob sb of sthg; **jm den Schlaf rauben** to deprive sb of their sleep.

Räuber, in (*mpl* -, *fpl* **-nen**) *der, die* robber.

Raub|mord *der* robbery with murder.

Raub|tier *das* predator.

Raubüber|fall *der* robbery.

Raub|vogel *der* bird of prey.

Rauch *der* smoke.

rauchen *vt* & *vi* to smoke.

Raucher (*pl* -) *der* smoker.

Raucherin (*pl* **-nen**) *die* smoker.

räuchern *vt* to smoke.

Rauch|verbot *das* ban on smoking.

rauf *fam* = **herauf**.

raufen *vi* to fight. ◆ **sich raufen** *ref* to fight.

Rauferei (*pl* **-en**) *die* fight.

rauh = **rau**.

Rauhreif = **Raureif**.

Raum (*pl* **Räume**) *der* - **1.** [Zimmer] room - **2.** [Platz & PHYS] space - **3.** *(ohne pl)* GEOGR area.

räumen *vt* - **1.** [Wohnung] to vacate - **2.** [Platz, Posten] to clear.

Raum|fahrt *die* space travel.

Raum|inhalt *der* volume.

räumlich ◇ *adj* spatial. ◇ *adv* spatially.

Raum|schiff *das* spaceship.

Räumung (*pl* **-en**) *die* clearing *(U)*; [von Wohnung] vacation *(U)*; [vor Gefahr] evacuation.

Raupe (*pl* **-n**) *die* [Insekt] caterpillar.

Raureif *der* hoarfrost.

raus *adv fam* - **1.** = **heraus** - **2.** [hinaus] out; **raus hier!** get out!

Rausch (*pl* **Räusche**) *der* - **1.** [das Betrunkensein] intoxication; **einen Rausch haben** to be drunk - **2.** [Ekstase] ecstasy; **im Rausch** in ecstasy.

rauschen (*perf* **hat/ist gerauscht**) *vi* - **1.** *(hat)* [Bäume] to rustle; [Bach] to murmur; **es rauscht** [im Telefon] there's a crackle; [in den Ohren] there's a buzz - **2.** *(ist) fam* [gehen] to rush.

rauschend *adj*: **ein rauschendes Fest** a glittering party; **rauschender Beifall** loud applause.

Rausch|gift *das* drug.

rauschgiftsüchtig *adj* addicted to drugs.

raus|fliegen (*perf* **ist rausgeflogen**) *vi (unreg) fam* [aus Schule] to be thrown out; [aus Firma] to be fired.

raus|halten *vt (unreg) fam* [nach draußen] to hold out. ◆ **sich raushalten** *ref fam*: **sich aus etw raushalten** to keep out of sthg.

raus|kriegen *vt fam* to find out.

räuspern ◆ **sich räuspern** *ref* to clear one's throat.

raus|rücken (*perf* **hat/ist rausgerückt**) *fam* ◇ *vi (ist)*: **mit etw rausrücken** [ausdrücken] to come out with sthg; [herausgeben] to hand over sthg. ◇ *vt (hat)* [herausgeben] to hand over.

raus|schmeißen *vt (unreg) fam* to throw out.

Raute (*pl* **-n**) *die* diamond (shape).

Rạzzia (*pl* **Rạzzien**) *die* (police) raid.

rd. *abk für* **rund**.

reagieren *vi* to react; **auf etw** *(A)* **reagieren** to react to sthg.

Reaktion (*pl* **-en**) *die* reaction; **die Reaktion auf etw** *(A)* the reaction to sthg.

Reạktor (*pl* **-toren**) *der* (nuclear) reactor.

realịstisch ◇ *adj* realistic. ◇ *adv* realistically.

Realität (*pl* **-en**) *die* reality.

Real|schule *die secondary school for pupils up to the age of 16.*

Rebe (*pl* **-n**) *die* vine.

rebellieren *vi* to rebel; **gegen jn/etw rebellieren** to rebel against sb/sthg.

Rebellion (*pl* **-en**) *die* rebellion.

rebẹllisch *adj* rebellious.

Reb|huhn *das* partridge.

Reb|stock *der* vine.

Rẹchen (*pl* **-**) *der* rake.

Rẹchen|aufgabe *die* sum.

Rẹchen|fehler *der* miscalculation.

rẹchnen ◇ *vi* - **1.** [berechnen] to calculate - **2.** [schätzen] to estimate - **3.** [erwarten]: **mit jm/etw rechnen** to expect sb/sthg - **4.** [sich verlassen]: **auf jn/etw rechnen** to count on sb/sthg; **mit jm rechnen** to rely on sb - **5.** [bedenken]: **mit jm/etw rechnen** to reckon with sb/sthg; **im Urlaub mit gutem Wetter rechnen** to reckon on having good weather on holiday. ◇ *vt* [berechnen] to work out. ◆ **sich rechnen** *ref* to be profitable.

Rẹchner (*pl* **-**) *der* EDV computer.

Rẹchnung (*pl* **-en**) *die* - **1.** WIRTSCH bill; [im Restaurant] bill *UK*, check *US*; **eine Rechnung begleichen** to pay a bill - **2.** [Rechenaufgabe] calculation; **eine Rechnung begleichen** to settle a score.

rẹcht ◇ *adj* - **1.** [korrekt, passend] right; **recht und billig** *fig* right and proper; **zur rechten Zeit am rechten Ort** at the right place at the right time; **ist es dir recht, wenn ich morgen vorbeikomme?** is it all right with you if I come by tomorrow? - **2.** [besonders] particular; **es macht keinen rechten Spaß** it's not really much fun. ◇ *adv* [ziemlich] quite; **man kann ihm nichts recht machen** there's no pleasing him; **jetzt erst recht** even more.

Rẹcht (*pl* **-e**) *das* - **1.** RECHT law; **Recht sprechen** to administer justice; **im Recht sein** to be in the right; **jm Recht geben** to admit sb is right - **2.** [Anrecht] right; **ein Recht auf etw** *(A)* **haben** to have a right to sthg. ◆ **mit** ODER **zu Recht** *adv* rightly.

rẹchte, r, s *adj* - **1.** [Seitenangabe] right - **2.** [rechtspolitisch] right-wing.

Rẹchte (*pl* **-n**) ◇ *die* - **1.** [rechte Hand] right hand; **zur Rechten** on the right - **2.** POL: **die Rechte** the Right. ◇ *der, die* right-winger. ◇ *das*: **nach dem Rechten sehen** to see to things.

Rẹchteck (*pl* **-e**) *das* rectangle.

rẹchteckig *adj* rectangular.

rẹchtfertigen *vt* to justify; **etw vor jm rechtfertigen** to justify sthg to sb. ◆ **sich rechtfertigen** *ref*: **sich (vor jm) rechtfertigen** to justify o.s. (to sb).

Rẹchtfertigung (*pl* **-en**) *die* justification.

rẹchthaberisch *adj abw* opinionated; **er ist immer so rechthaberisch** he always thinks he's right.

rẹchtlich ◇ *adj* legal. ◇ *adv* legally.

rẹchtmäßig ◇ *adj* lawful. ◇ *adv* lawfully.

rẹchts ◇ *adv* - **1.** [Angabe der Seite, Richtung] on the right; **rechts abbiegen** turn right; **nach/von rechts** to/from the right; **rechts von jm** to one's right; **rechts von etw** to the right of sthg - **2.** [Angabe der politischen Richtung] right wing; **rechts eingestellt sein** to have right-wing leanings. ◇ *präp (+ G)* [Angabe der Seite] to the right of.

Rẹchts|anwalt *der* lawyer.

Rẹchts|anwältin *die* lawyer.

rechtsbündig *adj* right justified.

Rechtschreib|fehler *der* spelling mistake.

Recht|schreibung *die* spelling.

rechtsextrem *adj*: **rechtsextreme Jugendliche** young right-wing extremists.

Rechts|extremist, in *der, die abw* right-wing extremist.

rechtsgerichtet *adj* right-wing.

rechtsgültig *adj* legally valid.

Rechtshänder, in (*mpl* -, *fpl* **-nen**) *der, die* right-hander.

rechtsherum *adv* to the right.

rechtskräftig ◇ *adj* final; **rechtskräftig sein** to be legally effective. ◇ *adv*: **jn rechtskräftig verurteilen** to pass a final sentence on sb.

Rechts|kurve *die* right-hand bend.

Rechts|lage *die* legal situation.

Rechtsprechung (*pl* **-en**) *die* administration of justice *(U)*.

rechtsradikal *adj* extreme right-wing.

Rechts|radikale *der, die* right-wing extremist.

rechtsseitig *adj* of the right side.

Rechts|staat *der* state based upon the rule of law.

Rechts|verkehr *der* - **1.** [Straßenverkehr] driving on the right - **2.** RECHT law.

Rechts|weg *der* legal action; **der Rechtsweg ist ausgeschlossen** no legal action may be taken.

rechtwinklig, rechtwinkelig ◇ *adj* right-angled. ◇ *adv* at a right angle.

rechtzeitig ◇ *adj* timely. ◇ *adv* in time; **rechtzeitig da sein/eintreffen** to be/get there in time.

Reck (*pl* **-e** *ODER* **-s**) *das* horizontal bar.

recyclen [ri'saikəln] *vt* to recycle.

Recycling [ri'saikliŋ] *das* recycling.

Recycling|papier *das* recycled paper.

Redakteur, in [redak'tøːɐ̯, rın] (*mpl* **-e**, *fpl* **-nen**) *der, die* editor.

Redaktion (*pl* **-en**) *die* - **1.** [Team] editorial staff - **2.** [von Texten] editing.

Rede (*pl* **-n**) *die* - **1.** [Ansprache] speech; **eine Rede halten** to make a speech - **2.** *(ohne pl)* [das Reden] talk; **die Rede ist von jm/etw** we are talking about sb/sthg - **3.** GRAMM [gebundene] verse; [ungebundene] prose; **wörtliche/indirekte Rede** direct/indirect speech; **jn zur Rede stellen** to demand an explanation from sb.

Rede|freiheit *die* freedom of speech.

reden ◇ *vi* - **1.** [gen] to talk; **deutlich/langsam reden** to speak clearly/slowly; **(mit jm) über jn/etw reden** to talk (to sb) about sb/sthg - **2.** [eine Rede halten] to speak; **du hast gut reden** *fam* it's easy for you to talk; **jn zum Reden bringen** to get sb to talk; **von sich reden machen** to cause a stir. ◇ *vt*: **Unsinn reden** to talk nonsense.

Redens|art *die* saying; **das ist doch nur eine Redensart** it's just an expression.

Rede|wendung *die* idiom.

Redner, in (*mpl* -, *fpl* **-nen**) *der, die* speaker.

redselig *adj* talkative.

reduzieren *vt* - **1.** [verringern] to reduce - **2.** [vereinfachen]: **etw auf etw** *(A)* **reduzieren** to reduce sthg to sthg. ◆ **sich reduzieren** *ref* to decrease.

Reederei (*pl* **-en**) *die* shipping company.

Referat (*pl* **-e**) *das* - **1.** [Abhandlung] paper; **ein Referat halten** to give a paper - **2.** [Abteilung] department.

Referendar (*pl* **-e**) *der person undergoing "Referendariat"*; [in Schule] student teacher.

Referendariat (*pl* **-e**) *das period of practical training in teaching or legal professions, undertaken on completion of first "Staatsexamen".*

Referendarin (*pl* **-nen**) *die person undergoing "Referendariat"*; [in Schule] student teacher.

Referenz (*pl* **-en**) *die* reference.

reflektieren ◇ *vt* - **1.** [Licht] to reflect - **2.** *geh* [Problem] to reflect on. ◇ *vi geh*: **über etw** *(A)* **reflektieren** to reflect on sthg.

Reflex (*pl* **-e**) *der* - **1.** [Reaktion] reflex - **2.** [Lichtreflex] reflection.

Reflexion (*pl* **-en**) *die* reflection.

reflexiv ◇ *adj* GRAMM reflexive. ◇ *adv* GRAMM reflexively.

Reflexiv|pronomen *das* GRAMM reflexive pronoun.

Reform (*pl* **-en**) *die* reform.

Reformations|tag *der* RELIG Reformation Day, *31 October, day on which the Reformation is celebrated.*

Reform|haus *das* health food shop.

reformieren *vt* to reform.

Reform|kost *die* health food.

Refrain [rə'frɛ̃ː] (*pl* **-s**) *der* refrain.

Regal (*pl* **-e**) *das* shelves *Pl*.

Regatta (*pl* **Regatten**) *die* regatta.

rege ◇ *adj* lively; [Verkehr] busy; [Handel] brisk. ◇ *adv*: **sich rege an etw** *(D)* **beteiligen** to take a lively interest in sthg.

Regel (*pl* **-n**) *die* - **1.** [Norm] rule; **in aller** *ODER* **der Regel** as a rule - **2.** [Periode] period.

Regel|blutung *die* period.

Regel|fall *der* rule.

regelmäßig ◇ *adj* regular. ◇ *adv* regularly.

Regelmäßigkeit (*pl* **-en**) *die* regularity.

regeln *vt* [Temperatur, Geschwindigkeit] to regulate; [Angelegenheit] to settle; [Nachlass] to put in order; [Verkehr] to direct. ◆ **sich regeln** *ref* to sort itself out; **sich von selbst regeln** to sort itself out.

regelrecht *adj* - **1.** *fam* [richtig] proper - **2.** [ordnungsgemäß] correct.

Regelung (*pl* **-en**) *die* regulation.

regen *vt* to move. ◆ **sich regen** *ref* to move; [Gefühl, Hoffnung] to stir.

Regen *der* rain; **saurer Regen** acid rain.

Regen|bogen *der* rainbow.

Regen|mantel *der* raincoat.

Regen|rinne *die* gutter.

Regen|schauer *der* shower.

Regen|schirm *der* umbrella.

Regen|tropfen *der* raindrop.

Regen|wald *der* rain forest.

Regen|wurm *der* earthworm.

Regie [re'ʒiː] *die* direction; **Regie führen** to direct; **etw in eigener Regie tun** ODER **durchführen** to do sthg on one's own account.

regieren ◇ *vt* to rule. ◇ *vi* to rule; **über jn/etw regieren** to rule over sb/sthg.

Regierung (*pl* **-en**) *die* government.

Regierungs|chef, in *der, die* head of government.

Regierungs|sitz *der* seat of government.

Regierungs|sprecher, in *der, die* government spokesperson.

Regime [re'ʒiːm] (*pl* -) *das* regime.

Regiment (*pl* **-e** ODER **-er**) *das* - **1.** *(pl Regimenter)* MIL regiment - **2.** *(pl Regimente)* [Leitung] rule; **ein strenges Regiment führen** to be strict.

Region (*pl* **-en**) *die* region.

regional ◇ *adj* regional. ◇ *adv* regionally; **regional verschieden** different from region to region.

Regisseur, in [reʒɪ'søːɐ̯, rɪn] (*mpl* **-e**, *fpl* **-nen**) *der, die* director.

Register (*pl* -) *das* - **1.** [Verzeichnis - in Buch] index; [- amtlich] register - **2.** [MUS - von Orgel] stop; [- von Stimme] register.

registrieren *vt* - **1.** [wahrnehmen] to notice - **2.** [eintragen] to register.

reglos ◇ *adj* motionless. ◇ *adv* motionlessly.

regnen ◇ *vi*: **es regnet** it's raining. ◇ *vt*: **es regnet Konfetti** confetti is raining down.

regnerisch *adj* rainy.

regulär ◇ *adj* - **1.** [Preis, Arbeit] normal; [Wahl, Spiel] in accordance with the rules - **2.** MIL regular. ◇ *adv* [arbeiten] normally; [zum normalen Preis] at the normal price.

regulieren *vt* - **1.** [regeln - Preis, Schaden, Verkehr] to regulate - **2.** [Temperatur, Lautstärke] to adjust - **3.** [Gewässer] to straighten.

Regung (*pl* **-en**) *die* - **1.** [Bewegung] movement - **2.** *geh* [Gefühl] stirring.

regungslos ◇ *adj* motionless. ◇ *adv* motionlessly.

Reh (*pl* **-e**) *das* deer.

Reha-|Klinik *die* rehab clinic.

Reh|bock (*pl* **-böcke**) *der* roebuck.

Reh|kitz (*pl* **-e**) *das* fawn.

Reibe (*pl* **-n**) *die* grater.

Reibe|kuchen *der small pancake made from grated potatoes.*

reiben (*prät* **rieb**, *perf* **hat gerieben**) ◇ *vt* - **1.** [Körperteile] to rub; **sich** *(D)* **die Hände/die Nase/das Auge reiben** to rub one's hands/nose/eye; **jm die Hände/Wangen reiben** to rub sb's hands/cheeks - **2.** [Käse, Karotten] to grate. ◇ *vi* to rub.

Reiberei (*pl* **-en**) *die* friction.

Reibung *die* - **1.** PHYS friction - **2.** [das Reiben] rubbing.

reibungslos ◇ *adj* smooth. ◇ *adv* smoothly.

reich ◇ *adj* - **1.** [wohlhabend] rich; **reich an etw** *(D)* **sein** [Bodenschätzen] to be rich in sthg; [Erfahrungen] to have a wealth of sthg - **2.** [Erdölvorkommen, Ernte] rich; [Erfahrung] extensive. ◇ *adv* [geschmückt] richly.

Reich (*pl* **-e**) *das* - **1.** POL empire - **2.** [Bereich] world.

Reiche (*pl* **-n**) *der, die* rich person.

reichen ◇ *vi* - **1.** [Geld, Zeit] to be enough; [Vorrat] to last; **das reicht!** that's enough!; **mir reichts** *fam fig* I've had enough - **2.**: **(von bis zu) reichen** [Grundstück, Gebiet] to extend (from to); [Kleidungsstück] to reach (from to). ◇ *vt*: **jm etw reichen** to pass sb sthg; **sich** *(D)* **die Hände reichen** to shake hands.

reichhaltig *adj* rich.

reichlich ◇ *adj* [Essen, Zeit] ample; [Trinkgeld] generous. ◇ *adv* - **1.** [viel] amply - **2.** [ziemlich] rather.

Reichs|tag ['raiçstaːk] *der* [Gebäude] Reichstag.

Reichtum (*pl* **-tümer**) *der* - **1.** [Vermögen] wealth - **2.** [Fülle]: **der Reichtum an etw** *(D)* the abundance of sthg. ◆ **Reichtümer** *Pl* riches.

Reich|weite *die* - **1.** [greifbare Nähe, von Boxern] reach - **2.** TECH range. ◆ **außer Reichweite** *adv* out of reach. ◆ **in Reichweite** *adv* within reach.

reif *adj* - **1.** [gen] ripe; **reif fürs Irrenhaus sein** to belong in the madhouse - **2.** [erwachsen] mature.

Reife *die* - **1.** [von Person] maturity; **mittlere Reife** SCHULE intermediate school-leaving certificate *(for those leaving at 16)* - **2.** [von Obst] ripeness.

Reifen (*pl* -) *der* - **1.** [von Fahrzeugen] tyre - **2.** [Ring] hoop.

Reifen|druck *der* tyre pressure.

Reifen|panne *die* flat tyre.

Reife|prüfung *die final examination at a German "Gymnasium", required for university entrance.*

Reife|zeugnis *das certificate awarded to people who have passed the "Reifeprüfung".*

reiflich <> *adj* very careful. <> *adv* very carefully.

Reihe (*pl* **-n**) *die* - **1.** [Linie, Sitzreihe] row - **2.** [Menge]: **eine Reihe von etw** a number of sthg - **3.** [Reihenfolge]: **du bist an der Reihe** it's your turn; **jn außer der Reihe drannehmen** to take sb out of turn; **er kommt an die Reihe** it is his turn. ◆ **der Reihe nach** *adv* in turn.

reihen *vt* - **1.** [nebeneinander stellen] to line up - **2.** [auffädeln]: **etw auf etw** *(A)* **reihen** to string sthg on sthg - **3.** [nähen] to tack.

Reihen|folge *die* order; **alphabetische Reihenfolge** alphabetical order.

Reihen|haus *das* terraced house *UK*, row house *US*.

Reiher (*pl* -) *der* heron.

Reim (*pl* **-e**) *der* rhyme.

reimen <> *vt* to rhyme. <> *vi* to make up rhymes. ◆ **sich reimen** *ref* to rhyme; **'Bein' reimt sich auf 'klein'** 'Bein' rhymes with 'klein'.

rein <> *adj* - **1.** [ohne Zusätze, nicht gemischt] pure; **eine reine Arbeitergegend** a wholely working-class area - **2.** [nicht als] sheer - **3.** [sauber] clean; **etw ins Reine bringen** to clear sthg up; **mit jm ins Reine kommen** to sort things out with sb. <> *adv* - **1.** [ausschließlich] purely; **rein zeitlich geht es nicht** there's simply not enough time to do it - **2.** *fam* [völlig] absolutely; **er wusste auch rein gar nichts** he didn't know anything - **3.** *fam* = **herein**.

Rein|fall *der fam* disaster.

rein|fallen (*perf* **ist reingefallen**) *vi (unreg) fam* - **1.** [hineinfallen] to fall in - **2.** [getäuscht werden] to fall for it; **auf jn/etw reinfallen** to be taken in by sb/sthg; **mit jm/etw reinfallen** to have nothing but trouble with sb/sthg.

reinigen *vt* to clean; **ein Kleidungsstück chemisch reinigen lassen** to have a garment dry-cleaned. ◆ **sich reinigen** *ref* to clean o.s.

Reinigung (*pl* **-en**) *die* - **1.**: **die (chemische) Reinigung** the (dry) cleaner's - **2.** [Säubern] cleaning.

Reinigungs|mittel *das* cleaner.

rein|legen *vt fam* - **1.** [hineinlegen] to put in - **2.** [übertölpeln] to take for a ride.

reinrassig *adj* purebred; [Pferd] thoroughbred.

rein|reden *vi fam* - **1.** [ins Wort fallen] to butt in - **2.** [sich einmischen]: **jm reinreden** to tread on sb's toes; **sich von niemandem reinreden lassen** not to take orders from anybody.

Reis *der* rice.

Reise (*pl* **-n**) *die* [lang] journey; [kurz] trip; **auf Reisen sein/gehen** to be/go away; **eine Reise machen** to go on a journey/trip. ◆ **gute Reise** *interj* have a good journey/trip!

Reise|apotheke *die* first-aid kit.

Reise|begleiter, in *der, die* travelling companion.

Reise|büro *das* travel agent's.

Reise|bus *der* bus, coach *UK*.

Reise|führer *der* - **1.** [Mensch] guide, courier - **2.** [Buch] guide book.

Reise|führerin *die* guide, courier.

Reise|gepäck *das* luggage.

Reise|gesellschaft *die* - **1.** [Reisegruppe] group of tourists - **2.** [Veranstalter] tour operator.

Reise|gruppe *die* group of tourists.

Reise|leiter, in *der, die* guide, courier.

reisen (*perf* **ist gereist**) *vi* to travel; **nach Athen/Schottland reisen** to go to Athens/Scotland.

Reisende (*pl* **-n**) *der, die* [Fahrgast] passenger.

Reisepass (*pl* **-pässe**) *der* passport.

Reise|route *die* route.

Reise|ruf *der emergency message for a driver, broadcast over the radio.*

Reise|tasche *die* travel bag.

Reise|verkehr *der* holiday traffic.

Reisever|sicherung *die* travel insurance.

Reise|zeit *die* - **1.** [Fahrtdauer] journey time - **2.** [Saison] holiday season.

Reise|ziel *das* destination.

Reiß|brett *das* drawing board.

reißen (*prät* **riss**, *perf* **hat/ist gerissen**) <> *vi* - **1.** *(ist)* [abreißen - Papier, Stoff] to tear; [- Seil, Kette] to snap - **2.** *(hat)* [ziehen]: **an etw** *(D)* **reißen** to pull at sthg. <> *vt (hat)* - **1.** [zerreißen]: **etw in Stücke reißen** to tear sthg into pieces - **2.** [herunterreißen] to pull - **3.** [herausreißen]: **sie wurde aus dem Schlaf gerissen** she was rudely awakened; **etw aus dem Zusammenhang reißen** to take sthg out of context - **4.** [wegreißen]: **jm etw aus der Hand reißen** to snatch sthg from sb; **etw an sich** *(A)* **reißen** [Paket, Macht] to seize sthg; [Gespräch] to monopolize sthg; **hin und her gerissen sein** *fig* to be torn - **5.** [töten] to kill. ◆ **sich reißen** *ref*: **sich um etw reißen** to fight to get sthg.

reißend *adj* - **1.** [Gewässer] raging - **2.** [schnell]: **reißenden Absatz finden** to sell like hot cakes - **3.** [Tier] rapacious - **4.** [Schmerzen] searing.

Reißverschluss (*pl* **-schlüsse**) *der* zip *UK*, zipper *US*.

Reiß|zwecke *die* drawing pin *UK*, thumbtack *US*.

reiten (*prät* **ritt**, *perf* **hat/ist geritten**) <> *vi (ist)* to ride; **im Schritt/Trab/Galopp reiten** to ride at a walk/trot/gallop. <> *vt (hat)* to ride.

Reiter, in (*mpl* -, *fpl* **-nen**) *der, die* rider.

Reit|hose *die* jodhpurs *Pl.*

Reit|pferd *das* horse *(for riding).*

Reit|sport *der* riding.

Reit|stiefel *der* riding boot.

Reit|weg *der* bridle path.

Reiz (*pl* **-e**) *der* - **1.** [Impuls] stimulus - **2.** [Verlockung, Schönheit] appeal *(U)*; **die Reize einer schönen Frau** the charms of a beautiful woman.

reizbar *adj* irritable; **sie ist leicht reizbar** she is very irritable.

reizen *vt* - **1.** [interessieren] to appeal to - **2.** [provozieren] to provoke - **3.** [Augen, Magen] to irritate - **4.** [Neugier] to arouse.

reizend ◇ *adj* charming. ◇ *adv* charmingly.

reizlos ◇ *adj* unattractive. ◇ *adv* unattractively.

Reizung (*pl* **-en**) *die* irritation.

reizvoll ◇ *adj* [verlockend] attractive; [reizend] charming. ◇ *adv* attractively.

rekeln = räkeln.

Reklamation (*pl* **-en**) *die* complaint.

Reklame *die* - **1.** [Werbung] advertising; **für jn/etw Reklame machen** to advertise sb/sthg; *fig* to sing sb's/sthg's praises - **2.** [Werbemittel] advertisement.

reklamieren ◇ *vt* - **1.** [beanstanden] to complain about - **2.** [einklagen] to claim. ◇ *vi* [Einspruch erheben]: **gegen etw reklamieren** to object to sthg.

rekonstruieren *vt* to reconstruct.

Rekọrd (*pl* **-e**) *der* [Bestleistung, Spitzenwert] record; **einen Rekord aufstellen/brechen** to set/break a record.

Rekrut (*pl* **-en**) *der* MIL recruit.

rekrutieren *vt* to recruit.

Rẹktor (*pl* **-toren**) *der* - **1.** [von Schulen] head teacher *UK*, principal *US* - **2.** [von Hochschulen] vice-chancellor *UK*, president *US*.

relativ, rẹlativ ◇ *adj* relative. ◇ *adv* relatively.

Relativ|pronomen *das* GRAMM relative pronoun.

Relativ|satz *der* GRAMM relative clause.

relạxen [ri'lɛksn̩] *vi fam* to take it easy.

relevạnt [rele'vant] *adj* relevant.

Religion (*pl* **-en**) *die* - **1.** [Anschauung] religion - **2.** *(ohne pl)* [Schulfach] religious education.

religiös ◇ *adj* religious. ◇ *adv* in a religious way; **jn religiös erziehen** to give sb a religious upbringing.

Relịkt (*pl* **-e**) *das* relic.

Reling (*pl* **-s** ODER **-e**) *die* SCHIFF rail.

remis [rə'mi:] *adv* SPORT: **remis enden** to end in a draw.

Remoulade (*pl* **-n**) *die* remoulade.

Renaissance [rənɛ'sɑ̃:s] *die* Renaissance.

Rẹnn|bahn *die* SPORT racetrack; [Pferdesport] racecourse.

rẹnnen (*prät* **rạnnte**, *perf* **ist gerạnnt**) *vi* to run; **sie kommt immer zu mir gerannt, wenn sie etwas braucht** she's always running to me when she needs something; **gegen etw rennen** to run into sthg.

Rẹnnen (*pl* **-**) *das* [Wettkampf] race; **das Rennen machen** to win.

Rẹnner (*pl* **-**) *der fam* in-thing.

Rẹnn|fahrer, in *der, die* racing driver.

Rẹnn|rad *das* racing bike.

Rẹnn|sport *der* racing.

Rẹnn|wagen *der* racing car.

renovieren [reno'vi:rən] *vt* to renovate.

Renovierung [reno'vi:rʊŋ] (*pl* **-en**) *die* renovation.

Rẹnte (*pl* **-n**) *die* pension; **auf** ODER **in Rente gehen** to retire.

Rẹntenver|sicherung *die* pension scheme.

Rẹn|tier, Rentier *das* reindeer.

rentieren ◆ **sich rentieren** *ref* [rentabel sein] to be profitable; [sich lohnen] to be worthwhile.

Rẹntner, in (*mpl* **-**, *fpl* **-nen**) *der, die* pensioner.

Reparatur (*pl* **-en**) *die* repair; **in Reparatur sein** to be being repaired.

Reparatur|werkstatt *die* [für Autos] garage.

reparieren *vt* to repair.

Reportage [repɔr'tɑ:ʒə] (*pl* **-n**) *die* report.

Repọrter, in (*mpl* **-**, *fpl* **-nen**) *der, die* reporter.

Repräsentạnt, in (*mpl* **-en**, *fpl* **-nen**) *der, die* representative.

repräsentativ ◇ *adj* - **1.** [ausgewogen, stellvertretend] representative - **2.** [vorzeigbar] imposing. ◇ *adv* - **1.** [ausgewogen, stellvertretend] representatively - **2.** [vorzeigbar] imposingly.

repräsentieren ◇ *vt* to represent. ◇ *vi* [öffentlich] to perform official duties.

Reproduktion (*pl* **-en**) *die* reproduction.

reproduzieren *vt* to reproduce.

Reptil (*pl* **-ien** ODER **-e**) *das* reptile.

Republik (*pl* **-en**) *die* republic.

Republikaner, in (*mpl* **-**, *fpl* **-en**) *der, die* [Anhänger der Republik] republican.

Requiem ['re:kvi̯ɛm] (*pl* **-s** ODER **Requien**) *das* requiem.

Resẹrve [re'zɛrvə] (*pl* **-n**) *die* - **1.** [Vorrat] reserve; **jn/etw in Reserve haben** ODER **halten** to have sb/sthg in reserve - **2.** *(ohne pl)* [Zurückhaltung] reserve - **3.** *(ohne pl)* [beim Militär] reserves *Pl.*

Resẹrve|kanister *der* spare can.

Resẹrve|rad *das* spare wheel.

Resẹrve|reifen *der* spare tyre.

Reservelspieler, in *der, die* substitute.
reservieren [rezɛr'viːrən] *vt* to reserve.
reserviert [rezɛr'viːɐ̯t] *adj* reserved.
Reservierung [rezɛr'viːrʊŋ] (*pl* **-en**) *die* reservation.
Residenz (*pl* **-en**) *die* [Wohnsitz] residence; [Stadt] royal seat.
Resignation (*pl* **-en**) *die* resignation *(U)*.
resignieren *vi* to give up.
Resonanz (*pl* **-en**) *die* - **1.** [Widerhall] response; **die Resonanz auf etw** *(A)* the response to sthg - **2.** [akustisch] resonance.
Respekt *der* respect; **Respekt vor jm haben** to have respect for sb; **Respekt!** well done!; **sich** *(D)* **Respekt verschaffen** to make o.s. respected.
respektieren *vt* to respect.
respektlos ◇ *adj* disrespectful. ◇ *adv* disrespectfully.
respektvoll ◇ *adj* respectful. ◇ *adv* respectfully.
Rest (*pl* **-e**) *der* - **1.** [von Mahlzeit, Gebäude, Leichnam] remains *Pl*; [von Stoff] remnant - **2.** [von Tag, Urlaub, Erzählung] rest; **jm/etw den Rest geben** *fam fig* to finish sb/sthg off.
Restaurant [rɛsto'rɑ̃ː] (*pl* **-s**) *das* restaurant.
restaurieren *vt* to restore.
Restaurierung (*pl* **-en**) *die* restoration.
Restlbetrag *der* balance.
restlich *adj* remaining.
restlos *adv* totally.
Resultat (*pl* **-e**) *das* result.
Retorte (*pl* **-n**) *die* CHEM retort; **aus der Retorte** *abw* artificial; **ein Kind aus der Retorte** a test-tube baby.
Retortenlbaby *das* test-tube baby.
Retrospektive [retrospɛk'tiːvə] (*pl* **-n**) *die* - **1.** *geh* [Rückblick] retrospective view - **2.** [Ausstellung] retrospective.
retten *vt* to save; [aus einer Gefahr] to rescue; **jn/etw vor jm/etw retten** to save sb/sthg from sb/sthg. ◆ **sich retten** *ref* to escape; **sich vor jm/etw nicht mehr retten können** *fam fig* to be besieged by sb/swamped with sthg.
Retter, in (*mpl* -, *fpl* **-nen**) *der, die* rescuer.
Rettich (*pl* **-e**) *der* radish *(of large red or white variety)*.
Rettung *die (ohne pl)* rescue; **jd/etw ist js (letzte) Rettung** *fig* sb/sthg is sb's salvation.
Rettungslboot *das* lifeboat.
Rettungsldienst *der* rescue service.
Rettungslring *der* lifebelt.
Rettungslwagen *der* ambulance.
Revanche [re'vɑ̃ːʃ(e)] (*pl* **-n**) *die* - **1.** [Gegenleistung]: **als Revanche für etw** in return for sthg - **2.** [Vergeltung] revenge *(U)* - **3.** [beim Spiel] return game.
Revier [re'viːɐ̯] (*pl* **-e**) *das* - **1.** [von Tieren] territory - **2.** [Polizeirevier - Wache] (police) station; [- Bezirk] district - **3.** [Bereich] domain - **4.** [von Jäger, Förster] area.
Revolte [re'vɔltə] (*pl* **-n**) *die* revolt.
Revolution [revolu'tsi̯oːn] (*pl* **-en**) *die* revolution.
revolutionär [revolutsi̯o'nɛːɐ̯] *adj* revolutionary.
Revolutionär, in [revolutsi̯o'nɛːɐ̯, rɪn] (*mpl* **-e**, *fpl* **-nen**) *der, die* revolutionary.
Revolver [re'vɔlvɐ] (*pl* -) *der* revolver.
Revue [re'vyː] (*pl* **-n**) *die* - **1.** [Show] revue - **2.** [Zeitschrift] review.
Rezension (*pl* **-en**) *die* review.
Rezept (*pl* **-e**) *das* - **1.** [ärztlich] prescription - **2.** [für Speisen] recipe.
rezeptfrei *adj* available without a prescription.
Rezeption (*pl* **-en**) *die* reception.
rezeptpflichtig *adj* available only on prescription.
R-lGespräch *das* TELEKOM reverse charge *UK* *ODER* collect *US* call.
Rhabarber *der* rhubarb.
Rhein *der*: **der Rhein** the (River) Rhine.
rheinisch *adj* Rhenish.
Rheinland *das*: **das Rheinland** the Rhineland.
Rheinland-Pfalz *nt* Rhineland-Palatinate.
Rhesuslfaktor *der* MED rhesus factor.
rhetorisch *adj* rhetorical.
Rheuma *das* rheumatism.
Rheumatismus (*pl* **-tismen**) *der* rheumatism *(U)*.
Rhododendron (*pl* **-dendren**) *der* rhododendron.
rhythmisch ◇ *adj* rhythmic. ◇ *adv* rhythmically.
Rhythmus (*pl* **Rhythmen**) *der* rhythm.
richten ◇ *vt* - **1.** [hinwenden] to point; **etw auf jn/etw richten** [Waffe] to point sthg at sb/sthg; [Aufmerksamkeit] to turn sthg to sb/sthg - **2.** [Brief, Appell]: **etw an jn richten** to address sthg to sb - **3.** [reparieren] to fix - **4.** [Essen, Zimmer] to prepare. ◇ *vi* [urteilen] to judge; **über jn/etw richten** *geh* to judge sb/sthg. ◆ **sich richten** *ref* - **1.** [sich einstellen auf]: **sich nach jm/etw richten** to fit in with sb/sthg - **2.** [abhängen von]: **sich nach etw richten** to depend on sthg - **3.** [sich wenden]: **sich gegen jn/etw richten** to be directed at sb/sthg.
Richter, in (*mpl* -, *fpl* **-nen**) *der, die* judge.
richterlich *adj* judicial.
richtig ◇ *adj* - **1.** [nicht falsch, passend] right; **bin ich hier richtig?** am I in the right place?; **sehr richtig!** quite right! - **2.** [echt - Person] real, true; [- Sache] real - **3.** [vollwertig] proper. ◇ *adv* - **1.** [nicht falsch] correctly; **meine Uhr**

geht richtig my watch is right ODER accurate; **das hast du richtig gemacht!** you were right to do it! - **2.** [passend]: **er kam gerade richtig** he came at just the right moment - **3.** *fam* [wirklich] really.

Richtige (*pl* **-n**) <> *das* right thing; **genau das Richtige** just the right thing; **nichts Richtiges** nothing much. <> *der, die* right person.

richtig gehend *adj* [Uhr] accurate.

Richtigkeit *die* correctness.

rieb *prät* ▷ **reiben**.

riechen (*prät* **roch**, *perf* **hat gerochen**) <> *vi* to smell. <> *vt* [Duft] to smell.

rief *prät* ▷ **rufen**.

Riemen (*pl* -) *der* - **1.** [Band] strap; **sich am Riemen reißen** *fam fig* to pull o.s. together - **2.** [Ruder] oar.

Riese (*pl* **-n**) *der* giant.

rieseln (*perf* **ist gerieselt**) *vi* [Flüssigkeit] to trickle; [Schnee] to float down; [Putz, Kalk] to crumble.

Riesen|erfolg *der* huge success.

riesengroß *adj* enormous.

Riesen|rad *das* big wheel.

Riesen|slalom *der* giant slalom.

riesig <> *adj* - **1.** [groß] enormous - **2.** *fam* [toll] fantastic. <> *adv fam* [sehr] enormously.

riet *prät* ▷ **raten**.

Riff (*pl* **-e**) *das* reef.

Rille (*pl* **-n**) *die* groove.

Rind (*pl* **-er**) *das* - **1.** [Tier] cow - **2.** [Fleisch] beef.

Rinde (*pl* **-n**) *die* - **1.** [von Bäumen] bark - **2.** [von Käse] rind - **3.** [von Brot] crust.

Rinder|braten *der* [roh] joint of beef; [gebraten] roast beef.

Rinder|wahnsinn, Rinderwahn *der (ohne pl)* mad cow disease.

Rind|fleisch *das* beef.

Ring (*pl* **-e**) *der* - **1.** [gen] ring - **2.** [Gruppe] group - **3.** [Straße] ring road. ◆ **Ringe** *Pl* SPORT rings.

Ring|buch *das* ring binder.

Ringel|natter *die* grass snake.

ringen (*prät* **rang**, *perf* **hat gerungen**) <> *vi* - **1.** SPORT to wrestle - **2.** [sich anstrengen] to struggle; **mit etw ringen** *geh* to wrestle with sthg. <> *vt*: **die Hände ringen** to wring one's hands.

Ringer, in (*mpl* -, *fpl* **-nen**) *der, die* wrestler.

Ring|finger *der* ring finger.

Ring|kampf *der* SPORT wrestling match.

Ring|richter, in *der, die* referee.

rings *adv*: **rings um jn/etw (herum)** all around sb/sthg.

ringsherum *adv* all around.

ringsumher *adv* all around.

Rinne (*pl* **-n**) *die* - **1.** [Vertiefung] channel - **2.** [Abflussrinne] gutter.

Rinn|stein *der* gutter.

Rippchen (*pl* -) *das* KÜCHE *lightly smoked pork rib.*

Rippe (*pl* **-n**) *die* - **1.** [Knochen] rib - **2.** [von Heizkörper] fin.

Risiko (*pl* **Risiken**) *das* risk; **auf eigenes Risiko** at one's own risk; **ein Risiko eingehen** to take a risk.

riskant <> *adj* risky. <> *adv* riskily.

riskieren *vt* to risk.

riss *prät* ▷ **reißen**.

Riss (*pl* **-e**) *der* [in Stoff, Kleidungsstück] tear; [in Gestein, Wand] crack; [in Gesellschaft] rift.

rissig *adj* cracked.

ritt *prät* ▷ **reiten**.

Ritt (*pl* **-e**) *der* ride.

Ritter (*pl* -) *der* knight.

Ritual (*pl* **-e**) *das* ritual.

rituell *adj* ritual.

Ritze (*pl* **-n**) *die* crack.

ritzen *vt* [gravieren] to carve. ◆ **sich ritzen** *ref* [verletzen] to scratch o.s.

Rivale [ri'vaːlə] (*pl* **-n**) *der* rival.

Rivalin [ri'vaːlɪn] (*pl* **-nen**) *die* rival.

Rivalität [rivali'tɛːt] (*pl* **-en**) *die* rivalry.

Robbe (*pl* **-n**) *die* seal.

robben (*perf* **ist gerobbt**) *vi* to crawl.

Roboter (*pl* -) *der* robot.

robust *adj* robust.

roch *prät* ▷ **riechen**.

röcheln *vi* to breathe with a wheezing sound; [Sterbender] to give the death rattle.

Rock *der* rock.

Rocker, in (*mpl* -, *fpl* **-nen**) *der, die abw* rocker.

Rock|musik *die* rock music.

Rodel|bahn *die* toboggan run.

rodeln (*perf* **hat/ist gerodelt**) *vi* to toboggan.

roden *vt* to clear.

Roggen *der* rye.

Roggen|brot *das* rye bread *(U)*.

roh <> *adj* - **1.** [ungekocht] raw - **2.** [grob, unbearbeitet] rough; **rohe Gewalt** brute force. <> *adv* - **1.** [ungekocht]: **etw roh essen** to eat sthg raw - **2.** [behandeln, entwerfen] roughly.

Roh|bau (*pl* **-ten**) *der* shell.

Roh|kost *die (ohne pl)* raw fruit and vegetables *Pl*.

Roh|material *das* raw material.

Rohr (*pl* **-e**) *das* - **1.** [Röhre] pipe - **2.** [Pflanze] reed.

Rohr|bruch *der* burst pipe.

Röhre (*pl* **-n**) *die* - **1.** TECH pipe - **2.** ELEKTR valve *UK*, tube *US* - **3.** [Backofen] oven.

Rohr|zucker *der* cane sugar.

Roh|stoff *der* raw material.

Rokoko *das* rococo.

Rolladen *der* = **Rollladen**.
Roll|bahn *die* runway.
Rolle (*pl* **-n**) *die* - **1.** [in Theater, in Gesellschaft] role - **2.** [von Garn] reel *UK*, spool *US* - **3.** [von Möbeln] castor - **4.** SPORT roll; **eine/keine Rolle spielen** to/not to matter.
rollen (*perf* **hat/ist gerollt**) <> *vi (ist)* to roll. <> *vt (hat)* - **1.** [Zigarette] to roll; [Teig] to roll out; [Papier, Fleisch] to roll up - **2.** [fortbewegen] to roll. ◆ **sich rollen** *ref* [Papier, Foto] to curl up; [sich wälzen] to roll around.
Roller (*pl* -) *der* scooter.
Rollerblades® (*pl* -) *Pl* roller blades, inline skates.
Roll|kragen *der* polo neck.
Rollladen (*pl* **-läden**) *der* (rolling) shutters *Pl*.
Roll|mops *der* rollmop, *rolled-up pickled herring*.
Rollo (*pl* **-s**) *das* roller blind.
Roll|schuh *der* roller skate; **Rollschuh laufen** to roller-skate.
Roll|splitt *der (ohne pl)* loose chippings *Pl*.
Roll|stuhl *der* wheelchair.
Rollstuhl|fahrer, in *der, die* wheelchair user.
Roll|treppe *die* escalator.
Rom *nt* Rome.
Roma *Pl* Romanies.
Roman (*pl* **-e**) *der* - **1.** [Buch] novel - **2.** *fam* [lange Geschichte] long rigmarole.
romanisch *adj* - **1.** [in Bezug auf Sprache] Romance - **2.** [der Romanik] Romanesque.
Romanistik *die* Romance languages and literature.
Romantik *die* - **1.** [Gefühl] romance - **2.** [Epoche] Romantic period.
romantisch <> *adj* - **1.** [gefühlvoll] romantic - **2.** KUNST & MUS Romantic. <> *adv* romantically.
Romanze (*pl* **-n**) *die* romance.
Römer, in (*mpl* -, *fpl* **-nen**) *der, die* Roman.
römisch *adj* Roman.
römisch-katholisch *adj* Roman Catholic.
Rommee (*pl* **-s**)**, Rommé** (*pl* **-s**) *das* rummy *(U)*.
röntgen *vt* to X-ray.
Röntgen|aufnahme *die* X-ray.
Röntgenbild (*pl* **-bilder**) *das* = **Röntgenaufnahme**.
Röntgenstrahlen *Pl* X-rays.
rosa *adj (unver)* pink.
Rosa *das* pink.
Rose (*pl* **-n**) *die* rose.
Rosen|kohl *der (ohne pl)* (Brussels) sprouts *Pl*.
Rosen|montag (*pl* **-e**) *der day before Shrove Tuesday which marks the height of the carnival season*.
rosig *adj* rosy.
Rosine (*pl* **-n**) *die* raisin.
Rosmarin *der* rosemary.
Rost (*pl* **-e**) *der* - **1.** [Eisenoxyd] rust - **2.** [Gitter - zum Braten] grill; [- zum Abdecken] grating.
Rostbrat|wurst *die*: **Nürnberger Rostbratwurst** Nuremberg grilled sausage.
rosten (*perf* **hat/ist gerostet**) *vi* to rust.
rösten *vt* & *vi* to roast.
rostfrei *adj* [Stahl] stainless; [Messer] stainless steel; [Blech] rustproof.
Rösti *Pl Schweiz potato pancake made from grated fried potatoes*.
rostig *adj* rusty.
rot (*kompar* **röter** ODER **roter**, *superl* **röteste** ODER **roteste**) *adj* - **1.** [Farbe] red; **rot werden** to blush - **2.** *fam* POL Red.
Rot *das (ohne pl)* red. ◆ **bei Rot** *adv* at red.
Röte *die* redness.
Rote Kreuz *das*: **das Rote Kreuz** the Red Cross.
Röteln *Pl* MED German measles *(U)*.
Rote Meer *das*: **das Rote Meer** the Red Sea.
rothaarig *adj* red-haired.
rotieren (*perf* **hat/ist rotiert**) *vi* - **1.** *(hat)* [sich drehen, wechseln] to rotate - **2.** *(hat, ist) fam* [durchdrehen] to be in a flap.
Rot|käppchen *das* Little Red Riding Hood.
Rot|kehlchen (*pl* **Rotkehlchen**) *das* robin.
Rot|kohl *der* red cabbage.
rötlich *adj* reddish.
Rötung (*pl* **-en**) *die* reddening.
Rot|wein *der* red wine.
Rot|wild *das* red deer *Pl*.
Roulade [ru'la:də] (*pl* **-n**) *die* ≃ beef olive.
Roulette [ru'lɛ:t] (*pl* **-s**) *das* roulette *(U)*.
Route ['ru:tə] (*pl* **-n**) *die* route.
Routine [ru'ti:nə] (*pl* **-n**) *die* - **1.** [Gewohnheit] routine; **zur Routine werden** to become routine - **2.** [Erfahrung]: **Routine haben** to have experience.
routiniert [ruti'ni:ɐt] <> *adj* [Autofahrer, Redner] experienced; [Betrüger, Stil] skilful. <> *adv* skilfully.
rubbeln *vt* [abrubbeln] to rub.
Rübe (*pl* **-n**) *die* - **1.** [Pflanze] turnip - **2.** *fam* [Kopf] nut.
Rubel (*pl* -) *der* rouble.
rüber *fam* = **herüber, hinüber**.
Rubin (*pl* **-e**) *der* ruby.
Rubrik (*pl* **-en**) *die* - **1.** [Kategorie] category - **2.** [von Zeitung] section.
Ruck (*pl* **-e**) *der* - **1.** [Bewegung] jerk; **sich** *(D)* **einen Ruck geben** *fam fig* to make the effort - **2.** [politisch] swing.
Rück|antwort *die* reply.

Rück|blick *der* look back; **im Rückblick** looking back; **ein Rückblick auf etw** *(A)* a look back at sthg.

rücken ◇ *vt* (*perf* **hat gerückt**) to move. ◇ *vi* (*perf* **ist gerückt**) to move.

Rücken (*pl* -) *der* - **1.** [gen] back; [von Buch] spine; [von Nase] bridge - **2.** SPORT [Schwimmen] backstroke.

Rücken|lehne *die* backrest.

Rücken|mark *das (ohne pl)* spinal cord.

Rücken|schmerzen *Pl* backache *(sg)*.

Rücken|schwimmen *das* backstroke.

Rücken|wind *der*: **Rückenwind haben** to have a following wind.

rück|erstatten *vt* to reimburse; **jm etw rückerstatten** to reimburse sb for sthg.

Rückfahr|karte *die* return (ticket) *UK*, round-trip ticket *US*.

Rück|fahrt *die* return journey.

rückfällig *adj*: **rückfällig werden** to relapse.

Rück|flug *der* return flight.

Rück|frage *die* query.

Rück|gabe *die* return *(U)*.

Rück|gang *der* decrease.

rückgängig ◇ *adj* decreasing. ◇ *adv*: **etw rückgängig machen** [Geschäft] to cancel sthg; [Entschluss] to reverse sthg.

Rück|gewinnung *die* recovery.

Rück|grat *das* spine; **jm das Rückgrat brechen** *fig* [Widerstand brechen] to break sb; **Rückgrat haben** *fig* to have fight in one; **Rückgrat zeigen** to show fight.

Rück|griff *der*: **Rückgriff auf etw** *(A)* [Methode] recourse to sthg; [Mode, Musik] throwback to sthg.

Rückkehr *die* return.

Rück|kopplung, Rückkoppelung *die* feedback *(U)*.

rückläufig ◇ *adj* declining; [Trend] downward; **rückläufige Entwicklung** decline. ◇ *adv*: **sich rückläufig entwickeln** to decline.

Rück|licht (*pl* **-er**) *das* rear light.

Rück|reise *die* return journey.

Rück|ruf *der* return call.

Ruck|sack *der* rucksack, pack; [für Reisen] backpack.

Rück|schlag *der* setback.

Rückschluss (*pl* **-schlüsse**) *der* conclusion; **aus etw Rückschlüsse ziehen** to draw conclusions from sthg.

Rück|schritt *der* backward step.

Rück|seite *die* back.

Rück|sicht *die* - **1.** [auf Person, Umstand] consideration; **aus Rücksicht auf jn/etw** out of consideration for sb/sthg; **auf jn/etw Rücksicht nehmen** to show consideration for sb/sthg - **2.** [nach hinten] rear view.

rücksichtslos ◇ *adj* [unhöflich] inconsiderate; [verantwortungslos] reckless; [erbarmungslos] ruthless. ◇ *adv* [unhöflich] inconsiderately; [verantwortungslos] recklessly; [erbarmungslos] ruthlessly.

rücksichtsvoll ◇ *adj* considerate. ◇ *adv* considerately.

Rück|sitz *der* back seat.

Rück|spiegel *der* rear-view mirror.

Rück|spiel *das* SPORT return game.

Rück|stand *der* - **1.** WIRTSCH arrears *Pl*; **(mit etw) im Rückstand sein** to be in arrears (with sthg) - **2.** SPORT: **in Rückstand geraten** to fall behind; **(mit etw) im Rückstand sein** to be trailing (by sthg) - **3.** [von Gift] residue - **4.** [Abstand] gap.

rückständig *abw adj* - **1.** [Person, Politik] outdated - **2.** [Land, Technik] backward.

Rück|stau *der* [von Autos] tailback *UK*, backup *US*; [von Flüssigkeiten] backing up *(U)*.

Rück|stoß *der* - **1.** PHYS thrust *(U)* - **2.** [von Gewehr] recoil.

Rück|tritt *der* - **1.** [aus Amt] resignation - **2.** *fam* [von Fahrrad] backpedal brake.

Rück|wand *die* back.

rückwärts *adv* backwards; **rückwärts einparken** to reverse into a parking space.

Rückwärts|gang *der* reverse gear; **im Rückwärtsgang** in reverse.

Rück|weg *der* way back.

rückwirkend ◇ *adj* [Zahlung] backdated; [Datierung, Gesetz] retrospective. ◇ *adv*: **die Gehaltserhöhung ist rückwirkend vom 1.1. wirksam** the salary increase is backdated to 1.1.

Rück|zahlung *die* repayment.

Rück|zug *der (ohne pl)* retreat.

Rudel (*pl* -) *das* [von Wölfen] pack; [von Hirschen] herd.

Ruder (*pl* -) *das* - **1.** [zum Rudern] oar - **2.** [zum Steuern] rudder.

Ruder|boot *das* rowing boat *UK*, rowboat *US*.

Ruderer, in (*mpl* -, *fpl* **-nen**) *der, die* oarsman (oarswoman *die*).

rudern (*perf* **hat/ist gerudert**) ◇ *vi* - **1.** *(hat)* SPORT to row; **mit den Armen rudern** to flail one's arms - **2.** *(ist)* [in bestimmte Richtung] to row. ◇ *vt (hat)* to row.

Ruf (*pl* **-e**) *der* - **1.** *(ohne pl)* [Leumund] reputation - **2.** *(ohne pl)* [Aufruf] call - **3.** UNI offer of a chair - **4.** [von Tier] call.

rufen (*prät* **rief**, *perf* **hat gerufen**) ◇ *vi* to call; **nach jm/etw rufen** to call for sb/sthg. ◇ *vt* - **1.** [herbeirufen, nennen] to call; **jd/etw kommt (jm) wie gerufen** sb/sthg comes at just the right moment; **jn zu Hilfe rufen** to call on sb to help - **2.** [schreien] to shout.

Ruf|nummer *die amt* telephone number.

Rüge (*pl* **-n**) *die* reprimand.

rügen *vt* - **1.** [Person] to reprimand - **2.** [Mängel] to complain about.

Rügen *nt* Rügen.

Ruhe *die* - **1.** [Stille] silence; **Ruhe bitte!** quiet please! - **2.** [Erholung] rest - **3.** [das Ungestörtsein] peace; **ich will jetzt meine Ruhe (haben)** I want a bit of peace and quiet; **in Ruhe** in peace; **jn (mit etw) in Ruhe lassen** *fam* to stop bothering sb (with sthg); **keine Ruhe geben** to keep pestering - **4.** [Gelassenheit] calm; **sie ist durch nichts aus der Ruhe zu bringen** she won't let anything disturb her composure; **(die) Ruhe bewahren** to keep calm; **zur Ruhe kommen** to calm down.

ruhen *vi* - **1.** [stillstehen - Verkehr, Arbeit, Maschinen] to be at a standstill; [- Waffen] to be silent - **2.** *geh* [liegen] to lie; [schlafen] to sleep - **3.** [lasten, verweilen] to rest.

Ruhe|stand *der* retirement; **in den Ruhestand gehen** ODER **treten** to retire; **in den Ruhestand versetzt werden** to be retired.

Ruhe|störung *die*: **jn wegen Ruhestörung anzeigen** to report sb for disturbing the peace; **nächtliche Ruhestörung** disturbance of the peace *(at night)*.

Ruhe|tag *der* closing day; **'montags Ruhetag!'** 'closed on Mondays'.

ruhig ◇ *adj* - **1.** [still] quiet - **2.** [unbewegt] calm - **3.** [gelassen - Mensch, Stimme] calm; [- Hand] steady; [- Gewissen] clear - **4.** [geruhsam] peaceful. ◇ *adv* - **1.** [still - liegen] still; [- wohnen] in a quiet area; **sich ruhig verhalten** to keep quiet - **2.** [gelassen] calmly - **3.** *fam* [gerne]: **mach ruhig mit!** join in if you like!

Ruhm *der* fame.

Ruhr *die (ohne pl)* [Krankheit] dysentery.

Rühr|ei *das* scrambled eggs *Pl*.

rühren ◇ *vt* - **1.** [gen] to move; **sie war gerührt** she was moved - **2.** [umrühren] to stir. ◇ *vi* [ansprechen]: **an etw *(A)* rühren** to touch on sthg. ◆ **sich rühren** *ref* - **1.** [sich bewegen] to move; **rührt euch!** stand at ease! - **2.** *fam* [sich melden] to be in touch.

Ruhrgebiet *das*: **das Ruhrgebiet** the Ruhr.

Rühr|teig *der* cake mixture.

Ruin *der* ruin.

Ruine (*pl* **-n**) *die* ruin.

ruinieren *vt* to ruin. ◆ **sich ruinieren** *ref* to ruin o.s.

rülpsen *vi* to burp.

Rülpser (*pl* -) *der* burp.

rụm *fam* = **herum**.

Rụm (*pl* **-s**) *der* rum.

Rumäne (*pl* **-n**) *der* Romanian.

Rumänien *nt* Romania.

Rumänin (*pl* **-nen**) *die* Romanian.

rumänisch *adj* Romanian.

rụm|gammeln *vi fam* to laze about.

rụm|hängen *vi (unreg) fam* to hang around.

rụm|kriegen *vt fam* - **1.** [Person] to talk round - **2.** [Zeit] to get through.

Rụmmel (*pl* -) *der* - **1.** [Jahrmarkt] fair - **2.** *fam* [Umstände]: **um jn/etw viel Rummel machen** to make a big fuss about sb/sthg.

Rụmpf (*pl* **Rụ̈mpfe**) *der* - **1.** [Oberkörper] trunk - **2.** TECH [von Schiff] hull; [von Flugzeug] fuselage - **3.** [Rest] remnant.

rụ̈mpfen *vt* ▷ **Nase**.

Rump|steak ['rʊmpsteːk] *das* rump steak.

rụnd ◇ *adj* - **1.** [Form, Summe] round - **2.** [ungefähr]: **eine runde Woche** a good week. ◇ *adv* - **1.** [ungefähr] about; **rund gerechnet** at a rough estimate - **2.** [ohne Ecken] in a round shape; [laufen] smoothly - **3.** [um herum]: **rund um jn/etw** [räumlich] round sb/sthg; [thematisch] all about sb/sthg.

Rụnde (*pl* **-n**) *die* - **1.** [gen] round - **2.** SPORT [bei Rennen] lap; [bei Boxkampf] round - **3.** [Personen] group; **etw macht die Runde** sthg is doing the rounds; **über die Runden kommen** *fam* to get by.

Rụnd|fahrt *die* tour.

Rụnd|flug *der* sightseeing flight.

Rụnd|funk *der* - **1.** [Institution] radio - **2.** [Radiosender] radio station.

Rụndfunk|gebühr *die* radio licence fee.

Rụnd|gang *der* [Spaziergang] walk; [von Wächter] round.

rụnd|gehen (*perf* **ist rụndgegangen**) *vi (unreg)*: **es geht rund** it's all go.

rụndheraus *adv* straight out.

rụndherụm *adv* - **1.** [ganz] completely - **2.** [ringsherum] all round.

rụndlich *adj* [Mensch] plump.

Rụnd|reise *die* tour.

rụndum *adv* completely.

rụndweg *adv* flatly.

rụnter *fam* = **herunter**, **hinunter**.

rụnter|hauen *fam vt*: **jm eine runterhauen** to slap sb.

rụnzeln *vt* ▷ **Stirn**.

rụpfen *vt* [Unkraut] to pull up; [Blätter] to pull off; [Huhn] to pluck.

rụppig ◇ *adj* [unfreundlich] gruff. ◇ *adv* [unfreundlich] gruffly.

Rüsche (*pl* **-n**) *die* frill.

Ruß *der* soot.

Rụsse (*pl* **-n**) *der* Russian.

Rüssel (*pl* -) *der* [von Elefant] trunk; [von Schwein] snout; [von Fliege] proboscis.

rußig *adj* sooty.

Rụssin (*pl* **-nen**) *die* Russian.

rụssisch *adj* Russian.

Rụssisch(e) *das* Russian; *siehe auch* **Englisch(e)**.

Rụssland *nt* Russia.

rüstig *adj* sprightly.

rustikal *adj* rustic.

Rüstung (*pl* **-en**) *die* - **1.** *(ohne pl)* [von Staat] armaments *Pl* - **2.** [von Ritter] armour.

Rutsch (*pl* **-e**) *der*: **in einem** ODER **auf einen** Rutsch in one go. ◆ **guten Rutsch** *interj* Happy New Year!

Rutsch|bahn *die* [auf dem Spielplatz] slide; [spiralförmig] helter-skelter; [Wasserröhre] flume.

Rutsche (*pl* **-n**) *die* - **1.** [Rutschbahn] slide - **2.** [zum Schütten] chute.

rutschen (*perf* **ist gerutscht**) *vi* [gleiten - ausrutschen, fallen] to slip; [- mit dem Auto] to skid; **auf dem Stuhl hin und her rutschen** to shift around on one's chair; **rutsch mal ein Stück** move up a bit.

rutschfest *adj* non-slip.

rutschig *adj* slippery.

rütteln ◇ *vt* to shake. ◇ *vi*: **an etw** *(D)* **rütteln** to rattle sthg.

S

s (*pl* -), **S** (*pl* -) [ɛs] *das* s, S. ◆ **S** (*abk für* **Süd**) S.

Saal (*pl* **Säle**) *der* hall.

Saar *die*: **die Saar** the (River) Saar.

Saarbrücken *nt* Saarbrücken.

Saar|land *das* Saarland.

saarländisch *adj* of/from Saarland.

Saat (*pl* **-en**) *die* - **1.** [das Säen] sowing - **2.** [Körner] seed.

Säbel (*pl* -) *der* sabre.

Sabotage [sabo'taːʒə] (*pl* **-n**) *die* sabotage *(U)*.

sabotieren *vt* to sabotage.

Sach|bearbeiter, in *der, die employee in charge of a particular matter.*

Sach|buch *das* non-fiction book.

Sache (*pl* **-n**) *die* - **1.** *(ohne pl)* [Angelegenheit] matter; **das ist (nicht) deine Sache** that's (none of) your business; **bei der Sache bleiben** to keep to the point; **zur Sache kommen** to get to the point; **nicht bei der Sache sein** not to be with it; **das tut nichts zur Sache** *fig* that is beside the point - **2.** *(ohne pl)* RECHT [Rechtssache] case; **das ist so eine Sache** *fam* it's a bit of a problem; **mit jm gemeinsame Sache machen** *fam* to join forces with sb; **seiner Sache sicher sein** to know what one is doing. ◆ **Sachen** *Pl* - **1.** [gen] things - **2.** *fam* [Stundenkilometer]: **100 Sachen draufhaben** to be doing a hundred; **mit 180 Sachen** *salopp* at 180; **du machst vielleicht Sachen!** the things you do!; **in Sachen** in the matter of.

Sach|gebiet *das* subject area.

Sach|kenntnis *die* expertise *(U)*.

sachkundig ◇ *adj* knowledgeable. ◇ *adv* knowledgeably.

Sach|lage *die (ohne pl)* situation.

sachlich ◇ *adj* - **1.** [Person, Diskussion] objective - **2.** [Fehler, Unterschied] factual. ◇ *adv* - **1.** [diskutieren, bleiben] objectively - **2.** [richtig, falsch] factually.

Sach|schaden *der* material damage.

Sachsen ['zaksn̩] *nt* Saxony.

Sachsen-Anhalt [zaksn̩'anhalt] *nt* Saxony-Anhalt.

sächsisch ['zɛksɪʃ] *adj* Saxon.

sacht, sachte ◇ *adj* - **1.** [sanft, langsam] gentle - **2.** [vorsichtig] cautious. ◇ *adv* gently; **sachte!** *fam* steady on!

Sach|verstand *der* expertise.

Sach|verständige (*pl* **-n**) *der, die* expert.

Sack (*pl* **Säcke** ODER -) *der* - **1.** *(pl Säcke, Sack)* [Behälter] sack - **2.** *(pl Säcke) salopp* [Mensch] bastard - **3.** *(pl Säcke) salopp* [Hodensack] balls *Pl*.

Sack|gasse *die* dead end; [in Wohngebiet] cul-de-sac.

Sadismus *der* sadism.

säen *vt* to sow.

Safe [seːf] (*pl* **-s**) *der* safe.

Saft (*pl* **Säfte**) *der* - **1.** [Fruchtsaft, Strom] juice - **2.** [Pflanzensaft] sap.

saftig *adj* - **1.** [Obst, Fleisch] juicy - **2.** *fam* [Rechnung, Ohrfeige] hefty.

Sage (*pl* **-n**) *die* legend.

Säge (*pl* **-n**) *die* saw.

sagen *vt* - **1.** [gen] to say; **jm etw sagen** to tell sb sthg; **sich** *(D)* **etw sagen** to tell o.s. sthg; **das kann jeder sagen!** that's easy to say!; **das hat nichts zu sagen** that doesn't mean anything; **was sagst du (denn) dazu?** (so) what do you think about it? - **2.** [befehlen]: **etwas/nichts zu sagen haben** to have a/no say in things; **jm etwas/nichts zu sagen haben** to have sthg/nothing to say to sb; **er lässt sich nichts sagen** you can't tell him anything; **das Sagen haben** to be in charge; **das sage ich dir** *fam* I'm telling you; **das kann man wohl sagen!** *fam* you can say that again!; **dagegen ist nichts zu sagen** it's perfectly all right; **man sagt** it is said; **wem sagst du das!** you're telling me! ◆ **du sagst es** *interj* you said it! ◆ **sag bloß** *interj* you don't say. ◆ **sag mal** *interj* tell me. ◆ **wie gesagt** *interj* as I've said.

sägen *vt* & *vi* to saw.

sagenhaft ◇ *adj* fantastic. ◇ *adv* fantastically.

Säge|späne *Pl* wood shavings.

sah *prät* ▷ **sehen**.

Sahne *die* cream.

Sahne|torte *die* gâteau.

sahnig *adj* creamy.

Saison [sɛ'zɔŋ] (*pl* **-s**) *die* season.

Saite (*pl* **-n**) *die* string.

Saiten|instrument *das* stringed instrument.

Sakko (*pl* **-s**) *der ODER das* jacket.

Sakrament (*pl* **-e**) *das* RELIG sacrament.

Sakristei (*pl* **-en**) *die* sacristy.

Salamander (*pl* -) *der* salamander.

Salami (*pl* **-s**) *die* salami.

Salat (*pl* **-e**) *der* **- 1.** [Gericht] salad; **grüner Salat** green salad **- 2.** [Produkt] lettuce **- 3.** *fam*: **da haben wir den Salat!** *fam* I said we'd end up in this mess!

Salat|schüssel *die* salad bowl.

Salat|soße *die* salad dressing.

Salbe (*pl* **-n**) *die* ointment.

Salbei *der* sage.

Salmonellen|vergiftung *die* salmonella poisoning.

Salon [sa'lɔŋ] (*pl* **-s**) *der* [Zimmer] drawing room.

salopp ◇ *adj* casual; [Ausdrucksweise] slangy. ◇ *adv* casually; [sich ausdrücken] slangily.

Salto (*pl* **-s**) *der* somersault.

Salz (*pl* **-e**) *das* salt.

Salzburg *nt* Salzburg.

salzen (*perf* **hat gesalzen**) *vt* to put salt in/on.

salzig *adj* salty.

Salz|kartoffeln *Pl* boiled potatoes.

Salz|säure *die* hydrochloric acid.

Salz|stange *die* pretzel stick.

Salz|streuer (*pl* **Salzstreuer**) *der* salt cellar.

Salz|wasser *das* **- 1.** [Meerwasser] saltwater **- 2.** [Kochwasser] salted water.

Samen (*pl* -) *der* **- 1.** [Sperma] sperm **- 2.** [Pflanzensamen] seed.

sämig *adj* thick.

Sammel|band (*pl* **-bände**) *der* omnibus edition.

sammeln *vt* **- 1.** [Eindrücke, Anhänger, Kräuter] to gather **- 2.** [Geld, Briefmarken] to collect. ◆ **sich sammeln** *ref* [sich konzentrieren] to collect one's thoughts.

Sammel|stelle *die* collection point.

Sammler, in (*mpl* -, *fpl* **-nen**) *der, die* collector.

Sammlung (*pl* **-en**) *die* **- 1.** [gen] collection **- 2.** [Ruhe] composure.

Samstag (*pl* **-e**) *der* Saturday; **am Samstag** on Saturday; **(am) nächsten Samstag kommt sie** she's coming next Saturday; **Samstag, den 31. Dezember** Saturday, 31 December.

Samstag|abend (*pl* **-e**) *der* Saturday evening; **Samstagabend muss ich nach Köln** I have to go to Cologne on Saturday evening.

Samstag|morgen (*pl* -) *der* Saturday morning; **Samstagmorgen muss ich nach Köln** I have to go to Cologne on Saturday morning.

Samstag|nacht (*pl* -) *die* Saturday night; **Samstagnacht hat es stark geregnet** it rained hard on Saturday night.

samstags *adv* on Saturdays; **samstags morgens/abends** on Saturday mornings/evenings.

samt *präp*: **samt jm/einer Sache** (together) with sb/sthg.

Samt (*pl* **-e**) *der* velvet.

sämtlich ◇ *adj* all; **sämtliche Fehler verbessern** to correct all the mistakes; **er hat sämtlichen Mut verloren** he lost all his courage. ◇ *adv*: **sie waren sämtlich erschienen** they all turned up.

Sanatorium [zana'to:ri̯ʊm] (*pl* **-torien**) *das* sanatorium.

Sand *der* sand; **die Straßen mit Sand streuen** to grit the roads; **im Sand verlaufen** *fig* to come to nothing.

Sandale (*pl* **-n**) *die* sandal.

Sand|bank (*pl* **-bänke**) *die* sandbank.

sandig *adj* sandy.

Sand|kasten *der* sandpit *UK*, sandbox *US*.

Sand|korn (*pl* **-körner**) *das* grain of sand.

Sand|männchen *das* sandman.

Sand|papier *das* sandpaper.

Sand|stein *der* sandstone.

Sand|strand *der* sandy beach.

sandte *prät* ▷ **senden**.

Sand|uhr *die* hourglass.

sanft ◇ *adj* **- 1.** [gen] gentle **- 2.** [Hände, Stimme, Licht] soft **- 3.** [Geburt] natural; [Energie, Tourismus] sustainable; [Tod] peaceful. ◇ *adv* **- 1.** [gen] gently **- 2.** [entschlafen] peacefully.

sanftmütig ◇ *adj* gentle. ◇ *adv* gently.

sang *prät* ▷ **singen**.

Sänger, in (*mpl* -, *fpl* **-nen**) *der, die* singer.

sanieren *vt* **- 1.** [Gebäude, Viertel] to renovate **- 2.** [Firma] to turn around **- 3.** [Finanzen] to sort out. ◆ **sich sanieren** *ref* [Person] to get o.s. out of the red.

Sanierung (*pl* **-en**) *die* **- 1.** [von Gebäude, Viertel] renovation **- 2.** [von Firma] turning round **- 3.** [von Finanzen] sorting out.

sanitär *adj* sanitary; **sanitäre Anlagen** sanitation *(U)*.

Sanitäter, in (*mpl* -, *fpl* **-nen**) *der, die* **- 1.** MED paramedic **- 2.** MIL medical orderly.

sank *prät* ▷ **sinken**.

Sankt Gallen *nt* St Gallen.

Sankt Gotthard *der* St Gotthard.

Sanktion (*pl* **-en**) *die* sanction; **Sanktionen verhängen** to impose sanctions.

Sankt Petersburg *nt* St Petersburg.

Saphir (*pl* **-e**), **Saphir** (*pl* **-e**) *der* sapphire.

Sardelle (*pl* **-n**) *die* anchovy.

Sardine (*pl* **-n**) *die* sardine.

Sardinien [zar'diːniən] *nt* Sardinia.

Sarg (*pl* **Särge**) *der* coffin, casket *US*.

Sarkasmus (*pl* **-men**) *der* **- 1.** [Spott] sarcasm **- 2.** [spöttische Bemerkung] sarcastic comment.

saß *prät* ▷ **sitzen**.

Satan (*pl* **-e**) *der* **- 1.** [Teufel] Satan **- 2.** *abw* [Mensch] fiend.

Satellit (*pl* **-en**) *der* satellite.

Satelliten|schüssel *die* satellite dish.

Satire (*pl* **-n**) *die* satire.

satt ◇ *adj* **- 1.** [Mensch, Tier] full; **satt sein** to be full (up); **bist du satt?** have you had enough (to eat)?; **diese Knödel machen satt** these dumplings are filling; **davon werde ich nicht satt** I won't have enough to eat with that **- 2.** [Farbe, Klang] rich. ◇ *adv*: **sich satt essen** to eat one's fill; **jn/etw satt haben** *fam* to be fed up with sb/sthg.

Sattel (*pl* **Sättel**) *der* saddle.

satteln *vt* to saddle.

Satz (*pl* **Sätze**) *der* **- 1.** [grammatikalische Einheit] sentence **- 2.** [Sprung] leap **- 3.** [SPORT - bei Tennis] set; [- bei Badminton, Tischtennis] game **- 4.** [von Text - das Setzen] setting; [- das Gesetzte] type **- 5.** MUS movement **- 6.** MATH theorem **- 7.** [von Reifen, Unterwäsche] set **- 8.** [Tarif] rate.

Satz|bau *der* syntax.

Satz|teil *der* sentence part.

Satzung (*pl* **-en**) *die* statutes *Pl*.

Satz|zeichen *das* punctuation mark.

Sau (*pl* **Säue** ODER **-en**) *die* **- 1.** *(pl Säue)* [Schwein] sow **- 2.** *(pl Sauen)* [Wildschwein] female wild boar **- 3.** *(pl Säue) salopp abw* [Mensch] pig.

sauber ◇ *adj* **- 1.** [rein] clean **- 2.** *fam iron* [fein] fine **- 3.** [Arbeit] neat; [Darbietung] faultless. ◇ *adv* **- 1.** [gut] neatly **- 2.** [fehlerfrei] faultlessly.

Sauberkeit *die* cleanliness.

sauber machen *vt* to clean.

säubern *vt* **- 1.** [reinigen] to clean **- 2.** [Institution] to purge.

Sauce ['zoːsə] (*pl* **-n**) *die* sauce; [Bratensoße] gravy.

Saudi (*pl* **-s**) *der* Saudi.

Saudi-Arabien *nt* Saudi Arabia.

sauer ◇ *adj* **- 1.** [Essen] sour; **saure Gurken** (pickled) gherkins; **ein saurer Wein** an acidic wine **- 2.** [Stimmung] annoyed, cross; **sauer auf jn sein** *fam* to be annoyed ODER cross with sb; **ein saures Gesicht machen** to pull a sour face **- 3.** CHEM acidic. ◇ *adv* **- 1.** [reagieren] crossly **- 2.** [nicht süß]: **sauer schmecken** to taste sour **- 3.** CHEM acidically.

Sauer|braten *der* sauerbraten, *braised beef marinated in vinegar*.

Sauerei (*pl* **-en**) *die salopp* **- 1.** [Schmutz] damn mess **- 2.** [Gemeinheit] damn disgrace.

Sauer|kirsche *die* sour cherry.

Sauer|kraut *das* sauerkraut.

säuerlich ◇ *adj* **- 1.** [Essen] slightly sour **- 2.** [Stimmung] annoyed, cross. ◇ *adv* **- 1.** [nicht süß]: **säuerlich schmecken** to taste slightly sour **- 2.** [reagieren] crossly.

Sauer|stoff *der* oxygen.

saufen (*präs* **säuft**, *prät* **soff**, *perf* **hat gesoffen**) ◇ *vt* **- 1.** [Subj: Tier] to drink **- 2.** *salopp* [trinken] to knock back; **sie gehen einen saufen** they're going on the booze **- 3.** *fam* [verbrauchen]: **mein Auto säuft zu viel** my car's a real gas-guzzler. ◇ *vi* **- 1.** [Tier] to drink **- 2.** *salopp* [Mensch] to booze.

Säufer (*pl* **-**) *der salopp abw* boozer.

Sauferei (*pl* **-en**) *die salopp abw* booze-up.

Säuferin (*pl* **-nen**) *die salopp abw* boozer.

säuft *präs* ▷ **saufen**.

saugen (*prät* **sog** ODER **saugte**, *perf* **hat gesogen** ODER **gesaugt**) ◇ *vt* **- 1.** [heraussaugen] to suck; **etw aus etw saugen** to suck sthg out of sthg **- 2.** *(reg)* [mit Staubsauger] to vacuum. ◇ *vi* **- 1.** [ziehen] to suck; **an etw** *(D)* **saugen** to suck at sthg **- 2.** *(reg)* [mit Staubsauger] to vacuum.

säugen *vt* to suckle.

Säuge|tier *das* mammal.

Säugling (*pl* **-e**) *der* baby.

Säule (*pl* **-n**) *die eigtl* & *fig* pillar.

Saum (*pl* **Säume**) *der* hem.

säumen *vt* **- 1.** [Stoff] to hem **- 2.** *geh* [Weg] to line.

Sauna (*pl* **-s** ODER **Saunen**) *die* sauna.

Säure (*pl* **-n**) *die* **- 1.** CHEM acid **- 2.** [von Wein] acidity; [von Zitrone] sourness.

Saurier ['zauriɐ] (*pl* **-**) *der* dinosaur.

säuseln ◇ *vi* [Wind] to murmur. ◇ *vt* [sprechen] to purr.

sausen (*perf* **hat/ist gesaust**) *vi (ist) fam* [schnell]: **zum Bäcker sausen** to dash over to the baker's; **mit dem Fahrrad um die Ecke sausen** to hurtle round the corner on one's bike.

Saxofon (*pl* **-e**), **Saxophon** (*pl* **-e**) *das* saxophone.

SB *abk für* **Selbstbedienung**.

S-|Bahn *die* suburban railway.

S-Bahn|hof *der* suburban railway station.

SBB (*abk für* **Schweizerische Bundesbahn**), *Swiss federal railway company*.

Schabe (*pl* **-n**) *die* cockroach.

schaben *vt* & *vi* to scrape.

schäbig *abw* <> *adj* - **1.** [Kleidung, Möbel] shabby - **2.** [Bezahlung] paltry - **3.** [Person] mean. <> *adv* - **1.** [angezogen, eingerichtet] shabbily - **2.** [ausnützen] shamelessly.

Schablone (*pl* **-n**) *die* - **1.** [zum Ausmalen] stencil; [zum Rundherummalen] template - **2.** [Schema] mould.

Schach (*pl* **-s**) *das* chess; **Schach!** check!

Schach|brett *das* chessboard.

schachmatt *adj* [beim Spiel] checkmate.

Schacht (*pl* **Schächte**) *der* shaft.

Schachtel (*pl* **-n**) *die* - **1.** [Behälter] box; **eine Schachtel Zigaretten** a packet *UK* ODER pack *US* of cigarettes - **2.** *salopp abw* [Frau] bag.

Schach|zug *der eigtl* & *fig* move.

schade *adj*: **es ist schade (um jn/etw)** it's a shame (about sb/sthg); **(wie) schade!** what a shame!; **zu schade für jn/etw sein** to be too good for sb/sthg.

Schädel (*pl* -) *der* - **1.** [Knochen] skull - **2.** *fam* [Kopf] nut; **mir brummt der Schädel** *fam* my head is killing me.

Schädel|bruch *der* skull fracture.

schaden *vi* [Sache] to damage; [Person] to harm; **das schadet nichts** it won't do any harm.

Schaden (*pl* **Schäden**) *der* - **1.** [an Sachen] damage *(U)* - **2.** [an Menschen] injury; **jm (einen) Schaden zufügen** to cause sb harm - **3.** [Nachteil]: **es soll dein Schaden nicht sein** I'll make it worth your while.

Schaden|ersatz *der* compensation.

Schaden|freude *die* malicious pleasure.

schadenfroh *adj* gloating; **schadenfroh sein** to gloat.

Schadens|fall *der*: **einen Schadensfall melden** to make a claim; **im Schadensfall** in the event of damage.

schadhaft *adj* [mit Fabrikationsfehler] defective; [beschädigt] damaged.

schädigen *vt* to damage; [Person] to harm.

schädlich *adj* harmful; **Rauchen ist schädlich für die Gesundheit** smoking damages your health.

Schädling (*pl* **-e**) *der* pest.

Schad|stoff *der* [im Boden, in der Luft] pollutant; [im Essen] harmful substance.

Schaf (*pl* **-e**) *das* - **1.** [Tier] sheep - **2.** *fam abw* [Mensch] dope; **ein schwarzes Schaf** *abw* a black sheep.

Schäfer (*pl* -) *der* shepherd.

Schäfer|hund *der* [Hirtenhund] sheepdog.

Schäferin (*pl* **-nen**) *die* shepherdess.

schaffen[1] <> *vt* - **1.** [beenden, bewältigen] to manage; **es schaffen, etw zu tun** to manage to do sthg; **er schafft drei Teller Spagetti zum Abendbrot** he gets through three plates of spaghetti for his dinner; **bis wann schaffst du das?** when can you have it ready by?; **du schaffst es!** you can do it!; **das wäre geschafft!** that's that done! - **2.** [Prüfung] to get through - **3.** [Ärger, Unruhe] to cause - **4.** [transportieren]: **etw an einen Ort schaffen** to take sthg somewhere; **jn ins Bett schaffen** to put sb to bed; **den Verletzten vom Spielfeld schaffen** to carry the injured player off the pitch - **5.** [erschöpfen] to wear out; **du schaffst mich!** you'll be the death of me! - **6.** *fam* [erreichen]: **den Bus gerade noch schaffen** only just to make it in time for the bus. <> *vi* - **1.** [tun]: **mit jm/etw nichts zu schaffen haben** to have nothing to do with sb/sthg; **jm zu schaffen machen** to give sb trouble; **sich an etw *(D)* zu schaffen machen** to busy o.s. with sthg - **2.** *Süddt* [arbeiten] to work. ◆ **geschafft** *interj* that's it!; [geglückt] done it!

schaffen[2] (*prät* **schuf**, *perf* **hat geschaffen**) *vt* to create; **Platz schaffen** to make room; **Ordnung schaffen** to restore order; **wie geschaffen für jn sein** to be made for sb.

Schaffner, in (*mpl* -, *fpl* **-nen**) *der, die* [in Bus] conductor; [in Zug] ticket collector.

Schafs|fell *das* - **1.** [an Tier] fleece - **2.** [Material, Teppich] sheepskin.

Schafs|käse *der* ewe's milk cheese.

Schaft (*pl* **Schäfte**) *der* - **1.** [von Speer, Pfeil] shaft; [von Messer] handle - **2.** [von Stiefel] leg.

Schakal (*pl* **-e**) *der* jackal.

schäkern *vi fam* [flirten] to flirt.

schal *adj* [Bier] flat; [Geschmack] stale.

Schal (*pl* **-s** ODER **-e**) *der* scarf.

Schale (*pl* **-n**) *die* - **1.** [von Zwiebel, Banane, Tomate] skin; [von Apfel, Orange, Kartoffel] peel; **Kartoffelschalen** potato peelings - **2.** [von Krebs, Ei, Kokosnuss] shell - **3.** [Gefäß] bowl; [flach] dish.

schälen *vt* to peel; [Ei, Nüsse, Erbsen] to shell. ◆ **sich schälen** *ref* to peel.

Schall (*pl* **-e** ODER **Schälle**) *der* sound.

Schall|dämpfer *der* - **1.** [von Auto] silencer *UK*, muffler *US* - **2.** [von Waffe] silencer - **3.** [von Musikinstrument] mute.

schalldicht *adj* soundproof; **etw schalldicht machen** to soundproof sthg.

schallen (*prät* **schallte** ODER **scholl**, *perf* **hat geschallt**) *vi* to resound.

schallend <> *adj* resounding. <> *adv*: **schallend lachen** to roar with laughter.

Schall|mauer *die* sound barrier.

Schall|platte *die* record.

schalten <> *vi* - **1.** [den Gang wechseln] to change gear; **in den vierten Gang schalten** to change into fourth gear - **2.** [umschalten]: **auf das zweite Programm schalten** to turn to channel two; **wir schalten jetzt nach Hamburg** we're now going over to Hamburg - **3.** *fam* [reagieren] to catch on - **4.** [tun]: **schalten und**

walten to do as one pleases. ◇ *vt* [anschließen] to connect; **etw parallel/in Serie schalten** ELEKTR to connect sthg in parallel/series.

Schalter (*pl* -) *der* - **1.** [Schaltknopf] switch - **2.** [für Auskunft, Verkauf] counter.

Schalt|hebel *der* AUTO gear lever.

Schalt|jahr *das* leap year.

Schaltung (*pl* **-en**) *die* - **1.** [Gangschaltung] gear change - **2.** ELEKTR circuit - **3.** TV link-up.

Scham *die* shame; **Scham empfinden** to be ashamed.

schämen ◆ **sich schämen** *ref* to be ashamed; **schäm dich!** shame on you!; **sich für jn schämen** to be ashamed for sb; **ich schäme mich seinetwegen** I'm ashamed of him.

schamlos ◇ *adj* - **1.** [gen] shameless - **2.** [Lüge] barefaced. ◇ *adv* shamelessly.

Schande *die* disgrace; **zu js Schande** to sb's shame.

schändlich ◇ *adj* disgraceful. ◇ *adv* disgracefully.

Schand|tat *die* - **1.** [Verbrechen] heinous crime - **2.** *fam hum* [Aktion]: **zu jeder Schandtat bereit sein** to be game for anything.

Schanze (*pl* **-n**) *die* ski jump.

Schar (*pl* **-en**) *die* [von Kindern] group; [von Vögeln] flock; **Scharen von** swarms of. ◆ **in Scharen** *adv* [von Menschen] in droves; [von Tieren] in swarms.

scharen *vt*: **jn/etw um sich scharen** to gather sb/sthg around o.s. ◆ **sich scharen** *ref*: **sich um jn scharen** to gather round sb.

scharf (*kompar* **schärfer**, *superl* **schärfste**) ◇ *adj* - **1.** [gen] sharp - **2.** [Geschmack] hot, spicy - **3.** *fam* [toll] great; [erotisch] hot; **scharf auf etw sein** to be dead keen on sthg - **4.** [Tempo] high; [Wind] biting - **5.** [Geräusch] piercing; [Geruch] pungent - **6.** [Säure] caustic - **7.** [Hund, Angriff] fierce - **8.** [Munition] live - **9.** [Prüfer] tough. ◇ *adv* [gen] sharply; **scharf geschliffen** keenly whetted; **scharf gewürzt** hot, spicy; **scharf riechen** to be pungent; **scharf beobachten** to watch closely; **scharf nachdenken** to think hard; **jn scharf angreifen** to attack sb fiercely.

Schärfe (*pl* **-n**) *die* - **1.** [von Messer, Sinnen] sharpness; [von Verstand] keenness - **2.** [Bildschärfe] focus - **3.** [von Ton, Streit] severity - **4.** [von Geschmack] spiciness - **5.** [von Prüfer] toughness.

scharf|machen *vt fam* [aggressiv machen] to rouse.

Scharf|schütze, schützin *der, die* marksman (markswoman *die*).

Scharf|sinn *der* astuteness.

Scharlach *der* scarlet fever.

Scharm *der* = **Charme**.

scharmant *adj* = **charmant**.

Scharnier (*pl* **-e**) *das* hinge.

scharren *vi* to scrape; [Hund, Pferd] to paw; **mit den Füßen scharren** to shuffle one's feet.

Schaschlik (*pl* **-s**) *der ODER das* shish kebab.

Schatten (*pl* -) *der* - **1.** [Bereich ohne Sonne] shade; **im Schatten** in the shade - **2.** [Silhouette, Fleck] shadow; **über seinen Schatten springen** to force o.s.

Schatten|seite *die* - **1.** [von Berg, Haus] dark side - **2.** [Nachteil] drawback.

Schattierung (*pl* **-en**) *die* - **1.** [dunkle Stelle] shading - **2.** [Farbe] shade.

schattig *adj* shady.

Schatz (*pl* **Schätze**) *der* - **1.** [Reichtum] treasure - **2.** *fam* [Liebling] darling.

schätzen *vt* - **1.** [Wert, Alter, Schaden] to estimate - **2.** [glauben, meinen] to think - **3.** [mögen]: **jn/etw schätzen** to value sb/sthg; **jn/etw zu schätzen wissen** to appreciate sb/sthg.

Schatz|kammer *die* treasure chamber.

Schätzung (*pl* **-en**) *die* estimate; [das Schätzen] estimation; [von Gebäuden, Grundstücken] valuation.

schätzungsweise *adv* approximately.

Schätz|wert *der* estimated value.

Schau (*pl* **-en**) *die* show; **eine Schau abziehen** *fam* to put on a show; **jn zur Schau stellen** to exhibit sb.

Schauder (*pl* -) *der* shudder; [vor Kälte] shiver.

schauderhaft ◇ *adj* terrible. ◇ *adv*: **schauderhaft aussehen** to look terrible.

schauen *vi* - **1.** [blicken] to look; **zu Boden schauen** to stare at the ground; **auf jn/etw schauen** to look at sb/sthg; **schau mal!** look! - **2.** [sich kümmern]: **nach jm/etw schauen** to look after sb/sthg - **3.** [kontrollieren] to check.

Schauer (*pl* -) *der* - **1.** [Regen] shower - **2.** [vor Angst] shudder; [vor Kälte] shiver.

Schaufel (*pl* **-n**) *die* shovel.

schaufeln *vt* - **1.** [Erde, Kies] to shovel; [Loch] to dig - **2.** *fam* [essen] to shovel down.

Schau|fenster *das* shop window.

Schaufenster|bummel *der* window-shopping trip.

Schaufenster|puppe *die* mannequin.

Schau|kasten *der* display case.

Schaukel (*pl* **-n**) *die* swing.

schaukeln ◇ *vi* - **1.** [gen] to rock - **2.** [auf einer Schaukel] to swing. ◇ *vt* - **1.** [Baby, Wiege] to rock - **2.** *fam* [erledigen]: **ich werde das schon schaukeln** I'll sort it out.

Schaukel|stuhl *der* rocking chair.

Schaulustige (*pl* **-n**) *der, die* onlooker.

Schaum (*pl* **Schäume**) *der* foam; [von Bier] head; **Schaum vor dem Mund haben** to be foaming at the mouth.

schäumen *vi* - **1.** [Flüssigkeit] to foam; [Bier] to froth - **2.** *fam* [vor Wut] to fume.

Schaum|gummi *der* foam rubber.

schaumig <> *adj* foamy. <> *adv*: **etw schaumig rühren** to beat sthg until light and fluffy.

Schaum|stoff *der* plastic foam.

Schaum|wein *der* sparkling wine.

Schau|platz *der* [von Ereignis] scene; [von Erzählung] setting.

Schau|spiel *das* - **1.** [Bühnenstück] play - **2.** [Gattung] drama - **3.** *fam* [Spektakel] spectacle.

Schau|spieler, in *der, die* actor (actress *die*).

Schauspiel|haus *das* theatre.

Schau|steller, in (*mpl* **Schausteller**, *fpl* **-nen**) *der, die* showman (showwoman *die*).

Schau|tafel *die* wall chart *(often made of plastic, wood, etc)*.

Scheck (*pl* **-s**) *der* cheque; **mit Scheck bezahlen** to pay by cheque; **ungedeckter Scheck** bad cheque.

Scheck|heft *das* chequebook.

Scheck|karte *die* cheque card.

Scheibe (*pl* **-n**) *die* - **1.** [Glas] pane (of glass); [Fensterscheibe] window pane; [von Auto] window - **2.** [von Brot, Käse, Wurst] slice.

Scheiben|wischer (*pl* **Scheibenwischer**) *der* windscreen *UK* ODER windshield *US* wiper.

Scheich (*pl* **-s** ODER **-e**) *der* sheikh.

Scheide (*pl* **-n**) *die* - **1.** [Vagina] vagina - **2.** [von Messer] sheath.

scheiden (*prät* **schied**, *perf* **hat/ist geschieden**) <> *vt (hat)* [Ehe] to dissolve; **sich scheiden lassen** to get divorced. <> *vi (ist) geh* - **1.** [fortgehen] to part - **2.** [entlassen werden]: **aus dem Amt scheiden** to resign from office.

Scheidung (*pl* **-en**) *die* divorce; **die Scheidung einreichen** to file for divorce.

Schein (*pl* **-e**) *der* - **1.** [Lichtschein] light; **im Schein einer Taschenlampe** by torchlight - **2.** *(ohne pl)* [Anschein] appearances *Pl*; **der Schein trügt** appearances can be deceptive - **3.** UNI ≃ credit, *certificate issued to students on successful completion of a course in a specific subject* - **4.** [Geldschein] note.

scheinbar <> *adj* apparent. <> *adv* apparently, seemingly.

scheinen (*prät* **schien**, *perf* **hat geschienen**) *vi* - **1.** [leuchten] to shine - **2.** [den Eindruck erwecken] to seem, to appear; **es scheint, dass...** it seems ODER appears that...; **mir scheint, dass...** it seems to me that...; **das scheint dir nur so** it just seems that way to you.

scheinheilig *adj* [heuchlerisch] hypocritical.

scheintot *adj* MED: **scheintot sein** to be apparently dead.

Scheinwerfer (*pl* -) *der* - **1.** [am Auto] headlight - **2.** [im Theater] spotlight; [Suchscheinwerfer] searchlight.

Scheinwerfer|licht *das* [von Autos] headlights *Pl*; [im Theater] spotlight; **im Scheinwerferlicht** in the spotlight.

Scheiße <> *die salopp* [gen] shit; **nur Scheiße im Kopf haben** to be a piss-artist; **in der Scheiße sitzen** to be in the shit. <> *interj salopp* shit!

scheißen (*prät* **schiss**, *perf* **hat geschissen**) *vi salopp* to shit.

Scheitel (*pl* -) *der* [Frisur] parting *UK*, part *US*.

scheitern (*perf* **ist gescheitert**) *vi* - **1.** [Person - gen] to fail; [- Sport] to lose; **sie sind mit ihrem Plan am Widerstand der Bewohner gescheitert** their plan failed because of the opposition of the local population - **2.** [Versuch, Vorhaben] to fail; **an etw *(D)* scheitern** to fail because of sthg.

Schell|fisch *der* haddock.

Schema (*pl* **-s, -ta** ODER **Schemen**) *das* - **1.** [Darstellung] diagram - **2.** [Muster] routine.

schematisch <> *adj* - **1.** [grob] schematic - **2.** [routiniert] mechanical. <> *adv* - **1.** [grob] schematically - **2.** [routiniert] mechanically.

schemenhaft <> *adj* shadowy. <> *adv*: **etw schemenhaft erkennen** to make out the silhouette of sthg.

Schenkel (*pl* -) *der* - **1.** [Bein] thigh - **2.** MATH side.

schenken *vt* - **1.** [geben] to give *(as a present)*; **jm etw schenken** to give sb sthg - **2.** [erlassen]: **jm etw schenken** to let sb off sthg; **sich etw schenken** to spare o.s. sthg.

Schenkung (*pl* **-en**) *die* gift.

scheppern *vi* to clatter.

Scherbe (*pl* **-n**) *die* piece, fragment; **die Scherben zusammenkehren** to sweep up the broken pieces.

Schere (*pl* **-n**) *die* - **1.** [Werkzeug] pair of scissors, scissors *Pl* - **2.** [von Krebs] pincer, claw.

scheren (*prät* **scherte** ODER **schor**, *perf* **hat geschert** ODER **geschoren**) *vt (unreg)* - **1.** [Schaf] to shear; [Hund] to clip - **2.** [Hecke] to clip; [Haare] to crop - **3.** *(reg)* [kümmern]: **das schert mich nicht** I don't care. ◆ **sich scheren** *ref (reg)*: **sich um jn/etw scheren/nicht scheren** to care/not to care about sb/sthg.

Scherereien *Pl* trouble *(U)*; **das gibt Scherereien** that will lead to trouble.

Scherz (*pl* **-e**) *der* joke.

scherzen *vi geh* to joke.

scherzhaft *adv* jokingly.

scheu <> *adj* shy; **jn/etw scheu machen** to frighten sb/sthg. <> *adv* shyly.

Scheu *die* shyness; **ohne Scheu** uninhibitedly.

scheuchen *vt* to shoo.

scheuen <> *vt*: **keine Mühen/Kosten scheuen** to spare no effort/expense. <> *vi* [Pferd] to shy.

Scheuer|lappen *der* floorcloth.

scheuern ◇ *vt* - **1.** [putzen - Boden] to scrub; [- Töpfe] to scour - **2.** [reiben]: **sich** *(D)* **in seinen Schuhen die Fersen wund scheuern** to get sore heels because one's shoes are rubbing. ◇ *vi* to rub.

Scheuklappen *Pl* blinker.

Scheune (*pl* **-n**) *die* barn.

Scheusal (*pl* **-e**) *das fam abw* beast.

scheußlich *abw* ◇ *adj* - **1.** [Verhalten, Anblick, Wetter] terrible - **2.** [Aussehen, Geschmack] horrible. ◇ *adv* - **1.** [sich verhalten, kalt] terribly - **2.** [einrichten, dekorieren] horribly.

Schi = **Ski**.

Schịcht (*pl* **-en**) *die* - **1.** [Lage] layer - **2.** [Gesellschaftsschicht] (social) class; **alle Schichten der Bevölkerung** all strata of society - **3.** [Schichtarbeit] shift; **Schicht arbeiten** to work shifts.

schịchten *vt* to stack.

schịck *adj* - **1.** [modisch] stylish - **2.** [in] trendy - **3.** [toll] great.

schịcken *vt* to send; **jm etw schicken, etw an jn schicken** to send sb sthg, to send sthg to sb. ◆ **sich schicken** *ref geh* - **1.** [sich gehören] to be proper - **2.** [sich abfinden]: **sich in etw** *(A)* **schicken** to resign o.s. to sthg.

Schịcksal (*pl* **-e**) *das* fate; **jn/etw seinem Schicksal überlassen** to leave sb/sthg to his/her/its fate.

Schiebe|dach *das* sunroof.

schieben (*prät* **schob**, *perf* **hat geschoben**) *vt* - **1.** [wegschieben] to push; **die Schuld auf einen anderen schieben** to put the blame on sb else; **ein schlechtes Ergebnis auf etw** *(A)* **schieben** to blame a poor result on sthg - **2.** [hineinschieben] to put - **3.** *fam* [schmuggeln] to traffic in. ◆ **sich schieben** *ref* to move; **sich durch das Gewühl schieben** to push one's way through the crowd.

Schieber (*pl* **-**) *der* - **1.** [an Gerät] slider - **2.** *fam* [Mensch] black marketeer.

Schiebe|tür *die* sliding door.

Schiebung (*pl* **-en**) *die* fixing; **das ist Schiebung!** it's a fix!

schied *prät* ▷ **scheiden**.

Schieds|richter, in *der, die* SPORT referee; [bei Tennis] umpire.

schief ◇ *adj* - **1.** [krumm] crooked; [geneigt] leaning; [Blick] wry; [Absatz] worn - **2.** [falsch - Vergleich] false; **ein schiefes Bild abgeben** to present a lop-sided ODER distorted picture. ◇ *adv*: **das Sofa steht schief** the sofa is at an angle; **das Bild hängt schief** the picture isn't straight; **jn schief ansehen** to look at sb askance.

Schiefer (*pl* **-**) *der* slate.

schief gehen (*perf* **ist schief gegangen**) *vi (unreg)* to go wrong.

schief|lachen ◆ **sich schieflachen** *ref fam* to kill o.s. laughing.

schief liegen *vi (unreg) fam*: **mit einer Meinung schief liegen** to be out in one's opinion.

schielen *vi* - **1.** [wegen Augenfehler] to squint; **sie schielt mit einem Auge** she has a squint in one eye - **2.** *fam* [schauen] to glance; **nach jm/etw schielen** *fig* to have one's eye on sb/sthg.

schien *prät* ▷ **scheinen**.

Schien|bein *das* shin.

Schiene (*pl* **-n**) *die* - **1.** [Gleis] rail - **2.** MED splint - **3.** [Führungsschiene] runner.

schießen (*prät* **schọss**, *perf* **hat/ist geschọssen**) ◇ *vi* - **1.** *(hat)* [mit Gewehr] to shoot, to fire; **auf jn/etw schießen** to shoot ODER fire at sb/sthg - **2.** *(ist)* [wachsen] to shoot up - **3.** *(ist)* [sich schnell bewegen] to shoot; [Flüssigkeit] to gush - **4.** *(hat)* SPORT to shoot. ◇ *vt (hat)* - **1.** [gen] to shoot - **2.** [Tor] to score - **3.** [Foto] to take.

Schießerei (*pl* **-en**) *die* shoot-out.

Schịff (*pl* **-e**) *das* - **1.** [Wasserfahrzeug] ship; **mit dem Schiff** by ship - **2.** [von Kirche] nave.

Schịffahrt *die* = **Schifffahrt**.

Schịff|bruch *der* shipwreck.

Schịfffahrt *die* shipping.

Schịffs|reise *die* voyage.

Schịffs|verkehr *der* shipping traffic.

Schikane (*pl* **-n**) *die* harassment; **mit allen Schikanen** *fam fig* with all the extras.

schikanieren *vt abw* to harass.

Schikoree (*pl* **-s**) *die* ODER *der* = **Chicorée**.

Schịld (*pl* **-er** ODER **-e**) ◇ *das (pl Schilder)* sign; [an Auto] numberplate *UK*, license plate *US*; [Namensschild] nameplate. ◇ *der (pl Schilde)* shield; **etw im Schilde führen** *fig* to be up to sthg.

Schịld|drüse *die* thyroid gland.

schịldern *vt* to describe.

Schịlderung (*pl* **-en**) *die* description.

Schịld|kröte *die* [auf dem Land] tortoise; [im Wasser] turtle.

Schịlf (*pl* **-e**) *das* - **1.** [Pflanze] reed - **2.** *(ohne pl)* [Gebiet] reedbed.

schịllern *vi* to shimmer.

Schịlling (*pl* **-e** ODER **-**) *der* schilling.

Schịmmel (*pl* **-**) *der* - **1.** [Pilz] mould - **2.** [Pferd] white horse.

schịmmelig, schịmmlig *adj* mouldy.

schịmmeln (*perf* **hat/ist geschịmmelt**) *vi* to go mouldy.

Schịmmer (*pl* **-**) *geh der* - **1.** [Glanz] gleam - **2.** [Spur] glimmer.

schịmmern *vi* to glimmer.

schịmmlig = **schimmelig**.

Schimpạnse (*pl* **-n**) *der* chimpanzee.

schimpfen *vi* to grumble; **auf** ODER **über jn/etw schimpfen** to grumble about sb/sthg; **mit jm schimpfen** to tell sb off.

Schimpf|wort (*pl* **-wörter** ODER **-e**) *das* swearword.

schinden (*prät* **schund**, *perf* **hat geschunden**) *vt* - **1.** [quälen] to maltreat - **2.** [herausschlagen]: **Zeit schinden** to play for time; **Applaus schinden** to fish for applause; **Eindruck schinden** to try to impress. ◆ **sich schinden** *ref* to slave away.

Schinderei (*pl* **-en**) *die* - **1.** [Quälerei] maltreatment - **2.** [Strapaze] struggle.

Schinken (*pl* -) *der* - **1.** [Fleisch] ham - **2.** *fam* [Buch] enormous tome - **3.** *fam* FILM tacky epic saga.

Schirm (*pl* **-e**) *der* - **1.** [Regenschirm] umbrella - **2.** [Sonnenschirm] sunshade; [zum Tragen] parasol; [an Mütze] visor, peak.

schiss *prät* ▷ **scheißen**.

schlabberig, schlabbrig *abw adj* - **1.** [wässrig] watery - **2.** [Pullover] baggy.

Schlacht (*pl* **-en**) *die* battle.

schlachten *vt* to slaughter.

Schlachter (*pl* -) *der* butcher.

Schlacht|feld *das* [Kriegsschauplatz] battlefield.

Schlacht|hof *der* slaughterhouse.

Schlaf *der* sleep.

Schlafan|zug *der* pyjamas *Pl*.

Schläfe (*pl* **-n**) *die* temple.

schlafen (*präs* **schläft**, *prät* **schlief**, *perf* **hat geschlafen**) *vi* - **1.** [eingeschlafen sein] to sleep; **schlafen gehen, sich schlafen legen** to go to bed; **mit jm schlafen** to sleep with sb; **schlaf schön** ODER **gut!** sleep well! - **2.** [übernachten]: **bei jm schlafen** to stay the night with sb - **3.** *fam* [unaufmerksam sein] to be asleep.

schlaff ◇ *adj* - **1.** [nicht fest - Seil] slack; [- Penis, Händedruck] limp; [- Haut] loose; [- Muskeln] flabby - **2.** [müde] listless; **Mensch, bist du ein schlaffer Typ!** you're such a drip! ◇ *adv* - **1.** [lose] slackly - **2.** [energielos] listlessly.

Schlaf|lied *das* lullaby.

schlaflos ◇ *adj* sleepless. ◇ *adv* sleeplessly.

Schlaf|mittel *das* sleeping pill.

schläfrig ◇ *adj* sleepy. ◇ *adv* sleepily.

Schlaf|saal *der* dormitory.

Schlaf|sack *der* sleeping bag.

schläft *präs* ▷ **schlafen**.

Schlaf|tablette *die* sleeping pill.

schlaftrunken ◇ *adj* drowsy. ◇ *adv* drowsily.

Schlaf|wagen *der* sleeper.

schlafwandeln (*perf* **hat/ist schlafgewandelt**) *vi* to sleepwalk.

Schlaf|zimmer *das* - **1.** [Zimmer] bedroom - **2.** [Möbel] bedroom suite.

Schlag (*pl* **Schläge**) *der* - **1.** [Stoß] blow; [leicht] pat; [mit der Faust] punch; [mit der Hand] slap; **jm einen Schlag versetzen** [Hieb] to hit sb; [Schock] to be a blow to sb - **2.** [Geräusch - von Uhr] chime; *Süddt* [- Knall] crash; [- von Trommel] bang; **Schlag zwölf** on the stroke of twelve o'clock - **3.** *fam* [Stromstoß] (electric) shock - **4.** [Hose]: **eine Hose mit Schlag** flared trousers *UK*, flared pants *US*; **auf einen Schlag** in one go; **alle erschienen auf einen Schlag** they all turned up at once; **mich trifft der Schlag** *fam* I'm flabbergasted. ◆ **Schläge** *Pl*: **Schläge bekommen** to get a hiding.

Schlag|ader *die* artery.

Schlagan|fall *der* stroke.

schlagartig ◇ *adj* sudden. ◇ *adv* suddenly.

schlagen (*präs* **schlägt**, *prät* **schlug**, *perf* **hat/ist geschlagen**) ◇ *vt (hat)* - **1.** [prügeln] to hit; [regelmäßig] to beat; [mit der Faust] to punch; [mit der Hand] to slap; [leicht] to pat; **jm etw aus der Hand schlagen** to knock sthg out of sb's hand - **2.** [besiegen] to beat; **jn eins zu null schlagen** to beat sb one-zero - **3.** [befestigen]: **jn/etw an etw *(A)* schlagen** [mit Nägeln] to nail sb/sthg to sthg; **einen Nagel in die Wand schlagen** to bang a nail into the wall - **4.** [Ball - bei Fußball] to kick - **5.** [Eier, Sahne, Trommel] to beat - **6.** [legen]: **die Hände vor das Gesicht schlagen** to cover one's face with one's hands - **7.** [hinzufügen]: **etw zu etw schlagen** [Gebiet] to annex sthg to sthg; **etw auf etw *(A)* schlagen** to add sthg to sthg. ◇ *vi* - **1.** *(ist)* [aufprallen]: **gegen etw schlagen** [Regen] to beat against sthg; [Wellen] to pound against sthg; **er schlug mit dem Kopf gegen die Wand** he banged his head against the wall - **2.** *(hat)* [hauen] to hit; **jm auf die Schulter schlagen** to slap sb on the back; **nach jm schlagen** to hit out at sb; **mit der Hand auf den Tisch schlagen** to bang one's hand on the table; **gegen etw schlagen** [Tür] to bang on sthg; **um sich schlagen** to lash out - **3.** *(ist)* [sich auswirken]: **das fette Essen schlägt mir auf den Magen** greasy food affects my stomach - **4.** *(hat)* [Uhr] to strike; [mit Glocke] to chime - **5.** *(ist)* [ähneln]: **nach jm schlagen** to take after sb - **6.** *(hat)* [Herz, Puls] to beat - **7.** *(hat, ist)* [einschlagen]: **in etw *(A)* schlagen** to strike sthg - **8.** *(ist)* [Flammen] to leap. ◆ **sich schlagen** *ref* - **1.** [sich prügeln]: **sich (mit jm) schlagen** to fight (sb); **sich um etw schlagen** *fam* to fight for sthg; **die Gäste schlugen sich um das kalte Büfett** the guests fought over the cold buffet - **2.** [sich begeben]: **sich in die Büsche schlagen** to slip off into the bushes.

Schlager (*pl* -) *der* [Lied] hit.

Schläger (*pl* -) *der* - **1.** [für Tennis, Badminton] racquet; [für Tischtennis] bat; [für Golf] club; [für Hockey] stick - **2.** *abw* [Mensch] thug.

Schlägerei (*pl* **-en**) *die* fight.

schlagfertig ◇ *adj* quick-witted. ◇ *adv*: **schlagfertig antworten** to give a quick-witted reply.

Schlag|loch *das* pothole.

Schlag|sahne *die* whipped cream.

Schlag|seite *die (ohne pl)* list; **Schlagseite bekommen** [Schiff] to start to list; **er hatte Schlagseite** *fam fig* he was swaying from side to side.

schlägt *präs* ▷ **schlagen**.

Schlag|wort (*pl* **-e** ODER **-wörter**) *das* - **1.** *(pl Schlagworte) abw* [Gemeinplatz] catchword - **2.** *(pl Schlagwörter)* [Stichwort] key word.

Schlag|zeile *die* headline; **Schlagzeilen machen** to make the headlines.

Schlag|zeug (*pl* **-e**) *das* [in Band] drums *Pl*; [in Orchester] percussion.

Schlamạssel *der fam* mess.

Schlạmm (*pl* **-e** ODER **Schlạ̈mme**) *der* mud; [Ablagerung] sludge.

schlạmmig *adj* muddy.

Schlamperei (*pl* **-en**) *die fam* sloppiness.

schlạmpig *abw* ◇ *adj* - **1.** [Person] slovenly - **2.** [Arbeit] sloppy. ◇ *adv* - **1.** [sich anziehen] in a slovenly way - **2.** [arbeiten] sloppily.

schlạng *prät* ▷ **schlingen**.

Schlạnge (*pl* **-n**) *die* - **1.** [Tier] snake - **2.** [Reihe] queue *UK*, line *US*; **Schlange stehen** to queue *UK*, to stand in line *US*.

schlạ̈ngeln ◆ **sich schlängeln** *ref* to wind one's/its way.

schlạnk ◇ *adj* slim; [Hals, Beine] slender. ◇ *adv*: **das macht schlank** that's good for your figure.

schlạpp ◇ *adj* [müde] tired out; [energielos] listless. ◇ *adv* listlessly.

schlạpp|machen *vi fam*: **kurz vor dem Ziel schlappmachen** to pull out just before the finishing line.

schlau ◇ *adj* clever; [listig] cunning; **aus jm/etw nicht schlau werden** not to be able to work sb/sthg out. ◇ *adv* cleverly; [listig] cunningly.

Schlauch (*pl* **Schläuche**) *der* hose; [in Reifen] tube.

Schlauch|boot *das* rubber dinghy.

schlauchen *vt fam* to wear out.

Schlaufe (*pl* **-n**) *die* loop.

schlẹcht ◇ *adj* - **1.** [gen] bad, poor; [Zeiten] hard; **ein schlechtes Gedächtnis** a bad ODER poor memory; **(das ist) nicht schlecht!** *fam* (that's) not bad! - **2.** [gesundheitlich - Person] sick; **mir ist/wird schlecht** I feel sick; **schlecht aussehen** to look ill - **3.** [Lebensmittel] off; **schlecht werden** to go off. ◇ *adv* - **1.** [gen] badly, poorly; **die Geschäfte gehen schlecht** business is bad; **er sieht schlecht** he's got bad eyesight; **das Essen ist mir schlecht bekommen** the food didn't agree with me - **2.** [unangenehm - schmecken, riechen] bad - **3.** [kaum] hardly; **das kann schlecht sein** that's hardly possible.

schlẹcht machen *vt* to run down.

schlẹcken ◇ *vt* [lecken] to lick. ◇ *vi fam* [naschen] to eat sweet things.

schleichen (*prät* **schlịch**, *perf* **ist geschlịchen**) *vi* to creep; [Auto] to crawl. ◆ **sich schleichen** *ref* to creep.

schleichend ◇ *adj* - **1.** [vorsichtig] creeping - **2.** [allmählich - Inflation] creeping; [- Krankheit] insidious. ◇ *adv* [langsam]: **die Autos bewegten sich schleichend vorwärts** the cars crept forwards.

Schleier (*pl* -) *der* - **1.** [Stoff] veil - **2.** [von Dunst, Nebel] haze; **auf dem Foto ist ein Schleier** the photo is fogged.

schleierhaft *adj*: **es ist mir schleierhaft, wie du das gemacht hast** it's a mystery to me how you did that.

Schleife (*pl* **-n**) *die* - **1.** [Band] bow - **2.** [Biegung] bend.

schleifen (*prät* **schlịff** ODER **schleifte**, *perf* **hat geschlịffen** ODER **hat/ist geschleift**) ◇ *vt* - **1.** *(unreg) (hat)* [abschleifen - Diamanten, Glas] to cut; [- mit Sandpapier] to sand; [- optische Linsen] to grind - **2.** *(unreg) (hat)* [schärfen] to sharpen, to grind - **3.** *(unreg) (hat)* [drillen] to drill hard - **4.** *(reg) (hat)* [zerren] to drag. ◇ *vi (reg) (hat, ist)* to drag.

Schleim (*pl* **-e**) *der* [in der Nase] mucus; [im Rachen] phlegm; [einer Schnecke] slime.

Schleim|haut *die* mucous membrane.

schlẹmmen ◇ *vt* to feast on. ◇ *vi* to feast.

schlẹndern (*perf* **ist geschlẹndert**) *vi* to stroll.

schlẹppen *vt* - **1.** [tragen] to lug; [zerren] to drag - **2.** [Fahrzeug] to tow - **3.** *fam* [mitnehmen] to drag (along) - **4.** *fam abw* [schmuggeln] to smuggle. ◆ **sich schleppen** *ref* - **1.** [gehen] to drag o.s. - **2.** [sich hinziehen] to drag on.

Schlesien *nt* Silesia.

Schleswig-Họlstein *nt* Schleswig-Holstein.

Schleuder (*pl* **-n**) *die* - **1.** [Steinschleuder] sling; [Wurfmaschine] catapult - **2.** [Wäscheschleuder] spin-dryer.

schleudern (*perf* **hat/ist geschleudert**) ◇ *vt (hat)* - **1.** *fam* [werfen] to hurl - **2.** [zentrifugieren - Wäsche] to spin; [- Honig] to extract. ◇ *vi (ist)* to skid.

Schleudern *das*: **ins Schleudern kommen** ODER **geraten** [mit dem Fahrzeug] to go into a skid; *fam* [unsicher werden] to be thrown.

Schleuder|sitz *der* ejector seat.

schleunigst *adv fam* - **1.** [sofort] at once - **2.** [schnell] hastily.

Schleuse (*pl* **-n**) *die* - **1.** SCHIFF lock - **2.** [Zwischenkammer] airlock.

schlich *prät* ▷ **schleichen**.

schlicht ◇ *adj* simple. ◇ *adv* simply.

schlichten *vt* to settle.

schlief *prät* ▷ **schlafen**.

schließen (*prät* **schloss**, *perf* **hat geschlossen**) ◇ *vt* - **1.** [gen] to close; [Umschlag] to seal; [Stromkreis] to complete - **2.** [Laden, Firma] to close down - **3.** [einschließen]: **jn/etw in etw** *(A)* **schließen** to lock sb/sthg in sthg - **4.** [schlussfolgern] to conclude - **5.** [befestigen]: **etw an etw** *(A)* **schließen** to lock sthg to sthg - **6.** [umarmen]: **er schloss sie in seine Arme** he embraced her - **7.** [Vertrag] to conclude, to sign; [Bündnis] to form. ◇ *vi* - **1.** [zumachen] to close - **2.** [den Betrieb einstellen] to close down - **3.** [schlussfolgern] to conclude - **4.** [enden] to end. ◆ **sich schließen** *ref* - **1.** [anschließen]: **sich an etw** *(A)* **schließen** to follow sthg - **2.** [Wunde, Blüte, Kreis] to close.

Schließ|fach *das* [am Bahnhof] left-luggage *UK* ODER baggage *US* locker; [bei der Bank] safe-deposit box.

schließlich *adv* - **1.** [endlich] finally - **2.** [nun einmal] after all.

schliff *prät* ▷ **schleifen**.

Schliff (*pl* **-e**) *der* - **1.** [Zuschleifen - Vorgang] cutting *(U)*; [- Ergebnis] cut - **2.** [Schärfen - Vorgang] sharpening *(U)*; [- Ergebnis] edge - **3.** [Vollkommenheit]: **ihm fehlt noch der Schliff** he lacks polish - **4.** [Benehmen] refinement.

schlimm *adj* - **1.** [gen] bad; [Folgen] serious; **es ist schlimm, wie viele Leute jetzt arbeitslos werden** the number of people being made redundant at the moment is terrible; **halb so schlimm sein** to be not too bad; **halb so schlimm!** never mind! - **2.** [böse, inakzeptabel] wicked; **es ist eine schlimme Sache, wie er mit ihr umgeht** it's terrible the way he treats her.

schlimmstenfalls *adv* at worst.

Schlinge (*pl* **-n**) *die* - **1.** [Armschlinge] sling - **2.** [in Seil] loop; [zum Aufhängen] noose - **3.** [zum Jagen] snare.

Schlingel (*pl* -) *der fam* rascal.

schlingen (*prät* **schlang**, *perf* **hat geschlungen**) ◇ *vt* - **1.** [binden] to tie; **etw um/in etw** *(A)* **schlingen** to tie sthg round/in sthg - **2.** *fam* [essen] to gobble down - **3.** [legen]: **die Arme um jn/etw schlingen** to throw one's arms around sb/sthg. ◇ *vi fam* [essen] to gobble. ◆ **sich schlingen** *ref*: **sich um etw schlingen** to wind o.s./itself around sthg.

schlingern (*perf* **hat/ist geschlingert**) *vi* to roll.

Schlips (*pl* **-e**) *der* tie.

Schlitten (*pl* -) *der* - **1.** [Rodelschlitten] sledge *UK*, sled *US* - **2.** [Pferdeschlitten] sleigh - **3.** *fam* [Auto] wheels *Pl*.

schlittern (*perf* **ist geschlittert**) *vi* - **1.** [Fahrzeug] to skid - **2.** [Mensch] to slide - **3.** [geraten]: **in den Konkurs schlittern** to slide into bankruptcy.

Schlitt|schuh *der* ice skate; **Schlittschuh laufen** to ice-skate.

Schlitz (*pl* **-e**) *der* [für Geld, Briefe] slot; [Spalte] slit.

schloss *prät* ▷ **schließen**.

Schloss (*pl* **Schlösser**) *das* - **1.** [Burg] castle; [Palast] palace - **2.** [Verschluss] lock.

Schlosser, in (*mpl* -, *fpl* **-nen**) *der, die* metalworker; [Autoschlosser] mechanic; [für Türschlösser] locksmith.

Schlot (*pl* **-e**) *der* chimney.

schlottern *vi* - **1.** [zittern] to tremble - **2.** [zu groß sein] to hang loose.

Schlucht (*pl* **-en**) *die* ravine.

schluchzen *vi* to sob.

Schluck (*pl* **-e**) *der* - **1.** [Menge] drop; **ein kleiner Schluck** a sip; **einen Schluck trinken** to have a drop (to drink); **einen Schluck nehmen** ODER **tun** to take a gulp - **2.** [Schlucken] gulp.

Schluckauf *der*: **einen Schluckauf haben** to have hiccups.

schlucken ◇ *vt* - **1.** [Essen, Gefühle] to swallow - **2.** [übernehmen - Firma] to swallow up - **3.** *fam* [Alkohol, Benzin] to guzzle. ◇ *vi* to swallow.

schlug *prät* ▷ **schlagen**.

schlüpfen (*perf* **ist geschlüpft**) *vi* - **1.** [anziehen, ausziehen]: **aus etw schlüpfen** to slip sthg off; **in etw** *(A)* **schlüpfen** to slip sthg on - **2.** [sich schnell bewegen] to slip; **aus etw schlüpfen** to slip out of sthg - **3.** [Küken]: **(aus etw) schlüpfen** to hatch (out of sthg).

Schlüpfer (*pl* -) *der* knickers *Pl UK*, panties *Pl US*.

Schlupf|loch *das* - **1.** [Öffnung] hole - **2.** [Versteck] hideout.

schlüpfrig *adj* - **1.** [anzüglich] lewd - **2.** [rutschig] slippery.

schlurfen (*perf* **ist geschlurft**) *vi fam* to shuffle.

schlürfen *vt* & *vi* to slurp.

Schluss (*pl* **Schlüsse**) *der* - **1.** [Ende] end; **zum Schluss** at the end; **mit etw Schluss machen** to stop sthg; **mit jm Schluss machen** *fam* to break up with sb; **jetzt ist aber Schluss damit!** it's over now!; **damit mache ich Schluss für heute** with that, I'll finish for today - **2.** [Schlussfolgerung] conclusion; **Schlüsse aus etw ziehen** to draw conclusions from sthg - **3.** [Schlussstück] ending.

Schlüssel (*pl* -) *der* - **1.** [für Schloss, Auflösung] key; **der Schlüssel zu etw** *fig* the key to sthg - **2.** [Schraubenschlüssel] spanner - **3.** [Code] code - **4.** [Verteilungsschlüssel] allocation base.

Schlüssel|bein *das* collar bone.

Schlüssel|bund *der* bunch of keys.

Schlüssel|loch *das* keyhole.

Schlussfolgerung (*pl* **-en**) *die* conclusion.

schlüssig ◇ *adj* conclusive. ◇ *adv* conclusively.

Schlusslicht (*pl* **-er**) *das* - **1.** [Letzter]: **der Verein ist das Schlusslicht in der Tabelle** the club is bottom of the table - **2.** [Rücklicht] rear light, taillight.

Schlussstrich (*pl* **-e**) *der*: **einen Schlussstrich unter etw** *(A)* **ziehen** to draw a line under sthg.

Schlussverkauf (*pl* **-käufe**) *der* end-of-season sale.

schmächtig ◇ *adj* slight. ◇ *adv* [gebaut] slightly.

schmackhaft ◇ *adj* tasty. ◇ *adv* [kochen] appetizingly; **jm etw schmackhaft machen** to make sthg palatable to sb.

schmal ◇ *adj* [Straße, Treppe, Hüften] narrow; [Person] thin; [Figur] slender. ◇ *adv* [geschnitten] narrowly; [gebaut] slenderly; [zusammenkneifen] tightly.

schmälern *vt* to diminish.

Schmalz (*pl* **-e**) *der* - **1.** [Fett - zum Kochen] lard; [- zum Essen] dripping - **2.** *fam* [Gefühl] schmaltz.

schmalzig ◇ *adj* schmaltzy. ◇ *adv* schmaltzily.

schmarotzen *vi* - **1.** *abw* [Person] to sponge - **2.** BIOL to live as a parasite.

Schmarotzer, in (*mpl* **-**, *fpl* **-nen**) *der, die abw* sponger.

schmatzen *vi* to eat noisily; **mit den Lippen schmatzen** to smack one's lips.

schmecken ◇ *vi* to taste; **schmeckt es?** does it taste good?; **hat es geschmeckt?** did you enjoy your meal?; **es schmeckt mir** I like it; **nach etw schmecken** to taste of sthg; **es schmeckt gut/schlecht** it tastes good/bad; **lass es dir schmecken!** enjoy your meal! ◇ *vt* to taste.

Schmeichelei (*pl* **-en**) *die* flattery *(U)*.

schmeicheln *vi*: **jm schmeicheln** to flatter sb.

schmeißen (*prät* **schmiss**, *perf* **hat geschmissen**) *fam* ◇ *vt* - **1.** [werfen] to chuck - **2.** [spendieren]: **eine Runde schmeißen** to stand a round - **3.** [aufgeben] to pack in - **4.** [organisieren] to handle. ◇ *vi*: **er schmiss mit dem Geschirr nach mir** he chucked the crockery at me.

schmelzen (*präs* **schmilzt**, *prät* **schmolz**, *perf* **hat/ist geschmolzen**) ◇ *vi (ist)* to melt. ◇ *vt (hat)* to melt; [Erz] to smelt.

Schmelz|punkt *der* melting point.

Schmerz (*pl* **-en**) *der* - **1.** *(meist pl)* [körperlich] pain - **2.** [seelisch] grief.

schmerzen *vi* & *vt* to hurt.

schmerzhaft *adj* painful.

schmerzlos ◇ *adj* painless. ◇ *adv* painlessly.

Schmerz|mittel *das* painkiller.

Schmerz|tablette *die* painkiller.

Schmetterling (*pl* **-e**) *der* [Tier & SPORT] butterfly.

Schmied (*pl* **-e**) *der* blacksmith.

Schmiede|eisen *das* wrought iron.

schmieden *vt* - **1.** [bearbeiten] to forge - **2.** [befestigen]: **jn an etw** *(A)* **schmieden** to chain sb to sthg - **3.** [Pläne] to make.

schmiegen *vt* to nestle. ◆ **sich schmiegen** *ref*: **sich an jn/etw schmiegen** to snuggle up to sb/sthg.

Schmiere (*pl* **-n**) *die* - **1.** [Fett] grease - **2.** *fam* [Wache]: **Schmiere stehen** to act as a lookout.

schmieren ◇ *vt* - **1.** [mit Fett] to grease; [mit Öl] to oil - **2.** *fam* TECH to lubricate; [bestechen] to bribe - **3.** [streichen] to spread; **ein Butterbrot schmieren** ≃ to make a sandwich; **wie geschmiert** *fam* without a hitch. ◇ *vi* - **1.** [schreiben] to scribble - **2.** [klecksen] to smudge.

Schmier|geld *das fam* bribe.

schmierig ◇ *adj* - **1.** [ölig] greasy - **2.** *abw* [Witz, Anspielung] smutty - **3.** *abw* [Typ] smarmy. ◇ *adv* [angrinsen] smarmily; [lachen, anmachen] smuttily.

Schmier|mittel *das* lubricant.

Schmier|seife *die* soft soap.

schmilzt *präs* ▷ **schmelzen**.

Schminke (*pl* **-n**) *die* make-up.

schminken *vt* to make up. ◆ **sich schminken** *ref* to put on one's make-up.

schmirgeln *vt* to sand.

Schmirgel|papier *das* sandpaper.

schmiss *prät* ▷ **schmeißen**.

Schmöker (*pl* **-**) *der* tome *(of lightweight reading)*.

schmökern ◇ *vi*: **in einem Buch schmökern** to bury o.s. in a book. ◇ *vt* to bury o.s. in.

schmollen *vi* to sulk.

schmolz *prät* ▷ **schmelzen**.

schmoren ◇ *vt* to braise. ◇ *vi* - **1.** [braten] to braise - **2.** *fam* [in der Sonne] to roast - **3.** *fam* [warten]: **jn schmoren lassen** to leave sb to stew (in his/her own juice).

Schmuck *der* - **1.** [Gegenstand] jewellery - **2.** [Dekoration] decoration.

schmücken *vt* to decorate. ◆ **sich schmücken** *ref* to adorn o.s.

schmucklos ◇ *adj* plain, unadorned. ◇ *adv* plainly.

Schmuck|stück *das* - **1.** [Schmuck] piece of jewellery - **2.** [aus Sammlung, Ausstellung] jewel.

Schmuggel *der* smuggling.

schmuggeln *vt* & *vi* to smuggle.

Schmuggler, in (*mpl* -, *fpl* **-nen**) *der, die* smuggler.

schmunzeln *vi*: **(über etw** *(A)***) schmunzeln** to smile to o.s. (at sthg).

schmusen *vi*: **(mit jm) schmusen** to cuddle (sb); [Liebespaar] to kiss and cuddle (with sb).

Schmutz *der* dirt; **Schmutz abweisend** dirt-resistant.

schmutzen *vi* to get dirty.

Schmutz|fink *der fam* - **1.** [schmutziger Mensch - Erwachsener] dirty pig; [- Kind] mucky pup - **2.** [unsittlicher Mensch] creep.

schmutzig *adj* - **1.** [gen] dirty; **sich schmutzig machen** to get dirty - **2.** [Geschäftspraktiken] shady.

Schnabel (*pl* **Schnäbel**) *der* beak.

Schnalle (*pl* **-n**) *die* buckle.

schnallen *vt* - **1.** [festmachen] to strap; [Gürtel] to fasten, to buckle; **den Gürtel enger schnallen** to tighten one's belt; **etw auf etw** *(A)* **schnallen** to strap sthg to sthg - **2.** *fam* [kapieren] to get.

schnalzen *vi*: **mit der Zunge/den Fingern schnalzen** to click one's tongue/fingers; **mit der Peitsche schnalzen** to crack the whip.

Schnäppchen (*pl* -) *das* snip, bargain; **mit dem Hemd habe ich ein Schnäppchen gemacht** the shirt was a real snip ODER bargain.

schnappen (*perf* **hat/ist geschnappt**) ◇ *vt* *(hat)* - **1.** *fam* [festnehmen] to catch - **2.** *fam* [nehmen]: **sich** *(D)* **etw schnappen** to grab sthg - **3.** [packen] to grab. ◇ *vi* - **1.** *(hat)* [beißen]: **nach jm/etw schnappen** to snap at sb/sthg - **2.** *(ist)* [federn] to spring up.

Schnappschuss (*pl* **-schüsse**) *der* snapshot.

Schnaps (*pl* **Schnäpse**) *der* schnapps.

schnarchen *vi* [im Schlaf] to snore.

schnattern *vi* - **1.** [Gänse] to gabble; [Enten] to quack - **2.** *fam* [reden] to chatter - **3.** [zittern]: **er schnattert vor Kälte** his teeth are chattering with cold.

schnauben *vi eigtl* & *fig* to snort; **vor Wut schnauben** to snort with anger.

schnaufen *vi* to wheeze.

Schnauz|bart *der* - **1.** [Bart] moustache - **2.** *fam* [Mensch] guy with the 'tache.

Schnauze (*pl* **-n**) *die* - **1.** [Maul] muzzle; [von Schwein] snout - **2.** *salopp abw* [Mund] trap, gob *UK*; **jm eins auf die Schnauze hauen** to sock sb in the mouth; **halt die Schnauze!** *salopp* shut your trap!

schnäuzen ◆ **sich schnäuzen** *ref*: **sich (die Nase) schnäuzen** to blow one's nose.

Schnauzer (*pl* -) *der* - **1.** [Hunderasse] Schnauzer - **2.** [Schnurrbart] large moustache.

Schnecke (*pl* **-n**) *die* snail; [ohne Schneckenhaus] slug; **jn zur Schnecke machen** *fig* to give sb a dressing-down.

Schnecken|haus *das* snail shell.

Schnee *der* snow; **es liegt Schnee** there is snow (on the ground); **Schnee räumen** to clear snow.

Schnee|ball *der* snowball.

Schnee|besen *der* whisk.

Schnee|fall *der* snowfall.

Schnee|flocke *die* snowflake.

Schnee|gestöber (*pl* **Schneegestöber**) *das* [leicht] snow flurry; [stärker] snowstorm.

Schnee|glöckchen (*pl* **Schneeglöckchen**) *das* snowdrop.

Schnee|kette *die* snow chain.

Schnee|mann (*pl* **-männer**) *der* snowman.

Schnee|pflug *der* snowplough.

Schnee|schmelze *die* thaw.

Schnee|sturm *der* snowstorm.

Schnee|treiben *das* blizzard.

Schneewittchen *das* Snow White.

Schneide (*pl* **-n**) *die* [Klinge] blade.

schneiden (*prät* **schnitt**, *perf* **hat geschnitten**) ◇ *vt* - **1.** [gen] to cut; [Hecke] to trim; [Baum] to cut back; **sich** *(D)* **die Haare schneiden lassen** to have one's hair cut - **2.** [klein schneiden - in Stücke] to chop; [- in Scheiben] to slice; [- Braten] to carve; **etw in Würfel schneiden** to cube sthg - **3.** [zurechtschneiden - Foto] to cut to size - **4.** [ausschneiden] to cut out - **5.** [beim Überholen] to cut in on; **eine Kurve schneiden** to cut a corner - **6.** [ignorieren]: **jn schneiden** to ignore sb - **7.** [überschneiden] to cut across, to cross; MATH to intersect - **8.** [hinzufügen]: **Schnittlauch in die Suppe schneiden** to chop some chives and add them to the soup - **9.** SPORT [Ball] to put spin on. ◇ *vi* - **1.** [beschädigen]: **(mit etw) in etw** *(A)* **schneiden** to cut sthg (with sthg) - **2.** [Frisör, Messer, Schere] to cut. ◆ **sich schneiden** *ref* - **1.** [sich verletzen] to cut o.s.; **sich in den Finger schneiden** to cut one's finger - **2.** [sich überschneiden] to intersect - **3.** *fam* [sich täuschen]: **wenn du das glaubst, dann hast du dich aber geschnitten!** if you think that, you've got another think ODER thing coming!

schneidend ◇ *adj* - **1.** [Wind, Kälte] biting - **2.** [Stimme] piercing. ◇ *adv* piercingly.

Schneider (*pl* -) *der* tailor; [für Damen] dressmaker.

Schneiderin (*pl* **-nen**) *die* tailor; [für Damen] dressmaker.

schneidern ◇ *vt*: **(sich** *(D)***) etw schneidern** to make sthg. ◇ *vi* to make clothes.

Schneider|sitz *der*: **im Schneidersitz** cross-legged.

Schneide|zahn *der* incisor.

schneidig *adj* [Bursche] dashing; [Fahrstil] daring.

schneien *vi*: **es schneit** it's snowing.

schnell ◇ *adj* - **1.** [gen] quick - **2.** [Tempo] fast, quick - **3.** [Person, Gefährt] fast. ◇ *adv*

- **1.** [laufen] fast, quickly - **2.** [zügig] quickly; **schnell machen** to hurry up - **3.** [bald] soon - **4.** [gleich]: **kannst du mal schnell vorbeikommen?** could you just pop round quickly?; **sag doch mal schnell** just tell me again.

Schnelle *die*: **auf die Schnelle** quickly.

Schnell|hefter *der* loose-leaf binder.

Schnelligkeit *die* speed.

Schnellimbiss (*pl* **-e**) *der* snack bar.

schnellstens *adv* as quickly as possible.

Schnell|straße *die* expressway.

Schnell|zug *der* express train.

schneuzen *ref* = **schnäuzen**.

schnippisch ◇ *adj* pert. ◇ *adv* pertly.

Schnipsel (*pl* -) *der* scrap.

schnipsen ◇ *vt* to flick. ◇ *vi* to snap.

schnitt *prät* ▷ **schneiden**.

Schnitt (*pl* **-e**) *der* - **1.** [Öffnung] cut; [bei Operation] incision - **2.** [von Haar, Kleidung] cut; [Schnittmuster] pattern - **3.** [von Film] editing *(U)* - **4.** [Schneiden - von Baum] cutting back; [- von Hecke] trimming - **5.** *fam* [Durchschnitt] average; **im Schnitt** on average - **6.** *fam* [Gewinn] profit.

Schnitte (*pl* **-n**) *die* - **1.** [Scheibe] slice - **2.** [belegtes Brot] open sandwich.

Schnitt|fläche *die* - **1.** [angeschnittener Teil] cut end - **2.** MATH section.

Schnitt|lauch *der (ohne pl)* chives *Pl*.

Schnitt|punkt *der* point of intersection.

Schnitt|wunde *die* cut.

Schnitzel (*pl* -) *das* - **1.** [Fleisch] escalope - **2.** [aus Papier] scrap.

schnitzen *vt* & *vi* to carve.

Schnitzer (*pl* -) *der* - **1.** [Fehler] blunder - **2.** [Beruf] carver.

Schnitzerei (*pl* **-en**) *die* carving.

Schnorchel (*pl* -) *der* snorkel.

schnorcheln *vi* to snorkel.

schnüffeln ◇ *vi* - **1.** [riechen]: **an etw** *(D)* **schnüffeln** to sniff at sthg - **2.** [durchsuchen] to snoop. ◇ *vt fam* [einatmen] to sniff.

Schnuller (*pl* -) *der* dummy *UK*, pacifier *US*.

Schnupfen (*pl* -) *der* cold; **einen Schnupfen haben/bekommen** to have/get a cold.

schnuppern ◇ *vi* - **1.** [riechen]: **(an etw** *(D)***) schnuppern** to sniff (at sthg) - **2.** [testen]: **einige Stunden schnuppern** to try it out for a few classes. ◇ *vt* to sniff.

Schnur (*pl* **Schnüre**) *die* string; [Zugschnur] cord; [Kabel] lead.

Schnürchen *das*: **wie am Schnürchen** *fam* without a hitch.

schnüren ◇ *vt* - **1.** [gen] to tie; [Mieder] to lace up - **2.** [Bündel, Paket] to tie up; **etw um etw schnüren** to tie sthg around sthg. ◇ *vi*: **ins Fleisch schnüren** to bite into one's flesh.

schnurlos *Adjektiv* cordless.

Schnurr|bart *der* moustache.

schnurren (*perf* **hat geschnurrt**) *vi eigtl* & *fig* to purr.

Schnür|senkel (*pl* -) *der* shoelace.

schob *prät* ▷ **schieben**.

Schock (*pl* **-s**) *der* shock; **unter Schock stehen** to be in shock.

schockieren *vt* to shock.

schockiert ◇ *adj* shocked; **über etw** *(A)* **schockiert sein** to be shocked at sthg. ◇ *adv*: **schockiert reagieren** to react with shock.

Schokokopf *der* KÜCHE *chocolate-covered marshmallow*.

Schokolade (*pl* **-n**) *die* - **1.** [Süßigkeit] chocolate - **2.** [Getränk ◆ heiß] hot chocolate; [- kalt] chocolate drink.

Scholle (*pl* **-n**) *die* [Fisch] plaice.

schon *adv* - **1.** [bereits] already; **wir essen heute schon um elf Uhr** we're eating earlier today, at eleven o'clock; **schon damals** even then; **schon 1914** as early as 1914; **er ist schon lange hier** he's been here for a long time; **schon jetzt** already; **schon wieder** again - **2.** [inzwischen] yet; **warst du schon auf der Post?** have you been to the post office yet?; **schon längst** a long time ago; **schon oft** often - **3.** [zwar]: **es gefällt mir schon, aber** I **do** like it, but; **ja schon, aber** yes of course, but - **4.** [endlich]: **komm schon!** come on!; **nun rede schon!** come on say something! - **5.** [zur Beruhigung]: **du machst das schon** don't worry, I'm sure you'll manage it!; **es wird schon gehen** it will work out all right; **schon gut!, schon recht!** all right!, OK! - **6.** [allein] just; **schon der Gedanke daran macht mich nervös** just thinking about it makes me nervous.

schön ◇ *adj* - **1.** [Frau, Kind, Sache] beautiful; [Mann] handsome - **2.** [angenehm] good; **schönes Wochenende!** have a nice weekend! - **3.** [erheblich] considerable; **es ist noch ein schönes Stück** it's still quite a way; **schönen Dank!** many thanks!, thanks a lot! ◇ *adv* - **1.** [gen] well; [gekleidet] beautifully - **2.** [verstärkend]: **schön langsam** nice and slowly; **sei schön brav!** be a good boy/girl! ◆ **ganz schön** *adv fam* really. ◆ **na schön** *interj fam* all right!

Schöne (*pl* **-n**) *der, die, das*: **die Schöne** the beauty; **der Schöne** the handsome man; **das Schöne** the beautiful; **das Schöne daran** the nice thing about it; **da hast du was Schönes angerichtet!** *fam* you've gone and done it now!

schonen *vt* - **1.** [pfleglich behandeln - Kleider, Auto, Möbel] to be careful with, to treat gently - **2.** [schützen - Augen, Umwelt] to protect - **3.** [weniger verlangen von] to go easy on; **er schont den Stürmer für das nächste Spiel** he's saving ODER resting the forward for the next game. ◆ **sich schonen** *ref* to take it easy.

schonend <> *adj* gentle. <> *adv* gently; **jm etw schonend beibringen** to break sthg to sb gently.

Schonfrist *die* period of grace.

Schönheit (*pl* **-en**) *die* - **1.** [gen] beauty - **2.** [Sehenswürdigkeit] attraction.

schön machen *vt* - **1.** [hübsch machen]: **etw schön machen** to make sthg look nice - **2.** [angenehm machen] to make agreeable; **es sich** *(D)* **schön machen** to make things nice. ◆ **sich schön machen** *ref* to do o.s. up.

Schonung (*pl* **-en**) *die* - **1.** [Baumschule] young plantation - **2.** [pflegliche Behandlung] careful ODER gentle treatment; [Schützen] protection; [verschonen] to spare; **jn um Schonung bitten** [weniger verlangen von] to ask sb to go easy on one.

schonungslos <> *adj* ruthless; [Offenheit] brutal. <> *adv* ruthlessly; [offen] brutally.

Schonzeit *die* close season.

Schopf (*pl* **Schöpfe**) *der* [Haar] shock of hair; **die Gelegenheit beim Schopf packen** to grasp the opportunity with both hands.

schöpfen *vt* - **1.** [auftun] to scoop; [mit Löffel, Kelle] to ladle; **etw aus etw schöpfen** to scoop/ladle sthg out of sthg - **2.** [Mut, Kraft, Atem] to draw; **Verdacht schöpfen** to become suspicious.

Schöpfer (*pl* -) *der* [Gott] Creator.

schöpferisch <> *adj* creative. <> *adv* creatively; **schöpferisch veranlagt sein** to have creative tendencies.

Schöpfkelle *die* ladle.

Schöpfung (*pl* **-en**) *die* - **1.** [Welterschaffung] Creation - **2.** *geh* [Werk] creation.

schor *prät* ▷ **scheren**.

Schorf *der (ohne pl)* scab.

Schornstein *der* chimney.

Schornsteinfeger, in (*mpl* -, *fpl* **-nen**) *der, die* chimney sweep.

schoss *prät* ▷ **schießen**.

Schoß (*pl* **Schöße**) *der* - **1.** [Körperteil] lap; **auf js Schoß sitzen** to sit on sb's lap; **der Erfolg ist mir nicht in den Schoß gefallen** success wasn't handed to me on a plate - **2.** *geh* [Schutz] bosom - **3.** *geh* [Mutterleib] womb - **4.** [von Jacke] tail.

Schotte (*pl* **-n**) *der* Scotsman, Scot.

Schottin (*pl* **-nen**) *die* Scotswoman, Scot.

schottisch *adj* Scottish.

Schottland *nt* Scotland.

schraffieren *vt* to hatch.

schräg <> *adj* - **1.** [schief] sloping; [Linie] diagonal - **2.** *fam* [eigenartig] offbeat - **3.** *fam* [falsch] dodgy. <> *adv* - **1.** [schief] at an angle; [diagonal] diagonally; **jn schräg ansehen** *fam* to look askance at sb - **2.** *fam* [falsch]: **das klingt schräg** that sounds dodgy.

Schräge (*pl* **-n**) *die* slope; [Wand] sloping ceiling.

Schramme (*pl* **-n**) *die* scratch.

Schrank (*pl* **Schränke**) *der* [für Geschirr, Vorräte] cupboard; [für Kleider] wardrobe *UK*, closet *US*; [für Bücher] bookcase.

Schranke (*pl* **-n**) *die* barrier. ◆ **Schranken** *Pl* [Grenzen] limits.

schrankenlos *adj* [Freiheit] boundless.

Schrankwand *die* wall unit.

Schraube (*pl* **-n**) *die* - **1.** [zum Befestigen] screw; [ohne Spitze] bolt - **2.** SPORT twist.

schrauben *vt*: **etw (auf/in etw** *(A)***) schrauben** to screw sthg (onto/into sthg); **etw an etw** *(A)* **schrauben** to screw sthg to sthg; **etw aus** ODER **von etw schrauben** to unscrew sthg from sthg; **den Deckel von der Flasche schrauben** to screw the lid off the bottle; **etw nach oben/unten schrauben** *fig* to raise/lower sthg.

Schraubenschlüssel *der* spanner *UK*, wrench *US*.

Schraubenzieher (*pl* **Schraubenzieher**) *der* screwdriver.

Schrebergarten *der* ≃ allotment.

Schreck *der* fright; **vor Schreck** in fear ODER fright; **einen Schreck kriegen** *fam* to get a fright; **jm einen Schreck einjagen** to give sb a fright.

Schrecken (*pl* -) *der* terror; **die Schrecken des Krieges** the horrors of war; **er ist der Schrecken der Nachbarschaft** he's the terror of the neighbourhood.

schreckhaft *adj* easily scared.

schrecklich <> *adj* terrible. <> *adv* terribly.

Schrei (*pl* **-e**) *der* shout; [von Tier, Baby] cry; [aus Angst, vor Schmerz, Lust] scream; **der letzte Schrei** *fam fig* the latest thing.

schreiben (*prät* **schrieb**, *perf* **hat geschrieben**) <> *vt* - **1.** [gen] to write; [mit Schreibmaschine] to type - **2.** [orthografisch] to spell; **wie schreibt man das?** how do you spell that?, how's that spelt? - **3.** [Klassenarbeit, Test] to do - **4.** [Rechnung] to make out; **die Firma schreibt rote Zahlen** the company is in the red. <> *vi* - **1.** [gen] to write; **an jn schreiben** to write to sb; **an etw** *(D)* **schreiben** to be writing sthg - **2.** [tippen] to type; *siehe auch* **großschreiben, kleinschreiben, krankschreiben**. ◆ **sich schreiben** *ref* - **1.** [korrespondieren] to correspond - **2.** [sich buchstabieren] to be spelt.

Schreiben (*pl* -) *das* letter.

Schreibkraft *die* clerical assistant; [Stenotypistin] shorthand typist.

Schreibmaschine *die* typewriter.

Schreibschrift *die* cursive script.

Schreibtisch *der* desk.

Schreibtischlampe *die* desk lamp.

Schreibwarengeschäft *das* stationery shop.

schreien (*prät* **schrie**, *perf* **hat geschrie(e)n**) *vi* [gen] to shout; [Tier, Baby] to cry; [aus Angst, vor Schmerz, Lust] to scream; **vor Schmerz schreien** to scream with pain; **schrei nicht so!** stop shouting!; **nach etw schreien** *eigtl* & *fig* to cry out for sthg.

Schreien *das* crying; [gellend] screaming; [Brüllen] shouting; **zum Schreien sein** *fam* to be a scream.

Schrei|hals *der fam* bawler.

Schreiner, in (*mpl* -, *fpl* **-nen**) *der, die* joiner.

schrie *prät* ▷ **schreien**.

schrieb *prät* ▷ **schreiben**.

Schrift (*pl* **-en**) *die* - **1.** [Handschrift] handwriting *(U)* - **2.** [das Geschriebene] writing *(U)* - **3.** [Alphabet] script - **4.** type. ◆ **Schriften** *Pl* texts; [kurze Abhandlungen] papers; [Werke] works.

schriftlich ◇ *adj* written. ◇ *adv* in writing.

Schriftsteller, in (*mpl* -, *fpl* **-nen**) *der, die* writer.

schrill *adj* shrill.

Schrimp (*pl* **-s**), **Shrimp** (*pl* **-s**) [ʃrɪmp] *der* shrimp.

Schritt (*pl* **-e**) *der* - **1.** [gen] step; **er ist mir immer einen Schritt voraus** he's always a step ahead of me; **jn am Schritt erkennen** to recognize sb's step - **2.** [von Hose] crotch - **3.** [zur Angabe der Entfernung] pace; **drei Schritte von mir entfernt** three paces away from me - **4.** [Gangart] walk; **im Schritt reiten** to ride at a walk; **Schritt für Schritt** step by step; **mit jm/etw Schritt halten** to keep up with sb/sthg.

Schritt|macher (*pl* **Schrittmacher**) *der* - **1.** [Vorreiter] pacesetter - **2.** [im Sport] pacemaker.

schrittweise *adv* gradually.

schroff ◇ *adj* - **1.** [Verhalten, Antwort, Wechsel] abrupt - **2.** [Felsen, Abhang] sheer - **3.** [Gegensatz] stark. ◇ *adv* [abweisen, antworten] abruptly.

schröpfen *vt fam* [ausnehmen] to rip off.

Schrot *der ODER das* - **1.** [Munition] shot - **2.** [Getreide] meal; [von Weizen] wholemeal *UK*, wholewheat *US*.

Schrott *der* - **1.** [altes Metall] scrap metal - **2.** *fam* [Plunder] junk - **3.** *fam* [Blödsinn] rubbish.

Schrott|platz *der* scrapyard *UK*, junkyard *US*.

schrottreif *adj* fit for the scrapheap.

schrubben *vt* to scrub.

Schrubber (*pl* -) *der* hard-bristled broom *(for scrubbing floors)*.

schrumpelig, schrumplig *adj* [Haut] wrinkled; [Apfel] shrivelled.

schrumpfen (*perf* **ist geschrumpft**) *vi* to shrink.

schrumplig = **schrumpelig**.

Schub (*pl* **Schübe**) *der* - **1.** [Kraft] thrust - **2.** [Anfall] bout - **3.** [Ladung, Menschengruppe] batch.

Schub|karre (*pl* **-n**) *die* wheelbarrow.

Schubkarren (*pl* -) *der* wheelbarrow.

Schub|lade (*pl* **-n**) *die* drawer.

Schubs (*pl* **-e**) *der* push.

schubsen *vt* to push.

schüchtern ◇ *adj* [Person, Blick] shy; [Versuch, Frage] timid. ◇ *adv* [lächeln, schauen] shyly; [sich benehmen, fragen] timidly.

Schüchternheit *die* shyness.

schuf *prät* ▷ **schaffen**.

Schuft (*pl* **-e**) *der abw* scoundrel.

schuften *vi fam* to slave away.

Schuh (*pl* **-e**) *der* shoe; **jm etw in die Schuhe schieben** *fig* to pin the blame for sthg on sb.

Schuh|creme, Schuhkrem *die* shoe polish.

Schuh|geschäft *das* shoe shop.

Schuh|größe *die* shoe size.

Schuh|macher, in (*mpl* **Schuhmacher**, *fpl* **-nen**) *der, die* cobbler, shoemaker.

Schulabschluss (*pl* **-schlüsse**) *der* school-leaving qualification.

Schul|anfang *der* - **1.** [Einschulung] first day of school - **2.** [nach den Ferien] beginning of term.

Schul|aufgabe *die* homework *(U)*.

Schul|besuch *der* school attendance.

Schul|bildung *die* school education, schooling.

Schul|bus *der* school bus.

schuld *adj*: **an etw** *(D)* **schuld sein** to be to blame for sthg; **er ist schuld daran** it's his fault.

Schuld (*pl* **-en**) *die* - **1.** [Verantwortung, Ursache] blame; **es war seine Schuld** it was his fault; **an etw Schuld haben** to be to blame for sthg; **jm (an etw** *(D)***) Schuld geben** to blame sb (for sthg) - **2.** [Unrecht] guilt; **sich** *(D)* **keiner Schuld bewusst sein** to be unaware of having done anything wrong; *siehe auch* **zuschulden**. ◆ **Schulden** *Pl* debts; **Schulden haben** to be in debt; **12 Milliarden Euro Schulden haben** to have debts of 12 billion euros; **Schulden machen** to run up debts.

schuldbewusst ◇ *adj* guilty. ◇ *adv* guiltily.

schulden *vt*: **jm etw schulden** to owe sb sthg.

schuldig ◇ *adj* - **1.** [verantwortlich] guilty; **an etw** *(D)* **schuldig sein** to be to blame for sthg - **2.** [nicht bezahlt] due; **jm etw schuldig sein** ODER **bleiben** to owe sb sthg. ◇ *adv*: **sich schuldig bekennen** to admit one's guilt.

schuldlos *adj* innocent.

Schule (*pl* **-n**) *die* school; **in der Schule** at school; **zur** ODER **in die Schule gehen** to go to school; **Schule machen** *fig* to set a precedent.

schulen *vt* to train.
Schüler (*pl* -) *der* pupil.
Schüler|austausch *der* (school) exchange.
Schüler|ausweis *der pupil's ID card entitling them to concessions etc.*
Schülerin (*pl* **-nen**) *die* pupil.
Schüler|karte *die* school season ticket.
Schul|ferien *Pl* school holidays.
schulfrei *adj*: **morgen ist schulfrei** there's no school tomorrow; **schulfrei haben** to be off school.
Schul|hof *der* school playground.
schulisch *adj* & *adv* at school.
Schul|jahr *das* - **1.** [Jahr] school year - **2.** [Klasse] year.
Schul|klasse *die* class.
Schul|leiter, in *der, die* headmaster (headmistress *die*) *UK*, principal *US*.
schulpflichtig *adj* required to attend school; **im schulpflichtigen Alter** of school age.
Schulschluss *der*: **nach Schulschluss** after school.
Schul|stunde *die* period.
Schul|tasche *die* schoolbag.
Schulter (*pl* **-n**) *die* shoulder.
Schulter|blatt *das* shoulder blade.
Schulung (*pl* **-en**) *die* - **1.** [gen] training - **2.** [Lehrveranstaltung] training course.
Schul|zeit *die* schooldays *Pl*.
Schul|zeugnis *das* school report.
schummeln *vi* to cheat.
Schund *der abw* trash.
schunkeln (*perf* **hat geschunkelt**) *vi* - **1.** [sich wiegen] to link arms and sway in time to the music - **2.** [Schiff] to rock.
Schuppe (*pl* **-n**) *die* - **1.** [von Fischen] scale - **2.** [Hautstück] flake - **3.** [Kopfschuppe] dandruff *(U)*.
schuppen *vt* to scale. ◆ **sich schuppen** *ref* to flake.
schürfen ◇ *vi* [schleifen] to scrape. ◇ *vt*: **sich** *(D)* **das Knie schürfen** to graze one's knee.
Schürf|wunde *die* graze.
Schurke (*pl* **-n**) *der abw* villain.
Schürze (*pl* **-n**) *die* apron.
Schuss (*pl* **Schüsse**) *der* - **1.** [mit Schusswaffe, beim Fußball] shot - **2.** [ein wenig] dash; **ein Schuss Whisky** a dash of whisky - **3.** [beim Skifahren]: **Schuss fahren** to schuss; **gut in Schuss sein** *fam* to be in good shape.
Schüssel (*pl* **-n**) *die* bowl.
schusselig *adj fam* scatterbrained.
Schusswaffe (*pl* **-n**) *die* firearm.
Schuster, in (*mpl* -, *fpl* **-nen**) *der, die* shoemaker.
Schutt *der* rubble.
Schuttablade|platz *der* rubbish *UK* ODER garbage *US* dump.
Schüttelfrost *der*: **Schüttelfrost haben** to be shivering.
schütteln *vt* to shake; **den Kopf schütteln** to shake one's head; **'vor Gebrauch schütteln'** 'shake before use'; **es schüttelte ihn bei dem Gedanken** the thought made him shudder. ◆ **sich schütteln** *ref* to shake o.s.; **sich vor etw** *(D)* **schütteln** [Lachen, Kälte] to shake with sthg; [Ekel, Entsetzen] to be filled with sthg.
schütten ◇ *vt* [Flüssigkeit] to pour; [Mehl, Kartoffeln] to tip. ◇ *vi*: **es schüttet** *fam* it's pouring (down).
Schutz *der* protection; **jn in Schutz nehmen** to stand up for sb.
Schutz|blech *das* mudguard.
Schutz|brief *der* travel insurance certificate.
Schütze (*pl* **-n**) *der* - **1.** ASTROL Sagittarius; **Schütze sein** to be a Sagittarius - **2.** [Sportschütze] marksman - **3.** [bei Ballsport] scorer - **4.** [Soldat] private.
schützen *vt*: **jn/etw (vor jm/etw) schützen** to protect sb/sthg (from sb/sthg). ◆ **sich schützen** *ref*: **sich gegen etw** ODER **vor etw** *(D)* **schützen** to protect o.s. against sthg ODER from sthg.
Schützen|fest *das shooting festival.*
Schutz|gebiet *das* - **1.** [Naturschutzgebiet] protected area - **2.** [Kolonie] protectorate.
Schutz|impfung *die* vaccination.
Schützling (*pl* **-e**) *der* [Kind in Obhut] charge; [Protegé] protégé (protégée *die*).
schutzlos ◇ *adj* defenceless. ◇ *adv*: **jm schutzlos ausgeliefert sein** to be completely at sb's mercy.
Schutz|maßnahme *die* precaution.
Schutz|patron, in *der, die* patron saint.
Schutzum|schlag *der* dust jacket.
schwabbelig *adj* [Körperteil] flabby; [Pudding] wobbly.
Schwabe (*pl* **-n**) *der* Swabian.
Schwaben *nt* Swabia.
Schwäbin (*pl* **-nen**) *die* Swabian.
schwäbisch *adj* Swabian.
schwach (*kompar* **schwächer**, *superl* **schwächste**) ◇ *adj* - **1.** [gen] weak; **bei Kuchen werde ich immer schwach** I have no willpower when it comes to cakes - **2.** [Konstitution] delicate - **3.** [leicht - Brise, Wärme, Ahnung, Gefühl] faint; [- Druck] light; [- Versuch, Entschuldigung] feeble - **4.** [Selbstbewusstsein] low - **5.** FILM [Leistung, Schüler] weak, poor; [Gehör, Gedächtnis] poor; **ein schwacher Trost sein** to be cold comfort - **6.** [Beteiligung] poor. ◇ *adv* - **1.** [eingeschränkt, schlecht, wenig] poorly - **2.** [leicht - wehen, strahlen, sich erinnern]

faintly; [- drücken] lightly; [- protestieren] feebly - 3. GRAMM: **das Verb wird schwach konjugiert** it is a weak verb.

Schwäche (*pl* **-n**) *die* - 1. [gen] weakness; **eine Schwäche für jn/etw haben** to have a weakness for sb/sthg - 2. [von Geräusch] faintness - 3. [von Druck] lightness.

schwächen *vt* to weaken.

Schwach|kopf *der fam abw* dummy.

schwächlich *adj* delicate.

Schwächling (*pl* **-e**) *der abw* weakling.

Schwach|sinn *der* - 1. *fam* [Unsinn] nonsense - 2. MED mental deficiency.

schwachsinnig ◇ *adj* - 1. *fam* [unsinnig] stupid, ridiculous - 2. MED mentally deficient. ◇ *adv fam* stupidly.

Schwächung (*pl* **-en**) *die* weakening.

Schwaden *Pl* clouds.

schwafeln *fam abw* ◇ *vi* to talk drivel. ◇ *vt* to drivel on about.

Schwager (*pl* **Schwäger**) *der* brother-in-law.

Schwägerin (*pl* **-nen**) *die* sister-in-law.

Schwalbe (*pl* **-n**) *die* swallow.

schwamm *prät* ▷ **schwimmen**.

Schwamm (*pl* **Schwämme**) *der* - 1. [Tier, Haushaltsschwamm] sponge - 2. [Schimmel] dry rot.

schwammig ◇ *adj* - 1. [Definition, Worte] woolly; [Kontur] vague, blurred - 2. [Gesicht] pasty - 3. [Material] spongy. ◇ *adv* [unklar] vaguely.

Schwan (*pl* **Schwäne**) *der* swan.

schwang *prät* ▷ **schwingen**.

schwanger *adj* pregnant; **schwanger werden** to get pregnant; **im dritten Monat schwanger sein** to be in the third month of pregnancy.

Schwangere (*pl* **-n**) *die* pregnant woman.

schwängern *vt* to make pregnant.

Schwangerschaft (*pl* **-en**) *die* pregnancy.

schwanken (*perf* **hat/ist geschwankt**) *vi* - 1. *(ist)* [sich schwankend bewegen] to sway - 2. *(hat)* [unentschlossen sein] to waver - 3. *(hat)* [instabil sein] to fluctuate.

Schwankung (*pl* **-en**) *die* fluctuation.

Schwanz (*pl* **Schwänze**) *der* - 1. [von Tieren] tail; **den Schwanz einziehen** *fam fig* to back down - 2. *vulg* [männliches Glied] dick - 3. *fam* [Serie] series.

schwänzen ◇ *vi fam* to skive *UK*, to play hookey *US*. ◇ *vt* [Unterricht, Stunde] to skip; **die Schule schwänzen** to skive off *UK* ODER play hookey *US* from school.

schwappen (*perf* **hat/ist geschwappt**) ◇ *vi* - 1. *(ist)* [überlaufen] to spill - 2. *(hat)* [sich bewegen] to slosh. ◇ *vt (hat)* to splash.

Schwarm (*pl* **Schwärme**) *der* - 1. [von Kindern, Bienen] swarm; [von Fischen] shoal; [von Vögeln] flock - 2. *fam* [Idol] heartthrob.

schwärmen (*perf* **hat/ist geschwärmt**) *vi* - 1. *(hat)* [begeistert sein]: **für jn/etw schwärmen** to be mad about sb/sthg - 2. *(hat)* [erzählen]: **von jm/etw schwärmen** to rave about sb/sthg - 3. *(ist)* [im Schwarm fliegen] to swarm.

Schwärmer, in (*mpl* -, *fpl* **-nen**) *der, die* dreamer.

Schwarte (*pl* **-n**) *die* - 1. [von Speck] rind; [von Schweinebraten] crackling *(U)* - 2. *fam abw* [Buch] tome.

schwarz (*kompar* **schwärzer**, *superl* **schwärzeste**) ◇ *adj* - 1. [gen] black - 2. POL pro-CDU/CSU - 3. [Geschäfte] illicit. ◇ *adv*: **der Stift schreibt schwarz** the pen writes in black; **schwarz auf weiß** *fig* in black and white; *siehe auch* **schwarz sehen**.

Schwarz *das* black.

Schwarz|afrika *nt* Black Africa.

Schwarz|arbeit *die* work on the black market; [als Nebentätigkeit] moonlighting.

Schwarz|brot *das* black bread.

Schwarze (*pl* **-n**) ◇ *der, die* black person. ◇ *das (ohne pl)* black; **ins Schwarze treffen** to hit the bull's-eye.

Schwärze *die* blackness.

Schwarze Markt *der* black market.

Schwarze Meer *das* Black Sea.

schwärzen *vt* to blacken.

schwarz|fahren (*perf* **ist schwarzgefahren**) *vi (unreg)* to travel without a ticket.

Schwarz|händler, in *der, die* black marketeer.

schwärzlich *adj* blackish.

Schwarz|markt *der* black market.

schwarz sehen *vi (unreg)*: **(für jn/etw) schwarz sehen** to be pessimistic (about sb/sthg).

Schwarz|wald *der* Black Forest.

schwarz-weiß ◇ *adj* black and white. ◇ *adv* in black and white.

Schwarz-Weiß-|Film *der* black and white film.

schwatzen, schwätzen ◇ *vi* - 1. [sich unterhalten] to chat - 2. [in der Schule] to talk. ◇ *vt abw*: **dummes Zeug schwatzen** to talk rubbish.

Schwätzer, in (*mpl* -, *fpl* **-nen**) *der, die abw*: **ein Schwätzer sein** to talk a load of nonsense.

schwatzhaft *adj abw*: **ein schwatzhafter Mensch** a person who can't keep their mouth shut.

Schwebe *die*: **in der Schwebe** in the balance.

Schwebe|bahn *die* overhead monorail.

Schwebe|balken *der* SPORT beam.

schweben *vi* - 1. [fliegen, in Wasser] to float; [Vögel] to hover; [Staubteilchen] to hang - 2. [unentschieden sein] to hover - 3. [Duft, Verdacht] to hang.

Schwede (*pl* **-n**) *der* Swede.

Schweden *nt* Sweden.

Schwedin (*pl* **-nen**) *die* Swede.

schwedisch *adj* Swedish.

Schwedisch(e) *das* Swedish; *siehe auch* **Englisch(e)**.

Schwefel *der* sulphur.

Schwefel|säure *die* sulphuric acid.

Schweif (*pl* **-e**) *der* tail.

schweigen (*prät* **schwieg**, *perf* **hat geschwiegen**) *vi* to be silent; **wenn du schweigen kannst, verrate ich dir etwas** if you can keep a secret, I'll tell you something; **von jm/etw ganz zu schweigen** to say nothing of sb/sthg.

Schweigen *das* silence; **jn zum Schweigen bringen** to silence sb.

Schweige|pflicht *die* professional duty to maintain confidentiality.

schweigsam *adj* taciturn; **du bist heute schweigsam** you're rather quiet today.

Schwein (*pl* **-e**) *das* - **1.** [Tier] pig - **2.** [Schweinefleisch] pork - **3.** *salopp abw* [Mensch] bastard; **armes Schwein** *salopp* poor bastard; **Schwein haben** *fam* to be jammy.

Schweine|braten *der* roast pork.

Schweine|fleisch *das* pork.

Schweinerei (*pl* **-en**) *die fam* - **1.** [schlimme Sache] goddamn scandal; **das neue Abtreibungsgesetz ist eine Schweinerei!** the new law on abortion is bloody *UK* ODER goddamn *US* disgraceful! - **2.** [Schmutz] mess - **3.** [Unanständiges]: **Schweinereien** filth *(U)*.

Schweine|stall *der eigtl* & *fig* pigsty *UK*, pigpen *US*.

Schweiß *der* sweat; **ihr brach der Schweiß aus** she broke out in a sweat.

schweißen *vt* & *vi* to weld.

schweißgebadet *adj* & *adv* bathed in sweat.

Schweiß|tropfen *der* drop of sweat.

Schweiz *die*: **die Schweiz** Switzerland.

Schweizer (*pl* -) *der* & *adj (unver)* Swiss.

Schweizer|deutsch *das* Swiss German; *siehe auch* **Englisch(e)**.

Schweizerin (*pl* **-nen**) *die* Swiss.

schweizerisch *adj* Swiss.

Schweizerische Eidgenossenschaft *die*: **die Schweizerische Eidgenossenschaft** the Swiss Confederation.

schwelen *vi* [Rauch entwickeln] to smoulder.

Schwelle (*pl* **-n**) *die* - **1.** [Türschwelle] threshold; **an der Schwelle einer Sache** *(D) fig* on the threshold of sthg - **2.** [der Eisenbahn] sleeper *UK*, tie *US*.

schwellen (*präs* **schwillt**, *prät* **schwoll**, *perf* **ist geschwollen**) *vi* to swell.

Schwellung (*pl* **-en**) *die* swelling.

schwenken *vt* - **1.** [Kran] to swing; [Kamera] to pan - **2.** [Fahne] to wave - **3.** KÜCHE to toss.

schwer ◇ *adj* - **1.** [Gewicht] heavy; **wie schwer bist du/ist der Koffer?** how heavy are you/is the suitcase? - **2.** [schwierig] difficult; [beschwerlich] hard; **es schwer haben mit** to have a hard time with - **3.** [schlimm - Krankheit, Schaden, Unfall] serious; [- Enttäuschung] huge, great - **4.** [stark - Mahlzeit, Sturm] heavy. ◇ *adv* - **1.** [an Gewicht] heavily - **2.** [unter Mühen]: **schwer atmen** to breathe with difficulty; **schwer hören** to be hard of hearing - **3.** [arbeiten] hard - **4.** [schwerlich] hardly - **5.** [schlimm - verletzt, krank] seriously; [- bestrafen] severely - **6.** *fam* [sehr] really; **er ist schwer in Ordnung** he's all right.

Schwer|arbeit *die* heavy work.

schwerbehindert, schwer behindert *adj* severely disabled.

schwer beschädigt *adj* [beschädigt] badly damaged.

schwer bewaffnet *adj* heavily armed.

Schwere ◇ *die* - **1.** [gen] heaviness - **2.** [von Krankheit, Schaden, Unfall] seriousness; [von Enttäuschung] enormity - **3.** [Schwierigkeitsgrad] difficulty. ◇ *das*: **Schweres durchmachen** to have a difficult time (of it).

schwerelos ◇ *adj* weightless. ◇ *adv* weightlessly.

schwer erziehbar *adj* difficult.

schwer fallen (*perf* **ist schwer gefallen**) *vi (unreg)*: **es fiel ihm schwer, Abschied zu nehmen** he found it difficult to say goodbye.

schwerfällig ◇ *adj* ponderous. ◇ *adv* ponderously.

schwerhörig *adj* hard of hearing.

Schwer|industrie *die* heavy industry.

Schwer|kraft *die* gravity.

schwer machen *vt*: **jm etw schwer machen** to make sthg difficult for sb.

schwermütig ◇ *adj* melancholy. ◇ *adv* in a melancholy way.

schwer nehmen *vt (unreg)*: **etw schwer nehmen** to take sthg hard.

Schwer|punkt *der* - **1.** [Hauptsache] main focus - **2.** PHYS centre of gravity.

Schwert (*pl* **-er**) *das* sword.

schwer tun ◆ **sich schwer tun** *ref (unreg)*: **sich mit etw schwer tun** to have difficulty with sthg.

Schwer|verbrecher, in *der, die* person who has committed a serious crime.

schwer verletzt *adj* seriously injured.

schwerwiegend *adj* serious.

Schwester (*pl* **-n**) *die* - **1.** [Verwandte] sister - **2.** [Krankenschwester] nurse - **3.** [Ordensschwester] nun, sister.

schwieg *prät* ▷ **schweigen**.

Schwieger|eltern *Pl* parents-in-law.

Schwieger|mutter *die* mother-in-law.

Schwieger|sohn *der* son-in-law.

Schwieger|tochter *die* daughter-in-law.
Schwieger|vater *der* father-in-law.
Schwiele (*pl* **-n**) *die* callus.
schwierig ◇ *adj* difficult. ◇ *adv* with difficulty.
Schwierigkeit (*pl* **-en**) *die* difficulty; **ohne Schwierigkeiten** without difficulty; **in Schwierigkeiten geraten/stecken** to get into/be in trouble.
schwillt *präs* ▷ **schwellen**.
Schwimm|bad *das* swimming pool.
Schwimm|becken *das* (swimming) pool.
schwimmen (*prät* **schwamm**, *perf* **hat/ist geschwommen**) *vi* & *vt (hat, ist)* to swim.
Schwimmen *das* swimming.
Schwimmer, in (*mpl* **-**, *fpl* **-nen**) *der, die* swimmer.
Schwindel *der* **- 1.** [Gleichgewichtsstörung] dizziness **- 2.** *abw* [Betrug] swindle.
schwindelig, schwindlig *adj*: **mir wird (es) schwindelig** I feel dizzy; *fig* my head is spinning.
Schwindler, in (*mpl* **-**, *fpl* **-nen**) *der, die* **- 1.** [Betrüger] swindler **- 2.** [Lügner] liar.
schwindlig = **schwindelig**.
schwingen (*prät* **schwang**, *perf* **hat/ist geschwungen**) ◇ *vi* **- 1.** *(hat)* [vibrieren] to vibrate **- 2.** [pendeln] to swing. ◇ *vt (hat)* to wave.
schwitzen *vi* [Person] to sweat.
schwoll *prät* ▷ **schwellen**.
schwor *prät* ▷ **schwören**.
schwören (*prät* **schwor**, *perf* **hat geschworen**) *vt* & *vi* to swear.
schwul *adj fam* gay.
schwül *adj* [Wetter] close, muggy.
Schwung (*pl* **Schwünge**) *der* **- 1.** [Bewegung] swing **- 2.** [Elan] zest, verve **- 3.** [Menge] stack.
Schwur (*pl* **Schwüre**) *der* oath.
scratchen *vi* to scratch.
sechs [zɛks] ◇ *num* [als Zahl, Anzahl] six; **sechs Mal** six times; **um sechs (Uhr)** at six (o'clock); **fünf vor/nach sechs** five to/past *UK* ODER after *US* six; **mit sechs kommen die Kinder in die Schule** children start school at the age of six; **sechs zu null** six-zero. ◇ *pron* six; **sie waren sechs** there were six of them; **ein Tisch für sechs** a table for six.
Sechs (*pl* **-en**) *die* **- 1.** [Zahl, Spielkarte] six **- 2.** [Spieler, Bus] number six **- 3.** [Schulnote] ≃ F, *mark of 6 on a scale from 1 to 6*.
sechsfach ◇ *adj*: **die sechsfache Menge** six times as much; **in sechsfacher Größe** six times as big; **die Formulare in sechsfacher Ausfertigung abgeben** to provide six copies of the forms; **der sechsfache Gewinner** the six-times winner. ◇ *adv* sixfold.
sechshundert *num* six hundred.
sechsmal *adv* six times.
sechstausend *num* six thousand.
sechste, r, s ['zɛkstə, ɐ, s] *adj* sixth; **der sechste Juni** the sixth of June, June the sixth; **auf dem sechsten Rang sein** to be sixth in the rankings.
Sechste (*pl* **-n**) ◇ *der, die, das* [in einer Reihenfolge] sixth; **Heinrich der Sechste** Henry the Sixth, Henry VI; **sie ist die Sechste im Weitsprung** she is sixth in the long jump. ◇ *der* [Angabe des Datums] sixth; **am Sechsten** on the sixth; **ich fahre Freitag, den Sechsten** I'm going on Friday the sixth.
sechstel *adj (unver)* sixth; **ein sechstel Liter** a sixth of a litre.
Sechstel (*pl* **-**) *das* sixth; **etw in Sechstel teilen** to divide sthg in six ODER into sixths.
sechzehn *num* sixteen; *siehe auch* **sechs**.
sechzehntel *adj* sixteenth.
Sechzehntel (*pl* **-**) *das* sixteenth.
sechzig *num* sixty; *siehe auch* **sechs**.
Sechzig *die* sixty; *siehe auch* **Sechs**.
Sechzigerjahre, sechziger Jahre *Pl*: **die Sechzigerjahre** the sixties.
See (*pl* **-n**) ◇ *der* lake. ◇ *die* sea; **an die See fahren** to go to the seaside; **auf hoher See** out at sea.
See|gang *der*: **leichter/hoher Seegang** calm/rough seas *Pl*.
See|hund *der* [Robbe] seal.
See|igel *der* sea urchin.
seekrank *adj* seasick.
Seele (*pl* **-n**) *die* [gen] soul; **etw auf der Seele haben** to have sthg on one's mind.
seelenruhig *adv* calmly.
Seeleute *Pl* ▷ **Seemann**.
seelisch ◇ *adj* psychological. ◇ *adv* mentally.
See|löwe *der* sea lion.
Seelsorge *die* pastoral care.
See|mann (*pl* **-leute**) *der* sailor.
See|meile *die* nautical mile.
See|not *die*: **in Seenot geraten/sein** to get into/be in distress.
See|räuber *der* pirate.
See|rose *die* [Pflanze] water lily.
seetüchtig *adj* seaworthy.
See|weg *der*: **auf dem Seeweg** by sea.
See|zunge *die* sole.
Segel (*pl* **-**) *das* sail.
Segel|boot *das* sailing boat.
segelfliegen *vi* to glide.
Segel|flugzeug *das* glider.
segeln (*perf* **hat/ist gesegelt**) *vi* to sail.
Segel|schiff *das* sailing ship.
Segen (*pl* **-**) *der* blessing.
segnen *vt* to bless.
sehbehindert *adj* visually impaired.

sehen (*präs* **sieht**, *prät* **sah**, *perf* **hat gesehen**) ◇ *vt* - **1.** [gen] to see; [willkürlich] to watch; **etw gerne/ungerne sehen** to like/dislike sthg; **das werden wir ja gleich sehen** we'll soon see; **das kann sich sehen lassen** that's remarkable - **2.** [treffen] to see, to meet. ◇ *vi* - **1.** [gen] to see; **gut/schlecht sehen** to have good/bad eyesight; **sieh mal!** look!; **jm ähnlich sehen** to look like sb - **2.** [hervorstehen]: **das Wrack sieht aus dem Wasser** the wreck sticks out of the water - **3.** [mit Präpositionen]: **auf jn/etw sehen** to look at sb/sthg; **nach jm/etw sehen** to look after sb/sthg. ◆ **sich sehen** *ref* - **1.** [treffen] to meet - **2.** [sich fühlen]: **sich betrogen sehen** to see o.s. cheated; **sich gezwungen sehen, etw zu tun** to feel obliged to do sthg. ◆ **mal sehen** *interj* we'll see! ◆ **sieh mal** *interj* look! ◆ **siehste, siehst du** *interj* there you are!

sehenswert *adj* worth seeing.

Sehenswürdigkeit (*pl* **-en**) *die* attraction; **Sehenswürdigkeiten** sights.

Sehkraft *die* sight.

Sehne (*pl* **-n**) *die* - **1.** [vom Muskel] tendon - **2.** [vom Bogen] string.

sehnen ◆ **sich sehnen** *ref*: **sich nach jm/etw sehnen** to long for sb/sthg.

sehnig *adj* - **1.** [Fleisch] stringy - **2.** [Körper] sinewy.

Sehnsucht (*pl* **-süchte**) *die* longing; **Sehnsucht nach jm/etw haben** to long for sb/sthg.

sehnsüchtig ◇ *adj* [Blick] longing. ◇ *adv* longingly.

sehr *adv* very; [mit Verben] a lot, very much; **das gefällt mir sehr** I like it a lot; **zu sehr** too much; **sehr viel Geld** an awful lot of money; **bitte sehr!** you're welcome!; **danke sehr!** thank you very much!

seicht *adj* shallow.

seid *präs* ▷ **sein**.

Seide (*pl* **-n**) *die* silk.

seidig *adj* silky.

Seife (*pl* **-n**) *die* soap.

Seifen|blase *die* soap bubble.

Seil (*pl* **-e**) *das* rope.

Seil|bahn *die* cable railway.

sein (*präs* **ist**, *prät* **war**, *perf* **ist gewesen**) ◇ *aux* - **1.** [im Perfekt] to have; **sie ist gegangen** she has gone - **2.** [im Konjunktiv]: **sie wäre gegangen** she would have gone. ◇ *vi* - **1.** [gen] to be; **Lehrer sein** to be a teacher; **aus etw sein** to be made of sthg; **aus Indien/Zürich sein** to be from India/Zurich; **du warst es!** it was you! - **2.** [mit Infinitiv, müssen]: **mein Befehl ist sofort auszuführen** my order is to be carried out immediately - **3.** [mit Infinitiv, können]: **das ist nicht zu ändern** there's nothing that can be done about it; **dieses Spiel ist noch zu gewinnen** this game can still be won - **4.** [mit Dativ]: **mir ist schlecht/kalt** I'm sick/cold - **5.** [mit unpersönlichem Pronomen] to be; **es ist zwölf Uhr** it's twelve o'clock; **es ist dunkel** it's dark; **wie wäre es mit...?** what about...?; **was ist?** what's up?; **das wärs** that's all; **etw sein lassen** to give sthg up; **lass es gut sein!** leave it!; **ist was?** is there anything wrong?

sein, e *det* his.

seine, r, s *pron* [bei Personen] his; [bei Sachen, Tieren] its.

Seine [sɛːn(ə)] *die*: **die Seine** the (River) Seine.

seiner *pron (Genitiv von er, es)*: **wir gedenken seiner** we remember him.

seinerseits *adv* - **1.** [er selbst] for his part; [es selbst] for its part - **2.** [von ihm - Person] on his part; [- Tier, Sache] on its part.

seinerzeit *adv* at that time.

seinesgleichen *pron abw* [Person] the likes of him; [Tier, Sache] the likes of it.

seinetwegen *adv* - **1.** [ihm zuliebe - Person] for his sake; [- Tier, Sache] for its sake - **2.** [wegen ihm - Person] because of him; [- Tier, Sache] because of it - **3.** [von ihm aus - Person] as far as he's concerned; [- Tier] as far as it's concerned.

seinetwillen ◆ **um seinetwillen** *adv* [Person] for his sake; [Tier] for its sake.

sein lassen *vt (unreg) fam*: **lass das sein!** stop that!; **sie kann es einfach nicht sein lassen** she just can't help herself.

seit ◇ *präp (+ D)* - **1.** [zur Angabe des Zeitpunktes] since; **seit wann?** since when? - **2.** [zur Angabe der Dauer] for; **ich wohne hier seit drei Jahren** I've lived here for three years; **seit langem** for a long time. ◇ *konj* since.

seitdem ◇ *adv* since then. ◇ *konj* since.

Seite (*pl* **-n**) *die* - **1.** [gen] side; **etw zur Seite legen** to put sthg to one side; **zur Seite gehen** ODER **treten** to move aside; **auf der linken/rechten Seite** on the left-hand/right-hand side - **2.** [von Buch, Heft, Zeitung] page; **auf beiden Seiten** on both sides; **jedes Ding hat seine guten und schlechten Seiten** there's a good and a bad side to everything; **jm zur Seite stehen** to stand by sb; **jn von der Seite ansehen** to look at sb askance; **jn zur Seite nehmen** to take sb aside. ◆ **auf Seiten** *präp (+ G)* on the part of. ◆ **Seite an Seite** *adv* side by side. ◆ **von Seiten** *präp (+ G)* on the part of.

Seiten|sprung *der* affair; **einen Seitensprung machen** to have an affair.

Seiten|stechen *das* stitch; **Seitenstechen haben** to have a stitch.

Seiten|straße *die* side street.

seither *adv* since then.

seitlich *adj* [Fenster, Eingang] side; [Zusammenstoß] side-on; **ein seitlicher Wind** a crosswind.

seitwärts *adv* - **1.** [zur Seite] sideways - **2.** [auf der Seite] to one side.

Sekretär (*pl* **-e**) *der* - **1.** [Person] secretary - **2.** [Möbelstück] bureau.

Sekretariat (*pl* **-e**) *das* secretary's office.

Sekretärin (*pl* **-nen**) *die* secretary.

Sekt (*pl* **-e**) *der German sparkling wine similar to champagne.*

Sekte (*pl* **-n**) *die* sect.

Sekt|glas *das* champagne glass.

Sekundar|stufe *die* SCHULE secondary *UK* *ODER* high *US* school level; **Sekundarstufe I** ≃ junior high school *US*; **Sekundarstufe II** ≃ sixth form *UK*, ≃ senior high school *US*.

Sekunde (*pl* **-n**) *die* second.

selber *pron (unver)* = **selbst**.

selbst ◇ *pron (unver)*: **er selbst** himself; **sie selbst** herself, themselves *Pl*; **ich selbst** myself; **wir selbst** ourselves; **Sie selbst** yourself, yourselves *Pl*; **ich selbst** I myself; **du bist selbst schuld** it's your own fault; **das versteht sich von selbst** that goes without saying. ◇ *adv* even; **selbst wenn** even if. ◆ **von selbst** *adv* - **1.** [freiwillig] of one's own accord - **2.** [automatisch] automatically, by itself.

Selbst|achtung *die* self-respect.

selbständig = **selbstständig**.

Selbständigkeit = **Selbstständigkeit**.

Selbst|bedienung *die* self-service; **Restaurant mit Selbstbedienung** self-service restaurant.

Selbst|befriedigung *die* masturbation.

Selbst|beherrschung *die* self-control.

Selbst|beteiligung *die* [bei Versicherungen] excess.

selbstbewusst ◇ *adj* self-confident. ◇ *adv* self-confidently.

Selbstbewusstsein *das* self-confidence.

Selbst|gespräch *das*: **Selbstgespräche führen** *ODER* **halten** to talk to o.s.

Selbstkosten|preis *der* cost price; **zum Selbstkostenpreis** at cost.

selbstlos ◇ *adj* unselfish, selfless. ◇ *adv* unselfishly, selflessly.

Selbst|mord *der* suicide; **Selbstmord begehen** to commit suicide.

selbstsicher ◇ *adj* self-confident. ◇ *adv* self-confidently.

selbstständig ◇ *adj* - **1.** [unabhängig] independent - **2.** [im Beruf] self-employed; **sich selbstständig machen** to set up on one's own. ◇ *adv* [unabhängig] independently.

Selbstständigkeit *die* independence.

selbsttätig ◇ *adj* automatic. ◇ *adv* automatically.

selbstverständlich ◇ *adj* natural; **das ist doch selbstverständlich!** that goes without saying! ◇ *adv* naturally.

Selbst|verteidigung *die* self-defence.

Selbst|vertrauen *das* self-confidence.

Selbst|zweck *der* end in itself.

selig ◇ *adj* - **1.** [glücklich - Person, Lächeln] blissfully happy; [- Schlummer] blissful - **2.** [heilig gesprochen] blessed - **3.** *geh* [tot] late. ◇ *adv* [glücklich] blissfully.

Seligkeit *die* bliss.

Sellerie *der* celery.

selten ◇ *adj* rare. ◇ *adv* - **1.** [kaum] rarely - **2.** [besonders] exceptionally.

Selters (*pl* **-**) *das* sparkling mineral water.

seltsam ◇ *adj* strange. ◇ *adv* strangely.

Semester (*pl* **-**) *das* semester; **im achten Semester sein** to be in the second half of one's fourth year.

Semikolon (*pl* **-s**) *das* semicolon.

Semmel (*pl* **-n**) *die Österr & Süddt* (bread) roll.

Senat (*pl* **-e**) *der* - **1.** [gen & UNI] senate - **2.** [von Berlin, Bremen, Hamburg] *government of one of the three German cities that have "Land" status* - **3.** RECHT panel of judges.

Senator (*pl* **-en**) *der* [gen & UNI] senator.

Senatorin (*pl* **-nen**) *die* [gen & UNI] senator.

senden (*prät* **sendete** *ODER* **sandte**, *perf* **hat gesendet** *ODER* **gesandt**) ◇ *vt* - **1.** *(reg)* [ausstrahlen] to broadcast - **2.** *(reg)* [funken] to transmit, to send - **3.** *(reg) (unreg)* [schicken] to send; **etw an jn senden** to send sb sthg. ◇ *vi* *(reg)* [übertragen] to broadcast.

Sende|pause *die* interval.

Sender (*pl* **-**) *der* - **1.** [Station] station - **2.** [Gerät] transmitter.

Sendung (*pl* **-en**) *die* - **1.** [das Senden] dispatch - **2.** [Postsendung - von Waren] consignment; [- Brief] letter; [- Paket] parcel - **3.** [ausgestrahltes Programm] programme - **4.** [Übertragung] broadcasting; **auf Sendung gehen** to go on (the) air.

Senegal *der* Senegal.

Senf (*pl* **-e**) *der* mustard.

sengend *adj* scorching.

Senior (*pl* **Senioren**) *der* - **1.** [gen] senior - **2.** [von Mannschaft, Gruppe] oldest member. ◆ **Senioren** *Pl* - **1.** [Alte] senior citizens - **2.** SPORT seniors.

Senioren|heim *das* old people's home.

Seniorin (*pl* **-nen**) *die* - **1.** [gen] senior - **2.** [von Mannschaft, Gruppe] oldest member.

senken *vt* - **1.** [gen] to lower; **beschämt senkte er den Kopf** he hung his head in shame - **2.** [Preis, Steuern] to cut. ◆ **sich senken** *ref* - **1.** [Wasserspiegel] to drop; [Erdreich] to subside - **2.** [Schranken, Vorhang] to come down.

senkrecht ◇ *adj* vertical. ◇ *adv* vertically.

Senk|rechte *die* - **1.** [Linie] vertical line - **2.** [Lot] perpendicular.

Sense (*pl* **-n**) *die* [Gerät] scythe.

sensibel ◇ *adj* sensitive. ◇ *adv* sensitively.

sentimental ◇ *adj* sentimental. ◇ *adv* sentimentally.

Seoul [se'u:l] *nt* Seoul.

separat ◇ *adj* separate; [Wohnung] self-contained. ◇ *adv* separately.

September *der* September; **am siebten September** on the seventh of September, on September the seventh; **Sonntag, den 1. September** Sunday, 1 September; **im September** in September; **Anfang/Ende September** at the beginning/end of September; **Mitte September** in mid-September.

Serbe (*pl* **-n**) *der* Serb.

Serbien *nt* Serbia.

Serbin (*pl* **-nen**) *die* Serb.

serbisch *adj* Serbian.

Serie ['ze:ri̯ə] (*pl* **-n**) *die* **- 1.** [Reihe, Sendereihe] series **- 2.** [Satz] set **- 3.** [von Produkten] line.

serienmäßig ◇ *adj* standard. ◇ *adv* [konstruieren, anfertigen] on a mass scale; [mit etw ausgestattet] as standard.

seriös ◇ *adj* **- 1.** [vertrauenswürdig] reliable **- 2.** [würdevoll, solide] respectable. ◇ *adv* [vertrauenswürdig] reliably; [würdevoll, solide] respectably.

Serum (*pl* **Seren**) *das* serum.

servieren [zɛr'vi:rən] *vt* [Speisen, Getränke] to serve.

Serviette [zɛr'vi̯ɛtə] (*pl* **-n**) *die* serviette.

Servo|lenkung ['zɛrvolɛŋkuŋ] *die* power steering *(U)*.

Sesam *der* sesame seeds *Pl*.

Sessel (*pl* **-**) *der* armchair.

Sessel|lift *der* chairlift.

setzen (*perf* **hat/ist gesetzt**) ◇ *vt (hat)* **- 1.** [gen] to put; **etw in jn/etw setzen** to put sthg in sb/sthg **- 2.** [Denkmal, Grabmal] to put up **- 3.** [Frist, Belohnung, Text] to set **- 4.** [Pflanzen] to plant **- 5.** [wetten]**: etw auf etw *(A)* setzen** to put sthg on sthg; **es setzt was** *fam* there'll be trouble. ◇ *vi* **- 1.** *(hat)* [wetten] to bet; **auf jn/etw setzen** to bet on sb/sthg **- 2.** *(hat, ist)* [befördern]**: über etw *(A)* setzen** [Fluss] to cross sthg; [Hindernis] to get over sthg. ◆ **sich setzen** *ref* **- 1.** [hinsetzen] to sit down; **sich zu jm setzen** to sit with sb **- 2.** [Kaffeesatz] to settle.

Seuche (*pl* **-n**) *die* epidemic.

seufzen *vi* to sigh.

Seufzer (*pl* **-**) *der* sigh.

Sex *der* sex.

Sexualität *die* sexuality.

sexuell ◇ *adj* sexual. ◇ *adv* sexually.

sexy *fam* ◇ *adj (unver)* sexy. ◇ *adv* sexily.

sezieren *vt & vi* to dissect.

sfr. (*abk für* **Schweizer Franken**) *Swiss francs*.

Shampoo ['ʃampu] (*pl* **-s**) *das* shampoo.

Shareware *die* EDV shareware.

Sherry ['ʃɛrɪ] (*pl* **-s**) *der* sherry.

Shorts ['ʃo:ɐ̯ts] *Pl* shorts.

Show [ʃo:] (*pl* **-s**) *die* show.

Showmaster, in ['ʃo:ma:stɐ, rɪn] (*mpl* **-**, *fpl* **-nen**) *der, die* compere *UK*, emcee *US*.

Shrimp *der* = **Schrimp**.

Sibirien [zi'bi:ri̯ən] *nt* Siberia.

sich *pron* **- 1.** [Reflexivpronomen - unbestimmt] oneself; [- Person] himself (herself *die*), themselves *Pl*; [- Ding, Tier] itself, themselves *Pl*; [- bei Höflichkeitsform] yourself, yourselves *Pl*; **sich *(D)* etw kaufen** to buy (o.s.) sthg **- 2.** [reziprokes Pronomen] each other.

Sichel (*pl* **-n**) *die* sickle.

sicher ◇ *adj* **- 1.** [ungefährdet] safe; **in sicherem Abstand** at a safe distance; **vor jm/etw sicher sein** to be safe from sb/sthg **- 2.** [zuverlässig] reliable **- 3.** [überzeugt, gewiss] sure, certain; **sich *(D)* einer Sache *(G)* sicher sein** to be sure ODER certain about sthg **- 4.** [selbstbewusst] self-confident. ◇ *adv* **- 1.** [ungefährdet] safely **- 2.** [zuverlässig] reliably; **etw sicher wissen** to know sthg for sure; **langsam aber sicher** slowly but surely **- 3.** [sicherlich] certainly, definitely; **das ist sicher richtig, aber** that may be true, but; **Sie haben es sicher gemerkt** you must have noticed it **- 4.** [selbstbewusst] self-confidently. ◆ **aber sicher** *interj* of course!

sicher|gehen (*perf* **ist sichergegangen**) *vi (unreg)* to play safe.

Sicherheit (*pl* **-en**) *die* **- 1.** [Schutz - persönliche, öffentliche, im Straßenverkehr] safety; [- soziale, wirtschaftliche, innere] security; **in Sicherheit (vor jm/etw) sein** to be safe (from sb/sthg) **- 2.** [Bestimmtheit] certainty **- 3.** [Fundiertheit, Zuverlässigkeit] reliability **- 4.** [Selbstbewusstsein] confidence **- 5.** [Bürgschaft] surety.

Sicherheits|gurt *der* seat belt.

sicherheitshalber *adv* to be on the safe side.

Sicherheits|nadel *die* safety pin.

sicherlich *adv* certainly.

sichern *vt* to secure. ◆ **sich sichern** *ref* **- 1.** [sich absichern] to secure o.s.; **sich gegen etw sichern** to protect o.s. against sthg **- 2.** [sich verschaffen]**: sich *(D)* etw sichern** to secure sthg.

sicher|stellen *vt* **- 1.** [beschlagnahmen - Geld, Fund] to seize; [- Spuren] to secure **- 2.** [gewährleisten] to safeguard.

Sicherung (*pl* **-en**) *die* **- 1.** [Schutz] safeguarding **- 2.** ELEKTR fuse **- 3.** [Schutzmaßnahme] safeguard.

Sicht *die* **- 1.** [Aussicht] visibility; **außer Sicht** out of sight **- 2.** [Betrachtungsweise] point of view; **aus meiner Sicht** from my point of view. ◆ **auf lange Sicht** *adv* long-term. ◆ **in Sicht** *adv* in sight; **Land in Sicht!** land ahoy!

sichtbar ◇ *adj* **- 1.** [deutlich] clear **- 2.** [wahrnehmbar] visible. ◇ *adv* [deutlich] clearly.

sichten *vt* - **1.** [einsehen] to sift through - **2.** *geh* [sehen] to sight.

sichtlich ◇ *adj* obvious. ◇ *adv* obviously.

Sicht|weite *die* visibility *(U)*; **außer/in Sichtweite sein** to be out of/in sight.

sickern (*perf* **ist gesickert**) *vi* [fließen] to seep.

sie *pron* - **1.** [Singular - Nominativ] she; [- Akkusativ] her; **sie wars!** it was her! - **2.** [Plural - Nominativ] they; [- Akkusativ] them - **3.** [Tier, Gegenstand] it.

Sie *pron (Singular und Plural)* you.

Sieb (*pl* **-e**) *das* [Küchensieb] sieve; [Teesieb] strainer.

sieben[1] ◇ *vt* - **1.** [durchsieben] to sieve - **2.** [auswählen] to weed out. ◇ *vi* [auswählen] to pick and choose.

sieben[2] *num* seven; *siehe auch* **sechs**.

Sieben (*pl* - ODER **-en**) *die* seven; *siehe auch* **Sechs**.

siebenfach *adj* & *adv* sevenfold.

siebenhundert *num* seven hundred.

siebenmal *adv* seven times.

siebentausend *num* seven thousand.

siebte, r, s, siebente, r, s *adj* seventh; *siehe auch* **sechste**.

Siebte (*pl* **-n**) *der, die, das* seventh; *siehe auch* **Sechste**.

siebtel *adj (unver)* seventh; *siehe auch* **sechstel**.

Siebtel (*pl* -) *das* seventh; *siehe auch* **Sechstel**.

siebzehn *num* seventeen; *siehe auch* **sechs**.

Siebzehn (*pl* **-en**) *die* seventeen; *siehe auch* **Sechs**.

siebzig *num* seventy; *siehe auch* **sechs**.

Siebzigerjahre, siebziger Jahre *Pl*: **die** Siebzigerjahre the seventies.

sieden (*prät* **siedete** ODER **sott**, *perf* **hat gesiedet** ODER **hat gesotten**) ◇ *vi (reg)* [Flüssigkeit] to boil. ◇ *vt* to boil.

Siedler, in (*mpl* -, *fpl* **-nen**) *der, die* settler.

Siedlung (*pl* **-en**) *die* [Häusergruppe] housing estate *UK* ODER development *US*.

Sieg (*pl* **-e**) *der* victory; **der Sieg über jn/etw** the victory over sb/sthg.

Siegel (*pl* -) *das* seal.

siegen *vi* to win; **über jn/etw siegen** to beat sb/sthg.

Sieger (*pl* -) *der* winner.

Sieger|ehrung *die* medals ceremony.

Siegerin (*pl* **-nen**) *die* winner.

siehe *vi* [in Text]: **siehe oben** see above; **siehe Seite 15** see page 15.

sieht *präs* ▷ **sehen**.

siezen *vt* to address as "Sie". ◆ **sich siezen** *ref* to address each other as "Sie".

Signal (*pl* **-e**) *das* signal; **das Signal zu etw geben** to give the signal for sthg.

Silbe (*pl* **-n**) *die* syllable; **jn/etw mit keiner Silbe erwähnen** *fig* not to say a word about sb/sthg.

Silben|trennung *die* syllabification *(U)*.

Silber *das* silver.

Silberhoch|zeit *die* silver wedding (anniversary).

Silber|medaille *die* silver medal.

silbern ◇ *adj* [aus Silber] silver. ◇ *adv* [wie Silber - glänzen] with a silvery sheen.

Silo (*pl* **-s**) *der ODER das* silo.

Silvester [zɪl'vɛstɐ] (*pl* -) *der ODER das* New Year's Eve; **Silvester feiern** to see the New Year in.

simsen *vi* to text.

Simulation (*pl* **-en**) *die* EDV simulation.

simultan ◇ *adj* simultaneous. ◇ *adv* simultaneously.

sind *präs* ▷ **sein**.

Sinfonie *die* = **Symphonie**.

Sinfoniker, in *der, die* = **Symphoniker**.

Singapur *nt* Singapore.

singen (*prät* **sang**, *perf* **hat gesungen**) ◇ *vi* - **1.** [musizieren] to sing - **2.** *salopp abw* [aussagen] to squeal. ◇ *vt* to sing; **jn in den Schlaf singen** to sing sb to sleep.

Single ['sɪŋ(g)l] (*pl* - ODER **-s**) ◇ *der* single person. ◇ *die* single.

Singular *der* GRAMM singular.

Sing|vogel *der* songbird.

sinken (*prät* **sank**, *perf* **ist gesunken**) *vi* - **1.** [einsinken, versinken] to sink - **2.** [abnehmen, niedersinken] to fall.

Sinn (*pl* **-e**) *der* - **1.** [Bedeutung, Wahrnehmungsfähigkeit] sense; **im übertragenen Sinn** figuratively - **2.** [Gefühl]: **einen/keinen Sinn für etw haben** to have a/no feeling for sthg; **er hat keinen Sinn für Humor** he has no sense of humour.

Sinn|bild *das* symbol.

Sinnes|organ *das* sense organ.

sinngemäß ◇ *adj*: **eine sinngemäße Übersetzung von etw** a translation which conveys the general meaning of sthg. ◇ *adv*: **etw sinngemäß wiedergeben** to give the gist of sthg.

sinnig ◇ *adj* clever. ◇ *adv* cleverly.

sinnlich ◇ *adj* - **1.** [körperlichen Genuss betreffend] sensual - **2.** [Sinneswahrnehmung betreffend] sensory. ◇ *adv* - **1.** [körperlichen Genuss betreffend] sensually - **2.** [Sinneswahrnehmung betreffend] through the senses.

sinnlos ◇ *adj* - **1.** [unsinnig] pointless - **2.** *abw* [maßlos] blind *(vor Subst)*. ◇ *adv* - **1.** [unsinnig] pointlessly - **2.** *abw* [maßlos - zerstören] in a blind rage; **sich sinnlos betrinken** to get blind drunk.

Sịnnlosigkeit (*pl* **-en**) *die* - **1.** [Wesen] pointlessness - **2.** [Handlung] pointless action.

sịnnvoll ◇ *adj* - **1.** [befriedigend] meaningful - **2.** [zweckmäßig] sensible. ◇ *adv* - **1.** [befriedigend] meaningfully - **2.** [zweckmäßig] sensibly.

Sịnt|flut *die* - **1.** [biblisch] Flood - **2.** [Übermaß - von Post, Anrufen] flood.

Sịppe (*pl* **-n**) *die* clan.

Sirene (*pl* **-n**) *die* siren.

Sirup *der* - **1.** [für Saft] syrup - **2.** [aus Zucker] treacle *UK*, molasses *US*.

Sịtte (*pl* **-n**) *die* - **1.** [Gepflogenheit] custom; **etw ist (bei jm) Sitte** sthg is the custom (with sb) - **2.** *(ohne pl) fam* [Sittenpolizei] vice squad. ◆ **Sitten** *Pl* - **1.** [Benehmen] manners - **2.** [Moral] morals.

sịttenwidrig ◇ *adj* morally offensive. ◇ *adv* in a morally offensive way.

sịttlich ◇ *adj* moral. ◇ *adv* morally.

Situation (*pl* **-en**) *die* situation.

Sịtz (*pl* **-e**) *der* - **1.** [in Parlament, Möbelstück] seat - **2.** *(ohne pl)* [von Institution, Firma] headquarters *Pl*; [von Regierung] seat - **3.** *(ohne pl)* [von Kleidung] fit.

sịtzen (*prät* **saß**, *perf* **hat gesẹssen**) *vi* - **1.** [gen] to sit; **bleiben Sie doch bitte sitzen!** please don't get up!; **auf etw** *(D)* **sitzen** to be sitting on sthg - **2.** [Mitglied sein]**: im Vorstand sitzen** to sit on the board (of directors); **im Parlament sitzen** to have a seat in parliament - **3.** [sich befinden] to be; [Firma] to be based - **4.** [passen] to fit - **5.** *fam* [im Gefängnis sein] to be inside - **6.** *fam* [Gelerntes]**: das Gedicht sitzt** the poem has stuck; **bei dem Meister sitzt jeder Handgriff** the expert can do every move in his sleep - **7.** *fam* [nicht loswerden]**: auf etw** *(D)* **sitzen** to be stuck with sthg.

sịtzen bleiben (*perf* **ist sịtzen geblieben**) *vi (unreg)* - **1.** [in Schule] to have to repeat a year - **2.** [auf Waren]**: auf etw** *(D)* **sitzen bleiben** to be stuck with sthg.

sịtzen lassen *vt (unreg) fam* [Person]**: jn sitzen lassen** [versetzen] to stand sb up; [verlassen] to walk out on sb.

Sịtz|gelegenheit *die* seat.

Sịtz|ordnung *die* seating plan.

Sịtz|platz *der* seat.

Sịtzung (*pl* **-en**) *die* [Konferenz - von Vorstand, Abteilung] meeting; [- von Bundestag] sitting.

Sizilien [zi'tsiːli̯ən] *nt* Sicily.

Skala (*pl* **-s** ODER **-len**) *die* scale; [von Farben] range.

Skalpẹll (*pl* **-e**) *das* scalpel.

Skandal (*pl* **-e**) *der* scandal.

skandalös ◇ *adj* scandalous. ◇ *adv* scandalously.

Skandinavien [skandi'nɑːvi̯ən] *nt* Scandinavia.

Skandinavier, in [skandi'nɑːvi̯ɐ, rɪn] (*mpl* **-**, *fpl* **-nen**) *der, die* Scandinavian.

skandinavisch [skandi'nɑːvɪʃ] *adj* Scandinavian.

Skat *der* skat; **Skat spielen** to play skat.

Skelẹtt (*pl* **-e**) *das* skeleton.

Skẹpsis *die* scepticism.

skẹptisch ◇ *adj* sceptical. ◇ *adv* sceptically.

Ski (*pl* **-** ODER **-er**)**, Schi** (*pl* **-** ODER **-er**) [ʃiː] *der* ski; **auf Skiern** on skis; **Ski fahren** ODER **laufen** to ski.

Ski|fahren *das* skiing.

Skifahrer, in (*mpl* **-**, *fpl* **-innen**) *der & die* skier.

Ski|gebiet *das* skiing area.

Skilạng|lauf *der (ohne Pl)* cross-country skiing.

Ski|läufer, in *der, die* skier.

Ski|lehrer, in *der, die* skiing instructor.

Ski|lift *der* ski lift.

Ski|piste *die* ski run.

Ski|urlaub *der* skiing holiday *UK* ODER vacation *US*.

Skịzze (*pl* **-n**) *die* - **1.** [Zeichnung] sketch - **2.** [Text] outline.

skizzieren *vt* - **1.** [zeichnen] to sketch - **2.** [schreiben] to outline.

Sklave ['sklɑːvə] (*pl* **-n**) *der* slave.

Sklavin ['sklɑːvɪn] (*pl* **-nen**) *die* slave.

Skorpion (*pl* **-e**) *der* - **1.** [Tier] scorpion - **2.** ASTROL [Sternzeichen, Person] Scorpio; **Skorpion sein** to be a Scorpio.

Skrupel (*pl* **-**) *der* scruple.

skrupellos ◇ *adj* unscrupulous. ◇ *adv* unscrupulously.

Skulptur (*pl* **-en**) *die* sculpture.

Slalom (*pl* **-s**) *der* slalom *(U)*.

Slawe (*pl* **-n**) *der* Slav.

Slawin (*pl* **-nen**) *die* Slav.

slawisch *adj* Slavonic.

Slịp (*pl* **-s**) *der* briefs *Pl*.

Slowakei *die* Slovakia.

Slowenien *nt* Slovenia.

Smoking (*pl* **-s**) *der* dinner jacket *UK*, tuxedo *US*.

SMS *die (ohne Pl) (abk für* **Short Message System**) SMS, text (message).

Snowboard (*pl* **-s**) *das* snowboard; **Snowboard fahren** to go snowboarding.

so ◇ *adv* - **1.** [auf diese Art] like this; [auf jene Art] like that; **lass es so, wie es ist** leave it as it is; **so ist es!** *fam* that's right!; **weiter so!** keep it up!; **gut so!** *fam* good; **so was** something like that - **2.** [mit Adjektiv, Adverb] so; **eine so schwierige Prüfung** such a difficult exam - **3.** [mit Substantiv, Pronomen]**: so einer/**

eine/eins such a; **so ein Pech!** what bad luck!; **so ein Unsinn!** what nonsense!; **so eine Art Jacke** a sort of jacket; **so mancher** many (people) - **4.** [mit Geste] this; **er war so groß** he was this big - **5.** *fam* [etwa] about, around - **6.** [bei Zitaten]:**..., so der Minister...,** said the minister - **7.** *fam* [ohne etwas] as it is - **8.** *fam* [kostenlos] for free - **9.** *fam* [im Allgemeinen]: **was hast du sonst noch so gemacht?** what else did you do, then? ◇ *konj* as; **laufen, so schnell man kann** to run as fast as one can; **so, dass** so that. ◇ *interj*: **so, das wars** so, that's it; **ach so!** oh, I see! ◆ **so dass** *konj* = **sodass.** ◆ **oder so** *adv fam* or so.

s. o. (*abk für* **siehe oben**), *see above*.

SO (*abk für* **Südost**) SE.

sobald *konj* as soon as.

Socke (*pl* **-n**) *die* sock.

Sockel (*pl* -) *der* [von Denkmal] plinth; [von Haus] base.

sodass, so dass *konj* so that.

soeben *adv* just.

Sofa (*pl* **-s**) *das* sofa.

soff *prät* ▷ **saufen.**

sofort *adv* - **1.** [unverzüglich] immediately, straight away - **2.** *fam* [gleich] in a moment.

Software|paket *das* EDV bundled software *(U)*, software package.

sog *prät* ▷ **saugen.**

sogar *adv* even.

Sohle (*pl* **-n**) *die* [Fuß-, Schuhsohle] sole.

Sohn (*pl* **Söhne**) *der* son.

solang, solange *konj* as long as.

solche, r, s *det* such.

Soldat (*pl* **-en**) *der* soldier.

Solidaritäts|zuschlag *der special tax levied to help finance the reconstruction of former East Germany.*

sollen (*perf* **hat gesollt** ODER **sollen**) ◇ *aux (perf hat sollen)* - **1.** [als Aufforderung] to be supposed to; **soll ich das Fenster aufmachen?** shall I open the window? - **2.** [als Vermutung]: **er soll 108 Jahre alt sein** he is said to be 108 years old; **was soll das heißen?** what's that supposed to mean? - **3.** [konjunktivisch] should, ought to - **4.** [als Bedingung]: **sollte sie noch kommen, sag ihr ...** if she should turn up, tell her ... ◇ *vi (perf hat gesollt)*: **die Ware soll nach München** the goods are meant to go to Munich; **soll er doch!** *fam* let him!; **was soll das?** *fam* what's all this?; **was solls!** *fam* what the hell! ◇ *vt (perf hat gesollt)*: **warum soll ich das?** why should I?

solo *adv* - **1.** [im Solo] solo - **2.** *fam* [allein] on one's own.

Somalia *nt* Somalia.

Sommer (*pl* -) *der* summer.

Sommer|ferien *Pl* summer holiday *UK* ODER vacation *US*.

Sommer|sprosse *die* freckle.

Sommer|zeit *die* summertime.

Sonate (*pl* **-n**) *die* MUS sonata.

Sonderan|gebot *das* special offer; **im Sonderangebot** on special offer.

sonderbar ◇ *adj* strange. ◇ *adv* strangely.

Sonder|fahrt *die amt* [Zugfahrt] special train; [Busfahrt] special bus.

Sonder|fall *der* special case.

sondergleichen *adj* unparalleled.

sonderlich ◇ *adj* - **1.** [besondere] particular - **2.** [sonderbar] peculiar. ◇ *adv*: **nicht sonderlich** not particularly.

Sonder|müll *der* hazardous waste.

sondern *konj* but.

Sonder|schule *die* special school.

Sonett (*pl* **-e**) *das* sonnet.

Sonn|abend (*pl* **-e**) *der* Saturday; *siehe auch* **Samstag.**

sonnabends *adv* on Saturdays; *siehe auch* **samstags.**

Sonne (*pl* **-n**) *die* sun; **die Sonne geht auf/unter** the sun rises/sets; **die Sonne scheint** the sun is shining; **in der prallen Sonne** in the blazing sun.

sonnen ◆ **sich sonnen** *ref* - **1.** [sich bräunen] to sun o.s. - **2.** [in Erfolg, Ruhm]: **sich in etw** *(D)* **sonnen** *fig* to bask in sthg.

Sonnenauf|gang *der* sunrise.

Sonnen|blume *die* sunflower.

Sonnen|brand *der* sunburn *(U)*.

Sonnen|brille *die* sunglasses *Pl*.

Sonnen|creme *die* sun cream.

Sonnen|energie *die* solar energy.

Sonnen|finsternis *die* solar eclipse.

Sonnen|licht *das* sunlight.

Sonnen|schein *der* sunshine.

Sonnen|schirm *der* sunshade.

Sonnenschutz *der* protection against the sun.

Sonnen|stich *der* sunstroke.

Sonnen|strahl *der* sunbeam.

Sonnen|system *das* solar system.

Sonnen|uhr *die* sundial.

Sonnenunter|gang *der* sunset.

Sonnen|wende *die* solstice.

sonnig *adj* sunny.

Sonntag (*pl* **-e**) *der* Sunday; *siehe auch* **Samstag.**

sonntags *adv* on Sundays; *siehe auch* **samstags.**

sonst ◇ *adv* - **1.** [außerdem] else; **sonst nichts** nothing else; **sonst noch etwas/jemand?** *fam* anything/anybody else?; **sonst noch Fragen?** any more questions? - **2.** [abgesehen hiervon] otherwise, apart from that; **wer/was (denn) sonst?** who/what else? - **3.** [gewöhnlich] usually. <> *konj* or (else).

sonstig *adj* other.

sonst wo *adv fam* somewhere else; [in Fragen] anywhere else.

sonst woher *adv fam* somewhere else; [in Fragen] anywhere else; **die Leute kamen (von) sonst woher** people came from all over; **das könnte sonst woher stammen** that could be from anywhere.

sonst wohin *adv fam* somewhere else; [in Fragen] anywhere else.

sooft *konj* whenever.

Sopran (*pl* **-e**) *der* - **1.** [Stimmlage - Frau] soprano; [- Knabe] treble - **2.** *(ohne pl)* [Stimme im Chor - Frauen] sopranos *Pl*; [- Knaben] trebles *Pl* - **3.** [Sängerin] soprano; [Sänger] treble.

Sorge (*pl* **-n**) *die* - **1.** [Problem] worry; **sich um jn/etw Sorgen machen** to worry about sb/sthg - **2.** [Pflege] care; **Sorge dafür tragen, dass...** to make sure that... ◆ **keine Sorge** *interj* [keine Angst] don't worry!

sorgen *vi*: **für etw sorgen** to see to sthg; **für jn sorgen** to look after sb. ◆ **sich sorgen** *ref*: **sich um jn/etw sorgen** to be worried about sb/sthg.

Sorgen|kind *das* problem child.

Sorge|recht *das* custody.

Sorgfalt *die* care.

sorgfältig <> *adj* careful. <> *adv* carefully.

sorglos <> *adj* carefree. <> *adv* in a carefree way.

Sorte (*pl* **-n**) *die* sort, type. ◆ **Sorten** *Pl* WIRTSCH foreign currency *(sg)*.

sortieren *vt* to sort.

Sortiment (*pl* **-e**) *das* range.

sosehr *konj* however much.

Soße (*pl* **-n**) *die* [für Nudeln, Pudding] sauce; [für Braten] gravy; [für Salat] dressing.

Sound|karte *die* EDV sound card.

Souvenir [suvəˈniːɐ̯] (*pl* **-s**) *das* souvenir.

souverän [zuvəˈrɛːn] <> *adj* - **1.** POL sovereign - **2.** [überlegen] masterful. <> *adv* - **1.** POL: **souverän herrschen** *ODER* **regieren** to have sovereign power - **2.** [überlegen] masterfully.

soviel *konj* as far as; **soviel ich weiß** as far as I know.

so viel *adv* so much; **so viel du willst** as much as you want; **noch einmal so viel** as much again; **dreimal so viel** three times as much; **so viel wie** as much as; **halb so viel (wie)** half as much/many (as).

soweit *konj* as far as; **soweit ich weiß** as far as I know.

so weit <> *adj*: **so weit sein** to be ready; **es ist so weit** it is time. <> *adv* on the whole; **so weit wie möglich** as far as possible; **so weit ich weiß** as far as I know.

so wenig *adv*: **so wenig wie möglich** as little as possible.

sowie *konj* as well as.

sowieso *adv* anyway.

Sowjet|union *die*: **die ehemalige Sowjetunion** the former Soviet Union.

sowohl *konj*: **sowohl A als auch B** A as well as B, both A and B.

sozial <> *adj* social; [Einstellung] socially aware; **sozialer Beruf** caring profession. <> *adv* socially; [handeln] in a socially aware manner; **sozial eingestellt** socially aware.

Sozial|abgaben *Pl* social security contributions.

Sozial|amt *das* social security office.

Sozial|arbeiter, in *der, die* social worker.

Sozial|demokrat, in *der, die* Social Democrat.

Sozial|fall *der*: **ein Sozialfall sein** to be dependent on state benefit.

Sozialhilfe *die* ≃ income support *UK*, ≃ welfare *US*.

Sozialismus *der* socialism.

sozialkritisch *adj* socially critical.

Sozial|leistungen *Pl* social security benefits.

Sozial|minister, in *der, die* social services minister.

Sozial|pädagogik *die* social education.

Sozialpolitik *die* social policy.

Sozial|staat *der* welfare state.

Sozialsystem (*pl* **-e**) *das* social system.

Sozialver|sicherung *die* social security.

Sozial|wohnung *die* ≃ council flat *UK*, ≃ low-rent apartment *US*.

Soziologie *die* sociology.

sozusagen *adv* so to speak.

Spachtel (*pl* -) *die ODER der* spatula.

spachteln *vt* [mit Spachtelmasse] to fill.

Spagat (*pl* **-e**) *der* - **1.** SPORT: **einen Spagat machen** to do the splits - **2.** *fig* balancing act.

Spagetti, Spaghetti *Pl* spaghetti *(U)*.

Spalt (*pl* **-e**) *der* crack; **etw einen Spalt weit** *ODER* **breit öffnen** to open sthg a crack.

Spalte (*pl* **-n**) *die* - **1.** [Öffnung] crack - **2.** column.

spalten *vt* [gen, CHEM & PHYS] to split; [Substanz, Verbindung] to break down.

Spaltung (*pl* **-en**) *die* - **1.** [Teilen - von Land, Partei] splitting up *(U)*; [Teilung - von Land, Partei] split - **2.** CHEM & PHYS splitting *(U)*; [von Substanz] breaking down *(U)* - **3.** MED split.

Span (*pl* **Späne**) *der* shaving.

Span|ferkel *das* KÜCHE suckling pig.

Spange (*pl* **-n**) *die* - **1.** [Schmuckstück] slide *UK*, barrette *US* - **2.** [Zahnspange] brace.

Spanien *nt* Spain.

Spanier, in ['ʃpaːni̯ɐ, rɪn] (*mpl* -, *fpl* **-nen**) *der, die* Spaniard.

spanisch <> *adj* Spanish. <> *adv*: **spanisch sprechen** to speak Spanish.

Spanisch(e) *das* Spanish; *siehe auch* **Englisch(e)**.

spann *prät* ▷ **spinnen**.

Spannbetttuch (*pl* **-tücher**) *das* fitted sheet.

Spanne (*pl* **-n**) *die* period; **in der/einer Spanne von... bis...** between... and...

spannen <> *vt* [Bogen] to draw; [Muskeln] to tense; [Schnur] to tighten; [Netz] to stretch out. <> *vi* - **1.** *fam* [heimlich zusehen] to take a peep - **2.** [zu eng sein] to be too tight. ◆ **sich spannen** *ref*: **sich über etw** *(A)* **spannen** to span sthg.

spannend <> *adj* exciting. <> *adv* excitingly.

Spann|kraft *die* vigour.

Spannung (*pl* **-en**) *die* - **1.** [gen] tension - **2.** [elektrisch] voltage; **unter Spannung stehen** to be live. ◆ **Spannungen** *Pl* tension *(sg)*.

Spannungs|gebiet *das* area of tension.

Spann|weite *die* wingspan.

Span|platte *die* chipboard *(U)*.

Spar|buch *das* savings book.

Spar|büchse *die* money box.

sparen <> *vt* to save; **spar dir deine dummen Bemerkungen** you can keep your silly remarks. <> *vi* to save; **an etw** *(D)* **sparen** to save on sthg; **für** ODER **auf etw** *(A)* **sparen** to save (up) for sthg.

Spargel (*pl* -) *der* asparagus *(U)*.

Spar|kasse *die* savings bank.

spärlich <> *adj* [Haare] sparse; [Beifall, Maßnahmen] meagre. <> *adv* [bekleidet] scantily; [bewachsen, wachsen] sparsely.

Spar|programm *das* economy drive.

sparsam <> *adj* economical; **mit etw sparsam sein** to be economical with sthg. <> *adv* economically; **mit etw sparsam umgehen** to be economical with sthg.

Sparsamkeit *die* economy.

Spar|schwein *das* piggy bank.

Sparte (*pl* **-n**) *die* - **1.** WIRTSCH line of business - **2.** [in Zeitungen] section.

Spaß (*pl* **Späße**) *der* - **1.** [Vergnügen] fun; **zum Spaß** for fun; **an etw** *(D)* **Spaß haben** to enjoy sthg; **jm den Spaß verderben** to spoil sb's fun; **es macht mir Spaß** I enjoy it; **Auto fahren macht mir keinen Spaß** I don't enjoy driving; **viel Spaß!** have fun!; **da hört der Spaß auf** I draw the line at that; **mir ist der Spaß vergangen** it's no fun any more - **2.** [Scherz] joke; [Streich] prank; **aus** ODER **im** ODER **zum Spaß** as a joke; **Spaß machen** [nicht ernst meinen] to be joking; **Spaß/keinen Spaß verstehen** to have a/no sense of humour.

spaßen *vi* to joke.

spät <> *adj* late; **bis in die späte Nacht** until late at night; **wie spät ist es?** what's the time? <> *adv* late; **sie kam mal wieder zu spät** she was late again; **von früh bis spät** from dawn to dusk.

Spaten (*pl* -) *der* spade.

später *adj* & *adv* later. ◆ **bis später** *interj* see you later!

spätestens *adv* at the latest.

Spät|lese (*pl* **-n**) *die* [Wein] late vintage.

Spätnach|mittag *der* late afternoon.

Spät|sommer *der* late summer.

Spätvor|stellung *die* late show.

Spatz (*pl* **-en**) *der* - **1.** [Tier] sparrow - **2.** *fam* [Anrede] pet.

Spätzle *Pl Süddt small round noodles, similar to macaroni.*

spazieren (*perf* **ist spaziert**) *vi* to stroll.

spazieren gehen (*perf* **ist spazieren gegangen**) *vi (unreg)* to go for a walk.

Spazier|gang *der* walk.

Spazier|gänger, in (*mpl* -, *fpl* **-nen**) *der, die* person going for a walk.

SPD [ɛspeː'deː] (*abk für* **Sozialdemokratische Partei Deutschlands**) *die* SPD.

Specht (*pl* **-e**) *der* woodpecker.

Speck *der* - **1.** [tierisch - von Schwein] pork fat; [- geräuchert, durchwachsen] bacon; [- von Wal, Robbe] blubber - **2.** *fam* [menschlich] flab.

Spediteur, in [ʃpedi'tøːɐ̯, rɪn] (*mpl* **-e**, *fpl* **-nen**) *der, die* haulier; [für Umzug] furniture mover.

Spedition [ʃpedi'tsi̯oːn] (*pl* **-en**) *die* haulage firm; [für Umzug] removal firm.

Speer (*pl* **-e**) *der* - **1.** SPORT javelin - **2.** [Waffe] spear.

Speiche (*pl* **-n**) *die* spoke.

Speichel *der* saliva.

Speicher (*pl* -) *der* - **1.** [Dachboden] loft - **2.** EDV memory.

speichern *vt* - **1.** [ansammeln, abspeichern] to store - **2.** EDV to save.

speien ['ʃpai̯ən] (*prät* **spie**, *perf* **hat gespie(e)n**) <> *vt* [Feuer, Lava] to spew; [Wasser] to spout. <> *vi* to vomit.

Speise (*pl* **-n**) *die* dish; **warme Speisen** hot food; **Speisen und Getränke** meals and drinks.

speisen *geh* <> *vt* - **1.** [essen] to dine on - **2.** [zu essen geben] to feed. <> *vi* to dine.

Speise|röhre *die* gullet.

Speise|saal *der* dining room.

Speise|wagen *der* dining car.

Spektakel (*pl* -) <> *das* [Aufführung, Ereignis] spectacle. <> *der* racket.

Spektrum (*pl* **Spektren**) *das* spectrum.

Spekulant, in (*mpl* **-en**, *fpl* **-nen**) *der, die* speculator.

Spekulation (*pl* **-en**) *die* speculation.

spekulieren *vi* - **1.** *fam* [hoffen]: **auf etw** *(A)* **spekulieren** to hope to get sthg - **2.** WIRTSCH: **(auf etw** *(A)***) spekulieren** to speculate (on sthg) - **3.** [mutmaßen]: **über etw** *(A)* **spekulieren** to speculate about sthg.

spendabel *adj fam* generous.

Spende (*pl* **-n**) *die* donation.

spenden ◇ *vt* to donate; [Blut] to give. ◇ *vi* to give.

Spender, in (*mpl* **-**, *fpl* **-nen**) *der, die* donor; **wer war der edle Spender?** who do I/we have to thank for this?

spendieren *vt*: **(jm) etw spendieren** to buy (sb) sthg.

Sperling (*pl* **-e**) *der* sparrow.

Sperma (*pl* **-ta** ODER **Spermen**) *das* sperm.

Sperre (*pl* **-n**) *die* - **1.** [Verbot & SPORT] ban; **eine Sperre verhängen/aufheben** to impose/lift a ban - **2.** [Absperrung] barrier - **3.** TECH locking device.

sperren *vt* - **1.** [einsperren]: **jn/etw in etw** *(A)* **sperren** to shut sb/sthg in sthg - **2.** [Konto, Kredit] to freeze; [Scheck] to stop - **3.** [Straße] to close - **4.** SPORT to ban. ◆ **sich sperren** *ref*: **sich (gegen etw) sperren** to resist (sthg).

Sperr|holz *das* plywood.

sperrig *adj* bulky.

Sperr|müll *der* bulky refuse *(collected separately from normal refuse)*.

Sperr|sitz *der* [in Zirkus] ringside seat.

Sperr|stunde *die* closing time.

Sperrung (*pl* **-en**) *die* - **1.** [von Straße] closing - **2.** [von Konto, Kredit] freezing; [von Scheck] stopping.

Spesen *Pl* expenses; **auf Spesen** on expenses.

Spezi (*pl* **-s**) *fam* ◇ *der Süddt* mate. ◇ *das* cola and orangeade.

spezialisieren ◆ **sich spezialisieren** *ref*: **sich auf etw** *(A)* **spezialisieren** to specialize in sthg.

Spezialist, in (*mpl* **-en**, *fpl* **-nen**) *der, die* specialist.

Spezialität (*pl* **-en**) *die* speciality *UK*, specialty *US*.

speziell ◇ *adj* special. ◇ *adv* specially.

spicken ◇ *vt* - **1.** KÜCHE: **etw mit etw spicken** to lard sthg with sthg - **2.** [ausstatten]: **etw mit etw spicken** [Text, Rede] to pepper sthg with sthg. ◇ *vi* to crib.

Spick|zettel *der fam* crib (sheet).

spie *prät* ▷ **speien**.

Spiegel (*pl* **-**) *der* - **1.** [Gegenstand] mirror - **2.** [von Gewässern] surface - **3.** MED level.

Spiegel|bild *das* reflection.

Spiegel|ei *das* fried egg.

spiegelglatt *adj* very slippery.

spiegeln *vi* to shine. ◆ **sich spiegeln** *ref*: **sich in etw** *(D)* **spiegeln** to be reflected in sthg.

Spiegelreflex|kamera *die* reflex camera.

Spiel (*pl* **-e**) *das* - **1.** [Vergnügen, Wettkampf] game; **machen wir noch ein Spiel?** shall we have another game?; **ein Spiel mit jm treiben** to play games with sb - **2.** [von Musiker] playing; [von Schauspieler] acting; [von Sportler, Mannschaft] game - **3.** TECH play - **4.** [Glücksspiel] gambling; **auf dem Spiel stehen** to be at stake; **etw aufs Spiel setzen** to risk sthg; **jn/etw aus dem Spiel lassen** to leave sb/sthg out of it.

Spiel|automat *der* slot machine, fruit machine *UK*.

spielen ◇ *vi* - **1.** [gen] to play; **mit jm/etw spielen** to play with sb/sthg - **2.** [als Schauspieler] to act - **3.** [Roman, Film] to be set - **4.** [Glücksspiel machen] to gamble; **um etw spielen** to play for sthg - **5.** [einsetzen]: **seine Beziehungen spielen lassen** to pull some strings; **seinen Charme spielen lassen** to use one's charm. ◇ *vt* to play; **Klavier/Saxofon spielen** to play the piano/saxophone; **Lotto spielen** to do the lottery; **den Unschuldigen spielen** to act ODER play the innocent.

spielend *adv* - **1.** [einfach] easily - **2.** [beim Spielen] through play.

Spieler (*pl* **-**) *der* - **1.** [Mitspieler] player - **2.** [Glücksspieler] gambler.

Spielerin (*pl* **-nen**) *die* - **1.** [Mitspielerin] player - **2.** [Glücksspielerin] gambler.

spielerisch ◇ *adj* - **1.** [locker] effortless - **2.** [Fähigkeit - in Sport, Musik] as a player; [- in Theater] as an actor. ◇ *adv* - **1.** [locker] effortlessly - **2.** [in Sport]: **eine spielerisch enttäuschende Mannschaft** a team that gave a disappointing performance.

Spiel|feld *das* [für Fußball, Hockey] field, pitch *UK*; [für Tennis, Federball, Volleyball] court.

Spiel|film *der* feature film.

Spielkonsole (*pl* **-n**) *die* game ODER video console.

Spiel|plan *der* - **1.** [von Theatern] programme - **2.** SPORT fixture list.

Spiel|platz *der* playground.

Spiel|raum *der* leeway.

Spiel|regel *die* rule.

Spiel|verderber, in (*mpl* **-**, *fpl* **-nen**) *der, die* spoilsport.

Spiel|waren *Pl* toys.

Spiel|zeug *das* - **1.** *(ohne pl)* [Spielsachen] toys *Pl* - **2.** [einzelnes Spielgerät] toy.

Spieß (*pl* **-e**) *der* spit; **am Spieß** spit-roasted; **den Spieß umdrehen** *fig* to turn the tables.

spießen *vt*: **etw auf etw** *(A)* **spießen** to skewer sthg with sthg.

Spießer, **in** (*mpl* **-**, *fpl* **-nen**) *der, die abw* (petit) bourgeois.

Spinat (*pl* **-e**) *der* spinach.

Spịnd *der* locker.

Spịnne (*pl* **-n**) *die* spider.

spịnnen (*prät* **spạnn**, *perf* **hat gespọnnen**) ◇ *vt* to spin. ◇ *vi* **- 1.** *fam* [verrückt sein] to be crazy; **du spinnst!, spinnst du?** are you crazy? **- 2.** [arbeiten] to spin.

Spịnnwebe (*pl* **-n**) *die* cobweb.

Spion (*pl* **-e**) *der* **- 1.** [Geheimagent] spy **- 2.** [Türspion] peephole.

Spionage [ʃpjoˈnɑːʒə] *die* spying; **Spionage betreiben** to spy.

spionieren *vi* **- 1.** [Spionage treiben] to spy **- 2.** *fam abw* [neugierig sein] to snoop.

Spionin (*pl* **-nen**) *die* spy.

Spirale (*pl* **-n**) *die* **- 1.** [gewundene Linie] spiral **- 2.** MED coil.

Spirituose (*pl* **-n**) *die amt* spirit.

Spịritus (*pl* **-se**) *der* spirit.

spịtz ◇ *adj* **- 1.** [Ende, Schuh, Bogen, Bemerkung] pointed; [Bleistift, Messer, Nadel] sharp **- 2.** [Winkel] acute **- 3.** *fam* [geil]: **auf jn spitz sein** to have the hots for sb; **spitz darauf sein, etw zu tun** to be dying to do sthg. ◇ *adv* **- 1.** [zulaufen] to a point **- 2.** [bemerken] pointedly.

Spịtze (*pl* **-n**) *die* **- 1.** [von Messer, Bleistift] point; [von Kirchturm, Baum] top; [von Berg] peak **- 2.** [Führung]: **an der Spitze** [in Betrieb, Partei] at the top; [in Rennen] in the lead **- 3.** [Höchstwert] maximum; **etw auf die Spitze treiben** *fig* to take sthg too far **- 4.** *fam* [besonders gut]: **Spitze sein** to be great **- 5.** [Bemerkung] gibe.

Spịtzel (*pl* **-**) *der* informer.

spịtzen *vt* **- 1.** [spitz machen] to sharpen **- 2.** [Ohren] to prick up.

Spịtzen|reiter, **in** *der, die* leader.

spịtzfindig *abw* ◇ *adj* hairsplitting. ◇ *adv*: **spitzfindig argumentieren** to split hairs.

Spịtz|name *der* nickname.

Splịtter (*pl* **-**) *der* [aus Holz, Glas] splinter; [von Bombe] fragment.

Splịtter|gruppe *die* splinter group.

splịttern (*perf* **hat/ist gesplịttert**) *vi* to splinter.

splịtternackt *adj* & *adv* stark naked.

SPÖ [ɛspeːˈø] (*abk für* **Sozialdemokratische Partei Österreichs**) *die Austrian Social Democratic Party*.

Spọnsor (*pl* **-soren**) *der* sponsor.

Sponsorin (*pl* **-nen**) *die* sponsor.

spontan ◇ *adj* spontaneous. ◇ *adv* spontaneously.

Spọrt *der* sport; **Sport treiben** to do sport.

Spọrt|art *die* sport.

Spọrt|halle *die* sports hall.

Spọrt|lehrer, **in** *der, die* sports teacher.

Spọrtler, **in** (*mpl* **-**, *fpl* **-nen**) *der, die* sportsman (sportswoman *die*).

spọrtlich ◇ *adj* **- 1.** [Leistung, Betätigung, Verhalten] sporting; [Person, Figur] sporty **- 2.** [leger] casual. ◇ *adv* **- 1.** [den Sport betreffend]: **sich sportlich betätigen** to do sport **- 2.** [leger] casually **- 3.** [fair] sportingly.

Spọrt|platz *der* playing field.

Spọrt|verein *der* sports club.

Spọrt|wagen *der* **- 1.** [Auto] sports car **- 2.** [Kinderwagen] pushchair *UK*, stroller *US*.

Spọtt *der* mockery.

spọttbillig *adj* & *adv* dirt-cheap.

spọtten *vi*: **(über jn/etw) spotten** to mock (sb/sthg).

spọ̈ttisch ◇ *adj* mocking. ◇ *adv* mockingly.

Spọtt|preis *der* knockdown price.

sprạch *prät* ▷ **sprechen**.

Sprache (*pl* **-n**) *die* [gen] language; **in deutscher Sprache** in German; **jm die Sprache verschlagen** to leave sb speechless; **raus mit der Sprache!** *fam* out with it!

Sprạch|kenntnisse *Pl* knowledge *(U)* of languages.

Sprạch|kurs *der* language course.

Sprạch|labor *das* language laboratory.

sprạchlich ◇ *adj* linguistic. ◇ *adv* linguistically.

sprachlos ◇ *adj* [Staunen] speechless; **sprachlos sein** to be speechless. ◇ *adv* [dastehen] speechlessly.

Sprạch|reise *die* language trip.

sprạng *prät* ▷ **springen**.

Spray [ʃpreː, spreː] (*pl* **-s**) *der ODER das* spray.

Sprẹch|anlage *die* intercom.

sprẹchen (*präs* **sprịcht**, *prät* **sprạch**, *perf* **hat gesprọchen**) ◇ *vi* **- 1.** [gen] to talk, to speak; **wer spricht da, bitte?** [am Telefon] who's speaking?; **mit jm sprechen** to talk to sb; **über jn/etw sprechen, von jm/etw sprechen** to talk about sb/sthg; **er sprach davon, dass...** he mentioned that...; **zu jm sprechen** to speak to sb; **auf jn/etw zu sprechen kommen** to discuss sb/sthg **- 2.** [als Redner auftreten] to speak; **frei sprechen** to speak without notes **- 3.** [urteilend]: **es spricht für ihn, dass...** it's in his favour that...; **alles spricht dafür, dass...** there is every reason to believe that... ◇ *vt* **- 1.** [gen] to speak; **deutsch sprechen** to speak German; **jn sprechen** to speak to sb **- 2.** [Gebet] to say **- 3.** [reden mit] to speak to.

Sprẹcher, **in** (*mpl* **-**, *fpl* **-nen**) *der, die* **- 1.** [von Gruppe] spokesperson **- 2.** [von Nachrichten] newsreader.

Sprẹch|stunde *die* [beim Arzt] surgery.

Sprechstunden|hilfe *die* (doctor's) receptionist.

Sprech|zimmer *das* consulting room.

spreizen *vt* to spread.

sprengen *vt* - **1.** [mit Sprengstoff - Brücke, Gebäude] to blow up; [- Tür] to blow open; **etw in die Luft sprengen** to blow sthg up - **2.** [mit Wasser - Rasen, Garten] to water; [- Wäsche] to sprinkle with water.

Spreng|satz *der* explosive charge.

Spreng|stoff *der* explosive.

spricht *präs* ▷ **sprechen**.

Sprich|wort (*pl* **-wörter**) *das* proverb.

sprießen (*prät* **spross**, *perf* **ist gesprossen**) *vi* to sprout.

Spring|brunnen *der* fountain.

springen (*prät* **sprang**, *perf* **hat/ist gesprungen**) ◇ *vi* - **1.** *(ist)* [hüpfen & SPORT] to jump; **auf etw** *(A)***/aus etw/von etw springen** to jump onto/out of/from sthg - **2.** [Ball] to bounce - **3.** *(ist)* [kaputtgehen] to crack; **mein Vater hat 20 Euro springen lassen** *fam* my dad gave me 20 euros. ◇ *vt (hat)* SPORT [Salto] to do.

Sprint (*pl* **-s**) *der* sprint.

Spritze (*pl* **-n**) *die* - **1.** [Injektion] injection - **2.** [Injektionsgerät, Küchengerät] syringe - **3.** [Wasserspritze] hose.

spritzen (*perf* **hat/ist gespritzt**) ◇ *vi* - **1.** *(hat)* [herumspritzen - Flüssigkeit, Person] to splash; [- Fett] to spit - **2.** *(ist)* [in bestimmte Richtung] to splash - **3.** *(hat)* [eine Spritze geben] to give an injection. ◇ *vt (hat)* - **1.** [gen] to spray; **jn nass spritzen** to splash sb - **2.** [Medikament, Droge] to inject; **sich/jm ein Schmerzmittel spritzen** to inject o.s./sb with a painkiller.

Spritzer (*pl* -) *der* splash.

spröde ◇ *adj* - **1.** [trocken] dry - **2.** [brüchig] brittle - **3.** [Mensch, Art] standoffish. ◇ *adv* [unzugänglich] standoffishly.

spross *prät* ▷ **sprießen**.

Sprosse (*pl* **-n**) *die* rung.

Spruch (*pl* **Sprüche**) *der* [Redensart] saying.

Sprudel (*pl* -) *der* sparkling mineral water.

sprudeln (*perf* **hat/ist gesprudelt**) *vi* - **1.** [gen] to bubble - **2.** [wenn Kohlensäure entweicht] to fizz.

Sprüh|dose *die* aerosol.

sprühen (*perf* **hat/ist gesprüht**) ◇ *vt (hat)* to spray. ◇ *vi* - **1.** *(ist)* [fliegen] to spray - **2.** *(hat)* [glänzen]: **vor Ideen sprühen** to be bubbling over with ideas; **vor Witz sprühen** to be sparklingly witty.

Sprüh|regen *der* drizzle.

Sprung (*pl* **Sprünge**) *der* - **1.** [Bewegung] jump - **2.** [Riss] crack; **einen Sprung haben** to be cracked.

Sprung|brett *das* springboard.

sprunghaft ◇ *adj* - **1.** [unstet] erratic - **2.** [abrupt steigend] rapid. ◇ *adv* - **1.** [unstet] erratically - **2.** [abrupt steigend] rapidly.

SPS [ɛs peː ɛs] (*abk für* **Sozialdemokratische Partei der Schweiz**) *die Swiss Social Democratic Party*.

Spucke *die* spit.

spucken ◇ *vi* - **1.** [ausspucken] to spit - **2.** *fam* [sich übergeben] to puke. ◇ *vt* [Olivenstein, Blut] to spit.

Spuk *der* haunting; **dem Spuk ein Ende machen** *fig* to return things to normal.

spuken *vi*: **in einem Haus spuken** to haunt a house; **spukt es hier?** is this place haunted?

Spule (*pl* **-n**) *die* - **1.** [Rolle] spool - **2.** ELEKTR coil.

Spüle (*pl* **-n**) *die* sink.

spülen ◇ *vt* - **1.** [Geschirr] to wash - **2.** [Wäsche] to rinse - **3.** [hinwegtragen]: **über Bord gespült werden** to be washed overboard. ◇ *vi* - **1.** [Geschirr reinigen] to do the dishes, to wash up *UK* - **2.** [Subj: Waschmaschine] to rinse - **3.** [hinunterspülen] to flush.

Spül|maschine *die* dishwasher.

Spül|mittel *das* washing-up liquid *UK*, dishwashing liquid *US*.

Spur (*pl* **-en**) *die* - **1.** [Anzeichen] clue - **2.** [Abdruck] track - **3.** [Fahrstreifen] lane; **die Spur wechseln** to change lanes - **4.** [kleine Menge - von Zutat] hint; [- von Substanz] trace; **eine heiße Spur** a strong lead; **jm/einer Sache auf der Spur sein** to be on sb's/sthg's track. ◆ **keine Spur** *interj* not at all!

spürbar ◇ *adj* - **1.** [fühlbar] noticeable - **2.** [deutlich] clear. ◇ *adv* - **1.** [fühlbar] noticeably - **2.** [sichtlich] clearly.

spüren *vt* - **1.** [fühlen] to feel; **du wirst die Konsequenzen zu spüren bekommen** you'll see what the consequences are - **2.** [ahnen] to sense.

Spuren|element *das* trace element.

spurlos *adv* - **1.** [verschwinden] without a trace - **2.** [ohne negative Auswirkungen]: **die Trennung ist nicht spurlos an ihr vorübergegangen** the separation has left its mark on her.

Spurt (*pl* **-s** ODER **-e**) *der* [Endspurt] sprint for the line; [Zwischenspurt] spurt.

sputen ◆ **sich sputen** *ref* to hurry up.

Squash [skvɔʃ] *das* squash.

Sri Lanka *nt* Sri Lanka.

s. S. (*abk für* **siehe Seite**) see p.

SS [ɛs'ɛs] *die* MIL (*abk für* **Schutzstaffel**) SS.

St. - **1.** (*abk für* **Sankt**) St - **2.** *abk für* **Stück**.

Staat (*pl* **-en**) *der* state; **die Staaten** *fam* the States.

Staaten|bund *der* confederation.

staatenlos *adj* stateless.

staatlich ◇ *adj* state. ◇ *adv* by the state; **staatlich anerkannt** government-approved; **staatlich geprüft** government-certified.
Staats|angehörigkeit *die* nationality; **doppelte Staatsangehörigkeit** dual nationality.
Staats|anwalt, anwältin *der, die* public prosecutor *UK*, district attorney *US*.
Staats|besuch *der* state visit.
Staats|bürger, in *der, die* citizen.
Staats|dienst *der* civil service.
staatseigen *adj* state-owned.
Staats|examen *das final exam taken by law and arts students at university.*
Staats|mann (*pl* **-männer**) *der* statesman.
Staatsober|haupt *das* head of state.
Staats|sekretär, in *der, die* ≃ permanent secretary.
Staats|sicherheitsdienst *der security service in former GDR.*
Staats|streich *der* coup (d'état).
staatstragend *adj* pro-government.
Staats|vertrag *der* international treaty.
Stab (*pl* **Stäbe**) *der* rod; [von Gitter] bar; [von Dirigent] baton; MIL [von Pilger] staff; [zum Stabhochsprung] pole.
Stäbchen (*pl* -) *das* stick; [Essstäbchen] chopstick.
Stabhochsprung *der* SPORT pole vault.
stabil *adj* - **1.** [Haus, Währung, Wetter] stable - **2.** [Person, Gesundheit] robust; [Möbel] solid.
stabilisieren *vt* to stabilize. ◆ **sich stabilisieren** *ref* to stabilize.
stach *prät* ▷ **stechen**.
Stachel (*pl* **-n**) *der* - **1.** [von Tier] sting - **2.** [von Pflanze] thorn.
Stachel|beere *die* gooseberry.
Stachel|draht *der* barbed wire *(U)*.
stachelig, stachlig *adj* prickly.
Stadion ['ʃtɑːdi̯ɔn] (*pl* **Stadien**) *das* stadium.
Stadium ['ʃtɑːdi̯ʊm] (*pl* **Stadien**) *das* stage.
Stadt (*pl* **Städte**) *die* - **1.** [Ort] town; [Großstadt] city; **die Stadt Köln** the city of Cologne - **2.** *fam* [Stadtverwaltung] town/city council.
stadtbekannt *adj* well-known throughout the town/city.
Stadt|bummel *der* stroll through town.
Städtebau *der* urban development; [Planung] town planning.
Stadt|gespräch *das*: **Stadtgespräch sein** to be the talk of the town.
städtisch *adj* - **1.** [der Stadtverwaltung] municipal - **2.** [der Stadt] urban.
Stadt|kern *der* town/city centre.
Stadt|plan *der* street map.
Stadt|rand *der* outskirts *Pl*.
Stadt|rat *der* - **1.** [Versammlung] town/city council - **2.** [Person] town/city councillor.
Stadt|rätin *die* town/city councillor.
Stadtrund|fahrt *die* city tour.
Stadt|staat *der* city state.
Stadt|teil *der* district.
Stadt|tor *das* city gate.
Stadt|viertel *das* district, quarter.
Stadt|zentrum *das* town/city centre, downtown area *US*.
Staffel (*pl* **-n**) *die* SPORT relay race.
Staffelei (*pl* **-en**) *die* easel.
staffeln *vt* to grade.
stahl *prät* ▷ **stehlen**.
Stahl (*pl* **Stähle**) *der* steel *(U)*.
Stahl|industrie *die* steel industry.
Stall (*pl* **Ställe**) *der* [gen] barn; [für Kühe] cowshed; [für Pferde] stable; [für Kaninchen] hutch; [für Schweine] sty; [für Hühner] coop.
Stamm (*pl* **Stämme**) *der* - **1.** [von Baum] trunk - **2.** [Volk] tribe - **3.** [Wortstamm] stem.
Stamm|baum *der* family tree; [von Tier] pedigree.
stammeln *vt* & *vi* to stammer.
stammen *vi* to come; **aus etw stammen** to come from sthg; **von jm stammen** [herrühren] to come from sb; [gemacht sein] to be made by sb; **das Bild stammt von meiner Nachbarin** the picture was painted by my neighbour; **aus etw stammen** [zeitlich] to date from sthg.
Stamm|gast *der* regular.
stämmig *adj* stocky.
Stamm|platz *der* usual seat.
Stamm|tisch *der* - **1.** [Personen] *group of regular customers at a pub* - **2.** [Treffen] *meeting of regular customers at a pub* - **3.** [Tisch] *regulars' table at a pub*.
stampfen (*perf* **hat/ist gestampft**) ◇ *vi* - **1.** *(hat)* [auftreten] to stamp; **mit den Füßen stampfen** to stamp one's feet - **2.** *(ist)* [gehen] to stomp. ◇ *vt (hat)* [Kartoffeln] to mash.
stand *prät* ▷ **stehen**.
Stand (*pl* **Stände**) *der* - **1.** [auf Messe, Markt] stand - **2.** *(ohne pl)* [das Stehen] standing position - **3.** *(ohne pl)* [Stellung - von Sonne] position; [- von Zähler] reading; [- von Entwicklung]: **der Stand der Dinge** the state of things; **auf dem neuesten Stand sein** to be right up-to-date; **einen schweren Stand (bei jm) haben** to have a tough time (with sb); = **instand, imstande, zustande**.
Standard (*pl* **-s**) *der* standard.
Stand-by [stɛnt'bai] (*pl* **-s**) ◇ *das* [bei Elektrogeräten] standby mode; **in Stand-by** in standby mode. ◇ *der* [bei Flugreisen] standby flight.
Ständchen (*pl* -) *das* serenade; **jm ein Ständchen bringen** to serenade sb.
Ständer (*pl* -) *der* [Gestell] stand.
Standes|amt *das* registry office.

stạndesamtlich ◇ *adj* registry-office. ◇ *adv* at the registry office.

stạndesgemäß ◇ *adj* in keeping with one's social status. ◇ *adv* according to one's social status.

stạndhaft ◇ *adj* steadfast. ◇ *adv*: **sich standhaft weigern** to refuse consistently.

stạnd|halten *vi (unreg)*: **einer Sache** *(D)* **standhalten** to withstand sthg.

stạ̈ndig ◇ *adj* [Schmerzen, Belästigung] constant; [Mitglied] permanent. ◇ *adv* constantly.

Stạnd|ort *der* - **1.** [von Firma] location; **der Standort Deutschland** Germany as an industrial location - **2.** [von Person, Pflanze] position.

Stạnd|punkt *der* point of view.

Stạnd|spur *die* hard shoulder *UK*, shoulder *US*.

Stạnge (*pl* **-n**) *die* pole; [aus Metall] rod; **eine Stange Zigaretten** a carton of cigarettes; **ein Anzug von der Stange** an off-the-peg suit; **eine Stange Geld** *fam fig* a fortune.

Stạ̈ngel (*pl* -) *der* stalk.

stạnk *prät* ▷ **stinken**.

stạnzen *vt* - **1.** [Formen, Teile] to press - **2.** [Löcher] to punch.

Stapel (*pl* -) *der* [Haufen] pile.

Stapel|lauf *der* launching (of a ship).

stapeln *vt* to pile up. ◆ **sich stapeln** *ref* [hingestellt werden] to be piled up; [sich türmen] to be piling up.

Star [ʃtaːɐ̯] (*pl* **-e** ODER **-s**) *der* - **1.** *(pl Stare)* [Vogel] starling - **2.** *(pl Stars)* [Person] star.

stạrb *prät* ▷ **sterben**.

stạrk (*kompar* **stạ̈rker**, *superl* **stạ̈rkste**) ◇ *adj* - **1.** [gen] strong - **2.** [Sturm, Schnupfen, Verkehr] heavy - **3.** *fam* [toll] great; **stark!** great! - **4.** [dick - Brille, Wände, Träger] thick; [- Figur, Beine] large - **5.** [mit Maßangabe] thick - **6.** [Beteiligung] good; [Interesse] strong - **7.** GRAMM: **starke Verben** strong verbs; **sich für jn/etw stark machen** to stand up for sb/sthg. ◇ *adv* - **1.** [intensiv - zuschlagen, schwanken, etw vermuten] strongly; [- regnen] heavily - **2.** [viel] a lot.

Stạ̈rke (*pl* **-n**) *die* - **1.** [gen] strength - **2.** [von Brett, Platte, Papier] thickness - **3.** [für Wäsche] starch; [Speisestärke] cornflour *UK*, cornstarch *US*.

stạ̈rken *vt* - **1.** [kräftigen] to strengthen - **2.** [Wäsche] to starch. ◆ **sich stärken** *ref* to fortify o.s.

Stạ̈rkung (*pl* **-en**) *die* - **1.** [Mahlzeit] refreshment - **2.** [Aufbau] strengthening.

stạrr ◇ *adj* - **1.** [unbeweglich - Glieder, Material] stiff; [- Blick] fixed - **2.** [System, Regeln] fixed. ◇ *adv* [unflexibel] doggedly.

stạrren *vi* - **1.** [sehen] to stare; **auf jn/etw starren** to stare at sb/sthg - **2.** [emporragen]: **aus etw starren** to rise up out of sthg; **vor** ODER **von Dreck starren** to be absolutely filthy.

stạrrsinnig *adj* obstinate.

Stạrt (*pl* **-s** ODER **-e**) *der* - **1.** [gen] start - **2.** [von Flugzeug] takeoff; [von Rakete] launch.

Stạrt|bahn *die* runway.

stạrten (*perf* **hat/ist gestạrtet**) ◇ *vi (ist)* - **1.** [Läufer, Pferd, Rennauto] to start - **2.** [Flugzeug] to take off - **3.** [abreisen] to set off. ◇ *vt (hat)* to start.

Stasi (*abk für* **Staatssicherheit**) *die ODER der* Stasi, *security service in former GDR*.

Statik *die* statics *(U)*.

Station (*pl* **-en**) *die* - **1.** [im Krankenhaus] ward - **2.** [Haltestelle, Halt] stop - **3.** [für Forschung] plant.

stationär *adv*: **stationär behandeln** to treat as an in-patient.

Statịst (*pl* **-en**) *der* extra.

Statịstik (*pl* **-en**) *die* statistics *Pl*.

Statịstin (*pl* **-nen**) *die* extra.

Stativ (*pl* **-e**) *das* tripod.

stạtt ◇ *konj* instead of; **statt früher aufzustehen,...** instead of getting up earlier,... ◇ *präp (+ G)* instead of.

stattdẹssen *adv* instead.

Stạ̈tte (*pl* **-n**) *die geh* place.

stạtt|finden *vi (unreg)* to take place.

stạttlich ◇ *adj* - **1.** [Erscheinung, Größe] imposing - **2.** [Summe, Anwesen] considerable. ◇ *adv* considerably.

Statue [ˈʃtaːtu̯ə, ˈstaːtu̯ə] (*pl* **-n**) *die* statue.

Stau (*pl* **-s** ODER **-e**) *der* - **1.** [von Autos] traffic jam; **im Stau stehen** to be stuck in a traffic jam - **2.** *(ohne pl)* [von Wasser] build-up.

Staub *der* dust; **Staub wischen** to dust; **sich aus dem Staub machen** *fam fig* to make one's getaway.

stauben *vi* to be dusty.

staubig *adj* dusty.

staubsaugen *vt* & *vi* to vacuum.

Staub|sauger (*pl* -) *der* vacuum cleaner.

Stau|damm *der* dam.

Staude (*pl* **-n**) *die* perennial.

stauen *vt* [Wasser] to dam; [Blut] to staunch. ◆ **sich stauen** *ref* - **1.** [Autos] to form a tailback - **2.** [sich ansammeln - Wut, Hitze] to build up; [- Luft] to accumulate.

staunen *vi* to be amazed; **über jn/etw staunen** to be amazed at sb/sthg.

Staunen *das* amazement.

Stau|see *der* reservoir.

Stauung (*pl* **-en**) *die* [von Wasser] damming *(U)*; [von Blut] staunching *(U)*.

Std. *abk für* **Stunde**.

Steak [ʃteːk, steːk] (*pl* **-s**) *das* KÜCHE steak.

stẹchen (*präs* **stịcht**, *prät* **stach**, *perf* **hat gestọchen**) ◇ *vt* - **1.** [verletzen - mit Stachel] to sting; [- mit Nadel] to prick; [- mit Spritze] to stick; [- mit Messer] to stab - **2.** [Spargel] to cut. ◇ *vi* - **1.** [Nadel, Dorn, Stachel] to prick; **mit etw in etw** *(A)* **stechen** to stick sthg in sthg - **2.** [Sonne] to beat down. ◆ **sich stechen** *ref* [sich verletzen] to prick o.s.

stẹchend *adj* - **1.** [Blick] piercing - **2.** [Geruch] pungent - **3.** [Schmerz] stabbing - **4.** [Sonne] burning.

Stẹck|brief *der* description *(of a criminal)*.

Stẹck|dose *die* socket.

stẹcken ◇ *vt* to put; **sich** *(D)* **etw in etw** *(A)* **stecken** to put sthg in sthg; **etw an etw** *(A)* **stecken** to put sthg on sthg; **die Kinder ins Bett stecken** *fam* to put the children to bed. ◇ *vi* [gen] to be; **wo steckst du?** where have you got to?; **hinter etw** *(D)* **stecken** *fam* to be behind sthg.

stẹcken bleiben (*perf* **ist stẹcken geblieben**) *vi (unreg)* to get stuck.

Stẹcker (*pl* -) *der* plug.

Stẹck|nadel *die* pin.

Steg (*pl* **-e**) *der* - **1.** [über Bach, Fluss] footbridge - **2.** [zu Boot] jetty.

stehen (*prät* **stạnd**, *perf* **hat gestạnden**) *vi* - **1.** [aufrecht sein] to stand - **2.** [sich befinden] to be; **die Vase steht auf dem Tisch** the vase is on the table; **du stehst mir im Weg** you're in the way; **vor Schwierigkeiten/einer Wahl stehen** to be faced with difficulties/a choice; **unter Alkohol stehen** to be under the influence (of alcohol); **es steht 15:3** the score is 15-3; **wie steht es mit deiner Gesundheit?** how is your health? - **3.** [geschrieben sein]: **auf dem Schild steht, dass...** the notice says that...; **in der Zeitung steht, dass...** it says in the paper that... - **4.** [Uhr, Motor, Zeiger] to have stopped - **5.** [Kleid, Farbe, Frisur]: **jm stehen** to suit sb; **jm gut/nicht stehen** to suit/not to suit sb - **6.** GRAMM: **mit Akkusativ/Dativ stehen** to take the accusative/dative; **das Substantiv steht im Plural** the noun is in the plural - **7.** *fam* [mögen]: **auf jn stehen** to fancy sb; **auf etw** *(A)* **stehen** to be into sthg - **8.** [stellvertretend]: **für etw stehen** to stand for sthg - **9.** [verantwortlich]: **zu jm/etw stehen** to stand by sb/sthg - **10.** [beurteilend]: **wie stehst du dazu?** what do you think about that?; **alles stehen und liegen lassen** to drop everything; **wie stehts?** *fam* how are things?; **die Arbeit steht mir bis hier** *fam* I've had it up to here with this job. ◆ **sich stehen** *ref fam* [verstehen]: **sich mit jm gut stehen** to get on with sb; **sich mit jm schlecht stehen** not to get on with sb.

Stehen *das*: **im Stehen** standing up.

stehen bleiben (*perf* **ist stehen geblieben**) *vi (unreg)* - **1.** [anhalten] to stop; **wo waren wir stehen geblieben?** where were we?; **die Zeit ist stehen geblieben** time has stood still - **2.** [nach Schlag, Erschütterung] to be left standing - **3.** [Satz] to stay.

stehen lassen (*perf* **hat stehen lassen** ODER **stehen gelassen**) *vt (unreg)* to leave.

Steh|lampe *die* standard lamp.

stehlen (*präs* **stiehlt**, *prät* **stahl**, *perf* **hat gestohlen**) *vt* [entwenden] to steal; **sie kann mir gestohlen bleiben** *fam* she can get lost.

Steiermark *die* Styria.

steif ◇ *adj* stiff; [Sahne] thick. ◇ *adv* stiffly; **Sahne/Eiweiß steif schlagen** to beat cream until thick/egg white until stiff; **steif und fest behaupten** *fig* to swear blind.

Steig|bügel *der* stirrup.

steigen (*prät* **stieg**, *perf* **ist gestiegen**) *vi* - **1.** [hinaufsteigen]: **auf etw** *(A)* **steigen** [auf Leiter, Berg, Baum] to climb sthg; [auf Stuhl, Pferd] to climb onto sthg; [auf Fahrrad, Motorrad] to get on sthg - **2.** [hineinsteigen]: **in etw** *(A)* **steigen** [Zug, Straßenbahn] to get on sthg; [Auto, Taxi] to get into sthg - **3.** [aussteigen]: **aus etw steigen** [Zug, Straßenbahn] to get off sthg; [Auto, Taxi] to get out of sthg - **4.** [absteigen]: **von etw steigen** to get off sthg - **5.** [Flugzeug, Preis, Temperatur, Wasser] to rise; [Nebel] to lift; **einen Drachen steigen lassen** to fly a kite - **6.** [Spannung, Misstrauen] to grow - **7.** *fam* [Fest] to take place; **ein Fest steigen lassen** to have a party.

Steigerung (*pl* **-en**) *die* - **1.** [von Preis, von Dosis] increase - **2.** [von Leistung] improvement - **3.** GRAMM comparison.

steil ◇ *adj* - **1.** [Wand, Berg, Weg] steep - **2.** [Karriere, Aufstieg] rapid. ◇ *adv* - **1.** [senkrecht] steeply - **2.** [schnell] rapidly.

Steil|hang *der* steep slope.

Stein (*pl* **-e**) *der* stone; **bei jm einen Stein im Brett haben** to be in sb's good books.

Stein|bock *der* - **1.** [Tier] ibex - **2.** ASTROL Capricorn; **Steinbock sein** to be a Capricorn.

Stein|bruch *der* quarry.

Steingut *das* earthenware.

steinig *adj* stony.

Stein|kohle *die* coal.

Stein|schlag *der* falling rocks *Pl*.

Stein|zeit *die* Stone Age.

steirisch *adj* Styrian.

Steiß (*pl* **-e**) *der* coccyx.

Stẹlle (*pl* **-n**) *die* - **1.** [Platz] place; [kleine Stelle] patch; [im Text] passage; **an vierter Stelle** in fourth place - **2.** [Arbeitsplatz] job - **3.** [Amt] office - **4.** MATH figure; **eine Zahl mit vier Stellen** a four-figure number; **zwei Stellen nach/hinter dem Komma** two decimal places; **an deiner Stelle** if I were you.

stẹllen *vt* - **1.** [hinstellen] to put - **2.** [aufrecht stellen] to place upright - **3.** [Gerät, Aufgabe] to set; **jm eine Frage stellen** to ask sb a question; **der Wecker auf drei Uhr stellen** to set the alarm clock for three o'clock; **das Radio lauter/leiser stellen** to turn the radio up/down - **4.** [zur Verfügung stellen]: **jm etw stellen** to provide sb with sthg - **5.** [Diagnose, Prognose, Bedingung] to make - **6.** [Forderung, Antrag] to submit - **7.** [Dieb, Täter] to catch - **8.** FOTO to pose - **9.** [konfrontieren mit]: **jn vor etw** *(A)* **stellen** to present sb with sthg; **gut/schlecht gestellt sein** to be well/badly off; **auf sich** *(A)* **(selbst) gestellt sein** to have to fend for o.s. ◆ **sich stellen** *ref* - **1.** [sich hinstellen] to go and stand; **sich auf einen Stuhl stellen** to stand on a chair - **2.** [nicht ausweichen]: **sich einer Sache** *(D)* **stellen** to face sthg - **3.** [ablehnen]: **sich gegen jn/etw stellen** to be against sb/sthg - **4.** [unterstützen]: **sich hinter jn/etw stellen** to back sb/sthg - **5.** [so tun als ob]: **sich krank/schlafend stellen** to pretend to be ill/asleep - **6.** [sich melden] to give o.s. up; **sich gut mit jm stellen** to get on good terms with sb.

Stellen|angebot *das* job offer.

Stellen|gesuch *das* 'situation wanted' advertisement.

stellenweise *adv* in places.

Stellung *(pl* **-en***)* *die* position; **in seiner Stellung als Vorsitzender** in his capacity as chairman; **(zu etw) Stellung nehmen** to comment (on sthg).

Stellungnahme *(pl* **-n***)* *die* statement.

Stell|vertreter, in *der, die* deputy.

stemmen *vt* - **1.** [drücken] to press - **2.** SPORT to lift; **ein Gewicht stemmen** to lift a weight above one's head; **den Körper hoch stemmen** to push one's body up. ◆ **sich stemmen** *ref* [sich drücken] to push o.s. up; **sich gegen etw stemmen** [sich abstemmen] to brace o.s. against sthg; [sich wehren] to resist sthg.

Stempel *(pl* **-***)* *der* [Gerät, Abdruck] stamp; [auf Briefmarke] postmark; [in Schmuckstück] hallmark.

stempeln ◇ *vt* [Stempel anbringen] to stamp; [Briefmarke] to cancel; [Post] to postmark; [Schmuckstück] to hallmark; **jn zu etw stempeln** [klassifizieren] to brand sb sthg. ◇ *vi*: **stempeln gehen** *fam* to be on the dole *UK* ODER welfare *US*.

Stengel *der* = **Stängel**.

Stenografie *(pl* **-n***)*, **Stenographie** *(pl* **-n***)* *die* shorthand.

Stepp|decke *die* quilt.

Steppe *(pl* **-n***)* *die* steppe.

steppen ◇ *vi* [tanzen] to tap dance. ◇ *vt* [nähen] to backstitch.

sterben *(präs* **stirbt**, *prät* **starb**, *perf* **ist gestorben***)* *vi* to die; **an etw** *(D)* **sterben** to die of sthg; **vor etw** *(D)* **sterben** *fam fig* to die of sthg.

sterblich *adj* mortal.

stereo ◇ *adj (unver)* stereo. ◇ *adv* in stereo.

Stereoan|lage *die* stereo (system).

steril *adj* sterile.

sterilisieren *vt* to sterilize.

Stern *(pl* **-e***)* *der* star.

Stern|bild *das* constellation.

Stern|schnuppe *(pl* **-n***)* *die* shooting star.

Stern|warte *(pl* **-n***)* *die* observatory.

Stern|zeichen *das* star sign, sign of the zodiac.

stetig ◇ *adj* steady; [Belästigungen, Wiederholung] constant. ◇ *adv* steadily; [wiederholen] constantly.

stets *adv* always.

Steuer *(pl* **-n** ODER **-***)* ◇ *die* - **1.** *(pl* **-n***)* [Abgabe] tax; **etw von der Steuer absetzen** to claim sthg against tax; **Steuern hinterziehen** to be guilty of tax evasion - **2.** *(pl* **-***)* *fam* [Steuerbehörde]: **die Steuer** the taxman. ◇ *das (pl* **-***)* [von Fahrzeug] (steering) wheel; [von Flugzeug] controls *Pl*; [von Schiff] helm.

Steuer|bord *das* starboard.

Steuerer|klärung *die* tax return.

Steuer|fahndung *die* [Behörde] *body responsible for carrying out investigations into cases of suspected tax evasion*.

Steuer|mann *(pl* **-männer***)* *der* helmsman.

steuern *vt* - **1.** [lenken - Schiff, Fahrzeug] to steer; [- Flugzeug] to fly; [- Spielzeugauto] to control - **2.** [beeinflussen] to guide, to steer - **3.** [organisieren] to organize - **4.** [kontrollieren & TECH] to control.

Steuer|oase *die* tax haven.

Steuer|rad *das* [von Auto] steering wheel; [von Flugzeug] wheel; [von Schiff] wheel, helm.

Steuerung *(pl* **-en***)* *die* - **1.** [Lenken - von Auto, Schiff] steering; [- von Flugzeug] flying; [- von Modellflugzeug] controlling - **2.** [Steuergerät] controls *Pl*.

Steuer|zahler, in *(mpl* **-**, *fpl* **-nen***)* *der, die* taxpayer.

Steward, Stewardess ['stjuːɐt ODER ʃtjuːɐt, 'stjuːɐdɛs ODER ʃtjuɐdɛs] *(mpl* **-s**, *fpl* **-en***)* *der, die* steward (stewardess *die*).

Stich *(pl* **-e***)* *der* - **1.** [Einstich - von Messer] stab; [- von Biene, Wespe] sting; [- von Mücke] bite - **2.** [Färbung] tinge - **3.** [beim Nähen & MED] stitch - **4.** [Schmerz] stabbing pain; [in der Seite] stitch - **5.** [Bemerkung] gibe - **6.** [beim Kartenspiel] trick - **7.** [Bild] engraving; **einen Stich haben** *salopp* [verrückt sein] to be nuts; [ungenießbar werden] to have gone ODER be off; **jn/etw im Stich lassen** [verlassen] to leave sb/sthg; [fallen lassen] to abandon sb/sthg; **wenn mich mein Orientierungssinn nicht im Stich lässt** if my sense of direction isn't deceiving me.

sticheln ◇ *vt* to tease. ◇ *vi* to make snide remarks.

stichhaltig <> *adj* valid; [Beweis] conclusive. <> *adv* validly; [beweisen, widerlegen] conclusively.
Stichlprobe *die* - **1.** [Menge] (random) sample - **2.** [Handlung] spot check.
sticht *präs* ▷ **stechen**.
Stichltag *der* effective date.
Stichlwahl *die* final ballot.
Stichlwort (*pl* **-e** ODER **-wörter**) *das* - **1.** [Notiz] note - **2.** [Eintrag] headword - **3.** [Schlüsselwort] keyword - **4.** *fig* [im Theater]: **das Stichwort geben** to give the cue.
sticken *vt* & *vi* to embroider.
Stickerei (*pl* **-en**) *die* embroidery.
stickig *adj* stuffy.
Sticklstoff *der* nitrogen.
Stieflbruder *der* stepbrother.
Stiefel (*pl* -) *der* boot.
Stieflkind *das* stepchild.
Stieflmutter *die* stepmother.
Stieflmütterchen (*pl* **Stiefmütterchen**) *das* pansy.
Stieflschwester *die* stepsister.
Stieflvater *der* stepfather.
stieg *prät* ▷ **steigen**.
Stiel (*pl* **-e**) *der* - **1.** [von Blume, Frucht, Trinkglas] stem - **2.** [Griff] handle; [von Lutscher, Eis] stick.
Stier (*pl* **-e**) *der* - **1.** [Tier] bull - **2.** [Sternzeichen, Person] Taurus; **Stier sein** to be a Taurus.
stieß *prät* ▷ **stoßen**.
Stift (*pl* **-e**) *der* - **1.** [Schreibutensil] pen; [Bleistift] pencil; [Buntstift] crayon - **2.** *fam* [Lehrling] *name given to apprentices during their first year* - **3.** TECH [aus Holz] peg; [aus Metall] pin.
stiften *vt* - **1.** [gründen] to found - **2.** [spenden] to donate; [ausgeben] to pay for - **3.** [hervorrufen - Unruhe, Aufregung] to cause - **4.** [spendieren] to buy.
Stiftung (*pl* **-en**) *die* - **1.** [Institution] foundation - **2.** [Schenkung] donation.
Stil (*pl* **-e**) *der* style; **in diesem Stil kann es nicht weitergehen!** it can't go on like this!; **im großen Stil** on a grand scale.
still <> *adj* - **1.** [ruhig, lautlos, stressfrei] quiet; **im Stillen** secretly - **2.** [bewegungslos] still - **3.** [ohne Worte - Protest, Gebet, Leiden] silent - **4.** [heimlich] secret. <> *adv* - **1.** [ruhig, lautlos, stressfrei] quietly - **2.** [bewegungslos] still; **sie stand still da** she was standing still - **3.** [ohne Worte - protestieren, beten, leiden] silently.
Stille *die* - **1.** [Ruhe] quiet - **2.** [Schweigen] silence; **in aller Stille heiraten** to get married in secret.
Stilleben *das* = **Stillleben**.
stillegen *vt* = **stilllegen**.
stillen <> *vt* - **1.** [die Brust geben] to breastfeed - **2.** [Schmerz] to stop - **3.** [Hunger, Bedürfnis] to satisfy; [Durst] to quench. <> *vi* to breastfeed.

Stille Ozean *der*: **der Stille Ozean** the Pacific (Ocean).
stillgestanden *pp* ▷ **stillstehen**.
stilllhalten *vi (unreg)* [sich nicht wehren] to offer no resistance.
still halten *vt* & *vi (unreg)* to keep still.
Stillleben (*pl* -) *das* still life.
stilllegen *vt* to close down.
stillschweigend <> *adj* tacit. <> *adv* tacitly.
stilllsitzen *vi (unreg)* [ruhig sein] to sit still.
Stilllstand *der* stopping; [von Maschine] stoppage; [von Verhandlung] deadlock; [von Entwicklung] halt; **zum Stillstand kommen** [Verkehr, Produktion] to come to a standstill; [Verhandlungen] to reach a deadlock; [Blutungen] to stop.
stilllstehen *vi (unreg)* - **1.** [Bewegung stoppen] to stand still; **stillgestanden!** MIL attention! - **2.** [Telefon]: **das Telefon stand keine Minute still** the phone never stopped ringing - **3.** [stillliegen - Verkehr, Produktion] to be at a standstill; [- Uhr, Maschine] to have stopped.
Stimmlband (*pl* **-bänder**) *das* vocal cord.
stimmberechtigt *adj* entitled to vote.
Stimmlbruch *der*: **er ist im Stimmbruch** his voice is breaking.
Stimme (*pl* **-n**) *die* - **1.** [gen] voice - **2.** [Wählerstimme] vote; **seine Stimme abgeben** to vote; **sich der Stimme enthalten** to abstain - **3.** MUS part.
stimmen <> *vi* - **1.** [richtig sein] to be right ODER correct; [Gerücht, Aussage] to be true ODER correct; **das stimmt nicht!** that's not true! - **2.** [wählen]: **für/gegen jn/etw stimmen** to vote for/against sb/sthg - **3.** [übereinstimmen] to be right; **stimmt so!** keep the change! <> *vt* MUS to tune.
Stimmlgabel *die* tuning fork.
stimmhaft *adj* voiced.
Stimmllage *die* voice; [beim Singen] register.
stimmlos *adj* voiceless, unvoiced.
Stimmlrecht *das* right to vote.
Stimmung (*pl* **-en**) *die* - **1.** [Laune] mood; **guter/schlechter Stimmung sein** to be in a good/bad mood - **2.** [Atmosphäre] atmosphere.
Stimmlzettel *der* ballot paper.
stinken (*prät* **stank**, *perf* **hat gestunken**) *vi* - **1.** *abw* [schlecht riechen]: **(nach etw) stinken** to stink (of sthg) - **2.** *salopp* [reichen]: **mir stinkt es** I'm fed up to the back teeth.
Stipendium (*pl* **-dien**) *das* [als Unterstützung] grant; [als Auszeichnung] scholarship.
stirbt *präs* ▷ **sterben**.
Stirn (*pl* **-en**) *die* forehead.
stöbern *vi* to rummage (around).
stochern *vi*: **(mit etw) in etw** *(A)* **stochern** to poke at sthg (with sthg); **im Essen stochern** to pick at one's food.

Stock (*pl* **Stöcke** ODER **-s**) *der* - **1.** *(pl Stöcke)* [Stab] stick; [von Dirigent] baton - **2.** *(pl -s)* [Stockwerk] floor, storey.

stockdunkel *adj* pitch-dark.

stocken *vi* [zum Stillstand kommen - Verkehr] to be held up; [- Gespräch] to falter; [- Produktion] to be interrupted; [- Verhandlungen] to break off.

stockend ◇ *adj* faltering; **es herrscht stockender Verkehr** traffic is moving slowly. ◇ *adv* falteringly.

Stockung (*pl* **-en**) *die* [Stillstand - von Verkehr] hold-up; [- von Verhandlungen] break; [- von Produktion] interruption.

Stock|werk *das* floor, storey.

Stoff (*pl* **-e**) *der* - **1.** [Tuch] material - **2.** [Inhalt] subject matter; [zu Roman, Film] material - **3.** [Substanz] substance.

Stoff|wechsel *der* metabolism.

stöhnen *vi* to groan.

Stollen (*pl* -) *der* - **1.** [Gang] gallery, tunnel - **2.** [Gebäck] stollen, *sweet bread loaf made with dried fruit and marzipan, eaten at Christmas.*

stolpern (*perf* **ist gestolpert**) *vi* to stumble; **über etw** *(A)* **stolpern** to trip over sthg.

stolz ◇ *adj* proud; **auf jn/etw stolz sein** to be proud of sb/sthg. ◇ *adv* proudly.

Stolz *der* pride.

stopfen ◇ *vt* - **1.** [ausbessern] to darn - **2.** [hineinstopfen] to stuff - **3.** [zustopfen] to plug - **4.** [füllen - Pfeife] to fill; [- Geflügel] to stuff. ◇ *vi* [Stuhlgang erschweren] to cause constipation.

stopp *interj* [halt] stop!

stoppen ◇ *vt* - **1.** [anhalten] to stop - **2.** [messen - Person, Lauf] to time. ◇ *vi* [anhalten] to stop.

Stopp|schild *das* stop sign.

Stopp|uhr *die* stopwatch.

Stöpsel (*pl* -) *der* [Gegenstand - von Becken] plug; [- von Flasche] stopper.

Storch (*pl* **Störche**) *der* stork.

stören ◇ *vt* - **1.** [belästigen] to disturb; [unterbrechen] to interrupt - **2.** [missfallen] to bother - **3.** [beeinträchtigen - Verhältnis] to spoil; [- Radioempfang, Fernsehempfang] to interfere with. ◇ *vi* [belästigend sein]: **darf ich mal kurz stören?** may I disturb you for a moment?; **'bitte nicht stören!'** 'do not disturb!'

Störung (*pl* **-en**) *die* - **1.** [Belästigung] disturbance; [von Zeremonie] disruption - **2.** [Funktionsstörung - von Gerät] fault; [- von Organ] disorder.

Stoß (*pl* **Stöße**) *der* - **1.** [Schlag] push, shove; [mit dem Fuß] kick; [in Auto, Schiff, Zug] jolt - **2.** [Stapel] pile.

stoßen (*präs* **stößt**, *prät* **stieß**, *perf* **hat/ist gestoßen**) ◇ *vt (hat)* - **1.** [schubsen] to push; [mit der Faust] to punch; [mit dem Fuß] to kick - **2.** SPORT [Kugel] to put; [Gewichte] to press - **3.** [aufmerksam machen]: **jn auf etw** *(A)* **stoßen** to point sthg out to sb. ◇ *vi* - **1.** *(ist)* [berühren]: **an etw** *(A)* **stoßen** to bang sthg; **gegen etw** *(A)* **stoßen** to bang into sthg; [Fahrzeug] to crash into sthg - **2.** *(ist)* [angrenzen]: **an etw** *(A)* **stoßen** [Grundstück] to border on sthg; [Zimmer] to be next to sthg - **3.** *(ist)* [finden]: **auf jn/etw stoßen** to come across sb/sthg; **auf Erdöl stoßen** to strike oil - **4.** *(ist)* [auf Reaktion]: **auf etw** *(A)* **stoßen** to meet with sthg - **5.** *(ist)* [sich treffen mit]: **zu jm stoßen** to meet up with sb. ◆ **sich stoßen** *ref* - **1.** [sich wehtun] to bang o.s. - **2.** [nicht mögen]: **sich an etw** *(D)* **stoßen** to take exception to sthg.

stößt *präs* ▷ **stoßen**.

stottern *vi* [sprechen] to stutter, to stammer.

Str. (*abk für* **Straße**) St.

Strafe (*pl* **-n**) *die* - **1.** [Bestrafung] punishment - **2.** [Geldbuße] fine - **3.** [in Gefängnis] sentence.

strafen *vt* to punish.

Straf|zettel *der* ticket.

Strahl (*pl* **-en**) *der* - **1.** [Wasserstrahl] jet - **2.** [Lichtstrahl] ray; [von Scheinwerfer, Licht, Laser] beam. ◆ **Strahlen** *Pl* [Energiewellen] rays.

strahlen *vi* - **1.** [lachen] to beam - **2.** [leuchten] to shine - **3.** [Strahlen abgeben] to radiate - **4.** [glänzen] to sparkle.

Strähne (*pl* **-n**) *die* strand.

Strand (*pl* **Strände**) *der* beach; **am Strand** on the beach.

Straße (*pl* **-n**) *die* - **1.** [in Stadt] street - **2.** [Landstraße] road; **auf der Straße sitzen** *fam* [arbeitslos sein] to be out of work; [ohne Wohnung sein] to be on the streets; **auf die Straße gehen** [demonstrieren] to take to the streets; [anschaffen gehen] to walk the streets. ◆ **auf offener Straße** *adv* in public.

Straßen|bahn *die* tram *UK*, streetcar *US*.

Straßen|karte *die* road map.

Straßen|schild *das* street sign.

Strategie (*pl* **-n**) *die* strategy.

sträuben ◆ **sich sträuben** *ref* - **1.** [Federn] to become ruffled; [Fell] to bristle - **2.** [sich wehren]: **sich gegen etw sträuben** to resist sthg.

Strauch (*pl* **Sträucher**) *der* bush.

Strauß (*pl* **Sträuße** ODER **-e**) *der* - **1.** *(pl Sträuße)* [Blumen] bunch of flowers - **2.** *(pl Strauße)* [Vogel] ostrich.

streben (*perf* **hat/ist gestrebt**) *vi (hat)* [trachten]: **nach etw streben** to strive for sthg.

Streber, in (*mpl* -, *fpl* **-nen**) *der, die abw* swot *UK*, grind *US*.

Strecke (*pl* **-n**) *die* - **1.** [Weg] route; **diese Strecke bin ich noch nie gefahren** I've never been this way before - **2.** [Entfernung] distance

- 3. [von Straße] stretch - 4. [von Eisenbahn] line; [von Schienen] track; **auf offener Strecke** between stations - 5. MATH (straight) line.

strecken *vt* - 1. [ausstrecken] to stretch - 2. [Hals] to crane - 3. [verdünnen] to thin down; [Droge] to cut. ◆ **sich strecken** *ref* - 1. [sich recken] to stretch - 2. [sich hinlegen] to stretch out.

streckenweise *adv* in places.

Streich (*pl* -e) *der* [zum Ärgern] trick; **jm einen Streich spielen** *eigtl* & *fig* to play a trick on sb.

streicheln ◇ *vt* to stroke. ◇ *vi*: **über etw** *(A)* **streicheln** to stroke sthg.

streichen (*prät* **strich**, *perf* **hat/ist gestrichen**) ◇ *vt (hat)* - 1. [mit Farbe] to paint; **'frisch gestrichen'** 'wet paint' - 2. [Satz, Passage] to delete; **etw von einer Liste streichen** to cross sthg off a list - 3. [schmieren] to spread - 4. [Subvention, Auftrag] to cancel. ◇ *vi* - 1. *(hat)*: **sich** *(D)* **über den Kopf streichen** to stroke one's head - 2. *(hat)* [mit Farbe] to paint.

Streicher, in (*mpl* -, *fpl* -nen) *der, die*: **die Streicher** the strings.

Streich|holz *das* match.

Streich|instrument *das* stringed instrument.

Streichung (*pl* -en) *die* - 1. [von Subvention, Auftrag] cancellation; **Streichungen** [an Etat] cuts - 2. [im Text] deletion.

Streife (*pl* -n) *die* patrol.

streifen (*perf* **hat/ist gestreift**) *vt (hat)* - 1. [berühren] to brush against - 2. [ziehen]: **etw über etw** *(A)* **streifen** to pull sthg over sthg; **etw von etw streifen** to pull sthg off sthg - 3. [Thema] to touch on.

Streifen (*pl* -) *der* - 1. [Stück, Band] strip - 2. [Strich] stripe; [auf Fahrbahn] line.

Streifen|wagen *der* patrol car.

Streik (*pl* -s) *der* strike; **in (den) Streik treten** to go on strike.

streiken *vi* - 1. [im Streik stehen] to strike - 2. [Motor, Maschine] to pack up.

Streit *der* argument; **Streit mit jm haben** to argue with sb.

streiten (*prät* **stritt**, *perf* **hat gestritten**) *vi* - 1. [sich auseinander setzen]: **(über etw** *(A)***) streiten** to argue (about sthg) - 2. *geh* [kämpfen]: **gegen/für etw streiten** to fight against/for sthg. ◆ **sich streiten** *ref*: **sich (mit jm/um etw) streiten** to argue (with sb/about sthg).

Streit|frage *die* contentious issue.

Streitigkeiten *Pl* disputes.

Streitkräfte *Pl* armed forces.

streitsüchtig *adj* quarrelsome.

streng ◇ *adj* - 1. [Eltern, Kontrolle, Diät, Regel] strict; [Blick] stern; [Maßnahme] stringent - 2. [Geruch, Geschmack] pungent - 3. [Gesicht, Frisur, Winter] severe. ◇ *adv* - 1. [erziehen, verbieten, einhalten] strictly; [überwachen] closely; [ansehen] sternly - 2. [durchdringend]: **streng riechen** to smell pungent.

Strenge *die* [von Erziehung, Kontrolle, Gesetz] strictness; [von Blick] sternness; [von Maßnahme] stringency.

streng genommen *adv* strictly speaking.

Stress *der* stress; **mach keinen Stress!** *fam* stay cool!

Streu *die* [aus Stroh] straw.

streuen ◇ *vt* [Salz, Gewürze] to sprinkle; [Dünger, Stroh, Gerüchte] to spread; [Futter, Samen] to scatter. ◇ *vi* [mit Sand] to grit; [mit Salz] to put down salt.

streunen (*perf* **hat/ist gestreunt**) *vi* - 1. [irgendwo] to roam around; [Hund, Katze] to stray - 2. *(ist)* [irgendwohin] to roam.

Streusel (*pl* -) *der ODER das* crumble topping.

strich *prät* ▷ **streichen**.

Strich (*pl* -e) *der* - 1. [Linie] line; [Gedankenstrich] dash; [von Pinsel] stroke - 2. [Streichen] stroke - 3. *fam* [Prostitution] prostitution; **auf den Strich gehen** *fam* to walk the streets; **jm einen Strich durch die Rechnung machen** to wreck sb's plans. ◆ **unter dem Strich** *adv* at the end of the day.

Strick (*pl* -e) *der* rope.

stricken *vt* & *vi* to knit.

Strick|jacke *die* cardigan.

Strick|leiter *die* rope ladder.

Strick|nadel *die* knitting needle.

Strickzeug *das (ohne pl)* [Handarbeit] knitting.

striegeln *vt* to groom.

Striemen (*pl* -) *der* weal.

Striptease ['ʃtrɪptiːs, 'strɪptiːs] *der ODER das* striptease.

stritt *prät* ▷ **streiten**.

strittig *adj* contentious.

Stroh *das* straw.

Stroh|dach *das* thatched roof.

Strolch (*pl* -e) *der* - 1. *abw* [Mann] ruffian - 2. *fam hum* [Schlingel] rascal.

Strom (*pl* **Ströme**) *der* - 1. [elektrisch] electricity - 2. [Fluss] river - 3. [Strömung] current - 4. [Menge] stream; **es regnet** ODER **gießt in Strömen** it's pouring down; **gegen den Strom schwimmen** to swim against the tide.

stromabwärts *adv* downstream.

stromaufwärts *adv* upstream.

Stromaus|fall *der* power failure.

strömen (*perf* **ist geströmt**) *vi* to stream.

Strom|kreis *der* (electrical) circuit.

Strom|stärke *die* current strength.

Strömung (*pl* -en) *die* - 1. [Strom] current - 2. [Bewegung] current of thought.

Strom|zähler *der* electricity meter.

Strophe (*pl* **-n**) *die* verse.

strotzen *vi*: **vor Gesundheit strotzen** to be bursting with health; **vor Dreck strotzen** to be filthy.

Strudel (*pl* -) *der* - **1.** [Wirbel] whirlpool - **2.** [Kuchen] strudel.

Struktur (*pl* **-en**) *die* - **1.** [von Systemen] structure - **2.** [von Material] texture.

Strumpf (*pl* **Strümpfe**) *der* - **1.** [beinlang] stocking - **2.** [Socke] sock.

Strumpf|hose *die* tights *Pl UK*, pantyhose *(U) US*.

struppig *adj* shaggy.

Stube (*pl* **-n**) *die* - **1.** *fam* [Wohnzimmer] living room - **2.** [Raum] room.

stubenrein *adj* house-trained.

Stück (*pl* **-e**) *das* [gen] piece; [von Butter, Zucker] lump.

stückeln *vi* to add patches.

Student (*pl* **-en**) *der* student.

Studentenwohn|heim *das* hall of residence.

Studentin (*pl* **-nen**) *die* student.

Studie ['ʃtuːdi̯ə] (*pl* **-n**) *die* study.

Studienabschluss (*pl* **-schlüsse**) *der* degree.

Studien|fach *das* subject.

Studiengang (*pl* **-gänge**) *der* course (of study).

Studien|platz *der* university/college place.

Studien|rat *der secondary school teacher*.

Studien|rätin *die secondary school teacher*.

studieren [ʃtu'diːrən] *vt* & *vi* to study.

Studio (*pl* **-s**) *das* studio.

Studium ['ʃtuːdi̯ʊm] (*pl* **Studien**) *das* - **1.** [gen] study - **2.** *(ohne pl)* [Ausbildung] studies *Pl*.

Stufe (*pl* **-n**) *die* - **1.** [von Treppen] step; **'Vorsicht Stufe!'** 'mind the step!' - **2.** [Stand] stage - **3.** [in einer Hierarchie] level - **4.** [Schaltstufe] setting - **5.** [Abstufung] degree.

Stuhl (*pl* **Stühle**) *der* [Sitzmöbel] chair.

Stuhlgang *der (ohne pl)* stool.

stülpen *vt*: **etw nach außen stülpen** to turn sthg inside out; **etw auf/über etw** *(A)* **stülpen** to put sthg onto/over sthg.

stumm ◇ *adj* - **1.** [sprechunfähig] dumb - **2.** [schweigend] silent. ◇ *adv* - **1.** [sprechunfähig] dumbly - **2.** [schweigend] silently.

Stummel (*pl* -) *der* [von Arm, Bein, Schwanz] stump; [von Zigarette] butt; [von Kerze, Bleistift] stub.

Stumm|film *der* silent movie.

Stümper (*pl* -) *der abw* bungler.

Stümperin (*pl* **-nen**) *die abw* bungler.

stumpf ◇ *adj* - **1.** [Messer, Spitze] blunt - **2.** [Fell, Haar, Lack] dull - **3.** [Person, Ausdruck] apathetic - **4.** MATH obtuse. ◇ *adv* - **1.** [leben, blicken] apathetically - **2.** [nicht scharf, nicht spitz] bluntly - **3.** [glanzlos] dully.

Stumpf (*pl* **Stümpfe**) *der* stump; [von Kerze] stub.

Stumpfsinn *der* - **1.** [Monotonie] monotony - **2.** [geistige Abwesenheit] apathy.

Stunde (*pl* **-n**) *die* - **1.** [Zeiteinheit] hour - **2.** [Unterrichtsstunde] lesson. ◆ **zu später Stunde** *adv geh* at a late hour.

stunden *vt*: **jm eine Zahlung stunden** to give sb longer to make a payment.

Stunden|geschwindigkeit *die*: **eine Stundengeschwindigkeit von 100 km** a speed of 100 km/h.

Stundenkilo|meter *Pl* kilometres per hour.

stundenlang ◇ *adj* lasting for hours; **nach stundenlangem Warten** after waiting for hours. ◇ *adv* for hours.

Stunden|lohn *der* hourly rate.

Stunden|plan *der* timetable.

Stunden|zeiger *der* hour hand.

stündlich ◇ *adv* - **1.** [jede Stunde] hourly, once an hour - **2.** [jeden Augenblick] at any moment. ◇ *adj* [jede Stunde] hourly.

Stups (*pl* **-e**) *der* nudge.

Stups|nase *die* snub nose.

stur *abw* ◇ *adj* pigheaded. ◇ *adv* pigheadedly; **stur geradeaus fahren** to drive straight on.

Sturm (*pl* **Stürme**) *der* - **1.** [Unwetter] storm - **2.** [von Begeisterung, Entrüstung] wave - **3.** [Andrang, Angriff] assault; **der Sturm auf die Bastille** the storming of the Bastille - **4.** [beim Fußball] forward line.

stürmen (*perf* **hat/ist gestürmt**) ◇ *vt (hat)* - **1.** [Geschäfte, Büfett] to besiege - **2.** [Festung, Stellung] to storm. ◇ *vi* - **1.** *(ist)* [rennen] to rush - **2.** *(hat)* [beim Fußball] to attack - **3.** *(hat)* [Sturm herrschen]: **es stürmt** it's blowing a gale.

Stürmer, in (*mpl* -, *fpl* **-nen**) *der, die* forward.

Sturm|flut *die* storm tide.

stürmisch ◇ *adj* - **1.** [windig] stormy - **2.** [Applaus] tumultuous; [Begeisterung] wild; [Protest] vehement - **3.** [leidenschaftlich] passionate. ◇ *adv* - **1.** [applaudieren] tumultuously - **2.** [leidenschaftlich] passionately - **3.** [wehen] stormily; [regnen] violently.

Sturz (*pl* **Stürze**) *der* fall.

stürzen (*perf* **hat/ist gestürzt**) ◇ *vi (ist)* - **1.** [fallen, zurückgehen] to fall - **2.** [eilen] to rush. ◇ *vt (hat)* - **1.** [Regierung, Herrscher] to bring down; [mit Gewalt] to overthrow - **2.** [Kuchen, Pudding] to turn out - **3.** [stoßen] to hurl. ◆ **sich stürzen** *ref* - **1.** [springen] to jump - **2.** [herfallen über]: **sich auf jn/etw stürzen** [bestürmen] to fall on sb/sthg; [angreifen] to pounce on sb/sthg - **3.** [sich begeben]: **sich in etw** *(A)* **stürzen** [springen] to plunge into sthg; [sich widmen] to throw o.s. into sthg.

Sturz|helm *der* crash helmet.

Stute (*pl* **-n**) *die* mare.

Stuttgart *nt* Stuttgart.

Stütze (*pl* **-n**) *die* [Vorrichtung] prop, support; [für Kopf, Rücken, Füße] rest.

stutzen ◇ *vt* [Bart, Haare, Hecke] to trim; [Pflanze, Baum] to cut back. ◇ *vi* [innehalten] to stop short.

stützen *vt* to support; **den Kopf in die Hände stützen** to prop one's head on one's hands; **die Ellbogen auf den Tisch stützen** to prop one's elbows on the table. ◆ **sich stützen** *ref*: **sich auf jn/etw stützen** [auf Stock, Möbel] to lean on sb/sthg; [auf Vermutung, Beweis] to be based on sb/sthg.

stutzig *adj*: **stutzig werden** to become suspicious.

Stütz|punkt *der* base.

Styropor® *das* polystyrene.

Subjekt (*pl* **-e**) *das* GRAMM subject.

subjektiv ◇ *adj* subjective. ◇ *adv* subjectively.

Substantiv (*pl* **-e**) *das* GRAMM noun.

Substanz (*pl* **-en**) *die* substance; **das geht an die Substanz** it wears you down.

subtrahieren *vt* & *vi* to subtract.

subventionieren [zʊpvɛntsi̯o'niːrən] *vt* to subsidize.

Suche (*pl* **-n**) *die* search; **auf der Suche nach jm/etw sein** to be looking for sb/sthg; [angestrengt] to be searching for sb/sthg; **sich auf die Suche (nach jm/etw) machen** to start looking (for sb/sthg).

suchen ◇ *vt* - **1.** [finden wollen] to look for; [angestrengt] to search for; **er/es hat hier nichts zu suchen** *fam* he/it has no business being here - **2.** [sich wünschen] to seek. ◇ *vi*: **(nach jm/etw) suchen** to look (for sb/sthg); [angestrengt] to search (for sb/sthg).

Such|maschine *die* EDV search engine.

Sucht (*pl* **Süchte**) *die* addiction.

süchtig *adj*: **(nach etw) süchtig sein** to be addicted (to sthg); **süchtig machen** to be addictive.

Such|trupp *der* search party.

Süd|afrika *nt* South Africa.

südafrikanisch *adj* South African.

Süd|amerika *nt* South America.

Süd|amerikaner, in *der, die* South American.

südamerikanisch *adj* South American.

süddeutsch *adj* South German.

Süden *der* south; **nach Süden** south; **im Süden** in the south.

Süd|europa *nt* Southern Europe.

Süd|frucht *die ordinary citrus fruits and certain tropical fruits, e.g. bananas.*

Süd|korea *nt* South Korea.

südländisch *adj* Mediterranean.

südlich ◇ *adj* [Gegend] southern; [Richtung, Wind] southerly. ◇ *präp*: **südlich einer Sache** *(G)* ODER **von etw** (to the) south of sthg.

Südosten *der* south-east.

Süd|pol *der* - **1.** GEOGR South Pole - **2.** PHYS south pole.

Süd|see *die*: **die Südsee** the South Seas *Pl.*

Süd|tirol *nt* South Tyrol.

Süd|westen *der* south-west.

Sues|kanal ['zuːɛskanaːl] *der* Suez Canal.

süffig *adj* very drinkable.

Sulfat (*pl* **-e**) *das* CHEM sulphate.

Sultan (*pl* **-e**) *der* sultan.

Sultanine (*pl* **-n**) *die* sultana.

Sülze (*pl* **-n**) *die* brawn *(U) UK*, headcheese *(U) US*.

Summe (*pl* **-n**) *die* sum.

summen (*perf* **hat/ist gesummt**) ◇ *vi (hat, ist)* to buzz. ◇ *vt (hat)* to hum.

summieren *vt* to add. ◆ **sich summieren** *ref* to add up.

Sumpf (*pl* **Sümpfe**) *der* [Sumpfgelände] marsh; [in Tropen] swamp.

sumpfig *adj* marshy.

Sünde (*pl* **-n**) *die* sin.

Sünden|bock *der* scapegoat.

super *fam* ◇ *adj (unver)* great. ◇ *adv* really well. ◇ *interj* great!

Super *das* four-star (petrol) *UK*, premium (gas) *US*.

Superlativ (*pl* **-e**) *der* GRAMM superlative.

Super|markt *der* supermarket.

Suppe (*pl* **-n**) *die* - **1.** [Essen] soup; **jm die Suppe versalzen** *fam fig* to put a spoke in sb's wheel - **2.** *fam* [Dunst, Nebel] pea souper.

Suppen|schüssel *die* tureen.

Suppen|teller *der* soup plate.

Suppen|würfel *der* stock cube.

Surf|brett ['sœːɐ̯fbrɛt] *das* - **1.** [zum Wellensurfen] surfboard - **2.** [zum Windsurfen] sailboard.

surfen ['sœːɐ̯fn̩] (*perf* **hat/ist gesurft**) *vi* - **1.** [gen & EDV] to surf - **2.** [mit Segel] to windsurf.

Surrealismus *der* surrealism.

surren (*perf* **hat/ist gesurrt**) *vi* - **1.** *(ist)* [Pfeil] to whizz - **2.** *(hat)* [Maschine] to whirr; [Insekt] to buzz.

suspekt *adj* suspicious; **jm suspekt sein** to make sb suspicious.

süß <> *adj* sweet. <> *adv*: **süß schmecken/aussehen** to taste/look sweet; **träume süß!** sweet dreams!

süßen *vt* to sweeten.

Süßigkeiten *Pl* sweets *UK*, candy *(U) US*.

süßlich <> *adj* - **1.** [süß] sweetish - **2.** [übertrieben freundlich] syrupy. <> *adv* - **1.** [süß]: **süßlich schmecken** to have a sweetish taste - **2.** [übertrieben freundlich] in a sickly-sweet way.

süßsauer <> *adj* sweet and sour. <> *adv*: **süßsauer schmecken** to have a sweet and sour taste.

Süß|speise *die* dessert.

Süß|wasser *das* fresh water.

SVP [ɛsfau'peː] (*abk für* **Schweizer Volkspartei**) *die (ohne pl) political party in Switzerland.*

SW (*abk für* **Südwest**) *abk für* **SW**.

Symbol (*pl* **-e**) *das* - **1.** [Zeichen] symbol - **2.** EDV [Icon] icon.

symbolisch <> *adj* symbolic. <> *adv* symbolically.

Symmetrie (*pl* **-n**) *die* symmetry.

symmetrisch <> *adj* symmetrical. <> *adv* symmetrically.

Sympathie (*pl* **-n**) *die* [Zuneigung] liking *(U)*; **sich** *(D)* **viele Sympathien verscherzen** to lose a lot of sympathy.

sympathisch <> *adj* nice; **sie ist mir sympathisch** I like her. <> *adv* nicely.

sympathisieren *vi*: **mit jm sympathisieren** to sympathize with sb.

Symphonie = **Sinfonie**.

Symphoniker = **Sinfoniker**.

Symptom (*pl* **-e**) *das* - **1.** MED symptom - **2.** [Anzeichen] sign.

Synagoge (*pl* **-n**) *die* synagogue.

synchron <> *adj* synchronous. <> *adv* synchronously.

synchronisieren *vt* FILM [Stimme] to dub; [Bewegungen, Abläufe] to synchronize.

Synonym (*pl* **-e**) *das* synonym.

Syntax (*pl* **-en**) *die* syntax.

Synthese (*pl* **-n**) *die*: **die Synthese aus etw** the synthesis of sthg.

synthetisch <> *adj* synthetic. <> *adv* synthetically.

Syrien *nt* Syria.

System [zys'teːm] (*pl* **-e**) *das* system.

systematisch <> *adj* systematic. <> *adv* systematically.

Szene (*pl* **-n**) *die* - **1.** [im Film, Theater] scene - **2.** [Vorfall] scene; **(jm) eine Szene machen** to make a scene (in front of sb) - **3.** [Milieu] scene.

T

t (*pl* **t** ODER **-s**), **T** (*pl* **T** ODER **-s**) [teː] *das* t, T. ◆ **t** *abk für* **Tonne**.

Tabak (*pl* **-e**), **Tabak** (*pl* **-e**) *der* tobacco *(U)*.

Tabak|laden *der* tobacconist's.

tabellarisch <> *adj* tabular. <> *adv* in tabular form.

Tabelle (*pl* **-n**) *die* - **1.** [Liste] table - **2.** SPORT (league) table.

Tablett (*pl* **-s** ODER **-e**) *das* tray.

Tablette (*pl* **-n**) *die* tablet, pill.

tabu *adj (unver)*: **etw ist tabu** sthg is taboo.

Tabu (*pl* **-s**) *das* taboo.

Tachometer (*pl* -) *der* speedometer.

Tadel (*pl* -) *der geh* rebuke.

tadellos <> *adj* impeccable. <> *adv* impeccably.

tadeln *vt* to rebuke.

Tafel (*pl* **-n**) *die* - **1.** [Schreibtafel] blackboard - **2.** *geh* [Tisch] table - **3.** [Stück]: **eine Tafel Schokolade** a bar of chocolate.

Tafel|wasser (*pl* **-wässer**) *das* mineral water.

Tag (*pl* **-e**) *der* - **1.** [24 Stunden] day; **in vierzehn Tagen** in a fortnight - **2.** [in seinem Verlauf] day; **am helllichtenTag** in broad daylight; **über/unter Tag(e)** above/below ground. ◆ **eines Tages** *adv* [irgendwann] one day. ◆ **guten Tag** *interj* hello!; [am Morgen] good morning!; [am Nachmittag] good afternoon! ◆ **Tag für Tag** *adv* [immer] day after day. ◆ **von Tag zu Tag** *adv* [immer mehr] day by day. ◆ **Tage** *Pl* - **1.** [Zeit] days; **js Tage sind gezählt** [muss sterben/weggehen] sb's days are numbered - **2.** *fam* [Periode] period *(sg)*; **sie hat/bekommt ihre Tage** *fam* she's got her period; *siehe auch* **zutage**.

tagaus *adv*: **tagaus, tagein** day in, day out.

Tag der Deutschen Einheit *der* Day of German Unity.

Tage|buch *das* diary.

tagelang <> *adj* lasting for days; **tagelanger Regen** days of rain. <> *adv* for days.

tagen *vi* - **1.** [Sitzung haben - gen] to meet; [- Gericht] to be in session - **2.** *geh* [hell werden]: **es tagt** day is breaking.

Tagesab|lauf *der* day.

Tagesan|bruch *der* dawn.

Tages|bedarf *der (ohne pl)* daily requirement.

Tages|fahrt *die* day trip.

Tages|gericht *das* dish of the day.

Tages|geschehen *das* day's events *Pl*.

Tages|karte *die* day ticket.

Tages|licht *das* daylight; **etw kommt ans Tageslicht** sthg comes to light.

Tages|ordnung *die* agenda.

Tages|schau *die* news.

Tages|zeit *die* time of day.

Tages|zeitung *die* daily newspaper.

täglich ◇ *adj* daily. ◇ *adv* every day; **dreimal täglich** three times a day.

tagsüber *adv* during the day.

tagtäglich *adj* daily.

Tagung (*pl* **-en**) *die* conference.

Taifun (*pl* **-e**) *der* typhoon.

Taille ['taljə] (*pl* **-n**) *die* waist.

tailliert [ta'jiːɐt] *adj* fitted.

Taiwan *nt* Taiwan.

Tạkt (*pl* **-e**) *der* - **1.** [musikalische Einheit] bar - **2.** *(ohne pl)* [Feingefühl] tact - **3.** *(ohne pl)* [Rhythmus] time; **jn aus dem Takt bringen** to put sb off.

Tạkt|gefühl *das* tact.

Tạktik (*pl* **-en**) *die* tactics *Pl*.

tạktisch ◇ *adj* [klug] tactical. ◇ *adv* tactically; **taktisch klug vorgehen** to use clever tactics.

tạktlos ◇ *adj* tactless. ◇ *adv* tactlessly.

Tạktlosigkeit (*pl* **-en**) *die* tactlessness.

Tạkt|stock *der* baton.

tạktvoll ◇ *adj* tactful. ◇ *adv* tactfully.

Tal (*pl* **Täler**) *das* valley.

Talẹnt (*pl* **-e**) *das* talent.

talentiert ◇ *adj* talented. ◇ *adv* with talent.

Tạlg (*pl* **-e**) *der* tallow; [von Menschen] sebum.

Talisman (*pl* **-e**) *der* talisman.

Talkshow ['tɔːkʃoː] (*pl* **-s**) *die* talk show.

Tampon ['tampɔn, tam'poːn] (*pl* **-s**) *der* tampon.

Tạndem (*pl* **-s**) *das* tandem.

Tạng (*pl* **-e**) *der* seaweed *(U)*.

Tangẹnte (*pl* **-n**) *die* MATH tangent.

Tạngo (*pl* **-s**) *der* tango.

Tạnk (*pl* **-s**) *der* tank.

Tạnk|deckel *der* fuel cap, petrol cap *UK*.

tạnken ◇ *vi* to get some petrol *UK* ODER gas *US*. ◇ *vt* - **1.** [auftanken]: **Benzin tanken** to get some petrol *UK* ODER gas *US* - **2.** [genießen] to get one's fill of.

Tạnker (*pl* -) *der* tanker.

Tạnk|stelle *die* petrol station *UK*, gas station *US*.

Tạnk|wart, in (*mpl* **-e**, *fpl* **-nen**) *der, die* petrol *UK* ODER gas *US* station attendant.

Tạnne (*pl* **-n**) *die* - **1.** [Baum] fir tree - **2.** *(ohne pl)* [Holz] fir.

Tạnnen|baum *der* - **1.** [Tanne] fir tree - **2.** [Weihnachtsbaum] Christmas tree.

Tạnnen|zapfen *der* fir cone.

Tansania *nt* Tanzania.

Tạnte (*pl* **-n**) *die* - **1.** [Verwandte] aunt - **2.** *fam* [als Anrede] auntie.

Tante-Ẹmma-|Laden *der* corner shop.

Tạnz (*pl* **Tạ̈nze**) *der* dance.

Tạnz|bein *das* *(ohne pl)*: **das Tanzbein schwingen** *fam hum* to hit the floor.

tạnzen *vt* & *vi* to dance; **komm, lass uns tanzen gehen** let's go dancing; **willst du mit mir tanzen?** would you like to dance?

Tạ̈nzer, in (*mpl* -, *fpl* **-nen**) *der, die* dancer.

Tạnz|fläche *die* dance floor.

Tạnz|schule *die* dancing school.

Tạnz|stunde *die* - **1.** [Kurs] dancing lessons *Pl* - **2.** [Unterrichtsstunde] dancing lesson.

Tapete (*pl* **-n**) *die* wallpaper *(U)*.

Tapeten|wechsel *der fig* change of scenery.

tapezieren *vt* & *vi* to wallpaper.

tạpfer ◇ *adj* brave. ◇ *adv* bravely.

Tạpferkeit *die* bravery.

tạppen (*perf* **ist getạppt**) *vi*: **durch das Zimmer tappen** to patter through the room.

tạpsig ◇ *adj* awkward. ◇ *adv* awkwardly.

Tarif (*pl* **-e**) *der* - **1.** WIRTSCH rate - **2.** [Gebühr] charge; [Verkehrstarif] fare.

Tarif|lohn *der* agreed rate of pay.

Tarifver|handlung *die* collective bargaining.

Tarif|vertrag *der* collective agreement.

tạrnen *vt* to camouflage. ◆ **sich tarnen** *ref* to camouflage o.s.; **sich als etw tarnen** to disguise o.s. as sthg.

Tạrnung *die* camouflage.

Tạsche (*pl* **-n**) *die* - **1.** [Tragetasche, Handtasche] bag - **2.** [Hosentasche] pocket; **etw aus eigener Tasche bezahlen** to pay for sthg o.s.; **etw (schon) in der Tasche haben** *fam* to have sthg in the bag; **jm auf der Tasche liegen** *fam* to live off sb.

Tạschen|buch *das* paperback.

Tạschen|dieb, in *der, die* pickpocket.

Tạschen|format *das*: **im Taschenformat** pocket-sized.

Tạschen|geld *das* pocket money.

Tạschen|lampe *die* torch *UK*, flashlight *US*.

Tạschen|messer *das* penknife, pocketknife

Tạschen|rechner *der* pocket calculator.

Tạschen|tuch (*pl* **-tücher**) *das* [aus Stoff] handkerchief; [aus Papier] tissue.

Tạschen|uhr *die* pocket watch.

Tạsse (*pl* **-n**) *die* cup; **nicht alle Tassen im Schrank haben** *fam fig* & *abw* to have a screw loose.

Tastatur (*pl* **-en**) *die* keyboard.

Taste (*pl* **-n**) *die* - **1.** [von Instrument, Computer] key - **2.** [von Geräten] button.

tasten ◇ *vi* to feel one's way; **nach etw tasten** to feel for sthg. ◇ *vt* to feel. ◆ **sich tasten** *ref* to feel one's way.

Tasten|instrument *das* keyboard instrument.

Tast|sinn *der* sense of touch.

tat *prät* ▷ **tun**.

Tat (*pl* **-en**) *die* action; **eine verbrecherische Tat** a criminal act; **eine gute Tat** a good deed; **jn auf frischer Tat ertappen** *fig* to catch sb in the act; **etw in die Tat umsetzen** to put sthg into action. ◆ **in der Tat** *adv* [tatsächlich] indeed.

Tatbe|stand *der* - **1.** RECHT: **der Tatbestand der Bestechung** the offence of bribery; **den Tatbestand des Betrugs erfüllen** to constitute fraud - **2.** [Tatsache] facts *Pl* (of the matter).

tatenlos ◇ *adj* idle. ◇ *adv* idly; **wir mussten tatenlos zusehen** we could only stand and watch.

Täter, in (*mpl* **-**, *fpl* **-nen**) *der, die* culprit.

tätig *adj* - **1.** [beschäftigt]: **tätig sein** to work - **2.** [aktiv] active; **tätig werden** to take action.

tätigen *vt geh* [von Geschäft] to transact.

Tätigkeit (*pl* **-en**) *die* [Arbeit] job; [Aktivität] activity.

tatkräftig ◇ *adj* active. ◇ *adv* actively.

tätlich ◇ *adj* physical; **tätlich werden** to become violent. ◇ *adv* physically.

Tat|ort *der* [von Verbrechen] scene of the crime.

Tätowierung (*pl* **-en**) *die* - **1.** [Vorgang] tattooing *(U)* - **2.** [Ergebnis] tattoo.

Tat|sache ◇ *die* fact; **jn vor vollendete Tatsachen stellen** *fig* to present sb with a fait accompli. ◇ *interj* it's true!

tatsächlich, tatsächlich ◇ *adj* real, actual. ◇ *adv* really; **du bist ja tatsächlich pünktlich!** you're actually on time!

tätscheln *vt* [liebkosen] to pat.

Tattoo [ta'tu:] (*pl* **-s**) *das* = **Tätowierung**.

Tatze (*pl* **-n**) *die* paw.

Tau (*pl* **-e**) ◇ *der* [Niederschlag] dew. ◇ *das* [Seil] rope.

taub *adj* - **1.** [nichts hörend] deaf; **sich taub stellen** *fam* to turn a deaf ear - **2.** [nichts fühlend] numb.

Taube (*pl* **-n**) ◇ *der, die* [Gehörlose] deaf person. ◇ *die* [Tier - gewöhnlich] pigeon; [- weiße] dove.

taubstumm *adj* deaf and dumb.

tauchen (*perf* **hat/ist getaucht**) ◇ *vi (hat, ist)* to dive. ◇ *vt (hat)* - **1.** [eintauchen] to dip - **2.** [drücken] to duck.

Taucher, in (*mpl* **-**, *fpl* **-nen**) *der, die* diver.

Taucher|brille *die* diving goggles *Pl*.

tauen (*perf* **hat/ist getaut**) ◇ *vi (hat, ist)* to melt; **es taut** it's thawing. ◇ *vt (hat)* to thaw.

Taufe (*pl* **-n**) *die* - **1.** [Vorgang] christening - **2.** *(ohne pl)* [Sakrament] baptism.

taufen *vt* - **1.** RELIG [Menschen] to baptize - **2.** [Tiere, Gegenstände] to name.

Tauf|pate *der* godfather.

Tauf|patin *die* godmother.

taugen *vi*: **nichts/wenig taugen** to be no/not much good; **zu** ODER **für etw taugen** to be suitable for sthg.

tauglich *adj* - **1.** [geeignet] suitable - **2.** MIL fit (for service).

Taumel *der (ohne pl)* - **1.** [Rausch] frenzy - **2.** [Schwindel] (feeling of) dizziness.

taumeln (*perf* **hat/ist getaumelt**) *vi* - **1.** *(ist)* [schwankend gehen] to stagger - **2.** *(hat)* [schwanken] to reel.

Tausch (*pl* **-e**) *der* exchange.

tauschen ◇ *vt* to swap. ◇ *vi*: **mit jm tauschen** [Arbeitszeit] to swap with sb; [an js Stelle sein, jd anderes sein] to swap places with sb.

täuschen ◇ *vt* to deceive; [Gegner] to trick. ◇ *vi* to be deceptive. ◆ **sich täuschen** *ref* to be wrong; **sich in jm täuschen** to be wrong about sb.

täuschend ◇ *adj* deceptive. ◇ *adv* deceptively.

Täuschung (*pl* **-en**) *die* - **1.** [Irreführung] deception - **2.** [Verwechslung] illusion.

Täuschungs|manöver *das* ploy.

tausend *num* a ODER one thousand; *siehe auch* **sechs**.

Tausend (*pl* **-** ODER **-e**) *das* thousand. ◆ **Tausende** *Pl* [sehr viele]: **zu Tausenden** by the thousand; *siehe auch* **Sechs**.

Tausender (*pl* **-**) *der* MATH thousand.

Tausend|füßler (*pl* **-**) *der* centipede.

tausendmal *adv* a thousand times.

tausendste, r, s *adj* thousandth; *siehe auch* **sechste**.

Tausendste (*pl* **-n**) *der, die, das* thousandth; *siehe auch* **Sechste**.

tausendstel *adj (unver)* thousandth; *siehe auch* **sechstel**.

Tausendstel (*pl* **-**) *das* thousandth; *siehe auch* **Sechstel**.

Tau|wetter *das* thaw.

Tau|ziehen *das* tug-of-war.

Taxi (*pl* **-s**) *das* taxi.

Technik (*pl* **-en**) *die* - **1.** *(ohne pl)* [Wissenschaft] technology - **2.** [Methode] technique - **3.** [Ausrüstung] equipment - **4.** *(ohne pl)* [Funktionsweise] workings *Pl*.

Techniker, in (*mpl* **-**, *fpl* **-nen**) *der, die* engineer; [im Sport, in Musik] technician.

technisch ◇ *adj* technical; [Fortschritt] technological. ◇ *adv* technically; [fortgeschritten] technologically.

Technische Hoch|schule *die technical college*.

Technische Überwachungs|verein *der amt institution charged with testing roadworthiness of cars and safety of consumer goods and installations.*

Techno *der* MUS techno.

Technologie (*pl* **-n**) *die* technology.

technologisch ◇ *adj* technological. ◇ *adv* technologically.

Teddy (*pl* **-s**)**, Teddybär** (*pl* **-en**) *der* teddy bear.

Tee (*pl* **-s**) *der* **- 1.** [gen] tea; **schwarzer Tee** black tea **- 2.** [Kräutertee] herbal tea.

Tee|beutel *der* teabag.

Tee|kanne *die* teapot.

Tee|löffel *der* teaspoon.

Teer *der* tar *(U)*.

teeren *vt* to tar.

Tee|sieb *das* tea strainer.

Teheran *nt* Teheran.

Teich (*pl* **-e**) *der* pond.

Teig (*pl* **-e**) *der* dough *(U)*.

Teigwaren *Pl amt* pasta *(U)*.

Teil (*pl* **-e**) ◇ *der* [Teilmenge] part. ◇ *der ODER das* [Anteil] share; **sich** *(D)* **seinen Teil denken** *fig* to keep one's thoughts to o.s. ◇ *das* [Bestandteil] part. ◆ **zum Teil** *adv* [teilweise] partly.

teilen ◇ *vt* [aufteilen] to share; [zerteilen] to divide; **etw mit jm teilen** to share sthg with sb; **sich** *(D)* **etw teilen** to share sthg. ◇ *vi* to share. ◆ **sich teilen** *ref* [Gruppe] to split up; [Straße] to fork; [Meinungen] to be divided.

teil|haben *vi (unreg)*: **an etw** *(D)* **teilhaben** to share in sthg.

Teilhaber, in (*mpl* **-**, *fpl* **-nen**) *der, die* partner.

Teilnahme (*pl* **-n**) *die* **- 1.** [Aufmerksamkeit, Beteiligung] participation *(U)* **- 2.** [an Kurs] attendance **- 3.** [Mitgefühl] sympathy.

teilnahmslos ◇ *adj* apathetic. ◇ *adv* apathetically.

teil|nehmen *vi (unreg)* **- 1.** [mitmachen]: **an etw** *(D)* **teilnehmen** to take part in sthg **- 2.** [mitfühlen]: **an etw** *(D)* **teilnehmen** *geh* to share in sthg.

Teilnehmer, in (*mpl* **-**, *fpl* **-nen**) *der, die* participant.

teils *adv fam* partly. ◆ **teils..., teils...** *adv* partly..., partly...

Teilung (*pl* **-en**) *die* division.

teilweise ◇ *adv* **- 1.** [zum Teil] partly **- 2.** [zeitweise] sometimes. ◇ *adj* partial.

Tel. (*abk für* **Telefon**) tel.

Tele|arbeit *die* teleworking.

Telefon (*pl* **-e**)**, Telefon** (*pl* **-e**) *das* **- 1.** [Gerät] telephone; **am Telefon** on the telephone **- 2.** *fam* [Anruf]: **Telefon für dich** there's a call for you.

Telefonan|ruf *der* telephone call.

Telefonat (*pl* **-e**) *das* telephone call.

Telefon|buch *das* telephone book.

Telefon|gespräch *das* telephone conversation.

telefonieren *vi* to make a telephone call; **mit jm telefonieren** to talk to sb on the telephone.

telefonisch ◇ *adj* telephone *(vor Subst)*. ◇ *adv* by telephone; **ich bin telefonisch erreichbar** you can reach me by telephone.

Telefon|karte *die* phonecard.

Telefon|nummer *die* telephone number.

Telefonver|bindung *die* telephone line.

Telefon|zelle *die* telephone box.

Telefon|zentrale *die* switchboard.

telegrafieren *vt* to telegraph.

telegrafisch ◇ *adj* telegraphic. ◇ *adv* by telegram.

Telegramm (*pl* **-e**) *das* telegram.

Telekom® *die German telecommunications company*.

Tele|objektiv *das* FOTO telephoto lens.

Telex (*pl* **-e**) *das* telex.

Teller (*pl* **-**) *der* [Gefäß] plate; **seinen Teller leer essen** to finish what's on one's plate.

Tempel (*pl* **-**) *der* temple.

Temperament (*pl* **-e**) *das* **- 1.** [Energie] liveliness; **Temperament haben** to be lively **- 2.** [Wesen] temperament.

temperamentvoll *adj* lively.

Temperatur (*pl* **-en**) *die* temperature.

Tempo[1] (*pl* **-s** ODER **Tempi**) *das* **- 1.** *(Pl Tempos)* [Geschwindigkeit] speed; **hier gilt Tempo 30** there's a 30 km speed limit here **- 2.** *(Pl Tempi)* MUS tempo.

Tempo®[2] (*pl* **-s**) *das fam* [Papiertaschentuch] tissue.

Tempo|limit *das* speed limit.

Tempotaschentuch® (*pl* **-tücher**) *das fam* tissue.

Tendenz (*pl* **-en**) *die* **- 1.** [Entwicklung] trend **- 2.** [Neigung] tendency.

tendieren *vi* to tend; **zu etw tendieren** to tend towards sthg.

Tennis *das* tennis.

Tennis|platz *der* tennis court.

Tennis|schläger *der* tennis racquet.

Tenor (*pl* **Tenöre**) *der* tenor.

Teppich (*pl* **-e**) *der* **- 1.** [Einzelstück] rug **- 2.** [Teppichboden] carpet.

Teppich|boden *der* carpet.

Termin (*pl* **-e**) *der* **- 1.** [Zeitpunkt] date; [Vereinbarung] appointment; **einen Termin vereinbaren** to make an appointment **- 2.** RECHT hearing.

Terminal ['tø:ɐminəl] (*pl* **-s**) ◇ *der ODER das* [Gebäude] terminal. ◇ *das* EDV terminal.

Termin|kalender *der* diary.

Termin|plan *der* schedule.
Terpentin (*pl* **-e**) *das* turpentine *(U)*.
Terrarium [tɛˈraːri̯ʊm] (*pl* **Terrarien**) *das* terrarium.
Terrasse (*pl* **-n**) *die* **- 1.** [am Haus] patio **- 2.** [am Berg] terrace.
Terrier [ˈtɛri̯ɐ] (*pl* -) *der* terrier.
Territorium [tɛriˈtoːri̯ʊm] (*pl* **-torien**) *das* territory.
Terror *der* **- 1.** [Gewalt] terrorism **- 2.** [Angst] terror **- 3.** *fam*: **Terror machen** *fam* to raise hell.
Terroran|schlag *der* terrorist attack.
terrorisieren *vt* to terrorize.
Terrorismus *der* terrorism.
Terrorist, in (*mpl* **-en**, *fpl* **-nen**) *der, die* terrorist.
Terz (*pl* **-en**) *die* MUS third.
Tesa® *das* Sellotape® *UK*, Scotch® tape *US*.
Tesafilm® *der* Sellotape® *UK*, Scotch® tape *US*.
Tessin *das* Ticino *(canton in south-east Switzerland)*.
Tessiner, in (*mpl* -, *fpl* **-nen**) *der, die* native/inhabitant of Ticino.
Test (*pl* **-e** ODER **-s**) *der* test.
Testament (*pl* **-e**) *das* **- 1.** [letzter Wille] will **- 2.** RELIG: **das Alte/Neue Testament** the Old/New Testament.
testamentarisch *adv*: **etw testamentarisch verfügen** to put sthg in one's will.
testen *vt* to test.
Tetanus|impfung *die* tetanus vaccination.
teuer ◇ *adj* **- 1.** [Preis] expensive **- 2.** *geh* [Freund] dear. ◇ *adv* dearly.
Teufel (*pl* -) *der* devil; **der Teufel ist los** *fam* all hell has broken loose; **zum Teufel mit jm/etw** *fam* [Schluss damit] to hell with sb/sthg.
Teufels|kreis *der* vicious circle.
teuflisch ◇ *adj* devilish. ◇ *adv* devilishly.
Text (*pl* **-e**) *der* **- 1.** [Geschriebenes] text; [von Lied] lyrics *Pl* **- 2.** [von Bild] caption.
texten *vt* to text.
Textilien *Pl* textiles.
Textil|industrie *die* textile industry.
Text|nachricht *die* text message.
Text|verarbeitung *die* EDV word processing *(U)*.
TH [teːˈhaː] *die abk für* **Technische Hochschule**.
Thailand *nt* Thailand.
Theater (*pl* -) *das* **- 1.** theatre; **Theater spielen** to act **- 2.** *fam* [Ärger] fuss; **Theater machen** to make a fuss; **so ein Theater!** such a fuss! **- 3.** *fam* [Vortäuschung] play-acting; **Theater spielen** to put on an act.
Theaterauf|führung *die* performance.
Theater|kasse *die* theatre box office.
Theater|stück *das* play.
theatralisch *adj* dramatic.
Theke (*pl* **-n**) *die* **- 1.** [in Kneipe] bar **- 2.** [in Geschäft] counter.
Thema (*pl* **Themen**) *das* subject; MUS theme; **etw ist für jn kein Thema** *fig* sthg is not important to sb; **etw ist kein Thema mehr** *fig* sthg is of no interest anymore.
Themenbe|reich *der* field.
Themse *die*: **die Themse** the (River) Thames.
Theologe (*pl* **-n**) *der* theologian.
Theologie (*pl* **-n**) *die* theology.
Theologin (*pl* **-nen**) *die* theologian.
Theoretiker, in (*mpl* -, *fpl* **-nen**) *der, die* theorist.
theoretisch ◇ *adj* theoretical. ◇ *adv* theoretically.
Theorie (*pl* **-n**) *die* theory.
therapeutisch ◇ *adj* therapeutic. ◇ *adv* therapeutically.
Therapie (*pl* **-n**) *die* therapy.
Thermal|bad *das* thermal bath.
Thermometer (*pl* -) *das* thermometer.
Thermos|flasche *die* thermos (flask).
Thermostat (*pl* **-e** ODER **-en**) *der* thermostat.
These (*pl* **-n**) *die* thesis.
Thron (*pl* **-e**) *der* throne.
thronen *vi* to sit imposingly.
Thron|folger, in (*mpl* -, *fpl* **-nen**) *der, die* heir to the throne.
Thunfisch, -fisch *der* tuna.
Thüringen *nt* Thuringia.
Thüringer (*pl* -) ◇ *der* native/inhabitant of Thuringia. ◇ *adj (unver)* of/from Thuringia.
Thüringerin (*pl* **-nen**) *die* native/inhabitant of Thuringia.
Thymian (*pl* **-e**) *der* thyme.
Tick (*pl* **-s**) *der* quirk; [nervös] tic.
ticken *vi* to tick.
Tide (*pl* **-n**) *die Norddt* tide.
tief ◇ *adj* **- 1.** [gen] deep; **ein tiefer Fall** a long fall; **zwei Meter tief** two metres deep; **im tiefsten Winter** in the depths of winter **- 2.** [niedrig] low. ◇ *adv* **- 1.** [nach unten] deep **- 2.** [niedrig] low; **zu tief singen** to sing flat **- 3.** [zeitlich]: **bis tief in die Nacht** far into the night **- 4.** [verletzt, atmen, bewegt] deeply; **tief schlafen** to be in a deep sleep.
Tief (*pl* **-s**) *das* depression.
Tiefdruck|gebiet *das* area of low pressure.
Tiefe (*pl* **-n**) *die* depth.
Tief|ebene *die* (lowland) plain.
tiefernst ◇ *adj* very serious. ◇ *adv* very seriously.
Tief|garage *die* underground car park *UK* ODER parking lot *US*.
tiefgefroren *adj* frozen.

tiefgekühlt <> *adj* frozen. <> *adv* in a freezer.

tief greifend <> *adj* radical. <> *adv* radically.

Tiefkühl|fach *das* freezer compartment.

Tiefkühl|kost *die* frozen food.

Tiefkühl|truhe *die* freezer.

Tief|punkt *der* low.

tief schürfend <> *adj* profound. <> *adv* profoundly.

tiefsinnig *adj* profound.

Tiefstand *der (ohne pl)* low.

Tier (*pl* -e) *das* animal; **ein großes** *ODER* **hohes Tier** *fam fig* a big shot.

Tier|art *die* species.

Tier|arzt, **ärztin** *der, die* vet.

Tier|garten *der* zoo.

Tier|handlung *die* pet shop.

Tier|heim *das* animal home.

tierisch <> *adj* - **1.** [von Tieren] animal - **2.** *fam* [groß]: **ich habe tierische Angst** I'm really frightened. <> *adv fam* really.

Tierkreis|zeichen *das* ASTROL star sign.

tierlieb *adj* animal-loving; **tierlieb sein** to be an animal lover.

Tier|park *der* zoo.

Tier|quälerei *die* cruelty to animals.

Tierschutz|verein *der* society for the prevention of cruelty to animals.

Tier|versuch *der* animal experiment.

Tiger, **in** (*mpl* -, *fpl* **-nen**) *der, die* tiger.

Tilde (*pl* **-n**) *die* tilde.

tilgen *vt* to repay.

Tilsiter (*pl* -) *der* [Käse] *strong cheese with small holes in it.*

Tinktur (*pl* **-en**) *die* tincture.

Tinte (*pl* **-n**) *die* ink; **in der Tinte sitzen** *fam fig* to be in the soup.

Tinten|fisch *der* octupus; [klein] squid; [Sepia] cuttlefish.

Tip = **Tipp**.

Tipp (*pl* **-s**) *der* - **1.** [Hinweis] tip - **2.** [Wette] bet.

tippen <> *vi* - **1.** [vorhersagen, wetten] to bet; **meistens tippe ich richtig** I'm usually right; **auf etw** *(A)* **tippen** to bet on sthg; **ich tippe darauf** I bet that - **2.** *fam* [Maschine schreiben] to type - **3.** [antippen] to tap; **an etw** *(A)* **tippen** to tap on sthg. <> *vt* - **1.** *fam* [Schreibmaschine schreiben] to type - **2.** [antippen] to tap.

tipptopp *fam adj (unver)* [von Person, Garten] immaculate; [von Haus] shipshape.

Tirol *nt* Tyrol.

Tiroler (*pl* -) *der* & *adj (unver)* Tyrolean.

Tirolerin (*pl* **-nen**) *die* Tyrolean.

tirolerisch *adj* Tyrolean.

Tisch (*pl* **-e**) *der* [Möbel] table; **den Tisch decken** to set the table; **unter den Tisch fallen** to fall by the wayside; **das ist vom Tisch** that's been done and dusted.

Tisch|decke *die* tablecloth.

Tischler, **in** (*mpl* -, *fpl* **-nen**) *der, die* carpenter.

Tisch|tennis *das* table tennis.

Tisch|tuch (*pl* **-tücher**) *das* tablecloth.

Titel (*pl* -) *der* title.

Titel|bild *das* cover picture.

Titel|seite *die* front page.

Titel|verteidiger, **in** *der, die* SPORT defending champion.

Toast [to:st] (*pl* **-e** *ODER* **-s**) *der* - **1.** [Brot] toast; [Scheibe] slice of toast - **2.** [Trinkspruch] toast.

Toast|brot *das* sliced white bread *(U)*.

toasten ['to:stn̩] *vt* to toast.

Toaster ['to:stɐ] (*pl* -) *der* toaster.

toben (*perf* **hat/ist getobt**) *vi* - **1.** *(hat)* [wild werden] to go berserk - **2.** *(ist)* [rennen] to charge about - **3.** *(hat)* [wüten] to rage.

Tochter (*pl* **Töchter**) *die* daughter.

Tod (*pl* -e) *der* death; **jn zum Tod(e) verurteilen** to condemn sb to death; **zu Tode erschreckt** scared to death.

todernst <> *adj* deadly serious. <> *adv* in a deadly serious way.

Todes|angst *die*: **eine Todesangst haben/ausstehen** to be scared to death.

Todes|anzeige *die* [in Zeitung] death notice.

Todes|fall *der* death.

Todes|kampf *der* death throes *Pl*.

Todes|opfer *das* casualty, fatality.

Todes|strafe *die* death penalty.

Todesur|sache *die* cause of death.

Todesur|teil *das* death sentence.

todkrank *adj* terminally ill.

tödlich <> *adj* - **1.** [Krankheit, Unfall] fatal; [Gift, Biss] lethal - **2.** *fam* [Angst, Langeweile, Sicherheit] deadly; [Beleidigung] mortal. <> *adv* - **1.** [verlaufen] fatally; [wirken] lethally - **2.** *fam* [langweilig] deadly; [beleidigt] mortally.

todmüde *adj* exhausted.

todschick *fam* <> *adj* dead smart. <> *adv* dead smartly.

todsicher *fam* <> *adj* [Sache, Gewinn] surefire; **das ist todsicher** it's dead certain. <> *adv* definitely.

Tofu *der* tofu.

toi, toi, toi ['tɔy 'tɔy 'tɔy] *interj* - **1.** [unberufen] touch wood! - **2.** [viel Glück] best of luck!

Toilette [to̩a'lɛtə] (*pl* **-n**) *die* toilet; **auf die Toilette gehen** to go to the toilet.

Toiletten|papier *das* toilet paper.

Tokio *nt* Tokyo.

tolerant <> *adj* tolerant. <> *adv* tolerantly.

Toleranz (*pl* **-en**) *die* tolerance.

tolerieren *vt* to tolerate.

toll *fam* ◇ *adj* - **1.** [schön] fantastic, brilliant - **2.** [unglaublich] far-out. ◇ *adv* - **1.** [wunderbar] fantastically, brilliantly - **2.** [sehr] like crazy; **er hat sich ganz toll gefreut** he was dead pleased.

tollen (*perf* **ist getollt**) *vi* to run around like crazy.

tollkühn ◇ *adj* reckless; **ein tollkühner Mensch** a daredevil. ◇ *adv* recklessly.

Tollpatsch (*pl* **-e**) *der* clumsy devil.

Toll|wut *die* rabies *(U)*.

Tolpatsch = **Tollpatsch**.

Tomate (*pl* **-n**) *die* tomato.

Tomaten|mark *das* tomato purée.

Ton (*pl* **-e** ODER **Töne**) *der* - **1.** *(pl Tone)* [Lehm] clay - **2.** *(pl Töne)* [Laut] note - **3.** *(pl Töne)* [Tonfall] tone; **hier herrscht ein rauer Ton!** the atmosphere's terrible here!; **sich im Ton vergreifen** to adopt the wrong tone - **4.** *(pl Töne)* [Farbton] shade, tone - **5.** [von Platte, Film] sound; **den Ton angeben** to be extremely influential; **zum guten Ton gehören** to be the done thing.

Ton|art *die* - **1.** MUS key - **2.** [Tonfall] tone.

Tonaus|fall *der* TV loss of sound.

Ton|band (*pl* **-bänder**) *das* - **1.** [Spule] tape - **2.** [Gerät] tape recorder.

Tonband|gerät *das* tape recorder.

tönen ◇ *vi* - **1.** [klingen] to sound - **2.** [prahlen] to boast. ◇ *vt* [Haare] to tint.

Ton|fall *der* - **1.** [Tonart] tone - **2.** [Sprachmelodie] intonation.

Ton|film *der* sound film.

Ton|lage *die* pitch.

Ton|leiter *die* scale.

Tonne (*pl* **-n**) *die* - **1.** [Behälter] barrel - **2.** [Gewicht] tonne.

top *fam* ◇ *adj (unver)*: **top sein** to be brilliant. ◇ *adv* brilliantly.

TOP [tɔp] (*pl* -) (*abk für* **Tagesordnungspunkt**) *der item on the agenda*.

Topf (*pl* **Töpfe**) *der* - **1.** [zum Kochen] pan - **2.** [für Vorräte, Blumen] pot - **3.** *fam* [Klo] loo *UK*, john *US*.

Töpfer (*pl* -) *der* potter.

Töpferei (*pl* **-en**) *die* pottery.

Töpferin (*pl* **-nen**) *die* potter.

töpfern ◇ *vt* to make *(pottery)*. ◇ *vi* to do pottery.

Topf|lappen *der* oven cloth.

Tor (*pl* **-e**) *das* - **1.** SPORT goal; **ein Tor schießen** to score a goal; **im Tor stehen** to be in goal - **2.** [Tür] gate; [von Garage, Scheune] door.

Torein|fahrt *die* entrance gate.

Torf *der* peat.

Tor|hüter, in (*mpl* -, *fpl* **-nen**) *der, die* goalkeeper.

torkeln (*perf* **hat/ist getorkelt**) *vi* to stagger.

Torpedo (*pl* **-s**) *das* torpedo.

Tor|schütze, schützin *der, die* goalscorer.

Torte (*pl* **-n**) *die* gâteau.

Tortenguss (*pl* **-güsse**) *der* glaze *(in fruit flan)*, jelly.

Tortur (*pl* **-en**) *die eigtl* & *fig* torture.

Torwart, in (*mpl* **-e**, *fpl* **-nen**) *der, die* goalkeeper.

tosen (*perf* **hat/ist getost**) *vi* to roar.

Toskana *die*: **die Toskana** Tuscany.

tot ◇ *adj eigtl* & *fig* dead; **ein toter Punkt** a standstill; *fig* a deadlock. ◇ *adv*: **tot umfallen** to drop dead; *siehe auch* **tot stellen**.

total ◇ *adj* total. ◇ *adv fam* totally; **total gut** dead good.

Total|schaden *der* write-off.

Tote (*pl* **-n**) *der, die* dead person; **es gab mehrere Tote** several people were killed.

töten *vt* & *vi* to kill.

Toten|kopf *der* - **1.** [auf Arzneimittel, Piratenflagge] skull and crossbones - **2.** [Schädel] skull.

Toten|schädel *der* skull.

Toten|schein *der* death certificate.

Toten|sonntag *der Sunday before Advent, day for commemoration of the dead in Protestant religion*.

totenstill *adj* deathly silent.

tot|lachen ◆ **sich totlachen** *ref fam* to kill o.s. laughing.

Totschlag *der* RECHT manslaughter.

tot|schlagen *vt (unreg)* [töten] to beat to death.

tot|schweigen *vt (unreg)* to hush up.

tot stellen ◆ **sich tot stellen** *ref* to play dead.

Toupet [tu'peː] (*pl* **-s**) *das* toupee.

toupieren [tu'piːrən] *vt* to backcomb.

Tour [tuːɐ̯] (*pl* **-en**) *die* - **1.** [Ausflug] tour; [kürzere Fahrt] trip - **2.** *fam* [Verhaltensweise] ploy; **es auf die sanfte Tour versuchen** *fam* to use the gentle approach - **3.** [Strecke] route - **4.** TECH revolution; **auf vollen** ODER **höchsten Touren laufen** [Motor, Maschine] to run at full speed; *fam* [Vorbereitungen] to be in full swing; **auf Touren kommen** *fam* to get going.

Tourismus [tu'rɪsmʊs] *der* tourism.

Tourist [tu'rɪst] (*pl* **-en**) *der* tourist.

Touristin [tu'rɪstɪn] (*pl* **-nen**) *die* tourist.

Trab *der* trot; **auf Trab sein** *fig* to be on the go; **jn in Trab halten** *fam fig* to keep sb on the go; **sich in Trab setzen** *fam fig* to get going.

Trabant® (*pl* **-s**) *der* AUTO Trabant®, *small car formerly manufactured in the GDR*.

traben (*perf* **ist getrabt**) *vi* to trot.

Trabi (*pl* **-s**) *der fam colloquial name for a* **Trabant**.

Trab|rennen *das* trotting.

Tracht (*pl* **-en**) *die* - **1.** [Kleidung] traditional costume - **2.** [Schläge]: **eine Tracht Prügel** *fam* a beating.

trachten *vi*: **nach etw trachten** to strive for sthg; **jm nach dem Leben trachten** to be after sb's blood.

trächtig *adj* pregnant.

Trackball [tr'ɛkbɔːl] (*pl* **-s**) *der* EDV trackball.

Tradition (*pl* **-en**) *die* tradition.

traditionell <> *adj* traditional. <> *adv* traditionally.

traf *prät* ▷ **treffen**.

tragbar *adj* - **1.** [Gerät] portable - **2.** [Zustand, Verhalten] acceptable; **finanziell tragbar sein** to be financially viable.

träge <> *adj* - **1.** [müde] lethargic - **2.** [langsam] sluggish. <> *adv* - **1.** [müde] lethargically - **2.** [langsam] sluggishly.

tragen (*präs* **trägt**, *prät* **trug**, *perf* **hat getragen**) <> *vt* - **1.** [schleppen] to carry - **2.** [am Körper haben] to wear - **3.** [bei sich haben]: **etw bei sich tragen** to carry sthg (on one) - **4.** [Früchte] to produce; [Zinsen] to yield - **5.** [Kosten, Schicksal, Leid] to bear; [Anteil] to pay - **6.** [Einrichtung, Schule] to support - **7.** [Verantwortung] to take; [Folgen] to suffer - **8.** [Namen, Unterschrift] to bear. <> *vi* - **1.** [Baum] to bear fruit - **2.** [Gewicht]: **das Eis trägt noch nicht** the ice won't bear any weight yet - **3.** [Reichweite haben] to carry - **4.** [stützen] to support; **an etw** *(D)* **schwer tragen** to find sthg hard to bear. ◆ **sich tragen** *ref fig* - **1.** [zu tragen sein]: **dieser Stoff trägt sich sehr angenehm** this material is very pleasant to wear; **der Koffer trägt sich schlecht** the suitcase is difficult to carry - **2.** [sich selbst finanzieren] to be self-supporting - **3.** *geh* [planen]: **sich mit etw tragen** to contemplate sthg. ◆ **Tragen** *das*: **zum Tragen kommen** to apply.

tragend *adj* load-bearing.

Träger, in (*mpl* -, *fpl* **-nen**) <> *der, die* - **1.** [Lastenträger] porter - **2.** [von Titel] holder - **3.** [Geldgeber] sponsor. <> *der* - **1.** ARCHIT girder - **2.** [an Kleidung] strap.

Trage|tasche *die* carrier bag.

tragfähig *adj* - **1.** [Kompromiss, Politik] tenable - **2.** [Konstruktion] solid, capable of supporting a load.

Trag|fläche *die* wing.

Trägheit *die* - **1.** [Faulheit] lethargy - **2.** PHYS inertia.

Tragik *die* tragedy.

tragisch <> *adj* tragic. <> *adv* tragically.

Tragödie [tra'gøːdjə] (*pl* **-n**) *die* tragedy.

trägt *präs* ▷ **tragen**.

Tragweite *die (ohne pl)* consequences *Pl*; **von großer Tragweite** of great consequence.

Trainer, in ['trɛːnɐ, rɪn] (*mpl* -, *fpl* **-nen**) *der, die* coach.

trainieren [trɛ'niːrən] <> *vt* [Verein, Sportler] to coach; [Pferd] to train; [Salto, Elfmeterschießen] to practise. <> *vi* to train.

Training ['trɛːnɪŋ] (*pl* **-s**) *das* training *(U)*.

Trainingsan|zug *der* tracksuit.

Traktor (*pl* **-toren**) *der* tractor.

trällern *vt* & *vi* to warble.

trampeln (*perf* **hat/ist getrampelt**) *vi* - **1.** *(ist) fam* [gehen] to stamp - **2.** *(hat)* [stampfen]: **mit den Füßen trampeln** to stamp one's feet.

trampen ['trɛmpn̩] (*perf* **hat/ist getrampt**) *vi (hat)* [an der Straße stehen] to hitchhike.

Tramper, in ['trɛmpɐ, rɪn] (*mpl* -, *fpl* **-nen**) *der, die* hitchhiker.

Trampolin (*pl* **-e**) *das* trampoline.

Tran (*pl* **-e**) *der* train oil; **im Tran sein** *fam* [unaufmerksam] to be out of it.

Träne (*pl* **-n**) *die* tear; **in Tränen ausbrechen** to burst into tears; **zu Tränen gerührt** moved to tears.

tränen *vi* to water.

Tränen|gas *das* tear gas.

trank *prät* ▷ **trinken**.

tränken *vt* to water.

Transformator (*pl* **-toren**) *der* transformer.

Transfusion (*pl* **-en**) *die* transfusion.

transitiv *adj* GRAMM transitive.

transparent *adj* transparent.

Transparent (*pl* **-e**) *das* banner.

Transport (*pl* **-e**) *der* transport.

transportabel *adj* portable.

transportfähig *adj*: **der Verletzte ist nicht transportfähig** the injured man cannot be moved.

transportieren <> *vt* - **1.** [befördern] to transport - **2.** FILM to wind on. <> *vi* [Kamera] to wind on; [Nähmaschine] to feed.

Transport|mittel *das* means *(sg)* of transport.

Transvestit [tansvɛs'tiːt] (*pl* **-en**) *der* transvestite.

Trapez (*pl* **-e**) *das* - **1.** [im Zirkus] trapeze - **2.** MATH trapezium *UK*, trapezoid *US*.

Trara *das fam*: **mit großem Trara** with a great hullabaloo; **Trara machen** to make a fuss.

trat *prät* ▷ **treten**.

Tratsch *der fam abw* gossip.

Traube (*pl* **-n**) *die* - **1.** [Obst] grape - **2.** BIOL raceme - **3.** [Menge] cluster.

Trauben|zucker *der* glucose.

trauen <> *vi*: **jm/einer Sache trauen** to trust sb/sthg. <> *vt* [Brautpaar] to marry; **sich trauen lassen** to be married. ◆ **sich trauen** *ref* to dare.

Trauer *die* - **1.** [Schmerz] sorrow - **2.** [Staatstrauer, Trauerkleidung] mourning.

Trauer|fall *der* death, bereavement.

trauern *vi*: **(um jn) trauern** to mourn (for sb).

Trauer|spiel *das*: **es ist ein Trauerspiel** *fam* it's tragic.

Trauer|zug *der* funeral procession.

Traufe (*pl* **-n**) *die*: **vom Regen in die Traufe kommen** to jump out of the frying pan into the fire.

träufeln *vt*: **etw auf/in etw** *(A)* **träufeln** to trickle sthg onto/into sthg.

Traum (*pl* **Träume**) *der* dream.

Trauma (*pl* **-ta**) *das* trauma.

träumen ◇ *vi* - **1.** [gen] to dream; **schrecklich/schön träumen** to have terrible/pleasant dreams; **von jm/etw träumen** *eigtl* & *fig* to dream about sb/sthg - **2.** [abwesend sein] to dream, to daydream. ◇ *vt* to dream about; **das hätte ich mir nicht träumen lassen** *fig* I'd never have imagined it possible.

Träumerei (*pl* **-en**) *die* daydream.

träumerisch ◇ *adj* [Mensch] dreamy; [Gedanken] wistful. ◇ *adv* dreamily.

traumhaft ◇ *adj* - **1.** [wunderschön] fabulous - **2.** [souverän] amazing. ◇ *adv* [wunderschön] fabulously.

traurig ◇ *adj* - **1.** [betrüblich] sad - **2.** [Rest, Zustand] sorry. ◇ *adv* sadly.

Traurigkeit *die* sadness.

Trau|schein *der* marriage certificate.

Trauung (*pl* **-en**) *die* wedding; **kirchliche/standesamtliche Trauung** church/civil wedding.

Trau|zeuge *der* witness *(at a wedding)*.

Trau|zeugin *die* witness *(at a wedding)*.

Traveller|scheck ['trɛvəlɐʃɛk] *der* traveller's cheque.

treffen (*präs* **trifft**, *prät* **traf**, *perf* **hat/ist getroffen**) ◇ *vt (hat)* - **1.** [begegnen] to meet - **2.** [Ziel] to hit; **auf dem Foto bist du gut getroffen** it's a good photo of you; **es gut/schlecht getroffen haben** *fig* to have been lucky/unlucky - **3.** [emotional verletzen] to affect - **4.** [Verabredung, Entscheidung] to make; [Maßnahmen] to take; **eine Vereinbarung treffen** to come to an agreement. ◇ *vi* - **1.** *(hat)* [ins Ziel treffen] to score; **der Schuss traf nicht** the shot missed - **2.** *(ist)* [begegnen]: **auf jn/etw treffen** to come across sb/sthg. ◆ **sich treffen** *ref* to meet; **sich mit jm treffen** to meet sb; **es trifft sich gut/schlecht, dass...** *fig* it's lucky/unlucky that...

Treffen (*pl* -) *das* meeting.

treffend ◇ *adj* fitting. ◇ *adv* fittingly.

Treffer (*pl* -) *der* - **1.** [Tor] goal; [beim Basketball] basket - **2.** [mit Schusswaffe] hit - **3.** [Boxhieb] blow - **4.** [Losgewinn] win.

Treff|punkt *der* meeting place.

treiben (*prät* **trieb**, *perf* **hat/ist getrieben**) ◇ *vt (hat)* - **1.** [gen] to drive; **jn in etw** *(A)***/zu etw treiben** to drive sb to sthg; **du treibst mich noch in den Wahnsinn** you're driving me mad; **die Strömung trieb das Boot an den Strand** the current carried the boat ashore; **durch Windkraft getrieben** wind-powered - **2.** *fam* [anstellen] to get up to; **was treibt ihr beiden denn da wieder?** what are you two up to now? - **3.** [ansetzen] to produce - **4.** [bohren - Schacht, Tunnel] to dig; **es zu bunt treiben** *fam* to overdo it. ◇ *vi* - **1.** *(ist)* [im Wasser] to drift; **sich treiben lassen** *fig* to drift - **2.** *(hat)* [ansetzen - Blüten] to flower; [- Wurzeln] to root - **3.** *(hat)* [Harndrang verursachen] to be a diuretic, to have a diuretic effect.

Treiben *das (ohne pl)* - **1.** [Durcheinander] bustle - **2.** *abw* [Tun] activities *Pl*.

Treib|haus *das* greenhouse.

Treibhaus|effekt *der* greenhouse effect.

Treib|jagd *die* shoot *(in which game is beaten)*.

Treib|stoff *der* fuel.

Trend (*pl* **-s**) *der* trend; **im Trend liegen** to be in vogue.

trennen *vt* - **1.** [gen] to separate - **2.** [unterscheiden] to distinguish. ◆ **sich trennen** *ref* - **1.** [Menschen] to separate; **sich von jm trennen** to leave sb; **sich von etw trennen** to part with sthg - **2.** [Wege, Leitungen *etc*] to divide.

Trennung (*pl* **-en**) *die* - **1.** [gen & CHEM] separation; **in Trennung leben** to be separated - **2.** [Unterscheidung] distinction - **3.** GRAMM end-of-line hyphenation.

Trenn|wand *die* partition.

Treppe (*pl* **-n**) *die* [in Gebäude] stairs *Pl*; [im Freien] steps *Pl*; **eine Treppe** [in Gebäude] a staircase; [im Freien] a flight of steps.

Treppenab|satz *der* half-landing.

Treppen|geländer *das* banister.

Treppen|haus *das* stairwell.

Tresen (*pl* -) *der* [Ausschank] bar; [Ladentisch] counter.

Tresor (*pl* **-e**) *der* safe; [Raum] strong room.

Tret|boot *das* pedal boat.

treten (*präs* **tritt**, *prät* **trat**, *perf* **hat/ist getreten**) ◇ *vt (hat)* - **1.** [mit dem Fuß] to kick; **jm auf den Fuß treten** to tread on sb's foot - **2.** [Kupplung, Bremse] to step on, to put one's foot down on - **3.** *fam* [antreiben]: **jn treten** to push sb. ◇ *vi* - **1.** *(hat)* [mit dem Fuß] to kick; **auf etw** *(A)* **treten** to step on sthg - **2.** *(ist)* [gehen]: **ins Zimmer treten** to enter ODER come into the room; **zu jm treten** to go up to sb; **treten Sie näher!** come closer! - **3.** [betätigen]: **auf die Bremse treten** to step on the brake, to brake - **4.** *(ist)* [hervor]: **aus etw treten** to issue from sthg - **5.** [beginnen]: **in den Streik treten** to go on strike.

treu ◇ *adj* faithful; [Anhänger, Kunde] loyal; **einer Sache** *(D)* **treu sein** to be true to sthg; **jm treu sein** [sexuell] to be faithful to sb; **jm/einer**

Sache treu bleiben to remain faithful to sb/ true to sthg. ◇ *adv* [verlässlich] faithfully; [unterstützen] loyally.

Treue *die* - **1.** [gen] faithfulness; [von Anhänger, Kunde] loyalty; **jm die Treue halten** to keep faith with sb - **2.** [sexuell] fidelity.

treuherzig ◇ *adj* trusting. ◇ *adv* trustingly.

treulos ◇ *adj* disloyal; [Liebhaber] unfaithful. ◇ *adv* disloyally; [Liebhaber] unfaithfully.

Tribüne (*pl* **-n**) *die* - **1.** [Sitzplätze] stand - **2.** [Rednertribüne] rostrum.

Trichine (*pl* **-n**) *die* trichina.

Trịchter (*pl* **-**) *der* - **1.** [Gerät] funnel - **2.** [nach Explosion] crater.

Trịck (*pl* **-s**) *der* trick.

Trịck|film *der* cartoon.

trieb *prät* ▷ **treiben**.

Trieb (*pl* **-e**) *der* - **1.** [biologisch] instinct - **2.** [psychologisch] urge - **3.** [pflanzlich] shoot.

triebhaft ◇ *adj* compulsive. ◇ *adv* compulsively.

Trieb|kraft *die* driving force; [von Handeln] motive.

Trieb|wagen *der* railcar.

Trieb|werk *das* FLUG engine.

triefen (*prät* **triefte** ODER **trọff**, *perf* **hat/ist getrieft**) *vi* - **1.** *(hat)* [nass sein]: **von** ODER **vor etw** *(D)* **triefen** *eigtl* & *fig* to drip with sthg; **eure Kleider triefen vor Nässe** your clothes are dripping wet - **2.** *(ist)* [fließen - in Tropfen] to drip; [- in Rinnsalen] to run.

trịfft *präs* ▷ **treffen**.

trịftig *adj* [Grund] good; [Argumente] valid.

Trikot (*pl* **-s**), **Trịkot** (*pl* **-s**) [tri'ko:, 'trɪko] *das* [von Radrennfahrer] jersey; [von Fußballspieler] shirt; [von Tänzer] leotard.

trịllern *vt* & *vi* to warble.

Trịller|pfeife *die* whistle.

Trimẹster (*pl* **-**) *das* [von Studienjahr] term; WIRTSCH quarter.

trịnkbar *adj* drinkable.

trịnken (*prät* **trạnk**, *perf* **hat getrụnken**) ◇ *vt* to drink; **einen trinken** *fam* to have a drink; **einen trinken gehen** *fam* to go for a drink. ◇ *vi* to drink; **auf jn/etw trinken** to drink to sb/sthg.

Trịnker, in (*mpl* **-**, *fpl* **-nen**) *der, die* alcoholic.

Trịnk|geld *das* tip.

Trịnk|halm *der* (drinking) straw.

Trịnk|wasser *das* drinking water.

Trio (*pl* **-s**) *das* trio.

trịppeln (*perf* **ist getrịppelt**) *vi* to trip along.

Trịpper (*pl* **-**) *der* gonorrhoea.

trịtt *präs* ▷ **treten**.

Trịtt (*pl* **-e**) *der* - **1.** [Fußtritt] kick; **jm einen Tritt (in den Bauch) versetzen** to kick sb (in the stomach) - **2.** [Schritt, Gang] step; **im Tritt** in step.

Trịtt|brett *das* step; [von Auto] running board.

Triụmph (*pl* **-e**) *der* triumph.

triumphieren *vi* - **1.** [siegen]: **über jn/etw triumphieren** to triumph over sb/sthg - **2.** [frohlocken]: **innerlich triumphieren** to be inwardly triumphant.

trivial [tri'vi̯a:l] *geh* ◇ *adj* - **1.** [banal] trite - **2.** [unbedeutend] trivial. ◇ *adv* - **1.** [banal] tritely - **2.** [unbedeutend] trivially.

trọcken ◇ *adj* - **1.** [gen] dry - **2.** [ohne Beilage] plain; [Brot] dry; **auf dem Trockenen sitzen** *fam* [keinen Alkohol mehr haben] to have nothing to drink; [kein Geld haben] to be broke. ◇ *adv* drily.

Trọckenheit (*pl* **-en**) *die* - **1.** [regenlose Zeit] drought - **2.** [Zustand] dryness.

trọcken|legen *vt* - **1.** [entwässern] to drain - **2.** [Windeln wechseln] to change.

trọcknen (*perf* **hat/ist getrọcknet**) ◇ *vt (hat)* to dry; **sich** *(D)* **die Tränen/Hände trocknen** to dry one's tears/hands. ◇ *vi (ist)* to dry.

Trọckner (*pl* **-**) *der* dryer.

Trödel *der* junk.

trödeln (*perf* **hat/ist getrödelt**) *vi* to dawdle.

trọff *prät* ▷ **triefen**.

trog *prät* ▷ **trügen**.

Trog (*pl* **Tröge**) *der* trough.

Trọmmel (*pl* **-n**) *die* drum; [von Revolver] cylinder; [für Kabel] reel.

Trọmmel|fell *das* MED eardrum.

trọmmeln ◇ *vi* - **1.** [Musik machen, Lärm machen] to drum; **sie trommelt sehr gut** she plays the drums very well - **2.** [schlagen] to beat. ◇ *vt* - **1.** [Rhythmus] to beat out - **2.** [mit Lärm wecken]: **jn aus dem Bett trommeln** to get sb up by hammering on the door.

Trọmmler, in (*mpl* **-**, *fpl* **-nen**) *der, die* drummer.

Trompete (*pl* **-n**) *die* trumpet.

Trompeter, in (*mpl* **-**, *fpl* **-nen**) *der, die* trumpeter.

Tropen *Pl*: **die Tropen** the tropics.

Trọpf (*pl* **-e** ODER **Trọ̈pfe**) *der* - **1.** *(pl Tropfe)* MED drip - **2.** *(pl Tröpfe)* [Mensch]: **armer Tropf!** poor devil!

trọ̈pfeln (*perf* **hat/ist getrọ̈pfelt**) ◇ *vi* - **1.** *(ist)* [tropfen] to drip - **2.** *(hat) fam* [regnen]: **es tröpfelt** it's spitting. ◇ *vt (hat)* to drip.

trọpfen (*perf* **hat/ist getrọpft**) ◇ *vi* to drip; **es tropft** it's spitting. ◇ *vt (hat)* to drip.

Trọpfen (*pl* **-**) *der* drop. ◆ **Tropfen** *Pl* MED drops.

Trophäe (*pl* **-n**) *die* [Jagdtrophäe] trophy.

tropisch ◇ *adj* tropical. ◇ *adv* tropically.
Trost *der (ohne pl)* consolation, comfort; **nicht ganz bei Trost sein** *fam* to be out of one's mind.
trösten *vt* to console, to comfort. ◆ **sich trösten** *ref*: **sich (mit etw) trösten** to console o.s. (with sthg); **sie tröstete sich mit ihrem Liebhaber** she found consolation in her lover; **tröste dich, mir geht es doch nicht besser!** if it's any consolation, I'm not much better!
tröstlich *adj* comforting.
trostlos *adj abw* - **1.** [deprimierend] dreary - **2.** [traurig] despairing.
Trost|preis *der* consolation prize.
Trott (*pl* **-e**) *der* - **1.** [Gangart] trot - **2.** *fam* [Gewohnheit] routine.
Trottel (*pl* -) *der fam abw* idiot.
trotten (*perf* **ist getrottet**) *vi* to trot.
trotz *präp (+ G)* despite, in spite of.
trotzdem *adv* nevertheless.
trotzig ◇ *adj* [Kind] difficult; [aus gutem Grund] defiant; [Gesicht, Antwort] contrary. ◇ *adv* [aus gutem Grund] defiantly; [uneinsichtig] contrarily.
Trotz|kopf *der* [sturer Mensch] pigheaded so-and-so.
trüb, trübe *adj* - **1.** [Flüssigkeit] cloudy; [Augen] dull - **2.** [Wetter, Tag, Stimmung] gloomy; **mit seinen Berufschancen siehts trüb aus** it's looking bleak as far as his career prospects are concerned.
Trubel *der* hurly-burly.
trüben *vt* - **1.** [verschlechtern] to mar; [gute Laune] to dampen - **2.** [Flüssigkeit, Denken, Urteilskraft] to cloud. ◆ **sich trüben** *ref* - **1.** [Wasser] to go cloudy; [Himmel] to cloud over - **2.** [Stimmung, Laune] to be dampened.
Trübsal *die geh* [Melancholie] melancholy; [Kummer] grief; **Trübsal blasen** *fig* to mope.
trübselig ◇ *adj* gloomy. ◇ *adv* gloomily.
trudeln (*perf* **ist getrudelt**) *vi* - **1.** [fliegen] to spin - **2.** [rollen] to roll.
Trüffel (*pl* -) *der* truffle.
trug *prät* ▷ **tragen**.
trügen (*prät* **trog**, *perf* **hat getrogen**) ◇ *vi* to be deceptive. ◇ *vt* to deceive.
trügerisch *adj* deceptive.
Trugschluss (*pl* **-schlüsse**) *der* misconception.
Truhe (*pl* **-n**) *die* chest.
Trümmer *Pl* [Ruinen] ruins; [Schutt] rubble *(U)*; [von Fahrzeug] wreckage *(U)*; **in Trümmern** *eigtl & fig* in ruins.
Trumpf (*pl* **Trümpfe**) *der* trump (card); **Karo ist Trumpf!** diamonds are trumps!; **Flexibilität ist Trumpf** flexibility is the order of the day.
Trunkenheit *die amt* inebriation.
Trunk|sucht *die* alcoholism.
Trupp (*pl* **-s**) *der* [von Soldaten, Polizisten] detachment, squad; [von Arbeitern] group.
Truppe (*pl* **-n**) *die* - **1.** [Einheit] unit - **2.** *(ohne pl)* [Streitkräfte] forces *Pl*; [Heer] army - **3.** [Gruppe] troupe. ◆ **Truppen** *Pl* troops.
Trut|hahn *der* turkey.
Tscheche (*pl* **-n**) *der* Czech.
Tschechien *nt* Czech Republic.
Tschechin (*pl* **-nen**) *die* Czech.
tschechisch *adj* Czech.
Tschechisch(e) *das* Czech; *siehe auch* **Englisch(e)**.
Tschechische Republik *die* Czech Republic.
Tschechoslowakei *die* Czechoslovakia.
tschüs, tschüss *interj fam* bye!
Tsd. *abk für* **Tausend**.
T-Shirt ['ti:ʃœ:ɐ̯t] (*pl* **-s**) *das* T-shirt.
TU [te:'u:] (*pl* **-s**) (*abk für* **Technische Universität**) *die university specializing in science and technology*.
Tuba (*pl* **Tuben**) *die* tuba.
Tube (*pl* **-n**) *die* tube.
Tuberkulose (*pl* **-n**) *die* tuberculosis.
Tuch (*pl* **-e** ODER **Tücher**) *das* [Stoffteil, Stoff] cloth; [Halstuch] scarf; **für jn ein rotes Tuch sein** *fig* to make sb see red.
tüchtig ◇ *adj* - **1.** [fleißig] hardworking; [fähig] competent - **2.** [groß] big; **ein tüchtiger Schreck** a real shock. ◇ *adv* - **1.** [fleißig] hard; [fähig] competently - **2.** *fam* [viel]: **tüchtig kalt** really cold.
Tücke (*pl* **-n**) *die* - **1.** [Eigenschaft] deceit - **2.** [Handlung] trick, ruse.
tückisch ◇ *adj* - **1.** [hinterhältig - Person] deceitful; [- Plan, Idee] underhand - **2.** [schwierig] devilishly difficult - **3.** [Auto, Gerät] temperamental - **4.** [gefährlich] treacherous. ◇ *adv* - **1.** [hinterhältig] deceitfully - **2.** [gefährlich] treacherously.
Tugend (*pl* **-en**) *die* virtue.
tugendhaft ◇ *adj* virtuous. ◇ *adv* virtuously.
Tulpe (*pl* **-n**) *die* tulip.
tummeln ◆ **sich tummeln** *ref* to romp around.
Tumor (*pl* **Tumore**), **Tumor** (*pl* **Tumore**) *der* tumour.
Tümpel (*pl* -) *der* pond.
Tumult (*pl* **-e**) *der* commotion.
tun (*prät* **tat**, *perf* **hat getan**) ◇ *vt* - **1.** [machen] to do; **was tust du denn da?** what are you doing?; **so etwas tut man nicht** you shouldn't do that; **was kann ich für Sie tun?** what can I do for you?; **das hat damit nichts zu tun** that's got nothing to do with it - **2.** [stellen, legen] to put - **3.** [antun]: **jm/sich etwas tun** to do something to sb/o.s. - **4.** *fam* [hinreichend sein]: **ich denke, das tut es** I think

that will do; **damit ist es nicht getan** that's not enough **- 5.** *fam* [funktionieren]**: das Auto tut es noch/nicht mehr** the car still works/has had it. ◇ *vi* **- 1.** [machen]**: zu tun haben** to be busy; **jm gut tun** to do sb good **- 2.** [vortäuschen]**: so tun, als ob** *fam* to act as if; **er tut nur so** he's only pretending **- 3.** [Ausdruck einer Beziehung]**: du bekommst es mit mir zu tun, wenn...** *fam* you'll have me to answer to if...; **mit jm dienstlich zu tun haben** to know sb professionally. ◆ **sich tun** *ref*: **es tut sich etwas/nichts** something/nothing is happening.

Tun *das (ohne pl)* actions *Pl*.

tünchen *vt* to whitewash.

Tunesien *nt* Tunisia.

Tunesier, in [tu'neːzi̯ɐ, rɪn] (*mpl* -, *fpl* **-nen**) *der, die* Tunisian.

tunesisch *adj* Tunisian.

Tunfisch *der* = **Thunfisch**.

tunken *vt* to dip; [Brot, Keks] to dunk.

tunlichst ['tuːnlɪçst] *adv* [unbedingt] at all costs; [möglichst] as far as possible.

Tunnel (*pl* -) *der* tunnel.

Tüpfelchen (*pl* -) *das* dot; **das Tüpfelchen auf dem i sein** to be the icing on the cake.

tupfen *vt* to dab; **etw auf etw** *(A)* **tupfen** to dab sthg onto sthg.

Tupfen (*pl* -) *der* spot; [kleiner] dot.

Tür (*pl* **-en**) *die* [gen] door; **Tür zu!** shut the door!; **jn vor die Tür setzen** *fam* [rauswerfen, entlassen] to kick sb out.

Turban (*pl* **-e**) *der* turban.

Turbine (*pl* **-n**) *die* turbine.

turbulent *adj* **- 1.** [ereignisreich] eventful **- 2.** [chaotisch] turbulent.

Tür|griff *der* doorhandle.

Türke (*pl* **-n**) *der* Turk.

Türkei *die*: **die Türkei** Turkey.

Türkin (*pl* **-nen**) *die* Turk.

türkis *adj* turquoise.

Türkis (*pl* **-e**) *der* ODER *das* turquoise.

türkisch *adj* Turkish.

Türkisch(e) *das* Turkish; *siehe auch* **Englisch(e)**.

Tür|klinke *die* door handle.

Turm (*pl* **Türme**) *der* **- 1.** [Bauwerk] tower **- 2.** [Schachfigur] rook, castle.

türmen (*perf* **hat/ist getürmt**) ◇ *vi (ist) fam* to beat it, to do a runner *UK*. ◇ *vt (hat)* to pile up. ◆ **sich türmen** *ref* to be piled up.

Turm|uhr *die* tower clock; [von Kirche] church clock.

turnen (*perf* **hat/ist geturnt**) ◇ *vt (hat)* to perform. ◇ *vi* **- 1.** *(hat)* [an einem Sportgerät] to do gymnastics; **an den Ringen/am Barren turnen** to exercise on the rings/on the parallel bars **- 2.** *(ist) fam* [klettern] to clamber about.

Turnen *das* [in der Schule] gym; [sport] gymnastics *(U)*.

Turn|halle *die* gymnasium.

Turn|hose *die* (gym) shorts *Pl*.

Turnier (*pl* **-e**) *das* tournament.

Turn|schuh *der* gym shoe *UK*, sneaker *US*.

Turn|verein *der* sports club.

Tür|rahmen *der* doorframe.

Türschloss (*pl* **-schlösser**) *das* lock.

Tür|schwelle *die* threshold.

Tusch (*pl* **-e**) *der* fanfare.

Tusche (*pl* **-n**) *die* Indian ink.

tuscheln *vt* & *vi* to whisper.

tut *präs* ▷ **tun**.

Tütchen (*pl* -) *das* sachet.

Tüte (*pl* **-n**) *die* bag; [mit Backpulver] packet.

tuten *vi* **- 1.** [hupen] to toot; **das Schiff tutet** the ship sounds its horn **- 2.** [tönen] to beep.

Tutor (*pl* **-en**) *der* tutor.

Tutorin (*pl* **-nen**) *die* tutor.

TÜV [tyf] (*abk für* **Technischer Überwachungsverein**) *der (ohne pl)*: **ein Auto zum TÜV bringen** ≃ to take a car for its MOT (test) *UK*.

TV (*abk für* **Fernsehen**) TV.

Typ (*pl* **-en**) *der* **- 1.** [Menschentyp, Art] type; **er ist der Typ eines Deutschen** he is a typical German; **(nicht) js Typ sein** *fam* (not) to be sb's type **- 2.** *fam* [Kerl] guy.

Typhus *der* MED typhoid.

typisch ◇ *adj* typical; **etw ist typisch für jn** sthg is typical of sb. ◇ *adv* typically. ◇ *interj*: **typisch!** typical!

Tyrann, in (*mpl* **-en**, *fpl* **-nen**) *der, die* tyrant.

tyrannisieren *vt abw* to tyrannize.

u (*pl* - ODER **-s**), **U** (*pl* - ODER **-s**) [uː] *das* u, U.

u. *abk für* **und**.

u. a. (*abk für* **unter anderem**), *among other things*.

u. a. m. (*abk für* **und anderes mehr**) etc.

U-|Bahn *die* underground *UK*, subway *US*.

übel (*kompar* **übler**, *superl* **übelste**) ◇ *adj* **- 1.** [Essen, Laune] bad; **nicht übel sein** *fam* to be not bad **- 2.** [moralisch] evil; **in übler Gesellschaft** in bad company **- 3.** [Zustand] nasty, bad; **übel dransein** *fam* to be in a bad way **- 4.** [unwohl]**: mir ist/wird übel** I feel sick.

◇ *adv* - **1.** [schlimm] badly - **2.** [unwirsch]: **übel gelaunt (sein)** (to be) in a bad mood *ODER* temper.

Übel (*pl* -) *das* evil; **von Übel sein** to be an evil.

übel nehmen *vt (unreg)*: **jm etw übel nehmen** to hold sthg against sb.

üben ◇ *vt* - **1.** [trainieren] to practise - **2.** *geh* [äußern]: **Nachsicht üben** to be lenient; **Kritik üben** to criticize. ◇ *vi* to practise.

über ◇ *präp* - **1.** *(+ A)* [eine Richtung anzeigend - oberhalb] over, above; [- quer über] over; [- bei Routen] via; **das Flugzeug flog über das Tal** the plane flew over the valley; **er breitete die Decke über das Bett** he spread the blanket over the bed; **über die Straße gehen** to cross the road - **2.** *(+ D)* [eine Position anzeigend] over, above; **die Lampe hängt über dem Tisch** the lamp hangs above *ODER* over the table - **3.** *(+ A)* [zeitlich] over; **über Wochen/Monate** for weeks/months; **über Nacht** overnight - **4.** *(+ A)* [mehr als] over; **über eine Stunde** over an hour - **5.** *(+ D)* [mehr als] above; **über dem Durchschnitt liegen** to be above average; **Kinder über zehn Jahren** children over ten (years of age); **seit über einem Jahr** for more than a year - **6.** *(+ A)* [mittels] through, via - **7.** *(+ A)* [stellt Bezug her] about; **ein Buch über Mozart** a book about *ODER* on Mozart - **8.** *(+ A)* [zur Angabe des Betrages] for; **eine Rechnung über 30 Euro** a bill for 30 euros - **9.** *(+ A) fig*: **ich bringe es nicht über mich** I can't bring myself to. ◇ *adv* - **1.** [mehr als] over - **2.** [zeitlich]: **den Winter über** all winter (long); **das ganze Jahr über** all (the) year round. ◇ *adj fam* - **1.** [überdrüssig]: **etw über haben** to have had enough of sthg - **2.** [übrig] left (over); **ich habe noch fünf Euro über** I still have five euros left.

überall, überạll *adv* everywhere.

überạnstrengen *vt* to overstrain. ◆ **sich überanstrengen** *ref* to overexert o.s.

überạrbeiten *vt* to revise. ◆ **sich überarbeiten** *ref* to overwork.

überbạcken (*präs* **überbạckt** *ODER* **überbạ̈ckt**, *prät* **überbạckte** *ODER* **überbuk**, *perf* **hat überbạcken**) *vt* to brown; **etw mit Käse überbacken** to bake sthg with a cheese topping.

überbelichten *vt* to overexpose.

überbieten (*prät* **überbot**, *perf* **hat überboten**) *vt*: **einen Preis (um etw) überbieten** to exceed a price (by sthg); **jn (um 5.000 Euro) überbieten** to outbid sb (by 5,000 euros); **einen Rekord (um 10 cm) überbieten** to break a record (by 10 cm). ◆ **sich überbieten** *ref geh* to surpass o.s.; [Konkurrenten] to vie with each other.

Überbleibsel (*pl* -) *das* [Spur] remnant; [Ruinen, Scherben] remains *Pl*.

Über|blick *der* - **1.**: **ein Überblick über etw** *(A)* [Übersicht] an overall perspective of sthg; [Zusammenfassung] a summary of sthg; **den Überblick verlieren** to lose perspective - **2.** [Aussicht]: **ein Überblick über etw** *(A)* a (panoramic) view of sthg.

überblịcken *vt* - **1.** [einschätzen] to assess - **2.** [sehen] to overlook.

überbrịngen (*prät* **überbrạchte**, *perf* **hat überbrạcht**) *vt*: **jm etw überbringen** to deliver sthg to sb.

überbrụcken *vt* [Zeit] to fill in; [Gegensätze] to reconcile.

überdauern *vt geh* to survive.

überdehnen *vt* to strain.

überdẹnken (*prät* **überdạchte**, *perf* **hat überdạcht**) *vt* to think over.

Überdruss *der* weariness; **sie haben bis zum Überdruss Karten gespielt** *fam fig* they played cards till they got fed up with it.

übereilen *vt* to rush; **nur nichts übereilen** don't rush things, take your time.

übereilt ◇ *adj* hasty. ◇ *adv* hastily.

übereinạnder *adv* - **1.** [Dinge] on top of each other - **2.** [Menschen - reden, nachdenken] about each other.

übereinạnder schlagen *vt (unreg)*: **die Beine übereinander schlagen** to cross one's legs.

Übereinkunft (*pl* **-künfte**) *die geh* agreement.

überein|stimmen *vi* - **1.** *geh* [einig sein]: **mit jm (in etw** *(D)***) übereinstimmen** to agree with sb (about sthg) - **2.** [gleich sein - Zahlen, Messwerte] to tally; [- Aussagen] to correspond.

Überein|stimmung *die* - **1.** [Einigung] agreement *(U)* - **2.** [Gleichheit] correspondence *(U)*; **etw (mit etw) in Übereinstimmung bringen** to bring sthg into line (with sthg).

überfahren (*präs* **überfährt**, *prät* **überfuhr**, *perf* **hat überfahren**) *vt* - **1.** [töten] to run over - **2.** [Kreuzung, Schild] to drive through.

Über|fahrt *die* crossing.

Über|fall *der* attack; **Überfall auf jn/etw** attack on sb/sthg.

überfạllen (*präs* **überfạ̈llt**, *prät* **überfiel**, *perf* **hat überfạllen**) *vt* - **1.** [ausrauben - gen] to attack; [- Bank] to raid; [- eine Frau] to assault - **2.** *fam* [überraschen] to descend on.

überfällig *adj* overdue.

überfliegen (*prät* **überflog**, *perf* **hat überflogen**) *vt* - **1.** [fliegen] to fly over - **2.** *fig* [lesen] to glance over.

Überfluss *der* [viel] abundance; [zu viel] surplus; **im Überfluss leben** to live affluently; **etw im Überfluss haben** to have sthg in abundance.

überflüssig *adj* [überzählig] superfluous; [frei] spare; [unnötig] unnecessary.

überfọrdern *vt* to overtax; **jn (mit etw** *(D)***) überfordern** to ask too much of sb (with sthg); **die junge Mutter war überfordert** the young mother couldn't cope.

überfragt *adj*: **da bin ich überfragt** I can't help you there.

Über|führung *die* - **1.** [Transport] transfer; [von Toten] transportation - **2.** [Brücke] bridge.

überfüllt *adj* overcrowded.

Über|gabe *die* - **1.** [von Gegenstand, Besitz] handing over; **die Übergabe (einer Sache *(G)*) an jn** the handing over (of sthg) to sb - **2.** MIL surrender.

Übergang (*pl* **-gänge**) *der* - **1.** *(ohne pl)* [Provisorium] temporary arrangement - **2.** [Kontrast] contrast - **3.** [Weg] crossing; [Brücke] bridge - **4.** [Phase] transition.

übergeben (*präs* **übergibt**, *prät* **übergab**, *perf* **hat übergeben**) *vt* - **1.** [überreichen, weitergeben]: **jm etw übergeben** to hand sthg over to sb; [feierlich überreichen] to present sthg to sb - **2.** [überantworten]: **jm etw/jn übergeben** to hand sthg/sb over to sb - **3.** [freigeben] to open. ◆ **sich übergeben** *ref* to vomit.

übergehen[1] (*prät* **überging**, *perf* **hat übergangen**) *vt* - **1.**: **jn/etw übergehen** [nicht beachten] to ignore sb/sthg; [überspringen] to skip sb/sthg - **2.** [nicht berücksichtigen]: **jn bei etw übergehen** to pass sb over for sthg.

über|gehen[2] (*perf* **ist übergegangen**) *vi (unreg)* - **1.** [wechseln]: **zu etw übergehen** to proceed to sthg; **dazu übergehen, etw zu tun** to proceed to do sthg - **2.** [den Besitzer wechseln]: **an jn übergehen** to pass to sb.

Über|gewicht *das* - **1.** [von Personen]: **Übergewicht haben** to be overweight - **2.** [von Gegenständen] excess weight *(U)*.

übergießen (*prät* **übergoß**, *perf* **hat übergossen**) *vt*: **jn/etw mit etw übergießen** to pour sthg over sb/sthg.

über|greifen *vi (unreg)*: **auf etw *(A)* übergreifen** to spread to sthg.

überhand nehmen *vi (unreg)* to get out of hand.

überhäufen *vt*: **jn/etw mit etw überhäufen** to inundate sb/sthg with sthg.

überhaupt ◇ *adv* - **1.** [verstärkend] at all; **gibt es überhaupt eine Hoffnung?** is there any hope at all?; **überhaupt nicht** not at all; **überhaupt nichts** nothing at all - **2.** [eigentlich] anyway; **wie gehts dir überhaupt?** so, how are you, anyway? - **3.** [im Allgemeinen] on the whole. ◇ *interj* [Ausdruck der Ungeduld, des Missfallens]: **und überhaupt** anyway.

überheblich ◇ *adj* arrogant. ◇ *adv* arrogantly.

überholen ◇ *vt* - **1.** [vorbeifahren] to overtake - **2.** *fam* [übertreffen] to leave behind - **3.** [warten] to overhaul. ◇ *vi* to overtake.

überholt *adj* outdated.

überhören *vt* - **1.** [nicht hören] not to hear - **2.** [ignorieren] to ignore.

überirdisch *adj* supernatural.

überladen (*präs* **überlädt**, *prät* **überlud**, *perf* **hat überladen**) *vt* to overload.

überlassen (*präs* **überläßt**, *prät* **überließ**, *perf* **hat überlassen**) *vt* - **1.** [leihen]: **jm etw überlassen** to let sb have sthg - **2.** [sich nicht einmischen]: **jm etw überlassen** to leave sthg to sb - **3.** [allein lassen]: **jn sich *(D)* selbst überlassen** to leave sb to his/her own devices.

überlastet *adj* - **1.** [belastet] overloaded - **2.** [überfordert]: **mit etw überlastet sein** to be overburdened with sthg.

über|laufen[1] (*perf* **ist übergelaufen**) *vi (unreg)* - **1.** [überfließen] to overflow - **2.** [überwechseln] to go over to the other side; **zu jm/etw überlaufen** to go over to sb/sthg.

überlaufen[2] (*präs* **überläuft**, *prät* **überlief**, *perf* **hat überlaufen**) *vt* - **1.** [überkommen]: **es überläuft mich** shivers run down my spine - **2.** SPORT [hinter sich lassen] to outrun; [zu weit laufen] to overshoot.

überlaufen[3] *adj*: **überlaufen sein** to be overcrowded; [Kurs] to be oversubscribed.

überleben ◇ *vt* - **1.** [lebend überstehen] to survive - **2.** [länger leben als]: **jn überleben** to outlive sb. ◇ *vi* to survive.

Überlebende (*pl* **-n**) *der, die* survivor.

überlegen[1] ◇ *vt* to think about, to consider; **sich *(D)* etw überlegen** [über etw nachdenken] to think sthg over; [sich etw ausdenken] to think of sthg. ◇ *vi* to think.

überlegen[2] ◇ *adj* [besser] superior; [arrogant] patronizing; **jm überlegen sein** to be superior to sb. ◇ *adv* [siegen] convincingly; [lächeln] patronizingly.

Überlegenheit *die* superiority.

Überlegung (*pl* **-en**) *die* consideration *(U)*; **ohne Überlegung handeln** to act without thinking.

überliefern *vt* to hand down.

Über|lieferung (*pl* **-en**) *die* - **1.** [das Überliefern] handing down - **2.** [das Überlieferte] tradition.

Übermacht *die* superior strength; **in der Übermacht sein** to be stronger.

Übermaß *das* excess.

übermäßig ◇ *adj* excessive. ◇ *adv* excessively; **sich übermäßig anstrengen** to overexert o.s.; **übermäßig ehrgeizig** overambitious.

übermitteln *vt*: **jm etw übermitteln** to pass sthg on to sb.

übermorgen *adv* the day after tomorrow.

übermüdet *adj* overtired.

Übermut *der (ohne pl)* high spirits *Pl*.

übernachten *vi* to stay ODER spend the night; **bei jm übernachten** to stay the night with sb.

übernächtigt *adj* bleary-eyed.

Übernachtung (*pl* **-en**) *die* overnight stay; **eine Übernachtung mit Frühstück** bed and breakfast.

Übernahme (*pl* **-n**) *die* - **1.** [von Firma, Betrieb] takeover; [das Übernehmen] taking over *(U)* - **2.** [Eingliederung]: **die Übernahme in ein dauerhaftes Arbeitsverhältnis** the conversion to a permanent position - **3.** [von Kosten] meeting *(U)* - **4.** [von Wort, Brauch] adoption *(U)*.

übernehmen (*präs* **übernimmt**, *prät* **übernahm**, *perf* **hat übernommen**) *vt* - **1.** [Firma, Betrieb] to take over; **etw von jm übernehmen** to take sthg over from sb - **2.** [annehmen] to take on - **3.** [einstellen, weiterbeschäftigen] to keep on - **4.** [kopieren]: **etw von jm/etw übernehmen** [Verhaltensweise, Konzept] to adopt sthg from sb/sthg; [Text] to copy sthg from sb/sthg. ◆ **sich übernehmen** *ref* to overdo it.

überprüfen *vt* to inspect, to check; [Verdächtigen] to screen.

Über|prüfung (*pl* **-en**) *die* checking *(U)*; [von Verdächtigern] screening *(U)*.

überqueren *vt* to cross.

überragen *vt* - **1.** [größer sein] to tower above - **2.** [übertreffen] to surpass.

überragend ◇ *adj* outstanding. ◇ *adv* superbly.

überraschen *vt* to surprise; **jn mit etw überraschen** to surprise sb with sthg; **jn bei etw überraschen** to catch sb doing sthg; **von jm/etw überrascht werden** to be taken by surprise by sb/sthg; **vom Regen überrascht werden** to get caught in the rain.

Überraschung (*pl* **-en**) *die* surprise.

überreden *vt* to persuade; **jn zu etw überreden** to persuade sb to do sthg; **sich zu etw überreden lassen** to let o.s. be talked into (doing) sthg.

überreichen *vt*: **jm etw überreichen** to present sthg to sb.

überreizt ◇ *adj* tense; [nervös] edgy, jumpy. ◇ *adv* nervously.

Über|rest *der* remains *Pl*.

überrumpeln *vt*: **jn (mit etw) überrumpeln** to take sb by surprise (with sthg).

überrunden *vt* - **1.** SPORT to lap - **2.** [übertreffen] to outstrip.

übers *präp fam (über + das)*: **der Vogel fliegt übers Haus** the bird is flying over the house; **übers Jahr verteilt** spread over the year; **übers schlechte Wetter schimpfen** to complain about the bad weather.

übersät *adj*: **mit etw übersät sein** to be strewn with sthg.

Überschallgeschwindigkeit *die* supersonic speed.

überschatten *vt* to overshadow.

überschätzen *vt* to overestimate. ◆ **sich überschätzen** *ref* to overestimate o.s.

über|schäumen (*perf* **ist übergeschäumt**) *vi* - **1.** [überfließen] to froth over - **2.** *fig* [emotional - vor Begeisterung, Lebenslust] to brim over; [- vor Wut, Zorn] to boil over.

überschlagen (*präs* **überschlägt**, *prät* **überschlug**, *perf* **hat überschlagen**) *vt* - **1.** [rechnen] to estimate (roughly) - **2.** [überblättern] to skip. ◆ **sich überschlagen** *ref* - **1.** [Auto] to overturn; [Person] to fall head over heels - **2.** [Ereignisse] to follow one another thick and fast - **3.** [Stimme] to crack.

über|schnappen (*perf* **ist übergeschnappt**) *vi fam* to go crazy.

überschneiden (*prät* **überschnitt**, *perf* **hat überschnitten**) ◆ **sich überschneiden** *ref* - **1.** [räumlich] to intersect - **2.** [zeitlich] to coincide - **3.** [inhaltlich] to overlap.

überschreiben (*prät* **überschrieb**, *perf* **hat überschrieben**) *vt* - **1.** [übereignen]: **jm etw überschreiben** to make sthg over to sb - **2.** [betiteln] to head.

überschreiten (*prät* **überschritt**, *perf* **hat überschritten**) *vt* - **1.** [räumlich] to cross - **2.** [inhaltlich - gen] to exceed; [- Befugnis] to overstep - **3.** [zeitlich] to pass.

Über|schrift *die* heading; [in Fettdruck] headline.

Überschuss (*pl* **-schüsse**) *der* - **1.** [Gewinn] profit; **Überschuss erzielen** to make a profit - **2.** [ein Zuviel] surplus.

überschüssig *adj* surplus.

überschütten *vt*: **jn/etw mit etw überschütten** to cover sb/sthg with sthg; **jn mit Lob überschütten** to shower sb with praise; **jn mit Vorwürfen überschütten** to heap criticism on sb.

überschwänglich ◇ *adj* effusive. ◇ *adv* effusively.

überschwemmen *vt* - **1.** [nass machen] to flood - **2.** [überreich versehen]: **jn/etw mit etw überschwemmen** to inundate sb/sthg with sthg.

Überschwemmung (*pl* **-en**) *die* flood.

überschwenglich = **überschwänglich**.

übersehen (*präs* **übersieht**, *prät* **übersah**, *perf* **hat übersehen**) *vt* - **1.** [nicht sehen, ansehen] to overlook; [absichtlich] to ignore - **2.** [einschätzen] to assess.

übersetzen[1] *vt* [in Sprache] to translate; **in etw** *(A)* **übersetzen** to translate into sthg.

über|setzen[2] (*perf* **hat/ist übergesetzt**) ◇ *vi (ist)* [überqueren] to cross. ◇ *vt (hat)* [befördern] to take across.

Übersetzer, in (*mpl* **-**, *fpl* **-nen**) *der, die* translator.

Übersetzung (*pl* **-en**) *die* - **1.** [das Übersetzen] translation - **2.** TECH gear ratio.

Übersicht (*pl* **-en**) *die* - **1.** [Fähigkeit] overview - **2.** [Darstellung]: **eine Übersicht über etw** *(A)* an outline of sthg.

übersichtlich ◇ *adj* - **1.** [gut strukturiert] clear - **2.** [gut zu sehen] open. ◇ *adv* clearly.

überspitzt ◇ *adj* exaggerated. ◇ *adv* in an exaggerated way.

überspringen (*prät* **übersprang**, *perf* **hat übersprungen**) *vt* - **1.** [darüber hinwegspringen] to jump - **2.** [auslassen] to skip.

über|sprudeln (*perf* **ist übergesprudelt**) *vi* - **1.** [Person]: **vor etw** *(D)* **übersprudeln** to bubble over with sthg - **2.** [Flüssigkeit] to bubble over.

überstehen[1] (*prät* **überstand**, *perf* **hat überstanden**) *vt* [hinter sich bringen] to come through.

über|stehen[2] (*perf* **hat/ist übergestanden**) *vi (unreg)* [vorstehen] to jut out.

übersteigen (*prät* **überstieg**, *perf* **hat überstiegen**) *vt* - **1.** [zu viel sein] to exceed - **2.** [überklettern] to climb over.

überstimmen *vt* [Person] to outvote; [Antrag] to vote down.

Über|stunde *die*: **eine Überstunde** an hour's overtime.

überstürzen *vt* to rush into. ◆ **sich überstürzen** *ref* [Ereignisse] to follow in rapid succession.

übertragbar *adj* - **1.** [Fahrkarte, Recht] transferable; **nicht übertragbar** non-transferable - **2.** [anwendbar] applicable.

übertragen[1] (*präs* **überträgt**, *prät* **übertrug**, *perf* **hat übertragen**) *vt* - **1.** [anwenden]: **etw auf jn/etw übertragen** to apply sthg to sb/sthg - **2.** [senden] to broadcast - **3.** [übersetzen]: **etw in etw** *(A)* **übertragen** to translate sthg into sthg - **4.** [Krankheit] to transmit - **5.** [überantworten]: **jm etw übertragen** to assign sthg to sb. ◆ **sich übertragen** *ref*: **sich auf jn übertragen** *fig* & MED to infect sb.

übertragen[2] ◇ *adj* [nicht wörtlich] figurative. ◇ *adv* [nicht wörtlich] figuratively.

Übertragung (*pl* **-en**) *die* - **1.** [Sendung] broadcast; [das Senden] broadcasting - **2.** [von Krankheit] transmission - **3.** [Überantwortung] transfer.

übertreffen (*präs* **übertrifft**, *prät* **übertraf**, *perf* **hat übertroffen**) *vt* [Erwartungen] to surpass; [Rekord] to beat; **jn an Ausdauer/Schnelligkeit übertreffen** to have more stamina/be faster than sb.

übertreiben (*prät* **übertrieb**, *perf* **hat übertrieben**) ◇ *vt* [bei Darstellung] to exaggerate; [Handlung] to overdo. ◇ *vi* [bei Darstellung] to exaggerate; [bei Handlung] to overdo it.

Übertreibung (*pl* **-en**) *die* exaggeration.

übertreten[1] (*präs* **übertritt**, *prät* **übertrat**, *perf* **hat übertreten**) *vt* to break.

über|treten[2] (*perf* **hat/ist übergetreten**) *vi (unreg)* - **1.** *(ist)* [beitreten]: **zu etw** *(D)* **übertreten** [zu Partei] to go over to sthg; [zu Konfession] to convert to sthg - **2.** *(hat)* SPORT to overstep.

übertrieben ◇ *adj* [Darstellung] exaggerated; [Forderung, Ehrgeiz] excessive. ◇ *adv* [darstellen] in an exaggerated manner; [ernst, höflich] excessively.

überwachen *vt* to keep under surveillance; [Arbeit] to oversee.

überwältigen *vt* - **1.** [besiegen] to overpower - **2.** [überkommen] to overwhelm.

überwältigend ◇ *adj* overwhelming. ◇ *adv*: **überwältigend aussehen** to look stunning; **überwältigend viele Besucher** an overwhelming number of visitors.

überweisen (*prät* **überwies**, *perf* **hat überwiesen**) *vt* - **1.** [bezahlen] to pay; **jm etw überweisen, etw an jn überweisen** to pay sthg to sb; **Geld auf ein anderes Konto überweisen** to transfer money to another account; **Ihr Gehalt bekommen Sie überwiesen** your salary will be paid into your account - **2.** MED: **einen Patienten ins Krankenhaus überweisen** to have a patient admitted to hospital.

Überweisung (*pl* **-en**) *die* - **1.** [Zahlung] transfer; [Formular] money transfer form - **2.** MED referral.

überwiegen (*prät* **überwog**, *perf* **hat überwogen**) ◇ *vi* - **1.** [Skepsis, Zweifel] to prevail - **2.** [zahlenmäßig] to predominate. ◇ *vt* to outweigh.

überwinden (*prät* **überwand**, *perf* **hat überwunden**) *vt* to overcome; [Krise] to get over. ◆ **sich überwinden** *ref*: **sich zu etw überwinden** to force o.s. to do sthg; **sich nicht überwinden können, etw zu tun** not to be able to bring o.s. to do sthg.

Überwindung *die* - **1.** [gen] overcoming - **2.** [von Berg] conquering - **3.** [das Sichüberwinden]: **es ist für mich eine Überwindung** ODER **es kostet mich Überwindung, es zu tun** I have to force myself to do it.

überwintern *vi* - **1.** [Pflanze, Vogel] to spend the winter - **2.** [Winterschlaf halten] to hibernate - **3.** *hum* [Mensch] to winter.

Überzahl *die* majority; **in der Überzahl sein** SPORT to have a numerical advantage; [mehr sein] to be in the majority.

überzählig *adj* spare, surplus.

überzeugen *vt* to convince; **jn von etw überzeugen** to convince sb of sthg. ◆ **sich überzeugen** *ref*: **sich (von etw) überzeugen** to satisfy o.s. (of sthg); **überzeugen Sie sich selbst!** see for yourself!

überzeugt *adj* convinced; **davon überzeugt sein, dass...** to be convinced that...

Überzeugung (*pl* **-en**) *die* conviction; **gegen seine Überzeugung handeln** to go against one's convictions; **zur Überzeugung kommen** ODER **gelangen, dass...** to become convinced ODER come to believe that...

überziehen[1] (*prät* **überzog**, *perf* **hat überzogen**) ◇ *vi* - **1.** [bei Bank] to go overdrawn

- **2.** [zeitlich] to overrun. <> *vt* - **1.** [Konto] to overdraw - **2.** [nicht pünktlich beenden] to overrun - **3.** [übertreiben] to take too far.

über|ziehen[2] *vt (unreg)* [anziehen]: **sich** *(D)* **etw überziehen** to pull sthg on.

überzogen <> *adj* exaggerated. <> *adv*: **überzogen reagieren** to overreact.

Über|zug *der* - **1.** [Bezug] cover - **2.** [Belag] coating.

üblich *adj* usual; **wie üblich** as usual.

U-|Boot *das* submarine.

übrig <> *adj* remaining; **ist noch etwas übrig?** is there any left?; **die übrigen Autos** the rest of the cars, the remaining cars; **die Übrigen** the rest. <> *adv*: **für jn/etw viel/nichts übrig haben** to have a lot of/no time for sb/sthg. ◆ **im Übrigen** *adv* in addition.

übrig bleiben (*perf* **ist übrig geblieben**) *vi (unreg)* to be left over; **uns blieb nichts anderes** ODER **weiter übrig, als zuzustimmen** we had no alternative but to agree.

übrigens *adv* by the way.

Übung (*pl* **-en**) *die* - **1.** [das Üben] practice; **aus der Übung kommen/sein** to get/be out of practice - **2.** SPORT, SCHULE, MIL & MUS exercise - **3.** UNI seminar.

UdSSR [uːdeːɛsɛs'ɛr] (*abk für* **Union der sozialistischen Sowjetrepubliken**) *die* HIST USSR.

UEFA-Pokal *der* UEFA Cup.

Ufer (*pl* -) *das* [von Fluss] bank; [von See, Meer] shore; **am Ufer** [von Fluss] on the bank; [von See, Meer] on the shore.

UFO (*pl* **-s**), **Ufo** (*pl* **-s**) [ˈjuːfoː] *das* UFO.

Uhr (*pl* **-en**) *die* - **1.** [Zeitanzeiger] clock - **2.** [Armbanduhr] watch - **3.** [Zeit]: **es ist 3 Uhr** it is 3 o'clock; **um 3 Uhr** at 3 o'clock; **um wie viel Uhr?** (at) what time?; **wie viel Uhr ist es?** what time is it?; **rund um die Uhr** round the clock.

Uhrmacher, in (*mpl* -, *fpl* **-nen**) *der, die* [von Armbanduhren] watchmaker; [von größeren Uhren] clockmaker.

Uhr|zeiger *der* hand.

Uhrzeiger|sinn *der*: **im Uhrzeigersinn** clockwise; **gegen den Uhrzeigersinn** anticlockwise.

Uhr|zeit *die* time.

Uhu (*pl* **-s**) *der* eagle owl.

Ukraine *die* Ukraine.

Ukrainer, in (*mpl* -, *fpl* **-nen**) *der, die* Ukrainian.

ukrainisch *adj* Ukrainian.

Ukrainisch(e) *das* Ukrainian; *siehe auch* **Englisch(e)**.

UKW [uːkaː'veː] (*abk für* **Ultrakurzwelle**) *die* FM.

ulkig *adj* comical, funny.

Ulme (*pl* **-n**) *die* elm.

Ultimatum (*pl* **-ten**) *das* ultimatum; **jm ein Ultimatum stellen** to give sb an ultimatum.

Ultraschall *der* ultrasound.

um <> *präp (+ A)* - **1.** [räumlich] (a)round; **um jn/etw herum** around sb/sthg; **gleich um die Ecke** just around the corner; **um sich blicken** to look around - **2.** [zur Angabe der Uhrzeit] at; **um drei Uhr** at three o'clock - **3.** [zur Angabe einer Differenz] by; **die Preise steigen um 15%** prices are rising by 15% - **4.** [zur Angabe von Grund]: **um etw kämpfen** to fight for sthg - **5.** [zur Angabe einer Folge] after; **Tag um Tag** day after day - **6.** [ungefähr] about, around; **es kostet um die 300 Euro** it costs about ODER around 300 euros. <> *konj*: **um zu** (in order) to; **zu stolz, um nachzugeben** too proud to give in. <> *adv* [vorüber] up; **die zehn Minuten sind um** the ten minutes are up. ◆ **um so** *konj* = **umso**.

umarmen *vt* to hug. ◆ **sich umarmen** *ref* to hug.

Umbau (*pl* **-e** ODER **-ten**) *der* renovation.

um|bauen <> *vt* [verändern] to renovate; **etw zu etw umbauen** to convert sthg to sthg. <> *vi* to renovate.

um|binden *vt (unreg)*: **sich** *(D)* **etw umbinden** to put sthg on.

um|blättern <> *vt* to turn over. <> *vi* to turn over the page.

Um|bruch *der* - **1.** [Veränderung] radical change - **2.** [von Büchern] page make-up.

um|buchen *vt*: **einen Flug umbuchen** to change one's flight booking.

um|denken *vi (unreg)* to change one's way of thinking.

um|drehen (*perf* **hat/ist umgedreht**) <> *vt (hat)* - **1.** [Seite, Stein] to turn over; [Pulli] to turn round - **2.** [Auto, Stuhl, Schlüssel] to turn. <> *vi (ist, hat)* [umkehren] to turn back. ◆ **sich umdrehen** *ref* - **1.** [im Stehen] to turn round; **sich nach jm/etw umdrehen** to turn round to look at sb/sthg - **2.** [im Liegen] to turn over.

Um|drehung (*pl* **-en**) *die* - **1.** [um eigene Achse] turn - **2.** TECH revolution.

umeinander, umeinander *adv* [sich kümmern] about each other; [wickeln] around each other.

um|fahren[1] *vt (unreg)* [überfahren] to knock down.

umfahren[2] (*präs* **umfährt**, *prät* **umfuhr**, *perf* **hat umfahren**) *vt* [ausweichen] to go round.

um|fallen (*perf* **ist umgefallen**) *vi (unreg)* - **1.** [umkippen] to fall over; [auf den Boden] to fall down - **2.** [zusammenbrechen] to collapse - **3.** *fam abw* [nachgeben] to give in.

Umfang (*pl* **-fänge**) *der* - **1.** [Maß] circumference - **2.** [Ausmaß - von Projekt, Untersuchung] scale; [- von Buch, Zahlung] size; [- von Schaden] extent; [- von Stimme] range; **in vollem Umfang** fully.

umfangreich ◇ *adj* extensive. ◇ *adv* extensively, at length.

umfassen (*präs* **umfasst**, *prät* **umfasste**, *perf* **hat umfasst**) *vt* - **1.** [beinhalten] to cover; **das Buch umfasst 200 Seiten** the book contains 200 pages - **2.** [umschlingen]: **jn umfassen** to put one's arm around sb; **etw umfassen** to clasp sthg.

umfassend, umfassend ◇ *adj* comprehensive. ◇ *adv* comprehensively.

Um|feld *das* - **1.** [Umgebung] surroundings *Pl* - **2.** [Milieu] environment, milieu.

Um|frage *die* survey.

um|funktionieren *vt* to convert.

Umgang *der* contact; **der Umgang mit Kindern/Tieren** working with children/animals; **das ist kein Umgang für dich!** you shouldn't mix with people like that; **mit jm Umgang haben** ODER **pflegen** to associate with sb.

umgänglich *adj* [angenehm] friendly, affable; [gesellig] sociable.

Umgangs|formen *Pl* manners.

Umgangs|sprache *die* [informelle Sprache] colloquial speech; **in der Umgangssprache** colloquially.

umgeben (*präs* **umgibt**, *prät* **umgab**, *perf* **hat umgeben**) *vt* to surround.

Umgebung (*pl* **-en**) *die* - **1.** [Gebiet] surroundings *Pl*; **in der Umgebung von Heilbronn** in the vicinity of Heilbronn - **2.** [Umfeld] environment.

umgehen[1] (*präs* **umgeht**, *prät* **umging**, *perf* **hat umgangen**) *vt* - **1.** [Schwierigkeiten] to avoid; [Verordnung] to get round; [Antwort] to evade - **2.** [Stau, Ortschaft] to bypass.

um|gehen[2] (*perf* **ist umgegangen**) *vi (unreg)* - **1.** [Grippe, Gerücht, Nachricht] to go round - **2.** [behandeln]: **mit jm/etw umgehen (können)** [Maschine] to (know how to) handle sb/sthg; [Kind, Tier] to (know how to) treat sb/sthg; **kannst du mit einem Computer umgehen?** do you know how to use a computer?

umgehend ◇ *adj* immediate. ◇ *adv* immediately.

Umgehungs|straße *die* bypass.

umgekehrt ◇ *adj* [Vorzeichen, Fall] opposite; [Verhältnis] inverse; [Reihenfolge] reverse; **nein, es ist gerade umgekehrt!** no, the opposite is true! ◇ *adv* the other way round; **die Sache verhält sich genau umgekehrt** the opposite is true; **und umgekehrt** and vice versa.

um|graben *vt (unreg)* to dig over.

Um|hang *der* cape.

um|hängen *vt* - **1.** [woandershin hängen] to hang somewhere else - **2.** [umlegen]: **jm/sich etw umhängen** [Jacke, Decke] to put sthg round sb's/one's shoulders; [Kette] to hang sthg round sb's/one's neck.

um|hauen *vt (unreg)* - **1.** [fällen] to cut down - **2.** *fam* [überraschen]: **es hat mich umgehauen, als** I was bowled over when - **3.** *salopp* [Alkohol, Gestank] to knock out - **4.** *fam* [niederschlagen] to knock for six - **5.** *fam* [umwerfen] to knock over.

umher *adv* around.

umher|irren (*perf* **ist umhergeirrt**) *vi* to wander around.

um|hören ◆ **sich umhören** *ref*: **sich umhören** to ask around.

Umkehr *die* turning back.

um|kehren (*perf* **hat/ist umgekehrt**) ◇ *vi (ist)* to turn back. ◇ *vt (hat)* [Entwicklung, Reihenfolge, Situation] to reverse. ◆ **sich umkehren** *ref* to be reversed.

um|kippen (*perf* **ist umgekippt**) *vi* - **1.** [umfallen] to fall over; [Auto] to overturn - **2.** *fam* [bewusstlos werden] to keel over - **3.** [ökologisch] to become uninhabitable - **4.** [Stimmung] to take a turn for the worse.

Umkleide|kabine *die* [in Schwimmbad] changing cubicle; [auf Sportplatz] changing room; [in Kaufhaus] fitting room.

um|kommen (*perf* **ist umgekommen**) *vi (unreg)* to die; **vor Hunger** *(D)* **umkommen** *fig* to be dying of hunger.

Um|kreis *der* - **1.** *(ohne pl)* [Umgebung] vicinity; **im Umkreis von 50 km** within a 50 km radius - **2.** MATH circumcircle.

um|krempeln *vt* - **1.** [hochkrempeln] to roll up - **2.** *fam* [verändern - Mensch] to reform; [- Geschäft] to reorganize completely - **3.** *fam* [durchsuchen] to turn upside down.

Umland *das* surrounding area.

Um|lauf *der* [Zirkulation] circulation.

Umlauf|bahn *die* orbit.

Um|laut *der* umlaut.

um|legen *vt* - **1.** *salopp* [erschießen] to bump off - **2.** [verteilen - Kosten, Ausgaben]: **etw auf mehrere Personen umlegen** to share sthg between several people - **3.** [umhängen]: **sich/jm etw umlegen** [Jacke, Decke] to put sthg round one's/sb's shoulders; [Kette] to put sthg round one's/sb's neck - **4.** [verlegen - Termin] to change - **5.** [umklappen] to fold down - **6.** [Kippen] to knock down; [Baum] to fell.

um|leiten *vt* to divert.

Um|leitung *die* diversion.

umliegend *adj* surrounding.

um|rechnen *vt*: **etw (auf/in etw** *(A)***) umrechnen** to convert sthg (into sthg).

umringen *vt* to surround.

Umriss (*pl* **-e**) *der* outline; **etw in groben Umrissen darstellen** to give a rough outline of sthg.

um|rühren *vt* to stir.

um|rüsten ◇ *vt* - **1.** MIL to re-equip - **2.** [ändern] to adapt. ◇ *vi* to re-equip.

ụms *präp (um + das)* round the; **ums Viereck gehen** to go round the block; **ihm geht es dabei weniger ums Geld, als...** for him it is not so much a question of money, as...

Ụm|satz *der* turnover; **wir müssen den Umsatz steigern** we have to boost our sales ODER turnover.

Ụm|schlag *der* - **1.** [von Brief] envelope; [von Buch] dust jacket - **2.** [Wechsel] sudden change - **3.** MED compress - **4.** [an Ärmel] cuff; [an Hose] turn-up - **5.** [von Gütern] transfer - **6.** [Verkauf] sale.

ụm|schlagen (*perf* **hat/ist ụmgeschlagen**) *(unreg)* ◇ *vi (ist)* [Wetter, Stimmung] to change suddenly. ◇ *vt (hat)* - **1.** [umlegen - Kragen] to turn down; [- Hosenbeine] to turn up - **2.** [umblättern - Seite] to turn over - **3.** WIRTSCH to transfer - **4.** [verkaufen] to sell - **5.** [Baum] to fell.

umschreiben[1] (*prät* **umschrieb**, *perf* **hat umschrieben**) *vt* - **1.** [paraphrasieren] to paraphrase - **2.** [abgrenzen] to define - **3.** [schildern] to describe.

ụm|schreiben[2] *vt (unreg)* - **1.** [ändern] to rewrite - **2.** [übertragen]: **etw auf jn umschreiben lassen** to have sthg transferred to sb.

ụm|schulen ◇ *vt* - **1.** [ausbilden] to retrain - **2.** [Schule wechseln lassen] to move (to another school). ◇ *vi* to retrain.

Ụm|schwung *der* sudden change.

ụm|sehen ◆ **sich umsehen** *ref (unreg)*: **sich (nach jm/etw) umsehen** [suchen] to look around (for sb/sthg); [sich umdrehen] to look round (at sb/sthg).

ụm sein (*perf* **ist ụm gewesen**) *vi (unreg) fam* to be over.

Ụmsicht *die* prudence.

ụmso *konj (+ kompar)*: **umso schneller/mehr/wichtiger** all the faster/more/more important; **umso besser!** all the better!

umsọnst ◇ *adj*: **umsonst sein** [erfolglos] to be in vain; [gratis] to be free (of charge). ◇ *adv* - **1.** [erfolglos] in vain - **2.** [gratis] for free, for nothing.

Ụmstand (*pl* **-stände**) *der* - **1.** [Mühe]: **Umstände** trouble *(U)*; **wir wollen dir keine Umstände machen** we don't want to put you to any trouble; **nicht viele Umstände (mit jm/etw) machen** not to go to a great deal of trouble (over sb/sthg) - **2.** [Sachlage] circumstance; **unter Umständen** in certain circumstances; **unter allen Umständen** whatever happens; **in anderen Umständen sein** *fig* to be in the family way.

ụmständlich ◇ *adj* - **1.** [Methode, Arbeit] laborious - **2.** [im Denken] ponderous; [beim Sprechen] long-winded. ◇ *adv* - **1.** [mühevoll] laboriously - **2.** [denken] ponderously; [sprechen] long-windedly.

Ụmstands|kleid *das* maternity dress.

Ụmstands|wort (*pl* **-wörter**) *das* GRAMM adverb.

ụmstehend *adj* - **1.** [umgebend] standing round about; **die Umstehenden** the bystanders - **2.** [umseitig] overleaf.

ụm|steigen (*perf* **ist ụmgestiegen**) *vi (unreg)* - **1.** [beim Reisen] to change - **2.** [wechseln]: **auf etw (A) umsteigen** to switch to sthg.

ụm|stellen[1] *vt* - **1.** [anders ausrichten - Möbel] to switch round; [- Methode, Produktion, Weichen] to switch; [- Kabinett] to reshuffle; **heute Nacht werden die Uhren umgestellt** the clocks go forward/back tonight; **etw auf etw (A) umstellen** to switch sthg to sthg; **einen Betrieb auf EDV umstellen** to computerize a company - **2.** [Leben, Fahrplan, Mannschaft, Programm] to change. ◆ **sich umstellen** *ref* to change; **sich in der Ernährung umstellen** to change one's diet; **sich auf etw (A) umstẹllen** [sich anpassen] to adapt to sthg.

umstẹllen[2] *vt* [einkreisen] to surround.

Ụm|stellung *die* - **1.** [von Methode, Produktion, Weichen] switch; **Umstellung auf EDV** computerization - **2.** [Veränderung] change.

ụm|stimmen *vt*: **jn umstimmen** to make sb change his/her mind.

ụm|stoßen *vt (unreg)* - **1.** [Stapel, Vase, Stuhl] to knock over - **2.** [Plan, Testament, Berechnungen] to wreck.

umstrịtten *adj* controversial; **es ist umstritten, ob** it is disputed whether.

Ụm|sturz *der* coup (d'état); **der Umsturz der Regierung** the overthrow of the government.

ụm|stürzen (*perf* **hat/ist ụmgestürzt**) ◇ *vi (ist)* to fall over; [Auto] to overturn. ◇ *vt (hat)* - **1.** [umwerfen] to knock over; [Auto] to overturn - **2.** [vereiteln] to upset - **3.** [ablösen] to overthrow.

Ụmtausch *der* exchange; **'vom Umtausch ausgeschlossen'** 'no refunds or exchanges'.

ụm|tauschen *vt* - **1.** [auswechseln] to exchange; **etw gegen etw umtauschen** to exchange sthg for sthg - **2.** [Währung tauschen] to change.

ụm|wandeln *vt*: **etw in etw (A)/zu etw umwandeln** to convert sthg into sthg.

Ụm|weg *der* detour; **einen Umweg über etw (A) machen** to make a detour via sthg; **auf Umwegen** *fig* in a roundabout way.

Ụmwelt *die* environment.

Ụmwelt|belastung *die* environmental pollution ODER damage.

ụmweltbewusst ◇ *adj* environmentally aware. ◇ *adv* in an environmentally aware way.

ụmweltfreundlich ◇ *adj* environmentally friendly, eco-friendly. ◇ *adv* in an environmentally friendly ODER eco-friendly way.

Ụmwelt|papier *das* recycled paper.

Ụmwelt|schäden *Pl* ecological damage *(U)*.

Ụmwelt|schutz *der* environmental protection.

Ụmweltschützer, in (*mpl* -, *fpl* -nen) *der, die* environmentalist.

Ụmwelt|verschmutzung *die* pollution *(U)*.

ụm|werfen *vt (unreg)* - **1.** [umstürzen] to knock over - **2.** *fam*: **jn umwerfen** [Alkohol] to knock sb out; [Nachricht] to stun sb - **3.** [umhängen]: **sich** *(D)* **etw umwerfen** to put sthg round one's shoulders - **4.** [hinfällig machen] to upset.

ụm|ziehen (*perf* **hat/ist ụmgezogen**) *(unreg)* ◇ *vi (ist)* to move; **nach...umziehen** to move to... ◇ *vt (hat)* to change. ◆ **sich umziehen** *ref* to change, to get changed.

umzịngeln *vt* to surround.

Ụm|zug *der* - **1.** [Wohnungswechsel] move - **2.** [Festzug] parade.

ụnabhängig ◇ *adj* independent; **von jm/etw unabhängig sein** to be independent of sb/sthg. ◇ *adv* independently.

Ụnabhängigkeit *die* independence.

ụnabsichtlich ◇ *adj* unintentional. ◇ *adv* unintentionally.

ụnachtsam ◇ *adj* - **1.** [unaufmerksam] inattentive - **2.** [nicht sorgsam] careless. ◇ *adv* [nicht sorgsam] carelessly.

Ụnachtsamkeit (*pl* -en) *die* - **1.** [Unaufmerksamkeit] inattentiveness *(U)* - **2.** [fehlende Sorgfalt] carelessness *(U)*.

ụnangebracht *adj* inappropriate.

ụnangemessen ◇ *adj* inappropriate. ◇ *adv* inappropriately; **unangemessen hoch** disproportionately high.

ụnangenehm ◇ *adj* unpleasant; **etw ist jm unangenehm** sb feels embarrassed about sthg. ◇ *adv*: **unangenehm berührt** embarrassed; **unangenehm auffallen** to make a bad impression.

Ụnannehmlichkeiten *Pl* trouble *(U)*.

ụnansehnlich *adj* unattractive.

ụnanständig ◇ *adj* [obszön] indecent; [Wort, Witz] rude; **es ist unanständig, mit vollem Mund zu reden** it's rude to talk with your mouth full. ◇ *adv* [obszön] indecently; [unhöflich] rudely.

ụnauffällig ◇ *adj* unobtrusive. ◇ *adv* - **1.** [nicht auffällig] unobtrusively - **2.** [heimlich] without anyone noticing.

unauffịndbar, ụnauffindbar ◇ *adj*: **unauffindbar sein** to be nowhere to be found. ◇ *adv*: **etw unauffindbar verstecken** to hide sthg where it cannot be found.

ụnaufgefordert ◇ *adj* unasked-for. ◇ *adv* without being asked.

unaufhạltsam, ụnaufhaltsam ◇ *adj* inexorable. ◇ *adv* inexorably.

unaufhörlich, ụnaufhörlich ◇ *adj* constant. ◇ *adv* constantly.

ụnaufmerksam ◇ *adj* inattentive. ◇ *adv* inattentively.

ụnaufrichtig ◇ *adj* insincere; **jm gegenüber unaufrichtig sein** not to be open with sb. ◇ *adv* insincerely.

unausstehlich, ụnausstehlich ◇ *adj* unbearable. ◇ *adv* unbearably.

ụnbändig *adj* [Wut, Freude, Eifersucht] unbridled; [Temperament] boisterous.

ụnbeabsichtigt ◇ *adj* unintentional. ◇ *adv* unintentionally.

ụnbeachtet ◇ *adj* unnoticed. ◇ *adv* unnoticed.

ụnbedenklich ◇ *adj* safe. ◇ *adv* [Medikament einnehmen] safely; [annehmen, zustimmen] without hesitation.

ụnbedeutend ◇ *adj* - **1.** [nicht bedeutend] unimportant - **2.** [belanglos] slight. ◇ *adv* [belanglos] slightly.

ụnbedingt ◇ *adj* absolute. ◇ *adv* - **1.** [auf jeden Fall] definitely; **er will unbedingt Ski fahren** he is determined to go skiing; **du wolltest ja unbedingt Ski fahren** it was **you** that wanted to go skiing - **2.** [bedingungslos] absolutely.

ụnbefriedigend *adj* unsatisfactory.

ụnbefugt ◇ *adj* unauthorized. ◇ *adv* without authorization.

unbegreiflich, ụnbegreiflich ◇ *adj* incomprehensible. ◇ *adv* unbelievably.

ụnbegrenzt ◇ *adj* [Freiheit, Möglichkeiten] unlimited; [Vertrauen, Zustimmung] total. ◇ *adv* [vertrauen, zustimmen] totally; [nutzen, wohnen] indefinitely.

ụnbegründet ◇ *adj* unfounded. ◇ *adv* without foundation.

ụnbeholfen ◇ *adj* clumsy. ◇ *adv* clumsily.

ụnbekannt ◇ *adj* [Künstler, Substanz, Krankheit] unknown; [Flugobjekt] unidentified; **er ist mir unbekannt** I don't know him; **diese Änderung ist mir unbekannt** I don't know about this change; **Anzeige gegen unbekannt** RECHT charge against person or persons unknown. ◇ *adv*: **'unbekannt verzogen'** 'gone away, address unknown'.

ụnbekümmert, unbekụmmert ◇ *adj* [unbeschwert] carefree; [ohne Bedenken] casual. ◇ *adv* [unbeschwert] in a carefree way; [ohne Bedenken] casually.

ụnbeliebt *adj* unpopular.

ụnbequem ◇ *adj* - **1.** [nicht bequem] uncomfortable - **2.** [lästig] awkward. ◇ *adv* [nicht bequem] uncomfortably.

unberẹchenbar, ụnberechenbar ◇ *adj* unpredictable. ◇ *adv* unpredictably.

ụnberechtigt ◇ *adj* [Ansprüche, Vorwürfe] unjustified; [Zutritt] unauthorized. ◇ *adv* [entlassen, bestrafen] without justification; [ohne Erlaubnis] without authorization.

ụnberührt *adj* - **1.** [nicht berührt - Essen, Gegenstand] untouched; [- Schnee] undisturbed; [- Natur] unspoilt - **2.** [ohne Regung] unmoved - **3.** [jungfräulich]: **unberührt sein** to be a virgin.

unbeschreiblich, ụnbeschreiblich ◇ *adj* indescribable. ◇ *adv* indescribably; **sich unbeschreiblich freuen** to be overjoyed.

ụnbeschwert ◇ *adj* carefree. ◇ *adv* free from care.

ụnbeständig *adj* changeable.

unbestẹchlich, ụnbestechlich *adj* [durch Geld] incorruptible; [Kritiker] uncompromising; [Verfechter] unwavering.

ụnbestimmt ◇ *adj* [Zeitpunkt & GRAMM] indefinite; [Vorstellung, Äußerung] vague. ◇ *adv* vaguely.

ụnbeteiligt ◇ *adj* - **1.** [nicht verwickelt] uninvolved; **an etw** *(D)* **unbeteiligt sein** not to be involved in sthg - **2.** [nicht interessiert] uninterested. ◇ *adv* - **1.** [nicht verwickelt] without getting involved - **2.** [nicht interessiert] without taking an interest.

ụnbewacht *adj* [Haus, Gefangene] unguarded; [Gepäck, Parkplatz] unattended; **in einem unbewachten Moment** when no one was looking.

ụnbeweglich ◇ *adj* - **1.** [nicht beweglich, festgelegt] immovable - **2.** [unflexibel] inflexible - **3.** [steif] stiff - **4.** [unverändert] fixed. ◇ *adv* - **1.** [regungslos] motionlessly - **2.** [unverändert] fixedly.

ụnbewusst ◇ *adj* unconscious. ◇ *adv* unconsciously.

ụnbrauchbar *adj* useless.

ụnd *konj* - **1.** [gen] and; **und wenn** even if; **und aber** even though; **eins und eins ist zwei** one and one is two; **und so weiter** and so on - **2.** [Ausdruck von Ironie]: **der und sich entschuldigen?** him, say he's sorry? ◆ **und ob** *interj* of course! ◆ **und wie** *interj* and how!

ụndankbar *adj* - **1.** [unhöflich] ungrateful - **2.** [schwer] thankless.

undẹnkbar, ụndenkbar *adj* inconceivable.

ụndeutlich ◇ *adj* unclear. ◇ *adv* unclearly.

ụndicht *adj* leaky.

ụndurchsichtig *adj* - **1.** [Geschichte, Mensch] shady - **2.** [Glas, Strümpfe] opaque.

ụneben *adj* uneven.

ụnehelich ◇ *adj*: **uneheliches Kind** illegitimate child; **in einer unehelichen Beziehung leben** to live together. ◇ *adv* illegitimately.

ụnehrlich ◇ *adj* dishonest. ◇ *adv* dishonestly.

ụneigennützig ◇ *adj* unselfish. ◇ *adv* unselfishly.

ụneinig *adj* in disagreement; **sich** *(D)* **über etw** *(A)* **uneinig sein** to disagree about sthg.

ụnempfindlich *adj* - **1.** [robust - Stoff, Material] hardwearing *UK*, longwearing *US*; [- Gerät] sturdy; [- Pflanze] hardy - **2.** [nicht anfällig - Person] immune; [- Haut] insensitive.

unẹndlich ◇ *adj* [Raum, Mühe & MATH] infinite; [Weite, Arbeit, Wiederholung] endless; [Geschichte] never-ending. ◇ *adv* enormously.

Unẹndlichkeit *die* - **1.** [von Raum, Universum] infinity; [von Weite, Wüste] endlessness - **2.** *fam* [zeitlich] eternity.

unentbehrlich, ụnentbehrlich *adj* indispensable.

unentgẹltlich, ụnentgeltlich ◇ *adj* free. ◇ *adv* [benutzen] free of charge; [arbeiten, helfen] for nothing.

ụnentschieden ◇ *adj* - **1.** [nicht entschieden - Spiel] drawn; [- Angelegenheit] undecided; **bei unentschiedenem Wahlausgang** if the election result is inconclusive - **2.** [vor Entscheidung] undecided; [nicht entschlussfreudig] indecisive. ◇ *adv* - **1.** [nicht entschieden]: **unentschieden spielen** to draw; **im Spiel steht es unentschieden** so far the game is a draw - **2.** [unentschlossen] undecidedly.

ụnentschlossen ◇ *adj* [vor Entscheidung] undecided; [nicht entschlussfreudig] indecisive. ◇ *adv* [vor Entscheidung] undecidedly; [nicht entschlussfreudig] indecisively.

unerbịttlich, ụnerbittlich ◇ *adj* - **1.** [unnachgiebig] unrelenting - **2.** [gnadenlos] relentless. ◇ *adv* - **1.** [unnachgiebig] unrelentingly; **unerbittlich bleiben** to remain adamant - **2.** [gnadenlos] relentlessly.

ụnerfahren *adj* inexperienced.

ụnerfreulich *adj* unpleasant.

ụnerhört ◇ *adj* - **1.** [empörend] outrageous; **(das ist ja) unerhört!** that's outrageous! - **2.** [Glück, Leistung] tremendous; [Preis] exorbitant. ◇ *adv* - **1.** [ungeheuer] tremendously; **unerhört viel** a tremendous amount - **2.** [empörend] outrageously.

unerlạ̈sslich, ụnerlässlich *adj* essential.

ụnerlaubt ◇ *adj* unauthorized. ◇ *adv* without authorization.

unermẹsslich, ụnermesslich *geh* ◇ *adj* - **1.** [unendlich] immeasurable - **2.** [ungeheuer] immense. ◇ *adv* immensely.

unermüdlich, ụnermüdlich ◇ *adj* tireless. ◇ *adv* tirelessly.

unerschütterlich, ụnerschütterlich ◇ *adj* [Überzeugung, Wille] unshakeable; [Person] unflinching. ◇ *adv* unflinchingly.

unerschwịnglich, ụnerschwinglich ◇ *adj* [Preis] prohibitive; [Luxusartikel] prohibitively expensive; **für jn unerschwinglich sein** to be beyond sb's means. <> *adv* prohibitively.

unerträglich <> *adj* unbearable. <> *adv* unbearably.

unerwartet <> *adj* unexpected. <> *adv* unexpectedly.

unerwünscht *adj* [Gast] unwelcome; [Kind] unwanted; [Benehmen] undesirable.

UNESCO [u'nɛsko] (*abk für* **United Nations Educational, Scientific and Cultural Organization**) *die* UNESCO.

unfähig *adj* incompetent; **unfähig sein, etw zu tun** to be incapable of doing sthg.

Unfähigkeit *die* incompetence; **die Unfähigkeit, etw zu tun** the inability to do sthg.

unfair ['ʊnfɛːɐ̯] <> *adj* unfair. <> *adv* unfairly.

Un|fall *der* accident.

Unfall|flucht *die* RECHT failure to stop after an accident.

Unfall|stelle *die* scene of the/an accident.

Unfallver|sicherung *die* accident insurance.

unfehlbar, unfehlbar *adj* infallible.

unfreiwillig <> *adj* - **1.** [nicht freiwillig] compulsory - **2.** *hum* [unabsichtlich] unintentional. <> *adv* - **1.** [nicht freiwillig] without wanting to - **2.** *hum* [unabsichtlich] unintentionally.

unfreundlich <> *adj* - **1.** [nicht freundlich] unfriendly; **zu jm unfreundlich sein** to be unfriendly to sb - **2.** [unangenehm] unpleasant. <> *adv* [nicht freundlich] coldly.

unfruchtbar *adj* - **1.** [steril, trocken] infertile - **2.** [nutzlos] fruitless.

Ungar, in (*mpl* **-n**, *fpl* **-nen**) *der, die* Hungarian.

ungarisch *adj* Hungarian.

Ungarisch(e) *das* Hungarian; *siehe auch* **Englisch(e)**.

Ungarn *nt* Hungary.

ungeahnt, ungeahnt ['ʊngeɑːnt, ʊnge'ɑːnt] *adj* undreamt-of; [Schwierigkeiten] unsuspected.

ungebeten <> *adj* uninvited. <> *adv* without being invited.

ungebildet *adj* uneducated.

Ungeduld *die* impatience.

ungeduldig <> *adj* impatient. <> *adv* impatiently.

ungeeignet *adj* unsuitable.

ungefähr, ungefähr *adv* about; **wann kommst du denn ungefähr wieder?** about when will you be back?; **die Wohnung sieht ungefähr so aus** the flat looks something like this; **sowas kommt nicht von ungefähr** such a thing is no accident.

ungefährlich *adj* safe.

ungehalten <> *adj* indignant; **über jn/etw ungehalten sein** to be indignant about sb/sthg. <> *adv* indignantly.

ungeheuer, ungeheuer <> *adj* tremendous. <> *adv* tremendously.

Ungeheuer (*pl* -) *das* monster.

ungehörig <> *adj* [Benehmen] improper; [Antwort] impertinent. <> *adv* [sich benehmen] improperly.

ungehorsam *adj* disobedient.

Ungehorsam *der* disobedience.

ungeklärt *adj* - **1.** [nicht entschieden - Problem, Mord] unsolved; [- Frage] unsettled - **2.** [nicht gereinigt - Abwasser] untreated.

ungelegen *adj* inconvenient; **das kommt mir ungelegen** that's inconvenient for me.

ungelogen *adv fam* honestly.

ungemein, ungemein <> *adj* tremendous. <> *adv* tremendously.

ungemütlich <> *adj* - **1.** [nicht behaglich] uncomfortable; [Mensch] unfriendly - **2.** [unangenehm] unpleasant. <> *adv* uncomfortably.

ungenau <> *adj* [Ausführungen, Erklärung] imprecise; [Übersetzung, Messung] inaccurate; [Vorstellung] vague. <> *adv* [ausführen, erklären] imprecisely; [übersetzen, messen] inaccurately; [erkennbar] vaguely.

ungeniert, ungeniert <> *adj* uninhibited. <> *adv* without any inhibition; [sich äußern] openly.

ungenießbar, ungenießbar *adj* - **1.** [Essen] inedible; [Getränk] undrinkable - **2.** *fam* [schlecht gelaunt] unbearable.

ungenügend <> *adj* inadequate. <> *adv* inadequately.

ungerade *adj* MATH odd.

ungerecht <> *adj* unjust. <> *adv* unjustly.

Un|gerechtigkeit *die* injustice.

ungern *adv* reluctantly; **ich tue das nur ungern** I don't like doing this.

ungeschehen *adj*: **etw ungeschehen machen** to undo sthg.

ungeschickt <> *adj* - **1.** [nicht geschickt] clumsy; **es wäre ungeschickt, das jetzt schon zu erwähnen** it wouldn't be wise to mention that now - **2.** *Süddt fam* [ungelegen] inconvenient - **3.** *Süddt fam* [unpraktisch] impractical. <> *adv* [nicht geschickt] clumsily.

ungeschminkt <> *adj* - **1.** [nicht geschminkt] without make-up - **2.** [unverhüllt] unvarnished. <> *adv* - **1.** [nicht geschminkt] without make-up - **2.** [unverhüllt] openly.

ungestört *adj* & *adv* undisturbed.

ungesund <> *adj* unhealthy. <> *adv* unhealthily.

ungetrübt *adj* - **1.** [Glück] perfect; [Zeit] blissful; [Zukunft] unclouded - **2.** [Glas, Wasser] clear.

ungewiss *adj* uncertain.

ungewöhnlich <> *adj* - **1.** [unüblich] unusual - **2.** [erstaunlich] exceptional. <> *adv* - **1.** [unüblich] unusually - **2.** [erstaunlich] exceptionally.

ungewohnt <> *adj* [fremd] unfamiliar; [Tageszeit, Großzügigkeit] unaccustomed; **etw ist für jn ungewohnt** sb is not used to sthg. <> *adv* unusually.

Ungeziefer *das (ohne pl)* pests *Pl*; **der Hund hat Ungeziefer** the dog has fleas.

ungezogen <> *adj* naughty; [Benehmen] bad; [frech] cheeky. <> *adv* [frech] cheekily; [sich benehmen] badly.

ungezwungen <> *adj* [Atmosphäre, Unterhaltung] informal; [Verhalten, Art] natural; [Lachen] easy. <> *adv* [sich verhalten] naturally; [sich unterhalten] informally; [sich bewegen] easily.

ungläubig <> *adj* - **1.** [nicht gläubig] unbelieving - **2.** [zweifelnd] disbelieving. <> *adv* in disbelief.

unglaublich, unglaublich <> *adj* - **1.** [nicht zu glauben] unbelievable - **2.** [ungeheuer] incredible. <> *adv* incredibly.

unglaubwürdig *adj* [Mensch] untrustworthy; [Geschichte] implausible.

ungleich <> *adj* unequal; [Brüder] different. <> *adv* - **1.** [nicht gleich] unequally; [sich verhalten] differently - **2.** [bei weitem] far.

Un|glück *das* - **1.** [Vorfall] accident - **2.** [Pech] bad luck; **zu allem Unglück brach er sich auch noch den Arm** on top of everything he broke his arm as well.

unglücklich <> *adj* - **1.** [nicht glücklich] unhappy - **2.** [ungünstig] unfortunate - **3.** [ungeschickt] clumsy. <> *adv* - **1.** [nicht glücklich] unhappily - **2.** [ungeschickt] awkwardly - **3.** [ungünstig] badly.

unglücklicherweise *adv* unfortunately.

ungültig *adj* invalid.

Ungunsten *Pl*: **zu js Ungunsten** to sb's disadvantage.

ungünstig <> *adj* unfavourable; [Moment] inconvenient; [Witterung] bad. <> *adv* unfavourably.

ungut <> *adj* bad. <> *adv* badly; **nichts für ungut!** *fig* no offence!

unhaltbar, unhaltbar *adj* - **1.** [Argument, Lage, These] untenable - **2.** [Schuss] unstoppable.

Unheil *das geh* disaster.

unheimlich, unheimlich <> *adj* - **1.** [gruselig] eerie; **dieser Typ ist mir unheimlich** this guy makes my flesh creep; **mir wird unheimlich** I have an eerie feeling - **2.** *fam* [groß] terrible; [Menge] huge. <> *adv fam* [ungeheuer] dead; **unheimlich viel Geld** loads of money; **sich unheimlich freuen** to be dead pleased.

unhöflich <> *adj* impolite. <> *adv* impolitely.

Uni (*pl* -s) *die fam* uni.

Uniform (*pl* -en), **Uniform** (*pl* -en) *die* uniform.

Union (*pl* -en) *die* union.

Universität [univerzi'tɛ:t] (*pl* -en) *die* university.

Universum [uni'verzum] *das* universe.

unkaputtbar *adj fam* unbreakable.

unkenntlich *adj* unrecognizable.

Unkenntnis *die*: **etw in Unkenntnis einer Sache** *(G)* **tun** to do sthg out of ignorance of sthg.

unklar <> *adj* unclear; **jn (über etw** *(A)***) im Unklaren lassen** to leave sb in the dark (about sthg). <> *adv* - **1.** [unverständlich] unclearly - **2.** [vage] vaguely.

unklug <> *adj* unwise. <> *adv* unwisely.

Unkosten *Pl* expenses; **sich in Unkosten stürzen** *fig* to go to great expense.

Unkosten|beitrag *der* contribution towards expenses.

Un|kraut *das* - **1.** *(ohne pl)* [störende Pflanzen] weeds *Pl* - **2.** [Unkrautart] weed.

unleserlich <> *adj* illegible. <> *adv* illegibly.

unlogisch <> *adj* illogical. <> *adv* illogically.

Un|menge *die* masses *Pl*; **eine Unmenge Arbeit** masses of work.

Un|mensch *der abw* monster.

unmenschlich <> *adj* - **1.** [menschenunwürdig, brutal] inhuman - **2.** *fam* [unerträglich] terrible. <> *adv* - **1.** [menschenunwürdig, brutal] inhumanly - **2.** *fam* [ungeheuer] terribly.

unmerklich, unmerklich <> *adj* imperceptible. <> *adv* imperceptibly.

unmissverständlich <> *adj* unambiguous. <> *adv* unambiguously.

unmittelbar <> *adj* immediate; [Verbindung] direct; **in unmittelbarer Nähe** in the immediate vicinity. <> *adv* directly; **unmittelbar danach** immediately afterwards.

unmöglich, unmöglich <> *adj* [nicht möglich] impossible; **es ist mir unmöglich, das zu tun** it is impossible for me to do that; **sich unmöglich machen** to make a fool of o.s. <> *adv* - **1.** [nicht möglich, keinesfalls]: **das kann unmöglich stimmen** that can't possibly be right; **das kannst du unmöglich von ihm verlangen** you can't possibly ask that of him - **2.** *fam* [sich benehmen] impossibly.

unmoralisch <> *adj* immoral. <> *adv* immorally.

unnachgiebig <> *adj* inflexible. <> *adv* inflexibly.

unnahbar, unnahbar *adj* unapproachable.

unnötig <> *adj* unnecessary. <> *adv* unnecessarily.

unnütz <> *adj* useless. <> *adv* [unnötig] needlessly.

UNO ['u:no] (*abk für* **United Nations Organization**) *die* UN.

ụnordentlich ◇ *adj* untidy. ◇ *adv* untidily.

Ụnordnung *die* mess; **etw in Unordnung bringen** to mess sthg up; **in Unordnung geraten** to get messed up.

ụnparteiisch ◇ *adj* impartial. ◇ *adv* impartially.

ụnpassend ◇ *adj* inappropriate. ◇ *adv* inappropriately.

ụnpersönlich ◇ *adj* [gen & GRAMM] impersonal. ◇ *adv* [gen & GRAMM] impersonally.

ụnpraktisch ◇ *adj* impractical. ◇ *adv* impractically.

ụnpünktlich ◇ *adj* [Mensch] unpunctual; [Abfahrt, Zahlung] late. ◇ *adv* late.

ụnrecht ◇ *adj* - **1.** [Zeit, Moment] inconvenient - **2.** *geh* [Tat, Gedanke] wicked; **es ist unrecht, so etw zu denken** it is wrong to think like that. ◇ *adv* - **1.** [ungelegen] inconveniently - **2.** *geh* [handeln, sich benehmen] wrongly; **jm unrecht tun** to wrong sb.

Ụnrecht *das* wrong; **Unrecht haben, im Unrecht sein** to be wrong; **jn/sich ins Unrecht setzen** to put sb/o.s. in the wrong; **zu Unrecht** wrongly.

ụnrechtmäßig ◇ *adj* illegal. ◇ *adv* illegally.

ụnregelmäßig ◇ *adj* [gen & GRAMM] irregular. ◇ *adv* [gen & GRAMM] irregularly.

ụnreif *adj* - **1.** [Obst] unripe - **2.** [Person] immature.

Ụnruhe (*pl* -n) *die (ohne pl)* - **1.** [Treiben] commotion; **er sorgt ständig für Unruhe** he's always causing a commotion; **Unruhe stiften** to stir up trouble - **2.** [Ruhelosigkeit] unease; **jn in Unruhe versetzen** to make sb uneasy - **3.** [Aufregung] unrest, disquiet - **4.** [Bewegung]: **in Unruhe sein** to be moving restlessly. ◆ **Unruhen** *Pl* [Aufruhr] riots.

ụnruhig ◇ *adj* - **1.** [nicht ruhig] restless - **2.** [ruhelos] uneasy; **unruhig werden** to get anxious - **3.** [gestört - Schlaf] fitful; [- Nacht] disturbed - **4.** [Zeit] troubled - **5.** [laut] noisy - **6.** [Muster, Bild] busy. ◇ *adv* - **1.** [nicht ruhig] restlessly - **2.** [ruhelos] uneasily - **3.** [schlafen] fitfully.

ụns *pron* - **1.** [Personalpronomen - Akkusativ, Dativ] us; **er sagte es uns** he told us; **das gehört uns** this is ours, this belongs to us; **sie hat uns gesehen** she has seen us - **2.** [Reflexivpronomen] ourselves; **wir konnten uns das nicht vorstellen** we couldn't imagine that; **wir setzten uns** we sat down - **3.** [einander] each other, one another.

ụnsachlich ◇ *adj* subjective. ◇ *adv* subjectively.

ụnsanft ◇ *adj* rough. ◇ *adv* roughly.

ụnschädlich *adj* harmless; **jn/etw unschädlich machen** to put sb/sthg out of action.

ụnscharf ◇ *adj* - **1.** [nicht scharf] blurred - **2.** [ungenau] vague. ◇ *adv*: **unscharf sehen** to have blurred vision.

ụnscheinbar *adj* inconspicuous.

unschlạgbar, ụnschlagbar *adj* - **1.** [nicht zu schlagen] unbeatable - **2.** [nicht zu übertreffen] unsurpassable.

ụnschlüssig ◇ *adj* undecided; **(sich** *(D)***) über etw** *(A)* **unschlüssig sein** to be undecided about sthg. ◇ *adv* indecisively.

Ụnschuld *die* - **1.** [gen] innocence - **2.** [Jungfräulichkeit] virginity.

ụnschuldig ◇ *adj* - **1.** [gen] innocent; **an etw** *(D)* **unschuldig sein** not to be to blame for sthg - **2.** [jungfräulich]: **ein unschuldiges Mädchen** a virgin. ◇ *adv* - **1.** [gen] innocently - **2.** [verurteilen] wrongly.

ụnselbstständig *adj* dependent.

ụnser, e *det* our.

ụnsere, r, s ODER **ụnsers** ◇ *pron* ours. ◇ *det* = **unser**.

ụnsereins *pron fam* the likes of us.

ụnsererseits, ụnsrerseits *adv* - **1.** [wir selbst] for our part - **2.** [von uns] on our part.

ụnseretwegen, ụnsertwegen *adv* - **1.** [uns zuliebe] for our sake - **2.** [wegen uns] because of us - **3.** [von uns aus] as far as we are concerned.

ụnsicher ◇ *adj* - **1.** [gen] uncertain - **2.** [Stimme, Hand] unsteady; **ich bin mir unsicher, ob** I'm uncertain whether - **3.** [unverlässlich] unreliable - **4.** [gefährdet] insecure - **5.** [unbeständig] unsettled - **6.** [gefährlich] unsafe; **etw unsicher machen** *fam* [sich vergnügen] to hit sthg. ◇ *adv* [nicht sicher - gehen fahren] unsteadily; [- reden, auftreten] uncertainly.

Ụn|sicherheit *die* - **1.** [Ungewissheit] uncertainty; [Eigenschaft] insecurity - **2.** [von Handlung] lapse.

ụnsichtbar ◇ *adj* invisible; **sich unsichtbar machen** to make o.s. scarce. ◇ *adv* invisibly.

Ụnsinn *der* nonsense.

ụnsinnig ◇ *adj* - **1.** [blödsinnig] idiotic - **2.** *fam* [ungeheuer] tremendous. ◇ *adv* tremendously.

Ụn|sitte *die abw* bad habit.

ụnsportlich *adj* - **1.** [Person] unsporty - **2.** [Verhalten] unsporting.

unstẹrblich, ụnsterblich ◇ *adj* immortal; [Liebe] undying. ◇ *adv*: **unsterblich verliebt** madly in love; **sich unsterblich blamieren** to make an absolute fool of o.s.

unstịllbar *adj* insatiable.

Ụnstimmigkeiten *Pl* - **1.** [Differenzen] differences of opinion - **2.** [Abweichungen] discrepancies.

Ụn|summe *die* huge amount of money.

unsympathisch *adj* unpleasant; **er/es ist mir unsympathisch** I don't like him/it.

Un|tat *die* evil crime.

untätig <> *adj* idle. <> *adv* idly.

untauglich *adj* unsuitable; **für den Wehrdienst untauglich** unfit for military service.

unten *adv* - **1.** [räumlich - im unteren Teil] at the bottom; [- tiefer gelegen] below; [- an der Unterseite] underneath; **unten am Tisch** at the bottom of the table; **links/rechts unten im Bild** in the bottom left-hand/right-hand corner of the picture; **hier/dort unten** down here/there; **von unten** from below; **nach unten** down; [- im Haus] downstairs; **mit dem Gesicht nach unten** face down; **weiter unten** further down - **2.** [im Text] below; **siehe unten** see below - **3.** *fam* [im Süden]: **unten im Süden** down south - **4.** *fam* [rangniedriger]: **die da unten** those at the bottom of the pile; **der ist bei mir unten durch** *fam fig* I'm finished with him.

unter <> *präp* - **1.** *(+ D)* [räumlich] under; [an der Unterseite von] underneath; **unter dem Tisch liegen** to lie under the table; **unter uns wohnt Herr Braun** Mr Braun lives below ODER beneath us - **2.** *(+ A)* [räumlich] under; **unter den Tisch kriechen** to crawl under the table - **3.** *(+ D)* [weniger als] under; **Kinder unter 12 Jahren** children under the age of 12 - **4.** *(+ A)* [weniger als] below - **5.** *(+ D)* [zur Angabe einer Teilmenge] among; **einer unter vielen** one of many; **unter uns (gesagt)** between you and me; **unter anderem** among other things - **6.** *(+ D)* [zwischen] between; **sie haben es unter sich ausgemacht** they arranged it between themselves - **7.** *(+ A)* [zwischen]: **sich unter die Menge mischen** to mingle ODER mix with the crowd - **8.** *(+ D)* [zur Angabe einer Hierarchie, einer Bezeichnung] under; **unter der Aufsicht/Leitung von** under the supervision/leadership of; **unter dem Namen X bekannt sein** to be known by the name of X - **9.** *(+ D)* [zur Angabe des Umstands] under; **unter Umständen** under ODER in certain circumstances; **unter Berücksichtigung von** taking into consideration; **unter der Bedingung, dass...** on the condition that... <> *adj* lower; **der unterste Knopf** the bottom button.

Unter|arm *der* forearm.

unterbelichtet *adj* - **1.** [Foto, Film] underexposed - **2.** *salopp* [Mensch] dim.

Unterbewusstsein *das* subconscious.

unterbieten (*prät* **unterbot**, *perf* **hat unterboten**) *vt* - **1.** [Preis, Angebot, Konkurrenz] to undercut - **2.** SPORT to beat.

unterbrechen (*präs* **unterbricht**, *prät* **unterbrach**, *perf* **hat unterbrochen**) *vt* - **1.** [stören] to interrupt - **2.** [aufhören - Arbeit, Behandlung, Urlaub] to break off.

Unterbrechung (*pl* **-en**) *die* - **1.** [Störung] interruption - **2.** [Aufhören - von Arbeit, Behandlung, Urlaub] breaking off.

unter|bringen *vt (unreg)* - **1.** [an einem Platz] to fit - **2.** [über Nacht] to put up - **3.** [bei Firma] to get a job for - **4.** [in Gedächtnis] to place.

Unterbringung *die* [Unterkunft] accommodation.

unterdessen *adv* meanwhile.

unterdrücken *vt* - **1.** [Volk, Minderheit] to oppress - **2.** [Gefühl, Bemerkung, Information] to suppress.

untereinander *adv* - **1.** [unter sich] among ourselves/yourselves/themselves - **2.** [unter das andere] one below the other.

unterentwickelt *adj* underdeveloped.

unterernährt *adj* undernourished.

Unter|führung (*pl* **-en**) *die* underpass, subway *UK*.

Untergang (*pl* **-gänge**) *der* - **1.** [von Volk, Kultur] decline - **2.** [von Schiff] sinking - **3.** [von Sonne, Mond] setting.

Untergebene (*pl* **-n**) *der, die* subordinate.

unter|gehen (*perf* **ist untergegangen**) *vi (unreg)* - **1.** [Sonne, Mond] to set - **2.** [Schiff, Person] to sink - **3.** [Kultur, Volk] to decline.

untergeordnet *adj* - **1.** [unterstellt & GRAMM] subordinate - **2.** [Bedeutung, Rolle] secondary.

Unter|grenze *die* lower limit.

Unter|grund *der* - **1.** [Boden] subsoil - **2.** [Unterwelt] underground; **in den Untergrund gehen** to go underground - **3.** [für Farbe, Stellfläche] surface.

Untergrund|bahn *die* underground *UK*, subway *US*.

unter|haken *vt* to link arms with. ◆ **sich unterhaken** *ref*: **sich (bei jm) unterhaken** to link arms (with sb).

unterhalb <> *adv*: **unterhalb von** below. <> *präp*: **unterhalb einer Sache** *(G)* below sthg.

Unterhalt *der* - **1.** [Zahlung] maintenance - **2.** [von Familie, Kindern] keep - **3.** [von Gebäude, Park] upkeep.

unterhalten (*präs* **unterhält**, *prät* **unterhielt**, *perf* **hat unterhalten**) *vt* - **1.** [amüsieren] to entertain - **2.** [Kosten übernehmen für - Familie] to support; [- Haus, Büro] to pay for the upkeep of - **3.** [Kontakte] to maintain - **4.** [betreiben] to run. ◆ **sich unterhalten** *ref* - **1.** [reden]: **sich (mit jm/über etw** *(A)***) unterhalten** to talk (with sb/about sthg) - **2.** [sich amüsieren] to enjoy o.s.

unterhaltsam <> *adj* entertaining. <> *adv* entertainingly.

Unterhaltung (*pl* **-en**) *die* - **1.** [Gespräch] conversation - **2.** *(ohne Pl)* [Zeitvertreib] entertainment; **gute Unterhaltung!** enjoy yourselves! - **3.** *(ohne Pl)* [von Kontakten] maintenance - **4.** *(ohne Pl)* [Betreibung] running.

Unter|händler, in *der, die* negotiator.

Unter|hemd *das* vest *UK*, undershirt *US*.

Unter|hose *die* [für Herren] underpants *Pl*; [für Frauen] briefs *Pl*.

unterirdisch *adj* & *adv* underground.

Unter|kiefer *der* lower jaw.

unter|kriegen *vt fam* to get down; **sich nicht unterkriegen lassen** *fam* not to let things get one down.

unterkühlt ◇ *adj* - **1.** [Reaktion, Verhalten] frosty - **2.** [untertemperiert] suffering from hypothermia. ◇ *adv* - **1.** [reagieren, sich verhalten] frostily - **2.** [untertemperiert] suffering from hypothermia.

Unterkunft (*pl* **-künfte**) *die* accommodation *(U)*.

Unter|lage *die* [für Gymnastik] mat; [zum Schreiben] something to rest on. ◆ **Unterlagen** *Pl* [Urkunden] documents.

unterlassen (*präs* **unterlässt**, *prät* **unterließ**, *perf* **hat unterlassen**) *vt* to refrain from; **es unterlassen, etw zu tun** to refrain from doing sthg.

unterlaufen (*präs* **unterläuft**, *prät* **unterlief**, *perf* **ist unterlaufen**) *vt* [passieren]: **mir ist ein Fehler unterlaufen** I made a mistake.

unter|legen[1] *vt* [drunter legen] to put underneath.

unterlegen[2] *vt* - **1.** [Teppich] to underlay; [Kragen, Hosenbund] to line - **2.** FILM: **etw mit Musik unterlegen** to add background music to sthg.

unterlegen[3] *adj* inferior.

Unter|leib *der* abdomen.

unterliegen (*prät* **unterlag**, *perf* **hat/ist unterlegen**) *vi* - **1.** *(hat)* [ausgesetzt sein]: **einer Sache** *(D)* **unterliegen** to be subject to sthg - **2.** *(ist)* [verlieren] to be defeated.

Unter|lippe *die* lower lip.

Unter|miete *die*: **in** ODER **zur Untermiete wohnen** to be a subtenant.

unternehmen (*präs* **unternimmt**, *prät* **unternahm**, *perf* **hat unternommen**) *vt* [Versuch, Anstrengung] to make; [Reise, Ausflug] to go on; **etwas/nichts unternehmen** to do something/nothing.

Unternehmen (*pl* -) *das* - **1.** [Betrieb] business, company - **2.** [Vorhaben] undertaking.

Unternehmer, in (*mpl* -, *fpl* **-nen**) *der, die* entrepreneur.

unternehmungslustig *adj* enterprising.

unter|ordnen *vt* to subordinate. ◆ **sich unterordnen** *ref*: **sich (jm/einer Sache) unterordnen** to subordinate o.s. (to sb/sthg).

Unterredung (*pl* **-en**) *die* discussion.

Unterricht (*pl* **-e**) *der* lessons *Pl*; **jm Unterricht geben** ODER **erteilen** to teach sb; **jm Unterricht in Englisch geben** to teach sb English; **hast du morgen Unterricht?** do you have any classes tomorrow?; **Unterricht in Deutsch nehmen** to have German lessons.

unterrichten ◇ *vt* - **1.** [Unterricht geben] to teach; **sie unterrichtet Kinder im Zeichnen** she teaches children drawing - **2.** [informieren]: **sich/jn (über etw** *(A)***) unterrichten** to inform o.s./sb (about sthg). ◇ *vi* to teach.

Unterrichts|fach *das* subject.

Unter|rock *der* slip.

untersagen *vt* to forbid; **jm untersagen, etw zu tun** to forbid sb to do sthg.

unterschätzen *vt* to underestimate.

unterscheiden (*prät* **unterschied** ODER **hat unterschieden**) ◇ *vt* - **1.** [auseinander halten, bemerken] to distinguish; **jn/etw von jm/etw unterscheiden** to tell sb/sthg from sb/sthg - **2.** [abgrenzen] to distinguish between. ◇ *vi* - **1.** [abgrenzen] to distinguish - **2.** [differenzieren] to make a distinction. ◆ **sich unterscheiden** *ref*: **sich (durch etw** ODER **in etw** *(D)***) unterscheiden** to differ (in sthg).

Unter|schenkel *der* lower leg.

Unter|schicht *die* lower classes *Pl*.

Unterschied (*pl* **-e**) *der* - **1.** [Verschiedenheit] difference - **2.** [Unterscheidung] distinction; **im Unterschied zu jm/etw** unlike sb/sthg.

unterschiedlich ◇ *adj* different. ◇ *adv* differently; **unterschiedlich groß/schnell** of varying size/speed.

Unterschlagung (*pl* **-en**) *die* [von Geldern] misappropriation.

Unterschlupf (*pl* **-e**) *der* [Obdach] shelter; [Versteck] hiding place; **Unterschlupf suchen/finden** [Obdach] to seek/find shelter; [Versteck] to seek/find a hiding place.

unterschreiben (*prät* **unterschrieb**, *perf* **hat unterschrieben**) ◇ *vt* to sign. ◇ *vi* to sign.

Unter|schrift *die* signature.

unterschwellig ◇ *adj* subliminal. ◇ *adv* subliminally.

Unterseeboot *das* submarine.

Unter|seite *die* underside.

Untersetzer (*pl* -) *der* [für Glas] coaster; [für Topf] mat.

untersetzt *adj* stocky.

Unter|stand *der* [vor Regen, Gefahr] shelter; [für Soldaten] dugout.

unter|stellen[1] *vt* - **1.** [zum Schutz] to store - **2.** [unter Gegenstand] to put underneath. ◆ **sich unterstellen** *ref* [zum Schutz] to shelter.

unterstellen[2] *vt* - **1.** [in Hierarchie]: **sie ist direkt dem Regierungspräsidenten unterstellt** she is directly answerable to the president - **2.** [Behauptung] to assume.

unterstreichen (*prät* **unterstrich**, *perf* **hat unterstrichen**) *vt* to underline.

Unter|stufe *die* SCHULE lower school.

unterstützen *vt* to support.

Unterstützung (*pl* **-en**) *die* support *(U)*.

untersuchen *vt* to examine; [polizeilich] to investigate; **etw auf etw** *(A)* **(hin) untersuchen** to examine sthg for sthg.

Untersuchung (*pl* **-en**) *die* - **1.** [Untersuchen - ärztlich] examination; [- polizeilich] investigation - **2.** [Studie] study.

Untersuchungsausschuss (*pl* **-schüsse**) *der* committee of inquiry.

Untersuchungs|haft *die* imprisonment whilst awaiting trial.

Untertan (*pl* **-en**) *der* subject.

Unter|tasse *die* saucer; **fliegende Untertasse** *fig* flying saucer.

unter|tauchen (*perf* **hat/ist untergetaucht**) ◇ *vi (ist)* - **1.** [tauchen] to dive; [versinken] to sink - **2.** *fig* [in der Menge] to disappear; [Verbrecher] to go to ground. ◇ *vt (hat)* to duck.

Unterteilung (*pl* **-en**) *die* division *(U)*.

Unter|titel *der* subtitle; **mit Untertiteln** with subtitles.

Untertreibung (*pl* **-en**) *die* understatement.

unter|vermieten *vt* to sublet.

unterwandern *vt* to infiltrate.

Unter|wäsche *die* underwear.

unterwegs *adv* on the way; **unterwegs sein** to be away.

unterweisen (*prät* **unterwies**, *perf* **hat unterwiesen**) *vt geh*: **jn in etw** *(D)* **unterweisen** to instruct sb in sthg.

Unter|welt *die* underworld.

unterwerfen (*präs* **unterwirft**, *prät* **unterwarf**, *perf* **hat unterworfen**) *vt* to subjugate. ◆ **sich unterwerfen** *ref* to submit.

unterwürfig *abw* ◇ *adj* servile. ◇ *adv* servilely.

unterzeichnen *vt* to sign.

unterziehen (*prät* **unterzog**, *perf* **hat unterzogen**) *vt* [aussetzen] to subject. ◆ **sich unterziehen** *ref* [über sich ergehen lassen]: **sich einer Sache** *(D)* **unterziehen** to undergo sthg.

Un|tiefe *die* - **1.** [seichte Stelle] shallow - **2.** [sehr große Tiefe] depth.

untreu *adj* - **1.** [treulos] unfaithful; **jm untreu werden** to be unfaithful to sb - **2.** *geh* [illoyal] disloyal.

Untreue *die* [zu Liebhaber] infidelity; [Illoyalität] disloyalty.

untröstlich *adj*: **über etw** *(A)* **untröstlich sein** to be inconsolable about sthg.

untrüglich *adj* unmistakable.

unüberlegt ◇ *adj* rash. ◇ *adv* rashly.

unübersehbar ◇ *adj* [Gebiet, Weite] vast; [Schild, Hinweis, Kratzer] obvious; [Folgen] inestimable. ◇ *adv* [groß] extremely; [aufgestellt] conspicuously.

unumgänglich *adj* unavoidable.

ununterbrochen ◇ *adj* uninterrupted. ◇ *adv* nonstop.

unveränderlich *adj* unchanging.

unverantwortlich ◇ *adj* irresponsible. ◇ *adv* irresponsibly.

unverbesserlich *adj* incorrigible.

unverbindlich ◇ *adj* not binding. ◇ *adv* without obligation.

unverblümt ◇ *adj* blunt. ◇ *adv* bluntly.

unverfänglich ◇ *adj* harmless. ◇ *adv* harmlessly.

unverfroren ◇ *adj* impudent. ◇ *adv* impudently.

unvergesslich *adj* unforgettable.

unverheiratet *adj* unmarried.

unverkennbar ◇ *adj* unmistakable. ◇ *adv* unmistakably.

unvermeidlich *adj* unavoidable.

unvermittelt ◇ *adj* sudden. ◇ *adv* suddenly.

unvermutet ◇ *adj* unexpected. ◇ *adv* unexpectedly.

unvernünftig ◇ *adj* stupid. ◇ *adv* stupidly.

unverrichtet *adj*: **unverrichteter Dinge** without having achieved anything.

unverschämt ◇ *adj* - **1.** [Mensch, Äußerung, Benehmen] impertinent; [Lüge] barefaced - **2.** [enorm - Glück] incredible; [- Preis] outrageous. ◇ *adv* - **1.** [taktlos] impertinently - **2.** [sehr] incredibly.

Unverschämtheit (*pl* **-en**) *die* impertinence *(U)*.

unversehrt ◇ *adj* [Person] unscathed; [Sache] intact; **unversehrt sein/bleiben** [Person] to be/remain unscathed; [Sache] to be/remain intact. ◇ *adv* unscathed.

unverständlich *adj* - **1.** [nicht deutlich] unintelligible - **2.** [unbegreiflich]: **es ist mir unverständlich, wie...** I don't understand how...

unversucht *adj*: **nichts unversucht lassen** to try everything.

unverwüstlich *adj* [Material] durable; [Mensch, Natur] resilient; [Gesundheit] robust; [Humor] irrepressible.

unverzeihlich *adj* inexcusable.

unverzüglich ◇ *adj* immediate. ◇ *adv* immediately.

unvorbereitet *adj* unprepared; [Rede] improvised.

unvoreingenommen ◇ *adj* impartial. ◇ *adv* impartially.

unvorhergesehen ◇ *adj* [Ereignis, Problem] unforeseen; [Besuch] unexpected. ◇ *adv* unexpectedly.

unvorsichtig ◇ *adj* careless. ◇ *adv* carelessly.

unvorstellbar ◇ *adj* unimaginable. ◇ *adv* incredibly.

unvorteilhaft *adj* unflattering.

unwahrscheinlich <> *adj* - **1.** [nicht wahrscheinlich] unlikely - **2.** *fam* [enorm] incredible. <> *adv fam* [sehr] incredibly.

unweigerlich <> *adj* inevitable. <> *adv* inevitably.

Un|wetter *das* storm.

unwichtig *adj* unimportant.

unwiderruflich <> *adj* irrevocable. <> *adv* irrevocably.

unwiderstehlich, unwiderstehlich <> *adj* irresistible. <> *adv* irresistibly.

unwillig <> *adj* [widerwillig] reluctant; [verärgert] angry. <> *adv* [widerwillig] reluctantly; [verärgert] angrily.

unwillkürlich <> *adj* involuntary. <> *adv* involuntarily.

unwirsch <> *adj* surly. <> *adv* in a surly way.

Unwissenheit *die* ignorance.

unwohl *adj*: **jm ist unwohl** [krank] sb feels unwell; [unbehaglich] sb feels uneasy; **sich unwohl fühlen** [krank] to feel unwell; [unbehaglich] to feel uneasy.

Unwohlsein *das* indisposition.

unwürdig <> *adj* undignified; **einer Sache** *(G)* **unwürdig sein** to be unworthy of sthg. <> *adv* in an undignified manner.

unzählig, unzählig <> *adj* innumerable. <> *adv*: **unzählig viele** a huge number (of).

Unze (*pl* **-n**) *die* ounce.

unzertrennlich, unzertrennlich *adj* inseparable.

unzüchtig <> *adj* indecent. <> *adv* indecently.

unzufrieden *adj* dissatisfied; **mit etw unzufrieden sein** to be dissatisfied with sthg.

Unzufriedenheit *die* dissatisfaction.

unzulässig <> *adj* inadmissible. <> *adv* inadmissibly.

unzurechnungsfähig *adj* not responsible for one's actions; **jn für unzurechnungsfähig erklären** to certify sb insane.

unzureichend <> *adj* insufficient. <> *adv* insufficiently.

unzuverlässig *adj* unreliable.

üppig <> *adj* [Busen] full; [Frau] voluptuous; [Essen] lavish; [Haar] thick; [Vegetation] lush. <> *adv* [bewachsen] thickly; [speisen, leben] lavishly; **üppig geformt** voluptuous.

Urab|stimmung *die* strike ballot.

Uran *das* CHEM uranium.

Urauf|führung *die* premiere.

urbar *adj*: **urbar machen** [Sumpf] to reclaim; [Stück Land] to cultivate.

Ur|bevölkerung *die* original inhabitants *Pl.*

Ur|einwohner, in *der, die* original inhabitant.

Ur|enkel, in *der, die* great-grandson (great-granddaughter *die*).

Urgroß|mutter *die* great-grandmother.

Urgroß|vater *der* great-grandfather.

Urheber, in (*mpl* **-**, *fpl* **-nen**) *der, die* [von Kunstwerk] creator; [von Verbrechen] perpetrator.

Urin (*pl* **-e**) *der* urine *(U).*

Urkunde (*pl* **-n**) *die* certificate.

Urkunden|fälschung *die* forging of documents.

Urlaub (*pl* **-e**) *der* holiday *UK*, vacation *US*; **Urlaub machen/haben** to have a holiday *UK* ODER vacation *US*; **im** ODER **in Urlaub sein** to be on holiday *UK* ODER vacation *US*.

Urlauber, in (*mpl* **-**, *fpl* **-nen**) *der, die* holidaymaker *UK*, vacationer *US*.

Urlaubs|ort *der* holiday *UK* ODER vacation *US* resort.

Urlaubs|zeit *die* holiday *UK* ODER vacation *US* season.

Urne (*pl* **-n**) *die* - **1.** [Graburne] urn - **2.** [Wahlurne] ballot box.

Ur|sache *die* cause; **die Ursache für etw** the cause of sthg. ◆ **keine Ursache** *interj* don't mention it!

Ur|sprung *der* origin.

ursprünglich <> *adj* - **1.** [anfänglich] original - **2.** [naturhaft] natural. <> *adv* [zunächst] originally.

Ur|teil *das* - **1.** RECHT verdict - **2.** [Bewertung] opinion; **sich** *(D)* **ein Urteil bilden** to form an opinion.

urteilen *vi* to judge; **über jn/etw urteilen** to judge sb/sthg.

Urteils|kraft *die* judgement.

Urteils|spruch *der* verdict.

Uruguay *nt* Uruguay.

Ur|wald *der* primeval forest; [tropisch] jungle.

urwüchsig ['uːɐ̯vyːksɪç] *adj* [Garten, Gelände] natural; [Sprache, Humor] earthy; [Stärke] elemental.

USA [uːˈɛsfɑː] (*abk für* **United States of America**) *die* USA.

User ['juːzɐ̯] (*pl* **-**) *der* EDV user.

usw. (*abk für* **und so weiter**) etc.

Utensilien [utɛnˈziːli̯ən] *Pl* equipment *(U).*

Utopie [utoˈpiː] (*pl* **-n**) *die* utopia.

u. U. (*abk für* **unter Umständen**), *possibly.*

u. v. a. (*abk für* **und viele(s) andere**), *and many others.*

v (*pl* - *ODER* **-s**), **V** (*pl* - *ODER* **-s**) [fau̯] *das* v, V. ◆ **V** (*abk für* **Volt**) V.

v. *abk für* **von**.

vage ['vaːgə] (*kompar* **vager**, *superl* **vagste**), **vag** [vaːk] (*kompar* **vager**, *superl* **vagste**) <> *adj* vague. <> *adv* vaguely.

Vagina [va'giːna] (*pl* **-nen**) *die* MED vagina.

Vakuum ['vaːkuʊm] (*pl* **-kuen**) *das* vacuum.

vakuumverpackt ['vaːkuʊmfɛɐ̯pakt] *adj* vacuum-packed.

Vampir ['vampiːɐ̯] (*pl* **-e**) *der* vampire.

Vanille [va'nɪljə, va'nɪlə] *die* vanilla.

Vanille|eis *das* vanilla ice cream.

variieren [vari'iːrən] *vt* & *vi* to vary.

Vase ['vaːzə] (*pl* **-n**) *die* vase.

Vater (*pl* **Väter**) *der* father.

Vater|land *das* homeland.

väterlich <> *adj* - **1.** [des Vaters] paternal - **2.** [wohlwollend] fatherly. <> *adv* [wohlwollend] in a fatherly way.

väterlicherseits *adv* on one's father's side.

Vater|tag *der* Father's Day.

Vaterunser (*pl* -) *das* RELIG: **das Vaterunser** the Lord's Prayer.

Vatikan [vati'kaːn] *der*: **der Vatikan** the Vatican.

V-Aus|schnitt *der* V-neck.

v. Chr. (*abk für* **vor Christus**) BC.

Veganer (*pl* -) *der* vegan.

Vegetarier, in [vege'taːri̯ɐ, rɪn] (*mpl* -, *fpl* **-nen**) *der, die* vegetarian.

vegetarisch [vege'taːrɪʃ] <> *adj* vegetarian. <> *adv*: **vegetarisch leben/essen** to be a vegetarian.

vegetieren [vege'tiːrən] *vi abw* to live from hand to mouth.

Veilchen ['failçən] (*pl* -) *das* - **1.** [Blume] violet - **2.** *fam fig* [blaues Auge] black eye.

Vene ['veːnə] (*pl* **-n**) *die* MED vein.

Venedig [ve'neːdɪç] *nt* Venice.

Ventil [vɛn'tiːl] (*pl* **-e**) *das* valve.

Ventilator [vɛnti'laːtɔr] (*pl* **-toren**) *der* fan.

verabreden *vt* to arrange; **etw mit jm verabreden** to arrange sthg with sb. ◆ **sich verabreden** *ref* to arrange to meet; **sich mit jm verabreden** to arrange to meet sb.

Verabredung (*pl* **-en**) *die* - **1.** [Treffen - geschäftlich] appointment; [- mit Freund] date - **2.** [Übereinkommen] arrangement.

verabreichen *vt* to administer; **jm etw verabreichen** *amt* to administer sthg to sb.

verabscheuen *vt* to detest.

verabschieden *vt* - **1.** [zum Abschied] to say goodbye to - **2.** [Gesetz] to pass. ◆ **sich verabschieden** *ref* [Auf Wiedersehen sagen] to say goodbye; **sich von jm verabschieden** to say goodbye to sb.

verachten *vt* to despise.

verächtlich <> *adj* - **1.** [missbilligend] contemptuous - **2.** [verachtenswert] despicable. <> *adv* - **1.** [missbilligend] contemptuously - **2.** [verachtenswert] despicably.

Verachtung *die* contempt.

verallgemeinern *vt* & *vi* to generalize.

Verallgemeinerung (*pl* **-en**) *die* generalization.

veraltet *adj* obsolete.

Veranda [ve'randa] (*pl* **-den**) *die* veranda.

veränderlich *adj* [Wetter, Stimmung] changeable; [Größe] variable.

verändern *vt* to change. ◆ **sich verändern** *ref* - **1.** [anders werden] to change - **2.** [eine andere Stelle annehmen] to change one's job.

Veränderung (*pl* **-en**) *die* change.

verängstigt *adj* frightened.

Verankerung (*pl* **-en**) *die* [das Anbringen] fixing *(U)*; [Befestigung] fixture; [von Schiff] anchoring *(U)*.

veranlagt *adj*: **melancholisch veranlagt sein** to have a melancholic disposition; **homosexuell veranlagt sein** to have homosexual tendencies *Pl*.

Veranlagung (*pl* **-en**) *die* disposition; [künstlerisch] bent; **homosexuelle Veranlagung** homosexual tendencies *Pl*.

veranlassen *vt*: **jn veranlassen, etw zu tun, jn zu etw veranlassen** to make sb do sthg; **etw veranlassen** to arrange for sthg.

Veranlassung (*pl* **-en**) *die* - **1.** [Veranlassen] instigation; **auf js Veranlassung (hin)** at sb's instigation - **2.** [Anlass] reason; **keine Veranlassung haben, etw zu tun** to have no reason to do sthg.

veranschaulichen *vt* to illustrate.

veranstalten *vt* - **1.** [organisieren] to organize - **2.** *fam* [machen] to make.

Veranstalter, in (*mpl* -, *fpl* **-nen**) *der, die* organizer.

Veranstaltung (*pl* **-en**) *die* - **1.** [Ereignis] event - **2.** [Organisation] organization.

verantworten *vt* to take responsibility for. ◆ **sich verantworten** *ref*: **sich vor jm/etw verantworten** to answer to sb/sthg; **sich für** *ODER* **wegen etw verantworten** to answer for sthg.

verantwortlich *adj* responsible; **für jn/etw verantwortlich sein** to be responsible for sb/sthg; **jn für etw verantwortlich machen** to hold sb responsible for sthg.

Verantwortung (*pl* **-en**) *die* responsibility; **jn zur Verantwortung ziehen** to call sb to account; **auf eigene Verantwortung** on one's own responsibility.

verantwortungslos ◇ *adj* irresponsible. ◇ *adv* irresponsibly.

verarbeiten *vt* - **1.** [Material] to process; **etw zu etw verarbeiten** to make sthg into sthg - **2.** [Eindruck, Erlebnis] to digest; [Misserfolg] to come to terms with.

Verarbeitung (*pl* **-en**) *die* - **1.** [von Rohstoffen] processing *(U)* - **2.** [Qualität] quality - **3.** [psychisch] coming to terms with the past.

verärgern *vt* to annoy.

verarzten *vt* to treat.

Verb [verp] (*pl* **-en**) *das* GRAMM verb.

Verband (*pl* **-bände**) *der* - **1.** [für Wunden] bandage; **einen Verband anlegen** to apply a bandage - **2.** [Organisation] association - **3.** [Gruppe] unit.

Verband|kasten, Verbandskasten *der* first-aid box.

verbannen *vt* to exile.

verbarrikadieren *vt* to barricade. ◆ **sich verbarrikadieren** *ref* to barricade o.s. in.

verbergen (*präs* **verbirgt**, *prät* **verbarg**, *perf* **hat verborgen**) *vt* to hide; **etw vor jm verbergen** to hide sthg from sb. ◆ **sich verbergen** *ref* to hide.

verbessern *vt* - **1.** [Leistung] to improve - **2.** [Fehler] to correct. ◆ **sich verbessern** *ref* - **1.** [besser werden] to improve - **2.** [sich korrigieren] to correct o.s. - **3.** [sozial, finanziell] to better o.s.

Verbesserung (*pl* **-en**) *die* - **1.** [gen] improvement - **2.** [Korrigieren, Text] correction - **3.** [Aufstieg] betterment.

verbeugen ◆ **sich verbeugen** *ref* to bow.

Verbeugung (*pl* **-en**) *die* bow.

verbiegen (*prät* **verbog**, *perf* **hat verbogen**) *vt* to bend. ◆ **sich verbiegen** *ref* to bend.

verbieten (*prät* **verbot**, *perf* **hat verboten**) *vt* [Handlung] to forbid; [Partei] to ban; **jm verbieten, etw zu tun** to forbid sb to do sthg.

verbilligt ◇ *adj* reduced. ◇ *adv* at a reduced price.

verbinden (*prät* **verband**, *perf* **hat verbunden**) ◇ *vt* - **1.** [Wunde] to bandage - **2.** [Werkstücke, Material] to join - **3.** [Orte, Punkte] to connect - **4.** [am Telefon] to put through; **jn mit jm verbinden** to put sb through to sb - **5.** [zubinden]: **jm die Augen verbinden** to blindfold sb - **6.** [kombinieren]: **etw mit etw verbinden** to combine sthg with sthg - **7.** [Freunde, Bekannte] to unite - **8.** [Gedanken] to associate. ◇ *vi* [am Telefon]: **ich verbinde** I'll put you through; **falsch verbunden!** wrong number! ◆ **sich verbinden** *ref* - **1.** [Stoffe, Materialien] to combine - **2.** [zusammentreffen] to be combined.

verbindlich ◇ *adj* - **1.** [Person] friendly - **2.** [Zusage] binding. ◇ *adv* - **1.** [lächeln] in a friendly manner - **2.** [verpflichtend]: **er hat verbindlich zugesagt** he has firmly accepted.

Verbindung (*pl* **-en**) *die* - **1.** [Aneinanderfügen] joining *(U)* - **2.** [Kombination & CHEM] combination - **3.** [zwischen Orten, Punkten] link - **4.** [Zusammenhang, am Telefon, Verkehrsverbindung] connection - **5.** [mit Erinnerung] association - **6.** [zu Freund, Bekannten] contact; **sich mit jm in Verbindung setzen** to contact sb.

verbissen ◇ *adj* [Kampf, Person] dogged; [Miene] grim. ◇ *adv* [arbeiten, kämpfen] doggedly; [betrachten] grimly.

verbittert ◇ *adj* bitter. ◇ *adv* with bitterness.

verblassen (*präs* **verblasst**, *prät* **verblasste**, *perf* **ist verblasst**) *vi* to fade.

verbleiben (*prät* **verblieb**, *perf* **ist verblieben**) *vi* - **1.** [übereinkommen]: **wie seid ihr gestern verblieben?** what did you arrange yesterday? - **2.** [bleiben, übrig bleiben] to remain.

verbleit *adj*: **verbleites Benzin** leaded petrol; **verbleites Super** super leaded.

verblöden ◇ *vi* (*perf* **ist verblödet**) to turn into a moron. ◇ *vt* (*perf* **hat verblödet**) to turn into a moron.

verblüffen ◇ *vt* to amaze; **verblüfft sein** to be taken aback. ◇ *vi* to be amazing.

verbluten (*perf* **ist verblutet**) *vi* to bleed to death.

verbohrt ◇ *adj* stubborn. ◇ *adv* stubbornly.

verborgen ◇ *pp* ▷ **verbergen**. ◇ *adj* hidden.

Verbot (*pl* **-e**) *das* ban.

verboten ◇ *pp* ▷ **verbieten**. ◇ *adj* - **1.** [nicht erlaubt] banned; **verboten sein** to be forbidden; **'streng verboten!'** 'strictly prohibited!' - **2.** *fam* [schrecklich] horrendous; **verboten aussehen** *fam* to look a real sight.

Verbots|schild (*pl* **-er**) *das sign indicating a restriction, e.g. "no parking", "no entry", etc.*

Verbrauch *der* consumption; **der Verbrauch von** ODER **an etw** *(D)* the consumption of sthg.

verbrauchen *vt* to consume.

Verbraucher, in (*mpl* -, *fpl* **-nen**) *der, die* consumer.

Verbrechen (*pl* -) *das* crime; **ein Verbrechen begehen** to commit a crime.

Verbrecher, in (*mpl* -, *fpl* **-nen**) *der, die* criminal.

verbrecherisch *adj* criminal.

verbreiten *vt* to spread. ◆ **sich verbreiten** *ref* - **1.** [sich ausbreiten] to spread - **2.** *abw* [sich auslassen]: **sich über etw** *(A)* **verbreiten** to hold forth about sthg.

verbreitern *vt* to widen. ◆ **sich verbreitern** *ref* to widen.

verbrennen (*prät* **verbrannte**, *perf* **hat/ist verbrannt**) ◇ *vt (hat)* - **1.** [durch Feuer] to burn - **2.** [Kalorien] to convert. ◇ *vi (ist)* - **1.** [durch Feuer] to burn - **2.** [Kalorien] to be converted. ◆ **sich verbrennen** *ref* to burn o.s.

verbringen (*prät* **verbrachte**, *perf* **hat verbracht**) *vt* - **1.** [Zeit] to spend - **2.** *amt* [bringen] to take.

verbrüdern ◆ **sich verbrüdern** *ref*: **sich mit jm verbrüdern** to avow eternal brotherhood with sb; [mit Feind] to fraternize with sb.

verbrühen *vt* to scald. ◆ **sich verbrühen** *ref* to scald o.s.

verbuchen *vt* to enter; **einen Sieg für sich verbuchen können** to notch up a success; **der Betrag wurde auf ihrem Konto verbucht** the sum was credited to her account.

verbünden ◆ **sich verbünden** *ref* to form an alliance; **sich mit jm verbünden** to form an alliance with sb.

Verbündete (*pl* **-n**) *der, die* ally.

verbürgen *vt* to guarantee. ◆ **sich verbürgen** *ref*: **sich für jn/etw verbürgen** to vouch for sb/sthg.

verbüßen *vt* to serve.

Verdacht (*pl* **-e**) *der* suspicion; **im Verdacht stehen** to be under suspicion; **jn im** ODER **in Verdacht haben** to suspect sb.

verdächtig ◇ *adj* suspicious. ◇ *adv* suspiciously.

verdächtigen *vt* to suspect; **jn einer Sache** *(G)* **verdächtigen** to suspect sb of sthg.

verdammt *fam adj & adv* [übel] damned.

verdampfen (*perf* **ist verdampft**) *vi* to vaporize.

verdanken *vt*: **jm etw verdanken** to owe sthg to sb.

verdarb *prät* ▷ **verderben**.

verdauen *vt* to digest.

verdaulich *adj*: **leicht/schwer verdaulich** easy/hard to digest.

Verdauung *die* digestion.

Verdeck (*pl* **-e**) *das* [von Autos] hood.

verdecken *vt* [zudecken] to cover; [verbergen] to conceal; **jm die Sicht verdecken** to block sb's view.

verderben (*präs* **verdirbt**, *prät* **verdarb**, *perf* **hat/ist verdorben**) ◇ *vi (ist)* to go off. ◇ *vt (hat)* to spoil; [völlig] to ruin; **jm die Laune verderben** to put sb in a bad mood; **es sich** *(D)* **mit niemandem verderben wollen** *fig* not to want to fall out with anyone.

verderblich *adj* perishable.

verdeutlichen *vt*: **jm etw verdeutlichen** to explain sthg to sb.

verdienen ◇ *vt* - **1.** [Gehalt, Gewinn] to earn - **2.** [Lob, Strafe] to deserve. ◇ *vi* to earn; **gut/schlecht verdienen** to be well/poorly paid.

Verdienst (*pl* **-e**) ◇ *der* [Entgelt] earnings *Pl.* ◇ *das* [Leistung] achievement.

verdirbt *präs* ▷ **verderben**.

verdoppeln *vt* [Gewinn, Einsatz] to double; [Anstrengungen] to redouble. ◆ **sich verdoppeln** *ref* to double.

verdorben *pp* ▷ **verderben**.

verdrängen *vt* - **1.** [räumlich] to force out - **2.** [psychisch] to repress.

Verdrängung (*pl* **-en**) *die* - **1.** [psychisch] repression *(U)* - **2.** [Abdrängen - von Person] ousting.

verdrehen *vt* to twist; **die Augen verdrehen** to roll one's eyes.

verdreifachen *vt* to triple. ◆ **sich verdreifachen** *ref* to triple.

Verdruss *der* annoyance.

verdünnen *vt* to dilute; [Farbe, Soße] to thin; [Kaffee, Wein] to water down.

verdunsten (*perf* **ist verdunstet**) *vi* to evaporate.

verdursten (*perf* **ist verdurstet**) *vi* to die of thirst.

verdutzt *adj* nonplussed.

verehren *vt* - **1.** [Gottheit] to worship - **2.** *geh* [Person] to admire - **3.** *iron* [schenken]: **jm etw verehren** to present sb with sthg.

Verehrer, in (*mpl* -, *fpl* **-nen**) *der, die* admirer.

Verehrung *die* - **1.** [von Gottheit] worship - **2.** *geh* [für Person] admiration.

vereidigen *vt* to swear in.

Verein (*pl* **-e**) *der* [für Sport und Hobby] club; [gemeinnützig] society.

vereinbaren *vt* - **1.** [verabreden]: **etw mit jm vereinbaren** to agree sthg with sb; [Termin, Treffpunkt] to arrange sthg with sb - **2.** [vereinen]: **etw mit etw vereinbaren** to reconcile sthg with sthg.

Vereinbarung (*pl* **-en**) *die* agreement; [von Termin, Treffpunkt] arrangement; **eine Vereinbarung treffen** to come to an agreement.

vereinen *vt* [Gruppen, Länder] to unite; [Meinungen] to reconcile; [Eigenschaften] to combine. ◆ **sich vereinen** *ref* [Gruppen, Länder] to unite; [Eigenschaften] to be combined.

vereinfachen *vt* to simplify.

vereinheitlichen *vt* to standardize.

vereinigen *vt* [Länder, Gebiete] to unite; [Firmen] to merge; **mehrere Titel auf sich vereinigen** to hold several titles. ◆ **sich vereinigen** *ref* [Statten, Gruppen] to unite; [Flüsse] to join up.

Vereinigte Staaten (von Amerika) *Pl* United States (of America).

Vereinigung (*pl* **-en**) *die* - **1.** [Vereinigen - von Staaten] uniting *(U)*; [- von Firmen] merging *(U)* - **2.** [Gruppe] organization.

vereint <> *adj* united. <> *adv* together.

Vereinte Nationen *Pl* United Nations.

vereinzelt <> *adj* [Regen] occasional; [Person, Überreste] odd. <> *adv* occasionally.

vereist *adj* icy.

vereiteln *vt* to thwart.

verenden (*perf* **ist verendet**) *vi* to perish.

vererben *vt* [Güter]: **jm etw vererben** to leave sthg to sb.

Vererbung (*pl* **-en**) *die* heredity *(U)*; **wir untersuchen die Vererbung von bestimmten Eigenschaften** we are investigating the way in which certain characteristics are passed on.

verewigen *vt* to immortalize. ◆ **sich verewigen** *ref fam hum* to immortalize o.s.

verfahren (*präs* **verfährt**, *prät* **verfuhr**, *perf* **hat/ist verfahren**) *vi (ist)* to proceed; **mit jm/etw verfahren** to deal with sb/sthg. ◆ **sich verfahren** *ref* to get lost.

Verfahren (*pl* -) *das* - **1.** [Gerichtsverfahren] proceedings *Pl* - **2.** [Methode] procedure.

Verfall *der* - **1.** [Niedergang - von Gebäude] decay; [- von Person, Gesundheit] decline - **2.** [von Gutschein, Garantie] expiry.

verfallen (*präs* **verfällt**, *prät* **verfiel**, *perf* **ist verfallen**) *vi* - **1.** [Gebäude] to decay; [Person] to decline - **2.** [Gutschein, Garantie] to expire - **3.** [auf etw kommen]: **auf jn/etw verfallen** to hit on sb/sthg - **4.** [geraten]: **in etw** *(A)* **verfallen** to lapse into sthg - **5.** [hörig werden]: **jm/einer Sache verfallen** to become a slave to sb/sthg.

Verfalls|datum *das* sell-by date.

verfälschen *vt* [Aussage, Tatsachen] to distort; [Geschmack] to adulterate.

verfänglich *adj* awkward.

verfärben *vt* to discolour. ◆ **sich verfärben** *ref* to change colour; **sich blau/schwarz verfärben** to turn blue/black.

verfassen *vt* to write.

Verfasser, in (*mpl* -, *fpl* **-nen**) *der, die* author.

Verfassung (*pl* **-en**) *die* - **1.** [von Staaten] constitution - **2.** [von Person] condition; **in guter/schlechter Verfassung sein** in good/poor shape.

verfaulen (*perf* **ist verfault**) *vi* to rot.

verfehlen *vt* to miss.

verfeinern *vt* to refine.

verfilmen *vt*: **einen Roman verfilmen** to make a film of a novel.

verfliegen (*prät* **verflog**, *perf* **hat/ist verflogen**) *vi (ist)* - **1.** [Geruch] to disappear; [Flüssigkeit] to evaporate - **2.** [Zeit] to fly by.

verflixt *fam* <> *adj* - **1.** [verdammt] damned - **2.** [groß] incredible. <> *adv* [sehr] damned.

verfluchen *vt* to curse.

verflüchtigen ◆ **sich verflüchtigen** *ref* [Geruch] to disappear; [Gas] to disperse.

verfolgen *vt* - **1.** [folgen, beobachten] to follow - **2.** [Verbrecher, Ziel, Plan] to pursue - **3.** [unterdrücken] to persecute.

Verfolger, in (*mpl* -, *fpl* **-nen**) *der, die* pursuer.

Verfolgung (*pl* **-en**) *die* - **1.** [gen] pursuit *(U)* - **2.** [Unterdrückung] persecution.

Verfolgungs|wahn *der* persecution mania.

verfrachten *vt* - **1.** [verladen] to transport - **2.** *fam hum* [transportieren] to cart off.

verfrüht <> *adj* premature. <> *adv* prematurely.

verfügbar *adj* available.

verfügen <> *vt* to order. <> *vi*: **über jn/etw verfügen** [haben] to have sb/sthg at one's disposal; **über etw** *(A)* **(frei) verfügen können** [bestimmen] to be able to do as one likes with sthg.

Verfügung (*pl* **-en**) *die* - **1.** [Zugriff]: **jm etw zur Verfügung stellen** to put sthg at sb's disposal - **2.** [Erlass] order.

verführen *vt* - **1.** [verleiten]: **jn zu etw verführen** to tempt sb to do sthg; **jn zum Klauen verführen** to encourage sb to steal - **2.** [zum Geschlechtsverkehr] to seduce.

verführerisch <> *adj* - **1.** [anziehend] tempting - **2.** [erotisch] seductive. <> *adv* - **1.** [anziehend] temptingly - **2.** [erotisch] seductively.

Verführung (*pl* **-en**) *die* seduction *(U)*.

vergammelt *adj fam abw* - **1.** [verdorben] spoilt - **2.** [heruntergekommen] scruffy.

vergangen <> *pp* ▷ **vergehen**. <> *adj* [Zeiten] past; **vergangenen Dienstag** last Tuesday.

Vergangenheit *die* - **1.** [vergangene Zeit] past - **2.** GRAMM past tense.

Vergaser (*pl* -) *der* carburettor.

vergaß *prät* ▷ **vergessen**.

vergeben (*präs* **vergibt**, *prät* **vergab**, *perf* **hat vergeben**) <> *vi*: **jm vergeben** to forgive sb. <> *vt* - **1.** [verzeihen]: **jm etw vergeben** to forgive sb sthg - **2.** [geben] to award - **3.** [verpassen] to miss.

vergebens *adv* in vain.

vergeblich <> *adj* futile. <> *adv* in vain.

vergehen (*prät* **verging**, *perf* **hat/ist vergangen**) *vi (ist)* - **1.** [Zeit] to pass - **2.** [verschwinden] to disappear; **der Spaß ist mir vergangen** I'm not enjoying it any more; **vor etw** *(D)* **vergehen** *fig* to die of sthg.

Vergeltung *die* retaliation.

vergessen (*präs* **vergisst**, *prät* **vergaß**, *perf* **hat vergessen**) *vt* to forget.

Vergessenheit *die*: **in Vergessenheit geraten** to fall into oblivion.

vergesslich *adj* forgetful.

vergeuden *vt* to waste.

vergewaltigen *vt* [sexuell] to rape; [allgemein] to violate.

Vergewaltigung (*pl* **-en**) *die* rape.

vergewissern ◆ **sich vergewissern** *ref* to make sure.

vergießen (*prät* **vergoss**, *perf* **hat vergossen**) *vt* - **1.** [verschütten] to spill - **2.** [Blut, Tränen] to shed.

vergiften *vt* to poison. ◆ **sich vergiften** *ref* to poison o.s.

Vergiftung (*pl* **-en**) *die* poisoning *(U)*.

Vergissmeinnicht (*pl* **-e**) *das* forget-me-not.

vergisst *präs* ▷ **vergessen**.

verglasen *vt* to glaze.

Vergleich (*pl* **-e**) *der* - **1.** [Gegenüberstellung] comparison; **im Vergleich mit** ODER **zu jm/etw** compared to sb/sthg - **2.** RECHT settlement - **3.** SPORT friendly.

vergleichbar *adj* comparable.

vergleichen (*prät* **verglich**, *perf* **hat verglichen**) *vt* to compare; **jn/etw mit jm/etw vergleichen** to compare sb/sthg to sb/sthg.

vergnügen ◆ **sich vergnügen** *ref* to enjoy o.s.

Vergnügen (*pl* -) *das* - **1.** [Freude] pleasure; **Tanzen macht ihr großes Vergnügen** she really enjoys dancing; **mit Vergnügen!** with pleasure! - **2.** [Unterhaltung] fun *(U)*. ◆ **viel Vergnügen** *interj* have fun!

vergnügt ◇ *adj* - **1.** [Person] cheerful - **2.** [Stunden] enjoyable. ◇ *adv* cheerfully.

vergoldet *adj* gold-plated.

vergraben (*präs* **vergräbt**, *prät* **vergrub**, *perf* **hat vergraben**) *vt* to bury.

vergreifen (*prät* **vergriff**, *perf* **hat vergriffen**) ◆ **sich vergreifen** *ref*: **sich an jm vergreifen** [brutal werden] to assault sb; [sexuell] to assault sb (sexually); **sich an etw** *(D)* **vergreifen** [stehlen] to misappropriate sthg.

vergriffen ◇ *pp* ▷ **vergreifen**. ◇ *adj* out of print.

vergrößern ◇ *vt* to expand; [Foto] to enlarge; [Haus] to extend; [vermehren] to increase. ◇ *vi* to magnify. ◆ **sich vergrößern** *ref* - **1.** [größer werden] to expand; [zunehmen] to increase; [Tumor] to increase in size - **2.** [mehr Raum benutzen] to get more space.

Vergrößerung (*pl* **-en**) *die* - **1.** [Vergrößern] expansion *(U)*; [von Haus] extension *(U)*; [von Tumor] increase in size; [Vermehrung] increase - **2.** [Foto] enlargement.

Vergrößerungs|glas *das* magnifying glass.

Vergünstigung (*pl* **-en**) *die* concession.

vergüten *vt*: **jm etw vergüten** [Unkosten] to reimburse sb for sthg; [Arbeit] to remunerate sb for sthg.

verhaften *vt* to arrest.

Verhaftung (*pl* **-en**) *die* arrest.

verhallen (*perf* **ist verhallt**) *vi* to die away.

verhalten (*präs* **verhält**, *prät* **verhielt**, *perf* **hat verhalten**) ◆ **sich verhalten** *ref* - **1.** [sich benehmen] to behave - **2.** [sein] to be; **es verhält sich so** this is how matters stand.

Verhalten *das* behaviour.

Verhältnis (*pl* **-se**) *das* - **1.** [Relation] ratio; **im Verhältnis zum letzten Jahr** compared to last year - **2.** [persönliche Beziehung] relationship; **ein gutes Verhältnis zu jm haben** to have a good relationship with sb - **3.** [Liebesbeziehung] affair; **ein Verhältnis mit jm haben** to have an affair with sb. ◆ **Verhältnisse** *Pl* [Bedingungen] conditions; **über seine Verhältnisse leben** to live beyond one's means.

verhältnismäßig *adv* relatively.

verhandeln ◇ *vi* - **1.** [beraten]: **mit jm verhandeln** to negotiate with sb; **über etw** *(A)* **verhandeln** to negotiate sthg - **2.** [vor Gericht] to hear a case. ◇ *vt* - **1.** [aushandeln] to negotiate - **2.** [vor Gericht] to hear.

Verhandlung (*pl* **-en**) *die* - **1.** [Beratung] negotiation - **2.** RECHT hearing.

verhängen *vt* - **1.** [zuhängen] to cover - **2.** [Urteil, Verbot] to impose; **etw über jn/etw verhängen** to impose sthg on sb/sthg.

Verhängnis (*pl* **-se**) *das*: **jn zum Verhängnis werden** to be sb's downfall.

verhängnisvoll ◇ *adj* [Tag, Begegnung] fateful; [Fehler] disastrous. ◇ *adv* disastrously.

verharmlosen *vt* to play down.

verhärten (*perf* **hat/ist verhärtet**) ◇ *vi (ist)* to harden. ◇ *vt (hat)* to harden. ◆ **sich verhärten** *ref* to harden.

verheerend ◇ *adj* devastating. ◇ *adv* devastatingly.

verheilen (*perf* **ist verheilt**) *vi* to heal.

verheimlichen *vt* to keep secret; **jm etw verheimlichen** to keep sthg secret from sb.

verheiratet *adj* married; **mit jm verheiratet sein** [mit dem Ehepartner] to be married to sb; **mit etw verheiratet sein** *fam hum* [auf etw fixiert sein] to be married to sthg.

verhindern *vt* to prevent.

Verhör (*pl* **-e**) *das* interrogation.

verhören *vt* to interrogate. ◆ **sich verhören** *ref* to mishear.

verhungern (*perf* **ist verhungert**) *vi* to starve to death.

verhüten ◇ *vt* to prevent. ◇ *vi* to take precautions.

Verhütungs|mittel *das* contraceptive.

verirren ◆ **sich verirren** *ref* to get lost.

verjagen *vt* to chase away.

verjähren (*perf* **ist verjährt**) *vi* to come under the statute of limitations.

verjụngen *vt* [Aussehen, Haut] to rejuvenate; [Belegschaft] to introduce young blood into. ◆ **sich verjüngen** *ref* to taper.

verkạlkt *adj* - **1.** [verstopft] furred up - **2.** *fam* [senil] senile; **verkalkt sein** to be gaga.

Ver|kauf (*pl* **-käufe**) *der* - **1.** [das Verkaufen] sale - **2.** [Abteilung] sales *(U)*.

verkaufen *vt* - **1.** [Ware] to sell; **etw an jn verkaufen** to sell sb sthg; **'zu verkaufen!'** 'for sale' - **2.** *fam* [darstellen]: **(jm) etw als etw verkaufen** to sell (sb) sthg as sthg. ◆ **sich verkaufen** *ref*: **sich gut/schlecht verkaufen** [Ware] to sell well/poorly; [sich darstellen] to sell o.s. well/poorly.

Ver|käufer, in (*mpl* **-**, *fpl* **-nen**) *der, die* - **1.** [beruflich] sales assistant *UK* ODER clerk *US* - **2.** [Verkaufende] seller.

verkäuflich *adj*: **verkäuflich sein** to be for sale; **schwer verkäuflich sein** to be hard to sell.

Verkehr *der* - **1.** [Straßenverkehr] traffic; **dichter Verkehr** heavy traffic - **2.** [Gebrauch]: **etw aus dem Verkehr ziehen** [Geld] to withdraw sthg from circulation; [Produkt] to withdraw sthg from sale - **3.** *geh* [Umgang] contact - **4.** [Geschlechtsverkehr] intercourse.

verkehren (*perf* **hat/ist verkehrt**) ◇ *vi* - **1.** *(hat) geh* [Person]: **mit jm verkehren** to associate with sb; **in einem Lokal verkehren** to frequent a bar - **2.** [Zug, Bus] to run. ◇ *vt (hat)*: **etw ins Gegenteil verkehren** to reverse sthg.

Verkehrs|ampel *die* traffic lights *Pl*.

Verkehrs|aufkommen *das*: **dichtes** ODER **hohes Verkehrsaufkommen** heavy traffic.

Verkehrs|funk *der* traffic bulletin service.

Verkehrs|kontrolle *die* traffic check.

Verkehrs|mittel *das*: **die öffentlichen Verkehrsmittel** public transport *(U)*.

Verkehrs|polizei *die (ohne pl)* traffic police *Pl*.

Verkehrsun|fall *der* road accident.

Verkehrsver|bindung *die* connection.

Verkehrs|zeichen *das* road sign.

verkehrt ◇ *adj* wrong. ◇ *adv* wrongly; **verkehrt fahren** to go the wrong way. ◆ **verkehrt herum** *adv* the wrong way round.

verkẹnnen (*prät* **verkạnnte**, *perf* **hat verkạnnt**) *vt* [Situation] to misjudge; [Absicht] to mistake.

verklagen *vt* to sue.

verkleben (*perf* **hat/ist verklebt**) ◇ *vi (ist)* to become sticky. ◇ *vt (hat)* - **1.** [beschmieren] to make sticky - **2.** [Riss] to stick something over.

verkleiden *vt* - **1.** [mit Kostüm] to dress up - **2.** [Innenwand] to cover; [Gebäude] to face. ◆ **sich verkleiden** *ref* to dress up.

Verkleidung (*pl* **-en**) *die* - **1.** [Kostüm] costume - **2.** [das Verkleiden] dressing up - **3.** [von Innenwand] covering; [von Gebäude] facing.

verkleinern *vt* to reduce. ◆ **sich verkleinern** *ref* to decrease.

verklẹmmt *adj* inhibited.

verkneifen (*prät* **verknịff**, *perf* **hat verknịffen**) *vt*: **sich** *(D)* **etw verkneifen** to suppress sthg.

verknoten *vt* to tie together. ◆ **sich verknoten** *ref* to become knotted.

verknụpfen *vt* - **1.** [verknoten] to tie together - **2.** [verbinden]: **etw mit etw verknüpfen** to connect sthg with sthg.

verkọmmen (*prät* **verkam**, *perf* **ist verkọmmen**) *vi* - **1.** [verfallen] to become rundown - **2.** [verderben] to go bad - **3.** [verwahrlosen]: **jn verkommen lassen** to let sb go to the bad.

verkrạchen ◆ **sich verkrachen** *ref*: **sich mit jm verkrachen** to have a row with sb.

verkrạften *vt* to cope with.

verkriechen (*prät* **verkrọch**, *perf* **hat verkrọchen**) ◆ **sich verkriechen** *ref* [kriechen] to crawl; [sich verstecken] to hide.

verkrüppelt *adj* - **1.** [Mensch] crippled - **2.** [Baum] twisted, gnarled.

verkụ̈mmern (*perf* **ist verkụ̈mmert**) *vi* to wither (away).

verkụ̈nden *vt* to announce; [Urteil] to pronounce; [Prophezeiung] to make.

verkụ̈rzen *vt* to shorten; [Leben, Urlaub] to cut short; [Arbeitszeit] to reduce; **die Zeit verkürzen** to while away the time.

Verlag (*pl* **-e**) *der* publishing house.

verlagern *vt* [Gewicht, Schwerpunkt] to shift; [an einen anderen Ort] to move. ◆ **sich verlagern** *ref* to shift.

verlạngen ◇ *vt* - **1.** [fordern] to demand; [bitten] to ask for; **viel von jm verlangen** to ask a lot of sb - **2.** [erfordern] to call for - **3.** [Lohn] to ask - **4.** [Ausweis] to ask to see - **5.** [am Telefon]: **jn am Telefon verlangen** to ask to speak to sb on the phone. ◇ *vi*: **nach jm/etw verlangen** [um etw bitten] to ask for sb/sthg; *geh* [sich sehnen] to long for sb/sthg.

Verlạngen *das* - **1.** [Wunsch] desire - **2.** [Forderung] request. ◆ **auf Verlangen** *adv* on demand.

verlạ̈ngern *vt* - **1.** [zeitlich, räumlich] to extend; [Ausweis] to renew - **2.** [Rock, Ärmel] to lengthen - **3.** [Soße] to thin down. ◆ **sich verlängern** *ref* - **1.** [zeitlich] to be extended - **2.** [räumlich] to grow longer.

Verlängerung (*pl* **-en**) *die* - **1.** [von Zeitraum, Strecke] extension - **2.** [von Rock, Ärmel] lengthening; [von Ausweis] renewal - **3.** SPORT extra time.

Verlängerungs|schnur *die* ELEKTR extension lead *UK* ODER cord *US*.

verlangsamen *vt* to slow down; **das Tempo verlangsamen** to reduce speed. ◆ **sich verlangsamen** *ref* to slow down.

verlassen (*präs* **verlässt**, *prät* **verließ**, *perf* **hat verlassen**) *vt* to leave. ◆ **sich verlassen** *ref*: **sich auf jn/etw verlassen** to rely on sb/sthg.

verlässlich *adj* reliable.

Ver|lauf (*pl* **-läufe**) *der* course; **im Verlauf von etw/einer Sache** *(G)* in the course of sthg.

verlaufen (*präs* **verläuft**, *prät* **verlief**, *perf* **hat/ist verlaufen**) *vi (ist)* - **1.** [Weg, Strecke, Farbe] to run - **2.** [Operation, Prüfung] to go. ◆ **sich verlaufen** *ref* - **1.** [sich verirren] to get lost - **2.** [Menge] to disperse.

verlegen[1] *vt* - **1.** [verlieren] to mislay - **2.** [Termin] to postpone - **3.** [an anderen Ort] to move, to transfer - **4.** [Kabel, Teppichboden] to lay - **5.** [Buch] to publish.

verlegen[2] ◇ *adj* embarrassed; **um etw nicht verlegen sein** not to be short of sthg. ◇ *adv* in embarrassment.

Verlegenheit (*pl* **-en**) *die* - **1.** [Befangenheit] embarrassment; **jn in Verlegenheit bringen** to embarrass sb - **2.** [Notlage] difficulty; **in finanzieller Verlegenheit** in financial difficulties.

Verleih (*pl* **-e**) *der* - **1.** *(ohne pl)* [das Verleihen] hiring (out) - **2.** [Firma - von Videos, Fahrrädern] rental shop; [- von Autos] car hire *UK* ODER rental *US* company.

verleihen (*prät* **verlieh**, *perf* **hat verliehen**) *vt* - **1.** [leihen] to lend; [gegen Bezahlung] to hire out - **2.** [Orden, Titel]: **jm etw verleihen** to award sb sthg - **3.** [Reiz, Glanz] to give, to lend.

verleiten *vt*: **jn dazu verleiten, etw zu tun** to lead sb to do sthg.

verlernen *vt* to forget; **das Klavierspielen verlernen** to forget how to play the piano.

verletzen *vt* - **1.** [Mensch, Körperteil] to injure; **sich den Fuß verletzen** to injure one's foot - **2.** [Gefühle, Stolz] to hurt - **3.** [Grenze] to violate; [Abkommen] to break. ◆ **sich verletzen** *ref* to hurt o.s.; [schwer] to injure o.s.

verletzlich *adj* [verletzbar] vulnerable; [empfindlich] sensitive.

verletzt ◇ *pp* ▷ **verletzen**. ◇ *adj*: **verletzt sein** [eine Wunde haben] to be injured; [gekränkt sein] to be hurt.

Verletzte (*pl* **-n**) *der, die* injured person; **ein Unfall mit vielen Verletzten** an accident in which several people were injured.

Verletzung (*pl* **-en**) *die* - **1.** [Wunde] injury - **2.** [von Grenzraum] violation; [von Gesetz, Abkommen] infringement.

verleugnen *vt* to deny; [Freund] to disown.

Verleumdung (*pl* **-en**) *die* [mündlich] slander; [schriftlich] libel.

verlieben ◆ **sich verlieben** *ref*: **sich (in jn/etw) verlieben** to fall in love (with sb/sthg).

verliebt ◇ *adj* [Person] in love; [Blicke] amorous; **in jn verliebt sein** to be in love with sb. ◇ *adv* amorously.

verlieren (*prät* **verlor**, *perf* **hat verloren**) ◇ *vt* to lose; **du hast hier nichts verloren** *fam* you've no business here. ◇ *vi* - **1.** [nicht gewinnen] to lose; **gegen jn verlieren** to lose to sb - **2.** [einbüßen] to suffer; **an etw** *(D)* **verlieren** [Reiz, Schönheit] to lose sthg. ◆ **sich verlieren** *ref* - **1.** [Personen] to lose one another - **2.** [Angst, Begeisterung] to evaporate.

Verlierer, in (*mpl* **-**, *fpl* **-nen**) *der, die* loser.

verloben ◆ **sich verloben** *ref*: **sich (mit jm) verloben** to get engaged (to sb).

Verlobte (*pl* **-n**) *der, die* fiancé (fiancée *die*).

Verlobung (*pl* **-en**) *die* engagement.

verlockend *adj* tempting.

verlogen *adj* false.

verlor *prät* ▷ **verlieren**.

verloren ◇ *pp* ▷ **verlieren**. ◇ *adj* lost.

verloren gehen (*perf* **ist verloren gegangen**) *vi (unreg)* to go missing, to disappear; **der Geschmack geht durch das Kochen verloren** it loses its taste when you boil it; **an ihm ist ein Lehrer verloren gegangen** he would have made a good teacher.

verlosen *vt* [kleine Preise] to raffle; [große Gewinne] to give away *(in a prize draw)*.

Verlosung (*pl* **-en**) *die* [von kleinen Preisen] raffle; [von großen Gewinnen] prize draw.

Verlust (*pl* **-e**) *der* loss.

Vermächtnis (*pl* **-se**) *das* legacy.

vermasseln *vt fam*: **jm etw vermasseln** to ruin sthg for sb.

vermehren *vt* to increase. ◆ **sich vermehren** *ref* - **1.** [größer werden] to increase - **2.** [sich fortpflanzen] to reproduce.

vermeiden (*prät* **vermied**, *perf* **hat vermieden**) *vt* to avoid.

vermerken *vt* - **1.** [notieren] to make a note of - **2.** [feststellen] to note.

vermessen[1] (*präs* **vermisst**, *prät* **vermaß**, *perf* **hat vermessen**) *vt* to measure; [Land, Wand] to survey.

vermessen[2] *adj* presumptuous.

vermieten *vt*: **etw (an jn) vermieten** to rent sthg out (to sb); **'zu vermieten!'** 'to let'.

Ver|mieter, in (*mpl* **-**, *fpl* **-nen**) *der, die* landlord (landlady *die*).

vermindern *vt* to reduce.

Verminderung (*pl* **-en**) *die* reduction.

vermischen *vt* to mix. ◆ **sich vermischen** *ref* to mingle.

vermịssen *vt* - **1.** [sehnsüchtig] to miss - **2.** [suchen]: **ich vermisse meinen Regenschirm** my umbrella is missing.

vermịsst *adj* missing.

vermịtteln ◇ *vi* to mediate. ◇ *vt* - **1.** [Ehe, Kontakt] to arrange - **2.** [Job, Arbeitskraft]: **jm jn/etw vermitteln** to find sb/sthg for sb - **3.** [Gefühl, Eindruck] to convey; [Wissen, Erfahrung] to impart, to pass on.

Vermịttlung (*pl* **-en**) *die* - **1.** *(ohne pl)* [von Mitarbeitern, Jobs] finding; [von Kontakten, Ehen] arranging; **durch js Vermittlung eine Stelle bekommen** to get a job through sb - **2.** [Firma, Büro] agency - **3.** [Telefonzentrale] exchange.

Vermögen (*pl* -) *das* - **1.** [Besitz] fortune - **2.** *geh* [Fähigkeit] ability.

vermögend *adj* wealthy.

vermuten *vt* - **1.** [annehmen] to assume - **2.** [für wahrscheinlich halten] to suspect.

vermutlich ◇ *adj* probable. ◇ *adv* probably.

Vermụtung (*pl* **-en**) *die* - **1.** [Annahme] supposition - **2.** [Verdacht] suspicion.

vernachlässigen *vt* - **1.** [gen] to neglect - **2.** [nicht beachten] to ignore.

vernẹhmen (*präs* **vernịmmt**, *prät* **vernahm**, *perf* **hat vernọmmen**) *vt* - **1.** [verhören] to question; [vor Gericht] to examine - **2.** *geh* [hören] to hear.

Vernẹhmung (*pl* **-en**) *die* questioning; [vor Gericht] examination.

vernẹinen *vt* [Vorschlag] to reject; [Frage] to say no to.

vernẹtzen *vt* - **1.** to connect, to link - **2.** EDV to network, to connect to the Internet; **vernetzt sein** to be on the Internet ODER online.

vernịchten *vt* to destroy; [Schädlinge] to exterminate.

vernịchtend ◇ *adj* [Kritik, Niederlage] devastating; [Blick] withering. ◇ *adv* [kritisieren] devastatingly; **jn vernichtend ansehen** to give sb a withering look.

Vernịchtung (*pl* **-en**) *die* destruction; [von Insekten] extermination.

Vernụnft *die* reason; **mit/ohne Vernunft handeln** to act sensibly/foolishly; **das widerspricht jeder Vernunft** that goes against all common sense; **zur Vernunft kommen** to come to one's senses; **jn zur Vernunft bringen** to bring sb to his/her senses.

vernụ̈nftig ◇ *adj* - **1.** [klug] sensible - **2.** [ordentlich] decent; [Preis] reasonable. ◇ *adv* - **1.** [klug] sensibly - **2.** [ordentlich] decently.

verọ̈ffentlichen *vt* to publish.

Verọ̈ffentlichung (*pl* **-en**) *die* publication.

verọrdnen *vt*: **(jm) etw verordnen** to prescribe sthg (for sb).

Verọrdnung (*pl* **-en**) *die* - **1.** [von Medikament] prescription - **2.** [von Regel] regulation.

verpạcken *vt* [Waren] to pack; [Geschenk] to wrap (up).

Verpạckung (*pl* **-en**) *die* - **1.** [Hülle - von Ware] packaging; [- von Geschenk] wrapping paper - **2.** [Verpacken] packing.

verpạssen *vt* - **1.** [Bus, Gelegenheit, Film] to miss - **2.** *fam* [Schlag, Frisur] to give.

verpẹsten *vt abw* to pollute.

verpflạnzen *vt* to transplant; [Haut] to graft.

verpflegen *vt* to cater for.

Verpflegung *die* - **1.** [das Verpflegen] catering - **2.** [Essen] food.

verpflịchten ◇ *vt* - **1.** [auf etw festlegen] to oblige; [durch Eid] to bind; **jn zu sechs Wochen gemeinnütziger Arbeit verpflichten** to give sb six weeks' community service - **2.** [Schauspieler] to engage; [Mannschaftssportler] to sign. ◇ *vi*: **dieses Angebot verpflichtet nicht zum Kauf** no purchase necessary to take advantage of this offer. ◆ **sich verpflichten** *ref* to commit o.s.; **sich vertraglich verpflichten** to sign a contract.

Verpflịchtung (*pl* **-en**) *die* - **1.** [Pflichten] obligation; **seine gesellschaftlichen Verpflichtungen** his social commitments - **2.** [von Schauspieler] engaging; [von Mannschaftssportler] signing - **3.** [Schulden] commitment.

verprügeln *vt* to beat up.

Verrat *der* betrayal; [gegen Vaterland] treason.

verraten (*präs* **verrät**, *prät* **verriet**, *perf* **hat verraten**) *vt* - **1.** [Person, Gedanken] to betray; [Geheimnis, Versteck] to give away, to betray - **2.** [Gefühle] to show - **3.** [mitteilen]: **er hat mir den Preis nicht verraten** he didn't tell me the price. ◆ **sich verraten** *ref* to give o.s. away.

Verräter, in (*mpl* -, *fpl* **-nen**) *der, die* traitor.

verrẹchnen *vt* to include; **etw mit etw verrechnen** to offset sthg against sthg. ◆ **sich verrechnen** *ref* - **1.** [falsch rechnen] to make a mistake; **sich um fünf Euro verrechnen** to be five euros out - **2.** [sich täuschen] to miscalculate.

verregnet *adj* wet.

verreisen (*perf* **ist verreist**) *vi* to go away; **verreist sein** to be away.

verrẹnken *vt*: **sich** *(D)* **den Arm verrenken** to dislocate one's arm.

verriegeln *vt* to bolt.

verrịngern *vt* to reduce. ◆ **sich verringern** *ref* to decrease.

verrọsten (*perf* **ist verrọstet**) *vi* to rust.

verrụ̈cken *vt* to move.

verrụ̈ckt ◇ *adj* - **1.** [geistesgestört] mad; **verrückt spielen** [Person] to act crazy; [Computer, Auto] to play up; **nach jm/etw verrückt sein** *fam* to be crazy about sb/sthg - **2.** [ausgefallen] crazy. ◇ *adv* [ausgefallen] crazily. ◆ **wie verrückt** *adv fam* like mad.

Verrückte (*pl* **-n**) *der, die* lunatic.

Verruf *der*: **in Verruf bringen/kommen** to bring/fall into disrepute.

verrufen *adj* disreputable.

Vers (*pl* **-e**) *der* line; **in Versen** in verse.

versagen *vi* to fail.

Versagen *das* failure.

Versager, in (*pl* **-nen**) *die* failure.

versammeln *vt* to assemble, to gather. ◆ **sich versammeln** *ref* to assemble, to gather.

Versammlung (*pl* **-en**) *die* meeting; [im Freien] rally.

Versand *der* - **1.** [Versenden] dispatch - **2.** [Abteilung] dispatch department.

Versandhaus *das* mail order firm.

versäumen *vt* - **1.** [Zug, Termin] to miss - **2.** [Pflicht] to neglect.

verschaffen *vt*: **jm etw verschaffen** to get sb/sthg; **sich** *(D)* **etw verschaffen** to get (hold of) sthg; **sich** *(D)* **einen Vorteil verschaffen** to gain an advantage; **sich** *(D)* **Respekt verschaffen** to earn respect.

verschämt ◇ *adj* bashful. ◇ *adv* bashfully.

verschärfen *vt* [Kontrolle] to tighten up; [Lage, Krise] to aggravate. ◆ **sich verschärfen** *ref* [Gegensätze] to intensify; [Lage, Krise] to get worse.

verschätzen ◆ **sich verschätzen** *ref* to miscalculate.

verschenken *vt* - **1.** [weg geben] to give away - **2.** [als Geschenk] to give *(as present)* - **3.** [Punkte] to throw away; [Raum] to waste.

verscherzen *vt*: **sich** *(D)* **etw verscherzen** to throw sthg away.

verscheuchen *vt* [Tier] to chase away; [Angst machen] to scare away.

verschicken *vt* to send out.

verschieben (*prät* **verschob**, *perf* **hat verschoben**) *vt* - **1.** [Termin] to postpone - **2.** [Möbel] to move - **3.** [schmuggeln] to traffic in. ◆ **sich verschieben** *ref* - **1.** [Termin] to be postponed - **2.** [verrutschen] to slip.

Verschiebung (*pl* **-en**) *die* postponement.

verschieden ◇ *adj* - **1.** [unterschiedlich] different - **2.** [mehrere] various. ◇ *adv* [unterschiedlich] differently; **verschieden groß sein** to be different sizes; **die Aufgaben waren verschieden schwer** the tasks were of varying degrees of difficulty.

verschimmeln (*perf* **ist verschimmelt**) *vi* to go mouldy.

verschlafen (*präs* **verschläft**, *prät* **verschlief**, *perf* **hat verschlafen**) ◇ *vi* to oversleep. ◇ *vt* - **1.** [schlafend verbringen] to sleep through - **2.** *fam* [vergessen] to forget.

verschlagen *abw* ◇ *adj* sly. ◇ *adv* slyly.

verschlechtern *vt* to make worse. ◆ **sich verschlechtern** *ref* to get worse, to deteriorate.

Verschlechterung (*pl* **-en**) *die* deterioration.

Verschleiß *der* wear (and tear).

verschleißen (*prät* **verschliss**, *perf* **hat/ist verschlissen**) ◇ *vi (ist)* to wear out; **diese Teile sind verschlissen** these parts are worn out. ◇ *vt (hat)* to wear out.

verschleppen *vt* - **1.** [Person] to take away (by force) - **2.** [Gegenstand] to hide - **3.** [Verhandlung] to draw out - **4.** [Krankheit] to allow to drag on.

verschleudern *vt* - **1.** [billig verkaufen] to give away - **2.** *abw* [verschwenden] to throw away.

verschließen (*prät* **verschloss**, *perf* **hat verschlossen**) *vt* - **1.** [Haus, Tür, Schrank] to lock - **2.** [Kunststoffbehälter] to seal; [Flasche] to stop up.

verschlimmern *vt* to make worse. ◆ **sich verschlimmern** *ref* to get worse.

verschlingen (*prät* **verschlang**, *perf* **hat verschlungen**) *vt* to devour; **viel Geld verschlingen** to cost a fortune.

verschlossen *adj* [Mensch] reticent; [Raum, Tür] locked; [Umschlag] sealed.

verschlucken *vt* to swallow. ◆ **sich verschlucken** *ref* to choke.

Verschluss (*pl* **-schlüsse**) *der* fastener; [von Flasche] top. ◆ **unter Verschluss** *adv* under lock and key.

verschlüsseln *vt* to encode.

verschmelzen (*präs* **verschmilzt**, *prät* **verschmolz**, *perf* **ist verschmolzen**) *vi*: **mit etw verschmelzen** to blend with sthg.

verschmutzen (*perf* **hat/ist verschmutzt**) ◇ *vi (ist)* [Kleidung, Wohnung] to get dirty. ◇ *vt (hat)* [Kleidung, Wohnung] to get dirty; [Umwelt] to pollute.

verschnaufen *vi* to have a breather.

verschneit *adj* snow-covered.

verschnupft *adj*: **verschnupft sein** to have a cold.

verschollen *adj* missing.

verschonen *vt* to spare; **jn mit etw verschonen** to spare sb sthg.

verschränken *vt*: **die Arme verschränken** to fold one's arms; **die Beine verschränken** to cross one's legs.

verschreiben (*prät* **verschrieb**, *perf* **hat verschrieben**) *vt*: **jm etw verschreiben** to prescribe sb sthg. ◆ **sich verschreiben** *ref*: **ich habe mich verschrieben** I've written it down wrong.

verschreibungspflichtig *adj* available on prescription only.

verschrien *adj* notorious.

verschrotten *vt* to scrap.

verschuldet *adj* in debt.

verschütten *vt* - **1.** [Wasser, Getränk] to spill - **2.** [mit Erde] to bury.

verschweigen (*prät* **verschwieg**, *perf* **hat verschwiegen**) *vt* [Nachricht] to keep quiet about; [Wahrheit] to conceal; **jm etw verschweigen** to conceal sthg from sb.

verschwenden *vt* to waste.

verschwenderisch <> *adj* [mit Geld] extravagant; [mit Energie] wasteful. <> *adv* [mit Geld] extravagantly; [mit Energie] wastefully.

Verschwendung *die* squandering; **so eine Verschwendung!** what a waste!

verschwiegen <> *pp* ▷ **verschweigen**. <> *adj* - **1.** [Mensch] discreet - **2.** [Winkel] secluded.

Verschwiegenheit *die* discretion.

verschwinden (*prät* **verschwand**, *perf* **ist verschwunden**) *vi* to disappear.

verschwommen <> *adj* blurred. <> *adv* vaguely; **ohne Brille sieht sie alles verschwommen** without her glasses everything looks blurred to her.

verschwören (*prät* **verschwor**, *perf* **hat verschworen**) ◆ **sich verschwören** *ref*: **sich gegen jn verschwören** to conspire against sb.

Verschwörung (*pl* **-en**) *die* conspiracy.

verschwunden <> *pp* ▷ **verschwinden**. <> *adj* missing.

versehen (*präs* **versieht**, *prät* **versah**, *perf* **hat versehen**) *vt* - **1.** [ausrüsten]: **etw mit etw versehen** to equip sthg with sthg; **jn mit etw versehen** to provide sb with sthg - **2.** [erledigen] to perform.

Versehen (*pl* -) *das* accident. ◆ **aus Versehen** *adv* accidentally.

versehentlich <> *adj* accidental. <> *adv* accidentally.

versenden (*prät* **versandte** ODER **versendete**, *perf* **hat versandt** ODER **versendet**) *vt* to send.

versengen *vt* to scorch.

versenken *vt* [Schiff] to sink.

versetzen *vt* - **1.** [umstellen] to move; [Angestellten] to transfer, to move; [Schüler] to move up *UK*, to promote *US* - **2.** [in einen anderen Zustand]: **sich in die Lage eines anderen versetzen** to put o.s. in somebody else's position; **jn in Erstaunen/Angst versetzen** to astonish/frighten sb; **etw in Bewegung versetzen** to set sthg in motion - **3.** [verpfänden] to pawn - **4.** [bei einer Verabredung]: **jn versetzen** to stand sb up - **5.** [austeilen]: **jm einen Stoß versetzen** to give sb a push; **jm einen Schlag versetzen** to hit sb - **6.** [antworten] to retort.

Versetzung (*pl* **-en**) *die* - **1.** [beruflich] transfer - **2.** SCHULE moving up *UK*, promotion *US*.

verseuchen *vt* to contaminate.

versichern *vt* - **1.** [erklären] to affirm; **jm versichern, dass...** to assure sb that... - **2.** [bei Versicherung] to insure. ◆ **sich versichern** *ref* - **1.** [bei Versicherung] to insure o.s. - **2.** [Gewissheit]: **sich einer Sache** *(G)* **versichern** to assure o.s. of sthg.

Versicherung (*pl* **-en**) *die* - **1.** [vertraglicher Schutz] insurance *(U)*; [Vertrag] insurance policy; **eine Versicherung (über etw** *(A)***) abschließen** to take out insurance ODER an insurance policy (for sthg) - **2.** [Firma] insurance company - **3.** [Angabe] assurance.

versinken (*prät* **versank**, *perf* **ist versunken**) *vi* - **1.** [in Sumpf, Sand, Schnee]: **in etw** *(A)* **versinken** to sink into sthg - **2.** [Schiff, Sonne] to sink - **3.** [in Gedanken]: **in etw** *(A)* **versinken** to become immersed in sthg.

versöhnen *vt* [Feinde] to reconcile; [besänftigen] to appease. ◆ **sich versöhnen** *ref* to become reconciled; **sich mit jm versöhnen** to make it up with sb.

versöhnlich <> *adj* - **1.** [Antwort, Stimmung] conciliatory - **2.** [Ende, Ausgang] optimistic. <> *adv* in a conciliatory way.

Versöhnung (*pl* **-en**) *die* reconciliation; [Besänftigung] appeasement.

versorgen *vt* - **1.** [versehen]: **jn/sich mit etw versorgen** to provide sb/o.s. with sthg - **2.** [beliefern - mit Strom, Wasser] to supply - **3.** [pflegen] to look after - **4.** [ernähren] to provide for.

Versorgung (*pl* **-en**) *die* - **1.** [mit Lebensmitteln] supply - **2.** [von Patienten] care.

verspäten ◆ **sich verspäten** *ref* to be late; **sich um eine halbe Stunde verspäten** to be half an hour late.

verspätet <> *adj* late; [Gratulation] belated. <> *adv* late.

Verspätung (*pl* **-en**) *die* delay; **mit Verspätung ankommen** to arrive late; **Verspätung haben** to be delayed; **eine Stunde Verspätung haben** to be an hour late.

versperren *vt* to block; **jm den Weg/die Sicht versperren** to block sb's way/view.

verspielen *vt* [Geld] to gamble away; [Glück, Chance] to throw away, to squander.

verspielt *adj* [Kind] playful; [Muster] fanciful.

versprechen (*präs* **verspricht**, *prät* **versprach**, *perf* **hat versprochen**) *vt* - **1.** [zusagen] to promise; **jm etw versprechen** to promise sb sthg - **2.** [erwarten]: **sich** *(D)* **etw von jm/etw versprechen** to hope for sthg from sb/sthg. ◆ **sich versprechen** *ref* [etw Falsches sagen] to trip over one's words.

Versprechen (*pl* -) *das* promise.

Verstand *der (ohne pl)* [Urteilsvermögen] reason; [Intellekt] mind; [Vernunft] sense; **den Verstand verlieren** *fam fig* to go out of one's mind; **jn um den Verstand bringen** *fig* to drive sb mad.

verständigen *vt*: **jn (von etw** ODER **über etw** *(A)***) verständigen** to notify sb (of sthg).

◆ **sich verständigen** *ref* - **1.** [kommunizieren] to make o.s. understood; **sich mit jm verständigen** to communicate with sb - **2.** [übereinkommen]: **sich über etw** *(A)* **verständigen** to come to an agreement on sthg.

Verständigung (*pl* **-en**) *die* - **1.** [Benachrichtigung] notification - **2.** [Kommunikation] communication - **3.** [Übereinkunft] agreement.

verständlich ◇ *adj* - **1.** [klar - Worte, Antwort] audible - **2.** [begreiflich - Verhalten, Angst] understandable; [- Text] comprehensible; **sich verständlich machen** to make o.s. understood. ◇ *adv* [klar] clearly.

Verständnis *das* understanding.

verständnisvoll ◇ *adj* understanding. ◇ *adv* understandingly.

verstärken *vt* - **1.** [stärker machen] to strengthen - **2.** [intensivieren] to increase; [Bemühungen] to intensify; [Strom] to boost; [Signal, Ton] to amplify - **3.** [Truppen, Team] to reinforce. ◆ **sich verstärken** *ref* [stärker werden] to intensify.

Verstärkung (*pl* **-en**) *die* reinforcement; **Verstärkung anfordern** to call for reinforcements.

verstauchen *vt*: **sich** *(D)* **den Fuß verstauchen** to sprain one's ankle.

verstauen *vt* to pack.

Versteck (*pl* **-e**) *das* hiding place; [von Verbrechern] hideout.

verstecken *vt* to hide. ◆ **sich verstecken** *ref*: **sich (vor jm/etw) verstecken** to hide (from sb/sthg).

verstehen (*prät* **verstand**, *perf* **hat verstanden**) ◇ *vt* - **1.** [gen] to understand; **ich konnte kein Wort verstehen** I couldn't understand ODER make out a single word; **etw unter etw** *(D)* **verstehen** to understand sthg by sthg; **versteh mich nicht falsch** don't get me wrong - **2.** [vermögen] to know; **etwas/nichts verstehen von** to know a bit/nothing about. ◇ *vi* to understand; **jm zu verstehen geben, dass...** to give sb to understand that... ◆ **sich verstehen** *ref* [Personen] to get on; **sich (gut) mit jm verstehen** to get on well with sb; **das versteht sich von selbst!** that goes without saying!

versteigern *vt* to auction; **etw meistbietend versteigern** to sell sthg to the highest bidder.

verstellen *vt* - **1.** [verändern] to adjust - **2.** [falsch stellen] to set wrongly; [Stimme, Schrift] to disguise - **3.** [blockieren]: **jm den Weg/die Sicht verstellen** to block sb's path/view - **4.** [an einen falschen Ort] to put in the wrong place. ◆ **sich verstellen** *ref* - **1.** [zur Täuschung - im Wesen] to play-act - **2.** [sich anders einstellen] to be moved (out of position).

verstohlen ◇ *adj* furtive. ◇ *adv* furtively.

verstopfen (*perf* **hat/ist verstopft**) ◇ *vt (hat)* to plug (up); [Abfluss] to block. ◇ *vi (ist)* to be blocked (up).

verstört *adj* distraught.

Ver|stoß (*pl* **-stöße**) *der* infringement; **ein Verstoß gegen etw** [gegen Gesetz] an infringement of sthg; [gegen Anstand] an offence against sthg.

verstoßen (*präs* **verstößt**, *prät* **verstieß**, *perf* **hat verstoßen**) ◇ *vi*: **gegen etw verstoßen** [Regel, Gesetz] to infringe sthg; [Anstand, Geschmack] to offend against sthg. ◇ *vt* [Kind, Ehefrau] to disown; **jn aus einer Gruppe verstoßen** to throw sb out of a group.

verstreichen (*prät* **verstrich**, *perf* **hat/ist verstrichen**) ◇ *vt (hat)* [Butter] to spread; [Farbe] to apply. ◇ *vi (ist)* [Zeit] to pass.

verstreuen *vt* - **1.** [verteilen] to scatter - **2.** [verschütten] to spill - **3.** [Creme] to spread.

verstümmeln *vt* to mutilate.

Versuch (*pl* **-e**) *der* - **1.** [Handlung] attempt - **2.** [wissenschaftlich] experiment.

versuchen ◇ *vt* to try; [etwas Schwieriges] to attempt. ◇ *vi* [kosten]: **von etw versuchen** to try sthg.

Versuchs|kaninchen [fɛɐ̯'zuːxskaniːnçən] *das* guinea pig.

Versuchung (*pl* **-en**) *die* temptation.

versüßen *vt* [Leben, Befinden] to make more pleasant; [schlechte Situation] to sweeten.

vertagen *vt* [verschieben] to postpone; [später fortsetzen] to adjourn.

vertauschen *vt* [verwechseln] to mix up.

verteidigen *vt* to defend. ◆ **sich verteidigen** *ref* to defend o.s.

Verteidiger, in (*mpl* **-**, *fpl* **-nen**) *der, die* RECHT counsel for the defence.

Verteidigung (*pl* **-en**) *die* defence.

Verteidigung|minister, in *der, die* defence minister.

verteilen *vt* - **1.** [ausgeben] to distribute; [Prospekte] to hand out - **2.** [teilen] to share out - **3.** [Creme] to spread. ◆ **sich verteilen** *ref* to spread out.

Verteilung (*pl* **-en**) *die* distribution.

vertiefen *vt* to deepen. ◆ **sich vertiefen** *ref* - **1.** [Graben, Loch, Falten] to become deeper - **2.** [Gefühl, Freundschaft] to deepen - **3.** [sich konzentrieren]: **sich in etw** *(A)* **vertiefen** to become engrossed in sthg.

Vertrag (*pl* **Verträge**) *der* contract.

vertragen (*präs* **verträgt**, *prät* **vertrug**, *perf* **hat vertragen**) *vt* to stand, to bear; [Belastung, Kritik, Witz] to take; **sie verträgt keinen Kaffee** coffee doesn't agree with her. ◆ **sich vertragen** *ref*: **sich mit jm vertragen** to get on with sb.

vertraglich ◇ *adj* contractual. ◇ *adv* contractually.

verträglich *adj* [Person, Charakter] easy-going; **gut verträglich** [Essen] easily digestible; [Medikament] with few side-effects.

vertrauen *vi*: **jm/einer Sache vertrauen** to trust sb/sthg; **auf etw** *(A)* **vertrauen** to put one's trust in sthg; **auf sein Glück vertrauen** to trust to luck.

Vertrauen *das* trust; **zu jm Vertrauen haben** to trust sb. ◆ **im Vertrauen** *adv* in confidence. ◆ **Vertrauen erweckend** *adj*: **ein Vertrauen erweckender Mensch** a person who inspires confidence.

Vertrauens|lehrer, **in** *der, die teacher who represents the interests of the pupils.*

Vertrauens|sache *die* matter of trust.

vertrauenswürdig *adj* trustworthy.

vertraulich ◇ *adj* - **1.** [geheim] confidential - **2.** [herzlich] familiar. ◇ *adv* [geheim] confidentially.

verträumt ◇ *adj* dreamy. ◇ *adv* dreamily.

vertraut *adj* familiar; [Freund] close; **jm vertraut sein** to be familiar to sb; **mit etw vertraut sein** to be familiar with sthg; **sich mit etw vertraut machen** to familiarize o.s. with sthg.

vertreiben (*prät* **vertrieb**, *perf* **hat vertrieben**) *vt* - **1.** [verjagen] to drive away; [aus Land] to drive out; **jn aus einem Haus vertreiben** to turn sb out of a house - **2.** [verkaufen] to sell - **3.** [Zeit] to pass.

vertretbar *adj* [Meinung] tenable; [Kosten, Risiko] justifiable.

vertreten (*präs* **vertritt**, *prät* **vertrat**, *perf* **hat vertreten**) *vt* - **1.** [bei Urlaub, Krankheit] to stand in for - **2.** [Interessen, Firma, Land] to represent - **3.** [Standpunkt, These, Prinzip] to support - **4.** [anwesend]: **vertreten sein** to be present - **5.** [verletzen]: **sich** *(D)* **den Fuß vertreten** to twist one's ankle.

Vertreter, **in** (*mpl* -, *fpl* **-nen**) *der, die* - **1.** [Stellvertreter] stand-in; [von Arzt] locum - **2.** [von Firma, Gruppe] representative - **3.** [von Meinung, Interessen] advocate.

Vertretung (*pl* **-en**) *die* - **1.** [bei Urlaub, Krankheit] replacement - **2.** [von Interessen, Firma, Land] representation - **3.** [Person] representative - **4.** [Filiale] branch; **diplomatische Vertretung** diplomatic mission.

Vertrieb *der* - **1.** [Verkauf] sale - **2.** [Abteilung] sales department; **im Vertrieb arbeiten** to work in sales.

vertrocknen (*perf* **ist vertrocknet**) *vi* [Boden] to dry out; [Pflanze, Gras] to wither.

vertrödeln *vt* to waste.

vertrösten *vt* to put off; **jn auf später vertrösten** to put sb off until later.

vertun (*prät* **vertat**, *perf* **hat vertan**) *vt* to waste. ◆ **sich vertun** *ref* to get it wrong.

vertuschen *vt* [Skandal] to hush up; [Fehler, Wahrheit] to cover up.

verübeln *vt*: **jm etw verübeln** to hold sthg against sb.

verüben *vt* to commit.

verunglücken (*perf* **ist verunglückt**) *vi* to have an accident; **mit dem Zug verunglücken** to be in a train crash.

verunsichern *vt* to make uneasy.

verunstalten *vt* to disfigure.

veruntreuen *vt* RECHT to embezzle.

verursachen *vt* to cause.

verurteilen *vt* - **1.** [vor Gericht]: **jn zu etw verurteilen** to sentence sb to sthg - **2.** [kritisieren] to condemn.

Verur|teilung *die* - **1.** [vor Gericht] sentencing - **2.** [Missbilligung] condemnation.

vervielfachen *vt* to multiply. ◆ **sich vervielfachen** *ref* to multiply.

vervielfältigen *vt* to make copies of.

vervollkommnen *vt* to perfect.

vervollständigen *vt* to complete.

verwackelt *adj fam* blurred.

verwählen ◆ **sich verwählen** *ref* to dial the wrong number.

verwahren *vt* to keep (safe).

verwahrlosen (*perf* **ist verwahrlost**) *vi* to be neglected; [Garten] to run wild.

verwaist *adj* - **1.** [Kind] orphaned - **2.** [Ort] deserted.

verwalten *vt* [Gebäude, Besitz] to manage; [Altenheim, Geschäft] to run; [Amt] to hold; [Geld] to administer.

Verwalter, **in** (*mpl* -, *fpl* **-nen**) *der, die* manager; [von Geld] administrator.

Verwaltung (*pl* **-en**) *die* administration; [von Geschäft, Gebäude] management; **die städtische Verwaltung** the municipal authorities.

verwandeln *vt* to transform, to change; **etw in etw** *(A)* **verwandeln** to transform ODER change sthg into sthg. ◆ **sich verwandeln** *ref* to change.

Verwandlung (*pl* **-en**) *die* transformation; [Zoologie] metamorphosis.

verwandt ◇ *pp* ▷ **verwenden**. ◇ *adj* related; **mit jm verwandt sein** to be related to sb.

Verwandte (*pl* **-n**) *der, die* relative.

Verwandtschaft (*pl* **-en**) *die* - **1.** [alle Verwandte] family - **2.** [Verwandtsein] relationship.

Verwarnung (*pl* **-en**) *die* caution; **eine gebührenpflichtige Verwarnung** a fine.

verwechseln [fɛr'vɛksl̩n] *vt* to mix up; **jn/etw mit jm/etw verwechseln** to mistake sb/sthg for sb/sthg.

Verwechslung (*pl* **-en**), **Verwechselung** (*pl* **-en**) [fɛr'vɛks(ə)lʊŋ] *die* mixing up; **es gab eine Verwechslung** there was a mix-up.

verweigern ◇ *vt* to refuse; **die Annahme von etw verweigern** to refuse to take sthg; **einen Befehl verweigern** to refuse to obey an order; **den Kriegsdienst verweigern** to be a conscientious objector; **jm etw verweigern** to refuse sb sthg. ◇ *vi fam* [den Wehrdienst verweigern] to be a conscientious objector.

Verweigerung (*pl* -en) *die* refusal; **die Verweigerung eines Befehls** refusal to obey an order.

Verweis (*pl* -e) *der* [Tadel] reprimand.

verweisen (*prät* **verwies**, *perf* **hat verwiesen**) ◇ *vt* - **1.** [weiterleiten]: **jn/etw an jn/etw verweisen** to refer sb/sthg to sb/sthg - **2.** [ausweisen - von Schule] to expel; [- aus Raum] to throw out. ◇ *vi*: **auf etw** *(A)* **verweisen** to refer to sthg; **eine Tafel verweist auf den Eingang** a sign points to the entrance.

verwelken (*perf* **ist verwelkt**) *vi* to wilt.

verwenden (*prät* **verwendete** ODER **verwandte**, *perf* **hat verwendet** ODER **verwandt**) *vt* - **1.** [benutzen] to use - **2.** [einsetzen - Zeit, Geld] to spend; **etw für** ODER **zu etw verwenden** to use sthg for sthg; **Kraft auf etw verwenden** to put energy into sthg.

Verwendung (*pl* -en) *die* use.

verwerfen (*präs* **verwirft**, *prät* **verwarf**, *perf* **hat verworfen**) *vt* to reject.

verwerten *vt* - **1.** [Kenntnisse] to make use of - **2.** [Abfall, Altpapier] to re-use, to recycle.

verwest *adj* decomposed.

Verwesung *die* decomposition.

verwildern (*perf* **ist verwildert**) *vi* [Garten] to become overgrown; [Tier] to become wild.

verwirklichen *vt* [Traum] to realize; [Plan, Ziel] to achieve; [Idee] to put into practice. ◆ **sich verwirklichen** *ref* - **1.** [Hoffnung, Traum, Befürchtung] to come true - **2.** [Person]: **sich selbst verwirklichen** to fulfil o.s.

Verwirklichung (*pl* -en) *die* [von Traum] realization; [von Plan, Ziel] achievement; [von Idee] putting into practice.

verwirren *vt* - **1.** [Fäden] to tangle up - **2.** [Person] to confuse.

Verwirrung (*pl* -en) *die* confusion.

verwischen *vt* [Spur] to cover over; [Schrift] to smudge; [Farbe] to smear; [Kontur] to blur.

verwitwet *adj* widowed.

verwöhnen *vt* to spoil.

verworren ◇ *adj* confused. ◇ *adv* [erzählen] in a confusing manner.

verwunden *vt* to wound.

Verwunderung *die* surprise.

Verwundete (*pl* -n) *der, die* wounded person; **die Verwundeten** the wounded.

Verwundung (*pl* -en) *die* [Wunde] wound.

verwünschen *vt* - **1.** [verfluchen] to curse - **2.** [verzaubern] to bewitch.

verwüsten *vt* to devastate.

Verwüstung (*pl* -en) *die* devastation *(U)*.

verzählen ◆ **sich verzählen** *ref* to miscount.

verzaubern *vt* to enchant; **einen Prinz in einen Frosch verzaubern** to turn a prince into a frog.

verzeichnen *vt* to record; [Erfolg] to notch up; **ist diese Stadt auf der Landkarte verzeichnet?** is this town (marked) on the map?

Verzeichnis (*pl* -se) *das* - **1.** [Liste] list; [Katalog] catalogue; [mit Namen] index - **2.** EDV directory.

verzeihen (*prät* **verzieh**, *perf* **hat verziehen**) *vt* to forgive; **jm etw verzeihen** to forgive sb for sthg; **verzeihen Sie bitte!** excuse me, please!; **verzeihen Sie bitte, dass ich stören muss!** please forgive the intrusion!

Verzeihung *die* forgiveness; **jn um Verzeihung bitten** to apologize to sb. ◆ **Verzeihung** *interj* sorry!

verzerren *vt* - **1.** [Gesicht] to contort - **2.** [Bild, Klang] to distort. ◆ **sich verzerren** *ref* [Gesicht] to contort.

Verzicht (*pl* -e) *der*: **der Verzicht auf Süßigkeiten fällt ihm schwer** he finds it hard to go without sweets.

verzichten *vi* to do without; **auf jn/etw verzichten** to do without sb/sthg; **wir werden zukünftig auf ihre Dienste verzichten** we will be dispensing with her services; **auf eine Bemerkung verzichten** not to make ODER to refrain from making a comment; **er verzichtete darauf, sich zu beschweren** he refrained from making a complaint; **zugunsten eines anderen auf eine Stelle verzichten** to let sb have a job instead of o.s.; **danke, ich verzichte** I'll pass (on that one), thanks.

verzieh *prät* ▷ **verzeihen**.

verziehen (*prät* **verzog**, *perf* **hat/ist verzogen**) ◇ *pp* ▷ **verzeihen**. ◇ *vt (hat)* - **1.** [Miene, Mund] to screw up; **das Gesicht verziehen** to pull a face - **2.** [Kind] to spoil. ◇ *vi (ist)* [fortziehen] to move. ◆ **sich verziehen** *ref* - **1.** [Gesicht, Mund] to contort - **2.** [Tür, Holz] to warp - **3.** [Nebel, Rauch] to disperse; [Unwetter] to pass - **4.** *fam* [fortgehen] to disappear; **verzieh dich** get lost!

verzieren *vt* to decorate.

verzögern *vt* - **1.** [verschieben] to delay - **2.** [verlangsamen] to slow down. ◆ **sich verzögern** *ref* [sich verspäten] to be delayed.

Verzögerung (*pl* -en) *die* [Verspätung] delay.

verzollen *vt* to declare; **haben Sie etwas zu verzollen?** do you have anything to declare?

Verzug *der* delay. ◆ **im Verzug** *adv*: **mit etw im Verzug sein** to be behind with sthg; **Gefahr ist im Verzug** danger is imminent.

verzweifeln (*perf* **ist verzweifelt**) *vi* to despair; **an etw** *(D)***/über etw** *(A)* **verzweifeln** to despair of/at sthg.

verzweifelt ◇ *adj* desperate; [Blick] despairing. ◇ *adv* [kämpfen, versuchen] desperately; [sagen, anblicken] despairingly.

Verzweiflung (*pl* **-en**) *die* despair; **vor Verzweiflung** in despair.

Veto ['ve:to] (*pl* **-s**) *das* veto.

Vetter (*pl* **-n**) *der* cousin.

vgl. (*abk für* **vergleiche**) cf.

VHS [fauhaː'ɛs] *die abk für* **Volkshochschule**.

vibrieren [vi'briːrən] *vi* to vibrate; [Stimme] to quiver.

Video ['viːdeo] (*pl* **-s**) *das* video.

Video|film *der* video.

Video|kamera *die* video camera.

Video|kassette *die* video (tape).

Video|rekorder *der* video (recorder) *UK*, VCR *US*.

Video|spiel *das* video game.

Video|text *der* videotext.

Vieh *das* - **1.** [alle Tiere] livestock - **2.** [Rinder] cattle.

viel (*kompar* **mehr**, *superl* **meiste**), **vieles** (*kompar* **mehr**, *superl* **meiste**) ◇ *adj*: **das viele Geld** all the money; **das Kleid mit den vielen Knöpfen** the dress with all the buttons; **vielen Dank!** thank you very much! ◇ *det* - **1.** [Menge] much, a lot of; **zu viel** too much - **2.** [Anzahl] many, a lot of, lots of; **zu viel** too many; **viele Menschen** many ODER a lot of people. ◇ *adv* - **1.** [intensiv, oft] a lot; **viel arbeiten** to work a lot; **sie ist viel allein** she is alone a lot of the time - **2.** [zum Ausdruck der Verstärkung] much; **viel mehr** much more; **viel zu** much too, far too; **nicht viel anders** not very different. ◇ *pron* a lot; **er sagt viel** he says a lot; **er sagt nicht viel** he doesn't say much. ◆ **nicht viel** ◇ *det* not much. ◇ *adv* not much; **er schläft nicht viel** he doesn't sleep much. ◆ **nicht viele** *det* not many. ◆ **vieles** *pron* a lot of things. ◆ **viel zu viel** *det* & *adv* much too much. ◆ **viel zu viele** *det* far too many; *siehe auch* **zu viel**.

vielfach ◇ *adj* [mehrfach, wiederholt] multiple; **auf vielfachen Wunsch** by popular demand; **das vielfache Gewicht** many times the weight. ◇ *adv* - **1.** [mehrfach, wiederholt] several times - **2.** [häufig] often.

Vielfache *das* [von Zahl] multiple; **um ein Vielfaches** many times over.

Vielfalt *die* diversity, great variety.

vielfältig *adj* diverse.

vielleicht *adv* - **1.** [eventuell] perhaps - **2.** *fam* [wirklich, außerordentlich] really; **der ist vielleicht gerannt!** he didn't half run! - **3.** [Ausdruck der Höflichkeit]: **wären Sie vielleicht so freundlich, den Termin zu bestätigen?** could you possibly confirm the date for me? - **4.** [ungefähr] about - **5.** *fam* [etwa]: **hast du vielleicht gedacht, ich würde da mitmachen?** you didn't think I would join in, did you? - **6.** *fam* [Ausdruck der Ungeduld]: **vielleicht kannst du dich mal beeilen!** do you think you could possibly get a move on!

vielmals *adv*: **danke vielmals** thank you very much.

vielsagend, viel sagend ◇ *adj* meaningful. ◇ *adv* meaningfully.

vielseitig ◇ *adj* - **1.** [Person] versatile - **2.** [umfassend] varied. ◇ *adv*: **vielseitig begabt** multitalented; **vielseitig einsetzbar** versatile.

vielversprechend, viel sagend ◇ *adj* promising. ◇ *adv* promisingly.

vier [fiːɐ̯] *num* four; **auf allen vieren** *fam* on all fours; *siehe auch* **sechs**.

Vier (*pl* **-en**) *die* - **1.** [Zahl] four - **2.** [Schulnote] ≃ D, *mark of 4 on a scale from 1 to 6; siehe auch* **Sechs**.

Viereck (*pl* **-e**) *das* four-sided figure; [Rechteck] rectangle; [Quadrat] square.

viereckig *adj* four-sided; [rechteckig] rectangular; [quadratisch] square.

vierfach ◇ *adj*: **die vierfache Menge** four times as much; **in vierfacher Größe** four times as big; **der vierfache Gewinner** the four-times winner. ◇ *adv* four times.

vierhundert *num* four hundred.

viermal *adv* four times.

vierspurig *adj* four-lane.

viertausend *num* four thousand.

vierte, **r**, **s** *adj* fourth; *siehe auch* **sechste**.

Vierte (*pl* **-n**) *der, die, das* fourth; *siehe auch* **Sechste**.

viertel *adj (unver)* quarter; *siehe auch* **sechstel**.

Viertel (*pl* **-**) *das* - **1.** [Teil] quarter; **Viertel vor/nach drei** a quarter to/past *UK* ODER after *US* three - **2.** MUS crotchet *UK*; *siehe auch* **Sechstel**.

Viertel|finale *das* quarter-final.

Viertel|jahr (*pl* **-e**) *das* quarter.

Viertel|stunde (*pl* **-n**) *die* quarter of an hour.

vierzehn *num* fourteen; *siehe auch* **sechs**.

Vierzehn (*pl* **-en**) *die* fourteen; *siehe auch* **Sechs**.

vierzehntägig ◇ *adv* every fortnight, fortnightly. ◇ *adj* - **1.** [alle zwei Wochen] fortnightly - **2.** [zwei Wochen lang] two-week, fortnight-long.

vierzig *num* forty; *siehe auch* **sechs**.

Vierzigerjahre, vierziger Jahre *Pl*: **die Vierzigerjahre** the forties.

Vierzimmer|wohnung *die* four-room flat *UK* ODER apartment *US*.

Vietnam [viɛt'nam] *nt* Vietnam.

Vikar, in [vi'kaːɐ̯, rɪn] (*mpl* **-e**, *fpl* **-nen**) *der, die* [evangelisch] ≃ curate.

Vịlla ['vɪla] (*pl* **Vịllen**) *die* villa.

violẹtt [vi̯o'lɛt] *adj* purple.

Violịne [vi̯o'liːnə] (*pl* **-n**) *die* violin.

Violin|schlüssel *der* treble clef.

Viper ['viːpɐ] (*pl* **-n**) *die* viper.

virtuẹll ◇ *adj* virtual; **virtuelle Realität** virtual reality. ◇ *adv* virtually.

Virus ['viːrʊs] (*pl* **Viren**) *der ODER das* MED & EDV virus.

Virus|infektion *die* viral infection.

Visier [vi'ziːɐ] (*pl* **-e**) *das* - **1.** [von Helm] visor - **2.** [von Gewehr] sight; **jn/etw im Visier haben** [es auf jn abgesehen haben] to have it in for sb/sthg; [anpeilen] to have one's eye on sb/sthg.

Visite [vi'ziːtə] (*pl* **-n**) *die* [privat, geschäftlich] visit; [Besuch des Arztes]: **Visite machen** to do one's rounds.

Visiten|karte *die* visiting card.

Viskose [vɪs'koːzə] *die* viscose.

Visum ['viːzʊm] (*pl* **Visa** ODER **Visen**) *das* visa.

Vitamịn [vita'miːn] (*pl* **-e**) *das* vitamin.

Vitrine [vi'triːnə] (*pl* **-n**) *die* - **1.** [Schrank] display cabinet - **2.** [Ausstellungskasten] display case.

Vize|kanzler, in *der, die* vice-chancellor.

Vize|präsident, in *der, die* vice-president.

Vogel (*pl* **Vögel**) *der* - **1.** [Tier] bird - **2.** *fam* [Person]: **ein komischer Vogel** an odd customer; **einen Vogel haben** *salopp abw* to be off one's head; **jm einen Vogel zeigen** *fam* to tap one's forehead at sb *(to indicate that he/she is crazy)*.

Vogelscheuche (*pl* **-n**) *die* scarecrow.

Vokabel [vo'kaːbl̩] (*pl* **-n**) *die* word; **Vokabeln** vocabulary *(U)*.

Vokabular [vokabu'laːɐ̯] (*pl* **-e**) *das* vocabulary.

Vokal [vo'kaːl] (*pl* **-e**) *der* vowel.

Vọlk (*pl* **Vọ̈lker**) *das* - **1.** [gen] people *Pl*; **das deutsche Volk** the German nation ODER people - **2.** *(ohne pl) fam* [viele Personen] crowd.

Vọ̈lker|bund *der* HIST League of Nations.

Vọ̈lker|kunde *die* ethnology.

Vọ̈lker|recht *das* international law.

Vọ̈lker|wanderung *die* HIST migration of the peoples.

Vọlksab|stimmung *die* referendum.

Vọlks|fest *das* festival.

Vọlkshoch|schule *die* ≃ college of adult education.

Vọlks|lied *das* folk song.

Vọlks|musik *die* folk music.

Vọlks|tanz *der* folk dance.

vọlkstümlich ◇ *adj* - **1.** [traditionell] traditional - **2.** [populär] popular. ◇ *adv* [populär] in plain language.

Vọlks|wirtschaft *die* - **1.** [Wissenschaft] economics *(U)* - **2.** [Wirtschaft] economy.

vọll ◇ *adj* - **1.** [gen] full; **voll von** ODER **mit etw sein** to be full of sthg; **halb voll** half full; **mit vollem Recht** with every justification; **in vollem Ernst** in all seriousness - **2.** *fam* [gesättigt]: **voll sein** to be full (up) - **3.** *salopp* [betrunken]: **voll sein** to be plastered - **4.** [vollwertig]: **jn nicht für voll nehmen** *fam fig* not to take sb seriously. ◇ *adv* - **1.** [völlig] totally, completely; **voll und ganz** completely - **2.** *salopp* [verstärkend] really.

vollauf *adv* completely.

Vọll|bart *der* full beard.

Vọll|blut (*pl* **-blüter**) *das* thoroughbred.

vollẹnden *vt* to complete.

vollẹndet ◇ *pp* ▷ **vollenden**. ◇ *adj* - **1.** [perfekt] perfect - **2.** [fertig] completed. ◇ *adv* perfectly.

vọllends *adv* completely.

Vollẹndung (*pl* **-en**) *die* - **1.** [Perfektion] perfection - **2.** [Vollenden] completion.

vọller *adj (unver)* full of.

Vọlley|ball ['vɔlibal] *der* volleyball.

Vọll|gas *das*: **mit Vollgas** at full throttle; **Vollgas geben** to put one's foot down *UK*, to step on the gas *US*.

vọ̈llig ◇ *adj* complete. ◇ *adv* completely.

vọlljährig *adj*: **volljährig sein** to be of age.

Vọllkaskover|sicherung *die* comprehensive insurance.

vollkọmmen ◇ *adj* - **1.** [perfekt] perfect - **2.** [absolut] complete. ◇ *adv* - **1.** [perfekt] perfectly - **2.** [absolut] completely.

Vọllkorn|brot *das* wholemeal *UK* ODER whole wheat *US* bread.

vọll machen *vt fam* - **1.** [Bett] to wet; [Windel, Hose] to dirty - **2.** [füllen] to fill - **3.** [vervollständigen] to complete.

Vọll|macht (*pl* **-en**) *die* - **1.** *(ohne pl)* [Befugnis] authority; RECHT power of attorney; **jm (die) Vollmacht geben** ODER **erteilen** to authorize sb; RECHT to give sb power of attorney - **2.** [Schreiben] letter of authorization; **schriftliche Vollmacht** written authorization.

Vọll|milch *die* full-fat milk.

Vọll|mond *der* full moon.

Vọll|pension *die* full board.

vọllständig ◇ *adj* complete. ◇ *adv* completely.

vollstrẹcken *vt* - **1.** RECHT [Testament] to execute; [Urteil] to carry out - **2.** SPORT to score from, to convert.

vọll tanken *vi* to fill up; **bitte einmal voll tanken!** fill it up, please!

Vọll|treffer *der* [Schuss] direct hit; **ein Volltreffer sein** to be a hit.

vọllwertig *adj* - **1.** [gleichwertig] fully-fledged - **2.** [Speisen] wholefood.

Vọllwertkost *die* wholefood.

vollzählig ◇ *adj* entire. ◇ *adv*: **sie sind vollzählig erschienen** they all turned up.

Vollzug *der* - **1.** [von Urteil, Beschlagnahmung] carrying out - **2.** [von Ehe] consummation - **3.** *fam* [Gefängnis] clink.

Vollzugs|anstalt *die* prison, penitentiary *US*.

Volt [vɔlt] (*pl* -) *das* volt.

Volumen [vo'luːmən] (*pl* -) *das* volume.

vom *präp* - **1.** *(von + dem)* from the; **vom Bahnhof** from the station - **2.** *(untrennbar)*: **vom Fach sein** to be an expert; **müde vom Arbeiten sein** to be tired from working.

von *präp (+ D)* - **1.** [räumlich] from; [von... weg] off, from; **von nach** from to; **etw vom Tisch nehmen** to take sthg from ODER off the table - **2.** [zeitlich] from; **von Montag bis Freitag** from Monday to Friday, Monday through Friday *US*; **von heute an** from today - **3.** [stellt Bezug her]: **die Zeitung von gestern** yesterday's paper; **von wem hast du das?** who gave it to you?; **ist das Buch von dir?** is the book yours?; **das war dumm/nett von dir** that was stupid/nice of you - **4.** [in Passivsätzen] by; **von einem Hund gebissen werden** to be bitten by a dog; **von Hand hergestellt** made by hand - **5.** [zur Angabe der Ursache] from; **müde von der Reise** tired from the journey - **6.** [drückt Eigenschaften aus] of; **ein Sack von 25 kg** a 25 kg bag; **eine Fahrt von 3 Stunden** a 3-hour journey - **7.** [zur Angabe einer Teilmenge] of; **ein Stück von der Torte** a piece of the cake; **neun von zehn** nine out of ten; **von mir aus** *fam* I don't mind; **von sich aus** *fam* by oneself. ◆ **von an** *präp* from; **von hier an** from here; **von jetzt an** from now on. ◆ **von aus** *präp* from; **von hier aus** from here.

voneinander *adv* from one another; **sie sind voneinander unabhängig** they are independent of one another.

vor ◇ *präp* - **1.** *(+ D)* [räumlich] in front of; **vor dem Haus stehen** to stand in front of the house; **vor Gericht erscheinen** to appear before a court - **2.** *(+ A)* [räumlich] in front of - **3.** *(+ D)* [zeitlich - zuvor] ago; **heute vor fünf Jahren** five years ago today; **vor kurzem** recently - **4.** [zur Angabe der Uhrzeit] to *UK*, before *US*; **fünf vor zwölf** five to twelve *UK*, five before twelve *US*; **fünf vor halb neun** twenty-five past eight *UK*, twenty-five after eight *US* - **5.** *(+ D)* [wegen] with; **vor Kälte/Angst zittern** to tremble with cold/fear; **vor Freude in die Luft springen** to jump for joy; **vor Hunger sterben** to die of hunger - **6.** [stellt Bezug her]: **Schutz vor etw** protection from sthg; **jn vor etw warnen** to warn sb about sthg; **vor sich hin murmeln/singen** to mutter/sing to oneself. ◇ *adv* forwards. ◆ **vor allem** *adv* above all.

Vor|abend *der* evening before.

voran *adv* - **1.** [vorweg] at the front - **2.** [vorwärts] forwards.

voran|gehen (*perf* **ist vorangegangen**) *vi (unreg)* - **1.** [Arbeit, Projekt] to advance, to progress - **2.** [vorne gehen] to go on ahead - **3.** [vorher passieren]: **jm/etw vorangehen** to precede sb/sthg.

voran|kommen (*perf* **ist vorangekommen**) *vi (unreg)* to make progress; [Arbeit, Projekt] to advance, to progress; **gut vorankommen** to make good progress; **nicht vorankommen** not to make any progress.

vor|arbeiten *vi*: **einen Tag vorarbeiten** to work an extra day *(in order to have a day off later)*. ◆ **sich vorarbeiten** *ref* to work one's way forward.

voraus *adv* in front; **jm in etw voraus sein** *fig* to be ahead of sb in sthg; **seiner Zeit voraus** ahead of one's time.

voraus|gehen (*perf* **ist vorausgegangen**) *vi (unreg)* - **1.** [vorher, früher gehen] to go on ahead - **2.** [vorher passieren]: **einer Sache** *(D)* **vorausgehen** to precede sthg.

vorausgesetzt ◇ *pp* ▷ **voraussetzen**. ◇ *konj* provided (that).

voraus|haben *vt (unreg)*: **jm etw voraushaben** to have the advantage of sthg over sb.

voraus|sagen *vt* to predict.

voraus|sehen *vt (unreg)* to foresee; **es war vorauszusehen, dass..** it was to be expected that...

voraus|setzen *vt* - **1.** [erfordern] to require - **2.** [für selbstverständlich halten] to take for granted; **wir müssen voraussetzen, dass...** we must assume that...; **etw als bekannt voraussetzen** to assume sthg is known.

Voraussetzung (*pl* **-en**) *die* - **1.** [Erfordernis] requirement; **ihm fehlen die nötigen Voraussetzungen** he lacks the necessary qualifications; **unter der Voraussetzung, dass...** on condition that... - **2.** [Annahme] assumption.

Voraussicht *die* foresight; **aller Voraussicht nach** in all probability.

voraussichtlich ◇ *adj* expected. ◇ *adv* probably.

Voraus|zahlung *die* advance payment.

Vorbehalt (*pl* **-e**) *der* reservation; **etw unter** ODER **mit Vorbehalt annehmen** to accept sthg with reservations.

vor|behalten *vt (unreg)*: **sich etw vorbehalten** to reserve o.s. sthg; **der Swimmingpool ist den Hotelgästen vorbehalten** the swimming pool is reserved for hotel guests only.

vorbei *adv* - **1.** [räumlich] past, by; **an mir vorbei** past me - **2.** [zeitlich] over; **die Schmerzen sind vorbei** the pain has gone; **mit etw ist es vorbei** *fam* sthg is over.

vorbei|gehen (*perf* **ist vorbeigegangen**) *vi (unreg)* - **1.** [entlanggehen, vergehen] to pass; **an**

jm/etw vorbeigehen to pass sb/sthg - **2.** [hingehen] to drop in. ◆ **im Vorbeigehen** *adv* in passing.

vorbei|kommen (*perf* **ist vorbeigekommen**) *vi (unreg)* - **1.** [an etw vorüber]: **(an etw** *(D)***) vorbeikommen** to pass (sthg) - **2.** [besuchen]: **(bei jm) vorbeikommen** to drop in (on sb); **komm mal vorbei!** come round some time! - **3.** [vorbeikönnen] to get past.

vorbei|reden *vi*: **aneinander vorbeireden** to talk at cross purposes.

vor|bereiten *vt* to prepare; **jn/etw auf etw** *(A)* **vorbereiten** to prepare sb/sthg for sthg. ◆ **sich vorbereiten** *ref*: **sich (auf etw** *(A)***) vorbereiten** to prepare o.s. (for sthg).

Vor|bereitung *die* preparation; **in Vorbereitung sein** to be in preparation.

vor|bestellen *vt* to order in advance.

vorbestraft *adj*: **vorbestraft sein** to have previous convictions, to have a criminal record.

vor|beugen ◇ *vi*: **einer Sache** *(D)* **vorbeugen** to prevent sthg. ◇ *vt* to bend forward. ◆ **sich vorbeugen** *ref* to lean forward.

Vor|beugung *die* prevention.

Vor|bild *das* model.

vorbildlich ◇ *adj* exemplary. ◇ *adv* in exemplary fashion.

vor|bringen *vt (unreg)* - **1.** [Wunsch, Bedenken] to express; [Bitte, Beschwerde] to make; **etw gegen etw vorbringen** to raise sthg as an objection to sthg; **etw gegen jn vorbringen** to say sthg against sb - **2.** [Beweise] to produce.

vordere, r, s *adj* front.

Vorder|grund *der* foreground; **etw in den Vordergrund stellen** ODER **rücken** to place special emphasis on sthg; **im Vordergrund stehen** to be to the fore.

Vorder|mann *der*: **der Läufer überholte seinen Vordermann** the runner overtook the man in front of him.

Vorder|rad *das* front wheel.

Vorder|sitz *der* front seat.

vor|drängen ◆ **sich vordrängen** *ref* to push in.

vor|dringen (*perf* **ist vorgedrungen**) *vi (unreg)* to advance; [in Menschenmenge] to push forward.

Vor|druck *der* form.

voreilig ◇ *adj* rash. ◇ *adv* rashly.

voreinander *adv* - **1.** [in Bezug aufeinander]: **Angst voreinander haben** to be afraid of one another - **2.** [räumlich] one in front of the other.

voreingenommen ◇ *adj* biased; **gegen jn/etw voreingenommen sein** to be biased against sb/sthg. ◇ *adv* in a biased way.

vor|enthalten *vt (unreg)*: **jm etw vorenthalten** to withhold sthg from sb; [Nachricht] to keep sthg from sb.

vorerst *adv* for the time being.

Vorfahr (*pl* **-en**), **Vorfahre** (*pl* **-n**) *der* ancestor.

vor|fahren (*perf* **hat/ist vorgefahren**) ◇ *vi (ist)* - **1.** [nach vorn fahren] to drive forward - **2.** [vorausfahren] to drive on ahead - **3.** [vor Gebäude] to drive up. ◇ *vt (hat)* - **1.** [nach vorn] to drive forward - **2.** [vor Gebäude] to drive up.

Vor|fahrt *die* right of way; **Vorfahrt haben** to have right of way.

Vorfahrts|straße *die* major road.

Vor|fall *der* [Geschehnis] occurrence, incident.

vor|fallen (*perf* **ist vorgefallen**) *vi (unreg)* to happen, to occur.

vor|finden *vt (unreg)* to find.

vor|führen *vt* - **1.** [zeigen - FILM] to show; [- Kunststück] to perform; [- Funktionsweise] to demonstrate; **jm etw vorführen** to show sb sthg - **2.** *fam* [blamieren] to show up.

Vor|führung *die* - **1.** [im Theater, Kino, Zirkus] performance - **2.** [von Maschine] demonstration.

Vor|gang *der* event, occurrence.

Vorgänger, in (*mpl* **-**, *fpl* **-nen**) *der, die* predecessor.

vorgefertigt *adj* prefabricated.

vorgegeben *adj* set in advance.

vor|gehen (*perf* **ist vorgegangen**) *vi (unreg)* - **1.** [vorhergehen] to go on ahead - **2.** [passieren] to go on - **3.** [handeln] to proceed; **gegen jn/etw vorgehen** to take action against sb/sthg - **4.** [Uhr] to be fast - **5.** [vorne gehen] to go first.

Vor|geschichte *die* - **1.** [vorherige Entwicklung] history - **2.** [Prähistorie] prehistory.

Vorgesetzte (*pl* **-n**) *der, die* superior.

vorgestern *adv* [vor zwei Tagen] the day before yesterday.

vor|haben *vt (unreg)* to plan; **was habt ihr am Wochenende vor?** what have you got planned for the weekend?

Vorhaben (*pl* **-**) *das* plan.

vor|halten *(unreg)* ◇ *vt*: **jm etw vorhalten** [halten] to hold sthg up to sb; [vorwerfen] to hold sthg against sb. ◇ *vi* [ausreichen] to last.

vorhanden *adj* existing; [Vorräte, Mittel] available; **vorhanden sein** to exist; [Vorräte, Mittel] to be available; **davon ist nichts mehr vorhanden** there's none of it left.

Vor|hang *der* curtain; **der eiserne Vorhang** the Iron Curtain.

Vorhängeschloss (*pl* **-schlösser**) *das* padlock.

Vor|haut *die* foreskin.

vorher *adv* - **1.** [früher] before; **am Tag vorher** the day before - **2.** [im Voraus] before(hand).

vorherig *adj* previous.

vor|herrschen *vi* to prevail.

Vorher|sage *die* - **1.** [für Wetter] forecast - **2.** [des Schicksals] prediction.

vorher|sehen *vt (unreg)* [wahrsagen] to foresee; [voraussehen] to predict; [Wetter] to forecast.

vorhin, vorhin *adv* just now.

vorig *adj* last.

Vorkehrungen *Pl*: **Vorkehrungen treffen** to take precautions.

Vor|kenntnisse *Pl* previous experience *(U)*.

vor|kommen (*perf* **ist vorgekommen**) *vi (unreg)* - **1.** [passieren] to happen - **2.** [auftreten] to be found, to occur - **3.** [scheinen]: **jm verdächtig vorkommen** to seem suspicious to sb; **es kommt mir vor, als sei heute Sonntag** today feels like Sunday to me; **sich überflüssig vorkommen** to feel unwanted - **4.** [nach vorne kommen] to come forward.

Vorkommen (*pl* -) *das* - **1.** [an Bodenschätzen] deposit - **2.** [Existieren] presence - **3.** [Auftreten] occurrence.

Vor|ladung *die* summons *(sg)*.

Vor|lage *die* - **1.** [Muster] pattern - **2.** [Vorlegen] presentation - **3.** [Gesetzesvorlage] bill - **4.** SPORT [bei Fußball] assist, pass *(leading to a goal)*.

vor|lassen *vt (unreg)*: **jn vorlassen** to let sb go first.

Vor|läufer, in *der, die* forerunner.

vorläufig ◇ *adj* provisional. ◇ *adv* provisionally; **ich wohne vorläufig bei ihm** I'm staying with him for the time being; **die Polizei nahm sie vorläufig fest** the police held them.

vorlaut ◇ *adj*: **vorlaut sein** to make comments out of turn. ◇ *adv* out of turn.

vor|legen *vt* to present; [Ausweis] to show; [Zeugnis] to submit; **jm etw vorlegen** to present sb with sthg.

vor|lesen *vt (unreg)* to read out; **jm etw vorlesen** to read sthg to sb.

Vor|lesung *die* UNI lecture.

vorletzte, r, s *adj* penultimate, last but one.

Vorliebe (*pl* -n) *die* preference; **eine Vorliebe für jn/etw haben** to be particularly fond of sb/sthg.

vor|liegen *vi (unreg)* [vorgelegt sein]: **der Antrag liegt vor** the application has been received; **die Ergebnisse liegen noch nicht vor** the results are not yet available; **gegen ihn liegt nichts vor** no charges have been brought against him.

vor|machen *vt* - **1.** *fam* [zeigen]: **jm etw vormachen** to show sb how to do sthg - **2.** [vortäuschen]: **jm etwas vormachen** to fool sb.

Vormacht|stellung *die* supremacy *(U)*.

Vor|marsch *der*: **auf dem Vormarsch sein** *fig* to be gaining ground.

vor|merken *vt* - **1.** [Termin] to make a note of - **2.** [Person]: **jn für einen Kurs vormerken** to put sb's name down for a course.

Vor|mittag *der* morning; **gestern/heute/morgen Vormittag** yesterday/this/tomorrow morning.

vormittags *adv* in the morning.

Vormund (*pl* **-e** ODER **-münder**) *der* guardian.

vorn, vorne *adv* in front, at the front; **da vorn** over there; **nach vorn** forwards. ◆ **von vorn** *adv* [von Anfang an] from the beginning.

Vor|name *der* first name.

vornehm ◇ *adj* - **1.** [fein - Charakter] noble; [der Oberschicht angehörend] distinguished - **2.** [elegant] upmarket. ◇ *adv* [elegant] elegantly.

vor|nehmen *vt (unreg)* - **1.** [durchführen] to carry out; [Auswahl] to make - **2.** [sich beschäftigen mit]: **sich** *(D)* **etw vornehmen** *fam* to tackle sthg - **3.** [sich entschließen]: **sich** *(D)* **vornehmen, etw zu tun** to resolve to do sthg; **sich** *(D)* **etw fest vorgenommen haben** to have made up one's mind to do sthg.

vornherein ◆ **von vornherein** *adv* from the start.

Vor|ort *der* suburb.

Vor|platz *der* forecourt.

Vorrang *der*: **vor jm Vorrang haben** to take precedence over sb.

vorrangig ◇ *adj* of prime importance. ◇ *adv*: **etw vorrangig behandeln** to treat sthg as a matter of priority.

Vorrat (*pl* **-räte**) *der* supply; [Reserve] store; **Vorräte** [von Geschäft] stocks; **ein Vorrat an etw** *(D)* a supply/store of sthg. ◆ **auf Vorrat** *adv*: **etw auf Vorrat einkaufen** to stock up on sthg.

vorrätig *adj* in stock.

Vor|raum *der* anteroom.

Vor|recht *das* privilege.

Vor|richtung *die* device.

vor|rücken (*perf* **hat/ist vorgerückt**) ◇ *vt (hat)* to move forward. ◇ *vi (ist)* - **1.** [räumlich] to move forward - **2.** [in Hierarchie] to move up.

Vorruhe|stand *der* early retirement; **in den Vorruhestand gehen** to take early retirement.

vor|sagen ◇ *vt*: **jm etw vorsagen** to tell sb sthg. ◇ *vi*: **jm vorsagen** to tell sb the answer.

Vor|saison *die* low season.

Vor|satz *der* resolution; **einen Vorsatz fassen, etw zu tun** to resolve to do sthg.

vorsätzlich ◇ *adj* RECHT premeditated. ◇ *adv* intentionally, on purpose.

Vor|schau *die* preview.

Vorschein *der*: **zum Vorschein kommen** to turn up.

vor|schieben *vt (unreg)* - **1.** [schieben] to push forward; [Riegel] to push across; **das Kinn vorschieben** to stick one's chin out - **2.** [Vorwand] to put forward as an excuse - **3.** [Stellvertreter] to use as a front man.

Vor|schlag *der* suggestion.

vor|schlagen *vt (unreg)* to suggest; **jm etw vorschlagen** to suggest sthg to sb; **er schlug vor, ins Kino zu gehen** he suggested going to the cinema.

vorschnell ◇ *adj* rash. ◇ *adv* rashly.

vor|schreiben *vt (unreg)* [Subj: Gesetz] to stipulate; **sein Vater versucht ihm alles vorzuschreiben** his father is always trying to tell him what to do.

Vor|schrift *die* regulation.

Vor|schule *die* nursery school.

Vor|schuss (*pl* **-schüsse**) *der* advance.

vor|sehen *vt (unreg)* - **1.** [planen] to plan; **die Feier ist für nächste Woche vorgesehen** the celebration is scheduled ODER planned for next week; **das ist nicht vorgesehen** there are no plans for that; **jn für etw vorsehen** to have sb in mind for sthg - **2.** [vorschreiben] to provide for. ◆ **sich vorsehen** *ref*: **sich vor jm/etw vorsehen** [achtsam sein] to beware of sb/sthg.

vor|setzen *vt*: **jm etw vorsetzen** to serve sb sthg.

Vorsicht ◇ *die* care. ◇ *interj* look out!; **Vorsicht, Stufe!** mind the step!

vorsichtig ◇ *adj* careful. ◇ *adv* carefully.

vorsichtshalber *adv* as a precaution.

Vorsichts|maßnahme *die* precaution; **Vorsichtsmaßnahmen treffen** to take precautions.

Vor|silbe *die* prefix.

Vor|sitz *der* chairmanship.

Vorsitzende (*pl* **-n**) *der, die* chairperson.

Vor|sorge *die (ohne pl)* [gegen Krankheit, Gefahr] precautions *Pl*; [für das Alter] provisions *Pl*; **Vorsorge treffen** to take precautions; [für das Alter] to make provisions.

vor|sorgen *vi*: **für etw vorsorgen** to make provisions for sthg.

vorsorglich ◇ *adj* precautionary. ◇ *adv* as a precaution.

Vor|speise *die* starter.

vor|spielen ◇ *vt* - **1.** [auf einem Instrument]: **jm ein Stück vorspielen** to play a piece for sb - **2.** [vortäuschen] to put on an act. ◇ *vi* [auf einem Instrument]: **jm vorspielen** to play for sb.

Vor|sprung *der* - **1.** [von Läufer, Auto] lead - **2.** [von Wand] ledge.

Vor|stadt *die* suburb.

Vor|stand *der* [von Firma] board of directors; [von Verein] committee; [von Partei] executive.

vor|stehen *vi (unreg)* - **1.** to jut out; [Backenknochen] to be prominent; [Zähne] to protrude - **2.** [einer Gruppe, Institution]: **jm/etw vorstehen** to be in charge of sb/sthg.

vor|stellen *vt* - **1.** [bekannt machen] to introduce; **jn jm vorstellen** to introduce sb to sb - **2.** [sich ausdenken]: **sich** *(D)* **etw vorstellen** to imagine sthg - **3.** [Uhr] to put forward. ◆ **sich vorstellen** *ref* - **1.** [bekannt machen]: **sich jm vorstellen** to introduce o.s. to sb - **2.** [sich bewerben]: **sich bei jm vorstellen** to go for an interview with sb.

Vor|stellung *die* - **1.** [Idee] idea; **etw entspricht (nicht) js Vorstellungen** sthg is (not) as sb imagined it - **2.** [im Theater] performance - **3.** [das Vorstellen] presentation.

Vorstellungs|gespräch *das* interview.

Vor|strafe *die* RECHT previous conviction.

vor|strecken *vt* - **1.** [Arme, Beine] to stretch out - **2.** [Geld]: **jm etw vorstrecken** to advance sb sthg.

vor|täuschen *vt* to feign; **jm etw vortäuschen** to pretend sthg to sb.

Vor|teil *der* advantage; **zu js Vorteil** to sb's advantage; **jm gegenüber im Vorteil sein** to have an advantage over sb.

vorteilhaft *adj* [Geschäft, Lage] advantageous; [Haarschnitt] flattering.

Vortrag (*pl* **-träge**) *der* talk; **ein Vortrag über jn/etw** a talk about sb/sthg; **einen Vortrag halten** to give a talk.

vor|tragen *vt (unreg)* - **1.** [darbieten] to perform; [Gedicht] to recite - **2.** [darlegen] to present.

Vortritt *der*: **jm den Vortritt lassen** to let sb go first.

vorüber *adj*: **vorüber sein** to be over.

vorüber|gehen (*perf* **ist vorübergegangen**) *vi (unreg)* - **1.** [Person] to pass by; **an jm/etw vorübergehen** to pass by sb/sthg - **2.** [Schmerzen] to come to an end.

vorübergehend ◇ *adj* temporary. ◇ *adv* temporarily.

Vorur|teil *das* prejudice.

Vorver|kauf *der* advance booking; **Karten im Vorverkauf bekommen** to buy tickets in advance.

Vor|wahl *die* - **1.** [telefonisch] dialling code *UK*, area code *US* - **2.** [von Wahlen] primary *US, candidate selection procedure*.

Vorwand (*pl* **-wände**) *der* excuse; **unter dem Vorwand** under the pretext.

vorwärts *adv* forwards.

vorwärts gehen (*perf* **ist vorwärts gegangen**) *vi (unreg)* to progress; **mit dem Experiment geht es nicht vorwärts** the experiment isn't getting anywhere.

vorwärts kommen (*perf* **ist vorwärts gekommen**) *vi (unreg)* to make progress.

vorwẹg *adv* - **1.** [vorher] beforehand - **2.** [voraus] in front.

vorwẹg|nehmen *vt (unreg)* to anticipate.

vor|weisen *vt (unreg)* - **1.** [vorzeigen] to show - **2.** [bieten]: **etw vorweisen können** to possess sthg.

vor|werfen *vt (unreg)*: **jm etw vorwerfen** to accuse sb of sthg.

vorwiegend *adv* mainly.

Vor|wort *das* preface.

Vor|wurf *der* accusation.

vorwurfsvoll ◇ *adj* reproachful. ◇ *adv* reproachfully.

Vor|zeichen *das* - **1.** [Anzeichen] omen - **2.** MATH sign - **3.** MUS key signature.

vor|zeigen *vt*: **(jm etw) vorzeigen** to show (sb sthg).

vorzeitig ◇ *adj* early; [Altern, Wehen] premature. ◇ *adv* prematurely; **vorzeitig in Rente gehen** to take early retirement.

vor|ziehen *vt (unreg)* - **1.** [lieber mögen] to prefer; **etw einer Sache** *(D)* **vorziehen** to prefer sthg to sthg - **2.** [Termin] to bring forward - **3.** [nach vorn ziehen] to pull forward.

Vor|zug *der* - **1.** [Vorrang] advantage; **jm/etw den Vorzug geben** to give sb/sthg preference - **2.** [gute Eigenschaft] virtue.

vorzüglich ◇ *adj* excellent. ◇ *adv* excellently.

vorzugsweise *adv* mainly.

vulgär *adj* vulgar.

Vulkan *(pl* **-e)** *der* volcano.

W

w *(pl* - ODER **-s)**, **W** *(pl* - ODER **-s)** [veː] *das* w, W. ◆ **W** *(abk für* **West, Watt)** W.

Waage *(pl* **-n)** *die* - **1.** [Gerät] scales *Pl* - **2.** ASTROL Libra; **Waage sein** to be Libra.

waagerecht, waagrecht ◇ *adj* horizontal. ◇ *adv* horizontally.

Wabe *(pl* **-n)** *die* honeycomb.

wạch *adj* - **1.** [nicht schlafend] awake; **jn wach machen** to wake sb; **wach halten** [Person] to keep awake; [Erinnerung] to keep alive; **wach sein** to be awake; **wach werden** to wake up - **2.** [Geist] alert.

Wạche *(pl* **-n)** *die* - **1.** *(ohne pl)* [Wachdienst] guard duty; **Wache halten** to be on guard - **2.** [Wächter] guard - **3.** [Polizeiwache] police station.

Wạch|hund *der* guard dog.

Wachọlder *(pl* **-)** *der* juniper.

Wạchs [vaks] *(pl* **-e)** *das* wax *(U)*.

wạchsam [ˈvaxzaːm] *adj* vigilant.

wạchsen [vaksn̩] *(präs* **wạ̈chst** ODER **wạchst**, *prät* **wuchs** ODER **wạchste**, *perf* **ist gewạchsen** ODER **hat gewạchst)** ◇ *vi (unreg) (ist)* - **1.** [größer werden] to grow - **2.** [entsprechen]: **einer Sache** *(D)* **gewachsen sein** to be up to sthg. ◇ *vt (reg) (hat)* [mit Wachs] to wax.

Wạchsmal|stift [ˈvaksmaːlʃtɪft] *der* wax crayon.

wạ̈chst [vɛkst] *präs* ▷ **wachsen**.

Wạchs|tuch *das* oilcloth.

Wạchstum [ˈvakstuːm] *das* growth.

Wạchtel *(pl* **-n)** *die* quail.

Wạ̈chter, in *(mpl* **-**, *fpl* **-nen)** *der, die* guard.

Wạcht|posten *der* guard.

Wạch|turm, Wạchtturm *der* watchtower.

wạckelig, wạcklig *adj* - **1.** [nicht fest] wobbly - **2.** *fam* [gefährdet] shaky.

Wạckel|kontakt *der* ELEKTR loose contact.

wạckeln *(perf* **hat/ist gewạckelt)** *vi* - **1.** *(hat)* [nicht fest sein] to be wobbly - **2.** *(hat)* [hin und her bewegen]: **mit etw wackeln** to shake sthg - **3.** *(ist) fam* [gehen] to totter - **4.** *(hat) fam* [Posten] to be shaky.

wạcker ◇ *adj* - **1.** [anständig] upright - **2.** [tüchtig] hearty. ◇ *adv* valiantly.

Wade *(pl* **-n)** *die* calf.

Wạffe *(pl* **-n)** *die* weapon.

Wạffel *(pl* **-n)** *die* waffle.

Wạffel|eisen *das* waffle iron.

Wạffen|gewalt *die*: **mit Waffengewalt** by force of arms.

Wạffen|schein *der* firearms licence.

Wạffenstill|stand *der* armistice.

wagen *vt* to risk; **einen Versuch wagen** to risk an attempt; **es wagen, etw zu tun** to dare to do sthg. ◆ **sich wagen** *ref* to dare; **sich nachts nicht auf die Straße wagen** not to dare to go out on the street at night; **sich an etw** *(A)* **wagen** to attempt sthg.

Wagen *(pl* **-)** *der* - **1.** [Auto] car - **2.** [von Zug, Straßenbahn] carriage *UK*, car *US* - **3.** [mit Pferd] carriage. ◆ **der Große Wagen** *der* ASTRON the Plough. ◆ **der Kleine Wagen** *der* ASTRON the Little Bear.

Wagen|heber *(pl* **Wagenheber)** *der* jack.

Waggon *(pl* **-s)**, **Wagon** *(pl* **-s)** [vaˈgɔŋ] *der* carriage *UK*, car *US*.

waghalsig *adj* reckless.

Wagnis *(pl* **-se)** *das* risk.

Wagọn = **Waggon**.

Wahl *(pl* **-en)** *die* - **1.** *(ohne pl)* [Auswahl] choice; **die Wahl haben** to have the choice; **eine Wahl treffen** to make a choice; **erste/**

zweite Wahl first/second class; **in die engere Wahl kommen** to be short-listed - **2.** [Abstimmung] election; **geheime Wahl** secret ballot; **zur Wahl gehen** to vote.

wahlberechtigt *adj* entitled to vote.

wählen ◇ *vt* - **1.** [aussuchen] to choose - **2.** [am Telefon] to dial - **3.** [politisch] to elect. ◇ *vi* - **1.** [aussuchen] to choose; **zwischen etw** *(D)* **und etw** *(D)* **wählen** to choose between sthg and sthg - **2.** [am Telefon] to dial - **3.** [politisch] to vote.

Wähler, in (*pl* -) *der* voter.

wählerisch *adj* choosy.

Wähler|stimme *die* vote.

Wahl|fach *das* SCHULE optional subject.

Wahl|gang *der* ballot.

Wahl|heimat *die* adopted home.

Wahl|kabine *die* polling booth.

Wahl|kampf *der* election campaign.

Wahl|kreis *der* constituency.

Wahl|lokal *das* polling station.

wahllos *adv* at random.

Wahlnieder|lage *die* election defeat.

Wahl|recht *das* right to vote; **allgemeines Wahlrecht** universal suffrage.

Wahl|rede *die* election speech.

Wahl|sieg *der* election victory.

Wahl|spruch *der* motto.

wahlweise *adv*: **zum Frühstück gibt es wahlweise Kaffee oder Tee** for breakfast there's a choice of coffee or tea.

Wahn *der (ohne pl)* delusion.

Wahnsinn *der* madness; **Wahnsinn!** amazing!

wahnsinnig ◇ *adj* - **1.** [verrückt] mad - **2.** [groß] incredible. ◇ *adv fam* [sehr] incredibly.

wahr *adj* true; **wahre Liebe/Freundschaft** true love/friendship; **das darf doch nicht wahr sein!** *fam* that can't be true!; **etw wahr machen** *fig* to carry out sthg. ◆ **nicht wahr** *interj*: **du warst doch gestern auch hier, nicht wahr?** you were here yesterday too, weren't you?; **das stimmt doch, nicht wahr?** that's right, isn't it?

während ◇ *konj* [zeitlich, gegensätzlich] while. ◇ *präp* during.

währenddessen *adv* in the meantime.

wahrhaben *vt*: **etw nicht wahrhaben wollen** not to want to accept sthg.

Wahrheit (*pl* -en) *die* truth *(U)*. ◆ **in Wahrheit** *adv* in reality.

wahrheitsgemäß ◇ *adj* truthful. ◇ *adv* truthfully.

wahr|nehmen *vt (unreg)* - **1.** [Veränderung, Geräusch] to notice - **2.** [Gelegenheit] to avail oneself of - **3.** [Interessen] to protect.

Wahrnehmung (*pl* -en) *die* - **1.** [Spüren] awareness *(U)* - **2.** [von Gelegenheit] seizing - **3.** [von Geschäft] representation.

wahr|sagen *vi* to predict the future.

Wahrsager, in (*mpl* -, *fpl* -nen) *der, die* fortune-teller.

wahrscheinlich ◇ *adj* probable. ◇ *adv* probably.

Wahrscheinlichkeit (*pl* -en) *die* probability; **aller Wahrscheinlichkeit nach** in all probability.

Wahrung *die* protection.

Währung (*pl* -en) *die* currency; **eine harte Währung** a hard currency.

Währungs|einheit *die* currency unit.

Währungsre|form *die* HIST & WIRTSCH currency reform.

Währungs|system *das* monetary system.

Wahr|zeichen *das* symbol.

Waise (*pl* -n) *die* orphan.

Waisen|haus *das* orphanage.

Waisen|kind *das* orphan.

Wal (*pl* -e) *der* whale.

Wald (*pl* **Wälder**) *der* wood; [groß] forest.

Wald|brand *der* forest fire.

Wäldchen (*pl* -) *das* copse.

Wald|gebiet *das* wooded area.

Waldmeister *der* woodruff.

Wald|sterben *das* forest dieback.

Wald|weg *der* forest track.

Wales ['weɪls] *nt* Wales.

Walkman® ['wɔːkmən] (*pl* -men) *der* Walkman®.

Wall (*pl* **Wälle**) *der* rampart.

Wall|fahrt *die* pilgrimage.

Wallis *das* Valais.

Walliser (*pl* -) ◇ *der* native/inhabitant of Valais. ◇ *adj (unver)* of/from Valais.

Walliserin (*pl* -nen) *die* native/inhabitant of Valais.

walliserisch *adj* of/from Valais.

Wallonien *nt* Wallonia.

wallonisch *adj* Walloon.

Walnuss (*pl* -nüsse) *die* walnut.

Walross (*pl* -rösser) *das* walrus.

walten *vi geh* to reign; **etw walten lassen** to exercise sthg.

Walze (*pl* -n) *die* roller.

walzen *vt* to roll.

wälzen *vt* - **1.** [rollen] to roll - **2.** [Buch] to pore over. ◆ **sich wälzen** *ref* to roll around.

Walzer (*pl* -) *der* waltz; **Walzer tanzen** to waltz.

Wälzer (*pl* -) *der fam* tome.

wand *prät* ▷ **winden**.

Wand (*pl* **Wände**) *die* - **1.** [Mauer] wall *(inside)* - **2.** [Felswand] rock face - **3.** [von Schrank] side;

in den eigenen vier Wänden in one's own home; **jn an die Wand stellen** *fam* to send sb before the firing squad.

Wandel *der* change; **im Wandel begriffen** to be in a state of flux.

wandeln (*perf* **hat/ist gewandelt**) *geh* ◇ *vi (ist)* to stroll. ◇ *vt (hat)* to change. ◆ **sich wandeln** *ref* to change.

Wanderer (*pl* -), **Wandrer** (*pl* -) *der* hiker.

Wanderin (*pl* **-nen**), **Wandrerin** (*pl* **-nen**) *die* hiker.

Wander|karte *die* walking map.

wandern (*perf* **ist gewandert**) *vi* - **1.** [als Sport] to go hiking - **2.** [ziellos] to wander - **3.** *fam* [gebracht werden]: **ins Gefängnis wandern** to end up in prison.

Wander|schuh *der* hiking ODER walking boot.

Wander|tag *der* school outing.

Wanderung (*pl* **-en**) *die* hike.

Wander|weg *der* trail.

Wand|gemälde *das* fresco.

Wandlung (*pl* **-en**) *die* change.

Wand|malerei *die* mural.

Wandrer = **Wanderer**.

Wandrerin = **Wanderin**.

Wand|schrank *der* built-in cupboard *UK* ODER closet *US*; [Kleiderschrank] built-in wardrobe *UK* ODER closet *US*.

wandte *prät* ▷ **wenden**.

Wand|teppich *der* tapestry.

Wand|uhr *die* wall clock.

Wange (*pl* **-n**) *die geh* cheek.

wanken (*perf* **hat/ist gewankt**) *vi* - **1.** *(ist)* [Betrunkener] to stagger - **2.** *(hat)* [Boden, Mauer] to sway - **3.** *(hat) geh* [Macht] to be under threat; [Entschluss] to waver.

wann *adv* when; **bis wann?** until when?, till when?; **seit wann lebst du schon hier?** how long have you been living here?; **von wann bis wann?** when?; **wann du willst** whenever you want.

Wanne (*pl* **-n**) *die* - **1.** [Badewanne] bath - **2.** [Becken] tub.

Wanze (*pl* **-n**) *die* bug.

Wappen (*pl* -) *das* coat of arms.

war *prät* ▷ **sein**.

warb *prät* ▷ **werben**.

Ware (*pl* **-n**) *die* product.

Waren|haus *das* department store.

Waren|lager *das* warehouse.

Waren|zeichen *das*: **eingetragenes Warenzeichen** registered trademark.

warf *prät* ▷ **werfen**.

warm (*kompar* **wärmer**, *superl* **wärmste**) ◇ *adj* warm; **es ist warm** it's warm; **mir ist/wird warm** I'm warm/warming up; **draußen ist es 30°C warm** it's 30°C outside; **mit jm warm werden** *fam fig* to get on well with sb; **warme Miete** *rent including heating bills.* ◇ *adv* warmly; **warm essen** to have a hot meal.

Wärme *die* warmth.

wärmedämmend *adj* insulating.

wärmen *vt* & *vi* to warm. ◆ **sich wärmen** *ref* to warm o.s.

Wärm|flasche *die* hot-water bottle.

warmherzig *adj* warm-hearted.

warm laufen (*perf* **hat/ist warm gelaufen**) *vi (unreg) (ist)* to warm up. ◆ **sich warm laufen** *ref* to warm up.

Warm|miete *die rent including heating bills.*

Warm|wasser *das* hot water.

Warnblinkan|lage *die* AUTO hazard lights *Pl.*

Warn|dreieck *das* AUTO warning triangle.

warnen *vt* to warn; **jn vor jm/etw warnen** to warn sb about sb/sthg.

Warn|schild (*pl* **-er**) *das* warning sign.

Warnung (*pl* **-en**) *die* warning.

Warschau *nt* Warsaw.

warten ◇ *vi* to wait; **auf jn/etw warten** to wait for sb/sthg; **mit etw warten** to put sthg on hold. ◇ *vt* TECH to service.

Wärter, in (*mpl* -, *fpl* **-nen**) *der, die* [im Zoo, Leuchtturm] keeper; [im Gefängnis] warder.

Warte|saal *der* waiting room.

Warte|zimmer *das* waiting room.

Wartung (*pl* **-en**) *die* servicing *(U)*.

warum *adv* why.

Warze (*pl* **-n**) *die* wart.

was ◇ *pron* - **1.** [Interrogativpronomen] what; **was ist?** what is it?; **was ist sie (von Beruf)?** what does she do (for a living)? - **2.** [wie viel] how much, what; **was kostet das?** how much is it? - **3.** *fam* [warum] why; **was fragst du?** why do you ask? - **4.** *fam* [nicht wahr]: **da freust du dich, was?** you're pleased, aren't you?; **es ist schön, was?** it's nice, isn't it?; **gut, was?** not bad, eh? - **5.** [Relativpronomen] which, that; **das, was** what; **alles, was** everything (that); **das Beste, was ich je gehört habe** the best I've ever heard - **6.** *fam* [etwas] something; **was für** what sort ODER kind of; **was sind das für Tiere?** what sort ODER kind of animals are those?; **was für ein Lärm!** what a noise!; **was weiß ich!** *fam* don't ask me. ◇ *interj fam* [wie bitte] what? ◆ **ach, was** *interj* no it's/etc not! ◆ **so was** *interj*: **na** ODER **also so was!** really!

Waschan|lage *die* carwash.

waschbar *adj* washable.

Wasch|becken *das* washbasin.

Wäsche (*pl* **-n**) *die* - **1.** [schmutzige Wäsche] laundry - **2.** [Unterwäsche] underwear - **3.** [Waschen] wash.

waschecht *adj* - **1.** [Stoff] colourfast - **2.** [typisch] true.

Wäschelklammer *die* clothes peg *UK*, clothespin *US*.

Wäschelkorb *der* laundry basket.

Wäschelleine *die* washing line.

waschen (*präs* **wäscht**, *prät* **wusch**, *perf* **hat gewaschen**) *vt* to wash; **sich** *(D)* **die Haare/die Hände waschen** to wash one's hair/hands. ◆ **sich waschen** *ref* to have a wash; **er bekam eine Abreibung, die sich gewaschen hatte** he got one hell of a hiding.

Wäscherei (*pl* **-en**) *die* laundrette.

Wäschelständer *der* clotheshorse.

Wäscheltrockner *der* **- 1.** [Maschine] tumble-dryer **- 2.** [Wäscheständer] clotheshorse.

Waschlgelegenheit *die* washing facilities *Pl*.

Waschllappen *der* **- 1.** [Lappen] facecloth **- 2.** *fam abw* [Person] wimp.

Waschlmaschine *die* washing machine.

Waschlmittel *das* detergent.

Waschlpulver *das* washing powder.

Waschlraum *der* washroom.

Waschlsalon *der* laundrette.

wäscht *präs* ▷ **waschen**.

Wasser (*pl* - ODER **Wässer**) *das* **- 1.** [gen] water; **Wasser abstoßend** water-repellent; **unter Wasser stehen** to be under water **- 2.** *(ohne pl)* [Körperflüssigkeit] fluid; **mir läuft das Wasser im Mund zusammen** my mouth is watering; **sich über Wasser halten** to keep one's head above water. ◆ **am Wasser** *adv* by the water.

wasserabstoßend ▷ **Wasser**.

Wasserlbad *das* KÜCHE bain-marie.

wasserdicht *adj* **- 1.** [Bekleidung, Uhr] waterproof **- 2.** *fam* [Alibi] watertight.

Wasserlfarbe *die* watercolours *Pl*.

Wasserlgraben *der* ditch; [Burggraben] moat.

Wasserlhahn *der* tap *UK*, faucet *US*.

Wasserkraftlwerk *das* hydroelectric power station.

Wasserlleitung *die* water pipe.

wasserlöslich *adj* soluble.

Wasserlmann (*pl* **-männer**) *der* ASTROL Aquarius; **Wassermann sein** to be an Aquarius.

Wasserlmelone *die* watermelon.

wässern *vt* **- 1.** [Pflanze, Beet] to water **- 2.** KÜCHE to soak.

Wasserlpflanze *die* aquatic plant.

Wasserlratte *die* **- 1.** [Tier] water rat **- 2.** *fam* [Person] waterbaby.

wasserscheu *adj* scared of water.

Wasserlschutzpolizei *die* river police.

Wasserlski ◇ *der* [Gerät] water ski. ◇ *nt* water-skiing.

Wasserlspiegel *der* water level.

Wasserlsport *der* water sport.

Wasserlspülung (*pl* **-en**) *die* flush.

Wasserlstand *der* water level.

Wasserlstoff *der* CHEM hydrogen.

Wasserlversorgung *die (ohne pl)* water supply.

Wasserlwaage *die* spirit level.

Wasserlwerk *das* waterworks *Pl*.

Wasserlzeichen *das* watermark.

wässrig *adj* watery.

waten (*perf* **ist gewatet**) *vi* to wade.

watscheln (*perf* **ist gewatschelt**) *vi* to waddle.

Watt (*pl* **-en** ODER -) *das* **- 1.** *(pl Watten)* [Küstengebiet] mudflats *Pl* **- 2.** *(pl Watt)* PHYS & TECH [Maßeinheit] watt.

Watte *die* cotton wool.

Wattelbausch *der* wad of cotton wool.

Wattenlmeer *das* mudflats *Pl*.

Wattelstäbchen *das* cotton bud.

wattiert *adj* padded.

WC [veːˈtseː] (*pl* **-s**) (*abk für* **water closet**) *das* WC.

weben (*prät* **wob**, *perf* **hat gewoben**) *vt* to weave.

Weblseite [ˈwebsaitə] *die* EDV web page, website.

Weblstuhl *der* loom.

Wechsel [ˈvɛksl̩] (*pl* -) *der* **- 1.** [Tausch] change **- 2.** [Zahlungsmittel] exchange. ◆ **im Wechsel** *adv* in turns.

Wechsellbeziehung *die* correlation.

Wechsellgeld *das* change.

wechselhaft [ˈvɛksl̩haft] *adj* changeable.

Wechseljahre *Pl* menopause *(U)*.

Wechselkurs *der* exchange rate.

wechseln [ˈvɛksl̩n] (*perf* **hat/ist gewechselt**) ◇ *vt (hat)* **- 1.** [Thema, Kleidung, Arbeitsplatz, Geld] to change; **etw gegen** ODER **in etw** *(A)* **wechseln** to change sthg for sthg **- 2.** [tauschen] to exchange. ◇ *vi* **- 1.** *(hat)* [sich verändern] to change **- 2.** *(ist)* [an anderen Ort] to move.

wechselseitig ◇ *adj* mutual. ◇ *adv* mutually.

Wechsellstrom *der (ohne pl)* ELEKTR alternating current.

Wechsellstube *die* bureau de change.

Wechsellwirkung *die* interaction.

wecken *vt* **- 1.** [Person] to wake **- 2.** [Neugier, Wunsch] to awaken.

Wecker (*pl* -) *der* alarm clock; **jm auf den Wecker fallen** *fam fig* to get on sb's nerves.

wedeln (*perf* **hat/ist gewedelt**) *vi*: **mit etw wedeln** to wave sthg; **mit dem Schwanz wedeln** to wag its tail.

weder ◆ **weder... noch...** *konj* neither... nor...

weg *adv* away; **er ist schon weg** he has already gone; **nichts wie weg hier!** *fam* let's get out of here!; **weg damit!** *fam* take it away!; **Hände weg!** hands off!; **weit weg** far away; **über etw** *(A)* **weg sein** *fam fig* to have got over sthg.

Weg (*pl* **-e**) *der* - **1.** [Pfad] path - **2.** [Strecke, Methode] way; **ein weiter Weg** a long way; **jm im Weg stehen** *ODER* **sein** to be in sb's way; **jm über den Weg laufen** to bump into sb; **(jn) nach dem Weg fragen** to ask (sb) the way; **sich auf den Weg machen** to be on one's way; **jm/etw aus dem Weg gehen** to avoid sb/sthg; **jm nicht über den Weg trauen** not to trust sb an inch.

wegen *präp (+ G, D)* because of; **wegen Umbau geschlossen** closed for refurbishment. ◆ **von wegen** *interj fam* far from it!

weg|fahren (*perf* **hat/ist weggefahren**) *(unreg)* ◇ *vi (ist)* to leave; [verreisen] to go away; **er stieg ins Auto und fuhr weg** he got in the car and drove off. ◇ *vt (hat)* [transportieren] to move; [entsorgen] to take away.

weg|gehen (*perf* **ist weggegangen**) *vi (unreg)* - **1.** [fortgehen] to leave; [ausgehen] to go out; **geh weg!** go away! - **2.** [verschwinden] to go away - **3.** [Ware] to sell well.

weg|jagen *vt* to chase away.

weg|kommen (*perf* **ist weggekommen**) *vi (unreg)* - **1.** [fortgehen können] to get away; **von etw wegkommen** to get away from sthg; [Drogen] to get off sthg - **2.** [verschwinden] to disappear - **3.** [behandelt werden]: **gut/schlecht bei etw wegkommen** to do well/badly out of sthg.

weg|lassen *vt (unreg)* - **1.** [Person] to let go - **2.** [Abschnitt, Teil] to leave out.

weg|laufen (*perf* **ist weggelaufen**) *vi (unreg)* to run away; **vor** *ODER* **von jm/etw weglaufen** to run away from sb/sthg.

weg|legen *vt* to put down.

weg|machen *vt fam* to get rid of.

weg|müssen *vi (unreg)* to have to go.

weg|nehmen *vt (unreg)* to take away; **jm etw wegnehmen** to take sthg away from sb.

weg|räumen *vt* to clear away.

weg|schaffen *vt* [sich einer Sache entledigen] to get rid of; [woandershin bringen] to move.

weg|schicken *vt* [Person] to send away; [Päckchen] to send.

weg|sehen *vi (unreg)* to look away.

weg|tun *vt (unreg)* - **1.** [weglegen] to put away - **2.** [wegwerfen] to throw away.

Weg|weiser (*pl* -) *der* signpost.

weg|werfen *vt (unreg)* to throw away.

Wegwerf|gesellschaft *die abw* throwaway society.

weg|wischen *vt* to wipe away.

weg|ziehen (*perf* **hat/ist weggezogen**) *(unreg)* ◇ *vi (ist)*: **aus etw wegziehen** [Stadt] to move away from sthg; [Wohnung, Haus] to move out of sthg. ◇ *vt (hat)* to pull away; [Vorhang, Decke] to pull back.

weh *adj* painful; *siehe auch* **wehtun**. ◆ **oh weh** *interj* oh dear!

wehen (*perf* **hat/ist geweht**) ◇ *vi* - **1.** *(hat)* [blasen] to blow; [flattern] to flutter - **2.** *(ist)* [geweht werden - Blatt, Schneeflocken] to blow about; [- Duft, Geruch] to waft. ◇ *vt (hat)* to blow.

Wehen *Pl* contractions.

wehleidig *adj abw* self-pitying.

wehmütig ◇ *adj* melancholy. ◇ *adv* melancholically.

Wehr (*pl* **-e**) ◇ *die*: **sich zur Wehr setzen** to defend o.s. ◇ *das (pl Wehre)* weir.

Wehr|dienst *der* military service.

Wehr|dienstverweigerer (*pl* -) *der* conscientious objector.

wehren ◆ **sich wehren** *ref* to defend o.s.

wehrlos ◇ *adj* defenceless. ◇ *adv*: **jm wehrlos ausgeliefert sein** to be defenceless against sb.

Wehr|pflicht *die* compulsory military service.

wehrpflichtig *adj* liable for military service.

weh|tun *vi*: **jm wehtun** to hurt sb; **mir tun die Füße weh** my feet hurt. ◆ **sich wehtun** *ref* to hurt o.s.

Weib (*pl* **-er**) *das fam abw* [Frau] woman.

Weibchen (*pl* -) *das* female.

weiblich *adj* - **1.** [Person, Tier, Geschlecht] female - **2.** [Kleidung, Verhalten & GRAMM] feminine.

weich ◇ *adj* soft; **weich werden** *fam* to soften. ◇ *adv* [landen] softly; [bremsen] gently; [liegen] comfortably; **weich gekocht** soft-boiled; **jn weich machen** to soften sb up.

Weiche (*pl* **-n**) *die* points *Pl UK*, switch *US*.

weichgekocht *adj* ⊳ **weich**.

Weich|käse *der* soft cheese.

weichlich *adj abw* weak.

Weichling (*pl* **-e**) *der abw* weakling.

Weichsel ['vaiksl̩] *die*: **die Weichsel** the (River) Vistula.

Weich|spüler ['vaiçʃpy:lɐ] (*pl* -) *der* fabric conditioner.

Weide (*pl* **-n**) *die* - **1.** [für Vieh] meadow - **2.** [Baum] willow tree.

weiden *vi* to graze.

weigern ◆ **sich weigern** *ref*: **sich weigern, etw zu tun** to refuse to do sthg.

Weigerung (*pl* **-en**) *die* refusal.

weihen *vt* to consecrate.

Weiher (*pl* -) *der* pond.

Weihnachten (*pl* -) *(ohne Artikel)* Christmas; **Weihnachten feiern** to celebrate Christmas. ◆ **frohe Weihnachten** *interj* Merry Christmas!

weihnachtlich ◇ *adj* Christmassy. ◇ *adv* for Christmas.

Weihnachts|abend *der* Christmas Eve.

Weihnachts|baum *der* Christmas tree.

Weihnachts|geld *das (ohne pl)* Christmas bonus.

Weihnachts|geschenk *das* Christmas present.

Weihnachts|lied *das* Christmas carol.

Weihnachts|mann (*pl* **-männer**) *der* Father Christmas.

Weihnachts|markt *der* Christmas market.

Weihnachts|tag *der*: **erster/zweiter Weihnachtstag** Christmas/Boxing Day.

Weih|rauch *der* incense.

Weih|wasser *das* holy water.

weil *konj* because.

Weile ◆ **eine Weile** *adv* a while.

Weimarer Republik *die* Weimar Republic.

Wein (*pl* **-e**) *der* - **1.** [Getränk] wine - **2.** *(ohne pl)* [Pflanze] vine.

Wein|bau *der* wine-growing.

Wein|berg *der* vineyard.

Wein|brand *der* brandy.

weinen ◇ *vi* to cry; **über etw** *(A)* **weinen** to cry over sthg; **um jn weinen** to cry for sb; **vor etw** *(D)* **weinen** to cry with sthg; **wegen etw weinen** to cry because of sthg. ◇ *vt* to cry.

weinerlich *adj* tearful.

Wein|flasche *die* wine bottle.

Wein|keller *der* wine cellar.

Wein|lese (*pl* **-n**) *die* grape harvest.

Wein|probe *die* wine tasting.

Wein|stube *die* wine bar.

Wein|traube *die* grape.

weise ◇ *adj* wise. ◇ *adv* wisely.

Weise (*pl* **-n**) ◇ *die* - **1.** [Art] way - **2.** [Melodie] tune. ◇ *der, die* wise man (wise woman *die*).

weisen (*prät* **wies**, *perf* **hat gewiesen**) *geh* ◇ *vt* [zeigen]: **jm etw weisen** to show sb sthg. ◇ *vi* to point.

Weisheit (*pl* **-en**) *die* wisdom; **kannst du deine Weisheiten nicht für dich behalten?** can't you keep your pearls of wisdom to yourself?

Weisheits|zahn *der* wisdom tooth.

weis|machen *vt fam*: **jm etw weismachen** to make sb believe sthg.

weiß ◇ *präs* ▷ **wissen**. ◇ *adj* white.

Weiß *das* white.

Weiß|brot *das* white bread *(U)*.

Weiße (*pl* **-n**) ◇ *der, die* [Person] white person. ◇ *das* [Farbe] white. ◇ *die*: **Berliner Weiße mit Schuss** *type of wheat beer, with a shot of raspberry syrup*.

Weiß|glut *die*: **jn zur Weißglut bringen** *fam fig* to send sb into a rage.

Weiß|kohl *der* white cabbage.

Weiß|wein *der* white wine.

weit ◇ *adj* [gen] wide; [Reise, Fahrt] long; **wie weit ist es bis?** how far is it to?; **ist es weit?** is it far?; **im weitesten Sinne** in the broadest sense; **mit seinen Kenntnissen ist es nicht weit her** he doesn't know enough; **bist du so weit?** are you ready?; **es ist so weit** the time has come. ◇ *adv* - **1.** [beträchtlich] far; **weit besser** far better; **weit weg** far away; **ihre Meinungen gehen weit auseinander** they differ widely in their opinions; **weit geöffnet** wide open; **weit verbreitet** widespread; **weit nach Mitternacht** long after midnight - **2.** [gehen, fahren] a long way; **zwei Kilometer weit fahren** ODER **gehen** to go two kilometres; **das geht zu weit!** that's going too far!; **so weit, so gut** so far, so good. ◆ **bei Weitem** *adv* by far; **bei Weitem nicht genug** not nearly enough. ◆ **von Weitem** *adv* from far away.

weitaus *adv* by far.

Weite (*pl* **-n**) *die* - **1.** *(ohne pl)* [weite Fläche] expanse; **das Weite suchen** *fig* to make o.s. scarce - **2.** SPORT distance - **3.** [von Kleidungsstücken] width.

weiter *adv* further; **was geschah weiter?** what happened then?; **immer weiter** further and further. ◆ **nicht weiter** *adv* [nicht weiter fort] no further; [nicht mehr] no longer; **es hat mich nicht weiter interessiert** I wasn't really interested in it. ◆ **und so weiter** *adv* and so on. ◆ **weiter nichts** *adv* nothing more.

weiter|arbeiten *vi* to carry on working.

weitere, r, s *adj* further.

weiter|empfehlen *vt (unreg)* to recommend; **jm etw weiterempfehlen** to recommend sthg to sb.

weiter|geben *vt (unreg)* to pass on; **etw an jn weitergeben** to pass on sthg to sb.

weiter|gehen (*perf* **ist weitergegangen**) *vi (unreg)* - **1.** [gehen] to go on - **2.** [sich fortsetzen] to continue.

weiterhin *adv* - **1.** [immer noch] still - **2.** [künftig] in future.

weiter|machen *vi* to carry on.

weiter|wissen *vi (unreg)*: **nicht mehr weiterwissen** to be at one's wits' end.

weitgehend, weit gehend *adj* considerable.

weitläufig ◇ *adj* - **1.** [Haus, Grundstück] spacious - **2.** [Verwandtschaft] distant - **3.** [Schilderung] long-winded. ◇ *adv* - **1.** [angelegt] spaciously - **2.** [verwandt] distantly - **3.** [schildern] at great length.

weiträumig ◇ *adj* spacious. ◇ *adv*: **etw weiträumig umfahren** to give sthg a wide berth.

weitsichtig *adj* - **1.** [sehbehindert] long-sighted - **2.** [umsichtig] farsighted.

Weitsprung *der* SPORT long jump.

weitverbreitet, weit verbreitet *adj* common.

Weizen *der* wheat.

Weizen|bier *das* wheat beer.

wẹlche, r, s ◇ *det* which. ◇ *pron* - **1.** [Interrogativpronomen] which (one); **welcher von ihnen?** which (one) of them? - **2.** [Relativpronomen - Person] who, that; [- Sache] which, that - **3.** [Indefinitpronomen - in Aussagesätzen] some; [- in Frage- und Konditionalsätzen] any; **hast du welche?** have you got any?

wẹlk *adj* [Blumen] wilted; [Haut] withered.

wẹlken (*perf* **ist gewẹlkt**) *vi* to wilt.

Wẹll|blech *das* corrugated iron *(U)*.

Wẹlle (*pl* **-n**) *die* - **1.** [im Wasser] wave - **2.** [beim Rundfunk] wavelength; **Wellen schlagen** to create a stir.

wẹllen ◆ **sich wellen** *ref* [Papier] to wrinkle; [Haar] to become wavy; [Teppich] to ruck up.

Wẹllenbe|reich *der* waveband.

Wẹllen|gang *der*: **hoher Wellengang** heavy seas *Pl.*

Wẹllen|länge *die* PHYS wavelength.

Wẹllen|linie *die* wavy line.

Wẹllen|sittich *der* budgerigar.

wẹllig *adj* [Haar] wavy; [Papier] wrinkled; [Gelände] undulating.

Wẹll|pappe *die* corrugated cardboard *(U)*.

Wẹlpe (*pl* **-n**) *der* [von Hund] puppy; [von Fuchs, Wolf] cub.

Wẹlt (*pl* **-en**) *die* world; **auf der Welt** in the world; **die Dritte Welt** the Third World; **alle Welt** the whole world; **auf die** ODER **zur Welt kommen** to come into the world.

Wẹlt|all *das (ohne pl)* universe.

Wẹlt|anschauung *die* world view.

Wẹltaus|stellung *die* world fair.

wẹltberühmt *adj* world-famous.

wẹltfremd *adj* unworldly.

Wẹlt|krieg *der* HIST: **der Erste/Zweite Weltkrieg** the First/Second World War.

wẹltlich *adj* worldly.

Wẹlt|macht *die* world power.

Wẹlt|meister, in *der, die* world champion.

Wẹlt|rang *der*: **von Weltrang** world-class.

Wẹltrang|liste *die* SPORT world rankings *Pl.*

Wẹlt|raum *der* space.

Wẹlt|reise *die* round-the-world trip.

Wẹlt|rekord *der* world record.

Wẹlt|stadt *die* cosmopolitan city.

Wẹlt|untergang *der* end of the world.

wẹltweit *adj* worldwide.

wem *pron (Dativ von wer)* (to) who, (to) whom; **wem gehört die Tasche?** whose bag is it?; **mit wem spreche ich?** who's speaking?; **von wem hast du das?** who did you get it from?

wen *pron (Akkusativ von wer)* who, whom; **für wen ist das?** who is that for?

Wẹnde (*pl* **-n**) *die* - **1.** [Veränderung] change - **2.** SPORT turn - **3.** HIST: **die Wende** the fall of the Berlin Wall.

Wẹnde|kreis *der* - **1.** [von Auto] turning circle - **2.** GEOGR tropic.

Wẹndel|treppe *die* spiral staircase.

wẹnden (*prät* **wẹndete** ODER **wạndte**, *perf* **hat gewẹndet** ODER **gewạndt**) ◇ *vt (reg)* [umdrehen] to turn; [Kleidungsstück] to reverse. ◇ *vi (reg)* to turn around; **'bitte wenden'** 'please turn over'. ◆ **sich wenden** *ref* - **1.** *(reg)* [sich ändern]: **sich zum Besseren/Schlechteren wenden** to take a turn for the better/worse - **2.** [sich richten]: **sich an jn/etw wenden** [hilfesuchend] to turn to sb/sthg; [appellierend] to address sb/sthg; **sich gegen jn/etw wenden** to oppose sb/sthg.

Wẹnde|punkt *der* turning point.

Wẹndung (*pl* **-en**) *die* - **1.** [Redewendung] idiom - **2.** [Drehung] turn.

wẹnig ◇ *det* - **1.** [Anzahl] a few; **mit wenigen Worten** in few words - **2.** [Menge] little. ◇ *pron* - **1.** [Anzahl] a few; **es ist nur wenigen bekannt, dass...** only a few people know that... - **2.** [Menge] little. ◇ *adv* a little; **wenig bekannt** little known; **wenig erfreulich** not very pleasant. ◆ **ein wenig** *det, pron* & *adv* a little. ◆ **nur wenig** ◇ *det* - **1.** [Anzahl] only a few - **2.** [Menge] only a little; **er hat nur wenig Zeit** he hasn't got much time. ◇ *adv* only a little. ◆ **zu wenig** ◇ *det* - **1.** [Anzahl] too few - **2.** [Menge] too little. ◇ *adv* & *pron* too little.

weniger ◇ *adv* less. ◇ *konj*: **sieben weniger drei** seven minus three.

wenigste *adj* ▷ **wenig.** ◆ **am wenigsten** *adv* least.

wenigstens *adv* at least.

wẹnn *konj* - **1.** [zeitlich] when - **2.** [konditional] if; **wenn ich das gewusst hätte** if I had known, had I known; **wenn er nur käme!** if only he would come! ◆ **wenn auch** *konj* even if. ◆ **wenn bloß** *konj* if only.

wer *pron* - **1.** [Interrogativpronomen] who; **wer von euch?** which of you? - **2.** [Relativpronomen] anyone ODER anybody who; **wer mitkommen will** anyone who wants to come - **3.** *fam* [Indefinitpronomen - in Aussagesätzen] somebody, someone; [- in Frage- und Konditionalsätzen] anybody, anyone; **ist da wer?** is there anyone there?

Wẹrbe|fernsehen *das* television advertising.

wẹrben (*präs* **wịrbt**, *prät* **wạrb**, *perf* **hat gewọrben**) ◇ *vi* to advertise. ◇ *vt* to attract.

Wẹrbung (*pl* **-en**) *die* advertising.

Wẹrde|gang *der* development; **der berufliche Werdegang** professional development.

wẹrden (*präs* **wịrd**, *prät* **wụrde**, *perf* **ist gewọrden** ODER **wọrden**) ◇ *aux* - **1.** [zur Bildung des Futurs] will; **sie wird kommen** she will come, she'll come; **sie wird nicht kommen** she won't come; **es wird warm werden** it is going to be warm - **2.** [zur Bildung des Konjunktivs] would; **würdest du/würden Sie?** would you?; **ich würde gerne** I would like to; **ich würde lieber noch bleiben** I would prefer to stay a bit longer - **3.** *(perf ist worden)* [zur Bildung des Passivs] to be; **sie wurde kritisiert** she was criticised; **nebenan wird gelacht** there's someone laughing next door. ◇ *vi (perf ist geworden)* - **1.** [gen] to become; **Vater werden** to become a father; **er will Lehrer werden** he wants to be a teacher; **alt werden** to grow ODER get old; **rot werden** to turn ODER go red; **verrückt werden** to go mad; **krank werden** to fall ill; **schlecht werden** to go off; **ich werde morgen 25** I'll be 25 tomorrow; **es wird Nacht** it's getting dark; **daraus wird nichts** nothing will come of it; **zu Stein werden** to turn to stone; **zum Mann werden** to become a man; **(na,) wirds bald!** *fam* get a move on! - **2.** *fam* [gelingen, sich erholen]: **sind die Fotos was geworden?** did the photos come out?; **es wird schon wieder werden** *fam* it will be all right.

wẹrfen (*präs* **wịrft**, *prät* **wạrf**, *perf* **hat gewọrfen**) ◇ *vt* - **1.** [Ball, Stein] to throw - **2.** [Tor, Korb] to score. ◇ *vi* to throw; **mit etw werfen** to throw sthg. ◆ **sich werfen** *ref* to throw o.s.

Wẹrft (*pl* **-en**) *die* shipyard.

Wẹrk (*pl* **-e**) *das* - **1.** [gen] work - **2.** [Betrieb] plant.

Wẹrk|statt (*pl* **-stätten**) *die* workshop.

Wẹrk|tag *der* working day.

wẹrktags *adv* on working days.

wẹrktätig *adj* working.

Wẹrkzeug (*pl* **-e**) *das* tool.

Wẹrkzeug|kasten *der* tool box.

Wermut (*pl* **-s**) *der* vermouth *(U)*.

wert *adj*: **wert sein** to be worth; **nichts wert sein** to be worthless; **viel/tausend Euro wert sein** to be worth a lot/a thousand euros; **werte Gäste!** dear guests!

Wert (*pl* **-e**) *der* value; **auf etw (A) Wert legen** to attach importance to sthg; **im Wert steigen/fallen** to increase/decrease in value; **das hat keinen Wert!** *fam* it's pointless.

werten *vt* [benoten] to rate; [beurteilen] to judge; [einschätzen]: **etw als Erfolg werten** to consider sthg a success.

Wertgegen|stand *der* valuable object.

wertlos *adj* worthless.

Wert|papier *das* WIRTSCH bond.

Wertung (*pl* **-en**) *die* judgement.

wertvoll *adj* valuable.

Wesen (*pl* **-**) *das* - **1.** [Charakter] nature - **2.** [Mensch] being - **3.** [Lebewesen] creature.

wesentlich ◇ *adj* essential. ◇ *adv* considerably. ◆ **im Wesentlichen** *adv* essentially.

weshạlb *adv* why.

Wẹspe (*pl* **-n**) *die* wasp.

wẹssen *pron (Genitiv von wer)* whose.

Wẹssi (*pl* **-s**) *der fam citizen of the former West Germany.*

Wẹst|deutschland *nt* western Germany; [frühere BRD] West Germany.

Wẹste (*pl* **-n**) *die* waistcoat *UK*, vest *US*.

Wẹsten *der* - **1.** [gen] west; **aus Westen** from the west; **nach Westen** west; **im Westen** in the west; **der Wilde Westen** the Wild West - **2.** POL West.

Wẹst|europa *nt* Western Europe.

Westfalen *nt* Westphalia.

Wẹst|küste *die* West Coast.

wẹstlich ◇ *adj* western. ◇ *präp*: **westlich einer Sache** *(G)* ODER **von etw** (to the) west of sthg.

weswegen *adv* why.

Wẹttbewerb (*pl* **-e**) *der* competition.

Wẹtte (*pl* **-n**) *die* bet. ◆ **um die Wette** *adv*: **um die Wette laufen** to have a race; **um die Wette jodeln** to have a yodelling competition.

wẹtten ◇ *vi* to bet; **mit jm wetten** to bet sb; **um etw wetten** to bet sthg. ◇ *vt* to bet. ◆ **wetten, dass?** *interj* do you want to bet?

Wẹtter (*pl* **-**) *das* [Klima] weather; **schönes/schlechtes Wetter** good/bad weather.

Wẹtter|amt *das* meteorological office.

Wẹtter|bericht *der* weather report.

wẹtterfest *adj* weatherproof.

Wẹtter|karte *die* weather map.

Wẹtter|lage *die* general weather situation.

wẹttern *vi*: **gegen jn/etw wettern** to curse sb/sthg.

Wẹttervorher|sage *die* weather forecast.

Wẹtt|kampf *der* contest.

Wẹtt|lauf *der* race.

wẹtt|machen *vt* to make up for.

Wẹtt|rennen *das* race.

wẹtzen (*perf* **hat gewẹtzt**) *vt* to sharpen.

WG [veːˈgeː] (*pl* **-s**) *die abk für* **Wohngemeinschaft**.

Whg. *abk für* **Wohnung**.

Whirlpool ['wœrlpu:l] *der* Jacuzzi®.

Whiskey (*pl* **-s**), **Whisky** (*pl* **-s**) ['vɪski] *der* whisky.

wichtig *adj* important; **etw wichtig nehmen** to take sthg seriously.

Wichtigkeit *die* importance.

Wichtigtuer (*pl* -) *der fam abw* bighead.

wickeln *vt* to wind; **etw um etw wickeln** to wrap sthg around sthg; **jn/etw in etw** *(A)* **wickeln** to wrap sb/sthg in sthg; **ein Baby wickeln** to change a baby's nappy *UK* ODER diaper *US*.

Widder (*pl* -) *der* - **1.** [Tier] ram - **2.** ASTROL Aries; **Widder sein** to be an Aries.

wider *präp geh* against.

widerlegen *vt* [Argument, Behauptung] to refute; **jn widerlegen** to prove sb wrong.

widerlich *adj abw* revolting.

widerrechtlich ◇ *adj* illegal. ◇ *adv* illegally.

Wider|ruf *der* [von Aussage] retraction *(U)*; [von Befehl] revocation. ◆ **bis auf Widerruf** *adv* until further notice.

widerrufen (*prät* **widerrief**, *perf* **hat widerrufen**) *vt* [von Aussage] to retract; [von Befehl] to revoke.

wider|setzen ◆ **sich widersetzen** *ref*: **sich einer Sache** *(D)* **widersetzen** to oppose sthg; **sich einem Befehl widersetzen** to refuse to comply with an order.

widerspenstig ◇ *adj* unruly. ◇ *adv* in an unruly manner.

wider|spiegeln *vt* to reflect. ◆ **sich widerspiegeln** *ref* to be reflected.

widersprechen (*präs* **widerspricht**, *prät* **widersprach**, *perf* **hat widersprochen**) *vi* to contradict; **jm widersprechen** to contradict sb; **einer Sache/sich** *(D)* **widersprechen** to contradict sthg/o.s.

Wider|spruch *der* - **1.** [von Personen] protest - **2.** [in Aussage] contradiction.

Wider|stand *der* - **1.** [Ablehnung & ELEKTR] resistance *(U)*; **Widerstand gegen jn/etw** resistance against sb/sthg; **Widerstand leisten** to put up resistance; **auf Widerstand stoßen** to meet with resistance - **2.** [Hindernis] obstacle.

widerstandsfähig *adj* resilient.

widerstehen (*prät* **widerstand**, *perf* **hat widerstanden**) *vi*: **jm/einer Sache widerstehen** to resist sb/sthg.

widerstrebend ◇ *adj* reluctant. ◇ *adv* reluctantly.

widerwärtig ◇ *adj* revolting. ◇ *adv*: **sich widerwärtig verhalten** to behave offensively.

Widerwille, Widerwillen *der* reluctance; **Widerwillen gegen jn/etw empfinden** to be disgusted by sb/sthg.

widmen *vt* - **1.** [zueignen]: **jm etw widmen** to dedicate sthg to sb - **2.** [aufwenden] to dedicate. ◆ **sich widmen** *ref* [sich zuwenden]: **sich jm/einer Sache widmen** to devote o.s. to sb/sthg.

Widmung (*pl* **-en**) *die* dedication.

wie ◇ *adv* how; **wie heißen Sie?** what's your name?; **sie fragte ihn, wie alt er sei** she asked him how old he was; **wie war das Wetter?** what was the weather like?; **wie gehts?** how are you?; **wie spät ist es?** what's the time?, what time is it?; **wie oft?** how often?; **wie bitte?** sorry?, excuse me?; **wie war das?** *fam* come again?; **wie nett von dir!** how kind of you!; **wie schade!** what a pity! ◇ *interj*: **er kam wohl nicht, wie?** he didn't come, did he? ◇ *konj* - **1.** [vergleichend - vor Substantiv] like; [- vor Adjektiv, Verb, Partikel] as; **wie sein Vater** like his father; **so... wie...** as... as...; **so viel, wie du willst** as much as you want; **so groß wie du** as big as you; **weiß wie Schnee** as white as snow - **2.** [zum Beispiel] such as, like - **3.** [dass]: **ich hörte, wie mein Nachbar Klavier spielte** I heard my neighbour playing the piano.

wieder *adv* - **1.** [gen] again; **immer wieder, wieder und wieder** again and again; **hin und wieder** now and again; **nie wieder** never again; **was hast du denn (jetzt) wieder angestellt?** what have you done this time?; **er ist wieder da** he is back; **er ging wieder ins Haus** he went back into the house - **2.** *fam* [wiederum] on the other hand.

wieder|bekommen *vt (unreg)* to get back.

wieder beleben, wiederbeleben *vt* to revive.

wieder|bringen *vt (unreg)* to bring back.

wieder erkennen, wiedererkennen *vt (unreg)* to recognize.

Wieder|gabe *die* [Bericht] account; [von Bild, Ton, Farben] reproduction; [von Musikstück, Gedicht] rendition.

wieder|geben *vt (unreg)* - **1.** [zurückgeben]: **jm etw wiedergeben** to give sthg back to sb - **2.** [mit Worten] to give an account of - **3.** [technisch] to reproduce.

wieder gut|machen, wiedergut|machen *vt* [Schaden] to compensate for; [Fehler] to put right; [Unrecht] to repair.

wiederher|stellen *vt* to restore; [Kontakt] to reestablish.

wiederholen *vt* - **1.** [gen] to repeat - **2.** [lernen] to revise. ◆ **sich wiederholen** *ref* - **1.** [Sprecher] to repeat o.s. - **2.** [Ereignis] to recur - **3.** [Muster] to reappear.

Wiederholung (*pl* **-en**) *die* repetition.

Wiederhören ◆ **auf Wiederhören** *interj* goodbye! *(on telephone)*.

wiedersehen *vt (unreg)* to see again.

Wiedersehen (*pl* -) *das* reunion. ◆ **auf Wiedersehen** *interj* goodbye!

wiederum *adv* - **1.** [von neuem] again - **2.** [andererseits] on the other hand.

Wiederver|einigung *die* HIST reunification *(U)*.

wieder verwerten, wiederverwerten *vt* to reuse.

Wiege (*pl* **-n**) *die* cradle.

wiegen (*prät* **wiegte** ODER **wog**, *perf* **hat gewiegt** ODER **gewogen**) *vt* - **1.** *(unreg)* [abwiegen] to weigh - **2.** *(reg)* [schaukeln] to rock.

Wiegen|lied *das* lullaby.

wiehern *vi* to neigh.

Wien *nt* Vienna.

Wiener (*pl* -) ◇ *der* Viennese. ◇ *adj (unver)*: **Wiener Schnitzel** Wiener schnitzel, *escalope of veal coated with breadcrumbs*; **Wiener Würstchen** Wiener, *small sausage made of beef, pork or veal*.

Wienerin (*pl* **-nen**) *die* Viennese.

wies *prät* ▷ **weisen**.

Wiese (*pl* **-n**) *die* meadow; **auf der grünen Wiese** outside town.

Wiesel (*pl* -) *das* weasel.

wieso *pron* why.

wie viel *pron* - **1.** [Anzahl] how many - **2.** [Menge] how much; **wie viel ist zwei mal drei?** what is two times three?; **wie viel Uhr ist es?** what's the time?, what time is it?; **wie viel älter/schneller?** how much older/faster?; **wie viel Geld das kostet!** what a lot of money it costs!

wievielt *adj* which. ◆ **zu wievielt** *adv*: **zu wievielt seid ihr in Urlaub gefahren?** how many of you went on holiday?

wieweit *konj* how far.

wịld ◇ *adj* - **1.** [gen] wild - **2.** [unzivilisiert] savage - **3.** [illegal] illegal. ◇ *adv* - **1.** [gen] wildly - **2.** [illegal] illegally.

Wịld *das* game.

wịldern ◇ *vi* [jagen - Mensch] to poach; [- Tier] to hunt. ◇ *vt* to poach.

wịldfremd *adj* completely strange; **ein wildfremder Mensch** a complete stranger.

Wịld|leder *das* suede *(U)*.

Wịldnis (*pl* **-se**) *die* wilderness.

Wịld|schwein *das* wild boar.

wịll *präs* ▷ **wollen**.

Wịlle (*pl* **-n**), **Wịllen** *der* will; **beim besten Willen** with the best will in the world.

wịllen *präp*: **um js/einer Sache willen** for the sake of sb/sthg.

wịllenlos *adj* & *adv* with a total lack of will.

wịllensstark *adj* strong-willed.

wịllig ◇ *adj* willing. ◇ *adv* willingly.

willkọmmen *adj* welcome; **ihr seid uns jederzeit willkommen** you are always welcome. ◆ **herzlich willkommen** *interj* welcome!

Willkọmmen (*pl* -) *das* welcome.

wịllkürlich ◇ *adj* arbitrary. ◇ *adv* arbitrarily.

wịmmeln *vi*: **es wimmelt von ...** it's crawling with ...

wịmmern *vi* to whimper.

Wịmper (*pl* **-n**) *die* eyelash; **ohne mit der Wimper zu zucken** *fig* without batting an eyelid.

Wịmpern|tusche *die* mascara *(U)*.

Wịnd (*pl* **-e**) *der* wind; **bei Wind und Wetter** in all weathers; **Wind von etw bekommen** *fam fig* to get wind of sthg.

Wịnde (*pl* **-n**) *die* - **1.** [Hebevorrichtung] winch - **2.** [Pflanze] bindweed *(U)*.

Wịndel (*pl* **-n**) *die* nappy *UK*, diaper *US*.

wịnden (*prät* **wạnd**, *perf* **hat gewụnden**) *vt* *geh* [flechten] to wind; [Kranz] to make; **etw um etw winden** to wind sthg around sthg. ◆ **sich winden** *ref* - **1.** [sich schlängeln - Schlange, Aal] to slither; [- vor Schmerz] to writhe - **2.** *geh* [Pflanze] to wind o.s. - **3.** [Weg] to wind - **4.** [vor Verlegenheit] to squirm.

wịndig *adj* - **1.** [Wetter] windy - **2.** *fam abw* [Person, Ausrede] dodgy.

Wịnd|mühle *die* windmill.

Wịnd|pocken *Pl* chickenpox *(U)*.

Wịndschutz|scheibe *die* windscreen *UK*, windshield *US*.

wịndstill *adj* [Tag] still; [Ecke] sheltered.

Wịnd|stoß *der* gust of wind.

Wịndung (*pl* **-en**) *die* winding.

Wịnk (*pl* **-e**) *der* - **1.** [Geste] sign - **2.** [Bemerkung] hint; **jm einen Wink geben** to give sb a tip.

Wịnkel (*pl* -) *der* - **1.** MATH angle; **ein stumpfer/spitzer/rechter Winkel** an obtuse/an acute/a right angle; **toter Winkel** *fig* blind spot - **2.** [Ecke] corner - **3.** [Platz] spot.

wịnken (*perf* **hat gewịnkt** ODER **gewụnken**) ◇ *vi* - **1.** [zur Begrüßung, zum Abschied] to wave; **jm winken** to wave to sb - **2.** [als Aufforderung]: **einem Taxi winken** to hail a taxi; **dem Kellner winken** to call the waiter - **3.** [Belohnung] to get. ◇ *vt*: **jn zu sich (hin) winken** to beckon sb over; **jn an einen Ort winken** to direct sb to a place.

wịnseln *vi* - **1.** [Tier] to whine - **2.** *abw* [Person] to whimper.

Wịnter (*pl* -) *der* winter; **den Winter über** for the winter; **im Winter** in winter.

wịnterlich ◇ *adj* wintery; [Kleidung, Landschaft] winter. ◇ *adv*: **winterlich kalt** cold and wintery.

Wịnter|reifen *der* winter tyre.

Wịnter|schlaf *der* hibernation.

Wịnterschlussverkauf (*pl* **-käufe**) *der* January sale.

Wịnter|semester *das* UNI winter semester.

Wịnter|spiele *Pl*: **Olympische Winterspiele** Winter Olympics.

Wịnter|sport *der* winter sport.

Wịnzer, in (*mpl* **-**, *fpl* **-nen**) *der, die* wine grower.

wịnzig *adj* tiny.

wịppen *vi* to rock.

wir *pron* we; **wir beide** both of us; **wir waren es** it was us.

Wịrbel (*pl* -) *der* - **1.** [von Wasser] whirlpool; [von Wind] whirlwind - **2.** [Aufregung] stir; **viel Wirbel um etw machen** to make a big fuss about sthg - **3.** [im Haar] cowlick - **4.** [im Rücken] vertebra.

wịrbeln (*perf* **hat/ist gewịrbelt**) ◇ *vi (ist)* to whirl; [Schneeflocken, Blätter] to swirl. ◇ *vt (hat)* to whirl; [Schneeflocken, Blätter] to swirl.

Wịrbel|säule *die* spine.

Wịrbel|tier *das* BIOL vertebrate.

wịrbt *präs* ▷ **werben**.

wịrd *präs* ▷ **werden**.

wịrft *präs* ▷ **werfen**.

wịrken *vi* - **1.** [erscheinen] to seem; **sie wirkt auf jeden sympathisch** everybody finds her nice - **2.** [wirksam sein] to have an effect; **beruhigend wirken** to have a calming effect; **gegen etw wirken** to be effective against sthg - **3.** [beruflich, Bild, Muster] to work.

wịrklich ◇ *adj* real. ◇ *adv* really.

Wịrklichkeit (*pl* **-en**) *die* reality.

wịrksam ◇ *adj* effective. ◇ *adv* effectively.

Wịrkung (*pl* **-en**) *die* effect.

wịrkungslos *adj* ineffective.

wịrkungsvoll *adj* effective.

wịrr ◇ *adj* - **1.** [unordentlich] tangled - **2.** [konfus] confused. ◇ *adv* - **1.** [unordentlich] in a tangle - **2.** [konfus] in a confused way.

Wịrrwarr *der ODER das* confusion.

Wịrt, in (*mpl* **-e**, *fpl* **-nen**) *der, die* landlord (landlady *die*).

Wịrtschaft (*pl* **-en**) *die* - **1.** [Ökonomie] economy; **die freie Wirtschaft** the private sector - **2.** [Gaststätte] pub *UK*, bar *US*.

wịrtschaften *vi* [leiten]: **Gewinn bringend wirtschaften** to run things at a profit; **wer wirtschaftet auf diesem Gut?** who runs this estate?; **mit Geld wirtschaften** to manage finances.

wịrtschaftlich ◇ *adj* - **1.** [materiell] economic - **2.** [sparsam] economical. ◇ *adv* economically.

Wịrtschafts|krise *die* economic crisis.

Wịrtschafts|ministerium *das* economics ministry.

Wịrtschafts|politik *die (ohne pl)* economic policy.

Wịrtschafts|system *das* economic system.

Wịrtschafts|zweig *der* economic sector.

Wịrts|haus *das pub, often with accommodation.*

Wịrts|leute *Pl* landlord and landlady.

Wịrts|stube *die* bar.

wịschen ◇ *vt* [Boden, Mund] to wipe; [Dreck] to wipe away; [putzen] to clean. ◇ *vi*: **mit der Hand über die Stirn wischen** to wipe one's hand across one's brow.

wịspern *vt* & *vi* to whisper.

wịssbegierig *adj* thirsty for knowledge.

wịssen (*präs* **weiß**, *prät* **wụsste**, *perf* **hat gewụsst**) ◇ *vt* to know; **etw über jn/etw wissen** to know sthg about sb/sthg; **immer alles besser wissen** to always know better; **weißt du was?** *fam* you know what?; **ich will nichts von ihm/davon wissen** I don't want to have anything to do with him/it; **das musst du wissen** that's up to you; **was weiß ich!** *fam* don't ask me! ◇ *vi* to know; **ich weiß!** I know!; **soviel** ODER **soweit ich weiß** as far as I know; **nicht, dass ich wüsste** *fam* not as far as I know; **von/um etw wissen** to know about sthg; **man kann nie wissen** you never know.

Wịssen *das* knowledge; **nach bestem Wissen und Gewissen** to the best of one's knowledge and ability; **meines Wissens** to my knowledge.

Wịssenschaft (*pl* **-en**) *die* science.

Wịssenschaftler, in (*mpl* **-**, *fpl* **-nen**) *der, die* scientist; [in Geisteswissenschaften] academic.

wịssenschaftlich ◇ *adj* academic; [naturwissenschaftlich] scientific. ◇ *adv* academically; [naturwissenschaftlich] scientifically.

wịssenswert *adj* worth knowing; [Fakten] valuable.

Wịssenswerte *das* useful knowledge.

wịttern *vt* - **1.** [riechen] to scent - **2.** [vermuten] to sense.

Wịtterung (*pl* **-en**) *die* - **1.** [Wetter] weather - **2.** [Geruch] scent.

Wịtwe (*pl* **-n**) *die* widow.

Wịtwer (*pl* -) *der* widower.

Wịtz (*pl* **-e**) *der* - **1.** [Scherz] joke; **Witze machen** ODER **reißen** *fam* to crack jokes; **du machst wohl Witze!** you can't be serious! - **2.** [Humor] wit.

Wịtzbold (*pl* **-e**) *der fam* joker.

wịtzeln *vi*: **über jn/etw witzeln** to make fun of sb/sthg.

wịtzig ◇ *adj* funny; [Idee] original. ◇ *adv* [lustig] funnily.

wịtzlos *adj* - **1.** [langweilig] dull - **2.** *fam* [überflüssig] pointless.

wo ◇ *adv* where; **von wo kam das Geräusch?** where did that noise come from?

◇ *pron* where. ◇ *konj fam* - **1.** [obwohl] when - **2.** [da] since; **jetzt, wo alles vorbei ist** now that it's all over.

woạnders *adv* somewhere else.

wob *prät* ▷ **weben**.

wobei *pron* - **1.** [als Frage]: **wobei ist es passiert?** how did it happen?; **wobei hast du ihn gestört?** what was he doing when you disturbed him? - **2.** [zeitlich]: **sie stürzte von der Leiter, wobei sie sich den Arm brach** she fell off the ladder and broke her arm - **3.** [allerdings] although.

Wọche (*pl* **-n**) *die* week; **vorige** ODER **letzte Woche** last week; **diese/nächste Woche** this/next week.

Wọchen|ende *das* weekend; **am Wochenende** at the weekend. ◆ **schönes Wochenende** *interj* have a nice weekend!

Wọchen|karte *die* weekly ticket.

wọchenlang ◇ *adj* lasting for weeks; **nach wochenlangem Warten** after waiting for weeks. ◇ *adv* for weeks.

Wọchen|markt *der* weekly market.

Wọchen|tag *der* weekday.

wọ̈chentlich *adj* & *adv* weekly.

Wọdka (*pl* **-s**) *der* vodka.

wodụrch, wodurch *pron* - **1.** [als Frage] how - **2.** [Relativpronomen] as a result of which.

wofür, wofür *pron* - **1.** [als Frage] what... for? - **2.** [Relativpronomen] for which.

wog *prät* ▷ **wiegen**.

wogegen, wogegen ◇ *pron* - **1.** [als Frage] against what - **2.** [Relativpronomen] against which. ◇ *konj* [wohingegen] whereas.

woher, woher *pron* - **1.** [als Frage] where... from; **woher kommen Sie?** where do you come from?; **woher weißt du das?** how do you know that? - **2.** [Relativpronomen] from where.

wohịn, wohin *pron* - **1.** [als Frage] where; **wohin damit?** *fam* where shall I put it? - **2.** [Relativpronomen] where.

wohl (*kompar* **wohler** ODER **bẹsser**, *superl* **am wohlsten** ODER **bẹsten**) *adv* - **1.** *(kompar wohler, superl am wohlsten)* [zufrieden] well; **sich wohl fühlen** [gesundheitlich] to feel well; [angenehm] to feel at home; **wohl oder übel** *fig* like it or not - **2.** [wahrscheinlich] probably; **das ist wohl möglich** quite possibly; **du bist wohl wahnsinnig!** you must be crazy! - **3.** [zum Ausdruck der Unbeantwortbarkeit]: **ob sie wohl gut angekommen sind?** I wonder if they have arrived safely - **4.** *(kompar besser, superl am besten) geh* [gut] well; **er weiß sehr wohl, dass...** he knows perfectly well that... ◆ **wohl aber** *konj* but.

Wohl *das* well-being; **zum Wohle der Allgemeinheit** for the common good; **zum Wohl!** cheers!

wohlbehalten *adv* safe and sound.

Wohlfahrt *die* welfare.

wohlhabend *adj* well-to-do.

wohlig ◇ *adj* [Wärme, Gefühl] pleasant; [Seufzer] contented. ◇ *adv* contentedly.

Wohl|stand *der* affluence.

wohltätig *adj* charitable.

wohlverdient *adj* well-earned.

wohlwollend ◇ *adj* benevolent. ◇ *adv* benevolently.

wohnen *vi* to live; **wir wohnen vorübergehend bei Freunden** we're staying with friends at the moment; **zur Miete wohnen** to rent, to live in rented accommodation.

Wohn|gemeinschaft *die* shared flat/house; **in einer Wohngemeinschaft wohnen** to share a flat/house.

wohnhaft *adj amt* resident.

Wohn|haus *das* house.

Wohn|heim *das* [für Studenten] hall of residence; [für Obdachlose] hostel.

wohnlich ◇ *adj* homely. ◇ *adv* in a homely way.

Wohn|mobil (*pl* **-e**) *das* camper *UK*, RV *US*.

Wohn|ort *der* place of residence.

Wohn|sitz *der* place of residence.

Wohnung (*pl* **-en**) *die* flat *UK*, apartment *US*.

Wohnungs|bau *der* housebuilding.

Wohnungs|not *die* housing shortage.

Wohnungs|suche *die* flat-hunting.

Wohn|viertel *das* residential area.

Wohn|wagen *der* caravan *UK*, trailer *US*.

Wohn|zimmer *das* living room.

Wọ̈lbung (*pl* **-en**) *die* [von Himmel] dome; [von Oberfläche] curvature.

Wolf (*pl* **Wọ̈lfe**) *der* - **1.** [Tier] wolf - **2.** *fam* [Fleischwolf] mincer; **jn durch den Wolf drehen** *fig* to give sb a hard time.

Wọlke (*pl* **-n**) *die* cloud; **aus allen Wolken fallen** *fig* to be astounded.

Wọlken|bruch *der* cloudburst.

Wọlken|kratzer *der* skyscraper.

wọlkig *adj* cloudy.

Wọll|decke *die* blanket.

Wọlle *die* wool; **aus Wolle** woollen; **sich in die Wolle kriegen** *fam fig* to start arguing.

wọllen (*präs* **will**, *prät* **wọllte**, *perf* **hat gewọllt** ODER **wọllen**) ◇ *aux (perf hat wollen)*: **er will anrufen** he wants to make a call; **wollen wir aufstehen?** shall we get up?; **ich wollte gerade gehen, da ...** I was just about to go when ...; **was willst du damit sagen?** what do you mean by that?; **diese Entscheidung will überlegt sein** this decision needs to be thought through. ◇ *vi (perf hat gewollt)*: **das Kind will nicht** the child doesn't want to; **sie will nach Hause** she wants to go home; **ich wollte, es wäre nur schon vorbei** I wish it were over; **dann wollen wir mal!** *fam* let's do it!; **ganz wie du willst** *fam* it's up to you! ◇ *vt (perf hat gewollt)* - **1.** [gen] to want; **ich will ein Eis** I want an ice-cream; **mach, was du willst** do as you like; **wollen, dass jd etw tut** to want sb to do sthg; **was willst du mit dem Messer?** what do you want a knife for?; **von jm etwas wollen** *fam* to fancy sb - **2.** *fam* [brauchen] to need; **da ist nichts (mehr) zu wollen** *fam* there's nothing that we/*etc* can do about it.

Woll|knäuel *das* ball of wool.

womit *pron* [Interrogativpronomen] what... with; **womit habe ich das verdient?** what did I do to deserve that?

womöglich *adv* possibly.

wonach *pron* [als Frage] for what; **wonach suchst du?** what are you looking for?; **wonach schmeckt es?** what does it taste of?

woran *pron* [Interrogativpronomen] what... on; **woran denkst du?** what are you thinking about?

worauf *pron* [Interrogativpronomen] what... on; **worauf wartest du?** what are you waiting for?

woraus *pron* [Interrogativpronomen] what... from; **woraus ist die Tasche?** what is the bag made of?

worin *pron* [Interrogativpronomen] what... in; **worin besteht der Unterschied?** what's the difference?

Workout *das* SPORT workout.

World Wide Web [wɜ:ld waɪd web] *das* EDV World Wide Web; **im World Wide Web** on the (World Wide) Web.

Wort (*pl* **-e** ODER **Wörter**) *das* - **1.** *(pl Wörter)* [sprachliche Einheit] word; **Wort für Wort** word for word - **2.** *(pl Worte)* [Äußerung] word; **etw aufs Wort glauben** to believe every word of sthg; **kein Wort sagen/glauben** not to say/believe a word; **mir fehlen die Worte!** I'm speechless!; **mit anderen Worten** in other words; **sie ließ mich nicht zu Wort kommen** she wouldn't let me speak ODER have my say - **3.** *(pl Worte)* [Zitat] quotation - **4.** *(pl Worte) geh* [Text] words *Pl* - **5.** *(ohne pl)* [Zusage] word; **jm sein Wort geben** to give sb one's word; **das Wort haben/erteilen/ergreifen** to have/give/take the floor; **ein geflügeltes Wort** a well-known quotation; **für jn ein gutes Wort einlegen** to put in a good word for sb.

Wort|art *die* GRAMM part of speech.

wortbrüchig *adj*: **wortbrüchig werden** to break one's word.

Wörter|buch *das* dictionary.

wortgewandt ◇ *adj* eloquent. ◇ *adv* eloquently.

wortkarg ◇ *adj* laconic. ◇ *adv* laconically.

wörtlich ◇ *adj* word-for-word. ◇ *adv* [übersetzen] word for word; **etw wörtlich nehmen** to take sthg literally.

wortlos ◇ *adj* silent. ◇ *adv* without a word.

Wort|spiel *das* pun.

worüber *pron* [Interrogativpronomen] what... about; **worüber lachst du?** what are you laughing about?

worum *pron* [Interrogativpronomen] what... about; **worum geht es?** what's it about?

worunter *pron* [Interrogativpronomen] under what; **worunter hat er gelitten?** what did he suffer from?

wovor *pron* [Interrogativpronomen] what... of; **wovor hast du Angst?** what are you frightened of?

wozu *pron* [Interrogativpronomen] why; **wozu dient dieser Schalter?** what's this switch for?

Wrack (*pl* **-s** ODER **-e**) *das* wreck.

WS *abk für* **Wintersemester**.

WSV *abk für* **Winterschlussverkauf**.

Wucher *der abw* extortion; **fünf Euro für ein Sandwich? das ist Wucher!** five euros for a sandwich? that's daylight robbery!

wuchern (*perf* **hat/ist gewuchert**) *vi* - **1.** *(ist)* [wild wachsen] to grow uncontrollably - **2.** *(hat)* [Wucher treiben] to profiteer.

Wucher|preis *der abw* extortionate price.

wuchs [vu:ks] *prät* ▷ **wachsen**.

Wuchs [vu:ks] *der* - **1.** [Wachstum] growth - **2.** [Gestalt] stature.

Wucht *die* force; **mit voller Wucht gegen einen Baum fahren** to smash into a tree.

wuchtig *adj* - **1.** [plump] massive - **2.** [Schlag, Stoß] violent.

wühlen *vi* - **1.** [graben] to dig - **2.** [stöbern] to rummage; **in etw** *(D)* **wühlen** *fam* to rummage through sthg. ◆ **sich wühlen** *ref* [sich graben] to burrow; **sich in etw** *(A)* **wühlen** to dig into sthg.

Wulst (*pl* **Wülste**) *der* roll.

wund ◇ *adj* sore. ◇ *adv*: **sich die Füße wund laufen** to walk until one's feet are sore.

Wunde (*pl* **-n**) *die* wound.

Wunder (*pl* -) *das* miracle; **Wunder wirken** to work wonders; **kein Wunder!** no wonder!; **er glaubt, er sei Wunder was für ein toller Kerl** *fam* he thinks he's God's gift.

wunderbar ◇ *adj* - **1.** [großartig] wonderful - **2.** [übernatürlich] miraculous. ◇ *adv* [großartig] wonderfully.

Wunder|kind *das* child prodigy.

wunderlich ◇ *adj* strange. ◇ *adv* strangely.

wundern *vt* to surprise. ◆ **sich wundern** *ref*: **sich (über jn/etw) wundern** to be surprised (at sb/sthg); **du wirst dich noch wundern** you're in for a nasty surprise.

wunderschön ◇ *adj* beautiful. ◇ *adv* beautifully.

Wunsch (*pl* **Wünsche**) *der* wish; **nach Wunsch verlaufen** to go as planned; **die besten Wünsche für etw** best wishes for sthg.

wünschen *vt* - **1.** [haben wollen]: **sich** *(D)* **etw wünschen** to want sthg; **was wünschst du dir zum Geburtstag?** what would you like for your birthday?; **wünsch dir etwas** make a wish; **(sich** *(D)***) wünschen, dass...** to hope that...; **ich wünschte, das wäre schon zu Ende** I wish it was already over - **2.** [erhoffen]: **jm etw wünschen** to wish sb sthg - **3.** [verlangen] to want; **ich wünsche eine Auskunft** I would like some information; **wie viel Kilo wünschen Sie?** how many kilos would you like?; **ich wünsche das nicht, dass du so spät heimkommst** I don't want you coming home so late; **was wünschen Sie?** can I help you?; **wünschen, dass jd etw macht** to want sb to do sthg - **4.** [zu erhoffen]: **es ist zu wünschen, dass...** it is to be hoped that... - **5.** [an einen Ort]: **jn weit weg wünschen** to wish sb far away; **zu wünschen übrig lassen** to leave a lot to be desired; **ganz wie Sie wünschen!** certainly!

wünschenswert *adj* desirable.

Wunsch|traum *der* dream.

Wunsch|zettel *der* ≃ letter to Santa Claus *(asking for presents)*.

wurde *prät* ▷ **werden**.

Würde (*pl* **-n**) *die* [Selbstachtung] dignity; **unter js Würde sein** to be beneath sb.

würdig ◇ *adj* - **1.** [würdevoll] dignified - **2.** [entsprechend] worthy; **einer Sache** *(G)* **würdig sein** to be worthy of sthg. ◇ *adv* - **1.** [würdevoll] with dignity - **2.** [entsprechend] appropriately.

würdigen *vt* - **1.** [mit Auszeichnung] to honour; [in Ansprache] to pay tribute to - **2.** [schätzen] to appreciate.

Wurf (*pl* **Würfe**) *der* - **1.** [Werfen] throw - **2.** [bei Säugetieren] litter.

Würfel (*pl* -) *der* - **1.** [Kubus] cube - **2.** [Spielwürfel] dice.

würfeln ◇ *vi* [Würfel werfen] to throw the dice. ◇ *vt* - **1.** [mit dem Würfel] to throw - **2.** [in Würfel schneiden] to dice.

Würfel|zucker *der (ohne pl)* sugar cubes *Pl*.

würgen ◇ *vt* [Subj: Person] to strangle; [Subj: Krawatte] to choke. ◇ *vi* - **1.** [schlucken]: **an etw** *(D)* **würgen** to choke on sthg - **2.** [Brechreiz haben] to retch.

Wurm (*pl* **Würmer**) *der* worm.

wurmstichig *adj* worm-ridden.

Wurst (*pl* **Würste**) *die* - **1.** [gen] sausage - **2.** [Aufschnitt] cold meats *Pl*; **es ist mir Wurst** *fam* I couldn't care less.

Würstchen (*pl* -) *das* - **1.** [kleine Wurst] frankfurter-style sausage - **2.** *fam* [unwichtige Person] nobody; **ein armes Würstchen** a poor thing.

Würze (*pl* **-n**) *die* seasoning; *fig* spice.

Wurzel (*pl* **-n**) *die* [gen & MATH] root; **Wurzeln schlagen** *eigtl* & *fig* to put down roots.

würzen *vt* - **1.** [Speise] to season - **2.** [Bericht] to spice up.

würzig *adj* [gut gewürzt] well-seasoned; [Bier] rich; [stark duftend] aromatic.

wusch *prät* ▷ **waschen**.

wusste *prät* ▷ **wissen**.

wüst ◇ *adj* - **1.** [vereinsamt - Gegend] desolate - **2.** [wirr - Haare] wild; [- Durcheinander] chaotic - **3.** *abw* [Schlägerei, Beschimpfung] savage. ◇ *adv* - **1.** [wirr] chaotically - **2.** *abw* [fluchen, schimpfen] savagely.

Wüste (*pl* **-n**) *die* desert.

Wut *die* rage; **eine Wut auf jn haben** to be furious with sb; **seine Wut an jm/etw auslassen** to vent one's anger on sb/sthg.

wüten *vi* to rage.

wütend ◇ *adj* furious; **auf** ODER **über jn wütend sein** to be furious with sb. ◇ *adv* furiously.

WWW *abk für* **World Wide Web**.

x (*pl* -), **X** (*pl* -) [ɪks] *das* x, X.

X-Beine *Pl* knock-knees.

x-beliebig *adj fam* any old.

x-mal *adv fam* countless times.

y (*pl* - ODER **-s**), **Y** (*pl* - ODER **-s**) ['ypsilɔn] *das* y, Y.

Yacht [jaxt] (*pl* **-en**) *die* = **Jacht**.

Yoga, Joga ['joːga] *der ODER das* yoga.

Z

z (*pl* - ODER **-s**), **Z** (*pl* - ODER **-s**) [tsɛt] *das* z, Z.

zack *interj fam* pow!

Zacke (*pl* **-n**) *die* [von Gabel, Harke] prong; [von Stern] point.

zackig ◇ *adj* - **1.** [gezackt - Felsen, Kante, Blatt] jagged; [- Stern] pointed - **2.** *fam* [forsch] brisk. ◇ *adv* - **1.** [gezackt] jaggedly - **2.** *fam* [forsch] briskly.

zaghaft ◇ *adj* hesitant. ◇ *adv* hesitantly.

zäh ◇ *adj* - **1.** [widerstandsfähig] tough - **2.** [zähflüssig] thick - **3.** [hartnäckig] tenacious. ◇ *adv* - **1.** [langsam] slowly - **2.** [hartnäckig] firmly.

Zähigkeit *die* - **1.** [von Material] toughness - **2.** [von Mensch] tenacity.

Zahl (*pl* **-en**) *die* number; **römische Zahlen** Roman numerals; **wir haben keine genauen Zahlen** we don't have exact figures; **eine gerade/ungerade Zahl** an even/odd number; **in den roten/schwarzen Zahlen sein** *fig* to be in the red/black.

zahlbar *adj* payable; **zahlbar an/in** payable to/in.

zahlen ◇ *vt* - **1.** [gen] to pay - **2.** [Taxi, Hotelzimmer, Reparatur] to pay for. ◇ *vi* to pay; **bitte zahlen!** the bill, please! *UK*, the check, please! *US*

zählen ◇ *vt* - **1.** [die Anzahl ermitteln] to count - **2.** [rechnen]: **etw zu etw zählen** to count sthg as sthg - **3.** [wert sein] to be worth. ◇ *vi* - **1.** [gen] to count - **2.** [gehören]: **Monet zählt zu meinen Lieblingsmalern** Monet is one of my favourite painters - **3.** [vertrauen]: **auf jn/etw zählen** to count on sb/sthg.

zahlenmäßig ◇ *adj* numerical. ◇ *adv*: **zahlenmäßig überlegen sein** to have a numerical advantage.

Zähler (*pl* -) *der* - **1.** [Gerät] meter - **2.** MATH numerator.

Zahl|grenze *die* fare stage.

zahllos *adj* innumerable.

zahlreich ◇ *adj* numerous. ◇ *adv* in great numbers.

Zahlung (*pl* **-en**) *die* payment.

Zählung (*pl* **-en**) *die* count; [der Bevölkerung] census.

Zahlungsan|weisung *die* money transfer order.

zahlungsfähig *adj* solvent.

Zahl|wort (*pl* **-wörter**) *das* GRAMM numeral.

zahm ◇ *adj* tame. ◇ *adv* tamely.

zähmen *vt* - **1.** [Tier, Natur] to tame - **2.** *geh* [Neugier, Ungeduld] to curb; [Kinder] to control.

Zähmung (*pl* **-en**) *die* - **1.** [von Tier] taming - **2.** [von Neugier, Ungeduld] curbing.

Zahn (*pl* **Zähne**) *der* [im Mund] tooth; **einen Zahn ziehen** to extract a tooth; **sich einen Zahn ziehen lassen** to have a tooth out; **sich** *(D)* **die Zähne putzen** to clean ODER brush one's teeth; **die dritten Zähne** [Gebiss] false teeth; **die Zähne zusammenbeißen** *fam* to grit one's teeth; **jm einen Zahn ziehen** to pour cold water on sb's idea.

Zahn|arzt *der* dentist.

Zahn|ärztin *die* dentist.

Zahn|bürste *die* toothbrush.

Zahn|ersatz *der (ohne pl)* false teeth *Pl*.

Zahn|fleisch *das (ohne pl)* gums *Pl*.

Zahn|lücke *die* gap in one's teeth.

Zahn|pasta (*pl* **-pasten**), **Zahnpaste** (*pl* **-n**) *die* toothpaste.

Zahn|rad *das* cog.

Zahnrad|bahn *die* cog railway.

Zahn|schmelz *der* (tooth) enamel.

Zahn|schmerzen *Pl* toothache *(U)*; **Zahnschmerzen haben** to have toothache.

Zahn|seide *die* dental floss.

Zahn|spange *die* brace.

Zahn|stein *der* tartar.

Zahn|stocher (*pl* **Zahnstocher**) *der* toothpick.

Zange (*pl* **-n**) *die* pliers *Pl*; [Beißzange, von Insekt] pincers *Pl*; [für Kohlen, Zucker] tongs *Pl*; MED forceps *Pl*; **jn in die Zange nehmen** *fam fig* to put the screws on sb.

zanken ◆ **sich zanken** *ref*: **sich (mit jm um etw) zanken** to quarrel (with sb about sthg).

Zäpfchen (*pl* -) *das* [Medikament] suppository.

zapfen *vt*: **ein großes Bier zapfen** ≃ to pull a pint.

Zapfen (*pl* -) *der* - **1.** [aus Holz] tenon - **2.** [von Bäumen] cone - **3.** [aus Eis] icicle.

Zapfenstreich *der*: **um 23 Uhr ist Zapfenstreich** lights out is at eleven o'clock.

Zapf|säule *die* petrol *UK* ODER gas *US* pump.

zappeln *vi* to wriggle; **auf seinem Stuhl zappeln** to fidget in one's chair; **jn zappeln lassen** *fam fig* to let sb sweat.

zappen *vi* to channel-hop.

zart ◇ *adj* - **1.** [gen] delicate - **2.** [weich - Haut] soft; [- Fleisch, Gemüse, Pflänzchen] tender - **3.** [Gebäck] fine - **4.** [Berührung, Kuss] gentle; [Farbton] soft. ◇ *adv* [berühren, küssen, lächeln] gently.

zart besaitet *adj* very sensitive.

zartbitter *adj* [Schokolade] dark.

zärtlich ◇ *adj* tender, affectionate; [Fürsorge] loving; **zu jm zärtlich sein** to be tender ODER affectionate towards sb. ◇ *adv* tenderly, affectionately.

Zärtlichkeit (*pl* **-en**) *die* [Gefühl] tenderness. ◆ **Zärtlichkeiten** *Pl* [Liebkosungen] caresses.

Zauber (*pl* -) *der* magic; **das ist doch fauler Zauber!** *fam abw* that's a con!

Zauberei (*pl* **-en**) *die* magic.

Zauberer (*pl* -) *der* magician.

Zauber|formel *die* [Zauberspruch] (magic) spell.

zauberhaft ◇ *adj* enchanting. ◇ *adv* enchantingly.

Zauberin (*pl* **-nen**) *die* magician.

Zauber|künstler, **in** *der, die* magician.

Zauberkunst|stück *das* magic trick.

zaubern ◇ *vi* to do magic. ◇ *vt*: **etw aus etw zaubern** *fig* to conjure sthg from sthg.

Zauber|spruch *der* (magic) spell.

Zauber|stab *der* magic wand.

Zaum (*pl* **Zäume**) *der* bridle; **sich/etw im Zaum halten** *fig* to keep o.s./sthg in check.

zäumen *vt* to bridle.

Zaumzeug (*pl* **-e**) *das* bridle.

Zaun (*pl* **Zäune**) *der* fence.

Zaun|pfahl *der* fencepost.

z. B. (*abk für* **zum Beispiel**) e.g.

ZDF [tsɛtdeːˈɛf] (*abk für* **Zweites Deutsches Fernsehen**) *das second German public television channel*.

Zebra (*pl* **-s**) *das* zebra.

Zebra|streifen *der* zebra crossing *UK*, crosswalk *US*.

Zeder (*pl* **-n**) *die* cedar.

Zeh (*pl* **-en**) *der* toe.

Zehe (*pl* **-n**) *die* - **1.** [Fußglied] toe; **jm auf die Zehen treten** *fam fig* to tread on sb's toes - **2.** [Knoblauchzehe] clove.

Zehen|nagel *der* toenail.

Zehen|spitze *die* tip of one's toes; **auf Zehenspitzen** on tiptoe.

zehn *num* ten; *siehe auch* **sechs**.

Zehn (*pl* **-en**) *die* ten; *siehe auch* **Sechs**.

Zehner|karte *die* book of ten tickets.

Zehneuro|schein *der* ten-euro note *UK* ODER bill *US*.

zehnfach ◇ *adj* tenfold. ◇ *adv* ten times.

Zehn|kampf *der* SPORT decathlon.

zehnmal *adv* ten times.

zehntausend *num* ten thousand; *siehe auch* **sechs**.

zehnte, **r**, **s** *adj* tenth; *siehe auch* **sechste**.

Zehnte (*pl* **-n**) *der, die, das* tenth; *siehe auch* **Sechste**.

zehntel *adj (unver)* tenth; *siehe auch* **sechstel**.

Zehntel (*pl* -) *das* tenth; *siehe auch* **Sechstel**.

Zehntel|sekunde *die* tenth of a second.

zehren *vi*: **von etw zehren** to live on sthg.

Zeichen (*pl* -) *das* - **1.** [gen] sign; **jm ein Zeichen geben** to give sb a signal ODER sign; **zum Zeichen seiner Dankbarkeit** as a token of his appreciation; **zum Zeichen, dass sie ihm folgen solle** to let her know that she should follow him - **2.** [Symbol] symbol - **3.** [Tierkreiszeichen] (star) sign - **4.** EDV character.

Zeichen|block (*pl* **-blöcke** ODER **-s**) *der* drawing pad.

Zeichener|klärung *die* key.

Zeichen|papier *das* drawing paper.

Zeichen|setzung *die* punctuation.

Zeichen|sprache *die* sign language.

Zeichentrick|film *der* cartoon.

zeichnen ◇ *vt* - **1.** [darstellen] to draw - **2.** [kennzeichnen] to mark; **das Fell ist interessant gezeichnet** its coat has interesting markings - **3.** [unterzeichnen - Scheck] to sign; [- Aktien, Anleihe] to subscribe. ◇ *vi* to draw.

Zeichner, **in** (*mpl* -, *fpl* **-nen**) *der, die* draughtsman (draughtswoman *die*).

Zeichnung (*pl* **-en**) *die* - **1.** [Bild] drawing - **2.** [von Fell, Tier, Blüte] markings *Pl*.

Zeige|finger *der* index finger.

zeigen ◇ *vt* - **1.** [gen] to show; **jm etw zeigen** to show sb sthg; **den Gästen die neue Wohnung zeigen** to show the guests round the new flat; **der habe ich es gezeigt!** *fam* I showed her! - **2.** [Uhr] to say; [Waage] to read. ◇ *vi* to point; **nach Südost zeigen** to point south-east; **auf jn/etw zeigen** to point at sb/sthg. ◆ **sich zeigen** *ref* - **1.** [sich verhalten] to show o.s.; **sich nachsichtig zeigen** to show lenience, to show o.s. to be lenient - **2.** [sich präsentieren]: **sich in der Öffentlichkeit zeigen** to appear in public - **3.** [erkennbar werden]: **schon zeigen sich die ersten Fehler** the first mistakes are already starting to appear; **es hat sich gezeigt, dass...** it has been shown ODER demonstrated that...; **es wird sich zeigen, ob...** time will tell whether...

Zeiger (*pl* -) *der* hand.

Zeile (*pl* **-n**) *die* - **1.** [von Texten] line - **2.** [Nachricht]: **jm ein paar Zeilen schreiben** to drop sb a line.

Zeit (*pl* **-en**) *die* - **1.** [gen] time; **in letzter Zeit** lately; **im Laufe der Zeit** in the course of time; **von Zeit zu Zeit** from time to time; **die Zeit stoppen** to stop the clock; **Zeit raubend** time-consuming; **Zeit sparend** time-saving; **sich** *(D)* **für jn/etw Zeit nehmen** to spend time on sb/sthg; **sich** *(D)* **die Zeit (mit Kartenspielen) vertreiben** to pass the time (playing cards); **sich** *(D)* **Zeit lassen** to take one's time - **2.** GRAMM tense - **3.** [Zeitung]: **Die Zeit** *weekly German* newspaper. ◆ **auf Zeit** *adv* temporarily. ◆ **eine Zeit lang** *adv* for a while. ◆ **mit der Zeit** *adv* - **1.** in time - **2.** = **zurzeit**.

Zeit|alter *das* age.

Zeitan|sage *die* speaking clock.

Zeit|arbeit *die* temporary work.

Zeit|bombe *die eigtl & fig* time bomb.

Zeit|druck *der*: **in Zeitdruck sein, unter Zeitdruck stehen** to be under time pressure.

Zeit|geist *der* spirit of the times, zeitgeist.

zeitgemäß *adj* contemporary, modern.

Zeit|genosse *der* contemporary.

Zeit|genossin *die* contemporary.

Zeit|geschehen *das (ohne pl)* current affairs *Pl*.

zeitig *adj & adv* early.

zeitlebens *adv* all my/his/her/*etc* life.

zeitlich ◇ *adj* chronological. ◇ *adv*: **zeitlich begrenzt sein** to be of limited duration.

Zeitliche *das*: **das Zeitliche segnen** to give up the ghost.

zeitlos *adj* timeless.

Zeit|lupe ◆ **in Zeitlupe** *adv* TV in slow motion.

Zeit|punkt *der* time; **etw zum richtigen Zeitpunkt tun** to do sthg at the right moment ODER time; **zu diesem Zeitpunkt** at this point in time.

Zeit|raffer *der* time-lapse photography.

Zeit|raum *der* period.

Zeit|rechnung *die*: **vor unserer Zeitrechnung** Before Christ; **nach unserer Zeitrechnung** Anno Domini.

Zeit|schrift *die* [Illustrierte] magazine; [wissenschaftlich] journal.

Zeit|soldat *der soldier who enlists for a fixed period of time.*

Zeit|spanne *die* timespan.

Zeitung (*pl* **-en**) *die* newspaper.

Zeitungs|annonce *die* newspaper advertisement.

Zeitungsaus|schnitt *der* newspaper cutting.

Zeitungs|bericht *der* newspaper report.

Zeitungs|kiosk *der* newspaper kiosk.

Zeitungs|papier *das* newspaper.

Zeit|unterschied *der* time difference.

Zeit|verlust *der* lost time.

Zeit|verschiebung *die* time difference.

Zeit|verschwendung *die* waste of time.

Zeit|vertrag *der* fixed-term ODER temporary contract.

Zeit|vertreib (*pl* **-e**) *der* pastime; **zum Zeitvertreib** to pass the time.

zeitweilig ◇ *adj* temporary. ◇ *adv* from time to time, on and off.

zeitweise *adv* - **1.** [gelegentlich] occasionally - **2.** [vorübergehend] temporarily.

Zelle (*pl* **-n**) *die* cell.

Zell|stoff *der* cellulose.

Zelt (*pl* **-e**) *das* tent; **die Zelte abbrechen** *fig* to up sticks; **die Zelte aufschlagen** *fig* to settle.

zelten *vi* to camp.

Zelt|lager *das* camp.

Zelt|platz *der* campsite.

Zelt|stange *die* tent pole.

Zement *der* cement.

zensieren ◇ *vt* - **1.** [benoten] to mark - **2.** [kontrollieren] to censor. ◇ *vi* to mark.

Zensur (*pl* **-en**) *die* - **1.** [Benotung] mark - **2.** [Kontrolle] censorship - **3.** [Behörde] censorship board, censors *Pl*.

Zenti|liter (*pl* -) *der* centilitre.

Zenti|meter (*pl* -) *der* centimetre.

Zentimeter|maß *das* tape measure.

Zentner (*pl* -) *der unit of measurement equivalent to 50 kg in Germany and 100 kg in Austria and Switzerland.*

zentral ◇ *adj* central. ◇ *adv* [wohnen, gelegen] centrally.

Zentral|afrika *nt* Central Africa.

Zentrale (*pl* **-n**) *die* - **1.** [zentrale Stelle] headquarters *Pl* - **2.** [Telefonzentrale] switchboard.

Zentral|heizung *die* central heating.

Zentrifuge (*pl* **-n**) *die* centrifuge.

Zentrum (*pl* **Zentren**) *das* centre.

Zeppelin (*pl* **-e**) *der* zeppelin.

zerbrechen (*präs* **zerbricht**, *prät* **zerbrach**, *perf* **hat/ist zerbrochen**) ◇ *vi (ist)* [Glas, Vase] to break into pieces, to smash; [Freundschaft, Ehe] to break up; **an etw** *(D)* **zerbrechen** *fig* to be broken by sthg. ◇ *vt (hat)* to smash.

zerbrechlich *adj* fragile.

zerdrücken *vt* [Kartoffeln, Bananen] to mash; [Knoblauch, Insekt] to crush.

Zeremonie (*pl* **-n**) *die* ceremony.

Zerfall *der* [von Gebäude, Denkmal] decay; [von Moral, Diktatur] decline.

zerfallen (*präs* **zerfällt**, *prät* **zerfiel**, *perf* **ist zerfallen**) *vi* to disintegrate; [Mauer, Kuchen, Reich] to crumble; [Molekül] to decay; **in etw** *(A)* **zerfallen** [Molekül] to decay into sthg; [Mauer, Kuchen] to crumble into sthg.

zerfetzen *vt* to tear to pieces; [Brief] to tear up.

zerfleddern *vt* to make tatty.

zerfließen (*prät* **zerfloss**, *perf* **ist zerflossen**) *vi* - **1.** [schmelzen] to melt - **2.** [auseinander fließen] to run.

zergehen (*prät* **zerging**, *perf* **ist zergangen**) *vi* to melt; **etw im Mund zergehen lassen** to allow sthg to dissolve in one's mouth.

zerkleinern *vt* to cut up; [mit Gabel] to mash.

zerklụftet *adj* [Landschaft, Tal] rugged; [Felsen] jagged.

zerknịrscht *adj* remorseful; **über etw** *(A)* **zerknirscht sein** to be full of remorse for sthg.

zerknịttern *vt* to crumple.

zerkrạtzen *vt* to scratch.

zerlegen *vt* - **1.** [auseinander nehmen] to take apart; **etw in (seine) Einzelteile zerlegen** to dismantle sthg into its constituent parts - **2.** [Geflügel, Wild] to carve up.

zermụrben *vt* to wear down.

zerquẹtschen *vt* to crush; [Kartoffeln] to mash.

zerreißen (*prät* **zerrịss**, *perf* **hat/ist zerrịssen**) ◇ *vt (hat)* - **1.** [in Stücke] to tear to pieces; [Brief] to tear up - **2.** [Strümpfe, Hose] to tear. ◇ *vi (ist)* to tear.

zẹrren ◇ *vt* to drag; **sich** *(D)* **einen Muskel zerren** to pull a muscle. ◇ *vi*: **an etw** *(D)* **zerren** to pull on sthg.

zerrịnnen (*prät* **zerrọnn**, *perf* **ist zerrọnnen**) *vi* - **1.** [Butter] to melt - **2.** [Träume] to fade away - **3.** [Zeit] to slip by.

Zẹrrung (*pl* **-en**) *die* pulled muscle ODER ligament.

zerrụttet *adj* [Gesundheit] ruined; [Ehe] broken; **aus zerrütteten Verhältnissen** from a broken home.

zerschlagen *adj* shattered.

zerschneiden (*prät* **zerschnịtt**, *perf* **hat zerschnịtten**) *vt* - **1.** [in Stücke] to cut up - **2.** [verletzen] to cut.

zersẹtzen *vt* - **1.** [Subj: Säure, Rost] to corrode; [Subj: Fäulnis] to decompose - **2.** [untergraben] to undermine. ◆ **sich zersetzen** *ref* [durch Säure, Rost] to corrode; [durch Fäulnis] to decompose.

zersplịttern (*perf* **ist zersplịttert**) *vi* [Holz, Knochen] to splinter; [Glas, Fenster] to shatter.

zerspringen (*prät* **zersprạng**, *perf* **ist zersprụngen**) *vi* to shatter.

zerstäuben *vt* to spray.

Zerstäuber (*pl* -) *der* atomizer.

zerstẹchen (*präs* **zerstịcht**, *prät* **zerstach**, *perf* **hat zerstọchen**) *vt* - **1.** [beschädigen] to puncture - **2.** [Subj: Insekten] to bite all over.

zerstören *vt* to destroy.

zerstörerisch *adj* destructive.

Zerstörung (*pl* **-en**) *die* destruction.

zerstreuen *vt* - **1.** [Blätter] to scatter - **2.** [Demonstranten] to disperse - **3.** [vom Alltag ablenken] to distract - **4.** [Zweifel] to dispel. ◆ **sich zerstreuen** *ref* - **1.** [Menschenmenge] to disperse - **2.** [sich vom Alltag ablenken] to distract o.s.

zerstreut ◇ *adj* absent-minded. ◇ *adv* absent-mindedly.

Zerstreuung (*pl* **-en**) *die* distraction.

Zertifikat (*pl* **-e**) *das* certificate.

zertreten (*präs* **zertrịtt**, *prät* **zertrat**, *perf* **hat zertreten**) *vt* [Insekt] to stamp on; [Zigarettenkippe] to stub out with one's foot.

zertrụmmern *vt* [Schrank, Felsbrocken] to smash up; [Spiegel] to smash.

zerzaust *adj* [Haare] dishevelled.

Zẹttel (*pl* -) *der* piece of paper; [Nachricht] note; [Einkaufszettel] (shopping) list.

Zeug *das fam* [Sachen] stuff; [Kleidung] gear; **das Zeug zu etw haben** *fam fig* to have the makings of sthg; **wir müssen uns ins Zeug legen** we're going to have to put our backs into it. ◆ **dummes Zeug** *interj fam* rubbish!

Zeuge (*pl* **-n**) *der* witness.

zeugen ◇ *vi*: **von etw zeugen** *geh* to show sthg. ◇ *vt* to father.

Zeugenaus|sage *die* statement.

Zeugin (*pl* **-nen**) *die* witness.

Zeugnis (*pl* **-se**) *das* - **1.** [von Arbeitgeber] reference - **2.** [von Prüfung] certificate - **3.** SCHULE report.

z. H. (*abk für* **zu Händen**) attn.

Zịckzack (*pl* **-e**) *der* zigzag. ◆ **im Zickzack** *adv*: **im Zickzack laufen/fahren** to zigzag.

Ziege (*pl* **-n**) *die* - **1.** [Tier] goat - **2.** *fam* [als Schimpfwort] cow.

Ziegel (*pl* -) *der* - **1.** [Stein] brick - **2.** [Dachziegel] tile.

Ziegel|stein *der* brick.

Ziegen|bock *der* billy goat.

Ziegen|käse *der* goat's cheese.

ziehen (*prät* **zog**, *perf* **hat/ist gezogen**) ◇ *vt (hat)* - **1.** [gen] to pull; [Subj: Tier - Karren] to draw; **etw durch etw ziehen** to pull sthg through sthg; **etw von etw ziehen** to pull sthg off sthg; **jn am Ärmel ziehen** to tug sb's sleeve; **jn an den Haaren ziehen** to pull sb's hair - **2.** [herausziehen - Zahn, Korken] to pull out; [- Rüben, Unkraut] to pull up - **3.** MED [Fäden] to take out - **4.** [Brieftasche, Waffe] to take out; [Hut] to doff; **etw aus etw ziehen** to take sthg out of sthg - **5.** [zeichnen] to draw - **6.** [züchten - Pflanzen] to grow; [- Tiere] to breed - **7.** [anziehen]: **Aufmerksamkeit auf sich** *(A)* **ziehen** to draw attention to o.s. - **8.** [zur Folge haben]: **etw nach sich ziehen** to lead to sthg; **Probleme nach sich ziehen** to cause problems - **9.** [aus dem Automaten] to get *(from a vending machine)* - **10.** [anlegen - Mauer, Zaun] to put up; [- Graben] to dig; [- Grenze] to draw. ◇ *vi* - **1.** *(hat)* [zerren] to pull; **an etw** *(D)* **ziehen** to pull sthg; **der Hund zog an der Leine** the dog was pulling on the lead *UK* ODER leash *US* - **2.** *(ist)* [umziehen, sich bewegen] to move; **durch die Straßen ziehen** to wander through the streets; **eine Blaskapelle zog durchs Dorf** a brass band trooped through the village; **die Vögel ziehen nach Süden** the birds are going ODER flying south - **3.** *(hat)* [saugen]: **an etw** *(D)* **ziehen** [Pfeife, Zigarette] to take a puff on sthg

- **4.** *(hat)* [Auto, Motor] to run - **5.** *(ist)* [dringen]: **der Duft zog durchs ganze Haus** the scent floated throughout the house; **in etw** *(A)* **ziehen** [Flüssigkeit] to soak into sthg - **6.** *(hat)* [Kaffee, Tee] to brew - **7.** *(hat)* [bei Brettspiel] to move; **du musst ziehen!** it's your move! - **8.** *(hat) fam* [Eindruck machen] to go down well; **das zieht bei mir nicht!** that doesn't wash with me! - **9.** *(hat)* [Luftzug haben]: **es zieht** there's a draught. ◆ **sich ziehen** *ref* - **1.** [nicht enden wollen] to drag on - **2.** [sich erstrecken] to stretch.

Ziehlharmonika *die* concertina.

Ziehung (*pl* **-en**) *die*: **die Ziehung der Lottozahlen** the lottery draw; **die Ziehung der Lose** the drawing of lots.

Ziel (*pl* **-e**) *das* - **1.** [Zielort] destination - **2.** SPORT finish - **3.** [Zweck] goal; **sich** *(D)* **ein Ziel setzen** to set o.s. a goal *ODER* target.

zielen *vi* to aim; **auf jn/etw zielen** to aim at sb/sthg.

Ziellgruppe *die* target group.

ziellos ◇ *adj* aimless. ◇ *adv* aimlessly.

Ziellscheibe *die* - **1.** [beim Schießen] target - **2.** [Opfer] butt.

zielstrebig ◇ *adj* single-minded. ◇ *adv* single-mindedly.

ziemlich ◇ *adj fam*: **mit ziemlicher Genugtuung/Sicherheit** with some satisfaction/certainty; **das war eine ziemliche Gemeinheit** that was a rather mean thing to do. ◇ *adv* - **1.** [sehr] quite; **ziemlich viel** quite a lot - **2.** *fam* [fast] almost.

Zierde (*pl* **-n**) *die* decoration.

zieren ◆ **sich zieren** *ref* to be coy.

zierlich ◇ *adj* [Person] petite; [Hände] dainty; [Porzellanfigur] delicate. ◇ *adv* daintily.

Zierlpflanze *die* ornamental plant.

Zịffer (*pl* **-n**) *die* figure.

Zịfferlblatt *das* face.

zịg *adj fam* umpteen.

Zigarẹtte (*pl* **-n**) *die* cigarette.

Zigarẹttenlautomat *der* cigarette machine.

Zigarẹttenlschachtel *die* cigarette packet.

Zigarịllo (*pl* **-s**) *der ODER das* cigarillo.

Zigạrre (*pl* **-n**) *die* cigar.

Zigeuner, in (*mpl* **-**, *fpl* **-nen**) *der, die* gypsy.

zịgmal *adv fam* umpteen times.

Zịmmer (*pl* **-**) *das* room; **'Zimmer frei!'** 'vacancies'.

Zịmmerllautstärke *die*: **in Zimmerlautstärke** at low volume.

Zịmmerlmädchen *das* chambermaid.

Zịmmerlmann (*pl* **-leute**) *der* carpenter.

zịmmern ◇ *vt* to make *(from wood)*. ◇ *vi* to do carpentry.

Zịmmerlpflanze *die* house plant.

Zịmmerlsuche *die*: **auf Zimmersuche sein** to be looking for a room.

Zịmmerlvermittlung *die* accommodation service.

zịmperlich *abw* ◇ *adj*: **sei nicht so zimperlich!** don't be such a wimp!; **sie ist nicht gerade zimperlich** she doesn't exactly hold back. ◇ *adv*: **nicht zimperlich mit jm umgehen** not to treat sb with kid gloves.

Zịmt *der* cinnamon.

Zịnk *das* zinc.

Zịnke (*pl* **-n**) *die* [von Gabel] prong; [von Kamm] tooth.

Zịnn *das* - **1.** [Metall] tin - **2.** [Gegenstände] pewter.

Zịns (*pl* **-en**) *der*: **Zinsen** interest *(U)*.

zịnslos *adj* interest-free.

Zịnslsatz *der* interest rate.

Zịpfel (*pl* **-**) *der* corner.

Zịpfellmütze *die* pointed hat.

zippen *vt* EDV to zip.

zịrka, cịrca ['tsɪrka] *adv* about, approximately; **zirka 1900** circa 1900.

Zịrkel (*pl* **-**) *der* - **1.** [Gerät] compasses *Pl* - **2.** [Gruppe] circle.

Zịrkus (*pl* **-se**) *der* circus.

zịschen (*perf* **hat/ist gezịscht**) ◇ *vi* - **1.** *(hat)* [Geräusch] to hiss - **2.** *(ist)* [Fahrzeug] to whizz. ◇ *vt (hat)* - **1.** [sagen] to hiss - **2.** *salopp* [trinken] to knock back.

Zitạt (*pl* **-e**) *das* quotation, quote.

zitieren ◇ *vt* - **1.** [wiedergeben] to quote - **2.** [rufen]: **jn zu jm/vor etw** *(A)* **zitieren** to summon sb to sb/before sthg. ◇ *vi*: **aus etw zitieren** to quote from sthg.

Zitronat *das* KÜCHE candied lemon peel.

Zitrone (*pl* **-n**) *die* lemon.

Zitronenlsaft *der* lemon juice.

zịtterig, zịttrig *adj* shaky.

zịttern *vi* - **1.** [vibrieren - Hände, Körper] to tremble; [- Stimme] to shake; **vor Kälte zittern** to shiver with cold - **2.** [Angst haben]: **vor jm/etw zittern** to be terrified of sb/sthg - **3.** [sich sorgen]: **um** *ODER* **für jn/etw zittern** to be very worried about sb/sthg.

Zịvi ['tsi:vi] (*pl* **-s**) *der fam man doing his "Zivildienst"*.

zivil [tsi'vi:l] ◇ *adj* - **1.** [Bevölkerung, Leben] civilian - **2.** *fam* [Preise] reasonable. ◇ *adv fam* [anständig] reasonably.

Zivil [tsi'vi:l] ◆ **in Zivil** *adv* [Soldat] in civilian clothes; [Polizist] in plain clothes.

Zivillbevölkerung *die* civilian population.

Zivillcourage *die* courage of one's convictions.

Zivilldienst *der community service done by conscientious objectors.*

Zivilisation [tsiviliza'tsio:n] *(pl* **-en**) *die* civilization.

zivilisiert [tsivili'zi:ɐt] *adj* civilized.

Zivilist, in [tsivi'lɪst, ɪn] *(mpl* **-en**, *fpl* **-nen**) *der, die* civilian.

Zivil|recht *das* RECHT civil law.

zog *prät* ▷ **ziehen**.

zögern *vi* to hesitate; **mit etw zögern** to delay sthg.

Zölibat *das* & *der* RELIG celibacy.

Zoll (*pl* **Zölle** ODER **-**) *der* - **1.** *(pl Zölle)* [Abgabe] duty - **2.** *(ohne pl)* [Behörde] customs *Pl* - **3.** *(pl Zoll)* [Maßeinheit] inch.

Zollab|fertigung *die* customs clearance.

Zoll|amt *das* customs office.

Zoll|beamte *der* customs officer.

Zoll|beamtin *die* customs officer.

zollfrei *adj* duty-free.

Zoll|kontrolle *die* customs check.

Zöllner (*pl* -) *der* customs officer.

zollpflichtig *adj* liable for duty.

Zoll|stock *der* folding rule.

Zone (*pl* **-n**) *die* zone.

Zoo [tso:] (*pl* **-s**) *der* zoo.

Zoologie [tsoolo'gi:] *die* zoology.

Zopf (*pl* **Zöpfe**) *der* plait *UK*, braid *US*; **Zöpfe flechten** to plait *UK* ODER braid *US* one's hair.

Zorn *der* anger. ◆ **im Zorn** *adv* in anger.

zornig ◇ *adj* angry; **auf jn/über etw** *(A)* **zornig sein** to be angry with sb/about sthg. ◇ *adv* angrily.

zottig *adj* shaggy.

z. T. (*abk für* **zum Teil**) partly.

zu ◇ *präp (+ D)* - **1.** [räumlich - Richtung] to; [- Position] at; **zu jm/etw hin** towards sb/sthg; **zu Hause** (at) home; **zu beiden Seiten** on both sides - **2.** [zeitlich] at; **zu Beginn** at the beginning; **zu Ostern/Weihnachten** at Easter/Christmas - **3.** [modal]: **zu Pferd** by horse; **zu Fuß** on foot; **zu Fuß gehen** to walk; **zu meiner großen Enttäuschung** to my great disappointment - **4.** [stellt Bezug her] about - **5.** [in Kombination mit] with; **stell das Glas zu den anderen** put that glass with the others - **6.** [für einen bestimmten Zweck] for - **7.** [mit Nennung eines Endzustandes] into; **zu Eis werden** to turn into ice - **8.** [aus einem bestimmten Anlass] on - **9.** [in Mengenangaben]: **zu viert** in fours; **wir sind zu viert** there are four of us; **zu Tausenden** in thousands; **Säcke zu 50 kg** 50 kg bags; **Orangen zu 25 Cent das Stück** oranges at 25 cents each - **10.** SPORT: **3 zu 2** 3:2. ◇ *adv* - **1.** [übermäßig] too; **zu alt** too old; **zu sehr** too much - **2.** *fam* [zumachen]: **Tür zu!** shut the door! - **3.** [zur Angabe der Richtung] towards. ◇ *konj* - **1.** *(+ Infinitiv)* to; **etwas zu essen** something to eat; **es fängt an zu schneien** it's starting to snow; **zu verkaufen** for sale; **ohne zu fragen** without asking - **2.** *(+ pp)* to; **die zu erledigende Sache** the matter to be dealt with. ◆ **nur zu** *interj* go ahead!; *siehe auch* **zu sein**.

zuallererst, zuallererst *adv* first of all.

zuallerletzt, zuallerletzt *adv* last of all.

Zubehör (*pl* **-e**) *das* accessories *Pl*.

zu|beißen *vi (unreg)* to bite.

zu|bekommen *vt (unreg)* [Tür, Koffer] to get shut.

zu|bereiten *vt* to prepare.

zu|bewegen *vt*: **etw auf jn/etw zubewegen** to move sthg towards sb/sthg. ◆ **sich zubewegen** *ref*: **sich auf jn/etw zubewegen** to make one's way towards sb/sthg.

zu|binden *vt (unreg)* to tie up.

zu|bleiben (*perf* **ist zugeblieben**) *vi (unreg) fam* to stay shut.

zu|blinzeln *vi*: **jm zublinzeln** to wink at sb.

Zubringer (*pl* -) *der* feeder road.

Zucchini [tsʊ'ki:ni] (*pl* **-s**) *die* courgette *UK*, zucchini *US*.

Zucht (*pl* **-en**) *die* - **1.** [Züchten - von Tieren] breeding; [- von Pflanzen] growing; [- von Perlen] cultivation - **2.** *geh* [Disziplin] discipline.

züchten *vt* [Tiere] to breed; [Pflanzen] to grow; [Bakterien, Perlen] to cultivate.

Züchtung (*pl* **-en**) *die* [Züchten - von Tieren] breeding; [- von Pflanzen] growing; [- von Bakterien, Perlen] cultivation; [Zuchtergebnis - Tiere] breed; [- Pflanzen] variety.

zucken (*perf* **hat/ist gezuckt**) *vi* - **1.** *(hat)* [unwillkürlich] to twitch; **mit den Schultern zucken** to shrug (one's shoulders) - **2.** *(ist)* [in eine Richtung - Flamme] to leap up; [- Blitz] to flash.

zücken *vt* - **1.** *geh* [Waffe] to draw - **2.** *hum* [Portmonee, Notizbuch] to whip out.

Zucker *der* - **1.** [Nahrungsmittel] sugar *(U)* - **2.** *fam* [Krankheit] diabetes; **Zucker haben** to be diabetic.

Zuckerguss (*pl* **-güsse**) *der* icing.

zuckerkrank *adj* diabetic.

Zucker|rohr *das* sugarcane.

Zucker|rübe *die* sugar beet.

Zucker|watte *die* candyfloss *UK*, cotton candy *US*.

zu|decken *vt* to cover; **sich/jn/etw mit etw zudecken** to cover o.s./sb/sthg with sthg.

zu|drehen *vt* - **1.** [schließen] to turn off - **2.** [zuwenden]: **jm den Rücken zudrehen** to turn one's back on sb.

zudringlich *adj* pushy.

zu|drücken *vt* [Auge, Koffer] to close; [Tür] to push shut.

zueinander *adv* to each other; **zueinander passen** to go together.

zueinander halten *vi (unreg)* to stick together.

zuerst *adv* - **1.** [als Erstes] first - **2.** [am Anfang] at first - **3.** [zum ersten Mal] for the first time.

zu|fahren (*perf* **ist zugefahren**) *vi (unreg)* - **1.** [sich zubewegen]: **auf jn/etw zufahren** to drive towards sb/sthg - **2.** *fam*: **fahr zu!** get a move on!

Zu|fahrt *die* [Zufahrtsweg] access road; [zu einem Haus] drive.

Zufahrts|straße *die* access road.

Zu|fall *der* coincidence; **etw dem Zufall überlassen** to leave sthg to chance. ◆ **durch Zufall** *adv* by chance.

zu|fallen (*perf* **ist zugefallen**) *vi (unreg)* - **1.** [Tür, Deckel] to slam shut; [Augen] to close - **2.**: **jm zufallen** [Preis] to go to sb; [Aufgabe] to fall to sb.

zufällig ◇ *adj* chance *(vor Subst)*. ◇ *adv* by chance.

zu|fassen *vi*: **fest zufassen** to grip tightly.

Zu|flucht *die* refuge.

zu|flüstern *vt*: **jm etw zuflüstern** to whisper sthg to sb.

zufolge *präp*: **jm/einer Sache zufolge** according to sb/sthg.

zufrieden ◇ *adj* contented; [mit Befriedigung] satisfied; **mit jm/etw zufrieden sein** to be satisfied with sb/sthg. ◇ *adv* contentedly.

zufrieden geben ◆ **sich zufrieden geben** *ref (unreg)*: **sich mit etw zufrieden geben** to be satisfied with sthg.

zufrieden lassen *vt (unreg)* to leave in peace.

zufrieden stellen *vt* to satisfy.

zu|fügen *vt*: **jm Schaden/Unrecht zufügen** to do sb harm/an injustice.

Zufuhr *die* [von Energie] supply; [von Luft] influx.

Zug (*pl* **Züge**) *der* - **1.** [Bahn] train; **mit dem Zug fahren** to go by train - **2.** [Schar] procession - **3.** [Bewegung - von Vögeln] migration; [- von Wolken] drifting - **4.** [mit Spielfigur] move; **er ist am Zug** *eigtl* & *fig* it is his move - **5.** [Schluck] gulp; **in einem Zug** in one go - **6.** [beim Rauchen] puff - **7.** [Atemzug] breath; **in vollen Zügen** in deep breaths; *fig* to the full - **8.** *(ohne pl)* [Durchzug] draught - **9.** [Gesichtszug]: **Züge** features - **10.** [Charakterzug] characteristic - **11.** [beim Schwimmen] stroke; **in groben Zügen** in broad outline; **zum Zug(e) kommen** to get a chance.

Zu|gabe *die* - **1.** [Zugeben] addition - **2.** [Zugegebenes] free gift.

Zugab|teil *das* compartment.

Zu|gang *der* - **1.** [gen & EDV] access; **Zugang zu etw haben** to have access to sthg - **2.** [Zugangsweg] entrance.

zugänglich *adj* - **1.** [Raum, Ort] accessible - **2.** [Information] available; **jm etw zugänglich machen** to make sthg available to sb - **3.** [Person] approachable.

Zug|brücke *die* drawbridge.

zu|geben *vt (unreg)* - **1.** [hinzugeben] to add - **2.** [gestehen] to admit.

zu|gehen (*perf* **ist zugegangen**) *vi (unreg)* - **1.** [sich zubewegen]: **auf jn/etw zugehen** to approach sb/sthg - **2.** [verlaufen]: **auf der Party gehts lustig zu** the party is going with a swing - **3.** *fam* [schneller gehen]: **geh zu!** get a move on! - **4.** [sich schließen - Tür, Koffer] to close; [- Knopf, Reißverschluss] to do up.

zugehörig *adj* that belongs with it/them; **sich jm/einer Sache zugehörig fühlen** to feel a part of sb/sthg.

Zugehörigkeit *die* [zu Verein, Familie] membership.

zugeknöpft *adj* buttoned up.

Zügel (*pl* -) *der* reins *Pl*.

zügellos ◇ *adj* unrestrained. ◇ *adv* in an unrestrained manner.

zügeln *vt* - **1.** [Pferd] to rein in - **2.** [Gefühl] to restrain.

Zu|geständnis *das* concession.

zu|gestehen *vt (unreg)*: **jm etw zugestehen** [gestatten] to grant sb sthg; [zugeben] to admit sthg to sb.

Zug|führer, in *der, die* senior guard *UK* ODER conductor *US*.

zugig *adj* draughty.

zügig ◇ *adj* rapid. ◇ *adv* rapidly.

zugleich *adv* at the same time.

Zug|luft *die (ohne pl)* draught.

Zug|personal *das (ohne pl)* train crew.

zu|greifen *vi (unreg)* - **1.** [zufassen] to grab it/them - **2.** [sich bedienen] to help o.s. - **3.** [mithelfen] to do one's bit.

zugrunde, zu Grunde *adv*: **an etw** *(D)* **zugrunde gehen** [sterben] to perish from sthg; [ruiniert werden] to be wrecked by sthg; **einer Sache** *(D)* **zugrunde liegen** to form the basis of sthg; **jn zugrunde richten** to ruin sb.

Zug|schaffner, in *der, die* ticket inspector.

Zug|unglück *das* train accident.

zugunsten, zu Gunsten ◇ *präp*: **zugunsten js/einer Sache** in favour of sb/sthg. ◇ *adv*: **zugunsten von jm/etw** in favour of sb/sthg.

zugute *adv*: **jm/etw zugute kommen** to prove beneficial to sb/sthg.

Zugver|bindung *die* train connection.

Zug|verkehr *der (ohne pl)* train services *Pl*.

zu|haben *vi (unreg) fam* to be shut.

Zuhälter (*pl* -) *der* pimp.

zuhause *adv Schweiz & Österr* at home; *siehe auch* **Haus**.

Zuhause *das* home.

zu|hören *vi* to listen; **jm/einer Sache zuhören** to listen to sb/sthg.

Zu|hörer, in *der, die* listener.

zu|kehren *vt*: **jm den Rücken zukehren** to turn one's back on sb.

zu|knöpfen *vt* to button up.

zu|kommen (*perf* **ist zugekommen**) *vi (unreg)* - **1.** [sich bewegen]: **auf jn/etw zukommen** to approach sb/sthg; **etw auf sich** *(A)* **zukommen lassen** *fig* to take sthg as it comes - **2.** [zustehen]: **jm zukommen** to befit sb - **3.** *geh* [zuteil werden]: **etw kommt jm zu** sb receives sthg; **jm etw zukommen lassen** to send sb sthg.

Zukunft *die* [künftige Zeit & GRAMM] future. ◆ **in Zukunft** *adv* in future.

zukünftig ◇ *adj* future. ◇ *adv* in future.

zu|lächeln *vi*: **jm zulächeln** to smile at sb.

Zu|lage *die* bonus.

zu|lassen *vt (unreg)* - **1.** [erlauben] to allow - **2.** [amtlich - Medikament] to license; [- Auto] to register; **jn zu einer Prüfung zulassen** to permit sb to take an examination.

zulässig *adj* permissible.

Zulassung (*pl* **-en**) *die* - **1.** [Zulassen - von Medikament] licensing; [- von Arzt, Auto] registration; **die Zulassung zum Studium** acceptance to study at university; **die Zulassung zur Prüfung** permission to take an examination - **2.** AUTO [Schein] vehicle registration document.

zu|laufen (*perf* **ist zugelaufen**) *vi (unreg)* - **1.** [sich bewegen]: **auf jn/etw zulaufen** to run towards sb/sthg - **2.** [Tier]: **jm zulaufen** to adopt sb - **3.** [auslaufen] to taper; **spitz zulaufen** to end in a point.

zu|legen *vt* [anschaffen]: **sich** *(D)* **etw zulegen** to get o.s. sthg.

zuletzt *adv* - **1.** [gen] last - **2.** [am Ende] in the end.

zuliebe *präp*: **jm zuliebe** for sb's sake; **einer Sache** *(D)* **zuliebe** for the sake of sthg.

zum *präp* - **1.** *(zu + dem)* to the; **zum Friseur gehen** to go to the hairdresser's - **2.** *(untrennbar)*: **zum Tanzen gehen** to go dancing; **zum Teil** partly; **zum Beispiel** for example; **zum Thema** on the subject of; **Fenster zum Garten** window overlooking the garden; *siehe auch* **zu**.

zu|machen *vt* & *vi* to close; [Mantel] to do up.

zumindest *adv* at least.

zumutbar *adj* reasonable.

zu|muten *vt*: **jm etw zumuten** to expect sthg of sb; **das kannst du ihr nicht zumuten** you can't ask her to do that.

Zumutung (*pl* **-en**) *die*: **etw als Zumutung empfinden** to feel that sthg is unreasonable; **eine Zumutung sein** to be unreasonable.

zunächst [tsu'nɛːçst] *adv* - **1.** [zuerst] first - **2.** [einstweilen] for the moment.

zu|nähen *vt* to sew up.

Zunahme (*pl* **-n**) *die* increase.

zünden ◇ *vt* [Bombe, Sprengladung] to detonate; [Triebwerk] to fire. ◇ *vi* [Triebwerk] to fire; [Treibstoff] to ignite.

zündend *adj fig* [Aussprache] rousing; [Idee] exciting.

Zünder (*pl* -) *der* detonator.

Zünd|kerze *die* AUTO spark plug.

Zünd|schlüssel *der* AUTO ignition key.

Zünd|schnur *die* fuse.

Zünd|stoff *der fig* dynamite *(U)*.

Zündung (*pl* **-en**) *die* - **1.** [Zünden] detonation - **2.** AUTO ignition.

zu|nehmen *(unreg)* ◇ *vi* - **1.** [gewinnen]: **an etw** *(D)* **zunehmen** to gain in sthg - **2.** [dicker werden] to put on weight. ◇ *vt*: **5 Kilo zunehmen** to put on 5 kilos.

Zuneigung *die* affection; **Zuneigung zu jm/etw** affection for sb/sthg.

Zunft (*pl* **Zünfte**) *die* HIST guild.

zünftig ◇ *adj* proper. ◇ *adv* properly.

Zunge (*pl* **-n**) *die* tongue; **auf der Zunge zergehen** to melt in the mouth; **die Zunge herausstrecken** to stick one's tongue out; **es liegt mir auf der Zunge** *fig* it's on the tip of my tongue.

Zungen|spitze *die* tip of the tongue.

zunichte *adj*: **etw zunichte machen** to ruin sthg.

zu|nicken *vi*: **jm zunicken** to nod to sb.

zunutze, zu Nutze *adj*: **sich** *(D)* **etw zunutze machen** to take advantage of sthg.

zuoberst *adv* on top.

zu|ordnen *vt*: **jn/etw jm/einer Sache zuordnen** to assign sb/sthg to sb/sthg; **Katzen werden den Raubtieren zugeordnet** cats are classified as carnivores.

zu|packen *vi* - **1.** [greifen] to grab it/them - **2.** [mitarbeiten] to knuckle down to it.

zupfen ◇ *vi*: **an etw** *(D)* **zupfen** to tug at sthg. ◇ *vt* - **1.** [Unkraut] to pull up - **2.** [Instrument, Augenbrauen, Haar] to pluck.

zur *präp* - **1.** *(zu + der)* to the; **zur Post gehen** to go to the post office - **2.** *(untrennbar)*: **zur Zeit** at the moment; **zur Straße liegen** to face the street; **zur allgemeinen Verwunderung** to everyone's amazement; *siehe auch* **zu**.

zurechnungsfähig *adj* of sound mind.

zurecht|finden ◆ **sich zurechtfinden** *ref (unreg)* to find one's way around.

zurecht|kommen (*perf* **ist zurechtgekommen**) *vi (unreg)* to get on; **mit jm zurechtkommen** to get on with sb; **mit etw zurechtkommen** to cope with sthg.

zurecht|legen *vt* - **1.** [Kleidung, Werkzeug] to lay out ready - **2.** [Ausrede] to get ready.

zurẹcht|machen *vt* [herrichten] to get ready. ◆ **sich zurechtmachen** *ref* [schminken] to put one's make-up on.

zurẹcht|weisen *vt (unreg)* to reprimand.

Zurẹcht|weisung *die* reprimand.

zu|reden *vi*: **jm zureden** to persuade sb; **jm gut zureden** to talk nicely to sb.

Zürich *nt* Zurich.

zu|richten *vt* to mess up; **jn übel zurichten** to beat sb up.

zurụck *adv* - **1.** [gen] back; **ich bin um 5 Uhr zurück** I'll be back at 5 o'clock; **einmal Berlin und zurück** a return to Berlin *UK*, a round-trip ticket to Berlin *US* - **2.** [im Rückstand] behind.

zurụck|bekommen *vt (unreg)* to get back.

zurụck|bleiben (*perf* **ist zurụckgeblieben**) *vi (unreg)* - **1.** [nicht folgen] to stay behind; **hinter jm/etw zurückbleiben** to fall behind sb/sthg - **2.** [sich nicht nähern] to keep back - **3.** [mit Leistung, Ergebnis] to fall behind - **4.** [Erinnerung, Schaden] to be left.

zurụck|blicken *vi* to look back; **auf etw** *(A)* **zurückblicken** to look back at sthg; *fig* to look back on sthg.

zurụck|bringen *vt (unreg)* to bring/take back.

zurụck|erhalten *vt (unreg)* to get back.

zurụck|erstatten *vt*: **jm etw zurückerstatten** to refund sb sthg.

zurụck|fahren (*perf* **hat/ist zurụckgefahren**) *(unreg)* ◇ *vi (ist)* - **1.** [zurückkehren] to go back - **2.** [rückwärts fahren] to drive back. ◇ *vt (hat)* to drive back.

zurụck|fallen (*perf* **ist zurụckgefallen**) *vi (unreg)* - **1.** [gen] to fall back - **2.** [in Rückstand geraten] to fall behind - **3.** [zurückgegeben werden]: **an jn zurückfallen** to revert to sb - **4.** [zurückgeführt werden]: **auf jn zurückfallen** to reflect on sb.

zurụck|fordern *vt*: **etw zurückfordern** to ask for sthg back.

zurụck|führen ◇ *vt* - **1.** [von etwas herleiten]: **etw auf etw** *(A)* **zurückführen** to put sthg down to sthg - **2.** [Person, Sache] to take back. ◇ *vi* [Weg] to lead back.

zurụck|geben *vt (unreg)* - **1.** [wiedergeben - Geliehenes, Führerschein] to give back; [- Ware] to return; [- Mandat] to give up; **jm etw zurückgeben** to give sb sthg back - **2.** [antworten] to answer - **3.** [zurückspielen] to return.

zurụckgeblieben *adj* retarded.

zurụck|gehen (*perf* **ist zurụckgegangen**) *vi (unreg)* - **1.** [gen] to go back - **2.** [weniger werden] to go down - **3.** [zurückzuführen sein]: **auf jn/etw zurückgehen** to go back to sb/sthg - **4.** [zurückgesandt werden]: **etw zurückgehen lassen** to send sthg back.

zurụckgezogen ◇ *adj* [Mensch] retiring; [Leben] secluded. ◇ *adv* in seclusion.

zurụck|greifen *vi (unreg)*: **auf jn/etw zurückgreifen** to fall back on sb/sthg.

zurụck|halten *vt (unreg)* - **1.** [Person, Meinung, Gefühl] to hold back - **2.** [Nachricht, Sendung] to withhold - **3.** [an etw hindern]: **jn von etw zurückhalten** to stop sb from doing sthg. ◆ **sich zurückhalten** *ref* [sich bremsen] to restrain o.s.; **sich mit dem Trinken zurückhalten** to watch what one drinks.

zurụckhaltend ◇ *adj* [Mensch] reserved; [Beifall, Äußerung] restrained. ◇ *adv* with restraint.

Zurụckhaltung *die* restraint.

zurụck|holen *vt* to fetch back.

zurụck|kehren (*perf* **ist zurụckgekehrt**) *vi geh* to return.

zurụck|kommen (*perf* **ist zurụckgekommen**) *vi (unreg)* - **1.** [zurückkehren] to come back - **2.** [zurückgreifen]: **auf jn/etw zurückkommen** to come back to sb/sthg.

zurụck|lassen *vt (unreg)* - **1.** [hinterlassen] to leave behind - **2.** [zurückgehen lassen] to let go back.

zurụck|legen *vt* - **1.** [wieder hinlegen] to put back - **2.** [Kopf] to lean back - **3.** [Geld, Ware] to put aside - **4.** [Strecke] to cover. ◆ **sich zurücklegen** *ref* [sich zurücklehnen] to lie back.

zurụck|liegen *vi (unreg)* - **1.** [vergangen sein]: **es liegt zwei Jahre zurück** it was two years ago - **2.** [im Rückstand sein] to be behind.

zurụck|müssen *vi (unreg)* to have to go back.

zurụck|nehmen *vt (unreg)* - **1.** [Ware] to take back - **2.** [widerrufen - Äußerung, Vorwurf] to take back; [- Antrag] to withdraw; [- Entscheidung, Befehl] to rescind.

zurụck|rufen *(unreg)* ◇ *vt* to call back; **sich etw ins Bewusstsein zurückrufen** to recall sthg. ◇ *vi* [am Telefon] to call back.

zurụck|schrecken (*perf* **ist zurụckgeschreckt**) *vi* - **1.** [vor Schreck] to start back in fright - **2.** [sich scheuen]: **vor etw** *(D)* **zurückschrecken** to shy away from sthg; **vor nichts zurückschrecken** to stop at nothing.

zurụck|stellen *vt* - **1.** [wieder zurück] to put back - **2.** [nach hinten] to move back - **3.** [Heizung, Lautstärke] to turn down - **4.** [verschieben - Plan, Projekt] to put off; [- Wünsche, Zweifel] to set aside.

zurụck|stoßen *vt (unreg)* - **1.** [wieder zurück] to push back - **2.** [wegstoßen] to push away.

zurụck|treten (*perf* **ist zurụckgetreten**) *vi (unreg)* - **1.** [nach hinten] to step back - **2.** [von Amt] to resign.

zurụck|weichen (*perf* **ist zurụckgewichen**) *vi (unreg)* to shrink back; **vor jm/etw zurückweichen** to shrink away from sb/sthg; **vor etw zurückweichen** to shrink from sthg.

zurụck|weisen *vt (unreg)* - **1.** [abweisen] to reject - **2.** [Vorwurf] to repudiate.

zurụ̈ck|zahlen *vt* to pay back; **jm etw zurückzahlen** [Schulden] to pay sb back sthg; *fam* [aus Rache] to pay sb back for sthg.

zurụ̈ck|ziehen (*perf* **hat/ist zurụ̈ckgezogen**) *(unreg)* ◇ *vt (hat)* - **1.** [gen] to withdraw - **2.** [nach hinten] to pull back. ◇ *vi (ist)* [umziehen] to move back. ◆ **sich zurückziehen** *ref* [sich isolieren] to withdraw.

Zu|ruf *der* shout.

zu|rufen *vt (unreg)* to shout.

zurzeit *adv* at present.

Zu|sage *die* - **1.** [zu Einladung] acceptance *(U)* - **2.** [Versprechen] promise.

zu|sagen ◇ *vt* [versprechen] to promise; **jm etw zusagen** to promise sb sthg. ◇ *vi* - **1.** [bei Einladung] to accept - **2.** [gefallen]**: jm zusagen** to appeal to sb.

zusạmmen *adv* - **1.** [gen] together - **2.** [insgesamt] altogether; **das macht zusammen 10 Euro** that's 10 euros altogether.

Zusạmmen|arbeit *die* collaboration.

zusạmmen|arbeiten *vi* to work together.

zusạmmen|brauen *vt fam* to concoct. ◆ **sich zusammenbrauen** *ref* to be brewing.

zusạmmen|brechen (*perf* **ist zusạmmengebrochen**) *vi (unreg)* - **1.** [gen] to collapse - **2.** [Verkehr] to come to a standstill.

zusạmmen|bringen *vt (unreg)* - **1.** [beschaffen] to get together - **2.** [Personen] to bring together - **3.** [Gelerntes] to manage.

Zusạmmen|bruch *der* collapse.

zusạmmen|fahren (*perf* **ist zusạmmengefahren**) *vi (unreg)* [erschrecken] to start.

zusạmmen|fallen (*perf* **ist zusạmmengefallen**) *vi (unreg)* - **1.** [einsinken]**: (in sich) zusammenfallen** to collapse - **2.** [abmagern] to become emaciated - **3.** [Termine, Flächen] to coincide.

zusạmmen|fassen *vt* to summarize.

Zusạmmen|fassung *die* summary.

zusạmmen|gehören *vi* to belong together.

zusạmmen|halten *(unreg)* ◇ *vi* - **1.** [Personen] to stick together - **2.** [Teile] to hold together. ◇ *vt* - **1.** [verbunden halten] to hold together - **2.** [beisammenhalten - Herde, Gruppe] to keep together; [- Geld] to hang on to.

Zusạmmen|hang *der* connection; **etw in Zusammenhang mit etw bringen** to make a connection between sthg and sthg; **im Zusammenhang mit etw stehen** to be connected with sthg.

zusạmmen|hängen *vi (unreg)* - **1.** [befestigt sein] to be joined (together) - **2.** [ursächlich]**: mit etw zusammenhängen** to be connected with sthg.

zusạmmenhängend *adj* coherent.

zusạmmenhanglos, zusạmmenhangslos ◇ *adj* incoherent. ◇ *adv* incoherently.

zusạmmen|kommen (*perf* **ist zusạmmengekommen**) *vi (unreg)* - **1.** [Personen] to meet - **2.** [Ereignisse, Unglück] to happen together; **heute kam wirklich alles zusammen** everything that could go wrong today, did go wrong - **3.** [sich sammeln - Spenden] to be collected; [- Unkosten, Verluste] to mount up.

zusạmmen|legen ◇ *vt* - **1.** [sammeln, zusammen unterbringen] to put together - **2.** [falten] to fold up - **3.** [Termine, Gruppen] to combine. ◇ *vi* [gemeinsam bezahlen] to club together.

zusạmmen|nehmen *vt (unreg)* to summon up. ◆ **sich zusammennehmen** *ref* to pull o.s. together.

zusạmmen|passen *vi* [Farben, Kleidungsstücke] to go together; [Menschen] to suit each other.

zusạmmen|prallen (*perf* **ist zusạmmengeprallt**) *vi* to collide.

zusạmmen|rechnen *vt* to add up.

zusạmmen|reißen *(unreg)* ◆ **sich zusammenreißen** *ref fam* to pull o.s. together.

zusạmmen|schlagen (*perf* **hat/ist zusạmmengeschlagen**) *(unreg)* ◇ *vt (hat)* - **1.** [gegeneinanderschlagen - Hände] to clap; [- Absätze] to click - **2.** *fam* [niederschlagen] to beat up. ◇ *vi (ist)*: **über jm/etw zusammenschlagen** to engulf sb/sthg.

zusạmmen|schließen *vt (unreg)* to lock together. ◆ **sich zusammenschließen** *ref* to join forces.

Zusạmmenschluss (*pl* **-schlüsse**) *der* joining together *(U)*.

Zusạmmensein *das* being together.

zusạmmen|setzen *vt* to put together. ◆ **sich zusammensetzen** *ref* - **1.** [bestehen]: **sich aus etw zusammensetzen** to be composed of sthg - **2.** [zusammentreffen] to get together; **sich mit jm zusammensetzen** to get together with sb.

Zusạmmensetzung (*pl* **-en**) *die* composition.

zusạmmen|stellen *vt* to put together.

Zusạmmen|stoß *der* [von Fahrzeugen] crash; *fig* [von Menschen] clash.

zusạmmen|stoßen (*perf* **ist zusạmmengestoßen**) *vi (unreg)* to crash.

zusạmmen|treffen (*perf* **ist zusạmmengetroffen**) *vi (unreg)* - **1.** [Personen] to meet; **mit jm zusammentreffen** to meet sb - **2.** [Ereignisse] to coincide.

Zusạmmen|treffen *das* [mit Freunden] meeting; [von Ereignissen] coincidence.

zusạmmen|tun *vt (unreg) fam* to put together. ◆ **sich zusammentun** *ref* to get together; **sich mit jm zusammentun** to get together with sb.

zusạmmen|zählen *vt* to count up.

zusạmmen|ziehen (*perf* **hat/ist zusạmmengezogen**) *(unreg)* <> *vt (hat)* - **1.** [enger machen - Schlinge, Netz] to pull tight; [- Augenbrauen] to knit - **2.** [sammeln] to mass. <> *vi (ist)* [in eine Wohnung] to move in together; **mit jm zusammenziehen** to move in with sb. ◆ **sich zusammenziehen** *ref* [enger, kleiner werden] to contract.

zusạmmen|zucken (*perf* **ist zusạmmengezuckt**) *vi* to give a start.

Zu|satz *der* addition; [in Nahrungsmittel] additive; [in Vertrag] rider.

Zusatz|gerät *das* attachment.

zusätzlich <> *adj* additional. <> *adv* in addition.

Zuschauer, in (*mpl* **-**, *fpl* **-nen**) *der, die* [im Theater, Kino] member of the audience; [im Stadion] spectator; [bei Unfall, Prügelei] onlooker. ◆ **Zuschauer** *Pl* [im Theater, Kino] audience *(sg)*.

zu|schicken *vt*: **jm etw zuschicken** to send sthg to sb.

zu|schieben *vt (unreg)* - **1.** [schließen] to push shut - **2.** [hinschieben]: **jm etw zuschieben** to push sthg over to sb - **3.** [Schuld]: **jm etw zuschieben** to push sthg onto sb.

Zu|schlag *der* - **1.** [zusätzlicher Betrag - auf Lohn] additional pay *(U)*; [- auf Ware] surcharge - **2.** [zur Fahrkarte] supplement - **3.** [Zusage]: **den Zuschlag erhalten** [Firma] to be awarded the contract; [Gebot] to be successful.

zu|schlagen (*perf* **hat/ist zugeschlagen**) *(unreg)* <> *vi* - **1.** *(ist)* [Tür, Deckel] to slam shut - **2.** *(hat)* [Person] to hit out - **3.** *(hat)* [Einsatztruppe, Terrorist] to strike - **4.** *(hat) fam* [kaufen] to go for it. <> *vt (hat)* - **1.** [Tür, Deckel] to slam shut - **2.** [zusprechen]: **jm etw zuschlagen** [einem Bieter] to knock sthg down to sb; [einer Firma] to award sthg to sb.

zu|schließen *(unreg)* <> *vt* to lock. <> *vi* to lock up.

zu|schnappen (*perf* **hat/ist zugeschnappt**) *vi* - **1.** *(hat)* [Hund] to snap - **2.** *(ist)* [Fälle, Tür] to click shut.

zu|schneiden *vt (unreg)* [Stoff, Kleidungsstück] to cut out; [Brett] to cut to size.

zu|schrauben *vt* [Flasche, Glas] to screw the top on; [Deckel] to screw on.

zu|schreiben *vt (unreg)*: **jm etw zuschreiben** to attribute sthg to sb.

Zu|schrift *die* reply.

zuschụlden, zu Schụlden *adv*: **sich** *(D)* **etwas zuschulden kommen lassen** to do wrong.

Zuschuss (*pl* **-schüsse**) *der* [öffentlich] grant; [privat] contribution.

zu|sehen *vi (unreg)* - **1.** [zuschauen] to watch; **jm bei etw zusehen** to watch sb doing sthg; **bei etw zusehen** to watch sthg - **2.** [veranlassen]: **zusehen, dass...** to make sure that...; **sieh zu, dass du wegkommst!** *fam* go away!

zu sein (*perf* **ist zu gewesen**) *vi (unreg)* to be closed.

zu|setzen <> *vt* - **1.** [Zutat] to add - **2.** [Geld] to pay out. <> *vi* [schaden]: **jm zusetzen** to take it out of sb.

zu|sichern *vt*: **jm etw zusichern** to assure sb of sthg.

zu|spitzen ◆ **sich zuspitzen** *ref* to intensify.

Zu|stand *der* state; [Gesundheitszustand] condition; **in gutem/schlechten Zustand** in good/bad condition. ◆ **Zustände** *Pl* situation.

zustạnde, zu Stạnde *adv*: **etw zustande bringen** to bring sthg about; **zustande kommen** to come about.

zuständig *adj* relevant.

zu|stehen *vi (unreg)*: **etw steht jm zu** sb is entitled to sthg.

zu|steigen (*perf* **ist zugestiegen**) *vi (unreg)* to get on.

zu|stimmen *vi* to agree; **jm zustimmen** to agree with sb.

Zu|stimmung *die* agreement; **zu etw seine Zustimmung geben** to give one's consent to sthg.

zu|stoßen (*perf* **hat/ist zugestoßen**) *(unreg)* <> *vt (hat)* [schließen] to push shut. <> *vi* - **1.** *(hat)* [mit Waffe] to make a stab - **2.** *(ist)* [geschehen]: **jm zustoßen** to happen to sb.

Zustrom *der (ohne pl)* stream.

zutage, zu Tage *adv*: **zutage treten** ODER **kommen** to come to the surface; *fig* to come to light.

Zutaten *Pl* ingredients.

zutiefst *adv* deeply.

zu|trauen *vt*: **jm/sich etw zutrauen** to think sb/one is capable of sthg; **ich hätte ihm mehr Geschick zugetraut** I would have expected him to show more skill.

zutraulich <> *adj* trusting. <> *adv* trustingly.

zu|treffen *vi (unreg)* to be correct; **auf jn/etw zutreffen** to apply to sb/sthg.

Zutritt *der* entry; **Zutritt haben** to have access; **'Zutritt verboten!'** 'no entry'.

Zutun *das*: **ohne js Zutun** without sb's involvement.

zuverlässig <> *adj* reliable. <> *adv* reliably.

Zuverlässigkeit *die* reliability.

Zuversicht *die* confidence.

zuversichtlich <> *adj* confident. <> *adv* confidently.

zu viel *pron* too much.

zuvor *adv* before.

zuvor|kommen (*perf* **ist zuvorgekommen**) *vi (unreg)*: **jm zuvorkommen** to beat sb to it.

zuvorkommend *adj* obliging.

Zuwachs ['tsu:vaks] *der* growth; **etw auf Zuwachs kaufen** to buy sthg big enough to allow room for growth.

zu|wachsen ['tsu:vaksn̩] (*perf* **ist zugewachsen**) *vi (unreg)* to become overgrown.

zuwege, zu Wege *adv*: **etw zuwege bringen** to bring sthg about.

zu|weisen *vt (unreg)*: **jm etw zuweisen** to allocate sthg to sb.

zu|wenden *vt*: **jm den Rücken zuwenden** to turn one's back on sb. ◆ **sich zuwenden** *ref*: **sich jm/etw zuwenden** to turn to sb/sthg.

Zu|wendung *die* - **1.** [Aufmerksamkeit] attention - **2.** [Geld] contribution.

zu wenig *pron* not enough.

zuwider *adv*: **mir sind Würmer zuwider** I find worms revolting.

zu|winken *vi*: **jm zuwinken** to wave to sb.

zu|ziehen (*perf* **hat/ist zugezogen**) *(unreg)* ◇ *vt (hat)* - **1.** [schließen - Tür, Fenster] to pull shut; [- Vorhang, Reißverschluss] to close; [- Schlinge, Knoten] to pull tight - **2.** [Spezialist] to bring in - **3.** [verschaffen]: **sich** *(D)* **etw zuziehen** [Erkältung] to catch sthg; [Zorn, Neid] to incur sthg. ◇ *vi (ist)* [an einen Ort ziehen] to move into the area/town/*etc*.

zuzüglich *präp (+G, D)* plus.

ZVS [tsɛtfau'ɛs] (*abk für* **Zentralstelle für die Vergabe von Studienplätzen**) *die* ≃ UCAS *UK, German organization responsible for the allocation of student places.*

zwang *prät* ▷ **zwingen**.

Zwang (*pl* **Zwänge**) *der* [körperlich] force; [Druck] pressure; [gesellschaftlich] constraint; [innerer] compulsion.

zwängen *vt* to force; **sich/etw in etw** *(A)* **zwängen** to force o.s./sthg into sthg.

zwanglos ◇ *adj* informal. ◇ *adv* informally.

Zwangs|lage *die* predicament.

zwangsläufig ◇ *adj* inevitable. ◇ *adv* inevitably; **etw zwangsläufig tun müssen** to be bound to do sthg.

zwanzig *num* twenty; *siehe auch* **sechs**.

Zwanzig *die (ohne pl)* twenty; *siehe auch* **Sechs**.

Zwanzigeuro|schein *der* twenty-euro note *UK* ODER bill *US*.

zwanzigste, r, s *adj* twentieth; *siehe auch* **sechste**.

Zwanzigste (*pl* **-n**) *der, die, das* twentieth; *siehe auch* **Sechste**.

zwar *adv*: **das ist zwar schön, aber viel zu teuer** it's nice but far too expensive; **und zwar** to be exact; **ihr geht jetzt ins Bett, und zwar sofort!** go to bed right now, and I mean right now!

Zweck (*pl* **-e**) *der* - **1.** [Ziel] purpose; **für einen guten Zweck** for a good cause; **seinen Zweck erfüllen** to serve its purpose; **zu diesem Zweck** for this purpose - **2.** [Sinn] point.

zwecklos *adj* pointless.

zwei *num* two; **für zwei essen** *fig* to eat enough for two; *siehe auch* **sechs**.

Zwei (*pl* **-en**) *die* - **1.** [Zahl] two - **2.** [Schulnote] ≃ B, *mark of 2 on a scale from 1 to 6*; *siehe auch* **Sechs**.

Zweibett|zimmer *das* twin room.

zweideutig ◇ *adj* - **1.** [mehrdeutig] ambiguous - **2.** [frivol] suggestive. ◇ *adv* - **1.** [mehrdeutig] ambiguously - **2.** [frivol] suggestively.

Zweieuro|stück *das* two-euro piece.

zweierlei *num* - **1.** [zwei verschiedene] odd - **2.** [etwas anderes]: **es ist zweierlei** it is two different things.

zweifach ◇ *adj* double; **die zweifache Menge** twice as much; **in zweifacher Ausfertigung** in duplicate; **der zweifache Gewinner** the two-times winner. ◇ *adv* twice.

Zweifel (*pl* -) *der* doubt; **Zweifel an etw** *(D)* doubts *Pl* about sthg; **ohne Zweifel** without doubt.

zweifelhaft *adj* - **1.** [unsicher] doubtful - **2.** [anrüchig] dubious.

zweifellos *adv* undoubtedly.

zweifeln *vi* to doubt; **an etw** *(D)* **zweifeln** to doubt sthg.

Zweifels|fall *der*: **im Zweifelsfall** in case of doubt.

Zweig (*pl* **-e**) *der* branch.

Zweig|stelle *die* branch.

zweihundert *num* two hundred.

zweimal *adv* twice.

Zwei|rad *das* two-wheeler.

zweiseitig *adj* - **1.** [zwei Seiten umfassend] two-page *(vor Subst)* - **2.** [gegenseitig] bilateral.

zweisprachig ◇ *adj* bilingual. ◇ *adv* [aufwachsen] bilingually; [geschrieben] in two languages.

zweistellig *adj* two-figure *(vor Subst)*.

zweistöckig *adj* two-storey *(vor Subst)*.

zweit ◆ **zu zweit** *adv*: **sie waren zu zweit** there were two of them; **wir sind zu zweit ins Kino gegangen** two of us went to the cinema.

zweitausend *num* two thousand.

zweitbeste, r, s *adj* second best.

zweite, r, s *adj* second; *siehe auch* **sechste**.

Zweite (*pl* **-n**) *der, die, das* second; **wie kein Zweiter** like nobody else; *siehe auch* **Sechste**.

zweiteilig *adj* [Kleid, Badeanzug] two-piece *(vor Subst)*; FILM two-part *(vor Subst)*; [Ausgabe] two-volume *(vor Subst)*.

zweitens *adv* secondly.

zweitrangig *adj* [Frage, Aufgabe] of secondary importance; [Bedeutung] secondary.

Zweit|wagen *der* second car.

Zweizimmer|wohnung *die* two-room flat *UK* ODER apartment *US*.

Zwerch|fell *das* diaphragm.

Zwerg (*pl* **-e**) *der* dwarf.

Zwetsche (*pl* **-n**), **Zwetschge** (*pl* **-n**) *die* plum.

zwicken *vt* & *vi* to pinch.

Zwieback (*pl* **Zwiebäcke** ODER **-e**) *der* rusk.

Zwiebel (*pl* **-n**) *die* onion.

zwielichtig *adj* shady.

zwiespältig *adj* [Gefühle] conflicting; [Charakter] contradictory.

Zwilling (*pl* **-e**) *der* - **1.** [Person] twin - **2.** ASTROL Gemini; **Zwilling sein** to be a Gemini. ◆ **Zwillinge** *Pl* ASTROL Gemini *(sg)*.

Zwillings|bruder *der* twin brother.

Zwillings|schwester *die* twin sister.

zwingen (*prät* **zwang**, *perf* **hat gezwungen**) *vt* to force; **jn zu etw zwingen** to force sb to do sthg. ◆ **sich zwingen** *ref* to force o.s.; **sich zu etw zwingen** to force o.s. to do sthg.

zwinkern *vi* [als Reflex] to blink; [als Zeichen] to wink.

Zwirn (*pl* **-e**) *der* thread.

zwischen *präp (+D, A)* - **1.** [gen] between - **2.** [inmitten] amongst.

zwischendurch *adv* - **1.** [zeitlich] in the meantime - **2.** [räumlich] here and there.

Zwischen|fall *der* incident. ◆ **Zwischenfälle** *Pl* clashes.

Zwischen|landung *die* stopover.

Zwischen|prüfung *die* UNI intermediate examination.

Zwischen|raum *der* gap.

Zwischen|ruf *der* interjection.

Zwischenzeit *die* time in between; **in der Zwischenzeit** in the meantime.

zwitschern *vi* to twitter.

zwölf *num* twelve; *siehe auch* **sechs**.

Zwölf (*pl* **-en**) *die* twelve; *siehe auch* **Sechs**.

zwölfte, **r**, **s** *adj* twelfth; *siehe auch* **sechste**.

Zwölfte (*pl* **-n**) *der, die, das* twelfth; *siehe auch* **Sechste**.

zwölftel *adj (unver)* twelfth; *siehe auch* **sechstel**.

Zwölftel (*pl* **-**) *das* twelfth; *siehe auch* **Sechstel**.

Zyankali [tsy̆aːn'kaːli] *das* potassium cyanide.

Zylinder [tsi'lɪndɐ] (*pl* **-**) *der* - **1.** [Hut] top hat - **2.** MATH & TECH cylinder.

Zynismus [tsy'nɪsmʊs] *der* cynicism.

Zypern *nt* Cyprus.

Zypresse [tsy'prɛsə] (*pl* **-n**) *die* cypress.

Zyste ['tsʏstə] (*pl* **-n**) *die* MED cyst.

z. Z. = **zurzeit**.

ENGLISH-GERMAN
ENGLISCH-DEUTSCH

a[1] (*pl* **as** *OR* **a's**), **A** (*pl* **As** *OR* **A's**) [eɪ] *n* [letter] a *das*, A *das*; **to get from A to B** von A nach B kommen. ◆ **A** *n* - **1.** MUS [note] A *das* - **2.** SCH [mark] ≃ eins.

a[2] *(stressed* [eɪ], *unstressed* [ə], *before vowel or silent 'h'* **an**, *weak form stressed* [æn], *unstressed* [ən]*) indef art* - **1.** [gen] ein(e); **a woman** eine Frau; **a restaurant** ein Restaurant; **a friend** ein Freund (eine Freundin); **an apple** ein Apfel - **2.** [referring to occupation]: **I'm a doctor** ich bin Arzt - **3.** [instead of the number one] ein(e); **a hundred** hundert; **a hundred and twenty** hundertzwanzig; **for a week** eine Woche lang - **4.** [in prices, ratios] pro; **£2 a kilo** £2 pro Kilo; **£10 a head** £10 pro Kopf; **twice a week/year** zweimal in der Woche/im *OR* pro Jahr; **50 km an hour** 50 km pro Stunde - **5.**: **not a** kein(e); **not a soul** kein Mensch; **I haven't understood a (single) word** ich habe kein (einziges) Wort verstanden.

AA *n* (*abbr of* **Automobile Association**) ≃ ADAC *der*.

AAA *n* (*abbr of* **American Automobile Association**) ≃ ADAC *der*.

AB *n US* (*abbr of* **Bachelor of Arts**), *Hochschulabschluss in einem geisteswissenschaftlichen Fach nach drei- oder vierjährigem Studium*.

aback [ə'bæk] *adv*: **to be taken aback (by sthg)** schockiert sein (über etw *(A)*).

abandon [ə'bændən] ◇ *vt* - **1.** [leave, desert] verlassen - **2.** [give up] auf|geben. ◇ *n (U)*: **with abandon** ausgelassen.

abashed [ə'bæʃt] *adj* verlegen, beschämt.

abate [ə'beɪt] *vi fml* nach|lassen.

abattoir ['æbətwɑːʳ] *n* Schlachthaus *das*.

abbey ['æbɪ] *n* Abtei *die*.

abbot ['æbət] *n* Abt *der*.

abbreviate [ə'briːvɪeɪt] *vt* ab|kürzen.

abbreviation [əˌbriːvɪ'eɪʃn] *n* Abkürzung *die*.

ABC *n* - **1.** [alphabet] ABC *das* - **2.** *fig* [basics]: **the ABC of** das ABC *(+ G)*.

abdicate ['æbdɪkeɪt] ◇ *vi* ab|danken. ◇ *vt* [responsibility] von sich schieben.

abdomen ['æbdəmən] *n* [of person] Unterleib *der*; [of animal, insect] Hinterleib *der*.

abduct [əb'dʌkt] *vt* entführen.

aberration [ˌæbə'reɪʃn] *n* Abweichung *die*.

abet [ə'bet] *vt* ▷ **aid**.

abeyance [ə'beɪəns] *n fml*: **to be in abeyance** [law] außer Kraft sein.

abhor [əb'hɔːʳ] *vt* verabscheuen.

abide [ə'baɪd] *vt* aus|stehen. ◆ **abide by** *vt insep* sich halten an *(+ A)*.

ability [ə'bɪlətɪ] *n* - **1.** *(U)* [capability] Fähigkeit *die* - **2.** [capability] Fähigkeit *die*, Gabe *die*; [talent] Begabung *die*.

abject ['æbdʒekt] *adj* - **1.** [poverty] bitter; **abject misery** tiefes Elend - **2.** [person] unterwürfig, demütig; **to offer an abject apology** unterwürfig um Entschuldigung bitten.

ablaze [ə'bleɪz] *adj* [on fire] in Flammen.

able ['eɪbl] *adj* - **1.** [capable] fähig; **to be able to do sthg** etw tun können; [due to circumstances] imstande *OR* in der Lage sein, etw zu tun - **2.** [competent] tüchtig; [gifted] begabt.

ably ['eɪblɪ] *adv* geschickt, gekonnt.

abnormal [æb'nɔːml] *adj* [behaviour] abnorm; [interest] krankhaft; [workload] übermäßig.

aboard [ə'bɔːd] ◇ *adv* [on ship, plane] an Bord; **to go aboard** an Bord gehen. ◇ *prep*: **aboard the ship/plane** an Bord des Schiffes/Flugzeugs; **aboard the bus/train** im Bus/Zug.

abode [ə'bəʊd] *n fml*: **of no fixed abode** ohne festen Wohnsitz.

abolish [ə'bɒlɪʃ] *vt* ab|schaffen.

abolition [ˌæbə'lɪʃn] *n* Abschaffung *die*.

abominable [ə'bɒmɪnəbl] *adj* [behaviour, treatment] abscheulich; [performance] furchtbar.

aborigine [ˌæbə'rɪdʒənɪ] *n* Ureinwohner *der*, -in *die*; [Australiens] Aborigine *der*.

abort [ə'bɔ:t] *vt* - **1.** [pregnancy] ab|brechen; [baby] ab|treiben - **2.** *fig* [plan, mission] ab|brechen - **3.** COMPUT ab|brechen.

abortion [ə'bɔ:ʃn] *n* [of pregnancy] Abtreibung *die*; **she's going to have an abortion** sie wird eine Abtreibung vornehmen lassen.

abortive [ə'bɔ:tɪv] *adj* misslungen.

abound [ə'baʊnd] *vi* - **1.** [be plentiful] in großer Fülle vorhanden sein - **2.** [be full]: **to abound with** OR **in sthg** reich an etw *(D)* sein.

about [ə'baʊt] ◇ *adv* - **1.** [approximately] ungefähr, etwa; **about 50** ungefähr 50; **at about six o'clock** gegen sechs Uhr - **2.** [referring to place] herum; **to walk about** herum|laufen; **is Mr Smith about?** ist Herr Smith da?; **there's a lot of flu about** die Grippe geht um - **3.** [on the point of]: **to be about to do sthg** im Begriff sein, etw zu tun. ◇ *prep* - **1.** [concerning] um, über *(+ A)*; **a book about Scotland** ein Buch über Schottland; **what's it about?** worum gehts?; **to talk about sthg** über etw sprechen; **to quarrel about sthg** sich wegen etw streiten; **what about a drink?** wie wärs mit etwas zu trinken? - **2.** [referring to place] herum; **to wander about the streets** in den Straßen umherschlendern.

about-turn *esp UK*, **about-face** *esp US* *n* - **1.** MIL Kehrtwendung *die* - **2.** *fig* [change of attitude] Wendung *die* um hundertachtzig Grad.

above [ə'bʌv] ◇ *prep* - **1.** [higher than] über *(+ A, D)*; **to fly above the clouds** über den Wolken fliegen - **2.** [more than] über *(+ A)*; **children above the age of twelve** Kinder über zwölf Jahre. ◇ *adv* - **1.** [on top, higher up] oben; **the flat above** die Wohnung oben; **see above** [in text] siehe oben - **2.** [more]: **children aged ten and above** Kinder ab zehn Jahren. ◆ **above all** *adv* vor allem.

aboveboard [əˌbʌv'bɔ:d] *adj* ehrlich.

abrasive [ə'breɪsɪv] *adj* - **1.** [for cleaning] Scheuer- - **2.** *fig* [person] ungehobelt; [manner] grob.

abreast [ə'brest] *adv* nebeneinander. ◆ **abreast of** *prep*: **to keep abreast of sthg** in Bezug auf etw *(A)* auf dem Laufenden bleiben.

abridged [ə'brɪdʒd] *adj* gekürzt.

abroad [ə'brɔ:d] *adv* [live] im Ausland; [travel, go] ins Ausland.

abrupt [ə'brʌpt] *adj* - **1.** [sudden] abrupt - **2.** [person] kurz angebunden; [manner] brüsk.

abscess ['æbsɪs] *n* Abszess *der*.

abscond [əb'skɒnd] *vi* [from detention centre] entfliehen; [from boarding school] weg|laufen.

abseil ['æbseɪl] *vi* sich ab|seilen.

absence ['æbsəns] *n* - **1.** [of person] Abwesenheit *die* - **2.** [lack] Mangel *der*.

absent ['æbsənt] *adj* [not present]: **absent (from)** abwesend (von).

absentee [ˌæbsən'ti:] *n* Abwesende *der*, *die*.

absent-minded [-'maɪndɪd] *adj* zerstreut.

absolute ['æbsəlu:t] *adj* - **1.** [complete, utter] absolut, vollkommen; **it's an absolute disgrace** es ist eine ausgesprochene Schande - **2.** [ruler, power] absolut.

absolutely [æbsə'lu:tlɪ] ◇ *adv* [completely, utterly] vollkommen, ausgesprochen; **I'm absolutely starving** ich bin ausgesprochen hungrig. ◇ *excl* [expressing agreement] genau!

absolve [əb'zɒlv] *vt*: **to absolve sb (from sthg)** [from crime] jn (von etw) frei|sprechen; [from sin] jn (von etw) los|sprechen; [from responsibility] jn (von etw) entbinden.

absorb [əb'zɔ:b] *vt* - **1.** [liquid] auf|saugen; [gas, heat] absorbieren - **2.** *fig* [learn] auf|nehmen - **3.** [interest] fesseln; **to be absorbed in sthg** in etw *(A)* vertieft OR versunken sein - **4.** [take over] übernehmen.

absorbent [əb'zɔ:bənt] *adj* absorbierend.

abstain [əb'steɪn] *vi* - **1.**: **to abstain from sthg** [drinking, smoking] sich einer Sache *(G)* enthalten; [sex, food] auf etw *(A)* verzichten - **2.** [in vote] sich der Stimme enthalten.

abstention [əb'stenʃn] *n* [in vote] Enthaltung *die*.

abstract ['æbstrækt] ◇ *adj* abstrakt. ◇ *n* [summary] Abstract *der*.

absurd [əb'sɜ:d] *adj* absurd.

abundant [ə'bʌndənt] *adj* reichlich.

abundantly [ə'bʌndəntlɪ] *adv* [extremely]: **it's abundantly clear** es ist mehr als klar.

abuse ◇ *n* [ə'bju:s] - **1.** *(U)* [offensive remarks] Beschimpfungen *Pl*, Schimpfworte *Pl* - **2.** [maltreatment] Missbrauch *der* - **3.** [of alcohol, drugs, power] Missbrauch *der*. ◇ *vt* [ə'bju:z] - **1.** [insult] beschimpfen - **2.** [maltreat, misuse] missbrauchen.

abusive [ə'bju:sɪv] *adj* ausfallend.

abysmal [ə'bɪzml] *adj* [behaviour, performance, weather] miserabel; [failure] erbärmlich.

abyss [ə'bɪs] *n* Abgrund *der*; *fig* [between people, groups] Kluft *die*, Abgründe *Pl*.

a/c (*abbr of* **account (current)**) Kto.

AC *n abbr of* **alternating current**.

academic [ˌækə'demɪk] ◇ *adj* - **1.** [of college, university] wissenschaftlich - **2.** [studious] intellektuell - **3.** [hypothetical] theoretisch ◇ *n* Akademiker *der*, -in *die*.

academy [ə'kædəmɪ] *n* Akademie *die*.

accede [æk'siːd] *vi* - **1.** *fml* [agree]: **to accede to sthg** in etw *(A)* ein|willigen - **2.** [monarch]: **to accede to the throne** den Thron besteigen.

accelerate [ək'seləreɪt] ◇ *vt* [pace, rhythm, decline, event] beschleunigen. ◇ *vi* - **1.** [car, driver] beschleunigen - **2.** [inflation, growth] sich beschleunigen, zu|nehmen.

acceleration [əkˌselə'reɪʃn] *n* Beschleunigung *die*.

accelerator [ək'seləreɪtəʳ] *n* Gaspedal *das*.

accent ['æksent] *n* [gen] Akzent *der*.

accept [ək'sept] *vt* - **1.** [gift, advice, apology, invitation, offer] an|nehmen - **2.** [change, situation] akzeptieren, hin|nehmen - **3.** [defeat, blame] ein|gestehen; [responsibility] übernehmen - **4.** [person - as part of group] akzeptieren; [- for job] nehmen; [- as member of club] auf|nehmen - **5.** [admit]: **to accept that...** zugeben, dass...; **it is generally accepted that...** es ist allgemein anerkannt, dass... - **6.** [subj: shop, bank] akzeptieren; [subj: machine] nehmen.

acceptable [ək'septəbl] *adj* akzeptabel.

acceptance [ək'septəns] *n* - **1.** [of gift, piece of work] Annahme *die* - **2.** [of change, situation] Hinnahme *die* - **3.** [of defeat, blame] Eingeständnis *das*; [of responsibility] Übernehmen *das* - **4.** [of person - as part of group] Akzeptierung *die*; [- for job] Anstellung *die*; [- as member of club] Aufnahme *die*.

access ['ækses] *n (U)* - **1.** [entry, way in] Zutritt *der*, Zugang *der* - **2.** [opportunity to use, see]: **to have access to sthg** zu etw Zugang haben - **3.** [to Internet] Zugang *der*.

accessible [ək'sesəbl] *adj* - **1.** [place] zugänglich - **2.** [available] verfügbar.

accessory [ək'sesərɪ] *n* - **1.** [extra part, device] Extra *das*; **accessories** Zubehör *das* - **2.** LAW Helfershelfer *der*, -in *die*.

accident ['æksɪdənt] *n* - **1.** [unpleasant event] Unfall *der*; [more serious] Unglück *das*; [mishap] Missgeschick *das*; **to have an accident** [in car] einen Autounfall haben - **2.** [unintentional act] Versehen *das* - **3.** *(U)* [chance]: **we met by accident** wir haben uns zufällig getroffen.

accidental [ˌæksɪ'dentl] *adj* [meeting, discovery] zufällig.

accidentally [ˌæksɪ'dentəlɪ] *adv* [meet, find, discover] zufällig.

accident-prone *adj*: **he is accident-prone** er ist vom Pech verfolgt.

acclaim [ə'kleɪm] ◇ *n* Anerkennung *die*, Beifall *der*. ◇ *vt* feiern.

acclimatize [ə'klaɪmətaɪz], **-ise** [ə'klaɪmətaɪz], **acclimate** *US* ['ækləmeɪt] *vi*: **to acclimatize (to sthg)** sich (in etw *(D)*) akklimatisieren.

accommodate [ə'kɒmədeɪt] *vt* - **1.** [subj: building, car] Platz bieten für; [subj: person] unter|bringen - **2.** [oblige] entgegegen|kommen *(+ D)*, berücksichtigen.

accommodating [ə'kɒmədeɪtɪŋ] *adj* entgegenkommend.

accommodation *UK* [əˌkɒmə'deɪʃn] *n* [lodging] Unterkunft *die*.

accommodations *US* [əˌkɒmə'deɪʃnz] *npl* = **accommodation**.

accompany [ə'kʌmpənɪ] *vt* - **1.** [gen] begleiten - **2.** MUS: **to accompany sb (on sthg)** jn (auf etw *(D)*) begleiten.

accomplice [ə'kʌmplɪs] *n* Komplize *der*, -zin *die*.

accomplish [ə'kʌmplɪʃ] *vt* [achieve] erreichen, leisten; [complete] vollbringen.

accomplishment [ə'kʌmplɪʃmənt] *n* - **1.** [feat, deed] Leistung *die* - **2.** [action] Vollendung *die*. ◆ **accomplishments** *npl* Fähigkeiten *Pl*.

accord [ə'kɔːd] *n* - **1.** [settlement] Einigung *die* - **2.** [agreement, harmony]: **to be in accord (with sthg)** (mit etw) im Einklang sein; **to do sthg of one's own accord** etw aus eigenem Antrieb tun, etw aus freien Stücken tun.

accordance [ə'kɔːdəns] *n*: **in accordance with** entsprechend *(+ D)*, gemäß *(+ D)*; **in accordance with your wishes** Ihren Wünschen entsprechend.

according to [ə'kɔːdɪŋ-] *prep* - **1.** [as stated or shown by] zufolge *(+ D)*, laut *(+ D)*; **to go according to plan** nach Plan gehen - **2.** [with regard to, depending on] entsprechend *(+ D)*.

accordingly [ə'kɔːdɪŋlɪ] *adv* - **1.** [appropriately] (dem)entsprechend - **2.** [consequently] folglich, demgemäß.

accordion [ə'kɔːdjən] *n* Akkordeon *das*.

accost [ə'kɒst] *vt* belästigen.

account [ə'kaʊnt] *n* - **1.** [with bank, building society] Konto *das* - **2.** [with shop, company] Kundenkonto *das* - **3.** [report] Bericht *der* - **4.** *phr*: **to take account of sthg, to take sthg into account** etw berücksichtigen; **to be of no account** ohne Bedeutung sein; **on no account** auf keinen Fall. ◆ **accounts** *npl* [of business] Buchführung *die*. ◆ **by all accounts** *adv* nach allem, was man hört. ◆ **on account of** *prep* aufgrund *(+ G)*. ◆ **account for** *vt insep* - **1.** [explain] erklären; **all the missing people have been accounted for** der Verbleib aller vermissten Personen ist geklärt worden - **2.** [represent] aus|machen.

accountable [ə'kaʊntəbl] *adj*: **accountable (for sb/sthg)** verantwortlich (für jn/etw).

accountancy [ə'kaʊntənsɪ] *n* Buchhaltung *die*, Buchführung *die*.

accountant [ə'kaʊntənt] *n* Buchhalter *der*, -in *die*.

accounts department *n* Buchhaltungsabteilung *die*, Buchführungsabteilung *die*.

accrue [ə'kruː] *vi* FIN sich an|sammeln.

accumulate [ə'kjuːmjʊleɪt] ◇ *vt* [money, belongings] an|häufen; [evidence] sammeln. ◇ *vi* [money, belongings] sich an|häufen.

accuracy ['ækjʊrəsɪ] *n* - **1.** [truth, correctness] Korrektheit *die*, Richtigkeit *die* - **2.** [precision - of weapon, marksman] Präzision *die*; [- of typing, typist] Fehlerlosigkeit *die*; [- of figures, estimate] Genauigkeit *die*.

accurate ['ækjʊrət] *adj* - **1.** [true] korrekt, richtig - **2.** [precise - weapon, marksman] präzis(e); [- typing, typist] fehlerlos; [- figures, estimate] genau.

accurately ['ækjʊrətlɪ] *adv* - **1.** [truthfully] korrekt, richtig - **2.** [precisely - aim, estimate] genau; [- type] fehlerlos.

accusation [ˌækjuː'zeɪʃn] *n* - **1.** [charge, criticism] Vorwurf *der*, Beschuldigung *die* - **2.** LAW [formal charge] Anklage *die*.

accuse [ə'kjuːz] *vt* - **1.** [charge, criticize]: **to accuse sb of sthg** jn einer Sache *(G)* beschuldigen; **to accuse sb of doing sthg** jn beschuldigen, etw getan zu haben - **2.** LAW: **to be accused of murder/fraud** des Mordes/Betrugs angeklagt sein *OR* werden; **to be accused of doing sthg** beschuldigt werden, etw getan zu haben.

accused [ə'kjuːzd] *n* LAW: **the accused** der/die Angeklagte.

accustomed [ə'kʌstəmd] *adj*: **to be accustomed to sthg** etw gewohnt sein, an etw *(A)* gewöhnt sein; **to be accustomed to doing sthg** gewohnt sein, etw zu tun.

ace [eɪs] *n* [gen] Ass *das*.

ache [eɪk] ◇ *n* [dull pain] (dumpfer) Schmerz. ◇ *vi* - **1.** [be painful] weh tun, schmerzen; **my head aches** mein Kopf tut mir weh - **2.** *fig* [want]: **to be aching for sthg** sich nach etw sehnen; **to be aching to do sthg** sich danach sehnen, etw zu tun.

achieve [ə'tʃiːv] *vt* [success] erzielen; [goal] erreichen; [ambition] verwirklichen; [victory] erringen; [fame] erlangen.

achievement [ə'tʃiːvmənt] *n* [feat, deed] Leistung *die*.

acid ['æsɪd] *n* - **1.** Säure *die* - **2.** *inf* [LSD] Acid *das*.

acid rain *n* saurer Regen.

acknowledge [ək'nɒlɪdʒ] *vt* - **1.** [accept, admit] ein|gestehen, zu|geben - **2.** [recognize]: **to acknowledge sb as sthg** jn als etw an|erkennen - **3.** [letter]: **to acknowledge (receipt of) sthg** den Eingang *OR* Empfang von etw bestätigen - **4.** [greet] grüßen.

acknowledg(e)ment [ək'nɒlɪdʒmənt] *n* - **1.** [thanks] Anerkennung *die* - **2.** [acceptance] Eingeständnis *das* - **3.** [letter] Empfangsbestätigung *die*. ◆ **acknowledg(e)ments** *npl* [in book] Danksagungen *Pl*.

acne ['æknɪ] *n* Akne *die*.

acorn ['eɪkɔːn] *n* Eichel *die*.

acoustic [ə'kuːstɪk] *adj* akustisch. ◆ **acoustics** *npl* [of room] Akustik *die*.

acquaint [ə'kweɪnt] *vt*: **to acquaint sb with sthg** [information] jn über etw *(A)* informieren; [method, technique] jn mit etw vertraut machen; **to be acquainted with sb** mit jm bekannt sein.

acquaintance [ə'kweɪntəns] *n* [personal associate] Bekannte *der*, *die*.

acquire [ə'kwaɪəʳ] *vt* - **1.** [house, company, book] erwerben; [information, document] erhalten - **2.** [habit] an|nehmen; [skill, knowledge] erwerben; **to acquire a taste for sthg** Gefallen an etw *(D)* finden.

acquisitive [ə'kwɪzɪtɪv] *adj* habgierig.

acquit [ə'kwɪt] *vt* - **1.** LAW: **to acquit sb (of sthg)** jn (von etw) frei|sprechen - **2.** [conduct]: **to acquit o.s. well/badly** seine Sache gut/schlecht machen.

acquittal [ə'kwɪtl] *n* LAW Freispruch *der*.

acre ['eɪkəʳ] *n* ≃ Morgen *der*, *= 4047,9 m²*.

acrid ['ækrɪd] *adj* [smoke, smell] beißend; [taste] bitter.

acrimonious [ˌækrɪ'məʊnjəs] *adj* erbittert.

acrobat ['ækrəbæt] *n* Akrobat *der*, -in *die*.

across [ə'krɒs] ◇ *adv* - **1.** [to the other side] hinüber; [from the other side] herüber - **2.** [in measurements] breit; [of circle] im Durchmesser - **3.** [in crossword] waag(e)recht. ◇ *prep* - **1.** [from one side to the other] über *(+ A)* - **2.** [on the other side of] auf der anderen Seite *(+ G)*. ◆ **across from** *prep* gegenüber von.

acrylic [ə'krɪlɪk] ◇ *adj* Acryl-, aus Acryl. ◇ *n* Acryl *das*.

act [ækt] ◇ *n* - **1.** [action, deed] Tat *die*, Akt *der*; **an act of mercy** ein Gnadenakt - **2.** LAW Gesetz *das* - **3.** [of play, opera] Akt *der*; [in cabaret *etc*] Nummer *die* - **4.** *fig* [pretence] Komödie *die*, Schau *die*; **to put on an act** Komödie spielen - **5.** *phr*: **get your act together!** reiß dich mal am Riemen! ◇ *vi* - **1.** [take action] handeln - **2.** [behave] sich benehmen - **3.** [in play, film] spielen - **4.** *fig* [pretend] Komödie spielen; **to act innocent** unschuldig tun - **5.** [take effect] wirken - **6.** [fulfil function]: **to act as sthg** als etw fungieren. ◇ *vt* [role] spielen.

acting ['æktɪŋ] ◇ *adj* [interim] stellvertretend. ◇ *n (U)* [performance] Spiel *das*; [profession] Schauspielerei *die*.

action ['ækʃn] *n* - **1.** *(U)* [fact of doing sthg] Handeln *das*; **to take action** etwas unternehmen; **to put sthg into action** etw in die Tat um|setzen; **in action** [person] in Aktion; [machine] in Betrieb; **out of action** [person] nicht in Aktion; [machine] außer Betrieb - **2.** [deed] Tat *die* - **3.** *(U)* [in battle, war] Gefecht *das* - **4.** LAW [trial] Prozess *der*; [charge] Klage *die* - **5.** [in play, book, film] Handlung *die* - **6.** [effect] Wirkung *die*.

action replay *n* Wiederholung *die*.

activate ['æktɪveɪt] *vt* [device, machine] in Gang setzen; [alarm] ausllösen.

active ['æktɪv] *adj* aktiv; [mind, interest] rege.

actively ['æktɪvlɪ] *adv* aktiv.

activity [æk'tɪvətɪ] *n* - **1.** *(U)* [movement, action] Geschäftigkeit *die* - **2.** [pastime, hobby] Betätigung *die*. ◆ **activities** *npl* Aktivitäten *Pl*.

actor ['æktəʳ] *n* Schauspieler *der*.

actress ['æktrɪs] *n* Schauspielerin *die*.

actual ['æktʃʊəl] *adj* eigentlich; [cost, amount, cause] tatsächlich, wirklich.

actually ['æktʃʊəlɪ] *adv* - **1.** [really, in truth] wirklich - **2.** [by the way] übrigens.

acumen ['ækjʊmen] *n*: **business acumen** Geschäftssinn *der*.

acupuncture ['ækjʊpʌŋktʃəʳ] *n* Akupunktur *die*.

acute [ə'kjuːt] *adj* - **1.** [pain, shortage] akut; [embarrassment, anxiety] groß - **2.** [observer, mind] scharf; [analysis, judgement, person] scharfsinnig - **3.** [sight] scharf; [hearing, sense of smell] fein - **4.** MATHS spitz.

ad [æd] (*abbr of* **advertisement**) *n inf* [in newspaper] Inserat *das*, Annonce *die*; [on TV] Werbung *die*; [in shop window] Angebot *das*.

AD (*abbr of* **Anno Domini**) A. D.

adamant ['ædəmənt] *adj*: **to be adamant (about sthg)** (in Bezug auf etw *(A)*) unnachgiebig sein; **to be adamant that...** darauf bestehen, dass...

Adam's apple ['ædəmz-] *n* Adamsapfel *der*.

adapt [ə'dæpt] ◇ *vt* - **1.** [adjust, modify] anlpassen; [machine, system] umlstellen; [text, materials] umlarbeiten - **2.** [book, play] adaptieren. ◇ *vi*: **to adapt to sthg** sich etw *(D)* anlpassen; [idea] sich mit etw anlfreunden.

adaptable [ə'dæptəbl] *adj* anpassungsfähig.

adapter, adaptor [ə'dæptəʳ] *n* [for foreign plug] Adapter *der*; [for several plugs] Mehrfachstecker *der*.

add [æd] *vt* - **1.** [gen]: **to add sthg (to)** etw hinzulfügen (zu) - **2.** [total] addieren. ◆ **add on** *vt sep* - **1.** [build on, attach]: **to add sthg on (to sthg)** etw (an etw *(A)*) anlbauen - **2.** [include]: **to add sthg on (to sthg)** etw (zu etw) hinzulfügen; [number, amount] etw (zu etw) dazulrechnen. ◆ **add to** *vt insep* [increase] vergrößern, vermehren. ◆ **add up** *vt sep* [total up] zusammenlrechnen. ◆ **add up to** *vt insep* [represent] ergeben.

adder ['ædəʳ] *n* [snake] Viper *die*.

addict ['ædɪkt] *n* - **1.** [taking drugs] Süchtige *der, die*, Abhängige *der, die* - **2.** *fig* [fan]: **to be a chocolate addict** süchtig nach Schokolade sein; **to be an exercise addict** ein Sportfanatiker sein.

addicted [ə'dɪktɪd] *adj liter* & *fig*: **addicted (to)** süchtig (nach).

addiction [ə'dɪkʃn] *n liter* & *fig*: **addiction (to)** Sucht *die* (nach).

addictive [ə'dɪktɪv] *adj*: **to be addictive** [drug] süchtig machen; *fig* [exercise, food, TV] zu einer Sucht werden können.

addition [ə'dɪʃn] *n* - **1.** MATHS Addition *die* - **2.** [extra thing] Zusatz *der*, Ergänzung *die* - **3.** [act of adding] Hinzufügen *das*; **in addition** außerdem; **in addition to** zusätzlich zu.

additional [ə'dɪʃənl] *adj* zusätzlich.

additive ['ædɪtɪv] *n* Zusatz *der*.

address [ə'dres] ◇ *n* - **1.** [location] Adresse *die* - **2.** [speech] Ansprache *die*. ◇ *vt* - **1.** [letter, parcel] adressieren - **2.** [meeting, conference] eine Ansprache halten bei - **3.** [person] anlsprechen; **to address sb as sthg** jn etw nennen.

address book *n* [gen & COMPUT] Adressbuch *das*.

adenoids ['ædɪnɔɪdz] *npl* Polypen *Pl*.

adept ['ædept] *adj*: **to be adept (at sthg)** (in etw *(D)*) geschickt sein.

adequate ['ædɪkwət] *adj* - **1.** [sufficient] ausreichend - **2.** [good enough] adäquat.

adhere [əd'hɪəʳ] *vi* - **1.** [stick]: **to adhere (to)** kleben (an *(+ D)*) - **2.** [observe]: **to adhere to sthg** sich an etw *(A)* halten, etw befolgen - **3.** [uphold]: **to adhere to sthg** an etw *(D)* festlhalten.

adhesive [əd'hiːsɪv] ◇ *adj* klebend; **adhesive label** Haftetikett *das*. ◇ *n* Klebstoff *der*.

adhesive tape *n* Klebestreifen *der*.

adjacent [ə'dʒeɪsənt] *adj* angrenzend, Neben-; **to be adjacent to sthg** an etw *(A)* anlgrenzen.

adjective ['ædʒɪktɪv] *n* Adjektiv *das*.

adjoining [ə'dʒɔɪnɪŋ] *adj* angrenzend.

adjourn [ə'dʒɜːn] ◇ *vt*: **to adjourn sthg (until)** etw vertagen (auf *(+ A)*). ◇ *vi* sich vertagen.

adjudicate [ə'dʒuːdɪkeɪt] *vi* als Preisrichter fungieren; **to adjudicate on** OR **upon sthg** entscheiden OR urteilen bei etw.

adjust [ə'dʒʌst] ◇ *vt* regulieren; [settings] einlstellen; [clothing] zurechtlrücken. ◇ *vi*: **to adjust (to sthg)** sich (auf etw *(A)*) einlstellen.

adjustable [ə'dʒʌstəbl] *adj* [machine] regulierbar; [chair] verstellbar.

adjustment [ə'dʒʌstmənt] *n* - **1.** [gen] Regulierung *die*; [of settings] Einstellung *die* - **2.** [to situation]: **adjustment (to)** Anpassung *die* (an *(+ A)*).

ad lib [,æd'lɪb] ◇ *adv* [freely] aus dem Stegreif. ◇ *n* [improvised joke] Stegreifwitz *der*. ◆ **ad-lib** *vi* improvisieren.

administer [əd'mɪnɪstəʳ] *vt* - **1.** [company] verwalten - **2.** [punishment] verhängen; **to administer justice** Recht sprechen - **3.** [drug, medication] verabreichen.

administration [əd,mɪnɪ'streɪʃn] *n* - **1.** [gen] Verwaltung *die* - **2.** [of punishment] Verhängung *die*; **the administration of justice** die Rechtssprechung.

administrative [əd'mɪnɪstrətɪv] *adj* Verwaltungs-, administrativ.

admirable ['ædmərəbl] *adj* [worthy of admiration] bewundernswert; [excellent] großartig.

admiral ['ædmərəl] *n* Admiral *der*.

admiration [,ædmə'reɪʃn] *n* Bewunderung *die*.

admire [əd'maɪəʳ] *vt* bewundern; **to admire sb for sthg** jn wegen etw *(G)* bewundern.

admirer [əd'maɪərəʳ] *n* - **1.** [suitor] Verehrer *der*, -in *die* - **2.** [enthusiast, fan] Bewunderer *der*, -in *die*.

admission [əd'mɪʃn] *n* - **1.** [permission to enter] Zulassung *die*; [to museum *etc*] Eintritt *der* - **2.** [cost of entrance] Eintrittspreis *der* - **3.** [confession - of crime] Geständnis *das*; [- of guilt, mistake] Eingeständnis *das*.

admit [əd'mɪt] ◇ *vt* - **1.** [crime] gestehen; [mistake] ein|gestehen; **to admit that** zugeben, dass; **to admit doing sthg** zu|geben, etw getan zu haben; **to admit defeat** *fig* auf|geben - **2.** [allow to enter] herein|lassen, hinein|lassen; **to be admitted to hospital** *UK* OR **to the hospital** *US* ins Krankenhaus eingeliefert werden - **3.** [allow to join]: **to admit sb (to sthg)** jn (in etw *(A)*) auf|nehmen. ◇ *vi*: **to admit to sthg** etw zu|geben.

admittance [əd'mɪtəns] *n*: **'no admittance'** 'kein Zutritt'.

admittedly [əd'mɪtɪdlɪ] *adv* zugegebenermaßen.

admonish [əd'mɒnɪʃ] *vt fml* ermahnen.

ad nauseam [,æd'nɔ:zɪæm] *adv* bis zum Überdruss.

ado [ə'du:] *n*: **without further** OR **more ado** ohne weitere Umstände.

adolescence [,ædə'lesns] *n* Jugend *die*.

adolescent [,ædə'lesnt] ◇ *adj* - **1.** [teenage] jugendlich - **2.** *pej* [immature] unreif. ◇ *n* [teenager] Jugendliche *der*, Jugendliche *die*.

adopt [ə'dɒpt] *vt* - **1.** [child] adoptieren - **2.** [plan, method] übernehmen; [attitude, mannerism, recommendation] an|nehmen.

adoption [ə'dɒpʃn] *n* - **1.** [of child] Adoption *die* - **2.** *(U)* [of plan, method] Übernahme *die*; [of recommendation] Annahme *die*.

adore [ə'dɔ:ʳ] *vt* über alles lieben; **I adore these chocolate biscuits** ich esse diese Schokoladenkekse für mein Leben gern.

adorn [ə'dɔ:n] *vt* schmücken.

adrenalin [ə'drenəlɪn] *n* Adrenalin *das*.

Adriatic [,eɪdrɪ'ætɪk] *n*: **the Adriatic (Sea)** die Adria.

adrift [ə'drɪft] *adj* [boat, ship] treibend.

adult ['ædʌlt] ◇ *adj* erwachsen; [animal] ausgewachsen; [book, film] für Erwachsene. ◇ *n* [person] Erwachsene *der*, *die*.

adultery [ə'dʌltərɪ] *n (U)* Ehebruch *der*.

advance [əd'vɑ:ns] ◇ *n* - **1.** [of army] Vorrücken *das* - **2.** [improvement, progress] Fortschritt *der* - **3.** [money] Vorschuss *der*. ◇ *comp*: **advance booking** Vorbestellung *die*; **advance payment** Vorauszahlung *die*; **advance warning** Vorwarnung *die*. ◇ *vt* - **1.** [improve - cause] voran|bringen, fördern; [- interest] fördern - **2.** [bring forward in time] vor|verlegen - **3.**: **to advance sb sthg** [money] jm etw vor|schießen. ◇ *vi* - **1.** [go forward - army] vor|rücken - **2.** [improve] Fortschritte machen. ◆ **advances** *npl*: **to make advances to sb** [sexual] bei jm Annäherungsversuche machen. ◆ **in advance** *adv* im Voraus.

advanced [əd'vɑ:nst] *adj* - **1.** [developed - plan] weit entwickelt; [- stage] vorgerückt - **2.** [student, pupil] fortgeschritten.

advantage [əd'vɑ:ntɪdʒ] *n* Vorteil *der*; **to be to one's advantage** für jn von Vorteil sein; **to have** OR **hold the advantage (over sb)** (jm gegenüber) im Vorteil sein; **to take advantage of** aus|nutzen.

advent ['ædvənt] *n* [of invention] Aufkommen *das*; [of period] Beginn *der*. ◆ **Advent** *n* RELIG Advent *der*.

adventure [əd'ventʃəʳ] *n* Abenteuer *das*.

adventure playground *n* Abenteuerspielplatz *der*.

adventurous [əd'ventʃərəs] *adj* - **1.** [person] abenteuerlustig - **2.** [life, project] abenteuerlich.

adverb ['ædvɜ:b] *n* Adverb *das*.

adverse ['ædvɜ:s] *adj* [weather] schlecht; [conditions] ungünstig; [criticism] negativ, nachteilig; [effect] nachteilig.

advert ['ædvɜ:t] *n UK* = **advertisement**.

advertise ['ædvətaɪz] *vt* [job, product] Reklame OR Werbung machen für; **to advertise for sb/sthg** jn/etw per Anzeige suchen.

advertisement [əd'vɜ:tɪsmənt] *n* - **1.** [in newspaper] Inserat *das*; [on TV] Werbung *die*; [in shop window] Angebot *das* - **2.** *fig* [recommendation] Aushängeschild *das*.

advertising ['ædvətaɪzɪŋ] *n (U)* - **1.** [advertisements] Werbung *die*, Reklame *die* - **2.** [industry] Werbebranche *die*.

advice [əd'vaɪs] *n (U)* Rat *der*; **to give sb advice** jm einen Rat geben; **to take sb's advice** js Rat befolgen; **a piece of advice** ein Ratschlag.

advisable [əd'vaɪzəbl] *adj* ratsam.

advise [əd'vaɪz] ◇ *vt* - **1.** [give advice to]: **to advise sb to do sthg** jm raten, etw zu tun; **to advise sb against sthg** jm von etw ab|raten; **to advise sb against doing sthg** jm davon ab|-

raten, etw zu tun - 2. [professionally]: **to advise sb on sthg** jn in etw *(D)* beraten - 3. *fml* [inform]: **to advise sb of sthg** jn über etw *(A)* unterrichten. <> *vi*: **to advise against sthg** von etw ab|raten; **to advise against doing sthg** davon ab|raten, etw zu tun.

advisedly [əd'vaɪzɪdlɪ] *adv* mit Bedacht.

adviser *UK*, **advisor** *US* [əd'vaɪzəʳ] *n* Berater *der*, -in *die*.

advisory [əd'vaɪzərɪ] *adj* [group, organization] beratend.

advocate <> *n* ['ædvəkət] - 1. *Scotland* LAW (Rechts)anwalt *der*, -wältin *die* - 2. [supporter] Befürworter *der*, -in *die*, Verfechter *der*, -in *die*. <> *vt* ['ædvəkeɪt] befürworten.

Aegean [iː'dʒiːən] *n*: **the Aegean (Sea)** die Ägäis.

aeon *UK*, **eon** *US* ['iːən] *n* Äon *der*; *fig* [very long time] Ewigkeit *die*.

aerial ['eərɪəl] <> *adj* Luft-; **aerial photograph** Luftaufnahme *die*. <> *n UK* [antenna] Antenne *die*.

aerobics [eə'rəʊbɪks] *n (U)* Aerobic *das*.

aerodynamic [ˌeərəʊdaɪ'næmɪk] *adj* aerodynamisch. ◆ **aerodynamics** <> *n (U)* [science] Aerodynamik *die*. <> *npl* [aerodynamic qualities] Aerodynamik *die*.

aeroplane *UK* ['eərəpleɪn], **airplane** *US n* Flugzeug *das*.

aerosol ['eərəsɒl] *n* Spraydose *die*.

aesthetic, esthetic *US* [iːs'θetɪk] *adj* ästhetisch.

afar [ə'fɑːʳ] *adv*: **from afar** aus der Ferne.

affable ['æfəbl] *adj* umgänglich.

affair [ə'feəʳ] *n* - 1. [event, concern] Angelegenheit *die*, Sache *die* - 2. [extramarital relationship] Verhältnis *das*.

affect [ə'fekt] *vt* - 1. [influence] beeinflussen; [health] beeinträchtigen - 2. [move emotionally] berühren - 3. [feign] vor|täuschen.

affection [ə'fekʃn] *n* Zuneigung *die*.

affectionate [ə'fekʃnət] *adj* liebevoll.

affirm [ə'fɜːm] *vt* - 1. [declare] versichern - 2. [confirm] bestätigen.

affix [ə'fɪks] *vt* [stamp] kleben.

afflict [ə'flɪkt] *vt* plagen; **to be afflicted with sthg** von etw geplagt sein.

affluence ['æfluəns] *n* Wohlstand *der*.

affluent ['æfluənt] *adj* wohlhabend.

afford [ə'fɔːd] *vt* - 1. [gen]: **to be able to afford sthg** sich *(D)* etw leisten können; **to be able to afford the time (to do sthg)** die Zeit haben (etw zu tun); **I can't afford two weeks off work** ich kann mir zwei Wochen Urlaub nicht leisten; **we can't afford to let this happen** wir können es uns nicht leisten, dies geschehen zu lassen - 2. *fml* [provide - protection, shelter] gewähren; [- assistance] leisten.

affront [ə'frʌnt] <> *n* Beleidigung *die*, Affront *der*. <> *vt* beleidigen.

Afghanistan [æf'gænɪstæn] *n* Afghanistan *nt*.

afield [ə'fɪəld] *adv*: **far afield** weit weg.

afloat [ə'fləʊt] *adj* - 1. [above water] schwimmend - 2. *fig* [out of debt]: **to stay afloat** sich über Wasser halten.

afoot [ə'fʊt] *adj*: **there's something afoot** da ist irgendetwas im Gange.

afraid [ə'freɪd] *adj* - 1. [frightened, reluctant]: **to be afraid (of sb/sthg)** (vor jm/etw) Angst haben; **to be afraid of doing** OR **to do sthg** Angst (davor) haben, etw zu tun - 2. [in apologies]: **I'm afraid we can't come** wir können leider nicht kommen; **I'm afraid so/not** leider ja/nicht.

afresh [ə'freʃ] *adv*: **to start afresh** noch einmal von vorn an|fangen; **to look at sthg afresh** etw erneut betrachten.

Africa ['æfrɪkə] *n* Afrika *nt*.

African ['æfrɪkən] <> *adj* afrikanisch. <> *n* Afrikaner *der*, -in *die*.

aft [ɑːft] *adv* achtern; **to go aft** nach achtern gehen.

after ['ɑːftəʳ] <> *prep* - 1. [in time] nach; **day after day** Tag für Tag; **time after time** immer wieder; **the day after tomorrow** übermorgen; **the week after next** übernächste Woche - 2. [in order] nach; **after you!** nach Ihnen!; **shut the door after you** schließe die Tür hinter dir - 3. [in search of]: **to be after sb/sthg** jn/etw suchen - 4. [with the name of] nach; **he is named after his father** er ist nach seinem Vater benannt - 5. [directed at sb moving away]: **to call (sthg) after sb** jm (etw) nach|rufen - 6. [enquiring]: **to ask after sb/sthg** sich nach jm/etw erkundigen - 7. [telling the time] nach; **a quarter after ten** *US* Viertel nach zehn. <> *adv* danach. <> *conj* nachdem; **I came after he had gone** ich kam, nachdem er gegangen war. ◆ **afters** *npl UK inf* Nachtisch *der*. ◆ **after all** *adv* - 1. [in spite of everything] doch - 2. [it should be remembered] schließlich.

aftereffects ['ɑːftərɪˌfekts] *npl* [of war, storm] Folgen *Pl*.

afterlife ['ɑːftəlaɪf] (*pl* **-lives** [-laɪvz]) *n* Leben *das* nach dem Tode.

aftermath ['ɑːftəmæθ] *n* Nachwirkungen *Pl*; **in the aftermath of sthg** nach etw.

afternoon [ˌɑːftə'nuːn] *n* Nachmittag *der*; **in the afternoon** am Nachmittag; **good afternoon** guten Tag. ◆ **afternoons** *adv esp US* nachmittags.

after-sales service *n* Kundendienst *der*.

aftershave ['ɑːftəʃeɪv] *n* Rasierwasser *das*.

aftersun (lotion) ['ɑːftəsʌn-] *n* Aftersunlotion *die*.

aftertaste ['ɑːftəteɪst] *n liter & fig* Nachgeschmack *der*.

afterthought ['ɑːftəθɔːt] *n* nachträgliche Idee.

afterwards ['ɑːftəwədz], **afterward** *esp US* ['ɑːftəwəd] *adv* danach; **three weeks afterwards** drei Wochen später.

again [ə'gen] *adv* - **1.** [one more time] wieder; **again and again** immer wieder; **time and again** immer wieder; **never again** nie wieder; **all over again** noch einmal von vorn - **2.** [once more as before] wieder; **he was ill, but he's well again now** er ist krank gewesen, aber jetzt ist er wieder gesund - **3.** [asking for repetition] wieder, noch einmal; **what is his name again?** wie heißt er noch gleich? - **4.** [besides] außerdem; **again, we must remember his age** außerdem müssen wir sein Alter berücksichtigen - **5.** *phr*: **half as much again** noch mal halb so viel; **(twice) as much again** doppelt so viel; **come again?** *inf* wie bitte?; **then** OR **there again** andererseits.

against [ə'genst] <> *prep* - **1.** [gen] gegen; **he was leaning against the wall** er stand an die Wand gelehnt; **against the law** rechtswidrig - **2.** [in contrast to]: **as against** verglichen mit. <> *adv*: **are you for or against?** bist du dafür oder dagegen?

age [eɪdʒ] (*cont* **ageing** OR **aging**) <> *n* - **1.** [gen] Alter *das*; **she's 20 years of age** sie ist 20 Jahre alt; **he's about my age** er ist ungefähr mein Alter; **he was still writing at the age of 80** mit 80 schrieb er immer noch; **what age are you?** wie alt sind Sie?; **to come of age** volljährig werden; **to be under age** minderjährig sein - **2.** [of history] Zeitalter *das*. <> *vt* altern lassen. <> *vi* [person] altern; [wine] reifen. ◆ **ages** *npl* [a long time]: **ages ago** schon ewig her; **I haven't seen her for ages** ich habe sie eine Ewigkeit nicht gesehen.

aged <> *adj* - **1.** [eɪdʒd] [of the stated age]: **a girl aged 5** ein fünfjähriges Mädchen - **2.** ['eɪdʒɪd] [very old] betagt. <> *npl* ['eɪdʒɪd]: **the aged** die alten Menschen.

age group *n* Altersgruppe *die*.

agency ['eɪdʒənsɪ] *n* - **1.** [business] Agentur *die* - **2.** [organization] Organisation *die*.

agenda [ə'dʒendə] (*pl* **-s**) *n* Tagesordnung *die*; **what's on the agenda for today?** was steht heute auf dem Programm?

agent ['eɪdʒənt] *n* - **1.** COMM [representative] Agent *der*, -in *die* - **2.** [spy] Agent *der*, -in *die*.

aggravate ['ægrəveɪt] *vt* - **1.** [make worse] verschlimmern - **2.** [annoy] ärgern.

aggregate ['ægrɪgət] <> *adj* Gesamt-; **aggregate earnings** Gesamtverdienst *der*. <> *n* [total] Gesamtsumme *die*; **on aggregate** insgesamt.

aggressive [ə'gresɪv] *adj* - **1.** [belligerent - person] aggressiv - **2.** [forceful - person] energisch; [- campaign] aggressiv.

aggrieved [ə'griːvd] *adj* gekränkt.

aghast [ə'gɑːst] *adj*: **aghast (at)** entsetzt (über *(+ A)*).

agile [*UK* 'ædʒaɪl, *US* 'ædʒəl] *adj* [person] beweglich, agil; [body] gelenkig.

agitate ['ædʒɪteɪt] <> *vt* - **1.** [disturb, worry] auf|regen - **2.** [shake] schütteln. <> *vi* [campaign actively]: **to agitate for/against sthg** für/gegen etw Propaganda machen.

AGM (*abbr of* **annual general meeting**) *n UK* JHV *die*.

agnostic [æg'nɒstɪk] <> *adj* agnostisch. <> *n* Agnostiker *der*, -in *die*.

ago [ə'gəʊ] *adv* vor; **that was a long time ago** das ist schon lange her; **three days/years ago** vor drei Tagen/Jahren.

agog [ə'gɒg] *adj* gespannt.

agonizing ['ægənaɪzɪŋ] *adj* qualvoll.

agony ['ægənɪ] *n* Qual *die*; **to be in agony** Qualen erleiden.

agony aunt *n UK inf* Kummerkastentante *die*.

agree [ə'griː] <> *vi* - **1.** [concur - two or more people] einer Meinung sein; [- one person] der gleichen Meinung sein; *phrase*: **to agree with sb/sthg** jm/etw zulstimmen; **to agree on sthg** sich auf etw *(A)* einigen - **2.** [consent] einlwilligen; **to agree to sthg** sich mit etw einverstanden erklären - **3.** [statements] übereinlstimmen - **4.** [food]: **curries don't agree with me** Currygerichte bekommen mir nicht - **5.** GRAM: **to agree (with)** übereinlstimmen (mit). <> *vt* - **1.** [price, terms] vereinbaren - **2.** [concur]: **I agree that...** ich bin auch der Meinung, dass...; **it was agreed that...** man einigte sich darauf, dass... - **3.** [consent]: **to agree to do sthg** sich bereit OR einverstanden erklären, etw zu tun - **4.** [concede]: **to agree that...** zugeben, dass...

agreeable [ə'grɪəbl] *adj* - **1.** [weather, experience] angenehm; [person] nett - **2.** [willing]: **to be agreeable to sthg** mit etw einverstanden sein.

agreed [ə'griːd] *adj*: **to be agreed on sthg** sich über etw *(A)* einig sein.

agreement [ə'griːmənt] *n* - **1.** [accord] Einigkeit *die*; **to be in agreement with sb/sthg** mit jm/etw übereinlstimmen - **2.** [settlement] Vereinbarung *die*; [contract] Vertrag *der* - **3.** [consent] Einwilligung *die* - **4.** GRAM Übereinstimmung *die*.

agricultural [,ægrɪ'kʌltʃərəl] *adj* landwirtschaftlich.

agriculture ['ægrɪkʌltʃə'] *n* Landwirtschaft *die*.

aground [ə'graʊnd] *adv*: **to run aground** auf Grund laufen, stranden.

ahead [ə'hed] *adv* - **1.** [in front]: **the road ahead** die Straße vor uns/ihnen/*etc*; **straight ahead** geradeaus - **2.** [in competition, game]: **to**

be ahead führen - 3. [indicating success]: **to get ahead** vorwärts kommen - 4. [in time]: **to plan ahead** vorauslplanen; **the weeks ahead are going to be difficult** die nächsten Wochen werden schwierig sein. ◆ **ahead of** *prep* - 1. [in front of] vor *(+ D)*; **the road ahead of them** die Straße vor ihnen - 2. [in competition, game]: **they are 10 points ahead of the other teams** sie sind den anderen Mannschaften um 10 Punkte voraus - 3. [in time] vor; **ahead of schedule** früher als geplant.

aid [eɪd] *vt* - 1. [help] unterstützen - 2. LAW: **to aid and abet** Beihilfe leisten *(+ D)*.

AIDS, Aids [eɪdz] (*abbr of* **acquired immune deficiency syndrome**) <> *n* Aids *das*. <> *comp*: **AIDS patient** Aidspatient *der*, -in *die*.

ailing ['eɪlɪŋ] *adj liter* & *fig* kränkelnd.

ailment ['eɪlmənt] *n* Leiden *das*.

aim [eɪm] <> *n* - 1. [objective] Ziel *das* - 2. [in firing gun, arrow] Zielen *das*; **to take aim at sthg** auf etw *(A)* zielen. <> *vt* - 1.: **to aim a gun at sb/sthg** mit einem Gewehr auf jn/etw zielen; **to aim a camera at sb/sthg** eine Kamera auf jn/etw richten - 2. [plan, programme]: **to be aimed at doing sthg** darauf ausgerichtet sein, etw zu tun - 3. [remark, criticism]: **to be aimed at sb** gegen jn gerichtet sein. <> *vi* - 1. [point weapon]: **to aim (at)** zielen (auf *(+ A)*) - 2. [intend]: **to aim at** OR **for sthg** etw anlstreben; **to aim to do sthg** vorlhaben, etw zu tun.

aimless ['eɪmlɪs] *adj* [person, life] ziellos; [task, activity] planlos.

ain't [eɪnt] *inf abbr of* **am not**, **are not**, **is not**, **have not**, **has not**.

air [eəʳ] <> *n* - 1. [gen] Luft *die*; **to throw sthg into the air** etw in die Luft werfen; **by air** [travel] mit dem Flugzeug; **to be (up) in the air** *fig* ungewiss sein - 2. [look] Aussehen *das*; [facial expression] Miene *die* - 3. RADIO & TV: **to be on the air** [programme] gesendet werden. <> *comp* Luft-. <> *vt* - 1. [washing] nachtrocknen lassen - 2. [room, bed] lüften - 3. [feelings, opinions] äußern - 4. [broadcast] senden. <> *vi* [washing] nachltrocknen.

air bag *n* AUT Airbag *der*.

airbase ['eəbeɪs] *n* Luftstützpunkt *der*.

airbed ['eəbed] *n UK* Luftmatratze *die*.

airborne ['eəbɔːn] *adj* - 1. [troops, regiment] Luftlande- - 2. [plane] in der Luft.

air-conditioned [-kən'dɪʃnd] *adj* klimatisiert.

air-conditioning [-kən'dɪʃnɪŋ] *n* [device] Klimaanlage *die*; [process] Klimatisierung *die*.

aircraft ['eəkrɑːft] (*pl inv*) *n* Flugzeug *das*.

aircraft carrier *n* Flugzeugträger *der*.

airfield ['eəfiːld] *n* Flugplatz *der*.

airforce ['eəfɔːs] *n* Luftwaffe *die*.

air freshener [-ˌfreʃnəʳ] *n* Raumspray *das*.

airgun ['eəgʌn] *n* Luftgewehr *das*.

airhostess ['eəˌhəʊstɪs] *n* Stewardess *die*.

airlift ['eəlɪft] <> *n* Luftbrücke *die*. <> *vt* über eine Luftbrücke befördern.

airline ['eəlaɪn] *n* Fluglinie *die*.

airliner ['eəlaɪnəʳ] *n* Verkehrsflugzeug *das*.

airmail ['eəmeɪl] *n* Luftpost *die*; **by airmail** mit OR per Luftpost.

airplane ['eəpleɪn] *n US* = **aeroplane**.

airport ['eəpɔːt] *n* Flughafen *der*.

air raid *n* Luftangriff *der*.

air rifle *n* Luftgewehr *das*.

airsick ['eəsɪk] *adj*: **I often get airsick** im Flugzeug wird mir leicht übel.

airspace ['eəspeɪs] *n* Luftraum *der*.

air steward *n* Steward *der*.

airstrip ['eəstrɪp] *n* Start- und Landebahn *die*.

air terminal *n* Terminal *der ODER das*.

airtight ['eətaɪt] *adj* luftdicht.

air-traffic controller *n* Fluglotse *der*, -sin *die*.

airy ['eərɪ] *adj* - 1. [room] luftig - 2. [notions] abstrus; [promises] vage - 3. [nonchalant] lässig, nonchalant.

aisle [aɪl] *n* - 1. [in church - central] Mittelgang *der*; [- at side] Seitenschiff *das* - 2. [in plane, theatre, shop] Gang *der*.

ajar [ə'dʒɑːʳ] *adj* angelehnt.

aka (*abbr of* **also known as**) alias.

akin [ə'kɪn] *adj*: **akin to** vergleichbar mit.

alacrity [ə'lækrətɪ] *n fml* [eagerness] Eifer *der*; **she accepted our offer with alacrity** sie nahm unser Angebot ohne zu zögern an.

alarm [ə'lɑːm] <> *n* - 1. [fear] Beunruhigung *die* - 2. [device] Alarmanlage *die*; **to raise** OR **sound the alarm** [by activating device] Alarm geben; [by shouting] Alarm schlagen. <> *vt* [scare] beunruhigen, alarmieren.

alarm clock *n* Wecker *der*.

alarming [ə'lɑːmɪŋ] *adj* beunruhigend.

alas [ə'læs] *excl liter* leider.

Albania [æl'beɪnjə] *n* Albanien *nt*.

Albanian [æl'beɪnjən] <> *adj* albanisch. <> *n* [person] Albaner *der*, -in *die*.

albeit [ɔːl'biːɪt] *conj fml* wenn auch.

albino [æl'biːnəʊ] (*pl* **-s**) *n* Albino *der*.

album ['ælbəm] *n* Album *das*.

alcohol ['ælkəhɒl] *n* Alkohol *der*.

alcoholic [ˌælkə'hɒlɪk] <> *adj* [drink] alkoholisch. <> *n* Alkoholiker *der*, -in *die*.

alcove ['ælkəʊv] *n* [in room] Alkoven *der*; [in wall] Nische *die*.

ale [eɪl] *n* Ale *das*.

alert [ə'lɜːt] <> *adj* - 1. [vigilant] wachsam - 2. [perceptive] aufmerksam; [as character trait] aufgeweckt - 3. [aware]: **to be alert to sthg** sich *(D)* einer Sache *(G)* bewusst sein. <> *n* Alarm *der*; **on the alert** [watchful] auf der Hut;

MIL in Gefechtsbereitschaft. ◇ *vt* - **1.** [police, fire brigade] alarmieren; [to imminent danger] warnen - **2.** [make aware]: **to alert sb to sthg** jm etw bewusst machen.

A level (*abbr of* **Advanced level**) *n einzelne Prüfung des Schulabschlusses weiterführender Schulen in England, Wales und Nordirland.*

alfresco [æl'freskəʊ] *adj* & *adv* im Freien.

algae ['ældʒiː] *npl* Algen *Pl.*

algebra ['ældʒɪbrə] *n* Algebra *die.*

Algeria [æl'dʒɪərɪə] *n* Algerien *nt.*

alias ['eɪlɪəs] (*pl* **-es**) ◇ *adv* alias. ◇ *n* Deckname *der.*

alibi ['ælɪbaɪ] *n* Alibi *das.*

alien ['eɪljən] ◇ *adj* - **1.** [foreign] ausländisch - **2.** [from outer space] außerirdisch - **3.** [unfamiliar] fremd. ◇ *n* - **1.** [from outer space] Außerirdische *der, die* - **2.** LAW [foreigner] Ausländer *der*, -in *die.*

alienate ['eɪljəneɪt] *vt* [voters, supporters] verärgern, entfremden.

alight [ə'laɪt] (*pt & pp* **-ed** OR **alit**) ◇ *adj*: **to be alight** brennen; **to set sthg alight** etw an|zünden. ◇ *vi fml* - **1.** [bird, insect] sich nieder|lassen - **2.** [from train, bus] aus|steigen.

align [ə'laɪn] *vt* [line up] aus|richten.

alike [ə'laɪk] *adj* & *adv* [similar] ähnlich; [identical] gleich; **to look alike** [similar] ähnlich aus|sehen; [identical] gleich aus|sehen.

alimony ['ælɪmənɪ] *n* Unterhaltszahlung *die.*

alive [ə'laɪv] *adj* [living, lively] lebendig; **is he still alive?** lebt er noch?; **to keep a tradition alive** eine Tradition aufrecht|erhalten.

alkali ['ælkəlaɪ] (*pl* **-s** OR **-es**) *n* Alkali *das.*

all [ɔːl] ◇ *adj* - **1.** [the whole of with sg noun] ganze; **all the money** das ganze Geld; **all the time** immer; **all day/evening** den ganzen Tag/Abend; **all his life** sein ganzes Leben lang - **2.** [every one of with pl noun] alle(r) (s); **all the people** alle Menschen; **all three died** alle drei starben; **at all hours** zu jeder Tages- und Nachtzeit. ◇ *pron* - **1.** [everything]: **all of the cake** der ganze Kuchen; **is that all?** [in shop] ist das alles?; **she ate it all, she ate all of it** sie aß alles auf; **it's all gone** es ist nichts mehr da - **2.** [everybody] alle; **all of us went, we all went** wir sind alle gegangen - **3.** *(with superl)*: **the best of all** der/die/das Allerbeste; **the biggest of all** der/die/das Allergrößte; **he is the cleverest of all** er ist der Klügste von allen; **and, best of all,...** und (was) das Beste ist,... ◇ *adv* - **1.** [completely] ganz; **all alone** ganz allein; **dressed all in red** ganz in rot gekleidet; **the water spilled all over the carpet** das Wasser ergoss sich über den Teppichboden; **I'd forgotten all about that** das hatte ich völlig vergessen; **all told** [in total] insgesamt - **2.** [in scores] beide; **it's two all** es steht zwei beide - **3.** *(with compar)*: **you'll feel all the better for it** du wirst dich danach umso besser fühlen; **to run all the faster** noch schneller laufen - **4.** *phr*: **all over** [finished] alles vorbei. ◆ **above all** *adv* = **above**. ◆ **after all** *adv* = **after**. ◆ **all but** *adv* fast; **all but empty** fast leer. ◆ **all in all** *adv* alles in allem. ◆ **at all** *adv* = **at**. ◆ **in all** *adv* [in total] zusammen; [in summary] alles in allem.

Allah ['ælə] *n* Allah.

all-around *adj US* = **all-round**.

allay [ə'leɪ] *vt fml* [fears, doubts] weitgehend zerstreuen; [anger] vermindern.

all clear *n* - **1.** [signal] Entwarnung *die* - **2.** *fig* [go-ahead] Bewilligung *die.*

allegation [ˌælɪ'geɪʃn] *n* Behauptung *die.*

allege [ə'ledʒ] *vt* behaupten; **he is alleged to have passed on the information** er soll die Informationen weitergegeben haben.

allegedly [ə'ledʒɪdlɪ] *adv* angeblich.

allergic [ə'lɜːdʒɪk] *adj*: **allergic (to)** allergisch (gegen).

allergy ['ælədʒɪ] *n* Allergie *die*; **to have an allergy to sthg** eine Allergie gegen etw haben.

alleviate [ə'liːvɪeɪt] *vt* mildern.

alley(way) ['ælɪ(weɪ)] *n* [street] (enge) Gasse *die*; [in garden] Weg *der.*

alliance [ə'laɪəns] *n* Bündnis *das.*

allied ['ælaɪd] *adj* - **1.** MIL verbündet, alliiert - **2.** [related] verwandt.

alligator ['ælɪgeɪtəʳ] (*pl inv* OR **-s**) *n* Alligator *der.*

all-important *adj* [crucial] entscheidend.

all-in *adj UK* [price] Pauschal-. ◆ **all in** ◇ *adj* [tired] völlig OR total erledigt. ◇ *adv UK* [inclusive] alles inklusive.

all-night *adj* [party, session] die ganze Nacht dauernd; [shop] nachts durchgehend geöffnet.

allocate ['æləkeɪt] *vt*: **to allocate sthg to sb** [money, resources] jm etw zur Verfügung stellen; [task, seats] jm etw zu|weisen; [tickets] etw an jn verteilen.

allot [ə'lɒt] *vt* [task] zu|weisen; [money, resources] zur Verfügung stellen; [time] vor|sehen.

allotment [ə'lɒtmənt] *n* - **1.** *UK* [garden] Schrebergarten *der* - **2.** [sharing out - of task] Zuweisung *die*; [- of money, resources] Verteilung *die*; [- of time] Vorsehen *das* - **3.** [share - of money, resources] Anteil *der*; [- of time] Zeitrahmen *der.*

all-out *adj* [effort] äußerst; [war] total; [attack] massiv.

allow [ə'laʊ] *vt* - **1.** [permit] erlauben; **to allow sb to do sthg** jm erlauben, etw zu tun; **to be allowed to do sthg** etw tun dürfen - **2.** [allocate - money] ein|rechnen; [- time] ein|planen - **3.** [admit]: **to allow that...** ein|räumen, dass... ◆ **allow for** *vt insep* ein|kalkulieren.

allowance [ə'laʊəns] *n* - 1. [grant] finanzielle Unterstützung; **travel allowance** Reisekostenzuschuss *der*; **clothing allowance** Kleidungsgeld *das* - 2. *US* [pocket money] Taschengeld *das* - 3. [excuse]: **to make allowances for sb** mit jm Nachsicht haben; **to make allowances for sthg** etw berücksichtigen.

alloy ['ælɔɪ] *n* Legierung *die*.

all right <> *adv* - 1. [healthy, unharmed]: **to feel all right** sich ganz gut fühlen; **did you get home all right?** bist du gut nach Hause gekommen? - 2. *inf* [acceptably] ganz gut - 3. *inf* [indicating agreement] okay - 4. *inf* [certainly]: **it's pneumonia all right** es ist sicher Lungenentzündung - 5. [do you understand?]: **all right?** okay? - 6. [now then]: **all right, let's go** okay, auf gehts. <> *adj* - 1. [healthy, unharmed]: **are you all right?** bist du in Ordnung? - 2. *inf* [acceptable]: **it was all right** es war ganz ordentlich; **that's all right** [never mind] das ist schon in Ordnung - 3. [permitted]: **is it all right if I make a phone call?** haben Sie etwas dagegen, wenn ich (kurz) telefoniere?

all-round *UK*, **all-around** *US adj* [athlete] Allround-; [worker] vielseitig begabt.

all-time *adj* [record, best] absolut.

allude [ə'lu:d] *vi*: **to allude to sthg** auf etw *(A)* an|spielen.

alluring [ə'ljʊərɪŋ] *adj* verführerisch.

allusion [ə'lu:ʒn] *n* Anspielung *die*.

ally *n* ['ælaɪ] Verbündete *der, die*.

almighty [ɔ:l'maɪtɪ] *adj inf* [noise, fuss] Riesen-.

almond ['ɑ:mənd] *n* Mandel *die*.

almost ['ɔ:lməʊst] *adv* fast, beinahe; **I almost missed the bus** ich hätte beinahe den Bus verpasst.

alms [ɑ:mz] *npl dated* Almosen *Pl*.

aloft [ə'lɒft] *adv* [in the air]: **to hold sthg aloft** etw in die Höhe halten.

alone [ə'ləʊn] <> *adj* allein(e). <> *adv* - 1. [without others] allein(e) - 2. [only] nur, allein; **you alone can help me** nur du OR du allein kannst mir helfen - 3. [untouched, unchanged]: **to leave sthg alone** etw in Ruhe lassen; **leave me alone!** lass mich in Ruhe! ◆ **let alone** *conj* geschweige denn.

along [ə'lɒŋ] <> *adv* - 1. [indicating movement]: **to stroll along** dahin|schlendern; **they went along to the demonstration** sie gingen zu der Vorführung - 2. [with others]: **to take sb/sthg along** jn/etw mit|nehmen; **to come along** mit|kommen. <> *prep* entlang *(+ A)*; **they walked along the river** sie liefen den Fluss entlang; **they walked along the forest path** sie folgten dem Waldweg; **the trees along the path** die Bäume neben dem Weg. ◆ **all along** *adv* die ganze Zeit. ◆ **along with** *prep* zusammen mit.

alongside [əˌlɒŋ'saɪd] <> *prep* neben *(+ D)*; [with verbs of motion] neben *(+ A)*. <> *adv* daneben.

aloof [ə'lu:f] <> *adj* unnahbar. <> *adv*: **to remain aloof (from)** sich fern halten (von).

aloud [ə'laʊd] *adv* laut.

alphabet ['ælfəbet] *n* Alphabet *das*.

alphabetical [ˌælfə'betɪkl] *adj* alphabetisch.

Alps [ælps] *npl*: **the Alps** die Alpen *Pl*.

already [ɔ:l'redɪ] *adv* schon.

alright [ˌɔ:l'raɪt] *adv* & *adj* = **all right**.

Alsatian [æl'seɪʃn] *n* [dog] (deutscher) Schäferhund.

also ['ɔ:lsəʊ] *adv* auch.

altar ['ɔ:ltər] *n* Altar *der*.

alter ['ɔ:ltər] <> *vt* ändern; [appearance] verändern; [text] ab|ändern. <> *vi* sich ändern; [appearance] sich verändern.

alteration [ˌɔ:ltə'reɪʃn] *n* Änderung *die*; [of appearance] Veränderung *die*; [of text] Abänderung *die*.

alternate <> *adj* [*UK* ɔ:l'tɜ:nət, *US* 'ɔ:ltərnət] - 1. [by turns] abwechselnd - 2. [every other]: **on alternate days** jeden zweiten Tag. <> *vt* ['ɔ:ltərneɪt] ab|wechseln. <> *vi* ['ɔ:ltərneɪt]: **to alternate (with)** sich ab|wechseln (mit); **to alternate between sthg and sthg** zwischen etw *(D)* und etw *(D)* (ab)|wechseln.

alternately [ɔ:l'tɜ:nətlɪ] *adv* abwechselnd.

alternating current ['ɔ:ltəneɪtɪŋ-] *n* ELEC Wechselstrom *der*.

alternative [ɔ:l'tɜ:nətɪv] <> *adj* - 1. [different, other] andere(r) (s) - 2. [nontraditional] alternativ. <> *n* Alternative *die*; **an alternative to sb/sthg** eine Alternative zu jm/etw; **to have no alternative (but to do sthg)** keine (andere) Wahl haben (als etw zu tun).

alternatively [ɔ:l'tɜ:nətɪvlɪ] *adv* oder aber, aber auch.

alternative medicine *n (U)* alternative Heilmethoden *Pl*.

alternator ['ɔ:ltəneɪtər] *n* ELEC Wechselstromgenerator *der*; [in car] Lichtmaschine *die*.

although [ɔ:l'ðəʊ] *conj* obwohl.

altitude ['æltɪtju:d] *n* Höhe *die*.

altogether [ˌɔ:ltə'geðər] *adv* - 1. [completely] vollkommen - 2. [in general, in total] insgesamt.

aluminium *UK* [ˌælju'mɪnɪəm], **aluminum** *US* [ə'lu:mɪnəm] <> *n* Aluminium *das*. <> *comp* Aluminium-.

always ['ɔ:lweɪz] *adv* immer; **you can always stay at my place** du kannst auch bei mir übernachten.

am [æm] *vb* ▷ **be**.

a.m. (*abbr of* **ante meridiem**) vormittags; **at 3 a.m.** um 3 Uhr morgens *OR* früh; **12 a.m.** 12 Uhr.

amalgamate [əˈmælgəmeɪt] <> *vt* mischen. <> *vi* sich verbinden.

amass [əˈmæs] *vt* [fortune, power, information] anlhäufen.

amateur [ˈæmətəʳ] <> *adj* - **1.** [nonprofessional] Amateur- - **2.** *pej* [unprofessional] dilettantisch. <> *n* [nonprofessional] Amateur *der*, -in *die*.

amateurish [ˈæmətəːrɪʃ] *adj pej* [unprofessional] dilettantisch.

amaze [əˈmeɪz] *vt* erstaunen, verblüffen.

amazed [əˈmeɪzd] *adj* erstaunt, verblüfft.

amazement [əˈmeɪzmənt] *n* Erstaunen *das*.

amazing [əˈmeɪzɪŋ] *adj* erstaunlich.

Amazon [ˈæməzn] *n* - **1.** [river]: **the Amazon** der Amazonas - **2.** [region]: **the Amazon (Basin)** das Amazonasbecken; **the Amazon rainforest** der Regenwald am Amazonas.

ambassador [æmˈbæsədəʳ] *n* Botschafter *der*, -in *die*.

amber [ˈæmbəʳ] *n* - **1.** [substance] Bernstein *der* - **2.** *UK* [colour of traffic light] Gelb *das*.

ambiguous [æmˈbɪgjʊəs] *adj* [two possible meanings] zweideutig; [many possible meanings] mehrdeutig.

ambition [æmˈbɪʃn] *n* - **1.** Ehrgeiz *der* - **2.** [objective, goal] Ambition *die*.

ambitious [æmˈbɪʃəs] *adj* ehrgeizig.

amble [ˈæmbl] *vi* schlendern.

ambulance [ˈæmbjʊləns] *n* Krankenwagen *der*, Ambulanz *die*.

ambush [ˈæmbʊʃ] <> *n* Hinterhalt *der*. <> *vt* [attack] aus dem Hinterhalt überfallen.

amenable [əˈmiːnəbl] *adj*: **amenable (to sthg)** (etw *(D)*) zugänglich.

amend [əˈmend] *vt* [change] abländern. ◆ **amends** *npl*: **to make amends (for sthg)** Entschädigungen (für etw) bieten.

amendment [əˈmendmənt] *n* Änderung *die*.

amenities [əˈmiːnətɪz] *npl* Einrichtungen *Pl*.

America [əˈmerɪkə] *n* Amerika *nt*.

American [əˈmerɪkn] <> *adj* amerikanisch. <> *n* Amerikaner *der*, -in *die*.

American football *n UK* American Football *der*.

American Indian *n* Indianer *der*, -in *die*.

amiable [ˈeɪmjəbl] *adj* freundlich.

amicable [ˈæmɪkəbl] *adj* freundschaftlich; [agreement] gütlich.

amid(st) [əˈmɪd(st)] *prep fml* inmitten *(+ G)*.

amiss [əˈmɪs] <> *adj*: **is there anything amiss?** stimmt etwas nicht? <> *adv*: **to take sthg amiss** etw übel nehmen.

ammonia [əˈməʊnjə] *n* Ammoniak *der*.

ammunition [ˌæmjʊˈnɪʃn] *n* Munition *die*.

amnesia [æmˈniːzjə] *n* Amnesie *die*.

amnesty [ˈæmnəstɪ] *n* Amnestie *die*.

amok [əˈmɒk] *adv*: **to run amok** Amok laufen.

among(st) [əˈmʌŋ(st)] *prep* unter *(+ D)*; **amongst other things** unter anderem; **I count him amongst my friends** ich zähle ihn zu meinen Freunden; **they were talking amongst themselves** sie unterhielten sich.

amoral [ˌeɪˈmɒrəl] *adj* amoralisch.

amorous [ˈæmərəs] *adj* amourös.

amount [əˈmaʊnt] *n* - **1.** [quantity] Menge *die* - **2.** [sum of money] Betrag *der*. ◆ **amount to** *vt insep* - **1.** [total] sich belaufen auf *(+ A)* - **2.** [be equivalent to] hinauslaufen auf *(+ A)*.

amp [æmp] *n abbr of* **ampere**.

ampere [ˈæmpeəʳ] *n* Ampere *das*.

amphibious [æmˈfɪbɪəs] *adj* amphibisch.

ample [ˈæmpl] *adj* - **1.** [enough] reichlich - **2.** [large] großzügig.

amplifier [ˈæmplɪfaɪəʳ] *n* Verstärker *der*.

amputate [ˈæmpjʊteɪt] *vt* & *vi* amputieren.

Amsterdam [ˌæmstəˈdæm] *n* Amsterdam *nt*.

amuck [əˈmʌk] *adv* = **amok**.

amuse [əˈmjuːz] *vt* - **1.** [make laugh] amüsieren - **2.** [entertain] unterhalten; **to amuse o.s. (with sthg)** sich *(D)* (mit etw) die Zeit vertreiben.

amused [əˈmjuːzd] *adj* amüsiert; **to be amused at** *OR* **by sthg** von etw erheitert sein; **to keep o.s. amused** sich die Zeit vertreiben.

amusement [əˈmjuːzmənt] *n* - **1.** [enjoyment] Vergnügen *das* - **2.** [diversion, game] Unterhaltungsmöglichkeit *die*.

amusement arcade *n* Spielhalle *die*.

amusement park *n* Vergnügungspark *der*.

amusing [əˈmjuːzɪŋ] *adj* [funny] amüsant.

an *(stressed* [æn], *unstressed* [ən]*) indef art* ▷ **a²**.

anaemic *UK*, **anemic** *US* [əˈniːmɪk] *adj* [suffering from anaemia] anämisch.

anaesthetic *UK*, **anesthetic** *US* [ˌænɪsˈθetɪk] *n* Anästhetikum *das*, Narkosemittel *das*; **under anaesthetic** unter Narkose, in der Narkose.

analogue *UK*, **analog** *US* [ˈænəlɒg] *adj* analog.

analogy [əˈnælədʒɪ] *n* Analogie *die*; **by analogy** analog dazu.

analyse *UK*, **-lyze** *US* [ˈænəlaɪz] *vt* analysieren.

analysis [əˈnæləsɪs] (*pl* **-ses** [əˈnæləsiːz]) *n* [gen] Analyse *die*.

analyst [ˈænəlɪst] *n* - **1.** [political, computer, statistics] Analytiker *der*, -in *die* - **2.** [psychoanalyst] Psychoanalytiker *der*, -in *die*.

analytic(al) [ˌænəˈlɪtɪk(l)] *adj* analytisch.
analyze *vt US* = **analyse**.
anarchist [ˈænəkɪst] *n* Anarchist *der*, -in *die*.
anarchy [ˈænəkɪ] *n* Anarchie *die*.
anathema [əˈnæθəmə] *n* Anathema *das*.
anatomy [əˈnætəmɪ] *n* Anatomie *die*.
ancestor [ˈænsestəʳ] *n* [person] Vorfahr *der*.
anchor [ˈæŋkəʳ] ◇ *n* - **1.** NAUT Anker *der*; **to drop/weigh anchor** Anker werfen/lichten - **2.** TV Moderator *der*, -in *die*. ◇ *vt* - **1.** [secure] sichern - **2.** TV moderieren. ◇ *vi* NAUT ankern.
anchovy [ˈæntʃəvɪ] (*pl inv* OR **-ies**) *n* Sardelle *die*.
ancient [ˈeɪnʃənt] *adj* - **1.** [dating from distant past] alt - **2.** *hum* [very old] alt, uralt.
ancillary [ænˈsɪlərɪ] *adj* [staff, device] Hilfs-.
and (*stressed* [ænd], *unstressed* [ənd] [ən]) *conj* - **1.** [gen] und; **and you?** und du/Sie?; **my wife and I** meine Frau und ich; **nice and warm** schön warm - **2.** [in numbers]: **a hundred and one** hunderteins; **an hour and a quarter** eineinviertel Stunden - **3.** [with repetition]: **more and more** immer mehr; **for days and days** tagelang - **4.** *(with infinitive)* [in order to]: **to try and do sthg** versuchen, etw zu tun; **wait and see!** warte es ab!, warten Sie es ab! ◆ **and all that** *adv* und dergleichen. ◆ **and so on, and so forth** *adv* und so weiter, und so fort.
Andes [ˈændi:z] *n*: **the Andes** die Anden *Pl*.
anecdote [ˈænɪkdəʊt] *n* Anekdote *die*.
anemic *adj US* = **anaemic**.
anesthetic *etc US* = **anaesthetic** *etc* .
anew [əˈnju:] *adv* von neuem.
angel [ˈeɪndʒəl] *n liter & fig* Engel *der*.
anger [ˈæŋgəʳ] ◇ *n* Zorn *der*. ◇ *vt* ärgern.
angina [ænˈdʒaɪnə] *n* Angina pectoris *die*.
angle [ˈæŋgl] *n* - **1.** MATHS [corner] Winkel *der* - **2.** [point of view] Standpunkt *der* - **3.** [slope] Schräge *die*; **at an angle** im schrägen Winkel.
angler [ˈæŋgləʳ] *n* Angler *der*, -in *die*.
Anglican [ˈæŋglɪkən] ◇ *adj* anglikanisch. ◇ *n* Anglikaner *der*, -in *die*.
angling [ˈæŋglɪŋ] *n* Angeln *das*.
angry [ˈæŋgrɪ] *adj* böse; **to be angry (with sb)** (jm) böse sein; **to get angry (with sb)** böse werden (auf jn).
anguish [ˈæŋgwɪʃ] *n* Qual *die*.
angular [ˈæŋgjʊləʳ] *adj* [face, jaw, body] kantig; [furniture, car] eckig.
animal [ˈænɪml] ◇ *adj* - **1.** [gen] Tier- - **2.** [physical] animalisch. ◇ *n* - **1.** [living creature] Tier *das* - **2.** *inf pej* [brutal person] Bestie *die*.
animate [ˈænɪmət] *adj* [alive] lebend.
animated [ˈænɪmeɪtɪd] *adj* [lively] lebhaft.
aniseed [ˈænɪsi:d] *n* Anis *der*.
ankle [ˈæŋkl] ◇ *n* Knöchel *der*. ◇ *comp* Knöchel-; **ankle socks** Söckchen *Pl*.
annex [ˈæneks] *vt* annektieren.
annexe [ˈæneks] *n* [building] Anbau *der*.
annihilate [əˈnaɪəleɪt] *vt* vernichten.
anniversary [ˌænɪˈvɜ:sərɪ] *n* Jahrestag *der*.
announce [əˈnaʊns] *vt* - **1.** [make public] ankündigen - **2.** [state, declare] verkünden.
announcement [əˈnaʊnsmənt] *n* [public statement] Bekanntmachung *die*; **government announcement** Regierungserklärung *die*.
announcer [əˈnaʊnsəʳ] *n* Ansager *der*, -in *die*; **television announcer** Fernsehansager *der*, -in *die*; **radio announcer** Radioansager *der*, -in *die*.
annoy [əˈnɔɪ] *vt* ärgern.
annoyance [əˈnɔɪəns] *n* Ärgernis *das*.
annoyed [əˈnɔɪd] *adj* verärgert; **to be annoyed at sthg/with sb** über etw/jn verärgert sein; **to get annoyed** sich ärgern.
annoying [əˈnɔɪɪŋ] *adj* ärgerlich.
annual [ˈænjʊəl] ◇ *adj* jährlich, Jahres-. ◇ *n* - **1.** [plant] einjährige Pflanze - **2.** [book] Jahrbuch *das*.
annual general meeting *n* Jahreshauptversammlung *die*.
annul [əˈnʌl] *vt* annullieren.
annulment [əˈnʌlmənt] *n* Annullierung *die*.
annum [ˈænəm] *n*: **per annum** pro Jahr.
anomaly [əˈnɒməlɪ] *n* Anomalie *die*.
anonymous [əˈnɒnɪməs] *adj* anonym.
anorak [ˈænəræk] *n esp UK* Anorak *der*.
anorexia (nervosa) [ˌænəˈreksɪə(nɜ:ˈvəʊsə)] *n* Anorexie *die*, Magersucht *die*.
anorexic [ˌænəˈreksɪk] ◇ *adj* magersüchtig. ◇ *n* Magersüchtige *der*, *die*.
another [əˈnʌðəʳ] ◇ *adj* - **1.** [additional] noch eine(r) (s); **in another few minutes** in einigen Minuten - **2.** [different] ein anderer, eine andere, ein anderes. ◇ *pron* - **1.** [an additional one] noch eine(r) (s); **one after another** einer/eine/eines nach dem/der anderen - **2.** [a different one] etwas anderes; **they love one another** sie lieben einander, sie lieben sich; **they are always arguing with one another** sie streiten immer miteinander, sie streiten (sich) immer.
answer [ˈɑ:nsəʳ] ◇ *n* - **1.** [reply] Antwort *die*; **in answer to** als Antwort auf *(+ A)* - **2.** [solution] Lösung *die*. ◇ *vt* - **1.** [reply to - question, letter, advertisement] beantworten - **2.** [respond to]: **to answer the door** die Tür öffnen; **to answer the phone** den Hörer abnehmen. ◇ *vi* [reply] antworten. ◆ **answer back** *vt sep & vi* widersprechen *(+ D)*. ◆ **answer for** *vt insep* verantworten.
answerable [ˈɑ:nsərəbl] *adj* [accountable] verantwortlich; **answerable to sb/for sthg** jm gegenüber/für etw verantwortlich.
answering machine [ˈɑ:nsərɪŋ-] *n* Anrufbeantworter *der*.

ant [ænt] *n* Ameise *die*.

antagonism [æn'tægənɪzm] *n* Feindlichkeit *die*, Feindseligkeit *die*.

antagonize, -ise [æn'tægənaɪz] *vt*: **to antagonize sb** jn gegen sich auf|bringen.

Antarctic [æn'tɑːktɪk] <> *n*: **the Antarctic** die Antarktis. <> *adj* antarktisch.

antelope ['æntɪləʊp] (*pl inv* OR **-s**) *n* Antilope *die*.

antenatal [,æntɪ'neɪtl] *adj* Schwangerschafts-.

antenatal clinic *n* Sprechstunde *die* für Schwangere.

antenna [æn'tenə] *n* - **1.** (*pl* **-nae** [-niː]) [of insect, lobster] Fühler *der* - **2.** (*pl* **-s**) *US* [aerial] Antenne *die*.

anthem ['ænθəm] *n* Hymne *die*.

anthology [æn'θɒlədʒɪ] *n* Anthologie *die*.

anthrax ['ænθræks] *n* Milzbrand *der*.

antibiotic [,æntɪbaɪ'ɒtɪk] *n* Antibiotikum *das*.

antibody ['æntɪ,bɒdɪ] *n* Antikörper *der*.

anticipate [æn'tɪsɪpeɪt] *vt* - **1.** [expect] erwarten, voraus|sehen - **2.** [preempt]: **to anticipate sb** jm zuvor|kommen.

anticipation [æn,tɪsɪ'peɪʃn] *n* Erwartung *die*; **in anticipation of** in Erwartung von.

anticlimax [æntɪ'klaɪmæks] *n* Enttäuschung *die*.

anticlockwise *UK* [,æntɪ'klɒkwaɪz] <> *adj* [direction] Links-. <> *adv* gegen den Uhrzeigersinn, nach links.

antics ['æntɪks] *npl* - **1.** [of children, animals] Possen *Pl* - **2.** *pej* [of politician *etc*] Eskapaden *Pl*.

anticyclone [,æntɪ'saɪkləʊn] *n* Hoch *das*.

antidepressant [,æntɪdɪ'presnt] *n* Antidepressivum *das*.

antidote ['æntɪdəʊt] *n liter* & *fig*: **antidote (to)** Gegenmittel *das* (gegen).

antifreeze ['æntɪfriːz] *n* Frostschutzmittel *das*.

antihistamine [,æntɪ'hɪstəmɪn] *n* Antihistamin *das*.

antiperspirant [,æntɪ'pɜːspərənt] *n* Deodorant *das*.

antiquated ['æntɪkweɪtɪd] *adj* antiquiert.

antique [æn'tiːk] <> *adj* antik. <> *n* Antiquität *die*.

antique shop *n* Antiquitätenhandlung *die*.

anti-Semitism [,æntɪ'semɪtɪzəm] *n* Antisemitismus *der*.

antiseptic [,æntɪ'septɪk] <> *adj* steril, desinfiziert. <> *n* Antiseptikum *das*.

antisocial [,æntɪ'səʊʃl] *adj* - **1.** [damaging to society] unsozial - **2.** [unsociable] ungesellig; [working hours] unsozial.

antlers ['æntləz] *npl* Geweih *das*.

anus ['eɪnəs] *n* After *der*.

anvil ['ænvɪl] *n* Amboss *der*.

anxiety [æŋ'zaɪətɪ] *n* - **1.** [worry, cause of worry] Sorge *die* - **2.** [keenness] Ungeduld *die*.

anxious ['æŋkʃəs] *adj* - **1.** [worried] besorgt; **to be anxious about sb/sthg** sich um jn/etw sorgen - **2.** [keen]: **to be anxious to do sthg** darauf brennen, etw zu tun.

any ['enɪ] <> *adj* - **1.** *(in questions)*: **have you got any money?** hast du Geld?; **have you got any postcards?** haben Sie Postkarten?; **can I be of any help?** kann ich Ihnen irgendwie behilflich sein? - **2.** *(with negatives)*: **I haven't got any money** ich habe kein Geld; **we don't have any rooms** wir haben keine Zimmer frei; **he never does any housework** er tut nie etwas im Haushalt - **3.** [no matter which] irgendein(e); **take any one you like** nimm, welches du willst; **any beer will do** jedes Bier ist recht; **at any time** jederzeit. <> *pron* - **1.** *(in questions)* welche; **I'm looking for a hotel – are there any nearby?** ich suche ein Hotel – gibts hier welche in der Nähe?; **can any of you change a tyre?** kann jemand von euch einen Reifen wechseln? - **2.** *(with if)*: **if any** wenn überhaupt; **few foreign films, if any, are successful here** nur wenige ausländische Filme haben hier Erfolg - **3.** *(with negatives)*: **I don't want any (of them)** ich möchte keinen/keines/keine (von denen) - **4.** [no matter which one] jede(r) (s); **take any you like** nimm, welches du willst; **you can sit at any of the tables** Sie können sich an jeden beliebigen Tisch setzen. <> *adv* - **1.** *(in questions)*: **is there any more ice cream?** ist noch Eis da?; **is that any better?** ist das besser? - **2.** *(with negatives)*: **we can't wait any longer** wir können nicht mehr länger warten; **I can't see it any more** ich kann es nicht mehr sehen.

anybody ['enɪ,bɒdɪ] *pron* = **anyone**.

anyhow ['enɪhaʊ] *adv* - **1.** [in spite of that] trotzdem - **2.** [carelessly] durcheinander, wahllos - **3.** [returning to topic] jedenfalls.

anyone ['enɪwʌn] *pron* - **1.** [any person] jeder; **anyone can tell you that** (ein) jeder kann dir das sagen; **anyone else would have given up** jeder andere hätte es aufgegeben; **if anyone asks, you haven't seen me** wenn jemand fragt, du hast mich nicht gesehen - **2.** *(in questions)* irgendjemand; **has anyone seen my book?** hat irgendjemand mein Buch gesehen?; **do you know anyone else?** kennst du sonst noch jemanden? - **3.** *(in negative statements)*: **there wasn't anyone in** niemand war zu Hause; **I didn't see anyone else** ich habe sonst niemanden gesehen; **there was hardly anyone there** es war kaum jemand dort.

anyplace ['enɪpleɪs] *adv US* = **anywhere**.

anything ['enɪθɪŋ] *pron* - **1.** [no matter what] alles; **he eats anything** er isst alles; **if anything**

should happen to him falls ihm irgendetwas zustoßen sollte - **2.** *(in questions)* irgendetwas; **would you like anything else?** darf es noch etwas sein? - **3.** *(in negative statements)*: **I don't want anything at all** ich möchte überhaupt nichts (haben); **he didn't tell me anything** er hat mir nichts gesagt; **hardly anything** kaum etwas; **not for anything** um keinen Preis.

anyway ['enɪweɪ] *adv* - **1.** [in any case] sowieso - **2.** [in spite of that] trotzdem - **3.** [in conversation] jedenfalls; **anyway, there we were** nun ja, jedenfalls standen wir da.

anywhere ['enɪweəʳ] *adv* - **1.** [any place] überall; **sit anywhere you like** setz dich einfach irgendwohin; **anywhere else** woanders, anderswo - **2.** *(in questions)* irgendwo; **have you seen my jacket anywhere?** hast du meine Jacke irgendwo gesehen?; **did you go anywhere else?** bist du/seid Ihr noch irgendwo anders hingegangen? - **3.** *(in negative statements)*: **I can't find it anywhere** ich kann es nirgends finden; **we didn't see anywhere interesting** wir haben nichts Interessantes gesehen.

apart [ə'pɑːt] *adv* - **1.** [separated in space] getrennt; **she stood apart from the group** sie hielt sich abseits der Gruppe - **2.** [in several pieces] auseinander; **to fall apart** auseinander fallen; **to take sthg apart** etw auseinander nehmen - **3.** [aside, excepted] beiseite; **joking apart** Spaß beiseite. ◆ **apart from** ◇ *prep* [except for] mit Ausnahme von. ◇ *conj* [in addition to] abgesehen von.

apartheid [ə'pɑːtheɪt] *n* Apartheid *die*.

apartment [ə'pɑːtmənt] *n esp US* Wohnung *die*.

apartment building *n US* Wohnblock *der*.

apathy ['æpəθɪ] *n* Teilnahmslosigkeit *die*.

ape [eɪp] ◇ *n* [animal] Menschenaffe *der*. ◇ *vt pej* [imitate] nach|äffen.

aperitif [əperə'tiːf] *n* Aperitif *der*.

aperture ['æpəˌtjʊəʳ] *n* - **1.** [hole, opening] Öffnung *die* - **2.** PHOT Blende *die*.

apex ['eɪpeks] (*pl* **-es** OR **apices**) *n liter* [top] Spitze *der*; *fig* Gipfel *der*.

APEX ['eɪpeks] (*abbr of* **advance purchase excursion**) *n UK zeitlich reglementierter Vorverkauf verbilligter Flugtickets und Bahnfahrkarten.*

apices ['eɪpɪsiːz] *Pl* ▷ **apex**.

apiece [ə'piːs] *adv* [object] pro Stück.

apocalypse [ə'pɒkəlɪps] *n* Apokalypse *die*.

apologetic [əˌpɒlə'dʒetɪk] *adj* entschuldigend; **to be apologetic (about sthg)** sich (für etw OR wegen etw *(G)*) entschuldigen.

apologize, -ise [ə'pɒlədʒaɪz] *vi* sich entschuldigen; **to apologize to sb for sthg** sich bei jm für etw entschuldigen.

apology [ə'pɒlədʒɪ] *n* Entschuldigung *die*.

apostle [ə'pɒsl] *n* RELIG Apostel *der*.

apostrophe [ə'pɒstrəfɪ] *n* GRAM Apostroph *der*.

appal *UK*, **appall** *US* [ə'pɔːl] *vt* entsetzen.

appalling [ə'pɔːlɪŋ] *adj* entsetzlich.

apparatus [ˌæpə'reɪtəs] (*pl inv* OR **-es**) *n* Apparat *der*; [device] Gerät *das*; [in gym] Geräte *Pl*.

apparel [ə'pærəl] *n US* Kleidung *die*.

apparent [ə'pærənt] *adj* - **1.** [evident] offensichtlich - **2.** [seeming] scheinbar.

apparently [ə'pærəntlɪ] *adv* - **1.** [according to rumour] anscheinend - **2.** [seemingly] scheinbar.

appeal [ə'piːl] ◇ *vi* - **1.** [request] (dringend) bitten; **to appeal to sb for sthg** jn (dringend) um etw bitten; **to appeal to the public to do sthg** die Öffentlichkeit dazu auf|rufen, etw zu tun - **2.** [to sb's honour, common sense]: **to appeal to** appellieren an *(+ A)* - **3.** LAW: **to appeal (against)** Berufung ein|legen (gegen) - **4.** [attract, interest]: **to appeal to sb** jm gefallen, jm zusagen. ◇ *n* - **1.** [for help, money] Aufruf *der*, Appell *der*; [for mercy] Gesuch *das* - **2.** LAW Berufung *die* - **3.** [charm, interest] Reiz *der*.

appealing [ə'piːlɪŋ] *adj* [person] ansprechend; [baby] süß; [idea] reizvoll.

appear [ə'pɪəʳ] ◇ *vi* - **1.** [gen] erscheinen - **2.** [in play] auf|treten. ◇ *vt* [seem] scheinen; **it would appear that...** es hat den Anschein,... OR es scheint, als ob...

appearance [ə'pɪərəns] *n* - **1.** [gen] Erscheinen *das*; [of symptoms] Auftreten *das* - **2.** [outward aspect] äußere Erscheinung; [facial features] Aussehen *das* - **3.** [in play, film, on TV] Auftritt *der*.

appease [ə'piːz] *vt* [person, anger] (durch Zugeständnisse) beschwichtigen.

append [ə'pend] *vt fml*: **to append sthg (to)** [add] etw hinzu|fügen (zu); [enclose] etw bei|fügen *(+ D)*.

appendices [ə'pendɪsiːz] *Pl* ▷ **appendix**.

appendicitis [əˌpendɪ'saɪtɪs] *n (U)* Blinddarmentzündung *die*.

appendix [ə'pendɪks] (*pl* **-dixes** OR **-dices**) *n* - **1.** MED Blinddarm *der*; **to have one's appendix out** OR **removed** sich *(D)* den Blinddarm heraus|nehmen lassen - **2.** [in book] Anhang *der*.

appetite ['æpɪtaɪt] *n*: **appetite (for)** Appetit *der* (auf *(+ A)*).

appetizer, -iser ['æpɪtaɪzəʳ] *n* (appetitanregendes) Häppchen; [starter] Vorspeise *die*.

appetizing, -ising ['æpɪtaɪzɪŋ] *adj* appetitlich.

applaud [ə'plɔːd] ◇ *vt* - **1.** [person] applaudieren *(+ D)* - **2.** *fig* [effort] loben; [decision] begrüßen. ◇ *vi* applaudieren.

applause [ə'plɔːz] *n* Applaus *der*.

apple ['æpl] *n* Apfel *der*.

apple tree *n* Apfelbaum *der*.

appliance [ə'plaɪəns] *n* Gerät *das*.

applicable [ə'plɪkəbl] *adj* zutreffend; **delete where not applicable** Nichtzutreffendes streichen; **to be applicable to sb/sthg** auf jn/etw zu|treffen.

applicant ['æplɪkənt] *n*: **applicant (for)** [for job] Bewerber *der*, -in *die* (um OR für); [for state benefit] Antragsteller *der*, -in *die* (für).

application [ˌæplɪ'keɪʃn] *n* - **1.** [for job, college]: **application (for)** Bewerbung *die* (um OR für) - **2.** [for club]: **application (for)** Antrag *der* (auf *(+ A)*) - **3.** [of knowledge, rule] Anwendung *die*; [of invention] Einsatz *der* - **4.** [use] Verwendung *die* - **5.** [diligence] Fleiß *der* - **6.** COMPUT: **application (program)** Anwendungsprogramm *das*.

application form *n* [for job] Bewerbungsformular *das*; [for state benefit, club] Antragsformular *das*.

applied [ə'plaɪd] *adj* [science] angewandt.

apply [ə'plaɪ] ◇ *vt* - **1.** [rule, skill] an|wenden - **2.** [paint, ointment] auf|tragen; **to apply the brakes** bremsen. ◇ *vi* - **1.** [for work, grant]: **to apply (for)** sich bewerben (um OR für); **to apply to sb for sthg** sich bei jm um OR für etw bewerben - **2.** [be relevant]: **to apply (to)** zu|treffen (auf *(+ A)*).

appoint [ə'pɔɪnt] *vt* [to job, position] ein|stellen; [to office] ernennen.

appointment [ə'pɔɪntmənt] *n* - **1.** *(U)* [to job, position] Einstellung *die*; [to office] Ernennung *die* - **2.** [job, position] Stelle *die* - **3.** [with doctor, hairdresser, in business] Termin *der*; **to have an appointment** einen Termin haben; **to make an appointment** einen Termin vereinbaren.

apportion [ə'pɔːʃn] *vt* [money] auf|teilen; [blame] zu|weisen.

appraisal [ə'preɪzl] *n* Beurteilung *die*.

appreciable [ə'priːʃəbl] *adj* [difference] merklich; [amount] beträchtlich.

appreciate [ə'priːʃɪeɪt] ◇ *vt* - **1.** [value] schätzen; **her books were not appreciated at the time** ihre Bücher wurden damals nicht gewürdigt - **2.** [recognize, understand] sich *(D)* bewusst sein *(+ G)* - **3.** [help, advice] dankbar sein für; **thanks, I really appreciate it!** danke schön, sehr nett von dir/Ihnen! ◇ *vi* FIN im Wert steigen.

appreciation [əˌpriːʃɪ'eɪʃn] *n* - **1.** [liking] Anerkennung *die* - **2.** [understanding] Verständnis *das* - **3.** [gratitude] Dankbarkeit *die*.

appreciative [ə'priːʃjətɪv] *adj* [person, audience] dankbar; **to be appreciative of sthg** etw zu schätzen wissen.

apprehensive [ˌæprɪ'hensɪv] *adj*: **apprehensive (about)** besorgt (wegen *(+ G)*).

apprentice [ə'prentɪs] *n* Lehrling *der*; **an apprentice mechanic** ein Mechanikerlehrling.

apprenticeship [ə'prentɪsʃɪp] *n* Lehre *die*.

approach [ə'prəʊtʃ] ◇ *n* - **1.** [arrival] (Heran)nahen *das* - **2.** [access] Zugang *der*; [road] Zufahrt *die* - **3.** [method] Ansatz *der* - **4.** [proposal]: **to make an approach to sb** an jn heran|treten. ◇ *vt* - **1.** [come near to] sich nähern *(+ D)*; **temperatures approaching 35°C** Temperaturen von bis zu 35°C - **2.** [speak to]: **to approach sb about sthg** wegen etw an jn heran|treten *(G)* - **3.** [problem, task] an|gehen. ◇ *vi* sich nähern.

approachable [ə'prəʊtʃəbl] *adj* - **1.** [person] umgänglich - **2.** [place] erreichbar.

appropriate ◇ *adj* [ə'prəʊprɪət] angemessen; [clothing, moment] passend. ◇ *vt* [ə'prəʊprɪeɪt] - **1.** LAW [steal] sich an|eignen - **2.** [allocate] bestimmen.

approval [ə'pruːvl] *n* - **1.** [liking, admiration] Anerkennung *die* - **2.** [official agreement] Genehmigung *die* - **3.** COMM: **on approval** zur Probe.

approve [ə'pruːv] ◇ *vi*: **to approve of sb** von jm etwas halten; **to approve of sthg** mit etw einverstanden sein; **I don't approve of him** ich halte nichts von ihm. ◇ *vt* genehmigen.

approx. [ə'prɒks] *abbr of* **approximately**.

approximate *adj* [ə'prɒksɪmət] ungefähr.

approximately [ə'prɒksɪmətlɪ] *adv* ungefähr, circa.

apricot ['eɪprɪkɒt] *n* [fruit] Aprikose *die*.

April ['eɪprəl] *n* April *der*; *see also* **September**.

April Fools' Day *n* der erste April.

apron ['eɪprən] *n* [clothing] Schürze *die*.

apt [æpt] *adj* - **1.** [pertinent] treffend - **2.** [likely]: **to be apt to do sthg** dazu neigen, etw zu tun.

aptitude ['æptɪtjuːd] *n* Begabung *die*; **to have an aptitude for sthg** eine Begabung für etw haben.

aptly ['æptlɪ] *adv* treffend.

aqualung ['ækwəlʌŋ] *n* Presslufttauchgerät *das*.

aquarium [ə'kweərɪəm] (*pl* **-riums** OR **-ria** [-rɪə]) *n* Aquarium *das*.

Aquarius [ə'kweərɪəs] *n* Wassermann *der*.

aquatic [ə'kwætɪk] *adj* Wasser-.

aqueduct ['ækwɪdʌkt] *n* Aquädukt *der ODER das*.

Arab ['ærəb] ◇ *adj* arabisch. ◇ *n* [person] Araber *der*, -in *die*.

Arabian [ə'reɪbjən] *adj* arabisch.

Arabic ['ærəbɪk] ◇ *adj* arabisch. ◇ *n* [language] Arabisch(e) *das*.

Arabic numeral *n* arabische Ziffer.

arable ['ærəbl] *adj*: **arable land** Ackerland *das*.

arbitrary ['ɑːbɪtrərɪ] *adj* willkürlich.

arbitration [ˌɑːbɪ'treɪʃn] *n* Schlichtungsverfahren *das*; **to go to arbitration** vor eine Schlichtungskommission gehen.

arcade [ɑː'keɪd] *n* - **1.** [for shopping] Passage *die* - **2.** ARCHIT [covered passage] Arkade *die*.

arch [ɑːtʃ] ◇ *adj* [knowing] schelmisch. ◇ *n* - **1.** ARCHIT Bogen *der*; [arched entrance] Torbogen *der* - **2.** [of foot] Wölbung *die*. ◇ *vt* [back] krümmen. ◇ *vi* sich wölben.

archaeologist [ˌɑːkɪ'ɒlədʒɪst] *n* Archäologe *der*, -in *die*.

archaeology [ˌɑːkɪ'ɒlədʒɪ] *n* Archäologie *die*.

archaic [ɑː'keɪɪk] *adj* [language] veraltet.

archbishop [ˌɑːtʃ'bɪʃəp] *n* Erzbischof *der*.

archenemy [ˌɑːtʃ'enɪmɪ] *n* Erzfeind *der*, -in *die*.

archeology *etc* [ˌɑːkɪ'ɒlədʒɪ] = **archaeology** *etc* .

archer ['ɑːtʃəʳ] *n* Bogenschütze *der*.

archery ['ɑːtʃərɪ] *n* Bogenschießen *das*.

archetypal [ˌɑːkɪ'taɪpl] *adj* typisch.

architect ['ɑːkɪtekt] *n* - **1.** [of buildings] Architekt *der*, -in *die* - **2.** *fig* [of plan, event] Urheber *der*, -in *die*.

architecture ['ɑːkɪtektʃəʳ] *n* - **1.** [gen & COMPUT] Architektur *die* - **2.** [style of building] Baustil *der*.

archives ['ɑːkaɪvz] *npl* [of documents] Archiv *das*.

archway ['ɑːtʃweɪ] *n* Torbogen *der*.

Arctic ['ɑːktɪk] ◇ *adj* - **1.** GEOG arktisch - **2.** *inf* [cold] eiskalt. ◇ *n*: **the Arctic** die Arktis.

ardent ['ɑːdənt] *adj* leidenschaftlich; [desire] brennend.

arduous ['ɑːdjʊəs] *adj* [task] mühselig; [climb, journey] anstrengend.

are *(weak form* [əʳ], *strong form* [ɑːʳ]*)* *vb* ▷ **be**.

area ['eərɪə] *n* - **1.** [region] Gegend *die*; [in town] Viertel *das*; **in the Bristol area** im Raum Bristol - **2.** *fig* [approximate size, number]: **in the area of** im Bereich von - **3.** [surface size] Fläche *die* - **4.** [space] Bereich *der*; **a parking area** ein Parkplatz - **5.** [of knowledge, interest, subject] Gebiet *das*.

area code *n US* Vorwahl *die*.

arena [ə'riːnə] *n liter* & *fig* Arena *die*.

aren't [ɑːnt] *abbr of* **are not**.

Argentina [ˌɑːdʒən'tiːnə] *n* Argentinien *nt*.

Argentine ['ɑːdʒəntaɪn], **Argentinian** [ˌɑːdʒən'tɪnɪən] ◇ *adj* argentinisch. ◇ *n* Argentinier *der*, -in *die*.

arguably ['ɑːgjʊəblɪ] *adv* möglicherweise.

argue ['ɑːgjuː] ◇ *vi* - **1.** [quarrel]: **to argue (with sb about sthg)** sich (mit jm über etw *(A)*) streiten - **2.** [reason] argumentieren; **to argue for/against sthg** für/gegen etw einltreten. ◇ *vt*: **to argue the case for sthg** für etw einltreten; **to argue that** die Meinung vertreten, dass.

argument ['ɑːgjʊmənt] *n* - **1.** [quarrel] Streit *der*; **to have an argument (with sb)** sich (mit jm) streiten - **2.** [reason] Argument *das* - **3.** *(U)* [reasoning] Diskussion *die*.

argumentative [ˌɑːgjʊ'mentətɪv] *adj* streitsüchtig.

arise [ə'raɪz] (*pt* **arose**, *pp* **arisen** [ə'rɪzn]) *vi* [problems, difficulties] aufltreten; [opportunities] sich ergeben; **to arise from sthg** sich aus etw ergeben; **if the need arises** falls sich die Notwendigkeit ergibt.

aristocrat [*UK* 'ærɪstəkræt, *US* ə'rɪstəkræt] *n* Aristokrat *der*, -in *die*, Adlige *der, die*.

arithmetic [ə'rɪθmətɪk] *n* Arithmetik *die*, Rechnen *das*; [calculation] Rechnung *die*.

ark [ɑːk] *n* [ship] Arche *die*.

arm [ɑːm] ◇ *n* - **1.** [of person] Arm *der*; **arm in arm** Arm in Arm; **to keep sb at arm's length** *fig* jn auf Distanz halten - **2.** [of garment] Ärmel *der* - **3.** [of chair] Armlehne *die*. ◇ *vt* [with weapons] bewaffnen. ◆ **arms** *npl* [weapons] Waffen *Pl*; **to take up arms** zu den Waffen greifen; **to be up in arms (about sthg)** (wegen etw *(G)*) aufgebracht sein.

armaments ['ɑːməmənts] *npl* Waffen *Pl*.

armband ['ɑːmˌbænd] *n* Armbinde *die*; [for swimming] Schwimmflügel *der*.

armchair ['ɑːmtʃeəʳ] *n* Sessel *der*.

armed [ɑːmd] *adj* - **1.** [police, thieves] bewaffnet - **2.** *fig* [with information]: **armed with sthg** mit etw ausgestattet.

armed forces *npl* Streitkräfte *Pl*.

armhole ['ɑːmhəʊl] *n* Armloch *das*.

armour *UK*, **armor** *US* ['ɑːməʳ] *n* - **1.** [for person] Rüstung *die* - **2.** [for military vehicle] Panzerung *die*.

armoured car *n* MIL Panzerwagen *der*.

armoury *UK*, **armory** *US* ['ɑːmərɪ] *n* Arsenal *das*.

armpit ['ɑːmpɪt] *n* Achselhöhle *die*.

armrest ['ɑːmrest] *n* Armlehne *die*.

arms control ['ɑːmz-] *n* Rüstungskontrolle *die*.

army ['ɑːmɪ] *n* - **1.** MIL Heer *das*, Armee *die*; **to be in the army** beim Militär sein - **2.** *fig* [large group] Heer *das*.

A road *n UK* ≃ Bundesstraße *die*.

aroma [ə'rəʊmə] *n* Duft *der*.

arose [ə'rəʊz] *pt* ▷ **arise**.

around [ə'raʊnd] ◇ *adv* - **1.** [here and there] herum; **to travel around** herumlreisen; **to sit around doing nothing** untätig herumlsitzen - **2.** [on all sides] herum; **all around** auf allen Seiten - **3.** [present, nearby]: **is she around?** ist sie da?; **around here** [in the area] hier in der

Gegend; **cars have been around for over a century** Autos gibt es schon seit über hundert Jahren - **4.** [in a circle]: **to go around** sich drehen; **to spin around (and around)** sich im Kreis drehen - **5.** [to the other side]: **to go around** herum|gehen; **to turn around** sich um|drehen; **to look around** sich um|sehen - **6.** *phr*: **to have been around** *inf* [travelled a lot] (viel) herumgekommen sein. ◇ *prep* - **1.** [surrounding] um herum - **2.** [near]: **around here/there** hier/dort in der Nähe; **is there a bank anywhere around here?** gibt es hier irgendwo eine Bank? - **3.** [all over]: **150 offices around the world** 150 Büros in der ganzen Welt; **all around the country** im ganzen Land; **we walked around the town** wir spazierten durch die Stadt - **4.** [in a circle]: **we walked around the lake** wir gingen um den See herum; **to go/drive around sthg** um etw herum|gehen/herum|fahren; **around the clock** *fig* rund um die Uhr - **5.** [approximately] ungefähr - **6.** [in circumference]: **she measures 30 inches around the waist** um die Taille misst sie 75 cm - **7.** [so as to avoid] um herum; **to get around an obstacle** um ein Hindernis herum|gehen; **to find a way around a problem** einen Ausweg für ein Problem finden.

arouse [ə'raʊz] *vt* - **1.** [excite] erregen; [interest, suspicion] erwecken - **2.** [wake] (auf)|wecken.

arrange [ə'reɪndʒ] *vt* - **1.** [flowers] arrangieren; [books, objects] (an)|ordnen; [furniture] (um)|stellen - **2.** [event] planen; [meeting] vereinbaren; [party] arrangieren; **to arrange to do sthg** vereinbaren, etw zu tun - **3.** MUS bearbeiten, arrangieren.

arrangement [ə'reɪndʒmənt] *n* - **1.** [agreement] Vereinbarung *die*; **to come to an arrangement** eine Einigung erzielen - **2.** [of objects] Anordnung *die* - **3.** MUS Bearbeitung *die*, Arrangement *das*. ◆ **arrangements** *npl* [preparations] Vorbereitungen *Pl*; **please make your own arrangements for accommodation** bitte arrangieren Sie Ihre Unterkunft selbst.

array [ə'reɪ] ◇ *n* [of objects, people, ornaments] Aufgebot *das*. ◇ *vt* [ornaments] auf|stellen.

arrears [ə'rɪəz] *npl* [money owed] Rückstände *Pl*; **to be paid in arrears** rückwirkend bezahlt werden; **to be in arrears** im Rückstand sein.

arrest [ə'rest] ◇ *n* [by police] Verhaftung *die*; **to be under arrest** verhaftet sein. ◇ *vt* - **1.** [subj: police] verhaften - **2.** *fml* [sb's attention] erregen - **3.** *fml* [stop - development] hemmen; [- spread of disease] auf|halten.

arrival [ə'raɪvl] *n* - **1.** [at place] Ankunft *die*; **on arrival** bei der Ankunft; **late arrival** [of train, bus, mail] verspätete Ankunft - **2.** [of new system, technology] Aufkommen *das* - **3.** [person] Ankömmling *der*; **new arrival** [person] Neuankömmling *der*.

arrive [ə'raɪv] *vi* - **1.** [gen] an|kommen; **to arrive at a conclusion/decision** zu einem Schluss/einer Entscheidung kommen - **2.** [moment, event] kommen.

arrogant ['ærəgənt] *adj* arrogant.

arrow ['ærəʊ] *n* Pfeil *der*.

arse *UK* [ɑːs], **ass** *US* [æs] *n vulg* [buttocks] Arsch *der*.

arsenic ['ɑːsnɪk] *n* Arsen *das*.

arson ['ɑːsn] *n* Brandstiftung *die*.

art [ɑːt] ◇ *n* Kunst *die*. ◇ *comp* Kunst-. ◆ **arts** *npl* - **1.** SCH & UNIV [humanities] Geisteswissenschaften *Pl* - **2.** [fine arts]: **the arts** die schönen Künste *Pl*.

artefact ['ɑːtɪfækt] *n* = **artifact**.

artery ['ɑːtərɪ] *n* Arterie *die*.

art gallery *n* Kunstgalerie *die*.

arthritis [ɑː'θraɪtɪs] *n* Arthritis *die*.

artichoke ['ɑːtɪtʃəʊk] *n* Artischocke *die*.

article ['ɑːtɪkl] *n* - **1.** [item] Gegenstand *der*; COMM Ware *die*, Artikel *der*; **article of clothing** Kleidungsstück *das* - **2.** [in newspaper, magazine] Artikel *der* - **3.** [in agreement, contract] Paragraph *der*; [in constitution] Artikel *der* - **4.** GRAM Artikel *der*.

articulate ◇ *adj* [ɑː'tɪkjʊlət] [speech] leichtverständlich; **to be articulate** [person] sich gut aus|drücken können. ◇ *vt* [ɑː'tɪkjʊleɪt] [thought, wish] zum Ausdruck bringen, artikulieren.

articulated lorry [ɑː'tɪkjʊleɪtɪd-] *n UK* Sattelschlepper *der*.

artifact ['ɑːtɪfækt] *n* Artefakt *das*.

artificial [ˌɑːtɪ'fɪʃl] *adj* - **1.** [non-natural] künstlich - **2.** [insincere] gekünstelt.

artillery [ɑː'tɪlərɪ] *n* Artillerie *die*.

artist ['ɑːtɪst] *n* Künstler *der*, -in *die*.

artistic [ɑː'tɪstɪk] *adj* - **1.** [gen] künstlerisch; [person] künstlerisch begabt - **2.** [attractive] kunstvoll.

artistry ['ɑːtɪstrɪ] *n* Kunstwertigkeit *die*.

as *(unstressed* [əz], *stressed* [æz]*)* ◇ *conj* - **1.** [referring to time] als - **2.** [referring to manner] wie; **as expected** wie erwartet; **do as I say** tu, was ich dir sage; **it's hard enough as it is** es ist ohnehin schon schwierig genug - **3.** [introducing a statement] wie; **as I told you** wie ich dir bereits gesagt habe; **as you know** wie du weißt - **4.** [because] weil, da. ◇ *adv (in comparisons)*: **as ... as** so ... wie; **he's as tall as I am** er ist so groß wie ich; **as many as** so viele wie; **as much as** so viel wie. ◇ *prep* als; **she works as a nurse** sie arbeitet als Krankenschwester; **to consider sb as a friend** jn als Freund betrachten. ◆ **as for** *prep*: **as for me** was mich betrifft. ◆ **as from, as of** *prep* ab; **as from** OR **of Monday** ab Montag. ◆ **as if, as though** *conj* als ob, als wenn; **he looked at me as if I were mad** er sah mich an, als ob ich verrückt wäre; **as if by chance** wie durch Zufall. ◆ **as to** *prep UK*: **she questioned him as to his motives** sie fragte ihn nach seinen Beweggründen.

a.s.a.p. (*abbr of* **as soon as possible**) baldmöglichst.

asbestos [æs'bestəs] *n* Asbest *der*.

ASBO ['æzbɔ] *n* (*abbr of* **antisocial behaviour order**) *Verwarnung gegen asoziales Verhalten*.

ascend [ə'send] ◇ *vt* [hill] besteigen; [staircase] hinauf|gehen; [ladder] hinauf|steigen. ◇ *vi* [climb] auf|steigen; [subj: path, road *etc*] an|steigen.

ascendant [ə'sendənt] *n*: **to be in the ascendant** im Aufstieg begriffen sein.

ascent [ə'sent] *n* - **1.** [gen] Aufstieg *der* - **2.** [upward slope] Steigung *die*.

ascertain [ˌæsə'teɪn] *vt* ermitteln.

ascribe [ə'skraɪb] *vt*: **to ascribe sthg to sthg** einer Sache *(D)* etw zu|schreiben; **to ascribe sthg to sb** jm etw zu|schreiben.

ash [æʃ] *n* - **1.** [from cigarette, fire] Asche *die* - **2.** [tree] Esche *die*.

ashamed [ə'ʃeɪmd] *adj* beschämt; **to be ashamed of sb/sthg** sich js/etw *(G)* schämen; **to be ashamed to do sthg** sich schämen, etw zu tun.

ashore [ə'ʃɔːʳ] *adv* [go, swim] an Land.

ashtray ['æʃtreɪ] *n* Aschenbecher *der*.

Ash Wednesday *n* Aschermittwoch *der*.

Asia [*UK* 'eɪʃə, *US* 'eɪʒə] *n* Asien *nt*.

Asian [*UK* 'eɪʃn, *US* 'eɪʒn] ◇ *adj* asiatisch. ◇ *n* [from Far East] Asiat *der*, -in *die*.

aside [ə'saɪd] ◇ *adv* - **1.** [to one side] beiseite, zur Seite; **step aside!** treten Sie zur Seite!; **to take sb aside** jn beiseite nehmen - **2.** [apart]: **joking aside** Spaß beiseite; **aside from** abgesehen von. ◇ *n* - **1.** [in play] Apart *das* - **2.** [remark] beiläufige Bemerkung.

ask [ɑːsk] ◇ *vt* - **1.** [gen] fragen; **to ask a question** eine Frage stellen; **to ask sb sthg** jn etw fragen - **2.** [request - permission, forgiveness] bitten um; *(phrase)*: **to ask sb for sthg** jn um etw bitten; **to ask sb for advice** jn um Rat fragen; **to ask sb to do sthg** jn (darum) bitten, etw zu tun - **3.** [invite] ein|laden; **to ask sb (round) to dinner** jn zum Abendessen ein|laden - **4.** [price] verlangen. ◇ *vi* - **1.** [enquire] fragen - **2.** [request] bitten. ◆ **ask after** *vt insep* sich erkundigen nach. ◆ **ask for** *vt insep* - **1.** [ask to talk to] verlangen; **he's asking for you** er will Sie sprechen - **2.** [request] bitten um.

askance [ə'skæns] *adv*: **to look askance at sb** jn missbilligend an|schauen; **to look askance at sthg** etw *(D)* ablehnend gegenüber|stehen.

askew [ə'skjuː] *adj* schief.

asking price ['ɑːskiŋ-] *n* Verkaufspreis *der*.

asleep [ə'sliːp] *adj* schlafend; **to fall asleep** ein|schlafen.

asparagus [ə'spærəgəs] *n* Spargel *der*.

aspect ['æspekt] *n* - **1.** [facet] Aspekt *der* - **2.** [appearance] Aussehen *das*.

aspersions [ə'spɜːʃnz] *npl*: **to cast aspersions (on sthg)** abfällige Bemerkungen (über etw *(A)*) machen.

asphalt ['æsfælt] *n (U)* Asphalt *der*.

asphyxiate [əs'fɪksɪeɪt] *vt* ersticken.

aspiration [ˌæspə'reɪʃn] *n* [desire, ambition] Bestrebung *die*.

aspire [ə'spaɪəʳ] *vi*: **to aspire to sthg** nach etw streben; **to aspire to do sthg** danach streben, etw zu tun.

aspirin ['æsprɪn] *n* Aspirin® *das*.

ass [æs] *n* - **1.** Esel *der* - **2.** *US vulg* = **arse**.

assailant [ə'seɪlənt] *n* Angreifer *der*, -in *die*.

assassin [ə'sæsɪn] *n* Attentäter *der*, -in *die* *(dessen Mordanschlag glückt)*.

assassinate [ə'sæsɪneɪt] *vt* ermorden; **to be assassinated** einem Attentat zum Opfer fallen.

assassination [əˌsæsɪ'neɪʃn] *n* (geglücktes) Attentat, (politischer) Mord.

assault [ə'sɔːlt] ◇ *n* - **1.** MIL: **assault (on sthg)** Sturmangriff *der* (auf etw *(A)*) - **2.** [physical attack]: **assault (on sb)** (tätlicher) Angriff (auf jn). ◇ *vt* [attack - physically] (tätlich) an|greifen; [- sexually] belästigen.

assemble [ə'sembl] ◇ *vt* - **1.** [gather - people] zusammen|rufen; [- evidence, material] zusammen|tragen; [- Parliament] ein|berufen - **2.** [fit together] zusammen|bauen. ◇ *vi* [people] sich versammeln; [Parliament] zusammen|treten.

assembly [ə'semblɪ] *n* - **1.** [gen] Versammlung *die*; [at school] Morgenandacht *die* - **2.** *(U)* [fitting together] Zusammenbau *der*; [of device, machine] Montage *die*.

assembly line *n* Fließband *das*.

assent [ə'sent] ◇ *n* Zustimmung *die*. ◇ *vi* zu|stimmen; **to assent to sthg** etw *(D)* zu|stimmen.

assert [ə'sɜːt] *vt* - **1.** [conviction, belief] behaupten; [innocence] beteuern - **2.** [authority] geltend machen.

assertive [ə'sɜːtɪv] *adj* [person, tone] energisch; [attitude] selbstbewusst.

assess [ə'ses] *vt* - **1.** [judge] ein|schätzen, beurteilen - **2.** [estimate - value] schätzen; [- damages] fest|setzen.

assessment [ə'sesmənt] *n* - **1.** [judgement] Einschätzung *die* - **2.** [estimate - of value] Schätzung *die*; [- of damages] Festsetzung *die*.

asset ['æset] *n* - **1.** [valuable quality] Vorteil *der* - **2.** [valuable person] Stütze *die*. ◆ **assets** *npl* COMM Vermögen *das*.

assign [ə'saɪn] *vt* - **1.** [allot]: **to assign sthg (to sb/sthg)** (jm/etw) etw zu|teilen *OR* zu|weisen

- **2.** [appoint]: **to assign sb (to sthg)** jn (etw *(D)*) zuteilen *OR* zulweisen; **to assign sb to do sthg** jn damit beauftragen, etw zu tun.

assignment [ə'saɪnmənt] *n* - **1.** [task] Aufgabe *die*; [at school] Projekt *das*; [job] Auftrag *der* - **2.** [act of appointing] Zuteilung *die*; [to task] Betrauung *die*; [to post] Berufung *die*.

assimilate [ə'sɪmɪleɪt] *vt* - **1.** [gen] auflnehmen - **2.** [people]: **to assimilate sb (into sthg)** jn (in etw *(A)*) integrieren.

assist [ə'sɪst] *vt* helfen *(+ D)*; **to assist sb with sthg** jm bei etw helfen; **to assist sb in doing sthg** jm helfen, etw zu tun.

assistance [ə'sɪstəns] *n (U)* Hilfe *die*; **to be of assistance (to sb)** (jm) helfen *OR* behilflich sein.

assistant [ə'sɪstənt] <> *n* - **1.** [helper] Assistent *der*, -in *die* - **2.** [in shop] Verkäufer *der*, -in *die*. <> *comp* stellvertretend; **assistant editor** Redaktionsassistent *der*, -in *die*.

associate <> *adj* [ə'səʊʃɪət] [member] außerordentlich. <> *n* [ə'səʊʃɪət] [business partner] Partner *der*, -in *die*. <> *vt* [ə'səʊʃɪeɪt] [connect] in Verbindung bringen, assoziieren; **to associate sb/sthg with sb/sthg** jn/etw mit jm/etw in Verbindung bringen; **to be associated with sb/sthg** mit jm/etw in Verbindung gebracht werden. <> *vi* [ə'səʊʃɪeɪt]: **to associate with sb** mit jm verkehren.

association [ə,səʊsɪ'eɪʃn] *n* - **1.** [organization] Verband *der* - **2.** *(U)* [relationship] Verkehr *der*, Umgang *der*; **in association with sb/sthg** in Zusammenarbeit mit jm/etw.

assorted [ə'sɔːtɪd] *adj* [colours, sizes] verschieden; [sweets] gemischt.

assortment [ə'sɔːtmənt] *n* [mixture - of people] Mischung *die*; [- of goods] Auswahl *die*.

assume [ə'sjuːm] *vt* - **1.** [suppose, adopt] anlnehmen - **2.** [undertake] übernehmen.

assumed name [ə'sjuːmd-] *n* falscher Name.

assuming [ə'sjuːmɪŋ] *conj*: **assuming (that)...** vorausgesetzt(, dass)...

assumption [ə'sʌmpʃn] *n* [supposition] Annahme *die*.

assurance [ə'ʃʊərəns] *n* - **1.** [promise] Zusicherung *die* - **2.** [confidence] Selbstsicherheit *die* - **3.** *(U)* FIN [insurance] Versicherung *die*.

assure [ə'ʃʊəʳ] *vt* [reassure] versichern *(+ D)*; **to assure sb of sthg** jn einer Sache *(G)* versichern; **to be assured of sthg** [be certain] sich *(D)* einer Sache *(G)* sicher sein.

assured [ə'ʃʊəd] *adj* selbstsicher.

asterisk ['æstərɪsk] *n* Sternchen *das*.

asthma ['æsmə] *n* Asthma *das*.

astonish [ə'stɒnɪʃ] *vt* erstaunen.

astonished [ə'stɒnɪʃd] *adj* erstaunt.

astonishment [ə'stɒnɪʃmənt] *n* Erstaunen *das*.

astound [ə'staʊnd] *vt* verblüffen.

astray [ə'streɪ] *adv*: **to go astray** [object] verloren gehen; [animal] sich verirren; **to lead sb astray** *fig* jn vom rechten Weg ablbringen.

astride [ə'straɪd] <> *adv* rittlings. <> *prep* rittlings auf *(+ D)*.

astrology [ə'strɒlədʒɪ] *n* Astrologie *die*.

astronaut ['æstrənɔːt] *n* Astronaut *der*, -in *die*.

astronomical [,æstrə'nɒmɪkl] *adj liter* & *fig* astronomisch.

astronomy [ə'strɒnəmɪ] *n* Astronomie *die*.

astute [ə'stjuːt] *adj* clever.

asylum [ə'saɪləm] *n* - **1.** *dated* [mental hospital] psychiatrische Anstalt - **2.** *(U)* [protection] Asyl *das*.

at *(unstressed* [ət], *stressed* [æt]*) prep* - **1.** [indicating place, position]: **there was a knock at the door** es klopfte an der Tür; **he studies at Cambridge** er studiert in Cambridge; **at the bottom of the hill** am Fuß(e) des Hügels; **at my father's** bei meinem Vater; **at home** zu Hause; **at school** in der Schule; **at work** bei der Arbeit - **2.** [indicating direction]: **to aim at sb/sthg** auf jn/etw zielen; **to smile at sb** jn anllächeln; **to look at sb/sthg** jn/etw anlsehen - **3.** [indicating a particular time]: **at midnight/noon/eleven o'clock** um Mitternacht/zwölf Uhr mittags/elf Uhr; **at Christmas/Easter** zu *OR* an Weihnachten/Ostern; **at night** bei Nacht, nachts - **4.** [indicating age, speed, rate]: **at your age** in deinem Alter; **at 52 (years of age)** mit 52 (Jahren); **at 100 miles per hour** mit 100 Meilen pro Stunde; **at high speed** mit hoher Geschwindigkeit - **5.** [indicating price]: **at £50 (a pair)** für 50 Pfund (das Paar) - **6.** [indicating particular state, condition]: **at peace/war** im Frieden/Krieg; **at lunch** beim Mittagessen - **7.** *(after adjectives)*: **amused/appalled/puzzled at sthg** über etw *(A)* belustigt/entsetzt/verblüfft; **to be bad/good at sthg** in etw *(D)* schlecht/gut sein. ◆ **at all** *adv* - **1.** *(with negative)*: **not at all** [when thanked] keine Ursache; [when answering a question] überhaupt nicht; **she's not at all happy** sie ist überhaupt nicht glücklich - **2.** [in the slightest]: **have you done anything at all today?** hast du heute überhaupt irgendetwas gemacht?; **do you know her at all?** kennst du sie überhaupt?

ate [*UK* et, *US* eɪt] *pt* ▷ **eat**.

atheist ['eɪθɪɪst] *n* Atheist *der*, -in *die*.

Athens ['æθɪnz] *n* Athen *nt*.

athlete ['æθliːt] *n* Leichtathlet *der*, -in *die*.

athletic [æθ'letɪk] *adj* - **1.** [relating to athletics] athletisch - **2.** [sporty] sportlich. ◆ **athletics** *npl* Leichtathletik *die*.

Atlantic [ət'læntɪk] <> *adj* atlantisch. <> *n*: **the Atlantic (Ocean)** der Atlantik.

atlas ['ætləs] *n* Atlas *der*.

atmosphere ['ætmə,sfɪəʳ] *n* - **1.** [gen] Atmosphäre *die* - **2.** [in room] Luft *die*.

atmospheric [,ætməs'ferɪk] *adj* - **1.** [pressure, pollution] atmosphärisch - **2.** [music, place, film] stimmungsvoll.

atom ['ætəm] *n* TECH Atom *das*.

atom bomb *n* Atombombe *die*.

atomic [ə'tɒmɪk] *adj* Atom-.

atone [ə'təʊn] *vi*: **to atone for sthg** [crime, sin] (für) etw büßen; [mistake, behaviour] etw wieder gut|machen.

A to Z *n* Stadtplan *der* (im Buchformat).

atrocious [ə'trəʊʃəs] *adj* grauenhaft.

atrocity [ə'trɒsətɪ] *n* Gräueltat *die*.

attach [ə'tætʃ] *vt* - **1.** [fasten] befestigen; [document] bei|heften; **to attach sthg to sthg** einer Sache an etw *(D)* befestigen; [document] einer Sache *(D)* etw bei|heften - **2.** [attribute]: **to attach sthg to sthg** [importance] etw *(D)* etw bei|messen; [blame] etw *(D)* etw zu|schreiben - **3.** COMPUT an|heften, an|hängen.

attaché case *n* Aktenkoffer *der*.

attached [ə'tætʃt] *adj* [fond]: **to be attached to sb/sthg** an jm/etw hängen.

attachment [ə'tætʃmənt] *n* - **1.** [device] Zusatzgerät *das* - **2.** COMPUT Attachment *das*, Anhang *der*.

attack [ə'tæk] ◇ *n* - **1.** [physical]: **attack (on sb)** [on person] Überfall *der* (auf jn); [on enemy] Angriff *der* (auf jn) - **2.** [verbal]: **attack (on sthg)** Angriff *der* (auf etw *(A)*) - **3.** [of illness] Anfall *der*. ◇ *vt* - **1.** [physically - person] überfallen; [- enemy] an|greifen - **2.** [verbally] an|greifen - **3.** [affect] befallen - **4.** [deal with] in Angriff nehmen. ◇ *vi* an|greifen.

attacker [ə'tækəʳ] *n* Angreifer *der*, -in *die*.

attain [ə'teɪn] *vt* [rank, objectives] erreichen; [success, happiness] erlangen.

attainment [ə'teɪnmənt] *n* [skill] Fertigkeit *die*.

attempt [ə'tempt] ◇ *n* Versuch *der*; **an attempt at a smile** ein Versuch, zu lächeln; **to make an attempt on sb's life** einen Mordanschlag auf jn verüben. ◇ *vt* [try] versuchen; **to attempt to do sthg** versuchen, etw zu tun.

attend [ə'tend] ◇ *vt* - **1.** [meeting] teil|nehmen an *(+ D)*; [party] gehen zu - **2.** [school, church] besuchen. ◇ *vi* - **1.** [be present] anwesend sein - **2.** [pay attention]: **to attend (to sthg)** auf|passen (bei etw). ◆ **attend to** *vt insep* - **1.** [deal with] sich kümmern um - **2.** [look after - customer] bedienen; [- patient] behandeln.

attendance [ə'tendəns] *n* - **1.** [number present - at meeting] Teilnehmerzahl *die*; [- at concert, cinema] Besucherzahl *die* - **2.** [presence] Anwesenheit *die*, Teilnahme *die*; **to have a poor attendance record** oft fehlen.

attendant [ə'tendənt] *n* [at museum] Aufseher *der*, -in *die*; [at petrol station] Tankwart *der*; **car park attendant** Parkplatzwächter *der*, -in *die*.

attention [ə'tenʃn] ◇ *n (U)* - **1.** [awareness, interest] Aufmerksamkeit *die*; **to attract sb's attention** jn auf sich *(A)* aufmerksam machen; **to bring sthg to sb's attention, to draw sb's attention to sthg** jn auf etw *(A)* aufmerksam machen; **to pay attention to sb/sthg** jm/etw Aufmerksamkeit schenken; **to pay attention** auf|passen - **2.** [care] Fürsorge *die* - **3.** COMM: **for the attention of** zu Händen (von). ◇ *excl* MIL stillgestanden!

attentive [ə'tentɪv] *adj* aufmerksam.

attic ['ætɪk] *n* Dachboden *der*.

attitude ['ætɪtjuːd] *n* - **1.** [way of thinking]: **attitude (to** OR **towards sb/sthg)** Einstellung *die* (gegenüber jm/zu etw) - **2.** [behaviour, posture] Haltung *die*.

attn (*abbr of* **for the attention of**) z. Hd.

attorney [ə'tɜːnɪ] *n* *US* [lawyer] (Rechts)anwalt *der*, -wältin *die*.

attorney general (*pl* **attorneys general**) *n* ≃ Generalbundesanwalt *der*.

attract [ə'trækt] *vt* - **1.** [draw, cause to come near] an|ziehen, an|locken - **2.** [be attractive to] anziehend wirken auf *(+ A)* - **3.** [support] gewinnen; [criticism] auf sich *(A)* ziehen - **4.** [magnetically] an|ziehen.

attraction [ə'trækʃn] *n* - **1.** [liking] Anziehungskraft *die*; **to feel an attraction to sb** sich zu jm hingezogen fühlen - **2.** *(U)* [appeal, charm] Reiz *der* - **3.** [attractive feature, event] Attraktion *die*.

attractive [ə'træktɪv] *adj* - **1.** [person] anziehend - **2.** [thing, idea] attraktiv.

attribute ◇ *vt* [ə'trɪbjuːt] - **1.** [ascribe]: **to attribute sthg to sb/sthg** etw jm/etw zu|schreiben - **2.** [work of art, remark]: **to attribute sthg to sb** jm etw zuschreiben. ◇ *n* ['ætrɪbjuːt] [quality] Eigenschaft *die*.

aubergine ['əʊbəʒiːn] *n UK* Aubergine *die*.

auburn ['ɔːbən] *adj* [hair] rotbraun.

auction ['ɔːkʃn] ◇ *n* Auktion *die*, Versteigerung *die*; **at** OR **by auction** bei einer Auktion OR Versteigerung; **to put sthg up for auction** etw zur Versteigerung an|bieten. ◇ *vt* versteigern. ◆ **auction off** *vt sep* versteigern.

auctioneer [,ɔːkʃə'nɪəʳ] *n* Auktionator *der*.

audacious [ɔː'deɪʃəs] *adj* [daring] kühn; [impudent] dreist.

audible ['ɔːdəbl] *adj* hörbar.

audience ['ɔːdjəns] *n* [gen] Publikum *das*; [of TV programme] Zuschauer *Pl*; [of radio programme] Zuhörer *Pl*.

audio-visual *adj* audiovisuell.

audit ['ɔːdɪt] ◇ *n* Buchprüfung *die*. ◇ *vt* prüfen.

audition [ɔːˈdɪʃn] *n* [of actor] Vorsprechen *das*; [of singer] Probesingen *das*; [of musician] Probespiel *das*.

auditor [ˈɔːdɪtəʳ] *n* Buchprüfer *der*, -in *die*.

auditorium [ˌɔːdɪˈtɔːrɪəm] (*pl* **-riums** *OR* **-ria** [-rɪə]) *n* Zuschauerraum *der*.

augur [ˈɔːgəʳ] *vi*: **to augur well/badly** etwas Gutes/nichts Gutes verheißen.

August [ˈɔːgəst] *n* August *der*; *see also* **September**.

aunt [ɑːnt] *n* Tante *die*.

auntie, aunty [ˈɑːntɪ] *n inf* Tantchen *das*.

au pair [ˌəʊˈpeəʳ] *n* Aupairmädchen *das*.

aura [ˈɔːrə] *n* Aura *die*.

aural [ˈɔːrəl] *adj* SCH: **aural comprehension** Hörverständnis *das*.

auspices [ˈɔːspɪsɪz] *npl*: **under the auspices of** unter der Schirmherrschaft *(+ G)*.

auspicious [ɔːˈspɪʃəs] *adj* [start] vielversprechend; [day, occasion] günstig.

Aussie [ˈɒzɪ] *inf* ◇ *adj* australisch. ◇ *n* Australier *der*, -in *die*.

austere [ɒˈstɪəʳ] *adj* - **1.** [person] streng; [life] asketisch - **2.** [room, building] karg.

austerity [ɒˈsterətɪ] *n* - **1.** [of person] Strenge *die*; [of life - for religious reasons] Entsagung *die*; [- for economic reasons] Entbehrung *die* - **2.** [of room, building] Kargheit *die*.

Australia [ɒˈstreɪljə] *n* Australien *nt*.

Australian [ɒˈstreɪljən] ◇ *adj* australisch. ◇ *n* Australier *der*, -in *die*.

Austria [ˈɒstrɪə] *n* Österreich *nt*.

Austrian [ˈɒstrɪən] ◇ *adj* österreichisch. ◇ *n* Österreicher *der*, -in *die*.

authentic [ɔːˈθentɪk] *adj* authentisch.

author [ˈɔːθəʳ] *n* Autor *der*, -in *die*; [by profession] Schriftsteller *der*, -in *die*.

authoritarian [ɔːˌθɒrɪˈteərɪən] *adj* autoritär.

authoritative [ɔːˈθɒrɪtətɪv] *adj* - **1.** [person, voice] Respekt einflößend - **2.** [report] verlässlich.

authority [ɔːˈθɒrətɪ] *n* - **1.** [official organization] Behörde *die*, Amt *das* - **2.** *(U)* [power] Autorität *die*; **to have authority over sb** Weisungsbefugnis gegenüber jm haben; **in authority** verantwortlich - **3.** [permission] Erlaubnis *die* - **4.** [expert] Autorität *die*. ◆ **authorities** *npl*: **the authorities** die Behörden.

authorize, -ise [ˈɔːθəraɪz] *vt* genehmigen; [biography] autorisieren; [money] bewilligen; **to authorize sb to do sthg** jn ermächtigen, etw zu tun.

autistic [ɔːˈtɪstɪk] *adj* autistisch.

auto [ˈɔːtəʊ] (*pl* **-s**) *n US* Auto *das*.

autobiography [ˌɔːtəbaɪˈɒgrəfɪ] *n* Autobiografie *die*.

autocratic [ˌɔːtəˈkrætɪk] *adj* autokratisch.

autograph [ˈɔːtəgrɑːf] ◇ *n* Autogramm *das*. ◇ *vt* signieren.

automate [ˈɔːtəmeɪt] *vt* automatisieren.

automatic [ˌɔːtəˈmætɪk] ◇ *adj* automatisch. ◇ *n* - **1.** [car] Wagen *der* mit Automatikgetriebe - **2.** [gun] automatische Waffe - **3.** [washing machine] Waschautomat *der*.

automatically [ˌɔːtəˈmætɪklɪ] *adv* automatisch.

automobile [ˈɔːtəməbiːl] *n US* Auto(mobil) *das*.

autonomy [ɔːˈtɒnəmɪ] *n (U)* Autonomie *die*.

autopsy [ˈɔːtɒpsɪ] *n* Autopsie *die*.

autumn [ˈɔːtəm] *n* Herbst *der*.

auxiliary [ɔːgˈzɪljərɪ] ◇ *adj* - **1.** [providing assistance] Hilfs-; **auxiliary nurse** Schwesternhelferin *die* - **2.** GRAM [verb] Hilfs-. ◇ *n* [in hospital] Hilfskraft *die*.

Av. *abbr of* **avenue**.

avail [əˈveɪl] ◇ *n*: **to no avail** vergeblich, ohne Erfolg. ◇ *vt*: **to avail o.s. of sthg** von etw Gebrauch machen.

available [əˈveɪləbl] *adj* verfügbar; [product] lieferbar; *(phrase)*: **to be available** [person] zur Verfügung stehen.

avalanche [ˈævəlɑːnʃ] *n liter & fig* Lawine *die*.

avarice [ˈævərɪs] *n* Habgier *die*.

Ave. *abbr of* **avenue**.

avenge [əˈvendʒ] *vt* rächen.

avenue [ˈævənjuː] *n* Allee *die (in der Stadt)*.

average [ˈævərɪdʒ] ◇ *adj* - **1.** [mean] durchschnittlich - **2.** [typical]: **the average Englishman** der Durchschnittsengländer - **3.** *pej* [mediocre] durchschnittlich, mittelmäßig. ◇ *n* Durchschnitt *der*; **on average** im Durchschnitt. ◇ *vt*: **we averaged 80 miles per hour** wir sind durchschnittlich 80 Meilen pro Stunde gefahren. ◆ **average out** *vi*: **to average out at** durchschnittlich betragen.

aversion [əˈvɜːʃn] *n* [dislike]: **aversion (to)** Abneigung *die* (gegen).

avert [əˈvɜːt] *vt* - **1.** [problem] vermeiden; [accident, disaster] verhindern - **2.** [eyes, glance] ab|wenden.

aviary [ˈeɪvjərɪ] *n* Vogelhaus *das*.

avid [ˈævɪd] *adj* begeistert, passioniert; **avid for sthg** begierig auf etw *(A)*.

avocado [ˌævəˈkɑːdəʊ] (*pl* **-s** *OR* **-es**) *n*: **avocado (pear)** Avocado *die*.

avoid [əˈvɔɪd] *vt* - **1.** [problem, accident, mistake] vermeiden; **to avoid doing sthg** vermeiden, etw zu tun - **2.** [keep away from] meiden.

await [əˈweɪt] *vt* erwarten.

awake [əˈweɪk] (*pt* **awoke** *OR* **awaked**, *pp* **awoken**) ◇ *adj* [not sleeping] wach. ◇ *vt* - **1.** [person] wecken - **2.** *fig* [memories, feelings] erwecken. ◇ *vi* auf|wachen.

awakening [əˈweɪknɪŋ] *n* Erwachen *das*.

award [əˈwɔːd] ◇ *n* [prize] Preis *der*; [for bravery] Auszeichnung *die*. ◇ *vt*: **to award sb**

sthg, to award sthg to sb [prize] jm etw verleihen; [free kick, penalty] jm etw geben; [damages, compensation] jm etw zu|sprechen.

aware [əˈweəʳ] *adj* - **1.** [conscious]: **to be aware of sthg** sich *(D)* einer Sache *(G)* bewusst sein; **to be aware that...** sich *(D)* bewusst sein, dass... - **2.** [informed, sensitive] (gut) informiert; **to be aware of sthg** über etw *(A)* informiert sein.

awareness [əˈweənɪs] *n* Bewusstsein *das*.

away [əˈweɪ] ◇ *adv* - **1.** [indicating movement] weg; **to walk away (from)** weg|gehen (von); **to run away (from)** weg|laufen (von); **to look away (from)** weg|sehen (von); **to turn away (from)** sich ab|wenden (von) - **2.** [at a distance]: **far away** weit entfernt; **10 miles away (from here)** 10 Meilen (von hier) entfernt; **it's still two weeks away** bis dahin sind es noch zwei Wochen - **3.** [absent] weg; [not at home or in the office] nicht da; **Mr Stone is away on a business trip** Herr Stone ist auf Geschäftsreise - **4.** [in a safe place]: **to put sthg away** etw weg|räumen - **5.** [indicating removal or disappearance]: **to fade away** verblassen; **to take sthg away (from sb)** (jm) etw weg|nehmen; **to give sthg away** [as a present] etw verschenken - **6.** [continuously]: **to work away** in einem fort arbeiten - **7.** *phr*: **straight** OR **right away** sofort. ◇ *adj* SPORT: **away game** Auswärtsspiel *das*.

awe [ɔː] *n* Ehrfurcht *die*; **to be in awe of sb** Ehrfurcht vor jm haben.

awesome [ˈɔːsəm] *adj* - **1.** [impressive] Ehrfurcht gebietend - **2.** *inf* [fantastic] irre.

awful [ˈɔːfʊl] *adj* - **1.** [terrible] furchtbar, schrecklich - **2.** *inf* [very great]: **an awful lot** sehr viel; **an awful lot of time/money/books** eine Menge Zeit/Geld/Bücher.

awfully [ˈɔːflɪ] *adv inf* [very] furchtbar.

awkward [ˈɔːkwəd] *adj* - **1.** [clumsy - movement] ungeschickt, unbeholfen; [- position] ungünstig; [- person] unbeholfen - **2.** [embarrassed - person] verlegen; [- silence] betreten; [- situation, questions] peinlich - **3.** [uncooperative] unkooperativ - **4.** [inconvenient] ungünstig - **5.** [difficult, delicate] schwierig.

awning [ˈɔːnɪŋ] *n* - **1.** [of tent] Vordach *das* - **2.** [of shop] Markise *die*.

awoke [əˈwəʊk] *pt* ▷ **awake**.

awoken [əˈwəʊkn] *pp* ▷ **awake**.

awry [əˈraɪ] ◇ *adj* schief. ◇ *adv*: **to go awry** schief gehen.

axe *UK*, **ax** *US* [æks] ◇ *n* Axt *die*. ◇ *vt* [project] auf|geben; [jobs] streichen, kürzen.

axes [ˈæksiːz] *Pl* ▷ **axis**.

axis [ˈæksɪs] (*pl* **axes**) *n* Achse *die*.

axle [ˈæksl] *n* Achse *die*.

aye [aɪ] ◇ *adv* - **1.** *Scotland* [yes] ja - **2.** NAUT [yes] zu Befehl, jawohl. ◇ *n* [vote] Jastimme *die*.

Azores [əˈzɔːz] *npl*: **the Azores** die Azoren *Pl*.

B

b (*pl* **b's** OR **bs**), **B** (*pl* **B's** OR **Bs**) [biː] *n* [letter] b *das*, B *das*. ◆ **B** *n* - **1.** MUS H *das* - **2.** SCH [mark] ≃ zwei.

BA *n abbr of* **Bachelor of Arts**.

babble [ˈbæbl] ◇ *n* [noise] Gemurmel *das*. ◇ *vi* plappern.

baboon [bəˈbuːn] *n* Pavian *der*.

baby [ˈbeɪbɪ] *n* Baby *das*; **don't be such a baby!** benimm dich nicht wie ein Baby!

baby buggy *n* - **1.** *UK* [pushchair] Sportwagen *der* - **2.** *US* = **baby carriage**.

baby carriage *n US* Kinderwagen *der*.

baby food *n* Babynahrung *die*.

baby-sit *vi* babysitten.

baby-sitter [-ˌsɪtəʳ] *n* Babysitter *der*, -in *die*.

bachelor [ˈbætʃələʳ] *n* Junggeselle *der*.

Bachelor of Arts *n* [degree] *erster akademischer Grad der Geisteswissenschaften an Universitäten in englischsprachigen Ländern*.

Bachelor of Science *n* [degree] *erster akademischer Grad der Naturwissenschaften an Universitäten in englischsprachigen Ländern*.

back [bæk] ◇ *adv* - **1.** [backwards] zurück; **stand back (please)!** (bitte) zurücktreten!; **to tie back** zurück|binden; **to push back** [shove] zurück|schieben - **2.** [to former position or state] zurück; **when will you be back?** wann bist du wieder da?; **back and forth** hin und her; **to give sthg back** etw zurück|geben; **we went back to sleep** wir sind wieder eingeschlafen; **back home** bei uns zu Hause - **3.** [earlier]: **two weeks back** vor zwei Wochen; **it dates back to 1960** es stammt aus dem Jahr(e) 1960; **I found out back in January** ich habe es schon im Januar erfahren; **to think back to sthg** an etw *(A)* zurück|denken - **4.** [in reply, in return]: **to write/phone/pay back** zurück|schreiben/-rufen/-zahlen - **5.** [in fashion again]: **to be back (in fashion)** wieder modern sein. ◇ *n* - **1.** [of person, animal, hand] Rücken *der*; [of chair] Lehne *die*; **to do sthg behind sb's back** etw hinter js Rücken tun; **to put one's back into sthg** sich bei etw an|strengen; **get off my back!** *inf* lass mich in Ruhe! - **2.** [opposite or reverse side - of bank note, page] Rückseite *die*; **back of the head** Hinterkopf *der* - **3.** [not front - inside car] Rücksitz *der*; [- of room] hinterer Teil; **at the back of, in back of** *US* hinter *(+ D)*; **at the back of the cupboard** hinten im Schrank - **4.** SPORT [player] Verteidiger *der*; [in rugby] Spieler *der* der Hintermannschaft. ◇ *adj (in compounds)* - **1.** [at the back - wheels, legs, door] Hinter- - **2.** [overdue - rent] überfällig.

◇ *vt* - **1.** [reverse] zurück|setzen - **2.** [support] unterstützen - **3.** [bet on]: **to back a horse** (Geld) auf ein Pferd setzen. ◇ *vi* [car, driver] rückwärts fahren. ◆ **back to back** *adv* [stand] Rücken an Rücken. ◆ **back to front** *adv* [the wrong way round] verkehrt herum. ◆ **back down** *vi* nach|geben. ◆ **back out** *vi* [of arrangement] aus|steigen. ◆ **back up** ◇ *vt sep* - **1.** [support] unterstützen - **2.** [confirm] bestätigen - **3.** [reverse] zurück|setzen - **4.** COMPUT ein Backup machen von. ◇ *vi* [car, driver] zurück|setzen.

backache ['bækeɪk] *n (U)* Rückenschmerzen *Pl.*

backbencher [ˌbæk'bentʃəʳ] *n UK* POL parlamentarischer Hinterbänkler.

backbone ['bækbəʊn] *n liter & fig* Rückgrat *das.*

backcloth ['bækklɒθ] *n UK* = **backdrop**.

backdate [ˌbæk'deɪt] *vt* zurück|datieren.

back door *n* Hintertür *die.*

backdrop ['bækdrɒp] *n liter & fig* Hintergrund *der.*

backfire [ˌbæk'faɪəʳ] *vi* - **1.** [motor vehicle] Fehlzündungen haben - **2.** [plan] fehl|schlagen; **to backfire on sb** auf jn zurück|fallen.

backgammon ['bækˌgæmən] *n* Backgammon *das.*

background ['bækgraʊnd] *n* - **1.** [gen] Hintergrund *der*; **in the background** *liter & fig* im Hintergrund - **2.** [upbringing] Herkunft *die.*

backhand ['bækhænd] *n* Rückhand *die.*

backhanded ['bækhændɪd] *adj fig* [compliment] zweifelhaft.

backhander ['bækhændəʳ] *n UK inf* [bribe] Schmiergeld *das.*

backing ['bækɪŋ] *n* - **1.** *(U)* [support] Unterstützung *die* - **2.** [lining] Verstärkung *die.*

backing group *n* MUS Begleitband *die.*

backlash ['bæklæʃ] *n* Gegenschlag *der.*

backlog ['bæklɒg] *n* Rückstände *Pl*; **to have a backlog of work** mit der Arbeit im Rückstand sein.

back number *n* alte Ausgabe.

backpack ['bækpæk] *n* Rucksack *der.*

back pay *n* ausstehender Lohn.

back seat *n* [in car] Rücksitz *der*; **to take a back seat** *fig* sich im Hintergrund halten.

backside [ˌbæk'saɪd] *n inf* Hintern *der.*

backstage [ˌbæk'steɪdʒ] *adv* hinter den Kulissen.

back street *n UK* kleine Seitenstraße.

backstroke ['bækstrəʊk] *n* Rückenschwimmen *das.*

backup ['bækʌp] *n* - **1.** *(U)* [support] Unterstützung *die* - **2.** COMPUT Sicherungskopie *die.*

backward ['bækwəd] ◇ *adj* - **1.** [gen] rückwärts gerichtet; **a backward glance** ein Blick über die Schulter - **2.** *pej* [child, country] zurückgeblieben. ◇ *adv US* = **backwards**.

backwards ['bækwədz], **backward** *US* ['bækwəd] *adv* [towards the rear] rückwärts; **to fall backwards** nach hinten fallen; **backwards and forwards** hin und her; **to look backwards** zurück|blicken.

backwater ['bækˌwɔːtəʳ] *n* [place] Kaff *das.*

backyard [ˌbæk'jɑːd] *n* - **1.** *UK* [yard] Hinterhof *der* - **2.** *US* [garden] Garten *der* hinter dem Haus.

bacon ['beɪkən] *n (U)* Schinkenspeck *der.*

bacteria [bæk'tɪərɪə] *npl* Bakterien *Pl.*

bad [bæd] (*comp* **worse**, *superl* **worst**) ◇ *adj* - **1.** [unpleasant, unfavourable - gen] schlecht; [- smell] übel; **bad breath** Mundgeruch *der*; **he is in a bad way** es geht ihm gar nicht gut; **smoking is bad for you** Rauchen ist schädlich; **too bad!** Pech! - **2.** [serious] schwer; **to have a bad cold** einen starken Schnupfen haben - **3.** [inadequate - eyesight, excuse] schwach; **to be bad at sthg** etw schlecht können; **he's bad at English** er ist schlecht in Englisch; **not bad** nicht schlecht - **4.** [injured, unhealthy] schlimm; **my bad leg** mein schlimmes Bein; **he has a bad heart** er hat ein schwaches Herz - **5.** [naughty] ungezogen; [wicked] böse, übel; **he's a bad lot** er ist ein übler Bursche - **6.** [food - rotten, off] verdorben; **to go bad** verderben - **7.** [guilty]: **he really feels bad about it** es tut ihm wirklich leid. ◇ *adv US* = **badly**.

baddy ['bædɪ] (*pl* **-ies**) *n inf* Böse *der.*

badge [bædʒ] *n* - **1.** [for fun] Button *der* - **2.** [for employee, visitor] Schild(chen) *das* - **3.** [sewn-on] Abzeichen *das* - **4.** [on car] Emblem *das.*

badger ['bædʒəʳ] ◇ *n* Dachs *der.* ◇ *vt* [pester]: **to badger sb** jm keine Ruhe lassen.

badly ['bædlɪ] (*comp* **worse**, *superl* **worst**) *adv* - **1.** [poorly] schlecht; **to treat sb badly** jn schlecht behandeln - **2.** [wounded, beaten, affected] schwer - **3.** [very much]: **to be badly in need of sthg** etw dringend benötigen.

badly-off *adj* [poor] nicht gut gestellt.

badminton ['bædmɪntən] *n (U)* Federball *das*; SPORT Badminton *das.*

bad-tempered [-'tempəd] *adj* - **1.** [by nature] übellaunig - **2.** [in a bad mood] schlecht gelaunt.

baffled [bæfld] *adj* ratlos.

bag [bæg] ◇ *n* - **1.** [container] Tasche *die*; [for shopping] Tüte *die*; [large, for coal, cement] Sack *der*; [of tea, rice] Beutel *der*; **to pack one's bags** *fig* [leave] seine Sachen packen - **2.** [handbag] Handtasche *die*; [when travelling] Reisetasche *die* - **3.** [bagful]: **a bag of crisps** *UK* eine Tüte Chips; **a bag of potatoes** ein Sack Kartoffeln - **4.** *v inf pej* [nasty woman] Ziege *die.*

◇ *vt* - **1.** *UK inf* [get] sich *(D)* schnappen - **2.** *UK inf* [reserve] belegen, besetzen. ◆ **bags** *npl* - **1.** [under eyes] Tränensäcke *Pl* - **2.** [lots]: **bags of time/room** *inf* eine Menge OR jede Menge Zeit/Platz.

bagel ['beɪgəl] *n kleines ringförmiges Brötchen.*

baggage ['bægɪdʒ] *n* Gepäck *das.*

baggage reclaim *n* Gepäckausgabe *die.*

baggy ['bægɪ] *adj* weit (geschnitten).

bagpipes ['bægpaɪps] *npl* Dudelsack *der.*

Bahamas [bə'hɑːməz] *npl*: **the Bahamas** die Bahamas.

bail [beɪl] *n (U)* LAW Kaution *die*; **on bail** gegen Kaution. ◆ **bail out** ◇ *vt sep* - **1.** LAW [pay bail for] (die) Kaution stellen für - **2.** [rescue] aus der Klemme helfen *(+ D)* - **3.** [boat] auslschöpfen. ◇ *vi* [from plane] ablspringen.

bailiff ['beɪlɪf] *n* [in charge of repossession] Gerichtsvollzieher *der*; [in court] Gerichtsdiener *der.*

bait [beɪt] ◇ *n (U)* Köder *der.* ◇ *vt* - **1.** [hook, trap] mit einem Köder versehen - **2.** [torment - person] piesacken; [- bear, badger] quälen.

bake [beɪk] ◇ *vt* - **1.** [bread, cake *etc*] backen - **2.** [ground] ausldörren; [clay, brick] brennen. ◇ *vi* backen.

baked beans [beɪkt-] *npl* weiße Bohnen *Pl* in Tomatensoße.

baked potato *n* in der Schale gebackene Kartoffel.

baker ['beɪkəʳ] *n* Bäcker *der*, -in *die*; **baker's (shop)** Bäckerei *die*, Bäckerladen *der.*

bakery ['beɪkərɪ] *n* Bäckerei *die.*

baking ['beɪkɪŋ] *n* [cooking] Backen *das.*

balaclava [mbælə'klɑːvə] *n UK eng anliegende Kopfbedeckung, die nur das Gesicht frei lässt.*

balance ['bæləns] ◇ *n* - **1.** [equilibrium] Gleichgewicht *das*; **to keep/lose one's balance** das Gleichgewicht halten/verlieren; **off balance** aus dem Gleichgewicht - **2.** *fig* [counterweight] Ausgleich *der* - **3.** *fig* [weight, force]: **balance of power** Gleichgewicht *das* der Kräfte - **4.** [scales] Waage *die* - **5.** [remainder] Rest *der* - **6.** [of bank account] Kontostand *der.* ◇ *vt* - **1.** [keep in balance] im Gleichgewicht halten - **2.** [compare]: **to balance sthg against sthg** etw gegen etw ablwägen - **3.** [in accounting]: **to balance the books/the budget** die Bilanz machen. ◇ *vi* - **1.** [maintain equilibrium] das Gleichgewicht halten - **2.** [in accounting] sich auslgleichen. ◆ **on balance** *adv* alles in allem.

balanced diet [,bælənst-] *n* ausgewogene Ernährung.

balance of payments *n* Zahlungsbilanz *die.*

balance of trade *n* Handelsbilanz *die.*

balance sheet *n* Bilanz *die.*

balcony ['bælkənɪ] *n* - **1.** [on building] Balkon *der* - **2.** [in theatre] oberster Rang.

bald [bɔːld] *adj* - **1.** [head, man] glatzköpfig, kahl(köpfig) - **2.** [tyre] völlig abgenutzt - **3.** *fig* [unadorned] nüchtern, unverblümt.

bale [beɪl] *n* Ballen *der.* ◆ **bale out** *UK* ◇ *vt sep* [boat] auslschöpfen. ◇ *vi* [from plane] ablspringen.

Balearic Islands [,bælɪ'ærɪk-], **Balearics** [,bælɪ'ærɪks] *npl*: **the Balearic Islands** die Balearen.

balk [bɔːk] *vi*: **to balk (at)** zurücklschrecken (vor *(+ D)*).

Balkans ['bɔːlkənz], **Balkan States** *npl*: **the Balkans** der Balkan.

ball [bɔːl] *n* - **1.** [in game] Ball *der*; [in snooker, bowling] Kugel *die*; **to be on the ball** auf Draht sein; **to play ball** *fig* mitlmachen - **2.** [of wool] Knäuel *das* - **3.** [of foot] Ballen *der* - **4.** [dance] Ball *der.* ◆ **balls** *v inf* ◇ *n (U)* [nonsense] Schwachsinn *der.* ◇ *npl* [testicles] Eier *Pl.* ◇ *excl* Scheiße!

ballad ['bæləd] *n* Ballade *die.*

ballast ['bæləst] *n* Ballast *der.*

ball bearing *n* Kugellager *das.*

ball boy *n* Balljunge *der.*

ballerina [,bælə'riːnə] *n* Ballerina *die.*

ballet ['bæleɪ] *n* Ballett *das.*

ballet dancer *n* Balletttänzer *der*, -in *die.*

ball game *n* - **1.** *US* [baseball match] Baseballspiel *das* - **2.** *fig* [situation]: **it's a whole new ball game** *inf* das ist eine ganz neue Lage.

balloon [bə'luːn] *n* - **1.** [toy] Luftballon *der* - **2.** [hot-air balloon] Heißluftballon *der.*

ballot ['bælət] ◇ *n* [voting process] Abstimmung *die.* ◇ *vt* [members] abstimmen lassen.

ballot box *n* Wahlurne *die.*

ballot paper *n* Stimmzettel *der.*

ball park *n US* Baseballstadion *das.*

ballpoint (pen) ['bɔːlpɔɪnt-] *n* Kugelschreiber *der.*

ballroom ['bɔːlrʊm] *n* Ballsaal *der.*

ballroom dancing *n (U)* Gesellschaftstanz *der.*

balmy ['bɑːmɪ] *adj* [evening] mild.

balsawood ['bɒlsəwʊd] *n* Balsaholz *das.*

Baltic ['bɔːltɪk] ◇ *adj* [port, coast] Ostsee-, baltisch. ◇ *n*: **the Baltic (Sea)** die Ostsee.

Baltic State *n*: **the Baltic States** die Baltischen Staaten.

bamboo [bæm'buː] *n* Bambus *der.*

bamboozle [bæm'buːzl] *vt inf* verwirren.

ban [bæn] ◇ *n* Verbot *das*; **ban on smoking** Rauchverbot *das.* ◇ *vt* verbieten; **to ban sb from doing sthg** jm etw verbieten.

banal [bə'nɑːl] *adj pej* banal.

banana [bə'nɑːnə] *n* Banane *die.*

band [bænd] *n* - **1.** [musical - pop] Gruppe *die*; [- traditional, classical] Kapelle *die*; [- jazz] Band *die* - **2.** [gang] Bande *die* - **3.** [of colour, metal] Streifen *der* - **4.** [range] Klasse *die*. ◆ **band together** *vi* sich zusammen|schließen.

bandage ['bændɪdʒ] ◇ *n* Verband *der*. ◇ *vt* verbinden.

Band-Aid® *n* Heftpflaster *das*.

bandit ['bændɪt] *n* Bandit *der*.

bandstand ['bændstænd] *n* Musikpavillon *der*.

bandwagon ['bændwægən] *n*: **to jump on the bandwagon** auf den fahrenden Zug auf|springen.

bandy ['bændɪ] *adj* [bandy-legged] krummbeinig. ◆ **bandy about, bandy around** *vt sep* [words] um sich werfen mit.

bang [bæŋ] ◇ *adv* [right]: **bang in the middle** genau in der Mitte; **his description was bang on** seine Beschreibung passte aufs Haar; **bang on time** auf die Minute pünktlich. ◇ *n* - **1.** [blow] Schlag *der* - **2.** [loud noise] Knall *der*. ◇ *vt* - **1.** [hit] an|schlagen - **2.** [door] zu|schlagen. ◇ *vi* - **1.** [knock]: **to bang on the door/wall** [once] gegen die Tür/die Wand schlagen; [more than once] gegen die Tür/die Wand hämmern - **2.** [make a loud noise] (herum)|poltern - **3.** [crash]: **to bang into sb/sthg** gegen jn/etw stoßen. ◇ *excl* peng! ◆ **bangs** *npl US* Pony *der*.

banger ['bæŋər] *n UK* - **1.** *inf* [sausage] Würstchen *das* - **2.** *inf* [old car] alte Kiste - **3.** [firework] Knallkörper *der*.

bangle ['bæŋgl] *n* Armreif *der*.

banish ['bænɪʃ] *vt liter & fig* verbannen.

banister ['bænɪstər] *n* Geländer *das*.

banisters ['bænɪstəz] *npl* = **banister**.

bank [bæŋk] ◇ *n* - **1.** FIN Bank *die* - **2.** [of data, blood *etc*] Bank *die* - **3.** [of river, lake] Ufer *das* - **4.** [slope] Böschung *die* - **5.** [of fog, cloud] Bank *die*; **a bank of snow** eine Schneeverwehung. ◇ *vt* FIN ein|zahlen. ◇ *vi* - **1.** FIN: **who do you bank with?** bei welcher Bank sind Sie? - **2.** [plane] sich in die Kurve legen. ◆ **bank on** *vt insep* sich verlassen auf *(+ A)*.

bank account *n* Bankkonto *das*.

bank balance *n* Kontostand *der*.

bank card *n* = **banker's card**.

bank charges *npl* Bankgebühren *Pl*.

bank draft *n* Banküberweisung *die*.

banker ['bæŋkər] *n* FIN Bankier *der*.

banker's card *n UK* Scheckkarte *die*.

bank holiday *n UK* Feiertag *der*.

banking ['bæŋkɪŋ] *n* Bankwesen *das*.

bank manager *n* Filialleiter *der*, -in *die*.

bank note *n* Banknote *die*, Geldschein *der*.

bank rate *n* Diskontsatz *der*.

bankrupt ['bæŋkrʌpt] *adj* bankrott; **to go bankrupt** bankrott machen, in Konkurs gehen.

bankruptcy ['bæŋkrəptsɪ] *n* Bankrott *der*.

bank statement *n* Kontoauszug *der*.

banner ['bænər] *n* Transparent *das*.

bannister *n* = **banister**.

bannisters *npl* = **banister**.

banquet ['bæŋkwɪt] *n* Festessen *das*.

banter ['bæntər] *n (U)* Frotzeleien *Pl*.

bap [bæp] *n UK* weiches Brötchen.

baptism ['bæptɪzm] *n* Taufe *die*.

Baptist ['bæptɪst] *n* Baptist *der*, -in *die*.

baptize, -ise [*UK* bæp'taɪz, *US* 'bæptaɪz] *vt* taufen.

bar [bɑːr] ◇ *n* - **1.** [of wood, metal] Stange *die*; [of gold] Barren *der*; [of soap] Stück *das*; [of chocolate - slab] Tafel *die*; [- long and thin] Riegel *der*; *(phrase)*: **to be behind bars** hinter Gittern sitzen; **the bar** [in gymnastics] der Balken - **2.** *fig* [obstacle] Hindernis *das* - **3.** [in hotel] Bar *die*; [pub] Kneipe *die* - **4.** [counter] Theke *die* - **5.** MUS Takt *der*. ◇ *vt* - **1.** [door, window] verriegeln - **2.** [block] (ver)sperren; **to bar sb's way** jm den Weg versperren. ◇ *prep* [except] ausgenommen, außer *(+ D)*; **bar none** ohne Ausnahme. ◆ **Bar** *n*: **to be called to the Bar** *UK* als Anwalt zugelassen werden.

barbaric [bɑː'bærɪk] *adj* barbarisch.

barbecue ['bɑːbɪkjuː] *n* - **1.** [grill] Grill *der* - **2.** [party] Barbecue *das*, Grillparty *die*.

barbed wire [bɑːbd-] *n* Stacheldraht *der*.

barber ['bɑːbər] *n* (Herren)friseur *der*; **barber's (shop)** (Herren)friseursalon *der*.

barbiturate [bɑː'bɪtjʊrət] *n* Barbiturat *das*.

bar code *n* Strichkodierung *die*.

bare [beər] ◇ *adj* - **1.** [feet, legs, body] nackt, bloß; [rock, branches, landscape] kahl - **2.** [basic]: **the bare facts** die reinen Tatsachen; **the bare minimum** das strikte Minimum - **3.** [room, cupboard] leer. ◇ *vt* entblößen; **to bare one's teeth** die Zähne fletschen.

barefaced ['beəfeɪst] *adj* schamlos, frech.

barefoot(ed) [,beə'fʊt(ɪd)] ◇ *adj* barfüßig. ◇ *adv* barfuß.

barely ['beəlɪ] *adv* [scarcely] kaum, knapp.

bargain ['bɑːgɪn] ◇ *n* - **1.** [agreement] Geschäft *das*; **into the bargain** obendrein - **2.** [good buy] Schnäppchen *das*. ◇ *vi* (ver)handeln; **to bargain with sb for sthg** mit jm um etw handeln OR feilschen. ◆ **bargain for, bargain on** *vt insep* erwarten, rechnen mit.

barge [bɑːdʒ] ◇ *n* Schleppkahn *der*, Lastkahn *der*. ◇ *vi inf*: **to barge into a room** in ein Zimmer herein|platzen; **to barge past sb/sthg** an jm/etw vorbei|stürmen. ◆ **barge in** *vi*: **to barge in (on sb)** herein|platzen (bei jm).

baritone ['bærɪtəʊn] *n* Bariton *der*.

bark [bɑːk] ◇ *n* - **1.** [of dog] Bellen *das* - **2.** [on tree] Rinde *die*, Borke *die*. ◇ *vi* [dog] bellen; **to bark at sb/sthg** jn/etw an|bellen.

barley ['bɑːlɪ] *n* Gerste *die*.

barley sugar *n UK* Malzbonbon *der ODER das*.

barmaid ['bɑːmeɪd] *n* Bardame *die*.

barman ['bɑːmən] (*pl* **-men** [-mən]) *n* Barkeeper *der*.

barn [bɑːn] *n* Scheune *die*.

barometer [bə'rɒmɪtə^r] *n liter & fig* Barometer *das*.

baron ['bærən] *n* Baron *der*; **oil baron** Ölmagnat *der*; **press baron** Pressezar *der*.

baroness ['bærənɪs] *n* Baronin *die*; [not married] Baronesse *die*.

barrack ['bærək] *vt UK* aus|pfeifen, aus|buhen. ◆ **barracks** *npl* Kaserne *die*.

barrage ['bærɑːʒ] *n* - **1.** [of firing] Sperrfeuer *das*; **a barrage of complaints/questions** eine Flut von Beschwerden/Fragen - **2.** *UK* [dam] Staudamm *der*.

barrel ['bærəl] *n* - **1.** [for beer, wine] Fass *das* - **2.** [for oil] Tonne *die*; [as measure] Barrel *das* - **3.** [of gun] Lauf *der*.

barren ['bærən] *adj* [woman, land, soil] unfruchtbar.

barricade [ˌbærɪ'keɪd] *n* Barrikade *die*.

barrier ['bærɪə^r] *n* Barriere *die*; [at car park, level crossing] Schranke *die*.

barring ['bɑːrɪŋ] *prep*: **barring accidents** falls nichts passiert.

barrister ['bærɪstə^r] *n UK* Rechtsanwalt *der*, -wältin *die*.

barrow ['bærəʊ] *n* [market stall] Karren *der*.

bartender ['bɑːtendə^r] *n US* Barkeeper *der*.

barter ['bɑːtə^r] ◇ *n* Tauschhandel *der*. ◇ *vt & vi* tauschen.

base [beɪs] ◇ *n* - **1.** [of post, lamp, mountain] Fuß *der*; [of triangle] Basis *die*; [of box] Boden *der* - **2.** [of food, paint] Basis *die* - **3.** [centre of activities - gen] Standort *der*; [- military, in mountaineering] Stützpunkt *der* - **4.** [in baseball] Mal *das*. ◇ *vt* - **1.** [locate - MIL] stationieren; *(phrase)*: **he's based in Paris** sein Büro ist in Paris - **2.** [use as starting point]: **to base sthg (up)on sthg** etw auf etw *(A)* gründen *OR* basieren. ◇ *adj pej* [dishonourable] niederträchtig.

baseball ['beɪsbɔːl] *n (U)* Baseball *der*.

baseball cap *n* Baseballkappe *die*.

basement ['beɪsmənt] *n* [of house] Keller *der*; [of department store] Untergeschoss *das*.

base rate *n* Leitzins *der*.

bases ['beɪsiːz] *Pl* ▷ **basis**.

bash [bæʃ] *inf* ◇ *n* - **1.** [blow] (heftiger) Schlag - **2.** [attempt]: **to have a bash (at sthg)** (etw) mal probieren. ◇ *vt* [hit] schlagen; **to bash one's head** sich *(D)* den Kopf an|hauen.

bashful ['bæʃfʊl] *adj* schüchtern.

basic ['beɪsɪk] *adj* grundlegend, wesentlich; [vocabulary, principle] Grund-; [meal, accommodation] einfach. ◆ **basics** *npl*: **the basics** die Grundlagen *Pl*.

basically ['beɪsɪklɪ] *adv* grundsätzlich.

basil ['bæzl] *n* Basilikum *das*.

basin ['beɪsn] *n* - **1.** [sink] Waschbecken *das* - **2.** *UK* [bowl] Schüssel *die*.

basis ['beɪsɪs] (*pl* **-ses**) *n* - **1.** [reason] Grundlage *die*, Basis *die*; **on the basis that...** in der Annahme, dass... - **2.** [foundation, arrangement] Basis *die*; **on a weekly basis** wöchentlich; **on the basis of** auf der Grundlage *(+ G)*.

bask [bɑːsk] *vi* sich aalen.

basket ['bɑːskɪt] *n* Korb *der*.

basketball ['bɑːskɪtbɔːl] *n* Basketball *der*.

bass [beɪs] *adj* [part, singer] Bass-.

bass drum [beɪs-] *n* große Trommel.

bass guitar [beɪs-] *n* Bassgitarre *die*.

bassoon [bə'suːn] *n* Fagott *das*.

bastard ['bɑːstəd] *n* - **1.** [illegitimate child] Bastard *der* - **2.** *v inf pej* [unpleasant person] Scheißkerl *der*; *phrase*: **the poor bastard** die arme Sau.

bastion ['bæstɪən] *n fig* Bastion *die*.

bat [bæt] *n* - **1.** [animal] Fledermaus *die* - **2.** [for cricket, baseball] Schlagholz *das*; [for table tennis] Schläger *der* - **3.** *phr*: **to do sthg off one's own bat** etw auf eigene Faust tun.

batch [bætʃ] *n* - **1.** [of papers, letters, work] Stapel *der* - **2.** [of products] Ladung *die* - **3.** [of people] Schwung *der*.

bated ['beɪtɪd] *adj*: **with bated breath** mit angehaltenem Atem.

bath [bɑːθ] ◇ *n* Bad *das*; [bathtub] (Bade)wanne *die*; **to have** *OR* **take a bath** ein Bad nehmen, baden. ◇ *vt* baden. ◆ **baths** *npl UK* Bad *das*.

bathe [beɪð] ◇ *vt* - **1.** [wound] (aus)|waschen, baden - **2.** [in light, sweat] baden. ◇ *vi* baden.

bathing ['beɪðɪŋ] *n* Baden *das*.

bathing cap *n* Badekappe *die*.

bathing costume, bathing suit *n* Badeanzug *der*.

bathrobe ['bɑːθrəʊb] *n* Bademantel *der*.

bathroom ['bɑːθrʊm] *n* - **1.** *UK* [room with bath] Badezimmer *das* - **2.** *US* [toilet] Toilette *die*.

bath towel *n* Badetuch *das*.

bathtub ['bɑːθtʌb] *n* Badewanne *die*.

baton ['bætən] *n* - **1.** [of conductor] Taktstock *der* - **2.** [in relay race] Staffelstab *der* - **3.** *UK* [of policeman] Schlagstock *der*.

batsman ['bætsmən] (*pl* **-men** [-mən]) *n* Schlagmann *der*.

battalion [bə'tæljən] *n* Bataillon *das*.

batter ['bætəʳ] <> *n* CULIN Teig *der*. <> *vt* [person] schlagen, verprügeln. <> *vi* [on door, wall] hämmern, trommeln.

battered ['bætəd] *adj* - **1.** [person] verprügelt - **2.** [car, hat, suitcase] verbeult - **3.** CULIN im Teigmantel.

battery ['bætərı] *n* Batterie *die*.

battle ['bætl] <> *n* - **1.** [in war] Schlacht *die* - **2.** [struggle]: **battle (for/against)** Kampf *der* (für/gegen); **that's half the battle** damit ist schon eine Menge gewonnen. <> *vi*: **to battle (for/against)** kämpfen (für/gegen).

battlefield ['bætlfi:ld], **battleground** [-graʊnd] *n liter* & *fig* Schlachtfeld *das*.

battlements ['bætlmənts] *npl* Zinnen *Pl*.

battleship ['bætlʃıp] *n* Schlachtschiff *das*.

bauble ['bɔ:bl] *n* Christbaumkugel *die*.

baulk [bɔ:k] *vi* = **balk**.

bawdy ['bɔ:dı] *adj* derb.

bawl [bɔ:l] <> *vt* [shout] brüllen. <> *vi* - **1.** [shout] brüllen - **2.** [weep] heulen.

bay [beı] *n* - **1.** GEOG Bucht *die* - **2.** [for loading] Ladeplatz *der* - **3.** [for parking] Parkbucht *die* - **4.** *phr*: **to keep sb at bay** jn auf Abstand halten.

bay leaf *n* Lorbeerblatt *das*.

bay window *n* Erkerfenster *das*.

bazaar [bə'zɑ:ʳ] *n* - **1.** [market] Basar *der* - **2.** *UK* [charity sale] Wohltätigkeitsbasar *der*.

B & B *n abbr of* **bed and breakfast**.

BBC (*abbr of* **British Broadcasting Corporation**) *n* BBC *die*.

BC (*abbr of* **before Christ**) v. Chr.

Bcc [ˌbi:si:'si:] *n* (*abbr of* **blind carbon copy**) Bcc.

be [bi:] (*pt* **was** OR **were**, *pp* **been**) <> *vi* - **1.** [exist] sein; **there is/are** es ist/sind da, es gibt; **are there any shops near here?** gibt es hier in der Nähe irgendwelche Geschäfte?; **there is someone in the room** es ist jemand im Zimmer; **be that as it may** wie dem auch sei - **2.** [referring to location] sein; **the hotel is near the airport** das Hotel befindet sich in der Nähe des Flughafens; **he will be here tomorrow** er kommt morgen - **3.** [referring to movement] sein; **have you ever been to California?** warst du schon mal in Kalifornien?; **I'll be there in ten minutes** ich komme in zehn Minuten; **where have you been?** wo bist du gewesen? - **4.** [occur] sein; **my birthday is in June** mein Geburtstag ist im Juni - **5.** [identifying, describing] sein; **he's a doctor** er ist Arzt; **I'm British** ich bin Brite/Britin; **I'm hot/cold** mir ist heiß/kalt; **you are right** du hast Recht; **be quiet!** sei still!, seid still!; **one and one are two** eins und eins ist zwei - **6.** [referring to health]: **how are you?** wie geht es Ihnen?; **I'm fine** mir geht es gut; **she is ill** sie ist krank - **7.** [referring to age]: **how old are you?** wie alt bist du?; **I am 14 (years old)** ich bin 14 (Jahre alt) - **8.** [referring to cost] kosten; **how much is it?** wie viel kostet es?; **it's £10** es kostet 10 Pfund - **9.** [referring to time, dates] sein; **what time is it?** wie viel Uhr ist es?, wie spät ist es?; **it's ten o'clock** es ist zehn Uhr; **today is February 17th** heute haben wir den 17. Februar - **10.** [referring to measurement] sein; **it's ten metres long/high** es ist zehn Meter lang/hoch; **I'm 8 stone** ich wiege 50 Kilo - **11.** [referring to the weather] sein; **it's hot/cold** es ist heiß/kalt - **12.** [for emphasis] sein; **is that you?** bist du das?; **yes, it's me** ja, ich bins. <> *aux vb* - **1.** *(in combination with present participle to form continuous tense)*: **I'm learning German** ich lerne Deutsch; **what is he doing?** was macht er?; **it's snowing** es schneit; **we've been visiting the museum** wir waren im Museum; **I've been living in London for 10 years** ich wohne seit 10 Jahren in London; **he is going on holiday next week** nächste Woche fährt er in Urlaub - **2.** *(forming passive)* werden; **they were defeated** sie wurden geschlagen; **the flight was delayed** das Flugzeug hatte Verspätung; **it is said** man sagt - **3.** *(with infinitive to express an order)*: **all rooms are to be vacated by 10.00 a.m.** alle Zimmer müssen bis 10 Uhr geräumt sein; **you are not to tell anyone** das darfst du niemandem erzählen - **4.** *(with infinitive to express future tense)*: **the race is to start at noon** das Rennen ist für 12 Uhr angesetzt - **5.** *(in tag questions)*: **it's cold, isn't it?** es ist kalt, nicht wahr?; **you're not going now, are you?** willst du schon gehen?

beach [bi:tʃ] *n* Strand *der*.

beacon ['bi:kən] *n* - **1.** [fire, lighthouse] Leuchtfeuer *das* - **2.** [radio beacon] Funkfeuer *das*.

bead [bi:d] *n* [of glass, wood, sweat] Perle *die*.

beak [bi:k] *n* [of bird] Schnabel *der*.

beaker ['bi:kəʳ] *n* Becher *der*.

beam [bi:m] <> *n* - **1.** [of wood] Balken *der*; [of steel] Träger *der* - **2.** [of light] Strahl *der* - **3.** *US* AUT: **high/low beams** Fern-/Abblendlicht *das*. <> *vt* [signal, news] aus|strahlen. <> *vi* strahlen.

bean [bi:n] *n* Bohne *die*; **to be full of beans** *inf* voller Tatendrang sein; **to spill the beans** *inf* [confess] singen.

beanbag ['bi:nbæg] *n* [seat] Sitzsack *der*.

beanshoot ['bi:nʃu:t], **beansprout** [-spraʊt] *n* (Soja)bohnensprosse *die*.

bear [beəʳ] (*pt* **bore**, *pp* **borne**) <> *n* [animal] Bär *der*. <> *vt* - **1.** [gen] tragen - **2.** [tolerate] ertragen, aus|halten - **3.** [ill will, hatred] hegen. <> *vi* - **1.** [turn]: **to bear left/right** sich links/rechts halten - **2.** [have effect]: **to bring pressure/influence to bear on sb** bei jm Druck/Einfluss geltend machen. ◆ **bear down** *vi*: **to bear down on sb/sthg** auf jn/etw zu|steuern. ◆ **bear out** *vt sep* bestätigen. ◆ **bear up** *vi*: **to bear up well** sich tapfer halten. ◆ **bear with** *vt insep*: **bear with me for a minute, will you?** einen Moment Geduld, bitte.

beard [bɪəd] *n* Bart *der*.

bearer ['beərəʳ] *n* - **1.** [of stretcher, coffin] Träger *der* - **2.** [of news, letter] Überbringer *der*, -in *die* - **3.** [of cheque, passport] Inhaber *der*, -in *die* - **4.** [of name, title] Träger *der*, -in *die*.

bearing ['beərɪŋ] *n* - **1.** [relevance] Bedeutung *die*; **to have a bearing on sthg** bei etw eine Rolle spielen - **2.** [deportment] (Körper)haltung *die* - **3.** TECH Lager *das* - **4.** [on compass]: **to take a bearing** die Richtung bestimmen; **to get one's bearings** *fig* sich orientieren; **to lose one's bearings** *fig* die Orientierung verlieren.

beast [bi:st] *n* - **1.** [animal] Tier *das* - **2.** *inf pej* [person - unpleasant] Ekel *das*; [- evil] Bestie *die*.

beat [bi:t] (*pt* **beat**, *pp* **beaten**) ◇ *n* - **1.** [of drum, heart, pulse] Schlag *der* - **2.** [MUS - rhythm] Rhythmus *der*; [- measure] Takt *der* - **3.** [of policeman] Runde *die*. ◇ *vt* - **1.** [gen] schlagen; **to beat a record** einen Rekord brechen; **it beats me** *inf* ich habe keine Ahnung - **2.** MUS: **to beat time** (den) Takt schlagen OR an|geben - **3.** *phr*: **beat it!** *inf* [go away] verschwinde!, hau ab! ◇ *vi* - **1.** [rain - on roof] trommeln - **2.** [heart, pulse] schlagen. ◆ **beat off** *vt sep* [resist] ab|wehren. ◆ **beat up** *vt sep inf* [person] zusammen|schlagen.

beating ['bi:tɪŋ] *n* - **1.** [punishment] Prügel *Pl*; **to give sb a beating** jm eine Tracht Prügel verabreichen - **2.** [defeat] Niederlage *die*.

beautiful ['bju:tɪfʊl] *adj* - **1.** [person] schön - **2.** [picture, music, weather] wundervoll, herrlich - **3.** *inf* [goal, player] herrlich, toll.

beautifully ['bju:təflɪ] *adv* - **1.** [dressed, decorated] wunderschön - **2.** *inf* [cook, sing, play] wunderbar.

beauty ['bju:tɪ] *n* Schönheit *die*.

beauty parlour *n* Schönheitssalon *der*.

beauty salon *n* = **beauty parlour**.

beauty spot *n* - **1.** [place] schönes Fleckchen - **2.** [on skin] Schönheitsfleck *der*.

beaver ['bi:vəʳ] *n* Biber *der*.

became [bɪ'keɪm] *pt* ▻ **become**.

because [bɪ'kɒz] *conj* weil. ◆ **because of** *prep* wegen (+ *G*, *D*).

beck [bek] *n*: **to be at sb's beck and call** nach js Pfeife tanzen.

beckon ['bekən] ◇ *vt* [make a signal to] zu|winken (+ *D*). ◇ *vi*: **to beckon to sb** jm zu|winken.

become [bɪ'kʌm] (*pt* **became**, *pp* **become**) *vt* werden; **to become old/rich/famous** alt/reich/berühmt werden; **to become accustomed to sthg** sich an etw (*A*) gewöhnen.

becoming [bɪ'kʌmɪŋ] *adj* - **1.** [attractive]: **it's very becoming** es steht ihr/dir/*etc* gut - **2.** [appropriate] schicklich.

bed [bed] *n* - **1.** [to sleep on] Bett *das*; **to go to bed** zu OR ins Bett gehen; **to get out of bed** auf|stehen; **to go to bed with sb** *euph* mit jm ins Bett gehen - **2.** [flowerbed] Beet *das* - **3.** [of sea] Meeresgrund *der*; [of river] Flussbett *das*.

bed and breakfast *n* Zimmer *das* mit Frühstück.

bedclothes ['bedkləʊðz] *npl* Bettzeug *das*.

bedlam ['bedləm] *n* Chaos *das*.

bed linen *n* Bettwäsche *die*.

bedraggled [bɪ'drægld] *adj* schmutzig und nass.

bedridden ['bed,rɪdn] *adj* bettlägerig.

bedroom ['bedrʊm] *n* Schlafzimmer *das*.

bedside ['bedsaɪd] *n*: **at sb's bedside** an js Bett.

bedside table *n* Nachttisch *der*.

bed-sit(ter) *n UK* Wohnschlafzimmer *das*.

bedsore ['bedsɔ:ʳ] *n* wund gelegene Stelle.

bedspread ['bedspred] *n* Tagesdecke *die*.

bedtime ['bedtaɪm] *n* Schlafenszeit *die*.

bee [bi:] *n* Biene *die*.

beech [bi:tʃ] *n* - **1.** [tree] Buche *die* - **2.** [wood] Buchenholz *das*.

beef [bi:f] *n* Rindfleisch *das*.

beefburger ['bi:f,bɜ:gəʳ] *n* Hamburger *der*.

beefsteak ['bi:f,steɪk] *n* Beefsteak *das*.

beehive ['bi:haɪv] *n* Bienenstock *der*.

beeline ['bi:laɪn] *n*: **to make a beeline for sb/sthg** *inf* geradewegs auf jn/etw zu|steuern.

been [bi:n] *pp* ▻ **be**.

beer [bɪəʳ] *n* Bier *das*.

beer garden *n* Biergarten *der*.

beermat ['bɪə,mæt] *n* Bierdeckel *der*.

beet [bi:t] *n* - **1.** [sugar beet] Zuckerrübe *die* - **2.** *US* [beetroot] rote Rübe, Rote Bete.

beetle ['bi:tl] *n* Käfer *der*.

beetroot ['bi:tru:t] *n* rote Rübe, Rote Bete.

before [bɪ'fɔ:ʳ] ◇ *prep* - **1.** [in time] vor (+ *D*); **they arrived before us** sie sind vor uns angekommen; **the week before last** vorletzte Woche; **the day before yesterday** vorgestern; **the day before** der Tag zuvor; **before long** bald - **2.** [in front of, facing] vor (+ *D*); **before my (very) eyes** vor meinen Augen; **we have a difficult task before us** wir haben eine schwierige Aufgabe vor uns. ◇ *adv* [previously] schon einmal; **never before** noch nie. ◇ *conj* bevor.

beforehand [bɪ'fɔ:hænd] *adv* vorher.

befriend [bɪ'frend] *vt* sich an|freunden mit.

beg [beg] ◇ *vt* - **1.** [money, food] betteln um - **2.** [favour, forgiveness] bitten um; **to beg sb for sthg** jn um etw bitten; **to beg sb to do sthg** jn bitten, etw zu tun. ◇ *vi* - **1.** [for money, food]: **to beg (for)** betteln (um) - **2.** [for favour, forgiveness]: **to beg (for)** bitten (um).

began [bɪ'gæn] *pt* ▻ **begin**.

beggar ['begəʳ] *n* Bettler *der*, -in *die*.

begin [bɪ'gɪn] (*pt* **began**, *pp* **begun**, *cont* **-ning**) <> *vt* beginnen, anlfangen; **to begin doing** *OR* **to do sthg** beginnen *OR* anlfangen, etw zu tun. <> *vi* beginnen, anlfangen; **to begin with** zunächst, zu Anfang.

beginner [bɪ'gɪnəʳ] *n* Anfänger *der*, -in *die*.

beginning [bɪ'gɪnɪŋ] *n* Anfang *der*; **from the beginning** von Anfang an.

begrudge [bɪ'grʌdʒ] *vt* - **1.** [envy]: **to begrudge sb sthg** jm etw missgönnen - **2.** [do unwillingly]: **to begrudge doing sthg** etw widerwillig tun.

begun [bɪ'gʌn] *pp* ▷ **begin**.

behalf [bɪ'hɑːf] *n*: **on** *UK* *OR* **in** *US* **behalf of** im Namen *(+ G)*, im Auftrag *(+ G)*.

behave [bɪ'heɪv] <> *vt*: **to behave o.s.** sich benehmen. <> *vi* sich verhalten; [with good manners] sich benehmen.

behaviour *UK*, **behavior** *US* [bɪ'heɪvjəʳ] *n* Benehmen *das*.

behead [bɪ'hed] *vt* enthaupten, köpfen.

beheld [bɪ'held] *pt & pp* ▷ **behold**.

behind [bɪ'haɪnd] <> *prep* - **1.** [at the back of] hinter *(+ D)*; [with verbs of motion] hinter *(+ A)* - **2.** [causing, responsible for] hinter *(+ D)*; **what's behind this campaign?** was hat es mit dieser Kampagne auf sich?; **what's behind it?** was steckt dahinter? - **3.** [supporting]: **to be behind sb** *fig* jn unterstützen - **4.** [indicating deficiency, delay]: **behind schedule** im Rückstand. <> *adv* - **1.** [at, in the back] hinten; **the others followed behind** die anderen kamen hinterher; **to leave sthg behind** etw zurücklassen; **to stay behind** (da)bleiben - **2.** [late]: **to be behind (with sthg)** (mit etw) im Verzug sein. <> *n inf* Hintern *der*.

behold [bɪ'həʊld] (*pt & pp* **beheld**) *vt liter* erblicken.

beige [beɪʒ] <> *adj* beige. <> *n* Beige *das*.

being ['biːɪŋ] *n* - **1.** [creature] Wesen *das*, Geschöpf *das* - **2.** [existence]: **in being** existierend, vorhanden; **to come into being** entstehen.

belated [bɪ'leɪtɪd] *adj* verspätet.

belch [beltʃ] <> *n* Rülpser *der*. <> *vt* [smoke, fire] (aus)lspeien. <> *vi* [person] rülpsen.

beleaguered [bɪ'liːgəd] *adj liter & fig* belagert.

Belgian ['beldʒən] <> *adj* belgisch. <> *n* Belgier *der*, -in *die*.

Belgium ['beldʒəm] *n* Belgien *nt*.

Belgrade [ˌbel'greɪd] *n* Belgrad *nt*.

belief [bɪ'liːf] *n* - **1.** [gen]: **belief (in)** Glaube *der* (an *(+ A)*) - **2.** [opinion] Meinung *die*; **it's my belief that...** ich bin davon überzeugt, dass...

believe [bɪ'liːv] <> *vt* glauben; **to believe sb** jm glauben; **I believe so** ich glaube ja; **I don't believe it!** das darf (ja wohl) nicht wahr sein!; **believe it or not** ob du/Sie es glaubst/glauben oder nicht. <> *vi* glauben; **to believe in sb/sthg** an jn/etw glauben.

believer [bɪ'liːvəʳ] *n* RELIG Gläubige *der, die*; **I'm a great believer in corporal punishment** ich halte viel von der Prügelstrafe.

belittle [bɪ'lɪtl] *vt* schmälern.

bell [bel] *n* Glocke *die*; [of phone, door, bike] Klingel *die*.

belligerent [bɪ'lɪdʒərənt] *adj* - **1.** [at war] kriegführend - **2.** [aggressive] angriffslustig.

bellows ['beləʊz] *npl* Blasebalg *der*.

belly ['belɪ] *n* Bauch *der*.

bellyache ['belɪeɪk] *n* Bauchschmerzen *Pl*.

belly button *n inf* Bauchnabel *der*.

belong [bɪ'lɒŋ] *vi* gehören; **to belong to sb** jm gehören; **to belong to a party/club** einer Partei/einem Verein anlgehören.

belongings [bɪ'lɒŋɪŋz] *npl* Sachen *Pl*.

beloved [bɪ'lʌvd] *adj* geliebt.

below [bɪ'ləʊ] <> *adv* - **1.** [in a lower position] unten; **they live on the floor below** sie wohnen ein Stockwerk tiefer; **see below** [in text] siehe unten - **2.** [with numbers, quantities]: **children of 5 and below** Kinder bis zu 5 Jahre - **3.** NAUT: **to go below** unter Deck gehen. <> *prep* - **1.** [lower than] unter *(+ D)*; [with verbs of motion] unter *(+ A)* - **2.** [in rank, status] unter *(+ D)*; **a sergeant is below a captain** ein Feldwebel steht unter einem Hauptmann - **3.** [less than] unter *(+ D)*; **10 degrees below (zero)** 10 Grad unter Null; **below average** unter dem Durchschnitt.

belt [belt] <> *n* - **1.** [for clothing] Gürtel *der* - **2.** TECH Riemen *der*. <> *vt inf* [hit] verprügeln.

beltway ['beltˌweɪ] *n* *US* Umgehungsstraße *die*.

bemused [bɪ'mjuːzd] *adj* verwirrt.

bench [bentʃ] *n* - **1.** POL [seat] Bank *die* - **2.** [in workshop] Werkbank *die*; [in laboratory] Labortisch *der*.

benchmark ['bentʃmɑːk] *n* [standard] Standard *der*; [standard & COMPUT] Benchmark *die*.

bend [bend] (*pt & pp* **bent**) <> *n* - **1.** [in river, pipe] Biegung *die*; [in road] Kurve *die* - **2.** *phr*: **round the bend** *inf* verrückt. <> *vt* [arm, leg, knee] beugen; [back] krümmen; [head] neigen; [wire, fork, tube] (ver)biegen. <> *vi* - **1.** [arm, leg] beugen; [branch, tree] biegen - **2.** [person] sich bücken - **3.** [road] eine Kurve machen; [river] eine Biegung machen. ◆ **bend down** *vi* sich bücken. ◆ **bend over** *vi* sich bücken; **to bend over backwards for sb** alles für jn tun.

beneath [bɪ'niːθ] <> *adv* [below] unten. <> *prep* - **1.** [under] unter *(+ D)*; [with verbs of motion] unter *(+ A)*; **she shoved it beneath the bed** sie schob es unter das Bett - **2.** [unworthy of]: **that is beneath him** das ist unter seiner Würde.

benefactor ['benɪfæktəʳ] *n* Wohltäter *der*, -in *die*.

beneficial [ˌbenɪ'fɪʃl] *adj* nützlich; **to be beneficial to sb/sthg** jm/etw zugute kommen.

beneficiary [ˌbenɪ'fɪʃərɪ] *n* LAW [of will] Begünstigte *der, die*.

benefit ['benɪfɪt] ◇ *n* - **1.** *(U)* [advantage] Nutzen *der*; **to be to sb's benefit, to be of benefit to sb** zu js Nutzen sein; **for the benefit of** zum Nutzen von; **to give sb the benefit of the doubt** jm trotz Zweifels Glauben schenken - **2.** [good point] Vorteil *der* - **3.** [allowance of money] Unterstützung *die*. ◇ *vt* nützen *(+ D)*. ◇ *vi*: **to benefit from sthg** von etw profitieren.

Benelux ['benɪlʌks] *n*: **the Benelux countries** die Beneluxstaaten, die Beneluxländer.

benevolent [bɪ'nevələnt] *adj* wohlwollend.

benign [bɪ'naɪn] *adj* - **1.** [influence] gut; [climate] mild - **2.** MED gutartig.

bent [bent] ◇ *pt* & *pp* ▷ **bend**. ◇ *adj* - **1.** [wire, bar] gebogen, verbogen - **2.** [person, body] gebeugt - **3.** *UK inf* [dishonest] korrupt - **4.** [determined]: **to be bent on sthg** etw unbedingt wollen/haben wollen; **to be bent on doing sthg** etw unbedingt tun wollen. ◇ *n* [natural aptitude]: **bent (for)** Neigung *die* (zu).

bequeath [bɪ'kwi:ð] *vt liter* & *fig* hinterlassen.

bequest [bɪ'kwest] *n* Nachlass *der*.

berate [bɪ'reɪt] *vt* schelten.

bereaved [bɪ'ri:vd] *(pl inv)* ◇ *adj*: **to be bereaved** trauern. ◇ *npl*: **the bereaved** die Hinterbliebenen *Pl*.

beret ['bereɪ] *n* Baskenmütze *die*.

berk [bɜ:k] *n UK inf* Dussel *der*.

Berlin [bɜ:'lɪn] *n* Berlin *nt*.

berm [bɜ:m] *n US* Grünstreifen *der*.

Bermuda [bə'mju:də] *n* Bermudainseln *Pl*.

Bern [bɜ:n] *n* Bern *nt*.

berry ['berɪ] *n* Beere *die*.

berserk [bə'zɜ:k] *adj*: **to go berserk** wild werden.

berth [bɜ:θ] ◇ *n* - **1.** [in harbour] Liegeplatz *der* - **2.** [on ship] Koje *die*; [on train] Schlafwagenplatz *der*. ◇ *vi* [ship] anlegen.

beseech [bɪ'si:tʃ] *(pt & pp* **besought** *OR* **beseeched**) *vt liter* [implore]: **to beseech sb (to do sthg)** jn an|flehen (, etw zu tun).

beset [bɪ'set] *(pt & pp inv)* ◇ *adj*: **beset with** *OR* **by sthg** von etw heimgesucht. ◇ *vt* heim|suchen.

beside [bɪ'saɪd] *prep* - **1.** [next to] neben *(+ A, D)* - **2.** [compared with] verglichen mit - **3.** *phr*: **to be beside o.s. with joy/anger** vor Freude/Wut außer sich sein.

besides [bɪ'saɪdz] ◇ *adv* außerdem. ◇ *prep* außer *(+ D)*; **besides being expensive, it's also ugly** es ist nicht nur teuer, sondern auch hässlich.

besiege [bɪ'si:dʒ] *vt liter* & *fig* belagern.

besotted [bɪ'sɒtɪd] *adj*: **besotted (with sb)** vernarrt (in jn).

besought [bɪ'sɔ:t] *pt* & *pp* ▷ **beseech**.

best [best] ◇ *adj* beste(r) (s); **my best friend** mein bester Freund/meine beste Freundin. ◇ *adv* am besten; **which car do you like best?** welches Auto gefällt dir am besten?; **what type of beer do you like best?** welches Bier magst du am liebsten? ◇ *n* - **1.** Beste *der, die, das*; **to do one's best** sein Bestes tun - **2.** *phr*: **to make the best of sthg** das Beste aus etw machen; **for the best** nur zum Guten; **all the best!** alles Gute! ◆ **at best** *adv* bestenfalls.

best man *n* Trauzeuge *der*.

bestow [bɪ'stəʊ] *vt fml*: **to bestow sthg on sb** jm etw gewähren.

best-seller *n* [book] Bestseller *der*.

bet [bet] *(pt & pp inv OR* **-ted**) ◇ *n* - **1.** [wager] Wette *die*; **to have a bet on sthg** auf etw *(A)* wetten - **2.** *fig* [prediction]: **it's a safe bet that...** man kann sicher sein, dass... ◇ *vt* wetten. ◇ *vi* - **1.** [gamble]: **to bet (on sthg)** (auf etw *(A)*) wetten - **2.** *fig* [predict]: **to bet on sthg** sich auf etw *(A)* verlassen.

betray [bɪ'treɪ] *vt* verraten; [trust] missbrauchen.

betrayal [bɪ'treɪəl] *n* Verrat *der*.

better ['betəʳ] ◇ *adj (compar of good, well)* besser; **to get better** besser werden; **I hope you get better soon** ich hoffe, es geht dir bald besser; **to get better and better** immer besser werden. ◇ *adv* besser; [like] lieber. ◇ *n* [best one] Bessere *der, die, das*; **to get the better of sb** die Oberhand über jn gewinnen; **my curiosity got the better of me** meine Neugier war stärker. ◇ *vt* [improve] verbessern; **to better o.s.** sich verbessern.

better off *adj* besser dran.

betting ['betɪŋ] *n (U)* - **1.** [bets] Wetten *das* - **2.** [odds] Wetten *Pl*.

betting shop *n UK* Wettannahmestelle *die*.

between [bɪ'twi:n] ◇ *prep* zwischen *(+ D)*; [with verbs of motion] zwischen *(+ A)*; **between now and next month** bis nächsten Monat; **we had only twenty pounds between us** wir hatten (zusammen) nur zwanzig Pfund. ◇ *adv*: **(in)between** zwischen.

beverage ['bevərɪdʒ] *n fml* Getränk *das*.

beware [bɪ'weəʳ] *vi* sich in Acht nehmen; **to beware of sthg** sich vor etw in Acht nehmen; **'beware of the dog'** 'Vorsicht bissiger Hund'.

bewildered [bɪ'wɪldəd] *adj* verwirrt.

beyond [bɪ'jɒnd] ◇ *prep* - **1.** [in space] jenseits *(+ G)*, über *(+ A)* hinaus; **it's just beyond**

the park es ist direkt auf der anderen Seite des Parks - 2. [in time]: **beyond the year 2010** über das Jahr 2010 hinaus; **beyond midnight** bis nach Mitternacht; **beyond the age of five** ab dem fünften Lebensjahr - 3. [outside the range of] über *(+ A, D)*; **the town has changed beyond all recognition** die Stadt hat sich bis zur Unkenntlichkeit verändert. ◇ *adv* - 1. [in space] jenseits (davon) - 2. [in time] darüber hinaus, danach.

bias ['baɪəs] *n* - 1. [prejudice] Voreingenommenheit *die* - 2. [tendency] Tendenz *die*.

biased ['baɪəst] *adj* - 1. [person]: **to be biased (against)** voreingenommen sein (gegenüber) - 2. [system]: **to be biased against/towards sb** jn benachteiligen/bevorteilen.

bib [bɪb] *n* [for baby] Latz *der*, Lätzchen *das*.

Bible ['baɪbl] *n* Bibel *die*.

bicarbonate of soda [baɪ'kɑːbənət-] *n* Natron *das*.

biceps ['baɪseps] *(pl inv) n* Bizeps *der*.

bicker ['bɪkər] *vi* sich zanken.

bicycle ['baɪsɪkl] *n* Fahrrad *das*.

bicycle path *n* Fahrradweg *der*.

bicycle pump *n* Luftpumpe *die*.

bid [bɪd] ◇ *n* - 1. [attempt] Versuch *der* - 2. [at auction] Gebot *das* - 3. COMM Angebot *das*. ◇ *vt* (*pt* **bid**) [at auction] bieten. ◇ *vi* (*pt* **bid**) [at auction]: **to bid (for)** bieten (für).

bidder ['bɪdər] *n* Bietende *der, die*.

bidding ['bɪdɪŋ] *n* [at auction] Bieten *das*.

bide [baɪd] *vt*: **to bide one's time** (eine Gelegenheit) ab|warten.

bifocals [ˌbaɪ'fəʊklz] *npl* Brille *die* mit Bifokalgläsern.

big [bɪg] *adj* - 1. [gen] groß; **how big is it?** wie groß ist es?; **my big brother** mein großer Bruder; **big ideas** hochfliegende Ideen - 2. [important] bedeutend; **the big day** der große Tag - 3. [conceited]: **to have a big head** eingebildet sein - 4. *inf* [phr]: **he's into motorbikes in a big way** er ist vernarrt in Motorräder.

bigamy ['bɪgəmɪ] *n* Bigamie *die*.

big deal *inf* ◇ *n*: **it's no big deal** das ist kein Problem; **what's the big deal?** was ist schon dabei? ◇ *excl* und wenn schon!

Big Dipper [-'dɪpər] *n* - 1. *UK* [rollercoaster] Achterbahn *die* - 2. *US* ASTRON: **the Big Dipper** der Große Bär.

bigheaded [ˌbɪg'hedɪd] *adj inf* eingebildet.

bigot ['bɪgət] *n* bigotter Mensch.

bigoted ['bɪgətɪd] *adj* bigott.

bigotry ['bɪgətrɪ] *n* Bigotterie *die*.

big time *n inf*: **to make** OR **hit the big time** ganz groß raus|kommen.

big toe *n* großer Zeh.

big top *n* Zirkuszelt *das*.

big wheel *n UK* [at fairground] Riesenrad *das*.

bike [baɪk] *n inf* - 1. [cycle] Rad *das* - 2. [motorcycle] Motorrad *das*.

bikeway ['baɪkweɪ] *n US* Radweg *der*.

bikini [bɪ'kiːnɪ] *n* Bikini *der*.

bile [baɪl] *n* Galle *die*.

bilingual [baɪ'lɪŋgwəl] *adj* zweisprachig.

bill [bɪl] ◇ *n* - 1. [statement of cost] Rechnung *die* - 2. [in parliament] Gesetzentwurf *der* - 3. [of show, concert] Programm *das* - 4. *US* [bank note] Geldschein *der*, Banknote *die* - 5. [poster]: **'post** OR **stick no bills'** 'Plakate ankleben verboten' - 6. [of bird] Schnabel *der*. ◇ *vt*: **to bill sb (for sthg)** jm eine Rechnung (für etw) schicken.

billboard ['bɪlbɔːd] *n* Plakatwand *die*.

billet ['bɪlɪt] *n* Quartier *das*.

billfold ['bɪlfəʊld] *n US* Brieftasche *die*.

billiards ['bɪljədz] *n (U)* Billard *das*.

billion ['bɪljən] *num* - 1. [thousand million] Milliarde *die* - 2. *UK dated* [million million] Billion *die*.

bimbo ['bɪmbəʊ] (*pl* **-s** OR **-es**) *n inf pej* Tussi *die*.

bin [bɪn] *n UK* [for rubbish] Abfalleimer *der*.

bind [baɪnd] (*pt & pp* **bound**) *vt* - 1. [gen] binden - 2. [bandage] verbinden - 3. [constrain] verpflichten.

binder ['baɪndər] *n* [cover] Ordner *der*.

binding ['baɪndɪŋ] ◇ *adj* verbindlich, bindend. ◇ *n* [of book] Einband *der*.

binge [bɪndʒ] *inf* ◇ *n*: **to go on a binge** [on drink] auf Sauftour gehen; [on food] eine Fresstour machen. ◇ *vi*: **to binge on sthg** [drink] etw saufen; [food] etw fressen.

bingo ['bɪŋgəʊ] *n* Bingo *das*.

binoculars [bɪ'nɒkjʊləz] *npl* Fernglas *das*.

biochemistry [ˌbaɪəʊ'kemɪstrɪ] *n* Biochemie *die*.

biodegradable [ˌbaɪəʊdɪ'greɪdəbl] *adj* biologisch abbaubar.

biography [baɪ'ɒgrəfɪ] *n* Biografie *die*.

biological [ˌbaɪə'lɒdʒɪkl] *adj* biologisch.

biological weapon *n* biologische Waffe *die*.

biology [baɪ'ɒlədʒɪ] *n* Biologie *die*.

biotechnology [ˌbaɪəʊtek'nɒlədʒɪ] *n* Biotechnologie *die*.

bioterrorism [ˌbaɪəʊ'terərɪzm] *n* Bioterrorismus *der*.

birch [bɜːtʃ] *n* [tree] Birke *die*.

bird [bɜːd] *n* - 1. [creature] Vogel *der* - 2. *inf* [woman] Braut *die*.

birdie ['bɜːdɪ] *n* [in golf] Birdie *das*.

bird's-eye view *n* Vogelperspektive *die*.

bird-watcher [-ˌwɒtʃər] *n* Vogelbeobachter *der*, -in *die*.

Biro® ['baɪərəʊ] *n* Kugelschreiber *der*.

birth [bɜ:θ] *n* - **1.** [of baby] Geburt *die*; **to give birth (to)** gebären - **2.** *fig* [of idea, system, country] Geburtsstunde *die*.

birth certificate *n* Geburtsurkunde *die*.

birth control *n (U)* Geburtenregelung *die*; **to use birth control** verhüten.

birthday ['bɜ:θdeɪ] *n* Geburtstag *der*.

birthmark ['bɜ:θmɑ:k] *n* Muttermal *das*.

birthrate ['bɜ:θreɪt] *n* Geburtenrate *die*.

biscuit ['bɪskɪt] *n* - **1.** *UK* [thin dry cake] Keks *der* - **2.** *US* [bread-like cake] *Hefebrötchen, das üblicherweise mit Bratensaft gegessen wird.*

bisect [baɪ'sekt] *vt* - **1.** GEOM halbieren - **2.** [cut in two] durch|schneiden.

bishop ['bɪʃəp] *n* - **1.** [in church] Bischof *der* - **2.** [in chess] Läufer *der*.

bison ['baɪsn] (*pl inv* OR **-s**) *n* Bison *der*.

bit [bɪt] ◇ *pt* ▷ **bite**. ◇ *n* - **1.** [small piece] Stück *das*; **bits and pieces** *UK* [objects] Krimskrams *der*; **to fall to bits** kaputt|gehen, auseinander fallen - **2.** [unspecified amount]: **a bit of** ein bisschen; **quite a bit of** eine ganze Menge - **3.** [short time]: **for a bit** für ein Weilchen - **4.** [of drill] Bohrer *der* - **5.** [of bridle] Trensengebiss *das* - **6.** COMPUT Bit *das*. ◆ **a bit** *adv* [tired, late, confused] ein bisschen. ◆ **bit by bit** *adv* Stück für Stück.

bitch [bɪtʃ] *n* - **1.** [female dog] Hündin *die* - **2.** *v inf pej* [woman] Miststück *das*.

bitchy [bɪtʃɪ] *adj inf* gehässig, gemein.

bite [baɪt] (*pt* **bit**, *pp* **bitten**) ◇ *n* Biss *der*; **to have a bite (to eat)** einen Happen essen. ◇ *vt* beißen. ◇ *vi* - **1.** [animal, person, insect] beißen; **to bite into sthg** in etw (hinein)|beißen - **2.** [tyres, clutch] greifen - **3.** *fig* [sanction, law] greifen.

biting ['baɪtɪŋ] *adj* - **1.** [wind, cold] schneidend, beißend - **2.** [caustic - comment] bissig.

bitmap [bɪtmæp] *n* COMPUT Bitmap *das*.

bitten ['bɪtn] *pp* ▷ **bite**.

bitter ['bɪtər] ◇ *adj* - **1.** [gen] bitter; **it's bitter (weather) today** es ist heute bitterkalt - **2.** [argument, war] erbittert - **3.** [resentful] verbittert. ◇ *n UK* [beer] *dem Altbier ähnliches Bier.*

bitterness ['bɪtənɪs] *n* Bitterkeit *die*.

bizarre [bɪ'zɑ:r] *adj* exzentrisch; [house, landscape] bizarr.

blab [blæb] *vi inf* quatschen.

black [blæk] ◇ *adj* - **1.** [gen] schwarz - **2.** [future] finster, düster. ◇ *n* - **1.** [colour] Schwarz *das*; **in black and white** [in writing] schwarz auf weiß; **in the black** [solvent] in den schwarzen Zahlen - **2.** [person] Schwarze *der, die*. ◇ *vt UK* [boycott] boykottieren. ◆ **black out** *vi* [faint] ohnmächtig werden.

blackberry ['blækbərɪ] *n* Brombeere *die*.

blackbird ['blækbɜ:d] *n* Amsel *die*.

blackboard ['blækbɔ:d] *n* Tafel *die*.

blackcurrant [,blæk'kʌrənt] *n* schwarze Johannisbeere.

blacken ['blækn] ◇ *vt* [in colour] schwärzen. ◇ *vi* [sky] sich verdunkeln.

black eye *n* schwarzes Auge.

Black Forest *n* Schwarzwald *der*.

blackhead ['blækhed] *n* Mitesser *der*.

black ice *n (U)* Glatteis *das*.

blackleg ['blækleg] *n pej* Streikbrecher *der*, -in *die*.

blacklist ['blæklɪst] ◇ *n* schwarze Liste. ◇ *vt* auf die schwarze Liste setzen.

blackmail ['blækmeɪl] ◇ *n* Erpressung *die*. ◇ *vt* erpressen.

black market *n* Schwarzmarkt *der*.

blackout ['blækaʊt] *n* - **1.** [in wartime] Verdunkelung *die* - **2.** [power cut] Stromausfall *der* - **3.** [suppression of news] Nachrichtensperre *die* - **4.** [fainting] Ohnmachtsanfall *der*.

black pudding *n UK* Blutwurst *die*.

Black Sea *n*: **the Black Sea** das Schwarze Meer.

black sheep *n* schwarzes Schaf.

blacksmith ['blæksmɪθ] *n* Schmied *der*, -in *die*.

black spot *n* [for road accidents] Gefahrenstelle *die*.

bladder ['blædər] *n* ANAT Blase *die*.

blade [bleɪd] *n* - **1.** [of knife, razor] Klinge *die* - **2.** [of propeller, saw, oar] Blatt *das* - **3.** [of grass] Halm *der*.

blame [bleɪm] ◇ *n* Schuld *die*; **to take the blame for sthg** die Schuld für etw auf sich *(A)* nehmen. ◇ *vt* beschuldigen; **to blame sthg on sb/sthg** jm/etw die Schuld an etw *(D)* geben; **they blamed her for the defeat** sie gaben ihr die Schuld an der Niederlage; **to be to blame for sthg** an etw *(D)* schuld sein.

bland [blænd] *adj* - **1.** [person] farblos - **2.** [food] fad - **3.** [music, style] nichtssagend.

blank [blæŋk] ◇ *adj* leer. ◇ *n* - **1.** [empty space] Leere *die*, leere Stelle - **2.** MIL [cartridge] Platzpatrone *die*.

blank cheque *n* Blankoscheck *der*; **to give sb a blank cheque to do sthg** *fig* jm freie Hand lassen, etw zu tun.

blanket ['blæŋkɪt] *n* - **1.** [bed cover] Decke *die* - **2.** [layer] Schicht *die*.

blare [bleər] *vi* plärren.

blasphemy ['blæsfəmɪ] *n* Blasphemie *die*.

blast [blɑ:st] ◇ *n* - **1.** [of bomb] Explosion *die* - **2.** [of air] Windstoß *der*. ◇ *vt* [hole, tunnel] sprengen. ◇ *excl UK inf* verdammt. ◆ **(at) full blast** *adv* - **1.** [maximum volume] auf höchster Lautstärke - **2.** [maximum effort, speed] auf Hochtouren.

blasted ['blɑ:stɪd] *adj inf* verdammt.

blast-off *n* [space] Start *der*.

blatant ['bleɪtənt] *adj* [shameless] unverhohlen.

blaze [bleɪz] ◇ *n* - **1.** [fire] Brand *der* - **2.** *fig* [of colour, light] Pracht *die*. ◇ *vi* - **1.** [fire] lodern - **2.** *fig* [with colour, emotion] brennen.

blazer ['bleɪzəʳ] *n* Blazer *der*.

bleach [bli:tʃ] ◇ *n (U)* [for clothes] Bleichmittel *das*; [for cleaning] Reinigungsmittel *das*. ◇ *vt* [hair, clothes] bleichen.

bleachers ['bli:tʃəz] *npl US* SPORT *nicht überdachte Zuschauertribüne*.

bleak [bli:k] *adj* - **1.** [weather] trüb, trostlos; [place] trostlos - **2.** [future, face, person] trüb.

bleary-eyed [ˌblɪərɪ'aɪd] *adj* verschlafen.

bleat [bli:t] *vi* - **1.** [sheep] blöken; [goat] meckern - **2.** *fig* [person] meckern.

bleed [bli:d] (*pt & pp* **bled** [bled]) ◇ *vt* [drain] entlüften. ◇ *vi* bluten.

bleeper ['bli:pəʳ] *n* Piepser *der*.

blemish ['blemɪʃ] *n liter & fig* Makel *der*.

blend [blend] ◇ *n liter & fig* Mischung *die*. ◇ *vt* (ver)mischen; **to blend sthg with sthg** etw mit etw mischen. ◇ *vi* [colours, sounds] sich (ver)mischen.

blender ['blendəʳ] *n* [food mixer] Mixer *der*.

bless [bles] (*pt & pp* **-ed** OR **blest**) *vt* - **1.** RELIG segnen - **2.** *phr*: **bless you!** [after sneezing] Gesundheit!; [thank you] du bist ein Engel!

blessing ['blesɪŋ] *n liter & fig* Segen *der*.

blest [blest] *pt & pp* ▷ **bless**.

blew [blu:] *pt* ▷ **blow**.

blight [blaɪt] *vt* beeinträchtigen.

blimey ['blaɪmɪ] *excl UK inf* herrje!

blind [blaɪnd] ◇ *adj* [gen] blind; **to be blind to sthg** *fig* gegenüber einer Sache *(D)* OR für etw blind sein. ◇ *n* [for window] Jalousie *die*. ◇ *npl*: **the blind** die Blinden *Pl*. ◇ *vt* blenden; **to blind sb to sthg** *fig* jn für etw blind machen.

blind alley *n liter & fig* Sackgasse *die*.

blind date *n Rendezvous mit einem oder einer Unbekannten*.

blinders ['blaɪndəz] *npl US* Scheuklappen *Pl*.

blindfold ['blaɪndfəʊld] ◇ *adv* mit verbundenen Augen. ◇ *n* Augenbinde *die*. ◇ *vt*: **to blindfold sb** jm die Augen verbinden.

blindingly ['blaɪndɪŋlɪ] *adv* [obvious] völlig.

blindly ['blaɪndlɪ] *adv liter & fig* blindlings.

blindness ['blaɪndnɪs] *n* Blindheit *die*.

blind spot *n* - **1.** [when driving] toter Winkel - **2.** *fig* [inability to understand]: **to have a blind spot about sthg** (überhaupt) keine Begabung für etw haben.

blink [blɪŋk] ◇ *n phr*: **to be on the blink** *inf* [machine] eine Macke haben. ◇ *vt* [eyes] an|blinzeln. ◇ *vi* [light] auf|scheinen.

blinkered ['blɪŋkəd] *adj fig* [view, attitude] engstirnig.

blinkers ['blɪŋkəz] *npl UK* [for horse] Scheuklappen *Pl*.

bliss [blɪs] *n* Glück *das*, (Glück)seligkeit *die*; **it was sheer bliss** es war die reinste Wonne.

blissful ['blɪsfʊl] *adj* herrlich; **in blissful ignorance** in völliger Ahnungslosigkeit.

blister ['blɪstəʳ] ◇ *n* Blase *die*. ◇ *vi* - **1.** [skin] Blasen bekommen - **2.** [paint] Blasen werfen.

blithely ['blaɪðlɪ] *adv* unbekümmert.

blitz [blɪts] *n* MIL Luftangriff *der*.

blizzard ['blɪzəd] *n* Schneesturm *der*.

bloated ['bləʊtɪd] *adj* - **1.** [body, face] aufgedunsen - **2.** [with food] übersatt.

blob [blɒb] *n* - **1.** [of paint] Klecks *der*; [of cream] Klacks *der* - **2.** [indistinct form] Fleck *der*.

block [blɒk] ◇ *n* - **1.** [building]: **block (of flats)** Wohnhaus *das*; **office block** Bürohaus *das* - **2.** [of ice, wood, stone] Klotz *der* - **3.** *US* [of buildings] Block *der* - **4.** [mental] geistige Sperre. ◇ *vt* - **1.** [road, path, law] blockieren; [pipe] verstopfen - **2.** [view] versperren.

blockade [blɒ'keɪd] ◇ *n* Blockade *die*. ◇ *vt* blockieren, sperren.

blockage ['blɒkɪdʒ] *n* Verstopfung *die*.

blockbuster ['blɒkbʌstəʳ] *n inf* Kassenschlager *der*.

block capitals *npl* Blockschrift *die*.

block letters *npl* Blockschrift *die*.

blog [blɒg] *n* Blog *der*.

bloke [bləʊk] *n UK inf* Typ *der*.

blond [blɒnd] *adj* blond.

blonde [blɒnd] ◇ *adj* blond. ◇ *n* [woman] Blondine *die*.

blood [blʌd] *n* Blut *das*; **in cold blood** kaltblütig.

bloodbath ['blʌdbɑ:θ] *n* Blutbad *das*.

blood cell *n* Blutzelle *die*.

blood donor *n* Blutspender *der*.

blood group *n* Blutgruppe *die*.

bloodhound ['blʌdhaʊnd] *n* Bluthund *der*.

blood poisoning *n* Blutvergiftung *die*.

blood pressure *n* Blutdruck *der*.

bloodshed ['blʌdʃed] *n* Blutvergießen *das*.

bloodshot ['blʌdʃɒt] *adj* [eyes] blutunterlaufen.

bloodstream ['blʌdstri:m] *n* Blutstrom *der*.

blood test *n* Blutprobe *die*.

bloodthirsty ['blʌdˌθɜ:stɪ] *adj* blutrünstig.

blood transfusion *n* Transfusion *die*.

bloody ['blʌdɪ] ◇ *adj* - **1.** [gen] blutig - **2.** *UK v inf* [for emphasis] verdammt; **bloody hell!** verdammt noch mal! ◇ *adv UK v inf* verdammt.

bloody-minded [-'maɪndɪd] *adj UK inf* stur.

bloom [blu:m] ◇ *n* Blüte *die*. ◇ *vi* blühen.

blooming ['blu:mɪŋ] ◇ *adj UK inf* [for emphasis] verflixt. ◇ *adv UK inf* verflixt.

blossom ['blɒsəm] ◇ *n* Blüte *die*; **in blossom** in Blüte. ◇ *vi* - **1.** [tree] blühen - **2.** *fig* [person] auf|blühen.

blot [blɒt] ◇ *n* - **1.** [of ink *etc*] (Tinten)klecks *der* - **2.** *fig* [blemish] Makel *der*; **a blot on the landscape** ein Schandfleck in der Landschaft. ◇ *vt* - **1.** [dry] ab|löschen - **2.** [spot with ink] beklecksen. ◆ **blot out** *vt sep* [memory] aus|löschen.

blotchy ['blɒtʃɪ] *adj* fleckig.

blotting paper ['blɒtɪŋ-] *n (U)* Löschpapier *das*.

blouse [blaʊz] *n* Bluse *die*.

blow [bləʊ] (*pt* **blew**, *pp* **blown**) ◇ *vi* - **1.** [wind] wehen; [stronger] blasen - **2.** [move in the wind] wehen; **the door blew open/shut** die Tür flog auf/zu - **3.** [person] blasen - **4.** [fuse] durch|brennen - **5.** [whistle] ertönen. ◇ *vt* - **1.** [subj: wind] wehen; [stronger] blasen - **2.** [clear]: **to blow one's nose** sich *(D)* die Nase putzen - **3.** [whistle, horn, trumpet] blasen. ◇ *n* Schlag *der*. ◆ **blow away** *vi* weg|fliegen. ◆ **blow out** ◇ *vt sep* aus|blasen. ◇ *vi* - **1.** [candle] aus|gehen - **2.** [tyre] platzen. ◆ **blow over** *vi* - **1.** [storm] sich legen - **2.** [argument] in Vergessenheit geraten. ◆ **blow up** ◇ *vt sep* - **1.** [inflate] auf|blasen; [with pump] auf|pumpen - **2.** [with bomb] in die Luft jagen - **3.** [photograph] vergrößern. ◇ *vi* [explode] explodieren.

blow-dry ◇ *n* Fönen *das*; **a cut and blow-dry** Schneiden und Fönen. ◇ *vt* fönen.

blowlamp *UK* ['bləʊlæmp], **blowtorch** *esp US* ['bləʊtɔːtʃ] *n* Lötlampe *die*.

blown [bləʊn] *pp* ▷ **blow**.

blowout ['bləʊaʊt] *n* [of tyre]: **he had a blowout** ihm platzte ein Reifen.

blowtorch *n esp US* = **blowlamp**.

blubber ['blʌbər] ◇ *n* Walfischspeck *der*. ◇ *vi pej* flennen, heulen.

bludgeon ['blʌdʒən] *vt* prügeln.

blue [bluː] ◇ *adj* - **1.** [in colour] blau - **2.** *inf* [sad] trübsinnig - **3.** [film] Porno-; [joke] unanständig. ◇ *n* Blau *das*; **out of the blue** aus heiterem Himmel. ◆ **blues** *npl* - **1.** MUS: **the blues** der Blues - **2.** *inf* [sad feeling]: **the blues** ein Anfall von Melancholie.

bluebell ['bluːbel] *n* Glockenblume *die*.

blueberry ['bluːbərɪ] *n* Heidelbeere *die*.

blue cheese *n* Blauschimmelkäse *der*.

blue-collar *adj*: **blue-collar worker** Arbeiter *der*, -in *die*.

blue jeans *npl US* (Blue) Jeans *die*.

blueprint ['bluːprɪnt] *n* - **1.** CONSTR Blaupause *die* - **2.** *fig* [plan, programme] Entwurf *der*.

bluff [blʌf] ◇ *adj* [person, manner] raubeinig. ◇ *n* - **1.** [deception] Bluff *der*; **to call sb's bluff** jn dazu auf|fordern, seine Drohung wahr zu machen - **2.** [cliff] Steilhang *der*. ◇ *vi* bluffen.

blunder ['blʌndər] ◇ *n* Schnitzer *der*. ◇ *vi* [make mistake] einen Schnitzer machen; [socially] sich blamieren.

blunt [blʌnt] ◇ *adj* - **1.** [knife, pencil, instrument] stumpf - **2.** [person] geradeheraus; [manner, question] unverblümt. ◇ *vt fig* [enthusiasm] dämpfen; [impact] ab|schwächen.

blur [blɜːr] ◇ *n* verschwommener Fleck; **he couldn't remember anything about the accident, it was all a blur** er konnte sich an nichts bezüglich des Unfalls erinnern, alles war verschwommen. ◇ *vt* - **1.** [outline, photograph] unscharf machen - **2.** [distinction] undeutlich machen.

blurb [blɜːb] *n inf* [on book] Klappentext *der*.

blurt [blɜːt] ◆ **blurt out** *vt sep* heraus|platzen mit.

blush [blʌʃ] ◇ *n* Röte *die*. ◇ *vi* rot werden.

blusher ['blʌʃər] *n* Rouge *das*.

blustery ['blʌstərɪ] *adj* stürmisch.

BMX (*abbr of* **bicycle motorcross**) *n*: **BMX bike** BMX-Rad *das*.

BO *n abbr of* **body odour**.

boar [bɔːr] *n* - **1.** [male pig] Eber *der* - **2.** [wild pig] Keiler *der*.

board [bɔːd] ◇ *n* - **1.** [plank] Brett *das* - **2.** [for notices - large] schwarzes Brett; [- small] Pinnwand *die* - **3.** [for games] Spielbrett *das* - **4.** [blackboard] Tafel *die* - **5.** ADMIN: **board (of directors)** Vorstand *der*; **board of examiners** Prüfungskommission *die*; **board of enquiry** Untersuchungsausschuss *der* - **6.** *UK* [at hotel, guesthouse] Verpflegung *die*; **board and lodging** Unterkunft und Verpflegung; **full/half board** Voll-/Halbpension *die* - **7.** *phr*: **above board** offen. ◇ *vt* [train, bus] ein|steigen in *(+ A)*; **to board a ship/aircraft** an Bord eines Schiffes/Flugzeugs gehen. ◆ **across the board** ◇ *adj* [increase] generell. ◇ *adv* [apply] überall. ◆ **on board** ◇ *prep* [ship, plane] an Bord *(+ G)*; [bus, train] in *(+ D)*. ◇ *adv*: **to be on board** [on ship, plane] an Bord sein; [on train] im Zug sein; **to take sthg on board** [knowledge] etw berücksichtigen; [advice] etw an|nehmen. ◆ **board up** *vt sep* mit Brettern vernageln.

boarder ['bɔːdər] *n* - **1.** [lodger] Pensionsgast *der* - **2.** [at school] Internatsschüler *der*, -in *die*.

boarding card ['bɔːdɪŋ-] *n* Bordkarte *die*.

boarding house ['bɔːdɪŋhaʊs] (*pl* [-haʊzɪz]) *n* Pension *die*.

boarding school ['bɔːdɪŋ-] *n* Internat *das*.

Board of Trade *n UK*: **the Board of Trade** das Handelsministerium.

boardroom ['bɔːdrʊm] *n* Sitzungssaal *der*.

boast [bəʊst] ◇ *n* Prahlerei *die*. ◇ *vi* prahlen; **to boast about sthg** mit etw prahlen.

boastful ['bəʊstfʊl] *adj* prahlerisch.

boat [bəʊt] *n* Boot *das*; [large] Schiff *das*; *(phrase)*: **by boat** mit dem Boot; [large] mit dem Schiff.

boater ['bəʊtəʳ] *n* [hat] steifer Strohhut.

boatswain ['bəʊsn] *n* NAUT Bootsmann *der*.

bob [bɒb] ◇ *n* - **1.** [hairstyle] Bubikopf *der* - **2.** *UK inf dated* [shilling] Schilling *der* - **3.** [bobsleigh] Bob *der*. ◇ *vi* [boat, ship] auf und ab schaukeln.

bobbin ['bɒbɪn] *n* Spule *die*.

bobby ['bɒbɪ] *n UK inf* [policeman] Polizist *der*.

bobsleigh ['bɒbsleɪ] *n* Bob *der*.

bode [bəʊd] *vi liter*: **to bode well/ill (for sb/sthg)** ein gutes/schlechtes Zeichen (für jn/etw) sein.

bodily ['bɒdɪlɪ] ◇ *adj* körperlich; **bodily functions** Körperfunktionen *Pl*. ◇ *adv* [carry, lift] mit dem ganzen Körper.

body ['bɒdɪ] *n* - **1.** [of human, animal] Körper *der* - **2.** [corpse] Leiche *die* - **3.** [organization] Organisation *die* - **4.** [of car] Karosserie *die*; [of plane] Rumpf *der* - **5.** [group] Gruppe *die* - **6.** [of wine] Körper *der* - **7.** [of hair] Volumen *das* - **8.** [garment] Body *der*.

body building *n* Bodybuilding *das*.

bodyguard ['bɒdɪgɑːd] *n* [one person] Leibwächter *der*; [group of people] Leibwache *die*.

body odour *n* Körpergeruch *der*.

bodywork ['bɒdɪwɜːk] *n* Karosserie *die*.

bog [bɒg] *n* - **1.** [marsh] Sumpf *der* - **2.** *UK inf* [toilet] Klo *das*.

bogged down [ˌbɒgd-] *adj*: **bogged down (in sthg)** *liter* & *fig* (in etw *(D)*) festgefahren.

boggle ['bɒgl] *vi*: **the mind boggles!** es übersteigt den Verstand!

bog-standard *adj inf* stinknormal.

bogus ['bəʊgəs] *adj* [identity] falsch; [emotion] geheuchelt.

boil [bɔɪl] ◇ *n* - **1.** [on skin] Furunkel *der ODER das* - **2.** [boiling point]: **to bring sthg to the boil** etw zum Kochen bringen; **to come to the boil** zu kochen beginnen. ◇ *vt* kochen; **to boil the kettle** Wasser auf|setzen. ◇ *vi* kochen; **the kettle is boiling** das Wasser im Kessel kocht. ◆ **boil down to** *vt insep fig* hinaus|laufen auf *(+ A)*. ◆ **boil over** *vi* - **1.** [liquid] über|kochen - **2.** *fig* [feelings] ihren Höhepunkt erreichen.

boiled ['bɔɪld] *adj* gekocht; **boiled potatoes** Salzkartoffeln *Pl*; **boiled sweets** Bonbons *Pl*; **boiled egg** gekochtes Ei.

boiler ['bɔɪləʳ] *n* Boiler *der*.

boiler suit *n UK* Overall *der*, Blaumann *der*.

boiling ['bɔɪlɪŋ] *adj* [hot liquid] kochend heiß; [weather] wahnsinnig heiß; **I'm boiling (hot)!** mir ist fürchterlich heiß!

boiling point *n* Siedepunkt *der*.

boisterous ['bɔɪstərəs] *adj* ungestüm.

bold [bəʊld] *adj* - **1.** [person, plan] kühn, mutig - **2.** ART [lines, colour] kräftig; [design] kühn - **3.** TYPO: **bold type** *OR* **print** Fettdruck *der*.

bollard ['bɒlɑːd] *n* Poller *der*.

bollocks ['bɒləks] *UK v inf* ◇ *npl* Eier *Pl*. ◇ *excl* Scheiße!

bolster ['bəʊlstəʳ] ◇ *n* Nackenrolle *die*. ◇ *vt* [confidence] stärken.

bolt [bəʊlt] ◇ *n* - **1.** [on door, window] Riegel *der* - **2.** [type of screw] Bolzen *der*. ◇ *adv*: **bolt upright** kerzengerade. ◇ *vt* - **1.** [fasten together] verschrauben - **2.** [close] verriegeln - **3.** [food] hinunter|schlingen. ◇ *vi* [run - horse] durch|gehen; [- person] flüchten.

bomb [bɒm] ◇ *n* Bombe *die*. ◇ *vt* [from the air] bombardieren; [on the ground] einen Bombenanschlag verüben auf *(+ A)*.

bombard [bɒm'bɑːd] *vt* [from the air] bombardieren; [from gun] beschießen; **to bombard sb with sthg** *fig* jn mit etw bombardieren.

bomb disposal squad *n* Bombenräumkommando *das*.

bomber ['bɒməʳ] *n* - **1.** [plane] Bomberflugzeug *das* - **2.** [person] Bombenleger *der*, -in *die*.

bombing ['bɒmɪŋ] *n* [from the air] Bombardierung *die*; [on the ground] Bombenanschlag *der*.

bombshell ['bɒmʃel] *n fig* schwerer Schlag.

bona fide [ˌbəʊnə'faɪdɪ] *adj* [genuine] echt.

bond [bɒnd] ◇ *n* - **1.** [emotional link] enge Beziehung; **bonds of friendship** freundschaftliche Bande *Pl* - **2.** [binding promise]: **my word is my bond** was ich verspreche, halte ich auch - **3.** FIN Obligation *die*. ◇ *vt* - **1.** [glue]: **to bond sthg to sthg** etw an etw *(A)* kleben - **2.** *fig* [people]: **the experience bonded them together** die Erfahrung band sie aneinander.

bone [bəʊn] ◇ *n* Knochen *der*; [of fish] Gräte *die*; **bones** [of skeleton] Gebeine *Pl*. ◇ *vt* [meat] von den Knochen lösen; [fish] entgräten.

bone-dry *adj* knochentrocken.

bone-idle *adj inf* stinkfaul.

bonfire ['bɒnˌfaɪəʳ] *n* großes Feuer *(im Freien)*.

bonfire night *n UK 5. November, Jahrestag der Pulververschwörung*.

bonk *vt* & *vi UK v inf* bumsen.

Bonn [bɒn] *n* Bonn *nt*.

bonnet ['bɒnɪt] *n* - **1.** *UK* [of car] Kühlerhaube *die*; Motorhaube *die* - **2.** [hat - for woman] Haube *die*; [- for baby] Häubchen *das*.

bonny ['bɒnɪ] *adj Scotland* [baby] prächtig; [girl] hübsch.

bonus ['bəʊnəs] (*pl* **-es**) *n* - **1.** [extra money] Prämie *die*; **Christmas bonus** Weihnachtsgratifikation *die* - **2.** *fig* [added advantage] Pluspunkt *der*.

bony ['bəʊnɪ] *adj* [person, hand, face] knochig.

boo [buː] (*pl* **-s**) ◇ *excl* buh! ◇ *n* Buhruf *der*. ◇ *vt* aus|buhen, aus|pfeifen. ◇ *vi* buhen.

boob [buːb] *n inf* [mistake] Schnitzer *der*. ◆ **boobs** *npl UK v inf* [breasts] Möpse *Pl*.

booby trap ['buːbɪ-] *n* - **1.** [bomb] getarnte Bombe - **2.** [prank] Falle *die (mit deren Hilfe ein Streich gespielt wird)*.

book [bʊk] ◇ *n* - **1.** [for reading] Buch *das* - **2.** [of stamps, matches, tickets] Heftchen *das*; [of cheques] Heft *das*. ◇ *vt* - **1.** [table, room] reservieren lassen; [ticket] bestellen; [performer] engagieren; [plane seat] buchen; **to be fully booked** [restaurant, hotel] ausgebucht sein; [performance] ausverkauft sein - **2.** *inf* [subj: police] auf|schreiben - **3.** *UK* FTBL verwarnen. ◇ *vi* [book table, room] reservieren lassen; [book ticket] vor|bestellen; [book plane seat] buchen. ◆ **books** *npl* COMM Bücher *die*. ◆ **book up** *vt sep* buchen; **to be booked up** [restaurant, hotel] ausgebucht sein; [performance] ausverkauft sein.

bookcase ['bʊkkeɪs] *n* Bücherregal *das*.

bookie ['bʊkɪ] *n inf* Buchmacher *der*.

booking ['bʊkɪŋ] *n* - **1.** *esp UK* [of seat, room] Reservierung *die*; [of ticket] Bestellung *die* - **2.** FTBL Verwarnung *die*.

booking office *n esp UK* [in station] Fahrkartenschalter *der*.

bookkeeping ['bʊkˌkiːpɪŋ] *n* COMM Buchhaltung *die*.

booklet ['bʊklɪt] *n* Broschüre *die*.

bookmaker ['bʊkˌmeɪkəʳ] *n* Buchmacher *der*.

bookmark ['bʊkmɑːk] ◇ *n* [gen & COMPUT] Lesezeichen *das*. ◇ *vt* COMPUT [web page] Bookmark *die ODER das*.

bookseller ['bʊkˌseləʳ] *n* Buchhändler *der*, -in *die*.

bookshelf ['bʊkʃelf] (*pl* **-shelves** [-ʃelvz]) *n* Bücherbord *das*.

bookshop *UK* ['bʊkʃɒp], **bookstore** *US* ['bʊkstɔːʳ] *n* Buchhandlung *die*.

book token *n esp UK* Büchergutschein *der*.

boom [buːm] ◇ *n* - **1.** [of cannons, guns] Donnern *das*; [of voice] Dröhnen *das* - **2.** [in business, economy] Boom *der*, Aufschwung *der* - **3.** NAUT Baum *der* - **4.** [for TV camera, microphone] Galgen *der*. ◇ *vi* - **1.** [cannons, guns] donnern; [voice] dröhnen - **2.** [business, economy] einen Aufschwung nehmen.

boon [buːn] *n* Segen *der*.

boost [buːst] ◇ *n* - **1.** [in profits, production] Zunahme *die* - **2.** [in popularity] Steigerung *die*; [in spirits, morale] Verbesserung *die*; **to give sb a boost** [encourage] jm Auftrieb geben. ◇ *vt* - **1.** [profits, production] an|kurbeln - **2.** [popularity] steigern; [morale, spirits] heben.

booster ['buːstəʳ] *n* [vaccine] Auffrischimpfung *die*.

boot [buːt] ◇ *n* - **1.** [footwear] Stiefel *der*; [for football, rugby] Schuh *der* - **2.** *UK* [of car] Kofferraum *der*. ◇ *vt* - **1.** *inf* [kick] einen Tritt geben *(+ D)*; [ball] kicken - **2.** COMPUT booten, hochfahren. ◆ **to boot** *adv* noch dazu. ◆ **boot up** *vi* COMPUT booten.

booth [buːð] *n* - **1.** [at fair] (Markt)bude *die* - **2.** [for telephone] Telefonzelle *die* - **3.** [for voting] Kabine *die*.

booty ['buːtɪ] *n liter* Beute *die*.

booze [buːz] *inf* ◇ *n* [alcohol] Alkohol *der*. ◇ *vi* saufen.

bop [bɒp] *inf* ◇ *n* [dance]: **to have a bop** rocken. ◇ *vi* [dance] rocken.

border ['bɔːdəʳ] ◇ *n* - **1.** [between countries] Grenze *die* - **2.** [of dress, handkerchief] Bordüre *die*; [of plate] Rand *der* - **3.** [outer limit] Rand *der* - **4.** [in garden] Rabatte *die*. ◇ *vt* - **1.** [country] grenzen an *(+ A)* - **2.** [field, garden] umschließen; [path] säumen. ◆ **border on** *vt insep* [verge on] grenzen an *(+ A)*.

borderline ['bɔːdəlaɪn] ◇ *adj*: **borderline case** Grenzfall *der*. ◇ *n fig* Grenze *die*.

bore [bɔːʳ] ◇ *pt* ▷ **bear**. ◇ *n* - **1.** [person] Langweiler *der*; [situation, event] Plage *die* - **2.** [of gun] Kaliber *das*; **a 12-bore shotgun** eine Flinte vom Kaliber 12. ◇ *vt* - **1.** [not interest] langweilen; **to bore sb stiff** OR **to tears** OR **to death** jn zu Tode langweilen - **2.** [drill] bohren.

bored [bɔːd] *adj* gelangweilt; **she is bored with always staying in** es langweilt sie, immer zu Hause zu bleiben.

boredom ['bɔːdəm] *n* Langeweile *die*.

boring ['bɔːrɪŋ] *adj* langweilig.

born [bɔːn] *adj*: **to be born** geboren werden; **I was born in London/1968** ich bin OR wurde in London/1968 geboren; **a born entertainer** ein geborener Entertainer.

borne [bɔːn] *pp* ▷ **bear**.

borough ['bʌrə] *n Regierungsbezirk, der entweder eine Stadt oder einen Stadtteil umfasst.*

borrow ['bɒrəʊ] *vt* sich *(D)* leihen; [book from library] aus|leihen; **to borrow sthg from sb** sich *(D)* etw von jm leihen OR borgen.

Bosnia ['bɒznɪə] *n* Bosnien *nt*.

Bosnian ['bɒznɪən] ◇ *adj* bosnisch. ◇ *n* Bosnier *der*, -in *die*.

bosom ['bʊzəm] *n* - **1.** [breasts] Busen *der*; [of dress] Brustteil *der* - **2.** *fig* [of family] Schoß *der*; **bosom friend** Busenfreund *der*, -in *die*.

boss [bɒs] *n* - **1.** [gen] Chef *der*, -in *die* - **2.** *fig* [of gang] Boss *der*. ◆ **boss about, boss around** *vt sep pej* herum|kommandieren.

bossy ['bɒsɪ] *adj* herrisch.

bosun ['bəʊsn] *n* = **boatswain**.

botany ['bɒtənɪ] *n* Botanik *die*.

botch [bɒtʃ] ◆ **botch up** *vt sep inf* mehr schlecht als recht machen.

both [bəʊθ] ◇ *pron* beide; **both of us** wir beide; **both of them speak German** sie sprechen beide Deutsch; **do you prefer music or painting? – I like them both** bevorzugst du Musik oder Malerei? – ich mag beides. ◇ *adj* beide. ◇ *adv*: **both my sister and I** sowohl meine Schwester als auch ich.

bother ['bɒðəʳ] ◇ *vt* - **1.** [worry, hurt] stören; **what you told me yesterday has been bothering me** was du mir gestern gesagt hast, hat mich beschäftigt; **she can't be bothered to do it** sie hat keine Lust, das zu tun - **2.** [annoy] ärgern; [pester] belästigen; **I'm sorry to bother you** entschuldigen Sie die Störung. ◇ *vi* sich bemühen; **no, don't bother!** nein, das ist nicht nötig!; **to bother about sthg** sich um etw kümmern; **don't bother to phone me** Sie brauchen mich nicht anzurufen; **I didn't bother to lock up** ich habe mir nicht die Mühe gemacht abzuschließen; **don't bother getting up** bleiben Sie doch sitzen. ◇ *n* Mühe *die*; **no bother at all** überhaupt kein Problem; **if it isn't too much of a bother** wenn es Ihnen nichts ausmacht. ◇ *excl* verflixt!

bothered ['bɒðəd] *adj* [annoyed] verärgert.

Botox® ['bəʊtɒks] *n* Botox *das*.

bottle ['bɒtl] ◇ *n* - **1.** [container, quantity] Flasche *die* - **2.** [for baby] Fläschen *das*, Flasche *die* - **3.** *(U) UK inf* [courage] Mumm *der*. ◇ *vt* - **1.** [wine] in Flaschen ab|füllen - **2.** [fruit] ein|machen. ◆ **bottle up** *vt sep* [feelings] in sich *(D)* auf|stauen.

bottle bank *n* Altglascontainer *der*.

bottleneck ['bɒtlnek] *n* Engpass *der*.

bottle-opener *n* Flaschenöffner *der*.

bottom ['bɒtəm] ◇ *adj* - **1.** [lowest] unterste(r) (s) - **2.** [least successful] schlechteste(r) (s); **to be bottom in sthg** [subject] der Schlechteste in etw *(D)* sein. ◇ *n* - **1.** [of glass, bottle, bag] Boden *der*; [of page, list, ladder] unteres Ende; [of sea, lake] Grund *der*; [of hill, mountain] Fuß *der*; *(phrase)*: **at the bottom** unten - **2.** [of street, garden]: **at the bottom of** am Ende *(+ G)* - **3.** [of organization] unteres Ende; **he worked his way up from the bottom** er hat sich hoch gearbeitet - **4.** [buttocks] Hintern *der* - **5.** [cause]: **to get to the bottom of sthg** einer Sache *(D)* auf den Grund gehen. ◆ **bottom out** *vi* den Tiefstand erreichen.

bottom line *n fig* [result]: **the bottom line** das Endergebnis.

bough [baʊ] *n* Ast *der*.

bought [bɔːt] *pt* & *pp* ▷ **buy**.

boulder ['bəʊldəʳ] *n* (gerundeter) Felsbrocken *der*.

bounce [baʊns] ◇ *vi* - **1.** [ball] springen; **the ball bounced onto the car** der Ball prallte auf das Auto - **2.** [person - with energy, enthusiasm] hüpfen; **to bounce on sthg** [jump up and down] auf etw *(D)* springen - **3.** *inf* [cheque] platzen. ◇ *vt* [ball] aufprallen lassen. ◇ *n* [rebound] Aufprall *der*.

bouncer ['baʊnsəʳ] *n inf* Rausschmeißer *der*.

bound [baʊnd] ◇ *pt* & *pp* ▷ **bind**. ◇ *adj* - **1.** [certain]: **to be bound to do sthg** etw bestimmt tun; **it was bound to happen** das musste so kommen; **he's bound to win** er gewinnt hundertprozentig - **2.** [forced, morally obliged]: **bound by sthg** durch etw gebunden; **bound to do sthg** gezwungen, etw zu tun; **I'm bound to say** OR **admit** ich muss sagen OR zugeben - **3.** [en route]: **to be bound for** unterwegs sein nach. ◇ *n* [leap] Sprung *der*. ◇ *vt* [border]: **to be bounded by** begrenzt sein von. ◆ **bounds** *npl* Grenzen *Pl*; **out of bounds** verboten.

boundary ['baʊndrɪ] *n* Grenze *die*.

bourbon ['bɜːbən] *n* Bourbon *der*.

bout [baʊt] *n* - **1.** [attack, session] Anfall *der* - **2.** [boxing match] Kampf *der*.

bow[1] [baʊ] ◇ *n* - **1.** [act of bowing] Verbeugung *die* - **2.** [of ship] Bug *der*. ◇ *vt* [lower] beugen. ◇ *vi* - **1.** [make a bow] sich verbeugen - **2.** [defer]: **to bow to sthg** sich einer Sache *(D)* beugen.

bow[2] [bəʊ] *n* - **1.** [weapon, for musical instrument] Bogen *der* - **2.** [knot] Schleife *die*.

bowels ['baʊəlz] *npl liter* & *fig* Eingeweide *Pl*.

bowl [bəʊl] ◇ *n* Schüssel *die*; [of pipe] Kopf *der*. ◇ *vi* [in cricket] den Ball werfen. ◆ **bowls** *n britische Variante des französischen Boulespiels, bei der die Spielkugeln gerollt werden.* ◆ **bowl over** *vt sep* um|werfen.

bow-legged [ˌbəʊ'legɪd] *adj* o-beinig.

bowler ['bəʊləʳ] *n* - **1.** [in cricket] Werfer *der*, -in *die* - **2.** [headgear]: **bowler (hat)** Melone *die*.

bowling ['bəʊlɪŋ] *n*: **(tenpin) bowling** Bowling *das*.

bowling alley *n* Bowlingbahn *die*.

bowling green *n Rasen- oder Kunstrasenfläche, auf der "bowls" gespielt wird.*

bow tie [bəʊ-] *n* Fliege *die*.

box [bɒks] ◇ *n* - **1.** [made of wood or metal] Kiste *die*; [smaller] Kasten *der*; [made of cardboard] Karton *der*; [smaller] Schachtel *die*; **a box of chocolates** eine Schachtel Pralinen - **2.** [in theatre] Loge *die* - **3.** [on form] Kästchen *das* - **4.** *UK inf* [television]: **the box** die Glotze. ◇ *vi* [fight] boxen.

boxer ['bɒksəʳ] *n* - **1.** [fighter] Boxer *der* - **2.** [dog] Boxer *der*, -hündin *die*.

boxer shorts *npl* Boxershorts *Pl*.

boxing ['bɒksɪŋ] *n* Boxen *das*.

Boxing Day *n* Zweiter Weihnachtsfeiertag.

boxing glove *n* Boxhandschuh *der*.

box office *n* Kasse *die (von Kino, Theater, bei Konzert).*
boy [bɔɪ] ◇ *n* [young male, son] Junge *der.* ◇ *excl*: **(oh) boy!** *inf* oh, Mann!
boycott [ˈbɔɪkɒt] ◇ *n* Boykott *der.* ◇ *vt* boykottieren.
boyfriend [ˈbɔɪfrend] *n* Freund *der.*
boyish [ˈbɔɪɪʃ] *adj* jungenhaft.
bra [brɑː] *n* Büstenhalter *der*, BH *der.*
brace [breɪs] ◇ *n* - **1.** [on teeth] Klammer *die* - **2.** [on leg] Stützapparat *der.* ◇ *vt* - **1.** [steady, support]: **to brace o.s.** sich festlhalten - **2.** *fig* [mentally prepare]: **to brace o.s. (for sthg)** sich (auf etw *(A)*) gefasst machen. ◆ **braces** *npl UK* [for trousers] Hosenträger *der.*
bracelet [ˈbreɪslɪt] *n* Armband *das.*
bracken [ˈbrækn] *n (U)* Farnkraut *das.*
bracket [ˈbrækɪt] ◇ *n* - **1.** [support] Halterung *die*; **(angle) bracket** Winkelträger *der* - **2.** [parenthesis] Klammer *die*; **in brackets** in Klammern - **3.** [group] Klasse *die.* ◇ *vt* [enclose in brackets] einlklammern, in Klammern setzen.
brag [bræg] *vi* prahlen.
braid [breɪd] ◇ *n* - **1.** *(U)* [on uniform] Tresse *die* - **2.** *esp US* [hairstyle] Zopf *der.* ◇ *vt esp US* flechten.
brain [breɪn] *n* - **1.** [organ] Gehirn *das* - **2.** [mind, person] Kopf *der.* ◆ **brains** *npl* [intelligence] Grips *der*, Intelligenz *die.*
brainchild [ˈbreɪntʃaɪld] *n* Geistesprodukt *das.*
brainwash [ˈbreɪnwɒʃ] *vt*: **to brainwash sb** jn einer Gehirnwäsche unterziehen.
brainwave [ˈbreɪnweɪv] *n* Geistesblitz *der.*
brainy [ˈbreɪnɪ] *adj inf* gescheit.
brake [breɪk] ◇ *n* - **1.** [on vehicle] Bremse *die* - **2.** *fig* [restraint] Zurückhaltung *die.* ◇ *vi* bremsen.
brake light *n* Bremslicht *das.*
bramble [ˈbræmbl] *n* [bush] Brombeerbusch *der*; [fruit] Brombeere *die.*
bran [bræn] *n (U)* Kleie *die.*
branch [brɑːntʃ] ◇ *n* - **1.** [of tree] Zweig *der*, Ast *der* - **2.** [of river] Arm *der*; [of railway] Nebenstrecke *die* - **3.** [of company, bank, organization] Zweigstelle *die* - **4.** [of subject] Zweig *der.* ◇ *vi* [road] sich teilen. ◆ **branch out** *vi* sein Tätigkeitsfeld erweitern.
brand [brænd] ◇ *n* - **1.** COMM [make] Marke *die* - **2.** *fig* [type, style] Sorte *die*, Art *die.* ◇ *vt* - **1.** [cattle] mit einem Brandzeichen versehen - **2.** *fig* [classify]: **to brand sb (as) sthg** jn als etw brandmarken.
brandish [ˈbrændɪʃ] *vt* schwingen.
brand name *n* Markenname *der.*
brand-new *adj* nagelneu, brandneu.
brandy [ˈbrændɪ] *n* Brandy *der.*
brash [bræʃ] *adj pej* [person, manner] laut.
brass [brɑːs] *n* - **1.** [metal] Messing *das* - **2.** MUS: **the brass** die Blechbläser *Pl.*
brass band *n* Blaskapelle *die.*
brat [bræt] *n inf pej* Balg *das.*
bravado [brəˈvɑːdəʊ] *n* Wagemut *der.*
brave [breɪv] ◇ *adj* mutig, tapfer. ◇ *n* [warrior] Krieger *der.* ◇ *vt* [weather] trotzen *(+ D)*; [anger, displeasure, punishment] über sich *(A)* ergehen lassen.
bravery [ˈbreɪvərɪ] *n* Mut *die.*
brawl [brɔːl] *n* Handgemenge *das.*
brawn [brɔːn] *n (U)* - **1.** [muscle] Muskelkraft *die* - **2.** *UK* [meat] Schweinskopfsülze *die.*
bray [breɪ] *vi* [donkey] schreien.
brazen [ˈbreɪzn] *adj* unverschämt, frech. ◆ **brazen out** *vt sep*: **to brazen it out** sich *(D)* nichts anmerken lassen.
brazier [ˈbreɪzjəʳ] *n* Kohlenbecken *das.*
Brazil [brəˈzɪl] *n* Brasilien *nt.*
Brazilian [brəˈzɪljən] ◇ *adj* brasilianisch. ◇ *n* Brasilianer *der*, -in *die.*
brazil nut *n* Paranuss *die.*
breach [briːtʃ] ◇ *n* - **1.** [of law, agreement] Bruch *der*; **to be in breach of sthg** gegen etw verstoßen; **breach of contract** Vertragsbruch *der* - **2.** [opening, gap] Bresche *die.* ◇ *vt* - **1.** [disobey] verletzen - **2.** [make hole in] durchbrechen.
breach of the peace *n* öffentliche Ruhestörung.
bread [bred] *n (U)* [food] Brot *das*; **bread and butter** [food] Butterbrot *das*; *fig* [main income] Lebensunterhalt *der.*
bread bin *UK*, **bread box** *US n* Brotkasten *der.*
breadcrumbs [ˈbredkrʌmz] *npl* Brotkrümel *Pl*; [for coating food] Paniermehl *das.*
breadline [ˈbredlaɪn] *n*: **to be on the breadline** am Existenzminimum leben.
breadth [bretθ] *n* - **1.** [in measurements] Breite *die* - **2.** *fig* [scope] Spektrum *das.*
breadwinner [ˈbred,wɪnəʳ] *n* Ernährer *der*, -in *die.*
break [breɪk] (*pt* **broke**, *pp* **broken**) ◇ *n* - **1.** [gap, interruption] Unterbrechung *die*; **break in sthg** Unterbrechung in etw *(D)* - **2.** [fracture, rupture, change] Bruch *der*; **break with sthg** Bruch *der* mit etw - **3.** [pause, rest] Unterbrechung *die*; SCH Pause *die*; **weekend break** Urlaubswochenende *das*; **to take** OR **have a break** eine (kurze) Pause machen; **to have a break from sthg** mit etw pausieren; **without a break** ohne Unterbrechung - **4.** *inf* [luck, chance] Chance *die.* ◇ *vt* - **1.** [gen] brechen; [smash] zerbrechen; [windows] einlschlagen - **2.** [cause to stop working] kaputtlmachen - **3.** [interrupt - journey, silence] unterbrechen; *(phrase)*: **to break sb's fall** js

Fall bremsen - **4.** [tell]: **to break the news of sthg to sb** jm etw mit|teilen. ◇ *vi* - **1.** [gen] brechen - **2.** [stop working] kaputt|gehen - **3.** [pause] eine Pause machen - **4.** [weather] um|schlagen - **5.** [escape]: **to break loose** OR **free** los|brechen - **6.** [voice] brechen - **7.** [news] bekannt werden - **8.** *phr*: **to break even** seine Kosten decken. ◆ **break away** *vi* [escape] weg|laufen. ◆ **break down** ◇ *vt sep* - **1.** [destroy] ein|schlagen - **2.** [analyse] auf|schlüsseln. ◇ *vi* [gen] zusammen|brechen; **the car has broken down** das Auto hat eine Panne. ◆ **break in** ◇ *vi* - **1.** [enter by force] ein|brechen - **2.** [interrupt]: **to break in (on sb/sthg)** (jn/etw) unterbrechen. ◇ *vt sep* - **1.** [horse] zu|reiten - **2.** [person] ein|arbeiten. ◆ **break into** *vt insep* - **1.** [enter by force] ein|brechen in *(+ A)* - **2.** [begin suddenly] aus|brechen in *(+ A)*. ◆ **break off** *vt sep* & *vi* ab|brechen. ◆ **break out** *vi* - **1.** [begin suddenly] aus|brechen - **2.** [escape]: **to break out (of)** aus|brechen (aus). ◆ **break up** ◇ *vt sep* - **1.** [object] zerbrechen; [ice, soil] auf|brechen - **2.** [bring to an end]: **the police broke up the party** die Polizei sprengte die Party; **she broke up the fight** sie trennte die Kämpfenden. ◇ *vi* - **1.** [object] auseinander brechen - **2.** [relationship] in die Brüche gehen; [fight, party] enden; **to break up with sb** sich von jm trennen - **3.** [crowd] auseinander treiben - **4.** [school] enden; [pupils, teachers] in die Ferien gehen.

breakage ['breɪkɪdʒ] *n* Bruchschaden *der*.

breakdown ['breɪkdaʊn] *n* - **1.** [of system] Zusammenbruch *der*; [of car] Panne *die*; [of machine] Störung *die*; [in talks] Scheitern *das* - **2.** [analysis] Aufschlüsselung *die*.

breakfast ['brekfəst] *n* Frühstück *das*; **to have breakfast** frühstücken.

break-in *n* Einbruch *der*.

breakneck ['breɪknek] *adj*: **at breakneck speed** in halsbrecherischem Tempo.

breakthrough ['breɪkθruː] *n* Durchbruch *der*.

breakup ['breɪkʌp] *n* [of relationship] Scheitern *das*.

breast [brest] *n* Brust *die*.

breast-feed *vt* & *vi* stillen.

breaststroke ['breststrəʊk] *n* Brustschwimmen *das*.

breath [breθ] *n* Atem *der*; **bad breath** Mundgeruch *der*; **he took a deep breath** er holte tief Atem; **out of breath** außer Atem; **to get one's breath back** Luft holen.

breathalyse *UK*, **-yze** *US* ['breθəlaɪz] *vt* (ins Röhrchen) blasen lassen.

breathe [briːð] ◇ *vi* atmen. ◇ *vt* [inhale] ein|atmen. ◆ **breathe in** *vt sep* & *vi* ein|atmen. ◆ **breathe out** *vi* aus|atmen.

breather ['briːðəʳ] *n inf* Atempause *die*.

breathing ['briːðɪŋ] *n* Atmen *das*.

breathless ['breθlɪs] *adj* atemlos.

breathtaking ['breθˌteɪkɪŋ] *adj* atemberaubend.

breed [briːd] (*pt & pp* **bred** [bred]) ◇ *n* - **1.** [of animal] Rasse *die* - **2.** *fig* [sort, style] Art *die*. ◇ *vt* - **1.** [animals, plants] züchten - **2.** *fig* [suspicion] säen. ◇ *vi* züchten.

breeding ['briːdɪŋ] *n (U)* - **1.** [of animals] Aufzucht *die*; [of plants] Züchtung *die* - **2.** [manners] Erziehung *die*.

breeze [briːz] *n* Brise *die*.

breezy ['briːzɪ] *adj* - **1.** [windy] windig - **2.** [cheerful] leichtherzig, fröhlich.

brevity ['brevɪtɪ] *n* Kürze *die*.

brew [bruː] ◇ *vt* [beer] brauen; [tea, coffee] auf|gießen. ◇ *vi* - **1.** [tea, coffee] ziehen - **2.** *fig* [trouble, storm] sich zusammen|brauen.

brewery ['bruːərɪ] *n* Brauerei *die*.

bribe [braɪb] ◇ *n* Bestechung *die*. ◇ *vt*: **to bribe sb (to do sthg)** jn bestechen(, etw zu tun).

bribery ['braɪbərɪ] *n (U)* Bestechung *die*.

brick [brɪk] *n* Ziegelstein *der*, Backstein *der*.

bricklayer ['brɪkˌleɪəʳ] *n* Maurer *der*.

bridal ['braɪdl] *adj* Braut-.

bride [braɪd] *n* Braut *die*.

bridegroom ['braɪdgrʊm] *n* Bräutigam *der*.

bridesmaid ['braɪdzmeɪd] *n* Brautjungfer *die*.

bridge [brɪdʒ] ◇ *n* - **1.** [gen] Brücke *die* - **2.** [card game] Bridge *das*. ◇ *vt fig* [gap] überbrücken.

bridle ['braɪdl] *n* Zaum *der*.

bridle path *n* Reitweg *der*.

brief [briːf] ◇ *adj* - **1.** [short] kurz - **2.** [skimpy, concise] knapp; **please be brief** fassen Sie sich kurz; **in brief** kurz (gesagt). ◇ *n* - **1.** LAW [statement] Unterlagen *Pl* - **2.** *UK* [instructions] Auftrag *der*. ◇ *vt*: **to brief sb (on sthg)** jn (über etw *(A)*) unterrichten. ◆ **briefs** *npl* [underwear] Slip *der*; **a pair of briefs** ein Slip.

briefcase ['briːfkeɪs] *n* Aktentasche *die*.

briefing ['briːfɪŋ] *n* Einsatzbesprechung *die*.

briefly ['briːflɪ] *adv* kurz.

brigade [brɪ'geɪd] *n* - **1.** MIL Brigade *die* - **2.** [organization] Truppe *die*.

brigadier [ˌbrɪgə'dɪəʳ] *n UK* Brigadegeneral *der*.

bright [braɪt] *adj* - **1.** [room, light] hell - **2.** [colour] leuchtend - **3.** [lively, cheerful] strahlend - **4.** [intelligent] klug, gescheit; **a bright girl** ein aufgewecktes Mädchen - **5.** [future, prospects] glänzend. ◆ **brights** *npl US inf* AUT Fernlicht *das*.

brighten ['braɪtn] *vi* sich auf|hellen. ◆ **brighten up** ◇ *vt sep* - **1.** [room, house] auf|hellen - **2.** [situation, prospects] auf|heitern.

◇ *vi* - **1.** [become more cheerful] fröhlicher werden; [face] sich auf|hellen - **2.** [weather] sich auf|hellen.

brilliance ['brɪljəns] *n* - **1.** [cleverness] Großartigkeit *die* - **2.** [of colour, light] Strahlen *das*.

brilliant ['brɪljənt] *adj* - **1.** [gen] glänzend, brilliant - **2.** [colour, light] strahlend - **3.** *inf* [wonderful, enjoyable] toll; **oh brilliant!** *iro* na toll!

brim [brɪm] ◇ *n* - **1.** [edge] Rand *der* - **2.** [of hat] Krempe *die*. ◇ *vi* - **1.** [with liquid]: **to brim with sthg** randvoll mit etw sein - **2.** [with feeling]: **to brim with ideas** vor Ideen über|sprudeln; **to brim with self-confidence** vor Selbstbewusstsein strotzen.

brine [braɪn] *n (U)* Sole *die*, Lake *die*.

bring [brɪŋ] (*pt & pp* **brought**) *vt* - **1.** [take along] mitbringen; [move] bringen; **to bring sb good luck** jm Glück bringen - **2.** [cause] führen zu; **to bring sthg to an end** etw zu Ende bringen; **to bring sthg into being** etw ins Leben rufen. ◆ **bring about** *vt sep* verursachen. ◆ **bring around** *vt sep* [make conscious] zu Bewusstsein bringen. ◆ **bring back** *vt sep* - **1.** [return] zurück|bringen - **2.** [shopping, gift] mit|bringen - **3.** [reinstate - custom] wieder ein|führen; [- government] wieder an die Macht bringen - **4.** [cause to remember]: **to bring back memories** Erinnerungen wach|rufen. ◆ **bring down** *vt sep* - **1.** [shoot down - plane] ab|schießen - **2.** [government, tyrant] stürzen - **3.** [prices] senken - **4.** THEAT: **to bring the house down** stürmischen Beifall ernten. ◆ **bring forward** *vt sep* - **1.** [meeting, election] vor|verlegen - **2.** [in bookkeeping] übertragen. ◆ **bring in** *vt sep* - **1.** [introduce] ein|führen - **2.** [earn] ein|bringen - **3.** [involve] ein|schalten. ◆ **bring off** *vt sep* [plan] in die Tat um|setzen; [deal] zustande bringen; **you'll never bring it off** das schaffst du nie. ◆ **bring out** *vt sep* - **1.** [new product, book] heraus|bringen - **2.** [reveal - flavour] betonen; **to bring sthg out in sb** [characteristic] etw in jm wach|rufen. ◆ **bring round, bring to** *vt sep* = **bring around**. ◆ **bring up** *vt sep* - **1.** [child] erziehen; **I was brought up in Liverpool** ich bin in Liverpool aufgewachsen - **2.** [subject] an|sprechen - **3.** [food] erbrechen.

brink [brɪŋk] *n*: **on the brink of** am Rand(e) *(+ G)*.

brisk [brɪsk] *adj* - **1.** [walk, swim] flott - **2.** [manner, tone] forsch.

bristle ['brɪsl] ◇ *n* Borste *die*. ◇ *vi* - **1.** [hair] sich sträuben - **2.** [person]: **to bristle (at sthg)** zornig reagieren (auf etw *(A)*).

Britain ['brɪtn] *n* Großbritannien *nt*.

British ['brɪtɪʃ] ◇ *adj* britisch. ◇ *npl*: **the British** die Briten *Pl*.

British Isles *npl*: **the British Isles** die Britischen Inseln.

Briton ['brɪtn] *n* Brite *der*, -tin *die*.

brittle ['brɪtl] *adj* [china] zerbrechlich; [material] spröde; [bones] schwach.

broach [brəʊtʃ] *vt* [subject] an|schneiden.

broad [brɔːd] ◇ *adj* - **1.** [wide] breit - **2.** [wide-ranging, extensive] weit - **3.** [introduction, description] umfassend - **4.** [hint] deutlich - **5.** [accent] stark. ◇ *n US inf* [woman] Braut *die*. ◆ **in broad daylight** *adv* am helllichten Tag.

B road *n UK* ≃ Landstraße *die*.

broadband ['brɔːdbænd] *n* COMPUT Breitband *das*.

broad bean *n* dicke Bohne, Saubohne *die*.

broadcast ['brɔːdkɑːst] (*pt & pp inv*) ◇ *n* RADIO & TV Sendung *die*, Übertragung *die*. ◇ *vt* RADIO & TV senden, übertragen.

broaden ['brɔːdn] ◇ *vt* - **1.** [make wider] verbreitern, erweitern - **2.** [make more wide-ranging] vergrößern; **to broaden one's mind** seinen Horizont erweitern. ◇ *vi* [become wider] sich verbreitern.

broadly ['brɔːdlɪ] *adv* [generally] allgemein.

broadminded [,brɔːd'maɪndɪd] *adj* tolerant.

broccoli ['brɒkəlɪ] *n* Brokkoli *der*.

brochure ['brəʊʃəʳ] *n* Prospekt *der*.

broil [brɔɪl] *vt US* grillen.

broke [brəʊk] ◇ *pt* ▻ **break**. ◇ *adj inf* [penniless] pleite.

broken ['brəʊkn] ◇ *pp* ▻ **break**. ◇ *adj* - **1.** [damaged, in pieces] zerbrochen - **2.** [fractured] gebrochen - **3.** [not working] kaputt - **4.** [interrupted] unterbrochen - **5.** [marriage, home] kaputt, zerrüttet - **6.** [hesitant, inaccurate] gebrochen.

broker ['brəʊkəʳ] *n* [of shares, commodities] Broker *der*, -in *die*; **(insurance) broker** Versicherungsmakler *der*, -in *die*.

brolly ['brɒlɪ] *n UK inf* (Regen)schirm *der*.

bronchitis [brɒŋ'kaɪtɪs] *n (U)* Bronchitis *die*.

bronze [brɒnz] *n* Bronze *die*.

brooch [brəʊtʃ] *n* Brosche *die*.

brood [bruːd] ◇ *n* Brut *die*. ◇ *vi*: **to brood (over** OR **about sthg)** (über etw *(D)*) brüten.

brook [brʊk] *n* Bach *der*.

broom [bruːm] *n* [brush] Besen *der*.

broomstick ['bruːmstɪk] *n* Besenstiel *der*.

Bros, bros (*abbr of* **brothers**) Gebr.

broth [brɒθ] *n* Brühe *die*.

brothel ['brɒθl] *n* Bordell *das*.

brother ['brʌðəʳ] *n* Bruder *der*.

brother-in-law (*pl* **brothers-in-law**) *n* Schwager *der*.

brought [brɔːt] *pt & pp* ▻ **bring**.

brow [braʊ] *n* - **1.** [forehead] Stirn *die* - **2.** [eyebrow] Braue *die* - **3.** [of hill] Bergkuppe *die*.

brown [braʊn] ◇ *adj* - **1.** [colour] braun; **brown bread** Graubrot *das* - **2.** [tanned] braun. ◇ *n* [colour] Braun *das*. ◇ *vt* [food] bräunen.

Brownie (Guide) ['braʊnɪ-] *n* Pfadfinderin *die*.

brown paper *n (U)* Packpapier *das*.

brown rice *n* brauner Reis.

brown sugar *n* brauner Zucker.

browse [braʊz] ◇ *vt* COMPUT: **to browse the Web** im Web surfen. ◇ *vi* - **1.** [in shop] sich um|sehen - **2.** [read]: **to browse through sthg** in etw *(D)* blättern - **3.** [graze] weiden.

browser ['braʊzəʳ] *n* COMPUT Browser *der*.

bruise [bruːz] ◇ *n* Bluterguss *der*, blauer Fleck. ◇ *vt* - **1.** [part of body] sich prellen; [fruit] beschädigen; **she bruised her arm** sie holte sich einen blauen Fleck am Arm - **2.** *fig* [pride, feelings] verletzen.

brunch [brʌntʃ] *n* Brunch *der*.

brunette [bruː'net] *n* Brünette *die*.

brunt [brʌnt] *n*: **to bear** OR **take the brunt of sthg** die Hauptlast von etw tragen.

brush [brʌʃ] ◇ *n* - **1.** [with bristles] Bürste *die*; [for painting] Pinsel *der* - **2.** [encounter]: **to have a brush with the law** mit dem Gesetz in Konflikt kommen. ◇ *vt* - **1.** [clean with brush - hair] bürsten; [- teeth] putzen - **2.** [touch lightly] berühren. ◆ **brush aside** *vt sep* [disregard] vom Tisch wischen. ◆ **brush off** *vt sep* [dismiss] zurück|weisen; **to brush sb off** jn abblitzen lassen. ◆ **brush up** ◇ *vt sep fig* [revise] auf|frischen. ◇ *vi*: **to brush up (on sthg)** (etw) auf|frischen.

brush-off *n inf*: **to give sb the brush-off** jm eine Abfuhr erteilen.

brusque [bruːsk] *adj* brüsk.

Brussels ['brʌslz] *n* Brüssel *nt*.

brussels sprouts *npl* Rosenkohl *der*.

brutal ['bruːtl] *adj* brutal.

brute [bruːt] ◇ *adj*: **brute force** rohe Gewalt. ◇ *n* Tier *das*, Vieh *das*.

BSc *n abbr of* **Bachelor of Science**.

BSE (*abbr of* **bovine spongiform encephalopathy**) *n* BSE *das*.

bubble ['bʌbl] ◇ *n* (Luft)bläschen *das*. ◇ *vi* - **1.** [produce bubbles] Bläschen bilden - **2.** [make a bubbling sound] blubbern - **3.** *fig* [person]: **to bubble with sthg** vor etw *(D)* sprühen.

bubble bath *n (U)* Schaumbad *das*.

bubble gum *n (U)* Kaugummi *der ODER das*.

bubblejet printer ['bʌbldʒet-] *n* Tintenstrahldrucker *der*.

Bucharest [ˌbjuːkə'rest] *n* Bukarest *nt*.

buck [bʌk] ◇ *n* - **1.** (*pl inv*) [male animal - rabbit, hare] Rammler *der*; [- deer] Bock *der* - **2.** (*pl* **-s**) *esp US inf* [dollar] Dollar *der* - **3.** (*pl* **-s**) *inf* [responsibility]: **to pass the buck** die Verantwortung weiter|reichen. ◇ *vi* [horse] bocken. ◆ **buck up** *inf vi* - **1.** [hurry up] sich beeilen - **2.** [cheer up] auf|leben.

bucket ['bʌkɪt] *n* Eimer *der*.

buckle ['bʌkl] ◇ *n* Schnalle *die*, Spange *die*. ◇ *vt* - **1.** [fasten] zu|schnallen - **2.** [bend] ein|dellen, verbeulen. ◇ *vi* [wheel] sich verbiegen; [knees, legs] nach|geben.

bud [bʌd] ◇ *n* Knospe *die*. ◇ *vi* Knospen treiben, aus|schlagen.

Budapest [ˌbjuːdə'pest] *n* Budapest *nt*.

Buddha ['bʊdə] *n* Buddha *der*.

Buddhism ['bʊdɪzm] *n* Buddhismus *der*.

budding ['bʌdɪŋ] *adj* [aspiring] angehend.

buddy ['bʌdɪ] *n esp US inf* [friend] Kumpel *der*.

budge [bʌdʒ] ◇ *vt* - **1.** [move] bewegen - **2.** [change mind of] beeinflussen. ◇ *vi* - **1.** [move] sich rühren - **2.** [change mind] nach|geben.

budgerigar ['bʌdʒərɪgɑːʳ] *n* Wellensittich *der*.

budget ['bʌdʒɪt] ◇ *adj* [cheap - travel, holiday] kostengünstig; [- prices] niedrig. ◇ *n* Budget *das*. ◆ **budget for** *vt insep* ein|planen.

budgie ['bʌdʒɪ] *n inf* Wellensittich *der*.

buff [bʌf] ◇ *adj* [brown] braun. ◇ *n inf* [expert] Kenner *der*, -in *die*.

buffalo ['bʌfələʊ] (*pl inv*, **-es** OR **-s**) *n* Büffel *der*, Buffalo *der*.

buffer ['bʌfəʳ] *n* - **1.** [gen] Puffer *der* - **2.** [for trains] Prellbock *der*.

buffet[1] ['bʊfeɪ] *n* - **1.** [meal] Buffet *das* - **2.** [cafeteria] Stehimbiss *der*.

buffet[2] ['bʌfɪt] *vt* [physically] rütteln.

buffet car ['bʊfeɪ-] *n* Speisewagen *der*.

bug [bʌg] ◇ *n* - **1.** *esp US* [small insect] Insekt *das*; [beetle] Käfer *der* - **2.** *inf* [germ] Bazillus *der* - **3.** *inf* [listening device] Wanze *die* - **4.** COMPUT Programmfehler *der*. ◇ *vt inf* - **1.** [room, phone] verwanzen - **2.** [annoy] nerven.

bugger ['bʌgəʳ] *UK v inf* ◇ *n* [unpleasant person] Scheißkerl *der*; **he's a lazy bugger!** er ist ein fauler Sack!; **the poor bugger!** der arme Kerl! ◇ *excl* Scheiße! ◆ **bugger off** *vi*: **bugger off!** hau ab!

buggy ['bʌgɪ] *n* Kinderwagen *der*.

bugle ['bjuːgl] *n* Signalhorn *das*.

build [bɪld] (*pt & pp* **built**) ◇ *vt* - **1.** [construct] bauen - **2.** *fig* [form, create] auf|bauen. ◇ *n (U)* Statur *die*. ◆ **build on** ◇ *vt insep* [further] auf|bauen. ◇ *vt sep* [base on]: **to build sthg on sthg** etw auf etw *(D)* auf|bauen. ◆ **build up** ◇ *vt sep* [strengthen] auf|bauen. ◇ *vi* [increase] zu|nehmen. ◆ **build upon** *vt insep* & *vt sep* = **build on**.

builder ['bɪldəʳ] *n* Bauarbeiter *der*, -in *die*.

building ['bɪldɪŋ] *n* - **1.** [structure] Gebäude *das* - **2.** *(U)* [profession] Bau *der*.

building and loan association *n US* Bausparkasse *die*.

building site *n* Baustelle *die*.

building society *n UK* Bausparkasse *die*.

buildup ['bɪldʌp] *n* [increase] Steigerung *die*, Zunahme *die*.

built [bɪlt] *pt* & *pp* ▷ **build**.

built-in *adj* - **1.** CONSTR eingebaut - **2.** [inherent] automatisch.

built-up *adj*: **built-up area** bebautes Gebiet.

bulb [bʌlb] *n* - **1.** [for lamp] (Glüh)birne *die* - **2.** [of plant] Zwiebel *die*.

Bulgaria [bʌl'geərɪə] *n* Bulgarien *nt*.

Bulgarian [bʌl'geərɪən] ◇ *adj* bulgarisch. ◇ *n* - **1.** [person] Bulgare *der*, -rin *die* - **2.** [language] Bulgarisch(e) *das*.

bulge [bʌldʒ] ◇ *n* [lump] Beule *die*. ◇ *vi*: **to bulge (with sthg)** (mit etw) voll gestopft sein.

bulk [bʌlk] ◇ *n* - **1.** [mass] Ausmaß *das* - **2.** [of person] Masse *die* - **3.** COMM: **in bulk** en gros - **4.** [majority]: **the bulk of** der Großteil *(+ G)*. ◇ *adj* en gros, Groß-.

bulky ['bʌlkɪ] *adj* sperrig, unhandlich; [garment] unhandlich.

bull [bʊl] *n* [male cow] Stier *der*, Bulle *der*.

bulldog ['bʊldɒg] *n* Bulldogge *die*.

bulldozer ['bʊldəʊzəʳ] *n* Bulldozer *der*.

bullet ['bʊlɪt] *n* [for gun] Kugel *die*.

bulletin ['bʊlətɪn] *n* - **1.** [brief report] Bericht *der* - **2.** [regular publication] Bulletin *das*.

bullet-proof *adj* kugelsicher.

bullfight ['bʊlfaɪt] *n* Stierkampf *der*.

bullfighter ['bʊl,faɪtəʳ] *n* Torero *der*.

bullfighting ['bʊl,faɪtɪŋ] *n (U)* Stierkampf *der*.

bullion ['bʊljən] *n (U)* Barren *der*.

bullock ['bʊlək] *n* Ochse *der*.

bullring ['bʊlrɪŋ] *n* Stierkampfarena *die*.

bull's-eye *n* Schwarze *das*, Zentrum *das*.

bully ['bʊlɪ] ◇ *n* Tyrann *der*. ◇ *vt* drangsalieren, tyrannisieren; **to bully sb into doing sthg** jn so drangsalieren, dass er/sie etw tut.

bum [bʌm] *n* - **1.** *esp UK v inf* [bottom] Hintern *der* - **2.** *US inf pej* [tramp] Gammler *der*, -in *die*.

bum bag *n inf* Gürteltasche *die*.

bumblebee ['bʌmblbiː] *n* Hummel *die*.

bump [bʌmp] ◇ *n* - **1.** [lump] Beule *die*; [in road] Unebenheit *die*, Hubbel *der* - **2.** [knock, blow] Delle *die* - **3.** [noise] Bums *der*. ◇ *vt* [knock, damage] an|schlagen. ◆ **bump into** *vt insep* [meet by chance] treffen.

bumper ['bʌmpəʳ] ◇ *adj* Riesen-; **bumper harvest** Rekordernte *die*. ◇ *n* - **1.** [on car] Stoßstange *die* - **2.** *US* RAIL Rammbohle *die*.

bumpy ['bʌmpɪ] *adj* holp(e)rig.

bun [bʌn] *n* - **1.** [cake] süße Stückchen *das* - **2.** [bread roll] Milchbrötchen *das* - **3.** [hairstyle] Knoten *der*.

bunch [bʌntʃ] ◇ *n* [group - of people] Traube *die*, Haufen *der*; [- of flowers] Strauß *der*; [- of grapes] Traube *die*; [- of parsley, asparagus, keys] Bund *der*. ◇ *vi* sich bauschen. ◆ **bunches** *npl* [hairstyle] Zöpfe *Pl*.

bundle ['bʌndl] ◇ *n* Bündel *das*. ◇ *vt* stopfen.

bung [bʌŋ] ◇ *n* Stöpsel *der*, Zapfen *der*. ◇ *vt UK inf* [put] schmeißen.

bungalow ['bʌŋgələʊ] *n* Bungalow *der*.

bungle ['bʌŋgl] *vt* verpfuschen.

bunion ['bʌnjən] *n* Ballen *der*.

bunk [bʌŋk] *n* - **1.** [bed] Koje *die*; [in dorm] Bett *das* - **2.** = **bunk bed**.

bunk bed *n* Etagenbett *das*.

bunker ['bʌŋkəʳ] *n* Bunker *der*.

bunny ['bʌnɪ] *n*: **bunny (rabbit)** Häschen *das*.

bunting ['bʌntɪŋ] *n (U)* Wimpel *Pl*.

buoy [*UK* bɔɪ, *US* 'buːɪ] *n* Boje *die*. ◆ **buoy up** *vt sep* [encourage] beleben, stärken.

buoyant ['bɔɪənt] *adj* - **1.** [able to float] schwimmfähig - **2.** [optimistic] beschwingt.

burden ['bɜːdn] ◇ *n* Bürde *die*, Last *die*; **to be a burden on sb** eine Last für jn sein. ◇ *vt*: **to burden sb with sthg** jn mit etw belasten.

bureau ['bjʊərəʊ] (*pl* **-x**) *n* - **1.** [office, branch] Büro *das* - **2.** *UK* [desk] Sekretär *der* - **3.** *US* [chest of drawers] Kommode *die*.

bureaucracy [bjʊə'rɒkrəsɪ] *n* Bürokratie *die*.

bureau de change (*pl* **bureaux de change**) *n* Wechselstube *die*.

bureaux ['bjʊərəʊz] *Pl* ▷ **bureau**.

burger ['bɜːgəʳ] *n* Hamburger *der*.

burglar ['bɜːgləʳ] *n* Einbrecher *der*, -in *die*.

burglar alarm *n* Alarmanlage *die*.

burglarize *vt US* = **burgle**.

burglary ['bɜːglərɪ] *n* Einbruch *der*.

burgle ['bɜːgl], **burglarize** *US* ['bɜːgləraɪz] *vt* ein|brechen in *(+ A)*.

burial ['berɪəl] *n* Begräbnis *das*.

burly ['bɜːlɪ] *adj* stämmig, kräftig.

Burma ['bɜːmə] *n* Birma *nt*.

burn [bɜːn] (*pt* & *pp* **burnt** OR **-ed**) ◇ *vt* - **1.** [gen] verbrennen; [house] ab|brennen - **2.** [overcook] anbrennen lassen - **3.** [use as fuel] verbrauchen - **4.** [with chemical] verätzen - **5.** [CD] brennen. ◇ *vi* - **1.** [gen] brennen - **2.** [food] an|brennen - **3.** [face, cheeks] glühen - **4.** [get sunburned] einen Sonnenbrand bekommen. ◇ *n* - **1.** [wound, injury] Brandwunde *die* - **2.** [mark - on carpet, sofa] Brandfleck *der*. ◆ **burn down** ◇ *vt sep* niederlbrennen. ◇ *vi* [building, town] ablbrennen.

burner ['bɜ:nəʳ] *n* [on cooker] Brenner *der*.

burnt [bɜ:nt] *pt* & *pp* ▷ **burn**.

burp [bɜ:p] *inf* ◇ *n* Rülpser *der*. ◇ *vi* auflstoßen.

burrow ['bʌrəʊ] ◇ *n* Bau *der*. ◇ *vi* - **1.** [dig] graben - **2.** *fig* [search] wühlen.

bursar ['bɜ:səʳ] *n* Schatzmeister *der*.

bursary ['bɜ:sərɪ] *n UK* Stipendium *das*.

burst [bɜ:st] (*pt & pp inv*) ◇ *vi* - **1.** [break open] platzen - **2.** [explode] explodieren - **3.** [go suddenly]: **to burst in** hineinlplatzen. ◇ *vt* [tyre, balloon, bubble] platzen lassen; [dam, river bank] durchlbrechen. ◇ *n* [bout] Explosion *die*. ◆ **burst into** *vt insep* auslbrechen in (+ *A*); *(phrase)*: **the house burst into flames** im Haus brach Feuer aus. ◆ **burst out** *vt insep* - **1.** [say suddenly] loslplatzen - **2.** [begin suddenly]: **to burst out laughing/crying** in Gelächter/Tränen auslbrechen.

bursting ['bɜ:stɪŋ] *adj* [eager]: **to be bursting to do sthg** darauf brennen, etw zu tun.

bury ['berɪ] *vt* - **1.** [in ground - person] begraben; [- thing] vergraben - **2.** [hide] vergraben.

bus [bʌs] *n* Bus *der*; **by bus** mit dem Bus.

bush [bʊʃ] *n* - **1.** [gen] Busch *der* - **2.** *phr*: **to beat about the bush** um den heißen Brei herumlreden.

bushy ['bʊʃɪ] *adj* buschig.

business ['bɪznɪs] *n* - **1.** *(U)* [commerce] Geschäft *das*; **on business** geschäftlich; **to mean business** *inf* es ernst meinen; **to go out of business** zulmachen, schließen - **2.** [company] Firma *die* - **3.** *(U)* [concern] Angelegenheit *die*; **mind your own business!** *inf* kümmere dich um deine eigenen Sachen! - **4.** [affair, matter] Sache *die*.

businesslike ['bɪznɪslaɪk] *adj* sachlich.

businessman ['bɪznɪsmæn] (*pl* **-men** [-men]) *n* Geschäftsmann *der*.

business trip *n* Geschäftsreise *die*.

businesswoman ['bɪznɪs,wʊmən] (*pl* **-women** [-,wɪmɪn]) *n* Geschäftsfrau *die*.

busker ['bʌskəʳ] *n UK* Straßenmusikant *der*, -in *die*.

bus shelter *n* Wartehäuschen *das*.

bus station *n* Busbahnhof *der*.

bus stop *n* Bushaltestelle *die*.

bust [bʌst] (*pt & pp inv* OR **-ed**) ◇ *adj inf* - **1.** [broken] kaputt - **2.** [bankrupt]: **to go bust** pleite gehen. ◇ *n* - **1.** [bosom] Busen *der* - **2.** [statue] Büste *die*. ◇ *vt inf* [break] kaputt machen. ◇ *vi inf* kaputt gehen.

bustle ['bʌsl] ◇ *n* [activity] reges Treiben. ◇ *vi*: **to bustle about** OR **around** hin und her eilen.

busy ['bɪzɪ] ◇ *adj* - **1.** [active] (viel) beschäftigt - **2.** [hectic - life] bewegt; [- week] hektisch; [- place] belebt; [- office] geschäftig; *(phrase)*: **to be busy doing sthg** damit beschäftigt sein, etw zu tun - **3.** *esp US* TELEC [engaged] besetzt. ◇ *vt*: **to busy o.s. doing sthg** sich damit beschäftigen, etw zu tun.

busybody ['bɪzɪ,bɒdɪ] *n pej* Wichtigtuer *der*, -in *die*.

busy signal *n US* TELEC Besetztzeichen *das*.

but [bʌt] ◇ *conj* aber; [with negatives] sondern; **we were poor but happy** wir waren arm, aber glücklich; **she owns not one but two houses** sie hat nicht nur eins, sondern zwei Häuser. ◇ *prep* [except] außer; **he has no one but himself to blame** das hat er sich *(D)* selbst zuzuschreiben; **the last but one** der/die/das Vorletzte; **anyone but him would have helped** jeder andere hätte geholfen. ◇ *adv fml* [only] nur. ◆ **but for** *prep* ohne.

butcher ['bʊtʃəʳ] ◇ *n* - **1.** [shopkeeper] Fleischer *der*, Metzger *der*; **butcher's (shop)** Fleischerei *die*, Metzgerei *die* - **2.** *fig* [killer] Schlächter *der*. ◇ *vt* - **1.** [kill for meat] schlachten - **2.** *fig* [massacre] ablschlachten.

butler ['bʌtləʳ] *n* Butler *der*.

butt [bʌt] ◇ *n* - **1.** [of cigarette] Kippe *die*; [of cigar] Stummel *der* - **2.** [of rifle] Kolben *der* - **3.** [for water] Fass *das* - **4.** [target] Zielscheibe *die* - **5.** *esp US inf* [bottom] Hintern *der*. ◇ *vt* [hit with head] mit dem Kopf stoßen. ◆ **butt in** *vi* [interrupt] sich einlmischen, dazwischenlplatzen; **to butt in on sb/sthg** sich bei jm/etw einlmischen.

butter ['bʌtəʳ] ◇ *n* Butter *die*. ◇ *vt* buttern, mit Butter bestreichen.

buttercup ['bʌtəkʌp] *n* Butterblume *die*.

butter dish *n* Butterdose *die*.

butterfly ['bʌtəflaɪ] *n* - **1.** [insect] Schmetterling *der* - **2.** *(U)* [swimming style] Schmetterlingsstil *der*.

buttocks ['bʌtəks] *npl* Hintern *der*.

button ['bʌtn] ◇ *n* - **1.** [on clothes, machine] Knopf *der* - **2.** *US* [badge] Anstecker *der*. ◇ *vt* = **button up**. ◆ **button up** *vt sep* zulknöpfen.

button mushroom *n* junger Champignon.

buttress ['bʌtrɪs] *n* Stützpfeiler *der*.

buxom ['bʌksəm] *adj* vollbusig.

buy [baɪ] (*pt & pp* **bought**) ◇ *vt* - **1.** [purchase] kaufen; [company] auflkaufen; **to buy sthg from sb** etw von jm kaufen - **2.** *fig* [bribe] kaufen, bestechen. ◇ *n* Kauf *der*. ◆ **buy out** *vt sep* - **1.** [in business] auslzahlen - **2.** [from army]: **to buy o.s. out** sich freilkaufen. ◆ **buy up** *vt sep* auflkaufen.

uyer *n* - **1.** [purchaser] Käufer *der*, -in *die* **2.** [profession] Einkäufer *der*, -in *die*.

buyout ['baɪaʊt] *n* Aufkauf *der*.

buzz [bʌz] <> *n* [noise - of insect, machinery] Summen *das*; [- of conversation] Gemurmel *das*; **to give sb a buzz** *inf* TELEC jn anlrufen. <> *vi* - **1.** [insect, machinery] summen - **2.** *fig* [place]: **the office was buzzing with excitement** im Büro herrschte große Aufregung - **3.** *fig*: **my head was buzzing** mir schwirrte der Kopf. <> *vt* [on intercom] rufen.

buzzer ['bʌzəʳ] *n* Summer *der*.

buzzword ['bʌzwɜːd] *n inf* Modewort *das*.

by [baɪ] <> *prep* - **1.** [expressing cause, agent] von; **he was hit by a car** er ist von einem Auto angefahren worden; **by Mozart** von Mozart - **2.** [indicating method, means, manner] mit; **by car/train** mit dem Auto/Zug; **to pay by credit card** mit Kreditkarte bezahlen; **to take sb by the hand** jn an der Hand nehmen; **made by hand** handgemacht; **he got rich by buying land** er wurde durch Grundstückskäufe reich - **3.** [near to, beside] an *(+ D)*; **by the sea** am Meer; **by my side** an meiner Seite, neben mir - **4.** [past] an *(+ D)* vorbei; **a car went by the house** ein Auto fuhr am Haus vorbei - **5.** [via] durch; **exit by the door on the left** Ausgang durch die Tür auf der linken Seite; **we came by way of Paris** wir kamen über Paris - **6.** [with time]: **it will be ready by tomorrow** bis morgen wird es fertig sein; **be there by nine** sei spätestens um neun da; **she should be there by now** sie müsste inzwischen da sein; **by then it was too late** zu diesem Zeitpunkt war es bereits zu spät; **by day** tagsüber; **by night** nachts - **7.** [expressing quantity]: **sold by the dozen** im Dutzend verkauft; **prices fell by 20%** die Preise fielen um 20%; **by the day/week/month/hour** pro Tag/Woche/Monat/Stunde - **8.** [expressing meaning]: **what do you mean by that?** was meinst du damit? - **9.** [in division] durch; [in multiplication] mit; **two metres by five** zwei mal fünf Meter - **10.** [according to] nach; **by law** nach dem Gesetz; **it's fine by me** ich bin damit einverstanden; **by nature** von Natur aus; **by profession** von Beruf - **11.** [expressing gradual process]: **day by day** Tag für Tag; **they came out one by one** sie kamen einer nach dem anderen heraus; **little by little** nach und nach - **12.** *phr*: **by mistake** versehentlich; **by chance** durch Zufall; **by the way** übrigens. <> *adv* ▷ **go, pass** *etc*. ◆ **by and large** *adv* im Großen und Ganzen. ◆ **(all) by oneself** <> *adv* allein; **did you do it all by yourself?** hast du das ganz allein gemacht? <> *adj* allein; **I'm all by myself today** ich bin heute ganz allein.

bye(-bye) [baɪ(baɪ)] *excl inf* tschüs!

byelaw ['baɪlɔː] *n* = **bylaw**.

by-election *n* Nachwahl *die*.

bygone ['baɪgɒn] *adj* vergangen. ◆ **bygones** *npl*: **to let bygones be bygones** die Vergangenheit ruhen lassen.

bylaw ['baɪlɔː] *n* Verordnung *die*.

bypass ['baɪpɑːs] <> *n* - **1.** [road] Umgehungsstraße *die* - **2.** MED: **bypass (operation)** Bypassoperation *die*. <> *vt* - **1.** [place] umlfahren, umgehen - **2.** [issue, person] umgehen.

by-product *n liter & fig* Nebenprodukt *das*.

bystanders ['baɪˌstændəʳz] *npl*: **the bystanders** die Umstehenden *Pl*.

byte [baɪt] *n* COMPUT Byte *das*.

byword ['baɪwɜːd] *n* [symbol]: **to be a byword for sthg** ein Synonym für etw sein.

C

c *(pl* **c's** *OR* **cs)**, **C** *(pl* **C's** *OR* **Cs)** [siː] *n* [letter] c *das*, C *das*. ◆ **C** *n* - **1.** MUS C *das*; **C major** C-Dur - **2.** SCH [mark] ≃ drei - **3.** *(abbr of* **celsius, centrigrade)** C.

c., ca. *(abbr of* **circa)** ca.

cab [kæb] *n* - **1.** [taxi] Taxi *das* - **2.** [of lorry] Führerhaus *das*.

cabaret ['kæbəreɪ] *n* Varieté *das*.

cabbage ['kæbɪdʒ] *n* [vegetable] Kohl *der*.

cabin ['kæbɪn] *n* - **1.** [on ship, in aircraft] Kabine *die* - **2.** [house] Hütte *die*.

cabin crew *n* Begleitpersonal *das*.

cabinet ['kæbɪnɪt] *n* - **1.** [cupboard] Vitrine *die* - **2.** POL Kabinett *das*.

cable ['keɪbl] <> *n* - **1.** [rope] Seil *das* - **2.** [telegram] Telegramm *das* - **3.** ELEC Kabel *das* - **4.** TV = **cable television**. <> *vt* [telegraph] telegrafieren.

cable car *n* Drahtseilbahn *die*.

cable television, cable TV *n* Kabelfernsehen *das*.

cache [kæʃ] *n* - **1.** [store] geheimes Lager, Versteck *das* - **2.** COMPUT Zwischenspeicher *der*.

cackle ['kækl] *vi* [person] kichern.

cactus ['kæktəs] *(pl* **-tuses** *OR* **-ti** [-taɪ]) *n* Kaktus *der*.

cadet [kə'det] *n* [in police] Kadett *der*, -in *die*.

cadge [kædʒ] *UK inf* <> *vt*: **to cadge sthg (off** *OR* **from sb)** etw (von jm) schnorren. <> *vi*: **to cadge off** *OR* **from sb** von jm schnorren.

caesarean (section) [sə'zeərɪən-] *n UK* Kaiserschnitt *der*.

cafe, café ['kæfeɪ] *n* Café *das*.

cafeteria [ˌkæfɪ'tɪərɪə] *n* Cafeteria *die*.

caffeine ['kæfi:n] *n* Koffein *das*.

cage [keɪdʒ] *n* Käfig *der*.

cagey ['keɪdʒɪ] (*comp* **-ier**, *superl* **-iest**) *adj inf* zugeknöpft, verschlossen.

cagoule [kə'gu:l] *n UK* Regenjacke *die*.

cajole [kə'dʒəʊl] *vt* zulreden; **to cajole sb into doing sthg** jn überreden, etw zu tun.

cake [keɪk] *n* - **1.** [sweet food] Kuchen *der*; **a piece of cake** *inf fig* ein Kinderspiel - **2.** [of soap] Stück *das*.

caked [keɪkt] *adj*: **caked with sthg** verkrustet mit etw.

calcium ['kælsɪəm] *n* Kalzium *das*.

calculate ['kælkjʊleɪt] *vt* - **1.** [work out] auslrechnen - **2.** [plan, intend]: **to be calculated to do sthg** darauf ausgelegt sein, etw zu tun.

calculating ['kælkjʊleɪtɪŋ] *adj pej* berechnend.

calculation [,kælkjʊ'leɪʃn] *n* [sum] Berechnung *die*.

calculator ['kælkjʊleɪtə^r] *n* Taschenrechner *der*, Rechenmaschine *die*.

calendar ['kælɪndə^r] *n* - **1.** [gen] Kalender *der* - **2.** [list of events] Veranstaltungskalender *der*.

calf [kɑ:f] (*pl* **calves**) *n* - **1.** [young animal] Kalb *das* - **2.** [of leg] Wade *die*.

calibre, caliber *US* ['kælɪbə^r] *n* Kaliber *das*.

California [,kælɪ'fɔ:njə] *n* Kalifornien *nt*.

calipers *npl US* = **callipers**.

call [kɔ:l] ◇ *n* - **1.** [shout - of person, animal] Ruf *der*; **a call for help** Hilferuf *der* - **2.** [visit] Besuch *der*; **to pay sb a call** bei jm vorbeilgehen - **3.** [demand]: **she has a lot of calls on her time** ihre Zeit ist stark beansprucht; **there are calls for a referendum** verschiedentlich wird nach einem Referendum verlangt; **there's no call for that sort of behaviour!** das gehört sich nicht! - **4.** [telephone call] Anruf *der* - **5.** [for flight] Aufruf *der*. ◇ *vt* - **1.** [name, describe] nennen; **to be called** heißen; **what's he called?** wie heißt er?; **to call sb names** jn beschimpfen; **let's call it £10** sagen wir 10 Pfund - **2.** [shout] rufen - **3.** [telephone] anlrufen; [doctor] rufen - **4.** [meeting] einlberufen; [election] anlsetzen; [flight] auflrufen; [strike] auslrufen. ◇ *vi* - **1.** [shout] rufen - **2.** [telephone] anlrufen; **who's calling?** wie war der Name? - **3.** [visit] vorbeilkommen; **this train calls at...** dieser Zug hält in... ◆ **on call** *adj*: **to be on call** [doctor, nurse] Bereitschaftsdienst haben. ◆ **call back** ◇ *vt sep* zurücklrufen. ◇ *vi* - **1.** [phone again] zurücklrufen - **2.** [visit again] wiederlkommen. ◆ **call for** *vt insep* - **1.** [come to fetch] ablholen - **2.** [demand] verlangen; [require] erfordern. ◆ **call in** ◇ *vt sep* - **1.** [send for - army, riot police] einlsetzen - **2.** FIN [loan] einlfordern. ◇ *vi*: **to call in (on sb)** (bei jm) vorbeilschauen. ◆ **call off** *vt sep* - **1.** [cancel] ablsagen - **2.** [dog, attacker] zurücklrufen. ◆ **call on** *vt insep* - **1.** [visit] besuchen - **2.** [ask]: **to call on sb to do sthg** jn aufl-fordern, etw zu tun. ◆ **call out** ◇ *vt se* - **1.** [shout out] auslrufen - **2.** [doctor, fire bri-gade] rufen. ◇ *vi* [shout out] rufen. ◆ **cal round** *vi* vorbeilkommen. ◆ **call up** *vt se* - **1.** MIL einlberufen - **2.** [on telephone] anlrufen - **3.** COMPUT auflrufen.

call box *n UK* Telefonzelle *die*.

caller ['kɔ:lə^r] *n* - **1.** [visitor] Besucher *der* -in *die* - **2.** [on telephone] Anrufer *der*, -in *die*.

calling ['kɔ:lɪŋ] *n* - **1.** [profession, trade] Beruf *der* - **2.** [vocation] Berufung *die*.

calling card *n US* Visitenkarte *die*.

callipers *UK*, **calipers** *US* ['kælɪpəz] *np* - **1.** MATHS Taster *der*, Zirkel *der* - **2.** MED Beinschienen *die*.

callous ['kæləs] *adj* gefühllos, herzlos.

callus ['kæləs] (*pl* **-es**) *n* Schwiele *die*.

calm [kɑ:m] ◇ *adj* - **1.** [person, voice] ruhig - **2.** [weather, day] windstill - **3.** [water] still. ◇ *n* Ruhe *die*. ◇ *vt* beruhigen. ◆ **calm down** ◇ *vt sep* beruhigen. ◇ *vi* sich beruhigen.

Calor gas® ['kælə^r-] *n UK britische Handelsmarke für Butangas.*

calorie ['kælərɪ] *n* Kalorie *die*.

calves [kɑ:vz] *Pl* ▷ **calf**.

Cambodia [kæm'bəʊdjə] *n* Kambodscha *nt*.

camcorder ['kæm,kɔ:də^r] *n* Camcorder *der*.

came [keɪm] *pt* ▷ **come**.

camel ['kæml] *n* [animal] Kamel *das*.

cameo ['kæmɪəʊ] (*pl* **-s**) *n* - **1.** [piece of jewellery] Kamee *die* - **2.** [in film] *kleine Nebenrolle, in der ein berühmter Schauspieler zu sehen ist.*

camera ['kæmərə] *n* Kamera *die*. ◆ **in camera** *adv* LAW unter Ausschluss der Öffentlichkeit.

cameraman ['kæmərəmæn] (*pl* **-men** [-men]) *n* Kameramann *der*.

cameraphone ['kæmərəfəʊn] *n* Fotohandy *das*.

camouflage ['kæməflɑ:ʒ] ◇ *n* - **1.** MIL Tarnung *die* - **2.** [of bird] Tarngefieder *das*; [of animal] Tarnkleid *das*. ◇ *vt* MIL tarnen.

camp [kæmp] ◇ *n* - **1.** [for tents] Lagerplatz *der* - **2.** MIL Feldlager *das* - **3.** [for refugees, faction] Lager *das*. ◇ *vi* MIL lagern; [holiday] campen. ◆ **camp out** *vi* campen.

campaign [kæm'peɪn] ◇ *n* - **1.** [project, crusade] Kampagne *die* - **2.** [in war] Feldzug *der*. ◇ *vi*: **to campaign for sthg** sich für etw einlsetzen; **to campaign against sthg** gegen etw anlgehen.

camp bed *n* Feldbett *das*.

camper ['kæmpə^r] *n* - **1.** [person] Camper *der*, -in *die* - **2.** [vehicle]: **camper (van)** Wohnmobil *das*.

campground ['kæmpgraʊnd] *n US* Campingplatz *der*, Zeltplatz *der*.

camping ['kæmpɪŋ] *n* Camping *das*; **to go camping** zelten gehen.

camping site, campsite ['kæmpsaɪt] *n* Campingplatz *der*, Zeltplatz *der*.

campus ['kæmpəs] (*pl* **-es**) *n* Universitätsgelände *das*, Campus *der*.

can[1] (*pt & pp* **-ned**, *cont* **-ning**) (*weak form* [kən], *strong form* [kæn]) <> *n* [container] Dose *die*. <> *vt* konservieren, ein|dosen.

can[2] (*weak form* [kən], *strong form* [kæn], *conditional and preterite form* **could**; *negative form* **cannot** *and* **can't**) *aux vb* - **1.** [be able to] können; **can you help me?** können Sie mir helfen?; **I can see you** ich kann dich sehen, ich sehe dich; **can you see/hear anything?** sehen/hören Sie etwas?, können Sie etwas sehen/hören? - **2.** [know how to] können; **can you drive?** kannst du Auto fahren?; **I can speak German/play the piano** ich spreche Deutsch/spiele Klavier - **3.** [be allowed to] können, dürfen; **you can't smoke here** Sie können OR dürfen hier nicht rauchen; **you can use my car if you like** du kannst mein Auto nehmen - **4.** [in polite requests] können; **can you tell me the time?** können Sie mir sagen, wie viel Uhr es ist? - **5.** [indicating disbelief, puzzlement] können; **what can she have done with it?** was hat sie bloß damit gemacht?; **you can't be serious!** das ist doch wohl nicht dein Ernst! - **6.** [indicating possibility] können; **they could be lost** sie könnten sich verlaufen haben.

Canada ['kænədə] *n* Kanada *nt*.

Canadian [kə'neɪdjən] <> *adj* kanadisch. <> *n* Kanadier *der*, -in *die*.

canal [kə'næl] *n* Kanal *der*.

Canaries [kə'neərɪz] *npl*: **the Canaries** die Kanaren *Pl*.

canary [kə'neərɪ] *n* Kanarienvogel *der*.

cancel ['kænsl] (*UK*) (*US pt & pp* **-ed**, *cont* **-ing**) <> *vt* - **1.** [call off - event, party] aus|fallen lassen; [- appointment, meeting] ab|sagen; [- order, booking] stornieren; *(phrase)*: **the concert has been cancelled** das Konzert fällt aus; **the flight has been cancelled** der Flug ist gestrichen worden - **2.** [invalidate - stamp] entwerten; [- cheque] stornieren; [- debt] streichen; [- subscription] ab|bestellen. <> *vi*: **we had to cancel** wir mussten absagen. ◆ **cancel out** *vt sep*: **to cancel each other out** einander aus|gleichen.

cancellation [,kænsə'leɪʃn] *n* Stornierung *die*; [of meeting, visit] Absage *die*; [of subscription] Abbestellung *die*.

cancer ['kænsəʳ] *n* Krebs *der*. ◆ **Cancer** *n* Krebs *der*.

candelabra [,kændɪ'lɑːbrə] *n* Leuchter *der*.

candid ['kændɪd] *adj* offen, ehrlich.

candidate ['kændɪdət] *n* - **1.** [for job] Kandidat *der*, -in *die* - **2.** [for exam] Prüfling *der*.

candle ['kændl] *n* Kerze *die*.

candlelight ['kændllaɪt] *n* Kerzenlicht *das*.

candlelit ['kændllɪt] *adj* im Kerzenschein.

candlestick ['kændlstɪk] *n* Kerzenständer *der*.

candour *UK*, **candor** *US* ['kændəʳ] *n* Offenheit *die*.

candy ['kændɪ] *n esp US* - **1.** *(U)* [confectionery] Süßigkeiten *Pl* - **2.** [sweet] Bonbon *das*.

candy bar *n US* Schokoriegel *der*.

candyfloss *UK* ['kændɪflɒs], **cotton candy** *US n (U)* Zuckerwatte *die*.

cane [keɪn] <> *n* - **1.** *(U)* [for making furniture] Rohr *das* - **2.** [walking stick] Spazierstock *der* - **3.** [for punishment]: **the cane** der Rohrstock - **4.** [for supporting plant] Stock *der*. <> *vt* mit dem Rohrstock züchtigen.

canine ['keɪnaɪn] <> *adj* Hunde-. <> *n*: **canine (tooth)** Eckzahn *der*.

canister ['kænɪstəʳ] *n* Kanister *der*, Behälter *der*; [for tea, film] Dose *die*.

cannabis ['kænəbɪs] *n* Cannabis *der*.

canned [kænd] *adj* [food] Konserven-; [drink] Dosen-.

cannibal ['kænɪbl] *n* Kannibale *der*, -lin *die*.

cannon ['kænən] (*pl inv* OR **-s**) *n* - **1.** [on ground] Kanone *die* - **2.** [on aircraft] Bordkanone *die*.

cannonball ['kænənbɔːl] *n* Kanonenkugel *die*.

cannot ['kænɒt] *vb* = **can**[2].

canny ['kænɪ] *adj* umsichtig, sparsam.

canoe [kə'nuː] *n* Paddelboot *das*, Kanu *das*.

canoeing [kə'nuːɪŋ] *n* Kanufahren *das*.

canon ['kænən] *n* - **1.** [clergyman] Domherr *der* - **2.** [general principle] Grundregel *die*.

can opener *n* Dosenöffner *der*.

canopy ['kænəpɪ] *n* [over bed, seat] Baldachin *der*.

can't [kɑːnt] *abbr of* **cannot**.

cantankerous [kæn'tæŋkərəs] *adj* streitsüchtig.

canteen [kæn'tiːn] *n* - **1.** [restaurant - in workplace] Kantine *die*; [- in university] Mensa *die* - **2.** [box of cutlery] Besteckkasten *der*.

canter ['kæntəʳ] <> *n* Kanter *der*. <> *vi* im Handgalopp reiten.

canvas ['kænvəs] *n* - **1.** *(U)* [cloth] Segeltuch *das* - **2.** [art - for painting] Leinwand *die*; [- finished painting] Gemälde *das*.

canvass ['kænvəs] *vt* - **1.** POL: **to canvass voters** um Wählerstimmen werben - **2.** COMM: **to canvass opinion** eine Meinungsumfrage durch|führen.

canyon ['kænjən] *n* Cañon *der*.

cap [kæp] *vt* [outdo]: **to cap it all** als Krönung des Ganzen.

capability [,keɪpə'bɪlətɪ] *n* - **1.** [ability] Fähigkeit *die* - **2.** MIL Potenzial *das*.

capable ['keɪpəbl] *adj* - **1.** [able, having capacity]: **to be capable of sthg** zu etw fähig sein; **to be capable of doing sthg** fähig sein, etw zu tun - **2.** [competent, skilful] kompetent.

capacity [kə'pæsɪtɪ] *n* - **1.** *(U)* [limit] Fassungsvermögen *das*; [of room, hall] Sitzplätze *Pl*; **the theatre has a capacity of 200** das Theater fasst 200 Personen - **2.** [ability] Fähigkeit *die*; **capacity for sthg** die Fähigkeit zu etw; **capacity for doing** OR **to do sthg** die Fähigkeit, etw zu tun - **3.** [position] Stellung *die*; **in a capacity** in der Funktion *(+ G)*.

cape [keɪp] *n* - **1.** GEOG Kap *das* - **2.** [cloak] Cape *das*, Umhang *der*.

caper ['keɪpəʳ] *n* - **1.** [food] Kaper *die* - **2.** *inf* [escapade] Eskapade *die*.

capital ['kæpɪtl] ◇ *adj* - **1.**: **capital letter** Großbuchstabe *der* - **2.** [offence] Kapital-. ◇ *n* - **1.** [of country]: **capital (city)** Hauptstadt *die* - **2.** [letter] Großbuchstabe *der* - **3.** *(U)* [money] Kapital *das*; **to make capital out of sthg** *fig* aus etw Kapital schlagen.

capital expenditure *n* Kapitalaufwand *der*.

capital gains tax *n* Kapitalertragssteuer *die*.

capitalism ['kæpɪtəlɪzm] *n* Kapitalismus *der*.

capitalist ['kæpɪtəlɪst] ◇ *adj* kapitalistisch. ◇ *n* Kapitalist *der*, -in *die*.

capitalize, -ise ['kæpɪtəlaɪz] *vi*: **to capitalize on sthg** aus etw Nutzen ziehen.

capital punishment *n (U)* Todesstrafe *die*.

capitulate [kə'pɪtjʊleɪt] *vi*: **to capitulate (to sthg)** kapitulieren (vor etw *(D)*).

Capricorn ['kæprɪkɔːn] *n* Steinbock *der*.

capsize [kæp'saɪz] ◇ *vt* zum Kentern bringen. ◇ *vi* kentern.

capsule ['kæpsjuːl] *n* - **1.** [gen] Kapsel *die* - **2.** [on spacecraft] Raumkapsel *die*.

captain ['kæptɪn] *n* Kapitän *der*; [in army] Hauptmann *der*.

caption ['kæpʃn] *n* Bildunterschrift *die*.

captivate ['kæptɪveɪt] *vt* bezaubern.

captive ['kæptɪv] ◇ *adj* - **1.** [imprisoned] gefangen - **2.** *fig* [unable to leave]: **captive audience** unfreiwilliges Publikum. ◇ *n* Gefangene *der, die*.

captor ['kæptəʳ] *n Person, die jemanden gefangen nimmt.*

capture ['kæptʃəʳ] ◇ *vt* - **1.** [take prisoner - person] gefangen nehmen; [- animal] einfangen - **2.** [city, market, audience] erobern; [interest, imagination, votes] gewinnen - **3.** COMPUT erfassen. ◇ *n* Gefangennahme *die*; [of city] Eroberung *die*.

car [kɑːʳ] ◇ *n* - **1.** [motor car] Auto *das*, Wagen *der* - **2.** [on train] Wagen *der*. ◇ *comp* Automobil-, Auto-.

carafe [kə'ræf] *n* Karaffe *die*.

car alarm *n* Autoalarm *der*.

caramel ['kærəmel] *n* - **1.** [burnt sugar] Karamell *der* - **2.** [sweet] Karamellbonbon *das*.

carat ['kærət] *n UK* Karat *das*.

caravan ['kærəvæn] *n* - **1.** *UK* [vehicle - towed by car] Wohnwagen *der*, Caravan *der*; [- towed by horse] Pferdewagen *der* - **2.** [travelling group] Karawane *die*.

caravan site *n UK* Wohnwagenplatz *der*.

carbohydrate [ˌkɑːbəʊ'haɪdreɪt] *n (U)* Kohle(n)hydrat *das*. ◆ **carbohydrates** *npl* [food] Kohle(n)hydrate *Pl*.

carbon ['kɑːbən] *n* [element] Kohlenstoff *der*.

carbonated ['kɑːbəneɪtɪd] *adj* mit Kohlensäure versetzt.

carbon copy *n* - **1.** [document] Durchschlag *der* - **2.** *fig* [exact copy]: **she's a carbon copy of her mother** sie ist ihrer Mutter wie aus dem Gesicht geschnitten.

carbon dioxide [-daɪ'ɒksaɪd] *n* Kohlendioxyd *das*.

carbon monoxide *n* Kohlenmonoxid *das*.

carbon paper *n (U)* Kohlepapier *das*.

car-boot sale *n UK auf einem (Park)platz oder in einem Parkhaus stattfindender Trödelmarkt.*

carburettor *UK*, **carburetor** *US* [ˌkɑːbə'retəʳ] *n* Vergaser *der*.

carcass ['kɑːkəs] *n* [of animal] Kadaver *der*.

card [kɑːd] *n* - **1.** [playing card] Spielkarte *die* - **2.** [for identification] Karte *die* - **3.** [greetings card] Grußkarte *die* - **4.** [postcard] Postkarte *die* - **5.** *(U)* [cardboard] Pappe *die*. ◆ **cards** *npl* [game] Kartenspiel *das*; **to play cards** Karten spielen. ◆ **on the cards** *UK*, **in the cards** *US adv inf* durchaus möglich.

cardboard ['kɑːdbɔːd] ◇ *n (U)* Pappe *die*. ◇ *comp* Papp-.

cardboard box *n* Pappkarton *der*.

cardiac ['kɑːdɪæk] *adj* Herz-.

cardigan ['kɑːdɪgən] *n* Strickjacke *die*.

cardinal ['kɑːdɪnl] ◇ *adj* äußerste(r) (s); **cardinal sin** Todsünde *die*. ◇ *n* RELIG Kardinal *der*.

card index *n UK* Kartei *die*.

card table *n* Kartentisch *der*.

care [keəʳ] *vi* - **1.** [be concerned]: **you really don't care, do you?** dir ist das wohl ganz egal, wie?; **to care about sb/sthg** an jn/etw denken - **2.** [mind] sich kümmern; **I don't care if/that/how** es ist mir egal, ob/dass/wie; **who cares?** wen interessiert das schon?; **I don't honestly care what I look like** es kümmert OR interessiert mich ehrlich gesagt nicht, wie ich aussehe. ◆ **care of** *prep* bei. ◆ **care for** *vt insep* [like] Interesse haben für; **I don't much care for opera** ich mache mir nichts aus Oper;

does she still care for him? bedeutet er ihr noch immer viel?; would you care for a drink? möchtest du etwas trinken?

career [kə'rɪəʳ] <> *n* - **1.** [job] Beruf *der*; **to make a career out of sthg** etw zum Beruf machen - **2.** [working life] Laufbahn *die*; [in retrospect] Werdegang *der* - **3.** [very successful] Karriere *die*; **to make a career for o.s.** Karriere machen. <> *vi* rasen.

careers adviser *n* Berufsberater *der*, -in *die*.

carefree ['keəfriː] *adj* sorglos, sorgenfrei.

careful ['keəfʊl] *adj* - **1.** [cautious] vorsichtig; **to be careful with sthg** vorsichtig mit etw um|gehen; **to be careful to do sthg** darauf achten, etw zu tun - **2.** [thorough] gründlich.

carefully ['keəflɪ] *adv* - **1.** [cautiously] vorsichtig - **2.** [thoroughly] gründlich.

careless ['keəlɪs] *adj* - **1.** [inattentive] unaufmerksam - **2.** [unconcerned] nachlässig.

caress [kə'res] <> *n* Liebkosung *die*. <> *vt* liebkosen.

caretaker ['keəˌteɪkəʳ] *n UK* Hausmeister *der*, -in *die*.

car ferry *n* Autofähre *die*.

cargo ['kɑːgəʊ] (*pl* **-es** OR **-s**) *n* Ladung *die*.

car hire *n (U) UK* Autovermietung *die*.

Caribbean [*UK* kærɪ'biːən, *US* kə'rɪbɪən] *n* - **1.** [sea]: **the Caribbean (Sea)** das Karibische Meer, die Karibische See - **2.** [region]: **the Caribbean** die Karibik.

caring ['keərɪŋ] *adj* mitfühlend.

carnage ['kɑːnɪdʒ] *n (U)* Gemetzel *das*.

carnal ['kɑːnl] *adj liter* fleischlich.

carnation [kɑː'neɪʃn] *n* Nelke *die*.

carnival ['kɑːnɪvl] *n* - **1.** [festive occasion] Karneval *der* - **2.** [fair] Volksfest *das*.

carnivorous [kɑː'nɪvərəs] *adj* Fleisch fressend.

carol ['kærəl] *n*: **(Christmas) carol** Weihnachtslied *das*.

carousel [ˌkærə'sel] *n* - **1.** *esp US* [at fair] Karussel *das* - **2.** [at airport] Gepäckband *das*.

carp [kɑːp] (*pl inv* OR **-s**) <> *n* Karpfen *der*. <> *vi* nörgeln; **to carp about sb** über jn meckern.

car park *n UK* Parkplatz *der*.

carpenter ['kɑːpəntəʳ] *n* [working on buildings] Zimmermann *der*; [making furniture] Tischler *der*.

carpentry ['kɑːpəntrɪ] *n* [working on buildings] Zimmerhandwerk *das*; [making furniture] Tischlerhandwerk *das*.

carpet ['kɑːpɪt] <> *n* [floor covering] Teppich(boden) *der*. <> *vt* [floor] mit Teppich(boden) aus|legen.

carpet sweeper [-ˌswiːpəʳ] *n* Teppichkehrmaschine *die*.

car phone *n* Autotelefon *das*.

car radio *n* Autoradio *das*.

car rental *n (U) US* Autovermietung *die*.

carriage ['kærɪdʒ] *n* - **1.** [horsedrawn vehicle] Kutsche *die* - **2.** *UK* [railway coach] Wagen *der* - **3.** [transport of goods] Transport *der*; **carriage paid** OR **free** *UK* frachtfrei, frei Haus.

carriageway ['kærɪdʒweɪ] *n UK* Fahrbahn *die*.

carrier ['kærɪəʳ] *n* - **1.** COMM Spediteur *der* - **2.** [of disease] Überträger *der*, -in *die* - **3.** = **carrier bag**.

carrier bag *n* Tragetasche *die*.

carrot ['kærət] *n* - **1.** [vegetable] Möhre *die*, Karotte *die* - **2.** *inf* [incentive] Köder *der*.

carry ['kærɪ] <> *vt* - **1.** [transport] tragen - **2.** [be equipped with] dabei|haben, mit sich führen - **3.** [disease] übertragen - **4.** [involve] mit sich bringen - **5.** [motion, proposal] an|nehmen - **6.** [be pregnant with] tragen - **7.** MATHS: **5 carry 1** 5 Rest 1. <> *vi* [sound] tragen. ◆ **carry away** *vt insep*: **to get carried away** sich hinreißen lassen. ◆ **carry forward** *vt sep* übertragen. ◆ **carry off** *vt sep* - **1.** [plan, performance] schaffen - **2.** [prize] gewinnen. ◆ **carry on** <> *vt insep* [continue] fort|führen; **to carry on doing sthg** etw weiterhin tun. <> *vi* - **1.** [continue] weiter|machen; **to carry on with sthg** mit etw weiter|machen - **2.** *inf* [make a fuss] sich auf|führen. ◆ **carry out** *vt insep* [task, plan, order] aus|führen; [experiment, investigation] durch|führen; [promise, threat] wahr machen. ◆ **carry through** *vt sep* [accomplish] durch|führen.

carryall ['kærɪɔːl] *n US* Reisetasche *die*.

carrycot ['kærɪkɒt] *n esp UK* Babytragetasche *die*.

carry-out *n US Essen oder Getränke zum Mitnehmen*.

carsick ['kɑːˌsɪk] *adj* reisekrank.

cart [kɑːt] <> *n* - **1.** [vehicle] Wagen *der* - **2.** *US* [for shopping]: **(shopping** OR **grocery) cart** Einkaufswagen *der*. <> *vt inf* schleppen.

carton ['kɑːtn] *n* Karton *der*; [of cream, yoghurt] Becher *der*; [of milk] Tüte *die*.

cartoon [kɑː'tuːn] *n* - **1.** [satirical drawing] Karikatur *die* - **2.** [comic strip] Comic(strip) *der* - **3.** [film] Zeichentrickfilm *der*.

cartridge ['kɑːtrɪdʒ] *n* - **1.** [for gun, pen] Patrone *die* - **2.** [for camera] Film *der*.

cartwheel ['kɑːtwiːl] *n* Rad *das*; **to do cartwheels** Rad schlagen.

carve [kɑːv] <> *vt* - **1.** [wood] schnitzen; [stone] hauen - **2.** [meat] auf|schneiden - **3.** [cut] ritzen. <> *vi* den Braten/das Fleisch auf|schneiden. ◆ **carve out** *vt sep*: **to carve out a career** sich eine Karriere auf|bauen. ◆ **carve up** *vt sep* [divide] auf|teilen.

carving ['kɑːvɪŋ] *n* [object] Skulptur *die*.

carving knife *n* Tranchiermesser *das*.

car wash *n* [place] Autowaschanlage *die*.

case [keɪs] *n* - **1.** [gen] Fall *der*; **in that case** in dem Fall; **as** *OR* **whatever the case may be** je nachdem; **in case of emergency/doubt** im Notfall/Zweifelsfall - **2.** [argument] Angelegenheit *die*; **the case for the defence** die Verteidigung - **3.** [packing case] Kiste *die*; [small box] Kästchen *das*; [for glasses, cigarettes] Etui *das*; [for musical instrument] Kasten *der* - **4.** *UK* [suitcase] Koffer *der*. ◆ **in any case** *adv* wie dem auch sei. ◆ **in case** <> *conj* falls. <> *adv*: **(just) in case** für alle Fälle.

cash [kæʃ] <> *n (U)* - **1.** [notes and coins] Bargeld *das*; **to pay (in) cash** bar bezahlen - **2.** *inf* [money] Geld *das*; **I'm a bit short of cash** ich bin etwas knapp bei Kasse - **3.** [payment]: **cash in advance** Vorkasse *die*; **cash on delivery** zahlbar bei Empfang. <> *vt* einllösen.

cash and carry *n* [for retailers] Großhandelsmarkt *der*; [for public] Verbrauchermarkt *der*.

cash box *n* Geldkassette *die*.

cash card *n* Kontokarte *die*.

cash desk *n UK* Kasse *die*.

cash dispenser [-dɪˌspensəʳ] *n* Geldautomat *der*.

cashew (nut) [ˈkæʃuː-] *n* Cashewnuss *die*.

cashier [kæˈʃɪəʳ] *n* Kassierer *der*, -in *die*.

cash machine *n* = **cash dispenser**.

cashmere [kæʃˈmɪəʳ] *n* Kaschmir *der*.

cashpoint (machine) [ˈkæʃpɔɪnt-] *n* Geldautomat *der*.

cash register *n* Registrierkasse *die*.

casing [ˈkeɪsɪŋ] *n* Gehäuse *das*; [of cable] Hülle *die*; [of tyre] Mantel *der*.

casino [kəˈsiːnəʊ] (*pl* **-s**) *n* Kasino *das*.

cask [kɑːsk] *n* Fass *das*.

casket [ˈkɑːskɪt] *n* - **1.** [for jewels] (Schmuck)kästchen *das* - **2.** *US* [coffin] Sarg *der*.

casserole [ˈkæsərəʊl] *n* - **1.** [stew] Fleischeintopf *der* - **2.** [pan] Schmortopf *der*.

cassette [kæˈset] *n* Kassette *die*.

cassette player *n* Kassettenspieler *der*.

cassette recorder *n* Kassettenrekorder *der*.

cast [kɑːst] (*pt & pp inv*) <> *n* - **1.** [of play, film] Besetzung *die* - **2.** MED Gipsverband *der*. <> *vt* - **1.** [gen] werfen; **to cast one's eye over sthg** einen Blick auf etw *(A)* werfen; **to cast doubt on sthg** etw in Zweifel ziehen - **2.** [choose for play, film]: **she cast him in the role of Hamlet** sie gab ihm die Rolle des Hamlet - **3.** POL: **to cast one's vote** seine Stimme ablgeben - **4.** [metal, statue] gießen. ◆ **cast aside** *vt sep* fallen lassen. ◆ **cast off** *vi* - **1.** NAUT abllegen - **2.** [in knitting] Maschen ablnehmen. ◆ **cast on** *vi* [in knitting] Maschen anlschlagen.

castaway [ˈkɑːstəweɪ] *n* Schiffbrüchige *der, die*.

caster [ˈkɑːstəʳ] *n* Rolle *die*.

caster sugar *n UK* Feinkristallzucker *der*.

casting vote *n* entscheidende Stimme.

cast iron *n (U)* Gusseisen *das*.

castle [ˈkɑːsl] *n* - **1.** [fortress] Burg *die*; [mansion] Schloss *das* - **2.** [in chess] Turm *der*.

castor [ˈkɑːstəʳ] *n* = **caster**.

castrate [kæˈstreɪt] *vt* kastrieren.

casual [ˈkæʒʊəl] *adj* - **1.** [relaxed] gleichgültig - **2.** *pej* [offhand] nachlässig - **3.** [chance] zufällig - **4.** [clothes]: **casual clothes** zwanglose Kleidung - **5.** [work, worker] Gelegenheits-.

casually [ˈkæʒʊəlɪ] *adv* - **1.** [in a relaxed manner] gleichgültig - **2.** [dress] leger.

casualty [ˈkæʒjʊəltɪ] *n* - **1.** [dead person] Todesopfer *das*; [injured person] Unfallopfer *das* - **2.** = **casualty department**.

casualty department *n* Ambulanz *die*.

cat [kæt] *n* - **1.** [domestic] Katze *die* - **2.** [wild] Raubkatze *die*.

catalogue *UK*, **catalog** *US* [ˈkætəlɒg] <> *n* [of items] Katalog *der*. <> *vt* katalogisieren.

catalyst [ˈkætəlɪst] *n* - **1.** CHEM Katalysator *der* - **2.** *fig* [cause] Auslöser *der*.

catalytic converter [ˌkætəˈlɪtɪk-] *n* Katalysator *der*.

catapult *UK* [ˈkætəpʊlt] <> *n* - **1.** [handheld] Katapult *das* - **2.** HIST [machine] Katapult *das*. <> *vt* schleudern; **she was catapulted to fame** *fig* sie wurde über Nacht berühmt.

cataract [ˈkætərækt] *n* MED grauer Star.

catarrh [kəˈtɑːʳ] *n* Katarrh *der*.

catastrophe [kəˈtæstrəfɪ] *n* Katastrophe *die*.

catch [kætʃ] (*pt & pp* **caught**) <> *vt* - **1.** [ball, fish, animal] fangen - **2.** [criminal] fassen - **3.** [discover] überraschen; **to catch sb doing sthg** jn bei etw ertappen - **4.** [train, plane] erreichen - **5.** [hear clearly] hören - **6.** [interest] wecken; [imagination] anlregen; **I tried to catch his attention** ich versuchte, ihn auf mich aufmerksam zu machen - **7.** [sight]: **to catch sight of sb/sthg, to catch a glimpse of sb/sthg** jn/etw flüchtig zu Gesicht bekommen - **8.** [illness, disease]: **to catch malaria/measles** an Malaria/Masern erkranken; **to catch a cold** sich erkälten - **9.** [trap]: **to catch one's finger in the door** sich den Finger in der Tür (ein)lklemmen - **10.** [strike] treffen. <> *vi* - **1.** [clothing] hängen bleiben; [foot, limb] stecken bleiben - **2.** [fire] anlgehen. <> *n* - **1.** [of ball *etc*]: **good catch!** sehr gut gefangen! - **2.** [of fish] Fang *der* - **3.** [fastener] Verschluss *der* - **4.** [snag] Haken *der*. ◆ **catch on** *vi* - **1.** [become popular] Anklang finden - **2.** *inf* [understand] begreifen; **to catch on to sthg** hinter etw *(A)* kommen. ◆ **catch out** *vt sep* [trick] hereinllegen. ◆ **catch up** <> *vt sep* - **1.** [come level with] einlholen - **2.** [involve]: **to get caught up in sthg** in etw *(A)* verwickelt werden. <> *vi* auflholen; **to catch up on sthg** etw nachlholen. ◆ **catch up with** *vt insep* - **1.** [in race, work] ein|holen - **2.** [criminal] ausfindig machen.

catching ['kætʃɪŋ] *adj* ansteckend.

catchment area ['kætʃmənt-] *n* Einzugsgebiet *das*.

catchphrase ['kætʃfreɪz] *n* [of performer] Lieblingsspruch *der*.

catchy ['kætʃɪ] *adj*: **a catchy tune** ein Ohrwurm.

categorically [ˌkætɪ'gɒrɪklɪ] *adv* kategorisch.

category ['kætəgərɪ] *n* Kategorie *die*.

cater ['keɪtəʳ] *vi* [provide food]: **to cater for sb** jn mit Lebensmitteln versorgen. ◆ **cater for** *vt insep UK* [tastes, needs] befriedigen.

caterer ['keɪtərəʳ] *n* Lebensmittellieferant *der*, -in *die*.

catering ['keɪtərɪŋ] *n (U)* [industry] Gaststättengewerbe *das*; [at wedding, party] Essen *das*.

caterpillar ['kætəpɪləʳ] *n* Raupe *die*.

cathedral [kə'θiːdrəl] *n* Kathedrale *die*.

Catholic ['kæθlɪk] ◇ *adj* katholisch. ◇ *n* Katholik *der*, -in *die*. ◆ **catholic** *adj*: **to have very catholic tastes** vielseitig interessiert sein.

cat litter *n* Katzenstreu *das*.

Catseyes® ['kætsaɪz] *npl UK* Katzenaugen *Pl*.

cattle ['kætl] *npl* Vieh *das*.

catty ['kætɪ] *adj inf pej* [spiteful] gehässig.

catwalk ['kætwɔːk] *n* Laufsteg *der*.

caucus ['kɔːkəs] *n* - **1.** *US* POL Sitzung *die*, Versammlung *die* - **2.** *UK* POL Gremium *das*.

caught [kɔːt] *pt & pp* ▷ **catch**.

cauliflower ['kɒlɪˌflaʊəʳ] *n* Blumenkohl *der*.

cause [kɔːz] ◇ *n* - **1.** [reason why sthg happens] Ursache *die* - **2.** [grounds]: **cause (for)** Grund *der* (zu); **to have no cause to do sthg** keinen Grund haben, etw zu tun; **I have no cause for complaint** ich habe keinen Grund zur Klage - **3.** [movement, aim] Sache *die*; **for a good cause** für eine gute Sache. ◇ *vt* verursachen; **to cause sb to do sthg** jn veranlassen, etw zu tun.

caustic ['kɔːstɪk] *adj* - **1.** CHEM ätzend - **2.** *fig* [comment] bissig.

caution ['kɔːʃn] ◇ *n* - **1.** [care] Vorsicht *die*; [prudence] Umsicht *die*; **'proceed with caution'** 'vorsichtig vorgehen' - **2.** [warning] Warnung *die* - **3.** *UK* LAW Verwarnung *die*. ◇ *vt* - **1.** [warn]: **to caution sb against doing sthg** jn davor warnen, etw zu tun - **2.** *UK* LAW verwarnen.

cautious ['kɔːʃəs] *adj* [careful] vorsichtig; [prudent] umsichtig.

cavalry ['kævlrɪ] *n (U)* - **1.** [on horseback] Kavallerie *die* - **2.** [in armoured vehicles] motorisierte Truppen *Pl*.

cave [keɪv] *n* Höhle *die*. ◆ **cave in** *vi* [physically collapse] ein|stürzen.

caveman ['keɪvmæn] (*pl* **-men** [-men]) *n* Höhlenmensch *der*.

cavernous ['kævənəs] *adj* [room, building] höhlenartig.

caviar(e) ['kævɪɑːʳ] *n* Kaviar *der*.

cavity ['kævətɪ] *n* - **1.** [in object, structure] Hohlraum *der*; [in body] Höhle *die* - **2.** [in tooth] Loch *das*.

cavort [kə'vɔːt] *vi* herum|tollen.

CB *n* (*abbr of* **Citizens' Band**) CB.

CBI (*abbr of* **Confederation of British Industry**) *n britischer Unternehmerverband*.

cc ◇ *n* (*abbr of* **cubic centimetre**) cm^3. ◇ *abbr of* **carbon copy**.

CD *n* (*abbr of* **compact disc**) CD *die*.

CD player *n* CD-Player *der*, CD-Spieler *der*.

CD-ROM [ˌsiːdiː'rɒm] (*abbr of* **compact disc read-only memory**) *n* CD-ROM *die*.

CD-RW *n* (*abbr of* **compact disc rewriteable**) CD-RW *die*.

cease [siːs] *fml* ◇ *vt* beenden, ein|stellen; **to cease doing** OR **to do sthg** auf|hören, etw zu tun. ◇ *vi* auf|hören, enden.

cease-fire *n* Waffenruhe *die*.

ceaseless ['siːslɪs] *adj fml* unaufhörlich.

cedar (tree) ['siːdəʳ-] *n* Zeder *die*.

ceiling ['siːlɪŋ] *n* - **1.** [of room] Decke *die* - **2.** [limit] oberste Grenze.

celebrate ['selɪbreɪt] ◇ *vt* [victory, anniversary] feiern. ◇ *vi* feiern.

celebrated ['selɪbreɪtɪd] *adj* berühmt.

celebration [ˌselɪ'breɪʃn] *n* - **1.** *(U)* [activity] Feiern *das* - **2.** [event] Feier *die*.

celebrity [sɪ'lebrətɪ] *n* [star] Star *der*.

celery ['selərɪ] *n* Stangensellerie *die ODER der*.

celibate ['selɪbət] *adj* RELIG zölibatär; *fig* enthaltsam.

cell [sel] *n* - **1.** [gen] Zelle *die* - **2.** COMPUT Feld *das*.

cellar ['seləʳ] *n* - **1.** [basement] Keller *der* - **2.** [stock of wine] Weinkeller *der*.

cello ['tʃeləʊ] (*pl* **-s**) *n* Cello *das*.

Cellophane® ['seləfeɪn] *n* Zellophan *das*.

Celsius ['selsɪəs] *adj* Celsius-, Celsius; **20 degrees Celsius** 20 Grad Celsius.

Celt [kelt] *n* Kelte *der*, -tin *die*.

Celtic ['keltɪk] *adj* keltisch.

cement [sɪ'ment] ◇ *n (U)* [for concrete] Zement *der*. ◇ *vt* - **1.** [cover with cement] betonieren - **2.** *fig* [friendship] festigen.

cement mixer *n* Betonmischmaschine *die*.

cemetery ['semɪtrɪ] *n* Friedhof *der*.

censor ['sensəʳ] ◇ *n* Zensor *der*. ◇ *vt* zensieren.

censorship ['sensəʃɪp] *n* Zensur *die*.

censure ['senʃəʳ] <> *n* Tadel *der*. <> *vt* tadeln.

census ['sensəs] (*pl* **censuses**) *n* Volkszählung *die*.

cent [sent] *n* Cent *der*.

centenary *UK* [sen'ti:nəri], **centennial** *US* [sen'tenjəl] *n* Hundertjahrfeier *die*.

center *n, adj* & *vt US* = **centre**.

centigrade ['sentɪgreɪd] *adj* Celsius-; **16 degrees centigrade** 16 Grad Celsius.

centilitre *UK*, **centiliter** *US* ['sentɪ,li:təʳ] *n* Zentiliter *der*.

centimetre *UK*, **centimeter** *US* ['sentɪ,mi:təʳ] *n* Zentimeter *der*.

centipede ['sentɪpi:d] *n* Tausendfüßler *der*.

central ['sentrəl] *adj* zentral.

Central America *n* Mittelamerika *nt*.

central heating *n* Zentralheizung *die*.

centralize, -ise ['sentrəlaɪz] *vt* zentralisieren.

central locking [-'lɒkɪŋ] *n* Zentralverriegelung *die*.

central reservation *n UK* Mittelstreifen *der*.

centre *UK*, **center** *US* ['sentəʳ] <> *n* - **1.** [gen] Mitte *die*, Zentrum *das*; [of circle] Mittelpunkt *der* - **2.** [building, place] Zentrum *das* - **3.** [of event, activity] Zentrum *das*, Mittelpunkt *der*; **she always wants to be the centre of attention** sie will immer im Mittelpunkt stehen; **centre of gravity** Schwerpunkt *der* - **4.** POL Mitte *die* - **5.** [in basketball, netball] Center *der*. <> *adj* - **1.** [middle] Mittel-, mittlere(r)(s) - **2.** POL: **centre party** Partei der Mitte. <> *vt* [text, image] zentrieren.

centre forward *n* Mittelstürmer *der*, -in *die*.

century ['sentʃʊrɪ] *n* Jahrhundert *das*.

ceramic [sɪ'ræmɪk] *adj* keramisch. ◆ **ceramics** *npl* [objects] Keramik *die*.

cereal ['sɪərɪəl] *n* - **1.** [crop] Getreide *das* - **2.** *(U)* [breakfast food] Frühstücksflocken *Pl*.

ceremonial [,serɪ'məʊnjəl] *adj* feierlich.

ceremony ['serɪmənɪ] *n* - **1.** [event] Zeremonie *die* - **2.** [formality] Förmlichkeit *die*; **to stand on ceremony** sehr förmlich sein.

certain ['sɜ:tn] *adj* - **1.** [gen] sicher; **he is certain to be late** er kommt bestimmt zu spät; **to make certain** nach|prüfen; **I always make certain of being on time** ich achte immer darauf, pünktlich zu sein; **for certain** sicher - **2.** [particular, individual] gewiss; **to a certain extent** bis zu einem gewissen Grad.

certainly ['sɜ:tnlɪ] *adv* sicher(lich); **can I bring a friend along? – certainly!** kann ich einen Bekannten/eine Bekannte mitbringen? – na klar!; **do you dye your hair? – certainly not!** färbst du dir die Haare? – natürlich nicht!

certainty ['sɜ:tntɪ] *n* Sicherheit *die*; **it's a certainty that he will win the race** es steht fest, dass er das Rennen gewinnen wird.

certificate [sə'tɪfɪkət] *n* Bescheinigung *die*; [from school, college] Zeugnis *das*; [of birth] Urkunde *die*.

certified ['sɜ:tɪfaɪd] *adj* - **1.** [teacher, accountant] geprüft - **2.** [document] beglaubigt.

certified mail *n US* Einschreiben *das*.

certified public accountant *n US* Buchhalter *der*, -in *die*.

certify ['sɜ:tɪfaɪ] *vt* - **1.** [declare true] bescheinigen; **this is to certify that...** hiermit wird bescheinigt, dass... - **2.** [declare insane] für unzurechnungsfähig erklären.

cervical [sə'vaɪkl] *adj* Gebärmutter-.

cervical smear *n* Abstrich *der*.

cervix ['sɜ:vɪks] (*pl* **-ices** [-ɪsi:z]) *n* Gebärmutterhals *der*.

cesarean (section) *n US* = **caesarean section**.

cesspit ['sespɪt], **cesspool** ['sespu:l] *n* Senkgrube *die*.

cf. (*abbr of* **confer**) vgl.

CFC (*abbr of* **chlorofluorocarbon**) *n* FCKW *das*.

ch. (*abbr of* **chapter**) Kap.

chafe [tʃeɪf] *vt* [rub] scheuern.

chaffinch ['tʃæfɪntʃ] *n* Buchfink *der*.

chain [tʃeɪn] <> *n* Kette *die*; **a chain of events** eine Kette von Ereignissen. <> *vt* an|ketten.

chain reaction *n* Kettenreaktion *die*.

chain saw *n* Kettensäge *die*.

chain smoker *n* Kettenraucher *der*, -in *die*.

chain store *n* Filiale *die* einer Ladenkette.

chair [tʃeəʳ] <> *n* - **1.** [gen] Stuhl *der* - **2.** [university post] Lehrstuhl *der*. <> *vt* [meeting, discussion] den Vorsitz führen bei, leiten.

chair lift *n* Sessellift *der*.

chairman ['tʃeəmən] (*pl* **-men** [-mən]) *n* Vorsitzende *der*.

chairperson ['tʃeə,pɜ:sn] (*pl* **-s**) *n* Vorsitzende *der*, *die*.

chalet ['ʃæleɪ] *n* [in mountains] Chalet *das*.

chalk [tʃɔ:k] *n* - **1.** [for drawing] Kreide *die* - **2.** *(U)* [type of rock] Kalkstein *der*.

chalkboard ['tʃɔ:kbɔ:d] *n US* Tafel *die*.

challenge ['tʃælɪndʒ] <> *n* - **1.** [gen] Herausforderung *die* - **2.** [to authority] Infragestellung *die*. <> *vt* - **1.** [to fight, competition]: **to challenge sb (to sthg)** jn (zu etw) heraus|fordern - **2.** [question] in Frage stellen.

challenging ['tʃælɪndʒɪŋ] *adj* herausfordernd.

chamber ['tʃeɪmbəʳ] *n* Kammer *die*.

chambermaid ['tʃeɪmbəmeɪd] *n* Zimmermädchen *das*.

chamber music *n* Kammermusik *die*.

chamber of commerce *n* Handelskammer *die*.

chameleon [kə'miːljən] *n* Chamäleon *das*.

champagne [ˌʃæm'peɪn] *n* Champagner *der*.

champion ['tʃæmpjən] *n* - **1.** [of competition] Meister *der*, -in *die*, Champion *der* - **2.** [of cause] Verfechter *der*, -in *die*.

championship ['tʃæmpjənʃɪp] *n* Meisterschaft *die*.

chance [tʃɑːns] ◇ *n* - **1.** *(U)* [luck] Glück *das*; **by chance** zufällig; **by any chance** vielleicht - **2.** [likelihood] Chance *die*, Möglichkeit *die*; **she doesn't stand a chance of winning the match** sie hat keine Chance, das Spiel zu gewinnen; **on the off chance** auf gut Glück - **3.** [opportunity] Gelegenheit *die*, Chance *die* - **4.** [risk]: **to take a chance** es riskieren. ◇ *adj* [meeting] zufällig. ◇ *vt* [risk] riskieren; **he's chancing his luck a bit** er fordert sein Glück heraus.

chancellor ['tʃɑːnsələʳ] *n* Kanzler *der*.

Chancellor of the Exchequer *n UK* Schatzkanzler *der*.

chandelier [ˌʃændə'lɪəʳ] *n* Kronleuchter *der*.

change [tʃeɪndʒ] ◇ *n* - **1.** [alteration] Änderung *die*; [difference] Veränderung *die*; **change in sb/sthg** Veränderung in jm/etw; **a change for the better** eine Verbesserung; **a change for the worse** eine Verschlechterung - **2.** [contrast, for variety] Abwechslung *die*; **for a change** zur Abwechslung - **3.** [switch, replacement] Wechsel *der*; **a change of clothes** Kleidung zum Wechseln - **4.** *(U)* [money returned after payment] Wechselgeld *das* - **5.** *(U)* [coins] Kleingeld *das*; **have you got change for a £5 note?** können Sie mir einen Fünfpfundschein wechseln? ◇ *vt* - **1.** [alter, make different] ändern; **to change sthg into sthg** etw in etw *(A)* umlwandeln; **to change one's mind** seine Meinung ändern - **2.** [replace] auslwechseln; [product purchased] umltauschen - **3.** [switch] wechseln; **to change clothes, to get changed** sich umlziehen; **to change trains/planes** umlsteigen - **4.** [money] wechseln - **5.** [bed] wechseln; [baby] trockenllegen. ◇ *vi* - **1.** [alter, become different] sich ändern, sich verändern; **to change into sthg** sich in etw *(A)* verwandeln - **2.** [put on different clothes] sich umlziehen - **3.** [on train, bus] umlsteigen; **all change!** alles auslsteigen! ◆ **change over** *vi*: **to change over to sthg** auf etw *(A)* umlstellen.

changeable ['tʃeɪndʒəbl] *adj* - **1.** [mood] wechselnd - **2.** [weather] wechselhaft.

change machine *n* Geldwechselautomat *der*.

changeover ['tʃeɪndʒˌəʊvəʳ] *n*: **changeover (to sthg)** Umstellung *die* (auf etw *(A)*).

changing ['tʃeɪndʒɪŋ] *adj* sich (ver)ändernd, wechselnd.

changing room *n* [in sports] Umkleideraum *der*; [in shop] Umkleidekabine *die*.

channel ['tʃænl] *(UK) (US)* ◇ *n* - **1.** [gen] Kanal *der* - **2.** [route] Fahrrinne *die*. ◇ *vt* [water] leiten. ◆ **Channel** *n*: **the (English) Channel** der Ärmelkanal. ◆ **channels** *npl*: **to go through the proper channels** sich an die richtigen Stellen wenden.

Channel Islands *npl*: **the Channel Islands** die Kanalinseln *Pl*.

Channel Tunnel *n*: **the Channel Tunnel** der Kanaltunnel.

chant [tʃɑːnt] *n* - **1.** RELIG [song] Gesang *der* - **2.** [repeated words] Sprechchor *der*.

chaos ['keɪɒs] *n* Chaos *das*.

chaotic [keɪ'ɒtɪk] *adj* chaotisch.

chap [tʃæp] *n UK inf* [man] Kerl *der*.

chapel ['tʃæpl] *n* [part of church, small church] Kapelle *die*.

chaplain ['tʃæplɪn] *n* Hausgeistliche *der*.

chapped [tʃæpt] *adj* aufgesprungen.

chapter ['tʃæptəʳ] *n* Kapitel *das*.

char [tʃɑːʳ] *vt* [burn] verkohlen.

character ['kærəktəʳ] *n* - **1.** [nature - of place] Charakter *der*; [- of person] Wesen *das*; **in character** typisch - **2.** [unusual quality, style] Originalität *die* - **3.** [in film, book, play] Gestalt *die* - **4.** *inf* [unusual person] Original *das* - **5.** [letter, symbol] Schriftzeichen *das*.

characteristic [ˌkærəktə'rɪstɪk] ◇ *adj* charakteristisch. ◇ *n* Kennzeichen *das*.

characterize, -ise ['kærəktəraɪz] *vt* - **1.** [typify] kennzeichnen - **2.** [portray]: **to characterize sthg as sthg** etw als etw beschreiben.

charade [ʃə'rɑːd] *n* Farce *die*. ◆ **charades** *n (U)* Scharade *die*.

charcoal ['tʃɑːkəʊl] *n (U)* [for drawing] Kohle *die*; [for barbecue] Holzkohle *die*.

charge [tʃɑːdʒ] ◇ *n* - **1.** [cost] Gebühr *die*; **free of charge** gebührenfrei - **2.** LAW Anklage *die* - **3.** [command, control] Verantwortung *die*; **to take charge (of sthg)** [of organization, group of people] die Leitung (einer Sache *(G)*) übernehmen; **in charge** zuständig; **in charge of** verantwortlich für - **4.** ELEC Ladung *die* - **5.** MIL Sturmangriff *der*. ◇ *vt* - **1.** [customer] berechnen *(+ D)*; **to charge £10 for sthg** für etw 10 Pfund verlangen; **to charge sthg to sb** jm etw in Rechnung stellen - **2.** [suspect, criminal] anlklagen; **to charge sb with sthg** jn wegen etw anlklagen - **3.** [attack] anlgreifen - **4.** ELEC auflladen. ◇ *vi* - **1.** [rush] stürmen - **2.** [attack] anlgreifen.

charge card *n* Kundenkreditkarte *die*.

chargé d'affaires ['ʃɑːʒeɪdæ'feəʳ] (*pl* **chargés d'affaires**) *n Diplomat, der anstelle eines Botschafters ein Land vertritt*.

charger ['tʃɑːdʒəʳ] *n* [for batteries] Ladegerät *das*.

chariot ['tʃærɪət] *n* Streitwagen *der*.

charisma [kə'rɪzmə] *n* Charisma *das*.

charity ['tʃærətɪ] *n* - **1.** *(U)* [gifts, money] Spenden *Pl* - **2.** [organization] Wohltätigkeitsorganisation *die*, karitative Einrichtung - **3.** [kindness] Nächstenliebe *die*.

charm [tʃɑːm] <> *n* - **1.** *(U)* [appeal, attractiveness] Charme *der* - **2.** [spell] Bann *der* - **3.** [on bracelet] Anhänger *der*; **lucky charm** Glücksbringer *der*. <> *vt* bezaubern.

charming ['tʃɑːmɪŋ] *adj* bezaubernd; [person] charmant.

chart [tʃɑːt] <> *n* - **1.** [diagram] Diagramm *das*; [for weather forecast] Wetterkarte *die* - **2.** [map] Karte *die*. <> *vt* - **1.** [map - seas, skies] kartieren; [- movements] auf einer Karte erfassen - **2.** *fig* [record] auf|zeichnen. ◆ **charts** *npl*: **the charts** die Hitparade.

charter ['tʃɑːtəʳ] <> *n* [document - of organization] Charta *die*; [- of town] Gründungsurkunde *die*. <> *vt* [plane, boat] chartern.

chartered accountant [ˌtʃɑːtəd-] *n UK* Wirtschaftsprüfer *der*, -in *die*.

charter flight *n* Charterflug *der*.

charter plane *n* Charterflugzeug *das*.

chase [tʃeɪs] <> *n* Verfolgungsjagd *die*; [hunt] Jagd *die*. <> *vt* - **1.** [pursue] jagen; [criminal] verfolgen - **2.** [drive away] fort|jagen. <> *vi*: **to chase after sb/sthg** jm/etw nach|jagen.

chasm ['kæzm] *n* - **1.** [deep crack] tiefe Felsspalte - **2.** *fig* [divide] Kluft *die*.

chassis ['ʃæsɪ] (*pl inv*) *n* [of vehicle] Fahrgestell *das*.

chat [tʃæt] <> *n* Plauderei *die*; **to have a chat** plaudern. <> *vi* - **1.** plaudern - **2.** [on Internet] chatten. ◆ **chat up** *vt sep UK inf* sich heran|machen an *(+ A)*.

chat room *n* COMPUT Diskussionsforum *das*, Chatroom *der*.

chat show *n UK* Talkshow *die*.

chatter ['tʃætəʳ] <> *n* [of person] Geplapper *das*. <> *vi* - **1.** [person] plappern - **2.** [animal, bird] zwitschern - **3.** [teeth] klappern.

chatterbox ['tʃætəbɒks] *n inf* [child] Plappermäulchen *das*.

chatty ['tʃætɪ] *adj* - **1.** [person] gesprächig - **2.** [letter] im Plauderton geschrieben.

chauffeur ['ʃəʊfəʳ] *n* Chauffeur *der*.

chauvinist ['ʃəʊvɪnɪst] *n* Chauvinist *der*.

cheap [tʃiːp] <> *adj* - **1.** [inexpensive] billig - **2.** [reduced in price] preiswert - **3.** [poor-quality] billig - **4.** [vulgar] billig; **to feel cheap** sich schäbig fühlen. <> *adv* billig.

cheapen ['tʃiːpn] *vt* [degrade - thing or place] herab|setzen; [- person] erniedrigen.

cheaply ['tʃiːplɪ] *adv* billig.

cheat [tʃiːt] <> *n* - **1.** [person] Betrüger *der*, -in *die*; [in exam, game] Mogler *der*, -in *die* - **2.** [act] Betrug *der*. <> *vt* betrügen; **to cheat sb out of sthg** jn um etw betrügen. <> *vi* [in exam, game] mogeln. ◆ **cheat on** *vt insep inf* [be unfaithful to] betrügen.

check [tʃek] <> *n* - **1.** [inspection, test]: **check (on sthg)** Überprüfung *die* (von etw); **to keep a check on sthg** etw (regelmäßig) überprüfen - **2.** [restraint]: **to put a check on sthg** etw unter Kontrolle halten; **in check** unter Kontrolle - **3.** *US* [bill] Rechnung *die* - **4.** [pattern] Karomuster *das* - **5.** *US* = **cheque**. <> *vt* - **1.** [test, verify] kontrollieren - **2.** [restrain] unter Kontrolle halten; [advance] auf|halten; **to check o.s.** inne|halten. <> *vi* [have a look] nach|sehen; [ask sb] nach|fragen; **to check on sthg** etw überprüfen. ◆ **check in** <> *vt sep* [luggage] abfertigen lassen; [coat] ab|geben. <> *vi* - **1.** [at hotel] sich an|melden - **2.** [at airport] ein|checken. ◆ **check out** <> *vt sep* [investigate] überprüfen. <> *vi* [from hotel] sich ab|melden. ◆ **check up** *vi*: **to check up on sb** [supervise] jn kontrollieren; [investigate] über jn Nachforschungen an|stellen; **to check up on sthg** etw überprüfen.

checkbook *n US* = **chequebook**.

checked [tʃekt] *adj* [patterned] kariert.

checkered *adj US* = **chequered**.

checkers ['tʃekəz] *n (U) US* Damespiel *das*.

check-in *n* Abfertigung *die*; [check-in desk] Abfertigungsschalter *der*.

checking account ['tʃekɪŋ-] *n US* Girokonto *das*.

checkmate ['tʃekmeɪt] *n* Schachmatt *das*.

checkout ['tʃekaʊt] *n* [in supermarket] Kasse *die*.

checkpoint ['tʃekpɔɪnt] *n* Kontrollpunkt *der*.

checkup ['tʃekʌp] *n* Kontrolluntersuchung *die*, Vorsorgeuntersuchung *die*.

Cheddar (cheese) ['tʃedəʳ-] *n* Cheddar(käse) *der*.

cheek [tʃiːk] *n* - **1.** [of face] Backe *die*, Wange *die* - **2.** *inf* [impudence] Frechheit *die*.

cheekbone ['tʃiːkbəʊn] *n* Wangenknochen *der*, Backenknochen *der*.

cheeky ['tʃiːkɪ] *adj* frech.

cheer [tʃɪəʳ] <> *n* [shout] Hurraruf *der*; [cheering] Jubelgeschrei *das*; **three cheers for Linda!** ein dreifaches Hurra für Linda! <> *vt* - **1.** [shout approval, encouragement at] zu|jubeln *(+ D)* - **2.** [gladden] auf|muntern. <> *vi* jubeln. ◆ **cheers** *excl* - **1.** [said before drinking] prost! - **2.** *UK inf* [goodbye] tschüs! - **3.** *UK inf* [thank you] danke! ◆ **cheer up** <> *vt sep* auf|muntern. <> *vi* vergnügter werden; **cheer up!** Kopf hoch!

cheerful ['tʃɪəfʊl] *adj* heiter; [music, colour] fröhlich.

cheerio [ˌtʃɪərɪ'əʊ] *excl UK inf* tschüs!

cheese [tʃi:z] *n* Käse *der*.

cheeseboard ['tʃi:zbɔ:d] *n* - **1.** [board] Käsebrett *das* - **2.** [on menu] Käseplatte *die*.

cheeseburger ['tʃi:zˌbɜ:gəʳ] *n* Cheeseburger *der*.

cheesecake ['tʃi:zkeɪk] *n* Käsekuchen *der*.

cheetah ['tʃi:tə] *n* Gepard *der*.

chef [ʃef] *n* [cook] Koch *der*, Köchin *die*; [head cook] Chefkoch *der*, -köchin *die*.

chemical ['kemɪkl] ◇ *adj* chemisch. ◇ *n* Chemikalie *die*.

chemist ['kemɪst] *n* - **1.** *UK* [pharmacist] Apotheker *der*, -in *die*; **chemist's (shop)** [dispensing] Apotheke *die*; [non-dispensing] Drogerie *die* - **2.** [scientist] Chemiker *der*, -in *die*.

chemistry ['kemɪstrɪ] *n* [science] Chemie *die*.

cheque *UK*, **check** *US* [tʃek] *n* Scheck *der*.

chequebook *UK*, **checkbook** *US* ['tʃekbʊk] *n* Scheckheft *das*.

cheque (guarantee) card *n UK* Scheckkarte *die*.

chequered *UK* ['tʃekəd], **checkered** *US* ['tʃekerd] *adj* [varied] bewegt.

cherish ['tʃerɪʃ] *vt* [person] liebevoll sorgen für; [thing] hegen und pflegen; [hope] hegen.

cherry ['tʃerɪ] *n* - **1.** [fruit] Kirsche *die* - **2.**: **cherry (tree)** Kirschbaum *der*.

chess [tʃes] *n* Schach *das*.

chessboard ['tʃesbɔ:d] *n* Schachbrett *das*.

chest [tʃest] *n* - **1.** ANAT Brust *die* - **2.** [trunk] Truhe *die*.

chestnut ['tʃesnʌt] ◇ *adj* [colour] kastanienbraun. ◇ *n* - **1.** [nut] Kastanie *die* - **2.**: **chestnut (tree)** Kastanienbaum *der*.

chest of drawers (*pl* **chests of drawers**) *n* Kommode *die*.

chew [tʃu:] ◇ *n* [sweet] Kaubonbon *der ODER das*. ◇ *vt* - **1.** [food] kauen - **2.** [nails, pencil] kauen an (+ *D*). ◆ **chew up** *vt sep* zerkauen, zerbeißen.

chewing gum ['tʃu:ɪŋ-] *n (U)* Kaugummi *der*.

chic [ʃi:k] *adj* schick.

chick [tʃɪk] *n* - **1.** [baby bird] Junge *das*, Küken *das* - **2.** *inf* [girl] Braut *die*.

chicken ['tʃɪkɪn] *n* - **1.** [bird] Huhn *das* - **2.** *(U)* [food] Hähnchen *das* - **3.** *inf* [coward] Feigling *der*. ◆ **chicken out** *vi inf*: **to chicken out of sthg** vor etw *(D)* kneifen; **to chicken out of doing sthg** sich (aus Angst) davor drücken, etw zu tun.

chickenpox ['tʃɪkɪnpɒks] *n* Windpocken *Pl*.

chickpea ['tʃɪkpi:] *n* Kichererbse *die*.

chicory ['tʃɪkərɪ] *n* [vegetable] Chicorée *die ODER der*.

chief [tʃi:f] ◇ *adj* - **1.** [most important] Haupt- - **2.** [head] leitend. ◇ *n* - **1.** [of organization] Leiter *der*, -in *die*, Chef *der*, -in *die*; **chief of police** Polizeipräsident *der*, -in *die* - **2.** [of tribe] Häuptling *der*.

chief executive *n* [of company] Direktor *der*, -in *die*.

chiefly ['tʃi:flɪ] *adv* hauptsächlich.

chiffon ['ʃɪfɒn] *n* Chiffon *der*.

chilblain ['tʃɪlbleɪn] *n* Frostbeule *die*.

child [tʃaɪld] (*pl* **children**) *n* Kind *das*.

child benefit *n UK* Kindergeld *das*.

childhood ['tʃaɪldhʊd] *n* Kindheit *die*.

childish ['tʃaɪldɪʃ] *adj pej* kindisch.

childlike ['tʃaɪldlaɪk] *adj* kindlich.

childminder ['tʃaɪldˌmaɪndəʳ] *n UK* Tagesmutter *die*.

childproof ['tʃaɪldpru:f] *adj* kindersicher.

children ['tʃɪldrən] *Pl* ▷ **child**.

children's home *n* Kinderheim *das*.

Chile *n* Chile *nt*.

chili ['tʃɪlɪ] *n* = **chilli**.

chill [tʃɪl] ◇ *adj* kühl. ◇ *n* - **1.** [illness] Erkältung *die* mit leichtem Fieber - **2.** [in temperature]: **there's a chill in the air** es ist kühl draußen - **3.** [feeling of fear] Schauder *der*. ◇ *vt* - **1.** [drink] kühlen; [food] kalt stellen - **2.** [person - with cold]: **I'm chilled to the bone** ich bin bis auf die Knochen durchgefroren. ◇ *vi* [drink, food] kühl werden.

chilli ['tʃɪlɪ] (*pl* **-ies**) *n* [vegetable] Chili *der*; **chilli con carne** Chili con Carne.

chilling ['tʃɪlɪŋ] *adj* - **1.** [very cold] eisig - **2.** [frightening] schaudererregend.

chilly ['tʃɪlɪ] *adj* kühl.

chime [tʃaɪm] ◇ *n* [of bells] Geläut *das*; [of clock] Schlagen *das*; [of door bell] Läuten *das*. ◇ *vt* [time] schlagen. ◇ *vi* [bell] läuten; [clock] schlagen. ◆ **chime in** *vi* sich einlschalten.

chimney ['tʃɪmnɪ] *n* Schornstein *der*.

chimneypot ['tʃɪmnɪpɒt] *n* Schornsteinaufsatz *der*.

chimneysweep ['tʃɪmnɪswi:p] *n* Schornsteinfeger *der*.

chimp [tʃɪmp] *n inf* Schimpanse *der*.

chimpanzee [tʃɪmpən'zi:] *n* Schimpanse *der*.

chin [tʃɪn] *n* Kinn *das*.

china ['tʃaɪnə] *n* Porzellan *das*.

China ['tʃaɪnə] *n* China *nt*.

Chinese [ˌtʃaɪ'ni:z] ◇ *adj* chinesisch. ◇ *n* [language] Chinesisch(e) *das*. ◇ *npl*: **the Chinese** die Chinesen *Pl*.

chink [tʃɪŋk] *n* [narrow opening] Ritze *die*; **a chink of light** ein dünner Lichtstrahl.

chip [tʃɪp] ◇ *n* - **1.** *UK* [fried potato]: **chips** Pommes frites *Pl* - **2.** *US* [potato crisp] Chip *der* - **3.** [fragment - of wood] Span *der*; [- of stone, metal] Splitter *der* - **4.** [flaw] angeschlagene

Stelle - 5. [microchip, token] Chip *der*. ◇ *vt* [damage] an|schlagen. ◆ **chip in** *inf vi* - 1. [contribute] etwas bei|steuern - 2. [interrupt] sich ein|schalten. ◆ **chip off** *vt sep* ab|kratzen.

chipboard ['tʃɪpbɔ:d] *n (U)* Spanplatte *die*.

chip shop *n UK* Imbissbude *die*.

chiropodist [kɪ'rɒpədɪst] *n* Fußpfleger *der*, -in *die*.

chirp [tʃɜ:p] *vi* [bird] zwitschern.

chirpy ['tʃɜ:pɪ] *adj esp UK inf* munter.

chisel ['tʃɪzl] (*UK*) (*US*) ◇ *n* [for stone] Meißel *der*; [for wood] Beitel *der*. ◇ *vt* [in stone] meißeln; [in wood] stemmen.

chit [tʃɪt] *n* Zettel *der*.

chitchat ['tʃɪttʃæt] *n inf* Geplauder *das*.

chivalry ['ʃɪvlrɪ] *n* - 1. *liter* [of knights] Rittertum *das* - 2. [courtesy] Ritterlichkeit *die*.

chives [tʃaɪvz] *npl* Schnittlauch *der*.

chlorine ['klɔ:ri:n] *n* Chlor *das*.

choc-ice ['tʃɒkaɪs] *n UK Eis mit Schokoladenüberzug*.

chock [tʃɒk] *n* Keil *der*.

chock-a-block, chock-full *adj inf* überfüllt.

chocolate ['tʃɒkələt] ◇ *n* - 1. *(U)* [food] Schokolade *die* - 2. [sweet] Praline *die* - 3. [drink]: **(hot) chocolate** heiße Schokolade. ◇ *comp* [made of chocolate] Schokoladen-.

choice [tʃɔɪs] ◇ *n* - 1. [gen] Wahl *die* - 2. [variety, selection] Auswahl *die*. ◇ *adj* erlesen, ausgesucht.

choir ['kwaɪəʳ] *n* Chor *der*.

choirboy ['kwaɪəbɔɪ] *n* Chorknabe *der*.

choke [tʃəʊk] ◇ *n* AUT Choke *der*. ◇ *vt* - 1. [strangle] würgen; **to choke sb to death** jn erwürgen; **the fumes choked her** durch den Rauch bekam sie keine Luft mehr - 2. [block] verstopfen. ◇ *vi* keine Luft mehr kriegen; [on fishbone] sich verschlucken; **to choke to death** ersticken.

cholera ['kɒlərə] *n* Cholera *die*.

choose [tʃu:z] (*pt* **chose**, *pp* **chosen**) ◇ *vt* - 1. [select - career] wählen; [- cake, dress] aus|wählen - 2. [opt]: **to choose to do sthg** beschließen, etw zu tun. ◇ *vi* [select]: **to choose (from sthg)** eine Wahl treffen (zwischen etw *(D)*).

choos(e)y ['tʃu:zɪ] (*comp* **-ier**, *superl* **-iest**) *adj* wählerisch.

chop [tʃɒp] ◇ *n* [meat] Kotelett *das*. ◇ *vt* - 1. [wood] hacken; [food] schneiden - 2. *inf* [funding, budget] kürzen - 3. *phr*: **to chop and change** es sich *(D)* dauernd anders überlegen. ◆ **chop down** *vt sep* fällen. ◆ **chop up** *vt sep* [wood] klein hacken; [food] klein schneiden.

chopper ['tʃɒpəʳ] *n* - 1. [axe] Hackbeil *das* - 2. *inf* [helicopter] Hubschrauber *der*.

choppy ['tʃɒpɪ] *adj* kabbelig.

chopsticks ['tʃɒpstɪks] *npl* Stäbchen *Pl*.

chord [kɔ:d] *n* MUS Akkord *der*.

chore [tʃɔ:ʳ] *n* lästige Pflicht; **household chores** Hausarbeit *die*.

chorus ['kɔ:rəs] *n* - 1. [part of song] Refrain *der* - 2. [singers] Chor *der*.

chose [tʃəʊz] *pt* ▻ **choose**.

chosen ['tʃəʊzn] *pp* ▻ **choose**.

Christ [kraɪst] ◇ *n* Christus *der*. ◇ *excl* oh Gott!

christen ['krɪsn] *vt* taufen.

christening ['krɪsnɪŋ] *n* Taufe *die*.

Christian ['krɪstʃən] ◇ *adj* christlich. ◇ *n* Christ *der*, -in *die*.

Christianity [,krɪstɪ'ænətɪ] *n* Christentum *das*.

Christian name *n* Vorname *der*.

Christmas ['krɪsməs] *n* Weihnachten *das*; **Happy** OR **Merry Christmas!** Frohe Weihnachten!

Christmas card *n* Weihnachtskarte *die*.

Christmas Day *n* erster Weihnachtstag.

Christmas Eve *n* Heiligabend *der*.

Christmas pudding *n UK schwere Süßspeise mit Trockenfrüchten, die an Weihnachten gegessen wird*.

Christmas tree *n* Weihnachtsbaum *der*.

chrome [krəʊm], **chromium** ['krəʊmɪəm] ◇ *n* Chrom *das*. ◇ *comp* Chrom-.

chronic ['krɒnɪk] *adj* - 1. [illness, unemployment] chronisch - 2. [alcoholic] Gewohnheits-; [liar] chronisch.

chronicle ['krɒnɪkl] *n* Chronik *die*.

chronological [,krɒnə'lɒdʒɪkl] *adj* chronologisch.

chrysanthemum [krɪ'sænθəməm] (*pl* **-s**) *n* Chrysantheme *die*.

chubby ['tʃʌbɪ] *adj* mollig.

chuck [tʃʌk] *vt inf* - 1. [throw] schmeißen - 2. [job] hin|schmeißen; [girlfriend, boyfriend] Schluss machen mit. ◆ **chuck away, chuck out** *vt sep inf* weg|schmeißen.

chuckle ['tʃʌkl] *vi* in sich *(A)* hinein|lachen.

chug [tʃʌg] *vi* tuckern.

chum [tʃʌm] *n inf* [friend] Kumpel *der*.

chunk [tʃʌŋk] *n* - 1. [of bread, cheese] Stück *das* - 2. *inf* [large amount] großer Teil.

church [tʃɜ:tʃ] *n* Kirche *die*; **to go to church** in die Kirche gehen.

Church of England *n*: **the Church of England** die Anglikanische Kirche.

churchyard ['tʃɜ:tʃjɑ:d] *n* Friedhof *der*.

churlish ['tʃɜ:lɪʃ] *adj* [impolite] unhöflich; [loutish] ungehobelt.

churn [tʃɜ:n] ◇ *n* - 1. [for making butter] Butterfass *das* - 2. [for milk] Milchkanne *die*. ◇ *vt* [stir up] auf|wühlen. ◆ **churn out** *vt sep inf* am laufenden Band produzieren.

chute [ʃuːt] *n* Rutsche *die*; [for rubbish] Müllschlucker *der*.

chutney ['tʃʌtnɪ] *n* Chutney *das*.

CIA (*abbr of* **Central Intelligence Agency**) *n* CIA *die ODER der*.

CID (*abbr of* **Criminal Investigation Department**) *n* ≃ Kripo *die*.

cider ['saɪdəʳ] *n* Cidre *der*, Apfelwein *der*.

cigar [sɪ'gɑːʳ] *n* Zigarre *die*.

cigarette [ˌsɪgə'ret] *n* Zigarette *die*.

cinder ['sɪndəʳ] *n* Asche *die*.

Cinderella [ˌsɪndə'relə] *n* Aschenputtel *das*.

cinecamera [ˌcɪnɪˌkæmərə] *n* Filmkamera *die*.

cinema ['sɪnəmə] *n* Kino *das*.

cinnamon ['sɪnəmən] *n* Zimt *der*.

cipher ['saɪfəʳ] *n* [secret writing system] Chiffre *die*, Kode *der*.

circa ['sɜːkə] *prep* etwa, zirka.

circle ['sɜːkl] <> *n* - **1.** [gen] Kreis *der*; **to go round in circles** sich im Kreis bewegen - **2.** [in theatre, cinema] Balkon *der*. <> *vt* - **1.** [draw a circle round] ein|kreisen - **2.** [move round] umkreisen. <> *vi* kreisen.

circuit ['sɜːkɪt] *n* - **1.** ELEC Stromkreis *der* - **2.** [lap] Runde *die* - **3.** [motor racing track] Rennstrecke *die* - **4.** [series of venues] Tour *die*.

circuitous [sə'kjuːɪtəs] *adj* umständlich.

circular ['sɜːkjʊləʳ] <> *adj* - **1.** [in shape] rund, kreisförmig - **2.** [route] Rund-. <> *n* - **1.** [letter, memo] Rundschreiben *das* - **2.** [advertisement] Wurfsendung *die*.

circulate ['sɜːkjʊleɪt] <> *vi* - **1.** [gen] zirkulieren - **2.** [rumour, story] um|gehen, kursieren - **3.** [socialize] sich unter die Leute mischen. <> *vt* - **1.** [document] zirkulieren lassen - **2.** [rumour, story] in Umlauf setzen.

circulation [ˌsɜːkjʊ'leɪʃn] *n* - **1.** [of blood] Zirkulation *die*, Kreislauf *der* - **2.** [of money, document] Umlauf *der*; **in circulation** im Umlauf - **3.** [of magazine, newspaper] Auflage *die* - **4.** [of heat, air] Zirkulation *die*.

circumcision [ˌsɜːkəm'sɪʒn] *n* Beschneidung *die*.

circumference [sə'kʌmfərəns] *n* Umfang *der*.

circumflex ['sɜːkəmfleks] *n*: **circumflex (accent)** Zirkumflex *der*.

circumspect ['sɜːkəmspekt] *adj* umsichtig.

circumstances ['sɜːkəmstənsɪz] *npl* Umstände *Pl*; **under** OR **in no circumstances** unter keinen Umständen, auf keinen Fall; **under** OR **in the circumstances** unter diesen Umständen.

circumvent [ˌsɜːkəm'vent] *vt fml* um|gehen.

circus ['sɜːkəs] *n* Zirkus *der*.

cistern ['sɪstən] *n* - **1.** *UK* [in roof] Wassertank *der* - **2.** [in toilet] Spülkasten *der*.

cite [saɪt] *vt* - **1.** [mention, quote] zitieren - **2.** LAW vorladen.

citizen ['sɪtɪzn] *n* - **1.** [of country] Staatsbürger *der*, -in *die* - **2.** [of town] Bürger *der*, -in *die*.

Citizens' Advice Bureau *n* Bürgerberatungsstelle *die*.

Citizens' Band *n* CB-Funk *der*.

citizenship ['sɪtɪznʃɪp] *n* [nationality] Staatsangehörigkeit *die*.

citrus fruit ['sɪtrəs-] *n* Zitrusfrucht *die*.

city ['sɪtɪ] *n* Stadt *die*; [large] Großstadt *die*.
◆ **City** *n UK*: **the City** *Londoner Finanzviertel*.

city centre *n* Innenstadt *die*.

city hall *n US* Rathaus *das*.

civic ['sɪvɪk] *adj* - **1.** [leader, event] Stadt- - **2.** [duty, pride] bürgerlich, Bürger-.

civil ['sɪvl] *adj* - **1.** [disorder, marriage] zivil - **2.** [polite] höflich.

civil engineering *n* Hoch- und Tiefbau *der*.

civilian [sɪ'vɪljən] <> *n* Zivilist *der*, -in *die*. <> *comp* [government] Zivil-; [organization] zivil; **in civilian clothes** in Zivil.

civilization [ˌsɪvəlaɪ'zeɪʃn] *n* - **1.** [advanced world] Zivilisation *die* - **2.** [society, culture] Kultur *die*.

civilized ['sɪvəlaɪzd] *adj* zivilisiert.

civil law *n* bürgerliches Recht.

civil liberties *npl* Freiheitsrechte *Pl*.

civil rights *npl* Bürgerrechte *Pl*.

civil servant *n* Beamte *der*, -in *die* (im Staatsdienst).

civil service *n* Staatsdienst *der*.

civil war *n* Bürgerkrieg *der*.

CJD (*abbr of* **Creutzfeldt-Jakob disease**) *n* CJK *die*.

cl (*abbr of* **centilitre**) *n* cl.

clad [klæd] *adj liter* [dressed]: **clad in sthg** in etw *(D)* gekleidet.

claim [kleɪm] <> *n* - **1.** [for territory, expenses, refund] Anspruch *der*; [demand] Forderung *die*; **to lay claim to sthg** etw für sich beanspruchen - **2.** [assertion] Behauptung *die*. <> *vt* - **1.** [money] beantragen; [lost property] beanspruchen; [expenses] ein|reichen; [credit] für sich in Anspruch nehmen; **he claimed responsibility for it** er bekannte, dafür verantwortlich zu sein - **2.** [assert] behaupten. <> *vi*: **to claim for sthg** Ansprüche auf etw *(A)* geltend machen.

claimant ['kleɪmənt] *n* Antragsteller *der*, -in *die*; LAW Kläger *der*, -in *die*.

clairvoyant [kleə'vɔɪənt] *n* Hellseher *der*, -in *die*.

clam [klæm] *n* Klaffmuschel *die*.

clamber ['klæmbəʳ] *vi* klettern.

clammy ['klæmɪ] *adj inf* [skin] feucht und klamm; [weather] schwül.

clamour *UK*, **clamor** *US* ['klæmər] *vi*: **to clamour for sthg** etw lautstark fordern.

clamp [klæmp] ◇ *n* - **1.** [fastener] Schraubzwinge *die* - **2.** MED & TECH Klemme *die*. ◇ *vt* - **1.** [with fastener] fest|klemmen - **2.** [parked car] Parkkralle an|legen *(+ D)*. ◆ **clamp down** *vi*: **to clamp down (on)** durch|greifen (gegen).

clan [klæn] *n* Clan *der*.

clandestine [klæn'destɪn] *adj* geheim.

clang [klæŋ] *n* [of bell] lautes Tönen.

clap [klæp] ◇ *vt* Beifall klatschen *(+ D)*; **to clap one's hands** in die Hände klatschen; **to clap eyes on sb/sthg** jn/etw zu Gesicht bekommen. ◇ *vi* Beifall klatschen.

clapping ['klæpɪŋ] *n* Beifall *der*.

claret ['klærət] *n* [wine] roter Bordeaux.

clarify ['klærɪfaɪ] *vt* (näher) erläutern.

clarinet [,klærə'net] *n* Klarinette *die*.

clarity ['klærətɪ] *n* Klarheit *die*.

clash [klæʃ] ◇ *n* - **1.** [incompatibility]: **a clash of interests** ein Interessenkonflikt; **a clash of personalities** ein Zusammenprall verschiedener Persönlichkeiten - **2.** [fight] Zusammenstoß *der* - **3.** [disagreement] Meinungsverschiedenheit *die*. ◇ *vi* - **1.** [ideas, beliefs] aufeinander prallen; [colours] sich beißen - **2.** [fight]: **to clash (with sb)** (mit jm) zusammen|stoßen - **3.** [disagree]: **to clash (with sb)** (mit jm) aneinander geraten.

clasp [klɑːsp] ◇ *n* [on necklace, bracelet] Verschluss *der*; [on belt] Schnalle *die*. ◇ *vt* ergreifen.

class [klɑːs] ◇ *n* - **1.** [gen] Klasse *die* - **2.** [lesson] Stunde *die*; **an evening class** ein Abendkurs - **3.** [social group] Schicht *die*; **upper class** Oberschicht *die*; **the working class** die Arbeiterklasse. ◇ *vt* ein|stufen; **to class sb as sthg** jn als etw ein|stufen.

classic ['klæsɪk] ◇ *adj* [gen] klassisch. ◇ *n* Klassiker *der*.

classical ['klæsɪkl] *adj* - **1.** klassisch - **2.** [sculpture, architecture] klassizistisch.

classified ['klæsɪfaɪd] *adj* [secret]: **classified information** Verschlusssache *die*.

classified ad *n* Annonce *die*.

classify ['klæsɪfaɪ] *vt* klassifizieren.

classmate ['klɑːsmeɪt] *n* Klassenkamerad *der*, -in *die*.

classroom ['klɑːsrʊm] *n* Klassenzimmer *das*.

classy ['klɑːsɪ] *adj inf* [clothes, restaurant] nobel; [car] edel; [person] vornehm.

clatter ['klætər] *n* Geklapper *das*.

clause [klɔːz] *n* - **1.** [in legal document] Klausel *die* - **2.** GRAM Satz *der*.

claw [klɔː] ◇ *n* [of animal, bird] Kralle *die*. ◇ *vt* kratzen. ◇ *vi*: **to claw at sthg** sich an etw *(A)* krallen.

clay [kleɪ] *n* [soil] Lehm *der*; [for pottery] Ton *der*.

clean [kliːn] ◇ *adj* - **1.** [gen] sauber - **2.** [reputation, driving licence] tadellos - **3.** [joke] harmlos - **4.** [line, movement] klar - **5.** [break] glatt. ◇ *vt* sauber machen; **to clean one's teeth** *UK* sich *(D)* die Zähne putzen. ◇ *vi* putzen. ◆ **clean out** *vt sep* [room, cupboard] gründlich auf|räumen. ◆ **clean up** *vt sep* [mess] auf|räumen; [with cloth] sauber machen; **to clean o.s. up** sich waschen.

cleaner ['kliːnər] *n* - **1.** [person] Putzfrau *die* - **2.** [substance] Reiniger *der*.

cleaning ['kliːnɪŋ] *n*: **to do the cleaning** sauber machen.

cleanliness ['klenlɪnɪs] *n* Reinlichkeit *die*.

cleanse [klenz] *vt* [skin, wound] säubern.

cleanser ['klenzər] *n* - **1.** [for skin] Reinigungsmilch *die* - **2.** [detergent] Reinigungsmittel *das*.

clean-shaven [-'ʃeɪvn] *adj* glatt rasiert.

clear [klɪər] ◇ *adj* - **1.** [gen] klar; **to make sthg clear (to sb)** (jm) etw klar machen; **to make it clear that...** deutlich machen, dass...; **to make o.s. clear** sich klar aus|drücken - **2.** [obvious] eindeutig - **3.** [sound] deutlich; [speaker] deutlich hörbar - **4.** [skin, complexion, conscience] rein - **5.** [road, view] frei; **try and keep Friday clear** versuch dir Freitag freizuhalten. ◇ *adv*: **stand clear!** zurücktreten!; **to be clear of sthg** etw nicht berühren; **to stay clear of sb, to steer clear of sb** jm aus dem Wege gehen; **to stay clear of sthg, to steer clear of sthg** etw meiden. ◇ *vt* - **1.** [path, road] räumen; [pipe] reinigen; **to clear the table** den Tisch ab|räumen - **2.** [take out of the way] aus dem Weg räumen - **3.** [jump over] überspringen - **4.** [debt] begleichen - **5.** [authorize] genehmigen - **6.** [prove not guilty] frei|sprechen; **to clear one's name** seinen Namen rein|waschen; **to be cleared of sthg** von etw freigesprochen werden. ◇ *vi* [fog, smoke] sich verziehen; [weather] sich auf|klären. ◆ **clear away** *vt sep* weg|räumen. ◆ **clear off** *vi UK inf* ab|hauen. ◆ **clear out** ◇ *vt sep* [room, cupboard] gründlich auf|räumen. ◇ *vi inf* [leave] verschwinden. ◆ **clear up** ◇ *vt sep* - **1.** [tidy] auf|räumen; [toys, litter] weg|räumen - **2.** [mystery] auf|klären; [problem, confusion] klären. ◇ *vi* - **1.** [weather] sich auf|klären - **2.** [tidy up] auf|räumen.

clearance ['klɪərəns] *n (U)* [permission] Genehmigung *die*; [for takeoff] Starterlaubnis *die*.

clear-cut *adj* klar umrissen.

clearing ['klɪərɪŋ] *n* [in forest] Lichtung *die*.

clearly ['klɪəlɪ] *adv* - **1.** [speak, write] deutlich - **2.** [think, explain] klar - **3.** [obviously] eindeutig.

cleavage ['kliːvɪdʒ] *n* [between breasts] Dekolletee *das*.

cleaver ['kliːvər] *n* Hackbeil *das*.

clef [klef] *n* Notenschlüssel *der*.

cleft [kleft] *n* [in rock] Spalt *der*.

clench [klentʃ] *vt* umklammern; [fist] ballen; [teeth] zusammen|beißen.

clergy ['klɜ:dʒɪ] *npl*: **the clergy** die Geistlichkeit.

clergyman ['klɜ:dʒɪmən] (*pl* **-men** [-mən]) *n* Geistliche *der*.

clerical ['klerɪkl] *adj* - **1.** [in office] Büro- **2.** [in church] geistlich.

clerk [*UK* klɑ:k, *US* klɜ:rk] *n* - **1.** [in office] Büroangestellte *der, die* - **2.** [in court] Gerichtsschreiber *der*, -in *die* - **3.** *US* [shop assistant] Verkäufer *der*, -in *die*.

clever ['klevəʳ] *adj* - **1.** [person] klug; **to be clever with one's hands** geschickte Hände haben - **2.** [idea, device] raffiniert.

click [klɪk] ◇ *n* Klicken *das*. ◇ *vt* [fingers] schnippen mit; [tongue] schnalzen mit. ◇ *vi* [gen & COMPUT] klicken; **to click on sthg** COMPUT etw an|klicken; **suddenly it all clicked** plötzlich wurde alles klar.

client ['klaɪənt] *n* Kunde *der*, -din *die*; [of lawyer] Klient *der*, -in *die*.

cliff [klɪf] *n* [by sea] Klippe *die*.

climate ['klaɪmɪt] *n liter* & *fig* Klima *das*.

climax ['klaɪmæks] *n* [culmination] Höhepunkt *der*.

climb [klaɪm] ◇ *n* [of mountain] Aufstieg *der*. ◇ *vt* [tree, wall] hoch|klettern; [rope] hoch|klettern an *(+ D)*; [ladder, stairs] hinauf|steigen; [hill] steigen auf *(+ A)*; [mountain] besteigen. ◇ *vi* - **1.** [person, plant] klettern - **2.** [road, prices, costs] an|steigen; [plane] (auf)|steigen.

climber ['klaɪməʳ] *n* [person] Kletterer *der*, -rin *die*; [mountaineer] Bergsteiger *der*, -in *die*.

climbing ['klaɪmɪŋ] *n* Klettern *das*; [mountaineering] Bergsteigen *das*; **to go climbing** bergsteigen gehen.

clinch [klɪntʃ] *vt* [deal] ab|schließen.

cling [klɪŋ] (*pt & pp* **clung**) *vi* - **1.** [hold tightly]: **to cling to** sich klammern an *(+ A)* - **2.** [clothes]: **to cling (to sb)** sich (an jn) an|schmiegen.

clingfilm ['klɪŋfɪlm] *n (U) UK* Frischhaltefolie *die*.

clinic ['klɪnɪk] *n* Klinik *die*.

clinical ['klɪnɪkl] *adj* - **1.** MED klinisch - **2.** [coldly rational] nüchtern.

clink [klɪŋk] *vi* klirren.

clip [klɪp] ◇ *n* - **1.** [fastener] Klammer *die*; [on earring] Klipp *der* - **2.** [of film, video] Ausschnitt *der*, Clip *der*. ◇ *vt* - **1.** [fasten]: **to clip sthg onto sthg** [papers] etw an etw *(A)* heften - **2.** [cut] schneiden.

clipboard ['klɪpbɔ:d] *n* - **1.** Klemmbrett *das* - **2.** COMPUT Zwischenablage *die*.

clippers ['klɪpəz] *npl* - **1.** [for hair] Haarschneidemaschine *die* - **2.** [for nails] Nagelknipser *der*, Nagelzange *die*.

clipping ['klɪpɪŋ] *n* [newspaper cutting] Zeitungsausschnitt *der*.

cloak [kləʊk] *n* [garment] Umhang *der*.

cloakroom ['kləʊkrʊm] *n* - **1.** [for clothes] Garderobe *die* - **2.** *UK* [toilets] Waschraum *der*.

clock [klɒk] *n* - **1.** [gen] Uhr *die*; **round the clock** rund um die Uhr - **2.** [mileometer] Tachometer *der*. ◆ **clock in** *vi UK* [at work] (den Arbeitsbeginn) stechen. ◆ **clock off** *vi UK* [at work] (das Arbeitsende) stechen.

clockwise ['klɒkwaɪz] *adj* & *adv* im Uhrzeigersinn.

clockwork ['klɒkwɜ:k] ◇ *n*: **like clockwork** wie am Schnürchen. ◇ *comp* [toy, train] zum Aufziehen.

clog [klɒg] *vt* verstopfen. ◆ **clogs** *npl* Clogs *Pl*. ◆ **clog up** *vt sep* & *vi* verstopfen.

close[1] [kləʊs] ◇ *adj* - **1.** [near] nahe; **close to** nahe an *(+ D)*; [with verbs of motion] nahe an *(+ A)*; **the house is close to the river** das Haus steht nahe am Fluss; **she sat down close to me** sie setzte sich in meine Nähe; **don't get too close to the edge** geh nicht zu nahe an den Abgrund; **that was a close shave** OR **thing** OR **call** das war knapp; **when seen from close up** OR **to** aus der Nähe betrachtet - **2.** [friend, contact, link] eng; **to be close to sb** jm nahe stehen - **3.** [resemblance] stark - **4.** [examination, inspection] genau; **on closer examination** bei näherer Betrachtung - **5.** [weather] schwül - **6.** [race, contest] knapp. ◇ *adv* nah; **close by, close at hand** in der Nähe; **close behind** dicht dahinter; **to stand close together** nahe beieinander stehen. ◆ **close on, close to** *prep* [almost] beinahe.

close[2] [kləʊz] ◇ *vt* - **1.** [gen] schließen - **2.** [road] sperren - **3.** [meeting, event] beenden; [speech, novel] beschließen - **4.** [bank account] auf|lösen - **5.** [deal] ab|schließen. ◇ *vi* - **1.** [door, eyes, wound] sich schließen - **2.** [shop, office, book, share price] schließen - **3.** [deadline, offer] enden. ◇ *n* [end] Schluss *der*; **to draw to a close** zu Ende gehen. ◆ **close down** ◇ *vt sep* [shut] schließen. ◇ *vi* [shut down] stillgelegt werden.

closed [kləʊzd] *adj* geschlossen.

close-knit [ˌkləʊs-] *adj* eng verbunden.

closely ['kləʊslɪ] *adv* - **1.** [gen] eng; [resemble] stark - **2.** [watch, guard, listen] genau; [follow] dicht.

closet ['klɒzɪt] ◇ *adj inf* heimlich; **he's a closet socialist** er ist ein verkappter Sozialist. ◇ *n US* Schrank *der*.

close-up ['kləʊs-] *n* Nahaufnahme *die*.

closing time *n* [for pubs] Sperrstunde *die*; [for shops] Ladenschlusszeit *die*.

closure ['kləʊʒəʳ] *n* - **1.** [of business, company] Schließung *die* - **2.** [of road, railway line] Sperrung *die*.

clot [klɒt] ◇ *n* - **1.** [lump] Klumpen *der*; [of blood] Blutgerinnsel *das* - **2.** *UK inf* [fool] Hornochse *der*. ◇ *vi* [blood] gerinnen.

cloth [klɒθ] *n* - **1.** *(U)* [material] Stoff *der* - **2.** [for cleaning] Lappen *der* - **3.** [tablecloth] Tischtuch *das*.

clothe [kləʊð] *vt fml* [dress] kleiden.

clothes [kləʊðz] *npl* Kleider *Pl*; **to put one's clothes on** sich an|ziehen; **to take one's clothes off** sich aus|ziehen.

clothes brush *n* Kleiderbürste *die*.

clothesline ['kləʊðzlaɪn] *n* Wäscheleine *die*.

clothes peg *UK*, **clothespin** *US* ['kləʊðzpɪn] *n* Wäscheklammer *die*.

clothing ['kləʊðɪŋ] *n* Kleidung *die*; **a piece of clothing** ein Kleidungsstück.

cloud [klaʊd] *n* Wolke *die*. ◆ **cloud over** *vi* [sky] sich bewölken.

cloudy ['klaʊdɪ] *adj* - **1.** [day, sky] bedeckt - **2.** [beer, water] trüb.

clout [klaʊt] *inf* ◇ *n (U)* [influence] Schlagkraft *die*. ◇ *vt* [hit] schlagen.

clove [kləʊv] *n*: **a clove of garlic** eine Knoblauchzehe. ◆ **cloves** *npl* [spice] Gewürznelken *Pl*.

clover ['kləʊvəʳ] *n* Klee *der*.

clown [klaʊn] ◇ *n* - **1.** [performer] Clown *der* - **2.** [fool] Idiot *der*. ◇ *vi* herum|albern.

cloying ['klɔɪɪŋ] *adj* - **1.** [scent] süßlich - **2.** [sentimentality] kitschig.

club [klʌb] ◇ *n* - **1.** [association] Klub *der* - **2.** [nightclub] Nachtklub *der* - **3.** [weapon] Knüppel *der*, Prügel *der* - **4.** SPORT [equipment]: **(golf) club** (Golf)schläger *der*. ◇ *vt* [hit] prügeln. ◆ **clubs** *npl* [playing cards] Kreuz *das*; **the six of clubs** die Kreuzsechs. ◆ **club together** *vi UK* zusammen|legen.

clubhouse ['klʌbhaʊs] (*pl* [-haʊzɪz]) *n* Klubhaus *das*.

cluck [klʌk] *vi* [hen] gackern.

clue [klu:] *n* [hint] Hinweis *der*; [in crime] Spur *die*; [in crossword] Frage *die*; **I haven't (got) a clue (about)** ich habe keine Ahnung (von).

clued-up [klu:d-] *adj UK inf* gut informiert.

clump [klʌmp] *n* [of trees, flowers] Gruppe *die*.

clumsy ['klʌmzɪ] *adj* [person] tollpatschig; [movement, remark] ungeschickt.

clung [klʌŋ] *pt* & *pp* ▷ **cling**.

cluster ['klʌstəʳ] ◇ *n* Gruppe *die*; [of grapes] Traube *die*. ◇ *vi* - **1.** [people] sich scharen - **2.** [things] sich drängen.

clutch [klʌtʃ] ◇ *n* AUT Kupplung *die*. ◇ *vt* fest|halten. ◇ *vi*: **to clutch at sb/sthg** nach jm/etw greifen.

clutter ['klʌtəʳ] *n* Unordnung *die*.

cm (*abbr of* **centimetre**) *n* cm.

c/o (*abbr of* **care of**) = **care**.

Co. *abbr of* **Company**, **County**.

coach [kəʊtʃ] ◇ *n* - **1.** [bus] (Reise)bus *der* - **2.** RAIL Wagen *der* - **3.** [horsedrawn] Kutsche *die* - **4.** SPORT Trainer *der*, -in *die* - **5.** [tutor] Nachhilfelehrer *der*, -in *die*. ◇ *vt* - **1.** SPORT trainieren - **2.** [tutor]: **to coach sb (in sthg)** jm Nachhilfestunden (in etw *(D)*) geben.

coach station *n* Busbahnhof *der*.

coal [kəʊl] *n (U)* [mineral] Kohle *die*.

coalfield ['kəʊlfi:ld] *n* Kohlenrevier *das*.

coalition [ˌkəʊə'lɪʃn] *n* POL Koalition *die*; **coalition government** Koalitionsregierung *die*.

coalmine ['kəʊlmaɪn] *n* Kohlenbergwerk *das*.

coarse [kɔ:s] *adj* - **1.** [rough - hair] dick; [- skin] derb; [- sandpaper, fabric] grob - **2.** [vulgar - remark, laugh] ordinär; [- joke] derb; [- person] ordinär.

coast [kəʊst] ◇ *n* Küste *die*. ◇ *vi* [car] im Leerlauf fahren.

coastal ['kəʊstl] *adj* Küsten-.

coaster ['kəʊstəʳ] *n* Untersetzer *der*.

coastguard ['kəʊstgɑ:d] *n* - **1.** [person] Mitglied *das* der Küstenwache - **2.** [organization]: **the coastguard** die Küstenwache.

coastline ['kəʊstlaɪn] *n* Küste *die*.

coat [kəʊt] ◇ *n* - **1.** [garment] Mantel *der* - **2.** [of animal] Fell *das* - **3.** [of paint, varnish] Schicht *die*. ◇ *vt*: **to coat sthg (with sthg)** etw (mit etw) überziehen.

coat hanger *n* Kleiderbügel *der*.

coating ['kəʊtɪŋ] *n* [of chocolate] Überzug *der*; [of dust] Schicht *die*.

coat of arms (*pl* **coats of arms**) *n* Wappen *das*.

coax [kəʊks] *vt*: **to coax sb (to do** OR **into doing sthg)** jn überreden(, etw zu tun).

cob [kɒb] *n* ▷ **corn on the cob**.

cobbles ['kɒblz], **cobblestones** ['kɒblstəʊnz] *npl* Kopfsteinpflaster *das*.

cobweb ['kɒbweb] *n* Spinnennetz *das*.

cocaine [kəʊ'keɪn] *n* Kokain *das*.

cock [kɒk] ◇ *n* - **1.** [male chicken] Hahn *der* - **2.** [male bird] Männchen *das* - **3.** *vulg* [penis] Schwanz *der*. ◇ *vt* - **1.**: **to cock a gun** den Hahn einer Schusswaffe spannen - **2.** [head]: **to cock one's head (to one side)** den Kopf auf die Seite legen. ◆ **cock up** *vt sep UK v inf* versauen.

cockerel ['kɒkrəl] *n* junger Hahn.

cockle ['kɒkl] *n* Herzmuschel *die*.

Cockney ['kɒknɪ] (*pl* **-s**) *n* - **1.** [person] Cockney *der* - **2.** [dialect, accent] Cockney *das*.

cockpit ['kɒkpɪt] *n* Cockpit *das*.

cockroach ['kɒkrəʊtʃ] *n* Küchenschabe *die*.

cocktail ['kɒkteɪl] *n* Cocktail *der.*
cocktail party *n* Cocktailparty *die.*
cock-up *n v inf*: **to make a cock-up** Scheiße bauen; **to make a cock-up of sthg** etw versauen.
cocky ['kɒkɪ] *adj inf* überheblich.
cocoa ['kəʊkəʊ] *n* Kakao *der.*
coconut ['kəʊkənʌt] *n* Kokosnuss *die.*
cod [kɒd] (*pl inv* OR **-s**) *n* Kabeljau *der.*
COD *abbr of* **cash on delivery.**
code [kəʊd] ◇ *n* - **1.** [cipher] Kode *der* - **2.** [set of rules] Kodex *der*; **code of behaviour** Verhaltenskodex *der* - **3.** TELEC Vorwahl *die.* ◇ *vt* - **1.** [encode] verschlüsseln, chiffrieren - **2.** [give identifier to] kennzeichnen.
cod-liver oil *n* Lebertran *der.*
coerce [kəʊ'ɜːs] *vt* zwingen; **to coerce sb into doing sthg** jn dazu zwingen, etw zu tun.
C of E *n abbr of* **Church of England.**
coffee ['kɒfɪ] *n* Kaffee *der.*
coffee bar *n UK* Café *das.*
coffee break *n* Kaffeepause *die.*
coffee morning *n UK morgendliches Kaffeetrinken, das zu Wohltätigkeitszwecken organisiert wird.*
coffeepot ['kɒfɪpɒt] *n* Kaffeekanne *die.*
coffee shop *n* - **1.** *UK* [café] Café *das* - **2.** *US* [restaurant] Café *das* - **3.** [shop selling coffee] Kaffeegeschäft *das.*
coffee table *n* Couchtisch *der.*
coffin ['kɒfɪn] *n* Sarg *der.*
cog [kɒg] *n* [tooth on wheel] Zahn *der*; [wheel] Zahnrad *das.*
coherent [kəʊ'hɪərənt] *adj* [answer] folgerichtig; [theory, ideas, story, speech] schlüssig; [account] zusammenhängend.
cohesive [kəʊ'hiːsɪv] *adj* [united - group] einheitlich; [- image] stimmig.
coil [kɔɪl] ◇ *n* - **1.** [of rope, wire] Rolle *die*; [of hair] Locke *die*; [of smoke] Kringel *der* - **2.** ELEC Spule *die* - **3.** *UK* [contraceptive device] Spirale *die.* ◇ *vt* auf|rollen; **to coil sthg around sb/sthg** etw um jn/etw wickeln. ◇ *vi* sich ringeln. ◆ **coil up** *vt sep* auf|rollen.
coin [kɔɪn] ◇ *n* Münze *die.* ◇ *vt* [invent] prägen.
coincide [ˌkəʊɪn'saɪd] *vi* - **1.** [occur simultaneously]: **to coincide (with sthg)** (mit etw) zusammen|fallen - **2.** [be in agreement] überein|stimmen.
coincidence [kəʊ'ɪnsɪdəns] *n* Zufall *der.*
coincidental [kəʊˌɪnsɪ'dentl] *adj* zufällig.
coke [kəʊk] *n* - **1.** [fuel] Koks *der* - **2.** *drug sl* [cocaine] Koks *der.*
cola ['kəʊlə] *n* Cola *die ODER das.*
colander ['kʌləndəʳ] *n* Sieb *das.*
cold [kəʊld] ◇ *adj* - **1.** [gen] kalt; **I'm cold** mir ist kalt - **2.** [unfriendly - eyes, smile, voice] kalt; [- person] gefühlskalt. ◇ *n* - **1.** [illness] Erkältung *die*; **to catch (a) cold** sich erkälten - **2.** [low temperature] Kälte *die.*
cold-blooded [-'blʌdɪd] *adj* - **1.** [unfeeling - person] gefühllos; [- attitude] herzlos - **2.** [ruthless] kaltblütig.
cold calling *n* unaufgeforderte Telefonwerbung *die.*
cold sore *n* Bläschenausschlag *der.*
cold war *n*: **the cold war** der Kalte Krieg.
coleslaw ['kəʊlslɔː] *n (U)* Krautsalat *der.*
collaborate [kə'læbəreɪt] *vi* - **1.** [work together]: **to collaborate (with sb)** (mit jm) zusammen|arbeiten - **2.** *pej* [with enemy]: **to collaborate (with sb)** (mit jm) kollaborieren.
collapse [kə'læps] ◇ *n* - **1.** [destruction] Einsturz *der* - **2.** [failure - of marriage, government] Scheitern *das*; [- of empire] Untergang *der*; [- of system, business, company] Zusammenbruch *der* - **3.** MED Kollaps *der.* ◇ *vi* - **1.** [fall down, fall in - house, building, roof] ein|stürzen; [- stage, bridge] zusammen|brechen; [- lung] zusammen|fallen; *(phrase)*: **I collapsed into bed** ich ließ mich aufs Bett fallen - **2.** [fail - marriage, government] scheitern; [- system, business, company] zusammen|brechen - **3.** MED kollabieren - **4.** [folding table, chair] sich zusammenklappen lassen.
collapsible [kə'læpsəbl] *adj* zusammenklappbar.
collar ['kɒləʳ] ◇ *n* - **1.** [on clothes] Kragen *der* - **2.** [for dog] Halsband *das* - **3.** TECH Bund *der.* ◇ *vt inf* [detain] fassen.
collarbone ['kɒləbəʊn] *n* Schlüsselbein *das.*
collate [kə'leɪt] *vt* - **1.** [information, evidence] sammeln - **2.** [pages, photocopies] sortieren.
collateral [kə'lætərəl] *n* Sicherheit *die.*
colleague ['kɒliːg] *n* Kollege *der*, -gin *die.*
collect [kə'lekt] ◇ *vt* - **1.** [gen] sammeln; [empty glasses, bottles] ein|sammeln; [dust] an|ziehen; [one's belongings] zusammen|suchen; [taxes] ein|ziehen; **to collect o.s.** sich sammeln - **2.** [go to get, fetch] ab|holen. ◇ *vi* - **1.** [dust, dirt] sich an|sammeln - **2.** [for charity, gift] sammeln. ◇ *adv US* TELEC: **to call (sb) collect** ein R-Gespräch (mit jm) führen.
collection [kə'lekʃn] *n* - **1.** [gen] Sammlung *die* - **2.** *(U)* [of taxes] Einziehen *das*; [of rubbish] Abfuhr *die*; [of mail] Leerung *die.*
collective [kə'lektɪv] ◇ *adj* kollektiv. ◇ *n* Produktionsgenossenschaft *die.*
collector [kə'lektəʳ] *n* [as a hobby] Sammler *der*, -in *die.*
college ['kɒlɪdʒ] *n* - **1.** [for further education] ≃ Fachhochschule *die*; **college of technology** technische Hochschule - **2.** [of university] College *das.*
college of education *n* pädagogische Hochschule.

collide [kə'laɪd] *vi*: **to collide (with sb/sthg)** (mit jm/etw) zusammen|stoßen.
colliery ['kɒljərɪ] *n* Kohlengrube *die*.
collision [kə'lɪʒn] *n* [crash]: **collision (with sb/sthg)** Zusammenstoß *der* (mit jm/etw), Kollision *die* (mit jm/etw); **to be on a collision course with sb/sthg** *fig* mit jm/etw auf Kollisionskurs sein.
colloquial [kə'ləʊkwɪəl] *adj* umgangssprachlich.
collude [kə'lu:d] *vi*: **to collude with sb** mit jm gemeinsame Sache machen.
Colombia [kə'lɒmbɪə] *n* Kolumbien *nt*.
colon ['kəʊlən] *n* - **1.** ANAT Dickdarm *der* - **2.** [punctuation mark] Doppelpunkt *der*.
colonel ['kɜ:nl] *n* Oberst *der*.
colonial [kə'ləʊnjəl] *adj* kolonial-.
colonize, -ise ['kɒlənaɪz] *vt* kolonisieren.
colony ['kɒlənɪ] *n* Kolonie *die*.
color *etc n, adj, vt & vi US* = **colour** *etc* .
colossal [kə'lɒsl] *adj* gewaltig.
colour *UK*, **color** *US* ['kʌlə^r] ◇ *n* Farbe *die*; **in colour** in Farbe. ◇ *adj* [not black and white] Farb-. ◇ *vt* - **1.** [give colour to] färben; [with pen, crayon] kolorieren - **2.** *fig* [affect] beeinflussen. ◇ *vi* [blush] erröten.
colour bar *n* Rassenschranke *die*.
colour-blind *adj* farbenblind.
coloured *UK*, **colored** *US* ['kʌləd] *adj* farbig.
colourful *UK*, **colorful** *US* ['kʌləfʊl] *adj* - **1.** [brightly coloured] farbenfroh - **2.** [story] ereignisreich; [description] farbig - **3.** [person] schillernd.
colouring *UK*, **coloring** *US* ['kʌlərɪŋ] *n* - **1.** [dye] Farbstoff *der* - **2.** [complexion] Gesichtsfarbe *die*; [of hair] Farbe *die* - **3.** [colours] Farben *Pl*.
colour scheme *n* Farbzusammenstellung *die*.
colt [kəʊlt] *n* Hengstfohlen *das*.
column ['kɒləm] *n* - **1.** [structure, of smoke] Säule *die* - **2.** [of people, vehicles, numbers] Kolonne *die* - **3.** [of text] Spalte *die* - **4.** [article] Kolumne *die*.
columnist ['kɒləmnɪst] *n* Kolumnist *der*, -in *die*.
coma ['kəʊmə] *n* Koma *das*.
comb [kəʊm] ◇ *n* Kamm *der*. ◇ *vt* - **1.** [hair] kämmen - **2.** [search] durchkämmen.
combat ['kɒmbæt] ◇ *n* Kampf *der*. ◇ *vt* bekämpfen.
combination [,kɒmbɪ'neɪʃn] *n* - **1.** *(U)* [act of combining] Verbindung *die* - **2.** [mixture, for safe] Kombination *die*.
combine ◇ *vt* [kəm'baɪn] vereinigen; **to combine sthg with sthg** [two substances, activities] etw mit etw verbinden; [two qualities] etw mit etw vereinigen. ◇ *vi* [kəm'baɪn] [businesses, political parties]: **to combine (with sb/sthg)** sich (mit jm/etw) zusammen|schließen. ◇ *n* ['kɒmbaɪn] [group] Firmengruppe *die*.
combined *adj*: **combined with sb/sthg** zusammen mit jm/etw; **combined efforts** vereinte Anstrengungen *Pl*; **combined attack** gemeinsamer Angriff.
come [kʌm] (*pt* **came**, *pp* **come**) *vi* - **1.** [move] kommen; **come here!** komm her!; **coming!** ich komme schon! - **2.** [arrive] kommen; **to come home** nach Hause kommen; **the news came as a shock (to him)** die Nachricht war ein Schock (für ihn) - **3.** [in competition, in order]: **to come first/last** Erster/Letzter werden; **P comes before Q** P kommt vor Q - **4.** [become] werden; **to come true** wahr werden; **to come undone** auf|gehen - **5.** [be sold]: **they come in packs of six** es gibt sie im Sechserpack - **6.** [happen]: **come what may** was auch geschieht.- **7.** [begin gradually]: **we have come to think that** wir sind zu der Ansicht gekommen, dass; **he has come to like Baltimore** inzwischen gefällt ihm Baltimore recht gut - **8.** *inf* [have orgasm] kommen - **9.** *phr*: **come to think of it** wenn ich es mir recht überlege. ◆ **to come** *adv*: **for generations to come** auf Generationen hin; **in years to come we will look back on today with pride** wir werden später mit Stolz auf diesen Tag zurückblicken. ◆ **come about** *vi* [happen] geschehen; [come into being] entstehen; **how did it come about?** wie ist es dazu gekommen? ◆ **come across** *vt insep* [find] stoßen auf *(+ A)*. ◆ **come along** *vi* - **1.** [arrive] kommen - **2.** [progress] voran|kommen. ◆ **come apart** *vi* auseinander fallen. ◆ **come at** *vt insep* [attack] los|gehen auf *(+ A)*. ◆ **come back** *vi* - **1.** [gen] zurück|kommen; **to come back to sthg** auf etw *(A)* zurück|kommen - **2.** [memory]: **it will come back to me in a minute** es wird mir gleich einfallen. ◆ **come by** *vt insep* [get, obtain]: **to come by sthg** an etw *(A)* kommen; **they are hard to come by** sie sind schwer zu finden. ◆ **come down** *vi* - **1.** [price, rain] fallen - **2.** [descend] herunter|kommen. ◆ **come down to** *vt insep*: **it comes down to a choice between money and happiness** es läuft auf eine Entscheidung zwischen Geld und Glück hinaus; **it all comes down to profitability** letztlich ist die Rentabilität entscheidend. ◆ **come down with** *vt insep* [illness] bekommen. ◆ **come forward** *vi* sich melden. ◆ **come from** *vt insep* - **1.** [person]: **I come from Ireland** ich komme aus Irland; **my family comes from Belgium** meine Familie stammt aus Belgien - **2.** [originate from]: **caviar comes from sturgeon** Kaviar stammt vom Stör; **where is that noise coming from?** woher kommt dieses Geräusch? ◆ **come in** *vi* - **1.** [enter] herein|kommen; **come in!** herein! - **2.** [finish race] an|kommen; **to come in first**

Erste/Erster werden. ◆ **come in for** *vt insep* [criticism] einstecken müssen. ◆ **come into** *vt insep* - **1.** [inherit] erben - **2.** [begin to be]: **to come into being** entstehen. ◆ **come off** *vi* - **1.** [button, top] ab|gehen - **2.** [succeed] klappen - **3.** [dirt, mud] ab|gehen - **4.** *phr*: **come off it!** *inf* hör doch auf! ◆ **come on** *vi* - **1.** [start] an|fangen; **the rain came on** es fing an zu regnen - **2.** [start working - light, machine] an|gehen - **3.** [progress] voran|kommen - **4.** *phr*: **come on!** [as encouragement, hurry up] komm!; [in disbelief] hör doch auf! ◆ **come out** *vi* - **1.** [become known] heraus|kommen - **2.** [appear - book, record] erscheinen; [- stars] zu sehen sein - **3.** [go on strike] streiken - **4.** [declare publicly]: **to come out for/against sthg** sich für/gegen etw aus|sprechen - **5.** [stain] heraus|gehen. ◆ **come out with** *vt insep* [idea] an|kommen mit; [remark] machen. ◆ **come round** *vi* - **1.** [visit] vorbei|kommen - **2.** [regain consciousness] zu sich kommen. ◆ **come through** ◇ *vt insep* [war, illness, difficult situation] überstehen. ◇ *vi* [survive] durch|kommen. ◆ **come to** ◇ *vt insep* - **1.** [reach]: **to come to an end** zu Ende gehen; **to come to a decision** zu einer Entscheidung kommen - **2.** [amount to]: **the bill comes to £20** das macht 20 Pfund. ◇ *vi* [regain consciousness] zu sich kommen. ◆ **come under** *vt insep* - **1.** [be governed by - jurisdiction, rules] fallen unter *(+ A)*; **to come under sb's influence** unter js Einfluss geraten - **2.** [suffer]: **to come under attack (from)** angegriffen werden (von). ◆ **come up** *vi* - **1.** [go upstairs] herauf|kommen - **2.** [be mentioned] erwähnt werden; **to come up for discussion** zur Diskussion kommen - **3.** [happen] passieren - **4.** [job] frei werden - **5.** [sun, moon] auf|gehen - **6.** [be imminent] bevor|stehen; **my birthday is coming up** ich habe bald Geburtstag. ◆ **come up against** *vt insep* [difficulties, obstacles] stoßen auf *(+ A)*; [opponent] treffen auf *(+ A)*. ◆ **come up to** *vt insep* - **1.** [approach - person, object] kommen zu; **it's coming up to Christmas/six o'clock** es ist bald Weihnachten/gleich sechs Uhr - **2.** [reach]: **the water comes up to my waist** das Wasser reicht mir bis zur Taille. ◆ **come up with** *vt insep* [answer, idea, solution] sich *(D)* aus|denken.

comeback ['kʌmbæk] *n* [of person] Comeback *das*; **to make a comeback** [person] ein Come-back schaffen; [activity, style] wieder in Mode kommen.

comedian [kə'mi:djən] *n* Komiker *der*, -in *die*.

comedown ['kʌmdaʊn] *n inf* Abstieg *der*.

comedy ['kɒmədɪ] *n* - **1.** [play, film] Komödie *die* - **2.** [humour] Komik *die*.

comet ['kɒmɪt] *n* Komet *der*.

come-uppance [,kʌm'ʌpəns] *n inf*: **to get one's come-uppance** die Quittung kriegen.

comfort ['kʌmfət] ◇ *n* - **1.** [ease] Behaglichkeit *die* - **2.** [luxury] Komfort *der* - **3.** [solace] Trost *der*; **to take comfort from sthg** Trost in etw *(D)* finden. ◇ *vt* trösten.

comfortable ['kʌmftəbl] *adj* - **1.** [chair, shoes, sofa, life] bequem; [house, hotel, coach] komfortabel - **2.** [at ease]: **to be comfortable** sich wohl fühlen; **make yourself comfortable** machen Sie es sich bequem - **3.** [financially secure - income] ausreichend; **to be comfortable** keine finanziellen Sorgen haben - **4.** [after operation, accident]: **his condition is comfortable** ihm geht es (den Umständen entsprechend) gut - **5.** [lead] sicher; [victory] leicht.

comfortably ['kʌmftəblɪ] *adv* - **1.** [sit] bequem; [sleep] gut - **2.** [without financial difficulty] bequem - **3.** [win] mühelos.

comfort station *n US euph* Bedürfnisanstalt *die*.

comic ['kɒmɪk] ◇ *adj* komisch. ◇ *n* - **1.** [comedian] Komiker *der*, -in *die* - **2.** [magazine] Comicheft *das*.

comical ['kɒmɪkl] *adj* ulkig, komisch.

comic strip *n* Comicstrip *der*.

coming ['kʌmɪŋ] ◇ *adj* [future] kommend. ◇ *n*: **comings and goings** Kommen und Gehen *das*.

comma ['kɒmə] *n* Komma *das*.

command [kə'mɑ:nd] ◇ *n* - **1.** [order] Befehl *der*; MIL Kommando *das* - **2.** *(U)* [control] Kommando *das* - **3.** [mastery] Beherrschung *die*; **to have sthg at one's command** etw zur Verfügung haben - **4.** COMPUT Befehl *der*. ◇ *vt* - **1.** [order]: **to command sb (to do sthg)** jm befehlen(, etw zu tun) - **2.** MIL [control] befehligen - **3.** [deserve - respect, attention, admiration] verdienen.

commandeer [,kɒmən'dɪə'] *vt* MIL beschlagnahmen.

commander [kə'mɑ:ndə'] *n* - **1.** [in army] Kommandant *der*, Befehlshaber *der* - **2.** [in navy] Fregattenkapitän *der*.

commando [kə'mɑ:ndəʊ] (*pl* **-s** OR **-es**) *n* - **1.** [unit] Kommandotrupp *der* - **2.** [soldier] Angehörige *der, die* eines Kommandotrupps.

commemorate [kə'meməreɪt] *vt* - **1.** [honour] gedenken *(+ G)* - **2.** [subj: statue, plaque] erinnern an *(+ A)*.

commemoration [kə,memə'reɪʃn] *n*: **in commemoration of** zum Gedenken an *(+ A)*.

commence [kə'mens] *fml* ◇ *vt* beginnen; **to commence doing sthg** (damit) beginnen, etw zu tun. ◇ *vi* beginnen.

commend [kə'mend] *vt* - **1.** [praise]: **to commend sb (on** OR **for sthg)** jn (wegen etw) loben - **2.** [recommend]: **to commend sthg (to sb)** (jm) etw empfehlen.

commensurate [kə'menʃərət] *adj fml*: **to be commensurate with sthg** etw *(D)* entsprechen.

comment ['kɒment] ◇ *n* Bemerkung *die*; **no comment** kein Kommentar. ◇ *vt*: **to comment that...** bemerken OR äußern, dass... ◇ *vi*: **to comment (on sthg)** sich (über etw *(A)*) äußern.

commentary ['kɒməntrɪ] *n* - **1.** RADIO & TV Livereportage *die* - **2.** [written] Kommentar *der*.

commentator ['kɒmənteɪtəʳ] *n* RADIO & TV Reporter *der*, -in *die*.

commerce ['kɒmɜːs] *n* Handel *der*.

commercial [kə'mɜːʃl] ◇ *adj* - **1.** [regarding business - law, organization] Handels-; [- premises] Geschäfts- - **2.** [profit-making] kommerziell. ◇ *n* [advert] Werbespot *der*.

commercial break *n* Werbepause *die*.

commiserate [kə'mɪzəreɪt] *vi*: **to commiserate (with sb)** (jm) sein Mitgefühl ausl-sprechen.

commission [kə'mɪʃn] ◇ *n* - **1.** *(U)* [money] Provision *die* - **2.** [piece of work] Auftrag *der* - **3.** [investigative body] Kommission *die*. ◇ *vt* [work] in Auftrag geben; **to commission sb to do sthg** jn damit beauftragen(, etw zu tun).

commissionaire [kəˌmɪʃə'neəʳ] *n UK* Portier *der*.

commissioner [kə'mɪʃnəʳ] *n* [of police] Präsident *der*, -in *die*.

commit [kə'mɪt] *vt* - **1.** [crime, sin] begehen - **2.** [money, resources]: **to commit sthg to sthg** etw für etw bestimmen; **to commit o.s. (to sthg)** sich (auf etw *(A)*) festllegen; **to commit o.s. to doing sthg** sich verpflichten, etw zu tun - **3.** [consign] einlweisen; **to commit sthg to memory** sich *(D)* etw merken.

commitment [kə'mɪtmənt] *n* - **1.** [dedication] Engagement *das* - **2.** [responsibility] Verpflichtung *die*.

committee [kə'mɪtɪ] *n* Ausschuss *der*.

commodity [kə'mɒdətɪ] *n* [product] Produkt *das*.

common ['kɒmən] ◇ *adj* - **1.** [ordinary, widespread] häufig; [practice] weit verbreitet; **the common cold** die Erkältung; **the common man** der Normalbürger - **2.** [shared] gemeinsam; **it's common to us all** es ist uns allen gemein - **3.** *UK pej* [vulgar] gewöhnlich. ◇ *n* [land] Gemeinde *die*. ◆ **in common** *adv* gemein; **we've got a lot in common** wir haben viel gemein.

common-law *adj*: **she is his common-law wife** sie lebt mit ihm in eheähnlicher Gemeinschaft.

commonly ['kɒmənlɪ] *adv* [generally] allgemein.

Common Market *n*: **the Common Market** der Gemeinsame Markt.

commonplace ['kɒmənpleɪs] *adj* alltäglich.

common room *n* Aufenthaltsraum *der*.

Commons ['kɒmənz] *npl UK*: **the Commons** das (britische) Unterhaus.

common sense *n* gesunder Menschenverstand.

Commonwealth ['kɒmənwelθ] *n*: **the Commonwealth** das Commonwealth.

commotion [kə'məʊʃn] *n* [activity] Aufregung *die*; [noise] Lärm *der*; **to cause a commotion** für Aufregung sorgen.

communal ['kɒmjʊnl] *adj* [kitchen] Gemeinschafts-; [garden, ownership] gemeinsam.

commune *n* ['kɒmjuːn] Kommune *die*.

communicate [kə'mjuːnɪkeɪt] ◇ *vt* mitlteilen. ◇ *vi* sich verständigen; **to communicate with** kommunizieren mit.

communication [kəˌmjuːnɪ'keɪʃn] *n* - **1.** *(U)* [contact] Kommunikation *die*; **to be in communication with sb** Kontakt mit jm haben - **2.** [letter, phone call] Mitteilung *die*.

communication cord *n UK* Notbremse *die*.

Communion [kə'mjuːnjən] *n* [Protestant] Abendmahl *das*; [Catholic] Kommunion *die*.

Communism ['kɒmjʊnɪzm] *n* Kommunismus *der*.

Communist ['kɒmjʊnɪst] ◇ *adj* kommunistisch. ◇ *n* Kommunist *der*, -in *die*.

community [kə'mjuːnətɪ] *n* - **1.** [group] Gemeinschaft *die*; [local] Gemeinde *die*; [ethnic] Bevölkerungsgruppe *die* - **2.** [people in general]: **the community** die Gesellschaft.

community centre *n* Gemeindezentrum *das*.

commutation ticket [ˌkɒmjuː'teɪʃn] *n US* Zeitnetzkarte *die*.

commute [kə'mjuːt] ◇ *vt* LAW umlwandeln. ◇ *vi* [to work] pendeln.

commuter [kə'mjuːtəʳ] *n* Pendler *der*, -in *die*.

compact ◇ *adj* [kəm'pækt] kompakt; [style, text] gedrängt. ◇ *n* ['kɒmpækt] - **1.** [for face powder] Puderdose *die* - **2.** *US* AUT: **compact (car)** Kompaktauto *das*.

compact disc *n* Compactdisc *die*.

compact disc player *n* CD-Player *der*.

companion [kəm'pænjən] *n* [person] Gefährte *der*, -tin *die*.

companionship [kəm'pænjənʃɪp] *n (U)* Gesellschaft *die*.

company ['kʌmpənɪ] *n* - **1.** [business] Firma *die*; **insurance company** Versicherung *die* - **2.** [of actors] Schauspieltruppe *die* - **3.** *(U)* [companionship] Gesellschaft *die*; **she's good company** es ist schön, mit ihr zusammen zu sein; **to keep sb company** jm Gesellschaft leisten - **4.** [guests] Besuch *der* - **5.** MIL Kompanie *die* - **6.** NAUT Besatzung *die*.

comparable ['kɒmprəbl] *adj*: **comparable (to** OR **with)** vergleichbar (mit).

comparative [kəm'pærətɪv] *adj* - **1.** [relative] relativ - **2.** [study, literature] vergleichend - **3.** GRAM: **comparative form** Komparativ *der*.

comparatively [kəm'pærətɪvlɪ] *adv* [relatively] relativ, verhältnismäßig.

compare [kəm'peəʳ] ◇ *vt* vergleichen; **to compare sb/sthg with** *OR* **to** jn/etw vergleichen mit; **compared with** *OR* **to** verglichen mit, im Vergleich zu. ◇ *vi*: **to compare (with sb/ sthg)** sich (mit jm/etw) vergleichen lassen.

comparison [kəm'pærɪsn] *n* Vergleich *der*; **in comparison (with** *OR* **to)** im Vergleich (zu).

compartment [kəm'pɑːtmənt] *n* - **1.** [in fridge, desk, drawer] Fach *das* - **2.** RAIL Abteil *das*.

compass ['kʌmpəs] *n* [for finding direction] Kompass *der*. ◆ **compasses** *npl*: **(a pair of) compasses** ein Zirkel.

compassion [kəm'pæʃn] *n* Mitgefühl *das*.

compassionate [kəm'pæʃənət] *adj* mitfühlend.

compatible [kəm'pætəbl] *adj* - **1.** [people]: **to be compatible** zueinander passen - **2.** COMPUT kompatibel.

compel [kəm'pel] *vt* [force] zwingen; **to compel sb to do sthg** jn (dazu) zwingen, etw zu tun.

compelling [kəm'pelɪŋ] *adj* zwingend.

compensate ['kɒmpenseɪt] ◇ *vt*: **to compensate sb for sthg** [financially] jn für etw entschädigen. ◇ *vi*: **to compensate for sthg** etw gut|machen.

compensation [ˌkɒmpen'seɪʃn] *n*: **compensation (for sthg)** Entschädigung *die* (für etw).

compete [kəm'piːt] *vi* - **1.** [vie]: **to compete (for sthg)** (um etw) kämpfen - **2.** COMM: **to compete (with sb/sthg)** (mit jm/etw) konkurrieren; **to compete for sthg** [contract, business] um etw kämpfen - **3.** [take part] teil|nehmen.

competence ['kɒmpɪtəns] *n* Fähigkeit *die*.

competent ['kɒmpɪtənt] *adj* fähig.

competition [ˌkɒmpɪ'tɪʃn] *n* - **1.** [rivalry & COMM] Konkurrenz *die* - **2.** [race, contest] Wettbewerb *der*.

competitive [kəm'petətɪv] *adj* - **1.** [person] vom Konkurrenzdenken geprägt - **2.** [exam] Auswahl-; [sport] Wettkampf- - **3.** COMM [goods, prices, company] konkurrenzfähig.

competitor [kəm'petɪtəʳ] *n* - **1.** COMM Konkurrent *der*, -in *die* - **2.** [in race, contest] Teilnehmer *der*, -in *die*.

compile [kəm'paɪl] *vt* [programme, album] zusammen|stellen; [book, report] ab|fassen.

complacency [kəm'pleɪsnsɪ] *n* Selbstzufriedenheit *die*.

complain [kəm'pleɪn] *vi* - **1.** [moan]: **to complain (about)** sich beschweren (über *(+ A)*) - **2.** MED: **to complain of sthg** über etw *(A)* klagen.

complaint [kəm'pleɪnt] *n* - **1.** [gen] Beschwerde *die*; **to have no complaints** [be satisfied] sich nicht beklagen können - **2.** MED Leiden *das*.

complement ◇ *vt* ['kɒmplɪˌment] gut ergänzen; [food] vervollkommnen. ◇ *n* ['kɒmplɪmənt] [accompaniment & GRAM] Ergänzung *die*.

complementary [ˌkɒmplɪ'mentərɪ] *adj* [colour] (einander) ergänzend.

complete [kəm'pliːt] ◇ *adj* - **1.** [entire] vollständig; **complete with** komplett mit - **2.** [finished] abgeschlossen, fertig - **3.** [total - disaster, surprise] völlig; **she was a complete stranger to me** sie war mir völlig fremd. ◇ *vt* - **1.** [make whole] vervollständigen - **2.** [finish] beenden - **3.** [questionnaire, form] aus|füllen.

completely [kəm'pliːtlɪ] *adv* vollkommen.

completion [kəm'pliːʃn] *n* [finishing] Beendigung *die*.

complex ['kɒmpleks] ◇ *adj* [complicated] kompliziert. ◇ *n* - **1.** [of buildings] (Gebäude)komplex *der* - **2.** PSYCHOL Komplex *der*.

complexion [kəm'plekʃn] *n* - **1.** [of face] Teint *der* - **2.** [aspect] Aspekt *der*.

compliance [kəm'plaɪəns] *n* Einverständnis *das*; **compliance with sthg** [with rules] Einhalten *das* einer Sache *(G)*.

complicate ['kɒmplɪkeɪt] *vt* komplizieren.

complicated ['kɒmplɪkeɪtɪd] *adj* kompliziert.

complication [ˌkɒmplɪ'keɪʃn] *n* - **1.** [complexity] Kompliziertheit *die* - **2.** MED Komplikation *die*.

compliment ◇ *n* ['kɒmplɪmənt] Kompliment *das*. ◇ *vt* ['kɒmplɪˌment]: **to compliment sb (on sthg)** jm ein Kompliment/Komplimente (wegen etw *(G)*) machen. ◆ **compliments** *npl fml*: **with compliments** mit den besten Empfehlungen; **my compliments to the chef!** mein Kompliment an den Küchenchef!

complimentary [ˌkɒmplɪ'mentərɪ] *adj* - **1.** [admiring] schmeichelhaft; **to be complimentary** [person] sich bewundernd äußern - **2.** [drink] Frei-.

complimentary ticket *n* Freikarte *die*.

comply [kəm'plaɪ] *vi*: **to comply with sthg** [contract] etw erfüllen; [request] etw *(D)* nach|kommen; [law, standards] etw ein|halten.

component [kəm'pəʊnənt] *n* Teil *das*.

compose [kəm'pəʊz] *vt* - **1.** [constitute] bilden; **to be composed of sthg** sich aus etw zusammen|setzen - **2.** [poem] verfassen; [music] komponieren; [letter] ab|fassen - **3.** [make calm]: **to compose o.s.** sich fassen.

composed [kəm'pəʊzd] *adj* [calm] beherrscht, gelassen.

composer [kəm'pəʊzəʳ] *n* Komponist *der*, -in *die*.

composition [ˌkɒmpəˈzɪʃn] *n* - **1.** [piece of music] Komposition *die* - **2.** [contents] Zusammensetzung *die* - **3.** [essay] Aufsatz *der*.

compost [*UK* ˈkɒmpɒst, *US* ˈkɒmpəʊst] *n* Kompost *der*.

composure [kəmˈpəʊʒəʳ] *n* Beherrschung *die*, Fassung *die*.

compound *n* [ˈkɒmpaʊnd] - **1.** CHEM Verbindung *die* - **2.** [mixture] Mischung *die* - **3.** [enclosed area] umzäuntes Gelände - **4.** GRAM zusammengesetztes Wort.

comprehend [ˌkɒmprɪˈhend] *vt* [understand] begreifen, verstehen.

comprehension [ˌkɒmprɪˈhenʃn] *n* Verständnis *das*; **it's beyond my comprehension** es ist mir unbegreiflich.

comprehensive [ˌkɒmprɪˈhensɪv] *adj* - **1.** [wide-ranging] umfassend - **2.** [insurance] Vollkasko-.

comprehensive (school) *n UK* Gesamtschule *die*.

compress ◇ *n* [ˈkɒmpres] MED Kompresse *die*. ◇ *vt* [kəmˈpres] - **1.** [squeeze] zusammen|pressen; **compressed air** Pressluft *die* - **2.** [text] kürzen.

comprise [kəmˈpraɪz] *vt* - **1.** [consist of]: **to be comprised of** bestehen aus - **2.** [constitute] bilden.

compromise [ˈkɒmprəmaɪz] ◇ *n* Kompromiss *der*. ◇ *vt* kompromittieren. ◇ *vi* einen Kompromiss schließen.

compulsion [kəmˈpʌlʃn] *n* Zwang *der*.

compulsive [kəmˈpʌlsɪv] *adj* [behaviour, gambler, liar] zwanghaft.

compulsory [kəmˈpʌlsərɪ] *adj* [retirement] Zwangs-; **it is compulsory to do sthg** es ist Pflicht, etw zu tun; **attendance is compulsory** die Teilnahme ist verpflichtend.

computer [kəmˈpjuːtəʳ] ◇ *n* Computer *der*. ◇ *comp* Computer-.

computer game *n* Computerspiel *das*.

computerized [kəmˈpjuːtəraɪzd] *adj* computerisiert.

computer science *n* Informatik *die*.

computing [kəmˈpjuːtɪŋ] *n* elektronische Datenverarbeitung; [subject] Informatik *die*.

comrade [ˈkɒmreɪd] *n* - **1.** POL Genosse *der*, -sin *die* - **2.** [companion] Kamerad *der*, -in *die*.

con [kɒn] *inf* ◇ *n* [trick] Schwindel *der*. ◇ *vt* [trick] rein|legen; **to con sb out of sthg** jn um etw bringen; **to con sb into doing sthg** jn durch einen Trick dazu bringen, etw zu tun.

concave [ˌkɒnˈkeɪv] *adj* konkav.

conceal [kənˈsiːl] *vt (phrase)*: **to conceal sthg (from sb)** [object] etw (vor jm) verstecken; [feelings, information] etw (vor jm) verbergen.

concede [kənˈsiːd] *vt* [a point] zu|geben; [defeat] ein|gestehen.

conceit [kənˈsiːt] *n* Arroganz *die*.

conceited [kənˈsiːtɪd] *adj* eingebildet.

conceive [kənˈsiːv] ◇ *vt* - **1.** [plan, idea] sich *(D)* aus|denken - **2.** MED [child] empfangen. ◇ *vi* - **1.** MED empfangen - **2.** [imagine]: **to conceive of sthg** sich *(D)* etw vor|stellen.

concentrate [ˈkɒnsəntreɪt] ◇ *vt* konzentrieren. ◇ *vi*: **to concentrate (on)** sich konzentrieren (auf *(+ A)*).

concentration [ˌkɒnsənˈtreɪʃn] *n* Konzentration *die*.

concentration camp *n* Konzentrationslager *das*, KZ *das*.

concept [ˈkɒnsept] *n* [idea] Vorstellung *die*; [principle] Konzept *das*.

concern [kənˈsɜːn] ◇ *n* - **1.** [worry] Besorgnis *die*; [cause of worry] Sorge *die*; **to show concern for sb/sthg** sich um jn/etw Gedanken machen - **2.** COMM [company] Unternehmen *das*. ◇ *vt* - **1.** [worry] beunruhigen; **to be concerned (about)** besorgt sein (um) - **2.** [involve] an|gehen; **to be concerned with sthg** [subj: person] mit etw zu tun haben; **to concern o.s. with sthg** sich mit etw befassen; **as far as I'm concerned** was mich betrifft - **3.** [subj: book, film] handeln von.

concerning [kənˈsɜːnɪŋ] *prep* bezüglich *(+ G)*.

concert [ˈkɒnsət] *n* Konzert *das*.

concerted [kənˈsɜːtɪd] *adj* [effort] vereint.

concert hall *n* Konzerthalle *die*.

concertina [ˌkɒnsəˈtiːnə] *n* Konzertina *die*.

concerto [kənˈtʃɜːtəʊ] (*pl* **-s**) *n* Konzert *das*.

concession [kənˈseʃn] *n* - **1.** [allowance] Zugeständnis *das* - **2.** COMM [franchise] Konzession *die* - **3.** [special price] Preisermäßigung *die*.

concise [kənˈsaɪs] *adj* präzis(e), exakt.

conclude [kənˈkluːd] ◇ *vt* - **1.** [end] beenden - **2.** [deduce]: **to conclude (that)...** schließen(, dass)..., folgern(, dass)... - **3.** [agreement, deal] ab|schließen. ◇ *vi* [finish] enden, schließen.

conclusion [kənˈkluːʒn] *n* - **1.** [opinion] Schlussfolgerung *die* - **2.** [ending] Abschluss *der* - **3.** [of agreement, deal] Abschluss *der*.

conclusive [kənˈkluːsɪv] *adj* eindeutig.

concoct [kənˈkɒkt] *vt* - **1.** [story, excuse, alibi] sich *(D)* aus|denken - **2.** [meal] kreieren; [drink] zusammen|brauen.

concoction [kənˈkɒkʃn] *n* [meal] selbst kreiertes Gericht; [drink] Gebräu *das*.

concourse [ˈkɒŋkɔːs] *n* [hall] Eingangshalle *die*.

concrete [ˈkɒŋkriːt] ◇ *adj liter* & *fig* konkret. ◇ *n* Beton *der*. ◇ *comp* [made of concrete] Beton-.

concur [kənˈkɜːʳ] *vi* [agree]: **to concur (with sthg)** (etw *(D)*) zu|stimmen.

concurrently [kən'kʌrəntlɪ] *adv* gleichzeitig.

concussion [kən'kʌʃn] *n* Gehirnerschütterung *die*.

condemn [kən'dem] *vt* - **1.** [disapprove of]: **to condemn sb (for sthg)** jn (wegen etw *(G)*) verurteilen - **2.** [force] verdammen - **3.** LAW [sentence]: **to condemn sb to sthg** jn zu etw verurteilen - **4.** [building] für unbewohnbar erklären.

condensation [ˌkɒnden'seɪʃn] *n* [on windows *etc*] Kondenswasser *das*.

condense [kən'dens] *vt* [text] zusammen|fassen.

condensed milk [kən'denst-] *n* Kondensmilch *die*.

condescending [ˌkɒndɪ'sendɪŋ] *adj* herablassend.

condition [kən'dɪʃn] ◇ *n* - **1.** [of object, building] Zustand *der*; [of person, patient] Verfassung *die*; **out of condition** schlecht in Form - **2.** MED [illness] Leiden *das* - **3.** [requirement] Bedingung *die*, Voraussetzung *die*; **on condition that** unter der Bedingung, dass. ◇ *vt* - **1.** PSYCHOL konditionieren - **2.** [determine] bestimmen - **3.** [hair] pflegen.

conditional [kən'dɪʃənl] ◇ *adj* [provisional] vorbehaltlich. ◇ *n* GRAM Konditional *der*.

conditioner [kən'dɪʃnəʳ] *n* - **1.** [for hair] Pflegespülung *die* - **2.** [for clothes] Weichspüler *der*.

condolences [kən'dəʊlənsɪz] *npl* Beileid *das*.

condom ['kɒndəm] *n* Kondom *der ODER das*.

condominium [ˌkɒndə'mɪnɪəm] *n US* - **1.** [apartment] Eigentumswohnung *die* - **2.** [building] Apartmenthaus *das*.

condone [kən'dəʊn] *vt* hinweg|sehen über *(+ A)*.

conducive [kən'dju:sɪv] *adj*: **to be conducive to sthg** einer Sache *(D)* förderlich sein.

conduct ◇ *n* ['kɒndʌkt] - **1.** [behaviour] Verhalten *das* - **2.** [of business, talks] Durchführung *die*. ◇ *vt* [kən'dʌkt] - **1.** [carry out] durch|führen - **2.** [behave]: **to conduct o.s. well/badly** sich gut/schlecht benehmen - **3.** MUS dirigieren - **4.** PHYS [heat, electricity] leiten.

conducted tour [kən'dʌktɪd-] *n* Führung *die*.

conductor [kən'dʌktəʳ] *n* - **1.** MUS Dirigent *der*, -in *die* - **2.** [on bus] Schaffner *der*, -in *die* - **3.** *US* [on train] Zugführer *der*.

cone [kəʊn] *n* - **1.** [shape] Kegel *der* - **2.** [for ice cream] Eistüte *die* - **3.** [from tree] Zapfen *der* - **4.** [on roads] Pylon *der*, Pylone *die*.

confectionery [kən'fekʃnərɪ] *n (U)* Süßwaren *Pl*.

confederation [kənˌfedə'reɪʃn] *n* Bund *der*.

confer [kən'fɜ:ʳ] ◇ *vt fml*: **to confer sthg (on sb)** [title, degree] (jm) etw verleihen. ◇ *vi*: **to confer (with sb on** *OR* **about sthg)** sich (mit jm über etw *(A)*) beraten.

conference ['kɒnfərəns] *n* Konferenz *die*.

confess [kən'fes] ◇ *vt* - **1.** RELIG beichten - **2.** [admit] gestehen. ◇ *vi* [admit]: **to confess (to sthg)** (etw) gestehen.

confession [kən'feʃn] *n* - **1.** [of guilt] Geständnis *das* - **2.** *(U)* RELIG Beichte *die*.

confetti [kən'fetɪ] *n (U)* Konfetti *Pl*.

confide [kən'faɪd] *vi*: **to confide in sb** sich jm an|vertrauen.

confidence ['kɒnfɪdəns] *n* - **1.** *(U)* [self-assurance] Selbstvertrauen *das* - **2.** *(U)* [trust] Vertrauen *das*; **to have confidence in sb** Vertrauen zu jm haben - **3.** [secrecy]: **in confidence** im Vertrauen - **4.** [secret] vertrauliche Information.

confidence trick *n* Schwindel *der*.

confident ['kɒnfɪdənt] *adj* - **1.** [self-assured] selbstbewusst - **2.** [sure] überzeugt; **to be confident of sthg** von etw überzeugt sein.

confidential [ˌkɒnfɪ'denʃl] *adj* vertraulich.

confine *vt* [kən'faɪn] beschränken; **to be confined to** beschränkt sein auf *(+ A)*; **to confine o.s. to sthg** sich auf etw *(A)* beschränken; **to confine o.s. to doing sthg** sich darauf beschränken, etw zu tun. ◆ **confines** *npl* Grenzen *Pl*.

confined [kən'faɪnd] *adj* [space, area] beschränkt.

confinement [kən'faɪnmənt] *n* [state of imprisonment] Haft *die*.

confirm [kən'fɜ:m] *vt* - **1.** [gen] bestätigen - **2.** RELIG konfirmieren; [Roman Catholic] firmen.

confirmation [ˌkɒnfə'meɪʃn] *n (U)* - **1.** [ratification] Bestätigung *die* - **2.** RELIG Konfirmation *die*; [of Roman Catholic] Firmung *die*.

confirmed [kən'fɜ:md] *adj* [bachelor, spinster] überzeugt.

confiscate ['kɒnfɪskeɪt] *vt* beschlagnahmen, konfiszieren.

conflict ◇ *n* ['kɒnflɪkt] Konflikt *der*. ◇ *vi* [kən'flɪkt] [clash] sich *(D)* widersprechen; **to conflict with sb/sthg** im Widerspruch zu jm/etw stehen.

conflicting [kən'flɪktɪŋ] *adj* widersprüchlich.

conform [kən'fɔ:m] *vi* - **1.** [behave as expected] sich an|passen - **2.** [be in accordance]: **to conform (to** *OR* **with sthg)** sich (nach etw *(D)*) richten.

confound [kən'faʊnd] *vt* [confuse] verblüffen.

confront [kən'frʌnt] *vt* - **1.** [opponent, enemy, problem] sich stellen *(+ D)*; **to be confronted with a problem** mit einem Problem konfrontiert werden; **the problem that confronts us**

das Problem, das sich uns stellt - 2. [present]: **to confront sb (with sthg)** jn (mit etw) konfrontieren.

confrontation [ˌkɒnfrʌn'teɪʃn] *n* Konfrontation *die*, Auseinandersetzung *die*.

confuse [kən'fjuːz] *vt* - 1. [bewilder] verwirren - 2. [mix up]: **to confuse sb/sthg (with)** jn/etw verwechseln (mit) - 3. [complicate - situation] verworren machen.

confused [kən'fjuːzd] *adj* [person] verwirrt; [ideas, thoughts, situation] verworren; **to get confused** konfus werden.

confusing [kən'fjuːzɪŋ] *adj* verwirrend.

confusion [kən'fjuːʒn] *n* - 1. [perplexity] Verwirrung *die* - 2. [mixing up] Verwechslung *die* - 3. [bewilderment] Verlegenheit *die* - 4. [disorder] Durcheinander *das*.

congeal [kən'dʒiːl] *vi* [blood] gerinnen; [food] fest werden.

congenial [kən'dʒiːnjəl] *adj* angenehm.

congested [kən'dʒestɪd] *adj* [roads, nose] verstopft.

congestion [kən'dʒestʃn] *n (U)* - 1. [overcrowding] Stau *der* - 2. MED Blutandrang *der*.

conglomerate [ˌkən'glɒmərət] *n* COMM Großkonzern *der (aus mehreren Firmen bestehend)*.

congratulate [kən'grætʃʊleɪt] *vt*: **to congratulate sb (on sthg)** jm (zu etw) gratulieren.

congratulations [kənˌgrætʃʊ'leɪʃənz] ◇ *npl* Glückwunsch *der*, Glückwünsche *Pl*. ◇ *excl* herzlichen Glückwunsch!

congregate ['kɒŋgrɪgeɪt] *vi* [people] sich versammeln; [animals] sich sammeln.

congregation [ˌkɒŋgrɪ'geɪʃn] *n* RELIG Gemeinde *die*.

congress ['kɒŋgres] *n* [meeting] Kongress *der*. ◆ **Congress** *n US* POL der Kongress.

congressman ['kɒŋgresmən] (*pl* **-men** [-mən]) *n US* POL Kongressabgeordnete *der*.

conifer ['kɒnɪfəʳ] *n* Nadelbaum *der*.

conjugation [ˌkɒndʒʊ'geɪʃn] *n* GRAM Konjugation *die*.

conjunction [kən'dʒʌŋkʃn] *n* - 1. GRAM Konjunktion *die* - 2. [combination] Verbindung *die*; [of events] Zusammentreffen *das*.

conjunctivitis [kənˌdʒʌŋktɪ'vaɪtɪs] *n (U)* Bindehautentzündung *die*.

conjure ['kʌndʒəʳ] *vt & vi* zaubern. ◆ **conjure up** *vt sep* [evoke] herauf|beschwören.

conjurer ['kʌndʒərəʳ] *n* Zauberer *der*, -rin *die*.

conjuror ['kʌndʒərəʳ] *n* = **conjurer**.

conker ['kɒŋkəʳ] *n UK* (Ross)kastanie *die*.

conman ['kɒnmæn] (*pl* **-men** [-men]) *n* Betrüger *der*.

connect [kə'nekt] ◇ *vt* - 1. [join]: **to connect sthg (to sthg)** etw (mit etw) verbinden - 2. [on telephone] verbinden - 3. [associate] in Verbindung OR Zusammenhang bringen; **to connect sb/sthg to, to connect sb/sthg with** jn/etw in Verbindung bringen mit; **to be connected** [two things] miteinander zu tun haben - 4. ELEC [to power supply]: **to connect sthg (to sthg)** etw (an etw *(A)*) anlschließen. ◇ *vi* [train, plane, bus]: **to connect with** Anschluss haben an *(+ A)*.

connected [kə'nektɪd] *adj* [related]: **to be connected with sthg** mit etw in Zusammenhang stehen.

connection [kə'nekʃn] *n* - 1. [relationship]: **to have a connection with** in Zusammenhang stehen mit; **connection between** Zusammenhang zwischen; **in connection with** im Zusammenhang mit - 2. ELEC [between wires] Schaltung *die* - 3. [on telephone] Verbindung *die* - 4. [plane, train, bus] Anschluss *der* - 5. [professional acquaintance]: **connections** Beziehungen *Pl*.

connive [kə'naɪv] *vi* - 1. [plot]: **to connive (with sb)** sich (mit jm) verschwören - 2. [allow to happen]: **to connive at sthg** etw dulden.

connoisseur [ˌkɒnə'sɜːʳ] *n* Kenner *der*, -in *die*; **a connoisseur of wine** ein Weinkenner.

conquer ['kɒŋkəʳ] *vt* - 1. [take by force - land, city] erobern; [- people] besiegen - 2. *fig* [overcome] besiegen.

conqueror ['kɒŋkərəʳ] *n* [of land, city] Eroberer *der*, -in *die*; [of people] Sieger *der*, -in *die*.

conquest ['kɒŋkwest] *n* - 1. [act - of land, city] Eroberung *die*; [- of people] Sieg *der* - 2. [thing conquered] Eroberung *die*.

cons [kɒnz] *npl* - 1. *UK inf* (*abbr of* **conveniences**); **all mod cons** mit allem modernen Komfort - 2. ▷ **pro**.

conscience ['kɒnʃəns] *n* Gewissen *das*.

conscientious [ˌkɒnʃɪ'enʃəs] *adj* gewissenhaft.

conscious ['kɒnʃəs] *adj* - 1. [awake] bei Bewusstsein - 2. [aware]: **to be conscious of sthg** sich einer Sache *(G)* bewusst sein; **fashion-conscious** modebewusst; **to be money-conscious** sehr auf Geld achten - 3. [intentional - effort, decision] bewusst; [- insult] absichtlich.

consciousness ['kɒnʃəsnɪs] *n* Bewusstsein *das*.

conscript *n* MIL Wehrpflichtige *der*.

conscription [kən'skrɪpʃn] *n* Wehrpflicht *die*.

consecutive [kən'sekjʊtɪv] *adj* aufeinanderfolgend; [numbers] fortlaufend; **for four consecutive days** vier Tage hintereinander.

consent [kən'sent] ◇ *n (U)* - 1. [permission] Zustimmung *die* - 2. [agreement]: **he is, by common consent, a good minister** man hält ihn allgemein für einen guten Minister. ◇ *vi*: **to consent (to sthg)** (einer Sache *(D)*) zulstimmen.

consequence ['kɒnsɪkwəns] *n* - **1.** [result] Folge *die*; **to take the consequences** die Konsequenzen tragen; **in consequence** folglich - **2.** *(U)* [importance] Bedeutung *die*; **a person of consequence** eine bedeutende Person.

consequently ['kɒnsɪkwəntlɪ] *adv* folglich.

conservation [ˌkɒnsə'veɪʃn] *n* [of buildings] Schutz *der*, Erhaltung *die*; **nature conservation** Naturschutz *der*; **conservation of energy/water** sorgsamer Umgang mit Energie/Wasser.

conservative [kən'sɜːvətɪv] ◇ *adj* - **1.** [traditional] konservativ - **2.** [cautious] vorsichtig. ◇ *n* Konservative *der, die*. ◆ **Conservative** ◇ *adj* POL konservativ. ◇ *n* POL Konservative *der, die*.

Conservative Party *n*: **the Conservative Party** die Konservative Partei.

conservatory [kən'sɜːvətrɪ] *n* Wintergarten *der*.

conserve ◇ *n* ['kɒnsɜːv] Marmelade *die*. ◇ *vt* [kən'sɜːv] [energy, supplies, electricity] sorgsam um|gehen mit; [nature, wildlife] schützen.

consider [kən'sɪdəʳ] *vt* - **1.** [think about] erwägen - **2.** [take into account] berücksichtigen; **all things considered** alles in allem - **3.** [believe]: **I consider him (to be) an expert** ich halte ihn für einen Experten.

considerable [kən'sɪdrəbl] *adj* beträchtlich.

considerably [kən'sɪdrəblɪ] *adv* beträchtlich.

considerate [kən'sɪdərət] *adj* rücksichtsvoll.

consideration [kənˌsɪdə'reɪʃn] *n* - **1.** [thought] Überlegung *die*; **to take sthg into consideration** etw berücksichtigen - **2.** [thoughtfulness] Rücksichtnahme *die* - **3.** [factor] Gesichtspunkt *der* - **4.** [discussion]: **the matter is under consideration** die Angelegenheit wird zur Zeit geprüft.

considering [kən'sɪdərɪŋ] ◇ *prep* in Anbetracht *(+ G)*. ◇ *conj* wenn man bedenkt, dass. ◇ *adv* eigentlich; **the play was quite good, considering** das Stück war eigentlich ganz gut.

consign [kən'saɪn] *vt*: **to consign sthg to the attic/shed/*etc*** etw auf den Dachboden/in den Schuppen/*etc* verbannen; **to consign sthg to the scrapheap** *fig* etw raus|werfen.

consignment [ˌkən'saɪnmənt] *n* Sendung *die*; [bigger] Ladung *die*.

consist [kən'sɪst] ◆ **consist in** *vt insep*: **to consist in sthg** in etw *(D)* bestehen; **to consist in doing sthg** darin bestehen, etw zu tun. ◆ **consist of** *vt insep* bestehen aus.

consistency [kən'sɪstənsɪ] *n* - **1.** [coherence] Beständigkeit *die*; [of several things] Einheitlichkeit *die* - **2.** [texture] Konsistenz *die*.

consistent [kən'sɪstənt] *adj* - **1.** [constant] beständig - **2.** [steady] stetig - **3.** [coherent]: **to be consistent (with)** im Einklang stehen (mit).

consolation [ˌkɒnsə'leɪʃn] *n* Trost *der*.

console ◇ *n* ['kɒnsəʊl] [control panel] Bedienungsfeld *das*; [of computer game] Spielkonsole *die*. ◇ *vt* [kən'səʊl] trösten.

consonant ['kɒnsənənt] *n* Konsonant *der*.

consortium [kən'sɔːtjəm] (*pl* **-tiums** OR **-tia** [-tjə]) *n* Konsortium *das*.

conspicuous [kən'spɪkjʊəs] *adj* auffällig.

conspiracy [kən'spɪrəsɪ] *n* Verschwörung *die*.

conspire [kən'spaɪəʳ] *vt*: **to conspire to do sthg** heimlich planen, etw zu tun.

constable ['kʌnstəbl] *n UK* Wachtmeister *der*, -in *die*.

constant ['kɒnstənt] *adj* - **1.** [unvarying] konstant, beständig - **2.** [recurring] ständig.

constantly ['kɒnstəntlɪ] *adv* [always] dauernd, ständig.

consternation [ˌkɒnstə'neɪʃn] *n* Bestürzung *die*.

constipated ['kɒnstɪpeɪtɪd] *adj* verstopft.

constipation [ˌkɒnstɪ'peɪʃn] *n (U)* Verstopfung *die*.

constituency [kən'stɪtjʊənsɪ] *n* Wahlkreis *der*.

constituent [kən'stɪtjʊənt] *n* - **1.** [voter] Wähler *der*, -in *die* - **2.** [element] Bestandteil *der*.

constitute ['kɒnstɪtjuːt] *vt* - **1.** [represent] dar|stellen - **2.** [form] bilden - **3.** [set up] ein|richten.

constitution [ˌkɒnstɪ'tjuːʃn] *n* - **1.** [health] Konstitution *die* - **2.** [composition] Zusammensetzung *die*.

constraint [kən'streɪnt] *n* - **1.** [restriction] Beschränkung *die* - **2.** [coercion]: **under constraint** unter Zwang.

construct *vt* [kən'strʌkt] [build] bauen.

construction [kən'strʌkʃn] *n* - **1.** [act of building] Bau *der*; **under construction** im Bau - **2.** [building industry] Bauindustrie *die* - **3.** [structure] Konstruktion *die*.

constructive [kən'strʌktɪv] *adj* konstruktiv.

construe [kən'struː] *vt fml* [interpret]: **to construe sthg as** etw auf|fassen als.

consul ['kɒnsəl] *n* Konsul *der*.

consulate ['kɒnsjʊlət] *n* Konsulat *das*.

consult [kən'sʌlt] ◇ *vt* - **1.** [ask advice of - doctor, lawyer] konsultieren; [- friend] um Rat fragen - **2.** [refer to - dictionary] nach|schlagen in *(+ D)*; [- map] nach|sehen auf *(+ D)*. ◇ *vi*: **to consult with sb** sich mit jm beraten.

consultant [kən'sʌltənt] *n* - **1.** [expert] Berater *der*, -in *die* - **2.** *UK* [hospital doctor] Facharzt *der*, -ärztin *die*.

consultation [ˌkɒnsəl'teɪʃn] *n* [meeting, discussion] Beratung *die*.

consulting room [kən'sʌltɪŋ-] *n* Sprechzimmer *das*.

consume [kən'sjuːm] *vt* - **1.** [food, drink] zu sich nehmen - **2.** [fuel, energy] verbrauchen.

consumer [kən'sjuːməʳ] *n* Verbraucher *der*, -in *die*.

consumer goods *npl* Konsumgüter *Pl*.

consumer society *n* Konsumgesellschaft *die*.

consummate *vt* ['kɒnsəmeɪt] [marriage] vollziehen.

consumption [kən'sʌmpʃn] *n* *(U)* - **1.** [of food, drink] Konsum *der* - **2.** [of fuel, energy] Verbrauch *der*.

cont. (*abbr of* **continued**) Forts.

contact ['kɒntækt] ◇ *n* Kontakt *der*; **to be in contact with sthg** [touching] etw berühren; **to lose contact with sb** den Kontakt zu jm verlieren; **to make contact with sb** mit jm Kontakt auf|nehmen; **in contact (with sb)** in Kontakt (mit jm). ◇ *vt* sich in Verbindung setzen mit.

contact lens *n* Kontaktlinse *die*.

contagious [kən'teɪdʒəs] *adj liter* & *fig* ansteckend.

contain [kən'teɪn] *vt* - **1.** [hold, include] enthalten - **2.** *fml* [control - enthusiasm, anger, excitement] unter Kontrolle halten; [- epidemic, riot] unter Kontrolle bringen; [- enemy troops] in Schach halten; [- population growth] in Grenzen halten.

container [kən'teɪnəʳ] *n* - **1.** [box, bottle *etc*] Behälter *der* - **2.** COMM [for transporting goods] Container *der*.

contaminate [kən'tæmɪneɪt] *vt* [make impure] verunreinigen; [make poisonous] verseuchen.

cont'd (*abbr of* **continued**) Forts.

contemplate ['kɒntempleɪt] *vt* - **1.** [consider] erwägen - **2.** *liter* [look at] betrachten.

contemporary [kən'tempərərɪ] ◇ *adj* [life] zeitgenössisch. ◇ *n* Zeitgenosse *der*, -sin *die*.

contempt [kən'tempt] *n* *(U)* - **1.** [scorn]: **contempt (for)** Verachtung *die* (für) - **2.** LAW: **contempt (of court)** Missachtung *die* des Gerichts.

contemptuous [kən'temptʃʊəs] *adj* verächtlich; **to be contemptuous of sthg** etw verachten.

contend [kən'tend] ◇ *vi* - **1.** [deal]: **to contend with sthg** mit etw zu kämpfen haben - **2.** [compete]: **to contend for sthg** um etw kämpfen. ◇ *vt fml* [claim]: **to contend that...** behaupten, dass...

contender [kən'tendəʳ] *n* - **1.** [in fight, race] Konkurrent *der*, -in *die* - **2.** [in election] Kandidat *der*, -in *die*.

content ◇ *adj* [kən'tent]: **content (with)** zufrieden (mit); **to be content to do sthg** etw gerne tun. ◇ *n* ['kɒntent] - **1.** [amount contained] Gehalt *der* - **2.** [subject matter] Inhalt *der*. ◇ *vt* [kən'tent]: **to content o.s. with sthg** sich mit etw zufrieden geben. ◆ **contents** *npl* - **1.** [of container, document] Inhalt *der* - **2.** [at front of book] Inhaltsverzeichnis *das*.

contented [kən'tentɪd] *adj* zufrieden.

contention [kən'tenʃn] *n* - **1.** [assertion] Behauptung *die* - **2.** *(U)* [disagreement]: **to be a source of contention** ein Streitpunkt sein.

contest ◇ *n* ['kɒntest] - **1.** [competition] Wettkampf *der*; **a beauty contest** ein Schönheitswettbewerb - **2.** [for power, control] Kampf *der*. ◇ *vt* [kən'test] - **1.** [compete for] kämpfen um - **2.** [dispute - statement] bestreiten; [- decision] Einspruch erheben gegen; [- will] an|fechten.

contestant [kən'testənt] *n* [in sports] Wettkampfteilnehmer *der*, -in *die*; [in quiz, election] Kandidat *der*, -in *die*.

context ['kɒntekst] *n* - **1.** [of word, phrase] Kontext *der* - **2.** [of event, idea] Zusammenhang *der*.

continent ['kɒntɪnənt] *n* Kontinent *der*. ◆ **Continent** *n UK*: **the Continent** Kontinentaleuropa *das*.

continental [ˌkɒntɪ'nentl] *adj* kontinental.

continental breakfast *n Frühstück mit Kaffee oder Tee, Brötchen und Marmelade*.

continental quilt *n UK* Steppdecke *die*.

contingency [kən'tɪndʒənsɪ] *n* Eventualität *die*.

contingency plan *n* Ausweichplan *der*.

continual [kən'tɪnjʊəl] *adj* - **1.** [without interruption - noise] pausenlos; [- growth] ununterbrochen; [- jealousy] dauernd - **2.** [frequently repeated] ständig, dauernd.

continually [kən'tɪnjʊəlɪ] *adv* - **1.** [without interruption] ununterbrochen - **2.** [frequently] ständig.

continuation [kənˌtɪnjʊ'eɪʃn] *n* Fortsetzung *die*.

continue [kən'tɪnjuː] ◇ *vt* [carry on] fort|setzen; **to continue singing/working/*etc* OR to sing/work/*etc*** weiter|singen/weiter|arbeiten/*etc*; **"And now," he continued** "Und nun," fuhr er fort. ◇ *vi* - **1.** [carry on] an|dauern; **to continue with sthg** etw fort|setzen - **2.** [begin again - gen] weiter|gehen; [- people] weiter|machen - **3.** [resume speaking] fort|fahren - **4.** [resume travelling] weiter|fahren; [on foot] weiter|gehen.

continuous [kən'tɪnjʊəs] *adj* ununterbrochen.

continuously [kən'tɪnjʊəslɪ] *adv* ununterbrochen.

contort [kən'tɔ:t] *vt* [face, image] verzerren; [one's body] verrenken.

contortion [kən'tɔ:ʃn] *n* [position] Verrenkung *die*.

contour ['kɒn,tʊəʳ] *n* - **1.** [outline] Kontur *die* - **2.** [on map] Höhenlinie *die*.

contraband ['kɒntrəbænd] ◇ *adj* geschmuggelt. ◇ *n (U)* Schmuggelware *die*.

contraception [,kɒntrə'sepʃn] *n* Empfängnisverhütung *die*.

contraceptive [,kɒntrə'septɪv] ◇ *adj* Verhütungs-; [advice] zur Empfängnisverhütung. ◇ *n* Verhütungsmittel *das*.

contract ◇ *n* ['kɒntrækt] Vertrag *der*; **a contract of employment** ein Arbeitsvertrag. ◇ *vt* [kən'trækt] - **1.** [through legal agreement]: **to contract to do sthg** sich vertraglich verpflichten, etw zu tun - **2.** *fml* [disease] sich *(D)* zu|ziehen. ◇ *vi* [kən'trækt] [decrease in size, length] sich zusammen|ziehen.

contraction [kən'trækʃn] *n* [short form] Kontraktion *die*.

contractor [kən'træktəʳ] *n* [person] Auftragnehmer *der*, -in *die*; [company] beauftragte Firma.

contradict [,kɒntrə'dɪkt] *vt* widersprechen *(+ D)*.

contradiction [,kɒntrə'dɪkʃn] *n* Widerspruch *der*.

contraflow ['kɒntrəfləʊ] *n Umleitung auf die Gegenfahrbahn (bei Baustellen auf der Fahrbahn)*.

contraption [kən'træpʃn] *n* Apparat *der*.

contrary ['kɒntrərɪ] ◇ *adj* - **1.** [opposing] gegensätzlich; **to be contrary to sthg** im Gegensatz zu etw stehen - **2.** [kən'treərɪ] [stubborn] widerspenstig. ◇ *n* Gegenteil *das*; **on the contrary** im Gegenteil. ◆ **contrary to** *prep* im Gegensatz zu.

contrast ◇ *n* ['kɒntrɑ:st]: **contrast (with** OR **to)** Gegensatz *der* (zu); **the contrast between** der Unterschied zwischen; **by** OR **in contrast** im Gegensatz dazu; **in contrast with** OR **to sthg** im Gegensatz zu etw. ◇ *vt* [kən'trɑ:st]: **to contrast sthg with sthg** etw einer Sache *(D)* gegenüber|stellen. ◇ *vi* [kən'trɑ:st]: **to contrast (with sthg)** im Gegensatz (zu etw) stehen; [colours] sich (gegen etw) ab|heben.

contravene [,kɒntrə'vi:n] *vt* verstoßen gegen.

contribute [kən'trɪbju:t] ◇ *vt* [ideas] bei|tragen; [money] bei|steuern; [help, advice] zur Verfügung stellen. ◇ *vi* - **1.** [donate]: **to contribute (to sthg)** (für etw) spenden - **2.** [be part of cause]: **to contribute to sthg** zu etw bei|tragen - **3.** [write material]: **to contribute to sthg** für etw einen Beitrag/Beiträge schreiben.

contribution [,kɒntrɪ'bju:ʃn] *n*: **contribution (to sthg)** Beitrag *der* (zu etw).

contributor [kən'trɪbjʊtəʳ] *n* - **1.** [of money] Spender *der*, -in *die* - **2.** [to magazine, newspaper] freier Mitarbeiter, freie Mitarbeiterin; [regular] Mitarbeiter *der*, -in *die*.

contrive [kən'traɪv] *vt fml* - **1.** [engineer] entwickeln; [meeting] arrangieren - **2.** [manage]: **to contrive to do sthg** es zu Wege bringen, etw zu tun.

contrived [kən'traɪvd] *adj* gewollt.

control [kən'trəʊl] ◇ *n* - **1.** *(U)* [power to manage - of situation, language] Beherrschung *die*; [- of traffic] Regelung *die*; [- of disease, crowd, fire] Kontrolle *die*; [- of budget] Aufsicht *die*; *(phrase)*: **to be in control of** [situation, place] unter Kontrolle haben; **under control** unter Kontrolle; **to get a situation under control** eine Situation in den Griff bekommen - **2.** [of emotions] Beherrschung *die*; **to lose control** [become angry] die Beherrschung verlieren - **3.** [limit] Beschränkung *die* - **4.** COMPUT Control *die*. ◇ *vt* - **1.** [have power to manage - company] leiten; [- government] unter sich *(D)* haben; [- country] beherrschen; [- traffic] regulieren; [- crowds, rioters] unter Kontrolle haben - **2.** [operate - car, plane] steuern; [- machine] bedienen - **3.** [curb] unter Kontrolle bringen - **4.** [emotions] beherrschen; **to control o.s.** sich beherrschen. ◆ **controls** *npl* [of machine, plane] Bedienungsfeld *das*.

control panel *n* [of car] Armaturenbrett *das*; [of plane, machine] Bedienungsfeld *das*.

control tower *n* Kontrollturm *der*.

controversial [,kɒntrə'vɜ:ʃl] *adj* umstritten.

controversy ['kɒntrəvɜ:sɪ, *UK* kən'trɒvəsɪ] *n* Streit *der*.

convalesce [,kɒnvə'les] *vi* genesen.

convene [kən'vi:n] ◇ *vt* [meeting, conference] ein|berufen. ◇ *vi* sich versammeln; [court, parliament] zusammen|treten.

convenience [kən'vi:njəns] *n* - **1.** [ease of use]: **I like the convenience of it** ich finde es so praktisch; **for convenience** aus praktischen Gründen - **2.** [benefit]: **please reply at your earliest convenience** *fml* wir bitten um baldmöglichste Antwort; **a telephone is provided for your convenience** ein Telefon wird Ihnen zur Verfügung gestellt.

convenient [kən'vi:njənt] *adj* - **1.** [suitable] günstig; **to be convenient for sb** jm passen - **2.** [handy] praktisch; **to be convenient for the shops** günstig in der Nähe von Geschäften gelegen sein.

convent ['kɒnvənt] *n* Kloster *das* (für Frauen).

convention [kən'venʃn] *n* - **1.** [practice] Brauch *der*; [social rule] Konvention *die* - **2.** [agreement] Abkommen *das* - **3.** [assembly] Tagung *die*.

conventional [kən'venʃənl] *adj* - **1.** *pej* [dull] konventionell; [person] konventionsgebunden - **2.** [traditional] üblich - **3.** [weapon, war] konventionell.

converge [kən'vɜːdʒ] *vi* - **1.** [come together] zusammen|laufen; **to converge on sb/sthg** von überall her zu jm/etw strömen - **2.** [become similar] sich einander an|nähern.

conversant [kən'vɜːsənt] *adj fml*: **conversant with sthg** mit etw vertraut.

conversation [ˌkɒnvə'seɪʃn] *n* Gespräch *das*; **to have a conversation** sich unterhalten.

converse *vi* [kən'vɜːs] *fml* [talk]: **to converse (with sb)** sich (mit jm) unterhalten.

conversely [kən'vɜːslɪ] *adv fml* umgekehrt.

conversion [kən'vɜːʃn] *n* - **1.** [process] Umwandlung *die* - **2.** [converted building, room] Umbau *der* - **3.** RELIG [change in belief] Bekehrung *die* - **4.** [in rugby] Verwandlung *die*.

convert ◇ *vt* [kən'vɜːt] - **1.** [change]: **to convert sthg (in)to sthg** [miles, pounds] etw in etw *(A)* um|rechnen; [energy] etw in etw *(A)* um|wandeln - **2.** *fig* & RELIG: **to convert sb (to sthg)** jn (zu etw) bekehren - **3.** [building, room, ship]: **to convert sthg (in)to sthg** etw zu etw um|bauen. ◇ *vi* [kən'vɜːt]: **to convert from sthg to sthg** [gas, electricity] sich von etw auf etw *(A)* um|stellen; [religion] von etw zu etw konvertieren. ◇ *n* ['kɒnvɜːt] Bekehrte *der, die*.

convertible [kən'vɜːtəbl] *n* [car] Kabrio *das*.

convex [kɒn'veks] *adj* konvex.

convey [kən'veɪ] *vt* - **1.** *fml* [people, cargo] befördern - **2.** [feelings, thoughts] vermitteln; **to convey sthg to sb** jm etw vermitteln.

conveyor belt [kən'veɪəʳ-] *n* [in factory] Fließband *das*; [at airport] Förderband *das*.

convict ◇ *n* ['kɒnvɪkt] Strafgefangene *der, die*. ◇ *vt* [kən'vɪkt]: **to convict sb of sthg** jn wegen etw verurteilen.

conviction [kən'vɪkʃn] *n* - **1.** [gen] Überzeugung *die* - **2.** LAW [of criminal] Verurteilung *die*; **previous convictions** Vorstrafen *Pl*.

convince [kən'vɪns] *vt* [persuade] überzeugen; **to convince sb of sthg** jn von etw überzeugen; **to convince sb to do sthg** jn überreden, etw zu tun.

convincing [kən'vɪnsɪŋ] *adj* - **1.** [person, argument, speech] überzeugend - **2.** [win, victory] klar.

convoluted ['kɒnvəluːtɪd] *adj* [plot, reasoning] verwickelt; [sentence] gewunden.

convoy ['kɒnvɔɪ] *n* Konvoi *der*.

convulse [kən'vʌls] *vt*: **to be convulsed with laughter** sich vor Lachen schütteln; **to be convulsed with pain** sich vor Schmerzen krümmen.

convulsion [kən'vʌlʃn] *n* MED Konvulsion *die*.

cook [kʊk] ◇ *n* Koch *der*, Köchin *die*. ◇ *vt* - **1.** [food, meal] machen; [boil] kochen; [roast, fry] braten; **to cook sthg (in the oven)** etw im Ofen garen lassen - **2.** *inf* [falsify] frisieren. ◇ *vi* [boil] kochen; [roast, fry] braten.

cookbook ['kʊkˌbʊk] *n* = **cookery book**.

cooker ['kʊkəʳ] *n esp UK* [stove] Herd *der*.

cookery ['kʊkərɪ] *n* Kochen *das*.

cookery book *n* Kochbuch *das*.

cookie ['kʊkɪ] *n* - **1.** Keks *der*, Plätzchen *das* - **2.** COMPUT Cookie *das*.

cooking ['kʊkɪŋ] *n (U)* - **1.** [activity] Kochen *das* - **2.** [food] Küche *die*; **her cooking's awful** ihre Kochkünste sind grauenvoll.

cool [kuːl] ◇ *adj* - **1.** [gen] kühl; [dress] leicht - **2.** [person] ruhig; **to keep a cool head** einen kühlen Kopf behalten - **3.** *inf* [excellent, fashionable] cool. ◇ *vt* kühlen. ◇ *vi* ab|kühlen. ◇ *n inf* [calm]: **to keep one's cool** die Ruhe bewahren; **to lose one's cool** die Nerven verlieren. ◆ **cool down** *vi* [become less warm] ab|kühlen; [person] kühler werden.

cool bag *n* Kühltasche *die*.

cool box *UK*, **cooler** *US* ['kuːləʳ] *n* Kühlbox *die*.

coop [kuːp] *n* Käfig *der*. ◆ **coop up** *vt sep inf* ein|pferchen.

co-op ['kəʊˌɒp] *n abbr of* **cooperative**.

cooperate [kəʊ'ɒpəreɪt] *vi*: **to cooperate (with sb)** (mit jm) zusammen|arbeiten.

cooperation [kəʊˌɒpə'reɪʃn] *n (U)* - **1.** [collaboration] Zusammenarbeit *die* - **2.** [assistance] Mitarbeit *die*, Kooperation *die*.

cooperative [kəʊ'ɒpərətɪv] ◇ *adj* - **1.** [helpful] kooperativ - **2.** [collective] auf Genossenschaftsbasis. ◇ *n* [enterprise] Genossenschaft *die*, Kooperative *die*.

coordinate ◇ *n* [kəʊ'ɔːdɪnət] [on map, graph] Koordinate *die*. ◇ *vt* [kəʊ'ɔːdɪneɪt] koordinieren. ◆ **coordinates** *npl* [clothes] Kleidung *die* zum Kombinieren.

coordination [kəʊˌɔːdɪ'neɪʃn] *n* Koordination *die*.

cop [kɒp] *n inf* Polizist *der*, -in *die*.

cope [kəʊp] *vi* zurecht|kommen; **to cope with sthg** etw schaffen.

Copenhagen [ˌkəʊpən'heɪgən] *n* Kopenhagen *nt*.

copier ['kɒpɪəʳ] *n* [photocopier] Kopierer *der*.

cop-out *n inf* Rückzieher *der*.

copper ['kɒpəʳ] *n* - **1.** [metal] Kupfer *das* - **2.** *UK inf* [policeman] Polizist *der*, -in *die*.

copse [kɒps] *n* Wäldchen *das*.

copy ['kɒpɪ] ◇ *n* - **1.** [gen] Kopie *die* - **2.** [of book, magazine] Exemplar *das*. ◇ *vt* - **1.** [imitate] nach|ahmen - **2.** [photocopy] kopieren.

copyright ['kɒpɪraɪt] *n* Copyright *das*.

coral ['kɒrəl] *n (U)* Koralle *die*.

cord [kɔ:d] *n* - **1.** [string] Schnur *die* - **2.** [wire] Kabel *das* - **3.** *(U)* [fabric] Kord *der.* ◆ **cords** *npl inf* Kordhose *die.*

cordial ['kɔ:djəl] ◇ *adj* freundlich. ◇ *n* Fruchtsirup *der.*

cordon ['kɔ:dn] *n* Kette *die.* ◆ **cordon off** *vt sep* ab|sperren.

corduroy ['kɔ:dərɔɪ] *n (U)* Kord *der.*

core [kɔ:ʳ] *vt* entkernen.

coriander [ˌkɒrɪ'ændəʳ] *n* Koriander *der.*

cork [kɔ:k] *n* - **1.** [material] Kork *der* - **2.** [stopper] Korken *der.*

corkscrew ['kɔ:kskru:] *n* Korkenzieher *der.*

corn [kɔ:n] *n* - **1.** *(U) UK* [cereal] Korn *das,* Getreide *das* - **2.** *(U) esp US* [maize] Mais *der* - **3.** [callus] Hühnerauge *das.*

corned beef [kɔ:nd-] *n* Cornedbeef *das.*

corner ['kɔ:nəʳ] ◇ *n* Ecke *die;* **to cut corners** oberflächlich arbeiten. ◇ *vt* - **1.** *fig* [person, animal] in die Enge treiben - **2.** [market] monopolisieren.

corner shop *n* Laden *der* an der Ecke.

cornerstone ['kɔ:nəstəʊn] *n fig* Grundstein *der.*

cornet ['kɔ:nɪt] *n* - **1.** [instrument] Kornett *das* - **2.** *UK* [ice-cream cone] Hörnchen *das.*

cornflakes ['kɔ:nfleɪks] *npl* Cornflakes *Pl.*

cornflour *UK* ['kɔ:nflaʊəʳ], **cornstarch** *US* [-stɑ:tʃ] *n (U)* Stärkemehl *das.*

corn on the cob *n* Maiskolben *der.*

corny ['kɔ:nɪ] *adj inf* abgedroschen.

coronary ['kɒrənrɪ], **coronary thrombosis** [-θrɒm'bəʊsɪs] *(pl* **coronary thromboses** [-si:z]) *n* Herzinfarkt *der.*

coronation [ˌkɒrə'neɪʃn] *n* Krönung *die.*

coroner ['kɒrənəʳ] *n für die Untersuchung ungeklärter Todesfälle zuständiger Beamter.*

corporal ['kɔ:pərəl] *n* Hauptgefreite *der.*

corporal punishment *n (U)* körperliche Züchtigung *die,* Prügelstrafe *die.*

corporate ['kɔ:pərət] *adj* - **1.** [business] körperschaftlich - **2.** [collective] gemeinsam.

corporation [ˌkɔ:pə'reɪʃn] *n* - **1.** [council] Gemeindeverwaltung *die* - **2.** [large company] Handelsgesellschaft *die.*

corps [kɔ:ʳ] *(pl inv) n* Korps *das.*

corpse [kɔ:ps] *n* Leiche *die.*

correct [kə'rekt] ◇ *adj* - **1.** [right, accurate] korrekt, richtig; **you're quite correct** du hast ganz Recht - **2.** [appropriate, suitable] angemessen. ◇ *vt* korrigieren.

correction [kə'rekʃn] *n* - **1.** *(U)* [act of correcting] Korrigieren *das* - **2.** [change] Korrektur *die,* Berichtigung *die.*

correlation [ˌkɒrə'leɪʃn] *n (U)*: **correlation (between)** Wechselbeziehung *die* (zwischen).

correspond [ˌkɒrɪ'spɒnd] *vi* - **1.** [be equivalent]: **to correspond with** OR **to sthg** etw *(D)* entsprechen - **2.** [tally]: **to correspond (with** OR **to sthg)** (mit etw) überein|stimmen - **3.** [write letters]: **to correspond (with sb)** (mit jm) korrespondieren.

correspondence [ˌkɒrɪ'spɒndəns] *n* - **1.** [letters] Briefe *Pl* - **2.** *(U)* [letter-writing]: **correspondence with/between** Briefwechsel *der* mit/zwischen *(D).*

correspondence course *n* Fernkurs *der.*

correspondent [ˌkɒrɪ'spɒndənt] *n* Korrespondent *der,* -in *die.*

corridor ['kɒrɪdɔ:ʳ] *n* Gang *der.*

corroborate [kə'rɒbəreɪt] *vt* bestätigen.

corrode [kə'rəʊd] ◇ *vt* zerfressen. ◇ *vi* korrodieren.

corrosion [kə'rəʊʒn] *n (U)* Korrosion *die.*

corrugated iron *n* Wellblech *das.*

corrupt [kə'rʌpt] ◇ *adj* - **1.** [gen] korrupt - **2.** [depraved] verdorben. ◇ *vt* - **1.** [deprave] verderben - **2.** COMPUT [damage] beschädigen.

corruption [kə'rʌpʃn] *n (U)* - **1.** [dishonesty] Korruption *die* - **2.** [depravity] Verdorbenheit *die* - **3.** [debasement] Verführung *die.*

corset ['kɔ:sɪt] *n* Korsett *das.*

cosh [kɒʃ] *n* Knüppel *der.*

cosmetic [kɒz'metɪk] ◇ *adj fig* [superficial] kosmetisch. ◇ *n* Kosmetikum *das.* ◆ **cosmetics** *n* Kosmetik *die.*

cosmopolitan [kɒzmə'pɒlɪtn] *adj* [place] kosmopolitisch; [person] welterfahren.

cosset ['kɒsɪt] *vt* verhätscheln.

cost [kɒst] ◇ *n* - **1.** [price] Kosten *Pl* - **2.** *fig* [loss, damage] Preis *der;* **at the cost of his health** auf Kosten seiner Gesundheit; **at all costs** um jeden Preis. ◇ *vt* - **1.** *(pt & pp inv)* [gen] kosten - **2.** *(pt & pp* **-ed***)* COMM [estimate price of] die Kosten kalkulieren *(+ G).* ◆ **costs** *npl* LAW Kosten *Pl.*

co-star *n*: **to be the co-star in a film** eine der Hauptrollen in einem Film spielen.

Costa Rica [ˌkɒstə'ri:kə] *n* Costa Rica *nt.*

cost-effective *adj* kosteneffektiv.

costing ['kɒstɪŋ] *n* Kalkulation *die.*

costly ['kɒstlɪ] *adj* kostspielig, teuer.

cost of living *n*: **the cost of living** die Lebenshaltungskosten *Pl.*

cost price *n* Selbstkostenpreis *der.*

costume ['kɒstju:m] *n* - **1.** THEAT Kostüm *das* - **2.** *(U)* [dress] Tracht *die* - **3.** [swimming costume] Badeanzug *der.*

costume jewellery *n* Modeschmuck *der.*

cosy *UK,* **cozy** *US* ['kəʊzɪ] *adj* [warm and comfortable] gemütlich.

cot [kɒt] *n* - **1.** *UK* [for child] Kinderbett *das* - **2.** *US* [folding bed] Feldbett *das.*

cottage ['kɒtɪdʒ] *n* Häuschen *das.*

cottage cheese *n (U)* Hüttenkäse *der.*

cottage pie *n UK Hackfleisch mit einer Lage Kartoffelbrei, im Ofen überbacken.*

cotton ['kɒtn] ◇ *n (U)* - **1.** [fabric] Baumwolle *die* - **2.** [thread] Faden *der.* ◇ *comp* [fabric] Baumwoll-. ◆ **cotton on** *vi inf*: **to cotton on (to sthg)** (etw) kapieren.

cotton candy *n US* = **candyfloss**.

cotton wool *n* Watte *die.*

couch [kaʊtʃ] *n* - **1.** [sofa] Sofa *das,* Couch *die* - **2.** [in doctor's surgery] Liege *die.*

cough [kɒf] *n* Husten *der.*

cough mixture *n UK* Hustensaft *der.*

cough sweet *n UK* Hustenpastille *die.*

cough syrup *n* = **cough mixture**.

could [kʊd] *pt* ▷ **can²**.

couldn't ['kʊdnt] *abbr of* **could not**.

could've ['kʊdəv] *abbr of* **could have**.

council ['kaʊnsl] *n* - **1.** [local authority] Stadtverwaltung *die* - **2.** [group, organization] Rat *der* - **3.** [meeting] Beratung *die.*

council estate *n* Sozialsiedlung *die.*

council house *n UK* ≃ Sozialwohnung *die, mit öffentlichen Mitteln gebautes Einfamilienhaus für eine Familie mit niedrigem Einkommen.*

councillor ['kaʊnsələr] *n* Stadtrat *der,* -rätin *die.*

council tax *n UK* Gemeindesteuer *die.*

counsel ['kaʊnsəl] (*UK*) (*US*) *n* - **1.** *(U) fml* [advice] Rat *der* - **2.** [lawyer] Rechtsanwalt *der,* -wältin *die*; **counsel for the defence** Verteidiger *der,* -in *die*; **counsel for the prosecution** Anklagevertreter *der,* -in *die.*

counsellor *UK*, **counselor** *US* ['kaʊnsələʳ] *n* - **1.** [adviser] Berater *der,* -in *die* - **2.** *US* [lawyer] Rechtsanwalt *der,* -wältin *die.*

count [kaʊnt] ◇ *n* - **1.** [total] Zählung *die*; **to keep count of sthg** etw mit|zählen; **to lose count of sthg** den Überblick über etw *(A)* verlieren - **2.** [aristocrat] Graf *der.* ◇ *vt* - **1.** [add up] zählen - **2.** [consider, include]: **to count sb/sthg as sthg** jn/etw als etw an|sehen; **there are six, not counting the broken ones** es sind sechs, die zerbrochenen nicht mitgezählt. ◇ *vi* zählen; **to count (up) to** zählen bis; **to count for nothing** umsonst gewesen sein; **to count as sthg** als etw zählen. ◆ **count against** *vt insep* sprechen gegen. ◆ **count on** *vt insep* - **1.** [rely on] zählen auf *(+ A)* - **2.** [expect] rechnen mit. ◆ **count up** *vt insep* zusammen|zählen. ◆ **count upon** *vt insep* = **count on**.

countdown ['kaʊntdaʊn] *n* Countdown *der.*

counter ['kaʊntəʳ] ◇ *n* - **1.** [in shop] Ladentisch *der* - **2.** [in board game] Spielmarke *die* - **3.** *US* [in kitchen] Theke *die.* ◇ *vt*: **to counter sthg with sthg** etw *(D)* mit etw begegnen. ◇ *vi*: **to counter with sthg** mit etw reagieren. ◆ **counter to** *adv* entgegen *(+ D)*; **to run counter to sthg** etw *(D)* zuwider|laufen.

counteract [ˌkaʊntə'rækt] *vt* entgegen|wirken *(+ D).*

counterattack ['kaʊntərəˌtæk] *vi* einen Gegenangriff führen.

counterclockwise [ˌkaʊntə'klɒkwaɪz] *adj & adv US* gegen den Uhrzeigersinn.

counterfeit ['kaʊntəfɪt] *adj* gefälscht.

counterfoil ['kaʊntəfɔɪl] *n* Kontrollabschnitt *der.*

counterpart ['kaʊntəpɑːt] *n* Gegenstück *das.*

counterproductive [ˌkaʊntəprə'dʌktɪv] *adj* die entgegengesetzte Wirkung habend.

countess ['kaʊntɪs] *n* Gräfin *die.*

countless ['kaʊntlɪs] *adj* unzählig.

country ['kʌntrɪ] *n* - **1.** [nation] Land *das*; **the country** [countryside] das Land; **they live in the country** sie leben auf dem Land - **2.** [area of land, region] Gebiet *das.*

country house *n* Landhaus *das.*

countryman ['kʌntrɪmən] (*pl* **-men** [-mən]) *n* Landsmann *der.*

countryside ['kʌntrɪsaɪd] *n (U)* Landschaft *die.*

county ['kaʊntɪ] *n* Grafschaft *die.*

county council *n UK* Grafschaftsrat *der.*

coup [kuː] *n* - **1.** [rebellion]: **coup (d'état)** Staatsstreich *der* - **2.** [masterstroke] Coup *der.*

couple ['kʌpl] ◇ *n* - **1.** [in relationship] Paar *das* - **2.** [small number]: **a couple (of)** [two] zwei; [a few] ein paar. ◇ *vt* [join]: **to couple sthg (to sthg)** etw (an etw *(A)*) koppeln.

coupon ['kuːpɒn] *n* Gutschein *der.*

courage ['kʌrɪdʒ] *n* Mut *der*; **to take courage (from sthg)** sich (durch etw) ermutigt fühlen.

courgette [kɔː'ʒet] *n UK* Zucchini *die.*

courier ['kʊrɪəʳ] *n* - **1.** [on holiday tour] Reiseleiter *der,* -in *die* - **2.** [to deliver letters, packages] Kurier *der.*

course [kɔːs] *n* - **1.** [of study - for student] Kurs(us) *der*; [- for employee] Lehrgang *der*; *(phrase)*: **a course of lectures** eine Vorlesungsreihe - **2.** MED [of treatment] Reihe *die* - **3.** [path, route] Kurs *der*; **in the course of time** im Laufe der Zeit; **during the course of the negotiations** im Verlauf der Verhandlungen; **on course** *liter & fig* auf Kurs; **off course** vom Kurs abgewichen - **4.** [plan]: **course (of action)** Vorgehensweise *die* - **5.** [of time]: **in due course** zu gegebener Zeit; **in the course of** im Laufe *(+ G)* - **6.** [in meal] Gang *der* - **7.** SPORT [for horseracing] Bahn *die,* Strecke *die*; [for golf] Platz *der.* ◆ **of course** *adv* natürlich; **of course not** natürlich nicht.

coursebook ['kɔːsbʊk] *n* Lehrbuch *das.*

coursework ['kɔ:swɜ:k] *n (U)* Mitarbeit *die* im Unterricht.

court [kɔ:t] *n* - **1.** [for trial] Gericht *das*; *(phrase)*: **to take sb to court** jn verklagen - **2.** SPORT Platz *der* - **3.** [courtyard, of monarch] Hof *der*.

courteous ['kɜ:tjəs] *adj* höflich.

courtesy ['kɜ:tɪsɪ] *n* Höflichkeit *die*. ◆ **courtesy of** *prep* [thanks to] dank *(+ G)*.

courthouse ['kɔ:thaʊs] (*pl* [-haʊzɪz]) *n US* Gerichtsgebäude *das*.

court-martial (*pl* **-s** *OR* **courts-martial**) (*UK*) (*US*) *n* [trial] Kriegsgerichtsverhandlung *die*.

courtroom ['kɔ:trʊm] *n* Gerichtssaal *der*.

courtyard ['kɔ:tjɑ:d] *n* Hof *der*.

cousin ['kʌzn] *n* Cousin *der*, Kusine *die*.

cove [kəʊv] *n* Bucht *die*.

covenant ['kʌvənənt] *n* [of money] Zahlungsverpflichtung *die*.

cover ['kʌvər] <> *n* - **1.** [of machine, typewriter] Abdeckung *die*; [of seat, cushion] Überzug *der* - **2.** [lid] Deckel *der* - **3.** [of book, magazine] Einband *der* - **4.** [blanket] Decke *die* - **5.** *(U)* [protection, shelter, insurance] Schutz *der*; **to take cover** [from weather] sich unter|stellen; [from gunfire] in Deckung gehen; **under cover** [from weather] geschützt - **6.** [disguise] Tarnung *die*. <> *vt* - **1.** [gen] bedecken; **to be covered in blood** blutüberströmt sein - **2.** [insure]: **to cover sb (against sthg)** [subj: policy] jn (gegen etw) versichern - **3.** [report on] berichten über *(+ A)* - **4.** [deal with] behandeln - **5.** [pay for - damage] decken. ◆ **cover up** *vt sep fig* [to conceal] vertuschen.

coverage ['kʌvərɪdʒ] *n (U)* [of news] Berichterstattung *die*.

cover charge *n* Gedeckgebühr *die*.

covering ['kʌvərɪŋ] *n* Belag *der*.

covering letter *UK*, **cover letter** *US n* Begleitbrief *der*.

cover note *n UK* vorläufiger Versicherungsschein.

covert ['kʌvət] *adj* verdeckt, versteckt; [look, glance] verstohlen.

cover-up *n* Vertuschung *die*.

covet ['kʌvɪt] *vt fml* begehren.

cow [kaʊ] <> *n* Kuh *die*. <> *vt* ein|schüchtern.

coward ['kaʊəd] *n* Feigling *der*.

cowardly ['kaʊədlɪ] *adj* feige.

cowboy ['kaʊbɔɪ] *n* [cattlehand] Cowboy *der*.

cower ['kaʊər] *vi* sich ducken; [squat] kauern.

cox [kɒks], **coxswain** ['kɒksən] *n* Steuermann *der*.

coy [kɔɪ] *adj* kokett, neckisch.

cozy *adj* & *n US* = **cosy**.

crab [kræb] *n* Krabbe *die*, Krebs *der*.

crack [kræk] <> *n* - **1.** [fault] Riss *der*; [in cup, glass, mirror] Sprung *der* - **2.** [in curtains, door] Spalt *der*; [in wall] Ritze *die* - **3.** [sharp noise] Knall *der* - **4.** *inf* [attempt]: **to have a crack at sthg** sich an etw *(D)* versuchen - **5.** [cocaine] Crack *das*. <> *adj* toll, erstklassig. <> *vt* - **1.** [damage] einen Riss machen in *(+ D)*; [cup, glass, mirror] an|schlagen; [skin] rissig machen - **2.** [whip] knallen mit - **3.** [bang, hit] an|schlagen; **I cracked my head on the doorpost** ich habe mir den Kopf am Türrahmen gestoßen - **4.** [solve] lösen; [code] knacken - **5.** *inf* [make]: **to crack a joke** einen Witz reißen. <> *vi* - **1.** [be damaged] einen Riss bekommen; [cup, glass, mirror] springen; [skin] auf|springen - **2.** [person] zusammen|brechen. ◆ **crack down** *vi*: **to crack down (on sb/sthg)** (bei jm/etw) hart durch|greifen. ◆ **crack up** *vi* durch|drehen.

cracker ['krækər] *n* - **1.** [biscuit] Keks *der* - **2.** *UK* [for Christmas] Knallbonbon *das*.

crackers ['krækəz] *adj UK inf* [mad] verrückt.

crackle ['krækl] *vi* knacken.

cradle ['kreɪdl] <> *n* [bed, birthplace] Wiege *die*. <> *vt* an sich *(A)* drücken.

craft [krɑ:ft] *n* - **1.** [trade, skill] Handwerk *das* - **2.** (*pl inv*) [boat] Boot *das*.

craftsman ['krɑ:ftsmən] (*pl* **-men** [-mən]) *n* Handwerker *der*.

craftsmanship ['krɑ:ftsmənʃɪp] *n (U)* Handwerkskunst *die*.

crafty ['krɑ:ftɪ] *adj* schlau.

crag [kræg] *n* Felszacken *der*.

cram [kræm] <> *vt* - **1.** [stuff]: **to cram sthg into sthg** etw in etw *(A)* stopfen - **2.** [overfill]: **to be crammed (with sthg)** (mit etw) vollgestopft sein. <> *vi* [study] pauken, büffeln.

cramp [kræmp] <> *n* Krampf *der*; **I've got cramp** ich habe einen Krampf; **stomach cramps** Magenkrämpfe. <> *vt* [hinder] hemmen, behindern.

cranberry ['krænbərɪ] *n* Preiselbeere *die*.

crane [kreɪn] *n* [machine] Kran *der*.

crank [kræŋk] <> *n* - **1.** TECH Kurbel *die* - **2.** *inf* [eccentric] Spinner *der*, -in *die*. <> *vt* [handle, mechanism] kurbeln.

crankshaft ['kræŋkʃɑ:ft] *n* Kurbelwelle *die*.

cranny ['krænɪ] *n* ▷ **nook**.

crap [kræp] *n v inf* Scheiße *die*.

crash [kræʃ] <> *n* - **1.** [of car] Unfall *der*; [of plane] Absturz *der*; [of train] Unglück *das*; [collision] Zusammenstoß *der*; **to have a crash** verunglücken; [collide] zusammen|stoßen - **2.** [loud noise] Krachen *das*. <> *vt* [car] einen Unfall haben mit; **she crashed her car into a tree** sie krachte mit dem Auto gegen einen Baum. <> *vi* - **1.** [car driver] verunglücken; [plane] ab|stürzen; [collide] zusammen|stoßen;

to crash into sthg [in car] mit dem Auto gegen etw krachen - **2.** FIN [business, company] bankrott gehen; [stock market] zusammen|brechen.

crash course *n* Intensivkurs *der*.

crash helmet *n* Sturzhelm *der*.

crash-land *vi* eine Bruchlandung machen.

crass [kræs] *adj* dumm und geschmacklos.

crate [kreɪt] *n* Kiste *die*; [of milk bottles, beer] Kasten *der*.

crater ['kreɪtəʳ] *n* Krater *der*.

cravat [krə'væt] *n* Halstuch *das*.

crave [kreɪv] ◇ *vt* sich sehnen nach. ◇ *vi*: **to crave for sthg** sich nach etw sehnen; [subj: pregnant woman] Gelüste auf etw *(A)* haben.

crawl [krɔːl] ◇ *vi* - **1.** [gen] kriechen; [baby, insect] krabbeln; **to crawl along** [traffic] im Schneckentempo vorwärts|kommen - **2.** *inf* [be covered]: **to be crawling with** wimmeln von. ◇ *n* [swimming stroke]: **the crawl** das Kraulen; **to do the crawl** kraulen.

crayfish ['kreɪfɪʃ] (*pl inv* OR **-es**) *n* [saltwater] Languste *die*.

crayon ['kreɪɒn] *n* [pencil] Buntstift *der*; [of wax] Wachsmalstift *der*.

craze [kreɪz] *n* Mode *die (die gerade "in" ist)*; **the latest craze** der letzte Schrei.

crazy ['kreɪzɪ] *adj inf* - **1.** [mad] verrückt - **2.** [enthusiastic]: **to be crazy about sthg/sb** auf etw *(A)* /nach jm verrückt sein.

creak [kriːk] *vi* [door, floorboard] knarren; [bed, hinge, handle] quietschen.

cream [kriːm] ◇ *adj* [in colour] creme(farben). ◇ *n* - **1.** [food] Sahne *die*; [filling for chocolates, biscuits] Creme *die* - **2.** *(U)* [cosmetic] Creme *die*.

cream cake *n UK* Sahnetorte *die*; [bun] Sahnetörtchen *das*.

cream cheese *n* Frischkäse *der*.

cream cracker *n UK* Kräcker *der*.

cream tea *n UK Nachmittagstee mit Gebäck, Marmelade und Sahne*.

crease [kriːs] ◇ *n* [in fabric - deliberate] Bügelfalte *die*; [- accidental] Falte *die*. ◇ *vt* [deliberately] falten; [accidentally] zerknittern. ◇ *vi* [fabric] knittern.

create [kriː'eɪt] *vt* - **1.** [gen] schaffen; [the world] erschaffen - **2.** [noise, fuss] verursachen; [impression] machen; [difficulties] bereiten.

creation [kriː'eɪʃn] *n* - **1.** [gen] Schaffung *die*; [of the world] Erschaffung *die* - **2.** [work of art] Werk *das*; [dress, hat, hairstyle] Kreation *die*.

creative [kriː'eɪtɪv] *adj* kreativ.

creature ['kriːtʃəʳ] *n* [animal] Lebewesen *das*, Geschöpf *das*.

crèche [kreʃ] *n UK* (Kinder)hort *der*.

credence ['kriːdns] *n*: **to give** OR **lend credence to sthg** etw glaubwürdig machen.

credentials [krɪ'denʃlz] *npl* - **1.** [papers] (Ausweis)papiere *Pl* - **2.** *fig* [qualifications] Qualifikationen *Pl*.

credibility [ˌkredə'bɪlətɪ] *n* Glaubwürdigkeit *die*.

credit ['kredɪt] ◇ *n* - **1.** [financial aid] Kredit *der*; **to be in credit** im Plus sein; **on credit** auf Kredit - **2.** *(U)* [honour] Ehre *die*; [approval] Anerkennung *die*; **he was never given any credit for it** man hat ihm nie Anerkennung dafür gezollt - **3.** SCH & UNIV [mark] Auszeichnung *die*; [unit of work] Schein *der* - **4.** FIN [money credited] Guthaben *das*. ◇ *vt* - **1.** FIN gut|schreiben - **2.** *inf* [believe] glauben - **3.** [attribute]: **to credit sb with sthg** jm etw zulschreiben. ◆ **credits** *npl* CIN Nachspann *der*.

credit card *n* Kreditkarte *die*.

credit note *n* COMM & FIN Gutschrift *die*.

creditor ['kredɪtəʳ] *n* Gläubiger *der*, -in *die*.

creed [kriːd] *n* - **1.** [political] Kredo *das* - **2.** RELIG Konfession *die*.

creek [kriːk] *n* - **1.** [of sea] Meeresarm *der* - **2.** *US* [stream] Bach *der*.

creep [kriːp] (*pt & pp* **crept**) ◇ *vi* [gen] kriechen; [person] schleichen. ◇ *n inf* [loathsome person] widerlicher Typ; [groveller] Schleimer *der*. ◆ **creeps** *npl*: **to give sb the creeps** *inf* jm nicht geheuer sein.

creeper ['kriːpəʳ] *n* [plant - growing along ground] Kriechpflanze *die*; [- growing upwards] Kletterpflanze *die*.

creeping *adj* [gradual] schleichend.

creepy ['kriːpɪ] *adj inf* unheimlich.

creepy-crawly [-'krɔːlɪ] (*pl* **creepy-crawlies**) *n inf* Krabbeltier *das*.

cremate [krɪ'meɪt] *vt* einläschern.

cremation [krɪ'meɪʃn] *n* Einäscherung *die*.

crematorium *UK* [ˌkremə'tɔːrɪəm] (*pl* **-riums** OR **-ria** [-rɪə]), **crematory** *US* ['kremətrɪ] *n* Krematorium *das*.

crepe [kreɪp] *n* - **1.** [cloth] Krepp *der* - **2.** [rubber] Kreppgummi *der* - **3.** [thin pancake] Crêpe *die*.

crepe bandage *n UK* elastische Binde.

crepe paper *n* Krepppapier *das*.

crept [krept] *pt & pp* ▷ **creep**.

crescent ['kresnt] *n* - **1.** [shape] Halbmond *der* - **2.** [street] *halbkreisförmig verlaufende Straße*.

cress [kres] *n* Kresse *die*.

crest [krest] *n* - **1.** [of bird] Haube *die*; [of cock, hill, wave] Kamm *der* - **2.** [of school, noble family] Wappen *das*.

crestfallen ['krestˌfɔːln] *adj* geknickt.

Crete [kriːt] *n* Kreta *nt*.

cretin ['kretɪn] *n inf pej* Idiot *der*, -in *die*.

crevice ['krevɪs] *n* Spalte *die*.

crew [kruː] *n* - **1.** [of ship, plane] Besatzung *die*, Crew *die* - **2.** CIN & TV Crew *die*.

crew cut *n* Bürstenschnitt *der*.

crew-neck *n* runder Halsausschnitt.

crib [krɪb] ◇ *n* - **1.** [cradle] Krippe *die* - **2.** *US* [cot] Kinderbett *das*. ◇ *vt inf* [copy]: **to crib sthg off** *OR* **from sb** etw von jm ab|schreiben.

crick [krɪk] *n*: **I've got a crick in my neck** ich habe einen steifen Hals.

cricket ['krɪkɪt] *n* - **1.** [game] Kricket *das* - **2.** [insect] Grille *die*.

crime [kraɪm] *n* - **1.** [gen] Verbrechen *das*; **crime is on the decrease** die Zahl der Verbrechen nimmt ab - **2.** *fig* [shameful act] Schande *die*.

criminal ['krɪmɪnl] ◇ *adj* kriminell; [act, offence] strafbar. ◇ *n* Kriminelle *der, die*.

crimson ['krɪmzn] *adj* - **1.** [in colour] purpurrot - **2.** [with embarrassment] knallrot.

cringe [krɪndʒ] *vi* - **1.** [out of fear] zurück|weichen - **2.** *inf* [with embarrassment] schaudern; **to cringe at sthg** vor etw *(D)* zurück|schrecken.

crinkle ['krɪŋkl] *vt* [paper, clothes] zerknittern.

cripple ['krɪpl] ◇ *n offens* Krüppel *der*. ◇ *vt* - **1.** MED [disable] zum Krüppel machen - **2.** [ship, plane] aktionsunfähig machen - **3.** *fig* [country, industry] lähmen.

crisis ['kraɪsɪs] (*pl* **crises** ['kraɪsiːz]) *n* Krise *die*.

crisp [krɪsp] *adj* - **1.** [pastry, bacon] knusprig; [apple, vegetables] frisch und knackig - **2.** [weather] frisch. ◆ **crisps** *npl UK* Chips *Pl*.

crisscross ['krɪskrɒs] ◇ *adj* [pattern] gitterartig. ◇ *vt* [subj: roads] kreuz und quer führen durch.

criterion [kraɪ'tɪərɪən] (*pl* **-rions** *OR* **-ria** [-rɪə]) *n* Kriterium *das*.

critic ['krɪtɪk] *n* Kritiker *der*, -in *die*.

critical ['krɪtɪkl] *adj* kritisch; [illness] schwer; [crucial] entscheidend; **to be critical of sb/sthg** jn/etw kritisieren.

critically ['krɪtɪklɪ] *adv* kritisch; [ill] schwer; **to be critically important** von entscheidender Bedeutung sein.

criticism ['krɪtɪsɪzm] *n* - **1.** [gen] Kritik *die* - **2.** [unfavourable comment] Kritikpunkt *der*.

criticize, -ise ['krɪtɪsaɪz] *vt* & *vi* kritisieren.

croak [krəʊk] *vi* [frog] quaken; [raven, person] krächzen.

Croat ['krəʊæt] ◇ *adj* kroatisch. ◇ *n* [person] Kroate *der*, -tin *die*.

Croatia [krəʊ'eɪʃə] *n* Kroatien *nt*.

Croatian [krəʊ'eɪʃn] *adj* & *n* = **Croat**.

crochet ['krəʊʃeɪ] *n* Häkeln *das*.

crockery ['krɒkərɪ] *n* Geschirr *das*.

crocodile ['krɒkədaɪl] (*pl inv OR* **-s**) *n* Krokodil *das*.

crocus ['krəʊkəs] (*pl* **-cuses**) *n* Krokus *der*.

crony ['krəʊnɪ] *n inf* [friend] Kumpel *der*.

crook [krʊk] *n* [criminal] Gauner *der*.

crooked ['krʊkɪd] *adj* - **1.** [picture, tie, teeth] schief; [path] gewunden - **2.** *inf* [dishonest - person] unehrlich; [- deal] krumm.

crop [krɒp] *n* - **1.** [kind of plant] Feldfrucht *die* - **2.** [harvest] Ernte *die* - **3.** [whip] Reitpeitsche *die* - **4.** [haircut] Kurzhaarschnitt *der*. ◆ **crop up** *vi* [problem] auf|tauchen.

croquette [krɒ'ket] *n* Krokette *die*.

cross [krɒs] ◇ *adj* [angry] böse; **to be cross with sb** böse auf jn sein. ◇ *n* - **1.** [gen] Kreuz *das* - **2.** [hybrid] Kreuzung *die*. ◇ *vt* - **1.** [street, road, river] überqueren; [room, desert] durchqueren; **it crossed my mind that...** der Gedanke ging mir durch den Kopf, dass... - **2.** [place one across the other] (über)kreuzen; [arms] verschränken; [legs] übereinander schlagen - **3.** *UK* [cheque] als Verrechnungsscheck kennzeichnen. ◇ *vi* [intersect] sich kreuzen. ◆ **cross off** *vt sep* streichen. ◆ **cross out** *vt sep* aus|streichen.

crossbar ['krɒsbɑːʳ] *n* - **1.** [of goal] Querlatte *die* - **2.** [of bicycle] Stange *die*.

cross-Channel ferry *n* Fähre *die* über den Ärmelkanal.

cross-country ◇ *adj* [run] Querfeldein-; [skiing] Langlauf-. ◇ *n* Querfeldeinlauf *der*.

cross-examine *vt liter* & *fig* ins Kreuzverhör nehmen.

cross-eyed [-aɪd] *adj*: **to be cross-eyed** schielen.

crossfire ['krɒs,faɪəʳ] *n* Kreuzfeuer *das*.

crossing ['krɒsɪŋ] *n* - **1.** [place] Übergang *der* - **2.** [sea journey] Überfahrt *die*.

cross-legged [-legd] *adv* im Schneidersitz.

cross-purposes *npl*: **to talk at cross-purposes** aneinander vorbei|reden.

cross-reference *n* Querverweis *der*.

crossroads ['krɒsrəʊdz] (*pl inv*) *n* Kreuzung *die*.

cross-section *n* Querschnitt *der*.

crosswalk ['krɒswɔːk] *n US* Fußgängerüberweg *der*.

crossword (puzzle) ['krɒswɜːd-] *n* Kreuzworträtsel *das*.

crotch [krɒtʃ] *n* - **1.** [of man] Hodengegend *die*; [of woman] Schamgegend *die* - **2.** [of clothes] Schritt *der*.

crotchet ['krɒtʃɪt] *n* Viertel(note) *die*.

crotchety ['krɒtʃɪtɪ] *adj UK inf* griesgrämig.

crouch [kraʊtʃ] *vi* kauern.

crow [krəʊ] ◇ *n* Krähe *die*; **10 miles as the crow flies** 10 Meilen Luftlinie. ◇ *vi* - **1.** [cock] krähen - **2.** *inf* [gloat]: **to crow over sthg** sich mit etw brüsten.

crowbar ['krəʊbɑːʳ] *n* Brecheisen *das*.

crowd [kraʊd] ◇ *n* [mass of people] Menschenmenge *die*; **crowds of people** große

Menschenmengen. <> *vi* sich drängen. <> *vt* [streets, town] bevölkern; **we were crowded into a small room** wir wurden in ein kleines Zimmer gedrängt.

crowded ['kraʊdɪd] *adj* voll; [train, shop, bar] überfüllt; [timetable, flat] eng; **to be crowded with people** voller Menschen sein.

crown [kraʊn] <> *n* - **1.** [of monarch, tooth] Krone *die* - **2.** [top - of hat] oberes Ende; [- of head] Scheitel *der*; [- of hill] Kuppe *die*. <> *vt* - **1.** [king, queen] krönen - **2.** [tooth] überkronen - **3.** [top] bedecken. ◆ **Crown** *n*: **the Crown** [monarchy] die Krone.

crown jewels *npl* Kronjuwelen *Pl.*

crow's feet *npl* Krähenfüße *Pl.*

crucial ['kru:ʃl] *adj* entscheidend.

crucifix ['kru:sɪfɪks] *n* Kruzifix *das.*

Crucifixion [ˌkru:sɪ'fɪkʃn] *n*: **the Crucifixion** die Kreuzigung.

crude [kru:d] *adj* - **1.** [raw] Roh-, roh - **2.** [vulgar] derb, ordinär - **3.** [drawing] grob; [method, shelter] primitiv.

crude oil *n* Rohöl *das.*

cruel [krʊəl] *adj* grausam.

cruelty ['krʊəltɪ] *n* Grausamkeit *die*; **cruelty to children** Kindesmisshandlung *die*; **cruelty to animals** Tierquälerei *die.*

cruet ['kru:ɪt] *n* Menage *die.*

cruise [kru:z] <> *n* Kreuzfahrt *die.* <> *vi* [ship] kreuzen; [plane] fliegen.

cruiser ['kru:zəʳ] *n* - **1.** [warship] Kreuzer *der* - **2.** [cabin cruiser] Vergnügungsjacht *die.*

crumb [krʌm] *n* [of food] Krümel *der.*

crumble ['krʌmbl] <> *n mit Streuseln bedeckte überbackene Obstnachspeise.* <> *vt* zerkrümeln; [into larger pieces] zerbröckeln. <> *vi* - **1.** [plaster] bröckeln; [bread] krümeln; [building, wall] zerbröckeln - **2.** *fig* [society, empire] verfallen; [hopes] dahin|schwinden.

crumbly ['krʌmblɪ] *adj* [plaster] bröckelig; [bread, cake] krümelig.

crumpet ['krʌmpɪt] *n kleines rundes Hefeteigbrot zum Toasten.*

crumple ['krʌmpl] *vt* [clothes] zerknittern; [paper] zerknüllen.

crunch [krʌntʃ] <> *n (phrase)*: **if** OR **when it comes to the crunch** *inf* wenn es darauf an|kommt. <> *vt* [with teeth] (krachend) kauen.

crunchy ['krʌntʃɪ] *adj* [apple, vegetables] frisch und knackig; [chocolate bar] knusprig.

crusade [kru:'seɪd] *n liter* & *fig* Kreuzzug *der.*

crush [krʌʃ] <> *n* - **1.** [crowd] Gedränge *das* - **2.** *inf* [infatuation]: **to have a crush on sb** für jn schwärmen. <> *vt* - **1.** [squeeze - limb] quetschen; [- clothes, garlic] zerdrücken - **2.** [ice, tablet] zerstoßen - **3.** [destroy] zerquetschen; **to be crushed to death** zu Tode gequetscht werden - **4.** *fig* [army, hopes] vernichten; [opposition] nieder|schlagen.

crust [krʌst] *n* Kruste *die.*

crutch [krʌtʃ] *n* [stick] Krücke *die.*

crux [krʌks] *n* Kern *der*; **the crux of the matter** der springende Punkt.

cry [kraɪ] *n* - **1.** [shout] Ruf *der*; [louder] Schrei *der*; **a cry of pain** ein Schmerzensschrei; **a cry for help** ein Hilferuf - **2.** [of bird] Schrei *der.* ◆ **cry off** *vi* einen Rückzieher machen. ◆ **cry out** *vt sep* & *vi* schreien.

cryptic ['krɪptɪk] *adj* rätselhaft.

crystal ['krɪstl] *n* Kristall *der.*

cub [kʌb] *n* - **1.** [young animal] Junge *das* - **2.** [boy scout] Wölfling *der.*

Cuba ['kju:bə] *n* Kuba *nt.*

Cuban ['kju:bən] <> *adj* kubanisch. <> *n* Kubaner *der*, -in *die.*

cubbyhole ['kʌbɪhəʊl] *n* [room] Kabäuschen *das*; [compartment] Fach *das.*

cube [kju:b] <> *n* - **1.** [object, shape] Würfel *der* - **2.** MATHS dritte Potenz. <> *vt* MATHS in die dritte Potenz erheben; **3 cubed** 3 hoch 3.

cubic ['kju:bɪk] *adj* Kubik-.

cubicle ['kju:bɪkl] *n* Kabine *die.*

Cub Scout *n* Wölfling *der.*

cuckoo ['kʊku:] *n* Kuckuck *der.*

cuckoo clock *n* Kuckucksuhr *die.*

cucumber ['kju:kʌmbəʳ] *n* Gurke *die.*

cuddle ['kʌdl] <> *n*: **to give sb a cuddle** jn in den Arm nehmen. <> *vt* an sich *(A)* drücken; [doll, dog] knuddeln. <> *vi* schmusen.

cuddly toy *n* Knuddeltier *das.*

cue [kju:] *n* - **1.** RADIO, THEAT & TV Stichwort *das*; **on cue** wie gerufen - **2.** [in snooker, pool] Queue *das.*

cuff [kʌf] *n* - **1.** [of sleeve] Manschette *die* - **2.** *US* [of trouser] Aufschlag *der.*

cuff link *n* Manschettenknopf *der.*

cul-de-sac ['kʌldəsæk] *n* Sackgasse *die.*

cull [kʌl] <> *n Kontrolle der Größe eines Viehbestands durch das Töten der schwächsten Tiere.* <> *vt* - **1.** [kill]: **to cull seals** Robbenschlag betreiben - **2.** *fml* [gather] sammeln.

culminate ['kʌlmɪneɪt] *vi*: **to culminate in sthg** in etw *(D)* gipfeln.

culmination [ˌkʌlmɪ'neɪʃn] *n* Höhepunkt *der.*

culottes [kju:'lɒts] *npl* Hosenrock *der.*

culpable ['kʌlpəbl] *adj fml* [person] schuldig.

culprit ['kʌlprɪt] *n* Schuldige *der*, *die*; [guilty of a crime] Täter *der*, -in *die.*

cult [kʌlt] <> *n* - **1.** RELIG Kult *der* - **2.** [book, film] Kultsymbol *das.* <> *comp* [book, film] Kult-.

cultivate ['kʌltɪveɪt] *vt* - **1.** [farm - land] bebauen; [- crops] an|bauen - **2.** [develop - interest, taste] entwickeln; [- friendship] pflegen; [- image] kultivieren.

cultural ['kʌltʃərəl] *adj* kulturell.

culture ['kʌltʃəʳ] *n* Kultur *die*.

cultured ['kʌltʃəd] *adj* kultiviert.

cumbersome ['kʌmbəsəm] *adj* [object] unhandlich; [parcel] sperrig.

cunning ['kʌnɪŋ] ◇ *adj* [plan] schlau; [person] gerissen; [device] schlau ausgedacht. ◇ *n* [of plan] Schlauheit *die*; [of person] Gerissenheit *die*.

cup [kʌp] *n* - **1.** [gen] Tasse *die*; **a cup of tea** eine Tasse Tee - **2.** [trophy, competition] Pokal *der* - **3.** [of bra] Körbchen *das*.

cupboard ['kʌbəd] *n* Schrank *der*.

Cup Final *n*: **the Cup Final** das Pokalendspiel.

curate ['kjʊərət] *n* Vikar *der*.

curator [ˌkjʊə'reɪtəʳ] *n* [of museum] Kustos *der*.

curb [kɜ:b] ◇ *n* - **1.** [control]: **to put a curb on sthg** etw im Zaum halten - **2.** *US* [of road] Bordstein *der*. ◇ *vt* zügeln.

curdle ['kɜ:dl] *vi* gerinnen.

cure [kjʊəʳ] ◇ *n* - **1.** MED: **cure (for)** Heilmittel *das* (für) - **2.** [solution]: **cure (for sthg)** Mittel *das* (gegen etw). ◇ *vt* - **1.** MED [illness, person] heilen - **2.** [solve] beheben - **3.** [rid]: **to cure sb of sthg** *fig* jn von etw heilen - **4.** [preserve - smoke] räuchern; [- salt] pökeln; [- dry] trocknen.

cure-all *n* Allheilmittel *das*.

curfew ['kɜ:fju:] *n* Ausgangssperre *die*.

curio ['kjʊərɪəʊ] (*pl* **-s**) *n* Kuriosität *die*.

curiosity [ˌkjʊərɪ'ɒsətɪ] *n* - **1.** [inquisitiveness] Neugier *die* - **2.** [rarity] Kuriosität *die*.

curious ['kjʊərɪəs] *adj* - **1.** [inquisitive]: **curious (about)** neugierig (auf *(+ A)*) - **2.** [strange] merkwürdig, seltsam.

curl [kɜ:l] ◇ *n* [of hair] Locke *die*. ◇ *vt* - **1.** [hair] in Locken legen - **2.** [tail, ribbon] (ein)rollen. ◇ *vi* - **1.** [hair] sich locken - **2.** [paper, leaf] sich zusammen|rollen - **3.** [smoke, snake] sich schlängeln. ◆ **curl up** *vi* [person, animal] sich zusammen|rollen; **to curl up in bed** sich ins Bett kuscheln.

curler ['kɜ:ləʳ] *n* Lockenwickler *der*.

curling tongs *npl* Lockenstab *der*.

curly ['kɜ:lɪ] *adj* [hair] lockig.

currant ['kʌrənt] *n* Korinthe *die*.

currency ['kʌrənsɪ] *n* - **1.** [money] Währung *die* - **2.** *fml* [acceptability]: **to gain currency** sich verbreiten, Verbreitung finden.

current ['kʌrənt] ◇ *adj* gegenwärtig. ◇ *n* [flow - of water] Strömung *die*; [- of air] Luftströmung *die*; [- of electricity] Strom *der*.

current account *n UK* Girokonto *das*.

current affairs *npl* aktuelle Fragen *Pl*.

currently ['kʌrəntlɪ] *adv* gegenwärtig.

curriculum [kə'rɪkjələm] (*pl* **-lums** *OR* **-la** [-lə]) *n* Lehrplan *der*.

curriculum vitae [-'vi:taɪ] (*pl* **curricula vitae**) *n* Lebenslauf *der*.

curry ['kʌrɪ] *n* Currygericht *das*; **chicken curry** Huhn mit Curry(sauce).

curse [kɜ:s] ◇ *n* - **1.** [evil spell, swearword] Fluch *der* - **2.** [source of problems] Plage *die*. ◇ *vt* verfluchen. ◇ *vi* [swear] fluchen.

cursor ['kɜ:səʳ] *n* COMPUT Cursor *der*.

cursory ['kɜ:sərɪ] *adj* flüchtig.

curt [kɜ:t] *adj* barsch.

curtail [kɜ:'teɪl] *vt* [visit] ab|kürzen.

curtain ['kɜ:tn] *n* [gen] Vorhang *der*.

curts(e)y ['kɜ:tsɪ] (*pt & pp* **curtsied**) ◇ *n* Knicks *der*. ◇ *vi* knicksen.

curve [kɜ:v] ◇ *n* Kurve *die*. ◇ *vi* [road, river] einen Bogen machen; [surface] sich wölben.

cushion ['kʊʃn] ◇ *n* [for sitting on] Kissen *das*. ◇ *vt* dämpfen, ab|fangen.

cushy ['kʊʃɪ] *adj inf* bequem, lässig.

custard ['kʌstəd] *n* ≃ Vanillesoße *die*.

custody ['kʌstədɪ] *n* - **1.** [of child] Sorgerecht *das* - **2.** [of suspect]: **in custody** in Untersuchungshaft.

custom ['kʌstəm] *n* - **1.** [tradition] Brauch *der*; [habit] Gepflogenheit *die* - **2.** COMM [trade] Einkauf *der*. ◆ **customs** *n (U)* [place] Zoll *der*.

customary ['kʌstəmrɪ] *adj* üblich.

customer ['kʌstəməʳ] *n* Kunde *der*, -din *die*.

customize, -ise ['kʌstəmaɪz] *vt* - **1.** [make] individuell her|richten - **2.** [modify] an|passen, modifizieren.

Customs and Excise *n (U) UK britische Finanzbehörde, die indirekte Steuern (Ex- und Importsteuer, Mehrwertsteuer und Verbrauchssteuer) einzieht und verwaltet.*

customs duty *n (U)* Zoll *der*.

customs officer *n* Zollbeamte *der*, -tin *die*.

cut [kʌt] (*pt & pp inv*) ◇ *n* - **1.** [slit] Schnitt *der* - **2.** [wound] Schnittwunde *die* - **3.** [of meat] Fleischstück *das* - **4.** [in salary, film, article] Kürzung *die* - **5.** [style - of clothes, hair] Schnitt *der*. ◇ *vt* - **1.** [gen] schneiden; **to cut one's finger** sich *(D)* in den Finger schneiden - **2.** [salary, costs, expenditure] reduzieren - **3.** [grass] mähen - **4.** [cards] ab|heben - **5.** *inf* [lecture, class] schwänzen. ◇ *vi* - **1.** [gen] schneiden - **2.** [intersect] sich kreuzen. ◆ **cut back** ◇ *vt sep* - **1.** [prune] zurück|schneiden - **2.** [reduce] reduzieren. ◇ *vi*: **to cut back on sthg** etw ein|schränken. ◆ **cut down** ◇ *vt sep* - **1.** [chop down] fällen - **2.** [reduce] reduzieren. ◇ *vi*: **to cut down on sthg** etw ein|schränken. ◆ **cut in** *vi* - **1.** [interrupt]: **to cut in (on sb)** (jn) unterbrechen - **2.** [in car]: **to cut in on** *OR* **in front of sb** jn schneiden. ◆ **cut**

off *vt sep* - **1.** [sever] ab|schneiden - **2.** [disconnect - electricity, gas, telephone] ab|stellen; **I got cut off** [on telephone] das Gespräch wurde unterbrochen - **3.** [isolate]: **to be cut off (from sb/sthg)** (von jm/etw) abgeschnitten sein - **4.** [discontinue] stoppen. ◆ **cut out** *vt sep* - **1.** [article, photo] aus|schneiden; [tumour] heraus|schneiden - **2.** [sewing] zu|schneiden - **3.** [stop] auf|hören mit; **cut it out!** lass das sein! - **4.** [exclude] aus|schließen. ◆ **cut up** *vt sep* [vegetables] schneiden; [wood] hacken; [meat] auf|schneiden.

cutback ['kʌtbæk] *n*: **cutback (in)** Kürzung *die* (von).

cute [kjuːt] *adj* süß.

cuticle ['kjuːtɪkl] *n* Nagelhaut *die*.

cutlery ['kʌtlərɪ] *n (U)* Besteck *das*.

cutlet ['kʌtlɪt] *n* Kotelett *das*.

cutout ['kʌtaʊt] *n* - **1.** [on machine] Stoppschalter *der* - **2.** [shape] Ausschneidemodell *das*.

cut-price, cut-rate *US adj* Billig-.

cut-throat *adj* [ruthless] gnadenlos.

cutting ['kʌtɪŋ] ◇ *adj* [wit] scharf; [remark] spitz, verletzend; [person] sarkastisch. ◇ *n* - **1.** [of plant] Ableger *der* - **2.** [from newspaper] Ausschnitt *der* - **3.** *UK* [for road, railway] Durchstich *der*.

CV *n abbr of* **curriculum vitae**.

cwt. *abbr of* **hundredweight**.

cyanide ['saɪənaɪd] *n* Cyanid *das*.

cycle ['saɪkl] ◇ *n* - **1.** [series of events] Kreislauf *der*, Zyklus *der* - **2.** [of machine] Durchlauf *der*, Durchgang *der* - **3.** [bicycle] Fahrrad *das* - **4.** [of poems, songs] Zyklus *der*. ◇ *comp* Fahrrad-. ◇ *vi* Fahrrad fahren.

cycling ['saɪklɪŋ] *n* Fahrradfahren *das*.

cyclist ['saɪklɪst] *n* Fahrradfahrer *der*, -in *die*.

cylinder ['sɪlɪndəʳ] *n* - **1.** [gen] Zylinder *der* - **2.** [for gas, oxygen] Flasche *die*.

cymbals ['sɪmblz] *npl* Becken *das*.

cynic ['sɪnɪk] *n* Zyniker *der*, -in *die*.

cynical ['sɪnɪkl] *adj* zynisch.

cynicism ['sɪnɪsɪzm] *n* Zynismus *der*.

Cypriot ['sɪprɪət] *n* Zypriot *der*, -in *die*.

Cyprus ['saɪprəs] *n* Zypern *nt*.

cyst [sɪst] *n* Zyste *die*.

czar [zɑːʳ] *n* Zar *der*.

Czech [tʃek] ◇ *adj* tschechisch. ◇ *n* - **1.** [person] Tscheche *der*, -chin *die* - **2.** [language] Tschechisch(e) *das*.

Czechoslovakia [ˌtʃekəslə'vækɪə] *n* Tschechoslowakei *die*.

Czech Republic *n*: **the Czech Republic** die Tschechische Republik.

D

d (*pl* **d's** OR **ds**), **D** (*pl* **D's** OR **Ds**) [diː] *n* [letter] d *das*, D *das*. ◆ **D** *n* - **1.** MUS D *das*; *(phrase)*: **D flat** Des *das* - **2.** SCH [mark] ≃ vier.

DA *n abbr of* **district attorney**.

dab [dæb] ◇ *n* [small amount] Klecks *der*. ◇ *vt* - **1.** [skin, wound] ab|tupfen - **2.** [cream, ointment]: **to dab sthg on(to) sthg** etw auf etw *(A)* tupfen.

dabble ['dæbl] *vi*: **to dabble (in sthg)** [in politics etc] (mit etw *(D)*) sich nebenbei beschäftigen.

dachshund ['dækshʊnd] *n* Dackel *der*.

dad [dæd], **daddy** ['dædɪ] *n inf* Vati *der*.

daddy longlegs [-'lɒŋlegz] (*pl inv*) *n* Schnake *die*.

daffodil ['dæfədɪl] *n* Osterglocke *die*.

daft [dɑːft] *adj UK inf* doof, blöd.

dagger ['dægəʳ] *n* Dolch *der*.

daily ['deɪlɪ] ◇ *adj* täglich. ◇ *adv* täglich. ◇ *n* [newspaper] Tageszeitung *die*.

dainty ['deɪntɪ] *adj* zierlich.

dairy ['deərɪ] *n* - **1.** [on farm] Molkerei *die* - **2.** [shop] Milchgeschäft *das*.

dairy products *npl* Molkereiprodukte *Pl*.

dais ['deɪɪs] *n* Podium *das*.

daisy ['deɪzɪ] *n* Gänseblümchen *das*.

dam [dæm] ◇ *n* (Stau)damm *der*. ◇ *vt* (auf)stauen.

damage ['dæmɪdʒ] ◇ *n*: **damage (to sthg)** Schaden *der* (an etw *(D)*). ◇ *vt* - **1.** [physically] beschädigen - **2.** *fig* [chances, reputation] schaden *(+ D)*. ◆ **damages** *npl* LAW Schaden(s)ersatz *der*.

damn [dæm] ◇ *adj* & *adv inf* verdammt. ◇ *n inf*: **not to give** OR **care a damn (about sthg)** sich einen Dreck scheren (um etw). ◇ *vt* RELIG [condemn] verdammen. ◇ *excl inf* verdammt!, Mist!

damned [dæmd] *inf* ◇ *adj* verdammt; **well I'll be** OR **I'm damned!** Donnerwetter! ◇ *adv* verdammt.

damning ['dæmɪŋ] *adj* vernichtend.

damp [dæmp] ◇ *adj* feucht. ◇ *n* Feuchtigkeit *die*. ◇ *vt* an|feuchten.

dampen ['dæmpən] *vt* - **1.** [make wet] an|feuchten - **2.** *fig* [emotion] dämpfen.

damson ['dæmzn] *n* Damaszenerpflaume *die*.

dance [dɑːns] ◇ *n* - **1.** [gen] Tanz *der* - **2.** [social event] Tanzabend *der* - **3.** [art form] Tanzen *das*. ◇ *vi* tanzen.

dancer ['dɑːnsəʳ] *n* Tänzer *der*, -in *die*.
dancing ['dɑːnsɪŋ] *n* Tanzen *das*.
dandelion ['dændɪlaɪən] *n* Löwenzahn *der*.
dandruff ['dændrʌf] *n* Schuppen *Pl*.
Dane [deɪn] *n* Däne *der*, -nin *die*.
danger ['deɪndʒəʳ] *n* Gefahr *die*; **in danger** in Gefahr; **out of danger** außer Gefahr; **danger to sb/sthg** Gefahr für jn/etw; **to be in danger of doing sthg** Gefahr laufen, etw zu tun.
dangerous ['deɪndʒərəs] *adj* gefährlich.
dangle ['dæŋgl] ◇ *vt* baumeln lassen; **to dangle sthg in front of sb** *fig* jn mit etw locken. ◇ *vi* baumeln.
Danish ['deɪnɪʃ] ◇ *adj* dänisch. ◇ *n* [language] Dänisch(e) *das*.
Danish (pastry) *n* Hefeteilchen *das*.
dank [dæŋk] *adj* naßkalt.
dapper ['dæpəʳ] *adj* adrett.
dappled ['dæpld] *adj* scheckig.
dare [deəʳ] ◇ *vt* - **1.** [be brave enough]: **to dare to do sthg** sich trauen, etw zu tun - **2.** [challenge]: **to dare sb to do sthg** jn heraus|fordern, etw zu tun - **3.** *phr*: **I dare say** ich glaube schon. ◇ *vi* es wagen, sich trauen; **how dare you!** was fällt dir ein! ◇ *n* Mutprobe *die*.
daredevil ['deə,devl] *n* Draufgänger *der*, -in *die*.
daring ['deərɪŋ] ◇ *adj* [person, action] kühn, verwegen; [comment, clothes] gewagt. ◇ *n* Wagemut *der*, Kühnheit *die*.
dark [dɑːk] ◇ *adj* [gen] dunkel. ◇ *n* - **1.** [darkness]: **the dark** die Dunkelheit; **to be in the dark about sthg** *fig* keine Ahnung von etw haben - **2.** [night]: **before/after dark** vor/nach Einbruch der Dunkelheit.
darken ['dɑːkn] ◇ *vt* verdunkeln. ◇ *vi* [gen] sich verdunkeln.
dark glasses *npl* Sonnenbrille *die*.
darkness ['dɑːknɪs] *n* Dunkelheit *die*.
darkroom ['dɑːkrʊm] *n* Dunkelkammer *die*.
darling ['dɑːlɪŋ] ◇ *adj* [dear] lieb. ◇ *n* - **1.** [loved person, term of address] Schatz *der* - **2.** [favourite] Liebling *der*.
darn [dɑːn] ◇ *adj* & *adv inf* verdammt, verflixt. ◇ *vt* [repair] stopfen.
dart [dɑːt] ◇ *n* [arrow] (Wurf)pfeil *der*. ◇ *vi* [move quickly] flitzen. ◆ **darts** *n (U)* [game] Darts *Pl*.
dartboard ['dɑːtbɔːd] *n* Dartscheibe *die*.
dash [dæʃ] ◇ *n* - **1.** [of liquid] Schuss *der* - **2.** [in punctuation] Gedankenstrich *der* - **3.** [rush]: **to make a dash for sthg** sich auf etw *(A)* stürzen. ◇ *vt* - **1.** *liter* [throw] schleudern - **2.** [hopes] zerstören. ◇ *vi* stürzen.
dashboard ['dæʃbɔːd] *n* Armaturenbrett *das*.
dashing ['dæʃɪŋ] *adj* [man] schneidig, flott.
data ['deɪtə] *n* Daten *Pl*.
database ['deɪtəbeɪs] *n* Datenbank *die*.
data processing *n* Datenverarbeitung *die*.
date [deɪt] ◇ *n* - **1.** [in time] Datum *das*; **to bring sb up to date** jn über den Stand der Dinge informieren; **to bring sthg up to date** etw auf den neuesten Stand bringen; **out of date** [fashion, dictionary] veraltet; [passport] abgelaufen; **to keep sb/sthg up to date** jn/etw auf dem Laufenden halten; **to date** bis heute - **2.** [appointment, person] Verabredung *die* - **3.** [fruit] Dattel *die*. ◇ *vt* - **1.** [gen] datieren - **2.** [go out with] aus|gehen mit. ◇ *vi* [go out of fashion] altmodisch werden.
dated ['deɪtɪd] *adj* altmodisch.
date of birth *n* Geburtsdatum *das*.
daub [dɔːb] *vt*: **to daub sthg with sthg** etw mit etw beschmieren; **to daub sthg on sthg** etw auf etw *(A)* schmieren.
daughter ['dɔːtəʳ] *n* Tochter *die*.
daughter-in-law (*pl* **daughters-in-law**) *n* Schwiegertochter *die*.
daunting ['dɔːntɪŋ] *adj* überwältigend.
dawdle ['dɔːdl] *vi* trödeln.
dawn [dɔːn] ◇ *n* - **1.** [of day] Morgengrauen *das*, Tagesanbruch *der* - **2.** *fig* [of era, period] Beginn *der*. ◇ *vi liter* & *fig* an|brechen; **the day is dawning** es dämmert. ◆ **dawn (up)on** *vt insep*: **it finally dawned on me that...** mir dämmerte schließlich, dass...
day [deɪ] *n* - **1.** [gen] Tag *der*; **the day before/after** am Tag zuvor/danach; **the day before yesterday** vorgestern; **the day after tomorrow** übermorgen; **any day now** jeden Tag *(in Kürze)*; **one day, some day, one of these days** irgendwann, eines Tages; **to make sb's day** jn sehr erfreuen - **2.** [period]: **in those days** damals; **in my day** zu meiner Zeit. ◆ **days** *adv* [work] tagsüber.
daybreak ['deɪbreɪk] *n* Tagesanbruch *der*; **at daybreak** bei Tagesanbruch.
daycentre ['deɪsentəʳ] *n UK* [for old people] Altentagesstätte *die*; [for children] Kindertagesstätte *die*.
daydream ['deɪdriːm] *vi* [not concentrate] vor sich hin träumen; [be idealistic] Luftschlösser bauen.
daylight ['deɪlaɪt] *n* - **1.** [light] Tageslicht *das* - **2.** [dawn] Tagesanbruch *der*.
day off (*pl* **days off**) *n* arbeitsfreier Tag.
day return *n UK* Tagesrückfahrkarte *die*.
daytime ['deɪtaɪm] ◇ *n* Tag *der*. ◇ *comp*: **daytime job** Arbeit am Tage OR über Tag; **daytime television** *tagsüber ausgestrahlte Fernsehprogramme*.
day-to-day *adj* [routine, life] (all)täglich; **on a day-to-day basis** tageweise.
day trip *n* Tagesausflug *der*.
daze [deɪz] ◇ *n*: **in a daze** benommen, betäubt. ◇ *vt* benommen machen.

dazzle ['dæzl] *vt* blenden.

DC *n abbr of* **direct current**.

deacon ['diːkn] *n* Diakon *der*.

deactivate [ˌdiː'æktɪveɪt] *vt* entschärfen.

dead [ded] ◇ *adj* - **1.** [person, animal, flower] tot; **the dead man/woman** der/die Tote; **to shoot sb dead** jn erschießen - **2.** [battery] leer; [telephone line, radio] tot - **3.** [numb - arm, fingers] wie abgestorben, taub - **4.** [lifeless - town] wie ausgestorben; [- party] öde. ◇ *adv* - **1.** [precisely] genau; **it's dead ahead** es ist genau geradeaus; **dead on time** auf die Minute pünktlich - **2.** *inf* [very] total; **'dead slow'** 'Schrittgeschwindigkeit'; **dead tired** todmüde - **3.** [suddenly]: **to stop dead** [in car] plötzlich stehen bleiben. ◇ *npl*: **the dead** die Toten *Pl*.

deaden ['dedn] *vt* - **1.** [noise] dämpfen - **2.** [feeling] betäuben.

dead end *n liter & fig* Sackgasse *die*.

dead heat *n* totes Rennen.

deadline ['dedlaɪn] *n* letztmöglicher Termin.

deadlock ['dedlɒk] *n* Stillstand *der*.

dead loss *n inf* Reinfall *der*; **dead loss at sthg** Niete *die* in etw *(D)*.

deadly ['dedlɪ] ◇ *adj* tödlich; [enemy, sin] Tod-. ◇ *adv* tödlich.

deadpan ['dedpæn] *adj* [delivery, manner] ausdruckslos; [humour] trocken.

deaf [def] ◇ *adj* taub; **to be deaf to sthg** *fig* sich in Bezug auf etw *(A)* taub stellen. ◇ *npl*: **the deaf** die Gehörlosen *Pl*.

deaf-aid *n UK* Hörgerät *das*.

deaf-and-dumb *adj* taubstumm.

deafen ['defn] *vt* taub machen.

deafness ['defnɪs] *n* Taubheit *die*.

deal [diːl] (*pt & pp* **dealt**) ◇ *n* - **1.** [quantity]: **a good** OR **great deal** (sehr) viel; **a good** OR **great deal of** eine Menge - **2.** [business agreement] Geschäft *das*; **to do** OR **strike a deal with sb** ein Geschäft mit jm ab|schließen - **3.** *inf* [treatment]: **to give sb a fair/rough deal** jn fair/unfair behandeln. ◇ *vt* - **1.** [strike]: **to deal sb/sthg a blow, to deal a blow to sb/sthg** jm/etw einen Schlag versetzen - **2.** [cards] aus|teilen. ◇ *vi* - **1.** [in cards] geben - **2.** [in drugs, arms] handeln. ◆ **deal in** *vt insep* COMM handeln mit. ◆ **deal out** *vt sep* - **1.** [cards] aus|teilen - **2.** [share out] verteilen. ◆ **deal with** *vt insep* - **1.** [handle, cope with] sich kümmern um - **2.** [be concerned with] handeln von - **3.** [be faced with] es zu tun haben mit.

dealer ['diːlə^r] *n* - **1.** [trader] Händler *der*, -in *die* - **2.** [in cards] Kartengeber *der*, -in *die*.

dealing ['diːlɪŋ] *n* [trading] Handel *der*. ◆ **dealings** *npl* [relations] Umgang *der*; **to have dealings with sb** mit jm (geschäftlich) zu tun haben.

dealt [delt] *pt & pp* ▷ **deal**.

dean [diːn] *n* UNIV & RELIG Dekan *der*.

dear [dɪə^r] ◇ *adj* - **1.** [loved] lieb; **to be dear to sb** jm lieb und teuer sein - **2.** *esp UK* [expensive] teuer - **3.** [in letter]: **Dear Tony** Lieber Tony; **Dear Mr Blair** Sehr geehrter Herr Blair; **Dear Sir or Madam** Sehr geehrte Damen und Herren. ◇ *n*: **my dear** mein Lieber, meine Liebe. ◇ *excl*: **oh dear!** ach je!; **dear me!** du meine Güte!

dearly ['dɪəlɪ] *adv* [love] von ganzem Herzen; [hope, wish] sehr.

death [deθ] *n* Tod *der*; **to frighten/worry sb to death** jn zu Tode erschrecken; **to be sick to death of sthg** etw gründlich satt haben.

death certificate *n* Totenschein *der*.

death duty *UK*, **death tax** *US n* Erbschaftssteuer *die*.

deathly ['deθlɪ] *adj* [silence] tödlich.

death penalty *n* Todesstrafe *die*.

death rate *n* Sterblichkeitsrate *die*.

death tax *n US* = **death duty**.

death trap *n inf* Todesfalle *die*.

debar [diː'bɑːr] *vt* aus|schließen.

debase [dɪ'beɪs] *vt* [quality, value, concept] entwerten; **to debase o.s.** sich erniedrigen.

debate [dɪ'beɪt] ◇ *n* Debatte *die*; **to be open to debate** zur Debatte stehen. ◇ *vt* debattieren, diskutieren; **to debate whether to do sthg** darüber diskutieren, ob etw getan werden soll. ◇ *vi* debattieren, diskutieren.

debauchery [dɪ'bɔːtʃərɪ] *n* Ausschweifung *die*.

debit ['debɪt] ◇ *n* Soll *das*, Debet *das*. ◇ *vt* debitieren, belasten.

debris ['deɪbriː] *n (U)* Trümmer *Pl*.

debt [det] *n* Schuld *die*; **to be in debt** Schulden haben; **to be in sb's debt** in js Schuld stehen.

debt collector *n* Schuldeneintreiber *der*.

debtor ['detə^r] *n* Schuldner *der*, -in *die*.

debug [ˌdiː'bʌg] *vt* COMPUT [program] Fehler beseitigen in.

debunk [ˌdiː'bʌŋk] *vt* entlarven.

debut ['deɪbjuː] *n* Debüt *das*.

decade ['dekeɪd] *n* Jahrzehnt *das*.

decadence ['dekədəns] *n* Dekadenz *die*.

decadent ['dekədənt] *adj* dekadent.

decaffeinated [dɪ'kæfɪneɪtɪd] *adj* entkoffeiniert.

decanter [dɪ'kæntə^r] *n* Karaffe *die*.

decathlon [dɪ'kæθlɒn] *n* Zehnkampf *der*.

decay [dɪ'keɪ] ◇ *n* - **1.** [of body] Verwesung *die*; [of plant, wood] Verrotten *das*; **(tooth) decay** Karies *die* - **2.** *fig* [of building] Zerfall *der*; [of society] Untergang *der*. ◇ *vi* - **1.** [tooth] faulen; [body] verwesen; [plant, wood] verrotten - **2.** *fig* [building] zerfallen; [society] unter|gehen.

deceased [dɪ'siːst] (*pl inv*) *fml* ◇ *adj* verstorben. ◇ *n*: **the deceased** der/die Verstorbene.

deceit [dɪ'siːt] *n* Betrug *der*.

deceitful [dɪ'siːtfʊl] *adj* betrügerisch.

deceive [dɪ'siːv] *vt* [trick] betrügen; [subj: memory, eyes] täuschen; **to deceive o.s.** sich *(D)* selbst etwas vorlmachen.

December [dɪ'sembəʳ] *n* Dezember *der*; *see also* **September**.

decency ['diːsnsɪ] *n* [respectability] Anstand *der*; **he didn't have the decency to thank me** er hat es nicht für nötig gehalten, sich bei mir zu bedanken.

decent ['diːsnt] *adj* anständig; **are you decent?** [dressed] hast du was an?

deception [dɪ'sepʃn] *n* Täuschung *die*.

deceptive [dɪ'septɪv] *adj* irreführend.

decide [dɪ'saɪd] ◇ *vt* - **1.** [resolve] (sich) entscheiden, beschließen; **to decide to do sthg** (sich) entscheiden etw zu tun; **to decide that...** entscheiden, dass..., beschließen, dass... - **2.** [issue, case, match] entscheiden; **what finally decided you?** was hat dich schließlich dazu gebracht? ◇ *vi* [make up one's mind] (sich) entscheiden, (sich) entschließen. ◆ **decide (up)on** *vt insep* sich entscheiden für.

decided [dɪ'saɪdɪd] *adj* - **1.** [distinct] entschieden - **2.** [resolute] bestimmt.

decidedly [dɪ'saɪdɪdlɪ] *adv* - **1.** [distinctly] entschieden - **2.** [resolutely] bestimmt.

deciduous [dɪ'sɪdjʊəs] *adj* Laub-.

decimal ['desɪml] ◇ *adj* dezimal. ◇ *n* Dezimalzahl *die*.

decimal point *n* Dezimalpunkt *der*.

decimate ['desɪmeɪt] *vt* dezimieren.

decipher [dɪ'saɪfəʳ] *vt* entziffern.

decision [dɪ'sɪʒn] *n* [choice, judgement] Entscheidung *die*.

decisive [dɪ'saɪsɪv] *adj* - **1.** [person] entschlossen - **2.** [factor, event] entscheidend.

deck [dek] *n* - **1.** [of ship, bus, plane] Deck *das* - **2.** [of cards] Spiel *das* - **3.** *US* [of house] Terrasse *die*.

deckchair ['dektʃeəʳ] *n* Liegestuhl *der*.

declaration [ˌdeklə'reɪʃn] *n* - **1.** [statement, proclamation] Erklärung *die* - **2.** [to customs] Zollerklärung *die*.

Declaration of Independence *n*: **the Declaration of Independence** die (amerikanische) Unabhängigkeitserklärung.

declare [dɪ'kleəʳ] *vt* - **1.** [state, proclaim] erklären - **2.** [goods at customs, taxes] deklarieren.

decline [dɪ'klaɪn] ◇ *n* Niedergang *der*; **to be in decline** sich verschlechtern; **to be on the decline** (ab)lsinken. ◇ *vt* [offer, request] abllehnen; **to decline to do sthg** ablehnen, etw zu tun. ◇ *vi* - **1.** [deteriorate] sich verschlechtern - **2.** [refuse] abllehnen.

decode [ˌdiː'kəʊd] *vt* entschlüsseln.

decompose [ˌdiːkəm'pəʊz] *vi* [vegetable matter] verfaulen; [flesh] verwesen.

decongestant [ˌdiːkən'dʒestənt] *n* schleimlösendes Mittel.

decorate ['dekəreɪt] *vt* - **1.** [make pretty - cake, dessert] verzieren; [- with balloons, streamers, flags] dekorieren, schmücken - **2.** [with paint] streichen; [with wallpaper] tapezieren - **3.** [with medal] auslzeichnen.

decoration [ˌdekə'reɪʃn] *n* - **1.** [ornament] Dekoration *die*; [on cake] Verzierung *die*; **Christmas tree decorations** Christbaumschmuck *der* - **2.** [appearance of room, building] Dekor *das* - **3.** [medal] Auszeichnung *die*.

decorator ['dekəreɪtəʳ] *n* Maler *der*, -in *die*.

decoy ◇ *n* ['diːkɔɪ] - **1.** [for hunting] Köder *der* - **2.** [person] Lockvogel *der*. ◇ *vt* [dɪ'kɔɪ] anllocken.

decrease ◇ *n* ['diːkriːs]: **decrease (in sthg)** [crime, unemployment] Rückgang *der* (an etw *(D)*); [size, spending] Abnahme *die* (einer Sache *(G)*). ◇ *vt* [dɪ'kriːs] verringern; [price] herablsetzen. ◇ *vi* [dɪ'kriːs] [in size] ablnehmen; [of numbers] zurücklgehen, sinken.

decree [dɪ'kriː] ◇ *n* - **1.** [order, decision] Erlass *der* - **2.** *US* [judgment] Urteil *das*. ◇ *vt* verordnen.

decree nisi [-'naɪsaɪ] (*pl* **decrees nisi**) *n* *UK* LAW vorläufiges Scheidungsurteil.

decrepit [dɪ'krepɪt] *adj* [person] altersschwach; [house, car] heruntergekommen.

dedicate ['dedɪkeɪt] *vt* - **1.** [book, song, poem]: **to dedicate sthg to sb** jm etw widmen - **2.** [devote]: **to dedicate one's life to sthg** sein Leben etw *(D)* widmen.

dedication [ˌdedɪ'keɪʃn] *n* - **1.** [commitment] Hingabe *die* - **2.** [in book] Widmung *die*.

deduce [dɪ'djuːs] *vt* schließen; **to deduce sthg from sthg** etw aus etw schließen.

deduct [dɪ'dʌkt] *vt*: **to deduct sthg (from)** etw ablziehen (von).

deduction [dɪ'dʌkʃn] *n* - **1.** [conclusion] Folgerung *die* - **2.** [of money, number] Abzug *der*.

deed [diːd] *n* - **1.** [action] Tat *die* - **2.** LAW Urkunde *die*; **deed of sale** Kaufvertrag *der*.

deem [diːm] *vt fml* erachten; **to deem it wise to do sthg** es für sinnvoll erachten, etw zu tun.

deep [diːp] ◇ *adj* - **1.** [gen] tief - **2.** [colour] dunkel - **3.** [thoughts, feelings] stark - **4.** [sigh, breath] schwer. ◇ *adv* tief; **deep down** *fig* innerlich.

deepen ['diːpn] *vi* - **1.** [river, sea] tiefer werden - **2.** [crisis, recession, feeling] sich verstärken.

deep freeze *n* Tiefkühltruhe *die*.

deep-fry *vt* frittieren.

deeply ['di:plɪ] *adv* - **1.** [gen] tief - **2.** [grateful, sorry, regret, moving] zutiefst.

deep-sea *adj* Tiefsee-.

deer [dɪəʳ] (*pl inv*) *n* [male] Hirsch *der*; [female] Reh *das*.

deface [dɪ'feɪs] *vt* [poster] verunstalten.

defamatory [dɪ'fæmətrɪ] *adj fml* verleumderisch.

default [dɪ'fɔ:lt] ◇ *n* - **1.** [failure]: **to win by default** durch Nichtantreten des Gegners gewinnen - **2.** COMPUT Voreinstellung *die*. ◇ *vi* [in sports] nicht an|treten.

defeat [dɪ'fi:t] ◇ *n* Niederlage *die*; [of motion] Ablehnung *die*; **to admit defeat** sich geschlagen geben. ◇ *vt* - **1.** [team, opponent] schlagen - **2.** [motion, proposal] ab|lehnen.

defeatist [dɪ'fi:tɪst] ◇ *adj* defätistisch. ◇ *n* Defätist *der*.

defect ◇ *n* ['di:fekt] Mangel *der*, Fehler *der*. ◇ *vi* [dɪ'fekt] POL über|laufen.

defective [dɪ'fektɪv] *adj* defekt.

defence *UK*, **defense** *US* [dɪ'fens] *n* - **1.** [gen] Verteidigung *die*; **in my defence** zu meiner Verteidigung - **2.** [protective device, system] Abwehr *die*.

defenceless *UK*, **defenseless** *US* [dɪ'fenslɪs] *adj* schutzlos.

defend [dɪ'fend] *vt* verteidigen; **to defend sb against sb/sthg** jn gegen jn/etw verteidigen.

defendant [dɪ'fendənt] *n* Angeklagte *der, die*, Beklagte *der, die*.

defender [dɪ'fendəʳ] *n* Verteidiger *der*, -in *die*.

defense *n US* = **defence**.

defenseless *adj US* = **defenceless**.

defensive [dɪ'fensɪv] ◇ *adj* - **1.** [weapons, tactics] Verteidigungs- - **2.** [person] defensiv. ◇ *n*: **on the defensive** in der Defensive.

defer [dɪ'fɜ:ʳ] ◇ *vt* verschieben. ◇ *vi*: **to defer to sb** sich jm beugen, sich jm fügen.

deferential [ˌdefə'renʃl] *adj* respektvoll.

defiance [dɪ'faɪəns] *n* Trotz *der*; **in defiance of sb/sthg** jm/etw zum Trotz.

defiant [dɪ'faɪənt] *adj* trotzig.

deficiency [dɪ'fɪʃnsɪ] *n* - **1.** [lack] Mangel *der* - **2.** [inadequacy] Mangelhaftigkeit *die*.

deficient [dɪ'fɪʃnt] *adj* - **1.** [lacking]: **he is deficient in sthg** es mangelt ihm an etw *(D)* - **2.** [inadequate] ungenügend.

deficit ['defɪsɪt] *n* Defizit *das*.

defile [dɪ'faɪl] *vt* besudeln.

define [dɪ'faɪn] *vt* - **1.** [give meaning of] definieren - **2.** [describe] bestimmen, fest|legen.

definite ['defɪnɪt] *adj* - **1.** [plan, date] bestimmt, definitiv - **2.** [answer] eindeutig; [improvement, difference] deutlich - **3.** [confident - person] bestimmt.

definitely ['defɪnɪtlɪ] *adv* definitiv.

definition [defɪ'nɪʃn] *n* - **1.** [of word, expression, concept] Definition *die* - **2.** [of image] Bildschärfe *die*.

deflate [dɪ'fleɪt] ◇ *vt* [balloon, tyre] die Luft ablassen aus. ◇ *vi* [balloon, tyre] Luft verlieren.

deflation [dɪ'fleɪʃn] *n* ECON Deflation *die*.

deflect [dɪ'flekt] *vt* ab|lenken.

defogger [ˌdi:'fɒgəʳ] *n US* AUT Scheibenbelüftung *die*.

deformed [dɪ'fɔ:md] *adj* deformiert.

defraud [dɪ'frɔ:d] *vt* betrügen.

defrost [ˌdi:'frɒst] ◇ *vt* - **1.** [fridge] ab|tauen; [frozen food] auf|tauen - **2.** *US* AUT [de-ice] enteisen; [demist] belüften. ◇ *vi* - **1.** [fridge] ab|tauen - **2.** [frozen food] auf|tauen.

deft [deft] *adj* geschickt.

defunct [dɪ'fʌŋkt] *adj* [organization] nicht mehr bestehend.

defuse [ˌdi:'fju:z] *vt UK liter* & *fig* entschärfen.

defy [dɪ'faɪ] *vt* - **1.** [disobey] trotzen *(+ D)* - **2.** [challenge]: **to defy sb to do sthg** jn heraus|fordern, etw zu tun - **3.** *fig*: **that defies description** das spottet jeder Beschreibung.

degenerate ◇ *adj* [dɪ'dʒenərət] degeneriert, entartet. ◇ *vi* [dɪ'dʒenəreɪt]: **to degenerate (into)** aus|arten (zu).

degrading [dɪ'greɪdɪŋ] *adj* entwürdigend.

degree [dɪ'gri:] *n* - **1.** [unit of measurement] Grad *der* - **2.** [qualification] akademischer Grad; **to have/take a degree (in sthg)** einen akademischen Abschluss (in etw *(D)*) haben/machen - **3.** [amount - of risk, truth] Maß *das*; *(phrase)*: **to a (certain) degree** bis zu einem gewissen Grad; **by degrees** allmählich, nach und nach.

dehydrated [ˌdi:haɪ'dreɪtɪd] *adj* [person] ausgetrocknet.

de-ice [di:'aɪs] *vt* enteisen.

deign [deɪn] *vi*: **to deign to do sthg** sich herab|lassen, etw zu tun.

deity ['di:ɪtɪ] *n* Gottheit *die*.

dejected [dɪ'dʒektɪd] *adj* niedergeschlagen.

delay [dɪ'leɪ] ◇ *n* Verspätung *die*. ◇ *vt* - **1.** [plane, train, traveller] auf|halten; [start, operation, recovery] verzögern - **2.** [postpone - meeting, journey, decision] verschieben; *(phrase)*: **to delay doing sthg** es auf|schieben, etw zu tun. ◇ *vi* zögern.

delayed [dɪ'leɪd] *adj* verspätet.

delectable [dɪ'lektəbl] *adj* - **1.** [food] köstlich - **2.** [person] reizend.

delegate ◇ *n* ['delɪgət] Delegierte *der, die*. ◇ *vt* ['delɪgeɪt] delegieren; **to delegate sb to do sthg** jn beauftragen, etw zu tun; **to delegate sthg to sb** jn mit etw beauftragen.

delegation [ˌdelɪˈgeɪʃn] *n* - **1.** [group of people] Delegation *die* - **2.** *(U)* [act of delegating] Delegieren *das*.

delete [dɪˈliːt] *vt* [word, line, name] streichen; COMPUT löschen, entfernen.

deli [ˈdelɪ] *n abbr of* **delicatessen**.

deliberate ◇ *adj* [dɪˈlɪbərət] - **1.** [intentional] absichtlich - **2.** [slow] bedächtig. ◇ *vi* [dɪˈlɪbəreɪt] *fml* beraten.

deliberately [dɪˈlɪbərətlɪ] *adv* [on purpose] absichtlich.

delicacy [ˈdelɪkəsɪ] *n* - **1.** [of lace, china] Feinheit *die*; [of health, instrument] Empfindlichkeit *die* - **2.** *(U)* [tact] Feingefühl *das* - **3.** [food] Delikatesse *die*.

delicate [ˈdelɪkət] *adj* - **1.** [lace, china, flavour] fein; [fingers, colour] zart - **2.** [child, person, health, instrument] empfindlich - **3.** [situation, subject] heikel.

delicatessen [ˌdelɪkəˈtesn] *n* Delikatessengeschäft *das*.

delicious [dɪˈlɪʃəs] *adj* [tasty] köstlich.

delight [dɪˈlaɪt] ◇ *n* Freude *die*; **to take delight in doing sthg** Freude daran haben, etw zu tun. ◇ *vt* erfreuen. ◇ *vi*: **to delight in doing sthg** sich damit vergnügen, etw zu tun.

delighted [dɪˈlaɪtɪd] *adj* sehr erfreut; **delighted by** OR **with sthg** hocherfreut über etw *(A)*; **to be delighted to do sthg** etw mit Vergnügen tun.

delightful [dɪˈlaɪtfʊl] *adj* reizend; [meal] köstlich.

delinquent [dɪˈlɪŋkwənt] ◇ *adj* straffällig. ◇ *n* Straftäter *der*, -in *die*.

delirious [dɪˈlɪrɪəs] *adj* - **1.** MED im Delirium - **2.** [ecstatic] ekstatisch.

deliver [dɪˈlɪvəʳ] *vt* - **1.** [distribute]: **to deliver sthg (to sb)** [mail, newspaper] (jm) etw zustellen; COMM (jm) etw liefern - **2.** [give - speech, lecture] halten; [- message, warning] überbringen - **3.** [a blow, kick] versetzen - **4.**: **to deliver a woman's baby** eine Frau von ihrem Baby entbinden - **5.** *fml* [liberate]: **to deliver sb (from sthg)** jn (von etw) erlösen - **6.** *US* POL [votes] stellen.

delivery [dɪˈlɪvərɪ] *n* - **1.** [of goods] Lieferung *die*; [of letters] Zustellung *die* - **2.** *(U)* [way of speaking] Vortragsweise *die* - **3.** [birth] Entbindung *die*.

delude [dɪˈluːd] *vt* täuschen; **to delude o.s.** sich etwas vor|machen.

delusion [dɪˈluːʒn] *n* Täuschung *die*.

delve [delv] *vi* - **1.** [into mystery]: **to delve into sthg** sich in etw *(A)* vertiefen - **2.** [in bag, cupboard] greifen.

demand [dɪˈmɑːnd] ◇ *n* - **1.** [claim, firm request] Forderung *die*; **it makes great demands on my time** es nimmt viel von meiner Zeit in Anspruch; **on demand** bei Bedarf - **2.** *(U)* COMM: **demand (for)** Nachfrage *die* (nach); **in demand** [product, person] gefragt. ◇ *vt* - **1.** [request forcefully] fordern, verlangen; **to demand to do sthg** verlangen, etw zu tun - **2.** [enquire forcefully] zu wissen verlangen - **3.** [require] erfordern.

demanding [dɪˈmɑːndɪŋ] *adj* - **1.** [job] anstrengend - **2.** [person, public] anspruchsvoll.

demean [dɪˈmiːn] *vt* erniedrigen.

demeaning [dɪˈmiːnɪŋ] *adj* erniedrigend.

demeanour *UK*, **demeanor** *US* [dəmiːnəʳ] *n (U) fml* Verhalten *das*.

demented [dɪˈmentɪd] *adj* wahnsinnig.

demise [dɪˈmaɪz] *n (U) fml* - **1.** [death] Ableben *das* - **2.** *fig* [of company, custom] Ende *das*.

demister [ˌdiːˈmɪstəʳ] *n UK* AUT Scheibenbelüftung *die*.

demo [ˈdeməʊ] (*pl* **-s**) *n inf abbr of* **demonstration**.

democracy [dɪˈmɒkrəsɪ] *n* Demokratie *die*.

democrat [ˈdeməkræt] *n* Demokrat *der*, -in *die*. ◆ **Democrat** *n US Wähler bzw. Angehöriger der Demokratischen Partei der USA*.

democratic [ˌdeməˈkrætɪk] *adj* demokratisch. ◆ **Democratic** *adj US die Demokratische Partei der USA betreffend*.

Democratic Party *n US*: **the Democratic Party** die Demokraten.

demolish [dɪˈmɒlɪʃ] *vt* - **1.** [building] ab|reißen - **2.** [idea, argument] zunichte machen.

demonstrate [ˈdemənstreɪt] ◇ *vt* - **1.** [prove] beweisen - **2.** [appliance, machine] vor|führen - **3.** [ability, talent] zeigen. ◇ *vi*: **to demonstrate (for/against)** demonstrieren (für/gegen).

demonstration [demənˈstreɪʃn] *n* - **1.** [public meeting] Demonstration *die* - **2.** [of new appliance, machine] Vorführung *die* - **3.** *fml* [of feelings] Ausdruck *der*.

demonstrator [ˈdemənstreɪtəʳ] *n* [protester] Demonstrant *der*, -in *die*.

demoralized [dɪˈmɒrəlaɪzd] *adj* demoralisiert, entmutigt.

demote [ˌdiːˈməʊt] *vt* degradieren.

demure [dɪˈmjʊəʳ] *adj* sittsam.

den [den] *n* [of animal] Höhle *die*.

denial [dɪˈnaɪəl] *n* - **1.** [refutation] Leugnung *die* - **2.** *(U)* [refusal] Verweigerung *die*.

denier [ˈdenɪəʳ] *n* Denier *das*.

denigrate [ˈdenɪgreɪt] *vt fml* verunglimpfen.

denim [ˈdenɪm] *n (U)* Jeansstoff *der*. ◆ **denims** *npl* Jeans *Pl*.

denim jacket *n* Jeansjacke *die*.

Denmark [ˈdenmɑːk] *n* Dänemark *nt*.

denomination [dɪˌnɒmɪˈneɪʃn] *n* - **1.** RELIG Konfession *die* - **2.** FIN Nennwert *der*.

denounce [dɪˈnaʊns] *vt* [person] an|greifen; [actions] an|prangern.

dense [dens] *adj* - **1.** [thick] dicht - **2.** *inf* [stupid] schwer von Begriff.

dent [dent] <> *n* Beule *die*. <> *vt* einlbeulen.

dental ['dentl] *adj* Zahn-; **dental appointment** Termin *der* beim Zahnarzt.

dental floss *n* Zahnseide *die*.

dental surgeon *n* Zahnarzt *der*, -ärztin *die*.

dentist ['dentɪst] *n* Zahnarzt *der*, -ärztin *die*; **to go to the dentist('s)** zum Zahnarzt gehen.

dentures ['dentʃəz] *npl* Gebiss *das*.

deny [dɪ'naɪ] *vt* - **1.** [refute] bestreiten; [publicly] dementieren - **2.** *fml* [refuse] verweigern; **to deny sb sthg** jm etw verweigern.

deodorant [diː'əʊdərənt] *n* Deodorant *das*.

depart [dɪ'pɑːt] *vi fml* - **1.** [leave] weglgehen; [by car, bus *etc*] weglfahren; [on journey] ablreisen; **to depart from** [train] ablfahren von; [plane] ablfliegen von - **2.** [differ]: **to depart from sthg** von etw ablweichen.

department [dɪ'pɑːtmənt] *n* - **1.** [in organization, shop] Abteilung *die* - **2.** SCH & UNIV Fachbereich *der* - **3.** [in government] Ministerium *das*.

department store *n* Kaufhaus *das*.

departure [dɪ'pɑːtʃəʳ] *n* - **1.** [leaving - on journey] Abreise *die*; [- of train] Abfahrt *die*; [- of plane] Abflug *der*; **'departures'** [in airport] 'Abflug' - **2.** [variation]: **departure (from sthg)** Abweichung *die* (von etw).

departure lounge *n* Abflughalle *die*.

depend [dɪ'pend] *vi* - **1.**: **to depend on sb/sthg** [financially] von jm/etw ablhängen; [to rely on] auf jn/etw angewiesen sein; **I can depend on you** ich kann mich auf dich verlassen - **2.** [be determined]: **to depend on sb/sthg** von jm/etw ablhängen; **it depends on what happens/who is there** das hängt davon ab, was passiert/wer da ist; **depending on the weather** je nachdem, wie das Wetter wird.

dependable [dɪ'pendəbl] *adj* verlässlich.

dependant [dɪ'pendənt] *n* versorgungsabhängige Angehörige *der, die*.

dependent [dɪ'pendənt] *adj* - **1.** [reliant]: **to be dependent (on sb/sthg)** [financially] abhängig sein (von jm/etw); [rely on] angewiesen sein (auf jn/etw) - **2.** [addicted] abhängig - **3.** [determined by]: **to be dependent on sb/sthg** von jm/etw abhängig sein.

depict [dɪ'pɪkt] *vt* - **1.** [show in picture] darstellen - **2.** [describe]: **to depict sb/sthg as sthg** jn/etw als etw beschreiben.

deplete [dɪ'pliːt] *vt* vermindern.

deplorable [dɪ'plɔːrəbl] *adj* beklagenswert.

deplore [dɪ'plɔːʳ] *vt* verurteilen.

deploy [dɪ'plɔɪ] *vt* einlsetzen.

deport [dɪ'pɔːt] *vt* auslweisen.

depose [dɪ'pəʊz] *vt* [king, ruler] ablsetzen.

deposit [dɪ'pɒzɪt] <> *n* - **1.** GEOL [of gold, oil] Ablagerung *die* - **2.** [in wine] Bodensatz *der* - **3.** [payment into bank] Einzahlung *die* - **4.** [down payment] Anzahlung *die* - **5.** [returnable payment - on bottle] Pfand *das*; [- on hired goods] Kaution *die*. <> *vt* - **1.** [in bank] deponieren - **2.** [bag, case, shopping] ablegen.

deposit account *n UK* Sparkonto *das*.

depot ['depəʊ] *n* - **1.** [storage area - for buses] Depot *das*; [- for goods] Lagerhaus *das* - **2.** *US* [terminus - for trains] Bahnhof *der*; [- for buses] Busbahnhof *der*.

depreciate [dɪ'priːʃɪeɪt] *vi* an Wert verlieren.

depress [dɪ'pres] *vt* - **1.** [sadden] deprimieren - **2.** ECON [economy, market] sich hemmend auswirken auf *(+ A)*; [prices, share values] verringern.

depressed [dɪ'prest] *adj* - **1.** [person] deprimiert, niedergeschlagen - **2.** [area] unterentwickelt *(in wirtschaftlicher Hinsicht)*.

depressing [dɪ'presɪŋ] *adj* deprimierend.

depression [dɪ'preʃn] *n* - **1.** [sadness] Niedergeschlagenheit *die*; MED Depression *die* - **2.** ECON Depression *die* - **3.** *fml* [hollow] Vertiefung *die*.

deprivation [ˌdeprɪ'veɪʃn] *n* Entbehrung *die*; **sleep deprivation** Schlafentzug *der*.

deprive [dɪ'praɪv] *vt*: **to deprive sb of sthg** [to take sthg away] jn einer Sache *(G)* berauben; [to prevent sb from having sthg] jm etw vorlenthalten.

depth [depθ] *n* Tiefe *die*; **to be out of one's depth** [in water] nicht mehr stehen können; *fig* [unable to cope] überfordert sein; **in depth** eingehend. ◆ **depths** *npl*: **the depths of the sea** die Tiefen des Meeres; **in the depths of winter** im tiefsten Winter; **to be in the depths of despair** in tiefster Verzweiflung sein.

deputize, -ise ['depjʊtaɪz] *vi*: **to deputize for sb** jn vertreten *(eine Person höheren Rangs)*.

deputy ['depjʊtɪ] <> *adj* stellvertretend. <> *n* - **1.** [second-in-command] Stellvertreter *der*, -in *die* - **2.** *US* [deputy sheriff] Hilfssheriff *der*.

derail [dɪ'reɪl] *vt* [train] entgleisen lassen.

deranged [dɪ'reɪndʒd] *adj* geistesgestört.

derby [*UK* 'dɑːbɪ, *US* 'dɜːbɪ] *n* - **1.** [sports event] Derby *das* - **2.** *US* [hat] Melone *die*.

derelict ['derəlɪkt] *adj* verfallen.

deride [dɪ'raɪd] *vt* verhöhnen.

derisory [də'raɪzərɪ] *adj* - **1.** [ridiculous] lächerlich - **2.** [scornful] höhnisch.

derivative [dɪ'rɪvətɪv] <> *adj pej* nachgeahmt. <> *n* Derivat *das*.

derive [dɪ'raɪv] <> *vt* - **1.**: **to derive pleasure from sthg** Freude an etw *(D)* haben; **to derive satisfaction from sthg** Befriedigung aus etw ziehen - **2.**: **to be derived from sthg** [from language] aus etw stammen; [from word] von etw abgeleitet sein. ◇ *vi*: **to derive from sthg** [from language] aus etw stammen; [from word] von etw abgeleitet sein.

derogatory [dɪ'rɒgətrɪ] *adj* abfällig.

derv [dɜ:v] *n UK* Diesel *der*.

descend [dɪ'send] ◇ *vi* - **1.** *fml* [go down - person] herunter|gehen/hinunter|gehen; [- in vehicle] herunter|fahren/hinunter|fahren; [- from carriage, ladder *etc*] herunter|steigen/hinunter|steigen; [- plane] die Flughöhe verringern - **2.** [fall]: **to descend on sb/sthg** [silence] sich über jn/etw legen; [gloom] jn/etw befallen. ◇ *vt fml* [go down] hinunter|gehen.

descendant [dɪ'sendənt] *n* Nachkomme *der*.

descended [dɪ'sendɪd] *adj*: **to be descended from sb** von jm ab|stammen.

descent [dɪ'sent] *n* - **1.** [downwards movement]: **a steep descent** ein steiler Abstieg - **2.** *(U)* [origin] Abstammung *die*.

describe [dɪ'skraɪb] *vt* beschreiben.

description [dɪ'skrɪpʃn] *n* - **1.** [account] Beschreibung *die* - **2.** [type] Art *die*.

desecrate ['desɪkreɪt] *vt* entweihen.

desert ◇ *n* ['dezət] GEOG Wüste *die*. ◇ *vt* [dɪ'zɜ:t] [abandon - place] verlassen; [- person] im Stich lassen. ◇ *vi* [dɪ'zɜ:t] MIL desertieren. ◆ **deserts** *npl* [dɪ'zɜ:t]: **to get one's just deserts** bekommen, was man verdient hat.

deserted [dɪ'zɜ:tɪd] *adj* verlassen, öde.

deserter [dɪ'zɜ:tə^r] *n* Deserteur *der*.

desert island ['dezət-] *n* einsame Insel.

deserve [dɪ'zɜ:v] *vt* verdienen; **to deserve to do sthg** verdienen, etw zu tun.

deserving [dɪ'zɜ:vɪŋ] *adj* verdienstvoll.

design [dɪ'zaɪn] ◇ *n* - **1.** [plan, drawing] Entwurf *der* - **2.** [art] Design *das* - **3.** [pattern] Muster *das* - **4.** [shape] Konstruktion *die*; [of dress] Schnitt *der* - **5.** [intention] Absicht *die*; **by design** absichtlich; **to have designs on sb/sthg** es auf jn/etw abgesehen haben. ◇ *vt* entwerfen; **to be designed to do sthg** dafür vorgesehen sein, etw zu tun.

designate *vt* ['dezɪgneɪt] [appoint - area] bestimmen; [- person] ernennen; *(phrase)*: **to designate sb to do sthg** bestimmen, dass jd etw tut.

designer [dɪ'zaɪnə^r] ◇ *adj* [jeans, glasses] Designer-. ◇ *n* [in industry] Konstrukteur *der*; [in theatre] Bühnenbildner *der*, -in *die*; [of clothes] Modedesigner *der*, -in *die*.

desirable [dɪ'zaɪərəbl] *adj* - **1.** *fml* [appropriate] wünschenswert - **2.** [attractive] reizvoll - **3.** [sexually attractive] begehrenswert.

desire [dɪ'zaɪə^r] ◇ *n* - **1.** [wish]: **desire (for sthg/to do sthg)** der Wunsch (nach etw/etw zu tun) - **2.** *(U)* [sexual longing] Begierde *die*. ◇ *vt* - **1.** [want] wünschen - **2.** [feel sexual longing for] begehren.

desist [dɪ'zɪst] *vi fml*: **to desist (from doing sthg)** davon ab|sehen (etw zu tun).

desk [desk] *n* - **1.** [piece of furniture] Schreibtisch *der*; [in school] Pult *das* - **2.** [service point] Schalter *der*; [in hotel] Empfang *der*.

desk diary *n* Tischkalender *der*.

desktop ['desktɒp] *n* COMPUT Desktop *das*.

desktop publishing *n* Desktop-Publishing *das*.

desolate ['desələt] *adj* - **1.** [place] trostlos - **2.** [person] tieftraurig.

despair [dɪ'speə^r] ◇ *n* Verzweiflung *die*. ◇ *vi* verzweifeln; **to despair of sb/sthg** an jm/etw verzweifeln; **to despair of doing sthg** die Hoffnung auf|geben, etw zu tun.

despairing [dɪ'speərɪŋ] *adj* verzweifelt.

despatch [dɪ'spætʃ] *n* & *vt* = **dispatch**.

desperate ['desprət] *adj* - **1.** [reckless - criminal, person] zum Äußersten entschlossen; [- attempt, measures] verzweifelt - **2.** [serious, hopeless] hoffnungslos - **3.** [despairing] verzweifelt - **4.** [in great need]: **to be desperate for sthg** etw dringend benötigen.

desperately ['desprətlɪ] *adv* - **1.** [seriously, hopelessly] hoffnungslos - **2.** [very - busy, sorry] äußerst; *(phrase)*: **she desperately wants to travel** sie wünscht sich nichts mehr als zu reisen.

desperation [ˌdespə'reɪʃn] *n* Verzweiflung *die*; **in desperation** aus Verzweiflung.

despicable [dɪ'spɪkəbl] *adj* [person] verachtenswert; [behaviour, act] verabscheuungswürdig.

despise [dɪ'spaɪz] *vt* [person] verachten; [racism] verabscheuen.

despite [dɪ'spaɪt] *prep* trotz *(+ G)*.

despondent [dɪ'spɒndənt] *adj* verzagt.

dessert [dɪ'zɜ:t] *n* Dessert *das*.

dessertspoon [dɪ'zɜ:tspu:n] *n* Dessertlöffel *der*.

destination [ˌdestɪ'neɪʃn] *n* [of means of transport] Bestimmungsort *der*; [of traveller] Reiseziel *das*.

destined ['destɪnd] *adj* [intended]: **to be destined for sthg** zu etw bestimmt sein; **to be destined to do sthg** dazu bestimmt sein, etw zu tun.

destiny ['destɪnɪ] *n* Schicksal *das*.

destitute ['destɪtju:t] *adj* notleidend; **to be destitute** Not leiden.

destroy [dɪ'strɔɪ] *vt* [ruin] zerstören.

destruction [dɪ'strʌkʃn] *n (U)* Zerstörung *die*, Vernichtung *die*.

detach [dɪ'tætʃ] *vt* [remove] ab|nehmen; [tear off] ab|trennen; **to detach sthg from sthg** etw von etw ab|nehmen/ab|trennen.

detached [dɪ'tætʃt] *adj* [unemotional] distanziert, unbeteiligt.

detached house *n* Einfamilienhaus *das*.

detachment [dɪ'tætʃmənt] *n* [aloofness] Distanziertheit *die*.

detail ['diːteɪl] ◇ *n* - **1.** [small point] Detail *das*; [specific] Einzelheit *die* - **2.** *(U)* [collection of facts, points] Details *Pl*; **to go into detail** ins Detail gehen; **in detail** im Detail. ◇ *vt* [list] auf|listen. ◆ **details** *npl* [information] Informationen *Pl*; [personal information] Personalien *Pl*.

detailed ['diːteɪld] *adj* detailliert.

detain [dɪ'teɪn] *vt* - **1.** [in police station] in polizeilichem Gewahrsam behalten; [in hospital] zur stationären Behandlung behalten - **2.** [delay] auf|halten.

detect [dɪ'tekt] *vt* - **1.** [subj: person] bemerken - **2.** [subj: machine] ausfindig machen.

detection [dɪ'tekʃn] *n* - **1.** *(U)* [discovery] Entdeckung *die* - **2.** [investigation] Ermittlungsarbeit *die*.

detective [dɪ'tektɪv] *n* [private] Detektiv *der*, -in *die*; [police officer] Kriminalbeamte *der*, -tin *die*.

detective novel *n* Kriminalroman *der*.

detention [dɪ'tenʃn] *n* - **1.** [of suspect] Untersuchungshaft *die* - **2.** [at school] Nachsitzen *das*.

deter [dɪ'tɜːʳ] *vt* ab|halten; **to deter sb from doing sthg** jn ab|halten, etw zu tun.

detergent [dɪ'tɜːdʒənt] *n* [for clothes] Waschmittel *das*; [for dishes] Spülmittel *das*.

deteriorate [dɪ'tɪərɪəreɪt] *vi* sich verschlechtern.

determination [dɪˌtɜːmɪ'neɪʃn] *n* [resolve] Entschlossenheit *die*.

determine [dɪ'tɜːmɪn] *vt* - **1.** [establish, find out] bestimmen, ermitteln - **2.** [control] entscheiden - **3.** *fml* [resolve]: **to determine to do sthg** sich dazu entschließen, etw zu tun - **4.** [fix, establish] fest|legen.

determined [dɪ'tɜːmɪnd] *adj* - **1.** [person] resolut; **to be determined to do sthg** fest entschlossen sein, etw zu tun - **2.** [effort] angestrengt.

deterrent [dɪ'terənt] *n* Abschreckungsmittel *das*.

detest [dɪ'test] *vt* verabscheuen.

detonate ['detəneɪt] ◇ *vt* zur Detonation bringen. ◇ *vi* detonieren.

detour ['diːˌtʊəʳ] *n* Umweg *der*.

detract [dɪ'trækt] *vi*: **to detract from** [quality] beeinträchtigen; [enjoyment, achievement] schmälern.

detriment ['detrɪmənt] *n*: **to the detriment of sb/sthg** zum Schaden von jm/etw.

detrimental [ˌdetrɪ'mentl] *adj* [effect] schädlich; [consequences] nachteilig.

deuce [djuːs] *n* TENNIS Einstand *der*.

devaluation [ˌdiːvæljʊ'eɪʃn] *n* FIN Abwertung *die*.

devastated ['devəsteɪtɪd] *adj* - **1.** [area, city] verwüstet - **2.** *fig* [person] am Boden zerstört.

devastating ['devəsteɪtɪŋ] *adj* - **1.** [disastrous - hurricane, storm] verheerend; [- news, experience] niederschmetternd - **2.** [very effective - charm, wit] umwerfend; [- remark, argument] vernichtend; [- player, speaker] überragend.

develop [dɪ'veləp] ◇ *vt* - **1.** [land, area, resources] erschließen - **2.** [illness] bekommen; [habit] an|nehmen; **the machine developed a fault** an der Maschine ist ein Fehler aufgetreten - **3.** [industry, sector] fördern - **4.** [machine, weapon, product] weiter|entwickeln - **5.** [business, company] aus|bauen; [idea, argument, plot] entfalten - **6.** PHOT entwickeln. ◇ *vi* - **1.** [gen] sich entwickeln; [plot] sich entfalten - **2.** [fault, problem] auf|tauchen; [illness] sich entwickeln.

developing country [dɪ'veləpɪŋ-] *n* Entwicklungsland *das*.

development [dɪ'veləpmənt] *n* - **1.** [gen] Entwicklung *die*; [of business, company] Ausbau *der*; [of idea, argument, plot] Entfaltung *die* - **2.** *(U)* [of land, area, resources] Erschließung *die* - **3.** [developed land] Neubausiedlung *die*.

deviate ['diːvɪeɪt] *vi*: **to deviate (from sthg)** (von etw) ab|weichen.

device [dɪ'vaɪs] *n* - **1.** [apparatus] Gerät *das* - **2.** [plan, method] Mittel *das* - **3.** [bomb] Sprengkörper *der*.

devil ['devl] *n* - **1.** [evil spirit] Teufel *der* - **2.** *inf* [person] Teufel *der*; **poor devil!** armer Teufel!; **you silly devil!** du Trottel!; **you lucky devil!** du Glückspilz! - **3.** [for emphasis]: **who/where/why the devil ?** wer/wo/warum zum Teufel ? ◆ **Devil** *n* [Satan]: **the Devil** der Teufel.

devious ['diːvjəs] *adj* [plan, means] fragwürdig; [person] verschlagen.

devise [dɪ'vaɪz] *vt* entwerfen.

devoid [dɪ'vɔɪd] *adj fml*: **devoid of** bar *(+ G)*.

devolution [ˌdiːvə'luːʃn] *n* POL Dezentralisierung *die*.

devote [dɪ'vəʊt] *vt*: **to devote sthg to sthg** etw für etw verwenden.

devoted [dɪ'vəʊtɪd] *adj* [mother] hingebungsvoll; [husband, wife] liebevoll und treu; **to be devoted to sb/sthg** jn/etw innig lieben.

devotion [dɪ'vəʊʃn] *n*: **devotion (to sb/sthg)** Hingabe *die* (an jn/etw).

devour [dɪ'vaʊəʳ] *vt liter* & *fig* verschlingen.

devout [dɪ'vaʊt] *adj* RELIG fromm.

dew [djuː] *n* Tau *der*.

diabetes [ˌdaɪəˈbiːtiːz] *n* Diabetes *der*.

diabetic [ˌdaɪəˈbetɪk] ◇ *adj* [person] zuckerkrank. ◇ *n* Diabetiker *der*, -in *die*.

diabolic(al) [ˌdaɪəˈbɒlɪk(l)] *adj* - **1.** [evil] teuflisch - **2.** *inf* [very bad] sauschlecht.

diagnose [ˈdaɪəgnəʊz] *vt* [illness] diagnostizieren.

diagnosis [ˌdaɪəgˈnəʊsɪs] (*pl* **-oses** [-əʊsiːz]) *n* [of illness] Diagnose *die*.

diagonal [daɪˈægənl] ◇ *adj* diagonal. ◇ *n* Diagonale *die*.

diagram [ˈdaɪəgræm] *n* Schaubild *das*.

dial [ˈdaɪəl] (*UK*) (*US*) ◇ *n* - **1.** [of watch, clock] Zifferblatt *das*; [of meter] Skala *die* - **2.** [of radio] Skala *die* - **3.** [of telephone] Wählscheibe *die*. ◇ *vt* [number] wählen.

dialect [ˈdaɪəlekt] *n* Dialekt *der*.

dialling code [ˈdaɪəlɪŋ-] *n UK* Vorwahl *die*.

dialling tone *UK* [ˈdaɪəlɪŋ-], **dial tone** *US* *n* Amtszeichen *das*.

dialogue *UK*, **dialog** *US* [ˈdaɪəlɒg] *n* Dialog *der*.

dial tone *n US* = **dialling tone**.

dialysis [daɪˈælɪsɪs] *n* Dialyse *die*.

diameter [daɪˈæmɪtəʳ] *n* Durchmesser *der*.

diamond [ˈdaɪəmənd] *n* - **1.** [gem] Diamant *der* - **2.** [shape] Raute *die*. ◆ **diamonds** *npl* Karo *das*; **the six of diamonds** die Karosechs.

diaper [ˈdaɪəpəʳ] *n US* Windel *die*.

diaphragm [ˈdaɪəfræm] *n* [contraceptive] Diaphragma *das*.

diarrh(o)ea [ˌdaɪəˈrɪə] *n* Durchfall *der*.

diary [ˈdaɪərɪ] *n* - **1.** [appointment book] (Termin)kalender *der* - **2.** [personal record] Tagebuch *das*.

dice [daɪs] (*pl inv*) ◇ *n* [for games] Würfel *der*. ◇ *vt* würfeln.

dictate [dɪkˈteɪt] *vt* - **1.** [read out] diktieren - **2.** [impose] vor|schreiben.

dictation [dɪkˈteɪʃn] *n* Diktat *das*; **to take** OR **do dictation** ein Diktat auf|nehmen.

dictator [dɪkˈteɪtəʳ] *n* POL Diktator *der*, -in *die*.

dictatorship [dɪkˈteɪtəʃɪp] *n* Diktatur *die*.

dictionary [ˈdɪkʃənrɪ] *n* Wörterbuch *das*; [for a particular subject] Lexikon *das*.

did [dɪd] *pt* ▷ **do**.

diddle [ˈdɪdl] *vt inf* übers Ohr hauen.

didn't [ˈdɪdnt] *abbr of* **did not**.

die [daɪ] ◇ *vi* (*pt & pp* **died**, *cont* **dying**) - **1.** [person] sterben; [animal, plant] ein|gehen; **to be dying** im Sterben liegen; **to be dying for sthg** *inf* sich nach etw sehnen; **to be dying to do sthg** *inf* darauf brennen, etw zu tun - **2.** *fig* [love, anger] vergehen; [memory] schwinden. ◇ *n* (*pl* **dice** [daɪs]) *esp US* [dice] Würfel *der*. ◆ **die away** *vi* [sound] leiser werden. ◆ **die down** *vi* [wind] sich legen; [sound] leiser werden; [fire] herunter|brennen. ◆ **die out** *vi* aus|sterben.

diehard [ˈdaɪhɑːd] *n* Ewiggestrige *der, die*.

diesel [ˈdiːzl] *n* - **1.** [vehicle] Diesel *der* - **2.** [fuel] Dieselöl *das*.

diesel engine *n* - **1.** [of car] Dieselmotor *der* - **2.** RAIL Diesellokomotive *die*.

diesel fuel, diesel oil *n* Dieselkraftstoff *der*, Dieselöl *das*.

diet [ˈdaɪət] ◇ *n* - **1.** [eating pattern] Ernährung *die* - **2.** [to lose weight, for medical reasons] Diät *die*; **to be/go on a diet** eine Diät machen. ◇ *comp* [low-calorie] Diät-. ◇ *vi* [to lose weight] eine Diät machen.

differ [ˈdɪfəʳ] *vi* - **1.** [be different] verschieden sein; **to differ from sb/sthg** sich von jm/etw unterscheiden - **2.** [disagree]: **to differ with sb (about sthg)** mit jm (über etw (*D*)) verschiedener Meinung sein.

difference [ˈdɪfrəns] *n* Unterschied *der*; **it doesn't make any difference** es ist egal; **difference of opinion** Meinungsverschiedenheit *die*.

different [ˈdɪfrənt] *adj* - **1.** [not like before] anders; [not identical] verschieden, unterschiedlich; [various] verschieden; **to be different from** *UK* OR **than** *US* **sb/sthg** anders sein als jd/etw - **2.** [unusual] außergewöhnlich.

differentiate [ˌdɪfəˈrenʃɪeɪt] ◇ *vt*: **to differentiate sthg from sthg** etw von etw unterscheiden. ◇ *vi*: **to differentiate (between)** unterscheiden (zwischen (*+ D*)).

difficult [ˈdɪfɪkəlt] *adj* - **1.** [hard] schwierig; **to make life difficult for sb** jm das Leben schwer machen - **2.** [awkward] schwierig.

difficulty [ˈdɪfɪkəltɪ] *n* Schwierigkeit *die*; **to have difficulty (in) doing sthg** Schwierigkeiten haben, etw zu tun.

diffident [ˈdɪfɪdənt] *adj* schüchtern.

diffuse *vt* [dɪˈfjuːz] - **1.** [light] aus|strahlen - **2.** [information] verbreiten.

dig [dɪg] (*pt & pp* **dug**) ◇ *n* - **1.** *fig* [unkind remark] Seitenhieb *der* - **2.** ARCHAEOL Ausgrabung *die*. ◇ *vt* [hole] graben; [garden] um|graben. ◇ *vi* [in ground] graben. ◆ **dig up** *vt sep liter & fig* aus|graben.

digest *vt* [dɪˈdʒest] *liter & fig* verdauen.

digestion [dɪˈdʒestʃn] *n* Verdauung *die*.

digestive biscuit *n UK mürber Keks aus Vollkornmehl.*

digestive system *n* Verdauungsapparat *der*.

digger [ˈdɪgəʳ] *n* [machine] Bagger *der*.

digit [ˈdɪdʒɪt] *n* - **1.** [figure] Ziffer *die* - **2.** [finger] Finger *der*; [toe] Zehe *die*.

digital [ˈdɪdʒɪtl] *adj* digital.

digital camera *n* Digitalkamera *die*.

digital radio *n* Digitalradio *das*.

digital television *n* digitales Fernsehen.
digital watch *n* Digitaluhr *die*.
dignified ['dɪgnɪfaɪd] *adj* würdevoll.
dignity ['dɪgnətɪ] *n* Würde *die*.
digress [daɪ'gres] *vi*: **to digress (from sthg)** (von etw) ab|schweifen.
digs [dɪgz] *npl UK inf* Bude *die*.
dike [daɪk] *n* - **1.** [wall, bank] Damm *der* - **2.** *inf pej* [lesbian] Lesbe *die*.
dilapidated [dɪ'læpɪdeɪtɪd] *adj* baufällig.
dilemma [dɪ'lemə] *n* Dilemma *das*.
diligent ['dɪlɪdʒənt] *adj* sorgfältig.
dilute [daɪ'luːt] ◇ *adj* verdünnt. ◇ *vt*: **to dilute sthg (with sthg)** etw (mit etw) verdünnen.
dim [dɪm] ◇ *adj* - **1.** [room] halbdunkel; [light] trüb - **2.** [indistinct - shape, sight] undeutlich; [- sound, memory] schwach - **3.** [eyes] schwach - **4.** *inf* [stupid] beschränkt. ◇ *vt* dämpfen. ◇ *vi* [light, hope] schwinden.
dime [daɪm] *n US* Zehncentstück *das*.
dimension [dɪ'menʃn] *n* Dimension *die*. ◆ **dimensions** *Pl* [of room, object] Abmessungen *Pl*; **in three dimensions** dreidimensional.
diminish [dɪ'mɪnɪʃ] ◇ *vt* [subj: person] herab|setzen; [subj: thing] verringern. ◇ *vi* [importance, popularity] ab|nehmen.
diminutive [dɪ'mɪnjʊtɪv] ◇ *adj fml* winzig. ◇ *n* GRAM Verkleinerungsform *die*.
dimmer *n* Dimmer *der*. ◆ **dimmers** *npl US* - **1.** [dipped headlights] Abblendlicht *das* - **2.** [parking lights] Begrenzungsleuchten *Pl*.
dimmer switch ['dɪmər-] *n* = **dimmer**.
dimple ['dɪmpl] *n* Grübchen *das*.
din [dɪn] *n inf* Getöse *das*.
dine [daɪn] *vi fml* speisen. ◆ **dine out** *vi* auswärts speisen.
diner ['daɪnər] *n* - **1.** [person] Gast *der (in einem Restaurant)* - **2.** *US* [restaurant] Lokal *das*.
dinghy ['dɪŋgɪ] *n* [for sailing] kleines Segelboot; **(rubber) dinghy** Schlauchboot *das*.
dingy ['dɪndʒɪ] *adj* schmuddelig.
dining car ['daɪnɪŋ-] *n* Speisewagen *der*.
dining room ['daɪnɪŋ-] *n* - **1.** [in house] Esszimmer *das* - **2.** [in hotel] Speisesaal *der*.
dinner ['dɪnər] *n* - **1.** [meal - in the evening] (warmes) Abendessen; [- at noon] Mittagessen *das* - **2.** [formal event] (Abend)essen *das*.
dinner jacket *n* [jacket] Smokingjacke *die*; [suit] Smoking *der*.
dinner party *n* Abendgesellschaft *die* (mit Essen).
dinnertime ['dɪnətaɪm] *n* Essenszeit *die*.
dinosaur ['daɪnəsɔːr] *n* Dinosaurier *der*.
dint [dɪnt] *n fml*: **by dint of** mittels *(+ G)*.
dip [dɪp] ◇ *n* - **1.** [in road, ground] Senke *die* - **2.** [sauce] Dip *der* - **3.** [swim]: **to go for a dip** (kurz) schwimmen gehen. ◇ *vt* - **1.** [into liquid]: **to dip sthg in(to) sthg** etw in etw *(A)* (ein)|tauchen - **2.** *UK* [headlights] ab|blenden. ◇ *vi* [wing, road, ground] sich senken.
diploma [dɪ'pləʊmə] (*pl* **-s**) *n* Diplom *das*.
diplomacy [dɪ'pləʊməsɪ] *n* Diplomatie *die*.
diplomat ['dɪpləmæt] *n* [official] Diplomat *der*, -in *die*.
diplomatic [ˌdɪplə'mætɪk] *adj* diplomatisch.
dipstick ['dɪpstɪk] *n* AUT Ölmessstab *der*.
dire ['daɪər] *adj* [serious - warning] dringend; [- consequences] schwerwiegend; *(phrase)*: **to be in dire need of sthg** etw dringend brauchen.
direct [dɪ'rekt] ◇ *adj* - **1.** [gen] direkt - **2.** [exact] genau. ◇ *vt* - **1.** [aim]: **to direct sthg at sb** [question, remark] etw an jn richten; **the campaign is directed at teenagers** die Kampagne zielt auf Teenager ab - **2.** [person to place] den Weg erklären *(+ D)* - **3.** [manage, be in charge of] leiten - **4.** [TV programme] leiten; [film, play] Regie führen bei - **5.** [order]: **to direct sb to do sthg** jn an|weisen, etw zu tun. ◇ *adv* direkt.
direct current *n* Gleichstrom *der*.
direct debit *n UK* Dauerauftrag *der*.
direction [dɪ'rekʃn] *n* - **1.** [orientation] Richtung *die* - **2.** [of play, film] Regie *die*; [of TV programme] Leitung *die*. ◆ **directions** *npl* - **1.** [to place] Wegbeschreibung *die*; **to ask (sb) for directions** (jn) nach dem Weg fragen - **2.** [for use] Gebrauchsanweisung *die*.
directly [dɪ'rektlɪ] *adv* - **1.** [gen] direkt - **2.** [exactly] genau - **3.** [very soon] sofort.
director [dɪ'rektər] *n* - **1.** [of company] Direktor *der*, -in *die* - **2.** [of film, play] Regisseur *der*, -in *die*; [of TV programme] Leiter *der*, -in *die*.
directory [dɪ'rektərɪ] *n* - **1.** [book, list] Verzeichnis *das*; **(telephone) directory** Telefonbuch *das* - **2.** COMPUT Directory *das*.
directory enquiries *n UK* Fernsprechauskunft *die*.
dire straits *npl*: **in dire straits** in großen Nöten.
dirt [dɜːt] *n* - **1.** [mud, dust] Schmutz *der* - **2.** [earth] Erde *die*.
dirt cheap *inf adj* spottbillig.
dirty ['dɜːtɪ] ◇ *adj* - **1.** [not clean] schmutzig - **2.** [unfair] gemein; **to play a dirty trick on sb** jm übel mitspielen - **3.** [smutty] schmutzig, unanständig. ◇ *vt* beschmutzen.
disability [ˌdɪsə'bɪlətɪ] *n* Behinderung *die*.
disabled [dɪs'eɪbld] ◇ *adj* behindert. ◇ *npl*: **the disabled** die Behinderten *Pl*.
disadvantage [ˌdɪsəd'vɑːntɪdʒ] *n* Nachteil *der*; **to be at a disadvantage** im Nachteil sein.
disagree [ˌdɪsə'griː] *vi* - **1.** [with another person] nicht überein|stimmen; [two people] sich nicht einig sein; **to disagree with sb** mit jm

nicht übereinlstimmen; **to disagree with sthg** mit etw nicht einverstanden sein - **2.** [statements, accounts] nicht übereinlstimmen - **3.** [subj: food, drink]: **to disagree with sb** jm nicht bekommen.

disagreeable [ˌdɪsəˈgriːəbl] *adj* - **1.** [smell, job] unangenehm - **2.** [person] unfreundlich.

disagreement [ˌdɪsəˈgriːmənt] *n* - **1.** [of opinions] Uneinigkeit *die*; [of records] Diskrepanz *die* - **2.** [argument] Meinungsverschiedenheit *die*; **to be in disagreement about sthg** [people] verschiedener Ansicht in Bezug auf etw *(A)* sein.

disallow [ˌdɪsəˈlaʊ] *vt* - **1.** *fml* [appeal, claim] zurücklweisen - **2.** [goal] nicht anlerkennen.

disappear [ˌdɪsəˈpɪəʳ] *vi* verschwinden.

disappearance [ˌdɪsəˈpɪərəns] *n* Verschwinden *das*.

disappoint [ˌdɪsəˈpɔɪnt] *vt* enttäuschen.

disappointed [ˌdɪsəˈpɔɪntɪd] *adj*: **disappointed (in** OR **with sthg)** (von etw) enttäuscht.

disappointing [ˌdɪsəˈpɔɪntɪŋ] *adj* enttäuschend.

disappointment [ˌdɪsəˈpɔɪntmənt] *n* Enttäuschung *die*.

disapproval [ˌdɪsəˈpruːvl] *n* Missfallen *das*.

disapprove [ˌdɪsəˈpruːv] *vi*: **to disapprove of sthg** etw missbilligen; **to disapprove of sb** etwas gegen jn haben.

disarm [dɪsˈɑːm] *vi* ablrüsten.

disarmament [dɪsˈɑːməmənt] *n* Abrüstung *die*.

disarray [ˌdɪsəˈreɪ] *n*: **to be in disarray** *fml* [clothes, hair, room] in Unordnung sein; [group] schlecht organisiert sein.

disaster [dɪˈzɑːstəʳ] *n* Katastrophe *die*.

disastrous [dɪˈzɑːstrəs] *adj* katastrophal.

disband [dɪsˈbænd] <> *vt* auflösen. <> *vi* sich auflösen.

disbelief [ˌdɪsbɪˈliːf] *n*: **in** OR **with disbelief** ungläubig.

disc *UK*, **disk** *US* [dɪsk] *n* - **1.** [shape] Scheibe *die* - **2.** MED Bandscheibe *die* - **3.** [record] Platte *die*.

discard [dɪˈskɑːd] *vt* weglwerfen.

discern [dɪˈsɜːn] *vt* - **1.** [see] wahrlnehmen - **2.** [detect] erkennen.

discerning [dɪˈsɜːnɪŋ] *adj* kritisch.

discharge <> *n* [ˈdɪstʃɑːdʒ] - **1.** [of patient, prisoner, soldier] Entlassung *die* - **2.** [toxic emission] Ausstoß *der* - **3.** MED [from wound] Ausfluss *der*. <> *vt* [dɪsˈtʃɑːdʒ] - **1.** [patient, prisoner, soldier] entlassen - **2.** *fml* [fulfil] erfüllen - **3.** [emit] auslstoßen.

disciple [dɪˈsaɪpl] *n* - **1.** RELIG Jünger *der* - **2.** *fig* [follower] Anhänger *der*, -in *die*.

discipline [ˈdɪsɪplɪn] <> *n* Disziplin *die*. <> *vt* - **1.** [train] disziplinieren - **2.** [punish] bestrafen.

disc jockey *n* Diskjockei *der*.

disclose [dɪsˈkləʊz] *vt* enthüllen.

disclosure [dɪsˈkləʊʒəʳ] *n* Enthüllung *die*.

disco [ˈdɪskəʊ] (*pl* **-s**) *n abbr of* **discotheque**.

discomfort [dɪsˈkʌmfət] *n* - **1.** *(U)* [physical pain] Beschwerden *Pl*; **to be in discomfort** Beschwerden haben - **2.** [anxiety, embarrassment] Unbehagen *das*.

disconcert [ˌdɪskənˈsɜːt] *vt* verunsichern.

disconnect [ˌdɪskəˈnekt] *vt* - **1.** [detach] trennen - **2.** [remove plug of] den Stecker herauslziehen von; [from water/gas supply] von der Wasserzufuhr/Gaszufuhr trennen; **to disconnect sb's telephone** jm das Telefon ablstellen; **we've been disconnected** man hat uns das Telefon/das Gas/das Wasser/den Strom abgestellt - **3.** [when talking]: **we've been disconnected** die Verbindung wurde unterbrochen.

disconsolate [dɪsˈkɒnsələt] *adj* untröstlich.

discontent [ˌdɪskənˈtent] *n*: **discontent (with sthg)** Unzufriedenheit *die* (mit etw).

discontented [ˌdɪskənˈtentɪd] *adj*: **to be discontented (with sthg)** (mit etw) unzufrieden sein.

discontinue [ˌdɪskənˈtɪnjuː] *vt* [service, supply] einlstellen; [visits] beenden; [production] auslaufen lassen.

discord [ˈdɪskɔːd] *n* - **1.** *fml* [conflict] Uneinigkeit *die* - **2.** MUS Disharmonie *die*.

discotheque [ˈdɪskəʊtek] *n* Diskothek *die*.

discount <> *n* [ˈdɪskaʊnt] Rabatt *der*. <> *vt* [*UK* dɪsˈkaʊnt, *US* ˈdɪskaʊnt] - **1.** [disregard] verwerfen - **2.** COMM [product] zu einem geringeren Preis anlbieten.

discourage [dɪsˈkʌrɪdʒ] *vt* - **1.** [dishearten] entmutigen - **2.** [dissuade]: **to discourage sb from doing sthg** jn davon ablbringen, etw zu tun.

discover [dɪˈskʌvəʳ] *vt* - **1.** [find] entdecken; [cause of sthg] herauslfinden - **2.** [realize] festlstellen.

discovery [dɪˈskʌvərɪ] *n* Entdeckung *die*.

discredit [dɪsˈkredɪt] *vt* diskreditieren.

discreet [dɪˈskriːt] *adj* diskret.

discrepancy [dɪˈskrepənsɪ] *n*: **discrepancy (in/between)** Diskrepanz *die* (zwischen *(+ D)*).

discretion [dɪˈskreʃn] *n* - **1.** [tact] Diskretion *die* - **2.** [judgment]: **use your own discretion** handeln Sie nach eigenem Ermessen; **at the discretion of** nach Ermessen *(+ G)*.

discriminate [dɪˈskrɪmɪneɪt] *vi* - **1.** [distinguish]: **to discriminate (between)** unterscheiden (zwischen *(+ D)*) - **2.** [treat unfairly]: **to discriminate against sb** jn diskriminieren.

discriminating [dɪ'skrɪmɪneɪtɪŋ] *adj* [person, eye, audience] kritisch; [taste] fein.

discrimination [dɪˌskrɪmɪ'neɪʃn] *n* - **1.** [prejudice] Diskriminierung *die* - **2.** [good judgment] Urteilsvermögen *das*.

discus ['dɪskəs] (*pl* **-es**) *n* Diskus *der*.

discuss [dɪ'skʌs] *vt* besprechen; [in political, academic context] diskutieren; **to discuss sthg with sb** etw mit jm besprechen.

discussion [dɪ'skʌʃn] *n* - **1.** *(U)* [act of discussing] Besprechen *das*; [in political, academic context] Diskussion *die*; **to be under discussion** zur Diskussion stehen - **2.** [talk] Gespräch *das*; [in political, academic context] Diskussion *die*.

disdain [dɪs'deɪn] *fml n*: **disdain (for sb/sthg)** Verachtung *die* (für jn/etw).

disease [dɪ'zi:z] *n liter & fig* Krankheit *die*.

disembark [ˌdɪsɪm'bɑ:k] *vi* von Bord gehen.

disenchanted [ˌdɪsɪn'tʃɑ:ntɪd] *adj*: **disenchanted (with sthg)** (von etw) ernüchtert.

disengage [ˌdɪsɪn'geɪdʒ] *vt* - **1.** [release]: **to disengage o.s./sthg (from sthg)** sich/etw (von etw) los|machen - **2.** TECH [gears, mechanism] aus|rücken.

disfigure [dɪs'fɪgəʳ] *vt* verunstalten.

disgrace [dɪs'greɪs] ◇ *n* Schande *die*; **to be in disgrace** in Ungnade gefallen sein. ◇ *vt*: **to disgrace sb** jm Schande machen; **to disgrace o.s.** sich blamieren.

disgraceful [dɪs'greɪsfʊl] *adj* skandalös.

disgruntled [dɪs'grʌntld] *adj* verstimmt.

disguise [dɪs'gaɪz] ◇ *n* Verkleidung *die*; **in disguise** verkleidet. ◇ *vt* - **1.** [dress up] verkleiden - **2.** [voice, handwriting] verstellen - **3.** [disappointment, surprise] verbergen; [fact] verschleiern; [taste of sthg] überdecken.

disgust [dɪs'gʌst] ◇ *n*: **disgust (at sthg)** Abscheu *der* (vor etw *(D)*). ◇ *vt* anlekeln.

disgusting [dɪs'gʌstɪŋ] *adj* ekelhaft.

dish [dɪʃ] *n* - **1.** [bowl] Schüssel *die*; [shallow] Schale *die* - **2.** *US* [plate] Teller *der* - **3.** [food] Gericht *das*. ◆ **dishes** *npl* Geschirr *das*; **to do** OR **wash the dishes** Geschirr spülen OR ablwaschen. ◆ **dish out** *vt sep inf* aus|teilen. ◆ **dish up** *vt sep inf* [food] auf|tun.

dish aerial *UK*, **dish antenna** *US n* Parabolantenne *die*, Satellitenschüssel *die*.

dishcloth ['dɪʃklɒθ] *n* Spültuch *das*.

disheartened [dɪs'hɑ:tnd] *adj* entmutigt.

dishevelled *UK*, **disheveled** *US* [dɪ'ʃevəld] *adj* [hair] zerzaust; [person] unordentlich.

dishonest [dɪs'ɒnɪst] *adj* - **1.** [person] unehrlich; [trader] unredlich - **2.** [action] unredlich, unlauter.

dishonor *n* & *vt US* = **dishonour**.

dishonorable *adj US* = **dishonourable**.

dishonour *UK*, **dishonor** *US* [dɪs'ɒnəʳ] ◇ *n* Unehre *die*. ◇ *vt* entehren.

dishonourable *UK*, **dishonorable** *US* [dɪs'ɒnərəbl] *adj* unehrenhaft.

dish towel *n US* Geschirrtuch *das*.

dishwasher ['dɪʃˌwɒʃəʳ] *n* [machine] Geschirrspülmaschine *die*.

disillusioned [ˌdɪsɪ'lu:ʒnd] *adj* desillusioniert; **disillusioned with sb/sthg** von jm/etw enttäuscht.

disincentive [ˌdɪsɪn'sentɪv] *n* Abschreckungsmittel *das*.

disinclined [ˌdɪsɪn'klaɪnd] *adj*: **to be disinclined to do sthg** abgeneigt sein, etw zu tun.

disinfect [ˌdɪsɪn'fekt] *vt* desinfizieren.

disinfectant [ˌdɪsɪn'fektənt] *n* Desinfektionsmittel *das*.

disintegrate [dɪs'ɪntɪgreɪt] *vi* [object] zerfallen.

disinterested [ˌdɪs'ɪntrəstɪd] *adj* - **1.** [objective] unparteiisch - **2.** *inf* [uninterested]: **disinterested (in sb/sthg)** nicht interessiert (an jm/etw).

disjointed [dɪs'dʒɔɪntɪd] *adj* zusammenhanglos.

disk [dɪsk] *n* - **1.** COMPUT: **(floppy) disk** Diskette *die*; **(hard) disk** Festplatte *die* - **2.** *US* = **disc**.

disk drive *UK*, **diskette drive** *US n* COMPUT [for floppy disk] Diskettenlaufwerk *das*.

diskette [dɪs'ket] *n* COMPUT Diskette *die*.

diskette drive *n US* = **disk drive**.

dislike [dɪs'laɪk] ◇ *n*: **dislike (of)** Abneigung *die* (gegen); **to take a dislike to sb/sthg** eine Abneigung gegen jn/etw empfinden. ◇ *vt* nicht mögen.

dislocate ['dɪsləkeɪt] *vt* MED aus|renken.

dislodge [dɪs'lɒdʒ] *vt*: **to dislodge sb/sthg (from)** jn/etw entfernen (von OR aus).

disloyal [ˌdɪs'lɔɪəl] *adj*: **disloyal (to sb)** illoyal (gegenüber jm).

dismal ['dɪzml] *adj* - **1.** [gloomy, depressing] trist - **2.** [attempt, failure] kläglich.

dismantle [dɪs'mæntl] *vt* auseinander nehmen.

dismay [dɪs'meɪ] ◇ *n* Bestürzung *die*. ◇ *vt* bestürzen.

dismiss [dɪs'mɪs] *vt* - **1.** [employee, class, troops]: **to dismiss sb (from sthg)** jn (aus etw) entlassen - **2.** [refuse to take seriously] ab|tun - **3.** LAW [case] ab|weisen.

dismissal [dɪs'mɪsl] *n* [from job] Entlassung *die*.

dismount [ˌdɪs'maʊnt] *vi*: **to dismount (from sthg)** ab|steigen (von etw).

disobedience [ˌdɪsə'bi:djəns] *n* Ungehorsam *der*.

disobedient [ˌdɪsə'bi:djənt] *adj* ungehorsam.

disobey [ˌdɪsə'beɪ] *vt* [rule] übertreten; [person] nicht gehorchen *(+ D)*.

disorder [dɪs'ɔ:dəʳ] *n* - **1.** [disarray]: **in disorder** in Unordnung - **2.** [rioting] Unruhen *Pl* - **3.** MED Funktionsstörung *die*.

disorderly [dɪs'ɔ:dəlɪ] *adj* - **1.** [untidy] unordentlich - **2.** [unruly - behaviour] ungehörig.

disorganized, -ised [dɪs'ɔ:gənaɪzd] *adj* [person] unorganisiert; [system] unstrukturiert.

disorientated *UK* [dɪs'ɔ:rɪənteɪtɪd], **disoriented** *US* [dɪs'ɔ:rɪəntɪd] *adj* desorientiert.

disown [dɪs'əʊn] *vt* [son, daughter] verstoßen; [friend] verleugnen.

disparaging [dɪ'spærɪdʒɪŋ] *adj* geringschätzig.

dispassionate [dɪ'spæʃnət] *adj* objektiv.

dispatch [dɪ'spætʃ] <> *n* Bericht *der*. <> *vt* [person, troops, submarine] entsenden; [message, letter, parcel] senden.

dispel [dɪ'spel] *vt* [doubts, fears] zerstreuen; [illusions] nehmen.

dispense [dɪ'spens] *vt* - **1.** [advice] erteilen; **to dispense justice** Recht sprechen - **2.** [drugs, medicine] ab|geben. ◆ **dispense with** *vt insep* - **1.** [do without] verzichten auf *(+ A)* - **2.** [make unnecessary] unnötig machen.

dispensing chemist *UK*, **dispensing pharmacist** *US* [dɪ'spensɪŋ-] *n* Apotheker *der*, -in *die*.

disperse [dɪ'spɜ:s] <> *vt* [crowd] zerstreuen. <> *vi* [crowd] sich zerstreuen.

dispirited [dɪ'spɪrɪtɪd] *adj* entmutigt.

displace [dɪs'pleɪs] *vt* [supplant] ab|lösen.

display [dɪ'spleɪ] <> *n* - **1.** [of goods, merchandise] Auslage *die*; [in museum] Ausstellung *die* - **2.**: **it was a fine display of courage/skill from him** er zeigte viel Mut/Geschick - **3.** [performance] Vorführung *die* - **4.** COMPUT Display *das*. <> *vt* - **1.** [goods, merchandise] aus|stellen - **2.** [courage, skill, self-control] zeigen.

displease [dɪs'pli:z] *vt* verärgern; **to be displeased with sthg** mit etw unzufrieden sein.

displeasure [dɪs'pleʒəʳ] *n* Missfallen *das*.

disposable [dɪ'spəʊzəbl] *adj* - **1.** [to be thrown away after use] Wegwerf-; **disposable nappy** *UK*, **disposable diaper** *US* Wegwerfwindel *die* - **2.** [available] verfügbar.

diposable camera *n* Einmalkamera *die*.

disposal [dɪ'spəʊzl] *n (U)* - **1.** [removal] Beseitigung *die* - **2.** [availability]: **to be at sb's disposal** jm zur Verfügung stehen; **to put sthg at sb's disposal** jm etw zur Verfügung stellen.

disposed [dɪ'spəʊzd] *adj* - **1.** [willing]: **to be disposed to do sthg** geneigt sein, etw zu tun - **2.** [friendly]: **to be well disposed to** OR **towards sb** jm wohlwollend gegenüber stehen.

dispose ◆ **dispose of** *vt insep* [rubbish, problem] beseitigen.

disposition [ˌdɪspə'zɪʃn] *n* [temperament] Naturell *das*; **he has a cheerful disposition** er ist ein fröhlicher Mensch.

disprove [ˌdɪs'pru:v] *vt* widerlegen.

dispute [dɪ'spju:t] <> *n* - **1.** [quarrel] Streit *der* - **2.** *(U)* [disagreement] Meinungsverschiedenheit *die*; **they are in dispute** zwischen ihnen herrschen Unstimmigkeiten - **3.** INDUST Auseinandersetzung *die*. <> *vt* - **1.** [question, challenge] bestreiten - **2.** [fight for - championship] jm streitig machen; [- territory] beanspruchen.

disqualify [ˌdɪs'kwɒlɪfaɪ] *vt* - **1.** [subj: illness, criminal record]: **to disqualify sb from doing sthg** jn dafür ungeeignet machen, etw zu tun - **2.** SPORT disqualifizieren - **3.** *UK*: **to disqualify sb from driving** jm den Führerschein entziehen.

disquiet [dɪs'kwaɪət] *n* Unruhe *die*.

disregard [ˌdɪsrɪ'gɑ:d] <> *n*: **disregard (for sthg)** Geringschätzung *die* (für etw). <> *vt* ignorieren.

disrepair [ˌdɪsrɪ'peəʳ] *n* Baufälligkeit *die*; **to fall into disrepair** verfallen.

disreputable [dɪs'repjʊtəbl] *adj* in einem schlechten Ruf stehend.

disrepute [ˌdɪsrɪ'pju:t] *n*: **to bring sthg into disrepute** etw in Verruf bringen.

disrupt [dɪs'rʌpt] *vt* [meeting, lesson] stören; [transport system] behindern.

dissatisfaction ['dɪsˌsætɪs'fækʃn] *n* Unzufriedenheit *die*.

dissatisfied [ˌdɪs'sætɪsfaɪd] *adj*: **dissatisfied (with sthg)** unzufrieden (mit etw).

dissect [dɪ'sekt] *vt* MED [animal] sezieren; [plant] präparieren.

dissent [dɪ'sent] <> *n (U)* Nichtübereinstimmung *die*. <> *vi*: **to dissent from sthg** in Bezug auf etw anderer Meinung sein.

dissertation [ˌdɪsə'teɪʃn] *n* [for degree] schriftliche Abschlussarbeit; [for PhD] Dissertation *die*.

disservice [ˌdɪs'sɜ:vɪs] *n*: **to do sb a disservice** jm einen schlechten Dienst erweisen.

dissimilar [ˌdɪ'sɪmɪləʳ] *adj*: **dissimilar (to)** verschieden (von); **to be not dissimilar to sthg** etw *(D)* nicht unähnlich sein.

dissipate ['dɪsɪpeɪt] *vt* [efforts, money] verschwenden, vergeuden.

dissociate [dɪ'səʊʃɪeɪt] *vt*: **to dissociate o.s. from sthg** sich von etw distanzieren.

dissolute ['dɪsəlu:t] *adj* [way of life] ausschweifend; [person, behaviour] zügellos.

dissolve [dɪ'zɒlv] <> *vt* auf|lösen. <> *vi* [substance] sich auf|lösen.

dissuade [dɪ'sweɪd] *vt*: **to dissuade sb from doing sthg** jn davon ab|bringen, etw zu tun.

distance ['dɪstəns] *n* - **1.** [between two places] Entfernung *die*; [distance covered] Strecke *die* - **2.** [distant point]: **at a distance of five metres** in 5 Metern Entfernung; **to follow sb at a distance** jm in einiger Entfernung folgen; **from a distance** aus der Entfernung; **in the distance** in der Ferne.

distant ['dɪstənt] *adj* - **1.** [place]: **distant (from)** weit entfernt (von) - **2.** [future] fern; **it's all in the distant past** das ist alles schon lange her - **3.** [relative] entfernt - **4.** [manner] kühl.

distaste [dɪs'teɪst] *n (U)*: **distaste (for sthg)** Widerwille *der* (gegen etw).

distasteful [dɪs'teɪstfʊl] *adj* sehr unangenehm.

distended [dɪ'stendɪd] *adj* aufgebläht.

distil *UK*, **distill** *US* [dɪ'stɪl] *vt* - **1.** [water] destillieren; [whisky] brennen - **2.** *fig* [information] heraus|destillieren.

distillery [dɪ'stɪlərɪ] *n* Brennerei *die*.

distinct [dɪ'stɪŋkt] *adj* - **1.** [different]: **distinct (from)** verschieden (von); **as distinct from** im Unterschied zu - **2.** [clear] deutlich, klar.

distinction [dɪ'stɪŋkʃn] *n* - **1.** [difference] Unterschied *der*; **to draw** OR **make a distinction between** einen Unterschied machen zwischen *(+ D)* - **2.** *(U)* [excellence] Rang *der* - **3.** [in exam result] Auszeichnung *die*.

distinctive [dɪ'stɪŋktɪv] *adj* unverkennbar.

distinguish [dɪ'stɪŋgwɪʃ] <> *vt* - **1.** [tell apart]: **to distinguish sthg from sthg** etw von etw unterscheiden - **2.** [discern, perceive] erkennen - **3.** [make different] unterscheiden. <> *vi*: **to distinguish between** unterscheiden zwischen *(+ D)*.

distinguished [dɪ'stɪŋgwɪʃt] *adj* [visitor, politician] bedeutend; [career] glänzend.

distinguishing [dɪ'stɪŋgwɪʃɪŋ] *adj* charakteristisch.

distort [dɪ'stɔ:t] *vt* - **1.** [shape, face, sound] verzerren - **2.** [truth, facts] verzerrt dar|stellen.

distract [dɪ'strækt] *vt*: **to distract sb (from sthg)** jn (von etw) ab|lenken.

distracted [dɪ'stræktɪd] *adj* geistesabwesend.

distraction [dɪ'strækʃn] *n* [interruption, diversion] Ablenkung *die*.

distraught [dɪ'strɔ:t] *adj* verzweifelt.

distress [dɪ'stres] <> *n (U)* [suffering - mental] Kummer *der*; [- physical] Leiden *das*. <> *vt* [upset] Kummer machen *(+ D)*.

distressing [dɪ'stresɪŋ] *adj* bestürzend.

distribute [dɪ'strɪbju:t] *vt* - **1.** [gen] verteilen; [prizes] verleihen - **2.** COMM [goods] vertreiben.

distribution [ˌdɪstrɪ'bju:ʃn] *n* - **1.** [gen] Verteilung *die*; [of prizes] Verleihung *die* - **2.** COMM [of goods] Vertrieb *der*.

distributor [dɪ'strɪbjʊtər] *n* COMM & AUT Verteiler *der*.

district ['dɪstrɪkt] *n* - **1.** [of country] Gebiet *das*; [of city] Stadtteil *der* - **2.** [administrative area] Bezirk *der*.

district attorney *n US* LAW Bezirksstaatsanwalt *der*, -anwältin *die*.

district nurse *n UK* Gemeindeschwester *die*.

distrust [dɪs'trʌst] <> *n* Misstrauen *das* <> *vt* misstrauen *(+ D)*.

disturb [dɪ'stɜ:b] *vt* - **1.** [interrupt] stören - **2.** [upset, worry] beunruhigen - **3.** [alter - surface of water] bewegen; [- papers] durcheinander bringen.

disturbance [dɪ'stɜ:bəns] *n* - **1.** [fight] Krawall *der* - **2.** *(U)* [interruption, disruption] Störung *die*.

disturbed [dɪ'stɜ:bd] *adj* - **1.** [upset, ill] gestört - **2.** [worried] beunruhigt.

disturbing [dɪ'stɜ:bɪŋ] *adj* beunruhigend.

disuse [ˌdɪs'ju:s] *n*: **to fall into disuse** [regulation] außer Gebrauch kommen; [building, mine] nicht mehr genutzt werden.

disused [ˌdɪs'ju:zd] *adj* stillgelegt.

ditch [dɪtʃ] <> *n* Graben *der*. <> *vt inf* - **1.** [boyfriend, girlfriend] ab|servieren - **2.** [plan] fallen lassen - **3.** [old car] (einfach) zurück|lassen.

dither ['dɪðər] *vi* zaudern.

ditto ['dɪtəʊ] *adv* dito.

dive [daɪv] <> *vi* (*UK pt & pp* **-d**; *US pt & pp* **-d** OR **dove**) - **1.** [goalkeeper] hechten; [bird, aircraft] einen Sturzflug machen; [submarine] ab|tauchen - **2.** [as sport - from board] einen Kopfsprung machen; [- underwater] tauchen; **he dived into the water** er sprang kopfüber ins Wasser - **3.** [rush] stürzen. <> *n* - **1.** [of swimmer] Kopfsprung *der*; **to go into a dive** [bird, aircraft] einen Sturzflug machen; [submarine] ab|tauchen - **2.** *inf pej* [bar, restaurant] Kaschemme *die*.

diver ['daɪvər] *n* [from board] Springer *der*, -in *die*; [underwater] Taucher *der*, -in *die*.

diverge [daɪ'vɜ:dʒ] *vi* - **1.** [opinions, interests] voneinander ab|weichen; **to diverge from sthg** von etw ab|weichen - **2.** [roads, paths] sich trennen.

diversify [daɪ'vɜ:sɪfaɪ] *vt & vi* diversifizieren.

diversion [daɪ'vɜ:ʃn] *n* - **1.** [distraction] Ablenkung *die* - **2.** [of traffic, river] Umleitung *die* - **3.** [of funds] Umverteilung *die*.

diversity [daɪ'vɜ:sətɪ] *n* Mannigfaltigkeit *die*.

divert [daɪ'vɜ:t] *vt* - **1.** [traffic, river] um|leiten - **2.** [funds] um|verteilen - **3.** [person, attention] ab|lenken.

divide [dɪ'vaɪd] <> *vt* - **1.** [form barrier between] trennen - **2.** [share out, distribute] auflteilen - **3.** [split up]: **to divide sthg into** etw auflteilen in *(+ A)* - **4.** MATHS: **to divide 9 by 3, to divide 3 into 9** 9 durch 3 teilen *OR* dividieren - **5.** [disunite] spalten. <> *vi* [split into two] sich teilen.

dividend ['dɪvɪdend] *n* Dividende *die*.

divine [dɪ'vaɪn] *adj liter & fig* göttlich.

diving ['daɪvɪŋ] *n* [from board] Springen *das*; [underwater] Tauchen *das*.

divingboard ['daɪvɪŋbɔːd] *n* Sprungbrett *das*.

divinity [dɪ'vɪnətɪ] *n* - **1.** [godliness] Göttlichkeit *die* - **2.** [study] Theologie *die*.

division [dɪ'vɪʒn] *n* - **1.** [barrier] Trennung *die*; [of country, group] Teilung *die*; **division between** Trennung zwischen *(+ D)* - **2.** [sharing out, distribution] Teilung *die* - **3.** MATHS Division *die* - **4.** [disagreement] Uneinigkeit *die* - **5.** [department] Abteilung *die* - **6.** *UK* [in sports league] Liga *die*.

divorce [dɪ'vɔːs] <> *n* LAW Scheidung *die*. <> *vt* LAW [husband, wife] sich scheiden lassen von.

divorced [dɪ'vɔːst] *adj* - **1.** LAW geschieden; **to get divorced** sich scheiden lassen - **2.** *fig* [separated]: **to be divorced from sthg** keine Beziehung haben zu etw.

divorcee [dɪvɔː'siː] *n* geschiedener Mann (geschiedene Frau).

divulge [daɪ'vʌldʒ] *vt* preis|geben.

DIY *n UK abbr of* **do-it-yourself**.

dizzy ['dɪzɪ] *adj* [person] schwind(e)lig.

DJ *n abbr of* **disc jockey**.

DNA (*abbr of* **deoxyribonucleic acid**) *n* DNS *die*.

do [duː] (*pt* **did**, *pp* **done**, *pl* **dos** *OR* **do's**) <> *aux vb* - **1.** *(in negatives)*: **don't do that!** tu das nicht!; **she didn't listen** sie hat nicht zugehört; **don't park your car there** stell dein Auto nicht dort ab - **2.** *(in questions)*: **did he like it?** hat es ihm gefallen?; **how do you do it?** wie machst du das?; **what did he want?** was wollte er? - **3.** *(referring back to previous verb)*: **I eat more than you do** ich esse mehr als du; **no I didn't!** nein, habe ich nicht!; **so do I** ich auch - **4.** *(in question tags)*: **so, you like Denver, do you?** Sie mögen Denver also, nicht wahr?; **you come from Ireland, don't you?** Sie kommen aus Irland, oder?; **I like coffee – do you?** ich mag Kaffee – du auch? - **5.** *(for emphasis)*: **I do like this bedroom** das Schlafzimmer gefällt mir wirklich; **do come in!** kommen Sie doch herein! <> *vt* - **1.** [perform] machen, tun; **I've a lot to do** ich habe viel zu tun; **to do one's homework** seine Hausaufgaben machen; **what is she doing?** was macht sie?; **what can I do for you?** was kann ich für Sie tun?; **to do aerobics/gymnastics** Aerobik/Gymnastik machen; **to do the cooking** kochen; **well done!** bravo! - **2.** [clean, brush, cook *etc*]: **to do one's make-up** sich schminken; **to do one's teeth** sich *(D)* die Zähne putzen; **how would you like the steak done?** wie möchten Sie Ihr Steak (haben)? - **3.** [take action] tun, machen; **he couldn't do anything about it** er konnte nichts dagegen tun *OR* machen; **I'll do my best to help** ich helfe, so gut ich kann - **4.** [cause]: **the storm did a lot of damage** der Sturm hat viel Schaden angerichtet - **5.** [have as job]: **what do you do?** was machen Sie beruflich?; **what do you want to do when you leave school?** was willst du machen, wenn du mit der Schule fertig bist? - **6.** [provide, offer]: **do you do vegetarian food?** haben Sie vegetarisches Essen?; **we do pizzas for under £4** wir bieten Pizzas für weniger als 4 Pfund an - **7.** [study] studieren, machen; **I did physics at school** ich habe Physik in der Schule gehabt *OR* gemacht - **8.** [subj: vehicle] fahren; **the car can do 110 mph** das Auto schafft 175 km/h - **9.** *inf* [visit]: **we did Switzerland in a week** wir haben uns in einer Woche die Schweiz angesehen - **10.** [be good enough for] genügen *(+ D)*; **that'll do me nicely** das genügt mir - **11.** *inf* [cheat]: **to do sb** jn übers Ohr hauen. <> *vi* - **1.** [behave, act] tun; **do as I say** tu, was ich sage; **you would do well to reconsider** Sie sollten es sich lieber noch einmal überlegen - **2.** [progress, get on]: **to do well/badly** gut/schlecht voran|kommen; [in exam] gut/schlecht ab|schneiden; **he will do well** er wird Erfolg haben - **3.** [be sufficient] reichen, genügen; **will £5 do?** genügen 5 Pfund *OR* sind 5 Pfund genug?; **that will do (nicely)** das genügt *OR* reicht; **that will do!** [showing annoyance] das reicht! - **4.** *phr*: **how do you do?** Guten Tag!; **how are you doing?** wie gehts? <> *n* [party] Party *die*. ◆ **dos** *npl*: **dos and don'ts** was man tun und lassen sollte. ◆ **do away with** *vt insep* [law, practice] ab|schaffen. ◆ **do down** *vt sep*: **to do sb/o.s. down** jn/sich schlecht machen. ◆ **do out of** *vt sep*: **to do sb out of £10** jn um 10 Pfund betrügen. ◆ **do up** *vt sep* - **1.** [fasten] zu|machen; **do your shoes up** binde dir die Schuhe - **2.** [decorate] renovieren - **3.** [wrap up] ein|packen. ◆ **do with** *vt insep* - **1.** [need]: **I could do with a drink** ich könnte einen Drink gebrauchen; **the floor could do with a wash** der Boden könnte mal (wieder) geputzt werden - **2.** [have connection with]: **what has that got to do with it?** was hat das damit zu tun?; **that has nothing to do with you** das geht dich gar nichts an. ◆ **do without** <> *vt insep*: **to do without sthg** ohne etw auskommen; **I can do without your sarcasm** [expressing annoyance] Sie können sich Ihren Sarkasmus sparen. <> *vi*: **we'll just have to do without then** dann müssen wir eben so auskommen.

docile [*UK* 'dəusaɪl, *US* 'dɒsəl] *adj* fügsam.

dock [dɒk] <> *n* - **1.** [in harbour] Dock *das* - **2.** [in court] Anklagebank *die*. <> *vi* [ship] anllegen.

docker ['dɒkəʳ] *n* Hafenarbeiter *der*, -in *die*.

dockyard ['dɒkjɑːd] *n* Werft *die*.

doctor ['dɒktəʳ] <> *n* - **1.** [of medicine] Arzt *der*, Ärztin *die*; **to go to the doctor's** zum Arzt gehen - **2.** [holder of PhD] Doktor *der*. <> *vt* [tamper with - results] fälschen; [- text] verfälschen.

doctorate ['dɒktərət], **doctor's degree** *n* Doktorwürde *die*.

doctrine ['dɒktrɪn] *n* Doktrin *die*, Lehre *die*.

document *n* ['dɒkjʊmənt] Dokument *das*.

documentary [,dɒkjʊ'mentərɪ] <> *adj* dokumentarisch. <> *n* Dokumentarfilm *der*.

dodge [dɒdʒ] <> *n inf* Trick *der*. <> *vt* [avoid] auslweichen. <> *vi*: **to dodge out of the way/to one side** zur Seite springen.

dodgy ['dɒdʒɪ] *adj UK inf* [business, deal] windig; [plan] dubios.

doe [dəʊ] *n* [female deer - roe deer] Ricke *die*; [- red deer] Hirschkuh *die*.

does (*weak form* [dəz], *strong form* [dʌz]) *vb* ▷ **do**.

doesn't ['dʌznt] *abbr of* **does not**.

dog [dɒg] <> *n* [animal] Hund *der*. <> *vt* [subj: problems, bad luck]: **dogged by problems** von Problemen geplagt; **dogged by bad luck** von Pech verfolgt.

dog collar *n* - **1.** [of dog] Halsband *das* - **2.** [of clergyman] *steifer weißer Kragen*.

dog-eared [-ɪəd] *adj* mit Eselsohren.

dog food *n* Hundefutter *das*.

dogged ['dɒgɪd] *adj* beharrlich.

dogsbody ['dɒgz,bɒdɪ] *n UK inf* Mädchen *das* für alles.

doing ['duːɪŋ] *n*: **is this your doing?** ist das dein Werk? ◆ **doings** *npl* [activities] Taten *Pl*.

do-it-yourself *n* Heimwerken *das*.

doldrums ['dɒldrəmz] *npl*: **to be in the doldrums** *fig* [industry] in einer Flaute stecken; [person] Trübsal blasen.

dole [dəʊl] *n UK* [unemployment benefit] Arbeitslosenunterstützung *die*; **to be on the dole** Arbeitslosenunterstützung beziehen. ◆ **dole out** *vt sep* auslteilen.

doll [dɒl] *n* Puppe *die*.

dollar ['dɒləʳ] *n* Dollar *der*.

dollop ['dɒləp] *n inf* Klacks *der*.

dolphin ['dɒlfɪn] *n* Delfin *der*.

domain [də'meɪn] *n* [sphere of interest] Gebiet *das*.

dome [dəʊm] *n* ARCHIT Kuppel *die*.

domestic [də'mestɪk] <> *adj* - **1.** [internal - flight] Inland-; [- policy] Innen- - **2.** [household, home-loving] häuslich - **3.** [not wild] Haus-. <> *n* Hausangestellte *der, die*.

domestic science *n* Hauswirtschaftslehre *die*.

dominant ['dɒmɪnənt] *adj* [personality] dominant; [nation, group, colour] dominierend.

dominate ['dɒmɪneɪt] *vt* dominieren.

domineering [,dɒmɪ'nɪərɪŋ] *adj* herrisch.

domino ['dɒmɪnəʊ] (*pl* **-es**) *n* Dominostein *der*. ◆ **dominoes** *npl* [game] Domino *das*.

don [dɒn] *n UK* UNIV Universitätsdozent *der*, -in *die*.

donate [də'neɪt] *vt* spenden.

done [dʌn] <> *pp* ▷ **do**. <> *adj* - **1.** [finished] erledigt; **I'm nearly done** ich bin fast fertig - **2.** [cooked] gar. <> *excl* [to conclude deal] abgemacht!

donkey ['dɒŋkɪ] (*pl* **-s**) *n* Esel *der*.

donor ['dəʊnəʳ] *n* Spender *der*, -in *die*.

donor card *n* Organspenderausweis *der*.

don't [dəʊnt] *abbr of* **do not**.

doodle ['duːdl] <> *n* Kritzelei *die*. <> *vi* vor sich hin kritzeln.

doom [duːm] *n (U)* Verhängnis *das*.

doomed [duːmd] *adj* zum Scheitern verurteilt; **to be doomed to sthg** zu etw verurteilt sein.

door [dɔːʳ] *n* Tür *die*.

doorbell ['dɔːbel] *n* Türklingel *die*.

doorknob ['dɔːnɒb] *n* Türknauf *der*.

doorman ['dɔːmən] (*pl* **-men** [-mən]) *n* Portier *der*.

doormat ['dɔːmæt] *n liter & fig* Fußabtreter *der*.

doorstep ['dɔːstep] *n* Eingangsstufe *die*; **the supermarket's right on her doorstep** sie hat den Supermarkt direkt vor der Tür.

doorway ['dɔːweɪ] *n* Eingang *der*.

dope [dəʊp] <> *n* - **1.** *drug sl* [cannabis] Hasch *das* - **2.** [for athlete, horse] Aufputschmittel *das* - **3.** *inf* [fool] Trottel *der*. <> *vt* dopen.

dopey ['dəʊpɪ] (*comp* **-ier**, *superl* **-iest**) *adj inf* - **1.** [groggy] benommen - **2.** [stupid] blöd.

dormant ['dɔːmənt] *adj* - **1.** [volcano] untätig - **2.** *(phrase)*: **to lie dormant** [talents] schlummern.

dormitory ['dɔːmətrɪ] *n* - **1.** [room] Schlafsaal *der* - **2.** *US* [in university] Wohnheim *das*.

DOS [dɒs] (*abbr of* **disk operating system**) *n* DOS *das*.

dose [dəʊs] *n* - **1.** [of medicine, drug] Dosis *die* - **2.** [of illness] Anfall *der*.

dot [dɒt] <> *n* Punkt *der*. <> *vt* verstreuen. ◆ **on the dot** *adv*: **at four on the dot** Punkt vier Uhr; **to arrive on the dot** auf die Minute pünktlich (an)lkommen.

dote ◆ **dote upon** *vt insep* vernarrt sein in (+ *A*).

dotted line ['dɒtɪd-] *n* punktierte Linie.

double ['dʌbl] ◇ *adj* doppelt; [row, door] Doppel-; **to have a double meaning** doppeldeutig sein; **two double one** zwei eins eins; **Susanne with a double "n"** Susanne mit zwei "n". ◇ *adv* - **1.** [twice]: **double the amount/number** doppelt so viel/viele - **2.** [two of the same] doppelt; **to see double** doppelt sehen - **3.** [in two - fold] einmal; *(phrase)*: **to bend double** sich zusammen|krümmen. ◇ *n* - **1.** [twice the amount] Doppelte *das* - **2.** [of alcohol] Doppelter *der* - **3.** [look-alike] Ebenbild *das* - **4.** CIN Double *das.* ◇ *vt* [increase twofold] verdoppeln. ◇ *vi* [increase twofold] verdoppeln. ◆ **doubles** *npl* TENNIS Doppel *das.*

double-barrelled *UK*, **double-barreled** *US* [-'bærəld] *adj* - **1.** [shotgun] doppelläufig - **2.** [name] Doppel-.

double bass [-beɪs] *n* Kontrabass *der.*

double bed *n* Doppelbett *das.*

double-breasted [-'brestɪd] *adj* zweireihig.

double-check *vt* noch einmal überprüfen.

double chin *n* Doppelkinn *das.*

double-click ◇ *vt* & *vi* COMPUT doppelklicken. ◇ *n* COMPUT Doppelklick *der.*

double cream *n UK* Schlagsahne *die.*

double-cross *vt* doppeltes Spiel treiben mit.

double-decker [-'dekəʳ] *n* Doppeldecker *der.*

double-dutch *n UK hum* Kauderwelsch *das.*

double fault *n* TENNIS Doppelfehler *der.*

double-glazing [-'gleɪzɪŋ] *n* Doppelverglasung *die.*

double-park *vi* AUT in der zweiten Reihe parken.

double room *n* Doppelzimmer *das.*

double vision *n* doppeltes Sehen.

doubly ['dʌblɪ] *adv*: **doubly difficult/important/***etc* umso schwieriger/wichtiger/*etc.*

doubt [daʊt] ◇ *n* Zweifel *der*; **there is no doubt that...** es besteht kein Zweifel, dass...; **to cast doubt on sthg** etw in Zweifel ziehen; **no doubt** ohne Zweifel; **without (a) doubt/beyond (all) doubt** ohne Zweifel; **to be in doubt** ungewiss sein. ◇ *vt* - **1.** [distrust] zweifeln an *(+ D)* - **2.** [consider unlikely] bezweifeln.

doubtful ['daʊtfʊl] *adj* - **1.** [unlikely, dubious] zweifelhaft - **2.** [uncertain] ungewiss.

doubtless ['daʊtlɪs] *adv* ohne Zweifel.

dough [dəʊ] *n (U)* - **1.** [for baking] Teig *der* - **2.** *v inf* [money] Knete *die.*

doughnut ['dəʊnʌt] *n* ≃ Berliner *der.*

douse [daʊs] *vt* - **1.** [fire, light] löschen - **2.** [person] übergießen.

dove[1] [dʌv] *n* [bird] Taube *die.*

dove[2] [dəʊv] *pt US* ▷ **dive.**

dowdy ['daʊdɪ] *adj* ohne jeden Schick.

down [daʊn] ◇ *adv* - **1.** [towards the bottom] nach unten, hinunter/herunter; **to fall down** [person] hin|fallen; [thing] herunter|fallen; **to bend down** sich bücken; **head down** mit gesenktem Kopf - **2.** [along]: **I'm going down to the shops** ich gehe einkaufen - **3.** [downstairs] herunter; **I'll come down later** ich komme später herunter - **4.** [southwards] hinunter/herunter; **we're going down to London** wir fahren hinunter nach London - **5.** [reduced]: **prices are coming down** die Preise fallen - **6.** [as far as]: **down to the last detail** bis ins letzte Detail; **down to the present** bis in die heutige Zeit. ◇ *prep* - **1.** [towards the bottom of]: **they ran down the hill** sie liefen den Hügel hinunter; **to fall down the stairs** die Treppe hinunter|fallen - **2.** [along] entlang; **I was walking down the street when** ich lief gerade die Straße entlang, als. ◇ *adj* - **1.** *inf* [depressed] down - **2.** [not in operation]: **the computers are down again** die Computer tun es wieder (mal) nicht. ◇ *n (U)* [feathers] Daunen *Pl.* ◇ *vt* - **1.** [knock over] nieder|schlagen - **2.** [swallow] hastig trinken - **3.** *phr*: **to down tools** die Arbeit nieder|legen. ◆ **downs** *npl UK* Hügelland *das.* ◆ **down with** *excl*: **down with the King!** nieder mit dem König!

down-and-out ◇ *adj* heruntergekommen. ◇ *n* Landstreicher *der*, -in *die.*

down-at-heel *adj esp UK* heruntergekommen.

downbeat ['daʊnbi:t] *adj inf* [ending] undramatisch.

downcast ['daʊnkɑ:st] *adj fml* niedergeschlagen.

downfall ['daʊnfɔ:l] *n* - **1.** *(U)* [ruin - of dictator] Sturz *der*; [- of business] Ruin *der* - **2.** [cause of ruin] Ruin *der.*

downhearted [,daʊn'hɑ:tɪd] *adj* niedergeschlagen.

downhill [,daʊn'hɪl] ◇ *adj* [path] bergab führend. ◇ *adv* - **1.** [downwards] bergab, abwärts - **2.** *fig*: **her career went downhill after that** mit ihrer Karriere ging es danach bergab. ◇ *n* [skiing] Abfahrtslauf *der.*

Downing Street ['daʊnɪŋ-] *n Straße, in der sich der offizielle Wohnsitz des britischen Premierministers und des Schatzkanzlers befindet.*

down payment *n* Anzahlung *die.*

downpour ['daʊnpɔ:ʳ] *n* Platzregen *der.*

downright ['daʊnraɪt] ◇ *adj* [fool, cheat, cheek] ausgesprochen; [lie] glatt; [insult] grob. ◇ *adv* ausgesprochen.

downstairs [,daʊn'steəz] ◇ *adj*: **a downstairs flat** eine Parterre- OR Erdgeschosswohnung. ◇ *adv* [be, live] unten; **to go downstairs** (die Treppe) hinunter|gehen; **to come downstairs** (die Treppe) herunter|kommen.

downstream [,daʊn'stri:m] *adv* flussabwärts, stromabwärts.

down-to-earth *adj* sachlich, nüchtern.
downtown [ˌdaʊn'taʊn] *esp US* <> *adj*: **downtown New York** im Stadtzentrum von New York. <> *adv* [go] ins Stadtzentrum; [live] im Stadtzentrum.
downturn ['daʊntɜːn] *n*: **downturn (in sthg)** Abnahme *die* (von etw).
down under *adv UK* [live] in Australien/Neuseeland; [go] nach Australien/Neuseeland.
downward ['daʊnwəd] <> *adj* - **1.** [towards ground] abwärts gerichtet; **downward glance** Blick nach unten; **downward movement** Abwärtsbewegung *die* - **2.** [decreasing] abnehmend, fallend. <> *adv US* = **downwards**.
downwards ['daʊnwədz] *adv* [look, move] nach unten.
dowry ['daʊərɪ] *n* Mitgift *die*.
doz. *abbr of* **dozen**.
doze [dəʊz] <> *n* Nickerchen *das*. <> *vi* dösen. ◆ **doze off** *vi* ein|nicken.
dozen ['dʌzn] *n* Dutzend *das*; **a dozen eggs** ein Dutzend Eier. ◆ **dozens** *npl inf*: **dozens of** Dutzende (von); **dozens of times** x-mal.
dozy ['dəʊzɪ] *adj* - **1.** [sleepy] schläfrig - **2.** *UK inf* [stupid] blöd.
Dr. *abbr of* **Drive**, **Doctor**.
drab [dræb] *adj* - **1.** [colour, buildings] trist; [clothes] langweilig; [place] trostlos - **2.** [life] eintönig, farblos.
draft [drɑːft] <> *n* - **1.** [early version] Entwurf *der*; [picture, plan] Skizze *die* - **2.** [money order] Zahlungsanweisung *die* - **3.** *US* MIL: **the draft** die Einberufung - **4.** *US* = **draught**. <> *vt* - **1.** [write] entwerfen - **2.** *US* MIL ein|berufen, ein|ziehen - **3.** [recruit] rekrutieren.
draftsman *n US* = **draughtsman**.
drafty *adj US* = **draughty**.
drag [dræg] <> *vt* - **1.** [pull] ziehen - **2.** [lake, river] (mit dem Schleppnetz) ab|suchen. <> *vi* - **1.** [trail]: **to drag on the ground** auf dem Boden schleifen - **2.** [pass slowly] sich in die Länge ziehen. <> *n* - **1.** *inf* [bore] langweilige Sache/Person; **what a drag!** wie öde! - **2.** *inf* [on cigarette] Zug *der* - **3.** [cross-dressing]: **in drag** in Frauenkleidern. ◆ **drag on** *vi* sich in die Länge ziehen.
dragon ['drægən] *n liter & fig* Drache *der*.
dragonfly ['drægnflaɪ] *n* Libelle *die*.
drain [dreɪn] <> *n* - **1.** [pipe] Abflussrohr *das*; [grating in street] Gully *der*; **that's £50 down the drain** *fig* die 50 Pfund sind zum Fenster rausgeworfen - **2.** [depletion]: **drain on sthg** [resources, funds] Belastung *die* für etw; [energy, time] Verlust *der* von etw. <> *vt* - **1.** [remove water from - vegetables] ab|gießen; [- marsh, field] entwässern - **2.** [deplete - funds, resources] erschöpfen; [- strength, energy] entziehen; *(phrase)*: **to feel drained** sich ausgelaugt fühlen - **3.** [drink, glass] aus|trinken. <> *vi* [dry] ab|tropfen.
drainage ['dreɪnɪdʒ] *n* [ditches, channels] Entwässerungssystem *das*; [in city] Kanalisation *die*.
draining board *UK* ['dreɪnɪŋ-], **drainboard** *US* ['dreɪnbɔːrd] *n* Abtropfbrett *das*.
drainpipe ['dreɪnpaɪp] *n* Abflussrohr *das*.
drama ['drɑːmə] *n* - **1.** [play, genre, event] Drama *das* - **2.** [dramatic quality] Dramatik *die*.
dramatic [drə'mætɪk] *adj* dramatisch.
dramatist ['dræmətɪst] *n* Dramatiker *der*, -in *die*.
dramatize, -ise ['dræmətaɪz] *vt* dramatisieren.
drank [dræŋk] *pt* ▷ **drink**.
drape [dreɪp] *vt* drapieren; **to be draped with** OR **in sthg** mit etw drapiert sein. ◆ **drapes** *npl US* Vorhänge *Pl*.
drastic ['dræstɪk] *adj* drastisch.
draught *UK*, **draft** *US* [drɑːft] *n* - **1.** [air current] Luftzug *der*; **there's a draught in here** hier zieht es - **2.** [from barrel]: **on draught** [beer] vom Fass. ◆ **draughts** *n UK* Damespiel *das*; **to play draughts** Dame spielen.
draught beer *n UK* Fassbier *das*.
draughtsman *UK* (*pl* **-men** [-mən]), **draftsman** *US* (*pl* **-men** [-mən]) ['drɑːftsmən] *n* technischer Zeichner.
draughty *UK*, **drafty** *US* ['drɑːftɪ] *adj* zugig.
draw [drɔː] (*pt* **drew**, *pp* **drawn**) <> *vt* - **1.** [sketch] zeichnen - **2.** [pull, pull out] ziehen - **3.** [conclusion, comparison, distinction] ziehen - **4.** [criticism, support] hervor|rufen; **to draw sb's attention to sthg** js Aufmerksamkeit auf etw *(A)* lenken. <> *vi* - **1.** [sketch] zeichnen - **2.** [move]: **to draw away** weg|ziehen; **to draw near** heran|ziehen - **3.** SPORT unentschieden spielen; **to draw with sb** gegen jn unentschieden spielen. <> *n* - **1.** SPORT [result] Unentschieden *das* - **2.** [lottery] Ziehung *die* - **3.** [attraction] Anziehungspunkt *der*. ◆ **draw out** *vt sep* - **1.** [encourage] aus der Reserve locken - **2.** [prolong] in die Länge ziehen - **3.** [withdraw] ab|heben. ◆ **draw up** <> *vt sep* [draft] auf|setzen; [list] auf|stellen. <> *vi* [stop] an|halten.
drawback ['drɔːbæk] *n* Nachteil *der*.
drawbridge ['drɔːbrɪdʒ] *n* Zugbrücke *die*.
drawer [drɔːʳ] *n* Schublade *die*.
drawing ['drɔːɪŋ] *n* - **1.** [picture] Zeichnung *die* - **2.** [skill, act] Zeichnen *das*.
drawing pin *n UK* Reißzwecke *die*.
drawing room *n* Salon *der*.
drawl [drɔːl] *n* gedehntes Sprechen.
drawn [drɔːn] *pp* ▷ **draw**.
dread [dred] <> *n* Furcht *die*. <> *vt* fürchten; **to dread doing sthg** es schrecklich finden, etw tun zu müssen.
dreadful ['dredfʊl] *adj* schrecklich, furchtbar; *(phrase)*: **I feel dreadful** [guilty] es ist mir sehr peinlich.

dreadfully ['dredfulı] *adv* - **1.** [badly] furchtbar - **2.** [extremely] schrecklich.

dream [dri:m] (*pt & pp* **-ed** OR **dreamt**) <> *n* Traum *der*. <> *adj* Traum-. <> *vt* [during sleep] träumen. <> *vi*: **to dream (of** OR **about sthg)** (von etw) träumen; **I wouldn't dream of it** *fig* das würde mir nicht im Traum ein|fallen; **to dream of doing sthg** davon träumen, etw zu tun. ◆ **dream up** *vt sep* sich *(D)* einfallen lassen OR aus|denken.

dreamt [dremt] *pt & pp* ▷ **dream**.

dreamy ['dri:mı] *adj* - **1.** [distracted] verträumt - **2.** [languorous] traumhaft.

dreary ['drıərı] *adj* - **1.** [gloomy, depressing] trostlos - **2.** [dull, boring] langweilig, öde.

dredge [dredʒ] *vt* aus|baggern. ◆ **dredge up** *vt sep* - **1.** [from lake, river] herauf|holen, heraus|holen - **2.** *fig* [from past] aus|graben.

dregs [dregz] *npl* - **1.** [of liquid] (Boden)satz *der* - **2.** *fig* [of society] Abschaum *der*.

drench [drentʃ] *vt* durch|nässen; **to be drenched in** OR **with sweat** in Schweiß gebadet sein.

dress [dres] <> *n* - **1.** [frock] Kleid *das* - **2.** [type of clothing] Kleidung *die*. <> *vt* - **1.** [clothe] an|ziehen; **to be dressed** angezogen sein; **to be dressed in** gekleidet sein in *(+ D)*; **to get dressed** sich an|ziehen - **2.** [wound] verbinden - **3.** [salad] an|machen. <> *vi* sich an|ziehen, sich kleiden. ◆ **dress up** *vi* - **1.** [in costume] sich verkleiden - **2.** [in best clothes] sich festlich an|ziehen.

dress circle *n* THEAT erster Rang.

dresser ['dresəʳ] *n* - **1.** [for dishes] Küchenbüffet *das* (mit Tellerbord) - **2.** *US* [chest of drawers] Frisiertisch *der*, Frisierkommode *die*.

dressing ['dresıŋ] *n* - **1.** [bandage] Verband *der* - **2.** [for salad] Dressing *das*, Salatsoße *die* - **3.** *US* [for turkey *etc*] Füllung *die*.

dressing gown *n* Bademantel *der*.

dressing room *n* - **1.** SPORT Umkleidekabine *die* - **2.** THEAT Garderobe *die*.

dressing table *n* Frisiertisch *der*.

dressmaker ['dres,meıkəʳ] *n* Schneider *der*, -in *die*.

dress rehearsal *n* Generalprobe *die*.

dressy ['dresı] *adj* elegant.

drew [dru:] *pt* ▷ **draw**.

dribble ['drıbl] <> *n* [trickle] Rinnsal *das*. <> *vt* SPORT [footballer] dribbeln. <> *vi* - **1.** [drool] sabbern - **2.** [spill] tropfen - **3.** SPORT [ball] dribbeln.

dried [draıd] <> *pt & pp* ▷ **dry**. <> *adj* getrocknet; **dried milk** Trockenmilch *die*.

drier ['draıəʳ] *n* = **dryer**.

drift [drıft] <> *n* - **1.** [mass - of snow, leaves, sand] Verwehung *die* - **2.** [meaning]: **I get her general drift** ich verstehe, worauf sie hinaus will. <> *vi* [boat, snow, sand, leaves] treiben.

drill [drıl] <> *n* - **1.** [tool] Bohrer *der* - **2.** [exercise, training] Übung *die* (für den Ernstfall). <> *vt* - **1.** [metal, wood, hole] bohren - **2.** [instruct] drillen; **to drill sthg into sb** jm etw ein|bläuen.

drink [drıŋk] (*pt* **drank**, *pp* **drunk**) <> *n* - **1.** [gen] Getränk *das*; **a drink of water** ein Glas Wasser - **2.** [alcoholic beverage] Drink *der*; **to have a drink** etwas trinken - **3.** [alcohol] Alkohol *der*. <> *vt* trinken. <> *vi* trinken.

drink-driving *UK*, **drunk-driving** *US* *n* Trunkenheit *die* am Steuer.

drinker ['drıŋkəʳ] *n* Trinker *der*, -in *die*.

drinking water *n* Trinkwasser *das*.

drip [drıp] <> *n* - **1.** [drop] Tropfen *der* - **2.** MED Tropf *der*, Infusion *die*; **to be on a drip** am Tropf hängen. <> *vi* tropfen.

drip-dry *adj* bügelfrei.

drive [draıv] (*pt* **drove**, *pp* **driven**) <> *n* - **1.** [journey] Fahrt *die*; **an hour's drive** eine Stunde Fahrt; **to go for a drive** spazieren fahren - **2.** [urge] Trieb *der* - **3.** [campaign] Aktion *die* - **4.** *(U)* [energy] Energie *die* - **5.** [in front of house] Einfahrt *die* - **6.** [stroke - in golf] Treibschlag *der*; [- in tennis] Drive *der* - **7.** AUT: **left-/right-hand drive** Links-/Rechtslenkung *die* - **8.** COMPUT Laufwerk *das*. <> *vt* - **1.** [vehicle, passenger] fahren; **to drive sb home** jn nach Hause fahren - **2.** TECH [operate] an|treiben; **driven by electricity** mit elektrischem Antrieb - **3.** [chase - cattle, clouds, people] treiben; **they were driven from their homeland** sie wurden aus ihrer Heimat vertrieben - **4.** [motivate]: **driven by greed/ambition** von Gier/Ehrgeiz getrieben - **5.** [force]: **to drive sb to do sthg** jn dazu treiben, etw zu tun; **to drive sb hard** jn schinden; **to drive sb mad** OR **crazy** jn verrückt machen - **6.** [hammer] schlagen. <> *vi* fahren; **can you drive?** kannst du Auto fahren?

drivel ['drıvl] *n inf* Quatsch *der*.

driven ['drıvn] *pp* ▷ **drive**.

driver ['draıvəʳ] *n* [of vehicle] Fahrer *der*, -in *die*.

driver's license *n US* = **driving licence**.

driveway ['draıvweı] *n* Auffahrt *die*.

driving ['draıvıŋ] <> *adj* [rain] strömend; [wind] stürmisch. <> *n* Fahren *das*.

driving instructor *n* Fahrlehrer *der*, -in *die*.

driving lesson *n* Fahrstunde *die*.

driving licence *UK*, **driver's license** *US* *n* Führerschein *der*.

driving school *n* Fahrschule *die*.

driving test *n* Fahrprüfung *die*.

drizzle ['drızl] <> *n* Sprühregen *der*. <> *impers vb*: **it's drizzling** es nieselt.

drone [drəʊn] *n* - **1.** [sound - of machine, engine, loudspeaker] Dröhnen *das*; [- of insect] Summen *das* - **2.** [male bee] Drohne *die*.

drool [druːl] *vi* - **1.** [dribble] sabbern - **2.** *fig* [admire]: **he stood there drooling over the sports car** er konnte sich an dem Sportwagen nicht satt sehen.

droop [druːp] *vi* [hang down] herunter|hängen; [flower] den Kopf hängen lassen.

drop [drɒp] ◇ *n* - **1.** [of liquid] Tropfen *der* - **2.** [sweet] Drops *der ODER das* - **3.** [decrease]: **drop (in sthg)** Rückgang *der* (von etw); [in salary] Minderung *die* (von etw) - **4.** [vertical distance] Höhenunterschied *der*; **there's a 50 m drop** hier geht es 50 m (senkrecht) hinunter. ◇ *vt* - **1.** [gen] fallen lassen; **to drop (sb) a hint** (jm gegenüber) eine Anspielung machen - **2.** [decrease, lower] senken - **3.** [leave out] weg|lassen - **4.** [let out of car] ab|setzen - **5.** [write]: **to drop sb a line** OR **note** jm ein paar Zeilen schreiben. ◇ *vi* - **1.** [fall] fallen; [with exhaustion] um|fallen - **2.** [decrease] sinken - **3.** [voice] leiser werden. ◆ **drops** *npl* MED Tropfen *Pl*. ◆ **drop in** *vi inf*: **to drop in (on sb)** vorbei|kommen (bei jm). ◆ **drop off** ◇ *vt sep* [person] ab|setzen; [letter, package] ab|schicken. ◇ *vi* - **1.** [fall asleep] ein|nicken - **2.** [grow less] zurück|gehen. ◆ **drop out** *vi*: **to drop out (of** OR **from sthg)** aus|steigen (aus etw).

dropout ['drɒpaʊt] *n* - **1.** [from society] Aussteiger *der*, -in *die* - **2.** [from university] Studienabbrecher *der*, -in *die*.

droppings ['drɒpɪŋz] *npl* Kot *der*; [of horses] Äpfel *Pl*.

drought [draʊt] *n* Dürre *die*.

drove [drəʊv] *pt* ▷ **drive**.

drown [draʊn] ◇ *vt* [person, animal] ertränken. ◇ *vi* ertrinken.

drowsy ['draʊzɪ] *adj* schläfrig.

drudgery ['drʌdʒərɪ] *n* Schinderei *die*.

drug [drʌg] ◇ *n* - **1.** [medication] Arzneimittel *das* - **2.** [illegal substance] Droge *die*; **to be on drugs** drogen- OR rauschgiftabhängig sein. ◇ *vt* [person, animal] Drogen verabreichen *(+ D)*; [food, drink] mit Drogen versetzen.

drug abuse *n* Drogenmissbrauch *der*.

drug addict *n* Drogensüchtige *der, die*.

druggist ['drʌgɪst] *n US* Apotheker *der*, -in *die*.

drugstore ['drʌgstɔːʳ] *n US* Drugstore *der*.

drum [drʌm] ◇ *n* - **1.** [instrument, cylinder] Trommel *die* - **2.** [container] Tonne *die*. ◇ *vt* & *vi* trommeln. ◆ **drums** *npl* Schlagzeug *das*. ◆ **drum up** *vt sep* [business] an|kurbeln.

drummer ['drʌməʳ] *n* Schlagzeuger *der*, -in *die*.

drumstick ['drʌmstɪk] *n* - **1.** [for drum] Trommelschlägel *der* - **2.** [of chicken] Keule *die*.

drunk [drʌŋk] ◇ *pp* ▷ **drink**. ◇ *adj* [on alcohol] betrunken. ◇ *n* [on one occasion] Betrunkene *der, die*; [habitual] Trinker *der*, -in *die*.

drunkard ['drʌŋkəd] *n* Trinker *der*, -in *die*.

drunk-driving *n US* = **drink-driving**.

drunken ['drʌŋkn] *adj* [person] betrunken; **a drunken evening** ein feuchtfröhlicher Abend; **in a drunken stupor** sinnlos betrunken.

dry [draɪ] ◇ *adj* - **1.** [gen] trocken - **2.** [river, lake] ausgetrocknet - **3.** [thirsty] durstig; **to feel** OR **be dry** durstig sein, Durst haben. ◇ *vt* & *vi* trocknen. ◆ **dry up** ◇ *vt sep* [dishes] ab|trocknen. ◇ *vi* - **1.** [river, lake, well] aus|trocknen - **2.** [supplies, inspiration] zur Neige gehen - **3.** [actor, speaker] stecken bleiben - **4.** [dry dishes] ab|trocknen.

dry cleaner *n*: **dry cleaner's** chemische Reinigung.

dryer ['draɪəʳ] *n* [for clothes] Trockner *der*.

dry land *n* Festland *das*.

dry rot *n* Trockenfäule *die*.

dry ski slope *n* Sommerskihang *der*.

DSS (*abbr of* **Department of Social Security**) *n britisches Sozialamt*.

DTI (*abbr of* **Department of Trade and Industry**) *n* Handels- und Industrieministerium *das*.

DTP (*abbr of* **desktop publishing**) *n* DTP *das*.

dual ['djuːəl] *adj* doppelt, Doppel-.

dual carriageway *n UK* vierspurige Straße.

dubbed [dʌbd] *adj* - **1.** CIN synchronisiert - **2.** [nicknamed] genannt.

dubious ['djuːbjəs] *adj* - **1.** [suspect, questionable] dubios, zweifelhaft - **2.** [uncertain, undecided]: **to be dubious about doing sthg** nicht wissen, ob man etw tun soll.

Dublin ['dʌblɪn] *n* Dublin *nt*.

duchess ['dʌtʃɪs] *n* Herzogin *die*.

duck [dʌk] ◇ *n* Ente *die*. ◇ *vt* - **1.** [head] ducken, ein|ziehen - **2.** [responsibility, duty] aus|weichen *(+ D)*. ◇ *vi* sich ducken.

duckling ['dʌklɪŋ] *n* - **1.** [animal] Entenküken *das* - **2.** *(U)* [food] junge Ente.

duct [dʌkt] *n* - **1.** [pipe] Leitung *die*, Rohr *das* - **2.** ANAT Kanal *der*.

dud [dʌd] ◇ *adj* - **1.** [false] falsch - **2.** [useless] wertlos. ◇ *n* [bomb, shell] Blindgänger *der*.

dude [duːd] *n US inf* Typ *der*.

due [djuː] ◇ *adj* - **1.** [expected] fällig; **the book's due (out) in May** das Buch soll im Mai erscheinen - **2.** [proper] ordnungsgemäß, nötig; **in due course** zu gegebener Zeit - **3.** [owed, owing] fällig. ◇ *adv*: **due west** genau nach Westen. ◆ **dues** *npl* Abgaben *Pl*, Gebühren *Pl*. ◆ **due to** *prep* wegen *(+ G, D)*.

duel ['djuːəl] *n* Duell *das*.

duet [djuː'et] *n* Duett *das*.

duffel bag ['dʌfl-] *n* Seesack *der*.

duffel coat ['dʌfl-] *n* Dufflecoat *der*.

dug [dʌg] *pt & pp* ▻ **dig**.

duke [dju:k] *n* Herzog *der*.

dull [dʌl] ◇ *adj* - **1.** [boring] langweilig - **2.** [colour, light] matt - **3.** [day, weather] trüb - **4.** [noise, pain] dumpf. ◇ *vt* - **1.** [senses] ab|stumpfen; [pain] dämpfen - **2.** [make less bright - metal] stumpf werden lassen.

duly ['dju:lɪ] *adv* - **1.** [properly] ordnungsgemäß - **2.** [as expected] erwartungsgemäß.

dumb [dʌm] *adj* - **1.** [unable to speak] stumm; **to be struck dumb** sprachlos sein - **2.** *esp US inf* [stupid] dumm.

dumbfound [dʌm'faʊnd] *vt* verblüffen; **to be dumbfounded** verblüfft sein, sprachlos sein.

dummy ['dʌmɪ] ◇ *adj* unecht; **a dummy gun** eine Spielzeugpistole. ◇ *n* - **1.** [model of human figure - for tailoring] Schneiderpuppe *die*; [- for crash testing] Dummy *der*; [- in shop] Schaufensterpuppe *die* - **2.** [copy, fake object] Attrappe *die* - **3.** *UK* [for baby] Schnuller *der*.

dump [dʌmp] ◇ *n* - **1.** [for rubbish] Müllhalde *die* - **2.** [for ammunition] Munitionslager *das*. ◇ *vt* - **1.** *inf* [put down] ab|laden - **2.** [dispose of - waste, rubbish] weg|werfen; [- car] zurück|lassen - **3.** *inf* [jilt] in die Wüste schicken.

dumper (truck) *UK* ['dʌmpəʳ-], **dump truck** *US n* Kipper *der*, Kipplaster *der*.

dumping ['dʌmpɪŋ] *n* [of waste] Abladen *das*; **'no dumping'** 'Schutt abladen verboten'.

dumpling ['dʌmplɪŋ] *n* CULIN Kloß *der*.

dump truck *n US* = **dumper truck**.

dumpy ['dʌmpɪ] *adj inf* dicklich, untersetzt.

dunce [dʌns] *n* Ignorant *der*.

dune [dju:n] *n* Düne *die*.

dung [dʌŋ] *n* Dung *der*, Mist *der*.

dungarees [ˌdʌŋgə'ri:z] *npl UK* [for work] Arbeitshose *die*; [fashion garment] Segeltuch *das*.

dungeon ['dʌndʒən] *n* Verlies *das*.

duo ['dju:əʊ] *n* - **1.** [of singers, musicians] Duett *das*; [on stage] Duo *das* - **2.** [couple] Duo *das*.

duplex ['dju:pleks] *n US* - **1.** [apartment] Doppelapartment *das* - **2.** [house] Zweifamilienhaus *das*.

duplicate ◇ *adj* ['dju:plɪkət] [document] kopiert; **a duplicate key** ein Nachschlüssel. ◇ *n* ['dju:plɪkət] Kopie *die*; **in duplicate** in doppelter Ausfertigung. ◇ *vt* ['dju:plɪkeɪt] [copy - document] kopieren; [- key] nach|machen.

durable ['djʊərəbl] *adj* strapazierfähig.

duration [djʊ'reɪʃn] *n* Dauer *die*; **for the duration of** für die Dauer von.

duress [djʊ'res] *n*: **under duress** unter Zwang.

during ['djʊərɪŋ] *prep* während *(+ G)*.

dusk [dʌsk] *n* Abenddämmerung *die*.

dust [dʌst] ◇ *n* Staub *der*. ◇ *vt* - **1.** [clean] ab|stauben - **2.** [cover]: **to dust sthg with sthg** etw mit etw bestäuben.

dustbin ['dʌstbɪn] *n UK* Mülltonne *die*.

dustbin lorry *n UK* Müllwagen *der*.

duster ['dʌstəʳ] *n* [cloth] Staubtuch *das*.

dust jacket *n* [on book] Schutzumschlag *der*.

dust(bin)man ['dʌst(bɪn)mən] *(pl* **-men** [-mən]) *n UK* Müllmann *der*.

dustpan ['dʌstpæn] *n* Kehrschaufel *die*.

dusty ['dʌstɪ] *adj* staubig, verstaubt.

Dutch [dʌtʃ] ◇ *adj* niederländisch, holländisch. ◇ *n* [language] Niederländisch(e) *das*. ◇ *adv*: **to go Dutch** getrennt bezahlen.

dutiful ['dju:tɪfʊl] *adj* pflichtbewusst.

duty ['dju:tɪ] *n* - **1.** *(U)* [responsibility] Pflicht *die*; **to do one's duty** seine Pflicht tun - **2.** *(U)* [work] Dienst *der*; **to be on duty** Dienst haben; **to be off duty** dienstfrei haben - **3.** [tax] Zoll *der*. ◆ **duties** *npl* [tasks] Aufgaben *Pl*.

duty-free *adj (U)* zollfrei.

duvet ['du:veɪ] *n UK* Daunendecke *die*.

duvet cover *n UK* Bettbezug *der (für eine Daunendecke)*.

DVD *(abbr of* **Digital Versatile Disk**) *n* DVD *die*.

DVD player *n* DVD-Player *der*.

dwarf [dwɔ:f] *(pl* **-s** OR **dwarves** [dwɔ:vz]) ◇ *n* Zwerg *der*, -in *die*. ◇ *vt* [tower over] winzig erscheinen lassen.

dwell [dwel] *(pt & pp* **dwelt** OR **-ed**) *vi liter* [live] wohnen. ◆ **dwell on** *vt insep* [talk about] sich lange befassen mit; [think about] lange nach|denken über *(+ A)*.

dwelling ['dwelɪŋ] *n liter* Wohnung *die*.

dwelt [dwelt] *pt & pp* ▻ **dwell**.

dwindle ['dwɪndl] *vi* dahin|schwinden.

dye [daɪ] ◇ *n* Farbstoff *der*. ◇ *vt* färben.

dying ['daɪɪŋ] ◇ *cont* ▻ **die**. ◇ *adj* - **1.** [person, animal] sterbend - **2.** *fig* [tradition, language] aussterbend.

dyke [daɪk] *n* = **dike**.

dynamic [daɪ'næmɪk] *adj* dynamisch.

dynamite ['daɪnəmaɪt] *n (U)* - **1.** [explosive] Dynamit *das* - **2.** *inf fig* [story, news]: **to be dynamite** viel Zündstoff enthalten - **3.** *inf fig* [excellent]: **to be dynamite** eine Wucht sein.

dynamo ['daɪnəməʊ] *(pl* **-s**) *n* TECH Dynamo *der*; AUT Lichtmaschine *die*.

dynasty [*UK* 'dɪnəstɪ, *US* 'daɪnəstɪ] *n* Dynastie *die*.

dyslexia [dɪs'leksɪə] *n (U)* Legasthenie *die*.

dyslexic [dɪs'leksɪk] *adj* legasthenisch; **to be dyslexic** Legastheniker/Legasthenikerin sein.

E

e (*pl* **e's** OR **es**), **E** (*pl* **E's** OR **Es**) [iː] *n* [letter] e *das*, E *das*. ◆ **E** *n* - **1.** MUS E *das* - **2.** *abbr of* **east** - **3.** *inf* (*abbr of* **ecstasy**) E *das*.

each [iːtʃ] ◇ *adj* jede(r) (s). ◇ *pron*: **each (one)** jede(r) (s); **each other** einander; **separated from each other** voneinander getrennt; **they know each other** sie kennen sich; **they kissed each other on the cheek** sie küssten sich auf die Wange; **there's one each** es ist für jeden eins da; **I'd like one of each** ich möchte von jedem/jeder eins; **they cost £10 each** sie kosten je 10 Pfund.

eager [ˈiːgəʳ] *adj* [person] eifrig; *(phrase)*: **to be eager for sthg** auf etw *(A)* erpicht sein; **to be eager to do sthg** etw unbedingt tun wollen.

eagle [ˈiːgl] *n* Adler *der*.

ear [ɪəʳ] *n* - **1.** [of person, animal] Ohr *das*; **I'll play it by ear** ich werde es auf mich zukommen lassen - **2.** [of corn] Ähre *die*.

earache [ˈɪəreɪk] *n* Ohrenschmerzen *Pl*.

eardrum [ˈɪədrʌm] *n* Trommelfell *das*.

earl [ɜːl] *n* Graf *der*.

earlier [ˈɜːlɪəʳ] *adj* & *adv* früher; **earlier on** früher.

earliest [ˈɜːlɪəst] ◇ *adj* - **1.** [first] frühstmöglich; **at the earliest opportunity** so bald wie möglich - **2.** [most early] frühest. ◇ *adv*: **she'll not be back till four o'clock at the earliest** sie wird frühestens um vier Uhr wieder hier sein.

earlobe [ˈɪələʊb] *n* Ohrläppchen *das*.

early [ˈɜːlɪ] ◇ *adj* früh; **early death** vorzeitiger Tod; **at an early hour** zu früher Stunde; **at an early age** [early in life] schon früh; [as a child] im Kindesalter; **in the early afternoon** am frühen Nachmittag; **to have an early breakfast/night** früh frühstücken/zu Bett gehen. ◇ *adv* früh; **to leave early** [person] früher gehen; [bus, train] zu früh ab|fahren; **as early as next week** schon nächste Woche; **early on** früh.

early closing *n*: **today is early closing** heute schließen die Geschäfte früher.

early retirement *n*: **to take early retirement** in den vorzeitigen Ruhestand gehen.

earmark [ˈɪəmɑːk] *vt*: **to be earmarked for sthg** für etw vorgesehen sein.

earn [ɜːn] *vt* - **1.** [gen] verdienen - **2.** COMM erwirtschaften.

earnest [ˈɜːnɪst] *adj* ernsthaft. ◆ **in earnest** ◇ *adj*: **I'm in earnest** ich meine es ernst. ◇ *adv* ernsthaft; **to begin in earnest** richtig an|fangen.

earnings [ˈɜːnɪŋz] *npl* [of person] Einkommen *das*; [of business] Ertrag *der*.

earphones [ˈɪəfəʊnz] *npl* Kopfhörer *der*.

earpiece *n* [of telephone] Hörmuschel *die*; [of radio, mobile phone] ≃ Kopfhörer *der*.

earplugs [ˈɪəplʌgz] *npl* Ohropax® *Pl*.

earring [ˈɪərɪŋ] *n* Ohrring *der*.

earshot [ˈɪəʃɒt] *n*: **within/out of earshot** in/außer Hörweite.

earth [ɜːθ] ◇ *n* Erde *die*; **how/what/where/why on earth ?** wie/was/wo/warum um Himmels willen ?; **to cost the earth** *UK* ein Vermögen kosten. ◇ *vt UK*: **to be earthed** geerdet sein.

earthenware [ˈɜːθnweəʳ] *n (U)* Töpferwaren *Pl*.

earthquake [ˈɜːθkweɪk] *n* Erdbeben *das*.

earthy [ˈɜːθɪ] *adj* [humour, person] derb.

ease [iːz] ◇ *n* - **1.** [in doing sthg] Leichtigkeit *die*; **to do sthg with ease** etw mit Leichtigkeit tun - **2.** [comfort]: **a life of ease** ein komfortables Leben; **to put sb at ease** jm die Befangenheit nehmen; **I feel at ease (with him)** ich fühle mich (in seiner Gegenwart) wohl; **ill at ease** unbehaglich. ◇ *vt* - **1.** [make less severe - pain] lindern; [- restriction, problem] verringern - **2.** [move carefully]: **she eased herself out of the armchair** sie erhob sich behutsam aus dem Sessel; **she eased the window open** sie öffnete behutsam das Fenster. ◇ *vi* [pain, rain] nach|lassen; [grip] sich lockern. ◆ **ease off** *vi* [pain, rain] nach|lassen. ◆ **ease up** *vi* - **1.** [rain] nach|lassen - **2.** [relax] sich *(D)* mehr Ruhe gönnen.

easel [ˈiːzl] *n* Staffelei *die*.

easily [ˈiːzɪlɪ] *adv* - **1.** [without difficulty] leicht - **2.** [undoubtedly] zweifellos - **3.** [in a relaxed manner] entspannt.

east [iːst] ◇ *adj* Ost-, östlich; **east wind** Ostwind *der*. ◇ *adv* [travel, face] ostwärts, nach Osten; **east of** östlich von. ◇ *n* - **1.** [direction] Osten *der* - **2.** [region]: **the east** der Osten. ◆ **East** *n*: **the East** [Asia & POL] der Osten.

East End *n*: **the East End** *der Londoner Osten nördlich der Themse*.

Easter [ˈiːstəʳ] *n* Ostern *Pl*.

Easter egg *n* Osterei *das*.

easterly [ˈiːstəlɪ] *adj* östlich; **easterly wind** Ostwind *der*; **in an easterly direction** in östlicher Richtung.

eastern [ˈiːstən] *adj* Ost-. ◆ **Eastern** *adj* - **1.** [from Asia] östlich - **2.** POL Ost-.

East German ◇ *adj* ostdeutsch. ◇ *n* Ostdeutsche *der, die*.

East Germany *n*: **(the former) East Germany** Ostdeutschland *nt*.

eastward ['i:stwəd] <> *adj* (in) Richtung Osten. <> *adv* = **eastwards**.

eastwards ['i:stwədz] *adv* ostwärts.

easy ['i:zɪ] <> *adj* - **1.** [not difficult] leicht; [route] einfach - **2.** [comfortable] leicht; **an easy life** ein bequemes Leben - **3.** [relaxed] ungezwungen. <> *adv*: **to take it** OR **things easy** *inf* [ease up] sich *(D)* mehr Ruhe gönnen; [have a rest] eine ruhige Kugel schieben.

easy chair *n* [armchair] Sessel *der*.

easygoing [ˌi:zɪ'gəʊɪŋ] *adj* [person] unbekümmert; [manner] lässig.

eat [i:t] (*pt* **ate**, *pp* **eaten**) *vt* [subj: person] essen; [subj: animal] fressen. ◆ **eat away, eat into** *vt insep* - **1.** [subj: rust, acid] zerfressen - **2.** [savings] auf|zehren.

eaten ['i:tn] *pp* ▷ **eat**.

eaves ['i:vz] *npl* [of house] Dachvorsprung *der*.

eavesdrop ['i:vzdrɒp] *vi* lauschen; **to eavesdrop on sb** jn belauschen.

ebb [eb] <> *n* Ebbe *die*. <> *vi* [tide, sea] zurück|gehen.

ebony ['ebənɪ] *n* Ebenholz *das*.

EC (*abbr of* **European Community**) *n* EG *die*.

ECB (*abbr of* **Eurpean Central Bank**) *n* EZB *die*.

e-cash *n* COMPUT elektronisches Geld.

eccentric [ɪk'sentrɪk] <> *adj* exzentrisch. <> *n* Exzentriker *der*, -in *die*.

echo ['ekəʊ] (*pl* **-es**) <> *n* - **1.** [sound] Echo *das* - **2.** [reminder] Reminiszenz *die*. <> *vt* [repeat - opinion] wieder|geben. <> *vi* wider|hallen.

eclipse [ɪ'klɪps] <> *n* - **1.** [of sun, moon] Eklipse *die*, Finsternis *die* - **2.** *fig* [decline] Niedergang *der*. <> *vt fig* [overshadow] in den Schatten stellen.

eco-friendly *adj* umweltfreundlich.

ecological [ˌi:kə'lɒdʒɪkl] *adj* ökologisch; **an ecological group** eine Gruppe von Umweltschützern.

ecology [ɪ'kɒlədʒɪ] *n* Ökologie *die*.

economic [ˌi:kə'nɒmɪk] *adj* - **1.** [growth, system, policy] Wirtschafts- - **2.** [business] wirtschaftlich.

economical [ˌi:kə'nɒmɪkl] *adj* wirtschaftlich; [person] sparsam.

economics [ˌi:kə'nɒmɪks] <> *n (U)* [study] Wirtschaftswissenschaften *Pl*. <> *npl* [of plan, business, trade] Wirtschaftlichkeit *die*.

economize, -ise [ɪ'kɒnəmaɪz] *vi* sparen; **to economize on sthg** an etw *(D)* sparen.

economy [ɪ'kɒnəmɪ] *n* - **1.** [system] Wirtschaft *die* - **2.** [saving]: **it is a false economy** es hilft nicht zu sparen; **to make economies** Sparmaßnahmen treffen; **economy measure** Sparmaßnahme *die*.

economy class *n* Touristenklasse *die*.

ecstasy ['ekstəsɪ] *n* - **1.** [great happiness] Ekstase *die*; **to go into ecstasies about sthg** über etw *(A)* in Verzückung geraten - **2.** *(U)* [drug] Ecstasy *das*.

ecstatic [ek'stætɪk] *adj* ekstatisch.

eczema ['eksɪmə] *n (U)* Ekzem *das*.

edge [edʒ] <> *n* - **1.** [of cliff, path, forest] Rand *der*; [of table, coin, book] Kante *die* - **2.** [of blade] Schneide *die* - **3.** [advantage]: **to have an edge over sb, to have the edge on sb** jm gegenüber einen Vorteil haben; **to have an edge over sthg, to have the edge on sthg** etw *(D)* überlegen sein. <> *vi* [move slowly]: **to edge forwards** sich Stück für Stück vorwärts|bewegen; **to edge away** sich langsam zurück|ziehen. ◆ **on edge** *adj*: **to be on edge** [person] nervös sein; [nerves] gereizt sein.

edgeways ['edʒweɪz], **edgewise** ['edʒwaɪz] *adv* seitwärts.

edgy ['edʒɪ] *adj* nervös.

edible ['edɪbl] *adj* essbar.

Edinburgh ['edɪnbrə] *n* Edinburgh *nt*.

edit ['edɪt] *vt* - **1.** [correct, select material for] redigieren - **2.** CIN, RADIO & TV schneiden - **3.** [newspaper, magazine] heraus|geben - **4.** COMPUT editieren.

edition [ɪ'dɪʃn] *n* - **1.** [of book, newspaper] Ausgabe *die* - **2.** [broadcast] Sendung *die*.

editor ['edɪtəʳ] *n* - **1.** [of newspaper, magazine, book] Herausgeber *der*, -in *die* - **2.** [of section of newspaper, programme] Redakteur *der*, -in *die* - **3.** [copy editor] Lektor *der*, -in *die* - **4.** CIN, RADIO & TV Cutter *der*, -in *die* - **5.** COMPUT Editor *der*.

editorial [ˌedɪ'tɔ:rɪəl] <> *adj* redaktionell; **editorial department/staff** Redaktion *die*. <> *n* Leitartikel *der*.

educate ['edʒʊkeɪt] *vt* - **1.** SCH & UNIV aus|bilden; [subj: parents] erziehen - **2.** [inform] informieren.

education [ˌedʒʊ'keɪʃn] *n* Ausbildung *die*; [by parents] Erziehung *die*.

educational [ˌedʒʊ'keɪʃənl] *adj* - **1.** [establishment, policy] Bildungs-; **educational background** Ausbildung *die* - **2.** [toy] didaktisch; [experience] lehrreich.

EEC (*abbr of* **European Economic Community**) *n* EWG *die*.

eel [i:l] *n* Aal *der*.

eerie ['ɪərɪ] *adj* unheimlich.

efface [ɪ'feɪs] *vt* [mark, inscription] entfernen; [memory] aus|löschen.

effect [ɪ'fekt] <> *n* - **1.** [result] Wirkung *die*; **to have an effect on sb/sthg** eine Wirkung auf jn/etw haben; **to take effect** [law, rule] in Kraft treten; [drug] wirken; **to put sthg into effect** etw in Kraft setzen - **2.** [impression] Wirkung *die*, Effekt *der*; **for effect** aus Effekthascherei. <> *vt* bewirken. ◆ **effects** *npl* - **1.**:

(special) effects (Spezial)effekte *Pl* - **2.** [property] Habe *die.* ◈ **in effect** *adv* in Wirklichkeit.

effective [ɪ'fektɪv] *adj* - **1.** [successful] effektiv - **2.** [actual] eigentlich - **3.** [in operation] wirksam.

effectively [ɪ'fektɪvlɪ] *adv* - **1.** [successfully] effektiv - **2.** [in fact] in Wirklichkeit.

effectiveness [ɪ'fektɪvnɪs] *n* [success] Effektivität *die.*

effeminate [ɪ'femɪnət] *adj pej* weibisch.

effervescent [ˌefə'vesənt] *adj* sprudelnd.

efficiency [ɪ'fɪʃənsɪ] *n* [of person] Tüchtigkeit *die*; [of machine] Leistungsfähigkeit *die*; [of system] Effizienz *die.*

efficient [ɪ'fɪʃənt] *adj* [person] tüchtig; [machine] leistungsfähig; [method] effizient.

effluent ['efluənt] *n* Abwasser *das.*

effort ['efət] *n* - **1.** [exertion] Anstrengung *die*; **it's not worth the effort** es ist nicht der Mühe wert; **to make the effort to do sthg** sich bemühen, etw zu tun; **with effort** mit Mühe - **2.** [attempt] Versuch *der*; **to make an/no effort to do sthg** sich an|strengen/sich nicht an|strengen, etw zu tun.

effortless ['efətlɪs] *adj* mühelos.

effusive [ɪ'fju:sɪv] *adj* überschwänglich.

e.g. (*abbr of* **exempli gratia**) *adv* z. B.

egg [eg] *n* Ei *das.* ◈ **egg on** *vt sep* an|stacheln.

eggcup ['egkʌp] *n* Eierbecher *der.*

eggplant ['egplɑ:nt] *n US* Aubergine *die.*

eggshell ['egʃel] *n* Eierschale *die.*

egg white *n* Eiweiß *das.*

egg yolk *n* Eigelb *das.*

ego ['i:gəʊ] (*pl* **-s**) *n* [opinion of self] Selbstbewusstsein *das*; PSYCHOL Ego *das.*

egoism ['i:gəʊɪzm] *n* Egoismus *der.*

egoistic [ˌi:gəʊ'ɪstɪk] *adj* egoistisch.

egotistic(al) [ˌi:gə'tɪstɪk(l)] *adj* egoistisch.

Egypt ['i:dʒɪpt] *n* Ägypten *nt.*

Egyptian [ɪ'dʒɪpʃn] ◇ *adj* ägyptisch. ◇ *n* Ägypter *der*, -in *die.*

eiderdown ['aɪdədaʊn] *n esp UK* [bed cover] Daunendecke *die.*

eight [eɪt] *num* acht; *see also* **six.**

eighteen [ˌeɪ'ti:n] *num* achtzehn; *see also* **six.**

eighth [eɪtθ] *num* achte(r) (s); *see also* **sixth.**

eighty ['eɪtɪ] *num* achtzig; *see also* **sixty.**

Eire ['eərə] *n* Irland *nt.*

either ['aɪðəʳ, 'i:ðəʳ] ◇ *adj* - **1.** [one or the other]: **either will do** es ist egal, welches (von beiden); **either way I will lose** wie ich es auch mache, ich werde dabei verlieren - **2.** [each] beide; **on either side** auf beiden Seiten. ◇ *pron*: **I'll take either (of them)** ich nehme einen/eine/eins (von beiden); **I don't like either (of them)** ich mag keinen/keine/keins (von beiden). ◇ *adv (in negatives)*: **I can't either** ich auch nicht. ◇ *conj*: **either...or...** entweder...oder...; **I don't like either him or her** ich mag weder ihn noch sie; **without either writing or phoning** ohne zu schreiben oder anzurufen.

eject [ɪ'dʒekt] *vt* - **1.** [object] aus|stoßen - **2.** [person]: **to eject sb (from)** jn hinaus|werfen (aus).

eke ◈ **eke out** *vt sep* strecken.

elaborate ◇ *adj* [ɪ'læbrət] [explanation] ausführlich; [plan] ausgefeilt; [carving] kunstvoll; [ceremony] kompliziert. ◇ *vi* [ɪ'læbəreɪt]: **to elaborate (on sthg)** (etw) näher erläutern.

elapse [ɪ'læps] *vi* [time] verstreichen.

elastic [ɪ'læstɪk] ◇ *adj* - **1.** [stretchy] elastisch - **2.** *fig* [flexible] flexibel. ◇ *n (U)* [material] Gummiband *das.*

elasticated [ɪ'læstɪkeɪtɪd] *adj* [waistband] mit Gummizug.

elastic band *n UK* Gummiband *das.*

elated [ɪ'leɪtɪd] *adj* in Hochstimmung.

elbow ['elbəʊ] *n* Ellbogen *der.*

elder ['eldəʳ] ◇ *adj* ältere(r) (s). ◇ *n* - **1.** [older person]: **show respect to your elders** zeige Respekt gegenüber älteren Menschen - **2.** [of church] Presbyter *der.*

elderly ['eldəlɪ] ◇ *adj* ältere(r) (s). ◇ *npl*: **the elderly** ältere Menschen *Pl.*

eldest ['eldɪst] *adj* älteste(r) (s).

elect [ɪ'lekt] ◇ *adj*: **president elect** designierter Präsident. ◇ *vt* [by voting] wählen; **he was elected (as) party leader** er wurde zum Parteivorsitzenden gewählt.

election [ɪ'lekʃn] *n* Wahl *die*; **to have** OR **hold an election** eine Wahl ab|halten.

elector [ɪ'lektəʳ] *n* [voter] Wähler *der*, -in *die.*

electorate [ɪ'lektərət] *n*: **the electorate** die Wählerschaft.

electric [ɪ'lektrɪk] *adj* - **1.** [gen] elektrisch - **2.** *fig* [atmosphere] elektrisiert. ◈ **electrics** *npl UK inf* [in car, machine] Elektrik *die.*

electrical [ɪ'lektrɪkl] *adj* elektrisch; **electrical goods** Elektrowaren *Pl.*

electrical shock *n US* = **electric shock.**

electric blanket *n* Heizdecke *die.*

electric cooker *n* Elektroherd *der.*

electric fire *n* Heizstrahler *der.*

electrician [ˌɪlek'trɪʃn] *n* Elektriker *der*, -in *die.*

electricity [ˌɪlek'trɪsətɪ] *n* [current] Strom *der*; [in physics] Elektrizität *die.*

electric shock *UK*, **electrical shock** *US n* Stromschlag *der.*

electrify [ɪ'lektrɪfaɪ] *vt* - **1.** [railway line] elektrifizieren - **2.** *fig* [excite] elektrisieren.

electrocute [ɪ'lektrəkjuːt] *vt*: **to electrocute o.s., to be electrocuted** sich durch Stromschlag töten; **to be electrocuted** [executed] auf dem elektrischen Stuhl hingerichtet werden.

electrolysis [ˌɪlek'trɒləsɪs] *n* Elektrolyse *die*.

electron [ɪ'lektrɒn] *n* Elektron *das*.

electronic [ˌɪlek'trɒnɪk] *adj* elektronisch. ◆ **electronics** ◇ *n (U)* [technology] Elektronik *die*. ◇ *npl* [of car, machine] Elektronik *die*.

electronic data processing *n* elektronische Datenverarbeitung.

elegant ['elɪgənt] *adj* elegant.

element ['elɪmənt] *n* - **1.** [gen] Element *das*; [component] Bestandteil *der*; **an element of truth** ein Körnchen Wahrheit - **2.** [of heater, kettle] Heizelement *das*. ◆ **elements** *npl* - **1.** [basics] Grundlagen *Pl* - **2.** [weather]: **the elements** die Elemente *Pl*.

elementary [ˌelɪ'mentərɪ] *adj* [precautions, mistake, question] simpel; [education, maths] Elementar-.

elementary school *n US* Grundschule *die*.

elephant ['elɪfənt] (*pl inv* OR **-s**) *n* Elefant *der*.

elevate ['elɪveɪt] *vt* - **1.** [raise] heben - **2.** [give importance to] erheben; [promote] befördern.

elevator ['elɪveɪtə^r] *n US* Fahrstuhl *der*.

eleven [ɪ'levn] *num* elf; *see also* **six**.

elevenses [ɪ'levnzɪz] *n UK* zweites Frühstück.

eleventh [ɪ'levnθ] *num* elfte(r) (s); *see also* **sixth**.

elicit [ɪ'lɪsɪt] *vt fml*: **to elicit sthg (from sb)** (jm) etw entlocken.

eligible ['elɪdʒəbl] *adj* [suitable, qualified] geeignet; **to be eligible for sthg** für etw in Frage kommen.

eliminate [ɪ'lɪmɪneɪt] *vt* - **1.** [remove] aus|schließen; [disease, poverty] eliminieren - **2.** [from competition]: **to be eliminated from sthg** aus etw aus|scheiden.

elite [ɪ'liːt] ◇ *adj* Elite-. ◇ *n* Elite *die*.

elitist [ɪ'liːtɪst] *adj* elitär.

elk [elk] (*pl inv* OR **-s**) *n* Elch *der*; [Canadian] Elk *der*.

elm [elm] *n*: **elm (tree)** Ulme *die*.

elongated ['iːlɒŋgeɪtɪd] *adj* [face, shape] lang gezogen.

elope [ɪ'ləʊp] *vi* durch|brennen.

eloquent ['eləkwənt] *adj* - **1.** [speaker] wortgewandt - **2.** [speech, words] wohlgesetzt.

else [els] *adv*: **I don't want anything else** ich will nichts mehr; **anything else?** sonst noch etwas?; **everyone else** alle anderen; **nobody else** niemand anders; **nothing else** sonst nichts; **somebody else** [additional person] noch jemand anders; [different person] jemand anders; **anybody else (but you) would have given up** jeder andere (außer dir) hätte aufgegeben; **something else** [additional thing] noch etwas; [different thing] etwas anderes; **somewhere else** woanders; **to go somewhere else** woandershin gehen; **what else?** [in addition] was (sonst) noch?; [instead] was sonst?; **who else?** [in addition] wer (sonst) noch?; [instead] wer sonst? ◆ **or else** *conj* [or if not] sonst, oder; **come in or else go out** komm entweder herein oder geh hinaus.

elsewhere [els'weə^r] *adv* woanders.

elude [ɪ'luːd] *vt* - **1.** [police, pursuers] entwischen - **2.** [subj: fact, name] entfallen sein *(+ D)*.

elusive [ɪ'luːsɪv] *adj* [quality] schwer fassbar; [success] schwer erreichbar; **he is very elusive** er ist selten anzutreffen.

emaciated [ɪ'meɪʃɪeɪtɪd] *adj* stark abgemagert.

e-mail ◇ *n* E-Mail *die ODER das*; **by e-mail** per E-Mail. ◇ *vt*: **to e-mail sb** jm ein(e) E-Mail schicken.

e-mail address *n* COMPUT E-Mail-Adresse *die*.

emanate ['eməneɪt] *fml vi*: **to emanate from** [idea] stammen von; [smell] kommen von/aus.

emancipate [ɪ'mænsɪpeɪt] *vt* befreien; [women] emanzipieren.

embankment [ɪm'bæŋkmənt] *n* - **1.** [along road, path] Böschung *die* - **2.** [along river] Damm *der*; [along railway] Bahndamm *der*.

embark [ɪm'bɑːk] *vi* - **1.** [board ship] sich ein|schiffen - **2.** [start]: **to embark (up)on sthg** mit etw beginnen.

embarrass [ɪm'bærəs] *vt* in Verlegenheit bringen.

embarrassed [ɪm'bærəst] *adj* verlegen.

embarrassing [ɪm'bærəsɪŋ] *adj* peinlich.

embarrassment [ɪm'bærəsmənt] *n* Verlegenheit *die*; **to be an embarrassment to sb** jn in Verlegenheit bringen.

embassy ['embəsɪ] *n* Botschaft *die*.

embedded [ɪm'bedɪd] *adj* - **1.** [in rock, wood, mud]: **to be embedded in sthg** in etw *(D)* fest|stecken - **2.** *fig* [feeling] fest verwurzelt.

embellish [ɪm'belɪʃ] *vt* - **1.** [decorate]: **to embellish sthg with sthg** etw mit etw schmücken - **2.** *fig* [story] aus|schmücken.

embers ['embəz] *npl* Glut *die*.

embezzle [ɪm'bezl] *vt* unterschlagen.

embittered [ɪm'bɪtəd] *adj* verbittert.

emblem ['embləm] *n* Emblem *das*.

embody [ɪm'bɒdɪ] *vt* - **1.** [epitomize] verkörpern - **2.** [include] enthalten.

embossed [ɪm'bɒst] *adj* geprägt.

embrace [ɪm'breɪs] ◇ *n* Umarmung *die*. ◇ *vt* [hug] umarmen. ◇ *vi* sich umarmen.

embroider [ɪm'brɔɪdə^r] *vt* - **1.** [design] sticken; [tablecloth, blouse] besticken - **2.** [story] aus|schmücken.

embroidery [ɪm'brɔɪdərɪ] *n* - **1.** [skill] Sticken *das* - **2.** [designs] Stickerei *die*.

embroil [ɪm'brɔɪl] *vt*: **to get embroiled (in sthg)** (in etw *(A)*) verwickelt werden.

embryo ['embrɪəʊ] (*pl* **-s**) *n* Embryo *der*.

emerald ['emərəld] *n* Smaragd *der*.

emerge [ɪ'mɜːdʒ] ◇ *vi* - **1.** [come out] auf|tauchen; **to emerge from sthg** aus etw heraus|kommen - **2.** [facts, truth] heraus|kommen. ◇ *vt*: **it emerged that...** es stellte sich heraus, dass...

emergency [ɪ'mɜːdʒənsɪ] ◇ *adj* Not-. ◇ *n* Notfall *der*; **in an emergency** im Notfall.

emergency brake *n US* Notbremse *die*.

emergency exit *n* Notausgang *der*.

emergency landing *n* Notlandung *die*.

emergency room *n US* Unfallstation *die*.

emergency services *npl* Hilfsdienste *Pl*.

emigrant ['emɪgrənt] *n* Auswanderer *der*.

emigrate ['emɪgreɪt] *vi* aus|wandern.

eminent ['emɪnənt] *adj* berühmt und anerkannt.

emit [ɪ'mɪt] *vt fml* [light] aus|strahlen; [radiation, smoke] emittieren; [sound, heat] ab|geben.

emotion [ɪ'məʊʃn] *n* - **1.** [particular feeling] Gefühl *das*, Emotion *die* - **2.** *(U)* [strength of feeling] Gemütsbewegung *die*; **she showed no emotion** sie blieb vollkommen unbewegt; **to speak with emotion** ergriffen sprechen.

emotional [ɪ'məʊʃənl] *adj* - **1.** [person - by nature] gefühlsbetont; [- temporarily] emotional; *(phrase)*: **to get emotional** emotional werden - **2.** [scene, farewell] emotionsgeladen; [music] gefühlvoll; [appeal, speech] gefühlsbetont - **3.** [problems, needs, reaction] emotional.

emperor ['empərə^r] *n* Kaiser *der*.

emphasis ['emfəsɪs] (*pl* **-ases** [-əsiːz]) *n* Betonung *die*; **to lay** OR **place emphasis on sthg** großen Wert auf etw *(A)* legen.

emphasize, -ise ['emfəsaɪz] *vt* betonen; [point, feature] hervor|heben.

emphatic [ɪm'fætɪk] *adj* [forceful] entschieden.

emphatically [ɪm'fætɪklɪ] *adv* - **1.** [with emphasis] mit Nachdruck - **2.** [deny] entschieden.

empire ['empaɪə^r] *n* POL Reich *das*.

employ [ɪm'plɔɪ] *vt* - **1.** [give work to] beschäftigen; [recruit] an|stellen; **to be employed as a secretary** als Sekretär(in) arbeiten - **2.** *fml* [use] an|wenden.

employee [ɪm'plɔɪiː] *n* Angestellte *der, die*.

employer [ɪm'plɔɪə^r] *n* Arbeitgeber *der*, -in *die*.

employment [ɪm'plɔɪmənt] *n* *(U)* Arbeit *die*; [recruitment] Anstellung *die*; **to be in employment** eine Stelle haben.

employment agency *n* Stellenvermittlung *die*.

empower [ɪm'paʊə^r] *vt fml*: **to be empowered to do sthg** ermächtigt sein, etw zu tun.

empress ['emprɪs] *n* Kaiserin *die*.

empty ['emptɪ] ◇ *adj* leer; **on an empty stomach** MED auf nüchternen Magen. ◇ *vt* leeren; [bin] aus|leeren; [room] aus|räumen; **to empty sthg into/out of sthg** [pour] etw in etw *(A)*/aus etw schütten. ◇ *vi* [room, theatre] sich leeren. ◇ *n inf* [bottle] leere Flasche; [glass] leeres Glas.

empty-handed [-'hændɪd] *adv* unverrichteter Dinge.

EMU (*abbr of* **European Monetary Union**) *n* WWU *die*.

emulate ['emjʊleɪt] *vt* [person, example] nach|eifern *(+ D)*; [system] nach|ahmen.

emulsion [ɪ'mʌlʃn] *n*: **emulsion (paint)** Dispersionsfarbe *die*.

enable [ɪ'neɪbl] *vt*: **to enable sb to do sthg** es jm möglich machen, etw zu tun.

enact [ɪ'nækt] *vt* - **1.** LAW erlassen - **2.** [scene, play] auf|führen.

enamel [ɪ'næml] *n* - **1.** [on metal, glass] Email *das* - **2.** [on tooth] Zahnschmelz *der* - **3.** [paint] Emaillack *der*.

encapsulate [ɪn'kæpsjʊleɪt] *vt fig* zusammen|fassen.

enchanting [ɪn'tʃɑːntɪŋ] *adj* bezaubernd.

encircle [ɪn'sɜːkl] *vt* umgeben; [subj: troops] umringen.

enclose [ɪn'kləʊz] *vt* - **1.** [surround] umgeben; **enclosed space** abgeschlossener Raum; **to be enclosed by** OR **with sthg** von etw umgeben sein - **2.** [put in envelope] bei|legen; **please find enclosed** als Anlage senden wir Ihnen.

enclosure [ɪn'kləʊʒə^r] *n* - **1.** [place] eingezäuntes Grundstück; [for animals] Gehege *das* - **2.** [in letter] Anlage *die*.

encompass [ɪn'kʌmpəs] *vt fml* umfassen.

encore ['ɒŋkɔː^r] ◇ *n* Zugabe *die*. ◇ *excl* Zugabe!

encounter [ɪn'kaʊntə^r] ◇ *n* Begegnung *die*; [battle] Kampf *der*. ◇ *vt fml* - **1.** [meet] begegnen *(+ D)* - **2.** [experience] stoßen auf *(+ A)*.

encourage [ɪn'kʌrɪdʒ] *vt* - **1.** [person] ermutigen; **to encourage sb to do sthg** jn ermutigen OR ermuntern, etw zu tun - **2.** [foster] fördern.

encouragement [ɪn'kʌrɪdʒmənt] *n* Ermutigung *die*; [support] Förderung *die*.

encroach [ɪn'krəʊtʃ] *vi*: **to encroach (up)on sthg** [on territory] in etw *(A)* vor|dringen; [on rights, privacy] in etw *(A)* ein|greifen.

encyclop(a)edic [ɪn,saɪkləʊ'piːdɪk] *adj* enzyklopädisch.

end [end] <> *n* - **1.** [finish] Ende *das*; **from beginning to end** von vorn bis hinten; **at the end of May** Ende Mai; **at an end** zu Ende; **to come to an end** enden; **to put an end to sthg** etw *(D)* ein Ende setzen; **at the end of the day** *fig* schließlich und endlich; **in the end** [finally] schließlich - **2.** [extremity] Ende *das*; [of box] Seite *die*; [of finger, stick] Spitze *die*; **to make ends meet** [financially] zurecht|kommen - **3.** [leftover part] Rest *der*; [of candle] Stummel *der* - **4.** *fml* [purpose] Ziel *das* - **5.** *liter* [death] Ende *das*. <> *vt* beenden. <> *vi* enden; **to end in failure** in einem Misserfolg enden. ◆ **on end** *adv* - **1.** [upright] hochkant - **2.** [continuously]: **for days on end** tagelang. ◆ **end up** *vi*: **to end up in prison** im Gefängnis landen; **to end up doing sthg** schließlich etw tun.

endanger [ɪn'deɪndʒəʳ] *vt* gefährden.

endearing [ɪn'dɪərɪŋ] *adj* liebenswert.

endeavour *UK*, **endeavor** *US fml* [ɪn'devəʳ] <> *n* Bemühung *die*. <> *vt*: **to endeavour to do sthg** sich bemühen, etw zu tun.

ending ['endɪŋ] *n* - **1.** [of story, film] Ende *das*, Schluss *der* - **2.** GRAM Endung *die*.

endive ['endaɪv] *n* - **1.** [salad vegetable] Endivie *die* - **2.** [chicory] Chicorée *die ODER der*.

endless ['endlɪs] *adj* endlos; [possibilities, desert] unendlich.

endorse [ɪn'dɔːs] *vt* - **1.** [approve] billigen - **2.** [cheque] auf der Rückseite unterschreiben, indossieren.

endorsement [ɪn'dɔːsmənt] *n* - **1.** [approval] Billigung *die* - **2.** *UK* [on driving licence] Strafvermerk *der* (auf dem Führerschein).

endow [ɪn'daʊ] *vt* [equip]: **to be endowed with sthg** mit etw ausgestattet sein; **to be endowed with charm/talent** Charme/Talent haben.

endurance [ɪn'djʊərəns] *n* Durchhaltevermögen *das*; **it was beyond endurance** es war nicht auszuhalten.

endure [ɪn'djʊəʳ] <> *vt* ertragen. <> *vi fml* Bestand haben.

endways *UK* ['endweɪz], **endwise** *US* ['endwaɪz] *adv* - **1.** [lengthways] mit dem Ende nach vorn - **2.** [end to end] mit den Enden aneinander.

enemy ['enɪmɪ] <> *n* Feind *der*. <> *comp* feindlich.

energetic [ˌenə'dʒetɪk] *adj* - **1.** [lively] energiegeladen; **to feel/be energetic** viel Energie haben - **2.** [game, activity] viel Energie erfordernd - **3.** [supporter, campaigner] tatkräftig.

energy ['enədʒɪ] *n* [gen] Energie *die*.

enforce [ɪn'fɔːs] *vt* [high standards, discipline] sorgen für; **to enforce a law** für die Einhaltung eines Gesetzes sorgen.

enforced [ɪn'fɔːst] *adj* aufgezwungen.

engage [ɪn'geɪdʒ] <> *vt* - **1.** [attract - attention] in Anspruch nehmen; [- interest] fesseln - **2.** TECH [gear] ein|legen; **to engage the clutch** kuppeln - **3.** *fml* [employ] an|stellen; **to be engaged in** *OR* **on sthg** mit etw beschäftigt sein. <> *vi*: **to engage in sthg** sich mit etw befassen.

engaged [ɪn'geɪdʒd] *adj* - **1.** [couple]: **engaged (to sb)** (mit jm) verlobt; **to get engaged** sich verloben - **2.** [busy] beschäftigt - **3.** [toilet, telephone number] besetzt.

engaged tone *n UK* Besetztzeichen *das*.

engagement [ɪn'geɪdʒmənt] *n* - **1.** [of couple] Verlobung *die* - **2.** [appointment - gen] Verpflichtung *die*; [- business] Termin *der*.

engagement ring *n* Verlobungsring *der*.

engaging [ɪn'geɪdʒɪŋ] *adj* [manner, personality] einnehmend; [smile] gewinnend.

engender [ɪn'dʒendəʳ] *vt fml* erzeugen.

engine ['endʒɪn] *n* - **1.** [of car, plane] Motor *der*; [of ship] Maschine *die* - **2.** RAIL Lokomotive *die*.

engine driver *n UK* Lokomotivführer *der*.

engineer [ˌendʒɪ'nɪəʳ] *n* - **1.** [of roads, machines, bridges] Techniker *der*, -in *die*; [with degree] Ingenieur *der*, -in *die* - **2.** *US* [engine driver] Lokomotivführer *der*.

engineering [ˌendʒɪ'nɪərɪŋ] *n (U)* Technik *die*; [mechanical] Maschinenbau *der*.

England ['ɪŋglənd] *n* England *nt*.

English ['ɪŋglɪʃ] <> *adj* englisch. <> *n* Englisch(e) *das*. <> *npl*: **the English** die Engländer *Pl*.

English breakfast *n* englisches Frühstück.

English Channel *n*: **the English Channel** der Ärmelkanal.

Englishman ['ɪŋglɪʃmən] (*pl* **-men** [-mən]) *n* Engländer *der*.

Englishwoman ['ɪŋglɪʃˌwʊmən] (*pl* **-women** [-wɪmɪn]) *n* Engländerin *die*.

engrave [ɪn'greɪv] *vt* [metal, glass] gravieren; [design] eingravieren.

engraving [ɪn'greɪvɪŋ] *n* [design] Gravierung *die*; [print] Stich *der*.

engrossed [ɪn'grəʊst] *adj*: **to be engrossed (in sthg)** (in etw *(A)*) vertieft sein.

engulf [ɪn'gʌlf] *vt* [subj: fire, water] verschlingen; [subj: panic, fear] überwältigen.

enhance [ɪn'hɑːns] *vt* verbessern; [value, chances] steigern, erhöhen; [beauty] betonen.

enjoy [ɪn'dʒɔɪ] *vt* - **1.** [like] genießen; **she enjoyed the film/book** der Film/das Buch hat ihr gefallen; **did you enjoy it?** hast du es genossen?, hat es dir gefallen?; **to enjoy doing sthg** etw gern(e) tun; **to enjoy o.s.** sich amüsieren; **enjoy yourself!** viel Spaß! - **2.** *fml* [possess] genießen; **to enjoy good health** sich guter Gesundheit erfreuen.

enjoyable [ɪn'dʒɔɪəbl] *adj* [job, work, experience] angenehm; [holiday, day] schön; [film, book] unterhaltsam.

enjoyment [ɪn'dʒɔɪmənt] *n* [gen] Vergnügen *das.*

enlarge [ɪn'lɑːdʒ] *vt* vergrößern; [scope, interest, circle of friends] erweitern. ◆ **enlarge (up)on** *vt insep* sich genauer äußern über *(+ A).*

enlargement [ɪn'lɑːdʒmənt] *n* Vergrößerung *die.*

enlighten [ɪn'laɪtn] *vt fml* auf|klären.

enlightened [ɪn'laɪtnd] *adj* [person] aufgeklärt; [approach] fortschrittlich.

enlist [ɪn'lɪst] ◇ *vt* - **1.** MIL [recruit] ein|ziehen - **2.** [support, help] in Anspruch nehmen. ◇ *vi* MIL: **to enlist (in)** sich melden (zu).

enmity ['enmətɪ] *n* Feindschaft *die.*

enormity [ɪ'nɔːmətɪ] *n* ungeheueres Ausmaß.

enormous [ɪ'nɔːməs] *adj* ungeheuer groß.

enough [ɪ'nʌf] ◇ *adj* genug; **enough time** Zeit genug; **have you got enough money?** hast du genügend Geld? ◇ *pron* genug; **is that enough?** reicht das?; **to have had enough (of sthg)** genug (von etw) haben; **I've had enough!** [expressing annoyance] jetzt reichts mir aber!; **more than enough** mehr als genug; **it's enough to drive you crazy!** es ist zum Verrücktwerden! ◇ *adv* - **1.** [sufficiently] genug; **good enough** gut genug; **would you be good enough to open the door for me?** *fml* wärst du so gut und öffnest mir die Tür? - **2.** [rather]: **he seems a nice enough chap** er scheint ganz nett zu sein; **strangely enough** merkwürdigerweise; **sure enough** tatsächlich.

enquire [ɪn'kwaɪəʳ] *vt & vi* = **inquire.**

enquiry [ɪn'kwaɪərɪ] *n* = **inquiry.**

enraged [ɪn'reɪdʒd] *adj* wütend.

enrol, enroll *US* [ɪn'rəʊl] ◇ *vt* ein|schreiben; SCH an|melden. ◇ *vi*: **to enrol (on** *OR* **in)** sich ein|schreiben (für).

ensue [ɪn'sjuː] *vi fml* folgen.

ensure [ɪn'ʃʊəʳ] *vt* sicher|stellen; [safety, privacy] gewährleisten; **to ensure (that)** dafür sorgen, dass.

ENT (*abbr of* **Ear, Nose & Throat**) HNO.

entail [ɪn'teɪl] *vt* mit sich bringen.

enter ['entəʳ] ◇ *vt* - **1.** [house, room] ein|treten in *(+ A)*, betreten; [car, bus, train] ein|steigen in *(+ A)*; [subj: vehicle] fahren in *(+ A)*; [subj: ship] ein|laufen in *(+ A)*; [country] ein|reisen in *(+ A)* - **2.** [army] ein|treten in *(+ A)*; [competition, race] teil|nehmen an *(+ D)* - **3.** [horse, competitor] an|melden; [poem, story] ein|reichen - **4.** [write down] ein|tragen - **5.** COMPUT ein|geben. ◇ *vi* - **1.** [come or go in] ein|treten; [enter bus, train] ein|steigen; [enter country] ein|reisen - **2.** [register]: **to enter (for sthg)** sich (für etw) an|melden. ◆ **enter into** *vt insep* [negotiations] treten in *(+ A)*; **to enter into an agreement with sb** mit jm ein Abkommen schließen.

enter key *n* COMPUT Eingabetaste *die.*

enterprise ['entəpraɪz] *n* - **1.** [company, project] Unternehmen *das*; **private enterprise** Privatwirtschaft *die* - **2.** *(U)* [initiative] Initiative *die.*

enterprising ['entəpraɪzɪŋ] *adj* [person] einfallsreich; [plan, idea] innovativ.

entertain [ˌentə'teɪn] *vt* - **1.** [amuse] unterhalten - **2.** [dinner guest] bewirten - **3.** *fml* [idea, proposal] erwägen; [hopes] nähren; [suspicion, ambition] hegen.

entertainer [ˌentə'teɪnəʳ] *n* Unterhalter *der*, -in *die*, Entertainer *der*, -in *die.*

entertaining [ˌentə'teɪnɪŋ] *adj* unterhaltsam.

entertainment [ˌentə'teɪnmənt] *n* - **1.** [amusement] Unterhaltung *die* - **2.** [show] Darbietung *die.*

enthral *UK*, **enthrall** *US* [ɪn'θrɔːl] *vt* fesseln.

enthusiasm [ɪn'θjuːzɪæzm] *n* - **1.** [eagerness] Begeisterung *die*, Enthusiasmus *der* - **2.** [hobby] Leidenschaft *die.*

enthusiast [ɪn'θjuːzɪæst] *n* Enthusiast *der*, -in *die.*

enthusiastic [ɪnˌθjuːzɪ'æstɪk] *adj* begeistert, enthusiastisch.

entice [ɪn'taɪs] *vt* locken; **to entice sb away from sthg** jn von etw weg|locken.

entire [ɪn'taɪəʳ] *adj* ganz; [amount, population] gesamt; [confidence, attention] voll.

entirely [ɪn'taɪəlɪ] *adv* ganz; **I agree entirely** ich stimme voll und ganz zu.

entirety [ɪn'taɪrətɪ] *n fml*: **in its entirety** in seiner Gesamtheit.

entitle [ɪn'taɪtl] *vt* [allow]: **to entitle sb to sthg** jn zu etw berechtigen; **to entitle sb to do sthg** jn dazu berechtigen, etw zu tun.

entitled [ɪn'taɪtld] *adj* - **1.** [allowed] berechtigt; **to be entitled to sthg** das Recht auf etw *(A)* haben - **2.** [called]: **to be entitled** den Titel haben.

entitlement [ɪn'taɪtlmənt] *n* Berechtigung *die*; [to compensation, holiday] Anspruch *der.*

entrance ◇ *n* ['entrəns] - **1.** [way in]: **entrance (to)** Eingang *der* (zu) - **2.** [arrival] Eintritt *der*; [of actor] Auftritt *der* - **3.** [admission] Eintritt *der*; **to gain entrance to sthg** *fml* [building] Zutritt zu etw erhalten; [society, university] die Zulassung zu etw erhalten; **'no entrance'** 'Zutritt verboten'. ◇ *vt* [ɪn'trɑːns] [delight] bezaubern.

entrance examination *n* Aufnahmeprüfung *die.*

entrance fee *n* Eintrittsgeld *das*; [for club] Aufnahmegebühr *die.*

entrant ['entrənt] *n* [in competition, exam, race] Teilnehmer *der*, -in *die*.

entreat [ɪn'triːt] *vt*: **to entreat sb to do sthg** jn inständig bitten, etw zu tun; [plead with] jn an|flehen, etw zu tun.

entrenched [ɪn'trentʃt] *adj* (fest) verwurzelt.

entrepreneur [ˌɒntrəprə'nɜːʳ] *n* Unternehmer *der*, -in *die*.

entrust [ɪn'trʌst] *vt*: **to entrust sthg to sb** jm etw anvertrauen; **to entrust sb with sthg** jn mit etw betrauen.

entry ['entrɪ] *n* - **1.** [entrance, arrival]: **entry (into)** Eingang *der* (in *(+ A)*) - **2.** *(U)* [admission]: **entry (to)** [to country] Einreise *die* (in *(+ A)*); [to building] Zutritt *der* (zu); [to event] Einlass *der* (in *(+ A)*); **to gain entry to** [house] gelangen in *(+ A)*; [organization] bei|treten *(+ D)*; **'no entry'** 'Zutritt verboten'; AUT 'Durchfahrt verboten' - **3.** [for race] Nennung *die*; [for competition] Einsendung *die* - **4.** [in diary, dictionary, ledger] Eintragung *die*.

entry form *n* Anmeldeformular *das*.

entry phone *n* Türsprechanlage *die*.

envelop [ɪn'veləp] *vt*: **to envelop sb/sthg in sthg** jn/etw in etw *(A)* (ein)|hüllen.

envelope ['envələʊp] *n* Briefumschlag *der*.

envious ['envɪəs] *adj*: **envious (of sb/sthg)** neidisch (auf jn/etw).

environment [ɪn'vaɪərənmənt] *n* - **1.** [surroundings] Umgebung *die* - **2.** [natural world]: **the environment** die Umwelt.

environmental [ɪnˌvaɪərən'mentl] *adj* Umwelt-.

environmentally [ɪnˌvaɪərən'mentəlɪ] *adv* umwelt-; **environmentally friendly** umweltfreundlich.

envisage [ɪn'vɪzɪdʒ], **envision** *US* [ɪn'vɪʒn] *vt* sich vor|stellen.

envoy ['envɔɪ] *n* Gesandte *der, die*.

envy ['envɪ] <> *n* Neid *der*. <> *vt* beneiden; **to envy sb sthg** jn um etw beneiden.

eon *n US* = **aeon**.

epic ['epɪk] <> *adj* [poetry] episch; [journey] lang und abenteuerlich; [story] monumental. <> *n* [book, film] Epos *das*.

epidemic [ˌepɪ'demɪk] *n* Epidemie *die*.

epileptic [ˌepɪ'leptɪk] <> *adj* epileptisch. <> *n* Epileptiker *der*, -in *die*.

episode ['epɪsəʊd] *n* - **1.** [event] Episode *die* - **2.** [broadcast] Folge *die*.

epitaph ['epɪtɑːf] *n* Epitaph *das*.

epitome [ɪ'pɪtəmɪ] *n*: **the epitome of** der Inbegriff *(+ G)*.

epitomize, -ise [ɪ'pɪtəmaɪz] *vt* beispielhaft zeigen.

epoch ['iːpɒk] *n* Epoche *die*.

equal ['iːkwəl] *(UK)* *(US)* <> *adj* - **1.** [of the same quantity, size, shape, degree] gleich; **they're of equal size** sie sind gleich groß; **to be equal to sthg** [sum] etw *(D)* entsprechen - **2.** [in status] gleich(berechtigt); **equal rights** Gleichberechtigung *die* - **3.** [capable]: **to be equal to sthg** etw *(D)* gewachsen sein. <> *n* [person] Gleichgestellte *der, die*. <> *vt* - **1.** MATHS gleichen - **2.** [in standard] gleich|kommen *(+ D)*.

equality [iː'kwɒlətɪ] *n* Gleichheit *die*.

equalize, -ise ['iːkwəlaɪz] *vt* & *vi* SPORT aus|gleichen.

equalizer, -iser ['iːkwəlaɪzəʳ] *n* SPORT Ausgleich *der*.

equally ['iːkwəlɪ] *adv* - **1.** [to the same extent] ebenso - **2.** [divide, share] in gleiche Teile - **3.** [by the same token] gleichzeitig.

equal opportunities *npl* Chancengleichheit *die*.

equate [ɪ'kweɪt] *vt*: **to equate sthg with sthg** etw mit etw gleich|setzen.

equation [ɪ'kweɪʒn] *n* MATHS Gleichung *die*.

equator [ɪ'kweɪtəʳ] *n*: **the equator** der Äquator.

equilibrium [ˌiːkwɪ'lɪbrɪəm] *n* Gleichgewicht *das*.

equip [ɪ'kwɪp] *vt* - **1.** [provide with equipment] aus|statten; **to equip sb/sthg with sthg** jn/etw mit etw aus|rüsten - **2.** [prepare mentally]: **to equip sb for sthg** jn für etw vor|bereiten.

equipment [ɪ'kwɪpmənt] *n* *(U)* Ausrüstung *die*; **electrical equipment** Elektrogeräte *Pl*.

equity *n* *(U)* FIN [market value] Eigenkapital *das*. ◆ **equities** *npl* [stock exchange] Stammaktien *Pl*.

equivalent [ɪ'kwɪvələnt] <> *adj* entsprechend, äquivalent; **to be equivalent to sthg** etw *(D)* entsprechen. <> *n* Gegenstück *das*.

equivocal [ɪ'kwɪvəkl] *adj* [statement, remark] zweideutig.

er [ɜːʳ] *excl* äh.

era ['ɪərə] (*pl* **-s**) *n* Ära *die*.

eradicate [ɪ'rædɪkeɪt] *vt* aus|rotten.

erase [ɪ'reɪz] *vt* - **1.** [rub out] aus|radieren; [tape, recording] löschen - **2.** *fig* [memory] (aus dem Gedächtnis) tilgen.

eraser [ɪ'reɪzəʳ] *n esp US* Radiergummi *der*.

erect [ɪ'rekt] <> *adj* - **1.** [person, posture] aufrecht - **2.** [penis] erigiert. <> *vt* - **1.** [building, statue] errichten, bauen - **2.** [tent] auf|bauen; [roadblock, sign] auf|stellen.

erection [ɪ'rekʃn] *n* - **1.** *(U)* [of building, statue] Errichtung *die*, Bau *der* - **2.** [erect penis] Erektion *die*.

ERM (*abbr of* **Exchange Rate Mechanism**) *n* WUM *der*.

erode [ɪ'rəʊd] *vt* - **1.** GEOL erodieren - **2.** *fig* [destroy] unter|graben.

erosion [ɪ'rəʊʒn] *n* GEOL Erosion *die*.

erotic [ɪ'rɒtɪk] *adj* erotisch.

err [ɜːʳ] *vi* sich irren.

errand ['erənd] *n* Besorgung *die*; **to go on** OR **run an errand (for sb)** (für jn) eine Besorgung OR einen Botengang machen.

erratic [ɪ'rætɪk] *adj* wechselhaft; [movement, bus service] unregelmäßig; [performance] variabel; [player] unberechenbar.

error ['erəʳ] *n* - **1.** [mistake] Fehler *der* - **2.** *(U)* [making mistakes]: **in error** aus Versehen.

erupt [ɪ'rʌpt] *vi* aus|brechen.

eruption [ɪ'rʌpʃn] *n* Ausbruch *der*.

escalate ['eskəleɪt] *vi* eskalieren.

escalator ['eskəleɪtəʳ] *n* Rolltreppe *die*.

escapade [,eskə'peɪd] *n* Eskapade *die*.

escape [ɪ'skeɪp] ◇ *n* - **1.** [from person, place, situation]: **escape (from sb/sthg)** Flucht *die* (vor jn/vor OR aus etw); **there was no escape** es gab kein Entkommen; **to make an** OR **one's escape (from)** flüchten (aus) - **2.** [from danger]: **to have a narrow escape** mit knapper Not entkommen - **3.** [leakage] Ausströmen *das* - **4.** COMPUT Escape *das*. ◇ *vt* - **1.** [avoid] entkommen *(+ D)* - **2.** [subj: fact, name] entfallen; **her name escapes me just now** ihr Name fällt mir momentan nicht ein. ◇ *vi* - **1.** [from person, place, situation]: **to escape (from sb/sthg)** fliehen OR flüchten (vor jm/vor OR aus etw); **to escape from prison** aus dem Gefängnis fliehen - **2.** [from danger] davon|kommen - **3.** [leak] aus|strömen.

escapism [ɪ'skeɪpɪzm] *n* Realitätsflucht *die*.

escort ◇ *n* ['eskɔːt] - **1.** [guard] Geleitschutz *der*, Eskorte *die*; **under escort** unter Bewachung - **2.** [companion] Begleiter *der*, -in *die*. ◇ *vt* [ɪ'skɔːt] [accompany] begleiten; [for protection] eskortieren.

Eskimo ['eskɪməʊ] (*pl* **-s**) *n* [person] Eskimo *der*, -frau *die*.

especially [ɪ'speʃəlɪ] *adv* - **1.** [in particular, more than usually] besonders - **2.** [specifically] speziell.

espionage ['espɪə,nɑːʒ] *n* Spionage *die*.

Esquire [ɪ'skwaɪəʳ] *n* ≃ Herr/Herrn, *britische Höflichkeitsanrede in der Postanschrift*.

essay ['eseɪ] *n* - **1.** SCH Aufsatz *der* - **2.** LIT & UNIV Essay *der*.

essence ['esns] *n* - **1.** [nature] Wesentliche *das*, Kern *der*; **in essence** im Wesentlichen - **2.** *(U)* CULIN Essenz *die*.

essential [ɪ'senʃl] *adj* - **1.** [necessary]: **essential (to** OR **for sthg)** (unbedingt) notwendig (für etw) - **2.** [basic] wesentlich. ◆ **essentials** *npl* - **1.** [basic commodities] Notwendigste *das* - **2.** [most important elements] Grundlagen *Pl*.

essentially [ɪ'senʃəlɪ] *adv* im Grunde.

establish [ɪ'stæblɪʃ] *vt* - **1.** [create - company, organization] gründen; [- system, law, post] schaffen - **2.** [initiate]: **to establish contact with sb** Kontakt mit jm auf|nehmen - **3.** [ascertain] fest|stellen, ermitteln - **4.** [cause to be accepted] bestätigen.

establishment [ɪ'stæblɪʃmənt] *n* - **1.** *(U)* [creation, foundation] Gründung *die*, Errichtung *die* - **2.** [shop, business] Unternehmen *das*. ◆ **Establishment** *n*: **the Establishment** das Establishment.

estate [ɪ'steɪt] *n* - **1.** [land, property] Gut *das* - **2.** [for housing] Wohnsiedlung *die*; [for industry] Industriegebiet *das* - **3.** LAW [inheritance] Besitz *der*, Besitztümer *Pl*.

estate agent *n UK* Grundstücksmakler *der*, -in *die*; **estate agent's** Immobilienbüro *das*.

estate car *n UK* Kombiwagen *der*.

esteem [ɪ'stiːm] ◇ *n* Achtung *die*, Wertschätzung *die*. ◇ *vt* schätzen, achten.

esthetic *etc adj US* = **aesthetic** *etc*.

estimate ◇ *n* ['estɪmət] - **1.** [calculation, reckoning] Schätzung *die* - **2.** COMM Kostenvoranschlag *der*. ◇ *vt* ['estɪmeɪt] schätzen, ein|schätzen.

estimation [,estɪ'meɪʃn] *n (U)* - **1.** [opinion] Urteil *das*, Einschätzung *die*; **to go up/down in one's estimation** in js Achtung steigen/sinken - **2.** [calculation] Schätzung *die*.

Estonia [e'stəʊnɪə] *n* Estland *nt*.

estranged [ɪ'streɪndʒd] *adj* getrennt lebend.

estuary ['estjʊərɪ] *n* Flußmündung *die*.

etc. (*abbr of* **etcetera**) usw.

etching ['etʃɪŋ] *n* Radierung *die*.

eternal [ɪ'tɜːnl] *adj* ewig.

eternity [ɪ'tɜːnətɪ] *n* Ewigkeit *die*.

ethic ['eθɪk] *n* Ethik *die*. ◆ **ethics** ◇ *n* [study] Ethik *die*. ◇ *npl* [morals] Moral *die*.

ethical ['eθɪkl] *adj* ethisch.

Ethiopia [,iːθɪ'əʊpɪə] *n* Äthiopien *nt*.

ethnic cleansing [,eθnɪk'klenzɪŋ] *n* ethnische Säuberung.

etiquette ['etɪket] *n* Etikette *die*.

EU (*abbr of* **European Union**) *n* EU *die*.

euphemism ['juːfəmɪzm] *n* Euphemismus *der*.

euphoria [juː'fɔːrɪə] *n* Euphorie *die*.

euro ['jʊərəʊ] *n* Euro *der*.

Eurocheque ['jʊərəʊ,tʃek] *n* Euroscheck *der*.

euro cent *n* Eurocent *der*.

Euroland *n* Euroland *das*.

Euro MP *n* Europaabgeordnete *der, die*.

Europe ['jʊərəp] *n* Europa *nt*.

European [,jʊərə'piːən] ◇ *adj* europäisch. ◇ *n* Europäer *der*, -in *die*.

European Community *n*: **the European Community** die Europäische Gemeinschaft.

European Monetary System *n*: **the European Monetary System** das Europäische Währungssystem.

European Parliament *n*: **the European Parliament** das Europäische Parlament.

European Union *n*: **the European Union** die Europäische Union.

euro zone *n* Eurozone *die*.

euthanasia [ˌjuːθəˈneɪzjə] *n* Euthanasie *die*.

evacuate [ɪˈvækjueɪt] *vt* evakuieren.

evade [ɪˈveɪd] *vt* - **1.** [pursuers, capture] sich entziehen *(+ D)* - **2.** [issue, question] ausl-weichen *(+ D)* - **3.** [subj: love, success]: **love/success has always evaded him** ihm ist die Liebe/der Erfolg immer versagt geblieben.

evaluate [ɪˈvæljueɪt] *vt* bewerten.

evaporate [ɪˈvæpəreɪt] *vi* - **1.** [liquid] verdunsten - **2.** *fig* [feeling] schwinden.

evaporated milk [ɪˈvæpəreɪtɪd-] *n* Kondensmilch *die*.

evasion [ɪˈveɪʒn] *n* - **1.** [of responsibility, payment *etc*] Ausweichen *das*, Umgehen *das* - **2.** [lie] Ausflucht *die*.

evasive [ɪˈveɪsɪv] *adj* - **1.** [to avoid question, subject] ausweichend - **2.** [to avoid being hit]: **to take evasive action** ein Ausweichmanöver machen.

eve [iːv] *n* [day before] Vortag *der*.

even [ˈiːvn] <> *adj* - **1.** [rate, speed] gleichmäßig - **2.** [calm] ausgeglichen - **3.** [level, flat] eben - **4.** [teams] gleich stark; **the scores were even** es herrschte Gleichstand; **to get even with sb** es jm heimlzahlen - **5.** [number] gerade. <> *adv* - **1.** [for emphasis] sogar; **not even** nicht einmal; **without even thinking** ohne auch nur einen Moment nachzudenken; **even now** sogar jetzt; **even then** selbst dann - **2.** [in comparisons] noch; **even better** noch besser; **even more stupid** (sogar) noch dümmer. ◆ **even if** *conj* selbst OR auch wenn. ◆ **even out** <> *vt sep* - **1.** [gen] ausl-gleichen; **to even things out** das Kräfteverhältnis auslgleichen - **2.** [surface] ebnen. <> *vi* sich auslgleichen. ◆ **even so** *adv* trotzdem. ◆ **even though** *conj* obwohl.

evening [ˈiːvnɪŋ] *n* Abend *der*; **in the evenings** am Abend. ◆ **evenings** *adv US* am Abend.

evening class *n* Abendkurs *der*.

evening dress *n* - **1.** [formal clothes] Abendkleidung *die* - **2.** [woman's garment] Abendkleid *das*.

event [ɪˈvent] *n* - **1.** [happening] Ereignis *das* - **2.** SPORT Wettkampf *der* - **3.** [case] Fall *der*; **in the event of** im Falle *(+ G)*; **in the event of rain** bei Regen; **in the event that** falls. ◆ **in any event** *adv* [all the same] wie dem auch sei, wie auch immer. ◆ **in the event** *adv UK* letztlich.

eventful [ɪˈventfʊl] *adj* ereignisreich; [life] bewegt.

eventual [ɪˈventʃʊəl] *adj*: **the eventual winner/outcome was...** der Sieger/das Resultat war schließlich...

eventuality [ɪˌventʃʊˈælətɪ] *n* (möglicher) Fall, Eventualität *die*.

eventually [ɪˈventʃʊəlɪ] *adv* schließlich.

ever [ˈevəʳ] *adv* - **1.** [at any time] je, jemals; **the worst film I've ever seen** der schlechteste Film, den ich je gesehen habe; **have you ever been to Chicago?** sind Sie jemals in Chicago gewesen?; **don't ever speak to me like that again!** so redest du nicht noch einmal mit mir!; **hardly ever** fast nie - **2.** [all the time] immer; **for ever** [eternally] für immer; [for a long time] seit Ewigkeiten; **I'll love you for ever** ich werde dich immer lieben; **as ever** wie immer; **ever larger** immer größer - **3.** [for emphasis]: **why/how ever did you do it?** warum/wie hast du das bloß gemacht?; **what ever is the matter with you?** was ist denn mit dir los?; **he was ever so angry** er war sehr verärgert; **ever such a mess** ein fürchterliches Durcheinander. ◆ **ever since** <> *adv* seitdem. <> *prep & conj* seit.

evergreen [ˈevəgriːn] *n* [plant] immergrüne Pflanze; [tree] immergrüner Baum.

everlasting [ˌevəˈlɑːstɪŋ] *adj* ewig; [peace] immer während.

every [ˈevrɪ] *adj* [each] jede(r) (s); **every day** jeden Tag; **every few days** alle paar Tage; **one in every ten** eine(r) (s) von zehn. ◆ **every now and then, every so often** *adv* dann und wann, ab und zu. ◆ **every other** *adj*: **every other day/car** jeden zweiten Tag/Wagen. ◆ **every which way** *adv US* überallhin.

everybody [ˈevrɪˌbɒdɪ] *pron* = **everyone**.

everyday [ˈevrɪdeɪ] *adj* (all)täglich.

everyone *pron* alle; [each person] jeder; **as everyone knows** wie jeder weiß.

everyplace *adv US* = **everywhere**.

everything *pron* alles; **money isn't everything** Geld ist nicht alles.

everywhere, everyplace *US adv* überall; [go] überallhin.

evict [ɪˈvɪkt] *vt*: **to evict sb (from a house)** jn zur Räumung zwingen (eines Hauses).

evidence [ˈevɪdəns] *n (U)* - **1.** [proof] Beweis *der* - **2.** LAW Beweismaterial *das*; **piece of evidence** Beweisstück *das*; **to give evidence** (als Zeuge/Zeugin) auslsagen.

evident [ˈevɪdənt] *adj* offensichtlich.

evidently [ˈevɪdəntlɪ] *adv* offensichtlich.

evil [ˈiːvl] <> *adj* [morally bad] böse, schlecht; [practice] übel. <> *n* - **1.** [wickedness] Böse *das* - **2.** [wicked thing] Übel *das*.

evoke [ɪˈvəʊk] *vt* hervorlrufen.

evolution [ˌiːvəˈluːʃn] *n* - **1.** BIOL Evolution *die* - **2.** [development] Entwicklung *die*.

evolve [ɪˈvɒlv] ◇ *vt* entwickeln. ◇ *vi* - **1.** BIOL: **to evolve (into/from)** sich entwickeln (in *(+ D)*/aus) - **2.** [develop] sich entwickeln.

ewe [juː] *n* Mutterschaf *das*.

ex- [eks] *prefix* Ex-, ehemalige(r) (s).

exacerbate [ɪgˈzæsəbeɪt] *vt* verschlimmern.

exact [ɪgˈzækt] ◇ *adj* genau; **to be exact** um genau zu sein. ◇ *vt*: **to exact sthg (from sb)** etw (von jm) erzwingen OR erpressen.

exacting [ɪgˈzæktɪŋ] *adj* - **1.** [demanding, tiring] anspruchsvoll - **2.** [rigorous] streng.

exactly [ɪgˈzæktlɪ] ◇ *adv* genau, exakt; **not exactly** [not really] nicht gerade; [as reply] nicht wirklich. ◇ *excl* genau!

exaggerate [ɪgˈzædʒəreɪt] *vt* & *vi* übertreiben.

exaggeration [ɪgˌzædʒəˈreɪʃn] *n* Übertreibung *die*.

exalted [ɪgˈzɔːltɪd] *adj* [important - person] hoch gestellt; [- position] hoch.

exam [ɪgˈzæm] (*abbr of* **examination**) *n* Prüfung *die*; **to take** OR **sit an exam** eine Prüfung machen OR ab|legen.

examination [ɪgˌzæmɪˈneɪʃn] *n* - **1.** [test, inspection, consideration] Prüfung *die* - **2.** MED Untersuchung *die* - **3.** LAW [of witness, suspect] Vernehmung *die*, Verhör *das*.

examine [ɪgˈzæmɪn] *vt* - **1.** [look at, inspect] überprüfen - **2.** MED untersuchen - **3.** [consider, test knowledge of] prüfen - **4.** LAW vernehmen.

examiner [ɪgˈzæmɪnəʳ] *n* Prüfer *der*, -in *die*.

example [ɪgˈzɑːmpl] *n* - **1.** [instance] Beispiel *das*; **for example** zum Beispiel - **2.** [model] Vorbild *das*.

exasperate [ɪgˈzæspəreɪt] *vt* zum Verzweifeln bringen.

exasperation [ɪgˌzæspəˈreɪʃn] *n* Verzweiflung *die*.

excavate [ˈekskəveɪt] *vt* - **1.** ARCHAEOL aus|graben - **2.** CONSTR aus|heben.

exceed [ɪkˈsiːd] *vt* - **1.** [be bigger than] übersteigen - **2.** [go beyond, go over] übersteigen; [limit] überschreiten; [expectations] übertreffen.

exceedingly [ɪkˈsiːdɪŋlɪ] *adv* äußerst.

excel [ɪkˈsel] ◇ *vi*: **to excel (in** OR **at sthg)** sich hervor|tun (in etw *(D)*). ◇ *vt*: **to excel o.s.** *UK* sich selbst übertreffen.

excellence [ˈeksələns] *n* [high quality] hervorragende Qualität; [high performance] hervorragende Leistung.

excellent [ˈeksələnt] *adj* ausgezeichnet.

except [ɪkˈsept] ◇ *prep* außer; **everyone except her** alle außer ihr. ◇ *conj*: **he does nothing except sleep** er tut nichts anderes als schlafen; **I'll do anything except typing** ich mache alles, nur nicht Maschine schreiben. ◇ *vt*: **present company excepted** Anwesende ausgenommen. ◆ **except for** *prep* & *conj* abgesehen von.

excepting [ɪkˈseptɪŋ] *prep* & *conj* = **except**.

exception [ɪkˈsepʃn] *n* - **1.** [exclusion] Ausnahme *die*; **an exception to the rule** die Ausnahme von der Regel; **with the exception of** mit Ausnahme von - **2.** [offence]: **to take exception to sthg** an etw *(D)* Anstoß nehmen.

exceptional [ɪkˈsepʃənl] *adj* außergewöhnlich.

excerpt [ˈeksɜːpt] *n*: **excerpt (from)** [from text] Auszug *der* (aus); [from film, play, piece of music] Ausschnitt *der* (aus).

excess [ɪkˈses] ◇ *adj (before nouns* [ˈekses]*)* [fat in diet] überschüssig; [weight] über-. ◇ *n* Übermaß *das*.

excess baggage *n* Übergewicht *das*.

excess fare *n UK* Nachlösegebühr *die*.

excessive [ɪkˈsesɪv] *adj* übermäßig; [price] überhöht.

exchange [ɪksˈtʃeɪndʒ] ◇ *n* - **1.** [of information, students] Austausch *der*; **to be on an exchange** [student] Austauschstudent(in) sein - **2.** [swap] Tausch *der*; **in exchange** dafür; **in exchange for** im Tausch gegen - **3.** TELEC: **(telephone) exchange** Fernmeldeamt *das*. ◇ *vt* [houses, seats, jobs] tauschen; [addresses] aus|tauschen; [in shop] um|tauschen; **to exchange sthg for sthg** etw gegen etw ein|tauschen; [foreign currency] etw in etw *(A)* um|tauschen; [in shop] etw gegen etw um|tauschen; **to exchange sthg with sb** etw mit jm (aus)|tauschen.

exchange rate *n* FIN Wechselkurs *der*.

Exchequer [ɪksˈtʃekəʳ] *n UK*: **the Exchequer** das Schatzamt.

excise [ˈeksaɪz] *n (U)* Verbrauchssteuer *die*.

excite [ɪkˈsaɪt] *vt* - **1.** [person] begeistern - **2.** [interest, curiosity, feeling] erregen.

excited [ɪkˈsaɪtɪd] *adj* aufgeregt.

excitement [ɪkˈsaɪtmənt] *n* Aufregung *die*.

exciting [ɪkˈsaɪtɪŋ] *adj* aufregend; [story, race, film] spannend.

exclaim [ɪkˈskleɪm] ◇ *vt* aus|rufen. ◇ *vi*: **to exclaim in delight/horror** vor Freude/Entsetzen auf|schreien.

exclamation mark *UK*, **exclamation point** *US n* Ausrufezeichen *das*.

exclude [ɪkˈskluːd] *vt* - **1.** [not include]: **to exclude sb/sthg (from sthg)** jn/etw (von etw) aus|nehmen - **2.** [prevent from entering]: **to exclude sb (from)** jm den Zutritt verweigern (zu) - **3.** [reject, rule out] aus|schließen.

excluding [ɪkˈskluːdɪŋ] *prep* außer *(+ D)*.

exclusive [ɪkˈskluːsɪv] ◇ *adj* - **1.** [high-class] exklusiv - **2.** [sole] ausschließlich - **3.** PRESS Exklusiv-. ◇ *n* [interview] Exklusivinterview *das*; [report] Exklusivbericht *der*. ◆ **exclusive of** *prep* exklusive (+ G).

excrement ['ekskrɪmənt] *n (U) fml* Exkremente *Pl*.

excruciating [ɪk'skruːʃɪeɪtɪŋ] *adj* - **1.** [pain, headache] schrecklich - **2.** [embarrassment, experience] unerträglich.

excursion [ɪk'skɜːʃn] *n* Ausflug *der*.

excuse ◇ *n* [ɪk'skjuːs]: **excuse (for)** Entschuldigung *die* (für); **that's just an excuse** das ist nur eine Ausrede. ◇ *vt* [ɪk'skjuːz] - **1.** [justify] entschuldigen - **2.** [forgive] verzeihen; **to excuse sb for sthg** jm etw verzeihen - **3.** [let off]: **to excuse sb (from sthg)** jn (von etw) befreien - **4.** *phr*: **excuse me!** [to attract attention] entschuldigen Sie bitte!; [forgive me] Entschuldigung!; *US* [sorry] Verzeihung!

ex-directory *adj UK*: **to be ex-directory** nicht im Telefonbuch stehen.

execute ['eksɪkjuːt] *vt* - **1.** [kill] hin|richten - **2.** *fml* [order, plan, movement] aus|führen.

execution [ˌeksɪ'kjuːʃn] *n* [killing] Hinrichtung *die*.

executive [ɪg'zekjʊtɪv] ◇ *adj*: **executive position** leitende Position. ◇ *n* COMM leitende Angestellte *der, die*.

executor [ɪg'zekjʊtəʳ] *n* Testamentsvollstrecker *der*.

exemplify [ɪg'zemplɪfaɪ] *vt* [typify] ein typisches Beispiel sein für.

exempt [ɪg'zempt] ◇ *adj*: **exempt (from)** befreit (von). ◇ *vt*: **to exempt sb/sthg from** jn/etw befreien von.

exercise ['eksəsaɪz] ◇ *n* - **1.** *(U)* [physical movement] Bewegung *die* - **2.** [series of movements] gymnastische Übung - **3.** [activity]: **it's a pointless exercise** das ist eine sinnlose Übung. ◇ *vt* - **1.** [horse] bewegen; [dog] aus|führen - **2.** *fml* [power] aus|üben; [right] wahr|nehmen; [caution] walten lassen. ◇ *vi* sich bewegen.

exercise book *n* Heft *das*.

exert [ɪg'zɜːt] *vt* aus|üben; **to exert o.s.** sich an|strengen.

exertion [ɪg'zɜːʃn] *n* - **1.** [of influence, power] Ausübung *die* - **2.** [effort] Anstrengung *die*.

exhale [eks'heɪl] *vt* & *vi* aus|atmen.

exhaust [ɪg'zɔːst] ◇ *n* - **1.** *(U)* [fumes] Abgase *Pl* - **2.** [on car]: **exhaust (pipe)** Auspuff *der*. ◇ *vt* - **1.** [tire] erschöpfen - **2.** [use up] auf|brauchen; [subject] erschöpfen; **my patience is exhausted** meine Geduld ist zu Ende.

exhausted [ɪg'zɔːstɪd] *adj* erschöpft.

exhausting [ɪg'zɔːstɪŋ] *adj* anstrengend.

exhaustion [ɪg'zɔːstʃn] *n* Erschöpfung *die*.

exhaustive [ɪg'zɔːstɪv] *adj* [search, study] eingehend; [list] erschöpfend.

exhibit [ɪg'zɪbɪt] ◇ *n* - **1.** ART Ausstellungsstück *das* - **2.** LAW Beweisstück *das*. ◇ *vt* - **1.** *fml* [demonstrate] zeigen - **2.** ART aus|stellen.

exhibition [ˌeksɪ'bɪʃn] *n* - **1.** ART Ausstellung *die* - **2.** [demonstration]: **it was a fine exhibition of skill** er/sie zeigte viel Geschick - **3.** *phr*: **to make an exhibition of o.s.** *UK* sich lächerlich machen.

exhilarating [ɪg'zɪləreɪtɪŋ] *adj* aufregend.

exile ['eksaɪl] ◇ *n* - **1.** [condition] Exil *das*; **in exile** im Exil - **2.** [person] Person *die*, die im Exil lebt. ◇ *vt*: **to exile sb (to)** jn aus|weisen OR verbannen (nach).

exist [ɪg'zɪst] *vi* existieren.

existence [ɪg'zɪstəns] *n* - **1.** [state of being] Existenz *die*; **to be in existence** existieren; **to come into existence** entstehen - **2.** [life] Dasein *das*.

existing [ɪg'zɪstɪŋ] *adj* bestehend; [government] gegenwärtig.

exit ['eksɪt] ◇ *n* - **1.** [way out] Ausgang *der*; [from motorway] Ausfahrt *die* - **2.** [departure]: **to make an exit** hinaus|gehen. ◇ *vi* [from building] hinaus|gehen; [from stage] ab|gehen; [from motorway] ab|fahren.

exodus ['eksədəs] *n* Auszug *der*.

exonerate [ɪg'zɒnəreɪt] *vt*: **to exonerate sb (from)** jn entlasten (von).

exorbitant [ɪg'zɔːbɪtənt] *adj* [cost, price] übertrieben hoch; [demands] übertrieben.

exotic [ɪg'zɒtɪk] *adj* exotisch.

expand [ɪk'spænd] ◇ *vt* [department, influence, area] vergrößern; [business, production, knowledge] erweitern. ◇ *vi* sich vergrößern; [business] erweitern; [metal] sich aus|dehnen. ◆ **expand (up)on** *vt insep* weiter aus|führen.

expanse [ɪk'spæns] *n*: **an expanse of water/sand** eine Wasserfläche/Sandfläche.

expansion [ɪk'spænʃn] *n* [of business, production, knowledge] Erweiterung *die*; [of department, influence, area] Vergrößerung *die*.

expect [ɪk'spekt] ◇ *vt* - **1.** [anticipate] erwarten; [count on] rechnen mit; **to expect sthg from sb** etw von jm erwarten; **to expect to do sthg** damit rechnen, etw zu tun; **to expect sb to do sthg** erwarten, dass jd etw tut; **what do you expect?** was willst du denn? - **2.** [suppose]: **to expect (that)** glauben, dass...; **I expect so** ich denke schon - **3.** [be pregnant with]: **to be expecting a baby** ein Kind erwarten. ◇ *vi* [be pregnant]: **to be expecting** in anderen Umständen sein.

expectancy *n* ▷ **life expectancy**.

expectant [ɪk'spektənt] *adj* [crowd, person] erwartungsvoll.

expectant mother *n* werdende Mutter.

expectation [ˌekspek'teɪʃn] *n*: **they have no expectation of winning** sie erwarten nicht, dass sie gewinnen; **against** OR **contrary to all expectation(s)** wider Erwarten.

expedient [ɪk'spiːdjənt] *adj fml* angebracht.

expedition [ˌekspɪ'dɪʃn] *n* - **1.** [organized journey] Expedition *die* - **2.** [short trip] Tour *die*.

expel [ɪk'spel] *vt* - **1.** [person]: **to expel sb (from)** [country] jn auslweisen (aus); [school] jn verweisen (von) - **2.** [liquid, gas] auslstoßen.

expend [ɪk'spend] *vt*: **to expend sthg (on)** etw auflwenden (auf *(+ A)*).

expendable [ɪk'spendəbl] *adj* [person] entbehrlich.

expenditure [ɪk'spendɪtʃə^r] *n (U)* [of money] Ausgaben *Pl*.

expense [ɪk'spens] *n* - **1.** [amount spent] Ausgabe *die* - **2.** *(U)* [cost] Kosten *Pl*; **at the expense of** auf Kosten *(+ G)*; **at his expense** auf seine Kosten. ◆ **expenses** *npl* COMM Spesen *Pl*.

expense account *n* Spesenkonto *das*.

expensive [ɪk'spensɪv] *adj* - **1.** [financially] teuer - **2.** *fig* [mistake] schwerwiegend.

experience [ɪk'spɪərɪəns] ◇ *n* - **1.** *(U)* [knowledge, practice] Erfahrung *die* - **2.** [event] Erlebnis *das*. ◇ *vt* erfahren; [change] erleben.

experienced [ɪk'spɪərɪənst] *adj*: **experienced (at** OR **in)** erfahren (in *(+ D)*).

experiment [ɪk'sperɪmənt] ◇ *n* - **1.** [science] Experiment *das* - **2.** [exploratory attempt] Versuch *der*. ◇ *vi liter & fig*: **to experiment (with)** experimentieren (mit).

expert ['ekspɜːt] ◇ *adj* [player] ausgezeichnet; [advice] fachmännisch. ◇ *n* Fachmann *der*, -frau *die*.

expertise [ˌekspɜː'tiːz] *n* Sachkenntnis *die*.

expire [ɪk'spaɪə^r] *vi* [licence, passport] abllaufen.

expiry [ɪk'spaɪərɪ] *n* Ablauf *der*.

explain [ɪk'spleɪn] ◇ *vt* erklären; **"my car broke down", she explained** "mein Auto ist kaputtgegangen", sagte sie; **to explain o.s.** [justify o.s.] sich rechtfertigen; [clarify one's meaning] sich klar ausldrücken; **to explain sthg to sb** jm etw erklären. ◇ *vi* erklären.

explanation [ˌeksplə'neɪʃn] *n*: **explanation (for)** Erklärung *die* (für).

explicit [ɪk'splɪsɪt] *adj* - **1.** [clearly expressed] explizit - **2.** [graphic] eindeutig.

explode [ɪk'spləʊd] ◇ *vt* [bomb] explodieren. ◇ *vi* - **1.** [bomb] explodieren - **2.** *fig* [with feeling]: **to explode in anger** (vor Wut) explodieren.

exploit ◇ *n* ['eksplɔɪt] Heldentat *die*. ◇ *vt* [ɪk'splɔɪt] - **1.** [workers] auslbeuten; [friend] auslnutzen - **2.** [resources] auslschöpfen; [opportunity] nutzen.

exploitation [ˌeksplɔɪ'teɪʃn] *n* - **1.** [of workers] Ausbeutung *die*; [of friend] Ausnutzung *die* - **2.** [of resources] Ausschöpfung *die*.

exploration [ˌeksplə'reɪʃn] *n* - **1.** [of place] Erforschung *die* - **2.** [of idea, theory] Untersuchung *die*.

explore [ɪk'splɔː^r] ◇ *vt* - **1.** [place] erforschen - **2.** [idea, theory] untersuchen. ◇ *vi* auf Erkundungstour gehen.

explorer [ɪk'splɔːrə^r] *n* Erforscher *der*, -in *die*.

explosion [ɪk'spləʊʒn] *n liter & fig* Explosion *die*.

explosive [ɪk'spləʊsɪv] ◇ *adj* [material, situation] explosiv; [question] heikel; [temper] explosiv. ◇ *n* Sprengstoff *der*.

export ◇ *n* ['ekspɔːt] Export *der*, Ausfuhr *die*. ◇ *comp* ['ekspɔːt] Export-. ◇ *vt* [ɪk'spɔːt] *liter & fig* exportieren.

exporter [ek'spɔːtə^r] *n* Exporteur *der*; [country] Exportland *das*.

expose [ɪks'pəʊz] *vt* - **1.** [uncover - skin] entblößen; [- underlying layer] freillegen; **to be exposed to sthg** einer Sache *(D)* ausgesetzt sein - **2.** [crime] aufldecken; [criminal] entlarven - **3.** PHOT belichten.

exposed [ɪk'spəʊzd] *adj* [place] ungeschützt.

exposure [ɪk'spəʊʒə^r] *n* - **1.** [to light, sun, radiation]: **exposure (to)** Ausgesetztsein *das (+ D)* - **2.**: **to die from exposure** [hypothermia] erfrieren - **3.** [PHOT - time] Belichtung *die*; [- photograph] Aufnahme *die* - **4.** [publicity] Publicity *die*.

exposure meter *n* Belichtungsmesser *der*.

expound [ɪk'spaʊnd] *fml vt* darllegen.

express [ɪk'spres] ◇ *adj* - **1.** *UK* [letter, delivery] Eil- - **2.** *fml* [request] ausdrücklich; [purpose] bestimmt. ◇ *adv* [send] per Express. ◇ *n*: **express (train)** D-Zug *der*. ◇ *vt* [feeling, opinion] ausldrücken.

expression [ɪk'spreʃn] *n* - **1.** [gen] Ausdruck *der* - **2.** [of feeling, opinion] Äußerung *die* - **3.** [look on face] Gesichtsausdruck *der*.

expressive [ɪk'spresɪv] *adj* ausdrucksvoll.

expressly [ɪk'spreslɪ] *adv* ausdrücklich.

expressway [ɪk'spresweɪ] *n US* Schnellstraße *die*.

exquisite [ɪk'skwɪzɪt] *adj* [object, jewellery] exquisit; [food] köstlich; [painting, manners] ausgezeichnet; [taste] erlesen.

ext., extn. (*abbr of* **extension**) App.

extend [ɪk'stend] ◇ *vt* - **1.** [road, building] auslbauen - **2.** [visit, visa, deadline] verlängern - **3.** [authority, law] ausldehnen - **4.** *fml* [head, arm] auslstrecken - **5.** [offer - credit, help] gewähren; *(phrase)*: **to extend a welcome to sb** jn willkommen heißen. ◇ *vi* - **1.** [stretch - in space] sich erstrecken; [- in time] anldauern - **2.** [rule, law]: **to extend to sb/sthg** sich auf jn/etw erstrecken.

extension [ɪk'stenʃn] *n* - **1.** [new room, building] Anbau *der* - **2.** [of visit, visa, deadline] Verlängerung *die* - **3.** TELEC Nebenanschluss *der* - **4.** ELEC Verlängerungskabel *das*.

extension lead *n* [lead] Verlängerungsschnur *die*.

extensive [ɪk'stensɪv] *adj* - **1.** [damage] beträchtlich - **2.** [land, area] ausgedehnt - **3.** [discussions, tests] ausgedehnt; [use] häufig.

extensively [ɪk'stensɪvlɪ] *adv* - **1.** [modify, damage] beträchtlich - **2.** [discuss] ausführlich; [read] viel.

extent [ɪk'stent] *n* - **1.** [of land, area] Ausdehnung *die* - **2.** [of knowledge, damage] Umfang *der*; [of problem] Größe *die* - **3.** [degree]: **to what extent ?** inwieweit ?; **to the extent that** [in that, in so far as] insofern dass; [to the point where] derart, dass; **to a certain extent** in gewissem Maße; **to a large** OR **great extent** in hohem Maße; **to some extent** bis zu einem gewissen Grade.

extenuating circumstances [ɪk'stenjʊeɪtɪŋ-] *npl* mildernde Umstände *Pl*.

exterior [ɪk'stɪərɪəʳ] <> *adj* [wall, lights] Außen-. <> *n* [of house, car, person] Äußere *das*.

exterminate [ɪk'stɜ:mɪneɪt] *vt* auslrotten.

external [ɪk'stɜ:nl] *adj* - **1.** [outside] äußere(r) (s); **for external use only** nur äußerlich anzuwenden - **2.** [foreign - debt] Auslands-; [- affairs] auswärtig.

extinct [ɪk'stɪŋkt] *adj* - **1.** [species] ausgestorben - **2.** [volcano] erloschen.

extinguish [ɪk'stɪŋgwɪʃ] *vt fml* [fire] löschen; [cigarette] ausldrücken.

extinguisher [ɪk'stɪŋgwɪʃəʳ] *n*: **(fire) extinguisher** Feuerlöscher *der*.

extol, extoll *US* [ɪk'stəʊl] *vt* rühmen.

extort [ɪk'stɔ:t] *vt*: **to extort sthg from sb** etw von jm erpressen.

extortionate [ɪk'stɔ:ʃnət] *adj* [price] Wucher-; [demand] ungeheuer.

extra ['ekstrə] <> *adj* [additional] zusätzlich; **extra charge** Zuschlag *der*. <> *n* - **1.** [addition] Extra *das* - **2.** CIN & THEAT Statist *der*, -in *die*. <> *adv* [to pay, charge] extra. ◆ **extras** *npl* [in price] zusätzliche Kosten *Pl*.

extra- ['ekstrə] *prefix* besonders; **an extra-special present** ein ganz besonderes Geschenk.

extract <> *n* ['ekstrækt] - **1.** [from book] Auszug *der*; [from film, piece of music] Ausschnitt *der* - **2.** [substance] Extrakt *der*. <> *vt* [ɪk'strækt] - **1.** [pull out]: **to extract sthg (from)** etw ziehen (aus) - **2.** [information, confession]: **to extract sthg (from sb)** etw (aus jm) herauslholen - **3.** [coal, oil]: **to extract sthg (from)** etw gewinnen (aus).

extradite ['ekstrədaɪt] *vt*: **to extradite sb (from/to)** jn auslliefern (von/an).

extramural [,ekstrə'mjʊərəl] *adj* UNIV: **extramural studies** *Studium für Teilzeitstudenten*.

extraordinary [ɪk'strɔ:dnrɪ] *adj* - **1.** [very special] außergewöhnlich - **2.** [strange] merkwürdig.

extraordinary general meeting *n* außerordentliche Hauptversammlung.

extravagance [ɪk'strævəgəns] *n* - **1.** [excessive spending] Verschwendung *die* - **2.** [luxury] Extravaganz *die*.

extravagant [ɪk'strævəgənt] *adj* - **1.** [wasteful - person, use] verschwenderisch; [- tastes] kostspielig - **2.** [gift, party, behaviour] extravagant - **3.** [claim] übertrieben.

extreme [ɪk'stri:m] <> *adj* - **1.** [gen] äußerste(r) (s); **extreme heat** extreme Hitze - **2.** [conditions, views, politician] extrem. <> *n* [furthest limit] Extrem *das*.

extremely [ɪk'stri:mlɪ] *adv* [very] äußerst.

extremist [ɪk'stri:mɪst] <> *adj* extremistisch. <> *n* Extremist *der*, -in *die*.

extricate ['ekstrɪkeɪt] *vt*: **to extricate sthg (from)** etw befreien (aus); **to extricate o.s. (from)** sich herauslwinden (aus); *fig* sich befreien (aus).

extrovert ['ekstrəvɜ:t] <> *adj* extrovertiert. <> *n* extrovertierter Mensch.

exuberance [ɪg'zju:bərəns] *n* Ausgelassenheit *die*.

exultant [ɪg'zʌltənt] *adj* [person, crowd] jubelnd; [smile] triumphierend.

eye [aɪ] (*cont* **eyeing** OR **eying**) <> *n* - **1.** [gen] Auge *das*; **to cast** OR **run one's eye over sthg** etw überfliegen; **to catch the waiter's eye** den Kellner auf sich *(A)* aufmerksam machen; **to have one's eye on sb/sthg** ein Auge auf jn/etw haben; **to keep one's eyes open for, to keep an eye out for** Ausschau halten nach *(+ D)*; **to keep an eye on** auflpassen auf *(+ A)* - **2.** [of needle] Öhr *das*. <> *vt* [suspiciously] beäugen; [with desire] sehnsüchtig anlschauen.

eyeball ['aɪbɔ:l] *n* Augapfel *der*.

eyebath ['aɪbɑ:θ] *n* Augenbad *das*.

eyebrow ['aɪbraʊ] *n* Augenbraue *die*.

eyebrow pencil *n* Augenbrauenstift *der*.

eyedrops ['aɪdrɒps] *npl* Augentropfen *Pl*.

eyeglasses ['aɪ,glɑ:sɪz] *npl US* Brille *die*.

eyelash ['aɪlæʃ] *n* Augenwimper *die*.

eyelid ['aɪlɪd] *n* Augenlid *das*.

eyeliner ['aɪ,laɪnəʳ] *n* Eyeliner *der*.

eye-opener *n inf*: **it was an eye-opener for me** das hat mir die Augen geöffnet.

eye shadow *n* Lidschatten *der*.

eyesight ['aɪsaɪt] *n (U)* Sehkraft *die*; **to have good/bad eyesight** gute/schlechte Augen haben.

eyesore ['aɪsɔ:ʳ] *n* Schandfleck *der*.

eyestrain ['aɪstreɪn] *n* Überanstrengung *die* der Augen.

eyewitness [,aɪ'wɪtnɪs] *n* Augenzeuge *der*, -gin *die*.

F

f (*pl* **f's** OR **fs**), **F** (*pl* **F's** OR **Fs**) [ef] *n* [letter] f *das*, F *das*. ◆ **F** *n* - **1.** MUS F *das* - **2.** (*abbr of* **Fahrenheit**) F.

fable ['feɪbl] *n* Fabel *die*.

fabric ['fæbrɪk] *n* - **1.** [cloth] Stoff *der* - **2.** [of building] Bausubstanz *die* - **3.** [of society] Gefüge *das*.

fabrication [,fæbrɪ'keɪʃn] *n* [lie] Lüge *die*.

fabulous ['fæbjʊləs] *adj inf* [excellent] toll.

facade [fə'sɑːd] *n liter* & *fig* Fassade *die*.

face [feɪs] ◇ *n* - **1.** [of person] Gesicht *das*; **face to face** [with person] von Angesicht zu Angesicht; **to come face to face with sthg** mit etw konfrontiert werden; **to say sthg to sb's face** jm etw offen ins Gesicht sagen - **2.** [expression] Gesicht *das*; **to make** OR **pull a face** ein Gesicht ziehen - **3.** [of cliff] Wand *die*; [of coin] Vorderseite *die*; [of building] Fassade *die*; **on the face of it** auf den ersten Blick - **4.** [of clock, watch] Zifferblatt *das* - **5.** [respect]: **to lose face** das Gesicht verlieren; **to save face** das Gesicht wahren. ◇ *vt* - **1.** [look towards] gegenüber|stehen *(+ D)*; **my house faces south** mein Haus liegt nach Süden; **the hotel faces the harbour** das Hotel liegt gegenüber vom Hafen - **2.** [confront] sich stellen *(+ D)*; **to be faced with sthg** [problem, decision] mit etw konfrontiert werden - **3.** [facts, truth] ins Auge sehen *(+ D)*; **let's face it!** machen wir uns nichts vor! - **4.** *inf* [cope with]: **I can't face another omelette** ich kann kein Omelett mehr sehen!; **I can't face it!** ich bringe es einfach nicht über mich. ◆ **face down** *adv* [person] mit dem Gesicht nach unten; [playing card] mit der Bildseite nach unten. ◆ **face up** *adv* [person] mit dem Gesicht nach oben; [playing card] mit der Bildseite nach oben. ◆ **in the face of** *prep* [in spite of] trotz *(+ G)*. ◆ **face up to** *vt insep* [responsibility] auf sich *(A)* nehmen; [problem] sich stellen *(+ D)*.

facecloth ['feɪsklɒθ] *n UK* Waschlappen *der*.

face cream *n* Gesichtscreme *die*.

face-lift *n* - **1.** [on face] Gesichtsstraffung *die* - **2.** *fig* [on building]: **to give sthg a face-lift** etw verschönern.

face-saving [-,seɪvɪŋ] *adj*: **a face-saving agreement/measure** eine Vereinbarung/Maßnahme, um das Gesicht zu wahren.

facet ['fæsɪt] *n* - **1.** [aspect] Seite *die* - **2.** [of jewel] Facette *die*.

facetious [fə'siːʃəs] *adj* leicht spöttisch.

face value *n* [of coin, stamp] Nennwert *der*; **to take sthg at face value** *fig* etw für bare Münze nehmen.

facility [fə'sɪlətɪ] *n* [feature] Einrichtung *die*. ◆ **facilities** *npl* [amenities] Ausstattung *die*; **cooking facilities** Kochgelegenheiten *Pl*.

facing ['feɪsɪŋ] *adj* [opposite] gegenüber befindlich.

facsimile [fæk'sɪmɪlɪ] *n* - **1.** [message] Fax *das* - **2.** [exact copy] Faksimile *das*.

fact [fækt] *n* Tatsache *die*; **it is a fact that...** es steht fest, dass...; **to know sthg for a fact** etw genau wissen. ◆ **in fact** *adv* [in reality] tatsächlich; [moreover] sogar.

fact of life *n* Tatsache *die (mit der man sich abfinden muss)*. ◆ **facts of life** *npl euph*: **to tell sb the fact of lifes of life** jn auf|klären.

factor ['fæktə^r] *n* Faktor *der*.

factory ['fæktərɪ] *n* Fabrik *die*.

fact sheet *n UK* Informationsblatt *das*.

factual ['fæktʃʊəl] *adj* [account] auf Tatsachen beruhend.

faculty ['fækltɪ] *n* - **1.** [ability] Fähigkeit *die* - **2.** UNIV [section] Fakultät *die*; [staff] Lehrkörper *der*.

fad [fæd] *n* Tick *der*.

fade [feɪd] ◇ *vi* - **1.** [material, colour] verbleichen; [flower] verwelken - **2.** [light] nach|lassen - **3.** [sound] verklingen - **4.** [feeling, interest, smile] schwinden; [memory] verblassen. ◇ *vt* [material, colour] aus|bleichen.

faeces *UK*, **feces** *US* ['fiːsiːz] *npl* Fäkalien *Pl*.

fag [fæg] *n* - **1.** *UK inf* [cigarette] Glimmstengel *der* - **2.** *US pej* [homosexual] Schwuler *der*.

Fahrenheit ['færənhaɪt] *adj* Fahrenheit.

fail [feɪl] ◇ *vt* - **1.** [not succeed in]: **to fail to do sthg** etw nicht tun können; **you can't fail to notice it** du kannst es nicht übersehen; **he failed to persuade her** es gelang ihm nicht, sie zu überreden - **2.** [exam, test] durch|fallen; [candidate] durchfallen lassen. ◇ *vi* - **1.** [not succeed] scheitern - **2.** [in exam, test] durch|fallen - **3.** [brakes, engine, heart] versagen; [lights] aus|fallen - **4.** [eyesight] nach|lassen; [health] sich verschlechtern.

failing ['feɪlɪŋ] ◇ *n* [weakness] Schwäche *die*. ◇ *prep* wenn nicht; **failing any renewed fighting** wenn es keine neuen Kampfhandlungen gibt; **failing that** andernfalls.

failure ['feɪljə^r] *n* - **1.** [gen] Misserfolg *der* - **2.** [person] Versager *der* - **3.** [of engine, brakes, heart] Versagen *das*; [of lights] Ausfall *der*.

faint [feɪnt] ◇ *adj* - **1.** [slight] schwach; [image] kaum sichtbar; [chance] gering; **I haven't the faintest idea** ich habe keinen blassen Schimmer - **2.** [dizzy] schwindelig. ◇ *vi* ohnmächtig werden.

fair [feə^r] ◇ *adj* - **1.** [just - judge, person] gerecht; [- result, decision, trial] fair; *(phrase)*: **it's not fair!** das ist ungerecht! - **2.** [quite large] ziemlich groß - **3.** [quite good] ziemlich gut - **4.** [hair, person] blond - **5.** [skin, complexion] hell - **6.** [weather] schön. ◇ *n* - **1.** *UK* [funfair] Jahrmarkt *der* - **2.** [trade fair] Messe *die*. ◇ *adv* [play, fight] fair. ◆ **fair enough** *excl UK inf* na gut!

fair-haired [-'heəd] *adj* blond.

fairly ['feəlɪ] *adv* - **1.** [rather] ziemlich - **2.** [treat, distribute] gerecht; [describe, fight, play] fair.

fairy ['feərɪ] *n* Fee *die*.

fairy tale *n* Märchen *das*.

faith [feɪθ] *n* - **1.** [trust]: **faith (in)** Vertrauen *das* (zu); **in bad faith** mit böser Absicht; **I told you that in good faith** ich habe dir das im Vertrauen gesagt - **2.** [particular religion] Religion *die* - **3.** *(U)* [religious belief] Glaube *der*.

faithful ['feɪθfʊl] *adj* - **1.** [friend, dog, lover] treu - **2.** [account, translation] getreu, genau.

faithfully ['feɪθfʊlɪ] *adv (phrase)*: **Yours faithfully** *UK* [in letter] hochachtungsvoll.

fake [feɪk] ◇ *adj* [painting, passport] gefälscht; [gun, jewellery] unecht. ◇ *n* - **1.** [object, painting] [of painting, passport] Fälschung *die*; [of gun, jewellery] Imitation *die* - **2.** [person] Schwindler *der*, -in *die*. ◇ *vt* - **1.** [signature, results] fälschen - **2.** [simulate] vor|täuschen; [illness] simulieren. ◇ *vi*: **he's faking** er tut nur so.

falcon ['fɔ:lkən] *n* Falke *der*.

fall [fɔ:l] (*pt* **fell**, *pp* **fallen**) ◇ *vi* - **1.** [gen] fallen; [person] hin|fallen; [from great height, heavily, in sport] stürzen; [thing to ground] herunter-/hinunter|fallen; **the city fell to the enemy troops** die Stadt fiel in die Hände der feindlichen Truppen; **to fall flat** [joke] daneben gehen - **2.** [decrease - temperature] fallen; [- number] ab|nehmen; [- demand, wind] nach|lassen - **3.** [become - ill, silent, vacant] werden; *(phrase)*: **to fall asleep** ein|schlafen; **to fall in love** sich verlieben; **to fall open** sich öffnen; **to fall to bits** OR **pieces** auseinander fallen - **4.** [occur]: **to fall (on)** fallen (auf *(+ D)*); **they fall into two groups** sie lassen sich zwei Gruppen zuordnen. ◇ *n* - **1.** [accident, from power] Sturz *der*; **to have a fall** stürzen - **2.**: **fall of snow** Schneefall *der* - **3.** [of city, country] Eroberung *die* - **4.** [decrease]: **fall (in)** Abnahme *die (+ G)* - **5.** *US* [autumn] Herbst *der*. ◆ **falls** *npl* [waterfall] Wasserfall *der*. ◆ **fall apart** *vi* - **1.** [book, chair] auseinander fallen - **2.** *fig* [country, person] zusammen|brechen. ◆ **fall back** *vi* - **1.** [retreat] zurück|weichen - **2.** [lag behind] zurück|fallen. ◆ **fall back on** *vt insep* [resort to] zurück|greifen auf *(+ A)*. ◆ **fall behind** *vi* - **1.** [in race] zurück|fallen - **2.** [with rent, work] in Rückstand geraten. ◆ **fall for** *vt insep* - **1.** *inf* [fall in love with] sich verlieben in *(+ A)* - **2.** [trick] herein|fallen auf *(+ A)*. ◆ **fall in** *vi* [roof, ceiling] ein|stürzen. ◆ **fall off** *vi* - **1.** [drop off] herunter-/hinunter|fallen - **2.** [diminish] zurück|gehen. ◆ **fall out** *vi* - **1.** [hair, tooth] aus|fallen - **2.** [quarrel]: **to fall out (with sb)** sich (mit jm) zerstreiten. ◆ **fall over** ◇ *vt insep* [step, obstacle] fallen über *(+ A)*. ◇ *vi* [lose balance - person] hin|fallen; [- chair, jug] um|kippen. ◆ **fall through** *vi* [plan, deal] fehl|schlagen.

fallacy ['fæləsɪ] *n* Irrtum *der*.

fallen ['fɔ:ln] *pp* ⊳ **fall**.

fallible ['fæləbl] *adj* [person] fehlbar; [method, plan] nicht unfehlbar.

fallout ['fɔ:laʊt] *n* [radiation] radioaktiver Niederschlag.

fallow ['fæləʊ] *adj* [land] brach; **to lie fallow** brach|liegen.

false [fɔ:ls] *adj* - **1.** [gen] falsch - **2.** [fake - nose, eyelashes] künstlich; [- passport] gefälscht; *phrase*: **false ceiling** Einschubdecke *die*.

false alarm *n* falscher Alarm.

falsely ['fɔ:lslɪ] *adv* - **1.** [accused, imprisoned] zu Unrecht - **2.** [laugh] gekünstelt.

false teeth *npl* künstliches Gebiss.

falsify ['fɔ:lsɪfaɪ] *vt* [facts, accounts] verfälschen.

falter ['fɔ:ltə^r] *vi* - **1.** [move unsteadily] wankend - **2.** [voice] stocken - **3.** [hesitate] zögern.

fame [feɪm] *n* Ruhm *der*.

familiar [fə'mɪljə^r] *adj* - **1.** [known] vertraut - **2.** [conversant]: **to be familiar with sthg** sich mit etw aus|kennen - **3.** *pej* [overly informal] vertraulich.

familiarity [fəˌmɪlɪ'ærətɪ] *n* [gen] Vertrautheit *die*.

familiarize, -ise [fə'mɪljəraɪz] *vt*: **to familiarize o.s. with sthg** sich mit etw vertraut machen; **to familiarize sb with sthg** jn mit etw vertraut machen.

family ['fæmlɪ] *n* Familie *die*.

family credit *n (U) UK staatlicher Zuschuss an einkommensschwache Familien*.

family planning *n* Familienplanung *die*.

famine ['fæmɪn] *n* Hungersnot *die*.

famished ['fæmɪʃt] *adj inf* [very hungry]: **I'm famished** ich sterbe vor Hunger.

famous ['feɪməs] *adj*: **famous (for)** berühmt (für).

fan [fæn] ◇ *n* - **1.** [held in hand] Fächer *der* - **2.** [electric] Ventilator *der* - **3.** [enthusiast] Fan *der*. ◇ *vt* - **1.** [cool]: **to fan one's face** sich *(D)* das Gesicht fächeln - **2.** [stimulate - fire, flames] an|fachen; [- feelings] entfachen; [- fears] schüren. ◆ **fan out** *vi* [army, search party] aus|schwärmen.

fanatic [fə'nætɪk] *n* Fanatiker *der*, -in *die*.

fan belt *n* Keilriemen *der*.

fanciful ['fænsɪfʊl] *adj* - **1.** [odd] abstrus - **2.** [elaborate] fantastisch.

fancy ['fænsɪ] ◇ *adj* - **1.** [elaborate - clothes, design, restaurant, hotel] ausgefallen; [- food, cakes] fein - **2.** [expensive] exklusiv. ◇ *n* - **1.** [liking] Lust *die*; **to take a fancy to** angetan sein von; **to take sb's fancy** jm gefallen, jn an|sprechen - **2.** [whim] Laune *die*. ◇ *vt* - **1.** *inf* [want] Lust haben auf *(+ A)*; **to fancy doing sthg** Lust dazu haben, etw zu tun - **2.** [person] scharf sein auf *(+ A)*.

fancy dress *n* (Masken)kostüm *das*.

fancy-dress party *n* Kostümfest *das*.

fanfare ['fænfeəʳ] *n* MUS Fanfare *die*.

fang [fæŋ] *n* - **1.** [of snake] Giftzahn *der* - **2.** [of wolf] Reißzahn *der*.

fan heater *n* Heizlüfter *der*.

fanny ['fænɪ] *n US inf* [buttocks] Po *der*.

fantasize, -ise ['fæntəsaɪz] *vi* fantasieren; **to fantasize about doing sthg** sich vor|stellen, etw zu tun.

fantastic [fæn'tæstɪk] *adj inf* [gen] fantastisch.

fantasy ['fæntəsɪ] *n* Fantasie *die*.

fao (*abbr of* **for the attention of**) z. H. (von).

far [fɑːʳ] (*comp* **farther** OR **further**, *superl* **farthest** OR **furthest**) ◇ *adv* - **1.** [in distance, time] weit; **have you come far?** sind Sie von weit her gekommen?; **how far is it (to London)?** wie weit ist es (bis London)?; **as far as** [town, country] bis nach; [station, school] bis zu; **so far** [until now] bisher; **far and wide** überall; **he will go far** *fig* er wird es weit bringen - **2.** [in degree]: **far better/quicker** weitaus besser/schneller; **as far as I'm concerned** was mich betrifft; **as far as I know** so weit ich weiß; **far and away, by far** bei weitem; **far from it** keineswegs. ◇ *adj*: **at the far end** am anderen Ende; **the far right/left** [in politics] die extreme Rechte/Linke.

faraway ['fɑːrəweɪ] *adj* - **1.** [place, country] weit entfernt - **2.** [look] abwesend.

farce [fɑːs] *n fig* & THEAT Farce *die*.

farcical ['fɑːsɪkl] *adj* lächerlich.

fare [feəʳ] *n* - **1.** [payment] Fahrpreis *der*; [for flight] Flugpreis *der* - **2.** *fml* [food] Kost *die*.

Far East *n*: **the Far East** der Ferne Osten.

farewell [ˌfeə'wel] *n* Lebewohl *das*; **they said their farewells** sie verabschiedeten sich.

farm [fɑːm] ◇ *n* Bauernhof *der*. ◇ *vt* bewirtschaften.

farmer ['fɑːməʳ] *n* Bauer *der*, Bäuerin *die*.

farmhouse ['fɑːmhaʊs] (*pl* [-haʊzɪz]) *n* Bauernhaus *das*.

farming ['fɑːmɪŋ] *n* Landwirtschaft *die*.

farmland ['fɑːmlænd] *n (U)* Ackerland *das*.

farmstead ['fɑːmsted] *n US* Gehöft *das*.

farmyard ['fɑːmjɑːd] *n* Hof *der*.

far-reaching [-'riːtʃɪŋ] *adj* weitreichend.

farsighted [ˌfɑː'saɪtɪd] *adj* - **1.** [person] weitblickend; [plan] auf weite Sicht konzipiert - **2.** *US* [longsighted] weitsichtig.

fart [fɑːt] *inf* ◇ *n* [wind] Furz *der*. ◇ *vi* furzen.

farther ['fɑːðəʳ] *compar* ▷ **far**.

farthest ['fɑːðəst] *superl* ▷ **far**.

fascinate ['fæsɪneɪt] *vt* faszinieren.

fascinating ['fæsɪneɪtɪŋ] *adj* faszinierend.

fascination [ˌfæsɪ'neɪʃn] *n* Faszination *die*.

fascism ['fæʃɪzm] *n* Faschismus *der*.

fashion ['fæʃn] ◇ *n* - **1.** [current style] Mode *die*; **to be in/out of fashion** modern/unmodern sein - **2.** [manner] Art *die*; **after a fashion** so einiger maßen. ◇ *vt fml* [shape] formen.

fashionable ['fæʃnəbl] *adj* [clothes, hairstyle] modisch.

fashion show *n* Mode(n)schau *die*.

fast [fɑːst] ◇ *adj* - **1.** [rapid] schnell; [journey] kurz - **2.** [clock, watch]: **to be fast** vor|gehen - **3.** [dye] farbecht. ◇ *adv* - **1.** [rapidly] schnell - **2.** [firmly] fest; **to hold fast to sthg** [grip firmly] an etw *(D)* fest|halten; **to be fast asleep** fest schlafen. ◇ *n* [act] Fasten *das*; [period] Fastenzeit *die*. ◇ *vi* fasten.

fasten ['fɑːsn] ◇ *vt* - **1.** [coat, door, bag, window] zu|machen; **to fasten one's seat belt** sich an|schnallen - **2.** [attach]: **to fasten sthg to sthg** etw an etw *(D)* befestigen. ◇ *vi*: **to fasten on to sthg** an etw *(D)* befestigt werden.

fastener ['fɑːsnəʳ] *n* Verschluss *der*.

fastening ['fɑːsnɪŋ] *n* Verschluss *der*.

fast food *n* Fastfood *das*.

fastidious [fə'stɪdɪəs] *adj* sehr genau.

fat [fæt] ◇ *adj* [gen] dick. ◇ *n* Fett *das*.

fatal ['feɪtl] *adj* - **1.** [mistake, decision] fatal - **2.** [accident, illness] tödlich.

fatality [fə'tælətɪ] *n* [accident victim] Todesopfer *das*.

fate [feɪt] *n* Schicksal *das*.

fateful ['feɪtfʊl] *adj* verhängnisvoll.

father ['fɑːðəʳ] *n* Vater *der*.

Father Christmas *n UK* Weihnachtsmann *der*.

father-in-law (*pl* **father-in-laws** OR **fathers-in-law**) *n* Schwiegervater *der*.

fathom ['fæðəm] ◇ *n* Faden *der*. ◇ *vt*: **to fathom sb/sthg (out)** jn/etw ergründen.

fatigue [fə'tiːg] *n* - **1.** [exhaustion] Erschöpfung *die* - **2.** [in metal] Ermüdung *die*.

fatten ['fætn] *vt* mästen.

fattening ['fætnɪŋ] *adj* dick machend; **to be fattening** dick machen.

fatty ['fætɪ] *adj* - **1.** [food, meat] fett - **2.** BIOL [tissue, acid] Fett-.

fatuous ['fætjʊəs] *adj* albern.

faucet ['fɔːsɪt] *n US* Wasserhahn *der*.

fault ['fɔ:lt] ◇ *n* - **1.** [responsibility] Schuld *die*; **it's my fault** es ist meine Schuld; **whose fault is it?** wer ist schuld daran? - **2.** [error, defect, in tennis] Fehler *der*; **to find fault with sb/sthg** etwas an jm/etw auszusetzen haben; **at fault** im Unrecht - **3.** GEOL Verwerfung *die*. ◇ *vt*: **to fault sb (on sthg)** jm widerlegen (in Bezug auf etw *(A)*).

faultless ['fɔ:ltlɪs] *adj* fehlerfrei.

faulty ['fɔ:ltɪ] *adj* fehlerhaft.

fauna ['fɔ:nə] *n* Fauna *die*.

favorites ['feɪvrɪtz] *n* COMPUT Favoriten *Pl*.

favour *UK*, **favor** *US* ['feɪvəʳ] ◇ *n* - **1.** *(U)* [approval] Gunst *die*; **in sb's favour** zu js Gunsten; **to be in/out of favour (with sb)** (bei jm) beliebt/unbeliebt sein; **to curry favour with sb** sich bei jm ein|schmeicheln - **2.** [kind act] Gefallen *der*, Gefälligkeit *die*; **to do sb a favour** jm einen Gefallen tun. ◇ *vt* - **1.** [prefer] bevorzugen - **2.** [benefit] begünstigen. ◆ **in favour** *adv* [in agreement]: **to be in favour** dafür sein. ◆ **in favour of** *prep* - **1.** [in preference to] zugunsten *(+ G)* - **2.** [in agreement with]: **to be in favour of sthg** für etw sein; **to be in favour of doing sthg** dafür sein, etw zu tun.

favourable *UK*, **favorable** *US* ['feɪvrəbl] *adj* - **1.** [conditions, weather] günstig - **2.** [review, impression] positiv.

favourite *UK*, **favorite** *US* ['feɪvrɪt] ◇ *adj* Lieblings-. ◇ *n* - **1.** [person] Liebling *der*; **this jacket is my favourite** das ist meine Lieblingsjacke - **2.** [in race, contest] Favorit *der*, -in *die*.

favouritism *UK*, **favoritism** *US* ['feɪvrɪtɪzm] *n* Günstlingswirtschaft *die*.

fawn [fɔ:n] ◇ *adj* rehbraun. ◇ *vi*: **to fawn on sb** sich bei jm ein|schmeicheln.

fax [fæks] ◇ *n* - **1.** [device] Faxgerät *das* - **2.** [message] Fax *das*. ◇ *vt* [document] faxen; **to fax sb sthg** jm etw faxen.

fax machine *n* Faxgerät *das*.

FBI (*abbr of* **Federal Bureau of Investigation**) *n* FBI *das*.

fear [fɪəʳ] ◇ *n* - **1.** [gen] Angst *die*, Furcht *die* - **2.** [risk] Gefahr *die*; **for fear of waking him** aus Angst, dass er aufwachen könnte; **no fear!** *inf* auf keinen Fall! ◇ *vt* Angst haben vor *(+ D)*; **to fear the worst** das Schlimmste befürchten.

fearful ['fɪəful] *adj* - **1.** *fml*: **to be fearful of sthg** vor etw *(D)* Angst haben - **2.** [noise, temper] furchterregend.

fearless ['fɪəlɪs] *adj* furchtlos.

feasible ['fi:zəbl] *adj* [plan] durchführbar.

feast [fi:st] *n* Festessen *das*.

feat [fi:t] *n* Meisterleistung *die*.

feather ['feðəʳ] *n* Feder *die*.

feature ['fi:tʃəʳ] ◇ *n* - **1.** [characteristic - gen] Merkmal *das*; [- of personality] Charakterzug *der* - **2.** [facial] Gesichtszug *der* - **3.** [article] Reportage *die* - **4.** RADIO & TV [programme] Feature *das* - **5.** CIN Kinofilm *der*. ◇ *vt*: **the film features Brad Pitt** Brad Pitt spielt in dem Film mit; **the exhibition features the work of two young artists** die Ausstellung zeigt das Werk zweier junger Künstler. ◇ *vi*: **to feature (in)** vor|kommen (in *(+ D)*).

feature film *n* Spielfilm *der*.

February ['februərɪ] *n* Februar *der*; *see also* **September**.

feces *npl US* = **faeces**.

fed [fed] *pt* & *pp* ▷ **feed**.

federal ['fedrəl] *adj* Bundes-.

federation [ˌfedə'reɪʃn] *n* - **1.** [country] Föderation *die* - **2.** [association] Zusammenschluss *der*.

fed up *adj*: **to be fed up with sb/sthg** jn/etw satt haben; **I'm (feeling) fed up** ich habe keine Lust mehr.

fee [fi:] *n* [for service] Gebühr *die*; [for membership] Beitrag *der*; [for doctor] Honorar *das*; **school fees** Schulgeld *das*.

feeble ['fi:bəl] *adj* - **1.** [weak] schwach - **2.** [excuse, joke] lahm.

feed [fi:d] (*pt & pp* **fed**) ◇ *vt* - **1.** [baby, animal] füttern - **2.** [insert]: **to feed sthg into sthg** etw in etw *(A)* ein|führen; [coins] etw in etw *(A)* ein|werfen. ◇ *vi* [baby] essen; [animal] fressen. ◇ *n* - **1.** [for baby] Mahlzeit *die* - **2.** [for animal] Futter *das*.

feedback ['fi:dbæk] *n (U)* - **1.** [reaction] Feedback *das* - **2.** ELEC Rückkoppelung *die*.

feeding bottle ['fi:dɪŋ-] *n UK* Saugflasche *die*.

feel [fi:l] (*pt & pp* **felt**) ◇ *vt* - **1.** [touch] fühlen; [examine] befühlen - **2.** [be aware of - tension, presence] spüren - **3.** [think]: **to feel that** glauben, dass; **he felt it (to be) his duty** er hielt es für seine Pflicht - **4.** [experience - sensation] spüren, fühlen; [- emotion] empfinden; **I feel the cold a lot** ich leide sehr unter der Kälte; **I felt myself blushing** ich fühlte, wie ich rot wurde - **5.** *phr*: **I'm not feeling myself today** ich bin heute nicht ich selbst. ◇ *vi* - **1.** [happy, angry, sleepy] sein; [lonely, fit, uncomfortable] sich fühlen; **I feel cold** mir ist kalt; **I feel stupid** ich komme mir blöd vor; **I feel ill** ich fühle mich nicht gut; **to feel like sthg** Lust haben auf etw *(A)*; **I don't feel like it** ich habe keine Lust dazu - **2.** [seem - light, heavy, soft *etc*] sich an|fühlen - **3.** [by touch]: **to feel for sthg** nach etw *(D)* tasten. ◇ *n* - **1.** [of material]: **it has a soft feel** es fühlt sich weich an - **2.** [atmosphere] Atmosphäre *die*.

feeler ['fi:ləʳ] *n* [of insect, snail] Fühler *der*.

feeling ['fi:lɪŋ] *n* - **1.** [gen] Gefühl *das* - **2.** [impression] Eindruck *der*; [opinion] Meinung *die*. ◆ **feelings** *npl* Gefühle *Pl*; **to hurt sb's feelings** jn verletzen.

feet [fi:t] *Pl* ▷ **foot**.

feign [feɪn] *vt fml* vor|täuschen.

fell [fel] ◇ *pt* ▷ **fall**. ◇ *vt* - **1.** [tree] fällen - **2.** [person] niederlstrecken.

fellow ['feləʊ] ◇ *adj* Mit-; **fellow passenger** Mitreisende *der, die*; **fellow sufferer** Leidensgenosse *der*, -sin *die*; **fellow student** Kommilitone *der*, -nin *die*. ◇ *n* - **1.** *dated* [man] Kerl *der* - **2.** [comrade] Kamerad *der* - **3.** [of society] Mitglied *das*; [of college] Fellow *der*.

fellowship ['feləʊʃɪp] *n* - **1.** [organization] Vereinigung *die* - **2.** [UNIV - scholarship] Stipendium *das*; [- post] Stellung *die* eines Fellows.

felt [felt] ◇ *pt* & *pp* ▷ **feel**. ◇ *n* Filz *der*.

felt-tip pen *n* Filzstift *der*.

female ['fiːmeɪl] ◇ *adj* weiblich; **female worker** Arbeiterin *die*; **female student** Studentin *die*. ◇ *n* - **1.** [animal] Weibchen *das* - **2.** *inf pej* [woman] Weib *das*.

feminine ['femɪnɪn] ◇ *adj* feminin. ◇ *n* GRAM Femininum *das*.

feminist ['femɪnɪst] *n* Feminist *der*, -in *die*.

fence [fens] ◇ *n* Zaun *der*; **to sit on the fence** *fig* nicht Partei ergreifen. ◇ *vt* einlzäunen.

fencing ['fensɪŋ] *n* - **1.** SPORT Fechten *das* - **2.** [fences] Zäune *Pl*.

fend [fend] *vi*: **to fend for o.s.** für sich selbst sorgen. ◆ **fend off** *vt sep* ablwehren.

fender ['fendəʳ] *n* - **1.** [round fireplace] Kamingitter *das* - **2.** [on boat] Fender *der* - **3.** *US* [over car wheel] Kotflügel *der*.

ferment ◇ *n* ['fɜːment] [unrest] Aufruhr *der*. ◇ *vi* [fə'ment] [beer, wine] gären.

fern [fɜːn] *n* Farn *der*.

ferocious [fə'rəʊʃəs] *adj* [animal] wild; [attack, criticism] heftig.

ferret ['ferɪt] *n* Frettchen *das*. ◆ **ferret about, ferret around** *vi inf* herumlstöbern.

ferry ['ferɪ] ◇ *n* Fähre *die*. ◇ *vt* transportieren.

fertile ['fɜːtaɪl] *adj* - **1.** [gen] fruchtbar - **2.** [imagination] reich.

fertilizer ['fɜːtɪlaɪzəʳ] *n* Dünger *der*.

fervent ['fɜːvənt] *adj* leidenschaftlich.

fester ['festəʳ] *vi* [wound, sore] eitern.

festival ['festəvl] *n* - **1.** [series of organized events] Festival *das* - **2.** [holiday] Feiertag *der*.

festive ['festɪv] *adj* festlich.

festive season *n*: **the festive season** die Weihnachtszeit.

festivities [fes'tɪvətɪz] *npl* Feierlichkeiten *Pl*.

festoon [fe'stuːn] *vt* schmücken.

fetch [fetʃ] *vt* - **1.** [go and get] holen; [person from station, school *etc*] ablholen - **2.** [sell for] einlbringen; **to fetch a high price** einen hohen Preis erzielen.

fetching ['fetʃɪŋ] *adj* attraktiv.

fete, fête [feɪt] ◇ *n* Wohltätigkeitsbasar *der*. ◇ *vt* durch Feiern ehren.

fetish ['fetɪʃ] *n* - **1.** [sexual obsession] Fetisch *der* - **2.** [mania] Manie *die*.

fetus ['fiːtəs] *n* = **foetus**.

feud [fjuːd] ◇ *n* Fehde *die*. ◇ *vi* in Fehde liegen.

feudal ['fjuːdl] *adj* feudal; [system, lord] Feudal-.

fever ['fiːvəʳ] *n liter* & *fig* Fieber *das*.

feverish ['fiːvərɪʃ] *adj* - **1.** MED fiebrig - **2.** [frenzied] fieberhaft.

few [fjuː] ◇ *adj* wenige; **the first few times** die ersten paar Male; **in a few minutes** in einigen Minuten. ◇ *pron*: **a few** ein paar; **a few more** noch ein paar; **quite a few, a good few** eine ganze Menge; **few and far between** dünn gesät.

fewer ['fjuːəʳ] ◇ *adj* weniger. ◇ *pron* weniger; **there are far fewer (of them) now** heute gibt es weit weniger.

fewest ['fjuːəst] *adj*: **(the) fewest** die wenigsten.

fiancé [fɪ'ɒnseɪ] *n* Verlobte *der*.

fiancée [fɪ'ɒnseɪ] *n* Verlobte *die*.

fiasco [fɪ'æskəʊ] (*UK pl* **-s**) (*US pl* **-s** OR **-es**) *n* Fiasko *das*.

fib [fɪb] *inf* ◇ *n* Schwindelei *die*; **to tell fibs** schwindeln. ◇ *vi* schwindeln.

fibre *UK*, **fiber** *US* ['faɪbəʳ] *n* - **1.** [gen] Faser *die* - **2.** *(U)* [roughage] Ballaststoffe *Pl* - **3.** [strength]: **moral fibre** Charakterstärke *die*.

fibreglass *UK*, **fiberglass** *US* ['faɪbəglɑːs] *n* Fiberglas *das*.

fickle ['fɪkl] *adj* wankelmütig.

fiction ['fɪkʃn] *n* - **1.** *(U)* [literature] Belletristik *die* - **2.** [lie] Fiktion *die*.

fictional ['fɪkʃənl] *adj* [work] erzählend; [character] fiktiv; [event] erfunden.

fictitious [fɪk'tɪʃəs] *adj* frei erfunden.

fiddle ['fɪdl] ◇ *n* - **1.** [violin] Geige *die* - **2.** *UK inf* [fraud] Schiebung *die*; **tax fiddle** Steuermanipulation *die*. ◇ *vt UK inf* frisieren. ◇ *vi* - **1.** [fidget]: **to fiddle (about** OR **around)** (herum)lzappeln; **to fiddle (about** OR **around) with sthg** an etw *(D)* OR mit etw (herum)lspielen - **2.** [waste time]: **to fiddle about** OR **around** herumltrödeln.

fiddly ['fɪdlɪ] *adj UK inf* knifflig.

fidget ['fɪdʒɪt] *vi* zappeln.

field [fiːld] ◇ *n* - **1.** [gen] Feld *das*; **in the field** in der Praxis - **2.** [for sports] Spielfeld *das* - **3.** [of knowledge] Gebiet *das* - **4.** COMPUT Datenfeld *das*. ◇ *vt* [question] parieren.

field day *n*: **to have a field day** *fig* seinen großen Tag haben.

field marshal *n* Feldmarschall *der*.

field trip *n* Exkursion *die*.

fieldwork ['fi:ldwɜ:k] *n* Arbeit *die* im Gelände.

fiend [fi:nd] *n* - **1.** [cruel person] Teufel *der* - **2.** *inf* [fanatic] Fanatiker *der*, -in *die*.

fiendish ['fi:ndɪʃ] *adj* - **1.** [evil] teuflisch - **2.** *inf* [very difficult, complex] verteufelt schwer.

fierce [fɪəs] *adj* [dog] bissig; [lion, warrior] aggressiv; [storm, temper] heftig; [competition] hart; [criticism] scharf; [heat] glühend.

fiery ['faɪərɪ] *adj* - **1.** [burning] brennend - **2.** [speech] feurig; [temper] hitzig.

fifteen [fɪf'ti:n] *num* fünfzehn; *see also* **six**.

fifth [fɪfθ] *num* fünfte(r) (s); *see also* **sixth**.

Fifth Amendment *n US*: **to take the Fifth Amendment** *die Aussage verweigern*.

fifty ['fɪftɪ] (*pl* **-ies**) *num* fünfzig; *see also* **sixty**.

fifty-fifty *adj* & *adv* fifty-fifty.

fig [fɪg] *n* Feige *die*.

fight [faɪt] (*pt & pp* **fought**) ◇ *n* - **1.** [brawl] Schlägerei *die*; [between boxers] Kampf *der*; **to have a fight with sb** sich mit jm schlagen; **to put up a fight** sich heftig zur Wehr setzen - **2.** *fig* [struggle] Kampf *der* - **3.** [argument] Streit *der*; **to have a fight (with sb)** Streit (mit jm) haben - **4.** [fighting spirit]: **there was no fight left in him** er war kampfmüde. ◇ *vt* - **1.** [physically] sich schlagen mit; [in battle, war] kämpfen mit OR gegen - **2.** [battle] auslltragen; [war] führen - **3.** [prejudice, racism] bekämpfen. ◇ *vi* - **1.** [physically] sich schlagen; [in war] kämpfen - **2.** *fig* [struggle]: **to fight for/against sthg** für/gegen etw kämpfen - **3.** [argue] sich streiten; **to fight about** OR **over sthg** sich um OR über etw *(A)* streiten. ◆ **fight back** ◇ *vt insep* [tears, anger] zurücklhalten. ◇ *vi* sich zur Wehr setzen.

fighter ['faɪtə^r] *n* - **1.** [plane] Jagdflugzeug *das* - **2.** [soldier] Kämpfer *der* - **3.** [combative person] Kämpfernatur *die*.

fighting ['faɪtɪŋ] *n (U)* [in war] Kämpfe *Pl*; [brawling] Schlägereien *Pl*.

figment ['fɪgmənt] *n*: **a figment of your/his imagination** ein Hirngespinst von dir/ihm.

figurative ['fɪgərətɪv] *adj* - **1.** [language] bildlich - **2.** ART gegenständlich.

figure [*UK* 'fɪgə^r, *US* 'fɪgjər] ◇ *n* - **1.** [number] Zahl *die*; [digit] Ziffer *die*; **in single/double figures** in ein-/zweistelligen Zahlen - **2.** [outline of person] Gestalt *die* - **3.** [personality] Persönlichkeit *die*; **a father figure** eine Vaterfigur - **4.** [shape of body] Figur *die* - **5.** [diagram] Abbildung *die*. ◇ *vt esp US* [suppose] schätzen. ◇ *vi* [feature] auftauchen; **to figure prominently** eine wichtige Rolle spielen. ◆ **figure out** *vt sep* [answer] herauslbekommen; [puzzle, problem] lösen.

figurehead ['fɪgəhed] *n liter* & *fig* Galionsfigur *die*.

figure of speech *n* Redensart *die*.

file [faɪl] ◇ *n* - **1.** [folder] Aktenordner *der* - **2.** [report] Akte *die*; **on file, on the files** in der Akte, in den Akten - **3.** COMPUT Datei *die* - **4.** [tool] Feile *die* - **5.** [line]: **in single file** hintereinander. ◇ *vt* - **1.** [put in folder] ablheften - **2.** [complaint, petition, lawsuit] einlreichen - **3.** [wood, metal] feilen; **to file one's fingernails** sich *(D)* die Fingernägel feilen. ◇ *vi* - **1.** [walk in single file]: **to file in/out** nacheinander hinein-/hinauslgehen - **2.** LAW: **to file for divorce** die Scheidung einlreichen.

filet *n US* = **fillet**.

filing cabinet ['faɪlɪŋ-] *n* Aktenschrank *der*.

fill [fɪl] ◇ *vt* - **1.** [gen] füllen - **2.** [repair - crack] zulspachteln; [- hole in ground] zulschütten - **3.** [fulfil - role] spielen; [- vacancy] besetzen; [- need] befriedigen. ◇ *vi* sich füllen. ◇ *n*: **to eat one's fill** sich satt essen. ◆ **fill in** ◇ *vt sep* - **1.** [form, questionnaire] auslfüllen; [name, address] einlsetzen - **2.** [inform]: **to fill sb in (on sthg)** jn (über etw *(A)*) ins Bild setzen. ◇ *vi*: **to fill in for sb** für jn einlspringen. ◆ **fill out** ◇ *vt sep* [form, questionnaire] auslfüllen. ◇ *vi* [get fatter] fülliger werden. ◆ **fill up** ◇ *vt sep* voll füllen. ◇ *vi* sich füllen.

fillet *UK*, **filet** *US* ['fɪlɪt] *n* Filet *das*.

fillet steak *n* Filetsteak *das*.

filling ['fɪlɪŋ] ◇ *adj* [food] sättigend. ◇ *n* Füllung *die*.

filling station *n* Tankstelle *die*.

film [fɪlm] ◇ *n* - **1.** [movie, for camera] Film *der* - **2.** [layer] Schicht *die*. ◇ *vt* filmen; [book, play] verfilmen. ◇ *vi* drehen.

film star *n* Filmstar *der*.

Filofax® ['faɪləʊfæks] *n* Filofax® *der*.

filter ['fɪltə^r] ◇ *n* Filter *der*. ◇ *vt* filtern.

filter coffee *n* Filterkaffee *der*.

filter lane *n UK* Abbiegespur *die*.

filter-tipped [-'tɪpt] *adj* mit Filter.

filth [fɪlθ] *n (U)* - **1.** [dirt] Dreck *der* - **2.** [obscenity] Obszönitäten *Pl*.

filthy ['fɪlθɪ] *adj* - **1.** [very dirty] dreckig - **2.** [obscene] obszön.

fin [fɪn] *n* - **1.** [on fish] Flosse *die* - **2.** *US* [for swimmer] Schwimmflosse *die*.

final ['faɪnl] ◇ *adj* - **1.** [last] letzte(r) (s) - **2.** [at end]: **the final score** der Schlussstand - **3.** [decision, version, defeat] endgültig; **I said no, and that's final!** ich sagte nein, und damit basta! ◇ *n* [of ball games] Endspiel *das*; [of races] Endrunde *die*. ◆ **finals** *npl* UNIV Examen *das*.

finale [fɪ'nɑ:lɪ] *n* Finale *das*.

finalize, -ise ['faɪnəlaɪz] *vt* [arrangements, details, dates] endgültig festllegen; [deal] zum Abschluss bringen.

finally ['faınəliː] *adv* - **1.** [at last] schließlich; [with relief] endlich - **2.** [lastly] zum Schluss.

finance ◇ *n* ['faınæns] *(U)* - **1.** [money] Geldmittel *Pl* - **2.** [money management] Finanzwesen *das.* ◇ *vt* [faı'næns] finanzieren. ◆ **finances** *npl* Finanzen *Pl.*

financial [fı'nænʃl] *adj* finanziell.

find [faınd] (*pt & pp* **found**) ◇ *vt* - **1.** [gen] finden - **2.** [discover]: **to find that** festIstellen, dass; **I found myself back where I started** ich stellte fest, dass ich wieder da angekommen war, wo ich angefangen hatte - **3.** LAW: **to be found guilty/not guilty** für schuldig/nicht schuldig befunden werden. ◇ *n* Fund *der.* ◆ **find out** ◇ *vi* herausIfinden. ◇ *vt insep* [information, truth] herausIfinden. ◇ *vt sep* [person] auf die Schliche kommen *(+ D).*

findings ['faındıŋz] *npl* Ergebnis *das.*

fine [faın] ◇ *adj* - **1.** [good - food, work] ausgezeichnet; [- building] prächtig; [- weather, day] schön; *(phrase)*: **how are you? – fine, thanks** wie gehts? – gut, danke - **2.** [satisfactory] in Ordnung, gut; **everything OK? – yes, fine!** ist alles OK? – ja, alles in Ordnung!; **more tea? – no, I'm fine, thanks** noch mehr Tee? – danke, ich habe genug; **it's fine by me** ich habe nichts dagegen - **3.** [hair] fein; [thread, wire] dünn - **4.** [sand, powder, sandpaper] fein - **5.** [small, exact - detail] klein - **6.** [grand - clothes, people] vornehm. ◇ *adv* - **1.** [quite well] gut; **that suits me fine** das passt mir gut - **2.** [thinly] fein. ◇ *n* Geldstrafe *die.* ◇ *vt* zu einer Geldstrafe verurteilen.

fine arts *npl* schöne Künste *Pl.*

fine-tune *vt liter* & *fig* fein abIstimmen.

finger ['fıŋgəʳ] ◇ *n* Finger *der.* ◇ *vt* [feel] anIfassen.

fingernail ['fıŋgəneıl] *n* Fingernagel *der.*

fingerprint ['fıŋgəprınt] *n* Fingerabdruck *der.*

fingertip ['fıŋgətıp] *n* Fingerspitze *die*; **to have sthg at one's fingertips** etw parat haben.

finicky ['fınıkı] *adj pej* [eater] wählerisch; [person] pingelig; [task] knifflig.

finish ['fınıʃ] ◇ *n* - **1.** [end] Ende *das*; [of race] Finish *das* - **2.** [on furniture, pottery] Oberfläche *die.* ◇ *vt* - **1.** [complete] beenden; **to finish doing the ironing/eating breakfast/*etc*** mit dem Bügeln/dem Frühstück/*etc* fertig sein; **to finish writing a letter** einen Brief zu Ende schreiben - **2.** [food] aufIessen; [drink] ausItrinken; [supplies] aufIbrauchen; [cigarette] zu Ende rauchen; [book] ausIlesen - **3.** [work, school]: **I finish work at half past five** ich mache um halb sechs Feierabend; **I finish school at half past three** ich habe um halb vier Schule aus. ◇ *vi* - **1.** [end] zu Ende sein; **when do you finish?** [stop work] wann machst du Feierabend? - **2.** [complete task] fertig werden; **I haven't finished yet** ich bin noch nicht fertig - **3.** [in race, competition]: **to finish top of the league** Tabellenführer werden; **to finish fifth** Fünfter werden. ◆ **finish off** *vt sep* - **1.** [complete] beenden - **2.** [food] aufIessen; [drink] ausItrinken. ◆ **finish up** *vi*: **we finished up in a pub** wir sind schließlich in einer Kneipe gelandet; **she finished up running her own company** zum Schluss leitete sie ihre eigene Firma.

finishing line ['fınıʃıŋ-] *n* Ziellinie *die.*

finite ['faınaıt] *adj* - **1.** [limited] begrenzt - **2.** GRAM finit.

Finland ['fınlənd] *n* Finnland *nt.*

Finn [fın] *n* Finne *der*, -nin *die.*

Finnish ['fınıʃ] ◇ *adj* finnisch. ◇ *n* [language] Finnisch(e) *das.*

fir [fɜːʳ] *n* Tanne *die.*

fire ['faıəʳ] ◇ *n* - **1.** [gen] Feuer *das*; **to be on fire** brennen; **to catch fire** Feuer fangen; [forest, building] in Brand geraten; **to set fire to sthg** etw anIzünden; [deliberately] etw in Brand setzen - **2.** [in forest, of building] Brand *der* - **3.** *UK* [heater] Ofen *der* - **4.** *(U)* [shooting]: **under fire** unter Beschuss; **to open fire (on sb)** das Feuer eröffnen (auf jn). ◇ *vt* - **1.** [shoot - bullet, missile] abIfeuern; [- gun] abIschießen - **2.** [from job] feuern - **3.** [imagination] beflügeln - **4.** [pottery] brennen. ◇ *vi*: **to fire (on** OR **at sb/sthg)** (auf jn/etw) schießen OR feuern.

fire alarm *n* Feueralarm *der.*

firearm ['faıərɑːm] *n* Schusswaffe *die.*

firebomb ['faıəbɒm] *n* Brandbombe *die.*

fire brigade *UK*, **fire department** *US n* Feuerwehr *die.*

fire engine *n* Feuerwehrauto *das.*

fire escape *n* [stairs] Feuertreppe *die*; [ladder] Feuerleiter *die.*

fire extinguisher *n* Feuerlöscher *der.*

fireguard ['faıəgɑːd] *n* Kamingitter *das.*

firelighter ['faıəlaıtəʳ] *n* Feueranzünder *der.*

fireman ['faıəmən] (*pl* **-men** [-mən]) *n* Feuerwehrmann *der.*

fireplace ['faıəpleıs] *n* Kamin *der.*

fireproof ['faıəpruːf] *adj* feuerfest.

fireside ['faıəsaıd] *n*: **by the fireside** am Kamin.

fire station *n* Feuerwache *die.*

firewall ['faıəwɔːl] *n* COMPUT Firewall *die.*

firewood ['faıəwʊd] *n* Brennholz *das.*

firework ['faıəwɜːk] *n* Feuerwerkskörper *der*; *(phrase)*: **fireworks** Feuerwerk *das.*

firing squad *n* Exekutionskommando *das.*

firm [fɜːm] ◇ *adj* - **1.** [in texture] fest - **2.** [structure, shelf] stabil - **3.** [forceful, strong - pressure, hold, control] fest; [- leader, voice] energisch; *(phrase)*: **you must be firm with him** sie müssen ihm gegenüber bestimmt auftreten;

to stand firm standhaft bleiben - **4.** [belief] unerschütterlich; [answer] entschieden; [evidence] sicher. ◇ *n* Firma *die*.

first [fɜ:st] ◇ *adj* erste(r) (s); **for the first time** zum ersten Mal; **I'll do it first thing (in the morning)** das ist das Erste, was ich morgen tun werde; **at first sight** auf den ersten Blick; **in the first place** zunächst einmal. ◇ *adv* - **1.** [firstly] zuerst; [arrive, speak *etc*] als erste(r) (s); **first of all** zuallererst; **what should I do first?** was soll ich zuerst tun? - **2.** [for the first time] zum ersten Mal. ◇ *pron* erste *der, die, das*; **the first of January** der erste Januar. ◇ *n* - **1.** [event]: **the balloon race was a world first** der Ballonweltflug war der erste seiner Art auf der Welt - **2.** *UK* UNIV *Abschluss mit "sehr gut"* - **3.** AUT: **first (gear)** erster Gang. ◆ **at first** *adv* zuerst. ◆ **at first hand** *adv* aus erster Hand.

first aid *n* Erste Hilfe.

first-aid kit *n* Verbandskasten *der*.

first-class *adj* - **1.** [excellent] erstklassig - **2.** [ticket] erster Klasse; **first-class compartment** Erste-Klasse-Abteil *das*; [stamp] *für Briefe, die innerhalb Großbritanniens schneller befördert werden sollen*.

first course *n* erster Gang.

first floor *n* - **1.** *UK* [above ground level] erster Stock - **2.** *US* [at ground level] Erdgeschoss *das*.

firsthand [fɜ:st'hænd] *adj* & *adv* aus erster Hand.

first lady *n* POL First Lady *die*, *Frau des US-Präsidenten*.

firstly ['fɜ:stlɪ] *adv* zuerst; [followed by "secondly"] erstens.

first name *n* Vorname *der*.

first-rate *adj* erstklassig.

fish [fɪʃ] (*pl inv* OR **-es**) ◇ *n* Fisch *der*. ◇ *vi*: **to fish (for)** fischen; [with rod] angeln; **to fish for compliments** *fig* auf Komplimente aus sein.

fish and chips *npl UK frittierter Fisch mit Pommes frites*.

fish and chip shop *n UK Imbisstube, die hauptsächlich frittierten Fisch mit Pommes frites verkauft*.

fishcake ['fɪʃkeɪk] *n* Fischfrikadelle *die*.

fisherman ['fɪʃəmən] (*pl* **-men** [-mən]) *n* Fischer *der*; [angler] Angler *der*, -in *die*.

fish fingers *UK*, **fish sticks** *US npl* Fischstäbchen *das*.

fishing ['fɪʃɪŋ] *n* Fischen *das*; [with rod] Angeln *das*; [industry] Fischerei *das*; **to go fishing** auf Fischfang gehen; [with rod] angeln gehen.

fishing boat *n* Fischerboot *das*.

fishing rod *n* Angelrute *die*.

fishmonger ['fɪʃ,mʌŋgəʳ] *n esp UK* Fischhändler *der*, -in *die*; **fishmonger's (shop)** Fischgeschäft *das*.

fish shop *n* Fischgeschäft *das*.

fish sticks *npl US* = **fish fingers**.

fish tank *n* [in house] Aquarium *das*.

fishy ['fɪʃɪ] *adj* - **1.** [smell, taste] Fisch- - **2.** *fig* [suspicious]: **there's something fishy about it** daran ist etwas faul.

fist [fɪst] *n* Faust *die*.

fit [fɪt] ◇ *adj* - **1.** [suitable]: **fit (for)** geeignet (für); **to be fit to do sthg** die richtige Person sein, um etw zu tun; **he's not fit to drive** [drunk] er ist nicht mehr in der Lage, Auto zu fahren; **fit to eat** essbar - **2.** [healthy] fit; **to keep/get fit** fit bleiben/werden. ◇ *n* - **1.** [of clothes, shoes *etc*]: **to be a good fit** gut passen - **2.** [epileptic, of anger, coughing] Anfall *der*; **to have a fit** MED einen Anfall haben OR erleiden; *fig* [be angry] einen Wutanfall kriegen; **to work in fits and starts** die Arbeit mehrmals unterbrechen. ◇ *vt* - **1.** [subj: clothes, shoes] passen *(+ D)*; [subj: key] passen in *(+ A)* - **2.** [insert]: **to fit sthg into sthg** etw in etw *(A)* stecken - **3.** [install] ein|bauen; **to fit sthg with sthg** etw mit etw aus|statten - **4.** [correspond to] entsprechen *(+ D)*; **he fits the description** die Beschreibung passt auf ihn. ◇ *vi* passen. ◆ **fit in** ◇ *vt sep* [find time for - person] dazwischen|schieben; [- task] zusätzlich erledigen. ◇ *vi* [belong]: **he's never fitted in here** er hat hier nie hingepasst.

fitness ['fɪtnɪs] *n* - **1.** [health] Fitness *die*, Kondition *die* - **2.** [suitability - for job]: **fitness (for)** Eignung *die* (für).

fitted carpet *n* Teppichboden *der*.

fitted kitchen *n UK* Einbauküche *die*.

fitter ['fɪtəʳ] *n* [mechanic] Monteur *der*, -in *die*, Installateur *der*, -in *die*.

fitting ['fɪtɪŋ] ◇ *adj fml* angemessen. ◇ *n* - **1.** [part] Zubehörteil *das* - **2.** [for clothing] Anprobe *die*. ◆ **fittings** *npl* Ausstattung *die*; [electrical, pipes] Installation *die*.

fitting room *n* Umkleidekabine *die*.

five [faɪv] *num* fünf; *see also* **six**.

fiver ['faɪvəʳ] *n inf* - **1.** *UK* [amount] fünf britische Pfund *Pl*; [note] Fünfpfundschein *der* - **2.** *US* [amount] fünf Dollar *Pl*; [note] Fünfdollarschein *der*.

fix [fɪks] ◇ *vt* - **1.** [attach] befestigen; **to fix sthg to sthg** etw an etw *(D)* befestigen; **to fix one's eyes on sthg** seine Augen auf etw *(A)* heften - **2.** [decide - date, amount, price] fest|setzen; *(phrase)*: **I've fixed it with him** ich habe es mit ihm abgemacht; **how are you fixed for money?** wie sieht es bei dir mit dem Geld aus? - **3.** [repair] reparieren - **4.** *inf* [rig - race, fight] manipulieren - **5.** *esp US* [food, drink] machen. ◇ *n* - **1.** *inf* [difficult situation]: **to be in a fix** in der Patsche sitzen - **2.** *drug sl* Fix *der*. ◆ **fix up** *vt sep* - **1.** [provide]: **to fix sb up with sthg** jm etw besorgen - **2.** [arrange] arrangieren.

fixation [fɪk'seɪʃn] *n* Fixierung *die*.

fixed [fɪkst] *adj* - **1.** [attached] fest - **2.** [charge, rate] festgesetzt - **3.** [smile, stare, belief] starr.

fixture ['fɪkstʃəʳ] *n* - **1.** [in building] festes Inventar; **fixtures and fittings** *zu einer Wohnung gehörende Ausstattung und Installationen* - **2.** [sports event] Spiel *das*.

fizz [fɪz] *vi* [drink] sprudeln.

fizzle ['fɪzl] ◆ **fizzle out** *vi* [fire, enthusiasm] verpuffen.

fizzy ['fɪzɪ] *adj* kohlensäurehaltig.

flabbergasted ['flæbəgɑːstɪd] *adj* platt.

flabby ['flæbɪ] *adj* wabbelig.

flag [flæg] ◇ *n* Fahne *die*; [of country] Flagge *die*, Fahne *die*. ◇ *vi* [person] ermüden; [enthusiasm, energy] nachllassen. ◆ **flag down** *vt sep* anlhalten.

flagpole ['flægpəʊl] *n* Fahnenstange *die*.

flagrant ['fleɪgrənt] *adj* himmelschreiend.

flagstone ['flægstəʊn] *n* Steinplatte *die*; [on floors] Fliese *die*.

flair [fleəʳ] *n* - **1.** [talent]: **flair (for)** Talent *das* (für) - **2.** [stylishness - of person] Ausstrahlung *die*.

flak [flæk] *n inf* [criticism]: **to get a lot of flak** unter schweren Beschuss geraten.

flake [fleɪk] ◇ *n* [of snow] Flocke *die*; [of skin] Schuppe *die*. ◇ *vi* [paint] ablblättern; [skin] sich schuppen.

flamboyant [flæm'bɔɪənt] *adj* extravagant; [design, decoration] üppig.

flame [fleɪm] *n* Flamme *die*; **to be in flames** in Flammen stehen; **to burst into flames** in Brand geraten.

flamingo [flə'mɪŋgəʊ] (*pl* **-s** OR **-es**) *n* Flamingo *der*.

flammable ['flæməbl] *adj* leicht entflammbar.

flan [flæn] *n* [sweet] Torte *die*; [savoury] Quiche *die*.

flank [flæŋk] ◇ *n* Flanke *die*. ◇ *vt*: **to be flanked by sb/sthg** von jm/etw flankiert sein.

flannel ['flænl] *n* - **1.** [fabric] Flannel *der* - **2.** *UK* [facecloth] Waschlappen *der*.

flap [flæp] ◇ *n* - **1.** [of pocket] Klappe *die*; [of envelope] Lasche *die*; [of table] hochklappbarer Teil - **2.** *inf* [panic]: **in a flap** in Panik. ◇ *vt* [wings] schlagen mit; [arms] wedeln mit. ◇ *vi* [sail, flag, clothes] flattern.

flapjack ['flæpdʒæk] *n* - **1.** *UK* [biscuit] Haferflockenkeks *der* - **2.** *US* [pancake] Pfannkuchen *der*.

flare [fleəʳ] ◇ *n* [distress signal] Leuchtsignal *das*. ◇ *vi* - **1.** [fire]: **to flare (up)** (auf)llodern - **2.: to flare (up)** [war, violence, disease] auslbrechen - **3.** [trousers, skirt] ausgestellt sein - **4.** [nostrils] sich blähen. ◆ **flares** *npl UK* [trousers] Hose *die* mit Schlag.

flash [flæʃ] ◇ *n* - **1.** [of light - bright] Aufblitzen *das*; *(phrase)*: **a flash of lightning** ein Blitz; **a flash of inspiration** *fig* ein Geistesblitz; **in a flash** blitzartig - **2.** PHOT Blitz *der*. ◇ *vt* - **1.** [torch]: **to flash a torch on sthg** etw anlleuchten; **to flash one's headlights** die Lichthupe benutzen; **to flash sb a look/smile** jn plötzlich (kurz) anlschauen/anllächeln - **2.** [show briefly - passport, image] kurz zeigen. ◇ *vi* [light] auflblinken; **to flash by** OR **past** vorbeilsausen.

flashback ['flæʃbæk] *n* [in film] Rückblende *die*.

flashbulb ['flæʃbʌlb] *n* Blitzlicht *das*.

flashgun ['flæʃgʌn] *n* Blitzgerät *das*.

flashlight ['flæʃlaɪt] *n* [torch] Taschenlampe *die*.

flashy ['flæʃɪ] *adj inf* protzig.

flask [flɑːsk] *n* - **1.** [Thermos] Thermosflasche *die* - **2.** [hip flask] Flachmann *der*.

flat [flæt] ◇ *adj* - **1.** [gen] flach; [feet, tyre] platt; **flat roof** Flachdach *das* - **2.** [refusal, denial] glatt - **3.** [voice] monoton - **4.** [MUS - singer, instrument] zu tief; *(phrase)*: **C flat** Ces *das*; **D flat** Des *das*; **A flat** As *das*; **B flat** B *das* - **5.** COMM [fare, fee] Pauschal- - **6.** [drink] abgestanden - **7.** [battery] leer. ◇ *adv* - **1.** [level] flach - **2.** [exactly]: **in five minutes flat** in ganzen fünf Minuten. ◇ *n* - **1.** *UK* [apartment] Wohnung *die* - **2.** [MUS - note] erniedrigter Ton; [- symbol] Erniedrigungszeichen *das*. ◆ **flat out** *adv* [work] auf Hochtouren.

flatly ['flætlɪ] *adv* [refuse, deny] rundweg.

flatmate ['flætmeɪt] *n UK* Mitbewohner *der*, -in *die*.

flat rate *n* Pauschalpreis *der*.

flat screen *n* [TV, monitor] Flachbildschirm *der*.

flatten ['flætn] *vt* - **1.** [surface] glätten; [paper] glatt streichen - **2.** [destroy] dem Erdboden gleichmachen. ◆ **flatten out** ◇ *vi* eben(er) werden. ◇ *vt sep* [surface] glätten; [paper] glatt streichen.

flatter ['flætəʳ] *vt* schmeicheln *(+ D)*.

flattering ['flætərɪŋ] *adj* schmeichelhaft.

flattery ['flætərɪ] *n (U)* Schmeicheleien *Pl*.

flaunt [flɔːnt] *vt* zur Schau stellen.

flavour *UK*, **flavor** *US* ['fleɪvəʳ] ◇ *n* - **1.** [taste] Geschmack *der* - **2.** *fig* [atmosphere] Touch *der*. ◇ *vt* [food, drink] Geschmack verleihen *(+ D)*.

flavouring *UK*, **flavoring** *US* ['fleɪvərɪŋ] *n* Aroma *das*.

flaw [flɔː] *n* Fehler *der*.

flawless ['flɔːlɪs] *adj* fehlerlos.

flax [flæks] *n* [plant] Flachs *der*.

flea [fliː] *n* Floh *der*.

flea market *n* Flohmarkt *der*.

fleck [flek] ◇ *n* Tupfen *der*. ◇ *vt*: **flecked (with)** besprenkelt (mit).

fled [fled] *pt* & *pp* ▷ **flee**.

flee [fliː] (*pt & pp* **fled**) ◇ *vt* [country] fliehen aus; [enemy] fliehen vor *(+ D)*. ◇ *vi* fliehen.

fleece [fliːs] ◇ *n* - **1.** [of sheep] Schaffell *das* - **2.** [material] Fleece *das*; [jacket] Fleecejacke *die*. ◇ *vt inf* [cheat] ab|zocken.

fleet [fliːt] *n* - **1.** [of ships] Flotte *die* - **2.** [of cars, buses] Fuhrpark *der*.

fleeting ['fliːtɪŋ] *adj* flüchtig.

Flemish ['flemɪʃ] ◇ *adj* flämisch. ◇ *n* [language] Flämisch(e) *das*.

flesh [fleʃ] *n* Fleisch *das*; [of fruit] Fruchtfleisch *das*; [of vegetable] Mark *das*; **flesh and blood** [family] Fleisch und Blut.

flesh wound *n* Fleischwunde *die*.

flew [fluː] *pt* ▷ **fly**.

flex [fleks] ◇ *n* ELEC Kabel *das*. ◇ *vt* [arm, knee] beugen.

flexible ['fleksəbl] *adj* - **1.** [material, bar] biegsam - **2.** [person, system] flexibel.

flexitime ['fleksɪtaɪm] *n* Gleitzeit *die*.

flick [flɪk] ◇ *n* [with finger] Schnippen *das*. ◇ *vt* [switch - turn on] an|knipsen; [- turn off] aus|knipsen. ◆ **flick through** *vt insep* durch|blättern.

flicker ['flɪkəʳ] *vi* [light, candle] flackern; [TV, screen] flimmern; [shadow, eyelids] zucken.

flick knife *n UK* Klappmesser *das*.

flight [flaɪt] *n* - **1.** [of plane, bird] Flug *der* - **2.**: **a flight of steps/stairs** eine Treppe - **3.** [escape] Flucht *die*.

flight attendant *n* Flugbegleiter *der*, -in *die*.

flight deck *n* - **1.** [of aircraft carrier] Flugdeck *das* - **2.** [of aircraft] Cockpit *das*.

flight recorder *n* Flugschreiber *der*.

flimsy ['flɪmzɪ] *adj* - **1.** [material, clothes, shoes] dünn; [paper] hauchdünn; [structure] nicht sehr stabil - **2.** [excuse] schwach; [argument] fadenscheinig.

flinch [flɪntʃ] *vi* zurück|zucken.

fling [flɪŋ] (*pt & pp* **flung**) ◇ *n* [affair] Affäre *die*. ◇ *vt* [throw] schleudern.

flint [flɪnt] *n* Feuerstein *der*.

flip [flɪp] ◇ *vt* - **1.** [omelette, steak *etc*] wenden; **to flip a coin** eine Münze werfen; **to flip open** auf|klappen; **to flip over** um|drehen; **to flip through** [magazine] durch|blättern - **2.** [switch - turn on] an|knipsen; [- turn off] aus|knipsen. ◇ *vi inf* [become angry] aus|flippen. ◇ *n* [of coin]: **it was decided on the flip of a coin** wir haben eine Münze geworfen, um zu entscheiden.

flip-flops *npl UK* [shoe] Badelatschen *Pl*.

flippant ['flɪpənt] *adj* leichtfertig.

flipper ['flɪpəʳ] *n* - **1.** [of animal] Flosse *die* - **2.** [for swimmer, diver] Schwimmflosse *die*.

flirt [flɜːt] ◇ *n*: **he's a terrible flirt** er flirtet mit allen. ◇ *vi* [with person]: **to flirt (with)** flirten (mit).

flirtatious [flɜː'teɪʃəs] *adj* kokett.

flit [flɪt] *vi* [bird] flattern.

float [fləʊt] ◇ *n* - **1.** [for fishing] Schwimmer *der*; [for swimming] Schwimmbrett *das* - **2.** [in procession] Festwagen *der* - **3.** [money] Wechselgeld *das*. ◇ *vi* - **1.** [on water - not sink] schwimmen; [- move] treiben - **2.** [through air] schweben.

flock [flɒk] *n* [of birds] Schwarm *der*; [of sheep] Herde *die*; [of people] Schar *die*.

flog [flɒg] *vt* - **1.** [whip] aus|peitschen - **2.** *UK inf* [sell] verkloppen.

flood [flʌd] ◇ *n* Flut *die*. ◇ *vt* - **1.** [gen] überschwemmen; [kitchen] unter Wasser setzen - **2.** [with light] durchfluten.

flooding ['flʌdɪŋ] *n* Überschwemmung *die*.

floodlight ['flʌdlaɪt] *n* Scheinwerfer *der*.

floor [flɔː] ◇ *n* - **1.** [of room] Fußboden *der* - **2.** [storey] Stock *der* - **3.** [at meeting, debate] Publikum *das* - **4.** [for dancing] Tanzfläche *die*. ◇ *vt* - **1.** [knock down] zu Boden schlagen - **2.** [subj: comment, question]: **to floor sb** jm die Sprache verschlagen.

floorboard ['flɔːbɔːd] *n* Diele *die*.

flop [flɒp] *n inf* [failure] Flop *der*.

floppy ['flɒpɪ] *adj* schlaff herunterhängend.

floppy (disk) *n* Diskette *die*.

flora ['flɔːrə] *n* Flora *die*.

florid ['flɒrɪd] *adj* - **1.** [face, complexion] gerötet - **2.** [style] blumig.

florist ['flɒrɪst] *n* Florist *der*, -in *die*; **florist's (shop)** Blumengeschäft *das*.

flotsam ['flɒtsəm] *n*: **flotsam and jetsam** Treibgut und Strandgut.

flounder ['flaʊndəʳ] *vi* - **1.** [in water] sich ab|strampeln - **2.** [in conversation, speech] ins Schwimmen kommen.

flour ['flaʊəʳ] *n* Mehl *das*.

flourish ['flʌrɪʃ] ◇ *vi* - **1.** [plant, flower] prächtig gedeihen - **2.** [company, business] florieren. ◇ *vt* schwenken.

flout [flaʊt] *vt* missachten.

flow [fləʊ] ◇ *n* - **1.** [river, of liquid] Fluss *der*; [of words] Redefluss *der*; **flow of information/traffic** Informations-/Verkehrsfluss - **2.** [of tide] Flut *die*. ◇ *vi* - **1.** [gen] fließen; [air, people] strömen - **2.** [hair, dress] wallen.

flowchart ['fləʊtʃɑːt], **flow diagram** *n* Flussdiagramm *das*.

flower ['flaʊəʳ] ◇ *n* [plant] Blume *die*; [blossom] Blüte *die*; **in flower** in Blüte. ◇ *vi* blühen.

flowerbed ['flaʊəbed] *n* Blumenbeet *das*.

flowerpot ['flaʊəpɒt] *n* Blumentopf *der*.

flowery ['flaʊərɪ] *adj* - **1.** [dress, material] geblümt - **2.** *pej* [language] blumig.

flown [fləʊn] *pp* ▷ **fly**.
flu [fluː] *n (U)* Grippe *die*.
fluctuate ['flʌktʃʊeɪt] *vi* schwanken.
fluency ['fluːənsɪ] *n* - **1.** [in a foreign language] Gewandtheit *die* - **2.** [in speaking, writing] Flüssigkeit *die*.
fluent ['fluːənt] *adj* - **1.** [in a foreign language] fließend - **2.** [writing] flüssig; [speaker] gewandt.
fluffy ['flʌfɪ] *adj* [animal] flaumweich; [jumper] flauschig.
fluid ['fluːɪd] ◇ *n* Flüssigkeit *die*. ◇ *adj* - **1.** [movement] fließend; [style] flüssig - **2.** [situation] Veränderungen unterworfen.
fluid ounce *n* = *28,41 cm³*.
fluke [fluːk] *n inf* [chance]: **it was a fluke** das war reiner Dusel.
flummox ['flʌməks] *vt esp UK inf* durcheinander bringen.
flung [flʌŋ] *pt* & *pp* ▷ **fling**.
flunk [flʌŋk] *US inf vt* SCH & UNIV [- exam, test] fallen durch; [- student] durchfallen lassen.
fluorescent [flʊə'resənt] *adj* fluoreszierend.
fluoride ['flʊəraɪd] *n* Fluorid *das*.
flurry ['flʌrɪ] *n* [of snow] Gestöber *das*; *(phrase)*: **there was a flurry of activity** es herrschte eine rege Betriebsamkeit.
flush [flʌʃ] ◇ *adj* [level]: **to be flush with sthg** bündig mit etw ab|schließen. ◇ *n* - **1.** [in toilet] Spülung *die* - **2.** [blush] Röte *die*. ◇ *vt* [with water]: **to flush the toilet** spülen. ◇ *vi* - **1.** [toilet] spülen - **2.** [blush] erröten.
flushed [flʌʃt] *adj* - **1.** [face] gerötet - **2.** [excited]: **to be flushed with sthg** über etw *(A)* aufgeregt und glücklich sein.
flustered ['flʌstəd] *adj* konfus.
flute [fluːt] *n* MUS Querflöte *die*.
flutter ['flʌtəʳ] *vi* flattern.
flux [flʌks] *n*: **to be in a state of flux** im Fluss sein.
fly [flaɪ] ◇ *n* - **1.** [insect] Fliege *die* - **2.** [of trousers] Hosenschlitz *der*. ◇ *vt* - **1.** [plane] fliegen; [kite] steigen lassen; [model aircraft] fliegen lassen; [passengers, goods] fliegen; [airline] fliegen mit - **2.** [flag] gehisst haben. ◇ *vi* - **1.** [gen] fliegen; **the days flew by** OR **past** die Tage sind schnell verflogen - **2.** [flag] wehen. ◆ **fly away** *vi* weg|fliegen.
fly-fishing *n* Fliegenfischen *das*.
flying ['flaɪɪŋ] ◇ *adj* [animal] Flug-; **flying leap** großer Sprung. ◇ *n* Fliegen *das*.
flying colours *npl*: **to pass (sthg) with flying colours** (etw) glänzend bestehen.
flying saucer *n* fliegende Untertasse.
flying start *n*: **to get off to a flying start** einen glänzenden Start haben.
flying visit *n* Stippvisite *die*.
flyover ['flaɪˌəʊvəʳ] *n UK* Überführung *die*.
flysheet ['flaɪʃiːt] *n* Überzelt *das*.
FM (*abbr of* **frequency modulation**) UKW.
foal [fəʊl] *n* Fohlen *das*.
foam [fəʊm] ◇ *n* - **1.** [bubbles] Schaum *der* - **2.** [material]: **foam (rubber)** Schaumgummi *der*. ◇ *vi* schäumen.
fob [fɒb] ◆ **fob off** *vt sep*: **to fob sthg off on sb** jm etw an|drehen; **to fob sb off with sthg** jn mit etw ab|speisen.
focal point ['fəʊkl-] *n fig* Mittelpunkt *der*.
focus ['fəʊkəs] (*pl* **-cuses** OR **-ci** [-kaɪ]) ◇ *n* PHOT Fokus *der*; [of rays] Brennpunkt *der*; [of discussion] Mittelpunkt *der*; **in focus** [image] scharf; **out of focus** [image] unscharf. ◇ *vt* - **1.** [lens, camera]: **to focus sthg (on)** etw ein|stellen (auf *(+ A)*) - **2.** [mentally]: **to focus one's attention on sb/sthg** seine Aufmerksamkeit auf jn/etw richten. ◇ *vi*: **to focus on** [with eyes] den Blick richten auf *(+ A)*; [with camera] mit der Kamera scharf stellen auf *(+ A)*; *fig* [mentally] konzentrieren auf *(+ A)*.
focused, focussed ['fəʊkəst] *adj* [mentally] konzentriert.
fodder ['fɒdəʳ] *n* Futter *das*.
foe [fəʊ] *n liter* Feind *der*.
foetus ['fiːtəs] *n* Fötus *der*.
fog [fɒg] *n* Nebel *der*.
foggy ['fɒgɪ] *adj* neblig.
foghorn ['fɒghɔːn] *n* Nebelhorn *das*.
fog lamp *n* Nebelscheinwerfer *der*.
foible ['fɔɪbl] *n* Eigenheit *die*.
foil [fɔɪl] ◇ *n (U)* [material] Folie *die*. ◇ *vt* [criminal] einen Strich durch die Rechnung machen *(+ D)*; [plot, plan] vereiteln.
fold [fəʊld] ◇ *vt* - **1.** [sheet, blanket, paper] falten; **to fold one's arms** die Arme verschränken - **2.** [wrap] ein|wickeln. ◇ *vi* - **1.** [bed, chair, bicycle] sich zusammenklappen lassen - **2.** *inf* [business] ein|gehen. ◇ *n* [in material, paper] Falte *die*. ◆ **fold up** ◇ *vt sep* - **1.** [sheet, blanket, paper] zusammen|falten - **2.** [chair, bed, bicycle] zusammen|klappen. ◇ *vi* [chair, bed, bicycle] sich zusammenklappen lassen.
folder ['fəʊldəʳ] *n* [for papers] Mappe *die*.
folding ['fəʊldɪŋ] *adj* [chair, table] Klapp-.
foliage ['fəʊlɪɪdʒ] *n (U)* Blätter *Pl*.
folk [fəʊk] ◇ *adj* Volks-. ◇ *npl* [people] Leute *Pl*. ◆ **folks** *npl inf* [relatives]: **my folks** meine Leute.
folklore ['fəʊklɔːʳ] *n* Folklore *die*.
folk music *n* [popular] Folk *der*; [traditional] Volksmusik *die*.
folk song *n* [popular] Folksong *der*; [traditional] Volkslied *das*.
folksy ['fəʊksɪ] *adj US inf* gemütlich.
follow ['fɒləʊ] ◇ *vt* - **1.** [gen] folgen *(+ D)*; **a presentation, followed by a discussion** ein Vortrag, gefolgt von einer Diskussion

- 2. [pursue] verfolgen - 3. [advice, instructions] befolgen - 4. [news, sb's career] verfolgen; [fashion] sich interessieren für. ◇ *vi* folgen; **it follows that...** daraus folgt, dass...; **I don't quite follow** [understand] da komm ich nicht ganz mit. ◆ **follow up** *vt sep* - 1. [complaint] nach|gehen *(+ D)*; [suggestion] auf|greifen - 2. [supplement]: **to follow sthg up with sthg** etw auf etw *(A)* folgen lassen.

follower ['fɒləʊəʳ] *n* [disciple, believer] Anhänger *der*, -in *die*.

following ['fɒləʊɪŋ] ◇ *adj* folgend; **the following day** am nächsten Tag. ◇ *n* [supporters] Anhängerschaft *die*. ◇ *prep* [after] nach.

folly ['fɒlɪ] *n* [foolishness] Torheit *die*.

fond [fɒnd] *adj* [affectionate] liebevoll; **to be fond of sb** jn gerne haben; **to be fond of sthg/of doing sthg** etw gerne haben/tun.

fondle ['fɒndl] *vt* streicheln.

font [fɒnt] *n* - 1. [in church] Taufstein *der* - 2. COMPUT & TYPO Schrift *die*.

food [fu:d] *n* Essen *das*; [for animals] Futter *das*; **health foods** Reformkost *die*.

food poisoning [-ˌpɔɪznɪŋ] *n* Lebensmittelvergiftung *die*.

food processor [-ˌprəʊsesəʳ] *n* Küchenmaschine *die*.

foodstuffs ['fu:dstʌfs] *npl* Nahrungsmittel *Pl*.

fool [fu:l] ◇ *n* [idiot] Narr *der*. ◇ *vt* täuschen; **to fool sb into doing sthg** jn durch Tricks dazu bringen, etw zu tun. ◆ **fool about, fool around** *vi* - 1. [behave foolishly]: **to fool about (with sthg)** (mit etw) herum|albern - 2. [be unfaithful]: **to fool about (with sb)** (mit jm) eine Affäre haben - 3. *US* [tamper]: **to fool around with sthg** mit etw Blödsinn machen.

foolhardy ['fu:lˌhɑ:dɪ] *adj* tollkühn.

foolish ['fu:lɪʃ] *adj* - 1. [unwise, silly] töricht - 2. [laughable, undignified] dumm; **to look foolish** albern aus|sehen; **to feel foolish** sich *(D)* albern vor|kommen.

foolproof ['fu:lpru:f] *adj* absolut sicher.

foot [fʊt] ◇ *n* - 1. (*pl* **feet**) [gen] Fuß *der*; [of sheep, cow] Huf *der*; [of bed] Fußende *das*; [of page] Ende *das*; **to be on one's feet** auf den Beinen sein; **to get to one's feet** auf|stehen; **on** *OR* **by foot** zu Fuß; **to find one's feet** Fuß fassen; **to have/get cold feet** kalte Füße bekommen; **to put one's foot in it** ins Fettnäpfchen treten; **to put one's feet up** die Beine hoch|legen - 2. (*pl inv OR* **feet**) [measurement] Fuß *der*, = 30,48 cm. ◇ *vt inf*: **to foot the bill (for sthg)** die Rechnung (für etw) bezahlen.

foot-and-mouth disease *n* Maul- und Klauenseuche *die*.

football ['fʊtbɔ:l] *n* - 1. *UK* [soccer] Fußball *der* - 2. *US* [American football] Football *der* - 3. [ball - in soccer] Fußball *der*; [- in American football] Ball *der*.

footballer ['fʊtbɔ:ləʳ] *n UK* Fußballspieler *der*, -in *die*.

football player *n* Fußballspieler *der*, -in *die*.

footbridge ['fʊtbrɪdʒ] *n* Fußgängerbrücke *die*.

foothills ['fʊthɪlz] *npl* Gebirgsausläufer *Pl*.

foothold ['fʊthəʊld] *n* Halt *der*.

footing ['fʊtɪŋ] *n* - 1. [foothold] Halt *der*; **to lose one's footing** den Halt verlieren - 2. [basis] Basis *die*; **to be on a war footing** auf einen Krieg vorbereitet sein.

footlights ['fʊtlaɪts] *npl* Rampenlicht *das*.

footnote ['fʊtnəʊt] *n* Fußnote *die*.

footpath ['fʊtpɑ:θ] (*pl* [-pɑ:ðz]) *n* Fußweg *der*.

footprint ['fʊtprɪnt] *n* Fußabdruck *der*.

footstep ['fʊtstep] *n* [sound] Schritt *der*.

footwear ['fʊtweəʳ] *n* Schuhwerk *das*.

for [fɔ:ʳ] ◇ *prep* - 1. [expressing purpose, reason, destination] für; **this is for you** dieses Buch ist für dich; **a ticket for Manchester** eine Fahrkarte nach Manchester; **for this reason** aus diesem Grund; **a cure for sore throats** ein Mittel gegen Halsschmerzen; **what did you do that for?** wozu *OR* warum hast du das getan?; **to jump for joy** vor Freude an die Decke springen; **what's it for?** wofür ist das?; **to go for a walk** spazieren gehen; **it's time for bed** es ist Zeit schlafen *OR* ins Bett zu gehen; **'for sale'** 'zu verkaufen' - 2. [during] seit; **I've lived here for ten years** ich lebe seit zehn Jahren hier; **we talked for hours** wir redeten stundenlang - 3. [by, before] für; **be there for 8 p.m.** sei um acht Uhr abends da; **I'll do it for tomorrow** ich mache es bis morgen; **be there at 7.30 for 8 o'clock** versucht um 19.30 Uhr da zu sein, damit wir um 20.00 Uhr anfangen können - 4. [on the occasion of]: **I got socks for Christmas** ich habe Socken zu Weihnachten bekommen; **what's for dinner?** was gibt's zum Abendessen? - 5. [on behalf of] für; **to do sthg for sb** etw für jn tun - 6. [with time and space] für; **there's no room for it** dafür ist kein Platz; **to have time for sthg** für etw Zeit haben - 7. [expressing distance]: **we drove for miles** wir fuhren meilenweit; **road works for 20 miles** Straßenarbeiten auf 20 Meilen - 8. [expressing price] für; **I bought it for five pounds** ich habe es für fünf Pfund gekauft; **for free** gratis - 9. [expressing meaning]: **what's the German for "boy"?** wie heißt "boy" auf Deutsch?; **P for Peter** P wie Peter - 10. [with regard to] für; **it's warm for November** es ist warm für November; **it's too far for him to walk** zum Gehen ist es für ihn zu weit; **to feel sorry for sb** jn bemitleiden; **to be glad for sb** sich für jn freuen - **11.** [in favour of] für; **is she for or against it?** ist sie dafür oder dagegen?; **to vote for sthg** für etw stimmen; **I'm all for doing it** ich bin sehr dafür, dass wir das tun - **12.** [in ratios] für; **for every person who passes the test there are five who fail** auf jede Person, die die Prüfung besteht, kommen fünf, die durchfallen - **13.** *phr*: **you'll be for it when...** du kannst dich auf etwas gefasst machen, wenn... ◇ *conj liter* denn. ◆ **for all** ◇ *prep* - **1.** [in spite of] trotz; **for all that** trotzdem - **2.** [considering how little]: **for all the good it's done me** so wenig, wie es mir genützt hat. ◇ *conj*: **for all I care** meinetwegen; **for all I know** so viel ich weiß.

forage ['fɒrɪdʒ] *vi* [search] herum|stöbern; **to forage for sthg** nach etw stöbern.

foray ['fɒreɪ] *n* (Raub)überfall *der*.

forbad [fə'bæd], **forbade** [fə'beɪd] *pt* ▷ **forbid**.

forbid [fə'bɪd] (*pt* **-bade** *OR* **-bad**, *pp* **forbid** *OR* **-bidden**) *vt* verbieten; **to forbid sb to do sthg** jm verbieten, etw zu tun.

forbidden [fə'bɪdn] ◇ *pp* ▷ **forbid**. ◇ *adj* [activity] verboten; **forbidden subject** Tabuthema *das*.

forbidding [fə'bɪdɪŋ] *adj* [person] abweisend; [landscape] unwirtlich.

force [fɔ:s] ◇ *n* - **1.** [strength, magnitude] Stärke *die*; [of explosion, blow] Wucht *die*; **a force ten gale** ein Sturm mit Windstärke zehn - **2.** [violence] Gewalt *die*; **by force** mit Gewalt - **3.** PHYS Kraft *die* - **4.** [powerful person, influence] Macht *die* - **5.** [effect]: **to be in/come into force** in Kraft sein/treten. ◇ *vt* - **1.** [compel] zwingen; **to force sb to do sthg** jn zwingen, etw zu tun; **to force sthg on sb** jm etw auf|zwingen - **2.** [lock, door] auf|brechen - **3.** [push] pressen. ◆ **forces** *npl*: **the forces** die Streitkräfte *Pl*; **to join forces (with sb)** sich (mit jm) zusammen|tun.

force-feed *vt* zwangsernähren.

forceful ['fɔ:sfʊl] *adj* [person] energisch; [words] eindringlich; [speech] überzeugend.

forceps ['fɔ:seps] *npl* Zange *die*.

forcibly ['fɔ:səblɪ] *adv* [seize, enter, remove] gewaltsam.

ford [fɔ:d] *n* Furt *die*.

fore [fɔ:ʳ] ◇ *adj* NAUT vordere(r) (s); **fore deck** Vordeck *das*. ◇ *n*: **to come to the fore** *fig* [become well-known] bekannt werden; [become important] bedeutend werden.

forearm ['fɔ:rɑ:m] *n* Unterarm *der*.

foreboding [fɔ:'bəʊdɪŋ] *n* Vorahnung *die*.

forecast ['fɔ:kɑ:st] (*pt & pp inv OR* **-ed**) ◇ *n* Prognose *die*; **(weather) forecast** (Wetter)vorhersage *die*. ◇ *vt* vorher|sagen.

foreclose [fɔ:'kləʊz] *vt & vi*: **to foreclose (on) a mortgage** eine (durch eine Hypothek gesicherte) Schuldforderung geltend machen.

forecourt ['fɔ:kɔ:t] *n* Vorhof *der*.

forefront ['fɔ:frʌnt] *n*: **to be in** *OR* **at the forefront of sthg** [campaign, movement] an der Spitze einer Sache *(G)* stehen.

forego [fɔ:'gəʊ] *vt* = **forgo**.

foregone conclusion ['fɔ:gɒn-] *n*: **it's a foregone conclusion** es stand von vornherein fest.

foreground ['fɔ:graʊnd] *n* Vordergrund *der*.

forehand ['fɔ:hænd] *n* Vorhand *die*.

forehead ['fɔ:hed] *n* Stirn *die*.

foreign ['fɒrən] *adj* [gen] ausländisch; [correspondent, debt] Auslands-; [policy] Außen-; *(phrase)*: **foreign person** Ausländer *der*, -in *die*; **foreign holiday** Urlaub *der* im Ausland; **foreign country** fremdes Land; **foreign countries** das Ausland.

foreign affairs *npl* Außenpolitik *die*.

foreign currency *n (U)* Devisen *Pl*.

foreigner ['fɒrənəʳ] *n* Ausländer *der*, -in *die*.

foreign language *n* Fremdsprache *die*.

foreign minister *n* Außenminister *der*, -in *die*.

Foreign Office *n UK*: **the Foreign Office** das Außenministerium.

Foreign Secretary *n UK* Außenminister *der*, -in *die*.

foreman ['fɔ:mən] (*pl* **-men** [-mən]) *n* - **1.** [of workers] Vorarbeiter *der* - **2.** [of jury] Obmann *der*, -männin *die*.

foremost ['fɔ:məʊst] ◇ *adj* führend. ◇ *adv*: **first and foremost** vor allem.

forensic [fə'rensɪk] *adj* [examination] gerichtsmedizinisch.

forerunner ['fɔ:ˌrʌnəʳ] *n* [precursor] Vorläufer *der*, -in *die*.

foresee [fɔ:'si:] (*pt* **-saw** [-'sɔ:]) (*pp* **-seen**) *vt* vorher|sehen, voraus|sehen.

foreseeable [fɔ:'si:əbl] *adj* vorhersehbar; **for the foreseeable future** in absehbarer Zeit.

foreseen [fɔ:'si:n] *pp* ▷ **foresee**.

foreshadow [fɔ:'ʃædəʊ] *vt* ahnen lassen.

foresight ['fɔ:saɪt] *n (U)* Weitsicht *die*.

forest ['fɒrɪst] *n* Wald *der*.

forestall [fɔ:'stɔ:l] *vt* zuvor|kommen *(+ D)*.

forestry ['fɒrɪstrɪ] *n* Forstwirtschaft *die*; [science] Forstwissenschaft *die*.

foretaste ['fɔ:teɪst] *n* Vorgeschmack *der*.

foretell [fɔ:'tel] (*pt & pp* **-told**) *vt* vorher|sagen.

foretold [fɔ:'təʊld] *pt & pp* ▷ **foretell**.

forever [fə'revəʳ] *adv* [eternally] ewig; [disappear, exile] für immer.

forewarn [fɔ:'wɔ:n] *vt* vor|warnen.

foreword ['fɔ:wɜ:d] *n* Vorwort *das*.

forfeit ['fɔ:fɪt] <> *n* Strafe *die*. <> *vt* [deposit, chance] ein|büßen; [right] verwirken.

forgave [fə'geɪv] *pt* ▷ **forgive**.

forge [fɔ:dʒ] <> *n* [place] Schmiede *die*. <> *vt* - **1.** [metal] schmieden - **2.** [friendship, alliance] schließen; [relationship] knüpfen - **3.** [signature, passport, banknotes] fälschen. ◆ **forge ahead** *vi* voran|kommen.

forger ['fɔ:dʒəʳ] *n* Fälscher *der*, -in *die*.

forgery ['fɔ:dʒərɪ] *n* Fälschung *die*.

forget [fə'get] (*pt* **-got**, *pp* **-gotten**) <> *vt* vergessen; **to forget to do sthg** vergessen, etw zu tun; **to forget how to dance** das Tanzen verlernen; **forget it!** vergiss es! <> *vi* es vergessen; **to forget about sthg** etw vergessen.

forgetful [fə'getfʊl] *adj* vergesslich.

forgive [fə'gɪv] (*pt* **-gave**) (*pp* **-given** [-'gɪvən]) *vt* [person] verzeihen *(+ D)*; [sins] vergeben; **to forgive sb for sthg** jm etw verzeihen.

forgiveness [fə'gɪvnɪs] *n* Verzeihung *die*.

forgo [fɔ:'gəʊ] (*pt* **-went**) (*pp* **-gone** [-'gɒn]) *vt* verzichten auf *(+ A)*.

forgot [fə'gɒt] *pt* ▷ **forget**.

forgotten [fə'gɒtn] *pp* ▷ **forget**.

fork [fɔ:k] <> *n* - **1.** [for food, gardening] Gabel *die* - **2.** [in road, path, river] Gabelung *die*. <> *vi* [road, river] sich gabeln; **to fork left/right** [driver] nach links/rechts abbiegen. ◆ **fork out** *inf* <> *vt insep* blechen. <> *vi*: **to fork out (for sthg)** (für etw) blechen.

forklift truck ['fɔ:klɪft-] *n* Gabelstapler *der*.

forlorn [fə'lɔ:n] *adj* - **1.** [expression] betrübt; [cry] verzweifelt - **2.** [desolate - person] einsam und unglücklich; [- place] trostlos - **3.** [hope] schwach; [attempt] verzweifelt.

form [fɔ:m] <> *n* - **1.** [shape, type] Form *die*; [shape of person] Gestalt *die*; **in the form of** in Form von - **2.** [health & SPORT] Form *die*; **on form** *UK*, **in form** *US* in Form; **off form** nicht in Form; **according to form, true to form** wie erwartet - **3.** [piece of paper] Formular *das*; [application form] Bewerbungsbogen *der* - **4.** *UK* SCH [class] Klasse *die* - **5.** [etiquette]: **it is bad form to arrive late** es ist schlechtes Benehmen, zu spät zu kommen; **for form's sake** der Form halber. <> *vt* - **1.** [plan] entwerfen; [friendship] schließen; [character] formen; **to form an idea of sthg** sich *(D)* eine Vorstellung von etw machen - **2.** [circle, sentence, plural, government] bilden - **3.** [constitute] sein; **to form part of sthg** ein Teil von etw sein. <> *vi* sich bilden.

formal ['fɔ:ml] *adj* - **1.** [language] formell; [person] förmlich - **2.** [event] feierlich; **formal clothes** Gesellschaftskleidung *die* - **3.** [offer, decision] offiziell; **formal education** Ausbildung *die* in einer Institution.

formality [fɔ:'mælətɪ] *n* - **1.** *(U)* [correctness] Förmlichkeit *die* - **2.** [convention] Formalität *die*.

format ['fɔ:mæt] <> *n* - **1.** [size & COMPUT] Format *das* - **2.** [structure, arrangement] Struktur *die*. <> *vt* COMPUT formatieren.

formation [fɔ:'meɪʃn] *n* - **1.** *(U)* [of company] Gründung *die*; [of government] Bildung *die* - **2.** [arrangement] Formation *die*.

formative ['fɔ:mətɪv] *adj* prägend; **formative years** entscheidende Jahre.

former ['fɔ:məʳ] <> *adj* - **1.** [previous] früher, ehemalig; **in former times** früher - **2.** [first] erstere(r) (s). <> *n*: **the former** der/die/das Erstere.

formerly ['fɔ:məlɪ] *adv* früher.

formidable ['fɔ:mɪdəbl] *adj* Respekt einflößend; [task] gewaltig.

formula ['fɔ:mjʊlə] (*pl* **-as** OR **-ae** [-i:]) *n* [gen] Formel *die*.

formulate ['fɔ:mjʊleɪt] *vt* - **1.** [express] formulieren - **2.** [plan] aus|arbeiten.

forsake [fə'seɪk] (*pt* **-sook**, *pp* **-saken**) *vt liter* [person] verlassen; [habit] auf|geben.

forsook [fə'sʊk] *pt* ▷ **forsake**.

fort [fɔ:t] *n* Fort *das*.

forth [fɔ:θ] *adv liter* [outwards, onwards]: **to go/send forth** fort|gehen/-schicken; **to bring forth** hervor|bringen.

forthcoming [fɔ:θ'kʌmɪŋ] *adj* - **1.** [future - election, events] bevorstehend; [- book] in Kürze erscheinend - **2.** [willing to talk] mitteilsam.

forthright ['fɔ:θraɪt] *adj* [person, manner] direkt; [opinions] unverblümt.

forthwith [ˌfɔ:θ'wɪθ] *adv fml* unverzüglich.

fortified wine ['fɔ:tɪfaɪd-] *n* mit zusätzlichem Alkohol angereicherter Wein.

fortify ['fɔ:tɪfaɪ] *vt* - **1.** [place] befestigen - **2.** *fig* [person, resolve] bestärken.

fortnight ['fɔ:tnaɪt] *n* vierzehn Tage *Pl*.

fortnightly ['fɔ:tˌnaɪtlɪ] <> *adj* [visit, meeting] alle zwei Wochen stattfindend; [magazine] alle zwei Wochen erscheinend. <> *adv* alle vierzehn Tage, alle zwei Wochen.

fortress ['fɔ:trɪs] *n* Festung *die*.

fortunate ['fɔ:tju:nət] *adj* glücklich; **to be fortunate** Glück haben; **it's fortunate that...** es ist ein Glück, dass...

fortunately ['fɔ:tʃnətlɪ] *adv* zum Glück.

fortune ['fɔ:tʃu:n] *n* - **1.** [money] Vermögen *das*; **it costs a fortune** *inf* es kostet ein Vermögen - **2.** [luck] Glück *das* - **3.** [fate] Schicksal *das* - **4.** [future]: **to tell sb's fortune** jm die Zukunft voraus|sagen.

fortune-teller [-ˌteləʳ] *n* Wahrsager *der*, -in *die*.

forty ['fɔ:tɪ] *num* vierzig; *see also* **sixty**.

forward ['fɔ:wəd] ◇ *adj* - **1.** [movement] vorwärts- - **2.** [planning] Voraus-; **we're no further forward now than we were last year** wir sind jetzt nicht weiter als letztes Jahr - **3.** [impudent] dreist. ◇ *adv* - **1.** [in space - go, move] vorwärts; [- look, lean] nach vorn; [- fall] vornüber - **2.** [in time]: **to bring a meeting forward** ein Treffen vor|verlegen; **from this time forward** [now] von jetzt an; [then] seitdem; **to put a clock forward** eine Uhr vor|stellen. ◇ *n* SPORT Stürmer *der*, -in *die*. ◇ *vt* [letter, parcel] nach|senden; **'please forward'** 'bitte nachsenden'.

forwarding address ['fɔ:wədɪŋ-] *n* Nachsendeadresse *die*.

forwards ['fɔ:wədz] *adv* = **forward**.

forwent [fɔ:'went] *pt* ▷ **forgo**.

fossil ['fɒsl] *n* Fossil *das*.

forward slash *n* Schrägstrich *der*.

foster ['fɒstər] ◇ *adj* [family, mother] Pflege-. ◇ *vt* - **1.** [child] in Pflege nehmen - **2.** [idea, hope] hegen; [relations] fördern.

foster child *n* Pflegekind *das*.

foster parents *npl* Pflegeeltern *Pl*.

fought [fɔ:t] *pt* & *pp* ▷ **fight**.

foul [faʊl] ◇ *adj* - **1.** [water] faulig; [air] verpestet; [food] verdorben; [smell, taste] übel - **2.** [very unpleasant] schrecklich; **she's in a foul mood today** sie ist heute in sehr schlechter Stimmung - **3.** [language] unflätig. ◇ *n* SPORT Foul *das*. ◇ *vt* - **1.** [make dirty] verunreinigen - **2.** SPORT foulen.

found [faʊnd] ◇ *pt* & *pp* ▷ **find**. ◇ *vt* - **1.** [organization, town] gründen; [hospital, school] errichten - **2.** [base]: **to be founded on sthg** auf etw *(D)* basieren.

foundation [faʊn'deɪʃn] *n* - **1.** [basis] Grundlage *die*; **without foundation** unbegründet - **2.** [organization] Stiftung *die* - **3.** [cosmetic]: **foundation (cream)** Grundierungscreme *die*.
◆ **foundations** *npl* CONSTR Fundament *das*.

founder ['faʊndər] ◇ *n* [person] Gründer *der*, -in *die*. ◇ *vi* [sink] sinken.

foundry ['faʊndrɪ] *n* Gießerei *die*.

fountain ['faʊntɪn] *n* [man-made] Springbrunnen *der*.

fountain pen *n* Füllfederhalter *der*.

four [fɔ:r] *num* vier; **on all fours** auf allen vieren; *see also* **six**.

four-letter word *n* Vulgärausdruck *der*.

four-poster (bed) *n* Himmelbett *das*.

foursome ['fɔ:səm] *n* Quartett *das*.

fourteen [,fɔ:'ti:n] *num* vierzehn; *see also* **six**.

fourth [fɔ:θ] *num* vierte(r) (s); *see also* **sixth**.

Fourth of July *n*: **the Fourth of July** der vierte Juli, *Nationalfeiertag (Unabhängigkeitstag) in den USA*.

four-wheel drive *n* - **1.** [vehicle] Fahrzeug *das* mit Allradantrieb - **2.** [system] Allradantrieb *der*.

fowl [faʊl] (*pl inv* OR **-s**) *n* [chicken] Huhn *das*; [turkey] Truthahn *der*; [duck] Ente *die*.

fox [fɒks] ◇ *n* Fuchs *der*. ◇ *vt* - **1.** [outwit] täuschen - **2.** [baffle] vor ein Rätsel stellen.

foxcub ['fɒkskʌb] *n* Fuchswelpe *der*.

foyer ['fɔɪeɪ] *n* - **1.** [of hotel, theatre] Foyer *das* - **2.** *US* [of house] Diele *die*.

fracas ['frækɑ:, *US* 'freɪkəs] (*UK pl inv*) (*US pl* **fracases**) *n* Tumult *der*.

fraction ['frækʃn] *n* - **1.** MATHS Bruch *der* - **2.** [small part] Bruchteil *der*.

fractionally ['frækʃnəlɪ] *adv* geringfügig.

fracture ['fræktʃər] ◇ *n* Bruch *der*. ◇ *vt* brechen; **to fracture one's arm** sich *(D)* den Arm brechen.

fragile ['frædʒaɪl] *adj* zerbrechlich; [health] anfällig.

fragment *n* ['frægmənt] - **1.** [of china, glass] Scherbe *die* - **2.** [of text] Fragment *das*; [of conversation] Fetzen *der*.

fragrance ['freɪgrəns] *n* Duft *der*.

fragrant ['freɪgrənt] *adj* duftend.

frail [freɪl] *adj* - **1.** [person, health] zart - **2.** [structure] brüchig.

frame [freɪm] ◇ *n* - **1.** [gen] Rahmen *der*; [of glasses, bed] Gestell *das*; [of house, boat] Gerippe *das* - **2.** [physique] Körper *der* - **3.** *phr*: **frame of mind** Gemütsverfassung *die*. ◇ *vt* - **1.** [painting, photograph] rahmen - **2.** *fig* [surround] umrahmen - **3.** [thoughts, answer] formulieren - **4.** *inf* [falsely incriminate]: **to frame sb** jm eine Sache an|hängen.

framework ['freɪmwɜ:k] *n* - **1.** [of boat, house] Gerippe *das* - **2.** [of society, democracy] (Grund)struktur *die*; [of essay] Gliederung *die*; **within the framework of** im Rahmen *(+ G)*.

France [frɑ:ns] *n* Frankreich *nt*.

franchise ['fræntʃaɪz] *n* - **1.** POL Wahlrecht *das* - **2.** COMM Lizenz *die*.

frank [fræŋk] ◇ *adj* offen; **to be frank, ...** offen gestanden, ... ◇ *vt* [letter] (frei)|stempeln.

frankly ['fræŋklɪ] *adv* - **1.** [talk] offen - **2.** [to be honest] offen gestanden.

frantic ['fræntɪk] *adj* - **1.** [person] außer sich - **2.** [activity, day, pace] hektisch.

fraternity [frə'tɜ:nətɪ] *n* - **1.** [community]: **the medical/banking fraternity** die Mediziner/Bankfachleute - **2.** *US* [of students] Studentenverbindung *die*.

fraternize, -ise ['frætənaɪz] *vi*: **to fraternize (with sb)** sich (mit jm) verbrüdern; **to fraternize with the enemy** mit dem Feind fraternisieren.

fraud [frɔ:d] *n* - **1.** *(U)* [crime] Betrug *der* - **2.** [deceitful act] Schwindel *der* - **3.** *pej* [impostor] Betrüger *der*, -in *die*.

fraught [frɔ:t] *adj* - **1.** [full]: **fraught with danger** gefährlich; **fraught with problems** voller Probleme - **2.** *UK* [frantic - person] gestresst.

fray [freɪ] <> *vi* [clothing, fabric] aus|fransen; [rope] sich durch|scheuern. <> *n liter*: **to join in the fray** sich in den Kampf/Streit ein|mischen.

frayed [freɪd] *adj* - **1.** [clothing, fabric] ausgefranst; [rope] durchgescheuert - **2.** *fig* [nerves] strapaziert; **tempers were frayed** Gemüter waren erhitzt.

freak [fri:k] <> *adj* außergewöhnlich. <> *n* - **1.** [strange creature - in appearance] Missgeburt *die*; [- in behaviour] Irre *der*, *die* - **2.** [unusual event] außergewöhnliche Begebenheit - **3.** *inf* [fanatic]: **a fitness freak** ein Fitnessfanatiker; **a computer freak** ein Computerfreak.
◆ **freak out** *inf vi* - **1.** [get angry] aus|flippen - **2.** [panic] durch|drehen.

freckle ['frekl] *n* Sommersprosse *die*.

free [fri:] (*comp* **freer**, *superl* **freest**, *pt & pp* **freed**) <> *adj* - **1.** [gen] frei; **free period** SCH Freistunde *die*; **she is free to leave** es steht ihr frei, zu gehen; **feel free to disagree** sie sind nicht gezwungen, zuzustimmen; **feel free!** nur zu!; **to set sb/an animal free** jn/ein Tier frei|lassen; **if you have a free moment** wenn Sie einen Moment Zeit haben - **2.** [costing nothing] kostenlos; **'admission free'** 'Eintritt frei'; **free of charge** umsonst. <> *adv* - **1.** [without payment] kostenlos; **for free** umsonst - **2.** [without restraint]: **to cut free** los|schneiden; [from wrecked vehicle] befreien; **to work free** sich lockern. <> *vt* - **1.** [prisoner, animal] frei|lassen; [country, city] befreien - **2.** [make available] zur Verfügung stellen - **3.** [extricate - person] befreien; [- object] heraus|kriegen.

freedom ['fri:dəm] *n* Freiheit *die*; **freedom of speech** Redefreiheit *die*.

freefone ['fri:fəʊn] *adj UK*: **a freefone number** eine gebührenfreie Telefonnummer.

free-for-all *n* - **1.** [brawl] allgemeine Schlägerei - **2.** [argument] allgemeine lautstarke Auseinandersetzung.

free gift *n* Gratisgabe *die*.

freehand ['fri:hænd] <> *adj* [drawing] Freihand-. <> *adv* aus der Hand.

free house *n Wirtshaus, das keiner bestimmten Brauerei gehört und daher Bier verschiedener Marken ausschenken darf.*

free kick *n* Freistoß *der*.

freelance ['fri:lɑ:ns] <> *adj* [work] freiberuflich; [translator, journalist] freiberuflich tätig. <> *n* Freiberufler *der*, -in *die*.

freely ['fri:lɪ] *adv* - **1.** [available, move] frei; [admit, talk] offen; [travel] ungehindert - **2.** [generously] großzügig.

Freemason ['fri:,meɪsn] *n* Freimaurer *der*.

freepost ['fri:pəʊst] *adv* [send] portofrei.

free-range *adj UK* [eggs] von frei laufenden Hühnern; [hens] frei laufend.

freestyle ['fri:staɪl] *n* [in swimming] Freistil *der*.

free time *n* Freizeit *die*.

free trade *n* Freihandel *der*.

freeware ['fri:weəʳ] *n* COMPUT Freeware *die*.

freeway ['fri:weɪ] *n US* Autobahn *die*.

freewheel [,fri:'wi:l] *vi* [cyclist] (mit dem Fahrrad) rollen; [motorist] im Leerlauf fahren.

free will *n* freier Wille; **to do sthg of one's own free will** etw aus freien Stücken tun.

freeze [fri:z] (*pt* **froze**, *pp* **frozen**) <> *vt* ein|frieren; [pond, river] zufrieren lassen; [lock, pipes] einfrieren lassen. <> *vi* - **1.** [pond, river] zu|frieren; [pipes] ein|frieren - **2.** METEOR frieren - **3.** [stop moving] in der Bewegung erstarren; **freeze!** keine Bewegung! <> *n* - **1.** [cold weather] Frost *der* - **2.**: **wage/price freeze** Lohn-/Preisstopp *der*.

freezer ['fri:zəʳ] *n* [upright] Tiefkühlschrank *der*; [chest] Tiefkühltruhe *die*; [part of fridge] Gefrierfach *das*.

freezing ['fri:zɪŋ] <> *adj* eiskalt; **I'm freezing** mir ist eiskalt. <> *n inf*: **above/below freezing** über/unter dem Gefrierpunkt.

freezing point *n* Gefrierpunkt *der*.

freight [freɪt] *n* [goods] Fracht *die*.

freight train *n* Güterzug *der*.

French [frentʃ] <> *adj* französisch. <> *n* [language] Französisch(e) *das*. <> *npl*: **the French** die Franzosen *Pl*.

French bean *n* grüne Bohne.

French doors *npl* = **French windows**.

French dressing *n* - **1.** [in UK] Vinaigrette *die* - **2.** [in US] *Salatsoße mit Majonäse und Ketschup*.

French fries *npl esp US* Pommes frites *pl*.

Frenchman ['frentʃmən] (*pl* **-men** [-mən]) *n* Franzose *der*.

French stick *n UK* Baguette *das*.

French windows *npl große zweiflügelige Glastür*.

Frenchwoman ['frentʃ,wʊmən] (*pl* **-women** [-,wɪmɪn]) *n* Französin *die*.

frenetic [frə'netɪk] *adj* [activity] hektisch; [pace] rasend.

frenzy ['frenzɪ] *n*: **in a frenzy** hektisch.

frequency ['fri:kwənsɪ] *n* - **1.** [rate] Häufigkeit *die* - **2.** [radio wave] Frequenz *die*.

frequent <> *adj* ['fri:kwənt] häufig; **she is a frequent visitor** sie kommt häufig zu Besuch. <> *vt* [frɪ'kwent] häufig besuchen.

frequently ['fri:kwəntlɪ] *adv* häufig.

fresh [freʃ] *adj* - **1.** [gen] frisch; [information] neu; **fresh water** Süßwasser *das* - **2.** [new] neu; **to make a fresh pot of tea** noch einmal eine Kanne Tee machen; **to give sthg a fresh coat of paint** etw neu streichen - **3.** [refreshing] erfrischend; **to get some fresh air** an die frische Luft gehen - **4.** [original] originell.

freshen ['freʃn] *vi* [wind] auf|frischen. ◈ **freshen up** *vi* [person] sich frisch machen.

fresher ['freʃər] *n UK inf* Erstsemester *das*.

freshly ['freʃlɪ] *adv* frisch.

freshman ['freʃmən] (*pl* **-men** [-mən]) *n* Erstsemester *das*.

freshness ['freʃnɪs] *n* - **1.** [of food, air, taste] Frische *die* - **2.** [originality] Originalität *die*.

freshwater ['freʃ,wɔ:tər] *adj* Süßwasser-.

fret [fret] *vi* [worry] sich *(D)* Sorgen machen.

friction ['frɪkʃn] *n (U)* - **1.** [force] Reibung *die* - **2.** [rubbing] Reiben *das* - **3.** [conflict] Reibereien *Pl*.

Friday ['fraɪdɪ] *n* Freitag *der*; *see also* **Saturday**.

fridge [frɪdʒ] *n esp UK* Kühlschrank *der*.

fridge-freezer *n UK* Kühlgefrierkombination *die*.

fried [fraɪd] ◇ *pt & pp* ▷ **fry**. ◇ *adj* gebraten; **fried egg** Spiegelei *das*.

friend [frend] *n* [gen] Freund *der*, -in *die*; **to be friends (with sb)** (mit jm) befreundet sein; **to make friends (with sb)** sich (mit jm) an|freunden.

friendly ['frendlɪ] *adj* freundlich; [country] befreundet; **to be friendly with sb** mit jm befreundet sein.

friendship ['frendʃɪp] *n* Freundschaft *die*.

fries [fraɪz] *npl* = **French fries**.

frieze [fri:z] *n* ARCHIT Fries *der*; [on wallpaper] Bordüre *die*.

fright [fraɪt] *n* - **1.** *(U)* [fear] Angst *die*; **to take fright** es mit der Angst zu tun bekommen - **2.** [shock] Schreck *der*; **to give sb a fright** jn erschrecken, jm einen Schreck ein|jagen.

frighten ['fraɪtn] *vt* Angst machen *(+ D)*.

frightened ['fraɪtnd] *adj* [person] verängstigt; [voice, expression] angsterfüllt; **to be frightened (of)** Angst haben (vor *(+ D)*).

frightening ['fraɪtnɪŋ] *adj* beängstigend.

frightful ['fraɪtfʊl] *adj* schrecklich.

frigid ['frɪdʒɪd] *adj* [sexually] frigide.

frill [frɪl] *n* - **1.** [on clothes] Rüsche *die* - **2.** *inf* [extra]: **with no frills** ohne Extras.

fringe [frɪndʒ] *n* - **1.** [on clothes, curtain] Fransen *Pl* - **2.** *UK* [of hair] Pony *der* - **3.** [edge] Rand *der*.

frisk [frɪsk] *vt* [search] durchsuchen.

frisky ['frɪskɪ] *adj inf* quicklebendig.

fritter ['frɪtər] *n* CULIN *in Pfannkuchenteig getauchtes und gebratenes Obst-, Gemüse- oder Fleischstück*. ◈ **fritter away** *vt sep* vergeuden.

frivolous ['frɪvələs] *adj* frivol.

frizzy ['frɪzɪ] *adj* kraus.

fro [frəʊ] ▷ **to**.

frock [frɒk] *n dated* Kleid *das*.

frog [frɒg] *n* [animal] Frosch *der*; **to have a frog in one's throat** einen Frosch im Hals haben.

frolic ['frɒlɪk] (*pt & pp* **-ked**, *cont* **-king**) *vi* herum|tollen.

from *(weak form* [frəm], *strong form* [frɒm]*)* *prep* - **1.** [expressing origin, source] von; **where did you get that from?** woher hast du das?; **I'm from England** ich bin aus England; **I bought it from a supermarket** ich habe es in einem Supermarkt gekauft; **the train from Manchester** der Zug aus Manchester; **we moved from Boston to Denver** wir sind von Boston nach Denver umgezogen - **2.** [expressing removal, deduction] von; **away from home** weg von zu Hause; **to take sthg away from sb** jm etw weg|nehmen; **take 5 (away) from 9** ziehe 5 von 9 ab; **he took a notebook from his pocket** er nahm ein Notizbuch aus der Tasche; **to drink from a cup** aus einer Tasse trinken - **3.** [expressing distance] von; **five miles from London** fünf Meilen von London entfernt; **it's not far from here** es ist nicht weit von hier - **4.** [expressing position] von; **from here you can see the valley** von hier aus kann man das Tal sehen - **5.** [expressing starting time] von an; **open from nine to five** von neun bis fünf geöffnet; **from next year** ab nächstem Jahr; **from now on** von nun an - **6.** [expressing change] von; **the price has gone up from one to two pounds** der Preis ist von einem Pfund auf zwei Pfund gestiegen - **7.** [expressing range]: **tickets cost from $10** Karten gibt es ab 10 Dollar; **it could take from two to six months** es könnte zwischen zwei und sechs Monaten dauern - **8.** [as a result of] von; **I'm tired from walking** ich bin vom Gehen müde; **to suffer from asthma** an Asthma leiden - **9.** [expressing protection] vor *(+ D)*; **sheltered from the wind** windgeschützt - **10.** [in comparisons]: **different from** anders als; **to distinguish good from bad** gut und böse auseinander halten - **11.** [indicating material]: **made from wood/plastic** aus Holz/Kunststoff (gemacht) - **12.** [on the evidence of]: **to speak from experience** aus Erfahrung sprechen; **from what I can see** so wie ich es verstehe; **to judge from appearances** nach dem Äußeren urteilen.

front [frʌnt] ◇ *n* - **1.** [most forward part] Vorderseite *die*; [of house] Vorderfront *die*; **at the front** vorne; **at the front of the train** vorne im Zug; **on the front of her dress** vorn auf ihrem Kleid; **to lie on one's front** auf dem Bauch liegen - **2.** MIL & METEOR Front *die* - **3.** [by the sea] (Strand)promenade *die* - **4.** [outward appearance]: **it's all a front** es ist alles nur Fassade. ◇ *adj* Vorder-, vordere(r) (s); [row, page] erste(r) (s); **front garden** Vorgarten *der*. ◆ **in front** *adv* vorne; **the people front** die vorne sitzenden/stehenden Leute. ◆ **in front of** *prep* vor *(+ D)*.

frontbench [ˌfrʌnt'bentʃ] *n* POL *führende Mitglieder der Regierung oder der Opposition.*

front door *n* [of house] Haustür *die*.

frontier ['frʌnˌtɪəʳ, *US* frʌn'tɪər] *n liter* & *fig* Grenze *die*.

front room *n* Wohnzimmer *das*.

front-runner *n* SPORT Läufer *der*, -in *die* an der Spitze; *fig* Spitzenkandidat *der*, -in *die*.

frost [frɒst] *n* - **1.** *(U)* [layer of ice] Frost *der*, Reif *der* - **2.** [weather] Frost *der*.

frostbite ['frɒstbaɪt] *n (U)* Erfrierungen *Pl*.

frosted ['frɒstɪd] *adj* - **1.** [opaque]: **frosted glass** Milchglas *das* - **2.** *US* CULIN mit Zuckerguss überzogen.

frosting ['frɒstɪŋ] *n US* CULIN Zuckerguss *der*.

frosty ['frɒstɪ] *adj* - **1.** *liter* & *fig* [cold] frostig - **2.** [field] bereift; [ground] gefroren.

froth [frɒθ] *n* Schaum *der*.

frown [fraʊn] *vi* die Stirn runzeln. ◆ **frown (up)on** *vt insep* missbilligen.

froze [frəʊz] *pt* ▷ **freeze**.

frozen ['frəʊzn] ◇ *pp* ▷ **freeze**. ◇ *adj* - **1.** [ground] gefroren; [pipes] eingefroren; [lake] zugefroren - **2.** [food] tiefgefroren - **3.** [very cold] eiskalt; **I'm frozen** mir ist eiskalt.

frugal ['fruːgl] *adj* - **1.** [meal] einfach - **2.** [person] sparsam.

fruit [fruːt] (*pl inv* OR **-s**) *n* - **1.** [food] Obst *das*; [variety of fruit] Frucht *die* - **2.** *fig* [result] Frucht *die*.

fruitcake ['fruːtkeɪk] *n Kuchen mit Trockenfrüchten.*

fruiterer ['fruːtərəʳ] *n UK* Obsthändler *der*, -in *die*.

fruitful ['fruːtfʊl] *adj* fruchtbar.

fruition [fruː'ɪʃn] *n*: **to come to fruition** [plans] Wirklichkeit werden; [hopes] in Erfüllung gehen.

fruit juice *n* Fruchtsaft *der*.

fruitless ['fruːtlɪs] *adj* fruchtlos.

fruit machine *n UK* Spielautomat *der*.

fruit salad *n* Obstsalat *der*.

frumpy ['frʌmpɪ] *adj inf* [clothes] unmodisch; [person] unmodisch gekleidet.

frustrate [frʌ'streɪt] *vt* - **1.** [person] frustrieren - **2.** [plan, attempt] vereiteln.

frustrated [frʌ'streɪtɪd] *adj* - **1.** [person] frustriert - **2.** [poet, artist] gescheitert.

frustration [frʌ'streɪʃn] *n* Frustration *die*.

fry [fraɪ] ◇ *vt* [food] braten; **to fry an egg** ein Spiegelei machen. ◇ *vi* [food] braten.

frying pan ['fraɪɪŋ-] *n* Bratpfanne *die*.

ft. (*abbr of* **foot**) & (*abbr of* **feet**) ft.

fuck [fʌk] *vt* & *vi vulg* ficken. ◆ **fuck off** *excl vulg* verpiss dich!

fudge [fʌdʒ] *n (U)* [sweet] *weiches Bonbon aus Milch, Zucker und Butter.*

fuel [fjʊəl] (*UK*) (*US*) ◇ *n* [for fire] Brennmaterial *das*; [for aircraft, ship] Treibstoff *der*; [for vehicle] Benzin *das*. ◇ *vt* [argument, violence] anlheizen.

fuel tank *n* Benzintank *der*.

fugitive ['fjuːdʒətɪv] *n*: **to be a fugitive from justice** vor der Justiz auf der Flucht sein.

fulfil *UK*, **fulfill** *US* [fʊl'fɪl] *vt* - **1.** [carry out - duty] erfüllen; [- promise] halten; [- role] auslfüllen - **2.** [satisfy - need] befriedigen; [- requirement] entsprechen *(+ D)*; [- hope, ambition] erfüllen.

fulfilment *UK*, **fulfillment** *US* [fʊl'fɪlmənt] *n (U)* - **1.** [satisfaction] Befriedigung *die* - **2.** [carrying through - of ambition, dream] Erfüllung *die*; [- of need] Befriedigung *die*.

full [fʊl] ◇ *adj* - **1.** [filled] voll; **I'm full (up)** [after meal] ich bin satt; **the bus is full** der Bus ist voll besetzt; **the room was full of furniture** das Zimmer war voll mit Möbeln; **his pockets were full of sweets** er hatte die Taschen voller Süßigkeiten - **2.** [complete - day, amount] ganz; [- details] genau; [- report] ausführlich - **3.** [plump - face] voll; [- figure] mollig - **4.** [skirt, sleeve] weit - **5.** [flavour] voll. ◇ *adv* [very]: **he knows full well that...** er weiß ganz genau, dass... ◇ *n*: **in full** vollständig.

full-blown [-'bləʊn] *adj* [heart attack] groß; [war] richtig; **full-blown Aids** Vollbild-Aids *das*.

full board *n (U)* Vollpension *die*.

full-fledged *adj US* = **fully-fledged**.

full moon *n* Vollmond *der*.

full-scale *adj* - **1.** [life-size] in Originalgröße - **2.** [thorough - inquiry] umfassend; [- war] total.

full stop *n* Punkt *der*.

full time *n UK* SPORT Spielende *das*. ◆ **full-time** ◇ *adj* [job, employment] Ganztags-; [worker] Vollzeit-. ◇ *adv* ganztags.

full up *adj* - **1.** [after meal] satt - **2.** [bus, train] voll.

fully ['fʊlɪ] *adv* - **1.** [completely] vollkommen; **fully trained/automatic** vollausgebildet/-automatisch - **2.** [in detail - answer] ausführlich; [- describe] detailliert.

fully-fledged *UK*, **full-fledged** *US* [-'fledʒd] *adj fig* [doctor, lawyer] vollausgebildet.

fumble ['fʌmbl] *vi* [in bag, pocket] wühlen; **to fumble for sthg** [for light switch] nach etw tasten; [for words] nach etw suchen.

fume [fjuːm] *vi* [with anger] kochen. ◆ **fumes** *npl* Dämpfe *Pl*; [from car] Abgase *Pl*; [from fire] Rauch *der*.

fumigate ['fju:mɪgeɪt] *vt* [room, building] ausǀräuchern.

fun [fʌn] *n* - **1.** [gen] Spaß *der*; **it's good fun** es macht viel Spaß; **to have fun** sich amüsieren; **for fun, for the fun of it** aus OR zum Spaß - **2.** [ridicule]: **to make fun of sb, to poke fun at sb** sich über jn lustig machen.

function ['fʌŋkʃn] ◇ *n* - **1.** [gen] Funktion *die* - **2.** [social event] Veranstaltung *die*. ◇ *vi* - **1.** [work] funktionieren - **2.** [serve]: **to function as** dienen als.

functional ['fʌŋkʃnəl] *adj* - **1.** [practical] funktionell - **2.** [operational] funktionsfähig.

fund [fʌnd] ◇ *n* - **1.** [amount of money] Fonds *der* - **2.** *fig* [of knowledge, experience] Fundus *der*. ◇ *vt* finanzieren. ◆ **funds** *npl* Gelder *Pl*; **public funds** öffentliche Mittel *Pl*.

fundamental [ˌfʌndə'mentl] *adj* - **1.** [basic - idea] grundlegend; [- principle, change, error] fundamental - **2.** [vital]: **to be fundamental (to)** von fundamentaler Bedeutung sein (für).

funding ['fʌndɪŋ] *n* Gelder *Pl*.

funeral ['fju:nərəl] *n* Beerdigung *die*.

funeral parlour *n* Beerdigungsinstitut *das*.

funfair ['fʌnfeəʳ] *n* Kirmes *die*.

fungus ['fʌŋgəs] (*pl* **-gi** [-gaɪ] OR **-guses**) *n* BOT Pilz *der*.

funnel ['fʌnl] (*UK*) (*US*) *n* - **1.** [tube] Trichter *der* - **2.** [on ship] Schornstein *der*.

funny ['fʌnɪ] *adj* - **1.** [amusing] lustig - **2.** [odd] komisch - **3.** [ill]: **I feel funny** mir ist komisch. ◆ **funnies** *npl US* Cartoons *Pl*.

fur [fɜ:ʳ] *n* - **1.** [on animal] Fell *das* - **2.** [garment] Pelz *der*.

fur coat *n* Pelzmantel *der*.

furious ['fjʊərɪəs] *adj* - **1.** [very angry] wütend - **2.** [violent] heftig; **at a furious pace/speed** mit rasender Geschwindigkeit.

furlong ['fɜ:lɒŋ] *n* Achtelmeile *die*.

furnace ['fɜ:nɪs] *n* [for melting metal] Schmelzofen *der*.

furnish ['fɜ:nɪʃ] *vt* - **1.** [room, house] einǀrichten - **2.** *fml* [provide - proof, explanation] liefern; **to furnish sb with sthg** jm etw liefern.

furnished ['fɜ:nɪʃt] *adj* möbliert.

furnishings ['fɜ:nɪʃɪŋz] *npl* Einrichtungsgegenstände *Pl*.

furniture ['fɜ:nɪtʃəʳ] *n (U)* Möbel *Pl*; **a piece of furniture** ein Möbelstück.

furrow ['fʌrəʊ] *n* - **1.** [in field] Furche *die* - **2.** [on forehead] Runzel *die*.

furry ['fɜ:rɪ] *adj* - **1.** [animal] mit dichtem Fell - **2.** [material] flauschig; **furry toy** Plüschtier *das*.

further ['fɜ:ðəʳ] ◇ *compar* ▷ **far**. ◇ *adv* - **1.** [gen] weiter; **further back** weiter hinten; [in time] weiter zurück; **further on** weiter; **the police decided not to take the matter any further** die Polizei entschied, die Angelegenheit nicht weiterzuverfolgen - **2.** [in addition] darüber hinaus. ◇ *adj* [additional] weitere(r) (s); **until further notice** bis auf Weiteres. ◇ *vt* [career] voranǀbringen; [aim] unterstützen.

further education *n UK* Erwachsenenbildung *die*.

furthermore [ˌfɜ:ðə'mɔ:ʳ] *adv* außerdem.

furthest ['fɜ:ðɪst] ◇ *superl* ▷ **far**. ◇ *adj* am weitesten entfernt. ◇ *adv* am weitesten.

furtive ['fɜ:tɪv] *adj* [glance] verstohlen; [behaviour] heimlichtuerisch.

fury ['fjʊərɪ] *n* Wut *die*.

fuse *UK*, **fuze** *US* [fju:z] ◇ *n* - **1.** [of plug] Sicherung *die* - **2.** [of bomb, firework] Zünder *der*. ◇ *vt* [ideas, styles] verbinden. ◇ *vi* ELEC: **the lights have fused** die Sicherung (für das Licht) ist durchgebrannt.

fusebox ['fju:zbɒks] *n* Sicherungskasten *der*.

fused [fju:zd] *adj* [plug] gesichert.

fuselage ['fju:zəlɑ:ʒ] *n* (Flugzeug)rumpf *der*.

fuss [fʌs] ◇ *n* Theater *das*; **to make a fuss** Aufhebens machen. ◇ *vi* sich aufǀregen.

fussy ['fʌsɪ] *adj* - **1.** [person] pingelig - **2.** [design, dress] verspielt.

futile ['fju:taɪl] *adj* zwecklos.

futon ['fu:tɒn] *n* Futon *der*.

future ['fju:tʃəʳ] ◇ *n* - **1.** [time ahead] Zukunft *die*; **in future** in Zukunft; **in the future** in der Zukunft - **2.** GRAM: **future (tense)** Futur *das*. ◇ *adj* künftig; **at a future date** zu einem späteren Zeitpunkt.

fuze *n, vt* & *vi US* = **fuse**.

fuzzy ['fʌzɪ] *adj* - **1.** [hair] kraus - **2.** [image, photo] unscharf - **3.** [ideas] wirr.

G

g[1] (*pl* **g's** OR **gs**), **G** (*pl* **G's** OR **Gs**) [dʒi:] *n* [letter] g *das*, G *das*. ◆ **G** ◇ *n* MUS G *das*. ◇ *abbr of* **good**.

g[2] [dʒi:] (*abbr of* **gram**) g.

gab [gæb] *n* ▷ **gift**.

gabble ['gæbl] ◇ *vt* herunterǀrasseln. ◇ *vi* brabbeln. ◇ *n* Gebrabbel *das*.

gable ['geɪbl] *n* Giebel *der*.

gadget ['gædʒɪt] *n* Gerät *das*.

Gaelic ['geɪlɪk] ◇ *adj* gälisch. ◇ *n* Gälisch(e) *das*.

gag [gæg] ◇ *n* - **1.** [for mouth] Knebel *der* - **2.** *inf* [joke] Gag *der*. ◇ *vt* knebeln.

gage *n* & *vt US* = **gauge**.

gaiety ['geɪətɪ] *n* Fröhlichkeit *die*.

gaily ['geɪlɪ] *adv* [cheerfully] fröhlich; [dressed] in leuchtenden Farben; **gaily coloured** farbenfroh.

gain [geɪn] ◇ *n* - **1.** [profit] Gewinn *der*; [advantage] Vorteil *der* - **2.** [increase] Zunahme *die*. ◇ *vt* - **1.** [support] gewinnen; [advantage] sich verschaffen; [reputation] erwerben; [victory] erringen - **2.** [increase]: **to gain weight** zu|nehmen; **to gain speed** schneller werden; **to gain strength/popularity** an Stärke/Beliebtheit gewinnen. ◇ *vi* - **1.** [increase]: **to gain in sthg** an etw *(D)* gewinnen - **2.** [profit]: **to gain (from/by sthg)** (von/durch etw) profitieren - **3.** [watch, clock] vor|gehen. ◆ **gain on** *vt insep*: **to gain on sb** jm (immer) näher kommen.

gait [geɪt] *n* Gang *der*.

gala ['gɑːlə] *n* [celebration] Festveranstaltung *die*.

galaxy ['gæləksɪ] *n* Galaxis *die*.

gale [geɪl] *n* Sturm *der*.

gall [gɔːl] *n*: **to have the gall to do sthg** die Frechheit haben, etw zu tun.

gallant *adj* - **1.** ['gælənt] [courageous] mutig - **2.** [gə'lænt, 'gælənt] [polite to women] galant.

gall bladder *n* Gallenblase *die*.

gallery ['gælərɪ] *n* - **1.** [gen] Galerie *die* - **2.** THEAT dritter Rang.

galley ['gælɪ] (*pl* **-s**) *n* [kitchen - of ship] Kombüse *die*; [- of aircraft] Bordküche *die*.

Gallic ['gælɪk] *adj* gallisch.

galling ['gɔːlɪŋ] *adj* ärgerlich.

gallivant [,gælɪ'vænt] *vi inf* sich herum|treiben.

gallon ['gælən] *n* Gallone *die*.

gallop ['gæləp] ◇ *n* - **1.** [pace of horse] Galopp *der* - **2.** [horse ride] Galoppritt *der*. ◇ *vi* [horse] galoppieren.

gallows ['gæləʊz] (*pl inv*) *n* Galgen *der*.

gallstone ['gɔːlstəʊn] *n* Gallenstein *der*.

galore [gə'lɔːʳ] *adv* in Hülle und Fülle.

galvanize, -ise ['gælvənaɪz] *vt* - **1.** TECH galvanisieren - **2.** [impel]: **to galvanize sb into action** jn dazu veranlassen, aktiv zu werden.

gamble ['gæmbl] ◇ *n* [risk] Risiko *das*. ◇ *vi* - **1.** [bet] (um Geld) spielen - **2.** [take risk]: **to gamble on sthg** sich auf etw *(A)* verlassen.

gambler ['gæmbləʳ] *n* Spieler *der*, -in *die*.

gambling ['gæmblɪŋ] *n* Spielen *das (um Geld)*.

game [geɪm] ◇ *n* - **1.** [gen] Spiel *das*; **fancy a game of chess/cards?** hast du Lust auf eine Partie Schach/Karten? - **2.** [hunted animals, meat] Wild *das* - **3.** *phr*: **the game's up** das Spiel ist aus; **to give the game away** alles verderben; **to play games with sb** sein Spiel mit jm treiben. ◇ *adj* - **1.** [brave] mutig - **2.** [willing]: **to be game for sthg** für etw bereit sein; **to be game to do sthg** bereit sein, etw zu tun. ◆ **games** ◇ *n* SCH Sport *der*. ◇ *npl* [sporting event] Spiele *Pl*.

gamekeeper ['geɪm,kiːpəʳ] *n* Wildhüter *der*.

game reserve *n* Wildreservat *das*.

gammon ['gæmən] *n geräucherter und gekochter Vorderschinken*.

gamut ['gæmət] *n* Skala *die*.

gang [gæŋ] *n* [of criminals] Bande *die*, Gang *die*; [of young people] Clique *die*. ◆ **gang up** *vi inf* sich zusammen|tun; **to gang up on sb** sich gegen jn verbünden.

gangrene ['gæŋgriːn] *n* Wundbrand *der*.

gangster ['gæŋstəʳ] *n* Gangster *der*.

gangway ['gæŋweɪ] *n* - **1.** *UK* [aisle] Gang *der* - **2.** [gangplank] Gangway *die*.

gaol [dʒeɪl] *n* & *vt UK* = **jail**.

gap [gæp] *n* - **1.** [empty space, omission] Lücke *die* - **2.** [in time] Abstand *der* - **3.** *fig* [disparity] Kluft *die*.

gape [geɪp] *vi* - **1.** [person] gaffen; **to gape at sb/sthg** jn/etw begaffen - **2.** [hole, shirt, wound] klaffen.

gaping ['geɪpɪŋ] *adj* - **1.** [person] gaffend - **2.** [hole, shirt, wound] klaffend.

gap year *n einjährige Pause zwischen Schule und Studium*.

garage [*UK* 'gærɑːʒ, 'gærɪdʒ, *US* gə'rɑːʒ] *n* - **1.** [for keeping car] Garage *die* - **2.** *UK* [for fuel] Tankstelle *die* - **3.** [for car repair] Werkstatt *die* - **4.** [for selling cars] Autohändler *der*.

garbage ['gɑːbɪdʒ] *n esp US* - **1.** [refuse] Müll *der* - **2.** *inf* [nonsense] Unsinn *der*.

garbage can *n US* Mülltonne *die*.

garbage truck *n US* Müllauto *das*.

garbled ['gɑːbld] *adj* entstellt.

garden ['gɑːdn] ◇ *n* - **1.** [private] Garten *der* - **2.** [public] Grünanlage *die*. ◇ *vi* gärtnern.

garden centre *n* Gartencenter *das*.

gardener ['gɑːdnəʳ] *n* - **1.** [professional] Gärtner *der*, -in *die* - **2.** [amateur] Hobbygärtner *der*, -in *die*.

gardening ['gɑːdnɪŋ] *n* Gartenarbeit *die*.

gargle ['gɑːgl] *vi* gurgeln.

gargoyle ['gɑːgɔɪl] *n* Wasserspeier *der*.

garish ['geərɪʃ] *adj* grell.

garland ['gɑːlənd] *n* Girlande *die*.

garlic ['gɑːlɪk] *n* Knoblauch *der*.

garlic bread *n (U)* Knoblauchbrot *das*.

garment ['gɑːmənt] *n* Kleidungsstück *das*.

garnish ['gɑːnɪʃ] ◇ *n* CULIN Garnierung *die*. ◇ *vt* CULIN garnieren.

garrison ['gærɪsn] *n* Garnison *die*.

garter ['gɑːtəʳ] *n* - **1.** [around leg] Strumpfband *das* - **2.** *US* [suspender] Strumpfhalter *der*.

gas [gæs] (*pl* **gases** OR **gasses**) ◇ *n* - **1.** [gen] Gas *das* - **2.** *US* [fuel for vehicle] Benzin *das*; **to step on the gas** *inf* aufs Gas treten OR steigen. ◇ *vt* [poison] vergasen.

gas cooker *n UK* Gasherd *der*.

gas fire *n UK* Gasofen *der*.

gas gauge *n US* Benzinuhr *die*.

gash [gæʃ] ◇ *n* tiefe Schnittwunde. ◇ *vt*: **to gash one's hand/arm** sich in die Hand/den Arm schneiden.

gasket ['gæskɪt] *n* Dichtung *die*.

gas mask *n* Gasmaske *die*.

gas meter *n* Gaszähler *der*, Gasuhr *die*.

gasoline ['gæsəliːn] *n US* Benzin *das*.

gasp [gɑːsp] ◇ *n* Keuchen *das*. ◇ *vi* - **1.** [breathe quickly] keuchen - **2.** [in shock, surprise] nach Luft schnappen.

gas pedal *n US* Gaspedal *das*.

gas station *n US* Tankstelle *die*.

gas stove *n* = **gas cooker**.

gas tank *n US* Benzintank *der*.

gastroenteritis ['gæstrəʊˌentə'raɪtɪs] *n* Magen-Darm-Katarr *der*.

gastronomy [gæs'trɒnəmɪ] *n* Gastronomie *die*.

gasworks ['gæswɜːks] (*pl inv*) *n* Gaswerk *das*.

gate [geɪt] *n* - **1.** [in wall, fence] Tor *das* - **2.** [at airport] Flugsteig *der*.

gatecrash ['geɪtkræʃ] *vt inf* hereinlplatzen.

gateway ['geɪtweɪ] *n* Tor *das*.

gather ['gæðəʳ] ◇ *vt* - **1.** [collect] sammeln; **to gather together** sich versammeln - **2.** [speed]: **to gather speed** schneller werden - **3.** [understand]: **to gather that** annehmen, dass; **as far as I can gather** soweit ich weiß - **4.** [into folds] raffen, kräuseln. ◇ *vi* [come together - people] sich versammeln; [- crowd] sich anlsammeln; [- clouds] sich zusammenlziehen.

gathering ['gæðərɪŋ] *n* Versammlung *die*.

gaudy ['gɔːdɪ] *adj* grell.

gauge, gage *US* [geɪdʒ] ◇ *n* - **1.** [measuring instrument] Messinstrument *das* - **2.** [calibre] Kaliber *das* - **3.** RAIL Spurweite *die*. ◇ *vt* - **1.** [measure, calculate] messen - **2.** [judge, predict] beurteilen.

gaunt [gɔːnt] *adj* hager.

gauntlet ['gɔːntlɪt] *n* (*phrase*): **to run the gauntlet** Spießbruten laufen; **to throw down the gauntlet (to sb)** (jm) den Fehdehandschuh hinlwerfen.

gauze [gɔːz] *n* Gaze *die*.

gave [geɪv] *pt* ▷ **give**.

gawky ['gɔːkɪ] *adj* unbeholfen.

gawp [gɔːp] *vi* gaffen; **to gawp at sb/sthg** jn/etw anlgaffen.

gay [geɪ] ◇ *adj* - **1.** [homosexual] schwul - **2.** [cheerful, lively] fröhlich - **3.** [brightly coloured] bunt. ◇ *n* [homosexual] Schwule *der*.

gay rights *npl* Rechte *Pl* von Homosexuellen.

gaze [geɪz] ◇ *n* Blick *der*. ◇ *vi*: **to gaze (at sb/sthg)** (jn/etw) anlstarren.

GB (*abbr of* **Great Britain**) *n* GB.

GCSE (*abbr of* **General Certificate of Secondary Education**) *n Abschlussprüfung an weiterführenden Schulen in England, Wales und Nordirland*.

GDP (*abbr of* **gross domestic product**) *n* BIP *das*.

gear [gɪəʳ] ◇ *n* - **1.** TECH [mechanism] Zahnrad *das* - **2.** [on car, bicycle] Gang *der*; **out of gear** im Leerlauf; **in gear** mit eingelegtem Gang - **3.** *(U)* [equipment, clothes] Ausrüstung *die*. ◇ *vt*: **to gear sthg to sb/sthg** etw auf jn/etw auslrichten. ◆ **gear up** *vi*: **to gear up for sthg** sich für etw rüsten; **to gear up to do sthg** sich dafür rüsten, etw zu tun.

gearbox ['gɪəbɒks] *n* Getriebegehäuse *das*; **six-speed gearbox** Sechsganggetriebe *das*.

gear lever, gear stick *UK*, **gear shift** *US n* Schaltknüppel *der*.

geese [giːs] *Pl* ▷ **goose**.

gel [dʒel] ◇ *n* Gel *das*. ◇ *vi fig* [idea, plan] Gestalt anlnehmen.

gelatin ['dʒelətɪn], **gelatine** [ˌdʒelə'tiːn] *n* Gelatine *die*.

gelignite ['dʒelɪgnaɪt] *n* Plastiksprengstoff *der*.

gem [dʒem] *n* - **1.** [jewel] (geschliffener) Edelstein - **2.** *fig* [person] Juwel *das*.

Gemini ['dʒemɪnaɪ] *n* [sign] Zwillinge *Pl*.

gender ['dʒendəʳ] *n* Geschlecht *das*.

gene [dʒiːn] *n* Gen *das*.

general ['dʒenərəl] ◇ *adj* [gen] allgemein. ◇ *n* MIL General *der*. ◆ **in general** *adv* - **1.** [as a whole] im Allgemeinen - **2.** [usually] gewöhnlich.

general anaesthetic *n* Vollnarkose *die*.

general delivery *adv US* postlagernd.

general election *n* Parlamentswahlen *Pl*.

generalization [ˌdʒenərəlaɪ'zeɪʃn] *n* Verallgemeinerung *die*.

general knowledge *n* Allgemeinbildung *die*.

generally ['dʒenərəlɪ] *adv* - **1.** [usually] im Allgemeinen - **2.** [in a general way] allgemein.

general practitioner *n* Arzt *der*, Ärztin *die* für Allgemeinmedizin.

general public *n*: **the general public** die breite Öffentlichkeit.

general store *n* Gemischtwarenhandlung *die*.

general strike *n* Generalstreik *der*.

generate ['dʒenəreɪt] *vt* - **1.** [energy, power, heat] erzeugen - **2.** [interest, excitement] hervorlrufen; [jobs, employment] schaffen.

generation [,dʒenə'reɪʃn] *n* - **1.** [gen] Generation *die* - **2.** [of energy, power, heat] Erzeugung *die*.

generator ['dʒenəreɪtəʳ] *n* Generator *der*.

generosity [,dʒenə'rɒsətɪ] *n* Freigebigkeit *die*, Großzügigkeit *die*.

generous ['dʒenərəs] *adj* großzügig.

genetic [dʒɪ'netɪk] *adj* genetisch. ◆ **genetics** *n* Genetik *die*, Vererbungslehre *die*.

genetically modified *adj* genmanipuliert, gentechnisch verändert.

Geneva [dʒɪ'ni:və] *n* Genf *nt*.

genial ['dʒi:njəl] *adj* jovial.

genitals ['dʒenɪtlz] *npl* Genitalien *Pl*.

genius ['dʒi:njəs] (*pl* **-es**) *n* Genie *das*.

gent [dʒent] *n UK inf* Gentleman *der*. ◆ **gents** *n UK* [toilets] Herrentoilette *die*.

genteel [dʒen'ti:l] *adj* - **1.** [refined] vornehm - **2.** [affected] geziert.

gentle ['dʒentl] *adj* - **1.** [person] sanftmütig - **2.** [rain, breeze, movement] sanft, leicht - **3.** [slope, curve] sanft - **4.** [hint] zart.

gentleman ['dʒentlmən] (*pl* **-men** [-mən]) *n* - **1.** [well-bred man] Gentleman *der* - **2.** [man] Herr *der*.

gently ['dʒentlɪ] *adv* - **1.** [speak] sanft - **2.** [blow] leicht; [move, heat] behutsam - **3.** [slope, curve] allmählich.

genuine ['dʒenjʊɪn] *adj* - **1.** [real] echt - **2.** [sincere] aufrichtig.

geography [dʒɪ'ɒgrəfɪ] *n* [science] Geografie *die*; [in school] Erdkunde *die*.

geology [dʒɪ'ɒlədʒɪ] *n* Geologie *die*.

geometric(al) [,dʒɪə'metrɪk(l)] *adj* geometrisch.

geometry [dʒɪ'ɒmətrɪ] *n* Geometrie *die*.

geranium [dʒɪ'reɪnjəm] (*pl* **-s**) *n* Geranie *die*.

geriatric [,dʒerɪ'ætrɪk] *adj* - **1.** [of old people] geriatrisch - **2.** *pej* [very old, inefficient] veraltet, altersschwach.

germ [dʒɜ:m] *n liter* & *fig* Keim *der*.

German ['dʒɜ:mən] ◇ *adj* deutsch. ◇ *n* - **1.** [person] Deutsche *der, die* - **2.** [language] Deutsch(e) *das*.

German measles *n* Röteln *die*.

Germany ['dʒɜ:mənɪ] *n* Deutschland *nt*.

germinate ['dʒɜ:mɪneɪt] *vi liter* & *fig* keimen.

gesticulate [dʒes'tɪkjʊleɪt] *vi* gestikulieren.

gesture ['dʒestʃəʳ] ◇ *n* Geste *die*. ◇ *vi*: **to gesture to** *OR* **towards sb** auf jn deuten.

get [get] (*UK pt & pp* **got**; *US pt* **got**, *pp* **gotten**) ◇ *vt* - **1.** [obtain] bekommen; [buy] kaufen; **she got a job** sie hat eine Stelle gefunden; **he got us two tickets** er hat uns zwei Karten besorgt - **2.** [receive] bekommen; **I got a book for Christmas** ich habe zu Weihnachten ein Buch bekommen; **when did you get the news?** wann haben Sie die Nachricht bekommen? - **3.** [train, plane, bus] nehmen; **let's get a taxi** lass uns ein Taxi nehmen - **4.** [fetch] holen; **could you get me the manager?** [on phone] könnten Sie mir den Geschäftsführer geben?; **can I get you something to eat/drink?** möchtest du etwas essen/trinken? - **5.** [illness] bekommen; **I got this cold while I was on holiday** ich habe mir diese Erkältung im Urlaub zugezogen - **6.** [catch] fangen; **the police have got the killer** die Polizei hat den Mörder gefasst - **7.** [cause to be done]: **to get sthg done** etw machen lassen; **can I get my car repaired here?** kann ich mein Auto hier reparieren lassen? - **8.** [cause to become]: **she got the children ready for school** sie machte die Kinder für die Schule fertig; **I can't get the car started** ich kriege das Auto nicht an; **to get lunch** das Mittagessen zubereiten - **9.** [ask, tell]: **to get sb to do sthg** jn bitten, etw zu tun - **10.** [move]: **I can't get it through the door** ich bekomme es nicht durch die Tür - **11.** [understand] verstehen; **I don't get it** *inf* das verstehe ich nicht - **12.** [time, chance] haben; **we didn't get the chance to see everything** wir hatten nicht die Gelegenheit, uns alles anzuschauen; **I haven't got (the) time** ich habe keine Zeit - **13.** [idea, feeling] haben; **I get a lot of enjoyment from it** ich habe viel Spaß daran - **14.** [answer - phone]: **could you get the phone?** könntest du ans Telefon gehen? - **15.** *phr*: **we get a lot of German tourists here** zu uns kommen viele deutsche Touristen; **we get a lot of rain here in winter** hier regnet es viel im Winter. ◇ *vi* - **1.** [become] werden; **it's getting late** es wird spät; **to get lost** sich verirren; **get lost!** *inf* hau ab!; **to get ready** sich fertig machen - **2.** [into particular state, position]: **to get into trouble** in Schwierigkeiten geraten; **how do you get to the river from here?** wie kommt man von hier zum Fluss?; **to get dressed** sich anlziehen; **to get married** heiraten - **3.** [arrive] anlkommen; **when does the train get here?** wann kommt der Zug hier an? - **4.** [eventually succeed]: **I finally got to meet him last week** letzte Woche habe ich ihn endlich getroffen; **she got to like the class** allmählich gefiel ihr der Kurs; **to get to know sb** jn kennen lernen - **5.** [progress]: **how far have you got?** wie weit bist du gekommen?; **we're getting nowhere** so kommen wir nicht weiter. ◇ *aux vb* werden; **to get delayed** aufgehalten werden; **to get killed** getötet werden; **to get excited** aufgeregt werden; **let's get going** *OR* **moving !** also los! ◆ **get about** *vi* - **1.** [move from place to place] herumlkommen; **he gets about a lot** er kommt viel herum - **2.** [news, rumour] sich verbreiten. ◆ **get along** *vi* - **1.** [manage]: **to get along (without sb/sthg)** (ohne jn/etw) zurecht|kommen - **2.** [progress]: **how are you getting along?** wie kommst du voran? - **3.** [in relationship]: **to get along (with sb)** (mit jm) aus|kommen - **4.** [leave] gehen; **I must be getting along** ich muss jetzt gehen. ◆ **get around, get round** ◇ *vt insep* [problem] um|gehen. ◇ *vi* - **1.** [move from place to place] herum|kommen - **2.** [circulate - news] sich verbreiten - **3.** [eventually do]: **to get around to sthg/to doing sthg** dazu kommen, etw zu tun. ◆ **get at** *vt insep* - **1.** [reach] heran|kommen an *(+ A)*; [truth] heraus|bekommen - **2.** [imply]: **what are you getting at?** worauf willst du hinaus? - **3.** *inf* [nag]: **stop getting at me!** nörgel nicht dauernd an mir rum! ◆ **get away** ◇ *vt sep*: **get him away from here** bring ihn von hier weg. ◇ *vi* - **1.** [leave] weg|kommen; **I need to get away by five** ich muss um fünf Uhr gehen OR weg - **2.** [escape] entkommen. ◆ **get away with** *vt insep* durchkommen mit. ◆ **get back** ◇ *vt sep* - **1.** [recover, regain] zurück|bekommen - **2.** [take revenge on]: **to get sb back for sthg** jm etw heim|zahlen. ◇ *vi* - **1.** [return] zurück|kommen - **2.** [move away] zurück|treten. ◆ **get back to** *vt insep* - **1.** [return to previous state, activity]: **to get back to sleep** wieder ein|schlafen; **to get back to work** zur Arbeit zurück|kehren - **2.** [phone back]: **I'll get back to you later** ich rufe Sie später zurück. ◆ **get by** *vi* [manage, survive] zurecht|kommen; **to get by on sthg** mit etw aus|kommen. ◆ **get down** *vt sep* - **1.** [depress] deprimieren; **don't let it get you down** lass dich davon nicht unterkriegen - **2.** [fetch from higher level] herunter|holen - **3.** [write] auf|schreiben. ◆ **get down to** *vt insep*: **to get down to doing sthg** sich daran machen, etw zu tun; **to get down to sthg** sich an etw *(A)* machen. ◆ **get in** *vi* - **1.** [arrive] an|kommen - **2.** [into car, bus] ein|steigen. ◆ **get into** *vt insep* - **1.** [car] ein|steigen in *(+ A)* - **2.** [become involved in] geraten in *(+ A)*; **to get into an argument with sb** mit jm in Streit geraten - **3.** [enter into a particular situation, state] geraten in *(+ A)*; **to get into a panic** in Panik geraten; **to get into trouble** in Schwierigkeiten geraten. ◆ **get off** ◇ *vt sep* [remove - clothes, shoes] aus|ziehen; [- stain] heraus|bekommen; [- lid] ab|bekommen; **to get sb/sthg off one's hands** jn/etw los|werden. ◇ *vt insep* [bus, train] aus|steigen aus; [bicycle] ab|steigen von. ◇ *vi* - **1.** [from train, bus] aus|steigen; [from bicycle] ab|steigen - **2.** [leave] los|gehen; [in car] los|fahren - **3.** [escape punishment] davon|kommen. ◆ **get on** ◇ *vt insep* [bus, train] ein|steigen in *(+ A)*; [bicycle] steigen auf *(+ A)*. ◇ *vi* - **1.** [on train, bus] ein|steigen; [on bicycle] auf|steigen - **2.** [in relationship] sich verstehen; **how do you get on with his family?** wie kommst du mit seiner Familie aus? - **3.** [progress]: **how are you getting on?** wie kommst du voran? - **4.** [proceed]: **to get on (with sthg)** (mit etw) weiter|machen - **5.** [have success] Erfolg haben. ◆ **get out** ◇ *vt sep* - **1.** [take out] heraus|nehmen - **2.** [remove]: **how do you get wine stains out?** wie bekommt man Weinflecken heraus? ◇ *vi* - **1.** [from car, bus] aus|steigen - **2.** [become known - news] heraus|kommen. ◆ **get out of** *vt insep* - **1.** [car, bus, train] aus|steigen aus - **2.** [escape from] heraus|kommen aus; **to get out of a difficult situation** sich aus einer schwierigen Lage befreien - **3.** [avoid]: **to get out of sthg** um etw herum|kommen; **to get out of doing sthg** darum herum|kommen, etw zu tun. ◆ **get over** ◇ *vt insep* - **1.** [recover from] hinweg|kommen über *(+ A)* - **2.** [overcome] überwinden. ◇ *vt sep* [communicate] verständlich machen. ◆ **get round** *vt insep* & *vi* = **get around**. ◆ **get through** ◇ *vt insep* - **1.** [work, task] erledigen - **2.** [exam] bestehen - **3.** [food, drink] verbrauchen - **4.** [survive] überstehen. ◇ *vi* - **1.** [on phone] durch|kommen; **I couldn't get through to her** ich konnte sie nicht erreichen - **2.** [make oneself understood]: **I can't get through to her** ich konnte es ihr nicht verständlich machen. ◆ **get to** *vt insep inf* [annoy] auf die Nerven gehen; **don't let him get to you** lass dich von ihm nicht ärgern. ◆ **get together** ◇ *vt sep* - **1.** [organize - team, report] zusammen|stellen; [- demonstration] organisieren - **2.** [gather - people] zusammen|bringen; [- belongings] zusammen|packen. ◇ *vi* zusammen|kommen. ◆ **get up** ◇ *vi* auf|stehen. ◇ *vt insep* - **1.** [organize - petition etc] organisieren - **2.** [gather]: **to get up speed** in Fahrt kommen. ◆ **get up to** *vt insep inf* an|stellen; **I wonder what they're getting up to** ich frage mich, was die da treiben.

get-together *n inf* Zusammenkunft *die*.

ghastly ['gɑːstlɪ] *adj* - **1.** *inf* [very bad, unpleasant] scheußlich, grässlich - **2.** [horrifying, macabre] schrecklich, schauerlich.

gherkin ['gɜːkɪn] *n* Gewürzgurke *die*.

ghetto ['getəʊ] (*pl* **-s** OR **-es**) *n* Getto *das*.

ghetto blaster [-ˌblɑːstəʳ] *n inf* Gettoblaster *der*.

ghost [gəʊst] *n* Geist *der*, Gespenst *das*.

giant ['dʒaɪənt] ◇ *adj* riesig. ◇ *n* [very tall man] Riese *der*.

gibberish ['dʒɪbərɪʃ] *n* [meaningless] Unsinn *der*, Quatsch *der*; [hard to understand] Kauderwelsch *das*.

gibe [dʒaɪb] *n* Seitenhieb *der*.

Gibraltar [dʒɪ'brɔːltəʳ] *n* Gibraltar *nt*.

giddy ['gɪdɪ] *adj* [dizzy] schwindelig.

gift [gɪft] *n* - **1.** [present] Geschenk *das* - **2.** [talent] Talent *das*, Begabung *die*; **to have a gift for sthg** ein Talent OR eine Begabung für etw haben; **to have a gift for doing sthg** ein Talent OR eine Begabung haben, etw zu tun; **the gift of the gab** die Überzeugungsgabe.

gift certificate *n US* = **gift token**.

gifted ['gɪftɪd] *adj* talentiert, begabt.

gift token, gift voucher *UK*, **gift certificate** *US n* Geschenkgutschein *der*.

gift wrap *n* Geschenkpapier *das*.

gig [gɪg] *n inf* Gig *der*, Konzert *das*.

gigabyte [gɪgə'baɪt] *n* Gigabyte *das*.

gigantic [dʒaɪ'gæntɪk] *adj* gigantisch.

giggle ['gɪgl] *vi* [laugh] kichern.

gilded ['gɪldɪd] *adj* = **gilt**.

gills [gɪlz] *npl* Kiemen *Pl*.

gilt [gɪlt] ◇ *adj* vergoldet. ◇ *n* [gold layer] Vergoldung *die*.

gimmick ['gɪmɪk] *n pej* Spielerei *die*.

gin [dʒɪn] *n* Gin *der*; **gin and tonic** Gin Tonic *der*.

ginger ['dʒɪndʒəʳ] ◇ *adj UK* [colour - hair] rotblond; [- cat] rötlichbraun. ◇ *n* Ingwer *der*.

ginger ale *n* Ginger Ale *das*.

ginger beer *n* Ingwerbier *das*.

gingerbread ['dʒɪndʒəbred] *n (U)* [biscuit] *Pfefferkuchen mit Ingwergeschmack*.

gingerly ['dʒɪndʒəlɪ] *adv* vorsichtig.

gipsy ['dʒɪpsɪ] ◇ *adj* Zigeuner-. ◇ *n* Zigeuner *der*, -in *die*.

giraffe [dʒɪ'rɑːf] (*pl inv* OR **-s**) *n* Giraffe *die*.

girder ['gɜːdəʳ] *n* Träger *der*.

girdle ['gɜːdl] *n* [corset] Mieder *das*.

girl [gɜːl] *n* Mädchen *das*; [daughter] Tochter *die*, Mädchen *das*.

girlfriend ['gɜːlfrend] *n* Freundin *die*.

girl guide *UK*, **girl scout** *US n* Pfadfinderin *die*.

giro ['dʒaɪrəʊ] (*pl* **-s**) *n UK* [system] Giro *das*; **giro (cheque)** *Giroscheck für Sozialhilfeempfänger*.

gist [dʒɪst] *n* Wesentliche *das*; **to get the gist (of sthg)** das Wesentliche (einer Sache *(G)*) mit|bekommen.

give [gɪv] (*pt* **gave**, *pp* **given**) ◇ *vt* - **1.** [gen] geben; **to give sb sthg** jm etw geben; **to give sb a push/kiss** jm einen Schubs/Kuss geben; **to give sb a look/smile** jn an|sehen/an|lächeln; **to give a cry** auf|schreien - **2.** [as present]: **to give sb sthg** jm etw schenken; [as donation] jm etw spenden - **3.** [speech] halten - **4.** [attention, time]: **he gives the issue a lot of attention** er widmet der Sache viel Aufmerksamkeit - **5.** [communicate] geben; **when will you give me your decision?** wann werden Sie mir Ihre Entscheidung mitteilen?; **give her my regards** grüß sie schön von mir - **6.** [produce] machen; **to give sb a surprise** jm eine Überraschung bereiten; **to give sb pleasure/trouble** jm Freude/Probleme bereiten OR machen; **to give sb a fright** jn erschrecken; **what gave you that idea?** wie bist du auf diese Idee gekommen? ◇ *vi* [yield] nach|geben. ◇ *n* [elasticity] Nachgiebigkeit *die*. ◆ **give or take** *prep*: **5,000 people, give or take a few hundred** schätzungsweise 5000 Leute. ◆ **give away** *vt sep* - **1.** [hand over] weg|geben - **2.** [reveal] verraten; **to give the game away** alles verraten. ◆ **give back** *vt sep* zurück|geben. ◆ **give in** *vi* - **1.** [agree unwillingly] nach|geben; **to give in to sb/sthg** jm/etw nach|geben - **2.** [admit defeat] sich geschlagen geben. ◆ **give off** *vt insep* ab|geben. ◆ **give out** ◇ *vt sep* [distribute] aus|teilen. ◇ *vi* [fail - legs, machine] versagen; [- strength, supply] zu Ende gehen. ◆ **give up** ◇ *vt sep* - **1.** [stop, abandon] auf|geben; **to give up doing sthg** auf|hören, etw zu tun - **2.** [surrender]: **to give o.s. up (to sb)** sich (jm) ergeben. ◇ *vi* [admit defeat] auf|geben.

given ['gɪvn] ◇ *adj* - **1.** [fixed] bestimmt - **2.** [prone]: **to be given to sthg** zu etw neigen; **to be given to doing sthg** die Angewohnheit haben, etw zu tun. ◇ *prep* [taking into account] angesichts *(+ G)*; **given that...** angesichts der Tatsache, dass...

given name *n US* Vorname *der*.

glacier ['glæsjəʳ] *n* Gletscher *der*.

glad [glæd] *adj* - **1.** [happy] froh; **to be glad about sthg** sich über etw *(A)* freuen - **2.** [grateful]: **to be glad of sthg** dankbar für etw sein.

gladly ['glædlɪ] *adv* [willingly, eagerly] gern(e).

glamor *n US* = **glamour**.

glamorous ['glæmərəs] *adj* [film star, lifestyle] glamourös; [job] Traum-.

glamour *UK*, **glamor** *US* ['glæməʳ] *n* [of film star, lifestyle] Glamour *der*; [of job] Reiz *der*.

glance [glɑːns] ◇ *n* Blick *der*; **at a glance** auf einen Blick; **at first glance** auf den ersten Blick. ◇ *vi*: **to glance at sb** jn kurz an|sehen; **to glance at sthg** einen Blick auf etw *(A)* werfen. ◆ **glance off** *vt insep* [subj: ball, bullet] ab|prallen an *(+ D)*; [subj: light] reflektiert werden von.

gland [glænd] *n* Drüse *die*.

glandular fever [,glændjʊləʳ-] *n* Drüsenfieber *das*.

glare [gleəʳ] ◇ *n* - **1.** [scowl] langer wütender Blick - **2.** *(U)* [of light, sun] greller Schein; **the glare of publicity** das Rampenlicht der Öffentlichkeit. ◇ *vi* - **1.** [scowl] böse blicken; **to glare at sb/sthg** jn/etw böse an|starren - **2.** [light, sun] grell scheinen.

glaring ['gleərɪŋ] *adj* - **1.** [error, example] eklatant - **2.** [light, sun] grell.

glass [glɑːs] ◇ *n* - **1.** [gen] Glas *das*; **a glass of wine** ein Glas Wein - **2.** *(U)* [glassware] Glaswaren *Pl*. ◇ *comp* Glas-. ◆ **glasses** *npl* [spectacles] Brille *die*; [binoculars] Fernglas *das*; **a pair of glasses** eine Brille.

glaze [gleɪz] ◇ *n* Glasur *die*. ◇ *vt* [pottery & CULIN] glasieren.

glazier ['gleɪzjəʳ] *n* Glaser *der*, -in *die*.

gleam [gli:m] ◇ *n* [of surface] Schimmer *der*; [of light, sunset] Schein *der*. ◇ *vi* [surface, object] schimmern; [gold, brass] glänzen; [light] scheinen; [eyes] funkeln.

gleaming ['gli:mɪŋ] *adj* [surface, object] schimmernd; [gold, brass] glänzend; [light] scheinend; [eyes] funkelnd.

glean [gli:n] *vt* [gather] zusammen|tragen.

glee [gli:] *n* [joy] Freude *die*; [gloating] Schadenfreude *die*.

glen [glen] *n Ireland & Scotland* enges Tal.

glib [glɪb] *adj pej* - **1.** [answer, excuse] leichthin gesagt - **2.** [person] aalglatt.

glide [glaɪd] *vi* - **1.** [move smoothly - boat] gleiten; [- dancer] schweben - **2.** [fly] schweben.

glider ['glaɪdəʳ] *n* Segelflugzeug *das*.

gliding ['glaɪdɪŋ] *n* Segelfliegen *das*.

glimmer ['glɪməʳ] *n* - **1.** [faint light] schwacher Schein - **2.** *fig*: **she didn't show a glimmer of interest/understanding** sie zeigte nicht die leiseste Spur von Interesse/Verständnis.

glimpse [glɪmps] ◇ *n* [look] flüchtiger Blick. ◇ *vt* - **1.** [catch sight of] flüchtig OR kurz sehen - **2.** [perceive]: **to glimpse sb's true feelings** einen Eindruck von js wahren Gefühlen bekommen.

glint [glɪnt] ◇ *n* - **1.** [of metal, sunlight] Glitzern *das* - **2.** [in eyes]: **there was a glint of anger in his eyes** seine Augen funkelten böse. ◇ *vi* - **1.** [metal, sunlight] glitzern - **2.** [eyes] funkeln.

glisten ['glɪsn] *vi* [gold, lips] glänzen; [lake, raindrops] glitzern.

glitter ['glɪtəʳ] ◇ *n* - **1.** [of object, light] Glitzern *das*; [of diamonds, stars] Funkeln *das* - **2.** [decoration, make-up] Glitzerstaub *der*. ◇ *vi* glitzern; [diamonds, stars] funkeln.

gloat [gləʊt] *vi*: **to gloat (over sthg)** [over sb's misfortune] sich hämisch (über etw *(A)*) freuen; [over one's own success] sich selbstzufrieden (über etw *(A)*) freuen.

global ['gləʊbl] *adj* global; [economy, peace] Welt-.

global warming [-'wɔ:mɪŋ] *n* Erwärmung *die* der Erdatmosphäre.

globe [gləʊb] *n* - **1.** [Earth]: **the globe** die Erde - **2.** [sphere representing world] Globus *der*.

gloom [glu:m] *n* - **1.** [darkness] Düsterkeit *die* - **2.** [unhappiness] Trübsinn *der*.

gloomy ['glu:mɪ] *adj* - **1.** [place, landscape, weather] düster - **2.** [person, atmosphere] trübsinnig - **3.** [outlook] düster; [news] bedrückend.

glorious ['glɔ:rɪəs] *adj* - **1.** [illustrious] glorreich - **2.** [wonderful] herrlich.

glory ['glɔ:rɪ] *n* - **1.** [fame, honour] Ruhm *der* - **2.** [splendour] Herrlichkeit *die*.

gloss [glɒs] *n* - **1.** [shine] Glanz *der* - **2.**: **gloss (paint)** Lackfarbe *die*. ◆ **gloss over** *vt insep* [treat briefly] nur ganz kurz erwähnen; [hide] unter den Teppich kehren.

glossary ['glɒsərɪ] *n* Glossar *das*.

glossy ['glɒsɪ] *adj* glänzend; [photo, paper] Glanz-.

glove [glʌv] *n* Handschuh *der*; **to fit like a glove** [garment] wie angegossen passen.

glove compartment *n* Handschuhfach *das*.

glow [gləʊ] ◇ *n* [of fire, light, sunset] Schein *der*. ◇ *vi* [light] scheinen; [fire, sky] glühen.

glower ['glaʊəʳ] *vi* wütend drein|blicken; **to glower at sb/sthg** jn/etw wütend an|blicken.

glucose ['glu:kəʊs] *n* Glukose *die*.

glue [glu:] (*cont* **glueing** OR **gluing**) ◇ *n* Klebstoff *der*. ◇ *vt* kleben; **to glue sthg to sthg** etw an etw *(A)* kleben.

glum [glʌm] *adj* trübsinnig.

glut [glʌt] *n*: **glut (of sthg)** Überangebot *das* (an etw *(D)*).

glutton ['glʌtn] *n* Vielfraß *der*; **to be a glutton for punishment** ein Masochist sein.

GM *adj abbr of* **genetically modified**.

GMO (*abbr of* **genetically modified organism**) *n* GVO *der*.

gnarled [nɑ:ld] *adj* knorrig.

gnat [næt] *n* Mücke *die*.

gnaw [nɔ:] *vt* nagen an *(+ D)*; [fingernails] kauen an *(+ D)*; **to gnaw a hole in sthg** ein Loch in etw *(A)* nagen.

gnome [nəʊm] *n* Gnom *der*; [in garden] Gartenzwerg *der*.

GNP (*abbr of* **gross national product**) *n* BSP *das*.

go [gəʊ] (*pt* **went**, *pp* **gone**, *pl* **goes**) ◇ *vi* - **1.** [move] gehen; [by vehicle, travel] fahren; [by plane] fliegen; **to go shopping/for a walk** einkaufen/spazieren gehen; **I'll go and collect the cases** ich gehe die Koffer abholen; **to go home/to school** nach Hause/in die Schule gehen; **to go to Austria** nach Österreich fahren; **to go by bus** mit dem Bus fahren; **to go by plane** fliegen; **to go to work** zur Arbeit gehen - **2.** [leave] gehen; [in vehicle] fahren; **it's time we went** es wird Zeit, dass wir gehen; **let's go!** gehen wir!; **when does the bus go?** wann fährt der Bus ab?; **go away!** geh weg! - **3.** [lead]: **where does this path go?** wohin führt dieser Weg? - **4.** [time] vergehen - **5.** [progress - negotiations, preparations, business] laufen; **how are your studies going?** wie läuft es mit deinem Studium?; **how did the party go?** wie war die Party?; **to go well** gut gehen; **how's it going?** wie gehts? - **6.** [become] werden; **she went pale** sie wurde bleich; **to go bankrupt** Bankrott machen - **7.** [be]: **our cries went unheard** unsere Rufe blieben ungehört;

to go hungry hungern - **8.** [expressing future tense]: **to be going to do sthg** etw tun werden; **it's going to rain tomorrow** morgen wird es regnen; **we're going to go to Switzerland** wir fahren in die Schweiz; **she's going to have a baby** sie bekommt ein Baby - **9.** [function - gen] laufen; [- watch, clock] gehen - **10.** [become damaged] kaputt|gehen; **the fuse has gone** die Sicherung ist herausgesprungen - **11.** [bell, alarm] los|gehen; **the bell went** es klingelte - **12.** [match] zusammen|passen; **to go with** passen zu; **red wine doesn't go with fish** Rotwein passt nicht zu Fisch - **13.** [fit] passen, gehen; **it won't go into my case** es geht OR passt nicht in meinen Koffer - **14.** [belong] kommen; **the plates go in the cupboard** die Teller kommen in den Schrank - **15.** [in division] gehen; **three into two won't go** zwei durch drei geht nicht - **16.** *inf* [with negative - giving advice]: **now, don't go catching cold** erkälte dich bloß nicht - **17.** *inf* [expressing irritation]: **he's gone and broken my computer!** er hat doch tatsächlich meinen Computer kaputtgemacht!; **now what's he gone and done?** was hat er jetzt wieder gemacht?; **you've gone and done it now!** jetzt hast du es geschafft! ◇ *n* - **1.** [turn]: **it's your go** du bist dran - **2.** *inf* [attempt] Versuch *der*; **to have a go at sthg** etw versuchen; **to have a go on sthg** etw aus|probieren; **'50p a go'** 'jede Runde 50 Pence' - **3.** *phr*: **to have a go at sb** *inf* [criticize] jn zur Schnecke machen. ◆ **to go** *adv* [remaining]: **how long is there to go until Christmas?** wie lange ist es noch bis Weihnachten? ◆ **go about** ◇ *vt insep* [perform]: **to go about one's business** seinen Geschäften nach|gehen. ◇ *vi* = **go around**. ◆ **go ahead** *vi* - **1.**: **to go ahead (with sthg)** (mit etw) an|fangen OR beginnen; **go ahead!** bitte! - **2.** [take place] statt|finden. ◆ **go along** *vi*: **he was making it up as he went along** er sagte einfach, was ihm gerade in den Sinn kam. ◆ **go along with** *vt insep* [idea, plan] zul|stimmen *(+ D)*. ◆ **go around** *vi* - **1.** [associate]: **to go around with sb** mit jm herum|ziehen - **2.** [joke, illness, story] herum|gehen; [rumour] um|gehen. ◆ **go away** *vi* weg|gehen; [by vehicle] weg|fahren; **go away!** geh weg! ◆ **go back** *vi* - **1.** [return] zurück|gehen; [by vehicle] zurück|fahren - **2.** [to activity]: **to go back to work** [after interruption] die Arbeit wieder auf|nehmen; [after holiday] wieder arbeiten gehen; **to go back to sleep** wieder ein|schlafen - **3.** [date from]: **their friendship goes back to 1955** sie sind schon seit 1955 befreundet. ◆ **go back on** *vt insep*: **to go back on one's word** sein Wort nicht halten. ◆ **go by** ◇ *vi* [time] vergehen. ◇ *vt insep* - **1.** [be guided by - instincts] folgen *(+ D)*; [- instructions] befolgen - **2.** [judge by - appearances] gehen nach; **going by her accent, I'd say she was French** ihrem Akzent nach ist sie Französin. ◆ **go down** ◇ *vi* - **1.** [decrease - prices, value, temperature] sinken - **2.** [sun] unter|gehen - **3.** [tyre] platt werden - **4.** [be accepted]: **to go down well/badly** gut/schlecht an|kommen. ◇ *vt insep* [stairs, road] hinunter|gehen. ◆ **go for** *vt insep* - **1.** [choose] wählen; [buy] nehmen - **2.** [be attracted to]: **to go for sb/sthg** jn/etw bevorzugen - **3.** [attack]: **to go for sb** auf jn los|gehen - **4.** [try to obtain] aus sein auf *(+ A)*; **just go for it and ask her out!** frag sie einfach, ob sie mit dir ausgehen will! ◆ **go in** *vi* hinein|gehen. ◆ **go in for** *vt insep* - **1.** [enter - competition] mit|machen bei; [- exam] machen - **2.** *inf* [activity]: **he goes in for sports in a big way** er ist ein großer Sportfan. ◆ **go into** *vt insep* - **1.** [investigate] sich befassen mit - **2.** [take up as a profession]: **to go into teaching** Lehrer werden. ◆ **go off** ◇ *vi* - **1.** [alarm] los|gehen; [bomb] explodieren - **2.** [food] schlecht werden - **3.** [light, heating] aus|gehen. ◇ *vt insep inf* [lose interest in] nicht mehr mögen. ◆ **go on** ◇ *vi* - **1.** [happen] los sein; **what's going on next door?** was ist nebenan los? - **2.** [light, heating] an|gehen - **3.** [continue]: **to go on doing sthg** etw weiter tun - **4.** [pass - time] vergehen - **5.** [talk for too long]: **to go on (and on) about sthg** auf etw *(D)* herum|reiten; **don't go on about it!** hör doch mal (damit) auf! ◇ *vt insep* [be guided by]: **I've got nothing to go on** ich habe keine Anhaltspunkte. ◆ **go on at** *vt insep* [nag]: **to go on at sb** an jm herum|nörgeln. ◆ **go out** *vi* - **1.** [light, heating] aus|gehen - **2.** [move outside] hinaus|gehen; **to go out for a meal** essen gehen; **to go out for a walk** einen Spaziergang machen - **3.** [have relationship]: **to go out with sb** mit jm zusammen sein; **we've been going out for six years** wir sind seit sechs Jahren zusammen - **4.** [tide]: **the tide is going out** die Ebbe hat eingesetzt. ◆ **go over** *vt insep* - **1.** [check] überprüfen - **2.** [repeat]: **to go over sthg again** etw wiederholen. ◆ **go round** *vi* [revolve] sich drehen; *see also* **go around**. ◆ **go through** *vt insep* - **1.** [experience] durch|machen - **2.** [search] durchsuchen. ◆ **go through with** *vt insep*: **the government is going through with the plan** die Regierung setzt den Plan in die Tat um; **she couldn't go through with it** sie brachte es nicht fertig. ◆ **go towards** *vt insep* [contribute to] bestimmt sein für. ◆ **go under** *vi liter* & *fig* unter|gehen. ◆ **go up** ◇ *vi* - **1.** [increase] steigen - **2.** [move upwards - balloon] auf|steigen; [- person] auf|steigen. ◇ *vt insep* [stairs, hill] hinauf|steigen. ◆ **go without** *vt insep*: **to go without sthg** ohne etw aus|kommen.

goad [gəʊd] *vt* [provoke] provozieren.

go-ahead ◇ *adj* fortschrittlich. ◇ *n* Erlaubnis *die*.

goal [gəʊl] *n* - **1.** SPORT Tor *das*; **to score a goal** ein Tor erzielen - **2.** [aim] Ziel *das*.

goalkeeper [ˈgəʊlˌkiːpəʳ] *n* Torwart *der*.

goalpost ['gəʊlpəʊst] *n* Torpfosten *der*.

goat [gəʊt] *n* Ziege *die*.

goat's cheese *n* Ziegenkäse *der*.

gob [gɒb] *n UK inf* [mouth] Maul *das*.

gobble ['gɒbl] *vt* hinunter|schlingen.

go-between *n* Vermittler *der*, -in *die*.

gobsmacked ['gɒbsmækt] *adj UK inf* platt.

go-cart *n* = **go-kart**.

god [gɒd] *n* Gott *der*. ◆ **God** ◇ *n* Gott *der*; **God knows** keine Ahnung; **for God's sake!** um Gottes willen!; **thank God!** Gott sei Dank! ◇ *excl*: **(my) God!** (mein) Gott!

godchild ['gɒdtʃaɪld] (*pl* **-children** [-ˌtʃɪldrən]) *n* Patenkind *das*.

goddaughter ['gɒdˌdɔːtəʳ] *n* Patentochter *die*.

goddess ['gɒdɪs] *n* Göttin *die*.

godfather ['gɒdˌfɑːðəʳ] *n* Pate *der*.

godforsaken ['gɒdfəˌseɪkn] *adj* gottverlassen.

godmother ['gɒdˌmʌðəʳ] *n* Patin *die*.

godsend ['gɒdsend] *n* Geschenk *das* des Himmels.

godson ['gɒdsʌn] *n* Patensohn *der*.

goes [gəʊz] *vb* ▷ **go**.

goggles ['gɒglz] *npl* [in industry] Schutzbrille *die*; [for diving] Taucherbrille *die*; [for skiing] Skibrille *die*.

going ['gəʊɪŋ] ◇ *adj* - **1.** [rate, salary] üblich - **2.** *UK* [available]: **any jobs going?** gibt es freie Stellen? ◇ *n* - **1.** [progress]: **have you finished already? – that's good going** bist du schon fertig? – du bist gut OR schnell vorangekommen; **it was slow going** es ging nur langsam voran - **2.** [in horse racing] Geläuf *das*; **the going is good** die Bahn ist gut; **this novel is heavy going** dieser Roman liest sich schwer.

go-kart [-kɑːt] *n UK* Go-Kart *der*.

gold [gəʊld] ◇ *adj* [gold-coloured] golden. ◇ *n* [gen] Gold *das*. ◇ *comp* [made of gold] Gold-.

golden ['gəʊldən] *adj* - **1.** [made of gold] Gold- - **2.** [gold-coloured] golden.

goldfish ['gəʊldfɪʃ] (*pl inv*) *n* Goldfisch *der*.

gold leaf *n* Blattgold *das*.

gold medal *n* Goldmedaille *die*.

goldmine ['gəʊldmaɪn] *n* - **1.** [mine] Goldmine *die* - **2.** [profitable business] Goldgrube *die*.

gold-plated [-'pleɪtɪd] *adj* vergoldet.

goldsmith ['gəʊldsmɪθ] *n* Goldschmied *der*, -in *die*.

golf [gɒlf] *n* Golf *das*.

golf ball *n* [for golf] Golfball *der*.

golf club *n* - **1.** [place, society] Golfklub *der* - **2.** [equipment] Golfschläger *der*.

golf course *n* Golfplatz *der*.

golfer ['gɒlfəʳ] *n* Golfspieler *der*, -in *die*.

gone [gɒn] ◇ *pp* ▷ **go**. ◇ *adj* [no longe here] weg. ◇ *prep* [past] nach; **it's gon twelve (o'clock)** es ist zwölf Uhr vorbei.

gong [gɒŋ] *n* Gong *der*.

good [gʊd] (*comp* **better**, *superl* **best**) ◇ *ad* - **1.** [gen] gut; **it's good to see you again** schön Sie wieder zu sehen; **to have a good time** sich gut amüsieren; **to feel good** sich wohl fühlen **it tastes/smells good** es schmeckt/riecht gut **is this meat still good?** kann man das Fleisch noch essen?; **it's good for you** [beneficial] das wird dir gut tun; [food] das ist gesund; **a good opportunity** eine günstige Gelegenheit; **to be good at sthg** etw gut können; **good at French** gut in Französisch; **she's good with her hands** sie ist geschickt mit den Händen - **2.** [suitable] geeignet; **he would make a good president** er eignet sich zum Präsidenten - **3.** [kind] lieb; **that's very good of you** das ist sehr nett von Ihnen; **to be good to sb** gut zu jm sein; **would you be good enough to open the door?** wären Sie so liebenswürdig, mir die Tür zu öffnen? - **4.** [well-behaved] artig, brav; **be good!** sei brav! - **5.** [thorough] gründlich - **6.** [considerable]: **a good while/deal** ziemlich lange/viel; **a good ten minutes** gute zehn Minuten. ◇ *n* - **1.** [moral correctness] Gute *das*; **to be up to no good** nichts Gutes im Schilde führen - **2.** [use]: **it's no good** [there's no point] es hat keinen Zweck - **3.** [benefit]: **it will do him good** es wird ihm gut tun. ◆ **goods** *npl* Waren *Pl*. ◆ **as good as** *adv* so gut wie; **as good as new** so gut wie neu. ◆ **for good** *adv* für immer. ◆ **good afternoon** *excl* guten Tag! ◆ **good evening** *excl* guten Abend! ◆ **good morning** *excl* guten Morgen! ◆ **good night** *excl* gute Nacht!

goodbye [ˌgʊd'baɪ] ◇ *excl* auf Wiedersehen!; [on phone] auf Wiederhören! ◇ *n*: **to say goodbye** auf Wiedersehen sagen; **to wave goodbye** zum Abschied winken.

good deed *n* gute Tat.

good fortune *n* Glück *das*.

Good Friday *n* Karfreitag *der*.

good-humoured [-'hjuːməd] *adj* [person - temporarily] gut gelaunt; [- by nature] gutmütig; [rivalry] freundschaftlich.

good-looking [-'lʊkɪŋ] *adj* gut aussehend.

good-natured [-'neɪtʃəd] *adj* [person] gutmütig; [rivalry] freundschaftlich; [argument] friedlich.

goodness ['gʊdnɪs] ◇ *n* - **1.** [kindness] Güte *die* - **2.** [of food] Nährgehalt *der*. ◇ *excl*: **(my) goodness!** meine Güte!; **for goodness' sake!** um Himmels willen!; **thank goodness!** Gott sei Dank!

goods train *n UK* Güterzug *der*.

goodwill [ˌgʊd'wɪl] *n (U)* guter Wille; [between countries & COMM] Goodwill *der*.

goody ['gʊdɪ] ◇ *n inf* [in story] Gute *der*, Gute *die*. ◇ *excl* toll!, prima! ◆ **goodies** *npl inf* - **1.** [delicious food] Leckerbissen *Pl* - **2.** [desirable objects] schöne Dinge *Pl*.

goose [gu:s] (*pl* **geese**) *n* Gans *die*.

gooseberry ['gʊzbərɪ] *n* Stachelbeere *die*.

goosebumps *US* ['gu:sbʌmps] *npl* = **gooseflesh**.

gooseflesh ['gu:sfleʃ] *n* Gänsehaut *die*.

goose pimples *UK*, **goosebumps** *US* ['gu:sbʌmps] *npl* = **gooseflesh**.

gore [gɔ:ʳ] ◇ *n (U) liter* [blood] Blut *das*. ◇ *vt* [subj: bull] mit den Hörnern verletzen.

gorge [gɔ:dʒ] ◇ *n* Schlucht *die*. ◇ *vt*: **to gorge o.s. on** OR **with sthg** sich mit etw voll stopfen.

gorgeous ['gɔ:dʒəs] *adj* - **1.** [place, present, weather] herrlich, wunderschön - **2.** *inf* [person] toll aussehend; **to be gorgeous** toll aussehen.

gorilla [gə'rɪlə] *n* Gorilla *der*.

gormless ['gɔ:mlɪs] *adj UK inf* dämlich.

gory ['gɔ:rɪ] *adj* [story, film] blutrünstig.

gosh [gɒʃ] *excl inf* mein Gott!, Mensch!

go-slow *n UK* Bummelstreik *der*.

gospel ['gɒspl] *n* [doctrine] Lehre *die*. ◆ **Gospel** *n* [in Bible] Evangelium *das*.

gossip ['gɒsɪp] ◇ *n* - **1.** [conversation] Klatsch *der*; **to have a gossip** klatschen - **2.** [person] Klatschbase *die*. ◇ *vi* klatschen.

gossip column *n* Klatschspalte *die*.

got [gɒt] *pt* & *pp* ▷ **get**.

gotten ['gɒtn] *pp US* ▷ **get**.

goulash ['gu:læʃ] *n* Gulasch *das*.

gourmet ['gʊəmeɪ] *n* Feinschmecker *der*, -in *die*.

gout [gaʊt] *n* Gicht *die*.

govern ['gʌvən] ◇ *vt* - **1.** POL regieren - **2.** [determine] bestimmen. ◇ *vi* POL regieren.

governess ['gʌvənɪs] *n* Gouvernante *die*.

government ['gʌvnmənt] *n* Regierung *die*.

governor ['gʌvənəʳ] *n* - **1.** POL Gouverneur *der*, -in *die* - **2.** [of school] Mitglied *das* des Schulbeirats; [of bank] Mitglied *das* des Direktoriums - **3.** [of prison] Direktor *der*, -in *die*.

gown [gaʊn] *n* - **1.** [dress] Kleid *das*; [evening gown] Abendkleid *das* - **2.** UNIV & LAW Talar *der* - **3.** MED Kittel *der*.

GP *n abbr of* **general practitioner**.

grab [græb] ◇ *vt* - **1.** [with hands]: **to grab (hold of)** [person] packen; [object] schnappen; **to grab (hold of) sb's arm** jn am Arm packen - **2.** *fig* [opportunity] (beim Schopf) ergreifen; [sandwich, lunch] schnell essen - **3.** *inf* [appeal to]: **how does that grab you?** wie findest du das? ◇ *vi*: **to grab at sthg** [with hands] nach etw greifen.

grace [greɪs] ◇ *n* - **1.** *(U)* [elegance] Grazie *die*, Anmut *die* - **2.** [extra time]: **ten days' grace** zehn Tage Aufschub - **3.** [prayer] Tischgebet *das*. ◇ *vt* [adorn] schmücken.

graceful ['greɪsfʊl] *adj* [beautiful] graziös, anmutig; [line, curve] gefällig.

gracious ['greɪʃəs] ◇ *adj* [polite] höflich. ◇ *excl*: **(good) gracious!** ach du meine Güte!

grade [greɪd] ◇ *n* - **1.** [quality] Güteklasse *die*; **high-grade** hochwertig - **2.** [in company, organization]: **(salary) grade** Gehaltsstufe *die* - **3.** *US* [class] Klasse *die* - **4.** [in exam, test] Note *die* - **5.** *US* [gradient] Gefälle *das*. ◇ *vt* - **1.** [classify] klassifizieren - **2.** [test, exam] benoten.

grade crossing *n US* Bahnübergang *der*.

grade school *n US* Grundschule *die*.

gradient ['greɪdjənt] *n* [of road - upward] Steigung *die*; [- downward] Gefälle *das*.

gradual ['grædʒʊəl] *adj* allmählich.

gradually ['grædʒʊəlɪ] *adv* allmählich.

graduate ◇ *n* ['grædʒʊət] - **1.** [person with a degree] Graduierte *der*, *die* - **2.** *US* [of high school] ≃ Abiturient *der (mit bestandenem Abitur)*. ◇ *vi* ['grædʒʊeɪt] - **1.** [with a degree]: **to graduate (from)** seinen Hochschulabschluss machen (an *(+ D)*) - **2.** *US* [from high school]: **to graduate (from)** ≃ das Abitur machen (an *(+ D)*).

graduation [ˌgrædʒʊ'eɪʃn] *n* [university or school ceremony] Abschlussfeier *die*.

graffiti [grə'fi:tɪ] *n (U)* Graffiti *Pl*.

graft [grɑ:ft] ◇ *n* - **1.** [from plant] Pfropfreis *das* - **2.** MED Transplantat *das* - **3.** *UK inf* [hard work] Plackerei *die* - **4.** *US inf* [corruption] Schiebung *die*. ◇ *vt* - **1.** [plant]: **to graft sthg (onto)** etw pfropfen (auf *(+ A)*) - **2.** MED: **to graft sthg (onto)** etw transplantieren (in *(+ A)*).

grain [greɪn] *n* - **1.** [of corn, rice, salt, sand] Korn *das* - **2.** *(U)* [crops] Getreide *das*, Korn *das* - **3.** [in wood] Maserung *die*.

gram [græm] *n* Gramm *das*.

grammar ['græməʳ] *n* Grammatik *die*.

grammar school *n* - **1.** [in UK] ≃ Gymnasium *das* - **2.** [in US] ≃ Grundschule *die*.

grammatical [grə'mætɪkl] *adj* grammatisch; **it's not grammatical** es ist nicht grammatikalisch richtig.

gramme [græm] *n UK* = **gram**.

gramophone ['græməfəʊn] *n dated* Grammofon *das*.

gran [græn] *n UK inf* Oma *die*, Omi *die*.

grand [grænd] (*pl inv*) ◇ *adj* [house, style] prachtvoll; [design, plan] ehrgeizig; [person, job] bedeutend. ◇ *n inf* [thousand pounds] tausend Pfund *Pl*; [thousand dollars] tausend Dollar *Pl*.

grandad ['grændæd] *n inf* Opa *der*, Opi *der*.

grandchild ['græntʃaɪld] (*pl* **-children** [-ˌtʃɪldrən]) *n* Enkelkind *das*.

granddad ['grændæd] *n inf* = **grandad**.

granddaughter ['græn,dɔːtəʳ] *n* Enkelin *die*.

grandeur ['grændʒəʳ] *n* [of building] Pracht *die*; [of scenery] Herrlichkeit *die*.

grandfather ['grænd,fɑːðəʳ] *n* Großvater *der*.

grandma ['grænmɑː] *n inf* Oma *die*, Omi *die*.

grandmother ['græn,mʌðəʳ] *n* Großmutter *die*.

grandpa ['grænpɑː] *n inf* Opa *der*, Opi *der*.

grandparents ['græn,peərənts] *npl* Großeltern *Pl*.

grand piano *n* Flügel *der*.

grand slam *n* SPORT Grandslam *der*.

grandson ['grænsʌn] *n* Enkel *der*.

grandstand ['grændstænd] *n* (überdachte) Tribüne.

grand total *n* Endsumme *die*.

granite ['grænɪt] *n* Granit *der*.

granny ['grænɪ] *n inf* Oma *die*, Omi *die*.

grant [grɑːnt] ◇ *n* [money] Zuschuss *der*; [money] [for study] Stipendium *das*. ◇ *vt fml* - **1.** [request, right] gewähren; [appeal] nachkommen *(+ D)*; [wish] erfüllen - **2.** [admit] zugeben - **3.** *phr*: **to take sthg for granted** etw als selbstverständlich betrachten.

granule ['grænjuːl] *n* Körnchen *das*.

grape [greɪp] *n* (Wein)traube *die*.

grapefruit ['greɪpfruːt] (*pl inv* OR **-s**) *n* Grapefruit *die*, Pampelmuse *die*.

grapevine ['greɪpvaɪn] *n* Weinstock *der*; **we heard on the grapevine that...** *fig* wir haben gehört, dass...

graph [grɑːf] *n* Diagramm *das*.

graphic ['græfɪk] *adj* - **1.** [vivid] anschaulich - **2.** ART grafisch. ◆ **graphics** *npl* [pictures] grafische Darstellungen *Pl*.

graphic artist *n* Grafiker *der*, -in *die*.

graphite ['græfaɪt] *n* Graphit *das*.

graph paper *n* Millimeterpapier *das*.

grapple ['græpl] ◆ **grapple with** *vt insep liter* & *fig* ringen mit.

grasp [grɑːsp] ◇ *n* - **1.** [grip] Griff *der* - **2.** [understanding]: **to have a good grasp of sthg** [language] etw gut beherrschen; [situation] etw verstehen. ◇ *vt* - **1.** [with hands] ergreifen - **2.** [understand] begreifen.

grasping ['grɑːspɪŋ] *adj pej* [greedy] habgierig.

grass [grɑːs] *n* - **1.** [on ground] Gras *das*; [lawn] Rasen *der* - **2.** *drug sl* [marijuana] Gras *das*.

grasshopper ['grɑːs,hɒpəʳ] *n* Heuschrecke *die*.

grass roots ◇ *npl* [ordinary people] Basis *die*. ◇ *comp*: **grass roots opinion/support** Meinung/Unterstützung der Basis; **at grass roots level** an der Basis.

grass snake *n* Ringelnatter *die*.

grate [greɪt] ◇ *n* [in fireplace] (Kamin)rost *der*. ◇ *vt* [cheese, carrots] reiben. ◇ *vi* [irritate] auf die Nerven gehen.

grateful ['greɪtfʊl] *adj*: **to be grateful to sb (for sthg)** jm (für etw) dankbar sein.

grater ['greɪtəʳ] *n* Reibe *die*.

gratify ['grætɪfaɪ] *vt* [please]: **to be gratified to hear/discover that...** mit Genugtuung hören/entdecken, dass...

grating ['greɪtɪŋ] ◇ *adj* nervend. ◇ *n* [grille] Gitter *das*.

gratitude ['grætɪtjuːd] *n*: **gratitude (to sb)** Dankbarkeit *die* (gegenüber jm).

gratuitous [grə'tjuːɪtəs] *adj fml* unnötig.

grave [grɑːv] ◇ *adj* - **1.** [solemn] ernst - **2.** [serious - situation, threat, illness] ernst; [- news] schlimm. ◇ *n* Grab *das*.

gravel ['grævl] *n* Kies *der*.

gravestone ['greɪvstəʊn] *n* Grabstein *der*.

graveyard ['greɪvjɑːd] *n* Friedhof *der*.

gravity ['grævətɪ] *n (U)* - **1.** [force] Schwerkraft *die* - **2.** *fml* [seriousness] Ernst *der*.

gravy ['greɪvɪ] *n (U)* [meat juice] Bratensaft *der*; [sauce] Soße *die*.

gray *adj* & *n US* = **grey**.

graze [greɪz] ◇ *vt* - **1.** [cattle] grasen OR weiden lassen - **2.** [knee, elbow] aufschürfen - **3.** [touch lightly] streifen. ◇ *vi* [animals] grasen, weiden. ◇ *n* [wound] Schürfwunde *die*.

grease [griːs] ◇ *n (U)* - **1.** [animal fat] Fett *das* - **2.** [lubricant] Schmiere *die*. ◇ *vt* [engine, machine] schmieren; [baking tray] einfetten.

greaseproof paper [ˌgriːspruːf-] *n UK* Pergamentpapier *das*.

greasy ['griːsɪ] *adj* - **1.** [food, hair, hands] fettig - **2.** [clothes] schmierig.

great [greɪt] ◇ *adj* - **1.** [large] groß; **to a great extent** in hohem Maße; **the great majority** die überwiegende Mehrheit; **a great deal of money** eine Menge OR sehr viel Geld - **2.** [very good] großartig; **we had a great time** wir haben uns toll amüsiert. ◇ *excl*: **(that's) great!** (das ist) toll!

Great Britain *n* Großbritannien *nt*.

greatcoat ['greɪtkəʊt] *n langer schwerer Mantel*.

great-grandchild *n* Urenkel *der*, -in *die*.

great-grandfather *n* Urgroßvater *der*.

great-grandmother *n* Urgroßmutter *die*.

greatly ['greɪtlɪ] *adv* sehr.

greatness ['greɪtnɪs] *n* [importance] Bedeutung *die*; [size] Größe *die*.

Greece [griːs] *n* Griechenland *nt*.

greed [griːd] *n* - **1.** [for food] Gefräßigkeit *die* - **2.** *fig* [for money, power] Gier *die*.

greedy ['griːdɪ] *adj* - **1.** [for food] gefräßig - **2.** *fig*: **greedy for money/power** geld-/machtgierig.

Greek [griːk] <> *adj* griechisch. <> *n* - **1.** [person] Grieche *der*, -chin *die* - **2.** [language] Griechisch(e) *das*.

green [griːn] <> *adj* grün; **green (with envy)** blass OR grün (vor Neid). <> *n* - **1.** [colour] Grün *das* - **2.** [in village]: **(village) green** (Dorf)wiese *die* - **3.** GOLF Grün *das*. ◆ **Green** *n* POL Grüne *der, die*; **the Greens** die Grünen. ◆ **greens** *npl* [vegetables] Grüngemüse *das*.

greenback ['griːnbæk] *n US inf* [banknote] Dollarschein *der*.

green belt *n UK* Grüngürtel *der*.

green card *n* - **1.** *UK* [for insuring vehicle] grüne Versicherungskarte - **2.** *US* [resident's permit] Aufenthaltserlaubnis *die*.

greenfly ['griːnflaɪ] (*pl inv* OR **-ies**) *n* (grüne) Blattlaus.

greengrocer ['griːn,grəʊsəʳ] *n* Obst- und Gemüsehändler *der*, -in *die*; **greengrocer's (shop)** Obst- und Gemüsegeschäft *das*.

greenhouse ['griːnhaʊs] (*pl* [-haʊzɪz]) *n* Gewächshaus *das*, Treibhaus *das*.

greenhouse effect *n*: **the greenhouse effect** der Treibhauseffekt.

Greenland ['griːnlənd] *n* Grönland *nt*.

green salad *n* grüner Salat.

greet [griːt] *vt liter* & *fig* begrüßen; [say hello to in passing] grüßen.

greeting ['griːtɪŋ] *n* Gruß *der*; **to exchange greetings** sich grüßen. ◆ **greetings** *npl* [on card]: **Christmas greetings** Weihnachtsgrüße; **birthday greetings** Glückwünsche zum Geburtstag.

greetings card *UK*, **greeting card** *US n* Glückwunschkarte *die*.

grenade [grə'neɪd] *n*: **(hand) grenade** (Hand)granate *die*.

grew [gruː] *pt* ▷ **grow**.

grey *UK*, **gray** *US* [greɪ] <> *adj* grau; [life] trostlos; **to go grey** grau werden. <> *n* Grau *das*.

grey-haired [-'heəd] *adj* grauhaarig.

greyhound ['greɪhaʊnd] *n* Windhund *der*.

grid [grɪd] *n* - **1.** [grating] Gitter *das* - **2.** [for maps] Gitternetz *das*; ELEC Überlandleitungsnetz *das*.

griddle ['grɪdl] *n gusseiserne Platte zum Backen von Pfannkuchen*.

gridlock ['grɪdlɒk] *n* [in traffic] Zusammenbruch *der* des Verkehrs.

grief [griːf] *n* - **1.** [sorrow] Trauer *die* - **2.** *inf* [trouble] Ärger *der* - **3.** *phr*: **to come to grief** [in an accident] verunglücken; [plan] scheitern; **good grief!** ach du lieber Himmel!

grievance ['griːvns] *n* [complaint] Beschwerde *die*.

grieve [griːv] *vi*: **to grieve (for sb/sthg)** (um jn/etw) trauern.

grievous ['griːvəs] *adj fml* [wound] schlimm; [mistake] schwer wiegend.

grill [grɪl] <> *n* [of cooker] Grill *der*; [over fire] Bratrost *der*. <> *vt* - **1.** [cook] grillen - **2.** *inf* [interrogate - interviewee] aus|quetschen; [- prisoner, suspect] ins Verhör nehmen.

grille [grɪl] *n* Gitter *das*; **radiator grille** AUT Kühlergrill *der*.

grim [grɪm] *adj* - **1.** [face, smile] grimmig; [determination] eisern - **2.** [place, situation] trostlos; [prospect] düster; [news] grauenvoll.

grimace ['grɪməs] <> *n* Grimasse *die*. <> *vi* Grimassen schneiden; **to grimace with pain** vor Schmerz das Gesicht verziehen.

grime [graɪm] *n* Schmutz *der*; [soot] Ruß *der*.

grimy ['graɪmɪ] *adj* schmutzig; [sooty] verrußt.

grin [grɪn] <> *n* Grinsen *das*. <> *vi* grinsen; **to grin at sb/sthg** jn/etw an|grinsen.

grind [graɪnd] (*pt & pp* **ground**) <> *vt* [coffee, pepper, flour] mahlen. <> *vi* [car, gears] knirschen. <> *n* [hard, boring work] Schinderei *die*; **the daily grind** der tägliche Trott. ◆ **grind down** *vt sep* [oppress] unterdrücken. ◆ **grind up** *vt sep* zermahlen.

grinder ['graɪndəʳ] *n* [for coffee, pepper] Mühle *die*.

grip [grɪp] <> *n* - **1.** [physical hold]: **to release one's grip on sb/sthg** jn/etw los|lassen - **2.** [control]: **to have a (good) grip on a situation** eine Situation im Griff haben; **to get to grips with sthg** etw in den Griff bekommen; **to get a grip on o.s.** sich zusammen|reißen - **3.** [of tyres] Haftung *die*; [of shoes] Halt *der* - **4.** [handle] Griff *der*. <> *vt* - **1.** [grasp] fest|halten - **2.** [subj: tyres] haften auf *(+ D)* - **3.** [imagination, attention, audience] fesseln.

gripe [graɪp] *inf* <> *n* [complaint] Gemecker *das*. <> *vi*: **to gripe (about sthg)** (über etw *(A)*) meckern.

gripping ['grɪpɪŋ] *adj* [story, film] fesselnd.

grisly ['grɪzlɪ] *adj* grausig.

gristle ['grɪsl] *n* Knorpel *der*.

grit [grɪt] <> *n (U)* - **1.** [for roads, in winter] Streusand *der* - **2.** *inf* [courage] Schneid *der*. <> *vt* [road, steps] streuen.

groan [grəʊn] <> *n* Stöhnen *das*. <> *vi* - **1.** [moan] stöhnen - **2.** [door, table] ächzen - **3.** [complain] sich beklagen.

grocer ['grəʊsəʳ] *n* Lebensmittelhändler *der*, -in *die*; **grocer's (shop)** Lebensmittelgeschäft *das*.

groceries ['grəʊsərɪz] *npl* Lebensmittel *Pl*.

groggy ['grɒgɪ] *adj* geschwächt.

groin [grɔɪn] *n* Leiste *die*.

groom [gru:m] ◇ *n* - **1.** [of horses] Stallbursche *der*, Stallgehilfin *die* - **2.** [bridegroom] Bräutigam *der*. ◇ *vt* - **1.** [horse] striegeln; [dog] bürsten - **2.** [candidate]: **to groom sb (for)** jn vor|bereiten (auf *(+ A)*).

groomed [gru:md] *adj*: **well groomed** gepflegt.

groove [gru:v] *n* Rille *die*.

grope [grəʊp] *vi*: **to grope (about) for sthg** [object] nach etw tasten.

gross [grəʊs] (*pl inv* OR **-es**) ◇ *adj* - **1.** [weight, income] Brutto- - **2.** *fml* [error, misconduct] grob; [exaggeration] krass - **3.** *inf* [coarse, vulgar - person, behaviour] ordinär - **4.** *inf* [obese] fett. ◇ *n* Gros *das*.

grossly ['grəʊslɪ] *adv* [for emphasis] äußerst.

grotesque [grəʊ'tesk] *adj* grotesk.

grotto ['grɒtəʊ] (*pl* **-es** OR **-s**) *n* Grotte *die*.

grotty ['grɒtɪ] *adj UK inf* mies.

ground [graʊnd] ◇ *pt* & *pp* ▷ **grind**. ◇ *n* - **1.** [gen] Boden *der*; **above ground** über der Erde; **below ground** unter der Erde; **on the ground** auf dem Boden; *fig* vor Ort; **to gain/lose ground** an Boden gewinnen/verlieren; **to cut the ground from under sb's feet** jm den Boden unter den Füßen weg|ziehen; **to stand one's ground** nicht von der Stelle weichen; *fig* auf seinem Standpunkt beharren - **2.** SPORT Sportplatz *der*; [stadium] Stadion *das*; **football ground** Fußballplatz *der*; [stadium] Fußballstadion *das*. ◇ *vt* - **1.** [base]: **to be grounded on** OR **in sthg** basieren auf etw *(D)* - **2.** *inf* [aircraft, pilot] nicht fliegen lassen - **3.** *esp US* [child]: **to be grounded** Hausarrest haben - **4.** *US* ELEC: **to be grounded** geerdet sein. ◆ **grounds** *npl* - **1.** [reason] Grund *der*; **to have grounds for doing sthg** einen Grund dafür haben, etw zu tun; **on health grounds** aus gesundheitlichen Gründen - **2.** [of building] Gelände *das* - **3.**: **coffee grounds** Kaffeesatz *der*.

ground crew *n* Bodenpersonal *das*.

ground floor *n* Erdgeschoss *das*.

grounding ['graʊndɪŋ] *n*: **to have a grounding in sthg** Grundkenntnisse in etw *(D)* haben.

groundless ['graʊndlɪs] *adj* grundlos.

groundsheet ['graʊndʃi:t] *n* Bodenplane *die*.

ground staff *n UK* [at airport] Bodenpersonal *das*.

groundwork ['graʊndwɜ:k] *n (U)* Vorarbeit *Pl*.

group [gru:p] ◇ *n* [gen] Gruppe *die*. ◇ *vt* gruppieren; [classify] klassifizieren. ◇ *vi*: **to group (together)** sich zusammen|tun.

groupie ['gru:pɪ] *n inf* Groupie *das*.

grouse [graʊs] (*pl inv* OR **-s**) ◇ *n* [bird] Schottisches Moorschneehuhn. ◇ *vi inf* meckern.

grove [grəʊv] *n* Hain *der*.

grovel ['grɒvl] (*UK*) (*US*) *vi* kriechen; **to grovel to sb** vor jm kriechen.

grow [grəʊ] (*pt* **grew**, *pp* **grown**) ◇ *vi* - **1.** [gen] wachsen; [problem] sich vergrößern; [love] stärker werden; [idea] Formen an|nehmen; **to grow in popularity** an Beliebtheit gewinnen - **2.** [become] werden; **to grow old** alt werden; **to grow to do sthg** allmählich etw tun. ◇ *vt* [crops, vegetables] an|bauen; [flowers] züchten; **to grow one's hair/a beard** sich *(D)* die Haare/einen Bart wachsen lassen. ◆ **grow on** *vt insep inf* [subj: music, idea]: **it'll grow on you** es wird dir mit der Zeit immer besser gefallen. ◆ **grow out of** *vt insep* - **1.** [clothes, shoes] heraus|wachsen aus - **2.** [habit] ab|legen. ◆ **grow up** *vi* [person] auf|wachsen; [become adult] erwachsen werden; **grow up!** werd endlich erwachsen!

grower ['grəʊəʳ] *n* [of flowers] Züchter *der*, -in *die*; [of crops, vegetables] Anbauer *der*, -in *die*.

growl [graʊl] *vi* knurren; [bear, engine] brummen.

grown [grəʊn] ◇ *pp* ▷ **grow**. ◇ *adj* erwachsen.

grown-up ◇ *adj* [fully grown] ausgewachsen; [mature] erwachsen. ◇ *n* Erwachsene *der, die*.

growth [grəʊθ] *n* - **1.** [increase - of economy, company, population] Wachstum *das*; [- of research, opposition, nationalism] Zunahme *die* - **2.** [development - of person] Entwicklung *die* - **3.** MED Geschwulst *die*.

grub [grʌb] *n* - **1.** [insect] Larve *die* - **2.** *inf* [food] Futter *das*.

grubby ['grʌbɪ] *adj* [clothes] schmuddelig; [hands, child] schmutzig.

grudge [grʌdʒ] ◇ *n* Groll *der*; **to bear sb a grudge, to have a grudge against sb** einen Groll gegen jn hegen. ◇ *vt*: **to grudge sb sthg** jm etw missgönnen.

gruelling *UK*, **grueling** *US* ['grʊəlɪŋ] *adj* strapaziös.

gruesome ['gru:səm] *adj* grausig.

gruff [grʌf] *adj* - **1.** [voice] rau - **2.** [person, manner] barsch.

grumble ['grʌmbl] *vi* [complain]: **to grumble (about)** murren (über *(+ A)*).

grumpy ['grʌmpɪ] *adj inf* mürrisch.

grunt [grʌnt] ◇ *n* Grunzen *das*. ◇ *vi* grunzen.

G-string *n* - **1.** MUS G-Saite *die* - **2.** [clothing] Tangaslip *der*.

guarantee [ˌgærən'ti:] ◇ *n* Garantie *die*; [document] Garantieschein *der*; **to give sb a guarantee that...** jm garantieren, dass... ◇ *vt* - **1.** COMM Garantie geben auf *(+ A)* - **2.** [promise] garantieren.

guard [gɑːd] ◇ *n* - **1.** [person] Wachposten *der*; [for prisoner] Gefängniswärter *der*, -in *die*; [group of guards] Wache *die* - **2.** [supervision] Überwachung *die*; **to be on guard** Wache haben; **to catch sb off guard** jn überrumpeln - **3.** *UK* RAIL Schaffner *der*, -in *die* - **4.** [protective device] Schutz *der*; [for machine] Schutzvorrichtung *die*; [for fire] Schutzgitter *das* - **5.** [in boxing] Deckung *die*. ◇ *vt* bewachen.

guard dog *n* Wachhund *der*.

guarded ['gɑːdɪd] *adj* [reply, statement] vorsichtig.

guardian ['gɑːdjən] *n* - **1.** LAW [of child] Vormund *der* - **2.** [protector] Wächter *der*, -in *die*.

guardrail ['gɑːdreɪl] *n* Geländer *das*.

guard's van *n UK* Schaffnerabteil *das*.

guerilla [gə'rɪlə] *n* = **guerrilla**.

Guernsey ['gɜːnzɪ] *n* [place] Guernsey *nt*.

guerrilla [gə'rɪlə] *n* Guerillakämpfer *der*, -in *die*.

guerrilla warfare *n (U)* Guerillakrieg *der*.

guess [ges] ◇ *n* - **1.** [at facts, figures] Schätzung *die*; **at a guess** schätzungsweise - **2.** [hypothesis] Vermutung *die*. ◇ *vt* [answer, name] raten; [correctly] erraten, richtig schätzen; [figure, weight] schätzen; **guess what!** stell dir vor! ◇ *vi* - **1.** [gen] raten; **to guess at sthg** etw zu erraten versuchen - **2.** [suppose] glauben, denken; **I guess (so)** ich glaube (schon).

guesswork ['geswɜːk] *n (U)* (reine) Vermutung.

guest [gest] *n* Gast *der*; **be my guest!** nur zu!

guesthouse ['gesthaʊs] (*pl* [-haʊzɪz]) *n* Pension *die*.

guestroom ['gestrʊm] *n* Gästezimmer *das*.

guffaw [gʌ'fɔː] *vi* schallend lachen.

guidance ['gaɪdəns] *n (U)* - **1.** [help from teacher, parents] Anleitung *die*; [counselling] Beratung *die* - **2.** [leadership] Führung *die*.

guide [gaɪd] ◇ *n* - **1.** [for tourists] Fremdenführer *der*, -in *die*; **tour guide** Reiseleiter *der*, -in *die* - **2.** [guide book] Führer *der*; [manual] Handbuch *das* - **3.** [indication] Orientierungshilfe *die*; **to use sthg as a guide** etw als Vorbild nehmen - **4.** = **girl guide**. ◇ *vt* - **1.** [lead] führen; *(phrase)*: **to be guided by sb/sthg** [influenced] sich von jm/etw leiten lassen - **2.** [plane, missile] lenken.

guide book *n* Führer *der*.

guide dog *n* Blindenhund *der*.

guided tour ['gaɪdɪd-] *n* Führung *die*.

guideline ['gaɪdlaɪn] *n* Richtlinie *die*.

guild [gɪld] *n* [association] Vereinigung *die*.

guile [gaɪl] *n liter* List *die*.

guillotine ['gɪlə,tiːn] ◇ *n* - **1.** [for executions] Guillotine *die* - **2.** [for paper] Papierschneidemaschine *die*. ◇ *vt* [execute] guillotinieren.

guilt [gɪlt] *n* Schuld *die*.

guilty ['gɪltɪ] *adj* - **1.** [gen] schuldig; [smile, look] schuldbewusst - **2.**: **to be found guilty/not guilty** LAW für schuldig/nicht schuldig befunden werden.

guinea pig ['gɪnɪ-] *n* - **1.** [animal] Meerschweinchen *das* - **2.** [subject of experiment] Versuchskaninchen *das*.

guise [gaɪz] *n fml*: **to present sthg in a new guise** etw anders darlstellen; **under the guise of friendship** unter dem Deckmantel der Freundschaft.

guitar [gɪ'tɑːʳ] *n* Gitarre *die*.

guitarist [gɪ'tɑːrɪst] *n* Gitarrist *der*, -in *die*.

gulf [gʌlf] *n* - **1.** [sea] Golf *der* - **2.** *liter* & *fig* [gap] Kluft *die*. ◆ **Gulf** *n*: **the Gulf** der Golf.

gull [gʌl] *n* Möwe *die*.

gullet ['gʌlɪt] *n* Speiseröhre *die*.

gullible ['gʌləbl] *adj* leichtgläubig.

gully ['gʌlɪ] *n* - **1.** [valley] Schlucht *die* - **2.** [ditch] Graben *der*.

gulp [gʌlp] ◇ *n* Schluck *der*. ◇ *vt* hinunterlschlucken. ◇ *vi* schlucken. ◆ **gulp down** *vt sep* hinunterlschlucken.

gum [gʌm] ◇ *n* - **1.** [chewing gum] Kaugummi *der* - **2.** [adhesive] Klebstoff *der* - **3.** ANAT Zahnfleisch *das*. ◇ *vt* [stick] kleben.

gummed *adj* gummiert.

gun [gʌn] *n* - **1.** [weapon - revolver] Pistole *die*, Revolver *der*; [- rifle, shotgun] Gewehr *das*; [- cannon] Kanone *die* - **2.** SPORT [starting pistol] Startpistole *die* - **3.** [for paint, spraying] Pistole *die*. ◆ **gun down** *vt sep* [person, animal] niederlschießen.

gunfire ['gʌnfaɪəʳ] *n (U)* MIL Geschützfeuer *das*; [of small arms] Schießerei *die*.

gunman ['gʌnmən] (*pl* **-men** [-mən]) *n* (mit einer Schußwaffe) bewaffneter Mann.

gunpoint ['gʌnpɔɪnt] *n*: **to hold sb at gunpoint** jn mit einer Pistole/einem Gewehr bedrohen.

gunpowder ['gʌn,paʊdəʳ] *n* Schießpulver *das*.

gunshot ['gʌnʃɒt] *n* Schuss *der*.

gurgle ['gɜːgl] *vi* - **1.** [water] gluckern - **2.** [baby] glucksen.

guru ['gʊruː] *n* Guru *der*.

gush [gʌʃ] ◇ *n* Strahl *der*. ◇ *vi* - **1.** [flow out] herauslschießen - **2.** *pej* [enthuse] schwärmen.

gust [gʌst] *n* Windstoß *der*, Böe *die*.

gusto ['gʌstəʊ] *n*: **with gusto** mit Genuss.

gut [gʌt] ◇ *n* - **1.** MED Darm *der* - **2.** *inf* [stomach] Bauch *der*. ◇ *vt* - **1.** [animal, fish] auslnehmen - **2.** [building]: **the fire gutted the house** das Haus brannte völlig aus. ◆ **guts** *npl inf* - **1.** [intestines] Eingeweide *Pl*; **to hate sb's guts** jn absolut nicht ausstehen können - **2.** [courage] Mumm *der*.

gutter ['gʌtəʳ] *n* - **1.** [beside road] Rinnstein *der* - **2.** [on roof] Dachrinne *die*.

guy [gaɪ] *n* - **1.** *inf* [man] Typ *der* - **2.** *esp US* [person]: **are you ready, guys?** seid ihr fertig? - **3.** *UK* [dummy] *Puppe, die Guy Fawkes darstellt und in der "Guy Fawkes' Night" verbrannt wird.*

Guy Fawkes' Night *n Nacht des 5. November, Jahrestag der Pulververschwörung gegen König James I und das Parlament 1605.*

guzzle ['gʌzl] <> *vt* [food] hinunter|schlingen; [drink] hinunter|kippen. <> *vi* [eat] sich voll fressen.

gym [dʒɪm] *n inf* - **1.** [gymnasium - in school] Turnhalle *die*; [- in hotel] Fitnessraum *der*; [- health club] Fitnessstudio *das* - **2.** [exercises] Turnen *das*.

gymnasium [dʒɪm'neɪzjəm] (*pl* **-iums** OR **-ia** [-jə]) *n* [in school] Turnhalle *die*; [in hotel] Fitnessraum *der*; [health club] Fitnessstudio *das*.

gymnast ['dʒɪmnæst] *n* Turner *der*, -in *die*.

gymnastics [dʒɪm'næstɪks] *n (U)* [exercises] Gymnastik *die*; [discipline] Turnen *das*.

gym shoes *npl* Turnschuhe *Pl*.

gynaecologist *UK*, **gynecologist** *US* [ˌgaɪnə'kɒlədʒɪst] *n* Gynäkologe *der*, -gin *die*.

gynaecology, **gynecology** *US* [ˌgaɪnə'kɒlədʒɪ] *n* Gynäkologie *die*.

gypsy ['dʒɪpsɪ] *adj* & *n* = **gipsy**.

gyrate [dʒaɪ'reɪt] *vi* sich schnell drehen; [disco dancer] ausgelassen tanzen.

h (*pl* **h's** OR **hs**), **H** (*pl* **H's** OR **Hs**) [eɪtʃ] *n* [letter] h *das*, H *das*.

haberdashery ['hæbədæʃərɪ] *n (U)* [goods] Kurzwaren *Pl*.

habit ['hæbɪt] *n* - **1.** [usual practice] Gewohnheit *die*; **to get into the habit of doing sthg** sich *(D)* daran gewöhnen, etw zu tun - **2.** [drug addiction] Abhängigkeit *die* - **3.** [garment] Habit *das*.

habitat ['hæbɪtæt] *n* Lebensraum *der*.

habitual [hə'bɪtʃʊəl] *adj* - **1.** [customary] gewohnt - **2.** [offender, smoker, drinker] Gewohnheits-.

hack [hæk] <> *n pej* [writer] Schreiberling *der*. <> *vt* [cut] hacken; **to hack sthg to pieces** etw zerhacken. ◆ **hack into** *vt insep* COMPUT ein|dringen in *(+ A)*.

hacker ['hækəʳ] *n* COMPUT Hacker *der*.

hackneyed ['hæknɪd] *adj pej* abgedroschen.

hacksaw ['hæksɔ:] *n* Metallsäge *die*.

had *(weak form* [həd], *strong form* [hæd]*) pt* & *pp* ▷ **have**.

haddock ['hædək] (*pl inv*) *n* Schellfisch *der*.

hadn't ['hædnt] *abbr of* **had not**.

haemorrhage ['hemərɪdʒ] *n* & *vi* = **hemorrhage**.

haemorrhoids ['hemərɔɪdz] *npl* = **hemorrhoids**.

haggard ['hægəd] *adj* verhärmt.

haggis ['hægɪs] *n schottische Spezialität aus Schafsinnereien, im Schafsmagen gekocht.*

haggle ['hægl] *vi*: **to haggle (over** OR **about)** feilschen (um).

Hague [heɪg] *n*: **The Hague** Den Haag *nt*.

hail [heɪl] <> *n liter* & *fig* Hagel *der*; **a hail of bullets** ein Kugelhagel. <> *vt* - **1.** [call] rufen; [taxi] heran|winken, an|halten - **2.** [acclaim]: **to hail sb/sthg as sthg** jn/etw als etw feiern. <> *impers vb* METEOR hageln.

hailstone ['heɪlstəʊn] *n* Hagelkorn *das*.

hailstorm ['heɪlstɔ:m] *n* Hagelsturm *der*.

hair [heəʳ] <> *n* - **1.** *(U)* [on human head] Haare *Pl*, Haar *das*; [single hair] Haar *das*; **to have one's hair cut** sich *(D)* die Haare schneiden lassen; **to do one's hair** sich *(D)* die Haare machen - **2.** [on animal, insect, plant] Haar *das* - **3.** [on human skin] Haar *das*. <> *comp* Haar-.

hairbrush ['heəbrʌʃ] *n* Haarbürste *die*.

haircut ['heəkʌt] *n* Haarschnitt *der*; **to get a haircut** sich *(D)* die Haare schneiden lassen.

hairdo ['heədu:] (*pl* **-s**) *n inf* Frisur *die*.

hairdresser ['heəˌdresəʳ] *n* Friseur *der*, -seuse *die*; **hairdresser's (salon)** Friseur *der*.

hairdryer ['heəˌdraɪəʳ] *n* [handheld] Föhn *der*; [with hood] Trockenhaube *die*.

hair gel *n* Haargel *das*.

hairgrip ['heəgrɪp] *n UK* Haarklammer *die*.

hairpin ['heəpɪn] *n* Haarnadel *die*.

hairpin bend *n* Haarnadelkurve *die*.

hair-raising [-ˌreɪzɪŋ] *adj* haarsträubend.

hair remover [-rɪˌmu:vəʳ] *n* Enthaarungscreme *die*.

hairspray ['heəspreɪ] *n* Haarspray *das*.

hairstyle ['heəstaɪl] *n* Frisur *die*.

hairy ['heərɪ] *adj* - **1.** [animal, person, body] behaart - **2.** *inf* [dangerous] haarig.

half [*UK* hɑ:f, *US* hæf] <> *adj* halb(e) (er) (es); **half my life** mein halbes Leben (lang); **half a dozen** ein halbes Dutzend; **half an hour** eine halbe Stunde. <> *adv* halb; **half as big** halb so groß; **half as much again** noch einmal halb so viel; **half past ten** *UK*, **half after ten** *US* halb elf; **it's half past** es ist halb; **it isn't half cold** *UK inf* es ist unheimlich kalt; **half-and-half** halb und halb. <> *n* - **1.** (*pl* **halves**) [50%]

Hälfte *die*; **half of it** die Hälfte davon; **in half** [cut, tear] in zwei Hälften; **to go halves (with sb)** (mit jm) halbe-halbe machen - **2.** (*pl* **halves**) [fraction] Halbe(s) *das*; **four and a half** viereinhalb - **3.** (*pl* **halves**) SPORT [of sports match] Spielhälfte *die* - **4.** (*pl* **halves** OR **halfs**) [of beer] kleines Bier - **5.** (*pl* **halves** OR **halfs**) [child's ticket] Fahrkarte *die* zum halben Preis; **one and a half** ein Erwachsener und ein Kind.

half board *n (U) esp UK* Halbpension *die*.

half-caste [-kɑ:st] *pej* ◇ *adj* Halbblut-. ◇ *n* Mischling *der*.

half-fare *n* halber Fahrpreis.

half-hearted [-'hɑ:tɪd] *adj* halbherzig.

half hour *n* halbe Stunde.

half-mast *n UK*: **at half-mast** [flag] auf halbmast.

half moon *n* Halbmond *der*.

half note *n US* MUS halbe Note.

halfpenny ['heɪpnɪ] (*pl* **-pennies** OR **-pence**) *n* halber Penny.

half-price *adj* & *adv* zum halben Preis.

half term *n UK kurze Schulferien in der Mitte des Trimesters.*

half time *n* Halbzeit *die*.

halfway [hɑ:f'weɪ] ◇ *adj*: **at the halfway stage** OR **point of sthg** in der Mitte von etw. ◇ *adv*: **to go halfway** die Hälfte des Weges zurück|legen; **halfway through the holidays** mitten im Urlaub.

hall [hɔ:l] *n* - **1.** [in house] Diele *die*, Flur *der* - **2.** [meeting room] Saal *der* - **3.** [public building] Halle *die* - **4.** *UK* UNIV [hall of residence] Studentenwohnheim *das* - **5.** [country house] Herrensitz *der*.

hallmark ['hɔ:lmɑ:k] *n* - **1.** [typical feature] Kennzeichen *das* - **2.** [on metal] Feingehaltsstempel *der*.

hallo [hə'ləʊ] *excl* = **hello**.

hall of residence (*pl* **halls of residence**) *n UK* UNIV Studentenwohnheim *das*.

Hallowe'en, Halloween [,hæləʊ'i:n] *n Abend vor Allerheiligen, an dem sich Kinder oft als Gespenster verkleiden.*

hallucinate [hə'lu:sɪneɪt] *vi* halluzinieren.

hallway ['hɔ:lweɪ] *n* Diele *die*, Flur *der*.

halo ['heɪləʊ] (*pl* **-es** OR **-s**) *n* [of saint, angel] Heiligenschein *der*.

halt [hɔ:lt] ◇ *n*: **to come to a halt** *liter* & *fig* zum Stillstand kommen; **to call a halt to sthg** etw *(D)* Einhalt gebieten. ◇ *vt* [person] an|halten; [development, activity] zum Stillstand bringen. ◇ *vi* [vehicle] an|halten, halten; [person] stehen bleiben; [development, activity] still|stehen.

halve [*UK* hɑ:v, *US* hæv] *vt* - **1.** [reduce by half] halbieren - **2.** [divide] teilen.

halves [*UK* hɑ:vz, *US* hævz] *Pl* ▷ **half**.

ham [hæm] ◇ *n* [meat] Schinken *der*. ◇ *comp* [salad, sandwich] Schinken-.

hamburger ['hæmbɜ:gər] *n* - **1.** [burger] Hamburger *der* - **2.** *(U) US* [mince] Hackfleisch *das*.

hamlet ['hæmlɪt] *n* kleines Dorf.

hammer ['hæmər] ◇ *n* Hammer *der*. ◇ *vt* - **1.** [with tool - nail] ein|schlagen; [- panel] hämmern - **2.** *inf fig* [fact, order]: **to hammer sthg into sb** jm etw ein|bläuen - **3.** *inf fig* [team, player] ab|servieren. ◇ *vi*: **to hammer (on)** hämmern (an *(+ A)*). ◆ **hammer out** ◇ *vt insep* [agreement, solution] aus|arbeiten. ◇ *vt sep* [metal] aus|hämmern; [dent] aus|beulen.

hammock ['hæmək] *n* Hängematte *die*.

hamper ['hæmpər] ◇ *n* - **1.** [for picnic] Picknickkorb *der* - **2.** *US* [for laundry] Wäschekorb *der*. ◇ *vt* [impede] behindern.

hamster ['hæmstər] *n* Hamster *der*.

hand [hænd] ◇ *n* - **1.** [part of body] Hand *die*; **to hold hands** Händchen halten; **by hand** von Hand; **to get** OR **lay one's hands on sb/sthg** an jn/etw heran|kommen; **to have one's hands full** alle Hände voll zu tun haben; **to try one's hand at sthg** sich in etw *(D)* versuchen - **2.** [help] Hilfe *die*; **do you need a hand?** kann ich dir helfen?; **to give** OR **lend sb a hand** jm helfen - **3.** [worker] Arbeiter *der*, -in *die*; [on ship] Besatzungsmitglied *das* - **4.** [of clock, watch] Zeiger *der* - **5.** [handwriting] Handschrift *die* - **6.** [of cards] Blatt *das*. ◇ *vt*: **to hand sthg to sb, to hand sb sthg** jm etw geben OR reichen. ◆ **(close) at hand** *adv* nah in Reichweite. ◆ **in hand** *adv* - **1.** [time, money]: **I have ten pounds in hand** ich habe zehn Pfund übrig; **we have an hour in hand** es bleibt uns noch eine Stunde - **2.** [problem, situation]: **to have sthg in hand** etw in Bearbeitung haben. ◆ **on hand** *adv* zur Stelle. ◆ **on the one hand** *adv* einerseits. ◆ **on the other hand** *adv* andererseits. ◆ **out of hand** ◇ *adj* [situation]: **to get out of hand** außer Kontrolle geraten. ◇ *adv* [completely] rundweg. ◆ **to hand** *adv* zur Hand. ◆ **hand down** *vt sep* [heirloom] hinterlassen; [knowledge] weiter|geben. ◆ **hand in** *vt sep* [lost property] ab|geben; [essay, application] ein|reichen. ◆ **hand out** *vt sep* aus|teilen. ◆ **hand over** ◇ *vt sep* - **1.** [gen] übergeben - **2.** TELEC: **I'll hand you over to the manager** ich gebe Ihnen (mal) den Manager. ◇ *vi*: **to hand over (to sb)** (an jn) übergeben.

handbag ['hændbæg] *n* Handtasche *die*.

handball ['hændbɔ:l] *n* [game] Handball *der*.

handbook ['hændbʊk] *n* Handbuch *das*.

handbrake ['hændbreɪk] *n* Handbremse *die*.

handcuffs ['hændkʌfs] *npl* Handschellen *Pl*.

handful ['hændfʊl] *n* [gen] Hand *die* voll; [of grass, hair] Büschel *das*.

handgun ['hændgʌn] *n* Handfeuerwaffe *die*.

handheld PC ['hændheld-] *n* Palmtop *der*.

handicap ['hændɪkæp] ◇ *n* - **1.** [disability] Behinderung *die* - **2.** *fig* [disadvantage] Nachteil *der* - **3.** SPORT Handicap *das*. ◇ *vt* [hinder] behindern.

handicapped ['hændɪkæpt] *adj* [disabled] behindert.

handicraft ['hændɪkrɑːft] *n* [skill] Handwerk *das*.

handiwork ['hændɪwɜːk] *n (U)* Handarbeit *die*.

handkerchief ['hæŋkətʃɪf] (*pl* **-chiefs** OR **-chieves** [-tʃiːvz]) *n* Taschentuch *das*.

handle ['hændl] ◇ *n* Griff *der*; [of door] Klinke *die*; [of broom, spade, frying pan] Stiel *der*; [of jug, cup] Henkel *der*. ◇ *vt* - **1.** [with hands] an|fassen - **2.** [control - tool, machine, words] handhaben; [- car, ship] steuern - **3.** [process - orders, complaints] bearbeiten; [- stolen goods] verschieben - **4.** [cope with - situation, crisis, death] um|gehen mit.

handlebars ['hændlbɑːz] *npl* Lenker *der*.

handler ['hændlər] *n*: **(baggage) handler** Gepäckabfertiger *der*, -in *die*.

hand luggage *n (U) UK* Handgepäck *das*.

handmade [ˌhænd'meɪd] *adj* in Handarbeit hergestellt.

handout ['hændaʊt] *n* - **1.** [of money, food] Almosen *das* - **2.** [leaflet] Flugblatt *das* - **3.** [for lecture, discussion] Handout *das*.

handrail ['hændreɪl] *n* Geländer *das*.

handset ['hændset] *n* TELEC Hörer *der*.

handshake ['hændʃeɪk] *n* Händedruck *der*.

handsome ['hænsəm] *adj* - **1.** [man] gut aussehend - **2.** [reward] großzügig; [profit] groß.

handstand ['hændstænd] *n* Handstand *der*.

hand towel *n* Händehandtuch *das*.

handwriting ['hændˌraɪtɪŋ] *n* Handschrift *die*.

handy ['hændɪ] *adj inf* - **1.** [useful] praktisch; **to come in handy** nützlich sein - **2.** [person] geschickt - **3.** [near]: **the newsagent's is very handy** der Zeitungshändler ist gleich um die Ecke.

handyman ['hændɪmæn] (*pl* **-men** [-men]) *n* Heimwerker *der*.

hang [hæŋ] ◇ *vt* - **1.** (*pt & pp* **hung**) [suspend] auf|hängen; **to hang sthg on sthg** etw an etw *(A)* hängen - **2.** (*pt & pp* **hung** OR **hanged**) [execute] hängen. ◇ *vi* hängen. ◇ *n*: **to get the hang of sthg** *inf* kapieren, wie etw funktioniert. ◆ **hang about, hang around** *vi* - **1.** [loiter] herum|hängen - **2.** [wait] warten. ◆ **hang down** *vi* herunter|hängen. ◆ **hang on** *vi* - **1.** [keep hold]: **to hang on (to)** sich fest|halten (an *(+ D)*) - **2.** *inf* [continue waiting] warten; **hang on!** Moment mal!; [on telephone] bleiben Sie am Apparat! - **3.** [persevere] aus|halten. ◆ **hang out** *vi inf* [spend time] herum|hängen. ◆ **hang round** *vi* = **hang about**. ◆ **hang up** ◇ *vt sep* [suspend] auf|hängen. ◇ *vi* [on telephone] auf|hängen. ◆ **hang up on** *vt insep* TELEC: **he hung up on me** er hat einfach aufgelegt.

hangar ['hæŋər] *n* Hangar *der*.

hanger ['hæŋər] *n* [coat hanger] Kleiderbügel *der*.

hangers-on *npl* Gefolgsleute *Pl*.

hang gliding *n* Drachenfliegen *das*.

hangover ['hæŋˌəʊvər] *n* [from drinking] Kater *der*.

hang-up *n inf* PSYCHOL Komplex *der*.

hanker ['hæŋkər] ◆ **hanker after, hanker for** *vt insep* sich sehnen nach.

hankie, hanky ['hæŋkɪ] *n inf abbr of* **handkerchief**.

haphazard [ˌhæp'hæzəd] *adj* willkürlich.

happen ['hæpən] *vi* - **1.** [occur] geschehen, passieren; **to happen to sb** jm passieren - **2.** [chance]: **to happen to do sthg** zufällig etw *(A)* tun; **as it happens** zufälligerweise.

happening ['hæpənɪŋ] *n* Ereignis *das*.

happily ['hæpɪlɪ] *adv* - **1.** [contentedly]: **the children were playing happily** die Kinder spielten vergnügt - **2.** [fortunately] glücklicherweise - **3.** [willingly] gern.

happiness ['hæpɪnɪs] *n* Glück *das*.

happy ['hæpɪ] *adj* - **1.** [contented] glücklich - **2.** [causing contentment - life, day] glücklich; [- story] erfreulich; **Happy Christmas!** frohe OR fröhliche Weihnachten!; **Happy New Year!** frohes neues Jahr!; **Happy Birthday!** herzlichen Glückwunsch zum Geburtstag! - **3.** [satisfied] zufrieden; **to be happy with** OR **about sthg** glücklich OR zufrieden mit etw sein - **4.** [willing]: **to be happy to do sthg** etw gerne tun.

happy-go-lucky *adj inf* unbeschwert.

harangue [hə'ræŋ] ◇ *n* Standpauke *die*. ◇ *vt*: **to harangue sb** jm eine Standpauke halten.

harass ['hærəs] *vt* belästigen.

harbour *UK*, **harbor** *US* ['hɑːbər] ◇ *n* Hafen *der*. ◇ *vt* - **1.** [feeling] hegen - **2.** [person] versteckt halten.

hard [hɑːd] ◇ *adj* - **1.** [gen] hart; **to be hard on sb** streng mit jm sein - **2.** [difficult, strenuous] schwer; **it is hard to believe that...** es ist kaum zu glauben, dass...; **hard of hearing** schwerhörig - **3.** [kick, push] heftig - **4.** [fact] nackt - **5.** *UK* POL: **the hard left/right** der linke/rechte Flügel der Partei. ◇ *adv* - **1.** [work, hit] hart; **to try hard** sich *(D)* viel Mühe geben; **to listen hard** genau hin|hören - **2.** [rain] heftig - **3.** *phr*: **to be hard pushed** OR **put** OR **pressed**

to do sthg Schwierigkeiten haben, etw zu tun; **to feel hard done by** sich benachteiligt fühlen.

hardback ['hɑːdbæk] ◇ *adj* gebunden. ◇ *n* [book] gebundene Ausgabe.

hardboard ['hɑːdbɔːd] *n* Pressspanplatte *die*.

hard-boiled *adj* [egg] hart gekocht.

hard cash *n* Bargeld *das*.

hard copy *n* COMPUT Papierausdruck *der*.

hard disk *n* Festplatte *die*.

harden ['hɑːdn] ◇ *vt* - **1.** *fig* [person] ab|härten - **2.**: **to harden sb's opinion/attitude** jn in seiner Meinung/Einstellung bestärken. ◇ *vi* - **1.** [glue, concrete] härten - **2.** [attitude, ideas, opinion] sich verhärten.

hardheaded *adj* nüchtern.

hard-hearted [-'hɑːtɪd] *adj* hartherzig.

hard labour *n* Zwangsarbeit *die*.

hard-liner *n* Hardliner *der*, -in *die*.

hardly ['hɑːdlɪ] *adv* - **1.** [scarcely, not really] kaum; **hardly ever** fast nie; **hardly anything** fast nichts - **2.** [only just] gerade erst.

hardship ['hɑːdʃɪp] *n* Entbehrung *die*.

hard shoulder *n UK* AUT Standspur *die*.

hard up *adj inf* knapp bei Kasse.

hardware ['hɑːdweəʳ] *n (U)* - **1.** [tools, equipment] Eisenwaren *Pl* - **2.** COMPUT Hardware *die*.

hardware shop *n* Eisenwarenhandlung *die*.

hardwearing [ˌhɑːd'weərɪŋ] *adj UK* strapazierfähig.

hardworking [ˌhɑːd'wɜːkɪŋ] *adj* fleißig.

hardy ['hɑːdɪ] *adj* - **1.** [person, animal] abgehärtet - **2.** [plant] mehrjährig.

hare [heəʳ] *n* Hase *der*, Feldhase *der*.

haricot (bean) ['hærɪkəʊ-] *n* weiße Bohne.

harm [hɑːm] ◇ *n* [physical] Verletzung *die*; [psychological] Schaden *der*; **to do harm to sb/sthg, to do sb/sthg harm** jm/etw Schaden zu|fügen, jm/etw schaden; **she means no harm by it** sie meint es nicht böse; **to be out of harm's way** [person] in Sicherheit sein; [thing] aus dem Weg sein. ◇ *vt* [physically] verletzen; [psychologically] schädigen.

harmful ['hɑːmfʊl] *adj* schädlich.

harmless ['hɑːmlɪs] *adj* harmlos; [substance] unschädlich.

harmonica [hɑː'mɒnɪkə] *n* Mundharmonika *die*.

harmonize, -ise ['hɑːmənaɪz] ◇ *vt* [views, policies] in Einklang bringen. ◇ *vi* - **1.** [sounds, colours]: **to harmonize (with sthg)** harmonieren (mit etw) - **2.** MUS harmonisieren.

harmony ['hɑːmənɪ] *n* Harmonie *die*.

harness ['hɑːnɪs] ◇ *n* - **1.** [for horse] Geschirr *das* - **2.** [for person, child] Gurt *der*. ◇ *vt* - **1.** [horse] an|schirren - **2.** [energy, solar power] nutzbar machen.

harp [hɑːp] *n* MUS Harfe *die*. ◆ **harp on** *vi*: **to harp on (about sthg)** immer wieder an|fangen (von etw).

harpoon [hɑː'puːn] ◇ *n* Harpune *die*. ◇ *vt* harpunieren.

harpsichord ['hɑːpsɪkɔːd] *n* Cembalo *das*.

harrowing ['hærəʊɪŋ] *adj* grauenvoll.

harsh [hɑːʃ] *adj* - **1.** [person, criticism, treatment, words] hart, streng - **2.** [conditions, weather] rau - **3.** [voice] barsch; [cry] schrill - **4.** [colour, contrast, light] grell - **5.** [landscape] trostlos - **6.** [taste] streng.

harvest ['hɑːvɪst] ◇ *n* Ernte *die*. ◇ *vt* ernten.

has *(weak form* [həz], *strong form* [hæz]*)* *vb* ▷ **have**.

has-been *n inf pej* vergessene Größe.

hash [hæʃ] *n* - **1.** [meat] Haschee *das* - **2.** *inf* [mess]: **to make a hash of sthg** etw vermasseln.

hashish ['hæʃiːʃ] *n* Haschisch *das*.

hasn't ['hæznt] *abbr of* **has not**.

hassle ['hæsl] *inf* ◇ *n* Ärger *der*. ◇ *vt* ärgern.

haste [heɪst] *n* - **1.** [rush] Eile *die*; **to do sthg in haste** etw in Eile tun - **2.** [speed] Eile *die*.

hasten ['heɪsn] ◇ *vt* beschleunigen. ◇ *vi*: **to hasten (to do sthg)** sich beeilen(, etw zu tun).

hastily ['heɪstɪlɪ] *adv* - **1.** [rashly] übereilt - **2.** [quickly] hastig.

hasty ['heɪstɪ] *adj* - **1.** [rash] übereilt - **2.** [quick] hastig.

hat [hæt] *n* Hut *der*.

hatch [hætʃ] ◇ *vt* - **1.** [egg] aus|brüten - **2.** *fig* [scheme, plot] aus|hecken. ◇ *vi* [chick] aus|schlüpfen. ◇ *n* [for serving food] Durchreiche *die*.

hatchback ['hætʃˌbæk] *n* Schräghecklimousine *die*.

hatchet ['hætʃɪt] *n* Beil *das*.

hate [heɪt] ◇ *n* [emotion] Hass *der*. ◇ *vt* hassen, verabscheuen; **to hate doing sthg** es hassen, etw zu tun.

hateful ['heɪtfʊl] *adj* abscheulich.

hatred ['heɪtrɪd] *n* Hass *der*.

hat trick *n* SPORT Hattrick *der*.

haughty ['hɔːtɪ] *adj* hochmütig.

haul [hɔːl] ◇ *n* - **1.** [of drugs, stolen goods] Beute *die* - **2.** [distance]: **a long haul** ein langer Weg. ◇ *vt* [pull] ziehen.

haulage ['hɔːlɪdʒ] *n (U)* [business] Transportunternehmen *das*.

haulier *UK* ['hɔːlɪəʳ], **hauler** *US* ['hɔːlər] *n* [business] Spedition *die*.

haunch [hɔːntʃ] *n* - **1.** [of person] Gesäß *das* - **2.** [of animal] Keule *die*.

haunt [hɔːnt] ◇ *n* [place] Lieblingsort *der*; [pub] Stammlokal *das*. ◇ *vt* - **1.** [subj: ghost] spuken in *(+ D)*, umlgehen in *(+ D)* - **2.** [subj: memory, fear, problem] verfolgen.

have [hæv] (*pt & pp* **had**) ◇ *aux vb (to form perfect tenses)* haben/sein; **I have burnt it** ich habe es verbrannt; **he has come** er ist gekommen; **I have finished** ich bin fertig; **I have lived here for three years** ich wohne hier seit drei Jahren; **have you seen the film?** hast du den Film gesehen?; **have you been there? – no, I haven't/yes, I have** warst du schon mal dort? – nein, noch nie/ja; **she hasn't gone yet, has she?** sie ist noch nicht gegangen, oder?; **we had already left** wir waren schon gegangen; **I would never have gone if I'd known** ich wäre nie gegangen, wenn ich das gewusst hätte. ◇ *modal vb* [be obliged]: **to have (got) to do sthg** etw tun müssen; **do you have to go, have you got to go?** musst du wirklich gehen?; **I've got to go to work** ich muss arbeiten gehen; **do you have to pay?** muss man bezahlen? ◇ *vt* - **1.** [possess]: **to have (got)** haben; **I have no money, I haven't got any money** ich habe kein Geld; **she has (got) brown hair** sie hat braunes Haar - **2.** [illness] haben; **to have a cold** eine Erkältung haben - **3.** [need to deal with]: **to have (got)** haben; **I've got things to do** ich habe einiges zu erledigen - **4.** [receive - news, letter] bekommen; **we don't have many visitors** wir haben OR bekommen wenig Besuch - **5.** [instead of another verb] haben; **to have a read of sthg** etw lesen; **to have a bath** ein Bad nehmen; **to have breakfast** frühstücken; **to have a cigarette** eine Zigarette rauchen; **to have a game of chess** eine Partie Schach spielen; **to have lunch/dinner** zu Mittag/zu Abend essen; **to have a shower** duschen; **to have a swim** schwimmen; **I've had a bad day** heute ist alles schief gegangen - **6.** [give birth to]: **to have a baby** ein Kind bekommen - **7.** [cause to be done]: **to have sb do sthg** jn etw tun lassen; **to have sthg done** etw machen lassen; **I'm having the house decorated** ich lasse das Haus tapezieren; **to have one's hair cut** sich *(D)* die Haare schneiden lassen - **8.** [experience, suffer - accident] haben; **to have a good time** sich großartig amüsieren - **9.** [organize - party] machen; [- meeting] abhalten - **10.** *inf* [cheat]: **you've been had!** du bist reingelegt worden! - **11.** *phr*: **to have it in for sb** es auf jn abgesehen haben; **to have had it** [car, machine, clothes] hinüber sein; **I've had it** [be tired] ich kann nicht mehr; [be in trouble] ich bin geliefert. ◆ **have on** *vt sep* - **1.** [be wearing] anlhaben - **2.** [tease] anlführen; **you're having me on!** du willst mich wohl auf den Arm nehmen! ◆ **have out** *vt sep* - **1.** [appendix, tonsils] herausgenommen bekommen; **to have a tooth out** einen Zahn gezogen bekommen - **2.** [discuss frankly]: **to have it out with sb** sich mit jm auslsprechen.

haven ['heɪvn] *n* Zufluchtsort *der*.

haven't ['hævnt] *abbr of* **have not**.

havoc ['hævək] *n* Chaos *das*, Verwüstung *die*; **to play havoc with sthg** [health] etw ruinieren; [plans] etw über den Haufen werfen.

Hawaii [hə'waiː] *n* Hawaii *nt*.

hawk [hɔːk] *n liter & fig* Falke *der*.

hawker ['hɔːkə^r] *n* - **1.** [street vendor] Straßenhändler *der*, -in *die* - **2.** [door-to-door] Hausierer *der*, -in *die*.

hay [heɪ] *n* Heu *das*.

hay fever *n* Heuschnupfen *der*.

haystack ['heɪˌstæk] *n* Heuschober *der*.

haywire ['heɪˌwaɪə^r] *adj inf*: **to go haywire** [person] durchldrehen; [machine] verrückt spielen.

hazard ['hæzəd] ◇ *n* [danger] Gefahr *die*; [risk] Risiko *das*. ◇ *vt* - **1.** [life, reputation] riskieren - **2.** [guess, suggestion] wagen.

hazardous ['hæzədəs] *adj* [risky] riskant; [dangerous] gefährlich.

hazard warning lights *npl UK* Warnblinkanlage *die*.

haze [heɪz] *n* - **1.** [mist] Dunst *der* - **2.** [state of confusion] Verwirrtheit *die*.

hazelnut ['heɪzlˌnʌt] *n* Haselnuss *die*.

hazy ['heɪzɪ] *adj* - **1.** [misty] dunstig - **2.** [vague, confused] verwirrt.

he [hiː] *pers pron* er; **he's tall** er ist groß; **he doesn't care** ihm ist es egal; **there he is** dort ist er; **HE can't do it** DER kann das nicht tun.

head [hed] ◇ *n* - **1.** [part of body] Kopf *der*; **a** OR **per head** pro Kopf; **to laugh one's head off** sich totllachen; **to sing/shout one's head off** aus vollem Halse singen/schreien - **2.** [mind, brain] Verstand *der*; **to have a head for figures** eine Begabung für Zahlen haben; **to be off one's head** *UK*, **to be out of one's head** *US* [mad] verrückt OR durchgedreht sein; *inf* [drunk] besoffen sein; **to go to sb's head** [alcohol, success, praise] jm zu Kopf steigen; **to keep one's head** den Kopf nicht verlieren; **to lose one's head** den Kopf verlieren - **3.** [top, extremity - of stairs] oberer Absatz; [- of queue] Anfang *der*; [- of table, bed] Kopfende *das*; [- of procession, arrow] Spitze *die* - **4.** [of flower, cabbage] Kopf *der* - **5.** [leader - gen] Leiter *der*, -in *die*; [- of family] Oberhaupt *das* - **6.** [head teacher] Schulleiter *der*, -in *die*. ◇ *vt* - **1.** [procession, queue, list] anlführen - **2.** [organization, delegation] leiten - **3.** FTBL köpfen. ◇ *vi* [gen] gehen; [by car, bus, train] fahren; **where are you heading?** wohin gehst/fährst du? ◆ **heads** *npl* [on coin] Kopf *der*; **heads or tails?** Kopf oder Zahl? ◆ **head for** *vt insep* - **1.** [place]: **to head for Glasgow** Richtung Glasgow fahren - **2.** *fig* [trouble, disaster] zulsteuern auf *(+ A)*.

headache ['hedeɪk] *n* Kopfschmerzen *Pl*; **to have a headache** Kopfschmerzen haben.

headband ['hedbænd] *n* Stirnband *das*.

headdress ['hed,dres] *n* Kopfschmuck *der*.

header ['hedəʳ] *n* - **1.** FTBL Kopfball *der* - **2.** [at top of page] Kopfzeile *die*.

headfirst [,hed'fɜ:st] *adv* kopfüber.

heading ['hedɪŋ] *n* Überschrift *die*.

headlamp ['hedlæmp] *n UK* Scheinwerfer *der*.

headland ['hedlənd] *n* Landspitze *die*.

headlight ['hedlaɪt] *n* Scheinwerfer *der*.

headline ['hedlaɪn] *n* - **1.** [in newspaper] Schlagzeile *die* - **2.** [of news broadcast]: **the news headlines** die Kurznachrichten *Pl*.

headlong ['hedlɒŋ] *adv* - **1.** [at great speed] halsbrecherisch - **2.** [impetuously] blindlings - **3.** [dive, fall] kopfüber.

headmaster [,hed'mɑ:stəʳ] *n* Schulleiter *der*.

headmistress [,hed'mɪstrɪs] *n* Schulleiterin *die*.

head office *n* Hauptsitz *der*.

head-on <> *adj* [collision] frontal; [confrontation] direkt. <> *adv* frontal; [meet] direkt.

headphones ['hedfəʊnz] *npl* Kopfhörer *der*.

headquarters [,hed'kwɔ:təz] *npl* [of business, organization] Hauptniederlassung *die*; [of armed forces] Hauptquartier *das*.

headrest ['hedrest] *n* Kopfstütze *die*.

headroom ['hedrʊm] *n* [in car] Kopfraum *der*; [below bridge] lichte Höhe.

headscarf ['hedskɑ:f] (*pl* **-s** OR **-scarves** [-skɑ:vz]) *n* Kopftuch *das*.

headset ['hedset] *n* Kopfhörer *der*.

head start *n*: **head start (on** OR **over sb)** Vorsprung *der* (vor OR gegenüber jm).

headstrong ['hedstrɒŋ] *adj* eigenwillig.

head waiter *n* Oberkellner *der*.

headway ['hedweɪ] *n*: **to make headway** voranlkommen.

headword ['hedwɜ:d] *n* Stichwort *das*.

heady ['hedɪ] *adj* [exciting] aufregend.

heal [hi:l] <> *vt* - **1.** [person, wound] heilen - **2.** *fig* [breach, division] schlichten, beillegen. <> *vi* heilen.

healing ['hi:lɪŋ] <> *adj* heilend. <> *n (U)* Heilung *die*.

health [helθ] *n* Gesundheit *die*.

health centre *n* Ärztezentrum *das*.

health food *n* Reformkost *die*.

health food shop *n* Reformhaus *das*.

health service *n* Gesundheitsdienst *der*.

healthy ['helθɪ] *adj* - **1.** [gen] gesund - **2.** [profit, sum] ordentlich - **3.** [attitude] vernünftig; [respect] angebracht.

heap [hi:p] <> *n* Haufen *der*. <> *vt* [pile up] auflhäufen; **to heap sthg on(to) sthg** etw auf etw *(A)* häufen. ◆ **heaps** *npl inf*: **heaps of money/people/books** ein Haufen Geld/Leute/Bücher; **heaps of time** eine Menge Zeit.

hear [hɪəʳ] (*pt & pp* **heard** [hɜ:d]) <> *vt* - **1.** [perceive] hören - **2.** [learn of] hören; **to hear (that) ...** hören, dass ... - **3.** LAW [listen to] anlhören. <> *vi* - **1.** [gen] hören; **to hear from sb** von jm hören - **2.** [know]: **to hear about sthg** etw erfahren - **3.** *phr*: **to have heard of sb/sthg** von jm/etw gehört haben; **I won't hear of it!** ich möchte nichts davon hören!

hearing ['hɪərɪŋ] *n* - **1.** [sense] Gehör *das* - **2.** LAW [trial] Verhandlung *die*.

hearing aid *n* Hörgerät *das*.

hearsay ['hɪəseɪ] *n* Hörensagen *das*.

hearse [hɜ:s] *n* Leichenwagen *der*.

heart [hɑ:t] *n* - **1.** [gen] Herz *das*; **from the heart** von Herzen; **to break sb's heart** jm das OR js Herz brechen - **2.** *(U)* [courage] Mut *der*; **to lose heart** den Mut verlieren - **3.** [core - of city] Herz *das*; [- of problem] Kern *der*. ◆ **hearts** *npl* [playing cards] Herz *das*; **the six of hearts** die Herzsechs. ◆ **at heart** *adv* im Grunde. ◆ **by heart** *adv* auswendig.

heartache ['hɑ:teɪk] *n* Kummer *der*.

heart attack *n* Herzanfall *der*.

heartbeat ['hɑ:tbi:t] *n* Herzschlag *der*.

heartbroken ['hɑ:t,brəʊkn] *adj* untröstlich.

heartburn ['hɑ:tbɜ:n] *n* Sodbrennen *das*.

heart failure *n* Herzversagen *das*.

heartfelt ['hɑ:tfelt] *adj* tief empfunden.

hearth [hɑ:θ] *n* Kamin *der*.

heartless ['hɑ:tlɪs] *adj* herzlos.

heartwarming ['hɑ:t,wɔ:mɪŋ] *adj* herzerfreuend.

hearty ['hɑ:tɪ] *adj* - **1.** [laughter, praise, welcome] herzlich - **2.** [meal, appetite] herzhaft.

heat [hi:t] <> *n* - **1.** [warmth] Wärme *die* - **2.** *(U)* [specific temperature] Temperatur *die* - **3.** *(U)* [fire, source of heat] Feuer *das* - **4.** *(U)* [hot weather] Hitze *die* - **5.** *fig* [pressure]: **in the heat of the moment** in der Hitze des Gefechts - **6.** [eliminating round - in race] Vorlauf *der*; [- in competition] Vorrunde *die* - **7.** ZOOL: **on heat** *UK*, **in heat** *US* brünstig; [dog, cat] läufig; [horse] rossig. <> *vt* heiß machen, erhitzen; [house, pool] heizen. ◆ **heat up** <> *vt sep* heiß machen. <> *vi* sich erwärmen.

heated ['hi:tɪd] *adj* - **1.** [room, swimming pool] beheizt - **2.** [argument, discussion, person] hitzig.

heater ['hi:təʳ] *n* [in car] Heizung *die*; [in room, water tank] Heizgerät *das*.

heath [hi:θ] *n* Heide *die*.

heathen ['hi:ðn] <> *adj* heidnisch. <> *n* Heide *der*, -din *die*.

heather ['heðəʳ] *n* Heidekraut *das*.

heating ['hi:tɪŋ] *n* Heizung *die*.

heatstroke ['hi:tstrəʊk] *n* Hitzschlag *der*.

heat wave *n* Hitzewelle *die*.

heave [hi:v] ◇ *vt* - **1.** [pull] hieven; [push] schieben - **2.** *inf* [throw] schmeißen - **3.** [give out]: **to heave a sigh** einen Seufzer auslstoßen. ◇ *vi* - **1.** [pull] ziehen - **2.** [rise and fall] sich heben und senken - **3.** [retch] brechen.

heaven ['hevn] *n* [Paradise] Himmel *der*. ◆ **heavens** ◇ *npl*: **the heavens** *liter* der Himmel. ◇ *excl*: **(good) heavens!** du lieber Himmel!

heavenly ['hevnlı] *adj inf* [delightful] himmlisch, herrlich.

heavily ['hevılı] *adv* - **1.** [smoke, drink] stark; [rain] heftig - **2.** [built] solide - **3.** [breathe, sigh] schwer, laut - **4.** [fall, land] schwerfällig - **5.** [sleep] tief.

heavy ['hevı] *adj* - **1.** [in weight] schwer - **2.** [fighting, losses] schwer; [rain] heftig; [traffic, smoker, drinker] stark; **to be a heavy sleeper** immer tief und fest schlafen - **3.** [person - fat] dick; [- solidly built] untersetzt - **4.** [coat, sweater] dick - **5.** [food, responsibility] schwer - **6.** [breathing, step, fall] schwerfällig - **7.** [schedule, week] arbeitsreich - **8.** [work, job] anstrengend.

heavy cream *n US* Schlagsahne *die*.

heavy goods vehicle *n UK* Schwertransporter *der*.

heavyweight ['hevıweıt] ◇ *adj* SPORT Schwergewichts-. ◇ *n* - **1.** [boxer] Schwergewichtler *der* - **2.** [intellectual] Größe *die*.

Hebrew ['hi:bru:] ◇ *adj* hebräisch. ◇ *n* [language] Hebräisch(e) *das*.

heck [hek] *excl*: **what/where/why the heck ... ?** was/wo/warum zum Teufel ... ?; **a heck of a nice guy** ein wahnsinnig netter Kerl; **a heck of a lot of people** wahnsinnig viele Leute.

heckle ['hekl] ◇ *vt* (durch Zwischenrufe) unterbrechen. ◇ *vi* zwischenlrufen.

hectic ['hektık] *adj* hektisch.

he'd [hi:d] *abbr of* **he had**, **he would**.

hedge [hedʒ] ◇ *n* [shrub] Hecke *die*. ◇ *vi* [prevaricate] Ausflüchte machen.

hedgehog ['hedʒhɒg] *n* Igel *der*.

heed [hi:d] ◇ *n*: **to take heed of sthg** etw *(D)* Beachtung schenken. ◇ *vt fml* beachten.

heedless ['hi:dlıs] *adj*: **to be heedless of sthg** etw nicht beachten.

heel [hi:l] *n* - **1.** [of foot] Ferse *die* - **2.** [of shoe] Absatz *der*.

hefty ['heftı] *adj inf* - **1.** [person] kräftig - **2.** [fee, fine] saftig; [salary] dick.

heifer ['hefəʳ] *n* Färse *die*.

height [haıt] *n* - **1.** [gen] Höhe *die*; [of person] Größe *die*; **5 metres in height** 5 Meter hoch; **what height are you?** wie groß sind Sie? - **2.** [zenith] Höhepunkt *der*.

heighten ['haıtn] ◇ *vt* [feeling, awareness] verstärken; [anxiety] steigern. ◇ *vi* sich verstärken.

heir [eəʳ] *n* Erbe *der*, -bin *die*.

heiress ['eərıs] *n* Erbin *die*.

heirloom ['eəlu:m] *n* Erbstück *das*.

heist [haıst] *n inf* Raubüberfall *der*.

held [held] *pt* & *pp* ▷ **hold**.

helicopter ['helıkɒptəʳ] *n* Hubschrauber *der*.

hell [hel] ◇ *n* - **1.** [gen] Hölle *die* - **2.** *inf* [for emphasis]: **what/where/why the hell ... ?** was/wo/warum zum Teufel ... ?; **one** OR **a hell of a mess** ein wahnsinniges Durcheinander; **one** OR **a hell of a nice guy** ein wahnsinnig netter Kerl - **3.** *phr*: **to hell with the expense!** (es ist mir) egal, was es kostet!; **to do sthg for the hell of it** *inf* etw aus Jux machen; **to give sb hell** *inf* jm die Hölle heißmachen; **go to hell!** *v inf* hau ab! ◇ *excl inf* verdammt!

he'll [hi:l] *abbr of* **he will**.

hellish ['helıʃ] *adj inf* höllisch, schrecklich.

hello [hə'ləʊ] *excl* hallo.

helm [helm] *n liter* & *fig* Ruder *das*.

helmet ['helmıt] *n* Helm *der*.

help [help] ◇ *n* Hilfe *die*; **to be of help** behilflich sein; **to be a help** eine Hilfe sein; **with sb's help** mit js Hilfe; **with the help of sthg** mit Hilfe einer Sache *(G)*. ◇ *vt* - **1.** [assist] helfen *(+ D)*; **to help sb (to) do sthg** jm helfen, etw zu tun; **to help sb with sthg** jm bei etw helfen - **2.** [make easier for] erleichtern; **to help sb (to) do sthg** es jm erleichtern, etw zu tun - **3.** [contribute to]: **to help (to) do sthg** helfen, etw zu tun - **4.** [avoid]: **I can't help it** ich kann nichts dafür; **I couldn't help laughing** ich mußte einfach lachen - **5.** *phr*: **to help o.s.** sich bedienen; **to help o.s. to sthg** sich *(D)* etw nehmen. ◇ *vi* helfen; **to help with sthg** bei etw helfen. ◇ *excl* Hilfe! ◆ **help out** ◇ *vt sep* auslhelfen *(+ D)*. ◇ *vi* auslhelfen.

helper ['helpəʳ] *n* - **1.** [on any task] Helfer *der*, -in *die* - **2.** *US* [to do housework] Hausgehilfe *der*, -fin *die*.

helpful ['helpfʊl] *adj* - **1.** [willing to help] hilfsbereit - **2.** [useful] nützlich, hilfreich.

helping ['helpıŋ] *n* Portion *die*.

helpless ['helplıs] *adj* hilflos.

helpline ['helplaın] *n* Servicenummer *die*; COMPUT Hotline *die*.

Helsinki ['helsıŋkı] *n* Helsinki *nt*.

hem [hem] ◇ *n* Saum *der*. ◇ *vt* säumen. ◆ **hem in** *vt sep* einlengen.

hemisphere ['hemı,sfıəʳ] *n* Hemisphäre *die*.

hemline ['hemlaın] *n* Saum *der*.

hemorrhage ['hemərıdʒ] *n* Blutung *die*.

hemorrhoids ['hemərɔıdz] *npl* Hämorriden *Pl*.

hen [hen] *n* [female chicken] Huhn *das*.

hence [hens] *adv fml* - **1.** [therefore] folglich - **2.** [from now]: **ten years hence** in zehn Jahren.

henceforth [ˌhens'fɔ:θ] *adv fml* fortan.

henchman ['hentʃmən] (*pl* **-men** [-mən]) *n pej* Helfershelfer *der*.

henna ['henə] *n* Henna *die ODER das*.

henpecked ['henpekt] *adj pej*: **to be henpecked** unter dem Pantoffel stehen; **a henpecked husband** ein Pantoffelheld.

her [hɜ:ʳ] ◇ *pers pron (accusative)* sie; *(dative)* ihr; **I know her** ich kenne sie; **it's her** sie ist es; **send it to her** schick es ihr; **tell her ...** sag ihr ...; **he's worse than her** er ist schlimmer als sie; **she took her luggage with her** sie nahm ihr Gepäck mit. ◇ *poss adj* ihr; **her friend** ihr Freund/ihre Freundin; **her children** ihre Kinder; **she washed her hair** sie hat sich die Haare gewaschen.

herald ['herəld] *vt fml* ankünd(ig)en.

herb [hɜ:b] *n* Kraut *das*.

herd [hɜ:d] ◇ *n liter & fig* Herde *die*. ◇ *vt* treiben.

here [hɪəʳ] *adv* hier; **come here!** komm her!; **here you are!** [when giving sthg] bitte!; [greeting sb] da bist du ja!; **here we are** da sind wir; **here and there** hier und da; **here and now** sofort; **here's to you!** [in toast] auf Ihr Wohl!

hereabouts *UK* [ˌhɪərə'baʊts], **hereabout** *US* [ˌhɪərə'baʊt] *adv* in dieser Gegend.

hereafter [ˌhɪər'ɑ:ftəʳ] ◇ *adv fml* im Folgenden. ◇ *n*: **the hereafter** das Jenseits.

hereby [ˌhɪə'baɪ] *adv fml* hiermit.

hereditary [hɪ'redɪtrɪ] *adj* erblich, Erb-.

heresy ['herəsɪ] *n* Ketzerei *die*, Häresie *die*.

herewith [ˌhɪə'wɪð] *adv fml* anbei.

heritage ['herɪtɪdʒ] *n* Erbe *das*.

hermit ['hɜ:mɪt] *n* Einsiedler *der*, -in *die*.

hernia ['hɜ:nɪə] *n* Bruch *der*, Hernie *die*.

hero ['hɪərəʊ] (*pl* **-es**) *n* [gen] Held *der*.

heroic [hɪ'rəʊɪk] *adj* [person, deed] heldenhaft. ◆ **heroics** *npl pej* Heldenstücke *Pl*.

heroin ['herəʊɪn] *n* Heroin *das*.

heroine ['herəʊɪn] *n* Heldin *die*.

heron ['herən] (*pl inv* OR **-s**) *n* Reiher *der*.

herring ['herɪŋ] (*pl inv* OR **-s**) *n* Hering *der*.

hers [hɜ:z] *poss pron* ihre (r) (s); **a friend of hers** ein Freund von ihr; **these shoes are hers** diese Schuhe gehören ihr; **she ate my portion and hers** sie aß meine und ihre Portion.

herself [hɜ:'self] *pron* - **1.** *(reflexive)* sich; **she hurt herself** sie hat sich verletzt - **2.** *(after prep)* sich selbst; **she did it herself** [stressed] sie hat es selbst getan; **by herself** allein.

he's [hi:z] *abbr of* **he is**, **he has**.

hesitant ['hezɪtənt] *adj* [person] unentschlossen, zögerlich.

hesitate ['hezɪteɪt] *vi* zögern; **to hesitate to do sthg** Bedenken haben, etw zu tun.

hesitation [ˌhezɪ'teɪʃn] *n* Zögern *das*.

heterosexual [ˌhetərəʊ'sekʃʊəl] ◇ *adj* heterosexuell. ◇ *n* Heterosexuelle *der, die*.

het up [ˌhet-] *adj inf* aufgeregt.

hexagon ['heksəgən] *n* Sechseck *das*.

hey [heɪ] *excl* he!

heyday ['heɪdeɪ] *n* Glanzzeit *die*.

HGV (*abbr of* **heavy goods vehicle**) *n* Lkw *der*.

hi [haɪ] *excl inf* hallo!

hiatus [haɪ'eɪtəs] (*pl* **-es**) *n fml* Unterbrechung *die*.

hibernate ['haɪbəneɪt] *vi* Winterschlaf halten.

hiccough, hiccup ['hɪkʌp] ◇ *n* - **1.** [sound] Schluckauf *der*; **to have hiccoughs** (den) Schluckauf haben - **2.** *fig* [difficulty] kleines Problem. ◇ *vi* schlucksen.

hid [hɪd] *pt* ▷ **hide**.

hidden ['hɪdn] ◇ *pp* ▷ **hide**. ◇ *adj* versteckt; **hidden costs** verdeckte Unkosten.

hide [haɪd] (*pt* **hid**, *pp* **hidden**) ◇ *vt* - **1.** [conceal - person, item] verstecken; [- emotions, facts] verbergen; *(phrase)*: **to hide sthg (from sb)** etw (vor jm) verstecken/verbergen - **2.** [cover] verdecken. ◇ *vi* sich verstecken. ◇ *n* [animal skin] Haut *die*.

hide-and-seek *n* Versteckspiel *das*.

hideaway ['haɪdəweɪ] *n inf* Versteck *das*.

hideous ['hɪdɪəs] *adj* grässlich.

hiding ['haɪdɪŋ] *n* - **1.** [concealment]: **to be in hiding** sich verstecken - **2.** *inf* [beating]: **to give sb a (good) hiding** jm eine (ordentliche) Abreibung verpassen.

hiding place *n* Versteck *das*.

hierarchy ['haɪərɑ:kɪ] *n* Hierarchie *die*.

hi-fi ['haɪfaɪ] *n* Hi-Fi *das*.

high [haɪ] ◇ *adj* - **1.** [gen] hoch; *(before noun)* hohe (r) (s); **how high is it?** wie hoch ist es?; **it's 10 metres high** es ist 10 Meter hoch; **high winds** starker Wind - **2.** *inf* [from drugs] high. ◇ *n* - **1.** [weather front] Hoch *das* - **2.** [highest point] Höchststand *der*. ◇ *adv* hoch; **to aim high** hoch hinaus|wollen.

highbrow ['haɪbraʊ] *adj* intellektuell; [literature, tastes] anspruchsvoll.

high chair *n* (Kinder)hochstuhl *der*.

high-class *adj* [superior - hotel, restaurant] vornehm; [- performance] hochwertig.

High Court *n UK* LAW oberster Gerichtshof.

higher ['haɪəʳ] *adj* [exam, qualification] höher. ◆ **Higher** *n* SCH: **Higher (Grade)** *schottischer Abiturabschluss in einem Fach*.

higher education *n* Hochschulbildung *die*.

high jump *n* SPORT Hochsprung *der*.

Highlands ['haɪləndz] *npl*: **the Highlands** [of Scotland] das schottische Hochland.

highlight ['haɪlaɪt] ◇ *n* [of event, occasion] Höhepunkt *der*. ◇ *vt* hervor|heben. ◆ **highlights** *npl* [in hair] Strähnchen *Pl*.

highlighter (pen) ['haɪlaɪtəʳ-] *n* Textmarker *der*.

highly ['haɪlɪ] *adv* - **1.** [very, extremely] höchst - **2.** [very well] sehr gut - **3.** [at an important level]: **highly placed** hoch plaziert - **4.** [favourably] sehr gut; **I highly recommend it** ich kann es sehr empfehlen.

highly-strung [-'strʌŋ] *adj* nervös.

Highness ['haɪnɪs] *n*: **His/Her/Your (Royal) Highness** Seine/Ihre/Eure (Königliche) Hoheit.

high-pitched [-'pɪtʃt] *adj* [voice] hoch; [shout, scream] schrill.

high point *n* Höhepunkt *der*.

high-powered [-'paʊəd] *adj* [dynamic - activity, place] anspruchsvoll, leistungsorientiert; [- person] dynamisch.

high-ranking [-'ræŋkɪŋ] *adj* ranghoch.

high-rise *adj*: **high-rise building** Hochhaus *das*.

high school *n* höhere Schule.

high season *n* Hochsaison *die*.

high spot *n* Höhepunkt *der*.

high street *n UK* Hauptstraße *die*.

high-tech [-'tek] *adj* Hightech-.

high tide *n* Flut *die*.

highway ['haɪweɪ] *n* - **1.** *US* [main road between cities] Schnellstraße *die* - **2.** *UK* [any main road] Landstraße *die*.

Highway Code *n UK*: **the Highway Code** die Straßenverkehrsordnung.

hijack ['haɪdʒæk] ◇ *n* Entführung *die*. ◇ *vt* entführen.

hijacker ['haɪdʒækəʳ] *n* [of aircraft] Flugzeugentführer *der*, -in *die*; [of vehicle] Entführer *der*, -in *die*.

hike [haɪk] ◇ *n* Wanderung *die*. ◇ *vi* wandern.

hiker ['haɪkəʳ] *n* Wanderer *der*, -rin *die*.

hiking ['haɪkɪŋ] *n* Wandern *das*; **to go hiking** wandern gehen.

hilarious [hɪ'leərɪəs] *adj* urkomisch.

hill [hɪl] *n* - **1.** [mound] Hügel *der* - **2.** [slope] Hang *der*.

hillside ['hɪlsaɪd] *n* Hang *der*.

hilly ['hɪlɪ] *adj* hügelig.

hilt [hɪlt] *n* Heft *das*; **to support/defend sb to the hilt** jn voll und ganz unterstützen/verteidigen.

him [hɪm] *pers pron (accusative)* ihn; *(dative)* ihm; **I know him** ich kenne ihn; **it's him** er ist es; **send it to him** schick es ihm; **tell him** sag ihm; **she's worse than him** sie ist schlimmer als er; **he took his luggage with him** er nahm sein Gepäck mit.

Himalayas [ˌhɪmə'leɪəz] *npl*: **the Himalayas** der Himalaja.

himself [hɪm'self] *pron* - **1.** *(reflexive)* sich; **he hurt himself** er hat sich verletzt - **2.** *(after prep)* sich selbst; **he did it himself** [stressed] er hat es selbst getan; **by himself** allein.

hind [haɪnd] (*pl inv* OR **-s**) ◇ *adj*: **hind legs** Hinterbeine *Pl*. ◇ *n* Hirschkuh *die*.

hinder ['hɪndəʳ] *vt* behindern.

hindrance ['hɪndrəns] *n* - **1.** [obstacle] Hindernis *das* - **2.** *(U)* [delay] Behinderung *die*.

hindsight ['haɪndsaɪt] *n (U)*: **with the benefit of hindsight** im Nachhinein.

Hindu ['hɪnduː] (*pl* **-s**) ◇ *adj* Hindu-, hinduistisch. ◇ *n* Hindu *der*.

hinge [hɪndʒ] *n* [on door, window] Angel *die*; [on lid] Scharnier *das*. ◆ **hinge (up)on** *vt insep* [depend on] ab|hängen von.

hint [hɪnt] ◇ *n* - **1.** [indirect suggestion] Andeutung *die*; **to drop a hint** eine Andeutung machen - **2.** [useful suggestion, tip] Tipp *der* - **3.** [small amount, trace] Spur *die*. ◇ *vi*: **to hint at sthg** etw an|deuten. ◇ *vt*: **to hint that...** an|deuten, dass...

hip [hɪp] *n* [part of body] Hüfte *die*.

hippie ['hɪpɪ] *n* Hippie *der*.

hippo ['hɪpəʊ] (*pl* **-s**) *n* Nilpferd *das*.

hippopotamus [ˌhɪpə'pɒtəməs] (*pl* **-muses** OR **-mi** [-maɪ]) *n* Nilpferd *das*.

hippy ['hɪpɪ] *n* = **hippie**.

hire ['haɪəʳ] ◇ *n (U)* [of car, television, venue] Mieten *das*; [of suit] Leihen *das*; **'for hire'** 'zu vermieten'; [taxi sign] 'frei'. ◇ *vt* - **1.** [rent - car, television, venue] mieten; [- suit] leihen - **2.** [employ] an|stellen. ◆ **hire out** *vt sep* [car, television, venue] vermieten; [suit] verleihen.

hire car *n UK* Mietwagen *der*.

hire purchase *n* Ratenkauf *der*.

his [hɪz] ◇ *poss adj* sein; **his friend** sein Freund/seine Freundin; **his children** seine Kinder; **he has washed his hair** er hat sich die Haare gewaschen. ◇ *poss pron* seine (r) (s); **a friend of his** ein Freund von ihm; **these shoes are his** diese Schuhe gehören ihm; **he ate my portion and his** er aß meine und seine Portion.

hiss [hɪs] *vi* zischen; [cat] fauchen.

historic [hɪ'stɒrɪk] *adj* historisch.

historical [hɪ'stɒrɪkəl] *adj* historisch.

history ['hɪstərɪ] *n* - **1.** [gen] Geschichte *die* - **2.** [past record] Vorgeschichte *die*.

hit [hɪt] (*pt & pp inv*) ◇ *n* - **1.** [blow] Schlag *der* - **2.** [successful strike] Treffer *der* - **3.** [success] Erfolg *der*; [record] Hit *der* - **4.** COMPUT [of website] Treffer *der*. ◇ *comp* Erfolgs-; [record] Hit-. ◇ *vt* - **1.** [strike] schlagen - **2.** [subj: stones, bullet] treffen; [subj: vehicle -

tree, wall] fahren gegen; [- person] erwischen - 3. [reach] erreichen - 4. *phr*: **to hit it off (with sb)** sich gut (mit jm) verstehen.

hit-and-miss *adj* = **hit-or-miss**.

hit-and-run <> *n*: **hit-and-run (accident)** Unfall *der* mit Fahrerflucht. <> *adj* [driver] unfallflüchtig.

hitch [hɪtʃ] <> *n* [problem, snag] Problem *das*. <> *vt* - **1.** [solicit]: **to hitch a lift** trampen - **2.** [fasten]: **to hitch sthg on(to) sthg** etw an etw *(D)* befestigen. <> *vi* [hitchhike] trampen. ◆ **hitch up** *vt sep* [skirt, trousers] hochlziehen.

hitchhike ['hɪtʃhaɪk] *vi* trampen.

hitchhiker ['hɪtʃhaɪkəʳ] *n* Anhalter *der*, -in *die*, Tramper *der*, -in *die*.

hi-tech [ˌhaɪ'tek] *adj* = **high-tech**.

hitherto [ˌhɪðə'tuː] *adv fml* bisher.

hit-or-miss *adj* willkürlich.

HIV (*abbr of* **human immunodeficiency virus**) *n* HIV; **to be HIV-positive** HIV-positiv sein.

hive [haɪv] *n* [for bees] Bienenstock *der*; **to be a hive of activity** *fig* der reinste Bienenstock sein. ◆ **hive off** *vt sep* [separate] ablspalten, auslgliedern.

HNC (*abbr of* **Higher National Certificate**) *n britische Qualifikation in technischen Fächern.*

HND (*abbr of* **Higher National Diploma**) *n britische Hochschulqualifikation in technischen Fächern.*

hoard [hɔːd] <> *n* Vorrat *der*. <> *vt* horten.

hoarding ['hɔːdɪŋ] *n UK* Plakatwand *die*.

hoarse [hɔːs] *adj* heiser.

hoax [həʊks] *n* [joke] Streich *der*; [threat, alarm] blinder Alarm.

hob [hɒb] *n UK* [on cooker] Kochfläche *die*.

hobble ['hɒbl] *vi* humpeln.

hobby ['hɒbɪ] *n* Hobby *das*.

hobbyhorse ['hɒbɪhɔːs] *n* [favourite topic] Lieblingsthema *das*.

hobo ['həʊbəʊ] (*pl* **-es** *OR* **-s**) *n US* Landstreicher *der*, Penner *der*.

hockey ['hɒkɪ] *n* - **1.** [on grass] Hockey *das* - **2.** *US* [ice hockey] Eishockey *das*.

hockey stick *n* Hockeyschläger *der*.

hoe [həʊ] <> *n* Hacke *die*. <> *vt* hacken.

hog [hɒg] <> *n* - **1.** *US* [pig] Schwein *das* - **2.** *inf* [greedy person] Vielfraß *der* - **3.** *phr*: **to go the whole hog** aufs Ganze gehen. <> *vt inf* [monopolize - road] in Beschlag nehmen; [- attention] mit Beschlag belegen.

Hogmanay ['hɒgməneɪ] *n Scotland* Silvester *der ODER das*.

hoist [hɔɪst] <> *n* [device for lifting] Lastenaufzug *der*. <> *vt* - **1.** [load, person] heben, hieven - **2.** [sail, flag] hissen.

hold [həʊld] (*pt & pp* **held**) <> *vt* - **1.** [gen] halten; **to hold sb prisoner/hostage** jn gefangen halten/als Geisel festlhalten - **2.** [position, responsibility, title, driving licence] haben; [belief, principle] vertreten - **3.** [meeting, talks] ablhalten; [conversation] führen - **4.** *fml* [consider]: **to hold sthg to be necessary/important** etw für notwendig/wichtig erachten *OR* halten; **to hold (that)** der Meinung sein, dass; **to hold sb responsible for sthg** jn für etw verantwortlich machen - **5.** [on telephone]: **please hold the line** bitte bleiben Sie am Apparat - **6.** [attention, interest] fesseln - **7.** [support] tragen - **8.** [contain] enthalten; **what does the future hold for him?** was birgt die Zukunft für ihn? - **9.** [have space for] Platz haben für - **10.** *phr*: **hold it!, hold everything!** halt!; **to hold one's own** sich behaupten können. <> *vi* - **1.** [promise, objection] gelten; [weather] sich halten; **his luck held** das Glück blieb ihm treu; **to hold still** *OR* **steady** stillhalten - **2.** [on phone] am Apparat bleiben. <> *n* - **1.** [grip] Griff *der*; **to keep hold of sthg** [with hand] etw festlhalten; [save] etw behalten; **to take** *OR* **lay hold of sthg** etw fassen *OR* packen; **to get hold of sthg** [obtain] etw bekommen; **to get hold of sb** [find] jn erreichen - **2.** [of ship, aircraft] Laderaum *der*, Frachtraum *der* - **3.** [control, influence]: **to have a hold over sb** [person] jn in der Hand haben; [feeling, idea] von jm Besitz ergreifen. ◆ **hold back** *vt sep* [gen] zurücklhalten. ◆ **hold down** *vt sep*: **to hold down a job** sich in einer Stelle halten. ◆ **hold off** *vt sep* [fend off] ablwehren. ◆ **hold on** *vi* - **1.** [wait, on phone] warten; **hold on!** [on phone] einen Moment, bitte! - **2.** [grip]: **to hold on (to sthg)** sich (an etw *(D)*) festlhalten. ◆ **hold out** <> *vt sep* [hand] auslstrecken; [arms] auslbreiten. <> *vi* - **1.** [last] reichen - **2.** [resist]: **to hold out (against sb/sthg)** sich (gegen jn/etw) behaupten. ◆ **hold up** *vt sep* - **1.** [raise] hochlheben - **2.** [delay - traffic, production] auflhalten; [- plans] verzögern.

holdall ['həʊldɔːl] *n UK* Reisetasche *die*.

holder ['həʊldəʳ] *n* - **1.** [container] Halter *der*; [for cigarette] Spitze *die* - **2.** [owner] Inhaber *der*, -in *die*.

holding ['həʊldɪŋ] *n* - **1.** [investment] Aktienbesitz *der* - **2.** [farm] Gut *das*.

holdup ['həʊldʌp] *n* - **1.** [robbery] bewaffneter Raubüberfall - **2.** [delay] Verzögerung *die*; [of traffic] stockender Verkehr.

hole [həʊl] *n* - **1.** [gen] Loch *das*; **hole in one** [in golf] Ass *das* - **2.** *inf* [horrible place] Loch *das*; [town] Kaff *das* - **3.** *inf* [predicament]: **to get o.s. into a hole** in die Bredouille kommen; **to be in a hole** in der Bredouille sein.

holiday ['hɒlɪdeɪ] *n* - **1.** [vacation] Urlaub *der*; **holidays** Urlaub *der*; SCH Ferien *Pl*; **to be on holiday** im Urlaub sein; **to go on holiday** in Urlaub fahren - **2.** [public holiday] Feiertag *der*.

holiday camp *n UK* ≃ Feriendorf *das*.

holidaymaker ['hɒlɪdɪˌmeɪkəʳ] *n UK* Urlauber *der*, -in *die*.

holiday pay *n UK* Urlaubsgeld *das.*

holiday resort *n UK* Ferienort *der.*

holistic [həʊ'lɪstɪk] *adj* holistisch.

Holland ['hɒlənd] *n* Holland *nt.*

holler ['hɒlə^r] *vt & vi inf* brüllen.

hollow ['hɒləʊ] ◇ *adj* hohl; [cheeks] eingefallen; [victory, success] wertlos; [promise] leer. ◇ *n* - **1.** [in tree] Höhlung *die* - **2.** [in ground, pillow] Mulde *die*; **the hollow of one's hand/back** die hohle Hand/das Kreuz. ◆ **hollow out** *vt sep* aus|höhlen.

holly ['hɒlɪ] *n* Stechpalme *die.*

holocaust ['hɒləkɔ:st] *n*: **a nuclear holocaust** ein atomarer Holocaust. ◆ **Holocaust** *n*: **the Holocaust** der Holocaust.

holster ['həʊlstə^r] *n* Pistolenhalfter *das.*

holy ['həʊlɪ] *adj* heilig; [ground] geweiht.

Holy Ghost *n*: **the Holy Ghost** der Heilige Geist.

Holy Land *n*: **the Holy Land** das Heilige Land.

Holy Spirit *n*: **the Holy Spirit** der Heilige Geist.

home [həʊm] ◇ *n* - **1.** [place of residence, institution] Heim *das* - **2.** [place of origin] Heimat *die* - **3.** [family unit] Zuhause *das*; **to leave home** von zu Hause weg|gehen. ◇ *adj* - **1.** [market, product] inländisch - **2.** SPORT Heim-. ◇ *adv*: **to go home** nach Hause gehen; [from abroad] zurück|fahren/zurück|fliegen; **to be home** zu Hause sein. ◆ **at home** *adv* - **1.** [in one's house, flat] daheim, zu Hause - **2.** [comfortable]: **to feel at home somewhere** sich irgendwo wohl fühlen; **to make o.s. at home** es sich *(D)* bequem machen - **3.** [in one's own country]: **at home the shops close at five** bei uns machen die Geschäfte um fünf zu.

home address *n* Privatadresse *die.*

home brew *n (U)* selbst gebrautes Bier.

home computer *n* Heimcomputer *der.*

home cooking *n* bürgerliche Küche.

Home Counties *npl UK*: **the Home Counties** *die London umgebenden Grafschaften.*

home economics *n (U)* Hauswirtschaft(slehre) *die.*

home help *n UK* Haushaltshilfe *die.*

homeland ['həʊmlænd] *n* [country of birth] Heimatland *das.*

homeless ['həʊmlɪs] ◇ *adj* obdachlos. ◇ *npl*: **the homeless** die Obdachlosen.

homely ['həʊmlɪ] *adj* - **1.** [simple, unpretentious - place] schlicht; *(phrase)*: **homely fare** Hausmannskost *die* - **2.** [ugly] unattraktiv.

homemade [,həʊm'meɪd] *adj* selbst gemacht; [bread] selbst gebacken; [food] hausgemacht.

Home Office *n UK*: **the Home Office** das Innenministerium.

homeopathy [,həʊmɪ'ɒpəθɪ] *n* Homöopathie *die.*

home page *n* COMPUT Homepage *die.*

Home Secretary *n UK* Innenminister *der*, -in *die.*

homesick ['həʊmsɪk] *adj* heimwehkrank; **to be/feel homesick** Heimweh haben.

hometown ['həʊmtaʊn] *n* Heimatstadt *die.*

homework ['həʊmwɜ:k] *n (U)* - **1.** SCH Hausaufgaben *Pl* - **2.** *inf* [preparation]: **he's really done his homework** er hat sich gut vorbereitet.

homey, homy ['həʊmɪ] *adj US* [place, atmosphere] heimelig.

homicide ['hɒmɪsaɪd] *n* Mord *der.*

homogeneous [,hɒmə'dʒi:nɪəs] *adj* homogen.

homophobic [,hɒmə'fəʊbɪk] *adj* homosexuellenfeindlich, homophob.

homosexual [,hɒmə'sekʃʊəl] ◇ *adj* homosexuell. ◇ *n* Homosexuelle *der, die.*

homy *adj US* = **homey**.

hone [həʊn] *vt* - **1.** [knife, sword] schleifen, wetzen - **2.** [intellect, wit] schärfen.

honest ['ɒnɪst] ◇ *adj* - **1.** [trustworthy, legal] redlich - **2.** [truthful] ehrlich; **to be honest,** ehrlich gesagt,. ◇ *adv inf* ehrlich.

honestly ['ɒnɪstlɪ] ◇ *adv* - **1.** [in a trustworthy manner] redlich - **2.** [truthfully] ehrlich. ◇ *excl* also wirklich!

honesty ['ɒnɪstɪ] *n* - **1.** [trustworthiness] Redlichkeit *die* - **2.** [truthfulness] Ehrlichkeit *die.*

honey ['hʌnɪ] *n* - **1.** [food] Honig *der* - **2.** *esp US* [dear] Liebling *der.*

honeycomb ['hʌnɪkəʊm] *n* - **1.** [in wax] Bienenwabe *die* - **2.** [pattern] Wabenmuster *das.*

honeymoon ['hʌnɪmu:n] ◇ *n* - **1.** [after wedding] Flitterwochen *Pl*; [trip] Hochzeitsreise *die* - **2.** *fig* [initial trouble-free period] Schonzeit *die.* ◇ *vi* Hochzeitsreise machen.

Hong Kong [,hɒŋ'kɒŋ] *n* Hongkong *nt.*

honk [hɒŋk] ◇ *vi* [motorist] hupen. ◇ *vt*: **to honk one's horn** auf die Hupe drücken.

honor *etc US* = **honour** *etc* .

honorary [*UK* 'ɒnərərɪ, *US* ɒnə'reərɪ] *adj* - **1.** [given as an honour] Ehren-; **honorary degree** ehrenhalber verliehener akademischer Grad - **2.** [unpaid] ehrenamtlich.

honour *UK*, **honor** *US* ['ɒnə^r] ◇ *n* Ehre *die*; **a man of honour** ein Ehrenmann; **in her honour** zu ihren Ehren. ◇ *vt* - **1.** [fulfil - debt] begleichen; [- promise, agreement] erfüllen; [- cheque] akzeptieren - **2.** *fml* [bring honour to] ehren. ◆ **honours** *npl* - **1.** [tokens of respect] Ehren *Pl* - **2.** UNIV *der erste erreichbare akademische Grad, der in ein oder zwei Fächern erlangt wird.*

honourable *UK*, **honorable** *US* ['ɒnrəbl] *adj* ehrenhaft.

hood [hʊd] *n* - **1.** [on cloak, jacket] Kapuze *die*; [of robber] Maske *die* - **2.** [of cooker] Abzugshaube *die*; [of pram, convertible car] Verdeck *das* - **3.** *US* [car bonnet] Motorhaube *die*.

hoodlum ['hu:dləm] *n US inf* [youth] Rowdy *der*; [gangster] Gangster *der*.

hoof [hu:f] (*pl* **-s** OR **hooves**) *n* Huf *der*.

hook [hʊk] ◇ *n* Haken *der*. ◇ *vt* - **1.** [fasten with hook]: **to hook sthg on to sthg** etw an etw *(D)* festlhaken - **2.** [fish] an die Angel bekommen. ◆ **off the hook** *adv* - **1.** TELEC: **the telephone is off the hook** der Hörer ist abgenommen; **to leave the phone off the hook** den Hörer nicht aufllegen - **2.** [out of trouble]: **to be off the hook** aus dem Schneider sein. ◆ **hook up** *vt sep*: **to hook sthg up to sthg** COMPUT & TELEC etw an etw *(A)* anlschließen.

hooked [hʊkt] *adj* - **1.** [shaped like a hook] gebogen; **hooked nose** Hakennase *die* - **2.** *inf* [addicted]: **to be hooked on sthg** [on drugs] von etw abhängig sein; [on music, money, art] auf etw *(A)* ganz versessen sein.

hook(e)y ['hʊkɪ] *n US inf*: **to play hookey** (die Schule) schwänzen.

hooligan ['hu:lɪgən] *n* Rowdy *der*.

hoop [hu:p] *n* Reifen *der*.

hooray [hʊ'reɪ] *excl* = **hurray**.

hoot [hu:t] ◇ *n* - **1.** [of owl] Schrei *der* - **2.** [of horn] Hupen *das* - **3.** *UK inf* [amusing thing, person]: **to be a hoot** zum Schießen sein. ◇ *vi* - **1.** [owl] schreien - **2.** [horn] hupen. ◇ *vt* [horn]: **to hoot one's horn** hupen.

hooter ['hu:tə^r] *n* [horn - of car] Hupe *die*; [- of factory] Sirene *die*.

Hoover® ['hu:və^r] *n UK* Staubsauger *der*. ◆ **hoover** *vt* & *vi* (staub)saugen.

hooves [hu:vz] *Pl* ▷ **hoof**.

hop [hɒp] ◇ *n* [of person, animal, bird] Hüpfer *der*. ◇ *vi* - **1.** [jump] hüpfen - **2.** *inf* [move nimbly] springen; **to hop on a bus/train/plane** kurz entschlossen den Bus/den Zug/das Flugzeug nehmen. ◇ *vt inf phr*: **hop it!** verschwinde! ◆ **hops** *npl* [for making beer] Hopfen *der*.

hope [həʊp] ◇ *vi* hoffen; **to hope for sthg** auf etw *(A)* hoffen; **I hope so** hoffentlich; **I hope not** hoffentlich nicht. ◇ *vt*: **to hope (that)...** hoffen, dass...; **to hope to do sthg** hoffen, etw zu tun. ◇ *n* - **1.** *(U)* [belief, optimism] Hoffnung *die*; **to be beyond hope** [situation] aussichtslos OR hoffnungslos sein - **2.** [expectation, chance] Hoffnung *die*; **in the hope of doing sthg** in der Hoffnung, etw zu tun.

hopeful ['həʊpfʊl] *adj* - **1.** [person] hoffnungsvoll; **to be hopeful that...** zuversichtlich sein, dass...; **to be hopeful of doing sthg** zuversichtlich sein, etw zu tun - **2.** [sign, future] vielversprechend.

hopefully ['həʊpfəlɪ] *adv* - **1.** [in a hopeful way] hoffnungsvoll - **2.** [with luck] hoffentlich.

hopeless ['həʊplɪs] *adj* - **1.** [despairing, impossible] hoffnungslos - **2.** *inf* [useless] miserabel.

hopelessly ['həʊplɪslɪ] *adv* hoffnungslos.

horizon [hə'raɪzn] *n* [of sky] Horizont *der*; **on the horizon** *liter* & *fig* am Horizont.

horizontal [,hɒrɪ'zɒntl] ◇ *adj* horizontal. ◇ *n*: **the horizontal** die Horizontale.

hormone ['hɔ:məʊn] *n* Hormon *das*.

horn [hɔ:n] *n* - **1.** [gen] Horn *das* - **2.** [on car] Hupe *die*; [on ship] Signalhorn *das*.

hornet ['hɔ:nɪt] *n* Hornisse *die*.

horny ['hɔ:nɪ] *adj* - **1.** [scale, body] hornig; [hand] schwielig - **2.** *v inf* [sexually excited] geil.

horoscope ['hɒrəskəʊp] *n* Horoskop *das*.

horrendous [hɒ'rendəs] *adj* - **1.** [horrific] entsetzlich - **2.** *inf* [unpleasant - bill, amount] horrend; [- weather] scheußlich.

horrible ['hɒrəbl] *adj* schrecklich.

horrid ['hɒrɪd] *adj esp UK* fürchterlich; **don't be so horrid** sei nicht so gemein.

horrific [hɒ'rɪfɪk] *adj* entsetzlich.

horrify ['hɒrɪfaɪ] *vt* entsetzen.

horror ['hɒrə^r] *n* - **1.** [alarm, fear] Entsetzen *das* - **2.** [horrifying thing] Schrecken *der*; **the horrors of war** die Gräuel des Krieges.

horror film *n* Horrorfilm *der*.

horse [hɔ:s] *n* Pferd *das*.

horseback ['hɔ:sbæk] ◇ *adj*: **horseback riding** *US* Reiten *das*. ◇ *n*: **on horseback** zu Pferd.

horse chestnut *n* [tree, nut] Rosskastanie *die*.

horseman ['hɔ:smən] (*pl* **-men** [-mən]) *n* Reiter *der*.

horsepower ['hɔ:s,paʊə^r] *n (U)* Pferdestärke *die*.

horse racing *n* Pferderennen *das*.

horseradish ['hɔ:s,rædɪʃ] *n (U)* [plant] Meerrettich *der*.

horse riding *n* Reiten *das*.

horseshoe ['hɔ:sʃu:] *n* Hufeisen *das*.

horsewoman ['hɔ:s,wʊmən] (*pl* **-women** [-,wɪmɪn]) *n* Reiterin *die*.

horticulture ['hɔ:tɪ,kʌltʃə^r] *n* Gartenbau *der*.

hose [həʊz] ◇ *n* [hosepipe] Schlauch *der*. ◇ *vt* [garden] sprengen.

hosepipe ['həʊzpaɪp] *n* Schlauch *der*.

hosiery ['həʊzɪərɪ] *n (U)* Strumpfwaren *Pl*.

hospitable [hɒ'spɪtəbl] *adj* gastfreundlich.

hospital ['hɒspɪtl] *n* Krankenhaus *das*.

hospitality [,hɒspɪ'tælətɪ] *n* Gastfreundschaft *die*.

host [həʊst] <> *n* - **1.** [gen] Gastgeber *der*; **host country** Gastland *das* - **2.** [compere] Moderator *der* - **3.** *liter* [large number]: **a host of sthg** eine Schar von etw. <> *vt* moderieren.

hostage ['hɒstɪdʒ] *n* Geisel *die*.

hostel ['hɒstl] *n* Wohnheim *das*; **(youth) hostel** Jugendherberge *die*.

hostess ['həʊstes] *n* [at party] Gastgeberin *die*.

hostile [*UK* 'hɒstaɪl, *US* 'hɒstl] *adj* - **1.** [antagonistic, unfriendly]: **hostile (to sb/sthg)** feindselig (gegenüber jm/etw) - **2.** [weather conditions] widrig; [climate] unwirtlich - **3.** MIL [territory, forces] feindlich.

hostility [hɒ'stɪlətɪ] *n (U)* Feindseligkeit *die*. ◆ **hostilities** *npl* Feindseligkeiten *Pl*.

hot [hɒt] *adj* - **1.** heiß; **I'm hot** mir ist heiß - **2.** [cooked] warm - **3.** [spicy] scharf - **4.** *inf* [expert] stark; **to be hot on** OR **at sthg** super in etw *(D)* sein - **5.** [recent]: **a hot piece of news** das Neueste vom Neuesten - **6.** [temper] hitzig.

hot-air balloon *n* Heißluftballon *der*.

hotbed ['hɒtbed] *n* Brutstätte *die*.

hot-cross bun *n Rosinenbrötchen mit kleinem Teigkreuz, das um Ostern gegessen wird*.

hot dog *n* Hotdog *der ODER das*.

hotel [həʊ'tel] *n* Hotel *das*.

hot flush *UK*, **hot flash** *US n* Hitzewallung *die*; **hot flushes** fliegende Hitze.

hotheaded [ˌhɒt'hedɪd] *adj* hitzköpfig.

hothouse ['hɒthaʊs] *n* (*pl* [-haʊzɪz]) [greenhouse] Treibhaus *das*.

hot line *n* - **1.** [between government heads] heißer Draht - **2.** [for crisis, disaster] Hotline *die*.

hotly ['hɒtlɪ] *adv* - **1.** [argue, debate, deny] heftig - **2.** [pursue]: **they were hotly pursued by a policeman** ein Polizist war ihnen dicht auf den Fersen.

hotplate ['hɒtpleɪt] *n* Kochplatte *die*.

hot-tempered [-'tempəd] *adj* jähzornig.

hot-water bottle *n* Wärmflasche *die*.

hound [haʊnd] <> *n* Jagdhund *der*. <> *vt* verfolgen.

hour ['aʊəʳ] *n* Stunde *die*; **half an hour** eine halbe Stunde; **per** OR **an hour** pro OR die Stunde; **on the hour** zur vollen Stunde; **every hour, on the hour** jede volle Stunde. ◆ **hours** *npl* [of business] Geschäftszeiten *Pl*; [of pub, museum *etc*] Öffnungszeiten *Pl*; [of doctor] Sprechstunde *die*.

hourly ['aʊəlɪ] <> *adj* - **1.** [happening every hour] stündlich - **2.** [per hour] Stunden-. <> *adv* - **1.** [every hour] stündlich - **2.** [per hour] pro Stunde.

house <> *n* [haʊs] (*pl* ['haʊzɪz]) - **1.** [gen] Haus *das*; **to move house** umlziehen; **on the house** auf Kosten des Hauses; **to bring the house down** das Publikum zum Toben bringen - **2.** SCH *eine der traditionellen Schülergemeinschaften innerhalb einer Schule, die untereinander Wettbewerbe veranstalten*. <> *vt* [haʊz] [subj: person] unterlbringen; **the building houses three families/offices** im Gebäude sind drei Familien/Büros untergebracht. <> *adj* [haʊs] Haus-; **house style** hauseigener Stil; **house red/white** [wine] Hausmarke *die (Rot-/Weißwein)*.

houseboat ['haʊsbəʊt] *n* Hausboot *das*.

household ['haʊshəʊld] <> *adj* - **1.** [domestic] Haushalts- - **2.** [familiar]: **to be a household name** ein Begriff sein. <> *n* Haushalt *der*.

housekeeper ['haʊsˌkiːpəʳ] *n* Haushälterin *die*.

housekeeping ['haʊsˌkiːpɪŋ] *n* - **1.** [work] Haushaltsführung *die* - **2.** [budget]: **housekeeping (money)** Haushaltsgeld *das*.

house music *n* Hausmusik *die*.

House of Commons *n UK*: **the House of Commons** das britische Unterhaus.

House of Lords *n UK*: **the House of Lords** das britische Oberhaus.

House of Representatives *n US*: **the House of Representatives** das Repräsentantenhaus.

houseplant ['haʊsplɑːnt] *n* Zimmerpflanze *die*.

Houses of Parliament *npl UK*: **the Houses of Parliament** *Sitz des britischen Parlaments*.

housewarming (party) ['haʊsˌwɔːmɪŋ-] *n* Einzugsparty *die*.

housewife ['haʊswaɪf] (*pl* **-wives** [-waɪvz]) *n* Hausfrau *die*.

housework ['haʊswɜːk] *n* Hausarbeit *die*.

housing ['haʊzɪŋ] *n (U)* [accommodation] Wohnungen *Pl*; [act] Unterbringung *die*.

housing association *n UK* Wohnungsbaugesellschaft *die*.

housing benefit *n (U) UK* Wohngeld *das*.

housing estate *UK*, **housing project** *US n* Wohnsiedlung *die*.

hovel ['hɒvl] *n* armselige Hütte.

hover ['hɒvəʳ] *vi* [fly] schweben.

hovercraft ['hɒvəkrɑːft] (*pl inv* OR **-s**) *n* Luftkissenfahrzeug *das*.

how [haʊ] *adv* - **1.** [referring to way, manner] wie; **how do you get there?** wie kommt man dahin?; **tell me how to do it** sag mir, wie man das macht - **2.** [referring to health, general state] wie; **how are you?** wie gehts dir?; **how are you doing?, how are things?** wie gehts dir?; **how is your room?** wie ist dein Zimmer?; **how do you do?** guten Tag! - **3.** [referring to degree, amount] wie; **how far?** wie weit?; **how long?** wie lang?; **how many?** wie viele?; **how much?** wie viel?; **how much is it?** wie viel kostet es?; **how old are you?** wie alt bist du? - **4.** [in exclamations] wie; **how nice/awful!** wie schön/schrecklich!; **how I wish I could!** wenn ich doch nur könnte! ◆ **how about** *adv*: **how about a drink?** wie wäre es mit einem Drink?;

I could do with a night off, how about you? ich könnte einen freien Abend gebrauchen, du auch?

however [haʊ'evəʳ] <> *conj* [in whatever way] wie (immer). <> *adv* - **1.** [nevertheless] jedoch; **however, it was not to be** es sollte jedoch nicht sein - **2.** [no matter how] wie auch; **however difficult/good it is** wie schwierig/gut es auch ist; **however many/much you have** wie viele/viel du auch hast - **3.** [how] wie bloß; **however did you know?** woher hast du das bloß gewusst?

howl [haʊl] *vi* - **1.** [animal, wind] heulen - **2.** [person] schreien; **to howl with laughter** brüllen vor Lachen.

hp (*abbr of* **horsepower**) *n* PS.

HP *n* - **1.** (*abbr of* **hire purchase**); **to buy sthg on HP** etw auf Raten kaufen - **2.** = **hp**.

HQ (*abbr of* **headquarters**) *n* HQ *das*.

hr (*abbr of* **hour**) Std.

hrs (*abbr of* **hours**) Std.

hub [hʌb] *n* - **1.** [of wheel] (Rad)nabe *die* - **2.** [of activity] Zentrum *das*.

hubbub ['hʌbʌb] *n* Lärm *der*.

hubcap ['hʌbkæp] *n* Radkappe *die*.

huddle ['hʌdl] *vi* - **1.** [crouch, curl up] kauern - **2.** [crowd together]: **to huddle (together)** sich (zusammen)|drängen.

hue [hjuː] *n* [colour] Farbton *der*.

huff [hʌf] *n*: **in a huff** beleidigt.

hug [hʌg] <> *n* Umarmung *die*; **to give sb a hug** jn umarmen. <> *vt* - **1.** [embrace] umarmen - **2.** [hold - one's knees] umfassen - **3.** [stay close to]: **to hug the coast/kerb** dicht an der Küste/am Straßenrand entlang|fahren.

huge [hjuːdʒ] *adj* riesig; [subject] vielfältig.

hulk [hʌlk] *n* - **1.** [of ship] (Schiffs)rumpf *der* - **2.** [person] Koloss *der*.

hull [hʌl] *n* [of ship] Schiffskörper *der*.

hullo [hə'ləʊ] *excl* = **hello**.

hum [hʌm] <> *vi* - **1.** [bee] summen; [car, machine] brummen - **2.** [sing] summen - **3.** [be busy - place] voller Leben sein; [- office] voller Aktivität sein. <> *vt* [tune] summen.

human ['hjuːmən] <> *adj* menschlich. <> *n*: **human (being)** Mensch *der*.

humane [hjuː'meɪn] *adj* [compassionate] human.

humanitarian [hjuːˌmænɪ'teərɪən] *adj* humanitär.

humanity [hjuː'mænətɪ] *n* - **1.** [kindness, sympathy] Humanität *die* - **2.** [mankind] Menschheit *die*. ◆ **humanities** *npl*: **the humanities** die Geisteswissenschaften.

human race *n*: **the human race** die menschliche Rasse.

human resources *npl* Humankapital *das*.

human rights *npl* Menschenrechte *Pl*.

humble ['hʌmbl] <> *adj* [position, job, origins] niedrig; [clerk] einfach; [home, room, opinion] bescheiden; [person] demütig. <> *vt* demütigen.

humbug ['hʌmbʌg] *n UK* [sweet] Pfefferminzbonbon *der ODER das*.

humdrum ['hʌmdrʌm] *adj* [life] eintönig.

humid ['hjuːmɪd] *adj* feucht.

humidity [hjuː'mɪdətɪ] *n* (Luft)feuchtigkeit *die*.

humiliate [hjuː'mɪlɪeɪt] *vt* demütigen.

humiliation [hjuːˌmɪlɪ'eɪʃn] *n* Demütigung *die*.

humility [hjuː'mɪlətɪ] *n* Demut *die*.

humor *n* & *vt US* = **humour**.

humorous ['hjuːmərəs] *adj* [remark, story] lustig; [person] humorvoll.

humour *UK*, **humor** *US* ['hjuːməʳ] <> *n* [comedy] Humor *der*; [of situation, remark] Komik *die*. <> *vt*: **to humour sb** jm seinen Willen lassen.

hump [hʌmp] *n* - **1.** [hill] Hügel *der* - **2.** [of camel] Höcker *der*; [of person] Buckel *der*.

hunch [hʌntʃ] *n inf* Gefühl *das*, Ahnung *die*.

hunchback ['hʌntʃbæk] *n* Bucklige *der, die*.

hundred ['hʌndrəd] *num* hundert; **a** OR **one hundred** (ein)hundert; *see also* **six**. ◆ **hundreds** *npl* Hunderte *Pl*.

hundredth ['hʌndrəθ] *num* hundertste(r)(s); *see also* **sixth**.

hundredweight ['hʌndrədweɪt] *n* - **1.** [in UK] ≃ Zentner *der*, *= 50,8 kg* - **2.** [in US] ≃ Zentner *der*, *= 45,36 kg*.

hung [hʌŋ] *pt* & *pp* ▷ **hang**.

Hungarian [hʌŋ'geərɪən] <> *adj* ungarisch. <> *n* - **1.** [person] Ungar *der*, -in *die* - **2.** [language] Ungarisch(e) *das*.

Hungary ['hʌŋgərɪ] *n* Ungarn *nt*.

hunger ['hʌŋgəʳ] *n liter* & *fig* Hunger *der*.

hunger strike *n* Hungerstreik *der*.

hung over *adj inf* verkatert.

hungry ['hʌŋgrɪ] *adj* hungrig; **to be hungry** Hunger haben; **to be hungry for sthg** *fig* sich nach etw sehnen.

hung up *adj inf*: **to be hung up (on** OR **about)** sich verrückt machen (wegen *(+ G)*).

hunk [hʌŋk] *n* - **1.** [of bread, cheese] Stück *das* - **2.** *inf* [attractive man]: **he's a real hunk** er ist ein richtiger Mann.

hunt [hʌnt] <> *n* - **1.** SPORT Jagd *die*; *UK* [for foxes] Fuchsjagd *die*; [hunters] Jagdgesellschaft *die* - **2.** [search] Suche *die*. <> *vi* - **1.** [for food, sport] jagen - **2.** *UK* [for foxes] auf die Fuchsjagd gehen - **3.** [search]: **to hunt (for)** suchen (nach). <> *vt* - **1.** [animals, birds] jagen - **2.** [criminal] fahnden nach.

hunter ['hʌntəʳ] *n* [of animals, birds] Jäger *der*.

hunting ['hʌntɪŋ] *n (U)* - **1.** SPORT Jagd *die* - **2.** *UK* [foxhunting] Fuchsjagd *die*.

hurdle ['hɜːdl] *n liter & fig* Hürde *die.* ◆ **hurdles** *npl* SPORT Hürdenlauf *der.*

hurl [hɜːl] *vt* schleudern; **to hurl abuse at sb** jm Beschimpfungen an den Kopf werfen.

hurray [hʊ'reɪ] *excl* hurra!

hurricane ['hʌrɪkən] *n* Orkan *der*; [tropical] Hurrikan *der.*

hurried ['hʌrɪd] *adj* [meal] hastig; [departure] überstürzt; [glance] flüchtig; [note] eilig geschrieben.

hurriedly ['hʌrɪdlɪ] *adv* [eat] hastig; [leave, write] eilig.

hurry ['hʌrɪ] ◇ *vt* [person] (zur Eile) an|treiben; [process] beschleunigen; **don't hurry me** hetz mich nicht; **to hurry to do sthg** sich beeilen, etw zu tun. ◇ *vi* sich beeilen. ◇ *n* Eile *die*; **to be in a hurry** in Eile sein; **to do sthg in a hurry** etw in Eile tun. ◆ **hurry up** *vi* sich beeilen.

hurt [hɜːt] *(pt & pp inv)* ◇ *vt* - **1.** [cause physical pain to] wehltun *(+ D)*; **to hurt one's leg/arm** sich *(D)* am Bein/Arm wehltun; **to hurt o.s.** sich *(D)* wehltun - **2.** [injure, upset] verletzen; **to hurt sb's feelings** js Gefühle verletzen - **3.** [harm] schaden *(+ D).* ◇ *vi* - **1.** [gen] weh|tun - **2.** [harm] schaden. ◇ *adj* [leg, arm, feelings] verletzt; [look, voice] gekränkt.

hurtful ['hɜːtfʊl] *adj* verletzend.

hurtle ['hɜːtl] *vi* sausen.

husband ['hʌzbənd] *n* Ehemann *der*; **my husband** mein Mann.

hush [hʌʃ] ◇ *n* Schweigen *das.* ◇ *excl* still! ◆ **hush up** *vt sep* [affair] vertuschen.

husk [hʌsk] *n* [of seed] Hülse *die*; [of grain] Spelze *die.*

husky ['hʌskɪ] ◇ *adj* [voice] rau. ◇ *n* [dog] Husky *der*, Eskimohund *der.*

hustle ['hʌsl] ◇ *vt* [hurry]: **he hustled her out of the room** er drängte sie schnell aus dem Raum. ◇ *n*: **hustle and bustle** geschäftiges Treiben.

hut [hʌt] *n* Hütte *die*; [temporary building] Baracke *die.*

hutch [hʌtʃ] *n* Stall *der.*

hyacinth ['haɪəsɪnθ] *n* Hyazinthe *die.*

hydrant ['haɪdrənt] *n* Hydrant *der.*

hydraulic [haɪ'drɔːlɪk] *adj* hydraulisch.

hydroelectric [ˌhaɪdrəʊɪ'lektrɪk] *adj* hydroelektrisch; **hydroelectric power** durch Wasserkraft erzeugte Energie.

hydrofoil ['haɪdrəfɔɪl] *n* Tragflächenboot *das.*

hydrogen ['haɪdrədʒən] *n* Wasserstoff *der.*

hyena [haɪ'iːnə] *n* Hyäne *die.*

hygiene ['haɪdʒiːn] *n* Hygiene *die*; **personal hygiene** Körperpflege *die.*

hygienic [haɪ'dʒiːnɪk] *adj* hygienisch.

hymn [hɪm] *n* Kirchenlied *das.*

hype [haɪp] *inf* ◇ *n* Publicity *die.* ◇ *vt* Publicity machen für.

hyperactive [ˌhaɪpər'æktɪv] *adj* überaktiv.

hypermarket ['haɪpəˌmɑːkɪt] *n* Großmarkt *der.*

hyphen ['haɪfn] *n* Bindestrich *der*; [at end of line] Trennungsstrich *der.*

hypnosis [hɪp'nəʊsɪs] *n* Hypnose *die.*

hypnotic [hɪp'nɒtɪk] *adj* hypnotisch.

hypnotize, -ise ['hɪpnətaɪz] *vt* hypnotisieren.

hypocrisy [hɪ'pɒkrəsɪ] *n* Heuchelei *die.*

hypocrite ['hɪpəkrɪt] *n* Heuchler *der*, -in *die.*

hypocritical [ˌhɪpə'krɪtɪkl] *adj* heuchlerisch.

hypothesis [haɪ'pɒθɪsɪs] *(pl* **-theses** [-θɪsiːz]) *n* Hypothese *die.*

hypothetical [ˌhaɪpə'θetɪkl] *adj* hypothetisch.

hysteria [hɪs'tɪərɪə] *n* Hysterie *die.*

hysterical [hɪs'terɪkl] *adj* - **1.** [gen] hysterisch - **2.** *inf* [very funny] urkomisch.

hysterics [hɪs'terɪks] *npl* [panic] hysterischer Anfall; **to be in hysterics** *inf* [with laughter] sich aus|schütten vor Lachen.

I

i *(pl* **i's** OR **is**), **I** *(pl* **I's** OR **Is**) [aɪ] *n* [letter] i *das*, I *das.*

I [aɪ] *pers pron* ich; **I'm tall** ich bin groß; **she and I were at college together** ich war mit ihr zusammen im College.

ice [aɪs] ◇ *n* - **1.** *(U)* [gen] Eis *das*; [on pond] Eisschicht *die*; [on road] Glatteis *das* - **2.** *UK* [ice cream] (Speise)eis *das*, Eiscreme *die.* ◇ *vt UK* [cake] glasieren. ◆ **ice over, ice up** *vi* [windscreen] vereisen; [lake] zu|frieren.

iceberg ['aɪsbɜːg] *n* Eisberg *der.*

iceberg lettuce *n* Eisbergsalat *der.*

icebox ['aɪsbɒks] *n* - **1.** *UK* [in refrigerator] Eisfach *das* - **2.** *US* [refrigerator] Eisschrank *der.*

ice cream *n* Eis *das*, Eiscreme *die.*

ice cube *n* Eiswürfel *der.*

ice hockey *n* Eishockey *das.*

Iceland ['aɪslənd] *n* Island *nt.*

Icelandic [aɪs'lændɪk] ◇ *adj* isländisch. ◇ *n* [language] Isländisch(e) *das.*

ice lolly *n UK* Eis *das* am Stiel.

ice pick *n* Eispickel *der.*

ice rink *n* Schlittschuhbahn *die*.

ice skate *n* Schlittschuh *der*. ◆ **ice-skate** *vi* Schlittschuh laufen, Eis laufen.

ice-skating *n* Schlittschuhlaufen *das*, Eislaufen *das*; [sport] Eiskunstlauf *der*; **to go ice-skating** Schlittschuh laufen gehen.

icicle ['aɪsɪkl] *n* Eiszapfen *der*.

icing ['aɪsɪŋ] *n* [of cake] Zuckerguss *der*.

icing sugar *n UK* Puderzucker *der*.

icon ['aɪkɒn] *n* - **1.** RELIG Ikone *die* - **2.** COMPUT Icon *das*.

icy ['aɪsɪ] *adj* - **1.** [wind, cold, weather] eisig; **it's icy cold** es ist eiskalt - **2.** [road, pavement] vereist - **3.** *fig* [welcome, atmosphere] eisig.

I'd [aɪd] *abbr of* **I would**, **I had**.

ID *n* (*abbr of* **identification**) Ausweis *der*.

idea [aɪ'dɪə] *n* - **1.** [plan, suggestion] Idee *die* - **2.** [notion] Vorstellung *die*; **you have no idea how difficult it is** du kannst dir nicht vorstellen, wie schwer es ist; **can you give me an idea of the price?** können Sie mir einen ungefähren Preis nennen?; **to have an idea that...** glauben, dass...; **to have no idea** keine Ahnung haben - **3.** [intention] Absicht *die*; **what's the big idea?** *inf* was soll das (heißen)?

ideal [aɪ'dɪəl] ◇ *adj* ideal. ◇ *n* Ideal *das*.

ideally [aɪ'dɪəlɪ] *adv* - **1.** [located] ideal; **he was ideally suited to the job** er war perfekt geeignet für die Stelle - **2.** [preferably] idealerweise, im Idealfall.

identical [aɪ'dentɪkl] *adj* identisch.

identification [aɪ,dentɪfɪ'keɪʃn] *n* - **1.** [gen] Identifizierung *die* - **2.** *(U)* [documentation] Ausweispapiere *Pl*; **do you have any identification?** können Sie sich ausweisen?

identify [aɪ'dentɪfaɪ] ◇ *vt* - **1.** [gen] identifizieren; [cause, need] erkennen; **to identify o.s.** sich aus|weisen - **2.** [connect]: **to identify sb with sthg** jn mit etw in Verbindung bringen. ◇ *vi* [empathize]: **to identify with sb/sthg** sich mit jm/etw identifizieren.

identity [aɪ'dentətɪ] *n* Identität *die*.

identity card *n* Personalausweis *der*.

ideology [,aɪdɪ'ɒlədʒɪ] *n* Weltanschauung *die*; *pej* Ideologie *die*.

idiom ['ɪdɪəm] *n* - **1.** [phrase] Redewendung *die* - **2.** *fml* [style] Idiom *das*.

idiomatic [,ɪdɪə'mætɪk] *adj* idiomatisch.

idiosyncrasy [,ɪdɪə'sɪŋkrəsɪ] *n* [of person] Eigenheit *die*; [of thing] Besonderheit *die*.

idiot ['ɪdɪət] *n* Idiot *der*.

idiotic [,ɪdɪ'ɒtɪk] *adj* idiotisch.

idle ['aɪdl] ◇ *adj* - **1.** [person - inactive] untätig, müßig; [- lazy] faul - **2.** [machine, factory] stillstehend; [workers] unbeschäftigt - **3.** [threat] leer - **4.** [glance] flüchtig - **5.** [futile] sinnlos. ◇ *vi* [engine] im Leerlauf sein. ◆ **idle away** *vt sep* [time] vertrödeln.

idol ['aɪdl] *n* - **1.** [hero] Idol *das* - **2.** RELIG Götze *der*.

idolize, -ise ['aɪdəlaɪz] *vt* vergöttern.

idyllic [ɪ'dɪlɪk] *adj* idyllisch.

i.e. (*abbr of* **id est**) d. h.

if [ɪf] *conj* wenn, falls; *(in indirect questions after "know", "wonder")* ob; **if I were you** wenn ich du wäre; **pleasant weather, if rather cold** schönes Wetter, wenn auch ziemlich kalt; **as if** als ob. ◆ **if not** *conj* wenn nicht, falls nicht. ◆ **if only** ◇ *conj* - **1.** [expressing regret] wenn nur; **if only I had known** wenn ich das nur OR bloß gewusst hätte - **2.** [providing a reason] (und) sei es nur; **go and see him, if only to please me** geh ihn besuchen, und sei es nur mir zuliebe. ◇ *excl*: **if only!** das wäre schön!

igloo ['ɪglu:] (*pl* **-s**) *n* Iglu *der ODER das*.

ignite [ɪg'naɪt] ◇ *vt* entzünden; AUT zünden. ◇ *vi* sich entzünden; AUT zünden.

ignition [ɪg'nɪʃn] *n* [in car] Zündung *die*.

ignition key *n* Zündschlüssel *der*.

ignorance ['ɪgnərəns] *n* Unwissenheit *die*; [of particular subject, information *etc*] Unkenntnis *die*.

ignorant ['ɪgnərənt] *adj* - **1.** [uneducated] ungebildet; [lacking information] unwissend - **2.** *fml* [unaware]: **to be ignorant of sthg** von etw nichts wissen - **3.** *inf* [rude] ungehobelt.

ignore [ɪg'nɔ:ʳ] *vt* ignorieren.

ilk [ɪlk] *n*: **people of that ilk** solche Leute; **and others of that ilk** und seines-/ihresgleichen.

ill [ɪl] ◇ *adj* - **1.** [sick] krank; **to feel ill** sich unwohl OR krank fühlen; **to be taken ill, to fall ill** krank werden - **2.** [bad - omen, treatment] schlecht; [- effects] nachteilig; *(phrase)*: **ill at ease** unbehaglich. ◇ *adv* schlecht; **to speak/think ill of sb** schlecht über jn reden/denken.

I'll [aɪl] *abbr of* **I will**, **I shall**.

ill-advised [-əd'vaɪzd] *adj* unklug.

illegal [ɪ'li:gl] *adj* [action] gesetzwidrig; [organization] illegal.

illegible [ɪ'ledʒəbl] *adj* unleserlich.

illegitimate [,ɪlɪ'dʒɪtɪmət] *adj* - **1.** [child] unehelich - **2.** [activity] unzulässig.

ill-equipped [-ɪ'kwɪpt] *adj*: **to be ill-equipped to do sthg** [unsuited] nicht dafür geeignet sein, etw zu tun.

ill-fated [-'feɪtɪd] *adj* unglückselig.

ill feeling *n* Feindseligkeit *die*.

ill health *n* schwache Gesundheit.

illicit [ɪ'lɪsɪt] *adj* illegal.

illiteracy [ɪ'lɪtərəsɪ] *n* Analphabetentum *das*.

illiterate [ɪ'lɪtərət] ◇ *adj* - **1.** [unable to read] des Lesens und Schreibens unkundig; **to be illiterate** Analphabet(in) sein - **2.** [uneducated] ungebildet. ◇ *n* Analphabet *der*, -in *die*.

illness ['ɪlnɪs] *n* Krankheit *die*.

illogical [ɪ'lɒdʒɪkl] *adj* unlogisch.

ill-suited *adj* nicht zusammenpassend; **to be ill-suited to sthg** für etw ungeeignet sein.

ill-treat *vt* misshandeln; [worker] schlecht behandeln.

illuminate [ɪ'luːmɪneɪt] *vt* - **1.** [light up] beleuchten - **2.** [problem, subject] erhellen.

illumination [ɪˌluːmɪ'neɪʃn] *n* [lighting] Beleuchtung *die*. ◆ **illuminations** *npl UK* festliche Beleuchtung.

illusion [ɪ'luːʒn] *n* Illusion *die*; **to be under the illusion that...** sich einlbilden, dass...; **optical illusion** optische Täuschung.

illustrate ['ɪləstreɪt] *vt* illustrieren.

illustration [ˌɪlə'streɪʃn] *n* - **1.** [picture] Illustration *die* - **2.** [example] Beispiel *das*.

illustrious [ɪ'lʌstrɪəs] *adj fml* berühmt; [career] glanzvoll.

ill will *n* böses Blut; **he didn't bear anyone any ill will** er war niemandem feindlich gesinnt.

I'm [aɪm] *abbr of* **I am**.

image ['ɪmɪdʒ] *n* - **1.** [gen] Bild *das*; [in mirror] Spiegelbild *das* - **2.** [in mind] Vorstellung *die* - **3.** [of company, public figure] Image *das*.

imagery ['ɪmɪdʒrɪ] *n* [in writing] Metaphorik *die*; [in visual arts] Bildersymbolik *die*.

imaginary [ɪ'mædʒɪnrɪ] *adj* imaginär.

imagination [ɪˌmædʒɪ'neɪʃn] *n* - **1.** [ability, fantasy] Fantasie *die* - **2.** [mind] Einbildung *die*; **it's all in her imagination** das bildet sie sich nur ein.

imaginative [ɪ'mædʒɪnətɪv] *adj* fantasievoll; [concerning new ideas] einfallsreich.

imagine [ɪ'mædʒɪn] *vt* - **1.** [visualize] sich *(D)* vorstellen, sich *(D)* denken; **to imagine doing sthg** sich *(D)* vorstellen, etw zu tun; **imagine (that)!** stell dir das mal vor! - **2.** [dream] sich *(D)* einbilden; **you imagined it** du hast es dir (nur) eingebildet - **3.** [suppose] anlnehmen, vermuten.

imbalance [ˌɪm'bæləns] *n* Ungleichgewicht *das*.

imbecile ['ɪmbɪsiːl] *n* Idiot *der*.

IMF (*abbr of* **International Monetary Fund**) *n* IWF *der*.

imitate ['ɪmɪteɪt] *vt* nachlahmen.

imitation [ˌɪmɪ'teɪʃn] ◇ *n* - **1.** [gen] Nachahmung *die* - **2.** [copy] Kopie *die*. ◇ *adj* unecht, imitiert; **imitation leather** Kunstleder *das*.

immaculate [ɪ'mækjʊlət] *adj* - **1.** [clean and tidy] makellos - **2.** [behaviour] tadellos.

immaterial [ˌɪmə'tɪərɪəl] *adj* [irrelevant] unwichtig.

immature [ˌɪmə'tjʊəʳ] *adj* - **1.** [person, behaviour] unreif - **2.** BOT & ZOOL noch nicht voll entwickelt.

immediate [ɪ'miːdjət] *adj* - **1.** [response, attention] unverzüglich; [need, problem] dringend; **to take immediate action** sofort *OR* unverzüglich handeln - **2.** [future, neighbourhood] unmittelbar; **the immediate area** das Gebiet in unmittelbarer Nähe; **the immediate family** die engste Familie.

immediately [ɪ'miːdjətlɪ] ◇ *adv* - **1.** [at once] sofort - **2.** [directly] unmittelbar, direkt. ◇ *conj* [as soon as] sobald.

immense [ɪ'mens] *adj* enorm.

immerse [ɪ'mɜːs] *vt* - **1.** [in liquid]: **to immerse sthg in sthg** etw in etw *(A)* einltauchen - **2.** *fig* [involve]: **to immerse o.s. in sthg** sich in etw *(A)* stürzen.

immersion heater [ɪ'mɜːʃn-] *n* Heißwasserbereiter *der*.

immigrant ['ɪmɪgrənt] *n* Einwanderer *der*, -derin *die*.

immigration [ˌɪmɪ'greɪʃn] *n* Einwanderung *die*.

imminent ['ɪmɪnənt] *adj* [danger] drohend; [death, disaster] unmittelbar bevorstehend.

immobilize, -ise [ɪ'məʊbɪlaɪz] *vt* [machine, lift] lahm legen; [vehicle] gegen Wegfahren sichern.

immoral [ɪ'mɒrəl] *adj* unmoralisch.

immortal [ɪ'mɔːtl] *adj* unsterblich.

immortalize, -ise [ɪ'mɔːtəlaɪz] *vt* unsterblich machen.

immovable [ɪ'muːvəbl] *adj* - **1.** [fixed] unbeweglich - **2.** [obstinate] unnachgiebig.

immune [ɪ'mjuːn] *adj* - **1.** MED: **immune (to)** immun (gegen) - **2.** *fig*: **to be immune to criticism** gegen Kritik unempfindlich sein.

immunity [ɪ'mjuːnətɪ] *n* MED: **immunity (to)** Immunität *die* (gegen).

immunize, -ise ['ɪmjuːnaɪz] *vt*: **to immunize sb (against)** MED jn immunisieren (gegen).

impact *n* ['ɪmpækt] - **1.** [force of contact] Aufprall *der*; [of two moving objects] Zusammenprall *der* - **2.** [effect] Auswirkung *die*; **to make an impact on sb** Eindruck auf jn machen; **to make an impact on sthg** einen Einfluss auf etw *(A)* haben.

impair [ɪm'peəʳ] *vt* beeinträchtigen.

impart [ɪm'pɑːt] *vt fml* - **1.** [knowledge, skills]: **to impart sthg to sb** jm etw vermitteln - **2.** [feeling, quality]: **to impart sthg to sthg** etw *(D)* etw verleihen.

impartial [ɪm'pɑːʃl] *adj* [person] unparteiisch; [news report] objektiv.

impassable [ɪm'pɑːsəbl] *adj* unpassierbar.

impassive [ɪm'pæsɪv] *adj* unbewegt.

impatience [ɪm'peɪʃns] *n* Ungeduld *die*.

impatient [ɪm'peɪʃnt] *adj* ungeduldig; **to be impatient to do sthg** es nicht erwarten können, etw zu tun.

impeccable [ɪm'pekəbl] *adj* untadelig.

impede [ɪm'piːd] *vt* [person] hindern; [progress, activity] behindern.

impediment [ɪm'pedɪmənt] *n* - **1.** [obstacle] Hindernis *das* - **2.** [disability] Behinderung *die*.

impel [ɪm'pel] *vt*: **to impel sb to do sthg** jn (dazu) nötigen, etw zu tun.

impending [ɪm'pendɪŋ] *adj* [doom, disaster] drohend; [interview, test] bevorstehend.

imperative [ɪm'perətɪv] ◇ *adj* dringend notwendig. ◇ *n* - **1.** [necessity] dringende Notwendigkeit - **2.** GRAM Imperativ *der*.

imperfect [ɪm'pɜːfɪkt] ◇ *adj* [work, copy] fehlerhaft; [knowledge] mangelhaft. ◇ *n* GRAM: **imperfect (tense)** Imperfekt *das*.

imperial [ɪm'pɪərɪəl] *adj* - **1.** [of an empire] imperial; [of an emperor] kaiserlich - **2.** [measurement] britisch.

imperil [ɪm'perɪl] (*UK*) (*US*) *vt fml* gefährden.

impersonal [ɪm'pɜːsnl] *adj* - **1.** [unemotional] unpersönlich - **2.** GRAM: **impersonal verb** unpersönlich gebrauchtes Verb.

impersonate [ɪm'pɜːsəneɪt] *vt* - **1.** [mimic] imitieren, nachlahmen - **2.** [pretend to be] sich auslgeben als.

impersonation [ɪm,pɜːsə'neɪʃn] *n* [by mimic] Imitation *die*, Nachahmung *die*.

impertinent [ɪm'pɜːtɪnənt] *adj* unverschämt.

impervious [ɪm'pɜːvɪəs] *adj*: **to be impervious to charm** für Charme unempfänglich sein; **to be impervious to criticism** von Kritik unberührt sein.

impetuous [ɪm'petʃʊəs] *adj* impulsiv.

impetus ['ɪmpɪtəs] *n* - **1.** *(U)* [momentum] Schwung *der* - **2.** [stimulus] Impuls *der*.

impinge [ɪm'pɪndʒ] *vi*: **to impinge on sb/sthg** sich auf jn/etw auslwirken.

implant ◇ *n* ['ɪmplɑːnt] Implantat *das*. ◇ *vt* [ɪm'plɑːnt] - **1.** [instil]: **to implant sthg in sb** jm etw einlimpfen - **2.** MED: **to implant sthg in(to) sb** jm etw implantieren.

implausible [ɪm'plɔːzəbl] *adj* [story] unglaubwürdig.

implement ◇ *n* ['ɪmplɪmənt] [tool] Werkzeug *das*; [piece of equipment] Gerät *das*. ◇ *vt* ['ɪmplɪment] [plan] auslführen; [law] vollziehen; [policy] in die Praxis umlsetzen.

implication [,ɪmplɪ'keɪʃn] *n* - **1.** *(U)* [involvement] Verwicklung *die* - **2.** [inference] Auswirkung *die*; **by implication** implizit.

implicit [ɪm'plɪsɪt] *adj* - **1.** [inferred] implizit; [acknowledgement] stillschweigend; [criticism] unausgesprochen - **2.** [faith, belief] blind.

implore [ɪm'plɔːʳ] *vt*: **to implore sb (to do sthg)** jn inständig bitten(, etw zu tun).

imply [ɪm'plaɪ] *vt* - **1.** [suggest]: **I'm not implying that...** ich will damit nicht sagen, dass... - **2.** [responsibility] mit einlschließen.

impolite ['ɪmpə'laɪt] *adj* unhöflich.

import ◇ *n* ['ɪmpɔːt] - **1.** [product] Importware *die* - **2.** *(U)* [act of importing] Import *der*. ◇ *vt* [ɪm'pɔːt] - **1.** [goods] importieren - **2.** COMPUT importieren.

importance [ɪm'pɔːtns] *n* *(U)* Wichtigkeit *die*; [significance] Bedeutung *die*.

important [ɪm'pɔːtnt] *adj* wichtig; [significant] bedeutend; [person] einflussreich; **to be important to sb** für jn wichtig sein.

importer [ɪm'pɔːtəʳ] *n* [person, firm] Importeur *der*; [country] Importland *das*.

impose [ɪm'pəʊz] ◇ *vt*: **to impose sthg (on sb/sthg)** (jm/etw) etw auflerlegen; **to impose a tax on sb** jn besteuern. ◇ *vi*: **to impose (on sb)** (jm) zur Last fallen.

imposing [ɪm'pəʊzɪŋ] *adj* beeindruckend.

imposition [,ɪmpə'zɪʃn] *n* - **1.** [enforcement - gen] Auferlegung *die*; [- of tax] Erhebung *die* - **2.** [burden] Zumutung *die*.

impossible [ɪm'pɒsəbl] *adj* unmöglich.

impostor, imposter *US* [ɪm'pɒstəʳ] *n* Hochstapler *der*, -in *die*.

impotent ['ɪmpətənt] *adj* - **1.** [sexually] impotent - **2.** [powerless] machtlos.

impound [ɪm'paʊnd] *vt* beschlagnahmen.

impoverished [ɪm'pɒvərɪʃt] *adj liter & fig* verarmt.

impractical [ɪm'præktɪkl] *adj* praxisfern.

impregnable [ɪm'pregnəbl] *adj* [fortress, defences] uneinnehmbar; *fig* [person] unangreifbar; [position, argument] unanfechtbar.

impregnate ['ɪmpregneɪt] *vt* - **1.** [saturate]: **to impregnate sthg with sthg** etw mit etw tränken; [to protect material] etw mit etw imprägnieren - **2.** *fml* [fertilize] befruchten.

impress [ɪm'pres] *vt* - **1.** [make impression on] beeindrucken; [deliberately] imponieren *(+ D)*; **to be favourably/unfavourably impressed** einen guten/schlechten Eindruck haben - **2.** [make clear]: **to impress sthg on sb** jm etw einlschärfen.

impression [ɪm'preʃn] *n* - **1.** [gen] Eindruck *der*; **to make an impression** Eindruck machen; **to be under the impression (that)...** den Eindruck haben, dass... - **2.** [impersonation] Nachahmung *die*, Imitation *die*; **to do an impression of sb** jn imitieren OR nachlahmen - **3.** [of book] Nachdruck *der*.

impressive [ɪm'presɪv] *adj* beeindruckend.

imprint *n* ['ɪmprɪnt] [mark] Abdruck *der*.

imprison [ɪm'prɪzn] *vt* inhaftieren.

improbable [ɪm'prɒbəbl] *adj* [unlikely] unwahrscheinlich.

impromptu [ɪm'prɒmptjuː] *adj* improvisiert.

improper [ɪm'prɒpəʳ] *adj* - **1.** [unsuitable - treatment] unangebracht; [- behaviour] unpassend - **2.** [dishonest - actions] unehrenhaft; [- dealings] unlauter - **3.** [rude] unanständig.

improve [ɪm'pruːv] <> *vi* [weather, work, student] besser werden; [delinquent, health] sich bessern; [productivity] sich steigern; **to improve (up)on** übertreffen; [offer] überbieten. <> *vt* - **1.** [make better] verbessern - **2.** [increase - vocabulary, knowledge] erweitern; [- productivity] erhöhen, steigern - **3.** [cultivate]: **to improve one's mind** sich (weiter)|bilden; **to improve o.s.** an sich *(D)* arbeiten.

improvement [ɪm'pruːvmənt] *n* Verbesserung *die*; [in health, sb's behaviour, weather] Besserung *die*; [in productivity, sports] Steigerung *die*.

improvise ['ɪmprəvaɪz] <> *vt* improvisieren; [shelter] notdürftig erstellen. <> *vi* improvisieren.

impudence ['ɪmpjʊdəns] *n* Unverschämtheit *die*.

impudent ['ɪmpjʊdənt] *adj* unverschämt.

impulse ['ɪmpʌls] *n* Impuls *der*; **to do sthg on impulse** etw aus einem Impuls heraus tun.

impulsive [ɪm'pʌlsɪv] *adj* impulsiv.

impunity [ɪm'pjuːnətɪ] *n*: **with impunity** ungestraft.

impurity [ɪm'pjʊərətɪ] *n* Unreinheit *die*.

in [ɪn] <> *prep* - **1.** [indicating place, position] in *(+ D)*; *(with verbs of motion)* in *(+ A)*; **it's in the box/garden** es ist in der Schachtel/im Garten; **put it in the box/garden** leg es in die Schachtel/in den Garten; **in the street/world** auf der Straße/Welt; **in the country** auf dem Lande; **in the sky** am Himmel; **in Paris/Belgium** in Paris/Belgien; **to be in hospital/prison** im Krankenhaus/Gefängnis sein; **in here/there** hier/dort drinnen - **2.** [wearing] in *(+ D)*; **she was still in her nightclothes** sie war noch im Nachthemd; **(dressed) in red** rot gekleidet - **3.** [at a particular time, during] in *(+ D)*; **in April** im April; **she was born in 1999** sie wurde 1999 geboren; **in (the) spring/winter** im Frühling/Winter; **in the afternoon/morning** am Nachmittag/Morgen; **ten o'clock in the morning** zehn Uhr morgens - **4.** [within, after] in *(+ D)*; **he learned to type in two weeks** er lernte in zwei Wochen Maschine schreiben; **it'll be ready in an hour** es ist in einer Stunde fertig - **5.** [expressing time passed] seit; **it's my first decent meal in weeks** das ist meine erste anständige Mahlzeit seit Wochen - **6.** [indicating situation, circumstances]: **in the sun/rain** in der Sonne/im Regen; **to be in pain** Schmerzen haben; **in danger/difficulty** in Gefahr/Schwierigkeiten; **in these circumstances** unter diesen Umständen - **7.** [indicating manner]: **to write in ink** mit Tinte schreiben; **in a soft voice** mit sanfter Stimme; **they were talking in English** sie sprachen Englisch; **in writing** schriftlich - **8.** [indicating emotional state]: **in anger/delight/amazement/despair** wütend/entzückt/erstaunt/verzweifelt; **in my excitement** in meiner Aufregung - **9.** [specifying area of activity]: **advances in medicine** Fortschritte in der Medizin; **he's in computers** er ist in der Computerbranche - **10.** [referring to quantity]: **to buy sthg in large/small quantities** etw in großen/kleinen Mengen kaufen; **in (their) thousands** zu Tausenden - **11.** [referring to age]: **she's in her twenties** sie ist in den Zwanzigern - **12.** [describing arrangement] in *(+ D)*; **in a circle/line** im Kreis/in einer Reihe; **to stand in twos** zu zweit dastehen - **13.** [indicating colour] in *(+ D)*; **it comes in green or blue** es gibt es in grün oder blau - **14.** [as regards]: **a rise in prices** ein Preisanstieg; **to be 3 metres in length** 3 Meter lang sein; **a change in direction** ein Richtungswechsel - **15.** [in ratios]: **one in ten** jeder Zehnte; **an increase of five pence in the pound** eine Preiserhöhung von fünf Prozent - **16.** *(after superl)* in *(+ D)*; **the best in the world** der/die/das Beste in der Welt - **17.** *(+ present participle)*: **she made a mistake in accepting the offer** sie machte einen Fehler, indem sie das Angebot annahm. <> *adv* - **1.** [inside] herein/hinein; **you can go in now** du kannst jetzt hineingehen - **2.** [at home, work] da; **is Judith in?** ist Judith da?; **to stay in** zu Hause bleiben - **3.** [of train, boat, plane]: **to get in** an|kommen; **the train isn't in yet** der Zug ist noch nicht angekommen - **4.** [in shop]: **is my new TV in yet?** ist mein neuer Fernseher schon da? - **5.** [of tide]: **the tide is in** es ist Flut - **6.** *phr*: **you're in for a surprise** du wirst eine Überraschung erleben; **he's in for it** *inf* der kann sich auf etwas gefasst machen; **my luck is in** das Glück ist auf meiner Seite. <> *adj inf* in; **short skirts are in this year** kurze Röcke sind dieses Jahr in. ◆ **ins** *npl*: **she knows the ins and outs of the matter** sie ist mit allen Feinheiten der Sache vertraut.

in. *abbr of* **inch**.

inability [,ɪnə'bɪlətɪ] *n* Unfähigkeit *die*.

inaccessible [,ɪnək'sesəbl] *adj* - **1.** [place] unzugänglich - **2.** [book, film, music] schwer verständlich.

inaccurate [ɪn'ækjʊrət] *adj* [imprecise] ungenau; [incorrect] inkorrekt.

inadequate [ɪn'ædɪkwət] *adj* unzureichend.

inadvertently [,ɪnəd'vɜːtəntlɪ] *adv* [forget, break] aus Versehen; [discover] zufällig.

inadvisable [,ɪnəd'vaɪzəbl] *adj* nicht ratsam.

inane [ɪ'neɪn] *adj* dumm.

inanimate [ɪn'ænɪmət] *adj* leblos.

inappropriate [ɪnə'prəʊprɪət] *adj* unpassend.

inarticulate [,ɪnɑː'tɪkjʊlət] *adj* [person]: **to be inarticulate** sich nicht gut ausdrücken können.

inasmuch [,ɪnəz'mʌtʃ] ◆ **inasmuch as** *conj fml* [because] da; [to the extent that] insofern als.

inaudible [ɪ'nɔːdɪbl] *adj* unhörbar.

inaugural [ɪ'nɔːgjʊrəl] *adj* [meeting] Eröffnungs-; [speech] Antritts-.

inauguration [ɪˌnɔːgjʊ'reɪʃn] *n* - **1.** [of leader, president] Amtseinführung *die* - **2.** [of building] Einweihung *die*.

inborn [ˌɪn'bɔːn] *adj* angeboren.

inbound ['ɪnbaʊnd] *adj* ankommend.

inbox ['ɪnbɒks] *n* COMPUT Posteingang *der*.

inbred [ˌɪn'bred] *adj* [characteristic, quality] angeboren.

inbuilt [ˌɪn'bɪlt] *adj* [quality, defect] angeboren.

inc. (*abbr of* **inclusive**) inkl.

Inc. [ɪŋk] *abbr of* **incorporated**.

incapable [ɪn'keɪpəbl] *adj* - **1.** [unable]: **to be incapable of sthg** zu etw nicht fähig sein; **to be incapable of doing sthg** nicht fähig sein, etw zu tun - **2.** [incompetent] unfähig.

incapacitated [ˌɪnkə'pæsɪteɪtɪd] *adj* [for work] arbeitsunfähig.

incarcerate [ɪn'kɑːsəreɪt] *vt fml* ein|kerkern.

incendiary device [ɪn'sendjərɪ-] *n* Brandsatz *der*.

incense ◇ *n* ['ɪnsens] Weihrauch *der*. ◇ *vt* [ɪn'sens] [anger] erbosen, erzürnen.

incentive [ɪn'sentɪv] *n* Anreiz *der*.

incentive scheme *n* Anreizsystem *das*.

inception [ɪn'sepʃn] *n fml* Beginn *der*; [of institution] Gründung *die*.

incessant [ɪn'sesnt] *adj* unaufhörlich.

incessantly [ɪn'sesntlɪ] *adv* unaufhörlich.

incest ['ɪnsest] *n* Inzest *der*.

inch [ɪntʃ] ◇ *n* Zoll *der*, = *2,54 cm*. ◇ *vi*: **to inch forward/through** sich zentimeterweise vorwärts bewegen/hindurch|bewegen.

incidence ['ɪnsɪdəns] *n* Häufigkeit *die*.

incident ['ɪnsɪdənt] *n* - **1.** [event] Vorfall *der*; **the meeting went off without incident** das Treffen verlief ohne Zwischenfälle - **2.** POL Zwischenfall *der*.

incidental [ˌɪnsɪ'dentl] *adj* [minor] nebensächlich; **incidental expenses** Nebenausgaben *Pl*.

incidentally [ˌɪnsɪ'dentəlɪ] *adv* [by the way] übrigens.

incinerate [ɪn'sɪnəreɪt] *vt* verbrennen.

incipient [ɪn'sɪpɪənt] *adj fml* beginnend.

incisive [ɪn'saɪsɪv] *adj* [person] scharfsinnig; [comment, writing] pointiert.

incite [ɪn'saɪt] *vt* auf|hetzen; **to incite sb to do sthg** jn dazu auf|stacheln, etw zu tun.

incl. (*abbr of* **inclusive**) inkl.

inclination [ˌɪnklɪ'neɪʃn] *n* - **1.** [desire, slope] Neigung *die* - **2.** [tendency]: **to have an inclination to do sthg** die Neigung (dazu) haben, etw zu tun.

incline ◇ *n* ['ɪnklaɪn] [slope] Hang *der*; [angle] Neigung *die*. ◇ *vt* [ɪn'klaɪn] [head, body] neigen.

inclined [ɪn'klaɪnd] *adj* - **1.** [tending] geneigt; **to be inclined to do sthg** dazu neigen, etw zu tun - **2.** [wanting]: **to be inclined to do sthg** Lust haben, etw zu tun - **3.** [sloping] geneigt.

include [ɪn'kluːd] *vt* - **1.** [gen] (mit) ein|schließen; [contain] enthalten - **2.** [add, count] mit|rechnen.

included [ɪn'kluːdɪd] *adj* eingeschlossen; **service is not included** die Bedienung ist nicht inbegriffen.

including [ɪn'kluːdɪŋ] *prep* einschließlich (+ *G*); **up to and including last month** bis einschließlich des letzten Monats.

inclusive [ɪn'kluːsɪv] *adj* einschließlich, inklusive; **inclusive price** Pauschalpreis *der*; **from the 8th to the 16th inclusive** vom 8. bis einschließlich 16.; **inclusive of** einschließlich (+ *G*).

incoherent [ˌɪnkəʊ'hɪərənt] *adj* [speech] zusammenhanglos; **he was incoherent** er drückte sich unklar aus.

income ['ɪŋkʌm] *n* Einkommen *das*.

income support *n UK* Sozialhilfe *die*.

income tax *n* Einkommensteuer *die*.

incompatible [ˌɪnkəm'pætɪbl] *adj* [ideas, jobs, characters] unvereinbar; [computers] inkompatibel; **to be incompatible with sb** nicht zu jm passen.

incompetent [ɪn'kɒmpɪtənt] *adj* unfähig, inkompetent; [work] unzulänglich.

incomplete [ˌɪnkəm'pliːt] *adj* unvollständig; [story] nicht abgeschlossen.

incomprehensible [ɪnˌkɒmprɪ'hensəbl] *adj* unverständlich.

inconceivable [ˌɪnkən'siːvəbl] *adj* undenkbar, unvorstellbar.

inconclusive [ˌɪnkən'kluːsɪv] *adj* [meeting, debate] ergebnislos; [evidence, argument] nicht schlüssig.

incongruous [ɪn'kɒŋgrʊəs] *adj* [clothes, behaviour] unpassend.

inconsequential [ˌɪnkɒnsɪ'kwenʃl] *adj* [insignificant] unbedeutend.

inconsiderate [ˌɪnkən'sɪdərət] *adj* rücksichtslos.

inconsistency [ˌɪnkən'sɪstənsɪ] *n* Widersprüchlichkeit *die*.

inconsistent [ˌɪnkən'sɪstənt] *adj* widersprüchlich; [performance] schwankend; [work] unbeständig; [behaviour] inkonsequent; **to be inconsistent with sthg** mit etw nicht überein|stimmen.

inconspicuous [ˌɪnkən'spɪkjʊəs] *adj* unauffällig.

inconvenience [ˌɪnkən'viːnjəns] ◇ *n* Unannehmlichkeit *die*. ◇ *vt* Unannehmlichkeiten OR Umstände bereiten.

inconvenient [ˌɪnkən'viːnjənt] *adj* ungünstig; **to be inconvenient for sb** jm ungelegen kommen.

incorporate [ɪn'kɔːpəreɪt] *vt* ein|schließen; **to incorporate sb/sthg in(to) sthg** jn/etw in etw *(A)* auf|nehmen.

incorporated company *n* COMM (im Handelsregister) eingetragene Gesellschaft.

incorrect [ˌɪnkə'rekt] *adj* falsch; [behaviour] inkorrekt.

incorrigible [ɪn'kɒrɪdʒəbl] *adj* unverbesserlich.

increase ◇ *n* ['ɪnkriːs]: **increase (in)** [number, unemployment] Zunahme *die (+ G)*; [price, demand, speed] Erhöhung *die (+ G)*; [output] Steigerung *die (+ G)*; **to be on the increase** (ständig) zu|nehmen. ◇ *vt* [ɪn'kriːs] [price, wages, speed] erhöhen; [output] steigern; [fear, efforts] verstärken. ◇ *vi* [ɪn'kriːs] steigen; [unemployment, pain] zu|nehmen; [anxiety] wachsen.

increasing [ɪn'kriːsɪŋ] *adj* [number, use, frequency] zunehmend; [anxiety, demand] wachsend.

increasingly [ɪn'kriːsɪŋlɪ] *adv* zunehmend.

incredible [ɪn'kredəbl] *adj* - **1.** [wonderful] sagenhaft - **2.** [very large, unbelievable] unglaublich.

incredulous [ɪn'kredjʊləs] *adj* ungläubig.

increment ['ɪnkrɪmənt] *n* Zuwachs *der*; [of salary] Gehaltserhöhung *die*.

incriminating [ɪn'krɪmɪneɪtɪŋ] *adj* belastend.

incubator ['ɪnkjʊbeɪtəʳ] *n* [for baby] Brutkasten *der*.

incur [ɪn'kɜːʳ] *vt* [loss] erleiden; [expenses] haben; [debts] machen.

indebted [ɪn'detɪd] *adj* [grateful]: **to be indebted to sb** jm zu Dank verpflichtet sein.

indecent [ɪn'diːsnt] *adj* unanständig.

indecisive [ˌɪndɪ'saɪsɪv] *adj* - **1.** [person] unentschlossen - **2.** [result] unklar.

indeed [ɪn'diːd] *adv* wirklich, tatsächlich; [certainly] natürlich; **very big indeed** wirklich sehr groß; **thank you very much indeed** vielen herzlichen Dank; **indeed?** [in surprise] wirklich?, so?

indefinite [ɪn'defɪnɪt] *adj* - **1.** [period, number] unbestimmt - **2.** [answer] unklar.

indefinitely [ɪn'defɪnətlɪ] *adv* [wait] unbegrenzt lange; [closed] bis auf weiteres; [postpone] auf unbestimmte Zeit.

indent [ɪn'dent] *vt* [text] ein|rücken.

independence [ˌɪndɪ'pendəns] *n* - **1.** [gen] Unabhängigkeit *die* - **2.** [in character] Selbstständigkeit *die*.

Independence Day *n* (amerikanischer) Unabhängigkeitstag *(4. Juli)*.

independent [ˌɪndɪ'pendənt] *adj* - **1.** [gen]: **independent (of)** unabhängig (von) - **2.** [person - in character] selbstständig.

independent school *n UK* nicht staatliche Schule.

in-depth *adj* eingehend.

indescribable [ˌɪndɪ'skraɪbəbl] *adj* unbeschreiblich.

indestructible [ˌɪndɪ'strʌktəbl] *adj* unzerstörbar.

index ['ɪndeks] *n* - **1.** (*pl* **-es**) [of book] Register *das* - **2.** (*pl* **-es**) [in library] Kartei *die* - **3.** (*pl* **-es** OR **indices**) ECON Index *der*.

index card *n* Karteikarte *die*.

index finger *n* Zeigefinger *der*.

index-linked [-ˌlɪŋkt] *adj* der Inflationsrate angepasst.

India ['ɪndɪə] *n* Indien *nt*.

Indian ['ɪndɪən] ◇ *adj* - **1.** [from India] indisch - **2.** [from the Americas] indianisch, Indianer-. ◇ *n* - **1.** [from India] Inder *der*, -in *die* - **2.** [from the Americas] Indianer *der*, -in *die*.

Indian Ocean *n*: **the Indian Ocean** der Indische Ozean.

indicate ['ɪndɪkeɪt] ◇ *vt* - **1.** [with finger, pointer] zeigen auf *(+ A)*; [subj: dial, arrow, gauge] an|zeigen - **2.** [intention, fact] an|deuten - **3.** [mention - desire, preference] zum Ausdruck bringen - **4.** [suggest] hin|deuten auf *(+ A)*. ◇ *vi* [when driving] blinken.

indication [ˌɪndɪ'keɪʃn] *n* - **1.** [suggestion]: **can you give me an indication of when you will arrive?** können Sie mir ungefähr sagen, wann Sie ankommen? - **2.** [sign] (An)zeichen *das*; [hint] Hinweis *der*.

indicative [ɪn'dɪkətɪv] ◇ *adj*: **to be indicative of sthg** auf etw *(A)* hin|deuten, auf etw *(A)* schließen lassen. ◇ *n* GRAM Indikativ *der*.

indicator ['ɪndɪkeɪtəʳ] *n* - **1.** [sign] Indikator *der* - **2.** [on car] Blinker *der*.

indices ['ɪndɪsiːz] *Pl* ▷ **index**.

indict [ɪn'daɪt] *vt*: **to indict sb (for)** jn an|klagen (wegen *(+ G)*).

indictment [ɪn'daɪtmənt] *n* - **1.** LAW Anklageerhebung *die* - **2.** [criticism]: **an indictment of** ein Armutszeugnis für.

indifference [ɪn'dɪfrəns] *n* Gleichgültigkeit *die*.

indifferent [ɪn'dɪfrənt] *adj* - **1.** [uninterested] gleichgültig; **to be indifferent to sthg** sich für etw nicht interessieren - **2.** [mediocre] mittelmäßig.

indigenous [ɪn'dɪdʒɪnəs] *adj* [culture, traditions] einheimisch, landeseigen.

indigestion [ˌɪndɪ'dʒestʃn] *n (U)* Magenverstimmung *die*.

indignant [ɪn'dɪgnənt] *adj*: **to be indignant (at)** empört sein (über *(+ A)*).

indignity [ɪn'dɪgnətɪ] *n* Demütigung *die*.

indigo ['ɪndɪgəʊ] *adj* indigoblau.

indirect [,ɪndɪ'rekt] *adj* indirekt; **an indirect route** ein Umweg.

indiscreet [,ɪndɪ'skri:t] *adj* indiskret; [tactless] taktlos.

indiscriminate [,ɪndɪ'skrɪmɪnət] *adj* wahllos; [treatment] willkürlich; [person] unkritisch.

indispensable [,ɪndɪ'spensəbl] *adj* unentbehrlich.

indisputable [,ɪndɪ'spju:təbl] *adj* unbestreitbar; [evidence] unanfechtbar.

indistinguishable [,ɪndɪ'stɪŋgwɪʃəbl] *adj*: **to be indistinguishable (from sb/sthg)** (von jm/etw) nicht zu unterscheiden sein.

individual [,ɪndɪ'vɪdʒʊəl] ◇ *adj* - **1.** [single] einzeln; [tuition] Einzel-; **individual case** Einzelfall *der* - **2.** [distinctive] individuell. ◇ *n* Einzelne *der, die*, Individuum *das*.

individually [,ɪndɪ'vɪdʒʊəlɪ] *adv* einzeln.

Indonesia [,ɪndə'ni:zɪə] *n* Indonesien *nt*.

indoor ['ɪndɔ:ʳ] *adj* [swimming pool, sports] Hallen-; [plant] Zimmer-.

indoors [,ɪn'dɔ:z] *adv* [stay] drinnen; [go] nach drinnen.

induce [ɪn'dju:s] *vt* [persuade]: **to induce sb to do sthg** jn dazu bringen, etw zu tun.

inducement [ɪn'dju:smənt] *n* [incentive] Anreiz *der*.

induction course *n* Einführungskurs *der*.

indulge [ɪn'dʌldʒ] ◇ *vt* - **1.** [whim] nachgeben *(+ D)*; [passion] frönen *(+ D)* - **2.** [child, person] verwöhnen. ◇ *vi*: **to indulge in sthg** etw *(D)* frönen.

indulgence [ɪn'dʌldʒəns] *n* - **1.** *(U)* [tolerance, kindness] Nachsicht *die* - **2.** [special treat] Luxus *der*.

indulgent [ɪn'dʌldʒənt] *adj* nachsichtig; [giving way] nachgiebig.

industrial [ɪn'dʌstrɪəl] *adj* industriell; [city, area, society] Industrie-.

industrial action *n*: **to take industrial action** in den Ausstand treten.

industrial estate *UK*, **industrial park** *US* *n* Industriegebiet *das*.

industrialist [ɪn'dʌstrɪəlɪst] *n* Industrielle *der, die*.

industrial park *n US* = **industrial estate**.

industrial relations *npl* Beziehungen *Pl* zwischen Arbeitgebern und Gewerkschaften.

industrial revolution *n* industrielle Revolution.

industrious [ɪn'dʌstrɪəs] *adj* fleißig.

industry ['ɪndəstrɪ] *n* - **1.** [gen] Industrie *die*; **the tourist industry** die Tourismusbranche - **2.** [hard work] Fleiß *der*.

inebriated [ɪ'ni:brɪeɪtɪd] *adj fml* betrunken.

inedible [ɪn'edɪbl] *adj* - **1.** [unpleasant to eat] ungenießbar - **2.** [poisonous] nicht essbar.

ineffective [,ɪnɪ'fektɪv] *adj* unwirksam.

ineffectual [,ɪnɪ'fektʃʊəl] *adj* [person] unfähig; [plan] ineffizient.

inefficiency [,ɪnɪ'fɪʃnsɪ] *n* [of person] Unfähigkeit *die*; [of process] Unproduktivität *die*; [of machine] Unwirtschaftlichkeit *die*.

inefficient [,ɪnɪ'fɪʃnt] *adj* [person] unfähig, ineffizient; [process] unproduktiv; [machine] unwirtschaftlich.

ineligible [ɪn'elɪdʒəbl] *adj*: **to be ineligible for sthg** [promotion] für etw nicht infrage kommen; [benefits] auf etw *(A)* keinen Anspruch haben.

inept [ɪ'nept] *adj* [person] unfähig; [comment] unpassend; [performance, attempt] ungeschickt.

inequality [,ɪnɪ'kwɒlətɪ] *n* - **1.** [gen] Ungleichheit *die* - **2.** [difference] Unterschied *der*.

inert [ɪ'nɜ:t] *adj* [person] reglos.

inertia [ɪ'nɜ:ʃə] *n* [gen] Trägheit *die*.

inescapable [,ɪnɪ'skeɪpəbl] *adj* unausweichlich.

inevitable [ɪn'evɪtəbl] ◇ *adj* unvermeidlich. ◇ *n*: **the inevitable** das Unvermeidliche.

inevitably [ɪn'evɪtəblɪ] *adv* zwangsläufig.

inexcusable [,ɪnɪk'skju:zəbl] *adj* unverzeihlich, unentschuldbar.

inexhaustible [,ɪnɪg'zɔ:stəbl] *adj* unerschöpflich.

inexpensive [,ɪnɪk'spensɪv] *adj* preiswert.

inexperienced [,ɪnɪk'spɪərɪənst] *adj* unerfahren; **to be inexperienced in sthg** mit etw wenig vertraut sein.

inexplicable [,ɪnɪk'splɪkəbl] *adj* unerklärlich.

infallible [ɪn'fæləbl] *adj* unfehlbar.

infamous ['ɪnfəməs] *adj* berüchtigt.

infancy ['ɪnfənsɪ] *n* frühe Kindheit; **to be in its infancy** *fig* (noch) in den Kinderschuhen stecken.

infant ['ɪnfənt] *n* - **1.** [baby] Säugling *der* - **2.** [young child] Kleinkind *das*.

infantry ['ɪnfəntrɪ] *n* Infanterie *die*.

infant school *n UK* Vorschule *die (für 5- bis 7-Jährige)*.

infatuated [ɪn'fætjʊeɪtɪd] *adj*: **to be infatuated (with sb/sthg)** (in jn/etw) vernarrt sein.

infatuation [ɪn,fætjʊ'eɪʃn] *n*: **infatuation (with sb/sthg)** Vernarrtheit *die* (in jn/etw).

infect [ɪn'fekt] *vt* MED infizieren.

infection [ɪn'fekʃn] *n* MED Infektion *die*; **ear infection** Ohrenentzündung *die*.

infectious [ɪn'fekʃəs] *adj liter & fig* ansteckend.

infer [ɪn'fɜːʳ] *vt* - **1.** [deduce]: **to infer that...** folgern, dass...; **to infer sthg (from sthg)** etw (aus etw) folgern - **2.** *inf* [imply] an|deuten.

inferior [ɪn'fɪərɪəʳ] <> *adj* - **1.** [lower in status] untergeordnet; **to be inferior (to sb/sthg)** (jm/etw) untergeordnet sein - **2.** [lower in quality] minderwertig; **to feel inferior** sich unterlegen fühlen; **to be inferior to sthg** von geringerer Qualität als etw sein. <> *n* [in status] Untergebene *der, die*.

inferiority [ɪn,fɪərɪ'ɒrətɪ] *n* - **1.** [in status] untergeordnete Stellung - **2.** [in quality] Minderwertigkeit *die*.

inferiority complex *n* Minderwertigkeitskomplex *der*.

inferno [ɪn'fɜːnəʊ] (*pl* **-s**) *n* Flammenmeer *das*.

infertile [ɪn'fɜːtaɪl] *adj* unfruchtbar.

infested [ɪn'festɪd] *adj*: **infested with sthg** [vermin, insects] von etw befallen; [weeds] von etw überwuchert.

infighting ['ɪn,faɪtɪŋ] *n (U)* [rivalry] interne Machtkämpfe *Pl*; [quarrelling] interne Querelen *Pl*.

infiltrate ['ɪnfɪltreɪt] *vt* [territory] infiltrieren; [party, organization] unterwandern.

infinite ['ɪnfɪnət] *adj* unendlich.

infinitive [ɪn'fɪnɪtɪv] *n* Infinitiv *der*.

infinity [ɪn'fɪnətɪ] *n* - **1.** [unreachable point] Unendlichkeit *die* - **2.** MATHS Unendliche *das*.

infirm [ɪn'fɜːm] *adj* gebrechlich.

infirmary [ɪn'fɜːmərɪ] *n* - **1.** [hospital] Krankenhaus *das* - **2.** [room] Krankenzimmer *das*.

infirmity [ɪn'fɜːmətɪ] *n* - **1.** [individual weakness or illness] Gebrechen *das* - **2.** [state of being weak or ill] Gebrechlichkeit *die*.

inflamed [ɪn'fleɪmd] *adj* MED entzündet.

inflammable [ɪn'flæməbl] *adj* leicht entzündlich.

inflammation [,ɪnflə'meɪʃn] *n* MED Entzündung *die*.

inflatable [ɪn'fleɪtəbl] *adj* aufblasbar.

inflate [ɪn'fleɪt] *vt* - **1.** [fill with air - tyre] auf|pumpen; [- life-jacket, balloon] auf|blasen - **2.** ECON [increase] in die Höhe treiben.

inflation [ɪn'fleɪʃn] *n* ECON Inflation *die*.

inflationary [ɪn'fleɪʃnrɪ] *adj* ECON [policy, spiral] Inflations-; [trend, wage rise] inflationär.

inflation rate *n* ECON Inflationsrate *die*.

inflict [ɪn'flɪkt] *vt*: **to inflict sthg on sb** [pain] jm etw zulfügen; [problem] jn mit etw belasten; [punishment] jn mit etw belegen; [responsibility] jm etw übertragen.

influence ['ɪnflʊəns] <> *n*: **influence (on sb/sthg), influence (over sb/sthg)** Einfluss *der* (auf jn/etw); **under the influence of** unter dem Einfluss von. <> *vt* beeinflussen.

influential [,ɪnflʊ'enʃl] *adj* einflussreich.

influenza [,ɪnflʊ'enzə] *n fml* Grippe *die*.

influx ['ɪnflʌks] *n* Zustrom *der*.

inform [ɪn'fɔːm] *vt* benachrichtigen; [police] verständigen; **to inform sb of/about sthg** jm etw mit|teilen. ◆ **inform on** *vt insep* an|zeigen.

informal [ɪn'fɔːml] *adj* - **1.** [casual, relaxed - party, clothes] zwanglos; [- language] informell - **2.** [non-official] inoffiziell.

informant [ɪn'fɔːmənt] *n* Informant *der*, -in *die*.

information [,ɪnfə'meɪʃn] *n (U)*: **information (on** OR **about sthg)** Informationen *Pl* (über etw *(A)*); **to get information** sich informieren; **a piece of information** eine Auskunft, eine Information; **'Information'** 'Information', 'Auskunft'; **for your information** COMM zu Ihrer Kenntnisnahme OR Information.

information desk *n* Auskunftsschalter *der*.

information technology *n* Informationstechnologie *die*.

informative [ɪn'fɔːmətɪv] *adj* [person] auskunftsfreudig; [book, film] informativ.

informer [ɪn'fɔːməʳ] *n* [denouncer] Informant *der*, -in *die*.

infrared [,ɪnfrə'red] *adj* Infrarot-.

infrastructure ['ɪnfrə,strʌktʃəʳ] *n* Infrastruktur *die*.

infringe [ɪn'frɪndʒ] <> *vt* - **1.** [right] verletzen - **2.** [law, agreement] verstoßen gegen. <> *vi*: **to infringe on sb's rights** js Rechte verletzen.

infringement [ɪn'frɪndʒmənt] *n* - **1.** [of right] Verletzung *die* - **2.** [of law, agreement] Verstoß *der*.

infuriating [ɪn'fjʊərɪeɪtɪŋ] *adj*: **he/his behaviour is infuriating!** er/sein Benehmen macht mich rasend!

ingenious [ɪn'dʒiːnɪəs] *adj* genial; [device, method] raffiniert; [person] einfallsreich.

ingenuity [,ɪndʒɪ'njuːətɪ] *n* [of person] Genialität *die*, Einfallsreichtum *der*; [of device, method] Raffiniertheit *die*.

ingot ['ɪŋgət] *n* [of gold, silver] Barren *der*.

ingrained [,ɪn'greɪnd] *adj* - **1.** [dirt] tief sitzend - **2.** [belief] unerschütterlich; [hatred] tief.

ingratiating [ɪn'greɪʃɪeɪtɪŋ] *adj* [smile] zuckersüß; [person, manner] schmeichlerisch.

ingredient [ɪn'griːdɪənt] *n* - **1.** [in cooking] Zutat *die* - **2.** [element] Element *das*.

inhabit [ɪn'hæbɪt] *vt* bewohnen.

inhabitant [ɪn'hæbɪtənt] *n* [of country, city] Einwohner *der*, -in *die*; [of house] Bewohner *der*, -in *die*.

inhale [ɪn'heɪl] <> *vt* ein|atmen. <> *vi* [breathe in] ein|atmen; [smoker] Lungenzüge machen.

inhaler [ɪn'heɪlə^r] *n* MED Inhalationsapparat *der*.

inherent [ɪn'hɪərənt, ɪn'herənt] *adj*: **her inherent laziness** die ihr eigene Faulheit; **the dangers inherent in this sport** die mit diesem Sport verbundenen Gefahren.

inherently [ɪn'hɪərəntlɪ, ɪn'herəntlɪ] *adv* von Natur aus.

inherit [ɪn'herɪt] ◇ *vt*: **to inherit sthg (from sb)** etw (von jm) erben. ◇ *vi* erben.

inheritance [ɪn'herɪtəns] *n* Erbe *das*.

inhibit [ɪn'hɪbɪt] *vt* hemmen.

inhibition [ˌɪnhɪ'bɪʃn] *n* Hemmung *die*.

inhospitable [ˌɪnhɒ'spɪtəbl] *adj* - **1.** [person] ungastlich - **2.** [climate, area] unwirtlich.

in-house ◇ *adj* hausintern; **in-house staff** fest angestellte Mitarbeiter. ◇ *adv* im Hause.

inhuman [ɪn'hjuːmən] *adj* [cruel] unmenschlich.

initial [ɪ'nɪʃl] (*UK*) (*US*) ◇ *adj* - **1.** [early] anfänglich - **2.**: **initial letter** Initiale *die*. ◇ *vt* mit seinen Initialen unterschreiben; [as authorization] ab|zeichnen. ◆ **initials** *npl* Initialen *Pl*.

initially [ɪ'nɪʃəlɪ] *adv* anfangs.

initiate *vt* [ˌɪ'nɪʃɪeɪt] - **1.** [start] initiieren; [talks, scheme] in die Wege leiten - **2.** [teach]: **to initiate sb (into sthg)** [into mystery, secret] jn (in etw *(A)*) ein|weihen; [into group] jn (in etw *(A)*) feierlich auf|nehmen; [into skill] jn (in etw *(A)*) ein|führen.

initiative [ɪ'nɪʃətɪv] *n* Initiative *die*.

inject [ɪn'dʒekt] *vt* - **1.** MED: **to inject sb with sthg, to inject sthg into sb** jm etw spritzen OR injizieren - **2.** *fig* [add]: **to inject sthg into sthg** [fun, excitement] etw in etw *(A)* bringen; [money, funds] etw in etw *(A)* pumpen; [resources] etw zu etw bei|steuern.

injection [ɪn'dʒekʃn] *n* - **1.** MED Spritze *die*, Injektion *die* - **2.** [of funds] Zuschuss *der*.

injure ['ɪndʒə^r] *vt* [hurt physically, offend] verletzen.

injured [ɪn'dʒəd] ◇ *adj* [physically hurt, offended] verletzt. ◇ *npl*: **the injured** die Verletzten.

injury ['ɪndʒərɪ] *n (U)* - **1.** [physical harm] Verletzungen *Pl* - **2.** [wound, to one's feelings] Verletzung *die*; **to do o.s. an injury** sich verletzen.

injury time *n (U)* Nachspielzeit *die*.

injustice [ɪn'dʒʌstɪs] *n* Ungerechtigkeit *die*; **to do sb an injustice** jm unrecht tun.

ink [ɪŋk] *n (U)* [for writing] Tinte *die*; [for drawing] Tusche *die*; [for printing] Druckfarbe *die*.

ink-jet printer *n* Tintenstrahldrucker *der*.

inkling ['ɪŋklɪŋ] *n*: **to have an inkling of sthg** etw ahnen.

inlaid [ˌɪn'leɪd] *adj*: **inlaid (with sthg)** (mit etw) eingelegt.

inland ◇ *adj* ['ɪnlənd] Binnen-. ◇ *adv* [ɪn'lænd] landeinwärts.

Inland Revenue *n UK*: **the Inland Revenue** ≃ das Finanzamt.

in-laws *npl inf* angeheiratete Verwandte *Pl*; [parents-in-law] Schwiegereltern *Pl*.

inlet ['ɪnlet] *n* - **1.** [stretch of water - from lake] (schmale) Bucht; [- from sea] Meeresarm *der* - **2.** [way in] Zuleitung *die*.

inmate ['ɪnmeɪt] *n* Insasse *der*, -sin *die*.

inn [ɪn] *n* Wirtshaus *das*.

innate [ɪ'neɪt] *adj* angeboren.

inner ['ɪnə^r] *adj* - **1.** [most central] innere(r) (s); [room] innen liegend; [courtyard] Innen-; **inner ear** Innenohr *das*; **Inner London** Innenstadt *die* Londons - **2.** [unexpressed, secret] innere.

inner city *n*: **the inner city** die Innenstadt, *die Innenbezirke einer Stadt, in denen es oft soziale Probleme gibt*.

inner tube *n* Schlauch *der*.

innings ['ɪnɪŋz] (*pl inv*) *n UK* [in cricket] Durchgang *der*.

innocence ['ɪnəsəns] *n (U)* Unschuld *die*.

innocent ['ɪnəsənt] *adj* unschuldig; **to be innocent of sthg** an etw *(D)* unschuldig sein.

innocuous [ɪ'nɒkjʊəs] *adj* harmlos.

innovation [ˌɪnə'veɪʃn] *n* Innovation *die*.

innovative ['ɪnəvətɪv] *adj* innovativ.

innuendo [ˌɪnjuː'endəʊ] (*pl* **-es** OR **-s**) *n* - **1.** [individual remark] versteckte Andeutung, Anspielung *die* - **2.** *(U)* [style of speaking] Anspielungen *Pl*.

innumerable [ɪ'njuːmərəbl] *adj* unzählig.

inoculate [ɪ'nɒkjʊleɪt] *vt* impfen.

inordinately [ɪ'nɔːdɪnətlɪ] *adv fml* außerordentlich.

in-patient *n* stationärer Patient, stationäre Patientin.

input ['ɪnpʊt] (*pt & pp inv* OR **-ted**) ◇ *n (U)* - **1.** [contribution - money, resources] Investition *die*; [- labour, effort] Beitrag *der* - **2.** COMPUT Eingabe *die* - **3.** ELEC Energiezufuhr *die*. ◇ *vt* COMPUT ein|geben.

inquest ['ɪnkwest] *n* LAW gerichtliche Untersuchung der Todesursache.

inquire [ɪn'kwaɪə^r] ◇ *vt*: **to inquire when/whether** OR **if/how** sich erkundigen wann/ob/wie. ◇ *vi* [ask for information] sich erkundigen; **to inquire about sthg** sich nach etw erkundigen, nach etw fragen. ◆ **inquire after** *vt insep* sich erkundigen nach. ◆ **inquire into** *vt insep* untersuchen.

inquiry [ɪn'kwaɪərɪ] *n* - **1.** [question] Anfrage *die*; **to make inquiries** Erkundigungen ein|ziehen; [police] Nachforschungen an|stellen - **2.** [investigation] Untersuchung *die*.

inquisitive [ɪn'kwɪzətɪv] *adj* [curious] neugierig; [for knowledge] wissbegierig.

inroads ['ɪnrəʊdz] *npl*: **to make inroads into sthg** [savings, supplies] etw an|greifen; [field of knowledge] in etw *(A)* vor|dringen.

insane [ɪn'seɪn] *adj* - **1.** MED [mad] geisteskrank - **2.** *fig* [person, idea, jealousy] verrückt.

insanity [ɪn'sænətɪ] *n (U)* MED [madness] Geisteskrankheit *die*.

insatiable [ɪn'seɪʃəbl] *adj* unersättlich.

inscription [ɪn'skrɪpʃn] *n* - **1.** [on wall, headstone, plaque - written] Aufschrift *die*; [- cut] Inschrift *die* - **2.** [in book] Widmung *die*.

inscrutable [ɪn'skruːtəbl] *adj* unergründlich; [look] undurchdringlich.

insect ['ɪnsekt] *n* Insekt *das*.

insecticide [ɪn'sektɪsaɪd] *n (U)* Insektizid *das*.

insect repellent *n (U)* Insektenschutzmittel *das*.

insecure [,ɪnsɪ'kjʊəʳ] *adj* unsicher.

insensitive [ɪn'sensətɪv] *adj* - **1.** [unkind, thoughtless] unsensibel - **2.** [unresponsive]: **insensitive to sthg** unempfänglich für etw - **3.** [to pain, cold]: **insensitive to sthg** unempfindlich gegen etw.

inseparable [ɪn'seprəbl] *adj* - **1.** [subjects, facts]: **to be inseparable (from sthg)** (mit etw) untrennbar verbunden sein - **2.** [people] unzertrennlich.

insert ◇ *vt* [ɪn'sɜːt] - **1.** [put inside]: **to insert sthg (in** OR **into sthg)** etw (in etw *(A)*) ein|führen - **2.** [include, add]: **to insert sthg (in** OR **into sthg)** etw (in etw *(A)*) ein|fügen. ◇ *n* ['ɪnsɜːt] Einlage *die*.

insertion [ɪn'sɜːʃn] *n* - **1.** [act of inserting] Einführen *das* - **2.** [thing inserted - in text] Einfügung *die*.

in-service training *n UK* (berufsbegleitende) Fortbildung.

inshore ◇ *adj* ['ɪnʃɔːʳ] Küsten-. ◇ *adv* [ɪn'ʃɔːʳ] [be situated] in Küstennähe.

inside [ɪn'saɪd] ◇ *prep* - **1.** [indicating place, position] in *(+ D)*; *(with verbs of motion)* in *(+ A)*; **it's inside the box** es ist in der Schachtel; **put it inside the box** leg es in die Schachtel; **come inside the house!** komm ins Haus! - **2.** [indicating time, limit]: **inside three weeks** in weniger als drei Wochen; **he was just inside the record** er lag knapp unter der Rekordzeit. ◇ *adv* - **1.** [referring to place, object, building] innen; **to be inside** drinnen sein; **to come inside** herein|kommen; **to go inside** hinein|gehen; **there was something inside** es war etwas drin - **2.** [referring to body, mind] innerlich - **3.** *inf prison sl* im Kittchen OR Knast; **to be inside** sitzen. ◇ *adj* Innen-; **an inside toilet** eine Toilette im Haus; **inside information** vertrauliche Information. ◇ *n* [interior, inner part]: **the inside** das Innere; **lock the door from the inside** schließ die Tür von innen ab; **on the inside** innen; **inside out** [clothes] links (herum); **to turn sthg inside out** etw auf links drehen; **to know sthg inside out** *fig* etw in- und auswendig kennen. ◆ **insides** *npl inf* [intestines] Eingeweide *Pl*. ◆ **inside of** *prep US* [building, object] in.

inside lane *n* AUT [in UK] linke Fahrspur; AUT [in Europe, US *etc*] rechte Fahrspur.

insight ['ɪnsaɪt] *n* - **1.** *(U)* [wisdom]: **insight (into sthg)** Verständnis *das* (für etw) - **2.** [glimpse]: **insight (into sthg)** Einblick *das* (in etw *(A)*).

insignificant [,ɪnsɪg'nɪfɪkənt] *adj* unbedeutend.

insincere [,ɪnsɪn'sɪəʳ] *adj* [person, remark] unaufrichtig; [smile] falsch.

insinuate [ɪn'sɪnjʊeɪt] *vt pej* [imply]: **to insinuate (that)** an|deuten (dass).

insipid [ɪn'sɪpɪd] *adj pej* - **1.** [taste, colour, music] fade; [person, character] geistlos - **2.** [food, drink] fade, geschmacklos.

insist [ɪn'sɪst] ◇ *vt* - **1.** [state firmly]: **to insist that** darauf beharren, dass - **2.** [demand]: **to insist that** darauf bestehen, dass. ◇ *vi*: **to insist on sthg** auf etw *(D)* bestehen; **to insist on doing sthg** darauf bestehen, etw zu tun.

insistent [ɪn'sɪstənt] *adj* - **1.** [determined] beharrlich; **to be insistent on sthg** auf etw *(D)* beharren OR bestehen - **2.** [continual] anhaltend.

insofar [,ɪnsəʊ'fɑːʳ] ◆ **insofar as** *conj* insofern als.

insole ['ɪnsəʊl] *n* Einlegesohle *die*.

insolent ['ɪnsələnt] *adj* frech.

insolvent [ɪn'sɒlvənt] *adj* zahlungsunfähig, insolvent.

insomnia [ɪn'sɒmnɪə] *n* Schlaflosigkeit *die*.

inspect [ɪn'spekt] *vt* - **1.** [letter, person] genau betrachten - **2.** [factory, troops, premises] inspizieren; [machine] prüfen.

inspection [ɪn'spekʃn] *n* - **1.** [examination] Prüfung *die* - **2.** [of factory, troops, premises] Inspektion *die*; [of machine] Prüfung *die*.

inspector [ɪn'spektəʳ] *n* - **1.** [official] Inspektor *der*, -in *die*; [on bus, train] Kontrolleur *der*, -in *die* - **2.** [of police] ≃ Kommissar *der*.

inspiration [,ɪnspə'reɪʃn] *n* - **1.** *(U)* [source of ideas] Inspiration *die* - **2.** [brilliant idea] Eingebung *die*.

inspire [ɪn'spaɪəʳ] *vt* inspirieren; **to inspire sb with sthg, to inspire sthg in sb** [confidence, passion, enthusiasm] in jm etw wecken; [respect] jm etw ein|flößen.

install *UK*, **instal** *US* [ɪn'stɔːl] *vt* [machinery, equipment] installieren.

installation [,ɪnstə'leɪʃn] *n* - **1.** [base, site] Anlage *die* - **2.** *(U)* [act of fitting] Installation *die*.

instalment *UK*, **installment** *US* [ɪn'stɔːlmənt] *n* - **1.** [payment] Rate *die*; **to pay**

in instalments in Raten zahlen - 2. [episode - of story] Fortsetzung *die*; [- of TV, radio programme] Folge *die*.

instance ['ɪnstəns] *n* Fall *der*; **for instance** zum Beispiel.

instant ['ɪnstənt] <> *adj* - 1. [immediate] sofort, unmittelbar - 2. [food]: **instant coffee** Instant- *OR* Pulverkaffee *der*; **instant mashed potato** fertiges Kartoffelpüree. <> *n* [moment] Augenblick *der*, Moment *der*; **the instant (that)...** in dem Augenblick, in dem...; **this instant** sofort.

instantly ['ɪnstəntlɪ] *adv* sofort.

instead [ɪn'sted] *adv* stattdessen; **instead of** statt *(+ G)*; **instead of him** an seiner Stelle.

instep ['ɪnstep] *n* Spann *der*, Fußrücken *der*.

instigate ['ɪnstɪgeɪt] *vt* [discussions] den Anstoß geben zu; [meeting] in die Wege leiten; [investigation] ein|leiten; [strike, revolt] an|stiften zu.

instil *UK*, **instill** *US* [ɪn'stɪl] *vt*: **to instil sthg in(to) sb** jm etw bei|bringen.

instinct ['ɪnstɪŋkt] *n* - 1. *(U)* [natural ability] Instinkt *der*; **by instinct** instinktiv - 2. [impulse] Impuls *der*.

instinctive [ɪn'stɪŋktɪv] *adj* instinktiv.

institute ['ɪnstɪtju:t] <> *n* Institut *das*. <> *vt* - 1. [establish] ein|führen - 2. [proceedings] an|strengen.

institution [,ɪnstɪ'tju:ʃn] *n* - 1. [tradition, system, organization] Institution *die* - 2. [home] Heim *das*, Anstalt *die*.

instruct [ɪn'strʌkt] *vt* - 1. [tell, order]: **to instruct sb to do sthg** jn an|weisen, etw zu tun - 2. [teach] unterrichten; **to instruct sb in sthg** jn in etw *(D)* unterrichten.

instruction [ɪn'strʌkʃn] *n* - 1. [order] Anweisung *die* - 2. *(U)* [teaching] Unterricht *der*. ◆ **instructions** *npl* [for use] Gebrauchsanleitung *die*.

instructor [ɪn'strʌktəʳ] *n* Lehrer *der*, -in *die*.

instrument ['ɪnstrumənt] *n* - 1. [gen] Instrument *das* - 2. *liter* [means] Mittel *das*.

instrumental [,ɪnstru'mentl] *adj* [important, helpful]: **to be instrumental in sthg** eine entscheidende Rolle bei etw spielen.

instrument panel *n* Armaturenbrett *das*.

insubordinate [,ɪnsə'bɔ:dɪnət] *adj fml* aufsässig; MIL ungehorsam.

insubstantial [,ɪnsəb'stænʃl] *adj* - 1. [fragile] zerbrechlich - 2. [unsatisfying - meal] dürftig; [- book] ohne Substanz.

insufficient [,ɪnsə'fɪʃnt] *adj fml*: **insufficient (for sthg)** unzureichend (für etw); **to be insufficient to do sthg** nicht dafür aus|reichen, um etw zu tun.

insular ['ɪnsjuləʳ] *adj* [narrow-minded] engstirnig.

insulate ['ɪnsjuleɪt] *vt* - 1. [house, tank & ELEC] isolieren - 2. [protect] schützen; **to insulate sb against** *OR* **from sthg** jn gegen etw abschirmen.

insulating tape ['ɪnsjuleɪtɪŋ-] *n (U) UK* Isolierband *das*.

insulation [,ɪnsju'leɪʃn] *n (U)* [material] Isolierung *die*.

insulin ['ɪnsjulɪn] *n* Insulin *das*.

insult <> *vt* [ɪn'sʌlt] beleidigen. <> *n* ['ɪnsʌlt] Beleidigung *die*.

insuperable [ɪn'su:prəbl] *adj fml* unüberwindlich.

insurance [ɪn'ʃuərəns] *n liter* & *fig*: **insurance (against sthg)** Versicherung (gegen etw).

insurance policy *n* Versicherungspolice *die*.

insure [ɪn'ʃuəʳ] <> *vt* - 1. [against fire, accident, theft]: **to insure sb/sthg against sthg** jn/etw gegen etw versichern - 2. *US* [make certain] sicher stellen. <> *vi* [protect]: **to insure against sthg** sich gegen etw ab|sichern.

insurer [ɪn'ʃuərəʳ] *n* Versicherungsgeber *der*, -in *die*.

insurmountable [,ɪnsə'mauntəbl] *adj* unüberwindlich.

intact [ɪn'tækt] *adj* unversehrt, intakt.

intake ['ɪnteɪk] *n* - 1. [amount consumed] Aufnahme *die* - 2. [people recruited]: **this year's intake includes several overseas students** dieses Jahr wurden einige ausländische Studenten aufgenommen - 3. [inlet] Einlass *der*.

integral ['ɪntɪgrəl] *adj* [part, feature] wesentlich; **to be integral to sthg** für etw wesentlich sein.

integrate ['ɪntɪgreɪt] *vt* - 1. [include in a larger unit, combine] integrieren - 2. [minorities, marginalized people] integrieren, eingliedern.

integrity [ɪn'tegrətɪ] *n* - 1. [honour] Integrität *die* - 2. *fml* [wholeness] Einheit *die*.

intellect ['ɪntəlekt] *n* - 1. [ability to reason] Verstand *der* - 2. [mind, intelligence] Intellekt *der*.

intellectual [,ɪntə'lektjuəl] <> *adj* intellektuell. <> *n* Intellektuelle *der, die*.

intelligence [ɪn'telɪdʒəns] *n (U)* - 1. [ability to reason] Intelligenz *die* - 2. [information service] Nachrichtendienst *der* - 3. [information] Information *die*.

intelligent [ɪn'telɪdʒənt] *adj* intelligent.

intend [ɪn'tend] *vt* beabsichtigen; **to be intended as sthg** als etw gemeint sein; **it was intended to be a surprise** es sollte eine Überraschung sein; **to intend doing** *OR* **to do sthg** beabsichtigen, etw zu tun.

intended [ɪn'tendɪd] *adj* [result] beabsichtigt.

intense [ɪn'tens] *adj* - **1.** [competition, pain, emotion] heftig; [concentration] äußerst; [colour, light] intensiv; [heat] stark - **2.** [person - serious] ernsthaft; [- emotional] heftig.

intensely [ɪn'tenslɪ] *adv* äußerst.

intensify [ɪn'tensɪfaɪ] <> *vt* intensivieren. <> *vi* [cold, heat] zu|nehmen; [pressure, problem] sich verschärfen.

intensity [ɪn'tensətɪ] *n* - **1.** [of competition, pain, emotion] Heftigkeit *die*; [of colour, light, concentration] Intensität *die*; [of heat] Stärke *die* - **2.** [of person - seriousness] Ernsthaftigkeit *die*; [- of emotional nature] Heftigkeit *die*.

intensive [ɪn'tensɪv] *adj* intensiv.

intensive care *n*: **to be in intensive care** auf der Intensivstation sein.

intent [ɪn'tent] <> *adj* - **1.** [expression] gespannt - **2.** [determined]: **to be intent (up)on doing sthg** fest entschlossen sein, etw zu tun. <> *n fml* Absicht *die*; **to all intents and purposes** im Grunde, so gut wie.

intention [ɪn'tenʃn] *n* Absicht *die*.

intentional [ɪn'tenʃənl] *adj* absichtlich.

intently [ɪn'tentlɪ] *adv* konzentriert.

interact [,ɪntər'ækt] *vi* - **1.** [people]: **to interact (with sb)** (mit jm) Kontakt haben - **2.** [forces, ideas]: **to interact (with sthg)** (mit etw) in Wechselwirkung stehen.

intercede [,ɪntə'si:d] *vi fml*: **to intercede (with sb)** sich ein|setzen (bei jm).

intercept [,ɪntə'sept] *vt* ab|fangen.

interchange *n* ['ɪntətʃeɪndʒ] [road junction] Kreuzung *die*.

interchangeable [,ɪntə'tʃeɪndʒəbl] *adj*: **interchangeable (with sb/sthg)** austauschbar (mit jm/etw).

intercom ['ɪntəkɒm] *n* Gegensprechanlage *die*.

intercourse ['ɪntəkɔ:s] *n*: **(sexual) intercourse** (Geschlechts)verkehr *der*.

interest ['ɪntrəst] <> *n* - **1.** [enthusiasm, appeal, advantage] Interesse *das*; **interest in sb/sthg** Interesse an jm/etw - **2.** [hobby] Hobby *das* - **3.** *(U)* [financial charge] Zinsen *Pl* - **4.** [share in company] Anteil *der*. <> *vt* interessieren; **can I interest you in buying my car?** wären Sie interessiert, mein Auto zu kaufen?

interested ['ɪntrəstɪd] *adj* - **1.** [enthusiastic, curious] interessiert; *(phrase)*: **to be interested in sthg** [in job] Interesse haben an etw *(+ D)*; [in butterflies, films] sich für etw *(A)* interessieren; **to be interested in doing sthg** interessiert sein, etw zu tun - **2.** [concerned] beteiligt.

interesting ['ɪntrəstɪŋ] *adj* interessant.

interest rate *n* Zinssatz *der*.

interface *n* ['ɪntəfeɪs] COMPUT Schnittstelle *die*.

interfere [,ɪntə'fɪə^r] *vi* - **1.** [meddle]: **to interfere (in sthg)** sich (in etw *(A)*) ein|mischen - **2.** [cause disruption]: **to interfere with sthg** etw stören.

interference [,ɪntə'fɪərəns] *n (U)* - **1.** [meddling]: **interference (with** OR **in sthg)** Einmischung *die* (in etw *(A)*) - **2.** RADIO & TV Störung *die*.

interim ['ɪntərɪm] <> *adj* [measure] Übergangs-; [report] Zwischen-. <> *n*: **in the interim** in der Zwischenzeit.

interior [ɪn'tɪərɪə^r] <> *adj* Innen-. <> *n* [inside] Innere *das*.

interlock [,ɪntə'lɒk] *vi* TECH ineinander greifen; **to interlock with sthg** in etw *(A)* greifen.

interlude ['ɪntəlu:d] *n* [period of time] Zwischenzeit *die*.

intermediary [,ɪntə'mi:djərɪ] *n* Mittelsmann *der*, -person *die*.

intermediate [,ɪntə'mi:djət] *adj* - **1.** [transitional] Zwischen- - **2.** [post-beginner — course] für fortgeschrittene Anfänger.

interminable [ɪn'tɜ:mɪnəbl] *adj* endlos.

intermission [,ɪntə'mɪʃn] *n* Pause *die*.

intermittent [,ɪntə'mɪtənt] *adj* in Abständen auftretend.

intern <> *vt* [ɪn'tɜ:n] internieren. <> *n* ['ɪntɜ:n] *esp US* [trainee - teacher] Assistent *der*, -in *die*; [- doctor] Assistenzarzt *der*, -ärztin *die*.

internal [ɪn'tɜ:nl] *adj* - **1.** [within the body] innere(r) (s) - **2.** [within a country - flight] Inlands-; [- trade] Binnen- - **3.** [within an organization] intern.

internally [ɪn'tɜ:nəlɪ] *adv* - **1.** [within the body] innerlich - **2.** [within a country] landesintern - **3.** [within an organization] intern.

Internal Revenue *n US*: **the Internal Revenue** das Finanzamt.

international [,ɪntə'næʃənl] <> *adj* international. <> *n UK* - **1.** SPORT [match] Länderspiel *das* - **2.** SPORT [player] Nationalspieler *der*, -in *die*.

Internet ['ɪntənet] *n*: **the Internet** das Internet.

Internet service provider *n* COMPUT Internetprovider *der*.

interpret [ɪn'tɜ:prɪt] <> *vt* [understand] aus|legen, interpretieren; **to interpret sthg as** etw interpretieren als. <> *vi* dolmetschen.

interpreter [ɪn'tɜ:prɪtə^r] *n* [person] Dolmetscher *der*, -in *die*.

interpreting [ɪn'tɜ:prɪtɪŋ] *n* [occupation] Dolmetschen *das*.

interrelate [,ɪntərɪ'leɪt] *vi*: **to interrelate (with sthg)** (mit etw) in Beziehung stehen.

interrogate [ɪn'terəgeɪt] *vt* [question] verhören.

interrogation [ɪn,terə'geɪʃn] *n* Verhör *das*.

interrogation mark *n US* Fragezeichen *das*.

interrogative [ˌɪntəˈrɒgətɪv] <> *adj* GRAM Frage-. <> *n* - **1.** GRAM [form]: **the interrogative** die Frageform - **2.** GRAM [word] Fragefürwort *das*.

interrupt [ˌɪntəˈrʌpt] *vt* & *vi* unterbrechen.

interruption [ˌɪntəˈrʌpʃn] *n* Unterbrechung *die*.

intersect [ˌɪntəˈsekt] <> *vi* sich kreuzen. <> *vt* kreuzen.

intersection [ˌɪntəˈsekʃn] *n* [junction] Kreuzung *die*.

intersperse [ˌɪntəˈspɜːs] *vt*: **to be interspersed with sthg** von etw unterbrochen OR durchsetzt sein.

interstate (highway) [ˈɪntərsteɪt-] *n US* Interstate-Highway *der*, *Autobahn zwischen den US-Bundesstaaten*.

interval [ˈɪntəvl] *n* - **1.** [period of time]: **interval (between)** Abstand *der* (zwischen *(+ D)*); **at intervals of** in Abständen von - **2.** *UK* [at play, concert] Pause *die*.

intervene [ˌɪntəˈviːn] *vi* - **1.** [person, government] ein|greifen; **to intervene in sthg** in etw *(A)* ein|greifen - **2.** [event] dazwischen|kommen.

intervention [ˌɪntəˈvenʃn] *n* Eingreifen *das*.

interview [ˈɪntəvjuː] <> *n* - **1.** [for job] Vorstellungsgespräch *das* - **2.** PRESS Interview *das*. <> *vt* - **1.** [for job] ein Vorstellungsgespräch führen mit - **2.** PRESS interviewen.

interviewer [ˈɪntəvjuːəʳ] *n* - **1.** [for job] Leiter *der*, -in *die* des Vorstellungsgesprächs - **2.** PRESS Interviewer *der*, -in *die*.

intestine [ɪnˈtestɪn] *n* Darm *der*.

intimacy [ˈɪntɪməsɪ] *n* [closeness]: **intimacy (between/with)** Vertrautheit *die* (zwischen *(+D)*/mit). ◆ **intimacies** *npl* Vertraulichkeiten *Pl*.

intimate *adj* [ˈɪntɪmət] - **1.** [friend, relationship] vertraut; **to be on intimate terms with sb** mit jm auf vertrautem Fuße stehen - **2.** [place, atmosphere, dinner] intim - **3.** [thoughts, details] persönlich - **4.** [thorough - knowledge] gründlich.

intimately [ˈɪntɪmətlɪ] *adv* - **1.** [directly] direkt - **2.** [as close friends] vertraulich; **to know sb intimately** jn gut kennen - **3.** [thoroughly] gründlich.

intimidate [ɪnˈtɪmɪdeɪt] *vt* ein|schüchtern.

into [ˈɪntʊ] *prep* - **1.** [inside] in *(+ A)*; **to put sthg into sthg** [lying down] etw in etw *(A)* legen; [upright] etw in etw *(A)* stellen; **to put sthg into one's pocket** etw in die Tasche stecken; **to go into the house** ins Haus hinein|gehen - **2.** [against]: **to bump/crash into sthg** gegen etw stoßen/knallen - **3.** [indicating transformation, change] in *(+ A)*; **to change into sthg** [become] zu etw werden; [clothes] sich *(D)* etw an|ziehen; **to translate into German** ins Deutsche übersetzen - **4.** [concerning, about] über *(+ A)* - **5.** MATHS: **4 into 20 goes 5 (times)** 20 (geteilt) durch 4 ist 5 - **6.** [indicating elapsed time]: **I was a week into my holiday when...** in meiner zweiten Urlaubswoche...; **late into the night** bis tief in die Nacht hinein - **7.** *inf* [interested in]: **to be into sthg** etw mögen; **she's into jazz** sie ist ein Jazzfan.

intolerable [ɪnˈtɒlrəbl] *adj* unerträglich.

intolerance [ɪnˈtɒlərəns] *n* Intoleranz *die*.

intolerant [ɪnˈtɒlərənt] *adj* intolerant.

intoxicated [ɪnˈtɒksɪkeɪtɪd] *adj* - **1.** [drunk]: **to be intoxicated** berauscht sein - **2.** *fig* [excited]: **to be intoxicated by** OR **with sthg** von etw berauscht sein.

intractable [ɪnˈtræktəbl] *adj fml* [insoluble] hartnäckig.

intramural [ˌɪntrəˈmjʊərəl] *adj* innerhalb der Universität.

intransitive [ɪnˈtrænzətɪv] *adj* intransitiv.

intravenous [ˌɪntrəˈviːnəs] *adj* intravenös.

in-tray *n* Eingangsablage *die*.

intricate [ˈɪntrɪkət] *adj* knifflig.

intrigue <> *n* [ˈɪntriːg] Intrige *die*. <> *vt* [ɪnˈtriːg] faszinieren.

intriguing [ɪnˈtriːgɪŋ] *adj* faszinierend.

intrinsic [ɪnˈtrɪnsɪk] *adj* immanent.

introduce [ˌɪntrəˈdjuːs] *vt* - **1.** [one person to another] vor|stellen; **to introduce sb to sb** jm jn vor|stellen - **2.** RADIO & TV [programme] vor|stellen - **3.** [animal, plant, method]: **to introduce sthg (to OR into)** etw ein|führen (in *(+ D)*) - **4.** [to new experience]: **to introduce sb to sthg** jn in etw *(A)* ein|führen - **5.** [signal start of] ein|leiten.

introduction [ˌɪntrəˈdʌkʃn] *n* - **1.** [of method, technology] Einführung *die* - **2.** [preface]: **introduction to sthg** Einleitung zu etw.

introductory [ˌɪntrəˈdʌktrɪ] *adj* einleitend; **an introductory offer** ein Eröffnungsangebot.

introvert [ˈɪntrəvɜːt] *n* introvertierter Mensch.

introverted [ˈɪntrəvɜːtɪd] *adj* introvertiert.

intrude [ɪnˈtruːd] *vi* stören; **to intrude (up)on sb/sthg** jn/etw stören.

intruder [ɪnˈtruːdəʳ] *n* Eindringling *der*.

intrusive [ɪnˈtruːsɪv] *adj* aufdringlich.

intuition [ˌɪntjuːˈɪʃn] *n* - **1.** *(U)* [sense] Intuition *die* - **2.** [hunch] Vorahnung *die*.

inundate [ˈɪnʌndeɪt] *vt* - **1.** *fml* [flood] überschwemmen - **2.** [overwhelm]: **to be inundated with sthg** von etw überschwemmt werden.

invade [ɪnˈveɪd] *vt* - **1.** MIL ein|marschieren in *(+ A)* - **2.** [subj: shoppers, fans] ein|fallen - **3.** [privacy, calm] stören.

invalid <> *adj* [ɪnˈvælɪd] - **1.** [ticket, contract, vote] ungültig - **2.** [argument, theory] nicht schlüssig. <> *n* [ˈɪnvəlɪd] Invalide *der*, -din *die*.

invaluable [ɪn'væljʊəbl] *adj*: **invaluable (to sb/sthg)** unschätzbar (für jn/etw).

invariably [ɪn'veərɪəblɪ] *adv* stets.

invasion [ɪn'veɪʒn] *n* - **1.** MIL Invasion *die* - **2.** *fig* [intrusion] Eingriff *der*.

invent [ɪn'vent] *vt* erfinden.

invention [ɪn'venʃn] *n* - **1.** [creation, untruth] Erfindung *die* - **2.** *(U)* [inventiveness] Vorstellungsgabe *die*.

inventive [ɪn'ventɪv] *adj* einfallsreich.

inventor [ɪn'ventəʳ] *n* Erfinder *der*, -in *die*.

inventory ['ɪnvəntrɪ] *n* - **1.** [list] Inventar *das* - **2.** *US* [goods] Bestand *der*.

invert [ɪn'vɜːt] *vt fml* umldrehen.

inverted commas [ɪn,vɜːtɪd-] *npl UK* Anführungszeichen *die*.

invest [ɪn'vest] ◇ *vt* - **1.** [money]: **to invest sthg (in sthg)** etw (in etw *(A)*) investieren - **2.** [time, energy]: **to invest sthg in sthg** etw in etw *(A)* investieren. ◇ *vi* - **1.** [financially]: **to invest (in sthg)** (in etw *(A)*) investieren - **2.** *fig* [in sthg useful]: **to invest in sthg** in etw *(A)* investieren.

investigate [ɪn'vestɪgeɪt] *vt* untersuchen.

investigation [ɪn,vestɪ'geɪʃn] *n* Untersuchung *die*; **an investigation into sthg** eine Untersuchung von etw.

investment [ɪn'vestmənt] *n* - **1.** [gen] Investition *die* - **2.** [financial product, purchase] Anlage *die*.

investor [ɪn'vestəʳ] *n* Anleger *der*, -in *die*.

inveterate [ɪn'vetərət] *adj* [liar, gambler] unverbesserlich.

invidious [ɪn'vɪdɪəs] *adj* - **1.** [unfair] ungerecht - **2.** [unpleasant] unangenehm.

invigilate [ɪn'vɪdʒɪleɪt] *UK* ◇ *vt* Aufsicht führen bei. ◇ *vi* Aufsicht führen.

invigorating [ɪn'vɪgəreɪtɪŋ] *adj* erfrischend, belebend.

invincible [ɪn'vɪnsɪbl] *adj* unschlagbar.

invisible [ɪn'vɪzɪbl] *adj* unsichtbar.

invitation [,ɪnvɪ'teɪʃn] *n* [request to attend] Einladung *die*.

invite [ɪn'vaɪt] *vt* - **1.** [request to attend] einlladen; **to invite sb to sthg** jn zu etw einlladen - **2.** [ask politely]: **to invite sb to do sthg** jn ersuchen, etw zu tun - **3.** [trouble, criticism] herauslfordern.

inviting [ɪn'vaɪtɪŋ] *adj* einladend.

invoice ['ɪnvɔɪs] ◇ *n* Rechnung *die*. ◇ *vt* - **1.** [customer] eine Rechnung schicken an (+ *A*) - **2.** [goods] in Rechnung stellen.

invoke [ɪn'vəʊk] *vt* [feeling] hervorlrufen.

involuntary [ɪn'vɒləntrɪ] *adj* [movement] unwillkürlich.

involve [ɪn'vɒlv] *vt* - **1.** [entail, require - work, travelling] mit sich bringen; [- special equipment, knowledge] erfordern - **2.** [concern, affect] betreffen - **3.** [make part of sthg]: **to involve sb in sthg** jn in etw *(A)* hineinlziehen.

involved [ɪn'vɒlvd] *adj* - **1.** [complex] kompliziert - **2.** [participating]: **to be involved in sthg** an etw *(D)* beteiligt sein - **3.** [in a relationship]: **to be/get involved with sb** mit jm eine enge Beziehung haben/einlgehen - **4.** [entailed]: **what is involved (in it)?** worum geht es (dabei)?

involvement [ɪn'vɒlvmənt] *n* - **1.** [participation]: **involvement (in sthg)** Beteiligung (an etw *(D)*) - **2.** [commitment]: **involvement (in sthg)** Engagement (für etw).

inward ['ɪnwəd] ◇ *adj* - **1.** [feelings, satisfaction] innerlich - **2.** [flow, movement] nach innen gehend. ◇ *adv US* = **inwards**.

inwards ['ɪnwədz], **inward** *US adv* nach innen.

iodine [*UK* 'aɪədiːn, *US* 'aɪədaɪn] *n (U)* Jod *das*.

iota [aɪ'əʊtə] *n* Jota *das*.

IOU (*abbr of* **I owe you**) *n* Schuldschein *der*.

IQ (*abbr of* **intelligence quotient**) *n* IQ *der*.

IRA *n* (*abbr of* **Irish Republican Army**) IRA *die*.

Iran [ɪ'rɑːn] *n* Iran *der*.

Iranian [ɪ'reɪnɪən] ◇ *adj* iranisch. ◇ *n* [person] Iraner *der*, -in *die*.

Iraq [ɪ'rɑːk] *n* Irak *der*.

Iraqi [ɪ'rɑːkɪ] ◇ *adj* irakisch. ◇ *n* [person] Iraker *der*, -in *die*.

irate [aɪ'reɪt] *adj* zornig.

Ireland ['aɪələnd] *n* Irland *nt*.

iris ['aɪərɪs] (*pl* **-es**) *n* - **1.** [flower] Schwertlilie *die*, Iris *die* - **2.** [of eye] Iris *die*.

Irish ['aɪrɪʃ] ◇ *adj* irisch. ◇ *n* [language] Irisch(e) *das*. ◇ *npl*: **the Irish** die Iren.

Irishman ['aɪrɪʃmən] (*pl* **-men** [-mən]) *n* Ire *der*.

Irish Sea *n*: **the Irish Sea** die Irische See.

Irishwoman ['aɪrɪʃ,wʊmən] (*pl* **-women** [-,wɪmɪn]) *n* Irin *die*.

iron ['aɪən] ◇ *adj* - **1.** [made of iron] eisern; **iron bar** Eisenstange *die* - **2.** *fig* [very strict] eisern. ◇ *n* - **1.** [metal, golf club] Eisen *das* - **2.** [for clothes] Bügeleisen *das*. ◇ *vt* bügeln.

◆ **iron out** *vt sep* [problems] auslbügeln.

ironic(al) [aɪ'rɒnɪk(l)] *adj* - **1.** [using irony] ironisch - **2.** [paradoxical] paradox.

ironing ['aɪənɪŋ] *n* - **1.** [work] Bügeln *das* - **2.** [clothes] Bügelwäsche *die*.

ironing board *n* Bügelbrett *das*.

ironmonger ['aɪən,mʌŋgəʳ] *n UK* Eisenwarenhändler *der*, -in *die*; **ironmonger's (shop)** Eisenwarenhandlung *die*.

irony ['aɪrənɪ] *n* Ironie *die*.

irrational [ɪ'ræʃənl] *adj* irrational.

irreconcilable [ɪ,rekən'saɪləbl] *adj* [views, differences] unvereinbar.

irregular [ɪ'regjʊləʳ] *adj* [gen & GRAM] unregelmäßig; [surface] uneben.

irrelevant [ɪ'reləvənt] *adj* unwichtig.

irreparable [ɪ'repərəbl] *adj* irreparabel.

irreplaceable [ˌɪrɪ'pleɪsəbl] *adj* unersetzlich.

irrepressible [ˌɪrɪ'presəbl] *adj* unerschütterlich; **he's irrepressible** er ist nicht unterzukriegen.

irresistible [ˌɪrɪ'zɪstəbl] *adj* unwiderstehlich.

irrespective [ˌɪrɪ'spektɪv] ◆ **irrespective of** *prep* ungeachtet *(+ G)*.

irresponsible [ˌɪrɪ'spɒnsəbl] *adj* unverantwortlich.

irrigation [ˌɪrɪ'geɪʃn] ◇ *n* [of land] Bewässerung *die*. ◇ *comp* Bewässerungs-.

irritable ['ɪrɪtəbl] *adj* [person, mood] reizbar; [voice, reply] gereizt.

irritate ['ɪrɪteɪt] *vt* - **1.** [make angry] ärgern - **2.** [make sore] reizen.

irritated ['ɪrɪteɪtɪd] *adj* [angry, sore] gereizt.

irritating ['ɪrɪteɪtɪŋ] *adj* - **1.** [person, noise] ärgerlich - **2.** [substance, material] reizend.

irritation [ɪrɪ'teɪʃn] *n* - **1.** [anger] Ärger *der* - **2.** [cause of anger] Ärgernis *das* - **3.** [soreness] Reizung *die*.

IRS (*abbr of* **Internal Revenue Service**) *n US*: **the IRS** das Finanzamt.

is [ɪz] *vb* ▷ **be**.

Islam ['ɪzlɑːm] *n* [religion] Islam *der*.

island ['aɪlənd] *n liter & fig* Insel *die*.

islander ['aɪləndəʳ] *n* Inselbewohner *der*, -in *die*.

isle [aɪl] *n* Insel *die*.

Isle of Man *n*: **the Isle of Man** die Insel Man.

Isle of Wight [-waɪt] *n*: **the Isle of Wight** Wight.

isn't ['ɪznt] *abbr of* **is not**.

isobar ['aɪsəbɑːʳ] *n* METEOR Isobare *die*.

isolate ['aɪsəleɪt] *vt* isolieren.

isolated ['aɪsəleɪtɪd] *adj* - **1.** [place] abgelegen - **2.** [person] isoliert - **3.** [example, incident] einzeln.

Israel ['ɪzreɪəl] *n* Israel *nt*.

Israeli [ɪz'reɪlɪ] ◇ *adj* israelisch. ◇ *n* Israeli *der, die*.

issue ['ɪʃuː] ◇ *n* - **1.** [important subject] Frage *die*; **to make an issue of sthg** ein Problem aus etw machen - **2.** [edition] Ausgabe *die* - **3.** [of stamps, bank notes, shares] Ausgabe *die*. ◇ *vt* - **1.** [statement] ab|geben; [decree] erlassen; [warning] aus|sprechen - **2.** [stamps, bank notes, shares] aus|geben - **3.** [passport, documents] aus|stellen; [uniforms] aus|geben.

it [ɪt] *pron* - **1.** *(subj)* [referring to specific person or thing] er/sie/es; *(direct object)* ihn/sie/es; *(indirect object)* ihm/ihr; **it's big** er/sie/es ist groß; **she hit it** sie hat ihn/sie/es getroffen; **get the cat/dog and give it a drink** hole die Katze/den Hund und gib ihr/ihm etwas zu trinken - **2.** *(with prepositions)*: **tell me about it** erzähl mir davon; **you're good at it** du kannst das gut; **a table with a chair beside it** ein Tisch mit einem Stuhl daneben; **what did you learn from it?** was hast du daraus gelernt?; **put your hand in it** steck deine Hand hinein; **stand on top of it** stell dich darauf; **put the books on it** leg die Bücher darauf; **it had a sheet over it** darüber lag ein Tuch; **shall we go to it?** sollen wir hin|gehen?; **put the box under it** stell die Schachtel darunter; **a free book came with it** es war ein kostenloses Buch dabei - **3.** *(impersonal use)* es; **it's hot** es ist heiß; **it's raining** es regnet; **it's Sunday** es ist Sonntag; **it's six o'clock** es ist sechs Uhr; **it's the children that worry me most** am meisten mache ich mir um die Kinder sorgen; **it's said that...** man sagt, dass... - **4.** *(nonspecific)* es; **it's easy** es ist einfach; **it's a difficult question** das ist eine schwierige Frage; **who is it? – it's Mary/me** wer ist da? – Mary/ich bins.

IT *n abbr of* **information technology**.

Italian [ɪ'tæljən] ◇ *adj* italienisch. ◇ *n* - **1.** [person] Italiener *der*, -in *die* - **2.** [language] Italienisch(e) *das*.

italic [ɪ'tælɪk] *adj* kursiv. ◆ **italics** *npl* Kursivschrift *die*.

Italy ['ɪtəlɪ] *n* Italien *nt*.

itch [ɪtʃ] ◇ *n* Juckreiz *der*. ◇ *vi* [part of body] jucken; **I'm itching** es juckt mich; **I'm itching to do it** es juckt mich, das zu tun.

itchy ['ɪtʃɪ] *adj* juckend; **to be itchy** [part of body] jucken; **I feel itchy** es juckt mich.

it'd ['ɪtəd] *abbr of* **it would**, **it had**.

item ['aɪtəm] *n* - **1.** [object] Gegenstand *der*; [in shop] Artikel *der*; [on agenda] Punkt *der*; COMM Posten *der*; **item of clothing** Kleidungsstück *das* - **2.** [of news] Meldung *die*.

itemize, -ise ['aɪtəmaɪz] *vt* auf einer Liste einzeln auf|führen.

itinerary [aɪ'tɪnərərɪ] *n* Reiseroute *die*.

it'll [ɪtl] *abbr of* **it will**.

its [ɪts] *poss adj* [masculine, neuter subject] sein; [feminine subject] ihr; **the dog wagged its tail** der Hund wedelte mit dem Schwanz.

it's [ɪts] *abbr of* **it is, it has**.

itself [ɪt'self] *pron* - **1.** *(reflexive)* sich - **2.** *(after prep)* sich selbst; **by itself** allein; **in itself** an sich - **3.** *(stressed)* selbst; **the house itself is fine** das Haus selbst ist in Ordnung.

I've [aɪv] *abbr of* **I have**.

ivory ['aɪvərɪ] *n* Elfenbein *das*.

ivy ['aɪvɪ] *n* Efeu *der*.

Ivy League *n US Gruppe von alten, angesehenen Universitäten im Osten der USA*.

J

j (*pl* **j's** *OR* **js**), **J** (*pl* **J's** *OR* **Js**) [dʒeɪ] *n* [letter] j *das*, J *das*.

jab [dʒæb] ◇ *n* - **1.** [push] Stoß *der*; [with needle, knife] Stich *der* - **2.** *UK inf* [injection] Spritze *die*. ◇ *vt* [with sthg] stechen; **to jab sthg into sb/sthg** etw in jn/etw (hinein)|stoßen.

jabber ['dʒæbəʳ] *vi* plappern.

jack [dʒæk] *n* - **1.** [for car] Wagenheber *der* - **2.** [playing card] Bube *der*. ◆ **jack up** *vt sep* [car] auf|bocken.

jackal ['dʒækəl] *n* Schakal *der*.

jackdaw ['dʒækdɔ:] *n* Dohle *die*.

jacket ['dʒækɪt] *n* - **1.** [garment] Jacke *die*; [of suit] Jacket *das* - **2.** [of book] Schutzumschlag *der* - **3.** *US* [of record] Plattenhülle *die*.

jacket potato *n in der Schale gebackene Kartoffel*.

jack knife *n* Klappmesser *das*. ◆ **jackknife** *vi* [lorry] sich quer|stellen.

jack plug *n* Bananenstecker *der*.

jackpot ['dʒækpɒt] *n* Jackpot *der*.

jaded ['dʒeɪdɪd] *adj* abgestumpft.

jagged ['dʒægɪd] *adj* [metal] schartig; [edge] ausgezackt; [rocks] zerklüftet.

jail [dʒeɪl] ◇ *n* Gefängnis *das*; **in jail** im Gefängnis; **to go to jail** ins Gefängnis kommen. ◇ *vt* ein|sperren.

jailer ['dʒeɪləʳ] *n* Gefängniswärter *der*, -in *die*.

jam [dʒæm] ◇ *n* - **1.** [preserve] Marmelade *die* - **2.** [of traffic] Stau *der* - **3.** *inf* [difficult situation] Klemme *die*. ◇ *vt* - **1.** [mechanism, brakes] blockieren; **to get one's finger jammed** sich *(D)* den Finger ein|quetschen - **2.** [cram]: **to jam sthg into sthg** etw in etw *(A)* stopfen - **3.** [streets, town] verstopfen - **4.** TELEC: **thousands of callers jammed the switchboard** Tausende von Anrufern blockierten die Leitungen der (Telefon)zentrale - **5.** RADIO stören. ◇ *vi* [stick - window, door] klemmen; [- brakes, lever] sich verklemmen. ◆ **jam on** *vt sep*: **to jam the brakes on** eine Vollbremsung machen.

Jamaica [dʒə'meɪkə] *n* Jamaika *nt*; **in Jamaica** auf Jamaika.

jam-packed [-'pækt] *adj inf* proppenvoll.

jangle ['dʒæŋgl] *vt* [keys] klimpern mit.

janitor ['dʒænɪtəʳ] *n US & Scotland* [caretaker] Hausmeister *der*.

January ['dʒænjʊərɪ] *n* Januar *der*; *see also* **September**.

Japan [dʒə'pæn] *n* Japan *nt*.

Japanese [,dʒæpə'ni:z] (*pl inv*) ◇ *adj* japanisch. ◇ *n* [language] Japanisch(e) *das*. ◇ *npl* [people]: **the Japanese** die Japaner *Pl*.

jar [dʒɑ:ʳ] ◇ *n* Glas *das*. ◇ *vt* [shake] durch|schütteln. ◇ *vi* - **1.** [noise, voice]: **to jar (on sb)** unangenehm sein (für jn) - **2.** [colours] sich beißen.

jargon ['dʒɑ:gən] *n* Fachsprache *die*.

jaundice ['dʒɔ:ndɪs] *n* Gelbsucht *die*.

jaundiced ['dʒɔ:ndɪst] *adj fig* [attitude, view] verbittert.

jaunt [dʒɔ:nt] *n* Ausflug *der*.

jaunty ['dʒɔ:ntɪ] *adj* [hat, wave] flott; [person] munter.

javelin ['dʒævlɪn] *n* Speer *der*.

jaw [dʒɔ:] *n* [of person, animal] Kiefer *der*.

jawbone ['dʒɔ:bəʊn] *n* Kieferknochen *der*.

jay [dʒeɪ] *n* Eichelhäher *der*.

jaywalker ['dʒeɪwɔ:kəʳ] *n im Straßenverkehr unachtsamer Fußgänger*.

jazz [dʒæz] *n* MUS Jazz *der*. ◆ **jazz up** *vt sep inf* auf|peppen.

jazzy ['dʒæzɪ] *adj* [colour, clothes] poppig.

jealous ['dʒeləs] *adj* [envious]: **to be jealous (of)** neidisch sein (auf *(+ A)*).

jealousy ['dʒeləsɪ] *n* - **1.** [envy] Neid *der* - **2.** [possessiveness] Eifersucht *die*.

jeans [dʒi:nz] *npl* Jeans *Pl*.

Jeep® [dʒi:p] *n* Jeep® *der*.

jeer [dʒɪəʳ] ◇ *vt* verhöhnen. ◇ *vi* [crowd, fans] höhnisch johlen; **to jeer at sb** jn verhöhnen.

Jello® ['dʒeləʊ] *n US* Wackelpudding *der*.

jelly ['dʒelɪ] *n* - **1.** *UK* [dessert] Wackelpudding *der* - **2.** *US* [jam] Gelee *das*.

jellyfish ['dʒelɪfɪʃ] (*pl inv OR* **-es**) *n* Qualle *die*.

jeopardize, -ise ['dʒepədaɪz] *vt* gefährden.

jerk [dʒɜ:k] ◇ *n* - **1.** [movement] Ruck *der* - **2.** *inf pej* [fool] Trottel *der*. ◇ *vi* einen Satz machen.

jersey ['dʒɜ:zɪ] (*pl* **-s**) *n* - **1.** [sweater] Pullover *der* - **2.** *(U)* [cloth] Jersey *der*.

Jersey ['dʒɜ:zɪ] *n* Jersey *nt*; **in Jersey** auf Jersey.

jest [dʒest] *n* Scherz *der*; **in jest** im Spaß.

Jesus (Christ) ['dʒi:zəs-] ◇ *n* Jesus (Christus). ◇ *excl inf* Menschenskind!

jet [dʒet] *n* - **1.** [aircraft] Jet *der*, Düsenflugzeug *das* - **2.** [of liquid, gas, steam] Strahl *der*.

jet-black *adj* pechschwarz.

jet engine *n* Düsentriebwerk *das*.

jetfoil ['dʒetfɔɪl] *n* Tragflügelboot *das*.

jet lag *n* Jetlag *der*.

jetsam ['dʒetsəm] *n* ▷ **flotsam**.

jettison ['dʒetɪsən] *vt* - **1.** [cargo, bombs - from plane] ab|werfen; [- from ship] über Bord werfen - **2.** *fig* [discard - ideas, hope] über Bord werfen; [- unwanted possession] weg|werfen.

jetty ['dʒetɪ] *n* Landungssteg *der*.

Jew [dʒuː] *n* Jude *der*, Jüdin *die*.

jewel ['dʒuːəl] *n* Edelstein *der*; [in watch] Stein *der*; **jewels** [jewellery] Schmuck *der*.

jeweller *UK*, **jeweler** *US* ['dʒuːələʳ] *n* Juwelier *der*; **jeweller's (shop)** Juweliergeschäft *das*.

jewellery *UK*, **jewelry** *US* ['dʒuːəlrɪ] *n* Schmuck *der*; **piece of jewellery** Schmuckstück *das*.

Jewish ['dʒuːɪʃ] *adj* jüdisch.

jibe [dʒaɪb] *n* spöttische Bemerkung.

jiffy ['dʒɪfɪ] *n inf*: **in a jiffy** sofort.

Jiffy bag® *n* Versandtasche *die*.

jig [dʒɪg] *n* [dance] *lebhafter Schreittanz, vor allem auf dem Land früher beliebt*.

jigsaw (puzzle) ['dʒɪgsɔː-] *n* Puzzle(spiel) *das*.

jilt [dʒɪlt] *vt* sitzen lassen.

jingle ['dʒɪŋgl] <> *n* [in advertising] Jingle *der*. <> *vi* [bells] bimmeln; [keys] klimpern.

jinx [dʒɪŋks] *n*: **there's a jinx on it** es ist verhext.

jitters ['dʒɪtəz] *npl inf*: **the jitters** das große Zittern.

job [dʒɒb] *n* - **1.** [paid work] Stelle *die*; **to lose one's job** entlassen werden - **2.** [task] Arbeit *die*; **on the job** bei der Arbeit - **3.** [difficult time]: **to have a job doing sthg** (große) Mühe haben, etw zu tun - **4.** *phr*: **that's just the job** *UK inf* das ist genau das Richtige.

job centre *n UK* Arbeitsamt *das*.

jobless ['dʒɒblɪs] *adj* arbeitslos.

jobsharing ['dʒɒbʃeərɪŋ] *n* Jobsharing *das*.

jockey ['dʒɒkɪ] (*pl* **-s**) <> *n* Jockey *der*. <> *vi*: **to jockey for position** um eine gute Position kämpfen.

jocular ['dʒɒkjʊləʳ] *adj* witzig, lustig.

jodhpurs ['dʒɒdpəz] *npl* Reithose *die*.

jog [dʒɒg] <> *n* [run]: **to go for a jog** joggen gehen. <> *vt* [nudge - person] an|stoßen; [- table, sb's arm, elbow] stoßen gegen; **to jog sb's memory** js Gedächtnis nach|helfen. <> *vi* [run] joggen.

jogging ['dʒɒgɪŋ] *n* Joggen *das*; **to go jogging** joggen gehen.

john [dʒɒn] *n US inf* [toilet] Klo *das*.

join [dʒɔɪn] <> *n* Naht(stelle) *die*. <> *vt* - **1.** [connect] verbinden; **to join sthg to sthg** etw mit etw verbinden - **2.** [other people] sich an|schließen *(+ D)*; **I'll join you in a moment** [follow you] ich komme gleich nach - **3.** [club, organization] bei|treten *(+ D)*; [company] an|fangen bei; [army] gehen zu - **4.** [take part in] teil|nehmen an *(+ D)*; **to join the queue** *UK*, **to join the line** *US* sich in die Schlange ein|reihen. <> *vi* - **1.** [connect - rivers] ineinander fließen; [- edges, pieces] miteinander verbunden sein - **2.** [become a member] Mitglied werden. ◆ **join in** <> *vt insep* mit|machen bei. <> *vi* mit|machen. ◆ **join up** *vi* MIL zum Militär gehen.

joiner ['dʒɔɪnəʳ] *n* Tischler *der*, -in *die*.

joint [dʒɔɪnt] <> *adj* [effort] vereint; [responsibility] gemeinsam; [owner] Mit-. <> *n* - **1.** ANAT Gelenk *das* - **2.** [in structure] Verbindungsstelle *die*; [in carpentry] Fuge *die* - **3.** *UK* [of meat] Braten *der* - **4.** *inf pej* [place] Laden *der* - **5.** *drug sl* [cannabis cigarette] Joint *der*.

joint account *n* gemeinsames Konto.

jointly ['dʒɔɪntlɪ] *adv* gemeinsam.

joke [dʒəʊk] <> *n* Witz *der*; **to play a joke on sb** jm einen Streich spielen; **it's no joke** [not easy] das ist keine Kleinigkeit; **to be a joke** [person] eine Witzfigur sein. <> *vi* Witze machen; **to joke about sthg** über etw *(A)* Witze machen; **you must be joking!** das meinst du doch nicht im Ernst!

joker ['dʒəʊkəʳ] *n* - **1.** [person] Spaßvogel *der* - **2.** [playing card] Joker *der*.

jolly ['dʒɒlɪ] <> *adj* lustig, fröhlich. <> *adv UK* [very] super.

jolt [dʒəʊlt] <> *n* - **1.** [jerk] Ruck *der* - **2.** [shock]: **to give sb a jolt** jm einen Schock versetzen. <> *vt* - **1.** [jerk] durch|schütteln - **2.** [shock]: **to jolt sb into doing sthg** jn so auf|rütteln, dass er etw tut.

jostle ['dʒɒsl] <> *vt* an|rempeln. <> *vi* drängeln.

jot [dʒɒt] *n*: **there isn't a jot of truth in it** es ist kein Funken Wahrheit darin. ◆ **jot down** *vt sep* sich *(D)* notieren.

journal ['dʒɜːnl] *n* - **1.** [magazine] Zeitschrift *die* - **2.** [diary] Tagebuch *das*.

journalism ['dʒɜːnəlɪzm] *n* Journalismus *der*.

journalist ['dʒɜːnəlɪst] *n* Journalist *der*, -in *die*.

journey ['dʒɜːnɪ] (*pl* **-s**) *n* Reise *die*; **to go on a journey** verreisen; **an hour's journey** eine Stunde Fahrt.

jovial ['dʒəʊvɪəl] *adj* fröhlich.

joy [dʒɔɪ] *n* Freude *die*.

joyful ['dʒɔɪfʊl] *adj* [person] froh; [shout] freudig; [scene, news] erfreulich.

joystick ['dʒɔɪstɪk] *n* - **1.** [in aircraft] Steuerknüppel *der* - **2.** [for computers] Joystick *der*.

Jr. (*abbr of* **Junior**) jun.

jubilant ['dʒuːbɪlənt] *adj* [person, fans] überglücklich; [shout] Jubel-.

jubilee ['dʒuːbɪliː] *n* Jubiläum *das*.

judge [dʒʌdʒ] <> *n* - **1.** LAW Richter *der*, -in *die* - **2.** SPORT Schiedsrichter *der*, -in *die*; [of competition] Preisrichter *der*, -in *die*. <> *vt* - **1.** LAW [case] verhandeln - **2.** [competition] beurteilen - **3.** [estimate] (ein)lschätzen. <> *vi* [decide] (be)urteilen; **to judge from** *OR* **by sthg, judging from** *OR* **by sthg** nach etw zu urteilen.

judg(e)ment ['dʒʌdʒmənt] *n* - **1.** LAW Urteil *das* - **2.** [opinion] Urteil *das* - **3.** [ability to form opinion] Urteilsvermögen *das*.

judicial [dʒuː'dɪʃl] *adj* Gerichts-.

judiciary [dʒuː'dɪʃərɪ] *n*: **the judiciary** das Gerichtswesen.

judicious [dʒuː'dɪʃəs] *adj* klug.

judo ['dʒuːdəʊ] *n* Judo *das*.

jug [dʒʌg] *n* Krug *der*.

juggernaut ['dʒʌgənɔːt] *n* [truck] Laster *der*.

juggle ['dʒʌgl] *vt* & *vi* - **1.** [throw] jonglieren - **2.**: **to juggle (with) figures** die Zahlen so hinldrehen, wie man sie haben will.

juggler ['dʒʌglər] *n* Jongleur *der*, -in *die*.

juice [dʒuːs] *n* Saft *der*.

juicy ['dʒuːsɪ] *adj* [fruit] saftig.

jukebox ['dʒuːkbɒks] *n* Musikbox *die*.

July [dʒuː'laɪ] *n* Juli *der*; *see also* **September**.

jumble ['dʒʌmbl] <> *n* [mixture] Durcheinander *das*. <> *vt*: **to jumble (up)** [objects] durcheinander werfen; [words] durcheinander bringen.

jumble sale *n UK in Gemeinde- und Stadthallen abgehaltener Trödelmarkt, dessen Erlös wohltätigen Vereinen zugute kommt.*

jumbo jet ['dʒʌmbəʊ-] *n* Jumbojet *der*.

jumbo-sized [-saɪzd] *adj* Riesen-.

jump [dʒʌmp] <> *n* - **1.** [leap] Sprung *der* - **2.** [rapid increase] Sprung *der*. <> *vt* - **1.** [fence, stream] überlspringen; **to jump the queue** sich vorldrängen - **2.** *inf* [attack] überfallen. <> *vi* - **1.** [gen] springen; **to jump over sthg** über etw *(A)* springen - **2.** [with fright, surprise] einen Satz machen; **you made me jump!** du hast mich erschreckt! - **3.** [increase] sprunghaft anlsteigen. ◆ **jump at** *vt insep fig* [opportunity] ergreifen. ◆ **jump in** *vi* hereinlspringen; **jump in!** [get in car] spring rein! ◆ **jump out** *vi* herauslspringen; **to jump out (of) the window** aus dem Fenster springen. ◆ **jump up** *vi* [get up quickly] auflspringen.

jumper ['dʒʌmpər] *n* - **1.** *UK* [pullover] Pullover *der* - **2.** *US* [dress] Trägerkleid *das*.

jump leads *npl* Starthilfekabel *Pl*.

jump-start *vt* mit Starthilfe zünden.

jumpsuit ['dʒʌmpsuːt] *n* Overall *der*.

jumpy ['dʒʌmpɪ] *adj* nervös.

junction ['dʒʌŋkʃn] *n* [of roads] Kreuzung *die*; [of railway lines, pipes] Knotenpunkt *der*; [on motorway] Anschlussstelle *die*.

June [dʒuːn] *n* Juni *der*; *see also* **September**.

jungle ['dʒʌŋgl] *n liter* & *fig* Dschungel *der*.

junior ['dʒuːnɪər] <> *adj* - **1.** [younger] jünger - **2.** [lower in rank] untergeordnet; **junior partner** Juniorpartner *der* - **3.** *US* [after name] junior. <> *n* - **1.** [person of lower rank] *Person niedrigeren Ranges* - **2.** [younger person] Jüngere *der, die*; **he is two years my junior** er ist zwei Jahre jünger als ich - **3.** *US* SCH & UNIV *Schüler/Student im vorletzten Jahr*.

junior high school *n US Schule zwischen Grund- und Oberschule*.

junior school *n UK* Grundschule *die (für 7- bis 11-Jährige)*.

junk [dʒʌŋk] *n* - **1.** *inf* [unwanted things] Ramsch *der* - **2.** [boat] Dschunke *die*.

junk food *n pej ungesundes Essen wie Fast Food, Chips, Süßigkeiten*.

junkie ['dʒʌŋkɪ] *n drug sl* Junkie *der*, Fixer *der*, -in *die*.

junk mail *n (U) pej* Reklamemüll *der (der mit der Post kommt)*.

junk shop *n* Trödelladen *der*.

Jupiter ['dʒuːpɪtər] *n* [planet] Jupiter *der*.

jurisdiction [ˌdʒʊərɪs'dɪkʃn] *n* [of court] Zuständigkeitsbereich *der*.

juror ['dʒʊərər] *n* Geschworene *der, die*.

jury ['dʒʊərɪ] *n* - **1.** [in court of law]: **the jury** die Geschworenen *Pl* - **2.** [in contest] Jury *die*.

just [dʒʌst] <> *adv* - **1.** [recently] gerade; **to have just done sthg** gerade etw getan haben - **2.** [at this or that moment] gerade; **I was just about to pick up the phone, when...** ich wollte gerade den Hörer abnehmen, als...; **we were just leaving, when...** wir wollten gerade gehen, als...; **I'm just coming** ich komme schon - **3.** [exactly] genau; **just what I need** genau das, was ich brauche; **it's just as good** es ist genauso gut - **4.** [only] nur; **just a bit** nur ein bisschen; **just over an hour** etwas über eine Stunde; **just a minute!** einen Moment! - **5.** [simply] einfach; **'just add water'** 'nur Wasser zugeben' - **6.** [almost not]: **(only) just** gerade (noch) - **7.** [for emphasis]: **just look what you've done!** sieh nur, was du gemacht hast! - **8.** [in requests]: **could you just open your mouth?** können Sie mal den Mund auflmachen? <> *adj* [fair] gerecht; **it's only just** es ist nur recht und billig. ◆ **just about** *adv* [almost] fast. ◆ **just now** *adv* - **1.** [a short time ago] gerade; **I was speaking to her just now** ich habe gerade mit ihr gesprochen - **2.** [at this moment] im Moment.

justice ['dʒʌstɪs] *n (U)* - **1.** [fairness] Gerechtigkeit *die* - **2.** LAW [power of law] Justiz *die* - **3.** [of cause, claim] Rechtmäßigkeit *die*.

justify ['dʒʌstɪfaɪ] *vt* - **1.** [gen] rechtfertigen - **2.** TYPO justieren; COMPUT auslrichten.

justly ['dʒʌstlɪ] *adv* zu Recht, mit Recht.

jut [dʒʌt] *vi*: **to jut (out)** (her)vorlragen.

juvenile ['dʒu:vənaɪl] ◇ *adj* - **1.** LAW jugendlich; **juvenile crime** die Jugendkriminalität - **2.** *pej* [childish] infantil. ◇ *n* LAW Jugendliche *der, die*.

juxtapose [,dʒʌkstə'pəʊz] *vt*: **to juxtapose sthg with sthg** etw neben etw *(A)* stellen.

K

k (*pl* **k's** OR **ks**), **K** (*pl* **K's** OR **Ks**) [keɪ] *n* [letter] k *das*, K *das*. ◆ **K** *n* - **1.** (*abbr of* **kilobyte**) Kb *das* - **2.** (*abbr of* **thousand**) Tsd.

kaleidoscope [kə'laɪdəskəʊp] *n* Kaleidoskop *das*.

kangaroo [,kæŋgə'ru:] *n* Känguru *das*.

kaput [kə'pʊt] *adj inf* kaputt.

karaoke [kærɪ'əʊki:] *n* Karaoke *das*.

karat ['kærət] *n US* Karat *das*.

karate [kə'rɑ:tɪ] *n* Karate *das*.

kayak ['kaɪæk] *n* Kajak *der ODER das*.

KB (*abbr of* **kilobyte(s)**) *n* COMPUT Kb *das*.

kcal (*abbr of* **kilocalorie**) kcal.

kebab [kɪ'bæb] *n*: **(shish) kebab** Kebab *der*; **(doner) kebab** Gyros *der*.

keel [ki:l] *n* Kiel *der*; **to get sthg back on an even keel** etw wieder auf die Beine bringen. ◆ **keel over** *vi* [ship] kentern; [person] umlkippen.

keen [ki:n] *adj* - **1.** [enthusiastic] begeistert; **to be keen on sthg** etw sehr mögen; **to be keen to do** OR **on doing sthg** etw unbedingt tun wollen; **she wasn't keen on the idea** sie war von der Sache nicht angetan - **2.** [interest, desire, competition] stark - **3.** [edge] scharf; [eyesight, hearing] gut - **4.** [wind] scharf.

keep [ki:p] (*pt & pp* **kept**) ◇ *vt* - **1.** [retain] behalten; **please keep the change** bitte behalten Sie das Wechselgeld; **to keep a seat for sb** einen Platz für jn frei halten - **2.** [store] auflbewahren - **3.** [maintain] halten; **to keep sb waiting** jn warten lassen; **to keep sb awake** jn wach halten - **4.** [promise, appointment] einlhalten - **5.** [secret] für sich behalten; **to keep sthg from sb** etw vor jm geheim halten - **6.** [delay]: **what kept you?** wo bist du denn so lang gewesen? - **7.** [record, diary] führen; **to keep a note of sthg** etw auflschreiben - **8.** [prevent]: **to keep sb from doing sthg** jn davon ablhalten, etw zu tun; **the noise kept me from sleeping** der Lärm ließ mich nicht schlafen - **9.** [own - farm animals] halten - **10.** *phr*: **they keep themselves to themselves** sie bleiben für sich. ◇ *vi* - **1.** [remain] bleiben; **to keep fit** fit bleiben; **to keep silent** schweigen; **to keep warm** sich warm halten; **to keep clear of sthg** sich von etw fern halten - **2.** [continue]: **to keep doing sthg** [continuously] etw weiter tun; [repeatedly] etw dauernd tun; **to keep going** [walking] weiterlgehen; [driving] weiterlfahren; [working] weiterlmachen; **'keep left'** 'links fahren'; **keep straight on** [walking] gehen Sie immer geradeaus; [driving] fahren Sie immer geradeaus - **3.** [food] sich halten - **4.** *UK* [in health]: **how are you keeping?** wie geht es dir? ◇ *n* [food, lodging] Unterhalt *der*; **to earn one's keep** sein eigenes Brot verdienen. ◆ **for keeps** *adv* für immer. ◆ **keep back** ◇ *vt sep* - **1.** [information] verschweigen - **2.** [money] zurücklbehalten. ◇ *vi* [stand back] zurücklbleiben. ◆ **keep off** *vt insep* [subject, food, drink] vermeiden; **'keep off the grass'** 'Rasen betreten verboten'. ◆ **keep on** *vi* - **1.** [continue]: **to keep on doing sthg** [continuously] etw weiter tun; [repeatedly] etw dauernd tun - **2.** [talk incessantly]: **to keep on (about sthg)** dauernd (über etw *(A)*) reden. ◆ **keep out** ◇ *vt sep* nicht hereinllassen. ◇ *vi*: **'keep out!'** 'Betreten verboten!' ◆ **keep to** *vt insep* - **1.** [rule, promise, plan]: **to keep to sthg** sich an etw *(A)* halten - **2.** [not deviate from]: **to keep to the point** bei der Sache bleiben; **keep to the path!** auf dem Weg bleiben! ◆ **keep up** ◇ *vt sep* - **1.** [prevent from falling] halten - **2.** [maintain - standards, friendship] aufrechtlerhalten; [- house, garden] instand halten; **keep it up!** weiter so! - **3.** [prevent from going to bed]: **to keep sb up** jn vom Schlafen ablhalten. ◇ *vi* [maintain pace, level] mitlhalten; **to keep up with sb/sthg** mit jm/etw mithalten können; **to keep up with the news** sich auf dem Laufenden halten.

keeper ['ki:pəʳ] *n* - **1.** [in zoo] Wärter *der*, -in *die* - **2.** [of museum] Kustos *der*.

keep-fit *UK n* Fitness *die*.

keeping ['ki:pɪŋ] *n* - **1.** [care]: **in safe keeping** sicher verwahrt; **for safe keeping** zur Verwahrung - **2.** [conformity]: **to be in keeping with sthg** [regulations, decision] etw *(D)* entsprechen; [clothes, furniture, style] zu etw passen.

keepsake ['ki:pseɪk] *n* Andenken *das*.

kennel ['kenl] *n* - **1.** [for dog] Hundehütte *die*; [for many dogs] Zwinger *der* - **2.** *US* = **kennels**. ◆ **kennels** *npl UK* [for boarding pets] Tierpension *die*.

Kenya ['kenjə] *n* Kenia *nt*.

kept [kept] *pt & pp* ▷ **keep**.

kerb [kɜ:b] *n UK* Bordsteinkante *die*.

kernel ['kɜ:nl] *n* [of nut] Kern *der*.

kerosene ['kerəsiːn] *n* Petroleum *das*.

ketchup ['ketʃəp] *n* Ketschup *der ODER das*.

kettle ['ketl] *n* Kessel *der*; **to put the kettle on** Wasser auf|setzen.

key [kiː] ◇ *n* - **1.** [gen] Schlüssel *der* - **2.** [of typewriter, computer, piano] Taste *die* - **3.** MUS Tonart *die*. ◇ *adj* [main] Schlüssel-.

keyboard ['kiːbɔːd] *n* - **1.** [of typewriter, computer] Tastatur *die*, Keyboard *das* - **2.** [of piano] Klaviatur *die*; [of organ] Manual *das*.

keyed up [ˌkiːd-] *adj* aufgeregt, nervös.

keyhole ['kiːhəʊl] *n* Schlüsselloch *das*.

keynote ['kiːnəʊt] *n* [main point] Hauptgedanke *der*.

keypad ['kiːpæd] *n* COMPUT Tastenfeld *das*.

key ring *n* Schlüsselring *der*.

kg (*abbr of* **kilogram**) kg.

khaki ['kɑːkɪ] ◇ *adj* kakifarben. ◇ *n* [colour] Kaki *das*.

kHz (*abbr of* **kilohertz**) *n* kHz.

kick [kɪk] ◇ *n* - **1.** [with foot] (Fuß)tritt *der* - **2.** *inf* [excitement]: **to do sthg for kicks** etw aus Spaß tun; **to get a kick from sthg** an etw *(D)* Spaß haben. ◇ *vt* - **1.** [with foot - gen] treten; [- ball] kicken; **I could have kicked myself!** ich hätte mich ohrfeigen können! - **2.** *inf* [habit] auf|geben. ◇ *vi* [person] treten; [baby] strampeln; [animal] aus|schlagen, treten. ◆ **kick off** *vi* - **1.** FTBL an|stoßen - **2.** *inf fig* [start] an|fangen. ◆ **kick out** *vt sep inf* raus|schmeißen.

kid [kɪd] ◇ *n* - **1.** *inf* [child] Kind *das* - **2.** [young goat] Zicklein *das*. ◇ *comp inf* [brother, sister] kleine(r). ◇ *vt inf* - **1.** [tease] veralbern - **2.** [delude]: **to kid o.s.** sich *(D)* etwas vor|machen. ◇ *vi inf*: **to be kidding** Spaß machen; **you're kidding!** das ist nicht dein Ernst!

kidnap ['kɪdnæp] (*UK*) (*US pt & pp* **-ed**, *cont* **-ing**) *vt* entführen, kidnappen.

kidnapper *UK*, **kidnaper** *US* ['kɪdnæpəʳ] *n* Kidnapper *der*, -in *die*, Entführer *der*, -in *die*.

kidnapping *UK*, **kidnaping** *US* ['kɪdnæpɪŋ] *n* Kidnapping *das*.

kidney ['kɪdnɪ] (*pl* **kidneys**) *n* Niere *die*.

kidney bean *n* Kidneybohne *die*.

kill [kɪl] ◇ *vt* - **1.** [person, animal] töten; [murder] um|bringen; [plant] eingehen lassen; **to kill o.s.** sich um|bringen - **2.** *fig* [hope] zerstören; [conversation, desire] zum Erliegen bringen; [pain] ab|töten. ◇ *vi* töten.

killer ['kɪləʳ] *n* [person] Mörder *der*, -in *die*.

killing ['kɪlɪŋ] *n* - **1.** [murder] Tötung *die* - **2.** *inf* [profit]: **to make a killing** ein Riesengeschäft machen.

killjoy ['kɪldʒɔɪ] *n* Spielverderber *der*.

kiln [kɪln] *n* [for bricks, pottery] Brennofen *der*; [for hops] Darrofen *der*.

kilo ['kiːləʊ] (*pl* **-s**) (*abbr of* **kilogram**) *n* Kilo *das*.

kilobyte ['kɪləbaɪt] *n* Kilobyte *das*.

kilogram(me) ['kɪləgræm] *n* Kilogramm *das*.

kilohertz ['kɪləhɜːts] (*pl inv*) *n* Kilohertz *das*.

kilometre *UK* ['kɪləˌmiːtəʳ], **kilometer** *US* [kɪ'lɒmɪtər] *n* Kilometer *der*.

kilowatt ['kɪləwɒt] *n* Kilowatt *das*.

kilt [kɪlt] *n* Kilt *der*, Schottenrock *der*.

kin [kɪn] *n* ▷ **kith**.

kind [kaɪnd] ◇ *adj* nett; **that's very kind of you** das ist sehr nett von dir. ◇ *n* Art *die*; [of cheese, wine *etc*] Sorte *die*; **what kind of music do you like?** welche Musik magst du?; **what kind of car do you drive?** was für ein Auto hast du?; **kind of** *inf* irgendwie; **they're two of a kind** sie sind vom gleichen Schlag; **all kinds of animals** allerlei Tiere; **in kind** [payment] in Naturalien.

kindergarten ['kɪndəˌgɑːtn] *n* Kindergarten *der*.

kind-hearted [-'hɑːtɪd] *adj* gutherzig.

kindle ['kɪndl] *vt fig* [idea, feeling] entfachen.

kindly ['kaɪndlɪ] ◇ *adj* gütig, wohltätig. ◇ *adv* - **1.** [speak, smile] freundlich - **2.** [please] freundlicherweise.

kindness ['kaɪndnɪs] *n* - **1.** [gentleness] Freundlichkeit *die* - **2.** [helpful act] Gefälligkeit *die*.

kindred ['kɪndrɪd] *adj* ähnlich; **kindred spirit** verwandte Seele.

king [kɪŋ] *n* König *der*.

kingdom ['kɪŋdəm] *n* - **1.** [country] Königreich *das* - **2.** [of animals, plants] Reich *das*.

kingfisher ['kɪŋˌfɪʃəʳ] *n* Eisvogel *der*.

king-size(d) [-saɪz(d)] *adj* Kingsize-.

kinky ['kɪŋkɪ] *adj inf* abartig.

kiosk ['kiːɒsk] *n* - **1.** [small shop] Kiosk *der* - **2.** *UK* [telephone box] Telefonzelle *die*.

kip [kɪp] *UK inf* ◇ *n*: **to have a kip** eine Runde schlafen. ◇ *vi* eine Runde schlafen.

kipper ['kɪpəʳ] *n* Räucherhering *der*.

kiss [kɪs] ◇ *n* Kuss *der*; **to give sb a kiss** jm einen Kuss geben. ◇ *vt* küssen. ◇ *vi* sich küssen.

kiss of life *n*: **the kiss of life** die Mund-zu-Mund-Beatmung.

kit [kɪt] *n* - **1.** [set] Ausrüstung *die*, Satz *der*; **repair kit** Flickzeug *das* - **2.** *(U)* [sports clothes] Sportsachen *Pl* - **3.** [to be assembled] Bausatz *der*.

kitchen ['kɪtʃɪn] *n* Küche *die*.

kitchen roll *n* Küchenrolle *die*.

kitchen sink *n* Spülbecken *das*.

kitchen unit *n* Küchenelement *das*.

kite [kaɪt] *n* [toy] Drachen *der*.

kitesurfing ['kaɪtsɜːfɪŋ] *n* Drachenfliegen *das*.
kith [kɪθ] *n*: **kith and kin** Kind und Kegel.
kitten ['kɪtn] *n* Kätzchen *das*.
kitty ['kɪtɪ] *n* [for bills, drinks] Gemeinschaftskasse *die*; [in card games] Bank *die*.
kiwi ['kiːwiː] *n* [bird] Kiwi *der*.
kiwi fruit *n* Kiwi *die*.
km (*abbr of* **kilometre**) km.
km/h (*abbr of* **kilometres per hour**) km/h.
knack [næk] *n* Trick *der*; **to have a** *OR* **the knack of doing sthg** [ability] den Dreh rauslhaben, etw zu tun; **he has a** *OR* **the knack of turning up late** er hat das Talent, (immer) zu spät zu kommen.
knackered ['nækəd] *adj UK inf* kaputt.
knapsack ['næpsæk] *n* Rucksack *der*.
knead [niːd] *vt* [dough, clay] kneten.
knee [niː] *n* Knie *das*.
kneecap ['niːkæp] *n* Kniescheibe *die*.
kneel [niːl] (*UK pt & pp* **knelt**) (*US pt & pp* **knelt** *OR* **-ed**) *vi* knien. ◆ **kneel down** *vi* niederlknien.
knelt [nelt] *pt & pp* ▷ **kneel**.
knew [njuː] *pt* ▷ **know**.
knickers ['nɪkəz] *npl* - **1.** *UK* [underwear] Schlüpfer *der* - **2.** *US* [knickerbockers] Knickerbockers *Pl*.
knick-knacks ['nɪknæks] *npl* Nippes *Pl*.
knife [naɪf] (*pl* **knives**) ◇ *n* Messer *das*. ◇ *vt* einlstechen auf *(+ A)*.
knight [naɪt] ◇ *n* - **1.** [gen] Ritter *der* - **2.** [in chess] Springer *der*. ◇ *vt* in den Adelsstand erheben.
knighthood ['naɪthʊd] *n*: **to get** *OR* **be given a knighthood** in den Adelsstand erhoben werden.
knit [nɪt] (*pt & pp inv OR* **-ted**) ◇ *adj*: **closely** *OR* **tightly knit** *fig* eng verbunden. ◇ *vt* stricken. ◇ *vi* - **1.** [with wool] stricken - **2.** [join] zusammenlwachsen.
knitting ['nɪtɪŋ] *n (U)* - **1.** [activity] Stricken *das* - **2.** [thing being knitted] Strickzeug *das*.
knitting needle *n* Stricknadel *die*.
knitwear ['nɪtweəʳ] *n (U)* Strickwaren *Pl*.
knives [naɪvz] *Pl* ▷ **knife**.
knob [nɒb] *n* - **1.** [handle] Griff *der*, Knauf *der* - **2.** [on TV, radio] Knopf *der*.
knock [nɒk] ◇ *n* - **1.** [hit - on body] Schlag *der*; [- on door] Klopfen *das* - **2.** *inf* [piece of bad luck] Schlag *der*. ◇ *vt* - **1.** [hit] (an)lschlagen, (an)lstoßen - **2.** *inf* [criticize] stark kritisieren. ◇ *vi* - **1.** [on door]: **to knock (at** *OR* **on)** klopfen (auf *OR* an *(+ A)*) - **2.** [car engine] klopfen. ◆ **knock down** *vt sep* - **1.** [pedestrian] anlfahren - **2.** [building] niederlreißen. ◆ **knock off** *vi inf* [stop working] Feierabend machen. ◆ **knock out** *vt sep* - **1.** [make unconscious - subj: person, punch] k.o. schlagen; [- subj: drug] bewusstlos werden lassen - **2.** [from competition] auslscheiden. ◆ **knock over** *vt sep* - **1.** [push over] umlstoßen; [person] umlwerfen - **2.** [pedestrian] überfahren.
knocker ['nɒkəʳ] *n* [on door] Türklopfer *der*.
knock-on effect *n UK* Auswirkung *die*.
knockout ['nɒkaʊt] *n* - **1.** [in boxing] Knockout *der*, K.o. *der* - **2.** *inf* [sensation]: **she's a knockout** sie ist toll.
knot [nɒt] ◇ *n* - **1.** [in rope, string] Knoten *der*; **to tie/untie a knot** einen Knoten machen/lösen - **2.** [in wood] Ast *der* - **3.** [ship's speed] Knoten *der*. ◇ *vt* [rope, string] knoten.
know [nəʊ] (*pt* **knew**, *pp* **known**) ◇ *vt* - **1.** [fact, information] wissen; **as far as I know** so viel ich weiß; **to let sb know sthg** jn etw wissen lassen - **2.** [person, place] kennen; **to get to know sb** jn kennen lernen - **3.** [language, skill] können; **to know how to do sthg** etw tun können - **4.** [recognize] erkennen - **5.** [call]: **to be known as** bekannt sein als - **6.** [distinguish] unterscheiden können; **to know right from wrong** Gut und Böse unterscheiden können. ◇ *vi*: **I know** das weiß ich; **to know about sthg** [understand] sich mit etw auslkennen; [have heard about] etw wissen; **to know of** kennen, wissen von; **you know** [for emphasis] weißt du. ◇ *n*: **to be in the know** im Bilde sein.
know-all *n UK* Besserwisser *der*, -in *die*.
know-how *n* Know-how *das*.
knowing ['nəʊɪŋ] *adj* [look, smile] wissend.
knowingly ['nəʊɪŋlɪ] *adv* - **1.** [look, smile] wissend - **2.** [act] wissentlich.
know-it-all *n* = **know-all**.
knowledge ['nɒlɪdʒ] *n (U)* - **1.** [learning] Kenntnisse *Pl* - **2.** [awareness] Wissen *das*; **I had no knowledge of it** ich wusste nichts davon; **to the best of my knowledge** soweit *OR* soviel ich weiß.
knowledgeable ['nɒlɪdʒəbl] *adj* sachkundig.
known [nəʊn] *pp* ▷ **know**.
knuckle ['nʌkl] *n* ANAT (Finger)knöchel *der*.
koala (bear) [kəʊ'ɑːlə-] *n* Koala(bär) *der*.
Koran [kɒ'rɑːn] *n*: **the Koran** der Koran.
Korea [kə'rɪə] *n* Korea *nt*.
Korean [kə'rɪən] ◇ *adj* koreanisch. ◇ *n* - **1.** [person] Koreaner *der*, -in *die* - **2.** [language] Koreanisch(e) *das*.
kosher ['kəʊʃəʳ] *adj* koscher.
kung fu [ˌkʌŋ'fuː] *n* Kung-Fu *das*.
Kurd [kɜːd] *n* Kurde *der*, -din *die*.
Kuwait [kʊ'weɪt] *n* - **1.** [country] Kuwait *nt* - **2.** [city] Kuwait-City *nt*.

L

l[1] (*pl* **l's** *OR* **ls**), **L** (*pl* **L's** *OR* **Ls**) [el] *n* [letter] l *das*, L *das*.

l[2] [el] (*abbr of* **litre**) l.

lab [læb] *n inf* Labor *das*.

label ['leɪbl] (*UK*) (*US*) ◇ *n* - **1.** [on bottle, clothing] Etikett *das*; [tied on] Anhänger *der*; [stuck on] Aufkleber *der* - **2.** [of record] Label *das*. ◇ *vt* - **1.** [fix label to - bottle, clothing] etikettieren; [- with tied-on label] mit Anhänger versehen; [- with stuck-on label] mit Aufkleber versehen - **2.** [describe]: **to label sb (as) sthg** jn als etw ein|stufen.

labor *etc n US* = **labour** *etc* .

laboratory [*UK* lə'bɒrətrɪ, *US* 'læbrəˌtɔːrɪ] *n* Labor(atorium) *das*.

laborious [lə'bɔːrɪəs] *adj* mühsam.

labor union *n US* (Arbeiter)gewerkschaft *die*.

labour *UK*, **labor** *US* ['leɪbəʳ] ◇ *n* - **1.** [work] Arbeit *die* - **2.** *(U)* [workers] Arbeiterschaft *die*, Arbeiter *Pl* - **3.** MED (Geburts)wehen *Pl*. ◇ *vi* - **1.** [work] arbeiten - **2.** [struggle]: **to labour at** *OR* **over sthg** sich mit etw plagen. ◆ **Labour** *UK* ◇ *adj* POL Labour-. ◇ *n* POL Labour Party *die*.

laboured *UK*, **labored** *US* ['leɪbəd] *adj* [breathing] schwer; [style] schwerfällig.

labourer *UK*, **laborer** *US* ['leɪbərəʳ] *n* Arbeiter *der*, -in *die*.

Labour Party *n UK*: **the Labour Party** die Labour Party.

Labrador ['læbrədɔːʳ] *n* [dog] Labrador *der*.

labyrinth ['læbərɪnθ] *n* Labyrinth *das*.

lace [leɪs] ◇ *n* - **1.** *(U)* [material] Spitze *die* - **2.** [for shoe] Schnürsenkel *der*. ◇ *vt* - **1.** [shoe, boot] (zu)|schnüren - **2.** [drink] mit einem Schuss Alkohol versetzen. ◆ **lace up** *vt sep* zu|schnüren.

lack [læk] ◇ *n*: **lack (of)** Mangel *der* (an *(+ D)*); **for lack of money** aus Geldmangel; **there is no lack of** es mangelt nicht an *(+ D)*. ◇ *vt*: **he lacks confidence/intelligence** es mangelt ihm an Selbstvertrauen/Intelligenz. ◇ *vi*: **to be lacking** fehlen; **he is lacking in confidence/intelligence** es mangelt ihm an Selbstvertrauen/Intelligenz.

lackadaisical [ˌlækə'deɪzɪkl] *adj pej* lustlos.

lacklustre *UK*, **lackluster** *US* ['lækˌlʌstəʳ] *adj* [performance] glanzlos; [person, party] langweilig.

laconic [lə'kɒnɪk] *adj* lakonisch.

lacquer ['lækəʳ] *n* - **1.** [for wood, metal] Lack *der* - **2.** [for hair] Haarspray *das*.

lacrosse [lə'krɒs] *n* Lacrosse *das*.

lad [læd] *n inf* - **1.** [young boy] Junge *der* - **2.** [male friend] Kumpel *der*.

ladder ['lædəʳ] ◇ *n* - **1.** [for climbing] Leiter *die* - **2.** *UK* [in tights] Laufmasche *die*. ◇ *vt UK*: **I've laddered my tights** ich habe eine Laufmasche.

laden ['leɪdn] *adj*: **laden (with)** beladen (mit).

ladies *UK* ['leɪdɪz], **ladies room** *US n* Damentoilette *die*.

ladle ['leɪdl] *n* (Schöpf)kelle *die*.

lady ['leɪdɪ] ◇ *n* - **1.** [woman] Dame *die* - **2.** [by birth or upbringing] Lady *die*. ◇ *comp*: **lady doctor** Ärztin; **lady dentist** Zahnärztin. ◆ **Lady** *n* [member of nobility] Lady *die*.

ladybird *UK* ['leɪdɪbɜːd], **ladybug** *US* ['leɪdɪbʌg] *n* Marienkäfer *der*.

ladylike ['leɪdɪlaɪk] *adj* damenhaft.

lag [læg] ◇ *vi*: **to lag (behind)** zurück|bleiben. ◇ *vt* isolieren. ◇ *n* [time lag] zeitliche Verzögerung.

lager ['lɑːgəʳ] *n* helles Bier.

lagoon [lə'guːn] *n* Lagune *die*.

laid [leɪd] *pt* & *pp* ▷ **lay**.

laid-back *adj inf* gelassen.

lain [leɪn] *pp* ▷ **lie**.

lair [leəʳ] *n* Lager *das*.

lake [leɪk] *n* See *der*.

Lake District *n*: **the Lake District** der Lake District, *Seenlandschaft in Nordwestengland*.

lamb [læm] *n* Lamm *das*.

lambswool ['læmzwʊl] *n* Lambswool *die*.

lame [leɪm] *adj liter* & *fig* lahm.

lament [lə'ment] ◇ *n* Klage *die*; [song] Klagelied *das*. ◇ *vt* beklagen.

lamentable ['læməntəbl] *adj* beklagenswert.

laminated ['læmɪneɪtɪd] *adj* geschichtet.

lamp [læmp] *n* Lampe *die*; [on street] Laterne *die*.

lampoon [læm'puːn] *vt* verspotten.

lamppost ['læmppəʊst] *n* Laternenpfahl *der*.

lampshade ['læmpʃeɪd] *n* Lampenschirm *der*.

lance [lɑːns] ◇ *n* [spear] Lanze *die*. ◇ *vt* MED auf|schneiden.

land [lænd] ◇ *n* - **1.** [gen] Land *das* - **2.** [property] Land *das*. ◇ *vt* - **1.** [plane] landen - **2.** [cargo] löschen - **3.** [fish] an Land ziehen - **4.** *inf* [job, contract] kriegen - **5.** *inf* [put]: **to land sb in trouble/jail** jn in Schwierigkeiten/ins Gefängnis bringen - **6.** *inf* [encumber]: **to land sb with sb/sthg** jm jn/etw auf|halsen. ◇ *vi* - **1.** [plane, passenger] landen; [from ship] an Land gehen - **2.** [fall] fallen. ◆ **land up** *vi inf* [in place] landen; [in situation] enden.

landing ['lændɪŋ] *n* - **1.** [between stairs] Treppenabsatz *der* - **2.** [of aeroplane] Landung *die*.

landing card *n* Einreisekarte *die*.

landlady ['lænd,leɪdɪ] *n* - **1.** [of pub] Wirtin *die* - **2.** [of lodgings] Vermieterin *die*.

landlord ['lændlɔːd] *n* - **1.** [of pub] Wirt *der* - **2.** [of lodgings] Vermieter *der*.

landmark ['lændmɑːk] *n* - **1.** [prominent feature] Wahrzeichen *das* - **2.** *fig* [in history] Meilenstein *der*.

landowner ['lænd,əʊnəʳ] *n* Grundbesitzer *der*, -in *die*.

landscape ['lændskeɪp] *n* [scenery] Landschaft *die*.

landslide ['lændslaɪd] *n liter & fig* Erdrutsch *der*.

lane [leɪn] *n* - **1.** [country road] (enge) Landstraße - **2.** [division of road] Fahrspur *die*, Fahrstreifen *der*; **'get in lane'** 'Bitte einordnen'; **'keep in lane'** 'Auf der Fahrspur bleiben' - **3.** [in swimming pool, on racetrack] Bahn *die* - **4.** [for shipping] Schifffahrtsweg *der*; [for aircraft] Flugroute *die*.

language ['læŋgwɪdʒ] *n* Sprache *die*; **bad language** Kraftausdrücke *Pl*.

language laboratory *n* Sprachlabor *das*.

languid ['læŋgwɪd] *adj* [gesture] lässig; [person] träge.

languish ['læŋgwɪʃ] *vi* - **1.** [suffer] schmachten - **2.** [become weak - person, plant] verkümmern.

lank [læŋk] *adj* [hair] strähnig.

lanky ['læŋkɪ] *adj* schlaksig.

lantern ['læntən] *n* Laterne *die*.

lap [læp] ◇ *n* - **1.** [knees] Schoß *der* - **2.** SPORT Runde *die*. ◇ *vt* - **1.** [subj: animal] (auf)lschlecken - **2.** SPORT [runner, car] überrunden. ◇ *vi* [water, waves] plätschern.

lapel [lə'pel] *n* Revers *das*.

lapse [læps] ◇ *n* - **1.** [failing]: **lapse of concentration** Konzentrationsschwäche *die*; **memory lapse** Gedächtnislücke *die* - **2.** [in behaviour] Lapsus *der* - **3.** [of time]: **after a lapse of three years** nach drei Jahren. ◇ *vi* - **1.** [licence, passport] ablaufen; [law] nicht mehr gelten; [custom] auslsterben - **2.** [standards] verfallen; [quality] sich verschlechtern - **3.** [subj: person]: **to lapse into sthg** in etw *(A)* verfallen; [coma] in etw *(A)* fallen.

lap-top (computer) *n* Laptop *der*.

lard [lɑːd] *n* Schweineschmalz *das*.

larder ['lɑːdəʳ] *n* [room] Vorratsraum *der*; [cupboard] Vorratsschrank *der*.

large [lɑːdʒ] *adj* groß; [person] korpulent. ◆ **at large** ◇ *adj*: **to be at large** [prisoner] auf freiem Fuß sein; [animal] frei herumllaufen. ◇ *adv* [as a whole]: **society/the world at large** die ganze Gesellschaft/Welt.

largely ['lɑːdʒlɪ] *adv* zum größten Teil.

lark [lɑːk] *n* - **1.** [bird] Lerche *die* - **2.** *inf* [joke] Jux *der*. ◆ **lark about** *vi* herumlalbern.

laryngitis [,lærɪn'dʒaɪtɪs] *n (U)* Kehlkopfentzündung *die*.

lasagna, lasagne [lə'zænjə] *n (U)* Lasagne *Pl*.

laser ['leɪzəʳ] *n* Laser *der*.

laser printer *n* Laserdrucker *der*.

lash [læʃ] ◇ *n* - **1.** [eyelash] Wimper *die* - **2.** [blow with whip] Peitschenhieb *der*. ◇ *vt* - **1.** [whip as punishment] auslpeitschen - **2.** [subj: wind, rain, waves] peitschen gegen - **3.** [tie]: **to lash sthg to sthg** etw an etw *(D)* festlbinden. ◆ **lash out** *vi* - **1.** [physically] um sich schlagen; **to lash out at** OR **against sb** (auf jn) einlschlagen OR loslschlagen - **2.** [verbally]: **to lash out at** OR **against sb** Schimpftiraden auf jn losllassen, jn beschimpfen.

lass [læs] *n* Mädel *das*.

lasso [læ'suː] *(pl* **-s)** ◇ *n* Lasso *das*. ◇ *vt* mit dem Lasso einlfangen.

last [lɑːst] ◇ *adj* letzte(r) (s); **last Tuesday** letzten Dienstag; **last but one** vorletzte(r) (s); **that's the last thing I want** das ist das Letzte, was ich will. ◇ *adv* zuletzt. ◇ *pron*: **to be the last to arrive/sit down/***etc* als Letzte(r) anlkommen/sich hinlsetzen/*etc*; **I'm always the last to be told** ich bin immer der Letzte, der etwas erfährt; **to leave sthg till last** etw bis zuletzt auflschieben; **the Saturday before last** vorletzten Samstag; **the last but one** der/die/das Vorletzte. ◇ *n* [final thing]: **the last I saw/heard of him** das Letzte, was ich von ihm sah/hörte. ◇ *vi* - **1.** [continue to exist or function] dauern; [shoes] halten; [luck, feeling] anlhalten - **2.** [keep fresh] sich halten - **3.** [be enough for]: **this will last a week** das wird für eine Woche reichen. ◆ **at (long) last** *adv* endlich.

last-ditch *adj* allerletzte(r) (s).

lasting ['lɑːstɪŋ] *adj* [peace] dauerhaft; [effect, mistrust] anhaltend.

lastly ['lɑːstlɪ] *adv* zum Schluss.

last-minute *adj* in letzter Minute; [flight, ticket] Last-Minute-.

last name *n* Familienname *der*.

latch [lætʃ] *n* Riegel *der*. ◆ **latch onto** *vt insep inf* [idea] ablfahren auf; [person] sich hängen an.

late [leɪt] ◇ *adj* - **1.** [not on time]: **to be late** [person] zu spät dran sein; [train, bus] Verspätung haben; **to be late for sthg** zu etw zu spät kommen - **2.** [near end of]: **in the late evening/afternoon/morning** am späten Abend/Nachmittag/Vormittag; **he arrived in late December** er kam Ende Dezember - **3.** [later than normal] spät - **4.** [dead] verstorben - **5.** [former] vorige. ◇ *adv* - **1.** [not on time]: **to arrive (20 minutes) late** [bus, train] (20 Minuten) Verspätung haben; [person] (20 Minuten) zu spät kommen - **2.** [later than normal, near end of period] spät; **late in the afternoon** am späten Nachmittag; **late in August** Ende August; **I worked late** ich habe lange gearbeitet. ◆ **of late** *adv* in letzter Zeit.

latecomer ['leɪtˌkʌməʳ] *n* Zuspätkommende *der, die*.

lately ['leɪtlɪ] *adv* in letzter Zeit.

latent ['leɪtənt] *adj* latent vorhanden.

later ['leɪtəʳ] ◇ *adj* später. ◇ *adv*: **later (on)** später.

lateral ['lætərəl] *adj* seitlich.

latest ['leɪtɪst] ◇ *adj* [most recent] neueste(r) (s). ◇ *n*: **at the latest** spätestens.

lather ['lɑːðəʳ] ◇ *n* (Seifen)schaum *der*. ◇ *vt* ein|seifen.

Latin ['lætɪn] ◇ *adj* [studies, student] Latein-. ◇ *n* [language] Latein(ische) *das*.

Latin America *n* Lateinamerika *nt*.

Latin American *adj* lateinamerikanisch.

latitude ['lætɪtjuːd] *n* GEOG Breite *die*.

latter ['lætəʳ] ◇ *adj* - **1.** [later - years] spätere; **in the latter part of the century** in der zweiten Hälfte des Jahrhunderts - **2.** [second] zweite(r) (s); [opposed to former] letzte(r) (s). ◇ *n*: **the latter** der/die/das Letztere.

lattice ['lætɪs] *n* Gitter *das*.

Latvia ['lætvɪə] *n* Lettland *nt*.

laudable ['lɔːdəbl] *adj* lobenswert.

laugh [lɑːf] ◇ *n* - **1.** [sound] Lachen *das* - **2.** *inf* [fun, joke] Spaß *der*; **to do sthg for laughs** OR **a laugh** etw aus OR zum Spaß machen. ◇ *vi* lachen. ◆ **laugh at** *vt insep* [mock] sich lustig machen über *(+ A)*. ◆ **laugh off** *vt sep* [dismiss] mit einem Lachen ab|tun.

laughable ['lɑːfəbl] *adj pej* lächerlich.

laughing stock ['lɑːfɪŋstɒk] *n* Zielscheibe *die* des Spotts.

laughter ['lɑːftəʳ] *n* Gelächter *das*.

launch [lɔːntʃ] ◇ *n* - **1.** [of new ship] Stapellauf *der* - **2.** [into air - of missile] Abschuss *der* - **3.** [start] Beginn *der* - **4.** COMM [of new book, product] Lancieren *das* - **5.** [boat] Barkasse *die*. ◇ *vt* - **1.** [into water - boat] zu Wasser lassen; [- new ship] vom Stapel lassen - **2.** [into air - space rocket, satellite] in den Weltraum schießen; [- missile] ab|schießen - **3.** [start - campaign] beginnen; *(phrase)*: **to launch an attack** einen Angriff durch|führen - **4.** COMM [new book, product] lancieren.

launch(ing) pad ['lɔːntʃ(ɪŋ)-] *n* [for rocket, missile, satellite] Abschussrampe *die*.

launder ['lɔːndəʳ] *vt* - **1.** [clothes] waschen und bügeln - **2.** *inf* [money] waschen.

laund(e)rette [lɔːn'dret], **Laundromat**® *US* ['lɔːndrəmæt] *n* Waschsalon *der*.

laundry ['lɔːndrɪ] *n* - **1.** *(U)* [clothes] Wäsche *die* - **2.** [business] Wäscherei *die*.

laurel ['lɒrəl] *n* Lorbeer *der*.

lava ['lɑːvə] *n* Lava *die*.

lavatory ['lævətrɪ] *n* Toilette *die*.

lavender ['lævəndəʳ] *n* [plant] Lavendel *der*.

lavish ['lævɪʃ] ◇ *adj* - **1.** [generous] großzügig; **to be lavish with sthg** [with money, time] mit etw großzügig sein - **2.** [sumptuous - decoration] aufwendig; [- banquet] üppig. ◇ *vt*: **to lavish sthg on sb** [praise, attention, money] jn mit etw förmlich überhäufen.

law [lɔː] *n* - **1.** [legislation, rule, natural or scientific principle] Gesetz *das*; **to become law** rechtskräftig werden; **to break the law** das Gesetz brechen; **against the law** gesetzeswidrig; **law and order** Recht und Ordnung - **2.** *(U)* [legal system]: **(the) law** das Recht - **3.** [subject studied] Jura.

law-abiding [-əˌbaɪdɪŋ] *adj* gesetzestreu.

law court *n* Gericht *das*.

lawful ['lɔːfʊl] *adj fml* rechtmäßig.

lawn [lɔːn] *n* Rasen *der*.

lawnmower ['lɔːnˌməʊəʳ] *n* Rasenmäher *der*.

lawn tennis *n* Rasentennis *das*.

law school *n* juristische Fakultät.

lawsuit ['lɔːsuːt] *n* Klage *die*.

lawyer ['lɔːjəʳ] *n* (Rechts)anwalt *der*, -anwältin *die*.

lax [læks] *adj* lax; [discipline] lasch; [behaviour] locker.

laxative ['læksətɪv] *n* Abführmittel *das*.

lay [leɪ] (*pt & pp* **laid**) ◇ *pt* ▷ **lie**. ◇ *vt* - **1.** [in specified position] legen - **2.** [prepare - trap, snare] auf|stellen; **to lay the table** den Tisch decken - **3.** [carpet, cable, pipes] verlegen; [bricks, foundations] legen - **4.** [egg] legen - **5.**: **to lay the blame (for sthg) on sb** jm die Schuld (für etw) geben; **to lay emphasis on sthg** Wert auf etw *(A)* legen. ◇ *adj* - **1.** RELIG Laien- - **2.** [untrained, unqualified] laienhaft; **lay person** Laie *der*. ◆ **lay aside** *vt sep* - **1.** [save - food, money] zur Seite legen - **2.** [knitting, book] weg|legen. ◆ **lay down** *vt sep* - **1.** [regulations] auf|stellen - **2.** [arms, tools] nieder|legen. ◆ **lay off** ◇ *vt sep* [workers] entlassen. ◇ *vt insep inf* - **1.** [leave alone] in Ruhe lassen - **2.** [stop, give up]: **to lay off alcohol/cigarettes** mit dem Trinken/Rauchen auf|hören. ◆ **lay on** *vt sep UK* [provide, supply] sorgen für. ◆ **lay out** *vt sep* - **1.** [clothes, tools, ingredients] bereit|legen - **2.** [garden, house, town] planen.

layabout ['leɪəbaʊt] *n UK inf* Faulenzer *der*.

lay-by (*pl* **-s**) *n UK* [small] Parkbucht *die*; [large] Rastplatz *der*.

layer ['leɪəʳ] *n* - **1.** [of substance, material] Schicht *die* - **2.** *fig* [level] Ebene *die*.

layman ['leɪmən] (*pl* **-men** [-mən]) *n fig* & RELIG Laie *der*.

layout ['leɪaʊt] *n* [of house] Raumaufteilung *die*; [of garden] Anlage *die*; [of text] Layout *das*.

laze [leɪz] *vi*: **to laze (about** *OR* **around)** faulenzen.

lazy ['leɪzɪ] *adj* - **1.** [person] faul - **2.** [action] träge.

lazybones ['leɪzɪbəʊnz] (*pl inv*) *n* Faulpelz *der*.

lb *abbr of* **pound**.

LCD (*abbr of* **liquid crystal display**) *n* LCD; **LCD display** LCD-Anzeige *die*.

lead¹ [li:d] (*pt & pp* **led**) ◇ *n* - **1.** *(U)* [winning position] Führung *die*; **to be in** *OR* **have the lead** in Führung liegen - **2.** [amount ahead] Vorsprung *der* - **3.** *(U)* [initiative, example]: **to take the lead** [do sthg first] mit gutem Beispiel voran|gehen; **I followed his lead** ich folgte seinem Beispiel - **4.** *(U)* [stage or film role]: **the lead** die Hauptrolle - **5.** [clue] Anhaltspunkt *der* - **6.** [for dog] Leine *die* - **7.** [wire, cable] Kabel *das*. ◇ *adj* [most important]: **lead singer** Leadsänger *der*, -in *die*; **lead actor** Hauptdarsteller *der*; **lead story** Leitartikel *der*. ◇ *vt* - **1.** [procession, parade] an|führen - **2.** [person, existence] führen - **3.** [team, investigation] leiten; [political party] führen - **4.** [strike, campaign] organisieren - **5.** [cause, influence]: **to lead sb to do sthg** jn veranlassen, etw zu tun. ◇ *vi* - **1.** [go] führen - **2.** [give access to]: **to lead to/into sthg** zu etw/in etw *(A)* führen - **3.** [be winning] führen - **4.** [result in]: **to lead to sthg** zu etw führen. ◆ **lead up to** *vt insep* - **1.** [precede]: **the events that led up to the disaster** die Ereignisse, die der Katastrophe vorausgingen - **2.** [in conversation - topic] zu|steuern auf *(+ A)*; *(phrase)*: **what are you leading up to?** worauf willst du hinaus?

lead² [led] ◇ *n* - **1.** [metal] Blei *das* - **2.** [in pencil] Mine *die*. ◇ *comp* Blei-.

leaded ['ledɪd] *adj* [petrol] verbleit.

leader ['li:dəʳ] *n* - **1.** [head - of organization] Leiter *der*, -in *die*; [- of political party] Vorsitzende *der, die*; [- of gang] Anführer *der*, -in *die* - **2.** [in race, competition] Führende *der, die*; **to be the leader** in Führung liegen - **3.** *UK* [in newspaper] Leitartikel *der*.

leadership ['li:dəʃɪp] *n* [position, people in charge] Führung *die*; [quality] Führungsqualitäten *Pl*.

lead-free [led-] *adj* bleifrei.

leading ['li:dɪŋ] *adj* [prominent] führend.

leading light *n* herausragende Persönlichkeit.

leaf [li:f] (*pl* **leaves**) *n* - **1.** [of tree, plant, book] Blatt *das* - **2.** [of table] Platte *die (zur Vergrößerung eines Tisches)*. ◆ **leaf through** *vt insep* durch|blättern.

leaflet ['li:flɪt] *n* Broschüre *die*; [commercial] Prospekt *der*; [political] Flugblatt *das*.

league [li:g] *n* - **1.** [group - of people, countries] Bündnis *das*; *(phrase)*: **to be in league with sb** mit jm verbündet sein - **2.** SPORT Liga *die*.

leak [li:k] ◇ *n* - **1.** [in pipe, tank, roof] undichte Stelle; [in boat] Leck *das* - **2.** [disclosure]: **there has been a leak** es ist etwas durchgesickert. ◇ *vt* [make known] durch|sickern lassen. ◇ *vi* [pipe, tank, roof, shoe] undicht sein; [boat] lecken; [gas] aus|strömen; [liquid] aus|laufen; **to leak (out) from sthg** aus etw aus|strömen/aus|laufen. ◆ **leak out** *vi* [news, secret] durch|sickern.

lean [li:n] (*pt & pp* **leant** *OR* **-ed**) ◇ *adj* - **1.** [person - thin] dünn; [- slim] schlank - **2.** [meat, harvest, year] mager. ◇ *vt*: **to lean sthg against sthg** etw gegen *OR* an etw *(A)* lehnen. ◇ *vi* - **1.** [bend, slope - person] sich beugen; [- wall] sich neigen; *(phrase)*: **to lean forward** sich vor|beugen - **2.** [rest]: **to lean on/against sthg** sich an etw *(A)*/gegen etw lehnen. ◆ **lean back** *vi* sich zurück|lehnen.

leaning ['li:nɪŋ] *n*: **leaning (towards sthg)** Neigung *die* (zu etw).

leant [lent] *pt & pp* ▷ **lean**.

lean-to (*pl* **-s**) *n* angebauter Schuppen.

leap [li:p] (*pt & pp* **leapt** *OR* **-ed**) ◇ *n* - **1.** [jump] Sprung *der* - **2.** [increase] sprunghafter Anstieg. ◇ *vi* [jump] springen.

leapfrog ['li:pfrɒg] ◇ *n (U)* Bockspringen *das*. ◇ *vt fig* über|springen.

leapt [lept] *pt & pp* ▷ **leap**.

leap year *n* Schaltjahr *das*.

learn [lɜ:n] (*pt & pp* **-ed** *OR* **learnt**) ◇ *vt* - **1.** [acquire knowledge, skill of] (er)lernen; **to learn (how) to cook/read/***etc* kochen/lesen/*etc* lernen - **2.** [memorize] (auswendig) lernen - **3.** [hear] erfahren; **to learn that...** erfahren, dass... ◇ *vi* - **1.** [acquire knowledge, skill] lernen - **2.** [hear]: **to learn of** *OR* **about sthg** von etw erfahren.

learned ['lɜ:nɪd] *adj* - **1.** [person] gelehrt - **2.** [journal, paper, book] wissenschaftlich.

learner ['lɜ:nəʳ] *n*: **she's a quick learner** sie lernt schnell; **learners of English** Englischlerner *Pl*.

learner (driver) *n* Fahrschüler *der*, -in *die*.

learning ['lɜ:nɪŋ] *n (U)* [process] Lernen *das*; [knowledge] Wissen *das*; [result] Gelehrsamkeit *die*.

learnt [lɜ:nt] *pt & pp* ▷ **learn**.

lease [li:s] ◇ *n* LAW [of premises] Pacht *die*; [contract] Pachtvertrag *der*; [of car] Leasing *das*; [contract] Leasingvertrag *der*. ◇ *vt* [premises - to sb] verpachten; [- from sb] pachten; [- car] leasen.

leasehold ['li:shəʊld] *adj* [property] Pacht-.

leash [li:ʃ] *n* (Hunde)leine *die*.

least [li:st] (*superl of* **little**) ◇ *adj* wenigste(r) (s); **he earns the least money** er verdient am wenigsten. ◇ *pron*: **(the) least** das Wenigste; **it's the least I can do** das ist das Mindeste, was ich tun kann; **not in the least** nicht im Geringsten; **to say the least** gelinde gesagt. ◇ *adv* am wenigsten. ◆ **at least** *adv* wenigstens. ◆ **least of all** *adv* am allerwenigsten.

leather ['leðəʳ] ◇ *n* Leder *das*. ◇ *comp* Leder-.

leave [li:v] (*pt & pp* **left**) ◇ *vt* - **1.** [gen] verlassen; **leave the door open** lass die Tür offen; **let's leave it at that** lassen wir es dabei - **2.** [not take away] lassen - **3.** [not use, not eat] übrig lassen - **4.** [a mark, scar, message, in will] hinterlassen; **to leave one's money to sb** jm sein Geld hinterlassen - **5.** [space, gap] lassen - **6.** [entrust] überlassen; **he left it to her to decide** er hat ihr die Entscheidung überlassen. ◇ *vi* gehen; [train, bus] ab|fahren. ◇ *n (U)* - **1.** [time off work] Urlaub *der*; **on leave** auf Urlaub - **2.** *fml* [permission] Erlaubnis *die*. ◆ **leave behind** *vt sep* zurück|lassen. ◆ **leave out** *vt sep* aus|lassen.

leave of absence *n* Urlaub *der*.

leaves [li:vz] *Pl* ▷ **leaf**.

Lebanon ['lebənən] *n* Libanon *der*.

lecherous ['letʃərəs] *adj* lüstern.

lecture ['lektʃəʳ] ◇ *n* - **1.** [talk - at university] Vorlesung *die*; [- at conference] Vortrag *der* - **2.** [criticism, reprimand] Strafpredigt *die*. ◇ *vt* [scold]: **to lecture sb** jm eine Strafpredigt halten. ◇ *vi* [give talk]: **to lecture (on/in sthg)** eine Vorlesung/einen Vortrag (über etw *(A)*) halten.

lecturer ['lektʃərəʳ] *n* - **1.** [teacher] Dozent *der*, -in *die* - **2.** [speaker] Redner *der*, -in *die*.

led [led] *pt & pp* ▷ **lead**[1].

ledge [ledʒ] *n* [of window - outside] Fenstersims *der*; [- inside] Fensterbrett *das*.

ledger ['ledʒəʳ] *n* Hauptbuch *das*.

leek [li:k] *n*: **a leek** eine Stange Lauch.

leer [lɪəʳ] ◇ *n* lüsterner Blick. ◇ *vi*: **to leer at sb** jm einen lüsternen Blick zu|werfen.

leeway ['li:weɪ] *n* [room to manoeuvre] Spielraum *der*.

left [left] ◇ *pt & pp* ▷ **leave**. ◇ *adj* - **1.** [remaining] übrig; **to be left** übrig geblieben sein - **2.** [side, hand, foot] linke(r) (s). ◇ *adv* links. ◇ *n* [direction]: **on the left** auf der linken Seite; **to the left** [position] auf der linken Seite; [movement] auf die linke Seite; **keep to the left!** sich links halten! ◆ **Left** *n* POL: **the Left** die Linke.

left-hand *adj* linke(r) (s); **the left-hand side** die linke Seite.

left-hand drive *adj* mit Linkssteuer.

left-handed [-'hændɪd] *adj* [person] linkshändig.

left luggage (office) *n UK* Gepäckaufbewahrung *die*.

leftover ['leftəʊvəʳ] *adj* übrig geblieben. ◆ **leftovers** *npl* Reste *Pl*.

left wing *n* POL linker Flügel. ◆ **left-wing** *adj* POL linke(r) (s).

leg [leg] *n* - **1.** [gen] Bein *das*; *phrase*: **to pull sb's leg** jn auf den Arm nehmen - **2.** CULIN [of chicken] Schenkel *der*; [of lamb, pork] Keule *die* - **3.** [of journey] Etappe *die*; [of tournament] Runde *die*.

legacy ['legəsɪ] *n* - **1.** [gift of money] Erbschaft *die* - **2.** *fig* [consequence] Erbe *das*.

legal ['li:gl] *adj* - **1.** [concerning the law - system] Rechts-; [- advice] juristisch; *(phrase)*: **the legal profession** die Juristenschaft - **2.** [lawful] legal.

legalize, -ise ['li:gəlaɪz] *vt* legalisieren.

legal tender *n (U)* legales Zahlungsmittel.

legend ['ledʒənd] *n* - **1.** [myth] Sage *die* - **2.** *fig* [person] Legende *die*.

leggings ['legɪŋz] *npl* Leggings *Pl*.

legible ['ledʒəbl] *adj* lesbar.

legislation [ˌledʒɪs'leɪʃn] *n (U)* [laws] Gesetze *Pl*.

legislature ['ledʒɪsleɪtʃəʳ] *n* Legislative *die*.

legitimate [lɪ'dʒɪtɪmət] *adj* - **1.** [government] rechtmäßig; [business, action] legal - **2.** [argument] stichhaltig; [complaint, question] berechtigt - **3.** [child] ehelich.

legroom ['legrʊm] *n* Beinfreiheit *die*.

leg-warmers [-ˌwɔ:məz] *npl* Legwarmer *Pl*.

leisure [*UK* 'leʒəʳ, *US* 'li:ʒər] *n* Freizeit *die*; **do it at (your) leisure** machen Sie es, wenn Sie Zeit haben.

leisure centre *n* Freizeitzentrum *das*.

leisurely [*UK* 'leʒəlɪ, *US* 'li:ʒərlɪ] *adj & adv* gemächlich.

leisure time *n* Freizeit *die*.

lemon ['lemən] *n* [fruit] Zitrone *die*.

lemonade [ˌlemə'neɪd] *n* - **1.** *UK* [fizzy] Limonade *die* - **2.** [made with fresh lemons] Zitronensaftgetränk *(aus Zitronen, Zucker und Wasser bestehend)*.

lemon juice *n (U)* Zitronensaft *der*.

lemon sole *n* Seezunge *die*.

lemon squash *n (U) UK* Zitronengetränk *das*.

lemon squeezer [-ˌskwi:zəʳ] *n* Zitronenpresse *die*.

lemon tea *n* Zitronentee *der*.

lend [lend] (*pt & pp* **lent**) *vt* - **1.** [money, book]: **to lend sb sthg, to lend sthg to sb** jm etw leihen; **I don't like lending money** ich verleihe nicht gerne Geld - **2.** [support, assistance]: **to lend one's support to sb** jn unterstützen; **to lend one's assistance to sb** jm helfen - **3.** [credibility, quality]: **to lend sthg to sb/sthg** jm/einer Sache etw verleihen.

lending rate ['lendɪŋ-] *n* Darlehenszinssatz *der*.

length [leŋθ] *n* - **1.** [gen] Länge *die*; **in length** in der Länge, lang - **2.** [whole distance]: **we walked the length of the street** wir gingen die ganze Straße entlang - **3.** [of swimming pool] Länge *die* - **4.** [of string, wood, cloth] Stück *das* - **5.** *phr*: **he went to great lengths to achieve his goal** er tat alles Mögliche, um sein Ziel zu erreichen. ◆ **at length** *adv* - **1.** [eventually] endlich - **2.** [in detail] ausführlich.

lengthen ['leŋθən] ◇ *vt* verlängern. ◇ *vi* länger werden.

lengthways ['leŋθweɪz] *adv* der Länge nach, längs.

lengthy ['leŋθɪ] *adj* lang, langwierig; [stay, visit] ausgedehnt; [discussions] langwierig.

lenient ['liːnɪənt] *adj* [person] nachsichtig; [verdict, sentence] mild.

lens [lenz] *n* - **1.** PHOT & ANAT Linse *die*; [of glasses] Glas *das* - **2.** [contact lens] Kontaktlinse *die*.

lent [lent] *pt & pp* ▷ **lend**.

Lent [lent] *n* Fastenzeit *die*.

lentil ['lentɪl] *n* Linse *die*.

Leo ['liːəʊ] *n* Löwe *der*.

leopard ['lepəd] *n* Leopard *der*.

leotard ['liːətɑːd] *n* - **1.** [in ballet, circus] Trikot *das* - **2.** [in gymnastics] Gymnastikanzug *der*.

leper ['lepəʳ] *n* Leprakranke *der, die*.

leprosy ['leprəsɪ] *n* Lepra *die*.

lesbian ['lezbɪən] *n* Lesbe *die*, Lesbierin *die*.

less [les] *(compar of* **little***)* ◇ *adj* weniger; **less than** weniger als; **of less value** von geringerem Wert. ◇ *pron* weniger; **less than 20** weniger als 20. ◇ *adv* weniger; **less and less** immer weniger. ◇ *prep* [minus] weniger; **purchase price less 10%** Kaufpreis abzüglich 10%.

lessen ['lesn] ◇ *vt* [risk, chances, effect] verringern; [pain] lindern. ◇ *vi* nachllassen.

lesser ['lesəʳ] *adj* geringer; **to a lesser extent** OR **degree** in geringerem Umfang.

lesson ['lesn] *n* - **1.** [class] (Unterrichts)stunde *die* - **2.** [example]: **to teach sb a lesson** jm eine Lektion erteilen.

let [let] *(pt & pp inv) vt* - **1.** [allow] lassen; **to let sb do sthg** jn etw tun lassen; **she let her hair grow** sie ließ sich *(D)* die Haare wachsen; **to let go of sthg** etw losllassen; **to let sb go** [release] jn losllassen; **to let o.s. go** [neglect] sich gehen lassen; **to let sb have sthg** [permanently] jm etw überlassen; **he wouldn't let me have the book** er wollte mir das Buch nicht geben; **to let sb know sthg** jn etw wissen lassen; **let me know as soon as possible** sagen Sie mir so bald wie möglich Bescheid - **2.** [in verb forms]: **let's go!** gehen wir!; **let me see** lass mich überlegen - **3.** [rent out] vermieten; **'to let'** 'zu vermieten'. ◆ **let alone** *conj* geschweige denn. ◆ **let down** *vt sep* - **1.** [person - disappoint] enttäuschen; [- not help] im Stich lassen - **2.** [let air out of]: **to let sb's tyres down** jm die Luft aus den Reifen lassen. ◆ **let in** *vt sep* hereinllassen; **to let o.s. in for sthg** sich auf etw *(A)* einllassen; **to let sb in on sthg** [secret, plan] jn in etw *(A)* einlweihen. ◆ **let off** *vt sep* - **1.** [excuse] davonkommen lassen - **2.** [from vehicle] aussteigen lassen - **3.** [cannon, missile] ablfeuern; [firework] losllassen. ◆ **let on** *vi*: **to let on about sthg** etw verraten. ◆ **let out** *vt sep* heraus-/hinausllassen; **let me out!** lass mich heraus!; **to let out a scream** einen Schrei auslstoßen. ◆ **let up** *vi* nachllassen.

letdown ['letdaʊn] *n inf* Enttäuschung *die*.

lethal ['liːθl] *adj* tödlich.

lethargic [lə'θɑːdʒɪk] *adj* träge, lethargisch.

let's [lets] *abbr of* **let us**.

letter ['letəʳ] *n* - **1.** [written message] Brief *der* - **2.** [of alphabet] Buchstabe *der*.

letter bomb *n* Briefbombe *die*.

letterbox ['letəbɒks] *n UK* Briefkasten *der*.

lettuce ['letɪs] *n* Kopfsalat *der*.

letup ['letʌp] *n* Pause *die*.

leuk(a)emia [luː'kiːmɪə] *n* Leukämie *die*.

level ['levl] *(UK) (US)* ◇ *adj* - **1.** [equal in height]: **to be level (with sthg)** (mit etw) auf gleicher Höhe sein - **2.** [equal in standard] ebenbürtig - **3.** [flat] waagerecht; [teaspoon] gestrichen. ◇ *n* - **1.** [amount - gen] Niveau *das*; [- of noise] Pegel *der*; [- of temperature] Höhe *die* - **2.** [of liquid] Stand *der* - **3.** [standard] Niveau *das* - **4.** *US* [spirit level] Wasserwaage *die* - **5.** [storey] Geschoss *das*; [of multistorey car park] Ebene *die* - **6.** *phr*: **to be on the level** *inf* ehrlich sein. ◇ *vt* - **1.** [make flat] ebnen - **2.** [demolish] dem Erdboden gleichlmachen. ◆ **level off, level out** *vi* - **1.** [unemployment, inflation] aufhören zu steigen - **2.** AERON [aircraft] ablfangen. ◆ **level with** *vt insep inf* ehrlich sein mit.

level crossing *n UK* ebener Bahnübergang.

level-headed [-'hedɪd] *adj* vernünftig.

lever [*UK* 'liːvəʳ, *US* 'levər] *n* [handle, bar] Hebel *der*.

leverage [*UK* 'liːvərɪdʒ, *US* 'levərɪdʒ] *n (U)* - **1.** *fig* [influence] Einfluss *der* - **2.** [principle] Hebelwirkung *die*; [force] Hebelkraft *die*.

levy ['levɪ] *(pl* **levies***)* ◇ *n*: **levy (on sthg)** Steuer *die* (auf etw *(A)*). ◇ *vt* erheben.

lewd [ljuːd] *adj* [joke, song] unanständig; [remark] anzüglich.

liability [,laɪə'bɪlətɪ] *n* - **1.** [hindrance] Belastung *die* - **2.** LAW [legal responsibility]: **liability (for sthg)** Haftung *die* (für etw). ◆ **liabilities** *npl* FIN Verbindlichkeiten *Pl*, Schulden *Pl*.

liable ['laɪəbl] *adj* - **1.** [likely]: **to be liable to do sthg** die Neigung haben, etw zu tun - **2.** [prone]: **to be liable to sthg** für etw anfällig OR empfänglich sein - **3.** LAW: **to be liable (for**

sthg) [debt, accident, damage] (für etw) verantwortlich sein; **to be liable to sthg** [fine, arrest, imprisonment] für etw haftbar sein.

liaise [lɪ'eɪz] *vi*: **to liaise with** Kontakt auf|nehmen mit; **to liaise between** als Verbindungsperson agieren zwischen *(+ D)*.

liar ['laɪəʳ] *n* Lügner *der*, -in *die*.

libel ['laɪbl] (*UK*) (*US*) ◇ *n* (schriftliche) Verleumdung. ◇ *vt* (schriftlich) verleumden.

liberal ['lɪbərəl] *adj* - **1.** [tolerant] liberal - **2.** [generous] großzügig. ◆ **Liberal** ◇ *adj* POL liberal. ◇ *n* POL Liberale *der, die*.

Liberal Democrat ◇ *adj* liberaldemokratisch. ◇ *n* Liberaldemokrat *der*, -in *die*.

liberate ['lɪbəreɪt] *vt* befreien.

liberation [,lɪbə'reɪʃn] *n* Befreiung *die*.

liberty ['lɪbətɪ] *n* Freiheit *die*; **at liberty** auf freiem Fuß; **you are at liberty to leave** es steht dir frei zu gehen; **to take liberties (with sb)** sich *(D)* (jm gegenüber) Freiheiten heraus|nehmen.

Libra ['liːbrə] *n* Waage *die*.

librarian [laɪ'breərɪən] *n* Bibliothekar *der*, -in *die*.

library ['laɪbrərɪ] *n* Bibliothek *die*.

library book *n* Leihbuch *das*.

libretto [lɪ'bretəʊ] (*pl* **-s**) *n* Libretto *das*.

Libya ['lɪbɪə] *n* Libyen *nt*.

lice [laɪs] *Pl* ▷ **louse**.

licence ['laɪsəns] ◇ *n* - **1.** [permit - for dog] Genehmigung *die*; [- for TV] Anmeldung *die*; [- for driver] Führerschein *der*; [- for marriage] Erlaubnis *die*, Lizenz *die*; [- for bar, pub] Konzession *die*; [- for pilot] Pilotenschein *der* - **2.** COMM Lizenz *die*. ◇ *vt US* = **license**.

license ['laɪsəns] ◇ *vt* COMM: **to license sb to do sthg** jm eine Lizenz erteilen, etw zu tun; **to license sthg** eine Lizenz OR Konzession für etw erteilen. ◇ *n US* = **licence**.

licensed ['laɪsənst] *adj* - **1.** [person]: **to be licensed to do sthg** die Genehmigung haben, etw zu tun - **2.** [object] zugelassen - **3.** *UK* [premises] mit Schankerlaubnis OR Schankkonzession.

license plate *n US* Nummernschild *das*.

lick [lɪk] *vt* [with tongue] lecken.

licorice ['lɪkərɪʃ, 'lɪkərɪs] *n* = **liquorice**.

lid [lɪd] *n* - **1.** [cover] Deckel *der* - **2.** [eyelid] Augenlid *das*.

lie [laɪ] ◇ *n* Lüge *die*; **to tell lies** lügen. ◇ *vi* - **1.** (*pt* **lied**, *pp* **lied**, *cont* **lying**) [tell lie] lügen; **to lie to sb** jn an|lügen; **to lie about sthg** über etw *(A)* nicht die Wahrheit sagen - **2.** (*pt* **lay**, *pp* **lain**, *cont* **lying**) [be horizontal, be situated] liegen; **to lie in wait for sb** jm auf|lauern; **to lie idle** [machine] still|stehen - **3.** (*pt* **lay**, *pp* **lain**, *cont* **lying**) [lie down] sich legen - **4.** (*pt* **lay**, *pp* **lain**, *cont* **lying**) [difficulty, answer, responsibility *etc*] liegen - **5.** (*pt* **lay**, *pp* **lain**, *cont* **lying**) *phr*: **to lie low** sich versteckt halten. ◆ **lie about, lie around** *vi* herum|liegen. ◆ **lie down** *vi* sich hin|legen. ◆ **lie in** *vi UK* im Bett bleiben.

lie-down *n UK* Nickerchen *das*; **to have a lie-down** sich (kurz) hin|legen.

lie-in *n UK*: **to have a lie-in** richtig aus|schlafen.

lieutenant [*UK* lef'tenənt, *US* luː'tenənt] *n* [in army] Oberleutnant *der*; [in navy] Kapitänleutnant *der*.

life [laɪf] (*pl* **lives**) *n* - **1.** [gen] Leben *das*; **to come to life** zum Leben erwachen; **that's life!** so ist das Leben!; **he was sent to prison for life** er wurde zu einer lebenslänglichen Haftstrafe verurteilt; **to scare the life out of sb** jn zu Tode erschrecken - **2.** *inf* [life imprisonment] lebenslängliche Freiheitsstrafe; **to get life** *inf* lebenslänglich kriegen.

life assurance *n* = **life insurance**.

life belt *n* Rettungsring *der*.

lifeboat ['laɪfbəʊt] *n* Rettungsboot *das*.

life buoy *n* Rettungsboje *die*.

life cycle *n* Lebenszyklus *der*.

life expectancy [-ɪk'spektənsɪ] *n* Lebenserwartung *die*.

lifeguard ['laɪfgɑːd] *n* Rettungsschwimmer *der*, -in *die*.

life insurance *n* Lebensversicherung *die*.

life jacket *n* Schwimmweste *die*.

lifeless ['laɪflɪs] *adj* leblos.

lifelike ['laɪflaɪk] *adj* lebensecht.

lifeline ['laɪflaɪn] *n* - **1.** [rope] Rettungsleine *die* - **2.** *fig* [with outside] Verbindung *die* mit der Außenwelt.

life preserver [-prɪ,zɜːvəʳ] *n US* - **1.** [belt] Rettungsring *der* - **2.** [jacket] Schwimmweste *die*, Rettungsweste *die*.

life raft *n* Rettungsfloß *das*.

lifesaver ['laɪf,seɪvəʳ] *n* Lebensretter *der*.

life sentence *n* lebenslange Freiheitsstrafe.

life-size(d) [-saɪz(d)] *adj* lebensgroß.

lifespan ['laɪfspæn] *n* - **1.** [of person, animal] Lebenserwartung *die* - **2.** [of product, machine] Lebensdauer *die*.

lifestyle ['laɪfstaɪl] *n* Lebensstil *der*.

lifetime ['laɪftaɪm] *n* Lebenszeit *die*.

lift [lɪft] ◇ *n* - **1.** [ride]: **to give sb a lift** jn (im Auto) mit|nehmen - **2.** *UK* [elevator] Fahrstuhl *der*. ◇ *vt* - **1.** [hand, arm, leg] heben - **2.** [object] hoch|heben - **3.** [ban, embargo] auf|heben - **4.** [plagiarize - idea] stehlen; [- writing] ab|schreiben - **5.** *inf* [steal] klauen. ◇ *vi* - **1.** [lid, top] sich heben - **2.** [mist, fog, clouds] sich lichten.

lift-off *n* Abheben *das*.

light [laɪt] (*pt & pp* **lit** OR **-ed**) ◇ *adj* - **1.** [gen] leicht - **2.** [pale, bright] hell; **light blue** hellblau. ◇ *n* - **1.** *(U)* [brightness] Licht *das* - **2.** [device -

lamp] Lampe *die*; [- on car] Scheinwerfer *der*; [- in street] Laterne *die*; **to put** *OR* **turn the light on** das Licht ein|schalten - **3.** [for cigarette, pipe] Feuer *das*; **to set light to sthg** etw an|zünden - **4.** [perspective]: **in the light of** *UK*, **in light of** *US* angesichts *(+ G)* - **5.** *phr*: **to come to light** ans Licht kommen. ◇ *vt* - **1.** [ignite] an|zünden - **2.** [illuminate] erleuchten. ◇ *adv*: **to travel light** mit wenig Gepäck reisen. ◆ **light up** ◇ *vt sep* - **1.** [sky, room, stage] erleuchten - **2.** [cigarette, cigar, pipe] an|zünden. ◇ *vi* - **1.** [face, eyes] auf|leuchten - **2.** *inf* [start smoking] sich *(D)* eine an|zünden.

light bulb *n* Glühbirne *die*.

lighten ['laɪtn] ◇ *vt* - **1.** [make brighter - gen] heller machen; [- hair] auf|hellen - **2.** [make less heavy - load] leichter machen; [- workload] erleichtern. ◇ *vi* [mood, atmosphere] lockerer *OR* entspannter werden.

lighter ['laɪtəʳ] *n* Feuerzeug *das*.

light-headed [-'hedɪd] *adj* schwindlig.

light-hearted [-'hɑːtɪd] *adj* - **1.** [cheerful] heiter, unbeschwert - **2.** [amusing] fröhlich.

lighthouse ['laɪthaʊs] (*pl* [-haʊzɪz]) *n* Leuchtturm *der*.

lighting ['laɪtɪŋ] *n* Beleuchtung *die*.

light meter *n* PHOT Belichtungsmesser *der*.

lightning ['laɪtnɪŋ] *n (U)* Blitz *der*.

lightweight ['laɪtweɪt] ◇ *adj* [object] leicht. ◇ *n* Leichtgewicht *das*; **political lightweights** Schmalspurpolitiker *Pl*.

likable ['laɪkəbl] *adj* sympathisch.

like [laɪk] ◇ *prep* wie; **like this/that** so; **what's it like?** wie ist es?; **to look like sb/sthg** jm/etw ähnlich sehen; **it looks like rain** es sieht nach Regen aus. ◇ *vt* mögen; **to like doing sthg** etw gern tun; **do you like it?** gefällt es dir?; **as you like** wie Sie wollen/wie du willst; **I don't like to bother her** ich will sie nicht stören; **I'd like to sit down** ich würde mich gern hinsetzen; **I'd like a drink** ich würde gern etwas trinken; **we'd like you to come for dinner** wir möchten Sie zum Essen einladen. ◇ *n*: **and the like** und dergleichen.

likeable ['laɪkəbl] *adj* = **likable**.

likelihood ['laɪklɪhʊd] *n* Wahrscheinlichkeit *die*.

likely ['laɪklɪ] *adj* - **1.** [probable] wahrscheinlich; **they're likely to win** sie werden wahrscheinlich gewinnen; **a likely story!** *iro* na klar! - **2.** [suitable] geeignet.

liken ['laɪkn] *vt*: **to liken sb/sthg to** jn/etw vergleichen mit.

likeness ['laɪknɪs] *n* - **1.** [resemblance]: **likeness (to sb/sthg)** Ähnlichkeit *die* (mit jm/etw) - **2.** [portrait] Bildnis *das*, Porträt *das*.

likewise ['laɪkwaɪz] *adv* gleichfalls, ebenfalls; **to do likewise** das Gleiche tun.

liking ['laɪkɪŋ] *n*: **liking for sb/sthg** Vorliebe *die* für jn/etw; **to have a liking for sb/sthg** für jn/etw eine Vorliebe haben; **that's not to my liking** das ist nicht nach meinem Geschmack.

lilac ['laɪlək] ◇ *adj* [colour] lila. ◇ *n* - **1.** [tree] Flieder *der* - **2.** [colour] Lila *das*.

Lilo® ['laɪləʊ] (*pl* **-s**) *n UK* Luftmatratze *die*.

lily ['lɪlɪ] *n* Lilie *die*.

limb [lɪm] *n* - **1.** [of body] Glied *das*; **limbs** Glieder *Pl*, Gliedmaßen *Pl* - **2.** [of tree] Ast *der*.

limber ['lɪmbəʳ] ◆ **limber up** *vi* sich auf|lockern, Lockerungsübungen machen.

limbo ['lɪmbəʊ] (*pl* **-s**) *n* [uncertain state]: **to be in limbo** in der Schwebe sein.

lime [laɪm] *n* - **1.** [fruit] Limone *die*; **lime juice** Limonensaft *der* - **2.** [linden tree] Linde *die*.

limelight ['laɪmlaɪt] *n*: **the limelight** das Rampenlicht.

limerick ['lɪmərɪk] *n* Limerick *der*.

limestone ['laɪmstəʊn] *n* Kalkstein *der*.

limit ['lɪmɪt] ◇ *n* - **1.** [restriction] Begrenzung *die* - **2.** [boundary, greatest extent] Grenze *die*; **'off limits'** *esp US* 'Zutritt verboten'; **that subject is off limits** das Thema ist tabu; **within limits** [to a certain extent] innerhalb bestimmter Grenzen. ◇ *vt* begrenzen.

limitation [ˌlɪmɪ'teɪʃn] *n* - **1.** [restriction, control] Begrenzung *die* - **2.** [shortcoming]: **limitations** Grenzen *Pl*.

limited ['lɪmɪtɪd] *adj* begrenzt.

limited company, limited liability company *n* Gesellschaft *die* mit beschränkter Haftung.

limousine ['lɪməziːn] *n* luxuriöse Limousine.

limp [lɪmp] ◇ *adj* schlaff; [lettuce, flowers] welk. ◇ *n* Hinken *das*; **to walk with a limp** hinken. ◇ *vi* hinken.

line [laɪn] ◇ *n* - **1.** [mark] Linie *die*; **to draw the line at sthg** *fig* bei etw den Schlussstrich ziehen - **2.** [row] Reihe *die* - **3.** [queue] Schlange *die*; **to stand** *OR* **wait in line** Schlange stehen *OR* an|stehen - **4.** [direction of movement] Gerade *die*; **he can't walk in a straight line** er kann nicht (mehr) geradeaus gehen - **5.** [alignment]: **in line (with)** in einer Linie (mit); **to step out of line** [misbehave] aus der Reihe tanzen - **6.** [RAIL - railway track] Gleise *Pl*; [- route] Bahnlinie *die*; **the line was blocked** die Strecke war blockiert - **7.** [of poem, song, text] Zeile *die* - **8.** [wrinkle] Falte *die* - **9.** [rope] Leine *die*; [wire] Kabel *das*; [string] Schnur *die* - **10.** TELEC [telephone connection] Leitung *die*; **hold the line** bleiben Sie am Apparat - **11.** *inf* [short letter] kurze Nachricht; **to drop sb a line** jm ein paar Zeilen schreiben - **12.** *inf* [field of activity] Branche *die* - **13.** MIL: **enemy lines** feindliche Linien - **14.** [limit, borderline] Grenze *die* - **15.** COMM [type of product] Modell *das*; [group of products] Kollektion *die*. ◇ *vt* [cover inside surface of - drawer] aus|schlagen; [- garment, curtains] füttern. ◆ **out of line** *adj* fehl am Platz. ◆ **line up** ◇ *vt sep* - **1.** [in rows] auf|stellen - **2.** *inf* [organize] arrangieren. ◇ *vi* - **1.** [in a row] sich auf|stellen - **2.** [in a queue] sich an|stellen.

lined [laɪnd] *adj* - **1.** [paper] liniert - **2.** [face] faltig.

linen ['lɪnɪn] *(U) n (U)* - **1.** [cloth] Leinen *das* - **2.** [tablecloths etc] Wäsche *die*.

liner ['laɪnəʳ] *n* [ship] Linienschiff *das*.

linesman ['laɪnzmən] (*pl* **-men** [-mən]) *n* SPORT Linienrichter *der*.

linger ['lɪŋgəʳ] *vi* - **1.** [dawdle]: **we lingered over our meal** wir aßen in aller Gemütlichkeit; **she lingered behind after school** sie blieb nach Schulschluss noch da - **2.** [persist] zurück|bleiben.

lingo ['lɪŋgəʊ] (*pl* **-es**) *n inf* - **1.** [language] Sprache *die* - **2.** [specialist jargon] (Fach)jargon *der*.

linguist ['lɪŋgwɪst] *n* - **1.** [person good at languages] Sprachkundige *der, die* - **2.** [student or teacher of linguistics] Linguist *der*, -in *die*.

lining ['laɪnɪŋ] *n* - **1.** [of garment, curtains, box] Futter *das* - **2.** [of stomach, nose] Schleimhaut *die* - **3.** *(U)* AUT [of brakes] Belag *der*.

link [lɪŋk] ◇ *n* - **1.** [of chain] Glied *das* - **2.** [connection]: **link (between/with)** Verbindung *die* (zwischen *(+ D)*/mit OR zu). ◇ *vt* verbinden; **to link arms with sb** sich bei jm unterhaken. ◆ **link up** *vt sep* verbinden; *(phrase)*: **to link sthg up with sthg** etw mit etw verbinden.

lino ['laɪnəʊ], **linoleum** [lɪ'nəʊlɪəm] *n* Linoleum *das*.

lion ['laɪən] *n* Löwe *der*.

lip [lɪp] *n* - **1.** [of mouth] Lippe *die* - **2.** [of container] Rand *der*.

lip-read *vi* von den Lippen lesen.

lip salve [-sælv] *n UK* Lippenbalsam *der*.

lip service *n*: **to pay lip service to sthg** ein Lippenbekenntnis zu etw ab|legen.

lipstick ['lɪpstɪk] *n* Lippenstift *der*.

liqueur [lɪ'kjʊəʳ] *n* Likör *der*.

liquid ['lɪkwɪd] ◇ *adj* flüssig. ◇ *n* Flüssigkeit *die*.

liquidation [,lɪkwɪ'deɪʃn] *n* Liquidation *die*.

liquidize, -ise ['lɪkwɪdaɪz] *vt UK* CULIN mit dem Mixer pürieren.

liquidizer, -iser ['lɪkwɪdaɪzəʳ] *n UK* (elektrischer) Mixer.

liquor ['lɪkəʳ] *n esp US* [alcoholic drink] Alkohol *der*; [spirits] Spirituosen *Pl*.

liquorice ['lɪkərɪʃ, 'lɪkərɪs] *n* Lakritze *die*.

liquor store *n US* Wein- und Spirituosenhandlung *die*.

Lisbon ['lɪzbən] *n* Lissabon *nt*.

lisp [lɪsp] ◇ *n* Lispeln *das*. ◇ *vi* lispeln.

list [lɪst] ◇ *n* Liste *die*. ◇ *vt* - **1.** [in writing] auf|listen - **2.** [in speech] auf|führen.

listed building [,lɪstɪd-] *n UK unter Denkmalschutz stehendes Gebäude*.

listen ['lɪsn] *vi* - **1.** [give attention] zulhören; **to listen to sb/sthg** jm/etw zulhören; **to listen for sthg** auf etw *(A)* horchen - **2.** [heed advice] hören; **to listen to sb/sthg** auf jn/etw hören.

listener ['lɪsnəʳ] *n* Zuhörer *der*, -in *die*; [of radio] Hörer *der*, -in *die*.

listless ['lɪstlɪs] *adj* apathisch.

lit [lɪt] *pt* & *pp* ▷ **light**.

liter *n US* = **litre**.

literacy ['lɪtərəsɪ] *n (U)* Lese- und Schreibfähigkeit *die*.

literal ['lɪtərəl] *adj* wörtlich.

literally ['lɪtərəlɪ] *adv* - **1.** [for emphasis] im wahrsten Sinne des Wortes, buchstäblich - **2.** [not figuratively] wörtlich.

literary ['lɪtərərɪ] *adj* literarisch; **a literary critic** ein Literaturkritiker.

literate ['lɪtərət] *adj* - **1.** [able to read and write] des Lesens und Schreibens kundig - **2.** [well-read] gebildet.

literature ['lɪtrətʃəʳ] *n* - **1.** [novels, plays, poetry] Literatur *die* - **2.** [printed information] Informationsmaterial *das*.

lithe [laɪð] *adj* geschmeidig.

Lithuania [,lɪθjʊ'eɪnɪə] *n* Litauen *nt*.

litigation [,lɪtɪ'geɪʃn] *n (U) fml* Prozess *der*.

litre *UK*, **liter** *US* ['liːtəʳ] *n* Liter *der*.

litter ['lɪtəʳ] ◇ *n* - **1.** [waste material] Abfall *der* - **2.** [newborn animals] Wurf *der* - **3.** [for litter tray]: **(cat) litter** (Katzen)streu *die*. ◇ *vt*: **to be littered with sthg** mit etw übersät sein.

litterbin ['lɪtə,bɪn] *n UK* Mülleimer *der*.

little ['lɪtl] ◇ *adj* - **1.** [small, younger] klein; **the little ones** die Kleinen *Pl* - **2.** [in distance, time] kurz - **3.** (*comp* **less**, *superl* **least**) [not much] wenig; **he speaks little English** er spricht wenig Englisch; **he speaks a little English** er spricht ein bisschen Englisch. ◇ *pron* wenig; **a little** ein bisschen. ◇ *adv* wenig; **little by little** nach und nach; **as little as possible** so wenig wie möglich.

little finger *n* kleiner Finger.

live[1] [lɪv] ◇ *vi* - **1.** [have home] wohnen - **2.** [be alive] leben; **to live to a great age** ein hohes Alter erreichen - **3.** [survive] überleben. ◇ *vt* führen; **to live a happy life** ein glückliches Leben führen; **to live it up** *inf* in Saus und Braus leben. ◆ **live down** *vt sep*: **she'll never live this down** das wird ihr auf ewig anhängen. ◆ **live off** *vt insep* [savings, land] leben von. ◆ **live on** ◇ *vt insep* [savings] leben von; [food] sich ernähren von; **I have enough to live on** ich habe genug zum Leben. ◇ *vi* [continue] weiter|leben. ◆ **live together** *vi* zusammen|wohnen. ◆ **live up to** *vt insep* [reputation] gerecht werden *(+ D)*; [expectations] entsprechen *(+ D)*. ◆ **live with** *vt insep* - **1.** [in same house] zusammen|wohnen mit - **2.** *inf* [problem, situation] sich ab|finden mit.

live[2] [laɪv] *adj* - **1.** [alive] lebendig - **2.** [programme, performance] Live-; ELEC [wire] geladen - **3.** [ammunition] scharf.

livelihood ['laɪvlɪhʊd] *n* Lebensunterhalt *der*.

lively ['laɪvlɪ] *adj* lebhaft.

liven ['laɪvn] ◆ **liven up** ◇ *vt sep* beleben. ◇ *vi* [person] auf|leben.

liver ['lɪvəʳ] *n* Leber *die*.

lives [laɪvz] *Pl* ▻ **life**.

livestock ['laɪvstɒk] *n* Nutzvieh *das*.

livid ['lɪvɪd] *adj inf* [angry] wütend.

living ['lɪvɪŋ] ◇ *adj* - **1.** [person] lebend - **2.** [language] lebendig. ◇ *n* - **1.** [means of earning money] Lebensunterhalt *der*; **what do you do for a living?** was machen Sie beruflich? - **2.** [lifestyle] Leben *das*.

living conditions *npl* Lebensbedingungen *Pl*.

living room *n* Wohnzimmer *das*.

living standards *npl* Lebensstandard *der*.

living wage *n zum Leben ausreichender Lohn*.

lizard ['lɪzəd] *n* Eidechse *die*.

llama ['lɑːmə] (*pl inv* OR **-s**) *n* Lama *das*.

load [ləʊd] ◇ *n* - **1.** [something carried] Ladung *die* - **2.** [large amount]: **loads of, a load of** *inf* eine Menge; **what a load of rubbish!** *inf* was für ein Blödsinn! ◇ *vt* - **1.** [container, vehicle] beladen; **to load sthg with sthg** etw mit etw beladen - **2.** [gun, cannon]: **to load sthg (with sthg)** etw (mit etw) laden - **3.** [camera]: **to load a camera with a film** einen Film in eine Kamera ein|legen - **4.** COMPUT [program] laden. ◆ **load up** ◇ *vt sep* beladen. ◇ *vi* auf|laden.

loaded ['ləʊdɪd] *adj* - **1.** [question, statement] gewichtig - **2.** [gun] geladen; [camera] mit eingelegtem Film - **3.** *inf* [rich] stinkreich.

loaf [ləʊf] (*pl* **loaves**) *n* Laib *der*.

loan [ləʊn] ◇ *n* - **1.** [money lent] Darlehen *das*, Kredit *der* - **2.** [act of lending] Ausleihen *das*; **on loan** ausgeliehen. ◇ *vt*: **to loan sthg (to sb), to loan (sb) sthg** etw (an jn) verleihen.

loath [ləʊθ] *adj*: **to be loath to do sthg** etw nur ungern tun.

loathe [ləʊð] *vt* verabscheuen; **to loathe doing sthg** es verabscheuen, etw zu tun.

loaves [ləʊvz] *Pl* ▻ **loaf**.

lob [lɒb] ◇ *n* TENNIS Lob *der*. ◇ *vt* - **1.** [throw] (in hohem Bogen) werfen - **2.** TENNIS lobben.

lobby ['lɒbɪ] ◇ *n* - **1.** [anteroom] Vorraum *der*; [in hotel] Empfangshalle *die*; [in theatre] Foyer *das* - **2.** [pressure group] Lobby *die*. ◇ *vt* Einfluss nehmen auf *(+ A)*.

lobe [ləʊb] *n* [of ear] Ohrläppchen *das*.

lobster ['lɒbstəʳ] *n* Hummer *der*.

local ['ləʊkl] ◇ *adj* - **1.** [of the immediate area - tradition] örtlich; [- phone call] Orts-; [- hospital, shop, inhabitants] örtlich - **2.** ADMIN & POL [services, council] Kommunal-. ◇ *n inf* - **1.** [person]: **the locals** die Einheimischen *Pl* - **2.** *UK* [pub] Stammkneipe *die*.

local authority *n UK* Kommunalverwaltung *die*.

local call *n* Ortsgespräch *das*.

local government *n* Kommunalverwaltung *die*.

locality [ləʊ'kælətɪ] *n* Gegend *die*.

localized, -ised ['ləʊkəlaɪzd] *adj* örtlich begrenzt.

locally ['ləʊkəlɪ] *adv* [in region] am Ort; [in neighbourhood] in der Nachbarschaft.

locate [*UK* ləʊ'keɪt, *US* 'ləʊkeɪt] *vt* - **1.** [find] ausfindig machen, lokalisieren - **2.** [situate]: **to be located** sich befinden.

location [ləʊ'keɪʃn] *n* - **1.** [place] Ort *der* - **2.** CIN: **the film was shot on location in China** die Außenaufnahmen zu diesem Film wurden in China gemacht.

loch [lɒk, lɒx] *n Scotland* See *der*.

lock [lɒk] ◇ *n* - **1.** [of door, window, box] Schloss *das* - **2.** [on canal] Schleuse *die* - **3.** AUT [steering lock] Einschlag *der* - **4.** [of hair] Locke *die*. ◇ *vt* - **1.** [fasten securely] ab|schließen; [bicycle] an|schließen - **2.** [keep safely]: **to lock sthg in sthg** etw in etw *(A)* ein|schließen - **3.** [immobilize] sperren. ◇ *vi* - **1.** [fasten securely] verschließen - **2.** [become immobilized] blockieren. ◆ **lock away** *vt sep* weg|schließen. ◆ **lock in** *vt sep* ein|schließen. ◆ **lock out** *vt sep* aus|sperren. ◆ **lock up** *vt sep* - **1.** [person] ein|sperren - **2.** [house] ab|schließen - **3.** [valuables] weg|schließen.

locker ['lɒkəʳ] *n* [at gym, work] Spind *der*; [at station] Schließfach *das*.

locker room *n US* Umkleideraum *der*.

locket ['lɒkɪt] *n* Medaillon *das*.

locomotive [ˌləʊkə'məʊtɪv] *n* Lokomotive *die*.

locust ['ləʊkəst] *n* Heuschrecke *die*.

lodge [lɒdʒ] ◇ *n* - **1.** [caretaker's room, of Freemasons] Loge *die* - **2.** [of manor house] Pförtnerhaus *das* - **3.** [for hunting] Jagdhütte *die*. ◇ *vi* - **1.** [stay, live]: **to lodge with sb** bei jm (zur Untermiete) wohnen - **2.** [become stuck] stecken|bleiben - **3.** *fig* [in mind] sich fest|setzen. ◇ *vt fml* [register] ein|reichen.

lodger ['lɒdʒəʳ] *n* Untermieter *der*, -in *die*.

lodging ['lɒdʒɪŋ] *n* ⊳ **board**. ◆ **lodgings** *npl* möblierte Zimmer *Pl*.

loft [lɒft] *n* Dachboden *der*.

lofty ['lɒftɪ] *adj* - **1.** [noble] hoch; [feelings] erhaben; [aims] hoch gesteckt - **2.** *pej* [haughty] hochmütig - **3.** *liter* [high] hoch.

log [lɒg] ◇ *n* - **1.** [of wood] Holzscheit *das* - **2.** [written record - of ship] Logbuch *das*; [- of plane] Bordbuch *das*. ◇ *vt* - **1.** [information - on paper] ein|tragen; [- in computer] ein|geben - **2.** [speed, distance, time] zurück|legen. ◆ **log in** *vi* COMPUT (sich) ein|loggen. ◆ **log out** *vi* COMPUT (sich) aus|loggen.

logbook ['lɒgbʊk] *n* [of car] Fahrtenbuch *das*.

loggerheads ['lɒgəhedz] *n*: **to be at loggerheads** sich *(D)* in den Haaren liegen.

logic ['lɒdʒɪk] *n* Logik *die*.

logical ['lɒdʒɪkl] *adj* logisch.

logistics [lə'dʒɪstɪks] *n (U)* Logistik *die*.

logo ['ləʊgəʊ] (*pl* **-s**) *n* Logo *das*.

loin [lɔɪn] *n* Lende *die*.

loiter ['lɔɪtəʳ] *vi* - **1.** [hang about] herum|lungern - **2.** [dawdle] trödeln, bummeln.

loll [lɒl] *vi* [sit, lie about] (sich) lümmeln, herum|lümmeln.

lollipop ['lɒlɪpɒp] *n* Lutscher *der*, Lolli *der*.

lollipop lady *n UK meist ältere Dame in der Funktion eines Schülerlotsen.*

lollipop man *n UK meist älterer Herr in der Funktion eines Schülerlotsen.*

lolly ['lɒlɪ] *n* [lollipop] Lutscher *der*, Lolli *der*.

London ['lʌndən] *n* London *nt*.

Londoner ['lʌndənəʳ] *n* Londoner *der*, -in *die*.

lone [ləʊn] *adj* [lonely] einsam; [only] einzig.

loneliness ['ləʊnlɪnɪs] *n* Einsamkeit *die*.

lonely ['ləʊnlɪ] *adj* einsam.

loner ['ləʊnəʳ] *n* Einzelgänger *der*, -in *die*.

lonesome ['ləʊnsəm] *adj US inf* einsam.

long [lɒŋ] ◇ *adj* lang; **it's 2 metres long** es ist 2 Meter lang; **it's two hours long** es dauert zwei Stunden; **the book is 500 pages long** das Buch hat 500 Seiten; **how long is it?** [in distance] wie lang ist es?; [in time] wie lange dauert es?; **a long time** lange. ◇ *adv* lange; **I won't be long** ich komme gleich wieder; **how long will it take?** wie lange dauert es?; **all day long** den ganzen Tag; **before long** bald; **no longer** nicht mehr; **so long!** *inf* tschüs! ◇ *vt*: **to long to do sthg** sich danach sehnen, etw zu tun. ◆ **as long as, so long as** *conj* [if] solange. ◆ **long for** *vt insep* sich sehnen nach.

long-distance *adj*: **a long-distance race** ein Langstreckenrennen; **he's a long-distance lorry driver** er ist Fernfahrer.

long-distance call *n* Ferngespräch *das*.

longhand ['lɒŋhænd] *n* Langschrift *die*.

long-haul *adj*: **long-haul flight** Langstreckenflug *der*.

longing ['lɒŋɪŋ] ◇ *adj* sehnsüchtig. ◇ *n*: **longing (for sthg)** Sehnsucht *die* (nach etw).

longitude ['lɒndʒɪtjuːd] *n* GEOG (geografische) Länge.

long jump *n* Weitsprung *der*.

long-life *adj* [battery] mit langer Lebensdauer; **long-life milk** H-Milch *die*.

long-range *adj* - **1.** [missile, bomber] Langstrecken- - **2.** [plan, forecast] langfristig.

long shot *n fig*: **it's a long shot, but it might work** es ist ein gewagtes Unternehmen, aber es könnte klappen.

longsighted [ˌlɒŋ'saɪtɪd] *adj* weitsichtig.

long-standing *adj* (schon) lange bestehend.

longsuffering [ˌlɒŋ'sʌfərɪŋ] *adj* geduldig.

long term *n*: **in the long term** auf lange Sicht.

long wave *n* Langwelle *die*.

longwinded [ˌlɒŋ'wɪndɪd] *adj* langatmig.

loo [luː] (*pl* **-s**) *n UK inf* Klo *das*.

look [lʊk] ◇ *n* - **1.** [with eyes] Blick *der*; **to give sb a look** jm einen Blick zu|werfen; **to have a look at sthg** sich *(D)* etw an|sehen; **let me have a look!** lass mich mal sehen! - **2.** [search]: **to have a look (for sthg)** (etw) suchen - **3.** [appearance] Aussehen *das*; **by the look** OR **looks of it** allem Anschein nach. ◇ *vi* - **1.** [with eyes] sehen; **to look at sb/sthg** jn/etw an|sehen; **I'm just looking** [in shop] ich wollte mich nur umsehen - **2.** [search] suchen - **3.** [building, room]: **to look onto** gehen auf *(+ A)* - **4.** [seem] aus|sehen; **he looks as if he hasn't slept** er sieht aus, als hätte er nicht geschlafen; **it looks like rain** es sieht nach Regen aus; **she looks like her mother** sie sieht ihrer Mutter ähnlich. ◆ **looks** *npl*: **(good) looks** gutes Aussehen. ◆ **look after** *vt insep* [take care of] sich kümmern um. ◆ **look at** *vt insep* ansehen; **he looked at his watch** er sah OR schaute auf seine Uhr. ◆ **look down on** *vt insep* [condescend to] herab|sehen auf *(+ A)*. ◆ **look for** *vt insep* suchen. ◆ **look forward to** *vt insep* sich freuen auf *(+ A)*. ◆ **look into** *vt insep* [examine] untersuchen. ◆ **look on** *vi* [watch] zu|sehen. ◆ **look out** *vi* auf|passen; **look out!** Vorsicht! ◆ **look out for** *vt insep* [person, place] Ausschau halten nach; [opportunity] suchen nach. ◆ **look round** ◇ *vt insep* [city, museum] besichtigen; **to look round the shops** einen Einkaufsbummel machen. ◇ *vi* - **1.** [look at surroundings] sich um|sehen - **2.** [turn] sich um|drehen. ◆ **look to** *vt insep* - **1.** [depend on] sich verlassen auf *(+ A)*; **they looked to her**

for help sie verließen sich darauf, dass sie ihnen helfen würde - **2.** [think about] planen. ◆ **look up** ◇ *vt sep* - **1.** [in dictionary] nachl-schlagen; [in phone book] herauslsuchen - **2.** [visit]: **to look sb up** jn auflsuchen. ◇ *vi* sich bessern. ◆ **look up to** *vt insep* [admire]: **to look up to sb** zu jm auflsehen.

lookout ['lʊkaʊt] *n* - **1.** [place] Ausguck *der* - **2.** [person] Wachposten *der* - **3.** [search]: **to be on the lookout for sthg** nach etw Ausschau halten.

loom [luːm] *vi* - **1.** [rise up] (plötzlich) aufl-tauchen - **2.** *fig* [be imminent - date] bevorl-stehen; [- threat, difficulties] sich ablzeichnen.

loony ['luːnɪ] *inf* ◇ *adj* bekloppt, verrückt. ◇ *n* Bekloppte *der, die*, Verrückte *der, die*.

loop [luːp] *n* - **1.** [shape] Schleife *die*, Schlinge *die* - **2.** [contraceptive] Spirale *die*.

loophole ['luːphəʊl] *n fig* Schlupfloch *das*.

loose [luːs] *adj* - **1.** [not firmly fixed - joint, tooth, handle] lose, locker - **2.** [unpackaged - sweets, nails, paper] lose - **3.** [not tight-fitting - clothes, fit] locker sitzend, leger - **4.** [animal - free, not restrained] frei laufend; [- which has escaped] entlaufen; [hair] offen - **5.** [translation, definition] frei.

loose change *n* Kleingeld *das*.

loose end *n*: **to be at a loose end** *UK*, **to be at loose ends** *US* nichts zu tun haben.

loosely ['luːslɪ] *adv* - **1.** [hold, connect, tie] locker - **2.** [translate, define] frei.

loosen ['luːsn] *vt* lockern. ◆ **loosen up** *vi* - **1.** [before game, race] sich auflwärmen - **2.** *inf* [relax] sich entspannen.

loot [luːt] ◇ *n* Beute *die*. ◇ *vt* ausl-plündern, auslrauben.

looting ['luːtɪŋ] *n* Plündern *das*.

lop [lɒp] *vt* stutzen, beschneiden. ◆ **lop off** *vt sep* ablschneiden.

lop-sided [-'saɪdɪd] *adj* [uneven] schief.

lord [lɔːd] *n UK* Lord *der*. ◆ **Lord** *n* - **1.** RELIG: **the Lord** [God] der Herr; **good Lord!** *UK* Grundgütiger!, oh mein Gott! - **2.** [in titles] Lord *der*. ◆ **Lords** *npl UK* POL: **the (House of) Lords** das Oberhaus.

lorry ['lɒrɪ] *n UK* Lastkraftwagen *der*.

lorry driver *n UK* Lastkraftwagenfahrer *der*.

lose [luːz] (*pt & pp* **lost**) ◇ *vt* - **1.** [gen] verlieren; **to lose sight of sb/sthg** jn/etw aus den Augen verlieren; **to lose one's way** sich verirren - **2.** [waste - time] verschwenden; [- opportunity] versäumen - **3.** [subj: clock, watch] nachlgehen - **4.** [pursuers] ablschütteln. ◇ *vi* verlieren. ◆ **lose out** *vi*: **to lose out (on sthg)** (bei etw) den Kürzeren ziehen.

loser ['luːzəʳ] *n* - **1.** [of competition] Verlierer *der*, -in *die* - **2.** *pej* [unsuccessful person] Loser *der*.

loss [lɒs] *n* - **1.** [gen] Verlust *der*; **to make a loss** Verlust machen - **2.** [of match, competition] Niederlage *die* - **3.** *phr*: **I'm at a loss to explain it** ich weiß nicht, wie ich es erklären soll; **he was at a loss for words** ihm fehlten die Worte.

lost [lɒst] ◇ *pt & pp* ▷ **lose**. ◇ *adj* - **1.** [unable to find way] verirrt; **to get lost** sich verirren, sich verlieren; **get lost!** *inf* verschwinde!, hau ab! - **2.** [keys, wallet] verloren.

lost-and-found office *n US* Fundbüro *das*.

lost property office *n UK* Fundbüro *das*.

lot [lɒt] *n* - **1.** [large amount]: **a lot of, lots of** eine Menge - **2.** *inf* [group of things]: **put this lot in my office** bring das hier in mein Büro - **3.** [destiny] Los *das* - **4.** [at auction] Posten *der* - **5.** [entire amount]: **the lot** alles, das Ganze - **6.** *US* [of land] Parzelle *die*; [car park] Stellfläche *die*, Parkplatz *der* - **7.** *phr*: **to draw lots** losen. ◆ **a lot** *adv* (sehr) viel.

lotion ['ləʊʃn] *n* Lotion *die*.

lottery ['lɒtərɪ] *n* - **1.** [raffle] Lotterie *die* - **2.** [risky venture] Glücksspiel *das*.

loud [laʊd] ◇ *adj* - **1.** [not quiet, noisy] laut - **2.** [garish] grell. ◇ *adv* laut; **out loud** laut.

loudhailer [ˌlaʊd'heɪləʳ] *n UK* Megafon *das*.

loudly ['laʊdlɪ] *adv* [noisily] laut.

loudspeaker [ˌlaʊd'spiːkəʳ] *n* Lautsprecher *der*.

lounge [laʊndʒ] ◇ *n* - **1.** [in house] Wohnzimmer *das* - **2.** [in airport, hotel] Lounge *die* - **3.** *UK* = **lounge bar**. ◇ *vi* sich lümmeln.

lounge bar *n UK abgetrennter, meist gemütlicherer Teil eines Pubs, in dem die Getränke teurer sind.*

louse [laʊs] *n* - **1.** (*pl* **lice**) [insect] Laus *die* - **2.** (*pl* **-s**) *fig* [person] Laus *die*.

lousy ['laʊzɪ] *adj inf* [poor-quality] lausig.

lout [laʊt] *n* Flegel *der*, Lümmel *der*.

lovable ['lʌvəbl] *adj* liebenswert.

love [lʌv] ◇ *n* - **1.** [gen] Liebe *die*; **a love of** OR **for sthg** eine Liebe zu OR für etw; **give her my love** grüße sie herzlich von mir; **love from** [at end of letter] alles Liebe von; **to be in love** verliebt sein; **to fall in love (with sb)** sich (in jn) verlieben; **to make love** miteinander schlafen - **2.** *inf* [term of address] Schatz *der* - **3.** TENNIS Null. ◇ *vt* lieben; **to love to do sthg** OR **doing sthg** etw sehr OR wahnsinnig gern tun.

love affair *n* Affaire *die*.

love life *n* Liebesleben *das*.

lovely ['lʌvlɪ] *adj* - **1.** [in looks - child] reizend; [- person] sehr hübsch; [in character] reizend - **2.** [good, nice] wunderschön; **it was lovely to meet you** es war sehr nett, Sie kennen zu lernen.

lover ['lʌvəʳ] *n* - **1.** [sexual partner] Geliebte *der, die* - **2.** [enthusiast]: **a lover of** ein Liebhaber, eine Liebhaberin (+ *G*).

loving ['lʌvɪŋ] *adj* liebevoll.

low [ləʊ] ◇ *adj* - **1.** [gen] niedrig; **to keep a low profile** sich unauffällig benehmen

- 2. [standard, quality, opinion] schlecht - 3. [level, sound, note, neckline] tief - 4. [light, heat] schwach - 5. [supplies] knapp - 6. [voice] leise - 7. [depressed] niedergeschlagen. <> *adv* [fly, bend, sink] tief. <> *n* - 1. [low point] Tiefstand *der* - 2. [area of low pressure] Tief *das*.

low-calorie *adj* kalorienarm.

low-cut *adj* tief ausgeschnitten.

lower ['laʊəʳ] *vi* - 1. [sky] dunkel sein - 2. [frown]: **to lower at sb** jn finster an|blicken.

low-fat *adj* fettarm.

low-key *adj* [negotiations] informell; [approach] zurückhaltend.

low-lying *adj* tief gelegen.

loyal ['lɔɪəl] *adj*: **to be loyal to sb** [friend, supporter] jm treu sein; [king, boss] gegenüber jm loyal sein.

loyalty ['lɔɪəltɪ] *n* [of friend, supporter] Treue *die*; [to government] Loyalität *die*.

lozenge ['lɒzɪndʒ] *n* [tablet] Pastille *die*.

LP (*abbr of* **long-playing record**) *n* LP *die*.

L-plate *n UK Schild mit einem L, welches anzeigt, das der Fahrer des Wagens Fahrschüler ist.*

Ltd, ltd (*abbr of* **limited**) GmbH.

lubricant ['luːbrɪkənt] *n* Schmiermittel *das*.

lubricate ['luːbrɪkeɪt] *vt* schmieren.

luck [lʌk] *n*: **(good)luck** Glück *das*; **good luck!** viel Glück!; **bad luck** Pech *das*; **bad luck!, hard luck!** so ein Pech!; **to be in luck** Glück haben; **with (any) luck** mit (ein bisschen) Glück.

luckily ['lʌkɪlɪ] *adv* glücklicherweise.

lucky ['lʌkɪ] *adj* - 1. [fortunate] glücklich; **to be lucky** Glück haben; **it was a lucky guess** das war gut geraten - 2. [bringing good luck] Glück bringend; [number] Glücks-.

lucrative ['luːkrətɪv] *adj* lukrativ.

ludicrous ['luːdɪkrəs] *adj* lächerlich.

lug [lʌg] *vt inf* schleppen.

luggage ['lʌgɪdʒ] *n UK* Gepäck *das*.

luggage rack *n UK* [in train] Gepäckablage *die*; [on car] Dachgepäckträger *der*.

lukewarm ['luːkwɔːm] *adj* - 1. [tepid] lauwarm - 2. [unenthusiastic] lau.

lull [lʌl] <> *n* Pause *die*; **a lull in the fighting** eine Kampfpause. <> *vt* - 1. [make sleepy]: **to lull sb to sleep** jn in den Schlaf lullen - 2. [reassure]: **to lull sb into a false sense of security** jn in Sicherheit wiegen.

lullaby ['lʌləbaɪ] *n* Schlaflied *das*.

lumber ['lʌmbəʳ] *n (U)* - 1. *US* [timber] Bauholz *das* - 2. *UK* [bric-a-brac] Gerümpel *das*. ◆ **lumber with** *vt sep UK inf*: **to lumber sb with sthg** jm etw auf|halsen.

lumberjack ['lʌmbədʒæk] *n* Holzfäller *der*.

luminous ['luːmɪnəs] *adj* [armband] leuchtend; [dial, paint] Leucht-.

lump [lʌmp] <> *n* - 1. [piece - of earth, in sauce] Klumpen *der*; [- of coal, cheese] Stück *das* - 2. [MED - bump] Beule *die*; [- tumour] Knoten *der* - 3. [of sugar] Stück *das*. <> *vt*: **to lump together** [not differentiate between] in einen Topf werfen; **you'll just have to lump it** *inf* du musst dich damit abfinden.

lump sum *n* Pauschalbetrag *der*.

lunacy ['luːnəsɪ] *n* Wahnsinn *der*.

lunar ['luːnəʳ] *adj* Mond-.

lunatic ['luːnətɪk] *pej* <> *adj* wahnwitzig. <> *n* Wahnsinnige *der, die*, Irre *der, die*.

lunch [lʌntʃ] <> *n* Mittagessen *das*; **to have lunch** zu Mittag essen. <> *vi* zu Mittag essen.

luncheon meat *n Frühstücksfleisch.*

luncheon voucher *n UK* Essensbon *der*.

lunch hour *n* Mittagspause *die*.

lunchtime ['lʌntʃtaɪm] *n* Mittagszeit *die*.

lung [lʌŋ] *n* Lunge *die*.

lunge [lʌndʒ] *vi*: **to lunge forward** nach vorn springen; **to lunge at sb** sich auf jn stürzen.

lurch [lɜːtʃ] <> *n*: **to leave sb in the lurch** jn im Stich lassen. <> *vi* [person] taumeln; [drunkard] torkeln; [ship] schlingern; [car] sich ruckartig bewegen.

lure [ljʊəʳ] <> *n* [attraction] Reiz *der*. <> *vt* [tempt] locken.

lurid ['ljʊərɪd] *adj* - 1. [brightly coloured] grell; [clothes] in grellen Farben - 2. [sensational] reißerisch.

lurk [lɜːk] *vi* [person, danger] lauern.

luscious ['lʌʃəs] *adj* [fruit] saftig.

lush [lʌʃ] *adj* - 1. [grass] saftig; [vegetation] üppig - 2. *inf* [decorations] üppig.

lust [lʌst] *n* - 1. *(U)* [sexual desire] (sexuelle) Begierde - 2. [greed]: **lust for sthg** Gier *die* nach etw. ◆ **lust after, lust for** *vt insep* - 1. [money, power] gieren nach - 2. [person] begehren.

Luxembourg ['lʌksəmbɜːg] *n* Luxemburg *nt*.

luxurious [lʌg'ʒʊərɪəs] *adj* - 1. [expensive] luxuriös - 2. [voluptuous] üppig.

luxury ['lʌkʃərɪ] <> *n* Luxus *der*; [expensive item] Luxusartikel *der*. <> *comp* Luxus-.

LW (*abbr of* **long wave**) LW.

Lycra® ['laɪkrə] <> *n (U)* Lycra® *das*. <> *comp* aus Lycra®.

lying ['laɪɪŋ] <> *adj* lügnerisch, verlogen. <> *n* [dishonesty] Lügen *das*.

lynch [lɪntʃ] *vt* lynchen.

lyric ['lɪrɪk] *adj*: **lyric poetry** Lyrik *die*. ◆ **lyrics** *npl* [of song] Text *der*.

lyrical ['lɪrɪkl] *adj* - 1. [poetic] lyrisch - 2. [enthusiastic]: **to wax lyrical about sthg** von etw schwärmen.

m[1] (*pl* **m's** *OR* **ms**), **M** (*pl* **M's** *OR* **Ms**) [em] *n* [letter] m *das*, M *das*. ◆ **M** *UK abbr of* **motorway**.

m[2] *abbr of* **metre**, **million**, **mile**.

MA *n abbr of* **Master of Arts**.

mac [mæk] *n UK inf abbr of* **mackintosh**.

macaroni [ˌmækəˈrəʊnɪ] *n (U)* Makkaroni *Pl*.

machine [məˈʃiːn] *n* - **1.** [device] Maschine *die* - **2.** [organization] Apparat *der*.

machine gun [məˈʃiːngʌn] *n* Maschinengewehr *das*.

machinery [məˈʃiːnərɪ] *n (U)* - **1.** [machines] Maschinen *Pl* - **2.** *fig* [system] Maschinerie *die*.

macho [ˈmætʃəʊ] *adj inf* machohaft.

mackerel [ˈmækrəl] (*pl inv OR* **-s**) *n* Makrele *die*.

mackintosh [ˈmækɪntɒʃ] *n UK* Regenmantel *der*.

mad [mæd] *adj* - **1.** [insane, foolish] verrückt; **to go mad** verrückt werden - **2.** [furious] wütend; **to go mad at sb** auf jn sehr wütend werden - **3.** [very enthusiastic]: **to be mad about sb/sthg** ganz verrückt nach jm/auf etw *(A)* sein.

madam [ˈmædəm] *n fml* [form of address] gnädige Frau.

mad cow disease *n* Rinderwahnsinn *der*.

madden [ˈmædn] *vt* wahnsinnig machen.

made [meɪd] *pt* & *pp* ▷ **make**.

made-to-measure *adj* maßgeschneidert.

made-up *adj* - **1.** [face, eyes] geschminkt - **2.** [story, excuse] erfunden.

madly [ˈmædlɪ] *adv* [frantically] wie verrückt; **to be madly in love (with sb)** bis über beide Ohren (in jn) verliebt sein.

madman [ˈmædmən] (*pl* **-men** [-mən]) *n* Verrückte *der*, Irre *der*.

madness [ˈmædnɪs] *n* Wahnsinn *der*.

Mafia [ˈmæfɪə] *n*: **the Mafia** die Mafia.

magazine [ˌmægəˈziːn] *n* - **1.** [periodical] Zeitschrift *die*, Magazin *das* - **2.** [news programme, of gun] Magazin *das*.

maggot [ˈmægət] *n* Made *die*.

magic [ˈmædʒɪk] ◇ *adj* - **1.** [potion, spell, trick] Zauber- - **2.** *inf* [moment, feeling] wundervoll. ◇ *n* - **1.** [sorcery] Magie *die* - **2.** [conjuring] Zauberei *die* - **3.** [special quality] Zauber *der*.

magical [ˈmædʒɪkl] *adj* magisch.

magician [məˈdʒɪʃn] *n* Zauberer *der*.

magistrate [ˈmædʒɪstreɪt] *n* Friedensrichter *der*, -in *die*.

magnanimous [mægˈnænɪməs] *adj* großmütig.

magnate [ˈmægneɪt] *n* Magnat *der*.

magnesium [mægˈniːzɪəm] *n* Magnesium *das*.

magnet [ˈmægnɪt] *n liter* & *fig* Magnet *der*.

magnetic [mægˈnetɪk] *adj* - **1.** [force, object] magnetisch - **2.** *fig*: **to have a magnetic personality** ein sehr anziehendes Wesen haben.

magnificent [mægˈnɪfɪsənt] *adj* [building, gown] prächtig; [idea, book] großartig.

magnify [ˈmægnɪfaɪ] *vt* [TECH - image] vergrößern; [- sound] verstärken.

magnifying glass [ˈmægnɪfaɪɪŋ-] *n* Lupe *die*.

magnitude [ˈmægnɪtjuːd] *n (U)* - **1.** [size] Größe *die* - **2.** [importance] Bedeutung *die*.

magpie [ˈmægpaɪ] *n* Elster *die*.

mahogany [məˈhɒgənɪ] *n* [wood] Mahagoni *das*.

maid [meɪd] *n* [servant] Dienstmädchen *das*; [in hotel] Zimmermädchen *das*.

maiden [ˈmeɪdn] ◇ *adj* [voyage, flight] Jungfern-. ◇ *n liter* [young girl] Maid *die*.

maiden name *n* Mädchenname *der*.

mail [meɪl] ◇ *n (U)* Post *die*; **by mail** mit der Post. ◇ *vt esp US* (mit der Post) (ver)schicken *OR* senden.

mailbox [ˈmeɪlbɒks] *n US* - **1.** [for letters] Briefkasten *der* - **2.** COMPUT Mailbox *die*.

mailing list [ˈmeɪlɪŋ-] *n* Mailingliste *die*.

mailman [ˈmeɪlmən] (*pl* **-men** [-mən]) *n US* Postbote *der*, Briefträger *der*.

mail order *n* Versandhandel *der*.

mailshot [ˈmeɪlʃɒt] *n* - **1.** [material] Postwurfsendung *die* - **2.** [activity]: **to do a mailshot** Postwurfsendungen verschicken.

maim [meɪm] *vt* verstümmeln.

main [meɪn] ◇ *adj* Haupt-. ◇ *n* Hauptleitung *die*; **a gas main** eine Hauptgasleitung. ◆ **mains** *npl*: **to turn the water/gas off at the mains** den Haupthahn für das Wasser/Gas ab|drehen. ◆ **in the main** *adv* im Allgemeinen.

main course *n* Hauptgericht *das*.

mainframe (computer) [ˈmeɪnfreɪm-] *n* Großrechner *der*.

mainland [ˈmeɪnlənd] ◇ *adj*: **mainland Britain** das britische Festland. ◇ *n*: **the mainland** das Festland.

mainly [ˈmeɪnlɪ] *adv* hauptsächlich.

main road *n* Hauptstraße *die*.

mainstay [ˈmeɪnsteɪ] *n* [person] wichtigste Stütze; **tourism is the mainstay of the economy** der Tourismus ist der Hauptpfeiler der Wirtschaft.

mainstream [ˈmeɪnstriːm] *adj* vorherrschend; [music] Mainstream-.

maintain [meɪn'teɪn] *vt* - **1.** [friendship, order, image] aufrechterhalten - **2.** [speed, temperature] bei|behalten - **3.** [family, children] unterhalten - **4.** [vehicle, building] instand halten - **5.** [assert - one's innocence] beteuern; **to maintain (that)** behaupten, dass.

maintenance ['meɪntənəns] *n (U)* - **1.** [of vehicle, building] Instandhaltung *die* - **2.** [paid to ex-wife] Unterhalt *der* - **3.** [of law and order] Aufrechterhaltung *die*.

maize [meɪz] *n* Mais *der*.

majestic [mə'dʒestɪk] *adj* majestätisch.

majesty ['mædʒəstɪ] *n* Erhabenheit *die*. ◆ **Majesty** *n*: **His/Her/Your Majesty** Seine/Ihre/Eure Majestät.

major ['meɪdʒər] ◇ *adj* - **1.** [important] bedeutend; [problem]: **a major operation** eine größere Operation - **2.** [main] Haupt- - **3.** MUS [key, scale] Dur-; **C major** C-Dur. ◇ *n* Major *der*.

majority [mə'dʒɒrətɪ] *n* Mehrheit *die*; **in a** OR **the majority** in der Mehrzahl.

make [meɪk] (*pt & pp* **made**) ◇ *vt* - **1.** [produce] machen; [manufacture] her|stellen; **it's made of wood** es ist aus Holz - **2.** [prepare] machen; **to make lunch** das Mittagessen machen - **3.** [perform, do] machen; **to make a decision** eine Entscheidung treffen; **to make an effort** sich an|strengen; **to make a phone call** telefonieren; **to make a speech** eine Rede halten - **4.** [cause to be] machen; **to make sb happy/sad** jn glücklich/traurig machen; **to make sthg into sthg** etw zu etw machen - **5.** [cause to do]: **to make sb/sthg do sthg** jn/etw dazu|bringen OR veranlassen, etw zu tun - **6.** [force] zwingen; **to make sb do sthg** jn zwingen, etw zu tun - **7.** [add up to] machen; **that makes £5** das macht 5 Pfund - **8.** [calculate]: **I make it 50** ich komme auf 50; **what time do you make it?** wie spät hast du? - **9.** [earn] verdienen; **to make a profit/loss** einen Gewinn/Verlust machen - **10.** [reach, be able to attend]: **we didn't make the train** wir haben den Zug nicht geschafft - **11.** [gain - friend, enemy] machen; **to make friends with sb** mit jm Freundschaft schließen - **12.** *phr*: **to make it** es schaffen; **I won't be able to make it tonight** ich schaffe es heute Abend nicht; **to make do with sthg** mit etw aus|kommen. ◇ *n* [brand] Marke *die*. ◆ **make for** *vt insep* - **1.** [move towards] zu|halten auf *(+ A)* - **2.** [contribute to, enable] fördern. ◆ **make of** *vt sep* halten von. ◆ **make off** *vi* sich davon|machen. ◆ **make out** ◇ *vt sep* - **1.** *inf* [see] aus|machen; [hear, understand] verstehen - **2.** [cheque, receipt] aus|stellen; [application form] aus|füllen; [list] auf|stellen. ◇ *vt insep* [pretend, claim]: **to make out (that)...** vor|geben, dass... ◆ **make up** ◇ *vt sep* - **1.** [compose, constitute] bilden; **to be made up of sthg** aus etw bestehen - **2.** [invent] erfinden, sich *(D)* aus|denken; **she made it up** sie hat es erfunden - **3.** [face] schminken. ◇ *vi* [become friends again]: **to make up with sb** sich mit jm versöhnen.

make-up *n (U)* - **1.** [cosmetics] Make-up *das* - **2.** [composition] Beschaffenheit *die*; [of team] Zusammensetzung *die*.

making ['meɪkɪŋ] *n* [of product] Herstellung *die*; [of cake] Backen *das*.

malaria [mə'leərɪə] *n* Malaria *die*.

Malaysia [mə'leɪzɪə] *n* Malaysia *nt*.

male [meɪl] ◇ *adj* - **1.** [staff, members] männlich; **male cat** Kater *der* - **2.** [concerning men - problems] Männer-; [- hormone] männlich. ◇ *n* - **1.** [animal] Männchen *das* - **2.** [human] Mann *der*.

malevolent [mə'levələnt] *adj* boshaft; [intention, action] böswillig.

malfunction [mæl'fʌŋkʃn] ◇ *n* Fehlfunktion *die*. ◇ *vi* nicht richtig funktionieren.

malice ['mælɪs] *n* Boshaftigkeit *die*.

malicious [mə'lɪʃəs] *adj* boshaft; [act, intention] böswillig.

malign [mə'laɪn] ◇ *adj* [influence] schädlich; [behaviour] Unheil bringend. ◇ *vt* verleumden.

malignant [mə'lɪgnənt] *adj* MED bösartig.

mall [mɔ:l] *n esp US*: **(shopping) mall** Einkaufszentrum *das*.

mallet ['mælɪt] *n* [tool] Holzhammer *der*.

malnutrition [,mælnju:'trɪʃn] *n* Unterernährung *die*.

malpractice [,mæl'præktɪs] *n* LAW Amtsmissbrauch *der*.

malt [mɔ:lt] *n* [grain] Malz *das*.

mammal ['mæml] *n* Säugetier *das*.

mammoth ['mæməθ] ◇ *adj* ungeheuer groß. ◇ *n* Mammut *das*.

man [mæn] (*pl* **men** [men]) ◇ *n* - **1.** [gen] Mann *der* - **2.** [type]: **he's not a betting man** er macht sich nicht viel aus Wetten - **3.** *(U)* [human beings] Mensch *der*. ◇ *vt* [ship, spaceship] bemannen.

manage ['mænɪdʒ] ◇ *vi* zurecht|kommen; **thanks, I can manage!** danke, ich komme schon zurecht! ◇ *vt* - **1.** [succeed]: **to manage to do sthg** es schaffen, etw zu tun - **2.** [control - company, organization] leiten; [- popstar, boxer, football team] managen - **3.** [be available for]: **I could manage a few hours on Friday** Freitag hätte ich ein paar Stunden Zeit; **I can't manage four o'clock** vier Uhr schaffe ich nicht.

management ['mænɪdʒmənt] *n* - **1.** *(U)* [control - of company, organization] Leitung *die* - **2.** [people in control - of business] Geschäftsführung *die*; [- of operation] Leitung *die*.

manager ['mænɪdʒər] *n* [of company, shop] Geschäftsführer *der*, -in *die*; [of organization] Leiter *der*, -in *die*; [of popstar, boxer, football team] Manager *der*, -in *die*.

managerial [ˌmænɪ'dʒɪərɪəl] *adj* [post] leitend.
mandate ['mændeɪt] *n* - **1.** [elected right or authority] Mandat *das* - **2.** [task] Auftrag *der*.
mane [meɪn] *n* Mähne *die*.
mangle ['mæŋgl] *vt* [body, car] (übel) zu|richten.
mango ['mæŋgəʊ] (*pl* **-es** OR **-s**) *n* Mango *die*.
manhandle ['mænˌhændl] *vt* [person] grob behandeln.
manhole ['mænhəʊl] *n* Kanalschacht *der*.
mania ['meɪnɪə] *n* [excessive liking]: **mania (for)** Leidenschaft *die* (für).
maniac ['meɪnɪæk] *n* - **1.** [madman] Wahnsinnige *der, die* - **2.** [fanatic]: **a TV/sex maniac** ein Fernseh-/Sexbesessener, eine Fernseh-/Sexbesessene.
manic ['mænɪk] *adj* [overexcited - person] aufgedreht.
manicure ['mænɪˌkjʊə^r] *n* Maniküre *die*.
manifest ['mænɪfest] *fml vt* bekunden, zum Ausdruck bringen; **to manifest itself** sich zeigen.
manifesto [ˌmænɪ'festəʊ] (*pl* **-s** OR **-es**) *n* Manifest *das*.
manipulate [mə'nɪpjʊleɪt] *vt* - **1.** [people] manipulieren - **2.** [machine, controls] bedienen.
manipulative [mə'nɪpjʊlətɪv] *adj* manipulativ.
mankind [mæn'kaɪnd] *n* Menschheit *die*.
manly ['mænlɪ] *adj* [voice, bearing] männlich; [behaviour] mannhaft.
man-made *adj* [fibre] Kunst-; [environment] von Menschen geschaffen.
manner ['mænə^r] *n* - **1.** [method] Art *die*, Weise *die*; **in this manner** auf diese Art und Weise - **2.** [attitude] Auftreten *das*; **I don't like your manner!** mir gefällt nicht, wie Sie mit mir reden! ◆ **manners** *npl* Manieren *Pl*.
manoeuvre *UK*, **maneuver** *US* [mə'nuːvə^r] ◇ *n* [movement] Manöver *das*. ◇ *vt* [car, ship] manövrieren.
manor ['mænə^r] *n* Herrenhaus *das*.
manpower ['mænˌpaʊə^r] *n (U)* Arbeitskräfte *Pl*.
mansion ['mænʃn] *n* Villa *die*.
manslaughter ['mænˌslɔːtə^r] *n (U)* Totschlag *der*.
manual ['mænjʊəl] ◇ *adj* [work, system] manuell. ◇ *n* [handbook] Handbuch *das*.
manufacture [ˌmænjʊ'fæktʃə^r] *vt* [make] her|stellen.
manufacturer [ˌmænjʊ'fæktʃərə^r] *n* Hersteller *der*.
manure [mə'njʊə^r] *n* Dung *der*.
manuscript ['mænjʊskrɪpt] *n* [untyped copy] Manuskript *das*.
many ['menɪ] (*comp* **more**, *superl* **most**) ◇ *adj* viele; **many people** viele Leute. ◇ *pron* viele; **how many?** wie viele?
map [mæp] *n* (Land)karte *die*; [of town] Stadtplan *der*.
maple ['meɪpl] *n* Ahorn *der*.
marathon ['mærəθn] *n* Marathon(lauf) *der*.
marble ['mɑːbl] *n* [stone] Marmor *der*.
march [mɑːtʃ] ◇ *n* MIL Marsch *der*. ◇ *vi* - **1.** [soldiers, protesters] marschieren - **2.** [walk briskly]: **to march up to sb** schnurstracks auf jn zu|marschieren.
March [mɑːtʃ] *n* März *der*; *see also* **September**.
marcher ['mɑːtʃə^r] *n* [protester] Demonstrant *der*, -in *die*.
mare [meə^r] *n* Stute *die*.
margarine [ˌmɑːdʒə'riːn, ˌmɑːgə'riːn] *n* Margarine *die*.
margin ['mɑːdʒɪn] *n* - **1.** [in contest] Spielraum *der* - **2.** COMM: **profit margin** Gewinnspanne *die* - **3.** [edge - of page, wood] Rand *der*.
marginal ['mɑːdʒɪnl] *adj* [unimportant] von geringer Bedeutung; [effect, adjustment] geringfügig.
marigold ['mærɪgəʊld] *n* Ringelblume *die*.
marihuana, marijuana [ˌmærɪ'wɑːnə] *n* Marihuana *das*.
marine [mə'riːn] ◇ *adj* [plant] im Meer lebend. ◇ *n* Marineinfanterist *der*.
marital ['mærɪtl] *adj* [happiness, crisis] Ehe-; [sex, rights] ehelich.
marital status *n* Familienstand *der*.
maritime ['mærɪtaɪm] *adj* See-.
mark [mɑːk] ◇ *n* - **1.** [stain] Fleck *der*; [on person's skin] Mal *das* - **2.** [sign] Zeichen *das* - **3.** SCH & UNIV Note *die* - **4.** [stage, level]: **we've reached the halfway mark** wir haben die Hälfte hinter uns - **5.** [currency] Mark *die*. ◇ *vt* - **1.** [stain] fleckig machen; [scratch] zerkratzen - **2.** [label] kennzeichnen - **3.** SCH & UNIV korrigieren - **4.** [identify] markieren - **5.** [commemorate] begehen.
marked [mɑːkt] *adj* [noticeable] merklich.
market ['mɑːkɪt] ◇ *n* Markt *der*. ◇ *vt* vermarkten.
marketing ['mɑːkɪtɪŋ] *n* COMM Marketing *das*.
marketplace ['mɑːkɪtpleɪs] *n* [in a town] Marktplatz *der*.
marmalade ['mɑːməleɪd] *n (U)*: **(orange) marmalade** Orangenmarmelade *die*.
marriage ['mærɪdʒ] *n* - **1.** [wedding] Hochzeit *die*, Heirat *die*; [ceremony] Trauung *die* - **2.** [state] Ehe *die*.
marrow ['mærəʊ] *n* - **1.** *UK* [vegetable] Speisekürbis *der* - **2.** *(U)* [in bones] (Knochen)mark *das*.
marry ['mærɪ] ◇ *vt* - **1.** [become spouse of] heiraten; **to get married** heiraten - **2.** [subj: priest, minister, registrar] trauen. ◇ *vi* heiraten.
Mars [mɑːz] *n* [planet] Mars *der*.

marsh [mɑːʃ] *n* Sumpf *der*.

marshal ['mɑːʃl] (*UK*) (*US*) <> *n* MIL Marschall *der*. <> *vt* [support] sichern.

martial arts [ˌmɑːʃl-] *npl* Kampfsportarten *Pl*.

martial law [ˌmɑːʃl-] *n* Kriegsrecht *das*.

martyr ['mɑːtəʳ] *n* Märtyrer *der*, -in *die*.

marvel ['mɑːvl] (*UK*) (*US*) <> *n* Wunder *das*; **you're a marvel!** du bist ja unglaublich! <> *vi*: **to marvel (at sthg)** staunen (über etw *(A)*).

marvellous *UK*, **marvelous** *US* ['mɑːvələs] *adj* wunderbar.

Marxism ['mɑːksɪzm] *n* Marxismus *der*.

Marxist ['mɑːksɪst] <> *adj* marxistisch. <> *n* Marxist *der*, -in *die*.

masculine ['mæskjʊlɪn] *adj* - **1.** [typically male] männlich - **2.** GRAM [woman] maskulin.

mash [mæʃ] *vt* (zu Brei) zerdrücken.

mashed potatoes [mæʃt-] *npl* Kartoffelbrei *der*.

mask [mɑːsk] <> *n* Maske *die*. <> *vt* - **1.** [truth, feelings] verbergen - **2.** [smell, flavour] überdecken.

masochist ['mæsəkɪst] *n* Masochist *der*, -in *die*.

mason ['meɪsn] *n* - **1.** [stonemason] Steinmetz *der* - **2.** [Freemason] Freimaurer *der*.

mass [mæs] <> *n* - **1.** [gen & PHYS] Masse *die* - **2.** [large quantity] Unmenge *die*; **a mass of people** eine große Menschenmenge. <> *adj* [unemployment, protest etc] Massen-. ◆ **Mass** *n* RELIG Messe *die*.

massacre ['mæsəkəʳ] *n* Massaker *das*.

massage [*UK* 'mæsɑːʒ, *US* mə'sɑːʒ] <> *n* Massage *die*. <> *vt* massieren.

massive ['mæsɪv] *adj* riesig; [dose] sehr groß.

mass media *n* & *npl*: **the mass media** die Massenmedien.

mast [mɑːst] *n* - **1.** [on boat] Mast *der* - **2.** RADIO & TV Sendemast *der*.

master ['mɑːstəʳ] <> *n* - **1.** [gen] Herr *der* - **2.** *UK* [teacher] Lehrer *der*. <> *vt* [job, skill, language] beherrschen.

Master of Arts (*pl* **Masters of Arts**) *n* - **1.** [degree] ≃ Magister Artium *der* - **2.** [person] *Inhaber des "Master of Arts"*.

Master of Science (*pl* **Masters of Science**) *n* - **1.** [degree] ≃ Magister rerum naturalium *der* - **2.** [person] *Inhaber des "Master of Science"*.

masterpiece ['mɑːstəpiːs] *n liter* & *fig* Meisterwerk *das*.

master's degree *n* Magister(titel) *der*.

mat [mæt] *n* [on table] Untersetzer *der*; [on floor] (Fuß)matte *die*; [in sport] Matte *die*.

match [mætʃ] <> *n* - **1.** [game] Spiel *das*; [in boxing, wrestling] Kampf *der* - **2.** [for lighting] Streichholz *das* - **3.** [equal]: **to be no match for sb** jm nicht gewachsen sein; **to meet one's match** seinen Meister finden. <> *vt* - **1.** [views, feelings, ideas] übereinǀstimmen mit - **2.** [in colour, design] passen zu *(+ D)* - **3.** [be as good as] gleichǀkommen *(+ D)*. <> *vi* - **1.** [views, ideas] übereinǀstimmen - **2.** [in colour, design] zusammenǀpassen.

matchbox ['mætʃbɒks] *n* Streichholzschachtel *die*.

matching ['mætʃɪŋ] *adj* (dazu) passend.

mate [meɪt] <> *n* - **1.** *inf* [friend] Kumpel *der* - **2.** *UK inf* [term of address] Kumpel *der* - **3.** [of animal - male] Männchen *das*; [- female] Weibchen *das* - **4.** NAUT: **(first) mate** Maat *der*. <> *vi* [animals]: **to mate (with)** sich paaren (mit).

material [mə'tɪərɪəl] <> *adj* - **1.** [physical] materiell - **2.** [important] wesentlich. <> *n* - **1.** [substance] Material *das* - **2.** [fabric] Stoff *der* - **3.** *(U)* [ideas, information] Stoff *der*, Material *das*. ◆ **materials** *npl*: **building materials** Baumaterialien *Pl*; **writing materials** Schreibzeug *das*; **cleaning materials** Putzzeug *das*.

materialistic [məˌtɪərɪə'lɪstɪk] *adj* materialistisch.

materialize, -ise [mə'tɪərɪəlaɪz] *vi* - **1.** [happen - crisis] einǀtreten; [- threat] in die Tat umgesetzt werden - **2.** [appear] aufǀtauchen.

maternal [mə'tɜːnl] *adj* - **1.** [instinct] Mutter-; [person] mütterlich - **2.** [on mother's side]: **maternal grandparents** Großeltern mütterlicherseits.

maternity [mə'tɜːnətɪ] *n* Mutterschaft *die*.

maternity dress *n* Umstandskleid *das*.

maternity leave *n (U)* Mutterschaftsurlaub *der*.

maternity ward *n* Entbindungsstation *die*.

math *n US* = **maths**.

mathematical [ˌmæθə'mætɪkl] *adj* mathematisch.

mathematics [ˌmæθə'mætɪks] *n (U)* Mathematik *die*.

maths *UK* [mæθs], **math** *US* [mæθ] (*abbr of* **mathematics**) *inf n (U)* Mathe *die*.

matinée ['mætɪneɪ] *n* Nachmittagsvorstellung *die*.

matriculation [məˌtrɪkjʊ'leɪʃn] *n* UNIV Immatrikulation *die*.

matrimonial [ˌmætrɪ'məʊnɪəl] *adj* [problems, dispute] Ehe-; [harmony] ehelich.

matrimony ['mætrɪmənɪ] *n* Ehestand *der*.

matron ['meɪtrən] *n UK* [in hospital] Oberschwester *die*.

matt *UK*, **matte** *US* [mæt] *adj* matt.

matted ['mætɪd] *adj* verfilzt.

matter ['mætəʳ] <> *n* - **1.** [question, situation] Angelegenheit *die*; **that's quite another** OR **a different matter** das ist etwas ganz anderes; **that's a matter of opinion** das ist Ansichtssache; **to make matters worse** die Sache noch schlimmer machen; **and to make matters worse** zu allem Unglück, und obendrein; **as a**

matter of course selbstverständlich - **2.** [trouble]: **there's something the matter with my radio** etwas stimmt nicht mit dem Radio; **what's the matter?** was ist (denn) los?; **what's the matter with it/her?** was ist (los) damit/mit ihr? - **3.** [substance] Materie *die* - **4.** *(U)* [material] Stoff *der*; **reading matter** Lesestoff *der*. ◇ *vi* von Bedeutung sein; **it doesn't matter** das macht nichts; **it doesn't matter what I do** ganz gleich was ich tue. ◆ **as a matter of fact** *adv* sogar. ◆ **for that matter** *adv* eigentlich. ◆ **no matter** *adv*: **no matter how** ganz gleich wie; **no matter what** ganz egal was.

matter-of-fact *adj* sachlich, nüchtern.

mattress ['mætrɪs] *n* Matratze *die*.

mature [mə'tjʊəʳ] ◇ *adj* - **1.** [person] reif - **2.** [cheese] reif; [wine] ausgereift. ◇ *vi* - **1.** [child] erwachsen werden; [animal] zur vollen Größe heran|wachsen; [plant] die volle Größe erreichen - **2.** *fig* [grow up] reifer werden - **3.** [cheese] reifen; [wine] aus|reifen - **4.** [insurance policy] fällig werden.

mature student *n UK* UNIV *Person, die erst einige Jahre nach dem Schulabschluss ein Studium aufnimmt*.

maul [mɔːl] *vt* übel zu|richten.

mauve [məʊv] *adj* mauve.

max. [mæks] *abbr of* **maximum**.

maxim ['mæksɪm] *(pl* **-s***)* *n* Maxime *die*.

maxima ['mæksɪmə] *Pl* ▷ **maximum**.

maximum ['mæksɪməm] *(pl* **maxima** OR **-s***)* ◇ *adj* maximal; [speed, weight, temperature] Höchst-. ◇ *n* Maximum *das*.

may [meɪ] *aux vb* - **1.** [expressing possibility] können; **it may be done as follows** man kann wie folgt vorgehen; **it may rain** es könnte regnen; **they may have got lost** sie haben sich vielleicht verirrt; **be that as it may** wie dem auch sei; **come what may** komme, was wolle - **2.** [expressing permission] können; **may I smoke?** darf ich rauchen?; **you may sit, if you wish** Sie dürfen sich setzen, wenn Sie wollen - **3.** [when conceding a point]: **it may be a long walk, but it's worth it** es ist vielleicht ein langer Weg, aber es lohnt sich - **4.** *fml* [expressing wish, hope]: **may you be very happy!** ich wünsche dir, dass du glücklich wirst!

May [meɪ] *n* Mai *der*; *see also* **September**.

maybe ['meɪbiː] *adv* vielleicht.

May Day *n* der 1. Mai.

mayhem ['meɪhem] *n* Chaos *das*.

mayonnaise [ˌmeɪə'neɪz] *n* Majonäse *die*.

mayor [meəʳ] *n* Bürgermeister *der*.

mayoress ['meərɪs] *n* [female mayor] Bürgermeisterin *die*; [mayor's wife] Frau *die* des Bürgermeisters.

maze [meɪz] *n* - **1.** [system of paths] Irrgarten *der* - **2.** *fig* [of ideas] Wirrwarr *der*; [of streets] Labyrinth *das*.

MB *(abbr of* **megabyte***)* Mb *das*.

MD *n (abbr of* **Doctor of Medicine***)* Dr. med.

me [miː] *pers pron (accusative)* mich; *(dative)* mir; **she knows me** sie kennt mich; **it's me** ich bins; **send it to me** schick es mir; **tell me** sagen Sie mal, sag mal; **he's worse than me** er ist schlechter als ich.

meadow ['medəʊ] *n* Wiese *die*.

meagre *UK*, **meager** *US* ['miːgəʳ] *adj* dürftig.

meal [miːl] *n* - **1.** [occasion] Mahlzeit *die*; **to go out for a meal** essen gehen - **2.** [food] Essen *das*, Gericht *das*.

mealtime ['miːltaɪm] *n* Essenszeit *die*.

mean [miːn] *(pt & pp* **meant***)* ◇ *vt* - **1.** [signify] bedeuten; **the name means nothing to me** der Name sagt mir nichts - **2.** [intend] beabsichtigen; **to mean to do sthg** vor|haben, etw zu tun; **the bus was meant to leave at eight** der Bus hätte eigentlich um acht Uhr abfahren sollen; **it's meant to be good** das soll gut sein; **he means well** er meint es gut - **3.** [with remark] meinen; **what do you mean by that?** was meinst du damit? - **4.** [be serious about] ernst meinen; **I didn't mean it!** ich habe es nicht so gemeint!; **I mean it!** es ist mein Ernst!, ich meine es ernst! - **5.** *phr*: **Paul, I mean Peter** [when correcting o.s.] Paul, ich meine (natürlich) Peter. ◇ *adj* - **1.** [miserly] geizig - **2.** [unkind] gemein; **to be mean to sb** gemein zu jm sein - **3.** [average] durchschnittlich. ◇ *n* [average] Durchschnitt *der*.

meander [mɪ'ændəʳ] *vi* - **1.** [river, road] sich schlängeln - **2.** [person] schlendern.

meaning ['miːnɪŋ] *n* Bedeutung *die*; [of film, work of art, life] Sinn *der*; **what's the meaning of this?** was soll denn das?

meaningful ['miːnɪŋfʊl] *adj* - **1.** [look, comment] vielsagend - **2.** [discussion, relationship] ernsthaft.

meaningless ['miːnɪŋlɪs] *adj* - **1.** [word, lyrics] ohne Sinn - **2.** [futile] sinnlos.

means [miːnz] *(pl inv)* ◇ *n* [method] Mittel *das*; **means of transport** Verkehrsmittel *das*; **by means of** mittels *(+ G)*, durch. ◇ *npl* [money] Mittel *Pl*; **it is beyond my means** das kann ich mir nicht leisten; **can I have one? by all means!** darf ich eins haben? (aber) selbstverständlich! ◆ **by no means** *adv* keineswegs.

meant [ment] *pt & pp* ▷ **mean**.

meantime ['miːnˌtaɪm] *n*: **in the meantime** in der Zwischenzeit.

meanwhile ['miːnˌwaɪl] *adv* inzwischen.

measles ['miːzlz] *n*: **(the) measles** Masern *Pl*.

measly ['miːzlɪ] *adj inf* mick(e)rig.

measure ['meʒəʳ] ◇ *n* - **1.** [step, action] Maßnahme *die* - **2.** [of alcohol] ausgeschenkte Menge - **3.** [indication]: **to be a measure of sthg**

ein Zeichen für etw sein. ◇ *vt* messen; [room] aus|messen; [damage, harm] ab|schätzen.

measurement ['meʒəmənt] *n* - **1.** [figure] Maß *das* - **2.** *(U)* [act of measuring] Messung *die*. ◆ **measurements** *npl* [of sb's body] Maße *Pl*; **to take sb's measurements** bei jm Maß nehmen.

meat [miːt] *n* Fleisch *das*.

meatball ['miːtbɔːl] *n* Fleischklößchen *das*.

meat pie *n UK* Fleischpastete *die*.

meaty ['miːtɪ] *adj fig* [full of ideas] aussagehaltig.

Mecca ['mekə] *n* GEOG Mekka *nt*.

mechanic [mɪ'kænɪk] *n* Mechaniker *der*, -in *die*. ◆ **mechanics** ◇ *n (U)* [study] Mechanik *die*. ◇ *npl* [way sthg works] Funktionsweise *die*.

mechanical [mɪ'kænɪkl] *adj* [device, action, smile] mechanisch.

mechanism ['mekənɪzm] *n* - **1.** [of machine, behaviour] Mechanismus *der* - **2.** [procedure] Verfahren *das*.

medal ['medl] *n* Medaille *die*.

medallion [mɪ'dæljən] *n* Medaillon *das*.

meddle ['medl] *vi*: **to meddle (in/with sthg)** sich (in etw *(A)*) ein|mischen; **to meddle with sb** sich mit jm ein|lassen.

media ['miːdɪə] ◇ *Pl* ▷ **medium**. ◇ *n* & *npl*: **the media** die Medien *Pl*.

mediaeval [ˌmedɪ'iːvl] *adj* = **medieval**.

median ['miːdɪən] *n US* [of road] Mittelstreifen *der*.

mediate ['miːdɪeɪt] *vi*: **to mediate (for/between)** vermitteln (für/zwischen *(+ D)*).

mediator ['miːdɪeɪtə^r] *n* Vermittler *der*, -in *die*.

Medicaid ['medɪkeɪd] *n US staatliche Gesundheitsfürsorge für einkommensschwache US-Bürger*.

medical ['medɪkl] ◇ *adj* medizinisch. ◇ *n* ärztliche Untersuchung.

Medicare ['medɪkeə^r] *n US staatliche Gesundheitsfürsorge für ältere US-Bürger*.

medicated ['medɪkeɪtɪd] *adj* medizinisch.

medicine ['medsɪn] *n* - **1.** [treatment of illness] Medizin *die* - **2.** [substance] Medikament *das*.

medieval [ˌmedɪ'iːvl] *adj* mittelalterlich.

mediocre [ˌmiːdɪ'əʊkə^r] *adj* mittelmäßig.

meditate ['medɪteɪt] *vi* - **1.** [reflect, ponder]: **to meditate (on** *OR* **upon)** nach|denken (über *(+ A)*) - **2.** [practise meditation] meditieren.

Mediterranean [ˌmedɪtə'reɪnɪən] ◇ *n* - **1.** [sea]: **the Mediterranean (Sea)** das Mittelmeer - **2.** [area around sea]: **the Mediterranean** der Mittelmeerraum. ◇ *adj* Mittelmeer-, mediterran.

medium ['miːdɪəm] ◇ *adj* mittlere(r) (s). ◇ *n* Medium *das*.

medium-size(d) [-saɪz(d)] *adj* mittelgroß.

medium wave *n* Mittelwelle *die*.

medley ['medlɪ] (*pl* **medleys**) *n* - **1.** [mixture] Gemisch *das* - **2.** [selection of music] Medley *das*, Potpourri *das*.

meek [miːk] *adj* sanftmütig; [voice] sanft.

meet [miːt] (*pt & pp* **met**) ◇ *vt* - **1.** [by arrangement] sich treffen mit; [by chance] treffen; [get to know] kennen lernen; **to arrange to meet sb** sich mit jm verabreden; **pleased to meet you!** sehr erfreut! - **2.** [go to collect] ab|holen - **3.** [need, requirement] erfüllen - **4.** [cost, expense] begleichen - **5.** [join - subj: road, river] treffen auf *(+ A)*. ◇ *vi* - **1.** [by arrangement, by chance] sich treffen; [committee *etc*] zusammen|kommen - **2.** [get to know each other] sich kennen lernen - **3.** [intersect] aufeinander treffen - **4.** [join] zusammen|kommen. ◇ *n US* [sports meeting] Sportfest *das*. ◆ **meet up** *vi*: **to meet up (with sb)** sich (mit jm) treffen. ◆ **meet with** *vt insep* - **1.** [problems, resistance] stoßen auf *(+ A)* - **2.** [by arrangement] sich treffen mit.

meeting ['miːtɪŋ] *n* - **1.** [for discussions, business] Meeting *das*, Sitzung *die* - **2.** [coming together - by chance] Begegnung *die*; [- by arrangement] Treffen *das*.

megabyte ['megəbaɪt] *n* COMPUT Megabyte *das*.

megaphone ['megəfəʊn] *n* Megafon *das*.

melancholy ['melənkəlɪ] *adj* melancholisch; [facts, news] traurig.

mellow ['meləʊ] ◇ *adj* - **1.** [light] warm - **2.** [smooth, pleasant] angenehm; [sound, tones] lieblich, sanft; [wine] ausgereift; [whisky] mild - **3.** [gentle, relaxed] milde, sanft. ◇ *vi* [person] abgeklärt werden.

melody ['melədɪ] *n* Melodie *die*.

melon ['melən] *n* Melone *die*.

melt [melt] ◇ *vt* [make liquid - chocolate, snow] schmelzen; [butter] zerlassen. ◇ *vi* - **1.** [become liquid] schmelzen - **2.** *fig* [soften - person] dahin|schmelzen; [- heart] über|gehen - **3.** *fig* [disappear]: **to melt away** [savings, anger] dahin|schmelzen, weg|schmelzen. ◆ **melt down** *vt sep* ein|schmelzen.

meltdown ['meltdaʊn] *n* Kernschmelze *die*.

melting pot ['meltɪŋ-] *n fig* Schmelztiegel *der*.

member ['membə^r] *n* Mitglied *das*; **a member of staff** ein Firmenangehöriger, eine Firmenangehörige.

Member of Congress (*pl* **Members of Congress**) *n US* Kongressmitglied *das*.

Member of Parliament (*pl* **Members of Parliament**) *n* Parlamentsabgeordnete *der*, *die*.

membership ['membəʃɪp] *n (U)* - **1.** [fact of belonging] Mitgliedschaft *die* - **2.** [number of members] Mitgliederzahl *die* - **3.** [people]: **the membership** die Mitglieder.

membership card *n* Mitgliedskarte *die*.

memento [mɪ'mentəʊ] (*pl* **-s**) *n* Andenken *das*.

memo ['meməʊ] (*pl* **-s**) *n* Mitteilung *die*.

memoirs ['memwɑ:z] *npl* Memoiren *Pl*.

memorandum [,memə'rændəm] (*pl* **-da** [-də] *OR* **-dums**) *n fml* Memorandum *das*.

memorial [mɪ'mɔ:rɪəl] <> *adj* Gedenk-. <> *n* Denkmal *das*.

memorize, -ise ['meməraɪz] *vt* auswendig lernen.

memory ['memərɪ] *n* - **1.** [ability to remember] Gedächtnis *das* - **2.** *(U)* [things remembered] Erinnerung *die*; **I have no memory of it** ich kann mich nicht daran erinnern; **from memory** auswendig - **3.** [event, experience remembered] Erinnerung *die* - **4.** *(U)* [of dead person] Andenken *das* - **5.** COMPUT Speicher *der*.

men [men] *Pl* ▷ **man**.

menace ['menəs] <> *n* - **1.** [threat] Drohung *die*; [danger] drohende Gefahr - **2.** *(U)* [threatening quality] Bedrohung *die* - **3.** *inf* [nuisance, pest] Plage *die*. <> *vt* bedrohen.

menacing ['menəsɪŋ] *adj* bedrohlich.

mend [mend] <> *n inf*: **to be on the mend** auf dem Weg der Besserung sein. <> *vt* [repair] reparieren; [clothes] flicken.

menial ['mi:nɪəl] *adj* niedrig.

meningitis [,menɪn'dʒaɪtɪs] *n* MED Hirnhautentzündung *die*, Meningitis *die*.

menopause ['menəpɔ:z] *n (U)*: **the menopause** die Wechseljahre, die Menopause.

men's room *n US*: **the men's room** die Herrentoilette.

menstruation [,menstrʊ'eɪʃn] *n (U)* Menstruation *die*, Periode *die*.

menswear ['menzweəʳ] *n (U)* Herrenbekleidung *die*.

mental ['mentl] *adj* - **1.** [intellectual] geistig - **2.** [psychiatric] psychiatrisch; **mental illness** Geisteskrankheit *die*; **her mental health** ihr Geisteszustand - **3.** [performed in the mind] im Kopf; **mental arithmetic** Kopfrechnen *das*.

mental hospital *n* Nervenklinik *die*.

mentality [men'tælətɪ] *n (U)* Mentalität *die*.

mentally handicapped *npl*: **the mentally handicapped** die geistig Behinderten *Pl*.

mention ['menʃn] <> *vt* erwähnen; **to mention sthg to sb** etw jm gegenüber erwähnen; **not to mention** ganz zu schweigen von; **don't mention it!** gern geschehen! <> *n* Erwähnung *die*; **to get a mention** erwähnt werden.

menu ['menju:] *n* - **1.** [in restaurant - card] Speisekarte *die*; [- dishes] Menü *das* - **2.** COMPUT Menü *das*.

meow *n* & *vi US* = **miaow**.

MEP (*abbr of* **Member of the European Parliament**) *n* MdEP *das*.

mercenary ['mɜ:sɪnrɪ] <> *adj* - **1.** [only interested in money] gewinnsüchtig - **2.** MIL Söldner-. <> *n* [soldier] Söldner *der*.

merchandise ['mɜ:tʃəndaɪz] *n (U)* Ware *die*.

merchant ['mɜ:tʃənt] *n* Händler *der*, -in *die*.

merchant bank *n UK* Handelsbank *die*.

merchant navy *UK*, **merchant marine** *US* *n* Handelsmarine *die*.

merciful ['mɜ:sɪfʊl] *adj* [person] barmherzig.

merciless ['mɜ:sɪlɪs] *adj* gnadenlos.

mercury ['mɜ:kjʊrɪ] *n* Quecksilber *das*.

Mercury ['mɜ:kjʊrɪ] *n* [planet] Merkur *der*.

mercy ['mɜ:sɪ] *n* - **1.** [kindness, pity] Gnade *die*; **to be at the mercy of sb/sthg** *fig* jm/etw ausgeliefert sein - **2.** [blessing] Segen *der*.

mere [mɪəʳ] *adj*: **a mere £10 is all it costs** es kostet bloß *OR* nur 10 Pfund; **it took him a mere two hours** er brauchte bloß *OR* nur zwei Stunden; **she's a mere child!** sie ist ja noch ein Kind!

merely ['mɪəlɪ] *adv* bloß, nur.

merge [mɜ:dʒ] <> *vt* - **1.** COMM fusionieren - **2.** COMPUT mischen. <> *vi* - **1.** COMM: **to merge (with)** fusionieren (mit) - **2.** [roads, lines] zusammen|laufen - **3.** [blend] ineinander über|gehen; **to merge into the landscape/background** mit der Landschaft/dem Hintergrund verschmelzen.

merger ['mɜ:dʒəʳ] *n* COMM Fusion *die*.

meringue [mə'ræŋ] *n* Baiser *das*.

merit ['merɪt] <> *n (U)* [value] Wert *der*; **she was chosen for the post on merit** sie bekam die Stelle aufgrund ihrer guten Leistungen. <> *vt* verdienen. ◆ **merits** *npl* Vorteile *Pl*.

mermaid ['mɜ:meɪd] *n* Meerjungfrau *die*.

merry ['merɪ] *adj* - **1.** [party] fröhlich; **Merry Christmas!** frohe *OR* fröhliche Weihnachten! - **2.** *inf* [tipsy] angeheitert.

merry-go-round *n* Karussell *das*.

mesh [meʃ] *n (U)* [netting]: **(wire) mesh** Maschendraht *der*.

mesmerize, -ise ['mezməraɪz] *vt*: **to be mesmerized by sb/sthg** fasziniert *OR* gebannt sein von jm/etw.

mess [mes] *n* - **1.** [untidy state] Durcheinander *das* - **2.** [sthg spilt, knocked over] Schweinerei *die* - **3.** [muddle] Durcheinander *das*; [problematic situation] Schlamassel *der* - **4.** MIL Messe *die*. ◆ **mess about, mess around** *inf* <> *vt sep* an der Nase herum|führen. <> *vi* - **1.** [fool around, waste time] herum|gammeln - **2.** [interfere]: **to mess about with** [machine] herum|basteln an (+ *D*); [sb's papers] durcheinander bringen. ◆ **mess up** *vt sep* *inf* - **1.** [make dirty] verdrecken; [make untidy] in Unordnung bringen - **2.** [plan, evening] verderben.

message ['mesɪdʒ] *n* - **1.** [piece of information] Nachricht *die* - **2.** [idea, moral] Botschaft *die*.

messenger ['mesɪndʒəʳ] *n* Bote *der*.

messy ['mesɪ] *adj* - **1.** [untidy] unordentlich; [dirty] dreckig - **2.** *inf* [complicated, confused] kompliziert.

met [met] *pt* & *pp* ▷ **meet**.

metal ['metl] ◇ *n* Metall *das*. ◇ *adj* Metall-, metallen.

metallic [mɪ'tælɪk] *adj* - **1.** [sound] metallisch - **2.** [shiny]: **metallic paint** Metalliclackierung *die*; **metallic blue** metallicblau.

metalwork ['metəlwɜːk] *n (U)* [craft] Metallarbeit *die*.

metaphor ['metəfəʳ] *n* [symbol, image] Metapher *die*.

mete [miːt] ◆ **mete out** *vt sep*: **to mete sthg out to sb** jm etw zulmessen.

meteor ['miːtɪəʳ] *n* Meteor *der*.

meteorology [miːtɪə'rɒlədʒɪ] *n* Meteorologie *die*.

meter ['miːtəʳ] ◇ *n* - **1.** [device - for gas, electricity] Zähler *der*; [- in taxi] Uhr *die*; [- for parking] Parkuhr *die* - **2.** *US* = **metre**. ◇ *vt* messen.

method ['meθəd] *n* Methode *die*.

methodical [mɪ'θɒdɪkl] *adj* methodisch.

Methodist ['meθədɪst] ◇ *adj* Methodisten-. ◇ *n* Methodist *der*, -in *die*.

meths [meθs] *n (U) UK inf* Brennspiritus *der*.

methylated spirits [ˌmeθɪleɪtɪd-] *n (U)* Brennspiritus *der*.

meticulous [mɪ'tɪkjʊləs] *adj* genau.

metre *UK*, **meter** *US* ['miːtəʳ] *n* [unit of measurement] Meter *der*.

metric ['metrɪk] *adj* metrisch.

metronome ['metrənəʊm] *n* Metronom *das*.

metropolitan [ˌmetrə'pɒlɪtn] *adj* Stadt-.

mettle ['metl] *n (U)*: **to be on one's mettle** sein Bestes geben; **to show one's mettle** zeigen, was man kann.

mew [mjuː] *n* & *vi* = **miaow**.

mews [mjuːz] (*pl inv*) *n UK* [stables] Stallungen *Pl*; [street] *Gasse mit ehemaligen Stallungen*.

Mexican ['meksɪkn] ◇ *adj* mexikanisch. ◇ *n* Mexikaner *der*, -in *die*.

Mexico ['meksɪkəʊ] *n* Mexiko *nt*.

MI5 (*abbr of* **Military Intelligence 5**) *n* MI5 *der, britische Spionageabwehr*.

miaow *UK* [miː'aʊ], **meow** *US* [mɪ'aʊ] ◇ *n* Miau *das*. ◇ *vi* miauen.

mice [maɪs] *Pl* ▷ **mouse**.

mickey ['mɪkɪ] *n*: **to take the mickey out of sb** *UK inf* jn auf den Arm nehmen.

microchip ['maɪkrəʊtʃɪp] *n* Mikrochip *der*.

microcomputer [ˌmaɪkrəʊkəm'pjuːtəʳ] *n* Mikrocomputer *der*.

microfilm ['maɪkrəʊfɪlm] *n* Mikrofilm *der*.

microphone ['maɪkrəfəʊn] *n* Mikrofon *das*.

microscope ['maɪkrəskəʊp] *n* Mikroskop *das*.

microscopic [ˌmaɪkrə'skɒpɪk] *adj* [very small] mikroskopisch.

microwave (oven) [ˌmaɪkrəweɪv-] *n* Mikrowellenherd *der*.

mid- [mɪd] *prefix*: **in mid-June** Mitte Juni; **a mid-morning snack** ein zweites Frühstück; **he is in his mid-fifties** er ist Mitte fünfzig; **in the mid-20th century** Mitte des 20. Jahrhunderts.

midair [ˌmɪd'eəʳ] ◇ *adj*: **midair collision** Zusammenstoß in der Luft. ◇ *n*: **in midair** in der Luft.

midday [mɪd'deɪ] *n* Mittag *der*; **at midday** mittags.

middle ['mɪdl] ◇ *adj* [central] Mittel-, mittlere(r) (s). ◇ *n* - **1.** [gen] Mitte *die*; **in the middle (of sthg)** in der Mitte (von etw); **in the middle of the night** mitten in der Nacht; **to be in the middle of doing sthg** gerade dabei sein, etw zu tun - **2.** [waist] Taille *die*.

middle-aged [-'eɪdʒd] *adj* im mittleren Alter, mittleren Alters.

Middle Ages *npl*: **the Middle Ages** das Mittelalter.

middle-class *adj* Mittelklasse-.

middle classes *npl*: **the middle classes** die Mittelklasse.

Middle East *n*: **the Middle East** der Nahe Osten.

middleman ['mɪdlmæn] (*pl* **-men** [-men]) *n* - **1.** COMM Zwischenhändler *der* - **2.** [in negotiations] Vermittler *der*.

middle name *n* zweiter Vorname.

midfield [ˌmɪd'fiːld] *n* FTBL Mittelfeld *das*.

midge [mɪdʒ] *n* Mücke *die*.

midget ['mɪdʒɪt] *n* Zwerg *der*.

Midlands ['mɪdləndz] *npl*: **the Midlands** *Region im Zentrum von England*.

midnight ['mɪdnaɪt] *n* Mitternacht *die*; **at midnight** um Mitternacht.

midriff ['mɪdrɪf] *n* Bauch *der*.

midst [mɪdst] *n*: **in the midst of** mitten in *(+ D)*; **to be in the midst of doing sthg** gerade dabei sein, etw zu tun.

midsummer ['mɪdˌsʌməʳ] *n (U)* Hochsommer *der*.

midway [ˌmɪd'weɪ] *adv* - **1.** [in space]: **midway (between)** auf halbem Wege (zwischen) - **2.** [in time] in der Mitte; **midway through** mitten in *(+ D)*.

midweek ◇ *adj* ['mɪdwi:k]: **a midweek meeting/match** ein Mitte der Woche stattfindendes Treffen/Spiel. ◇ *adv* [,mɪd'wi:k] Mitte der Woche.

midwife ['mɪdwaɪf] (*pl* **-wives** [-waɪvz]) *n* Hebamme *die*.

might [maɪt] ◇ *modal vb* - **1.** [expressing possibility] können; **they might still come** sie könnten noch kommen; **they might have been killed** sie sind vielleicht umgekommen - **2.** [expressing suggestion]: **you might have told me!** das hättest du mir doch sagen können!; **it might be better to wait** sie sollten vielleicht lieber warten - **3.** *fml* [asking permission]: **might I have a few words?** könnte ich Sie mal sprechen?; **he asked if he might leave the room** er fragte, ob er das Zimmer verlassen dürfte - **4.** [when conceding a point]: **it might be expensive, but it's good quality** es ist zwar teuer, aber es ist eine gute Qualität - **5.** [would]: **I'd hoped you might come too** ich hatte gehofft, du würdest auch mitkommen - **6.** *phr*: **I might have known/guessed** das hätte ich eigentlich wissen/mir eigentlich denken können. ◇ *n (U)* Macht *die*; **with all one's might** mit aller Macht OR Kraft.

mighty ['maɪtɪ] ◇ *adj* [powerful] mächtig. ◇ *adv US inf* mächtig.

migraine ['mi:greɪn, 'maɪgreɪn] *n* Migräne *die*.

migrant ['maɪgrənt] *n* - **1.** [bird] Zugvogel *der* - **2.** [worker] Wanderarbeiter *der*, -in *die*.

migrate [*UK* maɪ'greɪt, *US* 'maɪgreɪt] *vi* - **1.** [bird] in den Süden ziehen - **2.** [person] ablwandern.

mike [maɪk] (*abbr of* **microphone**) *n inf* Mikro *das*.

mild [maɪld] *adj* - **1.** [gen] mild; [sedative, illness] leicht - **2.** [person, manner] sanft.

mildew ['mɪldju:] *n* [on books, walls] Schimmel *der*.

mildly ['maɪldlɪ] *adv* milde; **to put it mildly** gelinde gesagt.

mile [maɪl] *n* Meile *die*; **to be miles away** [distracted] (mit seinen Gedanken) ganz woanders sein. ◆ **miles** *adv (in comparisons)* weit; **miles better** weit besser.

mileage ['maɪlɪdʒ] *n* - **1.** [recorded] Meilenzahl *die* - **2.** *(U) inf* [advantage] Vorteil *der*.

mileometer [maɪ'lɒmɪtəʳ] *n* ≃ Kilometerzähler *der*.

milestone ['maɪlstəʊn] *n liter* & *fig* Meilenstein *der*.

militant ['mɪlɪtənt] ◇ *adj* militant. ◇ *n* militanter Student/Arbeiter/*etc*.

military ['mɪlɪtrɪ] ◇ *adj* Militär-, militärisch. ◇ *n*: **the military** das Militär.

militia [mɪ'lɪʃə] *n* Miliz *die*.

milk [mɪlk] ◇ *n* Milch *die*. ◇ *vt* - **1.** [cow, goat] melken - **2.** [company] schröpfen; *fig* [situation, scandal] auslnutzen.

milk chocolate *n* Milchschokolade *die*.

milkman ['mɪlkmən] (*pl* **-men** [-mən]) *n* Milchmann *der*.

milk shake *n* Milchshake *der*.

milky ['mɪlkɪ] *adj* - **1.** *UK* [coffee] Milch-; [tea] mit Milch - **2.** [complexion] milchig.

Milky Way *n*: **the Milky Way** die Milchstraße.

mill [mɪl] *n* - **1.** [flour mill, grinder] Mühle *die* - **2.** [cloth factory] Weberei *die*. ◆ **mill about, mill around** *vi* umherllaufen.

millennium [mɪ'lenɪəm] (*pl* **-nnia** [-nɪə]) *n* Millennium *das*.

millet ['mɪlɪt] *n (U)* Hirse *die*.

milligram(me) ['mɪlɪgræm] *n* Milligramm *das*.

millimetre *UK*, **millimeter** *US* ['mɪlɪ,mi:təʳ] *n* Millimeter *der*.

million ['mɪljən] *n* - **1.** [1,000,000] Million *die* - **2.** [enormous number]: **a million, millions of** zig.

millionaire [,mɪljə'neəʳ] *n* Millionär *der*, -in *die*.

milometer [maɪ'lɒmɪtəʳ] *n* = **mileometer**.

mime [maɪm] ◇ *n* - **1.** [acting, act] Pantomime *die* - **2.** [actor]: **mime (artist)** Pantomime *der*, -min *die*. ◇ *vt* mimen.

mimic ['mɪmɪk] (*pt & pp* **-ked**, *cont* **-king**) ◇ *n* Imitator *der*, -in *die*. ◇ *vt* nachlahmen.

min. *abbr of* **minute**, **minimum**.

mince [mɪns] ◇ *n (U) UK* Hackfleisch *das*. ◇ *vt* - **1.** [meat] durchldrehen - **2.**: **not to mince one's words** kein Blatt vor den Mund nehmen. ◇ *vi* [walk] trippeln.

mincemeat ['mɪnsmi:t] *n (U)* - **1.** [fruit] *Mischung aus Äpfeln, Rosinen, Fett und Gewürzen, die im Teigmantel gebacken wird* - **2.** *US* [minced meat] Hackfleisch *das*.

mince pie *n mit Mincemeat gefüllte Pastete*.

mincer ['mɪnsəʳ] *n* Fleischwolf *der*.

mind [maɪnd] ◇ *n* - **1.** [reason] Verstand *der*; **to be out of one's mind** nicht bei Sinnen OR verrückt sein; **no one in their right mind would do that** kein vernünftiger Mensch würde das tun; **state of mind** Geisteszustand *der* - **2.** [thoughts] Gedanken *Pl*; **I can't get her out of my mind** sie geht mir nicht aus dem Kopf; **to come into/cross sb's mind** jm in den Sinn kommen; **to have sthg on one's mind** etw auf dem Herzen haben - **3.** [intellect] Geist *der* - **4.** [attention]: **to keep one's mind on sthg** sich auf etw *(A)* konzentrieren; **if you put your mind to it** wenn du dich anstrengst - **5.** [opinion]: **to my mind** meiner Ansicht OR Meinung nach; **to change one's mind** seine Meinung ändern; **to keep an open mind** sich nicht festllegen; **to make one's mind up**

sich entschließen; **to speak one's mind** seine Meinung frei äußern; **to be in two minds about sthg** hinsichtlich einer Sache *(G)* unentschlossen sein - **6.** [memory] Gedächtnis *das*; **to bear sthg in mind** etw nicht vergessen - **7.** [intention]: **to have sthg in mind** an etw *(A)* denken; **to have a mind to do sthg** die Absicht haben, etw zu tun - **8.** [intelligent person, thinker] Geist *der*; **he is one of the greatest minds of the 19th century** er ist einer der größten Köpfe des 19. Jahrhunderts. ◇ *vi* - **1.** [object]: **I don't mind** ich habe nichts dagegen; **do you mind if ...?** macht es Ihnen etwas aus, wenn ...?, stört es Sie, wenn ...? - **2.** [care, worry]: **I don't mind if...** es macht mir nichts aus, wenn...; **never mind** [don't worry] mach dir nichts draus; [it's not important] es macht nichts. ◇ *vt* - **1.** [object to]: **I don't mind it/him** ich habe nichts dagegen/gegen ihn; **do you mind waiting?** macht es dir etwas aus, zu warten? - **2.** [bother about]: **I don't mind what he says** es ist mir gleichgültig, was er sagt - **3.** [pay attention to] achten auf *(+ A)* - **4.** [take care of] sich kümmern um. ◆ **mind you** *adv* allerdings.

minder ['maɪndəʳ] *n UK* [bodyguard] Leibwächter *der*, -in *die*.

mindful ['maɪndfʊl] *adj*: **to be mindful of sthg** sich *(D)* einer Sache *(G)* bewusst sein.

mindless ['maɪndlɪs] *adj* - **1.** [stupid] sinnlos - **2.** [not requiring thought] geistlos.

mine[1] [maɪn] ◇ *n* - **1.** [for excavating minerals] Bergwerk *das*; [for gold, diamond] Mine *die* - **2.** [bomb] Mine *die*. ◇ *vt* - **1.** [coal, gold] fördern - **2.** [lay mines in] verminen.

mine[2] [maɪn] *poss pron* meine(r) (s) (meine); **it's mine** es gehört mir; **a friend of mine** ein Freund von mir.

minefield ['maɪnfi:ld] *n liter* & *fig* Minenfeld *das*.

miner ['maɪnəʳ] *n* Bergarbeiter *der*, -in *die*.

mineral ['mɪnərəl] ◇ *adj* GEOL mineralisch. ◇ *n* GEOL Mineral *das*.

mineral water *n (U)* Mineralwasser *das*.

mingle ['mɪŋgl] *vi* - **1.** [combine]: **to mingle (with)** sich mischen (mit) - **2.** [at party]: **to mingle (with the guests)** sich unter die Gäste mischen.

miniature ['mɪnətʃəʳ] ◇ *adj* Miniatur-. ◇ *n* - **1.** [painting] Miniatur *die* - **2.** [of alcohol] Miniflasche *die* - **3.** [small scale]: **in miniature** im Kleinen, Miniatur-.

minibus ['mɪnɪbʌs] *(pl* **-es***)* *n* Kleinbus *der*.

minicab ['mɪnɪkæb] *n UK* Kleintaxi *das*.

minima ['mɪnɪmə] *Pl* ▷ **minimum**.

minimal ['mɪnɪml] *adj* minimal.

minimum ['mɪnɪməm] *(pl* **-mums** *OR* **-ma***)* ◇ *adj* Mindest-. ◇ *n* Minimum *das*.

mining ['maɪnɪŋ] ◇ *n* Bergbau *der*. ◇ *adj* Bergbau-; [accident] Gruben-.

miniskirt ['mɪnɪskɜ:t] *n* Minirock *der*.

minister ['mɪnɪstəʳ] *n* - **1.** POL: **minister (of** *OR* **for sthg)** Minister *der*, -in *die* (für etw) - **2.** RELIG Pastor *der*, -in *die*. ◆ **minister to** *vt insep* sich kümmern um; **to minister to sb's needs** js Bedürfnisse befriedigen.

ministerial [,mɪnɪ'stɪərɪəl] *adj* POL Ministerial-, ministerial.

minister of state *n*: **minister of state (for sthg)** Staatsminister *der*, -in *die* (für etw).

ministry ['mɪnɪstrɪ] *n* - **1.** POL Ministerium *das* - **2.** RELIG: **the ministry** das geistliche Amt.

mink [mɪŋk] *(pl inv)* *n* [fur, animal] Nerz *der*.

minor ['maɪnəʳ] ◇ *adj* - **1.** [unimportant] unbedeutend - **2.** MUS [key] Moll-; **in B minor** in H-Moll. ◇ *n* [in age] Minderjährige *der, die*.

minority [maɪ'nɒrətɪ] *n* Minderheit *die*.

mint [mɪnt] ◇ *n* - **1.** *(U)* [herb] Minze *die* - **2.** [sweet] Pfefferminzbonbon *das ODER der* - **3.** [for coins]: **the Mint** die Münze; **in mint condition** in neuwertigem *OR* tadellosem Zustand. ◇ *vt* [coins] prägen.

minus ['maɪnəs] *(pl* **-es***)* ◇ *prep* - **1.** MATHS minus, weniger - **2.** [in temperatures] minus. ◇ *adj* - **1.** MATHS negativ - **2.** SCH [in grades] minus. ◇ *n* - **1.** MATHS Minus *das* - **2.** [disadvantage] Nachteil *der*.

minus sign *n* Minuszeichen *das*.

minute[1] ['mɪnɪt] *n* - **1.** [period of 60 seconds] Minute *die* - **2.** [moment] Moment *der*; **at any minute** jederzeit; **this minute** sofort, auf der Stelle. ◆ **minutes** *npl* [of meeting] Protokoll *das*.

minute[2] [maɪ'nju:t] *adj* [tiny] winzig.

miracle ['mɪrəkl] *n* Wunder *das*.

miraculous [mɪ'rækjʊləs] *adj* - **1.** RELIG wundersam - **2.** *fig* [recovery, escape] wunderbar.

mirage [mɪ'rɑ:ʒ] *n* [in desert] Fata Morgana *die*.

mire [maɪəʳ] *n* Morast *der*, Schlamm *der*.

mirror ['mɪrəʳ] ◇ *n* Spiegel *der*. ◇ *vt* [copy] wider|spiegeln.

misadventure [,mɪsəd'ventʃəʳ] *n* [unfortunate accident] Missgeschick *das*.

misapprehension [,mɪsæprɪ'henʃn] *n* Missverständnis *das*.

misbehave [,mɪsbɪ'heɪv] *vi* sich schlecht benehmen.

miscalculate [,mɪs'kælkjʊleɪt] ◇ *vt* - **1.** [amount, time, distance] falsch berechnen - **2.** *fig* [misjudge] falsch ein|schätzen. ◇ *vi* - **1.** MATHS sich verrechnen - **2.** *fig* [misjudge] sich verschätzen.

miscarriage [,mɪs'kærɪdʒ] *n* Fehlgeburt *die*.

miscarriage of justice *n* Justizirrtum *der*.

miscellaneous [,mɪsə'leɪnɪəs] *adj* verschieden.

mischief ['mɪstʃɪf] *n (U)* - **1.** [naughty behaviour] Unfug *der* - **2.** [harm] Schaden *der*.

mischievous ['mɪstʃɪvəs] *adj* - **1.** [playful] schelmisch - **2.** [naughty] unartig.

misconception [ˌmɪskən'sepʃn] *n* falsche Vorstellung, falsche Auffassung.

misconduct [ˌmɪs'kɒndʌkt] *n* [bad behaviour] schlechtes Benehmen.

miscount [ˌmɪs'kaʊnt] ◇ *vt* falsch zählen. ◇ *vi* sich verzählen.

misdemeanour *UK*, **misdemeanor** *US* [ˌmɪsdɪ'miːnəʳ] *n* LAW Vergehen *das*.

miser ['maɪzəʳ] *n* Geizhals *der*.

miserable ['mɪzrəbl] *adj* - **1.** [person, life] elend; **don't look so miserable** guck nicht so jämmerlich - **2.** [conditions, pay, weather] miserabel; [evening, holiday] schrecklich - **3.** [failure] kläglich.

miserly ['maɪzəlɪ] *adj* geizig.

misery ['mɪzərɪ] *n* - **1.** [unhappiness] Kummer *der* - **2.** [poverty] Elend *das*, Armut *die*.

misfire [ˌmɪs'faɪəʳ] *vi* - **1.** [gun, car engine] fehl|zünden - **2.** [plan] fehl|schlagen.

misfit ['mɪsfɪt] *n* Außenseiter *der*, -in *die*.

misfortune [mɪs'fɔːtʃuːn] *n* - **1.** [bad luck] Pech *das* - **2.** [piece of bad luck] Unglück *das*.

misgivings [mɪs'gɪvɪŋz] *npl* Bedenken *Pl*.

misguided [ˌmɪs'gaɪdɪd] *adj* [opinion] töricht.

mishandle [ˌmɪs'hændl] *vt* - **1.** [person, animal] schlecht behandeln - **2.** [negotiations, business] falsch handhaben.

mishap ['mɪshæp] *n* [unfortunate event] Missgeschick *das*.

misinterpret [ˌmɪsɪn'tɜːprɪt] *vt* falsch aus|legen OR deuten.

misjudge [ˌmɪs'dʒʌdʒ] *vt* - **1.** [calculate wrongly] falsch ein|schätzen - **2.** [appraise wrongly] falsch beurteilen.

mislay [ˌmɪs'leɪ] *(pt & pp* **-laid** [-'leɪd]*)* *vt* verlegen.

mislead [ˌmɪs'liːd] *(pt & pp* **-led***)* *vt* irre|führen.

misleading [ˌmɪs'liːdɪŋ] *adj* irreführend.

misled [ˌmɪs'led] *pt & pp* ▷ **mislead**.

misplace [ˌmɪs'pleɪs] *vt* verlegen.

misprint ['mɪsprɪnt] *n* Druckfehler *der*.

miss [mɪs] ◇ *vt* - **1.** [person in crowd, film, turning, opportunity, train, flight] verpassen - **2.** [subj: bullet, ball, footballer] verfehlen - **3.** [wife, family, home] vermissen; **I miss reading English newspapers** ich vermisse es, englische Zeitungen zu lesen - **4.** [meeting, appointment, school] versäumen - **5.** [disaster] entkommen *(+ D)*; **I just missed being run over** ich wäre beinahe überfahren worden. ◇ *vi* [fail to hit] nicht treffen. ◇ *n*: **to give sthg a miss** *inf* sich *(D)* etw verkneifen. ◆ **miss out** ◇ *vt sep* [omit - by accident] übersehen; [- deliberately] aus|lassen. ◇ *vi*: **to miss out on sthg** etw verpassen.

Miss [mɪs] *n* Fräulein *nt*.

misshapen [ˌmɪs'ʃeɪpn] *adj* [hands, fingers, toes] missgebildet; [biscuits, cake] missraten.

missile [*UK* 'mɪsaɪl, *US* 'mɪsəl] *n* - **1.** [weapon] Rakete *die*, Flugkörper *der* - **2.** [thrown object] Wurfgeschoss *das*.

missing ['mɪsɪŋ] *adj* - **1.** [lost] verschwunden; **missing in action** vermisst; **sixty people are still missing** sechzig Personen werden immer noch vermisst - **2.** [not present] fehlend; **who's missing?** wer fehlt?

mission ['mɪʃn] *n* - **1.** [task, duty] Auftrag *der* - **2.** [delegation] Delegation *die*, Gesandtschaft *die* - **3.** ASTRON & MIL Mission *die* - **4.** [RELIG - building, teaching] Mission *die*.

missionary ['mɪʃənrɪ] *n* Missionar *der*, -in *die*.

misspend [ˌmɪs'spend] *(pt & pp* **-spent** [-'spent]*)* *vt* [money, talent, youth] vergeuden.

mist [mɪst] *n* Nebel *der*. ◆ **mist over, mist up** *vi* beschlagen.

mistake [mɪ'steɪk] *(pt* **-took**, *pp* **-taken***)* ◇ *n* Fehler *der*; **to make a mistake** [in writing, work] einen Fehler machen; [be mistaken] sich irren; **by mistake** irrtümlich. ◇ *vt* - **1.** [misunderstand] falsch verstehen, missverstehen - **2.** [fail to distinguish]: **to mistake sb/sthg for** jn/etw verwechseln mit.

mistaken [mɪ'steɪkn] ◇ *pp* ▷ **mistake**. ◇ *adj* - **1.** [person]: **to be mistaken** sich irren; **to be mistaken about sb/sthg** sich in jm/etw irren - **2.** [belief, idea] irrig, falsch.

mistletoe ['mɪsltəʊ] *n (U)* Mistel *die*.

mistook [mɪ'stʊk] *pt* ▷ **mistake**.

mistreat [ˌmɪs'triːt] *vt* schlecht behandeln.

mistress ['mɪstrɪs] *n* - **1.** [of house, situation] Herrin *die* - **2.** [female lover] Geliebte *die*.

mistrust [ˌmɪs'trʌst] ◇ *n* Misstrauen *das*. ◇ *vt* misstrauen *(+ D)*.

misty ['mɪstɪ] *adj* neblig.

misunderstand [ˌmɪsʌndə'stænd] *(pt & pp* **-stood***)* ◇ *vt* missverstehen. ◇ *vi* falsch verstehen.

misunderstanding [ˌmɪsʌndə'stændɪŋ] *n* - **1.** [lack of understanding, wrong interpretation] Missverständnis *das* - **2.** [disagreement] Meinungsverschiedenheit *die*.

misunderstood [ˌmɪsʌndə'stʊd] *pt & pp* ▷ **misunderstand**.

misuse ◇ *n* [ˌmɪs'juːs] Missbrauch *der*; [of funds] Zweckentfremdung *die*. ◇ *vt* [ˌmɪs'juːz] [abuse] missbrauchen; [funds] zweckentfremden.

mitigate ['mɪtɪgeɪt] *vt fml* lindern.

mitten ['mɪtn] *n* Fausthandschuh *der*.

mix [mɪks] <> *vt* - **1.** [substances] mischen; [activities] miteinander verbinden; **to mix sthg with sthg** etw mit etw vermischen - **2.** [drink, song] mixen; [cement] mischen. <> *vi* - **1.** [substances] sich vermischen - **2.** [socially]: **to mix with sb** mit jm verkehren, Umgang pflegen mit jm. <> *n* - **1.** [combination] Mischung *die* - **2.** MUS Mix *der*. ◆ **mix up** *vt sep* - **1.** [confuse] verwechseln - **2.** [disorder] durcheinander bringen.

mixed [mɪkst] *adj* gemischt.

mixed grill *n* gemischter Grillteller.

mixed up *adj* - **1.** [confused] verwirrt - **2.** [involved]: **to be mixed up in sthg** in etw *(A)* verwickelt sein.

mixer ['mɪksəʳ] *n* - **1.** [device] Mixer *der*; [cement] Mischer *der* - **2.** [soft drink] *alkoholfreies Getränk, wie z. B. Fruchtsaft, das zum Mischen mit Spirituosen verwendet wird.*

mixture ['mɪkstʃəʳ] *n* Mischung *die*.

mix-up *n inf* Verwechslung *die*.

ml (*abbr of* **millilitre**) ml.

mm (*abbr of* **millimetre**) mm.

MMR [,emem'ɑːʳ] *n* MED (*abbr of* **measles, mumps & rubella**) MMR.

moan [məʊn] <> *n* [of pain] Stöhnen *das*; [of sadness] Seufzer *der*. <> *vi* - **1.** [in pain] stöhnen; [in sadness] seufzen - **2.** *inf* [complain] jammern; **to moan about sb/sthg** jammern OR sich beklagen über jn/etw.

moat [məʊt] *n* [around castle] Burggraben *der*; [in zoo] Wassergraben *der*.

mob [mɒb] <> *n* Mob *der*. <> *vt* belagern.

mobile ['məʊbaɪl] <> *adj* - **1.** [able to move] beweglich - **2.** *inf* [having transport] motorisiert. <> *n* [phone] Handy *das*.

mobile home *n* Wohnmobil *das*.

mobile phone *n* Handy *das*.

mobilize, -ise ['məʊbɪlaɪz] <> *vt* - **1.** [support, workforce] mobilisieren - **2.** MIL mobil machen. <> *vi* MIL mobil machen.

mock [mɒk] <> *adj* [surprise] gespielt; [Georgian house] Pseudo-; [exam] Übungs-. <> *vt* [deride] verspotten.

mockery ['mɒkərɪ] *n* - **1.** [scorn] Spott *der* - **2.** [travesty] Farce *die*.

mode [məʊd] *n* [manner] Art (und Weise) *die*; **mode of transport** Transportmittel *das*.

model ['mɒdl] (*UK*) (*US*) <> *n* - **1.** [gen] Modell *das* - **2.** [basis for imitation] Vorlage *die*; [person, society] Vorbild *das* - **3.** [best example] Musterbeispiel *das*. <> *adj* - **1.** [miniature] Modell- - **2.** [exemplary] Muster-, musterhaft. <> *vt* - **1.** [shape] modellieren - **2.** [in fashion show] vorlführen - **3.** [copy]: **to model o.s. on sb** sich *(D)* jn zum Vorbild nehmen. <> *vi* [in fashion show] als Modell arbeiten, modeln.

modem ['məʊdem] *n* COMPUT Modem *das*.

moderate <> *adj* ['mɒdərət] - **1.** [views, habits] gemäßigt; [demands] bescheiden - **2.** [heat] mäßig; [quantity] angemessen; **of moderate height/size** mittelgroß - **3.** [success, ability] mittelmäßig. <> *n* ['mɒdərət] POL Gemäßigte *der, die*. <> *vt* ['mɒdəreɪt] mäßigen.

moderation [,mɒdə'reɪʃn] *n* Mäßigung *die*; **in moderation** in Maßen.

modern ['mɒdən] *adj* modern.

modernize, -ise ['mɒdənaɪz] *vt* & *vi* modernisieren.

modern languages *npl* neue Sprachen *Pl*.

modest ['mɒdɪst] *adj* bescheiden.

modesty ['mɒdɪstɪ] *n* Bescheidenheit *die*.

modicum ['mɒdɪkəm] *n fml*: **a modicum of** ein bisschen; **a modicum of truth** ein Körnchen Wahrheit.

modify ['mɒdɪfaɪ] *vt* - **1.** [alter] ändern, abländern - **2.** [tone down] mäßigen.

module ['mɒdjuːl] *n* - **1.** [unit] Modul *das*; SCH & UNIV *zu einem Kurs gehörende Unterrichtseinheit* - **2.** [of spacecraft] Raumkapsel *die*.

mogul ['məʊgl] *n* [magnate] Mogul *der*.

mohair ['məʊheəʳ] *n (U)* Mohair *der*.

moist [mɔɪst] *adj* feucht.

moisten ['mɔɪsn] *vt* befeuchten.

moisture ['mɔɪstʃəʳ] *n* Feuchtigkeit *die*.

moisturizer, -iser ['mɔɪstʃəraɪzəʳ] *n* Feuchtigkeitscreme *die*.

molar ['məʊləʳ] *n* Backenzahn *der*.

molasses [mə'læsɪz] *n (U)* Melasse *die*.

mold *etc n* & *vt US* = **mould**.

mole [məʊl] *n* - **1.** [animal] Maulwurf *der* - **2.** [on skin] Muttermal *das*, Leberfleck *der* - **3.** [spy] Spion *der*.

molecule ['mɒlɪkjuːl] *n* Molekül *das*.

molest [mə'lest] *vt* - **1.** [attack sexually] sexuell belästigen - **2.** [bother] belästigen.

mollusc, mollusk *US* ['mɒləsk] *n* Weichtier *das*.

mollycoddle ['mɒlɪ,kɒdl] *vt inf* verhätscheln, verzärteln.

molt *vt* & *vi US* = **moult**.

molten ['məʊltn] *adj* geschmolzen.

mom [mɒm] *n US inf* Mutter *die*; [within speaker's family] Mutti *die*.

moment ['məʊmənt] *n* - **1.** [very short period of time] Moment *der*, Augenblick *der* - **2.** [particular point in time] Zeitpunkt *der*; **at any moment** jeden Moment; **at the moment** im Moment; **for the moment** vorerst.

momentarily ['məʊməntərɪlɪ] *adv* - **1.** [for a short time] momentan - **2.** *US* [immediately] jeden Moment OR Augenblick.

momentary ['məʊməntrɪ] *adj* kurz.

momentous [mə'mentəs] *adj* bedeutsam.

momentum [mə'mentəm] *n* [speed] Schwung *der*; **to gain** *OR* **gather momentum** [object, campaign] in Fahrt kommen.

momma ['mɒmə], **mommy** ['mɒmɪ] *n US* Mama *die*, Mami *die*.

Monaco ['mɒnəkəʊ] *n* Monaco *nt*.

monarch ['mɒnək] *n* Monarch *der*, -in *die*.

monarchy ['mɒnəkɪ] *n* Monarchie *die*.

monastery ['mɒnəstrɪ] *n* Kloster *das*.

Monday ['mʌndɪ] *n* Montag *der*; *see also* **Saturday**.

monetary ['mʌnɪtrɪ] *adj* Währungs-.

money ['mʌnɪ] *n (U)* Geld *das*; **to make money** Geld machen; **to get one's money's worth** etw für sein Geld geboten bekommen.

moneybox ['mʌnɪbɒks] *n* Sparbüchse *die*.

money order *n* Zahlungsanweisung *die*.

mongrel ['mʌŋgrəl] *n* [dog] Mischling *der*.

monitor ['mɒnɪtə^r] ◇ *n* Monitor *der*. ◇ *vt* - **1.** [check] überwachen, kontrollieren - **2.** [listen in to] ab|hören, mit|hören.

monk [mʌŋk] *n* Mönch *der*.

monkey ['mʌŋkɪ] (*pl* **monkeys**) *n* [animal] Affe *der*.

mono ['mɒnəʊ] ◇ *adj* [with noun] Mono-; [with adj] mono-. ◇ *n inf* [sound] Mono *das*.

monochrome ['mɒnəkrəʊm] *adj* monochrom, schwarz-weiß.

monocle ['mɒnəkl] *n* Monokel *das*.

monologue, monolog *US* ['mɒnəlɒg] *n* Monolog *der*.

monopolize, -ise [mə'nɒpəlaɪz] *vt* monopolisieren; [conversation] beherrschen; [person] in Beschlag nehmen.

monopoly [mə'nɒpəlɪ] *n*: **monopoly (on** *OR* **of)** Monopol *das* (auf *(+ A)*).

monotonous [mə'nɒtənəs] *adj* monoton.

monotony [mə'nɒtənɪ] *n* Monotonie *die*.

monsoon [mɒn'suːn] *n* Monsun *der*.

monster ['mɒnstə^r] *n* Monster *das*.

monstrosity [mɒn'strɒsətɪ] *n* Monstrosität *die*, Ungeheuerlichkeit *die*.

monstrous ['mɒnstrəs] *adj* - **1.** [appalling] abscheulich - **2.** [hideous] scheußlich - **3.** [very large] riesig.

month [mʌnθ] *n* Monat *der*.

monthly ['mʌnθlɪ] ◇ *adj* monatlich; [magazine] Monats-. ◇ *adv* monatlich. ◇ *n* [magazine] Monatsmagazin *das*.

monument ['mɒnjʊmənt] *n* - **1.** [memorial] Monument *das* - **2.** [historic building] Denkmal *das*.

monumental [ˌmɒnjʊ'mentl] *adj* - **1.** [very large] monumental - **2.** [important] bedeutend - **3.** [extremely bad] ungeheuerlich.

moo [muː] (*pl* **-s**) *vi* muhen.

mood [muːd] *n* Stimmung *die*; [of person] Laune *die*; **to be in a (bad) mood** schlechte Laune haben; **to be in a good mood** gute Laune haben.

moody ['muːdɪ] *adj pej* - **1.** [changeable] launisch - **2.** [bad-tempered] schlecht gelaunt.

moon [muːn] *n* Mond *der*.

moonlight ['muːnlaɪt] (*pt & pp* **-ed**) *n* Mondlicht *das*.

moonlighting ['muːnlaɪtɪŋ] *n* [illegal work] Schwarzarbeit *die*.

moonlit ['muːnlɪt] *adj* [place] mondbeschienen; [night] mondhell.

moor [mɔː^r] ◇ *vt* vertäuen. ◇ *vi* an|legen.

moorland ['mɔːlənd] *n esp UK* Heideland *das*.

moose [muːs] (*pl inv*) *n* Elch *der*.

mop [mɒp] ◇ *n* - **1.** [for cleaning] Mopp *der* - **2.** *inf* [of hair]: **mop of hair** (Haar)mähne *die*. ◇ *vt* wischen. ◆ **mop up** *vt sep* [liquid, dirt] auf|wischen.

mope [məʊp] *vi pej* Trübsal blasen.

moped ['məʊped] *n* Moped *das*.

moral ['mɒrəl] ◇ *adj* - **1.** [relating to morals] moralisch - **2.** [behaving correctly] moralisch einwandfrei. ◇ *n* [lesson] Moral *die*. ◆ **morals** *npl* [principles] Moral *die*.

morale [mə'rɑːl] *n* Moral *die*.

morality [mə'rælətɪ] *n* Moralität *die*.

morbid ['mɔːbɪd] *adj* morbid.

more [mɔː^r] ◇ *adv* - **1.** *(in comparatives)*: **more difficult (than)** schwieriger (als); **speak more clearly, please** sprich bitte deutlicher; **much more quickly** viel schneller - **2.** [to a greater degree] mehr; **we ought to go to the cinema more** wir sollten öfters ins Kino gehen; **I couldn't agree more** ich stimme dem völlig zu; **she's more like a mother to me than a sister** sie ist mehr wie eine Mutter als wie eine Schwester; **we were more hurt than angry** wir waren eher verletzt als zornig; **we'd be more than happy to help** wir würden sehr gerne helfen; **more than ever** mehr denn je - **3.** [referring to time]: **once/twice more** noch einmal/zweimal; **I don't go there any more** ich gehe da nicht mehr hin. ◇ *adj* - **1.** [larger number, amount of] mehr; **there are more tourists than usual** es sind mehr Touristen als gewöhnlich da; **more than ten men** mehr als zehn Männer - **2.** [additional] mehr; **we need more money/time** wir brauchen mehr Geld/Zeit; **two more bottles** noch zwei Flaschen; **is there any more cake?** ist noch mehr Kuchen da?; **there's no more wine** es ist kein Wein mehr da; **have some more tea** nehmen Sie noch etwas Tee. ◇ *pron* - **1.** [larger number, amount] mehr; **I've got more than you** ich habe mehr als du; **more than 20** mehr als 20 - **2.** [additional amount] mehr; **we need more**

wir brauchen mehr; **I'd like two more** ich möchte noch zwei; **to see more of sb** jn öfter sehen; **is there any more?** ist noch mehr da?; **there's no more** es ist nichts mehr da; **I have no more (of them)** ich habe keine mehr; **have some more** nimm dir noch; **(and) what's more** außerdem; **the more he has, the more he wants** je mehr er hat, desto mehr will er haben. ◆ **more and more** ◇ *adv* - **1.** [increasingly] immer mehr; **more and more depressed/difficult** immer deprimierter/schwieriger - **2.** [increasingly often] immer mehr *OR* öfter. ◇ *adj* immer mehr; **there are more and more cars on the roads** es gibt immer mehr Autos auf den Straßen. ◇ *pron* immer mehr; **we are spending more and more on petrol** wir geben immer mehr für Benzin aus. ◆ **more or less** *adv* [almost] mehr oder weniger; **she more or less suggested I had stolen it** sie hat mehr oder weniger behauptet, dass ich es gestohlen hätte; **it cost $500, more or less** es kostete um die $500.

moreover [mɔːˈrəʊvəʳ] *adv fml* außerdem.

morgue [mɔːg] *n* Leichenhalle *die*.

morning [ˈmɔːnɪŋ] *n* - **1.** [first part of day] Morgen *der*, Vormittag *der*; **in the morning** [before lunch] morgens; [tomorrow morning] morgen - **2.** [between midnight and noon] Morgen *der*. ◆ **mornings** *adv US* morgens.

Morocco [məˈrɒkəʊ] *n* Marokko *nt*.

moron [ˈmɔːrɒn] *n inf* Bekloppte *der, die*.

morose [məˈrəʊs] *adj* griesgrämig.

morphine [ˈmɔːfiːn] *n* Morphium *das*.

Morse (code) [mɔːs-] *n (U)* Morsezeichen *Pl*.

morsel [ˈmɔːsl] *n* Bissen *der*, Happen *der*.

mortal [ˈmɔːtl] ◇ *adj* - **1.** [not eternal] sterblich - **2.** [causing death] tödlich - **3.** [danger, fear] Todes-; **mortal enemy** Todfeind *der*; **mortal combat** Kampf *der* um Leben und Tod. ◇ *n* Sterbliche *der, die*.

mortality [mɔːˈtælətɪ] *n* Sterblichkeit *die*.

mortar [ˈmɔːtəʳ] *n* - **1.** [cement mixture] Mörtel *der* - **2.** [gun, bowl] Mörser *der*.

mortgage [ˈmɔːgɪdʒ] ◇ *n* Hypothek *die*. ◇ *vt* mit einer Hypothek belasten.

mortified [ˈmɔːtɪfaɪd] *adj* beschämt.

mortuary [ˈmɔːtʃʊərɪ] *n* Leichenhalle *die*.

mosaic [məˈzeɪɪk] *n* Mosaik *das*.

Moscow [ˈmɒskəʊ] *n* Moskau *nt*.

Moslem [ˈmɒzləm] *adj* & *n* = **Muslim**.

mosque [mɒsk] *n* Moschee *die*.

mosquito [məˈskiːtəʊ] (*pl* **-es** *OR* **-s**) *n* Moskito *der*.

moss [mɒs] *n (U)* Moos *das*.

most [məʊst] *(superl of* **many** & **much***)* ◇ *adj* - **1.** [the majority of] die meisten; **most people agree** die meisten Leute sind dieser Meinung - **2.** [the largest amount of] der/die/das meiste; **I drank (the) most beer** ich habe das meiste Bier getrunken. ◇ *adv* - **1.** [in superlatives]: **she spoke (the) most clearly** sie sprach am deutlichsten; **the most expensive hotel in town** das teuerste Hotel in der Stadt - **2.** [to the greatest degree] am meisten; **I like this one most** mir gefällt dieses am besten - **3.** *fml* [very] äußerst, höchst; **it was a most pleasant evening** es war ein äußerst angenehmer Abend. ◇ *pron* - **1.** [the majority] die meisten *Pl*; **most of the villages** die meisten Dörfer; **most of the time** die meiste Zeit; **most of the work** der größte Teil der Arbeit - **2.** [the largest amount] das meiste; **she earns (the) most** sie verdient am meisten - **3.** *phr*: **at most** höchstens; **to make the most of sthg** das Beste aus etw machen; **to make the most of an opportunity** eine Gelegenheit voll ausnutzen.

mostly [ˈməʊstlɪ] *adv* hauptsächlich.

MOT *n* (*abbr of* **Ministry of Transport (test)**) ≃ TÜV *der*.

motel [məʊˈtel] *n* Motel *das*.

moth [mɒθ] *n* Nachtfalter *der*; [eating clothes] Motte *die*.

mothball [ˈmɒθbɔːl] *n* Mottenkugel *die*.

mother [ˈmʌðəʳ] ◇ *n* Mutter *die*. ◇ *vt pej* [spoil] bemuttern.

motherhood [ˈmʌðəhʊd] *n* Mutterschaft *die*.

mother-in-law (*pl* **mothers-in-law** *OR* **mother-in-laws**) *n* Schwiegermutter *die*.

motherly [ˈmʌðəlɪ] *adj* mütterlich.

mother-of-pearl *n* Perlmutt *das*.

mother-to-be (*pl* **mothers-to-be**) *n* werdende Mutter.

mother tongue *n* Muttersprache *die*.

motif [məʊˈtiːf] *n* [pattern] Muster *das*.

motion [ˈməʊʃn] ◇ *n* - **1.** [movement] Bewegung *die*; **to set sthg in motion** etw in Bewegung setzen - **2.** [proposal] Antrag *der*. ◇ *vt* & *vi*: **to motion (to) sb to do sthg** jm durch Zeichen zu verstehen geben, etw zu tun.

motionless [ˈməʊʃənlɪs] *adj* bewegungslos.

motion picture *n US* Film *der*.

motivated [ˈməʊtɪveɪtɪd] *adj* motiviert.

motivation [ˌməʊtɪˈveɪʃn] *n* Motivation *die*.

motive [ˈməʊtɪv] *n* Motiv *das*.

motor [ˈməʊtəʳ] ◇ *adj UK* [relating to cars] Auto-. ◇ *n* [engine] Motor *der*.

motorbike [ˈməʊtəbaɪk] *n inf* Motorrad *das*.

motorboat [ˈməʊtəbəʊt] *n* Motorboot *das*.

motorcar [ˈməʊtəkɑːʳ] *n UK fml* Automobil *das*.

motorcycle [ˈməʊtəˌsaɪkl] *n* Motorrad *das*.

motorcyclist [ˈməʊtəˌsaɪklɪst] *n* Motorradfahrer *der*, -in *die*.

motoring ['məʊtərɪŋ] *adj UK* [offence] Verkehrs-; [magazine] Auto-.

motorist ['məʊtərɪst] *n* Autofahrer *der*, -in *die*.

motor racing *n* Autorennen *das*.

motor scooter *n* Motorroller *der*.

motor vehicle *n* Kraftfahrzeug *das*.

motorway ['məʊtəweɪ] *n UK* Autobahn *die*.

mottled ['mɒtld] *adj* [leaf] gesprenkelt; [skin, face] fleckig.

motto ['mɒtəʊ] (*pl* **-s** OR **-es**) *n* [maxim] Motto *das*.

mould, mold *US* [məʊld] ◇ *n* - **1.** [growth] Schimmel *der* - **2.** [shape] Form *die*. ◇ *vt* formen.

mouldy, moldy *US* ['məʊldɪ] *adj* schimmelig.

moult, molt *US* [məʊlt] *vi* [bird] sich mausern; [animal] im Fellwechsel OR Haarwechsel sein.

mound [maʊnd] *n* - **1.** [small hill] Hügel *der* - **2.** [untidy pile] Haufen *der*; [of papers, blankets] Stapel *der*.

mount [maʊnt] ◇ *n* - **1.** [support, frame - for photograph] Rahmen *der*; [- for jewel] Fassung *die*; [- for machine] Sockel *der* - **2.** [horse, pony] Reittier *das* - **3.** [mountain]: **Mount Everest** Mount Everest; **Mount Etna** Etna. ◇ *vt* - **1.** [climb onto] besteigen - **2.** *fml* [climb up - stairs] hoch|steigen - **3.** [organize] organisieren - **4.** [fix in place - jewel] ein|fassen; [- photographic slide] rahmen; **to mount sthg on the wall** etw an die Wand hängen. ◇ *vi* [increase] sich erhöhen.

mountain ['maʊntɪn] *n liter & fig* Berg *der*.

mountain bike *n* Mountainbike *das*.

mountaineer [ˌmaʊntɪ'nɪəʳ] *n* Bergsteiger *der*, -in *die*.

mountaineering [ˌmaʊntɪ'nɪərɪŋ] *n* Bergsteigen *das*.

mountainous ['maʊntɪnəs] *adj* [full of mountains] bergig.

mourn [mɔːn] ◇ *vt* trauern um. ◇ *vi* trauern; **to mourn for sb** um jn trauern.

mourner ['mɔːnəʳ] *n* Trauernde *der, die*.

mournful ['mɔːnfʊl] *adj* traurig.

mourning ['mɔːnɪŋ] *n (phrase)*: **to be in mourning** [mourn] trauern; [wear mourning clothes] Trauerkleidung tragen.

mouse [maʊs] (*pl* **mice**) *n* [animal & COMPUT] Maus *die*.

mouse mat, mouse pad *n* COMPUT Mauspad *das*.

mousetrap ['maʊstræp] *n* Mausefalle *die*.

mousse [muːs] *n* - **1.** [food] Mousse *die* - **2.** [for hair] Schaumfestiger *der*.

moustache *UK* [mə'stɑːʃ], **mustache** *US* ['mʌstæʃ] *n* Schnurrbart *der*.

mouth *n* [maʊθ] - **1.** [of person] Mund *der* - **2.** [entrance - of cave, tunnel] Eingang *der*; [- of river] Mündung *die*.

mouthful ['maʊθfʊl] *n* [amount - of food] Bissen *der*; [- of drink] Schluck *der*.

mouthorgan ['maʊθˌɔːgən] *n* Mundharmonika *die*.

mouthpiece ['maʊθpiːs] *n* - **1.** [of telephone] Sprechmuschel *die* - **2.** [of musical instrument] Mundstück *das* - **3.** [spokesperson] Sprachrohr *das*.

mouthwash ['maʊθwɒʃ] *n (U)* Mundwasser *das*.

mouth-watering [-ˌwɔːtərɪŋ] *adj* appetitlich, appetitanregend.

movable ['muːvəbl] *adj* beweglich.

move [muːv] ◇ *n* - **1.** [movement] Bewegung *die*; **to get a move on** *inf* sich beeilen - **2.** [to new house] Umzug *der*; [to higher position in company] Aufstieg *der* - **3.** [in board game] Zug *der*; **it's your move** du bist am Zug - **4.** [course of action]: **it would be a good move** es wäre klug. ◇ *vt* - **1.** [arm, head] bewegen; [piece of furniture] rücken; [car] weg|fahren; [piece in board game] einen Zug machen mit - **2.** [change]: **to move house** um|ziehen; **to move sb to another job** jn versetzen - **3.** [affect emotionally] bewegen, rühren - **4.** [in debate]: **to move that...** beantragen, dass... - **5.** *fml* [cause]: **to move sb to do sthg** jn dazu bewegen, etw zu tun. ◇ *vi* - **1.** [shift] sich bewegen - **2.** [act] handeln - **3.** [to new house] um|ziehen. ◆ **move about** *vi* - **1.** [fidget] sich unruhig (hin und her) bewegen - **2.** [travel] unterwegs sein. ◆ **move along** ◇ *vt sep* [person, crowds] zum Weitergehen veranlassen. ◇ *vi* weiter|gehen; [in car] weiter|fahren. ◆ **move around** *vi* = **move about**. ◆ **move away** *vi* [go in opposite direction] weg|gehen; [car] weg|fahren. ◆ **move in** *vi* - **1.** [to new house] um|ziehen - **2.** [troops] ein|rücken; [competitors] auf den Plan treten. ◆ **move on** *vi* - **1.** [after stopping] weiter|gehen; [in car] weiter|fahren - **2.** [in discussion] fort|fahren. ◆ **move out** *vi* [from house] aus|ziehen. ◆ **move over** *vi* zur Seite rutschen OR rücken. ◆ **move up** *vi* [on seat] auf|rutschen, auf|rücken.

moveable ['muːvəbl] *adj* = **movable**.

movement ['muːvmənt] *n* - **1.** [motion, gesture, group] Bewegung *die* - **2.** [transportation] Beförderung *die* - **3.** [trend] Trend *der* - **4.** MUS Satz *der*.

movie ['muːvɪ] *n esp US* Film *der*; **to go to the movies** zum Kino gehen.

movie camera *n* Filmkamera *die*.

moving ['muːvɪŋ] *adj* - **1.** [touching] bewegend - **2.** [not fixed] beweglich.

mow [məʊ] (*pt* **-ed**, *pp* **-ed** OR **mown**) *vt* mähen. ◆ **mow down** *vt sep* nieder|mähen.

mower ['məʊəʳ] *n* [lawnmower] Rasenmäher *der*.

mown [məʊn] *pp* ▷ **mow**.

MP *n UK abbr of* **Member of Parliament**.

MP3 [ˌempiː'θriː] *n* (*abbr of* **MPEG-1 Audio Layer-3**) MP3.

MP3 player *n* MP3-Spieler *der*.

mpg (*abbr of* **miles per gallon**) *n*: **31 mpg** 9,1 l auf 100 km.

mph (*abbr of* **miles per hour**) *n*: **he was doing 50 mph** er fuhr 80 km/h (schnell).

Mr ['mɪstəʳ] *n* Herr.

Mrs ['mɪsɪz] *n* Frau, Fr.

MRSA [ˌemɑːres'eɪ] *n* MED (*abbr of* **methicillin resistant Staphylococcus aureus**) MRSA *der*.

Ms [mɪz] *n* Frau, Fr.

MS *n* (*abbr of* **multiple sclerosis**) MS.

MSc *n abbr of* **Master of Science**.

much [mʌtʃ] (*comp* **more**, *superl* **most**) ◇ *adj* viel; **I haven't got much money** ich habe nicht viel Geld; **as much food as you can eat** so viel du essen kannst; **how much is left?** wie viel ist übrig?; **we have too much work** wir haben zu viel Arbeit. ◇ *adv* - **1.** [to a great extent] viel; **it's much better** es ist viel besser; **I like it very much** es gefällt mir sehr gut; **it's not much good** *inf* es ist nicht besonders; **nothing much** nichts Besonderes; **thank you very much** vielen Dank; **much as I like him** so gern ich ihn auch mag; **much to my surprise** sehr zu meiner Überraschung; **much the same** ziemlich das Gleiche; **he's not so much stupid as lazy** er ist weniger dumm als faul; **he left without so much as a goodbye** er hat sich nicht einmal verabschiedet - **2.** [often] oft; **we don't go there much** wir gehen da nicht oft hin. ◇ *pron* viel; **I haven't got much** ich habe nicht viel; **as much as you like** so viel Sie wollen; **how much is it?** wie viel kostet es?; **you've got too much** du hast zu viel; **I don't think much of him** ich halte nicht viel von ihm; **I thought as much** das habe ich mir gedacht; **I'm not much of a cook** ich bin kein großer Koch; **so much for his friendship!** und das nennt sich Freundschaft!

muck [mʌk] *n (U) inf* - **1.** [dirt] Dreck *der* - **2.** [manure] Mist *der*. ◆ **muck about, muck around** *UK inf* ◇ *vt sep* an der Nase herum|führen. ◇ *vi* herum|albern. ◆ **muck up** *vt sep UK inf* vermasseln.

mucky ['mʌkɪ] *adj inf* dreckig.

mucus ['mjuːkəs] *n (U)* Schleim *der*.

mud [mʌd] *n* Schlamm *der*.

muddle ['mʌdl] ◇ *n* [disorder] Durcheinander *das*. ◇ *vt* - **1.** [put into disorder] durcheinander bringen - **2.** [confuse - person] verwirren. ◆ **muddle along** *vi* vor sich *(A)* hin wursteln. ◆ **muddle through** *vi* sich durch|wursteln *OR* durch|schlagen. ◆ **muddle up** *vt sep* durcheinander bringen.

muddy ['mʌdɪ] ◇ *adj* [floor, boots] schmutzig; [river] schlammig. ◇ *vt fig* [issue, situation] verworren machen.

mudguard ['mʌdgɑːd] *n* [on car] Kotflügel *der*; [on motorcycle] Schutzblech *das*.

muesli ['mjuːzlɪ] *n UK* Müsli *das*.

muff [mʌf] ◇ *n* [for hands] Muff *der*; [for ears] Ohrenwärmer *der*. ◇ *vt inf* verpatzen.

muffin ['mʌfɪn] *n* - **1.** *UK* [bread roll] *kleines flaches Milchbrötchen, das warm und mit Butter gegessen wird* - **2.** *US* [cake] *kleiner Kuchen*.

muffle ['mʌfl] *vt* [quieten] dämpfen.

muffler ['mʌflər] *n US* [for car] Auspuff *der*.

mug [mʌg] ◇ *n* - **1.** [cup, mugful] Tasse *die* - **2.** *inf* [fool] Trottel *der*. ◇ *vt* [attack and rob] überfallen und berauben.

mugging ['mʌgɪŋ] *n* Straßenraub *der*.

muggy ['mʌgɪ] *adj* schwül.

mule [mjuːl] *n* - **1.** [animal] Maultier *das* - **2.** [slipper] Schlappen *der*.

mull [mʌl] ◆ **mull over** *vt sep* gründlich durch|denken.

mulled [mʌld] *adj*: **mulled wine** Glühwein *der*.

multicoloured *UK*, **multicolored** *US* ['mʌltɪˌkʌləd] *adj* bunt, mehrfarbig.

multilateral [ˌmʌltɪ'lætərəl] *adj* multilateral.

multilingual [ˌmʌltɪ'lɪŋgwəl] *adj* mehrsprachig.

multinational [ˌmʌltɪ'næʃənl] *n* multinationales Unternehmen.

multiple ['mʌltɪpl] ◇ *adj* vielfach. ◇ *n* MATHS Vielfache *das*.

multiple sclerosis [-sklɪ'rəʊsɪs] *n (U)* multiple Sklerose.

multiplex (cinema) ['mʌltɪpleks-] *n großes Kino mit mehreren Vorführsälen*.

multiplication [ˌmʌltɪplɪ'keɪʃn] *n (U)* - **1.** MATHS Multiplikation *die* - **2.** [increase] Vervielfachung *die*, Vermehrung *die*.

multiply ['mʌltɪplaɪ] ◇ *vt* - **1.** MATHS multiplizieren - **2.** [increase] vermehren. ◇ *vi* - **1.** MATHS multiplizieren - **2.** [increase] sich vervielfältigen - **3.** [breed] sich vermehren.

multistorey *UK*, **multistory** *US* [ˌmʌltɪ'stɔːrɪ] *adj* mehrstöckig; **multistorey car park** Parkhaus *das*.

multitude ['mʌltɪtjuːd] *n* [large number] Vielzahl *die*.

mum [mʌm] *UK inf* ◇ *n* Mutter *die*; [within speaker's family] Mutti *die*. ◇ *adj*: **to keep mum** den Mund halten.

mumble ['mʌmbl] ◇ *vt* [response] murmeln; [words] nuscheln. ◇ *vi* vor sich *(A)* hin murmeln; **stop mumbling** hör auf zu nuscheln.

mummy ['mʌmɪ] *n* - **1.** *UK inf* [mother] Mami *die* - **2.** [preserved body] Mumie *die*.

mumps [mʌmps] *n (U)* Mumps *der*.

munch [mʌntʃ] *vt* & *vi* mampfen.

mundane [mʌn'deɪn] *adj* [ordinary] alltäglich.

municipal [mju:'nɪsɪpl] *adj* städtisch; [park, administration] Stadt-.

municipality [mju:ˌnɪsɪ'pælətɪ] *n* Stadt *die*.

mural ['mju:ərəl] *n* Wandgemälde *das*.

murder ['mɜ:dəʳ] ◇ *n* Mord *der*. ◇ *vt* ermorden.

murderer ['mɜ:dərəʳ] *n* Mörder *der*, -in *die*.

murderous ['mɜ:dərəs] *adj* [thugs] mordgierig; [attack] mörderisch.

murky ['mɜ:kɪ] *adj* - **1.** [dark - place] düster; [- water] trüb - **2.** [shameful] dunkel, finster.

murmur ['mɜ:məʳ] ◇ *n* - **1.** [low sound - of voices] Gemurmel *das*; [- of disapproving voices] Murmeln *das* - **2.** MED [of heart] Herzgeräusch *das*. ◇ *vt* & *vi* murmeln.

muscle ['mʌsl] *n* - **1.** [organ] Muskel *der* - **2.** *(U)* MED [tissue] Muskelgewebe *das* - **3.** *(U)* *fig* [power] Macht *die*. ◆ **muscle in** *vi* mitmischen.

muscular ['mʌskjʊləʳ] *adj* - **1.** [of muscles] Muskel- - **2.** [strong] muskulös.

muse [mju:z] ◇ *n* Muse *die*. ◇ *vi* sinnieren.

museum [mju:'zɪəm] *n* Museum *das*.

mushroom ['mʌʃrʊm] ◇ *n* [cultivated] Pilz *der*, Champignon *der*. ◇ *vi* [grow quickly - organization, movement] sehr schnell wachsen; [- houses] wie Pilze aus dem Boden schießen.

music ['mju:zɪk] *n* - **1.** [gen] Musik *die*; **a piece of music** ein Musikstück - **2.** [subject studied] Musik *die* - **3.** [written] Noten *Pl*.

musical ['mju:zɪkl] ◇ *adj* - **1.** [education, director] Musik- - **2.** [talented in music] musikalisch - **3.** [voice, sound] melodiös. ◇ *n* Musical *das*.

musical instrument *n* Musikinstrument *das*.

music centre *n* Kompaktanlage *die*.

music hall *n UK* Varieté *das*.

musician [mju:'zɪʃn] *n* Musiker *der*, -in *die*.

Muslim ['mʊzlɪm] ◇ *adj* moslemisch. ◇ *n* Moslem *der*, Moslemin *die*.

mussel ['mʌsl] *n* Miesmuschel *die*.

must [mʌst] ◇ *aux vb* müssen; [with negative] dürfen; **I must go** ich muss gehen; **you mustn't be late** du darfst nicht zu spät kommen; **do it, if you must** tu es, wenn es sein muss; **the room must be vacated by ten** das Zimmer ist bis zehn Uhr zu räumen; **you must have seen it** du musst es doch gesehen haben; **you must see that film** du musst dir diesen Film ansehen; **you must be joking!** das kann doch nicht dein Ernst sein! ◇ *n*: **it's a must** *inf* das ist ein Muss.

mustache *n US* = **moustache**.

mustard ['mʌstəd] *n* Senf *der*.

muster ['mʌstəʳ] ◇ *vt* - **1.** [summon - strength, courage] zusammen|nehmen; [- support] zusammen|bekommen - **2.** [assemble - volunteers, helpers] versammeln; [- troops] zusammen|ziehen. ◇ *vi* [troops] sich sammeln.

mustn't ['mʌsnt] *abbr of* **must not**.

must've ['mʌstəv] *abbr of* **must have**.

musty ['mʌstɪ] *adj* [smell, room, air] muffig; [books] moderig.

mute [mju:t] *adj* [person] stumm.

muted ['mju:tɪd] *adj* - **1.** [sound, colour] gedämpft - **2.** [protest] schwach.

mutilate ['mju:tɪleɪt] *vt* - **1.** [maim] verstümmeln - **2.** [damage, spoil] ruinieren.

mutiny ['mju:tɪnɪ] ◇ *n* Meuterei *die*. ◇ *vi* meutern.

mutter ['mʌtəʳ] ◇ *vt* murmeln. ◇ *vi* murmeln; [grumble] murren.

mutton ['mʌtn] *n* Hammelfleisch *das*.

mutual ['mju:tʃʊəl] *adj* - **1.** [aid] gegenseitig; **by mutual consent** in gegenseitigem Einverständnis - **2.** [friend, interest] gemeinsam.

mutually ['mju:tʃʊəlɪ] *adv* [reciprocally - beneficial, convenient] für beide Seiten; [- agreed] von beiden Seiten.

muzzle ['mʌzl] ◇ *n* - **1.** [dog's nose and jaws] Schnauze *die* - **2.** [for dog] Maulkorb *der* - **3.** [of gun] Mündung *die*. ◇ *vt* - **1.** [dog] einen Maulkorb anlegen *(+ D)* - **2.** *fig* [press, opposition] knebeln.

MW (*abbr of* **medium wave**) MW.

my [maɪ] ◇ *poss adj* mein; **my friend** mein Freund, meine Freundin; **my children** meine Kinder; **I washed my hair** ich habe mir die Haare gewaschen. ◇ *excl*: **(oh) my!** meine Güte!

myself [maɪ'self] *pron* - **1.** *(reflexive: accusative)* mich; *(reflexive: dative)* mir; **I have hurt myself** ich habe mich verletzt; **I bought myself some new clothes** ich habe mir neue Kleider gekauft - **2.** *(after prep: accusative)* mich selbst; *(after prep: dative)* mir selbst; **I did it myself** ich habe es selbst gemacht; **by myself** allein.

mysterious [mɪ'stɪərɪəs] *adj* - **1.** [puzzling - illness, sound] rätselhaft; [- disappearance] mysteriös - **2.** [secretive] geheimnisvoll.

mystery ['mɪstərɪ] *n* - **1.** [puzzle] Rätsel *das* - **2.** [secret] Geheimnis *das*.

mystical ['mɪstɪkl] *adj* mystisch.

mystified ['mɪstɪfaɪd] *adj* verwirrt.

mystifying ['mɪstɪfaɪɪŋ] *adj* [action] rätselhaft; [decision] unerklärlich.

mystique [mɪ'stiːk] *n (U)* geheimnisvoller Nimbus.

myth [mɪθ] *n* - **1.** [legend] Mythos *der* - **2.** [false belief] Irrglauben *der*.

mythical ['mɪθɪkl] *adj* - **1.** [legendary] mythisch - **2.** [imaginary - place, time] fiktiv.

mythology [mɪ'θɒlədʒɪ] *n* Mythologie *die*.

N

n (*pl* **n's** OR **ns**), **N** (*pl* **N's** OR **Ns**) [en] *n* [letter] n *das*, N *das*. ◆ **N** (*abbr of* **north**) N.

n/a, N/A - **1.** (*abbr of* **not applicable**) entf. - **2.** (*abbr of* **not available**) n. bez.

nab [næb] *vt inf* - **1.** [arrest] schnappen - **2.** [claim quickly] sich *(D)* schnappen.

nag [næg] ◇ *vt* [pester] keine Ruhe lassen *(+ D)*; [find fault with] herum|nörgeln an *(+ D)*; **to nag sb to do sthg** jm zu|setzen, damit er/sie etw tut. ◇ *n UK inf* [horse] Klepper *der*.

nagging ['nægɪŋ] *adj* [thought, doubt, pain] quälend.

nail [neɪl] ◇ *n* [gen] Nagel *der*. ◇ *vt*: **to nail sthg to sthg** etw an etw *(A)* nageln. ◆ **nail down** *vt sep liter & fig* fest|nageln.

nailbrush ['neɪlbrʌʃ] *n* Nagelbürste *die*.

nail clippers [-ˌklɪpəz] *npl* Nagelknipser *der*.

nail file *n* Nagelfeile *die*.

nail polish *n* Nagellack *der*.

nail scissors *npl* Nagelschere *die*.

nail varnish *n* Nagellack *der*.

nail varnish remover [-rɪ'muːvəʳ] *n* Nagellackentferner *der*.

naive, naïve [naɪ'iːv] *adj* naiv.

naked ['neɪkɪd] *adj* - **1.** [nude] nackt - **2.** [flame] offen; [light bulb] nackt; **with the naked eye** mit bloßem Auge - **3.** [truth, aggression] nackt.

name [neɪm] ◇ *n* - **1.** [gen] Name *der*; **what's your name?** wie heißen Sie?; **my name is** ich heiße; **to know sb by name** jn mit Namen kennen; **to know sb only by name** jn nur dem Namen nach kennen; **in the name of** im Namen *(+ G)*; **the account is in her name** das Konto läuft auf ihren Namen; **to call sb names** jn beschimpfen - **2.** [reputation] Name *der*, Ruf *der*; **to clear one's name** seine Unschuld beweisen. ◇ *vt* - **1.** [baby, place, ship] einen Namen geben *(+ D)*; **they named their daughter Kate** sie nannten ihre Tochter Kate; **I name this ship "Bounty"** ich taufe das Schiff auf den Namen "Bounty"; **to name sb after sb** *UK*, **to name sb for sb** *US* jn nach jm nennen; **to name sthg after sthg** *UK*, **to name sthg for sthg** *US* etw nach etw benennen - **2.** [reveal identity of]: **to name sb** js Namen nennen - **3.** [choose - price, date] nennen; [- successor] ernennen.

namely ['neɪmlɪ] *adv* nämlich.

namesake ['neɪmseɪk] *n* Namensvetter *der*, -in *die*.

nanny ['nænɪ] *n* [childminder] Kindermädchen *das*.

nap [næp] ◇ *n* [sleep] Nickerchen *das*; **to take** OR **have a nap** ein Nickerchen machen. ◇ *vi* [sleep] ein Nickerchen machen; **to be caught napping** *inf* überrumpelt werden.

nape [neɪp] *n*: **nape (of the neck)** Nacken *der*.

napkin ['næpkɪn] *n* [serviette] Serviette *die*.

nappy ['næpɪ] *n UK* Windel *die*.

narcotic [nɑː'kɒtɪk] *n* Betäubungsmittel *das*. ◆ **narcotics** *npl* Rauschgift *das*.

narrative ['nærətɪv] ◇ *adj* [ability, skill] erzählerisch; [poem] narrativ. ◇ *n* [account] Schilderung *die*.

narrator [*UK* nə'reɪtəʳ, *US* 'næreɪtər] *n* [in book] Erzähler *der*, -in *die*; [of documentary] Kommentator *der*, -in *die*.

narrow ['nærəʊ] ◇ *adj* - **1.** [not wide] schmal; [valley, lane] eng - **2.** [attitude, beliefs] engstirnig - **3.** [victory, defeat, majority] knapp. ◇ *vt* - **1.** [almost shut]: **to narrow one's eyes** die Augen zu Schlitzen verengen - **2.** [difference, gap] verringern. ◇ *vi* - **1.** [become less wide] sich verengen - **2.** [eyes] zu Schlitzen werden - **3.** [difference, gap] sich verringern. ◆ **narrow down** *vt sep* [restrict - choice] ein|schränken; [- possibilities] beschränken.

narrowly ['nærəʊlɪ] *adv* [just] knapp; [escape] mit knapper Not.

narrow-minded [-'maɪndɪd] *adj* engstirnig.

nasal ['neɪzl] *adj* - **1.** [sound] näselnd - **2.** ANAT Nasen-.

nasty ['nɑːstɪ] *adj* - **1.** [unkind - person, behaviour] gemein; [- remark] gehässig - **2.** [smell, taste, weather] scheußlich - **3.** [problem, question] schwierig - **4.** [injury, accident, fall] schlimm.

nation ['neɪʃn] *n* Nation *die*; [people] Volk *das*.

national ['næʃənl] ◇ *adj* - **1.** [nationwide - strike] national, landesweit; [- newspaper] überregional; [- library, debt] Staats- - **2.** [typical of nation] landestypisch; [custom] Volks-. ◇ *n* Staatsbürger *der*, -in *die*.

national anthem *n* Nationalhymne *die*.

national curriculum *n Programm, das die Fächer und zu erreichenden Standards in den staatlichen Schulen in England und Wales festlegt.*

national dress *n* Landestracht *die*.

National Health Service *n staatlicher britischer Gesundheitsdienst.*

National Insurance *n (U) UK* - **1.** [system] Sozialversicherung *die* - **2.** [payments] Sozialversicherungsbeiträge *Pl*.

nationalism [ˈnæʃnəlɪzm] *n* Nationalismus *der*.

nationalist [ˈnæʃnəlɪst] ◇ *adj* nationalistisch. ◇ *n* Nationalist *der*, -in *die*.

nationality [ˌnæʃəˈnælətɪ] *n* Nationalität *die*.

nationalize, -ise [ˈnæʃnəlaɪz] *vt* verstaatlichen.

national service *n* Wehrdienst *der*.

National Trust *n britische Organisation, die im Besitz historischer Bauwerke ist und diese unterhält.*

nationwide [ˈneɪʃənwaɪd] *adj* & *adv* landesweit.

native [ˈneɪtɪv] ◇ *adj* [customs, population, plant] einheimisch; **native country** Heimatland *das*; **a native Italian** ein gebürtiger Italiener; **native speaker** Muttersprachler *der*; **native language** Muttersprache *die*; *(phrase)*: **native to** [plant, animal] beheimatet in *(+ D)*. ◇ *n* [person] Einheimische *der, die*; *offens* [of colony] Eingeborene *der, die*.

Native American *n* Indianer *der*, -in *die*.

Nativity [nəˈtɪvətɪ] *n*: **the Nativity** die Geburt Christi.

NATO [ˈneɪtəʊ] (*abbr of* **North Atlantic Treaty Organization**) *n* NATO *die*.

natural [ˈnætʃrəl] *adj* - **1.** [gen] natürlich - **2.** [inborn - instinct, skill] angeboren; [- footballer, musician *etc*] geboren - **3.** [disaster, phenomenon] Natur-.

natural gas *n* Erdgas *das*.

naturalize, -ise [ˈnætʃrəlaɪz] *vt* [make citizen] ein|bürgern.

naturally [ˈnætʃrəlɪ] *adv* - **1.** [of course] natürlich - **2.** [behave, speak] natürlich - **3.** [cheerful, talented] von Natur aus.

natural yoghurt *n* Naturjogurt *der ODER das ODER die*.

nature [ˈneɪtʃəʳ] *n* - **1.** [gen] Natur *die* - **2.** [temperament] Wesen *das*; **by nature** von Natur aus - **3.** [type] Art *die*.

nature reserve *n* Naturschutzgebiet *das*.

naughty [ˈnɔːtɪ] *adj* - **1.** [child] ungezogen - **2.** [word, story] unanständig.

nausea [ˈnɔːsɪə] *n* Übelkeit *die*.

nauseating [ˈnɔːzɪeɪtɪŋ] *adj fig* [disgusting] abscheulich.

nautical [ˈnɔːtɪkl] *adj* nautisch; [map] See-; [term] seemännisch.

naval [ˈneɪvl] *adj* Marine-; [battle, forces] See-.

nave [neɪv] *n* Kirchenschiff *das*.

navel [ˈneɪvl] *n* Nabel *der*.

navigate [ˈnævɪgeɪt] ◇ *vt* [steer - plane, ship] navigieren. ◇ *vi* [in plane, ship] navigieren; **I'll drive, and you navigate** ich fahre, und du dirigierst mich.

navigation [ˌnævɪˈgeɪʃn] *n* Navigation *die*.

navigator [ˈnævɪgeɪtəʳ] *n* Navigator *der*.

navy [ˈneɪvɪ] *n* [armed force] (Kriegs)marine *die*.

navy (blue) ◇ *adj* marineblau. ◇ *n* Marineblau *das*.

Nazi [ˈnɑːtsɪ] (*pl* **-s**) *n* Nazi *der*.

NB (*abbr of* **nota bene**) NB.

near [nɪəʳ] ◇ *adj* nahe; **in the near future** demnächst; **the nearest hospital** das nächste Krankenhaus; **a near disaster** beinahe ein Unglück; **it was a near thing (for us)** wir sind gerade noch davongekommen. ◇ *adv* nahe; **near at hand** (ganz) in der Nähe; **to come** *OR* **draw near to sb/sthg** sich jm/etw nähern; **a near impossible task** eine nahezu unmögliche Aufgabe. ◇ *prep*: **near (to)** nahe an *(+ D)*; **near the door** bei der Tür; **near to death/despair** dem Tode/der Verzweiflung nahe. ◇ *vt* sich nähern *(+ D)*; **the road is nearing completion** die Straße ist fast fertig. ◇ *vi* sich nähern.

nearby [nɪəˈbaɪ] ◇ *adj* nahe gelegen. ◇ *adv* in der Nähe.

nearly [ˈnɪəlɪ] *adv* [almost] fast, beinahe; **I nearly fell** ich bin fast *OR* beinahe gefallen; **not nearly** bei weitem nicht.

near miss *n* [between aircraft] Beinahezusammenstoß *der*.

nearside [ˈnɪəsaɪd] *n* Beifahrerseite *die*.

nearsighted [ˌnɪəˈsaɪtɪd] *adj US* kurzsichtig.

neat [niːt] *adj* - **1.** [tidy] ordentlich; [sb's appearance] adrett - **2.** [skilful - solution] elegant; [- manoeuvre] geschickt - **3.** [whisky, vodka *etc*] pur - **4.** *US inf* [very good] super.

neatly [ˈniːtlɪ] *adv* - **1.** [tidily] ordentlich; [dress] adrett - **2.** [skilfully] geschickt.

necessarily [ˌnesəˈserɪlɪ, *UK* ˈnesəsrəlɪ] *adv* notwendigerweise; **not necessarily** nicht unbedingt.

necessary [ˈnesəsrɪ] *adj* - **1.** [required] notwendig, nötig; **to make it necessary for sb to do sthg** es erforderlich machen, dass jd etw tut - **2.** [inevitable] unausweichlich.

necessity [nɪˈsesətɪ] *n* - **1.** [need] Notwendigkeit *die*; **of necessity** notwendigerweise - **2.** [necessary thing] Notwendigkeit *die*.

neck [nek] *n* - **1.** [gen] Hals *der* - **2.** [of shirt] Kragen *der*; [of dress] Ausschnitt *der*. ◆ **neck**

and neck *adj* gleichauf; **the two horses are neck and neck** zwischen den beiden Pferden gibt es ein Kopf-an-Kopf-Rennen.

necklace ['neklɪs] *n* (Hals)kette *die*.

neckline ['neklaɪn] *n* Ausschnitt *der*.

necktie ['nektaɪ] *n US* Krawatte *die*.

nectarine ['nektərɪn] *n* Nektarine *die*.

need [ni:d] ◇ *n* - **1.** [requirement, necessity] Bedürfnis *das*; **to be in** OR **have need of sthg** etw brauchen; **in need of repair** reparaturbedürftig; **there is no need (for you) to cry** du brauchst nicht zu weinen; **if need be** notfalls - **2.** [distress, poverty] Not *die*. ◇ *vt* brauchen; **to need to do sthg** etw tun müssen; **you don't need to wait for me** du brauchst nicht auf mich zu warten; **that's all I need!** *fig* das hat mir gerade noch gefehlt! ◇ *aux vb*: **need we go?** müssen wir gehen?; **it need not happen** es muss nicht dazu kommen.

needle ['ni:dl] *n* Nadel *die*.

needless ['ni:dlɪs] *adj* unnötig; **needless to say** selbstverständlich.

needlework ['ni:dlwɜ:k] *n (U)* Handarbeit *die*.

needn't ['ni:dnt] *abbr of* **need not**.

needy ['ni:dɪ] *adj* bedürftig.

negative ['negətɪv] ◇ *adj* - **1.** [not affirmative] negativ - **2.** [pessimistic] pessimistisch. ◇ *n* - **1.** PHOT Negativ *das* - **2.** LING Verneinung *die*; [word] Verneinungswort *das*; **to answer in the negative** mit "Nein" antworten.

neglect [nɪ'glekt] ◇ *n* Vernachlässigung *die*. ◇ *vt* - **1.** [not take care of] vernachlässigen - **2.** [not do - duty] versäumen; [- task, work] unerledigt lassen; **to neglect to do sthg** es versäumen, etw zu tun.

negligee ['neglɪʒeɪ] *n* Negligee *das*.

negligence ['neglɪdʒəns] *n* Nachlässigkeit *die*; [causing danger & LAW] Fahrlässigkeit *die*.

negligible ['neglɪdʒəbl] *adj* unerheblich.

negotiate [nɪ'gəʊʃɪeɪt] ◇ *vt* - **1.** [agreement, deal] aus|handeln - **2.** [obstacle] überwinden; [bend] nehmen; [hill, rapids] passieren. ◇ *vi* verhandeln; **to negotiate with sb for sthg** mit jm über etw *(A)* verhandeln.

negotiation [nɪ,gəʊʃɪ'eɪʃn] *n* Verhandlung *die*.

neigh [neɪ] *vi* wiehern.

neighbor *etc n US* = **neighbour** *etc*.

neighbour *UK*, **neighbor** *US* ['neɪbəʳ] *n* Nachbar *der*, -in *die*; [at table] Tischnachbar *der*, -in *die*; [country] Nachbarland *das*.

neighbourhood *UK*, **neighborhood** *US* ['neɪbəhʊd] *n* [small area of town] Gegend *die*; [people] Nachbarschaft *die*; *(phrase)*: **it costs in the neighbourhood of £3,000** [approximately] es kostet so um die 3000 Pfund.

neighbouring *UK*, **neighboring** *US* ['neɪbərɪŋ] *adj* angrenzend.

neighbourly *UK*, **neighborly** *US* ['neɪbəlɪ] *adj* [relations, deed] gutnachbarlich.

neither ['naɪðəʳ, 'ni:ðəʳ] ◇ *adj*: **neither bag is big enough** keine der beiden Taschen ist groß genug. ◇ *pron*: **neither of us** keiner von uns beiden. ◇ *conj*: **neither do I** ich auch nicht; **neither nor** weder noch; **that's neither here nor there** *fig* das hat nichts mit der Sache zu tun.

neon light *n* Neonlicht *das*.

nephew ['nefju:] *n* Neffe *der*.

Neptune ['neptju:n] *n* [planet] Neptun *der*.

nerd [nɜ:d] *n inf*: **computer nerd** Computerfreak *der*.

nerve [nɜ:v] *n* - **1.** ANAT Nerv *der* - **2.** [courage] Mut *der*; **to lose/keep one's nerve** seine Nerven verlieren/behalten - **3.** [cheek] Frechheit *die*. ◆ **nerves** *npl* Nerven *Pl*; **to get on sb's nerves** jm auf die Nerven gehen.

nerve-racking [-,rækɪŋ] *adj* nervenaufreibend.

nervous ['nɜ:vəs] *adj* [condition, twitch] nervös; [tissue, illness] Nerven-; **to be nervous of** Angst haben vor *(+ D)*; **to be nervous about sthg** nervös wegen etw sein.

nervous breakdown *n* Nervenzusammenbruch *der*.

nest [nest] ◇ *n* - **1.** [gen] Nest *das* - **2.** [of tables] Satz *der*. ◇ *vi* [bird] nisten.

nest egg *n* [money] Notgroschen *der*.

nestle ['nesl] *vi* [make o.s. comfortable] es sich bequem machen.

net [net] ◇ *adj* - **1.** [profit, weight] Netto-, netto - **2.** [final] End-. ◇ *n* [gen] Netz *das*. ◇ *vt* - **1.** [catch] mit dem Netz fangen - **2.** *fig* [husband] sich *(D)* angeln; [criminal] fangen; [fortune] verdienen - **3.** [profit, sum - subj: deal] netto ein|bringen; [- subj: person] netto ein|nehmen. ◆ **Net** *n* COMPUT: **the Net** das Internet.

netball ['netbɔ:l] *n* Korbball *der*.

net curtains *npl* Tüllgardinen *Pl*.

Netherlands ['neðələndz] *npl*: **the Netherlands** die Niederlande *Pl*.

nett [net] *adj* = **net**.

netting ['netɪŋ] *n (U)* - **1.** [gen] Netz *das*; [metal] Maschendraht *der* - **2.** [fabric] Tüll *der*.

nettle ['netl] *n* Nessel *die*.

network ['netwɜ:k] *n* - **1.** [gen] Netz *das* - **2.** RADIO & TV [station] Sendenetz *das* - **3.** COMPUT Netzwerk *das*.

neurosis [,njʊə'rəʊsɪs] *(pl* **-ses** [si:z]) *n* Neurose *die*.

neurotic [,njʊə'rɒtɪk] ◇ *adj* neurotisch. ◇ *n* Neurotiker *der*, -in *die*.

neuter ['nju:təʳ] ◇ *adj* GRAM sächlich. ◇ *vt* [animal] kastrieren.

neutral ['nju:trəl] ◇ *adj* - **1.** POL & ELEC neutral - **2.** [inexpressive] ausdruckslos - **3.** [pale grey-brown] naturfarben - **4.** [colourless] farblos. ◇ *n (U)* AUT Leerlauf *der*; **in neutral** im Leerlauf.

neutrality [nju:'trælətı] *n* POL Neutralität *die*.

neutralize, -ise ['nju:trəlaız] *vt* [effects] neutralisieren.

never ['nevər] *adv* nie; *(simple negative)* nicht; **she's never late** sie kommt nie zu spät; **he never said a word about it** er hat gar nichts davon gesagt; **never mind!** macht nichts!; **you've never asked him to dinner!** [in disbelief] hast du ihn wirklich zum Essen eingeladen?; **well I never!** na so was!

never-ending *adj* endlos.

nevertheless [ˌnevəðə'les] *adv* trotzdem.

new *adj* [nju:] neu; **as good as new** so gut wie neu. ◆ **news** *n* [nju:z] *(U)* - **1.** [information] Nachricht *die*; **that's news to me** das ist mir neu - **2.** RADIO & TV Nachrichten *Pl*.

newborn ['nju:bɔ:n] *adj* neugeboren.

newcomer ['nju:ˌkʌmər] *n*: **newcomer (to sthg)** Neuling *der* (in etw *(D)*).

newfangled [ˌnju:'fæŋgld] *adj inf pej* neumodisch.

new-found *adj* [confidence, strength] neu gefunden.

newly ['nju:lı] *adv* neu; **newly painted** frisch gestrichen.

newlyweds ['nju:lıwedz] *npl* Frischvermählte *Pl*.

new moon *n* Neumond *der*.

news agency *n* Nachrichtenagentur *die*.

newsagent *UK* ['nju:zeıdʒənt], **newsdealer** *US* ['nju:zdi:lər] *n* Zeitungshändler *der*, -in *die*; **newsagent's (shop)** Zeitungshändler *der*.

newsflash ['nju:zflæʃ] *n* Kurzmeldung *die*.

newsletter ['nju:zˌletər] *n* Rundschreiben *das*, Mitteilungsblatt *das*.

newspaper ['nju:zˌpeıpər] *n* - **1.** [publication, company] Zeitung *die* - **2.** [paper] Zeitungspapier *das*.

newsreader ['nju:zˌri:dər] *n* Nachrichtensprecher *der*, -in *die*.

newsstand ['nju:zstænd] *n* Zeitungskiosk *der*.

newt [nju:t] *n* Wassermolch *der*.

New Year *n* Neujahr *das*; **Happy New Year!** frohes neues Jahr!

New Year's Day *n* Neujahrstag *der*.

New Year's Eve *n* Silvester *der ODER das*.

New York [-'jɔ:k] *n* New York *nt*.

New Zealand [-'zi:lənd] *n* Neuseeland *nt*.

New Zealander [-'zi:ləndər] *n* Neuseeländer *der*, -in *die*.

next [nekst] ◇ *adj* nächste(r) (s); **when does the next bus leave?** wann fährt der nächste Bus ab? ◇ *adv* - **1.** [afterwards] als nächstes, danach - **2.** [on next occasion] das nächste Mal; **the week after next** übernächste Woche - **3.** *(with superlatives)*: **the next most expensive** der/die/das nächstteuerste; **the next best thing to do would be to...** das nächstbeste wäre, zu... ◇ *pron*: **next please!** der Nächste bitte! ◆ **next to** *prep* - **1.** [near] neben - **2.** [in comparisons]: **next to music I like the theatre best** nach Musik mag ich Theater am liebsten - **3.** [almost] fast; **next to nothing** fast nichts; **I got it for next to nothing** ich habe es fast umsonst bekommen.

next door *adv* nebenan. ◆ **next-door** *adj*: **next-door neighbour** direkter Nachbar, direkte Nachbarin.

next of kin *n* nächste Angehörige *der, die*.

NHS *n abbr of* **National Health Service**.

NI *n abbr of* **National Insurance**.

nib [nıb] *n* Feder *die*.

nibble ['nıbl] *vt* knabbern.

nice [naıs] *adj* - **1.** [car, picture, weather] schön; [dress] hübsch; [food] gut; **to have a nice time** Spaß haben; **it's nice and warm** es ist schön warm - **2.** [kind, pleasant] nett, sympathisch; **to be nice to sb** nett zu jm sein.

nice-looking [-'lʊkıŋ] *adj* [person] gut aussehend; [car, house] schön.

nicely ['naıslı] *adv* - **1.** [well, attractively - dressed, decorated] hübsch; [- made] schön - **2.** [politely - ask] höflich; [- behave] gut - **3.** [satisfactorily] gut; **that will do nicely** das ist genau richtig.

niche [ni:ʃ] *n* [in wall] Nische *die*.

nick [nık] ◇ *n* - **1.** [cut] Kerbe *die*, Einkerbung *die* - **2.** *UK inf* [condition]: **to be in good/bad nick** [object] gut/schlecht erhalten sein; [person] in guter/schlechter Verfassung sein - **3.** *phr*: **in the nick of time** in letzter Minute. ◇ *vt* - **1.** [cut - wood] einlkerben - **2.** *UK inf* [steal] klauen - **3.** *UK inf* [arrest] schnappen.

nickel ['nıkl] *n* - **1.** [metal] Nickel *das* - **2.** *US* [coin] Fünfcentstück *das*.

nickname ['nıkneım] *n* Spitzname *der*.

nicotine ['nıkəti:n] *n* Nikotin *das*.

niece [ni:s] *n* Nichte *die*.

niggle ['nıgl] *vt* [worry] zu schaffen machen *(+ D)*.

night [naıt] *n* - **1.** [not day] Nacht *die*; **at night** nachts - **2.** [evening] Abend *der*; **at night** abends - **3.** *phr*: **to have an early/a late night** früh/spät ins Bett gehen. ◆ **nights** *adv* - **1.** *US* [at night] nachts - **2.** *UK* [night shift]: **to work nights** Nachtschicht arbeiten.

nightcap ['naıtkæp] *n* [drink] Schlummertrunk *der*.

nightclub ['naıtklʌb] *n* Nightclub *der*.

nightdress ['naıtdres] *n* Nachthemd *das*.

nightfall ['naɪtfɔ:l] *n*: **at nightfall** bei Einbruch der Dunkelheit.

nightgown ['naɪtgaʊn] *n* Nachthemd *das*.

nightie ['naɪtɪ] *n inf* Nachthemd *das*.

nightingale ['naɪtɪŋgeɪl] *n* Nachtigall *die*.

nightlife ['naɪtlaɪf] *n* Nachtleben *das*.

nightly ['naɪtlɪ] ◇ *adj* nächtlich. ◇ *adv* [every evening] jeden Abend; [every night] jede Nacht.

nightmare ['naɪtmeəʳ] *n liter* & *fig* Albtraum *der*.

night porter *n* Nachtportier *der*.

night school *n (U)* Abendschule *die*.

night shift *n* Nachtschicht *die*.

nightshirt ['naɪtʃɜ:t] *n* Nachthemd *das (für Herren)*.

nighttime ['naɪttaɪm] *n (U)* Nacht *die*.

nil [nɪl] *n* - **1.** [nothing] null - **2.** *UK* SPORT: **two nil** zwei zu null.

Nile [naɪl] *n*: **the Nile** der Nil.

nimble ['nɪmbl] *adj* - **1.** [person] wendig; [fingers] geschickt - **2.** [mind] beweglich.

nine [naɪn] *num* neun; *see also* **six**.

nineteen [ˌnaɪn'ti:n] *num* neunzehn; *see also* **six**.

ninety ['naɪntɪ] *num* neunzig; *see also* **sixty**.

ninth [naɪnθ] *num* neunte(r) (s); *see also* **sixth**.

nip [nɪp] ◇ *n* - **1.** [bite] leichter Biss; [pinch] Kniff *der* - **2.** [of drink] Schluck *der*. ◇ *vt* [bite] beißen; [pinch] kneifen.

nipple ['nɪpl] *n* - **1.** [of breast] Brustwarze *die* - **2.** [of baby's bottle] Schnuller *der*.

nit [nɪt] *n* - **1.** [in hair] Nisse *die* - **2.** *UK inf* [idiot] Blödmann *der*.

nitpicking ['nɪtpɪkɪŋ] *n inf (U)* Spitzfindigkeit *die*.

nitrogen ['naɪtrədʒən] *n* Stickstoff *der*.

nitty-gritty [ˌnɪtɪ'grɪtɪ] *n inf*: **to get down to the nitty-gritty** zur Sache kommen.

no [nəʊ] (*pl* **-es**) ◇ *adv* nein; **to answer no** mit einem Nein antworten; **I am no richer than he is** ich bin nicht reicher als er. ◇ *adj* kein; **I have no money left** ich habe kein Geld übrig; **it's no easy job** es ist keine leichte Aufgabe; **it's no good** OR **use** es nützt nichts; **in no time** im Nu; **'no smoking'** 'Rauchen verboten'; **no way!** *inf* auf keinen Fall! ◇ *n* Nein *das*; **she won't take no for an answer** sie lässt sich nicht davon abbringen.

No., no. (*abbr of* **number**) Nr.

nobility [nə'bɪlətɪ] *n* - **1.** [aristocracy]: **the nobility** der Adel - **2.** [nobleness] Vornehmheit *die*.

noble ['nəʊbl] *adj* - **1.** [aristocratic] adlig - **2.** [fine, distinguished] edel, nobel.

nobody ['nəʊbədɪ] ◇ *pron* niemand; **nobody else can do it** das kann sonst keiner. ◇ *n pej* Niemand *der*.

no-claim(s) bonus *n* Schadenfreiheitsrabatt *der*.

nocturnal [nɒk'tɜ:nl] *adj* - **1.** [at night] nächtlich - **2.** [animal] Nacht-.

nod [nɒd] ◇ *vt*: **to nod one's head** mit dem Kopf nicken. ◇ *vi* nicken; **to nod to sb** jm zu|nicken. ◆ **nod off** *vi* ein|nicken.

noise [nɔɪz] *n* - **1.** [sound] Geräusch *das* - **2.** *(U)* [unpleasant sound] Krach *der*.

noisy ['nɔɪzɪ] *adj* laut.

nominal ['nɒmɪnl] *adj* - **1.** [in name only] nominell - **2.** [very small] gering.

nominate ['nɒmɪneɪt] *vt* - **1.** [propose]: **to nominate sb (for/as sthg)** jn (für/als etw) nominieren - **2.** [appoint]: **to nominate sb to sthg** jn zu etw ernennen.

nominee [ˌnɒmɪ'ni:] *n* Kandidat *der*, -in *die*.

non- [nɒn] *prefix* [with noun] Nicht-; [with adj] nicht-.

nonalcoholic [ˌnɒnælkə'hɒlɪk] *adj* nicht alkoholisch, ohne Alkohol.

nonaligned [ˌnɒnə'laɪnd] *adj* blockfrei.

nonchalant [*UK* 'nɒnʃələnt, *US* ˌnɒnʃə'lɑ:nt] *adj* nonchalant, lässig.

noncommittal [ˌnɒnkə'mɪtl] *adj* [reply, attitude] unverbindlich; **he was noncommittal** er legte sich nicht fest.

nonconformist [ˌnɒnkən'fɔ:mɪst] ◇ *adj* nonkonformistisch. ◇ *n* Nonkonformist *der*, -in *die*.

nondescript [*UK* 'nɒndɪskrɪpt, *US* ˌnɒndɪ'skrɪpt] *adj* unscheinbar.

none [nʌn] ◇ *pron* [not any] keine(r) (s); **none of us** keiner von uns; **none of the money** nichts von dem Geld; **I'll have none of your nonsense** ich will nichts von dem Unsinn hören; **it is none of his business** es geht ihn gar nichts an. ◇ *adv*: **I'm none the wiser** ich bin um nichts schlauer geworden; **I like him none the worse for it** ich mag ihn deshalb nicht weniger. ◆ **none too** *adv*: **none too soon** keine Minute zu früh.

nonentity [nɒ'nentətɪ] *n* Null *die*.

nonetheless [ˌnʌnðə'les] *adv* nichtsdestoweniger.

non-event *n* Reinfall *der*.

nonexistent [ˌnɒnɪg'zɪstənt] *adj* nicht existierend; **to be nonexistent** nicht existieren.

nonfiction [ˌnɒn'fɪkʃn] *n (U)* Sachliteratur *die*.

no-nonsense *adj* sachlich.

nonpayment [ˌnɒn'peɪmənt] *n (U)* Nichtzahlung *die*.

nonplussed, nonplused *US* [ˌnɒn'plʌst] *adj* verblüfft.

nonreturnable [ˌnɒnrɪ'tɜ:nəbl] *adj* [bottle] Einweg-.

nonsense ['nɒnsəns] ◇ *n (U)* - **1.** [meaningless words, foolish idea] Unsinn *der* - **2.** [foolish behaviour] Dummheiten *Pl.* ◇ *excl* Unsinn!

nonsensical [nɒn'sensɪkl] *adj* unsinnig.

nonsmoker [ˌnɒn'sməʊkəʳ] *n* Nichtraucher *der*, -in *die*.

nonstick [ˌnɒn'stɪk] *adj* antihaftbeschichtet.

nonstop [ˌnɒn'stɒp] ◇ *adj* [flight, race] Nonstop-; [activity, rain] ohne Unterbrechung. ◇ *adv* ununterbrochen.

noodles ['nu:dlz] *npl* Nudeln *Pl.*

nook [nʊk] *n* [of room] Winkel *der*; **in every nook and cranny** in allen Ecken OR Winkeln.

noon [nu:n] *n* Mittag *der*.

no one *pron* = **nobody**.

noose [nu:s] *n* Schlinge *die*.

no-place *adv US* = **nowhere**.

nor [nɔ:ʳ] *conj* auch nicht; **nor do I** ich auch nicht; **I don't know, nor do I care** das weiß ich nicht, und es ist mir auch egal.

norm [nɔ:m] *n* Norm *die*.

normal ['nɔ:ml] *adj* normal.

normality [nɔ:'mælɪtɪ] *n* Normalität *die*.

normally ['nɔ:məlɪ] *adv* - **1.** [usually] normalerweise - **2.** [in a normal way] normal.

north [nɔ:θ] ◇ *adj* Nord-. ◇ *adv* nach Norden; **north of** nördlich von. ◇ *n* Norden *der*.

North Africa *n* Nordafrika *nt*.

North America *n* Nordamerika *nt*.

North American ◇ *adj* nordamerikanisch. ◇ *n* Nordamerikaner *der*, -in *die*.

northeast [ˌnɔ:θ'i:st] ◇ *n* Nordosten *der*. ◇ *adj* nordöstlich, Nordost-. ◇ *adv* nordostwärts; **northeast of** nordöstlich von.

northerly ['nɔ:ðəlɪ] *adj* [direction] nördlich; [area] im Norden; [wind] Nord-.

northern ['nɔ:ðən] *adj* [region, dialect] nördlich; [Europe] Nord-.

Northern Ireland *n* Nordirland *nt*.

northernmost ['nɔ:ðənməʊst] *adj* nördlichste(r) (s).

North Pole *n*: **the North Pole** der Nordpol.

North Sea *n*: **the North Sea** die Nordsee.

northward ['nɔ:θwəd] ◇ *adj* [migration] nördlich. ◇ *adv* = **northwards**.

northwards ['nɔ:θwədz] *adv* nach Norden.

northwest [ˌnɔ:θ'west] ◇ *n* Nordwesten *der*. ◇ *adj* nordwestlich, Nordwest-. ◇ *adv* nordwestwärts; **northwest of** nordwestlich von.

Norway ['nɔ:weɪ] *n* Norwegen *nt*.

Norwegian [nɔ:'wi:dʒən] ◇ *adj* norwegisch. ◇ *n* - **1.** [person] Norweger *der*, -in *die* - **2.** [language] Norwegisch(e) *das*.

nose [nəʊz] *n* [of person] Nase *die*; **it's under your nose** es ist vor deiner Nase; **to keep one's nose out of sthg** sich aus etw herauslhalten; **to look down one's nose at sb/sthg** *fig* von oben auf jn/etw herablschauen; **to poke** OR **stick one's nose into sthg** *inf* seine Nase in etw *(A)* stecken; **to turn up one's nose at sthg** seine Nase über etw *(A)* rümpfen. ◆ **nose about, nose around** *vi* herumlschnüffeln.

nosebleed ['nəʊzbli:d] *n* Nasenbluten *das*.

nosey ['nəʊzɪ] *adj* = **nosy**.

nostalgia [nɒ'stældʒə] *n (U)* Nostalgie *die*; **nostalgia for sthg** Sehnsucht *die* nach etw.

nostril ['nɒstrəl] *n* Nasenloch *das*.

nosy ['nəʊzɪ] *adj* neugierig.

not [nɒt] *adv* nicht; **she's not there** sie ist nicht da; **not any** kein; **not yet** noch nicht; **not at all** [pleased, interested] überhaupt nicht; [in reply to thanks] gern geschehen; **not that I'm afraid of him** nicht etwa, dass ich Angst vor ihm habe; **not to worry!** keine Sorge!

notable ['nəʊtəbl] *adj* [person] bedeutend; [success] bemerkenswert; [improvement] beachtlich, beträchtlich; **to be notable for sthg** durch etw auflfallen; **with the notable exception of** mit Ausnahme von.

notably ['nəʊtəblɪ] *adv* - **1.** [in particular] vor allem - **2.** [noticeably] deutlich.

notary ['nəʊtərɪ] *n*: **notary (public)** Notar *der*, -in *die*.

notch [nɒtʃ] *n* [cut] Kerbe *die*.

note [nəʊt] ◇ *n* - **1.** [short letter] Zettel *der* - **2.** [written reminder, record] Notiz *die*; **to take note of sthg** etw bemerken - **3.** [paper money] Geldschein *der*; **a £5 note** eine Fünfpfundnote - **4.** [MUS - symbol] Note *die*; [- sound] Klang *der* - **5.** [tone] Ton *der*. ◇ *vt* - **1.** [observe] bemerken - **2.** [mention] erwähnen. ◆ **notes** *npl* [in book] Anmerkungen *Pl.* ◆ **note down** *vt sep* auflschreiben.

notebook ['nəʊtbʊk] *n* - **1.** [for writing in] Notizbuch *das* - **2.** COMPUT Notebook *das*.

noted ['nəʊtɪd] *adj*: **noted (for sthg)** bekannt (für etw).

notepad ['nəʊtpæd] *n* Notizblock *der*.

notepaper ['nəʊtpeɪpəʳ] *n* Briefpapier *das*.

noteworthy ['nəʊtˌwɜ:ðɪ] *adj* bemerkenswert.

nothing ['nʌθɪŋ] ◇ *pron* nichts; **nothing new/interesting** nichts Neues/Interessantes; **for nothing** [for free] umsonst; [in vain] vergeblich; **she is nothing if not discreet** diskret ist sie auf jeden Fall; **nothing but** nichts als; **he does nothing but complain** er beschwert sich dauernd; **he thinks nothing of walking ten miles** es macht ihm nichts aus, zehn Meilen zu gehen. ◇ *adv*: **nothing like** [very unlike] ganz anders als; **nothing like enough** lange nicht genug; **nothing like as good** längst nicht so gut.

notice ['nəʊtɪs] ◇ *n* - **1.** [piece of paper - announcing sthg] Ankündigung *die*; [- informing of sthg] Mitteilung *die* - **2.** [attention]: **it es-**

caped her notice** es entging ihrer Aufmerksamkeit; **to take notice/no notice of sb/sthg** jn/etw beachten/nicht beachten - **3.** *(U)* [warning] Bescheid *der*; **at short notice** kurzfristig; **until further notice** bis auf Weiteres - **4.** [at work]: **to be given one's notice** gekündigt werden; **to hand in one's notice** seine Kündigung einlreichen. ◇ *vt* bemerken.

noticeable ['nəʊtɪsəbl] *adj* deutlich.

notice board *n* Anschlagbrett *das*.

notify ['nəʊtɪfaɪ] *vt*: **to notify sb (of sthg)** jn benachrichtigen (über etw *(A)*).

notion ['nəʊʃn] *n* [concept, idea] Idee *die*, Vorstellung *die*. ◆ **notions** *npl US* [haberdashery] Kurzwaren *Pl*.

notorious [nəʊ'tɔ:rɪəs] *adj* [person] berühmt; [criminal, event] berühmt-berüchtigt; [place] verrufen.

notwithstanding [,nɒtwɪθ'stændɪŋ] *fml* ◇ *prep* trotz (+ *G*). ◇ *adv* trotzdem.

nought [nɔ:t] *num* Null *die*; **noughts and crosses** Kreuzchen- und Kringelspiel *das*.

noun [naʊn] *n* Substantiv *das*.

nourish ['nʌrɪʃ] *vt* [feed] ernähren.

nourishing ['nʌrɪʃɪŋ] *adj* nahrhaft.

nourishment ['nʌrɪʃmənt] *n* Nahrung *die*.

novel ['nɒvl] ◇ *adj* neuartig. ◇ *n* Roman *der*.

novelist ['nɒvəlɪst] *n* Romanschriftsteller *der*, -in *die*.

novelty ['nɒvltɪ] *n* - **1.** [quality] Neuartigkeit *die* - **2.** [unusual object, event] Neuheit *die* - **3.** [cheap object] Krimskrams *der*.

November [nə'vembəʳ] *n* November *der*; *see also* **September**.

novice ['nɒvɪs] *n* - **1.** [inexperienced person] Neuling *der* - **2.** RELIG Novize *der*, -zin *die*.

now [naʊ] ◇ *adv* - **1.** [gen] jetzt; **just now** gerade eben; **right now** [at the moment] im Moment; [immediately] sofort; **by now** inzwischen; **from now on** von jetzt an; **three days from now** heute in drei Tagen; **any day/time now** jeden Tag/Moment; **(every) now and then** OR **again** hin und wieder; **for now** erst einmal - **2.** [introducing statement]: **now (then)** also. ◇ *conj*: **now (that)...** jetzt, wo...

nowadays ['naʊədeɪz] *adv* heutzutage.

nowhere *UK* ['nəʊweəʳ], **no-place** *US adv* nirgendwo, nirgends; **nowhere near** nicht annähernd; **dinner is nowhere near ready** das Abendessen ist noch lange nicht fertig; **to be getting nowhere** [achieve nothing] nichts erreichen; [make no progress] nicht voranlkommen.

nozzle ['nɒzl] *n* Düse *die*.

nuance [nju:'ɑ:ns] *n* Nuance *die*.

nuclear ['nju:klɪəʳ] *adj* nuklear, Nuklear-.

nuclear bomb *n* Atombombe *die*.

nuclear disarmament *n* nukleare Abrüstung.

nuclear energy *n* Atomenergie *die*.

nuclear power *n* Atomkraft *die*, Kernkraft *die*; **nuclear power station** Atomkraftwerk *das*.

nuclear reactor *n* Atomreaktor *der*.

nuclear war *n* Atomkrieg *der*.

nucleus ['nju:klɪəs] (*pl* **-lei** [-lɪaɪ]) *n* Kern *der*; **atomic nucleus** Atomkern *der*.

nude [nju:d] ◇ *adj* nackt. ◇ *n* [figure, painting] Akt *der*; **in the nude** nackt.

nudge [nʌdʒ] *vt* [with elbow] anlstupsen.

nudist ['nju:dɪst] ◇ *adj* Nudisten-; **nudist beach** Nacktbadestrand *der*. ◇ *n* Nudist *der*, -in *die*.

nugget ['nʌgɪt] *n* - **1.** [of gold] Nugget *das*, Goldklümpchen *das* - **2.** *fig*: **a nugget of information** ein wertvolles Stück Information.

nuisance ['nju:sns] *n* - **1.** [annoying thing, situation] Ärgernis *das*; **what a nuisance!** wie ärgerlich! - **2.** [annoying person] Nervensäge *die*; **to make a nuisance of o.s.** lästig werden.

null [nʌl] *adj*: **null and void** null und nichtig.

numb [nʌm] *adj* [shoulder, hand] taub, gefühllos; [person] benommen; **to be numb with sthg** [with cold, fear, shock] starr vor etw *(D)* sein; [with grief] benommen vor etw *(D)* sein.

number ['nʌmbəʳ] ◇ *n* - **1.** [numeral] Zahl *die*, Ziffer *die* - **2.** [of telephone, house, car] Nummer *die* - **3.** [quantity] Anzahl *die*, Zahl *die*; **a number of** mehrere; **any number of** unzählig - **4.** [song] Nummer *die*. ◇ *vt* - **1.** [amount to] zählen - **2.** [give a number to] nummerieren - **3.** [include]: **he is numbered among the greatest politicians of this century** er zählt zu den größten Politikern dieses Jahrhunderts.

number one ◇ *adj* [main] vorrangig. ◇ *n inf* [oneself] Nummer eins.

numberplate ['nʌmbəpleɪt] *n* Nummernschild *das*.

Number Ten *n*: **Number Ten (Downing Street)** *Sitz des britischen Premierministers*.

numeral ['nju:mərəl] *n* Ziffer *die*.

numerate ['nju:mərət] *adj UK* rechenkundig.

numerical [nju:'merɪkl] *adj* numerisch.

numerous ['nju:mərəs] *adj* zahlreich.

nun [nʌn] *n* Nonne *die*.

nurse [nɜ:s] ◇ *n* Krankenschwester *die*; [male] Krankenpfleger *der*. ◇ *vt* - **1.** MED [person] pflegen - **2.** [desire, dream, hope] hegen, nähren - **3.** [breast-feed] stillen.

nursery ['nɜ:sərɪ] *n* - **1.** [for children] Kinderzimmer *das* - **2.** [for plants] Gärtnerei *die*.

nursery rhyme *n* Kinderreim *der*.

nursery school *n* Kindergarten *der*.

nursing ['nɜ:sɪŋ] *n (U)* - **1.** [profession] Krankenpflege *die* - **2.** [care] Pflege *die*.

nursing home *n* [for old people] Pflegeheim *das*.

nurture ['nɜ:tʃəʳ] *vt* - **1.** [children] nähren; [plants] hegen - **2.** [hope, desire, plan] hegen.

nut [nʌt] *n* - **1.** [to eat] Nuss *die* - **2.** TECH Schraubenmutter *die* - **3.** *inf* [mad person] Spinner *der*, -in *die*. ◆ **nuts** *inf* ◇ *adj*: **to be nuts** verrückt sein. ◇ *excl US* verdammt!

nutcrackers ['nʌt,krækəz] *npl* Nussknacker *der*.

nutmeg ['nʌtmeg] *n* Muskatnuss *die*.

nutritious [nju:'trɪʃəs] *adj* nahrhaft.

nutshell ['nʌtʃel] *n*: **in a nutshell** kurz gefasst.

nuzzle ['nʌzl] *vi*: **to nuzzle (up) against sb/sthg** sich an jn/etw an|schmiegen OR drücken.

nylon ['naɪlɒn] ◇ *n* [fabric] Nylon *das*. ◇ *comp* Nylon-.

o (*pl* **o's** OR **os**), **O** (*pl* **O's** OR **Os**) [əʊ] *n* - **1.** [letter] o *das*, O *das* - **2.** [zero] Null *die*.

oak [əʊk] ◇ *n* - **1.** [tree] Eiche *die* - **2.** *(U)* [wood] Eichenholz *das*. ◇ *comp* Eichenholz-.

OAP *n abbr of* **old age pensioner**.

oar [ɔ:ʳ] *n* Ruder *das*.

oasis [əʊ'eɪsɪs] (*pl* **oases** [əʊ'eɪsi:z]) *n liter & fig* Oase *die*.

oath [əʊθ] *n* - **1.** [promise] Eid *der*; **on** OR **under oath** unter Eid - **2.** [swearword] Fluch *der*.

oatmeal ['əʊtmi:l] *n* [food] Hafermehl *das*.

oats [əʊts] *npl* Hafer *der*.

obedience [ə'bi:dɪəns] *n*: **obedience (to sb)** Gehorsam *der* (gegenüber jm).

obedient [ə'bi:dɪənt] *adj* gehorsam.

obese [əʊ'bi:s] *adj* fettleibig.

obey [ə'beɪ] ◇ *vt* [person] gehorchen *(+ D)*; [orders, command, law] befolgen. ◇ *vi* gehorchen.

obituary [ə'bɪtʃʊərɪ] *n* Nachruf *der*.

object ◇ *n* ['ɒbdʒɪkt] - **1.** [thing] Gegenstand *der* - **2.** [aim] Ziel *das*; **the object of the exercise** der Zweck der Übung - **3.** GRAM Objekt *das*. ◇ *vt* [ɒb'dʒekt]: **to object that...** ein|wenden, dass... ◇ *vi* [ɒb'dʒekt] dagegen sein; **to object to sthg** gegen etw sein; **to object to doing sthg** etwas dagegen haben, etw zu tun.

objection [əb'dʒekʃn] *n* Einwand *der*; **to have no objection to sthg** keinen Einwand gegen etw haben; **to have no objection to doing sthg** nichts dagegen haben, etw zu tun.

objectionable [əb'dʒekʃənəbl] *adj* [behaviour, language] anstößig; [person] unausstehlich, widerwärtig.

objective [əb'dʒektɪv] ◇ *adj* objektiv. ◇ *n* Ziel *das*.

obligation [,ɒblɪ'geɪʃn] *n* - **1.** [compulsion] Zwang *der* - **2.** [duty] Verpflichtung *die*.

obligatory [ə'blɪgətrɪ] *adj* obligatorisch; **to be obligatory** Pflicht sein.

oblige [ə'blaɪdʒ] *vt* - **1.** [force]: **to oblige sb to do sthg** jn zwingen, etw zu tun - **2.** *fml* [do a favour for]: **to oblige sb** jm einen Gefallen tun.

obliging [ə'blaɪdʒɪŋ] *adj* zuvorkommend.

oblique [ə'bli:k] ◇ *adj* - **1.** [look, compliment] indirekt; [hint] versteckt - **2.** [line] Schräg-, schräg. ◇ *n* TYPO Schrägstrich *der*.

obliterate [ə'blɪtəreɪt] *vt* aus|löschen.

oblivion [ə'blɪvɪən] *n* - **1.** [unconsciousness] Bewusstlosigkeit *die* - **2.** [state of being forgotten] Vergessenheit *die*, Vergessen *das*.

oblivious [ə'blɪvɪəs] *adj*: **to be oblivious to sthg** sich *(D)* einer Sache *(G)* nicht bewusst sein.

oblong ['ɒblɒŋ] ◇ *adj* rechteckig. ◇ *n* Rechteck *das*.

obnoxious [əb'nɒkʃəs] *adj* [smell] widerlich; [remark] gemein; [person] unausstehlich.

oboe ['əʊbəʊ] *n* Oboe *die*.

obscene [əb'si:n] *adj* obszön.

obscure [əb'skjʊəʳ] ◇ *adj* - **1.** [not well-known] unbekannt - **2.** [difficult to understand, see] unklar. ◇ *vt* - **1.** [make difficult to understand] unklar machen - **2.** [hide] verdecken.

observance [əb'zɜ:vəns] *n* *(U)* Einhaltung *die*.

observant [əb'zɜ:vnt] *adj* aufmerksam.

observation [,ɒbzə'veɪʃn] *n* - **1.** *(U)* [action of watching] Beobachtung *die* - **2.** [remark] Bemerkung *die*, Äußerung *die*.

observatory [əb'zɜ:vətrɪ] *n* Observatorium *das*, Sternwarte *die*.

observe [əb'zɜ:v] *vt* - **1.** *fml* [notice] bemerken - **2.** [watch carefully] beobachten - **3.** [obey] ein|halten - **4.** [remark] bemerken.

observer [əb'zɜ:vəʳ] *n* - **1.** [watcher] Zuschauer *der*, -in *die* - **2.** [commentator] Beobachter *der*, -in *die*.

obsess [əb'ses] *vt*: **to be obsessed by** OR **with sb/sthg** von jm/etw besessen sein.

obsessive [əb'sesɪv] *adj* obsessiv, zwanghaft.

obsolete ['ɒbsəli:t] *adj* veraltet, überholt.

obstacle ['ɒbstəkl] *n* Hindernis *das*.

obstetrics [ɒb'stetrɪks] *n* Geburtshilfe *die*.

obstinate ['ɒbstənət] *adj* - **1.** [person] verbohrt - **2.** [cough, resistance] hartnäckig.

obstruct [əb'strʌkt] *vt* - **1.** [road, path] blockieren, versperren - **2.** [progress, justice, traffic] behindern.

obstruction [əb'strʌkʃn] *n* - **1.** [in road, pipe] Blockierung *die* - **2.** [of justice] Behinderung *die* - **3.** SPORT Behinderung *die*.

obtain [əb'teɪn] *vt* erhalten.

obtainable [əb'teɪnəbl] *adj* erhältlich.

obtrusive [əb'truːsɪv] *adj* [person, behaviour] aufdringlich; [colour] auffällig; [smell] penetrant.

obtuse [əb'tjuːs] *adj* - **1.** *fml* [person] begriffsstutzig - **2.** GEOM [angle] stumpf.

obvious ['ɒbvɪəs] *adj* offensichtlich.

obviously ['ɒbvɪəslɪ] *adv* - **1.** [of course] selbstverständlich - **2.** [clearly] eindeutig.

occasion [ə'keɪʒn] *n* - **1.** [circumstance, time] Gelegenheit *die*; **on one occasion** einmal - **2.** [important event] Anlass *der*; **to rise to the occasion** sich der Lage gewachsen zeigen - **3.** *fml* [reason, motive] Grund *der*.

occasional [ə'keɪʒənl] *adj* gelegentlich.

occasionally [ə'keɪʒnəlɪ] *adv* gelegentlich.

occult [ɒ'kʌlt] *adj* okkult.

occupant ['ɒkjʊpənt] *n* - **1.** [of building, room] Bewohner *der*, -in *die* - **2.** [of chair] Inhaber *der*, -in *die*; [of vehicle] Insasse *der*, -sin *die*.

occupation [ˌɒkjʊ'peɪʃn] *n* - **1.** [job] Beruf *der* - **2.** [pastime] Beschäftigung *die* - **3.** MIL Besetzung *die*, Okkupation *die*.

occupational hazard *n* Berufsrisiko *das*.

occupier ['ɒkjʊpaɪəʳ] *n* Bewohner *der*, -in *die*.

occupy ['ɒkjʊpaɪ] *vt* - **1.** [house, room] bewohnen; [seat] belegen - **2.** MIL besetzen, okkupieren - **3.** [keep busy]: **to occupy o.s.** sich beschäftigen - **4.** [time, space] in Anspruch nehmen; **how do you occupy your evenings?** wie füllst du deine Abende aus?

occur [ə'kɜːʳ] *vi* - **1.** [happen] sich ereignen; [change] stattǀfinden; [difficulty] aufǀtreten - **2.** [exist, be found] vorǀkommen - **3.** [come to mind]: **to occur to sb** jm in den Sinn kommen.

occurrence [ə'kʌrəns] *n* [event] Vorkommnis *das*, Ereignis *das*.

ocean ['əʊʃn] *n* - **1.** [in names] Ozean *der* - **2.** *US* [sea] Meer *das*.

ochre *UK*, **ocher** *US* ['əʊkəʳ] *adj* ockerfarben.

o'clock [ə'klɒk] *adv* Uhr; **five o'clock** fünf Uhr.

octave ['ɒktɪv] *n* MUS Oktave *die*.

October [ɒk'təʊbəʳ] *n* Oktober *der*; *see also* **September**.

octopus ['ɒktəpəs] (*pl* **-puses** OR **-pi** [-paɪ]) *n* Tintenfisch *der*.

OD *abbr of* **overdose**.

odd [ɒd] *adj* - **1.** [strange] seltsam - **2.** [not part of pair] einzeln - **3.** [number] ungerade - **4.** [leftover] überzählig - **5.** [occasional] gelegentlich - **6.** *inf* [approximately] ungefähr; **twenty odd years** mehr als zwanzig Jahre.

◆ **odds** *npl* - **1.** [probability] Wahrscheinlichkeit *die*; **the odds are that** aller Wahrscheinlichkeit nach; **against all** OR **the odds** wider Erwarten - **2.** [bits]: **odds and ends** Krimskrams *der* - **3.** *phr*: **to be at odds with sb/sthg** sich mit jm/etw uneinig sein.

oddity ['ɒdɪtɪ] *n* - **1.** [strange person] Sonderling *der*; [strange thing] Kuriosität *die* - **2.** [strangeness] Eigenartigkeit *die*.

odd jobs *npl* Gelegenheitsarbeiten *Pl*.

oddly ['ɒdlɪ] *adv* seltsam.

oddments ['ɒdmənts] *npl* Einzelstücke *Pl*.

odds-on ['ɒdz-] *adj inf*: **the odds-on favourite** der klare Favorit; **it's odds-on that...** es ist sehr wahrscheinlich, dass...

odometer [əʊ'dɒmɪtəʳ] *n* Kilometerzähler *der*.

odour *UK*, **odor** *US* ['əʊdəʳ] *n* Geruch *der*.

of *(unstressed* [əv], *stressed* [ɒv]*) prep* - **1.** [gen] von *(the genitive case is often used instead of "von")*; **the cover of the book** der Umschlag des Buches; **the handle of the door** der Türgriff; **a friend of mine** ein Freund von mir; **the works of Shakespeare** die Werke Shakespeares OR von Shakespeare; **the Queen of England** die Königin von England; **the University of Leeds** die Universität Leeds; **south of Boston/the river** südlich von Boston/des Flusses - **2.** [expressing quantity, contents, age]: **a pound of sweets** ein Pfund Bonbons; **a piece of cake** ein Stück Kuchen; **a cup of coffee** eine Tasse Kaffee; **a rise of 20%** ein Anstieg um 20%; **a town of 50,000 people** eine Stadt mit 50 000 Einwohnern; **thousands of people** Tausende von Leuten; **a girl of six** ein sechsjähriges Mädchen; **both/one of us** beide/einer von uns; **a man of courage** ein mutiger Mann - **3.** [made from] aus; **a house of stone** ein Haus aus Stein; **it's made of wood** es ist aus Holz - **4.** [with emotions]: **a love of France** eine Liebe zu Frankreich; **a fear of flying** Angst vor dem Fliegen - **5.** [on the part of] von; **that was very kind of you** das war sehr nett von Ihnen - **6.** [referring to place names]: **the city of Birmingham** die Stadt Birmingham - **7.** [indicating resemblance] von; **it was the size of a pea** es war so groß wie eine Erbse, es hatte die Größe einer Erbse - **8.** [with dates, periods of time]: **the 26th of April** der 26. April; **the summer of 1969** der Sommer 1969; **in September of last year** im September letzten Jahres - **9.** [indicating cause of death]: **to die of sthg** an etw *(D)* sterben - **10.** *US* [in telling the time] vor; **it's ten of four** es ist zehn vor vier.

off [ɒf] ◇ *adv* - **1.** [away] weg; **to get off** [from bus, train, plane] auslsteigen; **we're off to Austria next week** wir fahren nächste Woche nach Österreich; **to go** *OR* **drop off to sleep** einlschlafen - **2.** [expressing removal] ab; **to take sthg off** [clothes, shoes] etw auslziehen; [lid, wrapper] etw ablnehmen; **with his shoes off** ohne Schuhe - **3.** [not working]: **to turn sthg off** [TV, radio, engine] etw auslschalten; [tap] etw zuldrehen - **4.** [expressing distance or time away]: **it's 10 miles off** es sind noch 10 Meilen bis dahin; **it's a long way off** [in distance] es ist noch ein weiter Weg bis dahin; [in time] bis dahin ist es noch lange hin - **5.** [not at work]: **I'm taking a week off** ich nehme mir eine Woche frei. ◇ *prep* - **1.** [away from] von; **to get off sthg** [bed, chair] von etw auflstehen; [bus, train, plane] aus etw auslsteigen; [ship] etw verlassen; **off the coast** vor der Küste; **it's just off the main road** es ist gleich in der Nähe der Hauptstraße - **2.** [absent from]: **to be off work** frei haben - **3.** *inf* [from] von; **I bought it off her** ich habe es von ihr gekauft - **4.** *inf* [no longer liking or needing]: **I'm off my food at the moment** ich habe zur Zeit keinen Appetit; **she's off drugs now** sie nimmt keine Drogen mehr. ◇ *adj* - **1.** [meat, cheese, milk, beer] schlecht - **2.** [not working] aus; [tap] zu - **3.** [cancelled] abgesagt; **the deal is off** die Sache ist abgeblasen - **4.** [not available]: **the soup's off** es ist keine Suppe mehr da.

offal [ˈɒfl] *n* Innereien *Pl*.

off-chance *n*: **on the off-chance** auf gut Glück.

off colour *adj* kränklich.

off duty *adv* außer Dienst, dienstfrei. ◆ **off-duty** *adj* außer Dienst.

offence *UK*, **offense** *US* [əˈfens] *n* - **1.** [crime] Verbrechen *das* - **2.** [displeasure, hurt] Beleidigung *die*; **to take offence** beleidigt sein.

offend [əˈfend] *vt* beleidigen.

offender [əˈfendəʳ] *n* - **1.** [criminal] Straftäter *der*, -in *die* - **2.** [culprit] Schuldige *der, die*.

offense *n US* = **offence**.

offensive [əˈfensɪv] ◇ *adj* - **1.** [causing offence] beleidigend; [behaviour] anstößig - **2.** [aggressive] Angriffs-, aggressiv. ◇ *n* - **1.** MIL Offensive *die*, Angriff *der* - **2.** *fig* [attack]: **to go on** *OR* **take the offensive** in die Offensive gehen.

offer [ˈɒfəʳ] ◇ *n* Angebot *das*; **on offer** [available] verkäuflich; [at a special price] im Angebot. ◇ *vt* anlbieten; **to offer sthg to sb, to offer sb sthg** jm etw anlbieten; **to offer to do sthg** anlbieten, etw zu tun. ◇ *vi* sich anlbieten.

offering [ˈɒfərɪŋ] *n* - **1.** [something offered] Gabe *die* - **2.** RELIG [sacrifice] Opfer *das*.

off guard *adv* unvorbereitet.

offhand [ˌɒfˈhænd] ◇ *adj* lässig. ◇ *adv* auf Anhieb.

office [ˈɒfɪs] *n* - **1.** [gen] Büro *das* - **2.** [government department] Behörde *die* - **3.** [position of authority] Amt *das*; **in office** im Amt.

office block *n* Bürogebäude *das*.

office hours *npl* Bürostunden *Pl*.

officer [ˈɒfɪsəʳ] *n* - **1.** MIL Offizier *der* - **2.** [in organization] Vertreter *der*, -in *die* - **3.** [in police force] Polizeibeamte *der*, -tin *die*.

office worker *n* Büroangestellte *der, die*.

official [əˈfɪʃl] ◇ *adj* offiziell. ◇ *n* Beamte *der*, -tin *die*; SPORT Funktionär *der*, -in *die*.

offing [ˈɒfɪŋ] *n*: **in the offing** in Sicht.

off-licence *n UK* Wein- und Spirituosenhandlung *die*.

off-line *adj* COMPUT offline.

off-peak *adj*: **off-peak electricity** Nachtstrom *der*; **off-peak fares** verbilligter Tarif; **during off-peak hours** außerhalb der Stoßzeiten.

off-putting [-ˌpʊtɪŋ] *adj* abstoßend.

off season *n*: **the off season** die Nebensaison.

offset [ˈɒfset] (*pt & pp inv*) *vt* auslgleichen.

offshore [ˌɒfˈʃɔːʳ] ◇ *adj* - **1.** [in or on the sea] Offshore- - **2.** [near coast] in Küstennähe; **offshore waters** Küstengewässer *Pl*. ◇ *adv* - **1.** [out at sea] offshore, im offenen Meer - **2.** [near coast] in Küstennähe.

offside ◇ *adv* [ˌɒfˈsaɪd] SPORT im Abseits. ◇ *n* [ˈɒfsaɪd] [of vehicle] Fahrerseite *die*.

offspring [ˈɒfsprɪŋ] (*pl inv*) *n* - **1.** *fml & hum* [of people] Nachwuchs *der* - **2.** [of animals] Junge(s) *das*.

offstage [ˌɒfˈsteɪdʒ] *adj & adv* hinter der Bühne, hinter den Kulissen.

off-the-cuff *adj & adv* unüberlegt.

off-the-peg *adj UK*: **off-the-peg suit** Anzug *der* von der Stange.

off-the-record *adj & adv* inoffiziell.

off-white *adj* gebrochen weiß.

often [ˈɒfn, ˈɒftn] *adv* oft; **how often do the buses run?** wie oft fährt der Bus?; **every so often** gelegentlich; **as often as not, more often than not** meistens.

ogle [ˈəʊgl] *vt pej* begaffen.

oh [əʊ] *excl* - **1.** [to introduce comment] ach! - **2.** [expressing hesitation, joy, surprise, fear] oh!; **oh no!** oh nein!

oil [ɔɪl] ◇ *n* Öl *das*. ◇ *vt* ölen, schmieren.

oilcan [ˈɔɪlkæn] *n* Ölkanne *die*.

oilfield [ˈɔɪlfiːld] *n* Ölfeld *das*.

oil filter *n* Ölfilter *der*.

oil-fired [-ˌfaɪəd] *adj* ölbefeuert; **oil-fired central heating** Ölheizung *die*.

oil painting *n* - **1.** [picture] Ölgemälde *das* - **2.** [art] Ölmalerei *die*.

oilrig [ˈɔɪlrɪg] *n* Ölbohrinsel *die*.

oil slick *n* Ölteppich *der*.

oil tanker *n* - **1.** [ship] Öltanker *der* - **2.** [lorry] Tankwagen *der*.

oil well *n* Ölquelle *die*.

oily ['ɔɪlɪ] *adj* [rag, clothes] ölig; [food] fettig.

ointment ['ɔɪntmənt] *n* Salbe *die*.

OK (*pt & pp* **OKed**, *cont* **OKing**), **okay** [ˌəʊ'keɪ] *inf* ◇ *adj* in Ordnung; **are you OK?** ist alles in Ordnung?; **is that OK with you?** ist dir das recht? ◇ *adv* [well] gut. ◇ *excl* - **1.** [expressing agreement] okay! - **2.** [to introduce new topic]: **OK, let's get started** Okay, fangen wir an. ◇ *vt* sein Okay geben zu.

old [əʊld] ◇ *adj* - **1.** [gen] alt; **how old are you?** wie alt bist du?; **I'm 36 years old** ich bin 36 (Jahre alt); **to get old** alt werden; **in the old days** früher - **2.** [for emphasis]: **any old thing** das Erstbeste; **good old George!** der gute alte Georg! ◇ *npl*: **the old** ältere Leute.

old age *n (U)* Alter *das*.

old age pensioner *n UK* Rentner *der*, -in *die*.

old-fashioned [-'fæʃnd] *adj* [person, clothes] altmodisch; [ideas] überholt.

old people's home *n* Altersheim *das*.

O level (*abbr of* **ordinary level**) *n UK* ≃ mittlere Reife, *früherer Schulabschluss in England und Wales, 1988 durch das GCSE ersetzt.*

olive ['ɒlɪv] *n* Olive *die*.

olive green *adj* olivgrün.

olive oil *n* Olivenöl *das*.

Olympic [ə'lɪmpɪk] *adj* olympisch. ◆ **Olympics** *npl*: **the Olympics** die Olympischen Spiele.

Olympic Games *npl*: **the Olympic Games** die Olympischen Spiele.

omelet(te) ['ɒmlɪt] *n* Omelett *das*.

omen ['əʊmən] *n* Omen *das*.

ominous ['ɒmɪnəs] *adj* ominös.

omission [ə'mɪʃn] *n* Auslassung *die*.

omit [ə'mɪt] *vt* aus|lassen; **to omit to do sthg** es unterlassen, etw zu tun; [unintentionally] es versäumen, etw zu tun.

on [ɒn] ◇ *prep* - **1.** [indicating position, location] auf *(+ D)*; *(with verbs of motion)* auf *(+ A)*; **it's on the table** es ist auf dem Tisch; **put it on the table** leg es auf den Tisch; **on the wall/ceiling** an der Wand/der Decke; **on page four** auf Seite vier; **on my left/right** zu meiner Linken/Rechten; **on the left/right** auf der linken/rechten Seite; **we stayed on a farm** wir übernachteten auf einem Bauernhof; **on the Rhine** am Rhein; **on the main road** an der Hauptstraße; **he had a scar on his face** er hatte eine Narbe im Gesicht; **do you have any money on you?** hast du Geld bei dir? - **2.** [indicating means] auf *(+ D)*; **recorded on tape** auf Band; **on TV/the radio** im Radio/Fernsehen; **it runs on unleaded petrol** es fährt mit bleifreiem Benzin; **he lives on fruit and yoghurt** er lebt von Obst und Joghurt; **to cut o.s. on sthg** sich an etw *(D)* schneiden - **3.** [indicating mode of transport]: **to be on the train/plane** im Zug/Flugzeug sein; **to travel on the bus/train** mit dem Bus/Zug fahren; **to get on a bus** in einen Bus ein|steigen; **on foot** zu Fuß - **4.** [using, supported by]: **to stand on one leg** auf einem Bein stehen; **he was lying on his back** er lag auf dem Rücken; **to be on medication** Medikamente nehmen; **to be on drugs** [addicted] drogensüchtig sein; **to be on social security** Sozialhilfe bekommen - **5.** [about] über *(+ A)*; **a book on Germany** ein Buch über Deutschland - **6.** [indicating time] an *(+ D)*; **on Tuesday** am Dienstag; **on Tuesdays** dienstags; **on 25 August** am 25. August; **on arrival** bei Ankunft; **on my return, on returning** bei meiner Rückkehr - **7.** [indicating activity]: **to work on sthg** an etw *(D)* arbeiten; **he's here on business** er ist geschäftlich hier; **on holiday** im Urlaub; **she's on the telephone** [talking] sie telefoniert gerade; **to be on fire** brennen - **8.** [according to]: **on good authority** aus guter Quelle; **on this evidence** aufgrund dieser Beweise - **9.** [indicating influence, effect] auf *(+ A)*; **the effect on Britain** die Auswirkungen auf Großbritannien; **a tax on imports** eine Steuer auf Importe - **10.** [earning]: **she's on £25,000 a year** sie verdient £25.000 pro Jahr; **to be on a low income** ein niedriges Einkommen haben - **11.** [referring to musical instrument] auf *(+ D)*; **on the violin/flute** auf der Geige/Flöte - **12.**: **on the cheap** billig; **on the sly** hintenherum - **13.** *inf* [paid by]: **the drinks are on me** die Drinks gehen auf mich. ◇ *adv* - **1.** [in place, covering]: **to have sthg on** [clothes, hat] etw an|haben; **put the lid on** mach den Deckel drauf; **to put one's clothes on** sich *(D)* (seine Kleider) an|ziehen - **2.** [film, play, programme]: **the news is on** die Nachrichten laufen; **what's on at the cinema?** was läuft im Kino?; **there's nothing on tonight** heute Abend kommt nichts - **3.** [working] an; **you left the heater on** du hast das Heizgerät angelassen; **to turn sthg on** [TV, radio, engine] etw ein|schalten; [tap] etw auf|drehen - **4.** [indicating continuing action] weiter; **to work on** weiter|arbeiten; **we talked on into the night** wir redeten noch bis in die Nacht hinein; **he kept on walking** er ging immer weiter - **5.** [forward]: **send my mail on (to me)** senden Sie mir die Post nach - **6.** [with transport]: **to get on** ein|steigen; **is everyone on?** sind alle eingestiegen? - **7.** *phr*: **earlier on** früher; **later on** später; **it's just not on!** *inf* das geht einfach nicht!; **to be** OR **go on at sb (to do sthg)** [pester] jm zulsetzen (, etw zu tun). ◆ **from on** *adv*: **from that moment on** von dem Moment an; **from now on** von jetzt an, ab jetzt; **from then on** von da an. ◆ **on and off** *adv* ab und zu. ◆ **on to, onto** *prep (written as onto for senses 4 and 5 only)* - **1.** [to a position on top of] auf *(+ A)*; **she**

jumped on to the chair sie sprang auf den Stuhl - **2.** [into a vehicle] in *(+ A)*; **she got on to the bus** sie stieg in den Bus ein - **3.** [wall, door] an *(+ A)*; **stick the photo on to the page** kleb das Foto auf die Seite - **4.** [aware of]: **to be onto sb** [subj: police] jm auf der Spur sein; **she's onto something** sie hat etwas entdeckt - **5.** [into contact with]: **to get onto sb** sich an jn wenden.

once [wʌns] <> *adv* einmal; **not once** kein einziges Mal; **for once** ausnahmsweise; **once more** [one more time] noch einmal; [again] wieder; **once and for all** ein für allemal; **once (upon a time) there was** es war einmal. <> *conj* wenn. ◆ **at once** *adv* - **1.** [immediately] sofort - **2.** [at the same time] gleichzeitig; **all at once** auf einmal.

oncoming ['ɒn,kʌmɪŋ] *adj*: **oncoming traffic** Gegenverkehr *der*.

one [wʌn] <> *num* - **1.** [the number 1] eins; **thirty-one** einunddreißig; **at one/one thirty** [time] um eins/halb zwei; **in ones and twos** vereinzelt - **2.** *(with masculine and neuter nouns)* ein; *(with feminine nouns)* eine; **one brother and one sister** ein Bruder und eine Schwester; **one hundred/thousand** (ein)hundert/(ein)tausend; **page one** Seite eins; **one-fifth** ein Fünftel; **one or two** einige. <> *adj* - **1.** [only] einzige(r) (s); **it's her one ambition** das ist ihr einziger Ehrgeiz - **2.** [indefinite]: **one day** [in past, future] eines Tages; **one of these days** irgendwann einmal; **one afternoon/night** an einem Nachmittag/Abend - **3.** *fml* [a certain] ein gewisser (eine gewisse); **one James Smith** ein gewisser James Smith. <> *pron* - **1.** [referring to a particular thing or person]: **the red/blue one** der/die/das Rote/Blaue; **the best ones** die besten; **the one on the table** der/die/das auf dem Tisch; **the one I told you about** der/die/das, von dem/der/dem ich dir erzählt habe; **the ones you want** die OR diejenigen, die du willst; **I like that one** ich mag den/die/das (da); **which one?** welche(r) (s) ?; **a red dot and a blue one** ein roter Punkt und ein blauer - **2.** [indefinite] eine/einer/eins; **there's only one left** es ist nur eine/einer/eins übrig; **have you got one?** hast du eine/einen/eins?; **one of my friends** einer meiner Freunde; **not one (of them)** keiner (von ihnen); **one by one** einer nach dem anderen - **3.** [referring to money]: **one fifty, please** eins fünfzig, bitte - **4.** *fml* [you, anyone] man; **one never knows** man weiß nie; **to give one's opinion** seine Meinung sagen; **to cut one's finger** sich *(D)* in den Finger schneiden. ◆ **for one** *adv*: **I for one will come** ich jedenfalls werde kommen.

one-armed bandit [-ɑːmd] *n* einarmiger Bandit.

one-man *adj* Einmann-.

one-off *inf* <> *adj* [event, offer, concert] einmalig; **one-off object/product** Einzelstück *das*. <> *n* - **1.** [unique event] einmalige Sache - **2.** [unique object, product] Einzelstück *das*.

one-on-one *adj US* = **one-to-one**.

one-parent family *n* Einelternfamilie *die*.

oneself [wʌn'self] *pron fml* - **1.** *(reflexive)* sich; **to make oneself comfortable** es sich *(D)* bequem machen - **2.** *(after prep)* sich selbst; **to look at oneself in the mirror** sich (selbst) im Spiegel betrachten - **3.** *(stressed)* selbst; **to do sthg oneself** etw selbst tun.

one-sided [-'saɪdɪd] *adj* einseitig.

one-to-one *UK*, **one-on-one** *US adj*: **one-to-one discussion** Diskussion *die* unter vier Augen; **one-to-one tuition** Einzelunterricht *der*.

one-way *adj*: **one-way street** Einbahnstraße *die*; **one-way traffic** Einbahnverkehr *der*; **one-way ticket** einfache Fahrkarte.

ongoing ['ɒn,gəʊɪŋ] *adj* [situation] andauernd; [project] laufend; [discussions] im Gang befindlich.

onion ['ʌnjən] *n* Zwiebel *die*.

online <> *adj* ['ɒnlaɪn] COMPUT Online-. <> *adv* [,ɒn'laɪn] COMPUT online.

online banking *n* COMPUT Onlinebanking *das*.

online shopping *n* COMPUT Onlineshopping *das*.

onlooker ['ɒn,lʊkər] *n* Zuschauer *der*, -in *die*; [at accident scene] Schaulustige *der, die*.

only ['əʊnlɪ] <> *adj* einzige(r) (s); **an only child** ein Einzelkind. <> *adv* nur; **I only want one** ich möchte nur einen/eine/eines; **I only wish I could** ich würde es wirklich gern tun; **only yesterday** erst gestern; **we've only just arrived** wir sind gerade erst angekommen; **there's only just enough** es ist gerade noch genug da; **not only** nicht nur. <> *conj* aber; **I would go, only I'm too tired** ich würde gehen, aber ich bin zu müde.

onset ['ɒnset] *n* Beginn *der*; [of war, illness] Ausbruch *der*.

onshore [,ɒn'ʃɔːr] *adv* an Land.

onslaught ['ɒnslɔːt] *n* - **1.** [physical] (heftiger) Angriff - **2.** [verbal] (verbale) Attacke.

onto *(stressed* ['ɒntuː], *unstressed before consonant* ['ɒntə], *unstressed before vowel* ['ɒntʊ]*) prep* ▻ **on**.

onus ['əʊnəs] *n*: **the onus is on him to convince us** es liegt an ihm, uns zu überzeugen.

onward ['ɒnwəd] <> *adj*: **onward journey** Weiterreise *die*. <> *adv* = **onwards**.

onwards ['ɒnwədz] *adv* [forwards] vorwärts; **to travel onwards** weiter|reisen; **from now onwards** von jetzt an; **from October onwards** ab Oktober.

ooze [uːz] <> *vt fig* [charm] aus|strahlen; [confidence] strotzen vor *(+ D)*. <> *vi* [liquid, blood] triefen; [mud] (heraus)|quellen.

opaque [əʊ'peɪk] *adj* - **1.** [not transparent] undurchsichtig - **2.** *fig* [text, meaning] unverständlich.

open ['əʊpn] ◇ *adj* - **1.** [gen] offen; **wide open** weit offen - **2.** [receptive - mind, person]: **to be open to sthg** [ready to accept] für etw offen sein; **open to question** fraglich; **two options are open to us** zwei Möglichkeiten stehen uns offen - **3.** [shop, office, library] geöffnet; **open to the public** der Öffentlichkeit zugänglich - **4.** [inaugurated] eröffnet - **5.** [unobstructed - road, passage] frei; [- view] weit - **6.** [not enclosed]: **open country** freies Land; **in the open air** im Freien. ◇ *n*: **in the open** [in the fresh air] im Freien; **to bring sthg out into the open** etw ans Licht bringen. ◇ *vt* - **1.** [gen] öffnen; **to open fire** das Feuer eröffnen - **2.** [bank account, meeting, event, new building] eröffnen. ◇ *vi* - **1.** [door, window, eyes, flower] sich öffnen - **2.** [begin business] öffnen - **3.** [commence] beginnen. ◆ **open on to** *vt insep* [subj: door] führen auf *(+ A)*. ◆ **open up** ◇ *vt sep* - **1.** [gen] öffnen - **2.** [for development - country, market] erschließen. ◇ *vi* - **1.** [unlock door] aufIschließen - **2.** [for business] öffnen - **3.** [become available - possibilities, chances] sich eröffnen - **4.** [become less reserved] offener werden.

opener ['əʊpnəʳ] *n* Öffner *der*.

opening ['əʊpnɪŋ] ◇ *adj* [speech, scene] Eröffnungs-. ◇ *n* - **1.** [beginning] Anfang *der* - **2.** [gap] Öffnung *die* - **3.** [opportunity] Möglichkeit *die* - **4.** [job vacancy] freie Stelle.

opening hours *npl* Öffnungszeiten *Pl*.

openly ['əʊpənlɪ] *adv* [frankly] offen; [publicly] öffentlich.

open-minded [-'maɪndɪd] *adj* aufgeschlossen.

open-plan *adj* [office] Großraum-.

Open University *n UK*: **the Open University** *britische Fernuniversität*.

opera ['ɒpərə] *n* Oper *die*.

opera house *n* Opernhaus *das*.

operate ['ɒpəreɪt] ◇ *vt* - **1.** [machine] bedienen - **2.** COMM [business] leiten, führen. ◇ *vi* - **1.** [law] sich ausIwirken; [system] funktionieren; [machine - function] funktionieren; [- be in operation] in Betrieb sein - **2.** COMM [business] arbeiten - **3.** MED: **to operate (on sb/sthg)** (jn/etw) operieren.

operating theatre *UK*, **operating room** *US* ['ɒpəreɪtɪŋ-] *n* Operationssaal *der*.

operation [,ɒpə'reɪʃn] *n* - **1.** [planned activity - MIL] Operation *die*; [- of police force] Einsatz *der*; **rescue operation** Rettungsaktion *die*; **relief operation** Hilfsaktion *die* - **2.** *(U)* [COMM - management] Leitung *die*; [- company, business] Unternehmen *das* - **3.** *(U)* [of machine - running] Betrieb *der*; [- control] Bedienung *die*; **to be in operation** [- machine] in Betrieb sein; [- law] in Kraft sein; [- system] angewendet werden - **4.** MED Operation *die*; **to have an operation** operiert werden.

operational [,ɒpə'reɪʃənl] *adj* [machine]: **to be operational** [ready for use] betriebsbereit sein; [in use] in Betrieb sein.

operator ['ɒpəreɪtəʳ] *n* - **1.** [TELEC - at telephone exchange] Vermittlung *die*; [- at switchboard] Telefonist *der*, -in *die* - **2.** [of machine] Maschinenarbeiter *der*, -in *die*; [of computer] Operator *der*, -in *die* - **3.** COMM [person in charge] Unternehmer *der*, -in *die*.

opinion [ə'pɪnjən] *n* Meinung *die*, Ansicht *die*; MED Gutachten *das*; **what's your opinion of him?** was halten Sie von ihm?; **to be of the opinion that** der Meinung *OR* Ansicht sein, dass; **to have a high/low opinion of sb** eine hohe/schlechte Meinung von jm haben; **in my opinion** meiner Meinung *OR* Ansicht nach.

opinionated [ə'pɪnjəneɪtɪd] *adj pej* rechthaberisch.

opinion poll *n* Meinungsumfrage *die*.

opponent [ə'pəʊnənt] *n* Gegner *der*, -in *die*.

opportune ['ɒpətjuːn] *adj* [moment] günstig.

opportunist [,ɒpə'tjuːnɪst] *n* Opportunist *der*, -in *die*.

opportunity [,ɒpə'tjuːnətɪ] *n* Gelegenheit *die*; **to take the opportunity to do** *OR* **of doing sthg** die Gelegenheit ergreifen, um etw zu tun.

oppose [ə'pəʊz] *vt* [resist] sich widersetzen *(+ D)*; [ideas, views] abIlehnen.

opposed [ə'pəʊzd] *adj*: **to be opposed to sthg** gegen etw sein; **as opposed to** im Gegensatz zu.

opposing [ə'pəʊzɪŋ] *adj* [points of view] entgegengesetzt; [teams] gegnerisch.

opposite ['ɒpəzɪt] ◇ *adj* - **1.** [facing] gegenüberliegend; **the houses opposite** die Häuser gegenüber - **2.** [very different] entgegengesetzt. ◇ *adv* gegenüber. ◇ *prep* [facing] gegenüber *(+ D)*. ◇ *n* Gegenteil *das*.

opposite number *n* Pendant *das*.

opposition [,ɒpə'zɪʃn] *n* - **1.** [disapproval] Widerstand *der*, Opposition *die* - **2.** [opposing team] Gegner *Pl*. ◆ **Opposition** *n UK* POL: **the Opposition** die Opposition.

oppress [ə'pres] *vt* - **1.** [persecute] unterdrücken - **2.** [subj: anxiety, atmosphere] bedrücken.

oppressive [ə'presɪv] *adj* - **1.** [regime, government, society] repressiv - **2.** [heat, weather] drückend - **3.** [situation, silence] bedrückend.

opt [ɒpt] ◇ *vt*: **to opt to do sthg** sich dafür entscheiden, etw zu tun. ◇ *vi*: **to opt for sthg** sich für etw entscheiden. ◆ **opt in** *vi*: **to opt in to sthg** etw *(D)* beiltreten. ◆ **opt out** *vi*: **to opt out (of)** [scheme, system] ausltreten (aus).

optical ['ɒptɪkl] *adj* optisch.

optician [ɒp'tɪʃn] *n* Optiker *der*, -in *die*; **to go to the optician's** zum Optiker gehen.

optimist ['ɒptɪmɪst] *n* Optimist *der*, -in *die*.

optimistic [ˌɒptɪ'mɪstɪk] *adj*: **she's optimistic about passing her driving test** sie ist optimistisch, dass sie die Fahrprüfung bestehen wird.

optimum ['ɒptɪməm] *adj* optimal.

option ['ɒpʃn] *n* [choice] Wahl *die*; [alternative to be chosen] (Wahl)möglichkeit *die*; **to have the option to do** *OR* **of doing sthg** die Möglichkeit haben, etw zu tun.

optional ['ɒpʃənl] *adj* [subject] Wahl-; [course] fakultativ; **optional extra** Extra *das*.

or [ɔːʳ] *conj* - **1.** [linking alternatives] oder; **either one or the other** entweder das eine oder das andere; **or (else)** [otherwise] sonst; **ten kilometres or so** [approximately] ungefähr zehn Kilometer - **2.** *(after negatives)* noch; **he cannot read or write** er kann weder lesen noch schreiben.

oral ['ɔːrəl] ◇ *adj* - **1.** [exam] mündlich - **2.** MED [medicine] zum Einnehmen; [hygiene] Mund-; **oral vaccine** Schluckimpfung *die*. ◇ *n* mündliche Prüfung.

orally ['ɔːrəlɪ] *adv* MED oral; **to take sthg orally** etw ein|nehmen.

orange ['ɒrɪndʒ] ◇ *adj* [colour] orange. ◇ *n* - **1.** [fruit] Orange *die*, Apfelsine *die* - **2.** *(U)* [colour] Orange *das*.

orator ['ɒrətəʳ] *n* Redner *der*, -in *die*.

orbit ['ɔːbɪt] ◇ *n* [in space] Umlaufbahn *die*. ◇ *vt* umkreisen.

orchard ['ɔːtʃəd] *n* Obstgarten *der*.

orchestra ['ɔːkɪstrə] *n* Orchester *das*.

orchid ['ɔːkɪd] *n* Orchidee *die*.

ordain [ɔː'deɪn] *vt* RELIG: **to be ordained** (zum Priester) geweiht werden.

ordeal [ɔː'diːl] *n* Tortur *die*.

order ['ɔːdəʳ] ◇ *n* - **1.** [instruction] Anweisung *die*; MIL Befehl *der*; **until further orders** bis auf weiteren Befehl; **to be under orders to do sthg** MIL den Befehl haben, etw zu tun - **2.** COMM [request, in restaurant] Bestellung *die*; **to place an order with sb for sthg** bei jm eine Bestellung für etw auf|geben; [contract to manufacture or supply goods] Auftrag *der*; **to place an order with sb for sthg** jm für etw einen Auftrag erteilen; **to order** auf Bestellung - **3.** *(U)* [sequence] Reihenfolge *die*; **arranged in order of importance** nach Wichtigkeit geordnet; **in alphabetical order** in alphabetischer Reihenfolge - **4.** *(U)* [neatness, discipline, system] Ordnung *die* - **5.** [fitness for use]: **in order** [valid] in Ordnung; **in working order** funktionstüchtig; **out of order** [machine, lift] außer Betrieb; **you're out of order!** *inf* pass auf, was du sagst/machst! - **6.** RELIG Orden *der* - **7.** *US* [portion] Portion *die*. ◇ *vt* - **1.** [command] anordnen; MIL befehlen *(+ D)*; [subj: court] verfügen; **to order sb to do sthg** jn an|weisen, etw zu tun; MIL jm befehlen, etw zu tun; **to order that...** an|ordnen, dass...; MIL befehlen, dass... - **2.** COMM [request] bestellen; [to be manufactured: suit, aircraft, ship] in Auftrag geben. ◆ **in the order of** *UK*, **on the order of** *US prep* etwa. ◆ **in order that** *conj* damit. ◆ **in order to** *conj* um zu; **in order to get a better view** um eine bessere Sicht zu bekommen. ◆ **order about, order around** *vt sep* herum|kommandieren.

order form *n* Bestellschein *der*.

orderly ['ɔːdəlɪ] ◇ *adj* ordentlich. ◇ *n* [in hospital] Pfleger *der*, -in *die*.

ordinarily ['ɔːdənrəlɪ] *adv* [normally] gewöhnlich, normalerweise.

ordinary ['ɔːdənrɪ] ◇ *adj* - **1.** [normal] gewöhnlich, normal; **ordinary people** einfache Leute - **2.** *pej* [unexceptional] gewöhnlich. ◇ *n*: **out of the ordinary** außergewöhnlich.

ore [ɔːʳ] *n* Erz *das*.

oregano [ˌɒrɪ'gɑːnəʊ] *n* Oregano *der*.

organ ['ɔːgən] *n* - **1.** ANAT Organ *das* - **2.** MUS Orgel *die*.

organic [ɔː'gænɪk] *adj* - **1.** [of animals, plants] organisch - **2.** [food] biodynamisch.

organization [ˌɔːgənaɪ'zeɪʃn] *n* - **1.** [gen] Organisation *die* - **2.** *(U)* [arrangement] Ordnung *die*.

organize, -ise ['ɔːgənaɪz] *vt* organisieren; [affairs, thoughts] ordnen.

organizer, -iser ['ɔːgənaɪzəʳ] *n* [person] Organisator *der*, -in *die*.

orgasm ['ɔːgæzm] *n* Orgasmus *der*.

orgy ['ɔːdʒɪ] *n* Orgie *die*.

oriental [ˌɔːrɪ'entl] *adj* orientalisch.

origami [ˌɒrɪ'gɑːmɪ] *n* Origami *das*.

origin ['ɒrɪdʒɪn] *n* - **1.** [starting point] Ursprung *der* - **2.** *(U)* [birth] Herkunft *die*; **country of origin** Herkunftsland *das*. ◆ **origins** *npl* Herkunft *die*.

original [ɒ'rɪdʒənl] ◇ *adj* - **1.** [first] ursprünglich - **2.** [document] Original-; **original painting** Original *das* - **3.** [new, unusual] originell. ◇ *n* Original *das*.

originally [ə'rɪdʒənəlɪ] *adv* [initially] ursprünglich.

originate [ə'rɪdʒəneɪt] ◇ *vt* [scheme, policy] ins Leben rufen; [new style] begründen. ◇ *vi*: **to originate in/from** seinen Ursprung haben in *(+ D)*.

ornament ['ɔːnəmənt] *n* - **1.** [object] Ziergegenstand *der* - **2.** *(U)* [decoration] Verzierungen *Pl*.

ornamental [ˌɔːnə'mentl] *adj* dekorativ; **ornamental garden** Ziergarten *der*.

ornate [ɔː'neɪt] *adj* reich verziert; [language] blumig.

ornithology [,ɔ:nɪ'θɒlədʒɪ] *n* Ornithologie *die*.

orphan ['ɔ:fn] ◇ *n* Waise *die*, Waisenkind *das*. ◇ *vt*: **to be orphaned** (zur) Waise werden.

orphanage ['ɔ:fənɪdʒ] *n* Waisenhaus *das*.

orthodox ['ɔ:θədɒks] *adj* - **1.** [conventional] konventionell - **2.** RELIG orthodox.

orthopaedic [,ɔ:θə'pi:dɪk] *adj* orthopädisch.

Oslo ['ɒzləʊ] *n* Oslo *nt*.

ostensible [ɒ'stensəbl] *adj* angeblich.

ostentatious [,ɒstən'teɪʃəs] *adj* [person] protzenhaft; [behaviour] betont auffällig.

osteopath ['ɒstɪəpæθ] *n* Osteopath *der*, -in *die*.

ostracize, -ise ['ɒstrəsaɪz] *vt* ächten.

ostrich ['ɒstrɪtʃ] *n* Strauß *der*.

other ['ʌðə^r] ◇ *adj* andere(r) (s); **the other one** der/die/das andere; **the other day** neulich; **every other day** jeden zweiten Tag; **any other questions?** sonst noch Fragen? ◇ *pron* andere(r) (s); **one or other (of us)** der eine oder andere (von uns); **one after the other** hintereinander. ◇ *adv*: **other than** außer; **it was none other than the king** es war kein anderer als der König.

otherwise ['ʌðəwaɪz] ◇ *adv* - **1.** [apart from that] ansonsten, sonst - **2.** [differently] anders; **to be otherwise engaged** anderweitig beschäftigt sein; **otherwise known as** auch bekannt als. ◇ *conj* [or else] sonst, andernfalls.

otter ['ɒtə^r] *n* Otter *der*.

ouch [aʊtʃ] *excl* au!, aua!

ought [ɔ:t] *aux vb*: **I ought to go now** ich sollte jetzt gehen; **you ought not to have said that** du hättest das nicht sagen sollen; **you ought to see a doctor** du solltest zum Arzt gehen; **the car ought to be ready by Friday** das Auto sollte Freitag fertig sein; **that ought to be enough for three** das dürfte für drei Personen genügen.

ounce [aʊns] *n* - **1.** [unit of measurement] Unze *die (= 28,35 g)* - **2.** *fig* [of truth, intelligence] Funken *der*.

our ['aʊə^r] *poss adj* unser; **our children** unsere Kinder; **we washed our hair** wir haben uns die Haare gewaschen; **a home of our own** ein eigenes Haus.

ours ['aʊəz] *poss pron* unsere(r) (s); **this suitcase is ours** dieser Koffer gehört uns; **a friend of ours** ein Freund von uns.

ourselves [aʊə'selvz] *pron (reflexive, after prep)* uns; **we did it ourselves** wir haben es selbst gemacht; **(all) by ourselves** (ganz) allein.

oust [aʊst] *vt fml*: **to oust sb from sthg** [position, job] jn aus etw verdrängen.

out [aʊt] ◇ *adj* [light, cigarette] aus. ◇ *adv* - **1.** [outside] draußen; **to come out (of)** herauslkommen (aus); **to get out (of)** auslsteigen (aus); **it's cold out today** es ist heute kalt draußen; **out you go!** raus mit dir!; **out here/there** hier/dort draußen - **2.** [not at home, work]: **she's out** sie ist nicht da; **to go out** auslgehen; **to go out for a walk** einen Spaziergang machen - **3.** [so as to be extinguished] aus; **put your cigarette out!** mach deine Zigarette aus! - **4.** [of tides]: **the tide is out** es ist Ebbe - **5.** [expressing removal]: **to take sthg out (of)** etw herauslnehmen (aus); [money] etw ablheben (von); **he poured the water out** er schüttete das Wasser aus - **6.** [expressing distribution]: **to hand sthg out** etw ausIteilen - **7.** [wrong]: **the bill's £10 out** die Rechnung stimmt um 10 Pfund nicht - **8.** [published, known]: **the book is just out** das Buch ist soeben erschienen; **the secret is out** das Geheimnis ist gelüftet - **9.** [in flower] aufgeblüht; **the roses are out** die Rosen blühen - **10.** [visible]: **the moon is out** der Mond scheint - **11.** [out of fashion] aus der Mode - **12.** *inf* [on strike]: **they've been out for months now** sie streiken schon seit Monaten - **13.** [determined]: **to be out for revenge** auf Rache aus sein; **I'm not out to make money** ich bin nicht darauf aus, Geld zu verdienen. ◆ **out of** *prep* - **1.** [away from, outside]: **stay out of the sun** bleib aus der Sonne; **I was out of the country** ich war im Ausland - **2.** [indicating cause, origin] aus *(+ D)*; **out of respect/curiosity** aus Respekt/Neugierde; **made out of wood** aus Holz (gemacht) - **3.** [without]: **I'm out of** OR **I've run out of cigarettes** ich habe keine Zigaretten mehr - **4.** [to indicate proportion]: **five out of ten** fünf von zehn - **5.** *phr*: **out of danger/control** außer Gefahr/Kontrolle. ◆ **out of doors** *adv* im Freien.

out-and-out *adj* [liar, fool, crook] ausgemacht.

outback ['aʊtbæk] *n*: **the outback** *weit abseits der Städte gelegener Teil Australiens.*

outboard (motor) ['aʊtbɔ:d-] *n* Außenbordmotor *der*.

outbreak ['aʊtbreɪk] *n* [of war, disease] Ausbruch *der*.

outburst ['aʊtbɜ:st] *n* [of emotion, violence] Ausbruch *der*.

outcast ['aʊtkɑ:st] *n* [socially] Außenseiter *der*, -in *die*; [from family, group] Verstoßene *der, die*.

outcome ['aʊtkʌm] *n* Ergebnis *das*.

outcry ['aʊtkraɪ] *n* Aufschrei *der* der Empörung.

outdated [,aʊt'deɪtɪd] *adj* [belief, concept, method] überholt; [language] antiquiert.

outdid [,aʊt'dɪd] *pt* ▷ **outdo**.

outdo [,aʊt'du:] (*pt* **-did**, *pp* **-done** [-'dʌn]) *vt* übertreffen.

outdoor ['aʊtdɔːʳ] *adj* [life, activity] im Freien; **outdoor swimming pool** Freibad *das*; **outdoor clothes** Straßenkleidung *die*.

outdoors [aʊt'dɔːz] *adv* draußen, im Freien; [go] nach draußen.

outer ['aʊtəʳ] *adj* [wall] Außen-; [layer] äußere(r) (s).

outer space *n* Weltraum *der*.

outfit ['aʊtfɪt] *n* - **1.** [clothes] Kleider *Pl*; [fancy dress] Kostüm *das* - **2.** *inf* [organization] Laden *der*, Verein *der*.

outgoing ['aʊt,gəʊɪŋ] *adj* - **1.** [from job] (aus dem Amt) scheidend - **2.** [friendly, sociable] kontaktfreudig. ◆ **outgoings** *npl UK* Ausgaben *Pl*.

outgrow [,aʊt'grəʊ] (*pt* **-grew** [-'gruː], *pp* **-grown** [-'grəʊn]) *vt* - **1.** [grow too big for] heraus|wachsen aus - **2.** [habit] ab|legen.

outhouse ['aʊthaʊs] (*pl* [-haʊzɪz]) *n* Nebengebäude *das*.

outing ['aʊtɪŋ] *n* [trip] Ausflug *der*.

outlandish [aʊt'lændɪʃ] *adj* sonderbar.

outlaw ['aʊtlɔː] ◇ *n* Geächtete *der, die*; [in the Wild West] Bandit *der*. ◇ *vt* [make illegal] verbieten.

outlay ['aʊtleɪ] *n* Kostenaufwand *der*.

outlet ['aʊtlet] *n* - **1.** [for feelings] Ventil *das* - **2.** [hole, pipe] Auslass *der* - **3.** [shop] Verkaufsstelle *die* - **4.** *US* ELEC Steckdose *die*.

outline ['aʊtlaɪn] ◇ *n* - **1.** [brief description] Abriss *der*; **in outline** in Grundzügen - **2.** [silhouette] Umriss *der*. ◇ *vt* [describe briefly] umreißen, skizzieren.

outlive [,aʊt'lɪv] *vt* [subj: person] überleben.

outlook ['aʊtlʊk] *n* - **1.** [attitude, disposition] Einstellung *die* - **2.** [prospect] Aussichten *Pl*.

outlying ['aʊt,laɪɪŋ] *adj* [villages] abgelegen; **outlying district** Außenbezirk *der*.

outmoded [,aʊt'məʊdɪd] *adj* überholt.

outnumber [,aʊt'nʌmbəʳ] *vt* zahlenmäßig überlegen sein *(+ D)*.

out-of-date *adj* [passport, season ticket] abgelaufen; [clothes] altmodisch; [belief] überholt.

out of doors *adv* draußen, im Freien; [go] nach draußen.

out-of-the-way *adj* [isolated] abgelegen.

outpatient ['aʊt,peɪʃnt] *n* ambulanter Patient, ambulante Patientin; **outpatients (department)** Ambulanz *die*.

output ['aʊtpʊt] *n (U)* - **1.** [production - of factory, writer] Produktion *die*; [- in agriculture] Ertrag *der* - **2.** [COMPUT - printing out] Ausdrucken *das*; [- printout] Ausdruck *der*.

outrage ['aʊtreɪdʒ] ◇ *n* - **1.** *(U)* [anger, shock] Empörung *die* - **2.** [atrocity] Verbrechen *das*. ◇ *vt* empören; [sense of morality] zuwider|laufen *(+ D)*.

outrageous [aʊt'reɪdʒəs] *adj* - **1.** [offensive, shocking - crime] verabscheuungswürdig; [- language] unflätig; [- behaviour] unerhört - **2.** [extravagant, wild - outfit, idea] exzentrisch.

outright ◇ *adj* ['aʊtraɪt] [refusal, denial] kategorisch; [disaster] total; [winner, victory] klar; [lie] glatt. ◇ *adv* [,aʊt'raɪt] [ask] ohne Umschweife; [deny] kategorisch; [win, fail] klar.

outset ['aʊtset] *n*: **at the outset** zu OR am Anfang; **from the outset** von Anfang an.

outside ◇ *adv* [,aʊt'saɪd] draußen; **to go outside** nach draußen gehen. ◇ *prep* ['aʊtsaɪd] - **1.** [gen] außerhalb *(+ G)*; **we live just outside London** wir wohnen gleich außerhalb Londons; **outside (office) hours** außerhalb der Dienststunden - **2.** [in front of] vor *(+ A, D)*; **outside the door** vor der Tür. ◇ *adj* ['aʊtsaɪd] - **1.** [exterior] Außen- - **2.** [help, advice] von außen; **outside influence** äußere Einflüsse - **3.** [unlikely]: **there's an outside chance** es besteht eine geringe Chance. ◇ *n* ['aʊtsaɪd] [of building, car, container] Außenseite *die*; **to open the door from the outside** die Tür von außen öffnen. ◆ **outside of** *prep* - **1.** *US* [on the outside of] außerhalb *(+ G)* - **2.** [apart from] außer.

outside lane *n* Überholspur *die*.

outside line *n* Amtsleitung *die*.

outsider [,aʊt'saɪdəʳ] *n* Außenseiter *der*, -in *die*.

outsize ['aʊtsaɪz] *adj* - **1.** [book, portion] überdimensional - **2.**: **outsize clothes** Kleidung *die* in Übergröße.

outskirts ['aʊtskɜːts] *npl*: **the outskirts** die Außenbezirke *Pl*; **on the outskirts** am Stadtrand.

outsource ['aʊtsɔːs] *vt* outsourcen.

outsourcing ['aʊtsɔːsɪŋ] *n* Outsourcing *das*.

outspoken [,aʊt'spəʊkn] *adj* freimütig.

outstanding [,aʊt'stændɪŋ] *adj* - **1.** [excellent - person] außergewöhnlich; [- performance, achievement] hervorragend - **2.** [very obvious, important] bemerkenswert - **3.** [not paid - money] ausstehend; [- bill] unbezahlt - **4.** [still to be done - work] unerledigt; [- problem] ungeklärt.

outstay [,aʊt'steɪ] *vt*: **to outstay one's welcome** länger bleiben als erwünscht.

outstretched [,aʊt'stretʃt] *adj* ausgestreckt.

outstrip [,aʊt'strɪp] *vt* - **1.** [do better than] übertreffen - **2.** [run faster than] überholen.

out-tray *n* Ablage *die* für Ausgänge.

outward ['aʊtwəd] ◇ *adj* - **1.** [going away]: **outward journey** Hinreise *die* - **2.** [external, visible]: **she maintained her outward composure** sie blieb äußerlich ruhig; **he shows no outward sign of his grief** nach außen hin zeigt er nichts von seinem Kummer. ◇ *adv US* = **outwards**.

outwardly ['aʊtwədlɪ] *adv* nach außen hin.

outwards *UK* ['aʊtwədz], **outward** *US adv* nach außen.

outweigh [ˌaʊt'weɪ] *vt* überwiegen.

outwit [ˌaʊt'wɪt] *vt* überlisten.

oval ['əʊvl] <> *adj* oval. <> *n* Oval *das*.

Oval Office *n*: **the Oval Office** *Büro des US-Präsidenten im Weißen Haus*.

ovary ['əʊvərɪ] *n* ANAT Eierstock *der*.

ovation [əʊ'veɪʃn] *n* Ovation *die*, begeisterter Beifall; **to give sb a standing ovation** jm stehende Ovationen darlbringen.

oven ['ʌvn] *n* [for cooking] Backofen *der*.

ovenproof ['ʌvnpru:f] *adj* feuerfest.

over ['əʊvər] <> *prep* - **1.** [directly above] über *(+ D)*; **a bridge over the road** eine Brücke über der Straße - **2.** [indicating place, position] über *(+ D)*; [indicating direction] über *(+ A)*; **she wore a veil over her face** sie trug einen Schleier vor dem Gesicht; **put your coat over the chair** leg deinen Mantel über den Stuhl - **3.** [across] über *(+ A)*; **to walk over sthg** über etw laufen; **he threw it over the wall** er warf es über die Mauer; **it's just over the road** es ist gleich gegenüber; **it's over the river** es ist auf der anderen Seite des Flusses; **with a view over the gardens** mit Blick auf die Gärten - **4.** [more than] über *(+ A)*; **it cost over $1,000** es hat über 1000 Dollar gekostet; **over and above this amount** über den Betrag hinaus - **5.** [about] über *(+ A)*; **an argument over the price** ein Streit über den Preis - **6.** [during]: **over the weekend** übers Wochenende; **over the past two years** in den letzten zwei Jahren; **to discuss sthg over lunch/a cup of coffee** etw beim Essen/bei einer Tasse Kaffee besprechen - **7.** [to do]: **he took a long time over it** er hat lange dazu gebraucht - **8.** [recovered from] über *(+ A)*; **to be over sthg** über etw *(A)* hinweg sein - **9.** [by means of] über *(+ A)*; **over the phone** am Telefon; **over the radio** im Radio. <> *adv* - **1.** [referring to distance away]: **over by the gate** drüben beim Tor; **over here/there** hier/da drüben - **2.** [across] herüber/hinüber; **to drive over** herüberlfahren/hinüberlfahren - **3.** [round to other side]: **to turn sthg over** etw umldrehen; **to roll over** sich umldrehen - **4.** [more]: **children aged 12 and over** Kinder ab 12; **sums of £100 and over** Summen von 100 Pfund und mehr - **5.** [remaining] übrig; **to be (left) over** übrig bleiben - **6.** [at/to sb's house]: **to invite sb over for dinner** jn zu sich zum Essen einlladen; **I was over at my mum's yesterday** ich war gestern bei meiner Mutter - **7.** RADIO over; **over and out!** over and out! - **8.** [involving repetitions]: **(all) over again** wieder von vorne; **over and over (again)** immer wieder. <> *adj* [finished]: **to be over** zu Ende sein.

overall <> *adj* ['əʊvərɔ:l] - **1.** [total] Gesamt- - **2.** [general] allgemein. <> *adv* [ˌəʊvər'ɔ:l] - **1.** [in total] insgesamt - **2.** [in general] im Großen und Ganzen. <> *n* ['əʊvərɔ:l] - **1.** [coat] Kittel *der* - **2.** *US* [with trousers] Overall *der*. ◆ **overalls** *npl* - **1.** [with long sleeves] Overall *der* - **2.** *US* [with bib] Latzhose *die*.

overawe [ˌəʊvər'ɔ:] *vt* [subj: person - make feel fear] einlschüchtern; [- make feel respect] Ehrfurcht einlflößen *(+ D)*; [subj: surroundings] überwältigen.

overbalance [ˌəʊvə'bæləns] *vi* das Gleichgewicht verlieren.

overbearing [ˌəʊvə'beərɪŋ] *adj pej* herrisch.

overboard ['əʊvəbɔ:d] *adv* NAUT: **to fall overboard** über Bord gehen.

overcame [ˌəʊvə'keɪm] *pt* ▷ **overcome**.

overcast [ˌəʊvə'kɑ:st] *adj* bedeckt.

overcharge [ˌəʊvə'tʃɑ:dʒ] *vt*: **to overcharge sb (for sthg)** jm zu viel berechnen (für etw).

overcoat ['əʊvəkəʊt] *n* Mantel *der*.

overcome [ˌəʊvə'kʌm] (*pt* **-came**, *pp* **-come**) *vt* - **1.** [control, deal with] überwinden - **2.** [overwhelm]: **to be overcome with emotion** gerührt sein; **to be overcome by fear** von Furcht ergriffen werden; **he was overcome by the fumes** die Dämpfe machten ihn bewusstlos.

overcrowded [ˌəʊvə'kraʊdɪd] *adj* [room, pub, prison] überfüllt; [town] übervölkert.

overcrowding [ˌəʊvə'kraʊdɪŋ] *n* [of room, pub, prison] Überfüllung *die*; [of town] Übervölkerung *die*.

overdo [ˌəʊvə'du:] (*pt* **-did** [-'dɪd], *pp* **-done** [-'dʌn]) *vt* - **1.** [exaggerate, do too much] es übertreiben mit; **to overdo it** es übertreiben; [work too hard] sich übernehmen - **2.** [overcook - vegetables] verkochen; [- steak] verbraten.

overdose *n* ['əʊvədəʊs] Überdosis *die*.

overdraft ['əʊvədrɑ:ft] *n* Kontoüberziehung *die*.

overdrawn [ˌəʊvə'drɔ:n] *adj* [account] überzogen; **I'm (£200) overdrawn** mein Konto ist (um 200 Pfund) überzogen.

overdue [ˌəʊvə'dju:] *adj* - **1.** [late - library book] überfällig; **the train is 20 minutes overdue** der Zug hat 20 Minuten Verspätung - **2.** [reform, rent, bill] überfällig.

overestimate [ˌəʊvər'estɪmeɪt] *vt* - **1.** [guess too high a value for] zu hoch einlschätzen - **2.** [overrate] überschätzen.

overflow <> *vi* [ˌəʊvə'fləʊ] - **1.** [bath] überlaufen; [river] über die Ufer treten - **2.** [place, container]: **to be overflowing (with sthg)** [room] überfüllt sein (mit etw); [drawer, box] überquellen (vor etw). <> *n* ['əʊvəfləʊ] [pipe, hole] Überlauf *der*.

overgrown [ˌəʊvə'grəʊn] *adj* [garden, path] überwuchert.

overhaul <> *n* ['əʊvəhɔ:l] - **1.** [service] Überholung *die* - **2.** [revision] Überarbeitung *die*. <> *vt* [ˌəʊvə'hɔ:l] - **1.** [service] überholen - **2.** [revise] überarbeiten.

overhead <> *adj* ['əʊvəhed]: **overhead cable** ELEC Hochspannungsleitung *die*; **overhead lighting** Deckenbeleuchtung *die*. <> *adv* [ˌəʊvə'hed] über uns/ihm/*etc*; **the clouds overhead** die Wolken am Himmel. <> *n* ['əʊvəhed] *(U) US* Gemeinkosten *Pl*. ◆ **overheads** *npl UK* Gemeinkosten *Pl*.

overhead projector *n* Overheadprojektor *der*.

overhear [ˌəʊvə'hɪə^r] (*pt & pp* **-heard** [-'hɜ:d]) *vt* [remark] zufällig hören; [conversation] zufällig mit|hören.

overheat [ˌəʊvə'hi:t] <> *vt* [room] überheizen. <> *vi* [engine, car] heiß laufen; [photocopier, toaster] zu heiß werden.

overjoyed [ˌəʊvə'dʒɔɪd] *adj*: **to be overjoyed (at sthg)** (über etw *(A)*) überglücklich sein.

overkill ['əʊvəkɪl] *n* [excess]: **to be overkill** zu viel des Guten sein.

overladen [ˌəʊvə'leɪdn] <> *pp* ▷ **overload**. <> *adj* zu schwer beladen.

overland ['əʊvəlænd] *adj & adv* auf dem Landweg.

overlap *vi* [ˌəʊvə'læp] - **1.** [cover each other] einander teilweise überdecken - **2.** [be similar]: **to overlap (with sthg)** [ideas, systems] sich teilweise decken (mit etw); [timetable, holiday] sich überschneiden (mit etw).

overleaf [ˌəʊvə'li:f] *adv* auf der Rückseite.

overload [ˌəʊvə'ləʊd] (*pp* **-loaded** OR **-laden**) *vt* - **1.** [put too much in] überladen - **2.** ELEC überlasten - **3.** [with work, problems]: **to be overloaded (with sthg)** überlastet sein (mit etw).

overlook [ˌəʊvə'lʊk] *vt* - **1.** [look over] eine Aussicht haben auf *(+ A)*; **a room overlooking the square** ein Zimmer mit Blick auf den Platz - **2.** [disregard, miss] übersehen - **3.** [excuse] hinweg|sehen über *(+ A)*.

overnight <> *adj* ['əʊvənaɪt]: **overnight stay** Übernachtung *die*; **overnight bag** kleine Reisetasche; **to be an overnight success** [person] über Nacht großen Erfolg haben; [play] über Nacht ein großer Erfolg sein. <> *adv* [ˌəʊvə'naɪt] über Nacht.

overpass ['əʊvəpɑ:s] *n US* Überführung *die*.

overpower [ˌəʊvə'paʊə^r] *vt* überwältigen.

overpowering [ˌəʊvə'paʊərɪŋ] *adj* [feeling] überwältigend; [heat] unerträglich; [smell] penetrant; [person] einschüchternd.

overran [ˌəʊvə'ræn] *pt* ▷ **overrun**.

overrated [ˌəʊvə'reɪtɪd] *adj*: **to be overrated** überschätzt werden.

override [ˌəʊvə'raɪd] (*pt* **-rode**, *pp* **-ridden** [-'rɪdn]) *vt* - **1.** [be more important than] Vorrang haben vor *(+ D)* - **2.** [overrule - decision] auf|heben.

overriding [ˌəʊvə'raɪdɪŋ] *adj* vorrangig.

overrode [ˌəʊvə'rəʊd] *pt* ▷ **override**.

overrule [ˌəʊvə'ru:l] *vt* [person] überstimmen; [decision] auf|heben; [objection] ab|weisen.

overrun [ˌəʊvə'rʌn] (*pt* **-ran**, *pp* **-run**) <> *vt* - **1.** MIL [occupy] ein|fallen in *(+ A)* - **2.** *fig*: **to be overrun with** [insects, rats] wimmeln von; [weeds] überwuchert sein von; [tourists] überlaufen sein von. <> *vi* [last too long] länger als vorgesehen dauern.

oversaw [ˌəʊvə'sɔ:] *pt* ▷ **oversee**.

overseas <> *adj* ['əʊvəsi:z] - **1.** [in or to foreign countries] Auslands-; **overseas aid** Entwicklungshilfe *die* - **2.** [from abroad] aus dem Ausland. <> *adv* [ˌəʊvə'si:z] [travel] nach Übersee; [study, live] in Übersee.

oversee [ˌəʊvə'si:] (*pt* **-saw**, *pp* **-seen** [-'si:n]) *vt* beaufsichtigen.

overshadow [ˌəʊvə'ʃædəʊ] *vt* - **1.** *fig* [outweigh, eclipse]: **to be overshadowed by sb/sthg** von jm/etw in den Schatten gestellt werden - **2.** *fig* [mar, cloud]: **to be overshadowed by sthg** [subj: party, victory] von etw überschattet werden; [subj: happiness, peace of mind] durch etw stark beeinträchtigt werden.

overshoot [ˌəʊvə'ʃu:t] (*pt & pp* **-shot** [-ʃɒt]) *vt* [go past - turning] vorbei|fahren an *(+ D)*; [- runway] hinaus|rollen über *(+ A)*.

oversight ['əʊvəsaɪt] *n* Versehen *das*.

oversleep [ˌəʊvə'sli:p] (*pt & pp* **-slept** [-'slept]) *vi* verschlafen.

overstep [ˌəʊvə'step] *vt* überschreiten; **to overstep the mark** zu weit gehen.

overt ['əʊvɜ:t] *adj* unverhohlen.

overtake [ˌəʊvə'teɪk] (*pt* **-took**, *pp* **-taken** [-'teɪkn]) <> *vt* - **1.** AUT überholen - **2.** [subj: disaster, misfortune] ereilen. <> *vi* überholen.

overthrow (*pt* **-threw** [-'θru:], *pp* **-thrown** [-'θrəʊn]) <> *n* ['əʊvəθrəʊ] [of government] Sturz *der*. <> *vt* [ˌəʊvə'θrəʊ] [government, president] stürzen.

overtime ['əʊvətaɪm] <> *n (U)* - **1.** [extra time worked] Überstunden *Pl* - **2.** *US* SPORT Verlängerung *die*. <> *adv*: **to work overtime** Überstunden machen.

overtones ['əʊvətəʊnz] *npl* Untertöne *Pl*.

overtook [ˌəʊvə'tʊk] *pt* ▷ **overtake**.

overture ['əʊvəˌtjʊə^r] *n* MUS Ouvertüre *die*.

overturn [ˌəʊvə'tɜ:n] <> *vt* - **1.** [turn over] um|werfen - **2.** [overrule] auf|heben - **3.** [overthrow] stürzen. <> *vi* [boat] kentern; [lorry] um|stürzen.

overweight [ˌəʊvə'weɪt] *adj* [person] übergewichtig.

overwhelm [ˌəʊvə'welm] *vt* überwältigen.

overwhelming [ˌəʊvə'welmɪŋ] *adj* - **1.** [feeling, quality] überwältigend - **2.** [victory, majority] überwältigend; [defeat] vernichtend.

overwork [ˌəʊvə'wɜ:k] <> *n (U)* Überlastung *die*. <> *vt* [give too much work to] mit Arbeit überlasten.

owe [əʊ] *vt*: **to owe sthg to sb, to owe sb sthg** [money, respect, gratitude] jm etw schulden; [good looks, success] jm etw verdanken.

owing ['əʊɪŋ] *adj*: **the amount owing** der ausstehende Betrag; **to be owing** auslstehen. ◆ **owing to** *prep* wegen *(+ G)*.

owl [aʊl] *n* Eule *die*.

own [əʊn] ◇ *adj* eigen; **I have my own bedroom** ich habe ein eigenes Zimmer; **she makes her own clothes** sie näht ihre Kleider selbst. ◇ *pron*: **it has a taste all of its own** es hat einen ganz eigenen Geschmack; **on my own** allein; **to get one's own back** *inf* sich revanchieren; **he can hold his own** er kann sich behaupten. ◇ *vt* [possess] besitzen; **who owns this car?** wem gehört dieses Auto? ◆ **own up** *vi*: **to own up (to sthg)** (etw) zulgeben.

owner ['əʊnər] *n* Besitzer *der*, -in *die*; [of firm, shop] Inhaber *der*, -in *die*.

ownership ['əʊnəʃɪp] *n* Besitz *der*.

ox [ɒks] (*pl* **oxen**) *n* Ochse *der*.

Oxbridge ['ɒksbrɪdʒ] *n die Universitäten Oxford und Cambridge*.

oxen ['ɒksn] *Pl* ▷ **ox**.

oxtail soup [,ɒksteɪl-] *n* Ochsenschwanzsuppe *die*.

oxygen ['ɒksɪdʒən] *n* Sauerstoff *der*.

oxygen mask *n* Sauerstoffmaske *die*.

oyster ['ɔɪstər] *n* Auster *die*.

oz. *abbr of* **ounce**.

ozone ['əʊzəʊn] *n* Ozon *das*.

ozone-friendly *adj* FCKW-frei.

ozone layer *n* Ozonschicht *die*.

P

p[1] (*pl* **p's** OR **ps**), **P** (*pl* **P's** OR **Ps**) [pi:] *n* [letter] p *das*, P *das*.

p[2] [pi:] *abbr of* **page, penny, pence**.

P45 [,pi:fɔ:tɪ'faɪv] *n UK* ≃ Lohnsteuerkarte *die, Steuerbescheinigung, die bei einem Arbeitsplatzwechsel dem neuen Arbeitgeber vorgelegt werden muss*.

pa [pɑ:] *n esp US inf* Papa *der*, Vati *der*.

p.a. (*abbr of* **per annum**) p. a.

PA *n* - **1.** *UK abbr of* **personal assistant** - **2.** (*abbr of* **public address system**) Lautsprecheranlage *die*.

pace [peɪs] ◇ *n* - **1.** [speed, rate] Tempo *das*; **to keep pace (with sb/sthg)** (mit jm/etw) Schritt halten - **2.** [step] Schritt *der*. ◇ *vi* [walk up and down] auf und ab gehen.

pacemaker ['peɪs,meɪkər] *n* MED Herzschrittmacher *der*.

Pacific [pə'sɪfɪk] ◇ *adj* pazifisch; [coast] Pazifik-. ◇ *n*: **the Pacific (Ocean)** der Pazifik.

pacifier ['pæsɪfaɪər] *n US* [for child] Schnuller *der*.

pacifist ['pæsɪfɪst] *n* Pazifist *der*, -in *die*.

pacify ['pæsɪfaɪ] *vt* - **1.** [person] beruhigen - **2.** [country, region] befriedigen.

pack [pæk] ◇ *n* - **1.** [bag - on back] Rucksack *der*; [- carried by animal] Last *die* - **2.** [packet - of cigarettes, tissues] Packung *die*; [- of washing powder] Paket *das* - **3.** [of cards] (Karten)spiel *das* - **4.** [group - of wolves] Rudel *das*; [- of hounds] Meute *die*; [- of thieves] Bande *die*. ◇ *vt* - **1.** [for journey, holiday - bag, suitcase] packen; [- clothes, toothbrush] einlpacken - **2.** [put in container, parcel] einlpacken; [product] verpacken - **3.** [crowd into] füllen; **to be packed into sthg** in etw *(A)* gezwängt sein. ◇ *vi* [for journey, holiday] packen. ◆ **pack in** ◇ *vt sep UK inf* [job] hinlschmeißen; [boyfriend] sausen lassen; [smoking] auflhören mit; **pack it in!** [stop annoying me, shut up] hör (doch) auf damit! ◇ *vi inf* [break down] den Geist auflgeben. ◆ **pack off** *vt sep inf* fortlschicken.

package ['pækɪdʒ] ◇ *n* - **1.** [gen & COMPUT] Paket *das* - **2.** *esp US* [packet - of cigarettes, tissues] Packung *die*; [- of washing powder] Paket *das*. ◇ *vt* [wrap up, pack up] verpacken.

package deal *n* Paket *das*.

package tour *n* Pauschalreise *die*.

packaging ['pækɪdʒɪŋ] *n (U)* [wrapping] Verpackung *die*.

packed [pækt] *adj* - **1.** [place]: **packed (with)** (über)voll (mit) - **2.** [magazine, information pack]: **packed with** voll mit.

packed lunch *n UK* Lunchpaket *das*.

packet ['pækɪt] *n* - **1.** [box, bag, contents - of biscuits, cigarettes] Packung *die*; [- of washing powder] Paket *das* - **2.** [parcel] Päckchen *das*.

packing ['pækɪŋ] *n (U)* - **1.** [protective material] Verpackungsmaterial *das* - **2.** [for journey, holiday] Packen *das*.

packing case *n* Kiste *die*.

pact [pækt] *n* Pakt *der*.

pad [pæd] ◇ *n* - **1.** [for garment] Polster *das* - **2.** [for protection] Schützer *der* - **3.** [notepad] Block *der* - **4.** [for absorbing liquid]: **pad of cotton wool** Wattebausch *der*; **sanitary pad** Damenbinde *die* - **5.** [space]: **(launch) pad** Abschussrampe *die* - **6.** *inf dated* [home] Bude *die*. ◇ *vt* [furniture] polstern; [clothing] wattieren.

padding ['pædɪŋ] *n (U)* - **1.** [protective material] Polsterung *die* - **2.** [in speech, essay, letter] Füllwerk *das*.

paddle ['pædl] ◇ *n* - **1.** [for canoe, dinghy] Paddel *das* - **2.** [wade]: **to have a paddle** durchs Wasser waten. ◇ *vi* - **1.** [in canoe, dinghy] paddeln - **2.** [wade] waten.

paddle boat, paddle steamer *n* Raddampfer *der*.

paddling pool ['pædlɪŋ-] *n* - **1.** [in park] Planschbad *das* - **2.** [inflatable] Planschbecken *das*.

paddock ['pædək] *n* - **1.** [small field] Koppel *die* - **2.** [at racecourse] Sattelplatz *der*.

paddy field ['pædɪ-] *n* Reisfeld *das*.

padlock ['pædlɒk] ◇ *n* Vorhängeschloss *das*. ◇ *vt* (mit einem Vorhängeschloss) verschließen.

paediatrics [,pi:dɪ'ætrɪks] *n* = **pediatrics**.

pagan ['peɪgən] ◇ *adj* heidnisch. ◇ *n* Heide *der*, -din *die*.

page [peɪdʒ] ◇ *n* - **1.** [side of paper] Seite *die* - **2.** [leaf, sheet of paper] Blatt *das*. ◇ *vt* [call out name of] ausrufen lassen; **paging Miss Smith!** Miss Smith, bitte!

pageant ['pædʒənt] *n* [show] historisches Schauspiel; [parade] Festumzug *der*.

pageantry ['pædʒəntrɪ] *n* Prunk *der*.

page break *n* COMPUT Seitenumbruch *der*.

paid [peɪd] ◇ *pt & pp* ▷ **pay**. ◇ *adj* bezahlt.

pail [peɪl] *n* Eimer *der*.

pain [peɪn] *n* - **1.** [ache] Schmerz *der* - **2.** *(U)* [physical suffering] Schmerzen *Pl*; **to be in pain** Schmerzen haben - **3.** *(U)* [mental suffering] Qualen *Pl*. ◆ **pains** *npl* [effort] Mühe *die*; **to be at pains to do sthg** sich *(D)* große Mühe geben, etw zu tun; **to take pains to do sthg** sich *(D)* Mühe geben, etw zu tun.

pained [peɪnd] *adj* [expression] gequält.

painful ['peɪnfʊl] *adj* - **1.** [physically] schmerzhaft; **to be painful** wehtun, schmerzen - **2.** [distressing] schmerzlich.

painfully ['peɪnfʊlɪ] *adv* - **1.** [physically] unter Schmerzen - **2.** [distressingly] schmerzlich.

painkiller ['peɪn,kɪlə^r] *n* schmerzstillendes Mittel.

painless ['peɪnlɪs] *adj* - **1.** [physically] schmerzlos - **2.** [unproblematic] unproblematisch; [exam, decision] leicht.

painstaking ['peɪnz,teɪkɪŋ] *adj* sorgfältig.

paint [peɪnt] ◇ *n* Farbe *die*; [on car, furniture] Lack *der*. ◇ *vt* - **1.** [picture, portrait] malen - **2.** [wall, room] streichen; [car, fingernails] lackieren; [lips, face] schminken. ◇ *vi* ART malen.

paintbrush ['peɪntbrʌʃ] *n* Pinsel *der*.

painter ['peɪntə^r] *n* Maler *der*, -in *die*.

painting ['peɪntɪŋ] *n* - **1.** [picture] Gemälde *das* - **2.** [artistic] Malen *das*; [activity] Malerei *die* - **3.** [by decorator] Anstreichen *das*.

paintwork ['peɪntwɜ:k] *n (U)* [on wall] Anstrich *der*; [on car] Lack *der*.

pair [peə^r] *n* Paar *das*; **in pairs** paarweise; **a pair of pliers** eine Zange; **a pair of scissors** eine Schere; **a pair of shorts** Shorts *Pl*; **a pair of spectacles** eine Brille; **a pair of tights** eine Strumpfhose; **a pair of trousers** eine Hose.

pajamas [pə'dʒɑ:məz] *npl US* = **pyjamas**.

Pakistan [*UK* ,pɑ:kɪ'stɑ:n, *US* ,pækɪ'stæn] *n* Pakistan *nt*.

Pakistani [*UK* ,pɑ:kɪ'stɑ:nɪ, *US* 'pækɪstænɪ] ◇ *adj* pakistanisch. ◇ *n* Pakistaner *der*, -in *die*.

pal [pæl] *n inf* Kumpel *der*; **be a pal!** sei so nett!

palace ['pælɪs] *n* Palast *der*; [of bishop, aristocracy] Palais *das*; [grand house] Schloss *das*.

palatable ['pælətəbl] *adj* - **1.** [food] wohlschmeckend - **2.** [suggestion, idea] annehmbar.

palate ['pælət] *n* Gaumen *der*.

palaver [pə'lɑ:və^r] *n inf* [fuss] Theater *das*.

pale [peɪl] *adj* [colour, face] blass; [clothes] hell; [light] fahl.

Palestine ['pælə,staɪn] *n* Palästina *nt*.

Palestinian [,pælə'stɪnɪən] ◇ *adj* palästinensisch. ◇ *n* [person] Palästinenser *der*, -in *die*.

palette ['pælət] *n* ART Palette *die*.

pall [pɔ:l] ◇ *n* - **1.**: **a pall of smoke** eine Rauchglocke - **2.** *US* [over coffin] Sargtuch *das*. ◇ *vi* an Reiz verlieren.

pallet ['pælɪt] *n* Palette *die*.

palm [pɑ:m] *n* - **1.** [tree] Palme *die* - **2.** [of hand] Handfläche *die*; **to read sb's palm** jm aus der Hand lesen. ◆ **palm off** *vt sep inf*: **to palm sthg off on sb** jm etw anǀdrehen; **to palm sb off with sthg** jn mit etw abǀspeisen.

Palm Sunday *n* Palmsonntag *der*.

palmtop [-'pɑ:mtɒp] *n* COMPUT Palmtopcomputer *der*.

palm tree *n* Palme *die*.

palpable ['pælpəbl] *adj* [obvious] offensichtlich.

paltry ['pɔ:ltrɪ] *adj* armselig.

pamper ['pæmpə^r] *vt* verhätscheln.

pamphlet ['pæmflɪt] *n* [for information] Broschüre *die*; [for publicity] (Werbe)prospekt *der*; [political] Pamphlet *das*.

pan [pæn] ◇ *n* - **1.** [for frying] Pfanne *die*; [saucepan] Topf *der* - **2.** *US* [for baking] Backform *die*. ◇ *vt inf* [criticize] verreißen. ◇ *vi* CIN schwenken.

panacea [,pænə'sɪə] *n* Allheilmittel *das*.

panama [,pænə'mɑ:] *n*: **panama (hat)** Panamahut *der*.

Panama Canal *n*: **the Panama Canal** der Panamakanal.

pancake ['pænkeɪk] *n* Pfannkuchen *der*.

Pancake Day *n UK* Fastnachtsdienstag *der*.

panda ['pændə] (*pl inv* OR **-s**) *n* Panda *der*.

pandemonium [,pændɪ'məʊnɪəm] *n* Chaos *das*.

pander ['pændəʳ] *vi*: **to pander to sb/sthg** jm/etw nach|geben.

pane [peɪn] *n* Scheibe *die*.

panel ['pænl] *n* - **1.** [of experts, interviewers] Gremium *das*; [on TV and radio programmes] Diskussionsrunde *die* - **2.** [of wood] Platte *die* - **3.** [of machine] Schalttafel *die*.

panelling *UK*, **paneling** *US* ['pænəlɪŋ] *n* Täfelung *die*.

pang [pæŋ] *n* [of guilt, fear, regret] Anfall *der*; **pangs of conscience** Gewissensbisse *Pl*.

panic ['pænɪk] (*pt & pp* **-ked**, *cont* **-king**) ◇ *n* Panik *die*. ◇ *vi* in Panik geraten; **don't panic!** keine Panik!

panicky ['pænɪkɪ] *adj* [feeling] panisch; **to feel panicky** Angst bekommen.

panic-stricken *adj* von Panik erfasst OR ergriffen.

panorama [,pænə'rɑːmə] *n* Panorama *das*.

pansy ['pænzɪ] *n* - **1.** [flower] Stiefmütterchen *das* - **2.** *inf pej* [man] Tunte *die*.

pant [pænt] *vi* keuchen; [dog] hecheln. ◆ **pants** *npl* - **1.** *UK* [underpants - for men] Unterhose *die*; [- for women] Schlüpfer *der* - **2.** *US* [trousers] Hose *die*.

panther ['pænθəʳ] (*pl inv* OR **-s**) *n* Panther *der*.

panties ['pæntɪz] *npl inf* Schlüpfer *der*.

pantihose ['pæntɪhəʊz] *npl US* = **panty hose**.

pantomime ['pæntəmaɪm] *n UK meist um die Weihnachtszeit aufgeführtes Märchenspiel*.

pantry ['pæntrɪ] *n* Speisekammer *die*.

panty hose ['pæntɪhəʊz] *npl US* Strumpfhose *die*.

papa [*UK* pə'pɑː, *US* 'pæpə] *n dated* [father] Papa *der*.

paper ['peɪpəʳ] ◇ *n* - **1.** [for writing on] Papier *das*; **a piece of paper** [scrap] ein Stück Papier; [sheet] ein Blatt Papier; **on paper** [written down] schriftlich; [in theory] auf dem Papier - **2.** [newspaper] Zeitung *die* - **3.** [exam] Klausur *die* - **4.** [essay] Arbeit *die* - **5.** [at conference] Referat *das*. ◇ *adj* - **1.** [cup, napkin, hat] Papier-, aus Papier - **2.** [qualifications] auf dem Papier; [profits] nominell. ◇ *vt* [with wallpaper] tapezieren. ◆ **papers** *npl* - **1.** [identity papers] Papiere *Pl* - **2.** [documents] Dokumente *Pl*, Unterlagen *Pl*.

paperback ['peɪpəbæk] *n*: **paperback (book)** Taschenbuch *das*.

paper bag *n* Papiertüte *die*.

paper clip *n* Büroklammer *die*.

paper handkerchief *n* Papiertaschentuch *das*.

paper shop *n UK* Zeitungsgeschäft *das*.

paperweight ['peɪpəweɪt] *n* Briefbeschwerer *der*.

paperwork ['peɪpəwɜːk] *n (U)* Schreibarbeit *die*.

paprika ['pæprɪkə] *n* Paprika *der*.

par [pɑːʳ] *n* - **1.**: **to be on a par with sb/sthg** [person] sich mit jm/etw messen können; [company, country] mit jm/etw vergleichbar sein - **2.** [in golf] Par *das*; **above/below par** *fig* über/unter dem Durchschnitt - **3.** [good health]: **to feel below** OR **under par** nicht ganz auf dem Posten OR Damm sein.

parable ['pærəbl] *n* RELIG Gleichnis *das*; [moral story] Parabel *die*.

parachute ['pærəʃuːt] ◇ *n* Fallschirm *der*. ◇ *vi* mit dem Fallschirm ab|springen.

parade [pə'reɪd] ◇ *n* - **1.** [procession] Umzug *der* - **2.** MIL Parade *die*. ◇ *vt* - **1.** [people - soldiers] marschieren lassen; [- captives] zur Schau stellen - **2.** [object] vor sich *(D)* her|tragen - **3.** *fig* [flaunt] zur Schau stellen. ◇ *vi* paradieren; [soldiers] marschieren.

paradise ['pærədaɪs] *n* Paradies *das*.

paradox ['pærədɒks] *n* Paradox(on) *das*.

paradoxically [,pærə'dɒksɪklɪ] *adv* paradoxerweise.

paraffin ['pærəfɪn] *n* Paraffin *das*.

paragon ['pærəgən] *n* Muster *das*.

paragraph ['pærəgrɑːf] *n* Absatz *der*.

parallel ['pærəlel] (*UK*) (*US*) ◇ *adj liter & fig*: **parallel (to** OR **with)** parallel (zu). ◇ *n* - **1.** [gen] Parallele *die* - **2.** GEOG Breitenkreis *der*; **the 38th parallel** der 38. Breitengrad.

paralyse *UK*, **paralyze** *US* ['pærəlaɪz] *vt* - **1.** MED lähmen - **2.** *fig* [immobilize] lahm legen.

paralysis [pə'rælɪsɪs] (*pl* **-lyses** [-lɪsiːz]) *n* MED Lähmung *die*.

paralyze *vt US* = **paralyse**.

paramedic [,pærə'medɪk] *n* Sanitäter *der*, -in *die*.

parameter [pə'ræmɪtəʳ] *n* Parameter *der*.

paramount ['pærəmaʊnt] *adj*: **to be paramount** Vorrang OR Priorität haben; **of paramount importance** von äußerster Wichtigkeit.

paranoid ['pærənɔɪd] *adj* - **1.** MED paranoid - **2.** [worried, suspicious]: **she's paranoid about being on time** sie hat ständig Angst, zu spät zu kommen; **you're getting paranoid!** dein Misstrauen ist ja krankhaft!

paraphernalia [,pærəfə'neɪlɪə] *n* Drum und Dran *das*.

parasite ['pærəsaɪt] *n liter & fig* Schmarotzer *der*, Parasit *der*.

parasol ['pærəsɒl] *n* Sonnenschirm *der*.

paratrooper ['pærətruːpə^r^] *n* Fallschirmjäger *der*.

parcel ['pɑːsl] *(UK) (US) n* Paket *das*. ◆ **parcel up** *vt sep* als Paket verpacken.

parched [pɑːtʃt] *adj* - **1.** [very dry - grass, plain] ausgetrocknet, verdorrt; [- throat, lips] trocken - **2.** *inf* [very thirsty]: **I'm parched** ich habe riesigen Durst.

parchment ['pɑːtʃmənt] *n* Pergament *das*.

pardon ['pɑːdn] ◇ *n* - **1.** LAW Begnadigung *die* - **2.** [forgiveness]: **I beg your pardon?** [showing surprise or offence] erlauben Sie mal!; [what did you say?] (wie) bitte?; **I beg your pardon!** [apologizing] Entschuldigung! ◇ *vt* - **1.** LAW begnadigen - **2.** [forgive] verzeihen, vergeben; **to pardon sb for sthg** jm etw verzeihen; **pardon?** [what did you say?] wie bitte?; **pardon me!** Entschuldigung!, Verzeihung!

parent ['peərənt] *n* [father] Vater *der*; [mother] Mutter *die*; **parents** Eltern *Pl*.

parental [pə'rentl] *adj* elterlich.

parenthesis [pə'renθɪsɪs] *(pl* **-theses** [-θɪsiːz]) *n*: **in parentheses** in Klammern.

Paris ['pærɪs] *n* Paris *nt*.

parish ['pærɪʃ] *n* Gemeinde *die*.

parity ['pærətɪ] *n* [state] Gleichheit *die*.

park [pɑːk] ◇ *n* Park *der*. ◇ *vt* parken; [bicycle] ab|stellen. ◇ *vi* parken.

parking ['pɑːkɪŋ] *n (U)* - **1.** [act] Parken *das*; **'no parking'** 'Parken verboten' - **2.** [space] Parkplätze *Pl*.

parking lot *n US* Parkplatz *der*.

parking meter *n* Parkuhr *die*.

parking ticket *n* Strafzettel *der*.

parlance ['pɑːləns] *n*: **in common/legal parlance** im allgemeinen/juristischen Sprachgebrauch.

parliament ['pɑːləmənt] *n* Parlament *das*.

parliamentary [ˌpɑːlə'mentərɪ] *adj* parlamentarisch.

parlour *UK*, **parlor** *US* ['pɑːlə^r^] *n* [cafe]: **ice cream parlour** Eisdiele *die*.

parochial [pə'rəʊkɪəl] *adj pej* [person] engstirnig; [view, approach] eng, beschränkt.

parody ['pærədɪ] ◇ *n* Parodie *die*; **a parody of** eine Parodie auf *(+ A)*. ◇ *vt* parodieren.

parole [pə'rəʊl] *n (U)* Bewährung *die*; **on parole** auf Bewährung.

parrot ['pærət] *n* Papagei *der*.

parry ['pærɪ] *vt liter & fig* ab|wehren.

parsley ['pɑːslɪ] *n* Petersilie *die*.

parsnip ['pɑːsnɪp] *n* Pastinak *der*.

parson ['pɑːsn] *n* Pfarrer *der*, -in *die*.

part [pɑːt] ◇ *n* - **1.** [gen] Teil *der*; **in this part of Germany** in dieser Gegend Deutschlands; **for the better part of two hours** fast zwei Stunden; **for the most part** zum größten Teil - **2.** [of TV serial] Fortsetzung *die* - **3.** [component] Teil *das*; **to form part of sthg** Teil von etw sein - **4.** [acting role] Rolle *die*; *fig* [involvement] Anteil *der*; **his part in the crime** seine Rolle bei dem Verbrechen; **to play an important part in sthg** eine wichtige Rolle bei etw spielen; **to take part in sthg** an etw *(D)* teil|nehmen; **for my/his/*etc* part** was mich/ihn/*etc* anbetrifft; **on the part of** vonseiten *(+ G)* - **5.** *US* [hair parting] Scheitel *der*. ◇ *adv* teils. ◇ *vt* - **1.** [separate] trennen - **2.** [curtains] öffnen; [branches] zur Seite schieben; [legs] auf|machen; [hair] scheiteln. ◇ *vi* - **1.** [people] sich trennen - **2.** [curtains, lips, legs] sich öffnen; [crowd, branches] sich teilen. ◆ **parts** *npl*: **in these parts** in dieser Gegend; **in foreign parts** in fremden Ländern. ◆ **part with** *vt insep* sich trennen von.

part exchange *n*: **in part exchange (for)** in Zahlung (für).

partial ['pɑːʃl] *adj* - **1.** [incomplete] Teil-, teilweise - **2.** [biased] parteiisch - **3.** [fond]: **to be partial to sthg** eine Schwäche für etw haben.

participant [pɑː'tɪsɪpənt] *n* Teilnehmer *der*, -in *die*.

participate [pɑː'tɪsɪpeɪt] *vi*: **to participate (in)** teil|nehmen (an *(+ D)*).

participation [pɑːˌtɪsɪ'peɪʃən] *n* Teilnahme *die*.

participle ['pɑːtɪsɪpl] *n* Partizip *das*.

particle ['pɑːtɪkl] *n* - **1.** [tiny piece] Teilchen *das* - **2.** GRAM Partikel *die*.

particular [pə'tɪkjʊlə^r^] *adj* - **1.** [specific] bestimmt - **2.** [special] besondere(r) (s) - **3.** [fussy] eigen. ◆ **particulars** *npl* Einzelheiten *Pl*. ◆ **in particular** *adv* besonders; **nothing in particular** nichts Besonderes.

particularly [pə'tɪkjʊləlɪ] *adv* [very] besonders.

parting ['pɑːtɪŋ] *n* - **1.** [farewell] Abschied *der* - **2.** *UK* [in hair] Scheitel *der*.

partisan [ˌpɑːtɪ'zæn] ◇ *adj* parteiisch. ◇ *n* [freedom fighter] Partisan *der*, -in *die*.

partition [pɑː'tɪʃn] ◇ *n* [wall, screen] Trennwand *die*. ◇ *vt* teilen.

partly ['pɑːtlɪ] *adv* zum Teil, teilweise.

partner ['pɑːtnə^r^] ◇ *n* - **1.** [gen] Partner *der*, -in *die* - **2.** [in a business] Geschäftspartner *der*, -in *die* - **3.** [in crime] Komplize *der*, -zin *die*. ◇ *vt*: **to partner sb** js Partner sein.

partnership ['pɑːtnəʃɪp] *n* - **1.** [relationship] Partnerschaft *die* - **2.** [business] (Personen)gesellschaft *die*.

partridge ['pɑːtrɪdʒ] *(pl inv* OR **-s**) *n* Rebhuhn *das*.

part-time ◇ *adj* Teilzeit-. ◇ *adv*: **to work part-time** Teilzeit arbeiten.

party ['pɑːtɪ] ◇ *n* - **1.** POL & LAW Partei *die* - **2.** [social gathering] Party *die*; **to have a party** eine Party geben - **3.** [group of people] Gruppe *die*. ◇ *vi inf* feiern.

party line *n* - **1.** POL Parteilinie *die* - **2.** TELEC Gemeinschaftsanschluss *der*.

pass [pɑːs] ◇ *vt* - **1.** [walk past] vorbei|gehen an *(+ D)*; [drive past] vorbei|fahren an *(+ D)* - **2.** AUT [overtake] überholen - **3.** [hand over] reichen; **to pass sthg to sb, to pass sb sthg** jm etw reichen - **4.** [in football, hockey *etc*]: **to pass sb the ball, to pass the ball to sb** jm den Ball zulspielen *OR* passen - **5.** [exam, test] bestehen - **6.** [candidate] bestehen lassen - **7.** [approve - law] verabschieden; [- motion] an|nehmen; **this product has been passed as fit for sale** dieses Produkt ist für den Verkauf freigegeben worden - **8.** [life, time] verbringen - **9.** [exceed] überschreiten - **10.** [judgement] fällen; [sentence] verhängen. ◇ *vi* - **1.** [walk past] vorbei|gehen; [drive past] vorbei|fahren; **to let sb pass** jn vorbei|lassen; **if you're passing this way** falls Sie hier vorbeikommen - **2.** AUT [overtake] überholen - **3.** [road, river, path] führen; [pipe, cable] verlaufen - **4.** [time, holiday, lesson] vergehen - **5.** [in test, exam] bestehen - **6.** [in football, hockey *etc*] einen Pass spielen. ◇ *n* - **1.** [document] Ausweis *der* - **2.** *UK* [in exam] Bestehen *das*; **to get a pass** bestehen - **3.** [between mountains] Pass *der* - **4.** [in football, hockey *etc*] Pass *der*; [in tennis] Passierschlag *der* - **5.** *phr*: **to make a pass at sb** *inf* bei jm Annäherungsversuche machen. ◆ **pass as** *vt insep* durch|gehen für. ◆ **pass away** *vi* entschlafen. ◆ **pass by** ◇ *vt insep* [walk past] vorbei|gehen an *(+ D)*; [drive past] vorbei|fahren an *(+ D)*. ◇ *vt sep fig* [subj: news, events] vorbei|gehen an *(+ D)*. ◇ *vi* [walk past] vorbei|gehen; [drive past] vorbei|fahren. ◆ **pass for** *vt insep* = **pass as**. ◆ **pass on** ◇ *vt sep liter & fig*: **to pass sthg on (to sb)** etw (an jn) weiter|geben. ◇ *vi* - **1.** [move on] weiter|machen; **let's pass on to the next question** gehen wir zur nächsten Frage über - **2.** = **pass away**. ◆ **pass out** *vi* - **1.** [faint] ohnmächtig werden - **2.** *UK* MIL ernannt werden. ◆ **pass over** *vt insep* [subject, problem] übergehen; **to be passed over for promotion** bei der Beförderung übergangen werden. ◆ **pass through** *vi* durch|kommen; **we're just passing through** wir sind nur auf der Durchreise. ◆ **pass up** *vt sep* [opportunity] vorübergehen lassen; [invitation, offer] ab|lehnen.

passable ['pɑːsəbl] *adj* - **1.** [satisfactory] passabel - **2.** [road, path] passierbar.

passage ['pæsɪdʒ] *n* - **1.** [corridor] Gang *der*; [between houses] Durchgang *der* - **2.** [through crowd] Weg *der* - **3.** ANAT Gang *der* - **4.** *(U) fml* [transition] Übergang *der*; **the passage of time** der Strom der Zeit - **5.** [sea journey] Überfahrt *die*.

passageway ['pæsɪdʒweɪ] *n* Gang *der*; [between houses] Durchgang *der*.

passbook ['pɑːsbʊk] *n* Sparbuch *das*.

passenger ['pæsɪndʒəʳ] *n* [gen] Passagier *der*; [in taxi] Fahrgast *der*; [in car] Insasse *der*, -sin *die*.

passerby [ˌpɑːsə'baɪ] (*pl* **passersby** [ˌpɑːsəz'baɪ]) *n* Passant *der*, -in *die*.

passing ['pɑːsɪŋ] *adj* [remark] beiläufig; [fashion, mood] vorübergehend. ◆ **in passing** *adv* [mention] beiläufig.

passion ['pæʃn] *n* Leidenschaft *die*.

passionate ['pæʃənət] *adj* leidenschaftlich.

passive ['pæsɪv] *adj* - **1.** [person] passiv - **2.** GRAM passivisch, Passiv-.

Passover ['pɑːsˌəʊvəʳ] *n* Passah *das*.

passport ['pɑːspɔːt] *n* (Reise)pass *der*.

passport control *n* Passkontrolle *die*.

password ['pɑːswɜːd] *n* Passwort *das*.

past [pɑːst] ◇ *adj* - **1.** [former] ehemalig - **2.** [earlier] vergangene(r) (s); **in past times** in früheren Zeiten - **3.** [most recent, last] letzte(r) (s); **the past month** der letzte Monat - **4.** [finished] vorbei. ◇ *n* - **1.** [time]: **the past** die Vergangenheit; **in the past** früher - **2.** [personal history] Vergangenheit *die* - **3.** GRAM Vergangenheit *die*. ◇ *adv* - **1.** [telling the time] nach; **it's ten/a quarter past** es ist zehn/viertel nach - **2.** [by] vorbei; **to run past** vorbei|laufen. ◇ *prep* - **1.** [telling the time] nach; **twenty past four** zwanzig nach vier; **at half/a quarter past eight** um halb/viertel neun - **2.** [by] an *(+ D)* vorbei; **he drove past the house** er fuhr am Haus vorbei - **3.** [beyond] hinter *(+ D)*.

pasta ['pæstə] *n (U)* Nudeln *Pl*.

paste [peɪst] ◇ *n* - **1.** [smooth mixture] Brei *der* - **2.** *(U)* CULIN Brotaufstrich *der* - **3.** [glue] Kleister *der*. ◇ *vt* kleben; COMPUT ein|fügen.

pastel ['pæstl] *adj* pastellfarben.

pasteurize, -ise ['pɑːstʃəraɪz] *vt* pasteurisieren.

pastille ['pæstɪl] *n* Pastille *die*.

pastime ['pɑːstaɪm] *n* Hobby *das*.

pastor ['pɑːstəʳ] *n* Pfarrer *der*, -in *die*.

past participle *n* Partizip Perfekt *das*.

pastry ['peɪstrɪ] *n* - **1.** [mixture] Teig *der* - **2.** [cake] Teilchen *das*.

past tense *n* Vergangenheit *die*.

pasture ['pɑːstʃəʳ] *n* [field] Weide *die*.

pasty ['pæstɪ] *n UK* CULIN Pastete *die*.

pat [pæt] ◇ *adv*: **to have sthg off pat** etw parat haben. ◇ *n* - **1.** [light stroke] Klaps *der* - **2.** [of butter] Portion *die*. ◇ *vt* [dog, hand] tätscheln; [back, shoulder] (leicht) klopfen auf *(+ A)*.

patch [pætʃ] ◇ *n* - **1.** [piece of material] Flicken *der* - **2.** [over eye] Augenklappe *die* - **3.** [small area] Fleck *der*; **there were still**

patches of snow es lag vereinzelt *OR* stellenweise noch Schnee; **a bald patch** eine kahle Stelle - **4.** [of land] Stück (Land) *das*; **vegetable patch** Gemüsebeet *das* - **5.** [period of time]: **to be going through a difficult patch** eine schwierige Zeit durch|machen. ◇ *vt* flicken. ◆ **patch up** *vt sep* - **1.** [mend] zusammen|flicken - **2.** *fig* [quarrel] bei|legen; [marriage] kitten.

patchy ['pætʃɪ] *adj* - **1.** [fog, sunshine] vereinzelt; [colour] fleckig - **2.** [knowledge] lückenhaft - **3.** [performance, game] unterschiedlich (in der Qualität).

pâté ['pæteɪ] *n (U)* Pastete *die*.

patent [*UK* 'peɪtənt, *US* 'pætənt] ◇ *adj* [obvious] offensichtlich. ◇ *n* Patent *das*. ◇ *vt* patentieren lassen.

patent leather *n* Lackleder *das*.

paternal [pə'tɜːnl] *adj* - **1.** [love, attitude] väterlich - **2.** [on father's side]: **paternal grandmother/grandfather** Großmutter *die*/Großvater *der* väterlicherseits.

path [pɑːθ] (*pl* [pɑːðz]) *n* - **1.** [track] Weg *der*; [narrower] Pfad *der* - **2.** [way ahead, course of action] Weg *der* - **3.** [trajectory] Bahn *die*.

pathetic [pə'θetɪk] *adj* - **1.** [causing pity] Mitleid erregend; **to be a pathetic sight** ein Bild des Jammers bieten - **2.** [useless - attempt, effort] erbärmlich; **she's pathetic** sie ist ein hoffnungsloser Fall.

pathological [ˌpæθə'lɒdʒɪkl] *adj* - **1.** MED pathologisch - **2.** [uncontrollable] krankhaft.

pathology [pə'θɒlədʒɪ] *n* Pathologie *die*.

pathos ['peɪθɒs] *n* Pathos *das*.

pathway ['pɑːθweɪ] *n* Weg *der*; [narrower] Pfad *der*.

patience ['peɪʃns] *n* - **1.** [quality] Geduld *die* - **2.** [card game] Patience *die*.

patient ['peɪʃnt] ◇ *adj* geduldig. ◇ *n* Patient *der*, -in *die*.

patio ['pætɪəʊ] (*pl* **-s**) *n* Terrasse *die*.

patriotic [*UK* ˌpætrɪ'ɒtɪk, *US* ˌpeɪtrɪ'ɒtɪk] *adj* patriotisch.

patrol [pə'trəʊl] ◇ *n* [of police] Streife *die*; [of soldiers] Patrouille *die*. ◇ *vt* [subj: police - in vehicle] Streife fahren in *(+ D)*; [- on foot] seine Runden machen in *(+ D)*; [subj: soldiers] patrouillieren.

patrol car *n* Streifenwagen *der*.

patrolman [pə'trəʊlmən] (*pl* **-men** [-mən]) *n* *US* (Streifen)polizist *der*.

patron ['peɪtrən] *n* - **1.** [sponsor] Förderer *der*, -derin *die* - **2.** *UK* [of charity, campaign] Schirmherr *der*, -in *die*.

patronize, -ise ['pætrənaɪz] *vt pej* [talk down to] von oben herab behandeln.

patronizing, -ising ['pætrənaɪzɪŋ] *adj pej* gönnerhaft.

patter ['pætəʳ] ◇ *n* - **1.** [of feet] Getrappel *das*; [of raindrops] Platschen *das* - **2.** [talk] Sprüche *Pl*. ◇ *vi* [dog, feet] trappeln; [rain] platschen.

pattern ['pætən] *n* - **1.** [design] Muster *das* - **2.** [of life, work] Ablauf *der* - **3.** [of distribution] Schema *das* - **4.** [for sewing] Schnittmuster *das*; [for knitting] Strickanleitung *die* - **5.** [model] Vorbild *das*.

paunch [pɔːntʃ] *n* Bauch *der*.

pauper ['pɔːpəʳ] *n* Arme *der*, *die*.

pause [pɔːz] ◇ *n* Pause *die*; **without a pause** ohne Unterbrechung. ◇ *vi* - **1.** [stop speaking] inne|halten - **2.** [stop doing sthg] eine Pause machen *OR* ein|legen.

pave [peɪv] *vt* pflastern; **to pave the way for sb/sthg** jm/etw den Weg ebnen.

pavement ['peɪvmənt] *n* - **1.** *UK* [at side of road] Bürgersteig *der* - **2.** *US* [road surface] Fahrbahnbelag *der*.

pavilion [pə'vɪljən] *n* - **1.** [at sports field] Klubhaus *das* - **2.** [at exhibition] Pavillon *der*.

paving stone *n* Pflasterstein *der*.

paw [pɔː] *n* Pfote *die*; [of lion, bear] Tatze *die*.

pawn [pɔːn] ◇ *n* - **1.** [chesspiece] Bauer *der* - **2.** [unimportant person] Schachfigur *die*. ◇ *vt* verpfänden.

pawnbroker ['pɔːnˌbrəʊkəʳ] *n* Pfandleiher *der*, -in *die*.

pawnshop ['pɔːnʃɒp] *n* Pfandhaus *das*.

pay [peɪ] (*pt & pp* **paid**) ◇ *vt* - **1.** [bill, debt, person] bezahlen; [fine, taxes, fare, sum of money] zahlen; **to pay sb for sthg** jm das Geld für etw geben; **how much did you pay for it?** wie viel hast du dafür gezahlt? - **2.** [be profitable, advantageous to]: **it won't pay you to sell the house just now** es wird sich für dich nicht lohnen, das Haus jetzt zu verkaufen; **it will pay you to keep quiet** es wird für dich von Vorteil sein, wenn du schweigst - **3.**: **to pay sb a compliment** jm ein Kompliment machen; **to pay a visit to sb/a place** jn/einen Ort besuchen. ◇ *vi* - **1.** [for services, work, goods] (be)zahlen; **to pay for sthg** etw bezahlen - **2.** [be profitable - crime] sich lohnen; [- work] sich rentieren - **3.** *fig* [suffer] bezahlen; **to pay dearly for sthg** teuer für etw bezahlen. ◇ *n* [wages] Lohn *der*; [salary] Gehalt *das*. ◆ **pay back** *vt sep* - **1.** [return money to]: **I'll pay you back (the money) tomorrow** ich zahle dir morgen das Geld zurück - **2.** [revenge o.s. on]: **I'll pay you back for that!** das werde ich dir heimzahlen! ◆ **pay off** ◇ *vt sep* - **1.** [debt] ab|bezahlen; [loan] tilgen - **2.** [employee] aus|zahlen - **3.** [informer, blackmailer] Schweigegeld zahlen *(+ D)*. ◇ *vi* [be successful] sich aus|zahlen. ◆ **pay up** *vi* zahlen.

payable ['peɪəbl] *adj* - **1.** [debt, loan]: **to be payable** fällig sein - **2.** [cheque]: **to be payable to sb** an jn zu zahlen sein; **to make a cheque payable to sb** einen Scheck auf jn aus|stellen.

paycheck ['peɪtʃek] *n US* [cheque] Lohnscheck *der*; [money] Lohn *der*.

payday ['peɪdeɪ] *n* Zahltag *der*.

payee [peɪ'iː] *n* Zahlungsempfänger *der*, -in *die*.

pay envelope *n US* Lohntüte *die*.

payment ['peɪmənt] *n* - **1.** [act of paying] Bezahlung *die* - **2.** [amount of money] Zahlung *die*.

pay packet *n UK* - **1.** [envelope] Lohntüte *die* - **2.** [wages] Lohn *der*.

pay-per-view *adj* Pay-per-View-.

pay phone, pay station *US n* Münzfernsprecher *der*.

payroll ['peɪrəʊl] *n*: **to be on the payroll** angestellt sein.

payslip *UK* ['peɪslɪp], **paystub** *US* ['peɪstʌb] *n* [for wages] Lohnstreifen *der*; [for salary] Gehaltsstreifen *der*.

pay station *n US* = **pay phone**.

paystub *n US* = **payslip**.

PC *n* - **1.** (*abbr of* **personal computer**) PC *der* - **2.** *abbr of* **police constable**.

PDA [,piːdiː'ei] *n* (*abbr of* **personal digital assistant**) PDA *der*.

PE *n abbr of* **physical education**.

pea [piː] *n* Erbse *die*.

peace [piːs] *n* - **1.** [tranquillity] Ruhe *die*; **peace of mind** Seelenfrieden *der*; **to be at peace with o.s.** mit sich selbst im Reinen sein - **2.** [no war] Frieden *der*; **to make (one's) peace with sb/sthg** mit jm/etw Frieden schließen - **3.** [law and order] Ruhe *die* und Ordnung.

peaceful ['piːsfʊl] *adj* friedlich.

peacetime ['piːstaɪm] *n (U)* Friedenszeiten *Pl*.

peach [piːtʃ] ◇ *adj* [in colour] pfirsichfarben. ◇ *n* [fruit] Pfirsich *der*.

peacock ['piːkɒk] *n* Pfau *der*.

peak [piːk] ◇ *n* - **1.** [mountain top] Gipfel *der* - **2.** [highest point] Höhepunkt *der*; **to be at one's peak** auf dem Höhepunkt seiner Leistungen sein - **3.** [of cap] Schirm *der*. ◇ *adj*: **in peak condition** in Höchstform. ◇ *vi* den Höchststand erreichen.

peaked [piːkt] *adj*: **peaked cap** Schirmmütze *die*.

peak hour *n* TELEC & ELEC Hauptbelastungszeit *die*; [for traffic] Hauptverkehrszeit *die*.

peak period *n* Hochsaison *die*.

peak rate *n* Höchsttarif *der*.

peal [piːl] ◇ *n* - **1.** [of bells] Glockenläuten *das* - **2.**: **peals of laughter** schallendes Gelächter; **peal of thunder** Donnerschlag *der*. ◇ *vi* [bells] läuten.

peanut ['piːnʌt] *n* Erdnuss *die*.

peanut butter *n* Erdnussbutter *die*.

pear [peəʳ] *n* Birne *die*.

pearl [pɜːl] *n* Perle *die*.

peasant ['peznt] *n* [in countryside] (armer) Bauer, (arme) Bäuerin.

peat [piːt] *n* Torf *der*.

pebble ['pebl] *n* Kiesel(stein) *der*.

peck [pek] ◇ *n* [kiss] Küsschen *das*. ◇ *vt* - **1.** [with beak - hand] picken nach - **2.** [kiss] ein Küsschen geben *(+ D)*.

peckish ['pekɪʃ] *adj UK inf* (etwas) hungrig.

peculiar [pɪ'kjuːljəʳ] *adj* - **1.** [odd] seltsam, eigenartig - **2.** [slightly ill]: **to feel peculiar** sich komisch fühlen - **3.** [characteristic]: **to be peculiar to sb/sthg** jm/etw eigentümlich sein.

peculiarity [pɪ,kjuːlɪ'ærətɪ] *n* - **1.** [strange habit] Eigenheit *die* - **2.** [individual characteristic] Charakteristikum *das* - **3.** [oddness] Eigenartigkeit *die*.

pedal ['pedl] (*UK*) (*US*) *n* Pedal *das*.

pedal bin *n* Treteimer *der*.

pedantic [pɪ'dæntɪk] *adj pej* pedantisch.

peddle ['pedl] *vt* - **1.** [drugs] handeln mit - **2.** [rumour, gossip] verbreiten.

pedestal ['pedɪstl] *n* Sockel *der*.

pedestrian [pɪ'destrɪən] ◇ *adj pej* langweilig. ◇ *n* Fußgänger *der*, -in *die*.

pedestrian crossing *n UK* Fußgängerüberweg *der*.

pedestrian precinct *UK*, **pedestrian zone** *US n* Fußgängerzone *die*.

pediatrics [,piːdɪ'ætrɪks] *n* Kinderheilkunde *die*, Pädiatrie *die*.

pedigree ['pedɪgriː] ◇ *adj* mit einem Stammbaum. ◇ *n* Stammbaum *der*.

pedlar *UK*, **peddler** *US* ['pedləʳ] *n*: **(drug) pedlar** Drogenhändler *der*, -in *die*.

pee [piː] *inf* ◇ *n* - **1.** [act of urinating]: **to have a pee** pinkeln; **to go for a pee** pinkeln gehen - **2.** [urine] Urin *der*. ◇ *vi* pinkeln.

peek [piːk] *inf* ◇ *n (phrase)*: **to have** OR **take a peek at sthg** einen kurzen Blick auf etw *(A)* werfen. ◇ *vi* gucken.

peel [piːl] ◇ *n (U)* Schale *die*. ◇ *vt* schälen. ◇ *vi* [walls, paint] ablblättern; [wallpaper] sich lösen; [skin, nose, back] sich schälen.

peelings ['piːlɪŋz] *npl* Schalen *Pl*.

peep [piːp] ◇ *n* - **1.** [look]: **to have** OR **take a peep at sthg** einen kurzen Blick auf etw *(A)* werfen - **2.** *inf* [sound] Piep(s) *der*; **I haven't heard a peep from them** ich habe keinen Pieps von ihnen gehört. ◇ *vi* [look] gucken.

peephole ['piːphəʊl] *n* [in door] Spion *der*.

peer [pɪəʳ] ◇ *n* - **1.** [noble] *Angehöriger des hohen Adels in Großbritannien* - **2.** [equal]: **he is respected by his peers** er ist sehr anerkannt bei seinesgleichen. ◇ *vi* angestrengt schauen.

peer group *n* Peergroup *die*.

peeved [piːvd] *adj inf* eingeschnappt.

peevish ['piːvɪʃ] *adj* [remark, mood] gereizt; [person - as characteristic] reizbar; [- temporarily] gereizt.

peg [peg] ◇ *n* - **1.** [hook] Haken *der* - **2.** [for washing line] (Wäsche)klammer *die* - **3.** [for tent] Hering *der*. ◇ *vt* [price] festlsetzen.

pejorative [pɪ'dʒɒrətɪv] *adj* abwertend.

pekinese [ˌpiːkə'niːz] (*pl inv* OR **-s**) *n* Pekinese *der*.

Peking [piː'kɪŋ] *n* Peking *nt*.

pelican ['pelɪkən] (*pl inv* OR **-s**) *n* Pelikan *der*.

pelican crossing *n UK* Ampelübergang *der*.

pellet ['pelɪt] *n* [for gun] Schrotkugel *die*.

pelt [pelt] ◇ *vt*: **to pelt sb (with sthg)** jn (mit etw) bewerfen. ◇ *vi* - **1.** [rain]: **it's pelting (with rain)** es schüttet - **2.** [run very fast] rasen.

pelvis ['pelvɪs] (*pl* **-vises**) *n* Becken *das*.

pen [pen] *n* - **1.** [for writing]: **(ballpoint) pen** Kugelschreiber *der*; **(fountain) pen** Füllfederhalter *der*; **(felt-tipped) pen** Filzstift *der* - **2.** [enclosure] Pferch *der*.

penal ['piːnl] *adj* LAW: **penal system** Strafrecht *das*; **penal reform** Strafrechtsreform *die*.

penalize, -ise ['piːnəlaɪz] *vt* - **1.** [punish & SPORT] bestrafen - **2.** [put at a disadvantage] benachteiligen.

penalty ['penltɪ] *n* - **1.** [punishment] Strafe *die*; **to pay the penalty (for sthg)** *fig* (für etw) büßen müssen - **2.** [fine] Geldstrafe *die* - **3.** SPORT: **penalty (kick)** FTBL Strafstoß *der*; RUGBY Straftritt *der*.

penance ['penəns] *n (U)* - **1.** RELIG Buße *die* - **2.** *fig* [punishment] Strafe *die*.

pence [pens] *UK Pl* ▷ **penny**.

penchant [*UK* pɑ̃ʃɑ̃, *US* 'pentʃənt] *n*: **to have a penchant for sthg** eine Schwäche OR Vorliebe für etw haben.

pencil ['pensl] (*UK*) (*US*) *n* Bleistift *der*; **in pencil** mit Bleistift. ◆ **pencil in** *vt sep* [person] vorlmerken; [date] vorläufig festlhalten.

pencil case *n* Federmäppchen *das*.

pencil sharpener [-'ʃɑːpnəʳ] *n* (Bleistift)spitzer *der*.

pendant ['pendənt] *n* [jewel on chain] Anhänger *der*.

pending ['pendɪŋ] *fml* ◇ *adj*: **to be pending** [about to happen] bevorlstehen; LAW [waiting to be dealt with] noch anhängig sein. ◇ *prep* bis zu; **pending further inquiries** bis weitere Untersuchungen durchgeführt worden sind.

pendulum ['pendjʊləm] (*pl* **-s**) *n* Pendel *das*.

penetrate ['penɪtreɪt] *vt* - **1.** [get into - subj: person] vorldringen in *(+ A)*; [- subj: wind, rain, light] durchldringen; [- subj: sharp object, bullet] einldringen in *(+ A)* - **2.** [infiltrate] sich einlschleusen in *(+ A)*.

pen friend *n* Brieffreund *der*, -in *die*.

penguin ['peŋgwɪn] *n* Pinguin *der*.

penicillin [ˌpenɪ'sɪlɪn] *n* Penizillin *das*.

peninsula [pə'nɪnsjʊlə] (*pl* **-s**) *n* Halbinsel *die*.

penis ['piːnɪs] (*pl* **penises** ['piːnɪsɪz]) *n* Penis *der*.

penitentiary [ˌpenɪ'tenʃərɪ] *n US* Gefängnis *das*.

penknife ['pennaɪf] (*pl* **-knives** [-naɪvz]) *n* Taschenmesser *das*.

pen name *n* Pseudonym *das*.

pennant ['penənt] *n* Wimpel *der*.

penniless ['penɪlɪs] *adj* mittellos.

penny ['penɪ] *n* - **1.** (*pl* **-ies**) *UK* [coin] Penny *der* - **2.** (*pl* **-ies**) *US* [coin] Centstück *das* - **3.** (*pl* **pence**) *UK* [value]: **30 pence** 30 Pence.

pen pal *n inf* Brieffreund *der*, -in *die*.

pension ['penʃn] *n* - **1.** Rente *die* - **2.** [disability pension] Erwerbsunfähigkeitsrente *die*.

pensioner ['penʃənəʳ] *n UK*: **(old-age) pensioner** Rentner *der*, -in *die*.

pensive ['pensɪv] *adj* nachdenklich.

pentagon ['pentəgən] *n* Fünfeck *das*. ◆ **Pentagon** *n US*: **the Pentagon** das Pentagon.

Pentecost ['pentɪkɒst] *n* - **1.** [Christian] Pfingsten *das* - **2.** [Jewish] Ernte(dank)fest *das*.

penthouse ['penthaʊs] (*pl* [-haʊzɪz]) *n* Penthouse *das*.

pent up ['pent-] *adj* [emotions] unterdrückt; [energy] angestaut.

penultimate [pe'nʌltɪmət] *adj* vorletzte(r) (s).

people ['piːpl] ◇ *n* [nation, race] Volk *das*. ◇ *npl* - **1.** [persons] Menschen *Pl*, Leute *Pl*; **a lot of people** viele Menschen OR Leute; **five people** fünf Personen OR Leute - **2.** [in indefinite uses] Leute *die*; **people say that** man sagt OR es heißt, dass - **3.** [inhabitants - of country] Bevölkerung *die*; [- of town, city] Einwohner *Pl* - **4.** POL: **the people** das Volk. ◇ *vt*: **to be peopled by** OR **with** bevölkert sein von.

pep [pep] *n inf* Schwung *der*. ◆ **pep up** *vt sep inf* - **1.** [person] munter machen - **2.** [party, event] in Schwung bringen.

pepper ['pepəʳ] *n* - **1.** [spice] Pfeffer *der* - **2.** [vegetable] Paprika *der*.

pepperbox *n US* = **pepper pot**.

peppermint ['pepəmɪnt] *n* - **1.** [sweet] Pfefferminz(bonbon) *das* - **2.** [herb] Pfefferminze *die*.

pepper pot *UK*, **pepperbox** *US* ['pepəbɒks] *n* Pfefferstreuer *der*.

pep talk *n inf*: **to give sb a pep talk** jm ein paar aufmunternde Worte sagen.

per [pɜːʳ] *prep* [expressing rate, ratio] pro; **as per instructions** gemäß Anweisung.

per annum [pər'ænəm] *adv* pro Jahr.

per capita [pə'kæpɪtə] *adv* pro Kopf.

perceive [pə'si:v] *vt* - **1.** [see] wahr|nehmen - **2.** [notice, realize] erkennen - **3.** [conceive, consider]: **to perceive sb/sthg as** jn/etw betrachten als.

per cent [pə'sent] *n* Prozent *das*.

percentage [pə'sentɪdʒ] *n* Prozentsatz *der*.

perception [pə'sepʃn] *n* - **1.** [of colour, sound, time] Wahrnehmung *die* - **2.** [insight] Auffassungsvermögen *das*.

perceptive [pə'septɪv] *adj* scharfsinnig.

perch [pɜ:tʃ] <> *n* [for bird] (Sitz)stange *die*. <> *vi* - **1.** [bird]: **to perch (on sthg)** sich (auf etw *(D)*) nieder|lassen - **2.** [person]: **to perch on (the edge of) a desk** sich auf die Kante eines Schreibtisches setzen.

percolator ['pɜ:kəleɪtəʳ] *n* Kaffeemaschine *die*.

percussion [pə'kʌʃn] *n* MUS: **percussion instrument** Schlaginstrument *das*.

perennial [pə'renɪəl] <> *adj* - **1.** [continual] immer wieder auftretend - **2.** BOT perennierend. <> *n* BOT perennierende Pflanze.

perfect <> *adj* ['pɜ:fɪkt] - **1.** [ideal, faultless] perfekt, vollkommen - **2.** [for emphasis - nuisance] ausgesprochen; **perfect strangers** wildfremde Leute. <> *n* ['pɜ:fɪkt] GRAM: **perfect (tense)** Perfekt *das*. <> *vt* [pə'fekt] vervollkommnen.

perfection [pə'fekʃn] *n* [faultlessness] Perfektion *die*; **to do sthg to perfection** etw perfekt machen.

perfectionist [pə'fekʃənɪst] *n* Perfektionist *der*, -in *die*.

perfectly ['pɜ:fɪktlɪ] *adv* - **1.** [for emphasis - honest, frank, ridiculous] absolut; **you know perfectly well** du weißt ganz genau - **2.** [to perfection] exakt, genau.

perforate ['pɜ:fəreɪt] *vt* [paper - with one hole] lochen; [- with row of holes] perforieren; [lung, eardrum] durchstechen.

perform [pə'fɔ:m] <> *vt* - **1.** [carry out - operation] durch|führen; [- miracle] vollbringen; [- service, function] erfüllen - **2.** [play, concert] auf|führen; [part] spielen; [dance] vor|tanzen. <> *vi* - **1.** [car, machine] laufen; [in exam] ab|schneiden; **he is performing well** [employee] er leistet gute Arbeit; [sportsman] er ist in Hochform - **2.** [actor, singer] auf|treten.

performance [pə'fɔ:məns] *n* - **1.** [of task, duty] Erfüllung *die*; [of operation] Durchführung *die* - **2.** [at cinema] Vorstellung *die*; [of play, concert] Aufführung *die* - **3.** [by actor, singer, of car, engine] Leistung *die*.

performer [pə'fɔ:məʳ] *n* Künstler *der*, -in *die*.

perfume ['pɜ:fju:m] *n* - **1.** [for woman] Parfüm *das* - **2.** [pleasant smell] Duft *der*.

perfunctory [pə'fʌŋktərɪ] *adj* [search, read] oberflächlich; [kiss, glance] flüchtig; [explanation, apology] der Form halber.

perhaps [pə'hæps] *adv* vielleicht; **perhaps so** (das) mag sein; **perhaps not** vielleicht nicht.

peril ['perɪl] *n (U) liter* Gefahr *die*.

perimeter [pə'rɪmɪtəʳ] *n* Begrenzung *die*; **perimeter fence** Umzäunung *die*.

period ['pɪərɪəd] <> *n* - **1.** [of time] Zeit *die*; **over a period of several years** über einen Zeitraum von mehreren Jahren - **2.** HIST Zeitalter *das*, Epoche *die*; **the Elizabethan period** die elisabethanische Zeit - **3.** SCH (Schul)stunde *die*; **free period** Freistunde *die* - **4.** [menstruation] Periode *die* - **5.** *US* [full stop] Punkt *der*. <> *comp* [dress, furniture] zeitgenössisch.

periodic [,pɪərɪ'ɒdɪk] *adj* [events] regelmäßig wiederkehrend; [visits] regelmäßig.

periodical [,pɪərɪ'ɒdɪkl] <> *adj* = **periodic**. <> *n* [magazine] Zeitschrift *die*.

peripheral [pə'rɪfərəl] <> *adj* - **1.** [of little importance] nebensächlich - **2.** [vision] peripher; [region, group] Rand-. <> *n* COMPUT Peripheriegerät *das*.

perish ['perɪʃ] *vi* - **1.** [die] um|kommen - **2.** [food] verderben; [rubber] verschleißen.

perishable ['perɪʃəbl] *adj* verderblich. ◆ **perishables** *npl* verderbliche Waren *Pl*.

perjury ['pɜ:dʒərɪ] *n (U)* LAW Meineid *der*.

perk [pɜ:k] *n inf* Vergünstigung *die*. ◆ **perk up** *vi* [become more energetic] munter werden; [become more cheerful] auf|leben.

perky ['pɜ:kɪ] *adj inf* munter.

perm [pɜ:m] *n* Dauerwelle *die*.

permanent ['pɜ:mənənt] <> *adj* - **1.** [not temporary] dauerhaft; [job] fest - **2.** [continuous] ständig; [constant] konstant. <> *n US* [perm] Dauerwelle *die*.

permeate ['pɜ:mɪeɪt] *vt liter* & *fig* durch|dringen.

permissible [pə'mɪsəbl] *adj* erlaubt.

permission [pə'mɪʃn] *n (U)* Erlaubnis *die*; [official] Genehmigung *die*.

permit <> *vt* [pə'mɪt] - **1.** [allow] erlauben; **to permit sb to do sthg** jm erlauben, etw zu tun; **to permit sb sthg** jm etw gestatten - **2.** [enable] zulassen. <> *n* ['pɜ:mɪt] Genehmigung *die*.

perpendicular [,pɜ:pən'dɪkjʊləʳ] <> *adj*: **perpendicular (to)** senkrecht (zu). <> *n* MATHS Senkrechte *die*.

perpetrate ['pɜ:pɪtreɪt] *vt fml* [crime, murder] begehen.

perpetual [pə'petʃʊəl] *adj* - **1.** *pej* [continuous] ständig - **2.** [everlasting] ewig.

perplexing [pə'pleksɪŋ] *adj* verblüffend.

persecute ['pɜ:sɪkju:t] *vt* verfolgen.

persevere [,pɜ:sɪ'vɪəʳ] *vi* - **1.** [with difficulty] durch|halten; **to persevere with sthg** [studies, job] mit etw weiter|machen; [search] etw nicht auf|geben - **2.** [with determination]: **to persevere in doing sthg** darauf beharren, etw zu tun.

Persian ['pɜ:ʃn] *adj* persisch.

persist [pəˈsɪst] *vi* - **1.** [problem, situation, rain] an|halten, fort|dauern - **2.** [person]: **to persist in doing sthg** etw unaufhörlich tun.

persistence [pəˈsɪstəns] *n* - **1.** [continuation] Fortdauer *die*, Anhalten *das* - **2.** [determination] Beharrlichkeit *die*.

persistent [pəˈsɪstənt] *adj* - **1.** [constant] fortdauernd - **2.** [determined] hartnäckig.

person [ˈpɜːsn] (*pl* **people** *OR* **persons**) *fml n* - **1.** [man or woman] Mensch *der*; **in person** persönlich - **2.** GRAM Person *die*.

personable [ˈpɜːsnəbl] *adj* von angenehmem Äußeren.

personal [ˈpɜːsənl] *adj* - **1.** [gen] persönlich - **2.** [letter, message] privat.

personal assistant *n* persönlicher Assistent, persönliche Assistentin.

personal column *n* Privatanzeigen *Pl*.

personal computer *n* Personal Computer *der*.

personality [ˌpɜːsəˈnælətɪ] *n* Persönlichkeit *die*.

personally [ˈpɜːsnəlɪ] *adv* persönlich.

personal organizer, -iser *n* Terminplaner *der*.

personal property *n (U)* LAW Privateigentum *das*.

personal stereo *n* Walkman® *der*.

personify [pəˈsɒnɪfaɪ] *vt* [represent] verkörpern; **she's evil personified** sie ist das Böse in Person.

personnel [ˌpɜːsəˈnel] ◇ *n (U)* [department] Personalabteilung *die*. ◇ *npl* [staff] Personal *das*.

perspective [pəˈspektɪv] *n* Perspektive *die*.

Perspex® [ˈpɜːspeks] *n UK* Plexiglas® *das*.

perspiration [ˌpɜːspəˈreɪʃn] *n* - **1.** [sweat] Schweiß *der* - **2.** [sweating] Schwitzen *das*.

persuade [pəˈsweɪd] *vt* [convince] überzeugen; **to persuade sb to do sthg** jn überreden, etw zu tun; **to persuade sb that...** jn davon überzeugen, dass...; **to persuade sb of sthg** jn von etw überzeugen.

persuasion [pəˈsweɪʒn] *n* - **1.** *(U)* [act of persuading] Überredung *die* - **2.** [belief] Überzeugung *die*.

persuasive [pəˈsweɪsɪv] *adj* überzeugend.

pertain [pəˈteɪn] *vi fml*: **to pertain to** gehören zu.

pertinent [ˈpɜːtɪnənt] *adj* relevant.

perturb [pəˈtɜːb] *vt fml* beunruhigen.

peruse [pəˈruːz] *vt* [read - thoroughly] sorgfältig durch|lesen; [- quickly] überfliegen.

pervade [pəˈveɪd] *vt* durchdringen.

perverse [pəˈvɜːs] *adj* pervers.

perversion [*UK* pəˈvɜːʃn, *US* pərˈvɜːrʒn] *n* [sexual deviation] Perversion *die*.

pervert ◇ *n* [ˈpɜːvɜːt] Perverse *der, die*. ◇ *vt* [pəˈvɜːt] - **1.** [distort - truth] verzerren; [- course of justice] behindern - **2.** [corrupt morally - person, mind] verderben.

pessimist [ˈpesɪmɪst] *n* Pessimist *der*, -in *die*.

pessimistic [ˌpesɪˈmɪstɪk] *adj* pessimistisch.

pest [pest] *n* - **1.** [in garden, on farm] Schädling *der* - **2.** *inf* [annoying person, thing] Pest *die*, Plage *die*.

pester [ˈpestə^r] *vt* belästigen.

pet [pet] ◇ *adj* [favourite] Lieblings-. ◇ *n* - **1.** [animal] Haustier *das* - **2.** [favourite person] Liebling *der*. ◇ *vt* [stroke] streicheln. ◇ *vi* [sexually] Petting machen.

petal [ˈpetl] *n* Blütenblatt *das*.

peter [ˈpiːtə^r] ◆ **peter out** *vi* [supply] versiegen; [path] aus|laufen.

petite [pəˈtiːt] *adj* zierlich.

petition [pɪˈtɪʃn] ◇ *n* - **1.** [supporting campaign] Petition *die* - **2.** LAW: **petition for divorce** Scheidungsantrag *der*. ◇ *vt* [lobby]: **to petition sb** eine Petition bei jm ein|reichen.

petrified [ˈpetrɪfaɪd] *adj* [terrified] verängstigt, gelähmt vor Angst.

petrol [ˈpetrəl] *n UK* Benzin *das*.

petrol bomb *n UK* Benzinbombe *die*.

petrol can *n UK* Benzinkanister *der*.

petrol pump *n UK* Zapfsäule *die*.

petrol station *n UK* Tankstelle *die*.

petrol tank *n UK* Benzintank *der*.

petticoat [ˈpetɪkəʊt] *n* Unterrock *der*.

petty [ˈpetɪ] *adj* - **1.** [small-minded] kleinlich - **2.** [trivial] geringfügig.

petty cash *n* Portokasse *die*.

petulant [ˈpetjʊlənt] *adj* mürrisch; [child] bockig.

pew [pjuː] *n* Kirchenbank *die*.

pewter [ˈpjuːtə^r] *n* Zinn *das*.

phantom [ˈfæntəm] ◇ *adj* [imaginary] Phantom-. ◇ *n* [ghost] Phantom *das*.

pharmaceutical [ˌfɑːməˈsjuːtɪkl] *adj* pharmazeutisch.

pharmacist [ˈfɑːməsɪst] *n* [in shop] Apotheker *der*, -in *die*.

pharmacy [ˈfɑːməsɪ] *n* [shop] Apotheke *die*.

phase [feɪz] *n* Phase *die*. ◆ **phase in** *vt sep* schrittweise *OR* allmählich ein|führen. ◆ **phase out** *vt sep* auslaufen lassen.

PhD (*abbr of* **Doctor of Philosophy**) *n* Dr. phil.

pheasant [ˈfeznt] (*pl inv OR* **-s**) *n* Fasan *der*.

phenomena [fɪˈnɒmɪnə] *Pl* ▷ **phenomenon**.

phenomenal [fɪˈnɒmɪnl] *adj* [remarkable] phänomenal.

phenomenon [fɪˈnɒmɪnən] (*pl* **-mena**) *n* Phänomen *das*.

philanthropist [fɪ'lænθrəpɪst] *n* Philanthrop *der*, Menschenfreund *der*.

philosopher [fɪ'lɒsəfəʳ] *n* Philosoph *der*, -in *die*.

philosophical [ˌfɪlə'sɒfɪkl] *adj* - **1.** [gen] philosophisch - **2.** [stoical] gelassen.

philosophy [fɪ'lɒsəfɪ] *n* Philosophie *die*.

phlegm [flem] *n (U)* [mucus] Schleim *der*.

phobia ['fəʊbɪə] *n* Phobie *die*.

phone [fəʊn] <> *n* Telefon *das*; **to be on the phone** [speaking] telefonieren, am Telefon sein; *UK* [connected to network] Telefon haben. <> *comp* Telefon-. <> *vt* & *vi* an|rufen. ◆ **phone back** *vt sep* & *vi* zurück|rufen. ◆ **phone up** *vt sep* & *vi* an|rufen.

phone book *n* Telefonbuch *das*.

phone booth *n UK* Telefonkabine *die*.

phone box *n UK* Telefonzelle *die*.

phone call *n* Telefonanruf *der*, Telefongespräch *das*; **to make a phone call** telefonieren.

phonecard ['fəʊnkɑːd] *n* Telefonkarte *die*.

phone-in *n Radio- oder TV-Programm, bei dem Zuhörer bzw. Zuschauer anrufen können, um ihre Meinung zu äußern*.

phone number *n* Telefonnummer *die*.

phonetics [fə'netɪks] *n (U)* Fonetik *die*.

phoney *UK*, **phony** *US inf* ['fəʊnɪ] <> *adj* - **1.** [false] falsch - **2.** [insincere] unaufrichtig. <> *n* [person] Hochstapler *der*, -in *die*.

photo ['fəʊtəʊ] *n* Foto *das*; **to take a photo (of)** ein Foto machen (von).

photocopier ['fəʊtəʊˌkɒpɪəʳ] *n* Fotokopierer *der*.

photocopy ['fəʊtəʊˌkɒpɪ] <> *n* Fotokopie *die*. <> *vt* fotokopieren.

photograph ['fəʊtəgrɑːf] <> *n* Fotografie *die*, Aufnahme *die*; **to take a photograph (of sb/sthg)** jn/etw fotografieren. <> *vt* fotografieren.

photographer [fə'tɒgrəfəʳ] *n* Fotograf *der*, -in *die*.

photography [fə'tɒgrəfɪ] *n (U)* Fotografie *die*.

phrasal verb [ˌfreɪzl-] *n* Verb *das* mit Präposition.

phrase [freɪz] <> *n* - **1.** [part of sentence] Satzglied *das* - **2.** [expression] Wendung *die*. <> *vt* [express] aus|drücken.

phrasebook ['freɪzbʊk] *n* Sprachführer *der*.

physical ['fɪzɪkl] <> *adj* - **1.** [relating to the body] körperlich - **2.** [world, object] fassbar, materiell - **3.** [relating to physics] physikalisch. <> *n* ärztliche Untersuchung.

physical education *n* Sportunterricht *der*.

physically ['fɪzɪklɪ] *adv* - **1.** [bodily] körperlich - **2.** [materially] materiell, physisch.

physically handicapped <> *adj* körperbehindert. <> *npl*: **the physically handicapped** die Körperbehinderten *Pl*.

physician [fɪ'zɪʃn] *n* Arzt *der*, Ärztin *die*.

physicist ['fɪzɪsɪst] *n* Physiker *der*, -in *die*.

physics ['fɪzɪks] *n (U)* Physik *die*.

physiotherapy [ˌfɪzɪəʊ'θerəpɪ] *n* Physiotherapie *die*.

physique [fɪ'ziːk] *n* Körperbau *der*.

pianist ['pɪənɪst] *n* Pianist *der*, -in *die*.

piano [pɪ'ænəʊ] (*pl* **-s**) *n* Klavier *das*.

pick [pɪk] <> *n* - **1.** [tool] Spitzhacke *die* - **2.** [selection]: **take your pick** such dir einen/eine/eins aus - **3.** [best]: **the pick of** das Beste von. <> *vt* - **1.** [choose] aus|suchen; [winner] aus|wählen - **2.** [fruit, flowers] pflücken - **3.** [remove] entfernen - **4.** [nose, teeth]: **to pick one's nose** in der Nase bohren; **to pick one's teeth** in seinen Zähnen stochern - **5.** [provoke]: **to pick a fight (with sb)** (mit jm) einen Streit an|fangen - **6.** [lock] knacken. ◆ **pick on** *vt insep* auf dem Kieker haben. ◆ **pick out** *vt sep* - **1.** [recognize] erkennen - **2.** [select] aus|suchen; [winner] aus|wählen. ◆ **pick up** <> *vt sep* - **1.** [lift up] hoch|heben; [after dropping] auf|heben - **2.** [collect - gen] ab|holen; [- hitchhiker] mit|nehmen - **3.** [acquire - habit] an|nehmen; [- tips] bekommen; [- skill, language] lernen; **to pick up speed** schneller werden - **4.** *inf* [man, woman] an|machen - **5.** RADIO & TELEC [signal] empfangen - **6.** [conversation, work] wieder auf|nehmen. <> *vi* - **1.** [improve] sich verbessern - **2.** [resume] weiter|machen.

pickaxe *UK*, **pickax** *US* ['pɪkæks] *n* Spitzhacke *die*.

picket ['pɪkɪt] <> *n* [at place of work] Streikposten *der*. <> *vt* [place of work] Streikposten auf|stellen vor *(+ D)*.

picket line *n* Streikpostenkette *die*.

pickle ['pɪkl] <> *n* - **1.** *(U)* [food] Pickles *Pl* - **2.** *inf* [difficult situation]: **to be in a pickle** in der Tinte sitzen. <> *vt* ein|legen.

pickpocket ['pɪkˌpɒkɪt] *n* Taschendieb *der*, -in *die*.

pick-up *n* - **1.** [of record player] Tonabnehmer *der* - **2.** [truck] Pick-up *der*.

picnic ['pɪknɪk] (*pt* & *pp* **-ked**, *cont* **-king**) <> *n* Picknick *das*. <> *vi* picknicken.

pictorial [pɪk'tɔːrɪəl] *adj* [illustrated] bebildert.

picture ['pɪktʃəʳ] <> *n* - **1.** [gen] Bild *das*; [painting] Gemälde *das*; **as pretty as a picture** bildhübsch - **2.** [movie] Film *der* - **3.** [in one's mind] Vorstellung *die* - **4.** [prospect] Aussicht *die* - **5.** *phr*: **to get the picture** *inf* kapieren; **to put sb in the picture** jn ins Bild setzen. <> *vt* - **1.** [in mind] sich *(D)* vor|stellen - **2.** [in photo] fotografieren; [in painting, drawing] dar|stellen. ◆ **pictures** *npl UK*: **the pictures** [cinema] das Kino.

picture book *n* Bilderbuch *das*.

picturesque [ˌpɪktʃə'resk] *adj* malerisch.

pie [paɪ] *n* - **1.** [sweet] Obstkuchen *der* - **2.** [savoury] Pastete *die*.

piece [piːs] *n* - **1.** [gen] Stück *das*; [component] Teil *das*; **a piece of news** eine Neuigkeit; **a piece of advice** ein Rat; **a piece of furniture** ein Möbelstück; **a fifty pence piece** ein Fünfzigpencestück; **to fall to pieces** auseinander|fallen; **to take sthg to pieces** etw auseinander nehmen; **in one piece** [intact, unharmed] heil - **2.** [in chess] Figur *die*; [in backgammon, draughts] Stein *der* - **3.** [of journalism] Artikel *der*. ◆ **piece together** *vt sep* [facts] zusammen|fügen.

piecemeal ['piːsmiːl] *adj* & *adv* stückweise.

piecework ['piːswɜːk] *n (U)* Akkordarbeit *die*.

pier [pɪəʳ] *n* [at seaside] Pier *der*.

pierce [pɪəs] *vt* [subj: bullet, noise, light] durch|dringen; [subj: needle] durch|stechen; **to have one's ears pierced** sich *(D)* Ohrlöcher stechen lassen.

piercing ['pɪəsɪŋ] ◇ *adj* [sound, voice] durchdringend; [wind] schneidend; [look, eyes] stechend. ◇ *n* Piercing *das*.

pig [pɪg] *n* - **1.** [animal] Schwein *das* - **2.** *inf pej* [greedy eater] Vielfraß *der* - **3.** *inf pej* [unkind person] Schwein *das*.

pigeon ['pɪdʒɪn] (*pl inv* OR **-s**) *n* Taube *die*.

pigeonhole ['pɪdʒɪnhəʊl] ◇ *n* [compartment] Fach *das*. ◇ *vt fig* [classify] in eine Kategorie ein|ordnen.

piggybank ['pɪgɪbæŋk] *n* Sparschwein *das*.

pigheaded [,pɪg'hedɪd] *adj* stur.

pigment ['pɪgmənt] *n* Pigment *das*.

pigpen *n US* = **pigsty**.

pigskin ['pɪgskɪn] *n* Schweinsleder *das*.

pigsty ['pɪgstaɪ], **pigpen** *US* ['pɪgpen] *n liter* & *fig* Schweinestall *der*.

pigtail ['pɪgteɪl] *n* Zopf *der*.

pilchard ['pɪltʃəd] *n* Sardine *die*.

pile [paɪl] ◇ *n* - **1.** [heap] Haufen *der*; **a pile** OR **piles of money/work** *inf* ein Haufen Geld/Arbeit - **2.** [neat stack] Stapel *der*, Stoß *der* - **3.** [of carpet, fabric] Flor *der*. ◇ *vt* stapeln; **to be piled high with sthg** mit etw voll gestapelt sein. ◆ **piles** *npl* MED Hämorriden *Pl*. ◆ **pile into** *vt insep inf* [car] sich zwängen in *(+ A)*; [room] drängen in *(+ A)*. ◆ **pile up** ◇ *vt sep* [books, boxes] auf|stapeln. ◇ *vi* [accumulate] sich an|häufen.

pileup ['paɪlʌp] *n* Massenkarambolage *die*.

pilfer ['pɪlfəʳ] *vt* & *vi* stehlen.

pilgrim ['pɪlgrɪm] *n* Pilger *der*, -in *die*.

pilgrimage ['pɪlgrɪmɪdʒ] *n* Pilgerfahrt *die*.

pill [pɪl] *n* Pille *die*; [contraceptive]: **the pill** die Pille; **to be on the pill** die Pille nehmen.

pillage ['pɪlɪdʒ] *vt* plündern.

pillar ['pɪləʳ] *n* Pfeiler *der*.

pillar box *n UK* Briefkasten *der*.

pillion ['pɪljən] *n* Soziussitz *der*; **to ride pillion** auf dem Soziussitz mit|fahren.

pillow ['pɪləʊ] *n* - **1.** [for bed] Kopfkissen *das* - **2.** *US* [on sofa, chair] Kissen *das*.

pillowcase ['pɪləʊkeɪs], **pillowslip** ['pɪləʊslɪp] *n* Kopfkissenbezug *der*.

pilot ['paɪlət] ◇ *n* - **1.** [of plane] Pilot *der*, -in *die* - **2.** NAUT Lotse *der* - **3.** TV Pilotfilm *der*. ◇ *comp* [trial] Pilot-. ◇ *vt* - **1.** [plane] führen, fliegen - **2.** NAUT lotsen - **3.** [scheme] testen.

pilot light *n* Zündflamme *die*.

pimp [pɪmp] *n inf* Zuhälter *der*.

pimple ['pɪmpl] *n* Pickel *der*.

pin [pɪn] ◇ *n* - **1.** [for sewing] Nadel *die*; **I've got pins and needles in my feet** *fig* meine Füße sind eingeschlafen - **2.** [drawing pin] Reißzwecke *die*; [safety pin] Sicherheitsnadel *die* - **3.** [of plug] Kontaktstift *der* - **4.** TECH Bolzen *der*, Stift *der* - **5.** *US* [brooch] Brosche *die*; [badge] Anstecknadel *die*. ◇ *vt*: **to pin sthg to** OR **on** etw *(A)* heften an *(+ A)*; **to pin sb to the wall/ground** jn gegen die Wand/auf den Boden drücken; **to pin the blame for sthg on sb** jm die Schuld an etw zu|schieben. ◆ **pin down** *vt sep* - **1.** [identify] bestimmen - **2.** [force to make a decision] fest|legen.

pinafore ['pɪnəfɔːʳ] *n* - **1.** [apron] Schürze *die* - **2.** *UK* [dress] Trägerkleid *das*.

pinball ['pɪnbɔːl] *n (U)* Flipper *der*.

pincers ['pɪnsəz] *npl* - **1.** [tool] Kneifzange *die* - **2.** [of crab, lobster] Schere *die*.

pinch [pɪntʃ] ◇ *n* - **1.** [nip] Kneifen *das* - **2.** [of salt, herbs *etc*] Prise *die*. ◇ *vt* - **1.** [nip] kneifen - **2.** *inf* [steal] klauen. ◆ **at a pinch** *UK*, **in a pinch** *US adv* zur Not.

pincushion ['pɪn,kʊʃn] *n* Nadelkissen *das*.

pine [paɪn] ◇ *n* - **1.** [tree] Kiefer *die* - **2.** [wood] Kiefernholz *das*. ◇ *vi*: **to pine for** sich sehnen nach.

pineapple ['paɪnæpl] *n* Ananas *die*.

ping [pɪŋ] *n* [sound] Ping *das*.

pink [pɪŋk] ◇ *adj* rosa; **to go pink** erröten. ◇ *n* [colour] Rosa *das*.

pinnacle ['pɪnəkl] *n fig* [of career, success] Höhepunkt *der*.

pinpoint ['pɪnpɔɪnt] *vt* bestimmen.

pin-striped [-,straɪpt] *adj* Nadelstreifen-.

pint [paɪnt] *n* - **1.** *UK* [unit of measurement] Pint *das*, = *0,568 l.* - **2.** *US* [unit of measurement] Pint *das*, = *0,473 l.* - **3.** *UK* [beer]: **let's go for a pint** lass uns ein Bier trinken gehen; **a pint of Guinness** ein großes (Glas) Guinness.

pioneer [,paɪə'nɪəʳ] *n* Pionier *der*.

pious ['paɪəs] *adj* - **1.** [religious] fromm - **2.** *pej* [sanctimonious] scheinheilig.

pip [pɪp] *n* - **1.** [seed] Kern *der* - **2.** *UK*: **the pips** [on radio] Zeitzeichen *das*; [on public telephone] *Warnton, der ertönt, wenn Geld nachgeworfen werden muss.*

pipe [paɪp] ◇ *n* - **1.** [for gas, water] Rohr *das*, Leitung *die* - **2.** [for smoking] Pfeife *die*. ◇ *vt* [liquid, gas] leiten. ◆ **pipes** *npl* MUS [bagpipes] Dudelsack *der*. ◆ **pipe down** *vi inf* still sein. ◆ **pipe up** *vi inf* sich (spontan) zu Wort melden.

pipe cleaner *n* Pfeifenreiniger *der*.

pipeline ['paɪplaɪn] *n* Pipeline *die*.

piper ['paɪpəʳ] *n* MUS [on bagpipes] Dudelsackspieler *der*, -in *die*.

piping hot [,paɪpɪŋ-] *adj* siedend heiß.

pirate ['paɪrət] ◇ *adj* [video, copy *etc*] Piraten-, Raub-. ◇ *n* [sailor] Pirat *der*. ◇ *vt* [copy illegally] Raubkopien machen von.

pirouette [,pɪrʊ'et] ◇ *n* Pirouette *die*. ◇ *vi* Pirouetten drehen.

Pisces ['paɪsi:z] *n* Fische *Pl*; **I'm (a) Pisces** ich bin Fisch.

piss [pɪs] *v inf* ◇ *n* [urine] Pisse *die*; **to have a piss** pissen gehen. ◇ *vi* pissen.

pissed [pɪst] *adj v inf* - **1.** *UK* [drunk] voll, besoffen - **2.** *US* [annoyed] stocksauer.

pissed off *adj v inf* stocksauer.

pistol ['pɪstl] *n* Pistole *die*.

piston ['pɪstən] *n* Kolben *der*.

pit [pɪt] ◇ *n* - **1.** [large hole, coalmine] Grube *die* - **2.** [for orchestra] Orchestergraben *der* - **3.** *US* [of fruit] Kern *der*. ◇ *vt*: **to be pitted against sb** [in game] gegen jn spielen (müssen); [in fight] gegen jn kämpfen (müssen). ◆ **pits** *npl* [in motor racing]: **the pits** die Boxen *Pl*.

pitch [pɪtʃ] ◇ *n* - **1.** SPORT Feld *das*, Platz *der* - **2.** MUS Tonhöhe *die*; [of voice] Stimmlage *die*; [of instrument] Tonlage *die* - **3.** [level, degree] Ausmaß *das* - **4.** [in market, on street] Standplatz *der* - **5.** *inf* [sales talk] Verkaufsvortrag *der* - **6.** [of roof] Neigung *die*. ◇ *vt* - **1.** [throw] werfen - **2.** [set level of] an|setzen - **3.** [camp, tent] auf|schlagen. ◇ *vi* - **1.** [fall] fallen; **to pitch forward** nach vorne fallen - **2.** [ship] stampfen; [plane] ab|sacken.

pitch-black *adj* stockfinster.

pitcher ['pɪtʃəʳ] *n US* - **1.** [jug] Krug *der* - **2.** [in baseball] Pitcher *der*.

pitchfork ['pɪtʃfɔ:k] *n* Mistgabel *die*.

pitfall ['pɪtfɔ:l] *n* [hazard] Falle *die*.

pith [pɪθ] *n* [of fruit] weiße Haut.

pithy ['pɪθɪ] *adj* prägnant.

pitiful ['pɪtɪfʊl] *adj* - **1.** [arousing pity] Mitleid erregend - **2.** [arousing contempt] jämmerlich.

pitiless ['pɪtɪlɪs] *adj* erbarmungslos.

pit stop *n* Boxenstopp *der*.

pittance ['pɪtəns] *n* Hungerlohn *der*.

pity ['pɪtɪ] ◇ *n* - **1.** [compassion] Mitleid *das*; **to take** *OR* **have pity on sb** Mitleid mit jm haben - **2.** [shame]: **it's a pity (that)...** (es ist) schade(, dass)...; **what a pity!** wie schade! ◇ *vt* bemitleiden.

pivot ['pɪvət] *n* - **1.** TECH [joint] Drehgelenk *das* - **2.** *fig* [crux] Dreh- und Angelpunkt *der*.

pizza ['pi:tsə] *n* Pizza *die*.

placard ['plækɑ:d] *n* Plakat *das*.

placate [plə'keɪt] *vt* beschwichtigen.

place [pleɪs] ◇ *n* - **1.** [location] Ort *der*; [spot, place in text & MATHS] Stelle *die*; **place of birth** Geburtsort; **to two decimal places** bis auf zwei Stellen nach dem Komma - **2.** [home] Zuhause *das*; **let's go to my place** gehen wir zu mir - **3.** [post, vacancy] Stelle *die* - **4.** [role, function] Rolle *die* - **5.** [table setting] Gedeck *das* - **6.** [instance]: **in the first place** am Anfang; **why didn't you say so in the first place?** warum hast du das nicht gleich *OR* direkt gesagt?; **in the first place..., and in the second place...** erstens..., zweitens... - **7.** *phr*: **to take place** statt|finden; **to take sb's place** js Platz ein|nehmen. ◇ *vt* - **1.** [put] stellen; [put flat] legen; **to place the blame on sb** jm die Schuld zu|schieben; **to place an ad in the paper** eine Anzeige in die Zeitung setzen - **2.** [identify] ein|ordnen - **3.** [make]: **to place an order** COMM eine Bestellung auf|geben; **to place a bet on sthg** auf etw *(D)* wetten - **4.** [be situated]: **the house is well placed for the tube** das Haus liegt ganz in der Nähe der U-Bahn; **how are we placed for money/time?** wie viel Geld/Zeit haben wir? - **5.** [in race]: **to be placed** sich platzieren. ◆ **all over the place** *adv* überall. ◆ **in place** *adv* - **1.** [in proper position] an seinem Platz - **2.** [established, set up] eingerichtet. ◆ **in place of** *prep* anstatt *(+ G)*. ◆ **out of place** *adv* - **1.** [in wrong position] nicht an seinem Platz - **2.** [unsuitable] unpassend.

place mat *n* Platzset *das*.

placement ['pleɪsmənt] *n* [work experience] Praktikum *das*.

placid ['plæsɪd] *adj* - **1.** [person, child, animal] ausgeglichen - **2.** [place] ruhig.

plagiarize, -ise ['pleɪdʒəraɪz] *vt* plagiieren.

plague [pleɪg] ◇ *n* - **1.** MED Seuche *die*; *(U)* [specific disease] Pest *die* - **2.** [nuisance] Plage *die*. ◇ *vt* plagen; **to be plagued by bad luck** vom Pech verfolgt sein.

plaice [pleɪs] *(pl inv)* *n* Scholle *die*.

plain [pleɪn] ◇ *adj* - **1.** [simple] einfach, schlicht; [paper] unliniert; [in colour] einfarbig; [unpatterned] uni; [yoghurt] Natur-; **in plain clothes** in Zivil - **2.** [clear] klar - **3.** [blunt - statement, answer] unverblümt; **the plain truth** die reine Wahrheit - **4.** [absolute - madness, stupidity] absolut, schier - **5.** [not pretty] unattraktiv. ◇ *adv inf* [completely] einfach. ◇ *n* GEOG Ebene *die*.

plain chocolate *n UK* Bitterschokolade *die*.

plain-clothes *adj* in Zivil.

plainly ['pleɪnlɪ] *adv* - **1.** [upset, angry] sichtlich; [remember, hear] deutlich - **2.** [frankly] offen - **3.** [simply] einfach, schlicht.

plaintiff ['pleɪntɪf] *n* Kläger *der*, -in *die*.

plait [plæt] ◇ *n* Zopf *der*. ◇ *vt* flechten.

plan [plæn] ◇ *n* - **1.** [gen] Plan *der*; **to make plans** Pläne machen; **have you got any plans for tonight?** hast du heute Abend etwas vor?; **to go according to plan** nach Plan verlaufen - **2.** [of story, project] Konzept *das*, Entwurf *der*. ◇ *vt* - **1.** [organize] planen - **2.** [intend]: **to plan to do sthg** vor|haben, etw zu tun - **3.** [design] entwerfen. ◇ *vi* planen; **to plan for sthg** Pläne für etw machen. ◆ **plan on** *vt insep*: **to plan on doing sthg** vor|haben, etw zu tun.

plane [pleɪn] *n* - **1.** [aircraft] Flugzeug *das* - **2.** GEOM Ebene *die* - **3.** *fig* [level] Niveau *das* - **4.** [tool] Hobel *der* - **5.** [tree] Platane *die*.

planet ['plænɪt] *n* Planet *der*.

plank [plæŋk] *n* [piece of wood] (langes) Brett.

planning ['plænɪŋ] *n* Planung *die*.

planning permission *n (U)* Baugenehmigung *die*.

plant [plɑːnt] ◇ *n* - **1.** BOT Pflanze *die* - **2.** [factory] Werk *das*, Fabrik *die* - **3.** *(U)* [heavy machinery] Maschinen *Pl*. ◇ *vt* - **1.** [tree, vegetable] pflanzen; [seed] säen; [field, garden] bepflanzen - **2.** [place firmly] auf|stellen; **he planted a kiss on her cheek** er gab ihr einen Kuss auf die Wange - **3.** [bomb, microphone, spy] platzieren, an|bringen; [thought, idea] pflanzen, setzen.

plantation [plæn'teɪʃn] *n* - **1.** [piece of land] Plantage *die* - **2.** [of trees] Anpflanzung *die*.

plaque [plɑːk] *n* - **1.** [plate] Gedenktafel *die* - **2.** *(U)* [on teeth] Zahnbelag *der*.

plaster ['plɑːstəʳ] ◇ *n* - **1.** [for wall, ceiling] Putz *der* - **2.** [for broken bones] Gips *der* - **3.** *UK* [for cut]: **(sticking) plaster** Pflaster *das*. ◇ *vt* - **1.** [wall, ceiling] verputzen - **2.** [cover] pflastern.

plaster cast *n* - **1.** [for broken bones] Gipsverband *der* - **2.** [model, statue] Gipsform *die*.

plastered ['plɑːstəd] *adj inf* [drunk] besoffen.

plasterer ['plɑːstərəʳ] *n* Putzer *der*, -in *die*.

plaster of paris *n* Gips *der*.

plastic ['plæstɪk] ◇ *adj* Plastik-. ◇ *n* [material] Plastik *das*.

Plasticine® *UK* ['plæstɪsiːn], **play dough** *US n* Plastilin *das*.

plastic surgery *n* plastische Chirurgie.

plate [pleɪt] ◇ *n* [dish] Teller *der*; **to have a lot on one's plate** *fig* viel um die Ohren haben. ◇ *vt*: **to be plated with silver/gold** versilbert/vergoldet sein.

plateau ['plætəʊ] (*pl* **-s** OR **-x** [-z]) *n* - **1.** GEOG Plateau *das* - **2.** *fig* [steady level]: **prices have reached a plateau** die Preise haben sich stabilisiert.

plate-glass *adj* Spiegelglas-.

platform ['plætfɔːm] *n* - **1.** [gen & COMPUT] Plattform *die*; [for speaker, performer] Podium *das* - **2.** [at railway station] Bahnsteig *der*; **platform 12** Gleis 12.

platinum ['plætɪnəm] *n* Platin *das*.

platoon [plə'tuːn] *n* Zug *der*.

platter ['plætəʳ] *n* [dish] Platte *die*.

plausible ['plɔːzəbl] *adj* [reason, excuse] plausibel; [person] überzeugend.

play [pleɪ] ◇ *n* - **1.** [gen] Spiel *das*; **in play** SPORT im Spiel; **out of play** SPORT im Aus; **to come into play** *fig* eine Rolle spielen; **play on words** Wortspiel *das* - **2.** [in theatre] Schauspiel *das*, Stück *das*; [on radio] Hörspiel *das*; [on television] Fernsehspiel *das*. ◇ *vt* spielen; [opposing player or team] spielen gegen; **to play the piano** Klavier spielen; **to play a trick on sb** jm einen Streich spielen; **to play a part** OR **role in sthg** *fig* eine Rolle in etw *(D)* spielen; **to play it cool** so tun, als sei nichts gewesen. ◇ *vi* spielen; **to play for time** versuchen, Zeit zu gewinnen; **to play safe** auf Nummer sicher gehen. ◆ **play along** *vi*: **to play along (with sb)** sich (jm) vorübergehend fügen. ◆ **play down** *vt sep* herunter|spielen. ◆ **play up** ◇ *vt sep* [emphasize] betonen. ◇ *vi* [machine, part of body] Schwierigkeiten machen; [children] sich wie wild gebärden.

play-act *vi* schauspielern.

playboy ['pleɪbɔɪ] *n* Playboy *der*.

play dough *n US* = **Plasticine**®.

player ['pleɪəʳ] *n* [gen] Spieler *der*, -in *die*.

playful ['pleɪfʊl] *adj* [comment] neckisch; [person, animal] verspielt.

playground ['pleɪgraʊnd] *n* [at school] Schulhof *der*; [in park] Spielplatz *der*.

playgroup ['pleɪgruːp] *n* Krabbelgruppe *die*.

playing card ['pleɪɪŋ-] *n* Spielkarte *die*.

playing field ['pleɪɪŋ-] *n* Sportplatz *der*.

playmate ['pleɪmeɪt] *n* Spielkamerad *der*, -in *die*.

play-off *n* Entscheidungsspiel *das*.

playpen ['pleɪpen] *n* Laufstall *der*.

playschool ['pleɪskuːl] *n* Krabbelgruppe *die*.

plaything ['pleɪθɪŋ] *n liter* & *fig* Spielzeug *das*.

playtime ['pleɪtaɪm] *n (U)* [at school]: **at playtime** in der großen Pause.

playwright ['pleɪraɪt] *n* Dramatiker *der*, -in *die*.

plc (*abbr of* **public limited company**) AG *die*.

plea [pliː] *n* - **1.** [appeal] Appell *der* - **2.** LAW Plädoyer *das*; **what's your plea?** wie plädieren Sie?

plead [pliːd] (*pt* & *pp* **-ed** OR **pled**) ◇ *vt* - **1.** LAW plädieren; **to plead guilty/not guilty** sich schuldig/nicht schuldig bekennen

- 2. sich berufen auf *(+ A)*. ◇ *vi* - 1. [beg] flehen; **to plead with sb to do sthg** jn anlflehen, etw zu tun; **to plead for sthg** um etw flehen - 2. LAW: **to plead sb's case** jn in einer Sache vertreten.

pleasant ['pleznt] *adj* angenehm; [smile] freundlich; [day] schön.

pleasantry ['plezntrı] *n*: **to exchange pleasantries** Nettigkeiten auslltauschen.

please [pliːz] ◇ *vt* gefallen *(+ D)*; **there's no pleasing him** man kann ihm nichts recht machen; **he's hard to please** er ist nicht leicht zufriedenzustellen; **please yourself!** wie du willst! ◇ *vi* gefallen; **may I? – please do!** darf ich? – bitte sehr!; **he does as he pleases** er macht, was ihm gefällt. ◇ *adv* bitte; **yes, please!** ja, bitte!

pleased [pliːzd] *adj* [happy] erfreut; [satisfied] zufrieden; **to be pleased about sthg** sich über etw *(A)* freuen; **to be pleased with sb/sthg** mit jm/etw zufrieden sein; **pleased to meet you!** angenehm!

pleasing ['pliːzıŋ] *adj* erfreulich.

pleasure ['pleʒəʳ] *n* - 1. [gen] Freude *die*; **with pleasure** gern(e); **it's a pleasure!, my pleasure !** gern geschehen! - 2. *(U)* [enjoyment] Vergnügen *das*.

pleat [pliːt] ◇ *n* Falte *die*. ◇ *vt* fälteln.

pled [pled] *pt* & *pp* ▷ **plead**.

pledge [pledʒ] ◇ *n* - 1. [promise] Versprechen *das* - 2. [token] Pfand *das*. ◇ *vt* - 1. [promise] versprechen - 2. [commit]: **to be pledged to sthg** zu etw verpflichtet werden; **to pledge o.s. to sthg** sich zu etw verpflichten - 3. [pawn] verpfänden.

plentiful ['plentıfʊl] *adj* reichlich.

plenty ['plentı] ◇ *n (U)* Überfluss *der*. ◇ *pron*: **we've got plenty** wir haben mehr als genug; **five will be plenty** fünf sind mehr als genug; **plenty of** viel, eine Menge. ◇ *adv US* [very] sehr.

pliable ['plaıəbl], **pliant** ['plaıənt] *adj* - 1. [metal] biegsam; [material] geschmeidig - 2. [person] anpassungsfähig.

pliers ['plaıəz] *npl* Zange *die*.

plight [plaıt] *n* Elend *das*.

plimsoll ['plımsəl] *n UK* Turnschuh *der*.

plinth [plınθ] *n* Plinthe *die*.

plod [plɒd] *vi* - 1. [walk slowly] schwerfällig gehen - 2. [work slowly] sich ablmühen.

plonk [plɒŋk] *n (U) UK inf* [wine] billiger Wein. ◆ **plonk down** *vt sep inf* hinlknallen.

plot [plɒt] ◇ *n* - 1. [conspiracy] Komplott *das* - 2. [of story, film, play] Handlung *die* - 3. [of land] Stück *das* Land; [allotment] Parzelle *die*. ◇ *vt* - 1. [conspire] planen; **to plot to do sthg** gemeinsam planen, etw zu tun - 2. [chart] einlzeichnen; MATHS auflzeichnen. ◇ *vi*: **to plot (against)** sich verschwören (gegen).

plough *UK*, **plow** *US* [plaʊ] ◇ *n* Pflug *der*. ◇ *vt* pflügen; **to plough money into sthg** Geld in etw *(A)* stecken. ◇ *vi* [crash]: **to plough into sthg** in etw *(A)* rasen.

ploughman's ['plaʊmənz] *(pl inv) n UK*: **ploughman's (lunch)** *Pubmahlzeit aus Käse, Brot und Pickles.*

plow *etc n* & *vb US* = **plough** *etc* .

ploy [plɔı] *n* Trick *der*.

pluck [plʌk] ◇ *vt* - 1. [flower, fruit] pflücken - 2. [pull] ziehen - 3. [chicken] rupfen - 4. [eyebrows, guitar, harp] zupfen. ◇ *n (U) dated* Mut *der*. ◆ **pluck up** *vt sep*: **to pluck up the courage to do sthg** den Mut auflbringen, etw zu tun.

plug [plʌg] ◇ *n* - 1. ELEC Stecker *der*; [socket] Steckdose *die* - 2. [for bath, sink] Stöpsel *der*. ◇ *vt* - 1. [hole, ears] verstopfen - 2. *inf* [advertise] Schleichwerbung für etw machen. ◆ **plug in** *vt sep* ELEC einlstecken.

plughole ['plʌghəʊl] *n* Abfluss *der*.

plum [plʌm] *n* [fruit] Pflaume *die*.

plumb [plʌm] ◇ *adv* - 1. *UK* [exactly] genau; **plumb in the middle** genau in der/die Mitte - 2. *US* [completely] völlig, komplett. ◇ *vt*: **to plumb the depths of sthg** den Tiefpunkt von etw erreichen.

plumber ['plʌməʳ] *n* Klempner *der*.

plumbing ['plʌmıŋ] *n (U)* - 1. [fittings] Leitungen *Pl* - 2. [work] Installieren *das* von Sanitäranlagen.

plume [pluːm] *n* - 1. [on bird, hat] Feder *die*; [on helmet] Federbusch *der* - 2. [column]: **a plume of smoke** eine Rauchfahne.

plummet ['plʌmıt] *vi* - 1. [plane, bird] (senkrecht) hinunterlstürzen - 2. [prices, value, shares] rapide fallen.

plump [plʌmp] ◇ *adj* rundlich, mollig. ◇ *vi*: **to plump for sthg** sich für etw entscheiden. ◆ **plump up** *vt sep* auflschütteln.

plunder ['plʌndəʳ] *vt* plündern.

plunge [plʌndʒ] ◇ *n* - 1. [rapid decrease] Sturz *der* - 2. [dive] Sprung *der*; [head-on] Kopfsprung *der*; **to take the plunge** den Schritt wagen. ◇ *vt* - 1. [immerse]: **to plunge sthg into sthg** etw in etw *(A)* werfen - 2. [thrust]: **to plunge sthg into sthg** etw in etw *(A)* treiben; **plunged into darkness** in Dunkelheit getaucht. ◇ *vi* - 1. [dive] springen; [out of control] stürzen - 2. [prices, value] fallen.

plunger ['plʌndʒəʳ] *n* [for sinks, drains] Saugglocke *die*.

pluperfect [ˌpluː'pɜːfıkt] *n*: **pluperfect (tense)** Plusquamperfekt *das*.

plural ['plʊərəl] ◇ *adj* GRAM im Plural. ◇ *n* Plural *der*; **in the plural** im Plural.

plus [plʌs] *(pl* **-es** *OR* **-ses***)* ◇ *adj* - 1. [over, more than]: **30 plus** mehr als 30, über 30 - 2. [in school marks] plus. ◇ *n* - 1. MATHS [sign] Pluszeichen *das* - **2.** *inf* [bonus] Plus *das.* ◇ *prep* - **1.** MATHS plus, und - **2.** [as well as] und. ◇ *conj* [moreover] und (außerdem).

plush [plʌʃ] *adj* luxuriös.

plus sign *n* Pluszeichen *das.*

Pluto ['plu:təʊ] *n* [planet] Pluto *der.*

plutonium [plu:'təʊnɪəm] *n* Plutonium *das.*

ply [plaɪ] *vt* - **1.** [work at]: **to ply a trade** ein Gewerbe betreiben - **2.**: **to ply sb with drink** jm Alkohol auf|drängen; **to ply sb with questions** jn mit Fragen bedrängen.

-ply [plaɪ] *adj*: **four-ply** [wood] vierschichtig; [wool] vierfädig.

plywood ['plaɪwʊd] *n* Sperrholz *das.*

p.m., pm (*abbr of* **post meridiem**) nachmittags; **at 9 p.m.** um 21 Uhr *OR* 9 Uhr abends.

PM *n abbr of* **prime minister**.

PMT *n abbr of* **premenstrual tension**.

pneumatic [nju:'mætɪk] *adj* pneumatisch.

pneumatic drill *n* Pressluftbohrer *der.*

pneumonia [nju:'məʊnɪə] *n (U)* Lungenentzündung *die.*

poach [pəʊtʃ] ◇ *vt* - **1.** [hunt illegally] wildern - **2.** [idea] kopieren - **3.** [egg] pochieren. ◇ *vi* wildern.

poacher ['pəʊtʃər] *n* [person] Wilderer *der.*

poaching ['pəʊtʃɪŋ] *n* Wildern *das.*

PO Box *n abbr of* **Post Office Box**.

pocket ['pɒkɪt] ◇ *n* - **1.** [in clothes] Tasche *die*; **to be out of pocket** drauf|zahlen; **to pick sb's pocket** jm etwas (aus der Tasche) stehlen - **2.** [of warm air, mineral] Einschluss *der*; **pocket of resistance** Widerstandsnest *das* - **3.** [of snooker, pool table] Loch *das.* ◇ *adj* Taschen-. ◇ *vt* ein|stecken.

pocketbook ['pɒkɪtbʊk] *n* - **1.** [notebook] Notizbuch *das* - **2.** *US* [handbag] Handtasche *die.*

pocketknife ['pɒkɪtnaɪf] (*pl* **-knives** [-naɪvz]) *n* Taschenmesser *das.*

pocket money *n* Taschengeld *das.*

pod [pɒd] *n* [of plants] Hülse *die.*

podcast ['pɒdkɑ:st] *n* Podcast *der.*

podgy ['pɒdʒɪ] *adj inf* pummelig.

podia ['pəʊdɪə] *npl* ▷ **podium**.

podiatrist [pə'daɪətrɪst] *n US* Fußpfleger *der*, -in *die.*

podium ['pəʊdɪəm] (*pl* **-diums** *OR* **-dia**) *n* Podium *das.*

poem ['pəʊɪm] *n* Gedicht *das.*

poet ['pəʊɪt] *n* Dichter *der*, -in *die.*

poetic [pəʊ'etɪk] *adj* poetisch.

poetry ['pəʊɪtrɪ] *n (U)* [poems] Dichtung *die.*

poignant ['pɔɪnjənt] *adj* [moving] ergreifend.

point [pɔɪnt] ◇ *n* - **1.** [tip] Spitze *die* - **2.** [in discussion, debate] Punkt *der*; **to make a point** eine Anmerkung machen; **to make one's point** seinen Standpunkt deutlich machen - **3.** [meaning] Sinn *der*; **you've missed the point of what he is trying to say** du hast nicht verstanden, worauf er hinauswill; **to get** *OR* **come to the point** zur Sache kommen; **that's beside the point** das tut hier nichts zur Sache - **4.** [feature]: **good** *OR* **strong point** Stärke *die*; **bad** *OR* **weak point** Schwäche *die* - **5.** [purpose] Zweck *der*; **there's no point** es hat keinen Sinn - **6.** MATHS Komma *das*; **five point seven** fünf Komma sieben - **7.** [in scores] Punkt *der* - **8.** *UK* ELEC Steckdose *die* - **9.** *US* [full stop] Punkt *der* - **10.** *phr*: **to make a point of doing sthg** etw bewusst tun. ◇ *vt*: **to point sthg (at)** etw richten (auf *(+ A)*). ◇ *vi* - **1.** [person]: **to point at** *OR* **to** zeigen auf *(+ A)* - **2.** *fig* [evidence, facts]: **to point to sb/sthg** auf jn/etw hin|weisen. ◆ **points** *npl UK* RAIL Weiche *die.* ◆ **on the point of** *prep*: **to be on the point of doing sthg** im Begriff sein, etw zu tun; **I was on the point of going** ich wollte gerade gehen. ◆ **up to a point** *adv* bis zu einem gewissen Punkt. ◆ **point out** *vt sep* - **1.** [indicate] zeigen - **2.** [call attention to] hin|weisen auf *(+ A)*.

point-blank *adv* - **1.** [directly] direkt; [ask] geradeheraus; [refuse] rundweg - **2.** [shoot] aus nächster Nähe.

pointed ['pɔɪntɪd] *adj* - **1.** [sharp] spitz - **2.** [meaningful] betont; [remark] spitz.

pointer ['pɔɪntər] *n* - **1.** [tip] Hinweis *der* - **2.** [needle on dial] Zeiger *der* - **3.** [stick] Zeigestock *der* - **4.** COMPUT Mauszeiger *der.*

pointless ['pɔɪntlɪs] *adj* zwecklos, sinnlos.

point of view (*pl* **points of view**) *n* [attitude] Standpunkt *der.*

poise [pɔɪz] *n (U)* [composure] Selbstsicherheit *die.*

poised [pɔɪzd] *adj* - **1.** [ready] bereit; **to be poised to do sthg** bereit sein, etw zu tun; **to be poised for sthg** bereit sein für etw *OR* zu etw - **2.** [composed] gefasst.

poison ['pɔɪzn] ◇ *n* Gift *das.* ◇ *vt* - **1.** [gen] vergiften - **2.** *fig* [corrupt] verschmutzen - **3.** [atmosphere, water] verderben.

poisoning ['pɔɪznɪŋ] *n* Vergiftung *die.*

poisonous ['pɔɪznəs] *adj* [gen] giftig.

poke [pəʊk] ◇ *vt* - **1.** [with finger, stick] stoßen; **to poke sb in the ribs** jm einen Stoß in die Rippen geben - **2.** [thrust] stecken; **he poked his head round the door** er steckte den Kopf zur Tür herein - **3.** [fire] schüren. ◇ *vi*: **to poke out of** hervor|schauen aus *(+ D)*. ◆ **poke about, poke around** *vi inf* herum|stochern.

poker ['pəʊkər] *n* - **1.** [game] Poker *das* - **2.** [for fire] Schürhaken *der.*

poker-faced [-ˌfeɪst] *adj* mit einem Pokerface.

poky ['pəʊkɪ] *adj pej* eng.

Poland ['pəulənd] *n* Polen *nt*.

polar ['pəulər] *adj* GEOG polar.

Polaroid® ['pəulərɔɪd] *n* - **1.** [camera] Polaroidkamera® *die* - **2.** [photograph] Polaroidfoto *das*.

pole [pəul] *n* - **1.** Stange *die*; [for electricity] Pfahl *der*; [for flag] Mast *der*; [for skiing] Stock *der* - **2.** GEOG & ELEC Pol *der*.

Pole [pəul] *n* Pole *der*, -lin *die*.

pole vault *n*: **the pole vault** der Stabhochsprung.

police [pə'liːs] <> *npl* - **1.** [police force]: **the police** die Polizei - **2.** [policemen] Polizisten *Pl*. <> *vt* [area] kontrollieren.

police car *n* Streifenwagen *der*.

police constable *n UK* Wachtmeister *der*, -in *die*.

police force *n* Polizei *die*.

policeman [pə'liːsmən] (*pl* **-men** [-mən]) *n* Polizist *der*.

police officer *n* Polizeibeamte *der*, -tin *die*.

police station *n UK* Polizeiwache *die*.

policewoman [pə'liːs,wumən] (*pl* **-women** [-,wɪmɪn]) *n* Polizistin *die*.

policy ['pɒləsɪ] *n* - **1.** [plan] Politik *die* - **2.** [for insurance] Police *die*.

polio ['pəulɪəu] *n (U)* Kinderlähmung *die*.

polish ['pɒlɪʃ] <> *n* - **1.** [cleaning material] Politur *die*; **window polish** Glasreiniger *der* - **2.** [shine] Glanz *der*; [of furniture] Politur *die* - **3.** *fig* [of performance] Brillianz *die*; [of style, manners] Schliff *der*. <> *vt* - **1.** [shine] polieren - **2.** *fig* [perfect]: **to polish sthg (up)** etw verfeinern. ◆ **polish off** *vt sep inf* - **1.** [meal] verputzen - **2.** [job] schnell erledigen; [book] verschlingen.

Polish ['pəulɪʃ] <> *adj* polnisch. <> *n* [language] Polnisch(e) *das*.

polished ['pɒlɪʃt] *adj* - **1.** [surface] poliert - **2.** [person, manners] geschliffen - **3.** [performance] brilliant.

polite [pə'laɪt] *adj* höflich.

political [pə'lɪtɪkl] *adj* politisch.

politically correct *adj* politisch korrekt.

politician [,pɒlɪ'tɪʃn] *n* Politiker *der*, -in *die*.

politics ['pɒlətɪks] <> *n (U)* Politik *die*. <> *npl* - **1.** [personal beliefs] politische Ansichten - **2.** [of a group, area] Politik *die*.

poll [pəul] <> *n* - **1.** [election] Wahl *die* - **2.** [survey] Umfrage *die*. <> *vt* - **1.** [people] befragen - **2.** [votes] erhalten. ◆ **polls** *npl*: **to go to the polls** wählen gehen.

pollen ['pɒlən] *n* Blütenstaub *der*.

polling booth *n* Wahlkabine *die*.

polling day *n UK* Wahltag *der*.

polling station *n* Wahllokal *das*.

pollute [pə'luːt] *vt* verschmutzen.

pollution [pə'luːʃn] *n* Verschmutzung *die*.

polo ['pəuləu] *n* Polo *das*.

polo neck *n UK* - **1.** [collar] Rollkragen *der* - **2.** [jumper] Rollkragenpullover *der*.

polo shirt *n* Polohemd *das*.

polyethylene *n US* = **polythene**.

polystyrene [,pɒlɪ'staɪriːn] *n* Styropor® *das*.

polytechnic [,pɒlɪ'teknɪk] *n UK* Polytechnikum *das*, ≃ technische Hochschule.

polythene *UK* ['pɒlɪθiːn], **polyethylene** *US* [,pɒlɪ'eθɪliːn] *n* Polyethylen *das*.

polythene bag *n UK* Plastiktüte *die*.

pomegranate ['pɒmɪ,grænɪt] *n* Granatapfel *der*.

pomp [pɒmp] *n* Pomp *der*.

pompom ['pɒmpɒm] *n* Pompon *der*.

pompous ['pɒmpəs] *adj* [pretentious] aufgeblasen; [speech] geschwollen.

pond [pɒnd] *n* Teich *der*.

ponder ['pɒndər] *vt* & *vi* nach|denken; **to ponder on** OR **over sthg** über etw *(A)* nach|denken.

ponderous ['pɒndərəs] *adj* schwerfällig.

pong [pɒŋ] *UK inf n* Gestank *der*, Mief *der*.

pontoon [pɒn'tuːn] *n* - **1.** [bridge] Ponton *der* - **2.** *UK* [game] Siebzehnundvier *das*.

pony ['pəunɪ] *n* Pony *das*.

ponytail ['pəunɪteɪl] *n* Pferdeschwanz *der*.

poodle ['puːdl] *n* Pudel *der*.

pool [puːl] <> *n* - **1.** [of water, blood] Lache *die*; [of light] Lichtkegel *der*; [of rain] Pfütze *die* - **2.** [swimming pool] Swimmingpool *der*; [small pond] Teich *der* - **3.** [game] Poolbillard *das*. <> *vt* zusammen|legen. ◆ **pools** *npl UK*: **the pools** das Fußballtoto.

poor [pɔːr] <> *adj* - **1.** [impoverished, unfortunate] arm - **2.** [not very good] schlecht. <> *npl*: **the poor** die Armen *Pl*.

poorly ['pɔːlɪ] <> *adj UK inf* krank. <> *adv* [badly] schlecht.

pop [pɒp] <> *n* - **1.** [music] Pop *der* - **2.** *UK inf* [fizzy drink] Brause *die* - **3.** *esp US inf* [father] Papa *der* - **4.** [noise] Knall *der*. <> *vt* - **1.** [balloon, bubble] platzen, zerplatzen - **2.** [put] stecken. <> *vi* [balloon] platzen; [cork] knallen; **my ears are popping** ich habe Druck auf den Ohren. ◆ **pop in** *vi* [visit] vorbei|schauen. ◆ **pop up** *vi* auf|tauchen.

pop concert *n* Popkonzert *das*.

popcorn ['pɒpkɔːn] *n* Popcorn *das*.

pope [pəup] *n* Papst *der*.

pop group *n* Popgruppe *die*.

poplar ['pɒplər] *n* Pappel *die*.

poppy ['pɒpɪ] *n* Mohn *der*.

Popsicle® ['pɒpsɪkl] *n US* Eis *das* am Stiel.

popular ['pɒpjʊləʳ] *adj* - **1.** [well-liked] populär, beliebt - **2.** [common] weit verbreitet - **3.** [newspaper, politics] volksnah; [entertainment] volkstümlich; [debate] öffentlich.

popularize, -ise ['pɒpjʊləraɪz] *vt* - **1.** [make popular] popularisieren - **2.** [simplify] vereinfachen.

population [,pɒpjʊ'leɪʃn] *n* [gen] Bevölkerung *die*.

porcelain ['pɔːsəlɪn] *n* Porzellan *das*.

porch [pɔːtʃ] *n* - **1.** [entrance] Windfang *der* - **2.** *US* [veranda] Veranda *die*.

porcupine ['pɔːkjʊpaɪn] *n* Stachelschwein *das*.

pore [pɔːʳ] *n* Pore *die*. ◆ **pore over** *vt insep* brüten über.

pork [pɔːk] *n* Schweinefleisch *das*.

pork pie *n* Schweinefleischpastete *die*.

pornography [pɔː'nɒgrəfɪ] *n* Pornografie *die*.

porous ['pɔːrəs] *adj* porös.

porridge ['pɒrɪdʒ] *n* Haferbrei *der*.

port [pɔːt] *n* - **1.** [coastal town] Hafenstadt *die*; [harbour] Hafen *der* - **2.** NAUT Backbord *das* - **3.** [drink] Portwein *der* - **4.** COMPUT Anschluss *der*.

portable ['pɔːtəbl] *adj* tragbar.

porter ['pɔːtəʳ] *n* - **1.** *UK* [at hotel, museum] Pförtner *der*, Portier *der* - **2.** [at station, airport] Gepäckträger *der* - **3.** *US* [on train] Schlafwagenschaffner *der*.

portfolio [,pɔːt'fəʊlɪəʊ] (*pl* **-s**) *n* - **1.** [case] Aktentasche *die* - **2.** [sample of work] Mappe *die* - **3.** FIN Portefeuille *das*.

porthole ['pɔːthəʊl] *n* Bullauge *das*.

portion ['pɔːʃn] *n* - **1.** [part, share] Teil *der* - **2.** [of food] Portion *die*.

portrait ['pɔːtreɪt] *n liter* & *fig* Porträt *das*.

portray [pɔː'treɪ] *vt* - **1.** [gen] dar|stellen - **2.** [subj: artist] porträtieren.

Portugal ['pɔːtʃʊgl] *n* Portugal *nt*.

Portuguese [,pɔːtʃʊ'giːz] (*pl inv*) ◇ *adj* portugiesisch. ◇ *n* - **1.** [person] Portugiese *der*, -sin *die* - **2.** [language] Portugiesisch(e) *das*. ◇ *npl*: **the Portuguese** die Portugiesen *Pl*.

pose [pəʊz] ◇ *n* - **1.** [position] Haltung *die* - **2.** *pej* [pretence] Pose *die*. ◇ *vt* - **1.** [problem, danger, threat] dar|stellen - **2.** [a question] stellen. ◇ *vi* - **1.** [for photo] posieren; [for painting] Modell stehen - **2.** *pej* [behave affectedly] posieren - **3.** [pretend to be]: **to pose as a tourist** sich als Tourist aus|geben.

posh [pɒʃ] *adj inf* nobel.

position [pə'zɪʃn] ◇ *n* - **1.** [place, situation] Lage *die* - **2.** [of plane, ship] Position *die* - **3.** [of body] Haltung *die* - **4.** [setting, rank] Stellung *die* - **5.** [in race, combat] Platz *der* - **6.** [job] Stelle *die* - **7.** [stance, opinion]: **position on sthg** Haltung gegenüber etw *(D)*. ◇ *vt* positionieren.

positive ['pɒzətɪv] *adj* - **1.** [gen] positiv - **2.** [sure, certain] sicher; **to be positive about sthg** sich einer Sache *(G)* sicher sein - **3.** [evidence, fact] definitiv - **4.** [for emphasis] total.

possess [pə'zes] *vt* besitzen; **what possessed you to do that?** was ist in Sie gefahren, dass Sie das gemacht haben?

possession [pə'zeʃn] *n* Besitz *der*. ◆ **possessions** *npl* Habe *die*; **his personal possessions** all seine Sachen.

possessive [pə'zesɪv] ◇ *adj* - **1.** *pej* [person] besitzergreifend - **2.** GRAM Possessiv-. ◇ *n* GRAM Possessivfunktion *die*.

possibility [,pɒsə'bɪlətɪ] *n* Möglichkeit *die*.

possible ['pɒsəbl] *adj* möglich; **would it be possible for me to see him?** könnte ich ihn vielleicht sehen?; **as soon as possible** so bald wie möglich; **as much as possible** so viel wie möglich; **if possible** wenn möglich.

possibly ['pɒsəblɪ] *adv* - **1.** [perhaps] möglicherweise - **2.** [conceivably] möglich; **I'll do all I possibly can** ich werde mein Möglichstes tun; **I can't possibly do that** das kann ich unmöglich tun.

post [pəʊst] ◇ *n* - **1.** [service, letters, delivery] Post *die*; **by post** per Post - **2.** [pole] Pfosten *der*; **to pip sb at the post** [in race] jn knapp schlagen; *fig* jm etw vor der Nase weg|schnappen - **3.** [job & MIL] Posten *der*. ◇ *vt* - **1.** [by mail] per OR mit der Post schicken - **2.** [employee] versetzen.

postage ['pəʊstɪdʒ] *n* Porto *das*; **postage and packing** Porto und Verpackung.

postal ['pəʊstl] *adj* Post-, postalisch.

postal order *n* Postanweisung *die*.

postbox ['pəʊstbɒks] *n UK* Briefkasten *der*.

postcard ['pəʊstkɑːd] *n* Postkarte *die*.

postcode ['pəʊstkəʊd] *n UK* Postleitzahl *die*.

postdate [,pəʊst'deɪt] *vt* vor|datieren.

poster ['pəʊstəʳ] *n* Poster *das*, Plakat *das*.

poste restante [,pəʊst'restɑːnt] *n (U) esp UK*: **to send sthg poste restante** etw postlagernd schicken.

posterior [pɒ'stɪərɪəʳ] ◇ *adj* [rear] hintere(r) (s). ◇ *n hum* Hinterteil *das*.

postgraduate [,pəʊst'grædjʊət] ◇ *adj* [studies, course] Aufbau-. ◇ *n*: **postgraduate (student)** *Student, der ein Aufbaustudium absolviert*.

posthumous ['pɒstjʊməs] *adj* postum.

postman ['pəʊstmən] (*pl* **-men** [-mən]) *n* Briefträger *der*, Postbote *der*.

postmark ['pəʊstmɑːk] ◇ *n* Poststempel *der*. ◇ *vt* stempeln.

postmortem [ˌpəʊstˈmɔːtəm] *n* - **1.** [autopsy]: **postmortem (examination)** Obduktion *die* - **2.** *fig* [analysis] Analyse *die*.

post office *n* Post *die*.

post office box *n* Postfach *das*.

postpone [ˌpəʊstˈpəʊn] *vt* verschieben; [decision] auf|schieben.

postscript [ˈpəʊstskrɪpt] *n* [to letter] Postskriptum *das*.

posture [ˈpɒstʃəʳ] *n liter* & *fig* Haltung *die*.

postwar [ˌpəʊstˈwɔːʳ] *adj* Nachkriegs-.

posy [ˈpəʊzɪ] *n* Blumensträußchen *das*.

pot [pɒt] ◇ *n* - **1.** [for cooking, flowers] Topf *der* - **2.** [for tea, coffee] Kanne *die* - **3.** [for paint] Büchse *die*; [for jam] Glas *das* - **4.** *(U) drug sl* [cannabis] Hasch *das*. ◇ *vt* [plant] ein|topfen.

potassium [pəˈtæsɪəm] *n* Kalium *das*.

potato [pəˈteɪtəʊ] (*pl* **-es**) *n* Kartoffel *die*.

potato peeler [-ˌpiːləʳ] *n* Kartoffelschäler *der*.

potent [ˈpəʊtənt] *adj* - **1.** [argument] stichhaltig - **2.** [drink, drug] stark.

potential [pəˈtenʃl] ◇ *adj* potenziell. ◇ *n (U)* [of person] Potenzial *das*; **to have potential** [person] das Potenzial haben; [scheme, plan, company, business] entwicklungsfähig sein.

potentially [pəˈtenʃəlɪ] *adv* potenziell.

pothole [ˈpɒthəʊl] *n* - **1.** [in road] Schlagloch *das* - **2.** [underground] Höhle *die*.

potholing [ˈpɒtˌhəʊlɪŋ] *n UK* Höhlenforschung *die*; **to go potholing** eine Höhle erforschen (gehen).

potion [ˈpəʊʃn] *n* Trank *der*.

potluck [ˌpɒtˈlʌk] *n*: **to take potluck** aufs Geratewohl aus|wählen; [at meal] mit dem vorlieb nehmen, was gerade da ist.

potshot [ˈpɒtˌʃɒt] *n*: **to take a potshot at sthg** aufs Geratewohl auf etw *(A)* schießen.

potted [ˈpɒtɪd] *adj* - **1.** [grown in pot] Topf- - **2.** [meat] eingemacht.

potter [ˈpɒtəʳ] *n* [craftsperson] Töpfer *der*, -in *die*. ◆ **potter about, potter around** *vi UK* [do minor work] herum|werkeln; [work slowly] herum|trödeln.

pottery [ˈpɒtərɪ] *n* - **1.** *(U)* [clay objects] Töpferwaren *Pl* - **2.** [craft] Töpfern *das*.

potty [ˈpɒtɪ] *UK inf* ◇ *adj* verrückt; **to be potty about sb/sthg** nach jm/etw verrückt sein. ◇ *n* Töpfchen *das*.

pouch [paʊtʃ] *n* Beutel *der*.

poultry [ˈpəʊltrɪ] ◇ *n* [meat] Geflügel *das*. ◇ *npl* [birds] Geflügel *das*.

pounce [paʊns] *vi*: **to pounce on** OR **upon** sich stürzen auf *(+ A)*.

pound [paʊnd] ◇ *n* - **1.** *UK* [unit of money, currency system] Pfund *das* - **2.** [unit of weight] ≃ Pfund *das (= 454g)* - **3.** [for cars] Abstellplatz *der (für abgeschleppte Fahrzeuge)*; [for dogs] Asyl *das*. ◇ *vt* [pulverize] pulverisieren. ◇ *vi* - **1.** [strike loudly]: **to pound on sthg** [wall, door] an OR gegen etw *(A)* hämmern; [table] auf etw *(A)* hämmern - **2.** [beat, throb - heart] pochen; [- head] brummen.

pound coin *n* Einpfundmünze *die*.

pound sterling *n* Pfund *das* Sterling.

pour [pɔːʳ] ◇ *vt* [cause to flow]: **to pour sthg (into sthg)** [liquid] etw (in etw *(A)*) gießen; [grain, sugar] etw (in etw *(A)*) schütten; **to pour sb a drink, to pour a drink for sb** jm einen Drink ein|gießen. ◇ *vi liter* & *fig* strömen; **sweat was pouring off him** ihm lief der Schweiß herunter. ◇ *impers vb* [rain hard] (wie aus Eimern) gießen. ◆ **pour in** *vi* (in großen Mengen) ein|treffen. ◆ **pour out** *vt sep* - **1.** [from container] aus|schütten - **2.** [drink] ein|schenken.

pouring [ˈpɔːrɪŋ] *adj* [rain] strömend.

pout [paʊt] *vi* schmollen.

poverty [ˈpɒvətɪ] *n (U)* [hardship] Armut *die*.

poverty-stricken [-ˌstrɪkən] *adj* verarmt.

powder [ˈpaʊdəʳ] ◇ *n* [for baking, washing] Pulver *das*; [for face, body] Puder *der*. ◇ *vt* [face, body] pudern.

powder compact *n* Puderdose *die*.

powdered [ˈpaʊdəd] *adj* - **1.** [in powder form]: **powdered milk** Trockenmilch *die*; **powdered eggs** Trockenei *das* - **2.** [covered in powder] gepudert.

powder puff *n* Puderquaste *die*.

powder room *n* Damentoilette *die*.

power [ˈpaʊəʳ] ◇ *n* - **1.** *(U)* [control, influence] Macht *die*; **to be in power** an der Macht sein; **to come to power** an die Macht kommen; **to take power** die Macht übernehmen - **2.** [ability, capacity] Vermögen *das*, Fähigkeit *die*; **to be (with)in one's power to do sthg** in js Macht liegen, etw zu tun - **3.** [legal authority] Macht *die*; **to have the power to do sthg** das Recht haben, etw zu tun - **4.** *(U)* [strength] Stärke *die* - **5.** *(U)* TECH [energy] Energie *die* - **6.** *(U)* [electricity] Strom *der* - **7.** [powerful person, group] Macht *die*. ◇ *vt* [machine] an|treiben.

powerboat [ˈpaʊəbəʊt] *n* Rennboot *das*.

power cut *n* Stromsperre *die*.

power failure *n* Stromausfall *der*.

powerful [ˈpaʊəfʊl] *adj* - **1.** [influential] mächtig - **2.** [strong] kräftig; [drug, smell] stark; [blow, kick] kraftvoll; [machine] leistungsstark - **3.** [very convincing, very moving - piece of writing, speech] überzeugend; [- work of art] überwältigend.

powerless [ˈpaʊəlɪs] *adj* machtlos; **he was powerless to help** es stand nicht in seiner Macht zu helfen.

power point *n UK* Steckdose *die*.

power station *n* Kraftwerk *das*.

power steering *n* Servolenkung *die*.

pp (*abbr of* **per procurationem**) pp.

p & p (*abbr of* **postage and packing**) *n Post- und Verpackungsgebühr.*

PR *n* - **1.** *abbr of* **proportional representation** - **2.** *abbr of* **public relations**.

practicable ['præktɪkəbl] *adj* durchführbar.

practical ['præktɪkl] <> *adj* - **1.** [gen] praktisch - **2.** [practicable] durchführbar, umsetzbar. <> *n* Praktikum *das*.

practicality [,præktɪ'kælətɪ] *n* Praxisbezogenheit *die*.

practical joke *n* Streich *der*.

practically ['præktɪklɪ] *adv* - **1.** [sensibly] praktisch - **2.** [almost] fast.

practice, practise *US* ['præktɪs] *n* - **1.** *(U)* [training] Übung *die*; [for sport] Training *das*; [for music] Üben *das*; **to be out of practice** aus der Übung sein - **2.** [training session - of choir] Probe *die*; [- of sport] Training *das* - **3.** [implementation]: **to put sthg into practice** etw in die Praxis umǀsetzen; **in practice** [in fact] in Wirklichkeit, tatsächlich - **4.** [habit, regular activity - of group] Brauch *der*; [- of person] Gewohnheit *die* - **5.** [business] Praxis *die*.

practicing *adj US* = **practising**.

practise, practice *US* ['præktɪs] <> *vt* - **1.** [musical instrument, movement in sport] üben; [foreign language] sprechen - **2.** [customs, beliefs] ausǀüben - **3.** [do as profession] praktizieren. <> *vi* - **1.** [train] üben - **2.** [doctor, lawyer] praktizieren.

practising, practicing *US* ['præktɪsɪŋ] *adj* praktizierend.

Prague [prɑːg] *n* Prag *nt*.

prairie ['preərɪ] *n* Prärie *die*.

praise [preɪz] <> *n* Lob *das*; **to sing sb's praises** ein Loblied auf jn singen. <> *vt* loben.

praiseworthy ['preɪz,wɜːðɪ] *adj* lobenswert.

pram [præm] *n UK* Kinderwagen *der*.

prance [prɑːns] *vi* - **1.** [vain person] (herum)ǀstolzieren; [child] herumǀhüpfen - **2.** [horse] tänzeln.

prank [præŋk] *n* Streich *der*.

prawn [prɔːn] *n* Garnele *die*.

pray [preɪ] *vi* RELIG beten; **to pray to God** zu Gott beten.

prayer [preəʳ] *n* - **1.** *(U)* [act of praying] Beten *das*, Gebet *das* - **2.** [set of words] Gebet *das* - **3.** *fig* [strong hope] starke Hoffnung.

prayer book *n* Gebetsbuch *das*.

preach [priːtʃ] <> *vt liter & fig* predigen. <> *vi* - **1.** RELIG predigen - **2.** *pej* [pontificate]: **to preach (at sb)** (jm) eine Predigt halten.

preacher ['priːtʃəʳ] *n* Prediger *der*, -in *die*.

precarious [prɪ'keərɪəs] *adj* wackelig; [situation] prekär.

precaution [prɪ'kɔːʃn] *n* Vorsichtsmaßnahme *die*.

precede [prɪ'siːd] *vt* vorausǀgehen *(+ D)*.

precedence ['presɪdəns] *n*: **to take precedence over sb/sthg** den Vorrang vor jm/gegenüber etw haben.

precedent ['presɪdənt] *n* Präzedenzfall *der*.

precinct ['priːsɪŋkt] *n* - **1.** *UK* [for pedestrians] Fußgängerzone *die*; [for shopping] verkehrsfreies Einkaufsviertel - **2.** *US* [district] Bezirk *der*; **police precinct** Polizeirevier *das*.
◈ **precincts** *npl* [around building] Umgebung *die*, Bereich *der*.

precious ['preʃəs] *adj* - **1.** [gen] kostbar - **2.** *inf iro* [damned] verflixt, verdammt - **3.** [affected] affektiert.

precipice ['presɪpɪs] *n* Steilwand *die*.

precise [prɪ'saɪs] *adj* genau.

precisely [prɪ'saɪslɪ] *adv* genau.

precision [prɪ'sɪʒn] *n (U)* Genauigkeit *die*.

preclude [prɪ'kluːd] *vt fml* [possibility, misunderstanding] ausǀschließen; [event, action] unmöglich machen; **to preclude sb from doing sthg** es jm unmöglich machen, etw zu tun.

precocious [prɪ'kəʊʃəs] *adj* frühreif.

preconceived [,priːkən'siːvd] *adj* vorgefasst.

precondition [,priːkən'dɪʃn] *n fml* (Vor)bedingung *die*.

predator ['predətəʳ] *n* [animal] Raubtier *das*; [bird] Raubvogel *der*.

predecessor ['priːdɪsesəʳ] *n* - **1.** [person] Vorgänger *der*, -in *die* - **2.** [thing] Vorläufer *der*.

predicament [prɪ'dɪkəmənt] *n* missliche Lage.

predict [prɪ'dɪkt] *vt* vorherǀsagen.

predictable [prɪ'dɪktəbl] *adj* [result, reaction] vorhersehbar; [person, behaviour] berechenbar.

prediction [prɪ'dɪkʃn] *n* [something foretold] Voraussage *die*.

predispose [,priːdɪs'pəʊz] *vt*: **to be predisposed to do sthg** dazu neigen, etw zu tun; **to be predisposed to sthg** zu etw neigen.

predominant [prɪ'dɒmɪnənt] *adj* vorherrschend.

predominantly [prɪ'dɒmɪnəntlɪ] *adv* überwiegend.

preempt [,priː'empt] *vt* zuvorǀkommen *(+ D)*.

preen [priːn] *vt* - **1.** [subj: bird] putzen - **2.** *fig* [subj: person]: **to preen o.s.** sich zurechtǀmachen.

prefab ['priːfæb] *n inf* Fertighaus *das*.

preface ['prefɪs] *n* [in book] Vorwort *das*; **preface to sthg** [to text] Vorwort einer Sache *(G)*; [to speech] Einleitung *die* einer Sache *(G)*.

prefect ['priːfekt] *n UK* [pupil] Aufsichtsschüler *der*, -in *die*.

prefer [prɪ'fɜːʳ] *vt* vor|ziehen, bevorzugen; **to prefer sthg to sthg** etw etw *(D)* vor|ziehen; **to prefer to do sthg** es vor|ziehen, etw zu tun.

preferable ['prefrəbl] *adj*: **to be preferable (to sthg)** (etw *(D)*) vorzuziehen sein.

preferably ['prefrəblɪ] *adv* vorzugsweise.

preference ['prefərəns] *n* - **1.** [liking]: **preference (for sthg)** Vorliebe *die* (für etw) - **2.** [precedence]: **to give sb/sthg preference, to give preference to sb/sthg** jm/etw den Vorzug geben.

preferential [ˌprefə'renʃl] *adj* [treatment] bevorzugt.

prefix ['priːfɪks] *n* GRAM Präfix *das*.

pregnancy ['pregnənsɪ] *n* Schwangerschaft *die*.

pregnant ['pregnənt] *adj* [woman] schwanger; [animal] trächtig.

prehistoric [ˌpriːhɪ'stɒrɪk] *adj* prähistorisch, vorgeschichtlich.

prejudice ['predʒʊdɪs] ◇ *n* [bias]: **prejudice (against)** Vorurteil *das* (gegen). ◇ *vt* [jeopardize] schaden *(+ D)*.

prejudiced ['predʒʊdɪst] *adj* voreingenommen.

prejudicial [ˌpredʒʊ'dɪʃl] *adj*: **to be prejudicial to sb** für jn schädlich sein; **to be prejudicial to sthg** einer Sache *(D)* abträglich sein.

preliminary [prɪ'lɪmɪnərɪ] *adj* [activity] vorbereitend; [talks, investigation] Vor-; [report, results] vorläufig.

prelude ['preljuːd] *n* [event]: **prelude to sthg** Auftakt *der* zu etw.

premarital [ˌpriː'mærɪtl] *adj* vor der Ehe.

premature ['preməˌtjʊəʳ] *adj* - **1.** [death, baldness] vorzeitig - **2.**: **premature birth/child** Frühgeburt *die* - **3.** *pej* [decision, action] übereilt.

premeditated [ˌpriː'medɪteɪtɪd] *adj* vorsätzlich.

premenstrual syndrome, premenstrual tension [priːˌmenstrʊəl-] *n* prämenstruelles Syndrom.

premier ['premjəʳ] ◇ *adj* führend. ◇ *n* Premierminister *der*, -in *die*.

premiere ['premɪeəʳ] *n* Premiere *die*.

premise ['premɪs] *n* Voraussetzung *die*. ◆ **premises** *npl* Räumlichkeiten *Pl*; **on the premises** im Hause.

premium ['priːmɪəm] *n* - **1.**: **to sell sthg at a premium** [above usual value] etw über Wert verkaufen; **to be at a premium** [in great demand] sehr gefragt sein - **2.** [insurance payment] Prämie *die*.

premium bond *n UK* Prämienanleihe *die*, *britische Staatsanleihe, die eine monatliche Verlosungsteilnahme beinhaltet*.

premonition [ˌpremə'nɪʃn] *n* Vorahnung *die*.

preoccupied [priː'ɒkjʊpaɪd] *adj* in Gedanken vertieft OR versunken; **to be preoccupied with sthg** mit etw beschäftigt sein.

prepaid ['priːpeɪd] *adj* [envelope] portofrei; [items] im Voraus bezahlt.

preparation [ˌprepə'reɪʃn] *n* - **1.** *(U)* [act of preparing] Vorbereitung *die* - **2.** [prepared mixture - food] Fertigmischung *die*; [- medicine, cosmetics] Präparat *das*. ◆ **preparations** *npl* [plans] Vorbereitungen *Pl*.

preparatory [prɪ'pærətrɪ] *adj* vorbereitend.

preparatory school *n* - **1.** [in UK] *private Grundschule, die auf die Aufnahme in eine Public School vorbereitet* - **2.** [in US] *private höhere Schule, die auf die Aufnahme in eine Hochschule vorbereitet*.

prepare [prɪ'peəʳ] ◇ *vt* - **1.** [make ready] vor|bereiten; **to prepare to do sthg** sich an|schicken, etw zu tun - **2.** [make, assemble] zu|bereiten. ◇ *vi*: **to prepare for sthg** sich auf etw *(A)* vor|bereiten.

prepared [prɪ'peəd] *adj* - **1.** [organized, done beforehand] vorbereitet - **2.** [willing]: **to be prepared to do sthg** bereit sein, etw zu tun - **3.** [ready]: **to be prepared for sthg** auf etw *(A)* vorbereitet sein.

preposition [ˌprepə'zɪʃn] *n* Präposition *die*.

preposterous [prɪ'pɒstərəs] *adj* absurd.

prep school *n abbr of* **preparatory school**.

prerequisite [ˌpriː'rekwɪzɪt] *n*: **prerequisite (of** OR **for)** Voraussetzung *die* (für).

prerogative [prɪ'rɒgətɪv] *n* Vorrecht *das*.

preschool [ˌpriː'skuːl] *adj* Vorschul-.

prescribe [prɪ'skraɪb] *vt* - **1.** MED verschreiben - **2.** [order] vor|schreiben.

prescription [prɪ'skrɪpʃn] *n* MED Rezept *das*.

presence ['prezns] *n* - **1.** [being present] Anwesenheit *die*, Gegenwart *die*; **in his presence** in seiner Gegenwart - **2.** *(U)* [personality, charisma] Ausstrahlung *die*.

presence of mind *n* Geistesgegenwart *die*.

present ◇ *adj* ['preznt] - **1.** [current] gegenwärtig, derzeitig - **2.** [in attendance] anwesend; **to be present at sthg** bei etw anwesend sein. ◇ *n* ['preznt] - **1.** [current time]: **the present** die Gegenwart; **at present** zur Zeit - **2.** [gift] Geschenk *das* - **3.** GRAM: **present (tense)** Präsens *das*, Gegenwart *die*. ◇ *vt* [prɪ'zent] - **1.** [gift, award] überreichen; **to present sb with sthg, to present sthg to sb** jm etw überreichen - **2.** [opportunity] bieten; [problem] auf|werfen - **3.** [introduce - person] vor|stellen; *(phrase)*: **to present sb to sb** jm jn vor|stellen - **4.** [TV, radio programme] moderieren - **5.** [facts, figures, report] vor|legen - **6.** [portray] dar|stellen - **7.** [arrive, go]: **to present o.s.** [at reception] sich melden; [for interview] erscheinen - **8.** [perform] dar|bieten.

presentable [prɪ'zentəbl] *adj* präsentabel.

presentation [ˌprezn'teɪʃn] *n* - **1.** *(U)* [publication, broadcasting] Präsentation *die* - **2.** *(U)* [of product] Aufmachung *die*; [of policy, text] Präsentation *die* - **3.** [ceremony] Verleihung *die* - **4.** [talk] Präsentation *die* - **5.** [performance] Darbietung *die*.

present day *n*: **the present day** der heutige Tag, jetzt. ◆ **present-day** *adj* heutig.

presenter [prɪ'zentəʳ] *n UK* Moderator *der*, -in *die*.

presently ['prezəntlɪ] *adv* - **1.** [soon] bald - **2.** [now] gegenwärtig, jetzt.

preservation [ˌprezə'veɪʃn] *n (U)* - **1.** [of democracy, law and order] Aufrechterhaltung *die*; [of building, wildlife, countryside] Erhaltung *die* - **2.** [of food] Konservierung *die*.

preservative [prɪ'zɜːvətɪv] *n* [in food] Konservierungsmittel *das*; [for wood] Schutzmittel *das*.

preserve [prɪ'zɜːv] ◇ *vt* - **1.** [democracy, peace, situation] aufrecht|erhalten; [building, wildlife, way of life] erhalten - **2.** [food] konservieren; [fruit] ein|wecken. ◇ *n* [jam] Konfitüre *die*.

preset [ˌpriː'set] *(pt & pp inv) vt* [oven] vor|heizen; [VCR] programmieren.

president ['prezɪdənt] *n* Präsident *der*, -in *die*.

presidential [ˌprezɪ'denʃl] *adj* [decision] des Präsidenten; [campaign, election] Präsidentschafts-; [staff, limousine] Präsidenten-.

press [pres] ◇ *n* - **1.** [push]: **to give sthg a press** etw drücken; **at the press of a button** auf Knopfdruck - **2.** [journalism]: **the press** die Presse - **3.** [printing machine, pressing machine] Presse *die*. ◇ *vt* - **1.** [push firmly] drücken; **to press sthg against sthg** etw gegen etw pressen - **2.** [squeeze] drücken; [grapes] keltern; [flowers] pressen - **3.** [iron] bügeln - **4.** [urge, force] drängen; **to press sb to do sthg** *OR* **into doing sthg** jn drängen *OR* zwingen, etw zu tun - **5.** [pursue - claim, point] beharren auf. ◇ *vi* - **1.** [push hard]: **to press (on)** drücken (auf *(+ A)*) - **2.** [surge] drängen. ◆ **press on** *vi* [continue]: **to press on with** weiter|machen (mit).

press agency *n* Presseagentur *die*.

press conference *n* Pressekonferenz *die*.

pressed [prest] *adj*: **to be pressed for time/money** unter Zeitdruck/finanziellem Druck stehen.

pressing ['presɪŋ] *adj* [urgent] dringend.

press officer *n* Pressesprecher *der*, -in *die*.

press release *n* Pressemitteilung *die*.

press-stud *n UK* Druckknopf *der*.

press-up *n UK* Liegestütz *der*.

pressure ['preʃəʳ] *n (U) liter & fig* Druck *der*; **to put pressure on sb (to do sthg)** auf jn Druck aus|üben (, etw zu tun).

pressure cooker *n* Schnellkochtopf *der*.

pressure gauge *n* Druckmesser *der*.

pressure group *n* Interessengruppe *die*.

pressurize, -ise ['preʃəraɪz] *vt* - **1.** TECH unter Druck setzen - **2.** *UK* [force]: **to pressurize sb to do** *OR* **into doing sthg** jn (dazu) drängen, etw zu tun.

prestige [pre'stiːʒ] *n* Prestige *das*.

presumably [prɪ'zjuːməblɪ] *adv* vermutlich.

presume [prɪ'zjuːm] *vt* [assume] an|nehmen; **to presume (that)...** an|nehmen, dass...; **he is presumed dead** es wird davon ausgegangen, dass er tot ist.

presumption [prɪ'zʌmpʃn] *n* - **1.** [assumption] Annahme *die* - **2.** *(U)* [audacity] Vermessenheit *die*.

presumptuous [prɪ'zʌmptʃʊəs] *adj* anmaßend.

pretence, pretense *US* [prɪ'tens] *n*: **he made no pretence of being interested** er gab nicht vor, interessiert zu sein; **under false pretences** unter Vortäuschung falscher Tatsachen.

pretend [prɪ'tend] ◇ *vt* - **1.** [make believe]: **to pretend to do sthg** vorgeben, etw zu tun; **to pretend (that)...** tun, als ob... - **2.** [claim]: **to pretend to do sthg** behaupten, dass man etw tut. ◇ *vi* [feign] nur so tun.

pretense *n US* = **pretence**.

pretension [prɪ'tenʃn] *n* [claim] Anspruch *der*.

pretentious [prɪ'tenʃəs] *adj* [person] wichtigtuerisch; [film, book] prätentiös.

pretext ['priːtekst] *n* Vorwand *der*; **on** *OR* **under the pretext that...** unter dem Vorwand, dass...; **on** *OR* **under the pretext of doing sthg** unter dem Vorwand, etw zu tun wollen.

pretty ['prɪtɪ] ◇ *adj* hübsch. ◇ *adv* [quite, rather] ziemlich; **pretty much** *OR* **well** so ziemlich.

prevail [prɪ'veɪl] *vi* - **1.** [be widespread] vor|herrschen; [custom] weit verbreitet sein - **2.** [triumph] sich durch|setzen; **to prevail over sb/sthg** sich gegen jn/etw durch|setzen - **3.** [persuade]: **to prevail (up)on sb to do sthg** jn dazu bringen, etw zu tun.

prevailing [prɪ'veɪlɪŋ] *adj* - **1.** [belief, opinion] vorherrschend; [fashion] aktuell - **2.** [wind] vorherrschend.

prevalent ['prevələnt] *adj* vorherrschend; [illness] weitverbreitet.

prevent [prɪ'vent] *vt* verhindern; [illness] vor|beugen *(+ D)*; **to prevent sb (from) doing sthg** jn daran hindern, etw zu tun.

preventive [prɪ'ventɪv] *adj* vorbeugend; [measures, medicine] Präventiv-.

preview ['priːvjuː] *n* - **1.** [early showing - of film, play] Voraufführung *die*; [- of exhibition] Vorbesichtigung *die* - **2.** [trailer for films] Vorschau *die*.

previous ['priːvɪəs] *adj* - **1.** [earlier, prior] früher; **previous conviction** Vorstrafe *die* - **2.** [with days and dates] vorhergehend; **in previous years** in früheren Jahren - **3.** [former] vorherig.

previously ['priːvɪəslɪ] *adv* - **1.** [formerly] vorher - **2.** [with days and dates] zuvor.

prewar [ˌpriː'wɔːʳ] *adj* Vorkriegs-.

prey [preɪ] *n (U)* Beute *die*. ◆ **prey on** *vt insep* - **1.** [subj: animal, bird] Beute machen auf *(+ A)* - **2.** [trouble]: **to prey on sb's mind** jn bedrücken.

price [praɪs] ◇ *n* - **1.** [cost] Preis *der* - **2.** [value] Wert *der*; **to be without price** (mit Geld) nicht zu bezahlen sein. ◇ *vt* [set cost of] den Preis fest|setzen von; **it was priced at £100** es sollte 100 Pfund kosten.

priceless ['praɪslɪs] *adj* - **1.** [very valuable] von unschätzbarem Wert - **2.** *inf* [funny] wahnsinnig komisch.

price list *n* Preisliste *die*.

price tag *n* [label] Preisschild *das*.

pricey ['praɪsɪ] (*comp* **-ier**, *superl* **-iest**) *adj inf* teuer.

prick [prɪk] ◇ *n* - **1.** [scratch, wound] Stich *der* - **2.** *vulg* [penis] Schwanz *der* - **3.** *vulg* [stupid person] Arschloch *das*. ◇ *vt* [jab, pierce] stechen in *(+ A)*; **to prick one's finger** sich *(D)* in den Finger stechen. ◆ **prick up** *vt sep*: **to prick up one's ears** *liter* & *fig* seine Ohren spitzen.

prickle ['prɪkl] ◇ *n* - **1.** [thorn] Stachel *der* - **2.** [sensation] Prickeln *das*. ◇ *vi* prickeln.

prickly ['prɪklɪ] *adj* - **1.** [thorny] stachelig - **2.** *fig* [touchy] reizbar.

pride [praɪd] ◇ *n* Stolz *der*; **to take pride in sthg** auf etw *(A)* stolz sein. ◇ *vt*: **to pride o.s. on sthg** auf etw *(A)* stolz sein.

priest [priːst] *n* Priester *der*.

priestess ['priːstɪs] *n* Priesterin *die*.

priesthood ['priːsthʊd] *n (U)* - **1.** [position, office]: **the priesthood** das Priesteramt - **2.** [priests collectively]: **the priesthood** die Priesterschaft.

prig [prɪg] *n* Tugendbold *der*.

prim [prɪm] *adj* [person, behaviour] sittsam.

primarily ['praɪmərɪlɪ] *adv* in erster Linie.

primary ['praɪmərɪ] ◇ *adj* [main - concern, aim, reason] Haupt-. ◇ *n US* POL Vorwahl *die (zur Bestimmung der Präsidentschaftskandidaten einer Partei)*.

primary school *n* Grundschule *die*.

primary teacher *n* [in UK] Grundschullehrer *der*, -in *die*.

primate ['praɪmeɪt] *n* - **1.** ZOOL Primat *der* - **2.** RELIG Primas *der*.

prime [praɪm] ◇ *adj* - **1.** [main - concern, aim, reason] Haupt- - **2.** [excellent] erstklassig. ◇ *n* [peak]: **to be in one's prime** in den besten Jahren sein. ◇ *vt* [paint] grundieren.

prime minister *n* Premierminister *der*, -in *die*.

primer ['praɪməʳ] *n* - **1.** [paint] Grundierung *die* - **2.** [textbook] Fibel *die*.

primitive ['prɪmɪtɪv] *adj* primitiv.

primrose ['prɪmrəʊz] *n* Himmelschlüssel *der*.

Primus stove® ['praɪməs-] *n* Campingkocher *der*.

prince [prɪns] *n* - **1.** [son of king, queen] Prinz *der* - **2.** [ruler] Fürst *der*.

princess [prɪn'ses] *n* Prinzessin *die*.

principal ['prɪnsəpl] ◇ *adj* Haupt-. ◇ *n* [of school, college] Direktor *der*, -in *die*.

principle ['prɪnsəpl] *n* - **1.** [gen] Prinzip *das* - **2.** [integrity] Prinzipien *Pl*; **to do sthg on principle** OR **as a matter of principle** etw aus Prinzip tun. ◆ **in principle** *adv* im Prinzip.

print [prɪnt] ◇ *n* - **1.** *(U)* [printed characters] Schrift *die*; [printed matter] Gedruckte *das*; **in large/small print** groß/klein gedruckt; **in print** [available] erhältlich; [in newspaper] gedruckt; **to be out of print** vergriffen sein - **2.** ART Druck *der* - **3.** [photograph] Abzug *der* - **4.** [fabric] bedruckter Stoff - **5.** [footprint, fingerprint] Abdruck *der*. ◇ *vt* - **1.** [gen] drucken - **2.** [write clearly] in Druckschrift schreiben. ◇ *vi* [printer] drucken. ◆ **print out** *vt sep* COMPUT aus|drucken.

printed matter ['prɪntɪd-] *n (U)* Drucksache *die*.

printer ['prɪntəʳ] *n* [person & COMPUT] Drucker *der*; [firm] Druckerei *die*.

printing ['prɪntɪŋ] *n (U)* - **1.** [act] Drucken *das* - **2.** [trade] Druckereigewerbe *das*.

printout ['prɪntaʊt] *n* Ausdruck *der*.

prior ['praɪəʳ] ◇ *adj* - **1.** [previous - agreement] vorherig; [- warning] Vor-; **a prior engagement** eine anderweitige Verpflichtung - **2.** [more important] vorrangig. ◇ *n* [monk] Prior *der*. ◆ **prior to** *prep* vor *(+ D)*; **prior to leaving** bevor ich/er/*etc* ging.

priority [praɪ'ɒrətɪ] *n* - **1.** [matter] vordringliche Sache - **2.** [urgency] Vorrang *der*; **to have** OR **take priority (over sthg)** Vorrang (vor etw *(D)*) haben.

prise [praɪz] *vt*: **to prise sthg open** etw auf|brechen.

prison ['prɪzn] *n* Gefängnis *das*.

prisoner ['prɪznəʳ] *n* Gefangene *der, die*.

prisoner of war (*pl* **prisoners of war**) *n* Kriegsgefangene *der, die*.

privacy [*UK* 'prɪvəsɪ, *US* 'praɪvəsɪ] *n (U)* Privatsphäre *die*.

private ['praɪvɪt] ◇ *adj* - **1.** [gen] privat; [hospital, house, industry, life] Privat- - **2.** [confidential] vertraulich - **3.** [personal - belongings, plans] persönlich - **4.** [secluded] abgelegen

- 5. [reserved] in sich zurückgezogen. ◇ n - 1. [soldier] einfacher Soldat; **Private Smith** Soldat Smith - 2. [secrecy]: **in private** [of conversation between two people] unter vier Augen; [of meeting] hinter geschlossenen Türen.

private enterprise *n (U)* freies Unternehmertum.

private eye *n* Privatdetektiv *der*, -in *die*.

privately ['praɪvɪtlɪ] *adv* - 1. [not by the state] privat; **privately owned** in Privatbesitz - 2. [confidentially - discuss between two people] unter vier Augen; [- discuss in meeting] hinter verschlossenen Türen; [- meet, agree] insgeheim - 3. [personally] persönlich.

private property *n (U)* Privatgrundstück *das*.

private school *n* Privatschule *die*.

privatize, -ise ['praɪvɪtaɪz] *vt* privatisieren.

privet ['prɪvɪt] *n (U)* Liguster *der*.

privilege ['prɪvɪlɪdʒ] *n* - 1. [special advantage] Privileg *das* - 2. [honour] Ehre *die*.

privy ['prɪvɪ] *adj*: **to be privy to sthg** *fml* in etw *(A)* eingeweiht sein.

prize [praɪz] ◇ *adj* - 1. [prizewinning] preisgekrönt - 2. [perfect]: **prize idiot** Vollidiot. ◇ *n* Preis *der*. ◇ *vt* [value] (hoch)|schätzen.

prize-giving [-ˌgɪvɪŋ] *n UK* Preisverleihung *die*.

prizewinner ['praɪzˌwɪnəʳ] *n* Preisträger *der*, -in *die*.

pro [prəʊ] *n* - 1. *inf* [professional] Profi *der* - 2. [advantage]: **the pros and cons** das Für und Wider.

probability [ˌprɒbə'bɪlətɪ] *n* [gen] Wahrscheinlichkeit *die*.

probable ['prɒbəbl] *adj* wahrscheinlich.

probably ['prɒbəblɪ] *adv* wahrscheinlich.

probation [prə'beɪʃn] *n (U)* - 1. [of prisoner] Bewährung *die*; **to put sb on probation** jm Bewährung geben - 2. [trial period] Probezeit *die*; **I'm on probation** ich bin in der Probezeit.

probe [prəʊb] ◇ *n* - 1. [investigation]: **probe (into)** Untersuchung *die (+ G)* - 2. MED & TECH Sonde *die*. ◇ *vt* - 1. [investigate] sondieren; [mystery] erforschen - 2. [prod - with stick] suchend herum|stochern in *(+ D)*.

problem ['prɒbləm] ◇ *n* Problem *das*; **no problem!** *inf* kein Problem! ◇ *comp* Problem-.

procedure [prə'siːdʒəʳ] *n* Verfahren *das*.

proceed ◇ *vt* [prə'siːd]: **to proceed to do sthg** dazu übergehen, etw zu tun. ◇ *vi* [prə'siːd] - 1. [continue] fort|fahren; [activity] fortgesetzt werden; [event] weiter|gehen; **to proceed with sthg** mit etw fort|fahren - 2. *fml* [go, advance - on foot] gehen; [- in vehicle] fahren; **to proceed somewhere** sich irgendwohin begeben. ◈ **proceeds** *npl* ['prəʊsiːdz] Erlös *der*.

proceedings [prə'siːdɪŋz] *npl* - 1. [series of actions] Vorgänge *Pl*; [event] Veranstaltung *die* - 2. [legal action] Verfahren *das*.

process ['prəʊses] ◇ *n* - 1. [series of actions] Prozess *der*; **electoral process** Wahlverfahren *das*; **in the process** dabei; **to be in the process of doing sthg** dabei sein, etw zu tun - 2. [method] Verfahren *das*. ◇ *vt* - 1. [treat - materials] verarbeiten; [- food] behandeln - 2. [examine, deal with - application] bearbeiten; [- information, data] verarbeiten.

processing ['prəʊsesɪŋ] *n (U)* - 1. [treating - of materials] Verarbeitung *die*; [- of food] Behandeln *das* - 2. [examining - of applications] Bearbeitung *die*; [- of information, data] Verarbeitung *die*.

procession [prə'seʃn] *n* Zug *der*; **in procession** in einem langen Zug.

proclaim [prə'kleɪm] *vt* [independence] proklamieren; [innocence, loyalty] beteuern; **to proclaim sb king** jn zum König ernennen.

procure [prə'kjʊəʳ] *vt* [tickets, supplies] beschaffen; [somebody's release] bewirken.

prod [prɒd] *vt* [push, poke - person] an|stupsen; [- ground, food] herum|stochern in *(+ D)*.

prodigy ['prɒdɪdʒɪ] *n* Wunderkind *das*.

produce ◇ *n* ['prɒdjuːs] *(U)* - 1. [goods] Erzeugnisse *Pl* - 2. [fruit and vegetables] Obst und Gemüse *das*. ◇ *vt* [prə'djuːs] - 1. [manufacture, make] produzieren; [work of art] schaffen - 2. [yield - raw materials] liefern; [- heat, crop, gas] erzeugen; [- interest, profit] ein|bringen - 3. [cause - results, agreements] erzielen; [- disaster] hervor|rufen - 4. [give birth to - subj: woman] gebären; [- subj: animal] werfen - 5. [leaves, flowers] hervor|bringen - 6. [present, show - evidence, argument] liefern; [- passport, letter] vor|zeigen - 7. [gen] produzieren.

producer [prə'djuːsəʳ] *n* - 1. [gen] Produzent *der*, -in *die* - 2. [manufacturer] Hersteller *der*, -in *die*.

product ['prɒdʌkt] *n* [thing manufactured or grown] Produkt *das*.

production [prə'dʌkʃn] *n* - 1. *(U)* [process - of goods] Produktion *die*; [- of electricity, heat] Erzeugung *die*; [- of blood cells] Bildung *die* - 2. *(U)* [output] Produktion *die* - 3. CIN, THEAT & TV Produktion *die*.

production line *n* Fertigungsstraße *die*.

productive [prə'dʌktɪv] *adj* - 1. [worker] produktiv; [land] ertragreich; [business] leistungsfähig - 2. [meeting, relationship, experience] Gewinn bringend.

productivity [ˌprɒdʌk'tɪvətɪ] *n* Produktivität *die*.

profane [prə'feɪn] *adj* [vulgar] gotteslästerlich.

profession [prə'feʃn] *n* - **1.** [career] Beruf *der*; **by profession** von Beruf - **2.** [body of people] Berufsstand *der*; **the medical/teaching profession** die Ärzteschaft/Lehrerschaft.

professional [prə'feʃənl] <> *adj* - **1.** [relating to a profession - qualifications] beruflich; [- advice, help, opinion] fachmännisch; **professional people** hochqualifizierte Personen - **2.** [full-time, of high standard] professionell; [army, actor] Berufs-; [footballer] Profi-. <> *n* - **1.** [full-time sportsperson] Profi *der*; [full-time actor] Berufsschauspieler *der* - **2.** [skilled person]: **he's a real professional** er ist ein echter Profi.

professor [prə'fesəʳ] *n* - **1.** *UK* [head of department] Professor *der*, -in *die* - **2.** *US & Canada* [teacher, lecturer] Dozent *der*, -in *die*.

proficiency [prə'fɪʃənsɪ] *n (U)*: **proficiency (in)** Kompetenz *die* (in *(+ D)*).

profile ['prəʊfaɪl] *n* - **1.** [outline of face] Profil *das*; **to keep a low profile** *fig* sich unauffällig verhalten - **2.** [biography] Porträt *das*.

profit ['prɒfɪt] <> *n* - **1.** [financial gain] Gewinn *der*, Profit *der* - **2.** [advantage]: **you may learn something to your profit** du könntest etwas lernen, was nützlich für dich ist. <> *vi*: **to profit (from** OR **by sthg)** (von etw) profitieren.

profitability [ˌprɒfɪtə'bɪlətɪ] *n* Rentabilität *die*.

profitable ['prɒfɪtəbl] *adj* Gewinn bringend.

profound [prə'faʊnd] *adj* - **1.** [intense - feeling, silence] tief; [- change] tief greifend; [- effect] nachhaltig - **2.** [penetrating, wise - idea, book] tiefgründig.

profusely [prə'fju:slɪ] *adv* - **1.** [bleed, sweat] sehr stark - **2.** [thank] überschwänglich; **to apologize profusely** sich vielmals entschuldigen.

profusion [prə'fju:ʒn] *n*: **profusion (of)** (Über)fülle *die* (von).

prognosis [prɒg'nəʊsɪs] (*pl* **-noses** [-'nəʊsi:z]) *n* Prognose *die*.

program ['prəʊgræm] (*pt & pp* **-med** OR **-ed**, *cont* **-ming** OR **-ing**) <> *n* - **1.** COMPUT Programm *das* - **2.** *US* = **programme**. <> *vt* - **1.** COMPUT programmieren - **2.** *US* = **programme**.

programer *n US* = **programmer**.

programme *UK*, **program** *US* ['prəʊgræm] <> *n* - **1.** [gen] Programm *das* - **2.** RADIO & TV Sendung *die*. <> *vt* programmieren.

programmer *UK*, **programer** *US* ['prəʊgræməʳ] *n* COMPUT Programmierer *der*, -in *die*.

programming ['prəʊgræmɪŋ] *n* COMPUT Programmieren *das*.

progress <> *n* ['prəʊgres] - **1.** [physical movement] Vorwärtskommen *das* - **2.** [headway] Voranschreiten *das*; **to make progress (in sthg)** (bei etw) Fortschritte machen; **in progress** im Gange - **3.** [evolution] Fortschritt *der*. <> *vi* [prə'gres] - **1.** [improve - science, technology, work] voran|kommen; [- patient, student] Fortschritte machen - **2.** [continue]: **as the journey/meeting progressed** im Laufe der Reise/des Treffens.

progressive [prə'gresɪv] *adj* - **1.** [forward-looking] fortschrittlich - **2.** [gradual] fortschreitend.

prohibit [prə'hɪbɪt] *vt* verbieten; **to prohibit sb from doing sthg** jm verbieten, etw zu tun.

project <> *n* ['prɒdʒekt] - **1.** [plan, idea] Vorhaben *das*, Projekt *das* - **2.** SCH [study] Projekt *das*. <> *vt* [prə'dʒekt] - **1.** [plan] planen - **2.** [estimate] voraus|sagen; [costs] überschlagen - **3.** [film, light] projizieren - **4.** [present] dar|stellen; [image] vermitteln. <> *vi* [prə'dʒekt] [jut out] hervor|ragen.

projectile [prə'dʒektaɪl] *n* Geschoss *das*.

projection [prə'dʒekʃn] *n* - **1.** [estimate] Voraussage *die*; [of costs] Überschlagen *das* - **2.** *(U)* [of film, light] Projektion *die*.

projector [prə'dʒektəʳ] *n* Projektor *der*.

proletariat [ˌprəʊlɪ'teərɪət] *n* Proletariat *das*.

prolific [prə'lɪfɪk] *adj* sehr produktiv.

prologue, prolog *US* ['prəʊlɒg] *n* - **1.** [introduction] Prolog *der* - **2.** *fig* [preceding event]: **to be the prologue to sthg** die Vorstufe für etw sein.

prolong [prə'lɒŋ] *vt* verlängern.

prom [prɒm] *n* - **1.** *UK inf* [at seaside] (*abbr of* **promenade**) Strandpromenade *die* - **2.** *US* [ball - at high school] Schulball *der*; [- at college] Studentenball *der*.

promenade [ˌprɒmə'nɑ:d] *n UK* [at seaside] Strandpromenade *die*.

prominent ['prɒmɪnənt] *adj* - **1.** [important - person] prominent; [- ideas, issues] wichtig - **2.** [noticeable - building, landmark] exponiert; [- features] markant.

promiscuous [prɒ'mɪskjʊəs] *adj* promiskuitiv.

promise ['prɒmɪs] <> *n* - **1.** [vow] Versprechen *das* - **2.** *(U)* [hope, prospect]: **promise (of)** Aussicht *die* (auf *(+ A)*). <> *vt* versprechen; **to promise sb sthg** jm etw versprechen; **to promise (sb) to do sthg** (jm) versprechen, etw zu tun. <> *vi* versprechen.

promising ['prɒmɪsɪŋ] *adj* vielversprechend.

promontory ['prɒməntrɪ] *n* Kap *das*.

promote [prəˈməʊt] *vt* - **1.** [foster] fördern - **2.** [push, advertise] Werbung machen für - **3.** [in job] befördern - **4.** SPORT: **to be promoted** auflsteigen.

promoter [prəˈməʊtəʳ] *n* - **1.** [of event, concert] Veranstalter *der*, -in *die* - **2.** [of cause, idea] Förderer *der*.

promotion [prəˈməʊʃn] *n* - **1.** [in job] Beförderung *die* - **2.** [advertising] Werbung *die* - **3.** [campaign] Werbekampagne *die*.

prompt [prɒmpt] ◇ *adj* - **1.** [quick] prompt; [action] sofortig - **2.** [punctual] pünktlich. ◇ *adv*: **at nine o'clock prompt** Punkt 9 Uhr. ◇ *vt* - **1.** [provoke, persuade]: **to prompt sb to do sthg** jn dazu veranlassen, etw zu tun - **2.** THEAT soufflieren *(+ D)*.

promptly [ˈprɒmptlɪ] *adv* - **1.** [quickly] prompt - **2.** [punctually] pünktlich.

prone [prəʊn] *adj* [susceptible]: **to be prone to sthg** zu etw neigen; **to be prone to do sthg** dazu neigen, etw zu tun.

prong [prɒŋ] *n* Zinke *die*.

pronoun [ˈprəʊnaʊn] *n* Pronomen *das*.

pronounce [prəˈnaʊns] *vt* - **1.** [say aloud] auslsprechen - **2.** [declare, state - verdict, opinion] verkünden; **to pronounce sb fit for work/dead** jn für arbeitsfähig/tot erklären.

pronounced [prəˈnaʊnst] *adj* [accent] stark; [improvement, deterioration] deutlich.

pronouncement [prəˈnaʊnsmənt] *n* Erklärung *die*.

pronunciation [prəˌnʌnsɪˈeɪʃn] *n* Aussprache *die*.

proof [pruːf] *n* - **1.** [evidence] Beweis *der* - **2.** PRESS [first copy] Korrekturfahne *die* - **3.** [of alcohol] Alkoholgehalt *der*.

prop [prɒp] ◇ *n liter & fig* Stütze *die*. ◇ *vt*: **to prop sthg against sthg** etw gegen etw lehnen. ◆ **props** *npl* [in film, play] Requisiten *Pl*. ◆ **prop up** *vt sep* - **1.** [support physically - wall] ablstützen; [- ladder] anllehnen - **2.** *fig* [sustain - regime] stützen; [- organization] unterstützen; [- company] vor dem Konkurs bewahren.

propel [prəˈpel] *vt* anltreiben.

propeller [prəˈpeləʳ] *n* [of plane] Propeller *der*; [of ship] Schraube *die*.

propensity [prəˈpensətɪ] *n fml*: **propensity for** OR **to sthg** Hang *der* zu etw; **to have a propensity to do sthg** dazu neigen, etw zu tun.

proper [ˈprɒpəʳ] *adj* - **1.** [real] richtig - **2.** [correct] korrekt - **3.** [decent] anständig.

properly [ˈprɒpəlɪ] *adv* - **1.** [satisfactorily, correctly] richtig - **2.** [decently] anständig.

proper noun *n* Eigenname *der*.

property [ˈprɒpətɪ] *n* - **1.** [possession] Eigentum *das* - **2.** [specific building] Haus *das*; [piece of land] Grundstück *das* - **3.** *(U)* [buildings, land] Immobilien *Pl* - **4.** [quality] Eigenschaft *die*.

property owner *n* [of house] Hausbesitzer *der*, -in *die*; [of land] Grundbesitzer *der*, -in *die*.

prophecy [ˈprɒfɪsɪ] *n* Prophezeiung *die*.

prophesy [ˈprɒfɪsaɪ] *vt* prophezeien.

prophet [ˈprɒfɪt] *n* RELIG Prophet *der*.

proportion [prəˈpɔːʃn] *n* - **1.** [part] Teil *der*, Anteil *der* - **2.** [ratio, comparison] Verhältnis *das* - **3.** *(U)* ART: **in proportion** in den richtigen Proportionen; **out of proportion** mit verschobenen Proportionen; **a sense of proportion** *fig* ein vernünftiger Maßstab.

proportional [prəˈpɔːʃənl] *adj* im Verhältnis stehend; MATHS proportional; **to be proportional to sthg** zu etw im Verhältnis stehen; MATHS zu etw proportional sein.

proportional representation *n (U)* Verhältniswahlsystem *das*.

proportionate [prəˈpɔːʃnət] *adj*: **proportionate (to sthg)** im Verhältnis (zu etw).

proposal [prəˈpəʊzl] *n* - **1.** [plan, suggestion] Vorschlag *der* - **2.** [offer of marriage] Heiratsantrag *der*.

propose [prəˈpəʊz] ◇ *vt* - **1.** [plan, solution, person] vorlschlagen; [toast] auslbringen - **2.** [motion] einlbringen, stellen - **3.** [intend]: **to propose doing** OR **to do sthg** vorlhaben OR beabsichtigen, etw zu tun. ◇ *vi*: **to propose (to sb)** (jm) einen Heiratsantrag machen.

proposition [ˌprɒpəˈzɪʃn] *n* - **1.** [statement of theory] These *die* - **2.** [suggestion] Vorschlag *der*.

proprietor [prəˈpraɪətəʳ] *n* Besitzer *der*, -in *die*.

propriety [prəˈpraɪətɪ] *n fml* [moral correctness] Anstand *der*.

pro rata [-ˈrɑːtə] *adj & adv* anteilig.

prose [prəʊz] *n* Prosa *die*.

prosecute [ˈprɒsɪkjuːt] *vt* LAW strafrechtlich verfolgen.

prosecution [ˌprɒsɪˈkjuːʃn] *n* - **1.** [criminal charge] strafrechtliche Verfolgung - **2.** [lawyers]: **the prosecution** die Anklage(vertretung).

prosecutor [ˈprɒsɪkjuːtəʳ] *n esp US* Ankläger *der*, -in *die*.

prospect ◇ *n* [ˈprɒspekt] Aussicht *die*. ◇ *vi* [prəˈspekt]: **to prospect (for sthg)** [gold] schürfen (nach etw); [oil] bohren (nach etw). ◆ **prospects** *npl*: **prospects (for sthg)** Aussichten *Pl* (auf etw *(A)*); **he has good prospects** er hat gute Erfolgschancen.

prospective [prəˈspektɪv] *adj* voraussichtlich.

prospectus [prəˈspektəs] *(pl* **-es**) *n* (Werbe)prospekt *der*.

prosper [ˈprɒspəʳ] *vi* [business, country] blühen; [person] Erfolg haben.

prosperity [prɒˈsperətɪ] *n* Wohlstand *der*.

prosperous ['prɒspərəs] *adj* [person] wohlhabend; [business, place] blühend.

prostitute ['prɒstɪtjuːt] *n* Prostituierte *die*; **(male) prostitute** Stricher *der*, Strichjunge *der*.

prostrate *adj* ['prɒstreɪt] [lying flat] (auf dem Bauch) ausgestreckt.

protagonist [prə'tægənɪst] *n* Hauptfigur *die*, Protagonist *der*, -in *die*.

protect [prə'tekt] *vt* schützen; **to protect sb/sthg from/against** jn/etw schützen vor *(+ D)*/gegen.

protection [prə'tekʃn] *n*: **protection (from/against)** Schutz *der* (vor *(+ D)*/gegen).

protective [prə'tektɪv] *adj* **- 1.** [layer, clothing] Schutz-, schützend **- 2.** [feelings, instinct] Beschützer-.

protein ['prəʊtiːn] *n* Protein *das*.

protest ◇ *n* ['prəʊtest] **- 1.** [complaint] Protest *der* **- 2.** [demonstration] Protestkundgebung *die*. ◇ *vt* [prə'test] **- 1.** [one's innocence] beteuern **- 2.** *US* [protest against] protestieren gegen. ◇ *vi* [prə'test] [complain]: **to protest (about/against sthg)** protestieren (gegen etw).

Protestant ['prɒtɪstənt] ◇ *adj* protestantisch. ◇ *n* Protestant *der*, -in *die*.

protester [prə'testəʳ] *n* [demonstrator] Protestierende *der*, *die*.

protest march *n* Protestmarsch *der*.

protocol ['prəʊtəkɒl] *n (U)* Protokoll *das*.

prototype ['prəʊtətaɪp] *n* Prototyp *der*.

protracted [prə'træktɪd] *adj* langwierig.

protrude [prə'truːd] *vi*: **to protrude (from sthg)** (aus etw) hervor|stehen.

protuberance [prə'tjuːbərəns] *n* Auswuchs *der*.

proud [praʊd] *adj* stolz; **to be proud of sb/sthg** auf jn/etw stolz sein.

prove [pruːv] (*pp* **-d** OR **proven**) *vt* **- 1.** [show to be true] beweisen **- 2.** [show o.s. to be]: **to prove (to be) sthg** sich als etw erweisen; **to prove o.s. to be sthg** sich als etw erweisen.

proven ['pruːvn, 'prəʊvn] ◇ *pp* ▷ **prove**. ◇ *adj* [fact] erwiesen, bewiesen; [liar] ausgewiesen.

proverb ['prɒvɜːb] *n* Sprichwort *das*.

provide [prə'vaɪd] *vt* [food, money, information] zur Verfügung stellen; [opportunity] bieten; **to provide sb with sthg, to provide sthg for sb** jm etw zur Verfügung stellen. ◆ **provide for** *vt insep* **- 1.** [support] sorgen für **- 2.** *fml* [make arrangements for] vor|sorgen für.

provided [prə'vaɪdɪd] ◆ **provided (that)** *conj* vorausgesetzt, dass.

providing [prə'vaɪdɪŋ] ◆ **providing (that)** *conj* vorausgesetzt, dass.

province ['prɒvɪns] *n* **- 1.** [part of country] Provinz *die* **- 2.** [specialist subject] Fachgebiet *das*; [area of responsibility] Aufgabenbereich *der*.

provincial [prə'vɪnʃl] *adj* **- 1.** [of a province] Provinz- **- 2.** *pej* [narrow-minded] provinziell.

provision [prə'vɪʒn] *n* **- 1.** [act of supplying] Bereitstellung *die* **- 2.** *(U)* [arrangement] Vorkehrung *die* **- 3.** [in agreement, law] Bestimmung *die*. ◆ **provisions** *npl* [supplies] Vorräte *Pl*.

provisional [prə'vɪʒənl] *adj* provisorisch.

proviso [prə'vaɪzəʊ] (*pl* **-s**) *n* Vorbehalt *der*; **with the proviso that...** unter dem Vorbehalt, dass...

provocative [prə'vɒkətɪv] *adj* **- 1.** [controversial] provokativ **- 2.** [sexy] aufreizend.

provoke [prə'vəʊk] *vt* **- 1.** [annoy] provozieren **- 2.** [cause - criticism, reaction] hervor|rufen, erregen; [- argument] provozieren.

prow [praʊ] *n* Bug *der*.

prowess ['praʊɪs] *n (U) fml* Erfahrenheit *die*.

prowl [praʊl] ◇ *n*: **to be on the prowl** (auf Beutezug) herum|streifen. ◇ *vt* durchstreifen. ◇ *vi* herum|streifen, umher|streifen.

prowler ['praʊləʳ] *n* Herumtreiber *der*, -in *die*.

proxy ['prɒksɪ] *n*: **by proxy** in Vertretung.

prudent ['pruːdnt] *adj* [person] umsichtig; [action] überlegt.

prudish ['pruːdɪʃ] *adj* prüde.

prune [pruːn] ◇ *n* [fruit] Backpflaume *die*. ◇ *vt* [hedge, tree] beschneiden.

pry [praɪ] *vi* neugierig sein; **to pry into sthg** seine Nase in etw stecken.

PS *n abbr of* **postscript**.

psalm [sɑːm] *n* Psalm *der*.

pseudonym ['sjuːdənɪm] *n* Pseudonym *das*.

psyche ['saɪkɪ] *n* Psyche *die*.

psychiatric [ˌsaɪkɪ'ætrɪk] *adj* [hospital, department] psychiatrisch; [illness, problem] psychisch.

psychiatrist [saɪ'kaɪətrɪst] *n* Psychiater *der*, -in *die*.

psychiatry [saɪ'kaɪətrɪ] *n (U)* Psychiatrie *die*.

psychic ['saɪkɪk] ◇ *adj* **- 1.** [clairvoyant - powers] übersinnlich; *(phrase)*: **she is psychic** sie hat übersinnliche Kräfte **- 2.** [mental] psychisch. ◇ *n* Person *die* mit übersinnlichen Kräften.

psychoanalysis [ˌsaɪkəʊə'næləsɪs] *n* Psychoanalyse *die*.

psychoanalyst [ˌsaɪkəʊ'ænəlɪst] *n* Psychoanalytiker *der*, -in *die*.

psychological [ˌsaɪkə'lɒdʒɪkl] *adj* psychologisch.

psychologist [saɪ'kɒlədʒɪst] *n* Psychologe *der*, -gin *die*.

psychology [saɪ'kɒlədʒɪ] *n* Psychologie *die*.

psychopath ['saɪkəpæθ] *n* Psychopath *der*, -in *die*.

psychotic [saɪ'kɒtɪk] ◇ *adj* psychotisch. ◇ *n* Psychotiker *der*, -in *die*.

pt - 1. *abbr of* **pint** - 2. (*abbr of* **point**) Pkt.

PTO (*abbr of* **please turn over**) b.w.

pub [pʌb] *n* Pub *der*, Bierlokal *das*.

puberty ['pju:bətɪ] *n* Pubertät *die*.

pubic ['pju:bɪk] *adj* Scham-.

public ['pʌblɪk] ◇ *adj* - 1. [of people in general, open to all] öffentlich - 2. [of, by the state] staatlich, Staats- - 3. [known to everyone]: **public figure** bekannte Persönlichkeit; **it's public knowledge that...** es ist allgemein bekannt, dass... ◇ *n*: **the public** die Öffentlichkeit; **in public** in der Öffentlichkeit.

public-address system *n* Lautsprecheranlage *die*.

publican ['pʌblɪkən] *n UK* Wirt *der*, -in *die*.

publication [ˌpʌblɪ'keɪʃn] *n* - 1. *(U)* [act of publishing] Veröffentlichung *die* - 2. [book, article] Publikation *die*.

public bar *n UK schlicht eingerichteter Teil eines Pubs, in dem die Getränke billiger als in der "Lounge Bar" sind.*

public company *n* Aktiengesellschaft *die*.

public convenience *n UK* öffentliche Toilette.

public holiday *n* gesetzlicher Feiertag.

public house *n UK fml* Gaststätte *die*.

publicity [pʌb'lɪsɪtɪ] *n (U)* - 1. [media attention] Publicity *die* - 2. [information] Werbung *die*, Reklame *die*.

publicize, -ise ['pʌblɪsaɪz] *vt* bekannt machen.

public limited company *n* ≃ Aktiengesellschaft *die*.

public opinion *n (U)* öffentliche Meinung.

public relations ◇ *n (U)* [work] Öffentlichkeitsarbeit *die*, Public Relations *Pl*. ◇ *npl*: **it would be good for public relations** es wäre gut für unser öffentliches Ansehen.

public school *n* - 1. *UK* [private school] höhere Privatschule - 2. *US & Scotland* [state school] staatliche Schule.

public transport *n (U)* öffentliche Verkehrsmittel *Pl*.

publish ['pʌblɪʃ] *vt* veröffentlichen.

publisher ['pʌblɪʃər] *n* - 1. [company] Verlag *der* - 2. [person] Verleger *der*, -in *die*.

publishing ['pʌblɪʃɪŋ] *n* Verlagswesen *das*.

pub lunch *n* Mittagessen *das* im Pub.

pucker ['pʌkər] *vt* [lips for kissing] spitzen.

pudding ['pʊdɪŋ] *n* - 1. [sweet food] Nachspeise *die* - 2. *(U) UK* [part of meal] Nachtisch *der*, Dessert *das*.

puddle ['pʌdl] *n* Pfütze *die*.

puff [pʌf] ◇ *n* - 1. [of cigarette, pipe] Zug *der* - 2.: **puff of wind** Windhauch *der*; **puff of smoke** Rauchwölkchen *das*. ◇ *vt* paffen. ◇ *vi* - 1. [smoke]: **to puff at** OR **on sthg** an etw *(D)* paffen - 2. [pant] keuchen, schnaufen. ◆ **puff out** *vt sep* [cheeks] auf|blasen; [chest] anschwellen lassen; [feathers] auf|plustern.

puffed [pʌft] *adj* [swollen]: **puffed up** angeschwollen.

puff pastry, puff paste *US n (U)* Blätterteig *der*.

puffy ['pʌfɪ] *adj* aufgedunsen.

pull [pʊl] ◇ *vt* - 1. [rope, hair] ziehen an *(+ D)*; [cart] ziehen; **to pull sthg to pieces** etw in Stücke reißen; *fig* etw scharf kritisieren - 2. [curtains - open] auf|ziehen; [- close] zu|ziehen - 3. [trigger] drücken; [lever] ziehen - 4. [take out - cork] heraus|ziehen; [- gun, tooth] ziehen - 5. [muscle, hamstring] sich *(D)* zerren - 6. [crowd, voters] an|ziehen. ◇ *vi* [tug with hand] ziehen. ◇ *n* - 1. [tug with hand] Ziehen *das*, Zug *der*; **to give the rope a pull** am Seil ziehen - 2. *(U)* [influence] Einfluss *der*. ◆ **pull apart** *vt sep* [separate] auseinander ziehen. ◆ **pull at** *vt insep* ziehen an *(+ D)*. ◆ **pull away** *vi* - 1. [from roadside]: **to pull away (from)** weg|ziehen (von) - 2. [in race]: **to pull away (from)** sich ab|setzen (von). ◆ **pull down** *vt sep* [demolish] ab|reißen. ◆ **pull in** *vi* [car, bus] an|halten; [train] ein|fahren. ◆ **pull off** *vt sep* - 1. [take off] aus|ziehen - 2. [succeed in - coup, robbery] landen; [- deal] an Land ziehen. ◆ **pull out** ◇ *vt sep* [withdraw] zurück|ziehen. ◇ *vi* - 1. [train] ab|fahren - 2. [vehicle - from kerb] ab|fahren; [- from lane] aus|scheren - 3. [withdraw] sich zurück|ziehen. ◆ **pull over** *vi* [vehicle, driver] an den Straßenrand fahren. ◆ **pull through** *vi* [patient] durch|kommen. ◆ **pull together** *vt sep*: **to pull o.s. together** sich zusammen|reißen. ◆ **pull up** ◇ *vt sep* - 1. [raise] hoch|ziehen - 2. [move closer] heran|ziehen. ◇ *vi* an|halten.

pulley ['pʊlɪ] (*pl* **-s**) *n* [wheel] Rolle *die*; [whole system] Flaschenzug *der*.

pullover ['pʊlˌəʊvər] *n* Pullover *der*.

pulp [pʌlp] ◇ *adj*: **pulp novel** Schundroman *der*; **pulp fiction** Schundliteratur *die*. ◇ *n* [soft mass] Brei *der*.

pulpit ['pʊlpɪt] *n* Kanzel *die*.

pulsate [pʌl'seɪt] *vi* pulsieren; [air, sound] vibrieren.

pulse [pʌls] ◇ *n* - 1. [in body] Puls *der* - 2. TECH Impuls *der*. ◇ *vi* [blood, music] pulsieren. ◆ **pulses** *npl* [food] Hülsenfrüchte *Pl*.

puma ['pju:mə] (*pl inv* OR **-s**) *n* Puma *der*.

pummel ['pʌml] (*UK*) (*US*) *vt* mit den Fäusten bearbeiten, ein|schlagen auf *(+ A)*.

pump [pʌmp] ◇ *n* - 1. [machine] Pumpe *die* - 2. [for petrol] Zapfsäule *die*, Tanksäule *die*.

◇ *vt* [convey by pumping] pumpen. ◇ *vi* [machine, person, heart] pumpen. ◆ **pumps** *npl* [shoes] Pumps *Pl*.

pumpkin ['pʌmpkɪn] *n* Kürbis *der*.

pun [pʌn] *n* Wortspiel *das*.

punch [pʌntʃ] ◇ *n* - **1.** [blow] (Faust)schlag *der* - **2.** [for making holes in paper] Locher *der* - **3.** *(U)* [drink - cold] Bowle *die*; [- hot] Punsch *der*. ◇ *vt* - **1.** [hit] (mit der Faust) schlagen - **2.** [perforate - ticket] lochen; *(phrase)*: **to punch a hole in sthg** ein Loch in etw machen.

Punch-and-Judy show [ˌpʌntʃən'dʒuːdɪ-] *n* Kasperletheater *das*.

punch ball *n* Punchingball *der*.

punch line *n* Pointe *die*.

punch-up *n UK inf* Schlägerei *die*.

punchy ['pʌntʃɪ] *adj inf* [style] prägnant; [slogan] durchschlagend.

punctual ['pʌŋktʃʊəl] *adj* pünktlich.

punctuation [ˌpʌŋktʃʊ'eɪʃn] *n* Zeichensetzung *die*, Interpunktion *die*.

punctuation mark *n* Satzzeichen *das*.

puncture ['pʌŋktʃər] ◇ *n* [in tyre, ball] (kleines) Loch; **I had a puncture** ich hatte einen Platten. ◇ *vt* - **1.** [tyre, ball] ein Loch machen in *(+ A)* - **2.** [lung, skin] punktieren.

pundit ['pʌndɪt] *n* Experte *der*, -tin *die*.

pungent ['pʌndʒənt] *adj* - **1.** [smell] stechend, beißend; [taste] scharf - **2.** *fig* [criticism, remark] scharf.

punish ['pʌnɪʃ] *vt* bestrafen; **to punish sb for sthg** jn für etw bestrafen.

punishing ['pʌnɪʃɪŋ] *adj* [work, schedule] strapaziös.

punishment ['pʌnɪʃmənt] *n* - **1.** *(U)* [act of punishing] Bestrafung *die* - **2.** [means of punishment] Strafe *die*.

punk [pʌŋk] ◇ *adj* Punker-. ◇ *n* - **1.** [music]: **punk (rock)** Punk(rock) *der* - **2.** [person]: **punk (rocker)** Punker *der*, -in *die* - **3.** *US inf* [lout] Rowdy *der*, Randalierer *der*.

punt [pʌnt] *n* - **1.** [boat] Stechkahn *der* - **2.** [Irish currency] Punt *das*.

punter ['pʌntər] *n UK inf* [customer] Kunde *der*, -din *die*.

puny ['pjuːnɪ] *adj* [person] kümmerlich; [limbs] schwächlich; [effort] erbärmlich.

pup [pʌp] *n* - **1.** [young dog] Hundejunge *das* - **2.**: **seal pup** Robbenjunge *das*.

pupil ['pjuːpl] *n* - **1.** [student, follower] Schüler *der*, -in *die* - **2.** [of eye] Pupille *die*.

puppet ['pʌpɪt] *n* - **1.** *fig* [string puppet] Marionette *die* - **2.** [glove puppet] Handpuppe *die*.

puppy ['pʌpɪ] *n* Hundejunge *das*.

purchase ['pɜːtʃəs] *fml* ◇ *n* - **1.** *(U)* [act of buying] Kauf *der* - **2.** [thing bought]: **purchases** Einkäufe *Pl*; **this was a good purchase** das war ein guter Kauf - **3.** *(U)* [grip] Halt *der*. ◇ *vt* kaufen.

purchaser ['pɜːtʃəsər] *n* Käufer *der*, -in *die*.

pure [pjʊər] *adj* - **1.** [unadulterated, untainted] rein - **2.** [voice, sound] klar - **3.** *liter* [chaste] rein - **4.** [science, maths] theoretisch - **5.** [for emphasis] pur.

puree ['pjʊəreɪ] *n* Püree *das*.

purely ['pjʊəlɪ] *adv* rein.

purge [pɜːdʒ] ◇ *n* POL Säuberungsaktion *die*. ◇ *vt* - **1.** POL säubern - **2.** [rid]: **to purge sthg/o.s. of sthg** etw/sich von etw befreien.

purify ['pjʊərɪfaɪ] *vt* [air, water] reinigen.

purist ['pjʊərɪst] *n* Purist *der*, -in *die*.

purity ['pjʊərətɪ] *n (U)* - **1.** [of air, water] Reinheit *die* - **2.** [of sound, voice] Klarheit *die*.

purple ['pɜːpl] ◇ *adj* violett, lila. ◇ *n* Violett *das*, Lila *das*.

purport [pə'pɔːt] *vi fml*: **to purport to do/be sthg** vor|geben, etw zu tun/sein.

purpose ['pɜːpəs] *n* - **1.** [objective, reason] Zweck *der* - **2.** [use]: **to no purpose** umsonst - **3.** [determination] Entschlossenheit *die*. ◆ **on purpose** *adv* absichtlich, mit Absicht.

purposeful ['pɜːpəsfʊl] *adj* zielbewusst.

purr [pɜːr] *vi* - **1.** [cat, person] schnurren - **2.** [engine, machine] summen.

purse [pɜːs] ◇ *n* - **1.** [for money] Portmonee *das* - **2.** *US* [handbag] Handtasche *die*. ◇ *vt* [lips] auf|werfen, schürzen.

purser ['pɜːsər] *n* Zahlmeister *der*, -in *die*.

pursue [pə'sjuː] *vt* - **1.** [criminal, car] verfolgen - **2.** [hobby, interest] nach|gehen *(+ D)*; [aim] verfolgen - **3.** [matter] weiter|verfolgen.

pursuer [pə'sjuːər] *n* Verfolger *der*, -in *die*.

pursuit [pə'sjuːt] *n* - **1.** *(U) fml* [attempt to obtain, achieve]: **the pursuit of sthg** das Streben nach etw - **2.** [chase] Verfolgung *die* - **3.** [occupation, activity] Beschäftigung *die*.

pus [pʌs] *n* Eiter *der*.

push [pʊʃ] ◇ *vt* - **1.** [press, move - button] drücken; [- bicycle, person] schieben; *(phrase)*: **to push the door open/to** die Tür auf|-/zu|machen - **2.** [encourage] (nachdrücklich) ermutigen; **to push sb to do sthg** jn (nachdrücklich) ermutigen, etw zu tun - **3.** [force] drängen; **to push sb into doing sthg** jn drängen, etw zu tun - **4.** *inf* [promote] Werbung machen für. ◇ *vi* - **1.** [shove] schieben; [in crowd] drängen - **2.** [on button, bell] drücken - **3.** [campaign]: **to push for sthg** auf etw *(A)* drängen. ◇ *n* - **1.** [shove] Stoß *der*, Schubs *der* - **2.** [on button, bell]: **to give sthg a push** etw drücken - **3.** [campaign] (groß angelegte) Aktion. ◆ **push around** *vt sep inf fig* [bully] herum|schubsen. ◆ **push in** *vi* [in queue] (sich) vor|drängen. ◆ **push off** *vi inf* [go away] verschwinden. ◆ **push on** *vi* [continue] weiter|machen. ◆ **push through** *vt sep* [new law, reform] durch|bringen.

pushchair ['pʊʃtʃeəʳ] *n UK* Sportwagen *der*.

pushed [pʊʃt] *adj inf*: **to be pushed for time** unter Zeitdruck stehen; **to be pushed for money** in Geldnöten sein; **to be hard pushed to do sthg** es schwer finden, etw zu tun.

pusher ['pʊʃəʳ] *n drug sl* Dealer *der*, -in *die*.

pushover ['pʊʃ,əʊvəʳ] *n inf* [sucker]: **he's a pushover** er lässt sich leicht reinlegen.

push-up *n esp US* Liegestütz *der*.

pushy ['pʊʃɪ] *adj pej* aufdringlich, aggressiv.

puss [pʊs], **pussy (cat)** ['pʊsɪ-] *n inf* Mieze(katze) *die*.

put [pʊt] *(pt & pp inv) vt* - **1.** [place] tun; [place upright] stellen; [lay flat] legen; **to put sthg into sthg** etw in etw *(A)* hinein|tun/hinein|stellen/hinein|legen; **he put his arm round her shoulder** er legte ihr den Arm um die Schulter; **I put the children first** bei mir kommen die Kinder zuerst; **he put his hand in his pocket** er steckte die Hand in die Tasche; **that puts me in a difficult position** das bringt mich in eine schwierige Lage - **2.** [send]: **to put sb in prison/hospital** jn ins Gefängnis stecken/ins Krankenhaus schicken; **to put a child to bed** ein Kind ins Bett bringen - **3.** [express] sagen - **4.** [ask]: **to put a question (to sb)** (jm) eine Frage stellen - **5.** [make]: **to put a proposal to sb** jm einen Vorschlag machen - **6.** [write] schreiben - **7.** [cause]: **to put sb to a lot of trouble** jm viel Mühe machen - **8.** [estimate]: **to put sthg at** etw schätzen auf *(+ A)* - **9.** [invest - money, time, energy]: **to put sthg into sthg** etw in etw *(A)* investieren - **10.** [apply]: **to put the blame on sb** jm die Schuld geben. ◆ **put across** *vt sep* [ideas] verständlich machen. ◆ **put away** *vt sep* - **1.** [tidy away] weg|räumen - **2.** *inf* [lock up] ein|sperren - **3.** *inf* [eat] verdrücken; [drink] schlucken. ◆ **put back** *vt sep* - **1.** [replace] zurück|legen; [upright] zurück|stellen; **put it back in the bag** stecke es wieder in die Tasche - **2.** [postpone] verschieben - **3.** [clock, watch] zurück|stellen. ◆ **put by** *vt sep* [money] zurück|legen. ◆ **put down** *vt sep* - **1.** [place] setzen; [place upright] (hin)|stellen; [lay flat] (hin)|legen - **2.** [passenger] ab|setzen - **3.** [deposit] an|zahlen - **4.** [riot, rebellion] nieder|schlagen - **5.** [write down] auf|schreiben; **to put sthg down in writing** etw schriftlich nieder|legen - **6.** *UK* [animal] ein|schläfern. ◆ **put down to** *vt sep*: **to put sthg down to sthg** etw einer Sache *(D)* zu|schreiben. ◆ **put forward** *vt sep* - **1.** [plan, theory, name] vor|schlagen; [proposal] machen - **2.** [meeting, date] vor|verlegen - **3.** [clock, watch] vor|stellen. ◆ **put in** *vt sep* - **1.** [spend - time] verwenden auf *(+ A)* - **2.** [submit] ein|reichen - **3.** [install] ein|bauen. ◆ **put in for** *vt insep* [request] sich bewerben um. ◆ **put off** *vt sep* - **1.** [postpone] verschieben; **to put off doing sthg** es verschieben, etw zu tun - **2.** [switch off] aus|schalten, aus|machen - **3.** [cause to wait] hin|halten - **4.** [discourage]: **to put sb off doing sthg** jn davon ab|bringen, etw zu tun - **5.** [distract] ab|lenken - **6.** [cause to dislike]: **to put sb off doing sthg** es jm verleiden, etw zu tun - **7.** [passenger] ab|setzen. ◆ **put on** *vt sep* - **1.** [clothes] an|ziehen; [hat, glasses] auf|setzen; [make-up] auf|legen; **put your clothes on!** zieh dich an! - **2.** [play, show] auf|führen; [exhibition] veranstalten - **3.** [gain in weight]: **to put on weight** zu|nehmen; **I've put on two kilos** ich habe zwei Kilo zugenommen - **4.** [TV, radio, light] an|schalten; [handbrake] an|ziehen - **5.** [CD, record] auf|legen; [tape] ein|legen; [music] an|stellen - **6.** [start cooking] auf|stellen; **to put the kettle on** Wasser auf|setzen - **7.** [feign] vor|täuschen - **8.** [add] auf|schlagen - **9.** [provide - bus, train] ein|setzen. ◆ **put out** *vt sep* - **1.** [place outside - milk bottles] hinaus|stellen; [- rubbish] hinaus|bringen; [- cat] hinaus|setzen - **2.** [issue - book, record] veröffentlichen; [- statement] ab|geben - **3.** [cigarette, fire, light] aus|machen - **4.** [hand, arm, leg] aus|strecken - **5.** [annoy]: **to be put out** verärgert sein - **6.** [inconvenience]: **to put sb out** jm Umstände machen. ◆ **put through** *vt sep* [phonecall] durch|stellen; **to put sb through to sb** jn mit jm verbinden. ◆ **put up** ◇ *vt sep* - **1.** [tent, statue, building] auf|stellen - **2.** [umbrella] auf|spannen; [flag] hoch|ziehen - **3.** [notice] an|schlagen; [sign] an|bringen; [curtains] auf|hängen - **4.** [provide - money] stellen - **5.** [propose - candidate] auf|stellen - **6.** [increase - price, cost] hoch|treiben - **7.** [provide accommodation for] unter|bringen. ◇ *vt insep* [resistance] leisten; **to put up a fight** sich wehren. ◇ *vi UK* [in hotel] unter|kommen. ◆ **put up with** *vt insep* dulden.

putrid ['pju:trɪd] *adj fml* [decayed] faulig.

putt [pʌt] ◇ *n* Schlag *der*. ◇ *vt & vi* putten, ein|lochen.

putty ['pʌtɪ] *n* Kitt *der*.

puzzle ['pʌzl] ◇ *n* - **1.** [game] Rätsel *das*; [toy] Geduldsspiel *das*; **(jigsaw) puzzle** Puzzle *das* - **2.** [mystery] Rätsel *das*. ◇ *vt* verblüffen. ◇ *vi*: **to puzzle over sthg** sich *(D)* über etw *(A)* den Kopf zerbrechen. ◆ **puzzle out** *vt sep* heraus|finden.

puzzling ['pʌzlɪŋ] *adj* verblüffend.

pyjamas [pə'dʒɑ:məz] *npl* Schlafanzug *der*.

pylon ['paɪlən] *n* ELEC Mast *der*.

pyramid ['pɪrəmɪd] *n* Pyramide *die*.

Pyrex® ['paɪreks] *n (U)* ≃ Jenaer Glas® *das*.

python ['paɪθn] *(pl inv* OR *-s) n* Pythonschlange *die*.

Q

q (*pl* **q's** *OR* **qs**), **Q** (*pl* **Q's** *OR* **Qs**) [kjuː] *n* q *das*, Q *das*.

quack [kwæk] *n* - **1.** [noise] Quaken *das* - **2.** *inf pej* [doctor] Quacksalber *der*.

quadrangle ['kwɒdræŋgl] *n* - **1.** [figure] Viereck *das* - **2.** [courtyard] (viereckiger) Hof.

quadruple [kwɒ'druːpl] ◇ *adj* vierfach. ◇ *vt* vervierfachen. ◇ *vi* sich vervierfachen.

quadruplets ['kwɒdrʊplɪts] *npl* Vierlinge *Pl*.

quail [kweɪl] (*pl inv OR* **-s**) *n* Wachtel *die*.

quaint [kweɪnt] *adj* [cottage] urig; [tradition] kurios.

quake [kweɪk] ◇ *n inf* (*abbr of* **earthquake**) Beben *das*. ◇ *vi* beben, zittern.

qualification [,kwɒlɪfɪ'keɪʃn] *n* - **1.** [examination, certificate, skill] Qualifikation *die* - **2.** [qualifying statement] Einschränkung *die*.

qualified ['kwɒlɪfaɪd] *adj* - **1.** [trained] ausgebildet - **2.** [able]: **to be qualified to do sthg** qualifiziert sein, etw zu tun - **3.** [limited] eingeschränkt.

qualify ['kwɒlɪfaɪ] ◇ *vt* - **1.** [statement] einlschränken - **2.** [entitle]: **to qualify sb to do sthg** jn berechtigen, etw zu tun. ◇ *vi* - **1.** [pass exams & SPORT] sich qualifizieren - **2.** [be entitled]: **to qualify for sthg** zu etw berechtigt sein.

quality ['kwɒlətɪ] ◇ *n* - **1.** [gen] Qualität *die* - **2.** [characteristic] Eigenschaft *die*. ◇ *comp* Qualitäts-.

qualms [kwɑːmz] *npl* Skrupel *Pl*.

quandary ['kwɒndərɪ] *n (phrase)*: **to be in a quandary about** *OR* **over sthg** in einer Zwickmühle stecken wegen etw *OR* in Bezug auf etw *(A)*.

quantify ['kwɒntɪfaɪ] *vt* in Zahlen auslrücken.

quantity ['kwɒntətɪ] *n* Menge *die*; **to be an unknown quantity** eine unbekannte Größe sein.

quarantine ['kwɒrəntiːn] ◇ *n* Quarantäne *die*. ◇ *vt* unter Quarantäne stellen.

quarrel ['kwɒrəl] (*UK*) (*US*) ◇ *n* Streit *der*. ◇ *vi* sich streiten; **to quarrel with sb** sich mit jm streiten; **to quarrel with sthg** an etw *(D)* etwas auszusetzen haben.

quarrelsome ['kwɒrəlsəm] *adj* streitsüchtig.

quarry ['kwɒrɪ] *n* - **1.** [place] Steinbruch *der* - **2.** [prey] Beute *die*.

quart [kwɔːt] *n UK* [unit of measurement] Quart *das (= 1,14 l)*; *US* Quart *das (= 0,95 l)*.

quarter ['kwɔːtər] *n* - **1.** [fraction, area in town] Viertel *das* - **2.** [in telling time]: **a quarter past (two)** *UK*, **a quarter after (two)** *US* Viertel nach (zwei); **a quarter to (two)** *UK*, **a quarter of (two)** *US* Viertel vor (zwei) - **3.** [of year] Vierteljahr *das*, Quartal *das* - **4.** *US* [coin] Vierteldollar *der* - **5.** [four ounces] ≃ Viertelpfund *das* - **6.** [direction] Richtung *die*; **from an unexpected quarter** von unerwarteter Seite. ◆ **quarters** *npl* [rooms] Quartier *das*. ◆ **at close quarters** *adv* aus der Nähe.

quarterfinal [,kwɔːtə'faɪnl] *n* Viertelfinalspiel *das*.

quarterly ['kwɔːtəlɪ] ◇ *adj* & *adv* vierteljährlich. ◇ *n* Vierteljahresschrift *die*.

quartet [kwɔː'tet] *n* Quartett *das*.

quartz [kwɔːts] *n (U)* Quarz *der*.

quartz watch *n* Quarzuhr *die*.

quash [kwɒʃ] *vt* - **1.** [decision, sentence] aufheben - **2.** [rebellion] unterdrücken.

quasi- ['kweɪzaɪ] *prefix* quasi-.

quaver ['kweɪvər] *n* MUS Achtelnote *die*.

quay [kiː] *n* Kai *der*.

quayside ['kiːsaɪd] *n* Kai *der*.

queasy ['kwiːzɪ] *adj* unwohl.

queen [kwiːn] *n* - **1.** [royalty, bee] Königin *die* - **2.** [in chess, playing card] Dame *die*.

queen mother *n*: **the queen mother** die Königinmutter.

queer [kwɪər] ◇ *adj* [odd] seltsam, eigenartig; **I'm feeling a bit queer** mir ist nicht ganz wohl. ◇ *n inf pej* [homosexual] Schwule *der*.

quell [kwel] *vt* unterdrücken.

quench [kwentʃ] *vt* stillen.

query ['kwɪərɪ] ◇ *n* Frage *die*. ◇ *vt* [decision] in Frage stellen; [invoice] beanstanden.

quest [kwest] *n liter*: **quest (for sthg)** Suche *die* (nach etw).

question ['kwestʃn] ◇ *n* Frage *die*; **to ask (sb) a question** (jm) eine Frage stellen; **to bring** *OR* **call sthg into question** etw in Frage stellen; **to be beyond question** außer Zweifel *OR* Frage stehen; **without question** ohne Zweifel; *(phrase)*: **there's no question of doing it** es kommt nicht in Frage, es zu tun. ◇ *vt* - **1.** [interrogate] befragen - **2.** [express doubt about] bezweifeln. ◆ **in question** *adv*: **the thing in question** der/die/das Betreffende. ◆ **out of the question** *adj* ausgeschlossen.

questionable ['kwestʃənəbl] *adj* - **1.** [uncertain] fraglich - **2.** [not right, not honest] fragwürdig.

question mark *n* Fragezeichen *das*.

questionnaire [,kwestʃə'neər] *n* Fragebogen *der*.

queue [kjuː] *UK* ◇ *n* Schlange *die*. ◇ *vi* Schlange stehen; **to queue (up) for sthg** für etw an|stehen.

quibble ['kwɪbl] *pej* ◇ *n* Spitzfindigkeit *die*. ◇ *vi* spitzfindig sein; **to quibble over** *OR* **about sthg** über etw *(A)* streiten.

quiche [kiːʃ] *n* Quiche *die*.

quick [kwɪk] *adj* & *adv* schnell.

quicken ['kwɪkn] ◇ *vt* [make faster] beschleunigen. ◇ *vi* [get faster] schneller werden.

quickly ['kwɪklɪ] *adv* schnell.

quicksand ['kwɪksænd] *n* Treibsand *der*.

quick-witted [-'wɪtɪd] *adj* [person] geistesgegenwärtig; [response] schlagkräftig.

quid [kwɪd] *(pl inv) n UK inf* Pfund *das*.

quiet ['kwaɪət] ◇ *adj* - **1.** [not noisy, calm] ruhig - **2.** [not talkative, silent] still; **to keep quiet about sthg** über etw *(A)* nichts sagen; **be quiet!** sei/seid still! - **3.** [discreet - clothes, colours] dezent; **to have a quiet word with sb** mit jm unter vier Augen reden - **4.** [wedding] im kleinen Kreis. ◇ *n* Ruhe *die*; **on the quiet** *inf* heimlich. ◇ *vt US* zum Schweigen bringen. ◆ **quiet down** *US* ◇ *vt sep* beruhigen. ◇ *vi* sich beruhigen.

quieten ['kwaɪətn] *vt* beruhigen. ◆ **quieten down** ◇ *vt sep* beruhigen. ◇ *vi* sich beruhigen.

quietly ['kwaɪətlɪ] *adv* - **1.** [without noise] leise - **2.** [without excitement] ruhig - **3.** [without fuss] in aller Stille.

quilt [kwɪlt] *n* Steppdecke *die*.

quintet [kwɪn'tet] *n* Quintett *das*.

quintuplets [kwɪn'tjuːplɪts] *npl* Fünflinge *Pl*.

quip [kwɪp] ◇ *n* geistreiche Bemerkung. ◇ *vt* witzeln.

quirk [kwɜːk] *n* - **1.** [habit] Marotte *die* - **2.** [strange event]: **a quirk of fate** eine Laune des Schicksals.

quit [kwɪt] *(UK pt & pp inv* *OR* **-ted**) (*US pt & pp inv*) ◇ *vt* - **1.** [resign from - job] auf|geben, kündigen; [- army] verlassen - **2.** [stop] auf|hören mit. ◇ *vi* - **1.** [resign] kündigen - **2.** [stop] auf|hören.

quite [kwaɪt] *adv* - **1.** [fairly] ziemlich; **quite a lot** ziemlich viel; **quite a few** ziemlich viele - **2.** [completely] ganz; **I quite agree** das finde ich auch - **3.** [after negative]: **not quite big enough** nicht groß genug; **I don't quite understand** ich verstehe nicht ganz - **4.** [for emphasis]: **it was quite a surprise** es war eine ziemliche Überraschung; **she's quite a singer** sie singt ganz gut - **5.** [to express agreement]: **quite (so)!** richtig!

quits [kwɪts] *adj inf*: **to be quits (with sb)** (mit jm) quitt sein; **we'll call it quits** [forget the debt] es ist schon in Ordnung; [stop doing sthg] lassen Sie uns jetzt aufhören.

quiver ['kwɪvəʳ] *vi* zittern.

quiz [kwɪz] *(pl* **-zes**) ◇ *n* - **1.** [competition, game] Quiz *das* - **2.** *US* SCH Prüfung *die*. ◇ *vt*: **to quiz sb (about sthg)** jn (über etw *(A)*) aus|fragen.

quizzical ['kwɪzɪkl] *adj* fragend.

quota ['kwəʊtə] *n* Quote *die*.

quotation [kwəʊ'teɪʃn] *n* - **1.** [citation] Zitat *das* - **2.** COMM Kostenvoranschlag *der*.

quotation marks *npl* Anführungszeichen *Pl*; **in quotation marks** in Anführungszeichen.

quote [kwəʊt] ◇ *n* - **1.** [citation] Zitat *das* - **2.** COMM Kostenvoranschlag *der*. ◇ *vt* [cite] zitieren. ◇ *vi* [cite] zitieren; **to quote from sthg** zitieren aus etw.

quotient ['kwəʊʃnt] *n* Quotient *der*.

R

r *(pl* **r's** *OR* **rs**), **R** *(pl* **R's** *OR* **Rs**) [ɑːʳ] *n* r *das*, R *das*.

rabbi ['ræbaɪ] *n* Rabbiner *der*.

rabbit ['ræbɪt] *n* Kaninchen *das*.

rabbit hutch *n* Kaninchenstall *der*.

rabble ['ræbl] *n* - **1.** [disorderly crowd] aufwieglerische Menge - **2.** [riffraff]: **the rabble** der Pöbel.

rabies ['reɪbiːz] *n* Tollwut *die*.

RAC *(abbr of* **Royal Automobile Club**) *n* ≃ ADAC *der*.

race [reɪs] ◇ *n* - **1.** [competition] Rennen *das* - **2.** *fig* [for power, control] Wettlauf *der*; **arms race** Wettrüsten *das* - **3.** [people, ethnic background] Rasse *die*. ◇ *vt* - **1.** [compete against]: **to race sb** mit jm um die Wette laufen/fahren/*etc* - **2.** [animal, vehicle] antreten lassen. ◇ *vi* - **1.** [compete]: **to race against sb** gegen jn an|treten - **2.** [rush] rennen - **3.** [heart, pulse] rasen - **4.** [engine] durch|drehen.

race car *n US* = **racing car**.

racecourse ['reɪskɔːs] *n* Rennbahn *die*.

race driver *n US* = **racing driver**.

racehorse ['reɪshɔːs] *n* Rennpferd *das*.

racetrack ['reɪstræk] *n* Rennbahn *die*.

racial ['reɪʃəl] *adj* Rassen-.

racial discrimination *n* Rassendiskriminierung *die*.

racing ['reɪsɪŋ] *n* [motor racing] Rennsport *der*; [horse racing] Pferderennsport *der*.

racing car *UK*, **race car** *US* *n* Rennwagen *der*.

racing driver *UK*, **race driver** *US* *n* Rennfahrer *der*, -in *die*.

racism ['reɪsɪzm] *n* Rassismus *der*.

racist ['reɪsɪst] ◇ *adj* rassistisch. ◇ *n* Rassist *der*, -in *die*.

rack [ræk] *n* - **1.** [frame] Ständer *der* - **2.** [for luggage] Ablage *die*.

racket ['rækɪt] *n* - **1.** [noise] Krach *der* - **2.** [illegal activity] Gaunerei *die* - **3.** SPORT Schläger *der*.

racquet ['rækɪt] *n* Schläger *der*.

racy ['reɪsɪ] *adj* feurig.

radar ['reɪdɑːr] *n* Radar *der*.

radiant ['reɪdɪənt] *adj* strahlend.

radiate ['reɪdɪeɪt] *vt* aus|strahlen.

radiation [ˌreɪdɪ'eɪʃn] *n (U)* [radioactive] radioaktive Strahlung.

radiator ['reɪdɪeɪtər] *n* - **1.** [in house] Heizkörper *der* - **2.** AUT Kühler *der*.

radical ['rædɪkl] ◇ *adj* - **1.** POL radikal - **2.** [fundamental] fundamental. ◇ *n* POL Radikale *der, die*.

radically ['rædɪklɪ] *adv* radikal.

radii ['reɪdɪaɪ] *Pl* ▷ **radius**.

radio ['reɪdɪəʊ] *(pl* **-s***)* ◇ *n* - **1.** [system of communication] Rundfunk *der* - **2.** [broadcasting, equipment] Radio *das*. ◇ *comp* Radio-. ◇ *vt* [message] funken; [person] an|funken.

radioactive [ˌreɪdɪəʊ'æktɪv] *adj* radioaktiv.

radio alarm *n* Radiowecker *der*.

radio-controlled [-kən'trəʊld] *adj* ferngesteuert.

radiology [ˌreɪdɪ'ɒlədʒɪ] *n* Radiologie *die*.

radish ['rædɪʃ] *n* Radieschen *das*.

radius ['reɪdɪəs] *(pl* **radii***)* *n* - **1.** MATHS Radius *der* - **2.** ANAT Speiche *die*.

RAF [ɑːreɪ'ef, ræf] *n abbr of* **Royal Air Force**.

raffle ['ræfl] ◇ *n* Tombola *die*. ◇ *vt* verlosen.

raffle ticket *n* Los *das*.

raft [rɑːft] *n* Floß *das*.

rafter ['rɑːftər] *n* Dachsparren *der*.

rag [ræg] *n* - **1.** [piece of cloth] Lumpen *der* - **2.** *pej* [newspaper] Käseblatt *das*. ◆ **rags** *npl* [clothes] Lumpen *Pl*.

rag-and-bone man *n* Lumpensammler *der*.

rag doll *n* Flickenpuppe *die*.

rage [reɪdʒ] ◇ *n* - **1.** [fury] Wut *die*; **to fly into a rage** in Rage geraten - **2.** *inf* [fashion]: **to be all the rage** der letzte Schrei sein. ◇ *vi* toben; [disease] wüten.

ragged ['rægɪd] *adj* - **1.** [person, clothes] zerlumpt - **2.** [coastline] zerklüftet - **3.** [performance] stümperhaft.

raid [reɪd] ◇ *n* - **1.** MIL [attack] Angriff *der* - **2.** [forced entry - by thieves] Überfall *der*; [- by police] Razzia *die*. ◇ *vt* - **1.** MIL [attack] an|greifen - **2.** [enter by force - subj: thieves] ein|brechen in *(+ A)*; [- subj: police] eine Razzia machen in *(+ D)*.

raider ['reɪdər] *n* - **1.** [attacker] Angreifer *der*, -in *die* - **2.** [thief] Einbrecher *der*, -in *die*.

rail [reɪl] ◇ *n* - **1.** [fence] Geländer *das*; [on ship] Reling *die* - **2.** [bar, of railway] Schiene *die* - **3.** *(U)* [form of transport] (Eisen)bahn *die*. ◇ *comp* Eisenbahn-, Bahn-.

railcard ['reɪlkɑːd] *n UK* ≃ Bahncard *die*.

railing ['reɪlɪŋ] *n* Geländer *das*; [on ship] Reling *die*.

railway *UK* ['reɪlweɪ], **railroad** *US* ['reɪlrəʊd] *n* - **1.** [track] Gleis *das* - **2.** [company, system] (Eisen)bahn *die*.

railway line *n* - **1.** [route] (Eisen)bahnlinie *die* - **2.** [track] Gleis *das*.

railwayman ['reɪlweɪmən] *(pl* **-men** [-mən]*)* *n UK* Eisenbahner *der*.

railway station *n* Bahnhof *der*.

railway track *n* Gleis *das*.

rain [reɪn] ◇ *n* Regen *der*. ◇ *impers vb & vi* regnen; **it's raining** es regnet.

rainbow ['reɪnbəʊ] *n* Regenbogen *der*.

rain check *n US*: **to take a rain check on sthg** etw auf ein andermal verschieben.

raincoat ['reɪnkəʊt] *n* Regenmantel *der*.

raindrop ['reɪndrɒp] *n* Regentropfen *der*.

rainfall ['reɪnfɔːl] *n (U)* Niederschlag *der*.

rain forest *n* Regenwald *der*.

rainy ['reɪnɪ] *adj* regnerisch.

raise [reɪz] ◇ *vt* - **1.** [lift up] heben; [window] hoch|ziehen; **to raise o.s.** sich auf|richten - **2.** [increase, improve] an|heben; **to raise one's voice** [make louder] seine Stimme heben; [in protest] seine Stimme erheben - **3.** [obtain - from donations] auf|bringen; [- by selling, borrowing] auf|treiben - **4.** [evoke] (herauf)|beschwören - **5.** [child, animal] auf|ziehen - **6.** [crop] an|bauen - **7.** [mention] auf|werfen. ◇ *n US* Erhöhung *die*.

raisin ['reɪzn] *n* Rosine *die*.

rake [reɪk] ◇ *n* [implement] Harke *die*, Rechen *der*. ◇ *vt* - **1.** [smooth] harken, rechen - **2.** [gather] zusammen|rechen.

rally ['rælɪ] ◇ *n* - **1.** [meeting] Versammlung *die* - **2.** [car race] Rallye *die* - **3.** SPORT [exchange of shots] Ballwechsel *der*. ◇ *vt* sammeln. ◇ *vi* - **1.** [come together] sich sammeln - **2.** [recover] sich erholen. ◆ **rally round** ◇ *vt insep* sich scharen um. ◇ *vi* sich seiner/ihrer/*etc* an|nehmen.

ram [ræm] ◇ *n* [animal] Widder *der*. ◇ *vt* rammen.

RAM [ræm] *(abbr of* **random access memory***)* *n* RAM.

ramble ['ræmbl] ◇ *n* Wanderung *die.* ◇ *vi* - **1.** [walk] wandern - **2.** [talk] schwafeln.

rambler ['ræmblə^r] *n* [walker] Spaziergänger *der*, -in *die*.

rambling ['ræmblɪŋ] *adj* - **1.** [building] weitläufig - **2.** [conversation, book] weitschweifig.

ramp [ræmp] *n* Rampe *die*.

rampage [ræm'peɪdʒ] *n*: **to go on the rampage** randalieren.

rampant ['ræmpənt] *adj* - **1.** [unrestrained] wuchernd; **to be rampant** wüten - **2.** [widespread] weit verbreitet.

ramparts ['ræmpɑːts] *npl* Schutzwall *der*.

ramshackle ['ræm,ʃækl] *adj* heruntergekommen.

ran [ræn] *pt* ▷ **run**.

ranch [rɑːntʃ] *n* Ranch *die*.

rancher ['rɑːntʃə^r] *n* Viehzüchter *der*, -in *die*.

rancid ['rænsɪd] *adj* ranzig.

rancour *UK*, **rancor** *US* ['ræŋkə^r] *n* Bitterkeit *die*.

random ['rændəm] ◇ *adj* willkürlich; **random sample** Stichprobe *die*. ◇ *n*: **at random** [choose, sample] willkürlich; [fire, hit out] ziellos.

random access memory *n (U)* COMPUT Arbeitsspeicher *der*.

randy ['rændɪ] *adj UK inf* scharf.

rang [ræŋ] *pt* ▷ **ring**.

range [reɪndʒ] ◇ *n* - **1.** [distance covered] Reichweite *die*; **at close range** auf kurze Entfernung - **2.** [variety] Auswahl *die*; **there was a wide range of people there** es waren ganz unterschiedliche Leute da - **3.** [bracket] Klasse *die* - **4.** [of mountains, hills] Kette *die* - **5.** [shooting area] Platz *der* - **6.** MUS [of voice] Stimmumfang *der*. ◇ *vt* [place in row] auf|stellen. ◇ *vi* - **1.** [vary]: **to range from ... to ...** reichen von ... bis ...; **to range between ... and ...** liegen zwischen ... und ... - **2.** [deal with, include]: **to range over sthg** sich erstrecken auf etw *(A)*.

ranger ['reɪndʒə^r] *n* [of park] Aufseher *der*, -in *die*; [of forest] Förster *der*, -in *die*.

rank [ræŋk] ◇ *adj* - **1.** [utter, absolute] ausgesprochen - **2.** [offensive] übel. ◇ *n* - **1.** [in army, police] Rang *der*; **the rank and file** MIL die Mannschaft; [of political party, organization] die Basis - **2.** [social class] Stand *der* - **3.** [row, line] Reihe *die*; **taxi rank** Taxistand *der*. ◇ *vt* [classify]: **to rank sb among the great writers** jn zu den großen Schriftstellern zählen; **he is ranked fourth in the world** er steht an vierter Stelle in der Weltrangliste. ◇ *vi*: **to rank as** gelten als; **to rank among** zählen zu. ◆ **ranks** *npl* - **1.** MIL: **the ranks** die einfachen Soldaten - **2.** *fig* [members] Reihen *Pl*.

rankle ['ræŋkl] *vi*: **it still rankles with me** es wurmt mich noch immer.

ransack ['rænsæk] *vt* - **1.** [plunder] plündern - **2.** [search] durch|wühlen.

ransom ['rænsəm] *n* Lösegeld *das*; **to hold sb to ransom** [keep prisoner] jn als Geisel halten; *fig* [put in impossible position] jn erpressen.

rant [rænt] *vi* schwadronieren.

rap [ræp] ◇ *n* - **1.** [knock] Klopfen *das* - **2.** MUS Rap *der*. ◇ *vt* [on table] klopfen auf *(+ A)*; **to rap sb on the knuckles** jm auf die Finger klopfen.

rape [reɪp] ◇ *n* - **1.** [crime, attack] Vergewaltigung *die* - **2.** *fig* [destruction]: **the rape of the countryside** der Raubbau an der Landschaft - **3.** [plant] Raps *der*. ◇ *vt* vergewaltigen.

rapid ['ræpɪd] *adj* rapide, schnell. ◆ **rapids** *npl* Stromschnelle *die*.

rapidly ['ræpɪdlɪ] *adv* schnell.

rapist ['reɪpɪst] *n* Vergewaltiger *der*.

rapport [ræ'pɔː^r] *n*: **a (good) rapport with/between** ein gutes Verhältnis mit/zwischen *(+ D)*.

rapture ['ræptʃə^r] *n*: **to go into raptures over** OR **about sb/sthg** über jn/etw in Verzückung geraten.

rapturous ['ræptʃərəs] *adj* begeistert.

rare [reə^r] *adj* - **1.** [scarce, infrequent] selten - **2.** [exceptional] rar - **3.** CULIN [underdone] blutig.

rarely ['reəlɪ] *adv* selten.

raring ['reərɪŋ] *adj*: **to be raring to go** in den Startlöchern sein.

rarity ['reərətɪ] *n* - **1.** [unusual object, person] Rarität *die* - **2.** *(U)* [scarcity] Seltenheit *die*.

rascal ['rɑːskl] *n* [mischievous child] Frechdachs *der*.

rash [ræʃ] ◇ *adj* [person] unbesonnen; [action, decision, promise] voreilig. ◇ *n* - **1.** MED Ausschlag *der* - **2.** [spate] Serie *die*.

rasher ['ræʃə^r] *n* Streifen *der*.

raspberry ['rɑːzbərɪ] *n* [fruit] Himbeere *die*.

rat [ræt] *n* - **1.** [animal] Ratte *die* - **2.** *pej* [person] Schwein *das*.

rate [reɪt] ◇ *n* - **1.** [speed] Tempo *das*; **at this rate** bei diesem Tempo - **2.** [ratio, proportion] Rate *die* - **3.** [of taxation, interest] Satz *der*. ◇ *vt* - **1.** [consider]: **to rate sb/sthg (as)** jn/etw ein|schätzen (als); **to rate sb/sthg among** jn/etw zählen zu - **2.** [deserve] verdienen. ◆ **at any rate** *adv* auf jeden Fall.

ratepayer ['reɪt,peɪə^r] *n UK* Steuerzahler *der*, -in *die*.

rather ['rɑːðə^r] *adv* - **1.** [slightly, a bit] ziemlich; **he's had rather too much to drink** er hat ziemlich viel getrunken - **2.** [for emphasis] recht; **I rather thought so** das habe ich mir fast gedacht; **I rather like him** ich mag ihn recht gern - **3.** [expressing a preference] lieber; **would you rather leave?** möchtest du lieber gehen?;

I'd rather not lieber nicht - 4. [more exactly]: or rather vielmehr - 5. [on the contrary]: (but) rather vielmehr. ◆ rather than *conj* statt.

ratify ['rætɪfaɪ] *vt* ratifizieren.

rating ['reɪtɪŋ] *n* [standing]: **popularity rating** Beliebtheitsgrad *der*; **what is her rating in the polls?** wie hoch ist ihr Beliebtheitsgrad?

ratio ['reɪʃɪəʊ] (*pl* **-s**) *n* Verhältnis *das*.

ration ['ræʃn] ◇ *n* Ration *die*. ◇ *vt* [goods] rationieren. ◆ **rations** *npl* Rationen *Pl*.

rational ['ræʃənl] *adj* - **1.** [reasonable] rational - **2.** [capable of reason] vernünftig.

rationale [ˌræʃə'nɑːl] *n* Gründe *Pl*.

rationalize, -ise ['ræʃənəlaɪz] *vt* rationalisieren.

rat race *n* ständiger Konkurrenzkampf.

rattle ['rætl] ◇ *n* [toy] Klapper *die*. ◇ *vt* - **1.** [make rattling noise with - keys] klimpern mit; [subj: wind - windows] rütteln an *(+ D)* - **2.** [unsettle] durcheinander bringen. ◇ *vi* [make rattling noise] klappern; [bottles] klirren.

rattlesnake ['rætlsneɪk], **rattler** *US* ['rætlə^r] *n* Klapperschlange *die*.

raucous ['rɔːkəs] *adj* [voice, laughter] rau; [behaviour] wüst.

ravage ['rævɪdʒ] *vt* verheeren, verwüsten. ◆ **ravages** *npl* Verheerung *die*.

rave [reɪv] ◇ *adj* glänzend. ◇ *n UK inf* [event] Rave *der ODER das*. ◇ *vi* - **1.** [talk angrily]: **to rave about/against sthg** über etw *(A)*/gegen etw wettern - **2.** [talk enthusiastically]: **to rave about sthg** von etw schwärmen.

raven ['reɪvn] *n* Rabe *der*.

ravenous ['rævənəs] *adj* ausgehungert; *(phrase)*: **I'm ravenous!** ich habe einen Bärenhunger!

ravine [rə'viːn] *n* Schlucht *die*.

raving ['reɪvɪŋ] *adj*: **he's a raving lunatic** er ist total verrückt.

ravioli [ˌrævɪ'əʊlɪ] *n (U)* Ravioli *Pl*.

ravishing ['rævɪʃɪŋ] *adj* hinreißend.

raw [rɔː] *adj* - **1.** [uncooked] roh - **2.** [untreated] roh, Roh- - **3.** [painful - wound] offen; [- skin] wund - **4.** [inexperienced] unerfahren.

raw deal *n*: **to get a raw deal** schlecht weg|kommen.

raw material *n* - **1.** [natural substance] Rohstoff *der* - **2.** *(U) fig* [basis] Grundlage *die*.

ray [reɪ] *n* - **1.** [beam] Strahl *der* - **2.** *fig* [glimmer] Schimmer *der*.

rayon ['reɪɒn] *n* Reyon *das*.

raze [reɪz] *vt (phrase)*: **the house was razed to the ground** das Haus wurde dem Erdboden gleichgemacht.

razor ['reɪzə^r] *n* Rasierapparat *der*.

razor blade *n* Rasierklinge *die*.

RC (*abbr of* **Roman Catholic**) *adj* röm.-kath.

Rd (*abbr of* **Road**) Str.

R & D (*abbr of* **research and development**) *n* F & E.

re [riː] *prep* betreffs *(+ G)*.

RE *n* (*abbr of* **religious education**) Religionsunterricht *der*.

reach [riːtʃ] ◇ *vt* - **1.** [arrive at] an|kommen in *(+ D)* - **2.** [be able to touch] heran|kommen an *(+ A)* - **3.** [contact, extend as far as, attain, achieve] erreichen. ◇ *vi* - **1.** [person, arm, hand] greifen; **to reach (out) for sthg** nach etw greifen - **2.** [land] reichen. ◇ *n* [of boxer] Reichweite *die*; **within sb's reach** [easily touched] innerhalb js Reichweite; **within easy reach of the station** vom Bahnhof leicht zu erreichen; **out of** OR **beyond sb's reach** [not easily touched] außerhalb js Reichweite.

react [rɪ'ækt] *vi* - **1.** [rebel]: **to react against sthg** sich gegen etw auf|lehnen - **2.** CHEM: **to react with sthg** auf etw *(A)* reagieren.

reaction [rɪ'ækʃn] *n* - **1.** [response & MED]: **reaction (to sthg)** Reaktion *die* (auf etw *(A)*) - **2.** [rebellion]: **reaction (against sthg)** Gegenreaktion *die* (auf etw *(A)*) - **3.** [reflex] Reaktionsfähigkeit *die*; **she's got very quick reactions** sie hat sehr gute Reflexe.

reactionary [rɪ'ækʃənrɪ] ◇ *adj* reaktionär. ◇ *n* Reaktionär *der*, -in *die*.

reactor [rɪ'æktə^r] *n* [nuclear reactor] Reaktor *der*.

read [riːd] (*pt & pp inv*) ◇ *vt* - **1.** [book, magazine, music] lesen; **to read music** Noten lesen - **2.** [say aloud]: **to read sb sthg** jm etw vor|lesen - **3.** [subj: sign, notice] besagen; [subj: gauge, meter, barometer] an|zeigen - **4.** [take reading from - meter, gauge] ab|lesen - **5.** [interpret] verstehen; [sb's thoughts] lesen - **6.** *UK* UNIV studieren. ◇ *vi* - **1.** [in book, magazine] lesen; **to read about sthg** von etw lesen - **2.** [out loud]: **to read to sb (from)** jm vor|lesen (aus). ◆ **read out** *vt sep* vor|lesen. ◆ **read over, read through** *vt sep* durch|lesen. ◆ **read up on** *vt insep* nach|lesen über *(+ A)*.

readable ['riːdəbl] *adj* [book] lesenswert.

reader ['riːdə^r] *n* [person who reads] Leser *der*, -in *die*.

readership ['riːdəʃɪp] *n* [total number of readers] Leser *Pl*.

readily ['redɪlɪ] *adv* - **1.** [willingly] bereitwillig - **2.** [easily] leicht.

reading ['riːdɪŋ] *n* - **1.** [act of reading] Lesen *das* - **2.** [reading material] Lektüre *die* - **3.** [recital] Lesung *die* - **4.** [taken from meter] Zählerstand *der*; [taken from thermometer] Thermometerstand *der* - **5.** [POL - of bill] Lesung *die*.

readjust [ˌriːə'dʒʌst] ◇ *vt* [mechanism, instrument] nach|stellen; [mirror] ein|stellen; [policy] neu an|passen. ◇ *vi*: **to readjust to sthg** sich wieder an etw *(A)* gewöhnen.

readout ['riːdaʊt] *n* COMPUT Anzeige *die*.

ready ['redɪ] ◇ *adj* - **1.** [prepared] fertig; **to be ready to do sthg** bereit sein, etw zu tun; **to be ready for sthg** für etw bereit sein; **to get ready** sich fertig machen; **to get sthg ready** etw fertig machen - **2.** [willing]: **to be ready to do sthg** bereit sein, etw zu tun - **3.** [in need of]: **to be ready for sthg** etw gebrauchen können; **I'm ready for bed** ich bin bettreif - **4.** [likely]: **to be ready to collapse** zum Umfallen müde sein; **she was ready to cry** sie war den Tränen nahe. ◇ *vt* vor|bereiten.

ready cash *n* Bargeld *das*.

ready-made *adj* - **1.** [product] Fertig- - **2.** *fig* [reply, excuse] vorgefertigt.

ready money *n* Bargeld *das*.

ready-to-wear *adj*: **ready-to-wear clothes** Konfektionskleidung *die*, Kleidung *die* von der Stange.

real ['rɪəl] ◇ *adj* - **1.** [authentic, for emphasis] echt; **this is the real thing!** [marvellous] das ist unglaublich toll!; **this time it's for real** diesmal ist es echt - **2.** [actually existing] real - **3.** [cost, value] tatsächlich; **in real terms** real. ◇ *adv US* wirklich.

real estate *n (U)* Immobilien *Pl*.

realign [ˌriːə'laɪn] *vt* [brakes] nach|stellen.

realism ['rɪəlɪzm] *n* Realismus *der*.

realistic [ˌrɪə'lɪstɪk] *adj* realistisch.

reality [rɪ'ælətɪ] *n* Realität *die*.

reality TV *n* Reality-TV *das*.

realization [ˌrɪəlaɪ'zeɪʃn] *n (U)* - **1.** [awareness, recognition] Realisation *die* - **2.** [achievement] Realisierung *die*.

realize, -ise ['rɪəlaɪz] *vt* - **1.** [become aware of, understand] begreifen - **2.** [achieve] verwirklichen - **3.** COMM erzielen.

really ['rɪəlɪ] ◇ *adv* - **1.** [for emphasis] wirklich; **really good/bad** wirklich gut/schlecht; **you really ought to see this film** du solltest dir den Film unbedingt ansehen - **2.** [actually] eigentlich; **not really** eigentlich nicht - **3.** [honestly] wirklich - **4.** [to sound less negative] eigentlich. ◇ *excl* - **1.** [expressing doubt, surprise]: **really?** wirklich? - **2.** [expressing disapproval]: **really!** also wirklich!

realm [relm] *n* - **1.** [field] Bereich *der* - **2.** [kingdom] Reich *das*.

realtor ['rɪəltər] *n US* Grundstücksmakler *der*, -in *die*.

reap [riːp] *vt liter* & *fig* ernten.

reappear [ˌriːə'pɪəʳ] *vi* wieder erscheinen.

rear [rɪəʳ] ◇ *adj* [wheel] Hinter-; **rear window** [of car] Heckscheibe *die*. ◇ *n* - **1.** [back] Rückseite *die*; **to bring up the rear** die Nachhut bilden - **2.** *inf* [buttocks] Hintern *der*. ◇ *vt* [children, animals, plants] auf|ziehen. ◇ *vi*: **to rear (up)** sich auf|bäumen.

rearm [riː'ɑːm] ◇ *vt* wieder bewaffnen. ◇ *vi* wieder auf|rüsten.

rearrange [ˌriːə'reɪndʒ] *vt* - **1.** [arrange differently] um|stellen - **2.** [reschedule] verlegen.

rearview mirror ['rɪəvjuː-] *n* Rückspiegel *der*.

reason ['riːzn] ◇ *n* - **1.** [cause]: **reason (for sthg)** Grund *der* (für etw); **for some reason** aus irgendeinem Grund - **2.** [justification]: **to have reason to do sthg** Grund haben, etw zu tun - **3.** [common sense] Vernunft *die*; **to listen to reason** auf die Stimme der Vernunft hören; **it stands to reason** es ist logisch. ◇ *vt* [conclude]: **to reason that...** folgern, dass... ◇ *vi* vernünftig denken. ◆ **reason with** *vt insep* vernünftig reden mit.

reasonable ['riːznəbl] *adj* - **1.** [sensible] vernünftig - **2.** [acceptable - decision, explanation] angemessen; [- work] ganz gut; [- offer] akzeptabel; [- price] vernünftig - **3.** [fairly large]: **a reasonable amount/number** ziemlich viel/viele.

reasonably ['riːznəblɪ] *adv* - **1.** [quite] ziemlich - **2.** [sensibly] vernünftig.

reasoned ['riːznd] *adj* durchdacht.

reasoning ['riːznɪŋ] *n (U)* Argumentation *die*.

reassess [ˌriːə'ses] *vt* [position, opinion] neu ein|schätzen.

reassurance [ˌriːə'ʃʊərəns] *n* - **1.** [comfort] Beruhigung *die* - **2.** [promise] Versicherung *die*.

reassure [ˌriːə'ʃʊəʳ] *vt* beruhigen.

reassuring [ˌriːə'ʃʊərɪŋ] *adj* beruhigend.

rebate ['riːbeɪt] *n* Nachlass *der*.

rebel ◇ *n* ['rebl] Rebell *der*, -in *die*. ◇ *vi* [rɪ'bel]: **to rebel (against)** rebellieren (gegen).

rebellion [rɪ'beljən] *n* Rebellion *die*.

rebellious [rɪ'beljəs] *adj* rebellisch.

rebound *vi* [rɪ'baʊnd] [ball] ab|prallen.

rebuff [rɪ'bʌf] *n* Abfuhr *die*.

rebuild [ˌriː'bɪld] (*pt & pp* **-built** [ˌriː'bɪlt]) *vt* wieder auf|bauen.

rebuke [rɪ'bjuːk] ◇ *n* Tadel *der*. ◇ *vt*: **to rebuke sb (for sthg)** jn (für etw) tadeln.

recall [rɪ'kɔːl] ◇ *n (U)* [memory] Erinnerung *die*. ◇ *vt* - **1.** [remember] sich erinnern an *(+ A)* - **2.** [summon back] zurück|rufen.

recap *inf vt* & *vi* [ˌriː'kæp] [summarize] zusammen|fassen.

recapitulate [ˌriːkə'pɪtjʊleɪt] *vt* & *vi* zusammen|fassen.

recd, rec'd *abbr of* **received**.

recede [rɪ'siːd] *vi* - **1.** [move away] zurück|weichen; **his hair is receding** er bekommt eine leichte Stirnglatze - **2.** *fig* [disappear, fade] schwinden.

receding [rɪ'siːdɪŋ] *adj* [chin] fliehend; [hairline] zurückweichend.

receipt [rɪ'siːt] *n* - **1.** [piece of paper] Quittung *die* - **2.** *(U)* [act of receiving] Empfang *der*. ◆ **receipts** *npl* [money taken] Einnahmen *Pl*.

receive [rɪ'siːv] *vt* - **1.** [gift, letter] erhalten - **2.** [news] erfahren - **3.** [setback] erfahren; **to receive an injury** verletzt werden - **4.** [visitor, guest] empfangen - **5.** [greet]: **to be well/badly received** gut/schlecht aufgenommen werden.

receiver [rɪ'siːvəʳ] *n* - **1.** [of telephone] Hörer *der* - **2.** [radio, TV set] Empfänger *der* - **3.** FIN [official] Konkursverwalter *der*, -in *die*.

recent ['riːsnt] *adj* neueste(r) (s).

recently ['riːsntlɪ] *adv* kürzlich.

receptacle [rɪ'septəkl] *n* Behälter *der*.

reception [rɪ'sepʃn] *n* Empfang *der*.

reception desk *n* Empfang *der*.

receptionist [rɪ'sepʃənɪst] *n* Empfangschef *der*, Empfangsdame *die*.

recess ['riːses, *UK* rɪ'ses] *n* - **1.** [vacation] Ferien *Pl*; **to be in/go into recess** eine Sitzungspause haben/beginnen - **2.** [alcove] Nische *die* - **3.** [of mind, memory] Winkel *der* - **4.** *US* SCH Pause *die*.

recession [rɪ'seʃn] *n* Rezession *die*.

recharge [ˌriː'tʃɑːdʒ] *vt* (auf)lladen.

recipe ['resɪpɪ] *n liter* & *fig* Rezept *das*.

recipient [rɪ'sɪpɪənt] *n* Empfänger *der*, -in *die*.

reciprocal [rɪ'sɪprəkl] *adj* wechselseitig.

recital [rɪ'saɪtl] *n* [of poetry] Vortrag *der*; [of music] Konzert *das*.

recite [rɪ'saɪt] *vt* - **1.** [perform aloud] vorltragen - **2.** [list] auflzählen.

reckless ['reklɪs] *adj* leichtsinnig.

reckon ['rekn] *vt* - **1.** *inf* [think]: **to reckon (that)** schätzen, dass - **2.** [consider, judge]: **to be reckoned to be sthg** als etw eingeschätzt werden - **3.** [calculate] schätzen. ◆ **reckon on** *vt insep* zählen auf *(+ A)*. ◆ **reckon with** *vt insep* [expect] rechnen mit.

reckoning ['rekənɪŋ] *n (U)* [calculation] Schätzung *die*.

reclaim [rɪ'kleɪm] *vt* - **1.** [claim back - lost item, luggage] ablholen; [- tax, expenses] zurückl-erlangen - **2.** [make fit for use] gewinnen.

recline [rɪ'klaɪn] *vi* [lie back] sich zurückllehnen.

reclining [rɪ'klaɪnɪŋ] *adj* verstellbar.

recluse [rɪ'kluːs] *n* Einsiedler *der*, -in *die*.

recognition [ˌrekəg'nɪʃn] *n (U)* - **1.** [identification] Erkennen *das*; **to have changed beyond** OR **out of all recognition** nicht wiederzuerkennen sein - **2.** [acknowledgement] Anerkennung *die*; **in recognition of** in Anerkennung *(+ G)*.

recognizable ['rekəgnaɪzəbl] *adj* erkennbar.

recognize, -ise ['rekəgnaɪz] *vt* - **1.** [gen] erkennen - **2.** [officially accept, approve] anlerkennen.

recoil ◇ *vi* [rɪ'kɔɪl] - **1.** [draw back] zurückl-weichen - **2.** *fig* [shrink from]: **to recoil from/at sthg** vor etw *(D)* zurücklschrecken. ◇ *n* ['riːkɔɪl] [of gun] Rückstoß *der*.

recollect [ˌrekə'lekt] *vt* sich erinnern an *(+ A)*.

recollection [ˌrekə'lekʃn] *n* Erinnerung *die*.

recommend [ˌrekə'mend] *vt* - **1.** [commend, speak in favour of]: **to recommend sb/sthg (to sb)** (jm) jn/etw empfehlen - **2.** [advise] raten zu.

recompense ['rekəmpens] ◇ *n*: **recompense (for sthg)** Entschädigung *die* (für etw). ◇ *vt*: **to recompense sb (for sthg)** jn (für etw) entschädigen.

reconcile ['rekənsaɪl] *vt* - **1.** [beliefs, ideas] (miteinander) vereinbaren; **to reconcile sthg with sthg** etw mit etw vereinbaren - **2.** [people] versöhnen - **3.** [resign]: **to reconcile o.s. to sthg** sich mit etw auslsöhnen.

reconditioned [ˌriːkən'dɪʃnd] *adj* überholt.

reconnaissance [rɪ'kɒnɪsəns] *n (U)* Erkundung *die*.

reconsider [ˌriːkən'sɪdəʳ] ◇ *vt* neu überdenken. ◇ *vi*: **it's not too late to reconsider** Sie können es sich noch einmal überlegen.

reconstruct [ˌriːkən'strʌkt] *vt* - **1.** [building, bridge, country] wieder auflbauen - **2.** [event, crime] rekonstruieren.

record ◇ *n* ['rekɔːd] - **1.** [written account] Aufzeichnung *die*; **off the record** inoffiziell - **2.** [vinyl disc] (Schall)platte *die* - **3.** [best achievement] Rekord *der* - **4.** [history]: **to have a good record** gute Leistungen aufweisen können; **to have a criminal record** vorbestraft sein. ◇ *adj* ['rekɔːd] Rekord-. ◇ *vt* [rɪ'kɔːd] - **1.** [write down] auflzeichnen - **2.** [put on tape etc] auflnehmen.

recorded delivery [rɪ'kɔːdɪd-] *n*: **to send sthg by recorded delivery** etw per Einschreiben schicken.

recorder [rɪ'kɔːdəʳ] *n* - **1.** [machine]: **(tape) recorder** Tonbandgerät *das*; **(cassette) recorder** Kassettenrekorder *der*; **(video) recorder** Videorekorder *der* - **2.** [musical instrument] Blockflöte *die*.

record holder *n* Rekordinhaber *der*, -in *die*.

recording [rɪ'kɔːdɪŋ] *n* - **1.** [individual recording] Aufnahme *die* - **2.** *(U)* [process of recording] Aufzeichnung *die*.

record player *n* Plattenspieler *der*.

recount ◇ *n* ['riːkaʊnt] Nachzählung *die*. ◇ *vt* - **1.** [rɪ'kaʊnt] [narrate] erzählen - **2.** [ˌriː'kaʊnt] [count again] nachlzählen.

recoup [rɪ'kuːp] *vt* [recover] wieder einlbringen.

recourse [rɪ'kɔːs] *n fml*: **to have recourse to sthg** Zuflucht zu etw nehmen.

recover [rɪ'kʌvəʳ] ◇ *vt* - **1.** [stolen goods, money] zurücklbekommen; **to recover sthg**

from sb/somewhere etw von jm/irgendwo zurück|bekommen - **2.** [one's strength, balance, senses] wieder|gewinnen. ◇ *vi* [from illness]: **to recover (from)** genesen (von etw).

recovery [rɪ'kʌvərɪ] *n* - **1.** [from illness]: **recovery (from)** Genesung *die* (von) - **2.** *fig* [of currency, economy] Erholung *die* - **3.** [of stolen goods, money] Wiedererlangung *die*.

recreation [,rekrɪ'eɪʃn] *n* [leisure] Erholung *die*.

recrimination [rɪ,krɪmɪ'neɪʃn] *n (U)* Gegenbeschuldigung *die*. ◆ **recriminations** *npl* gegenseitige Beschuldigungen *Pl*.

recruit [rɪ'kru:t] ◇ *n* [in armed forces] Rekrut *der*, -in *die*; [in company, organization] neues Mitglied. ◇ *vt* - **1.** [find, employ - in armed forces] rekrutieren; [- in company, organization] ein|stellen - **2.** [persuade to join] werben; **they recruited her to help out** sie haben sie zur Hilfe herangezogen. ◇ *vi* [look for new staff] ein|stellen.

recruitment [rɪ'kru:tmənt] *n (U)* [of staff] Einstellung *die*; [of soldiers] Rekrutierung *die*.

rectangle ['rek,tæŋgl] *n* Rechteck *das*.

rectangular [rek'tæŋgjʊlər] *adj* rechteckig.

rectify ['rektɪfaɪ] *vt fml* berichtigen.

rector ['rektər] *n* - **1.** [priest] Pfarrer *der* - **2.** *Scotland* [head - of school] Direktor *der*, -in *die*; [- of college, university] Rektor *der*, -in *die*.

rectory ['rektərɪ] *n* Pfarrhaus *das*.

recuperate [rɪ'ku:pəreɪt] *vi fml*: **to recuperate (from)** genesen (von).

recur [rɪ'kɜ:r] *vi* wieder|kehren; [problem, error] wieder auf|treten.

recurrence [rɪ'kʌrəns] *n fml* Wiederkehr *die*; [of problem, error] Wiederauftreten *das*.

recurrent [rɪ'kʌrənt] *adj* immer wiederkehrend; [problem, error] immer wieder auftretend.

recycle [,ri:'saɪkl] *vt* recyceln.

recycle bin *n* COMPUT Papierkorb *der*.

red [red] ◇ *adj* rot. ◇ *n* [colour] Rot *das*; **to be in the red** *inf* in den roten Zahlen sein.

red card *n* FTBL: **to be shown the red card, to get a red card** die rote Karte gezeigt bekommen.

red carpet *n*: **to roll out the red carpet for sb** für jn den roten Teppich aus|rollen.

Red Cross *n*: **the Red Cross** das Rote Kreuz.

redcurrant ['redkʌrənt] *n* (rote) Johannisbeere.

redden ['redn] *vi* [person, face] erröten.

redecorate [,ri:'dekəreɪt] *vt & vi* renovieren.

redeem [rɪ'di:m] *vt* - **1.** [save, rescue] retten - **2.** [from pawnbroker] ein|lösen.

redeeming [rɪ'di:mɪŋ] *adj*: **her one redeeming feature is...** ihre einzige positive Eigenschaft ist...

redeploy [,ri:dɪ'plɔɪ] *vt* [troops] umverlegen; [workers, staff] an anderer Stelle ein|setzen.

red-faced [-'feɪst] *adj* [with embarrassment] mit rotem Kopf.

red-haired [-'heəd] *adj* rothaarig.

red-handed [-'hændɪd] *adj*: **to catch sb red-handed** jn auf frischer Tat ertappen.

redhead ['redhed] *n* Rotkopf *der*.

red herring *n fig* falsche Spur.

red-hot *adj* - **1.** [extremely hot] rot glühend - **2.** *inf* [very good] klasse, super.

redid [,ri:'dɪd] *pt* ▷ **redo**.

redirect [,ri:dɪ'rekt] *vt* - **1.** [mail] nach|senden - **2.** [aircraft, aid] um|leiten; [one's energies] anders ein|setzen.

rediscover [,ri:dɪ'skʌvər] *vt* - **1.** [re-experience] wieder entdecken - **2.** [make popular, famous again]: **to be rediscovered** wieder entdeckt werden.

red light *n* [traffic signal] rote Ampel.

red-light district *n* Rotlichtviertel *das*.

redo [,ri:'du:] (*pt* **-did**, *pp* **-done**) *vt* [do again] noch einmal machen; [letter, essay] noch einmal schreiben.

redolent ['redələnt] *adj*: **to be redolent of sthg** *liter* [reminiscent] an etw *(A)* erinnern.

redone [,ri:'dʌn] *pp* ▷ **redo**.

redouble [,ri:'dʌbl] *vt*: **to redouble one's efforts (to do sthg)** seine Anstrengungen verdoppeln (etw zu tun).

redraft [,ri:'drɑ:ft] *vt* neu ab|fassen.

red tape *n fig* Bürokratie *die*.

reduce [rɪ'dju:s] ◇ *vt* - **1.** [make smaller, less] reduzieren - **2.** [force, bring]: **to be reduced to doing sthg** dazu gezwungen sein, etw zu tun; **to be reduced to tears** zum Weinen gebracht werden. ◇ *vi US* [lose weight] ab|nehmen.

reduction [rɪ'dʌkʃn] *n* - **1.** [decrease]: **reduction (in sthg)** Reduzierung *die* (einer Sache *(G)*) - **2.** [amount of decrease]: **reduction (of)** Ermäßigung *die* (um).

redundancy [rɪ'dʌndənsɪ] *n UK* - **1.** [job loss]: **redundancies** Entlassungen *Pl* - **2.** [jobless state] Arbeitslosigkeit *die*.

redundant [rɪ'dʌndənt] *adj* - **1.** *UK* [jobless]: **to be made redundant** den Arbeitsplatz verlieren - **2.** [superfluous] überflüssig.

reed [ri:d] *n* - **1.** [plant] Schilfrohr *das* - **2.** [of musical instrument] Rohrblatt *das*.

reef [ri:f] *n* [in sea] Riff *das*.

reek [ri:k] ◇ *n* Gestank *der*. ◇ *vi*: **to reek (of sthg)** (nach etw) stinken.

reel [ri:l] ◇ *n* - **1.** [roll] Spule *die* - **2.** [on fishing rod] Rolle *die*. ◇ *vi* [stagger] torkeln. ◆ **reel in** *vt sep* [fishing line] ein|rollen; [fish] ein|holen. ◆ **reel off** *vt sep* [list] ab|spulen.

reenact [ˌriːɪ'nækt] *vt* nachlspielen.

ref *n* - **1.** *inf* SPORT (*abbr of* **referee**) Schiri *der* - **2.** ADMIN *abbr of* **reference**.

refectory [rɪ'fektərɪ] *n* [in school, college] Speisesaal *der*.

refer [rɪ'fɜːʳ] *vt* - **1.** [person]: **to refer sb to sb** jn an jn verweisen; **to refer sb to sthg** [document, article] jn auf etw *(A)* verweisen - **2.** [report, case, decision]: **to refer sthg to sb/sthg** etw an jn/etw weiterlleiten. ◆ **refer to** *vt insep* - **1.** [mention] erwähnen; [as support for argument] sich beziehen auf *(+ A)* - **2.** [apply to, concern] betreffen - **3.** [consult] zu Rate ziehen.

referee [ˌrefə'riː] ◇ *n* - **1.** SPORT Schiedsrichter *der*, -in *die* - **2.** *UK* [for job application] Referenz *die*. ◇ *vt* SPORT leiten. ◇ *vi* SPORT Schiedsrichter sein.

reference ['refrəns] *n* - **1.** [act of mentioning]: **to make reference to sb/sthg** jn/etw erwähnen; **with reference to** *fml* mit Bezug auf *(+ A)* - **2.** [mention]: **reference (to)** Anspielung *die* (auf *(+ A)*) - **3.** [in catalogue, on map] Verweis *der* - **4.** COMM [in letter, for job application] Referenz *die*.

reference book *n* Nachschlagewerk *das*.

reference number *n* [for customer] Kundennummer *die*; [for member] Mitgliedsnummer *die*; [on file] Aktenzeichen *das*.

referendum [ˌrefə'rendəm] (*pl* **-s** OR **-da** [-də]) *n* POL Referendum *das*.

refill ◇ *n* ['riːfɪl] - **1.** [for pen, lighter] Nachfüllpatrone *die* - **2.** *inf* [drink]: **would you like a refill?** möchten Sie nachgeschenkt haben? ◇ *vt* [ˌriː'fɪl] nachlfüllen.

refine [rɪ'faɪn] *vt* - **1.** [oil, food] raffinieren - **2.** [details, speech] verfeinern.

refined [rɪ'faɪnd] *adj* - **1.** [genteel] fein - **2.** [highly developed, purified] raffiniert.

refinement [rɪ'faɪnmənt] *n* - **1.** [improvement]: **refinement (on sthg)** Verfeinerung *die* (von etw) - **2.** *(U)* [gentility] Feinheit *die*.

reflect [rɪ'flekt] ◇ *vt* - **1.** [show, be a sign of] widerlspiegeln - **2.** [throw back - light, heat] reflektieren; [- image] spiegeln - **3.** [think, consider]: **to reflect that...** daran denken, dass... ◇ *vi* [think, consider]: **to reflect (on** OR **upon sthg)** reflektieren (über etw *(A)*).

reflection [rɪ'flekʃn] *n* - **1.** [sign, consequence] Widerspiegelung *die* - **2.** [criticism]: **this is no reflection on your judgement** das ist keine Kritik an Ihrem Urteil - **3.** [image] Spiegelung *die* - **4.** *(U) liter* [thinking] Reflexion *die*; **on reflection** bei näherer Überlegung.

reflector [rɪ'flektəʳ] *n* Rückstrahler *der*.

reflex ['riːfleks] *n*: **reflex (action)** Reflex *der*.

reflexive [rɪ'fleksɪv] *adj* GRAM reflexiv.

reform [rɪ'fɔːm] ◇ *n* Reform *die*. ◇ *vt* - **1.** [change] reformieren - **2.** [improve behaviour of] bessern. ◇ *vi* [behave better] sich bessern.

Reformation [ˌrefə'meɪʃn] *n*: **the Reformation** die Reformation.

reformatory [rɪ'fɔːmətrɪ] *n US* Besserungsanstalt *die*.

reformer [rɪ'fɔːməʳ] *n* Reformer *der*, -in *die*.

refrain [rɪ'freɪn] ◇ *n* Refrain *der*. ◇ *vi fml*: **to refrain from doing sthg** es unterlassen, etw zu tun.

refresh [rɪ'freʃ] *vt* erfrischen.

refresher course [rɪ'freʃəʳ-] *n* Auffrischungskurs *der*.

refreshing [rɪ'freʃɪŋ] *adj* erfrischend.

refreshments [rɪ'freʃmənts] *npl* Erfrischungen *Pl*.

refrigerator [rɪ'frɪdʒəreɪtəʳ] *n* Kühlschrank *der*.

refuel [ˌriː'fjʊəl] (*UK*) (*US*) *vt* & *vi* aufltanken.

refuge ['refjuːdʒ] *n* - **1.** [place of safety] Zuflucht *die* - **2.** [safety]: **to seek** OR **take refuge** [hide] Zuflucht suchen; **to seek** OR **take refuge in sthg** *fig* in etw *(D)* Zuflucht suchen.

refugee [ˌrefjʊ'dʒiː] *n* Flüchtling *der*.

refund ◇ *n* ['riːfʌnd] Rückzahlung *die*. ◇ *vt* [rɪ'fʌnd]: **to refund sthg to sb, to refund sb sthg** etw an jn zurücklzahlen.

refurbish [ˌriː'fɜːbɪʃ] *vt* renovieren.

refusal [rɪ'fjuːzl] *n*: **refusal (to do sthg)** Weigerung *die* (etw zu tun).

refuse[1] [rɪ'fjuːz] ◇ *vt* - **1.** [withhold, deny]: **to refuse sb sthg, to refuse sthg to sb** jm etw verweigern - **2.** [decline] abllehnen; **to refuse to do sthg** sich weigern, etw zu tun. ◇ *vi* sich weigern.

refuse[2] ['refjuːs] *n* Müll *der*.

refuse collection ['refjuːs-] *n* Müllabfuhr *die*.

refute [rɪ'fjuːt] *vt fml* widerlegen.

regain [rɪ'geɪn] *vt* [recover] wiederlgewinnen; **to regain consciousness** wieder zu Bewusstsein kommen.

regal ['riːgl] *adj* majestätisch.

regard [rɪ'gɑːd] ◇ *n* - **1.** *(U) fml* [respect, esteem]: **to hold sb/sthg in high/low regard** jn/etw hoch/gering achten - **2.** [aspect]: **in this/that regard** in dieser/jener Hinsicht. ◇ *vt*: **to regard o.s./sb/sthg as** sich/jn/etw halten für; **to be highly regarded** hoch geachtet sein. ◆ **regards** *npl* [in greetings] Grüße *Pl*; **send her my regards** grüße sie von mir. ◆ **as regards** *prep* in Bezug auf *(+ A)*. ◆ **in regard to, with regard to** *prep* bezüglich *(+ G)*.

regarding [rɪ'gɑːdɪŋ] *prep* in Bezug auf *(+ A)*.

regardless [rɪ'gɑːdlɪs] *adv* trotzdem. ◆ **regardless of** *prep* ohne Rücksicht auf *(+ A)*.

regime [reɪ'ʒiːm] *n pej* Regime *das*.

regiment ['redʒɪmənt] *n* MIL Regiment *das*.

region ['riːdʒən] *n* - 1. [of country] Gebiet *das*, Region *die* - 2. [of body] Bereich *der* - 3. [range]: **in the region of** ungefähr.

regional ['riːdʒənl] *adj* regional.

register ['redʒɪstəʳ] ◇ *n* [of school class] Klassenbuch *das*. ◇ *vt* - 1. [record officially, show, measure] registrieren - 2. [express] zeigen. ◇ *vi* - 1. [enrol]: **to register as/for sthg** sich als/für etw (an)|melden - 2. [book in] sich ein|tragen - 3. *inf* [be properly understood]: **it didn't register (with her)** sie registrierte es gar nicht.

registered ['redʒɪstəd] *adj* - 1. [officially listed - company, charity] eingetragen - 2. [letter, parcel] eingeschrieben.

registered trademark *n* eingetragenes Warenzeichen.

registrar [,redʒɪ'strɑːʳ] *n* [keeper of records] Standesbeamte *der*, -tin *die*.

registration [,redʒɪ'streɪʃn] *n* - 1. [in records] Eintragung *die* - 2. [on course] Anmeldung *die* - 3. AUT = **registration number**.

registration number *n* AUT Kennzeichen *das*.

registry ['redʒɪstrɪ] *n* Registratur *die*.

registry office *n* Standesamt *das*.

regret [rɪ'gret] ◇ *n* Bedauern *das*; **I have no regrets about it** ich bedauere es nicht. ◇ *vt* bedauern; **to regret doing sthg** bedauern, etw getan zu haben.

regretfully [rɪ'gretfʊlɪ] *adv* mit Bedauern.

regrettable [rɪ'gretəbl] *adj* bedauerlich.

regroup [,riː'gruːp] *vi* sich neu gruppieren; [soldiers] sich neu formieren.

regular ['regjʊləʳ] ◇ *adj* - 1. [gen & GRAM] regelmäßig - 2. [usual] üblich - 3. *US* [in size] klein - 4. *US* [pleasant]: **he's a regular guy** er ist O.K. - 5. *US* [normal] normal. ◇ *n* [customer, client] Stammkunde *der*, -din *die*.

regularly ['regjʊləlɪ] *adv* regelmäßig.

regulate ['regjʊleɪt] *vt* - 1. [control] regulieren - 2. [adjust] regeln.

regulation [,regjʊ'leɪʃn] ◇ *adj* [standard] vorgeschrieben. ◇ *n* - 1. [rule] Vorschrift *die* - 2. *(U)* [control] Regulierung *die*.

rehabilitate [,riːə'bɪlɪteɪt] *vt* rehabilitieren.

rehearsal [rɪ'hɜːsl] *n* Probe *die*.

rehearse [rɪ'hɜːs] *vt* & *vi* proben.

reheat [,riː'hiːt] *vt* auf|wärmen.

reign [reɪn] ◇ *n liter* & *fig* Herrschaft *die*. ◇ *vi* - 1. [rule]: **to reign (over)** herrschen (über *(+ A)*) - 2. [prevail]: **to reign over** sich aus|breiten über *(+ D)*.

reimburse [,riːɪm'bɜːs] *vt* [person] entschädigen; [expenses] zurück|erstatten; **to reimburse sb for sthg** jm etw zurück|erstatten.

rein [reɪn] *n fig*: **to give sb (a) free rein** jm freie Hand lassen. ◆ **reins** *npl* [for horse] Zügel *Pl*.

reindeer ['reɪn,dɪəʳ] (*pl inv*) *n* Rentier *das*.

reinforce [,riːɪn'fɔːs] *vt* - 1. [ceiling, frame, cover]: **to reinforce sthg (with sthg)** etw (mit etw) verstärken - 2. [dislike, prejudice] bestärken - 3. [argument, claim] stützen.

reinforced concrete [,riːɪn'fɔːst-] *n* Stahlbeton *der*.

reinforcement [,riːɪn'fɔːsmənt] *n* [in construction] Verstärkung *die*. ◆ **reinforcements** *npl* MIL Verstärkung *die*.

reinstate [,riːɪn'steɪt] *vt* - 1. [employee] wieder ein|stellen - 2. [payment, policy] wieder auf|nehmen.

reissue [riː'ɪʃuː] ◇ *n* Neuausgabe *die*; [of book] Neuauflage *die*. ◇ *vt* neu heraus|geben; [book] neu auf|legen.

reiterate [riː'ɪtəreɪt] *vt fml* wiederholen.

reject ◇ *n* ['riːdʒekt]: **rejects** [from factory] Ausschuss *der*. ◇ *vt* [rɪ'dʒekt] ab|lehnen.

rejection [rɪ'dʒekʃn] *n* - 1. [of offer, values, religion] Ablehnung *die* - 2. [for job] Absage *die*.

rejoice [rɪ'dʒɔɪs] *vi*: **to rejoice (at** *OR* **in sthg)** sich freuen (über etw *(A)*).

rejuvenate [rɪ'dʒuːvəneɪt] *vt* verjüngen.

rekindle [,riː'kɪndl] *vt fig* wieder entflammen.

relapse [rɪ'læps] *n* Rückfall *der*.

relate [rɪ'leɪt] ◇ *vt* - 1. [connect]: **to relate sthg to sthg** etw zu etw in Beziehung bringen *OR* setzen - 2. [tell] erzählen. ◇ *vi* - 1. [connect]: **to relate to sthg** mit etw zusammen|hängen - 2. [concern]: **to relate to sb/sthg** jn/etw betreffen - 3. [empathize]: **to relate to sb/sthg** einen Bezug zu jm/etw haben. ◆ **relating to** *prep* im Zusammenhang mit.

related [rɪ'leɪtɪd] *adj* - 1. [in same family] verwandt; **to be related to sb** mit jm verwandt sein - 2. [connected] zusammenhängend; **to be related to sthg** mit etw zusammen|hängen.

relation [rɪ'leɪʃn] *n* - 1. *(U)* [connection]: **relation to/between** Beziehung *die* zu/zwischen *(+ D)* - 2. [family member] Verwandte *der, die*. ◆ **relations** *npl* [relationship]: **relations (between/with)** Beziehungen *Pl* (zwischen *(+ D)*/mit).

relationship [rɪ'leɪʃnʃɪp] *n* Beziehung *die*.

relative ['relətɪv] ◇ *adj* - 1. [gen] relativ - 2. [respective] jeweilig. ◇ *n* Verwandte *der, die*. ◆ **relative to** *prep fml* - 1. [compared to] im Vergleich zu - 2. [connected with] sich beziehend auf *(+ A)*.

relatively ['relətɪvlɪ] *adv* relativ.

relax [rɪ'læks] ◇ *vt* - 1. [mind, muscle, person] entspannen - 2. [grip, discipline, regulation] lockern. ◇ *vi* - 1. [person, body, muscle] sich entspannen - 2. [grip] sich lockern.

relaxation [,riːlæk'seɪʃn] *n (U)* [rest] Entspannung *die*.

relaxed [rɪ'lækst] *adj* entspannt.

relaxing [rɪ'læksɪŋ] *adj* entspannend.

relay <> *n* ['ri:leɪ] - **1.** SPORT: **relay (race)** Staffellauf *der*; **to work in relays** *fig* sich (bei der Arbeit) ab|lösen - **2.** RADIO & TV Relais *das*. <> *vt* - **1.** ['ri:leɪ] RADIO & TV [broadcast] übertragen - **2.** ['ri:leɪ] [message, news]: **to relay sthg (to sb)** (jm) etw aus|richten.

release [rɪ'li:s] <> *n* - **1.** *(U)* [from captivity] Freilassung *die* - **2.** *(U)* [from pain, suffering] Erlösung *die* - **3.** [statement] Verlautbarung *die* - **4.** [of gas, fumes] Freisetzen *das* - **5.** [of film, video, CD] Freigabe *die*; **the movie is on release from Friday** der Film ist von Freitag an im Kino (zu sehen) - **6.** [video, CD]: **new release** Neuerscheinung *die*; [film] neuer Film. <> *vt* - **1.** [set free] frei|lassen; **to release sb from prison/captivity** jm aus dem Gefängnis/der Gefangenschaft entlassen; **to release sb from sthg** [promise, contract] jn von etw befreien - **2.** [make available] frei|setzen - **3.** [from control, grasp] los|lassen - **4.** [brake, lever, handle] lösen - **5.** [let out, emit]: **to be released (from/into sthg)** freigesetzt werden (aus etw/in etw *(A)*) - **6.** [film, video, CD] heraus|bringen; [statement, news story] veröffentlichen.

relegate ['relɪgeɪt] *vt* - **1.** [lower status of]: **to relegate sb/sthg (to)** jn/etw verbannen (in *(+ A)*) - **2.** *UK* SPORT: **to be relegated** ab|steigen.

relent [rɪ'lent] *vi* [person] nach|geben.

relentless [rɪ'lentlɪs] *adj* erbarmungslos.

relevant ['reləvənt] *adj* - **1.** [connected]: **relevant (to)** relevant (für) - **2.** [important]: **relevant (to)** wichtig (für) - **3.** [appropriate] entsprechend.

reliable [rɪ'laɪəbl] *adj* zuverlässig.

reliably [rɪ'laɪəblɪ] *adv* zuverlässig.

reliant [rɪ'laɪənt] *adj*: **reliant on** abhängig von *(+ D)*.

relic ['relɪk] *n* - **1.** [old object, custom - still in use] Überbleibsel *das*; [- no longer in use] Relikt *das* - **2.** RELIG Reliquie *die*.

relief [rɪ'li:f] *n* - **1.** [comfort] Erleichterung *die* - **2.** *(U)* [for poor, refugees] Hilfe *die* - **3.** *US* [social security] Fürsorge *die*.

relieve [rɪ'li:v] *vt* - **1.** [ease, lessen] lindern; **to relieve sb of sthg** jn von etw befreien - **2.** [take over from]: **to relieve sb of sthg** jn einer Sache *(G)* entheben - **3.** [give help to] helfen *(+ D)*.

religion [rɪ'lɪdʒn] *n* - **1.** [belief in a god] Glaube *der* - **2.** [system of belief] Religion *die*.

religious [rɪ'lɪdʒəs] *adj* religiös.

relinquish [rɪ'lɪŋkwɪʃ] *vt* auf|geben.

relish ['relɪʃ] <> *n* - **1.** [enjoyment]: **with (great) relish** genüsslich - **2.** [pickle] Soße *die*. <> *vt* [enjoy] genießen; **to relish the idea** OR **thought of doing sthg** sich darauf freuen, etw zu tun.

relocate [,ri:ləʊ'keɪt] <> *vt* verlegen. <> *vi* den Standort wechseln.

reluctance [rɪ'lʌktəns] *n* Widerwille *der*.

reluctant [rɪ'lʌktənt] *adj* widerwillig; **to be reluctant to do sthg** abgeneigt sein, etw zu tun.

reluctantly [rɪ'lʌktəntlɪ] *adv* widerwillig.

rely [rɪ'laɪ] ◆ **rely on** *vt insep* - **1.** [count on] sich verlassen auf *(+ A)* - **2.** [be dependent on]: **to rely on sb/sthg for sthg** wegen etw auf jn/etw angewiesen sein.

remain [rɪ'meɪn] <> *vt*: **that remains to be done** das bleibt (noch) zu tun. <> *vi* bleiben. ◆ **remains** *npl* - **1.** [of meal, ancient civilization, building] Überreste *Pl* - **2.** [corpse] menschliche Überreste *Pl*.

remainder [rɪ'meɪndə^r] *n* Rest *der*.

remaining [rɪ'meɪnɪŋ] *adj* verbleibend.

remand [rɪ'mɑ:nd] <> *n* LAW: **on remand** in Untersuchungshaft. <> *vt (phrase)*: **to be remanded in custody** in Untersuchungshaft bleiben.

remark [rɪ'mɑ:k] <> *n* Bemerkung *die*. <> *vt*: **to remark that...** bemerken, dass...

remarkable [rɪ'mɑ:kəbl] *adj* bemerkenswert.

remarry [,ri:'mærɪ] *vi* wieder heiraten.

remedial [rɪ'mi:djəl] *adj* - **1.** SCH Förder- - **2.** [corrective - action] abhelfend.

remedy ['remədɪ] <> *n*: **remedy (for sthg)** [for ill health] Heilmittel *das* (für OR gegen etw); [solution] Lösung *die* (für etw). <> *vt* ab|helfen *(+ D)*.

remember [rɪ'membə^r] <> *vt* - **1.** [recollect] sich erinnern an *(+ A)*; **to remember doing sthg** sich daran erinnern, etw getan zu haben - **2.** [not forget] denken an *(+ A)*; **to remember to do sthg** daran denken, etw zu tun. <> *vi* sich erinnern.

remembrance [rɪ'membrəns] *n fml*: **in remembrance of** zur Erinnerung an *(+ A)*.

Remembrance Day *n nationaler britischer Trauertag zum Gedenken an die in den beiden Weltkriegen gefallenen Soldaten. Er wird an dem 11. November nächstliegenden Sonntag begangen.*

remind [rɪ'maɪnd] *vt* - **1.** [tell]: **to remind sb about sthg** jn an etw *(A)* erinnern; **to remind sb to do sthg** jn daran erinnern, etw zu tun - **2.** [be reminiscent of]: **to remind sb of sb/sthg** jn an jn/etw erinnern.

reminder [rɪ'maɪndə^r] *n* - **1.** [to jog memory]: **to give sb a reminder to do sthg** jn daran erinnern, etw zu tun - **2.** [for bill, membership, licence] Mahnung *die*.

reminisce [,remɪ'nɪs] *vi*: **to reminisce (about sthg)** in Erinnerungen (an etw *(A)*) schwelgen.

reminiscent [,remɪ'nɪsnt] *adj*: **to be reminiscent of sb/sthg** an jn/etw erinnern.

remiss [rɪ'mɪs] *adj* nachlässig.

remit <> *n* ['ri:mɪt] *UK* Aufgabenbereich *der*. <> *vt* [rɪ'mɪt] [send] überweisen.

remittance [rɪ'mɪtns] *n* Überweisung *die*.

remnant ['remnənt] *n* Rest *der*.

remorse [rɪ'mɔ:s] *n* Reue *die*.

remorseful [rɪ'mɔ:sfʊl] *adj* reuig.

remorseless [rɪ'mɔ:slɪs] *adj* - **1.** [pitiless] unbarmherzig - **2.** [unstoppable] unaufhaltsam.

remote [rɪ'məʊt] *adj* - **1.** [distant - place] abgelegen; [- time] entfernt - **2.** [aloof] unnahbar - **3.** [unconnected, irrelevant]: **remote from** entfernt von - **4.** [slight - resemblance] entfernt; [- chance, possibility] gering.

remote control *n* - **1.** *(U)* [system] Fernsteuerung *die* - **2.** [machine, device] Fernbedienung *die*.

remotely [rɪ'məʊtlɪ] *adv* - **1.** [slightly]: **not remotely** nicht im Entferntesten, nicht im Geringsten - **2.** [distantly] entfernt.

removable [rɪ'mu:vəbl] *adj* [detachable] abnehmbar.

removal [rɪ'mu:vl] *n* - **1.** *UK* [change of house] Umzug *der* - **2.** [act of removing] Entfernen *das*.

removal van *n UK* Möbelwagen *der*.

remove [rɪ'mu:v] *vt* - **1.** [take away, clean]: **to remove sthg (from)** etw entfernen (aus/von) - **2.** [clothes, hat] ab|legen - **3.** [from a job]: **to remove sb (from)** jn entfernen (von) - **4.** [problem] beseitigen; [suspicion] zerstreuen.

remuneration [rɪˌmju:nə'reɪʃn] *n fml* - **1.** [pay] Bezahlung *die* - **2.** [amount of money] Vergütung *die*.

render ['rendəʳ] *vt* - **1.** [make] machen - **2.** [give - help, service] leisten.

rendezvous ['rɒndɪvu:] (*pl inv*) *n* - **1.** [meeting] Rendezvous *das* - **2.** [place] Treffpunkt *der*.

renegade ['renɪgeɪd] *n* Abtrünnige *der, die*.

renew [rɪ'nju:] *vt* - **1.** [repeat, restart] wieder auf|nehmen - **2.** [extend validity of] verlängern - **3.** [increase]: **with renewed enthusiasm/interest** mit neuem Enthusiasmus/Interesse.

renewable [rɪ'nju:əbl] *adj* - **1.** [resources] erneuerbar - **2.** [contract, licence, membership] verlängerbar.

renewal [rɪ'nju:əl] *n (U)* [of contract, licence, membership] Verlängerung *die*.

renounce [rɪ'naʊns] *vt* - **1.** [reject] ab|schwören *(+ D)* - **2.** *fml* [relinquish] verzichten auf *(+ A)*.

renovate ['renəveɪt] *vt* renovieren.

renown [rɪ'naʊn] *n* Ruf *der*.

renowned [rɪ'naʊnd] *adj*: **renowned (for sthg)** berühmt (für etw).

rent [rent] <> *n* Miete *die*. <> *vt* - **1.** [subj: tenant, hirer] mieten - **2.** [subj: owner] vermieten.

rental ['rentl] <> *adj* Miet-. <> *n* [money] Leihgebühr *die*; [for house] Miete *die*.

rental car *n* Mietwagen *der*.

renunciation [rɪˌnʌnsɪ'eɪʃn] *n (U)* - **1.** [relinquishing]: **renunciation of sthg** Verzicht *der* auf etw *(A)* - **2.** [rejection]: **renunciation of sthg** Abschwörung *die* von etw.

reorganize, -ise [ˌri:'ɔ:gənaɪz] *vt* neu organisieren.

rep [rep] *n abbr of* **representative**, **repertory company**.

repaid [ˌri:'peɪd] *pt & pp* ▷ **repay**.

repair [rɪ'peəʳ] <> *n* Reparatur *die*; **in good/bad repair** in gutem/schlechtem Zustand. <> *vt* - **1.** [fix, mend] reparieren; [puncture, crack] aus|bessern - **2.** [make amends for] wieder gut|machen.

repair kit *n* Flickzeug *das*.

repartee [ˌrepɑ:'ti:] *n (U)* Schlagabtausch *der*.

repatriate [ˌri:'pætrɪeɪt] *vt* repatriieren.

repay [ˌri:'peɪ] (*pt & pp* **repaid**) *vt* - **1.** [money] zurück|zahlen; **to repay sb sthg, to repay sthg to sb** jm etw zurück|zahlen - **2.** [kindness] vergelten.

repayment [ri:'peɪmənt] *n* Rückzahlung *die*.

repeal [rɪ'pi:l] *vt* auf|heben.

repeat [rɪ'pi:t] <> *vt* wiederholen. <> *n* [broadcast] Wiederholung *die*.

repeatedly [rɪ'pi:tɪdlɪ] *adv* wiederholt.

repel [rɪ'pel] *vt* - **1.** [disgust] ab|stoßen - **2.** [drive away] ab|wehren.

repellent [rɪ'pelənt] <> *adj* abstoßend. <> *n*: **(insect) repellent** Insektenabwehrmittel *das*.

repent [rɪ'pent] <> *vt* bereuen. <> *vi*: **to repent of sthg** über etw *(A)* Reue empfinden.

repentance [rɪ'pentəns] *n* Reue *die*.

repercussions [ˌri:pə'kʌʃnz] *npl* Auswirkungen *Pl*.

repertoire ['repətwɑ:ʳ] *n* Repertoire *das*.

repertory ['repətrɪ] *n* [repertoire] Repertoire *das*.

repetition [ˌrepɪ'tɪʃn] *n* Wiederholung *die*.

repetitious [ˌrepɪ'tɪʃəs], **repetitive** [rɪ'petɪtɪv] *adj* monoton.

replace [rɪ'pleɪs] *vt* - **1.** [gen] ersetzen; **to replace sb/sthg with sb/sthg** jn/etw durch jn/etw ersetzen - **2.** [put back - upright] zurück|stellen; [- lying flat] zurück|legen.

replacement [rɪ'pleɪsmənt] *n* - **1.** [act of replacing] Ersetzen *das* - **2.** [new person, object]: **replacement (for sthg)** Ersatz *der* (für etw); **replacement (for sb)** [in job - temporary] Vertretung *die* (von jm); [- permanent] Nachfolger *der*, -in *die* (von jm).

replay <> *n* ['ri:pleɪ] - **1.** [recording]: **(action) replay** Wiederholung *die* - **2.** [game] Wiederholungsspiel *das*. <> *vt* [ˌri:'pleɪ] - **1.** [match, game] wiederholen - **2.** [film, tape] nochmals ab|spielen.

replenish [rɪ'plenɪʃ] *vt fml*: **to replenish sthg (with sthg)** etw (mit etw) wieder auf|füllen.

replica ['replɪkə] *n* Kopie *die*.

reply [rɪ'plaɪ] ◇ *n*: **reply (to sthg)** Antwort *die* (auf etw *(A)*). ◇ *vt* antworten. ◇ *vi* antworten; **to reply to sb/sthg** jm/auf etw *(A)* antworten.

reply coupon *n* Antwortschein *der*.

report [rɪ'pɔ:t] ◇ *n* - **1.** [description, account] Bericht *der* - **2.** PRESS Reportage *die* - **3.** *UK* SCH Zeugnis *das*. ◇ *vt* - **1.** [news, crime] melden - **2.** [make known]: **to report that...** berichten, dass...; **to report sthg (to sb)** (jm) etw berichten - **3.** [complain about]: **to report sb (to sb)** jn (bei jm) an|zeigen; **to report sb for sthg** jn wegen etw an|zeigen. ◇ *vi* - **1.** [give account]: **to report (on sthg)** (über etw *(A)*) berichten - **2.** PRESS: **this is John Smith, reporting from Moscow** John Smith (mit einem Bericht) aus Moskau; **to report on sthg** über etw berichten - **3.** [present o.s.]: **to report to...** sich melden bei...; **to report for duty** sich zum Dienst melden.

report card *n US* SCH Zeugnis *das*.

reportedly [rɪ'pɔ:tɪdlɪ] *adv* angeblich.

reporter [rɪ'pɔ:tə^r] *n* [in TV, radio, press] Reporter *der*, -in *die*, Berichterstatter *der*, -in *die*.

repossess [ˌri:pə'zes] *vt* wieder in Besitz nehmen.

reprehensible [ˌreprɪ'hensəbl] *adj fml* verwerflich.

represent [ˌreprɪ'zent] *vt* - **1.** [act for] vertreten - **2.** [constitute, symbolize] dar|stellen.

representation [ˌreprɪzen'teɪʃn] *n* [depiction] Darstellung *die*. ◆ **representations** *npl fml*: **to make representations to sb** sich mit einem Anliegen an jn wenden.

representative [ˌreprɪ'zentətɪv] ◇ *adj* - **1.** [acting for main group] stellvertretend - **2.** [typical]: **representative (of)** repräsentativ (für). ◇ *n* - **1.** [of company, organization, group] Vertreter *der*, -in *die* - **2.** *US* POL Abgeordnete *der, die*.

repress [rɪ'pres] *vt* unterdrücken.

repression [rɪ'preʃn] *n (U)* Unterdrückung *die*.

reprieve [rɪ'pri:v] ◇ *n* - **1.** [of death sentence] Begnadigung *die* - **2.** [respite] Gnadenfrist *die*. ◇ *vt* begnadigen.

reprimand ['reprɪmɑ:nd] ◇ *n* Tadel *der*. ◇ *vt* tadeln.

reprisal [rɪ'praɪzl] *n* - **1.** [counterblow] Vergeltungsmaßnahme *die* - **2.** [revenge]: **in reprisal (for)** als Vergeltung (für).

reproach [rɪ'prəʊtʃ] ◇ *n* Vorwurf *der*; **to be beyond reproach** über jeden Vorwurf erhaben sein. ◇ *vt*: **to reproach sb (for** OR **with sthg)** jm (wegen etw) Vorwürfe machen.

reproduce [ˌri:prə'dju:s] ◇ *vt* [copy] reproduzieren. ◇ *vi* BIOL sich fort|pflanzen.

reproduction [ˌri:prə'dʌkʃn] *n* - **1.** [replica] Reproduktion *die*; **reproduction furniture** Stilmöbel *Pl* - **2.** *(U)* [copying, simulation] Reproduktion *die*; **sound reproduction** Tonwiedergabe *die* - **3.** BIOL Fortpflanzung *die*.

reprove [rɪ'pru:v] *vt*: **to reprove sb (for sthg)** jn (wegen etw) tadeln.

reptile ['reptaɪl] *n* Reptil *das*.

republic [rɪ'pʌblɪk] *n* Republik *die*.

republican [rɪ'pʌblɪkən] ◇ *adj* republikanisch. ◇ *n* Republikaner *der*, -in *die*. ◆ **Republican** ◇ *adj* - **1.** [in USA] republikanisch; **the Republican Party** die Republikanische Partei - **2.** [in Northern Ireland] *bezeichnet einen Befürworter einer vereinten unabhängigen Republik Irland bzw. dessen Ideen*. ◇ *n* - **1.** [in USA] Republikaner *der*, -in *die* - **2.** [in Northern Ireland] *Befürworter einer vereinten unabhängigen Republik Irland*.

repulse [rɪ'pʌls] *vt* - **1.** [refuse] zurück|weisen; [person] verstoßen - **2.** MIL [drive back] ab|wehren.

repulsive [rɪ'pʌlsɪv] *adj* abstoßend.

reputable ['repjʊtəbl] *adj* seriös.

reputation [ˌrepjʊ'teɪʃn] *n* Ruf *der*.

repute [rɪ'pju:t] *n fml* [reputation]: **of good/ill repute** von gutem/schlechtem Ruf.

reputed [rɪ'pju:tɪd] *adj*: **he is a reputed expert/millionaire** er soll ein Fachmann/Millionär sein; **to be reputed to be sthg** als etw gelten.

reputedly [rɪ'pju:tɪdlɪ] *adv*: **he is reputedly the best surgeon** er gilt als der beste Chirurg.

request [rɪ'kwest] ◇ *n*: **request (for sthg)** Bitte *die* (um etw); **on request** auf Wunsch. ◇ *vt* bitten um; **to request sb to do sthg** jn bitten, etw zu tun.

require [rɪ'kwaɪə^r] *vt* erfordern; **to be required to do sthg** aufgefordert werden, etw zu tun.

requirement [rɪ'kwaɪəmənt] *n* - **1.** [condition] Erfordernis *das* - **2.** [need] Bedarf *der*.

reran [ˌri:'ræn] *pt* ▷ **rerun**.

rerun (*pt* **reran**, *pp* **rerun**) ◇ *n* ['ri:rʌn] Wiederholung *die*. ◇ *vt* [ˌri:'rʌn] [gen] wiederholen.

resat [ˌri:'sæt] *pt* & *pp* ▷ **resit**.

rescind [rɪ'sɪnd] *vt* LAW annulieren.

rescue ['reskju:] ◇ *n* Rettung *die*. ◇ *vt* retten; **to rescue sb/sthg from sb/sthg** jn/etw vor jm/aus etw retten.

rescuer ['reskjʊə^r] *n* Retter *der*, -in *die*.

research [ˌrɪ'sɜ:tʃ] ◇ *n (U)*: **research (on** OR **into sthg)** Forschung *die* (über etw *(A)*); **research and development** Forschung und Entwicklung. ◇ *vt* erforschen; [article, book] recherchieren.

researcher [rɪ'sɜːtʃəʳ] *n* Forscher *der*, -in *die*.

resemblance [rɪ'zembləns] *n*: **resemblance (to/between)** Ähnlichkeit *die* (mit/zwischen *(+ D)*).

resemble [rɪ'zembl] *vt* ähneln.

resent [rɪ'zent] *vt* sich ärgern über *(+ A)*; **I resent that!** das ärgert mich!

resentful [rɪ'zentfʊl] *adj* verärgert.

resentment [rɪ'zentmənt] *n* Groll *der*.

reservation [ˌrezə'veɪʃn] *n* - **1.** [booking] Reservierung *die* - **2.** [doubt]: **without reservation** ohne Vorbehalt - **3.** *US* [for Native Americans] Reservat *das*. ◆ **reservations** *npl* [doubts] Vorbehalte *Pl*.

reserve [rɪ'zɜːv] ◇ *n* - **1.** [supply] Reserve *die*; **in reserve** in Reserve - **2.** SPORT [substitute] Reservespieler *der*, -in *die* - **3.** [sanctuary] Reservat *das* - **4.** *(U)* [restraint, shyness] Reserve *die*. ◇ *vt* - **1.** [keep for particular purpose]: **to reserve sthg for sb/sthg** etw für jn/etw reservieren - **2.** [book] reservieren - **3.** [retain]: **to reserve the right to do sthg** sich das Recht vorbehalten, etw zu tun.

reserved [rɪ'zɜːvd] *adj* reserviert.

reservoir ['rezəvwɑːʳ] *n* [lake] Reservoir *das*.

reset [ˌriː'set] *(pt & pp inv) vt* - **1.** [clock] neu stellen; [meter] zurück|stellen - **2.** COMPUT rücksetzen.

reshape [ˌriː'ʃeɪp] *vt* [policy, thinking] um|formen.

reshuffle [ˌriː'ʃʌfl] ◇ *n* POL Umbildung *die*. ◇ *vt* POL um|bilden.

reside [rɪ'zaɪd] *vi fml* - **1.** [live] seinen Wohnsitz haben - **2.** [be located, found]: **to reside in sthg** in etw *(D)* liegen.

residence ['rezɪdəns] *n* [house] Wohnsitz *der*.

residence permit *n* Aufenthaltserlaubnis *die*.

resident ['rezɪdənt] ◇ *adj* - **1.** [settled, living] wohnhaft - **2.** [on-site, live-in] Haus-. ◇ *n* [of town, street] Bewohner *der*, -in *die*; [in hotel] Gast *der*.

residential [ˌrezɪ'denʃl] *adj*: **residential course** *Kurs, bei dem die Teilnehmer auf dem Schulgelände untergebracht werden*; **residential care** Pflege *die* im Haus.

residential area *n* Wohngebiet *das*.

residue ['rezɪdjuː] *n* CHEM Rückstand *der*.

resign [rɪ'zaɪn] ◇ *vt* - **1.** [give up - job] kündigen; [- post] zurück|treten von - **2.** [accept calmly]: **to resign o.s. to sthg** sich mit etw ab|finden. ◇ *vi* [from job] kündigen; [from post] zurück|treten.

resignation [ˌrezɪg'neɪʃn] *n* - **1.** [from job] Kündigung *die*; [from post] Rücktritt *der* - **2.** [calm acceptance] Resignation *die*.

resigned [rɪ'zaɪnd] *adj*: **to be resigned to sthg** sich mit etw abgefunden haben.

resilient [rɪ'zɪlɪənt] *adj* - **1.** [material] elastisch - **2.** [person] unverwüstlich.

resist [rɪ'zɪst] *vt* Widerstand leisten gegen; [temptation, offer] widerstehen *(+ D)*.

resistance [rɪ'zɪstəns] *n (U)*: **resistance (to sthg)** Widerstand *der* (gegen etw).

resit *(pt & pp* **resat***) UK* ◇ *n* ['riːsɪt] Wiederholungsprüfung *die*. ◇ *vt* [ˌriː'sɪt] wiederholen.

resolute ['rezəluːt] *adj* energisch.

resolution [ˌrezə'luːʃn] *n* - **1.** [motion, decision] Resolution *die* - **2.** [vow, promise] Vorsatz *der* - **3.** [determination] Entschlossenheit *die* - **4.** *(U)* [solution - of problem] Lösung *die*; [- of dispute, argument] Beilegung *die*.

resolve [rɪ'zɒlv] ◇ *n* [determination] Entschlossenheit *die*. ◇ *vt* - **1.** [vow, promise]: **to resolve that...** beschließen, dass...; **to resolve to do sthg** sich entschließen, etw zu tun - **2.** [solve - problem] lösen; [- dispute, argument] bei|legen.

resort [rɪ'zɔːt] *n* - **1.** [for holidays] Urlaubsort *der* - **2.** [solution]: **as a last resort** als letzte Möglichkeit; **in the last resort** im schlimmsten Fall. ◆ **resort to** *vt insep* [lying, begging] sich verlegen auf *(+ A)*; [violence] an|wenden.

resound [rɪ'zaʊnd] *vi* - **1.** [noise] schallen - **2.** [place]: **to resound with** wider|hallen von.

resounding [rɪ'zaʊndɪŋ] *adj* - **1.** [noise, voice] schallend - **2.** [success, victory] gewaltig.

resource [rɪ'zɔːs] *n* [asset] Ressourcen *Pl*; **natural resources** Naturschätze *Pl*.

resourceful [rɪ'zɔːsfʊl] *adj* einfallsreich.

respect [rɪ'spekt] ◇ *n* - **1.** *(U)* [admiration]: **respect (for)** Respekt *der* (vor); **with respect,** bei allem Respekt, - **2.** *(U)* [observance]: **respect for sthg** Achtung *die* vor etw - **3.** [aspect] Hinsicht *die*; **in this/that respect** in dieser/jener Hinsicht. ◇ *vt* - **1.** [admire] an|erkennen; **to respect sb for sthg** jn für etw respektieren - **2.** [observe] achten. ◆ **respects** *npl* Grüße *Pl*; **give my respects to your wife** grüßen Sie Ihre Frau von mir. ◆ **with respect to** *prep* in Bezug auf *(+ A)*.

respectable [rɪ'spektəbl] *adj* - **1.** [morally correct] ehrbar - **2.** [adequate, quite good] ansehnlich.

respectful [rɪ'spektfʊl] *adj* respektvoll.

respective [rɪ'spektɪv] *adj* jeweilig.

respectively [rɪ'spektɪvlɪ] *adv* beziehungsweise; **Jill and John are four and six years old respectively** Jill and John sind vier beziehungsweise sechs Jahre alt.

respite ['respaɪt] *n* - **1.** [pause] Atempause *die*; **without respite** ohne Unterbrechung - **2.** [delay] Aufschub *der*.

resplendent [rɪ'splendənt] *adj liter* prachtvoll.

respond [rɪ'spɒnd] *vi*: **to respond (to sthg)** antworten (auf etw *(A)*).

response [rɪ'spɒns] *n* Antwort *die*.

responsibility [rɪ,spɒnsə'bɪlətɪ] *n* - **1.** [charge, blame]: **responsibility (for sthg)** Verantwortung *die* (für etw) - **2.** [duty - of job, position] Aufgabe *die*; *phrase*: **responsibility (to sb)** Verantwortung *die* (jm gegenüber).

responsible [rɪ'spɒnsəbl] *adj* - **1.** [in charge, to blame]: **responsible (for sthg)** verantwortlich (für etw) - **2.** [answerable]: **responsible to sb** jm (gegenüber) verantwortlich - **3.** [sensible] vernünftig - **4.** [position, task] verantwortungsvoll.

responsibly [rɪ'spɒnsəblɪ] *adv* verantwortungsbewusst.

responsive [rɪ'spɒnsɪv] *adj*: **to be responsive** [audience] mit|gehen; [class] mit|machen.

rest [rest] ◇ *n* - **1.** [remainder]: **the rest** der Rest; **the rest of the cake/customers** der Rest des Kuchens/der Kunden - **2.** [relaxation] Ruhe *die* - **3.** [break] Pause *die* - **4.** [support] Stütze *die*. ◇ *vt* - **1.** [relax] aus|ruhen - **2.** [support, lean]: **to rest sthg on/against sthg** etw auf *(+ A)*/gegen etw lehnen - **3.** *phr*: **rest assured (that)...** seien Sie versichert, dass... ◇ *vi* - **1.** [relax, be still] sich aus|ruhen - **2.** [depend]: **to rest (up)on sb/sthg** von jm/etw ab|hängen - **3.** [be supported]: **to rest on sthg** auf etw *(D)* ruhen; **to rest against sthg** an etw *(D)* lehnen.

restaurant ['restərɒnt] *n* Restaurant *das*.

restful ['restfʊl] *adj* ruhig.

rest home *n* Pflegeheim *das*.

restive ['restɪv] *adj* unruhig.

restless ['restlɪs] *adj* - **1.** [bored, fidgety] rastlos - **2.** [sleepless] schlaflos.

restoration [,restə'reɪʃn] *n (U)* - **1.** [reestablishment] Wiederherstellung *die* - **2.** [renovation] Restaurierung *die*.

restore [rɪ'stɔːʳ] *vt* - **1.** [reestablish] wieder her|stellen; **the palace has been restored to its former glory** dem Palast ist seine alte Pracht wiedergegeben worden - **2.** [renovate] restaurieren - **3.** [give back] zurück|geben.

restrain [rɪ'streɪn] *vt* - **1.** [hold back] zurück|halten; **to restrain o.s. from doing sthg** sich zurück|halten (davon), etw zu tun - **2.** [dog, attacker] bändigen - **3.** [repress] unterdrücken.

restrained [rɪ'streɪnd] *adj* - **1.** [person] beherrscht - **2.** [tone] verhalten.

restraint [rɪ'streɪnt] *n* - **1.** [rule, check] Beschränkung *die* - **2.** [self-control] Selbstbeherrschung *die*.

restrict [rɪ'strɪkt] *vt* [limit] ein|schränken; **to restrict sb/sthg to sb/sthg** jn/etw auf jn/etw beschränken.

restriction [rɪ'strɪkʃn] *n* [limitation, regulation] Einschränkung *die*.

restrictive [rɪ'strɪktɪv] *adj* einschränkend.

rest room *n US* Toilette *die*.

result [rɪ'zʌlt] ◇ *n* - **1.** [gen] Ergebnis *das* - **2.** [consequence] Folge *die*; **as a result** folglich; **as a result of sthg** als Folge von etw. ◇ *vi*: **to result in sthg** zu etw führen; **to result from sthg** aus etw folgen.

resume [rɪ'zjuːm] ◇ *vt* [activity] wieder auf|nehmen. ◇ *vi* wieder beginnen.

résumé ['rezjuːmeɪ] *n* - **1.** [summary] Resümee *das*, Zusammenfassung *die* - **2.** *US* [of career, qualifications] Lebenslauf *der*.

resumption [rɪ'zʌmpʃn] *n* Wiederaufnahme *die*.

resurgence [rɪ'sɜːdʒəns] *n* Wiederaufleben *das*.

resurrection [,rezə'rekʃn] *n* [of policy, festival, legal case] Wiederbelebung *die*.

resuscitation [rɪ,sʌsɪ'teɪʃn] *n* Wiederbelebung *die*.

retail ['riːteɪl] ◇ *n* Einzelhandel *der*. ◇ *adv* im Einzelhandel. ◇ *vi*: **it retails at £10** es kostet im Einzelhandel 10 Pfund.

retailer ['riːteɪləʳ] *n* Einzelhändler *der*, -in *die*.

retail price *n* Einzelhandelspreis *der*.

retain [rɪ'teɪn] *vt* - **1.** [pride, power, independence] behalten - **2.** [heat] speichern.

retainer [rɪ'teɪnəʳ] *n* [fee] Vorschuss *der*.

retaliate [rɪ'tælɪeɪt] *vi* zurück|schlagen.

retaliation [rɪ,tælɪ'eɪʃn] *n* Vergeltung *die*.

retarded [rɪ'tɑːdɪd] *adj offens* [child] zurückgeblieben.

retch [retʃ] *vi* würgen.

reticent ['retɪsənt] *adj* zurückhaltend.

retina ['retɪnə] (*pl* **-nas** OR **-nae** [-niː]) *n* Netzhaut *die*, Retina *die*.

retinue ['retɪnjuː] *n* Gefolge *das*.

retire [rɪ'taɪəʳ] *vi* - **1.** [from work] in den Ruhestand treten - **2.** *fml* [to another place, to bed] sich zurück|ziehen.

retired [rɪ'taɪəd] *adj* pensioniert; **to be retired** im Ruhestand sein.

retirement [rɪ'taɪəmənt] *n (U)* - **1.** [act of retiring] Pensionierung *die* - **2.** [life after work] Ruhestand *der*.

retiring [rɪ'taɪərɪŋ] *adj* [shy] zurückhaltend.

retort [rɪ'tɔːt] ◇ *n* [sharp reply] (scharfe) Erwiderung. ◇ *vt*: **to retort that...** erwidern, dass...

retrace [rɪ'treɪs] *vt*: **to retrace one's steps** denselben Weg zurück|gehen.

retract [rɪ'trækt] ◇ *vt* - **1.** [take back] zurück|nehmen - **2.** [draw in] ein|ziehen. ◇ *vi* [be drawn in] eingezogen werden.

retrain [,riː'treɪn] *vt* um|schulen.

retreat [rɪ'triːt] ◇ *n* - **1.** MIL [withdrawal]: **retreat (from)** Rückzug *der* (aus) - **2.** [refuge] Zuflucht *die*. ◇ *vi* - **1.** [withdraw]: **to retreat (to)**

sich zurück|ziehen (in (+ A)); **she retreated hastily** sie wich hastig zurück - **2.** MIL: **to retreat (from)** den Rückzug an|treten (aus) - **3.** [from principle, policy, lifestyle]: **to retreat from sthg** etw auf|geben.

retribution [ˌretrɪ'bjuːʃn] *n* Vergeltung *die*.

retrieval [rɪ'triːvl] *n* COMPUT Wiederauffinden *das*.

retrieve [rɪ'triːv] *vt* - **1.** [get back] zurück|bekommen - **2.** COMPUT wiederauffinden - **3.** [situation] retten.

retriever [rɪ'triːvəʳ] *n* [dog] Apportierhund *der*; [of specific breed] Retriever *der*.

retrospect ['retrəspekt] *n*: **in retrospect** im Nachhinein.

retrospective [ˌretrə'spektɪv] *adj* - **1.** [mood] (zu)rückblickend - **2.** [law, pay rise] rückwirkend.

return [rɪ'tɜːn] <> *n* - **1.** [arrival back]: **return (to)** Rückkehr *die* (nach); **return to sthg** *fig* Rückkehr *die* zu etw - **2.** [giving back] Rückgabe *die* - **3.** TENNIS Return *der* - **4.** *UK* [ticket] Rückfahrkarte *die*; [for plane] Rückflugticket *das* - **5.** [profit] Ertrag *der* - **6.** COMPUT [on keyboard] Eingabetaste *die*. <> *vt* - **1.** [give back] zurück|geben; [loan] zurück|zahlen - **2.** [visit, compliment, love] erwidern - **3.** [replace] zurück|stellen - **4.** LAW [verdict] fällen - **5.** POL [candidate] wählen. <> *vi* [come back] zurück|kommen; [go back] zurück|gehen; [pain] wieder|kehren; **to return from Germany** aus Deutschland zurück|kehren OR zurück|kommen; **to return to London** nach London zurück|kehren OR zurück|kommen; **to return to work** wieder arbeiten; **to return to a subject** auf ein Thema zurück|kommen. ◆ **returns** *npl* - **1.** COMM Gewinn *der* - **2.** [on birthday]: **many happy returns (of the day)!** herzlichen Glückwunsch (zum Geburtstag)! ◆ **in return** *adv* dafür. ◆ **in return for** *prep* für.

return ticket *n UK* Rückfahrkarte *die*.

reunification [ˌriːjuːnɪfɪ'keɪʃn] *n* Wiedervereinigung *die*.

reunion [ˌriː'juːnjən] *n* - **1.** [party] Treffen *das* - **2.** *(U)* [meeting again] Wiedersehen *das*.

reunite [ˌriːjuː'naɪt] *vt* wieder vereinigen; **to be reunited with sb/sthg** mit jm/etw wieder vereint sein.

rev [rev] *inf* <> *n* (*abbr of* **revolution**) Umdrehung *die*. <> *vt*: **to rev the engine (up)** den Motor hoch drehen lassen.

revamp [ˌriː'væmp] *vt inf* - **1.** [reorganize] auf Vordermann bringen - **2.** [redecorate] auf|möbeln.

reveal [rɪ'viːl] *vt* enthüllen.

revealing [rɪ'viːlɪŋ] *adj* - **1.** [dress, blouse] offenherzig - **2.** [comment] aufschlussreich.

revel ['revl] (*UK*) (*US*) *vi*: **to revel in sthg** [freedom, success] etw in vollen Zügen genießen; [gossip] in etw *(D)* schwelgen.

revelation [ˌrevə'leɪʃn] *n* - **1.** [surprising fact] Enthüllung *die* - **2.** [surprising experience] Offenbarung *die*; **to be a revelation to sb** jm die Augen öffnen.

revenge [rɪ'vendʒ] <> *n* Rache *die*; [in game] Revanche *die*; **to take revenge (on sb)** sich (an jm) rächen. <> *vt* rächen; **to revenge o.s. on sb/sthg** sich an jm/etw rächen.

revenue ['revənjuː] *n* [income] Einnahmen *Pl*; [of State] Staatseinnahmen *Pl*.

reverberate [rɪ'vɜːbəreɪt] *vi* - **1.** [re-echo] wider|hallen; [shock wave] sich fort|setzen - **2.** [have repercussions] Auswirkungen haben.

reverberations [rɪˌvɜːbə'reɪʃnz] *npl* - **1.** [echoes] Widerhall *der* - **2.** [repercussions] Auswirkungen *Pl*.

revere [rɪ'vɪəʳ] *vt fml* verehren.

Reverend ['revərənd] *n*: **(the) Reverend Peter James** Pfarrer Peter James.

reversal [rɪ'vɜːsl] *n* - **1.** [of order, position, trend] Umkehrung *die*; [of decision] Umstoßung *die*; [of roles] Vertauschung *die* - **2.** [piece of ill luck] Rückschlag *der*.

reverse [rɪ'vɜːs] <> *adj* umgekehrt; [side] Rück-. <> *n* - **1.** AUT: **reverse (gear)** Rückwärtsgang *der* - **2.** [opposite]: **the reverse** das Gegenteil - **3.** [back]: **the reverse** die Rückseite; [of coin] die Kehrseite. <> *vt* - **1.** AUT rückwärts fahren mit - **2.** [order, position, trend] um|kehren; [decision] um|stoßen; [roles] tauschen - **3.** [turn over] um|drehen - **4.** *UK* TELEC: **to reverse the charges** ein R-Gespräch führen. <> *vi* AUT rückwärts fahren.

reverse-charge call *n UK* R-Gespräch *das*.

reversing light [rɪ'vɜːsɪŋ-] *n UK* Rückfahrscheinwerfer *der*.

revert [rɪ'vɜːt] *vi*: **to revert to sthg** zu etw zurück|kehren; **to revert to type** *fig* wieder in die alten Gewohnheiten verfallen.

review [rɪ'vjuː] <> *n* - **1.** [examination] Überprüfung *die* - **2.** [critique] Besprechung *die*, Rezension *die*. <> *vt* - **1.** [reassess] überprüfen - **2.** [write critique of] besprechen - **3.** [troops] inspizieren, mustern - **4.** *US* [study] wieder|holen.

reviewer [rɪ'vjuːəʳ] *n* Rezensent *der*, -in *die*.

revile [rɪ'vaɪl] *vt liter* schmähen.

revise [rɪ'vaɪz] <> *vt* - **1.** [alter] revidieren - **2.** [rewrite] überarbeiten - **3.** *UK* [study] wiederholen. <> *vi UK*: **to revise (for sthg)** (für etw) den Stoff wiederholen.

revision [rɪ'vɪʒn] *n* - **1.** [alteration] Revision *die* - **2.** *UK* [study]: **to do some revision** den Stoff wiederholen.

revitalize, -ise [ˌriː'vaɪtəlaɪz] *vt* wieder beleben.

revival [rɪ'vaɪvl] *n* [of economy, interest] Wiederbelebung *die*.

revive [rɪ'vaɪv] ◇ *vt* wieder beleben; [tradition, memories] wieder auflleben lassen; [play] wieder aufführen. ◇ *vi* - **1.** [regain consciousness] wieder zu sich kommen - **2.** [plant, economy, interest] wieder aufleben, wieder erblühen.

revolt [rɪ'vəʊlt] ◇ *n* Aufstand *der*, Revolte *die*. ◇ *vt* anlwidern. ◇ *vi*: **to revolt (against)** revoltieren (gegen).

revolting [rɪ'vəʊltɪŋ] *adj* widerlich.

revolution [ˌrevə'luːʃn] *n* - **1.** *fig* & POL Revolution *die* - **2.** TECH [circular movement] Umdrehung *die*.

revolutionary [ˌrevə'luːʃnərɪ] ◇ *adj liter* & *fig* revolutionär. ◇ *n* POL Revolutionär *der*, -in *die*.

revolve [rɪ'vɒlv] *vi* sich drehen; **to revolve (a)round** *liter* & *fig* sich drehen um.

revolver [rɪ'vɒlvəʳ] *n* Revolver *der*.

revolving [rɪ'vɒlvɪŋ] *adj* Dreh-.

revolving door *n* Drehtür *die*.

revue [rɪ'vjuː] *n* Revue *die*.

revulsion [rɪ'vʌlʃn] *n* Ekel *der*.

reward [rɪ'wɔːd] ◇ *n* Belohnung *die*. ◇ *vt* belohnen; **to reward sb for/with sthg** jn für/mit etw belohnen.

rewarding [rɪ'wɔːdɪŋ] *adj* lohnend; **it is a rewarding book** es lohnt sich, das Buch zu lesen.

rewind [ˌriː'waɪnd] (*pt* & *pp* **rewound**) *vt* [tape] zurücklspulen.

rewire [ˌriː'waɪəʳ] *vt* [house] neu verkabeln; [plug] neu anlschließen.

reword [ˌriː'wɜːd] *vt* neu formulieren.

rewound [ˌriː'waʊnd] *pt* & *pp* ▷ **rewind**.

rewrite [ˌriː'raɪt] (*pt* **rewrote** [ˌriː'rəʊt], *pp* **rewritten** [ˌriː'rɪtn]) *vt* neu schreiben.

Reykjavik ['rekjəvɪk] *n* Reykjavik *nt*.

rhapsody ['ræpsədɪ] *n* - **1.** MUS Rhapsodie *die* - **2.** [strong approval]: **to go into rhapsodies over sthg** von etw zu schwärmen beginnen.

rhetoric ['retərɪk] *n (U)* Rhetorik *die*.

rhetorical question [rɪ'tɒrɪkl-] *n* rhetorische Frage.

rheumatism ['ruːmətɪzm] *n* Rheuma *das*.

Rhine [raɪn] *n*: **the Rhine** der Rhein.

rhino ['raɪnəʊ] (*pl inv* OR **-s**) *n* = **rhinoceros**.

rhinoceros [raɪ'nɒsərəs] (*pl inv* OR **-es**) *n* Nashorn *das*, Rhinozeros *das*.

rhododendron [ˌrəʊdə'dendrən] *n* Rhododendron *der ODER das*.

rhubarb ['ruːbɑːb] *n* Rhabarber *der*.

rhyme [raɪm] ◇ *n* Reim *der*. ◇ *vi*: **to rhyme (with sthg)** sich (mit etw) reimen.

rhythm ['rɪðm] *n* Rhythmus *der*.

rib [rɪb] *n* [of body, framework] Rippe *die*.

ribbon ['rɪbən] *n* - **1.** [for decoration] Band *das* - **2.** [for typewriter] Farbband *das*.

rice [raɪs] *n* Reis *der*.

rice pudding *n* Milchreis *der*.

rich [rɪtʃ] ◇ *adj* - **1.** [gen] reich; **to be rich in sthg** reich an etw *(D)* sein - **2.** [soil] fruchtbar - **3.** [food, cake] schwer. ◇ *npl*: **the rich** die Reichen *Pl*. ◆ **riches** *npl* Reichtümer *Pl*.

richly ['rɪtʃlɪ] *adv* - **1.** [well - rewarded] reich - **2.** [abundantly] reichlich - **3.** [sumptuously, expensively] reich.

richness ['rɪtʃnɪs] *n (U)* - **1.** [of deposit] Reichtum *der* - **2.** [of soil] Fruchtbarkeit *die* - **3.** [of food] Schwere *die*.

rickety ['rɪkətɪ] *adj* wackelig.

ricochet ['rɪkəʃeɪ] (*pt* & *pp* **-ed** OR **-ted**, *cont* **-ing** OR **-ting**) ◇ *n* Abprall *der*. ◇ *vi*: **to ricochet (off sthg)** (von etw) ablprallen.

rid [rɪd] (*pt* **rid** OR **-ded**, *pp* **rid**) *vt*: **to rid sb/sthg of sthg** jn/etw von etw befreien; **to rid o.s. of sthg** sich von etw befreien.

ridden ['rɪdn] *pp* ▷ **ride**.

riddle ['rɪdl] *n* Rätsel *das*.

riddled ['rɪdld] *adj*: **to be riddled with holes** ganz durchlöchert sein; **to be riddled with errors** voller Fehler sein.

ride [raɪd] (*pt* **rode**, *pp* **ridden**) ◇ *n* - **1.** [on horseback] Ritt *der*; **to go for a ride** reiten gehen - **2.** [on bicycle, motorbike, in car] Fahrt *die*; **to go for a ride** eine Fahrt/Tour machen - **3.** *phr*: **to take sb for a ride** *inf* [trick] jn reinllegen. ◇ *vt* - **1.** [horse] reiten - **2.** [bicycle, motorbike] fahren; **to ride a bicycle/motorbike** Rad/Motorrad fahren - **3.** [distance - on horse] reiten; [- on bicycle, motorbike] fahren - **4.** *US* [train, bus, elevator] fahren mit. ◇ *vi* - **1.** [on horseback] reiten - **2.** [on bicycle, motorbike] fahren - **3.** [in car, bus]: **to ride in sthg** mit etw fahren.

rider ['raɪdəʳ] *n* - **1.** [on horseback] Reiter *der*, -in *die* - **2.** [on bicycle, motorbike] Fahrer *der*, -in *die*.

ridge [rɪdʒ] *n* - **1.** [on mountain] Kamm *der*, Rücken *der* - **2.** [on flat surface] Riffel *die*.

ridicule ['rɪdɪkjuːl] ◇ *n* Spott *der*. ◇ *vt* lächerlich machen, verspotten.

ridiculous [rɪ'dɪkjʊləs] *adj* lächerlich.

riding ['raɪdɪŋ] *n* Reiten *das*.

riding school *n* Reitschule *die*.

rife [raɪf] *adj*: **to be rife** grassieren.

riffraff ['rɪfræf] *n* Gesindel *das*.

rifle ['raɪfl] *n* Gewehr *das*.

rifle range *n* Schießstand *der*.

rift [rɪft] *n* - **1.** GEOL Spalt *der* - **2.** [quarrel]: **a rift between** eine Kluft zwischen *(+ D)*.

rig [rɪg] ◇ *n*: **(oil) rig** Bohrinsel *die*. ◇ *vt* [fix outcome of] manipulieren. ◆ **rig up** *vt sep* auflstellen, montieren.

rigging ['rɪgɪŋ] *n (U)* [on ship] Takelung *die*.

right [raɪt] ◇ *adj* - **1.** [gen] richtig; **have you got the right time?** haben Sie die genaue Zeit?; **to be right (about sthg)** (bezüglich etw) Recht haben; **to get the answer right** die richtige Antwort geben - **2.** [going well]: **things aren't right between them** sie kommen nicht gut miteinander aus - **3.** [not left] rechte(r) (s) - **4.** *UK inf* [idiot, mess] richtig, total. ◇ *n* - **1.** [moral correctness, entitlement] Recht *das*; **to be in the right** im Recht sein; **human rights** Menschenrechte *Pl*; **by rights** rechtmäßig, von Rechts wegen - **2.** [right-hand side] rechte Seite; **on your right** zu Ihrer Rechten; **on the right** rechts. ◇ *adv* - **1.** [correctly] richtig - **2.** [not left] rechts - **3.** [emphatic use] ganz; **stay right here** bleib hier; **to turn right round** sich ganz herum|drehen - **4.** [immediately] gleich; **right now** [immediately] (jetzt) gleich; [at this very moment] (jetzt) gerade; **right away** sofort. ◇ *vt* - **1.** [correct] wiedergut|machen - **2.** [make upright] auf|richten. ◇ *excl* gut!, O. K.! ◆ **Right** *n* POL: **the Right** die Rechte.

right angle *n* rechter Winkel; **at right angles to sthg** im rechten Winkel zu etw.

righteous ['raɪtʃəs] *adj* [person] rechtschaffen; [anger] selbstgerecht.

rightful ['raɪtfʊl] *adj* rechtmäßig.

right-hand *adj* [on the right] rechte(r) (s).

right-hand drive *adj* rechts gesteuert.

right-handed [-'hændɪd] *adj* rechtshändig.

right-hand man *n* rechte Hand.

rightly ['raɪtlɪ] *adv* - **1.** [correctly, without error] ganz richtig - **2.** [appropriately, aptly] korrekt, richtig - **3.** [justifiably] mit Recht.

right of way *n* - **1.** AUT Vorfahrt *die* - **2.** [access] Durchgangsrecht *das*.

right wing *n*: **the right wing** der rechte Flügel. ◆ **right-wing** *adj* rechtsgerichtet.

rigid ['rɪdʒɪd] *adj* - **1.** [hard, stiff, inflexible] starr - **2.** [strict] strikt.

rigor *n US* = **rigour**.

rigorous ['rɪgərəs] *adj* streng.

rigour *UK*, **rigor** *US* ['rɪgəʳ] *n* Strenge *die*. ◆ **rigours** *npl* Unbilden *Pl*.

rile [raɪl] *vt* ärgern.

rim [rɪm] *n* Rand *der*; [of spectacles] Fassung *die*; [of wheel] Felge *die*.

rind [raɪnd] *n* [of fruit] Schale *die*; [of cheese] Rinde *die*; [of bacon] Schwarte *die*.

ring [rɪŋ] ◇ *n* - **1.** [telephone call]: **to give sb a ring** jn an|rufen - **2.** [sound of bell] Klingeln *das* - **3.** [quality, tone]: **her excuse had a familiar ring (about it)** ihre Ausrede kam mir bekannt vor; **there's a ring of truth about it** es klingt sehr wahrscheinlich - **4.** [object, jewellery, for boxing] Ring *der* - **5.** [of people, trees] Kreis *der* - **6.** [people working together] Ring *der*; **crime ring** Verbrecherring *der*. ◇ *vt* (*pt* **rang**, *pp* **rung**) - **1.** *UK* [phone] an|rufen - **2.** [bell] läuten; **to ring the doorbell** (an der Tür) klingeln OR läuten - **3.** (*pt & pp* **-ed**) [draw a circle round] ein|kreisen - **4.** (*pt & pp* **-ed**) [surround] umringen; **to be ringed with sthg** von etw umringt sein. ◇ *vi* (*pt* **rang**, *pp* **rung**) - **1.** *UK* [phone] klingeln - **2.** [doorbell, person at door] klingeln, läuten - **3.** [to attract attention]: **to ring (for sb)** (nach jm) läuten. ◆ **ring back** *vt sep & vi UK* zurück|rufen. ◆ **ring off** *vi UK* auf|hängen. ◆ **ring up** *vt sep UK* an|rufen.

ring binder *n* Ringbuch *das*.

ringing ['rɪŋɪŋ] *n* [of bell] Läuten *das*; [of telephone] Klingeln *das*; [in ears] Klingen *das*.

ringing tone *n UK* TELEC Freizeichen *das*.

ringleader ['rɪŋ,liːdəʳ] *n* Anführer *der*, -in *die*.

ringlet ['rɪŋlɪt] *n* Ringellocke *die*.

ring road *n UK* Umgehungsstraße *die*.

ring tone *n* [on mobile phone] Klingelton *der*.

rink [rɪŋk] *n* [for ice-skating] Eisbahn *die*; [for roller-skating] Rollschuhbahn *die*.

rinse [rɪns] *vt* [clothes] spülen; [vegetables] waschen; **to rinse one's hands** die Hände ab|spülen; **to rinse one's mouth out** sich *(D)* den Mund aus|spülen.

riot ['raɪət] ◇ *n* Aufruhr *der*; **to run riot** [hooligans] randalieren; [children] außer Rand und Band sein; [plants] wuchern. ◇ *vi* einen Aufruhr machen.

rioter ['raɪətəʳ] *n* Aufrührer *der*, -in *die*.

riotous ['raɪətəs] *adj* [mob] randalierend; [party, behaviour] ausgelassen, wild.

riot police *npl* Bereitschaftspolizei *die*.

rip [rɪp] ◇ *n* Riss *der*. ◇ *vt* - **1.** [tear, shred] zerreißen - **2.** [remove]: **to rip sthg from** OR **off sthg** etw von etw ab|reißen. ◇ *vi* reißen.

RIP (*abbr of* **rest in peace**) R. I. P.

ripe [raɪp] *adj* [ready to eat] reif; **to be ripe for sthg** *fig* für etw reif sein.

ripen ['raɪpn] ◇ *vt* reifen lassen. ◇ *vi* reifen.

rip-off *n inf* [excessive charge] Wucher *der*.

ripple ['rɪpl] ◇ *n* - **1.** [in water] kleine Welle - **2.** [sound]: **a ripple of laughter** sanftes Gelächter; **a ripple of applause** kurzer Applaus. ◇ *vt* kräuseln.

rise [raɪz] (*pt* **rose**, *pp* **risen** ['rɪzn]) ◇ *n* - **1.** *UK* [increase in amount]: **rise (in sthg)** Anstieg *der* (einer Sache *(G)*) - **2.** *UK* [increase in salary] Gehaltserhöhung *die* - **3.** [to power, fame] Aufstieg *der* - **4.** [slope] Steigung *die* - **5.** *phr*: **to give rise to sthg** zu etw führen. ◇ *vi* - **1.** [go upwards, become higher, increase] steigen - **2.** [sun, bread] auf|gehen - **3.** [stand up, get out of bed] auf|stehen - **4.** [slope upwards] (an)|steigen - **5.** [become louder - voice] lauter werden - **6.** [become higher in pitch] höher werden - **7.** [prove o.s.]: **to rise to the occasion** der Lage gewachsen sein; **to rise to the challenge**

die Herausforderung anlnehmen - **8.** [rebel] sich erheben - **9.** [in status] auflsteigen; **to rise to power** an die Macht kommen.

rising ['raɪzɪŋ] <> *adj* - **1.** [sloping upwards] (an)steigend - **2.** [increasing, tide] steigend - **3.** [increasingly successful] aufsteigend. <> *n* [rebellion] Aufstand *der*, Erhebung *die*.

risk [rɪsk] <> *n* Risiko *das*; **to run the risk of doing sthg** Gefahr laufen, etw zu tun; **to take a risk** ein Risiko einlgehen; **at one's own risk** auf eigenes Risiko; **at risk** in Gefahr; **to put at risk** gefährden. <> *vt* - **1.** [put in danger] riskieren - **2.** [take the chance of]: **to risk doing sthg** riskieren, etw zu tun.

risky ['rɪskɪ] *adj* riskant.

risqué [rɪ'skeɪ] *adj* gewagt, schlüpfrig.

rite [raɪt] *n* Ritus *der*.

ritual ['rɪtʃʊəl] <> *adj* rituell. <> *n* Ritual *das*.

rival ['raɪvl] (*UK*) (*US*) <> *adj* Konkurrenz-, konkurrierend. <> *n* Rivale *der*, -lin *die*; COMM Konkurrent *der*, -in *die*. <> *vt* sich messen mit, konkurrieren mit.

rivalry ['raɪvlrɪ] *n* Rivalität *die*.

river ['rɪvər] *n* Fluss *der*; **the River Thames** *UK*, **the Thames River** *US* die Themse.

river bank *n* Flussufer *das*.

riverbed ['rɪvəbed] *n* Flussbett *das*.

riverside ['rɪvəsaɪd] *n*: **the riverside** das Flussufer.

rivet ['rɪvɪt] <> *n* Niete *die*. <> *vt* - **1.** [fasten with rivets] nieten - **2.** *fig* [fascinate]: **to be riveted by sthg** von etw gefesselt sein.

road [rəʊd] *n* Straße *die*; **by road** [send] per Spedition; [travel] mit dem Auto/Bus/*etc*; **on the road to victory/success/recovery** auf dem Weg zum Sieg/zum Erfolg/der Besserung.

roadblock ['rəʊdblɒk] *n* Straßensperre *die*.

road map *n* Straßenkarte *die*.

road safety *n* Verkehrssicherheit *die*.

roadside ['rəʊdsaɪd] *n*: **by the roadside** am Straßenrand.

road sign *n* Verkehrszeichen *das*.

road tax *n* Kraftfahrzeugsteuer *die*.

roadway ['rəʊdweɪ] *n* Fahrbahn *die*.

road works *npl* (Straßen)bauarbeiten *Pl*.

roam [rəʊm] <> *vt* [countryside] durchstreifen; [streets] herumlziehen in *(+ D)*. <> *vi* [in countryside] wandern; [in streets] heruml-ziehen.

roar [rɔːr] <> *vi* - **1.** [lion, person] brüllen; **to roar with laughter** vor Lachen brüllen - **2.** [wind, engine] heulen. <> *vt* brüllen. <> *n* - **1.** [of lion, person] Brüllen *das* - **2.** [of wind, engine] Heulen *das*; [of traffic] Lärm *der*.

roaring ['rɔːrɪŋ] <> *adj* - **1.** [traffic] lärmend; [wind, engine] heulend - **2.** [fire] prasselnd - **3.** [for emphasis]: **a roaring success** ein Riesenerfolg; **to do a roaring trade** ein Riesengeschäft machen. <> *adv*: **roaring drunk** sternhagelvoll.

roast [rəʊst] <> *adj*: **roast beef** Rinderbraten *der*, Roastbeef *das*; **roast chicken** Brathähnchen *das*; **roast pork** Schweinebraten *der*. <> *n* Braten *der*. <> *vt* - **1.** [meat] braten; [potatoes] *im Ofen in Fett backen* - **2.** [coffee beans, nuts] rösten.

rob [rɒb] *vt* [person] bestehlen; [bank, house] auslrauben; **to rob sb of sthg** [of money, goods] jm etw stehlen; *fig* [of opportunity, glory] jn einer Sache *(G)* berauben.

robber ['rɒbər] *n* Räuber *der*, -in *die*.

robbery ['rɒbərɪ] *n* Raub *der*.

robe [rəʊb] *n* - **1.** [of priest, judge, monarch] Robe *die* - **2.** *US* [dressing gown] Morgenrock *der*.

robin ['rɒbɪn] *n* Rotkehlchen *das*.

robot ['rəʊbɒt] *n* Roboter *der*.

robust [rəʊ'bʌst] *adj* [person, health] robust; [economy] stabil; [criticism, defence] stark.

rock [rɒk] <> *n* - **1.** *(U)* [substance] Stein *der* - **2.** [boulder] Fels(en) *der* - **3.** *US* [pebble] Stein *der* - **4.** [music] Rock *der* - **5.** *UK* [sweet]: **stick of rock** Zuckerstange *die*. <> *comp* [band, concert, singer] Rock-. <> *vt* - **1.** [cause to move] schaukeln; [baby] wiegen - **2.** [shock] erschüttern. <> *vi* [boat, cradle, in chair] schaukeln. ◆ **on the rocks** *adv* - **1.** [drink] mit Eis - **2.** [marriage, relationship] kaputt.

rock bottom *n*: **to be at rock bottom** auf dem Tiefpunkt sein; **to hit rock bottom** den Tiefpunkt erreichen. ◆ **rock-bottom** *adj* [prices] Schleuder-.

rockery ['rɒkərɪ] *n* Steingarten *der*.

rocket ['rɒkɪt] <> *n* Rakete *die*. <> *vi* hoch schießen.

rocket launcher [-ˌlɔːntʃər] *n* Raketenwerfer *der*.

rocking chair ['rɒkɪŋ-] *n* Schaukelstuhl *der*.

rocking horse ['rɒkɪŋ-] *n* Schaukelpferd *das*.

rocky ['rɒkɪ] *adj* - **1.** [full of rocks] steinig - **2.** [unsteady] wackelig.

Rocky Mountains *npl*: **the Rocky Mountains** die Rocky Mountains.

rod [rɒd] *n* Stange *die*; [for fishing] Angel *die*.

rode [rəʊd] *pt* ▷ **ride**.

rodent ['rəʊdənt] *n* Nagetier *das*.

roe [rəʊ] *n* [of fish] Rogen *der*.

rogue [rəʊg] *n* - **1.** [likable rascal] Frechdachs *der* - **2.** *dated* [dishonest person] Schurke *der*.

role [rəʊl] *n* Rolle *die*.

roll [rəʊl] <> *n* - **1.** [of material, paper, film] Rolle *die* - **2.** [of bread] Brötchen *das*; **a cheese roll** ein Käsebrötchen - **3.** [list] Liste *die*; **electoral roll** Wählerverzeichnis *das* - **4.** [sound - of thunder] Rollen *das*; [- of drums] Wirbel *der*.

◇ *vt* - **1.** [turn over] rollen - **2.** [make into cylinder] auf|rollen; [umbrella] zusammen|rollen; **rolled into one** *fig* in einem. ◇ *vi* - **1.** [gen] rollen - **2.** [make loud noise - thunder] rollen; [- drums] wirbeln. ◆ **roll about, roll around** *vi* herum|rollen; [person] sich wälzen. ◆ **roll over** *vi* [person] sich um|drehen. ◆ **roll up** ◇ *vt sep* - **1.** [make into cylinder] auf|rollen, zusammen|rollen - **2.** [sleeves] hoch|krempeln. ◇ *vi* - **1.** [vehicle] vor|fahren - **2.** *inf* [person] auf|kreuzen.

roll call *n* Namensaufruf *der*; MIL Appell *der*.

roller ['rəʊlər] *n* - **1.** [cylinder] Walze *die* - **2.** [curler] (Locken)wickler *der*.

roller blades *npl* Rollerblades *Pl*.

roller coaster *n* Achterbahn *die*.

roller skate *n* Rollschuh *der*.

rolling ['rəʊlɪŋ] *adj* - **1.** [hills] wellig - **2.** *phr*: **to be rolling in it** *inf* im Geld schwimmen.

rolling pin *n* Nudelholz *das*.

roll-on *adj* & *n*: **roll-on (deodorant)** Deoroller *der*.

ROM [rɒm] (*abbr of* **read only memory**) *n* ROM.

Roman ['rəʊmən] ◇ *adj* römisch. ◇ *n* Römer *der*, -in *die*.

Roman Catholic ◇ *adj* römisch-katholisch. ◇ *n* Katholik *der*, -in *die*.

romance [rəʊ'mæns] *n* - **1.** [romantic quality] Romantik *die* - **2.** [love affair] Romanze *die* - **3.** [novel] Liebesroman *der*.

Romania [ruː'meɪnjə] *n* Rumänien *nt*.

Romanian [ruː'meɪnjən] ◇ *adj* rumänisch. ◇ *n* - **1.** [person] Rumäne *der*, -nin *die* - **2.** [language] Rumänisch(e) *das*.

romantic [rəʊ'mæntɪk] *adj* - **1.** [gen] romantisch - **2.** [novel, film, play] Liebes-.

Rome [rəʊm] *n* Rom *nt*.

romp [rɒmp] ◇ *n*: **to have a romp** herum|toben, herum|tollen. ◇ *vi* [play noisily] herum|toben, herum|tollen.

rompers ['rɒmpəz] *npl* Strampelhose *die*.

romper suit ['rɒmpər-] *n* = **rompers**.

roof [ruːf] *n* - **1.** [of building, vehicle] Dach *das*; **to go through** OR **hit the roof** an die Decke gehen - **2.** [upper part - of cave] Gewölbe *das*; **roof of the mouth** Gaumen *der*.

roofing ['ruːfɪŋ] *n (U)* [material] Deckung *die*.

roof rack *n* Dachträger *der*.

rooftop ['ruːftɒp] *n* Dach *das*.

rook [rʊk] *n* - **1.** [bird] Krähe *die* - **2.** [chess piece] Turm *der*.

rookie ['rʊkɪ] *n US inf* Grünschnabel *der*.

room [ruːm, rʊm] *n* - **1.** [in house, hotel] Zimmer *das*; [in office, public building etc] Raum *der* - **2.** *(U)* [space] Platz *der*; **to make room for sb/sthg** für jn/etw Platz machen - **3.** *(U)* [opportunity, possibility]: **there is still room for improvement** es könnte besser sein; **there is no room for sentimentality in politics** Sentimentalität hat in der Politik nichts zu suchen.

roommate ['ruːmmeɪt] *n* Zimmergenosse *der*, -sin *die*.

room service *n (U)* Zimmerservice *der*.

roomy ['ruːmɪ] *adj* [house, car] geräumig; [garment] weit.

roost [ruːst] ◇ *n* Hühnerstange *die*. ◇ *vi* [hens] auf der Stange sitzen.

rooster ['ruːstər] *n* Hahn *der*.

root [ruːt] ◇ *n liter* & *fig* Wurzel *die*; **to take root** [plant] Wurzel fassen; [idea] Fuß fassen; **the root of the problem** die Ursache des Problems. ◇ *vi* [search] wühlen. ◆ **roots** *npl* [origins] Wurzeln *Pl*. ◆ **root for** *vt insep esp US inf* an|feuern. ◆ **root out** *vt sep* [eradicate] aus|rotten.

rope [rəʊp] ◇ *n* Seil *das*; **to know the ropes** sich aus|kennen. ◇ *vt*: **to rope together** zusammen|binden; [climbers] an|seilen. ◆ **rope in** *vt sep inf* [involve] ran|kriegen.

rosary ['rəʊzərɪ] *n* Rosenkranz *der*.

rose [rəʊz] ◇ *pt* ▷ **rise**. ◇ *adj* [pink] rosa. ◇ *n* [flower] Rose *die*.

rosé ['rəʊzeɪ] *n* Rosé *der*.

rose bush *n* Rosenstrauch *der*.

rosemary ['rəʊzmərɪ] *n* Rosmarin *der*.

rosette [rəʊ'zet] *n* Rosette *die*.

roster ['rɒstər] *n* Dienstplan *der*.

rostrum ['rɒstrəm] (*pl* **-trums** OR **-tra** [-trə]) *n* [for speaker, conductor] Pult *das*.

rosy ['rəʊzɪ] *adj liter* & *fig* rosig.

rot [rɒt] ◇ *n* - **1.** *(U)* [decay - of wood, food] Fäulnis *die*; [- in society, organization] Verfall *der*; **dry rot** Trockenfäule *die*; **to stop the rot** den Verfall auf|halten; **the rot set in** es ging abwärts - **2.** *UK dated* [nonsense] Quatsch *der*. ◇ *vt* faulen lassen. ◇ *vi* faulen.

rota ['rəʊtə] *n* Dienstplan *der*.

rotary ['rəʊtərɪ] ◇ *adj* rotierend, Rotations-. ◇ *n US* [roundabout] Kreisverkehr *der*.

rotate [rəʊ'teɪt] ◇ *vt* [turn] drehen. ◇ *vi* [turn] sich drehen, rotieren.

rotation [rəʊ'teɪʃn] *n* [turning movement] Drehung *die*, Rotation *die*.

rote [rəʊt] *n*: **by rote** auswendig.

rotten ['rɒtn] *adj* - **1.** [decayed] verfault - **2.** *inf* [poor-quality, unskilled] lausig - **3.** *inf* [mean] gemein - **4.** *inf* [unpleasant, unenjoyable] mies - **5.** *inf* [unwell]: **to feel rotten** sich mies fühlen.

rouge [ruːʒ] *n* Rouge *das*.

rough [rʌf] ◇ *adj* - **1.** [not smooth - surface] rau; [- road] uneben, holprig - **2.** [violent] grob, rau - **3.** [crude, basic - shelter, conditions] primitiv; [- people, manners] rau - **4.** [not detailed, not exact] grob; **rough draft** Rohentwurf *der*; **at a rough guess** grob geschätzt; **can you give me a rough idea of the cost?** können Sie mir sagen, wie viel es ungefähr kostet? - **5.** [unpleasant, tough - life, time] hart; [- journey] anstrengend; [- area] rau; **to be rough on sb** hart für jn sein - **6.** [stormy] stürmisch - **7.** [harsh - voice] rau; [- wine] sauer. ◇ *adv*: **to sleep rough** im Freien übernachten. ◇ *n* - **1.** GOLF: **the rough** das Rough - **2.** [draft]: **to write sthg in rough** ein Konzept für etw machen. ◇ *vt phr*: **to rough it** primitiv leben.

rough and ready *adj* primitiv; [person] rau(beinig).

roughen ['rʌfn] *vt* [surface] auf|rauen.

roughly ['rʌflɪ] *adv* - **1.** [gen] grob - **2.** [approximately] etwa.

roulette [ru:'let] *n* Roulette *das*.

round [raʊnd] ◇ *adj* rund. ◇ *prep* - **1.** [surrounding] um herum; **there were soldiers all round the building** rund um das Gebäude waren Soldaten - **2.** [near]: **round here/there** hier/dort in der Nähe; **is there a bank anywhere round here?** gibt es hier irgendwo eine Bank? - **3.** [all over]: **150 offices round the world** 150 Büros in der ganzen Welt; **all round the country** im ganzen Land; **to go round a museum** ein Museum besuchen; **to show sb round sthg** jn in etw *(D)* herum|führen - **4.** [in a circle]: **we walked round the lake** wir gingen um den See herum; **to go/drive round sthg** um etw herum|gehen/herum|fahren; **round the clock** *fig* rund um die Uhr - **5.** [in circumference]: **she measures 30 inches round the waist** um die Taille misst sie 75 cm - **6.** [on or to the other side of]: **to be/go round the corner** um die Ecke sein/gehen - **7.** [so as to avoid] um herum; **to get round an obstacle** um ein Hindernis herum|gehen; **to find a way round a problem** einen Ausweg für ein Problem finden. ◇ *adv* - **1.** [on all sides] herum; **all round** auf allen Seiten, rundherum - **2.** [near]: **round about** [in distance] in der Nähe; [approximately] rund; **round about ten o'clock** gegen zehn Uhr - **3.** [here and there] herum; **to travel round** herum|reisen - **4.** [in a circle]: **to go round** sich drehen; **to spin round (and round)** sich im Kreis drehen - **5.** [to the other side]: **to go round** herum|gehen; **to turn round** sich um|drehen; **to look round** sich um|sehen; **it's a long way round** das ist ein Umweg - **6.** [on a visit]: **why don't you come round?** warum kommst du nicht vorbei?; **I spent the day round at her house** ich war den ganzen Tag bei ihr (zu Hause) - **7.** [when sharing]: **to hand sthg round** etw herum|reichen - **8.** [continuously]: **all year round** das ganze Jahr über. ◇ *n* - **1.** [gen & SPORT] Runde *die*; **a round of applause** eine Runde Applaus - **2.** [of ammunition] Schuss *der* - **3.** [of drinks] Runde *die*; **it's my round** es ist meine Runde - **4.**: **a round of sandwiches** ein Sandwich - **5.** [of toast] Scheibe *die*. ◇ *vt* [turn]: **to round a bend** um eine Kurve fahren. ◆ **round off** *vt sep* ab|runden. ◆ **round up** *vt sep* - **1.** [animals] zusammen|treiben - **2.** [number] auf|runden.

roundabout ['raʊndəbaʊt] ◇ *adj* umständlich. ◇ *n UK* - **1.** [on road] Kreisverkehr *der* - **2.** [at fairground, playground] Karussell *das*.

rounders ['raʊndəz] *n (U) UK* Schlagball *der*.

roundly ['raʊndlɪ] *adv* [criticize] scharf; [defeated] vernichtend.

round trip *n* Rundreise *die*.

roundup ['raʊndʌp] *n* [summary] Zusammenfassung *die*.

rouse [raʊz] *vt* - **1.** [wake up] wecken - **2.** [impel]: **to rouse o.s. to do sthg** sich dazu auf|raffen, etw zu tun; **to rouse sb to action** jn zum Handeln bewegen - **3.** [subj: orator] in Erregung versetzen - **4.** [give rise to] hervor|rufen; [emotions, interest] wecken, wach|rufen.

rousing ['raʊzɪŋ] *adj* [speech] mitreißend; [cheer] stürmisch.

rout [raʊt] ◇ *n* Niederlage *die*. ◇ *vt* in die Flucht schlagen.

route [ru:t] ◇ *n* - **1.** [line of travel] Strecke *die*, Route *die* - **2.** [fixed itinerary]: **air/bus/shipping route** Flug-/Bus-/Schifffahrtslinie *die* - **3.** *fig* [to achievement] Weg *der*. ◇ *vt* [flight, traffic] legen; [goods] schicken.

route map *n* [for public transport] Streckenkarte *die*; [for holiday route] Tourenplan *der*.

routine [ru:'ti:n] ◇ *adj* routinemäßig, Routine-. ◇ *n* Routine *die*.

row[1] [rəʊ] ◇ *n* Reihe *die*; **in a row** nacheinander. ◇ *vt* & *vi* rudern.

row[2] [raʊ] ◇ *n* - **1.** [quarrel] Streit *der*, Krach *der* - **2.** *inf* [noise] Krach *der*, Krawall *der*. ◇ *vi* [quarrel] sich streiten.

rowboat ['rəʊbəʊt] *n US* Ruderboot *das*.

rowdy ['raʊdɪ] *adj* [person] wild, randalierend; [party, atmosphere] laut.

row house [rəʊ-] *n US* Reihenhaus *das*.

rowing ['rəʊɪŋ] *n* Rudern *das*.

rowing boat *n UK* Ruderboot *das*.

royal ['rɔɪəl] ◇ *adj* [regal] königlich. ◇ *n inf* Angehörige *der, die* der königlichen Familie.

Royal Air Force *n*: **the Royal Air Force** die Königliche Luftwaffe.

royal family *n* königliche Familie.

Royal Mail *n UK*: **the Royal Mail** die Königliche Post.

Royal Navy *n*: **the Royal Navy** die Königliche Marine.

royalty ['rɔɪəltɪ] *n (U)* [persons] Königshaus *das*. ◆ **royalties** *npl* Tantiemen *Pl*.

rpm (*abbr of* **revolutions per minute**) *npl* U/min.

RSPCA (*abbr of* **Royal Society for the Prevention of Cruelty to Animals**) *n britischer Tierschutzverein*.

RSVP (*abbr of* **répondez s'il vous plaît**) u.A.w.g.

rub [rʌb] ◇ *vt* reiben; **to rub one's hands together** sich *(D)* die Hände reiben; **he rubbed sun cream into her back** er rieb ihren Rücken mit Sonnencreme ein; **to rub sb up the wrong way** *UK*, **to rub sb the wrong way** *US fig* jn verstimmen. ◇ *vi*: **to rub against** *OR* **on sthg** an etw *(D)* reiben; [person, animal] sich an etw *(D)* reiben; **to rub together** sich reiben. ◆ **rub off on** *vt insep* [subj: quality] ablfärben auf *(+ A)*. ◆ **rub out** *vt sep* [erase] auslradieren.

rubber ['rʌbəʳ] ◇ *adj* [made of rubber] Gummi-. ◇ *n* - **1.** [substance] Gummi *der* - **2.** *UK* [eraser] Radiergummi *der* - **3.** [in cards] Robber *der* - **4.** *US inf* [condom] Gummi *der*.

rubber band *n* Gummiband *das*.

rubber plant *n* Gummibaum *der*.

rubber stamp *n* Stempel *der*. ◆ **rubber-stamp** *vt* stempeln.

rubbish ['rʌbɪʃ] ◇ *n (U)* - **1.** [refuse] Abfall *der*, Müll *der* - **2.** *inf fig* [worthless thing] Mist *der* - **3.** *inf* [nonsense] Quatsch *der*, Blödsinn *der*. ◇ *vt inf* [person, opinion] lächerlich machen; [play, book] verreißen. ◇ *excl inf* Quatsch!

rubbish bag *n UK* Müllsack *der*.

rubbish bin *n UK* Mülleimer *der*.

rubbish dump, rubbish tip *n UK* Müllabladeplatz *der*.

rubble ['rʌbl] *n* Schutt *der*.

ruby ['ru:bɪ] *n* [gem] Rubin *der*.

rucksack ['rʌksæk] *n* Rucksack *der*.

rudder ['rʌdəʳ] *n* Ruder *das*.

ruddy ['rʌdɪ] *adj* - **1.** [reddish] rot; [complexion] gesund - **2.** *UK dated* [for emphasis] verdammt.

rude [ru:d] *adj* - **1.** [impolite] unhöflich - **2.** [dirty, naughty] unanständig - **3.** [unexpected]: **rude awakening** böses Erwachen.

rudimentary [ˌru:dɪ'mentərɪ] *adj* [basic] elementar.

rueful ['ru:fʊl] *adj* reumütig; [smile] wehmütig.

ruffian ['rʌfjən] *n* Grobian *der*.

ruffle ['rʌfl] *vt* - **1.** [hair, fur] zersausen; [water] kräuseln - **2.** [pride] verletzen; **to ruffle sb's composure** jn aus der Ruhe bringen.

rug [rʌg] *n* - **1.** [carpet] kleiner Teppich; [by bed] Bettvorleger *der* - **2.** [blanket] Decke *die*.

rugby ['rʌgbɪ] *n* Rugby *das*.

rugged ['rʌgɪd] *adj* - **1.** [rocky, uneven - landscape] wild; [- cliffs] zerklüftet - **2.** [sturdy] stabil.

rugger ['rʌgəʳ] *n UK inf* Rugby *das*.

ruin ['ru:ɪn] ◇ *n* - **1.** [financial downfall] Ruin *der* - **2.** [ruined building] Ruine *die*. ◇ *vt* ruinieren; [chances, atmosphere] verderben. ◆ **in ruins** *adv*: **to be in ruins** [town, country] in Ruinen liegen; [building] eine Ruine sein; [marriage, career, plans] ruiniert sein.

rule [ru:l] ◇ *n* - **1.** [regulation, guideline] Regel *die* - **2.** [norm]: **the rule** die Regel; **as a rule** in der Regel - **3.** *(U)* [control] Herrschaft *die*. ◇ *vt* - **1.** [control, guide] beherrschen - **2.** [govern] regieren - **3.** [decide]: **to rule that...** entscheiden, dass... ◇ *vi* - **1.** [give decision] entscheiden - **2.** *fml* [be paramount] herrschen - **3.** [govern] regieren. ◆ **rule out** *vt sep* auslschließen.

ruled [ru:ld] *adj* [lined] liniert.

ruler ['ru:ləʳ] *n* - **1.** [for measurement] Lineal *das* - **2.** [leader] Herrscher *der*, -in *die*.

ruling ['ru:lɪŋ] ◇ *adj* [in control] herrschend. ◇ *n* [decision] Entscheidung *die*.

rum [rʌm] *n* Rum *der*.

Rumania [ru:'meɪnjə] *n* = **Romania**.

Rumanian [ru:'meɪnjən] *adj* & *n* = **Romanian**.

rumble ['rʌmbl] ◇ *n* [of thunder] Grollen *das*; [of lorry, train] Rumpeln *das*; [of stomach] Knurren *das*. ◇ *vi* [thunder] grollen; [train] rumpeln; [stomach] knurren.

rummage ['rʌmɪdʒ] *vi* wühlen, stöbern.

rumour *UK*, **rumor** *US* ['ru:məʳ] *n* Gerücht *das*.

rumoured *UK*, **rumored** *US* ['ru:məd] *adj*: **he is rumoured to be married already** er soll angeblich schon verheiratet sein.

rump [rʌmp] *n* - **1.** [of animal] Hinterteil *das* - **2.** *inf* [of person] Hinterteil *das*.

rump steak *n* Rumpsteak *das*.

rumpus ['rʌmpəs] *n inf* Spektakel *das*, Krach *der*.

run [rʌn] (*pt* **ran**, *pp* **run**) ◇ *n* - **1.** [on foot] Lauf *der*; **to go for a run** laufen gehen; **at a run** im Lauf; **on the run** auf der Flucht - **2.** [in car] Fahrt *die*; **to go for a run** einen Ausflug im Auto machen - **3.** [series] Reihe *die*; **a run of bad luck** eine Pechsträhne - **4.** THEAT: **it had an eight-week run on Broadway** es wurde für acht Wochen am Broadway gespielt - **5.** [great demand]: **a run on sthg** ein Ansturm auf etw *(A)* - **6.** [in tights] Laufmasche *die* - **7.** [in cricket, baseball] Lauf *der* - **8.** [for skiing] Abfahrt *die*; [for bobsleigh] Bahn *die* - **9.** [term, period]: **in the long/short run** auf lange/kurze Sicht (gesehen). ◇ *vt* - **1.** [on foot] rennen, laufen; **to run a race** ein Rennen laufen - **2.** [business, hotel] führen; [course, event] leiten - **3.** [operate - machine, film, computer program] laufen lassen; [- experiment] durch|führen - **4.** [have and use - car] halten - **5.** [water, tap] laufen lassen; **to run a bath** ein Bad ein|lassen - **6.** [article, headline] veröffentlichen - **7.** *inf* [drive] fahren; **I'll run you home** ich fahre dich nach Hause - **8.** [move, pass]: **to run one's hand along sthg/over sthg** mit der Hand an etw *(D)* entlang/über etw *(A)* fahren. ◇ *vi* - **1.** [on foot, in race] laufen; [fast] rennen; **we had to run for the bus** wir mussten rennen, um den Bus zu erwischen - **2.** [road, track] führen, verlaufen; [river] fließen; [pipe, cable] verlaufen; **the path runs along the coast** der Weg verläuft entlang der Küste - **3.** [in election]: **to run (for)** kandidieren (für) - **4.** [progress, develop] laufen; **to run smoothly** gut laufen - **5.** [operate - machine, engine] laufen; [- factory] arbeiten; **to run on unleaded petrol** mit bleifreiem Benzin fahren; **to run off mains electricity** mit Netzstrom laufen - **6.** [bus, train] fahren; **the bus runs every hour** der Bus fährt jede Stunde - **7.** [liquid, tears, tap] laufen - **8.** [eyes] tränen; **my nose is running** mir läuft die Nase - **9.** [colour] aus|laufen; [clothes] ab|färben - **10.** [continue - contract] gültig sein, laufen; [- play] laufen. ◆ **run about** *vi* herum|laufen. ◆ **run across** *vt insep* [meet] zufällig treffen. ◆ **run around** *vi* = **run about**. ◆ **run away** *vi* [flee]: **to run away (from)** weg|laufen (von); [fast] weg|rennen (von). ◆ **run down** ◇ *vt sep* - **1.** [in vehicle] überfahren - **2.** [criticize] herunter|machen - **3.** [allow to decline] ab|bauen. ◇ *vi* [battery] leer werden; [clock] ab|laufen. ◆ **run into** *vt insep* - **1.** [meet - person] zufällig treffen - **2.** [encounter - problem] stoßen auf *(+ A)*; **to run into debt** in Schulden geraten - **3.** [in vehicle] laufen *OR* fahren gegen. ◆ **run off** ◇ *vt sep* [copy] drucken. ◇ *vi*: **to run off (with sthg)** sich (mit etw) davon|machen; **to run off with sb** mit jm durch|brennen. ◆ **run out** *vi* - **1.** [supply, fuel] aus|gehen; **time is running out** die Zeit wird knapp - **2.** [licence, contract] ab|laufen. ◆ **run out of** *vt insep*: **we've run out of petrol/money** wir haben kein Benzin/Geld mehr. ◆ **run over** *vt sep* [knock down] überfahren. ◆ **run through** *vt insep* - **1.** [practise] durch|gehen - **2.** [read through] schnell durch|lesen. ◆ **run to** *vt insep* [amount to] sich belaufen auf *(+ A)*. ◆ **run up** *vt sep* [debt] machen; [bill] zusammenkommen lassen. ◆ **run up against** *vt insep* stoßen auf *(+ A)*.

runaway ['rʌnəweɪ] ◇ *adj* [child] ausgerissen; [horse] durchgegangen; [inflation] galoppierend; [victory] sehr überzeugend. ◇ *n* [escapee] Ausreißer *der*, -in *die*.

rundown ['rʌndaʊn] *n* - **1.** [report] Bericht *der* - **2.** [decline] Abbau *der*. ◆ **run-down** *adj* - **1.** [dilapidated] heruntergekommen - **2.** [tired] erschöpft.

rung [rʌŋ] ◇ *pp* ▷ **ring**. ◇ *n liter & fig* Sprosse *die*.

runner ['rʌnə^r] *n* - **1.** [athlete] Läufer *der*, -in *die* - **2.** [of sledge, skate] Kufe *die*; [of drawer] Schiene *die*.

runner bean *n UK* Stangenbohne *die*.

runner-up (*pl* **runners-up**) *n* Zweite *der, die*.

running ['rʌnɪŋ] ◇ *adj* - **1.** [continuous] ständig - **2.** [consecutive] hintereinander; **three weeks running** drei Wochen hintereinander - **3.** [water] fließend. ◇ *n* - **1.** SPORT Laufen *das* - **2.** [management, control] Leitung *die* - **3.** [of machine] Betrieb *der* - **4.** *phr*: **to be in the running (for sthg)** im Rennen (für etw) liegen; **to be out of the running (for sthg)** aus dem Rennen (für etw) sein.

runny ['rʌnɪ] *adj* - **1.** [food] flüssig - **2.** [nose] laufend; [eyes] wässerig; **he had a runny nose** ihm lief die Nase.

run-of-the-mill *adj* durchschnittlich, nullachtfünfzehn.

runt [rʌnt] *n* - **1.** [animal] *kleinstes Tier eines Wurfs* - **2.** *pej* [person] mickriger Kerl.

run-up *n* - **1.** [preceding time]: **in the run-up to** in der Zeit vor *(+ D)* - **2.** SPORT Anlauf *der*.

runway ['rʌnweɪ] *n* Start- und Landebahn *die*; [for takeoff] Startbahn *die*; [for landing] Landebahn *die*.

rupture ['rʌptʃə^r] *n* - **1.** MED Bruch *der* - **2.** [of relationship] (Ab)bruch *der*.

rural ['rʊərəl] *adj* ländlich.

ruse [ru:z] *n* List *die*.

rush [rʌʃ] ◇ *n* - **1.** [hurry] Eile *die*; **to be in a rush** es sehr eilig haben; **to make a rush for sthg** auf etw *(A)* zu|stürzen *OR* zu|eilen - **2.** [demand]: **rush (for** *OR* **on sthg)** Ansturm *der* (auf etw *(A)*) - **3.** [busiest period] Stoßzeit *die* - **4.** [surge - of blood] Andrang *der*; [- of water] Schwall *der*. ◇ *vt* - **1.** [hurry - work] hastig erledigen; [- meal] hastig essen; [- person] drängen - **2.** [send quickly - people] schnell bringen; [- supplies, troops] schnell schicken; **to rush sb to hospital** jn schnell ins Krankenhaus bringen - **3.** [attack suddenly] zu|stürmen auf *(+ A)*; [enemy, position] stürmen. ◇ *vi* - **1.** [hurry] sich beeilen - **2.** [crowd] stürzen; [air, blood, water] schießen. ◆ **rushes** *npl* BOT Binsen *Pl*.

rush hour *n* Hauptverkehrszeit *die*, Stoßzeit *die*.

rusk [rʌsk] *n* Zwieback *der*.

Russia ['rʌʃə] *n* Russland *nt*.

Russian ['rʌʃn] ◇ *adj* russisch. ◇ *n* - **1.** [person] Russe *der*, -sin *die* - **2.** [language] Russisch(e) *das*.

rust [rʌst] ◇ *n* [on metal] Rost *der*. ◇ *vi* rosten.

rustle ['rʌsl] ◇ *vt* - **1.** [paper] rascheln mit; [subj: wind - leaves] rascheln lassen - **2.** *US* [cattle] stehlen. ◇ *vi* [paper, leaves] rascheln.

rusty ['rʌstɪ] *adj* - **1.** [metal] rostig - **2.** *fig* [skill] eingerostet; **I'm rusty** ich bin aus der Übung.

rut [rʌt] *n* [furrow] Furche *die*; **to get into a rut** in einen Trott kommen.

ruthless ['ru:θlɪs] *adj* [person] rücksichtslos; [investigation, destruction] schonungslos; [murder] brutal.

RV *n US* (*abbr of* **recreational vehicle**) Wohnmobil *das*.

rye [raɪ] *n* [grain] Roggen *der*.

rye bread *n (U)* Roggenbrot *das*.

S

s (*pl* **ss** OR **s's**), **S** (*pl* **Ss** OR **S's**) [es] *n* [letter] s *das*, S *das*. ◆ **S** (*abbr of* **south**) S.

Sabbath ['sæbəθ] *n*: **the Sabbath** der Sabbat.

sabotage ['sæbətɑ:ʒ] ◇ *n* Sabotage *die*. ◇ *vt* sabotieren.

sachet ['sæʃeɪ] *n* [of shampoo, cream] Einzelpackung *die*; [of sugar, coffee] Portionspackung *die*.

sack [sæk] ◇ *n* - **1.** [bag] Sack *der* - **2.** *UK inf* [dismissal]: **to get** OR **be given the sack** rausgeschmissen werden. ◇ *vt UK inf* [dismiss] rauslschmeißen.

sacred ['seɪkrɪd] *adj liter* & *fig* heilig.

sacrifice ['sækrɪfaɪs] ◇ *n liter* & *fig* Opfer *das*. ◇ *vt liter* & *fig* opfern.

sacrilege ['sækrɪlɪdʒ] *n liter* & *fig* Sakrileg *das*.

sad [sæd] *adj* traurig.

sadden ['sædn] *vt* traurig machen; **I was saddened to hear of her death** die Nachricht von ihrem Tod machte mich sehr traurig.

saddle ['sædl] ◇ *n* Sattel *der*. ◇ *vt* - **1.** [put saddle on] satteln - **2.** *fig* [burden]: **to saddle sb with sthg** jm etw auflhalsen; **to be saddled with sthg** etw am Hals haben.

saddlebag ['sædlbæg] *n* Satteltasche *die*.

sadistic [sə'dɪstɪk] *adj* sadistisch.

sadly ['sædlɪ] *adv* - **1.** [sorrowfully] traurig - **2.** [regrettably] leider.

sadness ['sædnɪs] *n* - **1.** [sorrow] Trauer *die* - **2.** [distressing nature] Traurigkeit *die*.

s.a.e., sae *n abbr of* **stamped addressed envelope**.

safari [sə'fɑ:rɪ] *n* Safari *die*.

safe [seɪf] ◇ *adj* sicher; [product] ungefährlich; **it's not safe for young children** es ist gefährlich für kleine Kinder; **have a safe journey!** gute Reise!; **safe and sound** wohlbehalten; *phrase*: **it's safe to say that...** man kann mit Sicherheit sagen, dass...; **to be on the safe side** um sicher zu gehen. ◇ *n* Safe *der*.

safe-conduct *n* - **1.** [document giving protection] Geleitbrief *der* - **2.** [protection] sicheres Geleit.

safe-deposit box *n* Banksafe *der*.

safeguard ['seɪfgɑ:d] ◇ *n*: **safeguard (against sthg)** Schutz *der* (gegen etw). ◇ *vt*: **to safeguard sb/sthg (against sthg)** jn/etw (vor etw *(D)*) schützen.

safekeeping [,seɪf'ki:pɪŋ] *n* (sichere) Aufbewahrung.

safely ['seɪflɪ] *adv* sicher; [arrive] wohlbehalten; **I can safely say (that)** ich kann mit Sicherheit sagen, dass.

safe sex *n* Safersex *der*.

safety ['seɪftɪ] *n* Sicherheit *die*.

safety belt *n* Sicherheitsgurt *der*.

safety pin *n* Sicherheitsnadel *die*.

sag [sæg] *vi* [sink downwards] durchlhängen.

sage [seɪdʒ] ◇ *adj* [wise] weise. ◇ *n* - **1.** [herb] Salbei *der* - **2.** [wise man] Weise *der*.

Sagittarius [,sædʒɪ'teərɪəs] *n* Schütze *der*.

Sahara [sə'hɑ:rə] *n*: **the Sahara (Desert)** die (Wüste) Sahara.

said [sed] *pt* & *pp* ▷ **say**.

sail [seɪl] ◇ *n* - **1.** [of boat] Segel *das*; **to set sail** loslfahren - **2.** [journey by boat]: **to go for a sail** segeln gehen. ◇ *vt* - **1.** [ship] steuern; [sailing boat] segeln mit - **2.** [sea] befahren. ◇ *vi* - **1.** [person - travel] mit dem Schiff fahren; [- leave] ablfahren; SPORT segeln - **2.** [ship - move] fahren; [- leave] ablfahren - **3.** [sailing boat] segeln - **4.** *fig* [through air] segeln. ◆ **sail through** *vt insep* [exam] spielend bestehen.

sailboat *n US* = **sailing boat**.

sailing ['seɪlɪŋ] *n* - **1.** SPORT Segeln *das*; **plain sailing** ganz einfach - **2.** [trip by ship]: **there are ten sailings a day** das Schiff fährt zehnmal am Tag.

sailing boat *UK*, **sailboat** *US* ['seɪlbəʊt] *n* Segelboot *das*.

sailing ship *n* Segelschiff *das*.

sailor ['seɪlə^r] *n* Seemann *der*; [in navy] Matrose *der*; SPORT Segler *der*, -in *die*.

saint [seɪnt] *n* RELIG Heilige *der*, *die*.

saintly ['seɪntlɪ] *adj* [person] gütig.

sake [seɪk] *n* - **1.** [benefit, advantage]: **for the sake of sb** jm zuliebe; **for my/your sake** mir/dir zuliebe - **2.** [purpose]: **for the sake of peace/your health** um des Friedens/deiner Gesundheit willen; **let us say, for the sake of argument, that...** sagen wir spaßeshalber, dass... - **3.** *phr*: **for God's** OR **Heaven's sake!** um Gottes willen!

salad ['sæləd] *n* Salat *der*.

salad bowl *n* Salatschüssel *die*.

salad cream *n UK majonäseartige Salatsoße*.

salad dressing *n* Salatsoße *die*, Dressing *das*.

salami [sə'lɑːmɪ] *n* Salami *die*.

salary ['sælərɪ] *n* Gehalt *das*.

sale [seɪl] *n* - **1.** [instance of selling] Verkauf *der*; **to make a sale** etwas verkaufen - **2.** *(U)* [selling] Verkauf *der*; **to be on sale** verkauft werden; **to be for sale** zu verkaufen sein - **3.** [at reduced prices] Ausverkauf *der* - **4.** [auction] Auktion *die*. ◆ **sales** *npl* - **1.** [quantity sold] Absatz *der* - **2.** [at reduced prices]: **the sales** der Schlussverkauf.

saleroom *UK* ['seɪlrʊm], **salesroom** *US* ['seɪlzrʊm] *n* [for auction] Auktionsraum *der*.

sales assistant ['seɪlz-], **salesclerk** ['seɪlzklɜːrk] *US n* Verkäufer *der*, -in *die*.

salesman ['seɪlzmən] (*pl* **-men** [-mən]) *n* Verkäufer *der*; [representative] Vertreter *der*.

sales rep *n inf* Vertreter *der*, -in *die*.

salesroom *n US* = **saleroom**.

saleswoman ['seɪlzˌwʊmən] (*pl* **-women** [-ˌwɪmɪn]) *n* Verkäuferin *die*; [representative] Vertreterin *die*.

saliva [sə'laɪvə] *n* Speichel *der*.

salmon ['sæmən] (*pl inv* OR **-s**) *n* Lachs *der*.

salmonella [ˌsælmə'nelə] *n (U)*: **salmonella (poisoning)** Salmonellenvergiftung *die*.

salon ['sælɒn] *n* Salon *der*.

saloon [sə'luːn] *n* - **1.** *UK* [car] Limousine *die* - **2.** *US* [bar] Wirtschaft *die*; [in the Wild West] Saloon *der* - **3.** [on ship] Salon *der*.

salt [sɔːlt, sɒlt] ◇ *n* Salz *das*; **to take sthg with a pinch of salt** etw nicht wörtlich nehmen. ◇ *vt* - **1.** [food] salzen - **2.** [roads] streuen. ◆ **salt away** *vt sep inf* [money] auf die hohe Kante legen.

saltcellar *UK* ['sɔːltˌseləʳ], **salt shaker** *US* [-ˌʃeɪkəʳ] *n* Salzstreuer *der*.

saltwater ['sɔːltˌwɔːtəʳ] ◇ *n* Salzwasser *das*. ◇ *adj* Meeres-.

salty ['sɔːltɪ] *adj* [tasting of salt] salzig.

salute [sə'luːt] ◇ *n* - **1.** MIL [with hand] Gruß *der*; **to give a salute** salutieren - **2.** MIL [firing of guns] Salut *der* - **3.** [formal acknowledgement]: **salute (to sthg)** Würdigung *die* (von etw). ◇ *vt* - **1.** MIL salutieren vor *(+ D)* - **2.** [acknowledge formally, honour] würdigen; [person] ehren. ◇ *vi* MIL salutieren.

salvage ['sælvɪdʒ] ◇ *n (U)* - **1.** [rescue of ship] Bergung *die* - **2.** [property rescued] Bergungsgut *das*. ◇ *vt* - **1.** [rescue]: **to salvage sthg (from)** etw bergen (aus) - **2.** *fig*: **to salvage one's reputation** seinen Ruf retten.

salvation [sæl'veɪʃn] *n (U)* - **1.** [saviour] Rettung *die* - **2.** RELIG Erlösung *die*.

Salvation Army *n*: **the Salvation Army** die Heilsarmee.

same [seɪm] ◇ *adj* - **1.** [identical]: **the same** derselbe/dieselbe/dasselbe, dieselben *Pl*; **you've got the same book as me** du hast das gleiche Buch wie ich; **the same thing** dasselbe; **the same ones** dieselben; **at the same time** [simultaneously] zur gleichen Zeit; [nevertheless] andererseits; **one and the same** ein und derselbe/dieselbe/dasselbe - **2.** [unchanged]: **the same** der/die/das Gleiche, die Gleichen *Pl*; **the same ones** die Gleichen. ◇ *pron* - **1.** [identical]: **the same** derselbe/dieselbe/dasselbe, dieselben *Pl*; **I'll have the same as her** ich möchte das Gleiche wie sie; **all** OR **just the same** [nevertheless] trotzdem; **it's all the same to me** es ist mir gleich; **they are all the same** sie sind alle gleich; **the same to you** gleichfalls; **(the) same again, please** noch einen/eine/eins, bitte; **it's not the same** es ist nicht dasselbe - **2.** [unchanged]: **the same** der/die/das Gleiche, die Gleichen *Pl*; **her views are still the same** sie hat immer noch die gleichen Ansichten. ◇ *adv* [identically]: **to dress/feel the same** sich gleich an|ziehen/fühlen; **they look the same** sie sehen gleich aus.

sample ['sɑːmpl] ◇ *n* - **1.** [of product] Probe *die*; [of fabric] Muster *das* - **2.** [for analysis] Probe *die* - **3.** [representative portion - of work] Musterbeispiel *das*; [- of people in survey] Auswahl *die*. ◇ *vt* - **1.** [taste] kosten - **2.** [try out, test] aus|probieren.

sanatorium, sanitorium *US* (*pl* **-riums** OR **-ria** [-rɪə]) [ˌsænə'tɔːrɪəm] *n* Sanatorium *das*.

sanctimonious [ˌsæŋktɪ'məʊnjəs] *adj pej* frömmlerisch.

sanction ['sæŋkʃn] ◇ *n* - **1.** [formal approval] Billigung *die* - **2.** [punishment] Strafe *die*. ◇ *vt* [authorize] billigen.

sanctuary ['sæŋktʃʊərɪ] *n* - **1.** [for birds, wildlife] Schutzgebiet *das* - **2.** [safety, place of safety] Zufluchtsort *der*.

sand [sænd] ◇ *n* Sand *der*. ◇ *vt* [make smooth] schmirgeln.

sandal ['sændl] *n* Sandale *die*.

sandalwood ['sændlwʊd] *n* Sandelholz *das*.

sandbox *n US* = **sandpit**.

sandcastle ['sændˌkɑːsl] *n* Sandburg *die*.

sand dune *n* Sanddüne *die*.

sandpaper ['sændˌpeɪpəʳ] ◇ *n* Sandpapier *das*. ◇ *vt* mit Sandpapier ab|schmirgeln.

sandpit *UK* ['sændpɪt], **sandbox** *US* ['sændbɒks] *n* Sandkasten *der*.

sandwich ['sænwɪdʒ] ◇ *n* Sandwich *das*; **ham/cheese sandwich** Schinken-/Käsebrot *das*. ◇ *vt fig*: **to be sandwiched between** eingeklemmt sein zwischen *(+ D)*.

sandwich board *n zweiteilige Reklametafel zum Umhängen*.

sandwich course *n UK Kurs, bei dem sich Studium und Praktikum abwechseln*.

sandy ['sændɪ] *adj* - **1.** [beach] sandig - **2.** [sand-coloured] sandfarben.

sane [seɪn] *adj* - **1.** [not mad] normal, bei Verstand - **2.** [sensible] vernünftig.

sang [sæŋ] *pt* ▷ **sing**.

sanitary ['sænɪtrɪ] *adj* - **1.** [connected with health - officer, system] Gesundheits-; [- procedures] sanitär - **2.** [clean, hygienic] hygienisch.

sanitary towel, sanitary napkin *US n* Damenbinde *die*.

sanitation [ˌsænɪ'teɪʃn] *n (U)* sanitäre Einrichtungen *Pl*.

sanitorium *n US* = **sanatorium**.

sanity ['sænətɪ] *n (U)* - **1.** [saneness] Verstand *der* - **2.** [good sense] Vernunft *die*.

sank [sæŋk] *pt* ▷ **sink**.

Santa (Claus) ['sæntə (ˌklɔːz)] *n* der Weihnachtsmann.

sap [sæp] ◇ *n (U)* [of plant] Saft *der*. ◇ *vt* [weaken] schwächen.

sapling ['sæplɪŋ] *n* junger Baum.

sapphire ['sæfaɪə^r] *n* Saphir *der*.

sarcastic [sɑː'kæstɪk] *adj* sarkastisch.

sardine [sɑː'diːn] *n* Sardine *die*.

Sardinia [sɑː'dɪnjə] *n* Sardinien *nt*.

sardonic [sɑː'dɒnɪk] *adj* [smile, look] hämisch.

SAS (*abbr of* **Special Air Service**) *n Spezialeinheit der britischen Armee*.

SASE *n US abbr of* **self-addressed stamped envelope**.

sash [sæʃ] *n* [strip of cloth] Schärpe *die*.

sat [sæt] *pt & pp* ▷ **sit**.

SAT [sæt] *n* - **1.** (*abbr of* **Standard Assessment Task**), *Eignungstest für Schulkinder in England und Wales* - **2.** (*abbr of* **Scholastic Aptitude Test**), *Zulassungsprüfung an US-Universitäten*.

Satan ['seɪtn] *n* Satan *der*.

satchel ['sætʃəl] *n* Schultasche *die*.

satellite ['sætəlaɪt] ◇ *n liter & fig* Satellit *der*. ◇ *comp* Satelliten-.

satellite TV *n* Satellitenfernsehen *das*.

satin ['sætɪn] ◇ *n* Satin *der*. ◇ *comp* - **1.** [made of satin] Satin- - **2.** [wallpaper, paint, finish] seidenmatt.

satire ['sætaɪə^r] *n* Satire *die*.

satisfaction [ˌsætɪs'fækʃn] *n* - **1.** [pleasure] Befriedigung *die* - **2.** [something that pleases]: **the job has few satisfactions** die Arbeit ist nicht sehr befriedigend - **3.** [fulfilment - of need, demand] Befriedigung *die*; [- of criteria] Erfüllung *die*.

satisfactory [ˌsætɪs'fæktərɪ] *adj* befriedigend.

satisfied ['sætɪsfaɪd] *adj* [happy] zufrieden; **to be satisfied with sthg** mit etw zufrieden sein.

satisfy ['sætɪsfaɪ] *vt* - **1.** [make happy] zufrieden stellen - **2.** [convince] überzeugen; **to satisfy sb/o.s. that...** jn/sich davon überzeugen, dass... - **3.** [fulfil - need, demand] befriedigen; [- requirements] genügen *(+ D)*.

satisfying ['sætɪsfaɪɪŋ] *adj* befriedigend.

satsuma [ˌsæt'suːmə] *n* Satsuma *die*.

saturate ['sætʃəreɪt] *vt* - **1.** [drench] tränken; [subj: rain] durchnässen - **2.** [fill completely, swamp - area, town] überschwemmen; [- market] sättigen.

saturated *adj* - **1.** [drenched] getränkt; [with rain] durchnässt - **2.** [fat] gesättigt.

Saturday ['sætədɪ] ◇ *n* Samstag *der*; **what day is it? – it's Saturday** was ist heute? – es ist Samstag; **on Saturday** am Samstag; **on Saturdays** samstags; **last/this/next Saturday** letzten/diesen/nächsten Samstag; **every Saturday** jeden Samstag; **every other Saturday** jeden zweiten Samstag; **the Saturday before** den Samstag davor, am vorhergehenden Samstag; **the Saturday before last** vorletzten Samstag; **the Saturday after next, Saturday week, a week on Saturday** übernächsten Samstag, Samstag in einer Woche. ◇ *comp* Samstags-; **Saturday morning/afternoon/evening/night** Samstagmorgen *der*/-nachmittag *der*/-abend *der*/-nacht *die*.

sauce [sɔːs] *n* CULIN Soße *die*, Sauce *die*.

saucepan ['sɔːspən] *n* Kochtopf *der*.

saucer ['sɔːsə^r] *n* Untertasse *die*.

saucy ['sɔːsɪ] *adj inf* frech.

Saudi Arabia ['saʊdɪ-] *n* Saudi-Arabien *nt*.

sauna ['sɔːnə] *n* Sauna *die*; **to have a sauna** in die Sauna gehen.

saunter ['sɔːntə^r] *vi* schlendern.

sausage ['sɒsɪdʒ] *n* Wurst *die*.

sausage roll *n UK Würstchen in Blätterteig*.

sauté [*UK* 'səʊteɪ, *US* səʊ'teɪ] (*pt & pp* **sautéed** OR **sautéd**) ◇ *adj* [potatoes] Röst-, Brat-. ◇ *vt* [potatoes] rösten, braten; [meat] sautieren.

savage ['sævɪdʒ] ◇ *adj* [attack, criticism, person] brutal; [dog] bissig. ◇ *n* Wilde *der, die*. ◇ *vt* [attack physically] anlfallen.

save [seɪv] ◇ *vt* - **1.** [rescue] retten; **to save sb from sthg** jn vor etw *(D)* retten; **to save sb's life** jm das Leben retten - **2.** [money, time, space] sparen - **3.** [reserve] auflheben; **to save a seat for sb** jm einen Platz freihalten; **to save one's strength/voice** seine Kräfte/Stimme schonen - **4.** [make unnecessary - trouble, work] ersparen; [- expense] vermeiden; **to save sb from doing sthg** es jm ersparen, etw zu tun - **5.** SPORT ablwehren - **6.** COMPUT speichern. ◇ *vi* [save money] sparen. ◇ *n* SPORT Parade *die*. ◇ *prep fml*: **save (for)** außer *(+ D)*.
◆ **save on** *vt insep* sparen. ◆ **save up** *vi*: **to save up (for sthg)** (auf etw *(A)*) sparen.

savings ['seɪvɪŋz] *npl* Ersparnisse *Pl*.

savings account *n US* Sparkonto *das.*

savings and loan association *n US* Bausparkasse *die.*

savings bank *n* Sparkasse *die.*

saviour *UK*, **savior** *US* ['seɪvjəʳ] *n* Retter *der*, -in *die.*

savour *UK*, **savor** *US* ['seɪvəʳ] *vt* genießen.

savoury *UK*, **savory** *US* ['seɪvərɪ] ◇ *adj* - **1.** [not sweet] pikant - **2.** [respectable, pleasant] angenehm. ◇ *n* (pikantes) Häppchen.

saw [sɔ:] (*UK pt* **-ed**, *pp* **sawn**) (*US pt & pp* **-ed**) ◇ *pt* ▷ **see**. ◇ *n* Säge *die.* ◇ *vt* sägen.

sawdust ['sɔ:dʌst] *n* Sägemehl *das.*

sawed-off shotgun *n US* = **sawn-off shotgun**.

sawmill ['sɔ:mɪl] *n* Sägewerk *das.*

sawn [sɔ:n] *pp UK* ▷ **saw**.

sawn-off shotgun *UK*, **sawed-off shotgun** ['sɔ:d-] *US n Gewehr mit abgesägtem Lauf.*

saxophone ['sæksəfəʊn] *n* Saxofon *das.*

say [seɪ] (*pt & pp* **said**) ◇ *vt* - **1.** [gen] sagen; **to say sthg again** etw nochmal sagen, etw wiederholen; **who should I say it is?** wen darf ich melden?; **he's said to be good** er soll gut sein - **2.** [subj: clock, meter] an|zeigen; [subj: sign] besagen; **the letter says...** in dem Brief steht...; **it says here that...** hier heißt es, dass... - **3.** [assume]: **I'd say he's lying** meiner Meinung nach lügt er; **(let's) say you were to lose** nehmen wir an, du verlierst; **shall we say nine (o'clock)?** sagen wir um neun? - **4.** *phr*: **that goes without saying** das versteht sich von selbst; **that's not saying much** das will nicht viel heißen; **it has a lot to be said for it** es spricht vieles dafür. ◇ *n*: **to have a/no say (in sthg)** etw/nichts (bei etw) zu sagen haben; **to have one's say** seine Meinung äußern. ◆ **that is to say** *adv* das heißt.

saying ['seɪɪŋ] *n* Redensart *die.*

scab [skæb] *n* - **1.** [of wound] Schorf *der* - **2.** *pej* [non-striker] Streikbrecher *der*, -in *die.*

scaffold ['skæfəʊld] *n* - **1.** [frame] Gerüst *das* - **2.** [for executions] Schafott *das.*

scaffolding ['skæfəldɪŋ] *n (U)* Gerüst *das.*

scald [skɔ:ld] ◇ *n* Verbrühung *die.* ◇ *vt* [burn] verbrühen.

scale [skeɪl] ◇ *n* - **1.** [set of numbers] Skala *die*; [of pay] Tarif *der* - **2.** [of ruler, thermometer] Einteilung *die* - **3.** [size] Größe *die*; [extent] Ausmaß *das*; **on a small/large scale** im Kleinen/Großen; **the project is on a large scale** das Projekt ist groß angelegt - **4.** [size ratio] Maßstab *der*; **to scale** maßstab(s)getreu - **5.** MUS Tonleiter *die* - **6.** [of fish, snake] Schuppe *die* - **7.** *US* = **scales**. ◇ *vt* - **1.** [climb] erklimmen - **2.** [remove scales from] schuppen. ◆ **scales** *npl* Waage *die.* ◆ **scale down** *vt sep* [industry] ab|bauen; [investment] reduzieren; [production] drosseln.

scallop ['skɒləp] ◇ *n* [shellfish] Kammmuschel *die*; CULIN Jakobsmuschel *die.* ◇ *vt* [decorate] mit einem Bogenrand verzieren.

scalp [skælp] ◇ *n* - **1.** ANAT Kopfhaut *die* - **2.** [removed from head] Skalp *der.* ◇ *vt* skalpieren.

scalpel ['skælpəl] *n* Skalpell *das.*

scamper ['skæmpəʳ] *vi* [children, dog] flitzen; [mouse] huschen; **to scamper around** [children] herum|tollen.

scampi ['skæmpɪ] *n (U)* Scampi *Pl.*

scan [skæn] ◇ *n* MED & TECH Scan *der*; [on pregnant woman] Ultraschalluntersuchung *die.* ◇ *vt* - **1.** [examine carefully - map] studieren; [- area] ab|suchen; [- crowd] mit den Augen ab|suchen - **2.** [glance at] überfliegen - **3.** MED computertomografisch untersuchen - **4.** COMPUT & TECH scannen.

scandal ['skændl] *n* - **1.** [scandalous event, outrage] Skandal *der* - **2.** *(U)* [rumours] Skandalgeschichten *Pl.*

scandalize, -ise ['skændəlaɪz] *vt* schockieren.

Scandinavia [ˌskændɪ'neɪvjə] *n* Skandinavien *nt.*

Scandinavian [ˌskændɪ'neɪvjən] ◇ *adj* skandinavisch. ◇ *n* [person] Skandinavier *der*, -in *die.*

scant [skænt] *adj* wenig.

scanty ['skæntɪ] *adj* [amount, resources] dürftig, spärlich; [dress] knapp.

scapegoat ['skeɪpgəʊt] *n* Sündenbock *der.*

scar [skɑ:ʳ] *n liter & fig* Narbe *die.*

scarce ['skeəs] *adj* knapp.

scarcely ['skeəslɪ] *adv* kaum.

scare [skeəʳ] ◇ *n* - **1.** [sudden fright] Schreck(en) *der*; **to give sb a scare** jn erschrecken - **2.** [public panic] Panik *die*; **a bomb scare** ein Bombenalarm. ◇ *vt* [frighten] erschrecken. ◆ **scare away, scare off** *vt sep* verscheuchen.

scarecrow ['skeəkrəʊ] *n* Vogelscheuche *die.*

scared ['skeəd] *adj* - **1.** [very frightened] verängstigt; **to be scared** Angst haben; **to be scared stiff** OR **to death** fürchterliche Angst haben - **2.** [nervous, worried]: **to be scared that...** befürchten, dass...

scarf [skɑ:f] (*pl* **-s** OR **scarves**) *n* Schal *der*; [headscarf] Kopftuch *das.*

scarlet ['skɑ:lət] *adj* scharlachrot.

scarves [skɑ:vz] *Pl* ▷ **scarf**.

scathing ['skeɪðɪŋ] *adj* [remark, criticism] scharf.

scatter ['skætəʳ] ◇ *vt* [spread out] verstreuen; [seed] streuen. ◇ *vi* [crowd] sich zerstreuen; [birds] auf|fliegen.

scatterbrained ['skætəbreɪnd] *adj inf* zerstreut.

scenario [sɪ'nɑ:rɪəʊ] (*pl* **-s**) *n* Szenario *das.*

scene [siːn] *n* Szene *die*; [location] Ort *der*; **behind the scenes** hinter den Kulissen; **it's not my scene** das ist nicht mein Fall; **to set the scene** [give background information] Hintergrundinformationen geben; **to set the scene for sthg** den Nährboden für etw bilden.

scenery ['siːnərɪ] *n (U)* - **1.** [of countryside] Landschaft *die* - **2.** [in theatre] Kulissen *Pl*.

scenic ['siːnɪk] *adj* [view] schön.

scent [sent] *n* - **1.** [smell - of flowers] Duft *der*; [- of animal] Witterung *die* - **2.** [perfume] Parfüm *das*.

scepter *n US* = **sceptre**.

sceptic *UK*, **skeptic** *US* ['skeptɪk] *n* Skeptiker *der*, -in *die*.

sceptical *UK*, **skeptical** *US* ['skeptɪkl] *adj* skeptisch; **to be sceptical about sthg** bezüglich etw *(G)* skeptisch sein.

sceptre *UK*, **scepter** *US* ['septər] *n* Zepter *das*.

schedule [*UK* 'ʃedjuːl, *US* 'skedʒul] ◇ *n* - **1.** [plan] Plan *der*, Programm *das*; **ahead of/behind schedule** früher/später als geplant; **on schedule** pünktlich, planmäßig - **2.** [written list] Verzeichnis *das*. ◇ *vt*: **to schedule sthg (for)** etw planen OR an|setzen (für).

scheduled flight [*UK* 'ʃedjuːld-, *US* 'skedjʊld-] *n* Linienflug *der*.

scheme [skiːm] ◇ *n* - **1.** [plan] Programm *das*; **pension scheme** Altersversorgung *die* - **2.** *pej* [dishonest plan] raffinierter Plan - **3.** [arrangement, decoration - of room] Einrichtung *die*; **colour scheme** Farbzusammenstellung *die*. ◇ *vi pej* Pläne schmieden.

scheming ['skiːmɪŋ] *adj* raffiniert; [politician] intrigant.

schizophrenic [ˌskɪtsə'frenɪk] ◇ *adj* schizophren. ◇ *n* Schizophrene *der*, *die*.

scholar ['skɒlər] *n* - **1.** [expert] Gelehrte *der*, *die* - **2.** *dated* [school student] Schüler *der*, -in *die* - **3.** [holder of scholarship] Stipendiat *der*, -in *die*.

scholarship ['skɒləʃɪp] *n* - **1.** [grant] Stipendium *das* - **2.** [learning] Gelehrsamkeit *die*.

school [skuːl] *n* - **1.** [gen] Schule *die*; **to go to school** in die Schule gehen; **at school** in der Schule - **2.** UNIV [department] Fachbereich *der*; **school of medicine/law** medizinische/juristische Fakultät - **3.** *US* [university] Universität *die* - **4.** [group of fish, dolphins] Schwarm *der*.

schoolbook ['skuːlbʊk] *n* Schulbuch *das*.

schoolboy ['skuːlbɔɪ] *n* Schuljunge *der*, Schüler *der*.

schoolchild ['skuːltʃaɪld] (*pl* **-children** [-tʃɪldrən]) *n* Schulkind *das*.

schooldays ['skuːldeɪz] *npl* Schulzeit *die*.

schoolgirl ['skuːlgɜːl] *n* Schulmädchen *das*, Schülerin *die*.

schooling ['skuːlɪŋ] *n* [education] Ausbildung *die*.

school-leaver [-ˌliːvər] *n UK* Schulabgänger *der*, -in *die*.

schoolmaster ['skuːlˌmɑːstər] *n dated* Schulmeister *der*.

schoolmistress ['skuːlˌmɪstrɪs] *n dated* Schulmeisterin *die*.

schoolteacher ['skuːlˌtiːtʃər] *n* Lehrer *der*, -in *die*.

school year *n* Schuljahr *das*.

sciatica [saɪ'ætɪkə] *n* Ischias *der*.

science ['saɪəns] *n* - **1.** *(U)* [system of knowledge] Wissenschaft *die* - **2.** [branch of knowledge] Naturwissenschaft *die*.

science fiction *n* Science-Fiction *die*.

scientific [ˌsaɪən'tɪfɪk] *adj* wissenschaftlich.

scientist ['saɪəntɪst] *n* Wissenschaftler *der*, -in *die*; [of physical or natural sciences] Naturwissenschaftler *der*, -in *die*.

scintillating ['sɪntɪleɪtɪŋ] *adj* [conversation, speaker] vor Geist sprühend.

scissors ['sɪzəz] *npl* Schere *die*; **a pair of scissors** eine Schere.

scoff [skɒf] ◇ *vt UK inf* verputzen. ◇ *vi* [mock] spotten; **to scoff at sb/sthg** über jn/etw spotten.

scold [skəʊld] *vt* aus|schimpfen.

scone [skɒn, skəʊn] *n kleiner brötchenartiger Kuchen, der mit Butter oder Marmelade und Schlagsahne bestrichen gegessen wird.*

scoop [skuːp] ◇ *n* - **1.** [kitchen implement] Schaufel *die*; [for potato, ice-cream] Portionierer *der* - **2.** [scoopful] Kugel *die* - **3.** [news report] Exklusivbericht *der*. ◇ *vt* schaufeln; [liquid] schöpfen. ◆ **scoop out** *vt sep* [remove] heraus|löffeln.

scooter ['skuːtər] *n* - **1.** [toy] (Tret)roller *der* - **2.** [motorcycle] (Motor)roller *der*.

scope [skəʊp] *n (U)* - **1.** [opportunity] Möglichkeit *die* - **2.** [range] Umfang *der*.

scorch [skɔːtʃ] *vt* - **1.** [clothes] versengen; [food] an|brennen; [skin] verbrennen - **2.** [grass, fields] versengen.

scorching ['skɔːtʃɪŋ] *adj inf*: **scorching (hot)** [day, weather] knallheiß; [sun] sengend.

score [skɔːr] ◇ *n* - **1.** SPORT Spielstand *der*; [at end of game] Ergebnis *das*; **the score is 4-3** es steht 4 zu 3 - **2.** [in test, competition] Punkte *Pl* - **3.** *dated* [twenty] zwanzig - **4.** MUS Noten *Pl* - **5.** [subject]: **on that score** in dieser Hinsicht. ◇ *vt* - **1.** SPORT erzielen; [goal] schießen - **2.** [achieve - success] erzielen; [- victory] erringen; [- hit] landen - **3.** [win in an argument]: **to score a point over sb** jn aus|stechen - **4.** [cut - surface] ein|kerben; [- line] ein|ritzen. ◇ *vi* SPORT Punkte erzielen; **to score a goal** [in football] ein Tor schießen; [in handball] ein Tor werfen. ◆ **score out** *vt sep UK* durch|streichen.

scoreboard ['skɔːbɔːd] *n* Anzeigetafel *die*.

scorer ['skɔ:rəʳ] *n* - **1.** [official] Anschreiber *der*, -in *die* - **2.** [player]: **(goal)scorer** Torschütze *der*, -zin *die*.

scorn [skɔ:n] ◇ *n (U)* Verachtung *die*. ◇ *vt* - **1.** [despise] verachten - **2.** *fml* [refuse to accept] verschmähen.

scornful ['skɔ:nfʊl] *adj* [laugh, remark] verächtlich; **to be scornful of sthg** etw verachten.

Scorpio ['skɔ:pɪəʊ] (*pl* **-s**) *n* Skorpion *der*.

scorpion ['skɔ:pjən] *n* Skorpion *der*.

Scot [skɒt] *n* Schotte *der*, -tin *die*.

scotch [skɒtʃ] *vt* [idea, rumour] ein Ende setzen *(+ D)*.

Scotch [skɒtʃ] ◇ *adj* schottisch. ◇ *n* [whisky] Scotch *der*.

Scotch (tape)® *n US* Tesafilm® *der*.

scot-free *adj inf*: **to get off scot-free** ungeschoren davon|kommen.

Scotland ['skɒtlənd] *n* Schottland *nt*.

Scots [skɒts] ◇ *adj* schottisch. ◇ *n* [dialect] Schottisch *das*.

Scotsman ['skɒtsmən] (*pl* **-men** [-mən]) *n* Schotte *der*.

Scotswoman ['skɒtswʊmən] (*pl* **-women** [-ˌwɪmɪn]) *n* Schottin *die*.

Scottish ['skɒtɪʃ] *adj* schottisch.

scoundrel ['skaʊndrəl] *n dated* Schurke *der*.

scour [skaʊəʳ] *vt* - **1.** [clean] scheuern - **2.** [search] durchkämmen.

scourge [skɜ:dʒ] *n* Geißel *die*.

scout [skaʊt] *n* MIL Kundschafter *der*, -in *die*.
◆ **Scout** *n* [boy scout] Pfadfinder *der*.
◆ **scout around** *vi*: **to scout around (for sthg)** (nach etw) herum|suchen.

scowl [skaʊl] ◇ *n* finsterer OR böser Blick. ◇ *vi* ein finsteres OR böses Gesicht machen; **to scowl at sb** jn finster OR böse an|sehen.

scrabble ['skræbl] *vi* - **1.** [scramble] klettern - **2.** [feel around] herum|wühlen; **to scrabble around for sthg** nach etw wühlen.

scramble ['skræmbl] ◇ *n* [rush] Gedrängel *das*. ◇ *vi* - **1.** [climb] klettern - **2.** [struggle]: **to scramble for sthg** um etw kämpfen.

scrambled eggs ['skræmbld-] *npl* Rührei *das*.

scrap [skræp] ◇ *n* - **1.** [small piece] Stückchen *das*; [of paper, material, conversation] Fetzen *der*; **not a scrap of evidence** kein einziger Beweis - **2.** [metal] Schrott *der* - **3.** *inf* [fight] Rauferei *die*; [quarrel] Streit *der*. ◇ *vt* [plan, system] auf|geben; [car, ship] verschrotten.
◆ **scraps** *npl* [food] (Essens)reste *Pl*.

scrapbook ['skræpbʊk] *n* Erinnerungsalbum *das*.

scrape [skreɪp] ◇ *n* - **1.** [scraping noise] Kratzen *das* - **2.** *dated* [difficult situation]: **to get into a scrape** in die Klemme geraten. ◇ *vt* - **1.** [remove]: **to scrape sthg off sthg** etw von etw ab|schaben - **2.** [peel] schaben - **3.** [rub against - car, bumper] schrammen; [- glass] verkratzen; [- knee, skin] auf|schürfen. ◇ *vi* [rub]: **to scrape against sthg** etw streifen.
◆ **scrape through** *vt insep* [exam, test] mit knapper Not bestehen.

scraper ['skreɪpəʳ] *n* [for paint] Spachtel *der*.

scrap merchant *n UK* Schrotthändler *der*, -in *die*.

scrap paper *UK*, **scratch paper** *US n* Schmierpapier *das*.

scrapyard ['skræpjɑ:d] *n* Schrottplatz *der*.

scratch [skrætʃ] ◇ *n* - **1.** [on skin, surface] Kratzer *der* - **2.** *phr*: **to start sthg from scratch** etw ganz von vorne an|fangen; **to be up to scratch** den Erwartungen entsprechen. ◇ *vt* - **1.** [skin] kratzen; **to scratch o.s.** sich kratzen - **2.** [surface] verkratzen. ◇ *vi* - **1.** [branch, knife, thorn]: **to scratch at/against sthg** an etw *(D)*/gegen etw kratzen - **2.** [person, animal] sich kratzen.

scratch card *n* Rubbellos *das*.

scratch paper *n US* = **scrap paper**.

scrawl [skrɔ:l] ◇ *n* [scribble] Kritzelei *die*. ◇ *vt* [scribble] hin|kritzeln.

scrawny ['skrɔ:nɪ] *adj* [person, legs, arms] dürr; [animal] mager.

scream [skri:m] ◇ *n* [of person] Schrei *der*. ◇ *vt* schreien. ◇ *vi* [person] schreien.

scree [skri:] *n* Geröll *das*.

screech [skri:tʃ] ◇ *n* - **1.** [of person, bird] Kreischen *das* - **2.** [of tyres, brakes] Quietschen *das*. ◇ *vt* kreischen. ◇ *vi* - **1.** [person, bird] kreischen - **2.** [tyres] quietschen.

screen [skri:n] ◇ *n* - **1.** [viewing surface] Bildschirm *der*; [in cinema] Leinwand *die* - **2.** [films]: **the (big) screen** der Film - **3.** [protective panel] Wandschirm *der*. ◇ *vt* - **1.** [in cinema] zeigen - **2.** [on TV] aus|strahlen - **3.** [hide] ab|schirmen - **4.** [shield]: **to screen sthg (from sb/sthg)** etw (gegen jn/etw) ab|schirmen - **5.** [candidate, luggage] überprüfen.

screening ['skri:nɪŋ] *n* - **1.** [in cinema] Vorführung *die* - **2.** [on TV] Ausstrahlung *die* - **3.** *(U)* [for security] Überprüfung *die* - **4.** *(U)* MED [examination] Untersuchung *die*.

screenplay ['skri:npleɪ] *n* Drehbuch *das*.

screw [skru:] ◇ *n* [nail] Schraube *die*. ◇ *vt* - **1.** [fix with screws]: **to screw sthg to sthg** etw an etw *(A)* schrauben - **2.** [lid]: **to screw sthg on/off** etw zu-/auf|schrauben - **3.** *vulg* [have sex with] bumsen, vögeln. ◇ *vi* [lid]: **to screw on/off** sich zu-/aufschrauben lassen; **to screw together** sich zusammenschrauben lassen.
◆ **screw up** *vt sep* - **1.** [crumple up] zusammen|knüllen - **2.** [contort, twist - eyes] zusammen|kneifen; [- face] verziehen - **3.** *v inf* [ruin] vermasseln.

screwdriver ['skru:ˌdraɪvəʳ] *n* [tool] Schraubenzieher *der*.

scribble ['skrɪbl] ◇ *n* Gekritzel *das*. ◇ *vt* hin|kritzeln. ◇ *vi* [write] (vor sich hin)|schreiben; [messily] kritzeln.

script [skrɪpt] *n* - **1.** [of film] Skript *das* - **2.** [system of writing] Schrift *die* - **3.** [handwriting] Handschrift *die*.

scriptwriter ['skrɪpt,raɪtəʳ] *n* Textautor *der*, -in *die*; [of film] Filmautor *der*, -in *die*.

scroll [skrəʊl] *n* [roll of paper] Schriftrolle *die*. ◆ **scroll down** *vi* COMPUT hinunter|scrollen. ◆ **scroll up** *vi* COMPUT hinauf|scrollen.

scrounge [skraʊndʒ] *inf vt*: **to scrounge sthg (off sb)** etw (bei jm) ab|stauben *OR* schnorren.

scrounger ['skraʊndʒəʳ] *n inf* Schnorrer *der*, -in *die*.

scrub [skrʌb] ◇ *n* - **1.** [rub]: **to give sthg a (good) scrub** etw (gründlich) schrubben - **2.** [undergrowth] Gestrüpp *das*. ◇ *vt* schrubben.

scruff [skrʌf] *n*: **by the scruff of the neck** am Genick.

scruffy ['skrʌfɪ] *adj* [person, clothes] ungepflegt; [part of town] heruntergekommen.

scrum(mage) ['skrʌm(ɪdʒ)] *n* RUGBY Gedränge *das*.

scrunchy ['skrʌntʃɪ] *n* Zopfband *das*.

scruples ['skru:plz] *npl* Skrupel *Pl*.

scrutinize, -ise ['skru:tɪnaɪz] *vt* [genau] untersuchen; [face] prüfend an|sehen.

scrutiny ['skru:tɪnɪ] *n (U)* (genaue) Untersuchung *OR* Prüfung.

scuff [skʌf] *vt* - **1.** [drag]: **to scuff one's feet** schlurfen - **2.** [damage - shoes, floor] ab|wetzen; [- furniture] ab|nutzen.

scuffle ['skʌfl] *n* Rauferei *die*.

scullery ['skʌlərɪ] *n* Spülküche *die*.

sculptor ['skʌlptəʳ] *n* Bildhauer *der*, -in *die*.

sculpture ['skʌlptʃəʳ] ◇ *n* - **1.** [work of art] Skulptur *die*, Plastik *die* - **2.** *(U)* [art] Bildhauerei *die*, Skulptur *die*. ◇ *vt* formen; [in stone, wood] hauen.

scum [skʌm] *n* - **1.** [froth] Schaum *der* - **2.** *v inf pej* [worthless people] Abschaum *der*.

scupper ['skʌpəʳ] *vt* - **1.** NAUT [sink] versenken - **2.** *UK fig* [plan] zerschlagen; [chance] ruinieren.

scurrilous ['skʌrələs] *adj fml* verleumderisch.

scurry ['skʌrɪ] *vi* hasten; [mouse] huschen.

scuttle ['skʌtl] ◇ *n*: **(coal) scuttle** Kohleneimer *der*. ◇ *vi* [rush] hasten; [mouse] huschen.

scythe [saɪð] *n* Sense *die*.

SDLP (*abbr of* **Social Democratic and Labour Party**) *n gemäßigte pro-irische Partei Nordirlands*.

sea [si:] ◇ *n* [ocean] Meer *das*, See *die*; **to be at sea** [ship, sailor] auf See sein; **to be all at sea** *fig* [person] verwirrt sein; **by sea** [send] auf dem Seeweg; [travel] mit dem Schiff fahren; **by the sea** am Meer; **out to sea** aufs Meer hinaus. ◇ *comp* See-.

seabed ['si:bed] *n*: **the seabed** der Meeresgrund.

seafood ['si:fu:d] *n (U)* Meeresfrüchte *Pl*.

seafront ['si:frʌnt] *n* Strandpromenade *die*.

seagull ['si:gʌl] *n* Möwe *die*.

seal [si:l] ◇ *n* - **1.** (*pl inv*) [animal] Robbe *die* - **2.** (*pl* **-s**) [official mark] Siegel *das* - **3.** (*pl* **-s**) [official fastening] Versiegelung *die*; [on letter] Siegel *das*; [of metal] Plombe *die*. ◇ *vt* - **1.** [stick down] zu|kleben - **2.** [block up] ab|dichten. ◆ **seal off** *vt sep* ab|riegeln.

sea level *n* Meeresspiegel *der*.

sea lion (*pl inv OR* **-s**) *n* Seelöwe *der*.

seam [si:m] *n* - **1.** SEW Naht *die* - **2.** [of coal] Flöz *das*.

seaman ['si:mən] (*pl* **-men** [-mən]) *n* Seemann *der*.

seamy ['si:mɪ] *adj* anrüchig.

séance ['seɪɒns] *n* spiritistische Sitzung.

seaplane ['si:pleɪn] *n* Wasserflugzeug *das*.

seaport ['si:pɔ:t] *n* Seehafen *der*.

search [sɜ:tʃ] ◇ *n* - **1.** [for lost person, object]: **search (for)** Suche *die* (nach); **in search of** auf der Suche nach - **2.** [of person, luggage, house] Durchsuchung *die*. ◇ *vt* durchsuchen; [city] ab|suchen; [one's mind, memory] durch|forschen. ◇ *vi*: **to search (for)** suchen (nach).

search engine *n* COMPUT Suchmaschine *die*.

searching ['sɜ:tʃɪŋ] *adj* [look] prüfend, forschend; [question] tiefschürfend; [examination] gründlich.

searchlight ['sɜ:tʃlaɪt] *n* Suchscheinwerfer *der*.

search party *n* Suchmannschaft *die*.

search warrant *n* Durchsuchungsbefehl *der*.

seashell ['si:ʃel] *n* Muschel *die*.

seashore ['si:ʃɔ:ʳ] *n*: **the seashore** der Strand.

seasick ['si:sɪk] *adj* seekrank.

seaside ['si:saɪd] *n*: **the seaside** das Meer.

season ['si:zn] ◇ *n* - **1.** [time of year] Jahreszeit *die* - **2.** [for particular activity] Zeit *die* - **3.** [of holiday] Saison *die*; **out of season** außerhalb der Saison - **4.** [of food]: **strawberries are out of season** zu dieser Jahreszeit gibt es keine Erdbeeren - **5.** [series - of films] Saison *die*; [- of lectures] Reihe *die*. ◇ *vt* [food] würzen.

seasonal ['si:zənl] *adj* [change] saisonal; [work] Saison-.

seasoned ['si:znd] *adj* [experienced] erfahren.

seasoning ['si:znɪŋ] *n* [for food] Gewürz *das*.

season ticket *n* Dauerkarte *die*; [for train] Zeitkarte *die*; [for theatre] Abonnement *das*.

seat [si:t] ◇ *n* - **1.** [chair, part of chair, in parliament] Sitz *der* - **2.** [place to sit] (Sitz)platz *der*;

take OR have a seat nehmen Sie Platz - 3. [of skirt] Sitz *der*; [of trousers] Hosenboden *der*. <> *vt* [person, guests] setzen.

seat belt *n* Sicherheitsgurt *der*.

seawater ['siː,wɔːtəʳ] *n* Meerwasser *das*, Seewasser *das*.

seaweed ['siːwiːd] *n* Seetang *der*.

seaworthy ['siː,wɜːðɪ] *adj* seetüchtig.

sec. (*abbr of* **second**) *n* sek.

secede [sɪ'siːd] *vi fml*: **to secede (from sthg)** sich (von etw) ab|spalten.

secluded [sɪ'kluːdɪd] *adj* abgelegen.

seclusion [sɪ'kluːʒn] *n* Abgeschiedenheit *die*.

second ['sekənd] <> *n* - 1. [of time, of angle] Sekunde *die* - 2. UK UNIV *Note an britischen Universitäten, die dem deutschen "Gut" entspricht* - 3. [moment] Moment *der*; **wait a second!** einen Moment! - 4. AUT: **second (gear)** zweiter Gang. <> *num* zweite(r) (s); **the second** der/die/das Zweite; **on the second (of March)** am zweiten (März); **she's second only to him** nur er ist besser als sie; **to come second** den zweiten Platz belegen; *see also* **sixth**. ◆ **seconds** *npl* - 1. COMM Waren *Pl* zweiter Wahl - 2. [of food] zweite Portion.

secondary ['sekəndrɪ] *adj* - 1. SCH: **secondary education** höhere Schulbildung - 2. [less important - road, cause] Neben-; [- issue] nebensächlich; **to be secondary to sthg** weniger wichtig als etw sein.

secondary school *n* höhere Schule.

second-class ['sekənd-] *adj* - 1. *pej* [less important] zweitklassig; [citizen] zweiter Klasse - 2. [ticket, seat] Zweite-Klasse- - 3. [postage]: **second-class stamp** *billigere Briefmarke für Post, die weniger schnell befördert wird* - 4. UK UNIV *Note an britischen Universitäten, die dem deutschen "Gut" entspricht*.

second-hand ['sekənd-] <> *adj* - 1. [goods] gebraucht; [clothes] Secondhand- - 2. [shop] Gebrauchtwaren-; [selling clothes] Secondhand- - 3. *fig* [indirect] aus zweiter Hand. <> *adv* [not new] gebraucht.

second hand ['sekənd-] *n* [of clock] Sekundenzeiger *der*.

secondly ['sekəndlɪ] *adv* zweitens.

secondment [sɪ'kɒndmənt] *n UK* einstweilige Versetzung.

second-rate ['sekənd-] *adj pej* zweitklassig, zweitrangig.

second thought ['sekənd-] *n*: **to have second thoughts about sthg** sich *(D)* etw anders überlegen; **on second thoughts** *UK*, **on second thought** *US* nach nochmaligem Überlegen.

secrecy ['siːkrəsɪ] *n (U)* - 1. [being kept secret] Geheimhaltung *die* - 2. [secretiveness] Heimlichtuerei *die*.

secret ['siːkrɪt] <> *adj* geheim; [admirer] heimlich. <> *n* Geheimnis *das*; **in secret** im Geheimen.

secretarial [,sekrə'teərɪəl] *adj*: **secretarial staff** Büroangestellte *Pl*.

secretary [*UK* 'sekrətrɪ, *US* 'sekrə,terɪ] *n* - 1. [clerical worker] Sekretär *der*, -in *die* - 2. [head of organization] Geschäftsführer *der*, -in *die* - 3. POL [minister] Minister *der*, -in *die*.

Secretary of State *n* - 1. *UK* [minister]: **Secretary of State (for sthg)** Minister *der*, -in *die* (für etw) - 2. *US* [in charge of foreign affairs] Außenminister *der*, -in *die*.

secretive ['siːkrətɪv] *adj* [person] heimlichtuerisch.

secretly ['siːkrɪtlɪ] *adv* [privately] heimlich.

sect [sekt] *n* Sekte *die*.

sectarian [sek'teərɪən] *adj* konfessionsbedingt; [war, quarrel] Konfessions-.

section ['sekʃn] *n* - 1. [portion] Teil *der*; [of book, road] Abschnitt *der*; [of law] Absatz *der*; [of community] Gruppe *die*; [of fruit] Stück *das*; **the sports section of the newspaper** der Sportsteil der Zeitung - 2. GEOM Schnitt *der*.

sector ['sektəʳ] *n* Sektor *der*.

secular ['sekjʊləʳ] *adj* säkular, weltlich; [music] profan.

secure [sɪ'kjʊəʳ] <> *adj* - 1. [gen] sicher - 2. [building] einbruchssicher, sicher OR fest verschlossen. <> *vt* - 1. [obtain] sich *(D)* sichern; [agreement] erzielen - 2. [make safe] sichern - 3. [fasten] fest|machen; [door, window, lid] sicher verschließen.

security [sɪ'kjʊərətɪ] *n* Sicherheit *die*. ◆ **securities** *npl* FIN Wertpapiere *Pl*.

security guard *n* Wache *die*.

sedan [sɪ'dæn] *n US* Limousine *die*.

sedate [sɪ'deɪt] <> *adj* ruhig. <> *vt* Beruhigungsmittel geben *(+ D)*.

sedation [sɪ'deɪʃn] *n*: **they've got him under sedation** er hat Beruhigungsmittel bekommen.

sedative ['sedətɪv] *n* Beruhigungsmittel *das*.

sediment ['sedɪmənt] *n* (Boden)satz *der*; CHEM & GEOL Sediment *das*.

seduce [sɪ'djuːs] *vt* verführen; **to seduce sb into doing sthg** jn dazu verleiten, etw zu tun.

seductive [sɪ'dʌktɪv] *adj* verführerisch.

see [siː] (*pt* **saw**, *pp* **seen**) <> *vt* - 1. [gen] sehen; **as I see it** wie ich es sehe; **what do you see in him?** was findest du bloß an ihm?; **see p. 10** siehe S. 10; **do you see what I mean?** verstehst du, was ich meine? - 2. [visit] besuchen; [doctor, solicitor] gehen zu; **to see sb about sthg** jn wegen etw sprechen; **see you!** tschüs!; **see you soon/later!** bis bald!; **see you tomorrow/on Thursday!** bis morgen/Donnerstag! - 3. [accompany] begleiten - 4. [make sure]: **to see that...** dafür sorgen, dass... <> *vi* - **1.** [with eyes] sehen; **let me see** [have a look] lass mich mal sehen - **2.** [understand] verstehen; **I see** ich verstehe; **you see, it's not that far at all** du siehst ja, es ist gar nicht weit - **3.** [find out]: **I'll go and see** ich sehe mal nach; **let's see, let me see** [when thinking] warten Sie mal, also - **4.** [decide]: **I'll (have to) see** ich muss es mir überlegen. ◆ **seeing as, seeing that** *conj inf* da. ◆ **see about** *vt insep* - **1.** [organize] sich kümmern um - **2.** [expressing doubt]: **we'll see about that** das werden wir sehen. ◆ **see off** *vt sep* - **1.** [say goodbye to] verabschieden - **2.** *UK* [chase away] verjagen. ◆ **see through** <> *vt insep* [person, scheme] durchschauen. <> *vt sep* - **1.** [not abandon - deal, project] zu Ende bringen - **2.** [help to survive] durch|bringen. ◆ **see to** *vt insep* [deal with] sich kümmern um; [repair] reparieren; **I'll see to it that he gets it** ich sorge dafür, dass er es bekommt.

seed [siːd] *n* - **1.** [of plant] Samen *der*; [pip] Kern *der* - **2.** SPORT: **to be the top/fourth seed** als Nummer eins/vier gesetzt sein. ◆ **seeds** *npl fig* [beginnings] Keim *der*.

seedling ['siːdlɪŋ] *n* Sämling *der*.

seedy ['siːdɪ] *adj* [shabby] schäbig; [disreputable] zwielichtig.

seek [siːk] (*pt & pp* **sought**) *vt fml* suchen; **to seek sb's advice/help** jn um Rat fragen/Hilfe bitten; **to seek to do sthg** danach streben, etw zu tun.

seem [siːm] <> *vi* scheinen; **he seems better** es scheint ihm besser zu gehen; **they seem to believe that...** sie glauben anscheinend, dass...; **I seem to remember his name was John** ich glaube, er hieß John. <> *impers vb* scheinen; **it seems (that)...** anscheinend...; **it seems to me (that) you're right** mir scheint, du hast Recht; **so it would seem** so scheint es wenigstens.

seemingly ['siːmɪŋlɪ] *adv* scheinbar.

seen [siːn] *pp* ▻ **see**.

seep [siːp] *vi* sickern.

seesaw ['siːsɔː] *n* Wippe *die*.

seethe [siːð] *vi* - **1.** [person] vor Wut schäumen - **2.** [place]: **to be seething with sthg** von etw wimmeln.

see-through *adj* durchsichtig.

segment ['segmənt] *n* - **1.** [of report, audience] Teil *der*; [of market] Segment *das* - **2.** [of fruit] Stück *das*.

segregate ['segrɪgeɪt] *vt* trennen.

seize [siːz] *vt* - **1.** [grab] packen, greifen - **2.** [win - control, power] übernehmen; [- town] ein|nehmen - **3.** [arrest] fest|nehmen - **4.** [chance, opportunity] ergreifen. ◆ **seize (up)on** *vt insep* [suggestion, idea] sich stützen auf (+ *A*). ◆ **seize up** *vi* - **1.** [body] versagen - **2.** [engine] sich fest|fressen.

seizure ['siːʒəʳ] *n* - **1.** MED Anfall *der* - **2.** *(U)* [taking - of town] Einnahme *die*; [- of control, power] Übernahme *die*; [- of goods by customs] Beschlagnahme *die*.

seldom ['seldəm] *adv* selten.

select [sɪ'lekt] <> *adj* - **1.** [carefully chosen] auserlesen - **2.** [exclusive] exklusiv. <> *vt* aus|wählen.

selection [sɪ'lekʃn] *n* [choice, assortment, range] Auswahl *die*.

selective [sɪ'lektɪv] *adj* - **1.** [not general, limited] selektiv - **2.** [choosy] wählerisch.

self [self] (*pl* **selves**) *n* Selbst *das*; **she's her old self again** sie ist wieder ganz die Alte.

self-addressed stamped envelope [-ə'drest-] *n US* adressierter und frankierter Rückumschlag.

self-assured *adj* selbstbewusst.

self-catering *adj* mit Selbstversorgung.

self-centred [-'sentəd] *adj* egozentrisch.

self-confessed [-kən'fest] *adj* erklärt.

self-confidence *n* Selbstbewusstsein *das*.

self-confident *adj* selbstbewusst.

self-conscious *adj* verlegen, befangen.

self-contained [-kən'teɪnd] *adj* - **1.** [person - independent] unabhängig; [- reserved] reserviert - **2.** [flat] abgeschlossen.

self-control *n* Selbstbeherrschung *die*.

self-defence *n* Selbstverteidigung *die*.

self-discipline *n* Selbstdisziplin *die*.

self-employed [-ɪm'plɔɪd] *adj* selbstständig.

self-esteem *n* Selbstachtung *die*.

self-explanatory *adj* aus sich heraus verständlich.

self-important *adj pej* überheblich.

self-indulgent *adj pej* [person] genusssüchtig.

self-interest *n pej* Eigennutz *der*.

selfish ['selfɪʃ] *adj* selbstsüchtig, egoistisch.

selfishness ['selfɪʃnɪs] *n* Selbstsucht *die*, Egoismus *der*.

selfless ['selflɪs] *adj* selbstlos.

self-made *adj* [man] Selfmade-.

self-opinionated *adj pej* rechthaberisch.

self-pity *n pej* Selbstmitleid *das*.

self-portrait *n* Selbstporträt *das*.

self-possessed *adj* beherrscht.

self-preservation *n* Selbsterhaltung *die*; **instinct for self-preservation** Selbsterhaltungstrieb *der*.

self-raising flour *UK* [-ˌreɪzɪŋ-], **self-rising flour** *US n (U)* Mehl *das* mit Backpulverzusatz.

self-reliant *adj* selbstständig.

self-respect *n* Selbstachtung *die*.

self-respecting [-rɪsˈpektɪŋ] *adj*: **no self-respecting parent would dress their child so badly** Eltern, die etwas auf sich halten, würden ihr Kind nicht so furchtbar anziehen.

self-restraint *n* Selbstbeherrschung *die*.

self-righteous *adj pej* selbstgerecht.

self-rising flour *n US* = **self-raising flour**.

self-satisfied *adj pej* selbstzufrieden.

self-service *n* Selbstbedienung *die*.

self-sufficient *adj* [person, community]: **to be self-sufficient (in sthg)** sich selbst (mit etw) versorgen.

self-taught *adj* autodidaktisch.

sell [sel] (*pt & pp* **sold**) ◇ *vt* - **1.** [goods] verkaufen; **to sell sthg to sb, to sell sb sthg** etw an jn verkaufen, jm etw verkaufen; **I sold it for fifty pounds** ich habe es für fünfzig Pfund verkauft - **2.** [promote sale of]: **such a cover will sell the magazine** mit so einem Titelbild verkauft sich die Zeitschrift garantiert gut - **3.** *fig* [make enthusiastic about]: **to sell sthg to sb, to sell sb sthg** jm etw schmackhaft machen; **I'm not sold on the idea** ich bin von der Idee nicht begeistert. ◇ *vi* - **1.** [person] verkaufen - **2.** [product] sich verkaufen; **to sell for** OR **at** verkauft werden für OR zu. ◆ **sell off** *vt sep* verkaufen. ◆ **sell out** ◇ *vt sep* [performance]: **to be sold out** ausverkauft sein. ◇ *vi* - **1.** [shop, ticket office]: **we've sold out** wir sind ausverkauft; **we've sold out of bread** wir haben kein Brot mehr - **2.** [betray one's principles] sich verkaufen.

sell-by date *n UK* Verfallsdatum *das*.

seller [ˈseləʳ] *n* [vendor] Verkäufer *der*, -in *die*.

selling price *n* Verkaufspreis *der*.

Sellotape® [ˈseləteɪp] *n UK* Tesafilm® *der*, Klebeband *das*.

sell-out *n* [performance, match]: **to be a sell-out** ausverkauft sein.

selves [selvz] *Pl* ▷ **self**.

semaphore [ˈseməfɔːʳ] *n (U)* Flaggenzeichen *Pl*.

semblance [ˈsembləns] *n fml* Anschein *der*.

semen [ˈsiːmen] *n (U)* Samen *der*.

semester [sɪˈmestəʳ] *n* Semester *das*.

semicircle [ˈsemɪˌsɜːkl] *n* Halbkreis *der*.

semicolon [ˌsemɪˈkəʊlən] *n* Semikolon *das*.

semidetached [ˌsemɪdɪˈtætʃt] *adj* & *n UK*: **semidetached (house)** Doppelhaushälfte *die*.

semifinal [ˌsemɪˈfaɪnl] *n* Halbfinale *das*.

seminar [ˈsemɪnɑːʳ] *n* Seminar *das*.

seminary [ˈsemɪnərɪ] *n* RELIG Priesterseminar *das*.

semiskilled [ˌsemɪˈskɪld] *adj* angelernt.

semolina [ˌseməˈliːnə] *n* Grieß *der*.

Senate [ˈsenɪt] *n* POL: **the Senate** der Senat.

senator [ˈsenətəʳ] *n* Senator *der*, -in *die*.

send [send] (*pt & pp* **sent**) *vt* - **1.** [letter, message, money] schicken; [signal] senden; **to send sb sthg, to send sthg to sb** jm etw schicken, etw an jn schicken - **2.** [tell to go]: **to send sb (to)** jn schicken (zu); **to send sb for sthg** jn nach etw schicken - **3.** [into a specific state]: **to send sb to sleep** jn zum Einschlafen bringen; **to send sb into a rage** jn wütend machen. ◆ **send back** *vt sep* zurück|schicken. ◆ **send for** *vt insep* - **1.** [person] holen lassen - **2.** [by post] an|fordern. ◆ **send in** *vt sep* - **1.** [visitor] herein|schicken - **2.** [troops, police] entsenden, schicken - **3.** [submit] ein|reichen. ◆ **send off** *vt sep* - **1.** [by post] ab|schicken - **2.** SPORT [player] vom Platz verweisen. ◆ **send off for** *vt insep* [by post] schriftlich an|fordern. ◆ **send up** *vt sep inf UK* [imitate] parodieren.

sender [ˈsendəʳ] *n* Absender *der*, -in *die*.

send-off *n* Verabschiedung *die*.

senile [ˈsiːnaɪl] *adj* senil.

senior [ˈsiːnjəʳ] ◇ *adj* - **1.** [high-ranking - position, manager] leitend; [- official] höher; [- nurse, doctor] Ober-; [- police officer] ranghoch - **2.** [higher-ranking]: **to be senior to sb** höher als jd gestellt sein - **3.** SCH [classes] höher; [pupils] älter. ◇ *n* - **1.** [older person]: **I'm five years his senior, I'm his senior by five years** ich bin fünf Jahre älter als er - **2.** SCH *Schüler/Student im letzten Schul-/Studienjahr*.

senior citizen *n* Senior *der*, -in *die*.

sensation [senˈseɪʃn] *n* - **1.** [feeling] Gefühl *das* - **2.** [cause of excitement] Sensation *die*.

sensational [senˈseɪʃənl] *adj* [news, victory, show] sensationell; [person, appearance] toll.

sense [sens] ◇ *n* - **1.** [faculty] Sinn *der* - **2.** [feeling, sensation] Gefühl *das*; **sense of guilt** Schuldgefühl *das*; **sense of justice** Gerechtigkeitssinn *der* - **3.** [natural ability] Gefühl *das*; **business sense** Geschäftssinn *der*; **a sense of humour** Humor *der* - **4.** [wisdom, reason] Vernunft *die* - **5.** [meaning] Bedeutung *die*; **to make sense** [have clear meaning] Sinn haben; [be logical] sinnvoll sein; **to make no sense** keinen Sinn machen - **6.** *phr*: **to come to one's senses** [be sensible again] (wieder) zur Vernunft kommen; [regain consciousness] (wieder) zu Bewusstsein kommen. ◇ *vt* [feel] spüren; **to sense (that)...** spüren, dass... ◆ **in a sense** *adv* in gewissem Sinne.

senseless [ˈsenslɪs] *adj* - **1.** [stupid] sinnlos - **2.** [unconscious] bewusstlos.

sensibilities [ˌsensɪˈbɪlətɪz] *npl* [delicate feelings] Empfindlichkeit *die*.

sensible [ˈsensəbl] *adj* vernünftig.

sensitive [ˈsensɪtɪv] *adj* - **1.** [eyes, skin] empfindlich; **sensitive to heat/light** hitze-/lichtempfindlich - **2.** [understanding, aware]: **to be sensitive (to sthg)** (gegenüber etw) aufmerksam sein - **3.** [easily hurt, touchy]: **to be sensitive to sthg** gegenüber etw empfindlich sein; **to**

be sensitive about sthg wegen etw empfindlich sein - **4.** [controversial] heikel - **5.** [instrument] empfindlich.

sensual ['sensjʊəl] *adj* sinnlich.

sensuous ['sensjʊəs] *adj* sinnlich.

sent [sent] *pt* & *pp* ▷ **send**.

sentence ['sentəns] ◇ *n* - **1.** [group of words] Satz *der* - **2.** LAW [decision] Urteil *das*; **a sentence of five years** eine fünfjährige Haftstrafe. ◇ *vt*: **to sentence sb (to sthg)** jn (zu etw) verurteilen.

sentiment ['sentɪmənt] *n* [feeling] Gefühl *das*; [opinion] Meinung *die*.

sentimental [ˌsentɪ'mentl] *adj* sentimental.

sentry ['sentrɪ] *n* Wache *die*.

separate ◇ *adj* ['seprət] - **1.** [not joined, apart]: **separate (from sthg)** getrennt (von etw) - **2.** [individual, distinct] verschieden; **write on a separate piece of paper** schreiben Sie auf ein neues Blatt. ◇ *vt* ['sepəreɪt] - **1.** [keep or set apart]: **to separate (from)** trennen (von); **to separate sb/sthg into** jn/etw einlteilen in *(+ A)* - **2.** [distinguish] unterscheiden; **to separate sb/sthg from** jn/etw unterscheiden von. ◇ *vi* ['sepəreɪt] - **1.** [go different ways]: **to separate (from)** sich trennen (von) - **2.** [come apart, divide] auseinander gehen - **3.** [couple] sich trennen.

separately ['seprətlɪ] *adv* getrennt.

separation [ˌsepə'reɪʃn] *n* Trennung *die*; [division] Einteilung *die*.

September [sep'tembəʳ] *n* September *der*; **in September** im September; **last/this/next September** letzten/diesen/nächsten September; **by September** bis September; **every September** jeden September, jedes Jahr im September; **during September** im September; **at the beginning/end of September** Anfang/Ende September; **in the middle of September** Mitte September.

septic ['septɪk] *adj* eitrig; MED septisch.

septic tank *n* Klärgrube *die*.

sequel ['siːkwəl] *n* - **1.** [book, film]: **sequel (to sthg)** Fortsetzung *die* (von etw) - **2.** [consequence]: **sequel to sthg** Folge *die* von etw.

sequence ['siːkwəns] *n* - **1.** [series] Reihe *die* - **2.** *(U)* [order] Reihenfolge *die* - **3.** [of film] Sequenz *die*.

Serbia ['sɜːbjə] *n* Serbien *nt*.

serene [sɪ'riːn] *adj* [person] gelassen.

sergeant ['sɑːdʒənt] *n* - **1.** [in the army] Feldwebel *der* - **2.** [in the police] Wachtmeister *der*, -in *die*.

sergeant major *n* Hauptfeldwebel *der*.

serial ['sɪərɪəl] *n* [on TV] Serie *die*; [on radio] Sendereihe *die*; [in newspaper] Fortsetzungsroman *der*.

series ['sɪəriːz] (*pl inv*) *n* - **1.** [sequence] Reihe *die* - **2.** RADIO & TV Serie *die*.

serious ['sɪərɪəs] *adj* - **1.** [gen] ernst; [situation, problem, illness, loss] schwer; [shortage] groß - **2.** [newspaper] seriös; **are you serious?** ist das dein Ernst?

seriously ['sɪərɪəslɪ] *adv* - **1.** [earnestly] ernsthaft; **to take sb/sthg seriously** jn/etw ernst nehmen - **2.** [very badly - ill] schwer; [- lacking] sehr.

seriousness ['sɪərɪəsnɪs] *n* - **1.** [of person, expression, situation] Ernst *der* - **2.** [of illness, loss] Schwere *die*.

sermon ['sɜːmən] *n* - **1.** [in church] Predigt *die* - **2.** *fig* & *pej* [lecture] Moralpredigt *die*.

serrated [sɪ'reɪtɪd] *adj* gezackt.

servant ['sɜːvənt] *n* [in household] Diener *der*, -in *die*.

serve [sɜːv] ◇ *vt* - **1.** [work for] dienen *(+ D)* - **2.** [have effect]: **this only served to make him more angry** das führte nur dazu, dass er noch ärgerlicher wurde; **to serve a purpose** einem Zweck dienen - **3.** [provide - with gas, electricity, water] versorgen; **which motorways serve Birmingham?** welche Autobahnen führen nach Birmingham? - **4.** [food or drink]: **to serve sthg to sb, to serve sb sthg** jm etw servieren - **5.** [customer] bedienen - **6.** LAW: **to serve sb with a writ** jn vor Gericht laden - **7.** [complete, carry out - prison sentence] verbüßen; [- apprenticeship] absolvieren; **to serve a term of office** im Amt sein - **8.** SPORT auflschlagen - **9.** *phr*: **it serves you right** das geschieht dir recht. ◇ *vi* - **1.** [be employed - as soldier] dienen; [- in profession] arbeiten; **to serve on** [committee] anlgehören *(+ D)* - **2.** [function]: **to serve as sthg** als etw dienen - **3.** [with food, drink] servieren - **4.** [in shop, bar *etc*] bedienen - **5.** SPORT auflschlagen. ◇ *n* SPORT Aufschlag *der*. ◆ **serve out, serve up** *vt sep* [food] servieren.

service ['sɜːvɪs] ◇ *n* - **1.** [organization, system] Dienst *der*; **bus/train service** Bus-/Zugverbindung *die* - **2.** [amenity] Dienstleistung *die*, Service *der* - **3.** [employment - length of time] Dienstzeit *die* - **4.** *(U)* [in shop, bar *etc*] Bedienung *die*, Service *der*; **'service not included'** 'Trinkgeld nicht inbegriffen' - **5.** MIL Militärdienst *der* - **6.** [mechanical check - of car] Durchsicht *die*; [- of machine] Wartung *die* - **7.** RELIG Gottesdienst *der* - **8.** [set of tableware] Service *das* - **9.** [operation] Betrieb *der*; **in/out of service** in/außer Betrieb - **10.** SPORT Aufschlag *der* - **11.** [help]: **to be of service to sb** [person] jm behilflich sein; [thing] jm von Nutzen sein. ◇ *vt* [car, machine] warten. ◆ **services** *npl* - **1.** [on motorway] Raststätte *die (mit Tankstelle)* - **2.** [armed forces]: **the services** das Militär - **3.** [help] Hilfe *die*, Dienste *Pl*.

serviceable ['sɜːvɪsəbl] *adj* praktisch.

service area *n* Raststätte *die (mit Tankstelle)*.

service charge *n* Bedienungszuschlag *der*, Service *der*.

serviceman ['sɜːvɪsmən] (*pl* **-men** [-mən]) *n* MIL Militärangehörige *der*.

service provider *n* COMPUT Provider *der*.

service station *n* Raststätte *die (mit Tankstelle)*.

serviette [ˌsɜːvɪ'et] *n* Serviette *die*.

session ['seʃn] *n* - **1.** [of court, parliament] Sitzung *die* - **2.** [meeting] Treffen *das*; **recording session** Aufnahme *die* - **3.** *US* [school term] Semester *das*.

set [set] (*pt & pp inv*) <> *adj* - **1.** [specified, prescribed] festgelegt, festgesetzt; [book, text] vorgeschrieben - **2.** [fixed - phrase, expression] fest; [- ideas, routine] starr - **3.** [ready]: **to be (all) set (to do sthg)** startbereit sein(, etw zu tun) - **4.** [determined]: **to be set on doing sthg** entschlossen sein, etw zu tun; **to be dead set against sthg** völlig gegen etw sein. <> *n* - **1.** [collection, group] Satz *der*; **set of teeth** Gebiss *das*; **chess set** Schachspiel *das* - **2.** [television, radio] Apparat *der* - **3.** [of film] Filmkulisse *die*; [of play] Kulisse *die* - **4.** TENNIS Satz *der*. <> *vt* - **1.** [put in specified position, place] stellen; [lying down] legen - **2.** [fix, insert]: **to set sthg in(to) sthg** etw in etw *(A)* einllassen - **3.** [indicating change of state or activity]: **to set sb free** jn befreien; **to set sb's mind at rest** jn beruhigen; **to set sthg on fire** etw anlzünden; **her remark set me thinking** ihre Bemerkung brachte mich zum Nachdenken - **4.** [prepare in advance - trap] auflstellen; [- table] decken - **5.** [clock, meter] stellen - **6.** [time, deadline, minimum wage] festlsetzen, festllegen - **7.** [create - trend] setzen; [- example] geben; [- precedent] schaffen; [- record] auflstellen - **8.** [assign - target] setzen; [- essay, homework] auflgeben; [- exam] auslarbeiten - **9.** MED [bone, broken leg] richten - **10.** [story, film] spielen - **11.** [hair] legen. <> *vi* - **1.** [sun] unterlgehen - **2.** [jelly, cement] fest werden. ◆ **set about** *vt insep* [start]: **to set about sthg** etw in Angriff nehmen; **to set about doing sthg** sich daranmachen, etw zu tun. ◆ **set aside** *vt sep* - **1.** [keep, save - food] auflheben; [- money] beiseite legen; [- time] einlplanen - **2.** [not consider] außer Acht lassen. ◆ **set back** *vt sep* [delay] zurücklwerfen. ◆ **set off** <> *vt sep* - **1.** [initiate, cause] ausllösen - **2.** [trigger - bomb] zünden; [- alarm] ausllösen. <> *vi* [on journey] auflbrechen. ◆ **set out** <> *vt sep* - **1.** [arrange, spread out] zurechtllegen; [chairs] auflstellen; [food] anlrichten - **2.** [clarify, explain] darllegen. <> *vt insep* [intend]: **to set out to do sthg** sich *(D)* vorlnehmen, etw zu tun. <> *vi* [on journey] auflbrechen. ◆ **set up** *vt sep* - **1.** [establish, arrange - fund, organization] gründen; [- interview, meeting] anlsetzen - **2.** [erect - roadblock] errichten; **to set up camp** Zelte auflschlagen - **3.** [install] auflstellen - **4.** *inf* [incriminate] als Schuldigen hinlstellen.

setback ['setbæk] *n* Rückschlag *der*.

settee [se'tiː] *n* Sofa *das*, Couch *die*.

setting ['setɪŋ] *n* - **1.** [surroundings] Umgebung *die* - **2.** [of dial, control] Einstellung *die*.

settle ['setl] <> *vt* - **1.** [argument, differences] beillegen - **2.** [pay - bill, debt] begleichen; [- account] auslgleichen - **3.** [nerves, stomach] beruhigen. <> *vi* - **1.** [go to live] sich niederllassen - **2.** [make o.s. comfortable] es sich *(D)* bequem machen - **3.** [come to rest - dust] sich legen; [- sediment] sich setzen. ◆ **settle down** *vi* - **1.** [give one's attention]: **to settle down to work** sich an die Arbeit machen; **to settle down to doing sthg** sich daranlmachen, etw zu tun - **2.** [assume stable lifestyle] sesshaft werden - **3.** [make o.s. comfortable] es sich *(D)* bequem machen - **4.** [become calm] sich beruhigen. ◆ **settle for** *vt insep* sich zufriedenlgeben mit. ◆ **settle in** *vi* [in house] sich einlleben; [in job] sich einlgewöhnen. ◆ **settle on** *vt insep* [choose] sich entscheiden für. ◆ **settle up** *vi* [financially]: **to settle up (with sb)** ablrechnen (mit jm).

settlement ['setlmənt] *n* - **1.** [agreement] Übereinkunft *die*, Einigung *die* - **2.** [village] (An)siedlung *die* - **3.** [payment] Begleichung *die*, Bezahlung *die*.

settler ['setləʳ] *n* Siedler *der*, -in *die*.

set-up *n inf* - **1.** [system] System *das*; [organization] Organisation *die* - **2.** [deception to incriminate] Falle *die*.

seven ['sevn] *num* sieben; *see also* **six**.

seventeen [ˌsevn'tiːn] *num* siebzehn; *see also* **six**.

seventeenth [ˌsevn'tiːnθ] *num* siebzehnte (r) (s); *see also* **sixth**.

seventh ['sevnθ] *num* siebte (r) (s); *see also* **sixth**.

seventy ['sevntɪ] *num* siebzig; *see also* **sixty**.

sever ['sevəʳ] *vt* - **1.** [limb] abltrennen; [rope] durchlschneiden; [ligament] reißen - **2.** [relationship, ties] ablbrechen.

several ['sevrəl] <> *adj* [some] mehrere, einige. <> *pron* mehrere, einige.

severe [sɪ'vɪəʳ] *adj* - **1.** [shock, pain, gale] stark; [illness, injury] schwer; [problem] ernst - **2.** [stern - person] streng; [- criticism] heftig.

severity [sɪ'verətɪ] *n (U)* - **1.** [of storm] Stärke *die*; [of illness] Schwere *die*; [of problem] Ernst *der* - **2.** [sternness - of person] Strenge *die*; [- of criticism] Heftigkeit *die*.

sew [səʊ] (*UK pp* **sewn**) (*US pp* **sewed** OR **sewn**) *vt & vi* nähen. ◆ **sew up** *vt sep* [join] zusammenlnähen.

sewage ['suːɪdʒ] *n* Abwasser *das*.

sewer ['sʊəʳ] *n* Abwasserkanal *der*.

sewing ['səʊɪŋ] *n (U)* - **1.** [activity] Nähen *das* - **2.** [items] Näharbeit *die*.

sewing machine *n* Nähmaschine *die*.

sewn [səʊn] *pp* ▷ **sew**.

sex [seks] *n* - **1.** [gender] Geschlecht *das* - **2.** [sexual intercourse] Sex *der*; **to have sex (with sb)** (mit jm) Sex haben.

sexist ['seksɪst] ◇ *adj* sexistisch. ◇ *n* Sexist *der*, -in *die*.

sexual ['sekʃʊəl] *adj* - **1.** [of sexuality, sexual intercourse] sexuell; [disease, organ] Geschlechts- - **2.** [of gender]: **sexual equality/rivalry** Gleichheit/Rivalität zwischen den Geschlechtern.

sexual discrimination *n* Diskriminierung *die* aufgrund des Geschlechts.

sexual harassment *n (U)* sexuelle Belästigung.

sexual intercourse *n (U)* Geschlechtsverkehr *der*.

sexually transmitted disease *n* sexuell übertragbare Krankheit.

sexy ['seksɪ] *adj inf* sexy.

shabby ['ʃæbɪ] *adj* schäbig; [street] heruntergekommen.

shack [ʃæk] *n* Hütte *die*.

shackle ['ʃækl] *vt* - **1.** [chain] fesseln - **2.** *liter* [restrict] (be)hindern.

shade [ʃeɪd] ◇ *n* - **1.** *(U)* [shadow] Schatten *der* - **2.** [lampshade] Lampenschirm *der* - **3.** [colour] Farbton *der* - **4.** [nuance] Schattierung *die*. ◇ *vt* - **1.** [from light] beschatten - **2.** [drawing] schattieren. ◆ **shades** *npl inf* [sunglasses] Sonnenbrille *die*.

shadow ['ʃædəʊ] *n* Schatten *der*; **there's not a** OR **the shadow of a doubt** es gibt nicht den geringsten Zweifel.

shadow cabinet *n* Schattenkabinett *das*.

shadowy ['ʃædəʊɪ] *adj* - **1.** [dark] dunkel - **2.** [unknown, sinister] mysteriös.

shady ['ʃeɪdɪ] *adj* - **1.** [place] schattig - **2.** [tree] Schatten spendend - **3.** *inf* [dishonest, sinister] zweifelhaft.

shaft [ʃɑːft] *n* - **1.** [vertical passage] Schacht *der* - **2.** [rod - of tool] Stiel *der*; [- of column] Schaft *der*; [- of propeller] Welle *die* - **3.** [of light] Strahl *der*.

shaggy ['ʃægɪ] *adj* [hair, beard, dog] struppig; [carpet] verfilzt.

shake [ʃeɪk] (*pt* **shook**, *pp* **shaken**) ◇ *vt* - **1.** [move vigorously] schütteln; **to shake hands** sich *(D)* die Hände schütteln; **to shake sb's hand, to shake hands with sb** jm die Hand schütteln, js Hand schütteln; **to shake one's head** den Kopf schütteln - **2.** [upset, undermine] erschüttern. ◇ *vi* zittern. ◇ *n*: **to give sthg a shake** etw schütteln. ◆ **shake off** *vt sep* [police, pursuer] ab|schütteln; [illness] los|werden. ◆ **shake up** *vt sep* [upset] stark mit|nehmen.

shaken ['ʃeɪkn] *pp* ▷ **shake**.

shaky ['ʃeɪkɪ] *adj* - **1.** [unsteady - chair, table] wackelig; [- hand, writing, voice] zitternd; [- person] zitterig - **2.** [weak, uncertain] schwach; [finances] unsicher.

shall (*weak form* [ʃəl], *strong form* [ʃæl]) *aux vb* - **1.** *(1st person sg & 1st person pl)* [to express future tense] werden; **I shall be late tomorrow** morgen werde ich später kommen; **I shall be ready soon** ich bin bald fertig; **will you be there? – we shall** werdet ihr dort sein? – ja - **2.** *(esp 1st person sg & 1st person pl)* [in questions] sollen; **shall I buy some wine?** soll ich Wein kaufen?; **where shall we go?** wo gehen wir hin?; **I'll tell her too, shall I?** ich sag es ihr auch, okay? - **3.** [in orders] sollen; **you shall tell me what happened!** du wirst mir erzählen, was passiert ist!; **payment shall be made within a week** die Zahlung muss innerhalb einer Woche erfolgen.

shallow ['ʃæləʊ] *adj* - **1.** [in size] flach - **2.** *pej* [superficial] seicht.

sham [ʃæm] ◇ *adj* [feeling] vorgetäuscht. ◇ *n* [piece of deceit] Schein *der*.

shambles ['ʃæmblz] *n* - **1.** [disorder] Chaos *das* - **2.** [fiasco] Disaster *das*.

shame [ʃeɪm] ◇ *n* - **1.** [remorse] Scham *die* - **2.** [dishonour]: **to bring shame (up)on sb** Schande über jn bringen - **3.** [pity]: **it's a shame (that)...** schade, dass...; **what a shame!** (wie) schade! ◇ *vt* beschämen; **to shame sb into doing sthg** jn moralisch zwingen, etw zu tun.

shameful ['ʃeɪmfʊl] *adj* schändlich.

shameless ['ʃeɪmlɪs] *adj* schamlos.

shampoo [ʃæm'puː] (*pl* **-s**, *pt & pp* **-ed**, *cont* **-ing**) ◇ *n* - **1.** [liquid] Shampoo *das* - **2.** [act of shampooing]: **to give one's hair a shampoo** sich *(D)* das Haar schampunieren. ◇ *vt* [hair] schampunieren; [carpet] reinigen.

shamrock ['ʃæmrɒk] *n* Klee *der*.

shandy ['ʃændɪ] *n* [in Northern Germany] Alsterwasser *das*; [in Southern Germany] Radler *das*.

shan't [ʃɑːnt] *abbr of* **shall not**.

shantytown ['ʃæntɪtaʊn] *n* Slum *der*.

shape [ʃeɪp] ◇ *n* - **1.** [outer form] Form *die* - **2.** [figure, abstract structure] Gestalt *die*; **to take shape** Gestalt an|nehmen - **3.** [form, health]: **to be in good/bad shape** [person] in guter/schlechter Form sein; **his business is in bad shape** seine Geschäfte laufen schlecht. ◇ *vt* - **1.** [mould physically]: **to shape sthg (into)** etw formen (in *(+ A)*) - **2.** [influence - person, character] formen; [- ideas, life, future] beeinflussen. ◆ **shape up** *vi* [develop] sich entwickeln.

-shaped ['ʃeɪpt] *suffix* -förmig; **egg-shaped** eiförmig.

shapeless ['ʃeɪplɪs] *adj* formlos.

shapely ['ʃeɪplɪ] *adj* [legs] wohlproportioniert; [woman] wohlgeformt.

share [ʃeəʳ] ◇ *n*: **to do one's share of sthg** seinen Beitrag zu etw leisten. ◇ *vt* teilen. ◇ *vi* [share book] zusammen hinein|schauen; **there's only one room left – we'll have to share** es gibt nur noch ein Zimmer –

wir müssen es teilen; **to share in sthg** sich an etw *(D)* beteiligen. ◆ **shares** *npl* FIN Aktien *Pl.* ◆ **share out** *vt sep* verteilen.

shareholder ['ʃeə,həʊldəʳ] *n* Aktionär *der*, -in *die*.

shark [ʃɑːk] *(pl inv* OR **-s**) *n* [fish] Hai *der*.

sharp [ʃɑːp] ◇ *adj* - **1.** [not blunt] scharf; [needle, pencil] spitz - **2.** [well-defined] scharf - **3.** [intelligent, keen - person, mind] scharfsinnig; [- eyesight, hearing] scharf - **4.** [sudden - increase, fall] abrupt; [- turn] scharf; [- slope] steil - **5.** [angry, severe] scharf; **she was rather sharp with me** sie war recht schroff zu mir - **6.** [piercing, loud] schrill - **7.** [painful] schneidend - **8.** [bitter] herb - **9.** [MUS - raised a semitone] um einen Halbton erhöht; **C sharp** Cis *das*; **D sharp** Dis *das*; **A sharp** Ais *das*. ◇ *adv* - **1.** [punctually] pünktlich; **at eight o'clock sharp** Punkt acht Uhr - **2.** [quickly, suddenly]: **to turn sharp right/left** scharf nach rechts/links ab|biegen. ◇ *n* [MUS - note] erhöhter Ton; [- symbol] Kreuz *das*.

sharpen ['ʃɑːpn] *vt* [make sharp] schärfen; [pencil] (an)|spitzen.

sharpener ['ʃɑːpnəʳ] *n* [for pencil] Spitzer *der*; [for knife] Messerschärfer *der*.

sharply ['ʃɑːplɪ] *adv* - **1.** [distinctly] scharf - **2.** [suddenly - increase, fall] abrupt; [- turn] scharf; [- slope] steil - **3.** [harshly] scharf.

shatter ['ʃætəʳ] ◇ *vt* - **1.** [glass, window] zerschmettern - **2.** *fig* [beliefs, hopes, dreams] zerschlagen. ◇ *vi* [glass, window] zerspringen.

shattered ['ʃætəd] *adj* - **1.** [shocked, upset] niedergeschmettert - **2.** *UK inf* [very tired] völlig fertig.

shave [ʃeɪv] ◇ *n* [with razor] Rasur *die*; **to have a shave** sich rasieren. ◇ *vt* - **1.** [with razor] rasieren - **2.** [wood] ab|hobeln. ◇ *vi* sich rasieren.

shaver ['ʃeɪvəʳ] *n* Rasierapparat *der*.

shaving brush ['ʃeɪvɪŋ-] *n* Rasierpinsel *der*.

shaving cream ['ʃeɪvɪŋ-] *n* Rasiercreme *die*.

shaving foam ['ʃeɪvɪŋ-] *n* Rasierschaum *der*.

shawl [ʃɔːl] *n* Schultertuch *das*.

she [ʃiː] ◇ *pers pron* - **1.** [referring to woman, girl, animal] sie; **she's tall** sie ist groß; **there she is** da ist sie; **she can't do it** sie kann es nicht tun; **if I were** OR **was she** *fml* wenn ich sie wäre - **2.** [referring to boat, car, country] es; **she sails tomorrow** es fährt morgen ab. ◇ *comp*: **she-bear** Bärin *die*.

sheaf [ʃiːf] *(pl* **sheaves**) *n* - **1.** [of papers, letters] Bündel *das* - **2.** [of corn, grain] Garbe *die*.

shear [ʃɪəʳ] *(pt* **-ed**, *pp* **-ed** OR **shorn**) *vt* scheren. ◆ **shears** *npl* - **1.** [for garden] Heckenschere *die* - **2.** [for dressmaking] große Schere.

sheath [ʃiːθ] *(pl* **-s** [ʃiːðz]) *n* - **1.** [for knife] Scheide *die* - **2.** [for cable] Umhüllung *die*, Ummantelung *die* - **3.** *UK* [condom] Kondom *das*.

sheaves [ʃiːvz] *Pl* ▷ **sheaf**.

shed [ʃed] *(pt & pp inv)* ◇ *n* Schuppen *der*. ◇ *vt* - **1.** [gen] verlieren - **2.** [employees] entlassen; [inhibitions] überwinden - **3.** [tears, blood] vergießen.

she'd *(weak form* [ʃɪd], *strong form* [ʃiːd]) *abbr of* **she had**, **she would**.

sheen [ʃiːn] *n* Glanz *der*.

sheep [ʃiːp] *(pl inv)* *n* Schaf *das*.

sheepdog ['ʃiːpdɒg] *n* Hütehund *der*.

sheepish ['ʃiːpɪʃ] *adj* verlegen.

sheepskin ['ʃiːpskɪn] *n* Schaffell *das*.

sheer [ʃɪəʳ] *adj* - **1.** [absolute] rein - **2.** [very steep] senkrecht - **3.** [delicate] hauchdünn.

sheet [ʃiːt] *n* - **1.** [for bed] Bettuch *das*, Laken *das* - **2.** [of paper] Blatt *das* - **3.** [of glass] Scheibe *die*; [of metal] Blech *das*; [of wood] Platte *die*.

shelf [ʃelf] *(pl* **shelves**) *n* Regal *das*.

shell [ʃel] ◇ *n* - **1.** [of egg, nut] Schale *die* - **2.** [of tortoise] Panzer *der*; [of snail] Haus *das* - **3.** [on beach] Muschel *die* - **4.** [of building] Rohbau *der*; [of car] Karosserie *die*; [of boat] Rumpf *der* - **5.** MIL Granate *die*. ◇ *vt* - **1.** [remove covering from] schälen; [peas] enthülsen - **2.** MIL beschießen.

she'll [ʃiːl] *abbr of* **she will**, **she shall**.

shellfish ['ʃelfɪʃ] *(pl inv)* *n* - **1.** [creature] Schalentier *das* - **2.** *(U)* [food] Meeresfrüchte *Pl*.

shell suit *n UK* Jogginganzug *der (aus Nylon)*.

shelter ['ʃeltəʳ] ◇ *n* - **1.** [building, structure] Unterstand *der*; [against air raids] (Luftschutz)bunker *der*; [in mountains] Berghütte *die* - **2.** [cover, protection] Schutz *der* - **3.** [accommodation] Obdach *das*. ◇ *vt* - **1.** [from rain, sun, bombs]: **to be sheltered by/from sthg** von/vor etw *(D)* geschützt sein - **2.** [give asylum to - refugee] Obdach geben *(+ D)*; [- fugitive, criminal] Unterschlupf gewähren *(+ D)*. ◇ *vi*: **to shelter from/in sthg** vor/in etw *(D)* Schutz suchen.

sheltered ['ʃeltəd] *adj* - **1.** [place] geschützt - **2.** [life, childhood] behütet - **3.** [accommodation, housing] betreut.

shelve [ʃelv] *vt* [plan] auf|schieben.

shelves [ʃelvz] *Pl* ▷ **shelf**.

shepherd ['ʃepəd] ◇ *n* Schäfer *der*. ◇ *vt fig* führen.

shepherd's pie ['ʃepədz-] *n mit Kartoffelbrei überbackenes Hackfleisch*.

sheriff ['ʃerɪf] *n US* [law officer] Sheriff *der*.

sherry ['ʃerɪ] *n* Sherry *der*.

she's [ʃiːz] *abbr of* **she is**, **she has**.

shield [ʃiːld] ◇ *n* - **1.** [armour] Schild *der* - **2.** *UK* [sports trophy] Trophäe *die* - **3.** [protection]: **shield against sthg** Schutz *der* gegen etw. ◇ *vt*: **to shield sb/o.s. (from sthg)** jn/sich (vor etw *(D)*) schützen.

shift [ʃɪft] ◇ *n* - **1.** [slight change] Veränderung *die* - **2.** [period of work, workers] Schicht *die.* ◇ *vt* - **1.** [move, put elsewhere] verschieben - **2.** [change slightly] ändern - **3.** *US* AUT: **to shift gear** schalten. ◇ *vi* - **1.** [move] sich bewegen; [move up - person] rutschen; [- thing] verrutschen - **2.** [change slightly - attitude, opinion] sich ändern; [- wind] umlschlagen - **3.** *US* AUT schalten.

shifty ['ʃɪftɪ] *adj inf* verschlagen.

shilling ['ʃɪlɪŋ] *n UK* Shilling *der.*

shimmer ['ʃɪmər] ◇ *n* Schimmer *der;* [in heat] Flimmern *das.* ◇ *vi* schimmern; [in heat] flimmern.

shin [ʃɪn] *n* Schienbein *das.*

shinbone ['ʃɪnbəʊn] *n* Schienbein *das.*

shine [ʃaɪn] (*pt & pp* **shone**) ◇ *n* Glanz *der.* ◇ *vt* - **1.** [torch, lamp]: **to shine sthg on sthg** mit etw auf etw leuchten - **2.** [polish] polieren. ◇ *vi* [moon, sun] scheinen; [stars, light] leuchten; [eyes, metal, shoes] glänzen.

shingle ['ʃɪŋgl] *n* [on beach] Strandkies *der.* ◆ **shingles** *(U) n* MED Gürtelrose *die.*

shiny ['ʃaɪnɪ] *adj* glänzend.

ship [ʃɪp] ◇ *n* Schiff *das.* ◇ *vt* [send] versenden; [send by ship - people] befördern; [- goods] verschiffen.

shipbuilding ['ʃɪpˌbɪldɪŋ] *n* Schiffbau *der.*

shipment ['ʃɪpmənt] *n* - **1.** [cargo] Sendung *die;* [in ship] Ladung *die* - **2.** [act of shipping] Versand *der;* [by ship] Verschiffung *die.*

shipping ['ʃɪpɪŋ] *n (U)* - **1.** [transport] Versand *der;* [by ship] Verschiffung *die* - **2.** [ships] Schiffe *Pl.*

shipshape ['ʃɪpʃeɪp] *adj* tipptopp in Ordnung.

shipwreck ['ʃɪprek] ◇ *n* - **1.** [destruction of ship] Schiffbruch *der* - **2.** [wrecked ship] Schiffswrack *das.* ◇ *vt*: **to be shipwrecked** Schiffbruch erleiden.

shipyard ['ʃɪpjɑːd] *n* (Schiffs)werft *die.*

shirk [ʃɜːk] *vt* sich drücken vor *(+ D).*

shirt [ʃɜːt] *n* Hemd *das.*

shirtsleeves ['ʃɜːtsliːvz] *npl*: **to be in (one's) shirtsleeves** in Hemdsärmeln sein.

shit [ʃɪt] (*pt & pp inv*, **-ted** OR **shat**) *vulg* ◇ *n* [excrement, nonsense] Scheiße *die.* ◇ *vi* scheißen. ◇ *excl* Scheiße!

shiver ['ʃɪvər] ◇ *n* Schauder *der.* ◇ *vi*: **to shiver (with sthg)** (vor etw *(D)*) zittern.

shoal [ʃəʊl] *n* [of fish] Schwarm *der.*

shock [ʃɒk] ◇ *n* - **1.** [surprise, reaction] Schock *der* - **2.** MED: **to be suffering from shock, to be in (a state of) shock** unter Schock stehen - **3.** [impact] Wucht *die* - **4.** ELEC Schlag *der.* ◇ *vt & vi* [upset] schockieren.

shock absorber [-əbˌzɔːbər] *n* Stoßdämpfer *der.*

shocking ['ʃɒkɪŋ] *adj* - **1.** [very bad] miserabel - **2.** [scandalous, horrifying] schockierend.

shod [ʃɒd] ◇ *pt & pp* ▷ **shoe**. ◇ *adj*: **well/poorly shod** gut/schlecht beschuht.

shoddy ['ʃɒdɪ] *adj* schäbig.

shoe [ʃuː] (*pt & pp* **-d** OR **shod**) ◇ *n* [for person] Schuh *der.* ◇ *vt* [horse] beschlagen.

shoebrush ['ʃuːbrʌʃ] *n* Schuhbürste *die.*

shoehorn ['ʃuːhɔːn] *n* Schuhanzieher *der.*

shoelace ['ʃuːleɪs] *n* Schnürsenkel *der.*

shoe polish *n (U)* Schuh(putz)creme *die.*

shoe shop *n* Schuhgeschäft *das.*

shoestring ['ʃuːstrɪŋ] *n fig*: **on a shoestring** mit minimalen (finanziellen) Mitteln.

shone [ʃɒn] *pt & pp* ▷ **shine**.

shoo [ʃuː] ◇ *vt* verscheuchen. ◇ *excl* husch!

shook [ʃʊk] *pt* ▷ **shake**.

shoot [ʃuːt] (*pt & pp* **shot**) ◇ *vt* - **1.** [fire gun at - killing] erschießen; [- wounding] anlschießen; **to shoot o.s.** [kill o.s.] sich erschießen - **2.** *UK* [hunt] jagen - **3.** [arrow] ablschießen - **4.** CIN drehen. ◇ *vi* - **1.** [fire gun]: **to shoot (at sb/sthg)** (auf jn/etw) schießen - **2.** *UK* [hunt] jagen - **3.** [move quickly]: **to shoot in/out/past** herein-/heraus-/vorbeischießen - **4.** CIN drehen - **5.** SPORT schießen. ◇ *n* - **1.** *UK* [hunting expedition] Jagd *die* - **2.** [of plant] Trieb *der.* ◆ **shoot down** *vt sep* [plane, helicopter] ablschießen; [person] niederlschießen. ◆ **shoot up** *vi* - **1.** [grow quickly] schnell wachsen - **2.** [increase quickly] in die Höhe schießen.

shooting ['ʃuːtɪŋ] *n* - **1.** [killing] Schießerei *die* - **2.** [hunting] Jagd *die.*

shooting star *n* Sternschnuppe *die.*

shop [ʃɒp] ◇ *n* - **1.** [store] Geschäft *das,* Laden *der* - **2.** [workshop] Werkstatt *die.* ◇ *vi* einlkaufen; **to go shopping** einkaufen gehen.

shop assistant *n UK* Verkäufer *der,* -in *die.*

shop floor *n*: **the shop floor** [workers] die Arbeiter *Pl;* **on the shop floor** bei den Arbeitern.

shopkeeper ['ʃɒpˌkiːpər] *n* Ladenbesitzer *der,* -in *die.*

shoplifting ['ʃɒpˌlɪftɪŋ] *n (U)* Ladendiebstahl *der.*

shopper ['ʃɒpər] *n* Käufer *der,* -in *die.*

shopping ['ʃɒpɪŋ] *n (U)* - **1.** [purchases] Einkäufe *Pl* - **2.** [act of shopping] Einkaufen *das;* **to do the shopping** einkaufen (gehen).

shopping bag *n* Einkaufstasche *die.*

shopping centre *UK*, **shopping mall** *US*, **shopping plaza** *US* [-ˌplɑːzə] *n* Einkaufszentrum *das.*

shop steward *n* gewerkschaftliche Vertrauensperson.

shopwindow [ˌʃɒp'wɪndəʊ] *n* Schaufenster *das.*

shore [ʃɔːʳ] *n* Ufer *das*; **on shore** [not at sea] an Land. ◆ **shore up** *vt sep* - **1.** [prop up] ablstützen - **2.** *fig* [sustain] stützen.

shorn [ʃɔːn] ◇ *pp* ▷ **shear**. ◇ *adj* [head, sheep] geschoren; [hair] kurz geschoren.

short [ʃɔːt] ◇ *adj* - **1.** [gen] kurz - **2.** [in height] klein - **3.** [curt]: **to be short (with sb)** (zu jm) schroff *OR* barsch sein - **4.** [lacking] knapp; **we're £10 short** uns fehlen 10 Pfund; **he is short on intelligence/money** es mangelt ihm an Intelligenz/Geld - **5.** [abbreviated]: **to be short for sthg** die Kurzform von etw sein. ◇ *adv* - **1.** [lacking]: **we're running short of food** unsere Lebensmittelvorräte gehen langsam zur Neige - **2.** [suddenly, abruptly]: **to cut sthg short** etw vorzeitig ablbrechen; **to stop short** plötzlich stehenlbleiben. ◇ *n* - **1.** *UK* [alcoholic drink] Schnaps *der* - **2.** CIN Kurzfilm *der*. ◆ **shorts** *npl* - **1.** [short trousers] Shorts *Pl* - **2.** *US* [underwear] Boxershorts *Pl*. ◆ **for short** *adv*: **he's called Bob for short** er wird kurz Bob genannt. ◆ **in short** *adv* kurz gesagt. ◆ **nothing short of** *prep* nichts anderes als. ◆ **short of** *prep* [apart from]: **short of ringing up, I don't see how I can find out** ich kann es nur herausfinden, wenn ich anrufe.

shortage [ˈʃɔːtɪdʒ] *n* Mangel *der*, Knappheit *die*.

shortbread [ˈʃɔːtbred] *n (U)* Buttergebäck *das*.

short-change *vt* - **1.** [in shop, restaurant] zu wenig herauslgeben *(+ D)* - **2.** *fig* [reward unfairly] übers Ohr gehauen werden.

short circuit *n* Kurzschluss *der*.

shortcomings [ˈʃɔːtˌkʌmɪŋz] *npl* Unzulänglichkeiten *Pl*.

short cut *n* - **1.** [quick route] Abkürzung *die* - **2.** [quick method] schneller Weg.

shorten [ˈʃɔːtn] ◇ *vt* - **1.** [in time] verkürzen - **2.** [in length] kürzen. ◇ *vi* [days, nights] kürzer werden.

shortfall [ˈʃɔːtfɔːl] *n*: **shortfall (in/of sthg)** Defizit *das* (bei/von etw).

shorthand [ˈʃɔːthænd] *n (U)* [writing system] Stenografie *die*, Kurzschrift *die*.

shorthand typist *n UK* Stenotypist *der*, -in *die*.

short list *n UK* engere Wahl.

shortly [ˈʃɔːtlɪ] *adv* [soon] bald; **shortly before/after our arrival** kurz vor/nach unserer Ankunft.

shortsighted [ˌʃɔːtˈsaɪtɪd] *adj liter* & *fig* kurzsichtig.

short-staffed [-ˈstɑːft] *adj*: **to be short-staffed** an Personalmangel leiden.

short story *n* Kurzgeschichte *die*.

short-tempered [-ˈtempəd] *adj* reizbar.

short-term *adj* kurzfristig.

short wave *n* Kurzwelle *die*.

shot [ʃɒt] ◇ *pt* & *pp* ▷ **shoot**. ◇ *n* - **1.** [gunshot, injection, drink] Schuss *der*; **like a shot** [quickly] wie der Blitz - **2.** [marksman] Schütze *der*, -zin *die* - **3.** [SPORT - in football] Schuss *der*; [- in golf, tennis] Schlag *der* - **4.** [photograph] Aufnahme *die* - **5.** CIN Einstellung *die* - **6.** *inf* [try, go] Versuch *der*.

shotgun [ˈʃɒtgʌn] *n* Schrotflinte *die*.

should [ʃʊd] *aux vb* - **1.** [expressing desirability]: **we should leave now** wir sollten jetzt gehen; **you should have seen her!** du hättest sie sehen sollen! - **2.** [asking for advice, permission]: **should I go too?** soll ich auch gehen?; **should I do it now?** soll ich es jetzt tun? - **3.** [as suggestion]: **I should deny everything** ich würde alles abstreiten; **I shouldn't take too much notice** kümmern Sie sich nicht zu sehr darum - **4.** [expressing probability]: **she should be home soon** sie müsste bald zu Hause sein - **5.** [ought to]: **they should have won the match** sie hätten das Spiel gewinnen müssen; **that should do** das dürfte genügen - **6.** *fml* [expressing wish]: **I should like to come with you** ich würde gerne mit dir kommen - **7.** *(as conditional)*: **should you need anything, call reception** *fml* sollten Sie irgendetwas brauchen, rufen Sie die Rezeption an; **how should I know?** wie soll ich das wissen? - **8.** *(in subordinate clauses)*: **we decided that you should meet him** wir beschlossen, dass du ihn kennenlernen solltest - **9.** [expressing uncertain opinion]: **I should imagine he's about 50** meiner Meinung nach ist er etwa 50.

shoulder [ˈʃəʊldəʳ] ◇ *n* Schulter *die*. ◇ *vt* - **1.** [load] auf die Schulter(n) nehmen - **2.** [responsibility] übernehmen.

shoulder blade *n* Schulterblatt *das*.

shoulder strap *n* - **1.** [on dress] Träger *der* - **2.** [on bag] Schulterriemen *der*.

shouldn't [ˈʃʊdnt] *abbr of* **should not**.

should've [ˈʃʊdəv] *abbr of* **should have**.

shout [ʃaʊt] ◇ *n* Schrei *der*. ◇ *vt* schreien. ◇ *vi* schreien; **to shout at sb** jn anlschreien. ◆ **shout down** *vt sep* niederlschreien.

shouting [ˈʃaʊtɪŋ] *n* Geschrei *das*.

shove [ʃʌv] *inf* ◇ *n*: **to give sb a shove** jm einen Schubs geben; **to give sthg a shove** etw rücken; [car] etw anlschieben. ◇ *vt* [push - person] schubsen; [- thing] schieben; [stuff] stopfen. ◆ **shove off** *vi* - **1.** [in boat] (vom Ufer) ablstoßen - **2.** *inf* [go away] verschwinden.

shovel [ˈʃʌvl] *(UK)* *(US)* ◇ *n* Schaufel *die*. ◇ *vt* [with a shovel] schaufeln.

show [ʃəʊ] *(pt* **-ed**, *pp* **shown** *OR* **-ed***)* ◇ *n* - **1.** [entertainment] Show *die* - **2.** CIN Vorstellung *die* - **3.** [exhibition] Ausstellung *die* - **4.** [display - of strength] Zurschaustellen *das*; [- of temper] Anfall *der*, Ausbruch *der*. ◇ *vt* zeigen; [subj: thermometer, dial] anlzeigen; [profit, loss] auflweisen; [work of art] auslstellen; **to show sb sthg, to show sthg to sb** jm etw zeigen; **to show sb to the door/his table** jn zur Tür bringen/zu seinem Tisch führen. ◇ *vi* - **1.** [indicate, make clear] zeigen - **2.** [be visible] zu sehen sein - **3.** CIN: **what's showing tonight?** welcher Film läuft heute Abend? ◆ **show off** ◇ *vt sep* vor|führen. ◇ *vi* an|geben. ◆ **show up** ◇ *vt sep* [embarrass] blamieren. ◇ *vi* - **1.** [stand out] hervor|stehen, hervor|treten - **2.** [arrive] auf|tauchen.

show business *n* Showbusiness *das*, Showgeschäft *das*.

showdown ['ʃəudaun] *n*: **to have a showdown with sb** mit jm eine klärende Auseinandersetzung haben.

shower ['ʃauəʳ] ◇ *n* - **1.** [device] Dusche *die* - **2.** [wash]: **to have OR take a shower** duschen - **3.** [of rain] Schauer *der* - **4.** [of confetti, sparks] Regen *der*; [of insults, abuse] Flut *der*. ◇ *vt*: **to shower sb with sthg** jn mit etw überschütten. ◇ *vi* [wash] duschen.

shower cap *n* Duschhaube *die*.

showing ['ʃəuɪŋ] *n* CIN Vorstellung *die*.

show jumping [-ˌdʒʌmpɪŋ] *n* Springreiten *das*.

shown [ʃəun] *pp* ▷ **show**.

show-off *n inf* Angeber *der*, -in *die*.

showpiece ['ʃəupiːs] *n* [main attraction] Paradestück *das*.

showroom ['ʃəurum] *n* Ausstellungsraum *der*.

shrank [ʃræŋk] *pt* ▷ **shrink**.

shrapnel ['ʃræpnl] *n (U)* Granatsplitter *Pl*.

shred [ʃred] ◇ *n* - **1.** [of paper] Schnitzel *der*; [of fabric] Fetzen *der* - **2.** *fig* [of truth] Funken *der*; [of evidence] Hauch *der*. ◇ *vt* - **1.** CULIN [cabbage, lettuce] in Streifen schneiden - **2.** [paper in shredder] in den Reißwolf stecken.

shredder ['ʃredəʳ] *n* - **1.** CULIN [in food processor] Zerkleinerer *der* - **2.** [for documents] Aktenvernichter *der*.

shrewd [ʃruːd] *adj* scharfsinnig; [person] klug; [action, judgement, move] klug.

shriek [ʃriːk] ◇ *n* Schrei *der*. ◇ *vi*: **to shriek (with/in)** auf|schreien (vor *(+ D)*).

shrill [ʃrɪl] *adj* [high-pitched] schrill.

shrimp [ʃrɪmp] *n* Garnele *die*.

shrine [ʃraɪn] *n* Schrein *der*.

shrink [ʃrɪŋk] (*pt* **shrank**, *pp* **shrunk**) ◇ *vt* eingehen lassen. ◇ *vi* - **1.** [become smaller] schrumpfen; [person] kleiner werden; [clothing] ein|gehen - **2.** *fig* [contract, diminish] zusammen|schrumpfen; [of trade] zurück|gehen - **3.** [recoil]: **to shrink away from sb/sthg** vor jm/etw zurück|weichen. ◇ *n inf* [psychoanalyst] Nervenklempner *der*.

shrink-wrap *vt* ein|schweißen.

shrivel ['ʃrɪvl] (*UK*) (*US*) ◇ *vt*: **to shrivel (up)** [plant] welken lassen; [skin] runzelig werden lassen. ◇ *vi*: **to shrivel (up)** [plant] welken; [skin] runzelig werden.

shroud [ʃraud] ◇ *n* [cloth] Leichentuch *das*. ◇ *vt*: **to be shrouded in sthg** in etw *(A)* eingehüllt sein.

Shrove Tuesday ['ʃrəuv-] *n* Faschingsdienstag *der*, Fastnachtsdienstag *der*.

shrub [ʃrʌb] *n* Strauch *der*, Busch *der*.

shrubbery ['ʃrʌbərɪ] *n* Gebüsch *das*.

shrug [ʃrʌg] ◇ *vt*: **to shrug one's shoulders** mit den Achseln zucken. ◇ *vi* mit den Achseln zucken. ◆ **shrug off** *vt sep* beiseite schieben.

shrunk [ʃrʌŋk] *pp* ▷ **shrink**.

shudder ['ʃʌdəʳ] *vi* - **1.** [person]: **to shudder (with sthg)** (vor etw *(D)*) schauern OR schaudern - **2.** [machine, vehicle] beben.

shuffle ['ʃʌfl] *vt* - **1.**: **to shuffle one's feet** mit den Füßen scharren; [when walking] schlurfen - **2.** [cards] mischen - **3.** [papers] durch|sortieren.

shun [ʃʌn] *vt* meiden *(+ D)*.

shunt [ʃʌnt] *vt* RAIL rangieren.

shut [ʃʌt] (*pt & pp inv*) ◇ *adj* geschlossen. ◇ *vt* schließen, zu|machen. ◇ *vi* schließen; [eyes] zu|fallen. ◆ **shut away** *vt sep* - **1.** [criminal] ein|sperren - **2.** [valuables] ein|schließen. ◆ **shut down** *vt sep & vi* [factory, business] schließen. ◆ **shut out** *vt sep* [person, cat] aus|sperren; [light, noise] am Eindringen hindern. ◆ **shut up** ◇ *vt sep* - **1.** [lock up] ab|schließen - **2.** [silence] zum Schweigen bringen. ◇ *vi* - **1.** *inf* [be quiet] den Mund halten; **shut up!** halt den Mund! - **2.** [close] schließen.

shutter ['ʃʌtəʳ] *n* - **1.** [on window] Fensterladen *der* - **2.** [in camera] Blende *die*.

shuttle ['ʃʌtl] ◇ *adj*: **shuttle service** Shuttle-Service *der*, Pendelverkehr *der*. ◇ *n* [plane] Pendelflugzeug *das*; [train] Pendelzug *der*; [bus] Pendelbus *der*.

shuttlecock ['ʃʌtlkɒk] *n* Federball *der*.

shy [ʃaɪ] ◇ *adj* [timid] schüchtern. ◇ *vi* scheuen.

Siberia [saɪ'bɪərɪə] *n* Sibirien *nt*.

siblings ['sɪblɪŋz] *npl* Geschwister *Pl*.

Sicily ['sɪsɪlɪ] *n* Sizilien *nt*.

sick [sɪk] *adj* - **1.** [unwell] krank; **she's off sick this week** sie fehlt diese Woche wegen Krankheit - **2.** [nauseous]: **she felt sick** ihr war schlecht OR übel - **3.** [vomiting]: **to be sick** *UK* sich übergeben (müssen) - **4.** [fed up]: **to be sick of sthg** etw satt haben; **to be sick of doing sthg** es satt haben, etw zu tun - **5.** [offensive - joke] makaber; [- humour] schwarz.

sicken ['sɪkn] ◇ *vt* [disgust] krank machen. ◇ *vi UK*: **to be sickening for sthg** etw aus|brüten.

sickening ['sɪknɪŋ] *adj* - **1.** [disgusting] widerlich - **2.** *hum* [infuriating] unerträglich.

sickle ['sɪkl] *n* Sichel *die*.

sick leave *n*: **to be on sick leave** krankgeschrieben sein.

sickly ['sɪklɪ] *adj* - **1.** [unhealthy] kränklich - **2.** [nauseating] widerlich.

sickness ['sɪknɪs] *n* - **1.** [illness] Krankheit *die* - **2.** *UK* [nausea] Übelkeit *die*; [vomiting] Erbrechen *das*.

sick pay *n (U)* Lohnfortzahlung *die* im Krankheitsfall.

side [saɪd] <> *n* - **1.** [gen] Seite *die*; **on every side, on all sides** auf allen Seiten; **from side to side** von einer Seite auf die andere, hin und her; **at** OR **by sb's side** an js Seite; **side by side** Seite an Seite; **on one's mother's side** mütterlicherseits; **on one's father's side** väterlicherseits - **2.** [inner surface - of cave, crate, bathtub] Wand *die* - **3.** [of river, lake] Ufer *das*; [of road] Rand *der* - **4.** [team] Mannschaft *die* - **5.** [of argument] Standpunkt *der*; **to take sb's side** für jn Partei ergreifen - **6.** [aspect - of character, personality] Seite *die*; [- of situation] Aspekt *der*; **to be on the safe side** um sicherzugehen. <> *adj* [situated on side] Seiten-. ◆ **side with** *vt insep* Partei ergreifen für.

sideboard ['saɪdbɔ:d] *n* Anrichte *die*, Büfett *das*.

sideboards *UK* ['saɪdbɔ:dz], **sideburns** *US* ['saɪdbɜ:nz] *npl* Koteletten *Pl*.

side effect *n* - **1.** MED [secondary effect] Nebenwirkung *die* - **2.** [unplanned result] Nebeneffekt *der*.

sidelight ['saɪdlaɪt] *n* Seitenlicht *das*.

sideline ['saɪdlaɪn] *n* - **1.** [extra business] Nebenbeschäftigung *die* - **2.** SPORT [painted line] Seitenlinie *die*.

sidelong ['saɪdlɒŋ] <> *adj* Seiten-. <> *adv*: **to look sidelong at sb/sthg** jn/etw aus dem Augenwinkel anlschauen.

sidesaddle ['saɪd,sædl] *adv*: **to ride sidesaddle** im Damensitz reiten.

sideshow ['saɪdʃəʊ] *n* Nebenattraktion *die*.

sidestep ['saɪdstep] *vt liter* & *fig* auslweichen *(+ D)*.

side street *n* Nebenstraße *die*, Seitenstraße *die*.

sidetrack ['saɪdtræk] *vt*: **to be sidetracked** abgelenkt werden.

sidewalk ['saɪdwɔ:k] *n US* Bürgersteig *der*.

sideways ['saɪdweɪz] <> *adj* [movement] zur Seite; [look] Seiten-. <> *adv* seitwärts.

siding ['saɪdɪŋ] *n* Abstellgleis *das*.

siege [si:dʒ] *n* - **1.** [by army] Belagerung *die* - **2.** [by police] Umstellen *das*.

sieve [sɪv] <> *n* Sieb *das*. <> *vt* sieben.

sift [sɪft] <> *vt* - **1.** [sieve] sieben - **2.** *fig* [examine carefully] sichten, durchlsehen. <> *vi*: **to sift through sthg** etw durchlsehen OR durchlgehen.

sigh [saɪ] <> *n* Seufzer *der*. <> *vi* seufzen.

sight [saɪt] <> *n* - **1.** [vision] Sehvermögen *das*; **he has good/poor sight** er sieht gut/schlecht - **2.** [act of seeing]: **it was their first sight of their grandchild** sie haben ihr Enkelkind zum ersten Mal gesehen; **in sight** in Sicht; **out of sight** außer Sicht; **at first sight** auf den ersten Blick - **3.** [spectacle] Anblick *der* - **4.** [on gun] Visier *das*. <> *vt* [see] erspähen; [land] sichten. ◆ **sights** *npl* [on tour] Sehenswürdigkeiten *Pl*.

sightseeing ['saɪt,si:ɪŋ] *n* Sightseeing *das*; **to do some** OR **go sightseeing** Sehenswürdigkeiten besichtigen.

sightseer ['saɪt,si:əʳ] *n* Tourist *der*, -in *die*.

sign [saɪn] <> *n* - **1.** [written symbol, gesture] Zeichen *das* - **2.** [notice] Schild *das* - **3.** [indication] Anzeichen *das*; **there's no sign of him yet** von ihm ist noch nichts zu sehen. <> *vt* [letter] unterschreiben; [document] unterzeichnen; [painting] signieren; **to sign one's name** unterschreiben. ◆ **sign on** *vi* - **1.** [enrol - for course] sich einlschreiben; MIL sich verpflichten - **2.** [register as unemployed] sich beim Arbeitsamt melden. ◆ **sign up** <> *vt sep* [employee] einlstellen; [recruit] verpflichten. <> *vi* [enrol - for course] sich einlschreiben; MIL sich verpflichten.

signal ['sɪgnl] (*UK*) (*US*) <> *n* Signal *das*. <> *vt*: **to signal sb to do sthg** jm ein Zeichen geben, etw zu tun. <> *vi* - **1.** AUT blinken - **2.** [indicate]: **to signal to sb to do sthg** jm ein Zeichen geben, etw zu tun.

signature ['sɪgnətʃəʳ] *n* [name] Unterschrift *die*.

significance [sɪg'nɪfɪkəns] *n (U)* Bedeutung *die*.

significant [sɪg'nɪfɪkənt] *adj* - **1.** [large, important] bedeutend - **2.** [full of hidden meaning] bedeutsam.

signify ['sɪgnɪfaɪ] *vt* bedeuten.

signpost ['saɪnpəʊst] *n* Wegweiser *der*.

Sikh [si:k] <> *adj* Sikh-. <> *n* Sikh *der*, *die*.

silence ['saɪləns] <> *n* - **1.** [of person, on topic] Schweigen *das* - **2.** [of place] Stille *die*, Ruhe *die*. <> *vt* zum Schweigen bringen.

silencer ['saɪlənsəʳ] *n* Schalldämpfer *der*.

silent ['saɪlənt] *adj* - **1.** [speechless] still - **2.** [taciturn] schweigsam - **3.** [noiseless] ruhig, leise - **4.** CIN Stumm- - **5.** LING stumm.

silhouette [,sɪlu:'et] *n* Silhouette *die*.

silicon chip *n* Siliziumchip *der*.

silk [sɪlk] <> *n* Seide *die*. <> *comp* Seiden-.

silky ['sɪlkɪ] *adj* seidig; [voice] samtig.

sill [sɪl] *n* [of window] (Fenster)sims *der*.

silly ['sɪlɪ] *adj* - **1.** [foolish] dumm - **2.** [comical] komisch - **3.** [childish, ridiculous]: **don't be so silly!** sei nicht so albern!

silo ['saɪləʊ] (*pl* **-s**) *n* Silo *das*.

silt [sɪlt] *n* Schlick *der*, Schlamm *der*.

silver ['sɪlvəʳ] ◇ *adj* [greyish-white] silbern. ◇ *n (U)* - **1.** [metal, silverware] Silber *das* - **2.** [coins] Silbermünzen *Pl*. ◇ *comp* [made of silver] Silber-.

silver foil, silver paper *n (U)* Alufolie *die*.

silver-plated [-'pleɪtɪd] *adj* versilbert.

silverware ['sɪlvəweəʳ] *n* - **1.** [objects made of silver] Silber *das* - **2.** *US* [cutlery] Besteck *das*.

similar ['sɪmɪləʳ] *adj* ähnlich; **to be similar to sthg** so ähnlich wie etw sein.

similarly ['sɪmɪləlɪ] *adv* ebenso.

simmer ['sɪməʳ] *vt* & *vi* auf kleiner Flamme kochen.

simple ['sɪmpl] *adj* - **1.** [easy] einfach - **2.** [plain - clothing, furniture, style] schlicht; [- fact, truth] rein; [- way of life] einfach - **3.** [mentally retarded] einfältig.

simple-minded [-'maɪndɪd] *adj* [person] einfältig; [view] vereinfacht.

simplicity [sɪm'plɪsətɪ] *n* [ease] Einfachheit *die*; [plainness - of clothing, furniture, style] Schlichtheit *die*.

simplify ['sɪmplɪfaɪ] *vt* vereinfachen.

simply ['sɪmplɪ] *adv* - **1.** [merely] einfach - **2.** [for emphasis]: **you simply must go** du musst unbedingt gehen; **the weather is simply dreadful** das Wetter ist einfach scheußlich - **3.** [in an uncomplicated way - live] einfach; [- dress] schlicht.

simulate ['sɪmjʊleɪt] *vt* - **1.** [feign - gen] vor|täuschen; [- illness] simulieren - **2.** [produce effect, appearance of] simulieren.

simultaneous [*UK* ˌsɪməl'teɪnjəs, *US* ˌsaɪməl'teɪnjəs] *adj* gleichzeitig; [broadcast] direkt; [interpreting] Simultan-.

sin [sɪn] ◇ *n* Sünde *die*. ◇ *vi*: **to sin (against)** sündigen (gegen).

since [sɪns] ◇ *adv* seitdem; **I haven't seen them since** ich habe sie seitdem nicht mehr gesehen; **she has since moved to London** inzwischen ist sie nach London umgezogen; **since then** seitdem. ◇ *prep* seit; **I've been here since six o'clock** ich bin hier seit sechs Uhr. ◇ *conj* - **1.** [in time] seit; **it's ages since I saw her** ich habe sie schon seit langem nicht mehr gesehen - **2.** [because] da.

sincere [sɪn'sɪəʳ] *adj* aufrichtig.

sincerely [sɪn'sɪəlɪ] *adv* aufrichtig; **Yours sincerely** [at end of letter] mit freundlichen Grüßen.

sincerity [sɪn'serətɪ] *n* Aufrichtigkeit *die*.

sinew ['sɪnju:] *n* Sehne *die*.

sinful ['sɪnfʊl] *adj* sündig.

sing [sɪŋ] (*pt* **sang**, *pp* **sung**) ◇ *vt* singen. ◇ *vi* singen.

Singapore [ˌsɪŋə'pɔ:ʳ] *n* Singapur *nt*.

singe [sɪndʒ] *vt* versengen.

singer ['sɪŋəʳ] *n* Sänger *der*, -in *die*.

singing ['sɪŋɪŋ] *n (U)* Gesang *der*.

single ['sɪŋgl] ◇ *adj* - **1.** [sole] einzig; **every single** jede/jeder/jedes einzelne - **2.** [unmarried] ledig - **3.** *UK* [one-way] einfach. ◇ *n* - **1.** *UK* [one-way ticket] einfache Fahrkarte - **2.** MUS Single *die*. ◆ **singles** *npl* TENNIS Einzel *das*. ◆ **single out** *vt sep*: **to single sb out (for sthg)** jn (für etw) aus|suchen OR aus|wählen.

single bed *n* Einzelbett *das*.

single-breasted [-'brestɪd] *adj* einreihig.

single cream *n (U) UK Sahne mit niedrigem Fettgehalt*.

single file *n*: **in single file** im Gänsermarsch.

single-handed [-'hændɪd] *adv* eigenhändig.

single-minded [-'maɪndɪd] *adj* zielstrebig.

single parent *n* [mother] alleinerziehende Mutter; [father] alleinerziehender Vater.

single-parent family *n* Familie *die* mit nur einem Elternteil.

single room *n* Einzelzimmer *das*.

singlet ['sɪŋglɪt] *n* - **1.** *UK* [underwear] Unterhemd *das* - **2.** SPORT ärmelloses Trikot.

singular ['sɪŋgjʊləʳ] ◇ *adj* - **1.** GRAM im Singular, in der Einzahl - **2.** [unusual] eigentümlich; [unique] einzigartig. ◇ *n* Singular *der*, Einzahl *die*.

sinister ['sɪnɪstəʳ] *adj* finster, unheimlich.

sink [sɪŋk] (*pt* **sank**, *pp* **sunk**) ◇ *n* - **1.** [in kitchen] Spülbecken *das* - **2.** [in bathroom] Waschbecken *das*. ◇ *vt* - **1.** [in water] versenken - **2.** [teeth, claws]: **to sink sthg into sthg** etw in etw *(A)* graben. ◇ *vi* - **1.** [gen] sinken; [person - in water] unter|gehen; **to sink to one's knees** auf die Knie sinken - **2.** *fig* [heart, spirits]: **my heart sank when I heard the news** meine Stimmung sank, als ich die Nachricht hörte - **3.** [building, ground] sich senken. ◆ **sink in** *vi*: **it hasn't sunk in yet** ich habe/er hat/*etc* es noch nicht realisiert.

sink unit *n* Spüle *die*.

sinner ['sɪnəʳ] *n* Sünder *der*, -in *die*.

sinus ['saɪnəs] (*pl* **-es**) *n* Stirnhöhle *die*.

sip [sɪp] ◇ *n* kleiner Schluck. ◇ *vt* nippen an *(+ D)*, in kleinen Schlucken trinken.

siphon ['saɪfn] ◇ *n*: **(soda) siphon** Siphon *der*. ◇ *vt* - **1.**: **to siphon (off)** ab|saugen - **2.** *fig* [transfer] verlagern.

sir [sɜ:ʳ] *n* - **1.** [form of address] mein Herr - **2.** [in titles] Sir *der*.

siren ['saɪərən] *n* Sirene *die*.

sirloin (steak) ['sɜ:lɔɪn-] *n* Lendensteak *das*.

sissy ['sɪsɪ] *n inf* Waschlappen *der*.

sister ['sɪstəʳ] *n* - **1.** [gen] Schwester *die* - **2.** *UK* [senior nurse] Oberschwester *die*.

sister-in-law (*pl* **sisters-in-law** *OR* **sister-in-laws**) *n* Schwägerin *die*.

sit [sɪt] (*pt & pp* **sat**) ◇ *vt* - **1.** [place] setzen - **2.** *UK* [examination] ab|legen. ◇ *vi* - **1.** [be in seated position] sitzen - **2.** [sit down] sich hin|setzen - **3.** [be member]: **to sit on sthg** in etw (D) sitzen - **4.** [be in session] tagen. ◆ **sit about, sit around** *vi* herum|sitzen. ◆ **sit down** *vi* sich setzen. ◆ **sit in on** *vt insep* bei|wohnen (+ D). ◆ **sit through** *vt insep* bis zum Ende durch|halten. ◆ **sit up** *vi* - **1.** [be sitting upright] aufrecht sitzen; [move into upright position] sich auf|setzen - **2.** [stay up] auf|bleiben.

sitcom ['sɪtkɒm] *n inf* Situationskomödie *die*.

site [saɪt] ◇ *n* - **1.**: **archaeological site** Ausgrabungsstätte *die*; **building site** Baustelle *die* - **2.** [location, place] Ort *der*, Stelle *die* - **3.** [website] Website *die*. ◇ *vt*: **to be sited** gelegen sein.

sit-in *n* Sit-in *das*.

sitting ['sɪtɪŋ] *n* - **1.**: **dinner is served in two sittings** das Abendessen wird in zwei Schichten serviert - **2.** [session] Sitzung *die*.

sitting room *n* Wohnzimmer *das*.

situated ['sɪtjʊeɪtɪd] *adj* [located]: **to be situated** sich befinden.

situation [,sɪtjʊ'eɪʃn] *n* - **1.** [circumstances] Lage *die*, Situation *die* - **2.** [location] Lage *die* - **3.** [job] Stelle *die*; **'Situations Vacant'** *UK* 'Stellenangebote'.

six [sɪks] ◇ *num adj* - **1.** [numbering six] sechs - **2.** [referring to age]: **she's six (years old)** sie ist sechs (Jahre alt). ◇ *num pron* sechs; **I want six** ich möchte sechs (Stück); **there were six of us** wir waren zu sechst; **groups of six** [people] Sechsergruppen; [objects] Gruppen von jeweils sechs. ◇ *num n* - **1.** [the number six] Sechs *die*; **two hundred and six** zweihundertsechs - **2.** [six o'clock]: **at six** um sechs (Uhr) - **3.** [in addresses]: **six Peyton Place** Peyton Place sechs - **4.** [group of six]: **the batteries come in sixes** die Batterien werden im Sechserpack verkauft; **we need one more person to make a six** wir brauchen noch eine Person, um eine Sechsergruppe zu bilden - **5.** [in scores] sechs; **six-zero** sechs zu null - **6.** [in cards] Sechs *die*; **the six of hearts** die Herzsechs.

sixteen [sɪks'ti:n] *num* sechzehn; *see also* **six**.

sixteenth [sɪks'ti:nθ] *num* sechzehnte(r) (s); *see also* **sixth**.

sixth [sɪksθ] ◇ *num adj* sechste(r) (s). ◇ *num adv* [on list] an sechster Stelle; **he came sixth** er wurde Sechster. ◇ *num pron* [in series] Sechste(r) (s). ◇ *n* - **1.** [fraction] Sechstel *das* - **2.** [in dates] Sechste *der*; **the sixth of March** der sechste März.

sixth form *n UK* SCH ≃ Oberstufe *die*.

sixth form college *n UK zu den A-Levels führende Schule für Schüler ab 16 Jahren.*

sixty ['sɪkstɪ] *num* sechzig; *see also* **six**. ◆ **sixties** *npl* - **1.** [decade]: **the sixties** die Sechzigerjahre - **2.** [in ages]: **to be in one's sixties** in den Sechzigern sein.

size [saɪz] *n* Größe *die*; **to cut sb down to size** jn zurecht|stutzen. ◆ **size up** *vt sep* sich (D) eine Meinung bilden über (+ A).

sizeable ['saɪzəbl] *adj* ziemlich groß.

sizzle ['sɪzl] *vi* brutzeln.

skate [skeɪt] ◇ *n* - **1.** [ice skate] Schlittschuh *der* - **2.** [roller skate] Rollschuh *der* - **3.** (*pl inv OR* **-s**) [fish] Rochen *der*. ◇ *vi* - **1.** [on ice skates] Schlittschuh laufen - **2.** [on roller skates] Rollschuh laufen.

skateboard ['skeɪtbɔ:d] *n* Skateboard *das*.

skater ['skeɪtəʳ] *n* - **1.** [on ice] Schlittschuhläufer *der*, -in *die* - **2.** [on roller skates] Rollschuhläufer *der*, -in *die*.

skating ['skeɪtɪŋ] *n* - **1.** [on ice] Schlittschuhlaufen *das* - **2.** [on roller skates] Rollschuhlaufen *das*.

skeleton ['skelɪtn] *n* Skelett *das*.

skeleton key *n* Dietrich *der*.

skeptic *etc n US* = **sceptic** *etc* .

sketch [sketʃ] ◇ *n* - **1.** [drawing] Skizze *die* - **2.** [brief description] kurze Darstellung - **3.** [on TV, radio, stage] Sketch *der*. ◇ *vt* - **1.** [draw] skizzieren - **2.** [describe] kurz dar|legen.

sketchbook ['sketʃbʊk] *n* Skizzenbuch *das*.

sketchpad ['sketʃpæd] *n* Skizzenblock *der*.

sketchy ['sketʃɪ] *adj* oberflächlich.

skewer ['skjʊəʳ] ◇ *n* Spieß *der*. ◇ *vt* auf|spießen.

ski [ski:] (*pt & pp* **skied**, *cont* **skiing**) ◇ *n* Ski *der*. ◇ *vi* Ski fahren.

ski boots *npl* Skistiefel *Pl*.

skid [skɪd] ◇ *n* Schleudern *das*; **to go into a skid** ins Schleudern geraten. ◇ *vi* schleudern.

skier ['ski:əʳ] *n* Skiläufer *der*, -in *die*.

skiing ['ski:ɪŋ] *n* Skifahren *das*.

ski jump *n* - **1.** [slope] Sprungschanze *die* - **2.** [sporting event] Skispringen *das*.

skilful, skillful *US* ['skɪlfʊl] *adj* geschickt.

ski lift *n* Skilift *der*.

skill [skɪl] *n* - **1.** [expertise] Geschicklichkeit *die* - **2.** [craft, technique] Fertigkeit *die*.

skilled [skɪld] *adj* - **1.** [skilful] geschickt; **skilled in** *OR* **at doing sthg** geschickt darin sein, etw zu tun - **2.** [trained - worker] ausgebildet; [- work, labour] fachmännisch.

skillful *etc US* = **skilful** *etc* .

skim [skɪm] ◇ *vt* [remove] ab|schöpfen. ◇ *vi* - **1.** [bird]: **to skim over sthg** hinweg|gleiten über (+ A) - **2.** [read]: **to skim through sthg** etw überfliegen.

skim(med) milk [skɪm(d)-] *n* Magermilch *die*.

skimp [skɪmp] ◇ *vt* sparen an *(+ D)*. ◇ *vi*: **to skimp on sthg** an etw *(D)* sparen.

skimpy ['skɪmpɪ] *adj* dürftig; [clothes] knapp.

skin [skɪn] ◇ *n* - **1.** [of person, on liquid] Haut *die* - **2.** [of animal] Fell *das* - **3.** [of fruit, vegetable] Schale *die*. ◇ *vt* - **1.** [animal] häuten - **2.** [graze] auf|schürfen.

skin-deep *adj* oberflächlich.

skinny ['skɪnɪ] *adj inf* dürr.

skin-tight *adj* hauteng.

skip [skɪp] ◇ *n* - **1.** [little jump] Hüpfer *der* - **2.** *UK* [large container] Sperrmüllcontainer *der*. ◇ *vt* [miss - page] überspringen; [- meal] aus|lassen; **to skip school** die Schule schwänzen. ◇ *vi* - **1.** [move in little jumps] hüpfen - **2.** *UK* [jump over rope] seil|springen.

ski pants *npl* Skihosen *Pl*.

ski pole *n* Skistock *der*.

skipper ['skɪpəʳ] *n* Kapitän *der*.

skipping rope *n UK* Springseil *das*.

skirmish ['skɜ:mɪʃ] *n* - **1.** MIL Gefecht *das* - **2.** *fig* [disagreement] Auseinandersetzung *die*.

skirt [skɜ:t] ◇ *n* [garment] Rock *der*. ◇ *vt liter & fig* um|gehen.

ski tow *n* Skilift *der*.

skittle ['skɪtl] *n UK* Kegel *der*; **to have a game of skittles** kegeln (gehen).

skive [skaɪv] *vi UK inf*: **to skive (off)** [from school] schwänzen; [from work] blau machen.

skulk [skʌlk] *vi* - **1.** [hide] sich verstecken - **2.** [prowl] herum|schleichen.

skull [skʌl] *n* Schädel *der*.

skunk [skʌŋk] *n* Stinktier *das*.

sky [skaɪ] *n* Himmel *der*.

skylight ['skaɪlaɪt] *n* Dachfenster *das*.

skyscraper ['skaɪˌskreɪpəʳ] *n* Wolkenkratzer *der*.

slab [slæb] *n* - **1.** [of concrete, stone] Platte *die*; [of wood] Tafel *die* - **2.** [of meat, chocolate, cake] großes Stück.

slack [slæk] ◇ *adj* - **1.** [not taut] locker - **2.** [not busy] flau - **3.** [careless] nachlässig. ◇ *n*: **there is too much slack in the rope** das Seil ist nicht straff genug.

slacken ['slækn] ◇ *vt* - **1.** [make slower] verlangsamen - **2.** [make looser] lockern. ◇ *vi* [become slower] langsamer werden.

slagheap ['slæghi:p] *n* Halde *die*.

slam [slæm] ◇ *vt* - **1.** [shut] zu|knallen - **2.** [place roughly]: **to slam sthg on(to) sthg** etw auf etw *(A)* knallen. ◇ *vi* [shut] zu|knallen.

slander ['slɑ:ndəʳ] ◇ *n (U)* Verleumdung *die*. ◇ *vt* verleumden.

slang [slæŋ] *n* Slang *der*.

slant [slɑ:nt] ◇ *n* - **1.** [diagonal angle] Schräge *die* - **2.** [point of view] Blickwinkel *der*. ◇ *vt* [bias] zurecht|biegen. ◇ *vi* schräg sein.

slanting ['slɑ:ntɪŋ] *adj* schräg.

slap [slæp] ◇ *n* Schlag *der*; [in face] Ohrfeige *die*; [on back] Klaps *der*. ◇ *vt* - **1.** [person] schlagen; **to slap sb's face** jm eine Ohrfeige geben; **to slap sb on the back** jm auf den Rücken klopfen - **2.** [put]: **to slap sthg on(to) sthg** etw auf etw *(A)* knallen. ◇ *adv inf* [directly] direkt.

slapdash ['slæpdæʃ], **slaphappy** ['slæpˌhæpɪ] *adj inf* schlampig.

slapstick ['slæpstɪk] *n* Slapstick *der*.

slap-up *adj UK inf* Super-.

slash [slæʃ] ◇ *n* - **1.** [long cut] Schnitt *der* - **2.** *esp US* [oblique stroke] Schrägstrich *der*. ◇ *vt* - **1.** [cut - material] (zer)schneiden; [- tyres] zerschlitzen, auf|schlitzen; **to slash one's wrists** sich die Pulsadern auf|schneiden - **2.** *inf* [reduce drastically] stark reduzieren.

slat [slæt] *n* [in blind] Lamelle *die*; [in bench] Latte *die*.

slate [sleɪt] ◇ *n* - **1.** *(U)* [rock] Schiefer *der* - **2.** [on roof] Schieferplatte *die*. ◇ *vt* [criticize] verreißen.

slaughter ['slɔ:təʳ] ◇ *n* - **1.** [of animals] Schlachten *das* - **2.** [of people] Abschlachten *das*. ◇ *vt* - **1.** [animals] schlachten - **2.** [people] ab|schlachten.

slaughterhouse ['slɔ:təhaʊs] (*pl* [-haʊzɪz]) *n* Schlachthof *der*.

slave [sleɪv] ◇ *n* [servant] Sklave *der*, -vin *die*. ◇ *vi*: **to slave (over sthg)** sich (mit etw) ab|plagen.

slavery ['sleɪvərɪ] *n* Sklaverei *die*.

sleaze ['sli:z] *n* Korruption *die*.

sleazy ['sli:zɪ] *adj* [area, bar] schäbig; [behaviour] korrupt.

sledge [sledʒ], **sled** *US* [sled] *n* Schlitten *der*.

sledgehammer ['sledʒˌhæməʳ] *n* Vorschlaghammer *der*.

sleek [sli:k] *adj* - **1.** [hair, fur] seidig glänzend - **2.** [car, plane] schnittig.

sleep [sli:p] (*pt & pp* **slept**) ◇ *n* Schlaf *der*; **to go to sleep** [doze off, go numb] ein|schlafen. ◇ *vi* schlafen. ◆ **sleep in** *vi* [oversleep] verschlafen. ◆ **sleep with** *vt insep euph* schlafen mit.

sleeper ['sli:pəʳ] *n* - **1.** [person]: **to be a heavy/light sleeper** einen tiefen/leichten Schlaf haben - **2.** [sleeping compartment] Schlafwagenabteil *das* - **3.** [train] Schlafwagenzug *der* - **4.** *UK* [on railway track] Schwelle *die*.

sleeping bag ['sli:pɪŋ-] *n* Schlafsack *der*.

sleeping car ['sli:pɪŋ-] *n* Schlafwagen *der*.

sleeping pill ['sli:pɪŋ-] *n* Schlaftablette *die*.

sleepless ['sli:plɪs] *adj* schlaflos.

sleepwalk ['sli:pwɔ:k] *vi* schlafwandeln.

sleepy ['sli:pɪ] *adj* [person] schläfrig.

sleet [sli:t] ◇ *n* Schneeregen *der.* ◇ *impers vb*: **it's sleeting** es fällt Schneeregen.

sleeve [sli:v] *n* - **1.** [of garment] Ärmel *der* - **2.** [for record] Hülle *die.*

sleigh [sleɪ] *n* Schlitten *der.*

slender ['slendəʳ] *adj* - **1.** [thin] schlank - **2.** [scarce - resources] knapp; [- hope, chance] gering.

slept [slept] *pt* & *pp* ▷ **sleep**.

S-level *n UK* SCH S-Level *das (ergänzendes Fortgeschrittenenniveau).*

slice [slaɪs] ◇ *n* - **1.** [thin piece] Scheibe *die;* [of pizza] Stück *das* - **2.** [proportion] Teil *der* - **3.** SPORT Slice *der.* ◇ *vt* - **1.** [cut into slices] in Scheiben schneiden - **2.** SPORT slicen. ◆ **slice off** *vt sep* [sever] ab|trennen.

slick [slɪk] ◇ *adj* - **1.** [smoothly efficient] geschickt gemacht - **2.** *pej* [person] aalglatt; [answer, argument] glatt. ◇ *n*: **(oil) slick** Ölteppich *der.*

slide [slaɪd] (*pt & pp* **slid** [slɪd]) ◇ *n* - **1.** PHOT Dia(positiv) *das* - **2.** [in playground] Rutsche *die* - **3.** *UK* [for hair] Haarspange *die* - **4.** [decline - of person] Abrutschen *das;* [- in prices, standards] Absinken *das.* ◇ *vt* gleiten lassen. ◇ *vi* - **1.** [on ice, slippery surface] schlittern - **2.** [move quietly] gleiten - **3.** [decline - person] ab|rutschen; [- prices, standards] ab|sinken.

sliding door [ˌslaɪdɪŋ-] *n* Schiebetür *die.*

slight [slaɪt] ◇ *adj* - **1.** [minor] leicht; **not the slightest interest** nicht das geringste Interesse; **not in the slightest** nicht im Geringsten - **2.** [slender] schmal. ◇ *n* [insult] Kränkung *die.* ◇ *vt* [offend] kränken.

slightly ['slaɪtlɪ] *adv* [to small extent] etwas.

slim [slɪm] ◇ *adj* - **1.** [person] schlank - **2.** [object] schmal - **3.** [chance, possibility] gering. ◇ *vi* [lose weight] ab|nehmen; [diet] eine Diät machen.

slime [slaɪm] *n* Schleim *der.*

slimming ['slɪmɪŋ] *n* Abnehmen *das.*

sling [slɪŋ] (*pt & pp* **slung**) ◇ *n* - **1.** [for injured arm] Armschlinge *die* - **2.** [for carrying things] Trageriemen *der.* ◇ *vt* - **1.** [hang roughly]: **she slung the bag over her shoulder** sie hängte sich die Tasche über die Schulter - **2.** *inf* [throw] schleudern - **3.** [hang by both ends] spannen.

slip [slɪp] ◇ *n* - **1.** [mistake] Versehen *das;* **a slip of the tongue** ein Versprecher - **2.** [form] Abschnitt *der* - **3.** [of paper]: **slip (of paper)** Zettel *der* - **4.** [underwear] Unterrock *der* - **5.** *phr*: **to give sb the slip** *inf* jm entkommen. ◇ *vt* - **1.** [put, slide] stecken - **2.** [clothes]: **to slip sthg on/off** etw über|ziehen/aus|ziehen - **3.** [escape]: **it slipped my mind** ich habe es vergessen. ◇ *vi* - **1.** [lose balance] aus|rutschen - **2.** [move unexpectedly - hand, foot] rutschen; **it slipped out of my hand** es rutschte mir aus der Hand; **I let it slip** [revealed it] es ist mir herausgerutscht - **3.** [decline] sinken - **4.** [move discreetly] schlüpfen; **to slip into/out of sthg** [clothes] in etw *(A)*/aus etw schlüpfen. ◆ **slip away** *vi* [leave] sich davon|schleichen. ◆ **slip on** *vt sep* [clothes] über|ziehen; [shoes] an|ziehen. ◆ **slip up** *vi* sich vertun.

slipped disc [ˌslɪpt-] *n* Bandscheibenvorfall *der.*

slipper ['slɪpəʳ] *n* Hausschuh *der.*

slippery ['slɪpərɪ] *adj* - **1.** [surface, soap] rutschig - **2.** [person] windig.

slip road *n UK* [onto motorway] Auffahrt *die;* [leaving motorway] Ausfahrt *die.*

slip-up *n inf* Versehen *das.*

slit [slɪt] (*pt & pp inv*) ◇ *n* Schlitz *der.* ◇ *vt* auf|schlitzen.

slither ['slɪðəʳ] *vi* - **1.** [car, person] rutschen - **2.** [snake] gleiten.

sliver ['slɪvəʳ] *n* - **1.** [splinter] Splitter *der* - **2.** [slice] hauchdünne Scheibe.

slob [slɒb] *n inf* Dreckschwein *das.*

slog [slɒg] *inf* ◇ *n* [tiring work] Schinderei *die.* ◇ *vi* [work]: **to slog (away) at sthg** sich mit etw ab|plagen.

slogan ['sləʊgən] *n* Slogan *der.*

slop [slɒp] ◇ *vt* verschütten. ◇ *vi* über|schwappen.

slope [sləʊp] ◇ *n* - **1.** [of roof, ground] Neigung *die* - **2.** [hill] Hang *der.* ◇ *vi* [shelf, table] schräg sein.

sloping ['sləʊpɪŋ] *adj* schräg; [land] abfallend.

sloppy ['slɒpɪ] *adj* [careless] schlampig.

slot [slɒt] *n* - **1.** [opening] Schlitz *der* - **2.** [groove] Nut *die* - **3.** [place in broadcasting schedule] Sendezeit *die.*

slot machine *n* - **1.** [vending machine] Münzautomat *der* - **2.** [arcade machine] Spielautomat *der.*

slouch [slaʊtʃ] *vi* [when sitting] sich hin|lümmeln; [when standing] schlaff da|stehen.

Slovakia [slə'vækɪə] *n* Slowakei *die.*

slovenly ['slʌvnlɪ] *adj* schlampig.

slow [sləʊ] ◇ *adj* - **1.** [not fast] langsam - **2.** [clock, watch]: **to be slow** nach|gehen - **3.** [not intelligent] langsam. ◇ *adv*: **to go slow** [driver] langsam fahren; [workers] Bummelstreik machen. ◇ *vt* verlangsamen. ◇ *vi* [person] langsam werden; [car] langsamer fahren; [increase, progress] sich verlangsamen. ◆ **slow down, slow up** ◇ *vt sep* verlangsamen. ◇ *vi* langsamer werden; [car] langsamer fahren; [walker] langsamer gehen.

slowdown ['sləʊdaʊn] *n* Verlangsamung *die.*

slowly ['sləʊlɪ] *adv* langsam.

slow motion *n* Zeitlupe *die*.

sludge [slʌdʒ] *n* Schlamm *der*.

slug [slʌg] *n* - **1.** ZOOL Nacktschnecke *die* - **2.** *inf* [of alcohol] Schluck *der* - **3.** *US inf* [bullet] Kugel *die*.

sluggish ['slʌgɪʃ] *adj* träge; [business] flau.

sluice [slu:s] *n* Schleuse *die*.

slum [slʌm] *n* [area] Slum *der*.

slumber ['slʌmbəʳ] *liter* <> *n* Schlummer *der*. <> *vi* schlummern.

slump [slʌmp] <> *n* - **1.** [decline]: **slump (in sthg)** Abfall *der* (einer Sache *(G)*) - **2.** [period of economic depression] Konjunkturabschwung *der*. <> *vi* - **1.** [business, market] plötzlich zurück|gehen; [prices] stürzen - **2.** [person] sich fallen lassen.

slung [slʌŋ] *pt* & *pp* ⊳ **sling**.

slur [slɜ:ʳ] <> *n* [insult]: **slur (on sb/sthg)** Schande *die* (für jn/etw). <> *vt* [speech]: **to slur one's words** mit schwerer Zunge sprechen.

slush [slʌʃ] *n* Schneematsch *der*.

slut [slʌt] *n inf* Schlampe *die*.

sly [slaɪ] (*comp* **slyer** OR **slier**, *superl* **slyest** OR **sliest**) *adj* - **1.** [look, smile, grin] wissend - **2.** [cunning] listig.

smack [smæk] <> *n* [slap] Klaps *der*; [on face] Ohrfeige *die*. <> *vt* - **1.** [slap] einen Klaps geben *(+ D)*; [in the face] ohrfeigen - **2.** [put] knallen.

small [smɔ:l] <> *adj* klein; **a small number** eine geringe Anzahl; **a small matter** eine Kleinigkeit; **a small business** ein Kleinbetrieb; **to feel small** sich schämen. <> *adv*: **to chop sthg up small** etw klein schneiden.

small ads [-ædz] *npl UK* Kleinanzeigen *Pl*.

small change *n* Kleingeld *das*.

smallholder ['smɔ:l,həʊldəʳ] *n UK* Kleinbauer *der*, -bäuerin *die*.

small hours *npl* frühe Morgenstunden *Pl*.

smallpox ['smɔ:lpɒks] *n (U)* Pocken *Pl*.

small print *n*: **the small print** das Kleingedruckte.

small talk *n* Small Talk *der*.

smarmy ['smɑ:mɪ] *adj* schleimig.

smart [smɑ:t] <> *adj* - **1.** [elegant] elegant - **2.** *esp US* [clever] klug - **3.** [fashionable, exclusive] exklusiv - **4.** [rapid] flott. <> *vi* - **1.** [sting] brennen - **2.** [feel anger and humiliation] verletzt sein.

smarten ['smɑ:tn] ◆ **smarten up** *vt sep* [room] auf|räumen; **to smarten up one's appearance** sich her|richten.

smash [smæʃ] <> *n* - **1.** [sound] Krach *der* - **2.** *inf* [car crash] Unfall *der* - **3.** TENNIS Schmetterball *der*. <> *vt* - **1.** [break into pieces] zerschlagen - **2.** *fig* [defeat] zerschlagen. <> *vi* - **1.** [break into pieces] zerbrechen - **2.** [crash, collide]: **to smash through sthg** durch etw rasen; **the car smashed into the tree** das Auto krachte gegen den Baum.

smashing ['smæʃɪŋ] *adj inf* klasse, toll.

smattering ['smætərɪŋ] *n*: **to have a smattering of sthg** Grundkenntnisse in etw *(D)* haben; **I have a smattering of German** ich kann ein bisschen Deutsch.

smear [smɪəʳ] <> *n* - **1.** [dirty mark] Fleck *der* - **2.** MED Abstrich *der* - **3.** [slander] Verleumdung *die*. <> *vt* - **1.** [smudge - page, painting] verschmieren; [- paint, ink] verwischen - **2.** [spread]: **to smear sthg onto sthg** etw auf etw *(A)* schmieren - **3.** [slander] verleumden.

smell [smel] (*pt & pp* **-ed** OR **smelt**) <> *n* - **1.** [odour] Geruch *der*; [unpleasant] Gestank *der* - **2.** *(U)* [sense of smell] Geruchssinn *der* - **3.** [sniff]: **to have a smell of sthg** an etw *(D)* riechen. <> *vt* - **1.** [notice an odour of, sense] riechen - **2.** [sniff at] riechen an *(+ D)*; [subj: dog] schnuppern an *(+ D)*. <> *vi* - **1.** [have sense of smell] riechen - **2.** [have particular smell]: **to smell of sthg** nach etw riechen; **to smell like sthg** wie etw riechen; **to smell good/bad** gut/schlecht riechen - **3.** [smell unpleasantly] übel riechen.

smelly ['smelɪ] *adj* übel riechend.

smelt [smelt] *pt* & *pp* ⊳ **smell**.

smile [smaɪl] <> *n* Lächeln *das*. <> *vi* lächeln.

smiley ['smaɪlɪ] *n* COMPUT Smiley *der*.

smirk [smɜ:k] *n* Grinsen *das*.

smock [smɒk] *n* Kittel *der*.

smog [smɒg] *n* Smog *der*.

smoke [sməʊk] <> *n* [from fire] Rauch *der*. <> *vt* - **1.** [cigarette, cigar] rauchen - **2.** [fish, meat, cheese] räuchern. <> *vi* rauchen.

smoked [sməʊkt] *adj* [food] geräuchert.

smoker ['sməʊkəʳ] *n* - **1.** [person who smokes] Raucher *der* - **2.** RAIL [compartment] Raucherabteil *das*.

smoke shop *n US* Tabakladen *der*.

smoking ['sməʊkɪŋ] *n* Rauchen *das*; **'no smoking'** 'Rauchen verboten'.

smoky ['sməʊkɪ] *adj* rauchig.

smolder *vi US* = **smoulder**.

smooth [smu:ð] <> *adj* - **1.** [surface] glatt - **2.** [sauce, paste] sämig - **3.** [flow, pace, supply] gleichmäßig - **4.** [taste] weich - **5.** [flight, ride] ruhig; [takeoff, landing] weich; [engine] ruhig laufend - **6.** *pej* [person, manner] aalglatt - **7.** [trouble-free] glatt verlaufend; [transition] reibungslos. <> *vt* - **1.** [hair, skirt, tablecloth] glatt streichen - **2.** [rub]: **smooth the oil into your skin** reiben Sie ihre Haut mit dem Öl ein. ◆ **smooth out** *vt sep* - **1.** [skirt, sheet, crease] glatt streichen - **2.** [difficulties] aus dem Weg räumen.

smother ['smʌðəʳ] *vt* - **1.** [cover thickly]: **to smother sthg in** OR **with sthg** etw mit etw bedecken - **2.** [suffocate, extinguish] ersticken - **3.** *fig* [repress] unterdrücken - **4.** [suffocate with love] (mit Liebe) erdrücken.

smoulder *UK*, **smolder** *US* ['sməʊldəʳ] *vi liter* & *fig* schwelen.

SMS [,esem'es] *n* (*abbr of* **short message system**) SMS *die*.

smudge [smʌdʒ] ◇ *n* [dirty mark] Fleck *der*; [of ink] verwischte Stelle. ◇ *vt* [spoil - by blurring] verschmieren; [- outline, ink] verwischen; [- by dirtying] beschmutzen.

smug [smʌg] *adj pej* selbstzufrieden.

smuggle ['smʌgl] *vt* schmuggeln.

smuggler ['smʌgləʳ] *n* Schmuggler *der*, -in *die*.

smuggling ['smʌglɪŋ] *n* Schmuggel *der*.

smutty ['smʌtɪ] *adj inf pej* [lewd] schmutzig.

snack [snæk] *n* Snack *der*, Imbiss *der*.

snack bar *n* Snackbar *die*, Imbissstube *die*.

snag [snæg] ◇ *n* [problem] Haken *der*. ◇ *vi*: **to snag on sthg** an etw *(D)* hängen|bleiben.

snail [sneɪl] *n* Schnecke *die*.

snake [sneɪk] *n* Schlange *die*.

snap [snæp] ◇ *adj* spontan; [election] Spontan-. ◇ *n* - **1.** [of twig, branch] Knacken *das*; [of whip] Knallen *das* - **2.** *inf* [photograph] Schnappschuss *der* - **3.** [card game] Schnipp-schnappschnurr *das*. ◇ *vt* - **1.** [break - rope] zerreißen; **to snap one's fingers** mit den Fingern schnippen - **2.** [say sharply] hervor|stoßen. ◇ *vi* - **1.** [break] (zer)brechen; [rope] (zer)reißen - **2.** [attempt to bite]: **to snap (at sb/sthg)** (nach jm/etw) schnappen - **3.** [speak sharply]: **to snap at sb** jn an|fahren. ◆ **snap up** *vt sep* zu|schlagen bei *(+ D)*.

snappy ['snæpɪ] *adj inf* [stylish, quick] flott; **make it snappy!** mach hin!

snapshot ['snæpʃɒt] *n* Schnappschuss *der*.

snare [sneəʳ] ◇ *n* Falle *die*. ◇ *vt* in einer Falle fangen.

snarl [snɑːl] ◇ *n* Knurren *das*. ◇ *vi* knurren.

snatch [snætʃ] ◇ *n* [of song, conversation] Bruchstück *das*. ◇ *vt* [grab] schnappen.

sneak [sniːk] (*US pt* **snuck**) ◇ *n UK inf* Petze *die*. ◇ *vt* [bring secretly] schmuggeln; **to sneak a look at sb/sthg** jn/etw heimlich an|sehen. ◇ *vi* [move quietly] schleichen; **to sneak up on sb** sich an jn heran|schleichen.

sneakers ['sniːkəz] *npl US* Sportschuhe *Pl*.

sneaky ['sniːkɪ] *adj inf* hinterhältig.

sneer [snɪəʳ] ◇ *n* spöttisches Lächeln. ◇ *vi* [smile unpleasantly] spöttisch lächeln.

sneeze [sniːz] ◇ *n* Niesen *das*. ◇ *vi* niesen.

snide [snaɪd] *adj* abfällig.

sniff [snɪf] ◇ *vt* - **1.** [smell] riechen an *(+ D)* - **2.** [drug] schnüffeln. ◇ *vi* schniefen.

snigger ['snɪgəʳ] ◇ *n* hämisches Kichern. ◇ *vi* hämisch kichern.

snip [snɪp] ◇ *n inf* [bargain] Schnäppchen *das*. ◇ *vt* [cut] schnippeln.

sniper ['snaɪpəʳ] *n* Heckenschütze *der*.

snippet ['snɪpɪt] *n* Bruchstück *das*.

snob [snɒb] *n* Snob *der*.

snobbish ['snɒbɪʃ], **snobby** ['snɒbɪ] *adj* snobistisch.

snooker ['snuːkəʳ] *n* Snooker *das*.

snoop [snuːp] *vi inf* (herum)|schnüffeln.

snooty ['snuːtɪ] *adj* hochnäsig.

snooze [snuːz] ◇ *n* Nickerchen *das*; **to have a snooze** ein Nickerchen machen. ◇ *vi* ein Nickerchen machen.

snore [snɔːʳ] ◇ *n* Schnarchen *das*. ◇ *vi* schnarchen.

snoring ['snɔːrɪŋ] *n* Schnarchen *das*.

snorkel ['snɔːkl] *n* Schnorchel *der*.

snort [snɔːt] ◇ *n* Schnauben *das*. ◇ *vi* schnauben.

snout [snaʊt] *n* Schnauze *die*.

snow [snəʊ] ◇ *n* Schnee *der*. ◇ *impers vb*: **it's snowing** es schneit.

snowball ['snəʊbɔːl] ◇ *n* Schneeball *der*. ◇ *vi fig* lawinenartig an|wachsen.

snowdrift ['snəʊdrɪft] *n* Schneewehe *die*.

snowdrop ['snəʊdrɒp] *n* Schneeglöckchen *das*.

snowfall ['snəʊfɔːl] *n* Schneefall *der*.

snowflake ['snəʊfleɪk] *n* Schneeflocke *die*.

snowman ['snəʊmæn] (*pl* **-men** [-men]) *n* Schneemann *der*.

snowplough *UK*, **snowplow** *US* ['snəʊplaʊ] *n* [vehicle] Schneepflug *der*.

snowstorm ['snəʊstɔːm] *n* Schneesturm *der*.

SNP (*abbr of* **Scottish National Party**) *n nationalistische Partei in Schottland*.

Snr, snr (*abbr of* **senior**) sen.

snub [snʌb] ◇ *n* Abfuhr *die*. ◇ *vt*: **to snub sb** jm eine Abfuhr erteilen.

snuck [snʌk] *pt US* ▷ **sneak**.

snug [snʌg] *adj* - **1.** [person, feeling, place] gemütlich - **2.** [close-fitting] gut sitzend.

snuggle ['snʌgl] *vi*: **to snuggle up to sb** sich an jn kuscheln; **to snuggle down in bed** sich ins Bett kuscheln.

so [səʊ] ◇ *adv* - **1.** [to such a degree] so; **it's so difficult that** es ist so schwierig, dass; **don't be so stupid!** sei nicht so dumm!; **I (do) so hope you can come** ich hoffe so sehr, dass du kommen kannst; **so much money/many cars** so viel Geld/viele Autos; **I liked it so much that...** es gefiel mir so sehr OR gut, dass...; **so much so that...** dermaßen, dass... - **2.** [referring back]: **so what's the point then?** was soll das also?; **so you knew already?** du hast es also schon gewusst?; **I think so** ich glaube (schon); **I don't think so** ich glaube nicht; **I'm afraid so** leider ja; **I told you so** das habe ich dir gleich gesagt; **if so** falls ja; **is that so?** tatsächlich? - **3.** [also] auch; **so can I** ich auch; **so do I** ich auch; **he is clever and so is she** er ist intelligent und sie auch - **4.** [in this way] so - **5.** [in expressing agreement]: **so there is** ja, stimmt; **that's her car - so it is!** das ist ihr Auto - tatsächlich!; **so I see** das sehe ich - **6.** [referring to unspecified amount, limit]: **they pay us so much a week** sie zahlen uns so viel die Woche; **or so** oder so. ◇ *conj* - **1.** [consequently] also; **he said yes and so we got married** er sagte ja, also heirateten wir; **I'm away next week so I won't be there** ich bin nächste Woche weg, also werde ich nicht kommen - **2.** [to introduce a statement] also; **so what have you been up to?** na, was treibst du so?; **so that's who she is!** das ist sie also!; **so what?** *inf* na und?; **so there!** *inf* das wars! ◆ **and so on, and so forth** *adv* und so weiter. ◆ **so as** *conj* um; **we didn't knock so as not to disturb them** wir klopften nicht an, um sie nicht zu stören. ◆ **so that** *conj* damit.

soak [səʊk] ◇ *vt* - **1.** [leave immersed] ein|weichen - **2.** [wet thoroughly] durchnässen; **to be soaked with sthg** mit etw durchtränkt sein. ◇ *vi* - **1.** [become thoroughly wet]: **to leave sthg to soak, to let sthg soak** etw ein|weichen - **2.** [spread]: **to soak into sthg** in etw (A) ein|sickern; **to soak through sthg** durch etw (hindurch)|sickern. ◆ **soak up** *vt sep* [liquid] auf|saugen.

soaking ['səʊkɪŋ] *adj*: **soaking (wet)** durchnässt.

so-and-so *n inf* - **1.** [to replace a name]: **Mr So-and-so** Herr Soundso - **2.** [annoying person]: **you little so-and-so!** du Biest!

soap [səʊp] *n* - **1.** *(U)* [for washing] Seife *die* - **2.** TV Seifenoper *die*.

soap dish *n* Seifenschale *die*.

soap opera *n* Seifenoper *die*.

soap powder *n* Seifenpulver *das*.

soapy ['səʊpɪ] *adj* seifig.

soar [sɔːʳ] *vi* - **1.** [bird, kite, rocket] auf|steigen - **2.** [increase rapidly] rapide an|steigen.

sob [sɒb] *n* Schluchzer *der*.

sober ['səʊbəʳ] *adj* - **1.** [not drunk] nüchtern - **2.** [serious] ernsthaft - **3.** [plain] einfach. ◆ **sober up** *vi* nüchtern werden.

sobering ['səʊbərɪŋ] *adj* ernüchternd.

so-called [-kɔːld] *adj* so genannt.

soccer ['sɒkəʳ] *n (U)* Fußball *der*.

sociable ['səʊʃəbl] *adj* gesellig.

social ['səʊʃl] *adj* - **1.** [behaviour, background, conditions] sozial, gesellschaftlich - **2.** [gathering, drinking] gesellig.

socialism ['səʊʃəlɪzm] *n* Sozialismus *der*.

socialist ['səʊʃəlɪst] ◇ *adj* sozialistisch. ◇ *n* Sozialist *der*, -in *die*.

socialize, -ise ['səʊʃəlaɪz] *vi*: **to socialize with sb** mit jm gesellschaftlich verkehren; **she socializes a lot** sie geht viel aus.

social security *n (U)* Sozialversicherung *die*.

social services *npl* Sozialeinrichtungen *Pl*.

social worker *n* Sozialarbeiter *der*, -in *die*.

society [sə'saɪətɪ] *n* - **1.** [mankind, community] Gesellschaft *die* - **2.** [club, organization] Verein *der*, Klub *der*.

sociology [ˌsəʊsɪ'ɒlədʒɪ] *n* Soziologie *die*.

sock [sɒk] *n* Socke *die*, Socken *der*.

socket ['sɒkɪt] *n* - **1.** ELEC Steckdose *die* - **2.** ANAT [of joint] Gelenkpfanne *die*; [of eye] Augenhöhle *die*.

sod [sɒd] *n* - **1.** [of turf] Sode *die* - **2.** *v inf* [man] Scheißkerl *der*; [woman] Miststück *das*.

soda ['səʊdə] *n* - **1.** CHEM Soda *das*, Natron *das* - **2.** [soda water] Soda *das* - **3.** *US* [fizzy drink] Limonade *die*.

soda water *n* Sodawasser *das*.

sodden ['sɒdn] *adj* durchnässt.

sodium ['səʊdɪəm] *n* Natrium *das*.

sofa ['səʊfə] *n* Sofa *das*.

Sofia ['səʊfjə] *n* Sofia *nt*.

soft [sɒft] *adj* - **1.** [gen] weich - **2.** [breeze, sound, knock, nature] sanft - **3.** [light, colour, music] gedämpft - **4.** [not strict] mild.

softball ['sɒftbɔːl] *n* Softball *der*.

soft drink *n* alkoholfreies Getränk.

soften ['sɒfn] ◇ *vt* - **1.** [substance] weich machen; [water] enthärten - **2.** [punch, impact, effect, light] dämpfen; [blow, attitude] mildern. ◇ *vi* - **1.** [substance] weich werden - **2.** [eyes, voice, expression] sanft werden.

softhearted [ˌsɒft'hɑːtɪd] *adj* weichherzig.

softly ['sɒftlɪ] *adv* - **1.** [move, touch] sanft - **2.** [speak, sing, shine] leise - **3.** [smile, look] sanft.

soft return *n* COMPUT weicher Zeilenumbruch.

software ['sɒftweəʳ] *n* COMPUT Software *die*.

soggy ['sɒgɪ] *adj* durchnässt; [ground] matschig.

soil [sɔɪl] ◇ *n* - **1.** [earth] Erde *die*; [ground & GEOG] Boden *der* - **2.** *fig* [territory] Boden *der*. ◇ *vt* [dirty] beschmutzen.

soiled [sɔɪld] *adj* schmutzig.

solar ['səʊləʳ] *adj* Sonnen-.

solar energy *n* Solarenergie *die*.

sold [səʊld] *pt & pp* ▷ **sell**.

solder ['səʊldəʳ] ◇ *n (U)* TECH Lot *das*. ◇ *vt* löten.

soldier ['səʊldʒəʳ] *n* Soldat *der*.

sold out *adj* ausverkauft.

sole [səʊl] ◇ *adj* - 1. [only] einzig - 2. [exclusive] alleinig. ◇ *n* - 1. [of foot] Sohle *die* - 2. (*pl inv* OR **-s**) [fish] Seezunge *die*.

solemn ['sɒləm] *adj* - 1. [person, face, voice] ernst - 2. [agreement, promise, occasion, music] feierlich.

solicit [sə'lɪsɪt] ◇ *vt fml* [request] werben um. ◇ *vi* [prostitute] sich an|bieten.

solicitor [sə'lɪsɪtəʳ] *n UK* Rechtsanwalt *der*, -anwältin *die*.

solid ['sɒlɪd] ◇ *adj* - 1. [not liquid or gas] fest - 2. [gold, silver, wood] massiv - 3. [building, base, relationship, person] solide - 4. [support] einmütig; [evidence] handfest; [majority] solide - 5. [line] ununterbrochen, durchgängig; **two hours solid, two solid hours** zwei volle Stunden. ◇ *adv*: **to be packed solid** brechend voll sein. ◇ *n* [not liquid or gas] fester Stoff. ◆ **solids** *npl* [food] feste Nahrung.

solidarity [,sɒlɪ'dærətɪ] *n* Solidarität *die*.

solitaire [,sɒlɪ'teəʳ] *n* - 1. [jewel] Solitär *der* - 2. [board game] Solitaire *das* - 3. *US* [card game] Patience *die*.

solitary ['sɒlɪtrɪ] *adj* - 1. [involving one person, single] einzeln - 2. [enjoying solitude] einsam.

solitary confinement *n* Einzelhaft *die*.

solitude ['sɒlɪtju:d] *n* Einsamkeit *die*.

solo ['səʊləʊ] (*pl* **-s**) ◇ *adj* - 1. MUS Solo- - 2. [attempt, flight] Allein-. ◇ *n* MUS Solo *das*. ◇ *adv* - 1. MUS solo - 2. [fly, climb] allein.

soloist ['səʊləʊɪst] *n* Solist *der*, -in *die*.

soluble ['sɒljʊbl] *adj* - 1. [substance] löslich - 2. [problem] lösbar.

solution [sə'lu:ʃn] *n* Lösung *die*; **a solution to sthg** eine Lösung für etw.

solve [sɒlv] *vt* lösen.

solvent ['sɒlvənt] ◇ *adj* FIN solvent. ◇ *n* [substance] Lösungsmittel *das*.

Somalia [sə'mɑ:lɪə] *n* Somalia *nt*.

sombre *UK*, **somber** *US* ['sɒmbəʳ] *adj* düster.

some [sʌm] ◇ *adj* - 1. [a certain amount of] etwas; **some money** etwas Geld; **some meat** ein bisschen Fleisch; **would you like some (more) tea?** möchtest du (noch) Tee? - 2. [a certain number of] einige; **some people** einige Leute; **I bought some sweets** ich habe Bonbons gekauft; **can I have some sweets?** kann ich Bonbons haben?; **I've known her for some years** ich kenne sie schon seit einigen Jahren - 3. *(contrastive use)* [certain] manche; **some jobs are better paid than others** manche Jobs sind besser bezahlt als andere - 4. [in imprecise statements] irgendein(e); **she married some Italian (or other)** sie hat irgend so einen Italiener geheiratet; **there must be some mistake** das muss ein Irrtum sein - 5. *inf iro* [not very good]: **some welcome that was!** das war vielleicht ein enttäuschender Empfang; **some friend you are!** du bist mir vielleicht ein Freund! ◇ *pron* - 1. [a certain amount] etwas; **I've read some of the article** ich habe einen Teil des Artikels gelesen; **some of it is mine** ein Teil davon gehört mir; **take some bread - I've already got some** nimm dir Brot - ich habe schon - 2. [a certain number] einige; **have some strawberries - I've already got some** nimm dir Erdbeeren - ich habe schon welche; **some (of them) left early** einige (von ihnen) gingen vorher - 3. [some people] manche; **some say he lied** manche sagen, dass er gelogen hat. ◇ *adv* ungefähr; **there were some 7,000 people there** es waren ungefähr OR um die 7000 Leute da.

somebody ['sʌmbədɪ] *pron* jemand; **ask somebody else** frag jemand anders; **somebody or other** irgend jemand; **he really thinks he's somebody** [important person] er glaubt wirklich, er ist wer.

someday ['sʌmdeɪ] *adv* eines Tages.

somehow ['sʌmhaʊ], **someway** *US* ['sʌmweɪ] *adv* irgendwie.

someone ['sʌmwʌn] *pron* = **somebody**.

someplace *adv US* = **somewhere**.

somersault ['sʌməsɔ:lt] ◇ *n* Purzelbaum *der*; SPORT Salto *der*. ◇ *vi* einen Purzelbaum schlagen; SPORT einen Salto machen.

something ['sʌmθɪŋ] ◇ *pron* etwas; **I saw something moving** ich sah, wie sich etwas bewegte; **something nice** etwas Schönes; **there's something about him I don't like** er hat etwas an sich, das mir nicht gefällt; **something else** sonst etwas; **something or other** irgend etwas; **or something** *inf* oder so etwas; **well, at least that's something** nun, das ist immerhin etwas; **there's something in what you say** es ist schon etwas Wahres an dem, was du sagst; **it's really something!** es ist ganz toll!; **it came as something of a surprise to me** es war schon irgendwie eine Überraschung für mich. ◇ *adv* [in approximations]: **something like/in the region of** ungefähr; **it looks something like a rose** es sieht so ähnlich wie eine Rose aus.

sometime ['sʌmtaɪm] ◇ *adj* ehemalig. ◇ *adv* irgendwann.

sometimes ['sʌmtaɪmz] *adv* manchmal.

someway *adv US* = **somehow**.

somewhat ['sʌmwɒt] *adv* ziemlich.

somewhere *UK* ['sʌmweəʳ], **someplace** *US* ['sʌmpleɪs] *adv* - 1. [gen - with verbs of position] irgendwo; [- with verbs of motion] irgendwohin; **somewhere else** irgendwo anders/irgendwo andershin; **somewhere or other** irgendwo/irgendwohin - 2. [in approximations] ungefähr; **somewhere around** OR **in the region of 50** ungefähr 50.

son [sʌn] *n* Sohn *der*.

song [sɒŋ] *n* Lied *das*; [of bird] Gesang *der*.

sonic ['sɒnɪk] *adj* Schall-.

son-in-law (*pl* **sons-in-law** *OR* **son-in-laws**) *n* Schwiegersohn *der*.

soon [suːn] *adv* - **1.** [in a short time] bald; **soon after** *OR* **afterwards** kurz danach - **2.** [early]: **how soon can you be ready?** wie schnell kannst du fertig sein?; **too soon** zu früh; **not a minute too soon** keine Minute zu früh; **as soon as** sobald; **as soon as possible** so bald wie möglich.

sooner [ˈsuːnəʳ] *adv* - **1.** [earlier] früher; **no sooner than** kaum als (auch schon); **sooner or later** früher oder später; **the sooner the better** je früher, desto besser - **2.** [expressing preference] lieber.

soot [sʊt] *n* Ruß *der*.

soothe [suːð] *vt* - **1.** [pain] lindern - **2.** [person, fear] beruhigen.

sophisticated [səˈfɪstɪkeɪtɪd] *adj* - **1.** [stylish] hochelegant - **2.** [intelligent] kultiviert - **3.** [complicated] hoch entwickelt.

sophomore [ˈsɒfəmɔːʳ] *n US* Student *der*, -in *die* im zweiten Studienjahr.

soporific [ˌsɒpəˈrɪfɪk] *adj* einschläfernd.

sopping [ˈsɒpɪŋ] *adj*: **sopping (wet)** klatschnass.

soppy [ˈsɒpɪ] *adj inf pej* rührselig.

soprano [səˈprɑːnəʊ] (*pl* **-s**) *n* - **1.** [person] Sopranistin *die* - **2.** [voice] Sopran *der*.

sorbet [ˈsɔːbeɪ] *n* Sorbet *das*.

sordid [ˈsɔːdɪd] *adj* [desires, thoughts, past] schmutzig.

sore [sɔːʳ] ◇ *adj* - **1.** [painful] wund, entzündet; **to have a sore throat/head** Halsschmerzen/Kopfschmerzen haben - **2.** *US inf* [angry] sauer. ◇ *n* MED wunde *OR* entzündete Stelle.

sorrow [ˈsɒrəʊ] *n* - **1.** [feeling of sadness] Kummer *der* - **2.** [cause of sadness] Leid *das*.

sorry [ˈsɒrɪ] ◇ *adj* - **1.** [expressing apology]: **I'm sorry** es tut mir leid; **I'm sorry about the mess** entschuldige bitte die Unordnung; **I'm sorry for what I did** was ich getan habe, tut mir leid; **I'm sorry to bother you, but could you ...** Verzeihung, könnten Sie ... - **2.** [expressing disappointment]: **I'm sorry you couldn't come** schade, dass du nicht kommen konntest; **we were sorry about his resignation** wir bedauern seinen Rücktritt; **we're sorry to see you go** wir finden es schade, dass du gehst - **3.** [expressing regret]: **I'm sorry I ever came here** ich bereue, jemals hierhergekommen zu sein; **I'm sorry to have to announce ...** ich muss Ihnen leider mitteilen ... - **4.** [expressing sympathy]: **to be** *OR* **feel sorry for sb** jn bedauern *OR* bemitleiden - **5.** [expressing polite disagreement]: **I'm sorry, but ...** Entschuldigung *OR* Verzeihung, aber ... - **6.** [poor, pitiable] bedauernswert. ◇ *excl* - **1.** [expressing apology] Entschuldigung!, Verzeihung! - **2.** [asking for repetition] wie bitte? - **3.** [to correct o.s.] ich meine (natürlich).

sort [sɔːt] ◇ *n* [kind, type] Sorte *die*; **what sort of car have you got?** was für ein Auto hast du?; **a sort of** eine Art (von). ◇ *vt* [classify, separate] sortieren. ◆ **sort of** *adv* [rather] irgendwie. ◆ **sort out** *vt sep* - **1.** [into groups] sortieren - **2.** [tidy up - papers, clothes] weg|räumen; [- room] auf|räumen; [- affairs, finances] regeln - **3.** [work out, arrange] sich *(D)* überlegen.

SOS (*abbr of* **save our souls**) *n* SOS *das*.

so-so *adj* & *adv inf* so la la.

sought [sɔːt] *pt* & *pp* ▷ **seek**.

soul [səʊl] *n* - **1.** [gen] Seele *die* - **2.** [perfect example] Inbegriff *der*; **I'm the soul of discretion** ich bin die Verschwiegenheit in Person - **3.** [music] Soul *der*.

soul-destroying [-dɪˌstrɔɪɪŋ] *adj* [boring] geisttötend; [discouraging] sehr entmutigend.

sound [saʊnd] ◇ *adj* - **1.** [mind, body] gesund - **2.** [building, structure] intakt - **3.** [advice, investment] vernünftig - **4.** [thorough] ordentlich. ◇ *adv*: **to be sound asleep** tief *OR* fest schlafen. ◇ *n* - **1.** [noise] Geräusch *das*; [of music, voice, instrument] Klang *der*; [of person, animal] Laut *der* - **2.** *(U)* PHYS Schall *der* - **3.** [volume] Lautstärke *die* - **4.** [impression, idea] Gedanke *der*; **I don't like the sound of this new plan** der neue Plan behagt mir nicht; **by the sound of it** allem Anschein nach. ◇ *vt* ertönen lassen; [alarm] aus|lösen; [bell] läuten; [horn] hupen. ◇ *vi* - **1.** [make a noise] ertönen; **to sound like sthg** wie etw klingen - **2.** [seem] klingen, zu sein scheinen; **she sounds nice** sie scheint nett zu sein; **it sounds like a good investment** das hört sich nach einer guten Investition an. ◆ **sound out** *vt sep*: **to sound sb out** bei jm vor|fühlen; [furtively] jn aus|horchen.

sound barrier *n* Schallmauer *die*.

sound effects *npl* Klangeffekte *Pl*.

soundly [ˈsaʊndlɪ] *adv* - **1.** [beat, defeat] vernichtend - **2.** [sleep] tief, fest.

soundproof [ˈsaʊndpruːf] *adj* schalldicht.

soundtrack [ˈsaʊndtræk] *n* Soundtrack *der*.

soup [suːp] *n* Suppe *die*.

soup plate *n* Suppenteller *der*.

soup spoon *n* Suppenlöffel *der*.

sour [ˈsaʊəʳ] ◇ *adj* sauer; [relationship] erkalten. ◇ *vt* [person] verbittern; [relationship] erkalten lassen.

source [sɔːs] *n* Quelle *die*.

south [saʊθ] ◇ *adj* Süd-, südlich. ◇ *adv* nach Süden, südwärts; **south of** südlich von; **in the south of England** im Süden Englands. ◇ *n* - **1.** [direction] Süden *der* - **2.** [region]: **the south** der Süden.

South Africa *n* Südafrika *nt*.

South America *n* Südamerika *nt*.

southeast [ˌsaʊθ'iːst] ◇ *adj* südöstlich, Südost-. ◇ *adv* südostwärts, nach Südosten; **southeast of** südöstlich von. ◇ *n* [direction] Südosten *der*.

southerly ['sʌðəlɪ] *adj* - **1.** [direction] südlich; [area] im Süden - **2.** [wind] Süd-.

southern ['sʌðən] *adj* [region, dialect] südlich; [Europe] Süd-.

South Korea *n* Südkorea *nt*.

South Pole *n*: **the South Pole** der Südpol.

southward ['saʊθwəd] ◇ *adj* südlich, nach Süden. ◇ *adv* = **southwards**.

southwards ['saʊθwədz] *adv* nach Süden.

southwest [ˌsaʊθ'west] ◇ *adj* südwestlich, Südwest-. ◇ *adv* südwestwärts, nach Südwesten; **southwest of** südwestlich von. ◇ *n* Südwesten *der*.

souvenir [ˌsuːvə'nɪəʳ] *n* Souvenir *das*, Andenken *das*.

sovereign ['sɒvrɪn] *n* - **1.** [ruler] Herrscher *der*, -in *die* - **2.** [coin] Sovereign *der*.

soviet ['səʊvɪət] *n* Sowjet *der*. ◆ **Soviet** ◇ *adj* sowjetisch. ◇ *n* [person] Sowjetbürger *der*, -in *die*.

Soviet Union *n*: **the (former) Soviet Union** die (ehemalige) Sowjetunion.

sow¹ [səʊ] (*pt* **-ed**, *pp* **sown** OR **-ed**) *vt* - **1.** [seeds] säen, aus|säen - **2.** *fig* [doubt] säen.

sow² [saʊ] *n* [pig] Sau *die*.

sown [səʊn] *pp* ▷ **sow¹**.

soya ['sɔɪə] *n* Soja *das*.

soy(a) bean ['sɔɪ(ə)-] *n* Sojabohne *die*.

spa [spɑː] *n* [spring] Mineralquelle *die*; [place] Bad *das*.

space [speɪs] ◇ *n* - **1.** *(U)* [room] Raum *der*; **there isn't enough space in here** hier ist nicht genug Platz - **2.** [outer space] Weltraum *der* - **3.** [gap] Zwischenraum *der* - **4.** [area] Fläche *die*, Raum *der* - **5.** TYPO Leerzeichen *das* - **6.** [period of time] Zeitraum *der*; **within the space of ten minutes** innerhalb von zehn Minuten; **in a short space of time** [in future] in Kürze; [in past] nach kurzer Zeit - **7.** [seat, place] Platz *der*. ◇ *comp* Weltraum-. ◇ *vt* in regelmäßigen Abständen an|ordnen. ◆ **space out** *vt sep* [arrange] in regelmäßigen Abständen anlordnen.

spacecraft ['speɪskrɑːft] (*pl inv*) *n* Raumschiff *das*.

spaceman ['speɪsmæn] (*pl* **-men** [-men]) *n* [astronaut] Raumfahrer *der*.

spaceship ['speɪsʃɪp] *n* Raumschiff *das*.

space shuttle *n* Spaceshuttle *das*.

spacesuit ['speɪssuːt] *n* Raumanzug *der*.

spacious ['speɪʃəs] *adj* geräumig.

spade [speɪd] *n* - **1.** [tool] Spaten *der* - **2.** [playing card] Pik *das*. ◆ **spades** *npl* Pik *das*; **the six of spades** die Piksechs.

spaghetti [spə'getɪ] *n (U)* Spaghetti *Pl*.

Spain [speɪn] *n* Spanien *nt*.

spam [spæm] *n* COMPUT Spam *der*.

span [spæn] ◇ *pt* ▷ **spin**. ◇ *n* - **1.** [in time] Zeitraum *der*, Zeitspanne *die* - **2.** [range] Reihe *die* - **3.** [of hands, arms, wings, bridge] Spannweite *die*. ◇ *vt* - **1.** [encompass] umfassen - **2.** [cross] überspannen.

Spaniard ['spænjəd] *n* Spanier *der*, -in *die*.

spaniel ['spænjəl] *n* Spaniel *der*.

Spanish ['spænɪʃ] ◇ *adj* spanisch. ◇ *n* [language] Spanisch(e) *das*.

spank [spæŋk] *vt*: **to spank sb** [once] jm einen Klaps auf den Hintern geben; [several times] jm den Hintern versohlen.

spanner ['spænəʳ] *n* Schraubenschlüssel *der*.

spar [spɑːʳ] *vi* [boxing] sparren.

spare [speəʳ] ◇ *adj* - **1.** [surplus] zusätzlich, Ersatz-; **have you got a spare pencil?** hast du einen Bleistift übrig? - **2.** [free] frei. ◇ *n inf* [part] Ersatzteil *das*. ◇ *vt* - **1.** [make available] entbehren können, übrig haben; **can you spare five minutes?** hast du (mal) fünf Minuten Zeit?; **to spare** [extra] übrig, zur Verfügung; **we had an hour to spare** wir hatten (noch) eine Stunde Zeit - **2.** [not harm] verschonen - **3.** [effort, trouble] scheuen; **to spare no expense** keine Kosten scheuen - **4.** [save, protect from]: **to spare sb sthg** jm etw ersparen.

spare part *n* AUT Ersatzteil *das*.

spare time *n* Freizeit *die*.

spare wheel *n* Ersatzrad *das*.

sparing ['speərɪŋ] *adj*: **to be sparing with sthg** mit etw sparsam sein.

sparingly ['speərɪŋlɪ] *adv* sparsam.

spark [spɑːk] *n* - **1.** [from fire, electricity] Funke *der* - **2.** *fig* [of understanding, interest, humour] Funken *der*.

sparkle ['spɑːkl] ◇ *n* [of jewel, frost, stars, sea] Glitzern *das*; [of eyes] Funkeln *das*. ◇ *vi* [jewel, frost, stars, sea] glitzern; [eyes] funkeln.

sparkling ['spɑːklɪŋ] *adj* - **1.** [mineral water] sprudelnd - **2.** [wit] sprühend.

sparkling wine *n* Schaumwein *der*, Sekt *der*.

spark plug *n* Zündkerze *die*.

sparrow ['spærəʊ] *n* Spatz *der*, Sperling *der*.

sparse ['spɑːs] *adj* spärlich; [hair] schütter, dünn.

spasm ['spæzm] *n* - **1.** MED [muscular contraction] Krampf *der* - **2.** [fit] Anfall *der*.

spastic ['spæstɪk] *n* MED Spastiker *der*, -in *die*.

spat [spæt] *pt & pp* ▷ **spit**.

spate [speɪt] *n* Flut *die*.

spatter ['spætəʳ] *vt* bespritzen.

spawn [spɔːn] ◇ *n* Laich *der*. ◇ *vt fig* [produce] erzeugen. ◇ *vi* ZOOL laichen.

speak [spiːk] (*pt* **spoke**, *pp* **spoken**) ◇ *vt* sprechen. ◇ *vi* - **1.** [say words] sprechen; **to speak to** *OR* **with sb** mit jm sprechen *OR* reden; **to speak to sb about sthg** mit jm über etw *(A)* sprechen *OR* reden; **to speak about sb/sthg** über jn/etw sprechen *OR* reden - **2.** [make a speech] sprechen, reden; **to speak on sthg** über etw *(A)* sprechen - **3.** [in giving an opinion]: **generally speaking** im Allgemeinen, im Großen und Ganzen; **personally speaking** meiner Ansicht nach. ◆ **so to speak** *adv* sozusagen. ◆ **speak for** *vt insep* [represent] sprechen für. ◆ **speak up** *vi* - **1.** [say something] sprechen; **to speak up for sb/sthg** für jn/etw einltreten - **2.** [speak louder] lauter sprechen.

speaker ['spiːkəʳ] *n* - **1.** [person talking] Sprecher *der*, -in *die* - **2.** [in lecture] Redner *der*, -in *die* - **3.** [of a language]: **a German speaker** ein Sprecher/eine Sprecherin des Deutschen - **4.** [loudspeaker, in hi-fi] Lautsprecher *der*. ◆ **Speaker** *n UK* [in House of Commons] Präsident *der*, -in *die* des Unterhauses.

spear [spɪəʳ] *n* Speer *der*.

spearhead ['spɪəhed] *vt* anlführen.

spec [spek] *n UK inf*: **on spec** aufs Geratewohl.

special ['speʃl] *adj* - **1.** [specific, out of the ordinary] besondere (r) (s), spezielle (r) (s) - **2.** [valued]: **to be special to sb** jm viel bedeuten.

special delivery *n* Eilzustellung *die*.

specialist ['speʃəlɪst] ◇ *adj* Fach-. ◇ *n* [expert] Spezialist *der*, -in *die*; [doctor] Facharzt *der*, -ärztin *die*.

speciality [ˌspeʃɪ'ælətɪ], **specialty** *US* ['speʃltɪ] *n* - **1.** [field of knowledge] Spezialgebiet *das* - **2.** [service, product] Spezialität *die*.

specialize, -ise ['speʃəlaɪz] *vi*: **to specialize (in sthg)** sich (auf etw *(A)*) spezialisieren; [have special qualifications] (auf etw *(A)*) spezialisiert sein.

specially ['speʃəlɪ] *adv* - **1.** [on purpose, specifically] speziell - **2.** [really] besonders.

specialty *n US* = **speciality**.

species ['spiːʃiːz] (*pl inv*) *n* Spezies *die*, Art *die*.

specific [spə'sɪfɪk] *adj* bestimmt, spezifisch; **to be specific to sb/sthg** jn/etw eigen sein.

specifically [spə'sɪfɪklɪ] *adv* - **1.** [explicitly] ausdrücklich - **2.** [particularly, precisely] im Besonderen.

specify ['spesɪfaɪ] *vt* spezifizieren, herauslstellen; **to specify that...** deutlich machen, dass..., herauslstellen, dass...

specimen ['spesɪmən] *n* - **1.** [example] Exemplar *das* - **2.** [sample] Probe *die*.

speck [spek] *n* - **1.** [small stain] Fleck *der*; [of paint, mud] Spritzer *der* - **2.** [small particle - of dust] Körnchen *das*; [- of soot] Flocke *die*.

speckled ['spekld] *adj*: **speckled (with sthg)** gesprenkelt (mit etw).

specs [speks] *npl inf* Brille *die*.

spectacle ['spektəkl] *n* - **1.** [sight] Anblick *der*; **to make a spectacle of o.s.** sich unmöglich benehmen - **2.** [event] Spektakel *das*. ◆ **spectacles** *npl UK* [glasses] Brille *die*.

spectacular [spek'tækjʊləʳ] *adj* spektakulär.

spectator [spek'teɪtəʳ] *n* Zuschauer *der*, -in *die*.

spectre *UK*, **specter** *US* ['spektəʳ] *n* - **1.** *fml* [ghost] Gespenst *das* - **2.** *fig* [frightening prospect] Schreckgespenst *das*.

speculation [ˌspekjʊ'leɪʃn] *n* Spekulation *die*.

sped [sped] *pt* & *pp* ▷ **speed**.

speech [spiːtʃ] *n* - **1.** *(U)* [ability to speak, dialect] Sprache *die* - **2.** [formal talk] Rede *die* - **3.** THEAT Text *der* - **4.** [manner of speaking] Sprechweise *die*; **his speech is clear and precise** er spricht klar und deutlich - **5.** GRAM: **direct/indirect speech** direkte/indirekte Rede.

speechless ['spiːtʃlɪs] *adj*: **to be speechless (with sthg)** (vor etw *(D)*) sprachlos sein.

speed [spiːd] (*pt* & *pp* **-ed** *OR* **sped**) ◇ *n* - **1.** [pace, rapid rate] Geschwindigkeit *die*, Tempo *das*; **speed of light/sound** Licht-/Schallgeschwindigkeit *die*; **at high/low speed** mit hoher/niedriger Geschwindigkeit; **at top** *OR* **full speed** mit Höchstgeschwindigkeit - **2.** [gear] Gang *der* - **3.** PHOT [of film] Lichtempfindlichkeit *die*. ◇ *vi* - **1.** [move fast]: **to speed along/away/by** entlang-/davon-/vorbeiljagen - **2.** AUT [go too fast] zu schnell fahren. ◆ **speed up** ◇ *vt sep* beschleunigen; [person] auf Trab bringen. ◇ *vi* [worker] sich beeilen; [driver, vehicle] beschleunigen; [production] sich erhöhen.

speedboat ['spiːdbəʊt] *n* Rennboot *das*.

speed dating *n* Speed-Dating *das*.

speeding ['spiːdɪŋ] *n* zu schnelles Fahren; LAW Geschwindigkeitsüberschreitung *die*.

speed limit *n* Geschwindigkeitsbeschränkung *die*.

speedometer [spɪ'dɒmɪtəʳ] *n* Tachometer *der ODER das*.

speedway ['spiːdweɪ] *n* - **1.** SPORT Speedway-Rennen *das* - **2.** *US* [road] Schnellstraße *die*.

speedy ['spiːdɪ] *adj* schnell.

spell [spel] (*UK pt* & *pp* **spelt** *OR* **-ed**) (*US pt & pp* **-ed**) ◇ *n* - **1.** [period of time] Weile *die*; **with some sunny spells** mit sonnigen Abschnitten; **for a spell** eine Weile - **2.** [enchantment] Zauber *der*; **to cast** *OR* **put a spell on sb** jn verzaubern - **3.** [magic word] Zauberspruch *der*. ◇ *vt* - **1.** [word, name] schreiben; [aloud] buchstabieren - **2.** *fig* [signify] bedeuten; [aloud] buchstabieren; **it spells disaster**

das bedeutet Unglück. ◇ *vi*: **to be able to spell** fehlerfrei schreiben können. ◆ **spell out** *vt sep* - **1.** [read aloud] buchstabieren - **2.** [explain]: **to spell sthg out (for** OR **to sb)** (jm) etw klar|machen.

spellbound ['spelbaʊnd] *adj* gebannt.

spelling ['spelɪŋ] *n* - **1.** [of a particular word] Schreibweise *die* - **2.** [ability to spell] Rechtschreibung *die*.

spelt [spelt] *pt* & *pp UK* ▷ **spell**.

spend [spend] (*pt & pp* **spent**) *vt* - **1.** [pay out] aus|geben; **she spends a lot of money on clothes** sie gibt viel Geld für Kleidung aus - **2.** [time, life] verbringen; **he spent two hours shopping** er ist zwei Stunden lang einkaufen gewesen.

spent [spent] ◇ *pt* & *pp* ▷ **spend**. ◇ *adj* [fuel, matches] verbraucht; [ammunition] verschossen; [patience, energy] erschöpft.

sperm [spɜ:m] (*pl inv* OR **-s**) *n* - **1.** [cell] Spermium *das* - **2.** *(U)* [fluid] Sperma *das*.

spew [spju:] ◇ *vt* [flames, lava] speien. ◇ *vi*: **to spew (out) from sthg** aus etw hervor|schießen.

sphere [sfɪəʳ] *n* - **1.** [globe] Kugel *die* - **2.** [of interest, activity] Bereich *der*; **sphere of influence** Einflussbereich *der*.

spice [spaɪs] *n* - **1.** CULIN Gewürz *das* - **2.** *(U) fig* [excitement] Würze *die*.

spick-and-span [ˌspɪkən'spæn] *adj* blitzblank.

spicy ['spaɪsɪ] *adj* pikant.

spider ['spaɪdəʳ] *n* Spinne *die*.

spike [spaɪk] ◇ *n* - **1.** [on railings] Spitze *die*; [on shoe] Spike *der* - **2.** [on plant] Stachel *der*. ◇ *vt* [drink] einen Schuss (Alkohol) zu|geben.

spill [spɪl] (*UK pt & pp* **spilt** OR **-ed**) (*US pt & pp* **-ed**) ◇ *vt* - **1.** [liquid, salt] verschütten - **2.** [blood] vergießen. ◇ *vi* [liquid, salt] sich ergießen.

spilt [spɪlt] *pt* & *pp UK* ▷ **spill**.

spin [spɪn] (*pt* **span** OR **spun**, *pp* **spun**) ◇ *n* - **1.** [turn] Drehung *die* - **2.** AERON Trudeln *das*; **the plane went into a spin** das Flugzeug begann zu trudeln - **3.** *inf* [in car] Spritztour *die*; **to go for a spin** eine Spritztour machen - **4.** SPORT [on ball] Effet *der*. ◇ *vt* - **1.** [gen] schnell drehen - **2.** [in spin-dryer] schleudern; [coin in the air] hoch|werfen - **3.** [thread, cloth, wool] spinnen - **4.** SPORT [ball] einen Effet geben *(+ D)*. ◇ *vi* - **1.** [gen] sich schnell drehen; [plane] trudeln - **2.** [spinner of thread] spinnen - **3.** [in spin-dryer] schleudern. ◆ **spin out** *vt sep* [story, explanation] in die Länge ziehen; [money, food] strecken.

spinach ['spɪnɪdʒ] *n* Spinat *der*.

spinal column ['spaɪnl-] *n* Wirbelsäule *die*.

spinal cord ['spaɪnl-] *n* Rückenmark *das*.

spindly ['spɪndlɪ] *adj* [arms, legs] spindeldürr; [plant] zierlich.

spin-dryer *n UK* Wäscheschleuder *die*.

spine [spaɪn] *n* - **1.** ANAT Wirbelsäule *die* - **2.** [of book] Rücken *der* - **3.** [of hedgehog, plant] Stachel *der*.

spin-off *n* [by-product] Nebenprodukt *das*.

spinster ['spɪnstəʳ] *n* Unverheiratete *die*.

spiral ['spaɪərəl] (*UK*) (*US*) ◇ *adj* spiralförmig. ◇ *n liter* & *fig* Spirale *die*. ◇ *vi* [move in spiral curve - staircase, path] sich (hoch)|winden; [- smoke] spiralförmig auf|steigen.

spiral staircase *n* Wendeltreppe *die*.

spire ['spaɪəʳ] *n* Turmspitze *die*.

spirit ['spɪrɪt] *n* - **1.** [soul, ghost] Geist *der*; **to be with sb in spirit** in Gedanken bei jm sein - **2.** *(U)* [courage] Mut *der* - **3.** *(U)* [attitude] Geist *der*; [mood] Stimmung *die*; **fighting spirit** Kampfgeist *der* - **4.** [essence] Geist *der*, Sinn *der*. ◆ **spirits** *npl* - **1.** [mood] Stimmung *die*, Laune *die*; **to be in high/low spirits** guter/schlechter Laune sein - **2.** [alcohol] Spirituosen *Pl*.

spirited ['spɪrɪtɪd] *adj* [action, defence] beherzt; [performance] lebendig; [debate] lebhaft.

spirit level *n* Wasserwaage *die*.

spiritual ['spɪrɪtʃʊəl] *adj* - **1.** [of the spirit] geistig, spirituell - **2.** [religious] geistlich.

spit [spɪt] (*UK pt & pp* **spat**) (*US pt & pp inv*) ◇ *n* - **1.** [saliva] Spucke *die* - **2.** [skewer] Spieß *der*. ◇ *vi* [from mouth] spucken. ◇ *impers vb UK* [rain lightly] tröpfeln.

spite [spaɪt] ◇ *n (U)* Bosheit *die*. ◇ *vt* ärgern. ◆ **in spite of** *prep* trotz *(+ G)*.

spiteful ['spaɪtfʊl] *adj* boshaft.

spittle ['spɪtl] *n* Spucke *die*.

splash [splæʃ] ◇ *n* - **1.** [sound] Platschen *das* - **2.** [patch - of colour] Tupfen *der*; [- of light] Fleck *der*. ◇ *vt* - **1.** [subj: person] bespritzen - **2.** [subj: water] spritzen auf *(+ A)* - **3.** [apply haphazardly] klatschen. ◇ *vi* - **1.** [person]: **to splash about** OR **around** herum|spritzen - **2.** [water, liquid]: **to splash on/against sthg** klatschen an etw *(A)*/gegen etw.

spleen [spli:n] *n* - **1.** ANAT Milz *die* - **2.** *(U) fig* [anger]: **to vent one's spleen on sb** seine Wut OR schlechte Laune an jm aus|lassen.

splendid ['splendɪd] *adj* - **1.** [very good] großartig - **2.** [magnificent, beautiful] prachtvoll.

splint [splɪnt] *n* Schiene *die*.

splinter ['splɪntəʳ] ◇ *n* Splitter *der*. ◇ *vi* [glass, bone, wood] splittern.

split [splɪt] (*pt & pp inv, cont* **-ting**) ◇ *n* - **1.** [crack] Spalt *der* - **2.** [tear] Riss *der* - **3.** [division, schism] Spaltung *die*, Riss *der*. ◇ *vt* - **1.** [crack, divide] spalten; **the collision split the ship in two** bei dem Zusammenstoß zerbrach das Schiff in zwei Teile - **2.** [tear] zerreißen - **3.** [share] teilen; **we'll split the costs** wir werden uns die Kosten teilen; **to split the difference** sich in der Mitte treffen. <> *vi* - **1.** [crack - wood, stone] sich spalten; [- ship] auseinander|brechen - **2.** [tear - fabric] reißen; [- seam, trousers] platzen; **the bag split open** die Tasche platzte auf - **3.** [divide] sich teilen. ◆ **split up** *vi* sich trennen; **to split up with sb** sich von jm trennen.

split second *n* Bruchteil *der* einer Sekunde.

splutter ['splʌtəʳ] *vi* - **1.** [person speaking, engine] stottern - **2.** [fire, flames] zischen.

spoil [spɔɪl] (*pt & pp* **-ed** *OR* **spoilt**) *vt* - **1.** [ruin] verderben; **to spoil sb's fun** jm den Spaß verderben - **2.** [pamper] verwöhnen; **to be spoilt for choice** die Qual der Wahl haben. ◆ **spoils** *npl* Beute *die*.

spoiled [spɔɪld] *adj* = **spoilt**.

spoilsport ['spɔɪlspɔ:t] *n* Spielverderber *der*, -in *die*.

spoilt [spɔɪlt] <> *pt & pp* ▷ **spoil**. <> *adj* - **1.** [child] verzogen - **2.** [food, dinner] verdorben.

spoke [spəʊk] <> *pt* ▷ **speak**. <> *n* Speiche *die*.

spoken ['spəʊkn] *pp* ▷ **speak**.

spokesman ['spəʊksmən] (*pl* **-men** [-mən]) *n* Sprecher *der*.

spokeswoman ['spəʊks,wʊmən] (*pl* **-women** [-,wɪmɪn]) *n* Sprecherin *die*.

sponge [spʌndʒ] (*UK cont* **spongeing**) (*US cont* **sponging**) <> *n* - **1.** [for cleaning, washing] Schwamm *der* - **2.** [cake] Biskuitkuchen *der*. <> *vt* [face] ab|wischen; [wall, car] mit einem Schwamm ab|waschen. <> *vi inf*: **to sponge off sb** jm auf der Tasche liegen.

sponge bag *n UK* Kulturbeutel *der*.

sponge cake *n* Biskuitkuchen *der*.

sponsor ['spɒnsəʳ] <> *n* - **1.** [of team, film, TV programme] Sponsor *der* - **2.** [of student, museum, for charity] Förderer *der*, -in *die*. <> *vt* - **1.** [team, film, TV programme] sponsern - **2.** [student, museum, for charity] finanziell unterstützen - **3.** [bill, appeal, proposal] unterstützen.

sponsored walk [,spɒnsəd-] *n* Wohltätigkeitsmarsch *der*.

sponsorship ['spɒnsəʃɪp] *n (U)* finanzielle Unterstützung.

spontaneous [spɒn'teɪnjəs] *adj* spontan.

spooky ['spu:kɪ] *adj inf* unheimlich.

spool [spu:l] *n* Spule *die*.

spoon [spu:n] *n* Löffel *der*.

spoon-feed *vt* - **1.** [feed with spoon] füttern - **2.** *fig* [students, pupils] gängeln.

spoonful ['spu:nfʊl] (*pl* **-s** *OR* **spoonsful**) *n* Löffel *der*; **a spoonful of salt** ein Löffel Salz.

sporadic [spə'rædɪk] *adj* sporadisch; [showers, shooting] vereinzelt.

sport [spɔ:t] *n* - **1.** [games] Sport *der*; [type of sport] Sportart *die*; **she's good at sport** sie ist sportlich - **2.** *dated* [cheerful person]: **he's a (good) sport** er ist in Ordnung.

sporting ['spɔ:tɪŋ] *adj* - **1.** [relating to sport] sportlich; **sporting event** Wettkampf *der* - **2.** [generous, fair] anständig, fair.

sports car ['spɔ:ts-] *n* Sportwagen *der*.

sportsman ['spɔ:tsmən] (*pl* **-men** [-mən]) *n* Sportler *der*.

sportsmanship ['spɔ:tsmənʃɪp] *n* sportliche Fairness.

sportswear ['spɔ:tsweəʳ] *n (U)* [in sport] Sportbekleidung *die*; [for leisure] Freizeitkleidung *die*.

sportswoman ['spɔ:ts,wʊmən] (*pl* **-women** [-,wɪmɪn]) *n* Sportlerin *die*.

sporty ['spɔ:tɪ] *adj inf* sportlich.

spot [spɒt] <> *n* - **1.** [of blood, ink, paint] Fleck *der* - **2.** [pimple] Pickel *der* - **3.** *inf* [small amount]: **a few spots of rain** ein paar Regentropfen; **a spot of** ein bisschen, etwas; **to have a spot of lunch** eine Kleinigkeit zu Mittag essen; **to do a spot of work** ein bisschen arbeiten - **4.** [place] Stelle *die*; **what a lovely spot!** was für ein schönes Plätzchen!; **to do sthg on the spot** etw auf der Stelle tun. <> *vt* [notice] sehen; [mistake] finden.

spot check *n* Stichprobe *die*.

spotless ['spɒtlɪs] *adj* [clean] blitzsauber.

spotlight ['spɒtlaɪt] *n* [in theatre, TV] Scheinwerfer *der*; [at home] Spot *der*; **to be in the spotlight** *fig* im Rampenlicht stehen.

spotted ['spɒtɪd] *adj* [material, garment] gepunktet.

spotty ['spɒtɪ] *adj UK* [skin] pick(e)lig.

spouse [spaʊs] *n* Gatte *der*, -tin *die*.

spout [spaʊt] <> *n* - **1.** [of kettle, watering can] Schnabel *der* - **2.** [of water - from fountain, geyser] Strahl *der*. <> *vi*: **to spout from** *OR* **out of sthg** [liquid] aus etw hervor|spritzen; [flames] aus etw hervor|schießen.

sprain [spreɪn] <> *n* Verstauchung *die*. <> *vt*: **to sprain one's ankle/wrist** sich *(D)* den Knöchel/das Handgelenk verstauchen.

sprang [spræŋ] *pt* ▷ **spring**.

sprawl [sprɔ:l] *vi* - **1.** [person] sich aus|strecken - **2.** [city, suburbs] sich unkontrolliert aus|breiten.

spray [spreɪ] <> *n* - **1.** [droplets] Sprühnebel *der*; [of sea] Gischt *die* - **2.** [pressurized liquid] Spray *das* - **3.** [can, container] Sprühdose *die*. <> *vt* - **1.** [plant, field] besprühen; [crops] spritzen; **to spray one's hair** sich das Haar mit Haarspray stylen - **2.** [paint, perfume] sprühen.

spread [spred] (*pt & pp inv*) <> *n* - **1.** CULIN [paste] Brotaufstrich *der*; **cheese spread** Streichkäse *der* - **2.** [diffusion, growth] Ausbreitung *die* - **3.** [range] Umfang *der* - **4.** *US* [bedspread] Decke *die*. <> *vt* - **1.** [open out - map, tablecloth, arms] auslbreiten; [- fingers, legs] spreizen - 2. [apply]: **to spread sthg with butter** etw mit Butter bestreichen; **to spread butter/jam on one's bread** Butter/Marmelade aufs Brot streichen - 3. [diffuse, disseminate] verbreiten - 4. [over a surface, share evenly] verteilen. <> *vi* - 1. [disease, fire, rumour, news] sich auslbreiten - 2. [water, cloud] sich ausldehnen. ◆ **spread out** *vi* [disperse] sich verteilen.

spread-eagled [-ˌiːgld] *adj*: **to be** OR **lie spread-eagled** ausgestreckt dalliegen.

spreadsheet ['spredʃiːt] *n* COMPUT Tabelle *die*.

spree [spriː] *n*: **to go on a spending/shopping spree** groß einkaufen gehen.

sprightly ['spraɪtlɪ] *adj* [old person] rüstig.

spring [sprɪŋ] (*pt* **sprang**, *pp* **sprung**) <> *n* - 1. [season] Frühling *der*, Frühjahr *das*; **in (the) spring** im Frühling, im Frühjahr - 2. [coil] Feder *die* - 3. [water source] Quelle *die*. <> *vi* - 1. [leap] springen; **to spring to one's feet** auflspringen - 2. [be released]: **the branch sprang back** der Zweig schnellte zurück; **to spring shut** zulfallen; **to spring open** auflspringen - 3. [originate]: **to spring from sthg** aus etw entstehen. ◆ **spring up** *vi* - 1. [get up] auflspringen - 2. [grow in size, height] wachsen - 3. [appear - building] aus dem Boden schießen; [- wind] auflkommen; [- problem] aufltauchen.

springboard ['sprɪŋbɔːd] *n liter & fig* Sprungbrett *das*.

spring-clean *vt*: **to spring-clean the house** Frühjahrsputz machen.

spring onion *n UK* Frühlingszwiebel *die*.

springtime ['sprɪŋtaɪm] *n*: **in (the) springtime** im Frühling.

springy ['sprɪŋɪ] *adj* [carpet, mattress, step] federnd; [ground, rubber] elastisch.

sprinkle ['sprɪŋkl] *vt* [liquid] sprenkeln, sprengen; [powder, salt] streuen; **to sprinkle sthg with sthg** [liquid] etw mit etw (be)sprengen; [powder, salt] etw mit etw bestreuen.

sprinkler ['sprɪŋkləʳ] *n* - 1. [for gardens] Rasensprenger *der* - 2. [for extinguishing fires]: **a sprinkler system** Sprinkleranlage *die*.

sprint [sprɪnt] <> *n* SPORT [race] Lauf *der*, Sprint *der*; **to break into** OR **put on a sprint** loslspurten. <> *vi* rennen; SPORT sprinten.

sprout [spraʊt] <> *n* - 1. CULIN: **(brussels) sprouts** Rosenkohl *der* - 2. [shoot] Trieb *der*. <> *vt* - 1. [germinate] keimen lassen - 2. [grow - leaves, shoots] (aus)ltreiben; [- beard, moustache] sich *(D)* wachsen lassen. <> *vi* - 1. [germinate] keimen - 2. [grow] wachsen, sprießen.

spruce [spruːs] <> *adj* gepflegt. <> *n* [tree] Fichte *die*. ◆ **spruce up** *vt sep* [room, house] auf Vordermann bringen.

sprung [sprʌŋ] *pp* ⊳ **spring**.

spry [spraɪ] *adj* rüstig.

spun [spʌn] *pt & pp* ⊳ **spin**.

spur [spɜːʳ] <> *n* - 1. [incentive]: **spur (to sthg)** Ansporn *der* OR Antrieb *der* (für etw) - 2. [on rider's boot] Sporn *der*. <> *vt* - 1. [horse] die Sporen geben *(+ D)* - 2. [encourage]: **to spur sb to do sthg** jn anlspornen, etw zu tun. ◆ **on the spur of the moment** *adv* ganz spontan. ◆ **spur on** *vt sep* [encourage] anlspornen.

spurn [spɜːn] *vt* verschmähen.

spurt [spɜːt] <> *n* - 1. [of water, steam] Strahl *der* - 2. [of energy] Anfall *der* - 3. [burst of speed] Spurt *der*. <> *vi*: **to spurt (out of** OR **from sthg)** [water, steam, flames] (heraus)lschießen (aus etw).

spy [spaɪ] <> *n* Spion *der*, -in *die*. <> *vt* sichten. <> *vi* - 1. [work as spy] spionieren - 2. [watch secretly]: **to spy on sb** jm nachlspionieren.

spying ['spaɪɪŋ] *n* Spionage *die*.

Sq., sq. *abbr of* **square**.

squabble ['skwɒbl] <> *n* Zank *der*. <> *vi*: **to squabble (about** OR **over sthg)** sich (wegen etw) zanken.

squad [skwɒd] *n* - 1. [police department] Dezernat *das* - 2. MIL Trupp *der* - 3. SPORT Mannschaft *die*.

squadron ['skwɒdrən] *n* [of fighter planes] Staffel *die*; [of warships] Geschwader *das*.

squalid ['skwɒlɪd] *adj* - 1. [filthy - place] dreckig und verkommen; [- conditions] erbärmlich - 2. [base, dishonest] schmutzig.

squall [skwɔːl] *n* [storm] Bö(e) *die*.

squalor ['skwɒləʳ] *n* Schmutz *der*.

squander ['skwɒndəʳ] *vt* [money] verschwenden; [opportunity] vertun.

square [skweəʳ] <> *adj* - 1. [in shape] quadratisch; [face, brackets] eckig - 2. *UK* [MATHS - referring to area] Quadrat-; [- when each side is of same length] im Quadrat - 3. [not owing money]: **to be square** quitt sein. <> *n* - 1. [shape] Quadrat *das* - 2. [in town, city] Platz *der* - 3. *inf* [unfashionable person] Spießer *der*, -in *die*. <> *vt* - 1. MATHS [multiply by itself] quadrieren; **4 squared is 16** 4 hoch 2 ist 16, 4 (zum) Quadrat ist 16 - 2. [balance, reconcile]: **to square sthg with sthg** etw mit etw in Einklang bringen. ◆ **square up** *vi* [settle up]: **to square up with sb** mit jm ablrechnen.

squarely ['skweəlɪ] *adv* - 1. [directly] genau - 2. [honestly] offen und ehrlich.

squash [skwɒʃ] <> *n* - 1. SPORT Squash *das* - 2. *UK* [drink]: **lemon/orange squash** *Fruchtsaftgetränk mit Zitronen-/Orangengeschmack* - 3. *US* [vegetable] Kürbis *der*. <> *vt* [hat] zerdrücken; [box] zusammenldrücken; [fruit] zerquetschen.

squat [skwɒt] <> *adj* gedrungen. <> *vi* [crouch]: **to squat (down)** sich (hin)lhocken; **he was squatting** er hockte.

squatter ['skwɒtəʳ] *n UK* [in empty building] Hausbesetzer *der*, -in *die*.
squawk [skwɔːk] *n* [of bird] Kreischen *das*.
squeak [skwiːk] *n* - **1.** [of animal] Quieken *das* - **2.** [of door, hinge] Quietschen *das*.
squeal [skwiːl] *vi* [person] kreischen; [animal] quieken.
squeamish ['skwiːmɪʃ] *adj* zart besaitet.
squeeze [skwiːz] ◇ *n* [pressure]: **to give sthg a squeeze** etw drücken. ◇ *vt* - **1.** [press firmly] drücken; [orange, lemon] auslpressen - **2.** [extract, press out - juice] herauslpressen; **to squeeze sthg out of sthg** etw aus etw drücken - **3.** [cram]: **to squeeze sthg into sthg** etw in etw *(A)* hineinlpressen *OR* zwängen.
squelch [skweltʃ] *vi* [through mud] patschen.
squid [skwɪd] (*pl inv OR* **-s**) *n* Tintenfisch *der*.
squiggle ['skwɪgl] *n* Schnörkel *der*.
squint [skwɪnt] ◇ *n* MED: **to have a squint** schielen. ◇ *vi* - **1.** MED schielen - **2.** [half-close one's eyes]: **to squint at sthg** etw blinzelnd anlsehen.
squirm [skwɜːm] *vi liter & fig* sich winden.
squirrel [*UK* 'skwɪrəl, *US* 'skwɜːrəl] *n* Eichhörnchen *das*.
squirt [skwɜːt] ◇ *vt* [force out] spritzen. ◇ *vi*: **to squirt (out of sthg)** (heraus)lspritzen (aus etw).
Sr *abbr of* **senior**.
Sri Lanka [ˌsriː'læŋkə] *n* Sri Lanka *nt*.
St *abbr of* **saint**, **street**.
stab [stæb] ◇ *n* - **1.** [with knife] Stich *der* - **2.** *inf* [attempt]: **to have a stab at sthg** etw probieren - **3.** [twinge]: **a stab of pain** ein stechender Schmerz. ◇ *vt* - **1.** [with knife] einlstechen (auf *(+ A)*); **to stab sb to death** jn erstechen; **to stab sb in the back** *fig* jm in den Rücken fallen - **2.** [with fork] auflspießen.
stable ['steɪbl] ◇ *adj* - **1.** [steady, unchanging] stabil; [job] sicher - **2.** [solid, anchored - ladder, shelf] stabil; [- ship, aircraft] sicher - **3.** [person, personality]: **(mentally) stable** innerlich gefestigt. ◇ *n* [building] Reitstall *der*; [horses] Rennstall *der*.
stack [stæk] ◇ *n* [pile] Stoß *der*, Stapel *der*. ◇ *vt* [pile up] stapeln.
stadium ['steɪdjəm] (*pl* **-diums** *OR* **-dia** [-djə]) *n* Stadion *das*.
staff [stɑːf] ◇ *n* [employees] Personal *das*. ◇ *vt* mit Personal auslstatten.
stag [stæg] (*pl inv OR* **-s**) *n* [deer] Hirsch *der*.
stage [steɪdʒ] ◇ *n* - **1.** [period, phase] Stadium *das*, Phase *die*; **at this stage** zu diesem Zeitpunkt - **2.** [platform] Bühne *die*. ◇ *vt* - **1.** THEAT auflführen, inszenieren - **2.** [organize] veranstalten.
stagecoach ['steɪdʒkəʊtʃ] *n* Postkutsche *die*.
stage fright *n* Lampenfieber *das*.
stagger ['stægəʳ] ◇ *vt* - **1.** [astound] die Sprache verschlagen *(+ D)* - **2.** [arrange at different times] staffeln. ◇ *vi* [totter] schwanken.
stagnant ['stægnənt] *adj* - **1.** [water] stehend; [air] verbraucht - **2.** [business, career, economy] stagnierend.
stagnate [stæg'neɪt] *vi* - **1.** [water] stehen; [air] verbraucht werden - **2.** [business, career, economy] stagnieren.
stag night, stag party *n feucht-fröhlicher Männerabend, mit dem ein Bräutigam am Abend vor der Hochzeit sein Jungesellendasein beschließt.*
staid [steɪd] *adj* [person] seriös, gesetzt; [appearance, attitude] bieder.
stain [steɪn] ◇ *n* [mark] Fleck *der*. ◇ *vt* [discolour] Flecken hinterlassen auf *(+ D)*.
stained glass *n* farbiges Glas.
stainless steel ['steɪnlɪs-] *n* Edelstahl *der*.
stain remover [-ˌrɪmuːvəʳ] *n* Fleckenentferner *der*.
stair [steəʳ] *n* [step] Stufe *die*. ◆ **stairs** *npl* Treppe *die*.
staircase ['steəkeɪs] *n* Treppe *die*.
stairway ['steəweɪ] *n* Treppenaufgang *der*, Treppe *die*.
stairwell ['steəwel] *n* Treppenhaus *das*.
stake [steɪk] ◇ *n* - **1.** [share]: **to have a stake in sthg** einen Anteil an etw *(D)* haben - **2.** [wooden post] Pfahl *der* - **3.** [in gambling] Einsatz *der*. ◇ *vt* - **1.** [risk]: **to stake sthg on sthg** etw auf etw *(A)* setzen - **2.** [in gambling] setzen. ◆ **to be at stake** *adv* auf dem Spiel stehen.
stale [steɪl] *adj* [bread] altbacken; [cake] trocken; [water, beer, air] abgestanden.
stalemate ['steɪlmeɪt] *n* - **1.** [deadlock] Sackgasse *die* - **2.** CHESS Patt *das*.
stalk [stɔːk] ◇ *n* Stiel *der*; [of cabbage] Strunk *der*. ◇ *vt* [animal] sich heranlpirschen an *(+ A)*; [person] nachlstellen *(+ D)*.
stall [stɔːl] ◇ *n* - **1.** [table] Stand *der* - **2.** [in stable] Box *die*. ◇ *vt* AUT ablwürgen. ◇ *vi* - **1.** AUT ablsterben - **2.** [delay]: **to stall for time** versuchen, Zeit zu schinden. ◆ **stalls** *npl UK* [in theatre, cinema] Parkett *das*.
stallion ['stæljən] *n* Hengst *der*.
stamina ['stæmɪnə] *n* Ausdauer *die*.
stammer ['stæməʳ] ◇ *n* Stottern *das*; **to have a stammer** stottern. ◇ *vi* stottern.
stamp [stæmp] ◇ *n* - **1.** [postage stamp] Briefmarke *die* - **2.** [rubber stamp] Stempel *der*. ◇ *vt* - **1.** [produce by stamping] auflstempeln - **2.** [stomp]: **to stamp one's foot** auflstampfen (mit dem Fuß). ◇ *vi* - **1.** [walk] stampfen, trampeln - **2.** [with one foot]: **to stamp on sthg** auf etw *(A)* treten.
stamp album *n* Briefmarkenalbum *das*.

stamp-collecting [-kəˌlektɪŋ] *n* Briefmarkensammeln *das*.

stamped addressed envelope ['stæmptəˌdrest-] *n UK* frankierter Rückumschlag.

stampede [stæm'piːd] *n* - **1.** [of animals] panische Flucht - **2.** [of people] Massenandrang *der*.

stance [stæns] *n* - **1.** [posture] Haltung *die* - **2.** [attitude]: **stance (on)** Einstellung *die* (zu).

stand [stænd] (*pt & pp* **stood**) ◇ *n* - **1.** [stall] Stand *der* - **2.** [for umbrellas, coats, bicycle] Ständer *der* - **3.** [at sports stadium] Tribüne *die* - **4.** *fig* & MIL: **to make a stand** Widerstand leisten - **5.** [position] Standpunkt *der* - **6.** *US* LAW Zeugenstand *der*. ◇ *vt* - **1.** [place] stellen - **2.** [withstand - pressure, heat] ertragen; **I can't stand him** ich kann ihn nicht ausstehen - **3.** [put up with] auslhalten. ◇ *vi* - **1.** [gen] stehen; **to be standing** stehen - **2.** [rise to one's feet] auflstehen - **3.** *UK* POL [be a candidate] kandidieren. ◆ **stand back** *vi* zurückltreten. ◆ **stand by** ◇ *vt insep* - **1.** [person] halten zu - **2.** [promise] halten; [decision, offer] bleiben bei. ◇ *vi* - **1.** [in readiness] sich bereitlhalten - **2.** [not intervene] danebenstehen. ◆ **stand down** *vi* [resign] zurückltreten. ◆ **stand for** *vt insep* - **1.** [signify] stehen für - **2.** [tolerate] hinlnehmen. ◆ **stand in** *vi*: **to stand in for sb** für jn einlspringen. ◆ **stand out** *vi* - **1.** [be clearly visible] herauslstechen - **2.** [be superior] sich ablheben. ◆ **stand up** ◇ *vt sep inf* [boyfriend, girlfriend *etc*] versetzen. ◇ *vi* - **1.** [be on one's feet] stehen - **2.** [rise to one's feet] auflstehen - **3.** [be upright] aufrecht stehen. ◆ **stand up for** *vt insep* einltreten für. ◆ **stand up to** *vt insep* - **1.** [bad treatment] sich wehren gegen; [weather, heat] trotzen *(+ D)* - **2.** [person, boss] sich behaupten gegenüber.

standard ['stændəd] ◇ *adj* Standard-; [spelling, pronunciation] korrekt. ◇ *n* - **1.** [level] Niveau *das*; **up to standard** der Norm entsprechend - **2.** [point of reference] Maßstab *der* - **3.** [flag] Fahne *die*. ◆ **standards** *npl* [principles] Wertvorstellungen *Pl*.

standard lamp *n UK* Stehlampe *die*.

standard of living (*pl* **standards of living**) *n* Lebensstandard *der*.

standby ['stændbaɪ] (*pl* **standbys**) ◇ *n* [substitute] Ersatz *der*; **on standby** in Bereitschaft. ◇ *comp* [ticket] Stand-by-.

stand-in *n* - **1.** [replacement] Vertretung *die* - **2.** [stunt person] Double *das*.

standing ['stændɪŋ] ◇ *adj* [permanent] ständig; [army] stehend. ◇ *n* - **1.** [reputation] Ruf *der* - **2.** [duration] Dauer *die*.

standing order *n* Dauerauftrag *der*.

standing room *n (U)* Stehplätze *Pl*.

standoffish [ˌstænd'ɒfɪʃ] *adj* kühl.

standpoint ['stændpɔɪnt] *n* Standpunkt *der*.

standstill ['stændstɪl] *n*: **to come to a standstill** [stop moving] stehen bleiben; *fig* zum Erliegen kommen.

stand-up *adj*: **stand-up comedian** Komiker *der*, -in *die*; **stand-up comedy** Comedyshow *die*.

stank [stæŋk] *pt* ▷ **stink**.

staple ['steɪpl] ◇ *adj* [principal] Haupt-. ◇ *n* - **1.** [for paper] (Heft)klammer *die* - **2.** [principal commodity] Grundnahrungsmittel *das*. ◇ *vt* zusammenlheften.

stapler ['steɪplər] *n* Hefter *der*.

star [stɑːr] ◇ *n* - **1.** [gen] Stern *der* - **2.** [celebrity] Star *der*. ◇ *comp* [performer] Star-; **star attraction** Spitzenattraktion *die*. ◇ *vi* [actor]: **to star (in)** die Hauptrolle spielen (in *(+ D)*). ◆ **stars** *npl* [horoscope] Sterne *Pl*.

starboard ['stɑːbəd] ◇ *adj* Steuerbord-. ◇ *n*: **to starboard** nach Steuerbord.

starch [stɑːtʃ] *n* Stärke *die*.

stardom ['stɑːdəm] *n* Ruhm *der*.

stare [steər] ◇ *n* starrer Blick. ◇ *vi* starren; **to stare at sb/sthg** jn/etw anlstarren.

stark [stɑːk] ◇ *adj* - **1.** [landscape, room] kahl - **2.** [fact, truth] nackt; [contrast] scharf. ◇ *adv*: **stark naked** splitternackt.

starling ['stɑːlɪŋ] *n* Star *der*.

starry ['stɑːrɪ] *adj* sternenklar.

Stars and Stripes *n*: **the Stars and Stripes** das Sternenbanner.

start [stɑːt] ◇ *n* - **1.** [beginning] Anfang *der*, Beginn *der* - **2.** [jump] Schreck(en) *der* - **3.** SPORT Start *der* - **4.** [lead, advantage] Vorsprung *der*. ◇ *vt* - **1.** [begin] anlfangen, beginnen; **to start work** anlfangen zu arbeiten; **to start a race** ein Rennen starten; **to start doing** OR **to do sthg** anlfangen, etw zu tun; **it started me thinking** es gab mir zu denken - **2.** [engine, car] starten; [cassette player] einlschalten; **to start a fire** [arson] Feuer legen; [for warmth] Feuer machen - **3.** [business] gründen; [shop] auflmachen; [society] ins Leben rufen. ◇ *vi* - **1.** [begin] beginnen, anlfangen; **to start with sb/sthg** mit jm/etw beginnen; **starting from next week** ab nächster Woche; **to start with** [at first] zuerst; [in the first place] erstens; [when ordering meal] als Vorspeise - **2.** [car, engine] starten; [tape] laufen - **3.** [on journey] auflbrechen - **4.** [jump] zusammenlschrecken. ◆ **start off** ◇ *vt sep* [meeting, discussion] beginnen; [rumour] in Umlauf bringen; **this should be enough to start you off** das sollte für den Anfang reichen. ◇ *vi* - **1.** [begin] beginnen, anlfangen - **2.** [on journey] auflbrechen. ◆ **start out** *vi* - **1.** [in life, career] anlfangen; **to start out as sthg** ursprünglich etw sein - **2.** [on journey] auflbrechen. ◆ **start up** ◇ *vt sep* - **1.** [business] gründen; [shop] auflmachen; [society] ins

Leben rufen - **2.** [car, engine] starten. ◇ *vi* - **1.** [guns, music, noise] loslgehen - **2.** [car, engine] starten - **3.** [set up business] anlfangen.

starter ['stɑːtəʳ] *n* - **1.** *UK* [of meal] Vorspeise *die* - **2.** AUT Anlasser *der* - **3.** SPORT [official] Starter *der*, -in *die*; [competitor] Teilnehmer *der*, -in *die*.

starting point ['stɑːtɪŋ-] *n* Ausgangspunkt *der*.

startle ['stɑːtl] *vt* erschrecken.

startling ['stɑːtlɪŋ] *adj* überraschend.

starvation [stɑː'veɪʃn] *n* Hunger *der*; **to die of starvation** verhungern.

starve [stɑːv] ◇ *vt* [deprive of food] auslhungern. ◇ *vi* [have no food] hungern; [die of hunger] verhungern; **I'm starving!** ich habe einen Mordshunger.

state [steɪt] ◇ *n* - **1.** [condition] Zustand *der* - **2.**: **to get into a state** sich auflregen - **3.** [country, region] Staat *der*. ◇ *comp* Staats-. ◇ *vt* [declare] erklären; [specify] anlgeben. ◆ **State** *n* [government]: **the State** der Staat. ◆ **States** *npl* [USA]: **the States** die Vereinigten Staaten *Pl*.

State Department *n US* Außenministerium *das*.

stately ['steɪtlɪ] *adj* [building] stattlich; [person] würdevoll.

statement ['steɪtmənt] *n* - **1.** [declaration & LAW] Aussage *die* - **2.** [from bank] Kontoauszug *der*.

state of mind (*pl* **states of mind**) *n* [mood] Verfassung *die*.

statesman ['steɪtsmən] (*pl* **-men** [-mən]) *n* Staatsmann *der*.

static ['stætɪk] ◇ *adj* [unchanging] konstant. ◇ *n* [on TV, radio] Empfangsstörung *die*.

static electricity *n* Reibungselektrizität *die*.

station ['steɪʃn] ◇ *n* - **1.** [for trains] Bahnhof *der*; [for buses] Busbahnhof *der* - **2.** RADIO Sender *der* - **3.** [police or fire station] Wache *die* - **4.** [position] Platz *der*. ◇ *vt* - **1.** [position] auflstellen - **2.** MIL stationieren.

stationary ['steɪʃnərɪ] *adj* stehend.

stationer ['steɪʃnəʳ] *n*: **stationer's (shop)** Schreibwarenhandlung *die*.

stationery ['steɪʃnərɪ] *n (U)* Schreibwaren *Pl*.

stationmaster ['steɪʃn,mɑːstəʳ] *n* Bahnhofsvorsteher *der*, -in *die*.

station wagon *n US* Kombiwagen *der*.

statistic [stə'tɪstɪk] *n* [number] statistisches Ergebnis; **statistics** Statistik *die*. ◆ **statistics** *n (U)* [science] Statistik *die*.

statistical [stə'tɪstɪkl] *adj* statistisch.

statue ['stætʃuː] *n* Statue *die*.

stature ['stætʃəʳ] *n* - **1.** [height, size] Statur *die* - **2.** [importance] Format *das*.

status ['steɪtəs] *n* - **1.** [legal or social position] Status *der* - **2.** [prestige] Prestige *das*.

status symbol *n* Statussymbol *das*.

statute ['stætjuːt] *n* - **1.** [law] Gesetz *das* - **2.** [of organization] Statut *das*.

statutory ['stætjʊtrɪ] *adj* gesetzlich.

staunch [stɔːntʃ] ◇ *adj* treu. ◇ *vt* [blood] stillen; [flow] stauen.

stave [steɪv] (*pt & pp* **-d** OR **stove**) *n* MUS Notenlinien *Pl*. ◆ **stave off** *vt sep* [danger, disaster] ablwenden; [hunger] lindern.

stay [steɪ] ◇ *vi* bleiben; [as guest] übernachten; **I'm staying at the hotel/with friends** ich wohne im Hotel/bei Freunden; **to stay for dinner** zum Abendessen bleiben; **to stay the night** übernachten. ◇ *n* [visit] Aufenthalt *der*. ◆ **stay in** *vi* [stay at home] zu Hause bleiben. ◆ **stay on** *vi* bleiben. ◆ **stay out** *vi* - **1.** [not come home]: **he stayed out last night** er ist letzte Nacht nicht nach Hause gekommen - **2.** [not get involved]: **to stay out of sthg** sich aus etw rauslhalten. ◆ **stay up** *vi* - **1.** [not go to bed] auflbleiben - **2.** [shelf, picture] hängen bleiben; [socks] oben bleiben.

stead [sted] *n*: **to stand sb in good stead** jm zustattenkommen.

steadfast ['stedfɑːst] *adj* - **1.** [supporter] treu - **2.** [resolve] unerschütterlich - **3.** [gaze] unverwandt.

steadily ['stedɪlɪ] *adv* - **1.** [improve, increase] stetig - **2.** [breathe, move] gleichmäßig - **3.** [look, say] ruhig.

steady ['stedɪ] ◇ *adj* - **1.** [gradual] stetig - **2.** [regular, constant] konstant - **3.** [not shaking, calm] ruhig - **4.** [boyfriend, job] fest - **5.** [worker] zuverlässig. ◇ *vt* - **1.** [boat, camera] ins Gleichgewicht bringen - **2.** [voice, nerves] beruhigen.

steak [steɪk] *n* - **1.** [meat] Steak *das* - **2.** [fish] Fischsteak *das*.

steal [stiːl] (*pt* **stole**, *pp* **stolen**) ◇ *vt liter & fig* stehlen; **to steal sthg from sb** jm etw stehlen. ◇ *vi* [move stealthily] schleichen.

stealthy ['stelθɪ] *adj* verstohlen.

steam [stiːm] ◇ *n* Dampf *der*. ◇ *vt* CULIN dämpfen. ◇ *vi* dampfen. ◆ **steam up** ◇ *vt sep* [window] beschlagen lassen. ◇ *vi* [window, glasses] beschlagen.

steamboat ['stiːmbəʊt] *n* Dampfer *der*.

steam engine *n* Dampflok *die*.

steamroller ['stiːm,rəʊləʳ] *n* Dampfwalze *die*.

steamy ['stiːmɪ] *adj* - **1.** [room] voll Dampf - **2.** *inf* [erotic] heiß.

steel [stiːl] ◇ *n* Stahl *der*. ◇ *comp* Stahl-.

steelworks ['stiːlwɜːks] (*pl inv*) *n* Stahlwerk *das*.

steep [stiːp] ◇ *adj* - **1.** [gen] steil - **2.** *inf* [expensive] gesalzen. ◇ *vt* [soak] einlweichen.

steeple ['stiːpl] *n* Kirchturm *der*.

steer ['stɪəʳ] ◇ *n* [bullock] junger Ochse. ◇ *vt* - **1.** [boat] steuern; [car] lenken - **2.** [person] lotsen. ◇ *vi* steuern; **to steer clear of sb/sthg** *fig* einen großen Bogen um jn/etw machen.

steering ['stɪərɪŋ] *n* Lenkung *die*.

steering wheel *n* Lenkrad *das*.

stem [stem] ◇ *n* - **1.** [of plant, glass] Stiel *der* - **2.** [of pipe] Hals *der* - **3.** GRAM Stamm *der*. ◇ *vt* [stop] ein|dämmen. ◆ **stem from** *vt insep* her|rühren von.

stench [stentʃ] *n* Gestank *der*.

stencil ['stensl] (*UK*) (*US*) ◇ *n* Schablone *die*. ◇ *vt* [design, pattern] mit einer Schablone zeichnen; [words] mit einer Schablone schreiben.

step [step] ◇ *n* - **1.** [pace, stage] Schritt *der*; **to be in step/out of step with public opinion** *fig* im Einklang/nicht im Einklang mit der öffentlichen Meinung sein; **to keep in step with sthg** mit etw Schritt halten; **step by step** Schritt für Schritt - **2.** [measure] Maßnahme *die*; **it's a step in the right direction** das ist immerhin ein Anfang - **3.** [of staircase, ladder] Stufe *die*. ◇ *vi* treten; **step this way** folgen Sie mir bitte; **she stepped off the bus** sie stieg aus dem Bus; **to step on/in sthg** auf/in etw *(A)* treten; **to step on it** *inf* [drive fast] aufs Gas drücken; [hurry up] einen Zahn zulegen. ◆ **steps** *npl* - **1.** [stairs] Stufen *Pl* - **2.** *UK* [stepladder] Trittleiter *die*. ◆ **step down** *vi* [resign] zurück|treten. ◆ **step in** *vi* [intervene] ein|schreiten. ◆ **step up** *vt sep* [increase] steigern.

stepbrother ['stepˌbrʌðəʳ] *n* Stiefbruder *der*.

stepdaughter ['stepˌdɔːtəʳ] *n* Stieftochter *die*.

stepfather ['stepˌfɑːðəʳ] *n* Stiefvater *der*.

stepladder ['stepˌlædəʳ] *n* Trittleiter *die*.

stepmother ['stepˌmʌðəʳ] *n* Stiefmutter *die*.

stepping-stone ['stepɪŋ-] *n* - **1.** [in river] Trittstein *der* - **2.** *fig* [way to success] Sprungbrett *das*.

stepsister ['stepˌsɪstəʳ] *n* Stiefschwester *die*.

stepson ['stepsʌn] *n* Stiefsohn *der*.

stereo ['sterɪəʊ] (*pl* **-s**) ◇ *adj* Stereo-. ◇ *n* - **1.** [stereo system] Stereoanlage *die* - **2.** [stereo sound] Stereo *das*.

stereotype ['sterɪətaɪp] *n* Klischee *das*.

sterile ['steraɪl] *adj* - **1.** [germ-free] steril - **2.** [man, woman, animal] unfruchtbar.

sterilize, -ise ['sterəlaɪz] *vt* sterilisieren.

sterling ['stɜːlɪŋ] ◇ *adj* - **1.** [pound]: **£100 sterling** 100 Pfund Sterling - **2.** [excellent] gediegen. ◇ *n (U)* Pfund *das* Sterling.

sterling silver *n* Sterlingsilber *das*.

stern [stɜːn] ◇ *adj* streng. ◇ *n* Heck *das*.

steroid ['stɪərɔɪd] *n* Steroid *das*.

stethoscope ['steθəskəʊp] *n* Stethoskop *das*.

stew [stjuː] ◇ *n* Eintopf *der*. ◇ *vt* schmoren.

steward ['stjʊəd] *n* - **1.** *UK* [on plane, ship] Steward *der* - **2.** *UK* [at public event] Ordner *der*, -in *die*.

stewardess ['stjʊədɪs] *n* Stewardess *die*.

stick [stɪk] (*pt & pp* **stuck**) ◇ *n* - **1.** [piece of wood] Stock *der* - **2.** [of dynamite, celery, cinnamon, rhubarb] Stange *die*; [of chewing gum, chalk] Stück *das* - **3.** SPORT Schläger *der*. ◇ *vt* - **1.** [with adhesive] kleben; **to stick sthg on** OR **to sthg** etw an etw *(A)* kleben - **2.** [into pocket etc] stecken; **to stick sthg in(to) sthg** etw in etw *(A)* stecken - **3.** *inf* [put] tun - **4.** *UK inf* [tolerate] ertragen. ◇ *vi* - **1.** [arrow, dart, spear] stecken - **2.** [adhere]: **to stick (to)** kleben (an OR auf *(+ D)*) - **3.** [become jammed] klemmen. ◆ **stick out** ◇ *vt sep* - **1.** [extend - tongue, head] heraus|strecken; [- hand] aus|strecken - **2.** *inf* [endure]: **to stick it out** es durch|halten. ◇ *vi* - **1.** [protrude] vor|stehen; [ears] ab|stehen - **2.** *inf* [be noticeable] auf|fallen. ◆ **stick to** *vt insep* [person, decision] bleiben bei; [path] bleiben auf *(+ D)*; [promise] halten. ◆ **stick up** *vi* vor|stehen; [hair] hoch|stehen. ◆ **stick up for** *vt insep* ein|treten für.

sticker ['stɪkəʳ] *n* Aufkleber *der*.

sticking plaster ['stɪkɪŋ-] *n* Heftpflaster *das*.

stick shift *n US* - **1.** [gear lever] Schalthebel *der* - **2.** [car] Auto *das* mit Gangschaltung.

sticky ['stɪkɪ] *adj* - **1.** [hands] klebrig; **sticky tape** Klebeband *das*; **sticky label** Aufkleber *der* - **2.** *inf* [awkward] heikel.

stiff [stɪf] ◇ *adj* - **1.** [gen] steif; [rod, brush] hart; [shoes] fest; [drawer, door] widerspenstig - **2.** [resistance, drink] stark; [penalty] hart - **3.** [difficult] schwer. ◇ *adv inf*: **to be bored stiff** sich zu Tode langweilen; **to be scared stiff** starr vor Angst sein.

stiffen ['stɪfn] ◇ *vt* - **1.** [material] steif machen - **2.** [resistance, resolve] verstärken. ◇ *vi* - **1.** [gen] steif werden; [with horror] erstarren - **2.** [resistance, resolve] sich verstärken.

stifle ['staɪfl] ◇ *vt* - **1.** [suffocate] ersticken - **2.** [suppress] unterdrücken. ◇ *vi* [suffocate] ersticken.

stifling ['staɪflɪŋ] *adj* drückend.

stigma ['stɪgmə] *n* - **1.** [social disgrace] Schande *die* - **2.** BOT Stigma *das*.

stile [staɪl] *n* Zaunübertritt *der*.

stiletto [stɪ'letəʊ] *n UK* [shoe] Stöckelschuh *der*.

still [stɪl] ◇ *adv* - **1.** [gen] noch; **we've still got ten minutes** wir haben noch zehn Minuten; **I still haven't seen it** ich habe es noch nicht gesehen; **still bigger/more important** noch größer/wichtiger; **still more money** noch mehr Geld - **2.** [even now] immer noch; **she could still change her mind** sie könnte es sich immer noch anders überlegen - **3.** [nevertheless] trotzdem; **you still have to pay** Sie müssen trotzdem zahlen - **4.** [motionless]: **to stand still** stilllstehen; **sit still!** sitz still! <> *adj* - **1.** [motionless] bewegungslos; **please be still!** sitz/steh bitte still! - **2.** [calm, quiet] ruhig - **3.** [not windy] windstill - **4.** [not fizzy] ohne Kohlensäure. <> *n* - **1.** PHOT Standfoto *das* - **2.** [for making alcohol] Destillierapparat *der*.

stillborn ['stɪlbɔːn] *adj* tot geboren.

still life (*pl* **-s**) *n* Stillleben *das*.

stilted ['stɪltɪd] *adj* gespreizt.

stilts ['stɪlts] *npl* - **1.** [for person] Stelzen *Pl* - **2.** [for building] Pfähle *Pl*.

stimulate ['stɪmjʊleɪt] *vt* - **1.** [interest] anlregen; [growth, economy] anlkurbeln - **2.** [person - physically] erregen; [- mentally] stimulieren.

stimulating ['stɪmjʊleɪtɪŋ] *adj* - **1.** [physically] belebend - **2.** [mentally] stimulierend.

stimulus ['stɪmjʊləs] (*pl* **-li** [-laɪ]) *n* - **1.** [gen] Anreiz *der* - **2.** BIOL Reiz *der*.

sting [stɪŋ] (*pt & pp* **stung**) <> *n* - **1.** [wound, pain, mark] Stich *der* - **2.** [part of bee, wasp, scorpion] Stachel *der*. <> *vt* - **1.** [subj: bee, wasp, scorpion] stechen; **I was stung by the nettles** ich habe mich an den Brennnesseln verbrannt - **2.** *fig* [subj: remark, criticism] schmerzen. <> *vi* [bee, wasp, scorpion] stechen; [nettle, smoke, eyes, skin] brennen.

stingy ['stɪndʒɪ] *adj inf* geizig.

stink [stɪŋk] (*pt* **stank** OR **stunk**, *pp* **stunk**) <> *n* Gestank *der*. <> *vi* [smell] stinken.

stint [stɪnt] <> *n* [period of time] Zeit *die*; **he did a two-year stint as editor** er arbeitete zwei Jahre lang als Redakteur. <> *vi*: **to stint on sthg** mit etw sparen.

stipulate ['stɪpjʊleɪt] *vt* festllegen.

stir [stɜːʳ] <> *n* [excitement] Aufsehen *das*. <> *vt* - **1.** [mix] umlrühren - **2.** [subj: wind] spielen mit - **3.** [excite] bewegen. <> *vi* - **1.** [move] sich bewegen - **2.** [emotion] wach werden. ◆ **stir up** *vt sep* - **1.** [dust, mud] auflwühlen - **2.** [trouble, feelings, memories] wachlrufen.

stirrup ['stɪrəp] *n* Steigbügel *der*.

stitch [stɪtʃ] <> *n* - **1.** [in sewing, for wound] Stich *der*; [in knitting] Masche *die* - **2.** [pain]: **to have a stitch** Seitenstechen haben. <> *vt* nähen.

stoat [stəʊt] *n* Hermelin *das*.

stock [stɒk] <> *n* - **1.** [supply] Vorrat *der* - **2.** *(U)* COMM [of shop] Lagerbestand *der*; **in stock** vorrätig; **out of stock** nicht vorrätig - **3.** FIN: **stocks and shares** Wertpapiere und Aktien - **4.** *(U)* [ancestry] Herkunft *die* - **5.** CULIN Brühe *die* - **6.** [livestock] Nutzvieh *das* - **7.** *phr*: **to take stock (of)** Bilanz ziehen (über *(+ A)*). <> *adj* [typical] stereotyp. <> *vt* - **1.** [have in stock] auf Lager haben - **2.** [shelves] auflfüllen; [lake with fish] bestücken. ◆ **stock up** *vi*: **to stock up (on** OR **with)** sich einldecken (mit).

stockbroker ['stɒk,brəʊkəʳ] *n* Börsenmakler *der*, -in *die*.

stock cube *n UK* Brühwürfel *der*.

stock exchange *n* Börse *die*.

stockholder ['stɒk,həʊldəʳ] *n US* Aktionär *der*, -in *die*.

Stockholm ['stɒkhəʊm] *n* Stockholm *nt*.

stocking ['stɒkɪŋ] *n* Strumpf *der*.

stock market *n* Börse *die*.

stockpile ['stɒkpaɪl] <> *n* Lager *das*. <> *vt* horten.

stocktaking ['stɒk,teɪkɪŋ] *n (U)* Inventur *die*.

stocky ['stɒkɪ] *adj* stämmig.

stodgy ['stɒdʒɪ] *adj* [food] schwer.

stoical ['stəʊɪkl] *adj* stoisch.

stoke [stəʊk] *vt* [fire] schüren.

stole [stəʊl] *pt* ▷ **steal**.

stolen ['stəʊln] *pp* ▷ **steal**.

stolid ['stɒlɪd] *adj* stur.

stomach ['stʌmək] <> *n* - **1.** [organ] Magen *der* - **2.** [belly] Bauch *der*. <> *vt* [tolerate] ertragen.

stomachache ['stʌməkeɪk] *n* Magenschmerzen *Pl*.

stomach upset *n* Magenverstimmung *die*.

stone [stəʊn] <> *n* - **1.** [gen] Stein *der* - **2.** (*pl inv* OR **-s**) [unit of measurement] = *6,35 kg*. <> *comp* aus Stein; [bridge, wall] Stein-. <> *vt* mit Steinen bewerfen.

stone-cold *adj* eiskalt.

stonework ['stəʊnwɜːk] *n* Mauerwerk *das*.

stood [stʊd] *pt & pp* ▷ **stand**.

stool [stuːl] *n* [seat] Hocker *der*.

stoop [stuːp] <> *n* [bent back]: **to walk with a stoop** gebeugt gehen. <> *vi* - **1.** [bend forwards] sich bücken - **2.** [have a stoop] gebeugt gehen.

stop [stɒp] <> *n* - **1.** [of bus] Haltestelle *die*; [of train] Station *die* - **2.** [in journey] Halt *der*; [longer] Aufenthalt *der* - **3.** [standstill]: **to put a stop to sthg** einer Sache *(D)* ein Ende machen - **4.** [in punctuation] Punkt *der*. <> *vt* - **1.** [halt - person, car] anlhalten; [- machine, engine] ablstellen; [- ball] stoppen; **to stop doing sthg** auflhören, etw zu tun; **to stop smoking** mit dem Rauchen auflhören - **2.** [prevent] verhindern; **to stop sb from doing sthg** jn daran hindern, etw zu tun; **to stop sthg from happening** verhindern, dass etw geschieht - **3.** [hole, gap] stopfen. <> *vi* - **1.** [come to an end] auflhören - **2.** [halt] anlhalten; [walker, machine, watch] stehen bleiben; [on journey] Halt machen - **3.** [stay] bleiben. ◆ **stop off** *vi* Halt machen. ◆ **stop up** *vt sep* [block] zulstopfen.

stopgap ['stɒpgæp] *n* Notlösung *die*.

stopover ['stɒp,əʊvəʳ] *n* Zwischenstation *die*.

stoppage ['stɒpɪdʒ] *n* - **1.** [strike] Streik *der* - **2.** *UK* [deduction] Abzug *der*.

stopper ['stɒpəʳ] *n* Pfropfen *der*.

stopwatch ['stɒpwɒtʃ] *n* Stoppuhr *die*.

storage ['stɔ:rɪdʒ] *n* - **1.** [act of storing] Lagerung *die* - **2.** COMPUT Speichern *das*.

store [stɔ:ʳ] ◇ *n* - **1.** *esp US* [shop] Laden *der*, Geschäft *das*; [department store] Kaufhaus *das* - **2.** [supply]: **store of sthg** Vorrat *der* an etw *(D)* - **3.** [storage place] Lager *das*. ◇ *vt* - **1.** [keep, save - address, details] auflbewahren; [- goods, provisions] lagern; [- furniture] einlstellen - **2.** COMPUT speichern. ◆ **store up** *vt sep* [information] anlsammeln; **to store food** Lebensmittelvorräte anlegen.

storekeeper ['stɔ:,ki:pəʳ] *n US* Ladenbesitzer *der*, -in *die*.

storeroom ['stɔ:rʊm] *n* Lagerraum *der*.

storey *UK (pl* **-s)**, **story** *US (pl* **-ies)** ['stɔ:rɪ] *n* Stockwerk *das*.

stork [stɔ:k] *n* Storch *der*.

storm [stɔ:m] ◇ *n* - **1.** [bad weather] Sturm *der* - **2.** [violent reaction - of abuse, tears] Flut *die*; [- of protest] Sturm *der*. ◇ *vt* - **1.** MIL stürmen - **2.** [say angrily] toben. ◇ *vi* [go angrily] stürmen.

stormy ['stɔ:mɪ] *adj liter* & *fig* stürmisch.

story ['stɔ:rɪ] *n* - **1.** [tale, history] Geschichte *die* - **2.** [article - in newspaper] Artikel *der*; [- on TV/radio news] Bericht *der* - **3.** *euph* [lie] Märchen *das* - **4.** *US* = **storey**.

stout [staʊt] ◇ *adj* - **1.** [corpulent] korpulent - **2.** [strong] kräftig; [boots] fest - **3.** [brave] tapfer. ◇ *n* Starkbier *das*.

stove [stəʊv] ◇ *pt* & *pp* ▷ **stave**. ◇ *n* - **1.** [for cooking] Herd *der* - **2.** [for heating] Ofen *der*.

stow [stəʊ] *vt*: **to stow sthg (away)** etw verstauen.

stowaway ['stəʊəweɪ] *n* blinder Passagier.

straddle ['strædl] *vt* - **1.** [subj: person - chair] rittlings sitzen auf *(+ D)*; [- gap] breitbeinig stehen über *(+ D)* - **2.** [subj: bridge] überspannen; **the town straddles the border** der Ort erstreckt sich zu beiden Seiten der Grenze.

straggle ['strægl] *vi* - **1.** [buildings] verstreut liegen; [plant] wuchern - **2.** [person, group] zurücklbleiben.

straggler ['stræglәʳ] *n* Nachzügler *der*, -in *die*.

straight [streɪt] ◇ *adj* - **1.** [not curved, level, upright] gerade - **2.** [not curly] glatt - **3.** [honest, frank] ehrlich, offen - **4.** [tidy] ordentlich; **to put a room straight** ein Zimmer auflräumen - **5.** [simple - exchange] einfach; [- choice] klar - **6.** [undiluted] pur - **7.** *phr*: **to get sthg straight** etw klarlstellen. ◇ *adv* - **1.** [in a straight line, upright] gerade - **2.** [directly, immediately] direkt - **3.** [honestly, frankly] offen - **4.** [undiluted] pur. ◆ **straight off** *adv* sofort. ◆ **straight out** *adv* rundheraus.

straightaway [,streɪtə'weɪ] *adv* sofort.

straighten ['streɪtn] *vt* - **1.** [tidy - dress] gerade ziehen; [- room, desk] auflräumen - **2.** [make straight] begradigen - **3.** [make level] auslrichten. ◆ **straighten out** *vt sep* [sort out] klären.

straightforward [,streɪt'fɔ:wəd] *adj* - **1.** [easy] einfach - **2.** [honest, frank] offen, ehrlich.

strain [streɪn] ◇ *n* - **1.** [gen] Belastung *die* - **2.** MED [of muscle] Zerrung *die*; [of back] Überanstrengung *die*. ◇ *vt* - **1.** [work hard - eyes] überanstrengen - **2.** MED [injure]: **to strain a muscle/one's back** sich einen Muskel zerren/seinen Rücken überanstrengen - **3.** [overtax - resources] überbeanspruchen; [- patience] auf die Probe stellen - **4.** [drain] durch ein Sieb gießen - **5.** TECH [rope, girder, ceiling] belasten. ◇ *vi*: **to strain to do sthg** sich anlstrengen, etw zu tun. ◆ **strains** *npl liter* [of music] Klänge *Pl*.

strained [streɪnd] *adj* - **1.** [forced] angestrengt - **2.** [tense] angespannt - **3.** MED [sprained] gezerrt.

strainer ['streɪnəʳ] *n* Sieb *das*.

strait [streɪt] *n* GEOG Meerenge *die*. ◆ **straits** *npl*: **in dire** OR **desperate straits** in einer Notlage.

straitjacket ['streɪt,dʒækɪt] *n* Zwangsjacke *die*.

straitlaced [,streɪt'leɪst] *adj pej* spießig.

strand [strænd] *n* Faden *der*; [of hair] Strähne *die*.

stranded ['strændɪd] *adj* [person, car] festsitzend.

strange [streɪndʒ] *adj* - **1.** [unusual, unexpected] seltsam - **2.** [unfamiliar] fremd.

stranger ['streɪndʒəʳ] *n* - **1.** [unknown person] Unbekannte *der, die*; **she's a complete stranger to me** ich kenne sie überhaupt nicht - **2.** [person from elsewhere] Fremde *der, die*.

strangle ['stræŋgl] *vt* - **1.** [kill] erwürgen - **2.** *fig* [stifle] ersticken.

strap [stræp] ◇ *n* - **1.** [for carrying] Riemen *der* - **2.** [for fastening - of dress, bra] Träger *der*; [- of watch] Armband *das*. ◇ *vt* [fasten]: **to strap sthg (on)to sthg** etw auf etw *(A)* schnallen.

strapping ['stræpɪŋ] *adj* stramm.

strategic [strə'ti:dʒɪk] *adj* strategisch.

strategy ['strætɪdʒɪ] *n* Strategie *die*.

straw [strɔ:] *n* - **1.** [dried corn] Stroh *das* - **2.** [for drinking] Strohhalm *der*.

strawberry ['strɔ:bərɪ] ◇ *n* Erdbeere *die*. ◇ *comp* Erdbeer-.

stray [streɪ] ◇ *adj* - **1.** [cat, dog] streunend - **2.** [bullet] verirrt. ◇ *vi* - **1.** [person, animal] herum|streunen; **to stray from the path** vom Weg ab|weichen - **2.** [thoughts, mind] ab|schweifen.

streak [stri:k] ◇ *n* - **1.** [mark, line] Streifen *der*; **a streak of lightning** ein Blitz(strahl) - **2.** [in character] Zug *der*. ◇ *vi* [move quickly] sausen.

stream [stri:m] ◇ *n* - **1.** [gen] Strom *der* - **2.** [brook] Bach *der* - **3.** [of abuse, complaints] Flut *die* - **4.** *UK* SCH Leistungsgruppe *die*. ◇ *vt* *UK* SCH in Leistungsgruppen ein|teilen. ◇ *vi* strömen.

streamer ['stri:mər] *n* [for party] Luftschlange *die*.

streamlined ['stri:mlaɪnd] *adj* - **1.** [aerodynamic] stromlinienförmig - **2.** [efficient] rationalisiert.

street [stri:t] *n* Straße *die*.

streetcar ['stri:tkɑ:r] *n* *US* Straßenbahn *die*.

street lamp, street light *n* Straßenlaterne *die*.

street plan *n* Stadtplan *der*.

strength [streŋθ] *n* - **1.** [gen] Stärke *die* - **2.** *(U)* [confidence, courage] Kraft *die* - **3.** [solidity] Stabilität *die*.

strengthen ['streŋθn] *vt* - **1.** [gen] stärken - **2.** [team, structure, resolve] verstärken - **3.** [friendship, ties, bond] festigen - **4.** [make braver, more confident] bestärken.

strenuous ['strenjʊəs] *adj* [exercise] anstrengend; [effort] gewaltig.

stress [stres] ◇ *n* - **1.** [emphasis]: **to lay** OR **put stress on sthg** etw besonders betonen - **2.** [tension, anxiety] Stress *der* - **3.** TECH [physical pressure]: **stress (on sthg)** Druck *der* (auf etw *(A)*) - **4.** LING [on word, syllable] Betonung *die*. ◇ *vt* [emphasize & LING] betonen.

stressful ['stresfʊl] *adj* stressig.

stretch [stretʃ] ◇ *n* - **1.** [area] Stück *das* - **2.** [period of time] Zeitspanne *die*; **for a five-year stretch** für fünf Jahre. ◇ *vt* - **1.** [pull longer or wider] dehnen - **2.** [pull taut] spannen - **3.** [extend to full length] aus|strecken - **4.** [rules, meaning, truth]: **to stretch the rules** eine Ausnahme machen; **to stretch the truth** übertreiben - **5.** [budget, resources] strecken - **6.** [provide challenge for] fordern. ◇ *vi* - **1.** [area]: **to stretch over** sich aus|dehnen über *(+ A)*; **to stretch from to** reichen von bis - **2.** [person, animal] sich strecken - **3.** [material, elastic] sich dehnen. ◆ **stretch out** ◇ *vt sep* [hold out] aus|strecken. ◇ *vi* [lie down] sich aus|strecken.

stretcher ['stretʃər] *n* Trage *die*.

strew [stru:] (*pt* **-ed**, *pp* **strewn** [stru:n] OR **-ed**) *vt* [scatter untidily]: **to be strewn with sthg** [freckles, confetti] mit etw übersät sein; **the streets were strewn with litter** die Straßen waren voller Müll.

stricken ['strɪkn] *adj*: **to be stricken by** OR **with sthg** [doubt, horror, panic] von etw erfüllt sein; [illness] an etw *(D)* leiden.

strict [strɪkt] *adj* - **1.** [severe] streng - **2.** [exact, precise] genau; **in the strictest sense of a word** im engsten Sinne des Wortes.

strictly ['strɪktlɪ] *adv* - **1.** [severely, rigidly, absolutely] streng - **2.** [precisely, exactly] genau; **strictly speaking** genau genommen - **3.** [exclusively] ausschließlich.

stride [straɪd] (*pt* **strode**, *pp* **stridden** ['strɪdn]) ◇ *n* [step] Schritt *der*; **to take sthg in one's stride** *fig* mit etw leicht fertig werden. ◇ *vi* schreiten.

strident ['straɪdnt] *adj* - **1.** [voice, sound] durchdringend - **2.** [demand] lautstark.

strike [straɪk] (*pt & pp* **struck**) ◇ *n* - **1.** [refusal to work, do sthg] Streik *der*; **to be (out) on strike** streiken; **to go on strike** in Streik treten - **2.** MIL [attack] Angriff *der* - **3.** [find] Fund *der*. ◇ *vt* - **1.** [hit deliberately] schlagen; [hit accidentally - car] fahren gegen; [- boat] auf|laufen auf *(+ A)* - **2.** [subj: hurricane, disaster, lightning] treffen - **3.** [subj: thought]: **it strikes me that ...** mir fällt auf, dass ...; **he strikes me as very capable** er scheint mir sehr fähig zu sein - **4.** [bargain] aus|handeln - **5.** [match] an|zünden - **6.** [chime] schlagen. ◇ *vi* - **1.** [stop working] streiken - **2.** [happen suddenly - disaster, hurricane] los|brechen; [- lightning] ein|schlagen - **3.** [attack] an|greifen - **4.** [chime] schlagen. ◆ **strike down** *vt sep* nieder|schlagen. ◆ **strike out** ◇ *vt sep* durch|streichen. ◇ *vi* - **1.** [head out] los|ziehen - **2.** [do sthg different]: **to strike out on one's own** eigene Wege gehen. ◆ **strike up** *vt insep* - **1.** [friendship, conversation] an|fangen - **2.** [music] an|fangen zu spielen.

striker ['straɪkər] *n* - **1.** [person on strike] Streikende *der, die* - **2.** FTBL Stürmer *der*, -in *die*.

striking ['straɪkɪŋ] *adj* - **1.** [noticeable, unusual] auffallend - **2.** [attractive] umwerfend.

string [strɪŋ] (*pt & pp* **strung**) *n* - **1.** [gen] Schnur *die*; **to pull strings** Beziehungen spielen lassen - **2.** [of onions] Zopf *der*; **string of pearls** [necklace] Perlenkette *die* - **3.** [series] Reihe *die* - **4.** [for musical instrument, tennis racket] Saite *die*; [for bow] Sehne *die*. ◆ **strings** *npl* MUS: **the strings** die Streicher *Pl*. ◆ **string out** *vt sep* [disperse]: **to be strung out** verteilt sein. ◆ **string together** *vt sep fig* [words, sentences] aneinander|fügen.

string bean *n* Stangenbohne *die*.

stringent ['strɪndʒənt] *adj* streng.

strip [strɪp] ◇ *n* - **1.** [of fabric, paper, land, water] Streifen *der* - **2.** *UK* SPORT [clothes] Tri-

kot *das*. ◇ *vt* - **1.** [undress] auslziehen - **2.** [remove - paint] ablkratzen; [- wallpaper] ablziehen. ◇ *vi* [undress] sich auslziehen.
◆ **strip off** *vi* sich auslziehen.

strip cartoon *n UK* Comic *der*.

stripe [straɪp] *n* - **1.** [band of colour] Streifen *der* - **2.** [sign of rank] Ärmelstreifen *der*.

striped [straɪpt] *adj* gestreift.

stripper ['strɪpəʳ] *n* - **1.** [performer of striptease] Stripper *der*, -in *die* - **2.** [liquid] Entferner *der*; [tool] Spachtel *der*.

striptease ['stripti:z] *n* Striptease *der*.

strive [straɪv] (*pt* **strove**, *pp* **striven** ['strɪvn]) *vi fml*: **to strive for sthg** nach etw streben; **to strive to do sthg** bemüht sein, etw zu tun.

strode [strəʊd] *pt* ▷ **stride**.

stroke [strəʊk] ◇ *n* - **1.** MED Schlaganfall *der* - **2.** [of pen, brush] Strich *der* - **3.** [in swimming - movement] Zug *der*; [- style] Stil *der* - **4.** [in rowing, in ball game, of clock] Schlag *der* - **5.** *UK* TYPO [oblique] Schrägstrich *der* - **6.** [piece]: **a stroke of genius** ein Geniestreich; **a stroke of luck** ein Glücksfall; **at a stroke** mit einem Streich. ◇ *vt* streicheln.

stroll [strəʊl] ◇ *n* Spaziergang *der*. ◇ *vi* spazieren gehen.

stroller ['strəʊləʳ] *n US* [for baby] Sportwagen *der*.

strong [strɒŋ] *adj* - **1.** [gen] stark; **strong point** Stärke *die* - **2.** [physically powerful, healthy] kräftig - **3.** [solid, sturdy] stabil; [measures] energisch - **4.** [argument, case, evidence] überzeugend.

stronghold ['strɒŋhəʊld] *n fig* Hochburg *die*.

strongly ['strɒŋlɪ] *adv* - **1.** [sturdily, solidly] solide - **2.** [in degree or intensity] stark - **3.** [support] energisch; **do you feel strongly about it?** ist es Ihnen wichtig?

strong room *n* Tresorraum *der*.

strove [strəʊv] *pt* ▷ **strive**.

struck [strʌk] *pt* & *pp* ▷ **strike**.

structure ['strʌktʃəʳ] *n* - **1.** [organization, arrangement] Struktur *die* - **2.** [building, construction] Konstruktion *die*.

struggle ['strʌgl] ◇ *n* Kampf *der*; **a struggle for sthg** ein Kampf um etw; **it will be a struggle to finish on time** wir werden uns sehr anstrengen müssen, um rechtzeitig fertig zu werden. ◇ *vi* - **1.** [try hard, strive] kämpfen; **to struggle for sthg** um etw kämpfen; **she struggled to reach the switch** sie hatte Mühe, an den Schalter zu kommen - **2.** [fight]: **to struggle (with sb)** (mit jm) kämpfen.

strum [strʌm] *vt* klimpern; [guitar] klimpern auf *(+ D)*.

strung [strʌŋ] *pt* & *pp* ▷ **string**.

strut [strʌt] ◇ *n* CONSTR Strebe *die*. ◇ *vi* stolzieren.

stub [stʌb] ◇ *n* - **1.** [of cigarette, pencil] Stummel *der* - **2.** [of ticket, cheque] Abschnitt *der*. ◇ *vt*: **to stub one's toe** sich den Zeh stoßen.
◆ **stub out** *vt sep* ausldrücken.

stubble ['stʌbl] *n (U)* Stoppeln *Pl*.

stubborn ['stʌbən] *adj* - **1.** [person - resolute] hartnäckig; [- unreasonable] dickköpfig, stur - **2.** [stain] hartnäckig.

stuck [stʌk] ◇ *pt* & *pp* ▷ **stick**. ◇ *adj* - **1.** [fixed tightly, jammed - window, lid] verklemmt; [- finger, toe, garment] eingeklemmt - **2.** [stumped]: **I'm stuck** ich komme nicht weiter - **3.** [stranded]: **he got stuck in Birmingham** er saß in Birmingham fest - **4.** [in an unpleasant situation, trapped]: **to be stuck** festlsitzen.

stuck-up *adj inf pej* hochnäsig.

stud [stʌd] *n* - **1.** [metal decoration] Niete *die* - **2.** [earring] Ohrstecker *der* - **3.** *UK* [on boot, shoe] Stollen *der* - **4.** [place for breeding horses] Gestüt *das*.

studded ['stʌdɪd] *adj*: **studded with sthg** mit etw besetzt.

student ['stju:dnt] ◇ *n* - **1.** [at college, university] Student *der*, -in *die* - **2.** [scholar]: **to be a student of history/human nature** sich für Geschichte/die menschliche Natur interessieren. ◇ *comp* Studenten-.

student loan *n UK* Studentendarlehen *das*.

studio ['stju:dɪəʊ] (*pl* **-s**) *n* - **1.** [artist's workroom] Atelier *das* - **2.** CIN, RADIO & TV Studio *das*.

studio flat *UK*, **studio apartment** *US n* Atelierwohnung *die*.

studious ['stju:djəs] *adj* fleißig.

study ['stʌdɪ] ◇ *n* - **1.** *(U)* [learning] Studium *das* - **2.** [piece of research] Untersuchung *die* - **3.** [room] Arbeitszimmer *das*. ◇ *vt* & *vi* studieren.

stuff [stʌf] ◇ *n (U) inf* - **1.** [matter, things, substance] Zeug *das* - **2.** [belongings] Sachen *Pl*. ◇ *vt* - **1.** [push, put] stopfen - **2.** [fill, cram]: **to stuff sthg (with sthg)** etw (mit etw) vollstopfen - **3.** CULIN füllen.

stuffed [stʌft] *adj* - **1.** [filled, crammed]: **stuffed with sthg** mit etw vollgestopft - **2.** *inf* [with food] voll - **3.** CULIN gefüllt - **4.** [animal] ausgestopft.

stuffing ['stʌfɪŋ] *n (U)* - **1.** [for furniture] Polsterung *die* - **2.** [for toys & CULIN] Füllung *die*.

stuffy ['stʌfɪ] *adj* - **1.** [room] stickig - **2.** [formal, old-fashioned] spießig.

stumble ['stʌmbl] *vi* - **1.** [trip] stolpern - **2.** [hesitate, make mistake] stocken.
◆ **stumble across, stumble on** *vt insep* stoßen auf *(+ A)*; [person] stolpern über *(+ A)*.

stumbling block ['stʌmblɪŋ-] *n* Hindernis *das*.

stump [stʌmp] ◇ *n* [remaining part] Stumpf *der*. ◇ *vt* [subj: question, problem]: **to be stumped by a problem/question** keine Lösung/Antwort wissen.

stun [stʌn] *vt* - **1.** [knock unconscious] bewusstlos schlagen - **2.** [shock, surprise] verblüffen.

stung [stʌŋ] *pt & pp* ▷ **sting**.

stunk [stʌŋk] *pt & pp* ▷ **stink**.

stunning ['stʌnɪŋ] *adj* - **1.** [beautiful] atemberaubend - **2.** [shocking] schrecklich; [surprising] sensationell.

stunt [stʌnt] ◇ *n* - **1.** [for publicity] Werbetrick *der* - **2.** CIN Stunt *der*. ◇ *vt* hemmen.

stunt man *n* Stuntman *der*.

stupefy ['stju:pɪfaɪ] *vt* - **1.** [tire, bore] abstumpfen lassen - **2.** [surprise] verblüffen.

stupendous [stju:'pendəs] *adj inf* - **1.** [wonderful] toll - **2.** [very large] enorm.

stupid ['stju:pɪd] *adj* - **1.** [foolish] dumm - **2.** *inf* [wretched, damned] blöd.

stupidity [stju:'pɪdətɪ] *n* Dummheit *die*.

sturdy ['stɜ:dɪ] *adj* kräftig; [furniture, bridge] stabil.

stutter ['stʌtər] *vi* [in speaking] stottern.

sty [staɪ] *n* Schweinestall *der*.

stye [staɪ] *n* Gerstenkorn *das*.

style [staɪl] ◇ *n* - **1.** [gen] Stil *der*; **in style** im großen Stil; **that's not my style** das ist nicht meine Art - **2.** [fashion, design] Mode *die*. ◇ *vt* [hair] stylen.

stylish ['staɪlɪʃ] *adj* elegant.

stylist ['staɪlɪst] *n* [hairdresser] Stylist *der*, -in *die*.

stylus ['staɪləs] (*pl* **-es**) *n* [on record player] Nadel *die*.

suave [swɑ:v] *adj* gewandt; *pej* glatt.

sub [sʌb] *n inf* - **1.** SPORT (*abbr of* **substitute**) Ersatz *der* - **2.** *abbr of* **submarine** - **3.** *UK abbr of* **subscription**.

subconscious [ˌsʌb'kɒnʃəs] ◇ *adj* unterbewusst. ◇ *n*: **the subconscious** das Unterbewusstsein.

subcontract [ˌsʌbkən'trækt] *vt* an (ein) Subunternehmen vergeben.

subdue [səb'dju:] *vt* - **1.** [enemy, rioters, crowds] unterwerfen - **2.** [feelings, passions] unterdrücken.

subdued [səb'dju:d] *adj* - **1.** [person] ruhig - **2.** [sound, feelings, lighting, colour] gedämpft.

subject ◇ *adj* ['sʌbdʒekt] - **1.** [subordinate]: **subject to sthg** etw *(D)* unterworfen - **2.** [liable]: **subject to sthg** [disease] anfällig für etw; **subject to tax** steuerpflichtig; **prices subject to change** COMM Preisänderungen vorbehalten. ◇ *n* ['sʌbdʒekt] - **1.** [topic under consideration] Thema *das*; **he is the subject of an inquiry** es wird eine Untersuchung über ihn durchgeführt - **2.** GRAM Subjekt *das* - **3.** SCH & UNIV Fach *das* - **4.** [citizen] Staatsbürger *der*, -in *die*. ◇ *vt* [səb'dʒekt] - **1.** [subjugate] unterwerfen - **2.** [force to experience]: **to subject sb to sthg** [punishment, inquiry] jn einer Sache *(D)* unterziehen. ◆ **subject to** *prep* ['sʌbdʒekt] [depending on] abhängig von.

subjective [səb'dʒektɪv] *adj* subjektiv.

subject matter *n* Stoff *der*.

subjunctive [səb'dʒʌŋktɪv] *n* GRAM: **subjunctive (mood)** Konjunktiv *der*.

sublet [ˌsʌb'let] (*pt & pp inv*) *vt* untervermieten.

sublime [sə'blaɪm] *adj* [wonderful] erhaben.

submachine gun [ˌsʌbmə'ʃi:n-] *n* Maschinenpistole *die*.

submarine [ˌsʌbmə'ri:n] *n* U-Boot *das*.

submerge [səb'mɜ:dʒ] ◇ *vt* - **1.** [flood] überschwemmen - **2.** [plunge into liquid] ein|tauchen. ◇ *vi* tauchen.

submission [səb'mɪʃn] *n* - **1.** [obedience, capitulation] Unterwerfung *die* - **2.** [presentation] Einreichen *das*.

submissive [səb'mɪsɪv] *adj* unterwürfig.

submit [səb'mɪt] ◇ *vt* [present] ein|reichen. ◇ *vi* [admit defeat] sich ergeben; *(phrase)*: **to submit to sb/sthg** sich jm/etw unterwerfen.

subordinate ◇ *adj* [sə'bɔ:dɪnət] *fml* [less important]: **subordinate (to sthg)** (einer Sache *(D)*) untergeordnet. ◇ *n* [sə'bɔ:dɪnət] Untergebene *der, die*.

subpoena [sə'pi:nə] (*pt & pp* **-ed**) ◇ *n* LAW Vorladung *die*. ◇ *vt* LAW vor|laden.

subscribe [səb'skraɪb] *vi* - **1.** [to magazine, newspaper]: **to subscribe to sthg** etw abonnieren - **2.** [to view, belief]: **to subscribe to sthg** sich einer Sache *(D)* an|schließen.

subscriber [səb'skraɪbər] *n* - **1.** [to magazine, newspaper] Abonnent *der*, -in *die* - **2.** [to service] Teilnehmer *der*, -in *die*.

subscription [səb'skrɪpʃn] *n* [to newspaper, magazine] Abonnement *das*; [to club, organization] Mitgliedsbeitrag *der*.

subsequent ['sʌbsɪkwənt] *adj* nachfolgend.

subsequently ['sʌbsɪkwəntlɪ] *adv* anschließend.

subservient [səb'sɜ:vjənt] *adj* [servile]: **subservient (to sb)** (jm gegenüber) unterwürfig.

subside [səb'saɪd] *vi* - **1.** [grow less intense] nach|lassen - **2.** [grow quieter] leiser werden - **3.** [sink - building, ground] sich senken; [- river] sinken.

subsidence [səb'saɪdns, 'sʌbsɪdns] *n (U)* CONSTR Bodensenkung *die*.

subsidiary [səb'sɪdjərɪ] ◇ *adj* untergeordnet. ◇ *n*: **subsidiary (company)** Tochter(gesellschaft) *die*.

subsidize, -ise ['sʌbsɪdaɪz] *vt* subventionieren.

subsidy ['sʌbsɪdɪ] *n* Subvention *die*.

substance ['sʌbstəns] *n* - **1.** [material, tangibility] Substanz *die* - **2.** [essence, gist] Kern *der* - **3.** *(U)* [importance] Gewicht *das*.

substantial [səb'stænʃl] *adj* - **1.** [large, considerable] beträchtlich - **2.** [solid, well-built] solide.

substantially [səb'stænʃəlɪ] *adv* - **1.** [quite a lot] beträchtlich - **2.** [mainly] im Wesentlichen.

substitute ['sʌbstɪtju:t] ◇ *n* - **1.** [replacement]: **substitute (für)** Ersatz *der* (für) - **2.** SPORT Ersatzspieler *der*, -in *die*. ◇ *vt*: **to substitute sb/sthg for sb/sthg** jn/etw durch jn/etw ersetzen.

subtitle ['sʌb,taɪtl] *n* [of book] Untertitel *der*. ◆ **subtitles** *npl* CIN Untertitel *Pl*.

subtle ['sʌtl] *adj* - **1.** [nuance, difference] fein; [colour, music] zart - **2.** [comment, method] subtil.

subtlety ['sʌtltɪ] *n* - **1.** [of difference] Feinheit *die*; [of colour, music] Zartheit *die* - **2.** [of comment, method] Subtilität *die*.

subtotal ['sʌb,təʊtl] *n* Zwischensumme *die*.

subtract [səb'trækt] *vt*: **to subtract sthg (from sthg)** etw (von etw) subtrahieren OR abziehen.

subtraction [səb'trækʃn] *n* Subtraktion *die*.

suburb ['sʌbɜ:b] *n* Vorort *der*. ◆ **suburbs** *npl* Vororte *Pl*.

suburban [sə'bɜ:bn] *adj* - **1.** [of suburbs] Vorort- - **2.** *pej* [boring] spießig.

suburbia [sə'bɜ:bɪə] *n (U)* die Vororte *Pl*.

subversive [səb'vɜ:sɪv] *adj* subversiv.

subway ['sʌbweɪ] *n* - **1.** *UK* [underground walkway] Unterführung *die* - **2.** *US* [underground railway] U-Bahn *die*.

succeed [sək'si:d] ◇ *vt* nachlfolgen *(+ D)*; [thing, event] folgen *(+ D)*. ◇ *vi* [be successful] erfolgreich sein; **he succeeded in persuading her** es gelang ihm, sie zu überreden.

succeeding [sək'si:dɪŋ] *adj fml* nachfolgend.

success [sək'ses] *n* Erfolg *der*.

successful [sək'sesfʊl] *adj* erfolgreich.

succession [sək'seʃn] *n* [series] Folge *die*.

successive [sək'sesɪv] *adj* aufeinander folgend.

succinct [sək'sɪŋkt] *adj* prägnant.

succumb [sə'kʌm] *vi* [to a bad influence]: **to succumb to sthg** einer Sache *(D)* erliegen.

such [sʌtʃ] ◇ *adj* - **1.** [gen] solche(r) (s); **such people** solche Leute; **I've never heard such nonsense** ich habe noch nie so einen Unsinn gehört!; **shoplifting and such crimes** Ladendiebstahl und derartige Delikte; **there's no such thing** so etwas gibt es nicht; **countries such as Spain and France** Länder wie Spanien und Frankreich - **2.** [whatever]: **I've spent such money as I had** ich habe mein weniges Geld ausgegeben - **3.** [so great]: **there are such differences that...** die Unterschiede sind so groß, dass...; **such was their skill that...** sie waren so geschickt, dass... ◇ *adv*: **such big houses** so große Häuser, solche großen Häuser; **such a man** ein solcher Mann, so ein Mann; **it's such a lovely day** es ist so ein schöner Tag; **such a thing should never have happened** so etwas hätte nie passieren dürfen; **such a lot** so viel; **such a long time** so lange; **in such a way that...** auf solche Weise, dass... ◇ *pron*: **and such (like)** und dergleichen. ◆ **as such** *adv* als solche(r) (s). ◆ **such and such** *adj* das und das; **on such and such a day** an dem und dem Tag.

suck [sʌk] *vt* - **1.** [by mouth] saugen; [lollipop, thumb] lutschen - **2.** [draw in] einlsaugen.

sucker ['sʌkər] *n* - **1.** [suction pad] Saugnapf *der* - **2.** *inf* [gullible person] Depp *der*.

suction ['sʌkʃn] *n* - **1.** [drawing in] Sogwirkung *die* - **2.** [adhesion] Saugwirkung *die*.

Sudan [su:'dɑ:n] *n* Sudan *der*.

sudden ['sʌdn] *adj* plötzlich; **all of a sudden** plötzlich.

suddenly ['sʌdnlɪ] *adv* plötzlich.

sue [su:] *vt* verklagen; **to sue sb for sthg** [libel *etc*] jn wegen etw verklagen; [sum of money] jn auf etw *(A)* verklagen.

suede [sweɪd] *n* Wildleder *das*.

suet ['sʊɪt] *n* Nierenfett *das*.

suffer ['sʌfər] ◇ *vt* erleiden. ◇ *vi* leiden; **to suffer from sthg** MED an etw *(D)* leiden.

sufferer ['sʌfrər] *n*: **rheumatism sufferer** Rheumakranke *der, die*; **hay fever sufferer** an Heuschnupfen Leidende *der, die*.

suffering ['sʌfrɪŋ] *n* Leiden *das*.

suffice [sə'faɪs] *vi fml* genügen.

sufficient [sə'fɪʃnt] *adj* genügend.

sufficiently [sə'fɪʃntlɪ] *adv* genug.

suffocate ['sʌfəkeɪt] *vt & vi* ersticken.

suffuse [sə'fju:z] *vt*: **suffused with sthg** von etw durchdrungen.

sugar ['ʃʊgər] ◇ *n* Zucker *der*. ◇ *vt* zuckern.

sugar beet *n (U)* Zuckerrübe *die*.

sugarcane ['ʃʊgəkeɪn] *n* Zuckerrohr *das*.

sugary ['ʃʊgərɪ] *adj* [high in sugar] süß.

suggest [sə'dʒest] *vt* - **1.** [propose] vorlschlagen - **2.** [imply] anldeuten.

suggestion [sə'dʒestʃn] *n* - **1.** [proposal, idea] Vorschlag *der* - **2.** *(U)* [implication]: **there was no suggestion of corruption** nichts deutete auf Korruption hin.

suggestive [sə'dʒestɪv] *adj* - **1.** [implying sexual connotation] anzüglich - **2.** [implying a certain conclusion]: **to be suggestive of sthg** auf etw *(A)* hinldeuten - **3.** [reminiscent]: **to be suggestive of sthg** an etw *(A)* denken lassen.

suicide ['sʊɪsaɪd] *n liter & fig* Selbstmord *der*; **to commit suicide** Selbstmord begehen.

suit [suːt] <> *n* - **1.** [matching clothes] Anzug *der*; [for woman] Kostüm *das* - **2.** [in cards] Farbe *die* - **3.** LAW Prozess *der*. <> *vt* - **1.** [look attractive on] stehen *(+ D)* - **2.** [be convenient or appropriate to] passen *(+ D)*; **suit yourself!** mach, was du willst! <> *vi*: **does that suit?** passt dir das?

suitable ['suːtəbl] *adj*: **suitable (for)** geeignet (für).

suitably ['suːtəblɪ] *adv* [dressed] passend; [impressed] gehörig.

suitcase ['suːtkeɪs] *n* Koffer *der*.

suite [swiːt] *n* - **1.** [of rooms] Suite *die* - **2.** [of furniture] Garnitur *die*.

suited ['suːtɪd] *adj* - **1.** [suitable]: **to be suited to/for sthg** für etw geeignet sein - **2.** [compatible]: **to be well/ideally suited** gut/ideal zusammen|passen.

sulfur *n US* = **sulphur**.

sulk [sʌlk] *vi* schmollen.

sulky ['sʌlkɪ] *adj* [remark] beleidigt; [child] schmollend; **to be in a sulky mood** schmollen.

sullen ['sʌlən] *adj* missmutig.

sulphur *UK*, **sulfur** *US* ['sʌlfəʳ] *n* Schwefel *der*.

sultana [səl'tɑːnə] *n UK* [dried grape] Sultanine *die*.

sultry ['sʌltrɪ] *adj* - **1.** [weather, day] schwül - **2.** [woman] sinnlich.

sum [sʌm] *n* Summe *die*. ◆ **sum up** *vt sep* & *vi* [summarize] zusammen|fassen.

summarize, -ise ['sʌməraɪz] *vt* & *vi* zusammen|fassen.

summary ['sʌmərɪ] *n* Zusammenfassung *die*.

summer ['sʌməʳ] <> *n* Sommer *der*; **in (the) summer** im Sommer. <> *comp* Sommer-.

summerhouse ['sʌməhaʊs] (*pl* [-haʊzɪz]) *n* Gartenhaus *das*.

summer school *n* Ferienkurs *der*.

summertime ['sʌmətaɪm] *n*: **in (the) summertime** im Sommer.

summit ['sʌmɪt] *n* [mountain top, meeting] Gipfel *der*.

summon ['sʌmən] *vt* [to sb's office] herbei|zitieren; [doctor, fire brigade] rufen. ◆ **summon up** *vt sep* [courage, energy] auf|bringen.

summons ['sʌmənz] (*pl* **summonses**) <> *n* LAW Vorladung *die*. <> *vt* LAW vor|laden.

sumptuous ['sʌmptʃʊəs] *adj* [decor, fittings] prächtig; [meal] üppig; [hotel] luxuriös.

sun [sʌn] *n* Sonne *die*.

sunbathe ['sʌnbeɪð] *vi* sich sonnen.

sunbed ['sʌnbed] *n* Sonnenbank *die*.

sunburn ['sʌnbɜːn] *n (U)* Sonnenbrand *der*.

sunburned ['sʌnbɜːnd], **sunburnt** ['sʌnbɜːnt] *adj* sonnengebräunt; [excessively] sonnenverbrannt.

Sunday ['sʌndɪ] *n* Sonntag *der*; **Sunday lunch** Sonntagsessen *das*; *see also* **Saturday**.

Sunday school *n* Sonntagsschule *die*.

sundial ['sʌndaɪəl] *n* Sonnenuhr *die*.

sundown ['sʌndaʊn] *n* Sonnenuntergang *der*.

sundry ['sʌndrɪ] *adj fml* verschiedene; **all and sundry** jedermann. ◆ **sundries** *npl fml* Verschiedenes *nt*.

sunflower ['sʌn,flaʊəʳ] *n* Sonnenblume *die*.

sung [sʌŋ] *pp* ▷ **sing**.

sunglasses ['sʌn,glɑːsɪz] *npl* Sonnenbrille *die*.

sunk [sʌŋk] *pp* ▷ **sink**.

sunlight ['sʌnlaɪt] *n* Sonnenlicht *das*.

sunny ['sʌnɪ] *adj liter* & *fig* sonnig; **sunny side up** *US* [fried egg] einseitig gebraten.

sunrise ['sʌnraɪz] *n* Sonnenaufgang *der*.

sunroof ['sʌnruːf] *n* [of car] Schiebedach *das*.

sunset ['sʌnset] *n* Sonnenuntergang *der*.

sunshade ['sʌnʃeɪd] *n* Sonnenschirm *der*.

sunshine ['sʌnʃaɪn] *n* Sonnenschein *der*.

sunstroke ['sʌnstrəʊk] *n* Sonnenstich *der*.

suntan ['sʌntæn] *n* Sonnenbräune *die*.

super ['suːpəʳ] *adj inf* toll.

superb [suː'pɜːb] *adj* erstklassig.

supercilious [,suːpə'sɪlɪəs] *adj* hochnäsig.

superficial [,suːpə'fɪʃl] *adj* oberflächlich.

superfluous [suː'pɜːflʊəs] *adj* überflüssig.

superhuman [,suːpə'hjuːmən] *adj* übermenschlich.

superimpose [,suːpərɪm'pəʊz] *vt*: **to superimpose sthg on sthg** etw mit etw überlagern.

superintendent [,suːpərɪn'tendənt] *n* - **1.** *UK* [of police] Polizeikomissar *der*, -in *die* - **2.** *fml* [of department] Direktor *der*, -in *die*.

superior [suː'pɪərɪəʳ] <> *adj* - **1.** [better]: **superior (to)** besser (als) - **2.** [of high quality - goods] besonders hochwertig; **a person of superior intelligence** ein Mensch von überragender Intelligenz - **3.** [of higher rank]: **superior (to sb)** höher (als jd) - **4.** *pej* [arrogant] überheblich. <> *n* [senior] Vorgesetzte *der, die*.

superlative [suː'pɜːlətɪv] <> *adj* [of the highest quality - performance] unübertrefflich; [- player] überragend. <> *n* GRAM Superlativ *der*.

supermarket ['suːpə,mɑːkɪt] *n* Supermarkt *der*.

supernatural [,suːpə'nætʃrəl] *adj* übernatürlich.

superpower ['suːpə,paʊəʳ] *n* Supermacht *die*.

supersede [,suːpə'siːd] *vt* ab|lösen.

supersonic [,suːpə'sɒnɪk] *adj* Überschall-.

superstitious [,suːpə'stɪʃəs] *adj* abergläubisch.

superstore ['su:pəstɔ:ʳ] *n* Verbrauchermarkt *der*; **DIY superstore** Heimwerkermarkt *der*.

supervise ['su:pəvaɪz] *vt* beaufsichtigen.

supervisor ['su:pəvaɪzəʳ] *n* Aufsicht *die*; [of university students] Tutor *der*, -in *die*.

supper ['sʌpəʳ] *n* - **1.** [main evening meal] Abendessen *das* - **2.** [light evening meal] Abendbrot *das*.

supple ['sʌpl] *adj* - **1.** [person] beweglich - **2.** [material] geschmeidig.

supplement ◇ *n* ['sʌplɪmənt] - **1.** [addition - to charge] Zuschlag *der*; [- to diet] Ergänzung *die* - **2.** [of newspaper] Beilage *die*; [in book] Nachtrag *der*. ◇ *vt* ['sʌplɪment] ergänzen.

supplementary [ˌsʌplɪ'mentərɪ] *adj* [additional] zusätzlich.

supplier [sə'plaɪəʳ] *n* Lieferant *der*, -in *die*.

supply [sə'plaɪ] ◇ *n* - **1.** [store, reserve] Vorrat *der* - **2.** [network]: **the water/electricity supply** die Wasser-/Stromversorgung - **3.** *(U)* ECON Angebot *das*. ◇ *vt*: **to supply sthg (to sb)** [deliver] etw liefern (an jn); **to supply sb (with sthg)** [deliver] jn (mit etw) beliefern; **he supplied the police with the necessary information** er lieferte der Polizei die nötigen Informationen; **to supply sthg with sthg** etw mit etw versorgen. ◆ **supplies** *npl* Vorräte *Pl*; [for office] Bürobedarf *der*; [for army] Nachschub *der*.

support [sə'pɔ:t] ◇ *n* - **1.** [gen] Unterstützung *die* - **2.** [object, person] Stütze *die*. ◇ *vt* - **1.** [gen] unterstützen - **2.** [physically] stützen - **3.** [theory] untermauern.

supporter [sə'pɔ:təʳ] *n* - **1.** [of person, plan] Anhänger *der*, -in *die* - **2.** SPORT Fan *der*.

suppose [sə'pəʊz] ◇ *vt* [assume] an|nehmen. ◇ *vi* - **1.** [assume]: **I suppose (so)** das nehme ich an; **I suppose not** wahrscheinlich nicht - **2.** [agree]: **I suppose so** ja, gut; **I suppose not** wahrscheinlich nicht.

supposed [sə'pəʊzd] *adj* - **1.** [doubtful] angeblich - **2.** [intended]: **to be supposed to do sthg** etw tun sollen - **3.** [reputed]: **it is supposed to be good** es soll gut sein.

supposedly [sə'pəʊzɪdlɪ] *adv* angeblich.

supposing [sə'pəʊzɪŋ] *conj*: **supposing you are right** angenommen, dass Sie Recht haben; **supposing he came back?** wenn er nun zurückkäme?

suppress [sə'pres] *vt* unterdrücken.

supreme [sʊ'pri:m] *adj* - **1.** [highest in rank] Ober- - **2.** [great] größte(r) (s).

surcharge ['sɜ:tʃɑ:dʒ] *n*: **surcharge (on sthg)** Zuschlag *der* (auf etw *(A)*).

sure [ʃʊəʳ] ◇ *adj* sicher; **to be sure of sthg** sich einer Sache *(G)* sicher sein; **with such qualifications she can be sure of getting a job** mit so einer Qualifikation findet sie mit Sicherheit eine Stelle; **be sure to lock the door** denke daran, die Tür abzuschließen; **to make sure (that)...** sicherstellen, dass...; **I'm sure (that)...** ich bin (mir) sicher, dass...; **to be sure of o.s.** selbstsicher sein; [about specific matter] sich *(D)* seiner Sache sicher sein. ◇ *adv* - **1.** *esp US inf* [yes] sicher - **2.** *US* [really] wirklich. ◆ **for sure** *adv*: **I don't know for sure** da bin ich nicht ganz sicher; **she'll come for sure** sie kommt bestimmt. ◆ **sure enough** *adv* tatsächlich.

surely ['ʃʊəlɪ] *adv* [expressing surprise] sicherlich; **surely you can't be serious?** das ist doch nicht dein Ernst?

surf [sɜ:f] ◇ *n* Brandung *die*. ◇ *vt*: **to surf the Internet** im Internet surfen.

surface ['sɜ:fɪs] ◇ *n liter* & *fig* Oberfläche *die*; **on the surface** [of person] äußerlich; **to scratch the surface of sthg** *fig* etw oberflächlich behandeln. ◇ *vi liter* & *fig* auf|tauchen.

surface mail *n Post, die auf dem Land-/Seeweg befördert wird.*

surfboard ['sɜ:fbɔ:d] *n* Surfbrett *das*.

surfeit ['sɜ:fɪt] *n fml*: **surfeit of sthg** Übermaß *das* an etw *(D)*.

surfing ['sɜ:fɪŋ] *n* Surfen *das*.

surge [sɜ:dʒ] ◇ *n* [of water] Schwall *der*; [of electricity] Stoß *der*; [of interest, support] Woge *die*. ◇ *vi* strömen; [interest, support] an|schwellen; [sales, applications] in die Höhe schießen.

surgeon ['sɜ:dʒən] *n* Chirurg *der*, -in *die*.

surgery ['sɜ:dʒərɪ] *n* - **1.** MED [performing operations] Chirurgie *die*; **to have surgery** operiert werden - **2.** *UK* MED [place] Praxis *die*.

surgical ['sɜ:dʒɪkl] *adj* - **1.** [connected with surgery] chirurgisch - **2.** [worn as treatment] orthopädisch.

surgical spirit *n UK* Wunddesinfektionsmittel *das*.

surly ['sɜ:lɪ] *adj* mürrisch.

surmount [sɜ:'maʊnt] *vt* [overcome] überwinden.

surname ['sɜ:neɪm] *n* Nachname *der*.

surpass [sə'pɑ:s] *vt fml* [exceed] übertreffen.

surplus ['sɜ:pləs] ◇ *adj* überschüssig. ◇ *n*: **surplus (of sthg)** Überschuss *der* (an etw *(D)*).

surprise [sə'praɪz] ◇ *n* Überraschung *die*. ◇ *vt* überraschen.

surprised [sə'praɪzd] *adj* überrascht.

surprising [sə'praɪzɪŋ] *adj* überraschend.

surprisingly [sə'praɪzɪŋlɪ] *adv* überraschenderweise.

surrender [sə'rendəʳ] ◇ *n* Kapitulation *die*. ◇ *vi* - **1.** [stop fighting]: **to surrender (to sb)** sich (jm) ergeben - **2.** *fig* [give in]: **to surrender (to sthg)** (etw *(D)*) nach|geben.

surreptitious [ˌsʌrəp'tɪʃəs] *adj* heimlich.

surrogate ['sʌrəgeɪt] ◇ *adj* Ersatz-. ◇ *n* Ersatz *der*.

surrogate mother *n* Leihmutter *die*.

surround [sə'raʊnd] *vt* - **1.** [gen] um|geben - **2.** [trap] umzingeln.

surrounding [sə'raʊndɪŋ] *adj* [area, countryside] umliegend. ◆ **surroundings** *npl* Umgebung *die*.

surveillance [sɜː'veɪləns] *n* *(U)* Überwachung *die*; **to keep sb under surveillance** jn überwachen.

survey ◇ *n* ['sɜːveɪ] - **1.** [statistical investigation] Untersuchung *die*; [of public opinion] Umfrage *die* - **2.** [physical examination - of land] Vermessung *die*; [- of building] Begutachtung *die*. ◇ *vt* [sə'veɪ] - **1.** [contemplate] betrachten - **2.** [investigate statistically] untersuchen - **3.** [examine, assess - land] vermessen; [- building] begutachten.

surveyor [sə'veɪəʳ] *n* [of land] Landvermesser *der*, -in *die*; [of building] Baugutachter *der*, -in *die*.

survival [sə'vaɪvl] *n* [continuing to live] Überleben *das*.

survive [sə'vaɪv] ◇ *vt* überleben. ◇ *vi* - **1.** [continue to exist] überleben - **2.** *inf* [cope successfully] es aus|halten.

survivor [sə'vaɪvəʳ] *n* - **1.** [person who escapes death] Überlebende *der, die* - **2.** *fig* [fighter] Kämpfernatur *die*.

susceptible [sə'septəbl] *adj* - **1.** [likely to be influenced]: **susceptible to sthg** empfänglich für etw - **2.** MED: **susceptible to sthg** anfällig für etw.

suspect ◇ *adj* ['sʌspekt] verdächtig. ◇ *n* ['sʌspekt] Verdächtige *der, die*. ◇ *vt* [sə'spekt] - **1.** [distrust] zweifeln an *(+ D)* - **2.** [think likely] vermuten - **3.** [consider guilty]: **to suspect sb (of sthg)** jn (einer Sache *(G)*) verdächtigen.

suspend [sə'spend] *vt* - **1.** [hang] auf|hängen - **2.** [temporarily discontinue] zeitweilig ein|stellen - **3.** [temporarily remove - from job] suspendieren; [- from school] zeitweilig von der Schule verweisen.

suspender belt [sə'spendəʳ-] *n UK* Strumpfhaltergürtel *der*.

suspenders [sə'spendəz] *npl* - **1.** *UK* [for stockings] Strumpfhalter *Pl*, Strapse *Pl* - **2.** *US* [for trousers] Hosenträger *Pl*.

suspense [sə'spens] *n* *(U)* Spannung *die*.

suspension [sə'spenʃn] *n* - **1.** [temporary discontinuation] Einstellung *die* - **2.** [removal - from job] Suspendierung *die*; [- from school] zeitweiliger Schulverweis - **3.** AUT Federung *die*.

suspension bridge *n* Hängebrücke *die*.

suspicion [sə'spɪʃn] *n* - **1.** *(U)* [distrust] Misstrauen *das* - **2.** [idea, theory] Verdacht *der*.

suspicious [sə'spɪʃəs] *adj* - **1.** [having suspicions] misstrauisch - **2.** [causing suspicion] verdächtig.

sustain [sə'steɪn] *vt* - **1.** [maintain - interest, opposition, activity] aufrecht|erhalten; [- hope] bewahren; [- rate, speed] bei|behalten - **2.** [nourish physically] ernähren - **3.** [injury, damage] davon|tragen - **4.** [withstand - weight] aus|halten.

sustenance ['sʌstɪnəns] *n* *(U)* *fml* Nahrung *die*.

SW (*abbr of* **short wave**) UW.

swab [swɒb] *n* [cotton wool] Tupfer *der*.

swagger ['swægəʳ] *vi* stolzieren.

swallow ['swɒləʊ] ◇ *n* [bird] Schwalbe *die*. ◇ *vt* - **1.** [food, drink] schlucken - **2.** *fig* [accept] schlucken - **3.** *fig* [anger, tears] hinunter|schlucken. ◇ *vi* schlucken.

swam [swæm] *pt* ▷ **swim**.

swamp [swɒmp] ◇ *n* Sumpf *der*. ◇ *vt* - **1.** [flood] unter Wasser setzen - **2.** [overwhelm]: **to swamp sb/sthg (with sthg)** jn/etw (mit etw) überfluten.

swan [swɒn] *n* [bird] Schwan *der*.

swap [swɒp] *vt* - **1.** [exchange]: **to swap sthg (with sb)** etw (mit jm) tauschen; **to swap sthg (over** OR **round)** etw (aus)|tauschen - **2.** [replace]: **to swap sthg for sthg** etw gegen etw ein|tauschen.

swarm [swɔːm] *n* Schwarm *der*.

swarthy ['swɔːðɪ] *adj* dunkel.

swastika ['swɒstɪkə] *n* Hakenkreuz *das*.

swat [swɒt] *vt* tot|schlagen.

sway [sweɪ] ◇ *vt* [influence] beeinflussen. ◇ *vi* sich wiegen; [drunk person] schwanken.

swear [sweəʳ] (*pt* **swore**, *pp* **sworn**) ◇ *vt* schwören; **to swear to do sthg** schwören, etw zu tun. ◇ *vi* - **1.** [state emphatically] schwören - **2.** [use swearwords] fluchen.

swearword ['sweəwɜːd] *n* Kraftausdruck *der*.

sweat [swet] ◇ *n* [perspiration] Schweiß *der*. ◇ *vi liter* & *fig* schwitzen.

sweater ['swetəʳ] *n* Pullover *der*.

sweatshirt ['swetʃɜːt] *n* Sweatshirt *das*.

sweaty ['swetɪ] *adj* [clothes] verschwitzt; [skin] schweißnass.

swede [swiːd] *n UK* Steckrübe *die*.

Swede [swiːd] *n* Schwede *der*, -din *die*.

Sweden ['swiːdn] *n* Schweden *nt*.

Swedish ['swiːdɪʃ] ◇ *adj* schwedisch. ◇ *n* [language] Schwedisch(e) *das*.

sweep [swiːp] (*pt* & *pp* **swept**) ◇ *n* - **1.** [of arm, hand] Schwung *der* - **2.** [with brush]: **to give sthg a sweep** etw kehren OR fegen - **3.** [chimneysweep] Schornsteinfeger *der*, -in *die*. ◇ *vt* - **1.** [with brush] fegen, kehren

- **2.** [scan] ab|suchen - **3.** [spread through] über|rollen. ◆ **sweep up** *vt sep* & *vi* [with brush] zusammen|kehren *OR* |-fegen.

sweeping ['swi:pɪŋ] *adj* - **1.** [effect, change] tief greifend - **2.** [statement] pauschal.

sweet [swi:t] ◇ *adj* - **1.** [gen] süß - **2.** [gentle, kind] lieb. ◇ *n UK* - **1.** [candy] Bonbon *das* - **2.** [dessert] Nachtisch *der*, Dessert *das*.

sweet corn *n* Mais *der*.

sweeten ['swi:tn] *vt* [add sugar to] süßen.

sweetheart ['swi:thɑ:t] *n* - **1.** [term of endearment] Liebling *der* - **2.** [boyfriend or girlfriend] Freund *der*, -in *die*.

sweetness ['swi:tnɪs] *n* - **1.** [gen] Süße *die* - **2.** [of character, voice] Liebenswürdigkeit *die*.

sweet pea *n* Wicke *die*.

swell [swel] (*pt* **-ed**, *pp* **swollen** *OR* **-ed**) ◇ *vi* - **1.** [become larger]: **to swell (up)** an|schwellen - **2.** [fill with air - lungs, balloons] sich füllen; [- sails] sich blähen - **3.** [increase in number] an|wachsen - **4.** [become louder] an|schwellen. ◇ *vt* [increase] steigern. ◇ *n* [of sea]: **there is a heavy swell** es herrscht starker Seegang. ◇ *adj US inf* klasse, prima.

swelling ['swelɪŋ] *n* [on body] Schwellung *die*.

sweltering ['sweltərɪŋ] *adj* [heat] drückend; [weather, day] drückend heiß.

swept [swept] *pt* & *pp* ▷ **sweep**.

swerve [swɜ:v] *vi* [vehicle, driver] aus|schwenken.

swift [swɪft] ◇ *adj* - **1.** [fast] schnell - **2.** [prompt] prompt. ◇ *n* [bird] Mauersegler *der*.

swig [swɪg] *inf n inf* Schluck *der*.

swill [swɪl] ◇ *n (U)* [pig food] Schweinefutter *das*. ◇ *vt UK* [wash] waschen; [glass, cup] aus|spülen.

swim [swɪm] (*pt* **swam**, *pp* **swum**) ◇ *n*: **to have a swim** schwimmen; **to go for a swim** schwimmen gehen. ◇ *vi* - **1.** [move through water] schwimmen - **2.** [feel dizzy]: **my head was swimming** mir war ganz schwindlig.

swimmer ['swɪmə^r] *n* Schwimmer *der*, -in *die*.

swimming ['swɪmɪŋ] *n* Schwimmen *das*; **to go swimming** schwimmen gehen.

swimming cap *n* Badekappe *die*.

swimming costume *n UK* Badeanzug *der*.

swimming pool *n* Schwimmbad *das*.

swimming trunks *npl* Badehose *die*.

swimsuit ['swɪmsu:t] *n* Badeanzug *der*.

swindle ['swɪndl] ◇ *n* Betrug *der*. ◇ *vt* betrügen; **to swindle sb out of sthg** jn um etw betrügen.

swine [swaɪn] *n inf pej* [person] Schwein *das*.

swing [swɪŋ] (*pt* & *pp* **swung**) ◇ *n* - **1.** [child's toy] Schaukel *die* - **2.** [change - in opinion, mood] Umschwung *der* - **3.** [swaying movement] Schwingen *das* - **4.** *inf* [blow]: **to take a swing at sb** nach jm schlagen - **5.** *phr*: **to be in full swing** in vollem Gange sein. ◇ *vt* - **1.** [move back and forth] hin und her schwingen; [arms] schwingen mit - **2.** [turn] schwenken. ◇ *vi* - **1.** [move back and forth] hin und her schwingen; [dangle - legs] baumeln - **2.** [turn]: **the door swung open** die Tür schwang auf; **he swung round** er drehte sich um - **3.** [change] um|schwenken; **the party has swung to the left** die Partei hat einen Linksschwenk gemacht.

swing bridge *n* Drehbrücke *die*.

swing door *n* Pendeltür *die*.

swingeing ['swɪndʒɪŋ] *adj esp UK* [cuts] drastisch; [criticism] scharf.

swipe [swaɪp] ◇ *vt* - **1.** *inf* [steal] klauen - **2.** [plastic card] durch|ziehen. ◇ *vi*: **to swipe at sb** nach jm schlagen.

swirl [swɜ:l] ◇ *n* Wirbel *der*. ◇ *vi* wirbeln.

swish [swɪʃ] ◇ *adj inf* [posh] schick. ◇ *vt* [tail] schlagen mit.

Swiss [swɪs] ◇ *adj* Schweizer, schweizerisch. ◇ *n* Schweizer *der*, -in *die*. ◇ *npl*: **the Swiss** die Schweizer *Pl*.

switch [swɪtʃ] ◇ *n* - **1.** [control device] Schalter *der* - **2.** [change - of policy] Änderung *die*; **the switch to a different system** die Umstellung auf ein anderes System. ◇ *vt* - **1.** [transfer] wechseln; **to switch sthg to sthg** [conversation, attention] etw auf etw *(A)* lenken; [allegiance] etw auf etw *(A)* übertragen - **2.** [swap, exchange] vertauschen; **to switch jobs** den Arbeitsplatz wechseln. ◆ **switch off** *vt sep* [device] aus|schalten. ◆ **switch on** *vt sep* [device] an|schalten.

switchboard ['swɪtʃbɔ:d] *n* Zentrale *die*.

Switzerland ['swɪtsələnd] *n* Schweiz *die*.

swivel ['swɪvl] (*UK*) (*US*) ◇ *vt* drehen. ◇ *vi* sich drehen.

swivel chair *n* Drehstuhl *der*.

swollen ['swəuln] ◇ *pp* ▷ **swell**. ◇ *adj* [part of body] geschwollen; [river] angeschwollen; **swollen with pride** stolzgeschwellt.

swoop [swu:p] ◇ *n* [raid] Razzia *die*. ◇ *vi* [plane] einen Sturzflug machen; [bird] herab|stoßen.

swop [swɒp] *n, vt* & *vi* = **swap**.

sword [sɔ:d] *n* Schwert *das*.

swordfish ['sɔ:dfɪʃ] (*pl inv OR* **-es**) *n* Schwertfisch *der*.

swore [swɔ:^r] *pt* ▷ **swear**.

sworn [swɔ:n] *pp* ▷ **swear**.

swot [swɒt] *UK inf* ◇ *n pej* Streber *der*, -in *die*. ◇ *vi*: **to swot (for sthg)** büffeln (für etw).

swum [swʌm] *pp* ▷ **swim**.

swung [swʌŋ] *pt* & *pp* ▷ **swing**.

sycamore ['sɪkəmɔːʳ] *n* Bergahorn *der*.

syllable ['sɪləbl] *n* Silbe *die*.

syllabus ['sɪləbəs] (*pl* **-buses** OR **-bi** [-baɪ]) *n* Lehrplan *der*.

symbol ['sɪmbl] *n* Symbol *das*.

symbolize, -ise ['sɪmbəlaɪz] *vt* symbolisieren.

symmetry ['sɪmətrɪ] *n (U)* Symmetrie *die*.

sympathetic [ˌsɪmpə'θetɪk] *adj* - **1.** [understanding] verständnisvoll - **2.** [willing to support] wohlgesinnt; **to be sympathetic to sthg** einer Sache *(D)* wohlwollend gegenüberstehen; [new ideas] für etw zugänglich sein.

sympathize, -ise ['sɪmpəθaɪz] *vi* - **1.** [feel sorry] mit|fühlen, Mitleid haben; **to sympathize with sb** mit jm mit|fühlen - **2.** [understand]: **to sympathize with sthg** für etw Verständnis haben - **3.** [support]: **to sympathize with sthg** mit etw sympathisieren.

sympathizer, -iser ['sɪmpəθaɪzəʳ] *n* [supporter] Sympathisant *der*, -in *die*.

sympathy ['sɪmpəθɪ] *n* [compassion] Mitgefühl *das*, Mitleid *das*; *(phrase)*: **to have sympathy for sb** Mitleid mit jm haben.

symphony ['simfənɪ] *n* Sinfonie *die*.

symposium [sɪm'pəʊzjəm] (*pl* **-siums** OR **-sia** [-zjə]) *n fml* Symposium *das*.

symptom ['sɪmptəm] *n liter & fig* Symptom *das*.

synagogue ['sɪnəgɒg] *n* Synagoge *die*.

syndicate *n* ['sɪndɪkət] Syndikat *das*.

syndrome ['sɪndrəʊm] *n* MED [set of symptoms] Syndrom *das*.

synonym ['sɪnənɪm] *n*: **synonym (for** OR **of sthg)** Synonym *das* (für OR von etw).

synopsis [sɪ'nɒpsɪs] (*pl* **-ses** [-siːz]) *n* Zusammenfassung *die*.

syntax ['sɪntæks] *n* LING Syntax *die*.

synthetic [sɪn'θetɪk] *adj* - **1.** [man-made] synthetisch; **synthetic fibre** Kunstfaser *die* - **2.** *pej* [insincere] künstlich.

syphilis ['sɪfɪlɪs] *n* Syphilis *die*.

syphon ['saɪfn] *n & vt* = **siphon**.

Syria ['sɪrɪə] *n* Syrien *nt*.

syringe [sɪ'rɪndʒ] *n* Spritze *die*.

syrup ['sɪrəp] *n (U)* - **1.** [sugar and water] Sirup *der* - **2.** *UK*: **(golden) syrup** Sirup *der (Brotaufstrich)* - **3.** [medicine]: **cough syrup** Hustensaft *der*.

system ['sɪstəm] *n* System *das*; **road/railway/transport system** Straßen-/Bahn-/Transportnetz *das*; **stereo system** Stereoanlage *die*; **to get sthg out of one's system** *inf* etw los|werden.

systematic [ˌsɪstə'mætɪk] *adj* systematisch.

systems analyst ['sɪstəmz-] *n* COMPUT Systemanalytiker *der*, -in *die*.

T

t (*pl* **t's** OR **ts**), **T** (*pl* **T's** OR **Ts**) [tiː] *n* t *das*, T *das*.

ta [tɑː] *excl UK inf* danke.

tab [tæb] *n* - **1.** [of maker] Etikett *das*; [bearing owner's name] Namensschild *das* - **2.** [for opening can] Verschluss *der* - **3.** *US* [bill] Rechnung *die*; **to pick up the tab** die Rechnung übernehmen - **4.** *phr*: **to keep tabs on sb** jn genau beobachten.

tabby ['tæbɪ] *n*: **tabby (cat)** getigerte Katze.

table ['teɪbl] ◇ *n* - **1.** [piece of furniture] Tisch *der* - **2.** [diagram] Tabelle *die*. ◇ *vt UK* [propose] ein|bringen.

tablecloth ['teɪblklɒθ] *n* Tischdecke *die*, Tischtuch *das*.

table football *n* Tischfußball *der*.

table lamp *n* Tischlampe *die*.

tablemat ['teɪblmæt] *n* Set *das*.

tablespoon ['teɪblspuːn] *n* Servierlöffel *der*.

tablet ['tæblɪt] *n* - **1.** [pill] Tablette *die* - **2.** [piece of stone] Tafel *die* - **3.** [of soap] Stück *das*.

table tennis *n* Tischtennis *das*.

tabloid ['tæblɔɪd] *n*: **tabloid (newspaper)** Boulevardzeitung *die*; **the tabloid press** die Boulevardpresse.

tacit ['tæsɪt] *adj* stillschweigend.

taciturn ['tæsɪtɜːn] *adj* schweigsam.

tack [tæk] ◇ *n* - **1.** [nail] kleiner Nagel - **2.** NAUT Kurs *der* - **3.** *fig* [course of action] Weg *der*. ◇ *vt* - **1.** [fasten with nail]: **to tack sthg to sthg** etw an etw *(A)* nageln - **2.** [in sewing] heften. ◇ *vi* NAUT kreuzen.

tackle ['tækl] ◇ *n* - **1.** FTBL Tackling *das* - **2.** RUGBY Fassen *das* - **3.** [equipment, gear] Ausrüstung *die* - **4.** [for lifting] Flaschenzug *der*. ◇ *vt* - **1.** [deal with] an|gehen - **2.** [attack & FTBL] an|greifen - **3.** RUGBY fassen.

tacky ['tækɪ] *adj* - **1.** *inf* [cheap] billig; [tasteless] geschmacklos - **2.** [sticky] klebrig.

tact [tækt] *n* Takt *der*; **he has no tact** er hat kein Taktgefühl.

tactful ['tæktfʊl] *adj* taktvoll.

tactic ['tæktɪk] *n* Taktik *die*. ◆ **tactics** *n (U)* MIL Taktik *die*.

tactical ['tæktɪkl] *adj* taktisch.

tactile *adj*: **a tactile person** eine Person, die Körperkontakt mag.

tactless ['tæktlɪs] *adj* taktlos.

tadpole ['tædpəʊl] *n* Kaulquappe *die*.

tag [tæg] *n* - **1.** [on clothing - of maker] Etikett *das*; [- bearing owner's name] Namensschild *das* - **2.** [of paper] Schild *das*; **price tag** Preisschild *das*; **luggage tag** Gepäckanhänger *der*. ◆ **tag along** *vi inf* mit|kommen.

tail [teɪl] ◇ *n* - **1.** [of animal, bird, fish] Schwanz *der* - **2.** [of coat] Schoß *der*; [of shirt] Zipfel *der*. ◇ *vt inf* [follow - person] beschatten; [- car] folgen *(+ D)*. ◆ **tails** ◇ *adv* [side of coin] Zahl *die*; **heads or tails?** Kopf oder Zahl? ◇ *npl* [formal dress] Frack *der*. ◆ **tail off** *vi* [decrease in volume] leiser werden.

tailback ['teɪlbæk] *n UK* Rückstau *der*.

tailcoat ['teɪlkəʊt] *n* Frack *der*.

tail end *n* Ende *das*.

tailgate ['teɪlgeɪt] *n* [of hatchback car] Heckklappe *die*.

tailor ['teɪlər] ◇ *n* Schneider *der*, -in *die*. ◇ *vt* [adjust]: **to tailor sthg to sthg** [plans, policy] etw auf etw *(A)* zu|schneiden; [product] etw auf etw *(A)* ab|stimmen.

tailor-made *adj fig*: **to be tailor-made for sb** [role, job] genau auf jn zugeschnitten sein.

tailwind ['teɪlwɪnd] *n* Rückenwind *der*.

tainted ['teɪntɪd] *adj* - **1.** [reputation] beschmutzt; [money] schmutzig - **2.** *US* [food] verdorben.

Taiwan [ˌtaɪ'wɑːn] *n* Taiwan *nt*.

take [teɪk] (*pt* **took**, *pp* **taken**) ◇ *vt* - **1.** [gen] nehmen; **she took my arm** sie nahm mich beim Arm; **to take the train/bus** den Zug/Bus nehmen; **to take a bath** ein Bad nehmen; **to take an exam/a photo/a walk** eine Prüfung/ein Foto/einen Spaziergang machen; **to take risks** Risiken ein|gehen; **to take a decision** eine Entscheidung treffen; **to take an interest in sthg** sich für etw interessieren; **to take pity on sb** Mitleid mit jm haben; **I take the view that...** ich bin der Meinung, dass...; **to take a seat** Platz nehmen; **to be taken ill** krank werden - **2.** [bring, accompany] bringen; [take along] mit|nehmen; **to take sthg to sb** jm etw bringen; **to take sb to the station** jn zum Bahnhof bringen; **he took her to the theatre** er ging mit ihr ins Theater - **3.** [remove, steal] (mit)|nehmen; **to take sthg from sb** jm etw (ab)|nehmen; [steal] jm etw weg|nehmen - **4.** [capture - city] ein|nehmen, erobern; [- prisoner] machen - **5.** [control, power] übernehmen; **to take charge** die Leitung übernehmen - **6.** [accept] an|nehmen; [subj: machine] nehmen; [opportunity] wahr|nehmen; [responsibility] übernehmen; **do you take travellers' cheques?** nehmen Sie Travellerschecks?; **to take sb's advice** js Rat *(D)* folgen - **7.** [receive - prize, praise] bekommen; **to take criticism** kritisiert werden - **8.** [contain] fassen; **the car can take six people** in dem Auto haben sechs Leute Platz - **9.** [size in clothes, shoes] haben; **what size do you take?** welche Größe haben Sie?; **I take a (size) 34** ich habe Größe 34 - **10.** [bear] ertragen; **I can't take any more** mir reichts - **11.** [require] erfordern; **how long will it take?** wie lange wird es dauern?, wie lange braucht es? - **12.** [react to] auf|nehmen; **to take sthg seriously** etw ernst nehmen; **to take sthg badly** etw schlecht auf|nehmen; **to take sthg the wrong way** etw falsch auf|fassen - **13.** [temperature, pulse] messen - **14.** [rent] mieten - **15.** [make - sum of money] ein|nehmen - **16.** GRAM: **this verb takes the dative** dieses Verb wird mit dem Dativ konstruiert - **17.** [assume]: **I take it (that)...** ich gehe davon aus, dass... ◇ *n* CIN Einstellung *die*. ◆ **take after** *vt insep* nach|schlagen *(+ D)*; **he takes after his mother/father** er schlägt nach seiner Mutter/seinem Vater. ◆ **take apart** *vt sep* [dismantle] auseinander|nehmen. ◆ **take away** *vt sep* - **1.** [remove]: **to take sthg away (from sb)** (jm) etw weg|nehmen; **is it to take away?** zum Mitnehmen? - **2.** [deduct] ab|ziehen. ◆ **take back** *vt sep* - **1.** [return] zurück|bringen - **2.** [faulty goods, statement] zurück|nehmen. ◆ **take down** *vt sep* - **1.** [pictures, curtains] ab|nehmen; [scaffolding, tent] ab|bauen - **2.** [from shelf] herunter|nehmen - **3.** [write down] auf|schreiben - **4.** [lower] herunter|lassen. ◆ **take in** *vt sep* - **1.** [bring inside - washing] herein|bringen - **2.** [deceive] herein|legen; **to be taken in (by sb/sthg)** (auf jn/etw) herein|fallen - **3.** [understand] auf|nehmen - **4.** [include] ein|schließen - **5.** [provide accommodation for] auf|nehmen - **6.** [clothes] enger machen. ◆ **take off** ◇ *vt sep* - **1.** [remove] ab|nehmen; [clothing] aus|ziehen; **to take one's clothes off** sich aus|ziehen - **2.** [have as holiday]: **to take time off** sich *(D)* frei|nehmen; **to take a week off** sich *(D)* eine Woche frei|nehmen - **3.** *UK inf* [imitate] nach|äffen. ◇ *vi* - **1.** [plane] ab|heben - **2.** [go away suddenly] verschwinden. ◆ **take on** *vt sep* - **1.** [job, responsibility] an|nehmen - **2.** [employ] an|stellen, ein|stellen - **3.** [confront] sich an|legen mit; [competitor, sports team] an|treten gegen. ◆ **take out** *vt sep* - **1.** [remove - from container] heraus|nehmen; [- tooth] ziehen; [- money from bank] ab|heben - **2.** [library book] aus|leihen - **3.** [loan] auf|nehmen; [insurance policy] ab|schließen; [patent] an|melden - **4.** [go out with] aus|gehen mit. ◆ **take over** ◇ *vt sep* [company, job] übernehmen. ◇ *vi* - **1.** [take control] die Kontrolle übernehmen - **2.** [in job]: **to take over from sb** jn ab|lösen. ◆ **take to** *vt insep* - **1.** [come to like] mögen - **2.** [begin]: **to take to doing sthg** an|fangen, etw zu tun; **she's taken to getting up earlier** sie steht nun früher auf; **to take to drink** zu trinken an|fangen. ◆ **take up** *vt sep* - **1.** [begin - post] an|treten; [- job] auf|nehmen; **to take up the clarinet** an|fangen, Klarinette zu spielen - **2.** [time, effort, space] in Anspruch nehmen - **3.** [trousers, dress] kürzen. ◆ **take up on** *vt sep* [accept]: **to take sb up on an offer** js Angebot an|nehmen.

takeaway *UK* ['teɪkə,weɪ], **takeout** *US* ['teɪkaʊt] ◇ *n* [food] Essen *das* zum Mitnehmen. ◇ *comp* [food] zum Mitnehmen.

taken ['teɪkn] *pp* ▷ **take**.

takeoff ['teɪkɒf] *n* [of plane] Start *der*.

takeout *n US* = **takeaway**.

takeover ['teɪk,əʊvəʳ] *n* Übernahme *die*.

takings ['teɪkɪŋz] *npl* Einnahmen *Pl*.

talc [tælk], **talcum (powder)** ['tælkəm-] *n* Talk *der*.

tale [teɪl] *n* Geschichte *die*.

talent ['tælənt] *n* Talent *das*.

talented ['tæləntɪd] *adj* talentiert.

talk [tɔ:k] ◇ *n* - **1.** [conversation] Gespräch *das*, Unterhaltung *die*; **to have a talk** sich unterhalten; [more formal] ein Gespräch führen - **2.** [gossip] Gerede *das* - **3.** [lecture] Vortrag *der*. ◇ *vi* - **1.** [speak] sprechen, reden; **to talk to sb** mit jm reden OR sprechen; **to talk to o.s.** Selbstgespräche führen; **to talk about sb/sthg** über jn/etw sprechen OR reden; **talking of him/that, ...** da wir gerade von ihm/davon sprechen ...; **he's talking of buying a car** er redet davon, dass er sich ein neues Auto kaufen will - **2.** [gossip] klatschen - **3.** [make a speech] eine Rede halten; **to talk on** OR **about sthg** über etw *(A)* sprechen. ◇ *vt* - **1.** [politics, sport, business] reden über *(+ A)* OR von - **2.** [nonsense] reden. ◆ **talks** *npl* Gespräche *Pl*. ◆ **talk into** *vt sep*: **to talk sb into doing sthg** jn dazu überreden, etw zu tun. ◆ **talk out of** *vt sep*: **to talk sb out of doing sthg** jm aus|reden, etw zu tun. ◆ **talk over** *vt sep* [discuss] bereden, besprechen.

talkative ['tɔ:kətɪv] *adj* gesprächig.

talk show *n US* Talkshow *die*.

tall [tɔ:l] *adj* - **1.** [person] groß; **I'm 5 feet tall** ich bin 1,50 m groß; **how tall are you?** wie groß bist du? - **2.** [building, tree] hoch.

tally ['tælɪ] ◇ *n* [record]: **to keep a tally of sthg** über etw *(A)* Buch führen. ◇ *vi* überein|stimmen.

talon ['tælən] *n* Kralle *die*.

tambourine [,tæmbə'ri:n] *n* Tamburin *das*.

tame [teɪm] ◇ *adj* - **1.** [animal, bird] zahm - **2.** *pej* [dull] lahm. ◇ *vt* - **1.** [animal, bird] zähmen; [lion] bändigen - **2.** [person] bändigen.

tamper ['tæmpəʳ] ◆ **tamper with** *vt insep* sich *(D)* zu schaffen machen an *(+ D)*.

tampon ['tæmpɒn] *n* Tampon *der*.

tan [tæn] ◇ *adj* [light brown] hellbraun. ◇ *n* [from sun] Bräune *die*; **to get a tan** braun werden. ◇ *vi* braun werden.

tangent ['tændʒənt] *n* GEOM Tangente *die*; **to go off at a tangent** *fig* plötzlich vom Thema ab|schweifen.

tangerine [,tændʒə'ri:n] *n* Mandarine *die*.

tangible ['tændʒəbl] *adj* [difference, benefit] merklich; [results] greifbar.

tangle ['tæŋgl] *n* - **1.** [mass] Gewirr *das* - **2.** *fig* [mess] Durcheinander *das*; **to get (o.s.) into a tangle** sich verstricken.

tank [tæŋk] *n* - **1.** [container] Tank *der*; **(fish) tank** Aquarium *das* - **2.** MIL Panzer *der*.

tanker ['tæŋkəʳ] *n* - **1.** [ship] Tanker *der* - **2.** [truck] Tankwagen *der*.

tanned [tænd] *adj* [suntanned] braun (gebrannt).

Tannoy® ['tænɔɪ] *n* Lautsprecheranlage *die*.

tantalizing ['tæntəlaɪzɪŋ] *adj* verlockend.

tantamount ['tæntəmaʊnt] *adj*: **to be tantamount to sthg** einer Sache *(D)* gleich|kommen.

tantrum ['tæntrəm] *(pl* **-s***)* *n* Wutanfall *der*.

Tanzania [,tænzə'nɪə] *n* Tansania *nt*.

tap [tæp] ◇ *n* - **1.** [device] Hahn *der*; **the hot(-water)/cold(-water) tap** der Warmwasser-/Kaltwasserhahn - **2.** [light blow] Klaps *der*; **she gave him a tap on the shoulder** sie klopfte ihm auf die Schulter; [on door] Klopfen *das*. ◇ *vt* - **1.** [knock] klopfen - **2.** [make use of] erschließen - **3.** [listen secretly to] ab|hören.

tap dance *n* Stepptanz *der*.

tape [teɪp] ◇ *n* - **1.** [magnetic tape] Magnetband *das* - **2.** [cassette] Kassette *die* - **3.** [adhesive material] Klebeband *das*. ◇ *vt* - **1.** [record] auf|nehmen - **2.** [fasten with adhesive tape] (mit Klebeband) verkleben OR zu|kleben; **to tape together** zusammen|kleben.

tape measure *n* Maßband *das*.

taper ['teɪpəʳ] *vi* [corridor] sich verengen; [trousers] nach unten enger werden.

tape recorder *n* Tonbandgerät *das*; [cassette recorder] Kassettenrekorder *der*.

tapestry ['tæpɪstrɪ] *n* [piece of work] Wandteppich *der*.

tar [tɑ:ʳ] *n* Teer *der*.

target ['tɑ:gɪt] ◇ *n* - **1.** [of missile, bomb] Ziel *das* - **2.** [for archery, shooting] Zielscheibe *die* - **3.** *fig* [butt of criticism] Zielscheibe *die* - **4.** *fig* [goal] Ziel *das*. ◇ *vt* - **1.** [aim weapon at] zielen auf *(+ A)* - **2.** [channel resources towards] sich *(D)* zum Ziel setzen; **to target the young** die Jugendlichen als Zielgruppe haben.

tariff ['tærɪf] *n* - **1.** [tax] Zoll *der* - **2.** *UK* [price list] Preisliste *die*.

Tarmac® ['tɑ:mæk] *n* [material] Makadam *der*. ◆ **tarmac** *n* AERON: **the tarmac** die Rollbahn.

tarnish ['tɑ:nɪʃ] *vt* - **1.** [make dull] stumpf werden lassen - **2.** *fig* [reputation] beflecken.

tarpaulin [tɑ:'pɔ:lɪn] *n* [sheet] Plane *die*.

tart [tɑ:t] ◇ *adj* - **1.** [bitter-tasting] herb; [fruit] sauer - **2.** [sarcastic] scharf. ◇ *n* - **1.** [sweet pastry] Kuchen *der*; [small] Törtchen *das*; **fruit tart** Obstkuchen/-törtchen - **2.** *UK v inf* [prostitute] Nutte *die*. ◆ **tart up** *vt sep UK inf pej* [building, room] auf|motzen; **to tart o.s. up** sich auf|takeln.

tartan ['tɑːtn] ◇ *n* - **1.** *(U)* [cloth] Schottenstoff *der* - **2.** [pattern] Schottenkaro *das*. ◇ *comp* im Schottenkaro.

task [tɑːsk] *n* Aufgabe *die*.

task force *n* - **1.** MIL Spezialeinheit *die* - **2.** [group of helpers] Kommando *das*.

tassel ['tæsl] *n* Quaste *die*.

taste [teɪst] ◇ *n* - **1.** [sense of taste] Geschmacksinn *der* - **2.** [flavour] Geschmack *der*; **to have a funny taste** komisch schmecken - **3.** [try] Kostprobe *die*; **to have a taste** probieren - **4.** *fig* [liking, preference]: **taste (for sthg)** Vorliebe *die* (für etw) - **5.** *fig* [experience]: **his first taste of success** sein erstes Erfolgserlebnis; **I've had a taste of power** ich habe erfahren, wie es ist, Macht zu haben - **6.** *(U)* [discernment] Geschmack *der*; **she has (good) taste** sie hat (guten) Geschmack; **in bad taste** geschmacklos; **in good taste** geschmackvoll. ◇ *vt* - **1.** [food - experience flavour of] schmecken; [- test, try] probieren, kosten - **2.** *fig*: **to taste success** ein Erfolgserlebnis haben. ◇ *vi* schmecken; **to taste of/like sthg** nach/wie etw schmecken.

tasteful ['teɪstfʊl] *adj* geschmackvoll.

tasteless ['teɪstlɪs] *adj liter* & *fig* geschmacklos.

tasty ['teɪstɪ] *adj* schmackhaft.

tatters ['tætəz] *npl*: **to be in tatters** [clothes] in Fetzen sein; *fig* [confidence, reputation] sehr angeschlagen sein.

tattoo [tə'tuː] (*pl* **-s**) ◇ *n* [design] Tätowierung *die*. ◇ *vt* tätowieren.

tatty ['tætɪ] *adj UK inf pej* schäbig.

taught [tɔːt] *pt* & *pp* ▷ **teach**.

taunt [tɔːnt] ◇ *vt* verspotten. ◇ *n* spöttische Bemerkung.

Taurus ['tɔːrəs] *n* Stier *der*; **I'm a Taurus** ich bin Stier.

taut [tɔːt] *adj* straff.

tawdry ['tɔːdrɪ] *adj pej* geschmacklos.

tax [tæks] ◇ *n* [money paid to government] Steuer *die*. ◇ *vt* - **1.** [gen] besteuern - **2.** [patience, ingenuity] strapazieren.

taxable ['tæksəbl] *adj* steuerpflichtig.

tax allowance *n* Steuerfreibetrag *der*.

taxation [tæk'seɪʃn] *n* - **1.** [system] Besteuerung *die* - **2.** [amount] Steuer *die*.

tax collector *n* Finanzbeamte *der*, -tin *die*.

tax disc *n UK* Steuermarke *die*.

tax-free *UK*, **tax-exempt** *US adj* steuerfrei.

taxi ['tæksɪ] ◇ *n* Taxi *das*. ◇ *vi* [plane] rollen.

taxi driver *n* Taxifahrer *der*, -in *die*.

tax inspector *n* Steuerprüfer *der*, -in *die*.

taxi rank *UK*, **taxi stand** *n* Taxistand *der*.

taxpayer ['tæks,peɪər] *n* Steuerzahler *der*, -in *die*.

tax return *n* Steuererklärung *die*.

TB (*abbr of* **tuberculosis**) *n* TB *die*.

tea [tiː] *n* - **1.** [drink] Tee *der* - **2.** *UK* [afternoon meal] Nachmittagstee *der* - **3.** *UK* [evening meal] Abendessen *das*.

teabag ['tiːbæg] *n* Teebeutel *der*.

tea break *n UK* Teepause *die*.

teach [tiːtʃ] (*pt* & *pp* **taught**) ◇ *vt* - **1.** [gen] unterrichten; **to teach sb sthg** jm Unterricht geben in etw *(D)*, jn in etw *(D)* unterrichten; **to teach sb to swim** jm das Schwimmen beibringen; **to teach (sb) that...** (jn)(be)lehren, dass... - **2.** [advocate] lehren; **to teach sb sthg, to teach sthg to sb** jn etw lehren; **to teach sb to do sthg** jn lehren, etw zu tun. ◇ *vi* unterrichten.

teacher ['tiːtʃər] *n* Lehrer *der*, -in *die*.

teaching ['tiːtʃɪŋ] *n* - **1.** [profession, work] Unterrichten *das* - **2.** [thing taught] Lehre *die*.

tea cloth *n* - **1.** [tablecloth] (kleine) Tischdecke *die* - **2.** [tea towel] Geschirrtuch *das*.

tea cosy *UK*, **tea cozy** *US n* Teewärmer *der*.

teacup ['tiːkʌp] *n* Teetasse *die*.

teak [tiːk] *n* Teakholz *das*.

team [tiːm] *n* - **1.** SPORT Team *das*, Mannschaft *die* - **2.** [group] Team *das*.

teammate ['tiːmmeɪt] *n* Mannschaftsmitglied *das*.

teamwork ['tiːmwɜːk] *n (U)* Teamarbeit *die*.

teapot ['tiːpɒt] *n* Teekanne *die*.

tear[1] [tɪər] *n* [when crying] Träne *die*.

tear[2] [teər] (*pt* **tore**, *pp* **torn**) ◇ *vt* - **1.** [rip] zerreißen - **2.** [remove roughly] reißen. ◇ *vi* - **1.** [rip] (zer)reißen - **2.** *inf* [move quickly] rasen. ◇ *n* [rip] Riss *der*. ◆ **tear apart** *vt sep* - **1.** [rip up] zerreißen - **2.** [upset greatly] fertig machen. ◆ **tear down** *vt sep* [building, poster] ab|reißen. ◆ **tear up** *vt sep* zerreißen.

teardrop ['tɪədrɒp] *n* Träne *die*.

tearful ['tɪəfʊl] *adj* [person] tränenüberströmt.

tear gas [tɪər-] *n* Tränengas *das*.

tearoom ['tiːrʊm] *n* Teestube *die*.

tease [tiːz] ◇ *n inf* - **1.** [joker] Witzbold *der* - **2.** [sexually] Schäker *der*, -in *die*. ◇ *vt*: **to tease sb (about sthg)** jn (wegen etw) auf|ziehen.

tea service, tea set *n* Teeservice *das*.

teaspoon ['tiːspuːn] *n* Teelöffel *der*.

teat [tiːt] *n* - **1.** [of animal] Zitze *die* - **2.** [of bottle] Sauger *der*.

teatime ['tiːtaɪm] *n (U) UK* [in evening] Abendessenszeit *die*; [in afternoon] Teezeit *die*.

tea towel *n* Geschirrtuch *das*.

technical ['teknɪkl] *adj* technisch; **technical term** Fachbegriff *der*.

technical college *n UK* ≃ Fachhochschule *die*.

technicality [ˌteknɪ'kælətɪ] *n* - **1.** [intricacy] technische Einzelheit - **2.** [petty rule] Formsache *die*.

technically ['teknɪklɪ] *adv* - **1.** [theoretically] theoretisch - **2.** [scientifically] technisch.

technician [tek'nɪʃn] *n* [worker] Techniker *der*, -in *die*.

technique [tek'niːk] *n* Technik *die*.

technological [ˌteknə'lɒdʒɪkl] *adj* technologisch.

technology [tek'nɒlədʒɪ] *n* Technologie *die*.

teddy ['tedɪ] *n*: **teddy (bear)** Teddy(bär) *der*.

tedious ['tiːdjəs] *adj* langweilig.

tee [tiː] *n* GOLF Tee *das*, Abschlag *der*.

teem [tiːm] *vi* - **1.** [rain] gießen - **2.** [be busy]: **to be teeming with** wimmeln von.

teenage ['tiːneɪdʒ] *adj* Teenager-; [children] halbwüchsig.

teenager ['tiːnˌeɪdʒər] *n* Teenager *der*.

teens [tiːnz] *npl*: **to be in one's teens** im Teenageralter sein.

tee shirt *n* T-Shirt *das*.

teeter ['tiːtər] *vi* - **1.** [wobble] schwanken - **2.** *fig* [be in danger]: **to be teetering on the brink of disaster** am Rande einer Katastrophe stehen.

teeth [tiːθ] *Pl* ▷ **tooth**.

teethe [tiːð] *vi* [baby] zahnen.

teething troubles *npl fig* Anfangsschwierigkeiten *Pl*.

teetotaller *UK*, **teetotaler** *US* [tiː'təʊtlər] *n* Abstinenzler *der*, -in *die*.

tel. (*abbr of* **telephone**) Tel.

telecommunications ['telɪkəˌmjuːnɪ'keɪʃnz] *npl* Telekommunikationswesen *das*.

telegram ['telɪgræm] *n* Telegramm *das*.

telegraph ['telɪgrɑːf] ◇ *n* Telegraf *der*. ◇ *vt* telegrafieren.

telegraph pole, telegraph post *UK n* Telegrafenmast *der*.

telepathy [tɪ'lepəθɪ] *n* Telepathie *die*.

telephone ['telɪfəʊn] ◇ *n* Telefon *das*; **to be on the telephone** *UK* [connected] Telefon haben; [speaking] am Telefon sein. ◇ *vt* anlrufen. ◇ *vi* telefonieren.

telephone book *n* Telefonbuch *das*.

telephone booth *n UK* Telefonkabine *die*.

telephone box *n UK* Telefonzelle *die*.

telephone call *n* Telfonanruf *der*, Telefongespräch *das*; **to make a telephone call** telefonieren.

telephone directory *n* Telefonbuch *das*.

telephone number *n* Telefonnummer *die*.

telephonist [tɪ'lefənɪst] *n UK* Telefonist *der*, -in *die*.

telescope ['telɪskəʊp] *n* Teleskop *das*.

teletext ['telɪtekst] *n* Videotext *der*.

televise ['telɪvaɪz] *vt* im Fernsehen übertragen.

television ['telɪˌvɪʒn] *n* - **1.** [medium, industry] Fernsehen *das*; **on television** im Fernsehen - **2.** [apparatus] Fernseher *der*.

television set *n* Fernseher *der*.

telex ['teleks] ◇ *n* Telex *das*. ◇ *vt* (ein) Telex schicken *(+ D)*; [message] telexen.

tell [tel] (*pt & pp* **told**) ◇ *vt* - **1.** [fact] sagen; [story, joke, lie] erzählen; **to tell sb (that)** jm sagen, dass; **to tell sb sthg, to tell sthg to sb** jm etw erzählen; **to tell the truth** die Wahrheit sagen; **to tell sb the time** jm sagen, wie spät es ist - **2.** [instruct, reveal] sagen; **to tell sb to do sthg** jm sagen, dass er/sie etw tun soll; **to tell sb (that)** jm sagen, dass - **3.** [judge, recognize] wissen; **to tell the time** die Uhr lesen können. ◇ *vi* - **1.** [reveal secret]: **he won't tell** er wird nichts sagen - **2.** [judge] beurteilen - **3.** [have effect] sich zeigen. ◆ **tell apart** *vt sep* unterscheiden. ◆ **tell off** *vt sep* auslschimpfen.

telling ['telɪŋ] *adj* - **1.** [effective] wirkungsvoll - **2.** [revealing] aufschlussreich.

telly ['telɪ] *n UK inf* - **1.** [medium] Fernsehen *das*; **on telly** im Fernsehen - **2.** [apparatus] Flimmerkiste *die*.

temp [temp] *UK inf* ◇ *n* (*abbr of* **temporary (employee)**) Zeitarbeitskraft *die*. ◇ *vi* als Zeitarbeitskraft arbeiten.

temper ['tempər] ◇ *n* - **1.** [state of mind, mood] Laune *die*; **to lose one's temper** die Beherrschung verlieren - **2.** [angry state]: **to be in a temper** wütend sein - **3.** [temperament] Temperament *das*. ◇ *vt fml* [moderate] mäßigen.

temperament ['temprəmənt] *n* Temperament *das*.

temperamental [ˌtemprə'mentl] *adj* launisch, launenhaft.

temperature ['temprətʃər] *n* Temperatur *die*; **to have a temperature** Fieber haben.

tempestuous [tem'pestjʊəs] *adj liter & fig* stürmisch.

template ['templɪt] *n* [of shape, letter] Schablone *die*.

temple ['templ] *n* - **1.** RELIG Tempel *der* - **2.** ANAT Schläfe *die*.

temporarily [ˌtempə'rerəlɪ] *adv* vorübergehend.

temporary ['tempərərɪ] *adj* vorübergehend; [job] befristet.

tempt [tempt] *vt* [entice]: **to tempt sb to do sthg** jn dazu verlocken, etw zu tun.

temptation [temp'teɪʃn] *n* - **1.** [state] Versuchung *die* - **2.** [tempting thing] Verlockung *die*.

tempting ['temptɪŋ] *adj* verlockend.

ten [ten] *num* zehn; *see also* **six**.

tenable ['tenəbl] *adj* [reasonable, credible] haltbar.

tenacious [tɪ'neɪʃəs] *adj* hartnäckig.

tenancy ['tenənsɪ] *n* - **1.** [period - of building] Mietdauer *die*; [- of land] Pachtzeit *die* - **2.** [possession - of building] Mieten *das*; [- of land] Pachten *das*.

tenant ['tenənt] *n* Mieter *der*, -in *die*.

tend [tend] *vt* - **1.** [have tendency]: **to tend to do sthg** [person] dazu neigen, etw zu tun - **2.** [look after] sich kümmern um.

tendency ['tendənsɪ] *n* - **1.** [trend]: **tendency towards sthg** Tendenz *die* zu etw - **2.** [leaning, habit] Neigung *die*; **to have the tendency to do sthg** die Neigung haben, etw zu tun.

tender ['tendəʳ] ◇ *adj* - **1.** [caring, gentle] zärtlich - **2.** [meat] zart - **3.** [sore] empfindlich. ◇ *n* COMM Angebot *das*. ◇ *vt fml* [offer - money] an|bieten; [- resignation] ein|reichen.

tendon ['tendən] *n* Sehne *die*.

tenement ['tenəmənt] *n* Mietshaus *das*.

tennis ['tenɪs] *n* Tennis *das*.

tennis ball *n* Tennisball *der*.

tennis court *n* Tennisplatz *der*.

tennis racket *n* Tennisschläger *der*.

tenor ['tenəʳ] *n* Tenor *der*.

tense [tens] ◇ *adj* angespannt. ◇ *n* GRAM Zeit(form) *die*. ◇ *vt* [muscles] an|spannen.

tension ['tenʃn] *n (U)* - **1.** [anxiety] Anspannung *die*; [between people] Spannung *die* - **2.** TECH [tightness] Spannung *die*.

tent [tent] *n* Zelt *das*.

tentacle ['tentəkl] *n* Fangarm *der*, Tentakel *der ODER das*.

tentative ['tentətɪv] *adj* - **1.** [person, step, smile] zögernd - **2.** [agreement, plan] vorläufig.

tenterhooks ['tentəhʊks] *npl*: **to be on tenterhooks** auf glühenden Kohlen sitzen.

tenth [tenθ] *num* zehnte(r) (s); *see also* **sixth**.

tent peg *n* Hering *der*, Zeltpflock *der*.

tent pole *n* Zeltstange *die*.

tenuous ['tenjʊəs] *adj* schwach.

tepid ['tepɪd] *adj liter* & *fig* lauwarm.

term [tɜːm] ◇ *n* - **1.** [word, expression] Begriff *der*, Ausdruck *der* - **2.** SCH & UNIV Trimester *das* - **3.** [period of time]: **a prison term** eine Haftstrafe; **in the long/short term** auf lange/kurze Sicht. ◇ *vt* bezeichnen; **to term sb/sthg sthg** jn/etw als etw bezeichnen. ◆ **terms** *npl* - **1.** [of contract, agreement] Konditionen *Pl* - **2.** [conditions]: **in international terms** im internationalen Vergleich; **in real terms** effektiv - **3.** [of relationship]: **to be on good terms (with sb)** (mit jm) gut aus|kommen - **4.** *phr*: **to come to terms with sthg** sich mit etw ab|finden. ◆ **in terms of** *prep* in Bezug auf *(+ A)*.

terminal ['tɜːmɪnl] ◇ *adj* MED unheilbar. ◇ *n* - **1.** RAIL Endbahnhof *der*; AERON Terminal *der* - **2.** COMPUT Terminal *das* - **3.** ELEC Pol *der*.

terminate ['tɜːmɪneɪt] ◇ *vt fml* beenden; [contract] auf|lösen; [pregnancy] ab|brechen. ◇ *vi* [bus, train] enden.

terminus ['tɜːmɪnəs] (*pl* **-ni** OR **-nuses**) *n* Endstation *die*.

terrace ['terəs] *n* - **1.** *UK* [of houses] Häuserreihe *die* - **2.** [patio] Terrasse *die*. ◆ **terraces** *npl* FTBL: **the terraces** die Ränge *Pl*.

terraced house *n UK* Reihenhaus *das*.

terrain [te'reɪn] *n* Gelände *das*.

terrible ['terəbl] *adj* furchtbar, schrecklich.

terribly ['terəblɪ] *adv* [extremely] furchtbar, schrecklich.

terrier ['terɪəʳ] *n* Terrier *der*.

terrific [tə'rɪfɪk] *adj* - **1.** [wonderful] großartig - **2.** [enormous] enorm.

terrified ['terɪfaɪd] *adj*: **to be terrified (of sb/sthg)** wahnsinnige Angst haben (vor jm/etw).

terrifying ['terɪfaɪɪŋ] *adj* fürchterlich.

territory ['terətrɪ] *n* - **1.** [political area] Territorium *das* - **2.** [terrain] Gelände *das*.

terror ['terəʳ] *n* - **1.** [fear] panische Angst - **2.** *inf* [rascal] Teufel *der*.

terrorism ['terərɪzm] *n* Terrorismus *der*.

terrorist ['terərɪst] *n* Terrorist *der*, -in *die*.

terrorize, -ise ['terəraɪz] *vt* terrorisieren.

terse [tɜːs] *adj* - **1.** [reply, remark] knapp - **2.** [person] kurz angebunden.

Terylene® ['terəliːn] *n* Trevira® *das*.

test [test] ◇ *n* - **1.** [trial] Test *der*; [of friendship, courage] Probe *die* - **2.** [examination of knowledge, skill - SCH] Klassenarbeit *die*; UNIV Klausur *die*; **driving test** Fahrprüfung *die* - **3.** MED [medical check] Test *der*. ◇ *vt* - **1.** [car, method] testen; [friendship, courage] auf die Probe stellen; **to have one's eyes tested** seine Augen testen lassen - **2.** [pupil] prüfen; **to test sb on sthg** jn in etw *(D)* prüfen.

test-drive *vt* Probe fahren.

testicles ['testɪklz] *npl* Hoden *Pl*.

testify ['testɪfaɪ] ◇ *vt*: **to testify that...** bezeugen, dass... ◇ *vi* - **1.** LAW aus|sagen - **2.** [be proof]: **to testify to sthg** von etw zeugen.

testimony [*UK* 'testɪmənɪ, *US* 'testəməʊnɪ] *n (U)* LAW Aussage *die*.

testing ['testɪŋ] *adj* [difficult] schwer.

test match *n UK internationales Cricket- oder Rugbyspiel*.

test tube *n* Reagenzglas *das*.

test-tube baby *n* Retortenbaby *das*.

tetanus ['tetənəs] *n* Tetanus *der*, Wundstarrkrampf *der*.

tether ['teðəʳ] ◇ *vt* an|binden. ◇ *n*: **to be at the end of one's tether** am Ende sein.

text [tekst] <> *n* - **1.** [gen] Text *der* - **2.** [of speech, interview] Wortlaut *der* - **3.** [on mobile phone] Textnachricht *die*. <> *vt* [with mobile phone] simsen.

textbook ['tekstbʊk] *n* Lehrbuch *das*.

textile ['tekstaɪl] *n* Textilie *die*.

text message *n* Textnachricht *die*.

texture ['tekstʃəʳ] *n* Beschaffenheit *die*.

Thai [taɪ] <> *adj* thailändisch. <> *n* - **1.** [person] Thailänder *der*, -in *die* - **2.** [language] Thai *das*.

Thailand ['taɪlænd] *n* Thailand *nt*.

Thames [temz] *n*: **the Thames** die Themse.

than *(weak form* [ðən], *strong form* [ðæn]*)* <> *prep* als; **you're better than me** du bist besser als ich; **more than ten** mehr als zehn. <> *conj* als; **I'd rather stay in than go out** ich bleibe lieber zu Hause als auszugehen; **no sooner had we arrived than the music began** kaum waren wir angekommen, da begann die Musik zu spielen.

thank [θæŋk] *vt*: **to thank sb (for sthg)** jm (für etw) danken; **thank God** OR **goodness** OR **heavens!** Gott sei Dank! ◆ **thanks** <> *npl* Dank *der*. <> *excl* danke. ◆ **thanks to** *prep* dank *(+ D)*.

thankful ['θæŋkfʊl] *adj* - **1.** [grateful]: **thankful (for sthg)** dankbar (für etw) - **2.** [relieved] erleichtert.

thankless ['θæŋklɪs] *adj* undankbar.

thanksgiving ['θæŋks,gɪvɪŋ] *n* Danksagung *die*. ◆ **Thanksgiving (Day)** *n amerikanisches Erntedankfest*.

thank you *excl* danke schön!; **thank you for ...** danke für ...

that [ðæt] (*pl* **those**) <> *pron* - **1.** *(demonstrative use)* das, die *Pl*; **who's/what's that?** wer/was ist das?; **that's interesting** das ist interessant; **is that Lucy?** [on phone] bist du das, Lucy?; [pointing] ist das Lucy?; **how much are those?** wieviel kosten die (da)?; **all those I saw** all die, die ich sah; **after that** danach; **what do you mean by that?** was willst du damit sagen? - **2.** *(referring to thing or person further away)* jene(r) (s), jene *Pl*; **this is new, that is old** dies ist neu, jenes ist alt; **I want those there** ich möchte die da - **3.** *(weak form* [ðət]*)* *(introducing relative clause: subject)* der/die/das, die *Pl*; **a shop that sells antiques** ein Geschäft, das Antiquitäten verkauft - **4.** *(weak form* [ðət]*)* *(introducing relative clause: object)* den/die/das, die *Pl*; **the film that I saw** der Film, den ich gesehen habe; **everything that I have done** alles, was ich gemacht habe; **the best that he could do** das Beste, was er machen konnte - **5.** *(weak form* [ðət]*)* *(introducing relative clause: after prep + D)* dem/der/dem, denen *Pl*; *(introducing relative clause: after prep + A)* den/die/das, die *Pl*; **the place that I'm looking for** der Ort, nach dem ich suche; **the envelope that I put it in** der Umschlag, in den ich es steckte; **the night that we went to the theatre** der Abend, an dem wir ins Theater gingen. <> *adj* - **1.** *(demonstrative use)* der/die/das, die *Pl*; **that film was good** der Film war gut; **who's that man?** wer ist der Mann?; **what's that noise?** was ist das für ein Lärm?; **those chocolates are delicious** die Pralinen da schmecken köstlich - **2.** *(referring to thing or person further away)* jene(r) (s), jene *Pl*; **I prefer that book** ich bevorzuge das Buch da; **I'll have that one** ich nehme das da. <> *adv* so; **it wasn't that bad/good** es war nicht so schlecht/gut. <> *conj (weak form* [ðət]*)* dass; **he recommended that I phone you** er empfahl mir, dich anzurufen. ◆ **that is (to say)** *adv* das heißt.

thatched [θætʃt] *adj*: **thatched roof** Reetdach *das*.

that's [ðæts] *abbr of* **that is**.

thaw [θɔ:] <> *vt* auftauen. <> *vi* - **1.** [ice, frozen food] tauen - **2.** *fig* [atmosphere] sich entspannen. <> *n* Tauwetter *das*.

the *(weak form* [ðə], *before vowel* [ðɪ], *strong form* [ði:]*)* *def art* - **1.** [gen] der/die/das, die *Pl*; **the man** der Mann; **the woman** die Frau; **the book** das Buch; **the girls** die Mädchen; **the Wilsons** die Wilsons; **to play the piano** Klavier spielen; **ten pence in the pound** zehn Pence pro Pfund; **you're not the Jack Straw, are you?** Sie sind nicht **der** Jack Straw, oder?; **it's the place to go to in Paris** da geht man in Paris hin - **2.** *(with an adj to form a noun)*: **the British/poor** die Briten/Armen; **the impossible** das Unmögliche - **3.** [in dates] der; **the twelfth (of May)** der Zwölfte (Mai); **the forties** die Vierziger - **4.** [in comparisons]: **the more I see of her, the less I like her** je mehr ich sie sehe, desto weniger mag ich sie; **the sooner the better** je eher, desto besser - **5.** [in titles]: **Elizabeth the Second** Elisabeth die Zweite.

theatre *UK*, **theater** *US* ['θɪətəʳ] *n* - **1.** [building] Theater *das* - **2.** [art, industry]: **the theatre** das Theater - **3.** [in hospital] Operationssaal *der* - **4.** *US* [cinema] Kino *das*.

theatregoer *UK*, **theatergoer** *US* ['θɪətə,gəʊəʳ] *n* Theaterbesucher *der*, -in *die*.

theatrical [θɪ'ætrɪkl] *adj* - **1.** [of the theatre] Theater- - **2.** *fig* [for effect] theatralisch.

theft [θeft] *n* Diebstahl *der*.

their [ðeəʳ] *poss adj* ihr; **their house** ihr Haus; **their children** ihre Kinder; **they brushed their teeth** sie putzten sich *(D)* die Zähne; **it wasn't their fault** das war nicht **ihre** Schuld.

theirs [ðeəz] *poss pron* ihre(r) (s); **that is theirs** das ist ihres; **this house is theirs** dieses Haus gehört ihnen; **a friend of theirs** ein Freund von ihnen; **it wasn't our fault, it was theirs** das war nicht unsere Schuld, es war ihre.

them *(weak form* [ðəm], *strong form* [ðem]*) pers pron* & *Pl (accusative)* sie; *(dative)* ihnen; **I know them** ich kenne sie; **I like them** sie gefallen mir; **it's them** sie sind es; **send it to them** schicke es ihnen; **tell them** sage ihnen; **he's worse than them** er ist schlimmer als sie; **if I were** *OR* **was them** wenn ich sie wäre; **you can't expect them to do it** du kannst nicht erwarten, dass **sie** das tun; **all of them** sie alle; **none of them** keiner von ihnen; **some/a few of them** einige von ihnen; **most of them** die meisten; **both of them** alle beide; **there are three of them** es gibt drei davon; [people] sie sind zu dritt; **neither of them** keiner/keine/keines von beiden.

theme [θi:m] *n* [gen] Thema *das*.

theme tune *n* [of film] Titelmelodie *die*; [of TV, radio programme] Erkennungsmelodie *die*.

themselves [ðem'selvz] *pron* sich; **they washed themselves** sie wuschen sich; **by themselves** [alone] allein; **they did it (by) themselves** sie machten es selbst; **they have the garden (all) to themselves** sie haben den Garten (ganz) für sich allein.

then [ðen] ◇ *adv* - **1.** [not now, next, afterwards] dann; [in the past] damals; **the film starts at eight – I'll see you then** der Film fängt um acht an – bis dann; **I had breakfast, then I went to work** ich frühstückte und ging dann zur Arbeit; **we were much younger then** wir waren damals viel jünger; **before then** vorher; **by/until then** bis dahin; **from then on** von da an; **since then** seitdem - **2.** [in that case] also; **go on, then** also machs!; **you knew all along, then?** du hast es also die ganze Zeit gewusst? - **3.** [therefore] also; **these, then, were the reasons for our failure** das waren also die Gründe für unser Versagen - **4.** [with "if" clauses] dann; **if you help me now, then I'll help you later** wenn Sie mir jetzt helfen, dann helfe ich Ihnen später - **5.** [furthermore, also] außerdem; **(and) then there are the children to consider** und dann müssen wir an die Kinder denken. ◇ *adj* damalig; **the then president** der damalige Präsident.

theoretical [θɪə'retɪkl] *adj* theoretisch.

theorize, -ise ['θɪəraɪz] *vi*: **to theorize (about sthg)** theoretisieren (über etw *(A)*).

theory ['θɪərɪ] *n* Theorie *die*; **in theory** theoretisch, in der Theorie.

therapist ['θerəpɪst] *n* Therapeut *der*, -in *die*.

therapy ['θerəpɪ] *n* Therapie *die*.

there [ðeə^r] ◇ *pron* [indicating existence]: **there is/are** es gibt; **are there any left?** sind noch welche übrig?; **there are three of us** wir sind zu dritt; **there's a page missing** es fehlt eine Seite; **there must be some mistake** das muss ein Irrtum sein. ◇ *adv* - **1.** [in existence, present] da; **is anyone there?** ist da jemand?; **is John there, please?** [on phone] ist John da? - **2.** [at/in that place] dort; [to that place] dorthin; **that man there** der Mann dort; **I'm going there next week** ich gehe nächste Woche hin; **we're there at last!** endlich sind wir da!; **it's 6 kilometres there and back** es sind 6 Kilometer hin und zurück; **there it/he is** da ist es/er; **in/over there** da drinnen/drüben; **up there** dort oben. ◇ *excl*: **there, I told you so!** ich habe es dir doch gleich gesagt!; **there, there (don't cry)** na, na (weine nicht). ◆ **there and then, then and there** *adv* auf der Stelle.

thereabouts [ðeərə'bauts], **thereabout** *US* [ðeərə'baut] *adv*: **at eight o'clock or thereabouts** so um acht Uhr herum; **fifty or thereabouts** so ungefähr fünfzig; **somewhere thereabouts** da irgendwo.

thereafter [,ðeər'ɑ:ftə^r] *adv fml* danach.

thereby [,ðeər'baɪ] *adv fml* damit.

therefore ['ðeəfɔ:^r] *adv* deshalb, deswegen.

there's [ðeəz] *abbr of* **there is**.

thermal ['θɜ:ml] *adj* [clothes] Thermo-.

thermometer [θə'mɒmɪtə^r] *n* Thermometer *das*.

Thermos (flask)® ['θɜ:məs-] *n* Thermosflasche® *die*.

thermostat ['θɜ:məstæt] *n* Thermostat *der*.

thesaurus [θɪ'sɔ:rəs] *(pl* **-es***)* *n* Thesaurus *der*.

these [ði:z] *Pl* ▷ **this**.

thesis ['θi:sɪs] *(pl* **theses** ['θi:si:z]*)* *n* - **1.** [argument] These *die* - **2.** [doctoral dissertation] Dissertation *die*, Doktorarbeit *die*.

they [ðeɪ] *pers pron* & *Pl* - **1.** [gen] sie; **they're happy** sie sind glücklich; **they're pretty earrings** das sind hübsche Ohrringe; **it is they who are responsible** sie sind es, die verantwortlich sind; **they can't do it die** können es nicht tun - **2.** [unspecified people] man; **they still haven't repaired the road** sie haben immer noch nicht die Straße repariert; **they say that...** man sagt, dass...

they'd [ðeɪd] *abbr of* **they had**, **they would**.

they'll [ðeɪl] *abbr of* **they shall**, **they will**.

they're [ðeə^r] *abbr of* **they are**.

they've [ðeɪv] *abbr of* **they have**.

thick [θɪk] ◇ *adj* - **1.** [gen] dick; **it is one metre thick** es ist einen Meter dick - **2.** [dense] dicht; **thick with smoke** voller Rauch - **3.** *inf* [stupid] dumm - **4.** [accent] stark. ◇ *n*: **to be in the thick of it** mittendrin sein.

thicken ['θɪkn] ◇ *vt* [soup, sauce] ein|dicken. ◇ *vi* [forest, crowd, fog] dichter werden; [soup, sauce] dicker werden.

thickness ['θɪknɪs] *n* - **1.** [width, depth] Dicke *die* - **2.** [density] Dichte *die* - **3.** [viscosity] Dickflüssigkeit *die*.

thickset [,θɪk'set] *adj* gedrungen.

thick-skinned [-'skɪnd] *adj* dickfellig.

thief [θi:f] (*pl* **thieves**) *n* Dieb *der*, -in *die*.

thieve [θi:v] *vt* & *vi* stehlen.

thieves [θi:vz] *Pl* ▷ **thief**.

thigh [θaɪ] *n* Oberschenkel *der*.

thimble ['θɪmbl] *n* Fingerhut *der*.

thin [θɪn] *adj* - **1.** [gen] dünn - **2.** [sparse] gering; [mist] leicht; [hair] dünn, schütter - **3.** [poor - excuse] fadenscheinig. ◆ **thin down** *vt sep* verdünnen.

thing [θɪŋ] *n* - **1.** [affair, item, subject] Sache *die*, Ding *das*; **the (best) thing to do would be...** das Beste wäre (es)...; **the thing is ...** die Sache ist die, dass ... - **2.** [anything]: **not a thing** gar nichts - **3.** [object, creature] Ding *das*; **the lucky thing!** der/die Glückliche!; **you poor thing!** du Armer/Arme! ◆ **things** *npl* - **1.** [clothes, possessions] Sachen *Pl* - **2.** *inf* [life] Dinge *Pl*.

think [θɪŋk] (*pt* & *pp* **thought**) ◇ *vt* - **1.** [believe]: **to think (that)...** denken(, dass)..., glauben(, dass)...; **I think so** ich glaube schon; **I don't think so** ich glaube nicht - **2.** [have in mind]: **to think (that)...** denken(, dass)...; **what are you thinking?** woran denkst du? - **3.** [imagine] sich *(D)* denken, sich *(D)* vor|stellen - **4.** [in polite requests]: **do you think you could help me?** könnten Sie mir vielleicht helfen? ◇ *vi* - **1.** [use mind] denken; **I thought for a long time** ich dachte lange nach - **2.** [have stated opinion]: **what do you think of** *OR* **about his new film?** was hältst du von seinem neuen Film?; **I don't think much of them/it** ich halte nicht viel von ihnen/davon; **to think a lot of sb/sthg** viel von jm/etw halten - **3.** *phr*: **to think twice before doing sthg** es sich *(D)* genau überlegen, bevor man etw tut. ◆ **think about** *vt insep* [consider] nach|denken über *(+ A)*; **to think about doing sthg** daran denken, etw zu tun. ◆ **think of** *vt insep* - **1.** [consider, remember, show consideration for] denken an *(+ A)*; **to think of doing sthg** daran denken, etw zu tun; **I can't think of her name** ich kann mich nicht an ihren Namen erinnern, ich komme nicht auf ihren Namen - **2.** [conceive] sich *(D)* aus|denken; **to think of doing sthg** die Idee haben, etw zu tun; **we'll think of sthg** wir werden uns *(D)* etwas einfallen lassen. ◆ **think over** *vt sep* überdenken. ◆ **think up** *vt sep* sich *(D)* aus|denken.

think tank *n* Expertenkommission *die*.

third [θɜ:d] ◇ *num* dritte(r) (s). ◇ *n* - **1.** [fraction] Drittel *das* - **2.** *UK* UNIV *Abschluss mit "Befriedigend"*; *see also* **sixth**.

thirdly ['θɜ:dlɪ] *adv* drittens.

third-rate *adj pej* drittklassig.

Third World *n*: **the Third World** die Dritte Welt.

thirst [θɜ:st] *n* Durst *der*; **a thirst for sthg** *fig* ein Durst nach etw; **thirst for adventure** Abenteuerlust *die*.

thirsty ['θɜ:stɪ] *adj*: **to be** *OR* **feel thirsty** Durst haben, durstig sein; **this is thirsty work** diese Arbeit macht durstig.

thirteen [,θɜ:'ti:n] *num* dreizehn; *see also* **six**.

thirty ['θɜ:tɪ] *num* dreißig; *see also* **sixty**.

this [ðɪs] (*pl* **these**) ◇ *pron* - **1.** *(referring to thing, person mentioned)* das; **this is for you** das ist für dich; **who's/what's this?** wer/was ist das?; **what are these?** was ist das?; **this is Daphne Logan** [introducing someone] das ist Daphne Logan; [introducing o.s. on phone] hier ist Daphne Logan; **before this** früher - **2.** *(referring to thing, person nearer speaker)* diese(r) (s), diese *Pl*; **which shoes do you want, these or those?** welche Schuhe wollen Sie, die hier oder die da?; **I want these here** ich möchte die hier. ◇ *adj* - **1.** *(referring to thing, person)* diese(r) (s), diese *Pl*; **I prefer this book** ich bevorzuge dieses Buch; **these chocolates are delicious** diese Pralinen schmecken köstlich; **I'll have this one/these ones** ich nehme dieses/diese; **this morning/evening** heute Morgen/Abend; **this week** diese Woche; **this Sunday/summer** diesen Sonntag/Sommer - **2.** *inf* [a certain]: **there was this man** da war dieser Mann; **this woman came over to my table** diese Frau kam an meinen Tisch. ◇ *adv* so; **it was this big** es war so groß; **this far** bis hier.

thistle ['θɪsl] *n* Distel *die*.

thorn [θɔ:n] *n* [prickle] Dorn *der*.

thorny ['θɔ:nɪ] *adj* - **1.** [prickly] dornig - **2.** *fig* [tricky, complicated] heikel.

thorough ['θʌrə] *adj* - **1.** [exhaustive, meticulous] gründlich; [worker] sorgfältig, gewissenhaft - **2.** [complete, utter] völlig; **that's a thorough nuisance** das ist wirklich lästig.

thoroughbred ['θʌrəbred] *n* [horse] Vollblut *das*.

thoroughfare ['θʌrəfeəʳ] *n fml* Durchgangsstraße *die*.

thoroughly ['θʌrəlɪ] *adv* - **1.** [fully, in detail] gründlich - **2.** [completely, utterly] durch und durch.

those [ðəʊz] *Pl* ▷ **that**.

though [ðəʊ] ◇ *conj* - **1.** [in spite of the fact that] obwohl, obgleich - **2.** [even if] wenn auch. ◇ *adv* [nevertheless] aber; **he's quite intelligent, though** er ist aber ziemlich intelligent.

thought [θɔ:t] ◇ *pt* & *pp* ▷ **think**. ◇ *n* - **1.** [notion] Gedanke *der* - **2.** *(U)* [act of thinking] Nachdenken *das*; **to give some thought to sthg** über etw *(A)* nach|denken; **after much thought** nach langem Überlegen - **3.** [philosophy] Denken *das* - **4.** [gesture]: **it's the thought that counts** der gute Wille zählt. ◆ **thoughts** *npl* Gedanken *Pl*.

thoughtful ['θɔ:tful] *adj* - **1.** [pensive - person, mood] nachdenklich - **2.** [considerate - person] rücksichtsvoll; [- action, remark] wohl überlegt.

thoughtless ['θɔ:tlɪs] *adj* [person, behaviour] rücksichtslos; [remark] unüberlegt.

thousand ['θaʊznd] *num* - **1.** [number] tausend; **a/one thousand** (ein)tausend; **five thousand and forty-two** fünftausend(und)zweiundvierzig; **thousands of** Tausende von - **2.** *fig* [umpteen]: **a thousand** tausend; **I have a thousand things to do** ich habe tausend Dinge zu tun; *see also* **six**.

thousandth ['θaʊzntθ] ◇ *num* tausendste(r) (s). ◇ *n* [fraction] Tausendstel *das*; *see also* **sixth**.

thrash [θræʃ] *vt* - **1.** [beat, hit] prügeln - **2.** *inf* [trounce] fertig machen. ◆ **thrash about, thrash around** *vi* sich hin und her werfen. ◆ **thrash out** *vt sep* durch|diskutieren.

thread [θred] ◇ *n* - **1.** [of cotton, wool] Faden *der* - **2.** [of screw] Gewinde *das* - **3.** *fig* [theme]: **to follow the thread of sb's argument** js Gedankengang *(D)* folgen; **she lost the thread (of what she was saying)** sie hat den Faden verloren. ◇ *vt* [needle] ein|fädeln; [beads] auf|ziehen.

threadbare ['θredbeəʳ] *adj* [garment] abgetragen; [carpet] abgewetzt.

threat [θret] *n* - **1.** [warning] Drohung *die* - **2.** [menace]: **threat (to sb/sthg)** Bedrohung *die* OR Gefahr *die* (für jn/etw) - **3.** [risk]: **the threat of war/inflation** die Gefahr eines Krieges/einer Inflation; **there is a threat of storms** es kann Stürme geben.

threaten ['θretn] ◇ *vt* - **1.** [issue threat]: **to threaten sb (with sthg)** jm (mit etw) drohen; **to threaten to do sthg** drohen, etw zu tun - **2.** [be likely]: **to threaten to do sthg** drohen, etw zu tun - **3.** [endanger] bedrohen, gefährden. ◇ *vi* drohen.

three [θri:] *num* drei; *see also* **six**.

three-dimensional [-dɪ'menʃənl] *adj* dreidimensional.

threefold ['θri:fəʊld] *adj* & *adv* dreifach.

three-piece *adj* dreiteilig.

three-ply *adj* [wool] dreifädig; [wood] dreischichtig.

thresh [θreʃ] *vt* dreschen.

threshold ['θreʃhəʊld] *n* - **1.** [doorway] Türschwelle *die* - **2.** [level] Schwelle *die*.

threw [θru:] *pt* ▷ **throw**.

thrift shop *n US Secondhandladen, dessen Erlöse einem wohltätigen Zweck zugute kommen.*

thrifty ['θrɪftɪ] *adj* [person] sparsam.

thrill [θrɪl] ◇ *n* - **1.** [sudden feeling] Erregung *die*; **a thrill of horror** ein Schauder des Entsetzens; **I felt a thrill of joy** ich war freudig erregt - **2.** [exciting experience] (aufregendes) Erlebnis. ◇ *vt* begeistern, mit|reißen.

thrilled [θrɪld] *adj*: **to be thrilled (with sthg)** (von etw) begeistert sein; **I was thrilled to meet her** ich fand es sehr aufregend, sie zu treffen.

thriller ['θrɪləʳ] *n* Thriller *der*.

thrilling ['θrɪlɪŋ] *adj* [match, book, film] spannend; [news] umwerfend.

thrive [θraɪv] (*pt* **-d** OR **throve**, *pp* **-d**) *vi* [person - be successful] erfolgreich sein; [plant] prächtig gedeihen; [business] blühen.

thriving ['θraɪvɪŋ] *adj* [person - successful] erfolgreich; [plant] prächtig gedeihend; [business] blühend.

throat [θrəʊt] *n* - **1.** [inside mouth] Hals *der* - **2.** [front of neck] Kehle *die*.

throb [θrɒb] *vi* - **1.** [beat - pulse, heart] pochen; [- blood] pulsieren; [- engine, machine, music] dröhnen - **2.** [be painful]: **my head is throbbing** ich habe pochende Kopfschmerzen.

throes [θrəʊz] *npl*: **to be in the throes of sthg** mitten in etw *(D)* stecken.

throne [θrəʊn] *n* Thron *der*.

throng [θrɒŋ] ◇ *n* [crowd] Menschenmenge *die*; **a throng of** Scharen *Pl* von. ◇ *vt* [place] belagern; [streets] sich drängen in *(+ D)*.

throttle ['θrɒtl] ◇ *n* - **1.** [valve] Drosselklappe *die* - **2.** [lever] Gashebel *der*; [Pedal] Gaspedal *das*; **at full throttle** mit Vollgas. ◇ *vt* [strangle] erwürgen.

through [θru:] ◇ *adj* - **1.** [finished]: **to be through (with sthg)** (mit etw) fertig sein - **2.** [referring to transport]: **through traffic** Durchgangsverkehr *der*; **a through train** ein durchgehender Zug. ◇ *adv* - **1.** [from one end to another] durch; **to let sb through** jn durch|lassen; **wet through** völlig durchnässt - **2.** [until]: **I slept through till ten** ich schlief bis zehn durch; **we stayed through till Friday** wir blieben bis Freitag. ◇ *prep* - **1.** [from one side to another] durch; **he went through the park** er ging durch den Park; **to drill through sthg** etw durch|bohren; **I'm halfway through this book** ich habe das Buch schon halb gelesen - **2.** [during, throughout] während *(+ G)*; **all through his life** sein ganzes Leben hindurch - **3.** [because of] wegen *(+ G)*; **absent through illness** wegen Krankheit abwesend; **through fear** aus Furcht - **4.** [by means of] durch; **I got the job through a friend** ich bekam die Stelle durch einen Freund - **5.** *US* [up until and including]: **Monday through Thursday** Montag bis Donnerstag. ◆ **through and through** *adv* - **1.** [completely] durch und durch - **2.** [thoroughly - know] gründlich.

throughout [θru:'aʊt] ◇ *prep* - **1.** [during]: **throughout the day/morning** den ganzen Tag/Morgen (über); **throughout the year** das ganze Jahr (hindurch); **throughout her life** ihr ganzes Leben lang - **2.** [everywhere in] überall in *(+ D)*; **throughout the country** im ganzen Land. ◇ *adv* - **1.** [all the time] die ganze Zeit (über) - **2.** [everywhere] überall; [completely] ganz.

throve [θrəʊv] *pt* ▷ **thrive**.

throw [θrəʊ] (*pt* **threw**, *pp* **thrown**) ◇ *vt* - **1.** [propel, put] werfen - **2.** [move suddenly]: **he threw himself to the floor/onto the bed** er warf sich auf den Boden/das Bett - **3.** [rider] ab|werfen - **4.** *fig* [force]: **to throw sb into confusion** jn durcheinander bringen - **5.** *fig* [confuse] aus dem Konzept bringen. ◇ *n* [toss, pitch] Wurf *der*. ◆ **throw away** *vt sep* - **1.** [discard] weg|werfen - **2.** *fig* [money, time] vergeuden; [opportunity] nicht nutzen. ◆ **throw out** *vt sep* - **1.** [discard] weg|werfen - **2.** *fig* [reject] ab|lehnen - **3.** [force to leave] hinaus|werfen. ◆ **throw up** *vi inf* [vomit] sich übergeben.

throwaway ['θrəʊə,weɪ] *adj* - **1.** [product, bottle] Wegwerf- - **2.** [remark] beiläufig.

throw-in *n UK* FTBL Einwurf *der*.

thrown [θrəʊn] *pp* ▷ **throw**.

thru [θruː] *adj, adv & prep US inf* = **through**.

thrush [θrʌʃ] *n* [bird] Drossel *die*.

thrust [θrʌst] (*pt & pp inv*) ◇ *n* - **1.** [forward movement - of knife, sword] Stoß *der*; MIL Vorstoß *der* - **2.** [main aspect] Tenor *der*. ◇ *vt* [jab, shove]: **to thrust sthg into sthg** [knife, stick] etw in etw *(A)* stoßen; **she thrust the money into her pocket** sie stopfte das Geld in ihre Tasche.

thud [θʌd] ◇ *n* dumpfer Aufschlag. ◇ *vi* dumpf auf|schlagen; [feet] stampfen.

thug [θʌg] *n* Schläger *der*.

thumb [θʌm] ◇ *n* [of hand] Daumen *der*. ◇ *vt inf* [hitch]: **to thumb a lift** per Anhalter fahren. ◆ **thumb through** *vt insep* durch|blättern.

thumbs down [,θʌmz-] *n*: **to get** OR **be given the thumbs down** abgelehnt werden.

thumbs up *n* [go-ahead]: **to get** OR **be given the thumbs up** grünes Licht bekommen.

thumbtack ['θʌmtæk] *n US* Reißzwecke *die*.

thump [θʌmp] ◇ *n* - **1.** [blow] Schlag *der* - **2.** [thud] Bums *der*. ◇ *vt* [punch] schlagen. ◇ *vi* [heart] heftig pochen.

thunder ['θʌndəʳ] ◇ *n (U)* - **1.** METEOR Donner *der* - **2.** *fig* [loud sound] Donnern *das*. ◇ *impers vb* METEOR: **it is thundering** es donnert.

thunderbolt ['θʌndəbəʊlt] *n* - **1.** METEOR Blitz *der* - **2.** *fig* [shock]: **the news was a thunderbolt** die Nachricht schlug wie ein Blitz ein.

thunderclap ['θʌndəklæp] *n* Donnerschlag *der*.

thunderstorm ['θʌndəstɔːm] *n* Gewitter *das*.

Thursday ['θɜːzdɪ] *n* Donnerstag *der*; *see also* **Saturday**.

thus [ðʌs] *adv fml* - **1.** [as a consequence] daher - **2.** [in this way] auf diese Weise - **3.** [as follows] folgendermaßen.

thwart [θwɔːt] *vt* vereiteln; [person] einen Strich durch die Rechnung machen *(+ D)*.

thyme [taɪm] *n* Thymian *der*.

tiara [tɪ'ɑːrə] *n* [piece of jewellery] Diadem *das*.

Tibet [tɪ'bet] *n* Tibet *nt*.

tic [tɪk] *n* Zucken *das*.

tick [tɪk] ◇ *n* - **1.** [written mark] Häkchen *das* - **2.** [sound] Ticken *das* - **3.** [insect] Zecke *die*. ◇ *vt* [name] ab|haken; [answer, box on form] an|kreuzen. ◇ *vi* [make ticking sound] ticken. ◆ **tick off** *vt sep* - **1.** [mark off] ab|haken - **2.** *inf* [tell off]: **to tick sb off (for sthg)** jn (wegen etw) rüffeln. ◆ **tick over** *vi* - **1.** [engine] im Leerlauf sein - **2.** [business, organization] ganz gut laufen.

ticket ['tɪkɪt] *n* - **1.** [for match, concert] Eintrittskarte *die*; [for bus, train, tram] Fahrkarte *die*, Fahrschein *der*; [for plane] Ticket *das*; [for lottery, raffle] Los *das*; [for library] Ausweis *der*; [for car park] Parkschein *der* - **2.** [on product]: **(price) ticket** Preisschild *das* - **3.** [notice of traffic offence] Strafzettel *der*.

ticket collector *n UK* [on train] Schaffner *der*, -in *die*; [in station] Fahrkartenkontrolleur *der*, -in *die*.

ticket inspector *n UK* [on bus, tram] Fahrkartenkontrolleur *der*, -in *die*; [on train] Schaffner *der*, -in *die*.

ticket machine *n* [for public transport] Fahrscheinautomat *der*; [in car park] Parkscheinautomat *der*.

ticket office *n* [at railway station] Fahrkartenschalter *der*; [at theatre] Theaterkasse *die*.

tickle ['tɪkl] ◇ *vt* [touch lightly] kitzeln; [subj: beard, wool] kratzen. ◇ *vi* [foot, back] jucken; [beard, wool] kratzen.

ticklish ['tɪklɪʃ] *adj* [sensitive to touch] kitzlig.

tidal ['taɪdl] *adj* Gezeiten-.

tidal wave *n* Flutwelle *die*.

tidbit ['tɪdbɪt] *n US* = **titbit**.

tiddlywinks ['tɪdlɪwɪŋks], **tiddledywinks** *US* ['tɪdldɪwɪŋks] *n (U)* [game] Flohhüpfspiel *das*.

tide [taɪd] *n* - **1.** [of sea] Gezeiten *Pl*; **high tide** Flut *die*; **low tide** Ebbe *die*; **the tide is in/out** es ist Flut/Ebbe - **2.** *fig* [trend]: **the tide of (public) opinion** der Trend der öffentlichen Meinung; **to swim with/against the tide** mit dem/gegen den Strom schwimmen - **3.** *fig* [large quantity]: **a tide of protest** eine Flut von Protesten.

tidy ['taɪdɪ] ◇ *adj* [gen] ordentlich; [appearance] gepflegt. ◇ *vt* auf|räumen. ◆ **tidy up** *vt sep & vi* auf|räumen.

tie [taɪ] (*pt & pp* **tied**, *cont* **tying**) ◇ *n* - **1.** [necktie] Krawatte *die* - **2.** [in game, competition] Unentschieden *das*. ◇ *vt* - **1.** [attach]: **to tie sthg (on)to sthg** etw an etw *(A)* binden; **to tie sthg round sthg** etw um etw binden; **my hands are tied** *fig* mir sind die Hände gebunden; **to tie sthg with sthg** etw mit etw zusammen|binden - **2.** [do up, fasten] binden; [knot] machen - **3.** *fig* [link]: **to be tied to sb/sthg** an jn/etw gebunden sein. ◇ *vi* [in sport] unentschieden spielen. ◆ **tie down** *vt sep fig* [restrict]: **to be tied down by sthg** durch etw eingeschränkt sein. ◆ **tie in with** *vt insep* passen zu. ◆ **tie up** *vt sep* - **1.** [parcel, papers] verschnüren; [person] fesseln; [animal] an|binden - **2.** [shoelaces] binden - **3.** *fig* [savings] fest anlegen - **4.** *fig* [link]: **to be tied up with sthg** mit etw zusammen|hängen.

tiebreak(er) ['taɪbreɪk(əʳ)] *n* - **1.** TENNIS Tiebreak *das* - **2.** [extra question] Entscheidungsfrage *die*.

tiepin ['taɪpɪn] *n* Krawattennadel *die*.

tier [tɪəʳ] *n* [of seats] Rang *der*; [of cake] Etage *die*.

tiff [tɪf] *n* Krach *der*.

tiger ['taɪgəʳ] *n* Tiger *der*.

tight [taɪt] ◇ *adj* - **1.** [close-fitting] eng; **the dress was a very tight fit** das Kleid war sehr eng - **2.** [secure - lid] fest sitzend; [- screw] fest angezogen; [- knot] fest - **3.** [taut] straff - **4.** [close together - bundle] fest zusammengebunden; **they stood in a tight group** sie standen eng zusammen - **5.** [schedule] eng; [money, match, finish] knapp - **6.** [rule, control] streng - **7.** [bend] scharf, eng - **8.** *inf* [drunk] voll - **9.** *inf* [miserly] knauserig. ◇ *adv* - **1.** [firmly, securely] fest; **to hold tight** fest|halten; **to shut** OR **close sthg tight** [eyes] etw fest schließen; [lid] etw fest verschließen - **2.** [tautly] straff. ◆ **tights** *npl* Strumpfhose *die*.

tighten ['taɪtn] ◇ *vt* - **1.** [knot, belt, screw] an|ziehen - **2.** [make tauter] straffen, spannen - **3.** [strengthen]: **to tighten one's hold** OR **grip on sthg** etw fester halten; *fig* [on party, country] seine Macht in etw *(D)* aus|bauen - **4.** [rule, control, security] verschärfen. ◇ *vi* [grip, hold] fester werden; [rope, chain] sich spannen.

tightfisted [ˌtaɪt'fɪstɪd] *adj inf pej* knauserig.

tightly ['taɪtlɪ] *adv* [firmly, securely] fest.

tightrope ['taɪtrəʊp] *n* Drahtseil *das*.

tile [taɪl] *n* - **1.** [on roof] Dachziegel *der* - **2.** [on floor, wall] Fliese *die*, Kachel *die*.

tiled [taɪld] *adj* [floor, wall, bath] gefliest.

till [tɪl] ◇ *prep* & *conj* bis. ◇ *n* Kasse *die*.

tilt [tɪlt] ◇ *vt* [object, chair] kippen; [head] neigen. ◇ *vi* [person, chair] kippen; [head] sich neigen.

timber ['tɪmbəʳ] *n* - **1.** *(U)* [wood] Holz *das* - **2.** [beam] Balken *der*.

time [taɪm] ◇ *n* - **1.** [gen] Zeit *die*; **at that time** zu der Zeit, damals; **now is the time to do it** jetzt ist der richtige Zeitpunkt OR die richtige Zeit, es zu tun; **it will take time** es wird einige Zeit dauern; **to have no time for sb/sthg** keine Zeit für jn/etw haben; **to pass the time** sich *(D)* die Zeit vertreiben; **to play for time** versuchen, Zeit zu gewinnen - **2.** [as measured by clock]: **what time is it?, what's the time?** wie spät ist es?, wie viel Uhr ist es?; **at this time of the day** zu dieser Tageszeit; **in a week's/year's time** in einer Woche/einem Jahr; **could you tell me the time?** können Sie mir sagen, wie spät es ist?; **can she tell the time?** kann sie schon die Uhr lesen? - **3.** [while, spell]: **it was a long time before...** es dauerte lange, bevor...; **in a short time** bald; **for a time** einige Zeit(lang) - **4.** [era] Zeit *die*; **in ancient times** zur Zeit der Antike; **in modern times** heutzutage - **5.** [occasion] Mal *das*; **this time** diesmal, dieses Mal; **(the) last time** letztes Mal, das letzte Mal; **three times a week** dreimal pro OR in der Woche; **from time to time** von Zeit zu Zeit; **time after time, time and again** immer wieder - **6.** [experience]: **we had a good time** es war schön; **to have a hard time** viel durch|machen; **to have a hard time doing sthg** Schwierigkeiten haben, etw zu tun - **7.** [degree of lateness]: **to be in good time** OR **ahead of time** früh dran sein; **on time** pünktlich; **did you get there on time?** warst du rechtzeitig dort? - **8.** MUS Takt *der*; **to beat time** den Takt an|geben; **in 4/4 time** im Viervierteltakt. ◇ *vt* - **1.** [schedule]: **the meeting was timed to start at nine o'clock** der Beginn der Sitzung war auf neun Uhr angesetzt - **2.** [measure - race, runner] die Zeit stoppen von; **I timed how long it took him** ich habe gestoppt, wie lange er gebraucht hat - **3.** [choose appropriate moment for] zeitlich ab|stimmen. ◆ **times** ◇ *npl*: **four times as much/many** viermal so viel/viele; **three times as big** dreimal so groß. ◇ *prep* MATHS mal; **10 times 4 is 40** 10 mal 4 ist 40. ◆ **about time** *adv*: **it's about time (that)...** es wird (langsam) Zeit, dass... ◆ **at a time** *adv*: **three/four at a time** drei/vier auf einmal; **one at a time** eine(r) (s) nach dem anderen; **for months at a time** monatelang. ◆ **at times** *adv* manchmal. ◆ **at the same time** *adv* - **1.** [simultaneously] gleichzeitig, zur gleichen Zeit - **2.** [equally] trotzdem, dennoch. ◆ **for the time being** *adv* vorläufig. ◆ **in time** *adv* - **1.** [not late] rechtzeitig; **to be in time for sthg** rechtzeitig für etw kommen - **2.** [eventually] schließlich; [over a long period] mit der Zeit.

time bomb *n liter* & *fig* Zeitbombe *die*.

time lag *n* Zeitabstand *der*.

timeless ['taɪmlɪs] *adj* zeitlos.

time limit *n* Frist *die*.

timely ['taɪmlɪ] *adj* rechtzeitig.

time off *n (U)* freie Zeit.

time-out (*pl* **time-outs**) *n* SPORT Auszeit *die*.

timer ['taɪmə^r] *n* [time switch] Schaltuhr *die*.

time scale *n* [for project] Zeitspanne *die*.

time-share *n UK Ferienwohnung, an der man einen Besitzanteil hat.*

time switch *n* Schaltuhr *die*.

timetable ['taɪm,teɪbl] *n* - **1.** SCH Stundenplan *der* - **2.** [of buses, trains] Fahrplan *der* - **3.** [schedule] Programm *das*.

time zone *n* Zeitzone *die*.

timid ['tɪmɪd] *adj* schüchtern.

timing ['taɪmɪŋ] *n (U)* - **1.** [of actor, musician, tennis player] Timing *das* - **2.** [chosen moment]: **the timing of the remark/election was unfortunate** der Zeitpunkt der Bemerkung/Wahlen war unglücklich gewählt - **3.** SPORT [measuring] Stoppen *das*.

tin [tɪn] *n* - **1.** *(U)* [metal] Blech *das* - **2.** *UK* [can] Dose *die* - **3.** [for storing] Dose *die*.

tin can *n* Blechdose *die*.

tinfoil ['tɪnfɔɪl] *n (U)* Alufolie *die*.

tinge [tɪndʒ] *n* Spur *die*.

tinged [tɪndʒd] *adj*: **tinged with sthg** mit einer Spur von etw.

tingle ['tɪŋgl] *vi* kribbeln.

tinker ['tɪŋkə^r] <> *n* Frechdachs *der*. <> *vi*: **to tinker (with sthg)** (an etw *(D)*) herum|basteln.

tinned [tɪnd] *adj UK* Dosen-.

tin opener *n UK* Dosenöffner *der*.

tinsel ['tɪnsl] *n* ≃ Lametta *das*.

tint [tɪnt] *n* Ton *der*.

tinted ['tɪntɪd] *adj* getönt.

tiny ['taɪnɪ] *adj* winzig.

tip [tɪp] <> *n* - **1.** [end] Spitze *die* - **2.** *UK* [dump] Müllkippe *die* - **3.** [gratuity] Trinkgeld *das* - **4.** [piece of advice] Tipp *der*. <> *vt* - **1.** [tilt] kippen - **2.** [spill] schütten - **3.** [give a gratuity to] Trinkgeld geben *(+ D)*. <> *vi* - **1.** [tilt] kippen - **2.** [spill] heraus|fallen; [liquid] sich ergießen. ◆ **tip over** *vt sep* & *vi* um|kippen.

tip-off *n* Tipp *der*.

tipped ['tɪpt] *adj* [cigarette] mit Filter.

tipsy ['tɪpsɪ] *adj inf* beschwipst.

tiptoe ['tɪptəʊ] <> *n*: **on tiptoe** auf Zehenspitzen. <> *vi* auf Zehenspitzen gehen.

tire ['taɪə^r] <> *n US* = **tyre**. <> *vt* ermüden. <> *vi* - **1.** [get tired] müde werden - **2.** [get fed up]: **to tire of sb/sthg** von jm/etw genug haben.

tired ['taɪəd] *adj* - **1.** [sleepy] müde - **2.** [fed up]: **to be tired of sthg** etw leid sein; **to be tired of doing sthg** es leid sein, etw zu tun.

tireless ['taɪəlɪs] *adj* unermüdlich.

tiresome ['taɪəsəm] *adj* lästig.

tiring ['taɪərɪŋ] *adj* ermüdend.

tissue ['tɪʃuː] *n* - **1.** [paper handkerchief] Tempo® *das*, Papiertaschentuch *das* - **2.** *(U)* BIOL Gewebe *das*.

tissue paper *n (U)* Seidenpapier *das*.

tit [tɪt] *n* - **1.** [bird] Meise *die* - **2.** *vulg* [breast] Titte *die*.

titbit *UK* ['tɪtbɪt], **tidbit** *US* ['tɪdbɪt] *n liter & fig* Leckerbissen *der*.

tit for tat [-'tæt] *n* wie du mir, so ich dir.

titillate ['tɪtɪleɪt] *vt* [person] an|regen.

title ['taɪtl] *n* Titel *der*.

titter ['tɪtə^r] *vi* kichern.

TM *abbr of* **trademark**.

to *(unstressed before consonant* [tə], *unstressed before vowel* [tʊ], *stressed* [tuː]*)* <> *prep* - **1.** [indicating direction] nach; **to go to Liverpool/Spain** nach Liverpool/Spanien fahren; **to go to the USA** in die USA fahren; **to go to school/the cinema** in die Schule/ins Kino gehen; **to go to university** auf die Universität gehen; **to go to work/the doctor's** zur Arbeit/zum Arzt gehen; **the road to Bakersfield** die Straße nach Bakersfield - **2.** [indicating position]: **I nailed it to the wall** ich habe es an die Wand genagelt; **to the left** links; **to the right** rechts; **to the east/west (of the river)** östlich/westlich (des Flusses) - **3.** *(to express indirect object)*: **to give sthg to sb** jm etw geben; **to talk to sb** mit jm sprechen; **to listen to the radio** Radio hören; **we added milk to the mixture** wir fügten Milch zu der Mischung hinzu - **4.** [as far as] bis; **from here to London** von hier bis London; **to count to ten** bis zehn zählen; **we work from nine to five** wir arbeiten von 9 bis 5; **a year to the day** ein Jahr auf den Tag genau - **5.** *UK* [in telling the time] vor; **it's ten to three** es ist zehn vor drei - **6.** [per] pro; **10 kilometres to the litre** 10 Kilometer pro Liter - **7.** [in ratios]: **six votes to four** sechs Stimmen gegen vier; **he's ten to one to win** es steht zehn zu eins, dass er gewinnt - **8.** [of, for]: **the key to the car** der Schlüssel für das Auto; **a letter to my daughter** ein Brief an meine Tochter - **9.** [indicating reaction, effect] zu; **to my surprise** zu meiner Überraschung; **it would be to your advantage** es wäre zu Ihrem Vorteil - **10.** [in stating opinion]: **to me, he's lying** meiner Meinung nach, lügt er; **it seemed quite unnecessary to me/him/*etc*** mir/ihm/*etc* erschien dies recht unnötig - **11.** [indicating process, change of state]: **to turn to ice** zu Eis werden; **it could lead to trouble** das könnte Ärger geben. <> *with inf* - **1.** *(forming simple infinitive)*: **to walk** gehen; **to laugh** lachen - **2.** *(following another vb)*: **to begin/try to do sthg** an|fangen/versuchen, etw zu tun; **to want to do sthg** etw tun wollen - **3.** *(following an adj)* zu; **difficult to do** schwer zu tun; **ready to go** bereit zu gehen - **4.** *(indicating purpose)* um zu; **we came here to look at the castle** wir sind hierher gekommen, um das Schloss anzuschauen - **5.** *(replacing a relative clause)*: **he is the first to complain** er ist der Erste, der sich beschwert; **to have a lot to do** viel zu tun haben; **he told me to leave** er sagte, ich solle gehen - **6.** *(to avoid repetition of infinitive)*: **I meant to call him, but I forgot to** ich wollte ihn eigentlich anrufen, vergaß es aber; **you ought to** du solltest es tun - **7.** [in comments]: **to be honest** um ehrlich zu sein; **to sum up** um zusammenzufassen. ◇ *adv* [shut]: **push the door to** drück die Tür zu. ◆ **to and fro** *adv* hin und her; **to go to and fro** kommen und gehen.

toad [təʊd] *n* Kröte *die*.

toadstool ['təʊdstu:l] *n* Giftpilz *der*.

toast [təʊst] ◇ *n (U)* [bread, drink] Toast *der*. ◇ *vt* - **1.** [bread] toasten - **2.** [person] trinken auf *(+ A)*.

toasted sandwich [ˌtəʊstɪd-] *n* getoastetes Sandwich.

toaster ['təʊstəʳ] *n* Toaster *der*.

tobacco [tə'bækəʊ] *n* Tabak *der*.

tobacconist [tə'bækənɪst] *n*: **tobacconist's (shop)** Tabakwarenhandlung *die*.

toboggan [tə'bɒgən] *n* Schlitten *der*.

today [tə'deɪ] *n* & *adv (U)* heute.

toddler ['tɒdləʳ] *n* Kleinkind *das*.

to-do (*pl* **-s**) *n inf dated* Getue *das*.

toe [təʊ] ◇ *n* - **1.** [of foot] Zeh *der*, Zehe *die* - **2.** [of sock, shoe] Spitze *die*. ◇ *vt*: **to toe the line** sich an die Regeln halten; [in political party] sich an die Parteilinie halten.

toenail ['təʊneɪl] *n* Zehennagel *der*.

toffee ['tɒfɪ] *n* - **1.** [sweet] Karamellbonbon *das* - **2.** [substance] Karamell *das*.

together [tə'geðəʳ] *adv* - **1.** [gen] zusammen; **to go together** [belong together] zusammen|gehören - **2.** [at the same time] zur gleichen Zeit. ◆ **together with** *prep* zusammen mit.

toil [tɔɪl] *fml* ◇ *n* Mühe *die*. ◇ *vi* sich ab|mühen.

toilet ['tɔɪlɪt] *n* Toilette *die*; **to go to the toilet** zur Toilette gehen.

toilet bag *n* Kulturbeutel *der*.

toilet paper *n* Toilettenpapier *das*.

toiletries ['tɔɪlɪtrɪz] *npl* Toilettenartikel *Pl*.

toilet roll *n* Rolle *die* Toilettenpapier.

token ['təʊkn] ◇ *adj* symbolisch. ◇ *n* - **1.** [voucher, disc] Gutschein *der* - **2.** [symbol] Zeichen *das*. ◆ **by the same token** *adv* ebenso.

told [təʊld] *pt* & *pp* ▷ **tell**.

tolerable ['tɒlərəbl] *adj* [reasonable] annehmbar.

tolerance ['tɒlərəns] *n* Toleranz *die*.

tolerant ['tɒlərənt] *adj* - **1.** [not bigoted]: **tolerant of sb/sthg** tolerant gegenüber jm/etw - **2.** [resistant]: **tolerant to sthg** unempfindlich gegen etw.

tolerate ['tɒləreɪt] *vt* - **1.** [put up with - noise, heat, behaviour] ertragen - **2.** [permit] dulden, tolerieren.

toll [təʊl] *n* - **1.** [number] Zahl *die*; **the death toll** die Zahl der Toten - **2.** [fee] Gebühr *die* - **3.** *phr*: **to take its toll** seinen Tribut fordern.

tomato [*UK* tə'mɑ:təʊ, *US* tə'meɪtəʊ] (*pl* **-es**) *n* Tomate *die*.

tomb [tu:m] *n* Grab *das*.

tomboy ['tɒmbɔɪ] *n*: **she was a bit of a tomboy** sie war wie ein Junge.

tombstone ['tu:mstəʊn] *n* Grabstein *der*.

tomcat ['tɒmkæt] *n* Kater *der*.

tomorrow [tə'mɒrəʊ] *n* & *adv* morgen.

ton [tʌn] (*pl inv* OR **-s**) *n* - **1.** *UK* [imperial unit of measurement] ≃ Tonne *die (= 1016 kg)* - **2.** *US* [unit of measurement] ≃ Tonne *die (= 907 kg)* - **3.** [metric unit of measurement] Tonne *die (= 1000 kg)*. ◆ **tons** *npl UK inf*: **tons of** ein Haufen *(+ G)*.

tone [təʊn] *n* [gen] Ton *der*; **to lower the tone** das Niveau senken. ◆ **tone down** *vt sep* mäßigen. ◆ **tone up** *vt sep* in Form bringen.

tone-deaf *adj*: **to be tone-deaf** kein musikalisches Gehör haben.

tongs [tɒŋz] *npl* - **1.** [for sugar] Zange *die* - **2.** [for hair] Lockenstab *der*.

tongue [tʌŋ] *n* - **1.** [gen] Zunge *die*; **to hold one's tongue** *fig* den Mund halten; **to have a sharp tongue** eine scharfe Zunge haben - **2.** *fml* [language] Sprache *die*.

tongue-in-cheek *adj* ironisch.

tongue-tied *adj*: **to be tongue-tied** kein Wort heraus|bringen.

tonic ['tɒnɪk] *n* - **1.** [tonic water] Tonic *das* - **2.** [medicine] Tonikum *das*.

tonic water *n* Tonic *das*.

tonight [tə'naɪt] *n* & *adv* heute Abend; [during night] heute Nacht.

tonne [tʌn] (*pl inv* OR **-s**) *n* Tonne *die*.

tonsil ['tɒnsl] *n* Mandel *die*.

tonsil(l)itis [ˌtɒnsɪ'laɪtɪs] *n (U)* Mandelentzündung *die*.

too [tu:] *adv* - **1.** [also] auch - **2.** [excessively] zu; **too many** zu viel; **it's too late to go out** es ist zu spät zum Ausgehen; **I know her all** OR **only too well** ich kenne sie nur zu gut; **it was none too comfortable** es war nicht gerade bequem; **not too good** nicht besonders gut; **how do you feel? not too bad** wie fühlst du dich? ganz gut; **I'd be only too happy to help** ich würde wirklich OR nur zu gerne helfen.

took [tʊk] *pt* ▷ **take**.

tool [tu:l] *n* - **1.** [implement] Werkzeug *das* - **2.** *fig* [means] Hilfsmittel *das.*

tool box *n* Werkzeugkasten *der.*

tool kit *n* Werkzeugsatz *der.*

toot [tu:t] ◇ *n*: **to give a toot** hupen. ◇ *vi* hupen.

tooth [tu:θ] (*pl* **teeth**) *n* Zahn *der.*

toothache ['tu:θeɪk] *n (U)* Zahnschmerzen *Pl.*

toothbrush ['tu:θbrʌʃ] *n* Zahnbürste *die.*

toothpaste ['tu:θpeɪst] *n* Zahnpasta *die.*

toothpick ['tu:θpɪk] *n* Zahnstocher *der.*

top [tɒp] ◇ *adj* - **1.** [highest] oberste(r) (s) - **2.** [most important, successful] Spitzen-; **she was top in the exam** sie war die Beste in der Prüfung - **3.** [maximum] Höchst-. ◇ *n* - **1.** [highest point - of road] Ende *das*; [- of stairs] oberste Stufe; [- of hill] Gipfel *der*; [- of tree] Krone *die*; **at the top of the page** oben auf der Seite; **from top to bottom** von oben bis unten; **on top** oben; **at the top of one's voice** aus vollem Halse - **2.** [lid, cap - of bottle, jar] Deckel *der*; [- of pen, tube] Kappe *die* - **3.** [upper side - of table] Platte *die*; [- of box] Oberseite *die* - **4.** [clothing] Oberteil *das* - **5.** [toy] Kreisel *der* - **6.** [in organization, league, table] Spitze *die*; **to be top of the class** Klassenbeste(r) sein. ◇ *vt* - **1.** [be first in - table, chart] an|führen; [- poll, league] an erster Stelle liegen in *(+ D)* - **2.** [better] übertreffen; [offer] überbieten - **3.** [exceed] übersteigen - **4.** [cover]: **to top with cream** Sahne geben auf *(+ A)*; **topped with** mit. ◆ **on top of** *prep* - **1.** [indicating position] auf *(+ D)*; [indicating direction] auf *(+ A)* - **2.** [in addition to] zusätzlich zu. ◆ **top up** *UK*, **top off** *US* *vt sep* nach|füllen.

top floor *n* oberstes Stockwerk.

top hat *n* Zylinder *der.*

top-heavy *adj* kopflastig.

topic ['tɒpɪk] *n* Thema *das.*

topical ['tɒpɪkl] *adj* aktuell.

topless ['tɒplɪs] *adj* [barebreasted] oben ohne.

topmost ['tɒpməʊst] *adj* oberste(r) (s).

topping ['tɒpɪŋ] *n* Garnierung *die.*

topple ['tɒpl] ◇ *vt* [government, leader] stürzen. ◇ *vi* fallen.

top-secret *adj* streng geheim.

topspin ['tɒpspɪn] *n (U)* Topspin *der.*

topsy-turvy [ˌtɒpsɪ'tɜ:vɪ] *adj* - **1.** [messy] durcheinander - **2.** [haywire] verkehrt.

torch [tɔ:tʃ] *n* - **1.** *UK* [electric] Taschenlampe *die* - **2.** [flaming stick] Fackel *die.*

tore [tɔ:ʳ] *pt* ▷ **tear^2**.

torment ◇ *n* ['tɔ:ment] Qual *die.* ◇ *vt* [tɔ:'ment] [worry, annoy] quälen.

torn [tɔ:n] *pp* ▷ **tear^2**.

tornado [tɔ:'neɪdəʊ] (*pl* **-es** OR **-s**) *n* Tornado *das.*

torpedo [tɔ:'pi:dəʊ] (*pl* **-es**) *n* Torpedo *der.*

torrent ['tɒrənt] *n* - **1.** [rushing water] reißender Strom - **2.** [of words] Schwall *der.*

torrid ['tɒrɪd] *adj liter* & *fig* heiß.

tortoise ['tɔ:təs] *n* Schildkröte *die.*

tortoiseshell ['tɔ:təʃel] ◇ *adj* [cat] Schildpatt-. ◇ *n* [material] Schildpatt *das.*

torture ['tɔ:tʃəʳ] ◇ *n* - **1.** *(U)* [punishment] Folter *die* - **2.** *fig* [cruel treatment] Qual *die.* ◇ *vt* foltern.

Tory ['tɔ:rɪ] ◇ *adj* Tory-, konservativ. ◇ *n* Tory *der, die*, Konservative *der, die.*

toss [tɒs] ◇ *vt* - **1.** [throw carelessly] werfen; **she tossed back her head** sie warf ihren Kopf zurück - **2.** [food] schwenken; [salad] mischen; [pancake] wenden - **3.** [coin] werfen; **I'll toss you for it** lass uns eine Münze werfen - **4.** [boat, passengers] hin und her werfen. ◇ *vi* [move about]: **to toss and turn** sich hin und her werfen. ◆ **toss up** *vi* eine Münze werfen.

tot [tɒt] *n* - **1.** *inf* [small child] kleines Kind - **2.** [of drink] Schluck *der.*

total ['təʊtl] *(UK) (US)* ◇ *adj* - **1.** [complete - dedication, despair, darkness] völlig; [- eclipse, failure] total; **total fool** Vollidiot *der* - **2.** [amount, number] Gesamt-. ◇ *n* Gesamtsumme *die*; **a total of 50 people** insgesamt 50 Leute. ◇ *vt* - **1.** [add up] zusammen|zählen - **2.** [amount to] sich belaufen auf *(+ A)*.

totally ['təʊtəlɪ] *adv* völlig.

totter ['tɒtəʳ] *vi* - **1.** [walk unsteadily] taumeln - **2.** *fig* [government] schwanken.

touch [tʌtʃ] ◇ *n* - **1.** *(U)* [act of touching] Berührung *die*; **to be soft to the touch** sich weich an|fühlen - **2.** [detail] Detail *das* - **3.** *(U)* [style] Note *die* - **4.** [contact]: **to get in touch with sb** sich mit jm in Verbindung setzen; **to keep in touch (with sb)** (mit jm) in Kontakt bleiben; **to lose touch with sb** jn aus den Augen verlieren; **to be out of touch with sthg** in Bezug auf etw *(A)* nicht auf dem Laufenden sein - **5.** [small amount]: **a touch (of sthg)** eine Spur (von etw) - **6.** SPORT: **in touch** im Aus. ◇ *vt* - **1.** [make contact with] an|fassen - **2.** [move emotionally] rühren - **3.** [eat, drink] an|rühren. ◇ *vi* - **1.** [make contact - people, things] sich berühren; **don't touch!** nicht anfassen! - **2.** [be in contact] aneinander stoßen. ◆ **touch down** *vi* [plane] auf|setzen. ◆ **touch on** *vt insep* rühren an *(+ A)*.

touch-and-go *adj* ungewiss.

touchdown ['tʌtʃdaʊn] *n* - **1.** [of plane] Aufsetzen *das* - **2.** [in American football] Touchdown *der.*

touched [tʌtʃt] *adj* - **1.** [moved] bewegt - **2.** *inf* [slightly mad] nicht ganz richtig im Kopf.

touching ['tʌtʃɪŋ] *adj* rührend.

touchline ['tʌtʃlaɪn] *n* Auslinie *die.*

touchy ['tʌtʃɪ] *adj* - **1.** [person] empfindlich - **2.** [subject, question] heikel.

tough [tʌf] *adj* - **1.** [gen] hart - **2.** [meat] zäh - **3.** [decision, life] schwer - **4.** [criminal, neighbourhood] rau.

toughen ['tʌfn] *vt* - **1.** [character] hart machen - **2.** [material] härten.

toupee ['tu:peɪ] *n* Toupet *das*.

tour [tʊəʳ] ◇ *n* - **1.** [trip] Tour *die* - **2.** [of building, town, museum] Rundgang *der* - **3.** [of pop group *etc*] Tournee *die*; **to be on tour** auf Tournee sein. ◇ *vt* - **1.** [visit - city, museum] besichtigen; [- country] reisen durch - **2.** SPORT & THEAT eine Tournee machen durch.

touring ['tʊərɪŋ] *n* Herumreisen *das*.

tourism ['tʊərɪzm] *n* Tourismus *der*, Fremdenverkehr *der*.

tourist ['tʊərɪst] *n* Tourist *der*, -in *die*.

tourist (information) office *n* Touristeninformation *die*, Fremdenverkehrsbüro *das*.

tournament ['tɔ:nəmənt] *n* Turnier *das*.

tour operator *n* Reiseveranstalter *der*.

tout [taʊt] ◇ *n* Schwarzhändler *der*, -in *die*. ◇ *vt* [tickets, goods] an|bieten. ◇ *vi*: **to tout for custom** auf Kundenfang sein.

tow [təʊ] ◇ *n*: **to give sb a tow** jn ab|schleppen; **to be on tow** *UK* abgeschleppt werden. ◇ *vt* ab|schleppen.

towards *UK* [tə'wɔ:dz], **toward** *US* [tə'wɔ:d] *prep* - **1.** [in the direction of] zu; **to run towards sb** auf jn zu|laufen; **efforts towards his release** Bemühungen um seine Freilassung - **2.** [facing] nach - **3.** [with regard to] gegenüber; **his feelings towards me** seine Gefühle mir gegenüber OR für mich - **4.** [in time] gegen; **towards nine o'clock** gegen neun Uhr - **5.** [in space]: **to sit towards the back/front** hinten/vorne sitzen - **6.** [as contribution] für; **he gave £20 towards the disaster relief fund** er spendete £20 für Katastrophenhilfsfonds.

towel ['taʊəl] *n* Handtuch *das*.

towelling *UK*, **toweling** *US* ['taʊəlɪŋ] *n (U)* Frotteestoff *der*.

towel rail *n* Handtuchhalter *der*.

tower ['taʊəʳ] ◇ *n* Turm *der*. ◇ *vi* hoch|ragen; **to tower over sb/sthg** jn/etw überragen.

tower block *n UK* Hochhaus *das*.

town [taʊn] *n* Stadt *die*; **to go out on the town** einen drauf|machen; **to go to town** *fig* [spend a lot] es sich *(D)* was kosten lassen; [take trouble] sich ins Zeug legen.

town centre *n* Stadtmitte *die*.

town council *n* Stadtrat *der*.

town hall *n* - **1.** [building] Rathaus *das* - **2.** *(U)* *fig* [council] Stadtrat *der*.

town plan *n* Stadtplan *der*.

town planning *n (U)* Stadtplanung *die*.

towpath ['təʊpɑ:θ] (*pl* [-pɑ:ðz]) *n* Leinpfad *der*.

towrope ['təʊrəʊp] *n* Abschleppseil *das*.

tow truck *n US* Abschleppwagen *der*.

toxic ['tɒksɪk] *adj* giftig.

toy [tɔɪ] *n* Spielzeug *das*. ◆ **toy with** *vt insep* spielen mit.

toy shop *n* Spielwarenladen *der*.

trace [treɪs] ◇ *n* Spur *die*. ◇ *vt* - **1.** [find] auf|spüren - **2.** [follow progress of] verfolgen - **3.** [mark outline of] nach|zeichnen; [with tracing paper] durch|pausen.

tracing paper *n (U)* Transparentpapier *das*.

track [træk] ◇ *n* - **1.** [path] Pfad *der* - **2.** SPORT Bahn *die* - **3.** RAIL Gleis *das* - **4.** [mark, trace] Spur *die* - **5.** [on record, tape, CD] Stück *das* - **6.** *phr*: **to lose track of sb/sthg** jn/etw aus den Augen verlieren; **to be on the right/wrong track** auf der richtigen/falschen Spur sein. ◇ *vt* [follow] nach|spüren *(+ D)*. ◆ **track down** *vt sep* [person, animal] auf|spüren; [book, address] auf|stöbern.

track record *n*: **to have a good track record** gute Erfolge aufzuweisen haben.

tracksuit ['træksu:t] *n* Trainingsanzug *der*.

traction ['trækʃn] *n (U)* PHYS Zugkraft *die*; **in traction** im Streckverband.

tractor ['træktəʳ] *n* Traktor *der*.

trade [treɪd] ◇ *n* - **1.** [commerce] Handel *der* - **2.** [job] Handwerk *das*; **by trade** von Beruf. ◇ *vt* [exchange] tauschen; **to trade sthg for sthg** etw gegen etw ein|tauschen. ◇ *vi* COMM [do business]: **to trade (with sb)** (mit jm) Handel treiben. ◆ **trade in** *vt sep* [exchange] in Zahlung geben.

trade fair *n* Messe *die*.

trade-in *n*: **they gave her a trade-in on her old cooker** sie nahmen ihren alten Herd in Zahlung.

trademark ['treɪdmɑ:k] *n* - **1.** COMM Warenzeichen *das* - **2.** *fig* [characteristic]: **honesty is his trademark** er ist für seine Ehrlichkeit bekannt.

trade name *n* COMM Handelsname *der*.

trader ['treɪdəʳ] *n* Händler *der*, -in *die*.

tradesman ['treɪdzmən] (*pl* **-men** [-mən]) *n* [shopkeeper, trader] Händler *der*.

trades union *n UK* = **trade union**.

Trades Union Congress *n UK*: **the Trades Union Congress** der Gewerkschaftsbund.

trade union *n* Gewerkschaft *die*.

trading ['treɪdɪŋ] *n* Handel *der*.

trading estate *n UK* Industriegebiet *das*.

tradition [trə'dɪʃn] *n* - **1.** *(U)* [system of customs] Tradition *die* - **2.** [established practice] Brauch *der*.

traditional [trə'dɪʃənl] *adj* traditionell.

traffic ['træfɪk] (*pt & pp* **-ked**, *cont* **-king**) ◇ *n* - **1.** [vehicles] Verkehr *der* - **2.** [illegal trade]

Handel *der*; **the traffic in drugs/arms** der Drogen-/Waffenhandel. <> *vi*: **to traffic in sthg** mit etw handeln.

traffic circle *n US* Kreisverkehr *der*.

traffic jam *n* Stau *der*.

trafficker ['træfɪkəʳ] *n* Händler *der*, -in *die*.

traffic lights *npl* Ampel *die*.

traffic warden *n UK* Hilfspolizist *der*, Politesse *die*.

tragedy ['trædʒədɪ] *n* Tragödie *die*.

tragic ['trædʒɪk] *adj* tragisch.

trail [treɪl] <> *n* - **1.** [path] Weg *der* - **2.** [traces] Spur *die*. <> *vt* - **1.** [drag behind, tow] hinter sich *(D)* her|schleifen - **2.** [lag behind] zurück|liegen hinter *(+ D)*. <> *vi* - **1.** [drag behind] schleifen - **2.** [move slowly] trotten - **3.** SPORT [lose] zurück|liegen. ◆ **trail away, trail off** *vi*: **his voice trailed away** seine Stimme wurde leiser und verstummte schließlich.

trailer ['treɪləʳ] *n* - **1.** [vehicle for luggage] Anhänger *der* - **2.** *esp US* [for living in] Wohnwagen *der* - **3.** CIN Trailer *der*.

train [treɪn] <> *n* - **1.** RAIL Zug *der*; **by train** mit dem Zug - **2.** [of dress] Schleppe *die* - **3.** [connected sequence]: **train of thought** Gedankengang *der*. <> *vt* - **1.** [teach - animal] dressieren; **to train sb to do sthg** jm beibringen, etw zu tun - **2.** [for job] aus|bilden; **to train sb as sthg** jn zu etw aus|bilden - **3.** SPORT trainieren - **4.** [gun, camera]: **to train sthg on sb/sthg** etw auf jn/etw richten. <> *vi* - **1.** [for job]: **to train (as)** eine Ausbildung machen (als) - **2.** SPORT: **to train (for sthg)** (für etw) trainieren.

train driver *n* Zugführer *der*, -in *die*.

trained [treɪnd] *adj* ausgebildet.

trainee [treɪ'niː] *n* Auszubildende *der, die*; [academic, technical] Praktikant *der*, -in *die*.

trainer ['treɪnəʳ] *n* - **1.** [of dogs] Dresseur *der*, -euse *die*; [of horses] Trainer *der*, -in *die* - **2.** SPORT Trainer *der*, -in *die*. ◆ **trainers** *npl UK* [shoes] Turnschuhe *Pl*.

training ['treɪnɪŋ] *n* - **1.** [for job] Ausbildung *die* - **2.** SPORT Training *das*.

training shoes *npl UK* Turnschuhe *Pl*.

traipse [treɪps] *vi* latschen.

trait [treɪt] *n* Charakterzug *der*.

traitor ['treɪtəʳ] *n*: **traitor (to sthg)** Verräter *der*, -in *die* (an etw *(D)*).

trajectory [trə'dʒektərɪ] *n* TECH Flugbahn *die*.

tram [træm] *n UK* Straßenbahn *die*.

tramp [træmp] <> *n* [homeless person] Landstreicher *der*, -in *die*. <> *vi* [trudge] trotten.

trample ['træmpl] *vt* nieder|trampeln.

trampoline ['træmpəliːn] *n* Trampolin *das*.

trance [trɑːns] *n* [hypnotic state] Trance *die*.

tranquil ['træŋkwɪl] *adj liter* friedlich.

tranquillizer *UK*, **tranquilizer** *US* ['træŋkwɪlaɪzəʳ] *n* Beruhigungsmittel *das*.

transaction [træn'zækʃn] *n* [piece of business] Transaktion *die*.

transcend [træn'send] *vt fml* [go beyond] hinaus|gehen über *(+ A)*.

transcript ['trænskrɪpt] *n* [of speech, conversation] Mitschrift *die*.

transfer <> *n* ['trænsfɜːʳ] - **1.** *(U)* [from one place to another - of money] Überweisung *die*; [- of prisoner] Überführung *die*; [- of patient] Verlegung *die* - **2.** *(U)* [from one person to another] Übertragung *die* - **3.** [for job] Versetzung *die* - **4.** SPORT Wechsel *der*, Transfer *der* - **5.** [design] Abziehbild *das*. <> *vt* [træns'fɜːʳ] - **1.** *(U)* [from one place to another - money] überweisen; [- prisoner] überführen; [- patient] verlegen - **2.** [from one person to another]: **to transfer sthg to sb** jm etw übertragen - **3.** [for job] versetzen - **4.** SPORT transferieren. <> *vi* [træns'fɜːʳ] [to different job *etc* & SPORT] wechseln.

transfix [træns'fɪks] *vt* [immobilize] erstarren lassen.

transform [træns'fɔːm] *vt*: **to transform sb/sthg (into)** jn/etw verwandeln (in *(+ A)*).

transfusion [træns'fjuːʒn] *n* Transfusion *die*.

transistor [træn'zɪstəʳ] *n* ELECTRON Transistor *der*.

transit ['trænsɪt] *n*: **in transit** [goods] auf dem Transport.

transition [træn'zɪʃn] *n*: **transition from sthg to sthg** Übergang *der* von etw zu etw.

transitive ['trænzɪtɪv] *adj* GRAM transitiv.

transitory ['trænzɪtrɪ] *adj* vergänglich.

translate [træns'leɪt] *vt* - **1.** [languages] übersetzen - **2.** *fig* [transform]: **to translate a plan into action** einen Plan in die Tat um|setzen.

translation [træns'leɪʃn] *n* Übersetzung *die*.

translator [træns'leɪtəʳ] *n* Übersetzer *der*, -in *die*.

transmission [trænz'mɪʃn] *n* - **1.** [passing on & ELECTRON] Übertragung *die* - **2.** RADIO & TV [programme] Sendung *die*.

transmit [trænz'mɪt] *vt* übertragen.

transmitter [trænz'mɪtəʳ] *n* ELECTRON Sender *der*.

transparency [trans'pærənsɪ] *n* - **1.** PHOT Dia(positiv) *das* - **2.** [for overhead projector] Folie *die*.

transparent [træns'pærənt] *adj* - **1.** [see-through] durchsichtig - **2.** [obvious] offensichtlich.

transpire [træn'spaɪəʳ] *fml* <> *vt*: **it transpires that ...** es stellt sich heraus, dass ... <> *vi* [happen] passieren.

transplant ◇ *n* ['trænsplɑːnt] [MED - operation] Transplantation *die*; [- organ, tissue] Transplantat *das*. ◇ *vt* [træns'plɑːnt] - **1.** MED transplantieren - **2.** BOT [seedlings] um|pflanzen.

transport ◇ *n* ['trænspɔːt] - **1.** [system] Verkehrsmittel *Pl* - **2.** [of goods, people] Beförderung *die*, Transport *der*. ◇ *vt* [træn'spɔːt] [goods, people] befördern, transportieren.

transportation [ˌtrænspɔː'teɪʃn] *n esp US* = **transport**.

transpose [træns'pəʊz] *vt* [change round] um|stellen.

trap [træp] ◇ *n* Falle *die*. ◇ *vt* - **1.** [animal, bird] fangen - **2.** *fig* [trick] eine Falle stellen *(+ D)* - **3.** [immobilize, catch]: **to be trapped in a relationship** in einer Beziehung gefangen sein - **4.** [energy] speichern.

trapdoor ['træp'dɔːʳ] *n* Falltür *die*.

trapeze [trə'piːz] *n* Trapez *das*.

trappings ['træpɪŋz] *npl* äußere Zeichen *Pl*.

trash [træʃ] *n* - **1.** *US* [refuse] Abfall *der* - **2.** *inf pej* [sthg of poor quality] Ramsch *der*; [book, film] Schund *der*.

trashcan ['træʃkæn] *n US* Abfalleimer *der*.

traumatic [trɔː'mætɪk] *adj* traumatisch.

travel ['trævl] (*UK*) (*US*) ◇ *n (U)* Reisen *das*. ◇ *vt* [distance] fahren; **to travel the world/country** durch die Welt/das Land reisen. ◇ *vi* - **1.** [journey] reisen - **2.** [go, move - train] fahren; [- light] sich fort|bewegen; [- current] fließen; [- news] sich verbreiten.

travel agency *n* Reisebüro *das*.

travel agent *n* Reiseveranstalter *der*, -in *die*; **travel agent's** Reisebüro *das*.

travelcard ['trævlkɑːd] *n* Zeitkarte *die*.

traveller *UK*, **traveler** *US* ['trævləʳ] *n* - **1.** [person on journey] Reisende *der, die* - **2.** [itinerant] Herumreisende *der, die*.

traveller's cheque *n* Travellerscheck *der*.

travelling *UK*, **traveling** *US* ['trævlɪŋ] *adj* - **1.** [itinerant] Wander- - **2.** [for taking on journeys, of travel] Reise-.

travelsick ['trævəlsɪk] *adj* reisekrank.

travesty ['trævəstɪ] *n*: **it was a travesty of justice** es war eine Verhöhnung der Gerechtigkeit.

trawler ['trɔːləʳ] *n* Trawler *der*.

tray [treɪ] *n* - **1.** [for carrying] Tablett *das* - **2.** [for papers, mail] Korb *der*.

treacherous ['tretʃərəs] *adj* - **1.** [person, behaviour] verräterisch - **2.** [rock, tides] tückisch.

treachery ['tretʃərɪ] *n* Verrat *der*.

treacle ['triːkl] *n UK* Sirup *der*.

tread [tred] (*pt* **trod**, *pp* **trodden**) ◇ *n* - **1.** [on tyre, shoe] Profil *das* - **2.** [sound or way of walking] Schritt *der*, Tritt *der*. ◇ *vi* [place foot]: **to tread on sthg** auf etw *(A)* treten.

treason ['triːzn] *n* Verrat *der*.

treasure ['treʒəʳ] ◇ *n* Schatz *der*. ◇ *vt* [memory] bewahren; [object] sorgfältig auf|bewahren.

treasurer ['treʒərəʳ] *n* Schatzmeister *der*, -in *die*.

treasury ['treʒərɪ] *n* [room] Schatzkammer *die*. ◆ **Treasury** *n*: **the Treasury** das Finanzministerium.

treat [triːt] ◇ *vt* - **1.** [gen] behandeln; **to treat sthg as a joke** etw als Witz an|sehen - **2.** [give sthg special]: **to treat sb (to sthg)** jn (zu etw) ein|laden. ◇ *n* [sthg special]: **what a treat!** was für ein Genuss!; **to give sb a treat** jm eine Freude bereiten; **this is my treat** ich lade dich ein.

treatment ['triːtmənt] *n* [gen] Behandlung *die*; [specific method of medical care] Behandlungsmethode *die*.

treaty ['triːtɪ] *n* Vertrag *der*.

treble ['trebl] ◇ *adj* [with numbers]: **treble 4** dreimal 4. ◇ *n* - **1.** *(U)* MUS [musical range] Oberstimme *die* - **2.** MUS [boy singer] Knabensopran *der*. ◇ *vt* verdreifachen. ◇ *vi* sich verdreifachen.

treble clef *n* Violinschlüssel *der*.

tree [triː] *n* [plant & COMPUT] Baum *der*.

treetop ['triːtɒp] *n* Baumkrone *die*.

tree-trunk *n* Baumstamm *der*.

trek [trek] ◇ *n* anstrengender Marsch. ◇ *vi* - **1.** [go on long journey]: **to trek through the jungle** durch den Urwald ziehen - **2.** *inf* [walk laboriously]: **I had to trek all the way home** ich musste den ganzen Weg nach Hause laufen.

tremble ['trembl] *vi* zittern.

tremendous [trɪ'mendəs] *adj* - **1.** [impressive, large] enorm - **2.** *inf* [really good] sagenhaft.

tremor ['treməʳ] *n* - **1.** [of body, voice] Zittern *das* - **2.** [small earthquake] Beben *das*.

trench [trentʃ] *n* - **1.** [channel] Graben *der* - **2.** MIL Schützengraben *der*.

trend [trend] *n* [tendency] Trend *der*, Tendenz *die*.

trendy ['trendɪ] *adj inf* in, angesagt.

trepidation [ˌtrepɪ'deɪʃn] *n (U) fml*: **in** OR **with trepidation** mit einem beklommenen Gefühl.

trespass ['trespəs] *vi*: **to trespass (on sb's land)** ein Grundstück unbefugt betreten; **'no trespassing'** 'Betreten verboten'.

trespasser ['trespəsəʳ] *n* Unbefugte *der*, Unbefugte *die*.

trial ['traɪəl] *n* - **1.** LAW Prozess *der*; **to be on trial (for sthg)** (wegen etw) vor Gericht stehen - **2.** [test, experiment] Versuch *der*; **on trial** zur Probe; **by trial and error** durch Ausprobieren - **3.** [unpleasant experience] Qual *die*.

triangle ['traɪæŋgl] *n* - **1.** [shape] Dreieck *das* - **2.** MUS Triangel *der*.

tribe [traɪb] *n* [social group] Stamm *der*.

tribunal [traɪ'bju:nl] *n* Tribunal *das*.

tributary ['trɪbjʊtrɪ] *n* GEOG Nebenfluss *der*.

tribute ['trɪbju:t] *n* - **1.** [respect] Tribut *der*; **to pay tribute to sb/sthg** jm/etw Tribut zollen - **2.** [evidence]: **it's a tribute to his strength of character that...** es ist ein Beweis für seine Charakterstärke, dass...

trice [traɪs] *n*: **in a trice** im Nu.

trick [trɪk] <> *n* - **1.** [to deceive] Streich *der*; **to play a trick on sb** jm einen Streich spielen - **2.** [to entertain] Trick *der* - **3.** [ability, knack] Trick *der*; **that will do the trick** damit ist das Problem gelöst. <> *vt* aus|tricksen; **to trick sb into doing sthg** jn durch List dazu bringen, etw zu tun.

trickery ['trɪkərɪ] *n* Betrug *der*.

trickle ['trɪkl] <> *n* [of liquid] Rinnsal *das*; [drip] Tröpfeln *das*. <> *vi* - **1.** [liquid] rinnen - **2.** [people]: **to trickle in/out** nach und nach herein-/heraus|kommen.

tricky ['trɪkɪ] *adj* [difficult] verzwickt.

tricycle ['traɪsɪkl] *n* Dreirad *das*.

tried [traɪd] *adj*: **tried and tested** erprobt, bewährt.

trifle ['traɪfl] *n* - **1.** CULIN *Dessert aus Biskuit, Früchten, Vanillecreme und Sahne in Schichten* - **2.** [unimportant thing] Kleinigkeit *die*. ◆ **a trifle** *adv fml* eine Spur.

trifling ['traɪflɪŋ] *adj pej* unbedeutend.

trigger ['trɪgə^r] <> *n* [on gun] Abzug *der*. <> *vt* aus|lösen. ◆ **trigger off** *vt sep* = **trigger**.

trill [trɪl] *n* - **1.** MUS Triller *der* - **2.** [of birds] Trällern *das*.

trim [trɪm] <> *adj* - **1.** [neat and tidy] gepflegt - **2.** [slim] schlank. <> *n* [cut]: **to give sb** *OR* **sb's hair a trim** jm die Haare nach|schneiden. <> *vt* - **1.** [cut - hedge] zurück|schneiden; [- hair] nach|schneiden; [- lawn] mähen; [- nails] schneiden - **2.** [decorate]: **to trim sthg (with sthg)** etw (mit etw) verzieren.

trinket ['trɪŋkɪt] *n* Schmuckstück *das*.

trio ['tri:əʊ] (*pl* **-s**) *n* Trio *das*.

trip [trɪp] <> *n* - **1.** [journey] Ausflug *der* - **2.** *drug sl* [experience] Trip *der*. <> *vt* [make stumble] ein Bein stellen *(+ D)*. <> *vi* [stumble]: **to trip (over sthg)** (über etw *(A)*) stolpern. ◆ **trip up** *vt sep* [make stumble] ein Bein stellen *(+ D)*.

tripe [traɪp] *n (U)* - **1.** CULIN Kaldaunen *Pl* - **2.** *inf* [nonsense] Quatsch *der*.

triple ['trɪpl] <> *adj* dreifach. <> *vt* verdreifachen. <> *vi* sich verdreifachen.

triple jump *n*: **the triple jump** der Dreisprung.

triplets ['trɪplɪts] *npl* Drillinge *Pl*.

tripod ['traɪpɒd] *n* Stativ *das*.

trite [traɪt] *adj pej* banal.

triumph ['traɪəmf] <> *n* Triumph *der*. <> *vi*: **to triumph (over)** triumphieren (über *(+ A)*).

trivia ['trɪvɪə] *n (U)* Belanglosigkeiten *Pl*.

trivial ['trɪvɪəl] *adj pej* trivial.

trod [trɒd] *pt* ▷ **tread**.

trolley ['trɒlɪ] (*pl* **trolleys**) *n* - **1.** *UK* [for shopping] Einkaufswagen *der*; [for luggage] Gepäckwagen *der* - **2.** *UK* [for food, drinks] Servierwagen *der* - **3.** *US* [vehicle] Straßenbahn *die*.

trombone [trɒm'bəʊn] *n* Posaune *die*.

troop [tru:p] <> *n* [large group] Schar *die*. <> *vi* strömen. ◆ **troops** *npl* MIL Truppen *Pl*.

trophy ['trəʊfɪ] *n* SPORT Trophäe *die*.

tropical ['trɒpɪkl] *adj* tropisch.

tropics ['trɒpɪks] *npl*: **the tropics** die Tropen.

trot [trɒt] <> *n* Trab *der*. <> *vi* traben. ◆ **on the trot** *adv inf* hintereinander.

trouble ['trʌbl] <> *n* - **1.** *(U)* [difficulty] Problem *das*; **to be in trouble** [having problems] in Schwierigkeiten stecken - **2.** [bother]: **it's no trouble** es macht mir keine Mühe; **to take the trouble to do sthg** sich *(D)* die Mühe machen, etw zu tun - **3.** *(U)* [pain, illness] Beschwerden *Pl*; **to have heart/kidney trouble** es mit dem Herzen/den Nieren haben - **4.** [fighting & POL] Unruhen *Pl*. <> *vt* - **1.** [worry, upset] beunruhigen - **2.** [interrupt, disturb] stören - **3.** [cause pain to] zu schaffen machen *(+ D)*. ◆ **troubles** *npl* - **1.** [worries] Sorgen *Pl* - **2.** POL [unrest] Unruhen *Pl*.

troubled ['trʌbld] *adj* - **1.** [worried, upset] besorgt - **2.** [disturbed - sleep] unruhig; [- place] von Unruhen geschüttelt; **troubled times** turbulente Zeiten.

troublemaker ['trʌbl,meɪkə^r] *n* Unruhestifter *der*, -in *die*.

troublesome ['trʌblsəm] *adj* lästig.

trough [trɒf] *n* - **1.** [for animals] Trog *der* - **2.** [low point] Tal *das*.

troupe [tru:p] *n* Truppe *die*.

trousers ['traʊzəz] *npl* Hose *die*; **a pair of trousers** eine Hose.

trout [traʊt] (*pl inv* *OR* **-s**) *n* Forelle *die*.

trowel ['traʊəl] *n* - **1.** [for the garden] Pflanzkelle *die* - **2.** [for cement, plaster] Kelle *die*.

truant ['tru:ənt] *n* [child] Schwänzer *der*, -in *die*; **to play truant** (die Schule) schwänzen.

truck [trʌk] *n* - **1.** *esp US* [lorry] Lastwagen *der* - **2.** RAIL Güterwagon *der*.

truck driver *n esp US* Lastwagenfahrer *der*, -in *die*.

trucker ['trʌkə^r] *n US* Lastwagenfahrer *der*, -in *die*.

truck farm *n US* Gemüsegärtnerei *die*.

trudge [trʌdʒ] *vi* sich schleppen; [through snow, mud] stapfen.

true [truː] *adj* - **1.** [factual] wahr; **to come true** wahr werden - **2.** [genuine] echt, wahr - **3.** [faithful] getreu - **4.** [precise, exact] gerade.

truffle ['trʌfl] *n* Trüffel *die*.

truly ['truːlɪ] *adv* - **1.** wirklich - **2.** *phr*: **yours truly** [at end of letter] mit freundlichen Grüßen; [me] ich.

trump [trʌmp] *n* [card] Trumpf *der*.

trumped-up ['trʌmpt-] *adj pej* konstruiert.

trumpet ['trʌmpɪt] *n* MUS Trompete *die*.

truncheon ['trʌntʃən] *n* Knüppel *der*.

trundle ['trʌndl] *vi* entlang|zockeln; [downhill] hinunter|zockeln.

trunk [trʌŋk] *n* - **1.** [of tree] Stamm *der* - **2.** ANAT Rumpf *der* - **3.** [of elephant] Rüssel *der* - **4.** [luggage] Schrankkoffer *der* - **5.** *US* [of car] Kofferraum *der*. ◆ **trunks** *npl* [for swimming] Badehose *die*.

trunk road *n UK* Fernstraße *die*.

truss [trʌs] *n* MED Bruchband *das*.

trust [trʌst] ◇ *vt* - **1.** [have confidence in] trauen *(+ D)*, vertrauen *(+ D)*; **to trust sb to do sthg** jm zu|trauen, etw zu tun - **2.** [entrust]: **to trust sb with sthg** jm mit etw vertrauen - **3.** *fml* [hope]: **I trust (that)** ich hoffe(, dass). ◇ *n* - **1.** *(U)* [faith] Vertrauen *das*; **trust in sb/sthg** Vertrauen zu jm/etw - **2.** *(U)* [responsibility] Verantwortung *die* - **3.** FIN Treuhandschaft *die* - **4.** COMM Trust *der*.

trusted ['trʌstɪd] *adj* bewährt.

trustee [trʌs'tiː] *n* - **1.** FIN & LAW Treuhänder *der*, -in *die* - **2.** [manager of institution] Verwalter *der*, -in *die*.

trust fund *n* Treuhandvermögen *das*.

trusting ['trʌstɪŋ] *adj* vertrauensvoll.

trustworthy ['trʌst,wɜːðɪ] *adj* vertrauenswürdig.

truth [truːθ] *n* Wahrheit *die*; **to tell the truth,...** um die Wahrheit zu sagen,...; **in (all) truth** in aller Aufrichtigkeit.

truthful ['truːθfʊl] *n* ehrlich.

try [traɪ] ◇ *vt* - **1.** [attempt] versuchen; **to try to do sthg** versuchen, etw zu tun - **2.** [sample] probieren; [test] aus|probieren - **3.** LAW [case] gerichtlich verhandeln; [criminal] vor Gericht stellen - **4.** [tax, strain] auf die Probe stellen. ◇ *vi* versuchen; **to try for sthg** sich um etw bemühen. ◇ *n* [attempt & SPORT] Versuch *der*; **to give sthg a try** etw mal versuchen. ◆ **try on** *vt sep* [clothes] an|probieren. ◆ **try out** *vt sep* aus|probieren.

trying ['traɪɪŋ] *adj* schwierig.

T-shirt *n* T-Shirt *das*.

tub [tʌb] *n* - **1.** [of margarine, ice cream] Becher *der* - **2.** *inf* [bath] Wanne *die*.

tubby ['tʌbɪ] *adj inf* rundlich.

tube [tjuːb] *n* - **1.** [hollow cylinder - inflexible] Röhrchen *das*, Rohr *das*; [- flexible] Schlauch *der* - **2.** [of toothpaste, glue] Tube *die* - **3.** *UK* [underground train] U-Bahn *die*; *(phrase)*: **by tube** mit der U-Bahn.

tuberculosis [tjuː,bɜːkjʊ'ləʊsɪs] *n* Tuberkulose *die*.

tubular ['tjuːbjʊlər] *adj* Röhren-.

TUC *n abbr of* **Trades Union Congress**.

tuck [tʌk] *vt* [place neatly] stecken. ◆ **tuck away** *vt sep* [store] verstecken. ◆ **tuck in** ◇ *vt sep* - **1.** [child, patient] zu|decken - **2.** [clothes] hinein|stecken. ◇ *vi inf* zu|langen. ◆ **tuck up** *vt sep* zu|decken.

tuck shop *n UK* Schulkiosk *der*.

Tuesday ['tjuːzdɪ] *n* Dienstag *der*; *see also* **Saturday**.

tuft [tʌft] *n* Büschel *das*.

tug [tʌg] ◇ *n* - **1.** [pull] Ruck *der* - **2.** [boat] Schleppkahn *der*. ◇ *vt* (ruckartig) ziehen; **she tugged his sleeve** sie zupfte ihn am Ärmel. ◇ *vi*: **to tug at sthg** (ruckartig) an etw *(D)* ziehen.

tug-of-war *n* Tauziehen *das*.

tuition [tjuː'ɪʃn] *n (U)* Unterricht *der*.

tulip ['tjuːlɪp] *n* Tulpe *die*.

tumble ['tʌmbl] ◇ *vi* - **1.** [person, prices] fallen - **2.** [water] stürzen. ◇ *n* Sturz *der*.

tumbledown ['tʌmbldaʊn] *adj* baufällig.

tumble-dryer [-,draɪər] *n* Wäschetrockner *der*.

tumbler ['tʌmblər] *n* [glass - short] Whiskyglas *das*; [- tall] Becherglas *das*.

tummy ['tʌmɪ] *n inf* - **1.** [outside of stomach] Bauch *der* - **2.** [inside of stomach] Magen *der*.

tumour *UK*, **tumor** *US* ['tjuːmər] *n* Tumor *der*.

tuna [*UK* 'tjuːnə, *US* 'tuːnə] *(pl inv* OR **-s**), **tuna fish** *(pl* **tuna fish**) *n* Tunfisch *der*.

tune [tjuːn] ◇ *n* [song, melody] Melodie *die*. ◇ *vt* - **1.** MUS stimmen - **2.** [engine, RADIO & TV] ein|stellen. ◆ **tune in** *vi* RADIO & TV ein|schalten; **to tune in to sthg** etw ein|schalten. ◆ **tune up** *vi* MUS stimmen. ◆ **in tune** ◇ *adj* MUS (richtig) gestimmt. ◇ *adv* - **1.** MUS richtig - **2.** [in agreement]: **to be in tune with sb/sthg** mit jm/etw im Einklang stehen. ◆ **out of tune** ◇ *adj* MUS verstimmt. ◇ *adv* - **1.** MUS falsch - **2.** [not in agreement]: **out of tune with sb/sthg** mit jm/etw nicht im Einklang stehen.

tuneful ['tjuːnfʊl] *adj* melodisch.

tuner ['tjuːnər] *n* - **1.** RADIO & TV Tuner *der* - **2.** MUS Stimmer *der*, -in *die*.

tunic ['tjuːnɪk] *n* [clothing] Hemdbluse *die*; [of uniform] Uniformjacke *die*.

tuning fork ['tjuːnɪŋ-] *n* Stimmgabel *die*.

Tunisia [tjuː'nɪzɪə] *n* Tunesien *das*.

tunnel ['tʌnl] *(UK) (US)* ◇ *n* Tunnel *der*. ◇ *vi* graben.

turban ['tɜ:bən] *n* [man's headdress] Turban *der*.

turbine ['tɜ:baɪn] *n* Turbine *die*.

turbocharged ['tɜ:bəʊtʃɑ:dʒd] *adj* mit Turboaufladung.

turbulence ['tɜ:bjʊləns] *n (U) liter & fig* Turbulenz *die*.

turbulent ['tɜ:bjʊlənt] *adj* - **1.** [period of time & PHYS] turbulent - **2.** [winds, weather] stürmisch - **3.** [crowd] ungestüm.

tureen [tə'ri:n] *n* Suppenterrine *die*.

turf [tɜ:f] (*pl* **-s** OR **turves**) ◇ *n* - **1.** *(U)* [grass surface] Rasen *der* - **2.** [clod] Grassode *die*. ◇ *vt* [with grass] mit Rollrasen bedecken. ◆ **turf out** *vt sep UK inf* [evict] raus|schmeißen.

Turk [tɜ:k] *n* Türke *der*, -kin *die*.

turkey ['tɜ:kɪ] (*pl* **turkeys**) *n* Truthahn *der*.

Turkey ['tɜ:kɪ] *n* Türkei *die*; **in Turkey** in der Türkei.

Turkish ['tɜ:kɪʃ] ◇ *adj* türkisch. ◇ *n* [language] Türkisch(e) *das*.

Turkish delight *n (U)* türkischer Honig.

turmoil ['tɜ:mɔɪl] *n (U)* Aufruhr *der*.

turn [tɜ:n] ◇ *n* - **1.** [in road, river] Kurve *die* - **2.** [of knob, key, switch] Drehung *die* - **3.** [change] Wendung *die* - **4.** [in game, order]: **it's my turn** ich bin an der Reihe, ich bin dran; **in turn** der Reihe nach - **5.** [performance] Nummer *die* - **6.** MED Anfall *der* - **7.** *phr*: **to do sb a good turn** jm etwas Gutes tun. ◇ *vt* - **1.** [key, head, wheel, chair] drehen - **2.** [corner] biegen um - **3.** [page, omelette] wenden - **4.** [direct]: **to turn one's attention to sb/sthg** jm/etw seine Aufmerksamkeit zu|wenden - **5.** [transform]: **to turn sthg into sthg** etw in etw *(A)* verwandeln - **6.** [make]: **to turn sthg red** etw rot werden lassen; **to turn sthg inside out** das Innere von etw nach außen drehen. ◇ *vi* - **1.** [change direction] wenden; **his thoughts turned to his family** er dachte an seine Familie - **2.** [wheel, knob, head, person] sich drehen - **3.** [in book]: **to turn to sthg** etw auf|schlagen - **4.** [for consolation, advice]: **to turn to sb/sthg** sich an jn/etw wenden - **5.** [become] werden; **to turn into sthg** sich in etw *(A)* verwandeln. ◆ **turn around** *vt sep & vi* = **turn round**. ◆ **turn away** ◇ *vt sep* [refuse entry to] ab|weisen. ◇ *vi* sich ab|wenden. ◆ **turn back** ◇ *vt sep* - **1.** [force to return] zurück|schicken - **2.** [fold back] auf|schlagen. ◇ *vi* [return] um|kehren. ◆ **turn down** *vt sep* - **1.** [reject] ab|weisen, ab|lehnen - **2.** [heating, lighting, sound] herunter|drehen. ◆ **turn in** *vi inf* [go to bed] sich aufs Ohr legen. ◆ **turn off** ◇ *vt insep* [leave - road, path] ab|biegen von. ◇ *vt sep* [switch off] ab|schalten. ◇ *vi* [leave path, road] ab|biegen. ◆ **turn on** ◇ *vt sep* - **1.** [make work] ein|schalten - **2.** *inf* [excite sexually] an|machen. ◇ *vt insep* [attack] los|gehen auf *(+ A)*. ◆ **turn out** ◇ *vt sep* - **1.** [switch off] aus|schalten - **2.** [empty] leeren. ◇ *vt insep*: **to turn out to be sthg** sich als etw erweisen; **it turns out that...** es stellt sich heraus, dass... ◇ *vi* - **1.** [end up]: **it will turn out all right** es wird (schon) alles in Ordnung kommen - **2.** [attend]: **to turn out (for sthg)** (zu etw) erscheinen. ◆ **turn over** ◇ *vt sep* - **1.** [playing card, stone, page] um|drehen - **2.** [consider] überdenken - **3.** [hand over]: **to turn sb/sthg over to sb** jm jn/etw über|geben. ◇ *vi* - **1.** [roll over] sich um|drehen - **2.** *UK* TV um|schalten. ◆ **turn round** ◇ *vt sep* - **1.** [rotate] um|drehen - **2.** [words, sentence] um|drehen - **3.** [quantity of work] bearbeiten. ◇ *vi* [person] sich um|drehen. ◆ **turn up** ◇ *vt sep* [heat, lighting, radio, TV] auf|drehen. ◇ *vi inf* - **1.** [appear, arrive, be found] auf|tauchen - **2.** [happen] sich ergeben.

turning ['tɜ:nɪŋ] *n* [side road] Abzweigung *die*.

turning point *n* Wendepunkt *der*.

turnip ['tɜ:nɪp] *n* Rübe *die*.

turnout ['tɜ:naʊt] *n* [attendance] Teilnahme *die*.

turnover ['tɜ:n,əʊvə^r] *n (U)* - **1.** [of personnel] Fluktuation *die* - **2.** FIN Umsatz *der*.

turnpike ['tɜ:npaɪk] *n US* gebührenpflichtige Autobahn.

turnstile ['tɜ:nstaɪl] *n* Drehkreuz *das*.

turntable ['tɜ:n,teɪbl] *n* [on record player] Plattenteller *der*.

turn-up *n UK* - **1.** [on trousers] Aufschlag *der* - **2.** *inf* [surprise]: **a turn-up for the books** eine echte Überraschung.

turpentine ['tɜ:pəntaɪn] *n (U)* Terpentin *das*.

turquoise ['tɜ:kwɔɪz] ◇ *adj* türkis. ◇ *n* - **1.** [mineral, gem] Türkis *der* - **2.** [colour] Türkis *das*.

turret ['tʌrɪt] *n* [on castle] Eckturm *der*.

turtle ['tɜ:tl] (*pl inv* OR **-s**) *n* Schildkröte *die*.

turtleneck ['tɜ:tlnek] *n* - **1.** [garment] Rollkragenpullover *der* - **2.** [neck] Rollkragen *der*.

turves [tɜ:vz] *Pl* ▷ **turf**.

tusk [tʌsk] *n* Stoßzahn *der*.

tussle ['tʌsl] ◇ *n* Gerangel *das*. ◇ *vi*: **to tussle over sthg** *liter* (sich) um etw *(A)* raufen; *fig* eine Auseinandersetzung wegen etw haben.

tutor ['tju:tə^r] *n* - **1.** [private] Privatlehrer *der*, -in *die* - **2.** UNIV Tutor *der*, -in *die*.

tutorial [tju:'tɔ:rɪəl] *n* Tutorium *das*.

tuxedo [tʌk'si:dəʊ] (*pl* **-s**) *n US* Smoking *der*.

TV (*abbr of* **television**) *n* - **1.** *(U)* [medium, industry] Fernsehen *das* - **2.** [apparatus] Fernseher *der*.

twang [twæŋ] *n* - **1.** [of spring, guitar string] vibrierender Ton; [of rubber band] schnappender Ton - **2.** [accent] Tonfall *der*.

tweed [twiːd] *n* Tweed *der.*

tweezers ['twiːzəz] *npl* Pinzette *die.*

twelfth [twelfθ] *num* zwölfte (r) (s); *see also* **sixth**.

twelve [twelv] *num* zwölf; *see also* **six**.

twentieth ['twentɪəθ] *num* zwanzigste (r) (s); *see also* **sixth**.

twenty ['twentɪ] *num* zwanzig; *see also* **sixty**.

twice [twaɪs] *adv* zweimal.

twiddle ['twɪdl] *vt* [knob, button] herum|drehen an *(+ D).*

twig [twɪg] *n* Zweig *der.*

twilight ['twaɪlaɪt] *n* [in evening] Dämmerung *die.*

twin [twɪn] ◇ *adj* - **1.** [child, sibling] Zwillings-; **twin girls** Zwillingsschwestern - **2.** [towns] Partner-; *(phrase)*: **twin beds** zwei Einzelbetten. ◇ *n* [sibling] Zwilling *der.*

twine [twaɪn] ◇ *n (U)* Schnur *die.* ◇ *vt*: **to twine sthg round sthg** etw um etw wickeln.

twinge [twɪndʒ] *n* Stich *der.*

twinkle ['twɪŋkl] *vi* funkeln.

twin room *n* Zweibettzimmer *das.*

twin town *n* Partnerstadt *die.*

twirl [twɜːl] ◇ *vt* - **1.** [spin] herum|wirbeln - **2.** [twist, moustache] zwirbeln. ◇ *vi* wirbeln.

twist [twɪst] ◇ *n* - **1.** [in road, staircase, river] Biegung *die* - **2.** *fig* [in plot] Wendung *die.* ◇ *vt* - **1.** [gen] verdrehen - **2.** [lid, knob, dial] drehen - **3.** MED [sprain]: **to twist one's ankle** sich *(D)* den Fuß verrenken. ◇ *vi* - **1.** [road, river] sich schlängeln - **2.** [body] sich winden; [face] sich verziehen.

twit [twɪt] *n UK inf* Trottel *der.*

twitch [twɪtʃ] ◇ *n* Zucken *das.* ◇ *vi* zucken.

two [tuː] *num* zwei; **in two** in zwei Teile; *see also* **six**.

twofaced [ˌtuː'feɪst] *adj pej* falsch.

twofold ['tuːfəʊld] *adj* & *adv* zweifach.

two-piece *adj* [suit, swimsuit] zweiteilig.

twosome ['tuːsəm] *n inf* Paar *das.*

two-way *adj* [in both directions] in beiden Richtungen.

tycoon [taɪ'kuːn] *n* Magnat *der.*

type [taɪp] ◇ *n* - **1.** [sort, kind] Art *die*; **what type of car are you looking for?** was für ein Auto suchen Sie denn? - **2.** [in classification] Gruppe *die* - **3.** *(U)* TYPO Schrift *die.* ◇ *vt* & *vi* tippen.

typecast ['taɪpkɑːst] (*pt* & *pp inv*) *vt* fest|legen (auf eine bestimmte Rolle).

typeface ['taɪpfeɪs] *n* TYPO Schrift *die.*

typescript ['taɪpskrɪpt] *n* Manuskript *das.*

typewriter ['taɪpˌraɪtəʳ] *n* Schreibmaschine *die.*

typhoid (fever) ['taɪfɔɪd-] *n (U)* Typhus *der.*

typhoon [taɪ'fuːn] *n* Taifun *der.*

typical ['tɪpɪkl] *adj* typisch; **typical of sb/sthg** typisch für jn/etw.

typing ['taɪpɪŋ] *n* Tippen *das,* Maschineschreiben *das.*

typist ['taɪpɪst] *n* Schreibkraft *die.*

typography [taɪ'pɒgrəfɪ] *n* Typografie *die.*

tyranny ['tɪrənɪ] *n (U)* [of person, government] Tyrannei *die.*

tyrant ['taɪrənt] *n* Tyrann *der,* -in *die.*

tyre *UK*, **tire** *US* ['taɪəʳ] *n* Reifen *der.*

tyre pressure *n (U)* Reifendruck *der.*

U

u (*pl* **u's** OR **us**), **U** (*pl* **U's** OR **Us**) [juː] *n* [letter] u *das,* U *das.*

U-bend *n* U-Bogen *der.*

udder ['ʌdəʳ] *n* Euter *der.*

UFO (*abbr of* **unidentified flying object**) *n* UFO *das.*

Uganda [juː'gændə] *n* Uganda *nt.*

ugly ['ʌglɪ] *adj* - **1.** [unattractive] hässlich - **2.** *fig* [unpleasant] unerfreulich.

UHF (*abbr of* **ultra-high frequency**) *n* UHF.

UK *n abbr of* **United Kingdom**.

Ukraine [juː'kreɪn] *n*: **the Ukraine** die Ukraine.

ulcer ['ʌlsəʳ] *n* - **1.** [in stomach] Geschwür *das* - **2.** [in mouth, stomach] Aphthe *die.*

Ulster ['ʌlstəʳ] *n* Ulster *nt.*

ulterior [ʌl'tɪərɪəʳ] *adj*: **an ulterior motive** Hintergedanke *der.*

ultimata [ˌʌltɪ'meɪtə] *Pl* ▷ **ultimatum**.

ultimate ['ʌltɪmət] ◇ *adj* - **1.** [final, long-term] letzte(r) (s) - **2.** [most powerful] absolut. ◇ *n*: **the ultimate in sthg** das Höchste an etw *(D).*

ultimately ['ʌltɪmətlɪ] *adv* [finally, in the long term] letztlich.

ultimatum [ˌʌltɪ'meɪtəm] (*pl* **-tums** OR **-ta** [-tə]) *n* Ultimatum *das.*

ultrasound ['ʌltrəsaʊnd] *n* Ultraschall *der.*

ultraviolet [ˌʌltrəˈvaɪələt] *adj* ultraviolett.

umbilical cord [ʌmˈbɪlɪkl-] *n* Nabelschnur *die*.

umbrella [ʌmˈbrelə] <> *n* - **1.** [portable] Regenschirm *der* - **2.** [fixed] Sonnenschirm *der*. <> *adj* Schirm-.

umpire [ˈʌmpaɪəʳ] <> *n* Schiedsrichter *der*, -in *die*. <> *vt* Schiedsrichter sein bei.

umpteen [ˌʌmpˈtiːn] *num adj inf* zigmal.

umpteenth [ˌʌmpˈtiːnθ] *num adj inf*: **for the umpteenth time** zum x-ten Mal.

UN (*abbr of* **United Nations**) *n* UNO *die*, UN *die*.

unabated [ˌʌnəˈbeɪtɪd] *adj* unvermindert.

unable [ʌnˈeɪbl] *adj*: **to be unable to do sthg** außer Stande sein, etw zu tun.

unacceptable [ˌʌnəkˈseptəbl] *adj* unannehmbar.

unaccompanied [ˌʌnəˈkʌmpənɪd] *adj* [luggage] aufgegeben; [child, song] ohne Begleitung.

unaccountably [ˌʌnəˈkaʊntəblɪ] *adv* [inexplicably] unerklärlicherweise.

unaccounted [ˌʌnəˈkaʊntɪd] *adj*: **unaccounted for** unauffindbar.

unaccustomed [ˌʌnəˈkʌstəmd] *adj* [unused]: **to be unaccustomed to sthg** an etw *(A)* nicht gewöhnt sein; **to be unaccustomed to doing sthg** nicht daran gewöhnt sein, etw zu tun.

unadulterated [ˌʌnəˈdʌltəreɪtɪd] *adj* rein.

unanimous [juːˈnænɪməs] *adj* einstimmig.

unanimously [juːˈnænɪməslɪ] *adv* einstimmig.

unanswered [ˌʌnˈɑːnsəd] *adj* unbeantwortet.

unappetizing, -ising [ˌʌnˈæpɪtaɪzɪŋ] *adj* unappetitlich.

unarmed [ˌʌnˈɑːmd] *adj* unbewaffnet.

unashamed [ˌʌnəˈʃeɪmd] *adj* schamlos.

unassuming [ˌʌnəˈsjuːmɪŋ] *adj* bescheiden.

unattached [ˌʌnəˈtætʃt] *adj* - **1.** [not fastened, linked]: **unattached to sthg** unabhängig von etw - **2.** [without partner] ungebunden.

unattended [ˌʌnəˈtendɪd] *adj* unbeaufsichtigt.

unattractive [ˌʌnəˈtræktɪv] *adj* unattraktiv.

unauthorized, -ised [ˌʌnˈɔːθəraɪzd] *adj* unrechtmäßig; [biography] nicht autorisiert.

unavailable [ˌʌnəˈveɪləbl] *adj* nicht verfügbar; [person] nicht zu erreichen.

unavoidable [ˌʌnəˈvɔɪdəbl] *adj* unvermeidlich.

unaware [ˌʌnəˈweəʳ] *adj*: **to be unaware of sthg** sich *(D)* einer Sache *(G)* nicht bewusst sein; **she was unaware of my presence** sie bemerkte mich nicht.

unawares [ˌʌnəˈweəz] *adv*: **to catch** OR **take sb unawares** jn überraschen.

unbalanced [ˌʌnˈbælənst] *adj* - **1.** [biased] unausgewogen - **2.** [deranged] psychisch labil.

unbearable [ʌnˈbeərəbl] *adj* unerträglich.

unbeatable [ˌʌnˈbiːtəbl] *adj* unschlagbar.

unbeknown(st) [ˌʌnbɪˈnəʊn(st)] *adv*: **unbeknownst to him** ohne sein Wissen.

unbelievable [ˌʌnbɪˈliːvəbl] *adj* unglaublich.

unbia(s)sed [ˌʌnˈbaɪəst] *adj* unvoreingenommen.

unborn [ˌʌnˈbɔːn] *adj* [child] ungeboren.

unbreakable [ˌʌnˈbreɪkəbl] *adj* unzerbrechlich.

unbridled [ˌʌnˈbraɪdld] *adj* ungezügelt.

unbutton [ˌʌnˈbʌtn] *vt* aufknöpfen.

uncalled-for [ˌʌnˈkɔːld-] *adj* unnötig.

uncanny [ʌnˈkænɪ] *adj* unheimlich.

unceasing [ˌʌnˈsiːsɪŋ] *adj fml* beständig.

unceremonious [ˈʌnˌserɪˈməʊnjəs] *adj* [abrupt] brüsk.

uncertain [ʌnˈsɜːtn] *adj* - **1.** [person, plans] unsicher; **in no uncertain terms** unmissverständlich - **2.** [weather] unvorhersehbar; [future] ungewiss - **3.** [cause, motive] unklar.

unchanged [ˌʌnˈtʃeɪndʒd] *adj* unverändert.

unchecked [ˌʌnˈtʃekt] *adj* & *adv* [unrestrained] uneingeschränkt.

uncivilized, -ised [ˌʌnˈsɪvɪlaɪzd] *adj* [barbaric] unzivilisiert.

uncle [ˈʌŋkl] *n* Onkel *der*.

unclear [ˌʌnˈklɪəʳ] *adj* - **1.** [meaning, instructions] unklar - **2.** [future, person] unsicher - **3.** [motives, details] undurchsichtig.

uncomfortable [ˌʌnˈkʌmftəbl] *adj* - **1.** [shoes, chair, clothes] unbequem - **2.** *fig* [fact, truth] unbequem - **3.** [person]: **to feel uncomfortable** [in physical discomfort] sich nicht wohl fühlen; [ill at ease] sich unbehaglich fühlen.

uncommon [ʌnˈkɒmən] *adj* - **1.** [rare] selten - **2.** *fml* [extreme] außergewöhnlich.

uncompromising [ˌʌnˈkɒmprəmaɪzɪŋ] *adj* unnachgiebig.

unconcerned [ˌʌnkənˈsɜːnd] *adj* [not anxious] unbesorgt.

unconditional [ˌʌnkənˈdɪʃənl] *adj* bedingungslos.

unconscious [ʌnˈkɒnʃəs] <> *adj* - **1.** [having lost consciousness] bewusstlos - **2.** *fig* [unaware]: **to be unconscious of sthg** sich *(D)* einer Sache *(G)* nicht bewusst sein - **3.** PSYCHOL unbewusst. <> *n* PSYCHOL: **the unconscious** das Unbewusste.

unconsciously [ʌnˈkɒnʃəslɪ] *adv* unbewusst.

uncontrollable [ˌʌnkən'trəʊləbl] *adj* - **1.** [irrepressible] unbezwingbar - **2.** [inflation, growth, epidemic] unkontrollierbar - **3.** [child, animal] nicht zu bändigen.

unconventional [ˌʌnkən'venʃənl] *adj* unkonventionell.

unconvinced [ˌʌnkən'vɪnst] *adj* nicht überzeugt.

uncouth [ʌn'ku:θ] *adj* ungehobelt.

uncover [ʌn'kʌvər] *vt liter & fig* auf|decken.

undecided [ˌʌndɪ'saɪdɪd] *adj* - **1.** [person] unentschlossen - **2.** [issue] unentschieden.

undeniable [ˌʌndɪ'naɪəbl] *adj* unbestreitbar.

under ['ʌndər] <> *prep* - **1.** [beneath, below] unter *(+ D)*; *(with verbs of motion)* unter *(+ A)*; **it's under the table** es ist unter dem Tisch; **put it under the table** leg es unter den Tisch - **2.** [less than] unter *(+ D)*; **children under ten** Kinder unter zehn; **in under two hours** in weniger als zwei Stunden - **3.** [indicating conditions or circumstances]: **under the circumstances** unter diesen Umständen; **to be under pressure** unter Druck sein - **4.** [undergoing]: **to be under review/discussion** revidiert/diskutiert werden; **under construction** im Bau - **5.** [directed, governed by] unter *(+ D)*; **Britain under Blair** Großbritannien unter Blair - **6.** [according to] nach; **under the terms of the will** nach dem Testament - **7.** [in classification, name, title] unter *(+ D)*. <> *adv* - **1.** [beneath] unten; **how long can you stay under?** [underwater] wie lange kannst du unter Wasser bleiben?; **she lifted the blanket and crawled under** sie hob die Decke hoch und kroch darunter - **2.** [less]: **children of 12 and under** Kinder bis zu 12 Jahren.

underage [ʌndər'eɪdʒ] *adj* minderjährig.

undercarriage ['ʌndəˌkærɪdʒ] *n* Fahrgestell *das*.

undercharge [ˌʌndə'tʃɑ:dʒ] *vt* zu wenig berechnen *(+ D)*.

underclothes ['ʌndəkləʊðz] *npl* Unterwäsche *die*.

undercoat ['ʌndəkəʊt] *n* [of paint] Grundierung *die*.

undercover ['ʌndəˌkʌvər] *adj* [agent] Geheim-.

undercurrent ['ʌndəˌkʌrənt] *n fig* [tendency] Unterton *der*.

undercut [ˌʌndə'kʌt] *(pt & pp inv) vt* [in price] unterbieten.

underdeveloped [ˌʌndədɪ'veləpt] *adj* unterentwickelt.

underdog ['ʌndədɒg] *n*: **the underdog** der/die Schwächere.

underdone [ˌʌndə'dʌn] *adj* nicht gar.

underestimate *vt* [ˌʌndər'estɪmeɪt] - **1.** [time, money, amount] zu niedrig schätzen - **2.** [strength, abilities] unterschätzen.

underfoot [ˌʌndə'fʊt] *adv* unter den Füßen.

undergo [ˌʌndə'gəʊ] *(pt* **-went**, *pp* **-gone** [-'gɒn]) *vt* [operation, examination] sich unterziehen *(+ D)*; [training] teilnehmen an *(+ D)*; [difficulties] durch|machen.

undergraduate [ˌʌndə'grædjʊət] *n* Student *der*, -in *die*.

underground <> *adj* ['ʌndəgraʊnd] - **1.** [below ground] unterirdisch - **2.** *fig* [secret, illegal] Untergrund-. <> *adv* [ˌʌndə'graʊnd]: **to go/be forced underground** in den Untergrund gehen/gedrängt werden. <> *n* ['ʌndəgraʊnd] - **1.** *UK* [transport system] U-Bahn *die* - **2.** [activist movement] Untergrund *der*.

undergrowth ['ʌndəgrəʊθ] *n (U)* Unterholz *das*.

underhand [ˌʌndə'hænd] *adj* hinterhältig.

underline [ˌʌndə'laɪn] *vt liter & fig* unterstreichen.

underlying [ˌʌndə'laɪɪŋ] *adj* zugrunde liegend.

undermine [ˌʌndə'maɪn] *vt fig* [weaken] untergraben.

underneath [ˌʌndə'ni:θ] <> *prep* [indicating location] unter *(+ D)*; [indicating movement] unter *(+ A)*; **from underneath sthg** unter etw *(D)* hervor. <> *adv* darunter. <> *n* [underside]: **the underneath** die Unterseite.

underpaid *adj* ['ʌndəpeɪd] unterbezahlt.

underpants ['ʌndəpænts] *npl* Unterhose *die*.

underpass ['ʌndəpɑ:s] *n* Unterführung *die*.

underprivileged [ˌʌndə'prɪvɪlɪdʒd] *adj* unterprivilegiert.

underrated [ˌʌndə'reɪtɪd] *adj* unterschätzt.

undershirt ['ʌndəʃɜ:t] *n US* Unterhemd *das*.

underside ['ʌndəsaɪd] *n*: **the underside** die Unterseite.

understand [ˌʌndə'stænd] *(pt & pp* **-stood**) <> *vt* - **1.** [gen] verstehen - **2.** *fml* [have heard]: **to understand that...** glauben, dass... <> *vi* verstehen.

understandable [ˌʌndə'stændəbl] *adj* verständlich.

understanding [ˌʌndə'stændɪŋ] <> *n* - **1.** [knowledge, insight] Kenntnis *die* - **2.** *(U)* [sympathy] Verständnis *das* - **3.** [interpretation, conception] Auffassung *die*; **it was my understanding that ...** ich dachte, dass ... - **4.** [informal agreement] Übereinkunft *die*. <> *adj* [sympathetic] verständnisvoll.

understated [ˌʌndə'steɪtɪd] *adj* untertrieben.

understatement [ˌʌndəˈsteɪtmənt] *n* - **1.** [inadequate statement] Untertreibung *die* - **2.** *(U)* [quality of understating] Understatement *das*.

understood [ˌʌndəˈstʊd] *pt* & *pp* ▷ **understand**.

understudy [ˈʌndəˌstʌdɪ] *n* zweite Besetzung.

undertake [ˌʌndəˈteɪk] (*pt* **-took**, *pp* **-taken** [-ˈteɪkn]) *vt* - **1.** [take on] auf sich *(A)* nehmen - **2.** [promise]: **to undertake to do sthg** sich verpflichten, etw zu tun.

undertaker [ˈʌndəˌteɪkəʳ] *n* Leichenbestatter *der*, -in *die*.

undertaking [ˌʌndəˈteɪkɪŋ] *n* - **1.** [task] Aufgabe *die* - **2.** [promise] Versprechen *das*.

undertone [ˈʌndətəʊn] *n* - **1.** [quiet voice] leise Stimme - **2.** [underlying feeling] Unterton *der*.

undertook [ˌʌndəˈtʊk] *pt* ▷ **undertake**.

underwater [ˌʌndəˈwɔːtəʳ] <> *adj* Unterwasser-. <> *adv* unter Wasser.

underwear [ˈʌndəweəʳ] *n* Unterwäsche *die*.

underwent [ˌʌndəˈwent] *pt* ▷ **undergo**.

underwriter [ˈʌndəˌraɪtəʳ] *n* Versicherer *der*.

undid [ˌʌnˈdɪd] *pt* ▷ **undo**.

undies [ˈʌndɪz] *npl inf* Unterwäsche *die*.

undisputed [ˌʌndɪˈspjuːtɪd] *adj* unbestritten.

undistinguished [ˌʌndɪˈstɪŋgwɪʃt] *adj* mittelmäßig.

undo [ˌʌnˈduː] (*pt* **-did**, *pp* **-done**) *vt* - **1.** [unfasten] auf|machen - **2.** [nullify] zunichte machen.

undoing [ˌʌnˈduːɪŋ] *n (U) fml* Verderben *das*.

undone [ˌʌnˈdʌn] <> *pp* ▷ **undo**. <> *adj* - **1.** [unfastened] offen - **2.** *fml* [not done] ungetan.

undoubted [ʌnˈdaʊtɪd] *adj* unbestritten.

undoubtedly [ʌnˈdaʊtɪdlɪ] *adv fml* zweifellos.

undress [ˌʌnˈdres] <> *vt* aus|ziehen. <> *vi* sich aus|ziehen.

undue [ˌʌnˈdjuː] *adj fml* unangemessen.

undulate [ˈʌndjʊleɪt] *vi fml* - **1.** [in movement - snake, road] sich schlängeln - **2.** [in shape - landscape] sich wellenförmig erstrecken.

unduly [ˌʌnˈdjuːlɪ] *adv fml* unnötig.

unearth [ˌʌnˈɜːθ] *vt* - **1.** [dig up] aus|graben - **2.** *fig* [discover] auf|stöbern.

unease [ʌnˈiːz] *n (U)* Unbehagen *das*.

uneasy [ʌnˈiːzɪ] *adj* - **1.** [person, feeling] unbehaglich - **2.** [silence] verlegen - **3.** [peace] unsicher.

uneconomic [ˈʌnˌiːkəˈnɒmɪk] *adj* unökonomisch.

uneducated [ˌʌnˈedjʊkeɪtɪd] *adj* - **1.** [person] ungebildet - **2.** [behaviour, manners, speech] unkultiviert.

unemployed [ˌʌnɪmˈplɔɪd] <> *adj* [out-of-work] arbeitslos. <> *npl*: **the unemployed** die Arbeitslosen *Pl*.

unemployment [ˌʌnɪmˈplɔɪmənt] *n* Arbeitslosigkeit *die*.

unemployment benefit *UK n (U)* Arbeitslosenunterstützung *die*.

unerring [ˌʌnˈɜːrɪŋ] *adj* untrüglich.

uneven [ˌʌnˈiːvn] *adj* - **1.** [not flat] uneben - **2.** [inconsistent] ungleichmäßig - **3.** [unfair] ungleich.

unexpected [ˌʌnɪkˈspektɪd] *adj* unerwartet.

unexpectedly [ˌʌnɪkˈspektɪdlɪ] *adv* unerwartet.

unfailing [ʌnˈfeɪlɪŋ] *adj* [loyalty, support, good humour] unerschöpflich.

unfair [ˌʌnˈfeəʳ] *adj* ungerecht.

unfaithful [ˌʌnˈfeɪθfʊl] *adj* [sexually] untreu.

unfamiliar [ˌʌnfəˈmɪljəʳ] *adj* - **1.** [not well-known] unbekannt - **2.** [not acquainted]: **to be unfamiliar with sb/sthg** jn/etw nicht kennen.

unfashionable [ˌʌnˈfæʃnəbl] *adj* unmodisch.

unfasten [ˌʌnˈfɑːsn] *vt* auf|machen; [rope] auf|knoten.

unfavourable *UK*, **unfavorable** *US* [ˌʌnˈfeɪvrəbl] *adj* - **1.** [not conducive] ungünstig - **2.** [negative] unvorteilhaft.

unfeeling [ʌnˈfiːlɪŋ] *adj* herzlos.

unfinished [ˌʌnˈfɪnɪʃt] *adj* unerledigt.

unfit [ˌʌnˈfɪt] *adj* - **1.** [not in good shape] nicht fit - **2.** [not suitable]: **unfit (for sthg)** ungeeignet (für etw).

unfold [ʌnˈfəʊld] <> *vt* [open out] auseinander|falten. <> *vi* [story, truth] an den Tag kommen.

unforeseen [ˌʌnfɔːˈsiːn] *adj* unvorhergesehen.

unforgettable [ˌʌnfəˈgetəbl] *adj* unvergesslich.

unforgivable [ˌʌnfəˈgɪvəbl] *adj* unverzeihlich.

unfortunate [ʌnˈfɔːtʃnət] *adj* - **1.** [unlucky] unglücklich - **2.** [regrettable] bedauernswert.

unfortunately [ʌnˈfɔːtʃnətlɪ] *adv* leider.

unfounded [ˌʌnˈfaʊndɪd] *adj* unbegründet.

unfriendly [ˌʌnˈfrendlɪ] *adj* unfreundlich.

unfurnished [ˌʌnˈfɜːnɪʃt] *adj* unmöbliert.

ungainly [ʌnˈgeɪnlɪ] *adj* unbeholfen.

ungrateful [ʌnˈgreɪtfʊl] *adj* undankbar.

unhappy [ʌnˈhæpɪ] *adj* - **1.** [sad] unglücklich - **2.** [not pleased]: **to be unhappy (about** OR **with sthg)** nicht glücklich (über etw *(A)* OR mit etw) sein - **3.** *fml* [unfortunate] unglückselig.

unharmed [ˌʌn'hɑːmd] *adj* unverletzt.

unhealthy [ʌn'helθɪ] *adj* ungesund.

unheard-of [ʌn'hɜːdɒv] *adj* - **1.** [unknown] unbekannt - **2.** [unprecedented] unerhört.

unhook [ˌʌn'hʊk] *vt* - **1.** [unfasten hooks of] auf|haken - **2.** [remove from hook] ab|haken, vom Haken nehmen.

unhurt [ˌʌn'hɜːt] *adj* unverletzt.

unhygienic [ˌʌnhaɪ'dʒiːnɪk] *adj* unhygienisch.

unidentified flying object *n* unbekanntes Flugobjekt.

unification [ˌjuːnɪfɪ'keɪʃn] *n (U)* Vereinigung *die*.

uniform ['juːnɪfɔːm] ◇ *adj* gleichförmig. ◇ *n* Uniform *die*.

unify ['juːnɪfaɪ] *vt* vereinen.

unilateral [ˌjuːnɪ'lætərəl] *adj* einseitig.

unimportant [ˌʌnɪm'pɔːtənt] *adj* unwichtig.

uninhabited [ˌʌnɪn'hæbɪtɪd] *adj* unbewohnt.

uninjured [ˌʌn'ɪndʒəd] *adj* unverletzt.

unintelligent [ˌʌnɪn'telɪdʒənt] *adj* nicht intelligent.

unintentional [ˌʌnɪn'tenʃənl] *adj* unabsichtlich.

union ['juːnjən] ◇ *n* - **1.** [trade union] Gewerkschaft *die* - **2.** [alliance] Union *die*. ◇ *comp* Gewerkschafts-.

Union Jack *n*: **the Union Jack** der Union Jack, *britische Nationalflagge*.

unique [juː'niːk] *adj* - **1.** [unparalleled] einzigartig - **2.** *fml* [peculiar, exclusive]: **this custom is unique to our country** diesen Brauch gibt es nur in unserem Land.

unison ['juːnɪzn] *n (U)* [agreement] Einklang *der*; **in unison** [simultaneously] unisono.

unit ['juːnɪt] *n* - **1.** [gen] Einheit *die* - **2.** [part of machine or system, piece of furniture] Element *das* - **3.** [department] Abteilung *die*.

unite [juː'naɪt] ◇ *vt* vereinigen. ◇ *vi* sich vereinigen.

united [juː'naɪtɪd] *adj* - **1.** [in harmony] vereint - **2.** [unified] vereinigt.

United Kingdom *n*: **the United Kingdom** das Vereinigte Königreich.

United Nations *n*: **the United Nations** die Vereinten Nationen *Pl*.

United States *n*: **the United States (of America)** die Vereinigten Staaten (von Amerika); **in the United States** in den Vereinigten Staaten.

unity ['juːnətɪ] *n* - **1.** [union] Einheit *die* - **2.** [harmony] Einigkeit *die*.

universal [ˌjuːnɪ'vɜːsl] *adj* universal.

universe ['juːnɪvɜːs] *n* ASTRON Universum *das*.

university [ˌjuːnɪ'vɜːsətɪ] ◇ *n* Universität *die*. ◇ *comp* Universitäts-; **university student** Student *der*, -in *die*.

unjust [ˌʌn'dʒʌst] *adj* ungerecht.

unkempt [ˌʌn'kempt] *adj* [hair, beard, appearance] ungepflegt.

unkind [ʌn'kaɪnd] *adj* [uncharitable] gemein.

unknown [ˌʌn'nəʊn] *adj* unbekannt.

unlawful [ˌʌn'lɔːfʊl] *adj* ungesetzlich.

unleaded [ˌʌn'ledɪd] *adj* bleifrei.

unleash [ˌʌn'liːʃ] *vt liter* entfesseln.

unless [ən'les] *conj* es sei denn, wenn nicht; **unless you know more** es sei denn, Sie wissen mehr; **you'll be late unless you set off at once** wenn du dich nicht gleich auf den Weg machst, wirst du zu spät kommen; **unless I'm mistaken** wenn ich mich nicht irre; **unless there's a miracle** falls nicht ein Wunder geschieht.

unlike [ˌʌn'laɪk] *prep* - **1.** [different from] nicht ähnlich *(+ D)* - **2.** [in contrast to] im Gegensatz zu - **3.** [not typical of]: **it's very unlike you to complain** es sieht dir gar nicht ähnlich, dich zu beschweren.

unlikely [ʌn'laɪklɪ] *adj* - **1.** [not probable] unwahrscheinlich - **2.** [bizarre] merkwürdig.

unlisted [ʌn'lɪstɪd] *adj US* [phone number]: **to be unlisted** nicht im Telefonbuch stehen.

unload [ˌʌn'ləʊd] *vt* - **1.** [remove] aus|laden - **2.** [remove load from] entladen.

unlock [ˌʌn'lɒk] *vt* auf|schließen.

unlucky [ʌn'lʌkɪ] *adj* - **1.** [unfortunate] unglücklich; [person] unglücksselig - **2.** [bringing bad luck] Unglücks-.

unmarried [ˌʌn'mærɪd] *adj* unverheiratet.

unmistakable [ˌʌnmɪ'steɪkəbl] *adj* unverwechselbar.

unmitigated [ʌn'mɪtɪgeɪtɪd] *adj* vollkommen.

unnatural [ʌn'nætʃrəl] *adj* - **1.** [unusual, strange] unnatürlich - **2.** [affected] aufgesetzt.

unnecessary [ʌn'nesəsərɪ] *adj* unnötig.

unnerving [ˌʌn'nɜːvɪŋ] *adj* [experience] verunsichernd; [silence] beunruhigend.

unnoticed [ˌʌn'nəʊtɪst] *adj*: **to go** OR **pass unnoticed** nicht bemerkt werden.

unobtainable [ˌʌnəb'teɪnəbl] *adj* nicht erhältlich.

unofficial [ˌʌnə'fɪʃl] *adj* inoffiziell.

unorthodox [ˌʌn'ɔːθədɒks] *adj* unorthodox.

unpack [ˌʌn'pæk] *vt* & *vi* aus|packen.

unparalleled [ʌn'pærəleld] *adj* einmalig.

unpleasant [ʌn'pleznt] *adj* unangenehm.

unplug [ʌn'plʌg] *vt* ELEC: **to unplug sthg** den Stecker von etw heraus|ziehen.

unpopular [ˌʌn'pɒpjʊlə^r] *adj* unpopulär.

unprecedented [ʌn'presɪdəntɪd] *adj* beispiellos.

unpredictable [ˌʌnprɪ'dɪktəbl] *adj* unvorhersehbar; [person] unberechenbar.

unprofessional [ˌʌnprə'feʃənl] *adj* unprofessionell.

unqualified [ˌʌn'kwɒlɪfaɪd] *adj* - **1.** [not qualified] unqualifiziert; [teacher, nurse] nicht ausgebildet - **2.** [total, complete - success, support] uneingeschränkt; [- denial] vollständig.

unquestionable [ʌn'kwestʃənəbl] *adj* unbestreitbar.

unquestioning [ʌn'kwestʃənɪŋ] *adj* bedingungslos.

unravel [ʌn'rævl] *(UK)* *(US)* *vt* - **1.** [undo - knitting] aufltrennen; [- threads] entwirren - **2.** *fig* [solve] lösen.

unreal [ˌʌn'rɪəl] *adj* [strange] unwirklich.

unrealistic [ˌʌnrɪə'lɪstɪk] *adj* unrealistisch.

unreasonable [ʌn'ri:znəbl] *adj* - **1.** [person]: **he's so unreasonable** mit ihm kann man überhaupt nicht vernünftig reden - **2.** [demand, decision] unangemessen.

unrelated [ˌʌnrɪ'leɪtɪd] *adj*: **to be unrelated (to sthg)** in keinem Zusammenhang (mit etw) stehen.

unrelenting [ˌʌnrɪ'lentɪŋ] *adj* [struggle, questions] unerbittlich; [pressure] unablässig.

unreliable [ˌʌnrɪ'laɪəbl] *adj* unzuverlässig.

unremitting [ˌʌnrɪ'mɪtɪŋ] *adj* [effort, activity] unablässig, unaufhörlich.

unrequited [ˌʌnrɪ'kwaɪtɪd] *adj* unerwidert.

unreserved [ˌʌnrɪ'zɜ:vd] *adj* [admiration, support, approval] uneingeschränkt.

unresolved [ˌʌnrɪ'zɒlvd] *adj* ungelöst.

unrest [ˌʌn'rest] *n (U)* Unruhen *Pl*.

unrivalled *UK*, **unrivaled** *US* [ʌn'raɪvld] *adj* unübertroffen.

unroll [ˌʌn'rəʊl] *vt* auflrollen.

unruly [ʌn'ru:lɪ] *adj* - **1.** [person, group] undiszipliniert; [child] unartig; [behaviour] ungezügelt - **2.** [hair] widerspenstig.

unsafe [ˌʌn'seɪf] *adj* - **1.** [dangerous] gefährlich - **2.** [in danger] nicht sicher.

unsaid [ˌʌn'sed] *adj*: **to leave sthg unsaid** etw unausgesprochen lassen.

unsatisfactory [ˌʌnsætɪs'fæktərɪ] *adj* unbefriedigend.

unsavoury, unsavory *US* [ˌʌn'seɪvərɪ] *adj* - **1.** [person] zwielichtig; [appearance] abstoßend; [reputation, behaviour, area] zweifelhaft - **2.** [smell] widerwärtig.

unscathed [ˌʌn'skeɪðd] *adj* unversehrt.

unscrew [ˌʌn'skru:] *vt* - **1.** [lid, bottle top] loslldrehen - **2.** [sign, mirror] ablschrauben.

unscrupulous [ʌn'skru:pjʊləs] *adj* skrupellos.

unseemly [ʌn'si:mlɪ] *adj* unpassend, unschicklich.

unselfish [ˌʌn'selfɪʃ] *adj* selbstlos.

unsettled [ˌʌn'setld] *adj* - **1.** [disturbed - person] beunruhigt; [- weather] unbeständig - **2.** [unfinished, unresolved - argument] nicht beigelegt; [- issue] ungeklärt - **3.** [account, bill] ausstehend.

unshak(e)able [ʌn'ʃeɪkəbl] *adj* [faith, belief] unerschütterlich; [decision] unumstößlich.

unshaven [ˌʌn'ʃeɪvn] *adj* unrasiert.

unsightly [ʌn'saɪtlɪ] *adj* unansehnlich.

unskilled [ˌʌn'skɪld] *adj* [worker] ungelernt; [work] einfach.

unsociable [ʌn'səʊʃəbl] *adj* ungesellig.

unsocial [ˌʌn'səʊʃl] *adj*: **to work unsocial hours** früh/morgens/nachts/am Wochenende arbeiten.

unsound [ˌʌn'saʊnd] *adj* - **1.** [conclusion, theory, decision] zweifelhaft - **2.** [building, structure] instabil.

unspeakable [ʌn'spi:kəbl] *adj* fürchterlich.

unstable [ˌʌn'steɪbl] *adj* - **1.** [structure, government] instabil; [weather] wechselhaft - **2.** [mentally, emotionally] labil.

unsteady [ˌʌn'stedɪ] *adj* wackelig.

unstoppable [ˌʌn'stɒpəbl] *adj* unaufhaltsam.

unstuck [ˌʌn'stʌk] *adj*: **to come unstuck** [notice, stamp, label] sich abllösen; *fig* [plan, system] schief gehen; [person] auf die Nase fallen.

unsuccessful [ˌʌnsək'sesfʊl] *adj* erfolglos; [attempt] vergeblich.

unsuccessfully [ˌʌnsək'sesfʊlɪ] *adv* erfolglos, vergeblich.

unsuitable [ˌʌn'su:təbl] *adj* unpassend; **to be unsuitable for sthg** für etw ungeeignet sein.

unsure [ˌʌn'ʃɔ:ʳ] *adj* - **1.** [not confident]: **to be unsure of o.s.** unsicher sein - **2.** [not certain]: **to be unsure (about/of sthg)** sich *(D)* (einer Sache *(G)*) nicht sicher sein.

unsuspecting [ˌʌnsə'spektɪŋ] *adj* nichts ahnend.

unsympathetic ['ʌnˌsɪmpə'θetɪk] *adj* [unfeeling] nicht mitfühlend.

untangle [ˌʌn'tæŋgl] *vt* entwirren.

untapped [ˌʌn'tæpt] *adj* ungenutzt; [mineral resources] unerschlossen.

untenable [ˌʌn'tenəbl] *adj* unhaltbar.

unthinkable [ʌn'θɪŋkəbl] *adj* undenkbar, unvorstellbar.

untidy [ʌn'taɪdɪ] *adj* unordentlich.

untie [ˌʌn'taɪ] *(cont* **untying***)* *vt* [string, knot, bonds] lösen; [package] auflbinden; [prisoner] loslbinden.

until [ən'tɪl] ◇ *prep* bis; **until the evening/end** bis zum Abend/Ende; **not until** erst; **she**

won't come until two o'clock sie kommt erst um zwei Uhr. <> *conj* bis; **wait until he comes** warte, bis er kommt; **she won't come until she is invited** sie kommt erst, wenn sie eingeladen wird.

untimely [ʌn'taɪmlɪ] *adj* - **1.** [premature] vorzeitig - **2.** [inopportune] ungelegen, unpassend.

untold [ˌʌn'təʊld] *adj* [amount] ungezählt; [wealth] unermesslich; [suffering, joy] unsäglich.

untoward [ˌʌntə'wɔ:d] *adj* [event] unglücklich; [behaviour] ungebührlich.

untrue [ˌʌn'tru:] *adj* [inaccurate] unwahr, falsch.

unused *adj* - **1.** [ˌʌn'ju:zd] [new] unbenutzt - **2.** [ʌn'ju:st] [unaccustomed]: **to be unused to sthg** an etw *(A)* nicht gewöhnt sein; **to be unused to doing sthg** nicht daran gewöhnt sein, etw zu tun.

unusual [ʌn'ju:ʒl] *adj* ungewöhnlich.

unusually [ʌn'ju:ʒəlɪ] *adv* außergewöhnlich.

unveil [ˌʌn'veɪl] *vt liter* & *fig* enthüllen.

unwanted [ˌʌn'wɒntɪd] *adj* [clothes, furniture] ausrangiert; [child, pregnancy] ungewollt; **to feel unwanted** das Gefühl haben, unerwünscht zu sein.

unwelcome [ʌn'welkəm] *adj* - **1.** [news, experience] unerfreulich - **2.** [visitor] unwillkommen.

unwell [ˌʌn'wel] *adj*: **to be/feel unwell** sich unwohl fühlen.

unwieldy [ʌn'wi:ldɪ] *adj* - **1.** [tool] unhandlich; [piece of furniture] sperrig - **2.** *fig* [system, method] umständlich; [organization] schwerfällig.

unwilling [ˌʌn'wɪlɪŋ] *adj* unwillig.

unwind [ˌʌn'waɪnd] (*pt & pp* **-wound**) <> *vt* ab|wickeln. <> *vi fig* [person] sich entspannen.

unwise [ˌʌn'waɪz] *adj* unklug.

unworkable [ˌʌn'wɜ:kəbl] *adj* undurchführbar.

unworthy [ʌn'wɜ:ðɪ] *adj*: **to be unworthy of sthg** einer Sache *(G)* unwürdig sein.

unwound [ˌʌn'waʊnd] *pt* & *pp* ▷ **unwind**.

unwrap [ˌʌn'ræp] *vt* aus|packen.

up [ʌp] <> *adv* - **1.** [towards higher position, level] hoch; **we walked up to the top** wir sind zum Gipfel gelaufen; **to throw sthg up** etw in die Höhe werfen; **prices are going up** die Preise steigen; **up and up** immer höher - **2.** [in higher position] oben; **she's up in her room** sie ist oben in ihrem Zimmer; **up here/there** hier/da OR dort oben - **3.** [into an upright position]: **to stand up** auf|stehen; **to sit up** [from lying position] sich auf|setzen; [sit straight] sich gerade hin|setzen; **help me up** hilf mir auf - **4.** [northwards]: **to live up north** oben im Norden wohnen; **I'm going up to York** ich fahre hoch nach York - **5.** [facing upwards] nach oben gerichtet; **he was lying face up** er lag mit dem Gesicht nach oben - **6.** [along river] oben; **their house is a little further up** ihr Haus liegt ein bisschen weiter in dieser Richtung - **7.** [ahead]: **to be two goals up** mit zwei Toren führen. <> *prep* - **1.** [towards higher position]: **to walk up a hill** einen Hügel hinauf|gehen; **I went up the stairs** ich ging die Treppe hinauf - **2.** [in higher position]: **to be up a hill** oben auf einem Hügel sein - **3.** [towards far end of]: **they live up the road from us** sie wohnen weiter oben in unserer Straße. <> *adj* - **1.** [out of bed] auf; **I was up at six today** ich war heute um sechs auf; **to be up all night** die ganze Nacht auf|bleiben - **2.** [at an end] um, zu Ende; **time's up** die Zeit ist um - **3.** *inf* [wrong]: **there's something up** es liegt etwas in der Luft; **what's up (with you)?** was ist (mit dir) los? <> *n*: **ups and downs** Höhen und Tiefen *Pl.* ◆ **up and down** <> *adv*: **to walk/jump up and down** auf und ab gehen/springen. <> *prep* [backwards and forwards]: **we walked up and down the avenue** wir gingen die Allee auf und ab. ◆ **up to** *prep* - **1.** [indicating position, level] bis zu; **the water came up to my knees** das Wasser reichte mir bis an die Knie; **up to this point** bis zu diesem Punkt; **up to six weeks/ten people** bis zu sechs Wochen/zehn Personen - **2.** [in time] bis; **I felt fine up to last month** bis letzten Monat ging es mir gut - **3.** [well or able enough for]: **my French isn't up to much** *inf* mein Französisch ist nicht besonders gut; **to be up to a task** einer Aufgabe gewachsen sein; **I'm not up to going out tonight** ich schaffe es heute Abend nicht auszugehen - **4.** *phr*: **what are you up to?** *inf* [doing] was machst du da?; [planning] was hast du vor?; **they're up to something** sie haben etwas vor; **it's up to you** das liegt bei dir. ◆ **up until** *prep* bis; **up until ten o'clock** bis um zehn Uhr.

up-and-coming *adj* [athlete, actor] kommend; [business] aufstrebend.

upbringing ['ʌpˌbrɪŋɪŋ] *n* Erziehung *die*.

update [ˌʌp'deɪt] *vt* aktualisieren.

upheaval [ʌp'hi:vl] *n* Aufruhr *der*.

upheld [ʌp'held] *pt* & *pp* ▷ **uphold**.

uphill [ˌʌp'hɪl] <> *adj* - **1.** [rising] ansteigend - **2.** *fig* [difficult] mühsam. <> *adv* bergauf.

uphold [ʌp'həʊld] (*pt & pp* **-held**) *vt* - **1.** [law] bei|behalten - **2.** [decision, system] unterstützen.

upholstery [ʌp'həʊlstərɪ] *n (U)* Polsterung *die*.

upkeep ['ʌpki:p] *n* Instandhaltung *die*; [of garden] Pflege *die*.

uplifting [ʌp'lɪftɪŋ] *adj* [cheering] erhebend.

up-market *adj* [hotel, restaurant, area] vornehm; [goods] edel.

upon [ə'pɒn] *prep fml* - **1.** [on, on top of - indicating place, position] auf *(+ D)*; [- indicating direction] auf *(+ A)*; *(phrase)*: **summer/the weekend is upon us** es ist beinahe Sommer/Wochenende - **2.** [when] als; **upon hearing the news, I rushed to the telephone** als ich die Neuigkeiten hörte, rannte ich sofort zum Telefon.

upper ['ʌpəʳ] <> *adj* - **1.** [physically higher & GEOG] obere(r) (s); **upper lip** Oberlippe *die* - **2.** [higher in order, rank] höher. <> *n* [of shoe] Obermaterial *das*.

upper class *n*: **the upper class** die Oberschicht. ◆ **upper-class** *adj* vornehm.

upper-crust *adj* vornehm.

upper hand *n*: **to have the upper hand** die Oberhand haben; **to gain** *OR* **get the upper hand** die Oberhand gewinnen.

Upper House *n* POL Oberhaus *das*.

uppermost ['ʌpəməʊst] *adj* - **1.** [highest] oberste(r) (s) - **2.** [most important]: **my father's illness is uppermost in my mind at the moment** die Krankheit meines Vaters beschäftigt mich momentan am meisten.

upright ['ʌpraɪt] <> *adj liter* & *fig* aufrecht. <> *adv* aufrecht. <> *n* [of goal] Pfosten *der*; [of bookshelf] Seitenteil *das*; [of door] Türpfosten *der*.

uprising ['ʌp,raɪzɪŋ] *n* Aufstand *der*.

uproar ['ʌprɔːʳ] *n* Aufruhr *der*.

uproot [ʌp'ruːt] *vt* entwurzeln.

upset [ʌp'set] *(pt & pp inv)* <> *adj* - **1.** [distressed] aufgeregt; [shocked] bestürzt; [offended] beleidigt - **2.** MED: **to have an upset stomach** eine Magenverstimmung haben. <> *n* - **1.** MED: **to have a stomach upset** eine Magenverstimmung haben - **2.** [surprise result] Überraschungsergebnis *das*. <> *vt* - **1.** [distress] auf|regen; **the news upset him** die Nachricht bestürzte ihn - **2.** [mess up] durcheinander bringen - **3.** [overturn, knock over] um|kippen, um|stoßen; [boat] zum Kentern bringen.

upshot ['ʌpʃɒt] *n* Ergebnis *das*.

upside down [,ʌpsaɪd-] <> *adj* [inverted] verkehrt herum. <> *adv* verkehrt herum; **to turn sthg upside down** *fig* [disorder] etw auf den Kopf stellen.

upstairs [,ʌp'steəz] <> *adj* oben, im oberen Stockwerk. <> *adv* - **1.** [not downstairs] oben; [with motion] nach oben - **2.** [on the floor above] oben, im oberen Stockwerk. <> *n* oberes Stockwerk.

upstart ['ʌpstɑːt] *n* Emporkömmling *der*.

upstream [,ʌp'striːm] <> *adj*: **upstream (from sthg)** stromaufwärts (von etw). <> *adv* stromaufwärts.

upsurge ['ʌpsɜːdʒ] *n*: **upsurge of/in sthg** Zunahme *die* an etw *(D)*.

uptake ['ʌpteɪk] *n*: **to be quick on the uptake** schnell verstehen; **to be slow on the uptake** schwer von Begriff sein.

uptight [ʌp'taɪt] *adj inf* verkrampft.

up-to-date *adj* - **1.** [machinery, methods] modern - **2.** [news, information] neueste(r) (s), aktuell; **to keep up-to-date with sthg** über etw *(A)* auf dem Laufenden bleiben.

upturn ['ʌptɜːn] *n*: **upturn (in sthg)** Aufschwung *der* (in etw *(D)*).

upward ['ʌpwəd] <> *adj* [movement, trend] Aufwärts-. <> *adv US* = **upwards**.

upwards ['ʌpwədz] *adv* - **1.** [to a higher place] nach oben - **2.** [to a higher number, degree, rate]: **to climb** *OR* **move upwards** an|steigen. ◆ **upwards of** *prep* über *(+ A)*, mehr als.

uranium [jʊ'reɪnjəm] *n* Uran *das*.

urban ['ɜːbən] *adj* städtisch; **urban development** Stadtentwicklung *die*.

urbane [ɜː'beɪn] *adj* gewandt.

Urdu ['ʊəduː] *n* Urdu *das*.

urge [ɜːdʒ] <> *n* Drang *der*; **to have an urge to do sthg** den Drang verspüren, etw zu tun. <> *vt* - **1.** [try to persuade]: **to urge sb to do sthg** jn drängen, etw zu tun - **2.** [advocate] eindringlich raten zu.

urgency ['ɜːdʒənsɪ] *n* Dringlichkeit *die*.

urgent ['ɜːdʒənt] *adj* - **1.** [pressing] dringend - **2.** [desperate] verzweifelt.

urinal [,jʊə'raɪnl] *n* [receptacle] Urinal *das*; [room] Pissoir *das*.

urinate ['jʊərɪneɪt] *vi* urinieren.

urine ['jʊərɪn] *n* Urin *der*.

urn [ɜːn] *n* - **1.** [for ashes] Urne *die* - **2.** [for tea, coffee] *Heißwasserbehälter mit Zapfhahn*.

Uruguay ['jʊərəgwaɪ] *n* Uruguay *nt*.

us [ʌs] *pers pron* uns; **they know us** sie kennen uns; **they like us** wir gefallen ihnen; **it's us** wir sinds; **send it to us** schicke es uns; **tell us** sag uns; **they're worse than us** sie sind schlimmer als wir; **you can't expect us to do it** du kannst nicht erwarten, dass **wir** das tun; **all of us** wir alle; **none of us** keiner von uns; **some/a few of us** einige von uns; **most of us** die meisten von uns; **both of us** wir beide; **there are three of us** wir sind zu dritt; **neither of us** keiner von uns.

US (*abbr of* **United States**) *n*: **the US** die USA *Pl*.

USA *n* (*abbr of* **United States of America**); **the USA** die USA *Pl*.

usage ['juːzɪdʒ] *n* - **1.** *(U)* [use of language] Gebrauch *der* - **2.** [meaning] Bedeutung *die* - **3.** *(U)* [treatment] Behandlung *die*; [handling] Gebrauch *der*.

use <> *n* [juːs] - **1.** [act of using] Gebrauch *der*, Benutzung *die*; [for specific purpose] Verwendung *die*; [of method] Anwendung *die*; **to be in/out of use** im/außer

Gebrauch sein; **to make use of sthg** von etw Gebrauch machen - **2.** [purpose, usefulness] Nutzen *der*; **can you find a use for this?** kannst du damit etwas anfangen?; **to be of use** nützlich sein; **it's no use!** es hat keinen Zweck!; **what's the use (of doing that)?** was hat es für einen Zweck(, das zu tun)? ◇ *aux vb* [ju:s]: **I used to go for a run every day** ich bin früher jeden Tag laufen gegangen; **he didn't use to be so fat** er war früher nicht so dick. ◇ *vt* [ju:z] - **1.** [utilize] gebrauchen, benutzen; [for specific purpose] verwenden; [method] an|wenden - **2.** *pej* [exploit] benutzen. ◆ **use up** *vt sep* auf|brauchen.

used *adj* - **1.** [ju:zd] [dirty] benutzt, schmutzig - **2.** [ju:zd] [second-hand] gebraucht, Gebraucht- - **3.** [ju:st] [accustomed]: **to be used to sthg** an etw *(A)* gewöhnt sein; **to be used to doing sthg** daran gewöhnt sein *OR* es gewöhnt sein, etw zu tun; **to get used to sthg** sich an etw *(A)* gewöhnen.

useful ['ju:sfʊl] *adj* [handy] nützlich.

useless ['ju:slɪs] *adj* - **1.** [unusable] nutzlos - **2.** [pointless] zwecklos, unnütz - **3.** *inf* [hopeless]: **to be useless** zu nichts zu gebrauchen sein.

user ['ju:zəʳ] *n* Benutzer *der*, -in *die*; **drug user** Drogenkonsument *der*, -in *die*.

user-friendly *adj* benutzerfreundlich.

usher ['ʌʃəʳ] ◇ *n* Platzanweiser *der*, -in *die*. ◇ *vt* führen.

usherette [,ʌʃə'ret] *n* Platzanweiserin *die*.

USSR (*abbr of* **Union of Soviet Socialist Republics**) *n* UdSSR *die*.

usual ['ju:ʒəl] *adj* üblich; **as usual** wie üblich.

usually ['ju:ʒəlɪ] *adv* normalerweise.

utensil [ju:'tensl] *n* Utensil *das*.

uterus ['ju:tərəs] (*pl* **-ri** [-raɪ] *OR* **-ruses**) *n* Uterus *der*, Gebärmutter *die*.

utility [ju:'tɪlətɪ] *n* - **1.** [usefulness] Nützlichkeit *die* - **2.** [company]: **(public) utility** (öffentlicher) Versorgungsbetrieb - **3.** COMPUT Dienstprogramm *das*.

utility room *n* ≃ Waschküche *die*.

utilize, -ise ['ju:təlaɪz] *vt* nutzen.

utmost ['ʌtməʊst] ◇ *adj* äußerste(r) (s). ◇ *n* - **1.** [best effort]: **to do one's utmost (to achieve sthg)** sein Möglichstes tun(, um etw zu erreichen) - **2.** [maximum] Äußerste *das*; **to the utmost** bis zum Äußersten.

utter ['ʌtəʳ] ◇ *adj* völlig, komplett. ◇ *vt* [sound, cry] aus|stoßen; [word] sagen.

utterly ['ʌtəlɪ] *adv* völlig.

U-turn *n* - **1.** [turning movement] Wende *die* - **2.** *fig* [complete change] Kehrtwendung *die*.

V

v^{1} (*pl* **v's** *OR* **vs**), **V** (*pl* **V's** *OR* **Vs**) [vi:] *n* [letter] v *das*, V *das*.

v^{2} *abbr of* **verse**, **versus**, **volt**.

vacancy ['veɪkənsɪ] *n* - **1.** [job, position] offene Stelle, freie Position - **2.** [room available] freies Zimmer; **'vacancies'** 'frei'; **'no vacancies'** 'belegt'.

vacant ['veɪkənt] *adj* - **1.** [house] leer stehend; [chair] unbesetzt; [toilet] nicht besetzt; [room] frei - **2.** [post, job] offen, frei - **3.** [look] leer.

vacant lot *n* Baugrundstück *das*.

vacate [və'keɪt] *vt* - **1.** [post, job] auf|geben - **2.** [seat] frei machen - **3.** [hotel, room] aus|ziehen aus.

vacation [və'keɪʃn] *n* - **1.** UNIV [period when closed] Ferien *Pl* - **2.** *US* [holiday] Ferien *Pl*, Urlaub *der*.

vacationer [və'keɪʃənəʳ] *n US* Urlauber *der*, -in *die*.

vaccinate ['væksɪneɪt] *vt*: **to vaccinate sb (against sthg)** jn (gegen etw) impfen.

vaccine [*UK* 'væksi:n, *US* væk'si:n] *n* Impfstoff *der*.

vacuum ['vækjʊəm] ◇ *n* - **1.** TECH Vakuum *das* - **2.** [cleaning machine] Staubsauger *der*. ◇ *vt* & *vi* Staub saugen.

vacuum cleaner *n* Staubsauger *der*.

vacuum-packed *adj* vakuumverpackt.

vagina [və'dʒaɪnə] *n* Scheide *die*, Vagina *die*.

vagrant ['veɪgrənt] *n* Landstreicher *der*, -in *die*.

vague [veɪg] *adj* - **1.** [imprecise, evasive] vage - **2.** [feeling] leicht - **3.** [absent-minded] zerstreut - **4.** [shape, outline] schemenhaft.

vaguely ['veɪglɪ] *adv* - **1.** [imprecisely] vage - **2.** [slightly, not very] leicht - **3.** [absent-mindedly] zerstreut - **4.** [indistinctly] undeutlich.

vain [veɪn] *adj* - **1.** *pej* [conceited] eitel - **2.** [attempt, hope] vergeblich. ◆ **in vain** *adv* vergeblich, vergebens.

valentine card ['væləntaɪn-] *n* Grußkarte *die* zum Valentinstag.

Valentine's Day ['væləntaɪnz-] *n*: **(St) Valentine's Day** Valentinstag *der*.

valet ['væleɪ, 'vælɪt] *n* Kammerdiener *der*.

valid ['vælɪd] *adj* - **1.** [argument] stichhaltig; [explanation] einleuchtend; [decision] begründet; [claim] berechtigt - **2.** [ticket, passport, driving licence] gültig; [contract] rechtsgültig.

valley ['vælɪ] (*pl* **valleys**) *n* Tal *das*.

valour *UK*, **valor** *US* ['vælər] *n fml & liter* Heldenmut *der*.

valuable ['væljuəbl] *adj* wertvoll. ◆ **valuables** *npl* Wertsachen *Pl*.

valuation [ˌvælju'eɪʃn] *n* - **1.** *(U)* [pricing] Schätzung *die* - **2.** [estimated price] Schätzwert *der*.

value ['vælju:] ◇ *n (U)* Wert *der*; **to be good value** preisgünstig sein; **to be value for money** ein gutes Preis-Leistungs-Verhältnis haben. ◇ *vt* schätzen. ◆ **values** *npl* [morals] Werte *Pl*, Wertvorstellungen *Pl*.

value-added tax [-ædɪd-] *n* Mehrwertsteuer *die*.

valued ['vælju:d] *adj* geschätzt.

valve [vælv] *n* - **1.** [in pipe, tube] Absperrhahn *der* - **2.** [on tyre] Ventil *das*.

van [væn] *n* - **1.** AUT Transporter *der*, Lieferwagen *der* - **2.** *UK* RAIL Wagon *der*, Wagen *der*.

vandal ['vændl] *n* Vandale *der*, -lin *die*.

vandalism ['vændəlɪzm] *n* Vandalismus *der*.

vandalize, -ise ['vændəlaɪz] *vt* mutwillig beschädigen.

vanguard ['væŋgɑ:d] *n*: **in the vanguard of sthg** an der Spitze einer Sache *(G)*.

vanilla [və'nɪlə] *n* Vanille *die*.

vanish ['vænɪʃ] *vi* - **1.** [no longer be visible] verschwinden - **2.** [no longer exist - race, species] auslsterben; [- hopes, chances] schwinden.

vanity ['vænətɪ] *n (U) pej* [of person] Eitelkeit *die*.

vapour *UK*, **vapor** *US* ['veɪpər] *n (U)* Dampf *der*.

variable ['veərɪəbl] *adj* - **1.** [changeable] unbeständig - **2.** [uneven - quality] unterschiedlich; [- performance] unbeständig.

variance ['veərɪəns] *n fml*: **to be at variance with sthg** mit etw nicht übereinlstimmen.

variation [ˌveərɪ'eɪʃn] *n* - **1.** *(U)* [fact of difference] Unterschied *der* - **2.** [change in level or quantity] Schwankung *die* - **3.** [different version & MUS] Variation *die*.

varicose veins ['værɪkəʊs-] *npl* Krampfadern *Pl*.

varied ['veərɪd] *adj* [life] bewegt; [group] gemischt; [work, diet] abwechslungsreich.

variety [və'raɪətɪ] *n* - **1.** *(U)* [difference in type] Abwechslung *die* - **2.** [selection] Auswahl *die* - **3.** [type] Art *die*, Sorte *die* - **4.** *(U)* THEAT Varietee *das*.

various ['veərɪəs] *adj* verschieden.

varnish ['vɑ:nɪʃ] ◇ *n* [for wood, fingernails] Lack *der*; [for pottery] Glasur *die*. ◇ *vt* [wood, fingernails] lackieren; [pottery] glasieren.

vary ['veərɪ] ◇ *vt* verändern, variieren. ◇ *vi* [differ] sich unterscheiden; [fluctuate] sich ändern; [prices] schwanken.

vase [*UK* vɑ:z, *US* veɪz] *n* Vase *die*.

vast [vɑ:st] *adj* riesig; [expense, difference] enorm.

vat [væt] *n* [open] Bottich *der*; [closed] Fass *das*.

VAT [væt, vi:eɪ'ti:] (*abbr of* **value added tax**) *n* Mehrwertsteuer *die*, MwSt.

Vatican ['vætɪkən] *n*: **the Vatican** der Vatikan.

vault [vɔ:lt] ◇ *n* - **1.** [in bank] Tresorraum *der* - **2.** [under church] Gruft *die* - **3.** [roof] Gewölbe *das*. ◇ *vt* springen über *(+ A)*. ◇ *vi*: **to vault over sthg** über etw *(A)* springen.

VCR (*abbr of* **video cassette recorder**) *n* Videorekorder *der*.

VD *n abbr of* **venereal disease**.

VDU (*abbr of* **visual display unit**) *n* Bildschirm *der*.

veal [vi:l] *n* Kalbfleisch *das*.

veer [vɪər] *vi* - **1.** [vehicle] auslscheren; [road] eine Kurve machen; [wind] (sich) drehen - **2.** *fig* [conversation, mood] schwanken.

vegan ['vi:gən] ◇ *adj* veganisch. ◇ *n* Veganer *der*, -in *die*.

vegetable ['vedʒtəbl] ◇ *n* Gemüse *das*. ◇ *adj* Gemüse-.

vegetarian [ˌvedʒɪ'teərɪən] ◇ *adj* vegetarisch. ◇ *n* Vegetarier *der*, -in *die*.

vegetation [ˌvedʒɪ'teɪʃn] *n* Vegetation *die*.

vehement ['vi:əmənt] *adj* heftig; [denial, protest, defence] vehement; [debate] hitzig.

vehicle ['vi:əkl] *n* [for transport] Fahrzeug *das*.

veil [veɪl] *n* Schleier *der*; **to draw a veil over sthg** *fig* etw verschweigen.

vein [veɪn] *n* [gen] Ader *die*.

velocity [vɪ'lɒsətɪ] *n* PHYS Geschwindigkeit *die*.

velvet ['velvɪt] *n* Samt *der*.

vendetta [ven'detə] *n* Blutrache *die*; [in the press] Hetzkampagne *die*.

vending machine ['vendɪŋ-] *n* Automat *der*.

vendor ['vendər] *n* Verkäufer *der*, -in *die*; **street vendor** Straßenhändler *der*, -in *die*.

veneer [və'nɪər] *n* - **1.** [of wood] Furnier *das* - **2.** *fig* [appearance]: **to give sthg a veneer of respectability** einer Sache *(D)* einen seriösen Anstrich geben.

venereal disease [vɪ'nɪərɪəl-] *n (U)* Geschlechtskrankheit *die*.

venetian blind [vɪˌni:ʃn-] *n* Jalousie *die*.

Venezuela [ˌvenɪz'weɪlə] *n* Venezuela *nt*.

vengeance ['vendʒəns] *n (U)* Vergeltung *die*, Rachung *die*; **with a vengeance** gewaltig; **to work with a vengeance** hart arbeiten.

venison ['venɪzn] *n (U)* Wild *das (Damwild)*.

venom ['venəm] *n* - **1.** [poison] Gift *das* - **2.** *fig* [spite, bitterness] Gehässigkeit *die*.

vent [vent] <> *n* Öffnung *die*; [in chimney, for ventilation] Abzug *der*; **to give vent to sthg** [feelings] etw *(D)* freien Lauf lassen; [anger] etw *(D)* Luft machen. <> *vt* [express - feelings] freien Lauf lassen *(+ D)*; [- anger] Luft machen *(+ D)*; **to vent one's anger on sb** seinen Ärger an jm aus|lassen.

ventilate ['ventɪleɪt] *vt* (be)lüften.

ventilator ['ventɪleɪtəʳ] *n* - **1.** [in room, building] Ventilator *der* - **2.** MED Beatmungsgerät *das*.

ventriloquist [ven'trɪləkwɪst] *n* Bauchredner *der*, -in *die*.

venture ['ventʃəʳ] <> *n* Unternehmen *das*. <> *vt* [proffer - opinion, advice] zu äußern wagen; [- guess] wagen; [- suggestion, remark] sich *(D)* erlauben; **to venture to do sthg** sich *(D)* erlauben, etw zu tun. <> *vi* - **1.** [go somewhere dangerous] sich wagen - **2.** [embark]: **to venture into politics** den Schritt in die Politik wagen.

venue ['venju:] *n* [for concert, conference] Veranstaltungsort *der*; [for match] Austragungsort *der*.

veranda(h) [və'rændə] *n* Veranda *die*.

verb [vɜ:b] *n* Verb *das*.

verbal ['vɜ:bl] *adj* - **1.** [spoken - agreement] mündlich; [- skills] sprachlich; **verbal abuse** Beschimpfung *die* - **2.** GRAM Verb-, verbal.

verbatim [vɜ:'beɪtɪm] *adj* & *adv* (wort)wörtlich.

verbose [vɜ:'bəʊs] *adj fml* langatmig.

verdict ['vɜ:dɪkt] *n* Urteil *das*; **what's your verdict on his new film?** was hältst du von seinem neuen Film?

verge [vɜ:dʒ] *n* - **1.** [edge, side] Rand *der*; [of road] Bankett *das* - **2.** [brink]: **to be on the verge of sthg** [ruin, mental breakdown] am Rand einer Sache *(G)* stehen; [success] kurz vor etw *(D)* stehen; **to be on the verge of doing sthg** kurz davor stehen, etw zu tun. ◆ **verge (up)on** *vt insep* grenzen an *(+ A)*.

verify ['verɪfaɪ] *vt* - **1.** [check] prüfen, überprüfen - **2.** [confirm] bestätigen.

veritable ['verɪtəbl] *adj fml* & *hum* wahr.

vermin ['vɜ:mɪn] *npl* - **1.** ZOOL [insects] Ungeziefer *das*; [rodents] Schädlinge *Pl* - **2.** *pej* [people] Abschaum *der*.

vermouth [vɜ:'mu:θ] *n* Wermut *der*.

versatile ['vɜ:sətaɪl] *adj* - **1.** [person] vielseitig - **2.** [machine, tool] vielseitig verwendbar.

verse [vɜ:s] *n* - **1.** *(U)* [poetry] Lyrik *die* - **2.** [stanza] Strophe *die* - **3.** [in Bible] Vers *der*.

version ['vɜ:ʃn] *n* [form, account of events] Version *die*.

versus ['vɜ:səs] *prep* - **1.** SPORT gegen - **2.** [as opposed to] im Gegensatz zu.

vertebra ['vɜ:tɪbrə] (*pl* **-brae** [-bri:]) *n* Rückenwirbel *der*.

vertical ['vɜ:tɪkl] *adj* senkrecht, vertikal.

vertigo ['vɜ:tɪgəʊ] *n (U)* Gleichgewichtsstörungen *Pl*.

verve [vɜ:v] *n* Schwung *der*.

very ['verɪ] <> *adv* sehr; **very much** sehr; **not very** nicht sehr. <> *adj* genau; **the very opposite** genau das Gegenteil; **the very person I was looking for!** nach Ihnen habe ich gerade gesucht!; **that very afternoon** am selben Nachmittag; **the very next day** gleich am nächsten Tag; **my very own room** mein eigenes Zimmer; **the very best** das Allerbeste; **for the very first/last time** zum allerersten/allerletzten Mal; **at the very beginning** ganz am Anfang; **the very thought makes me shudder** mich schauderts beim bloßem Gedanken. ◆ **very well** *adv* - **1.** [all right] schön, also gut - **2.** *phr*: **I/you/*etc* can't very well say no** ich kann/du kannst/*etc* wohl kaum nein sagen.

vessel ['vesl] *n fml* - **1.** [boat] Schiff *das* - **2.** [container] Gefäß *das*.

vest [vest] *n* - **1.** *UK* [undershirt] Unterhemd *das* - **2.** *US* [waistcoat] Weste *die*.

vestibule ['vestɪbju:l] *n fml* [entrance hall] Eingangshalle *die*.

vestige ['vestɪdʒ] *n fml* Spur *die*.

vestry ['vestrɪ] *n* Sakristei *die*.

vet [vet] <> *n UK abbr of* **veterinary surgeon**. <> *vt UK* [check] überprüfen.

veteran ['vetrən] <> *adj* [experienced] mit langjähriger Erfahrung. <> *n* Veteran *der*, -in *die*.

veterinarian [ˌvetərɪ'neərɪən] *n US* Tierarzt *der*, -ärztin *die*.

veterinary surgeon ['vetərɪnrɪ-] *n UK fml* Tierarzt *der*, -ärztin *die*.

veto ['vi:təʊ] (*pl* **-es**, *pt & pp* **-ed**, *cont* **-ing**) <> *n* Veto *das*. <> *vt* sein Veto ein|legen gegen.

vex [veks] *vt fml* [annoy] (ver)ärgern.

VHF (*abbr of* **very high frequency**) *n* UKW.

VHS (*abbr of* **video home system**) *n* VHS.

via ['vaɪə] *prep* - **1.** [travelling through] über *(+ A)*, via *(+ A)* - **2.** [by means of]: **via a friend** durch einen Freund; **via satellite** via OR per Satellit.

viable ['vaɪəbl] *adj* - **1.** [plan, programme, scheme] durchführbar - **2.** ECON lebensfähig.

Viagra® [vaɪ'ægrə] *n* Viagra® *das*.

vibrate [vaɪ'breɪt] *vi* vibrieren; PHYS schwingen.

vicar ['vɪkəʳ] *n* Pfarrer *der*, -in *die*.

vicarage ['vɪkərɪdʒ] *n* Pfarrhaus *das*.

vicarious [vɪ'keərɪəs] *adj* [enjoyment, pleasure] indirekt.

vice [vaɪs] *n* - **1.** [immorality, fault] Laster *das* - **2.** [tool] Schraubstock *der*.

vice-chairman *n* stellvertretender Vorsitzender.

vice-chancellor *n* UNIV *Leiter der Universitätsverwaltung und Vorsitzender des Senats.*

vice-president *n* Vizepräsident *der*, -in *die*.

vice versa [ˌvaɪsɪ'vɜːsə] *adv* umgekehrt.

vicinity [vɪ'sɪnətɪ] *n* - **1.** [neighbourhood] Umgebung *die*; **in the vicinity (of)** in der Nähe (von *OR* (+ *G*)) - **2.** [approximate figures]: **in the vicinity of £80,000 a year** um die £80 000 pro Jahr.

vicious ['vɪʃəs] *adj* - **1.** [attack, blow, killer] brutal - **2.** [person, gossip] boshaft, gehässig - **3.** [dog] bosärtig.

vicious circle *n* Teufelskreis *der*.

victim ['vɪktɪm] *n* Opfer *das*; **to fall victim to sb/sthg** jm/etw zum Opfer fallen.

victimize, -ise ['vɪktɪmaɪz] *vt* schikanieren.

victor ['vɪktəʳ] *n* Sieger *der*, -in *die*.

victorious [vɪk'tɔːrɪəs] *adj* [winning] siegreich.

victory ['vɪktərɪ] *n* Sieg *der*; **to win a victory over sb/sthg** jn/etw bezwingen.

video ['vɪdɪəʊ] (*pl* **-s**, *pt & pp* **-ed**, *cont* **-ing**) ◇ *n* - **1.** [gen] Video *das*; **I've got it on video** ich habe es auf Video - **2.** [machine] Videorekorder *der*. ◇ *comp* Video-. ◇ *vt* - **1.** [using videorecorder] (auf Video) auflnehmen - **2.** [using camera] filmen.

video camera *n* Videokamera *die*.

video cassette *n* Videokassette *die*.

video game *n* Videospiel *das*.

videorecorder ['vɪdɪəʊrɪˌkɔːdəʳ] *n* Videorekorder *der*.

video shop *n* Videothek *die*.

videotape ['vɪdɪəʊteɪp] *n* Videoband *das*.

vie [vaɪ] (*pt & pp* **vied**, *cont* **vying**) *vi*: **to vie (with sb) for sthg** (mit jm) um etw wetteifern; **to vie with sb to do sthg** mit jm darum wetteifern, etw zu tun.

Vienna [vɪ'enə] *n* Wien *nt*.

Vietnam [*UK* ˌvjet'næm, *US* ˌvjet'nɑːm] *n* Vietnam *nt*.

Vietnamese [ˌvjetnə'miːz] ◇ *adj* vietnamesisch. ◇ *n* [language] Vietnamesisch(e) *das*. ◇ *npl*: **the Vietnamese** die Vietnamesen.

view [vjuː] ◇ *n* - **1.** [opinion] Ansicht *die*, Meinung *die*; **in my view** meiner Ansicht *OR* Meinung nach - **2.** [vista] Aussicht *die*, Blick *der* - **3.** [ability to see] Sicht *die*; **to come into view** in Sicht kommen. ◇ *vt* - **1.** [consider] sehen; **he viewed her with suspicion** er betrachtete sie mit Argwohn - **2.** *fml* [house] besichtigen. ◆ **in view of** *prep* angesichts (+ *G*). ◆ **with a view to** *conj*: **with a view to doing sthg** mit der Absicht, etw zu tun.

viewer ['vjuːəʳ] *n* - **1.** [person] Zuschauer *der*, -in *die* - **2.** [for slides] Diabetrachter *der*.

viewfinder ['vjuːˌfaɪndəʳ] *n* Sucher *der*.

viewpoint ['vjuːpɔɪnt] *n* - **1.** [opinion] Standpunkt *der* - **2.** [place] Aussichtspunkt *der*.

vigilante [ˌvɪdʒɪ'læntɪ] *n* (militante) Bürgerwehr.

vigorous ['vɪgərəs] *adj* - **1.** [walk] flott; [shake, scrub] kräftig - **2.** [protest, denial, attempt] energisch.

vile [vaɪl] *adj* [act, person] abscheulich; [food] scheußlich.

villa ['vɪlə] *n* Villa *die*.

village ['vɪlɪdʒ] *n* Dorf *das*.

villager ['vɪlɪdʒəʳ] *n* Dorfbewohner *der*, -in *die*.

villain ['vɪlən] *n* - **1.** [of film, book, play] Bösewicht *der* - **2.** *dated* [criminal] Schurke *der*.

vindicate ['vɪndɪkeɪt] *vt* [confirm] bestätigen; [justify] rechtfertigen; **to vindicate o.s.** seine Unschuld beweisen.

vindictive [vɪn'dɪktɪv] *adj* rachsüchtig.

vine [vaɪn] *n* [grapevine] Weinrebe *die*.

vinegar ['vɪnɪgəʳ] *n* Essig *der*.

vineyard ['vɪnjəd] *n* Weinberg *der*.

vintage ['vɪntɪdʒ] ◇ *adj* [wine] erlesen. ◇ *n* [wine] Jahrgang *der*.

vinyl ['vaɪnɪl] *n* Vinyl *das*.

viola [vɪ'əʊlə] *n* - **1.** MUS Bratsche *die* - **2.** BOT Veilchen *das*.

violate ['vaɪəleɪt] *vt* - **1.** [human rights, law, treaty] verstoßen gegen - **2.** [peace, privacy] stören - **3.** [grave] schänden.

violence ['vaɪələns] *n (U)* - **1.** [physical force] Gewalt *die*; [of people] Gewalttätigkeit *die*; [of actions] Brutalität *die* - **2.** [of words, reaction] Heftigkeit *die*.

violent ['vaɪələnt] *adj* - **1.** [person] gewalttätig; [attack] heftig; [crime] Gewalt-; [death] gewaltsam - **2.** [intense] heftig.

violet ['vaɪələt] ◇ *adj* violett. ◇ *n* - **1.** [flower] Veilchen *das* - **2.** [colour] Violett *das*.

violin [ˌvaɪə'lɪn] *n* Violine *die*, Geige *die*.

violinist [ˌvaɪə'lɪnɪst] *n* Violinist *der*, -in *die*, Geiger *der*, -in *die*.

VIP (*abbr of* **very important person**) *n* Prominente *der, die*, VIP *der*.

viper ['vaɪpəʳ] *n* Viper *die*.

virgin ['vɜːdʒɪn] ◇ *adj* - **1.** [gen] jungfräulich - **2.** [forest, soil] unberührt. ◇ *n* Jungfrau *die*.

Virgo ['vɜːgəʊ] (*pl* **-s**) *n* Jungfrau *die*.

virile ['vɪraɪl] *adj* männlich.

virtually ['vɜːtʃʊəlɪ] *adv* [almost] so gut wie, praktisch.

virtual reality *n* virtuelle Realität.

virtue ['vɜːtjuː] *n* - **1.** [goodness] Tugendhaftigkeit *die* - **2.** [merit, quality] Tugend *die* - **3.** [benefit] Vorteil *der*. ◆ **by virtue of** *prep fml* aufgrund (+ *G*).

virtuous ['vɜːtʃʊəs] *adj* tugendhaft.

virus ['vaɪrəs] *n* MED & COMPUT Virus *das*.

visa ['viːzə] *n* Visum *das*; **entry/exit visa** Einreise-/Ausreisevisum *das*.

vis-à-vis *prep fml* [in comparison to] gegenüber *(+ D)*; [regarding] bezüglich *(+ G)*.

viscose ['vɪskəʊs] *n* Viskose *die*.

visibility [ˌvɪzɪ'bɪlətɪ] *n* - **1.** [being visible] Sichtbarkeit *die* - **2.** [range of vision] Sichtweite *die*; **good/poor visibility** gute/schlechte Sicht.

visible ['vɪzəbl] *adj* - **1.** [which can be physically seen] sichtbar - **2.** [evident] sichtlich.

vision ['vɪʒn] *n* - **1.** [ability to see] Sehvermögen *das* - **2.** *fig* [foresight] Weitblick *der*; **a man of vision** ein Mann mit Weitblick - **3.** [impression, dream] Vision *die*.

visit ['vɪzɪt] ◇ *n* Besuch *der*; [stay] Aufenthalt *der*. ◇ *vt* besuchen.

visiting hours ['vɪzɪtɪŋ-] *npl* Besuchszeiten *Pl*.

visitor ['vɪzɪtəʳ] *n* Besucher *der*, -in *die*; **she has visitors** sie hat Besuch.

visitors' book *n* Gästebuch *das*.

visor ['vaɪzəʳ] *n* [on helmet] Visier *das*.

vista ['vɪstə] *n* [view] Ausblick *der*.

visual ['vɪʒʊəl] *adj* Seh-; [joke, memory, image] visuell.

visual display unit *n* Bildschirm *der*.

visualize, -ise ['vɪʒʊəlaɪz] *vt* sich *(D)* vor|stellen.

vital ['vaɪtl] *adj* - **1.** [essential] unerlässlich, unbedingt notwendig; [essential to life] lebenswichtig - **2.** [full of life - person] vital.

vitally ['vaɪtəlɪ] *adv*: **vitally important** von entscheidender Bedeutung.

vitamin [*UK* 'vɪtəmɪn, *US* 'vaɪtəmɪn] *n* Vitamin *das*.

vivacious [vɪ'veɪʃəs] *adj* lebhaft, lebendig.

vivid ['vɪvɪd] *adj* - **1.** [colour] kräftig - **2.** [memory] lebhaft; [description] lebendig.

vividly ['vɪvɪdlɪ] *adv* - **1.** [painted] in kräftigen Farben - **2.** [remember] lebhaft; [describe] lebendig.

vixen ['vɪksn] *n* Füchsin *die*.

VLF (*abbr of* **very low frequency**) *n* VLF.

V-neck *n* - **1.** [sweater, dress] Pullover *der*/ Kleid *das* mit V-Ausschnitt - **2.** [neck] V-Ausschnitt *der*.

vocabulary [və'kæbjʊlərɪ] *n* - **1.** [gen] Wortschatz *der*, Vokabular *das* - **2.** [list of words] Wörterverzeichnis *das*.

vocal ['vəʊkl] *adj* - **1.** [outspoken] lautstark - **2.** [of the voice] stimmlich.

vocal cords *npl* Stimmbänder *Pl*.

vocation [vəʊ'keɪʃn] *n* [calling] Berufung *die*.

vocational [vəʊ'keɪʃənl] *adj* berufsbezogen.

vociferous [və'sɪfərəs] *adj fml* lautstark.

vodka ['vɒdkə] *n* Wodka *der*.

vogue [vəʊg] *n* Mode *die*; **to be in vogue** in Mode sein.

voice [vɔɪs] ◇ *n* [gen] Stimme *die*. ◇ *vt* [opinion, emotion] zum Ausdruck bringen.

void [vɔɪd] ◇ *adj* - **1.** [contract, result] ungültig, nichtig, ▷ **null** - **2.** *fml* [empty]: **void of interest** ohne jegliches Interesse. ◇ *n* - **1.** *liter* [feeling of emptiness]: **the void left by his death** die Lücke, die sein Tod hinterlassen hat - **2.** [chasm] Nichts *das*.

volatile [*UK* 'vɒlətaɪl, *US* 'vɒlətl] *adj* [situation] brisant; [person] aufbrausend; [market] unbeständig.

volcano [vɒl'keɪnəʊ] (*pl* **-es** OR **-s**) *n* Vulkan *der*.

volition [və'lɪʃn] *n fml*: **of one's own volition** aus freiem Willen.

volley ['vɒlɪ] (*pl* **volleys**) ◇ *n* - **1.** [of gunfire] Salve *die* - **2.** [of insults] Flut *die* - **3.** [in tennis] Volley *der*; [in football] Volleyschuss *der*. ◇ *vt* [in tennis] volley spielen; [in football] volley nehmen.

volleyball ['vɒlɪbɔːl] *n* SPORT Volleyball *das*.

volt [vəʊlt] *n* Volt *das*.

voltage ['vɒltɪdʒ] *n* Spannung *die*.

voluble ['vɒljʊbl] *adj fml* redselig.

volume ['vɒljuːm] *n* - **1.** [of sound] Lautstärke *die* - **2.** [of container, object] Volumen *das*, Rauminhalt *der* - **3.** [of work] Umfang *der*; **volume of traffic** Verkehrsaufkommen *das* - **4.** [book] Band *der*.

voluntarily [*UK* 'vɒləntrɪlɪ, *US* ˌvɒlən'terəlɪ] *adv* freiwillig; [work] ehrenamtlich.

voluntary ['vɒləntrɪ] *adj* - **1.** [not obligatory] freiwillig - **2.** [unpaid] ehrenamtlich.

voluntary work *n* freiwillige OR ehrenamtliche Tätigkeit.

volunteer [ˌvɒlən'tɪəʳ] ◇ *n* - **1.** [gen & MIL] Freiwillige *der, die* - **2.** [unpaid worker] freiwillige Helfer *der*, -in *die*. ◇ *vt* - **1.** [of one's free will]: **to volunteer to do sthg** sich bereit erklären, etw zu tun - **2.** [information] geben; **to volunteer advice** Ratschläge erteilen. ◇ *vi* sich freiwillig melden.

vomit ['vɒmɪt] ◇ *n* Erbrochene *das*. ◇ *vi* sich übergeben.

vote [vəʊt] ◇ *n* - **1.** [individual decision] Stimme *die*; **a vote for/against sb/sthg** eine Stimme für/gegen jn/etw - **2.** [session, ballot] Abstimmung *die* - **3.** [result of ballot]: **the vote** das Abstimmungsergebnis - **4.** [suffrage] Stimmrecht *das*. ◇ *vt* - **1.** [gen] wählen; **to vote to do sthg** (per Abstimmung) beschließen, etw zu tun - **2.** [suggest] vor|schlagen. ◇ *vi* wählen; **to vote for/against sb/sthg** für/gegen jn/ etw stimmen; **to vote on an issue** über eine Frage ab|stimmen.

voter ['vəʊtəʳ] *n* Wähler *die*, -in *die*.

voting ['vəʊtɪŋ] *n* Wahl *die*, Abstimmung *die*.

vouch [vaʊtʃ] ◆ **vouch for** *vt insep* - **1.** [person] bürgen für - **2.** [character, accuracy] sich verbürgen für.

voucher ['vaʊtʃəʳ] *n* Gutschein *der*.

vow [vaʊ] ◇ *n* Gelöbnis *das*; RELIG Gelübde *das*. ◇ *vt*: **to vow to do sthg** geloben, etw zu tun; **to vow (that)...** schwören(, dass)...

vowel ['vaʊəl] *n* Vokal *der*.

voyage ['vɔɪɪdʒ] *n* Reise *die*; [by sea] Seereise *die*; [through space] Flug *der*.

vs *abbr of* **versus**.

VSO (*abbr of* **Voluntary Service Overseas**) *n britische Hilfsorganisation, die Freiwillige mit Berufsausbildung in Entwicklungsländern einsetzt.*

vulgar ['vʌlgəʳ] *adj* - **1.** [tasteless - décor] geschmacklos; [- person] ordinär - **2.** [rude] vulgär.

vulnerable ['vʌlnərəbl] *adj* - **1.** [easily hurt - emotionally] verletzlich; [- physically] verwundbar - **2.** [easily influenced]: **vulnerable (to sthg)** anfällig (für etw).

vulture ['vʌltʃəʳ] *n liter* & *fig* Geier *der*.

w (*pl* **w's** OR **ws**), **W** (*pl* **W's** OR **Ws**) ['dʌblju:] *n* w *das*, W *das*. ◆ **W** (*abbr of* **west, watt**) W.

wad [wɒd] *n* - **1.** [of cotton wool] Bausch *der* - **2.** [of bank notes, documents] Bündel *das*.

waddle ['wɒdl] *vi* watscheln.

wade [weɪd] *vi* waten. ◆ **wade through** *vt insep fig* durchackern.

wading pool ['weɪdɪŋ-] *n US* Planschbecken *das*.

wafer ['weɪfəʳ] *n* [thin biscuit] Waffel *die*.

waffle ['wɒfl] ◇ *n* - **1.** CULIN Waffel *die* - **2.** *UK inf* [vague talk] Geschwafel *das*. ◇ *vi* schwafeln.

wag [wæg] ◇ *vt* [tail] wedeln mit. ◇ *vi* [tail] wedeln.

wage [weɪdʒ] ◇ *n* Lohn *der*. ◇ *vt*: **to wage war against sb/sthg** einen Kampf gegen jn/etw führen. ◆ **wages** *npl* Lohn *der*.

wage packet *n* - **1.** [envelope] Lohntüte *die* - **2.** [pay] Lohn *der*.

wager ['weɪdʒəʳ] *n* Wette *die*.

waggle ['wægl] *inf vt* [tail] wedeln mit; [ears] wackeln mit.

wagon, waggon *UK* ['wægən] *n* - **1.** [horse-drawn vehicle] Fuhrwerk *das* - **2.** *UK* RAIL Waggon *der*.

wail [weɪl] ◇ *n* - **1.** [of baby] Geschrei *das*; [of mourner] Klagen *das* - **2.** [of wind, siren] Heulen *das*. ◇ *vi* [baby] schreien; [mourner] klagen.

waist [weɪst] *n* Taille *die*.

waistcoat ['weɪskəʊt] *n UK* Weste *die*.

waistline ['weɪstlaɪn] *n* Taille *die*.

wait [weɪt] ◇ *n* Wartezeit *die*. ◇ *vi* warten; **to wait and see** abwarten(, was passiert). ◇ *vt* - **1.** [person]: **I/he/she can't wait to do it** ich/er/sie kann es kaum erwarten, es zu tun - **2.**: **to wait tables** kellnern. ◆ **wait for** *vt insep* warten auf *(+ A)*; **to wait for sb to do sthg** darauf warten, dass jd etw tut. ◆ **wait on** *vt insep* [serve food to] bedienen. ◆ **wait up** *vi* auf|bleiben.

waiter ['weɪtəʳ] *n* Kellner *der*.

waiting list ['weɪtɪŋ-] *n* Warteliste *die*.

waiting room ['weɪtɪŋ-] *n* Warteraum *der*; [at doctor's] Wartezimmer *das*; [at railway station] Wartesaal *der*.

waitress ['weɪtrɪs] *n* Kellnerin *die*, Serviererin *die*.

waive [weɪv] *vt fml* [entrance fee] verzichten auf *(+ A)*; [rule] nicht an|wenden.

wake [weɪk] (*pt* **woke** OR **-d**, *pp* **woken** OR **-d**) ◇ *n* [of ship, boat] Kielwasser *das*. ◇ *vt* wecken. ◇ *vi* auf|wachen. ◆ **wake up** ◇ *vt sep* auf|wecken. ◇ *vi* [wake] auf|wachen.

waken ['weɪkən] *fml* ◇ *vt* wecken. ◇ *vi* erwachen.

Wales [weɪlz] *n* Wales *nt*.

walk [wɔ:k] ◇ *n* - **1.** [stroll] Spaziergang *der*; **to go for a walk** einen Spaziergang machen; **to take the dog for a walk** mit dem Hund spazieren gehen; **it's quite a long walk to the station** zu Fuß ist es ganz schön weit bis zum Bahnhof - **2.** [gait] Gang *der*. ◇ *vt* - **1.** [escort]: **I'll walk you back to the car park** ich gehe mit dir bis zum Parkplatz - **2.** [dog] spazieren führen - **3.** [cover on foot] laufen, (zu Fuß) gehen. ◇ *vi* gehen, laufen; [hike] wandern; **he walks to work** er geht zu Fuß zur Arbeit. ◆ **walk out** *vi* - **1.** [leave suddenly] hinaus|gehen - **2.** [go on strike] in Streik treten. ◆ **walk out on** *vt insep* sitzen lassen.

walker ['wɔ:kəʳ] *n* [for pleasure] Spaziergänger *der*, -in *die*; [when hiking] Wanderer *der*, -derin *die*; SPORT Geher *der*, -in *die*.

walkie-talkie [ˌwɔ:kɪ'tɔ:kɪ] *n* Walkie-Talkie *das*.

walking ['wɔ:kɪŋ] *n* [for pleasure] Spazierengehen *das*; [hiking] Wandern *das*; SPORT Gehen *das*.

walking shoes *npl* Wanderschuhe *Pl*.

walking stick *n* Spazierstock *der*.

Walkman® ['wɔ:kmən] *n* Walkman® *der.*

walkout ['wɔ:kaʊt] *n* [of workers] Arbeitsniederlegung *die.*

walkover ['wɔ:kˌəʊvəʳ] *n UK inf* [victory] spielender Sieg.

walkway ['wɔ:kweɪ] *n* Fußweg *der.*

wall [wɔ:l] *n* - **1.** [inside building, of stomach, cell] Wand *die* - **2.** [outside] Mauer *die.*

wallchart ['wɔ:ltʃɑ:t] *n* Schautafel *die.*

walled [wɔ:ld] *adj* von Mauern umgeben.

wallet ['wɒlɪt] *n* [for money] Brieftasche *die*; [for documents] Etui *das.*

wallop ['wɒləp] *inf vt* [person] versohlen, verdreschen; [ball] dreschen.

wallow ['wɒləʊ] *vi* [in mud] sich wälzen, sich suhlen.

wallpaper ['wɔ:lˌpeɪpəʳ] <> *n (U)* Tapete *die.* <> *vt* tapezieren.

Wall Street *n* Wall Street *die.*

wally ['wɒlɪ] *n UK inf* Dussel *der.*

walnut ['wɔ:lnʌt] *n* - **1.** [nut] Walnuss *die* - **2.** [tree] Walnussbaum *der,* Nussbaum *der* - **3.** [wood] Nussbaumholz *das.*

walrus ['wɔ:lrəs] (*pl inv* OR **-es**) *n* Walross *das.*

waltz [wɔ:ls] <> *n* Walzer *der.* <> *vi* [dance] Walzer tanzen.

wan [wɒn] *adj* [person, complexion] bleich; [smile] matt.

wand [wɒnd] *n* Zauberstab *der.*

wander ['wɒndəʳ] *vi* - **1.** [person] herum|laufen, umher|wandern - **2.** [thoughts] schweifen, wandern.

wane [weɪn] *vi* - **1.** [popularity, enthusiasm] schwinden - **2.** [moon] abnehmen.

wangle ['wæŋgl] *vt inf* organisieren; **to wangle sthg out of sb** jm etw aus dem Kreuz leiern.

want [wɒnt] <> *vt* - **1.** [desire] wollen; **to want to do sthg** etw tun wollen; **to want sb to do sthg** wollen, dass jd etw tut; **what do you want to eat?** was möchtest du (zu) essen?; **you're wanted on the phone** Sie werden am Telefon verlangt - **2.** [need] brauchen; **you want to be more careful** du solltest vorsichtiger sein - **3.** [seek] suchen; **he is wanted by the police** er wird von der Polizei gesucht. <> *n* - **1.** [need] Bedürfnis *das* - **2.** [lack] Mangel *der*; **his want of understanding** seine mangelnde Einsicht; **for want of** aus Mangel an *(+ D)* - **3.** [poverty] Not *die*; **to be in want** Not leiden.

wanted ['wɒntɪd] *adj*: **to be wanted (by the police)** (polizeilich) gesucht werden.

wanton ['wɒntən] *adj fml* [destruction] mutwillig; [neglect] sträflich.

WAP [wæp] *n* (*abbr of* **wireless application protocol**) WAP *das.*

war [wɔ:ʳ] *n* Krieg *der*; **to be at war** sich im Kriegszustand befinden.

ward [wɔ:d] *n* - **1.** [part of hospital] Station *die*; [room in hospital] Krankensaal *der*; **maternity ward** Entbindungsstation *die* - **2.** *UK* POL Wahlbezirk *der* - **3.** LAW Mündel *das.* ◆ **ward off** *vt insep* [blow, evil spirits] ab|wehren; [disease] schützen vor *(+ D).*

warden ['wɔ:dn] *n* - **1.** [of park] Aufseher *der,* -in *die*; [of game reserve] Wildhüter *der,* -in *die* - **2.** *UK* [of youth hostel] Herbergsvater *der,* -mutter *die*; [of hall of residence] Heimleiter *der,* -in *die* - **3.** *US* [prison governor] Gefängnisdirektor *der,* -in *die.*

warder ['wɔ:dəʳ] *n* [in prison] Wärter *der,* -in *die.*

wardrobe ['wɔ:drəʊb] *n* - **1.** [piece of furniture] Kleiderschrank *der,* Schrank *der* - **2.** [collection of clothes] Garderobe *die.*

warehouse ['weəhaʊs] (*pl* [-haʊzɪz]) *n* Lagerhaus *das.*

warfare ['wɔ:feəʳ] *n (U)* [war] Krieg *der*; [technique] Kriegsführung *die.*

warhead ['wɔ:hed] *n* Sprengkopf *der.*

warily ['weərəlɪ] *adv* [carefully] vorsichtig; [suspiciously] misstrauisch.

warm [wɔ:m] <> *adj* - **1.** [gen] warm; **are you warm enough?** ist dir warm genug? - **2.** [friendly - person, feelings, welcome] herzlich; [- atmosphere] freundlich. <> *vt* [food, milk] warm machen. ◆ **warm to** *vt insep* [idea, place] Gefallen finden an *(+ D).* ◆ **warm up** <> *vt sep* - **1.** [heat - food] warm machen; [- room] heizen - **2.** [reheat] auf|wärmen. <> *vi* - **1.** [get warmer] wärmer werden - **2.** [machine, engine] warm laufen; [audience] in Stimmung kommen - **3.** [athlete, footballer] sich auf|wärmen; [orchestra, musician] sich ein|spielen.

warm-hearted [-'hɑ:tɪd] *adj* [person] warmherzig; [action, gesture] herzlich.

warmly ['wɔ:mlɪ] *adv* - **1.** [in warm clothes]: **to dress warmly** sich warm anziehen - **2.** [in a friendly way] herzlich.

warmth [wɔ:mθ] *n* - **1.** [of temperature, clothes] Wärme *die* - **2.** [of welcome, smile, support] Herzlichkeit *die.*

warn [wɔ:n] *vt* - **1.** [advise] warnen; **to warn sb of** OR **about sthg** jn vor etw *(D)* warnen - **2.** [inform] Bescheid geben *(+ D)*; **to warn sb that...** jn darauf hin|weisen, dass...

warning ['wɔ:nɪŋ] *n* - **1.** [cautionary advice] Warnung *die*; [from police, judge] Verwarnung *die* - **2.** [notice]: **to give sb warning** jm rechtzeitig Bescheid sagen.

warning light *n* Warnleuchte *die.*

warp [wɔ:p] <> *vt* - **1.** [wood]: **the sun will warp the wood** in der Sonne wird sich das Holz verziehen - **2.** [mind] psychisch schwer schädigen. <> *vi* [wood] sich verziehen.

warrant ['wɒrənt] <> *n* LAW [written order] Befehl *der*; [for arrest] Haftbefehl *der*; [for search] Durchsuchungsbefehl *der*. <> *vt fml* [justify] rechtfertigen.

warranty ['wɒrəntɪ] *n* [guarantee] Garantie *die*.

warren ['wɒrən] *n* Kaninchenbau *der*.

warrior ['wɒrɪəʳ] *n liter* Krieger *der*.

Warsaw ['wɔ:sɔ:] *n* Warschau *nt*.

warship ['wɔ:ʃɪp] *n* Kriegsschiff *das*.

wart [wɔ:t] *n* Warze *die*.

wartime ['wɔ:taɪm] *n* Kriegszeit *die*; **in wartime** in Kriegszeiten.

wary ['weərɪ] *adj* [careful] vorsichtig; [suspicious] misstrauisch; **to be wary of sthg** sich vor etw *(D)* in Acht nehmen.

was *(weak form* [wəz], *strong form* [wɒz]*)* *pt* ▷ **be**.

wash [wɒʃ] <> *n* - **1.** [act of washing]: **she/it needs a wash** sie/es muss gewaschen werden; **to have a wash** sich waschen; **to give sthg a wash** etw waschen - **2.** [clothes to be washed] Wäsche *die* - **3.** [from boat] Kielwasser *das*. <> *vt* [clean] waschen; [dishes] spülen, ab|waschen. <> *vi* [clean o.s.] sich waschen. ◆ **wash away** *vt sep* weg|spülen. ◆ **wash up** <> *vt sep UK* [dishes] ab|waschen, spülen. <> *vi* - **1.** *UK* [wash the dishes] ab|waschen, spülen - **2.** *US* [wash o.s.] sich waschen.

washable ['wɒʃəbl] *adj* waschbar.

washbasin *UK* ['wɒʃ,beɪsn], **washbowl** *US* ['wɒʃbəʊl] *n* Waschbecken *das*.

washcloth ['wɒʃ,klɒθ] *n US* Waschlappen *der*.

washer ['wɒʃəʳ] *n* - **1.** TECH Dichtungsring *der* - **2.** [washing machine] Waschmaschine *die*.

washing ['wɒʃɪŋ] *n* - **1.** [act] Waschen *das* - **2.** [clothes] Wäsche *die*.

washing line *n* Wäscheleine *die*.

washing machine *n* Waschmaschine *die*.

washing powder *n UK* Waschpulver *das*.

Washington ['wɒʃɪŋtən] *n* [city]: **Washington D.C.** Washington *nt*, *Hauptstadt der USA*.

washing-up *n* - **1.** *UK* [crockery, pans *etc*] Abwasch *der* - **2.** [act]: **to do the washing-up** spülen, den Abwasch machen.

washing-up liquid *n UK* Spülmittel *das*.

washout ['wɒʃaʊt] *n inf* Reinfall *der*.

washroom ['wɒʃrʊm] *n US* Toilette *die*.

wasn't ['wɒznt] *abbr of* **was not**.

wasp [wɒsp] *n* Wespe *die*.

wastage ['weɪstɪdʒ] *n (U)* [process] Verschwendung *die*; [amount] Verlust *der*.

waste [weɪst] <> *adj* [fuel] ungenutzt. <> *n* - **1.** [misuse] Verschwendung *die*; **a waste of time** eine Zeitverschwendung - **2.** [refuse] Abfall *der*. <> *vt* verschwenden; [opportunity] vertun.

wastebasket ['weɪst,bɑ:skɪt] *n US* Papierkorb *der*.

waste disposal unit *n* Müllschlucker *der*.

wasteful ['weɪstfʊl] *adj* verschwenderisch.

waste ground *n* Ödland *das*.

wastepaper basket, wastepaper bin [,weɪst'peɪpəʳ-], **wastebasket** *US* ['weɪst,bɑ:skɪt] *n* Papierkorb *der*.

watch [wɒtʃ] <> *n* - **1.** [timepiece] Uhr *die*, Armbanduhr *die* - **2.** [act of guarding]: **to keep watch** Wache halten; **to keep (a) watch on sb/sthg** auf jn/etw auf|passen - **3.** [guard - person] Wachmann *der*; [- group] Wache *die*. <> *vt* - **1.** [look at] beobachten; [game, event] zu|sehen OR zu|schauen bei; [film, play] sich *(D)* an|sehen - **2.** [spy on] beobachten - **3.** [be careful about] auf|passen auf *(+ A)*. <> *vi* [observe] zu|sehen, zu|schauen. ◆ **watch for** *vt insep* [person, thing] Ausschau halten nach; [opportunity] warten auf *(+ A)*. ◆ **watch out** *vi* - **1.** [be careful]: **to watch out (for sthg)** auf|passen (auf etw *(A)*), Acht geben (auf etw *(A)*); **watch out!** Achtung!, Vorsicht! - **2.** [keep a lookout]: **to watch out for sthg** nach etw Ausschau halten.

watchdog ['wɒtʃdɒg] *n* - **1.** [dog] Wachhund *der* - **2.** [organization] Aufsichtsbehörde *die*.

watchful ['wɒtʃfʊl] *adj* [vigilant] wachsam.

watchmaker ['wɒtʃ,meɪkəʳ] *n* Uhrmacher *der*, -in *die*.

watchman ['wɒtʃmən] *(pl* **-men** [-mən]*)* *n* Wächter *der*.

water ['wɔ:təʳ] <> *n* Wasser *das*. <> *vt* [plants] gießen; [garden, lawn] sprengen; [land, field] bewässern. <> *vi* - **1.** [eyes] tränen - **2.** [mouth]: **my mouth was watering** mir lief das Wasser im Munde zusammen. ◆ **waters** *npl* [territory at sea] Gewässer *Pl*. ◆ **water down** *vt sep* - **1.** [drink] verdünnen - **2.** [plan, criticism, novel] verwässern.

water bottle *n* Wasserflasche *die*.

watercolour ['wɔ:tə,kʌləʳ] *n* - **1.** [picture] Aquarell *das* - **2.** [paint] Aquarellfarbe *die*.

watercress ['wɔ:təkres] *n* Brunnenkresse *die*.

waterfall ['wɔ:təfɔ:l] *n* Wasserfall *der*.

water heater *n* Heißwassergerät *das*, Boiler *der*.

waterhole ['wɔ:təhəʊl] *n* Wasserstelle *die*.

watering can ['wɔ:tərɪŋ-] *n* Gießkanne *die*.

water lily *n* Seerose *die*.

waterline ['wɔ:təlaɪn] *n* NAUT Wasserlinie *die*.

waterlogged ['wɔ:təlɒgd] *adj* - **1.** [land, sports] (völlig) aufgeweicht - **2.** [vessel] voll Wasser.

water main *n* Hauptwasserleitung *die*.

watermark ['wɔːtəmɑːk] *n* - **1.** [in paper] Wasserzeichen *das* - **2.** [showing water level] Wasserstandsmarke *die*.

watermelon ['wɔːtəˌmelən] *n* Wassermelone *die*.

water polo *n* Wasserball *der*.

waterproof ['wɔːtəpruːf] ◇ *adj* [watch] wasserdicht; [anorak, shoes] wasserundurchlässig. ◇ *n*: **waterproofs** Regenkleidung *die*.

watershed ['wɔːtəʃed] *n* [turning point] Wendepunkt *der*.

water skiing *n* Wasserskilaufen *das*.

water tank *n* Wassertank *der*.

watertight ['wɔːtətaɪt] *adj* - **1.** [waterproof] wasserdicht - **2.** [faultless] hieb- und stichfest.

waterworks ['wɔːtəwɜːks] (*pl inv*) *n* [building] Wasserwerk *das*.

watery ['wɔːtərɪ] *adj* - **1.** [food, juice] wässrig; [coffee, tea] dünn - **2.** [light, sun] blass.

watt [wɒt] *n* Watt *das*.

wave [weɪv] ◇ *n* - **1.** [gen] Welle *die* - **2.** [gesture]: **to give sb a wave** jm zu|winken. ◇ *vt* - **1.** [flag, handkerchief] schwenken; [baton] schwingen; [gun, stick] fuchteln; **to wave one's hand at sb** jm winken - **2.** [gesture to]: **to wave sb on/over** jn weiter-/herüber|winken. ◇ *vi* - **1.** [with hand] winken; **to wave at** *OR* **to sb** jm zu|winken - **2.** [flag] wehen; [branches] sich hin und her bewegen, sich wiegen.

wavelength ['weɪvleŋθ] *n* Wellenlänge *die*; **to be on the same wavelength (as sb)** *fig* auf der gleichen Wellenlänge (wie jd) funken.

waver ['weɪvəʳ] *vi* - **1.** [person, resolve, confidence] wanken - **2.** [voice] zittern - **3.** [flame, light] flackern.

wavy ['weɪvɪ] *adj* - **1.** [hair] wellig - **2.** [line] Schlangen-.

wax [wæks] ◇ *n* - **1.** [in candles, polish, for skis] Wachs *das* - **2.** [in ears] Ohrenschmalz *das*. ◇ *vt* - **1.** [floor, table, skis] wachsen - **2.** [legs] mit Wachs enthaaren. ◇ *vi* [moon] zu|nehmen.

wax paper *n US* Wachspapier *das*.

waxworks ['wækswɜːks] (*pl inv*) *n* [museum] Wachsfigurenkabinett *das*.

way [weɪ] ◇ *n* - **1.** [means, method] Art und Weise *die*; **this/that way** so; **this is the best way to do it** man macht es am besten so - **2.** [manner, style] Art *die*; **I feel the same way as you** mir geht es wie Ihnen; **she's behaving in a very odd way** sie benimmt sich sehr seltsam; **if that's the way you feel** wenn du so denkst; **in the same way** auf die gleiche Weise - **3.** [thoroughfare, path] Weg *der*; **'give way'** *UK* AUT 'Vorfahrt beachten' - **4.** [route] Weg *der*; **which way is the station?** wie kommt man zum Bahnhof?; **what's the best way to the station?** wie kommt man am besten zum Bahnhof?; **to be in the way** im Weg sein; **to be in sb's way** jm im Wege stehen; **on the way (to the station)** auf dem Weg (zum Bahnhof); **on the way home/to school** auf dem Heimweg/Schulweg; **on the way back/there** auf dem Rückweg/Hinweg; **out of the way** [place] abgelegen; **get out of the** *OR* **my way!** geh mir aus dem Weg!; **to go out of one's way to do sthg** sich *(D)* besondere Mühe geben, etw zu tun; **to keep out of sb's way** jm aus dem Wege gehen; **to be under way** [ship] in Fahrt sein; [project, meeting] im Gange sein; **to get under way** [ship] in Fahrt kommen; [project, meeting] in Gang kommen; **to lose one's way** sich verlaufen; [in car] sich verfahren; **make your way to the exit** begeben Sie sich zum Ausgang; **to make way for sb/sthg** jm/einer Sache Platz machen; **to stand in sb's way** *fig* jn im Wege stehen - **5.** [direction] Richtung *die*; **which way are you going?** in welche Richtung gehst du?; **this/that way** hier/dort entlang; **look this way, please** sehen Sie bitte hierher; **way in** Eingang *der*; **way out** Ausgang *der* - **6.** [side]: **the right way round** richtig herum; **the wrong way round** verkehrt herum; **the right/wrong way up** richtig/verkehrt herum; **the other way round** anders herum - **7.** [distance] Weg *der*; **all the way** den ganzen Weg; **we're with you all the way** *fig* wir stehen voll und ganz hinter dir; **it's a long way (away) from here** es liegt weit weg *OR* entfernt; **I have a long way to go** ich habe einen weiten Weg vor mir; **he's not as clever as her by a long way** er ist bei Weitem nicht so klug wie sie - **8.** *phr*: **to give way** [under weight, pressure] nach|geben; **in many ways** in vieler Hinsicht; **no way!** auf keinen Fall! ◇ *adv inf* [far] viel; **way ahead** weit voraus; **way off** weit entfernt; **way back in 1930** damals, 1930. ◆ **ways** *npl* [customs, habits] Art *die*. ◆ **by the way** *adv* übrigens.

waylay [ˌweɪ'leɪ] (*pt & pp* **-laid** [-'leɪd]) *vt* ab|fangen.

wayward ['weɪwəd] *adj* eigenwillig.

WC (*abbr of* **water closet**) *n* WC *das*.

we [wiː] *pers pron* & *Pl* wir; **we British** wir Briten.

weak [wiːk] *adj* - **1.** [gen] schwach - **2.** [lacking knowledge, skill]: **to be weak on sthg** in etw *(D)* schwach sein.

weaken ['wiːkn] ◇ *vt* schwächen; [argument] entkräften. ◇ *vi* - **1.** [person] schwach werden - **2.** [influence, power & FIN] schwächer werden.

weakling ['wiːklɪŋ] *n pej* Schwächling *der*.

weakness ['wiːknɪs] *n* - **1.** [gen] Schwäche *die*; **to have a weakness for sthg** eine Schwäche für etw haben - **2.** [in plan, argument] Schwachpunkt *der*.

wealth [welθ] *n* - **1.** *(U)* [riches] Reichtum *der* - **2.** [abundance]: **a wealth of sthg** ein Reichtum an etw *(D)*.

wealthy ['welθɪ] *adj* reich.

weapon ['wepən] *n* Waffe *die*.

weaponry ['wepənrɪ] *n (U)* Waffen *Pl*.

wear [weəʳ] (*pt* **wore**, *pp* **worn**) ◇ *n* - **1.** [type of clothes] Kleidung *die* - **2.** [damage]: **wear (and tear)** Abnutzung *die*. ◇ *vt* - **1.** [clothes, shoes, jewellery, spectacles] tragen - **2.** [damage] ab|nutzen. ◇ *vi* - **1.** [deteriorate] sich ab|nutzen - **2.** [last]: **to wear well/badly** gut/nicht gut halten. ◆ **wear away** ◇ *vt sep* [steps] aus|treten; [inscription] verwittern; [grass] ab|nutzen. ◇ *vi* [steps] ausgetreten werden; [inscription] verwittern; [grass] abgenutzt werden. ◆ **wear down** *vt sep* - **1.** [reduce size of] ab|nutzen; [heel] ab|laufen - **2.** [weaken] aus|zehren; [resistance] zermürben. ◆ **wear off** *vi* nach|lassen. ◆ **wear out** ◇ *vt sep* - **1.** [clothing, machinery] ab|nutzen - **2.** [person, patience, strength] erschöpfen. ◇ *vi* [clothing, shoes] sich ab|nutzen.

weary ['wɪərɪ] *adj* - **1.** [exhausted] müde - **2.** [fed up]: **to be weary of sthg** etw satt haben; **to be weary of doing sthg** es satt haben, etw zu tun.

weasel ['wɪ:zl] *n* Wiesel *das*.

weather ['weðəʳ] ◇ *n* Wetter *das*; **to be under the weather** nicht ganz auf der Höhe sein. ◇ *vt* [survive] überstehen.

weather-beaten [-ˌbi:tn] *adj* [face, skin] wettergegerbt.

weather forecast *n* Wettervorhersage *die*.

weatherman ['weðəmæn] (*pl* **-men** [-men]) *n* Meterologe *der*.

weather vane [-veɪn] *n* Wetterfahne *die*.

weave [wi:v] (*pt* **wove**, *pp* **woven**) ◇ *vt* [using loom] weben. ◇ *vi* [move] sich durch|schlängeln.

weaver ['wi:vəʳ] *n* Weber *der*, -in *die*.

web [web] *n* - **1.** [cobweb] Spinnennetz *das* - **2.** *fig* [of lies, intrigue] Netz *das*. ◆ **Web** *n*: **the Web** COMPUT das Netz, das Web.

webcam ['webkæm] *n* Webcam *die*.

webcast ['webkɑ:st] *n* Webcast *der*.

website ['webˌsaɪt] *n* COMPUT Website *die*.

wed [wed] (*pt & pp inv* OR **-ded**) *liter* ◇ *vt* - **1.** [marry] heiraten - **2.** [subj: priest] trauen. ◇ *vi* heiraten.

we'd [wi:d] *abbr of* **we had, we would**.

wedding ['wedɪŋ] *n* Hochzeit *die*.

wedding anniversary *n* Hochzeitstag *der*.

wedding cake *n* Hochzeitskuchen *der*.

wedding dress *n* Hochzeitskleid *das*.

wedding ring *n* Ehering *der*.

wedge [wedʒ] ◇ *n* - **1.** [gen] Keil *der* - **2.** [of cheese, cake, pie] Stück *das*. ◇ *vt* - **1.** [secure] fest|klemmen - **2.** [squeeze, push] zwängen.

Wednesday ['wenzdɪ] *n* Mittwoch *der*; *see also* **Saturday**.

wee [wi:] ◇ *adj Scotland* klein. ◇ *n v inf*: **to do/have a wee** Pipi machen. ◇ *vi v inf* Pipi machen.

weed [wi:d] ◇ *n* - **1.** [wild plant] Unkraut *das* - **2.** *UK inf* [feeble person] Schwächling *der*. ◇ *vt*: **to weed the garden** im Garten Unkraut jäten.

weedkiller ['wi:dˌkɪləʳ] *n* Unkrautvertilgungsmittel *das*.

weedy ['wi:dɪ] *adj UK inf* [feeble] schwächlich.

week [wi:k] *n* Woche *die*; **in three weeks' time** in drei Wochen; **a week last Saturday** Samstag vor einer Woche.

weekday ['wi:kdeɪ] *n* Wochentag *der*.

weekend [ˌwi:k'end] *n* Wochenende *das*; **at the weekend** am Wochenende.

weekly ['wi:klɪ] ◇ *adj* wöchentlich; [newspaper] Wochen-. ◇ *adv* wöchentlich. ◇ *n* Wochenzeitung *die*.

weep [wi:p] (*pt & pp* **wept**) *vt & vi* weinen.

weeping willow [ˌwi:pɪŋ-] *n* Trauerweide *die*.

weigh [weɪ] ◇ *vt* - **1.** [find weight of] wiegen - **2.** [consider carefully] ab|wägen - **3.** [raise]: **to weigh anchor** den Anker lichten. ◇ *vi* [have specific weight] wiegen. ◆ **weigh down** *vt sep* - **1.** [physically]: **to be weighed down with sthg** mit etw beladen sein - **2.** [mentally]: **to be weighed down by** OR **with sthg** mit etw belastet sein. ◆ **weigh up** *vt sep* [situation, pros and cons] ab|wägen; [person, opposition] ein|schätzen.

weight [weɪt] *n* - **1.** [of person, package, goods & SPORT] Gewicht *das*; **to put on** OR **gain weight** zu|nehmen; **to lose weight** ab|nehmen - **2.** *fig* [power, influence]: **the weight of public opinion** die Übermacht der öffentlichen Meinung; **to throw one's weight about** sich auf|spielen - **3.** *liter & fig* [burden] Last *die*; **it took a weight off my mind** damit ist mir ein Stein vom Herzen gefallen - **4.** *phr*: **to pull one's weight** seinen Beitrag leisten.

weighted ['weɪtɪd] *adj*: **to be weighted in favour of/against sb/sthg** jn/etw bevorteilen/benachteiligen.

weighting ['weɪtɪŋ] *n (U)* Zulage *die*.

weight lifting *n* Gewichtheben *das*.

weighty ['weɪtɪ] *adj* [serious, important] schwerwiegend.

weir [wɪəʳ] *n* Wehr *das*.

weird [wɪəd] *adj* seltsam.

welcome ['welkəm] ◇ *adj* - **1.** [guest] willkommen - **2.** [free]: **to be welcome to do sthg** etw gerne tun können - **3.** [pleasant, desirable] angenehm - **4.** [in reply to thanks]: **you're welcome** bitte, gern geschehen. ◇ *n* Willkommen *das*; **to get/receive a warm welcome**

herzlich aufgenommen werden. ◇ *vt* - **1.** [receive] empfangen - **2.** [approve, support] willkommen heißen. ◇ *excl* willkommen!

weld [weld] ◇ *n* Schweißnaht *die*. ◇ *vt* schweißen.

welfare ['welfeəʳ] ◇ *adj* sozial; [work, worker] Sozial-. ◇ *n* - **1.** [state of wellbeing] Wohl *das* - **2.** *US* [income support] Sozialhilfe *die*.

well [wel] (*comp* **better**, *superl* **best**) ◇ *adj* - **1.** [in health] gesund; **how are you? – (I'm) very well, thanks** wie geht es Ihnen? – sehr gut, danke; **to feel well** sich wohl fühlen; **to get well** gesund werden; **get well soon!** gute Besserung! - **2.** [good]: **all's well** alles ist in Ordnung; **it's just as well you stayed** nur gut, dass du geblieben bist. ◇ *adv* - **1.** [gen] gut; **the patient is doing well** der Patient macht gute Fortschritte; **to do well out of sthg** von etw profitieren; **you did well to come immediately** gut, dass du sofort gekommen bist; **well done!** gut gemacht!; **to speak well of sb** jn lobend erwähnen; **well beaten** restlos geschlagen; **to go well** gut gehen - **2.** [definitely, certainly]: **well within one's rights** voll im Recht; **you know perfectly well that...** du weißt ganz genau, dass...; **it's well worth it** es lohnt sich unbedingt; **well after six o'clock** viel später als sechs Uhr; **well over 50** weit über 50 - **3.** [easily, possibly]: **it may well happen** es kann durchaus passieren; **you may well laugh** lachen Sie nur!; **that may well be true** das mag wahr sein. ◇ *n* - **1.** [for water] Brunnen *der* - **2.** [oil well] Ölquelle *die*. ◇ *excl* - **1.** [expressing hesitation]: **well, I don't really know** tja, das weiß ich nicht so recht - **2.** [expressing resignation]: **oh well!** na ja! - **3.** [expressing surprise]: **well, I didn't expect to see you here!** na so was, ich habe nicht erwartet, Sie hier zu sehen!; **well I never!** na, so was! - **4.** [after interruption]: **well, as I was saying** also, wie gesagt. ◆ **as well** *adv* [in addition] auch; **I might as well go home** ich könnte genauso gut nach Hause gehen. ◆ **as well as** *conj* sowohl ... als auch; **children as well as adults** sowohl Kinder als auch Erwachsene. ◆ **well up** *vi* [water] hochlquellen.

we'll [wiːl] *abbr of* **we shall, we will**.

well-advised [-əd'vaɪzd] *adj* klug; **he/you would be well-advised to do sthg** er täte/du tätest gut daran, etw zu tun.

well-behaved [-bɪ'heɪvd] *adj* artig.

wellbeing [ˌwel'biːɪŋ] *n* Wohl *das*.

well-built *adj* [person] gut gebaut.

well-done *adj* [thoroughly cooked] durchgebraten.

well-dressed [-'drest] *adj* gut gekleidet.

well-earned [-ɜːnd] *adj* wohlverdient.

wellington (boot) ['welɪŋtən-] *n* Gummistiefel *der*.

well-kept *adj* - **1.** [garden, village] gepflegt - **2.** [secret] wohl gehütet.

well-known *adj* bekannt.

well-mannered [-'mænəd] *adj*: **to be well-mannered** gute Manieren haben.

well-meaning *adj* [action, suggestion] gut gemeint; **she's very well-meaning** sie meint es gut.

well-nigh [-naɪ] *adv* nahezu.

well-off *adj* - **1.** [financially] wohlhabend - **2.** [in a good position]: **to be well-off for sthg** mit etw gut versorgt sein.

well-read [-'red] *adj* belesen.

well-rounded [-'raʊndɪd] *adj* [varied] vielseitig.

well-timed [-'taɪmd] *adj* gut abgepasst.

well-to-do *adj* wohlhabend.

well-wisher [-ˌwɪʃəʳ] *n* Symphatisant *der*, -in *die*.

Welsh [welʃ] ◇ *adj* walisisch. ◇ *n* [language] Walisisch(e) *das*.

Welshman ['welʃmən] (*pl* **-men** [-mən]) *n* Waliser *der*.

Welshwoman ['welʃˌwʊmən] (*pl* **-women** [-ˌwɪmɪn]) *n* Waliserin *die*.

went [went] *pt* ▷ **go**.

wept [wept] *pt* & *pp* ▷ **weep**.

were [wɜːʳ] *vb* ▷ **be**.

we're [wɪəʳ] *abbr of* **we are**.

weren't [wɜːnt] *abbr of* **were not**.

west [west] ◇ *n* Westen *der*; **the west** der Westen. ◇ *adj* - **1.** [area] West-, westlich - **2.** [wind] West-. ◇ *adv* nach Westen, westwärts; **west of** westlich von. ◆ **West** *n* POL: **the West** der Westen.

West Bank *n*: **the West Bank** das Westjordanland.

West Country *n*: **the West Country** *der Südwesten Englands*.

westerly ['westəlɪ] *adj* - **1.** [direction] westlich - **2.** [area] im Westen - **3.** [wind] West-.

western ['westən] ◇ *adj* - **1.** [part of country, continent] West- - **2.** POL [relating to the West] westlich. ◇ *n* [film] Western *der*.

West German ◇ *adj* westdeutsch. ◇ *n* [person] Westdeutsche *der, die*.

West Germany *n*: **(former) West Germany** (ehemaliges) Westdeutschland *nt*.

West Indies [-'ɪndiːz] *npl*: **the West Indies** die Westindischen Inseln.

Westminster ['westmɪnstəʳ] *n* - **1.** [area] Westminster *nt* - **2.** *fig* [British parliament] *britisches Parlament*.

westward ['westwəd] ◇ *adj* nach Westen. ◇ *adv* = **westwards**.

westwards ['westwədz] *adv* nach Westen, westwärts.

wet [wet] <> *adj* - **1.** [damp, soaked] nass - **2.** [rainy] regnerisch; [climate] feucht - **3.** [ink, concrete] feucht - **4.** *UK inf pej* [weak, feeble] lasch; **he's a wet** er ist ein Weichei. <> *n UK inf* POL Gemäßigte *der, die*. <> *vt* nass machen; **to wet the bed** ins Bett machen.

wet blanket *n inf pej* Spielverderber *der*.

wet suit *n* Taucheranzug *der*.

we've [wiːv] *abbr of* **we have**.

whack [wæk] *inf* <> *n* - **1.** [share] Teil *der* - **2.** [hit] Schlag *der*. <> *vt* einen Schlag geben *(+ D)*.

whale [weɪl] *n* [animal] Wal *der*.

wharf [wɔːf] (*pl* **-s** OR **wharves** [wɔːvz]) *n* Kai *der*.

what [wɒt] <> *adj* - **1.** *(in questions)* welche(r) (s); **what colour is it?** welche Farbe hat es?; **he asked me what colour it was** er fragte mich, welche Farbe es hatte; **what time is it?** wie viel Uhr OR wie spät ist es?; **what sort of (an) animal is that?** was ist das für ein Tier? - **2.** *(in exclamations)* was für; **what a surprise!** was für eine Überraschung!; **what a beautiful day!** was für ein schöner Tag! <> *pron* - **1.** *(in questions)* was; **what is going on?** was ist los?; **what are they doing?** was tun sie da?; **what's your name?** wie heißt du?; **she asked me what happened** sie fragte mich, was passiert war; **what is it for?** wofür ist das?; **what are they talking about?** worüber reden Sie?; **what if it rains?** was geschieht, wenn es regnet?; **what did you say?** wie bitte? - **2.** *(introducing relative clause)* was; **I didn't see what happened** ich habe nicht gesehen, was passiert ist; **you can't have what you want** du kannst nicht haben, was du willst - **3.** *phr*: **what for?** wozu?; **what about going for a meal?** wie wäre es mit essen gehen?; **so what?** *inf* na und? <> *excl* was!

whatever [wɒt'evəʳ] <> *adj*: **at whatever time you want** wann immer du willst; **they have no chance whatever** sie haben überhaupt keine Chance. <> *pron* - **1.** [no matter what]: **take whatever you want** nimm, was du willst; **whatever I do, I'll lose** was ich auch tue, ich verliere; **don't let go whatever happens** du darfst auf keinen Fall loslassen - **2.** [indicating vagueness]: **whatever that may be** was auch immer das sein mag - **3.** [indicating surprise]: **whatever did he say?** was hat er denn bloß gesagt? <> *excl US inf* von mir aus!

what's-his-name *n inf* Dingsda *der*, Dingsda *die*.

whatsit ['wɒtsɪt] *n inf* Dingsbums *das*.

whatsoever [ˌwɒtsəʊ'evəʳ] *adj*: **I had no interest whatsoever** ich hatte keinerlei Interesse; **nothing whatsoever** überhaupt nichts.

wheat [wiːt] *n* Weizen *der*.

wheedle ['wiːdl] *vt*: **to wheedle sb into doing sthg** jn dazu kriegen, etw zu tun; **to wheedle sthg out of sb** jm etw ab|schwatzen.

wheel [wiːl] <> *n* - **1.** [of bicycle, car, train] Rad *das* - **2.** AUT [steering wheel] Lenkrad *das*. <> *vt* schieben. <> *vi* [turn round]: **to wheel round** sich jäh um|drehen.

wheelbarrow ['wiːlˌbærəʊ] *n* Schubkarre *die*.

wheelchair ['wiːlˌtʃeəʳ] *n* Rollstuhl *der*.

wheel clamp *n* Parkkralle *die*. ◆ **wheelclamp** *vt*: **my car was wheel clamped** an meinem Auto war eine Parkkralle.

wheeze [wiːz] *vi* pfeifend atmen.

whelk [welk] *n* Wellhornschnecke *die*.

when [wen] <> *adv (in questions)* wann; **when does the plane arrive?** wann kommt das Flugzeug an?; **he asked me when I would be in London** er fragte mich, wann ich in London sei. <> *conj* - **1.** [specifying time] wenn; [in the past] als; **on the day when it happened** an dem Tag, als es geschah - **2.** [although, seeing as] wo doch; **you said it was black when in fact it was white** du hast gesagt, es wäre schwarz, wo es doch weiß war.

whenever [wen'evəʳ] <> *conj* [every time] (immer) wenn; **whenever you like** [no matter when] wann immer du willst. <> *adv*: **whenever did you find time to do it?** wann hast du bloß die Zeit dafür gefunden?; **next week or whenever** nächste Woche oder wann auch immer.

where [weəʳ] <> *adv (in questions)* wo; **where do you come from?** woher kommst du?; **where are you going?** wohin gehst du? <> *conj* - **1.** [referring to place, situation] wo; **at the place where it happened** dort, wo es passiert ist; **that's (just) where you're wrong** (genau) da irren Sie sich - **2.** [whereas] während.

whereabouts <> *adv* [ˌweərə'baʊts] wo. <> *npl* ['weərəbaʊts] Aufenthaltsort *der*.

whereas [weər'æz] *conj* während.

whereby [weə'baɪ] *conj fml* wodurch.

whereupon [ˌweərə'pɒn] *conj fml* woraufhin.

wherever [weər'evəʳ] <> *conj* wo immer; [from any place] woher auch immer; [to any place] wohin auch immer; [everywhere] überall wo; **wherever that may be** wo immer das sein mag. <> *adv*: **wherever did you hear that?** wo hast du das bloß gehört?

whet [wet] *vt*: **to whet sb's appetite (for doing sthg)** jn auf den Geschmack bringen(, etw zu tun).

whether ['weðəʳ] *conj* ob; **he didn't know whether to go or not** er wusste nicht, ob er gehen sollte oder nicht; **whether I want to or not** ob ich nun will oder nicht.

which [wɪtʃ] <> *adj (in questions)* welche(r) (s); **which room do you want?** welches Zimmer willst du?; **which one?** welches?; **she asked me which room I wanted** sie fragte mich, welches Zimmer ich wollte. <> *pron*

- 1. *(in questions – subject)* welche(r) (s); **which is the cheapest?** welches ist das billigste?; **he asked me which was the best** er fragte mich, welcher der beste sei - 2. *(in questions – object)* welche(n) (s); **which do you prefer?** welches gefällt dir besser?; **he asked me which I preferred** er fragte mich, welches ich bevorzugen würde - 3. *(in questions – after prep + A)* welche(n) (s); **which should I put the vase on?** auf welchen soll ich die Vase stellen? - 4. *(in questions – after prep + D)* welcher/welchem/welchem; **he asked me which I was talking about** er fragte mich, von welchem ich spreche - 5. *(introducing relative clause – after subject)* der/die/das, die *pl*; **the house which is on corner** das Haus, das an der Ecke steht - 6. *(introducing relative clause – object, after prep + A)* den/die/das, die *pl*; **the television which I bought** der Fernseher, den ich gekauft habe; **the book through which he became famous** das Buch, durch das er berühmt wurde - 7. *(introducing relative clause – object, after prep + D)* dem/der/dem, denen *pl*; **the settee on which I'm sitting** das Sofa, auf dem ich sitze; **ten apples, of which six are bad** zehn Äpfel, von denen OR wovon sechs faul sind - 8. *(introducing relative clause – object, after prep + G)* dessen/deren/dessen, deren *pl* - 9. *(referring back)* was; **he's late, which annoys me** er ist spät dran, was mich ärgert; **he's always late, which I don't like** er verspätet sich immer, was ich nicht leiden kann.

whichever [wɪtʃ'evəʳ] ◇ *adj* - 1. [any] welche(r) (s); **take whichever book you like** nehmen Sie welches Buch Sie (auch immer) wollen - 2. [no matter which] egal welche; **whichever way you look** wo man auch hinsieht. ◇ *pron* [the one which] welche(r) (s); **take whichever you like** nimm welches du (auch) willst.

whiff [wɪf] *n* [smell] Hauch *der*.

while [waɪl] ◇ *n*: **a while** eine Weile; **for a while** eine Weile, eine Zeit lang; **in a while** bald; **a short while ago** vor Kurzem; **once in a while** hin und wieder. ◇ *conj* - 1. [gen] während; **he fell asleep while (he was) reading** er schlief beim Lesen ein - 2. [although] obgleich, während. ◆ **while away** *vt sep*: **to while away the time** sich *(D)* die Zeit vertreiben.

whilst [waɪlst] *conj* = **while**.

whim [wɪm] *n* Laune *die*.

whimper ['wɪmpəʳ] *vi* [child] wimmern; [animal] winseln.

whimsical ['wɪmzɪkl] *adj* wunderlich.

whine [waɪn] *vi* [make sound] heulen; [dog] jaulen.

whinge [wɪndʒ] *vi UK*: **to whinge (about sb/sthg)** (über jn/etw) jammern.

whip [wɪp] ◇ *n* - 1. [for hitting] Peitsche *die* - 2. *UK* POL Einpeitscher *der*. ◇ *vt* - 1. [beat with whip] aus|peitschen - 2. [take quickly]: **to whip sthg out** etw zücken; **to whip sthg off** etw herunter|reißen - 3. CULIN [whisk] schlagen.

whipped cream [wɪpt-] *n* Schlagsahne *die*.

whip-round *n UK inf*: **to have a whip-round** eine Sammlung machen.

whirl [wɜːl] ◇ *n* - 1. [rotating movement] Wirbel *der* - 2. *fig* [of activity] Trubel *der*. ◇ *vt*: **to whirl sb/sthg round** jn etw herum|wirbeln. ◇ *vi* [move around] wirbeln.

whirlpool ['wɜːlpuːl] *n* Strudel *der*.

whirlwind ['wɜːlwɪnd] *n* Wirbelsturm *der*.

whirr [wɜːʳ] *vi* [of wings] schwirren; [machinery, camera] surren.

whisk [wɪsk] ◇ *n* CULIN Schneebesen *der*. ◇ *vt* - 1. [put or take quickly]: **she was whisked into hospital** sie wurde schnellstens ins Krankenhaus gebracht - 2. CULIN (mit dem Schneebesen) schlagen.

whisker ['wɪskəʳ] *n* [of animal] Schnurrhaar *das*. ◆ **whiskers** *npl* [of man] Backenbart *der*.

whisky *UK*, **whiskey** *US Ireland* (*pl* **whiskeys**) ['wɪskɪ] *n* Whisky *der*.

whisper ['wɪspəʳ] ◇ *vt* flüstern; **to whisper sthg to sb** jm etw zu|flüstern. ◇ *vi* flüstern.

whistle ['wɪsl] ◇ *n* - 1. [through lips, from whistle] Pfiff *der* - 2. [of kettle, train] Pfeifen *das* - 3. [object] Pfeife *die*. ◇ *vt* pfeifen. ◇ *vi*: **to whistle at sb** jm nach|pfeifen.

white [waɪt] ◇ *adj* - 1. [gen] weiß - 2. [coffee, tea] mit Milch - 3. [wine] Weiß-. ◇ *n* - 1. [colour] Weiß *das* - 2. [person] Weiße *der, die* - 3. [of egg] Eiweiß *das* - 4. [of eye] Weiße *das*.

white-collar *adj*: **white-collar worker** Büroangestellte *der, die*; *phrase*: **white-collar job** Schreibtischarbeit *die*.

white-hot *adj* weißglühend.

White House *n* [residence of president, US government]: **the White House** das Weiße Haus.

white lie *n* Notlüge *die*.

whiteness ['waɪtnɪs] *n* Weiße *die*.

white paper *n* POL Weißbuch *das*.

white sauce *n* Béchamelsoße *die*.

white spirit *n (U) UK* Terpentinersatz *der*.

whitewash ['waɪtwɒʃ] ◇ *n* - 1. *(U)* [paint] Tünche *die* - 2. *pej* [cover-up] Verschleierung *die*. ◇ *vt* [paint] tünchen.

Whitsun ['wɪtsn] *n* [day] Pfingstsonntag *der*.

whittle ['wɪtl] *vt* [reduce]: **to whittle sthg away** OR **down** etw allmählich reduzieren.

whiz, whizz [wɪz] *vi* sausen.

whiz(z) kid *n inf* Senkrechtstarter *der*, -in *die*.

who [huː] *pron* - 1. *(in questions)* wer; *(accusative)* wen; *(dative)* wem; **who are you?** wer bist du/sind Sie?; **who does he think he is?**

was bildet er sich eigentlich ein? - **2.** *(in relative clauses)* der/die/das, die *Pl*; **the friend who came yesterday** der Freund, der gestern kam.

who'd [hu:d] *abbr of* **who had**, **who would**.

whodu(n)nit [ˌhu:ˈdʌnɪt] *n inf* Krimi *der*.

whoever [hu:ˈevəʳ] *pron* [whichever person] wer immer; **whoever it is** wer es auch ist; **whoever could that be?** wer könnte das bloß sein?

whole [həʊl] ◇ *adj* - **1.** [entire, complete] ganz - **2.** *esp US* [for emphasis]: **a whole lot of questions** eine ganze Reihe von Fragen; **a whole lot bigger** viel größer. ◇ *adv esp US* [for emphasis] völlig. ◇ *n* - **1.** [all, entirety]: **the whole of the school** die ganze Schule; **the whole of the summer** den ganzen Sommer - **2.** [unit, complete thing] Ganze *das*. ◆ **as a whole** *adv* als Ganzes. ◆ **on the whole** *adv* im Großen und Ganzen.

whole-hearted [-ˈhɑ:tɪd] *adj* [support, agreement] voll.

wholemeal *UK* [ˈhəʊlmi:l], **whole wheat** *US adj* Vollkorn-.

wholesale [ˈhəʊlseɪl] ◇ *adj* - **1.** [bulk] Großhandels- - **2.** *pej* [excessive] Massen-. ◇ *adv* - **1.** [in bulk] im Großhandel - **2.** *pej* [excessively] massenhaft.

wholesaler [ˈhəʊlˌseɪləʳ] *n* Großhändler *der*, -in *die*.

wholesome [ˈhəʊlsəm] *adj* gesund.

whole wheat *adj US* = **wholemeal**.

who'll [hu:l] *abbr of* **who will**.

wholly [ˈhəʊlɪ] *adv* völlig.

whom [hu:m] *pron fml* - **1.** *(in direct, indirect questions)* wen; *(dative)* wem; **whom did you phone?** wen hast du angerufen?; **for/of/to whom?** nach/von/mit wem? - **2.** *(in relative clauses)* den/die/das, die *Pl*; *(dative)* dem/der/dem, denen *pl*; **the girl whom he married** das Mädchen, das er geheiratet hat; **the man to whom you were speaking** der Mann, mit dem du gesprochen hast; **several people came, none of whom I knew** es kamen verschiedene Leute, von denen ich keinen kannte.

whooping cough [ˈhu:pɪŋ-] *n (U)* Keuchhusten *der*.

whopping [ˈwɒpɪŋ] *adj inf* Mords-; [lie] faustdick.

whore [hɔ:ʳ] *n pej* Hure *die*.

who're [ˈhu:əʳ] *abbr of* **who are**.

whose [hu:z] ◇ *pron (in direct, indirect questions)* wessen; **whose is this?** wem gehört das?; **tell me whose this is** sag mir, wem das gehört. ◇ *adj* - **1.** *(in questions)* wessen; **whose car is that?** wessen Auto ist das? - **2.** *(in relative clauses)* dessen/deren/dessen, deren *pl*; **that's the boy whose father's an MP** das ist der Junge, dessen Vater Abgeordneter ist.

who've [hu:v] *abbr of* **who have**.

why [waɪ] ◇ *adv* warum; **why not?** warum nicht?; **I didn't ask why** ich habe nicht gefragt, weshalb. ◇ *conj* warum; **there are several reasons why he left** es gibt mehrere Gründe dafür, dass er wegging. ◇ *excl*: **why, it's David!** sieh da, (da kommt) David! ◆ **why ever** *adv*: **why ever did you do that?** warum hast du das bloß getan?

wick [wɪk] *n* [of candle] Docht *der*.

wicked [ˈwɪkɪd] *adj* - **1.** [evil] böse, schlecht - **2.** [mischievous] schelmisch.

wicker [ˈwɪkəʳ] *adj*: **wicker chair** Korbstuhl *der*.

wicket [ˈwɪkɪt] *n* - **1.** CRICKET [stumps] Mal *das*, Wicket *das* - **2.** CRICKET [pitch] Spielbahn *die* - **3.** CRICKET [dismissal] Wicket *das*.

wide [waɪd] ◇ *adj* - **1.** [broad] breit - **2.** [variety, selection, gap, difference] groß - **3.** [coverage, knowledge] umfassend - **4.** [far-reaching] weit reichend. ◇ *adv* - **1.** [as far as possible] weit - **2.** [off-target] daneben.

wide-awake *adj* hellwach.

widely [ˈwaɪdlɪ] *adv* - **1.** [broadly] breit - **2.** [extensively] weit; **widely read** belesen; **to be widely experienced** viel Erfahrung haben; **widely known** allgemein bekannt - **3.** [considerably] beträchtlich.

widen [ˈwaɪdn] *vt* - **1.** [road, hole] verbreitern - **2.** [search, activity, range] aus|weiten; [choice] erweitern - **3.** [gap, difference] vergrößern.

wide open *adj* - **1.** [window, door] weit offen - **2.** [eyes] weit aufgerissen.

wide-ranging [-ˈreɪndʒɪŋ] *adj* umfassend.

widescreen TV [ˈwaɪdskri:n-] *n* - **1.** Breitwandfernsehen *das* - **2.** [TV set] Breitwandfernseher *der*.

widespread [ˈwaɪdspred] *adj* weit verbreitet.

widow [ˈwɪdəʊ] *n* Witwe *die*.

widowed [ˈwɪdəʊd] *adj* verwitwet.

widower [ˈwɪdəʊəʳ] *n* Witwer *der*.

width [wɪdθ] *n* Breite *die*; **3 metres in width** 3 Meter breit.

wield [wi:ld] *vt* - **1.** [weapon] schwingen - **2.** [power] aus|üben.

wife [waɪf] *(pl* **wives***)* *n* Ehefrau *die*.

wig [wɪg] *n* Perücke *die*.

wiggle [ˈwɪgl] *inf vt*: **to wiggle one's ears/toes** mit seinen Ohren/Zehen wackeln.

wild [waɪld] *adj* - **1.** [gen] wild - **2.** [violent, dangerous] gewalttätig - **3.** [weather, sea] stürmisch - **4.** [hair, look] wirr. ◆ **wilds** *npl*: **the wilds** die Wildnis.

wilderness [ˈwɪldənɪs] *n* Wildnis *die*.

wild-goose chase *n inf* hoffnungslose Suche.

wildlife [ˈwaɪldlaɪf] *n* Tierwelt *die*.

wildly ['waɪldlɪ] *adv* - **1.** [gen] wild - **2.** [talk, throw] aufs Geratewohl - **3.** [very] äußerst.

wilful *UK*, **willful** *US* ['wɪlfʊl] *adj* - **1.** [determined] stur - **2.** [deliberate] beabsichtigt.

will[1] [wɪl] ◇ *n* - **1.** [gen] Wille *der*; **against his will** gegen seinen Willen; **will to live** Lebenswille *der* - **2.** [document] Testament *das*. ◇ *vt*: **to will sb to do sthg** (sich *(D)*) mit aller Kraft wünschen, dass jd etw tut.

will[2] [wɪl] *aux vb* - **1.** [expressing future tense] werden; **will you be here next Friday?** bist du nächsten Freitag hier?; **will you do that for me? – no I won't/yes I will** wirst du das für mich tun? – nein(, werde ich nicht)/ja(, werde ich); **when will you have finished it?** wann seid ihr damit fertig?; **I think he will come** ich glaube schon, dass er kommt - **2.** [expressing willingness] wollen, werden; **I won't do it** ich werde das nicht tun; **no one will do it** keiner wird das machen - **3.** [expressing polite question]: **will you have some more tea?** möchten Sie noch mehr Tee? - **4.** [in commands, requests]: **will you please be quiet!** sei bitte ruhig!; **close that window, will you?** mach doch bitte das Fenster zu - **5.** [expressing possibility]: **the hall will hold up to 1,000 people** die Halle fasst bis zu 1000 Leute; **pensions will be paid monthly** Pensionen werden monatlich ausgezahlt - **6.** [expressing an assumption]: **that'll be your father** das wird dein Vater sein; **as you will have gathered, ...** wie Sie sich wohl gedacht haben, ... - **7.** [indicating irritation]: **well, if you will leave your toys everywhere** na ja, wenn ihr auch dauernd eure Spielsachen überall herumliegen lasst; **she will keep phoning me** sie ruft mich aber auch dauernd an.

willful *adj US* = **wilful**.

willing ['wɪlɪŋ] *adj* - **1.** [prepared]: **to be willing (to do sthg)** bereit sein(, etw zu tun) - **2.** [eager] bereitwillig.

willingly ['wɪlɪŋlɪ] *adv* bereitwillig, gerne.

willow (tree) ['wɪləʊ-] *n* Weide *die*.

willpower ['wɪl,paʊəʳ] *n* Willenskraft *die*.

willy-nilly [,wɪlɪ'nɪlɪ] *adv* - **1.** [at random] aufs Geratewohl - **2.** [wanting to or not] wohl oder übel.

wilt [wɪlt] *vi* - **1.** [plant] verwelken - **2.** *fig* [person] schlapp werden.

wily ['waɪlɪ] *adj* listig.

wimp [wɪmp] *n inf pej* Waschlappen *der*.

win [wɪn] (*pt & pp* **won**) ◇ *n* Sieg *der*. ◇ *vt* gewinnen. ◇ *vi* gewinnen; [in battle] siegen.
◆ **win over, win round** *vt sep* für sich gewinnen.

wince [wɪns] *vi*: **to wince at/with sthg** bei/vor etw *(D)* zusammen|zucken.

winch [wɪntʃ] *n* Winde *die*.

wind[1] [wɪnd] ◇ *n* - **1.** METEOR Wind *der* - **2.** *(U)* [breath] Atem *der* - **3.** *(U)* [in stomach] Blähungen *Pl.* ◇ *vt* [knock breath out of]: **I was winded by the fall** durch den Sturz blieb mir die Luft weg.

wind[2] [waɪnd] (*pt & pp* **wound**) ◇ *vt* - **1.** [string, thread] wickeln - **2.** [clock] auf|ziehen. ◇ *vi* [river, road] sich schlängeln.
◆ **wind down** ◇ *vt sep* - **1.** [car window] herunter|kurbeln - **2.** [production] allmählich ein|stellen. ◇ *vi* [relax] entspannen.
◆ **wind up** *vt sep* - **1.** [finish - meeting] ab|schließen; [- business] auf|lösen - **2.** [clock] auf|ziehen - **3.** [car window] herauf|kurbeln - **4.** *UK inf* [deliberately annoy] auf|ziehen.

windfall ['wɪndfɔːl] *n* [unexpected gift] unerhoffter Gewinn.

winding ['waɪndɪŋ] *adj* kurvenreich; [river] gewunden.

wind instrument [wɪnd-] *n* Blasinstrument *das*.

windmill ['wɪndmɪl] *n* Windmühle *die*.

window ['wɪndəʊ] *n* - **1.** [gen & COMPUT] Fenster *das* - **2.** [of shop] Schaufenster *das* - **3.** [free time] freie Zeit.

window box *n* Blumenkasten *der*.

window cleaner *n* Fensterputzer *der*, -in *die*.

window ledge *n* [outside] Fenstersims *das*; [inside] Fensterbrett *das*.

windowpane ['wɪndəʊpeɪn] *n* Fensterscheibe *die*.

windowsill ['wɪndəʊsɪl] *n* [outside] Fenstersims *der ODER das*; [inside] Fensterbrett *das*.

windpipe ['wɪndpaɪp] *n* Luftröhre *die*.

windscreen *UK* ['wɪndskriːn], **windshield** *US* ['wɪndʃiːld] *n* Windschutzscheibe *die*.

windscreen washer *n* Scheibenwaschanlage *die*.

windscreen wiper *n* Scheibenwischer *der*.

windshield *n US* = **windscreen**.

windsurfing ['wɪnd,sɜːfɪŋ] *n* Windsurfen *das*.

windswept ['wɪndswept] *adj* [landscape] windgepeitscht.

windy ['wɪndɪ] *adj* windig.

wine [waɪn] *n* Wein *der*.

wine bar *n UK* Weinbar *die*.

wineglass ['waɪnglɑːs] *n* Weinglas *das*.

wine list *n* Weinkarte *die*.

wine tasting [-,teɪstɪŋ] *n* - **1.** [practice] Weinverkosten *das* - **2.** [event] Weinprobe *die*.

wine waiter *n* Weinkellner *der*.

wing [wɪŋ] *n* - **1.** [gen] Flügel *der* - **2.** [of plane] Tragfläche *die* - **3.** [of car] Kotflügel *der*.
◆ **wings** *npl* THEAT: **the wings** die Kulissen.

winger ['wɪŋəʳ] *n* SPORT Außenstürmer *der*, -in *die*.

wink [wɪŋk] ◇ *n* [of eye] Zwinkern *das*. ◇ *vi* [eye] zwinkern; **to wink at sb** jm zu|zwinkern.

winkle ['wɪŋkl] *n* Strandschnecke *die*. ◆ **winkle out** *vt sep* herausǀbekommen; **to winkle sthg out of sb** *fig* etw aus jm herausǀbekommen.

winner ['wɪnəʳ] *n* [person] Gewinner *der*, -in *die*; [in sport] Sieger *der*, -in *die*.

winning ['wɪnɪŋ] *adj* [victorious] siegreich; [successful] erfolgreich. ◆ **winnings** *npl* Gewinn *der*.

winning post *n* Zielpfosten *der*.

winter ['wɪntəʳ] ◇ *n* Winter *der*; **in winter** im Winter. ◇ *comp* Winter-.

winter sports *npl* Wintersport *der*.

wintertime ['wɪntətaɪm] *n* Winterzeit *die*.

wint(e)ry ['wɪntrɪ] *adj* winterlich.

wipe [waɪp] ◇ *n* [clean]: **he gave his face/the table a wipe** er wischte sein Gesicht/den Tisch ab. ◇ *vt* - **1.** [rub to clean - floor] wischen; [- face, table] abǀwischen - **2.** [rub to dry] abǀtrocknen. ◆ **wipe out** *vt sep* - **1.** [erase] wegǀwischen - **2.** [eradicate - gen] vernichten; [- race] ausǀrotten. ◆ **wipe up** ◇ *vt sep* aufǀwischen. ◇ *vi* [dry dishes] abǀtrocknen.

wire ['waɪəʳ] ◇ *n* - **1.** [gen] Draht *der*; [electrical] Leitung *die* - **2.** *esp US* [telegram] Telegramm *das*. ◇ *vt* - **1.** ELEC [plug] anǀschließen - **2.** *esp US* [send telegram to] ein Telegramm schicken.

wireless ['waɪəlɪs] *n dated* Radio *das*.

wireless network *n* Kabellose Netzwerk *das*.

wiring ['waɪərɪŋ] *n (U)* elektrische Leitungen *Pl*.

wiry ['waɪərɪ] *adj* - **1.** [hair] borstig - **2.** [body, man] drahtig.

wisdom ['wɪzdəm] *n* Weisheit *die*.

wisdom tooth *n* Weisheitszahn *der*.

wise [waɪz] *adj* [prudent] weise.

wish [wɪʃ] ◇ *n* Wunsch *der*; **wish to do sthg** der Wunsch, etw zu tun; **wish for sthg** der Wunsch nach etw *(D)*. ◇ *vt* - **1.** [want]: **to wish to do sthg** *fml* etw zu tun wünschen; **I wished (that) he'd come** wenn er nur käme - **2.** [desire, request by magic]: **I wish (that) I had a million pounds** ich wünschte, ich hätte eine Million Pfund - **3.** [in greeting]: **to wish sb sthg** jm etw wünschen. ◇ *vi* [by magic]: **to wish for sthg** sich etw herbeiǀwünschen. ◆ **wishes** *npl*: **best wishes** alles Gute; **(with) best wishes** [at end of letter] herzliche Grüße.

wishy-washy ['wɪʃɪˌwɒʃɪ] *adj inf pej* [person] kraftlos; [ideas] vage.

wisp [wɪsp] *n* - **1.** [tuft] Büschel *das* - **2.** [small cloud]: **wisp of smoke** Rauchfahne *die*.

wistful ['wɪstfʊl] *adj* wehmütig.

wit [wɪt] *n* - **1.** [humour] Witz *der* - **2.** [intelligence]: **to have the wit to do sthg** klug genug sein, etw zu tun. ◆ **wits** *npl* [intelligence, mind]: **to have** OR **keep one's wits about one** geistesgegenwärtig sein.

witch [wɪtʃ] *n* Hexe *die*.

with [wɪð] *prep* - **1.** [gen] mit; **come with me** komm mit mir; **a man with a beard** ein Mann mit Bart; **a room with a bathroom** ein Zimmer mit Bad; **be careful with that!** sei vorsichtig damit!; **bring it with you** bringen Sie es mit; **to argue with sb** (sich) mit jm streiten; **the war with Germany** der Krieg gegen Deutschland; **I can't do it with you watching me** ich kann es nicht tun, wenn du mir zuschaust - **2.** [at house of, in the hands of] bei; **we stayed with friends** wir haben bei Freunden übernachtet; **the decision rests with you** die Entscheidung liegt bei dir - **3.** [indicating emotion] vor *(+ D)*; **to tremble with fear** vor Angst zittern - **4.** [because of] bei; **with the weather as it is, we decided to stay at home** angesichts des Wetters beschlossen wir zu Hause zu bleiben; **with my luck, I'll probably lose** bei meinem Glück werde ich wahrscheinlich verlieren - **5.** *phr*: **I'll be with you in a moment** ich komme gleich; **I'm not quite with you** [I don't understand] ich komme nicht ganz mit; **I'm with you there** [I'm on your side] da bin ich ganz deiner Ansicht.

withdraw [wɪð'drɔː] (*pt* **-drew**, *pp* **-drawn**) ◇ *vt* - **1.** *fml* [remove] wegǀnehmen; **to withdraw sthg from sthg** etw von etw wegǀnehmen - **2.** FIN abǀheben - **3.** MIL [troops] zurückǀziehen - **4.** [retract] zurückǀnehmen. ◇ *vi* - **1.**: **to withdraw (from)** sich zurückǀziehen (aus) - **2.** [quit, give up] aufǀgeben; **to withdraw from sthg** aus etw ausǀscheiden.

withdrawal [wɪð'drɔːəl] *n* - **1.** [removal] Zurückziehen *das* - **2.** MIL Rückzug *der* - **3.** [retraction] Zurücknahme *die* - **4.** [leaving, quitting]: **withdrawal (from sthg)** Ausscheiden *das* (aus etw) - **5.** FIN Abheben *das*.

withdrawal symptoms *npl* Entzugserscheinungen *Pl*.

withdrawn [wɪð'drɔːn] ◇ *pp* ▷ **withdraw**. ◇ *adj* [shy, quiet] verschlossen.

withdrew [wɪð'druː] *pt* ▷ **withdraw**.

wither ['wɪðəʳ] *vi* - **1.** [dry up] verwelken - **2.** [become weak] schwinden.

withhold [wɪð'həʊld] (*pt & pp* **-held** [-'held]) *vt* [information] zurückǀhalten.

within [wɪ'ðɪn] ◇ *prep* innerhalb *(+ G)*; **within sight** in Sichtweite; **within the next week** innerhalb der nächsten Woche; **within 10 miles** im Umkreis von 10 Meilen. ◇ *adv* innen.

without [wɪð'aʊt] *prep* ohne; **without doing sthg** ohne etw zu tun; **I left without him seeing me** ich ging (weg), ohne dass er mich sah.

withstand [wɪð'stænd] (*pt & pp* **-stood** [-'stʊd]) *vt* standǀhalten *(+ D)*.

witness ['wɪtnɪs] ◇ *n* - **1.** [gen] Zeuge *der*, -gin *die* - **2.**: **to bear witness to sthg** [be proof of] von etw zeugen. ◇ *vt* - **1.**: **to witness sthg**

[murder, accident] Zeuge einer Sache *(G)* sein; [changes] etw erleben - **2.** [countersign] als Zeuge unterschreiben.

witness box *UK*, **witness stand** *US n* Zeugenstand *der*.

witticism ['wɪtɪsɪzm] *n* geistreiche Bemerkung.

witty ['wɪtɪ] *adj* geistreich und witzig.

wives [waɪvz] *Pl* ▷ **wife**.

wizard ['wɪzəd] *n* - **1.** [man with magic powers] Zauberer *der* - **2.** [skilled person] Genie *das*.

wobble ['wɒbl] *vi* wackeln.

woe [wəʊ] *n liter* Leid *das*.

woke [wəʊk] *pt* ▷ **wake**.

woken ['wəʊkn] *pp* ▷ **wake**.

wolf [wʊlf] (*pl* **wolves**) *n* [animal] Wolf *der*.

woman ['wʊmən] (*pl* **women** ['wɪmɪn]) ◇ *n* Frau *die*. ◇ *comp*: **woman doctor** Ärztin *die*; **woman teacher** Lehrerin *die*.

womanly ['wʊmənlɪ] *adj* fraulich.

womb [wuːm] *n* Gebärmutter *die*.

women ['wɪmɪn] *Pl* ▷ **woman**.

women's liberation *n* - **1.** [aim] Gleichstellung *die* der Frau - **2.** [movement] Frauenrechtsbewegung *die*.

won [wʌn] *pt* & *pp* ▷ **win**.

wonder ['wʌndəʳ] ◇ *n* - **1.** [amazement] Staunen *das* - **2.** [cause for surprise]: **it's a wonder that...** es ist ein Wunder, dass...; **no** *OR* **little** *OR* **small wonder** kein Wunder; **no wonder she left!** kein Wunder, dass sie gegangen ist! - **3.** [amazing thing] Wunder *das*. ◇ *vt* - **1.** [speculate] sich fragen; **to wonder if** *OR* **whether...** sich fragen, ob... - **2.** [in polite requests]: **I wonder whether you would mind shutting the window?** könnten Sie wohl bitte das Fenster schließen? ◇ *vi* [speculate] sich fragen; **to wonder about sthg** sich über etw *(A)* Gedanken machen.

wonderful ['wʌndəfʊl] *adj* wundervoll, wunderbar.

wonderfully ['wʌndəfʊlɪ] *adv* - **1.** [very well] wunderbar - **2.** [for emphasis] sehr.

won't [wəʊnt] *abbr of* **will not**.

woo [wuː] *vt* - **1.** *liter* [court - woman] den Hof machen *(+ D)* - **2.** *fig* [try to win over] umlwerben.

wood [wʊd] ◇ *n* - **1.** *(U)* [timber] Holz *das* - **2.** [group of trees] Wald *der*. ◇ *comp* Holz-. ◆ **woods** *npl* [forest] Wald *der*.

wooded ['wʊdɪd] *adj* [forested] bewaldet.

wooden ['wʊdn] *adj* - **1.** [of wood] Holz- - **2.** *pej* [actor] hölzern.

woodpecker ['wʊd,pekəʳ] *n* Specht *der*.

woodwind ['wʊdwɪnd] *n*: **the woodwind** die Holzbläser *Pl*.

woodwork ['wʊdwɜːk] *n* - **1.** [wooden objects] Holzarbeiten *Pl*; [part of house or room] Holzteile *Pl* - **2.** [craft] Tischlerei *die*.

wool [wʊl] *n* - **1.** [gen] Wolle *die* - **2.** *phr*: **to pull the wool over sb's eyes** *inf* jn hinters Licht führen.

woollen *UK*, **woolen** *US* ['wʊlən] *adj* [garment] Woll-. ◆ **woollens** *npl* Wollwaren *Pl*.

woolly ['wʊlɪ] *adj* [woollen] Woll-.

word [wɜːd] ◇ *n* - **1.** LING Wort *das*; **word for word** Wort für Wort; **in other words** mit anderen Worten; **in a word** kurz gesagt; **can I have a word (with you)?** kann ich Sie mal sprechen?; **I/you/*etc* couldn't get a word in edgeways** ich bin/du bist/*etc* nicht zu Wort gekommen - **2.** *(U)* [news] Nachricht *die*; **have you had word of John recently?** hast du in letzter Zeit etwas von John gehört? - **3.** [promise] Wort *das*; **to give sb one's word** jm sein Wort geben. ◇ *vt* formulieren.

wording ['wɜːdɪŋ] *n* Wortlaut *der*.

word processing *n* Textverarbeitung *die*.

word processor [-,prəʊsesəʳ] *n* Textverarbeitungssystem *das*.

wore [wɔːʳ] *pt* ▷ **wear**.

work [wɜːk] ◇ *n* - **1.** *(U)* [gen] Arbeit *die*; **to be in work** Arbeit haben; **to be out of work** arbeitslos sein - **2.** ART & LIT [created product] Werk *das*. ◇ *vt* - **1.** [person, staff]: **he works his staff too hard** er verlangt zu viel von seinen Angestellten - **2.** [machine] bedienen - **3.** [wood, clay, land] bearbeiten. ◇ *vi* - **1.** [do a job] arbeiten - **2.** [function, be successful] funktionieren - **3.** [gradually become]: **to work loose** sich lockern. ◆ **works** ◇ *n* [factory] Werk *das*. ◇ *npl* - **1.** [mechanism] Innere *das* - **2.** [digging, building] Bauarbeiten *Pl*. ◆ **work on** *vt insep* - **1.** [concentrate on] arbeiten an *(+ D)* - **2.** [principle, assumption, belief] auslgehen von - **3.** [try to persuade] bearbeiten. ◆ **work out** ◇ *vt sep* - **1.** [formulate] auslarbeiten - **2.** [calculate] auslrechnen. ◇ *vi* - **1.** [figure, total]: **that works out at £10 each** das macht 10 Pfund pro Person - **2.** [turn out]: **to work out in sb's favour** für jn vorteilhaft sein - **3.** [be successful] gut auslgehen - **4.** [train, exercise] trainieren. ◆ **work up** *vt sep* - **1.** [excite]: **to work o.s. up into** sich hineinlsteigern in *(+ A)* - **2.** [generate - enthusiasm, courage] auflbringen; [- appetite] entwickeln.

workable ['wɜːkəbl] *adj* [practicable] durchführbar.

workaholic [,wɜːkə'hɒlɪk] *n* Workaholic *der*.

worked up [,wɜːkt-] *adj* aufgeregt.

worker ['wɜːkəʳ] *n* [employee] Arbeiter *der*, -in *die*.

workforce ['wɜːkfɔːs] *n* Belegschaft *die*.

working ['wɜːkɪŋ] *adj* - **1.** [in operation] in Betrieb - **2.** [having employment] erwerbstätig - **3.** [relating to work] Arbeits-. ◆ **workings** *npl* [of system, machine] Funktionsweise *die*.

working class *n*: **the working class** die Arbeiterklasse. ◆ **working-class** *adj* Arbeiter-.

working order *n*: **in working order** funktionstüchtig.

workload ['wɜ:kləʊd] *n* Arbeitsvolumen *das*.

workman ['wɜ:kmən] (*pl* **-men** [-mən]) *n* [craftsman] Handwerker *der*; [worker] Arbeiter *der*.

workmanship ['wɜ:kmənʃɪp] *n (U)* handwerkliches Können.

workmate ['wɜ:kmeɪt] *n* Kollege *der*, -gin *die*.

work permit *n* Arbeitserlaubnis *die*.

workplace ['wɜ:kpleɪs] *n* Arbeitsplatz *der*.

workshop ['wɜ:kʃɒp] *n* - **1.** [room, building] Werkstatt *die* - **2.** [discussion] Workshop *der*.

workstation ['wɜ:kˌsteɪʃn] *n* COMPUT Workstation *die*.

worktop ['wɜ:ktɒp] *n UK* Arbeitsfläche *die*.

world [wɜ:ld] ◇ *n* - **1.** [gen]: **the world** die Welt; **to have the best of both worlds** die Vorteile beider Seiten genießen; **the next world** das Jenseits - **2.** [great deal]: **to think the world of sb** große Stücke auf jn halten; **a world of difference** ein himmelweiter Unterschied. ◇ *comp* Welt-.

world-class *adj* Weltklasse-.

world-famous *adj* weltberühmt.

worldly ['wɜ:ldlɪ] *adj* [not spiritual] weltlich.

World War I *n* Erster Weltkrieg.

World War II *n* Zweiter Weltkrieg.

worldwide ['wɜ:ldwaɪd] *adj & adv* weltweit.

World Wide Web *n*: **the World Wide Web** COMPUT das World Wide Web.

worm [wɜ:m] *n* [animal] Wurm *der*.

worn [wɔ:n] ◇ *pp* ▷ **wear**. ◇ *adj* - **1.** [threadbare - carpet] abgenutzt; [- clothes] abgetragen; [- tyre] abgefahren - **2.** [tired] erschöpft.

worn-out *adj* - **1.** [old, threadbare] ganz abgenutzt; [clothes, shoes] ganz abgetragen - **2.** [tired] ausgelaugt.

worried ['wʌrɪd] *adj* besorgt; **I was worried he'd be angry** ich hatte Angst, er würde böse sein.

worry ['wʌrɪ] ◇ *n* Sorge *die*. ◇ *vt* [cause to be troubled] Sorgen machen *(+ D)*. ◇ *vi*: **to worry about sb/sthg** sich um jn/etw sorgen OR Sorgen machen; **not to worry!** keine Sorge!

worrying ['wʌrɪɪŋ] *adj* beunruhigend.

worse [wɜ:s] ◇ *adj* - **1.** [not as good] schlechter; [situation] schlimmer; **to get worse** sich verschlechtern; [situation] sich verschlimmern - **2.** [sicker]: **he's worse** es geht ihm schlechter; **she seemed to get worse** ihr Zustand schien sich zu verschlechtern. ◇ *adv* [more badly] schlechter; **worse off** [having less money] schlechter dran; [in a more unpleasant situation] schlimmer dran. ◇ *n* Schlimmeres *das*; **a change for the worse** eine Verschlimmerung; [of health, weather] eine Verschlechterung.

worsen ['wɜ:sn] ◇ *vt* [situation, crisis] verschlimmern. ◇ *vi* [situation, crisis] sich verschlimmern; [weather, work] sich verschlechtern.

worship ['wɜ:ʃɪp] (*UK*) (*US*) ◇ *vt* - **1.** RELIG an|beten - **2.** [admire, adore] vergöttern. ◇ *n* - **1.** *(U)* RELIG Verehrung *die*; [service] Gottesdienst *der* - **2.** *(U)* [adoration] Vergötterung *die*. ◆ **Worship** *n*: **Your Worship** Euer Ehren; **Her/His Worship (the Mayoress/Mayor)** die sehr verehrte Frau Bürgermeister/der sehr verehrte Herr Bürgermeister.

worst [wɜ:st] ◇ *adj* schlimmste(r) (s), schlechteste(r) (s). ◇ *adv* am schlimmsten, am schlechtesten. ◇ *n*: **the worst** das Schlimmste; **if the worst comes to the worst** wenn alle Stricke reißen. ◆ **at (the) worst** *adv* schlimmstenfalls.

worth [wɜ:θ] ◇ *prep*: **how much is it worth?** wie viel ist das wert?; **it's worth £50** es ist 50 Pfund wert; **it's worth seeing** es ist sehenswert; **it's not worth it** es lohnt sich nicht; **he's worth millions** er besitzt Millionen; **to run for all one is worth** *fig* rennen, was man nur rennen kann. ◇ *n* - **1.** [amount]: **£50 worth of traveller's cheques** Reiseschecks im Wert von 50 Pfund; **a week's worth of groceries** Lebensmittel *Pl* für eine Woche - **2.** [value] Wert *der*; **he proved his worth** er hat sich bewährt.

worthless ['wɜ:θlɪs] *adj* - **1.** [object] wertlos - **2.** [person] nichtsnutzig.

worthwhile [ˌwɜ:θ'waɪl] *adj* lohnend; **to be worthwhile** sich lohnen.

worthy ['wɜ:ðɪ] *adj* - **1.** [deserving of respect] würdig; **for a worthy cause** für einen guten Zweck - **2.** [deserving]: **to be worthy of sthg** etw verdienen - **3.** *pej* [good but unexciting] ehrbar.

would [wʊd] *modal vb* - **1.** [in reported speech]: **she said she would come** sie sagte, sie würde kommen - **2.** [indicating condition]: **what would you do?** was würdest du tun?; **what would you have done?** was hättest du getan?; **I would be most grateful** ich wäre äußerst dankbar - **3.** [indicating willingness]: **she wouldn't go** sie wollte einfach nicht gehen; **he would do anything for her** er würde alles für sie tun - **4.** [in polite questions]: **would you like a drink?** möchtest du etwas trinken?; **would you mind closing the window?** könntest du das Fenster zumachen? - **5.** [indicating inevitability]: **he would say that** er musste das sagen; **I quite forgot! – you would!** das habe ich ganz vergessen! – das sieht dir ähnlich! - 6. [giving advice]: **I would report it if I were you** an deiner Stelle würde ich es melden - 7. [expressing opinions]: **I would prefer coffee** ich hätte lieber Kaffee; **I would prefer to go by bus** ich würde lieber mit dem Bus fahren; **I would have thought (that)...** ich hätte gedacht, dass... - 8. [describing habitual past actions]: **she would often come home tired out** oft kam sie total erschöpft nach Hause.

would-be *adj* angehend.

wouldn't ['wʊdnt] *abbr of* **would not**.

would've ['wʊdəv] *abbr of* **would have**.

wound¹ [wu:nd] ◇ *n* Wunde *die*. ◇ *vt* - 1. [physically] verwunden - 2. [emotionally] verletzen.

wound² [waʊnd] *pt* & *pp* ▷ **wind²**.

wove [wəʊv] *pt* ▷ **weave**.

woven ['wəʊvn] *pp* ▷ **weave**.

WP *n abbr of* **word processing**, **word processor**.

wrangle ['ræŋgl] ◇ *n* Streitigkeiten *Pl*. ◇ *vi* sich streiten; **to wrangle with sb (over sthg)** mit jm (über etw *(A)*) streiten.

wrap [ræp] *vt* [cover in paper or cloth] ein|wickeln; **to wrap sthg in sthg** etw in etw *(A)* ein|wickeln; **to wrap sthg (a)round sthg** etw um etw wickeln. ◆ **wrap up** ◇ *vt sep* [cover in paper or cloth] ein|wickeln. ◇ *vi* [put warm clothes on]: **wrap up well** OR **warmly!** zieh dich warm an!

wrapper ['ræpəʳ] *n* Hülle *die*; [of sweets] Papier *das*.

wrapping ['ræpɪŋ] *n* Verpackung *die*.

wrapping paper *n (U)* Geschenkpapier *das*.

wreak [ri:k] *vt* [destruction, havoc] an|richten; [revenge] üben.

wreath [ri:θ] *n* [circle of flowers] Kranz *der*.

wreck [rek] ◇ *n* Wrack *das*; **a nervous wreck** ein Nervenbündel; **a car wreck** *US* ein Autounfall. ◇ *vt* - 1. [break, destroy] demolieren; [car] zu Schrott fahren - 2. NAUT [cause to run aground] versenken; **to be wrecked** [person] Schiffbruch erleiden - 3. [spoil, ruin] ruinieren.

wreckage ['rekɪdʒ] *n* [of plane, building] Trümmer *Pl*; [of car] Wrack *das*.

wren [ren] *n* Zaunkönig *der*.

wrench [rentʃ] ◇ *n* [tool] Schraubenschlüssel *der*. ◇ *vt* - 1. [pull violently] reißen - 2. [twist and injure]: **to wrench one's arm/leg** sich den Arm/das Bein verrenken.

wrestle ['resl] *vi* - 1. [fight]: **to wrestle with sb** mit jm ringen - 2. *fig* [struggle]: **to wrestle with sthg** mit etw kämpfen.

wrestler ['resləʳ] *n* Ringer *der*, -in *die*; [as entertainer] Wrestler *der*, -in *die*.

wrestling ['reslɪŋ] *n* Ringen *das*; [as entertainment] Wrestling *das*.

wretch [retʃ] *n* [unhappy person]: **poor wretch!** armer Tropf!

wretched ['retʃɪd] *adj* - 1. [miserable] elend; [conditions] erbärmlich - 2. *inf* [damned] verflixt.

wriggle ['rɪgl] *vi* - 1. [move about - person] zappeln; [- worm] sich winden - 2. [twist]: **he wriggled under the fence** er wand sich unter dem Zaun hindurch; **to wriggle free** sich los|winden.

wring [rɪŋ] (*pt* & *pp* **wrung**) *vt* [squeeze out water from] aus|wringen.

wringing ['rɪŋɪŋ] *adj*: **wringing (wet)** tropfnass.

wrinkle ['rɪŋkl] ◇ *n* - 1. [on skin] Falte *die* - 2. [in cloth] Knitterfalte *die*. ◇ *vt* [screw up - nose] rümpfen; [- forehead] runzeln. ◇ *vi* [crease] knittern.

wrist [rɪst] *n* Handgelenk *das*.

wristwatch ['rɪstwɒtʃ] *n* Armbanduhr *die*.

writ [rɪt] *n* Verfügung *die*.

write [raɪt] (*pt* **wrote**, *pp* **written**) ◇ *vt* - 1. [gen] schreiben - 2. [cheque, prescription] aus|stellen - 3. COMPUT speichern. ◇ *vi* - 1. [gen] schreiben - 2. COMPUT ab|speichern. ◆ **write down** *vt sep* auf|schreiben. ◆ **write off** *vt sep* - 1. [project] auf|geben - 2. [debt, investment, person] ab|schreiben - 3. *UK inf* [vehicle] zu Schrott fahren. ◆ **write up** *vt sep* [notes] aus|arbeiten.

write-off *n* [car] Totalschaden *der*.

writer ['raɪtəʳ] *n* - 1. [as profession] Schriftsteller *der*, -in *die* - 2. [of letter, article, story] Verfasser *der*, -in *die*.

writhe [raɪð] *vi* sich winden; [with pain] sich krümmen.

writing ['raɪtɪŋ] *n* - 1. [gen] Schrift *die*; **in writing** schriftlich - 2. [activity] Schreiben *das*.

writing paper *n (U)* Briefpapier *das*.

written ['rɪtn] ◇ *pp* ▷ **write**. ◇ *adj* schriftlich.

wrong [rɒŋ] ◇ *adj* - 1. [amiss]: **there's nothing wrong with me** mir fehlt nichts; **is something wrong?** stimmt etwas nicht?; **what's wrong?** was ist los?; **there's something wrong with the car** mit dem Auto stimmt etwas nicht - 2. [not suitable] falsch - 3. [not correct - answer, decision, turning] falsch, verkehrt; **to be wrong** [person] Unrecht haben; **I was wrong to ask** ich hätte nicht fragen sollen - 4. [morally bad] unrecht. ◇ *adv* [incorrectly] falsch, verkehrt; **to get sthg wrong** sich mit etw vertun; **to go wrong** [make a mistake] einen Fehler machen; **the printer keeps going wrong** der Drucker spielt ständig verrückt. ◇ *n* Unrecht *das*; **to be in the wrong** Unrecht haben. ◇ *vt liter* Unrecht tun *(+ D)*.

wrongful ['rɒŋfʊl] *adj* [unjust] ungerecht.

wrongly ['rɒŋlɪ] *adv* - **1.** [unsuitably] falsch - **2.** [mistakenly] zu Unrecht.

wrong number *n* falsche Nummer; **you've got the wrong number** Sie haben sich verwählt.

wrote [rəʊt] *pt* ▷ **write**.

wrung [rʌŋ] *pt* & *pp* ▷ **wring**.

wry [raɪ] *adj* [amused] ironisch; [humour, remark] trocken.

x (*pl* **x's** OR **xs**), **X** (*pl* **X's** OR **Xs**) [eks] *n* - **1.** [letter] x *das*, X *das* - **2.** [unknown name] X - **3.** [quantity, in algebra] x - **4.** [to mark place]: **X marks the spot** ein Kreuzchen markiert die Stelle - **5.** [at end of letter] *ein Kreuzchen am Ende eines Briefes, das einen Kuss bedeutet*.

xenophobic [ˌzenə'fəʊbɪk] *adj* fremdenfeindlich, xenophob.

Xmas ['eksməs] *n* Weihnachten *das*.

X-ray ◇ *n* - **1.** [ray] Röntgenstrahl *der* - **2.** [picture] Röntgenbild *das*. ◇ *vt* röntgen.

xylophone ['zaɪləfəʊn] *n* Xylofon *das*.

y (*pl* **y's** OR **ys**), **Y** (*pl* **Y's** OR **Ys**) [waɪ] *n* [letter] y *das*, Y *das*.

yacht [jɒt] *n* Jacht *die*.

yachting ['jɒtɪŋ] *n* Segeln *das*.

yachtsman ['jɒtsmən] (*pl* **-men** [-mən]) *n* Segler *der*.

Yank [jæŋk] *n UK inf pej* Ami *der*.

Yankee ['jæŋkɪ] *n UK inf pej* [American] Ami *der*.

yap [jæp] *vi* [dog] kläffen.

yard [jɑːd] *n* - **1.** [unit of measurement] Yard *das*, *= 91,44 cm* - **2.** [enclosed area] Hof *der* - **3.** [place of work]: **ship yard** Schiffswerft *die*; **builder's yard** Bauhof *der* - **4.** *US* [attached to house] Garten *der*.

yardstick ['jɑːdstɪk] *n* Maßstab *der*.

yarn [jɑːn] *n (U)* [thread] Garn *das*.

yawn [jɔːn] ◇ *n* [when tired] Gähnen *das*. ◇ *vi* gähnen.

yd *abbr of* **yard**.

yeah [jeə] *adv inf* ja.

year [jɪəʳ] *n* Jahr *das*; **all (the) year round** das ganze Jahr über; **for seven years** sieben Jahre (lang). ◆ **years** *npl* [ages] Jahre *Pl*; **for years** jahrelang.

yearly ['jɪəlɪ] ◇ *adj* - **1.** [event, inspection, report] jährlich - **2.** [income, wage] Jahres-. ◇ *adv* jährlich.

yearn [jɜːn] *vi*: **to yearn for sthg** sich nach etw sehnen; **to yearn to do sthg** sich danach sehnen, etw zu tun.

yearning ['jɜːnɪŋ] *n*: **yearning (for sb/sthg)** Sehnsucht *die* (nach jm/etw).

yeast [jiːst] *n (U)* Hefe *die*.

yell [jel] ◇ *n* Schrei *der*. ◇ *vt* & *vi* schreien.

yellow ['jeləʊ] ◇ *adj* [in colour] gelb. ◇ *n* Gelb *das*.

yellow card *n* FTBL gelbe Karte.

yelp [jelp] *vi* auf|jaulen; [of person] auf|schreien.

yes [jes] ◇ *adv* - **1.** [gen] ja; **yes, please** ja, bitte; **to say yes to sthg** einer Sache *(D)* zustimmen - **2.** [to encourage further speech] so - **3.** [expressing disagreement] doch. ◇ *n* [vote in favour] Ja *das*.

yesterday ['jestədɪ] ◇ *n* Gestern *das*. ◇ *adv* gestern.

yet [jet] ◇ *adv* noch; *(in questions)* schon; **have you read the book yet?** hast du das Buch schon gelesen?; **not yet** noch nicht; **aren't you ready yet?** bist du bald fertig?; **as yet** bisher, bis jetzt; **I've yet to do it** ich muss es noch tun; **yet another delay** noch eine Verspätung; **yet again** schon wieder; **he'll win yet** er wird schon noch gewinnen. ◇ *conj* doch; **simple yet effective** einfach, aber wirksam; **and yet I like him** und doch OR dennoch mag ich ihn.

yew [juː] *n* Eibe *die*.

yield [jiːld] ◇ *n* Ertrag *der*. ◇ *vt* - **1.** [produce] hervor|bringen; [fruit] tragen; [profits] ab|werfen; [result, answer, clue] ergeben - **2.** [give up] ab|geben. ◇ *vi* - **1.** [open, give way, break] nach|geben - **2.** *fml* [give up, surrender] sich ergeben - **3.** *US* AUT [give way]: **'yield'** 'Vorfahrt beachten'.

YMCA (*abbr of* **Young Men's Christian Association**) *n* CVJM *der*.

yoga ['jəʊgə] *n* Yoga *der ODER das*.

yoghourt, yoghurt, yogurt [*UK* 'jɒgət, *US* 'jəʊgərt] *n* Jogurt *der ODER das ODER die*.

yoke [jəʊk] *n* Joch *das*.

yolk [jəʊk] *n* Dotter *der ODER das*, Eigelb *das*.

you [ju:] *pers pron* - **1.** *(subject – singular)* du; *(– plural)* ihr; *(– polite form)* Sie; **you Germans** ihr Deutschen; **I'm shorter than you** ich bin kleiner als du/Sie/ihr - **2.** *(direct object, after prep + A – singular)* dich; *(– plural)* euch; *(– polite form)* Sie; **I hate you!** ich hasse dich/Sie/euch!; **I did it for you** ich habe es für dich/Sie/euch getan - **3.** *(direct object, after prep + D – singular)* dir; *(– plural)* euch; *(– polite form)* Ihnen; **I told you!** ich habe es dir/Ihnen/euch gesagt; **after you!** nach Ihnen! - **4.** *(indefinite use – subject)* man; *(– object)* einen; *(– indirect object)* einem; **you never know** man kann nie wissen; **it does you good** es tut einem gut.

you'd [ju:d] *abbr of* **you had**, **you would**.

you'll [ju:l] *abbr of* **you will**.

young [jʌŋ] <> *adj* [not old] jung. <> *npl* - **1.** [young people]: **the young** die Jugend - **2.** [baby animals] Junge *Pl*.

younger ['jʌŋgəʳ] *adj* jünger.

youngster ['jʌŋstəʳ] *n* - **1.** [child] Kind *das* - **2.** [young person] Jugendliche *der, die*.

your [jɔ:ʳ] *poss adj* - **1.** *(singular subject)* dein(e), deine *Pl*; *(plural subject)* euer/eure, eure *Pl*; *(polite form)* Ihr(e), Ihre *Pl*; **your dog** dein/euer/Ihr Hund; **your house** dein/euer/Ihr Haus; **your children** deine/eure/IhreKinder - **2.** *(indefinite subject)*: **it's good for your teeth** es ist gut für die Zähne; **your average Englishman** der durchschnittliche Engländer.

you're [jɔ:ʳ] *abbr of* **you are**.

yours [jɔ:z] *poss pron (singular subject)* deiner/deine/deins, deine *Pl*; *(plural subject)* eurer/eure/eures, eure *Pl*; *(polite form)* Ihrer/Ihre/Ihres, Ihre *Pl*; **a friend of yours** ein Freund von dir/euch/Ihnen; **that money is yours** dieses Geld gehört dir/euch/Ihnen. ◆ **Yours** *adv* [in letter - gen] Dein/Deine; [- polite form] Ihr/Ihre.

yourself [jɔ:'self] (*pl* **-selves** [-'selvz]) *pron* - **1.** *(reflexive, after prep + A – singular)* dich; *(– plural)* euch; *(– polite form)* sich - **2.** *(reflexive, after prep + D – singular)* dir; *(– plural)* euch; *(– polite form)* sich; **did you do it yourself?** hast du/haben Sie das selbst gemacht?; **did you do it yourselves?** habt ihr/haben Sie das selbst gemacht?; **by yourself/yourselves** allein.

youth [ju:θ] *n* - **1.** [period of life, young people] Jugend *die* - **2.** [quality] Jugendlichkeit *die* - **3.** [boy] Junge *der*; [young man] junger Mann.

youth club *n* Jugendklub *der*.

youthful ['ju:θfʊl] *adj* jugendlich.

youth hostel *n* Jugendherberge *die*.

you've [ju:v] *abbr of* **you have**.

Yugoslavia [ˌju:gə'slɑ:vɪə] *n* Jugoslawien *das*.

Yugoslavian [ˌju:gə'slɑ:vɪən] <> *adj* jugoslawisch. <> *n* Jugoslawe *der*, -win *die*.

yuppie, yuppy ['jʌpɪ] *n* Yuppie *der*.

YWCA (*abbr of* **Young Women's Christian Association**) *n* CVJF *der*.

Z

z (*pl* **z's** *OR* **zs**), **Z** (*pl* **Z's** *OR* **Zs**) [*UK* zed, *US* zi:] *n* [letter] z *das*, Z *das*.

zany ['zeɪnɪ] *adj inf* verrückt.

zeal [zi:l] *n fml* Eifer *der*.

zebra [*UK* 'zebrə, *US* 'zi:brə] (*pl inv OR* **-s**) *n* Zebra *das*.

zebra crossing *n UK* Zebrastreifen *der*.

zenith [*UK* 'zenɪθ, *US* 'zi:nəθ] *n liter & fig* Zenit *der*.

zero [*UK* 'zɪərəʊ, *US* 'zi:rəʊ] (*pl* **-s** *OR* **-es**, *pt & pp* **-ed**, *cont* **-ing**) <> *adj* keinerlei; **zero growth** Nullwachstum *das*. <> *n* Null *die*.

zest [zest] *n* - **1.** [excitement] Schwung *der* - **2.** *(U)* [eagerness] Begeisterung *die* - **3.** *(U)* [of orange, lemon] Schale *die*.

zigzag ['zɪgzæg] *vi* [person, vehicle] im Zickzack laufen/fahren; [path] im Zickzack verlaufen.

Zimbabwe [zɪm'bɑ:bwɪ] *n* Simbabwe *nt*.

zinc [zɪŋk] *n* Zink *das*.

zip [zɪp] <> *n UK* [fastener] Reißverschluss *der*. <> *vt* COMPUT zippen. ◆ **zip up** *vt sep* den Reißverschluss zulmachen an (+ *D*).

zip code *n US* Postleitzahl *die*.

zip fastener *n UK* = **zip**.

zipper ['zɪpəʳ] *n US* = **zip**.

zodiac ['zəʊdɪæk] *n*: **the zodiac** Tierkreis *der*.

zone [zəʊn] *n* [district] Zone *die*.

zoo [zu:] *n* Zoo *der*.

zoom [zu:m] *vi inf* [move quickly] sausen. ◆ **zoom off** *vi inf* ablrauschen.

zoom lens *n* Zoomobjektiv *das*.

zucchini [zu:'ki:nɪ] (*pl inv OR* **-s**) *n US* Zucchini *die*.

Achevé d'imprimer par l'Imprimerie
Maury-Imprimeur - 45300 Malesherbes en janvier 2008
Dépôt légal : janvier 2008 - N° d'imprimeur : 133968/133969

Imprimé en France - (Printed in France)